Frommer's®

USA

11th Edition

Here's what the critics say about Frommer's:

"Amazingly easy to use. Very portable, very complete."
—BOOKLIST

"Detailed, accurate, and easy-to-read information for all price ranges."
—GLAMOUR MAGAZINE

"Hotel information is close to encyclopedic."
—DES MOINES SUNDAY REGISTER

"Frommer's Guides have a way of giving you a real feel for a place."
—KNIGHT RIDDER NEWSPAPERS

WILEY
Wiley Publishing, Inc.

Published by:

WILEY PUBLISHING, INC.

111 River St.
Hoboken, NJ 07030-5774

ISBN 978-0-470-38746-7
Editor: Kathleen Warnock, with Senior Editor Naomi Kraus
Production Editor: Katie Robinson
Cartographer: Guy Ruggiero
Photo Editor: Richard Fox
Production by Wiley Indianapolis Composition Services

Front cover photo: South Dakota, Black Hills: Mount Rushmore
Back cover photo: New York City: Times Square overview

For information on our other products and services or to obtain technical support, please contact our Customer Care Department within the U.S. at 800/762-2974, outside the U.S. at 317/572-3993 or fax 317/572-4002.

Wiley also publishes its books in a variety of electronic formats. Some content that appears in print may not be available in electronic formats.

Manufactured in the United States of America

5   4   3   2   1

CONTENTS

4 THE SOUTHEAST 213

5 FLORIDA 334

6 THE GULF SOUTH 415

11 THE SOUTHWEST 726

12 CALIFORNIA 819

13 THE PACIFIC NORTHWEST 929

14 ALASKA & HAWAII 984

APPENDIX A: THE BEST OF THE REST 1021

APPENDIX B: STATE TOURISM OFFICES 1038

APPENDIX C: FOR INTERNATIONAL VISITORS 1042

APPENDIX D: TOLL-FREE NUMBERS & WEBSITES 1052

INDEX 1055

USA

CONTENTS

LIST OF MAPS

ACKNOWLEDGMENTS

This book has been created from dozens of Frommer's guides covering the United States, and it couldn't exist without the tireless efforts of our many talented writers. They deserve special recognition for spending countless hours hitting the pavement, inspecting hotels, sampling restaurants, chasing down information, and visiting attractions so they can offer you their intelligent, informed insight.

Thanks for a job well done to: Lesley Abravamel, Harry Basch, Rich Beattie, Elizabeth Canning Blackwell, Leslie Brokaw, Elise Hartman Ford, Jeanette Foster, Bill Goodwin, Mary Herczog, Mark Hiss, Paul Karr, Lesley S. King, Erika Lenkert, Herbert Bailey Livesey, Laura Miller, Marie Morris, Eric Peterson, Laura M. Reckford, Linda Romine, Karl Samson, Neil E. Schlecht, Brian Silverman, Mary K. Tilghman, and Charles P. Wohlforth.

Special thanks also go to another group of contributors, who, often in addition to their Complete Guide duties, covered destinations especially for this guide: David Baird (Texas), Harry Basch (South Dakota), Amy Donohue (Atlantic City and Cape May), Amy Eckert (Pittsburgh, Michigan, Wisconsin, Minneapolis, and St. Paul), Bill McRae (Idaho), Lauren McCutcheon (Philadelphia), Matthew Richard Poole (Reno), Darwin Porter and Danforth Prince (Carolinas and Georgia), Beth Reiber (St. Louis, Kansas City, Branson, Oklahoma City, and Omaha), Linda Romine (Cleveland, Cincinnati, Kentucky, Tennessee, Alabama, and Mississippi), Karl Samson (Oregon), and Karen Snyder (Atlanta).

Major kudos to on-staff contributors Ian "Indy" Skinnari (who updated our Indianapolis section), and Naomi Kraus (who wrote and updated the Historic Hotels box, as well as using her considerable experience to fine-tune the Las Vegas and Orlando sections), and the other Frommer's editors who pitched in to edit and add their input to individual cities and regions: Stephen "Cheesesteak" Bassman, Linda Barth, Anuja Madar, and Marc Nadeau.

This book also owes much to the detailed, specific and frequently updated maps from our on-staff cartographers: Andrew Dolan, Andrew Murphy, Elizabeth Puhl, Guy Ruggiero, and Roberta Stockwell.

AN INVITATION TO THE READER

In researching this book, we discovered many wonderful places—hotels, restaurants, shops, and more. We're sure you'll find others. Please tell us about them, so we can share the information with your fellow travelers in upcoming editions. If you were disappointed with a recommendation, we'd love to know that, too. Please write to:

Frommer's USA, 11th Edition
Wiley Publishing, Inc. • 111 River St. • Hoboken, NJ 07030-5774

AN ADDITIONAL NOTE

Please be advised that travel information is subject to change at any time—and this is especially true of prices. We therefore suggest that you write or call ahead for confirmation when making your travel plans. The authors, editors, and publisher cannot be held responsible for the experiences of readers while traveling. Your safety is important to us, however, so we encourage you to stay alert and be aware of your surroundings. Keep a close eye on cameras, purses, and wallets, all favorite targets of thieves and pickpockets.

FROMMER'S ICONS & ABBREVIATIONS

This book uses **three feature icons** that point you to the great deals, family-friendly options, and top experiences that separate travelers from tourists. Throughout the book, look for:

(Kids)   Best bets for kids and advice for the whole family

(Value)   Great values—where to get the best deals

(Best)   The best hotel, restaurant, or attraction in the city or region

The following **abbreviations** are used for credit cards:

AE American Express	DISC Discover	V Visa
DC Diners Club	MC MasterCard	

FROMMERS.COM

Now that you have this guidebook to help you plan a great trip, visit our website at **www. frommers.com** for additional travel information on more than 4,000 destinations. We update features regularly to give you instant access to the most current trip-planning information available. At Frommers.com, you'll find scoops on the best airfares, lodging rates, and car rental bargains. You can even book your travel online through our reliable travel booking partners. Other popular features include:

- Online updates of our most popular guidebooks
- Vacation sweepstakes and contest giveaways
- Newsletters highlighting the hottest travel trends
- Podcasts, interactive maps, and up-to-the-minute events listings
- Opinionated blog entries by Arthur Frommer himself
- Online travel message boards with featured travel discussions

Planning Your Trip to the USA

You must remember, they are United States: 50 different places and states of mind, spread out over some 3.6 million square miles. It's 2,500 miles from New York to Los Angeles, and that again to Hawaii, so if you wake up in Louisiana, you'll see a different horizon, be in a different time zone, have a different major urban area, and have a different favorite team than if you wake up in Albuquerque.

While we think of ourselves as "American," despite the influence of TV, suburban sprawl, strip malls, and chain restaurants, the United States hasn't yet become a monolithic place. Each region still speaks with its own accent, enjoys its own favorite foods, and has its own political and social attitudes. Whatever you want to see, do, or eat, you're likely to find it within the vast and diverse confines of the United States of America.

As we go to press in uncertain economic times, after a summer in which gas prices shot up higher than they've ever been, with an accompanying rise in the price of everything else, and in which the term *staycation* entered people's vocabularies, we think you'll find you can still feed your spirit of adventure, and find something wonderful to see, whether it's just around the corner in your own home state or across the country. We list a range of accommodations, dining, activities, and events for travelers on a tight budget, as well as the people who want a bang for their buck when they decide to splurge.

In this chapter, we'll also give you some tips for getting the best value when you book a trip by air or reserve a hotel or motel room.

WHAT'S HERE & WHAT'S NOT

How can we possibly boil down the essence of such a huge, varied, complicated country in just over 1,000 pages? Impossible! No doubt, some of you will look at the table of contents and raise an eyebrow at what's missing. That's sure to be the case with any guide professing to cover the entire United States.

But . . . this book isn't meant to be a comprehensive guide to everything to see and do in every state. We did, however, concentrate on a select group of destinations that will appeal to a wide cross section of domestic travelers, be they road-trippers, business travelers, outdoor enthusiasts, history buffs, or museum lovers (along with the usual leavening of the opinionated Frommer's author). So we've narrowed the focus, in order to offer you in-depth, practical coverage you can really use.

Take, for example, the lovely islands off the coast of Massachusetts, Martha's Vineyard and Nantucket: We'd love to cover both, but we chose to focus on the Vineyard instead. Few travelers have time to visit both, so we used the space to include more detailed and useful information on the Vineyard, which is larger and easier to reach. We've applied the same sort of logic to our choices throughout. We do change them from edition to edition, based on reader response and our own observations, and those of our peripatetic authors. What you'll find in this book is information about destinations that's representative of the best this country has to offer—cities, national parks, beaches, resort areas, and more.

The USA—Major Interstate Routes

Legend

- 95 Interstate Highway
- ✪ National Capital
- – · – International Boundary
- – – – State Boundary
- **AL** State (abbreviation)

We do have all 50 states represented. In appendix A, we highlight the best offerings of five states that would otherwise get the (undeserved) short end of the stick. And if you're looking for Delaware, information about a couple of that state's top attractions is in between "Philadelphia" and "Maryland" in the Mid-Atlantic. For more visitor information on specific destinations in this book (or destinations we don't have room to cover), take a look at appendix B, which provides contact information for the state tourism offices in all 50 states and the District of Columbia.

International visitors, see appendix C for planning information tailored exclusively to you. Appendix D offers a handy list of contact information for the major airlines, hotel and motel chains, and rental car agencies.

We hope you'll discover your own America as you hit the road and start exploring. If you'd like more coverage of the destinations in this book, or if any of them prompt you to explore further, chances are good that we have a more dedicated, in-depth guidebook for you.

Our final advice to you here is to go somewhere great, have a marvelous time, and come home with some wonderful memories. Then start planning your next trip . . .

1 WHEN TO GO

Climate differences are dramatic across the United States. When it's bone cold in New England, the upper central states, and Alaska, it's sunny and warm in Florida, California, and Hawaii. When it's raining cats and dogs in the Pacific Northwest, it's dry as, well, a desert, in the Southwest desert. It can be a pleasant 75°F (24°C) on the beaches of Southern California in summer, yet 120°F (49°C) a few miles inland.

This works out well for travelers, because there isn't a nationwide high or low season: It's always shoulder season *somewhere*. In summer, room rates are highest on the Northeast and mid-Atlantic beaches but lowest on the sands of hot-and-humid Florida (though not in Central Florida, where rates can go sky-high in the Land of Theme Parks) and in the sticky climes of the Gulf South. Winter snows virtually close the great Rocky Mountain national parks and the major tourism centers of the northern Great Plains, but bring crowds to the nearby ski slopes. Alaska is usually well below freezing until summer, when the midnight sun smiles down on warm days and higher hotel rates greet the tourist crowds. Hawaii is warm year-round, but winter brings massive amounts of rain—and higher prices.

The Northeast and mid-Atlantic states have their summer beach season from June to Labor Day and their great fall foliage in September and October. Climate can vary wildly in these regions: One day can be warm and lovely, the next muggy and miserable. Winter storms are not an infrequent occurrence in these regions—New England is famous for its nor'easters—though some mid-Atlantic winters in the not-too-distant past have been very mild (and others have been frigid).

Summer can be brutally hot and humid in the Southeast (and is also prime hurricane season), but spring and fall last longer there, and winter is mild—with snow the exception rather than the rule. The Gulf South summers are often exceptionally hot and humid, though winters (except in the mountain areas) are generally mild, if rainy. Southern Florida's best season is from January to April, though cold snaps can turn it nippy for a few days.

The central states see harsh winters and scorching summers. Southwest weather varies from east Texas's hot, humid summers and mild winters to Arizona's dry, 110°F (43°C) summers and pleasant, dry winters. Nevada is similar, though it tends to get a bit chillier in winter. The mountains of Colorado, Utah, and the Northwest have dry, moderately hot summers and cold, snowy winters. The California coast is fine all year except early spring, when it rains; the Northwest coast is wet most of the time except July.

The long and the short of it: Late spring and early fall are the best times to visit most of the country. We note popular special events and celebrations in many of the following chapters.

2 MONEY & COSTS

ATMS

Nationwide, the easiest and best way to get cash away from home is from an ATM (automated teller machine), sometimes referred to as a "cash machine" or "cash-point." The **Cirrus** (© 800/424-7787; www.mastercard.com) and **PLUS** (© 800/843-7587; www.visa.com) networks span the country; you can find them even in remote regions. Look at the back of your bank card to see which network you're on, then call or check online for ATM locations at your destination. Be sure you know your personal identification number (PIN) and daily withdrawal limit before you depart. *Note:* Remember that many banks impose a fee every time you use a card at another bank's ATM, and that fee can be higher for international transactions (up to $5 or more) than for domestic ones (where they're rarely more than $2). In addition, the bank from which you withdraw cash may charge its own fee. To compare banks' ATM fees within the U.S., use **www.bankrate.com**. For international withdrawal fees, ask your bank.

CREDIT CARDS & DEBIT CARDS

Credit cards are the most widely used form of payment in the United States: **Visa** (Barclaycard in Britain), **MasterCard** (Eurocard in Europe, Access in Britain, Chargex in Canada), **American Express, Diners Club,** and **Discover.** They also provide a convenient record of all your expenses, and they generally offer relatively good exchange rates. You can withdraw cash advances from your credit cards at banks or ATMs, provided you know your PIN.

Visitors from outside the U.S. should inquire whether their bank assesses a 1% to 3% fee on charges incurred abroad.

It's highly recommended that you travel with at least one major credit card. You must have one to rent a car, and hotels and airlines usually require a credit card imprint as a deposit against expenses. (*Note:* Businesses in some U.S. cities may require a minimum purchase, usually around $10, before letting you use a credit card.)

ATM cards with major credit card backing, known as **"debit cards,"** are now a commonly acceptable form of payment in the same places that accept credit cards. In fact, many debit cards in the U.S. have a MasterCard or Visa logo. Debit cards draw money directly from your checking account. Some stores enable you to receive "cash back" on your debit card purchases as well. The same is true at most U.S. post offices.

TRAVELER'S CHECKS

Even with the advent of "instant money" from an ATM, many travelers still use traveler's checks, which are widely accepted in the U.S. Foreign visitors should make sure they're denominated in U.S. dollars; foreign-currency checks are often difficult to exchange.

You can buy traveler's checks at most banks. Most are offered in denominations of $20, $50, $100, $500, and sometimes $1,000. Generally, you'll pay a service charge ranging from 1% to 4%.

The most popular traveler's checks are offered by **American Express** (© 800/807-6233, or 800/221-7282 for cardholders—this number accepts collect calls, offers service in several foreign languages, and exempts Amex gold and platinum cardholders from the 1% fee); **Visa** (© 800/732-1322)—AAA members can obtain Visa checks for a $9.95 fee (for checks up to $1,500) at most AAA offices or by calling © 866/339-3378; and **MasterCard** (© 800/223-9920).

If you do choose to carry traveler's checks, keep a record of their serial numbers separate from your checks in the event that they are stolen or lost. You'll get a refund faster if you know the numbers.

3 TRAVEL INSURANCE

The cost of travel insurance varies widely, depending on the destination, the cost and length of your trip, your age and health, and the type of trip you're taking, but expect to pay between 5% and 8% of the vacation itself. You can get estimates from various providers through **InsureMyTrip. com**. Enter your trip cost and dates, your age, and other information for prices from more than a dozen companies.

TRIP-CANCELLATION INSURANCE

Trip-cancellation insurance will help retrieve your money if you have to back out of a trip or depart early, or if your travel supplier goes bankrupt. Trip cancellation traditionally covers such events as sickness, natural disasters, and State Department advisories. The latest news in trip-cancellation insurance is the availability of **expanded hurricane coverage** and the **"any-reason"** cancellation coverage—which costs more but covers cancellations made for any reason. You won't get back 100% of your prepaid trip cost, but you'll be refunded a substantial portion. **Travel-Safe** (© 888/885-7233; www.travelsafe. com) offers both types of coverage. Expedia also offers any-reason cancellation coverage for its air-hotel packages. For details, contact one of the following recommended insurers: **Access America** (© 866/807-3982; www.accessamerica. com), **Travel Guard International** (© 800/826-4919; www.travelguard.com), **Travel Insured International** (© 800/243-3174; www.travelinsured.com), and **Travelex Insurance Services** (© 888/457-4602; www.travelex-insurance.com).

MEDICAL INSURANCE

Although it's not required of travelers, health insurance is highly recommended. Most health insurance policies cover you if you get sick away from home—but verify that you're covered before you depart, particularly if you're insured by an HMO.

If you're ever hospitalized more than 150 miles from home, **MedjetAssist** (© 800/527-7478; www.medjetassistance. com) will pick you up and fly you to the hospital of your choice in a medically equipped and staffed aircraft 24 hours day, 7 days a week. Annual memberships are $225 individual, $350 family; you can also purchase short-term memberships.

LOST-LUGGAGE INSURANCE

On flights within the U.S., checked baggage is covered up to $2,800 per ticketed passenger. If you plan to check items more valuable than what's covered by the standard liability, see if your homeowner's policy covers your valuables, and consider

Travel in the Age of Bankruptcy

Airlines go bankrupt, so protect yourself by **buying your tickets with a credit card.** The Fair Credit Billing Act guarantees that you can get your money back from the credit card company if a travel supplier goes under (and if you request the refund within 60 days of the bankruptcy). **Travel insurance** can also help, but make sure it covers "carrier default" for your specific travel provider. And be aware that if a U.S. airline goes bust midtrip (not an unlikely happening these days!), federal law requires other carriers to take you to your destination (albeit on a space-available basis) for a fee of no more than $25, provided you rebook within 60 days of the cancellation.

getting baggage insurance as part of your comprehensive travel-insurance package. (Some of the companies mentioned in the section "Trip-Cancellation Insurance" above also offer baggage insurance.)

If your luggage is lost, immediately file a lost-luggage claim at the airport, detailing the luggage contents. Most airlines require that you report delayed, damaged, or lost baggage within 4 hours of arrival. The airlines are required to deliver luggage, once found, directly to your house or destination free of charge.

4 HEALTH & SAFETY

HEALTH

The United States doesn't present any unusual health hazards, provided travelers take reasonable precautions. **Lyme Disease,** carried by deer ticks, is a growing concern in the woodlands of the Northeast and mid-Atlantic, but you can minimize your risk by using insect repellent and by covering up when hiking in the deep woods. Should you get bitten by a tick or notice a bull's-eye-shaped rash after hiking or camping, consult a doctor immediately. Another insect-related illness that's become a nationwide issue is **West Nile Virus,** spread by mosquitoes. Again, use insect repellent and avoid swampy areas during the summer mosquito season, and you should encounter no problems. To keep from contracting **rabies,** avoid contact with wild animals, no matter how cute or friendly they appear. If you even think you may have been exposed, see a doctor at once.

In the Rocky Mountain states and the high elevations of the Southwest, one of the biggest health concerns is **altitude sickness.** Don't arrive in Denver planning to tackle the Rocky Mountains on the same day—the only thing that will happen is that you'll end up short of breath, exhausted, or worse. The best way to avoid this is to ease your transition into high-altitude climates, drink lots of water, and get plenty of rest; if you have breathing difficulties, your doctor may be able to prescribe medication to ease any difficulties.

If you plan on visiting some of the country's sun-soaked spots, limit the time you spend in direct sunlight and bring sunscreen with a high protection factor (at least 25). Apply it liberally—and often. This advice goes double if you're climbing at high altitudes, where the air is thinner and it's far easier to get a serious burn (even if the climate is actually cold). **Skin cancer** is one of the fastest-growing illnesses in the

United States and it doesn't take much time in the sun to do serious damage. Remember that children need more protection than adults do.

The other natural hazards for outdoor enthusiasts include **poison ivy** (learn to recognize and avoid it) and **hazardous wildlife** (never approach a wild animal or feed it). To minimize risks, never hike alone, notify someone of your planned hiking route, always carry a first-aid kit, and check in with park rangers to get the lowdown on possible hazards in the area in which you're hiking. If you're hiking in forested areas during hunting season, be sure to wear brightly colored clothing.

If you plan to head into the great outdoors, keep in mind that injuries often occur when people fail to follow instructions. Believe the experts who tell you to stay on the established ski trails and hike only in designated areas. Follow the marine charts if you're piloting your own boat. If you're rafting, wear a life jacket. If you're biking or rock climbing, be sure to use appropriate safety gear. Mountain weather can be fickle at any time of the year, so carry rain gear and pack a few warm layers. Watch out for summer thunderstorms that can leave you drenched or send bolts of lightning your way. In the Southwest, a summer storm can easily cause a flash flood, so be cautious and keep your wits about you.

When camping, always inquire if campfires are allowed in the area in which you are traveling. Some of the country's worst forest fires in recent years were started by campers who didn't follow proper safety protocols.

Tap water is safe to drink throughout the country, though you can get bottled water pretty much everywhere if you prefer it. Water in the wild should always be treated or boiled before drinking it.

The United States **Centers for Disease Control and Prevention** (© 800/311-3435; www.cdc.gov) provides up-to-date information on health hazards by region and offers tips on food safety.

If you suffer from a chronic illness, consult your doctor before your departure. For conditions like epilepsy, diabetes, or heart problems, wear a **MedicAlert identification tag** (© 888/633-4298; www.medicalert.org), which will immediately alert doctors to your condition and give them access to your records through MedicAlert's 24-hour hot line. If you have dental problems, a nationwide referral service known as **1-800-DENTIST** (© 800/336-8478; www.1800dentist.com) can give you the name of a nearby dentist or clinic.

Pack **prescription medications** in your carry-on luggage, in their original containers, with pharmacy labels—otherwise, they may not make it through airport security. Also bring along copies of your prescriptions in case you lose your pills or run out. Don't forget an extra pair of contact lenses or prescription glasses.

SAFETY

Although tourist areas are generally safe, U.S. urban areas have their fair share of crime. You should always stay alert; this is particularly true of large cities. If you're in doubt about which neighborhoods are safe, don't hesitate to inquire at the hotel's front desk or at the local tourist office.

Avoid deserted areas, especially at night, and don't go into public parks after dark unless there's a concert or similar occasion that will attract a crowd.

Avoid carrying valuables with you on the street, and keep expensive cameras or electronic equipment bagged up or covered when not in use. If you're using a map, try to consult it inconspicuously—or better yet, study it before you leave your room. Hold on to your pocketbook, and place your billfold in an inside pocket. In theaters, restaurants, and other public places, keep your possessions in sight.

Always lock your room door—don't assume that once you're inside the hotel you are automatically safe and no longer need to be aware of your surroundings. Hotels are open to the public, and in a large hotel, security may not be able to screen everyone who enters.

DRIVING SAFETY Driving safety is important, too, and carjacking is not unprecedented. Question your rental agency about personal safety, and ask for a traveler-safety brochure when you pick up your car. Obtain written directions—or a map with the route clearly marked—from the agency showing how to get to your destination. And, if possible, arrive and depart during daylight hours.

If you drive off a highway and end up in a dodgy-looking neighborhood, leave the area as quickly as possible. If you have an accident, even on the highway, stay in your car with the doors locked until you assess the situation or until the police arrive. If you're bumped from behind on the street or are involved in a minor accident with no injuries, and the situation appears to be suspicious, motion to the other driver to follow you. Never get out of your car in such situations. Go directly to the nearest police precinct, well-lit service station, or 24-hour store. Keep your cellphone with you, or if you find you don't have coverage with your own phone, consider buying a cheap pay-as-you-go phone, or rent one. One recommended wireless rental company is **InTouch USA** (© **800/872-7626;** www.intouchusa.com).

Park in well-lit and well-traveled areas whenever possible. Keep your car doors locked, whether the vehicle is attended or unattended. Never leave any packages or valuables in sight. If someone attempts to rob you or steal your car, don't try to resist the thief/carjacker. Report the incident to the police department immediately by calling © **911.**

5 SPECIALIZED TRAVEL RESOURCES

TRAVELERS WITH DISABILITIES

Most disabilities shouldn't stop anyone from traveling in the U.S. Thanks to provisions in the Americans with Disabilities Act, most public places are required to comply with disability-friendly regulations. Almost all public establishments (including hotels, restaurants, and museums, but not including certain National Historic Landmarks) and at least some modes of public transportation provide accessible entrances and other facilities for those with disabilities.

The **America the Beautiful—National Park and Federal Recreational Lands Pass—Access Pass** (formerly the **Golden Access Passport**) gives visually impaired or permanently disabled persons (regardless of age) free lifetime entrance to federal recreation sites administered by the National Park Service, including the Fish and Wildlife Service, the Forest Service, the Bureau of Land Management, and the Bureau of Reclamation. This may include national parks, monuments, historic sites, recreation areas, and national wildlife refuges.

The America the Beautiful Access Pass can be obtained only in person at any NPS facility that charges an entrance fee. You need to show proof of a medically determined disability. Besides free entry, the pass offers a 50% discount on some federal-use fees charged for such facilities as camping, swimming, parking, boat launching, and tours. For more information, go to www.nps.gov/fees_passes.htm or call the United States Geological Survey (USGS), which issues the passes, at © **888/ 275-8747.**

For more on organizations that offer resources to travelers with disabilities, go to **www.frommers.com/planning**.

GAY & LESBIAN TRAVELERS

The **International Gay and Lesbian Travel Association (IGLTA)** (© **800/448-8550** or 954/776-2626; www.iglta.org) is the trade association for the gay and lesbian travel industry, and offers an online directory of gay- and lesbian-friendly travel businesses; go to their website and click on "Members."

Many agencies offer tours and travel itineraries specifically for gay and lesbian travelers. Among them are **Above and Beyond Tours** (© **800/397-2681**; www.abovebeyondtours.com), **Now, Voyager** (© **800/255-6951**; www.nowvoyager.com), and **Olivia Cruises & Resorts** (© **800/631-6277**; www.olivia.com).

Gay.com Travel (© **800/929-2268** or 415/644-8044; www.gay.com/travel or www.outandabout.com) is an excellent online successor to the popular *Out & About* print magazine. It provides regularly updated information about gay-owned, gay-oriented, and gay-friendly lodging, dining, sightseeing, nightlife, and shopping establishments in every important destination worldwide.

The following travel guides are available at many bookstores, or you can order them from any online bookseller: *Spartacus International Gay Guide* (Bruno Gmünder Verlag; www.spartacusworld.com/gayguide) and the *Damron* guides (www.damron.com), with separate, annual books for gay men and lesbians.

SENIOR TRAVEL

Mention the fact that you're a senior when you make your travel reservations. Many hotels offer discounts for seniors. In most cities, people over the age of 60 qualify for reduced admission to theaters, museums, and other attractions, as well as discounted fares on public transportation.

Members of **AARP** (formerly known as the American Association of Retired Persons), 601 E St. NW, Washington, DC 20049 (© **888/687-2277**; www.aarp.org), get discounts on hotels, airfares, and car rentals. AARP offers members a wide range of benefits, including *AARP The Magazine* and a monthly newsletter. Anyone can join at the age of 50.

The U.S. National Park Service offers an **America the Beautiful—National Park and Federal Recreational Lands Pass—Senior Pass** (formerly the **Golden Age Passport**), which gives seniors 62 years or older lifetime entrance to all properties administered by the National Park Service—national parks, monuments, historic sites, recreation areas, and national

---

On Your Own or with a Furry Friend

Prefer to do your traveling alone? So long as you avoid all-inclusive resorts and vacation packages (which base their prices on double occupancy), you likely won't face the dreaded "single supplement," a penalty added to the base price of a room or package. For more information, pick up Eleanor Berman's latest edition of *Traveling Solo: Advice and Ideas for More Than 250 Great Vacations* (Globe Pequot, 2008), a guide with advice on traveling alone, either solo or as part of a group tour.

If, like John Steinbeck, you want to take your dog (or cat, or whatever) with you for companionship on your travels, many hotels across the U.S. (for example, all Motel 6 properties) will be happy to roll out the welcome mat for your pet. For travel tips and advice on traveling with Fido or Fluffy, head online to **www.petswelcome.com**, **www.pettravel.com**, and **www.travelpets.com**.

Frommers.com: The Complete Travel Resource

Planning a trip or just returned? Head to **Frommers.com,** voted Best Travel Site by *PC Magazine.* We think you'll find our site indispensable before, during, and after your travels—with expert advice and tips; independent reviews of hotels, restaurants, attractions, and preferred shopping and nightlife venues; vacation giveaways; and an online booking tool. We publish the complete contents of over 135 travel guides in our **Destinations** section, covering over 4,000 places worldwide. Each weekday, we publish original articles that report on **Deals and News** via our free **Frommers.com Newsletters.** What's more, **Arthur Frommer** himself blogs 5 days a week, with cutting opinions about the state of travel in the modern world. We're betting you'll find our **Events** listings an invaluable resource; it's an up-to-the-minute roster of what's happening in cities everywhere—including concerts, festivals, lectures, and more. We've also added weekly **podcasts, interactive maps,** and hundreds of new images across the site. Finally, don't forget to visit our **Message Boards,** where you can join in conversations with thousands of fellow Frommer's travelers and post your trip report once you return.

wildlife refuges—for a one-time processing fee of $10. The pass must be purchased in person at any NPS facility that charges an entrance fee. Besides free entry, the American the Beautiful Senior Pass offers a 50% discount on some federal-use fees charged for such facilities as camping, swimming, parking, boat launching, and tours. For more information, go to www. nps.gov/fees_passes.htm or call the United States Geological Survey (USGS), which issues the passes, at 🕿 **888/275-8747.**

For more information and resources on travel for seniors, see www.frommers.com/planning.

FAMILY TRAVEL

To locate accommodations, restaurants, and attractions that are particularly kid friendly, refer to the "Kids" icon throughout this guide.

Recommended family travel websites include **Family Travel Forum** (www.familytravelforum.com), a comprehensive site that offers customized trip planning; **Family Travel Network** (www.familytravel network.com), an award-winning site that offers travel features, deals, and tips; **Traveling Internationally with Your Kids** (www.travelwithyourkids.com), a comprehensive site offering sound advice for long-distance and international travel with children; and **Family Travel Files** (www.thefamilytravelfiles.com), which offers an online magazine and a directory of off-the-beaten-path tours and tour operators for families.

Frommer's and the Unofficial Guides both publish a "With Kids" series that features some of the major tourist destinations in the United States.

WOMEN TRAVELERS

More and more hotels in the United States are ratcheting up security measures for women traveling alone on business or for pleasure.

Check out the award-winning website **Journeywoman** (www.journeywoman.com), a "real life" women's travel-information network where you can sign up for a free e-mail newsletter and get advice on everything from etiquette and dress to safety; or the travel guide *Safety and Security for Women Who Travel,* by Sheila Swan and Peter Laufer (Travelers' Tales, Inc.), offering common-sense tips on safe travel.

MULTICULTURAL TRAVELERS

Soul of America (www.soulofamerica. com) is a comprehensive website, with travel tips, event and family-reunion postings, and sections on historically black beach resorts and active vacations.

Agencies and organizations that provide resources for black travelers include **Rodgers Travel** (© 800/825-1775; www. rodgerstravel.com) and the **African American Association of Innkeepers International** (© 877/422-5777; www.african americaninns.com). For more information, check out the following collections and guides: *Go Girl: The Black Woman's Guide to Travel & Adventure* (Eighth Mountain Press; **www.ugogurl.com**), a compilation of travel essays by writers including Jill Nelson and Audre Lorde; and *Pathfinders Magazine* (© 877/977-**PATH** [977-7284]; www.pathfinderstravel. com), which includes articles on everything from Rio de Janeiro to Ghana, as well as information on upcoming ski, diving, golf, and tennis trips.

6 SUSTAINABLE TOURISM

Sustainable tourism is conscientious travel. It means being careful with the environments you explore and respecting the communities you visit. Two overlapping components of sustainable travel are **eco-tourism** and **ethical tourism.** The **International Ecotourism Society** (TIES) defines eco-tourism as responsible travel to natural areas that conserves the environment and improves the well-being of local people. TIES suggests that eco-tourists follow these principles:

- Minimize environmental impact.
- Build environmental and cultural awareness and respect.
- Provide positive experiences for both visitors and hosts.
- Provide direct financial benefits for conservation and for local people.
- Raise sensitivity to host countries' political, environmental, and social climates.
- Support international human rights and labor agreements.

You can find some eco-friendly travel tips and statistics, as well as touring companies and associations—listed by destination under "Travel Choice"—at the **TIES** website, www.ecotourism.org. Also check out **Ecotravel.com,** which lets you search for sustainable touring companies in several categories (water-based, land-based, spiritually oriented, and so on).

While much of the focus of eco-tourism is about reducing impacts on the natural environment, ethical tourism concentrates on ways to preserve and enhance local economies and communities, regardless of location. You can embrace ethical tourism by staying at a locally owned hotel or shopping at a store that employs local workers and sells locally produced goods.

Sustainable Travel International (www. sustainabletravelinternational.org) promotes ethical tourism practices and manages an extensive directory of sustainable properties and tour operators around the world.

CELLPHONES

If you're not from the U.S., you'll be appalled at the poor reach of the **GSM (Global System for Mobile Communications) wireless network,** which is used by much of the rest of the world. Your phone will probably work in most major U.S. cities; it definitely won't work in many rural areas. To see where GSM phones work in the U.S., check out **www.t-mobile. com/coverage**. And you may or may not be able to send SMS (text messaging) home.

If you need to stay in touch at a destination where you know your phone won't work, **rent** a phone that does from **InTouch USA** (**©** 800/872-7626; www. intouchglobal.com) or a rental car location, but beware that you'll pay $1 a minute or more for airtime. Also consider buying a cheap pay-as-you-go phone in the city/region where you are staying.

If you're venturing deep into national parks, you may want to consider renting a **satellite phone ("satphone").** It's different from a cellphone, in that it connects to satellites rather than ground-based towers. Unfortunately, you'll pay at least $2 per minute to use the phone, and it works only where you can see the horizon (that is, usually not indoors). In North America, you can rent Iridium satellite phones from **RoadPost** (www.roadpost.com; **©** 888/ 290-1606 or 905/272-5665). InTouch USA (see above) offers a wider range of satphones but at higher rates.

VOICE-OVER INTERNET PROTOCOL (VOIP)

If you have Web access while traveling, consider a broadband-based telephone service (in technical terms, **Voice-over Internet protocol,** or **VoIP**) such as Skype (www.skype.com) or Vonage (www.vonage. com), which allow you to make free international calls from your laptop or in a cybercafe. Neither service requires the people you're calling to also have that service (though there are fees if they do not). Check the websites for details.

Online Traveler's Toolbox

Veteran travelers usually carry some essential items to make their trips easier. Following is a selection of handy online tools to bookmark and use.

- **Airplane Food** (www.airlinemeals.net)
- **Airplane Seating** (www.seatguru.com and www.airlinequality.com)
- **Foreign Languages for Travelers** (www.travlang.com)
- **Maps** (www.mapquest.com)
- **Subway Navigator** (www.subwaynavigator.com)
- **Time and Date** (www.timeanddate.com)
- **Travel Warnings** (http://travel.state.gov, www.fco.gov.uk/travel, www. voyage.gc.ca, www.smartraveller.gov.au)
- **Universal Currency Converter** (www.oanda.com)
- **Weather** (www.intellicast.com and www.weather.com)

INTERNET & E-MAIL
With Your Own Computer

To find public Wi-Fi hotspots at your destination, go to **www.jiwire.com**; its Hotspot Finder holds the world's largest directory of public wireless hotspots.

Aside from cybercafes, most **public libraries** in the United States offer Internet access free or for a small charge.

Most business-class hotels in the U.S. offer Wi-Fi or broadband Internet access (but check to see what the daily rate is).

Without Your Own Computer

Most major airports have **Internet kiosks** that provide basic Web access for a per-minute fee that's usually higher than cybercafe prices. Check out copy shops like **Kinko's** (FedEx Kinkos), which offers computer stations with fully loaded software (as well as Wi-Fi).

You'll also find cybercafes in most big cities and around university campuses; many hotels offer Internet access (sometimes for a fee) at terminals in their lobbies or business centers.

8 GETTING AROUND THE UNITED STATES

BY PLANE

For long-distance trips, the most efficient way to get around the United States is by plane, even in these days of increased security and poor airline service. See appendix D at the end of this book for a list of airlines, with their toll-free numbers and websites.

Getting Through the Airport

- Arrive at the airport 1 hour before a domestic flight and 2 hours before an international flight; if you show up late, tell an airline employee and he or she will probably whisk you to the front of the line.
- Beat the ticket-counter lines by using airport electronic kiosks or check in online, and print out your boarding passes at home before you leave for the airport. Curbside check-in is also a good way to avoid lines.
- Bring a current, government-issued photo ID such as a driver's license or passport. Children 17 and under do not need government-issued photo IDs for flights within the U.S., but they do for international flights.
- Speed up security by removing your jacket and shoes before you're screened.

Remember that laptop computers go in their own bin. In addition, remove metal objects such as big belt buckles. If you've got an internal pin or a plate, ask your doctor to give you a note of verification that you can show screeners.

- Use a TSA-approved lock for your checked luggage. Look for Travel Sentry–certified locks at luggage or travel shops and Brookstone stores (or online at **www.brookstone.com**).

BY CAR

Unless you plan to spend the bulk of your vacation in a city where walking is the best way to get around (read: New York City or New Orleans), the most cost-effective way to travel is by car. Even with skyrocketing gas prices in 2008, U.S. residents still pay less per gallon of gas than most of the rest of the world.

The interstate highway system connects cities and towns all over the country; in addition to these high-speed, limited-access roadways, there's an extensive network of federal, state, and local highways and roads. *Note:* To help you plan your driving routes, check out the map titled "The USA—Major Interstate Routes" at the beginning of this chapter.

Coping with Jet Lag

Jet lag is a pitfall of traveling across time zones. If you're flying north-south and you feel sluggish when you touch down, your symptoms will be the result of dehydration and the general stress of air travel. When you travel east-west or vice versa, your body becomes confused about what time it is, and everything from your digestive system to your brain is knocked for a loop. Traveling east is more difficult on your internal clock than traveling west because most people's bodies are more inclined to stay up late than to fall asleep early.

Here are some tips for combating jet lag:

- **Reset your watch** to your destination time before you board the plane.
- **Drink lots of water** before, during, and after your flight. Avoid alcohol.
- **Exercise and sleep well** for a few days before your trip.
- If you have trouble sleeping on planes, **fly eastward on morning flights.**
- **Daylight** is the key to resetting your body clock. At the website for **Outside In** (www.bodyclock.com), you can get a customized plan of when to seek and avoid light.

If you plan on driving your own car over a long distance, then automobile-association membership is recommended. **AAA,** the **American Automobile Association** (© **800/222-4357;** www.aaa.com), is the country's largest auto club and supplies its members with maps, insurance, and, most important, emergency road service. The cost of joining is $58 for a single member ($48, plus a $10 enrollment fee).

If your destination is too far from home to drive but will require a car once you arrive, see appendix D at the end of this book for a list of car-rental agencies, with their toll-free numbers and websites.

If you're visiting from abroad and plan to rent a car in the United States, keep in mind that foreign driver's licenses are usually recognized in the U.S., but you should get an international one if your home license is not in English.

Check out **Breezenet.com,** which offers domestic car-rental discounts with some of the most competitive rates around. Also worth visiting are Orbitz, Hotwire.com, Travelocity.com, and Priceline, all of which offer competitive online car-rental rates.

These national companies have offices at most airports and in many cities. You must have a valid credit card to rent a vehicle. Most also require a minimum age, ranging from 19 to 25 (some companies that will rent to the under-25 crowd will nevertheless assess underage driving fees of up to $25 per day extra), and some also set maximum ages. Others deny cars to anyone with a bad driving record. Ask about rental requirements and restrictions when you book, to avoid problems later.

Car-rental rates vary even more than airfares. The price you pay depends on the size of the car, where and when you pick it up and drop it off, the length of the rental period, where and how far you drive it, whether you purchase insurance, and a host of other factors. A few key questions could save you hundreds of dollars; you should comparison-shop and be persistent because reservations agents don't often volunteer money-saving strategies.

- Is a weekly rate cheaper than the daily rate? If you need to keep the car for 4 days, it may be cheaper to keep it for 5, even if you don't need it that long.

- Does the agency assess a drop-off charge if you do not return the car to the same location where you picked it up? Is it cheaper to pick up the car at the airport instead of a downtown location?
- How much tax will be added to the rental bill? Local tax? State use tax? Some states' rental-car taxes can top 25% of the base rate, so be sure you know exactly how much you'll be paying in total before making a decision. Recently, many online booking sites have begun posting the total rental price of a car instead of just the base rates.
- What is the cost of adding an additional driver's name to the contract?

Before you drive off in a rental car, be sure you're insured. Hasty assumptions about your personal auto insurance or a rental agency's additional coverage could end up costing you tens of thousands of dollars—even if you're involved in an accident that was clearly the fault of another driver.

If you already hold a private auto insurance policy, you are most likely covered for loss of or damage to a rental car, and liability in case of injury to any other party involved in an accident. Be sure to ask whether your policy extends to all persons who will be driving the rental car, how much liability is covered in case an outside party is injured in an accident, and whether the type of vehicle you are renting is included under your contract.

The basic insurance coverage offered by most car-rental companies, known as the **Loss/Damage Waiver (LDW)** or **Collision Damage Waiver (CDW),** can cost as much as $20 per day. It usually covers the full value of the vehicle with no deductible if an outside party causes an accident or other damage to the rental car. In many states, you will probably be covered in case of theft as well (ask before making any assumptions). **Liability coverage** varies according to the company policy and state law, but the minimum is usually at least

$15,000. If you are at fault in an accident, however, you will be covered for the full replacement value of the car but not for liability. Some states allow you to buy additional liability coverage for such cases. Most rental companies require a police report to process any claims you file, but your private insurer is not notified of the accident.

Most major credit cards offer some degree of coverage as well—if they were used to pay for the rental. Terms vary widely, so be sure to call your credit card company directly before you rent.

If you're uninsured, your credit card provides primary coverage as long as you decline the rental agency's insurance. That means the credit card will cover damage or theft of a rental car for the full cost of the vehicle. (In a few states, however, theft is not covered; ask specifically about state law where you will be renting and driving.) If you already have insurance, your credit card will provide secondary coverage—which basically covers your deductible.

Credit cards will not cover liability, the cost of injury to an outside party, and/or damage to an outside party's vehicle. If you do not hold an insurance policy, you may seriously want to consider purchasing additional liability insurance from your rental company, even if you decline collision coverage. Be sure to check the terms, however: Some rental agencies cover liability only if the renter is not at fault; even then, the rental company's obligation varies from state to state.

BY TRAIN

Long-distance trains in the United States are operated by **Amtrak** (© 800/USA-RAIL [872-7245]; www.amtrak.com), the national rail passenger corporation. Be aware, however, that with a few notable exceptions (for instance, the Northeast Corridor line btw. Boston and Washington, D.C.), intercity service is not particularly fabulous. An (expensive) exception is the high-speed **Acela Express** train that runs from Boston to Washington. Delays

Other Transportation Options

Traveling the U.S. in a **recreational vehicle (RV)** is an increasingly popular way of seeing the country. One good RV-rental agency with locations all over the country is **Cruise America** (www.cruiseamerica.com). It would take dozens of pages to thoroughly discuss the ins and outs of RV travel, so if you're thinking of hitting the road this way, check out *Frommer's Exploring America by RV* and *RV Vacations For Dummies.*

If you're more of the *Easy Rider* sort and have dreams of cruising the country on a **motorcycle,** know that you'll need a special motorcycle license and that almost every state also requires that riders wear a helmet. The best outfit for renting a bike nationwide is **EagleRider** (© 888/900-9901; www.eaglerider. com).

are common; routes are limited and often infrequently served. That said, if time isn't an issue, train travel can be a relaxing and scenic method of traveling. If you choose to travel by train, do it for the experience, not for the convenience.

Amtrak offers a **USA Rail Pass,** available for travel within three different regions, or the entire United States. Depending on the region, they offer 15-day and 30-day passes for unlimited travel. Travel must begin within 180 days of the date the pass is issued. They also offer a California and a Florida Rail Pass, and various regional tour packages.

You can also ride the "Auto Train," which is just what it sounds like: You drive your own car onboard a train in Sanford, Virginia, spend the trip in a standard train car, then drive off in Central Florida.

Amtrak also offers rail/fly packages that allow travelers to fly to their destination in one direction and to take the train in another.

BY BUS

Bus travel is often the most economical form of public transit for short hops between U.S. cities, but it can also be slow and uncomfortable—certainly not an option for everyone (particularly when Amtrak, which is far more luxurious, offers similar rates). **Greyhound/Trailways** (© 800/231-2222; www.greyhound.com), the sole nationwide bus line, offers several pass and discount options geared to domestic travelers. Their **Discovery Pass** (www.discoverypass.com) covers travel on all Greyhound routes in the U.S. and some in Canada.

9 SPECIAL-INTEREST VACATION PLANNER

Here's a sampling of companies that offer escorted adventures and tours, and some suggestions on where to go to enjoy your favorite activities. For information on the individual states mentioned below, see the appropriate destination chapter in the book.

ADVENTURE-TRAVEL COMPANIES

Scores of "soft" and "hard" adventure-travel companies have sprung up in recent years. Most travel agents have catalogs that list upcoming trips. More than 500 different tour operators are represented in the

Specialty Travel Index Online at **www. specialtytravel.com**. Another good source of up-to-date information is monthly *Outside* magazine, available in print and frequently updated online at **http://outsidemag.com**.

Mountain Travel—Sobek (© 888/687-6235 or 510/594-6000; www.mtsobek. com) is perhaps the granddaddy of adventure-travel companies, guiding its own trips and acting as an agent for other outfitters. It began with river rafting, which is still its strong suit. **Backroads** (© 800/462-2848 or 510/527-1555; www.backroads.com) originally sold bicycle tours but now has walking, hiking, cross-country skiing, trail running, and other trips. It's especially noteworthy for having options catering to adults traveling solo. **Bicycle Adventures** (© 800/443-6060 or 360/786-0989; www.bicycleadventures.com) offers biking, hiking, and cross-country skiing, as well as other multisport options in the West Coast states, the Rocky Mountain states, and Hawaii. Tours are tailored to ability levels; some are designed for families, others for solo travelers. The venerable **Sierra Club** (© 415/977-5522; www.sierraclub.com) also offers a number of trips each year.

These and other operators plan their adventures at least a year ahead of time, so call or e-mail them for schedules and catalogs as far in advance as possible.

WHERE SHOULD I GO FOR . . . ?

BEACHES Miami (chapter 5) and Southern California (chapter 12) have the best beaches in the continental United States, though they all pale in comparison to the spectacular sands on all the islands of Hawaii (chapter 14).

The entire **Atlantic** is lined with sand where you can sun and swim in the summer, and you'll find no shortage of resorts and beach motels. If you try hard enough, you can even find a little undeveloped solitude at the **Cape Cod National Seashore**

near Provincetown, Massachusetts (p. 57), and at **Cape Hatteras National Seashore** on North Carolina's Outer Banks (p. 285).

The **Maine coast** (chapter 2) is gorgeous but too cold for actual swimming. The same goes for the lovely, dramatic scenery in **Northern California** (chapter 12) and along the **Oregon coast** (chapter 13).

BIKING Biking is a great way to see the country up close and personal. Except for the interstate highways, you can bike on most roads in the United States. Among the best are the **Maine coast, Cape Cod,** and the hills of **New England**—especially Vermont (chapter 2); Virginia's rolling **Shenandoah Valley** (chapter 4); the combined **Skyline Drive** and **Blue Ridge Parkway** in Virginia and North Carolina (chapter 4); the **Outer Banks** of North Carolina (chapter 4); the dramatic **California coast** (chapter 12); the **Oregon coast** (chapter 13); the **San Juan Islands** near Seattle (p. 949); and the road circling the **Big Island** of Hawaii (p. 1015). Exceptional mountain biking is also available in most of **West Virginia's state parks** (p. 1033). Biking is an excellent way to see some national parks, especially **Shenandoah** (p. 232), **Yosemite** (p. 873), **Yellowstone** (p. 582), **Grand Tetons** (p. 579), and **Glacier** (p. 563).

An ongoing nationwide program is converting some 50,000 miles of abandoned railroad beds into biking-and-walking paths. For a list, contact the **Rails-to-Trails Conservancy,** 1100 17th St. NW, 10th Floor, Washington, DC 20005 (© 202/331-9696; www.railtrails. org), founded in 1986.

Several companies and organizations offer escorted bike excursions, including **Backroads** and **Bicycle Adventures** (see "Adventure-Travel Companies," above). **American Youth Hostels** (© 301/495-1240; www.hiusa.org) has trips for its members. **CrossRoads Cycling Adventures** (© 800/971-2453; www.crossroads cycling.com) offers nationwide excursions, including California to Massachusetts and Maine to Florida.

BIRDING The entire East Coast is on the Atlantic Flyway for migrating water birds and waterfowl. You can see them all the way from the Maine coast (chapter 2), particularly **Monhegan and Machias islands,** to the **Wellfleet Wildlife Sanctuary** on Cape Cod, and on south to Maryland's eastern shore, where **Chincoteague National Wildlife Refuge** (📞 757/336-6122; www.fws.gov/northeast/chinco), on the Maryland-Virginia line, is the best bet.

Shorebirds also migrate along the Pacific side of the country, with good viewing anywhere along the Washington and Oregon coasts, but especially in **Malheur National Wildlife Refuge** in southeastern Oregon.

Once endangered, the **bald eagle** is now widespread across the country. Dozens make their winter home at **Lake Cachuma** near Santa Barbara in California. In January they flock to the **Skagit River** north of Seattle to feast on salmon, and you can even spot them while riding a Washington State ferry through the **San Juan Islands** (p. 949). In September, look for them along **Alaska's southeastern coast** (chapter 14). Alaska also has many other birds not found in the lower 48 states.

In the Arizona (chapter 11) desert, **Ramsey Canyon Preserve** is internationally known as home to 14 species of **hummingbird,** more than anywhere else in the United States. **San Pedro Riparian National Conservation Area** is another good spot in Arizona, with more than 300 species.

For tropical species, head to **Florida** (chapter 5), especially to **Everglades National Park** (p. 390).

Hawaii's (chapter 14) tropical birds are found nowhere else on earth, including the rare **o'o,** whose yellow feathers Hawaiians once plucked to make royal capes. Large colonies of seabirds nest at **Kilauea**

National Wildlife Preserve and along the **Na Pali Coast** on Kauai, and **Molokai's Kamakou Preserve** is home to the Molokai thrust and Molokai creeper, found nowhere else.

For information about escorted bird-watching trips, contact **Field Guides** (📞 800/728-4953 or 512/263-4795; www.fieldguides.com) or **Victor Emanual Nature Tours** (📞 800/328-8368 or 512/328-5221; www.ventbird.com). The **National Audubon Society** (📞 212/979-3000; www.audubon.org) runs superb bird-watching programs for both aspiring and experienced naturalists.

CANOEING & KAYAKING There's a wide variety of rivers, streams, lakes, and sounds for canoeing and kayaking enthusiasts. In fact, most cities with rivers running through them now have a contingent of outfitters.

Out in the hinterlands, some of the best paddling takes place along **Maine's coast** (chapter 2) or through its 92-mile **Allagash Wilderness Waterway,** a series of remote rivers, lakes, and ponds.

In summer, it's hot and humid in **Florida's Everglades National Park** (p. 390), but winter offers great opportunities along a maze of well-marked trails. You can rent canoes at the main park center at **Flamingo.**

The peaceful lakes of Minnesota's **Boundary Waters Canoe Area** north of Minneapolis are another good choice.

Puget Sound's **San Juan Islands** (p. 949), near Seattle, are enchanting when seen by canoe or kayak. **San Juan Kayak Expeditions** (📞 360/378-4436; www.sanjuankayak.com) and **Shearwater Adventures** (📞 360/376-4699; www.shearwaterkayaks.com) both have multi-day trips to the islands, and biologists and naturalists lead educational expeditions sponsored by the nonprofit **Sea Quest Expeditions** (📞 888/549-4253 or 360/378-5767; www.sea-quest-kayak.com).

For a truly unique kayaking experience, you can paddle among the humpback whales taking their winter break in Hawaii. Contact **South Pacific Kayaks** (© **800/776-2326** or 808/661-8400; www.south pacifickayaks.com).

For general information, contact the **American Canoe Association,** 7432 Alban Station Blvd., Ste. B226, Springfield, VA 22150 (© **703/451-0141;** www. acanet.org), the nation's largest organization, for lists of trips and local clubs.

CIVIL WAR BATTLEFIELDS The Civil War started in 1861 at **Fort Sumter** in Charleston, South Carolina (p. 271). Battles raged all over the South during the next 4 years. Gen. Ulysses S. Grant took **Vicksburg,** Mississippi (p. 431), after a long siege, and Gen. William Tecumseh Sherman burned **Atlanta** (p. 239), but the most famous fighting took place within 100 miles of **Washington, D.C.** (p. 191). This area has more national battlefield parks than any other part of the country.

It won't be in chronological order, but when you are in Virginia, you can tour them by starting at the battles of **Fredericksburg, Chancellorsville,** and the **Wilderness** in and near Fredericksburg, Virginia. Proceed north to the two **Battles of Manassas** (or Bull Run) southwest of Washington, then north across the Potomac River to the **Battle of Antietam** at Sharpsburg, Maryland. From there, go northwest through Harpers Ferry, West Virginia, to the **Battle of Gettysburg** (p. 174), the turning point of the war, in south-central Pennsylvania. Gettysburg is perhaps the most moving and well preserved of the battlegrounds. You'll also pass several battlefields driving through the **Shenandoah Valley** (chapter 4).

FALL FOLIAGE Fall in **New England** (chapter 2) is one of the great natural spectacles on earth, with rolling hills blanketed in brilliant reds and stunning oranges. The colors start to peak in mid-September in the **Green and White** mountains of Vermont and New Hampshire, and then bleed down into the **Berkshires** of Massachusetts. The colors move progressively south down the East Coast, through New York's **Hudson River Valley** (p. 130), into October, when bumper-to-bumper traffic jams **Virginia's Skyline Drive** through Shenandoah National Park (p. 232). The precise dates for prime viewing vary from year to year, depending on temperatures and rainfall, but the local newspapers and TV stations closely track the coloration.

Fall is also quite spectacular in the Rockies, especially in **Colorado** (chapter 10), in West Virginia's mountains (p. 1033), and in the Wisconsin Dells (p. 519).

Tauck World Discovery (© **800/788-7885;** www.tauck.com), **Maupintour** (© **800/255-4266** or 913/843-1211; www.maupintour.com), and several other escorted tour operators have foliage tours; see your travel agent.

FISHING The United States can boast of record-setting catches and has every type of fishing invented—from surf-casting off **Cape Cod** or **Cape Hatteras** to flicking a fly in **Maine** or **Montana.**

Fly-fishing camps are as prolific as fish in the Maine woods. **Grant's Kennebago Camps** in Oquossoc has 18 of them, built on Kennebago Lake in 1905. Over in Vermont, **Orvis** (© **800/548-9548;** www. orvis.com) runs one of the top fly-fishing schools in the country. See chapter 2 for more on New England fishing.

The nation's other great fly-fishing area is in the Montana and Wyoming mountains near **Yellowstone National Park** (p. 582), made famous by *A River Runs Through It.* The top river out here is Montana's **Madison,** with headquarters starting in the park, but cutthroat trout make the **Snake River** over in Wyoming almost as good—and the resort of **Jackson Hole** offers luxury relief within casting distance (see chapter 8).

Most ports along the nation's seaboards have deep-sea charter-fishing fleets and less expensive party boats (all you have to do is show up for the latter). The best tropical strikes are in the **Florida Keys** (p. 392) and off the **Kona coast** of the **Big Island** in Hawaii (p. 1015). **Alaska** (chapter 14) is famous for summertime salmon and halibut fishing, with the biggest in the **Kenai River** and on **Kodiak Island,** which has the state's best roadside salmon fishing.

FLOWERS & GARDENS Flower lovers have many opportunities to stop and smell the roses, especially in **Portland, Oregon** (p. 962), which calls itself the City of Roses. Many other cities have gardens of note, including **Atlanta, Boston** (p. 28), **Denver** (p. 663), **New Orleans** (p. 437), **New York** (p. 104), **Seattle** (p. 929), and **Tucson** (p. 764). **Longwood Gardens** in the **Brandywine Valley** (p. 172) is noted for its greenhouses as well as its grounds. The **Biltmore Estate** in Asheville, North Carolina (p. 294), has a walled English garden on its 25 acres. **Magnolia Plantation** near Charleston, South Carolina (p. 272), is famed for its azaleas, camellias, and 60-acre cypress swamp. If you like gardens from the Elizabethan era, head for **Colonial Williamsburg,** Virginia (p. 220).

It's also a spectacular sight to see the commercial flower farms of **Washington State's Skagit Valley.** In the spring, tulips and daffodils carpet the farmlands surrounding the town of **La Conner** with great swaths of red, yellow, and white. In March and April, the town hosts an annual **Tulip Festival** (www.tulipfestival. org); the countryside erupts with color in a display that matches the legendary flower fields of the Netherlands. See chapter 13 for more on Washington State.

You may also be interested in seeing wildflowers in bloom out West. Springtime brings glorious color to the **Texas Hill Country** (p. 657), just north of San Antonio. The **deserts of New Mexico,** **Arizona, and Southern California** (chapters 11 and 12) are also magical in spring. Two of California's prettiest viewing areas are **Anza-Borrego Desert State Park,** near San Diego, and the **Antelope Valley Poppy Reserve,** in the high desert near L.A. There are also beautiful spring blooms in the Washington Cascades, especially in **Olympic National Park** (p. 953) and throughout the **Rocky Mountains** (chapter 10).

A few travel companies have escorted tours of gardens, others include them on their general sightseeing excursions, and still others organize trips for local botanical gardens or gardening and horticultural groups. Check with those in your hometown for upcoming trips, or try **Maupintour** (© **800/255-4266** or 913/843-1211; www.maupintour.com).

GOLF & TENNIS You can play golf and tennis almost anywhere in the country, although the southern tier of states, where the outdoor seasons are longest, offers the best opportunities. In the Southeast, top golfing destinations are **Pinehurst,** North Carolina; **Hilton Head Island** and **Myrtle Beach,** South Carolina (chapter 4); and almost anywhere in **Florida** (chapter 5). You can get information about most Florida courses, including current greens fees, and reserve tee times through **Tee Times USA** (© **888/465-3356** or 904/439-0001; www.teetimesusa.com). This company also publishes a vacation guide that includes stay-and-play golf packages.

In the Southwest, the twin desert cities of **Phoenix** and **Scottsdale,** Arizona (p. 751), have some of the country's most luxurious golf resorts. The same can be said of **Palm Springs** and the **Monterey coast** in California (chapter 12).

And **Hawaii** (chapter 14) has many famous and unique courses.

Most of the nation's top golf resorts also have excellent **tennis** facilities. For the top 50 tennis resorts, see *Tennis* magazine's rankings each November. Good choices include the **Ritz-Carlton Key Biscayne** in Key Biscayne, Florida (p. 384), the **Saddlebrook Resort—Tampa** (p. 410), and **Sea Pines Plantation** on Hilton Head, South Carolina (p. 263).

MOUNTAIN BIKING If mountain bikes are your thing, you'll find plenty of dirt roads and backcountry pathways to explore. Many national parks and forests have a good selection of trails—**Acadia National Park**'s (p. 99) carriage roads, for example, are unique. You can also take guided tours through 60 miles of connected trails in the **Sebago Lake area,** near the New Hampshire border, with **Back Country Excursions** (© 207/625-8189; www.bikebackcountry.com).

Out in Colorado (chapter 10), ski areas often open their lifts to bikers in the summer. **Winter Park** is considered the state's mountain-bike capital (© 800/903-**PARK** [903-7275] or 970/726-4118). The state's single-best route, the 30-mile **Tipperary Creek Trail,** ends at Winter Park. Another popular area is the **Bryce, Zion,** and **Canyonlands** regions of southern Utah (chapter 10). Contact **Rim Tours** (© 800/626-7335; www.rimtours.com) or **Escape Adventures** (© 800/596-2953; www.kaibabtours.com), based in the town of Moab.

West Virginia (p. 1033) is a top destination for mountain biking; especially good spots are **Canaan Valley Resort** and **Backwater Falls State Park.**

The companies mentioned under "Biking," above, also offer mountain-biking expeditions throughout the country and abroad.

NATURE & ECOLOGY TOURS Not just for bird-watchers, the **National Audubon Society** (© 212/979-3000; www.audubon.org) has its Ecology Camp on Hog Island off the Maine coast and another in the Grand Tetons of Wyoming, and it sponsors ecology excursions to such places as California's Death Valley. The **Sierra Club** maintains base camps in the Rockies and sponsors a variety of nature- and conservation-oriented trips (© 415/977-5500; www.sierraclub.com). On a tour sponsored by a conservation association, you'll learn more about our national parks than you could than just by driving through them. To find out what's available, contact the individual park you plan on visiting.

RIVER RAFTING The most famous place to run the rapids is the **Grand Canyon** (p. 780), with steep walls that tower above you as you race down the **Colorado River.** It's also the most popular spot, with bumper-to-bumper rafts in summer.

You may have less unwanted company on the Colorado upstream in **Utah**—which also has good rafting on the **Green River.** Call the **Utah Travel Council** (© 800/200-1160 or 801/538-1030; www.utah.com) and ask for a copy of *Raft Utah.* The **Snake River** south of Yellowstone National Park near Jackson Hole, Wyoming, is also a best bet. The Snake River flows into Idaho, where its wild Hells Canyon offers exciting rides—as do the Salmon and Middle Fork rivers. For more information, see chapter 8.

The **New River** cuts a dramatic, 2,000-foot-deep gorge through the Appalachian Mountains inside **New River Gorge National River Recreation Area** (p. 1036), near the town of Beckley, West Virginia, making it the most scenic rapids route in the east.

SCENIC DRIVES There are so many wonderful driving tours it's impossible to offer anything like a comprehensive list, but here are a few favorites.

In New England (chapter 2), the dramatic **Kancamagus Highway** (N.H. 112) cuts through New Hampshire's White Mountains between Lincoln and Conway. Nearby is the privately owned **Mount Washington Auto Road,** to the top of one of the tallest peaks in the east. The loop road in Maine's **Acadia National Park** is another beauty.

In the Southeast (chapter 4), you can't beat Virginia's **Skyline Drive** and the **Blue Ridge Parkway,** which continues south to North Carolina's Great Smoky Mountains near Asheville.

You'll traverse a wild and undeveloped portion of Monongahela National Forest on the **Highland Scenic Highway** in West Virginia (appendix A), a drive that's especially beautiful during fall foliage season.

The **Historic Coastal Highway** stretches along the eastern coast of Florida, offering up prime ocean views and lots of wildlife.

In the Gulf South (chapter 6), the **Natchez Trace Parkway** winds through forested beauty in the states of Mississippi, Tennessee, and Alabama on the way from Natchez to Nashville. Another good option in this region is the stunning beauty (including trees, rock formations, and waterfalls) along the **Red River Gorge Highway** in Kentucky. For picture-perfect views of marshlands and wildlife, look no further than the **Creole Nature Trail** in Louisiana.

In the Great Plains (chapter 8), a driving tour of Glacier Country in Montana puts you on **Going-to-the-Sun Road** through Glacier National Park, one of the great summertime drives in the country. Over the border in Wyoming, the **Beartooth Scenic Byway** (U.S. 212) from the northern part of Yellowstone National Park east to Red Lodge climbs over 10,947-foot **Beartooth Pass,** from where you can see mile upon mile of Wyoming and Montana mountains. Custer State Park in the **South Dakota Badlands** offers not one, but three scenic auto routes, though if you have time for only one, make it **Iron Mountain Road.**

In Colorado, a driving tour of the Western Slope follows the **Million Dollar Highway** (U.S. 550) across 11,008-foot **Red Mountain Pass,** an unforgettable drive. The **San Juan Skyway,** a 236-mile circuit that crosses five mountain passes, takes in the magnificent scenery of the San Juan Mountains, including some wonderful Old West towns. And visitors to Rocky Mountain National Park should not pass up a drive on the exceptionally scenic **Trail Ridge Road,** especially in spring when the wildflowers are in bloom and wildlife is out in force.

In the Southwest (chapter 11), the **Kaibab Plateau—North Rim Parkway** winds itself through the trees of Kaibab National Forest before landing at the scenic northern edge of the Grand Canyon. In the **Arizona desert,** the drive from Phoenix through Prescott and Sedona includes huge red rocks and the cool oasis of Oak Creek Canyon. The desert's most spectacular scenery is in **Monument Valley** on the Arizona-Utah border in Navajo and Hopi country and the nearby **Canyonlands.**

Out in California and the Pacific Northwest (chapters 12 and 13), driving doesn't get any more dramatic than it is along the **California** and **Oregon coasts.**

Up in Alaska (chapter 14), one of the world's great drives begins in Anchorage and leads roughly 50 miles south on the **Seward Highway** to Portage Glacier; chipped from the rocky Chugach Mountains, the **Turnagain Arm** provides a platform for viewing an untouched landscape full of wildlife.

Out in Hawaii (chapter 14), the drive from Honolulu to Oahu's Windward coast on **Hwy. 61** offers an unparalleled view down from the near-vertical Pali cliff. The narrow, winding **Hana Road** on Maui will reward your driving skills with wonderful seascapes.

For a comprehensive list of the major scenic byways and roads in the U.S., check out the U.S. Department of Transportation's **America's Byways** website at **www. byways.org**; while you're online, be sure to request their free *America's Byways* map.

SKIING New England may have started downhill skiing in the United States, but for the best, forget about the East altogether and head for the deep powder out West.

Colorado (chapter 10) is endowed with more than two dozen ski resorts, including world-renowned Aspen, Vail, Breckenridge, and Wolf Creek; **Utah** (chapter 10) is home to Alta, Beaver Mountain, Snowbasin, Park City, and Deer Valley; and **Taos** (p. 812) in New Mexico has well-known slopes. In California's Sierras, **Lake Tahoe** (p. 866) is home to Alpine Meadows, Heavenly Resort, and the famous Squaw Valley USA. And there's **Jackson Hole** (p. 573) in Wyoming, plus the Big Mountain and Big Sky resorts nearby in Montana (chapter 8).

New England (chapter 2) does have good cross-country skiing, especially at the **Trapp Family** (yes, *that* Trapp Family) **Lodge Cross-Country Ski Center** (© 800/826-7000 or 802/253-8511; www.trappfamily.com) in Stowe, Vermont, and the entire village of Jackson, New Hampshire, which is laced with a network of ski trails maintained by the **Jackson Ski Touring Foundation** (© 800/927-6697; www.jacksonxc.org). Moving south along the East Coast, you'll find good options in Lake Placid, New York (chapter 3), and Snowshoe in West Virginia (appendix A). Out West, many of the downhill resorts mentioned above have cross-country trails as well. The best are in **Yosemite** (p. 873), **Yellowstone** (p. 582), and **Glacier** (p. 563) national parks. The rims of the **Grand Canyon** (p. 780) and **Bryce Canyon** (p. 717) national parks also present some unusual skiing venues.

WHALE-&WILDLIFE-WATCHING The best whale-watching on the East Coast leaves from **Provincetown** on Cape Cod (p. 57), where some boats sight humpbacks and finbacks, claiming a 99% success rate from April to November.

On the West Coast, you can see Pacific gray whales during their spring and fall migrations from **Point Reyes National Seashore** north of San Francisco; **Depoe Bay** and other points on the Oregon coast; and the **San Juan Islands** near Seattle, which also have orcas. See chapters 12 and 13 for more information on these areas.

The port of **Sitka** (p. 989) in southeastern Alaska, **Kenai Fjords National Park,** and nearby **Seward** are great spots to watch humpbacks feeding in summer—plus a profusion of seals, otters, and other marine mammals.

For many humpbacks, the fall migration takes them south to sunny Hawaii (chapter 14), where they frolic in the warm waters from December to May. They are best seen here from **Maui's west coast.**

For wildlife-watching, you can see moose in **Rocky Mountain National Park** (p. 676) in Colorado, maybe a bear in the **Great Smoky Mountains** (p. 296), or alligators and other critters in **Florida's Everglades** (p. 390). But the best places to spot a variety of animals are undoubtedly the national parks out west and in Alaska. Without question, **Yellowstone** (p. 582) offers some of the top opportunities, with an abundance of elk and bison. Some of them will walk right up to your car. **Glacier** (p. 563) has this and more—mountain elk and the occasional grizzly bear. Alaska's **Denali** (p. 995) national park offers visitors a great chance to see grizzlies and other types of bears.

10 TIPS ON ACCOMMODATIONS

The United States has a wide range of accommodations, from roadside chain motels, to park lodges, to rental condos, to mammoth themed resorts, to historic inns (where George Washington really did sleep!). And there are many excellent public

How About House-Swapping?

House-swapping is becoming a more popular and viable means of travel; you stay in their place, they stay in yours, and you both get an authentic and personal view of the area, the opposite of the escapist retreat that many hotels offer. Try **HomeLink International** (Homelink.org), the largest and oldest home-swapping organization, founded in 1952, with over 11,000 listings worldwide ($75 for a yearly membership). **HomeExchange.org** ($49.95 for 6,000 listings) and **Inter-Vac.com** ($68.88 for over 10,000 listings) are also reliable. Many travelers find great housing swaps on **Craigslist** (www.craigslist.org), too, though the offerings cannot be vetted or vouched for. Swap at your own risk.

and private campgrounds all over the country.

For a list of the major hotel and motel chains' telephone numbers and websites, see appendix D. In the individual chapters in this book, we also provide information on local reservation services, if available. Most state tourism offices put out directories or other information on available accommodations—contact them and they'll be happy to send you the information. Much of the information is also available on the states' tourism websites. A list of all 50 state tourism bureaus is available in appendix B.

If you prefer the intimacy and character of a bed-and-breakfast, there are several reservation agencies and online websites that deal solely with B&Bs. A few of these B&B-only websites include **Inntravels. com**, **Bed & Breakfast Inns Online** (www.bbonline.com), **North American Bed & Breakfast Directory** (www.bb directory.com), and **BedandBreakfast. com**.

For historic lodging in the United States, look no further than the **Historic Hotels of America** (© 800/678-8946; www.historichotels.org), operated in conjunction with the National Trust for Historic Preservation. We've noted several hotels rich in American history throughout the book and have a box highlighting some of our favorites in the Florida chapter (chapter 5).

For information on campgrounds and RV parks in the United States, pick up the comprehensive *Frommer's RV & Tent Campgrounds in the U.S.A.* You can also contact the **National Association of RV Parks and Campgrounds** (www.gocamp ingamerica.com) or **KOA** (© 406/248-7444; www.koa.com), which operates numerous campgrounds and RV parks all over the country.

SAVING ON YOUR HOTEL ROOM

The **rack rate** is the maximum rate that a hotel charges for a room. Hardly anybody pays this price, however, except in high season or on holidays. To lower the cost of your room:

- **Ask about special rates or other discounts.** You may qualify for corporate, student, military, senior, frequent-flier, trade union, or other discounts.
- **Dial direct.** When booking a room in a chain hotel, you'll often get a better deal by calling the individual hotel's reservation desk rather than the chain's main number.
- **Book online.** Many hotels offer Internet-only discounts, or supply rooms to Priceline, Hotwire, or Expedia at rates much lower than the ones you can get through the hotel.

- **Remember the law of supply and demand.** Resort hotels are most crowded and, therefore, most expensive on weekends, so discounts are usually available for midweek stays. Business hotels in downtown locations are busiest during the week, so you can expect big discounts over the weekend. Many hotels have high-season and low-season prices, and booking even 1 day after high season ends can mean big discounts.

- **Look into group or long-stay discounts.** If you come as part of a large group, you should be able to negotiate a bargain rate. Likewise, if you're planning a long stay (at least 5 days), you might qualify for a discount. As a general rule, expect 1 night free after a 7-night stay.

- **Avoid excess charges and hidden costs.** When you book a room, ask whether the hotel charges for parking. Use a cellphone, pay phones, or prepaid phone cards instead of dialing direct from hotel phones, which usually have exorbitant rates. Don't be tempted by the room's minibar offerings: Most hotels overcharge for water, soda, and snacks. Finally, ask about local taxes and service charges, which can increase the cost of a room by 15% or more.

- **Book an efficiency.** A room with a kitchenette allows you to shop for groceries and cook your own meals. This is a big money saver, especially for families on long stays.

- **Consider enrolling in hotel "frequent-stay" programs**, which are upping the ante lately to win the loyalty of repeat customers. Frequent guests can now accumulate points or credits to earn free hotel nights, airline miles, in-room amenities, merchandise, tickets to concerts and events, discounts on sporting facilities—and even credit toward stock in the participating hotel, in the case of the Jameson Inn hotel group. Perks are awarded not only by many chain hotels and motels (Hilton HHonors, Marriott Rewards, Wyndham ByRequest, to name a few), but individual inns and B&Bs. Many chain hotels partner with other hotel chains, car-rental firms, airlines, and credit card companies to give consumers additional incentive to do repeat business.

LANDING THE BEST ROOM

Somebody has to get the best room in the house. It might as well be you. You can start by joining the hotel's frequent-guest program, which may make you eligible for upgrades. A hotel-branded credit card usually gives its owner "silver" or "gold" status in frequent-guest programs for free. Always ask about a corner room. They're often larger and quieter, with more windows and light, and they often cost the same as standard rooms. When you make your reservation, ask if the hotel is renovating; if it is, request a room away from the construction. Ask about nonsmoking rooms, rooms with views, or rooms with twin, queen- or king-size beds. If you're a light sleeper, request a quiet room away from vending machines, elevators, restaurants, bars, and discos. Ask for a room that has been most recently renovated or redecorated.

If you aren't happy with your room when you arrive, ask for another one. Most lodgings will be willing to accommodate you.

In resort areas, particularly in warm climates, ask the following questions before you book a room:

- What's the view like? Cost-conscious travelers may be willing to pay less for a back room facing the parking lot, especially if they don't plan to spend much time in their room. If, on the other hand, you can't do without that view of the ocean, the skyline, the Strip, whatever, then be prepared to pay extra for it.

- What's included in the price? Your room may be moderately priced, but if you're charged for beach chairs, towels, sports equipment, and other amenities, you could end up spending more than you bargained for.
- Is there a resort fee? These are recent and particularly heinous schemes ($5–$20 per day!) dreamed up by hotel executives trying to make an extra dime off travelers. They ostensibly cover items (local calls, a bottle of water, a newspaper, the electricity in your room) that used to be free but that you're now being charged for. And these extra charges are *never* included in the quoted rate. You'll find this sort of gouging mostly at resorts in the major resort destinations such as Florida and Hawaii, but we've seen even small chain hotels in some of these areas assessing this fee.

New England

One of the greatest challenges of traveling in New England is choosing from an abundance of superb restaurants, accommodations, and attractions. Do you want the mountains or the beach? Shining cities or quiet vistas? In this chapter, we give you an overview of one of the most historic regions of the United States, and still one of the most vital. We start in Massachusetts with Boston; go out to Cape Cod and Martha's Vineyard; swing through the Mystic seaport in Connecticut and then around to Rhode Island's glamorous Newport and revitalized Providence; and return to Massachusetts to the Berkshires. We head inland to the natural glories of southern Vermont and New Hampshire's White Mountains, then up the rocky, majestic Maine coast.

1 BOSTON & CAMBRIDGE

Boston greeted the 21st century by putting on a new face. The 2-decade, $15-billion highway-construction project known as the "Big Dig" wrapped up, leaving new parks, open spaces, surface roads, and buildings in place of the mile-long elevated expressway that had separated the waterfront from downtown for half a century. A subterranean highway now carries traffic through Boston, a modern metropolis that's also steeped in history. Rich in Colonial lore and 21st-century technology, it's a living landmark that changes every day. Cambridge and Boston are so close that many people believe they're the same—a notion both cities' residents are happy to dispel.

Take a few days (or weeks) to get to know the Boston area, or use it as a gateway to the rest of New England. Here's hoping your experience is memorable and delightful.

ESSENTIALS

GETTING THERE By Plane   Most major domestic carriers and many international carriers serve Boston's **Logan International Airport** (© **800/23-LOGAN** [235-6426]; www.massport.com/logan). You can get into town by bus, subway (the "T"), cab, van, or boat. The Silver Line **bus** stops at each airport terminal and runs directly to South Station. The **subway** takes 10 minutes to reach downtown, not including the shuttle-bus ride to the subway. Free **shuttle buses** run from each terminal to the Airport station on the Blue Line of the T daily from 5:30am to 1am. The fare for the bus or subway is $1.70 (with a pass or CharlieCard) or $2 (with a CharlieTicket or cash). A **cab** from the airport to downtown or the Back Bay costs about $20 to $35 and can be as high as $45 in bad traffic. The Logan Airport website lists numerous companies that operate **shuttle-van service** to local hotels. One-way prices start at $14 per person and are subject to fuel surcharges. The trip to the downtown waterfront (near cabstands and several hotels) in a weather-protected **boat** takes 7 minutes and costs $10 one-way. Some hotels have **limousines** or **shuttle vans;** ask when you make your reservations.

By Train   Amtrak (© **800/USA-RAIL** [872-7245] or 617/482-3660; www.amtrak.com) serves all three of Boston's three rail centers: **South Station,** on Atlantic Avenue;

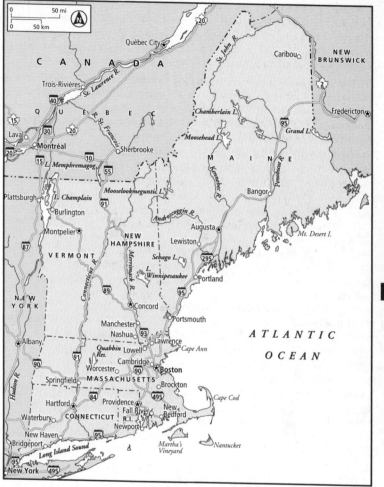

Back Bay Station, on Dartmouth Street across from the Copley Place mall; and **North Station,** on Causeway Street near the TD Banknorth Garden. Each train station is also a **rapid-transit** station (📞 **800/392-6100** outside Massachusetts, or 617/222-3200; www.mbta.com). A **commuter rail** serves Ipswich, Rockport, and Fitchburg from North Station, and points south and west, including Plymouth, from South Station.

By Car   Boston is 218 miles from New York; driving time is about $4^{1}/_{2}$ hours. From Washington, it takes about 8 hours to cover the 468 miles; the 992-mile drive from Chicago takes around 21 hours. Driving to Boston is not difficult, but you won't need a car to explore Boston and Cambridge.

The major highways are **I-90,** the Massachusetts Turnpike ("Mass. Pike"), an east-west toll road that leads to the New York State Thruway; **I-93/U.S. 1,** which extends north to Canada; and **I-93/Route 3,** the Southeast Expressway, which connects with the south, including Cape Cod. **I-95** (Mass. Rte. 128) is a beltway about 11 miles from downtown that connects to I-93 and to highways in Rhode Island, Connecticut, New York, New Hampshire, and Maine. The **Mass. Pike** extends into the city and connects with the **Central Artery** (the John F. Fitzgerald Expwy.).

By Bus   The **South Station Transportation Center,** on Atlantic Avenue next to the train station, is the city's bus-service hub. It's served by regional and national lines, including **Greyhound** (© **800/231-2222** or 617/526-1801; www.greyhound.com), **Bonanza** (© **800/556-3815** or 617/720-4110; www.bonanzabus.com), and **Peter Pan** (© **800/237-8747** or 800/343-9999; www.peterpanbus.com).

VISITOR INFORMATION   Contact the **Greater Boston Convention & Visitors Bureau,** 2 Copley Place, Ste. 105, Boston (© **888/SEE-BOSTON** [733-2678] or 617/536-4100, or 0171/431-3434 in the U.K.; www.bostonusa.com). It offers a comprehensive information kit ($10) with a planner, guidebook, map, and coupon book; and a *Kids Love Boston* guide ($5). Free smaller planners for specific seasons or events are often available.

The **Cambridge Office for Tourism,** 4 Brattle St., Ste. 208, Cambridge (© **800/862-5678** or 617/441-2884; www.cambridge-usa.org), distributes information about Cambridge. The **Massachusetts Office of Travel and Tourism,** 10 Park Plaza, Ste. 4510, Boston (© **800/227-6277** or 617/973-8500; www.massvacation.com), distributes the *Getaway Guide,* a free magazine with information on attractions and lodgings, a map, and a seasonal calendar.

The **Boston National Historical Park Visitor Center,** 15 State St. (© **617/242-5642;** www.nps.gov/bost), across the street from the Old State House and the State Street T, is a good place to start exploring. National Park Service rangers staff the center and lead free tours of the Freedom Trail. The audiovisual show provides basic information on 16 historic sites on the trail. The center is wheelchair accessible and has restrooms. It's open daily from 9am to 5pm.

The outdoor information booth at **Faneuil Hall Marketplace,** between Quincy Market and the South Market Building, is staffed in the spring, summer, and fall from 10am to 6pm Monday through Saturday, noon to 6pm Sunday.

The Freedom Trail begins at the **Boston Common Information Center,** 146 Tremont St., on the Common. The center is open Monday through Saturday from 8:30am to 5pm, Sunday from 9am to 5pm. The **Prudential Information Center,** on the main level of the Prudential Center, is open Monday through Friday from 8:30am to 6pm, Saturday and Sunday from 10am to 6pm. The **Greater Boston Convention & Visitors Bureau** (© **888/SEE-BOSTON** [733-2678] or 617/536-4100) operates both centers.

GETTING AROUND   When you reach your hotel, leave your car in the garage and walk or use public transportation. Free maps of downtown Boston and the transit system are available at visitor centers around the city.

By Public Transportation   The Massachusetts Bay Transportation Authority, or **MBTA** (© **800/392-6100** or 617/222-3200; www.mbta.com), is known as the "T," and its logo is the letter in a circle. It runs subways, trolleys, buses, and ferries in Boston and many suburbs, as well as the commuter rail. Its website includes maps, schedules, and other information.

MBTA (© **800/392-6100** or 617/222-3200; www.mbta.com) passengers pay their fares with stored-value CharlieTickets or CharlieCards. Buses and trolleys also accept cash. Fares are lower if you pay with a CharlieCard than if you use a Charli-eTicket or cash. The **CharlieCard** (a plastic "smart card" with an embedded chip) registers when you hold it in front of the rectangular fare reader; the **Charli-eTicket** (heavy paper with a magnetic strip) goes into and pops out of a slot on the turnstile or farebox. Self-service kiosks at the entrance to each subway station and in each terminal allow you to add value to CharlieTickets and Char-lieCards, using cash or a credit or debit card. They dispense CharlieTickets but not CharlieCards. To get a CharlieCard, ask a T employee, order one in advance, or visit a retail location (check the website for a list of convenience stores, news-stands, and other outlets). Consider ordering CharlieCards or CharlieTickets online before you leave home; at press time, shipping is free, and you won't have to buy one immediately upon arriving.

Newer stations on the Red, Blue, and Orange lines are wheelchair accessible; the Green Line is being converted. All T buses have lifts or kneelers; call © **800/LIFT-BUS** (543-8287) for information. To learn more, call the **Office for Transportation Access** (© **800/543-8287** or 617/222-5976, or TTY 617/222-5854).

Red, Blue, and Orange line **trains** and Green Line **trolleys** make up the **subway** system, which runs partly aboveground. The commuter rail to the suburbs is purple on system maps and is sometimes called the Purple Line. The Silver Line is a fancy name for a bus line; the Waterfront branch runs from South Station to the airport via the South Boston waterfront, including the convention center and the World Trade Center. The fare on the subway and Waterfront Silver Line is $1.70 with a CharlieCard, $2 with a CharlieTicket or cash. Transfers to local buses are free. Service begins around 5:15am and ends around 12:30am. On New Year's Eve, closing time is 2am and service is free after 8pm. A sign on the token booth in every station gives the time of the last train in either direction.

T buses and "trackless trolleys" (buses with electric antennae) provide service around town and to the suburbs. The fare for local buses and the Washington Street Silver Line is $1.25 with a CharlieCard (transferring to the subway costs 45¢), $1.50 with a Char-lieTicket or cash. Express-bus fares are higher. Important local routes include **no. 1** (Mass. Ave. from Dudley Sq. in Roxbury through the Back Bay and Cambridge to Har-vard Sq.), **nos. 92** and **93** (btw. Haymarket and Charlestown), and **no. 77** (Mass. Ave. from Harvard Sq. north to Porter Sq. and Arlington).

The MBTA Inner Harbor **ferry** connects Long Wharf (near the New England Aquarium) with the Charlestown Navy Yard—it's a good way to get back downtown from "Old Ironsides" and the Bunker Hill Monument. The fare is $1.70. Visit www.mbta.com or call © **617/227-4321** for information.

Taxis are expensive and not always easy to flag. To order one, try the **Independent Taxi Operators Association** (© 617/426-8700), **Boston Cab** (© 617/536-5100 or 262-2227), **Town Taxi** (© 617/536-5000; www.towntaxiboston.com), **City Cab** (© 617/536-5100), or **Metro Cab** (© 617/242-8000; www.boston-cab.com). In Cambridge, call **Ambassador Brattle** (© 617/492-1100) or **Yellow Cab** (© 617/547-3000). Boston Cab can dispatch a wheelchair-accessible vehicle; advance notice is recommended.

FAST FACTS   If you need medical attention, your hotel concierge should be able to help you. Hospital referral services include **Brigham and Women's** (© 800/294-9999), **Massachusetts General** (© 800/711-4MGH [711-4644]), and **Tufts New England Medical Center** (© 617/636-9700). An affiliate of Mass. General, **MGH Back Bay,** 388 Comm. Ave. (© 617/267-7171), offers walk-in service and honors most insurance plans.

Downtown Boston has no **24-hour pharmacy.** The CVS locations at 587 Boylston St., off Copley Square in the Back Bay (© 617/437-8414), and at the Porter Square Shopping Center, off Mass. Ave. in Cambridge (© 617/876-5519), are open 24/7, as are their pharmacies.

On the whole, Boston and Cambridge are **safe** cities for walking. As in any urban area, stay out of parks (including Boston Common, the Public Garden, and the Esplanade) at night unless you're in a crowd. Areas to avoid at night include Boylston Street between Tremont and Washington, and Tremont Street from Stuart to Boylston. Try not to walk alone late at night in the Theater District and around North Station. Public transportation is busy and safe, but service stops between 12:30 and 1am.

The 5% **sales tax** does not apply to food, prescription drugs, newspapers, or clothing that costs less than $175; the tax on meals and takeout food is 5%. The **lodging tax** in Boston and Cambridge is 12.45%.

SPECIAL EVENTS & FESTIVALS   Every March 17, a 5-mile parade salutes both **St. Patrick's Day** and the day British troops left Boston in 1776 (© 800/888-5515). **Patriot's Day,** the third Monday in April, features reenactments of the events of April 18 and 19, 1775, which signified the start of the Revolutionary War, as well as the running of the **Boston Marathon;** call the Boston Athletic Association (© 617/236-1652; www.bostonmarathon.org). The **Boston Pops Concert and Fireworks Display,** held at Hatch Memorial Shell on the Esplanade during Boston, Massachusetts, Independence Week, culminates in the famous Boston Pops's **Fourth of July** concert. The program includes Tchaikovsky's *1812 Overture* with actual cannon fire that segues into the fireworks. On the Web, head to **www.july4th.org**.

WHAT TO SEE & DO IN BOSTON

If you concentrate on the included attractions, a **CityPass** (© 888/330-5008; www.citypass.com) offers great savings. It's a booklet of tickets to the Harvard Museum of Natural History, Kennedy Library, Museum of Fine Arts, Museum of Science, New England Aquarium, and Prudential Center Skywalk Observatory. The price (at press time, $44 for adults, $24 for children 3–11) represents a 50% savings for adults who visit all six attractions, and having a ticket means you can go straight to the entrance without waiting in line. The passes, good for 1 year from the date of purchase, are on sale at participating attractions, from the website, through the **Greater Boston Convention & Visitors Bureau** (© 800/SEE-BOSTON [733-2678]; www.bostonusa.com), and from some hotel concierges and travel agents.

CityPass's main competition is the **Go Boston Card** (© 800/887-9103; www.gobostoncard.com). It includes admission to more than 60 Boston-area and New England attractions and a 2-day trolley pass. If you strategize wisely, this card can be a great value. It costs $55 for 1 day, $85 for 2 days, $115 for 3 days, $155 for 5 days, and $195 for 7 days, with discounts for children and winter travelers. A spinoff, the Explorer Pass, lets you select three of the nine included attractions and is good for 30 days. It costs $65 for adults and $39 for children—a potentially good deal, but do the math. Cards and passes are available through the website, at the Visitor Information Centers on Boston Common and at the Prudential Center, from the BosTix booths in Faneuil Hall Marketplace (closed Mon) and Copley Square, at many concierge desks, and as part of numerous hotel packages.

The Top Attractions

Faneuil Hall Marketplace (Kids)   Since Boston's most popular attraction opened in 1976, cities all over the country have imitated the "festival market" concept. The five-building complex incorporates brick-and-stone plazas that teem with crowds shopping, eating, performing, watching performers, and people-watching. In warm weather, it's busy from just after dawn until well past dark. **Quincy Market** is the Greek Revival–style central building; it contains an enormous food court. On either side, glass canopies cover restaurants, bars, and pushcarts that hold everything from crafts created by New England artisans to souvenirs. You'll also see a bar that replicates the set of the TV show *Cheers.* In the plaza between the **South Canopy** and the South Market building is an **information kiosk.** One constant since the year after the original market opened (1826) is **Durgin-Park,** a traditional New England restaurant with traditionally crabby waitresses. **Faneuil Hall** itself—nicknamed the "Cradle of Liberty"—sometimes gets overlooked, but it's worth a visit. National Park Service rangers give free 20-minute talks every half-hour from 9am to 5pm in the second-floor auditorium.

Btw. North, Congress, and State sts. and I-93. © 617/523-1300. www.faneuilhallmarketplace.com. Marketplace Mon–Sat 10am–9pm; Sun noon–6pm. Food court opens earlier; some restaurants and bars close later. T: Green or Blue Line to Government Center, Orange Line to Haymarket, or Blue Line to Aquarium or State.

Isabella Stewart Gardner Museum   Isabella Stewart Gardner (1840–1924) was an individualist long before such behavior was acceptable for a woman in polite society, and her legacy is a treasure for art lovers. "Mrs. Jack" designed her exquisite home in the style of a 15th-century Venetian palace and filled it with European, American, and Asian painting and sculpture. You'll see works by Titian, Botticelli, Raphael, Rembrandt, Matisse, and Mrs. Gardner's friends James McNeill Whistler and John Singer Sargent. The building holds a hodgepodge of furniture and architectural details imported from European churches and palaces. A special-exhibition gallery features two or three shows a year, often by contemporary artists in residence.

280 The Fenway. © 617/566-1401. www.gardnermuseum.org. Admission $12 adults, $10 seniors, $5 college students; free for children 17 and under and adults named Isabella with ID. Tues–Sun and some Mon holidays 11am–5pm. T: Green Line E to Museum.

John F. Kennedy Library and Museum (Kids)   The Kennedy era springs to life at this complex overlooking Dorchester Bay. It captures the 35th president's accomplishments in video and audio, as well as displays of memorabilia and photos. Far from being a static experience, it changes regularly, with temporary shows and displays that highlight and complement the permanent exhibits. A visit begins with a 17-minute film about Kennedy's early life. There's a film about the Cuban Missile Crisis, along with displays on Attorney General Robert F. Kennedy, the civil rights movement, the Peace Corps, the space program, First Lady Jacqueline Bouvier Kennedy, and the Kennedy family.

Columbia Point. © 866/JFK-1960 (535-1960) or 617/514-1600. www.jfklibrary.org. Admission $12 adults, $10 seniors and students with ID, $9 youths 13–17; free for children 12 and under. Surcharges may apply for special exhibitions. Daily 9am–5pm (last film at 3:55pm). T: Red Line to JFK/UMass, then free shuttle bus (every 20 min.). By car, take Southeast Expwy. (I-93/Rte. 3) south to exit 15 (Morrissey Blvd./ JFK Library), turn left onto Columbia Rd., and follow signs to free parking lot.

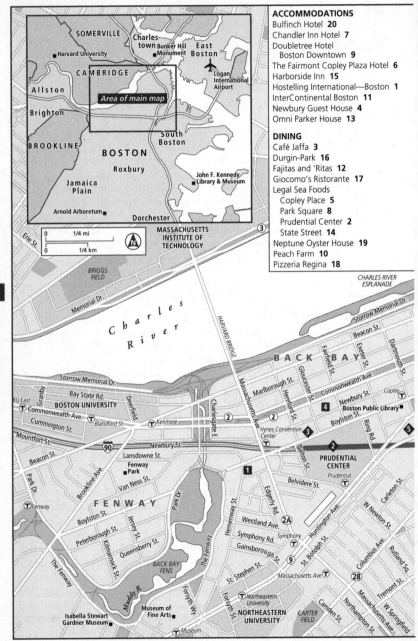

ACCOMMODATIONS
Bulfinch Hotel **20**
Chandler Inn Hotel **7**
Doubletree Hotel
  Boston Downtown **9**
The Fairmont Copley Plaza Hotel **6**
Harborside Inn **15**
Hostelling International—Boston **1**
InterContinental Boston **11**
Newbury Guest House **4**
Omni Parker House **13**

DINING
Café Jaffa **3**
Durgin-Park **16**
Fajitas and 'Ritas **12**
Giocomo's Ristorante **17**
Legal Sea Foods
  Copley Place **5**
  Park Square **8**
  Prudential Center **2**
  State Street **14**
Neptune Oyster House **19**
Peach Farm **10**
Pizzeria Regina **18**

NEW ENGLAND

2

BOSTON & CAMBRIDGE

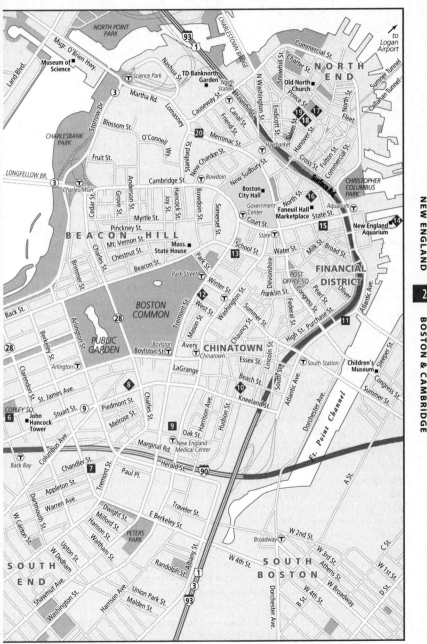

Museum of African American History The final stop on the **Black Heritage Trail** offers a comprehensive look at the history and contributions of blacks in Boston and Massachusetts. Exhibits incorporate art, artifacts, documents, historical photographs, and other objects—including many family heirlooms. The museum occupies the **Abiel Smith School** (1834), the first American public grammar school for African-American children, and the **African Meeting House,** 8 Smith Court. The oldest standing black church in the United States, the meetinghouse opened in 1806. Once known as the "Black Faneuil Hall," it also schedules lectures, concerts, and church meetings.

46 Joy St. ✆ **617/725-0022.** www.afroammuseum.org. Free admission; suggested donation $5. Mon-Sat 10am–4pm. T: Red or Green Line to Park St. or Red Line to Charles/MGH.

Museum of Fine Arts (Kids) One of the world's great museums. Every installation reflects an attitude that makes even those who go in with a feeling of obligation leave with a sense of discovery and wonder. That includes children, who can launch a scavenger hunt, admire the mummies, or participate in family-friendly programs. The MFA is noted for its **Impressionist paintings,** Asian and Old Kingdom Egyptian collections, Buddhist temple, and medieval sculpture and tapestries. The American and European paintings and sculpture are a remarkable assemblage that may seem as familiar as the face in the mirror or as unexpected as a comet. Pick up a floor plan at the information desk, or take a free **guided tour** (weekdays except Mon holidays at 10:30am–3pm; Wed at 6:15pm; Sat–Sun 11am–3pm). Note that the MFA's admission fees are among the highest in the country. A Boston CityPass is a great deal if you plan to visit enough of the other included attractions. An enormous expansion project began in 2005. While construction proceeds, the museum is rearranging some collections and closing some exhibition spaces. Check ahead before visiting if you have your heart set on seeing a particular work. And check out the dramatic revamped entrance from the Fenway, which reopened in 2008, 2 years ahead of schedule.

465 Huntington Ave. ✆ **617/267-9300.** www.mfa.org. Admission $17 adults, $15 seniors and students when entire museum is open ($2 discount when only West Wing is open); $6.50 children 7–17 on school days until 3pm, otherwise free. Admission good for 2 visits within 10 days. Voluntary contribution ($17 suggested) Wed 4–9:45pm. Surcharges may apply for special exhibitions. Free admission for museum shop, library, restaurants, and auditoriums. Entire museum Sat–Tues 10am–4:45pm; Wed 10am–9:45pm; Thurs–Fri 10am–5pm. West Wing only Thurs–Fri 5–9:45pm. T: Green Line E to Museum or Orange Line to Ruggles.

Museum of Science (Kids) For the ultimate pain-free educational experience, head to the Museum of Science. The demonstrations, experiments, and interactive displays introduce facts and concepts so effortlessly that everyone learns something. Among the hundreds of exhibits, you might find out how much you'd weigh on the moon, battle urban traffic (in a computer model), or climb into a space module. Activity centers focus on individual and interdisciplinary fields of interest—natural history (with live animals), computers, and the human body. The separate-admission theaters are worth planning for, even if you're skipping the exhibits. Buy all your tickets at once, because shows sometimes sell out. The **Mugar Omni Theater,** which shows IMAX movies on a five-story screen, is an intense experience. The **Charles Hayden Planetarium** takes you into space with daily star shows, as well as shows on special topics that change several times a year. On weekends, rock-music laser shows take over.

Science Park, off O'Brien Hwy. on bridge btw. Boston and Cambridge. ✆ **617/723-2500.** www.mos.org. Admission to exhibit halls $17 adults, $15 seniors, $14 children 3–11. Mugar Omni Theater, Hayden Planetarium, or laser shows $9 adults, $8 seniors, $7 children 3–11. Discounted combination tickets available.

New England Aquarium (Kids) This entertaining complex is home to more than 15,000 fish and aquatic mammals. At busy times, it seems to contain at least that many people—try to make this your first stop of the day, especially on weekends. Also consider buying a Boston CityPass; it allows you to skip the ticket line. The **Simons IMAX Theatre,** which has its own hours and admission fees, is worth planning ahead for, too. It shows 3-D films that concentrate on the natural world. The focal point of the main building is the four-story, 200,000-gallon **Giant Ocean Tank.** It holds a replica of a Caribbean coral reef, a vast assortment of sea creatures, and, twice a day, scuba divers who feed the sharks. Other exhibits focus on freshwater and tropical specimens, the Amazon, jellyfish, and the ecology of Boston Harbor. The hands-on **Edge of the Sea** exhibit contains a tide pool with sea stars, sea urchins, and horseshoe crabs, and the **Medical Center** is a working veterinary hospital.

Central Wharf (off Atlantic Ave. at State St.). © **617/973-5200.** www.newenglandaquarium.org. Admission $19 adults, $11 children 3–11. Free admission for outdoor exhibits, cafe, and gift shop. July to Labor Day Mon–Thurs 9am–6pm, Fri–Sun and holidays 9am–7pm; day after Labor Day to June Mon–Fri 9am–5pm, Sat–Sun and holidays 9am–6pm. Simons IMAX Theatre: © **866/815-4629** or 617/973-5206. Tickets $10 adults, $8 children 3–11. Thurs–Sat 10am–8pm; Sun–Mon 10am–6pm. T: Blue Line to Aquarium.

The Freedom Trail

A line of red paint or red brick down the center of the sidewalk, the 2^1/$_2$-mile Freedom Trail links 16 historic sights. Markers identify the stops, and plaques point the way from one to the next. The trail begins at **Boston Common,** where the Information Center, 148 Tremont St., distributes pamphlets that describe a self-guided tour. A 2-hour narrative commissioned by the **Freedom Trail Foundation** (© 617/357-8300; www.the freedomtrail.org) includes interviews, sound effects, and music, and allows visitors to tour the trail at their own pace. It costs $15 (credit cards only); buy it as an MP3 download, or rent a hand-held digital audio player, at the Boston Common Visitor Center. The foundation's costumed **Freedom Trail Players** lead 90-minute tours ($12 adults, $10 seniors and students, $6 children 12 and under) on two different routes. Make reservations online, allowing time to explore the interactive website.

You can also explore the 1.6-mile **Black Heritage Trail** from here. Two-hour guided tours start at the **Robert Gould Shaw Memorial,** on Beacon Street across from the State House. They're available Monday through Saturday from Memorial Day to Labor Day and by request at other times; contact the visitor center (© 617/742-5415; www.nps. gov/boaf) for starting times or to make a reservation. Or go on your own with a brochure available at the Museum of African American History and the Boston Common and State Street visitor centers that includes a map and descriptions.

As you follow the Freedom Trail, you'll come to the **Boston National Historical Park Visitor Center,** 15 State St. (© 617/242-5642; www.nps.gov/bost). From here, rangers lead free tours of the heart of the trail from April to September. The first-come, first-served tours are limited to 30 people and not offered in bad weather. It's open daily from 9am to 5pm.

The hard-core history fiend who peers at every artifact and reads every plaque along the trail will wind up at Bunker Hill some 4 hours later, weary but rewarded. The family with restless children will probably appreciate the 90-minute ranger-led tour.

The highlights of the trail include **Boston Common;** the **Massachusetts State House** (© 617/727-3676; www.sec.state.ma.us/trs); the **Old Granary Burying Ground,** which contains the graves of Samuel Adams, Paul Revere, and John Hancock; the **First Public School;** the **Old South Meeting House** (© 617/482-6439; www.oldsouth meetinghouse.org), the starting point of the Boston Tea Party; the **Boston Massacre Site;** the **Paul Revere House** (© 617/523-2338; www.paulreverehouse.org); **Old North Church** (© 617/523-6676; www.oldnorth.com), where Revere saw a signal in the steeple and set out on his "midnight ride"; the **USS** *Constitution* (© 617/242-5670; www.oldironsides.com), where active-duty sailors in 1812 dress uniforms give free tours of "Old Ironsides"; and the **Bunker Hill Monument** (© 617/242-5641; www.nps.gov/bost), the 221-foot granite obelisk that honors the memory of the men who died in the Battle of Bunker Hill on June 17, 1775.

The best-known **park** in Boston is the **Public Garden,** bordered by Arlington, Boylston, Charles, and Beacon streets. Something lovely is in bloom at least half of the year. For 5 months, the lagoon is home to the famous **swan boats** (© 617/522-1966; www.swanboats.com). The pedal-powered vessels—the attendants pedal, not the passengers—come out of hibernation in mid-April. The 15-minute ride costs $2.75 for adults, $2 for seniors, and $1.25 for children 15 and under.

Organized Tours

From May to October, **Boston by Foot** (© 617/367-2345, or 367-3766 for recorded info; www.bostonbyfoot.com) conducts historical and architectural walking tours that focus on neighborhoods or themes. Buy tickets ($12 adults, $8 children 6–12; Boston Underfoot $14 per person) from the guide; reservations are not required. The 90-minute tours take place rain or shine.

Historic New England (© 617/227-3956; www.historicnewengland.org) offers a fascinating tour that describes life in the mansions and garrets of Beacon Hill in 1800. "Magnificent and Modest" ($12, including museum tour) starts at the Otis House Museum, 141 Cambridge St., at 11am on Saturday from May to October. Reservations are recommended.

The most unusual and enjoyable way to see Boston is with **Boston Duck Tours** (© 800/226-7442 or 617/267-DUCK [267-3825]; www.bostonducktours.com). The tours, offered from late March to November, are pricey but great fun. Sightseers board a "duck," a reconditioned World War II amphibious landing craft, behind the Prudential Center on Huntington Avenue or at the Museum of Science. The 80-minute narrated tour begins with a quick but comprehensive jaunt around the city. Then the duck lumbers down a ramp, splashes into the Charles River, and takes a spin around the basin. Tickets cost $29 for adults, $25 for seniors and students, $19 for children 3 to 11, and $3 for children 2 and under.

The **sightseeing cruise** season runs from April to October, with spring and fall offerings often restricted to weekends. **Boston Harbor Cruises,** 1 Long Wharf (© 877/733-9425 or 617/227-4321; www.bostonharborcruises.com), is the largest company. Ninety-minute historic sightseeing cruises, which tour the Inner and Outer harbors, depart daily at 11am, 1pm, 3pm, and 6 or 7pm (the sunset cruise), with extra excursions at busy times. Tickets are $19 for adults, $17 for seniors, and $15 for children 4 to 12; sunset-cruise tickets are $1 more. The 45-minute USS *Constitution* cruise schedule gives you time to visit Old Ironsides. Tours leave Long Wharf hourly from 10:30am to 4:30pm, and on the hour from the Navy Yard from 11am to 5pm. Tickets are $14 for adults, $12 for seniors, and $10 for children.

Harvard Square is a people-watching paradise of students, instructors, commuters, and sightseers. Restaurants and stores pack the three streets that radiate from the center of the square and the streets that intersect them.

Harvard University is the oldest college in the country. Free student-led tours of the main campus leave from the **Events & Information Center,** in Holyoke Center, 1350 Mass. Ave. (© **617/495-1573**), during the school year twice a day Monday through Friday and once on Saturday (except during vacations), and during the summer four times a day Monday through Saturday and twice on Sunday. The Events & Information Center also has maps, illustrated booklets, and self-guided walking-tour directions. Before visiting, check out the university's website, www.harvard.edu.

Note: The **Boston Tea Party Ship & Museum** (© **617/269-7150;** www.bostontea partyship.com), closed after a fire in 2001, was scheduled to reopen in mid-2009. Chronically delayed plans called for the construction of two more ships and an added tearoom. Check at your hotel or call ahead before setting out.

Harvard Art Museum   In June 2008, Harvard's Fogg and Busch-Reisinger museums closed for renovations scheduled to last 5 years. In the interim, the Sackler Museum is showing highlights from all three institutions' collections. The **Arthur M. Sackler Museum** houses Harvard's world-famous collections of Asian, ancient, Islamic, and Later Indian art. Here you'll find internationally renowned Chinese jades, superb Roman sculpture, Greek vases, Korean ceramics, Japanese woodblock prints, and Persian minia-ture paintings and calligraphy. The **Fogg Museum**'s holdings include everything from 17th-century Dutch and Flemish landscapes to Impressionist masterpieces to contempo-rary sculpture. The **Busch-Reisinger Museum**'s specialty is the art of northern and central Europe, specifically Germany.

485 Broadway. © **617/495-9400.** www.artmuseums.harvard.edu. Admission $9 adults, $7 seniors, $6 students, free for children 17 and under; free to all before noon Sat. Mon–Sat 10am–5pm; Sun 1–5pm. Closed major holidays. T: Red Line to Harvard, cross Harvard Yard diagonally from the T station and exit onto Quincy St., turn left, and walk to the next corner. Or turn your back on the Coop and follow Mass. Ave. to Quincy St., then turn left and walk 1 long block.

Harvard Museum of Natural History and Peabody Museum of Archaeology & Ethnology   These museums house the university's collections of items and artifacts related to the natural world. On weekends, staffed "Investigation Stations" help visitors learn through hands-on activities. You'll certainly find something interesting here, be it a dinosaur skeleton, the largest turtle shell in the world, a Native American artifact, or the world-famous Glass Flowers. The **Glass Flowers** are 3,000 models of more than 840 plant species devised between 1887 and 1936 by the German father-and-son team of Leopold and Rudolph Blaschka. Children love the **zoological collections,** where dino-saurs share space with preserved and stuffed insects and animals that range in size from butterflies to giraffes. The **Peabody Museum** boasts the **Hall of the North American Indian,** which displays 500 artifacts representing 10 cultures.

Museum of Natural History: 26 Oxford St. © **617/495-3045.** www.hmnh.harvard.edu. Peabody Museum: 11 Divinity Ave. © **617/496-1027.** www.peabody.harvard.edu. Admission to both $9 adults, $7 seniors and students, $6 children 3–18; free to MA residents Sun until noon year-round and Wed 3–5pm. Daily 9am–5pm. T: Red Line to Harvard. Cross Harvard Yard, keeping John Harvard statue on right, and bear right before Science Center. First left is Oxford St. Check website for parking info.

Longfellow National Historic Site The books and furniture inside the yellow mansion have remained intact since the poet Henry Wadsworth Longfellow died here in 1882. During the siege of Boston in 1775 to 1776, the house served as the headquarters of Gen. George Washington. On the absorbing tour—the only way to see the house—you'll learn about the history of the building and its famous occupants.

105 Brattle St. © **617/876-4491.** www.nps.gov/long. Guided tours $3 adults, free for children 16 and under. Call ahead to confirm hours and tour times. June–Oct Wed–Sun 10am–4:30pm. Tours 10:30 and 11:30am and 1, 2, 3, and 4pm. Closed Nov–May. T: Red Line to Harvard, then follow Brattle St. about 7 blocks; house is on the right.

SPECTATOR SPORTS

BASEBALL No other experience in sports matches watching the **Boston Red Sox** play at **Fenway Park.** The **ticket office** (© **877/REDSOX-9** [733-7699]; www.redsox.com) is at 4 Yawkey Way, off Brookline Avenue. Tickets go on sale in December; order early. A few upper bleacher seats go for $12, but most are in the $25-to-$90 range. A limited number of same-day standing-room tickets ($20–$30) are available before each game. **Tours** (© **617/236-6666**) start on the hour Monday through Saturday from 9am to 4pm, Sunday from noon to 3pm (or 3 hr. before game time, whichever is earlier) in the summer; winter hours end 1 hour earlier, with no tours on Sunday. There are no tours on holidays or before day games. The cost is $12 for adults, $11 for seniors, and $10 for children 14 and under.

BASKETBALL The Boston Celtics' unlikely run to the 2008 NBA title captivated even the most jaded fans. The season runs from early October to April or May; especially when a top contender is visiting, you may have trouble getting tickets. Prices are as low as $10 for some games and top out at $275. For information, call **TD Banknorth Garden** (© **617/624-1000**; www.nba.com/celtics).

FOOTBALL The **New England Patriots** (© **800/543-1776**; www.patriots.com) play from August to December or January at Gillette Stadium on Route 1 in Foxboro. Tickets ($49–$169) sell out well in advance. Call or check the website for information on individual tickets and getting there.

HOCKEY Tickets to see the **Boston Bruins** are expensive ($19–$155) but worth it for serious fans. For information, call **TD Banknorth Garden** (© **617/624-1000;** www.boston bruins.com); for tickets, call **Ticketmaster** (© **617/931-2000;** www.ticketmaster.com).

THE BOSTON MARATHON Every year on Patriot's Day (the third Mon in Apr), the **Boston Marathon** rules the roads in Boston. For information, contact the **Boston Athletic Association** (© **617/236-1652;** www.bostonmarathon.org).

SHOPPING

The **Back Bay is** New England's premier shopping district. Dozens of upscale galleries, shops, and boutiques make **Newbury Street** a world-famous destination. Nearby, an enclosed walkway across Huntington Avenue links **Copley Place** (© 617/375-4400) and the **Shops at Prudential Center** (© 800/SHOP-PRU [746-7778]). This is where you'll find the tony department stores **Barneys New York** (© 617/385-3300), **Lord & Taylor** (© 617/262-6000), **Neiman Marcus** (© 617/536-3660), and **Saks Fifth Avenue** (© 617/262-8500). If you're passionate about art, set aside a couple of hours for strolling along Newbury Street. Besides being a prime location for upscale boutiques, it boasts an infinite variety of styles and mediums in the dozens of art galleries at street level and on the higher floors. (Remember to look up.) Most galleries are open Tuesday

(Best) Take Me Out to the Ballgame . . .

Millions worship at major league baseball's cathedrals (that is, stadiums) each year, hoping to catch a home run or celebrate a win over a hated rival. Here are our picks for the best places to watch the Boys of Summer duke it out:

1. Cubs fans have been crying "Maybe next year" since **Wrigley Field** opened in 1914, but it's the champ of baseball stadiums. From its famous Bleacher Bums and numerous day games to its old-fashioned scoreboard and classic seventh-inning-stretch rendition of "Take Me Out to the Ballgame" (which has lost only a little luster since the passing of legendary announcer Harry Carey), Wrigley is the class of the field. And a 2005 expansion added more than 1,800 bleacher seats and spruced things up, giving it a further leg up on the competition.

2. The oldest in the majors—it opened in 1912—**Fenway Park** is loaded with history and atmosphere. It's a national treasure. Sure, it's cramped, but it's a beauty, the fans are both knowledgeable and nice (provided you aren't sporting Yankee pinstripes), the hand-operated scoreboard is still in use, and the seats atop the famous Green Monster are the best in baseball.

3. Opened in 1992, **Oriole Park at Camden Yards** was the pioneer that inspired the building of more classic-style baseball parks, and for that alone, it deserves a standing O(r-i-o-l-e-s!). Architecturally, this beauty's still one of the best. Even better (though not for Baltimore), because the Orioles haven't had much to sing about lately, it's not that tough to get a seat to a game.

4. We argued long and hard over this last choice before finally settling on gorgeous **Coors Field** in Denver. The thin air (even if they've started keeping baseballs in a humidor) means the home runs fly out of the place. Watching batting practice here is a blast (or three or eight). Tack on the friendly crowds, the views of the Rocky Mountains, and good food, and this one's a winner.

In 2008, we saw the last of two major league ballyards: the classic **Yankee Stadium,** and (not-so-classic) **Shea Stadium** in the Bronx and Queens respectively. **New Yankee Stadium** will open in 2009 directly across from the old one, but whether it will live up to the legacy of the House That Ruth Built can be determined only in a few decades or so. The House That A-Rod Built? Hmmm . . .

through Sunday from 10 or 11am to 5:30 or 6pm. For specifics, pick up a copy of the free monthly *Gallery Guide* at businesses along Newbury Street.

Downtown, **Faneuil Hall Marketplace** (© 617/523-1300) is the busiest attraction in Boston not only for its smorgasbord of food, but for its shops, boutiques, and push-carts. Although it has more upscale chain outlets than only-in-Boston shops, it's fun. If the hubbub here is too much, stroll over to **Charles Street,** at the foot of Beacon Hill. A short but commercially dense (and picturesque) street, it's home to perhaps the best assortment of gift and antiques shops in the city. Be sure to check out the contemporary home accessories at **Koo De Kir,** 65 Chestnut St., just off Charles (© 617/723-8111; www.koodekir.com); the well-edited selection at **Upstairs Downstairs Antiques,** 93 Charles St. (© 617/367-1950); and the engagingly funky gifts at **Black Ink,** 101 Charles St. (© 617/723-3883).

One of Boston's oldest shopping areas is **Downtown Crossing.** Now a traffic-free pedestrian mall along Washington, Winter, and Summer streets near Boston Common, it's home to **Macy's;** tons of smaller clothing, shoe, and music stores; food and merchandise pushcarts; and a branch of **Borders.**

In **Cambridge** the bookstores, boutiques, and T-shirt shops of **Harvard Square** lie about 15 minutes from downtown Boston by subway. For a less generic experience, walk along **Mass. Ave.** in either direction to the next T stop. Bookworms flock to Cambridge. Check out the basement of the **Harvard Book Store,** 1256 Mass. Ave. (© **800/542-READ** [542-7323] outside the 617 area code, or 617/661-1515; www.harvard.com), for great deals on remainders and used books.

WHERE TO STAY

Boston has one of the busiest, most expensive hotel markets in the country. Rates at most downtown hotels are lower on weekends; leisure hotels offer discounts during the week. It's always a good idea to make a reservation, especially during foliage season and around college graduation time. The Convention & Visitors Bureau **Hotel Hot Line** (© **800/777-6001**) can help make reservations even at the busiest times. It's staffed Monday through Friday until 8pm, Saturday and Sunday until 4pm.

B&Bs are a popular form of lodging. The following organizations can help you find a B&B (most require a minimum stay of 2 nights): **Bed & Breakfast Agency of Boston** (© **800/248-9262** or 617/720-3540, or 0800/89-5128 in the U.K.; www.boston-bnb agency.com), **Host Homes of Boston** (© **800/600-1308** or 617/244-1308; www.host homesofboston.com), **Bed & Breakfast Reservations North Shore/Greater Boston/Cape Cod** (© **800/832-2632** outside MA, 617/964-1606, or 978/281-9505; www. bbreserve.com), and **Bed and Breakfast Associates Bay Colony** (© **888/486-6018** or 781/449-5302, or 08/234-7113 in the U.K.; www.bnbboston.com).

We've selected the recommended hotels below to give you a range of neighborhoods and prices from "very expensive" to "inexpensive."

Bulfinch Hotel One block from North Station, the Bulfinch abounds with details that enhance its "budget boutique" feel. Rooms are on the small side, but custom furnishings create the illusion of more space. Plush fabrics (including suede headboards), flatscreen TVs, and marble bathrooms set off the contemporary, uncluttered design. The hotel, new in 2004, offers business features such as work desks and cordless phones. The best units are junior suites—oversize doubles—known as "nose rooms" because they're in the pointed end of the triangular building.

107 Merrimac St., Boston, MA 02114. © **877/267-1776** or 617/624-0202. Fax 617/624-0211. www.bulfinch hotel.com. 80 units (most with shower only). $169–$399 double; $199–$489 junior suite. Children 17 and under stay free in parent's room. Packages and AAA, AARP, and military discounts available. AE, DC, DISC, MC, V. Parking $25 in nearby garage. T: Green or Orange Line to North Station. Pets accepted; $50 fee. **Amenities:** Restaurant and lounge; exercise room.

Chandler Inn Hotel The Chandler Inn is a bargain for its location, just 2 blocks from the Back Bay. Standard units are tastefully decorated in contemporary style and contain a queen-size or double bed or two twins, without enough room to squeeze in a cot. Bathrooms are tiny. The top three floors of the eight-story building hold deluxe guest rooms with plasma TVs and marble bathrooms. This is a gay-friendly hotel—Fritz, the bar next to the lobby, is a neighborhood hangout—that books up early for foliage season and events such as the Marathon and Boston Pride March.

26 Chandler St. (at Berkeley St.), Boston, MA 02116. (𝄞 **800/842-3450** or 617/482-3450. Fax 617/542-
3428. www.chandlerinn.com. 56 units. $109–$225 double; $179–$279 deluxe double. Children 11 and
under stay free in parent's room. AE, DC, DISC, MC, V. Parking $18 at nearby garage. T: Orange Line to Back
Bay. Pets under 25 lb. accepted; $50 fee. **Amenities:** Lounge; access to nearby health club ($10).

Doubletree Hotel Boston Downtown

Doubletree Hotel Boston Downtown   Within walking distance of downtown
and the Back Bay, the Doubletree is a better deal than most competitors in either neighborhood. The six-story building is a former high school with high ceilings and compact,
well-designed rooms. Ask for a unit that faces away from busy Washington Street, and
your view will be of a cityscape rather than of the hospital across the street. This Doubletree, which opened in 2000, adjoins the Wang YMCA of Chinatown, and room rates
include access to its extensive facilities.

821 Washington St., Boston, MA 02111. (𝄞 **800/222-TREE** (222-8733) or 617/956-7900. Fax 617/956-
7901. http://doubletree.hilton.com. 267 units (some with shower only). $129–$299 double; $189–$359
suite. Extra person $10. Children 16 and under stay free in parent's room. Packages and AAA, AARP, and
military discounts available. AE, DC, DISC, MC, V. Valet parking $36. T: Orange Line to New England
Medical Center. **Amenities:** Restaurant and lounge; cafe; access to YMCA w/Olympic-size pool.

The Fairmont Copley Plaza Hotel

The Fairmont Copley Plaza Hotel   The "grande dame of Boston" is a true grand
hotel with a well-earned reputation for excellent service. Built in 1912, the six-story
Renaissance Revival building faces Copley Square. The spacious guest rooms have a residential feel, thanks to a $34-million overhaul. The custom-made traditional furnishings
reflect the elegance of the opulent public spaces. Rooms that face the lovely square afford
better views than those that overlook busy Dartmouth Street.

138 St. James Ave., Boston, MA 02116. (𝄞 **800/441-1414** or 617/267-5300. Fax 617/247-6681. www.
fairmont.com/copleyplaza. 383 units. From $259 double; from $699 suite. Extra person $30. Packages
available. AE, DC, MC, V. Valet parking $32. T: Green Line to Copley, or Orange Line to Back Bay. Pets
accepted; $25 per day. **Amenities:** Restaurant; exercise room; access to nearby health club ($15).

Harborside Inn

Harborside Inn   The Harborside Inn offers an unbeatable combination of location
and value. The renovated 1858 warehouse is near Faneuil Hall Marketplace, the harbor,
and the Financial District. The nicely appointed guest rooms, renovated in 2007, have
hardwood floors and enough room for a table and chairs. City-view units are more
expensive than rooms that face the sky-lit atrium, but the former can be noisier. Rooms
on the upper floors have lower ceilings but better views.

185 State St. (btw. Atlantic Ave. and the Custom House Tower), Boston, MA 02109. (𝄞 **888/723-7565** or
617/723-7500. Fax 617/670-6015. www.harborsideinnboston.com. 54 units. $109–$299 double. Extra
person $15. Packages and long-term rates available. Rates may be higher during special events. AE, DC,
DISC, MC, V. Off-site parking $26. T: Blue Line to Aquarium or Orange Line to State. **Amenities:** Lounge;
access to nearby health club ($15).

Hostelling International–Boston

Hostelling International–Boston   This hostel near the Berklee College of Music
caters to students, youth groups, and other travelers in search of comfortable, no-frills
lodging. Accommodations are dorm-style, with six beds per room; a couple of private
units sleep one or two. The air-conditioned hostel has two kitchens, 29 bathrooms, and
a large common room. It provides linens, or you can bring your own; sleeping bags are
not permitted. The staff organizes free and inexpensive cultural, educational, and recreational programs. Open in summer only, **Hostelling International–Boston at Fenway,**
575 Commonwealth Ave. ((𝄞 **617/267-8599;** www.hifenway.org; T: Green Line B, C,
or D to Kenmore), holds 485 beds in a well-equipped building that's a Boston University
dorm during the school year. Rates are $35 per bed for HI-AYH members, $38 for nonmembers. Private rooms for one to three guests cost $89 to $99.

12 Hemenway St., Boston, MA 02115. ✆ **800/909-4776** or 617/536-9455. Fax 617/424-6558. www.bostonhostel.org. 205 beds. HI–American Youth Hostel members $28–$45 per bed; nonmembers $31–$48 per bed. Members $70–$100 per private unit; nonmembers $73–$106 per private unit. Children 3–12 half-price; children 2 and under free. Rates include continental breakfast. MC, V. T: Green Line B, C, or D to Hynes Convention Center. **Amenities:** Access to nearby health club ($6). *In room:* No phone.

The Inn at Harvard

The Inn at Harvard is adjacent to Harvard Yard in Cambridge, and its Georgian-style architecture would fit nicely on campus. The elegant hotel is popular with business travelers and university visitors. The guest rooms were renovated in 2006; they have pillow-top beds, and each has a work area with an Aeron chair. The four-story sky-lit atrium holds the "living room," a well-appointed lounge suitable for a meeting if you don't want to conduct business in your room.

1201 Mass. Ave. (at Quincy St.), Cambridge, MA 02138. ✆ **800/458-5886** or 617/491-2222. Fax 617/520-3711. www.theinnatharvard.com. 111 units (some with shower only). $179–$419 double; $1,500 presidential suite. AAA and AARP discounts available. AE, DC, DISC, MC, V. Valet parking $45. T: Red Line to Harvard. **Amenities:** Restaurant; Harvard Faculty Club dining privileges; fitness center.

InterContinental Boston

The 22-story glass-sheathed building (the hotel occupies the bottom 12 floors) faces the Rose Kennedy Greenway, near the Financial District, the convention center, and Boston Harbor. Guest rooms on the east (back) side have water views. All are decorated in contemporary style, with plush earth-tone fabrics and artwork. Rooms are large, with oversize work desks, and the bathrooms hold separate tubs and showers. The spa, health club, dining options, and upper-story condos amplify the residential feel. With top-notch service and amenities, this brand consistently earns repeat business from its predominantly corporate clientele.

510 Atlantic Ave., Boston, MA 02210. ✆ **800/424-6835** or 617/747-1000. Fax 617/747-5120. www.intercontinentalboston.com. 424 units. $350–$600 double; $800–$6,000 suite. Children 17 and under stay free in parent's room. Extra person $35. Packages available. AE, DC, DISC, MC, V. Valet parking $39. T: Red Line to South Station. Pets under 25 lb. accepted; $100/stay. **Amenities:** Restaurant (24-hr.); 2 bars; indoor pool; 24-hr. health club; spa.

Newbury Guest House

After a little shopping in the Back Bay, you'll appreciate what a find this cozy place is: a bargain on Newbury Street. The comfortably furnished, nicely appointed guest rooms take up three 1880s brick town houses. Largest and most expensive are the bay-window units, which overlook the street. This place operates near capacity all year: Reserve early!

261 Newbury St. (btw. Fairfield and Gloucester sts.), Boston, MA 02116. ✆ **800/437-7668** or 617/437-7666. Fax 617/670-6100. www.newburyguesthouse.com. 32 units (some with shower only). $135–$195 double. Extra person $20. Rates include continental breakfast and may be higher during special events. Minimum 2 nights on weekends. Packages available. AE, DC, DISC, MC, V. Parking $20. T: Green Line B, C, or D to Hynes Convention Center. **Amenities:** Access to nearby health club ($25).

Omni Parker House

The Parker House offers a great combination of over 150 years of history (since 1855!) and extensive renovations. Regular interior and exterior renovations keep the property in excellent shape. Guest rooms, a patchwork of more than 50 configurations, aren't huge, but they are thoughtfully laid out and nicely appointed. Business travelers can book a room with an expanded work area; sightseers can economize by requesting a smaller, less expensive unit.

60 School St., Boston, MA 02108. ✆ **800/THE-OMNI** [843-6664] or 617/227-8600. Fax 617/742-5729. www.omniparkerhouse.com. 551 units (some with shower only). $189–$289 double; $249–$399 suite. Children 17 and under stay free in parent's room. Packages and AARP discount available. AE, DC, DISC, MC, V. Valet parking $38. T: Green or Blue Line to Government Center, or Red Line to Park St. Pets accepted; deposit required. **Amenities:** 2 restaurants; bar; exercise room.

Travelers from around the world relish the variety of skillfully prepared seafood available in the Boston area. Lunch is an excellent, economical way to check out a fancy restaurant without breaking the bank. For those who like to dine alfresco, the **food court** at Faneuil Hall Marketplace is a great place to pick up picnic fare.

Baraka Café ALGERIAN/TUNISIAN/MEDITERRANEAN A tiny, aromatic destination for adventurous diners, Baraka Café specializes in flavorful, highly spiced (though not necessarily hot) cuisine. The drawbacks—no alcohol, cash only, tiny dining room, deliberate service—are insignificant when the food is this good. It's easy to fill up on housemade breads and appetizers, but save room for the likes of fork-tender lamb chops and eggplant stuffed with a tasty concoction of olives, spinach, scallions, and two cheeses. Daily specials show off the kitchen's considerable abilities better than the limited regular menu.

800½ Pearl St., Central Sq. ✆ **617/868-3951.** www.barakacafe.com. Reservations not accepted. Main courses $5–$9 at lunch, $9–$16 at dinner. No credit cards. Tues–Sat 11:30am–3pm; Tues–Sun 5:30–10pm. T: Red Line to Central.

The Blue Room ECLECTIC The Blue Room sits below plaza level in an office-retail complex, a slice of foodie paradise in high-tech heaven. The cuisine combines top-notch ingredients and aggressive flavors, and the crowded dining room isn't as noisy as it looks. Main courses tend to be grilled over a wood fire, roasted, or braised, with at least one well-conceived vegetarian choice. Chicken, roasted with Moroccan spices and served with garlic mashed potatoes, is fantastic. Seafood is always a good choice, and pork chops are juicy and succulent. In warm weather, there's patio seating.

1 Kendall Sq. ✆ **617/494-9034.** www.theblueroom.net. Reservations recommended. Main courses $21–$26. AE, DC, DISC, MC, V. Sun–Thurs 5:30–10pm; Fri–Sat 5:30–11pm; Sun brunch 11am–2:30pm. Closed 1st week of July. Validated parking available. T: Red Line to Kendall/MIT, then a 10-min. walk.

Café Jaffa MIDDLE EASTERN A long, narrow brick room with a glass front, Café Jaffa looks more like a snazzy pizza place than the excellent Middle Eastern restaurant it is. Reasonable prices, high quality, and large portions draw crowds for traditional dishes such as falafel, baba ghanouj, and hummus, as well as burgers and steak tips. For dessert, try the baklava if it's fresh (give it a pass if not).

48 Gloucester St. ✆ **617/536-0230.** Main courses $5–$18. AE, DC, DISC, MC, V. Mon–Thurs 11am–10:30pm; Fri–Sat 11am–11pm; Sun 1–10pm. T: Green Line B, C, or D to Hynes Convention Center.

Durgin-Park Kids NEW ENGLAND For huge portions of delicious food, a rowdy atmosphere where CEOs share tables with students, and famously cranky waitresses, Bostonians have flocked to Durgin-Park since 1827. The line stretches down the stairs to the first floor, and many diners are disappointed when the waitresses are nice (as they often are). Come here for prime rib the size of a hubcap, piles of fried seafood, fish dinners, and bounteous portions of roast turkey. This is the place to try Boston baked beans. For dessert, strawberry shortcake is justly celebrated.

340 Faneuil Hall Marketplace. ✆ **617/227-2038.** Reservations accepted for parties of 15 or more. Main courses $7–$25; daily specials $19–$40. Children's menu $8–$9. AE, DC, DISC, MC, V. Mon–Sat 11:30am–10pm; Sun 11:30am–9pm (lunch daily until 2:30pm). Validated parking available. T: Green or Blue Line to Government Center, or Orange Line to Haymarket.

Fajitas & 'Ritas TEX-MEX This colorful, entertaining restaurant serves nachos, quesadillas, burritos, and fajitas exactly the way you want them. Mark your food and drink selections on a checklist, and your server quickly returns with big portions of tasty food. Everything is superfresh, because this place is so popular that nothing sits around. As the name indicates, 'ritas (margaritas) are a specialty. Primarily a casual business destination at lunch, it's livelier at dinner (probably thanks to the margaritas) and a perfect stop before or after a movie at the AMC Loews Boston Common theater.

25 West St. (btw. Washington and Tremont sts.). ✆ **617/426-1222.** www.fajitasandritas.com. Reservations accepted only for parties of 8 or more. Main dishes $5–$9 at lunch, $6–$13 at dinner. AE, DC, DISC, MC, V. Mon–Tues 11:30am–9pm; Wed–Thurs 11:30am–10pm; Fri–Sat 11:30am–11pm; Sun noon–8pm. T: Red or Green Line to Park St., or Orange Line to Downtown Crossing.

Giacomo's Ristorante ITALIAN/SEAFOOD   No reservations, cash only, a tiny dining room with an open kitchen—what's the secret? Terrific food, plenty of it, and the "we're all in this together" atmosphere. To start, try fried calamari or mozzarella with marinara sauce. Put together your own main dish from the list of daily ingredients on a board on the wall. The best suggestion is salmon and sun-dried tomatoes in tomato cream sauce over fettuccine. Non-seafood offerings such as butternut squash ravioli are equally memorable. Service is friendly but incredibly swift. After a 40-minute dinner, dessert at a *caffe* is practically a necessity.

355 Hanover St. ✆ **617/523-9026.** Reservations not accepted. Main courses $14–$18; specials market price. No credit cards. Mon–Thurs 5–10pm; Fri–Sat 5–10:30pm; Sun 4–10pm. T: Green or Orange Line to Haymarket.

Legal Sea Foods SEAFOOD   This chain may not be the secret insider tip you were expecting, but trust me. The family-owned business enjoys an international reputation because it serves the freshest, best-quality fish and shellfish, which it processes at its own state-of-the-art plant. The menu includes regular selections plus whatever looked good at the market that morning, prepared in every imaginable way. The clam chowder is great, the fish chowder lighter but equally good. Entrees run the gamut from grilled fish served plain or with Cajun spices to seafood *fra diavolo* on fresh linguine to mammoth lobsters. The wine list is the best at any restaurant chain in the country.

255 State St. ✆ **617/227-3115.** www.legalseafoods.com. Reservations recommended. Main courses $11–$19 at lunch, $14–$35 at dinner; lobster market price. AE, DC, DISC, MC, V. Mon–Thurs 11am–10pm; Fri–Sat 11am–11pm; Sun noon–10pm. T: Blue Line to Aquarium. Also at 800 Boylston St., in the Prudential Center. ✆ **617/266-6800.** T: Green Line B, C, or D to Hynes Convention Center, or E to Prudential. 36 Park Place (btw. Columbus Ave. and Stuart St.), Park Sq. ✆ **617/426-4444.** T: Green Line to Arlington. Copley Place, 2nd level. ✆ **617/266-7775.** T: Orange Line to Back Bay or Green Line to Copley. 20 University Rd., behind the Charles Hotel, Cambridge. ✆ **617/491-9400.** T: Red Line to Harvard. 5 Cambridge Center, Cambridge. ✆ **617/864-3400.** T: Red Line to Kendall/MIT.

Neptune Oyster SEAFOOD   Tiny and cramped, Neptune feels like one of those off-the-radar places out-of-towners fantasize about—or it would, if it weren't so crowded. Superfresh, inventively prepared seafood keeps this restaurant busy and loud almost all the time; even in winter, I suggest planning for lunch or an early dinner on a weekday if you don't enjoy waiting. Check out the daily specials, then start with oysters. Main courses include some menu standards, and dishes that make good use of whatever's fresh that day. Neptune is just off the Freedom Trail and easy to find: Look for the lemons and oysters in the front window and the crowd inside.

63 Salem St. ✆ **617/742-3474.** www.neptuneoyster.com. Reservations not accepted. Main courses $13–$34; lobster market price. AE, MC, V. Sun–Wed 11:30am–10pm; Thurs–Sat 11:30am–midnight. T: Green or Orange Line to Haymarket.

Peach Farm SEAFOOD/CANTONESE/SZECHUAN   Chinatown's go-to place for fresh seafood is a subterranean hideaway with no decor to speak of and service so fast that just saying "calamari" seems to make spicy dry-fried salted squid appear on your table. Gobble it up while it's hot, then explore: delicious, messy clams with black-bean sauce; braised chicken hot pot; emerald-green stir-fried pea-pod stems. Spicy salt shrimp—you can eat them whole, shells, heads, and all—is addictive. Fresh fish steamed with ginger and scallions, a Cantonese classic, comes to your table thrashing in a plastic bucket and reappears moments later, perfectly cooked.

4 Tyler St. ⓒ **617/482-3332.** Reservations recommended for large groups at dinner. Main courses $5–$34 (most less than $15); fresh seafood market price. MC, V. Daily 11am–3am. T: Orange Line to Chinatown.

Pizzeria Regina PIZZA   In business since 1926, Regina's looks like a movie set, but it's the real thing. The line stretches up the street at busy times; even during off hours, business is seldom slow. Waitresses weave through the boisterous dining room, delivering pizza hot from the brick oven. The list of toppings includes nouveau ingredients such as sun-dried tomatoes, but that's not authentic. House-made sausage, maybe some pepperoni, and a couple of beers—now, *that's* authentic.

11½ Thacher St. ⓒ **617/227-0765.** www.pizzeriaregina.com. Reservations not accepted. Pizza $10–$17. AE, MC, V. Mon–Thurs 11am–11:30pm; Fri–Sat 11am–midnight; Sun noon–11pm. T: Green or Orange Line to Haymarket.

S&S Restaurant DELI   *Es* is Yiddish for "eat," and this Cambridge classic is as straightforward as its name ("eat and eat"). Founded in 1919 by the current owners' great-grandmother, the popular brunch spot draws crowds at busy times on weekends. It looks contemporary, but the brunch offerings are traditional: fantastic omelets, pancakes, waffles, fruit salad, cinnamon rolls. You'll also find traditional deli items, and breakfast anytime. Arrive early for brunch, or plan to spend a chunk of your Saturday or Sunday people-watching and getting hungry.

1334 Cambridge St., Inman Sq. ⓒ **617/354-0777.** www.sandsrestaurant.com. Main courses $4–$18. AE, MC, V. Mon–Wed 7am–11pm; Thurs–Fri 7am–11pm; Sat 8am–11pm; Sun 8am–10pm (brunch Sat–Sun until 4pm). T: Red Line to Central; 10-min. walk on Prospect St. Or Red Line to Harvard, then no. 69 (Harvard–Lechmere) bus to Inman Sq.

Upstairs on the Square ECLECTIC   Overlooking a park off Harvard Square, Upstairs on the Square is the perfect combination of comfort food and fine dining. It consists of two lovely spaces; I prefer the more casual Monday Club Bar, a dining room where firelight flickers on jewel-toned walls. The food—unusual salads and sandwiches, soups, fried chicken, inventive pastas, steak with ever-changing versions of potatoey goodness—is homey and satisfying. The top-floor Soirée Room, a jewel box of pinks and golds under a low, mirrored ceiling, is the place for that big anniversary dinner. In both rooms, you'll find outstanding wine selections and desserts.

91 Winthrop St. ⓒ **617/864-1933.** www.upstairsonthesquare.com. Reservations recommended. Main courses $10–$28 downstairs, $25–$42 upstairs; prix-fixe lunch (downstairs only) $20; tasting menus (upstairs only) $50–$86. AE, DC, DISC, MC, V. Downstairs Mon–Fri 11:30am–2:30pm; Sat–Sun brunch 10am–3pm; afternoon tea Fri–Sat 3–5pm; daily 5pm–2am (dinner until 11pm). Upstairs Mon–Thurs 5:30–10pm; Fri–Sat 5:30–11pm. Validated and valet parking available. T: Red Line to Harvard.

BOSTON & CAMBRIDGE AFTER DARK

For up-to-date entertainment listings, consult the "Sidekick" section of the daily *Boston Globe,* the "Edge" section of the Friday *Boston Herald,* or the daily arts sections of both papers. Four free publications, available at newspaper boxes around town, publish nightlife listings: the *Boston Phoenix,* the *Improper Bostonian, Stuff@Night* (a *Phoenix* offshoot), and the *Weekly Dig.* The *Phoenix* website (www.bostonphoenix.com) archives the paper's season preview issues; especially before a summer or fall visit, it's a worthwhile planning tool.

Gay- and lesbian-specific events and venues list what's happening in *Bay Windows* (**www.baywindows.com**), available at newsstands and at **Glad Day Bookstore,** 673 Boylston St., Back Bay (© **617/267-3010;** T: Copley).

GETTING TICKETS   Some companies and venues sell tickets over the phone or online. The major agencies that serve Boston are **Ticketmaster** (© **617/931-2000;** www.ticketmaster.com) and **Telecharge** (© **800/432-7250;** www.telecharge.com). Many smaller venues use independent companies that don't charge as much. For **discount tickets,** visit a **BosTix** (© **617/482-2849;** www.bostix.org) booth, at Faneuil Hall Marketplace or in Copley Square, where same-day tickets to musical and theatrical performances are half-price, subject to availability. Credit cards are not accepted, and there are no refunds or exchanges. Check the board or the website for the day's offerings. The booths, which are also Ticketmaster outlets, are open Tuesday through Saturday from 10am to 6pm (half-price tickets go on sale at 11am), Sunday from 11am to 4pm. The Copley Square location is open Monday from 10am to 6pm.

THE PERFORMING ARTS   The **Boston Symphony Orchestra,** one of the world's greatest, performs at Symphony Hall, 301 Mass. Ave. (© **617/266-1492;** www.bso.org; T: Green Line E to Symphony, or Orange Line to Mass. Ave.). The season runs from October to April. From May to July, members of the BSO lighten up. Tables and chairs replace the floor seats at Symphony Hall, and drinks and light refreshments are served. The famed **Boston Pops** (same contact info as the BSO) plays a range of music from light classical to show tunes to popular music, sometimes with celebrity guest stars. Its regular season ends with two **free outdoor concerts** along the Charles River: the July 3 rehearsal and the traditional Fourth of July concert.

The **Boston Ballet**'s reputation seems to jump a notch every time someone says, "So it's not just *The Nutcracker*." The country's fourth-largest dance company performs the holiday staple from Thanksgiving to New Year's. During the rest of the season (Oct–May), it presents an eclectic mix of classic ballets and contemporary work. Call © **617/695-6955** or check out **http://bostonballet.org**. Performances are held at the Wang Theatre, 270 Tremont St. (T: Green Line to Boylston).

The excellent local theater scene boasts the **Huntington Theatre Company,** which performs at the Boston University Theatre, 264 Huntington Ave. (© **617/266-0800;** www.huntington.org); and the **American Repertory Theatre,** which makes its home at Harvard University's Loeb Drama Center, 64 Brattle St., Cambridge (© **617/547-8300;** www.amrep.org).

You'll find most of the shows headed to or coming from Broadway in the **Theater District.** The promoter often is **Broadway Across America** (© **866/523-7469;** www.broadwayacrossamerica.com).

An excellent summer diversion is a free, top-quality performance on historic Boston Common. Bring a picnic, spread a blanket, and enjoy the sunset. The **Commonwealth Shakespeare Company** (© **617/482-9393;** www.commshakes.org) performs Tuesday through Sunday nights in July and early August. The **Boston Landmarks Orchestra** (© **617/520-2200;** www.landmarksorchestra.org) schedules "accessible classical" concerts in local parks on evenings from July to September.

THE CLUB SCENE   The Boston-area club scene changes constantly, and somewhere out there is a good time for everyone—or at least every early bird. Bars close at 1am, clubs at 2am. The subway shuts down between 12:30 and 1am. Check the "Sidekick" section

of the *Globe,* the *Phoenix,* the "Edge" section of the Friday *Herald, Stuff@Night,* or the
Improper Bostonian while you're planning.

For **dancing,** try the **Estate,** 1 Boylston Place (© **617/351-7000;** www.theestate boston.com; cover $10–$25; T: Green Line to Boylston). A can't-miss destination for visiting "celebrities," the Estate is a cavernous space with a balcony overlooking the large dance floor. It attracts a 20-something crowd with well-known local DJs and an excellent sound system. The lower level is the **Suite**—all house music, all the time. In both, the dress code is "casual chic and fashionable," which appears to mean shirts with collars on men and something tight and black on women. Open Thursday through Sunday (Thurs and Sun are gay nights); check ahead for specifics. The **Roxy,** in the Tremont Boston hotel, 279 Tremont St. (© **617/338-7699;** www.roxyplex.com; cover $10–$20; T: Green Line to Boylston), boasts excellent DJs and live music, a huge dance floor, a stage, and a balcony. Occasional concerts take good advantage of the sightlines. No jeans or athletic shoes. The Roxy is open Thursday through Saturday, plus some Wednesdays and Sundays.

FOLK & ECLECTIC Legendary coffeehouse **Club Passim,** at 47 Palmer St., Cambridge (© **617/492-7679;** www.clubpassim.org; cover $5–$25, most shows $15 or less; T: Red Line to Harvard), is where Joan Baez, Suzanne Vega, and Tom Rush started out. There's live music nightly, and coffee and food (no alcohol is served) until 10pm. It's open nightly.

JAZZ & BLUES On summer Thursdays at 6pm, the **Boston Harbor Hotel** (© 617/ **439-7000)** stages performances on the "Blues Barge," in the water behind the hotel. The theater at the Cambridge Multicultural Arts Center, 41 Second St., Cambridge (© **617/ 577-1400;** www.cmacusa.org; T: Green Line to Lechmere), becomes the **Real Deal Jazz Club & Cafe** a couple of times a month year-round.

Wally's Café, 427 Mass. Ave. (© **617/424-1408;** www.wallyscafe.com; T: Orange Line to Mass. Ave.), is a Boston institution. Opened in 1947 in the South End, it draws a diverse crowd—black, white, straight, gay, affluent, indigent—and features nightly live music by local ensembles, students and instructors from the Berklee College of Music, and the occasional international star. There's a one-drink minimum.

ROCK & ALTERNATIVE Big-name rock and pop artists play **TD Banknorth Garden,** 100 Legends Way (Causeway St.; © **617/624-1000;** www.tdbanknorthgarden.com), when it's not in use by the Bruins (hockey), the Celtics (basketball), the circus (in Oct), and touring ice shows.

The **Middle East,** one of the best clubs in town, books an impressive variety of progressive and alternative acts upstairs and downstairs every night at 472–480 Mass. Ave., Central Square, Cambridge (© **617/864-EAST** [864-3278]; www.mideastclub.com; cover $7–$15; T: Red Line to Central). Other venues are the **Paradise Rock Club,** which draws enthusiastic crowds for top local and national performers at 967 Comm. Ave. (© 617/ **562-8800,** or 423-NEXT [423-6398] for tickets; www.dlclive.com; T: Green Line B to Pleasant St.); and **T.T. the Bear's,** 10 Brookline St., Cambridge (© **617/492-0082;** www.ttthebears.com; T: Red Line to Central), a no-frills spot with bookings ranging from alternative rock to ska to up-and-coming pop acts.

BARS & LOUNGES If you want to go "where everybody knows your name," there's **Cheers,** 84 Beacon St. (© **617/227-9605;** www.cheersboston.com; T: Green Line to Arlington), the inspiration for the TV show *Cheers.* It really is a neighborhood bar with good pub grub, but it's better known for attracting legions of out-of-towners. Then there's an additional branch of **Cheers,** a bar that replicates the set of the TV show at Faneuil Hall Marketplace (© **617/227-0150;** www.cheersboston.com; T: Green or Blue lines to Government Center, or Orange Line to Haymarket).

At the **Black Rose,** 160 State St. (© **617/742-2286;** www.irishconnection.com; T: Orange or Blue lines to State), an always-jampacked pub and restaurant, you can sing along with the entertainment. (There's a cover, usually $5 or less). An excellent jukebox, food, and eavesdropping make **Casablanca,** 40 Brattle St., Cambridge (© **617/876-0999;** T: Red Line to Harvard), a legendary Harvard Square watering hole jammed with students and professors. At **Top of the Hub,** 800 Boylston St. (© **617/536-1775;** T: Green Line E to Prudential), the 52nd-story view of Boston from this lounge atop the Prudential Center is lovely at sunset. There's music and dancing nightly. Dress is casual but neat. There's a $24 minimum in the lounge after 8pm.

A SIDE TRIP TO CONCORD

Concord revels in its legacy as a center of groundbreaking thought and its role in the country's political and intellectual history. For an excellent overview of town history, start your explorations at the **Concord Museum.**

After just a little time in this lovely town, you may find yourself adopting the local attitude toward two of its most famous residents: Ralph Waldo Emerson, who comes across as a well-respected uncle figure; and Henry David Thoreau, everyone's favorite eccentric cousin. The first official battle of the Revolutionary War took place at the North Bridge, now part of Minute Man National Historical Park. By the middle of the 19th century, Concord was the center of the Transcendentalist movement. Homes of Emerson, Thoreau, Nathaniel Hawthorne, and Louisa May Alcott are open to visitors.

GETTING THERE   From Boston by **car** (30–40 min.), take Route 2 into Lincoln and stay in the right lane. Where the main road makes a sharp left, go straight onto Cambridge Turnpike and follow signs to HISTORIC CONCORD. To go directly to Walden Pond, use the left lane, take Route 2/2A another mile or so, and turn left onto Route 126. There's parking throughout town.

The **commuter rail** (© **800/392-6100** outside Massachusetts, or 617/222-3200; www.mbta.com) takes about 45 minutes from North Station in Boston, with a stop in Cambridge. The round-trip fare is $10.

VISITOR INFORMATION   The **chamber of commerce,** 15 Walden St., Ste. 7 (© **978/369-3120;** www.concordchamberofcommerce.org), maintains a visitor center at 58 Main St., next to Middlesex Savings Bank, 1 block south of Monument Square. It's open daily 9:30am to 4:30pm from April through October; public restrooms in the same building are open year-round. Guided walking tours are available. Weekday and group tours are available by appointment. The community (**www.concordma.com**) and town (**www.concordnet.org**) websites include visitor information. You can also contact the **Greater Merrimack Valley Convention & Visitors Bureau** (© **800/443-3332** or 978/459-6150; www.merrimackvalley.org).

WHAT TO SEE & DO

Concord Museum ⟨**Kids**⟩   This is a great place to start your visit. The **History Galleries** explore the question "Why Concord?" Artifacts, murals, films, maps, documents, and other presentations illustrate the town's role as a Native American settlement, Revolutionary War battleground, 19th-century intellectual center, and focal point of the 20th-century historic preservation movement. You'll also see the contents of Ralph Waldo

Emerson's study and a collection of Henry David Thoreau's belongings. Pick up a **family**
activity pack as you enter and use the games and reproduction artifacts (including a quill pen and powder horn) to give the kids a hands-on feel for life in the past.

Cambridge Tpk. at Lexington Rd. ✆ **978/369-9609** for recorded info, or 369-9763. www.concord museum.org. Admission $8 adults, $7 seniors and students, $5 children 15 and under. June–Aug daily 9am–5pm; Apr–May and Sept–Dec Mon–Sat 9am–5pm, Sun noon–5pm; Jan–Mar Mon–Sat 11am–4pm, Sun 1–4pm.

The Old Manse The history of this home touches on the military and the literary, but it's mostly the story of a family. The Rev. William Emerson built the Old Manse in 1770 and watched the Battle of Concord from his yard. For almost 170 years, the house was home to his descendants and to two famous friends. In 1842, Nathaniel Hawthorne and his bride, Sophia Peabody, moved in and stayed for 3 years. As a wedding present, Henry David Thoreau sowed the vegetable garden for them. This is also where William's grandson Ralph Waldo Emerson wrote the essay "Nature." Today you'll see mementos and memorabilia of the Emerson and Ripley families and of the Hawthornes.

269 Monument St. (at North Bridge). ✆ **978/369-3909**. www.oldmanse.org. Guided tour $8 adults, $7 seniors and students, $5 children 6–12, $25 families. Mid-Apr to Oct Mon–Sat 10am–5pm; Sun and holidays noon–5pm (last tour at 4:30pm). Closed Nov to mid-Apr.

Orchard House ⓑ**Best** *Little Women* (1868), Louisa May Alcott's most popular work, was written and set at Orchard House. Seeing the family home brings the Alcotts to life for legions of visitors. Fans won't want to miss the tour, illustrated with heirlooms. Check in advance for information on holiday programs and other special events. Louisa's father, Amos Bronson Alcott, created Orchard House by joining and restoring two homes. The family lived here from 1858 to 1877. Her mother, Abigail May Alcott, frequently assumed the role of breadwinner—Bronson, Louisa wrote in her journal, had "no gift for money making." *Note:* Call before visiting; an extensive preservation project is underway.

399 Lexington Rd. ✆ **978/369-4118**. www.louisamayalcott.org. Guided tour $8 adults, $7 seniors and students, $5 children 6–17, $20 families. Apr–Oct Mon–Sat 10am–4:30pm, Sun 1–4:30pm; Nov–Mar Mon–Fri 11am–2:45pm, Sat 10am–4:30pm, Sun 1–4:30pm. Closed Jan 1–15.

Ralph Waldo Emerson House Emerson, also an essayist and poet, lived here from 1835 until his death in 1882. He moved here after marrying his second wife, Lydia Jackson, whom he called "Lydian"; she called him "Mr. Emerson," as the staff still does. The tour gives a good look at his personal side and at the fashionably ornate interior decoration of the time. You'll see original furnishings and some of Emerson's personal effects.

28 Cambridge Tpk. ✆ **978/369-2236**. Guided tours $7 adults, $5 seniors and students. Call to arrange group tours (10 people or more). Mid-Apr to Oct Thurs–Sat 10am–4:30pm, Sun 1–4:30pm. Closed Nov to mid-Apr.

Sleepy Hollow Cemetery Follow the signs for AUTHOR'S RIDGE to the graves of some of the town's literary lights. Emerson's grave is marked by an uncarved quartz boulder. Thoreau's grave is nearby; at his funeral in 1862, Emerson concluded his eulogy with these words: "wherever there is knowledge, wherever there is virtue, wherever there is beauty, he will find a home."

Entrance on Rte. 62 W. ✆ **978/318-3233**. www.concordnet.org. Daily 7am–dusk, weather permitting. Call ahead for wheelchair access. No buses allowed.

The Wayside The Wayside was Nathaniel Hawthorne's home from 1852 until his death in 1864. The Wayside is part of Minute Man National Historical Park, and the fascinating 45-minute ranger-led tour illuminates the occupants' lives and the house's crazy-quilt architecture. The exhibit in the barn (free admission) consists of audio presentations and figures of the authors.

455 Lexington Rd. (C) **978/369-6975.** www.nps.gov/archive/mima/wayside/index1.htm. Guided tour $4 adults, free for children 16 and under. May–Oct; open days and hours vary. Closed Nov–Apr.

Minute Man National Historical Park

This 900-acre park preserves the scene of the first Revolutionary War battle, which took place on April 19, 1775. Encouraged by their victory at Lexington, the British continued to Concord in search of stockpiled arms (which the colonists had already moved). Warned of the advance, the Minutemen crossed the North Bridge, evading the "regulars" standing guard, and awaited reinforcements on a hilltop. The British searched nearby homes and burned any guns they found, and the Minutemen, seeing the smoke, mistakenly thought the soldiers were burning the town. The gunfire that ensued, the opening salvo of the Revolution, is remembered as "the shot heard round the world."

The park is open daily year-round. A visit can take as little as half an hour—for a jaunt to the North Bridge—or as long as half a day (or more), if you stop at both visitor centers and participate in a ranger-led program. To reach the bridge from Concord Center, follow Monument Street until you see the parking lot on the right. On one side of the bridge is a plaque commemorating the British soldiers who died in the Revolutionary War. On the other side is Daniel Chester French's *Minute Man* statue, engraved with a stanza of the poem Emerson wrote for the dedication ceremony in 1876.

You can also start at the **North Bridge Visitor Center,** 174 Liberty St., off Monument Street (C) **978/369-6993;** www.nps.gov/mima), which overlooks the Concord River and the bridge. A diorama and video illustrate the Battle of Concord; exhibits include uniforms, weapons, and tools of Colonial and British soldiers. Park rangers lead programs and answer questions. Outside, picnicking is allowed, and the scenery (especially the fall foliage) is lovely. The center is open daily from 9am to 5pm (until 4pm in winter).

At the Lexington end of the park, the **Minute Man Visitor Center** (C) **781/862-7753;** www.nps.gov/mima), off Route 2A, about ¹/₂ mile west of I-95, exit 30B, is open daily from 9am to 5pm (until 4pm in winter). You'll see a multimedia program on the Revolution, displays, and a 40-foot mural illustrating the battle. On summer weekends, rangers lead tours—call ahead for times. The **Battle Road Trail,** a 5.5-mile interpretive path, carries pedestrian, wheelchair, and bicycle traffic. Panels and granite markers display information about the area's history.

Also on the park grounds, on Old Bedford Road, is the **Hartwell Tavern.** Costumed interpreters demonstrate daily life on a farm and in a tavern in Colonial days. It's open from 9:30am to 5pm daily June through August and weekends only in April, May, September, and October. Admission is free.

Wilderness Retreats

Henry David Thoreau's first published works can serve as starting points: *A Week on the Concord and Merrimack Rivers* (1849) and *Walden* (1854).

To see the area from water level, rent a **canoe** at the **South Bridge Boathouse,** 496 Main St. (C) **978/369-9438**), about ³/₄ mile west of the center of town, and paddle to the North Bridge and back. Rates are about $12 per hour on weekends, less on weekdays.

At the **Walden Pond State Reservation,** 915 Walden St., Route 126 (C) **978/369-3254;** www.mass.gov/dcr), a pile of stones marks the site of the cabin where Thoreau lived from 1845 to 1847. Today the picturesque reservation is an extremely popular destination for walking (a path circles the pond), swimming, and fishing. Although crowded, it's well preserved and insulated from development, making it less difficult than you might expect to imagine Thoreau's experience. Call for the schedule of interpretive programs. No dogs or bikes are allowed. Parking costs $5. Call before setting out, because the rangers turn away visitors if the park has reached capacity (1,000). From Concord Center, take Walden Street (Rte. 126) south, cross Route 2, and follow signs to the parking lot.

2 CAPE COD

Curling some 75 miles into the Atlantic, Cape Cod offers miles of beaches, freshwater ponds, and historic New England villages; it's a popular summer destination, with plenty of activities after the sun goes down as well.

ESSENTIALS

GETTING THERE   By Car   From Providence and New York, cross the Cape Cod Canal on the Bourne Bridge; from Boston, cross on the Sagamore Bridge. Head east on **Route 6.** Exits are marked for all major destinations. Traffic can be a nightmare on peak weekends, so plan accordingly.

By Plane   The Cape's major hub is **Barnstable Municipal Airport,** Hyannis (© 508/775-2020), served by **US Airways** (© 800/428-4322; www.usair.com) and smaller airlines from Boston and New York. **Provincetown Airport** (© 508/487-0241) is served by **Cape Air** (© 800/352-0714; www.flycapeair.com) from Boston.

By Boat   **Bay State Cruises** (© 617/748-1428; www.baystatecruisecompany.com) runs a "fast ferry" to Provincetown from Boston, daily from mid-May through mid-October. The trip takes about 90 minutes and costs about $71 round-trip for an adult (discounts for children and seniors). The "excursion" service (on a slower boat) runs weekends only in the summer, takes 3 hours, and costs $33 round-trip for an adult.

HYANNIS

Hectic Hyannis is the commercial center and transportation hub of the Cape. It also has a diverse selection of restaurants, bars, and nightclubs. But if you were to confine your visit to this one town, you'd get a warped view of the Cape. Along routes 132 and 28, you could be visiting Anywhere, USA: The roads are lined with the standard chain stores and mired with maddening traffic.

The Kennedy Compound in Hyannisport is effectively screened from view. You'll see more at the **John F. Kennedy Hyannis Museum,** 397 Main St. (© 508/790-3077; www.hyannis.com/JFKMuseum.asp), with a multimedia display capturing the Kennedys during their glory days from 1934 to 1963. Admission is $5 adults, $2.50 for children ages 10 to 16. The museum is open April to October Monday to Saturday 9am to 4:30pm, Sunday and holidays noon to 4:30pm; last admission is at 3:30pm.

BREWSTER

With miles of placid Cape Cod Bay beaches and acres of state park, Brewster is an attractive place for families. Route 6A, the Old King's Highway, becomes Brewster's Main Street and houses a bevy of B&Bs, restaurants, and the Cape's finest **antiques** shops. Brewster also welcomes the tens of thousands of campers and day-trippers headed for **Nickerson State Park.**

VISITOR INFORMATION Contact the **Brewster Chamber of Commerce Visitor Center** behind Brewster Town Hall, 2198 Main St./Rte. 6A, Brewster (𝒞 **508/896-3500;** www.brewstercapecod.org).

Brewster's eight bay **beaches** have minimal facilities. When the tide is out, the beach extends as much as 2 miles, leaving behind tidal pools to splash in. On a clear day, you can see the whole curve of the Cape, from Sandwich to Provincetown. Purchase a beach parking sticker ($15 per day, $50 per week) at the **Visitor Center.**

The 25-mile **Cape Cod Rail Trail,** one of New England's most popular bike paths, intersects with the 8-mile **Nickerson State Park** trail system at the park entrance, where there's plenty of free parking; you could follow the Rail Trail back to Dennis (about 12 miles) or toward Wellfleet (13 miles). In season, **Idle Times** (𝒞 **508/255-8281**) provides bike rentals within the park. About ¹/₂ mile south of Route 6A, you'll find **Brewster Bicycle Rental,** 442 Underpass Rd. (𝒞 **508/896-8149**); and **Brewster Express,** which makes sandwiches to go. Just up the hill is **Rail Trail Bike & Blade,** 302 Underpass Rd. (𝒞 **508/896-8200**). Both shops offer free parking. Bicycle rentals start at around $14 for 4 hours and go up to about $22 for 24 hours.

Long before *ecology* became a buzzword, naturalist John Hay helped found the **Cape Cod Museum of Natural History,** 869 Rte. 6A (𝒞 **800/479-3867** in eastern Massachusetts, or 508/896-3867; www.ccmnh.org), dedicated to preserving Cape Cod's unique landscape. Children's exhibits include a "live hive"—like an ant farm, only with busy bees—and marine-room tanks. The bulk of the museum is outdoors. There's an on-site archaeology lab on Wing Island. Admission is $8 adults, $7 seniors, $3.50 children 3 to 12.

Where to Stay & Dine

Looking like an enormous seaside estate, **Ocean Edge Resort and Club** (2907 Main St./Rte. 6A; 𝒞 **800/896-9000;** www.oceanedge.com) offers many amenities, including beach, pools, tennis, and golf. Replete with New England–style charm—lovely quilts, sliding glass doors that lead to patios or balconies—hotel rooms off the mansion are large and comfortable. Summer rates range from $350 per night for doubles to $7,500 for a three-bedroom villa for a week. The reasonably priced, historic **Old Sea Pines Inn** (𝒞 **508/896-6114;** www.oldseapinesinn.com) is a great spot for families. The inn's former days as the Sea Pines School of Charm and Personality for Young Women can still be seen in the handful of rather minuscule boarding-school-scale rooms on the second floor. These bargain rooms share bathrooms and are the only ones in the house without air-conditioning, but at $105 per night in season, who cares!

One of the best restaurants on Cape Cod, the **Bramble Inn Restaurant,** 2019 Main St. (𝒞 **508/896-7544**), is one of the most expensive—but worth it. To get the gist of the expression "chow down," just observe the early-evening crowd happily doing so at the **Brewster Inn & Chowder House,** 1993 Rte. 6A (𝒞 **508/896-7771**), a century-old restaurant where the draw is hearty staples at prices geared to ordinary people.

CHATHAM

Chatham (say *Chatt*-um) is small-town America the way Norman Rockwell imagined it. Roses climb white picket fences in front of Cape cottages within a stone's throw of the ocean. Visit the **Chatham Chamber of Commerce,** 533 Main St., Chatham, MA 02633 (𝒞 **800/715-5567** or 508/945-5199; www.chathaminfo.com); or the new **Chatham Chamber booth** at the intersection of routes 137 and 28 (no phone).

Chatham has an unusual array of **beaches,** from the peaceful shores of Nantucket Sound to the shifting shoals along the Atlantic. For beach stickers ($15 per day, $60 per week), call the **Permit Department** on George Ryder Road in West Chatham (© **508/945-5180**). Among the beaches are **Cockle Cove Beach, Ridgevale Beach,** and **Hardings Beach;** lined up along the sound, each at the end of its namesake road south of Route 28, these pleasing beaches offer gentle surf and full facilities. **Oyster Pond Beach,** off Route 28, is only a block from Chatham's Main Street. This sheltered saltwater pond (with restrooms) swarms with children. **North Beach** extends all the way south from Orleans. This 5-mile barrier beach is accessible from Chatham only by boat; you can take the **Beachcomber** (© **508/945-5265**), a water taxi, which leaves from the fish pier. The round-trip costs $12 for adults, $8 for children 12 and under.

Though Chatham has no separate recreational paths, per se, a **biking/skating** lane makes a scenic 8-mile circuit of town, heading south onto "the Neck," east to the Chatham Light, up Shore Road to north Chatham, and back. A brochure prepared by the **chamber of commerce** (© **800/715-5567** or 508/945-5199) shows the route. Rentals are available at **Bikes & Blades,** 195 Crowell Rd. (© **508/945-7600**).

Chatham has five ponds and lakes that permit **fishing.** For saltwater fishing sans boat, try the fishing bridge on Bridge Street at the south end of Mill Pond. First, get a license at **Town Hall,** 549 Main St. (© **508/945-5101**). If you hear the deep sea calling, sign on with the *Headhunter* (© **508/430-2312;** www.capecodfishingcharters.com) or the *Banshee* (© **508/945-0403**), both berthed in Stage Harbor. Sportfishing rates average around $725 for 8 hours. Shellfishing licenses are available at the **Permit Department,** on George Ryder Road in West Chatham (© **508/945-5180**).

Heading southeast from the Hardings Beach parking lot, the 2-mile round-trip **Seaside Trail** offers beautiful parallel panoramas of Nantucket Sound and Oyster Pond River. Access to 40-acre Morris Island, southwest of the Chatham Light, is easy: Walk or drive across and start right in on a marked .75-mile trail.

The *Beachcomber* (© **508/945-5265**) runs seal-watching cruises out of Stage Harbor. Parking is behind the former Main Street School. Cruises cost $22 for adults, $20 for seniors, $16 for children 3 to 15, and are free for children 2 and under.

Uninhabited **Monomoy Island,** 2,750 acres of brush-covered sand favored by some 285 species of migrating birds, is the perfect pit stop along the Atlantic flyway. Harbor and gray seals carpet the coastline from late November to May. The **Wellfleet Bay Wildlife Sanctuary,** operated by the Audubon Society (© **508/349-2615**), and the **Cape Cod Museum of Natural History** (© **508/896-3867**) offer guided trips.

Seaworthy vessels, from surfboards to Sunfish, can be rented from **Monomoy Sail and Cycle,** 275 Rte. 28, North Chatham (© **508/945-0811**). Pleasant Bay is the best place to play for those with sufficient experience; if the winds don't seem to be going your way, try Forest Beach on the south Chatham shore.

Where to Stay

Chatham has several decent motels. The basic **Hawthorne,** 196 Shore Rd. (© **508/945-0372;** www.thehawthorne.com), is on the water, with views of Chatham Harbor, Pleasant Bay, and the Atlantic. The **Seafarer of Chatham,** 2079 Rte. 28, about ¹/₂ mile east of Route 137 in Chatham (© **800/786-2772** or 508/432-1739; www.chathamseafarer. com), lacks a pool but is close to Ridgevale Beach.

NEW ENGLAND

2

CAPE COD

Set above the beach in Chatham with commanding views, the grand **Chatham Bars Inn,** Shore Road (© **800/527-4884** or 508/945-0096; www.chathambarsinn.com), is the premier hotel on Cape Cod. The colonnaded 1914 brick building is surrounded by 26 shingled cottages. Take in the sweeping views on the breezy veranda. Amenities include an outdoor heated pool, putting green, public 9-hole golf course next door, tennis courts, basic fitness room, summer children's programs, shuffleboard, croquet, volleyball, and a complimentary launch to Nauset Beach. Cottage rooms are cheery with painted furniture and Waverly fabrics. Guests can take meals in the **Main Dining Room,** the **Tavern,** or the seasonal **Beach House Grill** right on the private beach.

The **Captain's House Inn,** 369–377 Old Harbor Rd. (© **800/315-0728** or 508/945-0127; www.captainshouseinn.com), is an 1839 Greek Revival house, along with a cottage and carriage house, a shining example of 19th-century style. Bedrooms are richly furnished with canopied four-posters, beamed ceilings, and, in some cases, brick hearths and Jacuzzis. Rates include full breakfast and afternoon tea. There are bikes for the guests to use, and many rooms have minifridges.

Across the street from Pleasant Bay, a few minutes' walk from a bay beach, **Pleasant Bay Village,** 1191 Orleans Rd./Rte. 28 (© **800/547-1011** or 508/945-1133; www.pleasantbayvillage.com), is one fancy motel. It's a Zen paradise, where waterfalls cascade through colorful rock gardens into a stone-edged pool surrounded by whimsical Oriental gardens. Many bathrooms in the lovely guest rooms feature marble countertops and stone floors. The suites have fully equipped kitchens, including microwave ovens. In summer, the restaurant serves three meals a day. You can order lunch from the grill without having to leave your place at the heated pool.

Where to Dine

We highly recommend the **Main Dining Room** at the Chatham Bars Inn (see above for location). This is not delicate food, but it is delicious—and the chowder may be the best on Cape Cod.

The **Chatham Wayside Inn,** 512 Main St. (© **508/945-5550**), is a good spot for a reasonably priced meal in town. Specialties include crab cakes, rack of lamb, and pesto cod. For something a little different, try the Portuguese-style chowder, with double-smoked bacon, fresh quahogs, and red bliss potatoes.

A major renovation has turned **28 Atlantic,** 2173 Rte. 28 at the Wequasett Inn, about 5 miles northwest of Chatham center, on Pleasant Bay (© **508/430-3000;** www.wequasett.com), into one of the top places to eat on Cape Cod. The elegant, spacious dining room overlooks Pleasant Bay through immense floor-to-ceiling glass panels. And the food stands out as superb, from the *amuse bouche* (a little taste teaser), to the exceptional desserts. Menu items use local provender as much as possible, but there are also delicacies from around the world.

Chatham After Dark

Chatham's free **band concerts** attract crowds in the thousands. This is small-town America at its most nostalgic, as the band plays old standards that never go out of style. Held in Kate Gould Park (off Chatham Bars Ave.) from July to early September, they kick off at 8pm every Friday. Call © **508/945-5199** for information.

A great leveler, the **Chatham Squire,** 487 Main St. (© **508/945-0942**), attracts CEOs, seafarers, and collegians alike. Great pub grub, too! The piano bar **Upstairs at Christian's,** 443 Main St. (© **508/945-3362**), has the air of a vintage frat house with scuffed leather couches and movie posters. Live music is offered nightly in season and weekends year-round.

PROVINCETOWN

You've made it all the way to the end of the Cape, to one of the most interesting spots on the eastern seaboard. Charles Hawthorne, the painter who "discovered" this near-derelict fishing town in the late 1890s and introduced it to the Greenwich Village intelligentsia, was besotted by this "jumble of color in the intense sunlight accentuated by the brilliant blue of the harbor."

The whole town, in fact, is dedicated to creative expression, both visual and verbal. That same open-mindedness may account for Provincetown's ascendancy as a gay and lesbian resort. The street life also includes families, art lovers, and gourmands. In short, Provincetown has something for just about everyone.

Contact the **Provincetown Chamber of Commerce,** 307 Commercial St., Province-town, MA 02657 (© **508/487-3424;** www.ptownchamber.com), or the gay-oriented **Provincetown Business Guild,** 115 Bradford St., P.O. Box 421, Provincetown, MA 02657 (© **800/637-8696** or 508/487-2313; www.ptown.org).

Beaches & Outdoor Pursuits

BEACHES With nine-tenths of its territory protected by the Cape Cod National Seashore, Provincetown has miles of beaches. The 3-mile bay beach that lines the harbor, though certainly swimmable, is not all that inviting compared to the ocean beaches overseen by the National Seashore. The two official access areas tend to be crowded; however, you can always find a less densely populated stretch if you're willing to hike down the beach a bit.

BICYCLING North of town is one of the more spectacular bike paths in New England, the 7-mile **Province Lands Trail,** a heady swirl of steep dunes anchored by wind-stunted scrub pines. With its free parking, the **Province Lands Visitor Center** (© **508/487-1256**) is a good place to start. Rentals are offered in season by **Nelson's Bike Shop,** 43 Race Point Rd. (© **508/487-8849**). In town, rentals are available at **Ptown Bikes,** 42 Bradford St. (© **508/487-8735**); reserve several days in advance.

BOATING **Flyer's Boat Rental,** 131 Commercial St., in the West End (© **508/487-0898**), offers all sorts of craft, from kayaks to sailboats; lessons and fishing-gear rentals are available.

MUSEUMS Anywhere you go in town, the **Pilgrim Monument & Provincetown Museum** on High Pole Hill Road (© **508/487-1310;** www.pilgrim-monument.org) looms. Climb the 60 gradual ramps interspersed with 116 steps and you'll get a gargoyle's-eye view of the spiraling coast and Boston against a backdrop of New Hampshire's mountains. Admission is $7 adults, $3.50 children 4 to 14. It's closed December to March. The **Provincetown Art Association & Museum,** 460 Commercial St. (© **508/487-1750;** www.paam.org), is an extraordinary cache of 20th-century American art begun by Charles Hawthorne. Founded in 1914, the museum was the site of innumerable "space wars," as classicists and modernists vied for square footage. Admission is $2 adults, free for children 11 and under.

TOURS **Art's Dune Tours** is at the corner of Commercial and Standish streets (© **800/894-1951** or 508/487-1950; www.artsdunetours.com). In 1946, Art Costa started driving sightseers out to ogle the "dune shacks" where Eugene O'Neill, Jack Kerouac, and Jackson Pollock found their respective muses. The tours typically take 1 to $1^1/_2$ hours. Tickets are $18 to $26 for adults, $13 to $16 for children 6 to 11. Additional tours offered include a sunset clambake dune tour ($66) and a barbecue tour ($56).

WHALE-WATCHING   Stellwagen Bank, 8 miles off Provincetown, is a feeding ground for whales. The **Dolphin Fleet** at MacMillan Wharf (© **800/826-9300** or 508/349-1900) was the first, and by most accounts is still the best, outfitter running whale-watching trips to Stellwagen. Tickets for the $3^1/_2$-hour trips are $28 for adults, $26 for seniors, and $22 for children 7 to 12. Call to reserve. Closed November through March.

Where to Stay

The **Brass Key Guesthouse,** 67 Bradford St. (© **800/842-9858** or 508/487-9005; www. brasskey.com), is the fanciest place in town. The innkeepers have thought of everything: down pillows, jetted showers, and iced tea and lemonade delivered poolside. Rooms in the 1828 Federal-style Captain's House and the Gatehouse are outfitted in a country style, while the Victorian-era building is elegant. Most deluxe rooms have gas fireplaces and whirlpool tubs. Rates include continental breakfast and afternoon wine and cheese. There's a heated outdoor pool, a Jacuzzi, and fridges and safes in the rooms. No children 17 and under.

   Carpe Diem, 12 Johnson St. (© **800/487-0132** or 508/487-4242; www.carpediem guesthouse.com), is a stylish 1884 house on a quiet side street that suits most P-town habitués to a T. Guest rooms are outfitted with antiques, down comforters, robes, and (most rooms) refrigerators. Two deluxe garden suites boast private entrances, Jacuzzis, and fireplaces. The cottage has a two-person whirlpool and a wet bar. The full breakfast features homemade pastries served at the dining-room table. On clear days, sun worshipers prefer the patio. Rates include continental breakfast.

   The **Masthead,** 31–41 Commercial St. (© **800/395-5095** or 508/487-0523; www. themasthead.com), is one of the few places in town, other than the impersonal motels, that actively welcomes families, and the placid 450-foot private beach will delight young splashers. The cottages are fun, some with wicker furniture and antiques. In the water-view rooms perched above the surf, with their 7-foot picture windows overlooking the bay and Long Point, you may feel as though you're on board a ship. All rooms have fridges; two share a bathroom.

   Look for the house with the bright yellow door in the East End; it's the very embodiment of Provincetown's bohemian mystique: the **White Horse Inn,** 500 Commercial St. (© **508/487-1790**). Frank Schaefer has been tinkering with this late-18th-century house since 1963; a number of his fellow artists helped him out in cobbling together the studio apartments out of salvage. Some units have shared bathrooms; there are no televisions or phones in the room, adding to the serenity.

Where to Dine

Spiritus, 190 Commercial St. (© **508/487-2808**), is an extravagant pizza parlor open until 2am. Peruse the scrumptious meat pies and pastries at the **Provincetown Portuguese Bakery,** 299 Commercial St. (© **508/487-1803**). Both establishments are closed November through March.

   Martin House, 157 Commercial St. (© **508/487-1327;** www.themartinhouse.com), is easily one of the most charming restaurants on the Cape. The chef favors local delicacies, such as the littlenecks that appear in a kafir-lime-tamarind broth with Asian noodles. Main courses might include grilled rack of pork with mango salsa and cactus-pear demi-glace on spicy masa.

Bubala's by the Bay, 183 Commercial St. (© **508/487-0773**), promises "serious food at sensible prices." And that's what it delivers: from buttermilk waffles to creative focaccia sandwiches to fajitas, Cajun calamari, and pad Thai. The huge patio facing Commercial Street is particularly popular in the morning. **Cafe Heaven,** 199 Commercial St. (© **508/ 487-9639**), is prized for its leisurely country breakfasts. The modern storefront also turns out substantial sandwiches, such as avocado and goat cheese on a French baguette.

The best gourmet takeout shop is **Angel Foods,** 467 Commercial St., in the East End (© **508/487-6666**), which offers Italian specialties and other prepared foods. The "rollwiches"—pita bread packed with a wide range of fillings—at **Box Lunch,** 353 Commercial St. (© **508/487-6026**), are ideal for a strolling lunch.

Provincetown After Dark

To order tickets for any of the shows at Provincetown's nightclubs and cabarets, call **Ptown Tix** (© **508/487-9793;** www.ptowntix.com).

An on-again, off-again contender for hottest club in town is **Club Euro,** 258 Commercial St., 2nd floor, beside Town Hall (© **508/487-8800**), the current home of "Two Fags and a Drag" and the ever-popular all-star musical comedy drag revue "Big Boned Barbies," starring Kandi Kane. Closed October to May.

Perhaps the nation's premier gay bar, the **Atlantic House,** 6 Masonic Place, off Commercial Street (© **508/487-3821**), is open year-round. The "A-house" welcomes straight folks, except in the leather-oriented Macho Bar upstairs. Come late afternoon; it's a safe bet that the crowds are at the gay-lesbian tea dance held daily in season from 3:30 to 6:30pm on the pool deck at the **Boatslip Beach Club,** 161 Commercial St. (© **508/ 487-1669**). The action then shifts to the **Pied,** 193A Commercial St. (© **508/487- 1527;** www.thepied.com), for its After Tea T-Dance from 5 to 10pm.

The women's bar **Vixen,** at the Pilgrim House, 336 Commercial St. (© **508/487- 6424**), occupies the lower floors of a former hotel. On the roster are jazz, blues, and comedy. There are also pool tables.

---

3 MARTHA'S VINEYARD

With 100 square miles, Martha's Vineyard is New England's largest island, yet each of its six communities is blessed with endearing small-town charm. Admire the sea captains' homes in **Edgartown.** Stroll down Circuit Avenue in **Oak Bluffs,** then ride the Flying Horses Carousel, said to be the oldest working carousel in the nation. Check out the cheerful "gingerbread" cottages behind Circuit Avenue. Then journey "up-island" to marvel at the red-clay cliffs of **Aquinnah.** Or bike the country roads of **West Tisbury** and **Chilmark.** Buy a lobster roll in the fishing village of **Menemsha.**

ESSENTIALS

GETTING THERE   By Ferry   Most visitors take ferries from the mainland to the Vineyard. It's easy to get a passenger ticket on almost any of the ferries, but space for cars is limited. We advise you to leave your car on the mainland. It's easy to take the shuttle buses from town to town or bike around.

From **Falmouth,** the **Steamship Authority** (© **508/477-8600;** www.islandferry. com) operates daily year-round, weather permitting. These ferries make the 45-minute trip to Vineyard Haven throughout the year; some boats go to Oak Bluffs from late May to late October. You can take your car on the ferry (though most visitors don't) or park your car in Woods Hole or Falmouth for $10 per day (arrive at least 45 min. ahead of time if you're leaving your car on the mainland). Free buses run regularly to the ferry terminal. The cost of a round-trip passenger ferry ticket is $14 for adults and $8 for children 5 to 12. Bringing a bike costs an extra $6 round-trip. You do not need a ferry reservation if you're traveling without a car.

From **Falmouth Inner Harbor,** you can board the *Island Queen* (© **508/548-4800;** www.islandqueen.com) for a 35-minute cruise to Oak Bluffs (passengers only). The **Falmouth–Edgartown Ferry Service,** 278 Scranton Ave. (© **508/548-9400;** www. falmouthferry.com), operates a 1-hour passenger ferry, called the *Pied Piper,* from Falmouth Inner Harbor to Edgartown. The boat runs from late May to mid-October; reservations are required. From **Hyannis,** May through October, **Hy-Line** (© **508/778-2600;** www.hy-linecruises.com) operates from the Ocean Street Dock to Oak Bluffs on Martha's Vineyard.

A fast ferry from Rhode Island to Oak Bluffs makes the trip in 90 minutes and avoids Cape Cod traffic jams. **Vineyard Fast Ferry Company** (© **401/295-4040;** www.vineyardfastferry.com) runs this seasonal high-speed catamaran, called *Millennium,* which leaves from Quonset Point in **North Kingston.** The round-trip cost is $72 for adults and $54 for children. Parking next to the ferry port is $8 per day.

Another option for Vineyard vacationers is a high-speed ferry from **New Bedford** to the island. A ticket costs $29 one-way and $58 round-trip for adults; free for children 12 and under traveling with a parent. Contact New England Fast Ferry for details (© **866/683-3779;** www.nefastferry.com).

By Plane   You can fly into **Martha's Vineyard Airport** (© **508/693-7022;** www. mvyairport.com), in West Tisbury, about 5 miles outside Edgartown.

Airlines serving the Vineyard include **Cape Air/Nantucket Airlines** (© **800/352-0714** or 508/771-6944) from Boston, Hyannis, Nantucket, and New Bedford; and **US Airways** (© **800/428-4322**), which has regular service from Boston and seasonal weekend service from LaGuardia.

By Bus   Bonanza Bus Lines (© **888/751-8800** or 508/548-7588; www.bonanzabus. com) connects the Woods Hole ferry port with Boston (from South Station and Logan Airport), New York City, and Providence, Rhode Island. Fares range from $30 to $93 round-trip, depending on your departure point.

GETTING AROUND   By Bicycle & Moped   The best way to explore the Vineyard is on two wheels. There's a little of everything for cyclists, from paved paths to hilly country roads. You need a driver's license to rent a moped.

Bike-, scooter-, and moped-rental shops are clustered throughout all three down-island towns. Bike rentals cost about $20 a day, scooters and mopeds $46 to $85. In Vineyard Haven, try **Strictly Bikes,** Union Street (© **508/693-0782**). In Edgartown, you'll find **Wheel Happy,** 204 Upper Main St. and 8 S. Water St. (© **508/627-5928**), which rents only bikes.

By Shuttle Bus   In season, shuttle buses certainly run often enough to make them a practical means of getting around. They are also cheap, dependable, and easy. The **Martha's Vineyard Regional Transit Authority** (© **508/693-9440;** www.vineyardtransit.com)

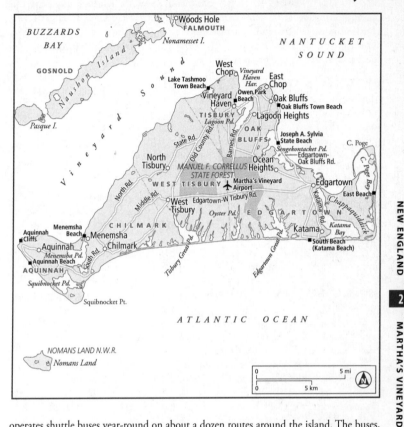

operates shuttle buses year-round on about a dozen routes around the island. The buses, which are white with purple logos, cost about $2 to $5, depending on distance. The formula is $1 per town. For example, Vineyard Haven to Oak Bluffs is $2, but Vineyard Haven to Edgartown (passing through Oak Bluffs) is $3. A 1-day pass is $6; a 3-day pass is $15.

For bus tours of the island, call **Island Transport** (© **508/693-0058**) or hop on one of the Island Transport buses that are stationed at the ferry terminals in Vineyard Haven and Oak Bluffs in the summer.

By Taxi You'll find taxis at all ferry terminals and the airport, as well as taxi stands in Oak Bluffs (at the Flying Horses Carousel) and Edgartown (next to the Town Wharf). Most taxi companies operate vans for larger groups and travelers with bikes. Cab companies on the island include **Accurate Cab** (© **888/557-9798** or 508/627-9798; the only 24-hr. service), and **All Island Taxi** (© **800/693-TAXI** [693-8294] or 508/693-2929). In summer, rates from town to town are generally flat fees based on distance and the number of passengers. Late-night revelers should keep in mind that rates double from midnight until 7am.

Contact the **Martha's Vineyard Chamber of Commerce,** Beach Road, in Vineyard Haven (© **508/693-0085;** www.mvy.com). There are also information booths at the ferry terminal in Vineyard Haven, across from the Flying Horses Carousel in Oak Bluffs, and on Church Street in Edgartown. For information on current events, check the newspapers *Vineyard Gazette* (www.mvgazette.com) and the *Martha's Vineyard Times* (www.mvtimes.com).

BEACHES & OUTDOOR PURSUITS

Most down-island **beaches** in Vineyard Haven, Oak Bluffs, and Edgartown are open to the public and just a walk or a short bike ride from town. In season, shuttle buses make stops at **State Beach,** between Oak Buffs and Edgartown. Most of the Vineyard's magnificent up-island shoreline is privately owned or restricted to residents, and thus off-limits to visitors. Renters in up-island communities can obtain a beach sticker (around $35–$50 for a season sticker) for those private beaches by applying for a lease at the relevant town hall.

The party boat *Skipper* (© **508/693-1238**) offers half-day **fishing** trips out of Oak Bluffs Harbor in season. Deep-sea excursions can be arranged aboard **Big Eye Charters** (© **508/627-3649**) out of Edgartown, or with **Summer's Lease** (© **508/693-2880**) out of Oak Bluffs.

About a fifth of the Vineyard's landmass has been set aside for conservation, and it's accessible to **bikers** and **hikers.** The **West Chop Woods,** off Franklin Street in Vineyard Haven, comprise 85 acres with marked trails. Midway between Vineyard Haven and Edgartown, the **Felix Neck Wildlife Sanctuary** includes a 6-mile network of trails over varying terrain.

The 633-acre **Long Point Wildlife Refuge,** off Waldron's Bottom Road in West Tisbury (© **508/693-7392** for gatehouse), offers heath and dunes, freshwater ponds, a beach, and interpretive nature walks for children.

Some remarkable botanical surprises can be found at the 20-acre **Polly Hill Arboretum,** 809 State Rd., West Tisbury (© **508/693-9426**). Horticulturist Polly Hill has developed this property over the past 40 years and allows the public to wander the grounds Thursday through Tuesday from 7am until 7pm. There's a requested donation of $5 for adults and $3 for children 11 and under.

Wind's Up, 199 Beach Rd., Vineyard Haven (© **508/693-4252**), rents canoes, kayaks, and various sailing craft, including windsurfers, and offers instruction on a placid pond. Canoes and kayaks rent for $20 per hour.

WHERE TO STAY

After a fire destroyed the 200-year-old Tisbury Inn in Vineyard Haven in 2001, the fate of the property was uncertain. But the three-story building has reopened as the **Mansion House Inn,** 9 Main St., Vineyard Haven (© **800/332-4112** or 508/693-2200; http://mvmansionhouse.com), a luxury 32-room inn that's a community hub with a restaurant, health club, and shops. The rooms range in size from cozy to spacious; many have kitchenettes, plasma-screen TVs, and extra-large bathtubs.

Linked by formal gardens, each of the 18th- and 19th-century houses at the **Charlotte Inn,** 27 S. Summer St., Edgartown (© **508/627-4751**), has a distinctive look and feel, though the predominant mode is English country. It's the best inn on the island. All but one of the rooms at this Relais & Châteaux property have TVs, but none have phones. Some of the luxurious bathrooms are bigger than those of most standard hotel rooms.

The inn's restaurant, **L'étoile,** is one of the island's finest. Rates include continental breakfast; full breakfast is offered for $15 extra. No children 13 and under.

With its graceful wraparound colonnaded front porch, the **Jonathan Munroe House,** 100 Main St., Edgartown (© 877/468-6763 or 508/627-5536; www.jonathanmunroe. com), stands out from the other inns and captains' homes on this stretch of upper Main Street. Guest rooms are immaculate, antiques-filled, and dotted with clever details. Many units have fireplaces. At breakfast (included in room rates, along with an afternoon wine hour), don't miss the homemade waffles and pancakes. No children 11 and under are permitted.

Do you long to stay at a reasonably priced inn that's bigger than a B&B but smaller than a Marriott? The **Victorian Inn,** 24 S. Water St., Edgartown (© 508/627-4784; www.thevic.com), is a freshened-up version of those old-style hotels that used to exist in every New England town. With three floors of long, graceful corridors, the Victorian could serve as a stage set for a 1930s romance. Several units have canopy beds and balconies. Rates include full breakfast and afternoon tea. Dogs are welcome. There are no phones in the rooms.

The **Edgartown Inn,** 56 N. Water St. (© 508/627-4794; www.edgartowninn.com), offers perhaps the best value on the island. It's a lovely 1798 Federal manse. Rooms are no-frills but traditional; some have TVs and harbor views. Modernists may prefer the cathedral-ceilinged quarters in the annex. Service is excellent. The inn does not accept credit cards, and there are no phones in the rooms.

WHERE TO DINE

Outside Oak Bluffs and Edgartown, all of Martha's Vineyard (including Vineyard Haven) is "dry," so bring your own bottle; some restaurants charge a small fee for uncorking.

Alchemy is a spiffy restaurant that's a little slice of Paris on 71 Main St. (© 508/627-9999). There's also a large selection of cocktails, liqueurs, and wines. In addition to lunch and dinner, a bar menu is served from 2:30 to 11pm.

Everything's appealing at **Among the Flowers Cafe** on Mayhew Lane (© 508/627-3233) near the dock. The breakfasts are the best around, and the comfort-food dinners are among the most affordable options in this pricey town.

At the **Newes from America,** 23 Kelly St. (© 508/627-4397), a subterranean tavern built in 1742, beers are a specialty: Try a rack of five brews, or let your choice of food—from a wood-smoked oyster "Island Poor Boy" sandwich to a porterhouse steak—dictate your draft.

The **Black Dog Tavern,** at the Beach Street Extension on the harbor (© 508/693-9223), is a national icon (with cool T-shirts). Soon after Robert Douglas decided in 1971 that this port could use a good restaurant, vacationers waiting for the ferry began to wander into this saltbox to tide themselves over with a bit of "blackout cake" or peanut-butter pie. The food is still home-cooking good. Come early, when it first opens, and sit on the porch, where the views are perfect.

MARTHA'S VINEYARD AFTER DARK

All towns except for Oak Bluffs and Edgartown are dry, and last call at bars and clubs is at midnight. Hit Oak Bluffs for the rowdiest bar scene and best nighttime street life. In Edgartown, you may have to hop around before you find the evening's most happening spot.

Young and loud are the buzzwords at the **Lamppost** and the **Rare Duck,** 111 Circuit Ave., Oak Bluffs (© 508/696-9352), a pair of clubs in the center of town. The Lamppost features live bands and a dance floor; the Rare Duck, acoustic acts. This is where the young folk go, and the performers could be playing blues, reggae, R&B, or '80s. The cover is $1 to $5.

4 THE BERKSHIRES

More than hills but less than mountains, the Taconic and Hoosac ranges that define this region at the western end of Massachusetts go by the collective name "the Berkshires." Mohawks and Mohegans lived and hunted here. Farmers, drawn to fertile flood plains of the Housatonic, were supplanted in the 19th century by manufacturers. Artists and writers came for the mild summers and seclusion offered by these hills and lakes. Nathaniel Hawthorne, Herman Melville, and Edith Wharton were among those who put down temporary roots. By the 1930s, theater, dance, and music performances had established themselves as regular summer fixtures. Tanglewood, Jacob's Pillow, and the Berkshire and Williamstown Theatre festivals draw tens of thousands of visitors every summer.

ESSENTIALS

GETTING THERE   The Massachusetts Turnpike (**I-90**) runs east-west from Boston to the Berkshires, with an exit near Lee and Stockbridge. From New York City, the scenic Taconic State Parkway connects with I-90 not far from Pittsfield.

Amtrak (© **800/USA-RAIL** [872-7245]; www.northeast.amtrak.com) operates several trains daily between Boston and Chicago, stopping in Pittsfield each way.

VISITOR INFORMATION   The **Berkshire Visitors Bureau,** Berkshire Common (off South St., near the entrance to the Hilton), Pittsfield (© **800/237-5747** or 413/443-9186), can assist with questions and lodging reservations. Also check out **www.berkshires.org**.

SHEFFIELD

Sheffield, known as the "Antiques Capital of the Berkshires," occupies a flood plain beside the Housatonic River, 11 miles south of Great Barrington. The canny, knowledgeable dealers know exactly what they have, so expect high quality and few bargains.

There are more than two dozen antiques dealers along Route 7. Most of them stock the **free directory** of the Berkshire County Antiques Dealers Association, which lists dealers from Sheffield to Cheshire and across the border in Connecticut and New York. Look, too, for the pamphlet called *The Antique Hunter's Guide to Route 7.*

GREAT BARRINGTON

Even with a population barely over 7,500, this pleasant retail center, 7 miles south of Stockbridge, is the largest town in the southernmost part of the county. Great Barrington has no sights of particular significance, leaving time to browse its many antiques galleries and specialty shops. Convenient as a home base for excursions to such nearby attractions as Monument Mountain, Bash-Bish Falls, Butternut Basin, Tanglewood concerts, and Stockbridge, it has a number of adequate motels north of the center along or near Route 7 that tend to fill up more slowly on weekends than the better-known inns in the area. It is something of a dining destination, too, with 55 eating places, including, at last count, 4 sushi bars! *Note:* The local board of health has banned smoking in *any* public space in town.

The **Southern Berkshire Chamber of Commerce** maintains an information booth at
362 Main St. (© **413/528-1510;** www.southernberkshires.com), near the town hall. It's
open Tuesday through Sunday from 10am to 5pm.

Head straight for Railroad Street. Start on the corner with Main Street, at **T. P. Saddle
Blanket & Trading Co.** (© **413/528-6500**). An unlikely emporium that looks lifted
whole from the Rockies, it's packed with boots, hats, Indian jewelry, blankets, and jars of
salsa. **Mistral's,** 6 Railroad St. (© **413/528-1618**), stocks Gallic tableware, linens, fancy
foods, and furniture. The **Chef's Shop,** 31 Railroad St. (© **413/528-0135**), still features
a bounty of gadgets and cookbooks, as well as cooking classes. At the north end of town,
just before Route 7 turns right across a short bridge, Route 41 goes straight, toward the
village of Housatonic. In about 4 miles you'll see a shed that houses the kiln of **Great
Barrington Pottery** (© **413/274-6259**). Owner Richard Bennett has been throwing
pots according to Japanese techniques for more than 30 years.

Where to Stay & Dine

There are several acceptable motels north of town on Route 7, the most desirable being
the **Holiday Inn Express,** 415 Stockbridge Rd. (© **413/528-1810;** www.hiexpress.
com), which has an indoor pool and whirlpool, and rooms with Jacuzzis and/or fireplaces; rates include breakfast. The **chamber of commerce** operates a lodging hot line at
© **800/269-4825** or 413/528-4006.

The **Old Inn on the Green** on Route 57, New Marlborough (© **413/229-7924;**
www.oldinn.com), comprised of a former 1760 tavern/general store and the adjacent
18th-century Thayer House, is under new management. The most desirable rooms are
in Thayer House, some with fireplaces and all with air-conditioning, VCRs, and whirlpool tubs. All five intimate dining rooms serve sophisticated cuisine and have fireplaces;
reservations are strongly advised. Rates ($205–$365 double) include breakfast, and there
is a courtyard pool at Thayer House.

A roadside lodging built in the middle of the 19th century in Federal style, the **Wind-
flower Inn,** 684 S. Egremont Rd. (© **800/992-1993** or 413/528-2720; www.windflower
inn.com), commands a large plot of land opposite the Egremont Country Club. Six
rooms have fireplaces; four have canopy beds. Rates ($100–$225 double) at the entirely
smoke-free property include breakfast and afternoon tea. There's an outdoor pool.

The **Castle Street Cafe,** 10 Castle St. (© **413/528-5244**), is a storefront bistro that
has ruled the Great Barrington roost for some time now and has expanded into the next
building. While a Francophilic inclination is apparent in the main room, what with duck
breast with potato galette and steak au poivre, it isn't overpowering. An award-winning
wine list is another reason to stop in. Main courses cost $20 to $28.

STOCKBRIDGE

Stockbridge's ready accessibility to Boston and New York (about $2^1/_2$ hr. from each
and reachable by rail since the mid–19th c.) transformed the frontier settlement into a
Gilded Age summer retreat for the rich. The town has long been popular with artists and
writers.

Stockbridge lies 7 miles north of Great Barrington and 6 miles south of Lenox. The
Stockbridge Chamber of Commerce (© **413/298-5200;** www.stockbridgechamber.
org) maintains an information booth opposite the row of stores depicted by Rockwell.
It's open May through October.

From June to August, the **Berkshire Theatre Festival,** Main Street (© 413/298-5576; www.berkshiretheatre.org), holds its season of classic and new plays, often with marquee names starring or directing. Kevin Kline and Al Pacino have been participants. Its venue is a "casino" built in 1887 to plans by architect Stanford White.

The striking **Norman Rockwell Museum,** Route 183 (© 413/298-4100; www.nrm. org), opened in 1993 to house the works of Stockbridge's favorite son. The illustrator used both his neighbors and the town to tell stories about an America now rapidly fading from memory. Most of Rockwell's paintings adorned covers of the *Saturday Evening Post:* warm and often humorous depictions of homecomings, first proms, and visits to the doctor. He addressed serious concerns, too, notably with his poignant portrait of a little African-American girl being escorted by U.S. marshals into a previously segregated school. The lovely 36-acre grounds also contain Rockwell's last studio (closed Nov–Apr). Admission is $13 adults, $7 students, free for children 18 and under.

Where to Stay

The **Inn at Stockbridge,** 30 East St. (© 888/466-7865 or 413/298-3337; www. stockbridgeinn.com), is a 1906 building with a grandly columned porch. It's set well back from the road on 12 acres. The innkeepers are eager to please, serving full breakfasts by candlelight and afternoon spreads of wine and cheese. Several bedrooms have fireplaces and whirlpools. There's an outdoor pool. No children 11 and under. Doubles run $140 to $345.

So well known that it serves as a symbol of the Berkshires, the **Red Lion Inn,** Main Street (© 413/298-5545; www.redlioninn.com), had its origins as a stagecoach tavern in 1773. The rocking chairs on the porch are the perfect place to while away an hour. An ancient bird-cage elevator carries guests up to halls and rooms filled with antiques ranging in styles of over 2 centuries. Six satellite buildings have been added, all within 3 miles of the inn. Jackets are required for men in the main dining room, but not in the casual **Widow Bingham Tavern** nor, in good weather, in the courtyard out back. The wine cellar has been recognized with important awards. The **Lion's Den** has nightly live entertainment, usually of the folk-rock variety. There are also an outdoor pool and an exercise room. Rooms cost $110 to $220 double.

LEE & JACOB'S PILLOW

While Stockbridge and Lenox were developing into luxurious recreational centers, Lee was a thriving paper-mill town and thus remained essentially a town of workers and merchants. The town's contribution to the Berkshire cultural calendar is the Jacob's Pillow Dance Festival, which first thrived as "Denishawn," a fabled alliance between founders Ruth St. Denis and Ted Shawn.

Lee is 5 miles southeast of Lenox. In summer and early fall, the **Lee Chamber of Commerce** (© 413/243-0852; www.leechamber.org) operates an **information center** on the town common, Route 20 (© 413/243-4929).

The **Jacob's Pillow Dance Festival,** George Carter Road, Becket (© 413/243-0745; www.jacobspillow.org), began in 1933 when Ted Shawn decided to put on a show in the barn. Jacob's Pillow is now to dance what Tanglewood is to classical music. The theater has long welcomed troupes of international reputation, including the Mark Morris Dance Group, Twyla Tharp, and the Paul Taylor Dance Company. The season runs from mid-June to late August, and tickets go on sale April 1. The growing campus includes a store, pub, dining room, tent restaurant, and exhibition space. Picnic lunches can be preordered 24 hours in advance.

Where to Stay

On the road to Lenox, the lakeside **Best Western Black Swan Inn,** 435 Laurel St./Rte. 20 (© **800/876-7926** or 413/243-2700; www.bestwestern.com), has a pool and restaurant; some of the 52 rooms have fireplaces.

Applegate, 279 W. Park St. (© **800/691-9012** or 413/243-4451; www.applegateinn. com), utilizes a gracious 1920s Georgian Colonial manse to full advantage. The top unit has a canopy bed, Queen Anne reproductions, a steam shower, and a fireplace (with real wood). Some rooms have Jacuzzis and/or gas fireplaces. Chocolates and brandy await guests at bedside. Breakfast is by candlelight, and the innkeepers set out wine and cheese in the afternoon. They are "flexible" on children. Rates run $120 to $350.

The **Chambéry Inn,** 199 Main St. (© **413/243-2221;** www.berkshireinns.com), was the Berkshires' first parochial school (1885), named for the French hometown of the nuns who ran it. The extra-large bedrooms were formerly classrooms. Six of them, with 13-foot ceilings and the original woodwork and blackboards, are equipped with whirlpool tubs and gas fireplaces. Some rooms have TV/VCRs, CD players, and fridges. A breakfast basket is delivered to your door each morning. No children 17 and under. Rooms cost $75 to $239.

LENOX & TANGLEWOOD

Stately homes and fabulous mansions mushroomed in this former agricultural settlement, and Lenox remains a repository of extravagant domestic architecture surpassed only in such resorts as Newport and Palm Beach. And because many of the cottages have been converted into inns and hotels, it is possible to get inside some of these beautiful buildings, if only for a cocktail or a meal.

The reason for so many lodgings in a town with a population of barely 5,000 is Tanglewood, a nearby estate where a series of concerts by the Boston Symphony Orchestra is held every summer.

Lenox lies 7 miles south of Pittsfield. The **Lenox Chamber of Commerce** (© **413/ 637-3646;** www.lenox.org) provides visitor information and lodging referrals.

Tanglewood Music Festival

Lenox is filled with music every summer, and the undisputed headliner is the **Boston Symphony Orchestra (BSO).** Concerts are given at Tanglewood estate, beginning in July, ending the weekend before Labor Day. The estate is on West Street (actually in Stockbridge township). From Lenox, take Route 183 1¹/₂ miles southwest of town.

The program features a menagerie of other performers and musical idioms. These run the gamut from popular artists (such as James Taylor and Bonnie Raitt) and jazz musicians (including Dave Brubeck and Wynton Marsalis) to such guest soloists as Itzhak Perlman and Yo-Yo Ma.

The **Koussevitzky Music Shed** is an open auditorium that seats 5,000, surrounded by a lawn where an audience lounges on folding chairs and blankets. Chamber groups and soloists appear in the smaller **Ozawa Hall.** Major performances are on Friday and Saturday nights and Sunday afternoons.

Tentative programs are available after January 1; the schedule is usually locked in by March. Tickets can sell out quickly, so get yours as far in advance as possible. If you decide to go at the last minute, take a blanket or lawn chair and get tickets for lawn seating, which is almost always available. You can also attend open rehearsals during the week, as well as the rehearsal for the Sunday concert on Saturday morning.

The estate itself (© 413/637-5165 June–Aug), with over 500 acres of lawns and gardens, was put together starting in 1849 by William Aspinwall Tappan. Admission to the grounds is free when concerts aren't scheduled. In 1851, a structure on the property called the Little Red Shanty was rented to Nathaniel Hawthorne, who stayed here long enough to write a children's book, *Tanglewood Tales,* and meet Herman Melville, who lived in nearby Dalton. The existing Hawthorne Cottage is a replica (and isn't open to the public). On the grounds is the original Tappan mansion, with fine views.

For recorded information, call © 617/266-1492 from September to June 10 (information on Tanglewood concerts is not available until the program is announced in Mar or Apr). Children 4 and under are not allowed in the Shed or Ozawa Hall. To order tickets by mail before June, write the Tanglewood Ticket Office at Symphony Hall, 301 Mass. Ave., Boston, MA 02115. After June 1, write the Tanglewood Ticket Office, 297 West St., Lenox, MA 01240. Tickets can be charged to a credit card through **Symphony Charge** (© 888/266-1200 outside Boston, or 617/266-1200; www.bso.org).

Other Attractions

The **Mount,** 2 Plunkett St. (© 413/637-1899; www.edithwharton.org), was the home of Edith Wharton, a member of the upper classes of the Gilded Age who won a Pulitzer for her novel detailing the strata of high society, *The Age of Innocence.* Wharton had her villa built on this 130-acre property in 1902 and lived here for 10 years. She took an active hand in its creation—one of the few designated National Historic Landmarks designed by a woman. A $25-million restoration campaign continues, with work so far completed on the terrace and greenhouse and continuing on the interior and gardens. Admission costs $18 adults; free for children 11 and under.

The repertory theater group **Shakespeare & Company,** 70 Kemble St. (© 413/637-3353; www.shakespeare.org), has long used buildings and amphitheaters on the grounds of the Mount to stage its May-to-October season of plays by the Bard, works by Edith Wharton and George Bernard Shaw, and works by new American playwrights. With the construction of a Founder's Theatre, the Spring Lawn Theatre, the tented Rose Footprint Theatre, and an administration building, and planned rehabilitation of other existing buildings, the Company now enjoys its very own campus devoted to the dramatic arts. Walking trails have been developed at the north end of the grounds, and a cafe in the theater lobby serves drinks and light fare. Free outdoor performances are staged before evening curtain times.

Where to Stay

The list of lodgings below is only partial, and most can accommodate only small numbers of guests. The Tanglewood concert season is a powerful draw, so prices are highest in summer as well as during the foliage season. Minimum 2- or 3-night stays are usually required during the Tanglewood weeks, foliage season, weekends, and holidays. Reserve well in advance for Tanglewood! Note that some lodgings are so crabby and rule-ridden, we say good riddance; others are open only 6 or 7 months a year and charge the world for a bed or a meal.

If all the area's inns are booked or if you want to be assured the full quota of 21st-century conveniences, routes 7 and 20 north and south of town harbor a number of motels, including the **Mayflower Motor Inn** (© 413/443-4468), the **Days Inn** (© 413/637-3560), the **Lenox Motel** (© 413/499-0324), and the **Comfort Inn** (© 413/443-4714).

Blantyre, 16 Blantyre Rd. (© **413/637-3556;** www.blantyre.com), is a Relais & Châteaux property ensconced in a 1902 Tudor-Norman mansion that used to be open only in the warmer months. Now it cossets its guests year-round in its undeniably luxurious public rooms, dining areas, and bedchambers. If any place is worth breathtaking tariffs, it's this one. Rates are $450 to $750 double, up to $1,050 for the top suite.

The **Canyon Ranch in the Berkshires,** 165 Kemble St. (© **800/742-9000** or 413/637-4100; www.canyonranch.com), is a one-of-a-kind spa/resort, with its core the 1897 mansion modeled after Le Petit Trianon at Versailles. Sweat away the pounds in the spa complex, with 40 exercise classes a day, weights, an indoor track, racquetball, squash, and all the equipment you might want. Canoeing and hiking are added possibilities. Guest rooms are in contemporary New England style, with every hotel convenience except minibars. After you've been steamed, exhausted, pummeled, and showered, the big events of each day are mealtimes: "nutritionally balanced gourmet," naturally. All-inclusive 3- to 7-night packages run from $1,580 to $5,290 double.

Harley Procter hitched up with a man called Gamble and made a bundle. In 1912, he built the current home of the totally smoke-free **Gateways Inn,** 51 Walker St., Lenox (© **888/492-9466** or 413/637-2532; www.gatewaysinn.com). The stunning staircase that winds down into the lobby is just the thing for a grand entrance. Eight rooms have working fireplaces. Dining here is one of Lenox's greater pleasures. The bar features 130 single-malt scotches and 55 grappas. Also, a terrace has been added for after-concert light meals and desserts. Rates run $100 to $295 double.

An inn off and on since 1775, the **Village Inn,** 16 Church St. (© **800/253-0917** or 413/637-0020; www.villageinn-lenox.com), hasn't a whiff of pretense. Its smoke-free rooms (all have VCRs) come in considerable variety. You'll find four-posters in the high-end rooms, some of which have fireplaces and/or Jacuzzis, and constricted quarters with double beds at the lower end. Claw-foot tubs are common. Ask about rooms on the renovated third floor. Afternoon tea and dinner are served in the restaurant, where prices are lower than the town average. Doubles run $109 to $269, including breakfast.

Where to Dine

See also "Where to Stay," above, as many inns have dining rooms. In particular, **Blantyre** (© **413/637-3556**) is worth a splurge. In high season, **Spigalina,** 80 Main St. (© **413/637-4455**), serves imaginative Mediterranean cooking. Note that the restaurants recommended below serve lunch, in a region where most of the better restaurants don't open until evening.

The **Church Street Café,** 65 Church St. (© **413/637-2745**), is the most popular place in town, delivering combinations that please the eye and pique the taste buds. Menus change with the seasons, but past options have included fried oysters with a lemony rémoulade sauce and sake-soy marinated shrimp with crabmeat wontons. Lunch is a busy time, with crab-cake sandwiches among the favorites. Main courses run about $19 to $30.

Dish, 37 Church St. (© **413/637-1800**), is a narrow storefront eatery that was packed from the day it opened. Since the decor is negligible and the accommodations cramped, the principal discernible reason for its furious popularity is the food. It comes from the kitchen in stuttering intervals, the uncertainty easily compensated by the startlingly high quality of what the creative chef-owner sends forth. At dinner, the char-broiled rainbow trout and herb-roasted baby rack of lamb au jus are stars. Another reason the locals like it—they don't need a bank loan to eat here. A main course will set you back $18 to $28.

This community and its prestigious college were named for Col. Ephraim Williams, killed in 1755 in the French and Indian War. He bequeathed the land for creation of a school and a town. Over the town's long history, buildings have been erected in several styles of the times. That makes Main Street a virtual museum of institutional architecture, with representatives of the Georgian, Federal, Gothic Revival, Romanesque, and Victorian modes, as well as a few yet to be labeled.

A free weekly newspaper, the *Advocate* (© 413/664-7900), produces useful guides to both the northern and southern Berkshires. For a copy, write to the *Advocate,* 87 Marshall St., North Adams, MA 01267. An **information booth,** at North Street (Rte. 7) and Main Street (Rte. 2), has an abundance of pamphlets and brochures free for the taking.

What to See & Do

The **Sterling and Francine Clark Art Institute,** 225 South St. (© **413/458-2303;** www.clarkart.edu), is a gem with canvases by Renoir (34 of them), and the Degas sculpture *Little Dancer.* There are also works by 15th- and 16th-century Dutch portraitists, European genre and landscape painters, and Americans Sargent and Homer, as well as porcelain, silver, and antiques. Adults pay $10 admission (kids enter free) mid-June to October; the museum is free to all on Tuesday and from November to June. It's open July to August daily 10am to 5pm, closed Monday the rest of the year.

The **Williams College Museum of Art,** 15 Lawrence Hall Dr. (© **413/597-2429;** www.williams.edu/WCMA), is the second leg of Williamstown's two prominent art repositories. It exists in large part thanks to the college's collection of almost 400 paintings by the American modernists Maurice and Charles Prendergast. The museum also has works by Gris, Léger, Whistler, Picasso, Warhol, and Hopper. Admission is free. The museum is open Tuesday through Saturday (and some Mon holidays) from 10am to 5pm, Sunday from 1 to 5pm.

Williamstown has long hosted one of the Berkshires' premier summer attractions, the **Williamstown Theatre Festival** (© 413/597-3400; www.wtfestival.org), and now it has a facility that provides a proper showcase: the **'62 Center for Theatre and Dance,** 1000 Main St. (© **413/597-2425** for box office; www.williams.edu/go/62center). This ambitious center opened in the fall of 2005 and hosts dramatic productions, as well as dance, music, and related cultural events, involving students and alumni as well as professionals. The schedule is usually announced by April. Tickets to the Festival itself range from about $20 to $55, while admission to other events is often free, and no more than $10.

---

5 MYSTIC

The spirit and texture of the maritime life and history of New England are captured in many ports along its indented coast, but nowhere more cogently than beside the Mystic River estuary and its harbor. The town is home to one of New England's most singular attractions, the Mystic Seaport museum village.

GETTING THERE By **car** from New York or Boston, take **I-95** to exit 90 at Mystic. **Amtrak** (© **800/USA-RAIL** [872-7245]) serves Mystic with several **trains** daily from New York (trip time: 3¹/₄ hr.) and Boston (1³/₄ hr.).

VISITOR INFORMATION Two helpful sources of information are **Mystic & More** (© 800/873-6569; www.mysticmore.com) and **Mystic Coast & Country** (© 800/692-6278; www.mycoast.com). A **visitor center** is in Building 1D of the Olde Mistick Village shopping center, at Route 27 and Coogan Boulevard, near the Interstate (© **860/536-1641**).

EXPLORING MYSTIC SEAPORT

The village of **Mystic Seaport,** 75 Greenmanville Ave., Route 27 (© **888/9-SEAPORT** [973-2767] or 860/572-5315; www.mysticseaport.org), encompasses an entire waterfront settlement, more than 60 buildings on and near a 17-acre peninsula. A useful map guide is available at the ticket counter in the **visitor center** in the building opposite the museum stores (which stay open later than the village most of the year, so make them your last stop).

Exit the visitor center and bear right along the path between the Galley Restaurant and the village green. It bends to the left, intersecting with a street of shops, public buildings, and houses. At that corner is an 1870s hardware and dry-goods store. Turning right here, you'll pass a schoolhouse, a chapel, and an 1830s home. Stop at the **children's museum,** which invites youngsters to play games characteristic of the seafaring era. It faces a small square that is the starting point for **horse-drawn wagon tours.**

From here, the three-masted barque *Charles W. Morgan,* built in 1841, one of the proudest possessions of the Seaport fleet of over 400 craft, is a few steps away.

If you're a fan of scrimshaw and ship models, continue along the waterfront until you reach the **Stillman Building,** which contains fascinating exhibits of both. Otherwise, head left toward the lighthouse. Along the way, you'll encounter a tavern, an 1833 bank, a cooperage, and other shops and services that did business with the whalers and clipper ships that put in at ports such as this.

The friendly docents in the village are highly competent at the crafts they demonstrate and always ready to impart information. The fact that they aren't dressed in period costumes enhances the village's feeling of authenticity by avoiding the contrived air of many such enterprises.

The next vessel is the iron-hulled square-rigger *Joseph Conrad,* which dates from 1881. Up ahead is a **lighthouse,** which looks out across the water toward the riverside houses that line the opposite shore. Round the horn, go past the boat sheds, the fishing shacks, and the ketches and sloops moored here in season until you come to the dock for the 1908 **SS Sabino.** This working ship gives half-hour river rides from mid-May to early October, daily from 11am to 4pm, and $1^{1}/_{2}$-hour evening excursions. A few steps away is the 1921 fishing schooner *L. A. Dunton.*

A few steps south is the **Henry B. Du Pont Preservation Shipyard,** where the boats are painstakingly restored. One recent project was the re-creation of the schooner *Amistad,* which inspired an exhibit exploring the historical incident.

Also on the grounds are the **Galley Restaurant,** which serves fish and chips, fried clam strips, and lobster rolls; and **Sprouter's Tavern,** which offers snacks and sandwiches. When you exit for the day, ask the gatekeeper to validate your ticket so you can come back the next day for free.

Across the courtyard with the giant anchor is a building containing several **museum stores** as well as an art gallery. These superior shops stock books, kitchenware, fresh-baked goods, nautical prints and paintings, and ship models.

A Casino in the Woods

What has been wrought in the woodlands north of the Mystic coast in the last decade is astonishing. There was little but trees here when the Mashantucket Pequot tribe received clearance to open a gambling casino on their ancestral lands in rural Ledyard. Virtually overnight, the tribal bingo parlor was expanded into a full-fledged casino, and a hotel was built.

That was in 1992. Within 3 years, **Foxwoods Resort & Casino** (© **800/369-9003;** www.foxwoods.com) had become the single-most profitable gambling operation in the world, with a reported 40,000 visitors a day. Money cascaded over the Pequot (pronounced *Pee*-kwat) in a seemingly endless torrent. Expansion was immediate—another hotel, then a third, more casinos, golf courses, and the $139-million **Mashantucket Pequot Museum and Research Center,** devoted to Native American arts and culture. The tribe bought up adjacent lands and at least four nearby inns and hotels, and then opened a ship works to build high-speed ferries. All that hasn't sopped up the cascades of money, and the tribe has made major contributions to the Mystic Aquarium and Smithsonian Museum of the American Indian.

And that isn't the end of it. The Mashantucket Pequot Tribal Nation has announced a new $700-million project, scheduled for completion in mid-2008. Included will be a fourth high-rise hotel, another parking garage, two new golf courses, and more shops, restaurants, and gambling spaces.

All this prosperity came to a tribe of fewer than 520 acknowledged members, nearly all of them of mixed ethnicity. Residents of surrounding communities were ambivalent, to put the best face on it. When it was learned that one of the tribe's corporate entities was to be called Two Trees Limited Partnership, a predictable query was, "Is that all you're going to leave us? Two trees?" But while there is a continuing danger of damage to the fragile character of this authentically picturesque corner of Connecticut, it is also a fact that because of

Admission to the shipyard is $17 adults, $9 for children 6 to 12 (second day included with validation). The ships and exhibits are open from April to October daily from 9am to 5pm, November to March daily from 10am to 4pm; the grounds are open 9am to 5pm.

While you're in town, check out the **Mystic Aquarium,** 55 Coogan Blvd. at exit 90 off I-95 (© **860/572-5955;** www.mysticaquarium.org). The 15-minute marine show here illuminates as it entertains. It features alternating dolphins, sea lions, and orcas. And there are a host of other exhibits featuring marine mammals and other creatures of the deep that will occupy at least another hour of your time. In the outdoor "Alaskan Coast," see five beluga whales squeal and twirl and otherwise perform for their trainers at feeding time. Next door is a facsimile of the Bering Strait's Pribilof Islands, home to fur seals and endangered Steller sea lions, and out back are African black-footed penguins, with underwater viewing windows. There's also a new re-creation of a Louisiana bayou stocked with "Swamp Things": frogs, turtles, carp, largemouth bass, and small alligators. Elsewhere, visitors are eye to eye with such creatures as sea horses, jellyfish, and the pugnacious

the recent development, thousands of non-Pequots have found employment in their various enterprises.

The complex is reached through forested countryside of quiet hamlets that give little hint of the behemoth rising above the trees in Ledyard Township. There are no signs screaming FOXWOODS. Instead, watch for plaques with the symbols of tree, wolf, and fire above the word RESERVATION. As you enter the property, platoons of attendants point the way to parking and hotels. Ongoing construction surrounds the glassy, turquoise-and-violet towers of the hotels and casino. Though bustling, it doesn't look like Vegas from the outside—happily, there are no sphinxes, no fake volcanoes, and no neon palm trees.

Inside, the glitz gap narrows, but it is still relatively restrained, as such temples to chance go. The gambling rooms have windows, for example, even though the prevailing wisdom among casino designers is that they should not give customers any idea of what time of day or night it is.

And no one is allowed to forget that this whole eye-popping affair is owned and operated by Native Americans. Prominently placed around the main buildings are larger-than-life sculptures by artists of Chiricahua and Chippewa descent, depicting Amerindians in a variety of poses and artistic styles. One other Indian-oriented display is *The Rainmaker,* a glass statue of an archer shooting an arrow into the air. Every hour on the hour, he is the focus of artificial thunder, wind-whipped rain, and lasers pretending to be lightning bolts, the action described in murky prose by a booming voice-of-Manitou narrator. That's as close as the chest thumping gets to going over-the-top.

Two dozen bus companies provide daily service to Foxwoods from numerous cities in the northeast and mid-Atlantic regions, including Boston, Providence, New York, and Philadelphia, among many other cities. For information on transit from particular destinations, call © **860/885-3000.**

yellow-head jaw fish, which spends its hours digging fortifications in the sand. Dozens of rays flutter like butterflies, and translucent jellyfish billow and flex in slow-motion dance, a hypnotic display. Admission to the aquarium is $18 adults, $13 children 3 to 12; the museum is open daily except Christmas and New Year's.

WHERE TO STAY & DINE

Mystic's most appealing lodging is the **Steamboat Inn,** 73 Steamboat Wharf (© **860/ 536-8300;** www.steamboatinnmystic.com), a yellow-clapboard structure that has apartment-size downstairs bedrooms, with Jacuzzis and wet bars, while the upstairs units have wood-burning fireplaces. Every room is decorated uniquely and has a fridge; all but one have water views. The inn commissioned the 97-foot yacht, *Valiant,* that is moored at its dock. The staterooms can be rented when the yacht isn't chartered. Rates ($140–$300 double) include breakfast. Children 10 and over are welcome.

There are plenty of adequate area motels. Pick of the litter may be the **Best Western Sovereign,** north of exit 90 (© **860/536-4281**), with a pool and restaurant. Nearby competitors are the **Comfort Inn** (© 860/572-8531), **Days Inn** (© 860/572-0574), and **Residence Inn** (© 860/536-5150).

For dining, **Abbott's Lobster in the Rough,** 117 Pearl St., Noank (© 860/536-7719), is a nitty-gritty lobster shack with plenty of picnic tables. The classic shore dinner rules. That means clam chowder, boiled shrimp, mussels, and a lobster, with coleslaw, chips, and drawn butter. Bring your own beer. Main courses run $16 to $34.

Similarly, **Kitchen Little,** on Route 27, 1 mile south of I-95 (© 860/536-2122), is not much more than a shack by the water, but the menu offers 45 distinct breakfast choices and some of the coast's tastiest clam and scallop dishes. At lunch, you must have the definitive clear broth clam chowder, maybe the whole belly clam rolls, and absolutely the fried scallop sandwich. Try to snare a table out back, in view of the tall ships. Main courses cost $4 to $13.

6 NEWPORT

Newport occupies the southern tip of Aquidneck Island in Narragansett Bay, and is connected to the mainland by three bridges and a ferry. Wealthy industrialists, railroad tycoons, coal magnates, financiers, and robber barons were drawn to the area in the 19th century. They bought up property at the ocean's rim to build what they called summer "cottages"—patterned after European palaces.

But despite Newport's prevailing image as a collection of ornate mansions and regattas, the city is, for the most part, middle class and moderately priced. Scores of inns and B&Bs assure lodging even during festival weeks, at rates and fixtures from budget to luxury level. In almost every respect, this is the "First Resort" of the New England coast.

GETTING THERE   From New York City, take **I-95** to the third Newport exit, picking up **Route 138** heading east (which joins briefly with Rte. 4) and crossing the Newport toll bridge slightly north of the downtown district. From Boston, take **Route 24** through Fall River, picking up **Route 114** into town.

T. F. Green/Providence Airport (© 401/737-8222; www.pvdairport.com), in Warwick, south of Providence (exit 13, I-95), handles national flights into the state on several major carriers. A few of the larger Newport hotels provide shuttle service, as does **Cozy Cab** (© 401/846-2500).

VISITOR INFORMATION   For advance information available 24 hours, call **visitor information** (© 800/976-5122 outside Rhode Island, or 800/556-2484; www.go Newport.com). In town, stop by the excellent **Newport Gateway Visitor Center,** 23 America's Cup Ave. (© 800/326-6030 or 401/849-8048). Open daily from 9am to 5pm (until 6pm Fri–Sat).

GETTING AROUND   Most of Newport's attractions, except for the mansions, can be reached on foot. If you'd prefer not to hoof it, the **Rhode Island Public Transit Authority,** or **RIPTA** (© 800/244-0444 or 401/781-9400; www.ripta.com), has a free shuttle bus that follows a roughly circular route through town, making stops at major sights.

SPECIAL EVENTS   Arrive any day in summer and expect to find at least a half-dozen festivals, competitions, or other events; for a comprehensive listing of the city's best waterfront festivals, check out **www.newportfestivals.com**. In the off season, there's the 2-week **Christmas in Newport** festival (© 401/849-6454; www.christmasinnewport. org), when candlelight tours of the city's magnificent homes are offered. In June, there's

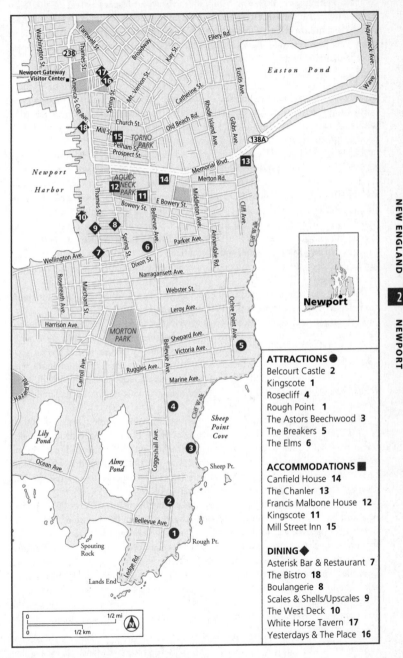

ATTRACTIONS ●
Belcourt Castle **2**
Kingscote **1**
Rosecliff **4**
Rough Point **1**
The Astors Beechwood **3**
The Breakers **5**
The Elms **6**

ACCOMMODATIONS ■
Canfield House **14**
The Chanler **13**
Francis Malbone House **12**
Kingscote **11**
Mill Street Inn **15**

DINING ◆
Asterisk Bar & Restaurant **7**
The Bistro **18**
Boulangerie **8**
Scales & Shells/Upscales **9**
The West Deck **10**
White Horse Tavern **17**
Yesterdays & The Place **16**

Great Chowder Cook-Off (© 401/846-1600), where 30 of the country's best chefs compete. During the middle 2 weeks in July, the **Newport Music Festival** (© **401/849-0700;** www.newportmusic.org) offers classical concerts daily at various venues. August brings the **Dunkin' Donuts Newport Folk Festival** (www.newportfolk.com) and the 4-day **JVC Jazz Festival—Newport** (© **866/468-7619;** www.festivalproductions.net), both held at Fort Adams State Park.

THE COTTAGES

That's what wealthy summer people called the sumptuous mansions they built in Newport. We suggest you visit only one or two per day: The sheer opulence can soon become numbing. Each residence requires 45 minutes to an hour for its guided tour. If at all possible, go during the week to avoid crowds and traffic.

Six of the mansions are maintained by the **Preservation Society of Newport County,** 424 Bellevue Ave. (© **401/847-1000;** www.newportmansions.org), which also operates the 1748 Hunter House, the 1860 Italianate Chepstow villa, the 1883 Isaac Bell House, and the Green Animals Topiary Gardens in Portsmouth. The Society sells a **combination ticket,** good for a year, to five of its properties; the cost is $31 for adults, $10 for children 6 to 17. Individual tickets for the Breakers are $15 for adults, $4 for children, and for Hunter House $25 for adults, $4 for children. Individual tickets for Kingscote, the Elms, Chateau-sur-mer, Marble House, and Rosecliff are $10 for adults, $4 for children. They can be purchased at any of the properties. Credit cards are accepted at most, but not all, of the cottages.

Mansions that aren't operated by the Preservation Society but are open to the public are **Belcourt Castle, Beechwood,** and **Rough Point.**

The cottages include **Kingscote** on Bowery Street (west of Bellevue Ave.), built in 1839, considered one of the Newport Cottages because it was acquired in 1864 by the sea merchant William Henry King, who furnished it with porcelains and textiles accumulated in the China trade. Architect Richard Upjohn designed the mansion in the same Gothic Revival style he used for Trinity Church in New York. The firm of McKim, Mead & White was commissioned to design the 1881 dining room, notable for its Tiffany glass panels.

Architect Horace Trumbauer is said to have been inspired by the Château d'Asnieres outside Paris, and a first look at the dining room of the **Elms,** on Bellevue Avenue, buttresses that claim. So, too, do the sunken gardens, laid out and maintained in the formal French manner. Trumbauer completed the cottage in 1901 and filled it with genuine Louis XIV and XV furniture as well as paintings and accessories true to the late 18th century. Visitors can opt for a self-guided audio tour.

If you have time to see only one cottage, make it the **Breakers** on Ochre Point Avenue. Architect Richard Morris Hunt was commissioned to create this replica of a Florentine Renaissance palazzo. The high iron entrance gates alone weigh over 7 tons. The 50×50-foot great hall has 50-foot-high ceilings, forming a giant cube, and is sheathed in marble. Such mind-numbing extravagance shouldn't really be surprising—Hunt's patron was Cornelius Vanderbilt II, grandson of railroad tycoon Commodore Vanderbilt. The mansion's foundation is approximately the size of a football field, and the Breakers took nearly 3 years to build (1892–95). Platoons of artisans were imported from Europe to apply gold leaf, carve wood and marble, and provide mural-size baroque paintings. The furnishings on view are original.

From the Breakers, return to Bellevue Avenue and turn left (south); **Rosecliff** is on the left. Stanford White thought the Grand Trianon of Louis XVI at Versailles a suitable model for this 1902 commission for heiress Tessie Fair Oelrichs. It has the largest ballroom of all the cottages, not to mention a storied heart-shaped grand staircase. It was used as a setting for some scenes in the Robert Redford movie of F. Scott Fitzgerald's *The Great Gatsby* (1974). On a humid summer day, keep in mind that this mansion is air-conditioned.

Mrs. William Backhouse Astor—*the* Mrs. Astor—was the arbiter of who constituted New York and Newport society. "The 400" list of socially acceptable folk was influenced or perhaps even drawn up by her. Being invited to the **Astors' Beechwood,** 580 Bellevue Ave. (© **401/846-3772;** www.astors-beechwood.com), was a coveted prize. Rebuilt in 1857 after a fire destroyed the original version, the mansion isn't as large or impressive as some of its neighbors. But it provides a little theatrical pizazz with a corps of actors who pretend to be friends, children, and servants of Mrs. Astor. In set pieces, they share details about life in the late Victorian era. Admission is $18 to $30 for adults, $8 to $15 for children 6 to 12, $45 per family.

OUTDOOR PURSUITS: THE BEACH & BEYOND

Fort Adams State Park, Harrison Avenue (© **401/841-0707;** www.fortadams.org), is on the thumb of land that partially encloses Newport Harbor. It can be seen from the downtown docks and reached by driving or biking south on Thames Street and west on Wellington Avenue (a section of Ocean Dr., which becomes Harrison Ave.). Boating, ocean swimming, fishing, and sailing are all possible in the park's 105 acres. The park is open from Memorial Day to Labor Day.

Farther along Ocean Drive is **Brenton Point State Park,** a scenic preserve that borders the Atlantic, with nothing to impede the waves rolling in and collapsing on the rock-strewn beach. Scuba divers are often seen surfacing offshore, anglers enjoy casting from the long breakwater, and on a windy day the sky is dotted with colorful kites.

On Ocean Drive, less than 2 miles from the south end of Bellevue Avenue, is **Gooseberry Beach,** which is privately owned but open to the public. Parking costs $8 Monday through Friday, $12 Saturday and Sunday.

Cliff Walk skirts the edge of the southern section of town where most of the cottages were built, and provides better views of many of them than can be seen from the street. The walk is open from 9am to 9pm daily.

Biking is one of the best ways to get around town, especially out to the mansions and along **Ocean Drive.** Among several rental shops are **Firehouse Bicycle,** 25 Mill St. (© **401/847-5700**); **Ten Speed Spokes,** 18 Elm St. (© **401/847-5609**); and **Scooters,** 411 Thames St. (© **401/619-0573**).

Adventure Sports Rentals, at the Inn on Long Wharf, 142 Long Wharf (© **401/849-4820**), rents not only bikes and mopeds, but also outboard boats, kayaks, and sailboats; parasailing outings can be arranged.

ORGANIZED TOURS Several organizations conduct tours of the mansions and the downtown historic district. Between May 15 and October 15, the **Newport Historical Society,** 82 Touro St. (© **401/846-0813**), offers a few different itineraries of considerable variety and length. Tickets cost as little as $4 and as much as $12. They can be purchased at the Society or at the Gateway Visitor Center. **Viking Tours,** based at the Gateway Visitor Center, 23 America's Cup Ave. (© **401/847-6921**), has narrated bus tours of the mansions and harbor cruises on the excursion boat *Viking Queen.* Bus tours—daily in summer, Saturdays from November to March—are 1¹/₂ to 4 hours and cost $22 to $47 for adults, $13 to $21 for children 5 to 11. Boat tours, from late May to early October, are 1 hour in length and cost $12 for adults, and $6 for kids.

The *Spirit of Newport,* 2 Bowen's Wharf (© **401/849-3575**), offers daily 1¹/₂-hour cruises of the bay and harbor from May 1 to Columbus Day; fares are $13 for adults, $7 for children ages 4 to 12. The **Newport Touring Company,** 19 America's Cup Ave. (© **800/398-7427** or 401/841-8700; www.newportdinnertrain.com), features 90-minute round-trip excursions in vintage railroad trains along the edge of the bay. Fares are $15 for adults; kids 10 and under are free, but only one per paying adult; additional kids are charged $7.95.

SHOPPING

For nautical shopping, try the shops along **Lower Thames Street.** For example, **J. T.'s Ship Chandlery** (no. 364) outfits recreational sailors with sea chests, ship lanterns, and foul-weather gear. **Aardvark Antiques** (no. 475) specializes in salvaged architectural components. **Spring Street** is noted for its antiques shops and purveyors of crafts, jewelry, and folk art. Antique boat models are displayed along with marine paintings and navigational instruments at **North Star Gallery** (no. 105). The **Drawing Room/**the **Zsolnay Store** (nos. 152–154) stocks estate furnishings and specializes in Hungarian Zsolnay ceramics. Folk art and furniture are the primary goods at **Liberty Tree** (no. 104).

WHERE TO STAY

The **Gateway Visitor Center** (© **800/976-5122** or 401/849-8040; www.gonewport. com) lists vacancies in motels, hotels, and inns. Most can be called from free direct-line phones located nearby. Less impulsive travelers should reserve in advance, especially on weekends (2 months ahead for weekends from Memorial Day to Labor Day). **Bed & Breakfast Newport, Ltd.** (© **800/800-8765** or 401/846-5408; www.bbnewport.com), claims to offer 350 choices of accommodations.

Many of the better motels are located in Middletown, about 2 miles north of downtown Newport. Possibilities include the **Courtyard by Marriott,** 9 Commerce Dr. (© **401/849-8000**); **Newport Ramada Inn,** 936 W. Main Rd. (© **401/846-7600**); **Newport Gateway Hotel,** 31 W. Main Rd. (© **401/847-2735**); and **Howard Johnson,** 351 W. Main Rd. (© **401/849-2000**). Newport itself has a **Marriott,** 25 America's Cup Ave. (© **401/849-1000**).

The innkeepers and hoteliers of Newport keep topping themselves, but it will be a long while before they can best the **Chanler,** 117 Memorial Blvd. (© **401/847-1300;** www.thechanler.com). A boutique hotel with only 20 units, the main structure dates from 1873. It stands above the northern end of the Cliff Walk, overlooking the surf that rolls through the bay and onto Eaton's Beach. All rooms are decorated in theme—Mediterranean, Renaissance, Tudor—and have DVD and CD players, gas fireplaces, two TVs (some are plasma), separate sitting areas, and, except for one suite, double Jacuzzis, supplemented by multinozzled shower stalls. Rates run $350 to $1,195 double.

At the **Francis Malbone House,** 392 Thames St. (© **800/846-0392** or 401/846-0392; www.malbone.com), several modern rooms were added in a wing attached to the original 1760 Colonial house. They are nice, with reproductions of period furniture and

CD players. Given a choice, take a room in the old section, where antiques outnumber
repros, Oriental rugs adorn buffed wide-board floors, and silks and linens are deployed
unsparingly. Rates include breakfast and afternoon tea. No children 11 and under. Rates
range from $99 to $345 double.

Mill Street Inn, 75 Mill St., 2 blocks east of Thames (© **800/392-1316** or 401/849-
9500; www.millstreetinn.com), is a 19th-century sawmill that was scooped out and
rebuilt from the walls in. Apart from exposed expanses of brick and an occasional wood
beam, all of it is new. An all-suite facility, even the smallest unit has a queen-size bed and
a sofa bed. The duplexes have private balconies, but everyone can use the rooftop decks,
where breakfast is served on warm days. Rates are $119 to $199 double.

WHERE TO DINE

There are far too many restaurants in Newport to give full treatment even to the best
among them. Equal in many ways to those recommended below are **Canfield House,**
5 Memorial Blvd. (© **401/847-0416**); **Yesterday's & the Place,** 28 Washington Sq.
(© **401/847-0116**); the **Bistro,** 41 Bowen's Wharf (© **401/849-7778**); and the **West
Deck,** 1 Waites Wharf (© **401/847-3610**). And for bargain dining in pricey Newport,
the bountiful pastas of **Salas,** 343 Thames St. (© **401/845-8772**), are a perfect choice
for hungry families.

Winter hours and days of operations vary considerably. Call ahead to avoid disappointment.

Still going strong after almost 330 years, the **White Horse Tavern,** 25 Marlborough
St. (© **401/849-3600**), makes a credible claim of being the oldest tavern in America.
On the ground floor are a bar and two dining rooms. The food is quite good, from the
daily lunch specials to the spice-rubbed venison with pears poached with rosemary.
About a third of the dishes involve seafood. Prices are significantly lower on the Pub
menu ($10–$24 for entrees) available from 5pm Sunday through Thursday. Otherwise,
main courses run $28 to $40. At **Scales & Shells,** 527 Lower Thames St. (© **401/846-
3474**), the graceless name reflects the uncompromising character of this clangorous fish
house. Diners who insist on a modicum of elegance should head for the upstairs room,
called **Upscales** (© **401/847-2000**). Myriad fish and shellfish, listed on the blackboard,
are offered in guileless preparations that allow the natural flavors to prevail. Main courses
downstairs cost $11 to $21; at Upscales it's $16 to $29.

NEWPORT AFTER DARK

The most likely places to spend an evening lie along **Thames Street.** One of the most
obvious possibilities, the **Red Parrot,** 348 Thames St., near Memorial Boulevard (© **401/
847-3140**), has the look of an Irish saloon and features jazz combos Thursday through
Sunday. **One Pelham East,** at Thames and Pelham streets (© **401/847-9460**), has a
cafe, a small dance floor, a pool table, and another bar upstairs, with mostly college-age
patrons attending to rockers on the stage at front. Free pizza is served some evenings.

A full schedule of live music is featured at the **Newport Blues Café,** 286 Thames St.,
at Green Street (© **401/841-5510**), plus a Sunday gospel brunch. With its fireplace,
dark wood, and massive steel back door that used to guard the safe of this former bank,
the cafe has a lot more class than most of the town's bars. Meals are available nightly in
summer, Thursday through Sunday nights off season.

Providence delights in its sobriquet, "Renaissance City." No question, this city is moving on up, counter to the trend of so many small and midsize New England cities. *Money* magazine even declared it the "Best Place to Live in the East." Revival is in the air and prosperity is returning, evident in the resurgent "downcity" business district. Rivers have been uncovered to form canals and waterside walkways; distressed buildings of the last century have been reclaimed; and continued construction has added a new hotel behind Union Station as well as Providence Place, a monster mall that brings national department stores to town for the first time. Adjacent to downcity is the Downtown Arts District, newly designated to the National Register of Historic Places, attracting restaurants, shops, a new boutique hotel, and several theater and repertory companies.

GETTING THERE   By Air   T. F. **Green/Providence Airport** (© **888/268-7222** or 401/737-8222; www.pvdairport.com) in Warwick, south of Providence (exit 13, I-95), is served by major airlines. The Rhode Island Public Transit Authority (RIPTA) provides transportation between the airport and the city center. Taxis are also available, costing about $20 for the 20-minute trip.

By Train   Amtrak (© **800/USA-RAIL** [872-7245]; www.amtrak.com) runs several trains daily between Boston and New York, stopping at the attractive station at 100 Gaspee St., near the State House.

By Car   **I-95,** which connects Boston and New York, runs right through the city. From Cape Cod, pick up **I-195 West.**

VISITOR INFORMATION   For advance information, contact the **Providence Warwick Convention & Visitors Bureau,** 1 W. Exchange St. (© **800/233-1636** or 401/ 274-1636; www.providencecvb.com). In town, consult the new visitor center in the Rhode Island Convention Center, 1 Sabin St. (© **800/233-1636** or 401/751-1177), or check with the helpful park rangers at the visitor center of the Roger Williams National Park, at the corner of Smith and North Main streets, open daily from 9am to 4:30pm.

EXPLORING PROVIDENCE
Strolling the Historic Neighborhoods
This is a city of manageable size—the population is about 170,000—that can easily occupy 2 or 3 days of a Rhode Island vacation. Two leisurely walks, one short, another longer, pass most of the prominent attractions and offer up a sense of the city's evolution from a colony of dissidents to a contemporary center of commerce and government.

Downtown, chart a route from the 1878 City Hall on Kennedy Plaza along Dorrance Street 1 block to Westminster. Turn left, then right in 1 block, past the Arcade, then left on Weybosset.

To extend this into a longer walk, follow Weybosset until it joins Westminster and continue across the Providence River. Turn right on the other side, walking along South Water Street as far as James Street, just before the I-195 overpass. Turn left, cross South Main, and then turn left on Benefit Street. This is the start of the so-called **Mile of History.** Lined with 18th- and 19th-century houses, it is enhanced by gas streetlamps and sections of brick herringbone sidewalks. Along the way are opportunities to visit, in sequence, the 1786 **John Brown House,** the **First Unitarian Church** (1816), the **Providence Athenaeum,** and the **Museum of Art, Rhode Island School of Design** (see below).

The **Rhode Island Historical Society** (© 401/438-0463; www.rihs.org) offers 90-minute guided tours of four different neighborhoods of interest.

Boosters are understandably proud of their **Waterplace Park & Riverwalk,** which encircles a tidal basin and borders the Woonasquatucket River down past where it joins the Moshassuck to become the Providence River. It incorporates an amphitheater, boat landings, landscaped walkways, and vaguely Venetian bridges that cross to the East Side. Summer concerts and other events are held here, among them the enormously popular **WaterFires** (© 401/272-3111), when 97 bonfires are set ablaze in the basin of Waterplace Park and along the river on New Year's Eve and on more than 20 other dates July through October, their roar accentuated by amplified music.

Nearby, in Kennedy Plaza, the **Fleet Skating Center** has an ice rink twice the size of the one in New York's Rockefeller Center, fully utilized almost every winter evening. Skate rentals, lockers, and a snack bar are available.

The prestigious **Museum of Art, Rhode Island School of Design,** 224 Benefit St., between Waterman and College streets (© 401/454-6500; www.risd.edu/museum.cfm), is an ingratiating center of fine and decorative arts that ranks near the top of New England's many fine university museums because of the sheer breadth of its collection. Those holdings include Chinese terra cotta, Greek statuary, French Impressionist paintings, works by masters such as Rodin and Picasso, and a wing containing paintings by American artists such as Gilbert Stuart and John Singer Sargent. The Gorham silver collection alone is nearly worth the admission ($8 adults, $2 children 5–18).

Constructed of Georgian marble that blazes in the sun, the **Rhode Island State House,** 82 Smith St. (© 401/277-2357), dominates the city center. This near-flawless example of neoclassical governmental architecture boasts one of the largest self-supported domes in the world. The gilded figure on top represents "Independent Man," the state symbol. Inside, a portrait of George Washington by native Rhode Islander Gilbert Stuart is given pride of place. Guided tours are available on weekday mornings by prior appointment only.

Situated in a 430-acre park that also contains a museum of natural history and a planetarium, the **Roger Williams Park Zoo,** 1000 Elmwood Ave., at exit 17 off I-95 (© 401/785-3510; www.rogerwilliamsparkzoo.org), is divided into three principal habitats: Tropical America, the Farmyard, and the Plains of Africa. A newer exhibit is devoted to Australia, with the zoo's first saltwater aquarium. A walk-through aviary and underwater viewing areas with polar bears, sea lions, and harbor seals are additional attractions. The facility has looked a bit bedraggled of late, but not enough to deter visits. Admission is $12 adults, $6 kids 3 to 12.

WHERE TO STAY & DINE

The clusters of motels around most of the exits from I-95 and I-195 offer decent value. Among these possibilities are the **Days Hotel,** 220 India St. (© 401/272-5577), and the **Ramada Inn,** 940 Fall River Ave., Seekonk, MA (© 508/336-7300). *Note:* Rates at most area inns and motels go up on alumni and parents' weekends and during graduation weeks.

At the **Providence Biltmore,** 11 Dorrance St. (© 800/294-7709 or 401/421-0700; www.providencebiltmore.com), a grand staircase beneath the stunning Art Deco bronze ceiling dates the centrally located building from the 1920s, and a plaque in the lobby shows the nearly 7-foot-high water level of the villainous 1938 hurricane. From the lobby, the dramatic glass elevator literally shoots skyward, exiting outdoors to scoot up the side of the building. Most guest rooms are large and some of the 20 suites have kitchenettes. An Elizabeth Arden Red Door Spa should be open by the time you read this. Rates run $249 to $289 double.

Easily the city's best hotel, the **Westin Providence,** 1 W. Exchange St. (© **800/937-8461** or 401/598-8000; www.westin.com), has a luxurious interior and a central downtown location. Skyways connect the hotel with the new Providence Place mall and the convention center. The architectural grandeur of the lobby rotunda and other public spaces is only enhanced by the sunny dispositions of the staff. Rooms are equipped with Westin's signature "Heavenly Bed." Rooms run $199 to $339 double. **Agora,** the main dining room, gets excellent reviews from critics.

Providence has a sturdy Italian heritage, resulting in a profusion of tomato-sauce and pizza joints, especially on Federal Hill, the district west of downtown and I-95. Because they are so obvious, the suggestions below focus on restaurants that break away from the red-gravy imperative.

One fruitful strip to explore for lower-cost dining options is that part of **Thayer Street** that borders the Brown University campus. It counts Thai, Tex-Mex, barbecue, and Indian restaurants among its possibilities.

The very steady **Cafe Nuovo,** 1 Citizens Plaza (access is from the Steeple St. bridge; © **401/421-2525**), occupies a spacious room of glass, marble, and burnished wood on the ground floor of a downtown office tower that overlooks the confluence of the Moshassuck and Woonasquatucket rivers. The kitchen here impresses with every course, from dazzling appetizers to stunning pastries. The fare is grounded in the Italian repertoire, but skips lightly among other inspirations, too—Thai, Greek, and Portuguese among them. There's music on weekends and outdoor dining in warm weather. Main courses cost $22 to $32.

XO Café, 125 N. Main St. (© **401/273-9090**), draws a young, casual crowd, which keeps the staff moving at a fast evening-long pace. Behind the copper-topped bar are female mixologists in clothes not meant to conceal their gender, though they serve almost as many meals as drinks. A note at the top of the varied menu insists "Life is short, order dessert first" and some diners happily take the advice (whatever you do, don't skip dessert). Slaves to tradition can order the "Pre Fixe"—their spelling—which on one occasion listed seared foie gras in brioche with candied shallots and citrus-honey glaze. Main courses cost $20 to $31.

Providence claims the invention of the diner, starting with a horse-drawn wagon transporting food down Westminster Street in 1872. The tradition is carried forward by the likes of the **Seaplane Diner,** 307 Allens Ave. (© **401/941-9547**), a silver-sided classic with tableside jukeboxes; and **Richard's Diner,** 377 Richmond St. (© **401/331-8541**), so small you can walk across it in six strides.

8 SOUTHERN VERMONT

ARLINGTON & MANCHESTER

Southwestern Vermont is the turf of Ethan Allen, Robert Frost, Grandma Moses, and Norman Rockwell. The rolling Green Mountains are rarely out of view from this region. And in midsummer, the lush green hereabouts give Ireland a good run for its money—verdant hues are found in the forests blanketing the hills, the valley meadows, and the mosses along the tumbling streams, making it obvious how these mountains earned their name.

These Vermont villages make an ideal destination for romantic getaways, antiquing, and outlet shopping. **Arlington** has a town center that borders on microscopic; with its auto-body shops and redemption center (remnants of a time when the main highway artery passed through town), it gleams a bit less than its sibling towns to the north.

To the north, **Manchester** and **Manchester Center** share a town line but maintain distinct characters. The more southerly Manchester has an old-world elegance with a campuslike town centered on the Equinox Hotel. Just to the north, Manchester Center is a major mercantile center with dozens of national outlets offering discounts on brand-name clothing, accessories, and housewares.

Essentials

GETTING THERE From **I-91** at Brattleboro, take **Route 9 west.** Arlington, Manchester, and Manchester Center are north of Bennington on Historic Route 7A, which runs parallel to and west of **Route 7. Vermont Transit** (② **800/552-8737;** www.vermonttransit. com) provides bus service to Manchester.

VISITOR INFORMATION The **Manchester and the Mountains Chamber of Commerce** (② **800/362-4144** or 802/362-2100; www.manchestervermont.net) maintains a year-round information center at 5080 Main St. (Rte. 7A) beside the small village green in Manchester Center. Hours are Monday through Saturday from 10am to 5pm; from Memorial Day weekend through October, it's also open Sundays from 10am to 5pm, and to 7pm Fridays and Saturdays.

For information on outdoor recreation, the **Green Mountain National Forest** maintains a district ranger office (② **802/362-2307**) in Manchester on routes 11 and 30 east of Route 7. It's open Monday through Friday from 8am to 4:30pm.

Exploring the Area

Arlington has long been associated with illustrator Norman Rockwell, who lived here from 1939 to 1953. Its residents were regularly featured in Rockwell covers for the *Saturday Evening Post.* "Moving to Arlington had given my work a terrific boost. I'd met one or two hundred people I wanted to paint . . . the sincere, honest, homespun types that I love to paint," Rockwell wrote. At press time, the small **Norman Rockwell Exhibition** (② **802/375-6423**) was up for sale and its status was in doubt.

Manchester has long been one of Vermont's moneyed resorts, attracting prominent summer residents. This town is worth visiting to wander its quiet streets, bordered by distinguished homes dating from the early Federal period. Be sure to note the sidewalks made of irregular marble slabs. The town is said to have 17 miles of such sidewalks, composed of the castoffs from Vermont's marble quarries.

Hildene, Route 7A (② **802/362-1788;** www.hildene.org), was built by Robert Todd Lincoln, the only son of Abraham and Mary Todd Lincoln to survive to maturity. Lincoln summered in this 24-room Georgian Revival mansion between 1905 and 1926 and delighted in showing off its features, including a sweeping staircase and a 1908 Aeolian organ with 1,000 pipes. Lincoln had formal gardens designed after the patterns in a stained-glass window and planted on a gentle promontory with outstanding views of the flanking mountains. The home is viewed on group tours that start at the visitor center; allow time following the tour to explore the grounds. Admission is $12 adults, $4 children 6 to 14. Tours are given from mid-May to October daily from 9:30am to 4pm; grounds close at 5:30pm.

Skiers head to **Bromley Mountain Ski Resort** in Manchester Center (② **800/865-4786** for lodging, or 802/824-5522; www.bromley.com) to learn to ski. Gentle and forgiving, the mountain also features long, looping intermediate runs tremendously popular with families. **Stratton** (☎ **800/STRATTON** [787-2886] for lodging, or 802/297-4000; www.stratton.com) is another popular resort, where new owners have added $25 million in improvements in recent years, mostly in snowmaking, with coverage now up over 80%. The slopes are especially popular for snowboarding, a sport invented here. Expert skiers should seek out Upper Middlebrook, a fine, twisting run off the summit.

Where to Stay & Dine

Owned and managed by the upscale Rockresorts, the **Equinox,** Route 7A, Manchester Village (☎ **800/362-4747** or 802/362-4700; www.equinoxresort.com), is a blue-blood favorite, with acres of white clapboard behind a long row of stately columns that define lovely Manchester Village. Its roots extend back to 1769, but don't be misled by its lineage: The Equinox is a full-blown modern resort, complete with the full-service spa. You'll find extensive sports facilities scattered about its 2,300 acres, four dining rooms, scheduled events (such as guided hikes up Mount Equinox), and a sense of settled graciousness. The rooms are tastefully appointed, though not terribly large. Rates run $279 to $449 double.

The **Arlington Inn,** Route 7A (☎ **800/443-9442** or 802/375-6532; www.arlington inn.com), is an 1848 Greek Revival that would be at home in the Virginia countryside. But it anchors this village well, on a lawn bordered with sturdy maples. Inside, unique wooden ceilings adorn the first-floor rooms and a tavern that borrows its atmosphere from an English hunt club. If you prefer modern comforts, ask for a room in the 1830 parsonage next door, where you'll find phones and TVs. The quietest units are in the detached carriage house. There's also a tennis court. Rates ($95–$315 double) include breakfast.

If you're looking for a bit of history with your lodging but are shell-shocked by area rates, consider the **Barnstead Inn,** Route 30, Manchester Center (☎ **800/331-1619** or 802/362-1619; www.barnsteadinn.com), a congenial place within walking distance of Manchester. All but two of the guest rooms are in an 1830s barn; many are decorated in a rustic style, some with exposed beams. Expect vinyl bathroom floors, industrial carpeting, and a mix of motel-modern and antique furniture. Among the more desirable units are room B, which is the largest, and the two rooms (nos. 12 and 13) above the office, each with original round beams. Children 13 and over are welcome. In the summer, there's a heated pool. Rates run $90 to $229 double.

If you like superbly prepared Continental fare but are put off by the stuffiness of highbrow restaurants, **Chantecleer** on Route 7A, 3¹/₂ miles north of Manchester Center (☎ **802/362-1616**), is the place for you. Rustic elegance is the best description for this century-old dairy barn. Chef Michel Baumann specializes in game and might feature veal with a roasted garlic, sage, and balsamic demi-glace. Especially good is the whole Dover sole, filleted tableside. Main courses cost $26 to $35.

The **Little Rooster Café,** Route 7A South, Manchester Center (☎ **802/362-3496**), is the best choice in town for breakfast or lunch. Start the day with flapjacks, a Cajun omelet, or a luscious corned-beef hash. Lunches feature a creative sandwich selection, such as a commendable roast beef with pickled red cabbage and a horseradish dill sauce. Menu items run from $4.50 to $6.75 at breakfast to a high of $8.25 at lunch.

THE SOUTHERN GREEN MOUNTAINS

The southern Green Mountains are New England writ large. If you've developed a notion in your head of what New England looks like, this may be the place you've envisioned. This region is known for its pristine, historic villages. Stop for a spell in Brattleboro to stock up on supplies, then head for the southern Green Mountains and continue your explorations on foot or by bike. In winter, you can plumb the snowy hills by cross-country ski or snowshoe.

Newfane & Townshend

These two villages, about 5 miles apart on Route 30, are the epitome of Vermont. Both are set within the serpentine West River Valley and built around open town greens. Both consist of impressive white-clapboard houses and public buildings that share the grace and scale of the surrounding homes. Both boast striking examples of Early American architecture, notably Greek Revival.

For visitors, inactivity is often the activity of choice. Guests find an inn or lodge that suits their temperament, then spend the days strolling, driving the back roads, soaking in a mountain stream, hunting for antiques, or striking off on foot for one of the rounded, wooded peaks that overlook villages and valleys.

Essentials

GETTING THERE   Newfane and Townshend are located on **Route 30** northwest of Brattleboro. The nearest interstate access is off exit 3 from **I-91.**

VISITOR INFORMATION   No formal information center serves these towns. Brochures are available at the **state visitor center** (© **802/254-4593**) on I-91 in Guilford, south of Brattleboro. The website **www.newfanevermontusa.com** provides good local information.

What to See & Do

Newfane was originally founded on a hill a few miles from the current village in 1774; in 1825, it was moved to its present location on a valley floor. Some of the original buildings were dismantled and rebuilt, but most date from the early to mid–19th century. The **National Historic District** comprises some 60 buildings around the green and on nearby side streets. You'll find styles ranging from Federal to Colonial Revival, although Greek Revival appears to carry the day. For more information on area buildings, get a copy of the free walking-tour brochure at the Moore Free Library on West Street or at the Historical Society.

Newfane's history is explored at the **Historical Society of Windham County,** on Route 30 across from the village common, in a 1930s Colonial Revival brick building. There's an assemblage of local artifacts (dolls, melodeons, rail ephemera), along with changing exhibits. It's open from late May to mid-October, Wednesday through Sunday from noon to 5pm; admission is by donation.

More than two dozen **antiques shops** are on or near Route 30 in the West River Valley. They provide good grazing and are a fine resource for collectors. At any of the shops, look for the brochure *Antiquing in the West River Valley.* Treasure hunters should time their visit to coincide with the **Newfane Flea Market** (© **802/365-7771**), which features 100-plus tables of assorted stuff, including some of the 12-tube-socks-for-$8 variety. The flea market is held on Sundays from May through October on Route 30 just north of Newfane Village.

A Little Mountain Music

The **Marlboro Music Festival** offers classical concerts by accomplished masters as well as talented younger musicians from mid-July to mid-August in Marlboro, in the foothills of southeastern Vermont on Route 9. The retreat was founded in 1951 and has hosted countless musicians, including Pablo Casals, who participated between 1960 and 1973.

Concerts are in the 700-seat auditorium at Marlboro College, and advance ticket purchases are recommended. Between September and June, contact the festival's winter office at Marlboro Music, 135 S. 18th St., Philadelphia, PA 19103 (© **215/569-4690**). In summer, write Marlboro Music, Marlboro, VT 05344; or call the box office (© **802/254-2394;** www.marlboromusic.org). Marlboro's about a 4-hour drive from New York City and 2 ¹/₂ hours from Boston.

On Route 30 between Townshend and Jamaica, you'll pass the **Scott Covered Bridge** below the Townshend Dam (closed to car traffic). It dates from 1870 and is an example of a Towne lattice-style bridge, with an added arch. At 166 feet long, it is the longest single-span bridge in the state.

Where to Stay & Dine

You can't help but notice the **Four Columns Inn,** West Street, Newfane (© **800/787-6633** or 802/365-7713; www.fourcolumnsinn.com). It's the regal white-clapboard building with four Ionic columns just off the green. Rooms in the Main House and Garden Wing are larger (and more expensive) than those above the restaurant. Four units have been made over as luxury suites. The best choice in the house is room no. 12, with a Jacuzzi, skylight, gas fireplace, and private deck with a view of a small pond. Low beams and white damask tablecloths characterize the inn's dining room, which features creative New American cooking. Rates include continental breakfast. There's an outdoor pool and hiking trails. Rates ($160–$225 double) include continental breakfast.

The **Windham Hill Inn,** Windham Hill Road, West Townshend (© **800/944-4080** or 802/874-4080; www.windhamhill.com), is about as good as it gets in this region. Situated on 160 acres at the end of a dirt road in a high upland valley, it was built in 1823 as a farmhouse. The guest rooms are appointed in an elegant country style; 6 have Jacuzzis or soaking tubs, 9 have balconies or decks, 13 have gas fireplaces, and all have views. The dining room features creative cooking with a strong emphasis on local ingredients. Rates ($245–$435) include breakfast. There are a heated pool, tennis court, and 6 miles of cross-country ski trails in winter. Children 13 and over are welcome.

WOODSTOCK

For more than a century, the resort community of Woodstock has been considered one of New England's most exquisite villages. The downtown is compact and neat, populated largely by galleries and boutiques. The village green is surrounded by handsome homes, creating what amounts to a comprehensive review of architectural styles of the 19th and early 20th centuries.

It was first settled in 1765, rose to some prominence as a publishing center in the mid–19th century, and began to attract wealthy families who summered here in the late 19th century. Much of the town is on the National Register of Historic Places, and the

Rockefeller family has deeded 500 acres surrounding Mount Tom to the National Park
Service.

Essentials

GETTING THERE   Woodstock is 13 miles west of White River Junction on **Route 4.**
(Take exit 1 off I-89.) From the west, Woodstock is 20 miles east of Killington on Route
4. **Vermont Transit** (© **800/451-3292;** www.vermonttransit.com) provides bus service
to Boston and Burlington.

VISITOR INFORMATION   The **Woodstock Area Chamber of Commerce,** 18 Central St. (© **888/496-6378** or 802/457-3555; www.woodstockvt.com), staffs an information booth on the green, open June through October daily from 9:30am to 5:30pm.

Exploring the Area

The heart of the town is the shady, elliptical green. To put local history in perspective,
stop by the **Woodstock Historical Society,** 26 Elm St. (© **802/457-1822**). Housed in
the beautiful 1807 Charles Dana House, it has rooms furnished in Federal, Empire, and
Victorian styles. It's open from late May to October, plus weekends in December. Hours
are Monday through Saturday from 10am to 5pm and Sunday from noon to 4pm.
Admission is $5.

The **Billings Farm and Museum** on Elm Street, about a half-mile north of town on
Route 12 (© **802/457-2355;** www.billingsfarm.org), was the creation of Frederick Billings, who is credited with completing the Northern Pacific Railroad. The 19th-century
dairy farm was once renowned for its scientific breeding of Jersey cows and its fine architecture, especially the gabled 1890 Victorian farmhouse. A tour includes hands-on
demonstrations of farm activities, exhibits of farm life, a look at an heirloom kitchen
garden, and a visit to active milking barns. Admission is $10 adults, $8 children 13 to
17, $6 children 5 to 12, and $3 children 3 to 4.

The Billings Farm and the National Park Service have teamed up to manage the
Marsh-Billings-Rockefeller National Historic Park (© **802/457-3368;** www.nps.gov/
mabi), focusing on the history of conservation. Visitors can tour the elaborate Victorian
mansion, walk the carriage roads surrounding Mount Tom, and view one of the oldest
professionally managed woodlands in the nation.

Admission to the grounds is free; mansion tours cost $6 adults, $3 children 16 and
under. Advance reservations are recommended for mansion tours.

Outdoor Pursuits

The rolling, hilly terrain around Woodstock is ideal for exploring by **bike.** Few roads
don't lead to great rides; just grab a map and go. Mountain bikes are available for rent at
Woodstock Sports, 30 Central St. (© **802/457-1568**).

Mount Tom is the prominent hill overlooking Woodstock, and its low summit has
great views over the village and to the Green Mountains to the west. You can ascend
the mountain right from the village: Start at Faulkner Park. To reach the trail head from
the green, cross Middle Covered Bridge and continue straight on Mountain Avenue. The
road soon arrives at the park at the base of Mount Tom.

The area's best **cross-country skiing** is at the **Woodstock Ski Touring Center** (© **800/
448-7900** or 802/457-6674), at the Woodstock Country Club, just south of town on
Route 106. The center maintains 36 miles of trails, including 12 miles of trails groomed
for skate-skiing. The full-day trail fee is $14 for adults.

Jackson House Inn, 114–3 Senior Lane (© **800/448-1890** or 802/457-2065; www. jacksonhouse.com), was built in 1890 by a lumber baron who hoarded the best wood for himself; the cherry and maple floors are so beautiful you'll feel guilty for not taking off your shoes. The guest rooms are well appointed with antiques, although some of the older rooms are rather small. A well-executed addition (1997) created four suites with fireplaces and Jacuzzis. The inn welcomes guests with complimentary evening hors d'oeuvres and champagne, and a 3-acre backyard with formal English gardens. Rates ($195–$260 double) include breakfast. Children 14 and over are welcome. The **Dining Room** (3-course prix-fixe dinner about $55) offers Continental fare in a modern addition to the original inn. Its centerpiece is a 16-foot-high stone fireplace, and it boasts soaring windows with views of the gardens. Men may feel most comfortable in a sports coat, though a jacket is not required.

The **Shire Motel,** 46 Pleasant St. (© **802/457-2211;** www.shiremotel.com), is within walking distance of the green and, with its Colonial decor, is better appointed than your average motel. The rooms are bright, with most facing the river that runs behind the property; all have fridges. (The downside: thin sheets and some scuffed walls.) Off a second-floor porch is an outdoor kitchen where you can sit on rockers overlooking the river and enjoy a cup of coffee. The yellow-clapboard house next door has three modern suites, all with gas fireplaces and Jacuzzis. Rates run $78 to $315 double.

The **Woodstock Inn & Resort,** 14 The Green (© **800/448-7900** or 802/457-1100; www.woodstockinn.com), is central Vermont's best full-scale resort. The inn appears to be a venerable and long-established institution at first glance. But it's not—it wasn't built until 1969, but adopted a dignified Colonial Revival look well suited for Woodstock. Guest rooms are decorated in either country pine or a Shaker-inspired style. The best units, in a wing built in 1991, feature plush carpeting, fridges, and fireplaces. There are two restaurants, indoor and outdoor pools, a Robert Trent Jones–designed golf course (at the inn-owned Woodstock Country Club), tennis courts, a free shuttle to a fitness center, bike rental, and cross-country ski trails. Rates run $149 to $434 double.

On the dining front, the **Prince and the Pauper,** 24 Elm St. (© **802/457-1818;** www.princeandpauper.com), takes a bit of sleuthing to find (located down Dana Alley, next to the Woodstock Historical Society's Dana House), but it's worth the effort. This is one of Woodstock's more inviting restaurants, with an intimate but informal setting. Ease into the evening with a libation in the taproom, then move over to the rustic but elegant dining room. The menu changes often; the house specialty is a boneless rack of lamb baked in puff pastry with spinach and mushroom duxelles. The fixed-price dinner (appetizer, salad, entree) is $43.

The setting of the **Simon Pearce Restaurant,** The Mill, Quechee (© **802/295-1470;** www.simonpearce.com), can't be beat. Housed in a restored 19th-century woolen mill with wonderful views of a waterfall (spotlighted at night), Simon Pearce is a collage of exposed brick, pine floorboards, and handsome wooden tables and chairs. Meals are served on Simon Pearce pottery and glassware—if you like your place setting, you can buy it afterward at the sprawling retail shop in the mill. The atmosphere is a wonderful concoction of formal and informal. At dinner, look for entrees such as roast duck with mango chutney, and pan-roasted wild salmon. Main courses cost $22 to $28.

KILLINGTON

Killington is not the Vermont pictured on calendars and place mats. But the region around the mountain boasts Vermont's most active winter scene. Those most content here are skiers, singles in search of mingling, and travelers who want a wide selection of amenities.

Essentials

GETTING THERE   Killington Road extends southward from **routes 4** and **100** (marked on some maps as Sherburne). It's about 12 miles east of Rutland on Route 4. Many inns offer shuttles to the Rutland airport. **Amtrak** (© 800/USA-RAIL [872-7245]; www.amtrak.com) offers service from New York to Rutland, with connecting shuttles to the mountain and various resorts. The **Marble Valley Regional Transit District** (© 802/773-3244; www.thebus.com) operates the **Skibus,** with $2 shuttle rides service between Rutland and Killington daily in winter.

VISITOR INFORMATION   The **Killington Chamber of Commerce** (© 800/773-4181 or 802/773-4181; www.killington-chamber.org) has information on lodging and travel packages, and staffs an information booth on Route 4 at the base of the access road, open Monday through Friday from 9am to 5pm, and Saturday through Sunday from 10am to 2pm. For information on accommodations in the area and travel to Killington, contact the **Killington Lodging and Travel Service** (© 877/4-K-TIMES [5-84637]).

Skiing & More

Killington (© 877/4-K-TIMES [5-84637] for lodging, or 800/734-9435; www.killington.com) is New England's largest ski area, offering greater vertical drop than any other New England mountain. You'll find the broadest selection of slopes, with trails ranging from long, narrow, old-fashioned runs to killer bumps high on its flanks. Thanks to this diversity, it has long been the destination of choice for serious skiers. That said, it's also a huge operation run with efficiency and not much of a personal touch. To avoid getting lost, ask about the free tours of the mountain, led by the ski ambassadors based at Snowshed. If you're looking for the big mountain experience, with lots of evening activities and plenty of challenging terrain, it's a good choice. Lift-ticket prices vary through the season, but they average around $70 adults and $50 for kids and seniors.

Nearest to the downhill ski area (just east of Killington Rd. on Rte. 100/Rte. 4) is **Mountain Meadows Cross Country Ski Resort** (© 800/221-0598 or 802/775-7077; www.xcskiing.net), with 34 miles of trails groomed for both skating and classic skiing. The trails are largely divided into three pods, with beginner trails closest to the lodge, an intermediate area a bit farther along, and an advanced 6-mile loop farthest away. Rentals and lessons are available. A 1-day pass is $18, a half-day pass (after 1pm) $15. The intricate network of trails at **Mountain Top Inn** (© 802/483-6089) has long had a loyal local following. The 66-mile trail network offers pastoral views through mixed terrain groomed for traditional and skate skiing. Adults pay $19 for 1-day trail passes, $16 for half-day passes (after 1pm). With more challenging and picturesque terrain, Mountain Top is the better value of the two options.

Where to Stay

Skiers headed to Killington for a week or so should consider the condo option. A number of condo developments spill down the hillside and along the low ridges flanking the access road. These vary in elegance, convenience, and size. **Highridge** features units with saunas and Jacuzzis, along with access to a compact health club. **Sunrise Village** has a more remote setting, along with a health club and access to the Bear Mountain lifts. The **Woods at Killington** is farthest from the slopes (free shuttle) but offers access to the finest health club and the best restaurant. Rates fluctuate, depending on time of year, number of guest rooms, and length of stay. But figure on prices ranging from around $100 to $130 and up per person per day, including lift tickets. You can line up a vacation—or request more information—by contacting the **Killington Lodging and Travel Bureau** (© **888/4-K-TIMES [5-84637]**; www.killington.com), which also arranges stays at area inns and motels.

The **Blueberry Hill Inn,** Goshen–Ripton Road, Goshen (© **800/448-0707** or 802/247-6735; www.blueberryhillinn.com), is along a quiet road about 45 minutes northwest of Killington. It's an extraordinary destination for those inclined toward spending time outdoors. The inn dates to 1813; one graceful addition is the greenhouse walkway, which leads to the cozy guest rooms. Family-style meals are served in a rustic dining room, with a great stone fireplace and homegrown herbs drying from the wooden beams. Rates ($110–$190 double) include breakfast and dinner. There's lake swimming nearby, a sauna, bike rental, and cross-country ski trails. There are no phones in the rooms.

Where to Dine

It's our impression that *every* Killington restaurant serves up chicken wings, and plenty of them. If you love wings, especially free wings, you'll be in heaven. Most restaurants are okay spots to carbo-load for a day on the slopes, and if you're with a group of friends, you may not mind the middling quality—but for the most part, don't expect much of a dining adventure.

One of the locally favored spots for consistently good, unpretentious fare is **Choices Restaurant and Rotisserie,** Killington Road at Glazebook Center (© **802/422-40300**), located on the access road across from the Outback. Full dinners come complete with salad or soup and bread and will amply restore calories lost on the slopes or the trail. Fresh pastas are a specialty (try the Cajun green-peppercorn fettuccine); other inviting entrees include meats from the rotisserie. The atmosphere is nothing to write home about and the prices are higher than at nearby burger joints, but the high quality of the food and the care in preparation make up for that. Main courses run $13 to $22.

Hemingway's, 4988 Rte. 4, between Route 100 North and Route 100 South (© **802/ 422-3886;** www.hemingwaysrestaurant.com), is an elegant spot—and one that ranks among the best restaurants in New England. Located in the 1860 Asa Briggs House, a former stagecoach stop, Hemingway's seats guests in three formal areas. The two upstairs rooms are sophisticatedly appointed with damask linen, crystal goblets, and fresh flowers. Diners tend to dress casually but neatly (no shorts or T-shirts). The three- or four-course dinners are offered at a price (fixed-price menu $42–$60) that turns out to be rather reasonable, given the quality of the kitchen and the unassailable service. The menu changes often to reflect available stock.

9 THE WHITE MOUNTAINS OF NEW HAMPSHIRE

The White Mountains are northern New England's outdoor-recreation capital. This cluster of ancient mountains is a sprawling, rugged playground that attracts kayakers, mountaineers, rock climbers, skiers, mountain bikers, bird-watchers, and especially hikers.

The **White Mountain National Forest** encompasses some 773,000 acres of rocky, forested terrain; more than 100 waterfalls; dozens of remote backcountry lakes, and miles of clear brooks and cascading streams. The center of the White Mountains—in spirit if not in geography—is its highest point: 6,288-foot **Mount Washington,** an ominous, brooding peak that's often cloud-capped and mantled with snow both early and late in the season.

JACKSON & MOUNT WASHINGTON

Jackson is a village in a picturesque valley just off Route 16, about 15 minutes north of North Conway. The village center, approached on a single-lane covered bridge, is tiny, but touches of old-world elegance remain—vestiges of a time when Jackson was a favored destination for the East Coast upper middle class.

Essentials

GETTING THERE   Jackson is off **Route 16** about 11 miles north of North Conway. Look for the covered bridge on the right when heading north.

VISITOR INFORMATION   The **Jackson Chamber of Commerce** (© **800/866-3334** or 603/383-9356; www.jacksonnh.com), based in offices at the Jackson Falls Marketplace, can answer questions about area attractions and make lodging reservations.

What to See & Do

Mount Washington, just north of Jackson, is the highest mountain in the Northeast, at 6,288 feet. It's also got some of the worst winter weather in the Northeast: It holds the world's record for the highest surface wind speed ever recorded—231 mph, in 1934. Mount Washington may also be the mountain with the most options for getting to the top. Visitors can ascend by cog railroad, by car, by guide-driven van, or on foot.

Despite the raw power of the weather, Mount Washington's summit is not the best destination for those seeking wilderness wild and untamed. The summit is home to a train platform, a snack bar, a gift shop, a museum, and a handful of outbuildings, some of which house the weather observatory. And there are the crowds, which can be thick on a clear day. Then again, on a clear day the views can't be beat, with vistas extending into four states and to the Atlantic Ocean.

The best place to learn about Mount Washington is rustic **Pinkham Notch Visitor Center** (© **603/466-2721**), operated by the Appalachian Mountain Club. At the crest of Route 16 between Jackson and Gorham, Pinkham Notch offers overnight accommodations and meals, maps, and advice from the helpful staff. A number of hiking trails depart from Pinkham Notch.

The **Mount Washington Auto Road** (© **603/466-3988;** www.mountwashingtonautoroad.com) opened in 1861 as a carriage road and has since remained one of the most popular White Mountain attractions. The steep, winding 8-mile road (with an average grade of 12%) is partially paved and incredibly dramatic. The ascent will test your iron will; the descent will test your car's brakes. The trip's not worth doing if the summit is in the clouds.

Van tours also ascend throughout the day, allowing you to relax, enjoy the views, and learn about the mountain from informed guides. The Auto Road, which is on Route 16 north of Pinkham Notch, is open from mid-May to late October from 7:30am to 6pm (limited hours early and late in the season). The cost is $20 for car and driver, $7 for each additional adult ($5 for children 5–12). The fee includes audiocassette narration pointing out sights along the way. Management has imposed some curious restrictions on cars; for instance, Acuras and Jaguars with automatic transmissions must show a "1" on the shifter to be allowed on the road; call or check the website for details before heading out.

One additional note: The average temperature atop the mountain is 30°F (–1°C). The record low was –43°F (–42°C), and the warmest temperature ever recorded atop the mountain, in August, was 72°F (22°C). Even in summer, visitors should come prepared for blustery, cold conditions.

Where to Stay & Dine

The **Covered Bridge Motor Lodge,** Route 16 (© 800/634-2911 or 602/383-9151; www.jacksoncoveredbridge.com), is a pleasant motel on 5 acres between Route 16 and the river next to Jackson's covered bridge. While pretty basic, the lodge features lovely gardens and other appealing touches that make it a good value. The best rooms have balconies that overlook the river. Ask about the two-bedroom apartments with kitchen and fireplace. Rates ($79–$139 double) include continental breakfast. There's an outdoor pool and a tennis court.

The **Inn at Thorn Hill,** Thorn Hill Road (© 603/383-4242; www.innatthornhill.com), is a great choice for a romantic getaway. Built in 1895, the inn sits outside the village center surrounded by hills. Inside, there's a Victorian feel and luxuriously appointed guest rooms. A favorite is Catherine's Suite, with a fireplace and two-person Jacuzzi. The hospitality is warm and top-notch, and the meals are among the best in the valley. The romantic **Inn at Thorn Hill Restaurant** is a great choice for a memorable meal. The candlelit dining room faces the forested hill behind the inn. Start with a glass of wine (the restaurant has won the *Wine Spectator* Award of Excellence), then browse the menu selections, which change weekly but often feature Asian accents. Rooms run $60 to $410 double, and rates include breakfast and dinner.

Thompson House Eatery, Route 16A, Jackson, near north intersection with Route 16 (© 603/383-9341), a friendly, old-fashioned spot in a 19th-century farmhouse at the edge of Jackson's golf course, attracts crowds not only for its well-prepared fare, but also for its reasonable prices. Dining is indoors and out, offering both lunch and dinner. Main courses cost $19 to $25.

For basic family dining, **Wilfred's,** 117 Main St. (© 603/466-2380), serves steaks, chops, and a variety of seafood. The **Moonbeam Café,** 19 Exchange St. (© 603/466-5549), has hearty meals such as potato pancakes and cups of coffee; a visit to the antique bathroom (complete with pull-chain) is mandatory. **Libby's Bistro,** at 115 Main St. (© 603/466-5330), is in a handsomely renovated bank and serves dinners better than any place in North Conway.

CRAWFORD NOTCH

Crawford Notch is a wild, rugged mountain valley that angles through the heart of the White Mountains. **Route 302** (which is wide and speedy on the lower sections) runs through it, becoming steeper as it approaches the narrow defile of the notch itself. The views up the cliffs from the road can be spectacular on a clear day; on an overcast or drizzly day, the effect is nicely foreboding.

The **Twin Mountain Chamber of Commerce** (© 800/245-8946; www.twinmountain.org) offers general information and lodging referrals at its booth near the intersection of routes 302 and 3.

What to See & Do

Much of the land flanking Route 302 falls under the jurisdiction of **Crawford Notch State Park,** established in 1911 to preserve land that elsewhere had been decimated by logging. The headwaters of the Saco River form in the notch, and what's generally regarded as the first permanent trail up Mount Washington also departs from here. The trail network on both sides of Crawford Notch is extensive; consult the *AMC White Mountain Guide* or *White Mountains Map Book* for detailed information.

The **Mount Washington Cog Railway,** Route 302, Bretton Woods (© **800/922-8825** or 603/846-5404; www.thecog.com), was a marvel of engineering when it opened in 1869. Part moving museum, part slow-motion roller-coaster ride, the cog railway steams to the summit at about 4 mph. Passengers enjoy the expanding view on this 3-hour round-trip. (There are stops to add water to the steam engine, to check the track switches, and to allow other trains to ascend or descend.) There's also a 20-minute stop at the summit. Be aware that the ride is noisy and sulfurous. Dress warmly and expect to acquire a patina of cinder and soot. The fare costs $57 adults, $37 children 6 to 12.

Where to Stay & Dine

The **Mount Washington Resort,** Route 302, Bretton Woods (© **800/258-0330** or 603/278-1000; www.mtwashington.com), was built in 1902. In its heyday, it attracted luminaries like Babe Ruth and Thomas Edison. Guest rooms vary in size and decor (not too lavish, though innkeepers are making improvements); many have grand views of the mountains and countryside. A 900-foot veranda makes for relaxing afternoons. Meals are enjoyed in an impressive octagonal dining room. Rates ($145–$525 double) include breakfast and dinner. This remains one of our favorite spots in the mountains, partly for the sheer improbability of it all, and partly for its direct link to a lost era.

Located off Route 302 in a wild section of Crawford Notch, **Notchland Inn,** Route 302, Hart's Location (© **800/866-6131** or 603/374-6131; www.notchland.com), would fit quite well in a Sir Walter Scott novel. Built of hand-cut granite in the mid-1800s, Notchland is classy yet informal, perfectly situated for exploring the wilds of the White Mountains. Guest rooms are outfitted with antiques, wood-burning fireplaces, high ceilings, and individual thermostats. All but three rooms have air-conditioning. The inn is also home to affable Bernese mountain dogs and llamas. You may want to add the five-course dinner to your plan ($30 per person). It's not just good value—the closest restaurant is a long, dark drive away. Rates ($245 double) include breakfast.

FRANCONIA NOTCH

Franconia Notch is rugged New Hampshire writ large. Most of the notch is included in a well-managed state park. Those seeking the sublime should plan on a leisurely trip through the notch, allowing enough time to get out of the car and explore forests and craggy peaks.

Essentials

GETTING THERE I-93 runs through Franconia Notch, gearing down from four lanes to two (where it becomes the Franconia Notch Pkwy.) in the most scenic and sensitive areas of the park. Several roadside turnoffs dot the route.

VISITOR INFORMATION Information on the park and surrounding area is available at the **Flume Information Center** (© 603/745-8391), at exit 1 off the parkway. It's open in summer daily from 9am to 4:30pm. North of the notch, the **Franconia Notch Chamber of Commerce** (© 603/823-5661; www.franconianotch.org), on Main Street next to town hall, is open spring through fall Tuesday through Sunday from 10am to 5pm. (Days and hours often vary.)

Franconia Notch State Park's 8,000 acres, nestled within the surrounding White Mountain National Forest, hosts an array of scenic attractions easily accessible from I-93 and the Franconia Notch Parkway. For information on any of the following, contact the park offices (© **603/745-8391**).

The **Flume** is a rugged gorge through which the Flume Brook tumbles. The gorge, a popular attraction in the mid–19th century, is 800 feet long, 90 feet deep, and as narrow as 20 feet at the bottom; visitors explore it on a 2-mile walk through a network of boardwalks and bridges. It's open May through October; admission is $8 for adults, $5 for children 6 to 12.

Echo Lake is a picturesquely situated recreation area, with a 28-acre lake, a handsome swimming beach, and picnic tables scattered within view of Cannon Mountain on one side and Mount Lafayette on the other. A bike path runs alongside the lake and meanders up and down the notch for a total of 8 miles. Mountain bikes, canoes, and paddle boats can be rented for $10 per hour. Admission to the park is $3 for all visitors 12 and over, $1 for visitors under 12. It's open from mid-June through Labor Day only.

Robert Frost lived in New Hampshire from the time he was 10 until he was 45. This humble farmhouse on Ridge Road (© **603/823-5510;** www.frostplace.org) is where Frost lived with his family. Wandering the grounds, it's not hard to see how his granite-edged poetry evolved at the fringes of the White Mountains. First editions of Frost's works are on display; a nature trail in the woods nearby is posted with excerpts from his poems. Admission costs $4 for adults, $2 for children 6 to 12.

Where to Stay & Dine

Sugar Hill Inn, Route 117, Franconia (© **800/548-4748** or 603/823-5621; www. sugarhillinn.com), is a classic inn, with wraparound porch and sweeping mountain panoramas occupying 16 acres on lovely Sugar Hill. This welcoming, comfortable spot is a great base for exploring the western White Mountains. Rooms are graciously appointed in antique country style, some influenced by Shaker sensibility. Most have gas Vermont Castings stoves for heat and atmosphere. The restaurant, one of the area's best, features upscale regional fare. Rates ($140–$290 double) include breakfast.

10 THE MAINE COAST

Maine's southern coast runs roughly for 60 miles from the state line at Kittery to Portland, and is the destination of most travelers to the state (including many day-trippers from the Boston area). While it takes some doing to find privacy and remoteness here, you'll find at least two excellent reasons for a detour: long, sandy beaches, the region's hallmark; and a sense of history in some of the coastal villages. It's not hard to find a relaxing sandy spot, whether you prefer dunes and the lulling sound of the surf or the carnival-like atmosphere of a festive beach town. Waves depend on the weather—during a good Northeast blow (especially prevalent in spring and fall), they pound the shores and threaten beach houses built decades ago. During balmy midsummer days, the ocean can be as gentle as a farm pond, barely audible waves lapping timidly at the shore.

One thing all beaches share in common: a season that is generally brief and intense, running from July 4th to Labor Day. While an increasing number of beach towns see visitors well into the fall, shorefront communities tend to adopt a slower, more somnolent pace after Labor Day.

KITTERY & THE YORKS

Kittery is the first town you'll come to if you're driving to Maine from the south on **I-95** or **Route 1.** Kittery was once famous for its naval yard, but regionally it's now better known for its dozens of factory outlets.

"The Yorks," to the north, are three towns that share a name but little else. In fact, it's rare to find three such well-defined and diverse New England archetypes in such a compact area. **York Village** is full of early (17th-c.) American history and architecture. **York Harbor** reached its zenith during America's Victorian era, when wealthy urbanites built cottages at the ocean's edge. **York Beach** has an early-20th-century beach-town feel, with loud amusements, taffy shops, and summer homes in crowded enclaves near the beach.

The **Kittery Information Center** (☎ 207/439-1319) is at a well-marked rest area on I-95. It's open daily from 8am to 6pm in summer, from 9am to 5:30pm the rest of the year. The **York Chamber of Commerce** (☎ 207/363-4422) operates an information center at 571 Rte. 1. It's open in summer daily from 9am to 5pm (until 6pm Fri), limited days and hours the rest of the year.

Fun On & Off the Beach

Kittery's consumer mecca is 4 miles south of York on Route 1. Some 120 **factory outlets** flank the highway, including Dansk, Eddie Bauer, Calvin Klein, and Polo/Ralph Lauren.

In summer, navigating the area can be frustrating. (A free shuttle bus links the outlets and lessens some of the frustration.) The selection of outlets is more diverse than in Freeport an hour north, which is more clothing oriented. But Freeport's quaint village setting is more appealing. Information on current outlets is available from the **Kittery Outlet Association** (☎ 888/KITTERY [548-8379]; www.thekitteryoutlets.com).

Learn about the area at the **Old York Historical Society,** 5 Lindsay Rd., York (☎ 207/363-4974). First settled in 1624, York Village has several early buildings open to the public. A good place to start is **Jefferds Tavern,** across from the handsome old burying ground. Changing exhibits here document various facets of early life. Next door is the **School House,** furnished as it might have been in the last century. A 10-minute walk along Lindsay Road will bring you to **Hancock Wharf,** which is next door to the **George Marshall Store.** Also nearby is the **Elizabeth Perkins House,** with its well-preserved Colonial Revival interiors. The one don't-miss structure is the intriguing **Old Gaol,** built in 1719 with musty dungeons for criminals. (The jail is the oldest surviving public building in the U.S.) Just down the knoll is the **Emerson-Wilcox House,** built in the mid-1700s. Added to periodically over the years, it's a virtual catalog of architectural styles and early decorative arts. Admission to the village costs $10 adults, $5 children 4 to 16.

York Beach consists of two beaches—**Long Sands Beach** and **Short Sands Beach**—separated by a rocky headland and a small island capped by scenic **Nubble Light.** Both offer plenty of room when the tide is out. When the tide is in, they're both cramped. Short Sands fronts the town of York Beach, with its candlepin bowling and video arcades. It's the better bet for families with kids. Long Sands runs along Route 1A, across from a profusion of motels and convenience stores. Changing rooms, restrooms, and parking (50¢ per hour) are available at both beaches.

York Beach has a number of motels facing Long Sands Beach. Reserve ahead during high season. Among those with simple accommodations on or near the beach are the **Anchorage Inn** (© 207/363-5112) and **Sea Latch** (© 800/441-2993 or 207/363-4400).

Dockside Guest Quarters, in York (© 888/860-7428 or 207/363-2868; www. docksidegq.com), was established by David and Harriet Lusty in 1954, and recent additions haven't changed the maritime flavor of the place. Situated on a 7-acre peninsula, the inn occupies grounds shaded with maples and white pines. Five rooms are in the main house (1885), but most of the accommodations are in small, modern, town house–style cottages. These are bright and airy, and all have private decks that overlook the entrance to York Harbor. Several rooms also have woodstoves and/or kitchenettes. Rates run $95 to $190.

Chauncey Creek Lobster Pier, on Chauncey Creek Road between Kittery Point and York off Route 103, Kittery Point (© 207/439-1030), is one of the best lobster pounds in the state, not least because the Spinney family, which has been selling lobsters here since the 1950s, takes such pride in the place. You reach the pound by walking down a wooden ramp to a broad deck on a tidal inlet, where some 42 festively painted picnic tables await. Lobster (served at market price) is the specialty, of course, but steamed mussels (in wine and garlic) and clams are also available. It's BYOB. Menu items run $1.50 to $9.

The **Goldenrod Restaurant,** Railroad Road and Ocean Avenue, York Beach (© 207/363-2621; www.thegoldenrod.com), has been an institution in York Beach since 1896. Visitors gawk at the ancient machines churning out taffy in volumes. Behind the taffy-and-fudge operation is the restaurant, short on gourmet fare but long on atmosphere. Diners sit around a stone fireplace or at the antique soda fountain. The meals are basic and filling; expect waffles, griddlecakes, club sandwiches, and deviled-egg-and-bacon sandwiches. Nothing on the menu costs more than $8.

THE KENNEBUNKS

"The Kennebunks" are the villages of **Kennebunk** and **Kennebunkport,** situated along the shores of small rivers, both claiming a portion of rocky coast. The region was settled in the mid-1600s and flourished after the American Revolution, when ship captains, boat builders, and merchants constructed imposing, solid homes.

The **Kennebunk-Kennebunkport Chamber of Commerce,** 17 Western Ave. (P.O. Box 740), Kennebunk, ME 04043 (© 800/982-4421 or 207/967-0857), can answer your questions year-round by phone or at its offices on Route 9 next to Meserve's Market. The **Kennebunkport Information Center** (© 207/967-8600), operated by an association of local businesses, is off Dock Square (next to Ben & Jerry's) and is open daily throughout the summer and fall.

A local "trolley" service (© 207/967-3686; www.intowntrolley.com)—actually, it's a bus with a tour narrator—makes stops in and around Kennebunkport and also serves the beaches. The fare, a day pass costing $11 per adult or $6 per child ages 3 to 14, includes unlimited trips.

Fun On & Off the Beach

Kennebunkport is the summer home of President George Bush the Elder, whose family has summered here for decades. As such, it's possessed of the tweedy, upper-crust feel that you might expect. The tiny downtown, whose streets were laid out during days of travel by boat and horse, is subject to traffic jams. If the municipal lot off the square is full, head north on North Street to the free long-term lot and catch the trolley back into town. Or go about on foot—it's a pleasant walk of about 10 to 15 minutes from the satellite lot to Dock Square.

Dock Square has an architecturally eclectic wharflike feel to it, with low buildings of mixed vintages and styles, but the flavor is mostly clapboard and shingles. Kennebunkport's deeper appeal is found in the surrounding blocks, where the side streets are lined with Federal-style homes.

For a clear view of the coast, sign up for a 2-hour sail aboard the *Schooner Eleanor* (at the Arundel Wharf Restaurant, Kennebunkport; © 207/967-8809), a 55-foot gaff-rigged schooner, built in Kennebunkport in 1999 after a classic Herreshoff design. If the weather's willing, you'll have a perfect view of the Bush compound and Cape Porpoise. Fare is $38 per person.

A bit farther afield, in the neighborhood around the Colony Hotel (about 1 mile east of Dock Sq. on Ocean Ave.), is a collection of homes of the uniquely American shingle style. Ocean Drive from Dock Square to **Walkers Point** and beyond is lined with summer homes overlooking surf and rocky shore. You'll likely recognize the former president's home at Walkers Point when you arrive (look for the shingle-style Secret Service booth). There's nothing to do here but park for a minute, take a picture of the house, then push on.

The **Seashore Trolley Museum,** 95 Log Cabin Rd. (© 207/967-2800; www.trolleymuseum.org), is a local marvel: a scrap yard masquerading as a museum. Founded in 1939 to preserve a disappearing way of life, today it contains one of the largest collections in the world—more than 200 trolleys, including specimens from Glasgow, Moscow, San Francisco, and Rome. (Naturally, there's a streetcar named *Desire.*) About 40 cars still operate, and admission includes rides on a 2-mile track. Admission is $8 adults, $5.50 children 6 to 16.

The area around Kennebunkport is home to several of the state's best **beaches.** Across the river are **Gooch's Beach** and **Kennebunk Beach. Goose Rocks Beach** is north of Kennebunkport off Route 9 (watch for signs) and is a good destination for those who like their crowds light. Offshore is a narrow barrier reef that has historically attracted flocks of geese. No restrooms are available here.

Where to Stay & Dine

Housed in a Federal-style home that peers down a shady lawn toward the river, the **Captain Lord Mansion,** Pleasant and Green streets (© 800/522-3141 or 207/967-3141), is one of New England's most architecturally distinguished inns. Check out the grandfather clocks and Chippendale highboys in the front hall. Guest rooms are furnished with antiques, and all feature gas fireplaces; there's not a single unappealing room. Among our favorites: Excelsior, a corner unit with a massive four-poster and a two-person Jacuzzi; and Hesper, the best of the lower-priced rooms. Children 12 and over are welcome. Rates ($248–$419 double) include breakfast.

One of the few resorts that have preserved intact the classic New England vacation experience, the **Colony Hotel,** 140 Ocean Ave. (© 800/552-2363 or 207/967-3331; www.thecolonyhotel.com/maine), is a mammoth Georgian Revival (1914) that lords over the ocean and the mouth of the Kennebunk River. All the bright and cheery rooms in the main inn have been renovated, though few have air-conditioning or TV. Rooms in two of the three outbuildings carry over the rustic elegance of the main hotel; the

(Best) Staying & Dining At the White Barn

Part of the exclusive Relais & Châteaux group, Kennebunkport's **White Barn Inn,** Beach Avenue (© **207/967-2321;** www.whitebarninn.com), pampers its guests like no other in Maine. The atmosphere is distinctly European, with an emphasis on service. The rooms are individually decorated in an upscale country style and offer many unexpected niceties, such as robes and fresh flowers in the rooms. Nearly half the rooms have wood-burning fireplaces, while the suites are truly spectacular; each is themed with a separate color, and most have plasma TVs, whirlpools, or similar perks. Guests can avail themselves of the inn's free bikes or take a cruise on its Hinckley charter yacht. You might also lounge around the beautiful outdoor pool. In 2003, the inn acquired a handful of cottages on the Kennebunk River. The wonderful cottages are cozy, are nicely equipped with modern kitchens and bathrooms, and will continue to see future upgrades; an adjacent "friendship cottage" is stocked at all times with snacks, wine, and the like. Rates ($280–$540 double; $565–$785 suite) include continental breakfast and afternoon tea.

The restaurant here is just as noteworthy as the accommodations, attracting gourmands from New York and Boston, and was selected as one of America's top inn restaurants by readers of *Travel + Leisure.* Housed in a rustic barn with a soaring interior and a collection of country antiques displayed in a hayloft, it's pricey but worth it. The setting is magical, the service is attentive, and the kitchen rarely produces a flawed dish. You might start with a lobster spring roll, then graduate to roasted pheasant breast with butternut squash. Anticipate a meal to remember. The fixed-price dinner is $89; a tasting menu costs $105 per person.

exception is the East House, a 1950s-era building with 20 uninteresting motel-style rooms. Staff encourages guests to socialize in the evening downstairs in the lobby, on the porch, or at the shuffleboard court, which is lighted for nighttime play. Rates ($145–$545 double) include breakfast.

The **Franciscan Guest House,** Beach Street (© **207/967-4865;** www.franciscan guesthouse.com), on the grounds of St. Anthony's Monastery, is a unique budget choice. The rooms are institutional, basic, and clean, with private bathrooms; guests can stroll the very attractive riverside grounds or walk to Dock Square, about 10 minutes away. It's not nearly as inexpensive as it used to be, but the place is still an outstanding bargain, especially given the fine walking trails. Rates run $50 to $144 double; credit cards are not accepted.

Prices for lobster in the rough tend to be a bit more expensive around Kennebunkport than farther up the coast. But if you can't wait, **Nunan's Lobster Hut,** on Route 9 north of Kennebunkport at Cape Porpoise (© **207/967-4362**), is a good choice.

Grissini, 27 Western Ave. (© **207/967-2211;** www.restaurantgrissini.com), is a handsome trattoria that Tuscan specialties. The mood is elegant but rustic. Italian advertising posters line the walls of the soaring, barnlike space, while the stone fireplace takes the chill

car is 45 to 60 minutes for J[ ] to 35 minutes for LaGuardia, and 35 to 50 minutes for Newark. Always allow extr[ ] though, especially during rush hour, during peak holiday travel times, and if you'[ ]g a bus.

Buses and shuttle services prov[ ]omfortable and less expensive option for airport transfers than taxis and car servi[ ] SuperShuttle (© 800/258-3826; www.super shuttle.com) serves all three area airp[ ]viding door-to-door service to Manhattan every 15 to 30 minutes round-the-clo[ ] don't need to reserve your ride from the airport; just go to the ground-transporta[ ][ ]. Pickups for your return require 24 to 48 hours' notice; you can reserve online. [ ] $13 to $22 per person, depending on the airport, with discounts for additional p[ ][ ]ur party.

New York Airport Service (© 718/87[ ][ ]ww.nyairportservice.com) buses travel from JFK and LaGuardia to the Port Au[ ]Terminal (42nd St. and Eighth Ave.), Grand Central Terminal (Park Ave. btw. [ ][ ]d sts.), and select Midtown hotels between 27th and 59th streets. Follow the[ ]e[ ]NSPORTATION signs to the curbside pickup, or look for the uniformed agent.[ ]the airport every 20 to 70 minutes between 6am and midnight. Buses to J[ ]ardia depart the Port

Authority and Grand Central Terminal on the Park Avenue side every 15 to 30 minutes, depending on the time of day and the day of the week. To request shuttle service from your hotel, call at least 24 hours in advance. One-way fare for JFK is $15, $27 round-trip; to LaGuardia it's $12 one-way and $21 round-trip.

Taxis are a convenient way to get to and from the airports. They're available at designated taxi stands outside the terminals, with uniformed dispatchers during peak hours at JFK and LaGuardia, round-the-clock at Newark. Follow the **ground transportation** or **taxi** signs. There may be a long line, but it generally moves quickly. Fares, whether fixed or metered, do not include bridge and tunnel tolls ($4–$6) or a tip for the cabbie (15%–20% is customary). They do include all passengers in the cab and luggage—never pay more than the metered or flat rate, except for tolls and a tip (8pm–6am a $1 surcharge also applies on New York yellow cabs).

BY TRAIN   Amtrak (② **800/USA-RAIL** [872-7245]; www.amtrak.com) runs frequent service to New York City's **Penn Station,** on Seventh Avenue between 31st and 33rd streets. If you're traveling to New York from a city along Amtrak's Northeast Corridor, you can take the **Acela.** The Acela Express trains cut travel time from D.C. down to $2^1/_2$ hours, and from Boston to 3 hours.

BY CAR   From the **New Jersey Turnpike** (I-95) and points west, there are three Hudson River crossings to Manhattan: the **Holland Tunnel** (lower Manhattan), the **Lincoln Tunnel** (Midtown), and the **George Washington Bridge** (Upper Manhattan). From **upstate,** take the **New York State Thruway** (I-87), which becomes the **Major Deegan Expressway** (I-87) through the Bronx. From **New England,** the **New England Thruway** (I-95) connects with the **Bruckner Expressway** (I-278), which leads to the Triborough Bridge (Robert F. Kennedy Bridge). You'll pay tolls along some of these roads and at most crossings.

Visitor Information

Before you leave home, your best information source (besides the current edition of *Frommer's New York City*) is **NYC & Company,** at 810 Seventh Ave., New York, NY 10019. You can call ② **800/NYC-VISIT** (692-8474) for the *Official NYC Guide* detailing hotels, restaurants, theaters, attractions, and events. The guide is free and will arrive in 7 to 10 days. (*Note:* We've received complaints that they sometimes take longer.)

You can find a wealth of free information on their website, **www.nycvisit.com.** To speak with a live travel counselor, call ② **212/484-1222** weekdays from 8:30am to 6pm EST, weekends from 8:30am to 5pm EST.

You will need a decent map of the city and also a transit map, which you can get at the **Times Square Visitors Center,** 1560 Broadway, between 46th and 47th streets (② **212/869-1890;** www.timessquarenyc.org), or at most larger subway stations.

Getting Around

Do not even think of driving in Manhattan. Traffic is horrendous, and you don't know the rules of the road or the arcane alternate-side-of-the-street parking regulations. If you do arrive in New York City by car, park it in a garage (expect to pay at least $25–$45 per day) and leave it there for the duration of your stay.

For the most part, you can get where you're going in Manhattan pretty quickly and easily using some combination of subways, buses, and cabs; this section will tell you how to do just that. But between traffic gridlock and subway delays, sometimes you just can't get there from here—unless you **walk.** During rush hours, you'll easily beat car traffic on foot. So pack your most comfortable shoes and hit the pavement—it's the best, cheapest, and most appealing way to experience the city.

BY SUBWAY   Run by the **Metropolitan Transit Authority** (**MTA;** www.mta.info/nyct/subway), the subway system is the fastest way to travel around New York, especially during rush hours. The subway is quick, inexpensive, relatively safe, and efficient, as well as being a genuine New York experience. It runs 24 hours a day, 7 days a week. The rush-hour crushes are roughly from 8 to 9:30am and from 5 to 6:30pm on weekdays; the rest of the time, the trains are much more manageable.

The **subway fare** is $2 (half-price for seniors and those with disabilities); children under 44 inches ride free (up to three per adult). People pay with the **MetroCard,** a magnetically encoded card that debits the fare when swiped through the turnstile (or the fare box on any city bus). Once you're in the system, you can transfer freely to any sub-way line that you can reach without exiting your station. MetroCards also allow you **free transfers** between the bus and subway within a 2-hour period. MetroCards can be pur-chased from staffed **token booths,** where you can pay only with cash; at the ATM-style vending machines in every subway station, which accept cash, credit cards, and debit cards; from a MetroCard merchant; or at the MTA information desk at the **Times Square Information Center,** 1560 Broadway, between 46th and 47th streets.

MetroCards come in a few different configurations: **Pay-Per-Ride MetroCards** can be used for up to four people by swiping up to four times (bring the entire family). You can put any amount from $4 (two rides) to $80 on your card. Every time you put $7 or more on your Pay-Per-Ride MetroCard, it's automatically credited 15%—that's one free ride for every $15 you spend. You can buy Pay-Per-Ride MetroCards at any subway station; most have MetroCard vending machines, which allow you to buy one using cash or a credit or debit card. MetroCards are also available from many shops and newsstands in $10 and $20 values. You can refill your card at any subway station.

Unlimited-Ride MetroCards, which can't be used for more than one person at a time or more frequently than 18-minute intervals, are available in four values: the **daily Fun Pass,** which allows you a day's worth of unlimited subway and bus rides for $7.50; the **7-Day MetroCard,** for $25; a **14-day MetroCard,** for $47; and the **30-Day Metro-Card,** for $81. Seven-, 14-, and 30-day Unlimited-Ride MetroCards can be purchased at any subway station or from a MetroCard merchant. Fun Passes can be purchased only at a station vending machine, from a MetroCard merchant, or at the MTA information desk at the Times Square Information Center. Unlimited-Ride MetroCards go into effect the first time you use them—so if you buy a card on Monday and don't use it until Wednesday, Wednesday is when the clock starts ticking.

A Fun Pass is good from the first time you use it until 3am the next day, while 7- and 30-day MetroCards run out at midnight on the last day. These MetroCards cannot be refilled. To locate the nearest MetroCard merchant, or for any other MetroCard ques-tions, call ✆ **800/METROCARD** (638-7622; out of NYC only) or 212/METRO-CARD (212/638-7622) Monday through Friday between 7am and 11pm, Saturday and Sunday from 9am to 5pm. Or go online to **www.mta.nyc.ny.us/metrocard,** which can give you a full rundown of MetroCard merchants in the tristate area.

BY TAXI   If you don't want to deal with public transportation, then take a taxi. The biggest advantages are, of course, that cabs can be hailed on any street and will take you right to your destination. We find they're best used at night when there's little traffic to keep them from speeding you to your destination and when the subway may seem a little daunting.

Subway Service Interruption Notes

Subway service is always subject to change, for reasons ranging from "a sick passenger" to regularly scheduled construction. Contact the **Metropolitan Transit Authority (MTA)** for details at ☏ **718/330-1234** or **www.mta.nyc.ny.us**, where you'll find system updates that are thorough, timely, and clear. (You can also sign up online to receive service advisories by e-mail.) Also read any posters that are taped up on the platform or notices written on the token booth's whiteboard.

The base fare on entering the cab is $2.50. The cost is 40¢ for every ¹/₅ mile or 40¢ per 60 seconds in stopped or slow-moving traffic (or for waiting time). There's no extra charge for each passenger or for luggage. However, you must pay bridge or tunnel tolls. You'll pay a $1 surcharge between 4 and 8pm and a 50¢ surcharge after 8pm and before 6am. A 15% to 20% tip is customary. Most taxis are now equipped with a device that allows you to pay by credit card.

Fast Facts

Walk-in service for nonemergency illnesses is available from **DOCS at New York Healthcare,** 55 E. 34th St., between Park and Madison avenues (☏ **212/252-6001;** subway: 6 to 33rd St.). Hospitals with emergency rooms include **Beth Israel Medical Center,** First Avenue and 16th Street (☏ **212/420-2000;** subway: L to First Ave.); **New York University Medical Center,** 560 First Ave., at 33rd Street (☏ **212/263-7300;** subway: 6 to 33rd St.); and many others. There are a number of 24-hour pharmacies in Manhattan; in Midtown; head for **CVS** at 630 Lexington Ave. (at 53rd St.; ☏ **917/369-8688**). **Sales tax** is 8.625% on meals, most goods, and some services. **Hotel tax** is 13.25% plus $2 per room per night (including sales tax). **Parking garage tax** is 18.25%.

Special Events & Festivals

For a complete New York City events schedule, point your browser to **www.nycvisit.com** and click on "Calendar of Events." Here are some favorites:

The ultimate purebred pooch fest and one of the oldest events in the nation (129 years and counting), **Westminster Kennel Club Dog Show** takes place in mid-February inside **Madison Square Garden.** Some 30,000 dog fanciers from all over the world show up at this "World Series of Dogdom."

More than 150,000 marchers participate in the **St. Patrick's Day Parade every** March 17, as Fifth Avenue from 44th to 86th streets rings with the sounds of bands and bagpipes. The parade usually starts at 11am, but go early if you want a good spot.

The **U.S. Open Tennis Championships** are held at the Arthur Ashe Stadium at the USTA National Tennis Center, the largest public tennis center in the world, at **Flushing Meadows Park** in Queens around Labor Day.

The **Greenwich Village Halloween Parade** is Halloween at its most outrageous. It's on October 31, of course. The **New York City Marathon** features some 30,000 hopefuls from around the world; more than a million fans will cheer them on as they follow a route that touches on all five New York boroughs and finishes at Central Park.

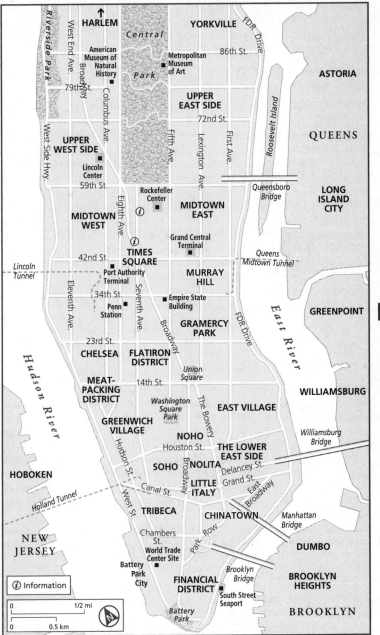

Macy's Thanksgiving Day Parade that proceeds from Central Park West and 77th Street and down Broadway to Herald Square at 34th Street continues to be a national tradition. The night before, you can usually see the big blow-up on Central Park West at 79th Street. On **New Year's Eve,** the biggest party of them all happens in **Times Square,** where thousands of raucous revelers count down in unison the year's final seconds until the new lighted ball drops at midnight.

WHAT TO SEE & DO
Some Top Attractions

In addition to the choices below, don't forget about **Central Park,** the great green swath that is, just by virtue of its existence, Manhattan's greatest marvel.

American Museum of Natural History   This is one of the hottest museum tickets in town, thanks to the **Rose Center for Earth and Space,** whose planetarium sphere hosts the Space Show "Are We Alone?" The diversity of the museum's holdings is astounding: some 36 million specimens ranging from microscopic organisms to the world's largest cut gem, the Brazilian Princess Topaz (21,005 carats). Rose Center aside, it would take you all day to see the entire museum, and then you *still* wouldn't get to everything. If you don't have a lot of time, you can see the best of the best on free **highlights tours** offered daily every hour at 15 minutes after the hour from 10:15am to 3:15pm. If you see only one exhibit, see the **dinosaurs,** which take up the entire fourth floor. The magical **Butterfly Conservatory,** a walk-in enclosure housing nearly 500 free-flying tropical butterflies, has developed into a can't-miss fixture from October through May; check to see if it's in the house while you're in town.

Central Park West (btw. 77th and 81st sts.). ✆ **212/769-5100** for information, or 769-5200 for tickets (tickets can also be ordered online for an additional $4 charge). www.amnh.org. Suggested admission $14 adults, $11 seniors and students, $8 children 2–12; Space Show and museum admission $22 adults, $17 seniors and students, $13 children 11 and under. Additional charges for IMAX movies and some special exhibitions. Daily 10am–5:45pm; Rose Center open 1st Fri of every month until 8:45pm. Subway: B, C to 81st St.; 1 to 79th St.

Bronx Zoo Wildlife Conservation Park ⓚ**ids**   Founded in 1899, the Bronx Zoo is the largest metropolitan animal park in the United States, with more than 4,000 animals living on 265 acres. One of the most impressive exhibits is the **Wild Asia Complex,** where you'll find an indoor re-creation of Asian forests, with birds, lizards, gibbons, and leopards; and the **Bengali Express Monorail** (open May–Oct), which takes you on a narrated ride high above free-roaming Siberian tigers, Asian elephants, Indian rhinoceroses, and other non-native New Yorkers. The **Himalayan Highlands** is home to some 17 extremely rare snow leopards, as well as red pandas and white-naped cranes. The **Children's Zoo** (open Apr–Oct) allows young humans to learn about their wildlife counterparts.

Fordham Rd. and Bronx River Pkwy., the Bronx. ✆ **718/367-1010.** www.bronxzoo.com. Admission $14 adults, $12 seniors, and $10 for children 2–12; discounted admission Nov–Mar; free Wed year-round. There may be nominal additional charges for some exhibits. Nov–Mar daily 10am–4:30pm (extended hours for Holiday Lights late Nov to early Jan); Apr–Oct Mon–Fri 10am–5pm, Sat–Sun 10am–5:30pm. Transportation: See "Getting There," above.

Brooklyn Bridge Ⓥ**alue**   Its Gothic-inspired stone pylons and intricate steel-cable webs have moved poets like Walt Whitman to sing the praises of this great span, completed in 1883. Walking the Brooklyn Bridge is one of our all-time favorite New York activities, although there's no doubt that the Lower Manhattan views from the bridge

(Value) A Money & Time-Saving Tip

CityPass may be New York's best sightseeing deal. Pay one price ($65, or $49 for kids 12–17) for admission to six major attractions: The American Museum of Natural History (admission only; does not include Space Show), the Guggenheim Museum, the Empire State Building, the Museum of Modern Art, the Metropolitan Museum of Art and the Cloisters, and a 2-hour Circle Line harbor cruise. Individual tickets would cost more than twice as much (though the Met is a "suggested" admission fee).

CityPass is not a coupon book. It contains actual tickets, so you can bypass lengthy lines. CityPass is good for 9 days from the first time you use it. It's sold at participating attractions and online at **http://citypass.com**. To avoid online service and shipping fees, you may wish to buy the pass at your first attraction. However, if you begin your sightseeing on a weekend or during holidays, when lines are longest, online purchase may be worthwhile.

For more information, call CityPass at ✆ **888/330-5008** (note, however, that CityPass is not sold over the phone).

now have a painful resonance as well as a joyous spirit. A wood-plank pedestrian walkway is elevated above the traffic, making it a relatively peaceful, and popular, walk. For Manhattan skyline views, take an A or C train to High Street, one stop into Brooklyn. From there, you'll be on the bridge in no time: Come aboveground, then walk through the little park to Cadman Plaza East and head downslope (left) to the stairwell that will take you up to the footpath. (Following Prospect Place under the bridge, then turning right onto Cadman Plaza E., will also take you directly to the stairwell.) It's a 20- to 40-minute stroll over the bridge to Manhattan.
Subway: A or C to High St.; 4, 5, or 6 to Brooklyn Bridge–City Hall.

The Cloisters This remote yet lovely spot is devoted to the art and architecture of medieval Europe. Atop a cliff overlooking the Hudson River, you'll find a 12th-century chapter house, parts of five cloisters from medieval monasteries, a Romanesque chapel, and a 12th-century Spanish apse brought intact from Europe. Surrounded by peaceful gardens, this is the one place on the island that can even approximate the kind of solitude suitable to such a collection. Inside you'll find extraordinary works that include the famed unicorn tapestries, sculpture, illuminated manuscripts, stained glass, ivory, and precious metalwork.
At the north end of Fort Tryon Park. ✆ **212/923-3700.** www.metmuseum.org. Suggested admission (includes same-day entrance to the Metropolitan Museum of Art) $20 adults, $15 seniors, $10 students, free for children 11 and under. Nov–Feb Tues–Sun 9:30am–4:45pm; Mar–Oct Tues–Sun 9:30am–5:15pm. Subway: A to 190th St., then a 10-min. walk north along Margaret Corbin Dr., or pick up the M4 bus at the station (1 stop to Cloisters). Bus: M4 Madison Ave. (Fort Tryon Park–The Cloisters).

Ellis Island Roughly 40% of Americans can trace their heritage back to an ancestor who came through Ellis Island. For the 62 years when it was America's main entry point for immigrants (1892–1954), Ellis Island processed some 12 million people. The **Immigration Museum** relates the story of immigration in America by placing the emphasis on personal experience. What might be the most poignant exhibit is *Treasures from Home,*

1,000 objects and photos donated by descendants of immigrants, including family heirlooms, religious articles, and rare clothing and jewelry. Outside, the **American Immigrant Wall of Honor** commemorates more than 500,000 immigrants and their families. *Touring tips:* Ferries run daily to Ellis Island and Liberty Island from Battery Park and Liberty State Park at frequent intervals; see the Statue of Liberty listing (p. 115) for details.

In New York Harbor. (C) **212/363-3200** (general info) or 269-5755 (ticket/ferry info). www.nps.gov/elis, www.ellisisland.org, or www.statuecruises.com. Free admission (ferry ticket charge). Daily 9:30am–5:15pm (last ferry departs around 3:30pm). For subway and ferry details, see the Statue of Liberty listing on p. 115 (ferry trip includes stops at both sights).

Empire State Building   It took 60,000 tons of steel, 10 million bricks, 2½ million feet of electrical wire, 120 miles of pipe, and 7 million worker-hours to build. On September 11, 2001, it once again regained its status as New York City's tallest building. And through it all, the Empire State Building has remained one of the city's favorite landmarks, and its signature high-rise. Completed in 1931, the limestone-and-stainless-steel streamline Deco dazzler climbs 102 stories (1,454 ft.); it harbors the offices of fashion firms and, in its upper reaches, a jumble of broadcast equipment. It glows every night, bathed in colored floodlights to commemorate events of significance—red, white, and blue for Independence Day, and so forth. The silver spire can be seen from all over the city. But the views that keep nearly three million visitors coming every year are the ones from the 86th- and 102nd-floor **observatories.** The lower one is best; the higher observation deck is glass enclosed and cramped.

350 Fifth Ave. (at 34th St.). (C) **212/736-3100.** www.esbnyc.com. Observatory admission $19 adults, $17 seniors and children 12–17, $13 children 6–11, free for children 5 and under. Daily 8am–2am (last elevator at 1:15am). Subway: B, D, F, N, R, Q, V, W to 34th St.; 6 to 33rd St.

Grand Central Terminal   The 1913 landmark has been reborn as one of the most magnificent public spaces in the country. Its restoration is an utter triumph, putting the "grand" back into Grand Central. The greatest visual impact comes when you enter the vast **main concourse.** The high windows once again allow sunlight to penetrate the space, glinting off the half-acre Tennessee marble floor. The masterful **sky ceiling,** again a brilliant greenish blue, depicts the constellations of the winter sky above New York. They're lit with 59 stars, surrounded by 24-carat gold and emitting light fed through fiber-optic cables, their intensities roughly replicating the magnitude of the actual stars as seen from earth. The **Municipal Art Society** ((C) **212/935-3960;** www.mas.org) offers a walking tour of Grand Central Terminal on Wednesday at 12:30pm, which meets at the information booth on the Grand Concourse (there is a $10 "suggested donation" for the tour).

42nd St. at Park Ave. (C) **212/340-2210** (events hot line). www.grandcentralterminal.com. Subway: S, 4, 5, 6, or 7 to 42nd St./Grand Central.

Metropolitan Museum of Art (Best)   Home of blockbuster after blockbuster exhibition, the Metropolitan Museum of Art attracts some five million people a year, more than any other spot in New York City. This is the largest museum in the Western Hemisphere. Nearly all the world's cultures are on display through the ages—from Egyptian mummies to Islamic carvings to Renaissance paintings to Native American masks to 20th-century decorative arts—and masterpieces are the rule. The newly renovated **Roman and Greek galleries** are overwhelming, but in a marvelous way. Unless you plan on spending your whole vacation here, you cannot see it all. Our recommendation is to give it a good day—or, better yet, 2 half-days so you don't burn out. One good way to get an overview is to take advantage of the **Museum Highlights Tour,** offered every day at various times throughout the day (usually 10:15am–3:15pm). The least overwhelming way to see the Met on your own is to pick up a map at the round desk in the entry hall and choose to concentrate on what you like, whether it's 17th-century paintings, American furniture, or the art of the South Pacific.

Fifth Ave. at 82nd St. © 212/535-7710. www.metmuseum.org. Suggested admission (includes same-day entrance to the Cloisters) $20 adults, $15 seniors and $10 students, free for children 11 and under when accompanied by an adult. Sun, holiday Mon (Memorial Day, Labor Day, and so on), and Tues–Thurs 9:30am–5:30pm; Fri–Sat 9:30am–9pm. Strollers are permitted in most areas—inquire at Information Desks for gallery limitations. Oversize and jogging strollers are prohibited. Subway: 4, 5, 6 to 86th St.

Morgan Library This New York treasure, boasting one of the world's most important collections of original manuscripts, rare books and bindings, master drawings, and personal writings has reopened after 2 years of extensive renovations. Those renovations include a welcoming entrance on Madison Avenue and new and renovated galleries so that more of the library's holdings can be exhibited. Some of the Library's recent exhibitions include one on the life of Bob Dylan through music, letters, and memorabilia, and an exhibit on illustrator Saul Steinberg. You can lunch in the intimate **Morgan Dining Room** as if you were dining in J. P.'s own quarters.

225 Madison Ave. (btw. 36th and 37th sts). © 212/685-0008. www.themorgan.org. $12 adults, $8 seniors and students, 11 and under free. Tues–Thurs 10:30am–5pm; Fri 10:30am–9pm; Sat 10am–6pm; Sun 11am–6pm. Subway: 6 to 33rd St.

Museum of Modern Art The newer, larger MoMA, after a 2-year renovation, is almost twice the space of the original. Its 630,000-square-foot quarters, designed by Yoshio Taniguchi, highlight space and light, with open rooms, high ceilings, and gardens—a beautiful work of architecture and a perfect complement to the art that resides within. This is where you'll find van Gogh's *Starry Night,* Cézanne's *Bather,* Picasso's *Les Demoiselles d'Avignon,* and the great sculpture by Rodin *Monument to Balzac.* We like to browse the fun "Architecture and Design" department, with examples of design for appliances, furniture, and even sports cars. But the heart of the museum remains the **Abby Aldrich Rockefeller Sculpture Garden.** Our big complaint: the *very* high ($20) admission charge for adults.

11 W. 53rd St. (btw. Fifth and Sixth aves.). © 212/708-9400. www.moma.org. Admission $20 adults, $16 seniors, $12 students, children 15 and under free if accompanied by an adult. Sat–Mon and Wed–Thurs 10:30am–5:30pm; Fri 10:30am–8pm. Subway: E, V to Fifth Ave.; B, D, F to 47th–50th/Rockefeller Center.

Rockefeller Center A streamlined modern masterpiece, Rockefeller Center is one of New York's central gathering spots for visitors and New Yorkers alike. A prime example of the city's skyscraper spirit and historical sense of optimism, it was erected mainly in the 1930s, when the city was deep in the Depression as well as its most passionate Art Deco phase. The **Rink at Rockefeller Center** (© 212/332-7654; www.rockefellercenter. com) is tiny but romantic, especially during the holidays, when the giant Christmas tree's multicolored lights twinkle from above. **NBC** television maintains studios throughout the complex, and the 70-minute **NBC Studio Tour** (© 212/664-3700; www.nbc superstore.com) will take you behind the scenes at the Peacock network. **Radio City Music Hall,** 1260 Sixth Ave., at 50th Street (© 212/247-4777; www.radiocity.com), is perhaps the most impressive architectural feat of the complex. Designed by Donald Deskey and opened in 1932, it's one of the largest indoor theaters, with 6,200 seats. But

Heading for the Top of the Rock

Giving the Empire State Building some friendly competition when it comes to spectacular views is the observation deck of 30 Rockefeller Plaza, **Top of the Rock.** The deck, which comprises floors 67 to 70, which had been closed since 1986, reopened in 2005. It was constructed in 1933 to resemble the grandeur of a luxury ocean liner. The views, though not quite as high, are as stunning. You might have just as much fun getting up there as you will on the deck; the sky-shuttle elevators with glass ceilings project images from the 1930s through the present day as they zoom upward. Reserved-time tickets help minimize the lines and are available online at **www.topoftherocknyc.com**. The observation deck is open daily from 8:30am to midnight; admission rates are $19 for adults, $16 for seniors, $11 for ages 6 to 11. For more information, call ✆ **877/NYC-ROCK** (692-7625) or 212/698-2000, or visit www.topoftherocknyc.com.

its true grandeur derives from its magnificent Art Deco appointments. The crowning touch is the stage's great proscenium arch, which evokes a faraway sun setting on the horizon of the sea. The theater hosts the annual **Christmas Spectacular,** starring the Rockettes. The 1-hour **Stage Door Tour** is offered Monday through Saturday from 10am to 5pm, Sunday from 11am to 5pm; tickets are $16 for adults, $10 for children 11 and under.

Btw. 48th & 50th sts., from Fifth to Sixth aves. ✆ **212/332-6868.** www.rockefellercenter.com. Subway: B, D, F, V to 47th–50th sts./Rockefeller Center.

Solomon R. Guggenheim Museum   It's been called a bun, a snail, a concrete tornado, and a giant wedding cake. Whatever description you choose to apply, Frank Lloyd Wright's only New York building, completed in 1959, is a brilliant work of architecture, which recently received a multimillion-dollar exterior overhaul. Inside, a spiraling rotunda circles over a slowly inclined ramp that leads you past changing exhibits. Permanent exhibits of 19th- and 20th-century art, including strong holdings of Kandinsky, Klee, Picasso, and French Impressionists, occupy a stark annex called the **Tower Galleries.**

1071 Fifth Ave. (at 89th St.). ✆ **212/423-3500.** www.guggenheim.org. Admission $18 adults, $15 seniors and students, free for children under 12, pay what you wish Fri 5:45–7:15pm. Sat–Wed 10am–5:45pm; Fri 10am–7:45pm. Subway: 4, 5, 6 to 86th St.

Staten Island Ferry Ⓥⓐⓛⓤⓔ   Here's New York's best freebie—especially if you just want to glimpse the Statue of Liberty and not climb its steps. You get an enthralling hour-long excursion (round-trip) into the world's biggest harbor. The old orange-and-green boats usually have open decks along the sides or at the bow and stern. Grab a seat on the right side of the boat for the best view. On the way out of Manhattan, you'll pass the Statue of Liberty, Ellis Island, Governor's Island, and the Verrazano Narrows Bridge spanning the distance from Brooklyn to Staten Island in the distance.

Departs from the Whitehall Ferry Terminal at the southern tip of Manhattan. ✆ **718/727-2508.** www. ci.nyc.ny.us/html/dot. Free admission. 24 hr.; every 20–30 min. weekdays, less frequently during off-peak and weekend hours. Subway: R, W to Whitehall St.; 4, 5 to Bowling Green; 1 to South Ferry (ride in one of the 1st 5 cars).

Statue of Liberty (Kids)   For the millions who first came by ship to America in the last century, Lady Liberty, standing in the Upper Bay, was their first glimpse of America. The statue was designed by sculptor Frédéric-Auguste Bartholdi and unveiled on October 28, 1886. After nearly 100 years of wind, rain, and exposure to the harsh sea air, Lady Liberty received a resoundingly successful $150-million face-lift in time for her centennial celebration on July 4, 1986. After September 11, 2001, access to the base of the statue was prohibited, but in the summer of 2004, access, albeit still somewhat limited (you can't climb to the statue's crown), was once again allowed. Now you can explore the Statue of Liberty Museum, peer into the inner structure through a glass ceiling near the base of the statue, and enjoy views from the observation deck on top of a 16-story pedestal.

Touring tips: Ferries leave daily every half-hour to 45 minutes from 9am to about 3:30pm (their clock), with more frequent ferries in the morning and extended hours in summer. Try to go early on a weekday to avoid the crowds as much as you can. You can **buy ferry tickets in advance** via **www.statuereservations.com**, which will allow you to board the boat without standing in the sometimes-long ticket line; however, there is an additional service charge.

On Liberty Island in New York Harbor. ℂ **212/363-3200** (general info), or 269-5755 (ticket/ferry info). www.nps.gov/stli or www.statuecruises.com. Free admission; ferry ticket to Statue of Liberty and Ellis Island $12 adults, $10 seniors, $5 children 3–17. Daily 9am–3:30pm (last ferry departs around 3:30pm); extended hours in summer. Subway: 4, 5 to Bowling Green; 1 to South Ferry. Walk south through Battery Park to Castle Clinton, the fort housing the ferry ticket booth.

United Nations   In the midst of New York City is this working monument to world peace. The UN headquarters occupies 18 acres of international territory—neither the city nor the United States has jurisdiction here—along the East River from 42nd to 48th streets. Designed by an international team of architects (led by American Wallace K. Harrison and including Le Corbusier) and finished in 1952, the complex along the East River weds the 39-story glass slab Secretariat with the free-form General Assembly on beautifully landscaped grounds donated by John D. Rockefeller, Jr. One hundred eighty nations use the facilities to arbitrate worldwide disputes. **Guided tours** leave every half-hour and last 45 minutes to an hour.

At First Ave. and 46th St. ℂ **212/963-8687**. www.un.org/tours. Guided tours $14 adults; $9 seniors, high school, and college students; $7.50 children 5–14. Children 4 and under not permitted. Daily tours every half-hour 9:30am–4:45pm; Jan–Feb Sat–Sun 10am–4:30pm; limited schedule may be in effect during the general debate (late Sept to mid-Oct). Subway: S, 4, 5, 6, 7 to 42nd St./Grand Central.

World Trade Center Site (Ground Zero)   Do you call a place where over 3,000 people lost their lives on September 11, 2001, an "attraction"? Or do you now call it a shrine? This is the quandary of the World Trade Center site. Though ground was broken for rebuilding in the summer of 2004, there is still controversy over what actually will be built. So don't expect to see much more than a big open hole for years to come. Now they are saying that the planned "Freedom Tower" will be built by 2012. In the meantime, you can see the site through a viewing wall on the Church Street side of the site; on that **"Wall of Heroes"** are the names of those who lost their lives that day along with the history of the site, including photos of the construction of the World Trade Center in the late 1960s and how, after it opened in 1972, it changed the New York skyline and downtown. The Tribute Center gives guided tours of the site. Call ℂ **212/422-3520,** or visit **www.tributewtc.org** for more information. Tours are given Monday to Friday at

11am and 1 and 3pm, Saturday and Sunday at noon, 1, 2, and 3pm. The fee is $10 for adults, 11 and under free.

Bounded by Church, Barclay, Liberty, and West sts. (℗ 212/484-1222. www.nycvisit.com or www. southstseaport.org for viewing information, or www.downtownny.com for lower-Manhattan area information and rebuilding updates. Subway: C or E to World Trade Center; N or R to Cortlandt St.

Organized Sightseeing Tours

Double-decker bus tours are one of the best ways to get an overview of Manhattan. Among the operators who offer tours narrated by a guide are **Gray Line New York Tours** (℗ **800/669-0051** or 212/445-0848; www.graylinenewyork.com), which has hop-on/hop-off privileges on tours day and night, uptown, downtown, and all around the town for about $49 adults, $39 children 5 to 11.

The **Circle Line** (℗ **212/563-3200;** www.circleline42.com, www.ridethebeast.com, or www.seaportmusiccruises.com) circumnavigates the entire 35 miles around Manhattan. The panorama is riveting, and the commentary isn't bad. The big boats are basic, with lots of deck room. Snacks, soft drinks, coffee, and beer are available on board. They depart from Pier 83, at West 42nd Street and Twelfth Avenue, and from Pier 16 at South Street Seaport. Sightseeing cruises range from $12 to $29 adults, $16 to $24 seniors, $13 to $16 children 12 and under.

Walking Tours

The **Municipal Art Society** (℗ **212/439-1049** or 935-3960; www.mas.org) offers historical and architectural walking tours aimed at individualistic travelers, not the mass market. Highly qualified guides give insights into the significance of buildings, neighborhoods, and history. Weekday walking tours are $12, weekend tours are $15. Reservations are required on some tours, so call ahead.

For a bit more whimsy on your tour, **Levy's Unique New York** (℗ **877/692-5869;** www.levysuniqueny.com) offers a lighter look at the city's history and landmarks. A few of their tours include the "Bohemians and Beats of Greenwich Village Literary Tours," and "Hey Ho! Let's Go! Punk Rock on the Bowery" tour. Tours of Coney Island and another called "Edible Ethnic Brooklyn Eats" are just a few that feature Brooklyn.

Top Shopping Streets & Neighborhoods

DOWNTOWN   Lower Manhattan continues to shine in the discount department. **Century 21,** the king of discount department stores, is across the street from the World Trade Center site. In **Chinatown, Canal Street** and **Mott Street,** between Pell Street and Chatham Square, boast the most interesting shopping. On the **Lower East Side,** there's the **Historic Orchard Street Shopping District,** where prices on leather bags, shoes, luggage, and fabrics on the bolt are still quite good.

People love to complain about **SoHo**—it's become too trendy, too tony, too Mall of America. But it is still one of the best shopping [']hoods in the city—and fun to browse. It's the epicenter of cutting-edge fashion and has plenty of unique boutiques.

Elizabeth Street is the star of the neighborhood known as **Nolita.** Its boutiques are largely the province of sophisticated shopkeepers specializing in high-quality, fashion-forward products and design.

The **East Village** personifies bohemian hip. **East 9th Street** between Second Avenue and Avenue A has become one of our favorite shopping strips. Up-and-coming designers sell excellent-quality and affordably priced original fashions for women here. If it's strange, illegal, or funky, it's probably available on **St. Marks Place,** which takes over for 8th Street, running east from Third Avenue to Avenue A.

Take Me Out to the Ballgame (at the New Stadiums)

The **Yankees** will be moving across the parking lot to new Yankee Stadium in 2009 (subway: C, D, or 4 to 161st St./Yankee Stadium). For tickets, call **Ticketmaster** (© 212/307-1212 or 307-7171; www.ticketmaster.com) or **Yankee Stadium** (© 718/293-6000; www.yankees.com). The **Mets** will also be heading to new digs, at Citi Field, across from their old ones in Flushing, Queens (subway: 7 to Willets Point/Shea Stadium). For tickets and information, call the **Mets Ticket Office** at © 718/507-TIXX (507-8499) or visit **www.mets.com**.

Lafayette Street has grown into a full-fledged Antiques Row, especially strong in mid-20th-century furniture. Prices are high, but so is quality. The **West Village** is great for browsing and gift shopping. Specialty book- and record stores, antiques and crafts shops, and gourmet food markets dominate.

West Chelsea has been transformed into the **Chelsea Art District,** where more than 200 galleries have sprouted up in a once-moribund enclave of repair shops and warehouses. The hottest shopping/eating/hanging-out neighborhood in the city may be **Union Square.** The **Flatiron District** off Sixth Avenue is the city's discount shopping center, with superstores and off-pricers filling up the renovated spaces.

MIDTOWN   **Herald Square**—where 34th Street, Sixth Avenue, and Broadway converge—is dominated by **Macy's,** the self-proclaimed world's biggest department store. At Sixth Avenue and 33rd Street is the **Manhattan Mall** (© 212/465-0500; www.manhattanmallny.com).

Times Square and the **Theatre District** have become increasingly family oriented. The massive **Toys "R" Us** has its own Ferris wheel. West 47th Street between Fifth and Sixth avenues is the city's famous **Diamond District.**

The heart of Manhattan retail is the corner of **Fifth Avenue and 57th Street. Tiffany & Co.** has long reigned supreme here, near **Niketown** and the **NBA Store.** In addition, a good number of mainstream retailers have flagships along Fifth. Still, you will find a number of big-name, big-ticket designers radiating from the crossroads, including **Versace, Chanel, Dior,** and **Cartier.** You'll also find big-name jewelers along here, as well as chichi department stores such as **Bergdorf Goodman, Henri Bendel,** and **Saks Fifth Avenue.**

UPTOWN   **Madison Avenue** from 57th to 79th streets has usurped Fifth Avenue as *the* tony shopping street in the city. This strip is home to the most luxurious designer boutiques in the world—with **Barneys New York** as the anchor.

The **Upper West Side**'s best shopping street is **Columbus Avenue.** Small shops catering to the neighborhood's mix of young hipsters and families line both sides of the pleasant avenue from 66th Street to about 86th Street. You won't lack for good browsing along here.

Boutiques also dot Amsterdam Avenue, but **Broadway** is most notable for its terrific gourmet edibles at **Zabar's,** 2445 Broadway, at 80th Street (© 212/787-2000; www.zabars.com), and **Fairway,** 2127 Broadway, at 74th Street (© 212/595-1888; www.fairwaymarket.com) markets.

New York hotel rooms give everybody a whole new perspective on "small." Space is the city's biggest asset, and getting space costs money (New York's rates are the highest in the United States). If you're traveling on a budget, don't be surprised if your room isn't much bigger than the bed that's in it and your cramped bathroom has a sink so small that it looks like it was manufactured for the Keebler elves. Even expensive rooms can be on the small side, or lack closet space, or have smallish bathrooms.

We've given you a choice of chain hotels and independent properties, traditional and avant-garde, in neighborhoods from fast-paced to quiet (well, for New York).

The Benjamin   When you enter the high-ceilinged marble lobby at the Benjamin, it's as if you've suddenly stepped into the jazz era of 1920s New York. But once you get to your spacious and luxurious room and notice the amenities, such as Bose Wave radios, Web TV, and ergonomic chairs, you will know you are definitely in the 21st century. How many hotels can claim a "sleep concierge" (choose from 11 pillow designs) or *guarantee* a good night's sleep? All rooms are airy, but the deluxe studios and one-bedroom suites are extra large. Bathrooms feature Frette robes, TV speakers, and water pressure from the shower head strong enough to make you think you've just experienced a deep-tissue massage. *Tip:* If you are a light sleeper, book a room off Lexington Avenue.

125 E. 50th St. (at Lexington Ave.), New York, NY 10022. ✆ **888/4-BENJAMIN** (423-6526), 212/320-8002, or 715-2500. Fax 212/715-2525. www.thebenjamin.com. 209 units. From $459 superior double; from $499 deluxe studio; from $559 suite. Call or check website for special weekend-stay offers. AE, DC, DISC, MC, V. Parking $45. Subway: 6 to 51st St.; E, F to Lexington Ave. Pets accepted. **Amenities:** Restaurant; exercise room; full-service spa. *In room:* Kitchenette.

The Carlyle: A Rosewood Hotel   This 34-story grande dame perfectly epitomizes the old-world, moneyed neighborhood where it stands. Service is white glove (literally); many celebrities and dignitaries sip tea in the hotel's cozy Gallery. The recently renovated lobby offers marble floors and columns, Baccarat light fixtures, a new reception desk, and an expanded concierge space. Guest rooms range from singles to seven-room suites. All have marble bathrooms with whirlpool tubs and all the amenities you'd expect from a hotel of this caliber. The English manor–style decor is luxurious but not excessive, creating the comfortably elegant ambience of an Upper East Side apartment. Many apartments have breathtaking views of either downtown or the West Side and Central Park.

35 E. 76th St. (at Madison Ave.), New York, NY 10021. ✆ **800/227-5737** or 212/744-1600. Fax 212/717-4682. www.thecarlyle.com. 180 units. $650–$950 double; from $950 1- or 2-bedroom suite. AE, DC, DISC, MC, V. Parking $48. Subway: 6 to 77th St. Pets under 25 lb. accepted. **Amenities:** 3 restaurants; high-tech fitness room; spa. *In room:* Pantry kitchenette or full kitchen (in some).

Casablanca Hotel ⓥ Value   Who wouldn't want a desert oasis in the middle of all the Times Square mayhem? And that's what the Casablanca Hotel really is: a calming refuge where you can escape from the noise and crowds. In the hotel's homey guest lounge, you can sit by a fire, read a paper, check your e-mail, watch television on the gargantuan-size screen, or sip a cappuccino from the serve-yourself cappuccino/espresso machine. Or you can just retreat to your well-outfitted room, which includes a ceiling fan, bathrobes, free bottles of water, and beautifully tiled bathrooms. Service is top-notch. Because of its location, moderate prices, and size, the Casablanca is in high demand, so book early.

147 W. 43rd St. (just east of Broadway), New York, NY 10036. ✆ **888/922-7225** or 212/869-1212. Fax 212/391-7585. www.casablancahotel.com. 48 units. $249–$299 double; from $399 suite. Rates include continental breakfast, all-day cappuccino, and weekday wine and cheese. Check website for Internet

Cosmopolitan Hotel—Tribeca (Value)

This is one of the best hotel deals in Manhattan for budget travelers who insist on a private bathroom. Everything is strictly budget, but nice. Beds are comfy, and sheets and towels are of good quality. Rooms are small but make the most of the limited space, and the place is pristine. The two-level minilofts have lots of character, but expect to duck on the second level. Management does a great job of keeping everything fresh. Services are kept at a bare minimum to keep costs down, so you must be a low-maintenance guest to be happy here.

95 W. Broadway (at Chambers St.), New York, NY 10007. **©** **888/895-9400** or 212/566-1900. Fax 212/566-6909. www.cosmohotel.com. 105 units. $200–$270 double. AE, DC, MC, V. Subway: 1, 2, 3, A, C to Chambers St.

Flatotel (Kids)

In the heart of Midtown the Flatotel (Flat, like an apartment combined with hotel amenities), offers *space.* The sleek, apartment-like rooms, especially the suites, are large by New York standards, and all feature refrigerators and microwaves, while suites have kitchenettes or full kitchens, two flatscreen televisions, and generous desks. The marble bathrooms are spacious and well equipped. The hotel features 60 one- to three-bedroom family suites with dining areas and full kitchens in each. In some suites on higher floors—the hotel is 47 stories—you have spectacular river-to-river views.

132 West 52nd St. (btw. Sixth and Seventh aves.), New York, NY 10019. **©** **800/FLATOTEL** (352-8683) or 212/887-9400. Fax 212/887-9795. www.flatotel.com. 288 units. From $399 double; from $549 suite. AE, DC, DISC, MC, V. Self-parking $30; valet parking $47. Subway: B, D, E to Seventh Ave. **Amenities:** Restaurant; fitness center. *In room:* Fridge, microwave; suites have kitchens/kitchenettes.

Hotel Metro (Value) (Kids)

The Metro is the best choice in Midtown for those who don't want to sacrifice either style or comfort for affordability. This Art Deco–style jewel's large rooms are outfitted with retro furnishings, refrigerators, and marble bathrooms. Only about half the bathrooms have tubs, but the others have shower stalls big enough for two (junior suites have whirlpool tubs). The "family room" is a two-room suite that has a second bedroom in lieu of a sitting area. The comfy library/lounge area off the lobby, where complimentary buffet breakfast is laid out and the coffeepot's on all day, is a popular hangout. The rooftop terrace boasts a breathtaking view of the Empire State Building.

45 W. 35th St. (btw. Fifth and Sixth aves.), New York, NY 10001. **©** **800/356-3870** or 212/947-2500. Fax 212/279-1310. www.hotelmetronyc.com. 179 units. $250–$365 double; $245–$420 triple or quad; $255–$425 family room; $275–$475 suite. Extra person $25. 1 child 12 and under stays free in parent's room. Rates include continental breakfast. Check with airlines and other package operators for great-value package deals. AE, DC, MC, V. Parking $20 nearby. Subway: B, D, F, V, N, R to 34th St. **Amenities:** Restaurant; fitness room. *In room:* Fridge.

Le Parker Meridien (Kids)

A stay at Le Parker Meridien is a New York experience in itself. Not many hotels in New York can rival the attributes of this hotel: Its location on 57th Street is practically perfect. The 17,000-square-foot state-of-the-art fitness center features a basketball and a racquetball court, a spa, and a rooftop pool; a gorgeous, bustling lobby that also serves as a public space; and elevators with televisions that continuously show cartoons and Charlie Chaplin shorts that are a wonder for the kids. The spacious hotel rooms, though a bit on the IKEA side, have a fun feel to them. Rooms have wood platform beds with feather beds, built-ins that include large work desks, stylish Aeron chairs, and 32-inch flatscreen televisions with VCR/CD and DVD players. The slate-and-limestone bathrooms are large but, unfortunately, come only with shower.

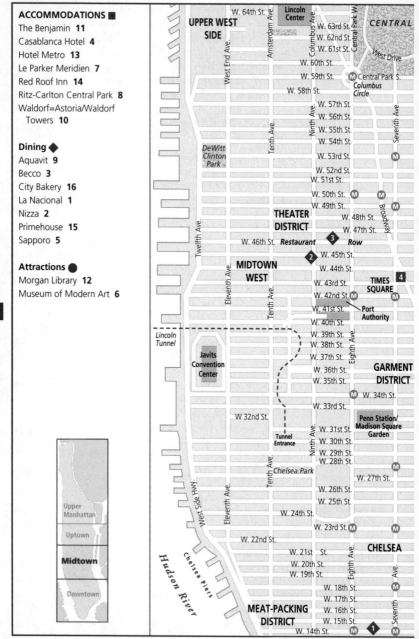

ACCOMMODATIONS ■
The Benjamin **11**
Casablanca Hotel **4**
Hotel Metro **13**
Le Parker Meridien **7**
Red Roof Inn **14**
Ritz-Carlton Central Park **8**
Waldorf=Astoria/Waldorf
   Towers **10**

Dining ◆
Aquavit **9**
Becco **3**
City Bakery **16**
La Nacional **1**
Nizza **2**
Primehouse **15**
Sapporo **5**

Attractions ●
Morgan Library **12**
Museum of Modern Art **6**

THE MID-ATLANTIC

3

NEW YORK CITY

UPPER WEST SIDE
CENTRAL
Lincoln Center
West End Ave.
Amsterdam Ave.
Columbus Ave.
Central Park W.
W. 64th St.
W. 63rd St.
W. 62nd St.
W. 61st St.
W. 60th St.
West Drive
W. 59th St.
Central Park S.
Columbus Circle
W. 58th St.
W. 57th St.
Ninth Ave.
Seventh Ave.
W. 56th St.
W. 55th St.
W. 54th St.
Tenth Ave.
DeWitt Clinton Park
W. 53rd St.
W. 52nd St.
W. 51st St.
W. 50th St.
W. 49th St.
Twelfth Ave.
THEATER DISTRICT
W. 48th St.
Broadway
W. 47th St.
W. 46th St. Restaurant Row **3**
2 W. 45th St.
W. 44th St.
Eleventh Ave.
MIDTOWN WEST
Tenth Ave.
W. 43rd St.
TIMES SQUARE **4**
W. 42nd St.
W. 41st St. Port Authority
W. 40th St.
Lincoln Tunnel
W. 39th St.
W. 38th St.
Eighth Ave.
W. 37th St.
Javits Convention Center
W. 36th St.
GARMENT DISTRICT
W. 35th St.
W. 34th St.
W. 33rd St.
W 32nd St.
Ninth Ave.
Penn Station/ Madison Square Garden
W. 31st St.
Tunnel Entrance
W. 30th St.
W. 29th St.
W. 28th St.
Tenth Ave.
Chelsea Park
W. 27th St.
West Side Hwy.
W. 26th St.
W. 25th St.
Eleventh Ave.
W. 24th St.
W. 23rd St.
W. 22nd St.
W. 21st St.
Eighth Ave.
CHELSEA
W. 20th St.
W. 19th St.
Hudson River
Chelsea Piers
W. 18th St.
W. 17th St.
Seventh Ave.
Ninth Ave.
MEAT-PACKING DISTRICT
W. 16th St.
W. 15th St.
1
W. 14th St.

Upper Manhattan
Uptown
Midtown
Downtown

THE MID-ATLANTIC

3

NEW YORK CITY

118 W. 57th St. (btw. Sixth and Seventh aves.), New York, NY 10019. ℂ **800/543-4300** or 212/245-5000. Fax 212/307-1776. www.parkermeridien.com. 731 units. $600–$800 double; from $780 suite. Extra person $30. Excellent packages and weekend rates often available (as low as $225 at press time). AE, DC, DISC, MC, V. Parking $45. Subway: F, N, Q, R to 57th St. Pets accepted. **Amenities:** 3 restaurants; rooftop pool; fitness center; spa.

The Lucerne   This magnificent 1903 landmark building on the Upper West Side (it was once a dormitory) has been transformed into a luxury boutique hotel, and that transformation has been a triumph on many levels. Service here is impeccable, especially for a moderately priced hotel; everything is fresh and immaculate. The rooms are all spacious and comfortable, with attractive bathrooms complete with travertine counters. Some of the rooms have views of the Hudson River. The suites are extra special and include kitchenettes, stocked minifridges, microwaves, and sitting rooms with sofas and extra TVs.

201 W. 79th St. (at Amsterdam Ave.), New York, NY 10024. ℂ **800/492-8122** or 212/875-1000. Fax 212/579-2408. www.thelucernehotel.com. 216 units. $330–$460 double or queen; $380–$500 king or junior suite; $420–$710 1-bedroom suite (check website for Internet specials and packages). Extra person $20. Children 15 and under stay free in parent's room. Check website for Internet specials. AE, DC, DISC, MC, V. Parking $29 nearby. Subway: 1 to 79th St. **Amenities:** Restaurant; fitness center. *In room:* Kitchenette (in suites only).

Red Roof Inn ⓥalue   Manhattan's first, and only, Red Roof Inn offers welcome relief from Midtown's high-priced hotel scene. The hotel occupies a former office building that was gutted and laid out fresh, allowing for more spacious rooms than you'll usually find in this price category. The high-ceilinged lobby feels smarter than most in this price range, and elevators are quiet and efficient. What's more, in-room amenities (including Wi-Fi) are better than most competitors', and furnishings are new and comfortable. The location—just a stone's throw from the Empire State Building and Herald Square—is excellent. A complimentary continental breakfast adds to the good value.

6 W. 32nd St. (btw. Broadway and Fifth Ave.), New York, NY 10001. ℂ **800/755-3194,** 800/RED-ROOF (733-7663), or 212/643-7100. Fax 212/643-7101. www.applecorehotels.com or www.redroof.com. 171 units. $89–$329 double (usually less than $189). Rates include continental breakfast. Children 12 and under stay free in parent's room. AE, DC, DISC, MC, V. Parking $26. Subway: B, D, F, N, R, V to 34th St. **Amenities:** Exercise room. *In room:* Fridge.

Ritz-Carlton New York, Central Park ⓑest ⓚids   This hotel features an enviable location overlooking Central Park, impeccable and personable service, and luxury galore—but it still manages to maintain a homey elegance. Rooms are spacious and decorated in traditional English-countryside style. Suites are larger than most New York City apartments. Rooms facing Central Park come with telescopes, and all have flatscreen TVs with DVD players. The marble bathrooms are also oversize and feature bathrobes and Frederic Fekkai bath amenities. For families who can afford the very steep prices, the hotel is extremely kid friendly. Children are given in-room cookies and milk. The Switzerland-based **La Prairie Spa** offers loads of pampering.

50 Central Park South (at Sixth Ave.), New York, NY 10019. ℂ **212/308-9100.** Fax 212/207-8831. www.ritzcarlton.com. 259 units. $650–$1,295 double; from $995 suite. Package and weekend rates available. AE, DC, DISC, MC, V. Parking $50. Subway: N, R, W to Fifth Ave. and F to 57th St. Pets under 60 lb. accepted. **Amenities:** Restaurant; fitness center; La Prairie spa.

Waldorf=Astoria and the Waldorf Towers   If you are looking for the epitome of old-school elegance, you can't do better than this Art Deco masterpiece—a genuine New York City landmark. No two rooms are exactly alike, yet all are airy, with high ceilings,

traditional decor, comfortable linens and beds, and spacious marble bathrooms. If you
crave more luxury, book a room on the **Astoria** level, which features huge suites, deluxe
bathroom amenities, access to the clubby Astoria Lounge for breakfast or afternoon hors
d'oeuvres, and free entry to the hotel's fitness club (other guests pay a fee). For even more
opulence, try a suite in the **Waldorf Towers,** where most rooms are bigger than most
New York City apartments.

301 Park Ave. (btw. 49th and 50th sts.), New York, NY 10022. ℭ **800/WALDORF** (925-3673), 800/774-
1500, or 212/355-3000. Fax 212/872-7272 (Astoria) or 212/872-4875 (Towers). www.waldorfastoria.com
or www.waldorf-towers.com. 1,245 units (180 in the Towers). Waldorf=Astoria $229–$585 double; from
$549 suite. Waldorf Towers $549–$959 double; from $799 suite. Extra person $35. Children 17 and under
stay free in parent's room. Corporate, senior, seasonal, and weekend discounts may be available (as low
as $189 at press time), as well as attractive package deals. AE, DC, DISC, MC, V. Parking $55. Subway: 6 to
51st St. **Amenities:** 4 restaurants; fitness center; spa. *In room:* Kitchenette or wet bar w/fridge (in some).

WHERE TO DINE

Reservations (where taken) are always a good idea in New York, and a virtual necessity if
your party is bigger than two or you want a special meal at a top restaurant. Do yourself
a favor and call ahead as a rule of thumb so you won't be disappointed.

Besides the restaurants listed below, also consider the legendary Central Park restaurant **Tavern on the Green,** Central Park West and West 67th Street (ℭ **212/873-3200**).
Food takes a back seat to dining in one of the city's best settings. Views over the park are
wonderful; in good weather, try for a seat in the outdoor garden, with its whimsical topiary shrubs and Japanese lanterns. It's also a great place to visit during the holidays.

For nonvegetarians and the non-health-minded, consider the cheapest, yet in some
ways, most comforting indulgence: **Gray's Papaya,** 2090 Broadway, at 72nd Street (ℭ **212/
799-0243**). This 24-hour hot-dog stand is a New York institution. The "Recession
Special"—two hot dogs and a drink (overly sweetened papaya, piña colada, or orange
juice)—is a whopping $3.50.

Note: Smoking is forbidden in every restaurant in the city. Tipping, however, is a
must—do as locals do and tip double the sales tax on your meal.

Aquavit SCANDINAVIAN This first-rate restaurant, which moved into a shiny new
home in 2005, is designed in sleek Scandinavian style with modernist furniture. In the
front of the restaurant is an informal and less expensive cafe, while past a long bar is the
dining room. The smoked fish—really, all the fish—is prepared perfectly. I often day-
dream about the herring plate: four types of herring accompanied by a tiny glass of
Aquavit, distilled liquor not unlike vodka flavored with fruit and spices, and a frosty
Carlsberg beer. The hot smoked arctic char on the main a la carte menu, served with
clams and bean purée in a mustard green broth, is also a winner. Most fixed-price menus
offer a well-chosen beverage accompaniment option.

65 E. 55th St. (btw. Park and Madison aves.). ℭ **212/307-7311.** www.aquavit.org. Reservations recommended. Cafe main courses $9–$32; 3-course fixed-price meal $24 at lunch, $35 at dinner; main dining
room fixed-price meal $39 at lunch, $82 at dinner ($39 for vegetarians); 3-course pre-theater dinner
(5:30–6:15pm) $55; tasting menus $58 at lunch, $115 at dinner ($90 for vegetarians); supplement for
paired wines $30 at lunch, $80 at dinner. AE, DC, MC, V. Mon–Fri noon–2:30pm; Sun–Thurs 5:30–10:30pm;
Fri–Sat 5:15–10:30pm. Subway: E, F to Fifth Ave.

Becco ITALIAN If you're a fan of Lidia Bastianich's PBS cooking shows, you be can
sample her simple, hearty Italian cooking here. The prices are not rock bottom, but in
terms of service, portions, and quality, you get tremendous bang for your buck. The main
courses can head north of the $20 mark, but the prix-fixe "Sinfonia de Pasta" menu ($18

at lunch, $23 at dinner), includes a Caesar salad or an antipasto plate, followed by unlimited servings of the three fresh-made daily pastas. There's also an excellent selection of Italian wines at $25 a bottle. For dessert, a tasting plate includes gelato, cheesecake, and whatever else the dessert chef has whipped up that day.

355 W. 46th St. (btw. Eighth and Ninth aves.). (C) **212/397-7597.** www.becconyc.com. Reservations recommended. Main courses lunch $13–$25, dinner $19–$35. AE, DC, DISC, MC, V. Mon noon–3pm and 5–10pm; Tues noon–3pm and 5pm–midnight; Wed 11:30am–2:30pm and 4pm–midnight; Thurs–Fri noon–3pm and 5pm–midnight; Sat 11:30am–2:30pm and 4pm–midnight; Sun noon–10pm. Subway: C, E to 50th St.

Big Wong King CHINESE/CANTONESE   For over 30 years, Big Wong has been an institution for workers from the nearby courthouses and Chinese families who come to feast on congee (rice porridge) and fried crullers for breakfast. They also come for the superb roasted meats, the pork and duck seen hanging in the window, the comforting noodle soups, and the terrific barbecued ribs. This is simple, down-home Cantonese food—lo mein, chow fun, bok choy in oyster sauce—cooked lovingly, and so cheap. If you don't mind sharing a table, Big Wong is a must at any time of day.

67 Mott St. (btw. Canal and Bayard sts.). (C) **212/964-0540.** Appetizers $1.50–$5; congee $1.50–$6; soups $3–$5; Cantonese noodles $5.25–$11. No credit cards. Daily 8:30am–9pm. Subway: N, R.

Chanterelle (Best) CONTEMPORARY FRENCH   This West Village spot is our favorite special-occasion restaurant (you don't dine here on the cheap). The dining room is a charmer, with widely spaced tables (a rarity in New York City) and gorgeous floral displays. Your server will work with you on your choices, pairing items that go best together. The French-themed menu is seasonal and changes every few weeks, but one signature dish appears on almost every menu: a marvelous grilled seafood sausage. Cheese lovers should opt for a cheese course—the presentation and selection can't be beat. The wine list is superlative but expensive.

2 Harrison St. (at Hudson St.). (C) **212/966-6960.** www.chanterellenyc.com. Reservations recommended well in advance. Fixed-price lunch $42; a la carte lunch $22–$30; 3-course fixed-price dinner $95; tasting menu $125. AE, DISC, MC, V. Mon–Wed 5:30–10:30pm; Mon–Sat noon–2:30pm; Thurs–Sat 5:30–11pm; Sun 5–10pm. Subway: 1 to Franklin St.

City Bakery (Kids) ORGANIC AMERICAN   City Bakery offers comfort food that manages to be delicious, nutritious, *and* eco-friendly. Its salad bar is unlike any other in the city, where the integrity of the ingredients is as important as the taste. This is health food, all right—roasted beets with walnuts, glistening sautéed greens, lavender eggplant tossed in miso—but with heart and soul, offering such favorites as French toast with artisanal bacon, mac 'n cheese, fried chicken, tortilla pie, even smoked salmon with all the trimmings on Sunday. The "bakery" refers to the plethora of sinful desserts; kids love the spinning wheel of chocolate and the homemade marshmallows. *One caveat:* It's a bit pricey for a salad bar, but oh, what good eats.

3 W. 18th St. (btw. Fifth and Sixth aves.). (C) **212/366-1414.** Salad bar $12 per pound; soups $4–$7; sandwiches $5–$10. AE, MC, V. Mon–Fri 7:30am–7pm; Sat 7:30am–6:30pm; Sun 9am–6pm. Subway: N, R, Q, 4, 5, 6 to Union Sq.

Katz's Delicatessen (Value) JEWISH DELI   Arguably the city's best Jewish deli. The motto is "There's Nothing More New York Than Katz's," and it's spot on. Founded in 1888, this cavernous, brightly lit place is suitably Noo Yawk, with dill pickles, Dr. Brown's cream soda, and old-world attitude to spare. But one word of caution: Katz's is a serious tourist destination, so if you see a tour bus parked in front, you might be in for

For the Perfect Pizza

Patsy's Pizzeria, 2287 First Ave., between 117th and 118th streets (© **212/534-9783**), is our favorite pizzeria in the city and was also the favorite of Frank Sinatra, who liked it so much he had pies flown out to Las Vegas. The coal oven here has been burning since 1932, and though the neighborhood in East Harlem, where it is located, has had its ups and downs, the quality of pizza at Patsy's has never wavered. Try the marinara pizza, a pie with fresh marinara sauce but no cheese that's so good you won't miss the mozzarella. Don't be fooled by imitators using Patsy's name; this is the original and the best.

a wait. (And remember to tip your carver, who gives you a plate with a sample of the succulent pastrami or corned beef as he prepares your sandwich!)

205 E. Houston St. (at Ludlow St.). © 212/254-2246. Reservations not accepted. Sandwiches $3–$10; other main courses $5–$18. AE, DC, DISC, MC, V ($20 minimum). Sun–Tues 8am–10pm; Wed 8am–11pm; Thurs 8am–midnight; Fri–Sat 8am–3am. Subway: F to Second Ave.

La Nacional SPANISH/TAPAS   It's not easy finding the oldest Spanish restaurant in New York. Once you find it, though, you will be rewarded. The grill turns out tasty tapas like sardines, octopus, and shrimp. There is a somewhat formal dining room in the front, while in the back, next to the open kitchen, there are a few tables and TVs usually tuned to soccer matches. Come and share a bottle of Spanish wine and make a meal out of the tapas—the *albondigas* (Spanish meatballs), *boquerones* (white anchovy filets), and the octopus are favorites—or you can order the excellent paella. Tapas range from $4 to $9, while no entree is more than $18.

239 W. 14th St. (btw. Seventh and Eighth aves.). © 212/243-9308. www.lanacionaltapas.com. Tapas $7–$9; main courses $16–$18. AE, DC, DISC, MC, V. Sun–Wed noon–10pm; Thurs–Sat noon–11pm. Subway: A, C, E, 1, 2, 3 to 14th St.

Nizza Value FRENCH/ITALIAN   New in 2007, Nizza offers the cuisine of the French Mediterranean, the city of Nice specifically, and its Ligurian-Italian influence. You can fill up on appetizers and salads, starting with the tapenade of black olives served with light, freshly baked focaccia chips and *socca,* a chickpea pancake cooked in a brick oven and sprinkled with fresh herbs. Or savor a glass of wine with a plate of *salumi,* a selection of cured meats such as *coppa, mortadella,* prosciutto, and a variety of salamis, including duck. It's is loud and seating is on the tight side, but you forgive Nizza once you sample the food and, especially, the easy-on-your-wallet prices.

630 Ninth Ave. (at 45th St.). © 212/956-1800. $8–$12. AE, MC, V. Tues–Sat 11:30am–2am; Sun–Mon 11:30am–midnight. Subway: A, C, E, 7 to 42nd St.

Primehouse STEAKHOUSE   There are many meanings of the word *prime,* and in the case of Primehouse, the newest (2007) from restaurateur Stephen Hanson, it means top-of-the-line meat, of which there are many cuts at Primehouse. The romaine, tomato, onion and Maytag blue cheese salad was crisp, even when smothered by the rich blue cheese dressing, but do not attempt to tackle it yourself—it will finish you before your steak arrives, and that would be a mistake, especially if you've splurged and ordered one of the special cuts aged in the restaurant's "Himalayan Salt Room."

381 Park Ave. S. (at 27th St.). ✆ **212/824-2600.** www.brguestrestaurants.com. Reservations recommended. Main courses $24–$62. AE, DC, DISC, MC, V. Mon–Fri 11:30am–4pm; Sat–Sun 11am–4pm; Mon–Wed 5–11pm; Thurs–Sat 5pm–midnight; Sun 5–10pm. Subway: N, R, Q, 6 to 28th St.

Sapporo (Value) JAPANESE NOODLES   If the mostly Japanese clientele at this long-time Theater District noodle shop doesn't convince you of Sapporo's authenticity, the constant din of satisfied diners slurping at huge bowls of steaming ramen (noodle soup with meat and vegetables) surely will. And though the ramen is Sapporo's well-deserved specialty, the *gyoza* (Japanese dumplings) and the *donburi* (pork or chicken over rice with soy-flavored sauce) are also terrific. Best of all, nothing on the menu is over $10, and that's not easy to accomplish in the oft-overpriced Theater District.

152 W. 49th St. (btw. Sixth and Seventh aves.). ✆ **212/869-8972.** Reservations not accepted. Main courses $6–$9. No credit cards. Mon–Sat 11am–11pm; Sun 11am–10pm. Subway: N, R to 49th St.

NEW YORK CITY AFTER DARK

For the latest, most comprehensive nightlife listings, the magazine *Time Out New York* (**www.timeoutny.com**) is our favorite weekly source; it comes out every Thursday. The free weekly *Village Voice*'s (**www.villagevoice.com**) arts and entertainment coverage is extensive, and just about every live-music venue advertises here. The *New York Times* (**www.nytoday.com**) features terrific entertainment coverage, particularly in the two-part Friday "Weekend" section. *New York* magazine's **www.nymetro.com** site is an excellent online source.

The Theater Scene

We can't tell you precisely what will be on while you're in town, so check the publications listed above for specifics. Another good source is the **Broadway Line** (✆ **888/BROAD-WAY** [276-2392]; www.livebroadway.com), where you can obtain details and descriptions on current Broadway shows, and choose to be transferred to TeleCharge or Ticketmaster. There's also **NYC/Onstage** (✆ **212/768-1818;** www.tdf.org), a recorded service providing complete schedules, descriptions, and other details on theater and the performing arts.

   Ticket prices vary dramatically. Expect to pay for good seats; the high end for any given show is likely to be between $60 and $100 (though it can be a lot more). Off-Broadway and Off-Off-Broadway shows tend to be cheaper, with tickets often as low as $10 or $15, though seats for the most established shows can command prices as high as $50 to $75.

TICKET-BUYING TIPS   Phone ahead or go online for tickets to the most popular shows as far in advance as you can. You need only call such general numbers as **TeleCharge** (✆ **212/239-6200;** www.telecharge.com) or **Ticketmaster** (✆ **212/307-4100;** www.ticketmaster.com).

   Theatre Direct International (TDI) is a ticket broker (minimum service charge of $15) that sells tickets to select Broadway and Off-Broadway shows. Check to see if they have seats to the shows you're interested in by calling ✆ **800/BROADWAY** (276-2392) or 212/541-8457; you can also order tickets via its website, **www.broadway.com**.

   Three competing sites—**Broadway.com** (**www.broadway.com**), **Playbill Online** (**www.playbill.com** or www.playbillclub.com), and **TheaterMania** (**www.theatermania.com**)—offer information on Broadway and Off-Broadway shows, with links to the ticket-buying agencies. Each offers an **online theater club** that's free to join and can yield substantial savings—as much as 50%—on advance-purchase theater tickets for select Broadway and Off-Broadway shows.

You should also try the **Broadway Ticket Center,** run by the League of American Theatres and Producers, at the Times Square Visitors Center, 1560 Broadway, between 46th and 47th streets (open Mon–Sat 10am–6pm, Sun 10am–3pm). They often have tickets available for otherwise sold-out shows, both for advance and same-day purchase, and charge only about $5 extra per ticket.

Even if saving money isn't an issue for you, check the boards at the **TKTS Booth** in Times Square (Broadway and 47th St.; open 3–8pm for evening performances, 10am–2pm for Wed and Sat matinees, 11am–8pm on Sun for all performances), for same-day discounted tickets. Tickets for the day's performances are usually offered at half-price, with a few reduced only 25%, plus a $2.50-per-ticket service charge. Boards outside the ticket windows list available shows. Only cash and traveler's checks are accepted (no credit cards). There's often a huge line, so show up early for the best availability and be prepared to wait—but frankly, the crowd is all part of the fun. Visit **www.tdf.org** or call **NYC/Onstage** at © 212/768-1818 and press 8 for the latest TKTS information.

The Performing Arts

In addition to the listings below, see what's happening at **Carnegie Hall,** 881 Seventh Ave. (© 212/247-7800; www.carnegiehall.org; subway: N, R, or W to 57th St.); and at the **92nd Street Y,** 1395 Lexington Ave., at 92nd Street (© 212/415-5500; www.92ndsty.org), which offers many excellent cultural events.

LINCOLN CENTER FOR THE PERFORMING ARTS   New York is the world's premier performing arts city, and **Lincoln Center,** at Broadway and 64th Street (© 212/546-2656 or 875-5456; www.lincolncenter.org; subway: 1 or 9 to 6th St.), is its premier institution. It's undergoing a massive renovation for its 50th birthday in 2009, and construction has also blocked off some of the entrances and public spaces, and may displace some of the companies for all or part of their 2008–09 seasons.

Resident companies include the **Chamber Music Society of Lincoln Center** (© 212/875-5788; www.chambermusicsociety.org); the **Film Society of Lincoln Center** (© 212/875-5600; www.filmlinc.com), which shows films at the Walter Reade Theater; **Jazz at Lincoln Center** (© 212/258-9800; www.jalc.org), led by Wynton Marsalis, which is actually located several blocks down Broadway in the Time-Warner Center; and **Lincoln Center Theater** (© 212/362-7600; www.lct.org), with the Vivian Beaumont Theater, a home to Broadway shows and the Mitzi E. Newhouse Theater, an Off-Broadway house.

Other renowned tenants are the **Metropolitan Opera** (© 212/362-6000; www.metopera.org), **New York City Opera** (© 212/870-5570; www.nycopera.com), **New York City Ballet** (© 212/870-5570; www.nycballet.com), **New York Philharmonic** (© 212/875-5656; www.newyorkphilharmonic.org), and **American Ballet Theatre** (**www.abt.org**).

Most of the companies' **major seasons** run from about September or October to April, May, or June. **Tickets** for all performances at Avery Fisher and Alice Tully halls can be purchased through **CenterCharge** (© 212/721-6500) or online at **www.lincoln center.org** (click on "Event Calendar"). Tickets for all Lincoln Center Theater performances can be purchased thorough **TeleCharge** (© 212/239-6200; www.telecharge.com). Tickets for New York State Theater productions (New York City Opera and Ballet companies) are available through **Ticketmaster** (© 212/307-4100; www.ticketmaster.com), while tickets for films showing at the Walter Reade Theater can be bought up to 7 days in advance by calling © 212/496-3809.

OTHER CONCERT HALLS & VENUES Modern dance takes center stage at **City Center,** 131 W. 55th St. between Sixth and Seventh avenues (© **212/247-0430** or 581-1212; www.citycenter.org.; subway: F, N, Q, R, or W to 57th St.; B, D, or E to Seventh Ave.); and at the **Joyce Theater,** one of the world's greatest modern dance institutions, located at 175 Eighth Ave., at 19th Street (© **212/242-0800;** www.joyce.org.; subway: C or E to 23rd St.; 1 or 9 to 18th St.).

The **Apollo Theatre,** 253 W. 125th St., between Adam Clayton Powell and Frederick Douglass boulevards (© **212/531-5300** or 531-5301; www.apollotheater.com; subway: 1 or 9 to 125th St.), is internationally renowned for its African-American acts of all musical genres and is in the middle of a major restoration project. The **Brooklyn Academy of Music** presents cutting-edge theater, opera, dance, and music at 30 Lafayette Ave., off Flatbush Avenue, Brooklyn (© **718/636-4100;** www.bam.org; subway: 2, 3, 4, 5, M, N, Q, R, or W to Pacific St./Atlantic Ave.).

Live Popular Music

A midsize venue for national acts is the **Bowery Ballroom,** 6 Delancey St., at the Bowery (© **212/533-2111;** www.boweryballroom.com), an atmospheric general admission space that holds about 500. Its bigger brother, the **Fillmore New York at Irving Plaza,** is another old hall near Union Square at 17 Irving Place (© **212/777-1224;** www.irvingplaza.com; subway: L, N, R, 4, 5, or 6 to 14th St.–Union Sq.).

B. B. King Blues Club & Grill anchors Times Square's "new" 42nd Street with pop, funk, and rock names, mainly from the past (© **212/997-4144,** or 307-7171 for tickets; www.bbkingblues.com; subway: A, C, E, Q, W, 1, 2, 3, 7, or 9 to 42nd St.). **S.O.B.'s** is a longtime favorite for Latin-flavored music and dancing at 204 Varick St. at Houston Street (© **212/243-4940;** www.sobs.com; subway: 1 to Houston St.). Folk rock's legendary **Bitter End,** 147 Bleecker St., between Thompson and LaGuardia streets (© **212/673-7030;** www.bitterend.com), is still going strong.

JAZZ **Smoke** is a superstar in the New York scene on the Upper East Side, 2751 Broadway, between 105th and 106th streets (© **212/864-6662;** www.smokejazz.com; subway: 1 to 103rd St.). Prices are astronomical, but the **Blue Note** attracts the biggest names to its intimate setting at 131 W. 3rd St., at Sixth Avenue (© **212/475-8592;** www.bluenote.net; subway: A, C, E, F, or V to W. 4th St.).

CABARET Cabaret doesn't get any better than at the **Cafe Carlyle.** It's at the Carlyle hotel, 781 Madison Ave., at 76th Street (© **212/744-1600;** subway: 6 to 77th St.). Closed from July to August. **Joe's Pub** is a popular cabaret and supper club at the Joseph Papp Public Theater, 425 Lafayette St., between Astor Place and 4th Street (© **212/539-8777;** www.joespub.com; subway: 6 to Astor Place).

COMEDY **Carolines on Broadway** presents today's headliners in its Theater District showroom at 1626 Broadway, between 49th and 50th streets (© **212/757-4100;** www.carolines.com; subway: N or R to 49th St.; 1 or 9 to 50th St.). The **Comedy Cellar** is the club of choice for stand-up fans in the know at 117 MacDougal St., between Bleecker and West 3rd streets (© **212/254-3480;** www.comedycellar.com; subway: A, C, E, F, V, or S to W. 4th St., use 3rd St. exit).

Bars & Cocktail Lounges

Ear Inn is one of many claimants to be the oldest bar in New York, sitting in SoHo since the 1870s at 326 Spring St., between Greenwich and Washington streets (© **212/226-9060;** subway: C, E to Spring St.)

(Value) Park It! Shakespeare, Music & Other Free Fun

As the weather warms, New York culture comes outdoors to play.

Shakespeare in the Park, held at Central Park's Delacorte Theater, is the city's most famous alfresco arts event. The schedule consists of one or two summertime productions, usually of the Bard's plays. Productions often feature big names and range from traditional to avant-garde interpretations. The theater itself, next to Belvedere Castle near 79th Street and West Drive, is a dream—on a beautiful starry night, there's no better stage in town. Tickets are given out free on a first-come, first-served basis (two per person), at 1pm on the day of the performance at the theater. The Delacorte might have 1,881 seats, but each is a hot commodity, so people generally line up about 2 to 3 hours in advance (even earlier for a big hit or a big star). You can also pick up same-day tickets between 1 and 3pm at the Public Theater, at 425 Lafayette St., or try your luck at the online lottery. For more information, call the Public Theater at ℂ **212/539-8500** or the Delacorte at ℂ **212/861-7277,** or visit **www.publictheater.org**.

Free concerts by the **New York Philharmonic** and the **Metropolitan Opera** are held under the stars on Central Park's Great Lawn and in parks throughout the five boroughs. For schedules, call the Philharmonic at ℂ **212/875-5656** or the Metropolitan Opera at ℂ **212/362-6000.** The Philharmonic lists its upcoming gigs at www.newyorkphilharmonic.org, under "Attend Concerts."

Central Park may be the most happening park in town, but the calendar of free events heats up throughout the city's parks in summertime. You can find out what's happening by calling the **Parks and Recreation Special Events Hot Line** at ℂ **888/NY-PARKS** (697-2757) or 212/360-3456, or pointing your browser to www.nycgovparks.org.

KGB Bar, at 85 E. 4th St. (ℂ **212/505-3360;** www.kgbbar.com; subway: 6 to Astor Place), in the East Village, is an old Ukranian social-club-turned-writer's-bar. There are free readings every night.

Near Gramercy Park, **Pete's Tavern,** 129 E. 18th St., at Irving Place (ℂ **212/473-7676;** www.petestavern.com; subway: L, N, R, 4, 5, or 6 to 14th St./Union Sq.), opened while Lincoln was president. There's Guinness on tap and a terrific happy hour.

On the West Side, at the **Oak Room at the Algonquin,** 59 W. 44th St., between Fifth and Sixth avenues (ℂ **212/840-6800;** subway: B, D, F, or V to 42nd St.), you can feel the spirit of Dorothy Parker and the legendary Algonquin Round Table. It's the comfiest hotel bar in town.

On the East Side, the **Campbell Apartment,** in Grand Central Terminal, 15 Vanderbilt Ave. (ℂ **212/953-0409;** subway: S, 4, 5, 6, 7 to 42nd St./Grand Central), is a high-ceilinged room restored to its full Florentine glory, and serves wines and champagnes by the glass, single-malt Scotches, fine stogies, and haute noshies to a well-heeled commuting crowd. There's a dress code.

The **All State Cafe,** 250 W. 72nd St., between Broadway and West End Avenue (© 212/874-1883; subway: 1, 2, 3, or 9 to 72nd St.), is a subterranean pub that's one of Manhattan's undiscovered treasures—the quintessential neighborhood "snugger."

On the Upper East Side, **Bemelmans Bar** at the Carlyle hotel, 35 E. 76th St. at Madison Avenue (© 212/744-1600; subway: 6 to 77th St.), is a luxurious spot for cocktails and the best hotel bar in the city. **Elaine's,** at 1703 Second Ave., between 88th and 89th streets (© 212/534-8103; subway: 4, 5, or 6 to 86th St.), is where the glittering literati still come for dinner and book parties.

Dance/Nightclubs
You go to Amy Sacco's still-hot **Bungalow 8,** 515 W. 27th St., between Tenth and Eleventh avenues. (© 212/629-3333; subway: C, E to 23rd St.) for the (very expensive) scene; you'll get past the doorman if you're glitterati or can convince him you are! At **Cain,** 544 W. 27th St., between Tenth and Eleventh aves. (© 212/947-8000; subway: C, E to 23rd St.), the theme is Africa—South Africa, to be specific. The front door, if you gain entry, has elephant-trunk handles, there are zebra hides everywhere, and the big game is celebrity-spotting. At **Cielo,** 18 Little W. 12th St., between Ninth Avenue and Washington Street (© 212/645-5700; www.cieloclub.com; subway: A, C, E, to 14th St.; L to Eighth Ave.), you'll find the best sound system of any small club in town. House is big here, and they bring in some of the best DJs from around the globe. There's a sunken dance floor and an authentic, glittering disco ball rotating above.

The Gay & Lesbian Scene
To get a thorough, up-to-date take on what's happening in GLBT nightlife, grab a copy of *HX* (www.hx.com), *Gay City News* (www.gaycitynews.com), the *New York Blade* (www.nyblade.com), *GONYC* (www.gomag.com), or *Next.* They're available for free in bars and clubs all around town or at the **Lesbian and Gay Community Center,** at 208 W. 13th St., between Seventh and Eighth avenues (© 212/620-7310; www.gaycenter.org).

Highlights of the bar scene include Chelsea's **Barracuda** (© 212/645-8613; subway: C, E, 1, or 9 to 23rd St.), a trendy, loungey place that's regularly voted "Best Bar" by the readers of *HX.* Look for the regular drag shows at 275 W. 22nd St., between Seventh and Eighth avenues. The **Stonewall Bar** (© 212/463-0950; subway: 1 or 9 to Christopher St.) is where it all started. A mixed gay and lesbian crowd makes this an easy place to begin.

2 HIGHLIGHTS OF THE HUDSON VALLEY

Just over 300 miles long, the **Hudson River Valley** spans eight counties along the east and west banks of the river, from Albany down to Yonkers. The entire valley is a National Heritage Area and one of the most beautiful regions in the eastern United States. The river valley's extraordinary landscapes gave birth to America's first art school, the Hudson River School of Painters, and writers such as Edith Wharton and Washington Irving set their stories and novels along the banks of the Hudson. And it was here that America's most legendary families—among them, the Livingstons, Vanderbilts, Roosevelts, and Rockefellers—shaped the face of American industry and politics, leaving legacies of grand country estates and the towns that grew up around them. When it comes to history, few areas can rival the Hudson.

ESSENTIALS

GETTING THERE   Most visitors traveling by air fly into one of the New York City area's three major airports. For information on those, see p. 104. Major rental-car companies (a car is by far the best way to tour the region) have representatives at all the major airports.

The Lower Hudson Valley begins just north of New York City, on either side of the river; take either **I-87** (New York State Thruway) north or the **Taconic State Parkway.** From Albany south, take I-87 south to 9W or **I-90** south to Route 9. Heading either east or west, the most direct route is along **I-84.**

Amtrak (𝓒 **800/USA-RAIL** [872-7245]; www.amtrak.com) has service to the Hudson Valley from New York City. The commuter **Metro-North Railroad** (𝓒 **800/638-7646;** www.mta.nyc.ny.us/mnr) travels up and down the Hudson out of Grand Central Station in New York City. The trip hugging the river on the east side is one of the prettier train trips in the U.S.

VISITOR INFORMATION   General tourist information is available by calling Hudson Valley Tourism, Inc. (𝓒 800/232-4782); visit the organization's website, **www.travel hudsonvalley.org**, for links to the very informative sites maintained by each of the eight counties that touch upon the Hudson River Valley. For information on the historic estates and sites, visit **www.hudsonvalley.org**.

FAMOUS HISTORIC ESTATES & SITES

The Lower Hudson Valley is lined with grand manor houses, but none compares to **Kykuit** (pronounced *kye*-cut), in Sleepy Hollow (𝓒 914/631-9491). John D. Rockefeller built his estate in its present classical Greek-Roman style in 1913. Take the guided tour of the mansion, which is loaded with Chinese ceramics and a fabulous collection of 20th-century modern art, including an outstanding series of tapestries executed by Pablo Picasso. The gardens (which boast a magnificent view of the Hudson) are loaded with works by Alexander Calder, Henry Moore, and Constantin Brancusi. The estate's coach barn features horse-drawn vehicles and classic automobiles from the family's collection. *Note:* Tours to the estate leave from another spot worth touring—**Phillipsburg Manor** (𝓒 914/631-3992), which transports visitors to a complicated time in history, when this estate functioned as one of the largest slave plantations in the North. The site still functions as a working farm, with horses and sheep, wool spinning, milling of flour, and harvesting of rye in June and July. It's a great educational outing for families.

Sunnyside, West Sunnyside Lane, Tarrytown (𝓒 914/591-8763), was the home of Washington Irving, the author who made Sleepy Hollow a household name and introduced the world to Rip van Winkle. Sunnyside, with its mélange of historical and architectural styles, including a Dutch stepped-gable roofline, a Spanish tower, and a master bedroom modeled after a Paris apartment, was Irving's personal retreat, a place to write and retire. Today the charming pastoral villa, swathed in vines and wisteria and nestled into the grounds along the Hudson, remains as he left it, with his books and writing papers in the study.

HIGHLIGHTS OF THE HUDSON VALLEY

Farther up the Hudson, in the town of Garrison, lies **Boscobel Restoration,** 1601 Rte. 9D (© 845/265-3638; www.boscobel.org), which features one of the best collections of Federal-period furnishings and decorative arts in the United States. The mansion, built in 1804 by a British Loyalist, is a neoclassical Georgian masterpiece that was rescued from government destruction (it was sold at auction for $35 in the 1950s) and moved piece by piece to its current location. For a truly breathtaking view of the Hudson, head through the lovely rose garden to the front of the mansion, in the direction of the river. The **Hudson Valley Shakespeare Festival** (advance reservations required; **www.hvshakespeare.org**) is held here in the summer.

One sight you'll see off to the right if you glance down the Hudson from Boscobel is the **U.S. Military Academy at West Point,** Route 218, Highland Falls (© 845/446-4724; www.usma.ed or www.westpointtours.com), the nation's oldest and foremost military college—which celebrated its 200th anniversary in 2002 and is the Hudson Valley's most popular attraction. The only way to visit is by organized 1- or 2-hour tour on a bus that, among other spots, stops at the famous Cadet Chapel, which possesses stained-glass windows and the largest church organ in the world, with more than 21,000 pipes. The massive campus, with its Gothic Revival buildings perched on the west side above the Hudson River, is undeniably handsome, especially in fall. Tickets for all tours must be purchased at the Visitor's Center.

Heading north into the middle section of the valley, you'll arrive in Hyde Park, site of several of the region's best attractions. First up is the **Vanderbilt Mansion National Historic Site** (© 845/229-9115; www.nps.gov/vama). Frederick Vanderbilt's lavish 54-room country palace (actually the smallest of the Vanderbilt mansions) in Hyde Park, built in 1898, is a no-holds-barred gem that epitomized the Gilded Age's nouveau riche. French in every respect, from Louise's Versailles-like bedroom to the grand dining room and Frederick's glittering master bedroom, it's impressively decorated in grand style and should not be missed. Nearby is the **Franklin Delano Roosevelt Presidential Library and Museum/FDR Home** (© 800/FDR-VISIT [337-8474] or 845/229-8114; www.nps.gov/hofr and www.fdrlibrary.marist.edu). FDR adored the Hudson River Valley and designed his own presidential library, the nation's first, while still in his second term; he built it next to his lifelong home in Hyde Park. It is the only presidential library to have been used by a sitting president. See his cluttered White House desk (left as it was the last day of his presidency), and exhibits on the FDR presidency and times. Two wings added in memory of his wife, Eleanor Roosevelt, make this the only presidential library to have a section devoted to a first lady. FDR and Eleanor are buried in the rose garden on the grounds. Also in the area is the **Eleanor Roosevelt National Historic Site (Val-Kill Cottage) & Top Cottage** (© 845/229-9115; www.nps.gov/elro), where you can visit the country retreats used by the Roosevelts to get away from it all and to entertain important guests (such as Winston Churchill and the queen of England). *Tip:* The National Park Service sells a pass to all three Hyde Park sites that offers a good discount off the regular single admission price (and those with valid National Parks passes can enter all three sites for free).

The best estate in the Upper Hudson area is the **Olana State Historic Site,** Route 9G, Hudson (© 518/828-0135; www.olana.org), the unique home of the accomplished Hudson River School painter Frederick Church (1826–1900), who designed both the building and the surrounding landscape. Named for a Persian treasure house, the home reflects Church's interest in Moorish design and is loaded with the knickknacks, furniture, tapestries, rugs, bronzes, paintings, sculptures, and the other objets d'art collected by Church during his travels. Everything you see looks exactly as it did when Church died in 1900,

WHERE TO STAY & DINE

Most of the sites above can be visited as day trips out of New York City, but why not do as New Yorkers do and spend a night or a weekend at one of the region's many charming and romantic inns? What follows are two great places to stay in the region and one exceptional place to dine; contact Hudson Valley Tourism (see above) for more info on accommodations in the area.

Castle on the Hudson, 400 Benedict Ave., Tarrytown (© **914/631-1980;** www. castleonthehudson.com), is a Relais & Châteaux property that offers some of the most extravagant accommodations along the Hudson Valley in a grand 45-room castle built in 1910 on a bluff overlooking the river (rates $340–$360 double). Even if you're not staying here, it's well worth dining at its **Equus** restaurant for a special four-course prix-fixe meal or one of the periodic wine-tasting dinners.

In the Middle Hudson region, for unrestrained luxury in a country inn setting, nothing comes close to the **Belvedere Mansion,** Route 9, Staatsburgh (© **845/889-8000;** www.belvederemansion.com). Doubles from $105 to $225. The elegant interiors feature 18th-century antiques, silk fabrics, rich colors, luxurious linens, and marble bathrooms. The seven main-house rooms are the biggest and most expensive; several have fantastic river views and such details as claw-foot tubs and canopied beds. Stick to the main building or the rooms in the new Hunting Lodge (these have fireplaces) for the best experience. The restaurant in the inn offers exquisitely prepared cuisine in a refined setting (try to reserve the private dining nook just up the main staircase for an especially romantic meal—many a proposal's been tendered there).

If you have a chance, while in Hyde Park, try to have at least one meal at the legendary **Culinary Institute of America,** 1946 Campus Dr., off Route 9, Hyde Park (© **845/ 471-6608;** www.ciachef.edu). The nation's foremost culinary arts college has four on-campus restaurants and a bakery cafe that are open to the public (reserve online well in advance!). No matter where you eat, you're guaranteed to have a meal worth savoring.

---

3 UPSTATE NEW YORK HIGHLIGHTS

THE ADIRONDACKS

The 'dacks (as locals know them) is an area you simply can't ignore. Its 600 million acres hold some 2,000 peaks, 100 of them taller than 3,000 feet. Nearly half of the park is forest preserve: vast forests of pine, maple, and birch. The park supports 500,000 acres of old-growth forest, 200,000 acres of which have never been logged. And water? You'll find some 2,500 lakes and ponds, along with more than 30,000 miles of rivers and streams. Ralph Waldo Emerson and other thinkers found refuge here in the mid–19th century, forming philosopher's camps and using the woods for inspiration. And the park formed the exploratory dreams of Theodore Roosevelt, who canoed in the St. Regis Wilderness Canoe Area at the age of 12 and often returned to seek refuge.

Make no mistake: Though the peaks of the Adirondacks don't have the rugged, jagged look of the Rockies, this can be harsh territory. But if you prepare well, it can be some of the most beautiful land to travel in. The region is well stocked with hotels, restaurants, and campsites, so you can get as much or as little civilization as you please.

GETTING THERE The Adirondack region is best appreciated by car. The New York State Thruway, **I-87,** a toll road from New York City to Albany, becomes the scenic, toll-free Adirondack Northway. It hugs the region's eastern border, with exits to Lake George (about 4 hr. from the Big Apple), Blue Mountain Lake, Ticonderoga, Lake Placid, and other areas of interest, eventually reaching Canada. The western side of the Adirondacks can be accessed from either **I-81** north at Watertown to **Route 3** or by following **I-90** east through Utica to **routes 8** and **12.** Inside the park, a sparse network of roads squeezes between mountain ranges and tunnels into dense forests. **Route 73,** which begins at exit 30 of the Northway and ends in Lake Placid, provides a particularly picturesque tour through the High Peaks region.

VISITOR INFORMATION The **Adirondack Regional Tourism Council** (© 518/846-8016; www.adk.org) has an information center on I-87 southbound between exits 41 and 40, which is open daily year-round, from 8am to 5pm; from Memorial Day to Labor Day, it's open until 8pm. For information on Lake George, you can also contact **Warren County Tourism,** Municipal Center, 1340 State Rte. 9, Lake George (© 800/95-VISIT [958-2728]; www.visitlakegeorge.com). Farther west, contact **Inlet Information** (© 866/GO-INLET [464-6538]; www.inletny.com) or **Old Forge Tourism** (© 315/369-6983; www.oldforgeny.com). For info on Lake Placid, contact the **Lake Placid/Essex County Visitors Bureau,** Olympic Center, 216 Main St., Lake Placid (© 800/447-5224 or 518/523-2445; www.lakeplacid.com). Other good sources of information are **www.adirondacks.com** and **www.adirondacklife.com**.

Exploring the Adirondacks

As an all-season destination, the Adirondack region has its highlights and its hazards. Icy roads and winter storms can make driving precarious, so call ahead to check road conditions. Visitors planning an outdoor excursion should anticipate unpredictable dips in temperature and unexpected precipitation year-round. For workshops on outdoor skills, such as paddling or mountain climbing, contact the **Adirondack Mountain Club** (© 800/395-8080 or 518/668-4447; www.adk.org).

THE OLYMPIC SIGHTS The 1932 Winter Olympics put Lake Placid in the international spotlight; hosting the Games again in 1980 cemented its legacy. You can see some of the sites where legends were made, including the "Miracle on Ice" hockey victory of the Americans over the Russians. the **Olympic Regional Development Authority** (© 518/523-1655; www.orda.org) handles it all.

Skip the Olympic Training Center, at 421 Old Military Rd.; there's not much open to the public. For downhill skiing on **Whiteface,** see below. You can see all of the following in 1 day. Start off at the **Olympic Sports Complex,** Route 73 (© 518/523-2811), 20 minutes west of Lake Placid, for cross-country skiing. In the same complex—and definitely something you should not miss—is the **bobsled/luge/skeleton track,** where you'll watch athletes bomb down on and in crazy machinery. You can even strap yourself into a bobsled and race down the half-mile track with a guide and brakeman ($55 summer, $65 winter)—you'll never watch the Olympics the same way. The sleds are on wheels in summer, but they go much faster on the winter ice. Then drive back toward town and you'll see the towering presence of the ski jump towers at the **MacKenzie-Intervale Ski Jumping Complex,** Route 73 (© 518/523-2202). December through March and June through October, watch athletes soar off these ramps. Ride the lift alongside it and take the 26-story elevator to the top of the 394-foot tower ($10) to get the skiers' terrifying perspective. From June to October you can watch them jump, too—into a 750,000-gallon pool at the adjacent **Kodak Sports Park.** Drive back into town and spend a half-hour in the **Winter Olympic Museum** (© **518/523-1655**) at the **Olympic Center;** it's $4 to check out a good history of the Games in Placid and tons of memorabilia. While there, go skating on the rinks where such legends as Sonja Henie and Eric Heiden made history.

Whiteface, Route 86, Wilmington (© **518/946-2223;** www.whiteface.com), is the east's only Olympic mountain (elevation 4,400 ft.), and it has the best skiing in the state. With the greatest vertical drop in the east (3,430 ft.), there's a variety of terrain that will appeal to all levels. In fact, 35% of the trails are rated for novices. There are 65 trails and 11 lifts in all. A 1-day lift ticket costs $65 to $67.

TOURING LAKE CHAMPLAIN   Lake Champlain doesn't offer much in the way of hotels or recreation, but it does have one must-see attraction.

Fort Ticonderoga, Route 74, Ticonderoga (© **518/585-2821;** www.fort-ticonderoga. org), was once a grimy, bloody stage for battle during the French and Indian War and the American Revolution. Military history buffs will be in heaven at this fort set right on Lake Champlain. Built by the French in 1755, the fort protected this narrow strip of water from its high perch, and since 1909 it's been open to the public, detailing the military history of the Lake Champlain and Lake George valleys. The collection is anything but dry; on view are nearly 1,000 muskets, bayonets, pistols, and swords from the 18th century, as well as a unique collection of uniforms. Not interested in the military stuff? There are gorgeous gardens for wandering. Allow 2 to 4 hours. Admission is $12 for adults, $6 for children 7 to 12, free for children 6 and under.

CENTRAL ADIRONDACKS   The wilderness in the heart of this region drew the likes of J. P. Morgan, Andrew Carnegie, and the Vanderbilts, who built elaborate rustic retreats, some accessible only by rail, during the Gilded Age. The Vanderbilts' estate, **Great Camp Sagamore,** 4 miles south of Raquette Lake (© **315/354-5311;** www. sagamore.org), is open to the public and is a spectacular achievement in rustic craftsmanship. Their 27-building summer retreat for more than 50 years even included a bowling alley.

Just about everything there is to learn about the Adirondacks can be absorbed at the **Adirondack Museum,** Route 30, Blue Mountain Lake, off routes 28 and 30 (© **518/ 352-7311;** www.adirondackmuseum.org), which celebrated its 50th birthday in 2007. History buffs will love the collection that traces the transportation, tourism, and past of the region, as well as a rundown of its flora and fauna. A couple of odd items—a canoe big enough to camp in, a bark-covered outhouse—will appeal to everyone, and the setting, overlooking **Blue Mountain Lake,** is spectacular. Allow 3 hours to see the exhibits and grounds, and bring a picnic lunch to enjoy the view. Admission is $15 adults, $8 children 7 to 17. It's open from Memorial Day weekend to mid-October.

THE SOUTHEASTERN REGION   James Fenimore Cooper had Lake George and environs in mind when he penned *Last of the Mohicans.* This area, once a battle zone, then a busy 18th-century port, and later a getaway for the elite, is now a lively, family-friendly vacation spot in summer and a sleepy, though lovely, destination in winter. There's historic Fort William Henry, kitschy arcades, minigolf courses, a local rodeo, an amusement park, and accommodations galore. Lake George village hosts a range of events, such as Americade (a huge biker rally), the Adirondack Balloon Festival, and Jazz Fest.

For lake excursions, try the **Lake George Steamboat Company,** Steel Pier, Lake George (© **800/553-BOAT** [553-2628] or 518/668-5777; www.lakegeorgesteamboat. com), where you can choose from 1- to 4-hour narrated cruises with or without a meal on their steamship paddle-wheeler or one of the other two old-time ships. Lake George is also a gorgeous place to paddle, with crystal-clear, spring-fed waters and a wealth of islands and small bays; at 32 miles long, you'd be better off in a kayak if you want to do some serious exploring. Get a canoe or kayak from **Mountainman Outdoor Supply Company,** Route 28 in both Inlet and Old Forge (© **877/CANOE-NY** [226-6369] or 315/357-6672; www.mountainmanoutdoors.com).

Lovers of kitschy minigolf shouldn't miss **Around the World Golf,** Route 9 (© **518/ 668-3223**), where you can choose to putt around the U.S. (complete with graffiti under the Brooklyn Bridge) or the world (with the Egyptian pyramids and a Japanese garden).

Where to Stay

In addition to the numerous hotels, B&Bs, and motels in the Adirondacks, the State of New York has a number of campgrounds, including some on 44 of the islands in Lake George, accessible only by boat. For information (and reservations), visit **http://new yorkstateparks.reserveamerica.com**.

The exclusive **Lake Placid Lodge,** Whiteface Inn Road (© **877/523-2700** or 518/ 523-2700; www.lakeplacidlodge.com), is a Relais & Châteaux member set right on Lake Placid, with an upscale rustic look (*very* Adirondack) and lots of privacy. It's the kind of place that could get away with an air of snootiness, but there's none—you're in the woods, after all. The service is helpful and friendly, and staffers will bend over backward to make your stay perfect. Birch branches are everywhere, from the hallway ceilings to the cozy bar to the funky, woodsy furnishings in the (nonsmoking) guest rooms. In fact, all the furniture, made by local artists, is for sale. Rooms and bathrooms are large, luxurious, and comfortable, but the cabins afford the ultimate in privacy—most are set right on the lake's shore, with stone fireplaces, sitting areas, and picture windows. Rates run $550 double. Children 11 and under are not permitted.

Well-heeled travelers have been drawn to the **Sagamore,** 110 Sagamore Rd. (© **800/ 358-3585** or 518/644-9400; www.thesagamore.com), since 1883. Drive onto its personal 72-acre island and up to its Colonial-style main building, and you'll see why: peace, quiet, and luxury. Jutting out into Lake George, this private getaway serves up a wealth of water activities, a great golf course, a full spa, and lakeside lounging. The common-area decor is more formal than comfy; luckily, that stuffiness doesn't carry over to the helpful staff. The restored main-building rooms—done in flowery patterns and muted tones—have the same formal furniture, but bathrooms give you plenty of room to navigate. Suites, with two full rooms and some with views in two directions, are well worth the extra money. There are several buildings and price options. The contemporary "lodge" rooms are not actually in the lodge but, with balconies and fireplaces, offer the best bang for the buck. An eye-popping, privately owned castle is also for rent. All rooms are nonsmoking. Rates run $229 to $410 double.

The gorgeous 1870 Victorian that's home to the **Lake Champlain Inn,** 428 County Rte. 3, Ticonderoga (© **518/547-9942;** www.tlcinn.com), has a prime location on Lake Champlain, and its rooms offer views of the lake, the Adirondacks, and even Vermont's Green Mountains. You're also just 2 miles from the northern end of Lake George. While rooms aren't the biggest, their views are among the best in the park. And they boast nice touches like wrought-iron beds, claw-foot tubs, and original woodwork. The one suite

(Best) Cooperstown: Hall of Fame Moments

For aficionados of America's national pastime, a pilgrimage to the **Baseball Hall of Fame** in the charming town of Cooperstown, a 5-hour drive north of New York City, is a must; for everyone else—it's still worth a trip. Yes, you'll find plenty of statistics-spouting baseball fanatics walking around. But this museum isn't just for passionate lovers of the game or its collectibles. After all, this *is* America's pastime, and a walk through the 30,000 exhibits shows just how important this sport has been to America's past and present. The hall collected its first artifact in 1937, and now you can find baseballs, bats, uniforms, ballpark artifacts, priceless trading cards, and a microcosm of American history. You'll learn about the Negro Leagues and the integration of baseball, find out the president who established the tradition of throwing out the first pitch on opening day, and, of course, see some of the greatest moments of the greatest players ever.

A 3-year, $20-million renovation was completed in 2005, adding 10,000 square feet of exhibit space and new technology, so depending on how big a fan you are, you could spend anywhere from an hour to a full day (or more) browsing, learning, and loving the game.

For more information on the hall, call (©) **888/HALL-OF-FAME** (425-5633) or 607/547-7200, or surf the Internet to **www.baseballhalloffame.org**. Admission to the hall costs $17 adults, $6 for kids ages 7 to 12.

Cooperstown is easiest to get to by car. From the New York State Thruway, take exit 30 at Herkimer and go south on State Hwy. 28 or State Hwy. 80—both will take you to Cooperstown. The hall is located at 25 Main St.

gives you two adjoining rooms. You'll also find a house with two rooms, called the Schoolhouse, a large modern Victorian-style house that's very modern inside and sits on 130 acres. The adjacent state land is perfect for hiking or cross-country skiing. The entire property is nonsmoking, and none of the rooms have phones. Rates include full breakfast and run $95 to $135 double.

CORNING

Corning is a charming destination in New York's southern tier, surrounded by the beauty of the Finger Lakes region. Quite literally, it's the town that Corning built; the company, the original makers of Corningware, Pyrex, and now high-tech materials such as fiber optics, has employed as much as half the town's population. Corning was once known as "crystal city" for its concentration of glassworks, and today glass is at the center of the town's attractions, at the world-renowned Corning Museum of Glass.

Essentials

GETTING THERE Easily accessible by car from most points in the northeast, Corning is directly off **Route 17/I-86** and a straight shot along **Route 414** south of Watkins Glen; from the south, take **Route 15.**

(Best) **Barreling Around Niagara Falls**

Okay, let's ignore the wedding and honeymoon thing and focus on the water at one of the most visited attractions in the United States, which happens to be in western New York. It flows down the Niagara River, picking up speed, reaching speeds of up to 30 mph before tumbling, hundreds of thousands of gallons at a time, over the rocks of Niagara Falls. You can get the view with your toes just inches from both sets of falls, the American Falls and the Horseshoe Falls; you can also check them out from way up high, from your hotel room, or from down below, with the mist spraying up in your face.

On the American side, the **Niagara Tourism and Convention Corporation** is at 345 Third St., Ste. 605, Niagara Falls (© **877/FALLS-US** [325-5787] or 716/282-8992; www.niagara-usa.com). Office hours are Monday to Friday from 8:30am to 5pm. In Canada, **Niagara Falls Tourism,** 5400 Robinson St., Niagara Falls, Ontario (© **800/563-2557;** www.niagarafallstourism.com), is open June to August Monday to Friday from 8am to 5pm, Saturday and Sunday from 10am to 5pm; rest of the year 9am to 5pm daily. Several of the top falls attractions, like *Maid of the Mist* and Cave of the Winds, operate only when the ice has melted, which could be in April or as late as May. The season usually runs through October.

Start off in the **Niagara Falls State Park** (© 716/278-1796; www.niagara fallsstatepark.com), the oldest state park in the United States. Designed by Frederick Law Olmsted, it's also the best thing about the American side of the falls. In winter it's quiet and serene; the summer brings a crush of people. You can walk or ride the trolley ($2 adults, $1 kids 6–12; operates year-round) along its 3-mile route. Parking is $10. Walk out onto the newly renovated **Observation Tower,** which stretches into the river ($1; open late Mar to Dec).

In the park, visit **Cave of the Winds** ($10 adults, $7 kids), where you'll take an elevator down 175 feet and emerge onto boardwalks to walk around the base of the American falls. They'll give you a raincoat and sandals.

Accessible from the New York Observation Tower and from the Canadian side is the *Maid of the Mist* boat ride (© 716/284-8897; www.maidofthemist. com; Apr or May–Oct; $13 adults, $7.30 kids). Hands down, this is the coolest way to see the falls. Board this famous boat and chug upriver toward the roar of both the American and the Horseshoe Falls. You'll sail up the base of both, with the mist in your face. Don't worry, they'll provide the slicker to keep you dry. The downside: The trip is only 30 minutes, and the boat will be packed.

If you plan on doing several of the falls attractions, consider buying a pass. On the American side, the Park Service's **Passport to the Falls** (© 716/278-1796) will gain you up to 35% off the *Maid of the Mist,* Cave of the Winds, and other nearby attractions, plus unlimited free rides on the Niagara Scenic Trolley ($28 adults, $21 for ages 6–12). Pick up your pass at the visitor center inside the park.

located at 1 W. Market St., Corning (© **866/946-3386** or 607/936-6544; www.corning
fingerlakes.com). The **Chemung County Chamber of Commerce** is at 400 E. Church
St., Elmira (© **800/MARK-TWAIN** [627-5892]; www.chemungchamber.org).

Exploring Corning

The **Corning Museum of Glass,** I-86, exit 46 (© **607/937-5371;** www.cmog.org), is
the premier and most comprehensive collection of historical and art glass in the world.
It is, quite literally, dazzling. On view are 35,000 glass pieces representing 35 centuries
of glass craftsmanship, beginning with a piece dating from 1411 B.C. There is also a gallery of glass sculpture and a glass innovation center, with ingeniously designed exhibits
that depict the use of glass in technology. The museum is anything but static; it offers
hot-glass demonstrations, glassmaking workshops, and some of the best shopping to be
found, with a sprawling array of shops dealing in glass, crystal, and jewelry. The museum
is especially well designed for children, who usually can't get enough of the interactive
science exhibits and opportunities to handle telescopes and peer out a periscope that
"sees" from the building's roof. A walk-in glass workshop allows visitors to make their
very own glass souvenirs. The museum is open daily. Admission is $13 for adults, free for
children 18 and under. A $17 combination ticket for adults includes admission to
CMoG and the Rockwell Museum (see below). The museum operates a free shuttle
service from the museum to Market Street, downtown.

The **Rockwell Museum of Western Art,** 111 Cedar St. (© **607/937-5386;** www.
rockwellmuseum.org), which occupies the former city hall, maintains an excellent collection of both historical and contemporary Western and Native American art. An inviting
design of bold colors and gorgeous woods inside the shell of a neo-Romanesque building,
the museum features daring juxtapositions that work surprisingly well, including a number of fantastic pieces by Native Americans. A neat idea for children is the color-coded
"art backpacks," which come equipped with games and lesson and drawing books, making the museum an especially interactive place. The museum is open daily. Admission is
$6.50 for adults, $5.50 for children 6 to 17, and free for children 5 and under. Allow an
hour or two.

Where to Stay

The best accommodations in town are at the **Hillcrest Manor,** 227 Cedar St. (© **607/
936-4548;** www.corninghillcrestmanor.com), one of the finest B&Bs we've seen. The
grand 1890 Greek Revival mansion, with massive pillars, porches, and terraces, sits in a
quiet residential neighborhood up the hill from downtown Corning. Rooms are huge
and impeccably decorated with great, luxurious taste. The house features stately parlors,
an elegant candlelit dining room, and a palatial cedar stairway. Some rooms have fireplaces and immense tubs; all offer excellent value for the money. We could relax here for
days. Rates include full breakfast and run $145 double.

The large and well-run **Radisson Hotel Corning,** 125 Denison Pkwy. (© **800/
333-3333** or 607/962-5000; www.radisson.com/corningny), is the only full-service
hotel in downtown Corning, a reason for its popularity with business travelers, though
its pool and on-site restaurant also make it a good place for families and other leisure
travelers. Rooms are spacious and attractively appointed. Rates run $118 to $174
double.

THE MID-ATLANTIC

3

UPSTATE NEW YORK HIGHLIGHTS

ATLANTIC CITY

One of America's oldest seaside resorts, Atlantic City is most famous these days as a weekend gambler's mecca and a town that's in the midst of an impressive rebirth. To wit: The town's new slogan is "Atlantic City: Always Turned On." It's the East Coast's answer to Las Vegas, and home to many of the same names: Caesars, Bally's, the Tropicana. Tourists come by the millions (more than 35 million per year) to try their luck at the city's 11 casinos, eight of which line the world's first oceanfront boardwalk, opened in 1870. The city itself began life in 1854 and celebrated its 150th anniversary in 2004 with a lot of fanfare, and two more glittering mega-casinos are planned to rise along the Boardwalk in the next 5 years.

Despite its historic pedigree, Atlantic City went to seed post–World War II, abandoned in the wake of cheap, easy air travel to Florida and the Caribbean. In the 1970s, in a last-ditch effort to reinvigorate this once-proud Victorian vacation resort, the state of New Jersey instituted casino gambling—and though the unconventional urban-renewal plan has had its rough spots, the past 5 years have seen an influx of luxury that has added a younger, moneyed visitor to the Atlantic City mix. With options including glossy hotel rooms going for $600 a night, a Wolfgang Puck eatery, and a Gucci boutique, Atlantic City is more upscale than ever before.

The city is in the midst of a multibillion-dollar renewal plan that has resulted in sparkling new convention and visitor centers, new bus and train terminals, a new outlet mall complex, and a generally more cleaned-up appearance. The opening of the **Borgata** in 2003 added quite a bit of luster to the city's revitalization efforts. In 2004, the Tropicana launched the **Quarter,** an Old Havana–themed complex consisting of added hotel space, restaurants, retail venues, and an IMAX theater. Meanwhile, Caesars debuted the **Pier at Caesars,** a multimillion-dollar retail-and-entertainment complex featuring fabulous Coach, Baccarat, and Tiffany & Co. boutiques. And in 2008, the opening of the **Water Club,** the Borgata's "boutique style" sister property, gave the Marina District an added dash of sophistication.

Atlantic City clearly has Vegas aspirations: It hopes to reemerge as a *luxe* playground catering to adults and has already succeeded in ratcheting up its cool factor enormously. We've yet to see if the Boardwalk is going to be as successful as Sin City in integrating families to the mix of visitors (though plenty of families do take advantage of the beach); few kids are seen with parents at the casinos, though a new boutique hotel on the Boardwalk, the Chelsea, is very kid friendly.

And clearly, this isn't Vegas. There's not a lot to do beyond the casino hotels, shopping, and the beach, and though the neighborhood in the immediate vicinity of the Boardwalk is looking better nowadays, we still don't recommend walking around that area after dark. If you're with the kids, Cape May, or Ocean City, New Jersey, are better options: These shore towns are cleaner, quieter, and safer.

Still, if you're looking for glitz, you'll find it in A.C. (baby)!

Essentials

GETTING THERE   By Plane   You can fly into **Atlantic City International Airport** (© **609/645-7895;** www.acairport.com), 10 miles from downtown. **Mutual Taxi & Limousine Service** (© **609/345-6111**) can whisk you to your hotel from the terminal

Do Not Pass Go . . .

Monopoly was created in 1933 by Pennsylvanian Charles Darrow, who used the streets of Atlantic City as the basis for his game board.

for $35; another good option is **A1 Action Taxi, Van and Limos** (© **609/839-9797**). There are also several car-rental agencies with desks at the airport.

By Car Atlantic City is on the southern New Jersey shoreline, 60 miles southeast of Philadelphia and 120 miles south of New York City. From Philadelphia, take **I-76** to **State Road 42,** which connects to the Atlantic City Expressway. From Manhattan, take the Lincoln or Holland tunnels or the George Washington Bridge to the New Jersey Turnpike **(I-95)** south; pick up the **Garden State Parkway** at Perth Amboy and follow it south to exit 38, which connects to the **Atlantic City Expressway.**

By Bus A car isn't necessary here, so if you prefer not to drive, bus service is available from Philadelphia and New York (trip time: about 1¹/₂ hr. from Philly, 2 hr. from New York) via **Greyhound** (© **800/231-2222;** www.greyhound.com) and **NJ Transit** (© **973/275-5555;** www.njtransit.com). Buses arrive at the relatively new bus station adjacent to the Convention Center at Atlantic and Michigan avenues, 2 blocks from the Boardwalk. **Academy Bus Lines** (© **800/442-7272** or 800/992-0451; www.academybus.com) offers direct service from New York's Port Authority to a number of Boardwalk casinos.

Most Atlantic City casinos offer **bus packages,** which often include such value-added premiums as $20 in coins or free meals, from major Northeast cities—including New York, Philadelphia, Baltimore, Pittsburgh, and Washington, D.C.—aboard casino-direct charters. They generally cater to day visitors. Call the casinos directly, or check your local paper to learn about current offers (see "The Casinos," below).

By Train NJ Transit's Atlantic City line (© **973/275-5555;** www.njtransit.com) offers frequent service from Philadelphia (trip time: 1¹/₂ hr.). And a new NJ Transit **"ACES" train** is scheduled to start service from New York City to A.C. in late 2008, courtesy of the casinos, who teamed up to purchase eight rail cars that the transit authority will operate. The ACES train originates at Penn Station (trip time: 2¹/₂ hr.). There's a free shuttle bus from the station to the casinos.

VISITOR INFORMATION Contact the **Atlantic City Convention & Visitors Authority** (© **888/AC-VISIT** [228-4748] or 609/449-7130; www.atlanticcitynj.com), and request its free visitor's guide. Their website is easy to navigate and helpful in planning a trip.

The **Atlantic City Visitor Welcome Center,** right on the Atlantic City Expressway, makes an ideal first stop. You can't miss this state-of-the-art resource center at the city's gateway, open from 9am to 5pm daily and from 9am to 8pm summer weekends. Another welcome center is located on the Boardwalk right next to Boardwalk Hall at Mississippi Avenue. The staff at the centers can give you a good map, brochures, and answers to specific questions.

GETTING AROUND If you don't want to walk from casino to casino along the mile-long stretch of the Boardwalk where most of the action is, you can catch a ride in an old-fashioned **rolling chair.** These shaded surreys are rolled up and down the length of

THE MID-ATLANTIC

3

HIGHLIGHTS OF THE NEW JERSEY SHORE

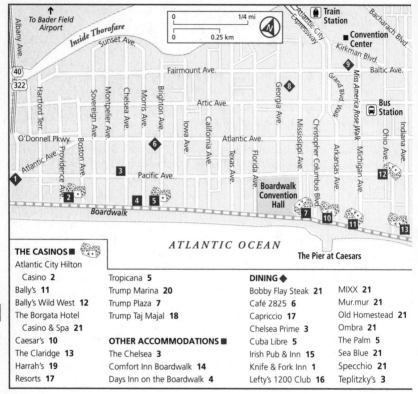

THE CASINOS ■

Atlantic City Hilton
  Casino **2**
Bally's **11**
Bally's Wild West **12**
The Borgata Hotel
  Casino & Spa **21**
Caesar's **10**
The Claridge **13**
Harrah's **19**
Resorts **17**

Tropicana **5**
Trump Marina **20**
Trump Plaza **7**
Trump Taj Majal **18**

OTHER ACCOMMODATIONS ■

The Chelsea **3**
Comfort Inn Boardwalk **14**
Days Inn on the Boardwalk **4**

DINING ◆

Bobby Flay Steak **21**
Café 2825 **6**
Capriccio **17**
Chelsea Prime **3**
Cuba Libre **5**
Irish Pub & Inn **15**
Knife & Fork Inn **1**
Lefty's 1200 Club **16**

MIXX **21**
Mur.mur **21**
Old Homestead **21**
Ombra **21**
The Palm **5**
Sea Blue **21**
Specchio **21**
Teplitzky's **3**

the Boardwalk by experienced guides, who are out soliciting riders day and night. The fee is based on the distance traveled, but expect a minimum fare of $5 plus tip.

You can also travel between the casinos along Pacific Avenue, which runs parallel to the Boardwalk 1 block inland, aboard the **Atlantic City Jitney** (©️ **609/344-8642;** www. jitneys.net), a fleet of minibuses that run 24 hours a day; the fare is $1.50. The baby-blue or green versions run to the Marina section of the city, where the Trump Marina and Harrah's casinos are located.

The Casinos

The casino hotels are Atlantic City's big draw, luring visitors to spend nearly $5 billion in 2007. First on the Boardwalk was **Resorts,** at Pennsylvania Avenue (©️ **800/336-6378** or 609/344-6000; www.resortsac.com), which boasts a sharp new look, thanks to a stylish $50-million renovation. It's bright, casual, and colorful, with a beachy vibe and an active showroom with top-flight rock, country, and pop headliners. Next door is Donald Trump's **Trump Taj Mahal,** at Virginia Avenue (©️ **800/825-8888** or 609/449-1000; www.trumptaj.com). With its *Arabian Nights* architecture, the Taj has a fun, funky vibe, and swanky, modern new rooms and amenities in its upscale **Chairman Tower,** which opened in Fall 2008 (see www.thenewtaj.com).

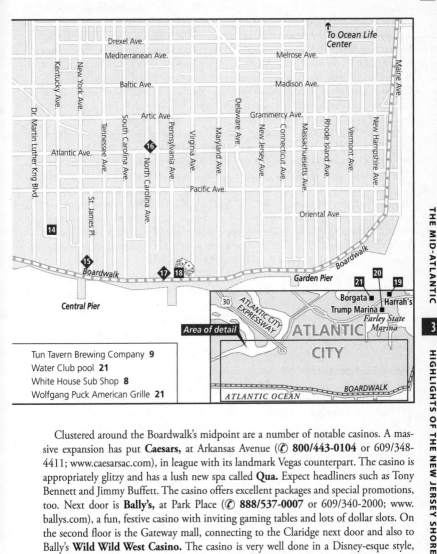

Tun Tavern Brewing Company **9**
Water Club pool **21**
White House Sub Shop **8**
Wolfgang Puck American Grille **21**

Clustered around the Boardwalk's midpoint are a number of notable casinos. A massive expansion has put **Caesars,** at Arkansas Avenue (📞 800/443-0104 or 609/348-4411; www.caesarsac.com), in league with its landmark Vegas counterpart. The casino is appropriately glitzy and has a lush new spa called **Qua.** Expect headliners such as Tony Bennett and Jimmy Buffett. The casino offers excellent packages and special promotions, too. Next door is **Bally's,** at Park Place (📞 888/537-0007 or 609/340-2000; www.ballys.com), a fun, festive casino with inviting gaming tables and lots of dollar slots. On the second floor is the Gateway mall, connecting to the Claridge next door and also to Bally's **Wild Wild West Casino.** The casino is very well done in a Disney-esque style, with faux red rocks and audio-animatronic figures (though we have to wonder about its obvious kid appeal, given the casino's stance on discouraging kids from entering).

All that glitters isn't gold at **Trump Plaza,** at Mississippi Avenue (📞 800/677-7378 or 609/441-6000; www.trumpplaza.com), but it sure is shiny. Behind the glitz, this is an Everyman's casino. The showroom often showcases big-name stars.

The **Tropicana,** at Brighton and the Boardwalk (📞 800/THE-TROP [843-8767]; www.tropicana.net), has undergone a revitalization with its "Quarter at Tropicana" addition. This glossy new shopping and dining complex with an Old Havana theme even has an IMAX theater (and a bluemercury Spa). The addition added 500 new hotel rooms, and some of the casino's old rooms have been updated. The Palm steakhouse and Carmine's, a classic Italian spot, are good dining options for families here.

Farther down, at the cleanest and quietest end of the Boardwalk, is the **Atlantic City Hilton** (© 800/257-8677 or 609/347-7111; www.hiltonac.com). The Hilton does what Atlantic City's other casino hotels don't dare (lest you leave the casino, of course): It provides full beach services to its guests, including beach chairs, cabanas, kayaks, on-the-sand volleyball, and more. It also features a headliner showroom and some surprisingly comfy rooms. It's hands-down the best casino for those who'd like to play at the beach and/or bring the kids, before returning to high-quality rooms.

At Farley State Marina, a quick drive from the Boardwalk via Brigantine Boulevard (Rte. 87), are three more casinos. **Harrah's** (© 800/HARRAHS [427-7247] or 609/441-5000; www.harrahs.com) has just unveiled a $550-million expansion that includes more than 900 new rooms, giving it a younger and hipper vibe; its sleek new Elizabeth Arden Spa, plus "the Pool," a Vegas-like scene with alfresco bars and cabanas, have added to its attractions. **Trump Marina** (© 800/777-8477 or 609/441-2000; www.trumpmarina. com) targets a younger crowd with rock-'n'-roll Muzak and headliners, but it otherwise seems like just another glittery Trump property. The best of the bunch is the **Borgata Casino Hotel & Spa** (see the box "A Vegas Resort in Atlantic City Expands!", below) and its more sophisticated (and brand-new) sister, the Water Club.

IN THE SHOWROOMS On any given night, Atlantic City's showrooms are peopled with acts ranging from Chris Rock and Aerosmith to Alicia Keys and Ringo Starr's All-Starr Band—and the quality just keeps getting better. Check with the visitor bureau at © 888/AC-VISIT (228-4748) or www.atlanticcitynj.com, or contact the casinos directly for current schedules. You can also find out what's on and buy tickets through **Ticketmaster** (© 856/338-9000; www.ticketmaster.com).

More to See & Do

The city has the usual tourist traps, but there are a number of places worth your time. At Gardner's Basin, at the top end of New Hampshire Avenue, is the **Ocean Life Center** (© 609/348-2880; www.oceanlifecenter.com), with the **Atlantic City Aquarium** (including a touch tank), shipwreck artifacts, and more marine-themed fun for the kids. You can't miss the **Absecon Lighthouse,** 31 S. Rhode Island Ave. (© 609/449-1360; www.abseconlighthouse.org), which was built in 1857 and is the tallest in New Jersey. On a clear day, it's worth climbing the 228 steps to the top to get a magnificent view of the Jersey shoreline. The free **Atlantic City Historical Museum,** New Jersey Avenue and the Boardwalk (© 609/344-1943; www.acmuseum.org), offers some interesting insights into the city's history through various exhibits and artifacts (including a larger-than-life Mr. Peanut). Do check out the interesting video that plays continuously in the museum. If you can make it through the crowds on the Boardwalk, skip the tattoo parlors and head north to **Steel Pier,** 1000 Boardwalk (© 609/345-4893), a classic amusement park with a Ferris wheel, bumper cars, games galore, and, of course, classic junk food such as funnel cake. Another hard-to-miss attraction is in nearby Margate: **Lucy the Elephant,** 9200 Atlantic Ave. (© 609/823-6473; www.lucytheelephant.org), is a 65-ton building built to look like—yep, you guessed it—an elephant. Built in 1881 and listed on the National Register of Historic Places, this is one of those curious pieces of Americana that you just don't see too much of anymore, so go ahead and take the 30-minute tour of its interior.

(Best) A Vegas Resort in Atlantic City Expands!

The multibillion-dollar **Borgata Hotel Casino & Spa,** One Borgata Way (☎ **866/ 692-6742;** www.theborgata.com), which debuted to great acclaim in summer 2003, is the undisputed champ of the city's casino hotels. And in 2008, it unveiled a 43-story, $400-million new addition: The **Water Club** is an ultraglam "boutique-style" tower with its own glossy pool and cabana scene where you can sip cocktails, flirt, and snack (guests also get full use of the Borgata's facilities). Perhaps the best compliment we can give these two celeb favorites— joint ventures of Boyd Gaming and MGM MIRAGE—is that they the only ones in Atlantic City to remind us of Vegas. The decor at each property is sleek and beautiful: The Borgata has a magnificent lobby with Dale Chihuly chandeliers and a lovely "Living Room" seating area for guests to relax in; the Water Club is an Asian Zen wonder with a top-floor spa that has to-die-for views of the ocean. The facilities are so extensive (fitness centers; spas; pools; classic barbershop; immense casino with reasonable table limits; and multiple retail, entertainment, and dining venues), you won't want to leave. The large rooms ($129–$509 double, $379–$679 at the Water Club) are luxurious, the nicest in town: Think Egyptian cotton sheets on the comfy beds; plenty of lighting; designer toiletries; fridges (minibars in the Water Club); and immense marble bathrooms, a separately enclosed toilet, and a huge, two-person temperature-controlled shower encased entirely in marble. The suites ($209–$18,000) are even more luxurious.

Dining here is the best of the casino hotels as well (you'll need to reserve well in advance to get in on the weekends). For Italian, there's **Specchio,** which features modern Italian cuisine in an upscale dining room loaded with cherrywood and the chef's antique mirror collection, and **Ombra,** a fabulous wine bar (over 14,000 bottles) with a vaulted Italian brick ceiling. If beef is more your thing, head to the branch of New York's famous **Old Homestead,** where superb steaks are served amid modern ambience. There's also chic **SeaBlue,** designed by Adam Tihany as a backdrop for chef Michael Mina's haute seafood menu (including 2-lb. Maine lobster potpie); **Wolfgang Puck's American Grille,** where the celebrated celebrity chef produces his signature Spago-style gourmet pizzas as well as an excellent grilled steak with blue cheese; and **Bobby Flay Steak,** where classic chopped salads and gigantic rib-eyes are as excellent as you would expect from the Food Network star. For mingling, hit the **Water Club pool,** or head to **MIXX,** a trendy restaurant/nightclub where the food is Latin-Asian fusion and the music is hip; for late-night partying, there's **mur.mur,** a sleek lounge with pricey bottle service starting at 10pm and lasting until morning, of course. (This is a casino, after all.)

If shopping is more your thing, you'll find plenty of souvenir shops on the Boardwalk and boutiques in many of the hotels; there are also some affordable but chic stores such as **White House/Black Market** in the Quarter at Tropicana.

Die-hard fashionistas will want to head straight to the **Pier at Caesar's** (www.thepier-atcaesars.com), an upscale retail mecca far more glamorous than could have been imagined here a decade ago. Here you'll find the jewels of **Tiffany & Co.,** the handbags and gorgeous luggage at **Louis Vuitton,** and men's and women's clothing and accessories at **Burberry. It's Sugar** is a wonderland of a candy store where there's even a replica of Lucy the Elephant made of millions of jelly beans.

Check out the Atlantic City Outlets—the **Walk,** at Michigan and Arctic avenues (© **609/343-0387;** www.acoutlets.com), is a welcome shopping, dining, and entertainment venue, with excellent Banana Republic, Gap, and Calvin Klein outlets. For the city's famous saltwater taffy (discovered here in 1883 after an ocean storm flooded a candy store), head straight to **James Salt Water Taffy,** 1519 Boardwalk (© **609/344-1519;** www.jamescandy.com), which has been in business since 1880; those whose tastes run more to chocolate should make a beeline for **Steel's Fudge,** 1633 Boardwalk (© **888/783-3571;** www.steelsfudge.com), the oldest continually operated fudge company in the world.

Where to Stay

There's no useful way to quote exact room rates at Atlantic City's casino hotels (see "The Casinos," above). Doubles vary from a low of about $95 to a high of $500 (or more at the new towers), and the hotels stay generally competitive across-the-board. Rates are usually highest on summer weekends and lowest midweek in winter, but they can go through the roof during certain events or if there's a major convention in town. Rooms in the summer are especially hard to come by at the newer resorts such as the Borgata. Always ask about packages and special promotions, which may be able to save you big bucks. And if you plan to visit again, sign up for the casino hotel's free slot clubs—members often get special rates and packages.

A fantastic new addition to A.C.'s hotel scene is the boutique hotel the **Chelsea,** at Chelsea and Pacific avenues (© **800/548-3030;** www.thechelsea-ac.com). From the smart, stylish team that owns Congress Hall hotel in Cape May, the Chelsea is a cool makeover of a former HoJo and Holiday Inn, which have been transformed into 300 modern rooms with a Miami-meets-L.A. vibe. It features a sprawling lounge space with two lushly landscaped pools, chic restaurants, and beach cabanas. *Bonus:* It's kid-friendly. Expect to pay from $100 to $400 per night. It's right on the Boardwalk.

If the big hotels are too expensive, you have some noncasino options. A few good motels are right on or just off the Boardwalk—although they can be subject to similarly dramatic pricing, with rates fluctuating between $64 and $310; always ask about packages. The **Days Inn on the Boardwalk,** 1 block over at Morris Avenue (© **800/325-2525** or 609/344-6101; www.atlanticcitydaysinn.com), has rooms with ocean views. Just off the Boardwalk, near the Sands, is the **Comfort Inn Boardwalk,** 154 S. Kentucky Ave. (© **800/228-5150** or 609/348-4000; www.comfortinn.com), whose well-kept rooms feature Jacuzzi tubs.

Where to Dine

If you're looking for something more sophisticated than theme restaurants (they are all over the Boardwalk), take heart. Under new ownership, the **Knife & Fork Inn,** Atlantic and Pacific avenues (© **609/344-1133;** www.knifeandforkinn.com), in its revamped, iconic Tudor brick structure that once housed a men's club, has a glam charm again, and where better to indulge in A.C. classics such as lobster thermidor?

For a romantic night out with Atlantic City flavor, head to **Lefty's 1200 Club** ((C) 609/348-5677), an old-style supper club featuring terrific Italian cuisine, seafood, and steaks served by a friendly staff. Housed in a historic 19th-century building, the club sports an elegant Renaissance theme and features live music in the nightclub in back.

The casual **Tun Tavern Brewing Company,** at the corner of Baltic and Michigan avenues ((C) 609/347-7800; www.tuntavern.com), serves upscale pub grub and first-rate microbrews in a festive, modern setting.

The best casino dining is at the **Borgata Hotel** and **Water Club** in the Marina District (see the box "A Vegas Resort in Atlantic City Expands!", above, for the lowdown on the hotel's best restaurants). A few other standouts are worth mentioning. **Cuba Libre** ((C) 609/348-6700; www.cubalibrerestaurant.com), in the Quarter at Tropicana, combines a cool Old Havana decor with spicy seviche, guava BBQ ribs, gaucho steak, *camarones* (shrimp) enchiladas, and the most refreshing mojitos this side of Miami; there's even salsa dancing. The **Palm** ((C) 609/344-7256; www.thepalm.com), also in the Quarter, draws a high-rolling, high-heeled, Armani-wearing crowd who like their caricatures on the walls—and great porterhouses the size of a Louis Vuitton handbag. **Capriccio,** the Italian jewel at Resorts ((C) 609/344-6000), has received Zagat's award of excellence for its array of pastas, seafood, and specialties such as *osso buco.* **Café 2825,** at 2825 Atlantic Ave., is classic, upscale Italian, with excellent homemade pasta and a posh crowd ((C) 609/344-6913). And the new restaurants at the Chelsea hotel, including **Chelsea Prime** and **Teplitzky's,** are sleek takes on the Frank Sinatra glory days of Atlantic City in the 1950s ((C) 800/548-3030).

The **Irish Pub & Inn,** just off the Boardwalk at 164 St. James Place ((C) 609/344-9063; www.theirishpub.com), is a true Atlantic City gem. It's appealingly old-fashioned, with friendly service and hearty fare that's the best cheap eats in town (nothing more than $7.95). Rooms above the pub are also a steal: Rates range from $25 (yes, $25) to $80 a night. And no Atlantic City visit is complete without a visit to the **White House Sub Shop,** 2301 Arctic Ave. ((C) 609/345-8599), where you will stand in line (so worth it) for one of its legendary immense sandwiches. Everyone from presidents to celebrities has sought out these yummy creations.

CAPE MAY

At the southern tip of the Garden State is the jewel of the Jersey shore: Cape May, a beautifully preserved Victorian beach resort that's popular with romance-seeking couples drawn by the impeccably restored inns and quaint vibe, and families that like the town's easygoing nature and fine collection of affordable beachfront motels. Visiting Cape May is like taking a step back in time to the glory days of the Jersey shore, before frenetic amusement piers and summer-break college crowds overtook the scene. Even at the height of the summer season, the town stays relaxed and friendly; after a lazy day at the beach, most folks' big activity is to retire to a wide veranda, glass of iced tea in hand, to sit back and watch the world stroll by.

Essentials

GETTING THERE & GETTING AROUND   Cape May, a spit stretching 20 miles offshore between the Atlantic Ocean and Delaware Bay, is at the southern tip of New Jersey, about 40 miles south of the Atlantic City Toll Plaza at the end of the Garden State Parkway. **NJ Transit** buses ((C) 973/275-5555; www.njtransit.com) arrive from Philadelphia and Atlantic City year-round, and from New York City in summer. If you're arriving from points south, you can take the 70-minute **Cape May–Lewes Ferry** (© **800/64-FERRY** [643-3779]; www.capemaylewesferry.com), which carries passengers and vehicles between Lewes, Delaware, and Cape May daily year-round (car fare costs $29–$34 one-way; passengers pay $3.75–$9.50).

Cape May can become quite traffic congested, and parking is hard to come by, particularly in summer, so most visitors park their cars for the length of their stay and walk or trolley around town. If you'd like to rent a bike or a four-wheeled surrey for two or for the entire family, stop into **Shields' Bike Rentals,** 11 Gurney St., just inland from Beach Drive (© **609/898-1818**), or the **Village Bicycle Shop,** 605 Lafayette St. (© **609/884-8500**). You can reserve in advance from **Cape Island Bicycle Center,** at Beach and Howard streets (© **609/898-7368;** www.capeislandbikerentals.com). Rentals start at $10 a day for a single-speed bicycle.

VISITOR INFORMATION   For more information, contact the **Chamber of Commerce of Greater Cape May** (© **609/884-5508;** www.capemaychamber.com), or the **Cape May County Chamber of Commerce** (© **609/465-7181;** www.capemaycounty-chamber.com). Information is also available online at **www.capemay.com**. A staffed **information center** is at the Ocean View Plaza Rest Area, 1½ miles beyond the Garden State Parkway's Cape May Toll Plaza. The chamber of commerce runs an excellent **visitor center** a few minutes' drive south, at exit 11 (on the right side of the road after the traffic light).

SPECIAL EVENTS & FESTIVALS   Highlights include the **Cape May Music Festival,** which draws distinguished classical performers from around the globe over 6 weeks in May and June; the **Cape May Food & Wine Festival,** where open-house food samplings at dozens of participating restaurants consume the better part of a week in late September; hugely popular **Victorian Week** in mid-October, celebrating the town's heritage with historic house tours and other nostalgic events; and **Christmas in Cape May,** a whole host of holiday-themed events (including special candlelight house tours) that start in mid-November. For more information on all of these events, call © **609/884-5404** or head online to **www.capemaymac.org**.

Exploring Cape May

One of the best ways to explore Cape May is to take one of the many **trolley tours** offered by the **Mid-Atlantic Center for the Arts (MAC),** Cape May's premier preservation organization (© **800/275-4278** or 609/884-5404; www.capemaymac.org). You can buy tickets at the booth at the entrance to the Washington Street Mall, at Ocean Street; tours generally run a half-hour to 45 minutes and concentrate on a specific area of town, so you may want to take more than one. They cost $10 for adults, $7 for children 3 to 12. MAC also offers **walking tours, train tours,** and **self-guided audio tours.**

Cape May's top attraction is the **Emlen Physick Estate,** 1048 Washington St. (© **609/884-5404**), a beautifully restored Victorian house museum. You can see the entire house on a great 45-minute living history tour, which can be combined with a trolley tour. In the carriage house on the estate is the **Carriage House Cafe,** serving lunch and elegant afternoon tea. Afternoon tea costs $19 per person. Call MAC for reservations.

The **Cape May Carriage Co.** (© **609/884-4466;** www.capemaycarriage.com) offers half-hour guided tours ($10 adults, $5 kids 2–11) in old-fashioned horse-drawn carriages that leave from Ocean Street and Washington Mall.

At the heart of town is the **Washington Street Mall,** 401 Washington St. (© **609/884-0555;** www.washingtonstreetmall.com), a 3-block-long pedestrian mall lined with clothing and gift boutiques. A block over from the mall is **Caroline,** 400 Carpenters Lane (© **609/884-5055**), a first-rate clothing boutique for women with lines such as Three Dot and Michael Stars. Another top shopping stop is **39 Degrees,** 251 Beach Ave. (© **609/884-6677**), in the Congress Hall hotel, which offers great casual dresses by Lilly Pulitzer, plus hip clothes for men. For a list of local antiques dealers, go online to **www. capemay.com**, or stop by one of the visitor centers listed above and ask for the *Antique Shops of Cape May* map.

No visit to Cape May is complete without a round of minigolf. The best local course is **Cape May Miniature Golf,** between Jackson and Perry streets (© **609/884-2222**).

BEACHES & NATURAL ATTRACTIONS   The big draws in summer are Cape May's calm waters and wide, white sandy beaches. The beach is accessible all along **Beach Drive,** with concessions and public restrooms available near Convention Hall (at Stockton Place) and at various points along the Promenade. In summer, **beach tags** are required on all Cape May beaches; virtually all inns and motels will provide beach tags (currently $4 per day, $13 per week, free for kids 11 and under) to their guests.

Locals usually head to **Sunset Beach** at Cape May Point (take W. Perry St. to Sunset Blvd.), which has a nice swimming cove, easy parking, and a beach grill. It's worth visiting any time of year to see the *Atlantus,* one of 12 experimental concrete ships built during World War I. Needless to say, this was not a good idea; the curious ship ran aground in 1926, and its remains poke through the waves just offshore.

The area's best beach is 2 miles south of town, at **Cape May Point State Park** (© **609/ 884-2159;** www.state.nj.us/dep/parksandforests), also accessible via Sunset Boulevard (turn left on Lighthouse Ave.). The quiet, noncommercial crescent of white sand has restrooms but no concessions, so pack a picnic. You can climb to the top of **Cape May Lighthouse** (© **609/884-5404;** www.capemaymac.org), the second-tallest operating lighthouse in the United States, for breathtaking coastline views. It's a grueling (and very narrow) 199 steps (about 14 1/2 stories), but exhibits give you an excuse to rest at various points along the way. Admission costs $5 for adults, $2 for children 11 and under. The park also has 3 miles of **hiking trails** through wetlands (some wheelchair accessible), which are great for birders.

Avid birders will want to visit the **Cape May Migratory Bird Refuge,** just before the park turnoff on Sunset Boulevard. This 212-acre refuge is one of the East Coast's premier birding areas. Call the New Jersey Audubon Society's **Cape May Bird Observatory** (© **609/884-2736**) for more information.

Where to Stay

Cape May has dozens of wonderful places to stay, ranging from small, lovely inns to grand hotels. Rates tend to fluctuate dramatically, even for different rooms in the same inn, so it's worth calling around. Rates are generally lowest in winter and highest over holiday and summer weekends. Most include both breakfast and afternoon tea. Many establishments require minimum stays in season and book up far in advance for the summer months.

Many of Cape May's historic homes have been wonderfully restored and converted into B&Bs. The **Mainstay Inn,** 635 Columbia Ave. (© **609/884-8690;** www.mainstay inn.com), housed in an immaculate 1872 Italianate villa, is widely regarded as the town's finest inn. Rates run from $175 to $360 double (the inn is open Apr–Nov). Nonguests can visit the main house by self-guided tour; call for details.

(Best) Simple, Relaxed Luxury

The most stylishly modernized of the Cape May grand hotels is **Congress Hall,** 251 Beach Ave. (© **888/941-1816** or 609/884-8421; www.congresshall.com). Its motto, "Simple, relaxed luxury," is apparent everywhere from the chic lobby with its yellow walls, sisal carpet, and black wicker furnishings to its sunny guest rooms with gaily striped carpets and Frette linens. In winter or summer, its zebra-carpeted **Brown Room** lounge is a perfect setting for a glass of wine and a good book (or a flirtation), and its pool and beachfront setting make the hotel the most desirable place for both couples and families. A huge colonnaded porch overlooks the lawn and ocean, and many rooms have balconies. Rooms range from $115 to $450 double.

The **Fairthorne,** 111 Ocean St. (© **800/438-8742** or 609/884-8791; www.fairthorne. com), is my favorite. This gorgeous Colonial Revival–style old sailing captain's home is impeccable without being too frilly or formal, and hosts Diane and Ed Hutchinson couldn't be more welcoming. Doubles run $230 to $265; a suite goes for $280. Around the corner is the **John F. Craig House,** 609 Columbia Ave. (© **877/544-0314** or 609/884-0100; www.johnfcraig.com), a beautifully restored Carpenter Gothic inn with a cozy, homey vibe. (*Warning:* Some rooms have tiny bathrooms.) Doubles and suites cost $145 to $265.

If you consider B&Bs too personal, consider the small, chic **Virginia Hotel,** 25 Jackson St. (© **800/732-4236** or 609/884-5700; www.virginiahotel.com), a large Victorian that's been a full-service hotel since 1879. Fresh off a complete renovation, rooms sport such modern, luxurious amenities as Bulgari toiletries, CD players, and bathrobes; doubles run $235 to $425. Or opt for the attractive and well-outfitted 32-unit, four-building complex known as the **Queen Victoria Bed & Breakfast,** 102 Ocean St. (© **609/ 884-8702;** www.queenshotel.com), whose innkeepers emphasize privacy and keep rates ($105–$495 double) low.

Beach Drive is lined with value-priced motels—all with pools—that are ideal for those who prefer to avoid the fussiness of historic properties. A good choice is **La Mer Beachfront Motor Inn,** 1317 Beach Dr. (© **609/884-9000;** www.lamermotorinn.com), whose new addition features comfortable rooms ($76–$369) that are big enough for budget-minded families. The rooms in the older building are cheaper but not nearly as spiffy. One floor is set aside solely for adults—a good choice for couples looking for peace and quiet. The **Marquis de Lafayette,** 501 Beach Ave. (© **609/884-3500**), has groovy architecture and sits right on the beach, with simple motel-style rooms and a huge pool. Pets are welcome (rates $109–$519). We're also fans of the **Montreal Inn,** Beach Drive at Madison Avenue (© **800/525-7011;** www.montreal-inn.com; rates $63–$369). The Hirsch family, who built the old-school beach motel in the mid-1960s, still runs it and keeps it in impeccable shape. They offer several styles of rooms, from doubles to suites with kitchens.

Where to Dine

Cape May boasts an excellent, if pricey, collection of restaurants. The best casual seafood joint is the rollicking, indoor-outdoor **Lobster House,** Fisherman's Wharf, Route 109

(© **609/884-8296**), where you dine on fresh steamed clams, crab cakes, or "port and
starboard" (surf and turf) on a dock overlooking the harbor, and have cocktails on the
restaurant's own schooner, the *America.*

If you're a seafood lover, drop your anchor at **Axelsson's Blue Claw Restaurant,** 991
Ocean Dr. (© **609/884-5878;** www.blueclawrestaurant.com), with its sophisticated
decor, nautical-style bar, and ocean views. The restaurant offers some great meat selections, but it's the fresh seafood (crab cakes, lobster tail) that draws diners. Start your meal
off with one of the many martini options and cap it with one of the excellent desserts
and specialty coffees.

Among Cape May's finest is the elegant **Washington Inn,** 801 Washington St., at
Jefferson Street (© **609/884-5697;** www.washingtoninn.com), whose winning New
American Cuisine includes such classics as rack of lamb and filet mignon, complemented
by faultless service and a super-romantic setting. Its 10,000-bottle wine list is the largest
in the region.

For classics such as clams casino, shrimp cocktail, and thick-cut steaks, head to the
Merion Inn, 106 Decatur St., at Columbia Avenue (© **609/884-8363;** www.merion
inn.com), somewhat less expensive than the Washington Inn but no less romantic. This
dimly lit, old-world restaurant features several theme rooms (we like the porch ones best)
and has an excellent mahogany bar with a jazz pianist in summer.

Island Grill, 311 Mansion St. (© **609/884-0200**), is a great addition to the local
dining scene. It's run by a mother-daughter team and has a beachy Key West feel, set in
a pretty old house with a modern decor and great pastas (like chicken and penne in
white-wine sauce) and just-caught fish; most entrees are under $22. It's a kid-friendly
place (coloring on the white-paper tablecloths) and it's BYOB.

For more affordable eats, a yellow striped awning signals the **Mad Batter,** 19 Jackson
St., just off Carpenters Lane (© **609/884-5970;** www.madbatter.com), a comfortable,
casual restaurant specializing in made-from-scratch breakfasts; fresh, leafy salads at lunch;
and unfussy European-style entrees at dinner (Mediterranean shrimp pasta, for example).
Several vegetarian options are always offered, and there's a sizeable selection of moderately priced wines (several available by the glass). On the Washington Mall, **Jackson
Mountain Café,** 400 Washington Ave. (© **609/884-5648**), is an easy place to grab a
good Philly cheesesteak, a burger, or a nice salad, and they've also added some excellent
raw bar selections such as jumbo shrimp.

If you want a quick, inexpensive lunch, your best bet is the **Depot Market Cafe,** 409
Elmira St., next to the Village Bike Shop on Ocean Street (© **609/884-8030**), an ultra-
casual sandwich shop with homemade everything and a pleasing alfresco patio.

5 PHILADELPHIA

Much of the story of America begins in Philadelphia in those revolutionary, horsefly-
filled days of the late 18th century: The Founding Fathers signed the Declaration of
Independence here (on July 4, 1776), managed the Revolutionary War, established the
U.S. Constitution (1787), and then governed the country until Washington, D.C., was
built (1793). Today you can view the Liberty Bell that proclaimed America's freedom
(and eventually cracked); Independence Hall, where these documents were signed, and
dozens of other historic treasures that fill the largest Colonial district in the country—as
well as newer, glossier tribute museums such as the National Constitution Center.

You'll find a lot more than history in Philadelphia. Its smart Center City core is a stroller's paradise and a working urban environment, with restored Georgian and Federal structures, sleek shops, and chic restaurants. Broad Street south of City Hall has been reconstituted as a first-class "Avenue of the Arts"; it's anchored by the Kimmel Center for the Performing Arts (home of the Philadelphia Orchestra), and two gleaming sports centers at the avenue's end. Though it is often referred to as "New York's 6th borough" (because of its proximity), the City of Brotherly Love is its own fiercely independent town—filled with art, dining, music, shopping, a vibrant "Gayborhood," and, of course, history for every age and taste.

ESSENTIALS

GETTING THERE By Plane Philadelphia International Airport (© 215/937-6937; www.phl.org) is at the southwest corner of the city. For up-to-the-minute flight information, call © **800/PHL-GATE** (745-4283). Thirty airlines are spread throughout seven terminals, with a shopping mall and food court between terminals B and C. You can pick up taxis and shuttles outside each terminal.

A **taxi** from the airport to Center City takes about 20 minutes and costs a flat rate of $26 plus tip, usually with a maximum of three passengers.

Airport limousine and shuttle services are provided by **Philadelphia Airport Shuttle** (© **215/333-1441**), **Lady Liberty** (© **215/724-8888**), or **Deluxe Limo** (© **215/463-8787**), for $8 to $20 from the airport to Center City. Philadelphia Airport Shuttle charges $175 from the airport to Atlantic City, New Jersey (p. 140).

By Train Amtrak (© **800/USA-RAIL** [872-7245]; www.amtrak.com) serves Philadelphia's **30th Street Station,** 1 N. 30th St. (© **215/349-3196;** www.30thstreetstation. com). There's frequent service from New York (trip time: 1¹/₂ hr.), Washington (1³/₄–2 hr.), and Boston (5¹/₂–7 hr.).

SEPTA commuter trains (© **215/580-7800;** www.septa.org) connect 30th Street Station and several Center City stations to Trenton, New Jersey, and Delaware. **New Jersey Transit** (© **800/772-2222;** www.njtransit.com) operates commuter trains from New York and Newark to Trenton, where you can switch to the Philadelphia-bound SEPTA train.

SEPTA also runs a **high-speed rail link** (R1), offering direct service between the airport and Center City; trains depart daily every 30 minutes from 5:09am to 12:09am from raised pedestrian bridges at the terminals. Trains to the airport depart from Market East (near the Convention Center), Suburban Station at 16th Street, and 30th Street Station. The 30-minute trip costs $5.50 for adults, $1.50 weekdays and 75¢ weekends for children ages 5 to 11, free for children 4 and under, and $17 for families (off-peak hours and holidays only).

By Car Philadelphia is some 300 miles from Boston and 100 miles from New York City. If you think of Center City as a rectangle, **I-95** whizzes by its bottom and right sides; **I-276,** the Pennsylvania Turnpike, is the top edge; and **I-76** splits off and snakes along the Schuylkill River along the left side into town. **I-676** traverses Center City under Vine Street, connecting I-76 to adjacent Camden, New Jersey, via the Ben Franklin Bridge ($3 inbound only) over the Delaware River. The "Blue Route" of **I-476** forms a left edge for the suburbs, about 15 miles west of town, connecting I-276 and I-76 at its northern end with I-95 to the south.

streets in the heart of historical Philadelphia (© **800/537-7676** or 215/965-7676; www. independencevisitorcenter.com), offers information on over 500 attractions, as well as package tours, Amtrak discounts, and more. The center is open 8:30am to 7pm daily during summer and until 5pm the rest of the year.

GETTING AROUND   Philadelphia is very pedestrian friendly, so we advise leaving your car in a garage. Center City is easily explored on foot or by taxi, and traffic, particularly around City Hall and near Rittenhouse Square, can be very congested. Many hotels offer reduced-rate parking to guests.

SEPTA (© **215/580-7800;** www.septa.org) operates a complicated and extensive network of trolleys, buses, commuter trains, and subways. The fare for any bus, trolley, or subway route is $2 cash or $1.30 by token, plus 60¢ for a transfer; exact change or tokens are required. A $5.50 **DayPass** is valid for buses, subways, trolleys, and a one-way trip on the commuter lines to most destinations, including the airport; a $19 weekly **TransPass** is good from Monday to the following Sunday and includes limited commuter train access on weekdays but unrestricted access on weekends and holidays.

Two **subway** lines crisscross the city, intersecting under City Hall. The Broad Street line connects directly to sporting events and concerts in the south. The Market-Frankford line stops at many popular destinations and stretches to the west and northeast. In addition, the Subway-Surface trolleys connect City Hall and 30th Street Station, stopping at 19th and 22nd streets along the way. West of 30th Street, the trolleys branch out to the north and south, moving aboveground.

Several **commuter trains,** known as the Regional Rail lines, service most suburban areas, including the posh Main Line area west of the city. Regional Rail trains depart Center City from 30th Street Station, Suburban Station at 16th Street and John F. Kennedy Boulevard, and the Market East Station at 10th and Market streets. Fares vary from $3 to $7, based on destination and time of day. Tickets should be purchased in advance at the station to avoid surcharges.

The **PATCO** rail line (© **215/922-4600;** www.drpa.org) begins at Locust and 16th streets, connects with SEPTA at 8th and Market, and crosses the Ben Franklin Bridge to New Jersey's Walter Rand Transportation Center in Camden for the bargain fare of $1.15. From there, you can take New Jersey Transit's River LINE (© **800/772-2222;** www.riverline.com) to the nearby Adventure Aquarium.

Philadelphia has 1,600 licensed cabs; try **Olde City Taxi** (© **215/338-0838**) or **Quaker City** (© **215/728-8000**). Fares are $2.70 for the first $1/7$ mile and 30¢ for each additional $1/7$ mile or minute of the motor running.

Most tourist destinations—from the waterfront and Independence Park in the east to the Museum of Art in the west—are also serviced by **PHLASH,** a purple bus that loops around the city from March through November, 10am to 6pm. Fares are $1 for adults; children 4 and under and seniors ride free. Discounted passes and maps are available at the Independence Visitor Center.

FAST FACTS   Call the **Philadelphia County Medical Society** (© **215/563-5343**) for a doctor referral, or © **215/925-6050** in a dental emergency. Major hospitals include **Children's Hospital of Philadelphia,** 34th Street and Civic Center Boulevard (© **215/ 590-1000**); **University of Pennsylvania Hospital,** 3400 Spruce St. (© **215/662-4000**); and **Thomas Jefferson,** 11th and Walnut streets (© **215/955-6000**).

THE MID-ATLANTIC

3

PHILADELPHIA

The only 24-hour pharmacy downtown is the **CVS** at 1826 Chestnut St., at the corner of 19th Street (© **215/972-0909**).

Philadelphia is generally safe if you concentrate on major tourist destinations, but stay alert, be aware of your surroundings, and keep a close eye on your possessions. Be especially careful at night and around college campuses in West Philadelphia.

Within city limits, there is a 7% **sales tax** on general sales and restaurant meals, but not on clothing. Liquor, including wine, beer, and hard liquor, is taxed at 10%. Lodging charges incur a 14% tax.

SPECIAL EVENTS & FESTIVALS   The all-day **Mummers Parade** (© 215/336-3050), held on New Year's Day, attracts 15,000 spangled strutters marching in feathered outfits while strumming banjos. You can line up on Broad Street between Oregon Avenue and City Hall to watch; the most exotically appointed groups, known as the Fancy Brigades, perform indoors at the Convention Center.

The **Philadelphia Flower Show** (© 215/988-8800; www.theflowershow.com) is the largest and most prestigious indoor exhibition of its kind. Acres of gardens, including exotic orchid displays and rustic settings, occupy the Convention Center in late February or early March.

Each March, **The Book and The Cook** festival (© 215/545-4543; www.thebook andthecook.com), combines the love of reading and eating. Food critics, cookbook authors, celebrity chefs, and restaurateurs create special menus at the city's best restaurants; food samplings and wine and beer tastings are held all over town. The list of participating restaurants is announced in January; many get booked quickly.

In the week leading up to the Fourth of July, the whole town turns out for the **Welcome America!** festival (© 215/683-2200; www.americasbirthday.com) to celebrate. There are dozens of free events, and the 4th brings special ceremonies to Independence Square, including a reading of the Declaration of Independence, and fireworks at the Philadelphia Museum of Art following a spectacular evening parade and concert on the Benjamin Franklin Parkway.

WHAT TO SEE & DO

The city's top attraction is **Independence National Historical Park** (SEPTA: buses or Market-Frankford Line to 5th St.), America's most historic square mile, centered at Independence Hall on Chestnut Street between 5th and 6th streets. The Declaration of Independence and U.S. Constitution were written here in the late 1700s, and the city served as the nation's capital for 10 years during the construction of the new capital in Washington, D.C.

The park is composed of 40 buildings on 45 acres of Center City real estate, including original sites such as **Independence Hall,** reconstructions such as **City Tavern** and **Declaration House,** and contemporary structures such as the **Liberty Bell Center** and the **National Constitution Center,** on the north side of the mall. Hours for most buildings are from 9am to 5pm daily except Christmas (the Visitor Center opens at 8:30am, the Constitution Center at 9:30am). Visitors to most historical attractions must pass through a security screening. You will need free timed tickets to enter **Independence Hall,** 500 Chestnut St. (© 877/444-6777 or www.nps.gov/inde/independence-hall.htm for advance tickets).

Make your first stop the **Independence Visitor Center,** 6th and Market streets (© 800/537-7676 or 215/965-7676), where you can pick up a map of the area, get tickets to tour Independence Hall, and reserve a spot on one of the frequent **ranger-led tours** of the Second Bank of the United States, Bishop White House, and Todd House.

Barnes Foundation (Best) The Barnes Foundation will stun you, if you are one of the lucky few who are able to get inside this quirky art gallery and education facility. In the 1920s, eccentric millionaire Albert Barnes crammed his French Provincial mansion with more than 1,000 masterpieces—180 Renoirs, 69 Cézannes, innumerable Impressionists and post-Impressionists, and a generous sampling of European art from the Italian primitives onward. Local zoning restricts the museum to only 1,200 visitors per week, so reserve months in advance. After a lengthy citywide debate and a couple of lawsuits, the collection will move to a central Philadelphia location, possibly as early as 2008. For now, the gallery resides in a leafy, upscale Main Line neighborhood.

300 N. Latches Lane, Merion Station. (C) 610/667-0290. www.barnesfoundation.org. Admission $10; audio tour $7. On-site parking $10. Reserve at least 2 months in advance by telephone. July–Aug Wed–Fri 9:30am–5pm; all other months Fri–Sun 9:30am–5pm. SEPTA: R5 (Paoli local train) to Merion; from station, turn right and walk up Merion Rd., turn left onto N. Latches Lane. Bus: 44 to the intersection of Old Lancaster Rd. and Latches Lane.

Betsy Ross House Elizabeth (Betsy) Ross was a Quaker needlewoman; some historians believe she sewed the original American flag of 13 stars and 13 stripes. Her tiny house takes only few minutes to walk through; it's a great picture of average Colonial life, from the low ceilings to the cellar kitchen and the model working areas for upholstering, making musket balls, and the like.

239 Arch St. (C) 215/686-1252. www.betsyrosshouse.org. Suggested contribution $3 adults, $2 children. Daily 10am–5pm (Oct–Mar closed Mon, except legal holidays). SEPTA: Market-Frankford 2nd St. Bus: 9, 17, 21, 32, 24, 48, 57, or PHLASH.

Christ Church (Value) This is the most beautiful Colonial building (1727–54) in Old City; its spire gleams white and can be seen from almost anywhere in the neighborhood. The interior spans one large arch, with galleries above the sides as demanded by the Anglican Church. The massive Palladian window behind the altar was the wonder of worshipers and probably the model for the one in Independence Hall. Seating is by pew—Washington's seat is marked with a plaque—and it's impossible to ignore the history etched in the church's stones and memorials.

2nd St. (a half-block north of Market St.). (C) 215/922-1695. Free admission; donations welcome. Mon–Sat 9am–5pm; Sun 1–5pm; Sun services at 9 and 11am. Closed Jan–Feb Mon–Tues. SEPTA: Market-Frankford 2nd St. Bus: 9, 17, 21, 32, 24, 48, 57, or PHLASH.

Elfreth's Alley The huge Benjamin Franklin Bridge shadows Elfreth's Alley, the oldest continuously inhabited street in the United States. Most of Colonial Philadelphia looked like this block does: cobblestone lanes between the major thoroughfares, small two-story homes, and pent eaves over doors and windows—a local trademark. A diverse population made this a miniature melting pot in the 18th and 19th centuries. Number 126, the 1755 **Mantua Maker's House** (cape maker), now serves as a museum. There is a gift shop with free brochures and information at no. 124.

Off 2nd St. (btw. Arch and Race sts.). (C) 215/574-0560. Street is public; Mantua Maker's House suggested admission $3 adults, $1 children ages 6–18, free for children 5 and under. Tues–Sat 10am–5pm; Sun noon–5pm. SEPTA: Market-Frankford 2nd St. Bus: 9, 17, 21, 32, 24, 48, 57, or PHLASH.

Franklin Court (Value) This imaginative, informative, and fun museum was designed under and around the site of Ben Franklin's home and is run by the National Park Service. The exhibits reflect Franklin's wide interests as scientist, inventor, statesman, printer, politician, and diplomat. Enter through arched passages from either Market or Chestnut

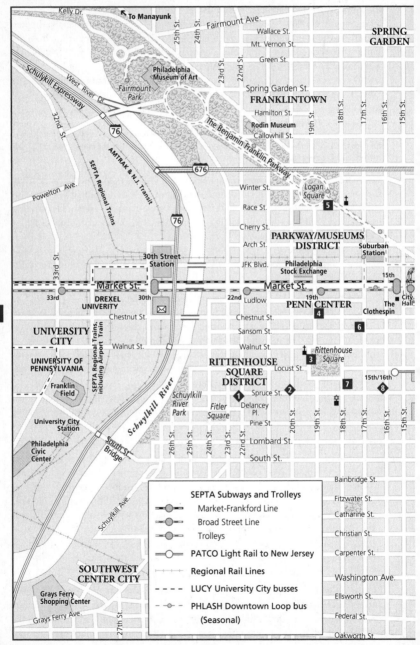

SPRING GARDEN

Kelly Dr.
To Manayunk
Fairmount Ave.
Wallace St.
Mt. Vernon St.
Green St.

Philadelphia Museum of Art
Fairmount Park

Spring Garden St.
FRANKLINTOWN
Hamilton St.
Rodin Museum
The Benjamin Franklin Parkway
Callowhill St.

Schuylkill Expressway
West River Dr.

AMTRAK & N.J. Transit
SEPTA Regional Trains

Powelton Ave.

Winter St.
Logan Square
Race St.

Cherry St.
Arch St.

PARKWAY/MUSEUMS DISTRICT

Suburban Station

30th Street Station
JFK Blvd.
Philadelphia Stock Exchange

15th

Market St.
33rd
DREXEL UNIVERITY
30th
22nd
Ludlow
19th
PENN CENTER
The Clothespin
City Hall

Chestnut St.
Chestnut St.
Sansom St.

UNIVERSITY CITY

UNIVERSITY OF PENNSYLVANIA
Franklin Field

Walnut St.
Walnut St.

RITTENHOUSE SQUARE DISTRICT
Rittenhouse Square

SEPTA Regional Trains, including Airport Train

Locust St.
Schuylkill River Park
Fitler Square
Spruce St.
Delancey Pl.
Pine St.
15th/16th

University City Station
Philadelphia Civic Center

South St. Bridge
Schuylkill River

26th 25th 24th 23rd 22nd
Lombard St.
South St.

Bainbridge St.
Fitzwater St.
Catharine St.
Christian St.
Carpenter St.
Washington Ave.

Schuylkill Ave.

SOUTHWEST CENTER CITY

Grays Ferry Shopping Center
Grays Ferry Ave.
27th St.

SEPTA Subways and Trolleys

Market-Frankford Line
Broad Street Line
Trolleys
PATCO Light Rail to New Jersey
Regional Rail Lines
LUCY University City busses
PHLASH Downtown Loop bus (Seasonal)

Ellsworth St.
Federal St.
Oakworth St.

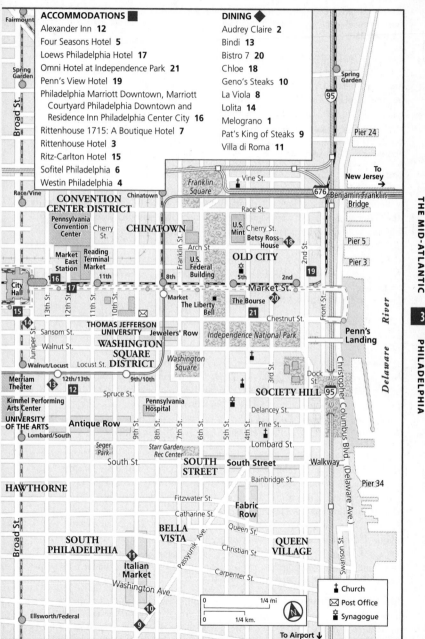

ACCOMMODATIONS ▪

Alexander Inn **12**

Four Seasons Hotel **5**

Loews Philadelphia Hotel **17**

Omni Hotel at Independence Park **21**

Penn's View Hotel **19**

Philadelphia Marriott Downtown, Marriott
Courtyard Philadelphia Downtown and
Residence Inn Philadelphia Center City **16**

Rittenhouse 1715: A Boutique Hotel **7**

Rittenhouse Hotel **3**

Ritz-Carlton Hotel **15**

Sofitel Philadelphia **6**

Westin Philadelphia **4**

DINING ◆

Audrey Claire **2**

Bindi **13**

Bistro 7 **20**

Chloe **18**

Geno's Steaks **10**

La Viola **8**

Lolita **14**

Melograno **1**

Pat's King of Steaks **9**

Villa di Roma **11**

Fairmount

Spring Garden

Broad St.

Race/Vine

CONVENTION CENTER DISTRICT

Pennsylvania Convention Center

Cherry St.

CHINATOWN

Chinatown

Market East Station

Reading Terminal Market

11th

City Hall

16 **17**

15

13th St.

12th St.

11th St.

10th St.

Sansom St.

Walnut St.

Juniper St.

THOMAS JEFFERSON UNIVERSITY

Jewelers' Row

WASHINGTON SQUARE DISTRICT

Walnut/Locust

Locust St.

Merriam Theater

13

12

12th/13th

9th/10th

Spruce St.

Kimmel Performing Arts Center

UNIVERSITY OF THE ARTS

Lombard/South

Antique Row

Pennsylvania Hospital

9th St.

8th St.

7th St.

6th St.

5th St.

4th St.

Pine St.

Delancey St.

Seger Park

Starr Garden Rec Center

South St.

Lombard St.

HAWTHORNE

SOUTH PHILADELPHIA

BELLA VISTA

Italian Market

11

Washington Ave.

Ellsworth/Federal

10

9

Passyunik Ave.

Christian St.

Carpenter St.

SOUTH STREET

South Street

Bainbridge St.

Fitzwater St.

Catharine St.

Queen St.

Fabric Row

QUEEN VILLAGE

Walkway

Franklin Square

Vine St.

676

Race St.

U.S. Mint

Cherry St.

Betsy Ross House

18

Arch St.

OLD CITY

U.S. Federal Building

8th

5th

2nd

Market St.

19

Market

The Liberty Bell

The Bourse

20

21

Chestnut St.

Independence National Park

Washington Square

SOCIETY HILL

3rd St.

Dock St.

95

Front St.

Penn's Landing

Christopher Columbus Blvd. (Delaware Ave.)

Swanson St.

Delaware River

Spring Garden

95

Pier 24

To New Jersey →

Benjamin Franklin Bridge

Pier 5

Pier 3

Pier 34

0 ___ 1/4 mi

0 ___ 1/4 km.

N

✝ Church

✉ Post Office

✡ Synagogue

To Airport ↓

streets; the Market entrance adjoins Franklin's reconstructed and fully operational post office, where employees still hand-stamp the marks.

Chestnut St. (btw. 3rd and 4th sts.), with another entrance at 316–318 Market St. Free admission, including the post office and postal museum. Daily 9am–5pm. SEPTA: Market-Frankford 2nd or 5th St. Bus: 21, 42, or PHLASH.

Franklin Institute Science Museum (Kids)

Set in an imposing, pillar-fronted limestone building, this museum explores the influence of science on our lives with an imaginative flair. It's a great spot for those traveling with kids. The complex includes a memorial to Ben Franklin; exhibitions such as a walk-through heart and antique airplanes; an outdoor science park; a newly renovated planetarium; and IMAX theater.

222 N. 20th St. (📞 **215/448-1200.** www.fi.edu. Sci-Pass (includes admission and 1 planetarium show) $14 adults, $11 children and seniors; Sci-Pass plus 1 IMAX movie $19 adults, $11 children and seniors. Daily 9:30am–5pm (Tuttleman IMAX Theater until 9pm Fri–Sat). Bus: 33 or PHLASH.

Independence Seaport Museum

This user-friendly maritime museum is the star of the city's waterfront. It's beautifully laid out, blending a first-class maritime collection with interactive exhibits for a trip through time that engages all ages. The **Workshop on the Water** lets you watch classes and amateurs undertake traditional wooden boat building and restoration throughout the year. The **Historic Ship Zone** includes the USS *Becuna,* a guppy-size submarine which served in Admiral Halsey's South Pacific fleet; and the USS *Olympia,* the only ship from the Spanish-American War still in existence.

Penn's Landing, at 211 S. Columbus Blvd. (📞 **215/925-5439.** www.phillyseaport.org. Admission $9 adults, $8 seniors, $6 children, free to all Sun 10am–noon. Daily 10am–5pm except major holidays. SEPTA: Market-Frankford 2nd St. Bus: 5,17, 21, 33, 42, 48, or PHLASH.

Liberty Bell Center

America's symbol of independence was commissioned in 1751 and hung in Independence Hall to "proclaim liberty throughout the land" as the Declaration of Independence was read aloud to the country's citizens (the quote engraved on the bell is from the Bible, not the Declaration). At some point in the 19th century, the bell cracked. The bell's new home, an interactive pavilion run by the National Park Service, is only 300 feet from its former glass pavilion, but moving the 2,080-pound bell required a team of engineers and a special steel cart.

501 Market St. (📞 **215/965-7676.** www.nps.gov/inde. Free admission. Daily 9am–5pm. SEPTA: Market-Frankford 5th St. Bus: 38, 44, 48, 121, or PHLASH.

National Constitution Center

A sprawling, dramatic, and unexpectedly modern steel-and-glass temple to the U.S. Constitution, the center at first seems rather unapproachable. But a multimedia theatrical show, *Freedom Rising,* which kicks off each visit, rallies adults and children into a patriotic mind-set for the more than 100 interactive exhibits that line this vast 160,000-square-foot building. Go ahead, take the Presidential Oath of Office, or test out a bench on the Supreme Court. *Tip:* Reserve your tickets by phone or on the website before you visit, to avoid long waits in line.

525 Arch St. (📞 **866/917-1787** or 215/409-6600. www.constitutioncenter.org. Admission $9 adults, $7 seniors and children, free for children 3 and under. Sun–Fri 9:30am–5pm; Sat 9:30am–6pm. SEPTA: Market-Frankford 5th St. Bus: 38, 44, 48, 121, or PHLASH.

Philadelphia Museum of Art (Best)

The third-largest art museum in the country is a resplendent Greco-Roman temple on a hill—approached, of course, by the "*Rocky* steps," made famous by the film. It houses one of the finest decorative arts collections in the country, featuring many American arts and crafts, including Philadelphia-made furniture and silver. Upstairs, spread over dozens of galleries, is a chronological sweep of European art from medieval times through 1900. The 19th- and 20th-century galleries highlight Cézanne's *The Large Bathers* and Marcel Duchamp's *Nude Descending a Staircase*—the museum is internationally renowned for its Duchamp collection. There are also many works by Philadelphia's Thomas Eakins.

26th St. and Ben Franklin Pkwy. (©) **215/763-8100,** or 684-7500 for 24-hr. information. www.phila museum.org. Admission $12 adults; $9 seniors; $8 students, seniors, and children 13–18; free for children 12 and under; on Sun, all ages pay what you wish. Tues–Sun 10am–5pm (until 8:45pm Fri). Bus: 7, 32, 38, 43, 48, or PHLASH.

Philadelphia Zoo (Kids) This 42-acre zoo, opened in 1874, was the nation's first and remains a leader, with 1,600-plus animals (including snow leopard cubs and other endangered cats in the brand-new Big Cat Falls). Other options include a Carnivore Kingdom (starring a white-nosed coati); a renovated Reptile House (Gaboon viper); a Primate Reserve (lowland gorillas); and the helium-filled Zooballoon, which carries you 400 feet in the air, with incredible views as far away as the New York skyline.

34th St. and Girard Ave. (©) **215/243-1100.** www.phillyzoo.org. Admission $17 adults, $14 children 2–11; free for children 1 and under. Parking $10. Mar–Nov daily 10am–5pm; Dec–Feb daily 10am–4pm. Bus: 32, 38, or PHLASH. Trolley: 15.

ORGANIZED TOURS

Philadelphia Trolley Works (©) 215/389-TOUR [8687]; www.phillytour.com) operates double-decker buses and buses decked out like old-fashioned trolleys. Guided tours of historic areas (all-day pass with unlimited on-and-off privileges: $27 adults, $25 seniors, $10 kids; $2 less if you purchase tickets online) leave from the northwest corner of 5th and Market streets on the edge of Independence Park.

To get the feel of Philadelphia as it once was, try a narrated horse-drawn carriage ride. Operated daily by Philadelphia Trolley Works sister tour operator, the **76 Carriage Co.** (©) 215/923-8516; www.phillytour.com), tours begin at 5th and Chestnut streets in front of Independence Hall from 10am to around 3:30pm, with later hours in summer. Reservations are not necessary. There are three tour options: The short tour is 15 to 20 minutes and costs $30, 35 minutes is $40, and an hour is $80. Prices include up to four passengers.

Several times a day from Memorial Day through Labor Day (and weekends in the spring and fall), the guided, 75-minute **Constitutional Walking Tour** (©) 215/525-1776; www.theconsitutional.com) covers 20 attractions in 1.25 miles in and around Independence National Historic Park. Tours begin at the Independence Visitor Center at 6th and Market: $18 adults, $13 kids 3 to 12, $55 family of four. The Constitutional Walking Tour's after-dark counterpart, **The Spirits of '76** (©) 215/525-1776; www. spiritsof76.com), bills itself as "equal parts history and haunts," and covers similar ground for the same price. From May to October, **Centipede Tours,** 1315 Walnut St. (©) 215/ 735-3123), leads Saturday-evening candlelit strolls of the historic Society Hill neighborhood; costumed guides leave from Welcome Park at Second and Walnut streets at 6:30pm, $5 per person. Call for reservations or customized tours. Also from May to October, the **Greater Philadelphia Tourism Marketing Corp.** (www.gophila.com) hosts tours of neighborhoods such as Chinatown and the Italian Market. Tours leave from the "ticket trolley" at 5th and Market streets (©) 215/389-TOUR [389-8687]). Tours cost $27 for adults; $20 for students, seniors, and kids 8 to 12 (the organizers do not recommend the 3-hr. tours for kids 7 and under).

The past few years have seen a surge of boutique culture in Center City. Along **Walnut Street** from **Broad Street** to **Rittenhouse Square,** you'll find Cole Haan and Lacoste, Burberry and Tiffany, Williams-Sonoma and Diesel, Anthropologie and J. Crew. But the haute local gems exist in between the big names: Joan Shepp and Knit Wit, Kimberly on 16th Street, and Echo Chic on Sansom Street for women's fashion; Born Yesterday and Piccolini for children's clothes and furnishings; bluemercury for beauty supplies; Kellmer for jewels; and, when you deserve a rest from all the bag-toting, the glamorous refuge of **Rescue Rittenhouse Spa Lounge,** 255 S. 17th St., 2nd floor (© 215/722-2766; www.rescuerittenhousespa.com).

Just a block or two on the other side of Broad, more finds can be, well, found at bustling little **Midtown Village,** which stretches eastward to 11th Street, and whose can't-miss stores include lifestyle boutique-cum-clothing-store-cum-hair-salon **Matthew Izzo,** 1109 Walnut St. (© 215/829-0606; www.matthewizzo.com); along 13th Street, friendly soap specialists **Duross & Langel,** no. 117 (© 215/592-7627; www.durossandlangel.com); and fantastic shelter and gift shop **Open House,** no. 107 (© 215/922-1415; www.openhouseliving.com).

Old City, known foremost for its history and more recently for its art galleries, has also become quite the shopping destination. Fans of modern design and newfangled kitchen trimmings will relish a trip to fantastic 10,000-square-foot **Foster's Homeware,** 399 Market St. (© 215/925-0950; www.shopfosters.com). On Third Street north of Market Street, you'll find up-and-coming (mostly women's) clothing designers at **Vagabond Boutique,** no. 37 (© 267/671-0737; www.vagabondboutique.com); **Sugarcube,** no. 124 (© 215/238-0825); **Third Street Habit,** no. 153 (© 215/925-5455); **Lost & Found,** no. 133 (© 215/928-1311); and more.

Pine Street from 9th to 12th streets is "Antiques Row," offering vintage-to-older items in additional to a handful of new home stores for more modern furniture and accessories, while **Sansom Street** from 7th to 9th streets is "Jeweler's Row," peppered with shops that attract ring-seeking couples and in-the-biz retailers.

South Street is the dividing line between Center City and South Philadelphia, and has long attracted the teen scene with sneaker shops, music stores, costume jewelry vendors, and junk food fuel. If fresher fare—and even more atmosphere—is what you're after, walk a few blocks south to wander through South Philly's **Italian Market,** on 9th Street between Christian and Wharton streets. It feels straight out of another era: gritty, colorful, and redolent of garlic and just-baked bread, with open stalls that sell fresh produce, just-made mozzarella, fresh pasta, and dry-cured olives, plus white-coated butchers that swear their homemade sausage is the best in town.

WHERE TO STAY

Center City has more than 10,000 hotel rooms, and packages and discounts abound. State and city surcharges will tack on an additional 14% to your lodging bill.

The **Independence Visitor Center,** 6th and Market streets (© 800/537-7676; www.independencevisitorcenter.com), can help with any questions. For information on B&Bs, try **Bed & Breakfast Connections of Philadelphia** (© 800/448-3619 or 610/687-3565; www.bnbphiladelphia.com).

Many of the city's more affordable options are chain hotels, including the **Best Western Independence Park Hotel,** 235 Chestnut St. (© 800/624-2988 or 215/922-4443; www.independenceparkhotel.com), and the **Hampton Inn Philadelphia Center City–Convention Center,** 1301 Race St. (© 215/665-9100; www.hamptoninn.com).

Alexander Inn (Value)   This midsize corner inn offers a refreshingly neighborhood-y respite from its nationally based brethren. The independent operation has all the comfort and charm of a bed-and-breakfast, with a classy 1930s Art Deco–cruise ship feel to the furnishings. Smallish rooms feature DirecTV with eight all-movie channels; individual artwork; and bathrooms that sparkle with cleanliness. Corner rooms are larger and brighter. Located at the edge of Center City's Gayborhood—and across the street from one of the city's best wine bars—the inn affably hosts clientele both straight and gay.

301 S 12th St., Philadelphia, PA, 19107. (C) **877/253-9466** or 215/923-3535. Fax 215/923-1004. www.alexanderinn.com. 48 units. From $109 double; $12 per additional person. Rates include breakfast buffet. AE, DC, DISC, MC, V. Garage parking at 12th and Walnut is $10 for guests. **Amenities:** 24-hr. fitness center.

Four Seasons Hotel (Best)   This refined, luxurious property sets the bar for hotel sophistication in Philadelphia, and it's perfect for weekday business or romantic weekend getaways. The elegant rooms have windows that open, or private balconies on the seventh floor boasting marvelous views of Logan Circle's Swann Fountain or the interior court-yard. Amenities include marble bathrooms with bathrobes and thick towels; down pil-lows; and general luxury. The **Fountain,** under executive chef Martin Hamann, is one of Philadelphia's best restaurants, with its inventive, French-accented American menu and service—come for the fabulous Sunday brunch. On the below-ground level, the tiny spa is a favorite among both longtime guests and local elite.

One Logan Sq., Philadelphia, PA 19103. (C) **866/516-1100** or 215/963-1500. Fax 215/963-9506. www.fourseasons.com/philadelphia. 372 units. $395–$550 double; from $455 suite. Children 17 and under stay free in parent's room. Weekend rates and discount packages available. AE, DC, MC, V. Valet parking $45. Bus: 33. Pets under 15 lb. permitted. **Amenities:** 2 restaurants; indoor pool; health club; spa. *In room:* Exercise equipment available.

Loews Philadelphia Hotel (Kids)   Beneath the landmark neon PSFS sign, this chic Convention Center–area hotel resides in the country's first International Style skyscraper, a glassy building outfitted with Cartier clocks and polished stone surfaces in a Deco interior preserved as a National Historic Landmark. Still, guests—especially families, even those traveling with pets—return for the chain's signature services, including con-cierges dedicated to kids, 'tweens, and teens—and dogs, too. Although some of the less expensive rooms are on the small side, most units boast marvelous city skyline views, but no view rivals that looking out from the top-floor lap pool.

1200 Market St., Philadelphia, PA 19107. (C) **877/235-6397** or 215/627-1200. Fax 215/231-7305. www.loewshotels.com. 581 units. From $189 double. Excellent weekend rates available. A maximum of 2 chil-dren 18 and under stay free in parents' room. AE, DC, MC, V. Valet parking (on 12th St. side of building) $38. Maximum of 2 pets permitted for $25 fee. **Amenities:** Restaurant; indoor pool; health club; spa.

Omni Hotel at Independence Park   This hotel has a terrific location in the middle of Independence National Historical Park and near Old City. All units have park views; you can watch horse-drawn carriages clip-clopping by, or walk a half-block to trendy bars and restaurants. The classic lobby features current newspapers, huge vases of flowers, and a piano bar. Rooms are cheery and equipped with marble bathrooms and handy conve-niences. You can catch an after-dinner flick at the Ritz Five movie theater tucked into the hotel's back corner, catch a romantic dinner at any number of nearby bistros, or brave the boisterous crowds at the bars of Old City.

401 Chestnut St., Philadelphia, PA 19106. (C) **800/843-6664** or 215/925-0000. Fax 215/931-1263. www.omnihotels.com. 150 units. $189–$529 double. Children 9 and under stay free in parent's room. Weekend rates available. AE, DC, DISC, MC, V. Valet parking $32 plus tax; self-parking at the Bourse garage next door $24. SEPTA: 5th St. **Amenities:** Restaurant; indoor pool; health club; spa.

Penn's View Hotel (Value)   Behind the Market Street ramp to I-95 in a renovated 1856 warehouse, this pretty boutique hotel offers roomy guest rooms with Chippendale-style furniture and modern amenities—and reasonable rates. The main concern is traffic noise, but rooms are well insulated; some offer fireplaces and Jacuzzi tubs. The hotel was developed by the Sena family, which runs the on-premises **Panorama,** a marvelous wine bar and trattoria, and the nearby La Familigia restaurant.

Front and Market sts., Philadelphia, PA 19106. (©) **800/331-7634** or 215/922-7600. Fax 215/922-7642. www.pennsviewhotel.com. 51 units. $159–$289. Rates include European continental breakfast. Weekend rates and discount packages available. AE, MC, V. Parking $20 at adjacent lot. SEPTA: 2nd St. **Amenities:** Restaurant.

Philadelphia Marriott Downtown, Marriott Courtyard Philadelphia Downtown and Residence Inn Philadelphia Center City   The biggest hotel in Pennsylvania, linked by a sky bridge to the Convention Center, is even bigger, thanks its additions of two neighboring buildings: the historic City Hall Annex converted into a 498-room Courtyard, and the Art Deco 269-suite Residence Inn, also across the street from City Hall. The main hotel's rooms and terraces provide plenty of natural light and views from the rooms on floors 6 to 23. The Courtyard property has restored bronze and copper details throughout. Although tastefully outfitted and equipped with spacious bathrooms, the rooms are slightly less elegant than those at the top hotels. Service is impeccable.

Marriott: 1201 Market St. (at 12th St.) and 21 N. Juniper St., Philadelphia, PA 19107. (©) **800/320-5744** or 215/625-2900. Fax 215/625-6000. www.marriott.com. 1,408 units. From $299 double. Weekend rates available. Valet parking $41. Courtyard by Marriott: 25 N. Juniper St., Philadelphia, PA 19107. (©) **888/887-8130** or 215/496-3200. Fax 215/496-3696. 498 units. From $269 double. Weekend rates available. Valet parking $35. Residence Inn: One East Penn Square, Philadelphia, PA 19107. (©) **800/331-3131** or 215/557-0005. Fax 215/557-1991. 269 units. From $249 double. Weekend rates available. Valet parking $42. AE, DC, DISC, MC, V. SEPTA: Direct internal connection to 11th St.–Market E. or 13th St. **Amenities:** 4 restaurants; pool; health club; spa.

Rittenhouse 1715: A Boutique Hotel   Steps from Rittenhouse Square, a pristine park ringed by million-dollar apartments and mansions, this boutique hotel incarnates a small, European-style luxury hotel. Set in two early-20th-century town houses on a leafy street 1 block from Walnut Street shopping, and 15 minutes' walk to the Convention Center, the hotel exudes modernized, haute-British style, with Frette linens, Berber carpets, and large guest rooms and suites with marble bathrooms stocked with Molton Brown products. Sip wine in the lobby each evening, and enjoy a lavish continental breakfast, but forget about bringing along children 11 and under.

1715 Rittenhouse Sq., Philadelphia, PA 19103. (©) **877/791-6500** or 215/546-6500. Fax 215/546-8787. www.rittenhouse1715.com. 23 units. From $249 double; from $309 suite. Rates include complimentary continental breakfast and nightly wine reception. AE, DC, DISC, MC, V. SEPTA: 17th St. Children 11 and under not permitted.

Rittenhouse Hotel (Best)   Among Philadelphia's luxury hotels, the Rittenhouse has the fewest and largest rooms, dramatic views of the flowers and trees in Rittenhouse Square, and a franchise on hosting movie stars: Tom Hanks, Demi Moore, and Denzel Washington have all roosted here while filming in Philly. Built in 1989, it's a jagged concrete-and-glass high-rise; the lobby is a peaceful oasis, with inlaid marble floors and frosted-glass chandeliers. The guest rooms have bay windows, reinforced walls, flatscreen TVs, oversize tubs, and separate showers. And everything else one requires for a wonderful vacation is on-premises: **Lacroix,** a world-class, treetop-level restaurant (see below); an outpost of the renowned Smith & Wollensky steakhouses; and the *luxe* Adolf Biecker spa, salon, and gym. (Just a half-block away: La Colombe, declared by *Food & Wine* to be the best coffee shop in the country.)

210 W. Rittenhouse Sq., Philadelphia, PA 19103. © **800/635-1042** or 215/546-9000. Fax 215/732-3364. www.rittenhousehotel.com. 98 units. $279–$500 double; $600–$800 suite. Discounts and packages available. AE, DC, MC, V. Valet parking $30. SEPTA: 19th St. Pets permitted. **Amenities:** 4 restaurants; indoor pool; health club; spa.

Ritz-Carlton Hotel   This luxury hotel is set inside a historic Broad Street bank building (itself designed to resemble the Pantheon in Rome) with a 140-foot-high white marble lobby and some of the city's loveliest rooms and suites. Rooms are traditionally decorated with exceptional city views and gorgeous marble bathrooms; some overlook neighboring City Hall. Splurge on one of the "club floors," and you'll be treated to champagne, brie, and a lavish breakfast in a paneled, 30th-floor former boardroom. The spa offers a full complement of treatments, sexy 10 Arts restaurant and lounge offer the gastronomic masterpieces of none other than *the* Eric Ripert, and the tucked-away Vault lounge is still the place to steal the night away.

10 S. Broad St. (Ave. of the Arts), Philadelphia, PA 19102. © **800/241-3333** or 215/523-8000. Fax 215/568-0942. www.ritzcarlton.com. 331 units. From $259 double; from $509 suite. Weekend packages available. AE, DC, DISC, MC, V. Valet parking $45. Dogs permitted under certain conditions for a $75 surcharge. **Amenities:** Restaurant; health club; spa.

Sofitel Philadelphia   This stateside take on France's premier hotel chain is hospitable and chic, with its modern-Deco vibe, classy bar off the marble lobby, and doormen who make a serious effort to greet you with an authentic "Bonjour." The location, half a block from the Walnut Street shopping corridor and between Rittenhouse Square and the Avenue of the Arts, is wonderful for business or pleasure visitors. Downstairs, the lobby is filled with marble, wood, and flower arrangements; upstairs, guest rooms are upscale and Deco-contemporary, with a glass coffee table, two armchairs, and an opulent bed with wall-mounted bedside lights on walls of checkerboard cherrywood. Bathrooms are huge, with travertine marble throughout.

120 S. 17th St., Philadelphia, PA 19103. © **800/763-4835** or 215/569-8300. www.sofitel.com. 306 units. From $215 double. Weekend rates available. AE, DC, DISC, MC, V. Valet parking $29. SEPTA: 17th St. Pets up to 25 lb. permitted for $50 surcharge. **Amenities:** Restaurant; health club.

Westin Philadelphia   This hotel, attached to Liberty One, one of the city's tallest buildings (and one of its very few indoor shopping centers), opened years ago to great fanfare as a gorgeous, Parisian-proper Ritz-Carlton. While its lineage makes it a bit higher priced than other Westins, it's a value compared to its luxury peers. A small *porte-cochere* and a ground-floor entrance on 17th Street lead to elevators that lift you up to the main lobby, which is a series of living-room-like sitting rooms that serve wine and cheese nightly. The guest rooms are outfitted with bedside walnut tables, desks, and armoires, but the beds, with their spindle-top headboards, triple sheeting, and luxurious five pillows, are the main attraction. (Baby guests will enjoy the bumper-protected, supersafe crib, too.) The modern bathrooms include an oversize, dual-head shower, magnifying mirrors, and Brazilian cotton towels.

99 S. 17 St., Philadelphia, PA 19103. © **800/228-3000** or 215/563-1600. Fax 215/564-9559. www.westin.com. 290 units. From $179 double. Weekend rates available. AE, DC, MC, V. Valet parking $32. **Amenities:** Restaurants; health club; spa.

Philadelphia's unsung culinary heroes are its bring-your-own-bottle restaurants, BYOBs. These typically smaller bistros often have quirky reservations policies, accept cash only, sell out of popular dishes on a Saturday night—and serve some of the best, least expensive food in town.

In the Rittenhouse Square neighborhood (west of Broad St.), try the gnocchi at little **La Viola,** 253 S. 16th St. (© 215/735-8630); the grilled Romaine salad and flatbreads at stylish **Audrey Claire,** 276 S. 20th St. (© 215/731-1222; www.audreyclaire.com); or anything at all at chic trattoria **Melograno,** 2201 Spruce St. (© 215/875-8116). In Midtown Village, don't miss the quirky-delicious Mexican fare—and the mix-your-own margaritas—at funky **Lolita,** 106 S. 13th St. (© 215/546-7100; www.lolitabyob.com), or the marvelously fused Indian fare across the street at **Bindi,** 105 S. 13th St. (© 215/ 922-6061; www.bindibyob.com). In Old City, head to a divine nouveau American dinner at pretty **Bistro 7,** 7 S. 3rd St. (© 215/931-1560; www.bistro7restaurant.com), or dig into modern comfort foods at neighborhood-y **Chloe,** 232 Arch St. (© 215/629-2337; www.chloebyob.com).

It's also worth exploring outside of Center City to eat, especially if you're headed to South Philly, where you'll run into lines at famously dueling 24-hour cheesesteak vendors **Pat's King of Steaks,** 1237 E. Passyunk Ave. (© 215/468-1546; www.patskingofsteaks), and **Geno's Steaks,** 1219 S. 9th St. (© 215/389-0659; www.genosteaks.com). (We say these aren't even the best in town; see "The Ultimate Cheesesteak Taste Test," p. 165.) For a slightly more serious meal, go for casual Italian restaurants like a casual (ca.-1927), pizza-friendly **Marra's,** 1734 E. Passyunk Ave. (© 215/463-9249; www.marras1.com), or the Italian Market's red-sauce-perfumed **Villa di Roma,** 932 S. 9th St. (© 215/592-1295).

Also worth the trip: The north-of-Old-City nabe of Northern Liberties, where hipsters indulge in the great tavern food and marvelous local beers of the exceedingly popular **Standard Tap,** 901 N. 2nd St. (© 215/238-0630; www.standardtap.com), and **North 3rd,** 801 N. 3rd St. (© 215/413-3666; www.norththird.com).

Amada CONTEMPORARY TAPAS   Antique sangria casks, a Spanish meat slicer, and a mini groceria set the scene for stunningly authentic, meant-for-sharing tapas in this popular Old City eatery. Reserve a table on a Wednesday or Saturday night, and enjoy flamenco performers while you nibble truffled Manchego with lavender honey, tissue-thin slices of cured pork, grilled octopus, warm fava-bean salad, pernil asada, overflowing bowls of paella, order-ahead roasted suckling pig, green plantain empanadas, and chocolate hazelnut and garlic dulce de leche spreads—washed down with the city's best sangria. (Or, if you're across town near Rittenhouse Square, try Spanish sister wine bar **Tinto** for elegant atmosphere and slightly more refined fare.)

217–219 Chestnut St. © **215/625-2450**. www.amadarestaurant.com. Reservations strongly recommended. Tapas $4–$18; larger dishes from $30. AE, DC, DISC, MC, V. Mon–Fri 11:30am–2:30pm; Mon–Thurs 5–11pm; Fri–Sat 5pm–midnight; Sun 4–11pm. **Tinto:** 114 S. 20th St. © **215/665-9150.** www.tinto restaurant.com. Reservations recommended. Small dishes $4–$22; chef's tasting $55. AE, DC, DISC, MC, V. Mon–Fri 11:30am–2:30pm; Sun–Thurs 5–11pm; Fri–Sat 5pm–midnight; Sun brunch 10:30am–2:30pm.

Buddakan ASIAN   With high ceilings, mod dining room, giant golden Buddha statue overlooking sleek tables of trendy couples and extended families, Buddakan could coast on its good looks. But its stellar made-for-sharing Pan-Asian cuisine—"angry lobster," wasabi mashed potatoes, sesame-crusted tuna, and chocolate pagodas—make this reserve-in-advance showplace more than just a pretty spot to dine.

The Ultimate Cheesesteak Taste Test

Hats off to Richard Rys at *Philadelphia Magazine,* who wolfed down 50 cheesesteaks in 34 days in a quest to crown a Cheesesteak King. Richard ordered steaks with American cheese but without onions, also known as an "American, widout": "A great steak shouldn't hide behind onions or condiments."

Here's a sample of his top picks closest to Center City.

Cosmi's Deli, 1501 S. 8th St. (© **215/468-6093**), is around the corner from famous rivals Pat's and Geno's, but Richard swears Cosmi's is the real king of steaks. "Fresh roll, meat chopped with a samurai's precision, and melted cheese embracing each piece like Mama giving Raj a bear hug on *What's Happening.*" Richard's rating: 5.

Tony Luke's, 39 E. Oregon Ave. (© **215/551-5725**), is in South Philly, near the Walt Whitman Bridge. "Strips of meat stuffed into a hearty, rugged roll that was built for handling a serious payload. My only complaint is that for all its mass, it's a little light on cheese." Rating: 4.5.

Jim's Steaks, 400 South St. (© 215/928-1911) is just south of Society Hill. "The roll looks like it just wandered in off the set of a Sally Struthers infomercial, the meat is only moderately chopped, and the cheese is barely melted. Yet the damn thing is inexplicably good." Rating: 3.5.

Geno's Steaks (p. 164) is a Philly landmark, but Richard gives it modest praise. "Decent amount of cheese. Good roll. The meat is another story. It's riddled with pockets and veins of fat and contains a rainbow of colors from brown to gray. Oddly enough, the taste isn't bad." Rating: 2.5.

Pat's King of Steaks (p. 164), Geno's rival around the corner, gets no special treatment, either. "The cheese distribution on my sandwich makes me think Stevie Wonder is working dairy duty on the grill line. It's spotty, leaving some regions bare. Like Geno's, a good roll, but a frightening amount of fat in the meat." Rating: 2.

—courtesy of Richard Rys and *Philadelphia Magazine*
(www.phillymag.com)

325 Chestnut St. © **215/574-9440.** www.buddakan.com. Reservations recommended. Main courses $19–$31. AE, DC, MC, V. Mon–Fri 11:30am–2:30pm; Mon–Thurs 5–11pm; Fri–Sat 5pm–midnight; Sun 4–10pm. SEPTA: 2nd St. or 5th St.

Fork CONTINENTAL   Set in a renovated warehouse, this warm 68-seat bistro, outfitted with tall banquettes and soft lighting, attracts gastronomic aesthetes. On the menu: seasonal, American-international sampling: heirloom tomato salad, lemon grass–touched baby back ribs, chimichurri steak with yucca fries, and tarragon-buttered scallops. Sunday brunch is known as much for its elegantly laid-back attitude as for its house-made baked goodies. Wednesday nights, the next-door market-cafe Fork Etc. offers fixed price meals served to neighbors at a tall community table.

306 Market St. (© **215/625-9425.** www.forkrestaurant.com. Reservations recommended. Main courses $19–$28. AE, DC, DISC, MC, V. Mon–Thurs 11:30am–10:30pm; Fri 11:30am–11:30pm; Sat 5–11:30pm; Sun 11am–2:30pm and 5–10:30pm. SEPTA: 2nd St. or 5th St.

Lacroix CONTINENTAL   Hidden on an upper floor of the refined Rittenhouse Hotel, this ethereal yet unstuffy destination with deep emerald-green armchairs shows off maverick chef Matt Levin's menu of interchangeable courses (choose from three to five dishes) that might include veal skirt steak with cauliflower, hand-rolled pasta, and black-strap molasses one night, and raw white belly fluke with black salt and watermelon fizz the next. At any time of day—as early as 6:30am—guests can order three meals' worth of delicacies that are slightly more familiar, but just as refined.

210 W. Rittenhouse Sq. (© **215/790-2533.** www.lacroixrestaurant.com. Reservations recommended. A la carte dinner entrees from $26; prix-fixe $69–$85 dinner; business lunch $31; brunch $56. AE, DC, DISC, MC, V. Daily 6am–2:30pm; Sun–Thurs 5:30–10pm; Fri–Sat 5:30–10:30pm.

Le Bec-Fin ⟨Best⟩ FRENCH   In short: The fanciest French restaurant in town, the progeny of Lyon-born chef-owner Georges Perrier, oft credited with transforming palates citywide. "Le Bec" is a special-occasion sort of place, with a multitude of silverware to choose from, a Versailles-worthy dessert cart, and plenty of properly elegant courses in between. A la carte service is available, but while you're here, you might as well go for broke and order the seven-course tasting menu.

1523 Walnut St. (© **215/567-1000.** www.lebecfin.com. Reservations required. 7-course dinner $140; a la carte entrees from $20. AE, DC, DISC, MC, V. Lunch seatings Fri–Sat 11:30am–1:30pm; dinner seatings Mon–Sat 5:30pm–9:30pm. Bar Lyonnais downstairs serves food and drink in a more casual setting. SEPTA: Walnut-Locust.

Osteria ITALIAN   North of City Hall, this buzz-worthy trattoria attracts gourmets galore, diners who've developed addictions to egg- or octopus-topped pizzas, sublime pork Milanese, rabbit doused in brown butter, and endless rustic Italian delights that turn the idea of spaghetti and meatballs on its head. Chef-owner Marc Vetri is in charge of this boisterous, "Big Night"–reminiscent affair, while simultaneously helming his smaller, more subdued bistro **Vetri** a few blocks south.

640 N. Broad St. (© **215/763-0920.** www.osteriaphilly.com. Reservations strongly recommended. Dinner entrees $24–$35. AE, DC, MC, V. Sun–Wed 5–10pm; Thurs–Sat 5–11pm; Thurs–Fri 11:30am–2pm. **Vetri:** 1312 Spruce St. (© **215/732-3478.** www.vetriristorante.com. Sept–May Mon–Sat from 6pm; June–Aug Mon–Fri from 6pm.

PHILADELPHIA AFTER DARK

The most up-to-date event listings are online. Visit **www.philly.com**, the site for both the *Philadelphia Daily News* and the *Philadelphia Inquirer,* and **www.phillyfunguide. com** for listings *and* discounts. Also pick up the free *City Paper* (www.citypaper.net) and *Philadelphia Weekly* (www.phillyweekly.com).

Event tickets may be purchased through the following vendors: **Upstages** (© **215/ 569-9700**), which specializes in local theater; **Ticket Philadelphia** (© **215/893-1999;** www.ticketphiladelphia.org), for larger cultural events; and **Ticketmaster** (© **215/336-2000;** www.ticketmaster.com), primarily for rock concerts.

THE PERFORMING ARTS   Broad Street south of City Hall is called the "Avenue of the Arts," home to several theaters and performance halls. The **Philadelphia Orchestra** (www.philorch.org), one of the "Big Five" American orchestras, performs at the stunning, accordion-shaped **Kimmel Center,** Broad and Spruce streets (© **215/893-1999**

from September to May. In summer, the orchestra moves outdoors to the **Mann Music Center,** near 52nd Street and Parkside Avenue (© **215/893-1999** for tickets; www. manncenter.org). The **Curtis Institute,** 1726 Locust St. (© **215/893-5252,** or 893-5261 for schedule; www.curtis.edu; SEPTA: Walnut–Locust), a world-famous conservatory, presents many free concerts, operas, and recitals during the school year.

The **Opera Company of Philadelphia** (© **215/928-2110;** www.operaphilly.com), hosts internationally renowned singers at the gorgeous (ca.-1857) Academy of Music (1420 Locust St.). The impeccable **Pennsylvania Ballet** (© **215/551-7014;** www.pa ballet.org) performs at the Academy of Music, Kimmel Center, and elsewhere from September to June.

Philadelphia is an attentive theater town. The acclaimed **Wilma Theater** stages modern plays in a state-of-the-art space at Broad and Spruce streets (© **215/546-7824;** www. wilmatheater.org; SEPTA: Walnut–Locust). Across Broad, the shockingly pink Suzanne Roberts Theatre hosts the **Philadelphia Theatre Company,** 480 S. Broad St. (© **215/985-0420** for tickets; www.philadelphiatheatrecompany.org; SEPTA: 15th–16th sts.), which combines fine regional talent with Tony Award–winning actors and directors. The popular **Arden Theatre Co.,** 40 N. 2nd St. (© **215/922-1122** for tickets; www.arden theatre.org; SEPTA: 2nd St.), presents diverse productions for adults and kids in an intimate setting in Old City.

Founded in 1809, the **Walnut Street Theatre,** 825 Walnut St. (© **215/574-3550;** www.wstonline.org; SEPTA: 8th–Market), stages large-scale plays and both classic and recent musicals. The **Prince Music Theater** (© **215/569-9700** for tickets; www.prince musictheater.org) presents opera, musical comedy, cabaret, and experimental theater at a dramatically renovated movie palace, at 1412 Chestnut St. (SEPTA: City Hall or 15th St.). The 2,000-seat, 1930s-built **Merriam Theater** (© **215/732-5446;** www.merriam theater.org) hosts major touring Broadway productions.

THE CLUB & MUSIC SCENE   The best nightlife areas are **Old City,** for young, low-cut types slugging down all manner of libations; **Walnut Street** between 15th and 18th streets and around **Rittenhouse Square** for sophisticated bars and lounges; and, for a more dressed-down night out, **Northern Liberties.**

For a low-key evening of good jazz and cheap drinks, opt for Center City's **Chris' Jazz Café,** 1421 Sansom St. (© **215/568-3131;** www.chrisjazzcafe.com), or Northern Liberties' slightly more out-of-the-way **Ortlieb's Jazzhaus,** 847 N. 3rd St. (© **215/922-1035;** www.ortliebsjazzhaus.com).

For concerts, check out the schedule for the often all-ages **Electric Factory** (the Roots, Bob Dylan), 421 N. 7th St. (© **215/336-2000** for tickets, 627-1332 for venue; www. ticketmaster.com); South Street's always packed **TLA** (Liz Phair, the Dandy Warhols), 334 South St. (for tickets © **215/336-2000** or for box office 922-1011; www.ticket master.com), the burlesque-hall-turned-concert-venue **Trocadero** (the Magnetic Fields, Bow Wow), 1003 Arch St. (for tickets © **215/336-2000,** for venue 922-6888; www. thetroc.com); singer-songwriter-centric **World Café** (Jimmy Dale Gilmore, Joan Osborne), 3025 Chestnut St. (© **215/222-1400;** www.worldcafelive.com); for more local sound, Old City's legendary little **Khyber,** 56 S. 2nd St. (© **215/238-5888;** www. thekhyber.com; SEPTA: 2nd St.); or **Johnny Brenda's,** 1201 Frankford Ave. (© **215/731-9684;** www.johnnybrendas.com; SEPTA: Girard)—the last two serve some great local beer, too.

THE BAR SCENE   From lunchtime until 2am, the who's who of Philadelphia come to Rittenhouse Square's chic **Parc,** 225 S. 18th St. (© **215/735-0110;** www.parcritten house.com), and **Rouge,** 205 S. 18th St. (© **215/732-6622**), to sip wine, gawk, and be gawked at. Another popular setting for the cocktail crowd is the roomy bar at **Brasserie Perrier,** 1619 Walnut St. (© **215/568-3000;** www.georgesperriergroup.com), a contemporary, colorful spot co-owned by Le Bec-Fin's Georges Perrier. All year long, the slightly younger set sees and is seen on the atomic-age roof deck of **Continental Midtown,** 1801 Chestnut St. (© **215/567-1800;** www.continentalmidtown.com), and gets its groove on in the white-bright **Denim Lounge,** 1710 Walnut St. (© **215/735-6700;** www.denim lounge.com).

Across town, Old City's effortful-ly stylish set gets going late—unless it's the first Friday of the month, when a gallery crawl attracts hordes early—to barhop: a mojito at **Cuba Libre,** 10 S. 2nd St. (© **215/627-0666;** www.cubalibrerestaurant.com); a shot-and-a-beer at **Drinker's Tavern,** 124 Market St. (© **215/351-0141;** www.drinkers tavern.com); a sugary martini at yet another **Continental,** 138 Market St. (© **215/923-6069;** www.continentalmartinibar.com); microbrews at **Triumph,** 138 Chestnut St. (© **215/625-0855;** www.triumphbrewing.com), and bottle service at **32 Degrees,** 32 S. 2nd St. (© **215/627-3132;** www.32lounge.com).

THE GAY & LESBIAN SCENE   Center City is gay friendly—doubly so in the "Gayborhood," from about 10th to 13th and Chestnut and Pine (SEPTA: Walnut–Locust). Find out what's going on in the *Philadelphia Gay News* (www.epgn.com). Or just drop by perennially popular **Woody's,** 202 S. 13th St. (© **215/545-1893;** www.woodysbar. com), with a bar downstairs and dance floor up. The **12th Air Command,** 254 S. 12th St. (© **215/545-8088;** www.12thair.com), has a lounge, game room, disco, and pub menu. Piano bar **Tavern on Camac,** 243 S. Camac St. (© **215/545-0900;** www.tavern oncamac.com), is all about the singalong. Dance clubbers stay late at **Pure,** 1221 St. James St. (© **215/735-5772;** www.purephilly.com). Women gather at **Sisters,** 1320 Chancellor St. (© **215/735-0735;** www.sistersnightclub.com). And everyone goes on first dates at **Valanni,** 1229 Spruce St. (© **215/790-9494;** www.valanni.com). Close to the 'hood you'll find the popular gay bookstore **Giovanni's Room,** 345 S. 12th St. (© **215/923-2960**).

---

6 SIDE TRIPS FROM PHILADELPHIA

THE AMISH COUNTRY

Fifty miles west of Philadelphia is a quietly beautiful region of rolling hills, winding creeks, neatly cultivated farms, covered bridges, and towns with picturesque names such as Paradise and Bird-in-Hand. The Amish community, which steadfastly retains a life of agrarian simplicity centered on religious worship and family cohesiveness, numbers 18,000. The preservation of their world evokes feelings of curiosity, nostalgia, amazement, and respect.

The area is relatively small, with good roads for motorist and bicyclist alike. The attention to the Amish has spurred lots of interesting facsimiles and even some authentic pathways into Amish life, although you have to sift through them if you want to avoid overt religious messages. Tourism has promoted excellence in quilting, antiques, and farm-based crafts. There are historical sites, pretzel and chocolate factories, covered bridges, and wonderful farmers' markets, as well as modern diversions such as movie

All Things Chocolate

Hershey (www.hersheypa.com), the adorable village founded by Milton Hershey in 1903 as his candy empire's company town, literally *smells* of chocolate. It bills itself as "the sweetest place on earth" and offers golf, gardens, rolling farmland, and lots of chocolate-related fun. Though it's best to visit in summer, the town has a huge holiday spirit. Beginning in mid-November, more than one million holiday "Sweet Lights" are draped around town (including on the Kiss-shaped street lanterns); there's also Santa, reindeer, music, and a Teddy Bear Jubilee.

The big attraction is the kid-friendly amusement park **HERSHEYPARK** (**www.hersheypark.com**). The 110-acre park sports 10 roller coasters (some of them, such as the SuperDooperLooper, are among the best in the country) and a host of water and kiddie rides. Oh, and lots and lots of chocolate! Live "candy characters" parade around daily, offering kids the chance to get a hug from some real Kisses and Hugs. Admission is $50 adults, $31 kids 3 to 8. There are flexpasses, combo tickets, and other discount admissions. Check the website.

Just outside the theme park is the free **Chocolate World** visitor center, where you can see how your Reese's Peanut Butter Cups and Mr. Goodbars are made (and get a free sample!). *Tip:* Ignore the 3-D film that costs extra; it's not worth the price.

The town offers several accommodations options, but the best is the national historic landmark **Hotel Hershey** (© **800/HERSHEY** [437-7439]; www.thehotel hershey.com), a Mediterranean-style luxury hotel (ca. 1933) where you're greeted with kisses. Chocolate kisses, of course. The hotel's Circular Dining Room is top-notch and the cozy Iberian Lounge offers chocolate martinis. The luxurious $7-million **Spa at the Hotel Hershey** overlooks a formal rose garden (Milton's wife, Catherine, loved roses) and incorporates chocolate in its treatments; soak in the Whipped Cocoa Bath or get a Chocolate Bean Polish.

Note: Guests staying at a Hershey resort can breakfast with larger-than-life Hershey's product characters and then get early admittance to some family-friendly rides in the amusement park with the Breakfast in the Park package.

Hershey, off Route 322, is a 2-hour drive from Philly (3 hr. from New York City) via I-76. For more information about the town, the theme park, and dining and accommodations options in Hershey, as well as detailed directions and maps, call © **800/HERSHEY** (437-7439) or head online to **www.hersheypa.com**.

theaters, amusement parks, and great outlet mall shopping. And, of course, the family-style, all-you-can-eat or gourmet Pennsylvania Dutch restaurants offer unique dining experiences as well as meals.

Essentials

GETTING THERE Lancaster County is 57 miles or a 90-minute drive west of Philadelphia, on Route 30. **From the Northeast,** take I-95 south from New York City onto the New Jersey Turnpike, then take exit 6 onto the Pennsylvania Turnpike (I-76), turning south to Lancaster City via exit 266 or 286 (trip time: 2¼ hr.). **From the south,** follow

I-83 north for 90 minutes from Baltimore, then head east on Route 30 from York into the county. **Amtrak** provides frequent service from 30th Street Station in Philadelphia to the great old Lancaster station (trip time: 70 min.).

VISITOR INFORMATION   The **Pennsylvania Dutch Convention & Visitors Bureau,** 501 Greenfield Rd., Lancaster, PA 17601 (© **800/PA-DUTCH** [723-8824]; www. padutchcountry.com), provides an excellent map and visitors' guide, along with answers to specific questions and interests. The office itself (off the Rte. 30 Bypass east of Lancaster) offers direct telephone links to many local hotels and an overview slide show. Many towns, such as Intercourse, Strasburg, and Lancaster, have local information centers.

What to See & Do

The suggestive name of **Intercourse** refers to the intersection of two old roads, the King's Highway (now Rte. 340 or Old Philadelphia Pike) and Newport Road (now Rte. 772). It's now the center of Amish life, set in the midst of the wedge of country east of Lancaster; unfortunately, the number of commercial attractions, ranging from schlock to good quality, about equals the places of genuine interest. One not-to-miss spot is the **People's Place,** 3518 Old Philadelphia Pike (© **800/390-8436** or 717/768-7171; www. thepeoplesplace.com), a bookshop and interpretive center with as much information on the Amish as you can handle. Of the commercial developments, try **Kitchen Kettle Village** (© **800/732-3538** or 717/768-8261; www.kitchenkettle.com), where over 30 stores selling crafts from decoys to fudge are grouped around the Burnleys' 1954 jam and relish kitchen.

Ephrata, near exit 286 off I-76, combines an 18th-century Moravian religious site with some pleasant country and the area's largest farmers' market and auction center. **Ephrata Cloister,** 632 W. Main St. (© **717/733-6600;** www.ephratacloister.org), near the junction of routes 222 and 322, was one of America's earliest communal societies and is an interesting group of medieval-style structures that includes a museum shop. The main street of Ephrata is pleasant for strolling, including an old rail car where the train line used to run. **Doneckers,** 318–324 N. State St. (© **717/738-9500;** www.doneckers. com), is a complex consisting of a hotel, sophisticated furniture and clothing boutiques, and a fine-dining restaurant (the boutiques and restaurant are closed Wed and Sun). Just outside of town is the **Green Dragon Market** (© **717/738-1117;** www.greendragon market.com), open Friday from 9am to 9pm. You might see goats and cows changing hands here. Summer brings fresh corn, fruit, and melons, which is one reason why local chefs shop for produce here.

Other charming towns in the region include **Lititz,** with its pretzel factory and a lovely park adjoining a purely 18th-century main street; **Strasburg,** with rides on its preserved iron steam locomotive and assorted rail-related attractions; and **Bird-in-Hand,** known for its farmers' market (Fri–Sat year-round, plus Wed Apr–Nov and Thurs July–Oct) and homemade ice cream. For antiquing, the Sunday fairs in **Adamstown,** 2 miles east of exit 286 off I-76, bring thousands of vendors to their enormous sites. The largest are **Stoudt's Black Angus Antiques Mall** (www.stoudtsbeer.com), with more than 350 permanent dealers (and a great on-site brewery and restaurant), and **Renningers Antique and Collectors Market** (www.renningers.com), with 375 permanent dealers.

There's less to do in the city of **Lancaster** itself than in the surrounding area, though this is slowly changing. In town, the one visitor highlight is **Central Market,** erected in 1889 just off Penn Square but operating since the 1730s as the nation's oldest farmers' market, with more than 80 stalls. You can savor regional produce and foods, from sweet bologna and scrapple to egg noodles and shoofly pie (Tues and Fri 6am–4:30pm; Sat 6am–2pm). Don't miss the brand-new **Clipper Magazine Stadium** for minor league baseball, featuring the **Lancaster Barnstormers** (© 717/509-HITS [509-4487]; www. lancasterbarnstormers.com). To the city's east on Route 30, the outlet centers of **Rockvale Square** (www.rockvalesquareoutlets.com) and **Tanger Outlets** (www.tangeroutlet. com) offer dozens of top brands.

Where to Stay & Dine

You're more apt to find solid, value-oriented quality than elegance in food and lodging in this family-oriented landscape. The **Best Western Eden Resort Inn & Suites,** 222 Eden Rd., routes 30 and 272 in Lancaster (© 800/528-1234 or 717/569-6444; www. edenresort.com), is a cut above, with three pools (one indoor and one children's wading pool), a tropically landscaped atrium, and kitchenettes in 40 of the 276 rooms (others come with fridges). Doubles run $129 to $159. **Country Inn of Lancaster,** 2133 Lincoln Hwy. E. (Rte. 30), Lancaster (© 877/393-3413 or 717/393-3413; www.country innoflancaster.com), is a 125-room hotel that lets you rock away on your back porch overlooking beautiful Amish farmland, with a heated pool, free breakfast, and refrigerators in the deluxe rooms. Doubles from $125. The Convention & Visitors Bureau (see above) or the website **www.authenticbandb.com** will provide information on dozens of B&Bs and a scattering of working farms taking in lodgers.

Pennsylvania Dutch meals or smorgasbords include German-style meats and potpies, starchy noodle dishes, boiled vegetables, and sweet desserts. Among the smorgasbords and family-style restaurants open Monday through Saturday, try **Miller's Smorgasbord,** Route 30 at Ronks Road, 5 miles east of Lancaster (© 800/669-3568 or 717/687-6621; www.millerssmorgasbord.com), which has served millions since 1929. In downtown Lancaster, try the premium homemade brews and great bar food at **Lancaster Brewing Company,** Walnut and Plum streets (© **717/391-6258;** www.lancasterbrewing.com).

VALLEY FORGE

Only 30 minutes from central Philadelphia today, Valley Forge was hours of frozen trails away in the winter of 1777–78. The Revolutionary forces had just lost the battles of Brandywine and Germantown. While the British occupied Philadelphia, Washington's forces repaired to winter quarters near an iron forge where the Schuylkill met Valley Creek, 18 miles northwest. A sawmill and gristmill were supposed to help provide basic requirements, but the British had destroyed them. Some 12,000 men and boys straggled into the encampment, setting up quarters and lines of defense.

Unfortunately, the winter turned bitter. Shortages of food and clothing, along with damp shelters, left nearly 4,000 men diseased and unfit for duty. Almost 2,000 perished, and others deserted. Congress, which had left Philadelphia hurriedly, couldn't persuade the colonies to give money to alleviate the conditions. Nevertheless, the forces slowly gained strength and confidence, thanks in part to the Prussian army veteran Baron von Steuben, appointed by Washington to retrain the Continental Army under his revised and distinctly American "Manual of Arms." By springtime the Continentals were an army on which their new allies, the French, could rely. Replicas of their huts, some of the officers' actual lodgings, dot the park today.

Admission to the park is free. Start your visit at the Valley Forge **National Historical Park Visitors Center,** at the junction of Pa. 23 and North Gulph Road (© **610/783-1077;** www.nps.gov/vafo). A short film depicting the encampment is shown at the visitor center every half-hour. Also at the visitor center is a museum containing Washington's tent, an extensive collection of Revolutionary War artifacts, and a bookstore.

Highlights in the park include the **National Memorial Arch;** an 1865 covered bridge; the **Isaac Potts House** (1770), which Washington commandeered as his headquarters; and the 1993 Monument to Patriots of African Descent. General Washington's Head-quarters and surrounding area are closed for construction/renovation from October 2008 through January 2009. A 1903 Gothic **Washington Memorial Chapel** is free, with Sunday carillon recitals in the bell tower at 2pm. A private-public partnership is working on an extensive **National Center for the American Revolution**—don't look for comple-tion before the late-2000s, though. A brand-new innovative "Cell Phone Tour" is avail-able for free, offering information on the park's attractions through a cellular phone call.

The park's facilities are open daily from 9am to 5pm, later in summer.

GETTING THERE   From Philadelphia, take exit 327, the Mall Boulevard exit, of the Pennsylvania Turnpike (I-76) to North Gulph Road. Follow the signs.

TWO PREMIER ATTRACTIONS IN THE BRANDYWINE VALLEY

The Brandywine Valley, bridging Pennsylvania and Delaware, is beautiful rolling country filled with Americana from Colonial days through the Gilded Age. Many of the farms that kept the Revolutionary troops fed have survived to this day. There are 15 covered bridges and scores of antiques stores in Chester County, with miles of country roads and horse trails between them. Though the area is filled with things to see and do, two par-ticular attractions stand out.

Tip: For more information on the region and its attractions, contact the **Brandywine Conference and Visitors Bureau (CVB)** (© **610/565-3679;** www.brandywinecvb.org) and request its free visitor's guide; the CVB also offers information on discounted weekend packages, including hotel and attractions tickets. Or try the **Chester County Conference and Visitors Bureau** (© **800/228-9933** or 610/719-1730; www.brandywinevalley.com) and ask for its official tourist guide.

Longwood Gardens (Best   One of the world's most celebrated horticultural dis-plays, Longwood Gardens marked its centennial in 2006. It showcases more than 11,000 different types of plants and flowers amid 1,050 acres of outdoor gardens and woodlands. For sheer size, Longwood is spectacular. But the ever-blooming displays throughout the grounds and conservatory are both creative and delightful. Everybody has a favorite spot: the tropical paradise of the **Conservatory;** the eye-popping seasonal displays; the flower-garden walk that explodes in seasonal color; the **Chimes Tower** (with carillon); the **Idea Garden** to inspire home gardeners; the **Flower Garden Fountains,** the **Italian Water Garden,** or the **Main Fountain Garden,** whose 380 fountains and spouts rise over 130 feet high during one of the 5-minute displays throughout the day. There are also illumi-nated displays in the fountain garden on Tuesday, Thursday, and Saturday evenings June through September, plus fireworks displays on several evenings in summer (check the website for a schedule). The recently restored **East Conservatory** is filled with water features among the plantings (serious gardeners will enjoy the audio-wand tours). Behind the ballroom is an organ museum with interactive displays for children. An enlarged **Indoor Children's Garden** with secret garden and bamboo maze opened in 2007.

Longwood's attractions also include seasonal plant displays (Christmas and Easter gardens are noteworthy) and hundreds of performances; check the website for a schedule. Facilities include the **Peirce–du Pont House,** open daily from 10am to 5pm; a large museum shop; and the **Terrace Restaurant,** which has both a cafeteria and full-service dining room. Both restaurants are open later during special events; reservations are recommended for the dining room.

Rte. 1 (just north of Rte. 52), Kennett Square, PA. ✆ **610/388-1000.** www.longwoodgardens.org. Admission $16 adults, $14 seniors, $6 ages 16–22, $2 ages 6–15. AE, DC, DISC, MC, V. Mid-Jan to Mar daily 9am–5pm; Apr–May daily 9am–6pm; Memorial Day to Labor Day Mon–Wed and Sun 9am–6pm, Thurs–Sat 9am–10pm; Sept–Oct daily 9am–6pm; early Nov to Thanksgiving daily 9am–5pm; Thanksgiving to early Jan daily 9am–9pm.

Winterthur Museum & Country Estate   Named after a town in Switzerland and pronounced "win-ter-tour," this eight-story mansion and country estate features one of the world's premier collections of American antiques and decorative arts. The estate was the country home of Henry Francis du Pont, a collector of furniture, who in 1951 turned the place into a museum for American decorative arts. The 85,000 objects made or used in America, including Chippendale furniture, silver tankards by Paul Revere, and a dinner service made for George Washington, are displayed in the 175 period rooms. A variety of 1-hour **Discovery Tours** focus on everything from entertaining to du Pont collections to seasonal topics. The introductory Elegant Entertaining tour, for instance, covers only one floor, highlighting the dining room, sitting rooms, and other period public rooms. The Winterthur Experience pass, good for 2 consecutive days, includes one Discovery Tour, admission to the galleries, and a tram tour of the 966-acre grounds. Additional hour-long tours can be added for $5 for adults. Reservations are recommended. An annual **Yuletide Tour** ($20 for adults, $10 for children) is offered from mid-November to December 31, and **iPod tours** of the first-floor galleries are also available—and can be downloaded from the website.

Children 7 and under are permitted on three of the tours, as well as the Yuletide Tour. Kids (and adults, too) will love the **Enchanted Woods,** a 3-acre fairy-tale garden filled with places to play, including a Faerie Cottage and Troll Bridge. Other facilities include two restaurants (afternoon tea is a special treat), a store, and a bookshop.

5105 Kennett Pike (Rte. 52), Winterthur, DE. ✆ **800/448-3883** or 302/888-4600. www.winterthur.org. Admission to galleries and garden $15 adults, $13 seniors and students, $5 children 5–11. Guided Discovery Tours of house and garden $20 adults, $18 seniors and students. Special-interest tours $15 additional. AE, DISC, MC, V. Tues–Fri 10am–5pm (last tour at 4pm). Closed Thanksgiving and Christmas. Located 6 miles northwest of Wilmington on Rte. 52 and 5 miles south of Rte. 1.

WHERE TO STAY & DINE   The **Brandywine River Hotel,** routes 1 and 100 in Chadds Ford (✆ **610/388-1200;** www.brandywineriverhotel.com), has adapted and expanded a historic inn. All units were updated in 2007 with traditional furnishings. From $129 to $139 double. The **Hamanassett Bed & Breakfast,** in Chester Heights (✆ **877/836-8212** for reservations, or 610/459-3000; www.hamanassett.com), is in a romantic 1856 country house with Palladian windows and a wide porch, about 20 minutes from the main Brandywine Valley attractions. Doubles from $150 to $200.

You can dine well at the 1758 **Dilworthtown Inn,** 1390 Old Wilmington Pike and Brinton Bridge Road, in West Chester (✆ **610/399-1390;** www.dilworthtown.com). The menu changes weekly and includes an array of fine-dining options.

The battle that took place in this small university town (about a 2-hr. drive from Philadelphia and an hour from Baltimore) in 1863 was the turning point of the Civil War. Over 3 broiling hot July days, Gen. Robert E. Lee's 75,000-man Confederate Army of Northern Virginia clashed thrice with Gen. George Meade's 83,000-strong Union troops, each time failing to deliver the decisive blow that would convince President Lincoln to end the war. More than 51,000 men died and over 40,000 others were wounded, making this the bloodiest battle in American history. The war didn't end until 2 years later, but after Gen. George E. Pickett's ill-fated charge up Cemetery Ridge on July 3, Lee realized he was beaten and began his retreat south.

Lincoln traveled to Gettysburg 4 months after the battle to dedicate the cemetery that held 3,706 casualties, a third of them unknown. "Four score and seven years ago," Lincoln began his brief address—the most famous speech by any American president.

The battle and Lincoln's address are commemorated at **Gettysburg National Military Park,** the country's premier battlefield shrine, with a monument to just about every company that served here (more than 1,000 in all) spread out along 40 scenic miles. Stop first at the Gettysburg National Military Park Visitor Center (© 717/334-1124; www. nps.gov/gett). In April 2008, a new 139,000-square-foot headquarters off the battlefield opened at 1195 Baltimore Pike (Rte. 97). The center features a Gettysburg in the Civil War museum, an interesting bookstore, and the much-loved Electric Map and Cyclorama (which are undergoing extensive restoration through Sept 2008). It is also be the starting point for bus tours, licensed guide tours, and ranger walks. Rangers are glad to answer questions and provide maps of the hiking trails and the 18-mile self-guided auto tour, which hits all the major sites. For security reasons, backpacks and large parcels are not allowed in the visitor center.

Admission to Gettysburg National Military Park is free. The cost of the Electric Map presentation is $4. The battlefield is open daily year-round from 6am to 10pm April through October, and from 6am to 7pm November through March. The visitor center is open daily from 8am to 5pm (until 6pm in summer), except Thanksgiving, Christmas, and January 1. The cemetery is open from dawn to dusk.

The busiest time to visit is during the 3-day reenactment every July 1 to July 3, when 350,000 people descend on Gettysburg. If you plan to come then, make hotel reservations at least 8 months in advance.

For information about accommodations, restaurants, shopping, and other local attractions, contact the **Gettysburg Convention and Visitors Bureau,** 89 Steinwehr Ave., Gettysburg, PA 17325 (© 717/334-2100; www.gettysburg.com).

WHERE TO STAY   Two new hotels have opened at the Gettysburg Gateway complex northwest of the battlefield on Route 15. The **Wyndham Gettysburg**, 95 Presidential Circle (© 717/339-0020), has 248 rooms, indoor and outdoor pools, and a contemporary style for $129 to $189 for doubles. The **Courtyard by Marriott,** 115 Presidential Circle (© 717/334-5600), has 152 rooms and an indoor pool. Doubles range from $109 to $169. If you'd like to sleep in a bit of history, the **Best Western Gettysburg Hotel,** 1 Lincoln Sq. (© 800/528-1234 or 717/337-2000; www.gettysburg-hotel.com), is on the town square and charges $94 to $350 double.

GETTING THERE   Gettysburg is about 125 miles west of Philadelphia, 180 miles east of Pittsburgh, and about 50 miles northwest of Baltimore. Take **I-76** (Pennsylvania Tpk.) west from Philadelphia or east from Pittsburgh to Harrisburg, then **U.S. 15** south to Gettysburg.

7 PITTSBURGH & WESTERN PENNSYLVANIA

PITTSBURGH

Steel mills played a big part in the creation of Pittsburgh, but gone are the days when you'll see any of those belching smokestacks marring the Steel City skyline. Modern glass office towers, contemporary public artworks, and theaters are more the norm these days. And Pittsburgh lies surrounded by natural beauty. The city's hilly landscape is sliced by the Ohio, Allegheny, and Monongahela rivers and bordered by the lovely Laurel Highlands, begging visitors to hit the trail, rent a canoe, or just set out on a pleasant evening stroll. Add to all of this some of the nation's friendliest residents, and you've got the makings of the perfect vacation getaway.

Essentials

GETTING THERE   By Plane   Pittsburgh International Airport (© **412/472-3525;** www.pitairport.com) is 15 miles west of downtown. **US Airways** is the dominant carrier. To get downtown from the airport, take the public **28X Airport Flyer bus** (© **412/442-2000;** www.portauthority.org) for $2.25. A cab ride costs $30. The airport is a 20-minute drive (45 min. during rush hour) from downtown.

By Train   Amtrak (© **800/USA-RAIL** [872-7245] or 412/471-6172; www.amtrak.com) provides daily service from Philadelphia (trip time: $7^1/_2$ hr.), Washington, D.C. ($7^3/_4$ hr.), Cleveland (3 hr.), and Chicago ($9^1/_2$ hr.) to its station at 1100 Liberty Ave.

By Car   **Major routes into the belt roads around Pittsburgh are **I-76 from the northwest (Cleveland) and east (Philadelphia), **I-70** from the west (Columbus) and southeast (Baltimore), and **I-79** from the north (Erie, Pennsylvania) and south (Charleston, West Virginia).

VISITOR INFORMATION   **The **Greater Pittsburgh Convention & Visitors Bureau, 425 6th Ave. (© **800/359-0758** or 412/281-7711; www.visitpittsburgh.com), operates several **Welcome Centers:** downtown, Liberty Avenue next to the Gateway Center; at the Airport Landside Terminal; and at the Senator John Heinz History Center in the Strip District.

GETTING AROUND   **The **Port Authority of Allegheny County (© **412/442-2000;** www.portauthority.org) operates subways and buses throughout Pittsburgh as well as the "T" Light Rail. Fares are free within the Golden Triangle downtown; prices vary outside that area but are generally less than $2. A weekly unlimited pass goes for $20 to $30, depending upon the zones; children ages 6 to 12 pay half-fare.

FAST FACTS   **For **medical services, call **Mercy Hospital** downtown, 1400 Locust St. (© **412/232-8111**). In the Oakland area, the major local hospital is **UPMC Presbyterian,** 200 Lothrop St. (© **412/647-8762**). The 7% city sales tax is not assessed on clothing, shoes, groceries, or prescriptions; hotel taxes total 14%.

What to See & Do

Pittsburgh's compact and walkable downtown is called the **Golden Triangle,** where the Allegheny and Monongahela rivers converge into the Ohio. Here you'll find 36-acre **Point State Park** (© **412/471-0235**), the historic site of Fort Pitt, now home to Pittsburgh's landmark 150-foot fountain and outdoor gathering and concert spaces. Until 2010, portions of Point State Park will be cordoned off as the city renovates lighting, benches, stage areas, and park infrastructure. Entrance is free to the park and the adjoining **Allegheny Riverfront Park.**

Your best perspective of Point State Park is from the **Mount Washington Overlook** (Grandview Ave.). The city's bridges, rivers, and Golden Triangle create a lovely panorama enjoyed from one of Mount Washington's observation decks, restaurants, or bars. Ascend the cliff face via either the 19th-century **Duquesne Incline,** 1220 Grandview Ave. (© 412/381-1665; http://incline.pghfree.net), where the fares are $4 for adults and $2 for children; or the **Monongahela Incline,** 8 Grandview Ave. (© 412/442-2000; www.portauthority.org), with fares of $2 for adults, $1 for children.

Many of Pittsburgh's cultural institutions bear the names of American industrial barons who amassed their fortunes here and said thanks with hefty endowments. In 1895, Andrew Carnegie endowed the **Carnegie Museums** (www.carnegiemuseums.org), among the city's finest: the **Carnegie Museum of Art,** 4400 Forbes Ave., Oakland (© 412/622-3131; www.cmoa.org), with contemporary exhibitions and Impressionist and post-Impressionist masterpieces; the **Carnegie Museum of Natural History,** 4400 Forbes Ave., Oakland (© 412/622-3131; www.carnegiemnh.org), renowned for its Dinosaur Hall; the **Carnegie Science Center,** 1 Allegheny Ave. (© 412/237-3400; www.carnegiesciencecenter.org), where kids experience hands-on science and Sports-Works next door; and the **Andy Warhol Museum,** 117 Sandusky St. (© 412/237-8300; www.warhol.org), devoted to the life and work of Pittsburgh's most colorful native artist.

The **Mattress Factory,** 500 Sampsonia Way (© 412/231-3169; www.mattress.org), is a museum of site-specific, room-size artworks by artists-in-residence. **Clayton,** the former home of Henry Clay Frick, shares a 6-acre site with the **Frick Art & Historical Center,** 7227 Reynolds St. (© 412/371-0600; www.frickart.org). Museums in the latter include artistic masterpieces and classic cars, as well as a floral conservatory. Many guests round out an afternoon of free chamber music with high tea on the grounds. Among the city's most unusual sights are the **Nationality Rooms** in the 42-story Cathedral of Learning on the University of Pittsburgh's campus, Fifth Avenue at Bigelow Boulevard (© 412/624-6000; www.pitt.edu/~natrooms). Twenty-four classrooms meticulously re-create the interior design styles of Pittsburgh's diverse immigrant settlers.

Pittsburghers love their sports teams, especially the **Steelers.** Join them at a football game in **Heinz Field,** North Shore Drive at Allegheny Avenue (© 412/323-1200; www.steelers.com). **PNC Park,** 115 Federal St. (© 800/BUY-BUCS [289-2827]; www.pirateball.com), on the shore of the Allegheny River, hosts the Pittsburgh Pirates. Views of Pittsburgh's skyline form a beautiful backdrop to the outfield. The Pittsburgh Penguins play at **Mellon Arena,** 66 Mario Lemieux Place (© 800/642-1842; www.pittsburgh penguins.com), right off I-579.

The **Pittsburgh Zoo & Aquarium,** 7340 Butler St. (© 800/474-4966; www.pittsburghzoo.com), set atop a hill in Pittsburgh's Shadyside neighborhood, is known for its large children's zoo. Other highlights include a walk-through bat flyaway, a rare Komodo dragon, and a well-stocked African savanna. Another family favorite is **Kennywood,** 4800 Kennywood Blvd. (© 412/461-0500; www.kennywood.com), a traditional amusement park 10 miles southeast of Pittsburgh in West Mifflin. The park features steel and wooden roller coasters, water rides, and dozens of spinning, twirling attractions for all ages.

The **Strip District** (© 412/201-4774; www.neighborsinthestrip.com), a warehouse district bounded roughly by 16th and 31st streets, between Smallman Street and Liberty

Avenue, was once Pittsburgh's waterfront market. Today the Strip draws locals and visitors to its ethnic grocery stores; fresh produce, meat, fish markets and bakeries; and specialty foods stores. Here you'll find the **Senator John Heinz History Center,** 1212 Smallman St. (© **412/454-6000;** www.pghhistory.org), housed in a massive renovated 1898 icehouse. A highlight is the Heinz 57 exhibit, featuring the pickled relishes, ketchup, and mustards made famous by the Pittsburgh-born Heinz family.

Where to Stay & Dine

The landmark **Omni William Penn,** 530 William Penn Place (© **888/444-6664** or 421/281-7100; www.omniwilliampenn.com), is Pittsburgh's historic grande dame. The luxurious downtown hotel is known for its crystalline lobby and romantic guest rooms. Rates start at $169 double. Another romantic downtown favorite is the **Renaissance Pittsburgh Hotel,** 107 6th St. (© **800/468-3571** or 412/562-1200; www.marriott. com), a 14-story copper-clad hotel known for its 30-foot glass atrium, marble lobby, upscale rooms, and fabulous views. Doubles begin at $179. The proximity of Mellon Arena and the David Lawrence Convention Center draw business and leisure travelers to the **Doubletree Hotel,** 1 Bigelow Sq. (© **800/222-TREE** [222-8733] or 412/281-5800; www.doubletree.com). Doubles begin at $169. The **Holiday Inn Select at University Center,** 100 Lytton Ave. (© **888/465-4329** or 412/682-6200; www.ihg.com), with doubles starting at $169, offers pleasant, affordable accommodations within blocks of Carnegie Mellon, the University of Pittsburgh, and the Carnegie Museums of Art and Natural History.

For upscale dining within walking distance of the Theater District and Heinz Hall, try **Opus,** inside the Renaissance Pittsburgh Hotel at 107 6th St. (© **412/992-2005;** www. dineatopus.com). The warm, intimate restaurant features a Continental menu with Mediterranean influences and a very impressive wine list. On the Strip, **Lidia's,** 1400 Smallman St. (© **412/552-0150;** www.lidiasitaly.com), serves homemade pasta and northern Italian specialties created by Lidia Bastianich, hostess of the PBS cooking show *Lidia's Italian Table.* For excellent German beer and food, visit Deutschtown's **Penn Brewery,** 800 Vinial St. (© **412/237-9402;** www.pennbrew.com). The Pastorius family, descendants of the oldest German family in America, brews award-winning beers and serves them alongside bratwurst and sauerbraten in a fun beer-hall atmosphere appropriate for the whole family.

Don't miss Pittsburgh's culinary original, **Primanti Brothers,** a 70-year-old institution famous for putting the fries and coleslaw inside their sandwiches, right along with the chopped meat, cheese, and sliced tomato. (Open wide!) The restaurant still churns out sandwiches in its original location in the Strip at 46 18th St. (© **412/263-2142;** www. primantibros.com), but you'll find Primanti's at a dozen locations around town, including PNC Park and Heinz Field.

Pittsburgh After Dark

PERFORMING ARTS Gilded and plush with red velvet, Italian marble, and Viennese crystal chandeliers, **Heinz Hall,** 600 Penn Ave. (© **412/392-4900;** www.pittsburgh symphony.org), endowed by Henry John Heinz, is the elegantly opulent home of the renowned **Pittsburgh Symphony.** The nearby **Benedum Center,** 719 Liberty Ave., houses performances by the **Pittsburgh Ballet** (© **412/281-0360;** www.pbt.org), **Pittsburgh Opera** (© **412/281-0912;** www.pittsburghopera.org), and **Pittsburgh CLO** (© **412/456-6666;** www.pittsburghclo.org), which produces a summer season of musicals. Pittsburgh is also home to several theater companies, including **PNC Broadway,**

719 Liberty Ave. (© **412/471-6070;** www.pgharts.org); **Pittsburgh Public Theatre,** 621 Penn Ave. (© **412/316-1600;** www.ppt.org); and **Pittsburgh City Theatre,** 1300 Bingham St. (© **412/431-2489;** www.citytheatrecompany.org).

THE BAR & CLUB SCENE   A good place to check out the nightlife is the **Strip District** (© **412/201-4774;** www.neighborsinthestrip.com), which becomes a club scene after dark. **Firehouse Lounge,** 2216 Penn Ave. (© **412/434-1230**), features a wide variety of music, includes plenty of drinking and dancing, and even offers a cocktail and dessert lounge. **Station Square** (© **800/859-8959;** www.stationsquare.com), across the Smithfield Street or Fort Pitt Bridges from downtown, is home to several after-hours restaurants and bars with nice city views.

OUTSIDE PITTSBURGH

The Laurel Highlands, 60 miles to the southeast, boasts historic sites and a wealth of outdoor activities, all set in some of Pennsylvania's loveliest countryside. The **Laurel Highlands Visitors Bureau,** 120 E. Main St., Ligionier (© **800/333-5661** or 724/238-5661; www.laurelhighlands.org), provides details about the entire area.

Active outdoor enthusiasts make time for **Ohiopyle State Park,** just east of Pa. 381 (© **888/PA-PARKS** [727-2757] or 724/329-8591; www.dcnr.state.pa.us), home of the Ohiopyle Falls and more than 19,000 acres of unspoiled wilderness bordering the Youghiogheny River gorge. Popular activities include hiking, biking, camping, fishing, and serious white-water rafting down the "Yough" (pronounced *yawk*).

Nearby, just off U.S. 40, **Fort Necessity National Battlefield** (© **724/329-5512;** www.nps.gov/fone) first tested George Washington's mettle during the French and Indian War in 1754. The 900-acre site includes a visitor center, the battlefield, the reconstructed Fort Necessity, and the Mount Washington Tavern.

For some childish good fun, spend a day at **Idlewild Park** in Ligonier (© **724/238-3666;** www.idlewild.com). Idlewild doesn't have America's sleekest, fastest rides; it's simply a great old amusement park, with a fresh new Soak Zone waterpark to refresh on hot days. Little ones will enjoy the park's Mister Rogers' Neighborhood of Make-Believe, inspired by the late Fred Rogers, who lived close by.

The Laurel Highlands feature prominently on the radar of Frank Lloyd Wright lovers. A number of the architectural innovator's masterworks sit within the area, chief among them **Fallingwater,** 1478 Mill Run Rd. (© **724/329-8501;** www.fallingwater.org). Three cantilevered house levels extend from the hillside, allowing the namesake waterfall to gush through the building. When Wright designed the house in 1936 for Pittsburgher Edgar Kaufmann, most engineers said it wouldn't stand. Extensive reinforcements were added 60 years later to prevent Fallingwater from rejoining the river that runs through it, but Fallingwater still stands and remains a national architectural treasure.

Tours of **Fallingwater** highlight the house Wright designed, its custom-made furniture, and the surrounding property. Take your pick from an array of options (including sunset, nature, and individualized tours), but tours are generally held from March to Thanksgiving with few exceptions. Standard 1-hour tours cost $16 for adults, $10 for ages 6 to 12 (5 and under prohibited). Two-hour in-depth tours, which include more interior rooms and thorough interpretation, cost $55 (children 8 and under prohibited). Advance reservations are essential.

When I. N. Hagan saw Fallingwater, he commissioned Wright to construct **Kentuck Knob,** 723 Kentuck Rd. (© **724/329-1901;** www.kentuckknob.com), a home smaller and less pivotal in architectural history but worth visiting. Guides lead tours on the hour from March through November, with a reduced schedule other months. Standard 1-hour tours cost $16 for adults, $10 for ages 6 to 12 (5 and under prohibited). In-depth 2-hour tours cost $55. Advance reservations are recommended.

Polymath Park, 1 Usonian Dr., Acme (© **877/833-7829;** www.polymathpark.com), marks the latest addition to Frank Lloyd Wright tours in the Laurel Highlands. The park's Wright-designed **Duncan House** can be explored on 60- to 90-minute tours, costing $16 for adults and $8 for ages 6 to 12 (5 and under not permitted). Thorough grounds tours cost $22 and last 1½ to 2 hours. Tour availability varies widely by the season. Call ahead for specific dates and times. Polymath Park's **Balter** and **Blum Houses** were designed by Wright apprentices. They are not available to tour. All three houses feature overnight lodging (see below).

WHERE TO STAY   For an unforgettable weekend, reserve lodging at **Polymath Park,** in the Wright-designed and -influenced Duncan, Balter, or Blum Houses, 1 Usonian Dr., Acme (© **877/833-7829;** www.polymathpark.com). The Duncan and Balter houses, which sleep as many as 12 and begin at $345, must be reserved in their entirety; the Blum house offers individual rooms beginning at $175. The luxury, rural **Nemacolin Woodlands Resort and Spa,** 1001 LaFayette Dr., Farmington (© **800/422-2736** or 724/329-8555; www.nemacolin.com), offers lodge rooms beginning at $309 and two-bedroom town houses starting at $379. The resort includes restaurants, pools, tennis courts, golf courses, and spas, and sits near Ohiopyle State Park, Fallingwater, and Kentuck Knob.

Look for more moderately priced lodging near Idlewild in Greensburg. **Four Points by Sheraton,** 100 Sheraton Dr. (© **888/625-5144** or 724/836-6060; www.fourpoints greensburg.com), offers an indoor pool; doubles begin at $110. In Uniontown, the **Holiday Inn,** 700 W. Main St. (© **888/465-4329** or 724/437-2816; www.hiunion town.com), also has an indoor pool; doubles start at $126.

GETTING THERE   To get to Idlewild from Pittsburgh, follow U.S. 30 east. To get to Fallingwater, Ohiopyle State Park, Farmington, and Chalk Hill, take I-76 east to exit 91. From there, take Pa. 31 East, then Pa. 381 South.

8 BALTIMORE

A combination of interesting tourist attractions, historical sites, and friendly people in such picturesque old neighborhoods as Fells Point, Mount Vernon, Canton, and Federal Hill makes Baltimore an increasingly popular destination. "Charm City" has welcomed visitors since 1729. It was founded as a shipping and ship-building town, so manufacturing has always been a big part of this city. General Motors and Bethlehem Steel have been a part of the east Baltimore landscape for decades. Domino Sugar's sign dominates the Inner Harbor. More recently, Baltimore has welcomed a new wave of service industries and nonprofits. Baseball fans flock to Oriole Park at Camden Yards, which has been instrumental in revitalizing the city's downtown area. Tourism plays an ever-increasing role in the city's economy, and a laid-back population welcomes its visitors with a friendly "Hello, hon!" in the unique Bawlamer accent.

GETTING THERE   By Plane   Baltimore/Washington International Thurgood Marshall Airport (☎ **800/I-FLY-BWI** [435-9294] or 410/859-7111; www.bwiairport. com) is 10 miles south of downtown Baltimore, off I-295 (the Baltimore–Washington Pkwy.). It's a major domestic and international hub. To drive to downtown Baltimore from the airport, take I-195 west to Route 295 North. **SuperShuttle** (☎ **800/258-3826;** www.supershuttle.com) operates vans between the airport and all major downtown hotels. Departures are scheduled every 30 minutes between 5:45am and 11:15pm, and the cost is $11 per person one-way. The **Light Rail** also connects the airport with downtown Baltimore and the Amtrak stations at BWI and at Penn Station.

By Car   **I-95** provides the easiest routes to Baltimore from the north and south. Take I-95 south to I-395 (exit 53), and follow signs to the Inner Harbor. If you're driving in from the north, you'll have to pass through the **Fort McHenry Tunnel** ($2 toll). From the west, take **I-70** east to exit 91, I-695 South (the **Baltimore Beltway**) heading toward Glen Burnie. Take exit 11A, I-95 to I-395, north to downtown.

Once you arrive, you'll find lots of parking garages, as well as metered on-street parking. Garages charge about $20 a day, or $8 to $12 for special events or evening visits. Parking meters must be fed $1 an hour (in quarters only).

By Train   Baltimore is a stop on **Amtrak**'s (☎ **800/872-7245;** www.amtrak.com) Northeast Corridor, between Wilmington, Delaware, and Washington, D.C. Trains arrive at and depart from Pennsylvania Station, 1500 N. Charles St. (north of the Inner Harbor), and BWI Airport Rail station, off Route 170 about 1½ miles from the airport (☎ **410/672-6169**). In addition, the **Maryland Area Rail Commuter Service** (**MARC;** ☎ **800/325-RAIL** [325-7245]; www.mtamaryland.com) provides rail service on two routes from Washington, D.C., stopping at BWI en route. One ends at Camden Station, closest to the Inner Harbor, and the other ends at Penn Station about 20 blocks north.

VISITOR INFORMATION   Contact the **Baltimore Area Convention and Visitors Association** at 100 Light St., Baltimore, MD 21202 (☎ **877/BALTIMORE** [225-8466]; www.baltimore.org), for maps, brochures, and water taxi schedules. In town, check out the new visitor center located between Harborplace and the Maryland Science Center. You can also pick up a copy of the *Baltimore Quick Guide,* a purse-size guide to what's happening in and around the city.

GETTING AROUND   Because so many of Baltimore's major attractions are clustered around the Inner Harbor, walking is often the easiest way to get around.

Baltimore's **Mass Transit Administration (MTA)** operates **Light Rail,** a 27-mile trolley system that travels north-south from the northern suburb of Timonium to Glen Burnie in the south, with a spur to Penn Station. The key stop within the city is Camden Station, next to the Orioles' ballpark. The Light Rail is the ideal way to get to a game or to travel within the downtown area between Camden Yards and the Inner Harbor to Lexington Market and the area around Mount Vernon Place. Tickets are $1.60 one-way and are dispensed at machines at each stop. Better yet, get a day pass covering all MTA transport for $3.50. Trains run Monday through Friday between 6am and 11pm, Saturday between 7am and 11pm, and Sunday between 11am and 7pm.

Baltimore's MTA also operates **Metro,** a subway system that connects downtown with the northwest suburbs, and an extensive **bus** system. The base fare is $1.60, and exact change is necessary, or you can buy a day pass for $3.50. For information and schedules

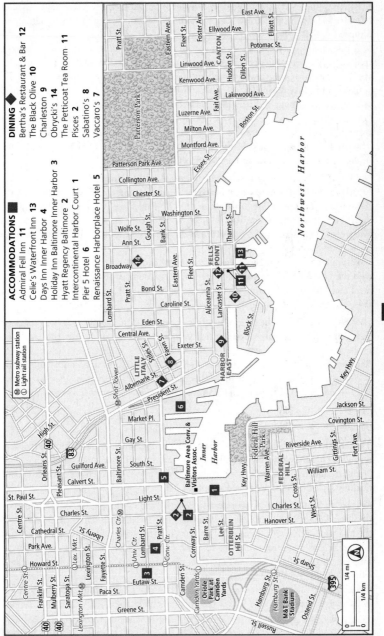

ACCOMMODATIONS ■

Admiral Fell Inn **11**
Celie's Waterfront Inn **13**
Days Inn Inner Harbor **4**
Holiday Inn Baltimore Inner Harbor **3**
Hyatt Regency Baltimore **2**
Intercontinental Harbor Court **1**
Pier 5 Hotel **6**
Renaissance Harborplace Hotel **5**

DINING ◆

Bertha's Restaurant & Bar **12**
The Black Olive **10**
Charleston **9**
Obrycki's **14**
The Petticoat Tea Room **11**
Pisces **2**
Sabatino's **8**
Vaccaro's **7**

Ⓜ Metro subway station
Ⓛ Light rail station

THE MID-ATLANTIC

3

BALTIMORE

for all MTA services, call ✆ **800/543-9809** or 410/539-5000, or visit the MTA website at **www.mtamaryland.com**.

All taxis in the city are metered; two reputable companies are **Yellow Checker Cab** (✆ **410/841-5573**) and **Arrow Cab** (✆ **410/261-0000**). For airport trips, call **Super-Shuttle** (✆ **410/258-3826**).

A ride on a water taxi is a pleasant way to visit Baltimore's attractions, or even to go to dinner. Two companies operate water taxi service, and both have different stops. But you can use either to get within walking distance of your waterfront destination. **Ed Kane's Water Taxi & Trolley** (✆ **800/658-8947** or 410/563-3901) runs a continual service between about a dozen Inner Harbor locations, including Harborplace, Fells Point, and Fort McHenry. The main stop at Harborplace is on the corner between the two pavilions. Tell the mate where you want to go; not all taxis stop at every destination. The cost is $8 for adults and $4 for children 10 and under for a full day's unlimited use of the water taxi and trolley to Fort McHenry.

FAST FACTS   City hospitals include **Johns Hopkins Hospital,** 600 N. Wolfe St. (✆ **410/955-5000**); **University of Maryland Medical Center,** 22 S. Greene St. (✆ **410/328-8667**); and **Mercy Medical Center,** 301 St. Paul Place (✆ **410/332-9000**). Two downtown pharmacies at are **Rite Aid,** 17 W. Baltimore St. (✆ **410/539-0838**), and **Walgreens,** 19 E. Fayette St. (✆ **410/625-1179**). The state sales tax is 5%. The hotel tax is an additional 7.5%.

Baltimore has a nagging problem with property and violent crime. More police, along with the Downtown Partnership's safety guides, are doing a pretty good job of keeping the Inner Harbor and Mount Vernon areas fairly safe. But be alert and use common-sense precautions.

SPECIAL EVENTS   The biggest and best-known event in Baltimore is the **Preakness Celebration** (www.preaknesscelebration.com), a weeklong, citywide party leading up to the Preakness Stakes, the middle jewel of horse racing's Triple Crown, held at Pimlico Racecourse in mid-May. Events include a 5K run, a music festival, hot-air balloon races, a golf tournament, and much more. For tickets to the horse race (they go on sale Jan 1—and they go fast), call ✆ **410/542-9400** or go on the Internet to **www.maryland racing.com**.

WHAT TO SEE & DO

The city's focal point for tourism is the **Inner Harbor,** home of the Baltimore Convention Center and Festival Hall Exhibit Center, the Harborplace shopping pavilions, the National Aquarium and other museums, Oriole Park at Camden Yards, M&T Bank Stadium, and the Pier 6 Concert Pavilion.

American Visionary Art Museum   Look for the "Whirligig," a 55-foot multicolored, wind-powered sculpture at the front of this curvaceous building housing some of the most interesting art you're bound to see. Visionary art is made by people who aren't trained as artists but feel compelled to draw, paint, or create something in an unusual medium. A 10-foot model of the *Lusitania* made from 193,000 matchsticks dominates a first-floor gallery. All the exhibits are fascinating, but some are disturbing and certainly too strong for children (alerts are posted). On Thursdays during June through August, a free movie is screened on the side of the museum's building.

800 Key Hwy. (take Light St. south, turn left onto Key Hwy. at the Maryland Science Center; museum is about 3 blocks farther on the right). ✆ **410/244-1900**. www.avam.org. Admission $12 adults; $8 seniors, students, and children. Tues–Sun 10am–6pm. Closed Thanksgiving and Christmas.

Babe Ruth Birthplace and Museum   George Herman "Babe" Ruth was born in this row house, where two rooms have been re-created to look as they would have when the Sultan of Swat was a boy. Other exhibits include a wall enumerating his home runs, plus memorabilia from his major league career and his days at St. Mary's Industrial School in Baltimore, where he learned to play the game.

216 Emory St. (from Camden Yards, follow the sidewalk baseballs from the Babe Ruth statue at the north end of the warehouse to the house on this tiny street, 3 blocks away). ℂ 410/727-1539. www.baberuth museum.com. Admission $6 adults, $4 seniors, $3 children 5–16. Combination tickets with Sports Legends available. Apr–Oct daily 10am–6pm (until 7:30pm on days of Orioles home games); Nov–Mar daily 10am–5pm. Closed Thanksgiving, Christmas, and New Year's Day.

Baltimore Museum of Art Best   The largest museum in Maryland, the BMA offers galleries dedicated to modern and contemporary art; European sculpture and painting; American painting and decorative arts; prints and photographs; and the arts of Africa, Asia, the Americas, and Oceania; there's also a 2³/₄-acre sculpture garden with 35 major works by Alexander Calder, Henry Moore, and others. The BMA is famous for its Matisse collection, assembled by Baltimore sisters Claribel and Etta Cone, who went to Paris in the 1920s and came back with Impressionist and modern art. The $4-million Cone Wing showcases their collection of paintings by Matisse, Cézanne, Gauguin, van Gogh, and Renoir. Visit the special room set up to remember these women, featuring drawers filled with their personal things, pieces of furniture, and a virtual tour of their Baltimore apartments.

10 Art Museum Dr. (at N. Charles St. and 31st St.; take Howard St. north and bear right onto Art Museum Dr., about 3 miles north of the harbor). ℂ 443/573-1700. www.artbma.org. Free except for special exhibits. Wed–Fri 11am–5pm; Sat–Sun 11am–6pm. Bus: 3 or 11.

Edgar Allan Poe's Grave Site and Memorial   Three modest memorials in this small old graveyard recall the poet who wrote "The Tell-Tale Heart" and "The Raven" (the only poem to inspire an NFL team's name). The main memorial features a bas-relief bust of Poe; a small gravestone adorned with a raven can be found at Poe's original burial lot; and there's also a plaque placed by the French, who, thanks to the poet Baudelaire, enjoy some of the best translations of Poe's works. The poet is remembered on his birthday every January when a mysterious visitor leaves half a bottle of cognac and roses at the grave. On the weekend closest to Poe's birthday, a party is held in his honor. A Halloween tour is also scheduled each year.

Westminster Hall and Burying Grounds, southeast corner of Fayette and Greene sts. ℂ 410/706-2072 (answered by a University of Maryland Law School staffer). Daily 8am–dusk. Closed major holidays.

Fort McHenry National Monument   The flag that flies at Fort McHenry is 30×42 feet, big enough for Francis Scott Key to see by the dawn's early light and write "The Star-Spangled Banner." The star-shaped fort, now a national park, looks much as it did in 1814, the year of the British attack. Its buildings, repaired in the days following that attack, still stand. Exhibits recall Baltimore under siege during the War of 1812, the fort's Civil War service, and its use as an army hospital during World War I. Visitors are invited to take part in the daily changing of the flag, so stop by at 9:30am or 4:30pm (7:30pm June–Aug) to join in. A visit takes about 90 minutes.

Fort McHenry National Monument, E. Fort Ave. ℂ 410/962-4290. www.nps.gov/fomc. Admission $7 adults, free for children 15 and under. Sept–May fort and grounds daily 8am–5pm; June to Labor Day grounds remain open daily until 8pm. Closed Thanksgiving, Christmas, and New Year's Day. Bus: 1. Water taxi stop.

(Value) Money-Saving Harbor Pass

Baltimore's top tourism spots have teamed up with **Harbor Pass.** For $49, adults can visit the National Aquarium, Maryland Science Center, Port Discovery, and Top of the World Observation Level—and ride Ed Kane's Water Taxi all day. Kids' passes are $35. The passes are valid for 3 consecutive days, but only one visit per location. They're also good for discounts at a few hotels and restaurants, an Orioles game, and other Inner Harbor attractions. Call ✆ **877/BALTIMORE** (225-8466) or visit **www.baltimore.org** to order passes; they're also available at the Inner Harbor visitor center.

Maryland Historical Society Museum (Kids)   You can find all kinds of stuff here: Cal Ripken's bat, recordings, correspondence, and sheet music of Broadway composer Eubie Blake. Francis Scott Key's manuscript of the "Star-Spangled Banner" is the centerpiece of an exhibit called "Looking for Liberty." Other collections represent Maryland's 350-plus years of history in a sprawling museum that takes up a city block and includes the town house of Baltimore philanthropist Enoch Pratt, which served as the MHS's first home. The museum store is part consignment store, part gift shop, and has plenty of antiques and other interesting items.

201 W. Monument St. ✆ **410/685-3750.** www.mdhs.org. Admission $4 adults, $3 seniors and children 13–17, free age 11 and under. Free admission 1st Thurs of month. Light Rail: Centre St.

Maryland Science Center (Kids)   This museum's three floors of exhibits include the popular Outer Space Place, home of the Hubble Space Telescope National Visitor Center. Sometimes the exhibits are too crowded or have limited interest, but the IMAX theater and planetarium are always worth a visit. The IMAX theater presents shows as diverse as *Beauty and the Beast* and *Space Station 3D.* IMAX is so popular, extra screenings are available Friday and Saturday evenings. The stars are on display at the David Planetarium and the Crosby Ramsey Memorial Observatory; the latter is free to the public on Friday nights, weather permitting (call for hours).

601 Light St. (south side of the Inner Harbor). ✆ **410/685-5225.** www.mdsci.org. Admission varies according to special exhibits: core experience with planetarium $15 adults, $10 children 3–12; core experience with planetarium and IMAX film $19 adults, $14 children 3–12; special exhibits additional charge. Labor Day to Memorial Day Tues–Thurs 10am–5pm, Fri 10am–8pm, Sat 10am–6pm, Sun 11am–5pm; Memorial Day to Labor Day Thurs–Sat 10am–8pm, Sun–Wed 10am–6pm. Call ahead, as hours change with some exhibits. Water taxi stop.

National Aquarium in Baltimore (Best)   Walk into a room surrounded by patrolling sharks, stroll among coral reefs, and visit a rainforest on the roof of one of the best aquariums in the country. **Animal Planet Australia: Wild Extremes,** set in a 120-foot-tall glass cube at the front of the aquarium, takes visitors to the floor of an Australian river gorge. In this immersion exhibit, wander past tanks filled with death adders, pythons, archer fish, and barramundi, while kookaburras, parrots, and lorikeets fly overhead—there are 1,800 animals in all, as well as plants native to Australia. Although you simply walk in front of most of the exhibits, you get to actually walk inside the doughnut-shaped coral reef and the shark tanks. At feeding time, the divers always draw a crowd. The **Marine Mammal Pavilion,** connected by covered bridge to the main hall, is where you'll find the dolphins. Don't miss the presentations—reserve a seat (at no additional fee) when you pay your admission. **4-D Immersion Theatre,** which opened in late 2007, shows 3-D movies, with the added sensations of movement, mist, and wind. *Tip:* The aquarium draws huge crowds in summer. Beat the crush by purchasing timed tickets in advance.

501 E. Pratt St. (on the harbor). ✆ **410/576-3800.** www.aqua.org. Admission to aquarium only $22 adults, $21 seniors, $13 children 3–11. Aquarium and dolphin presentation $28 adults, $25 seniors, $15 children. Aquarium and 4-D theater $26 adults, $25 seniors, $17 children. All 3 programs $29 adults, $28 seniors, $18 children. Mar–June and Sept–Oct daily 9am–5pm; Nov–Feb daily 10am–5pm; July–Aug daily 9am–5pm; year-round Fri until 8pm. Hours subject to change; call ahead. Exhibits are open 2 hr. after last ticket is sold.

USS *Constellation* (Kids) You can't miss the *Constellation,* docked for years at the Inner Harbor (predating Harborplace). A stunning triple-masted sloop-of-war launched in 1854, the *Constellation* is the last Civil War–era vessel afloat. Tour her gun decks, visit the wardrooms, see a cannon demonstration, and learn about the life of a sailor. Demonstrations begin with the raising of the colors at 10:30am and continue on the hour. "Powder Monkey" tours are directed at children 6 and over.

301 E. Pratt St. (Pier 1). ✆ **410/539-1797.** www.constellation.org. Admission (including audio tour) $8.75 adults, $7.50 seniors, $4.75 children 6–14. Apr–Oct daily 10am–5:30pm (extended hours June–Aug); Nov–Mar daily 10am–4:30pm. Closed Thanksgiving, Christmas, and New Year's Day.

Walters Art Museum (Value) The Walters, with its collections of ancient art, medieval armor, and French 19th-century painting, has always been one of Baltimore's great attractions. Walk through the galleries of sculpture, paintings, gold jewelry, mummies, and sarcophagi and see the progress of fine art through 50 centuries. The original Palazzo building features 1,500 works from mostly the Renaissance and baroque periods. Hackerman House features Asian art. The Palace of Wonders is the imaginary gallery of a 17th-century Flemish nobleman with art, collections from nature, and artifacts from around the world. Docents offer free tours Saturday at 11:30am and Sunday at 2pm. The cafe serves light fare.

600 N. Charles St. ✆ **410/547-9000.** www.thewalters.org. Free admission, though changes in city funding could reinstate admission fees; admission is charged for special exhibitions. Wed–Sun 11am–5pm. Closed July 4, Thanksgiving, and Dec 24–25. Bus: 3, 11, 31, 61, or 64. Light Rail: Centre St. Take Charles St. north to the Washington Monument.

WHERE TO STAY

Baltimore caters to the business traveler but loves families—there are about 7,000 hotel rooms downtown, with all the expected amenities—with more hotels due to open by 2010. A few bed-and-breakfasts around town offer unique style and comfort. *Note:* Every hotel listed in this section is accessible to travelers with disabilities, although specific amenities vary from place to place.

Admiral Fell Inn Updated and expanded over the years, this charming inn sits just a block from the harbor in the heart of Fells Point. It spans eight buildings, built between 1790 and 1996 and blending Victorian and Federal-style architecture. The inn features an antiques-filled lobby and library, and guest rooms individually decorated with Federal period furnishings (and offering luxe touches such as bottled water and bathrobes). Some have canopy beds and some have Jacuzzis. A more rustic loft room has sloping ceilings that tall guests might not like, but its three dormer windows offer some of the best views in the inn. There's a complimentary shuttle to downtown. The **Petticoat Tea Room** offers lunch, tea, and late-afternoon dining.

888 S. Broadway, Baltimore, MD 21231. © **866/583-4162** or 410/522-7377. Fax 410/522-0707. www. harbormagic.com. 80 units. $199–$249 double. Rates include breakfast. AE, DC, DISC, MC, V. Valet parking $25. Located across the street from a water taxi stop. Pets welcome. **Amenities:** Restaurant; access to nearby health club.

Celie's Waterfront Inn   This 18th-century town house is one of only a few bed-and-breakfasts in Baltimore, and it's delightful. Each of the rooms has its own charms: Two have a fireplace and whirlpool and harbor views. Two inside rooms are particularly quiet, as they overlook the courtyard filled with flowers in summer. New owners have added two suites (with living and dining rooms and full kitchens), which can accommodate four and six comfortably. Have breakfast in your room, on the deck, or in the garden. Furnishings throughout were chosen with comfort in mind, with big beds, private bathroom with bathrobes, and a homey parlor.

1714 Thames St., Baltimore, MD 21231. © **800/432-0184.** www.celieswaterfront.com. 9 units. $139–$239 double; $299–$349 suites. Rates include hearty continental breakfast. 2- or 3-night minimum stay may be required on weekends or holidays. AE, DISC, MC, V. On-street parking or $7 in nearby lot. Located across the street from a water taxi stop. *In room:* Fridge (by request).

Days Inn Inner Harbor ⓥ Value   If you're willing to give up proximity to the harbor (by 2 or 3 blocks), you can get a great deal at this modern nine-story hotel. It is located between the arena and convention center, and only 3 blocks from Camden Yards. "Work zone" rooms for business travelers offer large desks, a kitchenette, and plenty of room, but all rooms have the comfort you expect from this chain. Guest rooms offer standard chain-motel furnishings. Many rooms received fresh updates in 2007.

100 Hopkins Place (btw. Lombard and Pratt sts.), Baltimore, MD 21202. © **800/DAYS-INN** (329-7466) or 410/576-1000. Fax 410/576-9437. www.daysinnerharbor.com. 250 units. $99–$189 double. Children 16 and under stay free in parent's room. AE, DC, DISC, MC, V. Parking $15. **Amenities:** Restaurant; pool; fitness center.

Holiday Inn Baltimore Inner Harbor ⓚ Kids   For value and location, it's hard to beat this old-timer, the first major chain property in Baltimore. It's between the 1st Mariner Arena and the convention center, a block from Camden Yards, and 3 blocks from Harborplace. Renovations in 2006 renewed everything from the hotel's facade to the bedroom upholstery. Guest rooms are a good size, with traditional furniture and wide windows with skyline views. Some suites have whirlpool tubs.

301 W. Lombard St., Baltimore, MD 21201. © **800/HOLIDAY** (465-4329) or 410/685-3500. www.holiday-inn.com/bal-downtown. 375 units. $129–$189 double; $285 suite. Children 17 and under stay free in parent's room. AE, DC, DISC, MC, V. Self-parking $15. **Amenities:** Restaurant; indoor pool; health club.

Hyatt Regency Baltimore ⓑ Best   A $20-million renovation has made this convenient hotel the city's most stylish. Not only is the all-glass facade eye-catching, but you won't want to miss the distinctive blue-and-yellow modern decor inside. The most pleasing new feature is the chaise longues tucked under the picture windows. And the location is still the best. It's a short walk across a skywalk to the Inner Harbor, another skywalk to the convention center, and a few blocks to the stadiums.

300 Light St., Baltimore, MD 21202. © **800/233-1234** or 410/528-1234. Fax 410/685-3362. www. baltimore.hyatt.com. 488 units. $199–$399 double. Ask about packages and discounts. Children 17 and under stay free in parent's room. AE, DC, DISC, MC, V. Self-parking $27; valet parking $36. **Amenities:** Restaurant; outdoor pool; putting green; 2 tennis courts; 24-hr. fitness center.

Intercontinental Harbor Court   Baltimore's finest hotel, now part of the Intercontinental chain, was spruced up in 2008. When you spend the night, prepare to be pampered.

Accommodations are exquisitely furnished, from the large standard rooms to the suites, which boast hand-painted decor, marble bathrooms, kitchenettes, and canopy beds. The hotel over-looks the harbor, but only a few rooms have a clear harbor view. Breakfast, lunch, afternoon tea, and dinner are offered at the cheery **Brighton's,** which offers waterfront views, and the **Explorers Lounge** serves lunch, dinner, and late-night fare, as well as live entertainment every night but Monday.

550 Light St., Baltimore, MD 21202. ✆ **800/824-0076** or 410/234-0550. Fax 410/659-5925. www.harbor court.com. 195 units. $275–$305 double; $450–$3,800 suite. AE, DC, DISC, MC, V. Self-parking $21; valet parking $29. **Amenities:** 2 restaurants; indoor pool; tennis courts; health club.

Pier 5 Hotel Be prepared for something wild when you walk into the lobby of the Pier 5. It's bright and airy, and it's fun to settle back into those offbeat sofas. The rooms continue the lobby's purple, red, and yellow color scheme, though much quieter and more refined. Standard rooms are quite comfortable and have lots of conveniences, including bathrobes and bottled water. Suites are luxurious with one, two, or even three tiny balconies overlooking the harbor or the National Aquarium next door. Just about every room has a water view. They offer lots of discount packages for both families and couples.

711 Eastern Ave. (at the end of Pier 5), Baltimore, MD 21202. ✆ **866/583-4162** or 410/539-2000. Fax 410/783-1787. www.harbormagic.com. 65 units. $149–$399 double; $329–$1,500 suite. AE, DC, DISC, MC, V. Self-parking $21; valet parking $28. Located at a water taxi stop. Pets welcome. **Amenities:** 3 restau-rants; access to nearby health club. *In room:* Fridge.

Renaissance Harborplace Hotel The Renaissance is right in the middle of every-thing. It's part of the Gallery at Harborplace, five floors of shops and a food court topped by an office tower. Rooms are the biggest in Baltimore, with comfortable furniture, bathrobes, and wide windows that really open overlooking the Inner Harbor. Its views are good, especially on the upper floors. Special suites connect bedrooms to living room, dining room, and kitchenette. Some even have Murphy beds for extra guests. Public spaces, renovated in 2007, include the contemporary-styled **Water Table** restaurant and lounge.

202 E. Pratt St., Baltimore, MD 21202. ✆ **800/HOTELS-1** (468-3571) or 410/547-1200. Fax 410/783-9676. www.renaissanceharborplace.com. 622 units. $259–$309 double; $500–$5,000 suite. Children 16 and under stay free in parent's room. AE, DC, DISC, MC, V. Self-parking $27; valet parking $30. **Amenities:** Restaurant; indoor pool; health club.

WHERE TO DINE

"Crabtown" has always been known for good seafood, but Baltimore is also home to an increasing variety of ethnic and regional cuisines. There are plenty of good restaurants in Baltimore's main tourist area, with excellent choices in nearby Little Italy, Fells Point, and Mount Vernon.

Bertha's Restaurant & Bar INTERNATIONAL/SEAFOOD This Fells Point landmark is known for its mussels and music. The decor is shabby chic, with dark walls and plenty of accessories proud of their age. It's a perfect place for a traditional afternoon tea, a dinner featuring Bertha's mussels, or a night of jazz or blues. Mussels are prepared in a dozen different ways—they're delicious swimming in garlic butter. At lunch you can get salads, omelets, sandwiches, and burgers. Afternoon tea is served Monday through Saturday from 3 to 4:30pm. Brunch is served on Sunday.

734 S. Broadway. ✆ **410/327-5795.** www.berthas.com. Reservations accepted only for parties of 6 or more for lunch and dinner; reservations required 24 hr. in advance for afternoon tea. Main courses

$6.50–$19 lunch, $12–$22 dinner; afternoon tea $10. MC, V. Sun–Thurs 11:30am–11pm; Fri–Sat 11:30am–midnight. Bar open until 2pm.

The Black Olive GREEK/SEAFOOD This Greek taverna, just beyond the busier streets of Fells Point, is creating its own traffic. The combination of Greek fare and fresh seafood has made this place a standout. Choose whatever the catch of the day is and trust the chef to make it wonderful. The restaurant has four intimate dining rooms, so small that reservations are a must. The service here is smooth but friendly. Tea fans should try the iced tea made with Greek flowers—it's fragrant and spicy.

814 S. Bond St. ✆ 410/276-7141. www.theblackolive.com. Reservations required for dinner. Entrees $12–$22 lunch, $27–$40 dinner. AE, MC, V. Daily noon–2pm and 5–10pm. Valet parking for dinner.

The Brass Elephant (Value CONTINENTAL The Brass Elephant prides itself on well-prepared food in an elegant setting for reasonable prices. You can count on rockfish or soft-shell crabs in season, or hearty American dishes such as stuffed pork chops. And all of this comes in one of Baltimore's most elegant restaurant settings, an 1861 town house with fireplace, chandeliers, and gold-leaf trim. Upstairs in the **Tusk Lounge,** the atmosphere is more casual.

924 N. Charles St. ✆ 410/547-8480. www.brasselephant.com. Reservations recommended. Main courses $18–$28. AE, DC, DISC, MC, V. Mon–Thurs 5:30–9:30pm; Fri–Sat 5:30–11pm; Sun 4:30–8:30pm. Free valet parking.

Charleston (Best AMERICAN/SOUTHERN With a beautiful setting and imaginative menu, the Charleston is a top choice for a special night out and has the best food in Baltimore. The menu changes every day but might include pan-fried rockfish or bacon-wrapped tenderloin with seasonal vegetables. The cheese course, with about a dozen artisanal cheeses, remains popular. Portions aren't so big you can't enjoy one of the great desserts. Charleston offers a choice of three to six courses: A three-course dinner is $74; a six-course meal will run $109 (wine is extra). The chef's husband and co-owner, Tony Foreman, has selected 600 bottles for the restaurant's wine list, which wins accolades. The couple run a virtual chain in Baltimore nowadays—if you like Charleston, try **Pazo,** 1425 Aliceanna St. (✆ **410/534-7296**), for tapas, or **Cinghiale,** 822 Lancaster St. (✆ **410/547-8282**), for its wine bar and Italian food.

1000 Lancaster St. ✆ 410/332-7373. www.charlestonrestaurant.com. Reservations recommended. Prix-fixe dinners $74–$109. AE, DC, DISC, MC, V. Mon–Sat 5:30–10pm. Free valet parking.

Obrycki's SEAFOOD Food connoisseurs Craig Claiborne and George Lang have raved about this place in Upper Fells Point. The decor is charming, with stained-glass windows, wainscoting, and brick archways. It's the quintessential crab house, where you can crack open steamed crabs or choose crab soup, crab cocktail, crab balls, crab cakes, crab imperial, or soft-shell crabs. The rest of the menu is just as tempting, with options such as lobster, haddock, flounder, and steaks. Service is extremely attentive. Note that Obrycki's is open only during the local crab season.

1727 E. Pratt St. ✆ 410/732-6399. www.obryckis.com. Reservations recommended, but accepted only until 7pm Mon–Fri, 6pm Sat–Sun. Main courses $15–$29; lunch and light fare $6.50–$15. AE, DC, DISC, MC, V. Mon–Fri 11:30am–10pm; Sat 11:30am–11pm; Sun 11:30am–9:30pm. Closed late Nov to mid-Mar.

Pisces SEAFOOD In a city where lots of restaurants have good views, this one tops them all, literally. Overlooking the Inner Harbor, Camden Yards, and the downtown skyline, this rooftop restaurant spreads the city out before you. The interior is sleek and modern, while the menu features mostly seafood prepared with creative sauces and seasonings.

The well-spaced tables offer a pleasantly intimate dining experience; service is anything but hurried.

At the Hyatt Regency, 300 Light St., 15th floor. ✆ **410/528-1234.** Reservations recommended. Main courses $34–$48; Sun brunch $40. AE, DC, DISC, MC, V. Tues–Sat 6–10pm; Sun 10am–2pm.

The Prime Rib STEAKHOUSE   In the heart of Mount Vernon, this restaurant has been dishing out the beef since 1965. The prime rib is the best in town, the Caesar salad is dressed to perfection, and the lobster bisque is rich and creamy. If you want seafood, there are crab cakes and fish. Everything is a la carte. But tables are squeezed together, making intimate conversation impossible. In fact, the dining room—elegant and manly with black leather chairs—can be noisy, with live entertainment nightly.

1101 N. Calvert St. (btw. Biddle and Chase sts.). ✆ **410/539-1804.** www.theprimerib.com. Reservations required. Jackets are required for men. Main courses $21–$45. AE, DC, MC, V. Mon–Thurs 5–10pm; Fri–Sat 5pm–midnight; Sun 4–10pm. Bar fare until 1am. Free valet parking.

Sabatino's SOUTHERN ITALIAN   For 50 years, Sabatino's has been known for its exceptional cuisine. Everyone will tell you to get the house salad with the house dressing, which is thick and garlicky. Simple pasta dishes come in very large portions. The menu also has seafood and meat dishes—*brasciola,* a roll of beef, prosciutto, cheeses, and marinara, is heavenly. Dining rooms fill three floors of this narrow building. It's worth the wait to be seated upstairs, where it's quieter.

901 Fawn St. (at High St.). ✆ **410/727-9414.** www.sabatinos.com. Reservations recommended. Main courses $8–$15 lunch, $13–$30 dinner. AE, DC, DISC, MC, V. Sun–Thurs 11:30am–midnight; Fri–Sat 11:30am–3am.

Vaccaro's ITALIAN PASTRIES/DESSERTS   To top off a perfect day, stop at the always-busy Vaccaro's for dessert and coffee. The cannoli is famous, the pastries and tiramisu stand up to the competition, and if you love gelato, you'll be thrilled by the huge servings—just one scoop is plenty (really!). If dessert is your thing, come on Monday for the all-you-can-eat special. Vaccaro's also has an outlet in Harborplace's Light Street Pavilion (✆ **410/547-7169**).

222 Albemarle St. ✆ **410/685-4905.** www.vaccarospastry.com. Reservations not accepted. Desserts $3.30–$9.40. AE, MC, V. Mon 9am–10pm; Tues–Thurs and Sun 9am–11pm; Fri–Sat 9am–1am.

BALTIMORE AFTER DARK

Baltimore is jumping when the sun sets: The Inner Harbor, Federal Hill, Canton, and Mount Vernon have all developed lives after dark.

For major events, check the arts and entertainment sections of the *Baltimore Sun* and the *Washington Post.* The free weekly *City Paper* has very complete listings, down to the smallest bars and clubs. On the Web, try **www.baltimorefunguide.com.**

Tickets for most major venues are available at the individual box offices or through **Ticketmaster** (✆ **410/547-SEAT** [547-7328]; www.ticketmaster.com).

THE PERFORMING ARTS   The world-class **Baltimore Symphony Orchestra** (✆ **410/ 783-8000;** www.bsomusic.org) is led by renowned conductor Marin Alsop. The BSO performs classical and pops concerts at the Meyerhoff Symphony Hall, 1212 Cathedral St. In summer, you'll also find the BSO outside at Oregon Ridge Park, north of the city off I-83. Its Fourth of July concerts are terrific fun. Tickets are $25 to $75.

Baltimore has a busy theater scene. Regional theater standout **Center Stage,** 700 N. Calvert St. (✆ **410/332-0033;** www.centerstage.org), has developed many new American plays—including works by August Wilson and Eric Overmyer—as Maryland's state theater, presenting new and classic work since 1963.

Everyman Theatre, 1727 N. Charles St. (© **410/752-2208;** www.everymantheatre.org), earns rave reviews for its Equity productions of classics and new works. It plans to move to the renovated Town Theatre, 315 W. Fayette St., in 2009. The **Theatre Project,** 45 W. Preston St. (© **410/752-8558;** www.theatreproject.org), presents experimental and avant-garde work.

The city's prominent African-American theater company **Arena Players,** 801 McCulloh St., off Martin Luther King Boulevard (© **410/728-6500**), presents contemporary plays and romantic comedies.

Touring Broadway shows stop at the renovated 1914 **Hippodrome Theatre** at 10 N. Eutaw St. (© **410/837-7400,** or 547-SEAT [547-7328] for tickets; www.france-merrickpac.com), once a vaudeville house.

THE CLUB & MUSIC SCENE   National acts come to the **1st Mariner Arena** near the Inner Harbor and to the **Pier Six Concert Pavilion** at the Inner Harbor. A number of smaller local clubs welcome smaller touring acts and local performers, from rock to jazz to folk. Music venues include **Bertha's,** 734 S. Broadway (© **410/327-5795**), a great venue for live jazz and blues every day of the week; the **Cat's Eye Pub,** 1730 Thames St. (© **410/276-9085;** www.catseyepub.com), which features nightly live music ranging from traditional Irish music to bluegrass, zydeco, and jazz; and the **8x10,** 8–10 E Cross St. (© **410/625-2000;** www.the8x10.com), where blues, funk, and rock groups play regularly.

Two top dance clubs are **Baja Beach Club,** 55 Market Place, at East Lombard Street, Inner Harbor (© **410/727-0468**), which is popular with locals and draws a crowd of energetic 20-somethings; and **Sonar,** 407 E. Saratoga St. (© **410/327-8333;** www.sonarbaltimore.com), which has a DJ or concerts most nights, with an emphasis on techno and house music.

THE BAR SCENE   Baltimore locals like nothing better than to relax over a cold beer. The best drinking spots include the **Havana Club,** 600 Water St., upstairs from Ruth's Chris Steak House (© **410/468-0022;** www.serioussteaks.com), a sophisticated spot offering tapas, appetizers, desserts, and cigars; the cigar-friendly **Max's Taphouse,** 737 S. Broadway (© **410/675-MAXS** [675-6297]; www.maxs.com), a Baltimore institution known for its tremendous beer selection; and **Wharf Rat Pub & Restaurant,** 206 W. Pratt St., at Hanover Street across from the convention center (© **410/244-8900**), a small brewpub with excellent stouts and ales.

THE GAY & LESBIAN SCENE   For a complete listing of nightspots, check out *Gay Life,* published by the **Gay, Lesbian, Bisexual & Transgender Community Center of Baltimore** (© **410/837-5445;** www.glccb.org) and **www.outinbaltimore.com.** The gay scene centers around Charles Street in Mount Vernon. The popular disco the **Hippo,** 1 W. Eager St. (© **410/547-0069;** www.clubhippo.com), is a Baltimore mainstay. **Grand Central,** 1001 N. Charles St. (© **410/752-7133;** www.centralstationpub.com), offers jazz, drag, karaoke, and other theme nights. Its newest addition, Sapphos, is a ladies' lounge. There's dancing Wednesday through Sunday. Women gather at the friendly **Coconuts Café,** 311 W. Madison St., at Linden Avenue (© **410/383-6064;** www.coconutscafe.com). The **Creative Alliance** (© **410/276-3206;** www.creativealliance.org) hosts the Charm City Kitty Club, a troupe of lesbian, bi, and transgender performers. See the website for a schedule and ticket prices.

The nation's capital still commands center stage, whether it's an election year or not. Visitors continue to pour into town, although security is tighter and additional safeguards have been put into place, reflecting the changes in security everywhere since September 11, 2001, especially in one of the places that was attacked.

Washington continues to offer its own special brand of excitement. You can listen to Senate debates and hear the Supreme Court in session. Find inspiration in magnificent monuments, and wander the vast museums of the Smithsonian Institution and other scientific and cultural institutions. Here you can see firsthand just how the government of the United States works, and some of our great monuments and artistic treasures.

ESSENTIALS

GETTING THERE   By Plane   Washington is served by three major airports. **Ronald Reagan Washington National Airport** (© 703/417-8000; www.metwashairports.com) is just across the Potomac River in Virginia and a 15-minute drive from downtown. About a dozen major airlines and shuttles serve this airport, which has flights to 69 U.S. cities. Climate-controlled pedestrian bridges connect the terminal directly to a Metro station, whose Blue and Yellow lines stop here. The trip downtown via Metro takes about 20 minutes.

Washington Dulles International Airport (© 703/572-2700; www.metwashairports. com) is also in Virginia, about 45 minutes west of downtown. It's a big discount airline hub. The **Washington Flyer Express Bus** runs every 30 minutes between Dulles and the West Falls Church Metro station, where you can board a train for D.C. Buses cost $9 one-way. More convenient is the hourly Metrobus service that runs between Dulles and the L'Enfant Plaza Metro station, located near Capitol Hill and within walking distance of the National Mall. The bus departs hourly daily, costs only $3, and takes about 45 to 60 minutes.

Baltimore–Washington International Thurgood Marshall Airport (BWI) (© 800/435-9294; www.bwiairport.com) is northeast of the city near Baltimore, about 45 minutes from downtown. Southwest Airlines, with its bargain fares, commands a major presence here, pulling in nearly half of BWI's business. Both **Amtrak** (© 800/872-7245; www.amtrak.com; $12–$38 fare) and **Maryland Rural Commuter (MARC;** © 800/325-7245; $6 fare; weekdays only) trains link BWI to Washington's Union Station, about a 30-minute ride.

SuperShuttle (© 800/258-3826; www.supershuttle.com) offers shared-ride, door-to-door van service between National, Dulles, and BWI airports and your destination downtown or in the Maryland or Virginia suburbs. Expect to pay anywhere from $12 to $35, depending on distance. **Taxi** fares are $10 to $20 from National to downtown, $50 to $60 from Dulles, and $79 from BWI.

By Train   **Amtrak** (© 800/872-7245; www.amtrak.com) serves **Union Station,** 50 Massachusetts Ave. NE (© 202/371-9441; www.unionstationdc.com), a turn-of-the-20th-century Beaux Arts masterpiece conveniently located near the Capitol; it now houses shops and restaurants. There's daily service from New York (trip time: $2^{3}/_{4}$–$3^{1}/_{2}$ hr.), Philadelphia ($1^{3}/_{4}$–2 hr.), Boston (7–8 hr.), and Chicago (19 hr.). Amtrak also offers daily service from several points in the South, including Raleigh, Charlotte, Atlanta, cities in Florida, and New Orleans.

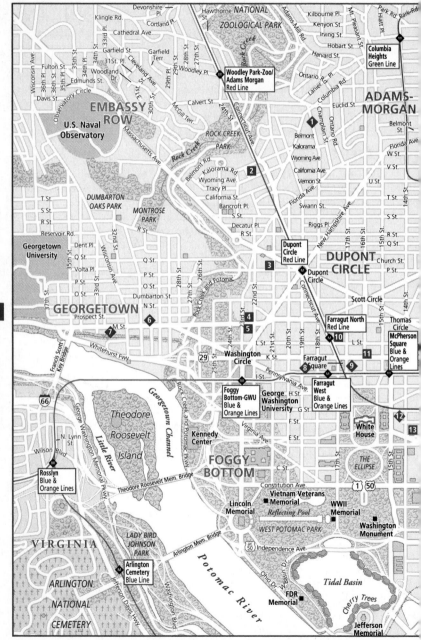

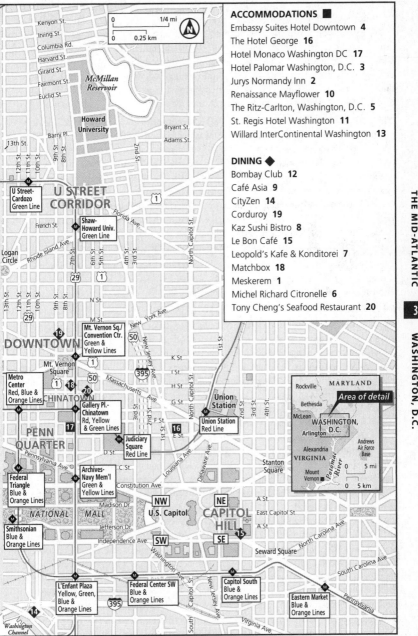

ACCOMMODATIONS ■

Embassy Suites Hotel Downtown **4**
The Hotel George **16**
Hotel Monaco Washington DC **17**
Hotel Palomar Washington, D.C. **3**
Jurys Normandy Inn **2**
Renaissance Mayflower **10**
The Ritz-Carlton, Washington, D.C. **5**
St. Regis Hotel Washington **11**
Willard InterContinental Washington **13**

DINING ◆

Bombay Club **12**
Café Asia **9**
CityZen **14**
Corduroy **19**
Kaz Sushi Bistro **8**
Le Bon Café **15**
Leopold's Kafe & Konditorei **7**
Matchbox **18**
Meskerem **1**
Michel Richard Citronelle **6**
Tony Cheng's Seafood Restaurant **20**

By Car   Major highways approach Washington, D.C., from all parts of the country. Specifically, these are **I-270, I-95,** and **I-295** from the north; **I-95** and **I-395, Route 1,** and **Route 301** from the south; **Route 50/301** and **Route 450** from the east; and **Route 7, Route 50, I-66,** and **Route 29/211** from the west.

No matter which road you take, there's a good chance you will have to navigate some portion of the **Capital Beltway** (I-495 and I-95) to gain entry to D.C. The Beltway girds the city, 66 miles around, with 56 interchanges or exits, and is nearly always congested, but especially during weekday morning and evening rush hours, roughly 6 to 9:30am and 3 to 7pm. Commuter traffic on the Beltway now rivals that of major L.A. freeways, and drivers can get a little crazy, weaving in and out of traffic.

VISITOR INFORMATION   Contact the **Washington, DC Convention & Tourism Corporation (WCTC),** 901 7th St. NW, Washington, DC 20001-3719 (© **800/422-8644** or 202/789-7000; www.washington.org), and ask for a free copy of the *Washington, D.C., Visitors Guide,* which details hotels, restaurants, sights, shops, and more, and is updated twice yearly. Consult the WCTC website for latest information, including upcoming events and anticipated closings of tourist attractions.

The **Smithsonian Information Center,** in the "Castle," 1000 Jefferson Dr. SW (© **202/633-1000,** or TTY 202/357-1729; www.si.edu), is open every day but Christmas from 8:30am to 5:30pm. Call or check the website for a free copy of the Smithsonian's "My Smithsonian," which is full of valuable tips, or stop at the Castle for a copy.

GETTING AROUND   If you're thinking about driving, bear in mind that traffic is thick during the week, parking spaces are sparse, and parking lots will cost you. Street signs and parking information are often confusing and illegible. We can't recommend using a car within the city. Metrorail is definitely the easiest way to go.

By Metro   Metrorail's 86 stations include locations at or near almost every sightseeing attraction and extend to suburban Maryland and northern Virginia. There are five lines—Red, Blue, Orange, Yellow, and Green. When entering a Metro station for the first time, go to the kiosk and ask for a free *Metro System Pocket Guide.*

To enter or exit a Metro station, you need a computerized **farecard,** available at vending machines near the entrance. Charts posted near the farecard machines explain the fares, which at press time started at $1.35. If you plan to take several Metrorail trips during your stay, put more value on the farecard to avoid having to buy a new card each time you ride. Discount passes include the **7-Day Fast Pass,** for $39 per person, which allows you unlimited travel, and the **1-Day Rail Pass,** for $7.80 per person, allowing you unlimited passage for the day, after 9:30am weekdays, and all day on Saturday, Sunday, and holidays. Passes are available for purchase at all Metro stations.

Metrorail opens at 5:30am weekdays and 7am Saturday and Sunday, operating until midnight Sunday through Thursday and until 3am Friday and Saturday. Call © **202/637-7000** or visit **www.wmata.com** for information.

The **D.C. Circulator**'s (© **202/962-1423;** www.dccirculator.com) fleet of red-and-gray buses travels three routes: the north-south route between the D.C. Convention Center and the waterfront; the east-west route between upper Georgetown and Union Station; and the Smithsonian/National Gallery route, which simply loops around the Mall, from 4th Street to Independence Avenue, to 17th Street, to Constitution Avenue, and back around. Buses stop at designated points (look for the red-and-gold sign, often topping a regular Metro sign) and operate daily between 7am and 9pm, except for the Smithsonian/National Gallery route, which operates from 10am to 6pm weekends only. The fare is $1 (35¢ with the use of a Metrorail transfer); you can order passes online, or bus ticket purchased at a street meter. For easy and fast transportation in the busiest parts of town, you can't beat it.

By Taxi   In May 2008, the D.C. taxi cab system switched from charging passengers by geographical zones to charging passengers according to time- and distance-based meters. Fares begin at $3, plus 25¢ per each additional $\frac{1}{6}$ mile, 25¢ per minute of wait time, and $1.50 per additional passenger. Expect to pay your fare in cash; very few cabbies accept credit cards. Try **Diamond Cab Company** (© 202/387-6200) or **Yellow Cab** (© 202/544-1212). Call © 202/645-6018 to inquire about fares within the District and © 202/331-1671 to find out the rate between any point in D.C. and an address in Virginia or Maryland. For more information, check out the D.C. Taxicab Commission's website, www.dctaxi.dc.gov.

FAST FACTS   Emergency room treatment is available at **Children's Hospital National Medical Center,** 111 Michigan Ave. NW (© 202/884-5000), and at **Georgetown University Medical Center,** 4000 Reservoir Rd. NW (© 202/444-3111). The **CVS** drugstore chain has two 24-hour locations—in the West End, at 2240 M St. NW (© 202/296-9877), and at Dupont Circle (© 202/785-1466). The sales tax on merchandise in the District is 5.75%, the tax on restaurant meals is 10%, and you pay a 14.5% hotel tax.

SPECIAL EVENTS & FESTIVALS   For more information, call © 202/789-7000 or go to www.washington.org.

In early April, the 3,700 Japanese cherry trees by the Tidal Basin in Potomac Park burst into spectacular bloom. The **Cherry Blossom Festival** features a major parade with floats, concerts, celebrity guests, and more. For information, call © 202/547-1500 or go to www.nps.gov/nacc/cherry.

The **White House Easter Egg Roll** takes place on Easter Monday. Entertainment on the White House South Lawn and the Ellipse might include clog dancers, clowns, puppet and magic shows, military drill teams, an egg-rolling contest, and a hunt for 1,000 or so wooden eggs, many of them signed by celebrities, astronauts, or the president. Call © 202/208-1631 for details.

At 11am on **Memorial Day,** a wreath-laying ceremony takes place at the Tomb of the Unknowns in Arlington National Cemetery, followed by military band music, a service, and an address by a high-ranking government official; call © 703/607-8000 for details. **Fourth of July** festivities include a massive parade down Constitution Avenue. A morning program in front of the National Archives includes military demonstrations, period music, and a reading of the Declaration of Independence. In the evening, the National Symphony Orchestra plays on the west steps of the Capitol. Big-name entertainment precedes the fabulous fireworks display behind the Washington Monument. Consult the *Washington Post* or call © 202/619-7222 for details. In early December, at the northern end of the Ellipse, the president lights the **national Christmas tree** to the accompaniment of orchestral and choral music. The lighting inaugurates the 4-week Pageant of Peace, a tremendous holiday celebration with seasonal music, caroling, a nativity scene, 50 state trees, and a burning Yule log. Call © 202/208-1631 for details.

WHAT TO SEE & DO

From the inauguration of a new president at the start of 2009 to the dedication of the Rev. Dr. Martin Luther King, Jr., Memorial at the end, one momentous event follows another in this city built on heroic American dreams and audacious hopes. It's a good time to visit.

Here's a crucial piece of advice: Call or check the website of the places you plan to tour before you set out. Many of Washington's government buildings, museums, memorials, and monuments are open to the general public nearly all the time—except when they're not. Because buildings like the Capitol, the Supreme Court, and the White House are offices as well as tourist destinations, the business of the day (as well as security concerns) always poses the potential for closing one of those sites, or at least sections, to sightseers. Want to avoid frustration and disappointment? Call ahead.

The Top Sights

Arlington National Cemetery   Since the Civil War, these 612 wooded acres on a ridge overlooking the Potomac River and Washington have been a cherished shrine to members of the U.S. armed forces. Upon arrival, head over to the **Visitor Center,** where you can view exhibits, pick up a detailed map, use the restrooms (there are no others until you get to Arlington House), and purchase a **Tourmobile ticket** ($7.50 per adult, $3.75 for children 3–11), which allows you to stop at all major sites in the cemetery and then reboard whenever you like.

Your first stop should be the **Women in Military Service for America Memorial** (© **800/222-2294** or 703/533-1155; www.womensmemorial.org), which honors the more than two million women who have served in the armed forces from the American Revolution to the present. High atop a hill at the center of the cemetery is **Arlington House** (© **703/235-1530;** www.nps.gov/arho), once the home of Robert E. Lee, who left here in 1861 to take command of the Confederate army (to spite him, the Union army buried its dead in his front yard). You can tour the house on your own. Below Arlington House is the **Gravesite of John Fitzgerald Kennedy.** Jacqueline Kennedy Onassis is buried next to her first husband, and Robert Kennedy is buried close by. America's most distinguished honor guard watches over the **Tomb of the Unknowns,** which contains the unidentified remains of service members from both world wars and the Korean War, and honors all Americans who gave their lives in war. Plan to see the changing of the guard, which takes place every half-hour April to September, every hour on the hour October to March, and every hour at night.

Just across the Memorial Bridge from the base of the Lincoln Memorial. © **703/607-8000.** www.arlington cemetery.org. Free admission. Apr–Sept daily 8am–7pm; Oct–Mar daily 8am–5pm. Metro: Arlington National Cemetery. If you come by car, parking is $1.75 an hour for the 1st 3 hr., $2 an hour thereafter. The cemetery is also accessible via Tourmobile.

The Capitol   The U.S. Congress has met here since 1800. The hub of the building is the **Rotunda,** under the soaring 180-foot-high Capitol dome. The adjoining **National Statuary Hall** was originally the House chamber. The Senate used to meet in the **Old Supreme Court Chamber,** now beautifully restored. You can obtain free tickets to the **House and Senate galleries** by contacting the office of your senator or representative. (Visitors who are not citizens can obtain a gallery pass by presenting a passport at the Senate or House appointments desk.) Check the weekday "Today in Congress" column in the *Washington Post* for details on times of the House and Senate sessions and committee hearings.

The guided tours are free, last 30 minutes, and are led by a Capitol Guide Service guide. The Capitol has quite a list of items it prohibits, and the recording that you listen to on the © **202/225-6827** number recites them for you, everything from large bags of any kind to food and drink. Leave everything possible back at the hotel.

The Opening of the Capitol Visitor Center

Under construction since mid-2002, a comprehensive, underground Capitol Visitor Center finally debuted in late 2008, years behind schedule. All visitors to the Capitol now queue up inside the visitor center, which offers exhibits, 26 restrooms, a dining facility, and an orientation film shown in two theaters. To find the visitor center, go to the East Front of the Capitol (along 1st St., across from the Library of Congress) and look for the signs pointing you to the entrance. As before, you and everyone in your party must have a timed pass to tour the Capitol; you can now order tickets online. Call ✆ **202/225-6827** in advance of your visit to find out whether the Capitol is open to the public the day you wish to visit and whether touring procedures have changed.

Try to visit when both the Senate and House are **in session.** The Senate Gallery is open to visitors only when it is in session, but the House Gallery is open to visitors whether or not it is in session. You must have a separate pass, one for each gallery. Once obtained, the passes are good through the remainder of the Congress. You can obtain visitor passes at the offices of your representative and senator, or in the case of District of Columbia and Puerto Rico residents, from the office of their delegate to Congress. Visit the Capitol's website, **www.aoc.gov**, or call your senator or congressperson's office for more exact information about obtaining passes.

Capitol and Capitol Visitor Center: On E. Capitol St. (at 1st St. NW). ✆ **202/225-6827**. www.aoc.gov, www.house.gov, and www.senate.gov. Free admission. Year-round Mon–Sat 9am–4:30pm, with first tour starting at 9:30am and last tour starting at 3:30pm. Closed for tours Sun and Thanksgiving, Christmas, and New Year's Day. Parking at Union Station or on neighborhood streets. Metro: Union Station (Massachusetts Ave. exit) or Capitol South (to walk to the Capitol Visitor Center located on the East Front of the Capitol).

Corcoran Gallery of Art   The first art museum in Washington, the Corcoran occupies a Beaux Arts building just west of the White House. The collection spans American art from 18th-century portraiture to works by 20th-century moderns such as Nevelson, Warhol, and Rothko. There's also an eclectic grouping of works by Dutch and Flemish masters and French Impressionists, plus Delft porcelains and a Louis XVI *salon doré* transported complete from Paris. Allow an hour for touring the collection.

500 17th St. NW (btw. E St. and New York Ave.). ✆ **202/639-1700**. www.corcoran.org. $6 general admission; admission to special exhibits is usually $12 adults, $10 seniors and students. Children 5 and under always free. Sun–Wed and Fri–Sat 10am–5pm; Thurs 10am–9pm. Closed Christmas and New Year's Day. Metro: Farragut West (17th St. exit) or Farragut North (K St. exit).

Franklin Delano Roosevelt Memorial   The FDR Memorial has become the most popular of the presidential memorials since it opened in 1997. Set amid waterfalls and quiet pools, "outdoor rooms" are devoted to each of Roosevelt's four terms in office (1933–45). Ten bronze sculptures honor Franklin and wife Eleanor and memorialize the struggles of the Great Depression and America's rise to world leadership. If you don't see a posting of tour times, look for a park ranger and request a tour; the rangers are happy to oblige. Thirty minutes is sufficient time to allot here.

On W. Basin Dr., alongside the Tidal Basin in West Potomac Park (across Independence Ave. SW from the Mall). ✆ **202/426-6841**. www.nps.gov/frde. Free admission. Ranger on duty daily 9:30am–11:30pm, except for Christmas. Limited parking. Metro: Smithsonian (12th St./Independence Ave.), with a 30-min. walk, or take Tourmobile.

International Spy Museum   Try to pace yourself through this 68,000-square-foot museum, immensely popular ever since its mid-2002 opening. Interactive and video exhibits offer a fun indoctrination into "Tricks of the Trade." Learn about the use of codes and code-breaking in spying, with one room of the museum devoted to the Enigma cipher machine used by the Germans (whose "unbreakable" codes the Allied cryptanalysts succeeded in deciphering) in World War II. An actual Enigma machine is displayed. Much more follows, including a re-created tunnel beneath the divided city of Berlin during the Cold War, the intelligence-gathering stories of those behind enemy lines and of those involved in planning D-day in World War II, and an exhibit on escape and evasion techniques in wartime. The museum's newest feature is **Operation Spy,** a 1-hour interactive immersion into espionage activities.

800 F St. NW (at 8th St. NW). (℃ **866/779-6873** or 202/393-7798. www.spymuseum.org. Admission $18 adults (ages 12–65), $17 for seniors, $15 for children ages 5–11. Operation Spy: $14 for ages 12 and up. Combined admission fee $25. Open daily, but hours vary; generally, the museum opens at 9am or 10am and closes most of the time at 6pm, but sometimes later, rarely earlier. Check website for details. Closed Thanksgiving, Christmas, and New Year's Day. Metro: Gallery Place/Chinatown (9th and G sts. exit) or Archives–Navy Memorial.

Jefferson Memorial   The domed interior of this beautiful columned rotunda in the style of the Pantheon in Rome contains a 19-foot bronze statue of Thomas Jefferson, the third U.S. president, who also served as ambassador to France, secretary of state, and vice president—and still found time to pen the Declaration of Independence, create the University of Virginia, and pursue wide-ranging interests, including architecture, astronomy, anthropology, music, and farming. A gift shop, a small museum, and a bookstore are located on the bottom floor of the memorial. Rangers present 20- to 30-minute programs throughout the day as time permits.

On Ohio Dr. SW, at the south shore of the Tidal Basin (in West Potomac Park). (℃ **202/426-6841.** www. nps.gov/thje. Free admission. Ranger on duty daily 9:30am–11:30pm, except Christmas. Limited parking. Metro: Smithsonian (12th St./Independence Ave. exit), with a 20- to 30-min. walk, or take Tourmobile.

Lincoln Memorial   This beautiful neoclassical temple–like structure, similar in design to the Parthenon in Greece, is a moving testament to the great Civil War president. Visitors are silently awed in the presence of Daniel Chester French's 19-foot-high seated statue of Lincoln in deep contemplation. Lincoln's enormously powerful Gettysburg Address is engraved on the interior walls. Especially at night, the view from the steps, across the Reflecting Pool to the Washington Monument and the Capitol beyond, is one of the city's most beautiful. An information booth, a small museum, and a bookstore are on the premises. Rangers present 20- to 30-minute programs as time permits throughout the day.

On the western end of the Mall, at 23rd St. NW (btw. Constitution and Independence aves.). (℃ **202/426-6842.** www.nps.gov/linc. Free admission. Ranger on duty daily 9:30am–11:30pm except Christmas. Limited parking. Metro: Foggy Bottom, then a 30-min. walk, or take Tourmobile, or catch the D.C. Circulator to 17th and Constitution and walk from there.

National Air and Space Museum (Kids)   A hit with kids of all ages, this museum chronicles the story of man's mastery of flight, from Kitty Hawk to outer space, including the Wright Brothers' first plane, Charles Lindbergh's *Spirit of St. Louis,* and the Apollo moon ships. Arrive before 10am to make a rush for the film-ticket line—the **IMAX films** are not to be missed (tickets are $8.50 adults, $7.50 seniors, $7 ages 2–12). One highlight is the *How Things Fly* gallery, which includes wind and smoke tunnels, a boardable

Cessna 150 airplane, and dozens of interactive exhibits that demonstrate principles of flight, aerodynamics, and propulsion. You'll also need tickets ($8.50 adults, $7.50 seniors, $7 ages 2–12) to attend a show at the **Albert Einstein Planetarium,** where projectors display blended space imagery upon a 70-foot diameter dome, making you feel as if you're traveling in 3-D through the cosmos.

At the Udvar-Hazy Center you'll find two hangars—one for aviation artifacts, the other for space artifacts—and a 164-foot-tall observation tower for watching planes leave and arrive at Dulles Airport.

On Independence Ave. SW (btw. 4th and 7th sts.; on the south side of the Mall, with entrances on Jefferson Dr. or Independence Ave.). © **202/633-1000** (for both locations), or 877/932-4629 for IMAX ticket information. www.nasm.si.edu. Free admission. Both locations daily 10am–5:30pm. The Mall museum often stays open until 7:30pm in summer, but call to confirm. Free 1¹/₂-hr. highlight tours daily at 10:30am and 1pm. Closed Christmas. Metro: L'Enfant Plaza (Smithsonian Museums/Maryland Ave. exit) or Smithsonian (The Mall/Jefferson Dr. exit). The Udvar-Hazy Center is located at 14390 Air and Space Museum Pkwy., Chantilly, VA.

National Archives   After a major restoration completed in 2004, visitors can now get a marvelous look at the nation's three most important documents—the Declaration of Independence, the Constitution of the United States, and the Bill of Rights. Exhibits in the newly renovated **Public Vaults** feature interactive technology and displays of documents and artifacts to explain our country's development in the use of records, from Indian treaties to presidential websites. A theater continually runs dramatic films during the day, illustrating the relationship between records and democracy in the lives of real people, and at night serves as a premier documentary film venue for the city. Anyone is welcome to use the National Archives center for genealogical research—this is where Alex Haley began his work on *Roots*—and it's all available for the perusal of anyone age 16 or over (call for details). The building itself is an impressive example of the Beaux Arts style, with 72 columns on each of the four facades.

700 Pennsylvania Ave. NW (btw. 7th and 9th sts. NW; tourists enter on Constitution Ave., researchers on Pennsylvania Ave.). © **202/357-5000.** www.archives.gov. Free admission. March 15 to Labor Day daily 10am–7pm; day after Labor Day to Mar 14 daily 10am–5:30pm. Call for research hours. Closed Christmas. Metro: Archives–Navy Memorial.

National Gallery of Art   Housing one of the world's foremost collections of Western painting, sculpture, and graphic arts from the Middle Ages through the 20th century, the National Gallery has a dual personality. You'll find the masters in the original **West Building,** a neoclassical marble masterpiece with a domed rotunda. This is your chance to see the works of the old masters, including several renowned Raphaels; about 1,000 paintings are on display at any one time. The ultramodern **East Building** appropriately houses an important collection of 20th-century art, including masterpieces by Picasso, Miró, Matisse, Pollock, and Rothko. Other exhibitions feature the decorative arts, drawings, and prints. The **National Gallery Sculpture Garden,** just across from the West Wing, features open lawns, a central pool with a spouting fountain (the pool is converted into an ice rink in winter), and an exquisite, glassed-in pavilion housing a cafe and an impressive sculpture garden. Allow a leisurely 2 hours to see everything here.

On Constitution Ave. NW (btw. 3rd and 7th sts. NW; on the north side of the Mall). © **202/737-4215.** www.nga.gov. Free admission. Gallery: Mon–Sat 10am–5pm; Sun 11am–6pm. Sculpture Garden: late May to mid-Sept Mon–Thurs and Sat 10am–7pm, Fri 10am–9:30pm, Sun 11am–7pm; mid-Sept to late May Mon–Sat 10am–5pm, Sun 11am–6pm. Closed Christmas and New Year's Day. Metro: Archives–Navy Memorial or Gallery Place/Verizon Center (Arena/7th and F sts. exit).

National Museum of Natural History (Kids) Another hit with kids, this fascinating museum contains more than 120 million artifacts and specimens—it's the largest museum of its kind in the world. Exhibits include everything from one of the largest African elephants to the Hope Diamond. Before you enter the museum, stop on the Ninth Street side of the building to visit the lovely butterfly garden. Inside, dinosaurs loom large, including a life-size model of the pterosaur, which had a 40-foot wingspan. Don't miss the **Discovery Center,** funded by the Discovery Channel, featuring the Johnson **IMAX theater** (requires separate admission) with a six-story-high screen for 2-D and 3-D movies. In 2008, the museum debuted a brand-new, 22,000-square-foot **Ocean Hall,** the largest, most diverse exhibit of its kind. Look for a model of a 45-foot-long North American right whale and a 1,500-gallon coral reef aquarium with more than 70 live animals and 674 specimens. November 2009 brings the opening of **"Origins: What Does It Mean to Be Human?",** probing the ecological and genetic connection that humans have had with the natural world.

On Constitution Ave. NW (btw. 9th and 12th sts.; on the north side of the Mall, with entrances on Madison Dr. and Constitution Ave.). ✆ **202/633-1000,** or 633-4629 for information about IMAX films. www.mnh. si.edu. Free admission. Daily 10am–5:30pm. In summer the museum often stays open until 7:30pm, but call to confirm. Closed Christmas. Free highlight tours Feb–July Tues–Fri 10:30am and 1:30pm. Metro: Smithsonian (The Mall/Jefferson Dr. exit) or Federal Triangle.

National Museum of the American Indian (Kids) This $219-million museum took 5 years to build before finally opening in September 2004. Very much a "living" museum, the museum has performances, events, and exhibits that aim at giving Native peoples the chance to tell their own stories. Exhibits explore Native life and history and specific themes, and showcase works of individual artists. Most importantly, the museum is a giant display case for a collection of precious objects representing 1,000 Native communities. About 8,000 of the collection's 800,000 pieces, including wood and stone carvings, masks, pottery, feather bonnets, and so on are on display at any given time. Three permanent exhibits, "Our Universes: Traditional Knowledge Shapes Our World," "Our Peoples: Giving Voice to Our Histories," and "Our Lives: Contemporary Life and Identities," use videos, interactive technology, and displays to help you learn about Native cosmologies, history, and contemporary cultural identity, both of Native Americans as a group and within certain individual tribes.

4th St. and Independence Ave. SW. ✆ **202/633-1000.** www.nmai.si.edu. Free admission. Daily 10am–5:30pm. Closed Christmas. Metro: Federal Center Southwest or L'Enfant Plaza (Smithsonian Museums/Maryland Ave. exit).

National World War II Memorial Thousands of World War II veterans and their families turned out when this memorial was dedicated on May 29, 2004. The 7½-acre memorial funded mostly by private donations features 56 granite pillars, each one 17 feet high, representing each state and territory, standing to either side of a central plaza and the Rainbow Pool. Likewise, 24 bas-relief panels illustrate seminal scenes from the war years as they relate to the Pacific and Atlantic theaters: Pearl Harbor, Normandy Beach, the Battle of the Bulge, and so on. Beyond the center Rainbow Pool is a wall of 4,000 gold stars, one star for every 100 soldiers who died in World War II. People often leave photos and mementos everywhere around the memorial, which the National Park Service gathers up daily. From the 17th Street entrance, walk south around the perimeter of the memorial to reach a ranger station, where there are brochures and registry kiosks, the latter for looking up names of veterans. Better information and faster service is available online at the memorial's website.

On 17th St., near Constitution Ave. NW. ℂ **800/639-4WW2** (639-4992) or 202/426-6841. www.nps.gov/ **201**
wwii. Free admission. Ranger on duty daily 9:30am–11:30pm, except Christmas. Limited parking. Metro:
Farragut West, Federal Triangle, or Smithsonian, with 20–25 min. walk, or take Tourmobile, or catch the
D.C. Circulator.

Phillips Collection   This charming museum is even more alluring now that its
expansion is complete. In an elegant 1890s Georgian Revival mansion (plus an added
wing) is the exquisite collection of Duncan and Marjorie Phillips, avid collectors and
proselytizers of modernism. The original building was once the Phillipses' elegant abode,
and it still has the warmth of a home. Among the highlights: superb Daumier, Dove, and
Bonnard paintings; some splendid small Vuillards; five van Goghs; Renoir's *Luncheon of
the Boating Party;* seven Cézannes; and six works by Georgia O'Keeffe. It's a collection no
art lover should miss.

   Note: The Phillips Collection's admission structure is a little confusing: You may tour
the permanent collection for free on weekdays. To tour the permanent collection on
weekends, and to tour whatever special exhibit is currently running, whatever day of the
week you are there, you pay the admission fee established for that special exhibition. This
fee can vary, anywhere from $10 to $12 per person. The Phillips almost always has a
special exhibition on view. You may order tickets in advance at the Phillips, or through
Ticketmaster at ℂ **800/551-SEAT** (551-7328) or online at www.ticketmaster.com.

1600 21st St. NW (at Q St.). ℂ **202/387-2151.** www.phillipscollection.org. Admission: See information in
the note above. Tues–Sat 10am–5pm year-round (Thurs until 8:30pm); Sun 11am–6pm. Admission: See
"Note:" above. Call ahead for information and admission prices on special exhibits. Closed federal holidays. Metro: Dupont Circle (Q St. exit).

The Supreme Court of the United States   The Supreme Court hears and decides
its cases in this stately Corinthian marble temple Monday through Wednesday from
10am to noon and from 1 to 2pm or 3pm, starting the first Monday in October through
late April. From mid-May to late June, you can attend brief sessions (about 15 min.) at
10am on Monday, when the justices release orders and opinions. Find out what cases are
on the docket by calling the Supreme Court (ℂ **202/479-3211**) or, better yet, by going
to the court's website, where the argument calendar and the "Merits Briefs" (case descriptions) are posted. Arrive at least 90 minutes early—and as early as 3 hours ahead in
March and April, when schools are often on spring break and students lengthen the
line—to line up for the 150 seats allotted to the general public. If the court is not in
session, you can attend a **free lecture,** given every hour on the half-hour from 9:30am to
3:30pm. After the talk, explore the Great Hall and go down a flight of steps to see the
24-minute film on the workings of the Court.

One 1st St. NE (btw. E. Capitol St. and Maryland Ave. NE). ℂ **202/479-3000.** www.supremecourtus.gov.
Free admission. Mon–Fri 9am–4:20pm. Closed all federal holidays. Metro: Capitol South or Union Station.

United States Holocaust Memorial Museum   This extraordinarily powerful
museum (it remains one of the city's top draws, sometimes hosting up to 10,000 visitors
in 1 day) reminds us of what can happen when civilization goes awry. An outer wall is
reminiscent of an extermination camp's exterior brickwork, and towers evoke the guard
towers of Auschwitz. A reconstructed Auschwitz barracks, the yellow stars that Jews were
forced to wear, instruments of genocide, and a gas-chamber door are among the artifacts
on display. As you enter, you'll be given the identity card of a real person living in Europe
in the 1930s; at the end of your visit, you'll learn that person's fate. A highlight is a
30-minute film called *Testimony,* in which Holocaust survivors tell their own stories. The

museum recommends not bringing children 10 and under; for older children, it's advisable to prepare them for what they'll see.

100 Raoul Wallenberg Place SW (formerly 15th St. SW; near Independence Ave., just off the Mall). *C* 202/488-0400. www.ushmm.org. Free admission. Daily 10am–5:30pm, staying open later in peak seasons. Closed Yom Kippur and Christmas. Metro: Smithsonian (12th St. and Independence Ave. SW exit).

Vietnam Veterans Memorial

The Vietnam Veterans Memorial is possibly the most poignant sight in Washington: two long black-granite walls in the shape of a V, each inscribed with the names of the men and women who gave their lives, or remain missing, in the longest war in American history. Even if no one close to you died in Vietnam, it's wrenching to watch visitors grimly studying the directories to find out where their loved ones are listed, or rubbing pencil on paper held against a name etched into the wall. The walls list close to 60,000 people, most of whom died very young. The National Park Service continues to add names as Vietnam veterans die of injuries sustained during the war.

Northeast of the Lincoln Memorial, east of Henry Bacon Dr. (btw. 21st and 22nd sts. NW, on the Constitution Ave. NW side of the Mall). *C* 202/426-6841. www.nps.gov/vive. Free admission. Ranger on duty daily 9:30am–11:30pm except Christmas. Limited parking. Metro: Foggy Bottom, with 25-min. walk, or take Tourmobile, or catch the D.C. Circulator to 17th and Constitution and walk from there.

Washington Monument

The 555-foot stark marble obelisk glowing under floodlights at night is the city's most visible landmark. You can't climb or descend the 897 steps, but a large elevator whisks visitors to the top in just 70 seconds. The 360-degree views are spectacular. Admission to the Washington Monument is free, but you still have to get a ticket. The ticket booth is located in the Monument Lodge, at the bottom of the hill from the monument, on 15th Street NW between Madison and Jefferson drives. It opens daily at 8:30am. Tickets are often gone by 9am, so plan to get there by 7:30 or 8am, especially in peak season. The tickets grant admission at half-hour intervals between the stated hours on the day you visit. If you want to get tickets in advance, call the National Park Reservation Service (*C* 877/444-6777) or go to www.recreation.gov. The tickets themselves are free, but you'll pay $1.50 per ticket, plus $2.85 for shipping and handling, if you're ordering 10 or more days in advance; otherwise, you pick up the tickets at the "will call" window at the ticket kiosk.

Directly south of the White House, on 15th St. (btw. Madison Dr. and Constitution Ave. NW). *C* 202/426-6841. www.nps.gov/wamo. Free admission. Daily 9am–4:45pm. Last elevators depart 15 min. before closing (arrive earlier). Closed Christmas, open until noon July 4th. Limited parking. Metro: Smithsonian (Mall/Jefferson Dr. exit), then a 10-min. walk, or take Tourmobile or the D.C. Circulator (takes you close, though not directly to it).

The White House

It's amazing when you think about it: This house has served as residence, office, reception site, and world embassy for every U.S. president since John Adams. The White House is the only private residence of a head of state that has opened its doors to the public for tours, free of charge. These days, the White House is available only for group tours arranged in advance. The White House is a repository of art and furnishings. Tours of the public areas include the gold-and-white **East Room,** scene of gala receptions and other dazzling events; the **Green Room,** used as a sitting room; the **Oval Blue Room,** where presidents and first ladies officially receive guests; the **Red Room,** used as a reception room and for afternoon teas; and the **State Dining Room,** a superb setting for state dinners and luncheons. There are no public restrooms or telephones in the White House, and picture-taking and videotaping are prohibited. *Best advice:* Leave everything but your wallet back at the hotel.

How to Arrange a White House Tour

The White House allows groups of 10 or more to tour the White House, Tuesday through Saturday, from 7:30am to 12:30pm. Tours are self-guided and most people take no more than an hour to go through. You must have a reservation. At least 2 months and as far as 6 months in advance, call your senator's or representative's office with the names of the people in your group and ask for a specific tour date. The tour coordinator consults with the White House on availability and, if your date is available, contacts you to obtain the names, birth dates, Social Security numbers (for those 14 and older), and other information for each of the people in your party. The Secret Service reviews the information and clears you for the tour, putting the names of the people in your group on a confirmed reservation list; you'll receive a confirmation number and the date and time of your tour usually about 1 month in advance of your trip. On the day of your tour, call ✆ **202/456-7041** to make sure that the White House is still open that day to the public. Then off you go, to the south side of East Executive Avenue, near the Southeast Gate of the White House, with photo IDs for everyone in your party who is 15 or older.

1600 Pennsylvania Ave. NW (visitor entrance gate at E St. and E. Executive Ave.). ✆ **202/456-7041** or 208-1631. www.whitehouse.gov. Free admission. Tours for groups of 10 or more who have arranged the tour through their congressional offices. Metro: Federal Triangle.

An Organized Tour

TOURMOBILE   Best known and least expensive, **Tourmobile Sightseeing** (✆ **888/ 868-7707** or 202/554-5100; www.tourmobile.com) is a good choice if you're looking for an easy-on/easy-off tour of major sites, especially since security concerns have made the already limited parking nearly nonexistent. The comfortable red, white, and blue sightseeing trams travel to as many as 24 attractions (the company changes its schedule and number of stops depending on whether sites are open for public tours), including Arlington National Cemetery. Tourmobile is the only narrated sightseeing shuttle tour authorized by the National Park Service. The 1-day American Heritage Tour, including Arlington, costs $27, $13 for children 3 to 11.

Parks, Gardens & the National Zoo

For the sight of lush, breathtakingly beautiful greenery and flowers year-round, stop in at the **United States Botanic Garden,** 100 Maryland Ave., at First Street SW, at the east end of the Mall (✆ **202/225-8333;** www.usbg.gov), at the foot of the Capitol, next door to the National Museum of the American Indian. The grand conservatory devotes half of its space to exhibits that focus on the importance of plants to people, and half to exhibits that focus on ecology and the evolutionary biology of plants. The new National Garden outside the conservatory includes a First Ladies Water Garden, formal rose garden, and lawn terrace. Admission is free; open daily from 10am to 5pm.

  West and East Potomac Parks, their 720 riverside acres divided by the Tidal Basin, are most famous for their spring display of cherry blossoms and all the hoopla that goes with it (check out **www.nps.gov/nacc/cherry** for info on the blossoms). West Potomac Park also encompasses Constitution Gardens; the Vietnam, Korean, Lincoln, Jefferson, and FDR memorials; and the Reflecting Pool.

Rock Creek Park (www.nps/gov.rocr), a 1,750-acre valley within the District of Columbia, extends 12 miles from the Potomac River to the Maryland border. It's one of the biggest and finest city parks in the nation. Adjacent to Rock Creek Park is the Smithsonian Institution's **National Zoological Park,** with its main entrance in the 3000 block of Connecticut Avenue NW (© **202/673-4800** or 673-4717; www.si.edu/natzoo). It's home to several thousand animals of some 500 species, many of them rare or endangered (including a pair of pandas). The zoo animals live in large, open enclosures—simulations of their natural habitats—along two easy-to-follow numbered paths: Olmsted Walk and the Valley Trail. Free admission; open daily.

SHOPPING HIGHLIGHTS

D.C. isn't a serious shopper's town, but it does have outstanding museum shops. The **National Gallery of Art** shop sells printed reproductions, stationery, and jewelry whose designs are based on works in the gallery's collections. It also has one of the largest selections of books on art history and architecture in the country. The largest museum shop is at the **National Air and Space Museum** (three floors!).

One of the most popular tourist attractions in the Washington area (it attracts more visitors than any other site) is **Potomac Mills Mall** (© **703/496-9301;** www.potomac mills.com), a collection of over 200 outlet and discount stores 30 miles south of Washington on I-95. You can take the Metro Franconia-Springfield (Blue Line) to Springfield (Virginia), and on weekdays the local OmniRide bus goes to the mall.

WHERE TO STAY

Washington, D.C., has just about every type of accommodations you can imagine. For ease in booking a reservation, try contacting one of two well-established local reservation services: **Capitol Reservations** (© **800/847-4832** or 202/452-1270; www.washington dchotels.com) or **Washington D.C. Accommodations** (© **800/503-3330** or 202/289-2220; www.dcaccommodations.com). Both services are free. Another free service is **Bed & Breakfast Accommodations, Ltd.** (© **877/893-3233** or 413/582-9888; www.bnb accom.com), which works with more than 30 homes, inns, guesthouses, and unhosted furnished apartments to find visitors lodging.

Embassy Suites Hotel Downtown ⟨Value⟩ ⟨Kids⟩ This well-placed hotel offers great value within walking distance of Georgetown and Dupont Circle. A tropical eight-story atrium is the setting for an ample complimentary breakfast every morning and complimentary cocktails and light snacks every evening. Every unit is a two-room suite. The living room holds a queen-size sofa bed, 32-inch plasma TV, easy chair, and table and chairs. The bedroom overlooks a quiet courtyard or the street. Between the living room and the bedroom are the bathroom, a small closet, and a kitchenette. Request a room on the eighth or ninth floor for views of Georgetown and beyond; request an "executive corner suite" for a slightly larger unit.

1250 22nd St. NW (btw. M and N sts.), Washington, DC 20037. © **800/EMBASSY** (362-2779) or 202/857-3388. Fax 202/293-3173. www.washingtondc.embassysuites.com. 318 suites. $159–$369 double. Rates include full breakfast and evening reception. Ask for AAA discounts or check the website for best rates. Extra person $20 weekdays, $25 weekends. Children 18 and under stay free in parent's room. AE, DC, DISC, MC, V. Parking $24. Metro: Foggy Bottom. **Amenities:** Restaurant; indoor pool; fitness center. *In room:* Kitchenette.

The Hotel George This is one of Washington's hippest places to stay, and one within easy reach of the Capitol. Clientele leans toward powerbrokers and celebrities, who often meet in the hotel's **Bistro Bis** restaurant. Decor in the oversize guest rooms is minimalist, all creamy white and modern, with 32-inch plasma-screen television, and shades nestled perfectly within the window frame. Fluffy comforters rest on over-large beds; an ergonomically designed chair draws up to the desk. Spacious bathrooms feature black granite and marble, and a speaker that broadcasts TV sounds from the other room. The smoke-free hotel has three one-bedroom suites.

15 E St. NW (at N. Capitol St.), Washington, DC 20001. ✆ **800/576-8331** or 202/347-4200. Fax 202/347-4213. www.hotelgeorge.com. 139 units. Weekdays $289–$659 double; weekends $169–$349 double; year-round $750–$1,050 suite. Ask about seasonal and corporate rates and the "Hot Dates, Great Rates" deal. Extra person $25. Children 17 and under stay free in parent's room. AE, DC, DISC, MC, V. Parking $36 plus tax overnight. Metro: Union Station (Massachusetts Ave. NW exit). Pets accepted. **Amenities:** Restaurant; fitness center.

Hotel Monaco Washington DC (Best)

The Monaco occupies a four-story, all-marble mid-19th-century building, half of which was designed by Robert Mills, the architect for the Washington Monument. The other half was designed by Thomas Walter, one of the architects for the U.S. Capitol. Spacious guest rooms feature vaulted ceilings and long windows. Eclectic furnishings include neoclassical armoires and three-legged desks. (The hotel's historic status precludes it from installing closets; hence, the armoires.) Interior rooms overlook the courtyard and the restaurant, **Poste;** exterior rooms view city sights on floors 2 through 4. Pets get VIP treatment, with their own registration cards, maps of nearby fire hydrants, and gourmet puppy and kitty treats.

700 F St. NW (at 7th St.), Washington, DC 20004. ✆ **800/649-1202** or 202/628-7177. Fax 202/628-7277. www.monaco-dc.com. 184 units. Weekdays $369–$609 double, $509–$1,200 suite; weekends $169–$369 double, $269–$800 suite. Extra person $20. Children 17 and under stay free in parent's room. Rates include complimentary organic coffee in morning and a hosted evening wine hour. AE, DC, DISC, MC, V. Parking $30 plus tax. Nonsmoking property. Metro: Gallery Place (7th and F sts. NW exit). Pets welcome. **Amenities:** Restaurant; fitness center.

Hotel Palomar Washington, D.C.

If you prefer a hotel to be more than simply a place to sleep, you'll love the Palomar. This Kimpton hotel is in the heart of the fun Dupont Circle neighborhood, full of galleries, boutiques, and restaurants; and it regularly invites local artists to pop in for the evening wine hour. The Palomar fancies itself a kind of art gallery, from its displays of decorative arts in the lobby, to the splashes of mulberry and magenta, zebrawood, and faux leather finishes in the guest rooms. These are spacious rooms and comfortably appointed. Specialty rooms include 18 "Tall" rooms (the beds are 90-in. kings) and 8 "Motion" rooms (each comes with your choice of in-room exercise equipment). **Urbana** is the hotel's popular restaurant.

2121 P St. NW (at 21st St.), Washington, DC 20037. ✆ **877/866-3070** or 202/448-1800. Fax 202/448-1801. www.hotelpalomar-dc.com. 335 units. $189–$469 double; from $500 suite. Book online for best rates. Extra person $25. Children 17 and under stay free in parent's room. Rates include hosted evening wine reception and morning coffee (in lobby). AE, DC, DISC, MC, V. Parking $36. Nonsmoking property. Metro: Dupont Circle (S. 19th St. NW exit). Pets welcome. **Amenities:** Restaurant; outdoor (seasonal) lap pool; 24-hr. fitness center.

Jurys Normandy Inn (Value)

This gracious hotel is a gem—a small gem, but a gem nonetheless. Situated in a neighborhood of architecturally impressive embassies, the six-floor hotel has small but pretty guest rooms (all remodeled in 2003), with tapestry-upholstered mahogany and cherrywood furnishings in 18th-century style, and pretty floral-print bedspreads covering firm beds. The Normandy is an easy walk from both Adams-Morgan and Dupont Circle, where many restaurants and shops await you. Complimentary wine and cheese are served from the antique oak sideboard on Tuesday evenings. In nice weather, you can lounge on the garden patio.

2118 Wyoming Ave. NW (at Connecticut Ave.), Washington, DC 20008. ✆ **800/424-3729** or 202/483-1350. Fax 202/387-8241. www.jurysdoyle.com. 75 units. $89–$239 double. Extra person $10. Children 11 and under stay free in parent's room. AE, DC, DISC, MC, V. Parking $15 plus tax. Metro: Dupont Circle (N. Q St. NW exit). **Amenities:** Access to the neighboring Courtyard by Marriott Northwest's pool and exercise room. *In room:* Fridge.

Renaissance Mayflower   The Mayflower is steeped in history: In 1925, it was the site of Calvin Coolidge's inaugural ball. President-elect FDR and family lived in room nos. 776 and 781 while waiting to move into the White House; this is where he penned the words "The only thing we have to fear is fear itself." Guest rooms feature silvery green bed coverings, embroidered drapes, silk wall coverings, pillow-top mattresses, and sink-into armchairs. Each guest room has its own marble foyer, high ceiling, combination of reproduction and contemporary furnishings, and Italian marble bathroom. In the lovely **Café Promenade,** lawyers and lobbyists continue to gather for weekday power breakfasts. At cocktail time, the clubby, mahogany-paneled **Town and Country Lounge** is a favorite spot for locals, thanks to complimentary hors d'oeuvres.

1127 Connecticut Ave. NW (btw. L and M sts.), Washington, DC 20036. ✆ **800/228-7697** or 202/347-3000. Fax 202/776-9182. www.renaissancemayflower.com. 657 units. Weekdays $299–$519 double, suites $499–$599; weekends $179–$299 double, suites $499–$599. Rates include complimentary coffee service in Town and Country. No charge for extra person in room. AE, DC, DISC, MC, V. Parking $35. Metro: Farragut North (L St. NW exit). **Amenities:** Restaurant; 24-hr. fitness center.

The Ritz-Carlton, Washington, D.C.   This Ritz-Carlton surpasses all other Washington hotels in service and amenities. It's built around a multitiered Japanese garden and courtyard with reflecting pools and cascading waterfall. Standard rooms are large and richly furnished with decorative inlaid wooden furniture and pretty artwork. The marble bathrooms are immense, with long counter space and a separate bathtub and shower stall. Don't pass up the evening turndown—the maid places a warm, freshly baked brownie upon your pillow instead of the usual mint. For a $15 fee, guests may use the two-level, 100,000-square-foot **Sports Club/LA,** the best hotel health club in the city. The hotel's **Westend Bistro** by Eric Ripert is one of the hottest restaurants in town.

1150 22nd St. NW (at M St.), Washington, DC 20037. ✆ **800/241-3333** or 202/835-0500. Fax 202/835-1588. www.ritzcarlton.com/hotels/washington_dc. 300 units. Weekday from $649 double, from $749 suite; weekend from $349 (on occasion, $249) double, from $449 suite. No charge for extra person in the room. Ask about discount packages. AE, DC, DISC, MC, V. Valet parking $28. Metro: Foggy Bottom. Pets accepted and pampered (no fee). **Amenities:** Restaurant; health club; spa.

St. Regis Hotel Washington   A glance to the right as you enter shows you the White House, staring back at you from the end of 16th Street. Inside the hotel, the ornate lobby and the paneled **Library** bar have been touched up but are otherwise, thankfully, unchanged by the recent 16-month, multimillion-dollar renovation. Already-elegant guest rooms are more so now, with built-in, handcrafted armoires hiding the 32-inch LCD TV, minibar, wine fridge, drawers, and closets. Don't miss ultracool amenities, like the television embedded behind the bathroom mirror—the picture appears within the glass. The cherries on top are the new restaurant, Alain Ducasse's **Adour,** and the 5,000-square-foot spa, scheduled to debut by early 2009.

926 16th and K St. NW, Washington, DC 20006. ✆ **202/638-2626** or 866/716-8116. Fax 202/638-4231. www.stregis.com. 175 units. In season $375–$795 double; $575–$1,495 junior suite; $635–$3,200 1-bedroom suites; specialty suite from $3,400. Call for holiday, off-peak, and promotional rates. 3rd person $75.

Children 11 and under stay free in parent's room. AE, DC, DISC, MC, V. Valet parking $40. Metro: Farragut West (17th St. NW exit) or Farragut North (K St. NW exit). Pets under 25 lb. allowed for $100 nonrefundable fee, plus $25 per day. **Amenities:** 2 restaurants; fitness center. *In room:* Fridge.

Willard InterContinental Washington   The classy Willard is a stone's throw from the White House and down the avenue from the Capitol. Rooms in this National Historic Landmark are handsome, if staid, and furnished with Edwardian- and Federal-style reproductions; amenities include bathrobes in the wonderful bathrooms. Those with the best views are the oval suites overlooking Pennsylvania Avenue to the Capitol. Stop in at the Round Robin Bar for a mint julep (introduced here), and listen to barman Jim Hewes spin tales about all the people who have stopped or stayed here, from Mark Twain to Bill Clinton. The hotel's **I Spa,** charming **Café du Parc,** and schedule of seasonal festivities offer further inducement to stop by.

1401 Pennsylvania Ave. NW (at 14th St.), Washington, DC 20004. ✆ **800/827-1747** or 202/628-9100. Fax 202/637-7326. www.washington.interconti.com. 332 units. $349–$1,149 double; $699–$4,199 suite. Ask about special promotions and packages. AE, DC, DISC, MC, V. Parking $35 per 24 hr. Metro: Metro Center (13th St. NW exit). Small pets accepted. **Amenities:** Restaurant; fitness center; spa.

WHERE TO DINE

Read through the descriptions; if a place beckons, call for **reservations,** especially for Saturday night. More and more restaurants are affiliated with the online reservation service **www.opentable.com,** so you can also reserve your table online.

Bombay Club INDIAN   The delightful Bombay Club pleases patrons who know their Indian food, as well as those who've never tried it. Dishes present an easy introduction to Indian food for the uninitiated and are sensitive to varying tolerances for spiciness. The spiciest item on the menu is the fiery green chili chicken ("not for the fainthearted," the menu warns). You can't go wrong ordering a tandoori entree. The Bombay Club is known for its vegetarian offerings (try the black lentils cooked overnight on a slow fire) and for its Sunday champagne brunch. Slow-moving ceiling fans and wicker furniture accentuate the colonial British ambience.

815 Connecticut Ave. NW. ✆ **202/659-3727.** www.bombayclubdc.com. Reservations recommended. Entrees $7.50–$32; Sun brunch $20. AE, DC, MC, V. Mon–Fri and Sun brunch 11:30am–2:30pm; Mon–Thurs 6–10:30pm; Fri–Sat 6–11pm; Sun 5:30–9pm. Metro: Farragut West (17th St. exit).

Café Asia ASIAN FUSION   It's easy to miss Café Asia, nestled between hair salons and offices on I Street near the White House. Inside is a different story. The decor and menu both stand out. The restaurant has three levels, set within an atrium. The menu here is Pan-Asian: Chinese, Indonesian, Japanese, Thai. If your waitress steers you to something "interesting," you can take that to mean "spicy." Have a glass of water handy, but do try the *nasi uduk,* which is a tasty Indonesian coconut rice platter with spicy beef, crispy anchovies, pickled vegetables, *emping* (acorn chips), chicken satay, and spicy prawn sauce. Young professionals throng Café Asia's happy hour, Monday through Saturday from 4 to 7:30pm, when nigiri sushi is available for $1.25 per piece and select draft beers are sold for $2.50.

1720 I St. NW. ✆ **202/659-2696.** www.cafeasia.com. Reservations accepted. Lunch and dinner entrees $9–$16. AE, DC, DISC, MC, V. Mon–Thurs 11:30am–11pm; Fri 11:30am–midnight; Sat noon–midnight; Sun noon–11pm. Metro: Farragut West (17th St. exit) or Farragut North (K St. exit).

CityZen MODERN AMERICAN   Chef Eric Ziebold, winner of the 2008 James Beard Foundation's "Best Chef for the Mid-Atlantic Region" award, continues to fill tables nightly at CityZen. In the Mandarin Oriental Hotel, CityZen's dining room is temple-like: cathedral ceiling, dimly lit, with a coterie of acolytes flitting back and forth between tables and kitchen. You choose among three prix-fixe menus: three courses for $75, a six-course vegetarian tasting menu for $80, or a six-course $110 tasting menu. Every taste is exquisite and out of the ordinary. The restaurant's 800-bottle wine selection concentrates on bordeaux, burgundy, and California cabernet.

In the Mandarin Oriental Hotel, 1330 Maryland Ave. SW (at 12th St.). ✆ **202/787-6868.** www.mandarin oriental.com/washington (then click on "Dining"). Reservations recommended. Open for dinner only: prix-fixe $75 for 3-course menu; 6-course tasting menus $80 (vegetarian) and $110. AE, DC, DISC, MC, V. Tues–Thurs 6–9:30pm; Fri–Sat 5:30–9:30pm. Metro: Smithsonian (12th St./Independence Ave. exit).

Corduroy AMERICAN   In March 2008, Corduroy, with chef Tom Power steady at the helm, moved from its perch inside the Four Points Sheraton Hotel to its own place in the up-and-coming convention center neighborhood. Power has built a following in this food-mad city, where diners can tell you exactly how many stars the best restaurants have been awarded by local food critics. Fans have followed Power to his new digs in a historic town house, where the rooms are cozy and the kitchen is on display. Winning dishes here include prime rib-eye with lyonnaise potatoes, and strawberry tart with strawberry creamsicle.

1122 9th St. NW. ✆ **202/589-0699.** www.corduroydc.com. Reservations recommended. Dinner entrees $20–$38. AE, DC, DISC, MC, V. Mon–Sat 5:30–10:30pm. Metro: Mt. Vernon Sq./7th St./Convention Center.

Kaz Sushi Bistro JAPANESE   Amiable chef/owner Kazuhiro ("Kaz") Okochi introduced Washington to sushi long ago, at a restaurant called Sushi-Ko. Since 1999, Kaz has run his sushi bistro in this handsome town house. Aficionados vie for one of the six chairs at the bar to watch Kaz and his staff do their thing, especially at lunch, when fellow diners are likely to be Japanese men in Washington on business and young Washingtonians. Besides sushi, Kaz is known for his briny lobster with wasabi mayo, sea trout napoleon, and his bento boxes. This is also the place for premium sakes and a large selection of teas.

1915 I St. NW. ✆ **202/530-5500.** Reservations recommended. www.kazsushibistro.com. Sushi a la carte $4–$9; lunch entrees $13–$20; dinner entrees $19–$27. AE, DC, DISC, MC, V. Mon–Fri 11:30am–2pm; Mon–Sat 6–10pm. Metro: Farragut West.

Le Bon Café AMERICAN   Pennsylvania Avenue and its town house–lined side streets compose a village, enlivened by the presence of young staffers who swarm here for lunch, dinner, coffee, or a drink. My favorite place is the tiny Le Bon Café, whose menu is short but sweet: homemade pumpkin gingerbread and scones, smoked turkey club sandwich on farm bread, grilled salmon Niçoise salad, and the like. And it's cheap: The most expensive item is that salmon salad for $9.85. Seating is minimal, with most people grabbing food to go; in good weather, you can sit at outdoor tables.

210 2nd St. SE (at Pennsylvania Ave. SE). ✆ **202/547-7200.** Breakfast items $2.25–$5; salads, sandwiches, and soups $3.85–$9.85. MC, V. Mon–Fri 7am–3:30pm; Sat–Sun 8am–2pm. Metro: Capitol South.

Leopold's Kafe & Konditorei AUSTRIAN   If you find yourself at the western end of Georgetown, caught in the maze of high-end shops collectively known as Cady's Alley, you owe it to yourself to track down Leopold's and treat yourself to a delicious taste of Sacher torte or veal schnitzel. This may be the only place in Washington that serves Austrian food; it is certainly one of the most adorable eateries, with its whimsically modern furniture and bright whites punched up with orange. The customers represent a cross section of Washington, from chic to bohemian, and offer an intriguing picture to con- template as you sip your Viennese coffee and enjoy your *apfelstrudel*. The cafe offers a full bar.

3315 Cady's Alley, #213 (off M St. NW). (Find the passageway at 3318 M St., btw. 33rd and 34th sts., and walk back to Leopold's.) © **202/965-6005.** www.kafeleopolds.com. No reservations. Breakfast items $1.75–$10; lunch and dinner entrees $13–$22. AE, DISC, MC, V. Sun–Tues 8am–10pm; Wed 8am–11pm; Thurs–Sat 8am–midnight.

Matchbox PIZZA/ITALIAN   This restaurant started out in 2003 as a skinny, three-level town house in Chinatown. By 2006, Matchbox had grown so popular that it expanded into an L-shaped structure that nearly triples its capacity and includes a patio. The key things here are the wood-fired brick ovens, which bake the thin pizza crust at temperatures as high as 900°F. You can choose a regularly featured pizza, like the "prosciutto white," which is topped with prosciutto, kalamata olives, fresh garlic, ricotta cheese, fresh mozzarella, and extra-virgin olive oil. Matchbox is a cut above a pizzeria, for it also serves super salads, appetizers, sandwiches, and entrees. Its full bar on the first floor is quite the social scene. Matchbox now has a second location in the Barracks Row section of Capitol Hill, 521 8th St. SE.

713 H St. NW. © **202/289-4441.** www.matchboxdc.com. Pizzas and sandwiches $11–$21; lunch and dinner entrees $10–$26. AE, DC, DISC, MC, V. Sun–Thurs 11am–10:30pm; Fri–Sat 11am–1am. Metro: Gallery Place/Chinatown (H and 7th sts. exit).

Meskerem ETHIOPIAN   Meskerem in Adams-Morgan was one of the first Ethiopian restaurants to open in Washington and remains among the best. It's attractive; the three-level high-ceilinged dining room has an oval skylight girded by a painted sunburst and yellow-washed walls hung with African art and musical instruments. On the mezzanine level, you sit at *messobs* (basket tables) on low, carved Ethiopian chairs or upholstered leather poufs. Diners share large platters of food, which they scoop up with a sourdough crepelike pancake called *injera* (no silverware here). You'll notice a lot of *watt* dishes, which refers to the traditional Ethiopian stew, made with your choice of beef, chicken, lamb, or vegetables, in varying degrees of hot and spicy; the *alicha watts* are milder and more delicately flavored. There's a full bar, and the wine list includes Ethiopian honey wine and beer.

2434 18th St. NW. © **202/462-4100.** www.ethiopianrestaurant.com. Reservations recommended. Lunch and dinner entrees $6.50–$15. AE, DC, MC, V. Sun–Thurs noon–11pm; Fri–Sat noon to midnight. Bar stays open later Fri–Sat.

Michel Richard Citronelle (Best)   I consider this Washington's best restaurant—and so does *Washingtonian* magazine, which named it #1 in 2008. You can chalk its success up to ebullient chef/owner Michel Richard. Each presentation is a work of art, with swirls of colorful sauce surrounding the main event. Citronelle's decor is also breathtaking and includes a wall that changes colors, a state-of-the-art wine cellar (a glass-enclosed room that encircles the dining room, displaying its 8,000 bottles), and a Provençal color scheme of mellow yellow and raspberry red. Also consider dining at Richard's French/American bistro, **Central,** 2008 winner of the James Beard Award for "Best New Restaurant." Central offers a less expensive, less elaborate, but every bit as delicious meal.

In the Latham Hotel, 3000 M St. NW. © **202/625-2150.** www.citronelledc.com. Reservations required. Jacket required, tie optional for men at dinner. Open for dinner only. Fixed-price 3-course dinner $95; 9-course tasting menu $175; 15-course tasting menu $225. Bar/lounge entrees $14–$42. AE, DC, MC, V. Mon–Sat 6–9:30pm; Sun 6–9pm.

Tony Cheng's Seafood Restaurant CHINESE/SEAFOOD Tony Cheng's is a good choice if you like Cantonese specialties and spicy Szechuan and Hunan cuisine. Downstairs is the Mongolian Barbecue eatery, where you have a choice of dipping your own vegetables, seafood, and meats in a "hot pot" of boiling broth or ordering a $18-per-person, all-you-can-eat spread of foods you select for the chef to barbecue over a huge grill. The second-floor Tony Cheng's Seafood Restaurant has been here for decades. It has earned a reputation for its Cantonese roast duck (see it for yourself before ordering, since it is displayed in a case at the back of the restaurant); lobster or Dungeness crab, stir-fried and served with either ginger and scallions or black-bean sauce. Dim sum is available at lunch daily, but during the week you order items off the menu rather than from rolling carts.

619 H St. NW (btw. 6th and 7th sts.). ✆ **202/842-8669** (Mongolian Barbecue) and **202/371-8669** (Seafood Restaurant). www.tonychengrestaurant.com Reservations recommended. Mongolian Barbecue entrees $18 all-you-can-eat, or $11–$20. Seafood restaurant lunch entrees $10–$15; dinner entrees $13–$19. AE, MC, V. Sun–Thurs 11am–11pm; Fri–Sat 11am–midnight. Metro: Gallery Place/Chinatown (7th and H sts. exit).

WASHINGTON AFTER DARK

To find out what's on when you're in town, check the Friday "Weekend" section of the *Washington Post.* The *City Paper,* available free at restaurants, bookstores, and other places around town, and online at **www.washingtoncitypaper.com**, is another source.

TICKETplace (✆ **202/842-5387** for information; www.ticketplace.org), Washington's discount, day-of-show ticket outlet, is at 407 7th St. NW, between D and E streets (Metro: Gallery Place/Verizon Center or Archives–Navy Memorial). It's open Tuesday through Friday from 11am to 6pm and Saturday from 10am to 5pm; half-price tickets for Sunday and Monday shows are sold on Saturday. Though tickets are half-price, you still have to pay a per-ticket service charge of 12% of the full face value of the ticket. You can also order some tickets online. TICKETplace accepts only credit and select debit cards.

You can buy full-price tickets for most performances in town through **Ticketmaster** (✆ **800/551-7328;** www.ticketmaster.com) if you're willing to pay a hefty service charge. You can purchase full-price Ticketmaster tickets at TICKETplace.

THE KENNEDY CENTER America's national performing-arts center, the hub of Washington's cultural and entertainment scene, is the **John F. Kennedy Center for the Performing Arts,** at the southern end of New Hampshire Avenue NW and Rock Creek Parkway (✆ **800/444-1324** or 202/467-4600; www.kennedy-center.org).

The center is actually made up of six different theaters: the Opera House, the Concert Hall, the Terrace Theater, the Eisenhower Theater, the Theater Lab, and the Family Theater. The **Washington National Opera** (www.dc-opera.org), under the direction of Placido Domingo, is resident in the Opera House. The **National Symphony Orchestra,** under the direction of Ivan Fischer, presents concerts in the Concert Hall from September to June. The **Theater Lab** continues by day as Washington's premier stage for children's theater and by night as a cabaret.

The Kennedy Center's very popular free concert series, the **"Millennium Stage"** (www.kennedy-center.org/millennium), features daily performances by national and local musicians, each evening at 6pm in the center's Grand Foyer.

Discounted tickets are usually offered to students, seniors, people with permanent disabilities, enlisted military personnel, and people with fixed low incomes (call ✆ **202/416-8340** for details).

anything on Broadway has been tried out here or will eventually come here. The city also
has several nationally acclaimed repertory companies and two companies specializing in
Shakespearean productions. Check the *Washington Post* or the *City Paper* for specific listings of what's going on. Among the best are **Arena Stage** (© 202/488-3300; www.
arenastage.org), **Ford's Theatre** (© 202/347-4833; www.fordstheatre.org), the **National
Theatre** (© 800/447-7400 or 202/628-6161; www.nationaltheatre.org), and the **Shakespeare Theatre Company** at the Lansburgh Theatre and Sidney Harman Hall (© 202/
547-1122; www.shakespearetheatre.org). The Shakespeare Theatre Company moved
into its new Harman Center for the Arts (comprised of the existing Lansburgh Theater
and the new Sidney Harman Hall) in 2007. Expansion at Arena Stage includes a third
theater, scheduled for a 2009 opening. Both companies remain in production throughout the various phases of construction.

THE CLUB & MUSIC SCENE The best nightlife districts are Adams-Morgan; the U
Street Corridor, 12th to 15th streets Northwest, a still-developing district that's in a
somewhat dangerous part of town; the Seventh Street Northwest corridor near Chinatown and the MCI Center; and Georgetown.

If you're in a dancing mood, stop in at **Eighteenth Street Lounge,** 1212 18th St. NW
(© 202/466-3922), for a mix of DJ tunes that includes acid jazz, hip-hop, reggae, or
Latin jazz; or **Madam's Organ Restaurant and Bar,** 2461 18th St. NW (© 202/667-
5370; www.madamsorgan.com), if live jazz, blues, or R&B turns you on. **Blues Alley,**
1073 Wisconsin Ave. NW, in an alley below M Street (© 202/337-4141; www.blues
alley.com), in Georgetown, has been Washington's top jazz club since 1965.

Clubs hosting a combination of big names and up-and-coming bands for live rock
include the **Black Cat,** 1811 14th St. NW, between S and T streets (© 202/667-7960;
www.blackcatdc.com); and the famous **9:30 Club,** 815 V St. NW, at Vermont Avenue
(© 202/393-0930; www.930.com). Many of these clubs have DJs on nights when live
acts aren't playing.

THE BAR SCENE Washington has a thriving and varied bar scene. Travel the triangle
formed by the intersections of Connecticut Avenue, 18th Street, and M Street, in
Dupont Circle, and you'll find the latest bunch. The **Big Hunt,** 1345 Connecticut Ave.
NW, between N Street and Dupont Circle (© 202/785-2333; www.thebighuntdc.
com), is a casual hangout for the 20- to 30-something crowd, with a kind of *Raiders of
the Lost Ark* jungle theme. If you like beer, head for **Brickskeller,** 1523 22nd St. NW
(© 202/293-1885), which has been around for about 50 years and offers more than
1,000 beers from all over the world. Capitol Hill staffers and their bosses, apparently at
ease in dive surroundings, have been coming to the **Tune Inn,** 33¹/₂ Pennsylvania Ave.
SE (© 202/543-2725), since 1955.

Gay nightlife centers around **Dupont Circle,** with at least 10 gay bars within easy
walking distance of one another. Younger men pack **J. R.'s Bar and Grill,** 1519 17th St.
NW (© 202/328-0090).

A SIDE TRIP TO MOUNT VERNON

Mount Vernon, George Washington's stunning Southern plantation, dates from a 1674
land grant given to his great-grandfather. The restoration by the Mount Vernon Ladies'
Association is an unmarred beauty; many of the furnishings are original pieces, and the
rooms have been repainted in the original colors. There are a number of family portraits,
and the rooms are appointed as if actually in day-to-day use. After leaving the house, you

can tour the kitchen, slave quarters, storeroom, smokehouse, overseer's quarters, coach house, stables, and a 4-acre exhibit area called "George Washington, Pioneer Farmer." Explore the grounds to see the wharf, the slave burial ground, the greenhouse and gardens, and the tomb containing George and Martha Washington's sarcophagi. There's no formal tour of the plantation, but attendants stationed throughout the house and grounds provide brief orientations and answer questions.

The **Ford Orientation Center** and **Donald W. Reynolds Museum and Education Center** opened in 2006 at the estate's main gate, much of it underground so as not to take away from the estate's pastoral setting. A 15-minute film in the orientation center fills you in on the life and character of George Washington. The education center's 23 galleries and theater presentations inform you further about Washington's military and presidential careers. Admission is $13 for adults, $6 for children 6 to 11. The house and grounds are open April to August daily from 8am to 5pm; March, September, and October daily from 9am to 5pm; and November to February daily from 9am to 4pm. For more information, call ⓒ **703/780-2000** or go to www.mountvernon.org.

GETTING THERE   Mount Vernon is 16 miles south of Washington via the George Washington Memorial Parkway (Va. 400). You can also get there by public transportation (the Metro Yellow Line and Fairfax Connector), by boat (**Potomac Riverboat Company,** in Old Town Alexandria (ⓒ **703/548-9000;** www.potomacriverboatco.com), and by Tourmobile (ⓒ **202/554-5100;** www.tourmobile.com).

4

The Southeast

The six states of the Southeast—Virginia, North and South Carolina, Kentucky, Tennessee, and Georgia—encompass a region that is among the most geographically diverse in the country. Topography ranges from the plains of Georgia and the gorgeous beaches of the Outer Banks to the misty peaks of the much-visited Great Smoky Mountains and the Bluegrass Country of Kentucky.

And the sights, tastes, and touring opportunities in this region are just as varied. History buffs can choose from famous sites from Revolutionary days to the Civil War. You can swing by Thomas Jefferson's Monticello on your way to Colonial Williamsburg, or you can head farther south to the beautiful port cities of Savannah and Charleston, or the Civil Rights District in Atlanta.

Outdoors enthusiasts will find opportunities to indulge in just about every form of recreation. Sports nuts will feel at home in sports-crazy Atlanta, or in horse-crazy Lexington, where the oldest continuous sports event in the country—the Kentucky Derby—still attracts hordes in May. If music moves you, then head for Tennessee's Memphis and Nashville, where country music and the blues rule, and the King still reigns supreme. And if your tastes run more in the culinary direction, don't head home before you've had some down-home Carolina barbecue or a slice of Virginia ham (with some fine Southern bourbon, like Jack Daniel's, or a mint julep).

With its good weather, hospitable people, thriving urban scenes, and down-home country destinations, along with a lot of wallet-friendly lodging and dining, the Southeast is a great place to come back now, hear?

1 JEFFERSON'S VIRGINIA

It was in Charlottesville that Thomas Jefferson built his famous mountaintop home, Monticello; selected the site for and helped plan James Monroe's Ash Lawn–Highland house near Monticello; designed his "academical village," the University of Virginia; and died at home. "All my wishes end where I hope my days will end," he wrote, "at Monticello." Situated in the rolling foothills of the Blue Ridge Mountains, Charlottesville is a vibrant cosmopolitan center, consistently ranked as one of America's best places to live. And at the center of it all are still Thomas Jefferson and his magnificent creations.

ESSENTIALS

GETTING THERE   US Airways, Delta, Northwest, and United fly commuter planes to **Charlottesville-Albemarle Airport (CHO),** 201 Bowen Loop (© **434/973-8341;** www.gocho.com), north of town off U.S. 29.

By Train   The **Amtrak** station is at 810 W. Main St. (© **800/872-7245;** www.amtrak. com), midway between the Downtown Mall and the university.

By Car   Charlottesville is on **I-64** from the east or west and **U.S. 29** from the north or south. I-64 connects with **I-81** at Staunton and with **I-95** at Richmond.

Contact the **Charlottesville/Albemarle Convention and Visitors Bureau,** P.O. Box 178, Charlottesville, VA 22902 (© **877/386-1102** or 434/977-1783; fax 434/977-6151; www.pursuecharlottesville.org). The bureau's main office is at 610 E. Market St., on the eastern end of the Downtown Mall. It also operates the **Monticello Visitors Center,** on Va. 20 at exit 121 off I-64, near Thomas Jefferson's home. The Monticello center is open March through October daily from 9am to 5:30pm; the rest of the year, daily until 5pm. The downtown center is open Monday to Saturday from 10am to 5pm. Both are closed New Year's Day, Thanksgiving, and Christmas.

WHAT TO SEE & DO

The Monticello Visitors Center (see above) sells a **Presidents' Pass,** a discount block ticket combining admission to Monticello, Michie Tavern, and Ash Lawn–Highland. It costs $26 for all ages. The three attractions are within 2 miles of each other on the south-eastern outskirts of town. The attractions validate the tickets when you show up, so there's no time limit on when you must use the pass.

Thomas Jefferson's architectural masterpiece, **Monticello** (© **434/984-9822** or 984-9800; www.monticello.org), is one of the highlights of any visit to Virginia. Jefferson designed it himself, combining the 16th-century Italian style of Andrea Palladio with features of the Parisian buildings that he knew and admired during his stint as U.S. minister (ambassador) to France.

Today the house has been restored as closely as possible to its appearance during Jefferson's retirement years. He or his family owned nearly all its furniture and other household objects. The garden has been extended to its original 1,000-foot length, and Mulberry Row—where slaves and free artisans lived and labored in light industrial shops such as a joinery, smokehouse/dairy, blacksmith shop/nailery, and carpenter's shop—has been excavated. Jefferson's grave is in the family burial ground, which is still in use. After visiting the graveyard, you can take a shuttle bus back to the visitor parking lot or walk through the woods via a delightful path.

Admission is $15 adults, $7 children 6 to 11, free for children 5 and under. You must take a 30-minute guided tour in order to go inside the house. These run March through October daily from 8am to 5pm, and November through February daily from 9am to 4:30pm. Tickets to Monticello have specific house tour times printed on them, which has reduced the long lines of people waiting to go through the mansion on spring and summer weekends and during the October "leaf season." It's a good idea to buy your tickets as early as possible so you'll have the widest choice of tour times. You can buy Monticello tickets in advance at **www.monticello.org**.

Ash Lawn–Highland, on C.R. 795 (James Monroe Pkwy.), 2½ miles past Monticello (© **434/293-9539;** www.ashlawnhighland.org), was the estate of America's fifth president, James Monroe. Today Monroe's 535-acre estate is owned and maintained as a working farm by his alma mater, the College of William and Mary. Livestock, vegetable and herb gardens, and Colonial crafts demonstrations recall daily life on the Monroes' plantation. Horses, sheep, and cattle graze in the fields, while peacocks roam the box-wood gardens. Five of the original rooms remain, along with the basement kitchen, the overseer's cottage, restored slave quarters, and the old smokehouse.

On the mandatory 30-minute house tour, you'll see some of the family's original fur-nishings and artifacts, and learn a great deal about the fifth president. Admission is $9

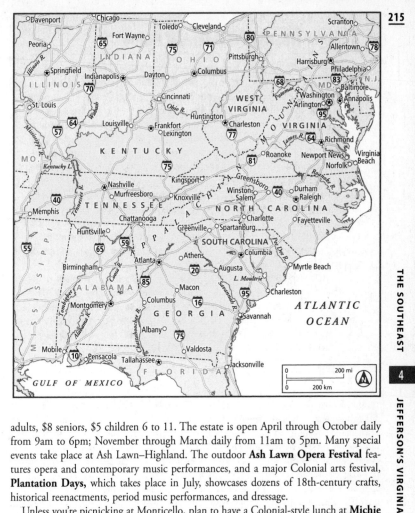

adults, $8 seniors, $5 children 6 to 11. The estate is open April through October daily from 9am to 6pm; November through March daily from 11am to 5pm. Many special events take place at Ash Lawn–Highland. The outdoor **Ash Lawn Opera Festival** features opera and contemporary music performances, and a major Colonial arts festival, **Plantation Days,** which takes place in July, showcases dozens of 18th-century crafts, historical reenactments, period music performances, and dressage.

Unless you're picnicking at Monticello, plan to have a Colonial-style lunch at **Michie Tavern ca. 1784,** 683 Thomas Jefferson Pkwy. (© **434/977-1234;** www.michietavern. com), which was built in 1784 and has been painstakingly reconstructed. Behind the tavern are reproductions of the "dependencies"—log kitchen, dairy, smokehouse, ice-house, root cellar, and "necessary" (note the not-so-soft corncobs). The re-created general store houses an excellent crafts shop. Mandatory 30-minute tavern-museum tours depart as needed from April to October (self-guided tours with recorded narratives are available other months). Admission is $8 adults, $7 seniors, $3 children 6 to 11. Buffet meals cost $15 for adults, $7.25 for children. The museum is open daily from 9am to 5pm (last tour 4:20pm). The restaurant serves food daily from 11:30am to 3pm.

Another Nearby Presidential Home

Twenty-five miles east of Charlottesville is **Montpelier,** 11407 Constitution Hwy. (Va. 20), Montpelier Station (© **540/672-2728;** www.montpelier.org), a 2,700-acre estate facing the Blue Ridge Mountains that was home to President James Madison and his wife, Dolley. They are buried here in the family cemetery. Two structures remain from their time: the main house and the "Ice House Temple" (built over a well and used to store ice). William du Pont, Sr., bought the estate in 1900; he enlarged the mansion and added barns, staff houses, a sawmill, a blacksmith shop, a train station, a dairy, and greenhouses, and his wife created a 22-acre formal garden.

The National Trust for Historic Preservation owns the property and is in the process of a meticulous multiyear restoration, which has stripped away the du Pont's additions to the mansion, reducing it to the 22-room brick version the Madisons occupied in 1820s. The house is open to the public during the project, with 30-minute tours explaining the near-archaeological aspects of the work.

Admission is $12 adults, $6 children ages 6 to 11. Open April through October daily from 9:30am to 5:30pm, November through March daily from 9:30am to 4:30pm. Call ahead for a schedule of special events, such as birthday celebrations for James (Mar 16) and Dolley (May 20). To get there from Charlottesville, go north on U.S. 29 to U.S. 33 at Ruckersville and head east; at Barboursville, turn left (north) onto Va. 20.

The **University of Virginia** (© **434/982-320;** www.virginia.edu), designed by Thomas Jefferson himself, is graced with spacious lawns, serpentine-walled gardens, colonnaded pavilions, and a classical rotunda inspired by the Pantheon in Rome. Jefferson was in every sense the university's father, since he conceived it, wrote its charter, raised money for its construction, drew the plans, selected the site, laid the cornerstone in 1817, supervised construction, served as the first rector, selected the faculty, and created the curriculum. His good friends Monroe and Madison sat with him on the first board. The focal point of the university is the **Rotunda** (at Rugby Rd.), today restored as Jefferson designed it. Some 600 feet of tree-dotted lawn extends from the south portico of the Rotunda to what is now Cabell Hall, designed at the turn of the 20th century by Stanford White. The room Edgar Allan Poe occupied when he was a student here is furnished as it would have been in 1826 and is open to visitors.

When school is in session, students lead 45-minute **campus tours** daily at 10 and 11am, and 2, 3, and 4pm from the Rotunda. The tours are first-come, first-served, but call © **434/982-3200** to make sure there will be one when you're here. Self-guided walking tour brochures are available in the Rotunda (© **434/924-3239**) and from the university's **Visitor Information Center** (© **434/924-7166**), which is located not on campus, but in the University Police Headquarters, on Ivy Road (U.S. 250 Business) just east of the U.S. 29/U.S. 250 bypass. The visitor center is open 24 hours a day. *Note:* The university is closed 3 weeks around Christmas.

Standing beside a picturesque lake, the **Boar's Head Inn,** 200 Ednam Dr. (© **800/476-1988** or 434/296-2181; www.boarsheadinn.com), is a university-owned property that's one of the best all-around resorts in Virginia. The focal point is a 19th-century gristmill that is loaded with antiques and art, and its plank flooring and huge old ceiling beams give ancient charm to the **Old Mill Room,** the resort's signature restaurant offering fine dining accompanied by an excellent selection of Virginia wines. The innlike guest rooms upstairs in the mill are charming and romantic, but if you want more space and a balcony, opt for a unit in one of the other lakeside structures. Guest quarters throughout are furnished with Colonial reproductions, and some units have kitchenettes. In addition to the full-service spa and the resort's own tennis courts, guests can use the adjacent Boar's Head Sports Club and the university's Birdwood Golf Course nearby. Rates run $150 to $325 double.

Also luxurious (and pricey) but slightly more formal is the 48-room **Keswick Hall at Monticello,** 701 Country Club Dr., in nearby Keswick (© **800/274-5391** or 804/979-3440; www.keswick.com). Many of the 1912-vintage Italianate rooms and suites have fireplaces, claw-foot tubs, and views over a golf course redesigned by Arnold Palmer. Dining here is gourmet all the way, and guests can also enjoy swimming pools, a fitness center, and tennis courts. Rates run $161 to $325 double.

Not as expensive, although still plenty upscale, are the **Silver Thatch Inn,** 3001 Hollymead Dr., Charlottesville (© **800/261-0720** or 434/978-4686; www.silverthatch.com; $155–$190 double), and the **Inn at Monticello,** 1188 Scottsville Rd. (Va. 20), Charlottesville (© **434/979-3593;** www.innatmonticello.com; $135–$235 double).

On the affordable end of the scale, one of Charlottesville's most reliable places is the **Hampton Inn & Suites,** 900 W. Main St., at 10th Street (© **800/HAMPTON** [426-7866] or 434/923-8600; www.hamptonsuites.com). Rates are $124 to $184 double. The commercial strip along U.S. 29 north of the U.S. 250 Bypass has an abundance of chain motels.

Guesthouses Reservation Service, Inc., P.O. Box 5737, Charlottesville, VA 22905 (© **434/979-7264;** www.va-guesthouses.com), handles bed-and-breakfast accommodations in elegant homes and private cottages. The office is open Monday through Friday from 9am to 5pm.

For a complete rundown, pick up a copy of *Bite & Sites,* a free restaurant guide supplement to *C-Ville Weekly* (www.c-ville.com), at the visitor centers. There are also lists and reviews in *The Hook* (www.readthehook.com), the other free newspaper found in boxes all over town.

Some of the area's finest dining is at the country inns, such as the **Boar's Head Inn** and the **Silver Thatch Inn** (see above). Another favorite is the **C&O Restaurant,** 515 E. Water St. (© **434/971-7044**), whose excellent menu ranges across the globe—from France to Thailand, from New Mexico to Louisiana.

For a caffeine fix, drop into the **Mudhouse,** 213 W. Main St. (© **434/984-6833**), a quintessential college-town coffeehouse. You can get a substantial breakfast at the **Nook,** 415 E. Main St. (© **434/295-6665**), which has been serving inexpensive meals for more than half a century. Also still going strong is the soda fountain in **Timberlake Drugs,** 322 E. Main St. (© **434/295-9155**), which has been around since 1890.

2 RICHMOND

Now a sprawling metropolitan area flanking the James River in the center of the state, Richmond supplanted the more militarily vulnerable Williamsburg as Virginia's capital in 1780, and it has been the scene of much of the state's history ever since. It was here in St. John's Church that Patrick Henry concluded his address to the second Virginia Convention with the stirring words "Give me liberty, or give me death!" But Richmond really made its mark on American history during the Civil War. This is where Jefferson Davis presided over the Confederate Congress, and Robert E. Lee accepted command of Virginia's armed forces.

ESSENTIALS

GETTING THERE By Plane   **Richmond International Airport (RIC),** Airport Drive off I-64, I-295, and Williamsburg Road (U.S. 60; © **804/226-3052;** www.fly richmond.com), known locally as Byrd Field, is about 15 minutes east of downtown. Several domestic carriers service the airport, and the major car-rental companies all have desks here.

By Train   Several daily **Amtrak** (© **800/872-7245;** www.amtrak.com) trains pull into two stations here. The main terminal is at 7519 Staples Mill Rd. (U.S. 33), north of I-64. There is no shuttle service from the Staples Mill Road station into tourist areas, so a better choice is the **Main Street Station** at 1500 E. Main St. in Shockoe Bottom. This restored French Renaissance–style building served as the city's transportation hub from 1901 until 1959 and is itself worth a look.

By Car   Richmond is at the junction of **I-64,** traveling east-west, and **I-95,** traveling north-south. **I-295** bypasses the city on its east and north sides. **U.S. 60** (east-west) and **U.S. 1** and **U.S. 301** (north-south) are other major arteries.

VISITOR INFORMATION   The **Richmond Visitors Center,** 401 N. 3rd St. (btw. Clay and Marshall sts.), Richmond, VA 23219 (© **888/742-4666;** www.visit.richmond.com), provides information and operates a same-day discounted hotel reservation service. It also shows a 10-minute orientation video. The center is in the Greater Richmond Convention Center and is open Monday through Friday from 9am to 5pm (to 6pm from Memorial Day weekend through Labor Day). There are free 20-minute parking spaces by the serpentine brick wall on 3rd Street between Clay and Marshall streets. Another comprehensive source of information is **www.discoverrichmond.com**, a community site operated by the *Richmond Times-Dispatch* newspaper.

EXPLORING RICHMOND

Richmond was probably the most important city in the South during the Civil War and was, therefore, a prime military target. The key sites are preserved by the **Richmond National Battlefield Park** (© **804/226-1981;** www.nps.gov/rich), whose visitor center is in the Tredegar Iron Works, Tredegar and 5th streets, at the western end of the city's **Riverfront Canal Walk,** a promenade running along the tow path of the old James River and Kanawha Canal. Rangers can give information on and driving directions to the several Civil War battlefields that lie on the city's eastern suburbs. The **Museum and White House of the Confederacy,** 1201 E. Clay St. (© **804/649-1861;** www.moc.org), houses the largest collection of Confederate objects in the country, many of them contributed by veterans and their descendants. Both the White House and museum are open

Monday through Saturday from 10am to 5pm and Sunday from noon to 5pm. A combined ticket for the museum and White House is $11 adults, $10 seniors, and $6 children 7 to 18.

But Richmond's history goes back even farther than the Civil War. **St. John's Episcopal Church,** 2401 E. Broad St. (② **804/648-5015;** www.historicstjohnschurch.org), dates from 1741 and was the site of the second Virginia Convention in 1775, with Thomas Jefferson, George Washington, and Richard Henry Lee in attendance. In support of a bill to assemble and train a militia to oppose Great Britain, Patrick Henry stood up and delivered his famous speech: "I know not what course others may take, but as for me, give me liberty or give me death!" Admission is free, but 20-minute tours are available for $6 adults, $5 seniors, and $4 children 7 to 18. Tours run Monday through Saturday from 10am to 3:30pm and Sunday from 1 to 3:30pm.

Designed by Thomas Jefferson, the **Virginia State Capitol,** 9th and Grace streets (② **804/698-1788;** http://legis.state.va.us), has been in continuous use since 1788. Jefferson modeled it on the Maison Carrée, a Roman temple built in Nîmes during the 1st century A.D. Admission is free; 1-hour grounds tours depart continuously Monday through Friday on the hour from 9am to 4pm, Saturday from 10am to 4pm, and Sunday from 1 to 4pm.

History buffs should also visit the **John Marshall House,** 818 E. Marshall St., at 9th Street (② **804/648-7998;** www.apva.org/marshall), the restored home of the first chief justice of the United States. It's open Tuesday through Saturday from 10am to 4:30pm and Sunday from noon to 5pm. Admission is $10 adults, $7 seniors, and $5 for students.

In addition, Richmond is home to the **Virginia Museum of Fine Arts,** Boulevard and Grove Avenue (② **804/340-1400;** www.vmfa.state.va.us), noted for the largest public Fabergé collection outside Russia—more than 300 objets d'art created at the turn of the 20th century for czars Alexander III and Nicholas II. Other highlights include the Goya portrait *General Nicholas Guye,* a rare life-size marble statue of Roman emperor Caligula, and Monet's *Iris by the Pond.* The museum is open Wednesday through Sunday from 11am to 5pm; admission is free, though a $5 donation is "suggested."

A great place to take the kids is **Paramount's Kings Dominion** (② **804/876-5000;** www.kingsdominion.com), north of the city in Doswell (take I-95 to Va. 30). This family-oriented theme park, one of the most popular in the East, offers a variety of rides and entertainment, mostly based on themes from Paramount movies and TV shows. Check the website for the park's ever-changing hours and admission costs.

WHERE TO STAY

The **Richmond Visitors Center** (see above) operates a free hotel reservation service. Top hotels in Richmond include the magnificent **Jefferson Hotel,** Franklin and Adams streets (② **800/484-8014** or 804/788-8000; www.jeffersonhotel.com), a stunning Beaux Arts sightseeing attraction in its own right (check out the rotunda in the lobby!), which has hosted countless presidents and celebrities over the years. Rates run $310 to $340 double.

Other options include the intimate, upscale the **Berkeley Hotel,** 1200 E. Cary St. (② **888/780-4422** or 804/780-1300; www.berkeleyhotel.com; $205–$225 double); and the more moderately priced **Linden Row Inn,** 100 E. Franklin St. (② **800/348-7424** or 804/783-7000; www.lindenrowinn.com; $89–$129 double), which is comprised of a row of seven small, separate 140-year-old Greek Revival town houses and their garden dependencies.

A Side Trip to Petersburg

The town of Petersburg, 23 miles south of Richmond on I-95, offers an excellent excursion for history buffs. Petersburg was the site of the siege that ended in the Civil War's last great battle, which resulted in Robert E. Lee's surrender. When you arrive, take Washington Street (exit 52) west and follow the Petersburg Tour signs to the **visitor center** at 425 Cockade Alley (© **800/368-3595** or 804/733-2400; www.petersburg-va.org), where you can get maps and literature, and buy a block ticket to local museums. **Block tickets** cover the Siege Museum, Centre Hill Mansion, and Old Blandford Church for $11 adults, $9 seniors and children 7 to 12. Otherwise, admission to each is $5 adults, $4 seniors and children. The center is open daily from 9am to 5pm.

Petersburg's Old Town holds many interesting historic sights and museums, all within a short walk of the visitor center. Ringing the eastern and southern outskirts of town, the impressive 2,600-acre-plus **Petersburg National Battlefield** (© **804/732-3531;** www.nps.gov/pete) preserves the key sites of the protracted siege that ended the war. The battlefield's visitor center is 2½ miles east of downtown on East Washington Street (Va. 36).

Chain motels are scattered throughout the suburbs. The Executive Center area, on West Broad Street (U.S. 33/250) at I-64 (exit 183), about 5 miles west of downtown, is a campuslike area convenient to the major attractions. The best of its hotels is the redwood-and-brick **Sheraton Richmond** (© **800/325-3535** or 804/285-1234).

WHERE TO DINE

East Cary Street between 12th and 15th streets is Richmond's premier dining mecca, with a bevy of good restaurants. Consistently popular with young professionals as a watering hole, **Siné Irish Pub & Restaurant,** 1327 E. Cary St. (© 804/649-7767), is anything but a typical Irish pub, offering a wide selection of seafood, steaks, and chicken in addition to the usual corned beef and cabbage. In warm weather you can dine and drink on the deck out back. Also on that stretch of Cary, you can get fresh sushi at **Ninanohena,** 1309 E. Cary St. (© 804/225-8801); excellent Italian at **La Grotta Restaurant,** 1218 E. Cary St. (© 804/644-2466); Chesapeake Bay seafood at the **Hard Shell,** 1411 E. Cary St. (© 804/643-2333); upscale American at **Sam Miller's Warehouse,** 1210 E. Cary St. (© 804/643-1301); and Spanish tapas and paella at **Europa,** 1409 E. Cary St. And for picnic fare, head to **Coppola's Delicatessen,** in the Carytown section at 2900 W. Cary St. (© 804/359-NYNY [359-6969]), with its aromatic clutter of cheeses, sausages, olives, pickles, and things marinated.

3 WILLIAMSBURG & COLONIAL VIRGINIA

The narrow peninsula between the James and York rivers saw the very beginnings of Colonial America and the rebellion that eventually created the United States. Visitors today can get an extensive history lesson in the beautifully restored 18th-century town of

Colonial Williamsburg, see the earliest permanent English settlement in North America at Jamestown, and walk the Yorktown ramparts where Washington decisively defeated Cornwallis, thus turning the colonists' dream of a new nation into a reality.

More than history, however, makes this one of America's family vacation meccas. There are also the Busch Gardens Williamsburg theme park with entertainment and rides, world-class shopping in the factory outlet stores near Williamsburg, and golf on some of Virginia's finest courses.

ESSENTIALS

GETTING THERE   By Plane   Several domestic carriers serve **Newport News/Williamsburg Airport** (© 757/877-0221; www.nnwairport.com), 14 miles east of Williamsburg. More flights (and certainly more jets) arrive at **Richmond International Airport** (see "Essentials" under "Richmond," above), about 45 miles west of town via I-64.

By Train   Amtrak trains (© 800/USA-RAIL [872-7245]; www.amtrak.com) serve the Transportation Center, 468 N. Boundary St., at Lafayette Street (© **757/229-8750**), within walking distance of the historic area.

By Car   **I-64** passes Williamsburg on its way between Richmond and Norfolk. For the historic area, take exit 238 (Va. 143) off I-64 and follow the signs. The **Colonial Parkway,** one of Virginia's most scenic routes, connects Williamsburg to Jamestown and Yorktown (it runs through a tunnel under the Historic Area).

VISITOR INFORMATION   You and a few million other persons who come here every year will begin your visit at the **Colonial Williamsburg Visitor Center,** off the U.S. 60 Bypass, just east of Va. 132 (© **800/HISTORY** [447-8679] or 757/220-7645; www.colonialwilliamsburg.com). You can't miss it; bright green signs point the way from all access roads to Williamsburg. This is where you buy your tickets for the dozens of attractions that make up Colonial Williamsburg. The center is open daily 9am to 5pm. Parking is free.

The best source for general information about the hotels, restaurants, and activities not operated by the foundation is the **Greater Williamsburg Chamber & Tourism Alliance,** 421 N. Boundary St., Williamsburg, VA 23187 (© **800/368-6511** or 757/229-6511; www.visitwilliamsburg.com), open Monday through Friday from 8:30am to 5pm.

GETTING AROUND   Since few cars are allowed into the Historic Area from 8am to 10pm daily, you must park elsewhere. The visitor center has ample parking and operates a **shuttle bus** to and from the Historic Area. It's free for holders of tickets to the Historic Area attractions. There's also a footpath from the visitor center to the Historic Area.

The easiest way to get around outside the Historic Area is by buses operated by **Williamsburg Area Transport** (© **757/259-4093;** www.williamsburgtransport.com). They depart the Colonial Williamsburg Visitor Center daily every 30 minutes from 9am to 3:30pm, with the final return trips departing Jamestown and Yorktown at 5:15pm. The rides cost $2 each way but are free with admission to Historic Jamestowne and Yorktown Battlefield. Save your admission tickets.

The buses follow U.S. 60 from the Williamsburg Pottery Factory in the west to Busch Gardens Williamsburg in the east, with a detour to the Bypass Road hotels.

The land is flat here, so getting around via bicycle is a great idea. **Bike and stroller rentals** are available from Easter through October at the **Woodlands Hotel & Suites,** at the Colonial Williamsburg Visitor Center (© **757/229-1000;** see "Visitor Information," above). For a taxi, call **Yellow Cab** (© 757/722-1111) or **Williamsburg Taxi** (© **757/566-3009**).

TICKETS   It costs nothing to stroll the streets of the Historic Area and perhaps debate revolutionary politics with the actors playing Thomas Jefferson or Patrick Henry, but you will need a **ticket** to enter the key buildings and the museums, see the 35-minute orientation film at the visitor center, use the Historic Area shuttle buses, and take a 30-minute Orientation Walk through the restored village.

The Colonial Williamsburg Foundation changes its system of tickets and passes so frequently that you should *definitely* call the visitor center or check the Colonial Williamsburg website (**www.colonialwilliamsburg.com**) for the latest information. With that caveat, this was the pass structure as it existed when we went to press.

A 1-day **Capital City Pass** ticket allowed access to most Historic Area attractions, but not the Governor's Palace or the walking tours. It cost $36 for adults, $18 for children 6 to 14, free for children 5 and younger. You could add the Governor's Palace for $9 adults, $4.50 children. It is good for the day you buy it, regardless of the time you purchased it. Much more useful is the **Governor's Key-to-the-City Pass,** which includes everything you're likely to see and is good for 2 days. At press time it was going for $49 adults, $24 children 6 to 17.

For longer stays, it's worth paying $59 per adult, $29 for children 6 to 17 for a **Freedom Pass,** which is good for 1 year and includes a 50% discount on the nighttime performances.

Tickets are available at the Colonial Williamsburg Visitor Center, a **ticket booth** at the Merchants Square shops on Henry Street at Duke of Gloucester Street, and **Lumber House** on Duke of Gloucester Street opposite the Palace Green.

American Express, Diners Club, MasterCard, and Visa credit cards are accepted at Colonial Williamsburg ticket outlets, attractions, hotels, and taverns.

Ⓥⁱ**Value**   **Saving Money on Tickets**

You can buy tickets to Colonial Williamsburg, Busch Gardens Europe, Water Country USA, Colonial Historical National Park, and other Historic Triangle attractions separately and pay full price, or you can do some shopping and come up with money-saving combination deals. For example, as I write this, the **Historic Triangle Pass** included admission to Colonial Williamsburg, Historic Jamestowne, Jamestown Settlement, Yorktown Battlefield, and the Yorktown Victory Center for $68 per person, regardless of age, good for 5 days. Be sure to check out **Flex Tickets,** which combine several area attractions for one price. They are available at the Colonial Williamsburg Visitor Center. Some hotels and motels offer discounted ticket prices to local attractions if you stay with them; it's worth asking when you call to make your reservation. The Williamsburg Hotel & Motel Association sponsors **"I Am a Williamsburg Vacation"** (© **800/211-7164;** www.go williamsburg.com), which lets you combine tickets and hotels into a one-price Flex Vacation Package.

In addition to the sights below, look for the numerous 18th-century crafts demonstrations on view throughout the Historic Area. You can stroll the Historic Area streets anytime, but in general, its attractions are open from April to October daily from 9am to 5pm, to 6pm Memorial Day to Labor Day. Some places are closed on specific days, and hours can vary, so check with the visitor center for current information.

The Colonial Buildings

BRUSH-EVERARD HOUSE   The Brush-Everard House was occupied without interruption from 1717—when Public Armorer and master gunsmith John Brush built it as a residence-cum-shop—to 1946. Its most distinguished owner was Thomas Everard, clerk of York County from 1745 to 1771 and two-time mayor of Williamsburg. Today the home is restored and furnished to its Everard-era appearance. The smokehouse and kitchen out back are original. Special programs here focus on African-American life in the 18th century.

THE CAPITOL   Virginia legislators met in the Capitol at the eastern end of Duke of Gloucester Street from 1704 to 1780. The House of Burgesses became a training ground for patriots and future governors such as George Washington, Thomas Jefferson, Richard Henry Lee, and Patrick Henry. The original Capitol burned down in 1747, was rebuilt in 1753, and succumbed to fire again in 1832. The reconstruction is of the 1704 building, complete with Queen Anne's coat of arms adorning the tower and the Great Union flag flying overhead. You must take a 30-minute **tour** to get inside the Capitol.

THE COURTHOUSE   An intriguing window on the criminal justice system of Colonial life is offered in the courthouse, which dominates Market Square. An original building, the courthouse was the scene of varying proceedings, ranging from dramatic criminal trials to the prosaic issuance of licenses. Visitors can participate in the administration of Colonial justice at the courthouse by sitting on a jury or acting as a defendant.

GEORGE WYTHE HOUSE   On the west side of the Palace Green is the elegant restored brick home of George Wythe (pronounced *With*), the first Virginia signer of the Declaration of Independence. On principle, Wythe did not sign the Constitution, however, because it did not contain a bill of rights or antislavery provisions. This house, in which he lived with his second wife, was Washington's headquarters before the siege of Yorktown and Rochambeau's after the surrender of Cornwallis. Open-hearth cooking is demonstrated in the outbuilding.

GOVERNOR'S PALACE   This building is a meticulous reconstruction of the Georgian mansion that was the residence and official headquarters of royal governors from 1714 until Lord Dunmore fled before dawn in the face of armed resistance in 1775, thus ending British rule in Virginia. The sumptuous surroundings, nobly proportioned halls and rooms, 10 acres of formal gardens and greens, and vast wine cellars all evoke splendor. **Tours,** given continuously throughout the day, wind up in the gardens, where you can explore at your leisure the elaborate geometric parterres, topiary work, bowling green, pleached *allées,* and a holly maze patterned after the one at Hampton Court. Plan at least 30 minutes to wander the stunning grounds and to visit the kitchen and stable yards.

JAMES GEDDY HOUSE & FOUNDRY   This two-story L-shaped 1762 home (with attached shops) is an original building. Here visitors can see how a comfortably situated middle-class family lived in the 18th century. Unlike the fancier abodes you'll visit, the

Hitting the Beach

A great antidote to the plethora of Colonial history is to head over to **Virginia Beach,** about 60 miles southwest of Williamsburg (take I-64 to I-264 East). Summertime vacationers flock to this resort area to enjoy over 20 miles of unbroken sand and surf, as well as the Virginia Marine Science Museum. A great choice for lodging is the **Cavalier Hotel,** oceanfront at 42nd Street, Virginia Beach (© **800/ 446-8199** or 757/425-8555; www.cavalierhotel.com), one of the best resorts on the beach. Doubles run about $89 to $289. All but a few of the major chains are present here, too, including Sheraton, Ramada, Comfort Inn, and Holiday Inn (see appendix D for their toll-free numbers).

Geddy House has no wallpaper or oil paintings; a mirror and spinet from England, however, indicate relative affluence. At a foundry on the premises, craftsmen cast silver, pewter, bronze, and brass items at a forge.

THE MAGAZINE & GUARDHOUSE   The magazine is a sturdy octagonal brick building constructed in 1715 to house ammunition and arms for the defense of the British colony. It has survived intact to the present day. Today the building is stocked with 18th-century equipment—British-made flintlock muskets, cannons and cannonballs, barrels of powder, bayonets, and drums, the latter for communication purposes. Children can join the militia here during the summer.

PEYTON RANDOLPH HOUSE   The Randolphs were one of the most prominent— and wealthy—families in Colonial Virginia. This house (actually two connected homes) dates to 1715. Robertson's Windmill, in back of the house, is a post mill of a type popular in the early 18th century.

THE PUBLIC GAOL   Imprisonment was not the usual punishment for crime in Colonial times, but people awaiting trial (at the Capitol in Williamsburg) and runaway slaves sometimes spent months in the Public Gaol. Beds were piles of straw; leg irons, shackles, and chains were used; and the daily diet consisted of "salt beef damaged, and Indian meal." This thick-walled red-brick building served as the Williamsburg city jail until 1910. The building today is restored to its 1720s appearance.

THE PUBLIC HOSPITAL   Opened in 1773, the "Public Hospital for Persons of Insane and Disordered Minds" was America's first "lunatic asylum." On a self-guided tour you'll see a 1773 cell—with a filthy straw-filled mattress on the floor, ragged blanket, and manacles—as well as rooms from later periods.

RALEIGH TAVERN   This most famous of Williamsburg taverns was named for Sir Walter Raleigh. After the Governor's Palace, it was the social and political hub of the town. Regulars included George Washington and Thomas Jefferson, who met here in 1774 with Patrick Henry, Richard Henry Lee, and Francis Lightfoot Lee to plot revolution.

The Museums

From the central hallway of the Public Hospital (see above), an elevator descends underground to Colonial Williamsburg's two fine museums.

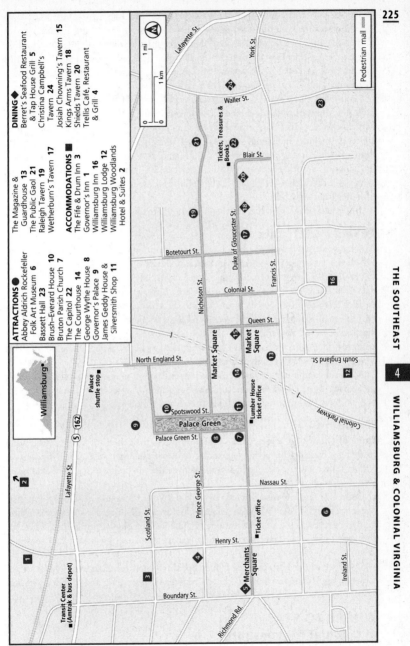

ATTRACTIONS ●

Abbey Aldrich Rockefeller Folk Art Museum **6**
Bassett Hall **23**
Brush–Everard House **10**
Bruton Parish Church **7**
The Capitol **22**
The Courthouse **14**
George Wythe House **8**
Governor's Palace **9**
James Geddy House & Silversmith Shop **11**
The Magazine & Guardhouse **13**
The Public Gaol **21**
Raleigh Tavern **19**
Wetherburn's Tavern **17**

ACCOMMODATIONS ■

The Fife & Drum Inn **3**
Governor's Inn **1**
Williamsburg Inn **16**
Williamsburg Lodge **12**
Williamsburg Woodlands Hotel & Suites **2**

DINING ◆

Berret's Seafood Restaurant & Tap House Grill **5**
Christina Campbell's Tavern **24**
Josiah Chowning's Tavern **15**
Kings Arms Tavern **18**
Shields Tavern **20**
Trellis Café, Restaurant & Grill **4**

The 62,000-square-foot **DeWitt Wallace Decorative Arts Museum** houses some 10,000 objects representing the highest achievement of American and English artisans from the 1640s to 1800. You'll see furnishings, ceramics, textiles, paintings, prints, silver, pewter, clocks, scientific instruments, mechanical devices, and weapons. Don't miss Charles Willson Peale's 1780 portrait of George Washington, which he patterned after the coronation portrait of George III of England, in the Masterworks Gallery.

Go through the Weldon Gallery on the upper level to the **Abby Aldrich Rockefeller Folk Art Museum,** with more than 2,600 folk-art paintings, sculptures, and art objects. Mrs. Rockefeller was a pioneer in this branch of collecting in the 1920s and 1930s. Her collection includes household ornaments and useful wares (hand-stenciled bed covers, butter molds, pottery, utensils, painted furniture, boxes), mourning pictures (embroideries honoring departed relatives and national heroes), family and individual portraits, shop signs, carvings, whittled toys, calligraphic drawings, weavings, quilts, and paintings of scenes from daily life.

A cafe here offers light fare, beverages, and a limited luncheon menu.

Theme Park Thrills

At some point you'll want to take a break from history, especially if you have kids in tow, and there's no better place here than **Busch Gardens Europe,** 1 Busch Gardens Blvd. (© 800/343-9746; www.buschgardens.com), on U.S. 60 about 3 miles east of the Historic Area. Here you can get a peek at European history, albeit fanciful, in authentically detailed 17th-century hamlets from England, Scotland, France, Germany, and Italy—but little mental effort is required to enjoy all the attractions you'll find here. Each village here has its own shops, crafts demonstrations, restaurants, rides, shows, and other entertainment. The sights are connected by trains pulled by reproductions of European steam locomotives, so you can easily skip around.

Admission and hours vary from year to year and season to season, so call ahead, check the website, or pick up a brochure at the visitor centers. At press time, it was $55 adults, $48 children 3 to 6 for unlimited rides, shows, and attractions

Shopping

Duke of Gloucester Street, in the Historic Area, is the center for 18th-century wares created by craftspeople plying the trades of American forefathers. You'll find hand-wrought silver jewelry, hats, hand-woven linens, leather-bound books, gingerbread cakes, and much more.

Don't miss **Craft House,** also run by Colonial Williamsburg, on Duke of Gloucester Street at Henry Street in Merchants Square. Featured at Craft House are exquisite works by master craftspeople and authentic reproductions of Colonial furnishings. There are also reproduction wallpapers, china, toys, games, maps, books, prints, and souvenirs aplenty.

Shopping in the Historic Area is fun, but the biggest merchandising draws are the outlets along **Richmond Road** (U.S. 60) between Williamsburg and Lightfoot, an area 5 to 7 miles west of the Historic Area.

WHERE TO STAY
In Colonial Williamsburg

The Colonial Williamsburg Foundation operates four hotels in the Historic Area, in all price categories. For advance reservations or information on all four hotels, call the **Visitor Center reservations service** (© 800/447-8679; www.colonialwilliamsburg.com).

Parking at all four properties is free for guests. Another advantage to staying at one of these four hotels is the option to purchase discounted Colonial Williamsburg Hotel Guest Tickets valid for the length of their stay (recently $29 adults, $15 children 6–17).

One of the nation's most distinguished hotels, the rambling white-brick Regency-style **Williamsburg Inn,** at 136 Francis St., has played host to 17 heads of state over its lifetime. All the large accommodations have marble bathrooms with separate tubs and showers. All are exquisitely furnished with reproductions, books, and photos of famous prior guests. The Regency Dining Room features classic American cuisine (coats and ties required after 6pm) and a view of one of the inn's three top-flight golf courses. Rates in the main inn run $319 to $579 double. Rooms in a modern building called **Providence Hall,** adjacent to the inn, are furnished in a contemporary blend of 18th-century and Asian style, with balconies or patios. Rates in this building range from $300 to $359. The Inn's fitness center is in Providence Hall. A full-service spa is located between this property and the Williamsburg Lodge.

Across the street from the Williamsburg Inn, the foundation's second-best hotel, the **Williamsburg Lodge,** South England Street, recently completed an extensive renovation that restored most of it to its original 1930s appearance, albeit with modern conveniences. Only the existing Tazewell Wing, a 1970s-vintage structure whose rooms have balconies facing landscaped courtyards, escaped serious surgery. The other more luxurious rooms are in five Colonial-style "Guest Houses" linked to the main building by covered brick walkways. The new units are notable for their Colonial Williamsburg–designed furniture and their retro 1930s bathrooms. Guests here share all of the Williamsburg Inn's facilities, including the luxurious spa. Rates run $129 to $239 double.

The **Williamsburg Woodlands Hotel & Suites,** 105 Visitors Center Dr., is the foundation's newest and third-best hotel. A separate building with a peaked roof and skylights holds the lodgelike lobby, where guests are treated to continental breakfast in a room with a fireplace. Interior corridors lead to the guest quarters in a U-shaped building around a courtyard. The suites have separate living and sleeping rooms divided by the bathroom and a wet bar with coffeemaker, fridge, and microwave oven. All units have Colonial-style pine furniture and photos of the Historic Area on their walls. The Huzzah! family restaurant (think Applebee's) is on the premises. There's plenty to keep kids occupied here, and when you couple that with the pullout sofa beds in the suites, it's a good choice for families of moderate means. Rates range from $69 to $159 double, $119 to $209 suite.

Least expensive of the foundation's hotels, the **Governor's Inn,** 506 Henry St. (Va. 132), at Lafayette Street, is a two- and three-story brick motel surrounded by parking lots. Natural wood furniture brightens the standard motel-style rooms, which have been spiffed up recently. There's a small outdoor pool for cooling off. It's near the visitor center on the northwest edge of the Historic Area. Rates include continental breakfast and run $49 to $109 double. *Note:* The Governor's Inn is near the Transportation Center, which means that trains come by during the night.

The foundation also has 77 rooms in the Historic Area in its **Colonial Houses.** Tastefully furnished with 18th-century antiques and reproductions, they all are variously equipped with canopied beds, kitchens, living rooms, fireplaces, and/or sizable gardens. Many of these are former laundries, workshops, small homes, and stand-alone kitchens that have been converted into one- and two-bedroom bungalows. Others are rooms in taverns, some of which have as many as 16 units. Some rooms are tiny; tell the reservation clerk precisely what size room and what bed configuration you want. Some units are close to Francis Street, whose traffic noise can easily penetrate the noninsulated walls. Rates run $179 to $269 double, while houses go for $199 to $459 per night. Reserve through the visitor center's reservations service (© **800/447-8679;** www.colonial williamsburg.com).

Other Area Accommodations

The area has more than 80 hotels and motels, including many chain options. You should be able to find a room on short notice except during the peak holiday periods.

One of the best of the chain entries is the 151-room **Courtyard By Marriott,** 470 McLaws Circle (© **800/321-2211** or 757/221-0700; www.courtyard.com), which enjoys an attractively landscaped setting of trees and shrubs on the eastern side of town near Busch Gardens. Rates run $119 to $169 double. A family-friendly choice is the 303-room **Crowne Plaza Williamsburg at Fort Magruder,** 6545 Pocahontas Trail (U.S. 60; © **877/227-6963** or 757/220-2250; www.crowneplaza.com), with a convenient location right between the Historic Area and Busch Gardens. Rates run $89 to $169 double.

The **Fife & Drum Inn,** 441 Prince George St. (© **888/838-1783** or 757/345-1776; www.fifeanddruminn.com), is a relaxed and interesting charmer that offers the only privately owned accommodations in the Historic Area. A sky-lit hallway with faux brick floor and clapboard siding leads to the B&B's seven medium-size rooms and two suites, some of which have dormer windows. Smokers need to look elsewhere. Rates include full breakfast and free parking; they run $165 to $190 double.

Nestled in a peaceful setting on beautifully landscaped grounds beside the James River, the luxurious, country-club-like **Kingsmill Resort & Spa,** 1010 Kingsmill Rd. (© **800/832-5665** or 757/253-1703; www.kingsmill.com), is one of Virginia's most complete resorts, offering three golf courses (the River Course is the highlight), a sports complex with 15 tennis courts, and the Williamsburg area's only full-service spa. Accommodations consist of standard guest rooms and one-, two-, and three-bedroom individually decorated suites with full kitchens and fireplaces. Kingsmill's main dining room offers fine cuisine with a terrific view of the James. Guests can take a complimentary shuttle to Colonial Williamsburg and Busch Gardens Williamsburg. Rates run $239 to $299 double.

WHERE TO DINE

The Colonial Williamsburg Foundation runs four popular reconstructed Colonial taverns: **Christiana Campbell's Tavern,** on Waller Street; and **Josiah Chowning's Tavern, Kings Arms Tavern,** and **Shields Tavern,** all on Duke of Gloucester Street. All are reconstructed 18th-century *ordinaries,* or taverns, and aim at authenticity in fare, ambience, and costuming of the staff. Although relatively expensive, dinner at one of the taverns is a necessary ingredient of the Williamsburg experience. Advance reservations for dinner at the taverns are essential during the summer and on spring and fall weekends. Except at Josiah Chowning's Tavern, which does not accept reservations, you can book tables up to 60 days in advance by dropping by or calling the visitor center (© **800/TAVERNS** [828-3767] or 757/229-2141). Lunch reservations are accepted only for major holidays.

There are benches throughout the restored area (lots of grass, too) if you feel like a picnic, and if you have a car, you can drive to nearby scenic overlooks along Colonial

Parkway (the parking areas along the James and York rivers are best, but they don't have picnic tables or other facilities). The **Cheese Shop,** 424 Prince George St., in Merchants Square (© **757/220-0298**), is a good place to purchase takeout sandwiches and other fixings.

Berret's Seafood Restaurant & Tap House Grill, 199 S. Boundary St., at Francis Street (© **757/253-1847;** www.berrets.com), is a congenial, casual place, with a dining room that features Canvas sailcloth shades, blue-trimmed china, and marine artifacts—an appropriate backdrop for excellent seafood. The Tap House is the best place in town to slake a thirst after schlepping around the Historic Area all day and also serves light fare. Main courses in the main dining room cost $25 to $30.

Executive chef Marcel Desaulniers has brought national recognition to the **Trellis, Café Restaurant & Grill,** Duke of Gloucester Street between Henry and Boundary streets (© **757/229-8610;** www.thetrellis.com), whose decor evokes California's wine country. The menu changes seasonally and combines the best in foods from different regions of the United States. If it's offered, try the exciting combination of grilled fish, thinly sliced Virginia country ham, pine nuts, and zinfandel-soaked raisins. And don't skip the sinful Death by Chocolate for dessert. If the weather is fine, you might dine alfresco on the planter-bordered brick terrace. Main courses cost $16 to $32; a complete, fixed-price dinner for $29 is a steal.

One of the great places to sample traditional, down-home Virginia cooking, the **Old Chickahominy House,** 1211 Jamestown Rd., at Va. 199 (© **757/229-4689**), is a reconstructed 18th-century house with mantels from old Gloucester homes and wainscoting from Carter's Grove. The entire effect is extremely cozy and charming, from the rocking chairs on the front porch to the blazing fireplaces within. This is the best place in town for hearty Southern plantation food. It's open only for breakfast and lunch; main courses run $4 to $9.

A SIDE TRIP TO JAMESTOWN

The story of Jamestown, the first permanent English settlement in the New World, is documented in a national park on the Jamestown Island site where they landed. Here you'll learn the exploits of Capt. John Smith, the colony's leader, rescued from execution by the American Indian princess Pocahontas; the arrival of the first African-American slaves; and how life was lived in 17th-century Virginia. Archaeologists have excavated more than 100 building frames, evidence of manufacturing ventures (pottery, winemaking, brick making, and glass blowing), wells, and roads. Opened prior to Jamestown's big 400th-anniversary bash in 2007, the Archaearium museum displays hundreds of thousands of artifacts of everyday life—tools, utensils, ceramic dishes, armor, keys, and the like—uncovered during the digs.

Next door at Jamestown Settlement, a state-run living-history museum complex, you can see re-creations of the three ships in which the settlers arrived in 1607, the colony they built, and a typical American Indian village of the time.

Allow at least half a day for your visit and consider packing a lunch. There is a cafe at Jamestown Settlement, but you may want to take advantage of the picnic areas at the National Park Service site.

GETTING THERE The scenic way here from Williamsburg is via the picturesque Colonial Parkway, or you can take Jamestown Road (Va. 31).

Jointly administered by the National Park Service and the Association for the Preservation of Virginia Antiquities (APVA; www.apva.org), **Historic Jamestowne** (© 757/898-2410 or 229-1773; www.nps.gov/colo) is the site of the actual colony. It was an island then; now an isthmus separates it from the mainland. At the Ranger Station entrance gate, you'll pay $10 for each person 16 years old and over; admission is good for 7 days. The price includes admission to Yorktown Battlefield and is good for 7 days. The gate is open daily from 8:30am to 4:30pm in summer. You can stay on the grounds until dusk.

After entering the park, stop first at the reconstructed **Glasshouse,** where costumed interpreters make glass in the ancient way used by the colonists in 1608 during their first attempt to create an industry (it failed). Then stop in at the **visitor center** before following the footpaths to the actual site of **"James Cittie,"** where rubbly brick foundations of 17th-century homes, taverns, shops, and statehouses are enhanced by artists' renderings, text, and audio stations. A short walk along the seawall past Confederate breastworks—built during the Civil War to protect this narrow part of the river—will take you to the fascinating **Archaearium,** which artfully displays the results of the archaeological digs, including the skeleton of one of the settlers and a resin cast reproduction of another belonging to a young man who apparently died of a musket shot to the right knee, giving rise to the theme of the interactive display: "Who Shot J. R.?"

A fascinating **5-mile loop drive** begins at the visitor center parking lot and winds through 1,500 wilderness acres of woodland and marsh that have been allowed to return to their natural state in order to approximate the landscape as 17th-century settlers found it. Illustrative markers interpret aspects of daily activities and industries of the colonists—tobacco growing, lumbering, silk and wine production, pottery making, farming, and so on.

Jamestown Settlement

Operated by the Commonwealth of Virginia, **Jamestown Settlement** (© 888/593-4682 or 757/253-4838; www.historyisfun.org), an indoor/outdoor museum, is open daily from 9am to 5pm (until 6pm June 15–Aug 15). Built in 1957 to celebrate Jamestown's 350th anniversary, this living history was a major focus of the 400th anniversary events in 2007, beginning with "The World of 1607," a major exhibit featuring rare treasures of the time. Admission is $14 adults, $6.25 children 6 to 12, free for children under 6, or you can buy a combination ticket with Yorktown Victory Center (see "A Side Trip to Yorktown," below) for $19 adults, $9.25 children 6 to 12, free for kids 5 and under.

After purchasing tickets, you can watch a 15-minute film that gives you an introduction to Jamestown. Beyond the theater, three large permanent galleries feature artifacts and dioramas relating to the Jamestown period. Leaving the museum complex, you'll come directly into the **Powhatan Indian Village,** representing the culture and technology of a highly organized chiefdom of 32 tribes that inhabited coastal Virginia in the early 17th century. There are several mat-covered lodges, or longhouses, which are furnished as dwellings, as well as a garden and a ceremonial dance circle. Historical interpreters tend gardens, tan animal hides, and make bone and stone tools and pottery. Triangular **James Fort** is a re-creation of the one constructed by the Jamestown colonists on their arrival in the spring of 1607. Interpreters are engaged in activities typical of early-17th-century life, such as agriculture, animal care, carpentry, blacksmithing, and meal preparation. A short walk from James Fort are reproductions of the three **ships,** the *Susan Constant, Godspeed,* and *Discovery,* that transported 104 colonists to Virginia in 1607. *Tip:* Exhibits here are hands-on and interactive, making them more enjoyable for kids than those at Historic Jamestowne.

A SIDE TRIP TO YORKTOWN

Yorktown, the setting for the last major battle of the American Revolution, is about 14 miles northeast of Williamsburg. Today the battlefield is a national park, and the Commonwealth of Virginia has built an interpretive museum explaining the road to revolution, the war itself, and the building of a new nation afterward. The old town of Yorktown itself is also worth seeing. For lunch, consider a picnic in a large tree-shaded area at the Victory Center or at a riverside picnic area with tables and grills on Water Street at the foot of Comte de Grasse Street.

GETTING THERE   From Williamsburg, drive to the eastern end of the Colonial Parkway. From Norfolk, take I-64 West to U.S. 17 North.

Yorktown National Battlefield

The **National Park Service Visitor Center** (© 757/898-2410 or 898-3400; www.nps. gov/colo) displays Washington's actual military headquarters tent, a replica (which you can board and explore) of the quarterdeck of HMS *Charon,* additional objects recovered from the York River in the excavations, exhibits about Cornwallis's surrender and the events leading up to it, and dioramas detailing the siege. Upstairs, an "on-the-scene" account of the Battle of Yorktown is given by a 13-year-old soldier in the Revolutionary army, his taped narrative accompanied by a sound-and-light show. National Park Service rangers are on hand to answer questions; they also give **free tours** of the British inner defense line.

The Park Service visitor center is the starting point for the 7-mile **Battlefield route** and the 10-mile **Encampment route** auto tours of the battlefield. You'll be given a map indicating both routes and detailing major sites. At each stop there are explanatory historical markers (sometimes taped narratives as well), but for the most interesting experience, rent a cassette player and tape at the visitor center. If you can do only one, make it the Battlefield route.

The center is open daily from 9am to 5pm, with extended hours from spring to fall. Admission is $10 per person age 16 and older, good for 7 days (including admission to Jamestown Island). Audiotape tours cost $3.95, CDs $4.95. National Park Service passports are accepted for admission.

Yorktown Victory Centre

Set on 21 acres overlooking part of the battlefield of 1781, the state-owned **Yorktown Victory Center** (© 888/593-4682 or 757/253-4838; www.historyisfun.org) offers an excellent orientation to Yorktown, including a film, a living-history program, and museum exhibits. In the outdoor Continental army encampment, costumed interpreters re-create the lives of men and women who took part in the American Revolution. Admission is $9.25 adults, $5 children 6 to 12. A combination ticket with Jamestown Settlement is $19 adults, $9.25 children 6 to 12. It's open daily from 9am to 5pm.

4 THE SHENANDOAH VALLEY

Native Americans called the 200-mile-long valley in northwestern Virginia *Shenandoah,* meaning "Daughter of the Stars." Today the Shenandoah National Park offers spectacular landscapes and a plethora of hiking and riding trails, and protects the beauty and peace of the Blue Ridge Mountains along the eastern boundary of the valley. Along the Blue

Ridge crest, the 105-mile-long Skyline Drive—one of America's great scenic drives—runs the full length of the park and connects directly with the Blue Ridge Parkway, which continues south into North Carolina. Pioneers moved west from the Tidewater in the early 1700s to found picturesque small towns on the rolling valley floor, which was later to play a major role in the Civil War.

SHENANDOAH NATIONAL PARK

Running for 105 miles down the spine of the Blue Ridge Mountains, Shenandoah National Park is a haven for plants and wildlife. Although long and skinny, the park encompasses some 300 square miles of mountains, forests, waterfalls, and rock formations. It has more than 60 mountain peaks higher than 2,000 feet, with Hawksbill and Stony Man exceeding 4,000 feet. From overlooks along the road through the park, called the Skyline Drive, you can see many of the park's wonders and enjoy panoramic views over the Piedmont to the east and the Shenandoah Valley to the west. The drive gives you access to the park's visitor facilities and to more than 500 miles of glorious hiking and horse trails, including the Appalachian Trail. Animals such as deer, bear, bobcat, and turkey live here; the park also boasts more than 100 species of trees.

Essentials

ENTRANCES & ORIENTATION   The park and its Skyline Drive have four entrances. Northernmost is at **Front Royal** on U.S. 340 near the junction of I-81 and I-66, about 1 mile south of Front Royal and 90 miles west of Washington, D.C. The two middle entrances are at **Thornton Gap,** 33 miles south of Front Royal on U.S. 211 between Sperryville and Luray, and at **Swift Run Gap,** 68 miles south of Front Royal on U.S. 33 between Standardsville and Elkton. The southern gate is at **Rockfish Gap,** 105 miles south of Front Royal at I-64 and U.S. 250, some 21 miles west of Charlottesville and 18 miles east of Staunton.

The Skyline Drive is marked with **Mileposts,** starting at zero at the Front Royal entrance and increasing as you go south, with Rockfish Gap on the southern end at Mile 105.

VISITOR INFORMATION   For information about attractions, accommodations, restaurants, and services in the entire region, contact the **Shenandoah Valley Travel Association (SVTA),** 277 W. Old Cross Rd. (P.O. Box 1040), New Market, VA 22844 (© 877/847-4878 or 540/740-3132; fax 540/740-3100; www.visitshenandoah.org). The SVTA operates a visitor center in New Market, just off I-81 at U.S. 211 (exit 264). The center, open daily from 9am to 5pm, has a free phone line for making hotel reservations.

NATIONAL PARK INFORMATION   For free information, call or write to Superintendent, Shenandoah National Park, 3655 U.S. Hwy. 211 East, Luray, VA 22835 (© **540/999-3500;** www.nps.gov/shen). The headquarters is 4 miles west of Thornton Gap and 5 miles east of Luray on U.S. 211.

Aramark Virginia Sky-Line Co., the park's major concessionaire (© **888/896-3833;** www.visitshenandoah.com), maintains an informative website on which you can book accommodations at the park's lodges and cabins.

American Park Network (www.americanparknetwork.com) publishes a helpful advertiser-supported guide to the park, and it has bountiful information on its website.

FEES, REGULATIONS & BACKCOUNTRY PERMITS   Entrance permits good for 7 consecutive days are $15 per car, $10 per motorcycle, $8 for each pedestrian or bicyclist from March through November. These fees are $10, $10, and $5, respectively, from December through February. An annual pass ($30) is good for 1 year. Park entrance is free to holders of America the Beautiful—National Parks and Federal Recreational Lands Passes and the National Park Service's Golden Eagle, Golden Access, and Golden Age passports.

The **speed limit** on Skyline Drive is 35 mph, although given the number of camper vans and rubberneckers creeping along this winding two-lane road, you'll be lucky to go that fast. This is no place to have a fit of road rage.

Plants and animals are protected, so all hunting is prohibited. Pets must be kept on a leash at all times and are not allowed on some trails. Wood fires are permitted only in fireplaces in developed areas. The Skyline Drive is a great bike route, but neither bicycles nor motor vehicles of any sort are allowed on the hiking trails.

Most of the park is open to backcountry camping. Permits, which are free, are required; get them at the entrance gates, at visitor centers, or by mail from park headquarters (see "National Park Information," above). Campers are required to leave no trace of their presence. No permits are necessary for backcountry hiking, but the same "no-trace" rule applies.

VISITOR CENTERS   There are two park visitor centers, **Dickey Ridge Visitor Center,** at Mile 4.6 in the Northern District, and **Byrd Visitor Center,** in the Central District at Mile 51 in Big Meadows. Both are open daily 8:30am to 5pm from mid-April through October (to 6pm on weekends from July through Labor Day) and on an intermittent schedule through Thanksgiving weekend in late November. Both provide information, maps of nearby hiking trails, interpretive exhibits, films, slide shows, and nature walks.

Operated by the town of Waynesboro, the **Rockfish Gap Information Center,** on U.S. 211 (at exit 99 off I-64) at the park's southern gate (© **540/943-5187**), has a room-size topographical map of the region (and a life-size statute of Robert E. Lee). Daily hours are 9am to 5pm (closed Thanksgiving, Christmas, and New Year's Day).

SEASONS   The park's high season is from mid- to late October, when the fall foliage peaks, and weekend traffic on the Skyline Drive can be bumper-to-bumper. Days also tend to be more clear in fall than in summer, when lingering haze can obscure the views. In spring, the green of leafing trees moves up the ridge at the rate of about 100 feet a day. Wildflowers begin to bloom in April, and by late May, the azaleas are brilliant and the dogwood is putting on a show. Nesting birds abound, and the normally modest waterfalls are at their highest during spring, when warm rains melt the highland snows. You'll find the clearest views across the distant mountains during winter, but many facilities are closed then, and snow and ice can shut down the Skyline Drive. Also, parts of the drive are closed at night during Virginia's hunting season from mid-November to early January.

SEEING THE HIGHLIGHTS

Unless you're caught in heavy traffic on fall foliage weekends, you can drive the entire length of the **Skyline Drive** in about 3 hours without stopping. But why rush? Give yourself at least a day for this drive and its 75 designated scenic overlooks. Better yet, get out of your car and take at least a short hike down one of the hollows to a waterfall.

If you have only a day, head to the **Central District** between Thornton Gap and Swift Run Gap, the most developed but also most interesting part of the park. It has the highest mountains, the best views, nearly half of the park's 500 miles of hiking trails, and the park's only stables and overnight accommodations. Most visitors make Big Meadows or

THE SOUTHEAST

4

THE SHENANDOAH VALLEY

Skyland their base for stays of more than a day, but if you plan to do this, place your lodge reservations early (see "Where to Camp & Stay," below).

Among the more interesting of the 75 designated overlooks along the drive are the **Shenandoah Valley Overlook** (Mile 2.8), with views west to the Signal Knob of Massanutten Mountain across the south fork of the river; **Range View Overlook** (Mile 17.1; elevation 2,800 ft.), providing views of the central section of the park, looking south; **Stony Man Overlook** (Mile 38.6), offering panoramas of Stony Man Cliffs, the valley, and the Alleghenies; **Thoroughfare Mountain Overlook** (Mile 40.5; elevation 3,595 ft.), one of the highest, with views from Hogback Mountain south to cone-shaped Robertson Mountain and the rocky face of Old Rag Mountain; **Old Rag View Overlook** (Mile 46.5), dominated by Old Rag, sitting all by itself in an eastern extremity of the park; **Franklin Cliffs Overlook** (Mile 49), offering a view of the cliffs and the Shenandoah Valley and Massanutten Mountain beyond; and **Big Run Overlook** (Mile 81.2), which looks down on rocky peaks and the largest watershed in the park.

Hiking

The number-one outdoor activity here is hiking. The park's 112 hiking trails total more than 500 miles, varying in length from short walks to a 101-mile segment of the Appalachian Trail running the entire length of the park. Access to the trails is marked along the Skyline Drive. There are parking lots at the major trail heads, but they fill quickly on weekends.

Free maps of many trails are available at the visitor centers, which also sell topographic maps published by the Potomac Appalachian Trail Conference, as well as a one-sheet map of all of the park's walks published by Trails Illustrated. See "Visitor Information," above, for addresses and phone numbers.

An alternative to doing it yourself is to take a guided outdoor adventure organized by **Aramark Virginia Sky-Line Co.** (© **888/896-3833;** www.visitshenandoah.com). Led by mountain guides, they include short hikes from the park lodges ($10 per person), 1-day hikes ($89–$178 per person), 2-day excursions ($178 per person), and rock-climbing expeditions ($99 per person). Call or check Aramark's website for schedules and reservations.

Try to take at least one of the short hikes on trails at Dickey Ridge Visitor Center (Mile 4.6), Byrd Visitor Center/Big Meadows (Mile 51), and Loft Mountain (Mile 79.5). There's an excellent 1.6-mile hike at Stony Man (Mile 41.7). The following are a few of the more popular trails:

LIMBERLOST ACCESSIBLE TRAIL   At Mile 43 south of Skyland, Limberlost is accessible to visitors in wheelchairs. The 1.3-mile loop runs through an old-growth forest of ancient hemlocks. The trail has a 5-foot-wide, hard-packed surface; crosses a 65-foot bridge; and includes a 150-foot boardwalk.

WHITE OAK CANYON   Beginning at Mile 42.6 just south of Skyland, this steep gorge is the park's scenic gem. The 7.3-mile trail goes through an area of wild beauty, passing no less than six waterfalls and cascades. The upper reaches to the first falls are relatively easy, but farther down the track can be rough and rocky. Total climb is about 2,160 feet, so allow 6 hours.

DARK HOLLOW FALLS   One of the park's most popular hikes is the 1.4-mile walk to Dark Hollow Falls, the closest cascade to the Skyline Drive. The trail begins at Mile 50.7 near the Byrd Visitor Center. Allow 1¼ hours for the round-trip.

CAMP HOOVER/MILL PRONG   Starting at the Milam Gap parking area (Mile 52.8), this 4-mile round-trip hike drops down the Mill Prong to the Rapidan River, where President Herbert Hoover, an avid fisherman, had a camp during his administration (sort of the Camp David of his day). The total climb is 850 feet. Allow 4 hours.

SOUTH RIVER FALLS   Third-highest in the park, South River Falls drops a total of 83 feet in two stages. From the parking lot at South River Overlook (Mile 62.7), the trail is a moderately easy 2.6 miles round-trip, with a total climb of about 850 feet. Allow $2^1/_2$ hours.

Access points to the **Appalachian Trail** are well marked at overlooks on the Skyline Drive. Along the trail, five backcountry shelters for day use each offer a table, fireplace, pit toilet, and water. The **Potomac Appalachian Trail Club,** 118 Park St. SE, Vienna, VA 22180 (© **703/242-0315;** www.patc.net), maintains huts and fully enclosed cabins that can accommodate up to 12 people. Use of the huts is free, but they are intended for long-distance hikers only. Cabins cost $10 to $20 on weekdays, $15 to $40 on weekends. You can reserve cabins by calling PATC Monday to Thursday between 7 and 9pm, Thursday and Friday from noon to 2pm (*only* during these hours). You'll have to submit a signed form (available on PATC's website), so you'll want to start the process as early as possible. PATC's website also shows cabin availabilities.

Where to Camp & Stay
The park has four campgrounds with tent and trailer sites (but no hookups anywhere). In the middle of the park's Central District, **Big Meadows** (Mile 51.2) has the best location and sites equipped for campers with disabilities. You can reserve Big Meadows sites in advance by calling © **800/365-2267** daily between 10am and 10pm, or on the Park Service's reservation website at http://reservations.nps.gov. They cost $20 per night. Big Meadows is open from early April to the end of October. Sites at **Mathews Arm** (Mile 22.2), **Lewis Mountain** (Mile 57.5), and **Loft Mountain** (Mile 79.5) are on a first-come, first-served basis at $15 per site per night. They are open from mid-May to late October. Lewis Mountain has only 31 sites and is often full during summer and early fall. Mathews Arm and Loft Mountain have 100 and 200 sites, respectively, and usually only fill on summer and fall weekends.

On the Skyline Drive in the Central District, **Big Meadows Lodge** and **Skyland Lodge** are the only hotels in the park. Lodge reservations should be made well in advance—up to a year ahead for the peak fall season. Make them through the **National Park Reservations** (© **866/875-8456;** www.nationalparkreservations.com) or directly through **Aramark Virginia Sky-Line Co.** (© **888/896-3833;** www.visitshenandoah. com), the concessionaire that operates both.

Big Meadows Lodge (Value)   Big Meadows is what you expect a historic mountain lodge to be. Built of stone and timber, the rustic main building sports a large guest lounge with a roaring fireplace, and its window walls present a spectacular view over the Shenandoah Valley. Accommodations consist of small rustic rooms in the main lodge, cabins, and multiunit lodges with suites spread out over the premises. You'll find plain but comfortable furnishings and a private bathroom. "Deluxe" units have air-conditioning and TVs; otherwise, you won't have such modern amenities. No unit has a phone, but your cellphone should work out on the lodge terrace, and there's wireless Internet access in public areas of the main lodge. The main-lodge dining room features traditional fare. Wine, beer, and cocktails are available. Live entertainment keeps the taproom busy during the season.

P.O. Box 727, Luray, VA 22835 (on Skyline Dr. at Mile 51.2). ℂ **800/999-4714** or 540/999-2221. Fax 540/999-2011. www.visitshenandoah.com. 97 units. $72–$135 double main lodge; $87–$127 double motel; $130–$165 suite; $92–$103 cabin room. Highest rates charged weekends and in Oct. AE, DISC, MC, V. Closed Nov to early May. **Amenities:** Restaurant. *In room:* No phone.

Skyland Lodge   Naturalist George Freeman Pollock built Skyland in 1894 as a summer retreat atop the highest point on the Skyline Drive. Encompassing 52 forested acres, the resort offers rustic wood-paneled cabins as well as motel-type accommodations with wonderful views (ask for a room with a view), but no major modern amenities. The central building has a lobby with a huge stone fireplace, seating areas, and a TV. Complete breakfast, lunch, and dinner menus are offered at reasonable prices. There's a fully stocked taproom.

P.O. Box 727, Luray, VA 22835 (on Skyline Dr. at Mile 41.8). ℂ **800/999-4714** or 540/999-2211. Fax 540/999-2231. www.visitshenandoah.com. 177 units. $87–$131 double lodge; $122–$189 suite; $66–$124 double cabin room; $223–$275 family cabin. Highest rates charged weekends and Oct. Packages available. AE, DISC, MC, V. Closed Nov to early May. **Amenities:** Restaurant. *In room:* No phone.

LEXINGTON

A lively college atmosphere prevails in Lexington, which consistently ranks as one of America's best small towns. Fine old homes line tree-shaded streets, among them the house where Stonewall Jackson lived when he taught at Virginia Military Institute (VMI). A beautifully restored downtown looks much like it did in the 1800s. Besides VMI, the town is home to Washington and Lee University, which has one of the oldest and most beautiful campuses in the country.

Essentials

GETTING THERE   Lexington lies about 60 miles south and west of the southern end of the Skyline Drive. From Washington, D.C., take I-66 West, then I-81 South. From Richmond, take I-64 West.

VISITOR INFORMATION   The **Lexington & Rockbridge Area Visitor Center,** 106 E. Washington St., Lexington, VA 24450 (ℂ **877/453-9822** or 540/463-3777; fax 540/463-1105; www.lexingtonvirginia.com), is a block east of Main Street. Begin your tour of Lexington here, for it offers displays about the town's history, has an accommodations gallery for making same-day hotel reservations, and distributes free walking-tour brochures (you can park in the center's lot while touring the town). The center is open daily from 8:30am to 6pm June through August, from 9am to 5pm the rest of the year.

What to See & Do

The **Lee Chapel and Museum,** near Letcher Avenue on the Washington and Lee University campus (ℂ **540/458-8768;** http://leechapel.wlu.edu), is a magnificent Victorian-Gothic chapel of brick and native limestone, built in 1867 at the request of General Lee. Lee's remains are in a crypt below the chapel. His office was in the lower level of the building, now part of the chapel museum and preserved just as he left it on September 28, 1870. His beloved horse, Traveller, is buried in a plot outside the office. Admission is free, and it's open Monday to Saturday 9am to 5pm (closes at 4pm Nov–Mar), Sunday 1 to 5pm.

     The fine **Virginia Military Institute Museum,** in the basement of Jackson Memorial Hall, VMI Campus (ℂ **540/464-7232;** www.vmi.edu/museum), displays uniforms, weapons, and memorabilia from cadets who attended the college and fought in numerous wars. Of special note is the bullet-pierced raincoat Stonewall Jackson was wearing when accidentally shot by his own men at Chancellorsville, and also, thanks to taxidermy, Jackson's unflappable war horse, Little Sorrel. Admission is free (a $3 donation is suggested). The museum is open daily 9am to 5pm.

Also on the VMI campus is the **George C. Marshall Museum and Research Library** (© 540/463-7103; www.marshallfoundation.org), with the archives and research library of General of the Army George C. Marshall, a 1901 graduate of VMI who served as army chief of staff during World War II and as secretary of state and secretary of defense under President Truman. He is best remembered for the Marshall Plan, which fostered the economic recovery of Europe after the war. For his role in promoting peace, he became the first career soldier to be awarded the Nobel Peace Prize. In contrast to the many Civil War shrines here, this is an excellent World War II museum. Admission is $5 adults, $4 seniors. The museum is open daily 9am to 5pm.

The **Stonewall Jackson House,** 8 E. Washington St. (btw. Main and Randolph sts.; © 540/463-2552; www.stonewalljackson.org), is where the legendary Confederate general lived from early 1859 until he answered General Lee's summons to Richmond in 1861. Appropriate period furnishings duplicate the items on the inventory of Jackson's estate made shortly after he died near Chancellorsville in 1863. His body was returned to Lexington and buried in **Stonewall Jackson Memorial Cemetery** on South Main Street. Admission is $6 adults, $3 children 6 to 17. The house is open Monday to Saturday from 9am to 6pm, Sunday 1 to 6pm.

An impressive attraction nearby is the **Natural Bridge** (© 800/533-1410 or 540/291-2121; www.naturalbridgeva.com), a limestone formation that Thomas Jefferson called "the most sublime of nature's works . . . so beautiful an arch, so elevated, so light and springing, as it were, up to heaven." This geological oddity rises 215 feet above Cedar Creek; its span is 90 feet long and spreads at its widest to 150 feet. The Monocan Indian tribes worshiped it as "the bridge of God" (the **Monacan Indian Living History Village** included in your admission price is definitely worth seeing). Today it is also the bridge of man, as U.S. 11 passes over it. The Natural Bridge is now a small tourist-industry enclave, with a cavern, department-store-size souvenir shop, restaurant, hotel, campground, wax museum, and zoo. The bridge is 12 miles south of Lexington on U.S. 11 (take exit 175 off I-81). Admission to the bridge, Monacan village, and show is $12 for adults, $6 for children 5 to 12. Tickets to the wax or toy museum or caverns cost $10 for adults, $5 for children 5 to 15. Combination tickets to any two of the attractions are $18 adults, $9 children 5 to 15. Any three attractions cost $23 adults, $12 for kids 5 to 15. The bridge is open daily from 8am to dusk. The attractions are open during summer daily from 8am to sunset; the rest of the year, daily from 8am to 5pm.

Lexington's charming 19th-century downtown offers many interesting shops, most on Main and Washington streets. Among the best is **Artists in Cahoots,** a cooperative venture run by local artists and craftspeople in the Alexander-Withrow House, at the corner of Main and Washington streets (© 540/464-1147). **Virginia Born & Bred,** 16 W. Washington St. (© 540/463-1832), has made-in-Virginia gifts.

The Maury River, which runs through Lexington, provides some of Virginia's best **white-water rafting** and **kayaking,** especially through the Goshen Pass, on Va. 39 northwest of town. The visitor center has information about several put-in spots, or you can rent equipment or go on expeditions on the Maury and James rivers with **Twin River Outfitters,** 917 Rockbridge Rd. (P.O. Box 99), Glasgow, VA 24455 (© 540/258-1999; www.canoevirginia.com).

A Side Trip to Warm Springs & Hot Springs

A scenic drive 42 miles from Lexington will bring you to the towns of Warm Springs and Hot Springs, famous for their thermal springs. The most famous are the **Jefferson Pools** (© **540/839-5346**), which sit in a grove of trees at the intersection of U.S. 220 and Va. 39. Opened in 1761, they're still covered by the octagonal white clapboard bathhouses built in the 19th century, so the only luxuries you'll get are a clean towel and a rudimentary changing room. Use of the pools costs $15 an hour. Reservations aren't taken; just walk in. The pools are open from June to October, daily from 10am to 7pm. Call for winter hours.

In the tiny town of Hot Springs is the acclaimed and pricey **Homestead** (© **800/838-1766** or 540/839-1776; www.thehomestead.com; $270–$550 double per person, per night), a famous spa and golf resort that has hosted everyone from FDR to John D. Rockefeller. The Homestead's historic Dining Room is a lush palm court, in which an orchestra performs every evening during six-course dinners. The resort boasts three outstanding golf courses, indoor and outdoor pools, a spa with full health club facilities, 12 tennis courts, hiking trails, horseback and carriage rides, ice-skating on an Olympic-size rink, and much more. **Note:** Nonguests can pay to use all of the Homestead's facilities.

There are several B&B inns in the area, including **Warm Springs Inn** (© **540/839-5351**), a converted courthouse across the road from the Jefferson Pools. In Hot Springs, **Vine Cottage Inn** (© **800/410-9755** or 540/839-2422; www.vinecottageinn.com) is a block from the Homestead.

The **Garth Newel Music Center** (© **877/558-1689** or 540/839-5018; www. garthnewel.org) is on U.S. 220 between Warm Springs and Hot Springs, and their summer-long chamber music festival has been drawing critical acclaim since the early 1970s.

For more information, contact the **Bath County Chamber of Commerce** (© **800/628-8092** or 540/839-5409; www.discoverbath.com), whose visitor center is 2 miles south of Hot Springs on U.S. 220.

Two linear parks connect to offer hikers and joggers nearly 10 miles of gorgeous trail between Lexington and Buena Vista, a railroad town 7 miles to the southeast. The major link is the **Chessie Nature Trail,** which follows an old railroad bed along the Maury River between Lexington and Buena Vista. No vehicles (including bicycles) are allowed, but you can cross-country-ski the trail during winter. The Chessie trail connects with a walking path in **Woods Creek Park,** which starts at the Waddell School on Jordan Street and runs down to the banks of the Maury. Both trails are open from dawn to dusk. The visitor center has maps and brochures.

There are excellent hiking, mountain-biking, and horseback-riding trails in the **George Washington National Forest,** which encompasses much of the Blue Ridge Mountains east of Lexington. Small children might not be able to make it, but the rest of the family will enjoy the 3-mile trail up to **Crabtree Falls,** a series of cascades tumbling 1,200 feet down the mountain (the highest waterfall in Virginia). Crabtree Falls is on Va.

56 east of the Blue Ridge Parkway; from Lexington, go north on I-81 to Steeles Tavern
(exit 205), then east on Va. 56.

Where to Stay & Dine

In town and just outside are three lovely and historic country inns: **Alexander-Withrow House** and **McCampbell Inn,** both at 11 N. Main St. (rates $105–$150 double), and **Maple Hall,** which lies 6 miles north of town on U.S. 11 (rates $105–$150 double). Make reservations for all three through **Historic Country Inns** (© 877/283-9680 or 540/463-2044; www.lexingtonhistoricinns.com).

Another good lodging choice is the **Hampton Inn Col Alto,** 401 E. Nelson St. (© 800/426-7866 or 540/463-2223; www.hamptoninnlexington.com), situated in an 1827 manor house with 10 bedrooms (rates $215–$269 double) built on a plantation that was then on the outskirts of town. Motel-style rooms are in a new L-shaped wing next door (rates $134–$169 double).

Lexington has several chain motels, especially at the intersection of U.S. 11 and I-64 (exit 55), 1¹/₂ miles north of downtown. The 100-unit **Best Western Inn at Hunt Ridge,** 25 Willow Springs Rd./Va. 39 (© 800/780-7234 or 540/464-1500; www.bestwestern. com/innathuntridge), is the only full-service hotel among them, offering a restaurant, indoor-outdoor pool, and fine mountain views. Try to get one of its six rooms with balconies. Rates are $100 to $130 double.

While you're walking around town, stop in at Lexington's famous **Sweet Things,** 106 W. Washington St., between Jefferson Street and Lee Avenue (© 540/463-6055), for a cone or cup of "designer" ice cream or frozen yogurt. For more substantial fare, head to the **Southern Inn,** 37 S. Main St. (© 540/463-3612), which offers excellent sandwiches such as Dijon and tarragon chicken salad, and the regular menu features comfort food such as an excellent rendition of Mom's meatloaf, but the real stars here are specials like sea scallops sautéed with garlic and herb butter, and braised lamb shanks with herb risotto. There's an excellent wine list featuring Virginia vintages. Main courses run $13 to $30.

THE SOUTHEAST

4

ATLANTA

5 ATLANTA

More than 38 million visitors a year decide Atlanta, Georgia, is a city worth visiting, and for good reason. With its international flavor and something-for-everyone reputation, Atlanta continues to redefine the South. It is the city of Martin Luther King, Jr., father of one of the country's most important social revolutions, and of Ted Turner, who brought the world a revolution of another sort. The dramatic downtown skyline, with its gleaming skyscrapers and continual new construction, is testimony to Atlanta's inability to sit still—even for a minute.

Consistently ranked as one of the best cities in the world in which to do business, Atlanta is fifth in the nation for the number of Fortune 500 companies headquartered here—nine, including Home Depot, United Parcel Service, Coca-Cola, and Delta. The metro area is vast and sprawling. With a population that in 2008 broke five million, the only limit to its growth appears to be awful traffic congestion (really, really awful!).

But commerce and development are not the only things that characterize this bustling metropolis. You'll still hear gentle Southern accents here, though at least half of Atlanta's citizens were born outside the South, with 1 of every 10 foreign born. Those transplants, though, find themselves bending to the local customs, waving to strangers, saying "hey" and "ma'am," and holding doors open for each other. And, yes, even eating grits on occasion.

ESSENTIALS

GETTING THERE   By Plane   Hartsfield-Jackson Atlanta International Airport (www.atlanta-airport.com), 10 miles south of downtown, is the world's busiest passenger airport and transfer hub, accommodating 89.4 million passengers and nearly one million flights a year. Despite its size, Hartsfield is well planned and easy to negotiate. Adding a fifth runway, upgrading the international concourse and terminal, and consolidating rental-car terminals has gone a long way to ease congestion. Delta, which is based at Hartsfield, is the major carrier, but most other major domestic and several international airlines also serve the airport.

A taxi from the airport to downtown costs $30 for one passenger, with a $2 fee for each additional person (fee applies to all destinations). Depending on the time of day, the ride should take about half an hour. To Midtown, the fare is $32 for one passenger. To Buckhead, the fare is $40 for one passenger. As of mid-2008, a $2 fuel surcharge is added to all fares. *Warning:* Be sure the taxi driver knows how to get to where you want to go before you leave the airport.

Several of the larger hotels offer free shuttle buses from the airport. **MARTA** (Metropolitan Atlanta Rapid Transit Authority; © 404/848-4711; www.itsmarta.com) rapid-rail trains run from a station inside the airport from 5am to 1am Monday through Friday and 6am to midnight Saturday and Sunday, with a one-way fare of $1.75.

By Train   Amtrak (© 800/USA-RAIL [872-7245]; www.amtrak.com) serves **Brookwood Station,** 1688 Peachtree Rd., providing daily service from Washington (trip time: 14 hr.), New York (18 hr.), and New Orleans (11 hr.).

By Car   Major routes into Atlanta are I-75 from the northwest (Chattanooga) and south (Miami), I-85 from the northeast (Charlotte) and southwest (Montgomery, Alabama), and I-20 from the east (Columbia, South Carolina) and west (Birmingham, Alabama).

VISITOR INFORMATION   Contact the **Atlanta Convention & Visitors Bureau (ACVB),** 233 Peachtree St. NE, Ste. 100, Atlanta, GA 30303 (© **404/521-6600;** www. atlanta.net), weekdays from 8:30am to 5:30pm. Once in town, you can visit ACVB information centers at the airport; Underground Atlanta, 65 Upper Alabama St.; the Georgia World Congress Center, 285 International Blvd.; and Lenox Square Shopping Center, 3393 Peachtree Rd.

GETTING AROUND   It's possible to reach most major Atlanta sites by the transit system (MARTA), but despite the growing problem of traffic jams, a car is preferable if flexibility is an issue. The system is efficient and, in light of today's fuel prices, is moving more people than ever.

The **Metropolitan Atlanta Rapid Transit Authority (MARTA;** © **404/848-5000;** www.itsmarta.com) operates subways and buses daily from about 5am to 1am. Regular fare is $1.75. Vending machines for the MARTA Breeze Card and Breeze Ticket passes are located at all stations, and transfers are free. A convenient feature on MARTA's website is a list of popular attractions, followed by the rail stations and buses necessary to get to each spot. Go to **www.itsmarta.com,** click on "Exploring Atlanta," then click on "Popular Destinations."

Downtown Atlanta

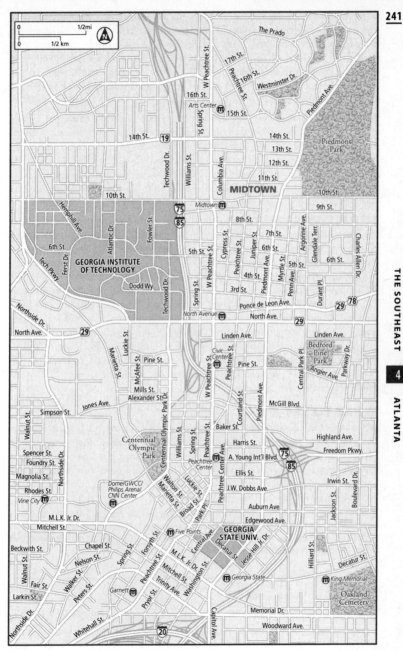

It's not possible to step outside anywhere and hail a cab. There are, however, always cabs outside the airport, major hotels, Underground Atlanta, and most MARTA stations, except those downtown. Taxis charge a flat rate based on travel between city zones. If you need to call for a taxi, try **Yellow Cab** (© 404/521-0200), **Checker Cab** (© 404/351-1111), or **Buckhead Safety Cab** (© 404/233-1152). *Warning:* Many Atlanta taxis are dirty, mechanically suspect, and operated by drivers not familiar with the city. Be sure they are familiar with your destination before setting off.

FAST FACTS   Major downtown hospitals are **Atlanta Medical Center,** 303 Parkway Dr. NE (© 404/265-4000; www.atlantamedcenter.com), and **Grady Memorial Hospital,** 80 Butler St. SE (© 404/616-1000; www.gradyhealthsystem.org). **CVS Pharmacy** has two centrally located pharmacies open 24 hours daily, at 1943 Peachtree Rd. (© 404/351-4932; www.cvs.com), across from Piedmont Hospital between downtown and Buckhead, and at 2350 Cheshire Bridge Rd. NE (© 404/486-7289), near Midtown, Buckhead, and Virginia–Highland.

SPECIAL EVENTS & FESTIVALS   The second week of January is King Week, honoring the late Rev. Martin Luther King, Jr., an Atlanta native. The week includes a variety of religious services, concerts, speeches, volunteer opportunities, and a parade. For details, contact the **King Center** (© 404/526-8900; www.thekingcenter.com).

Late January/early February brings the **Southeastern Flower Show** (© 404/351-1074; www.flowershow.org), followed in mid-April by the **Atlanta Dogwood Festival** (© 404/817-6642; www.dogwood.org). Also beginning in mid-April and running for 8 weekends is the **Georgia Renaissance Festival** (© 770/964-8575; www.garenfest.com), a re-creation of a 16th-century English country fair with a birds-of-prey show, jousting knights, jugglers, giant stilt-walkers, minstrels, and magicians. Other events include the May **Atlanta Jazz Festival** (© 404/853-4234; www.atlantafestivals.com), and in October, Stone Mountain's **Annual Scottish Festival and Highland Games** (© 770/498-5690; www.stonemountainpark.com).

WHAT TO SEE & DO

Atlanta Botanical Garden   This delightful garden, occupying 30 acres in Piedmont Park, includes a tranquil moon-gated Japanese garden, a rose garden, a fern glade, an orchid center, a camellia garden, a children's garden featuring a three-story treehouse, gurgling streams, beautiful statuary, and more. The Fuqua Conservatory houses rare and endangered tropical and desert plants—and a fascinating exhibit of carnivorous plants and poisonous dart frogs. Allow 2 to 3 hours.

1345 Piedmont Ave. NE (in Piedmont Park at Piedmont Ave. and The Prado). © **404/876-5859.** www. atlantabotanicalgarden.org. Admission $12 adults, $9 seniors and children 3–17, free for children 2 and under. Tues–Sun 9am–7pm (until 10pm Thurs and Tues–Sun until 5pm during daylight saving time); open same hours on holiday Mon. Closed Thanksgiving, Christmas, and New Year's Day.

A Note on Area Codes

In metro Atlanta, you must dial the area code (**404, 770,** or **678**) and the seven-digit telephone number, even if you are calling a number within the same area code. It is not, however, necessary to dial 1 before calling a different area code in metro Atlanta.

Atlanta History Center From the prehistory of the area that became Atlanta to the present, it's all here in vivid display in this vast museum. In addition to traveling exhibits, permanent exhibits focus on the Civil War, folk art, golf legend and Atlanta native Bobby Jones, the 1996 Atlanta Olympic Games, and the Atlanta Braves baseball team. On the grounds is recently renovated Swan House and Gardens, the finest residential design of architect Philip Trammel Schutze. This classical home—listed on the National Register of Historic Places—was constructed in 1928 by the Edward H. Inman family, heirs to a cotton fortune. Also on the grounds is a "plantation plain" home built around 1840, the Tullie Smith Farm. Here you can see how most Georgia farmers really lived. The grounds include two children's playhouses and 33 acres of gardens and nature trails. Allow 2 to 3 hours.

130 W. Paces Ferry Rd. (at Slaton Dr.). ✆ **404/814-4000.** www.atlhist.org. Admission $15 adults, $12 seniors and students 13 and up, $10 children 4–12, free for children 3 and under. Mon–Sat 10am–5:30pm; Sun noon–5:30pm. Closed Thanksgiving, Christmas Eve, Christmas, New Year's Day. MARTA: Lenox station, then bus 23 to Peachtree St. and W. Paces Ferry Rd., then a 3-block walk.

Birth Home of Martin Luther King, Jr. This Queen Anne–style house is where King was born on January 15, 1929. He was the eldest son of a Baptist minister and music teacher. The future civil rights leader lived here until he was 12. It has been restored to its appearance when young Martin lived here. A great deal of King memorabilia is displayed. *Note:* In summer, tickets often run out because of the crowds. Plan to visit the nearby Ebenezer Baptist Church and Martin Luther King, Jr., Center for Nonviolent Social Change while you're here. For all, allow 2 to 3 hours.

501 Auburn Ave. ✆ **404/331-6922.** www.nps.gov/malu. Free admission and parking (obtain tickets at 449 Auburn Ave.). Daily 9am–5pm (mid-June to mid-Aug until 6pm). Closed major holidays. MARTA: King Memorial, then bus 99 to King Memorial/North Ave.; or Five Points, then bus 1133 to Auburn Ave.

Centennial Olympic Park This is a living monument to the 1996 Olympic Summer Games. A 21-acre swath of green space and bricks, the park was carved out of a blighted downtown area. It's an oasis of rolling lawns crisscrossed by brick pathways and punctuated by artwork, rock gardens, pools, and fountains, and it often hosts festivals, artists' markets, concerts, and other performances. The best part of the park is the fountain in the shape of five interlocking Olympic Rings. If you're here in summer, you and the kids can frolic in the fountain. Allow 1 hour.

Andrew Young International Blvd. NW at Techwood Dr. ✆ **404/222-PARK** (222-7275). www.centennial park.com. Free admission. Daily 7am–11pm. MARTA: Philips Arena/Come/GWCC station, then walk 1 block (past CNN Center).

CNN Center This building anchors the city's dynamic entertainment, news, sports, and business core, and is adjacent to the Georgia Dome and the Georgia World Congress Center and near the Georgia Aquarium, Centennial Olympic Park, and the World of Coca-Cola. It houses the CNN, Headline News, and CNN International studios and offers guided, 50-minute tours of these facilities daily. *Note:* Reservations are highly recommended and should be made at least 1 day in advance. Allow 2 hours.

One CNN Center (Marietta St. at Techwood Dr.). ✆ **877/4CNN-TOUR** (426-6868). www.cnn.com/tour/ atlanta. Admission $12 adults, $11 seniors, $9 children 4–18 (children 3 and under are free but must have a ticket). Tours daily every 10 min. 9am–5pm. Closed Easter, Thanksgiving, and Christmas. MARTA: Philips Arena/Dome/GWCC station.

Cyclorama For a panorama of the Battle of Atlanta, go see the world's largest oil painting, a 42-foot-high, 356-foot-circumference 1880s painting with a three-dimensional foreground and special lighting, music, and sound effects. When you see the monumental work, you'll know why Union Gen. William Sherman, who burned Atlanta to the ground, said, "War is hell." One of only three cycloramas in the United States, it's an artistic and historical treasure that many visitors to Atlanta miss, erroneously thinking it's "strictly for kids." Allow 1 hour.

800 Cherokee Ave. in Grant Park. ⓒ **404/624-1071.** www.bcaatlanta.com. Admission $7 adults, $6 seniors, $5 children 6–12, free for children 5 and under. Tues–Sun 9am–4:30pm. Closed major holidays. Shows begin every half-hour. MARTA: Five Points, then bus 97 (Grant Park). Zoo Atlanta is next door.

Ebenezer Baptist Church   From 1960 to 1968, this Gothic Revival–style church, founded in 1886 and completed in 1922, became a center of world attention. Martin Luther King, Jr., served as co-pastor of the church. Martin Luther King, Sr., a civil rights leader before his son, was the pastor. A taped historical message and a 10-minute guided tour are available. Most church services are now conducted in a modern annex across the street. While here, visit the nearby Martin Luther King, Jr., Center for Nonviolent Social Change and the King Birth Home. Allow 2 to 3 hours total.

407 Auburn Ave. NE. ⓒ **404/688-7263.** www.nps.gov/malu. Free admission and parking (donations appreciated). Mon–Sat 9am–5pm; Sun 1–5pm; until 6pm during summer months. MARTA: King Memorial, then bus 99 to King Memorial/North Ave.; or Five Points, then bus 1133 to Auburn Ave.

Fernbank Museum of Natural History   This is the largest natural science museum in the Southeast, a $43-million complex featuring "Giants of the Mesozoic," which includes skeletons of the world's largest meat- and plant-eating dinosaurs. Permanent exhibits include a priceless collection of more than one million artifacts that retell the story of human habitation in Georgia as it unfolded on St. Catherine's Island, the best-understood aboriginal landscape in the American Southeast. In addition to other permanent and rotating exhibits, the museum has an IMAX Theater with a six-story screen and a cafe with great prices and often live piano jazz. Allow 2 hours.

767 Clifton Rd. NE (off Ponce de Leon Ave.). ⓒ **404/929-6300.** www.fernbank.edu. Admission to museum $15 adults, $14 students and seniors, $13 children 3–12, free for 2 and under. Admission to IMAX Theater $13 adults, $12 students and seniors, $11 children, free for 2 and under. Combined museum and theater admission $23 adults, $21 seniors and students, $19 children. Mon–Sat 10am–5pm; Sun noon–5pm. IMAX open Fri until 10pm. Free parking. MARTA: North Ave. station, then bus 2 for Ponce de Leon Ave., but ask the driver to drop you at the corner of Clifton Rd. Walk down Clifton; Fernbank Museum is the 1st driveway on the right.

Fox Theatre   This Moorish-Egyptian extravaganza began life as a Shriners' temple. It became a movie theater when movie mogul William Fox threw open its doors to the public. Its exotic lobby was decorated with lush carpeting; in the auditorium itself, a skyscape was transformed to sunrise, sunset, or starry night scenes as the occasion demanded, and a striped Bedouin canopy overhung the balcony. By the 1970s, the Fox was slated for demolition, but Atlantans raised $1.8 million to save their treasured movie palace. Restored to its former glory, it now thrives as a venue for live entertainment. Allow 1 hour.

660 Peachtree St. NE (at Ponce de Leon Ave.). ⓒ **404/688-3353** for tour info. www.foxtheatre.org. Tours $10 adults, $5 students and seniors. The Atlanta Preservation Center conducts walking tours of the Fox Theatre and surrounding area Mon and Wed–Thurs 10am, Sat 10 and 11am. Meet in Fox Theatre arcade for tickets and tour. Call early on day of tour, as they can be canceled based on production/performance schedules. MARTA: North Ave., then walk 2 blocks east.

Georgia Aquarium (Kids) Drawing massive crowds since it opened in 2005, the Georgia Aquarium is the world's largest, boasting 8 million gallons of fresh and marine water, and more than 100,000 animals representing 500 species from around the globe. The aquarium includes five stunning exhibits—Cold Water Quest, Georgia Explorer, Ocean Voyager, River Scout, and Tropical Diver—each featuring inhabitants of those environments. Crowds have been so big that tickets are issued based on your preferred time to enter the aquarium. The 4-D Theater features high-definition 3-D film, live action, and interactive seats. Several behind-the-scenes tours are available for an additional $35 to $50 above general admission. Advanced booking online is highly recommended. The on-site **Café Aquaria** features burgers, sandwiches, and pizza.

225 Baker St. ✆ **404/581-4000.** www.georgiaaquarium.org. Admission $26 adults, $22 seniors, $20 children ages 3–12; for 4-D Theater tickets, add about $2 each. Daily 9am–6pm; open certain dates until 8pm; spring and summer Sat 8am–8pm. MARTA: Omni/Dome/GWCC.

High Museum of Art An impressive $85-million expansion project gave this dazzling white porcelain-tiled building an equally pristine white interior that houses four floors of galleries featuring more than 10,000 pieces. Among them is a significant group of 19th- and 20th-century American paintings that feature work of the Hudson River School. There's also an extensive sub-Saharan African art collection and the Virginia Carroll Crawford Collection of American Decorative Arts, covering changing tastes from 1825 to 1917. Friday Jazz is held the third Friday of each month from 5 to 10pm. An unprecedented Louvre exhibit will run through fall 2009. Table 1280 is a delicious choice for dining. Allow 2 hours.

1280 Peachtree St. NE, at 16th St., part of the Woodruff Arts Center. ✆ **404/733-4400.** www.high.org. Admission $18 adults, $15 seniors and students, $11 children 6–17, free for children 5 and under. Tues–Sat 10am–5pm (until 8pm Thurs); Sun noon–5pm. MARTA: Arts Center.

Jimmy Carter Library and Museum Set on 35 acres of gardens, lakes, and waterfalls 2 miles east of the center of downtown Atlanta, the library-museum is part of the Carter Presidential Center. The library-museum houses Carter's Nobel Peace Prize as well as millions of documents, photographs, and videotapes from Jimmy Carter's White House years. You'll see an exact replica of the Oval Office during Carter's presidency, enhanced by a recording of Carter speaking about his experiences in that office. Allow 1 to 2 hours.

441 Freedom Pkwy. ✆ **404/865-7100.** www.jimmycarterlibrary.org. Admission $8 adults; $6 seniors, military, and students; free for children 16 and under. Mon–Sat 9am–4:45pm; Sun noon–4:45pm. Free parking. MARTA: Five Points station, then bus 16 Noble.

Margaret Mitchell House and Museum Restoration has saved the Tudor Revival apartment house (the birthplace of *Gone With the Wind*) where Margaret Mitchell, who called the place "The Dump," wrote most of her epic novel and lived from 1925 to 1932. Guided tours—60 and 90 minutes—feature a 17-minute film, a visit to the apartment, and an exhibit that celebrates Mitchell's life and examines the impact of her book and the subsequent movie. A museum shop offers all things *Gone With the Wind*. Allow 1 to 2 hours.

999 Peachtree St. (at 10th St.). ✆ **404/249-7015.** www.gwtw.org. Admission $12 adults, $9 seniors and students, $5 children 4–12, free for children 3 and under. Mon–Sat 9:30am–5pm; Sun noon–5pm. Shortened hours on minor holidays; closed major holidays. MARTA: Midtown station.

Martin Luther King, Jr., Center for Nonviolent Social Change (Best) The Nobel Prize winner's commitment to nonviolent social change lives on at this memorial and educational center. The self-guided tour includes the Freedom Hall complex and several sites nearby: Ebenezer Baptist Church, the King Birth Home, and the National Park Service Visitor's Center. The Freedom Hall portion includes memorabilia of King and the civil rights movement, including his Bible and clerical robe, a handwritten sermon, a photographic essay on his life and work, and, on a grim note, the suit he was wearing when a deranged woman stabbed him in New York City, as well as the key to his room at the Lorraine Motel in Memphis, Tennessee, where he was assassinated. In an alcove off the main exhibit area is a video display on King's life and work. There are other exhibits honoring Rosa Parks and Mahatma Gandhi. Outside in Freedom Plaza, the white marble crypts of Dr. King and wife, Coretta Scott King, rest surrounded by a five-tiered reflecting pool. An eternal flame burns in a small circular pavilion directly in front of the crypt. Allow 2 to 3 hours for all.

449 Auburn Ave. (btw. Boulevard and Jackson St.). © **404/524-1956.** www.thekingcenter.com. Free admission. Daily 9am–5pm. MARTA: King Memorial, then bus 99 to King Memorial/North Ave.; or Five Points, then bus 1133 to Auburn Ave.

Michael C. Carlos Museum of Emory University Four human mummies and a wealth of funerary art from ancient Egypt, beautiful objects from the ancient Mediterranean, stunning art from Africa, and pre-Columbian art are among this museum's rich collections. There are also special shows mounted from the museum's vast holdings, including exquisite drawings—some from the 1600s. There's nothing in Georgia to equal this collection. The 1916 Beaux Arts building housing the museum is a National Historic Landmark. Allow 1 to 2 hours.

571 S. Kilgo St. (near the intersection of Oxford and N. Decatur roads on the main quadrangle of campus). © **404/727-4282.** www.carlos.emory.edu. Admission $7. Tues–Sat 10am–5pm; Sun noon–5pm. MARTA: Candler Park or Lindbergh station, then bus 6 Emory; or Avondale or Arts Center station, then bus 36 N. Decatur.

Oakland Cemetery Margaret Mitchell, author of *Gone With the Wind,* is buried here; perhaps she's swapping stories after dark with the 50,000 Union and Confederate soldiers who share this 88-acre site. The cemetery opened 10 years before the Civil War and has become an outdoor museum of funerary architecture, including classic and Gothic Revival mausoleums. Many other notable Georgians are buried here, including golfing legend Bobby Jones, 25 Atlanta mayors, and six Georgia governors. The cemetery, covered with a canopy of old oaks, is actually a beautiful city park. People often bring picnic lunches and eat ham sandwiches among the dead or cross the street to eat at Six Feet Under. Allow 1 to 2 hours.

248 Oakland Ave. SE; main entrance at Oakland Ave. and Martin Luther King, Jr., Dr. © **404/688-2107.** www.oaklandcemetery.com. Free admission; self-guided tour maps $4. Daily dawn–dusk. Visitor center mid-Mar to Oct Mon–Fri 9am–5pm, Sat 9am–8pm, Sun 10am–8pm; Nov to mid-Mar Mon–Fri 9am–5pm, Sat–Sun 10am–4pm. Guided weekend tours Mar–Nov Sat 10am and 2pm, Sun 2pm. $10 adults; $5 seniors, students, and children. MARTA: King Memorial station, walk south on Grant St., turn left on Martin Luther King, Jr., Dr. to reach front gates.

Stone Mountain Park The world's largest granite outcropping, carved with a massive monument to the Confederacy, Stone Mountain is the focal point of a recreation area that covers 3,200 acres of lakes and beautiful wooded parkland. Over half a century in the making, Stone Mountain's neoclassical carving (90 ft. high and 190 ft. wide) depicts Confederate leaders Jefferson Davis, Robert E. Lee, and Stonewall Jackson galloping on horseback. A spectacular choreographed laser show and fireworks (nightly during the summer, Sat Apr–May, Sept–Oct) bring the mountain to life. Although the best view of the mountain is from below, the vistas from the top are spectacular. Visitors who are part mountain goat can take a walking trail up and down its moss-covered slopes, especially lovely in spring when they're blanketed in wildflowers. From the top, which you can also reach by cable car, you have an incredible view of Atlanta and the Appalachian Mountains. Other major park attractions include **Sky Hike,** a treetop family adventure course added in 2008; **Crossroads,** a re-creation of an 1870s Southern village plus a 3-D theater; the **Great Barn,** which offers four stories of children's activities such as rope nets to climb and the chance to play a character in a computer game; the **Stone Mountain Scenic Railroad,** which chugs around the 5-mile base of Stone Mountain and features a staged train robbery; the *Scarlett O'Hara,* a paddle-wheel riverboat that cruises the 363-acre Stone Mountain lake; the **Antique Car and Treasure Museum;** the **Antebellum Plantation and Farmyard;** a 36-hole golf course; miniature golf; 16 tennis courts built for the 1996 Summer Olympics; and a sandy lakefront beach with water slides, carillon concerts, boating, bicycle rental, fishing, hiking, campground, picnicking, and more. Allow at least 4 hours.

6867 Memorial Dr., Stone Mountain, 16 miles east of downtown on U.S. 78. (**©** **800/317-2006.** www.stonemountainpark.com. $25 adults, $22 seniors, $20 children 3–11, free for children 2 and under. Daily parking pass $8. Year-round gates open 6am–midnight daily, except Dec 24–25. Major attractions fall and winter 10am–5pm; spring and summer 10am–8pm. MARTA: Train to Avondale station, then bus 120 to Stone Mountain and walk about a block to the park.

The World of Coca-Cola It's a whole new World of Coca-Cola that opened in 2007 in the Pemberton Place complex that also includes the Georgia Aquarium and Centennial Olympic Park. Highlighting the history of what's been called "the world's most popular product," the facility includes Bottle Works, a real bottling line; the Secret Formula 4-D Theater; a Pop Culture Gallery celebrating Coke as an icon of popular culture; and everyone's favorite, Taste It!, stations of drink fountains featuring more than 70 different flavors or Coke products from around the world (nothing like getting the kids wired on caffeine and corn syrup). Exhibits, some new and some moved over from the old location, include tons of Coke memorabilia and a 1930s soda fountain, complete with a soda jerk. Allow 1 to 2 hours.

121 Baker St. NW. (**©** **770/578-4325,** ext. 1465. www.worldofcoca-cola.com. Admission $15 adults, $13 seniors, $9 children 3–12, free for children 2 and under. Mon–Sat 9am–5pm, Sun 10am–6pm; June–Aug Mon–Sat until 6pm. Closed major holidays. Parking in adjoining deck $10. MARTA: Peachtree Center or Dome/GWCC/Philips Arena/CNN Center.

SHOPPING

The stamping ground of well-to-do Atlanta, **Buckhead** is the ultimate shopping area, with two major malls and lots of little boutiques, antiques shops, and galleries. Start at the corner of Peachtree and Lenox roads, where two major malls—**Phipps Plaza** (www.phippsplaza.com) and **Lenox Square** (www.lenox-square.com)—face off against each other. If you have more time and are interested in art, antiques, or decorative accessories, head straight to nearby **Bennett Street** (www.buckhead.org/bennettstreet), where you'll find a healthy concentration of stores in a 2-block strip. There are also many shops in the **Buckhead West Village** (www.buckhead.org/westvillage), near the intersection of Peachtree and West Paces Ferry roads, but there are many more establishments up and down Peachtree and scattered along smaller side streets.

Atlantic Station (www.atlanticstation.com) is a mixed-use development, much of which includes shopping for everything from books and boots to furniture and furs. Covering 138 acres, the number of shops is vast and includes the Southeast's very first IKEA, a shopping experience in itself and the first of its kind to serve sweet tea and grits in its cafeteria-style restaurant (try the Swedish meatballs—delish *and* cheap). Additional options include all the popular retail names you'd expect, from Ann Taylor to American Eagle Outfitters, and hundreds in between.

The charming area of **Virginia–Highland,** centered on North Highland Avenue between University Drive and Ponce de Leon Avenue, boasts antiques shops, trendy boutiques, and art galleries. There are three major concentrations: on North Highland just south of University Drive, at the intersection of North Highland and Virginia avenues, and just north of Ponce de Leon around St. Charles Place. From one end to the other, it's about 1¹/₂ miles, but it's a nice walk and there are cafes where you can stop and take a break. For more info, check out **www.virginiahighland.com**.

An area similar to Virginia–Highland, but a lot funkier and much rougher around the edges, **Little Five Points** (www.l5p.com) is as much a happening as an offbeat shopping area. There are still authentic hippies here and enough young people with wildly colored hair and pierced body parts to give you a '60s flashback. A community-owned natural food store, Sevananda, is an interesting browse even if you aren't in the market for fresh organic wheat grass.

WHERE TO STAY

Many of the hotels are quite full during the business week, but they're usually not sold out on the weekend. Most of the major hotels that cater to business travelers, especially those downtown, offer reduced weekend rates. In addition to the 7% city sales tax, there is a 7% hotel and motel tax.

Bed & Breakfast Atlanta (☎ **800/967-3224** or 404/875-0525; www.bedandbreakfast atlanta.com) can book you into more than 30 carefully screened homes and inns. If you want to book your own B&B, be sure to ask if they are licensed and for how many rooms. There are only two licensed B&Bs currently operating in Fulton County (Atlanta proper)—Shellmont Inn and Beverly Hills Inn. And while they both market themselves as B&Bs, all others are technically "home stays" and may end up being less than acceptable for some travelers.

Four Seasons Hotel (Best)   Soaring 19 floors above midtown, the Four Seasons has the most attentive and sophisticated staff and the most dramatic lobby of any hotel in Georgia. Accommodations are as plush as you'd expect from this top-notch chain, each with comfortable chaise longues, deep mattresses, and bathrobes. Gourmet dining at the hotel's **Park 75** restaurant is hard to beat, and a full-service spa opened in 2008.

75 14th St. (btw. Peachtree and W. Peachtree sts.), Atlanta, GA 30309. ☎ **800/332-3442** or 404/881-9898. Fax 404/873-4692. www.fourseasons.com/atlanta. 244 units. From $410 double; from $750 suite. Children stay free in parent's room. Weekend packages and other special offers often available. AE, DC, DISC, MC, V. Valet parking $28. MARTA: Arts Center. Pets up to 25 lb. accepted at no charge. **Amenities:** Restaurant; indoor pool; health club.

Gaslight Inn   This 1913 Craftsman-style house is one of the most appealing B&Bs in Virginia–Highland—not to mention one of the most guest friendly in the city. The accommodations, especially the suites, are exquisitely decorated; some have four-poster

beds, while others have whirlpool tubs. Three units have full kitchens; the rest have access
to microwaves and refrigerators. The breakfast—named one of the best in the Southeast—is served in the formal dining room or outside on the front porch.

1001 St. Charles Ave. (btw. Frederica St. and N. Highland Ave.), Atlanta, GA 30306. © **404/875-1001.** Fax 404/876-1001. www.gaslightinn.com. 8 units. $115–$215 double. Rates include breakfast. AE, DC, DISC, MC, V. Free parking. MARTA: North Ave. station, then bus 2 Ponce to Frederica St.

Holiday Inn Express and Suites (Kids)   This is a good choice if you're looking for a great Buckhead location at less than the usual Buckhead price. It's within walking distance of several fine restaurants (Pricci is across the street and the Atlanta Fish Market a few blocks away) and close to Buckhead nightlife. There's good shopping in the area, and a park nearby. Accommodations include spacious one- or two-bedroom suites with queen-size beds, a separate living room, and a full kitchen. The complimentary full breakfast is served buffet-style in a bright room next to the lobby.

505 Pharr Rd. (about a block off Piedmont Rd.), Atlanta, GA 30305. © **888/465-4329** or 404/262-7880. Fax 404/262-3734. www.hiexpress.com. 88 units. $129 1-bedroom suite; $153 2-bedroom suite. Rates include full hot breakfast. AE, DISC, MC, V. Free parking. MARTA: Bus 5 from Lindbergh Station stops at the corner of Pharr and Piedmont roads, about a block away. **Amenities:** Outdoor pool; exercise room.

Hotel Indigo (Value)   This fun and funky boutique hotel has a welcoming foyer, hardwood floors, and beds with oversize pillows in funky color combinations. Also oversize are the Adirondack lobby chairs, sporting more funky pillows. The spa-style showers are the perfect treat after a long day of sightseeing, but the bathrooms are teeny tiny and only two rooms have bathtubs. This is the most pet-friendly place in town—no weight limit and no fee. The hotel is right across the street from the Fox Theatre, so you can just roll into bed after attending a performance.

683 Peachtree St. (btw. Third St. and Ponce de Leon Ave.), Atlanta, GA 30308. © **404/874-9200.** Fax 404/873-4245. www.hotelindigo.com. 139 units. $144–$204 double. Rates may be higher during conventions and special events. AE, DC, DISC, MC, V. Self-parking $18. MARTA: North Ave. **Amenities:** Fitness center.

Ritz-Carlton Atlanta   Downtown Atlanta's finest hotel is a bastion of luxury filled with antiques and fine art. The rooms are restful refuges decorated in traditional style, with bay windows, CD players, bathrobes, and fresh flowers. Bathrooms are large and luxurious. And the service is impeccable—you'll be cosseted as never before.

181 Peachtree St. NE (at Ellis St.), Atlanta, GA 30303. © **800/241-3333** or 404/659-0400. Fax 404/688-0400. www.ritzcarlton.com/hotels/atlanta_downtown. 444 units. From $249 double; $319 club level; $399–$1,200 suite. Rates include up to 4 people. Weekend packages available. AE, DC, DISC, MC, V. Valet parking $27. MARTA: Peachtree Center. **Amenities:** Restaurant; health club.

Ritz-Carlton Buckhead   A 22-story tower soaring above Buckhead, the elegant Ritz-Carlton has been likened to Claridges in London. Located between Lenox Square and Phipps Plaza, it's a convenient way station for "shop-'til-you-drop" guests, with a lavish afternoon tea to revive your flagging energy. The guest rooms are large, yet manage to feel cozy; amenities include bathrobes and CD players in some rooms.

3434 Peachtree Rd. NE (at Lenox Rd.), Atlanta, GA 30326. © **800/241-3333** or 404/237-2700. Fax 404/233-5168. www.ritzcarlton.com/hotels/atlanta_buckhead. 553 units. From $299 double; $439 club level; $419–$1,500 suite. Rates include up to 4 people. Weekend packages available. AE, DC, DISC, MC, V. Valet parking $30; self-parking $15. MARTA: Buckhead or Lenox stations, then a short walk. **Amenities:** 2 restaurants; indoor pool; health club.

Shellmont Inn   This charming two-story Victorian mansion dates to 1891, is on the National Register of Historic Places, and is a city landmark. Innkeepers Ed and Debbie McCord have done a superb job of restoring the place. Four rooms are available on the second floor, with a carriage house out back featuring a luxurious master bedroom, modern bathroom with whirlpool tub and steam shower, a fully equipped kitchen, and a living area with a second bed. Don't miss the gorgeous five-paneled stained-glass window on the landing, believed to be Tiffany.

Breakfast consists of fresh-squeezed juice, fresh and dried fruits, an entree (perhaps Belgian waffles or a frittata), cereals and granolas, and tea or coffee.

821 Piedmont Ave. NE (at Sixth St.), Atlanta, GA 30308. ✆ **404/872-9290.** Fax 404/872-5379. www.shellmont.com. 4 units, plus carriage house. $185–$225 standard double; $235–$275 whirlpool suite; $295–$350 carriage house double. Children 12 and under allowed in carriage house only. Rates include full breakfast. AE, DC, MC, V. Free parking. MARTA: Midtown.

Westin Peachtree Plaza   Atlanta's most famous contemporary hotel is also the tallest, with 73 soaring floors. A bank of 18 elevators will carry you to the roof with its revolving Sun Dial restaurant, a grand spectacle for a special evening on the town. The hotel is in tiptop shape, restored following extensive damage from a tornado that ripped through downtown in 2008. The elegant guest rooms are comfortably large, with all the expected luxuries, including Westin's Heavenly Bed, bathrobes, and roomy marble bathrooms. Ask for a room on a higher floor for a more panoramic view.

210 Peachtree St. NW (at International Blvd.), Atlanta, GA 30303. ✆ **800/228-3000** or 404/659-1400. Fax 404/589-7591. www.westin.com. 1,116 units. From $218 double; from $325 suite. AE, DISC, MC, V. Valet parking $23; self-parking $19. **Amenities:** 2 restaurants; indoor pool; fitness center.

WHERE TO DINE

Atlanta Fish Market ⓑest   SEAFOOD   This place serves up a great mix of whimsy (there's a three-story copper fish outside the entrance) and good food. The main dining area has been compared to an old train station; the Geechee Crab Lounge manages to be both upscale and comfortable. The seared sea scallops, with crab cake ravioli, asparagus, spinach, and more, are highly recommended. The extensive menu changes daily, and you can buy fresh seafood from their market to take home.

265 Pharr Rd. (btw. Peachtree and Piedmont roads). ✆ **404/262-3165.** www.buckheadrestaurants.com. Reservations recommended. Main courses $11–$26 lunch (served until 3pm), $20–$39 dinner. AE, DC, DISC, MC, V. Mon–Thurs 11:30am–11pm; Fri–Sat 11:30am–midnight; Sun 11:30am–10pm. MARTA: Buckhead.

Bacchanalia   INTERNATIONAL   Posh and upscale, this establishment combines a stylish and popular restaurant with a boutique-style gourmet food shop. The setting is in a former 1920s meatpacking plant, on an unlikely looking, drab commercial stretch at the edge of midtown. Menus change seasonally, but the unusual fruit-and-cheese pairings are hard to resist any time of the year. Wines are offered by the half-bottle.

1198 Howell Mill Rd. ✆ **404/365-0410,** ext. 22. www.starprovisions.com. Reservations recommended. Fixed-price dinner $75. AE, DISC, MC, V. Mon–Sat dinner starts at 6pm. MARTA: Tenth St.

Bone's   STEAK/SEAFOOD   In an atmosphere one food critic called "boardroom frat house," this is just the place to get that juicy rib-eye steak weighing in at 22 ounces. Fresh Maine lobster is flown in daily, and the corn-fed beef is cut into steaks on the premises.

Locals favor cheese grits fritters (yes, fritters made out of grits). A cigar humidor can be brought to your table at your request after dinner.

3130 Piedmont Rd. NE (a half-block past Peachtree Rd.). © **404/237-2663.** www.bonesrestaurant.com. Reservations required. Main courses $12–$40 lunch, $25–$40 dinner; all sides a la carte. AE, DISC, MC, V. Mon–Fri 11:30am–2:30pm; Sun–Fri 5:30–10pm; Sat 5:30–11pm. MARTA: Buckhead.

Buckhead Diner AMERICAN   Even though it sounds like a hash house for truckers, this award-winner is decidedly upscale. A highly theatrical venture, the interior is designed to look like the interior of the Orient Express's rail cars, and it has a gleaming stainless-steel exterior adorned with neon. Inside, the fare is contemporary: veal and wild mushroom meatloaf, for example, or Granny Smith apple pie with a candied pecan crust. Be sure to leave room for the white chocolate banana-cream pie.

3073 Piedmont Rd. (at E. Paces Ferry Rd.). © **404/262-3336.** www.buckheadrestaurants.com. Reservations not accepted, but you can call just before you go for "priority seating." Main courses $10–$20 lunch, $18–$24 dinner. AE, DC, DISC, MC, V. Mon–Sat 11am–midnight; Sun 10am–10pm. MARTA: Buckhead.

City Grill AMERICAN   One of Atlanta's most opulent restaurants, City Grill is a mecca for power-lunchers and couples seeking a special night out. The setting is the 1912 Hurt Building (originally a Federal Reserve Bank), with its rotunda lined in marble with a gold-leaf dome. The frequently changing menu incorporates many Southern standards such as chicken with oyster dressing, pork loin chop, or quail. A South Georgia dairy farm provides the choices for the nighttime cheese plates. The selection of French and California wines is about as good as Atlanta gets.

50 Hurt Plaza (at Edgewood Ave.). © **404/524-2489.** www.greathospitalityrestaurants.com. Reservations strongly recommended. Main courses $10–$19 lunch, $18–$42 dinner. AE, DC, DISC, MC, V. Mon–Fri 11:30am–2pm; Mon–Sat 5–10pm. MARTA: Peachtree Center.

The Colonnade SOUTHERN   An Atlanta favorite since 1927, this friendly joint offers great value, stiff drinks, and an authentic Southern-style meat-and-three. Inexpensively priced steaks, chops, seafood, and the inevitable Southern fried chicken round out the menu. Don't miss the yeast rolls. Now serving lunch on weekends only.

1879 Cheshire Bridge Rd. NE, btw. Wellborne Dr. and Manchester St. © **404/874-5642.** Reservations not accepted. Main courses $8–$10 lunch, slightly higher at dinner. No credit cards, but out-of-town personal checks accepted. Mon–Thurs 5–9pm; Fri 5–10pm; Sat noon–10pm; Sun 11:30am–9pm.

Floataway Café COUNTRY FRENCH/ITALIAN   Mediterranean-inspired and innovative, this airy restaurant's menu features top-quality ingredients. Hand-cut pastas are wonderful; locals rave about the hanger steak with pommes frites, and a salad of beets and avocados with a citrus dressing. You really can't get here using MARTA; if your cab pulls up to an old warehouse, don't worry—you're in the right place. Get out and follow the crowd. If the inside is too noisy, move to one of the outdoor tables.

1123 Zonolite Rd. NE (btw. Briarcliff and Lenox roads, near Emory University). © **404/892-1414.** www. starprovisions.com. Reservations recommended. Main courses $15–$30, extra for sides. AE, MC, V. Tues–Sat from 6pm.

Horseradish Grill SOUTHERN   This restaurant began life as a country store, then a horse barn, and retains much of that simple style. Eat in the romantic main dining room or on the patio outside. Organic vegetables and wildflowers are grown in a backyard garden, and everything is made from scratch, including the ice cream. The menu is upscale Southern, simply prepared. Start with the corn-bread-crusted Georgia mountain trout or jumbo shrimp and grits, and end with the Kentucky oatmeal spice cake topped with caramel ice cream.

4320 Powers Ferry Rd. (at W. Wieuca Rd.). (C) **404/255-7277.** www.horseradishgrill.com. Reservations recommended. Main courses $9–$14 lunch, $22–$25 dinner. AE, DC, DISC, MC, V. Mon–Fri 11:30am–2:30pm; Sat 11am–2:30pm; Mon–Thurs 5:30–9pm; Fri–Sat 5–10pm; Sun 5–9pm; Sun brunch 11am–2:30pm. MARTA: Buckhead.

Sotto Sotto TUSCAN   The best and most appealing restaurant in Inman Park occupies a former row of brick-fronted stores built around 1900. We recommend the wood-roasted whole fish or the seafood risotto. A favorite pasta is *tortelli di Michelangelo*, stuffed with minced veal, pork, and chicken, served with brown butter and sage sauce. Portions are generous and the service is friendly. Chocolate lovers *must* save room for the chocolate soup. If the wait is too long (and it can be 45 min., even with a reservation), get a Neapolitan pizza at next-door sister restaurant Fritti Fritti. *Note:* Sotto Sotto's name may mean "hush hush" in Italian, but the noise level here can be intense. If you're looking for an intimate, romantic meal, head elsewhere.

313 N. Highland Ave. (C) **404/523-6678.** www.sottosottorestaurant.com. Reservations recommended. Main courses $16–$34. AE, DC, MC, V. Mon–Thurs 5:30–11pm; Fri–Sat 5:30pm–midnight; Sun 5:30–10pm.

The Varsity AMERICAN   Some 16,000 people dine daily at this Atlanta institution, 30,000 if there's a home football game at nearby Georgia Tech. This is the world's largest drive-in, opened in 1928. Service is fast both car-side and inside, with seats and stand-up eating counters; the food is good and prices are definitely low. Ordering can be an adventure; counter workers greet you with a rapid-fire, "Whaddya have? Whaddya have?" Hot dogs are called "dawgs," and hamburgers are "steaks." *Tip:* If you want a cheeseburger, be sure to order it topped with pimento cheese. True, it's a mess, but you've never had anything like it.

For visitors staying closer to Buckhead or Virginia–Highland, there's a **Varsity Jr.** at 185 Lindbergh Dr. ((C) **404/261-8843**).

61 North Ave. (at Spring St.). (C) **404/881-1706.** www.thevarsity.com. All burgers and sandwiches under $5. No credit cards. Sun–Thurs 10am–11:30pm; Fri–Sat 10am–12:30am. MARTA: North Ave.

ATLANTA AFTER DARK

The biggest concentration of clubs and bars is in **Buckhead** (near the intersection of Peachtree and E. Paces Ferry roads); in **Virginia–Highland** (at the intersection of Virginia and N. Highland aves., on **North Highland** just north of Ponce de Leon Ave.); in **Little Five Points** (near the intersection of Moreland and Euclid aves.); and downtown near Peachtree Center. The Buckhead scene, for the most part, is like a huge frat party, especially on weekends. (*Warning:* Serious crime has risen here in recent years as the club scene grows.) Virginia–Highland is full of yuppie 20- and 30-somethings. Little Five Points is a mix of wildly, weirdly dressed folks and neighborhood regulars. Downtown has a large proportion of out-of-town visitors and conventiongoers.

To find out what's going on, consult the *Atlanta Journal-Constitution*'s Thursday "Big 'A' List" pullout section. Or pick up a free copy of *Creative Loafing*, available all over town.

THE PERFORMING ARTS   See "What to See & Do," earlier in this section, for details on the Fox Theatre, which hosts all kinds of performances.

The oldest continuously operating ballet company in the United States, the **Atlanta Ballet,** performs at the Cobb Energy Performing Arts Centre (© **404/892-3303;** www. atlantaballet.com).

The **Atlanta Symphony Orchestra,** Woodruff Arts, 1280 Peachtree St. NE, at 15th Street (© **404/733-5000;** www.atlantasymphony.org), is complemented by the 200-voice Atlanta Symphony Orchestra Chorus, enabling performances of large-scale symphonic/choral works. The season runs from September to May, plus summer concerts in Chastain Park Amphitheatre in Buckhead.

The **Alliance Theatre Company,** Woodruff Arts (© **404/733-5000;** www.alliance theatre.org), is the largest regional theater in the Southeast, but there are many other excellent companies, with performances ranging from experimental to classic. Watch each summer for performances by the **Georgia Shakespeare Festival** (© **404/264-0020;** www.gashakespeare.org), held at Oglethorpe University, 4484 Peachtree Rd. NE.

THE CLUB & MUSIC SCENE Atlanta's club scene is ephemeral; there's a good chance that the packed venue you visited on your last visit has since closed and reopened as something entirely different. Still, there are a few old reliables.

In Buckhead, **Johnny's Hideaway,** 3771 Roswell Rd., 2 blocks north of Piedmont Road (© **404/233-8026;** www.johnnyshideaway.com), has been one of Atlanta's top nightspots for more than 2 decades. The music sweeps through the decades, from the big-band era to the '80s, attracting a crowd of all ages. Original owner Johnny Esposito, who retired in 1999 and then unretired due to boredom, opened **Johnny's Side Door,** compared to a 1940s martini bar and part of the Landmark Diner, 3652 Roswell Rd., in Buckhead (© **404/844-0408**). An elegant cocktail lounge/dance club in its new location since 2008, **Tongue & Groove,** 2420 Piedmont Rd. (© **404/261-2325;** www.tongue andgrooveonline.com), attracts a chic crowd (there's a dress code). The DJ spins dance music with a different theme every night.

On the east side, closer to Emory, **Eddie's Attic,** 515-B N. McDonough St., Decatur (© **404/377-4976;** www.eddiesattic.com), is Atlanta's most popular venue for acoustic singer/songwriters. The Indigo Girls, Billy Pilgrim, and Shawn Mullins started their careers here.

In Virginia–Highland, the **Dark Horse Tavern,** 816 N. Highland Ave. (© **404/873-3607;** www.darkhorseatlanta.com), is known as the place for young professionals to meet. Those more interested in local bands than romance can visit 10 High Club in the Dark Horse basement.

East Atlanta Village, a newer, rougher version of Little Five Points but farther east at the intersection of Flat Shoals and Glenwood avenues, is home to several clubs featuring independent and underground acts. The **Earl,** 488 Flat Shoals Ave. SE (© **404/522-3950;** www.badearl.com), and **Eastside Lounge,** 485 Flat Shoals Ave. (© **404/521-9666;** www.eastsidelounge.net), are among the better known.

THE BAR & CAFE SCENE Atlanta's quintessential sports bar is **Jocks & Jills,** 5600 Roswell Rd. (© **770/209-0920;** www.jocks-frankies.com), whose more than 70 TVs will ensure you don't miss a minute of the big game. **Fadó,** 279 Buckhead Ave. (© **404/841-0066;** www.fadoirishpub.com), is divided into five pub areas: a cottage pub with a peat-burning fireplace, a Victorian pub with dark wood and stained glass, and so on. There's often traditional Irish or Celtic music. It's a good place to watch televised soccer.

Not far from Virginia–Highland and Little Five Points is **Manuel's Tavern,** 602 N. Highland Ave. NE, at North Avenue (© **404/525-3447;** www.manuelstavern.com), a regular watering hole for journalists, politicos, cops, students, and writers. Jimmy Carter often drops by with the Secret Service when he's in town. It's lots of fun to watch a Braves game on TV here.

A classic San Francisco–style coffeehouse, the **RedLight Cafe,** 553 W. Amsterdam Ave., between Monroe Drive and Piedmont Park (© **404/874-7828;** www.redlightcafe. com), is also a cybercafe, with tables and comfy sofas, offering a mix of art, music, conversation, and beverages.

6 SAVANNAH

Savannah's free spirit and hint of decadence give it more kinship with Key West or New Orleans than with the Bible Belt down-home interior of Georgia. Savannah—pronounce it with a drawl—conjures up all the clichéd images of the deep South: live oaks dripping with Spanish moss, antebellum mansions, and mint juleps sipped on the veranda. Old Savannah is beautifully restored and is the largest urban National Historic Landmark District in the country. *Forrest Gump* first put Savannah on the tourist map, but nothing changed the face of Savannah more than the 1994 publication of John Berendt's *Midnight in the Garden of Good and Evil.* It long ago disappeared from the bestseller lists but is still credited with launching mass tourism to this antebellum city.

ESSENTIALS

GETTING THERE **By Plane** **Savannah/Hilton Head International Airport** (© 912/964-0514; www.savannahairport.com) is about 8 miles west of downtown just off I-16. It's served by American, Delta, United, and US Airways, and all major car-rental agencies have desks here. Pre-arranged limousine service to downtown locations (© 800/845-5582) costs about $25. Taxi fare is about $25 for one person and $10 for each extra passenger.

By Train **Amtrak** (© 800/USA-RAIL [872-7245]; www.amtrak.com) provides service from Charleston (trip time: 1³/₄ hr.); Washington, D.C. (11 hr.); Jacksonville (2¹/₄ hr.); and Miami (12 hr.) to its station at 2611 Seaboard Coastline Dr., some 4 miles southwest of downtown. Cab fare into the city is around $8.

By Car Major routes into Savannah are **I-95** from the north (Richmond, Virginia) and south (Jacksonville), and **I-16** from the west (Atlanta).

VISITOR INFORMATION The **Savannah Information Visitor Center,** 301 Martin Luther King, Jr., Blvd., Savannah, GA 31401 (© 912/944-0455; www.savannah-visit. com), is open Monday through Friday from 8:30am to 5pm and Saturday and Sunday from 9am to 5pm. It offers organized tours and self-guided walking, driving, or bike tours with excellent maps.

GETTING AROUND The grid-shaped Historic District is best seen on foot; the real point of your visit is to take leisurely strolls with frequent stops in the many squares.

You can reach many points of interest outside the Historic District by bus, but your own wheels will be much more convenient, and they're absolutely essential for sightseeing outside the city proper.

The base rate for taxis is $2, with a $1.80 additional charge for each mile. For 24-hour taxi service, call **Yellow Cab Co.** at © 912/236-1133.

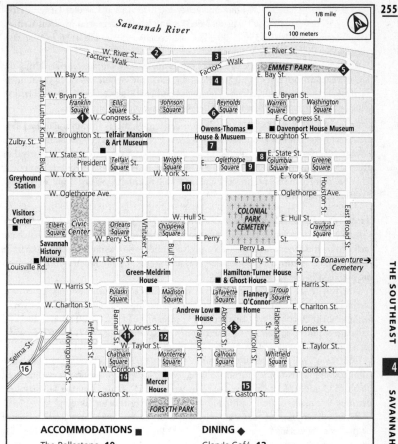

Savannah River

W. River St.
Factors' Walk **2**
E. River St.
Factors' Walk

3

W. Bay St.
E. Bay St.
EMMET PARK **5**

4

W. Bryan St.
E. Bryan St.

Franklin Square
Ellis Square
Johnson Square
Reynolds Square
Warren Square
Washington Square

1
W. Congress St.
E. Congress St.

6

W. Broughton St.
Telfair Mansion & Art Museum
Owens-Thomas House & Museum
Davenport House Museum
E. Broughton St.

Zulby St.

W. State St.
7
E. State St.

President
Telfair Square
St.
Wright Square
Oglethorpe Square
8
Columbia Square
Greene Square

9

W. York St.
W. York St.
E. York St.

10

Greyhound Station

W. Oglethorpe Ave.
E. Oglethorpe Ave.

Houston St.
East Broad St.

Visitors Center

W. Hull St.
COLONIAL PARK CEMETERY
E. Hull St.

Elbert Square
Civic Center
Orleans Square
Chippewa Square
Crawford Square

W. Perry St.
E. Perry
St.

Savannah History Museum
W. Liberty St.
Perry La.
E. Liberty St.

Whitaker St.
Bull St.
Price St.

Louisville Rd.

To Bonaventure Cemetery

Green-Meldrim House
Hamilton-Turner House & Ghost House

W. Harris St.
E. Harris St.

Pulaski Square
Madison Square
Lafayette Square
Flannery O'Connor Home
Troup Square

W. Charlton St.
E. Charlton St.

Jefferson St.
Barnard St.
Montgomery St.
Drayton St.
Abercorn St.
Lincoln St.
Habersham St.

Andrew Low House

W. Jones St.
11
12
13
E. Jones St.

16
Selma St.
W. Taylor St.
E. Taylor St.

Chatham Square
Monterrey Square
Calhoun Square
Whitfield Square

W. Gordon St.
E. Gordon St.

14

Mercer House

W. Gaston St.
15
E. Gaston St.

FORSYTH PARK

0   1/8 mile
0   100 meters

ACCOMMODATIONS ■

The Ballastone **10**

Bed and Breakfast Inn **14**

Eliza Thompson House **12**

The Gastonian **15**

Hampton Inn **4**

The Kehoe House **8**

The Marshall House **7**

River Street Inn **3**

17 Hundred 90 **9**

DINING ◆

Clary's Café **13**

45 South at the Pirate's House **5**

Huey's **2**

The Lady and Sons **1**

Mrs. Wilkes' Dining Room **11**

The Olde Pink House Restaurant **6**

Atlanta

Savannah

GEORGIA

There are 24-hour emergency-room services at **Candler General Hospital,** 5353 Reynolds St. (② **912/692-6637**), and at the **Memorial Medical Center,** 4700 Waters Ave. (② **912/350-8390**). The sales tax rate in Savannah is 6%; lodging sales taxes add an additional 6% to your bill.

Although it's reasonably safe to explore the Historic and Victorian districts during the day, the situation changes at night. The clubs, bars, and restaurants along the touristy riverfront seem reasonably safe, but muggings and robberies are frequently reported in some of the rougher neighborhoods. The usual discretion is always advised.

SPECIAL EVENTS & FESTIVALS   In mid-September, there's the **Savannah Jazz Festival,** featuring national and local jazz and blues legends. Contact Host South at **www. savannahjazzfestival.org** for details. December is especially festive, with the **Festival of Trees** at the Marriott Riverfront Hotel; **Christmas 1864,** a dramatic re-creation of the Civil War evacuation of Fort Jackson; and the **Annual Holiday Tour of Homes** (② **912/236-8362**).

SEEING THE SIGHTS

Virtually every tour group in town offers tours of the *Midnight* sites, many of which are included on their regular agenda. Reactions from readers vary, some complaining that the Berendt book "is a tired cliché," others proclaiming that touring the *Midnight* sites "was the highlight of my visit to Savannah."

One way to see Savannah is by horse-drawn carriage. An authentic antique carriage carries you over cobblestone streets as the coachman spins a tale of the town's history. The 1-hour tour ($20 adults, $10 children 5–11) covers 15 of the city's 20 squares. Reservations are required, so contact **Carriage Tours of Savannah** (② **912/236-6756;** www. carriagetoursofsavannah.com).

Old Town Trolley Tours (② **800/868-7482** or 912/233-0083; www.oldtowntrolley. com) operates tours of the Historic District, with pickups at most downtown inns and hotels ($23 adults, $10 children 4–12), as well as a 1¹/₂-hour **Haunted History** tour detailing Savannah's ghostly past (and present). Call to reserve for all tours.

Savannah Riverboat Cruises are offered aboard the *Savannah River Queen,* operated by the River Street Riverboat Co., 9 E. River St. (② **800/786-6404** or 912/232-6404; www.savannah-riverboat.com). The fare for adults is $18, children $11. More expensive dinner cruises are available, too, going for anywhere from $33 to $45, or else $19 to $28 for ages 12 and under.

Andrew Low House   After her marriage, Juliette Low lived in this 1848 house, and it was here that she founded the Girl Scouts. She died here in 1927. The classic mid-19th-century house facing Lafayette Square is of stucco over brick with elaborate iron-work, shuttered piazzas, carved woodwork, and crystal chandeliers. William Makepeace Thackeray visited here twice, and Robert E. Lee was entertained at a gala reception in the double parlors in 1870. Guided tours are offered every half-hour.

329 Abercorn St. ② **912/233-6854.** www.andrewlowhouse.com. Admission $8 adults; $4.50 students, children 12 and under, and Girl Scouts; free for children 5 and under. Mon–Wed and Fri 10am–4:30pm; Sat–Sun noon–4:30pm.

Davenport House Museum   This is where seven determined women started the Savannah restoration movement in 1954. They raised $22,500 and purchased the house, saving it from demolition. Built between 1815 and 1820 by master builder Isaiah

Davenport, this is one of the great Federal-style houses in the United States, with delicate ironwork and an elliptical stairway. Give yourself about an hour to explore.

324 E. State St. ✆ **912/236-8097.** www.davenporthousemuseum.org. Admission $8 adults, $5 children 6–17, free for children 5 and under. Mon–Sat 10am–4pm; Sun 1–4pm.

Fort Jackson   Georgia's oldest standing fort, with a 9-foot-deep tidal moat around its brick walls, was begun in 1808 and staffed during the War of 1812. It was enlarged and strengthened between 1845 and 1860, and saw its greatest use as headquarters for the Confederate river defenses during the Civil War. Its arched rooms, designed to support the weight of cannons mounted above, hold 13 exhibit areas. Allow 1 hour.

1 Fort Jackson Rd. (about 2¹⁄₂ miles east of Savannah via the Islands Expwy.). ✆ **912/232-3945.** www. chsgeorgia.org/jackson. Admission $4.25 adults, $3.75 seniors and children 7–18, free for children 6 and under. Daily 9am–5pm.

Fort McAllister   On the banks of the Great Ogeechee River stood this Confederate earthwork fortification. Constructed from 1861 to 1862, it withstood nearly 2 years of bombardment before it finally fell on December 13, 1864, in a bayonet charge that ended General Sherman's "March to the Sea." There's a visitor center with historical exhibits and also walking trails and campsites. A visit takes 45 minutes.

Richmond Hill, 10 miles southwest on U.S. 17. ✆ **912/727-2339.** www.gastateparks.org. Admission $4 adults, $2.50 children. Daily 8am–5pm.

Fort Pulaski   It cost $1 million and took 25 tons of brick and 18 years of toil to finish this fortress at the mouth of the Savannah River. Yet this National Monument was captured in just 30 hours by Union forces. Completed in 1847 with walls 7¹⁄₂ feet thick, it was taken by Georgia forces at the beginning of the war. However, on April 11, 1862, defense strategy changed worldwide when Union cannons, firing from more than a mile away on Tybee Island, overcame a masonry fortification. The effectiveness of rifled artillery (firing a bullet-shaped projectile with great accuracy at long range) was clearly demonstrated. The new Union weapon marked the end of the era of masonry fortifications. You can still find shells from 1862 embedded in the walls. Visits average 45 minutes.

15 miles east of Savannah off U.S. 80 on Cockspur and McQueen islands. ✆ **912/786-5787.** www.nps. gov/fopu. Admission $3 adults, free for 15 and under. Daily 9am–5pm.

Green-Meldrim Home   This impressive house was built on Madison Square for cotton merchant Charleston Green, but its moment in history came as the Savannah headquarters of Gen. William Tecumseh Sherman at the end of his 1864 "March to the Sea." It was from this Gothic-style house that the general sent a telegram to President Lincoln, offering him the city as a Christmas gift. Now the Parish House for St. John's Episcopal Church, the house is open to the public. A good look takes 30 minutes.

14 W. Macon St. ✆ **912/233-3845.** Admission $7 adults, $2 children. Tues and Thurs–Fri 10am–4pm; Sat 10am–1pm.

Owen-Thomas House & Museum   Famed as a place where Lafayette spent the night in 1825, this jewel box of a house evokes the heyday of Savannah's golden age. It was designed in 1816 by English architect William Jay, who instilled in it the grace of Georgian Bath in England and the splendor of Regency London. You can visit the bedchambers, kitchen, drawing and dining rooms, and garden in about 45 minutes.

124 Abercorn St. ✆ **912/233-9743.** Admission $9 adults, $8 seniors, $6 students, $5 children 6–12, free for children 5 and under. Tues–Sat 10am–5pm; Sun 2–5pm.

4

SAVANNAH

Savannah History Museum   Housed in the restored train shed of the old Central Georgia Railway station, this museum is a good introduction to the city. In the theater, *The Siege of Savannah* is replayed. In addition to theatrics, there's an exhibition hall displaying memorabilia from every era of Savannah's history. Allow 1 hour.

303 Martin Luther King, Jr., Blvd. ✆ **912/651-6825.** www.chsgeorgia.org/shm. Admission $4.25 adults; $3.75 seniors, students, and children 6 and older; free for children 5 and under. Mon–Fri 8:30am–5pm; Sat–Sun 9am–5pm.

Telfair Mansion and Art Museum   The oldest public art museum in the South, housing both American and European paintings, was designed and built in 1818 by William Jay, an English architect noted for introducing the Regency style to America. A sculpture gallery and rotunda were added in 1883, and Jefferson Davis attended the formal opening in 1886. William Jay's period rooms have been restored, and the Octagon Room and Dining Room are particularly outstanding. Visits last 45 minutes.

121 Bernard St. ✆ **912/232-1177.** www.telfair.org. Admission $10 adults, $5 seniors, $6 students, $4 children 5–12, free for children 4 and under. Mon noon–5pm; Wed–Sat 10am–5pm; Sun noon–5pm. Closed Tues.

LITERARY LANDMARKS

Long before John Berendt's *Midnight in the Garden of Good and Evil*, other writers were associated with Savannah.

Chief of them was **Flannery O'Connor** (1924–64), one of the South's greatest writers. Between October and May, an association dedicated to her offers readings, films, and lectures about her and other Southern writers. You can visit the **Flannery O'Connor Childhood Home** at 207 E. Charlton St. (✆ **912/233-6014;** www.flanneryoconnor home.org). The house is open Saturday and Sunday from 1 to 4pm. Admission is $5 or else free for ages 12 and under.

Conrad Aiken (1889–1973), the American poet, critic, writer, and Pulitzer Prize winner, was also born in Savannah. He lived at 228 and later at 230 E. Oglethorpe Ave.

Mercer House, 429 Bull St. (✆ **912/236-6352;** www.mercerhouse.com), used in *Midnight in the Garden of Good and Evil,* is open to the public, following a complete restoration. Currently, it is the star attraction of the city. The house is so spectacular it's been called "the envy of Savannah," and thousands of visitors stop by to photograph it. It was here in May 1981 that wealthy antiques dealer Jim Williams fatally shot his lover/ assistant, that blond "walking streak of sex," Danny Hansford, age 21. Mercer House is also where Williams gave his legendary Christmas parties each year. In January 1990, Jim Williams died of a heart attack at 59, in the same room where he'd killed Hansford. (And, no, Johnny Mercer never lived in this house, but it was built by his great-grandfather.) The house is sumptuously furnished with antiques, paintings, and objets d'art. It is still lived in by Dr. Dorothy Kingery, sister of the late Jim Williams, a distinguished academician. Open Monday through Saturday from 10:30am to 3:40pm and Sunday 12:30 to 4pm. Admission is $13 for adults and $8 for children and students (college-age students need ID).

All fans of The Book must pay a visit to **Bonaventure Cemetery,** filled with obelisks and columns and dense shrubbery and moss-draped trees. Bonaventure is open daily from 8am to 5pm. Take Wheaton Street east from downtown to Bonaventure Road. This cemetery lies on the grounds of what was once a great oak-shaded plantation. It was at the cemetery that John Berendt had martinis in silver goblets with Miss Harty, while they

sat on the bench-gravestone of Conrad Aiken. Songwriter Johnny Mercer is buried in
plot H-48.

SHOPPING

River Street is a shopper's delight, with some 9 blocks (including Riverfront Plaza) of
interesting shops, offering everything from crafts to clothing to souvenirs. The **City
Market,** between Ellis and Franklin squares on West St. Julian Street, boasts art galleries,
boutiques, and sidewalk cafes along with horse-and-carriage rides. Bookstores, boutiques,
and antiques shops are located between Wright Square and Forsyth Park.

J. D. Weed & Co., 102 W. Victory Dr. (© **912/234-8540;** www.jdweedco.com), is
one of our favorite antiques dealers. **Memory Lane,** 230 Bay St. (© **912/232-0975**),
offers more than 8,000 square feet of collectibles.

The leading art galleries include **Gallery 209,** 209 E. River St. (© **912/236-4583**);
John Tucker Gallery, 5 W. Charles St. (© **912/231-8161;** www.johntuckerfinearts.
com); **Morning Star Gallery,** 60 Jasper St. (© **912/233-4307**); and the **Village Craftsmen,** 223 W. River St. (© **912/236-7280;** www.thevillagecraftsmen.com).

WHERE TO STAY

Because many of Savannah's historic inns are in former converted residences, price ranges
can vary greatly. A very expensive hotel might also have some smaller and more moderately priced units—so it pays to ask.

The Ballastone (Best) This glamorous, award-winning B&B is a celeb favorite and
occupies a dignified 1838 building separated from the Juliette Gordon Low House by a
well-tended formal garden; it's richly decorated with hardwoods, elaborate draperies, and
antiques, and is ideal for romantic couples. There's an elevator, unusual for Savannah
B&Bs, but no closets (they were taxed as extra rooms in the old days). All rooms offer
bathrobes, deluxe toiletries, and VCRs; some have Jacuzzi tubs. The four suites are in a
clapboard town house that's a 5-minute walk away from the main building and is staffed
with its own live-in receptionists. A very good breakfast is served, as are afternoon tea and
evening hors d'oeuvres.

14 E. Oglethorpe Ave., Savannah, GA 31401. © **800/822-4553** or 912/236-1484. Fax 912/236-4626.
www.ballastone.com. 16 units. $235–$375 double; $395 suite. Rates include full breakfast, afternoon tea,
and evening hors d'oeuvres. AE, MC, V. Free parking. Pets accepted for $50 fee (under 25 lb. permitted).
No children age 15 and under. **Amenities:** Free passes to local health club; smoking not permitted.

Bed and Breakfast Inn In the oldest part of historic Savannah, this is a dignified
stone-fronted town house built in 1853 and is a suitable address for both families and
couples. You climb a gracefully curved front stoop to reach the cool high-ceilinged interior, outfitted with a combination of antique and reproduction furniture. Most rooms
offer four-poster beds.

117 W. Gordon St. (at Chatham Sq.), Savannah, GA 31401. © **888/230-0518** or 912/238-0518. Fax
912/233-2537. www.savannahbnb.com. 18 units. $149–$219 double. Children 7–13 stay in parent's room
for $25. Rates include full breakfast and afternoon tea. DISC, MC, V. Free parking. **Amenities:** Smoking not
permitted.

Eliza Thompson House The rooms of this stately home, attracting families and
couples, are divided between the original 1847 building and a converted carriage house.
Steve and Carol Day have completely redecorated, using original Savannah colors, beautiful antiques, and Oriental carpets. You'll find comfortable robes, fine linens, and well-kept,

elegant bathrooms. The inn is also graced with one of the most beautiful courtyards in the city. Breakfast is a lavish affair, usually served outdoors.

5 W. Jones St., Savannah, GA 31401. ✆ **800/348-9378** or 912/236-3620. Fax 912/238-1920. www. elizathompsonhouse.com. 25 units. $189–$259 double. Children 11 and under stay free in parent's room. Rates include full breakfast and evening hors d'oeuvres. AE, DC, DISC, MC, V. Free parking. **Amenities:** Smoking not permitted.

The Gastonian

One of the most posh B&Bs in Savannah, this Relais & Châteaux property, catering mainly to adults, incorporates a pair of Italianate Regency buildings constructed in 1868. Today everything is a testimonial to Victorian charm, except for a skillfully crafted serpentine bridge connecting the two buildings and curving above a verdant semitropical garden. Rooms are appropriately plush, comfortable, cozy, and beautifully furnished; some rooms have whirlpool tubs, others have working fireplaces. Afternoon tea is served in a formal drawing room.

220 E. Gaston St., Savannah, GA 31401. ✆ **800/322-6603** or 912/232-2869. Fax 912/232-0710. www. gastonian.com. 17 units. $205–$305 double; $395–$435 suite. Discount packages available. Rates include full breakfast and afternoon tea. AE, DISC, MC, V. Free parking. No children 11 and under.

Hampton Inn (Value (Kids

Opened in 1997, this family favorite rises above busy Bay Street, across from Savannah's Riverwalk and some of the city's most hopping nightclubs. Its lobby was designed to mimic an 18th-century Savannah salon, thanks to heart-of-pine flooring and antique Savannah bricks. Rooms are simple yet comfortable, with wall-to-wall carpeting and medium-size bathrooms.

201 E. Bay St., Savannah, GA. ✆ **800/576-4945** or 912/231-9700. Fax 912/231-0440. www.hotel savannah.com. 144 units. Sun–Thurs $120–$139 double; Fri–Sat $120–$179 double. Children 18 and under stay free in parent's room. Rates include continental breakfast. AE, DC, DISC, MC, V. Parking $10. **Amenities:** Pool; fitness room; smoking not permitted. *In room:* Fridge (in some), microwave (in some).

The Kehoe House

This is a spectacularly opulent B&B set in an 1892 mansion, with a museum-quality collection of fabrics and furniture, although it might be too flawless and formal for some tastes. Tom Hanks stayed in room no. 301 during the filming of *Forrest Gump*. Rooms are spacious, with 12-foot ceilings, and each is tastefully furnished in English period antiques. All units have well-kept bathrooms with plush bathrobes; some offer balconies.

123 Habersham St., Savannah, GA 31401. ✆ **800/820-1020** or 912/232-1020. Fax 912/231-0208. www. kehoehouse.com. 13 units. $239–$389 double. Children 12 and under stay free in parent's room. Rates include full breakfast, afternoon tea, and evening hors d'oeuvres. AE, DISC, MC, V. Free parking. **Amenities:** Smoking not permitted.

The Marshall House

After a $12-million renovation, this landmark antebellum hotel, having closed in the early 1960s, is once again a favorite. A luxurious decor, great iron verandas, and original features such as claw-foot tubs await guests, who range from business execs to families and couples. All the midsize-to-spacious bedrooms are modernized but still retain an aura of the 19th century with pinewood floors and rocking chairs resting under ceiling fans. Nice touches include bathrobes, Bath & Body Works toiletries, and bottled water.

123 E. Broughton St., Savannah, GA 31401. ✆ **800/589-6304** or 912/644-7896. Fax 912/234-3334. www. marshallhouse.com. 68 units. $185–$279 double; $249–$279 suite. Children 12 and under stay free in parent's room. Rates include breakfast. AE, DC, DISC, MC, V. Parking $10. **Amenities:** Restaurant; free membership in nearby health club.

River Street Inn This restored former cotton warehouse now has a dash of Colonial pizazz in its public areas, and the building's warren of brick-lined storerooms has been converted into some of the most comfortable and well-maintained rooms in town. All rooms offer a view of the Savannah River and bathrobes; some have four-poster beds. You'll be near tons of bars, restaurants, and nightclubs. A wine-and-cheese reception is held in the evening Monday through Saturday.

115 E. River St., Savannah, GA 31401. ℂ **800/253-4229** or 912/234-6400. Fax 912/234-1478. www. riverstreetinn.com. 86 units. $199–$249 double; $250–$299 suite. Children 11 and under stay free in parent's room. AE, DC, MC, V. Parking $6. **Amenities:** Smoking not permitted. *In room:* Fridge.

17 Hundred 90 The oldest inn in Savannah is in a clapboard house that was built in the year that gave the establishment its name. It's reminiscent of the kind of sea captain's house you might see emulated in a well-appointed private home. Most of the smallish but charming guest rooms have fireplaces. There's a basement-level restaurant with a beamed ceiling and original brickwork where locals come to eat and drink.

307 E. President St., Savannah, GA 31401. ℂ **800/487-1790** or 912/236-7122. Fax 912/236-7123. www.17hundred90.com. 14 units. $163–$215 double. AE, DC, DISC, MC, V. **Amenities:** Smoking not permitted.

WHERE TO DINE

Clary's Café AMERICAN Clary's, serving breakfast and lunch, has been a Savannah tradition since 1903, though the ambience today is decidedly 1950s. The place was famous long before it was featured in *Midnight in the Garden of Good and Evil.* John Berendt is still a frequent patron, as is the fabled drag diva Lady Chablis. Begin your day with the classic Hoppel Poppel (scrambled eggs with chunks of kosher salami, potatoes, onions, and green peppers), or drop in for fresh salads, stir-fries, homemade chicken soup, or flame-broiled burgers.

404 Abercorn St. (at Jones St.). ℂ **912/233-0402.** Breakfast $3.95–$9.95; main courses $5.95–$11. AE, DC, DISC, MC, V. Mon–Thurs 7am–4pm; Fri 8am–5pm; Sat 8am–5pm; Sun 8am–4pm.

Elizabeth on 37th (Best) MODERN SOUTHERN This restaurant is the most glamorous and upscale in town, and is the best choice for a romantic night out. It's housed in a palatial neoclassical-style 1900 villa ringed with semitropical landscaping and cascades of Spanish moss. Menu items change with the season and manage to retain their gutsy originality despite an elegant presentation. Their signature dish is grouper Celeste (sesame and almond–crusted grouper in a peanut sauce). The desserts are the best in Savannah.

105 E. 37th St. ℂ **912/236-5547.** www.elizabethon37th.net. Reservations required. Main courses $25–$35; 7-course fixed-price menu $90. AE, DC, DISC, MC, V. Daily 6–10pm.

45 South at the Pirate's House INTERNATIONAL/SEAFOOD Recommended by *Food & Wine, Southern Living,* and even *Playboy,* this ritzy restaurant has an ever-changing menu that might feature smoked North Carolina trout and other contemporary American food, including some of the best seafood caught off the Carolina coasts. The food has been called "gourmet Southern." The setting is softly lit with elegantly set tables and a cozy bar; the service is impeccable.

20 E. Broad St. ℂ **912/233-1881.** www.thepiratehouse.com. Reservations required. Jacket or tie preferred for men. Main courses $27–$34. AE, MC, V. Mon–Thurs 11am–9pm; Fri–Sat 11am–9:30pm.

Huey's (Kids) CAJUN/CREOLE This casual place overlooking the Savannah River even manages to please visitors from New Orleans—and that's saying a lot. It's usually packed with folks, especially families, enjoying dishes such as an oyster poor-boy, jambalaya with andouille sausage, crawfish étouffée, and crab-and-shrimp au gratin. The soups are homemade and the appetizers distinctive. Service is hectic but efficient.

Under the River Street Inn, 115 E. River St. (✆) **912/234-7385.** Reservations not accepted. Main courses $8.95–$11; sandwiches $6–$11. AE, DISC, MC, V. Mon–Fri 7am–10pm; Sat 8am–11pm; Sun 8am–10pm.

Johnny Harris Restaurant AMERICAN Started as a roadside diner in 1924, Johnny Harris is Savannah's oldest continuously operated restaurant. The place has a lingering aura of the 1950s and features all that great food so beloved back in the days of Elvis and Marilyn: barbecue, charbroiled steaks, and seafood. The barbecued pork is especially savory, and the prime rib is tender. Colonel Sanders never came anywhere close to equaling the fried chicken here. Guests can dine in the "kitchen" or in the main dining room, where you can dance under the "stars."

1651 E. Victory Dr. (Hwy. 80). (✆) **912/354-7810.** www.johnnyharris.com. Reservations recommended. Lunch items $7–$12; dinner main courses $12–$23. AE, DC, DISC, MC, V. Mon–Thurs 11:30am–9:30pm; Fri–Sat 11:30am–10:30pm.

The Lady & Sons (Value) SOUTHERN Paula Deen started this place in 1989 with $200; today she runs one of Savannah's most celebrated restaurants, a temple to greens and grits. The wonderful crab cakes and amazing chicken potpie topped with puff pastry best exhibit her style. The locals love her buffets, which are very Southern—with fried chicken, meatloaf, collard greens, and macaroni and cheese. Lunches are busy, with a loyal following; dinners are casual and inventive. Deen has numerous best-selling cookbooks in print and also hosts a top-rated cooking show, *Paula's Home Cooking*, on the Food Network.

102 W. Congress St. (✆) **912/233-2600.** www.ladyandsons.com. Reservations not accepted. Main courses $17–$28; all-you-can-eat buffet $14–$18; Sun buffet $18. AE, DISC, MC, V. Mon–Sat 11am–3pm; Mon–Sat 5–9pm; Sun 11am–5pm (buffet only).

Mrs. Wilkes' Dining Room (Value) SOUTHERN Remember the days of the boardinghouse, when everybody sat together and belly-busting food was served in big dishes at the center of the table? The late Sema Wilkes launched this former boardinghouse, now a restaurant, in the 1940s, and it's still going strong. You won't find a sign, but you probably will find a long line of people patiently waiting for a seat. The cooks believe in freshness and will fill you and your family with fried or barbecued chicken, red rice and sausage, corn on the cob, squash and yams, corn bread, collard greens, and other down-home favorites.

107 W. Jones St. (west of Bull St.). (✆) **912/232-5997.** www.mrswilkes.com. Reservations not accepted. Lunch $16. No credit cards. Mon–Fri 11am–2pm.

The Olde Pink House Restaurant SEAFOOD/AMERICAN Built in 1771 and painted pink, this house was once headquarters for one of Sherman's generals. Today its interior is severe and dignified, with stiff-backed chairs, bare wooden floors, and a Colonial ambience, ideal for a romantic date. The cuisine is steeped in the traditions of the Low Country—heavy on collards, grits, and seafood, especially shrimp dishes. The chef's signature dish is crispy sautéed flounder in an apricot sauce. You can enjoy your meal in the candlelit dining rooms or in the basement-level piano bar.

23 Abercorn St. (✆) **912/232-4286.** Reservations recommended. Main courses $15–$30. AE, MC, V. Sun–Thurs 5–10:30pm; Fri 5–11pm.

SAVANNAH AFTER DARK

To find out what's what on the Savannah nightlife scene, check **www.savannahunder ground.com.**

River Street, along the Savannah River, is the heart of the action. Many night owls stroll the waterfront until they hear the sound of music they like, and then follow their ears inside.

Savannah Civic Center's **Johnny Mercer Theater,** 301 W. Oglethorpe Ave. (© **800/ 351-7469** or 912/651-6656; www.savannahcivic.com), is home to ballet, musicals, and Broadway shows. Check locally to see what's on.

In summer, concerts of jazz, Big Band, and Dixieland music fill downtown **Johnson Square** with lots of foot-tapping sounds. Some of Savannah's finest musicians perform regularly.

Planters Tavern, in the Olde Pink House Restaurant, 23 Abercorn St. (© **912/232- 4286**), is a beloved local spot, graced with a sprawling and convivial bar, a pair of fire-places, and a decor of antique bricks and carefully polished hardwoods. You can listen to the melodies emanating from the sadder-but-wiser pianist, or perhaps you'll catch the endearingly elegant Gail Thurmond, one of Savannah's most legendary songstresses.

Most unpretentious is **Kevin Barry's Irish Pub,** 117 W. River St. (© **912/233-9626;** www.kevinbarrys.com), which is *the* place to be on St. Patrick's Day. The **Rail Pub,** 405 W. Congress St. (© **912/238-1311**), is sophisticated but low key.

On your nightly pub crawl, check out such local fun spots as **Mercury Lounge,** 125 W. Congress St. (© **912/447-6952**), with the biggest martinis in Savannah; the "high octane" **Monkey Bar,** 8 E. Broughton St. (© **912/232-0755**), with live music nightly, or the bar and grill; and **Bernies,** 115 E. River St. (© **912/236-1827;** www.bernies riverstreet.com), lying along the waterfront in a pre–Civil War cotton warehouse, with all the ambience today of an old portside pub.

Savannah's leading gay club is **Club One,** 1 Jefferson St. (© **912/232-0200**), where you can catch a drag show, sometimes starring Lady Chablis.

7 HILTON HEAD

The largest sea island between New Jersey and Florida, Hilton Head, South Carolina, offers broad, sandy beaches warmed by the Gulf Stream and fringed with palm trees and rolling dunes. The subtropical climate makes all this beauty the ideal setting for golf and saltwater fishing. Far more sophisticated and upscale than Myrtle Beach and the Grand Strand, Hilton Head feels like a luxurious planned community.

ESSENTIALS

GETTING THERE   It's easy to fly into Charleston, rent a car, and drive to Hilton Head (about 65 miles away). If you're driving from other points south or north, just take exit 8 off I-95 to U.S. 278, which runs over the bridge to the island. It's 52 miles northeast of Savannah and located directly on the Intracoastal Waterway.

VISITOR INFORMATION   The **Island Visitors Information Center,** on 71 Pope Ave. (© **888/271-7666** or 843/341-9184; www.enjoyhiltonhead.com), can be found just before you cross over from the mainland. It's open daily 10am to 7pm.

Hilton Head Visitors and Convention Bureau, 1 Chamber Dr. (© **800/523-3373** or 843/785-3673; www.hiltonheadisland.org), offers a free vacation guide with golf and tennis tips and planning advice. It's open Monday through Friday from 8:30am to 5:30pm.

SPECIAL EVENTS & FESTIVALS **Springfest,** a March festival, features seafood, live music, stage shows, and tennis and golf tournaments. Outstanding PGA golfers descend on the island in mid-April for the **Verizon Heritage** at the Harbour Town Golf Links. To herald fall, the **Hilton Head Celebrity Golf Tournament** is held on Labor Day weekend at several Island golf courses.

BEACHES, GOLF & OTHER OUTDOOR ACTIVITIES

BEACHES   Hilton Head's beaches possess extremely firm sand, providing a sound surface for biking, hiking, jogging, and beach games. In summer, watch for the endangered loggerhead turtles that lumber ashore at night to bury their eggs.

All beaches on Hilton Head are public but do not necessarily offer easy public access; sometimes land bordering the beaches is private property and you can't enter the public land unless you're a private guest. Most beaches are safe, although there's sometimes an undertow at the northern end of the island. Lifeguards are posted only at major beaches, and concessions are available at which to rent beach chairs, umbrellas, and watersports equipment.

We recommend four public entrances to Hilton Head's beaches. **Coligny Beach** at Coligny Circle and Pope Avenue and South Forest Beach Drive is the island's busiest strip of sands and our favorite; it offers toilets, sand showers, a playground, and changing rooms. (*Note:* Locals sometimes call Coligny "North and South Forest Beach.") **Alder Lane,** entered along South Forest Beach Road at Alder Lane, offers parking and public toilets, and is less crowded. Off the William Hilton Parkway, **Dreissen Beach Park** at Bradley Beach Road has toilets, sand showers, and plenty of parking, as well as a playground and picnic tables. On Starfish Road, **Folly Field Beach** has more limited parking but offers toilets and sand showers, and is our favorite of the beaches on the island's north side. The island also has a number of other less accessible and less desirable beaches.

BIKING   Hilton Head has 25 miles of bicycle paths. Some beaches are firm enough to support wheels, and every year cyclists seem to delight in dodging the waves or racing the fast-swimming dolphins in the nearby water.

Most hotels and resorts rent bikes to guests. If yours doesn't, try **Hilton Head Bicycle Company,** off Sea Pines Circle at 112 Arrow Rd. (© **800/995-4319** or 843/686-6888; www.hiltonheadbicycle.com). Rates start at around $28 weekly. Open Monday to Saturday 9am to 5pm, Sunday noon to 5pm.

CRUISES   To explore Hilton Head's waters, contact **Adventure Cruises, Inc.,** Shelter Cove Harbour, Ste. G, Harbourside III (© **843/785-4558;** www.hiltonheadisland.com/adventure/index.htm). Outings include a dolphin-watch and a sport crabbing cruise. A 1³/₄-hour cruise costs $25 adults, $15 kids ages 3 to 12. **Calibogue Cruises,** Broad Creek Marina (© **843/342-8687;** www.daufuskieislandtours.com), offers boat transportation to Daufuskie Island for $23 per adult (includes golf cart), half-price for children 2 to 12.

FISHING   No license is needed for saltwater fishing, although freshwater licenses are required for the island's lakes and ponds. The season for fishing offshore is April to October. Inland fishing is good between September and December. Crabbing is also popular; these crustaceans are easy to catch in low water from docks, from boats, or right off a bank.

Off Hilton Head you can go deep-sea fishing for amberjack, barracuda, sharks, and king mackerel. **Harbour Town Yacht Basin,** Harbour Town Marina (© **843/671-4534;** www.harbourtownyachtbasin.com), can set you up with personal service and a small boat. A cheaper way to go—for only $60 per adult, $50 per child—is aboard the *Drifter* (© **843/363-2900**), a party boat that departs from the South Beach Marina Village.

GOLF   With 22 challenging golf courses on the island, this area is a mecca for golfers. For information on the area's various courses, consult **www.hiltonheadgolf.com**.

Many of Hilton Head's championship courses are open to the public, including the **George Fazio Course** at Palmetto Dunes Resort (© **843/785-1130**), an 18-hole, 6,534-yard, par-70 course, named in the top 50 of *Golf Digest's* "75 Best American Resort Courses." Greens fees are $56 to $115, depending on time of day.

Old South Golf Links, 50 Buckingham Plantation Dr., Bluffton (© **800/257-8997** or 843/785-5353), is an 18-hole, 6,772-yard, par-72 course, recognized by *Golf Digest* for its panoramic views and lovely setting. Greens fees range from $80 to $95. The course lies on Hwy. 278, 1 mile before the bridge leading to Hilton Head.

Hilton Head National, Hwy. 278 (© **843/842-5900**), is a Gary Player Signature Golf Course, an 18-hole, 6,779-yard, par-72 course with gorgeous scenery that evokes Scotland. Greens fees are $85 to $95.

Island West Golf Club, Hwy. 278 (© **843/689-6660**), has a backdrop of oaks, elevated tees, and rolling fairways. It's a challenging but playable 18-hole, 6,803-yard, par-72 course. Greens fees are $58 to $68.

The **Robert Trent Jones Course** at the Palmetto Dunes Resort (© **843/785-1138**) is an 18-hole, 6,710-yard, par-72 course with a winding lagoon system that comes into play on 11 holes. Greens fees are $85 to $165.

HORSEBACK RIDING   Riding through beautiful maritime forests and nature preserves is reason enough to visit Hilton Head. We like **Lawton Fields Stables,** 190 Greenwood Dr., Sea Pines (© **843/671-2586**), offering rides for both adults and kids (kids 6 and under ride ponies) through the Sea Pines Forest Preserve. The cost is $50 per person for a ride lasting somewhat over an hour. Reservations are necessary.

NATURE PRESERVES   The **Audubon-Newhall Preserve,** Palmetto Bay Road (© **843/842-9246**), is a 50-acre preserve on the south end of the island. Here you can walk along marked trails to observe wildlife in its native habitat. Guided tours are available when plants are blooming. Open from sunrise to sunset; free admission.

Sea Pines Forest Preserve, Sea Pines Plantation (© **843/363-4530**), is a 605-acre public wilderness with marked walking trails. Nearly all the birds and animals known to live on Hilton Head can be seen here (yes, there are alligators, but there are also less fearsome creatures, such as egrets, herons, osprey, and white-tailed deer). All trails lead to public picnic areas in the center of the forest. The preserve is open from sunrise to sunset year-round except during the Heritage Golf Classic in early April. Maps and toilets are available. There is a $5-per-car fee to enter the plantation.

TENNIS   *Tennis* magazine has rated Hilton Head one of its "50 Greatest U.S. Tennis Resorts." No other domestic destination can boast such a concentration of tennis facilities, with more than 300 courts ideal for beginning, intermediate, and advanced players. The island has 19 tennis clubs, 7 of which are open to the public. A variety of tennis clinics and lessons are also found here, with the academy of famed tennis guru Dennis van der Meer being just one of the instructional centers. The top tennis facility is the **Sea Pines Racquet Club** (© **843/363-4495**), along with the **Port Royal Racquet Club**

(© 843/686-8803), the **Hilton Head Island Beach and Tennis Resort** (© 843/842-4402), and the **Palmetto Dunes Tennis Center** (© 843/785-1152).

WHERE TO STAY

Villa rentals are available from two secluded enclaves of privately owned condos. The **Palmetto Dunes Resort** (© 866/292-4148 or 843/785-1138; www.palmettodunes.com) has a wide variety of units available for rental and offers golf packages. It's ideal for families, with kitchens, washer/dryers, and balconies or patios. Facilities include a huge tennis center, five golf courses, 3 miles of beach, 20 restaurants, a 10-mile lagoon ideal for canoeing, and a 200-slip marina. The **Sea Pines Resort** (© 888/807-6873 or 843/785-3333; www.seapines.com) is a huge development that's best for overnight stays; it attracts hordes of golfers since it's the home of the Verizon Heritage, a major stop on the PGA tour.

Moderately priced and affordable chain choices include the **Holiday Inn Oceanfront,** 1 S. Forest Beach Dr. (© 800/423-9897 or 843/785-5126; www.hihiltonhead.com); **Days Inn Hilton Head**, 9 Marina Side Dr. (© 843/842-4800; fax 843/842-5388); and **Hampton Inn,** 1 Dillon Rd. (© 800/HAMPTON [426-7866] or 843/681-7900; fax 843/681-4330; www.hamptoninn.com).

Crowne Plaza Resort   This five-story hotel, set on 800 landscaped acres, gives the Westin (see below) stiff competition because of the sheer beauty of its landscaping, with a golf course praised by the National Audubon Society for its respect for local wildlife. Bedrooms don't quite match the style and comfort level of its competitor's, but they are neatly furnished and sport CD players. The attentive service is just another reason that a stay here is memorable.

130 Shipyard Dr., Shipyard Plantation, Hilton Head Island, SC 29928. © **877/227-6963** or 843/842-2400. Fax 843/785-8463. www.ichotelsgroup.com. 338 units. $119–$399 double; $459–$579 suite. Children 17 and under stay free in parent's room. AE, DC, DISC, MC, V. Valet parking $10; free self-parking. **Amenities:** 2 restaurants; 2 pools (1 indoor); fitness center. *In room:* Fridge ($10 per night).

Disney Hilton Head Island Resort (Kids)   This family-friendly resort is on a 15-acre island that rises above Hilton Head's widest estuary, Broad Creek. About 20 woodsy-looking buildings are arranged in a compound. Expect lots of pine trees and fallen pine needles, garlands of Spanish moss, and plenty of kids. All accommodations contain kitchenettes, simple wooden furniture, and well-kept bathrooms. There are lots of summer camp–style activities (dolphin-watching cruises, eco-tours, canoeing lessons, marshmallow roasts), though the ambience is more low key than what you'd expect from Disney.

22 Harbourside Lane, Hilton Head Island, SC 29928. © **800/500-3990** or 843/341-4100. Fax 843/341-4130. www.dvc.disney.go.com. 123 units. $110–$324 studio for 2; $164–$289 1-bedroom villa, $189–$335 2-bedroom villa. Resort fee $9 per night. Children 17 and under stay free in parent's room. AE, DC, DISC, MC, V. Free parking. **Amenities:** 2 pools; fitness center; spa. *In room:* Kitchenette in studios, kitchen in villas.

Hilton Oceanfront Resort (Kids)   We like the Hilton because of its hideaway position, tucked at the end of the main road through Palmetto Dunes. Its low-rise design has hallways that open to sea breezes at either end. Rooms are some of the largest on the island, all with ocean views and well-kept bathrooms. All the studio suites have kitchenettes, making this resort a favorite of families, which also like the children's activities such as a kids' camp.

23 Ocean Lane, Hilton Head Island, SC 29928. ✆ **800/845-8001** or 843/842-8000. Fax 843/341-8033.
www.hiltonoceanfrontresort.com. 324 units. $119–$390 double; $170–$550 junior suite; $219–$595
suite. Children 18 and under stay free in parent's room. AE, DC, DISC, MC, V. Parking $6. **Amenities:** 3
restaurants; 2 pools; fitness center. In room: Kitchenette.

Main Street Inn   Don't expect cozy Americana at this small, luxurious inn for
adults—it's grander and more European than its name would imply. Designed like a
small-scale villa that you might find in the south of France, it combines design elements
from both New Orleans and Charleston, including cast-iron balustrades and a formal
semitropical garden where guests are encouraged to indulge in afternoon tea. Inside you'll
find an artfully clipped topiary, French Provincial furnishings, and accommodations that
are more luxurious, and more richly appointed (marble bathrooms, bathrobes, the occasional fireplace), than any other hotel in Hilton Head.

2200 Main St., Hilton Head Island, SC 29926. ✆ **800/471-3001** or 843/681-3001. Fax 843/681-5541.
www.mainstreetinn.com. 33 units. $149–$239 double; $199–$249 suite. Rates include breakfast.
AE, DISC, MC, V. Free parking. **Amenities:** Pool; spa.

South Beach Marina Inn (Value)   Of the dozens of available accommodations in Sea
Pines Plantation, this complex of marina-front buildings is the only place offering traditional hotel-style rooms by the night. With lots of charm, it meanders over a labyrinth
of catwalks and stairways above a complex of shops and restaurants. The one- and two-
bedroom units each have a kitchenette and at least one bathroom, and are cozily outfitted
with country-style braided rugs and pine floors.

In the Sea Pines Plantation, 232 S. Sea Pines Dr., Hilton Head Island, SC 29938. ✆ **800/367-3909** or
843/671-6498. Fax 843/671-7495. www.sbinn.com. 17 units. $65–$175 1-bedroom apt; $109–$186
2-bedroom apt. Children 17 and under stay free in parent's room. AE, DISC, MC, V. Free parking. **Amenities:** Pool. In room: Kitchenette.

Westin Resort (Best)   Set near the isolated northern end of Hilton Head Island on 24
landscaped acres, this opulent European-style hotel is rather formal, although suitable for
families. Rooms, most with ocean views, are outfitted in Low Country Plantation style
with touches of Asian art. Each room has a private balcony and Westin's signature Heavenly Bed; refrigerators are available. Suites toss in Jacuzzi tubs and sleeper sofas.

2 Grasslawn Ave., Hilton Head Island, SC 29928. ✆ **800/937-8461** or 843/681-4000. Fax 843/681-1096.
www.starwoodhotels.com. 412 units. $199–$369 double; from $450 suite. Resort fee $10 per night.
Children 16 and under stay free in parent's room; children 4 and under eat free. Packages often available.
AE, DC, DISC, MC, V. Valet parking $9.50; free self-parking. Pet fee $100 (under 30 lb. permitted). **Amenities:** 3 restaurants; 3 pools (2 indoor); 3 golf courses; 16 tennis courts; fitness center; Heavenly spa. In
room: Fridge ($10 per night).

WHERE TO DINE
Charlie's L'Etoile Verte (Best)   INTERNATIONAL/SEAFOOD   Outfitted like a
Parisian bistro, our favorite Hilton Head restaurant is also a favorite of Bill Clinton. The
atmosphere is unpretentious but elegant, and it bursts with energy in an otherwise sleepy
shopping center. Begin with roasted portobello and crab, and move on to tilapia sautéed
in a Parmesan crust. The wine list is impressive and has won *Wine Spectator*'s Award of
Excellence 10 years running.

8 New Orleans Rd. ✆ **843/785-9277.** www.charliesofhiltonhead.com. Reservations recommended.
Main courses $14–$39. AE, DISC, MC, V. Tues–Sat 11:30am–2pm; Mon–Sat 6–9:30pm.

Hudson's Seafood House on the Docks SEAFOOD   Built as a seafood-processing factory in 1912, this family-run restaurant still processes fish, clams, and oysters for local distribution—so you know everything is fresh. We recommend the crab cakes, the steamed shrimp, or the especially appealing blackened catch of the day. Before dinner, stroll on the docks past shrimp boats and enjoy the sunset view of the mainland and nearby Parris Island.

1 Hudson Rd. ✆ **843/681-2772.** www.hudsonsonthedocks.com. Reservations not accepted. Main courses $13–$22. AE, DC, MC, V. Daily 11am–2:30pm and 5–10pm. Go to Skull Creek just off Squire Pope Rd. (signposted from U.S. 278).

Scott's Fish Market ⟨Kids⟩ SEAFOOD/AMERICAN   The largest full-service outdoor dining area at Hilton Head, this family favorite is known for its fresh seafood. In addition to fresh fish, a regular American menu of other dishes is offered. Tables overlook the boats bobbing at anchor along the waterfront. The Hurricane Harry's Wharf Bar offers live entertainment if you want to make an evening of it.

Shelter Cove Harbour. ✆ **843/785-7575.** Reservations recommended. Main courses $10–$24; children's menu $3–$5. AE, DC, DISC, MC, V. Mon–Sat 4:30–10pm. Closed Jan.

Waterfront Café CONTINENTAL/SEAFOOD   At the base of the Harbour Town Lighthouse, this restaurant opens onto a panoramic view of Calibogue Sound and Daufuskie Island. For nearly 3 decades, it was known as Cafe Europa. Even with a name change, owners have kept the popular dishes for which the restaurant is known, including the catch of the day, which can be poached, grilled, baked, or fried. Other dishes include Julia Child's favorite meatloaf and Southern spring roll.

Harbour Town, Sea Pines Plantation. ✆ **843/671-3399.** www.waterfrontcafehhi.com. Reservations recommended for dinner. Main courses $6–$12 lunch, $18–$29 dinner. AE, MC, V. Daily 11am–2:30pm and 5–10pm.

HILTON HEAD AFTER DARK

Nightlife starts with sunset cocktails and stays pretty mellow. There are lots of options in hotel bars and lounges. The **Quarterdeck,** Harbour Town, Sea Pines Plantation (✆ **843/842-1999**), is our favorite waterfront lounge, the best place on the island to watch sunsets. There's dancing every night to beach music and Top-40 hits. Soft guitar music or the strains of Jimmy Buffett records usually set the scene at the **Salty Dog Cafe,** South Beach Marina Village, Sea Pines Plantation (✆ **843/363-2198;** www.saltydog.com), where you can enjoy your beer outdoors under a sycamore.

8 CHARLESTON

If the Old South still lives all through South Carolina's Low Country—the term for the state's southern coastal communities—it positively thrives in Charleston. All romantic notions of antebellum days—stately homes, courtly manners, gracious hospitality, and, above all, gentle dignity—are facts of everyday life in this old city. In spite of earthquakes, hurricanes, fires, and Yankee bombardments, Charleston remains one of the best-preserved cities in America. It boasts 73 pre-Revolutionary buildings, 136 from the late 18th century, and more than 600 built before the 1840s. With its cobblestone streets and horse-drawn carriages, Charleston is a place of visual images and sensory pleasures. Tea, jasmine, and wisteria fragrances fill the air; the aroma of she-crab soup (the local favorite) wafts from sidewalk cafes; and antebellum architecture graces the historic cityscape.

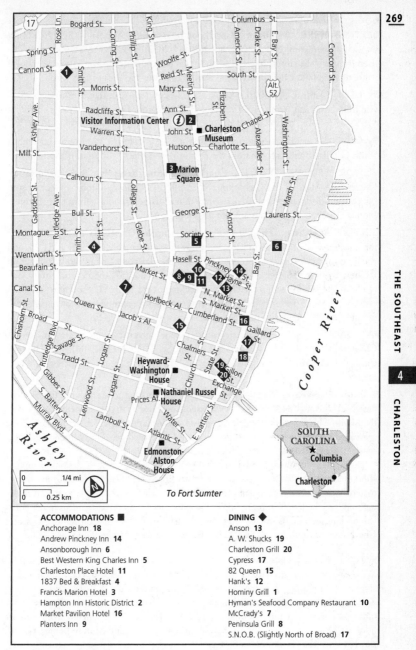

SOUTH CAROLINA
★
Columbia

Charleston

To Fort Sumter

ACCOMMODATIONS ■
Anchorage Inn **18**
Andrew Pinckney Inn **14**
Ansonborough Inn **6**
Best Western King Charles Inn **5**
Charleston Place Hotel **11**
1837 Bed & Breakfast **4**
Francis Marion Hotel **3**
Hampton Inn Historic District **2**
Market Pavilion Hotel **16**
Planters Inn **9**

DINING ◆
Anson **13**
A. W. Shucks **19**
Charleston Grill **20**
Cypress **17**
82 Queen **15**
Hank's **12**
Hominy Grill **1**
Hyman's Seafood Company Restaurant **10**
McCrady's **7**
Peninsula Grill **8**
S.N.O.B. (Slightly North of Broad) **17**

GETTING THERE **By Plane** Charleston International Airport (© 843/767-1100; www.chs-airport.com) is in north Charleston on I-26, about 12 miles west of the city. The fixed rate from the airport into the city is $9 per passenger, not to exceed $27 per trip. If you're driving, follow the airport access road to I-26 into the heart of Charleston.

By Train Amtrak (© 800/USA-RAIL [872-7245]; www.amtrak.com) provides service from Savannah (trip time: $1^3/_4$ hr.) and Washington, D.C. (9 hr.), to its station at 4565 Gaynor Ave., north Charleston.

By Car The main routes into Charleston are **I-26** from the northwest (Columbia, South Carolina), and **U.S. 17** from the north (Myrtle Beach) and south (Savannah).

VISITOR INFORMATION The **Charleston Visitor Reception & Transportation Center,** 375 Meeting St., Charleston, SC 29402 (© **800/774-0006;** www.charleston cvb.com), provides maps and advice. Numerous tours depart hourly from here. It's open Monday through Friday from 8:30am to 5:30pm.

GETTING AROUND The **Downtown Area Shuttle (DASH;** © 843/724-7420) is the quickest way to get around the main downtown area daily. The fare is $1.25, and you'll need exact change. A pass good for the whole day costs $4 and can be bought on the bus. Leading taxi companies are **Yellow Cab** (© 843/577-6565) and **Safety Cab** (© 843/722-4066); within the city, fares seldom exceed $6 to $12. You must call for a taxi—there are no pickups on the street. Don't try to drive around downtown; park your car and save it for day trips to outlying areas.

FAST FACTS For a physician referral or 24-hour emergency-room treatment, contact **Charleston Memorial Hospital,** 326 Calhoun St. (© 843/792-2300). Call **Doctor's Care** (© 843/556-5585) for the names of walk-in clinics. Sales tax in Charleston is 6%; the hotel tax is also 6%.

SPECIAL EVENTS & FESTIVALS Held from late May to early June, the **Spoleto Festival U.S.A.** (© 843/579-3100; www.spoletousa.org) is the premier cultural event in the South. This famous international festival, the American counterpart to the equally celebrated one in Spoleto, Italy, showcases world-renowned performers in drama, dance, music, and art in various venues throughout the city.

During the mid-January **Low-Country Oyster Festival** (© www.charlestonlowcountry. com), steamed buckets of oysters greet visitors at Boone Hall Plantation. Enjoy live music, oyster-shucking contests, and children's events. For nearly 50 years, people have been enjoying some of Charleston's most prestigious neighborhoods and private gardens in the **Festival of Houses and Gardens,** from mid-March to mid-April. Contact the **Historic Charleston Foundation** (© 843/722-3405; www.historiccharleston.org) for details.

WHAT TO SEE & DO

We always head for the **Battery** (officially White Point Gardens) to get into the feel of this city. It's right on the end of the peninsula, facing the Cooper River and the harbor. There's a landscaped park, shaded by palmettos and live oaks, with walkways lined with old monuments and other war relics. The view toward the harbor goes out to Fort Sumter. We like to walk along the seawall on East Battery and Murray Boulevard, and slowly absorb the Charleston ambience.

The **Old South Carriage Co.,** 14 Anson St. (© 843/723-9712; www.oldsouth carriagetours.com), offers narrated horse-drawn carriage tours through the historic district daily from 9am to 5pm, at $21 for adults and $13 for children 3 to 11.

Charleston Museum Founded in 1773, this is the first and oldest museum in **271**
America. The full-scale replica of the famed Confederate submarine *Hunley* standing outside the museum is one of the most photographed subjects in the city. The museum has the city's largest silver collection, plus early crafts, historical relics, costumes and textiles, and hands-on exhibits for children.

360 Meeting St. ✆ 843/722-2996. www.charlestonmuseum.org. Admission $10 adults, $5 children 3–12. Combination ticket to the museum, Joseph Manigault House, and Heyward-Washington House (see below) $22. Mon–Sat 9am–5pm; Sun 1–5pm.

Charles Towne Landing This 663-acre park is on the site of the city's first settlement (in 1670). There's a re-creation of a small village and a full-scale replica of a 17th-century trading ship. There's no flashy theme-park atmosphere: You'll walk under huge old oaks, past freshwater lagoons, and through the Animal Forest, seeing what those early settlers saw.

1500 Old Towne Rd. (S.C. 171, btw. U.S. 17 and I-126). ✆ 843/852-4200. www.southcarolinaparks.com. Admission $5 adults, $3.25 seniors, $3 children 6–15, free for travelers with disabilities and children 5 and under. Daily 9am–5pm.

Cypress Gardens Giant cypress trees draped with Spanish moss provide an unforgettable setting as you glide along in a flat-bottomed boat. Footpaths in the garden wind through a profusion of azaleas, camellias, and daffodils. Visitors share the swamp with alligators, woodpeckers, wood ducks, otters, and barred owls. The gardens are worth a visit at any time of year, but they're at their most colorful in March and April. Other features include a butterfly house and a small freshwater aquarium.

U.S. 52 (24 miles north of Charleston), Moncks Corner. ✆ 843/553-0515. www.cypressgardens.info. Admission $10 adults, $9 seniors, $5 children 6–12. Daily 9am–5pm.

Edmondston-Alston House This house, built in 1825, was one of the earliest constructed in the city in the late Federalist style; it was later modified in Greek Revival style. You can still see the Alston family's heirloom furnishings, silver, and paintings. At this house, in 1861, General Beauregard joined the Alstons to watch the bombardment of Fort Sumter. Robert E. Lee once found refuge here when his hotel uptown caught on fire.

21 E. Battery. ✆ 843/722-7171. www.middletonplace.org. Admission $10 adults, $8 children 7–15, free for children 6 and under. Guided tours Tues–Sat 10am–4:30pm; Sun–Mon 1:30–4:30pm.

Fort Sumter National Monument It was here that the first shot of the Civil War was fired on April 12, 1861, as Confederate forces launched a 34-hour bombardment. Union forces eventually surrendered, and the Rebels' occupation became a symbol of Southern resistance. This action led to a declaration of war in Washington. Amazingly, Confederate troops held on to Sumter for nearly 4 years, although it was almost continually bombarded. When evacuation finally came, the fort was nothing but a heap of rubble. Park rangers today are on hand to answer your questions, and you can explore gun emplacements and visit a museum filled with artifacts related to the siege. Expect to spend about 2 hours. *Tip:* We recommend the tour of the fort and harbor offered by **Fort Sumter Tours,** 360 Concord St., Ste. 201 (✆ 843/722-1691 or 881-7337; www.fort sumtertours.com). Sailing times change every month or so; call ahead.

In Charleston Harbor. ✆ 843/883-3123. www.nps.gov/fosu. Free admission to fort; boat trip $15 adults, $14 seniors, $9 children 6–11, free for children 5 and under. Daily 10am–5:30pm (in winter until 4pm).

Heyward-Washington House In a district called "Cabbage Row," this 1772 house was built by Daniel Heyward, "the rice king," and was also home to Thomas Heyward,

Jr., a signer of the Declaration of Independence. President George Washington bedded down here in 1791. Many of the fine period pieces in the house are the work of Thomas Elfe, one of America's most famous cabinetmakers. The restored 18th-century kitchen is the only historic kitchen in the city open to the public.

87 Church St. (btw. Tradd and Elliott sts.). © **843/722-0354.** www.charlestonmuseum.org. Admission $10 adults, $5 children 3–12. Mon–Sat 10am–5pm; Sun 1–5pm. Tours leave every half-hour until 4:30pm. Combination tickets with Charleston Museum available (see above).

Magnolia Plantation   Ten generations of the Drayton family have lived here continuously since the 1670s. They haven't had much luck keeping a roof over their heads: The first mansion burned just after the Revolution and the second was set afire by General Sherman. But you can't call its replacement "modern." A simple, pre-Revolutionary house was barged down from Summerville and set on the foundations of its unfortunate predecessors. It's been furnished with museum-quality Early American furniture. The gardens of camellias and azaleas—among the most beautiful in America—reach their peak bloom in March and April but are colorful year-round. You can tour the house, the gardens, a petting zoo, and a waterfowl refuge, or walk or bike through wildlife trails. The **Audubon Swamp Garden,** also on the grounds, is an independently operated 60-acre cypress swamp offering a close look at wildlife, such as alligators, otters, turtles, and herons.

3550 Ashley River Rd. © **800/367-3517** or 843/571-1266. www.magnoliaplantation.com. Admission to garden and grounds $15 adults, $14 seniors, $10 children 6–12. Tour of plantation house additional $7 for ages 6 and up; children 5 and under not allowed to tour the house. Admission to Audubon Swamp Garden $7 adults, $6 seniors, $5 children 6–12. Summer daily 8am–5:30pm; winter daily 9am–5pm.

Middleton Place   This National Historic Landmark was the home of Henry Middleton, president of the First Continental Congress. Today it includes America's oldest landscaped gardens, where ornamental lakes, terraces, and plantings of camellias, azaleas, magnolias, and crape myrtle accent the grand design. The Middleton Place House itself was built in 1755, but in 1865 all but the south flank was ransacked and burned by Union troops. It was restored in the 1870s as a family residence and today houses fine silver, furniture, rare first editions, and portraits. In the stable yards, craftspeople demonstrate life on a plantation of yesteryear.

4300 Ashley River Rd. (14 miles northwest of Charleston). © **843/556-6020.** www.middletonplace.org. Admission $25 adults, $5 children 7–15, free for children 6 and under. Tour of house additional $10. Gardens and stable yards daily 9am–5pm. House Mon 1:30–4:30pm; Tues–Sat 10am–4:30pm.

Nathaniel Russell House   One of America's finest examples of Federal architecture, this 1808 house was completed by Nathaniel Russell, one of Charleston's richest merchants. It is celebrated for its "free-flying" staircase, spiraling unsupported for three floors. The interiors are ornate with period furnishings, especially the elegant music room with its golden harp and neoclassical-style sofa.

51 Meeting St. © **843/805-6736.** www.historiccharleston.org. Admission $10 or $5 ages 6–16. Free 5 and under. Guided tours Mon–Sat 10am–5pm; Sun and holidays 2–5pm.

South Carolina Aquarium (Best) (Kids)   Visitors can explore Southern aquatic life in an attraction filled with thousands of enchanting creatures and plants in amazing habitats, from five major regions of the Appalachian Watershed. Jutting out into the Charleston Harbor for 2,000 feet, the focal point is a 93,000-square-foot aquarium featuring a two-story Great Ocean Tank Exhibition. Contained within are some 800 animals, including deadly sharks but also sea turtles and stingrays. Every afternoon at 4pm the aquarium offers a dolphin program, when bottle-nosed dolphins can be viewed from an open-air terrace. A major new exhibit exploring the aquatic life of the Amazon (including some piranha!) opened in 2004.

100 Aquarium Wharf. ✆ **843/720-1990.** www.scaquarium.org. Admission $17 adults (12–61), $16 seniors 62 and older, $10 children 2–11, free for children 1 and under. Apr 1–Aug 15 Mon–Sat 9am–6pm, Sun noon–6pm; Aug 16–Mar 31 Mon–Sat 9am–5pm, Sun noon–5pm.

BEACHES & OUTDOOR ACTIVITIES

BEACHES There are some great beaches within a 25-minute drive from Charleston. In the East Cooper area, both the **Isle of Palms** and **Sullivan's Island** offer miles of beaches, mostly bordered by beachfront homes. Windsurfing and jet-skiing are popular here. **Kiawah Island** has the area's most pristine beach at the **Beachwalker State Park,** on the southern end of the island. For more information on the beach scene, head online to **www.charlestonlowcountry.com/Beaches**.

GOLF Charleston is said to be the home of golf in America. **Wild Dunes Resort,** Isle of Palms (✆ **843/886-6000**), offers two championship golf courses designed by Tom Fazio. The **Links** is a 6,722-yard, par-72 layout ending with a pair of oceanfront holes once called "the greatest east of Pebble Beach." The course has been ranked in the top 100 in the world by *Golf Magazine.* The **Harbor Course** offers 6,402 yards of Low Country marsh and Intracoastal Waterway views. This par-70 layout challenges players with 2 holes that play from one island to another across Morgan Creek. Greens fees at these courses can range from $85 to $165, depending on the season.

If you'd like to play at any of the other Charleston-area golf courses, contact **Charleston Golf Inc.** (✆ **800/774-4444;** www.charlestongolfguide.com), representing 20 golf courses and offering packages that include greens fees and accommodations. (They can also arrange rental cars and airfares.)

SHOPPING

King Street is lined with many specialty shops and boutiques.

Two of the leading galleries are the **Waterfront Gallery,** 215 E. Bay St., across from the Custom House (✆ **843/722-1155;** www.waterfrontartgallery.com), and the **Wells Gallery,** 103 Broad St. (✆ **843/853-3233;** www.wellsgallery.com), both specializing in the works of local artists.

Charleston Crafts, 87 Hassell St. (✆ **843/723-2938;** www.charlestoncrafts.org), offers locally made jewelry, basketry, leather, traditional crafts, and soaps. **Clown's Bazaar,** 56 Broad St. (✆ **843/723-9769**), features hand-carvings, silks, and pewter from exotic locales, with proceeds going to benefit developing nations. Also supporting a good cause, **Historic Charleston Reproductions,** 105 Broad St. (✆ **843/723-8292**), aids local restoration projects. Licensed replica products range from furniture to jewelry. The pride of the store is its home furnishings collection, with most in lovely mahogany. It operates shops in several historic houses and runs the **Francis Edmunds Center Museum Shop,** at 108 Meeting St. (✆ **843/724-8484**). A local company, **Charleston Gift Company,** 239 1/2 King St. (✆ **843/577-7774**), specializes in all sorts of Charleston "things," including clothing, specialty gift baskets, handbags, and one-of-a-kind photo albums and frames.

WHERE TO STAY

For help with reservations, contact **Historic Charleston Bed & Breakfast** (✆ **800/743-3583** or 843/722-6606; www.historiccharlestonbedandbreakfast.com). During the major festivals, owners charge pretty much what the market will bear. Advance reservations are essential at those times.

Reliable moderately priced and affordable chain options include the **Hampton Inn Historic District,** 345 Meeting St. (© **800/HAMPTON** [426-7866] or 843/723-4000), across from the visitor center, and the **Best Western King Charles Inn,** 237 Meeting St. (© **866/546-4700** or 843/723-7451; www.kingcharlesinn.com).

Anchorage Inn   Built in the 1840s as a cotton warehouse, this inn, a favorite of couples, boasts the only decorative theme of its type in Charleston: a mock-Tudor interior with lots of dark paneling; references to Olde England; canopied beds with matching tapestries; leaded casement windows; and, in some places, half-timbering. Modern conveniences include satellite TV and Neutrogena toiletries. Each room's shape is different from that of its neighbors, and the expensive ones have bona fide windows overlooking the street outside.

26 Vendue Range, Charleston, SC 29401. © **800/421-2952** or 843/723-8300. Fax 843/723-9543. www.anchoragencharleston.com. 19 units. $129–$279 double; $179–$309 suite. Children 11 and under stay free in parent's room. Rates include continental breakfast and afternoon tea. AE, MC, V. Parking $10. **Amenities:** Smoking not permitted.

Andrew Pinckney Inn   This nonsmoking boutique hotel—housed in a converted 18th-century stable—has old-world charm but is completely up-to-date with modern amenities. Its special feature is a three-story plant-filled atrium, along with a beautiful courtyard, plus a rooftop terrace overlooking the Market District and the French Quarter. The hotel is decorated in an elegant yet casual West Indian style. Its St. Philip's Suite is one of the best places in Charleston for a romantic getaway.

40 Pinckney St., Charleston, SC 29401. © **800/505-8983** or 843/937-8800. Fax 843/937-8810. www.andrewpinckneyinn.com. 41 units. $139–$299 double; $199–$449 suite. Children 11 and under stay free in parent's room. Rates include continental breakfast. AE, DC, MC, V. Parking $12. **Amenities:** Smoking not permitted. *In room:* Fridge, microwave (in some).

Ansonborough Inn   Once past the not-very-promising exterior, most visitors (it's popular with both couples and families) really like the unusual configuration of the suites here. Set close to the waterfront, this former warehouse has a lobby that features exposed timbers and a soaring atrium filled with plants. All accommodations are suites with ceilings of 14 to 16 feet and, in many cases, sleeping lofts; five have fireplaces. They're outfitted with copies of 18th-century furniture. There's a panoramic terrace with a bar on the rooftop.

21 Hassell St., Charleston, SC 29401. © **800/522-2073** or 843/723-1655. Fax 843/577-6888. www.ansonboroughinn.com. 37 units. Mar–Nov $159–$379 double; off season $109–$289 double. Additional person $20 per night. Children 11 and under stay free in parent's room. Rates include continental breakfast. AE, DISC, MC, V. Parking $12. **Amenities:** Smoking not permitted. *In room:* Kitchenette.

Charleston Place Hotel (Best)   Charleston's premier hotel is an eight-story landmark in the historic district that looks like a postmodern French château. It's big-time, glossy, and urban, with prices to match, and can be both a romantic getaway for couples and a good choice for well-heeled families. Rooms are among the most spacious and handsomely furnished in town—stately, modern, and state-of-the-art. All units have well-maintained marble bathrooms with upscale amenities. Dine in the highly recommended upscale Charleston Grill (see "Where to Dine," below), then swim off the calories in the hotel's heated indoor pool.

205 Meeting St., Charleston, SC 29401. **©** **800/611-5545** or 843/722-4900. Fax 843/722-0728. www. charlestonplacehotel.com. 440 units. $259–$669 double; $700–$1,995 suite. Children 15 and under stay free in parent's room. Seasonal packages available. AE, DC, DISC, MC, V. Parking $12. Pet fee $75. **Amenities:** 2 restaurants; indoor pool; rooftop tennis court; fitness center; spa.

1837 Bed & Breakfast   Built in 1837 by a cotton planter, this place, which is best for couples, was restored and decorated by two artists. It's only a single room wide—which makes for some interesting room arrangements. Our favorite is no. 2 in the Carriage House, which has authentic designs, exposed brick walls, and a beamed ceiling. All the individually furnished rooms have separate entrances and canopied poster "rice beds." On one of the verandas (the piazza), you can sit under whirling ceiling fans and enjoy your breakfast or afternoon tea.

126 Wentworth St., Charleston, SC 29401. **©** **877/723-1837** or 843/723-7166. Fax 843/853-2186. www.1837bb.com. 9 units. $89–$205 double. Rates include full breakfast and afternoon tea. AE, DISC, MC, V. Free off-street parking. No children age 6 and under. **Amenities:** Smoking not permitted. *In room:* Fridge, no phone.

Francis Marion Hotel   A $14-million award-winning restoration has returned this historic hotel to its original 1920s elegance. Although the 12-story structure breaks from the standard Charleston decorative motif and has rooms furnished in traditional European style, it is not devoid of Charleston charm. Guest rooms feature a king-size, queen-size, or double bed, and the renovated bathrooms contain tub/shower combinations with brass fixtures. The hotel's restaurant, **Swamp Fox Restaurant & Bar,** serves breakfast, lunch, and dinner, and features classic Southern cuisine.

387 King St., Charleston, SC 29403. **©** **877/756-2121** or 843/722-0600. Fax 843/853-2186. www.francis marioncharleston.com. 226 units. $179–$269 standard double; $219–$309 deluxe double; $289–$359 suite. Children 11 and under stay free in parent's room. AE, DC, DISC, MC, V. Parking $10–$15. **Amenities:** Restaurant; spa.

Market Pavilion Hotel   In the Market District, this is Charleston's latest deluxe hotel. Its owners claim, with some degree of accuracy, that they are redefining the art of Southern hospitality. You don't even have to leave the premises at night, as the **Pavilion Bar** atop the hotel is a popular nightspot, offering a topiary-framed skyline view. The midsize-to-spacious bedrooms are beautifully furnished with marble-clad bathrooms (with bathrobes and Hermès toiletries), mahogany furniture, and such luxe touches as Frette linens and cashmere blankets on the poster beds—most often occupied by couples seeking a romantic getaway. Some rooms have balconies and/or Jacuzzi tubs.

225 E. Bay St., Charleston, SC 29401. **©** **877/440-2250** or 843/723-0500. www.marketpavilion.com. 66 units. $209–$239 double; from $450 suite. Rates include breakfast. AE, DISC, MC, V. Valet parking $20. **Amenities:** Restaurant; pool. *In room:* Kitchenette in suite.

Planters Inn   This distinguished brick-sided inn stands next to the City Market and is a tasteful enclave of Colonial charm best suited to couples. The spacious rooms have an 18th-century decor, and a number of them overlook the hotel's garden courtyard. Some of the rooms have working fireplaces; others have whirlpool tubs. Afternoon tea is served in the lobby, and there's a well-recommended restaurant, the Peninsula Grill (see "Where to Dine," below).

112 N. Market St., Charleston, SC 29401. **©** **800/845-7082** or 843/722-2345. Fax 843/577-2125. www. plantersinn.com. 64 units. $275–$425 double; $595–$825 suite. Children 15 and under stay free in parent's room. AE, DC, DISC, MC, V. Parking $18. Pet fee $75 (under 20 lb.). **Amenities:** Restaurant.

Anson LOW COUNTRY/MODERN AMERICAN   Anson is a hip, stylish place with a dash of Low Country charm, perfect for a romantic evening. The setting is a century-old brick-sided ice warehouse; the owners have added New Orleans–style iron balconies, Corinthian pilasters, and Victorian rococo. A well-trained staff offers sophisticated interpretations of traditional local dishes, including fried cornmeal oysters with potato cakes; and lobster, corn, and black-bean quesadillas. Our favorite is the crispy flounder.

12 Anson St. ✆ **843/577-0551.** www.ansonrestaurant.com. Reservations recommended. Main courses $19–$36. AE, DC, DISC, MC, V. Sun–Thurs 5–10pm; Fri–Sat 5–11pm.

A. W. Shucks SEAFOOD   This is a hearty oyster bar where thousands of crustaceans have been cracked open over the years. The menu highlights oysters and clams on the half-shell, tasty seafood chowders, deviled crab, shrimp Creole, and a selection of international beers. Nobody cares how you dress—just dig in.

70 State St. ✆ **843/723-1151.** www.a-w-shucks.com. Reservations not necessary. Main courses $14–$19. AE, DC, DISC, MC, V. Sun–Thurs 11am–10pm; Fri–Sat 11am–11pm.

Charleston Grill ⓑ**Best** LOW COUNTRY/FRENCH   You'll be surprised how well French and Low Country cuisine are wed at this pocket of posh in the city's best hotel, a perfect place for a romantic evening. The decor makes no concessions to Southern folksiness, with its marble floors, mahogany seating, and stained glass evoking the Gilded Age. In this old-world atmosphere, you dine on Charleston's most sophisticated cuisine, touted by everyone from the *New York Times* to *Wine Spectator.* Live jazz and Charleston's best cocktails help make this an enduring favorite.

In the Charleston Place Hotel, 224 King St. ✆ **843/577-4522.** www.charlestongrill.com. Reservations recommended. Main courses $27–$48. AE, DC, DISC, MC, V. Sun–Thurs 6–10pm; Fri–Sat 6–11pm.

Cypress LOW COUNTRY   Perhaps Charleston's trendiest dining spot, this place was hailed by local food critics for raising the bar for other eateries. One of South Carolina's best restaurants, it has also won the acclaim of *Wine Spectator* for its *carte.* Ideal for a romantic night out, Cypress offers a fresh modern take on classic Low Country cooking. From Carolina waters to its rich farmlands, the chefs pick the best products to turn into their distinctive, marvelous cuisine. A wood-burning grill is a feature in the dining room. What they do here with fresh oysters is reason enough to visit.

167 E. Bay St. ✆ **843/727-0111.** www.magnolias-blossom-cypress.com. Reservations required. Main courses $25–$32. AE, MC, V. Sun–Tues 5:30–10pm; Fri–Sat 5:30–11pm.

82 Queen LOW COUNTRY   Three 18th- and 19th-century houses are clustered around an ancient magnolia tree, with outdoor tables arranged in its shade. This is classic Charleston dining. Menu items filled with flavor and flair include an award-winning version of she-crab soup laced with sherry, a down-home barbecued shrimp-and-grits, and melt-in-the-mouth crab cakes. As one diner said, "We can't wait to tell the folks up North."

82 Queen St. ✆ **843/723-7591.** www.82queen.com. Reservations recommended for dinner. Main courses $19–$28. AE, DC, DISC, MC, V. Daily 11:30am–2:30pm and 5:30–10pm.

Hank's ⓚ**Kids** SEAFOOD/LOW COUNTRY   If a movie producer were seeking a setting for a 1940s Charleston fish house, Hank's would be at the top of the list. In its old-fashioned saloon-style bar, crowds of locals and visitors mingle happily. Near the City

Market, this family favorite occupies a 19th-century warehouse, with pine paneling and leather booths. Sometimes there's a big line waiting to get in to sample the chef's specialties, such as Charleston oyster stew, Hank's crab cakes, or an assortment from the raw bar, the town's best.

10 Hayne St. ✆ **843/723-3474.** www.hanksseafoodrestaurant.com. Reservations recommended. Main courses $18–$29. AE, DC, DISC, MC, V. Sun–Thurs 5–10:30pm; Fri–Sat 5–11:30pm.

Hominy Grill (Kids) LOW COUNTRY   This family favorite features beautifully prepared dishes, served in a friendly environment inside an 1897 historic building. A devoted local following comes here to feast on barbecued chicken sandwiches, shrimp and grits, and—a brunch favorite—smothered or poached eggs on homemade biscuits with mushroom gravy. The catfish stew with corn bread at lunch is a temptation on a cold and rainy day, and the banana bread is worth writing home about. There's also outdoor patio seating.

207 Rutledge Ave. ✆ **843/937-0930.** www.hominygrill.com. Reservations accepted for dinner only. Main courses $6.50–$14; brunch $4.50–$11. AE, MC, V. Mon–Fri 7:30am–8:30pm; Sat–Sun 9am–3pm (brunch).

Hyman's Seafood Company Restaurant (Value) (Kids) SEAFOOD   Hyman's was established a century ago and continues to be one of Charleston's all-time family favorites. It sprawls over most of a city block in the heart of Charleston's business district. Inside are at least six dining rooms and a take-away deli loaded with salmon, lox, and smoked herring. One sit-down section is devoted to deli-style sandwiches, chicken soup, and salads; another to a delectably messy choice of fish, shellfish, lobsters, and oysters.

215 Meeting St. ✆ **843/723-6000.** www.hymanseafood.com. Reservations not accepted. Main courses $7.95–$21. AE, DC, DISC, MC, V. Daily 11am–11pm.

McCrady's AMERICAN/FRENCH   In the historic district, Charleston's oldest eating establishment is where George Washington dined back in 1791. It is one of the finest kitchens in the Low Country. Entered from a mysterious-looking "Jack the Ripper alley," the restaurant—housed in the city's oldest tavern, built in 1778—looks like an elegant wine cellar with rough brick walls, exposed beams, and wide plank floors. Cooking times are unerringly accurate, and a certain charm and fragrance is given to every dish on the seasonally changing menu.

2 Unity Alley. ✆ **843/577-0025.** www.mccradysrestaurant.com. Reservations required. Main courses $25–$34. AE, MC, V. Daily 5:30–10pm.

Peninsula Grill LOW COUNTRY/INTERNATIONAL   The Peninsula Grill has caused quite a stir, though it's quaint and quiet, full of 19th-century charm. The multi-award-winner (*Food & Wine* has consistently included it among its top-50 hotel restaurants in America) is a good place for a special evening out. The menu changes frequently. Start with the James Island clams with wild mushroom bruschetta, and follow with the duo of Low Country quail and shrimp with crab. Finish up with the exceptional coconut cake. The kitchen does a marvelous job of bringing new cuisine to an old city.

In the Planters Inn, 112 N. Market St. ✆ **843/723-0700.** www.peninsulagrill.com. Reservations required. Main courses $23–$35. AE, DC, DISC, MC, V. Sun–Thurs 5:30–10pm; Fri–Sat 5:30–11pm.

S.N.O.B. (Slightly North of Broad) SOUTHERN   There's an exposed kitchen, a high ceiling crisscrossed with ventilation ducts, and a smattering of wrought iron in this snazzy rehabbed warehouse. The place was one of the first in town to put a sophisticated modern spin on traditional Southern dishes. Main courses can be ordered in medium and large sizes. Try the grilled barbecue tuna or the maverick grits. For dessert, make it the chocolate pecan torte, the best in town. Wine is available by the glass or bottle.

192 E. Bay St. (© 843/723-3424. www.slightlynorthofbroad.net. Reservations recommended. Main courses $9.95–$34. AE, DC, DISC, MC, V. Mon–Fri 11:30am–3pm; Sun–Thurs 5:30–10pm; Fri–Sat 5:30–11pm.

CHARLESTON AFTER DARK

THE PERFORMING ARTS   Charleston's major cultural venue is the **Dock Street Theatre,** 135 Church St. (© 843/577-7183; www.charlestonstage.com), a 463-seat theater that hosts various companies throughout the year, especially during the annual Spoleto Festival USA in May and June. The **Robert Ivey Ballet,** 1910 Savannah Hwy. (© 843/556-1343), offers both classical and contemporary dance, as well as children's ballet programs. The **Charleston Ballet Theatre,** 477 King St. (© 843/723-7334; www.charlestonballet.org), is one of the South's best professional ballet companies. The **Charleston Symphony Orchestra,** 160 E. Bay St. (© 843/723-7528; www.charlestonsymphony.com), performs throughout the state, but its main venues are the Gaillard Auditorium, Sottile Theater, and North Charleston Performing Arts Center. The season runs from September to May.

THE CLUB & MUSIC SCENE   **Henry's,** 54 N. Market St. (© 843/723-4363), also presents bands playing a wide range of music from Sunday to Thursday. There also is music upstairs on Friday and Saturday starting at 10pm. In a restored warehouse in the City Market area, **Tommy Condon's Irish Pub,** 160 Church St. (© 843/577-3818; www.tommycondons.com), features live Irish entertainment Wednesday through Sunday evenings. If your musical tastes run from the Delta blues to rock to reggae, head for **Cumberland's,** 301 King St. (© 843/577-9469), where people of all ages lift a glass together; music is the common bond. The **Music Farm,** 32 Ann St. (© 843/722-8904; www.musicfarm.com), covers nearly every taste in music, from country to rock, with a range of live acts.

THE BAR SCENE   Our favorite watering hole is the elegant and comfortable **First Shot Bar,** in the Mills House Hotel, 115 Meeting St. (© 843/577-2400); if you get hungry, the kitchen will whip you up some shrimp and grits. The **Griffon,** 18 Vendue Range (© 843/723-1700), is a popular place to share a pint. **Vickery's Bar & Grill,** 15 Beaufain (© 843/577-5300; www.vickerysbarandgrill.com), is one of the most frequented gathering places in Charleston for the younger crowd.

9 MYRTLE BEACH & THE GRAND STRAND

One of the most popular destinations along the East Coast, the Grand Strand area stretches south from the South Carolina state line at Little River to Georgetown. It's 98 miles north of Charleston, but a world away in ambience. Development, mostly in the form of theme parks, kiddie attractions, minigolf courses, and condos, has proceeded at a runaway pace.

The Grand Strand hosts more than twice as many visitors each year as Hawaii, mostly families and young singles from the Carolinas, who come year after year to enjoy the beach-party scene. It's become a rival to Branson and Nashville, with more than a dozen

ESSENTIALS

GETTING THERE   The closest airport is **Myrtle Beach International Airport**
(© 843/448-1589; www.myrtlebeachairport.com). If you're driving, major routes into
Myrtle Beach are **U.S. 17** from the north (Wilmington) and south (Charleston), and
U.S. 501 from the west (I-95).

VISITOR INFORMATION   The **Myrtle Beach Area Chamber of Commerce** is at
1200 N. Oak St., Myrtle Beach, SC 29578 (© **800/356-3016,** or 843/626-7444 to
order literature only; www.visitmyrtlebeach.com), open Monday to Friday 8:30am to
5pm, Saturday and Sunday 9am to 2pm. Ask for their free *Stay & Play* guide (or order it
in advance via the website).

THE BEACHES, THE LINKS & BEYOND

When you're ready to hit the beach, the main action is at Ocean Boulevard and Ninth
Avenue North. For more seclusion, head north of 79th Avenue for several miles. The
sands here are mostly hard packed and the color of brown sugar. The beach has lifeguards
and plenty of fast-food joints but, amazingly, no public toilets. However, South Carolina
law obligates hotels to allow beach buffs to use their facilities.

At the southern tier of the beach, **Myrtle Beach State Park** (© 843/238-5325; www.
southcarolinaparks.com) offers 312 acres of pine woods and a sandy beach. Admission to
the park is $4 adults, $2.50 seniors, $1.50 children 6 to 15. There are toilets, along with
pavilions, picnic tables, and a nature center. It's possible to fish from the pier for $4.50
adults, $2.92 seniors, 11 and under free. The park is full of nature trails and offers 350
campsites that rent quickly at $25 per site, so it's a good idea to book ahead.

Serious golfers will find plenty of places to play; the area has 120 golf courses. Many
golf packages are available, including accommodations and greens fees; call **Golf Holiday**
(© 800/845-4653; www.golfholiday.com). **Legends,** U.S. 501, Myrtle Beach (© **800/
552-2660** or 843/236-9318), designed by Pete Dye and Tom Doak, is a 54-hole, par-72
course, charging greens fees of $124. We also like **Arcadian Shores,** 701 Hilton Rd.,
Arcadian Shores (© **866/326-5275** or 843/449-5217), an 18-hole, par-72 course created by Rees Jones, charging greens fees ranging from $83 to $89. **Azalea Sands,** 2100
U.S. 17, in North Myrtle Beach (© **800/253-2312** or 843/272-6191), is an 18-hole
course with white sand traps and blue lakes; its greens fees range from $48 to $58.
Finally, **Beachwood,** 1520 U.S. 17, Crescent Section, North Myrtle Beach (© **800/526-
4889** or 843/272-6168), hosts the annual Dupont World Amateur Handicap Championships. At other times, it is open to the general public, charging greens fees of $55
to $71.

Anglers can go out after mackerel, amberjack, barracuda, sea bass, grouper, and red
snapper. You'll get great fishing aboard any boat of **Captain Dick's,** Business Hwy. 17,
at Myrtle Beach South Strand and Murrells Inlet (© **866/557-3474** or 843/651-3676;
www.captdicks.com), which provides half-day party boat outings that cost $44 for adults,
$26 for kids 12 and under. There are also sailings that are strictly for sightseeing, offering
stunning views of the Grand Strand.

You can spend a day at the **Myrtle Waves Water Park,** 10th Avenue at U.S. 17N
Bypass (© **843/913-9260;** www.myrtlewaves.com), enjoying the water slides, wave
pool, children's play pool, video arcade, and tanning deck. Its Turbo-Twisters is the

world's tallest water ride. Adults pay $28 and children ages 3 to 8 (and seniors 55 and older) are charged $20. The park is open daily from mid-May to mid-September, 10am to 6pm.

WHERE TO STAY

In addition to the listings below, other solid, moderately priced and affordable choices include the **Holiday Inn Oceanfront,** 415 S. Ocean Blvd. (© **800/211-7143** or 843/448-4481; www.hionthebeach.com); the **Landmark Resort,** 1501 S. Ocean Blvd. (© **843/448-9441;** www.landmarkresort.com); the **Coral Beach Hotel,** 1105 S. Ocean Blvd. (© **800/843-2684** or 843/448-8421; www.thecoralbeach.com); and **St. John's Inn,** 6803 N. Ocean Blvd. (© **800/845-0624** or 843/449-5251; www.stjohnsinn.com).

The Breakers Resort (Kids) This longtime family favorite is better than ever. With one of the best north beachfront locations, it occupies both a multistory complex and a 19-floor North Tower 7 blocks away. The accommodations range from tastefully furnished rooms to efficiencies with kitchenettes, and even one- to three-bedroom suites. Many rooms have balconies and refrigerators; some have microwaves. A rooftop lounge features nightly entertainment.

2006 N. Ocean Blvd., Myrtle Beach, SC 29578. © **800/952-4507** or 843/626-5000. Fax 843/626-5001. www.breakers.com. 612 units. $69–$219 double; $119–$349 suite. 7-night minimum in high season. Children 16 and under stay free in parent's room. Rates include breakfast. AE, DC, DISC, MC, V. Free parking. **Amenities:** Restaurant; 10 pools; fitness center. *In room:* Kitchenette in suite.

Kingston Plantation & The Embassy Suites at Kingston Plantation (Best

(Kids) This is the top choice along the strip, a 20-story main building along with two other high-rises opening onto its own 145 acres of oceanfront property. Suites with beach views have living/dining areas, kitchens, balconies, and tasteful furnishings. In addition, the hotel has two 18-story oceanfront condos and town-house villas, all with fully equipped kitchens, beautiful bathrooms, living rooms, and balconies or decks; they're great for families.

9800 Lake Dr., Myrtle Beach, SC 29572. © **800/876-0010** or 843/449-0006. Fax 843/497-1110. www. kingstonplantation.com. 255 suites, 595 condos and villas. $169–$394 suite; $154–$729 condo or villa. 5-night minimum June–Sept. Children 12 and under stay free in parent's room. AE, DC, DISC, MC, V. Free parking. **Amenities:** 2 restaurants; 12 pools (4 indoor); 4 tennis courts; fitness center; spa. *In room:* Kitchen.

Ocean Creek Resort One of the finest resorts along the beach, this first-class choice features studios and condos of varying sizes in half a dozen different complexes spread out on almost 57 acres. Units vary in size and are suitable for families or couples; all contain kitchenettes and well-kept bathrooms with tub/showers. The Beach Club on the ocean operates in summer.

10600 N. Kings Hwy., Myrtle Beach, SC 29572. © **877/844-3800** or 843/272-7724. Fax 843/272-9627. www.oceancreek.com. 750 units. $60–$393 studio or condo. Resort fee $7 per night. Children 17 and under stay free in parent's room. AE, DC, DISC, MC, V. Free parking. **Amenities:** Restaurant; 7 pools (1 indoor); 6 tennis courts; fitness center. *In room:* Kitchenette.

Ocean Reef Resort North of the bustling beach center, this 16-floor oceanfront resort is well maintained and better than most other moderately priced choices. All the rooms and efficiencies are well kept and tropically inspired. Most have two double beds, balconies, and kitchenettes, attracting both the family trade and couples.

7100 N. Ocean Blvd. (at 71st Ave. N.), Myrtle Beach, SC 29577. © **888/322-6411** or 843/449-4441. Fax 843/497-3041. www.oceanreefmyrtlebeach.com. 291 units. $140–$165 double; $150–$400 suite.

WHERE TO DINE

Murrells Inlet bills itself "The Seafood Capital of South Carolina." Just take U.S. 17 (Business) south 11 miles from Myrtle Beach, and prepare to dig in. Our favorite choices for a feast are the **Fisherman's Market** (☎ 843/651-6440) and **Drunken Jacks** (☎ 843/651-2044). Both of them are on U.S. 17 (Business), right along the water.

NASCAR Cafe AMERICAN   The most intriguing of Myrtle Beach's many theme restaurants, this one is set within a building that vaguely evokes a temple to some exotic high-tech god, and the dining room is prefaced with one of the most complete collections of NASCAR memorabilia in the world. The heavily American menu is relentlessly geared to the kind of fare you might expect at Indy on a superheated race day. Your waiter (who will identify him- or herself as a member of your "pit crew") will bring you heaping portions.

1808 21st Ave. N. ☎ 843/946-7223. www.nascarcafe.com. Reservations not accepted. Sandwiches and platters $9–$23. AE, DC, DISC, MC, V. Daily 11am–10pm (Fri–Sat until 11pm).

Sea Captain's House AMERICAN   In a 1930s beachfront home 1¹⁄₂ miles north of the center, this family-run restaurant is loved by locals. A glassed-in patio affords an ocean view. She-crab soup is a specialty. The seafood platter includes five different types of seafood served with slaw, potatoes, and hush puppies; and there's a selection of succulent charcoal-broiled steaks, flavorful pork chops, and Mama's Southern fried chicken.

3002 N. Ocean Blvd. ☎ 843/448-8082. www.seacaptains.com. Reservations not accepted. Main courses $7.95–$24. AE, DISC, MC, V. Daily 6–10:30am, 11:30am–2:30pm, and 5–10pm.

Thoroughbreds (Best) SEAFOOD/CONTINENTAL   This, one of the few places along the Grand Strand that truly specializes in fine dining, has been a hit ever since it opened in 1988. Guests are seated in one of four handsomely appointed rooms (mahogany, leather, fireplaces, and so on); it also has a garden terrace and a piano bar. The staff is among the best trained in the area, but the food is what keeps people coming back for more. The steaks are among the juiciest and most tender along the Strand. The wine list is long and varied.

9706 N. Kings Hwy. ☎ 843/497-2636. Reservations recommended. www.thoroughbredsrestaurant. com. Main courses $19–$40. AE, DC, DISC, MC, V. Sun–Wed 5–10:30pm; Thurs–Sat 5–11pm.

THE GRAND STRAND AFTER DARK

Tickets for most of the following variety shows and revues begin at $30 for adults. You can catch Alabama and other top country stars, or a variety show, at the **Alabama Theatre,** Barefoot Landing, North Myrtle Beach (☎ 800/342-2262 or 843/272-1111; www. alabama-theatre.com), which is part of a waterside shopping complex. The **Carolina Opry,** North Kings Highway at U.S. 17 (☎ 800/843-6779 or 843/913-4000; www. carolinaopry.com), might host country, bluegrass, big band, or patriotic music, plus comedy. The Christmas show is so popular that it's often sold out by June. The **Dixie Stampede Dinner and Show,** North Kings Highway at U.S. 17 (☎ 800/433-4401 or 843/497-9700; www.dixiestampede.com), owned by Dolly Parton's Dollywood Productions, is one of the most entertaining shows at the beach. Catch it if you have to skip the rest. **Legends in Concert,** 301 U.S. 17, Surfside Beach (☎ 800/960-SHOW [960-2469] or 843/238-7827; www.legendsinconcertsc.com), features an array of celebrity impersonators. The **Palace Theatre at Myrtle Beach,** 1420 Celebrity Circle (© **800/905-4228** or 843/448-9224; www.palacetheatremyrtlebeach.com), features "Le Grande Cirque" and a Dean Martin Tribute show.

Medieval Times & Dinner Complex, 2904 Fantasy Way (© **888/WE-JOUST** [935-6878] or 843/236-8080; www.medievaltimes.com), features falconry, sorcery, swordplay, and jousting, plus a four-course banquet (no utensils, of course). Catch this production only if you have nothing else to do.

Barefoot Landing, Hwy. 17 South (© **843/272-8349;** www.barefootlanding.com), offers 13 restaurants, the Alabama Theater, an endlessly popular nightlife venue—the House of Blues—and a reptilian theme park known as Alligator Adventure. Everything about this place, frankly, is well orchestrated except for parking, which can be very hard to come by. **Broadway at the Beach,** between 22nd and 29th boulevards (© **843/444-3200;** www.broadwayatthebeach.com), includes the Hard Rock Cafe, Ripley's Aquarium, and a collection of late-night bars and dance clubs that include everything from country-western line dancing to Latino salsa. The '50s live on at **Studebaker's,** 21st Avenue North and Hwy. 17 (© **843/448-9747;** www.studebakersclub.com), site of the National Shag Dance Championship held annually in March.

10 WILMINGTON & THE OUTER BANKS

WILMINGTON & CAPE FEAR

As the chief port of North Carolina, Wilmington is a major retail, trade, and manufacturing center, but tourism is looming larger than ever in its economy. Boasting one of the largest districts listed in the National Register of Historic Places, Wilmington is known for its preservation efforts, reflected in the restored grandeur of its antebellum, Victorian, Georgian, and Italianate homes.

Essentials

GETTING THERE **Wilmington International Airport,** 1740 Airport Blvd. (© **910/341-4333;** www.flyilm.com), is half a mile from the center of town. Taxis meet arriving planes. By car, Wilmington is reached via **I-40** from the north (Raleigh) and **U.S. 17** from the south (Charleston, South Carolina). A cab into town costs $10 to $14, but to get around and explore this part of the state, a car is recommended. Several major rental-car agencies have desks at the airport.

VISITOR INFORMATION The **Cape Fear Coast Convention and Visitors Bureau,** 24 N. 3rd St., Wilmington, NC 28401 (© **877/406-2356** or 910/341-4030; www.cape-fear.nc.us), is inside the Hanover County Courthouse and is open Monday through Friday from 8:30am to 5pm, Saturday from 9am to 4pm, and Sunday from 1 to 4pm. Staffers provide free information, maps, and brochures on the area.

What to See & Do

To get an overview of the historic Wilmington waterfront, hop aboard the *Henrietta III* (© **910/343-1611;** www.cfrboats.com), which departs from the foot of Market Street for a 5-mile loop of the Cape Fear River. The 45-minute narrated cruise (which runs Memorial Day to Labor Day) stops at the dock for passengers who want to tour the battleship USS *North Carolina* (see below). Tours cost $12 adults, $10 seniors, $6 kids ages 2 to 11.

The **Cotton Exchange,** in the 300 block of North Front Street (© **910/343-9896;**
www.shopcottonexchange.com), an in-town shopping center, is in the old exchange
building with 2-foot-thick brick walls and hurricane rods. The small shops and restaurants are a delight, and the wrought-iron lanterns and benches add to the setting's charm.
It's right on the riverfront, and there's an ample parking deck next door.

In Historic Wilmington, the old residential area bounded roughly by Nun, Princess,
Front, and 4th streets, the **Burgwin-Wright House,** 224 Market St. (© **910/762-0570;**
www.burgwinwrighthouse.com), was constructed in 1771 and used by British General
Cornwallis as his headquarters in 1781. You can tour the interior Tuesday to Saturday
10am to 4pm; $10 adults, $4 ages 5 to 12, free for 4 and under.

Airlie Gardens, Arlie Road off U.S. 76 (© **910/798-7700;** www.airliegardens.com),
grace the grounds of what was once the plantation home of a wealthy rice planter. These
huge lawns, serene lakes, and wooded gardens hold just about every kind of azalea in
existence. Admission is $5 adults, $3 children 6 to 12, free for 5 and under. Open daily
9am to 5pm.

The **USS *North Carolina* Battleship Memorial,** Eagle Island (© **910/251-5797;**
www.battleshipnc.com), is a memorial to the state's World War II dead. You can tour
most of the ship and an exhibit focusing on recollections of the battleship's former crew.
Tours are $12 adults, $10 seniors, $6 children 6 to 11; open Memorial Day through
Labor Day daily from 8am to 8pm, off season 8am to 5pm.

Fort Fisher State Historic Site, on U.S. 421, Kure Beach (© **910/458-5538;** www.
ncparks.gov/Visit/parks/fofi/main.php), one of the Confederacy's largest and most technically advanced forts, was the last stronghold of the Confederate Army. After withstanding two of the heaviest naval bombardments of the Civil War, the fort finally fell to
Union forces in what was the largest land-sea battle in U.S. history until World War II.
Costumed tour guides welcome visitors, and living-history events are held in summer. It's
open April to September Monday to Saturday 9am to 5pm and Sunday from 1 to 5pm,
October to March Tuesday to Saturday 10am to 4pm. Free admission.

Beaches & Outdoor Activities

Everyone flocks to **Wrightsville Beach,** 6 miles east of Wilmington on U.S. 74/76. The
island is separated from the mainland by a small drawbridge. This wide beach stretches
for a mile, with beige sands set against a backdrop of sea oats. There's also **Carolina
Beach State Park,** sprawling across 1,770 acres 10 miles north of Wilmington off U.S.
421. Flanked on one bank by the Cape Fear River and on the other by the Intracoastal
Waterway, it lies at the northern edge of aptly named Pleasure Island. The beach here,
however, is not for swimming; it's really for sunbathing and beachcombing. Facilities
include toilets, a marina, a picnic area, hiking trails, and a family campground.

At the southern tip of Pleasure Island is the small, family-friendly community of **Kure
Beach.** The white-sand beaches are generally uncrowded, the restaurants are informal,
and the Kure Beach fishing pier is great for anglers. You can wander through the remains
of Fort Fisher (see above).

The **Belvedere Plantation Golf & Country Club,** 2368 Country Club Dr., 14 miles
from Wilmington in Hampstead (© **910/270-2703;** www.thegolfcourses.net), is one of
the best courses, offering a par-71, 6,401-yard, 18-hole course. It charges greens fees of
$25 to $35, depending on the season and the use of carts. Reservations are requested. For
more information on golf in the area, contact the CVB or head online to **www.golf
carolina.com.**

THE SOUTHEAST

4

WILMINGTON & THE OUTER BANKS

The **Cape Fear Coast CVB** (see above) will send you its *Accommodations Guide* and can help find you an apartment or cottage to rent for a week or more if you contact them well in advance.

The smoke-free all-suite **Wilmingtonian,** 101 S. 2nd St. (© **800/525-0909** or 910/343-1800; www.thewilmingtonian.com), is Wilmington's premier inn. Some suites contain kitchenettes and washer/dryers. The "special occasion" suite—ideal for a honeymoon—has a fireplace, whirlpool tub, CD player, and VCR. There's an intimate dining room and a less formal bar and grill. Rates run $109 to $165 double.

In many ways, the **Graystone Inn,** 100 S. 3rd St. (© **888/763-4773** or 910/763-2000; www.graystoneinn.com), is the grandest of Wilmington's B&Bs. A neoclassical stone mansion from 1905, it offers 12- to 14-foot ceilings, Victorian period furnishings, and a grand staircase of hand-carved red oak. No children 11 and under are allowed. Rooms run $169 to $379 double.

Other choices include the moderately priced **Coastline Inn,** 503 Nutt St. (© **800/617-7732** or 910/763-2800; www.coastlineinn.com), and **C. W. Worth House Bed & Breakfast,** a Queen Anne confection at 412 S. 3rd St. (© **800/340-8559** or 910/762-8562; www.worthhouse.com). Nearby Wrightsville Beach has the expensive 150-room **Blockade Runner Resort Hotel & Conference Center,** 275 Waynick Blvd. (© **800/541-1161** or 910/256-2251; www.blockade-runner.com), a full-service resort with ocean views and a fine restaurant.

Where to Dine

The tiny town of **Calabash,** 35 miles south of Wilmington on U.S. 17, is renowned for its seafood restaurants—about 20 of them, vying with one another to serve the biggest platter of seafood at the lowest price. You can't miss, no matter which one you choose.

Moderately priced **Café Phoenix,** 9 S. Front St. (© **910/343-1395**), a block from the water in the center of town, is easily the best bistro in Wilmington. It has a light, open, and airy decor. Lunch choices include homemade soups, fresh salads, pasta, and sandwiches. Dinner becomes more elaborate, including spinach with prosciutto or chicken piccata. Many Wilmington artists dine here, and the place has a sizable gay following.

Elijah's, 2 Ann St., Chandler's Wharf (© **910/343-1448;** www.elijahs.com), is installed in a renovated maritime museum offering outdoor dining and a view of the river. Lunches tend to emphasize sandwiches and simple platters that always include a fine version of crab cakes. Dinners are more elaborate, with classic and well-prepared dishes that include soft-shell crabs. Sunday brunch here is a tradition in Wilmington. A children's menu is featured.

On the Cape Fear River in the historic and restored Craig House, the **Pilot House,** 2 Ann St., Chandler's Wharf (© **910/343-0200;** www.pilothouserest.com), is especially known for its Low Country specialties such as shrimp and grits or crunchy catfish. There are also prime cuts of beef. A children's menu is offered.

BEAUFORT

North Carolina's third-oldest town, Beaufort (pronounced *Bo*-fort) dates from 1713. Along its narrow streets are two 200-year-old houses and some hundred houses more than a century old. Access is on U.S. 70 just over the Grayden Paul Bridge from Morehead City. From New Bern, take U.S. 70 east. The **Beaufort Historical Association,** 138 Turner St. (© **252/728-5225;** www.historicbeaufort.com), is open Monday through Saturday from 9:30am to 5pm.

The **Beaufort Historic Site** in the 100 block of Turner Street includes the 1767 Joseph Bell House, the 1825 Josiah Bell House, the 1796 Carteret County Courthouse, the 1829 county jail, the 1859 apothecary shop and doctor's office, and the 1778 Samuel Leffers House, home of the town's first schoolmaster. Tours are given Monday through Saturday at 10am, 11:30am, 1pm, and 3pm. Adults pay $8 for the tour, and children age 6 and over are charged $4.

Divers are attracted to this area because of the many wrecks off the coast. If you want to get into this action, contact **Discovery Diving Co.,** 414 Orange St. (© **800/726-0321** or 252/728-2265; www.discoverydiving.com), whose staff knows the local waters best.

Our favorite local inns are the **Beaufort Inn,** 101 Ann St. (© **252/728-2600;** www.beaufort-inn.com); the **Cedars By the Sea,** 305 Front St. (© **252/728-7036;** www.cedarsinn.com); the **Old Seaport Inn,** 217 Turner St. (© **800/349-5823** or 252/728-4300; www.oldseaportinn.com); and the **Pecan Tree Inn Bed & Breakfast,** 116 Queen St. (© **800/728-7871** or 252/728-6733; www.pecantree.com).

CAPE HATTERAS NATIONAL SEASHORE

The Cape Hatteras National Seashore stretches 70 miles down the Outer Banks barrier islands. The drive along N.C. 12 (about 4½ hr.) takes you through a wildlife refuge and pleasant villages, past sandy beaches, and on to Buxton and the **Cape Hatteras Lighthouse** (www.nps.gov/caha), the tallest on the coast and a symbol of North Carolina. The light has stood here since 1870 as a beacon for ships passing through these treacherous waters that have claimed more than 1,500 victims of foul weather, strong rip currents, and shifting shoals. Preservation efforts have attempted to save the lighthouse, which is constantly battered by erosion.

From the little village of **Hatteras,** with its colorful fishing fleet and popular fishing pier, a car ferry crosses to **Ocracoke Island,** where more than 5,000 acres, including 16 miles of beach, are preserved by the National Park Service. **Pea Island Wildlife Refuge** (© **252/473-1131;** www.fws.gov/peaisland), on Hatteras Island (the northern part, south of Bonner Bridge), attracts birders from all over the country.

The National Seashore is best explored on an all-day trip, or on several half-day trips, from a Nags Head base (see "Nags Head & the Outer Banks," below, for lodging recommendations). Give yourself plenty of time for swimming, fishing, or just walking along the sand.

All along **N.C. 12,** you'll see places to pull off and park to reach the beaches, which are hidden from view by huge sand dunes. *Note: Don't* try to park anywhere else—the sand is soft and it's easy to get stuck. Keep in mind that tides and currents along the Outer Banks are *very* strong, and ocean swimming can be dangerous at times.

NAGS HEAD & THE OUTER BANKS

Nags Head has been one of North Carolina's most popular beach resorts for more than a century. The town itself is a collection of nondescript beach houses and motels, but it has one of the finest beaches in the state. Toilets, showers, bathhouses, and picnic shelters line some 70 miles of beaches here. Ferocious tides, strong currents, and fickle, constantly changing winds alter the beach scene from day to day on the Outer Banks. These very conditions also make ocean swimming hazardous at certain periods. If you're with children, stick to the beaches along the northern banks that have lifeguard protection; they include Kitty Hawk, Kill Devil Hills, and Nags Head, all lying along Beach Road paralleling N.C. 12. Signs direct you to the parking lots.

Learning to Fly

At Milepost 8 on U.S. 158 in Kill Devil Hills, you can visit the **Wright Brothers National Memorial** (📞 252/441-7430; www.nps.gov/wrbr) for $4 per person; seniors and children 16 and under are admitted free. Both the hangar and Orville's and Wilbur's living quarters have been restored, and the visitor center holds a replica of that first airplane, as well as exhibits that tell the story of the two brothers who came here on vacation from their Dayton, Ohio, bicycle business to turn their dream into reality. The memorial is open daily from 9am to 5pm. A park ranger gives tours at 11am and 3pm year-round.

From Virginia and points north, you can reach Nags Head via **U.S. 158;** from Raleigh, via **U.S. 64;** from Wilmington, via the Cedar Island ferry. **N.C. 12** runs the length of the Outer Banks, from Ocracoke to Duck. The nearest airport is 80 miles northwest in Norfolk, Virginia.

Contact the **Outer Banks Visitors Bureau,** in Manteo (📞 877/629-4386 or 252/473-2138; www.outerbanks.org), for information about accommodations and outdoor activities. It's open Monday to Friday from 8am to 6pm, Saturday and Sunday from 10am to 4pm.

Jockey's Ridge, north of Nags Head, is the highest sand dune on the East Coast. Its smooth, sandy, 138-foot-high slopes are part of a state park. Also north of Nags Head at **Kill Devil Hills,** the Wright brothers made that historic first air flight back in 1903.

From Whalebone Junction, U.S. 64/264 leads to Roanoke Island and the village of Manteo. Four miles west, you'll reach **Fort Raleigh National Historic Site,** where the old fort has been excavated and reconstructed just as it stood in 1585. The **visitor center** (📞 252/473-5772; www.nps.gov/fora) is a first stop, with a museum and an audiovisual program to acquaint visitors with the park's story. Most people visit Roanoke Island to see a performance of Paul Green's moving drama, *The Lost Colony,* presented from mid-June to late August Monday to Saturday at 8:30pm. It's the country's oldest outdoor drama, running since 1937. All seats are reserved (contact the **Waterside Theater** at 📞 866/468-7630 or 252/473-3414 to charge tickets). The nearby **Elizabethan Gardens** (www.elizabethangardens.org), as well as the Tudor-style auxiliary buildings, remind us that this was the first connection between Elizabethan England and what was to become the United States of America. The gardens charge an admission price of $8 adults, $7 seniors, and $5 for children ages 6 to 17; free for children 5 and under.

One of the top local golf courses is **Nags Head Golf Links,** 5615 S. Seachase Dr., Nags Head (📞 252/441-8073; www.nagsheadgolflinks.com), which boasts an 18-hole, 6,130-yard, par-71 course. Greens fees range from $40 to $130. Reservations are required.

Kitty Hawk Water Sports Center, Bypass Highway, Milepost 16, Nags Head (📞 252/441-2756; www.kittyhawkwatersports.com), offers watersports equipment, including windsurfers and kayaks.

Our favorite accommodations in the area include the **Sanderling Inn Resort and Spa,** 1461 Duck Rd., Duck (📞 877/650-4812 or 252/261-4111; www.thesanderling.com), the premier inn of the Outer Banks, bordering the 3,400-acre Pine Island National Audubon Sanctuary, where wild horses run free. Edenton's top choice is the **Lords**

Proprietors' Inn, 300 N. Broad St. (© 800/348-8933 or 252/482-3641; www.
edentoninn.com). Manteo has the lovely **Tranquil House Inn,** 405 Queen Elizabeth St.
(© 800/458-7069 or 252/473-1404; www.1587.com). In Nags Head, we suggest the
First Colony Inn, 6720 S. Virginia Dare Trail (© 800/368-9390 or 252/441-2343;
www.firstcolonyinn.com), or the **Nags Head Inn,** 4701 S. Virginia Dare Trail
(© 800/327-8881 or 252/441-0454; www.nagsheadinn.com).

11 PINEHURST: WHERE GOLF IS KING

Midland Road (N.C. 2), a highway divided by a stately 6-mile row of pine trees and
bordered by lavish homes and gardens, sets the tone for this golf mecca. About a third of
the area's more than 35 golf courses are accessible via this road. (Also on Midland Rd.
you'll pass a rambling white building, Midland Crafters, a virtual survey of American
crafts.) In addition to golf, this area offers some of America's best tennis facilities and
programs, and it's also known for its equestrian competitions. Most of these events are
free to spectators. *Horse Days,* a monthly publication about events, with calendar listings,
is available locally at information offices.

U.S. 1 runs north and south through Southern Pines; **N.C. 211** runs east and west;
U.S. 15/501 reaches Pinehurst from the north; there's direct area access to I-95, I-85,
and I-40. Raleigh/Durham is the nearest commercial airport. We strongly recommend
that you call ahead to the **Pinehurst Area Convention and Visitors Bureau,** P.O. Box
2270, Southern Pines, NC 28388 (© 800/346-5362 or 910/692-3330; www.home
ofgolf.com), to get information.

The town of Pinehurst has retained its New England village air, with a village green
and shaded residential streets. Moderate temperatures mean color through all seasons—
camellias, azaleas, wisteria, and dogwoods.

With its more than 35 superb championship golf courses, some of which are among
the highest rated in the world, Pinehurst represents golf's grandest era. Legends were
born and nurtured here, and some of the finest golf architects of the 20th century
designed courses in the area, including Donald Ross, Ellis Maples, Robert Trent Jones,
Jack Nicklaus, and Rees Jones.

There are too many courses here to list them all, but our favorites are **Longleaf Golf
and Country Club** (© 800/542-0450 or 910/692-6100; www.longleafgolf.com); the
Legacy Golf Links, U.S. 15/501 South, Aberdeen (© 800/314-7560 or 910/944-8825;
www.legacygolfnc.com), the only public course to receive *Golf Digest*'s four-star rating;
the **Pine Needles Resort,** Southern Pines (© 910/692-7111; www.pineneedles-
midpines.com), a Donald Ross masterpiece built in 1927; and the **Pinehurst Hotel &
Country Club,** Carolina Vista (© 800/ITS-GOLF [487-4653] or 910/235-8507; www.
pinehurst.com), a resort with eight courses that played host to golf's U.S. Open Championship in 1999 and 2005.

Tennis buffs will find nearly 100 public courts in the area (© 910/235-8556 for
locations, hours, and fees), but most resorts have their own courts.

About an hour's drive to the northwest on U.S. 220 is the little town of **Seagrove**
(© 336/873-7887 for information or search www.seagrovepotteryheritage.com), which
has been turning out pottery for more than 200 years. Many of the potters work in or
behind their homes, with only a small sign outside to identify their trade; just stop and
ask—everybody does, so don't be shy. While you're there, inquire about **Jugtown,** a

group of rustic, log-hewn buildings in a grove of pines where potters demonstrate their art Monday to Saturday. The **Museum of North Carolina Traditional Pottery** is at 250 East Ave., just off U.S. 220 and the intersection of N.C. 705 in Seagrove (© **336/873-7887**), or stop in at their visitor center at 120 Main St.

WHERE TO STAY

Pinehurst Hotel and Country Club, Carolina Vista (© **800/ITS-GOLF** [487-4653] or 910/235-8507; www.pinehurst.com), is one of America's premier golf and tennis resorts. Set on 10,000 acres of landscaped grounds, it's a white, four-story clapboard landmark, with porches lined with rocking chairs. Here the art of gracious living is still practiced, and service is superb. The resort's Carolina Dining Room is the finest in the area. The major attractions, of course, are the eight 18-hole golf courses, especially the world-famous No. 2, and the 24 tennis courts. Guests also enjoy trap and skeet fields; croquet and bowling lawns; bicycles; a huge pool and deck area; and 200 acres of fishing, boating, and swimming at Lake Pinehurst. Rates run $156 to $336 double.

Other hotels offer luxury and graciousness at more moderate prices. We like the intimate **Magnolia Inn,** 65 Magnolia Rd. (© **800/526-5562** or 910/295-6900; www.themagnoliainn.com), and the **Pine Crest Inn,** Dogwood Road (© **800/371-2545** or 910/295-6121; www.pinecrestinnpinehurst.com). For the ultimate golfer's haven, check into the **Carolina** hotel, Carolina Vista Drive, in the village of Pinehurst (© **800/ITS-GOLF** [487-4653] or 910/235-8507; www.pinehurst.com), a mecca for golfers with eight 18-hole courses designed by the sport's leading golf architects. In nearby Southern Pines, there's the lovely, old-fashioned, and affordable **Mid Pines Golf Club,** 1010 Midland Rd., Southern Pines (© **910/692-2114;** www.pineneedles-midpines.com), as well as several chain properties.

If there's a hotel in the area that *doesn't* arrange golf times for its guests, we couldn't find it.

12 CHARLOTTE

The second-ranked financial center in the United States (behind New York City) is home to thriving banking, insurance, and transportation industries, and does more than $900 billion worth of business each year. Suburban sprawl continues to grow, with landscaped housing developments, skyscrapers, and enormous strip malls springing up in every direction. This is the New South, built squarely on the foundation of the Old South. Though 4.5 million visitors arrive here annually (and business travelers in droves), there's not much here for the casual tourist, though the city does feature some wonderful spots for those who make the trip.

ESSENTIALS

GETTING THERE   By Plane   Charlotte–Douglas International Airport (© **704/359-4000** or www.charmeck.org) is served by most major U.S. carriers (US Airways has its hub in Charlotte—and the lion's share of flights). Taxis found outside the terminal will get you into town for about $25. If you plan on doing much exploring outside of the city proper, however, we suggest you rent a car from one of the many agencies with desks at the airport.

By Train   Amtrak (© 800/USA-RAIL [872-7245]; www.amtrak.com) provides daily service from Atlanta (trip time: 5¹/₂ hr.) and Washington, D.C. (8 hr.), to its station at 1914 N. Tryon St.

By Car   Major routes into Charlotte are **I-85** from the northeast (Greensboro, North Carolina) and southwest (Atlanta), and **I-77** from the north (Charleston, West Virginia) and south (Columbia, South Carolina).

VISITOR INFORMATION   Contact the **Charlotte Convention & Visitors Bureau,** 500 S. College St., Ste. 300, Charlotte, NC 28202 (© **800/722-1994** or 704/334-2282; www.visitcharlotte.com), open Monday through Friday from 8:30am to 5pm. For walk-in visits to pick up brochures once you're here, stop by **Visit Charlotte,** at 330 S. Tryon St.

GETTING AROUND   Those without rental cars can use the city's visitor-friendly **trolley system** (© **704/336-7433**), which runs across the city for a fare of $1.30. Trolleys operate Monday to Thursday 11am to 8pm, Friday and Saturday 10am to 11pm, and Sunday 11am to 6pm.

SPECIAL EVENTS   In late April, **Springfest** brings the streets alive with music and other entertainment, and street vendors dispense a wide variety of foods. In late October, the **Bank of America 500** (© **704/455-3200**) packs 'em in at the Charlotte Motor Speedway. For 6 full days in mid-September, the **Festival in the Park** in Freedom Park celebrates regional arts and crafts.

WHAT TO SEE & DO

The stately **Mint Museum of Art,** 2730 Randolph Rd. (© **704/337-2000;** www.mint museum.org), displays a fine survey of European and American art, as well as the internationally recognized Delhom Collection of porcelain and pottery. New galleries exhibit studio glass and pottery from North Carolina studios. Admission costs $6 adults, $5 students and seniors, $3 children ages 6 to 17. **Discovery Place,** 301 N. Tryon St. (© **800/935-0553** or 704/372-6261; www.discoveryplace.org), is one of the top hands-on science-and-technology museums in the region and also boasts an OMNIMAX theater. Admission is $10 adults (ages 14–59), $8 seniors and children 2 to 13. OMNIMAX tickets are $8 adults, $7 for seniors and children 2 to 13.

The **Wing Haven Gardens & Bird Sanctuary,** 248 Ridgewood Ave. (© **704/331-0664;** www.winghavengardens.com), is a 3-acre enclosed area in the heart of a residential neighborhood. Some 142 winged species have been sighted in the walled garden. The gardens are at their most splendid in the spring, when birds are returning from their winter migration. Donations are accepted.

Charlotte is ringed by nature preserves and parks, including the nearly 1,000-acre **McDowell Park and Nature Preserve,** about 12 miles south of the center on N.C. 49, 15222 York Rd. (© **704/588-5224**). Even bigger is **Latta Plantation Nature Preserve,** 5226 Sample Rd., Huntersville (© **704/875-2312;** www.lattaplantation.org), 12 miles northeast of the center. It's a favorite resting place for waterfowl. There are also stables where you can rent horses and ride along some 7 miles of trail. A nature center and picnic tables are available. Fishing is permitted, but there is no swimming. Admission to both preserves is free.

WHERE TO STAY & DINE

The modern 700-room **Westin Charlotte,** 601 S. College St. (© **704/375-2600;** www.starwoodhotels.com), offers exceedingly comfortable rooms, excellent service, and a location on the city's new trolley line. Other top hotels include the **Omni Charlotte Hotel,** 132 E. Trade St. (© **704/377-0400;** www.omnihotels.com); the **Hyatt Charlotte,** 5501 Carnegie Blvd., opposite South Park Mall (© **888/492-8847** or 704/554-1234; www.hyatt.com); the luxurious **Park Hotel,** 2200 Rexford Rd. (© **800/228-9290** or 704/364-8220; www.marriott.com); and the more moderately priced **Residence Inn by Marriott,** 8503 N. Tryon St. (© **800/228-9290** or 704/547-1122; www.marriott.com).

The **Coffee Cup,** 914 S. Clarkson St. (© **704/375-8855;** www.coffeecupsoul.com), a local favorite open for breakfast and lunch, is a roadside joint where—as they say in the South—"all God's children got chicken grease on their fingers." The more formal **La Bibliothèque,** in the Morrison Office Building, 1901 Roxborough Rd. (© **704/365-5000;** www.labibliotheque.net), serves the city's finest French cuisine; dine on the patio in good weather. One of the best places for seafood is **Upstream,** 6902 Phillips Place (© **704/556-7730**), which features a sushi and oyster bar. Try the sake-marinated Chilean sea bass or the jumbo lump crab cakes.

CHARLOTTE AFTER DARK

The **Charlotte Symphony Orchestra** (© **704/972-2000;** www.charlottesymphony.org) plays from September to July, **Opera Carolina** (© **704/332-7177;** www.operacarolina.org) performs from September to April, and the **Charlotte Pops** (© **704/972-2003**) gives outdoor concerts in Freedom Park on summer evenings. Classic plays are often performed by **Theatre Charlotte,** 501 Queens Rd. (© **704/376-3777;** www.theatrecharlotte.org). The immense **N.C. Blumenthal Performing Arts Center,** 130 N. Tryon St. (© **704/372-1000** for tickets; www.performingartsctr.org), presents headline acts, touring Broadway productions, and other theatrical performances.

Swing 1000, 1000 Central Ave. (© **704/334-4443**), is a nightclub/restaurant that's brought the neo-swing movement to town. The house band plays '30s and '40s big band, and the Continental cuisine is better than you'd expect. The same owners have another hot spot at 911 E. Morehead (© **704/347-4447**) called the **Big Chill,** featuring live R&B several nights a week. The venerable **Double Door Inn,** 1218 Charlotte Towne Ave. (© **704/376-1446;** www.doubledoorinn.com), is a legendary place to hear the blues. The popular lesbian and gay nightclub **Scorpio,** 2301 Freedom Dr. (© **704/373-9124;** www.scorpios.com), has been going strong for years.

13 THE BLUE RIDGE PARKWAY

One of America's most spectacular drives, the Blue Ridge Parkway takes up where Virginia's Skyline Drive (p. 233) leaves off, linking the southern end of Shenandoah National Park in Virginia with the eastern entrance of the Great Smoky Mountains National Park in North Carolina. It winds and twists along the mountain crests for 469 miles, offering panoramic views along the way. October brings incredible fall foliage that paints the valleys and slopes in vivid hues of scarlet, orange, and gold (expect big crowds and lots of traffic, though). At many overlooks you'll see a rifle-and-powder-horn symbol and the word TRAIL, which means there are marked walking trails through the woods.

There are frequent exits to nearby towns, plus 11 visitor centers, 9 campgrounds (open May–Oct only; no reservations) with drinking water and comfort stations (but no shower or utility hookups), restaurants, and gas stations. Before you set out, get maps and

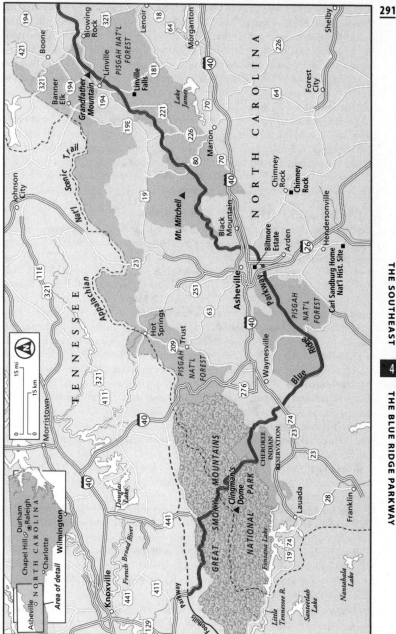

detailed information from the Superintendent, **Blue Ridge Parkway Headquarters,** 199 Hemphill Knob Rd., Asheville, NC 28803 (© 828/271-4779; www.nps.gov/blri).

Don't plan to hurry down the Blue Ridge: If you don't have time to amble and drink in the beauty, you'll only be frustrated. If you want to drive the entire length of the parkway, allow at least 2 or 3 days. On the first day, drive the Virginia half, then stop for the night at Boone, North Carolina, not far from the state border. The final two legs of the trip (from Boone to Asheville and from there to Fontana Village) can easily be accomplished in another day's drive.

You can veer off the parkway to see a number of attractions, including **Linville Falls,** with parking at Milepost 316 on the parkway. The falls plunge into the 2,000-foot-deep Linville Gorge. A 1-mile round-trip hike leads to the upper falls; other trails lead to more views. Another stop, **Linville Caverns,** lies at Milepost 382 on the parkway, just off U.S. 221 between Linville and Marion (© 828/756-4171). The only caverns in North Carolina, these chilly tunnels go 2,000 feet underground.

TOWNS JUST OFF THE PARKWAY

BOONE   Boone has been called "the coolest spot in the South," with average temperatures around 68°F (20°C) in summer. It's a great place for golf, swimming, fishing, skiing, mountain biking, canoeing, and white-water rafting. It lies an hour from **I-77, I-81,** and **I-40,** and is accessible by three major highways, **U.S. 321, U.S. 421,** and **U.S. 221. N.C. 105** provides access from U.S. 221. The **Boone Area Convention and Visitors Bureau,** 208 Howard St., Boone, NC 28607 (© 800/852-9506 or 828/262-3516; www.visit boonenc.com), is open Monday to Friday 9am to 4pm.

Kermit Hunter's *Horn in the West* is presented in the Daniel Boone Theatre, 591 Horn in the West Dr. (© 828/264-2120), every night except Monday from late June to mid-August. It tells a vivid story of pioneer efforts to win freedom during the American Revolution. (Reserve tickets in advance.) Next door to the theater are the **Daniel Boone Native Gardens** (© 828/264-6390; www.danielboonegardens.org) and the **Hickory Ridge Homestead Museum** (© 828/264-2120; www.blueridgeheritage.com), an 18th-century living-history museum in a re-created log cabin.

The **Tweetsie Railroad Theme Park,** Blowing Rock Road, halfway between Boone and Blowing Rock (© 800/526-5740 or 828/264-9061; www.tweetsie.com), is hokey but fun for kids.

Boone Golf Club, U.S. 321/221 South, Blowing Rock Road (© 828/264-8760; www.boonegolfclub.com), is the standard all High Country public courses are measured against. Greens fees are $35 to $45.

Wahoo's Adventures, on U.S. 321 between Boone and the Tweetsie Railroad Theme Park (© 800/444-RAFT [444-7238] or 828/262-5774; www.wahoosadventures.com), is the best all-around outfitter to get you out there white-water rafting, tubing, or fishing.

For overnight stays, we recommend the **Lovill House Inn,** 404 Old Bristol Rd. (© 800/849-9466 or 828/264-4204; www.lovillhouseinn.com). Families might prefer the **Holiday Inn Express,** 1943 Blowing Rock Rd. (© 800/HOLIDAY [465-4329] or 828/264-2451), the best motel in the area.

BANNER ELK & GRANDFATHER MOUNTAIN   The **Avery/Banner Elk Chamber of Commerce,** 4539 Tynecastle Hwy., no. 2 in the shops of Tynecastle (© 800/972-2183 or 828/898-5605; www.averycounty.com), is open Monday to Friday 9am to 4pm, Saturday 10am to 4pm, and Sunday noon to 4pm.

Kilt-clad revelers gather here early in July for the annual **Highland Games and Gathering of the Clans.** Bagpipe music, dancing, wrestling, and tossing the caber make this a spectacle not to miss.

Grandfather Mountain, on U.S. 221 near Linville, a mile off the Blue Ridge Parkway (© **828/733-4337;** www.grandfather.com), is the highest peak in the Blue Ridge. You can see as far as 100 miles from the **Mile High Swinging Bridge,** and the **Environmental Habitat** is home to Mildred the Bear and her black bear friends. Grandfather Mountain is open daily except Thanksgiving and Christmas; admission is $14 adults, $12 seniors, $6 children 4 to 12.

There's an excellent golf course at the **Hawksnest Golf & Ski Resort,** 2853 Skyland Dr., off N.C. 105, Seven Devils (© **800/822-4295** or 828/963-6561; www.hawksnest-resort.com); greens fees are $30 to $50, including cart.

Our favorite lodging in the area is the intimate **Banner Elk Inn Bed and Breakfast,** N.C. 407, Main Street East (© **828/898-6223;** www.bannerelkinn.com). Another recommended option is **Archers Mountain Inn,** 2489 Beech Mountain Pkwy., Beech Mountain (© **888/827-6155** or 828/898-9004; www.archersinn.com), which has an excellent restaurant, the Jackalope's View.

BLOWING ROCK   Blowing Rock is filled with little B&Bs, inns, and galleries. To get here from Boone, take U.S. 321 South directly into Blowing Rock. The **Blowing Rock Chamber of Commerce,** 132 Park Ave. (© **800/295-7851** or 828/295-7851; www.blowingrock.com), is open Monday to Saturday from 9am to 5pm.

The area's biggest attraction is **Blowing Rock,** on U.S. 321, 2 miles south of town (© **828/295-7111**), rising 4,000 feet above John's River Gorge. Its strong updraft returns any light object (such as a handkerchief) thrown into the void. The observation tower, gazebos, and gardens offer panoramic views. Admission is $6 adults, $1 children 4 to 11.

Shoppers can check **Expressions Craft Guild & Gallery,** Main Street (© **828/295-7839**), a cooperative gallery featuring contemporary local crafts. The **Parkway Craft Center,** at Milepost 294 on the Bridge Ride Parkway in the Moses Cone Manor just off Route 221 (© **828/295-7938**), offers the finest-quality mountain crafts.

For luxurious lodgings in a panoramic setting, there's the **Hound Ears Club,** off N.C. 105 South near Boone (© **828/963-4321;** www.houndears.com). We also like the time-worn charm of **Crippen's Country Inn,** 239 Sunset Dr. (© **828/295-3487;** www.crippens.com), a National Historic Landmark with a good restaurant.

14 ASHEVILLE

Asheville, once just a tiny mountain trading village at the confluence of the French Broad and Swannanoa rivers, has grown up and turned into a year-round resort, complete with architectural gems from several eras and a lively cultural scene.

ESSENTIALS

GETTING THERE   The **Asheville Airport** (© **828/687-2226;** www.flyavl.com) is just off I-26. Major routes into Asheville are **I-40** from the east (Raleigh and Wilmington) and west (Knoxville), and **I-26** from the southeast (Charleston).

VISITOR INFORMATION The **Asheville Convention and Visitors Bureau,** 35 Montford Ave., Asheville, NC 28802 (© **800/257-1300** or 828/258-6101; www. ashevillechamber.org or www.exploreasheville.com), is open Monday to Friday from 8:30am to 5:30pm and Saturday and Sunday from 9am to 5pm.

SPECIAL EVENTS & FESTIVALS Special happenings at Biltmore Estate include a spring **Festival of Flowers.** Fiddlers, banjo pickers, and clog dancers entertain during the first weekend of August at the **Annual Mountain Dance and Folk Festival.** Most every Saturday night in summer, there's a **Shindig-on-the-Green** downtown, with mountain musicians and dancers having an old-fashioned wingding. In Brevard, 27 miles southwest of Asheville, a major music festival is held from late June to mid-August at the **Brevard Music Center** (© **888/384-8682** or 828/862-2105; www.brevardmusic.org), with symphony, chamber music, band, and choral concerts, as well as musical comedy and opera.

WHAT TO SEE & DO

Biltmore Village is a cluster of some 24 cottages housing boutiques, crafts shops, and restaurants. The best of them is the **New Morning Gallery,** 7 Boston Way (© **828/274-2831;** www.newmorninggallerync.com), one of the South's largest galleries of arts and crafts. Asheville is also home to more than 50 other galleries around town. The **Kress Emporium,** 19 Patton Ave. (© **828/281-2252;** www.asheville.com), serves as a showcase for more than 80 local artists and craftspeople.

Some 5 miles east of downtown Asheville, at Milepost 382 on the Blue Ridge Parkway, the **Folk Art Center** (© **828/298-7928**) displays the finest handicrafts and runs a terrific crafts shop.

Thomas Wolfe, a native of Asheville, immortalized the town in *Look Homeward, Angel.* His mother's boardinghouse at 48 Spruce St. is maintained as a literary shrine (© **828/253-8304** for information; www.wolfememorial.com). An arsonist set the house on fire in 1998, but it has been restored. Wolfe lived here from 1906 to 1916. Family furnishings and original manuscripts are on display. Both Wolfe and short-story writer **O. Henry** (William Sydney Porter) are buried in Riverside Cemetery (entrance on Birch St. off Pearson Dr.).

The rolling terrain around Asheville offers golfers hundreds of uncrowded fairways. Our favorite course, which opened in 1899, is at the **Grove Park Inn Resort & Spa,** 290 Macon Ave. (© **800/438-5800** or 828/252-2711; www.groveparkinn.com). The par-70 course was redesigned in 1924 by master golf architect Donald Ross. Seasonal greens fees range from $50 to $149. The Grove Park is also ranked one of the country's 50 greatest tennis resorts by *Tennis* magazine. Courts can be booked by the hour ($25 indoor, $20 outdoor).

Biltmore Estate (**Best**) This French Renaissance château, built by George W. Vanderbilt, has 250 rooms, and every inch of them is extraordinary. The largest private residence in the country, the National Historic Landmark is now owned by Vanderbilt's grandson. The elder Vanderbilt journeyed through Europe and Asia purchasing paintings, porcelains, bronzes, carpets, and antiques, along with artwork by Renoir, Sargent, and Whistler, and furniture by Chippendale and Sheraton. Vanderbilt also hired Frederick Law Olmsted to create one of the most lavish formal gardens you'll ever see, ablaze with more than 200 varieties of azaleas.

1 Approach Rd. (on U.S. 25, 2 blocks north of I-40). **©** **800/624-1575** or 828/225-1333. www.biltmore. com. House and gardens $29–$49 adults, half-price children 10–16. Jan–Mar daily 9am–4pm; Apr–Dec daily 8:30am–5pm.

WHERE TO STAY

In the heart of downtown, the elegant all-suite **Haywood Park Hotel,** 1 Battery Park Ave. (**©** **800/228-2522** or 828/252-2522; www.haywoodpark.com), is tops. Outstanding historic B&B choices include the **Beaufort House Victorian Inn,** 61 N. Liberty St. (**©** **800/261-2221** or 828/254-8334; www.beauforthouse.com); the **Lion and the Rose Bed & Breakfast,** 276 Montford Ave. (**©** **800/546-6988** or 828/255-7673; www. lion-rose.com); and the **Old Reynolds Mansion,** 100 Reynolds Heights (**©** **800/709-0496** or 828/254-0496; www.oldreynoldsmansion.com).

Cedar Crest Victorian Inn This Queen Anne mansion is one of the largest and most opulent residences surviving Asheville's 1890s boom. The mansion has a captain's walk, projecting turrets, and expansive verandas; inside it's a fantasy of leaded glass, ornately carved fireplaces, antiques, and a massive oak staircase. Rooms are romantic and whimsical; some sport canopy beds, ideal for couples. A few bathrooms have either claw-foot or whirlpool tubs.

674 Biltmore Ave., Asheville, NC 28803. **©** **877/251-1389** or 828/252-1389. Fax 828/253-7667. www. cedarcrestinn.com/index.html. 12 units. $190–$255 double; $230–$300 suite. Rates include breakfast. AE, DC, DISC, MC, V. Free parking. No children 9 and under allowed. *In room:* Shared kitchenettes in cottages.

The Greystone Inn Henry Ford and John D. Rockefeller once whiled away their summers here at this fabled all-inclusive inn that appeals to both couples and families. Set on a wooded peninsula along the lake, this Swiss Revival mansion is a National Historic Landmark. For dedicated do-nothings, there are wicker rocking chairs on the glassed-in sun porch overlooking the lake. The midsize rooms are beautifully maintained; some offer Jacuzzis and working fireplaces. Complimentary midafternoon tea is served with cakes.

Greystone Lane, Lake Toxaway, NC 28747. **©** **800/824-5766** or 828/966-4700. Fax 828/862-5689. www. greystoneinn.com. 33 units. Nov–Apr $290–$440 double, $490 suite. May–Oct Sun–Thurs $360–$440 double, $590 suite; Fri–Sat $410–$490 double, $640 suite. Rates include breakfast, dinner, champagne cruise, afternoon tea, and sports activities except golf. MC, V. Free parking. **Amenities:** Restaurant; pool; golf course; 6 tennis courts; fitness center; spa.

The Grove Park Inn Resort & Spa ⓑest With panoramic views and old-world charm, this resort, built in 1913, is one of the oldest and most famous in the South, and our favorite choice in all of western North Carolina. A National Historic Landmark, it's hosted F. Scott Fitzgerald, Thomas Edison, Henry Ford, and a couple of presidents, and today shelters everybody from honeymooners to families. The large, recently refurbished guest rooms are bastions of luxury. **Horizons Restaurant** is the finest in the area, and the **Blue Ridge Dining Room** has a legendary outdoor dining veranda.

290 Macon Ave., Asheville, NC 28804. **©** **800/438-5800** or 828/252-2711. Fax 828/253-7053. www. groveparkinn.com. 510 units. High season $325–$675 double, $1,300 suite; off season $265–$525 double, $750 suite. Children 16 and under stay free in parent's room. AE, DC, DISC, MC, V. Valet parking $15; free self-parking. **Amenities:** 3 restaurants (nonsmoking); 2 pools (1 indoor); golf course; 6 tennis courts; fitness center; spa. *In room:* Fridge, microwave.

Richmond Hill Inn This inn is Asheville's premier remaining example of Queen Anne–style architecture. The interior is graced with family heirloom portraits and original oak paneling. Rooms are charming, with balconies, canopied beds, refrigerators, fireplaces, and bathrooms containing showers and claw-foot tubs. Ideal for families, nine cottages, containing rooms and suites, all with small porches and rockers, are across the way. The inn has an exceptional restaurant, **Gabrielle's,** featuring American contemporary cuisine.

87 Richmond Hill Dr., Asheville, NC 28806. ✆ **800/545-9238** or 828/252-7313. Fax 828/252-8726. www. richmondhillinn.com. 36 units. $195–$325 double; $275–$525 suite. Children 16 and under stay free in parent's room. Rates include full breakfast and afternoon tea. AE, MC, V. Free parking. **Amenities:** Restaurant; fitness center.

WHERE TO DINE

The **Richmond Hill Inn** and the **Grove Park Inn Resort** have outstanding restaurants; see above.

Charlotte St. Grill AMERICAN   Downstairs is an authentic-looking English pub, and upstairs is a restaurant with a Victorian decor offering more intimate dining and suitable for families. The pub keeps the longest hours and is noted for serving one of the best-value lunches in Asheville, including freshly made pastas and house salads that are meals in themselves. No matter where you eat, the food will be well prepared and based on fresh ingredients.

157 Charlotte St. ✆ **828/253-5348.** Reservations recommended. Main courses $15–$25 dinner; pub lunches $14–$16. AE, MC, V. Restaurant Mon–Thurs 11:30am–2pm and 5–9pm, Fri–Sat 5–10pm. Pub daily 11:30am–2am.

The Market Place CONTINENTAL   This upscale casual restaurant with candlelit tables—ideal for a romantic evening—offers impeccable service. The chef uses extra-fresh ingredients, and all herbs and vegetables are grown locally. Many dishes are nouvelle in style and preparation, and the staff is knowledgeable about the extensive wine list.

20 Wall St. ✆ **828/252-4162.** www.marketplace-restaurant.com. Reservations recommended. Main courses $24–$30. AE, DC, MC, V. Mon–Sat 5:30–9:30pm.

15 GREAT SMOKY MOUNTAINS NATIONAL PARK

The Great Smoky Mountains are the oldest mountains in the world, composed of peaks that range in elevation from 840 to 6,642 feet. The oval-shaped national park, bisected by the North Carolina–Tennessee border, encompasses more than 520,000 acres of forests, streams, rivers, waterfalls, and hiking trails. More than 200 kinds of birds and 70 species of mammals live in the park, including the lumbering black bear, the white-tailed deer, groundhogs, wild turkeys, and bobcats. Abundant wildflowers offer a kaleidoscope of colors in spring and early summer and a blanket of lush greenery in later summer.

See the section "Eastern Tennessee," later in this chapter, for information on Gatlinburg, a convenient gateway town on the western side of the park.

CHEROKEE: THE NORTH CAROLINA GATEWAY TO THE PARK

From the southern end of the Blue Ridge Parkway and points south, U.S. 441 leads to Cherokee; U.S. 19 runs east and west through the town. Asheville is 48 miles southwest.

www.cherokee-nc.com), is open daily from 8:15am to 5pm.

Oconaluftee Indian Village, U.S. 441 North (© **828/497-7000;** www.about
cherokee.com), is a living museum of the mid-1750s Cherokee people. You'll see men
and women shaping clay into pottery, chipping arrowheads, and firing blowguns. Lectures on all facets of Cherokee life are held at the Ceremonial Grounds and at the Council House. Admission is $13 adults, $6 children; it's open from mid-May to mid-October
daily from 9am to 5:30pm.

Unto These Hills, the most popular outdoor drama in America, is staged in Cherokee
each summer, relating the story of the Cherokees from 1540 until the "Trail of Tears"
exodus to Oklahoma in 1838, when thousands died. As you watch the first encounter
with Hernando de Soto, you'll hear voices echoing off the surrounding mountainside, the
very mountainside that became a hiding place for Cherokee determined to remain in
their homeland instead of joining the long march to exile. Performances are at the 2,800-
seat **Mountainside Theater,** off U.S. 441 (© **828/497-7000;** www.untothesehills.com).
Opening night is around June 10, and the curtain goes down for the last time at August's
end. Tickets cost $22 for reserved seating or $18 for general admission; children are
charged $8 to $10. No shows on Sunday.

The major outdoor pursuit on the reservation is fishing, with 30 miles of streams
stocked with 400,000 trout annually. A tribal permit is required.

Cherokee's major hotel, **Harrah's Cherokee Casino & Hotel,** 777 Casino Dr. (© **800/
HARRAHS** [427-7247] or 828/497-7777; www.harrahscherokee.com), is a 576-room,
15-story luxury hotel connecting directly to a casino. Local Indian crafts are on display on
each floor. Harrah's is under contract with the tribe to run the casino. When Tower II
opens during the lifetime of this edition, the number of rooms will be doubled.

Cherokee also has an abundance of motels, including the **Holiday Inn–Cherokee,**
U.S. 19 South (© **800/HOLIDAY** [465-4329] or 828/497-9181); the **Hampton Inn,**
185 Tsalagi Rd. (© **800/HAMPTON** [426-7866] or 828/497-3115); the **Newfound
Lodge,** 34 U.S. 441 N. (© **828/497-2746**); and the **Riverside Motel,** U.S. 441 South
at Old Route 441 (© **877/643-1439** or 828/497-9311; www.riversidemotelnc.com).

PARK ESSENTIALS

ACCESS POINTS & ORIENTATION   Take I-40 from Asheville to U.S. 19, then U.S.
441 to the park's southern entrance near Cherokee, 50 miles west.

Although there are several side roads into the park, the best routes are through one of
the three main entrances, two of which are on Newfound Gap Road, U.S. 441, a 33-mile
road that stretches north-south through the park. The southern entrance is near Cherokee, North Carolina; the northern entrance is miles away near Gatlinburg, Tennessee
(p. 312). The third main entrance is on the western side of the park at Townsend, Tennessee. Other access points are from the campgrounds at the edge of the park. The park
is open year-round, and admission is free.

VISITOR CENTERS   At each of the three main entrances are visitor centers for the
park. Each center offers information on road, weather, camping, and backcountry conditions. You'll also find books, maps, and first-aid information.

The **Sugarlands Visitor Center and Park Headquarters** (© **865/436-1291** for park
headquarters and all three visitor centers; www.nps.gov/grsm) is at the northern entrance,
near Gatlinburg, Tennessee. The smaller **Oconaluftee Visitor Center** is at the southern
entrance. Both of these offer useful exhibits to help you understand what you're seeing.

The **Cades Cove Visitor Center,** at the western end of the park, on Laurel Creek Road about 12 miles southwest of Townsend, Tennessee, is set among a cluster of historic 19th-century farms and buildings (see "Seeing the Park's Highlights," below).

The visitor centers are open year-round.

WHEN TO GO   From late March to June, spring brings great bursts of color from the wildflowers, with mild daytime temperatures and cool evenings. As summer begins, the lush greenery comes into its full splendor and the weather gets warm and humid. Although the higher elevations offer milder temperatures, ranging from the low 50s (teens Celsius) to the mid-60s (late teens Celsius), the lower ones can bring on days that are in the 90s (30s Celsius). Around the beginning of October, elevations above a mile have seen the end of fall, but lower elevations are just coming into their own with brilliant reds, yellows, oranges, purples, and browns. The best time to experience this change is from mid- to late October.

Throughout the year, weather can change rapidly. During the course of a day, you can witness several thunderstorms, with breaks of clear, bright skies, while temperatures change from cool and comfortable to hot and humid. The wettest months are generally March and July.

The height of the tourist season lasts from late May to late August. As autumn approaches, the park is swamped on weekends, but the crowds are more manageable during weekdays. Early-morning hours are always a good bet to avoid the hordes.

SEEING THE PARK'S HIGHLIGHTS

If you have only 2 days to see the park, start early in the morning to avoid the crowds. When crossing the park on the **Newfound Gap Road** (U.S. 441), you should allow, at the very least, 1 hour. The speed limit does not rise above 45 mph anywhere in the park. When ascending the mountain slopes, you can rarely go over 25 to 30 mph because of the winding roads. Pack a lunch—there are no restaurants in the park, but picnic sites abound.

Your best strategy is to visit the sights along the Newfound Gap Road. Begin at the Oconaluftee Visitor Center, where you can pick up park information and get a weather report. Today the **Oconaluftee Mountain Farm Museum,** a replica of a pioneer farmstead, operates here within a collection of original log buildings. Park staff, dressed in period costumes, make it a living-history farm from April to October. About half a mile north on the Newfound Gap Road is the Mingus Mill, constructed in 1886 and still grinding wheat and corn from mid-April to October.

As you travel north, you'll come to a turnoff for **Clingmans Dome,** the highest peak in the park, soaring 6,642 feet. Once you turn onto this road, you travel 7 miles southwest to a parking lot where you can walk a steep half-mile to a viewing platform featuring one of the park's best views. Next comes **Newfound Gap,** which, at 5,048 feet, is the center of the park. If the sky is clear, you can see for miles around; on other days you find yourself literally in the clouds.

The drive across the park leads you to the Sugarlands Visitor Center, where you can stroll through the nature exhibit, view a slide show, or browse through the gift shop. At this point, you can either head into Gatlinburg for the night or go west about 5 miles on Little River Road to Elkmont Campground. It's best to make reservations (accepted only mid-May to Nov).

On Day 2, continue your journey west on Little River Road to **Cades Cove,** where you'll find more pioneer structures than at any other location in the park. Plan to spend half a day exploring the many attractions along the 11-mile **Cades Cove Loop.** Stop at the visitor center for a pamphlet containing a key for the numbered sights. Founded in 1818, the cove was a thriving, self-supporting community for more than 100 years. Original home sites, smokehouses, and barns still stand today, giving visitors a glimpse into the lives of the original settlers. You'll also find cemeteries with such epitaphs as one from the Civil War that reads BAS SHAW—KILLED BY REBELS. Cades Cove offers several nature trails. **Note:** The loop is closed to cars and open to pedestrians and cyclists on select days from May to September.

Once you've completed the Cades Cove Loop, head toward the Sugarlands Visitor Center to the Newfound Gap Road to recross the park, this time taking advantage of the numerous pull-off areas dotting the roadside, all offering good photo opportunities. At most of them you'll find "Quiet Walkways," short paths created for moments of solitude to experience nature. Don't be discouraged if a pull-off is full, because another one will appear within a mile.

OUTDOOR ACTIVITIES IN THE PARK

FISHING   The park contains more than 700 miles of streams suitable for fishing. Anglers must have a valid North Carolina or Tennessee state fishing license, which can be purchased in the gateway towns at sporting goods stores. The optimum seasons are spring and fall. Popular fishing areas include Abrams Creek, Big Creek, Fontana Lake, and Little River.

HIKING   With more than 850 miles of trails, the park offers folks of all fitness levels a chance to experience the great outdoors. (Before setting out, make sure to check the weather forecast; carry rain gear, because sudden storms are common.)

Laurel Falls Trail, the most popular waterfall and dramatic trail in the park, is an easy, flat walk; it's 1.25 miles to the falls from the Laurel Falls parking area, a few miles from the Sugarlands Visitor Center. The **Abrams Falls Trail** has an elevation gain of 340 feet. You travel 2.5 miles from the Abrams Falls parking lot at the west end of Cades Cove Loop Road to a 20-foot-high waterfall. The trail follows a clear stream and is relatively flat. The **Ramsay Cascades Trail** has a total elevation gain of 2,375 feet and is 8 miles long round-trip. This trail also leads to Ramsay Cascades, a 100-foot-high waterfall—the park's highest. From Greenbrier Cove, follow the signs to the trail head.

The **Appalachian Trail** stretches from Maine to Georgia and has 68 of its 2,100 miles situated in the park, following the Smokies' ridgeline from east to west almost the entire length of the park. Access points are at Newfound Gap, Clingmans Dome, the end of Tenn. 32 just north of the Big Creek Campground, and the Fontana Dam. The most popular, if strenuous, section is from Newfound Gap to Charlies Bunion.

Self-guided nature trails offer even couch potatoes an opportunity to commune with nature. These trails are staked and keyed to pamphlets with descriptions of points of interest along the way. You can get a keyed pamphlet from one of the visitor centers or stands at the trail heads. There are about a dozen such trails, ranging in length from .3 mile to 6 miles. All offer easy walks through peaceful surroundings.

HORSEBACK RIDING   The park offers some of the state's most beautiful scenery for equestrians. Off-trail and cross-country riding, as well as use of hiking trails, are prohibited. The following five drive-in horse camps offer easy access to designated horse trails: Anthony Creek, Big Creek, Cataloochee, Round Bottom, and Towstring. Reservations can be made 30 days in advance with the **Backcountry Reservations Office** by calling ⓒ 865/436-1231.

Horses can be rented for $22 an hour, from mid-March to late November. Ask for details at the individual concessions within the park at **Cades Cove** (© 865/448-6286); **Sugarlands Riding Stables** (© 865/436-3885); **Smokemont Campground** (© 828/497-2373); and **Smoky Mountains Riding Stables,** U.S. 321 (© 865/436-5634). The Park Service requires that a guide accompany all rental treks.

WHITE-WATER RAFTING   Starting at the Waterville Power Plant, a 5-mile stretch of the Big Pigeon River has 10 rapids and offers some of the most challenging white-water rafting in the South. **Rafting in the Smokies** (© **800/776-7238** or 865/436-5008; www.raftinginthesmokies.com) rafts the Big Pigeon, Nantahala, and Ocoee rivers. A trip on the Pigeon costs $39 per person, on the Nantahala $30, and on the Ocoee River $38 to $47.

WHERE TO CAMP

The park contains 10 campgrounds with picnic tables, fire grills, cold running water, and flush toilets, but no showers or water and electrical hookups. There are three major campgrounds. **Cades Cove,** 159 sites, features a camp store, bike rentals, a disposal station, wood for sale, and naturalist programs held in the small amphitheater. **Elkmont,** 220 sites, offers a disposal station, firewood for sale, vending machines, and a phone. **Smokemont,** 142 sites, has a disposal station and firewood for sale.

Reservations (© **800/365-CAMP** [365-2267]) can be made up to 5 months in advance. The campgrounds are full on weekends beginning in April, and daily from July to October. The busiest months are July and October, and you should make reservations at least 4 weeks in advance. From mid-May to October, there's a 7-day maximum stay; from November to mid-May, with limited sites available, the maximum stay is 14 days. The charge is $17 to $25 per day. The seven smaller campgrounds, open from mid-May to October, are along the boundaries of the park and cost $14 to $25 per day.

WHERE TO STAY

See also "Cherokee: The North Carolina Gateway to the Park," above, and the section "Eastern Tennessee," later in this chapter, for information on Gatlinburg, Tennessee, which borders the other side of the park and also makes an excellent base.

Offering the only accommodations in the park itself, **LeConte Lodge** (© 865/429-5704; www.leconte-lodge.com) is on top of Mount LeConte, and it's very back-to-basics—no electricity, TV, phone, or indoor plumbing, although there are four flush toilets in outhouses. You have to hike in on a 4-mile one-way trip. Lodgings include private bedrooms in cabins with shared living rooms as well as private cabins. The rates include breakfast, dinner (served family style), and lunch for those staying more than 1 night. There are seven rooms to rent, costing $128 per adult. A two-bedroom lodge rents for $512 for up to eight people, plus $64 extra per person for meals. Reservations are difficult to come by if you don't make them in October for the following year. It's open from the last week in March to late November. No credit cards.

In Bryson City, there's the highly recommended and moderately priced **Fryemont Inn,** Fryemont Road (© **800/845-4879** or 828/488-2159; www.fryemontinn.com). In Maggie Valley, the **Cataloochee Ranch,** Fie Top Road, 119 Ranch Dr. (© **800/868-1401** or 828/926-1401; www.cataloocheeranch.com), is a 1,000-acre spread offering loads of activities.

16 HIGHLIGHTS OF KENTUCKY

LEXINGTON & THE BLUEGRASS REGION

Often called the Heart of Kentucky, the centrally located Bluegrass region offers much of what Kentucky is all about—thoroughbred horses, bourbon, basketball, natural beauty, history, and Southern hospitality.

Ringed by the stunning horse farms that give this area its reputation and personality is Lexington, the state's second-largest city and a growing urban area that has just the right mix of big-city excitement and small-town charm.

Essentials

GETTING THERE   By Plane   Major airlines fly into **Blue Grass Airport** (© 859/425-3100; www.bluegrassairport.com), 10 minutes from downtown. There's frequent service from most Midwest hubs. Most major car-rental agencies have desks at the airport.

By Car   The major routes into Lexington are I-75 from the north (Cincinnati) and south (Knoxville), and I-64 from the east (Charleston, West Virginia) and west (Louisville).

VISITOR INFORMATION   Contact the **Lexington Convention and Visitors Bureau,** 301 E. Vine St., Lexington, KY 40507 (© 800/84-LEX-KY [845-3959] or 859/233-1221; www.visitlex.com). For statewide information and trip-planning resources, call © **800/225-TRIP** [225-8747] or visit www.kytravel.com or www.kentuckytourism. com.

Exploring the Area

HORSE FARMS   Calumet Farms (www.calumetfarm.com) is the granddaddy of 'em all, breeder of nine Kentucky Derby champions, including three Triple Crown winners. It is not open to the public. **Claiborne Farm,** Winchester Road, Paris (© 859/233-4252; www.claibornefarm.com), was the birthplace of Seabiscuit. It's also known in part for its association with Secretariat, the 1973 Triple Crown winner considered by many to be the greatest thoroughbred of all time. The horse once stood at stud at the farm and is buried here. Tour schedules vary, so call in advance to arrange an appointment. Tours are free, but tips for the guides are customary.

Triple Crown winner Seattle Slew (in 1977) once stood at stud at **Three Chimneys Farm,** Old Frankfort Parkway, Versailles (© 859/873-7053), as well as 2008 Derby and Preakness winner Big Brown. Barbaro's sire is also at this popular farm. Tours are free but should be booked 6 months to a year in advance.

Part museum, part equestrian arena, the state-run **Kentucky Horse Park,** 4089 Iron Works Pike, Lexington (© 800/568-8813 or 859/233-4303; www.kyhorsepark.com), is a mecca for horse lovers, drawing more than 700,000 visitors yearly. A gravesite statue of Man o' War, who lost only one race in his career, welcomes visitors. Seasonal horse and pony rides please the kids. Open daily from 9am to 5pm (Nov–Mar discounted rates; closed Mon and Tues). Admission is $15 for adults, $8 for kids ages 7 to 12. Through the park, you can also book narrated 2¹/₂-hour tours of off-premises, Lexington-area horse farms. Tickets are $25 for adults and $15 for children 4 to 12; not recommended for kids 3 and under.

Meanwhile, Kentucky Horse Park is gearing up for a major international event in 2010, when the **Alltech FEI (Federation Equestre Internationale) World Equestrian Games** will be held here September 25 to October 10. It will be the first time the competition, billed as the world's largest equine sporting event, is being held outside Europe. For more information, visit www.feigames2010.org.

Keeneland, 4201 Versailles Rd., Lexington (© 800/456-3412 or 859/254-3412; www.keeneland.com), a meticulously manicured racetrack, may not be as famous as Churchill Downs, but most folks think it's one of the prettiest courses in America. Much of the film *Seabiscuit* was shot here. Races are held only 6 weeks a year: 3 in April, including the Blue Grass Stakes, a major Kentucky Derby tune-up, and 3 more in October. Post time is 1:10pm. A reserved seat in the grandstand costs $6 weekdays, $8 weekends. Order tickets in advance for major stakes races.

BOURBON DISTILLERY TOURS Bourbon, a whiskey made from at least 51% corn, is distilled in several Bluegrass region towns, but ironically, none are in Bourbon County, which is dry. (You can, however, buy bourbon in Christian County.) A number of the distilleries within easy driving distance of Lexington offer tours. For general information, contact the Kentucky Distillers Association's **Kentucky Bourbon Trail** (© 859/336-9612; www.kybourbontrail.com). From here, you can download interactive maps and get detailed driving directions to the region's main distilleries, including the ones listed below. Most of the distilleries offer free guided tours, and some end with sample sips of bourbon and/or bourbon-spiked chocolates.

One of the oldest and largest is the **Wild Turkey Distillery,** 1525 Tyrone Rd., Lawrenceburg (© 502/839-4544; www.wildturkeybourbon.com). It's the closest to Lexington. Free tours are conducted weekdays at 9am, 10:30am, 12:30pm, and 2:30pm. The distillery is closed the first week of January and the last 2 weeks of July.

Visit **Heaven Hill Distilleries Bourbon Heritage Center,** 1311 Gilkey Run Rd., Bardstown (© 502/337-1000; www.bourbonheritagecenter.com), to see where Evan Williams and other brands are produced. Photomurals, bourbon-making artifacts, antiques, handmade quilts, and other crafts are showcased. There's also a gift shop brimming with bourbon merchandise.

Family-owned **Maker's Mark Distillery,** 3350 Burks Spring Rd., Loretto (© 270/865-2099; www.makersmark.com), a small-batch distillery (peak capacity is a mere 38 barrels), has attracted a devoted following. Its silky-smooth bourbon has garnered numerous awards. Free tours are offered on the half-hour from 10:30am to 3:30pm Monday through Saturday; closed Saturdays in January and February.

The oldest operating distillery in Kentucky is **Woodford Reserve Distillery** (© 859/879-1812; www.woodfordreserve.com), 7855 McCracken Pike, Versailles, in Woodford County, a short drive from Lexington. This picturesque distillery is located among lush, rolling horse farms. There's a lunchtime cafe with indoor and alfresco seating, offering lovely views of the grounds. Tours cost $5 and are held Tuesday through Saturday on the hour from 10am to 4pm, with a break at noon, and Sunday at 1, 2, and 3pm.

In nearby Frankfort, a 25-minute drive from Lexington, is **Buffalo Trace Distillery,** 1001 Wilkinson Blvd., Franklin County (© 502/223-7641; www.buffalotrace.com). Bourbon making on this 110-acre site dates from 1787. In the last decade the distillery has won more international awards than any other in North America. Free tours are held every day except Sunday and holidays.

Other popular bourbon distilleries offering tours include the **Jim Beam American Outpost,** 149 Happy Hollow Rd., Clermont (© 502/543-9877; www.jimbeam.com),

Kentucky Celebrates Lincoln's Bicentennial: 1809–2009

If you're a history or Civil War buff, you're probably already aware of the major anniversary celebrations taking place in Kentucky, Illinois, and other parts of the USA in 2009, the 200th anniversary of the birth of President Abraham Lincoln. For its part, the **Kentucky Abraham Lincoln Bicentennial 1809–2009** has a clever tag line: "His first address wasn't Gettysburg" underscores the fact that Abe was born in the Bluegrass State. You can download interactive maps of the **Kentucky Lincoln Heritage Trail** (www.kylincoln.org), a scenic route through central Kentucky with 16 designated sites, including the following:

- Ashland: The Henry Clay Estate, Lexington
- Camp Nelson Civil War Heritage Park, Jessamine County
- Downtown Springfield (stamp site Opera House)
- Farmington Historic Plantation, Louisville
- Hardin County Museum, Elizabethtown
- Jefferson Davis State Historic Site, Fairview
- Kentucky Historical Society, Frankfort
- Kentucky State Capitol Rotunda, Frankfort
- Lincoln Birthplace National Historic Site, Hodgenville
- Lincoln Boyhood Home, Hodgenville
- Lincoln Museum, Hodgenville
- Lincoln Homestead State Park, Springfield
- Lincoln Marriage Temple, Harrodsburg
- Mary Todd Lincoln House, Lexington
- Perryville Battlefield State Historic Site
- White Hall State Historic Site, Richmond

located about 25 miles south of Louisville, and the Spanish mission-style **Four Roses,** 1224 Bonds Mill Rd., Lawrenceburg (© **502/839-3436;** www.fourroses.us).

MORE ATTRACTIONS Downtown Lexington is home to several historic buildings. Maps for these as well as a self-driving tour of the area and horse farms are available at the visitor center, 301 E. Vine (© **800/845-3959**). **Mary Todd Lincoln House,** 578 W. Main St. (© **859/233-9999;** www.mtlhouse.org), was the first American historic site restored to honor a first lady. Tours are offered from April to mid-December Tuesday through Saturday from 10am to 4pm. Admission is $7 for adults, $4 for ages 6 to 12. **Ashland,** 120 Sycamore Rd. (© **859/266-8581;** www.henryclay.org), is the beautiful 20-acre estate of famous 19th-century statesman and emancipationist Henry Clay. It's open Tuesday through Saturday from 10am to 4:30pm, Sunday from 1 to 4:30pm; closed during January and February. Admission is $7 for adults and $3 for ages 6 to 18.

A scenic 25-mile drive southwest of Lexington takes you to **Shaker Village of Pleasant Hill,** 3501 Lexington Rd., Harrodsburg (© **800/734-5611** or 859/734-5411; www.shakervillageky.org), the largest historic community of its kind in America. The National

Historic Landmark features 33 original 19th-century buildings and 2,800 acres of farm-land. Self-guided tours, horseback riding, and riverboat excursions are offered. Dining, lodging, and two crafts shops are also on the premises. It's open daily year-round except December 24 and 25. Admission for village tours is $14 for adults, $7 for youth 12 to 17, and $5 for children 6 to 11.

For a culturally rich retail therapy experience, be sure to stop by the impressive **Kentucky Artisan Center at Berea** (© **859/985-5448;** www.kentuckyartisancenter.ky.gov). Located about 40 miles south of Lexington off I-75 in Berea, the state's folk arts and crafts capital, this modern, museum-like center combines exhibits, artist demonstrations, and tourist services, along with a world-class gift shop featuring fine Appalachian pottery, textiles, furniture, jewelry, and basketry. There's also a good selection of books and music by noted Kentucky authors, including Bobbie Ann Mason, Sue Grafton, Barbara Kingsolver, and the late Hunter S. Thompson. Admission is free. A sunny cafe features sandwiches as well as slow-cooked comfort foods. For more information, contact the Berea Tourism Center, 3 Artist Circle (in the old train depot at 201 N. Broadway), at © **800/598-5263** or 859/986-2540 (www.berea.com).

Where to Stay

Griffin Gate Marriott Resort and Spa, 1800 Newtown Pike, at the intersection of I-64 and I-75, Lexington (© **800/228-9290** or 859/231-5100; www.griffingatemarriott.com), is a favorite of golf fanatics and spa divas alike. In addition to an acclaimed 18-hole golf course, the resort offers a new full-serve day spa and salon, along with a lighted tennis court, indoor and outdoor swimming pools and hot tubs, and a fitness center. Two restaurants and two bars keep guests entertained any time of day or night. Doubles run $169 to $419.

Across the street, another popular property offering first-class service is the **Embassy Suites Lexington,** 1801 Newtown Pike (© **800/362-2779** or 859/455-5000; www.embassysuites.com). The upscale 230-suite hotel offers amenities including a fitness center, lap pool, jogging track, and restaurant and lounge. Guests receive a complimentary breakfast and evening reception. Suites cost $199 to $329.

In downtown Lexington, you can't beat the boutique-style **Gratz Park Inn,** 120 W. Second St. (© **800/752-4166** or 859/231-1777; www.gratzparkinn.com), for its convenient location and attentive concierge service. Each room is individually decorated with antiques and other historic pieces. Rates run $169 to $249 double.

The wrought-iron furniture, live jazz performances on weekends, and Cajun restaurant in the lobby of the **Doubletree Guest Suites** (formerly Sheraton Suites), 2601 Richmond Rd. (© **800/262-3774** or 859/268-0060), make you feel like you're in New Orleans. With its shift from the Sheraton to the Hilton/Doubletree brand, the property just completed a $7-million renovation in 2008. Each suite ($149–$199 double) offers a hot tub and refrigerator. There's also an outdoor pool and a fitness center.

If you just want a comfortable, affordable chain hotel, two safe options are the **Best Western Regency of Lexington,** 2241 Elkhorn Rd., Lexington (© **800/528-1234** or 859/293-2202), and the **Best Western South,** 5532 Athens-Boonesboro Rd., Lexington (© **859/263-5241**), a family-style motel that's big on facilities and welcomes pets. Both have swimming pools. Rates at both hotels range between $60 and $100 double.

B&Bs tend to come and go, but my favorite is still thriving. A cozy retreat nestled on a secluded 300-acre organic farm southeast of Lexington, **Snug Hollow Farm Bed and Breakfast,** 790 McSwain Branch, Irvine (© **606/723-4786;** www.snughollow.com), is a rustic slice of heaven. Guests may stay in the antiques-filled two-story farmhouse or in the comfortably furnished and fully restored chestnut-log cabin. Hearty breakfasts and gourmet vegetarian meals are a specialty of the chef/owner. Rates range from $100 to $195 double.

A new Lexington-area B&B earning raves is **A Storybook Inn,** 277 Rose Hill Ave., Versailles (© **877/279-2563** or 859/879-9993; www.storybook-inn.com). Oil paintings, antiques and ultra-luxurious queen-size and king-size beds are signature traits of this elegantly restored 1853 white farmhouse. Rates range from $189 to $345.

LOUISVILLE

Kentucky's largest city, Louisville (say it either *Loo*-uh-vul or *Looey*-ville) sits on the southeast bank of the Ohio River across from Indiana. It's about 100 miles west of Lexington.

Louisville is best known for hosting the Kentucky Derby, held on the first Saturday in May every year. It's all but impossible to get tickets to the Derby, but Churchill Downs is open other times of the year when it's not nearly as crowded.

Essentials

GETTING THERE   By Plane   Major airlines fly into **Louisville International Airport** (© **502/368-6524;** www.flylouisville.com), 10 minutes from downtown. There's frequent service from all major Midwest hubs. The flat rate for a taxi downtown is $20 (except during Derby week, when it runs about $35).

By Car   The major routes into Louisville are I-71 from the northeast (Cincinnati), I-65 from the north (Indianapolis) and south (Nashville), and I-64 from the east (Lexington) and west (St. Louis).

VISITOR INFORMATION   Contact the **Louisville and Jefferson County Convention and Visitors Bureau,** 400 S. First St., Louisville, KY 40202 (© **800/626-5646** or 502/584-2121; www.gotolouisville.com). There's also an **Information Booth** at the airport (© **502/367-4636**). To find out what's happening around town, pick up a copy of the *Courier-Journal* newspaper's free entertainment tabloid, *Velocity* (www.velocity weekly.com), or the LEO Weekly (www.leoweekly.com), an alternative weekly that's also free at newsstands around town.

What to See & Do

Louisville celebrates its lazily idyllic waterfront with a 7-mile **RiverWalk** along the shore. Anchoring an ongoing downtown revitalization effort is the new **Muhammad Ali Center,** 144 N. Sixth St. (© **502/584-9254;** www.alicenter.org), a $60-million museum-like conflict-resolution center inspired by the life of boxing's "Greatest," Louisville native, Ali. Brad Pitt and Angelina Jolie (she funded one of the galleries) were among the celebs who attended the star-studded grand opening in November 2005. Interactive displays (see any Ali fight on demand) and exhibits trace Ali's life, his boxing career, and his accomplishments as a peace activist and humanitarian. Admission is $9 for adults, $8 for seniors, $5 for students, and $4 for children. The center is open Monday through Saturday from 9:30am to 5pm, and Sunday from noon to 5pm.

Churchill Downs, 700 Central Ave. (© **502/636-4400;** www.churchilldowns.com), has hosted the Kentucky Derby, which runs the first Saturday in May, since it was first run in 1875. The season runs from late April to early July and from late October to November; post times vary. General admission is $3 for adults, $1 for seniors, and free for children 12 and under when accompanied by an adult. Parking is free in certain areas, $3 in a lot near Gate 17, or $5 for valet.

On the same grounds is the **Kentucky Derby Museum** (ⓒ **502/637-1111;** www.derbymuseum.org), with photos, films, exhibits, and even a chance to sit on a saddle in a real starting gate. It's open year-round Monday through Saturday from 8am to 5pm, and Sunday from noon to 5pm. Admission is $10 for adults, $9 for seniors, $8 for students, and $5 for children ages 5 to 12; guided tours are available every half-hour.

The **Six Flags Kentucky Kingdom Amusement Park,** 937 Phillips Lane, Kentucky Fair and Exposition Center (ⓒ **800/SCREAMS** [727-3267] or 502/366-2231; www.sixflags.com), boasts one of the largest wooden roller coasters in the world and a 750,000-gallon wave pool among its 60-plus rides and attractions. Different parts of the park are open at different times of year, so call before you arrange to spend the entire day. It's open from April to October. Admission is $40 for adults, $25 for seniors and children shorter than 48 inches, free for children 2 and under.

The **Louisville Slugger Museum and Factory,** 800 W. Main St. (ⓒ **502/588-7228;** www.sluggermuseum.org), offers fun for all ages. Look for the giant bat (the world's tallest) standing outside the door. Inside, you can see a bat used by Babe Ruth, as well as miniature souvenir bats, and feel what it's like to stare down the stitches of a 90-mph fastball. The Hillerich & Bradsby factory here is where they turn out thousands of bats for Major Leaguers every year. It's open Monday through Saturday from 9am to 5pm and Sunday noon to 5pm, with 90-minute tours of the factory every 20 minutes from 9am to 3:30pm. Admission is $9 for adults, $8 for seniors, $4 for children ages 6 to 12, and free for children 5 and under.

Gun enthusiasts and history buffs alike will find plenty to ponder at the new **Frazier International History Museum,** 829 W. Main St. (ⓒ **866/886-7103** or 502/412-2280; www.frazierarmsmuseum.org). The interactive museum, which opened in spring 2004 as the Frazier Historical Arms Museum, changed its name a few years later but not its focus. It features the largest collection of arms, armor, and related historical artifacts in the world. Hours are Monday through Saturday 9am to 5pm, and Sunday noon to 5pm. Admission, which includes an audio guide, is $12 for adults, $11 for military, $10 for seniors, $9 for students and children, and $3 for children 4 and under.

The *Belle of Louisville,* moored at Fourth Street and River Road (ⓒ **502/574-2355;** www.belleoflouisville.org), is the oldest operating steamboat on the Mississippi River system. The stern-wheeler was built in 1914 and is now a National Historic Landmark. There's even an old-fashioned calliope on board. The *Belle* and a larger, more modern paddle-wheeler, *Spirit of Jefferson,* carry passengers along the Ohio River. Admission for a 2-hour sightseeing cruise is $16 for adults, $15 for seniors, and $8 for ages 3 to 12.

Where to Stay & Dine

The two grande dames of Louisville hotels are the **Camberley Brown,** Fourth Street and West Broadway (ⓒ **502/583-1234;** www.thebrownhotel.com; $119–$225 double), and the **Seelbach Hilton,** 500 Fourth St. (ⓒ **502/585-3200;** www.seelbachhilton.com; $239–$284 double). The Seelbach opened in 1905, the Camberley Brown in 1923; both are downtown (within boasting distance of each other). Both also have top-flight formal restaurants: the English Grill at the Camberley Brown, and the Oakroom at the Seelbach Hilton.

Along the Ohio River, the gigantic **Galt House,** Fourth Street and River Road (ⓒ **800/626-1814** or 502/589-5200; www.galthouse.com; $165–$210 double), is Louisville's only riverfront, full-service hotel. A few blocks away, the new **Louisville Marriott**

Downtown, is a 616-room high-rise at 280 W. Jefferson St. (© **800/533-0127** or 502/627-5045; www.marriott.com; $139–$249 double).

The chic **21c Museum Hotel,** 700 W. Main (© **877/217-6400** or 502/217-6300; www.21chotel.com), is downtown Louisville's first cutting-edge boutique hotel, featuring a 9,000-square-foot contemporary art gallery and ultramodern furnishings in its 90 rooms. Rates range from $159 to $279 double. Proof on Main is the hotel's upscale restaurant, serving Tuscan-inspired American food, including Kentucky bison and various bourbon-spiked specialty dishes. Open daily for breakfast, lunch, and dinner; entrees start at $18.

Holiday Inn (© **800/HOLIDAY** [465-4329]; www.holiday-inn.com) alone has more than a dozen different properties in the Louisville area. A **Jameson Inn** can be found at 1301 Kentucky Mills Dr. (© **502/267-8100**).

Everybody's favorite restaurant is **Lilly's Lapeche,** 1147 Bardstown Rd., east of downtown (© **502/451-0447;** www.lillyslapeche.com). Owner-chef Kathy Cary, a frequent guest chef at New York's James Beard House, combines local meats and homegrown organic vegetables to create innovative cuisine that changes with the seasons. Main courses run from $10 to $15 for lunch, and $28 to $35 for dinner. **Lynn's Paradise Cafe,** 984 Barrett Ave. (© **502/583-3447;** www.lynnsparadisecafe.com), is considerably more downscale. Folks go here for the melt-in-your-mouth buttermilk biscuits and the famed breakfast burrito. Lunch and dinner are served Tuesday through Sunday. An entree costs about $15.

NORTHERN KENTUCKY

One of the fastest-growing areas of Kentucky is the northern tip, across the Ohio River from Cincinnati. Its many riverfront restaurants and hotels provide spectacular views of the river and the Cincinnati skyline.

Essentials

GETTING THERE   See "Cincinnati," on p. 490.

VISITOR INFORMATION   Contact the **Northern Kentucky Convention and Visitors Bureau,** 50 E. River Center Blvd., Ste. 40, Covington, KY 41011 (© **800/STAYNKY** [782-9659]; www.nkycvb.com).

What to See & Do

One of the newest attractions in Northern Kentucky is the **Creation Museum,** 2800 Bullittsburg Church Rd., Petersburg (© **888/582-4253;** www.creationmuseum.org), a controversial museum that opened in 2006 in the countryside about 7 miles west of the Cincinnati/Northern Kentucky International Airport.

A decidedly Christian endeavor, the 70,000-square-foot museum features state-of-the-art exhibits, interactive sensory theater experiences, and a stellar planetarium show—all designed to entertain visitors while bringing the Bible to life. Scientific and evolution theories are examined in great detail. For example, displays suggest that dinosaurs roamed the Garden of Eden along with Adam and Eve, and that God literally made the entire universe in 6 days, resting on the seventh day.

A magnet for families and church groups, the Creation Museum also offers a Bible-themed restaurant and cafe with outdoor seating, and an extensive gift shop. Surrounded by farmland, the bucolic grounds outside the museum include a petting zoo, a small lake, and landscaped walking trails and picnic sites. Admission is $20 for adults, $15 for seniors, $9.95 for children 5 to 12, and free to children 4 and under. Planetarium admission is an additional $7, and the petting zoo is an extra $2 (children 1 and under are free).

Back in the Covington/downtown Cincinnati area, the **Newport Aquarium,** One Aquarium Way, Newport (© **800/406-3474** or 859/491-FINS [491-3467]; www. newportaquarium.com), is another top regional tourist destination. Located on the banks of the Ohio River, with stunning views of the Cincinnati skyline, the aquarium displays 11,000 marine animals, including 50 sharks and 16 king penguins. It also offers 200 feet of clear, seamless tunnels that put visitors literally face-to-face with sharks and other creatures of the deep. The aquarium is open 365 days a year, from 10am to 7pm Memorial Day to Labor Day, from 10am to 6pm the rest of the year. Admission is $19 for adults, $12 for children ages 3 to 12. Late afternoon and early evening are the best times to avoid crowds.

Leaving the aquarium, head west on Fourth Street, across the Licking River, and in about 2 miles you'll come to Main Street, Covington. A left turn takes you into **Main Strasse Village,** a neighborhood that recalls northern Kentucky's German heritage. Over several blocks, visitors will find an inviting and interesting collection of shops, antiques stores, restaurants, art galleries, pubs, and neighborhood taverns. It's rarely overcrowded and great for a late-afternoon stroll and window-shopping, followed by dinner in a local haunt.

BB Riverboats, 1 Madison Ave., Covington (© **800/261-8586** or 859/261-8500; www.bbriverboats.com), offers short afternoon and evening excursions up and down the Ohio River past the city's skyline, particularly beautiful from the water at night. Call or check the website for information on the numerous options and prices.

Where to Stay

Northern Kentucky has become a popular alternative overnight destination for business and leisure travelers visiting Cincinnati. Most hotels offer shuttle buses to the city or other locations in northern Kentucky. The traffic is not as bad as Cincinnati's, and guests are close to nightlife and restaurants on the south side of the Ohio River.

The **Cincinnati Marriott at RiverCenter** (© **859/261-2900;** http://marriott.com) is a new high-rise hotel right on the river at the foot of Madison Avenue in Covington, directly across from the Northern Kentucky Convention Center. It's a favorite of business travelers; weekend packages are available for leisure visitors. Rates run $159 to $249 double.

A local landmark known for its circular style, the **Radisson Hotel Cincinnati Riverfront** (© **859/491-1200;** www.radisson.com/covingtonky) sits hard against I-75—the major north-south route through Ohio and Kentucky—along Covington's Fifth Street. Rooms cost $99 to $199 double. Other riverfront hotels include **Comfort Suites Hotel** (© **859/291-6700;** www.choicehotels.com), on Newport's Riverboat Row; **Embassy Suites** (© **888/EMBASSY** [362-2779] or 859/261-8400; www.embassysuites.com), at Covington's RiverCenter; **Hampton Inn/Cincinnati Riverfront,** 200 Crescent Ave., Covington (© **800/HAMPTON** [426-7866] or 859/581-7800; www.hamptoninn. com); and **Holiday Inn/Riverfront,** 600 W. Third St., Covington (© **859/291-4300;** www.holidayinn.com).

Northern Kentucky's historic riverfront neighborhoods also offer some quaint bed-and-breakfasts. Two of the best are the **Amos Shinkle Townhouse B&B,** 215 Garrard St., Covington (© **859/431-2118;** www.amosshinkle.net), which is just 2 blocks from the river near the Mike Fink restaurant; and **Christopher's Bed and Breakfast,** 604

located in a restored turn-of-the-20th-century church that features the intriguing combination of whirlpool tubs and stained-glass windows in the guest rooms. Rates at both B&Bs run $105 to $179 double.

Where to Dine

For great views of the Cincinnati skyline and the Ohio River, you can't beat the restaurants along the shorelines in Covington and Newport.

One of the best restaurants in Kentucky is found in Covington's Main Strasse. **Dee Felice Food & Spirits Café,** Sixth and Main streets (© **859/261-2365;** www.deefelice. com), mixes live jazz and spicy New Orleans–style cuisine. Main courses cost $10 to $35.

Just upriver on the east side of the Roebling Suspension Bridge—a Civil War–era span that connects Kentucky with downtown Cincinnati—is **Mike Fink's** (© **859/261-4212;** www.mikefink.com). Named for a legendary riverman, the restaurant is housed in a paddle-wheeler replica at the foot of Greenup Street. Known for its seafood and raw bar, this is a fun place with moderate to expensive prices (main courses $19–$51). (At press time, Mike Fink's was closed for renovations.)

Though it's not directly on the river, **Behle Street Café,** adjacent to the Embassy Suites Hotel just off the riverfront in Covington (© **859/291-4100**), offers the rare combination of good food and low prices (main courses $11–$24). This is a great place to hit for a quick meal or drink before a Reds game or other evening event.

Newport, just east of Covington across the Licking River, has a whole strip of restaurants along an area known as **Riverboat Row.** Most are family friendly and offer outdoor docks and decks that provide wonderful views of the city and give the kids a chance to feed the ducks.

At Newport on the Levee, near the aquarium, I heartily recommend the **Hofbrauhaus** (© **859/491-7200;** www.hofbrauhausnewport.com), a friendly German-American restaurant serving up hearty Bavarian favorites. Main courses run $9 to $13. Try the appetizer sampler, a hefty platter of deep-fried sauerkraut balls, potato pancakes, and two-fisted pretzels with warm beer-cheese dip, among other goodies.

MAMMOTH CAVE NATIONAL PARK

This is the world's longest system of caves and one of America's most popular national parks, drawing almost two million visitors a year. They come not just for the miles and miles of underground exploring, but also for the 53,000 acres of pristine hardwood forest aboveground, where you can hike, ride horses, canoe, go boating, go birding, or camp.

The best way to see everything Mammoth Cave has to offer is by taking a cave tour and then hiking the surface afterward. The parks department runs several cave tours for all ability levels, including one that's open to visitors in wheelchairs. All tours sell out quickly, especially in summer, so reserve in advance.

Essentials

GETTING THERE Mammoth Cave is in western Kentucky, about 100 miles south of Louisville. From Louisville, take I-65 south to Cave City; from Lexington, take the Bluegrass Parkway to I-65, then I-65 south to Cave City. From Cave City, take Ky. 70 west to the East Entrance Road. From Nashville, take I-65 north to Park City, then Ky. 255 north to the South Entrance Road.

VISITOR INFORMATION Entrance to Mammoth Cave National Park (© **270/758-2328;** www.nps.gov/maca) is free. All entrances converge at the visitor center in the southeastern corner of the park. It's open year-round, usually from 8am to 5pm (from 9am Jan–Feb). Ranger-led tours of the caves leave from the visitor center at different times throughout the day.

Cave Tours

Rangers lead a host of different tours through the cave, varying in difficulty from a moderate walk to an all-day affair involving crawling on hands and knees. Call the park or check the website for a complete list. Reservations are strongly recommended for all cave tours. Tours range in price from $5 to $48.

Other Activities in the Park

A variety of hiking trails are available throughout the park. Pick up a hiking map and a schedule of ranger-led walks, and campfire and evening programs at the visitor center. Mammoth Cave has more than 30 miles of canoeing along the Green and Nolin rivers. Pick up a map at the visitor center.

Where to Stay

There are three campgrounds in the park, as well as a dozen backcountry campsites where you might not see another soul. Permits are required for both types of camping. Fees range from $5 to $17 for the campgrounds; backcountry permits are free. All campgrounds have toilets, grills, and drinking water. For more information, contact the campgrounds office (ℓ **270/758-2424**).

The **Mammoth Cave Hotel** (ℓ **270/758-2225;** www.mammothcavehotel.com) is the only lodging within the park boundaries. Accommodations run $55 for basic cabins with shared bathrooms to $94 for rooms with the usual modern conveniences. Cave City is the primary gateway to the park. Here you'll find an assortment of inexpensive chains, such as **Comfort Inn** (ℓ **270/773-2030**) and a **Super 8 Motel** (ℓ **270/773-2500**).

DANIEL BOONE NATIONAL FOREST & KENTUCKY STATE PARKS

When Daniel Boone first crossed into what is now Kentucky more than 200 years ago, he found a naturally beautiful yet rugged landscape: a place of deep forests, high mountains, steep cliffs, pristine lakes, lush valleys, and abundant wildlife. Today these attributes draw millions of tourists each year. The antithesis of eastern Tennessee's traffic-congested, overdeveloped tourist traps, the southeastern highlands of Kentucky are picturesque and unspoiled, marked by small towns and winding, two-lane roads dotted with old barns, country stores, and the occasional antiques shop.

The **Daniel Boone National Forest,** headquartered in Winchester (ℓ **859/745-3100;** www.danielboonecountry.com), covers 21 Kentucky counties. Hiking, camping, rock climbing, fishing, caving, horseback riding, boating, exploring, and hunting are among the activities available to visitors. In addition to the 269-mile Sheltowee Trace National Recreation Trail, there are hundreds of shorter hiking trails to explore.

The park has several campgrounds (© 877/444-6777), but for lodges and cabins (as well as campsites), take advantage of the magnificent **Kentucky State Parks** (© 800/225-8747; www.parks.ky.gov), regarded as the nation's best. Resort parks such as **Cumberland Falls** (© 800/325-0063 or 606/528-4121) and **Pine Mountain** (© 606/337-3066) are revered for their scenic beauty, all-ages recreation, and ranger-led nature activities, as well as for clean, comfortable accommodations and lodge restaurants. Hiking is excellent in all state parks, where maps are available at each park's main Activities Center.

The **Black Mountain ATV Park**, located in Harlan County in the southeastern part of the state, offers 6,000 acres of terrain for motor-happy enthusiasts to traverse. For more information, call **Cumberland Tourism** (© 606/589-5812).

Another family-oriented attraction in the area is the **Big South Fork Scenic Railway** (© 800/462-5664 or 606/376-5330; www.bsfsry.com), located in the Big South Fork National River and Recreation Area along the south-central Kentucky and Tennessee border. The slow-moving, scenic train ride departs from the small-town depot at Stearns and takes passengers to an abandoned coal-mining village and back. Tickets are $18 for adults, $17 for seniors, and $9 for children ages 3 to 12.

For detailed information about the scenic back roads and off-the-beaten path discoveries to be found throughout southern and eastern Kentucky, call © 877/TOUR-SEKY (868-7735) or visit www.tourseky.com.

BLUEGRASS & COAL MINES

The **Kentucky Music Hall Of Fame and Museum** (© 606/256-1000; www.kentuckymusicmuseum.com), in Renfro Valley (south of Lexington, along I-75), honors the rich history of Kentucky performers. The log-cabin-like venue showcases home-state natives from Rosemary Clooney and Ricky Skaggs to the Backstreet Boys. Hours are 10am to 6pm Tuesday through Saturday, and 9am to 5pm Sunday. Admission is $7.50 for adults, $7 for seniors, and $4.50 for children.

Down-home music and variety shows are offered March through December at the nearby **Renfro Valley Entertainment Center** (© 800/765-7464; www.renfrovalley.com). Gospel, bluegrass, country, and comedy acts take the stage at the 1,500-seat New Barn Theater (open since 1990) and the weathered 500-seat Old Barn Theater, where the barn dances began in 1939. (Ticket prices vary.) The area has an RV park, restaurant, and gift shop, as well as several motels.

In the breathtaking highlands of southeastern Kentucky, along the Kingdom Come Scenic Parkway in the tiny town of Benham, lies the **Kentucky Coal Mining Museum,** 221 Main St. (© 606/848-1530; www.kingdomcome.org). Antiques and exhibits pack four levels in this historic commissary, offering a somber glimpse of life in this coal-mining town around the 1940s. Kids can don lighted helmets to explore a simulated mine. Country music fans will lap up all the Loretta ("Coal Miner's Daughter") Lynn memorabilia, including a replica of Butcher Holler, the log cabin where she was raised. Hours are 10am to 5pm Monday through Saturday, and 1 to 4pm Sunday. Admission is $5 for adults, $4 for seniors, and $2 for students and children.

In the northwestern Kentucky river town of Owensboro, the state-of-the-art **International Bluegrass Music Museum,** 207 E. Second St. (© 270/926-7891; www.bluegrass-museum.org), is a must-see for fans of the genre. Bill Monroe and other pioneers are honored through educational, interactive exhibits and artifacts. Hours are 10am to 5pm Tuesday through Friday, and 1 to 5pm Saturday and Sunday. Admission is $5 for adults, $2 for youths, and free to children 6 and under. For more information, contact the Owensboro Tourist Commission, 215 E. Second St. (© **800/489-1131** or 270/926-1100; www.visitowensboro.com).

17 EASTERN TENNESSEE

There's much to see and do on the outskirts of majestic Smoky Mountain National Park, where strip malls and fast-food joints compete with quaint historic towns. So when you tire of bargain shopping in Pigeon Forge's outlet malls or scaling the pedestrian-friendly cliffs of Rock City near Chattanooga, get out and explore the rural countryside, where time seems to stand still.

GATLINBURG

Just 7 miles south of Pigeon Forge on U.S. 321 is Gatlinburg, which borders the Great Smoky Mountains National Park. For more information, contact the **Department of Tourism** at 811 E. Parkway (© **800/267-7088** or 865/436-2392; www.gatlinburg. com).

Gatlinburg is a great place to base yourself if you're interested in being near Great Smoky Mountains National Park (see earlier in this chapter) and want to enjoy a wide range of outdoor activities. As for the town itself, well, despite an aerial tramway/amusement park calling itself **Ober Gatlinburg** (© **865/436-5423;** www.obergatlinburg.com; admission $9.50 adults, $6.50 ages 7–11) with admittedly superb views of the surrounding mountains, this is no little Switzerland. Though not as strip-malled as Pigeon Forge, crowded Gatlinburg is still lined with hotels, restaurants, and other tourist traps.

Most of Gatlinburg's attractions line the Parkway (U.S. 441). In addition to the rides and views available at the Ober Gatlinburg amusement park, the **Space Needle Family Fun Center** (© **865/436-4629;** www.gatlinburgspaceneedle.com) offers a great overview of the town and a fun trip for $7.25 adults, $5 seniors, and $3 children (free for 5 and under with paid adult admission). Believe it or not, **Ripley's Aquarium of the Smokies** (© **888/240-1358;** www.ripleysaquariumofthesmokies.com) isn't the most impressive aquarium you'll ever see, but it can be a fun way to spend an afternoon. One-day admission is $22 for ages 12 and up, $12 for children 6 to 11, and $5.55 for children ages 2 to 5. The museum is open 365 days a year.

Gatlinburg is packed with chain hotels and motels. All the big names, such as **Days Inn, Comfort Inn,** and **Fairfield Inn,** have links here. Or try the **Greystone Lodge,** 559 Parkway (© **800/451-9202** or 865/436-5621; www.greystonelodgetn.com), where the standard motel rooms come with balconies overlooking a stream and free breakfast ($75–$145 double; one- and two-bedroom cottages $125–$225).

For more upscale accommodations with spectacular mountain views, book a room or suite at the Lodge at Buckberry Creek, 961 Campbell Lead Rd. (© 865/430-8030 or 866/30-LODGE [305-6343]; www.buckberrycreek.com). Dubbed "The Great Camp of the Smokies," this elegant, Adirondack-style retreat and restaurant opened in 2005. Rates range from $200 to $360.

For hearty traditional dishes, such as moonshine chicken and barbecue ribs, try the **Park Grill Steakhouse** 1100 Parkway (© **865/436-2300;** www.parkgrillgatlinburg. com), where entrees run $18 to $39. Hickory-grilled ribs and steaks, as well as a large salad bar and full bar, have kept the crowds coming here.

Its sister restaurant, the **Peddler Steakhouse,** 820 River Rd. (© 865/436-5794; www.peddlergatlinburg.com), was built around an authentic pioneer log cabin, rustic yet romantic. Blackened seafood, steaks, and chicken, as well as the dessert known as mud pie, are signature dishes. Entrees range from $18 to $28.

PIGEON FORGE

The interactive **Pigeon Forge Welcome Center,** 1950 Parkway (© 800/251-9100 or 865/453-8574; www.mypigeonforge.com), is a good starting point for exploration in the area.

Pigeon Forge is honky-tonk development run amok. What it lacks in charm and beauty, though, it makes up for with its shopping bargains. There are more than 200 stores in an array of outlet malls, offering discounts of up to 75% for popular brand names like Big Dog Sportswear, Nike, and Black & Decker, as well as Bibles, Christmas decorations, quilts, and cowboy boots.

For shopping that's more quaintly "Tennessee" in tone, check out the Old Mill at 160 Old Mill Ave. (© 888/453-6455 or 865/453-4628; www.old-mill.com). Just look for the sign that says Traffic Light No. 7. (In Pigeon Forge, you'll soon find that most addresses are designated by traffic light stops rather than numbered street addresses.) It may look out of place on Pigeon Forge's relentlessly overdeveloped strip, but it's a good place to pick up locally made gifts like jams and candy and stone-ground products for your own baking. Next door, the restaurant of the same name serves hearty Southern meals at breakfast, lunch, and dinner.

No trip to this part of Tennessee would be complete without a visit to **Dollywood,** 1020 Dollywood Lane (© 865/428-9488; www.dollywood.com), the amusement park owned by Pigeon Forge's beloved daughter, Dolly Parton. The park has been credited with putting Pigeon Forge on the map as a major tourist attraction and almost single-handedly turning around the city's economy. The park's souvenir stands, rides, and cheesy attractions are redeemed somewhat by Dollywood's tribute to Appalachia and the singer's own origins. Demonstrations showcase regional crafts such as basket making, pottery making, and glass blowing, and shops provide an outlet for these traditional skills that might otherwise be lost. New in 2008 is River Battle through Timber Canyon, a family-style white-water-rafting ride. One-day park admission is $50 for ages 12 to 59, $47 seniors, and $37 ages 4 to 11. Closed January through March.

Nightlife in Pigeon Forge focuses on family-oriented, Branson, Missouri–style musical theater. Long-running favorites include the family-oriented **Smoky Mountain Jubilee,** Hwy. 441 at Music Road (© 865/428-1836; www.smokymtnjubilee.com), and **Dolly Parton's Dixie Stampede,** 3849 Parkway (© 800/356-1676 or 865/453-4400; www. dixiestampede.com), a dinner-theater show. Christian themes dominate some programs, such as the 2-hour Broadway-style musical about Jesus, showcasing a large cast and live animals, at the **Miracle Theater** (formerly the Louise Mandrell Theater), 2046 Parkway (© 800/768-1170 or 865/453-3534; www.miracletheater.com). It's open from April to December.

There's no shortage of places to stay in Pigeon Forge. All the major chains are represented. If you want to be in the thick of it all, try the **Best Western Plaza Inn,** 3755 Parkway (© 800/223-9715 or 865/453-5538). If you prefer to be a little farther away from the crowds, try **Mainstay Suites,** 410 Pine Mountain Rd. (© 888/428-8350 or 865/428-8350), which has full kitchens. Both hotels have indoor and outdoor pools, and rates (about $83–$130 double, at both hotels) include breakfast.

Essentials

GETTING THERE   By Plane   You can fly directly into Knoxville's **McGhee Tyson Airport** (© 865/342-3000; www.tys.org).

By Car   Major routes into Knoxville are I-40 from the east (Winston-Salem, North Carolina) and west (Nashville), I-75 from the north (Lexington, Kentucky) and south (Chattanooga and Atlanta), and I-81 from the northeast.

VISITOR INFORMATION   For information on the region, visit the **Gateway Regional Visitor Center,** 301 S. Gray St. (© 800/727-8045; www.knoxville.org). If you're interested in country music, pick up the "Cradle of Country Music" walking tour of downtown Knoxville; if you prefer your sights vintage, try the "Historic Homes" driving tour.

What to See & Do

Your one can't-miss attraction is the **Knoxville Zoo,** 3333 Woodbine Ave., off I-40, near Rutledge Pike, exit 392 (© 865/637-5331; www.knoxville-zoo.org). In particular, watch for the sweet-looking (but apparently ill-tempered) red pandas, and the otter exhibit, where you can see the otters swimming underwater. The zoo is justifiably popular, but unfortunately a little too close to the road; it's a little odd to watch a wrinkly baby rhino eating grass against a backdrop of whizzing cars. Admission is $17 adults, $13 seniors, and $6.95 children 4 and over. Parking is $4.

Fans of *Roots* will want to visit the larger-than-life-size **Alex Haley statue** at 1600 Dandridge Ave., in Morningside Park near downtown Knoxville. The writer was a native of Tennessee and adopted Knoxville as his home. The park is charming, and the seated figure provides a great photo op for those wanting to clamber into the storyteller's welcoming bronze lap.

If it's raining, head over to the **Knoxville Museum of Art,** 1050 World's Fair Park Dr. (© 865/525-6101; www.knoxart.org). The museum features about 12 exhibitions a year, as well as a permanent collection that focuses on postmodern works. Admission is $5 adults and seniors, and free for children 12 and under.

Or visit the new **Women's Basketball Hall of Fame,** 700 Hall of Fame Dr. (© 865/633-9000; www.wbhof.com), downtown; just look for the world's biggest basketball, an orange orb that stands 30 feet tall and weighs 10 tons. Admission is $7.95 adults, $5.95 seniors and children ages 6 to 15.

Where to Stay & Dine

Try to stay downtown, where you'll be close to all major attractions. The **Marriott Knoxville,** 500 Hill Ave. (© 800/836-8031 or 865/637-1234), is adjacent to the Women's Basketball Hall of Fame. The hotel has an outdoor pool (necessary in summer), a restaurant, lounge, and small fitness center. Rates run $119 to $169 double. The **Holiday Inn Select Downtown Convention Center,** 525 Henley St. (© 800/HOLIDAY [465-4329] or 865/522-2800), has almost identical facilities, but its pool is indoors. Rooms cost $119 to $139 double.

CHATTANOOGA

Chattanooga is a great family destination, with historic districts, Civil War sites, and interactive museums, plus a whole range of outdoor activities.

GETTING THERE By Plane Major airlines serve the **Chattanooga Metropolitan Airport** (© 423/855-2200; www.chattairport.com) from Atlanta, Cincinnati, Memphis, and Charlotte. To reach the city center, take Hwy. 153 south to I-75, and then go west on I-24. Exits 1A, 1B, and 1C all get you downtown.

By Car Major routes into Chattanooga are **I-75** from the north (Knoxville) and south (Atlanta), **I-24** from the northwest (Nashville), and **I-59** from the southwest (Birmingham, Alabama).

VISITOR INFORMATION Start your visit at the **Chattanooga Visitors Center,** 2 Broad St. (© 800/322-3344 or 423/756-8687; www.chattanoogafun.com), open daily from 8:30am to 5:30pm, where you can pick up some helpful brochures and maps. Here you can buy discount ticket packages, which get you into several of Chattanooga's most popular attractions. A free electric shuttle from the visitor center makes touring downtown attractions a snap.

What to See & Do

Adjacent to the visitor center is the **Tennessee Aquarium and IMAX 3D Theatre,** 1 Broad St. (© 800/262-0695 or 423/265-0698; www.tnaqua.org), the world's largest freshwater aquarium, with exhibits designed to take you on a journey from the Tennessee River's source in the Appalachian high country, down through the Mississippi Delta. Should you tire of watching the 9,000 critters here busily swimming, flying, and crawling, you can check out the IMAX theater. Open daily from 10am to 6pm (to 8pm some summer evenings). Admission is $20 adults, $13 ages 3 to 12, free for children 11 and under. Combination tickets, which include the aquarium and IMAX theater, are $25 for adults and $17 for children.

The **Creative Discovery Museum,** 321 Chestnut St. (© 423/756-2738; www.cdm fun.org), just 2 blocks from the aquarium, caters to toddlers as young as 18 months while also enthralling the older set with such interactive exhibits as the Artist's and Musician's Studios and the Inventor's Workshop. Hours are daily from 10am to 6pm Memorial Day to Labor Day; otherwise, they are Tuesday through Sunday from 10am to 5pm, and Sunday from noon to 5pm. Admission is $8.95 adults (including children ages 13 and older), $6.95 children 2 to 12.

Culture vultures flock to the **Bluff View Art District** (© 423/265-5033; www.bluffview.com), located just east of the Walnut Street Pedestrian Bridge. Spend some time ambling through the free Sculpture Garden, perched scenically on a bluff overlooking the Tennessee River. The **Houston Museum of Decorative Arts,** 201 High St. (© 423/267-7176), houses an impressive glass collection. It's open Monday through Saturday from 9:30am to 4pm, summer Sunday from noon to 4pm. Admission is $9. Reopened in 2005 after a yearlong renovation, the **Hunter Museum of American Art,** 10 Bluff View (© 423/267-0968; www.huntermuseum.org), showcases paintings, sculpture, decorative arts, and contemporary studio glass—not to mention spectacular river views. Just across the Walnut Street bridge is Coolidge Park, with its beautiful hand-carved carousel, and Frasier Street, where you'll find some funky shops and cafes.

Exploring Around Lookout Mountain

From downtown, Lookout Mountain can be reached quickly and easily via Broad Street to Tenn. 58. Don't miss historic **Incline Railway,** 827 E. Brow Rd. (© 423/821-4224;

www.lookoutmountainattractions.com), the steepest passenger railway in the world, with panoramic views of the city and the Great Smoky Mountains 100 miles away. Round-trips cost $14 adults and $6 ages 3 to 12. Open daily.

Also on Lookout Mountain is **Ruby Falls,** 1720 S. Scenic Hwy. (© **423/821-2544;** www.rubyfalls.com), a 145-foot waterfall located 1,100 feet inside the mountain. If you're at all claustrophobic, or simply don't want to be herded through a cave with a large group of people, skip it. Open daily at 8am. Admission is $15 adults and $7.95 ages 3 to 12.

Best among Lookout Mountain's main attractions is **Rock City Gardens,** 1400 Patten Rd. (© **800/854-0675** or 706/820-2531; www.seerockcity.com), where you'll have a view of seven states on a clear day. Rock City's unique sandstone formations are striking, and younger kids will be fascinated by the displays based on classic fairy tales and nursery rhymes. Open daily year-round. Admission is $16 adults and $8.95 for ages 3 to 12.

If you want to save some money, here's a tip: Discounted tickets to all three Lookout Mountain Attractions (Incline Railway, Ruby Falls, and Rock City Gardens) are $42 for adults and $21 for children.

Civil War buffs should check out the **Battles for Chattanooga Museum,** 1110 E. Brow Rd. (© **423/821-2812;** www.battlesforchattanooga.com). Just 3 blocks from the Incline Railroad's upper station at the entrance to **Point Park** (site of the "Battle above the Clouds" in 1863), this museum features a three-dimensional electronic battle map that presents details of major battles in Chattanooga's Civil War history. It's open daily; admission is $6.95 adults, $4.95 ages 3 to 12.

Where to Stay & Dine

If the name *Chattanooga* makes you yearn for the days of leisurely train travel, there's no better place to stay than the **Chattanooga Choo Choo/Holiday Inn,** 1400 Market St. (© **800/TRACK-29** [872-2529] or 423/266-5000; www.choochoo.com), formerly Chattanooga's main railway terminal. Reserve the motel-issue rooms in the main build-ing for all the comforts of a chain, or if you've got a sense of whimsy or are traveling with kids, try one of the converted train cars. Rates run $139 to $179 double. Alternatively, the Sheraton **Read House Hotel Chattanooga,** Martin Luther King Boulevard and Broad Street (© **800/325-3535** or 423/266-4121; www.readhousehotel.com), is a lovely National Historic Landmark. Rates run $159 to $289 double. Both hotels are on the shuttle route downtown.

After a day spent touring Lookout Mountain attractions, you can't go wrong with a meal at **Mount Vernon,** 3509 Broad St. (© **423/266-6591**), a family-friendly, white-tablecloth restaurant. Besides their signature fried green tomatoes, the locally owned landmark serves delicious salads along with steaks, seafood, and burgers. An entree will set you back about $10.

If you prefer a B&B atmosphere, head to the **Bluff View Inn,** 412 E. 2nd St. (© **423/ 265-5033**), in the Bluff View Arts District, where rooms are spread across three historic houses and rates run $105 to $240 double. There are several dining options in the dis-trict, including the **Back Inn Café,** which has a lovely outdoor patio overlooking the river. Other options are **Tony's Pasta Shop and Trattoria** and **Rembrandt's Coffee House** (try the hand-dipped chocolates or the lemon tarts).

18 NASHVILLE

Nashville may be the capital of Tennessee, but it's better known as Music City USA, the country music capital of the world. At its epicenter, Nashville is still the city where unknown musicians can become overnight sensations, where the major record deals are cut and music-publishing fortunes are made, and where the *Grand Ole Opry* still takes center stage.

ESSENTIALS

GETTING THERE   By Plane   Nashville International Airport (© 615/275-1600) is about 8 miles east of downtown Nashville and is just south of I-40. It takes about 15 minutes to reach downtown Nashville from the airport. Many hotels near the airport offer a complimentary shuttle service, while others slightly farther away have their own fee shuttles; check with your hotel when you make your reservation. The **Gray Line Airport Express** (© 615/883-5555) operates shuttles between the airport and downtown and West End hotels. They run every 15 to 20 minutes daily between 5am and 11pm, and will cost you. Rates are $11 one-way and $17 round-trip.

By Car   Nashville is a hub city intersected by three interstate highways. **I-65** runs north to Louisville, Kentucky, and south to Birmingham, Alabama. **I-40** runs west to Memphis and east to Knoxville, Tennessee. **I-24** runs northwest toward St. Louis and southeast toward Atlanta.

VISITOR INFORMATION   Before heading to Music City, you can get more information on the city by contacting the **Nashville Convention & Visitors Bureau,** 211 Commerce St. (© 800/657-6910 or 615/259-4700; www.visitmusiccity.com).

GETTING AROUND   Because the city and its attractions are spread out, the best way to get around Nashville is by car.

Though it won't get you everywhere you need to go, Nashville is served by the Metropolitan Transit Authority (MTA) bus system (© 615/862-5950). The MTA information center and ticket booth is on Deaderick Street at Fifth Avenue. Adult **bus fares** are $1.25 ($1.75 for express buses); children 3 and under ride free. Exact change is required. You can purchase a weekly pass good for unlimited local rides from Sunday to Saturday for $17 per adult or $10 per youth age 19 and under; a picture ID is required. Seniors and riders with disabilities qualify for a 60¢ fare with an MTA Golden Age, Medicare, Tennesenior, or Special Service card. Call © 615/862-5950 to register for this discount.

For a quick way to get around downtown on weekdays, look for the LunchLINE shuttles. It's a free trolley that loops through the heart of downtown weekdays from 11am to 1:30pm. Riders may hop on or off at any of the 15 stops. No tickets are required. Just look for the yellow LunchLINE signs.

The **downtown route** passes by many points of interest in downtown Nashville and is a good way to get acquainted with the city. For more information, look at this website: **www.nashvilledowntown.com**.

For cab service, call **American Music City Taxi** (© 615/262-0451), **Checker Cab** (© 615/256-7000), or **Allied and Nashville Cab** (© 615/244-7433). The flag-drop rate is $3; after that it's $2 per mile, plus $1 for each additional passenger.

Country Music Hall of Fame and Museum (Best) If you're a fan of country music, this is *the* museum in Nashville. Even if you aren't, almost anyone with an appreciation for American popular music will thrill to such sights as Bob Dylan's barely legible inscription scrawled across a lyric sheet, Emmylou Harris's petite bejeweled cowboy boots, and Elvis's gold-leafed Cadillac (a gift from Priscilla). Savvy multimedia exhibits let visitors explore displays on bluegrass, cowboy music (a la Roy Rogers), country swing, rockabilly, Cajun, honky-tonk, and contemporary country music through personalized CD listening posts, interactive jukeboxes, and computer stations. Nashville resident Vince Gill is said to be a regular here, and other legends have been known to drop by for impromptu concerts.

222 Fifth Ave. S. (at Demonbreun). © **800/852-6437** or 615/416-2001. www.countrymusichalloffame. com. Admission $18 adults; $16 seniors, military, and college students; $9.95 children 6–17. Daily 9am–5pm.

Grand Ole Opry Museum Adjacent to the Grand Ole Opry House, these exhibits are tributes to the performers who have appeared on the famous radio show over the years: Patsy Cline, Hank Snow, George Jones, Jim Reeves, Marty Robbins, and other longtime stars of the show. There are also about a dozen other exhibits on more recent performers. The museum is best visited in conjunction with a night at the *Opry*, so you might want to arrive early. Allow 20 to 30 minutes (just right for browsing before attending a performance of the *Grand Ole Opry*).

2804 Opryland Dr. © **615/871-OPRY** (871-6779). www.gaylordopryland.com. Free admission. Daily 10am to varied closing hours, depending on performance schedule. Closes for special events; call ahead. At the Grand Ole Opry House (it's within the same complex).

The Hermitage (Kids) Andrew Jackson, whose visage graces the $20 bill, built the Hermitage, a stately Southern plantation home. Originally built in the Federal style in 1821, the Hermitage was expanded and remodeled in 1831, and acquired its current appearance in 1836. Recordings that describe each room and section of the grounds accompany tours through the mansion and around it. In addition to the main house, you'll visit the kitchen, the smokehouse, the garden, Jackson's tomb, an original log cabin, the spring house (a cool storage house built over a spring), and, nearby, the Old Hermitage Church and Tulip Grove mansion. You can tour the museum and grounds in a few hours.

Old Hickory Blvd., Nashville. © **615/889-2941.** www.thehermitage.com. Admission $15 adults, $13 seniors, $11 for students 13–18, $7 children 6–12, free for children 5 and under. Daily 9am–5pm. Closed Thanksgiving, Christmas, and 3rd week of Jan. Take I-40 east to exit 221, then head north 4 miles.

The Parthenon This full-size replica of the Athens Parthenon was the centerpiece of the Tennessee Centennial Exposition of 1897. The original structure was meant to be only temporary, but the city opted to reconstruct a permanent Parthenon in 1931. The building now duplicates the floor plan of the original Parthenon in Greece. Inside stands the 42-foot statue of Athena Parthenos, the goddess of wisdom, prudent warfare, and the arts. Newly gilded with 8 pounds of gold leaf, she is the tallest indoor sculpture in the country. A more recent renovation of the building included air-conditioning, which makes for pleasant viewing on muggy summer days.

Centennial Park, West End Ave. (at West End and 25th aves.). © **615/862-8431.** www.parthenon.org. Admission $5 adults, $2.50 seniors and children. Oct–Mar Tues–Sat 9am–4:30pm; Apr–Sept Tues–Sat 9am–4:30pm, Sun 12:30–4:30pm. (Closed Sun after Labor Day.)

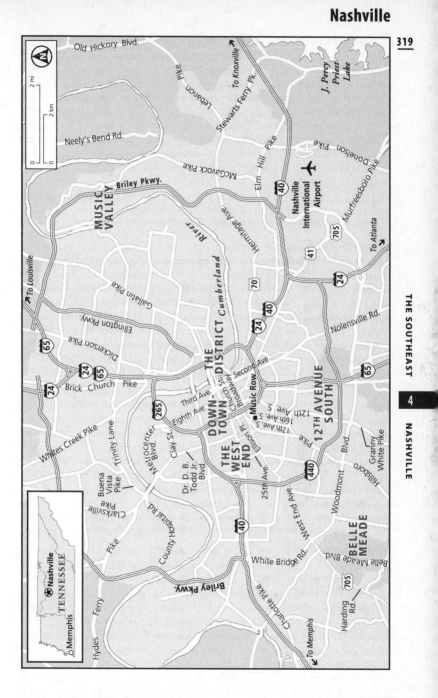

Ryman Auditorium & Museum   The site of the *Grand Ole Opry* from 1943 to 1974, the Ryman Auditorium is known as the "Mother Church of Country Music," the single most historic site in the world of country music. Originally built in 1892, its stage has seen the likes of Enrico Caruso, Katharine Hepburn, Will Rogers, and Elvis Presley. The *Grand Ole Opry* began broadcasting from here in 1943 and hosted the most famous country music radio show in the world until 1974. Since its meticulous renovation in 1994, the Ryman has regained its prominence as a temple of bluegrass and country music. Its peerless acoustics make it a favored venue of rock's best singer-songwriters and classical musicians as well. Acts as diverse as Yo-Yo Ma, Coldplay, and Keith Urban have performed here. Allow at least an hour for a self-guided tour, or opt for a live show instead.

116 Fifth Ave. N. (btw. Commerce and Broadway). (📞 **615/458-8700** or 889-3060. www.ryman.com. Self-guided tours admission $13 adults, $6.25 children 4–11, free for children 3 and under; add $3.75 for backstage tour. Daily 9am–4pm. Closed Thanksgiving, Christmas, and New Year's Day.

WHERE TO STAY

National and regional chain motels in the area are increasing exponentially. Some good choices include the following (see appendix D for toll-free reservation numbers): **Alexis Inn and Suites,** 600 Ermac Dr. (📞 **615/889-4466**), charging $59 to $109; **Doubletree Guest Suites,** 2424 Atrium Way (📞 **615/889-8889**), charging $129 to $179 for a double; and **Drury Inn & Suites,** 555 Donelson Pike (📞 **615/902-0400**), charging $109 to $130. Other budget bets include such old standbys as **Best Western Airport,** 701 Stewart's Ferry Pike (📞 **615/889-9199**), charging $60 to $70 for a double; **Days Inn–Nashville East,** 3445 Percy Priest Dr. (📞 **615/889-8881**), charging $59 to $72 for a double; and **Red Roof Inn–Nashville East,** 510 Claridge Dr. (📞 **615/872-0735**), charging $50 to $60 for a double.

Embassy Suites Nashville (Kids)   This all-suite hotel makes a great choice and a good value for families as well as business travelers. Not only do you get a two-room suite, but breakfast and evening cocktails are included in the rates. The centerpiece of the hotel is its large atrium, which is full of tropical plants, including palm trees. The casual restaurant is located amid the tropical plants in the atrium and serves moderately priced meals. Also in the atrium are the lounge where the evening manager's reception is held and a dining area where complimentary breakfast is served.

10 Century Blvd., Nashville, TN 37214. (📞 **800/EMBASSY** (362-2779) or 615/871-0033. Fax 615/883-9245. www.embassy-suites.com. 296 units. $99–$179 suite. Rates include cooked-to-order breakfast. AE, DC, DISC, MC, V. Free parking. **Amenities:** Restaurant; indoor pool; exercise room. *In room:* Fridge.

The Hermitage Hotel (Best)   This historic downtown hotel, built in 1910 in the classic Beaux Arts style, is Nashville's grand hotel. Reopened in 2003 after an $18-million restoration, this is the city's top choice if you crave both space and elegance. The lobby, with its marble columns, gilded plasterwork, and stained-glass ceiling, is the most magnificent in the city. Afternoon tea is served here Thursday through Saturday. Guest rooms (all of which are suites) are recently upgraded, spacious, and comfortable, with down-filled duvets and pillows on the beds. North-side rooms have good views of the capitol.

231 6th Ave. N., Nashville, TN 37219. (📞 **888/888-9414** or 615/244-3121. Fax 615/254-6909. www.thehermitagehotel.com. 123 suites. $299–$399 suite; $950 2-bedroom suite. AE, DC, DISC, MC, V. Valet parking $18 plus tax. Pets allowed ($25 daily fee). **Amenities:** Restaurant.

Holiday Inn Express   With an inviting, spacious lobby and simple yet elegant furnishings, this above-ordinary property offers a slightly less expensive alternative to the historic Union Station Hotel across the street. In fact, rooms with westward views of the **321**

Union Station's Gothic beauty are an added plus—and though you'll still be able to see and hear the trains rumbling down the railroad tracks, they're not right outside your window as they are at Union Station. This hotel is across the street from the Frist Center for the Arts and a short hike (about 5 blocks straight down Broadway) to bars and night-clubs in the District. Rooms are bright, clean, and reasonably spacious. Free Wi-Fi and continental breakfast are other amenities.

920 Broadway, Nashville, TN 37203. © **800/258-2466** or 615/244-0150. Fax 615/244-0445. www.holiday-inn.com. 287 units, including 14 suites. $149–$179 double; $244–$299 suite. AE, DISC, MC, V. Self-parking $14. **Amenities:** Outdoor pool; exercise room. *In room:* Fridges and microwaves in suites and in all rooms on the 6th and 7th floors.

Opryland Hotel (Kids) What Graceland is to Memphis, Opryland is to Nashville. Whether you're into country music or not, a tour of this palatial property with its 85-foot water fountains, tropical foliage, shops, restaurants, and winding "rivers" has become almost obligatory. The Opryland has the look and feel of a massive theme park, and it does attract thousands of visitors daily (on top of the numbers who are actually staying at this massive hotel). Guest rooms, while modern and comfortable, don't quite live up to the promise of the public areas. There's something here for all tastes and budgets. The hotel's new spa, **Relâche,** provides an extensive array of salon and fitness services. Gift shops, cafes, and food specialty stores are scattered throughout. From family-style Italian dining and a build-your-own burger joint to upscale steak and seafood restaurants, there's something here for all tastes and budgets. Opryland has recently begun charging overnight hotel guests an additional $10-per-day resort fee, which includes the H_2O and Wi-Fi.

2800 Opryland Dr., Nashville, TN 37214-1297. © **888/777-OPRY** (777-6779) or 615/889-1000. Fax 615/871-5728. www.gaylordhotels.com. 2,881 units. $199–$274 double; $319–$3,500 suite. AE, DC, DISC, MC, V. Valet parking $18 plus tax; self-parking $10 plus tax. **Amenities:** 14 restaurants; 3 pools (1 indoor); golf club; fitness center; salon/spa. *In room:* Kitchen or kitchenette (in suites), fridge in some units.

Sheraton Music City Big, elegant, and set on 23 acres in a modern business park near the airport, this large convention hotel has a commanding vista of the surrounding area. In the elegant lobby, you'll find marble floors and burnished cherrywood paneling. Off to one side is a lounge with the feel of a conservatory. Following a recent $8-million renovation, all guest rooms have been updated with an eye toward the business traveler; each room has three phones, large work desks, and plenty of closet space, as well as a couple of comfortable chairs. And here's good news for big-dog owners: Pets up to 80 pounds are accepted with a security deposit but no daily fee. The hotel reserves 20 rooms on the ground-floor level specifically for pet owners.

777 McGavock Pike, Nashville, TN 37214-3175. © **800/325-3535** or 615/885-2200. Fax 615/231-1134. www.sheratonmusiccity.com. 410 units. $109–$189 double; $300–$600 suite. AE, DC, DISC, MC, V. Valet parking $7; free self-parking. **Amenities:** Restaurant; 2 pools (1 indoor/1 outdoor); health club.

Union Station: A Wyndham Historic Hotel Housed in the Romanesque Gothic former Union Station railway terminal, built in 1900, this hotel is a grandly restored National Historic Landmark. Following a $10-million renovation completed in 2007, all guest rooms and public spaces have been updated. The lobby is the former main hall of the railway station and has a vaulted ceiling of Tiffany stained glass. In contrast to the historic atmosphere, decor in the public spaces such as the lobby is contemporary. Although guest rooms offer exterior views, some also have the disadvantage of overlooking the railroad tracks, a plus for railroad buffs but perhaps less endearing to those who

THE SOUTHEAST

4

NASHVILLE

can't sleep with the clang-and-roar that continues day and night. Take a tip that I learned the hard way: Go ahead and splurge on valet parking, because self-parking is inconvenient and down several flights of outdoor stairs.

1001 Broadway, Nashville, TN 37203. © **800/996-3426** or 615/726-1001. Fax 615/248-3554. www.wyndham.com. 125 units. $169–$239 double; $349–$499 suite. AE, DC, DISC, MC, V. Valet parking $20. **Amenities:** Restaurant; exercise room.

WHERE TO DINE

When you just need a quick pick-me-up, a rich pastry, or some good rustic bread for a picnic, there are good cafes, coffeehouses, and bakeries scattered around the city.

In hip Hillsboro Village, you'll find **Fido,** 1812 21st Ave. S. (© **615/385-7959**), a big place with an artsy, urban feel. No, it's not one of those upscale dog bakeries. Though the space used to be a pet shop, it is the friendliest coffeehouse in Nashville. Across the street, you'll find **Provence Breads & Café,** 1705 21st Ave. S. (© **615/386-0363;** www.provencebreads.com), which bakes the best breads and pastries in town and also serves sandwiches and salads. Provence also has a stylish bistro in the new downtown library, 601 Church St. (© **615/644-1150**).

Downtown, in the sunny lobby of the Country Music Hall of Fame and Museum, you can order cocktails or coffee with lunch at **SoBro Grill,** 222 5th Ave. S. (© **615/254-9060;** www.sobrogrill.com). The stretch of 12th Avenue South is where you'll find the funky **Frothy Monkey,** 2509 12th Ave. S. (© **615/292-1808;** www.frothymonkey nashville.com), a bungalow with hardwood floors and a skylight, not to mention free wireless access.

Blackstone Restaurant & Brewery BURGERS/NEW AMERICAN   At this glitzy brewpub, brewing tanks in the front window silently crank out half a dozen different beers ranging from a pale ale to a dark porter. Whether you're looking for a quick bite of pub grub (pizzas, soups, pub-style burgers) or a more formal dinner (a meaty pork loin well complemented by apple chutney and a smidgen of rosemary, garlic, and juniper berries), you'll be satisfied with the food here, especially if you're into good microbrews.

1918 West End Ave. © **615/327-9969.** www.blackstonebrewpub.com. Sandwiches, pizza, main courses $8–$20. AE, DC, DISC, MC, V. Mon–Thurs 11am–midnight; Fri–Sat 11am–1am; Sun noon–10pm.

Bound'ry (Best) NEW AMERICAN/NEW SOUTHERN   With its colorful murals and chaotic angles (seemingly inspired by Dr. Seuss), this Vanderbilt campus–area eatery is a fun yet sophisticated bastion of trendiness, popular with everyone from college students to families to businesspeople in suits. Add some jazz to the wild interior design, and you have a very energetic atmosphere. In addition to signature salads such as the Bound'ry, which combines endive and radish relish with crispy ham, tomatoes, and black-eyed peas, "large platter" entrees include vegetarian dishes such as polenta stacked with eggplant, portobello mushrooms, and cheeses to meaty pork chops and steaks, including the 16-ounce porterhouse. Wine and beer choices are extensive.

911 20th Ave. S. © **615/321-3043.** www.pansouth.net. Reservations recommended, except Fri–Sat after 6:30pm, when it's first-come, first-served. Tapas $4.75–$11; main courses $15–$30. AE, DC, DISC, MC, V. Restaurant daily 5pm–1am. Bars daily 4pm–2:30am.

Cock of the Walk SOUTHERN   No, roosters aren't on the menu. The restaurant takes its unusual name from an old flatboatman's term for the top boatman. This big, barnlike eatery near the Opryland Hotel is well known around Nashville for having the best seafood in town. Like the catfish filets and dill pickles on the menu, the shrimp and chicken are fried in peanut oil. Rounding out the hearty platters are sides such as beans and turnip greens brought to the table in big pots.

2624 Music Valley Dr. ✆ **615/889-1930.** www.cockofthewalkrestaurant.com. Reservations accepted for groups of 20 or more. Main courses $9–$12. AE, DISC, MC, V. Mon–Thurs 5–9pm; Fri–Sat 5–10pm; Sun 11am–9pm.

Harper's AMERICAN/SOUTHERN   If the thought of slow-simmered turnip greens, crispy fried chicken, tender sweet potatoes, and fluffy yeast rolls makes your mouth water, wipe off your chin and immediately head to the Jefferson Street district for Nashville's best soul food. Be sure to save room for a slice of pie or a heaping bowl of banana pudding. Popular with white-collar professionals and blue-collar laborers alike, Harper's attracts a friendly, diverse clientele. Unlike seamier soul-food haunts, this immaculate cafeteria accepts credit cards but (thankfully) does not allow smoking.

2610 Jefferson St. ✆ **615/329-1909.** Main courses $4–$7. AE, DISC, MC, V. Mon–Fri 6am–8pm; Sat–Sun 11am–6pm.

Loveless Café SOUTHERN   For some of the best country cooking in the Nashville area, take a trip to this old-fashioned roadhouse and popular Nashville institution. People rave about the cooking here—and with good reason. Southern specialties are made just the way Granny used to make them back when the Loveless opened nearly 40 years ago. This restaurant may be a little out-of-the-way, but it's well worth it if you like down-home cookin'—and if you're prepared to endure a long wait to get one of the few available tables inside.

8400 Tenn. 100, about 7½ miles south of Belle Meade and the turnoff from U.S. 70 S. ✆ **615/646-9700.** www.lovelesscafe.com. Reservations recommended. Main courses $7–$17. AE, DISC, MC, V. Daily 7am–9pm.

Noshville DELICATESSEN   When the deli craving strikes in Nashville, head for Noshville. The deli cases in this big, bright, and antiseptic place are filled to overflowing with everything from beef tongue to pickled herring to corned beef to chopped liver. Make Mama happy: Start your meal with some good matzo-ball soup. Then satisfy the kid inside you by splurging on a hefty, two-fisted chocolate-and-vanilla-iced shortbread cookie.

1918 Broadway. ✆ **615/329-NOSH** (329-6674). www.noshville.com. Main courses $6–$16. AE, DC, DISC, MC, V. Mon 6:30am–2:30pm; Tues–Thurs 6:30am–9pm; Fri 6:30am–10:30pm; Sat 7:30am–10:30pm; Sun 7:30am–9pm.

The Old Spaghetti Factory ⓚ Kids ITALIAN   With its ornate Victorian elegance, you'd never guess that this restaurant was once a warehouse. Where boxes and bags were stacked, diners now sit surrounded by burnished wood. There's stained and beveled glass all around, antiques everywhere, and plush seating in the waiting area. The front of the restaurant is a large and very elegant bar. Now if they'd just do something about that trolley car someone parked in the middle of the dining room. A great spot to bring the family, this is one of the cheapest places to get a meal in the District.

160 Second Ave. N. ✆ **615/254-9010.** www.osf.com. Main courses $4.60–$10. AE, DISC, MC, V. Mon–Fri 11:30am–2pm; Mon–Thurs 5–10pm; Sat noon–11pm; Sun noon–10pm.

Whitt's Barbecue ⓥ Value BARBECUE   Walk in, drive up, or get it delivered. Whitt's serves some of the best barbecue in Nashville. There's no seating here, so take it back to your hotel or plan a picnic. You can buy barbecued pork, beef, and even turkey by the

pound, or order sandwiches and plates with the extra fixins. The pork barbecue sandwiches, topped with zesty coleslaw, get my vote for the best in town. Among the many
other locations are those at 2535 Lebanon Rd. (© **615/883-6907**), and 114 Old
Hickory Blvd. E. (© **615/868-1369**).

5310 Harding Rd. © **615/356-3435.** www.whittsbarbecue.com. Meals $3–$8; barbecue $6.60 per
pound. AE, DC, DISC, MC, V. Mon–Sat 10:30am–8pm.

NASHVILLE'S COUNTRY MUSIC SCENE

Nashville nightlife happens all around town but predominates in two main entertainment areas—the District and Music Valley. The **District,** an area of renovated warehouses and old bars, is the livelier of the two, whereas **Music Valley** offers a more
family-oriented, suburban nightlife scene.

The *Nashville Scene* is the city's arts-and-entertainment weekly. It comes out on
Thursday and is available at restaurants, clubs, convenience stores, and other locations.
Just keep your eyes peeled. Every Friday, the *Tennessean,* Nashville's morning daily,
publishes the *Opry* lineup, and on Sunday it publishes a guide to the coming week's
entertainment. *Jazz & Blues News* is a free monthly newsletter featuring news and event
listings of interest to music buffs of these genres. It can be found at local bookstores and
cafes such as Café One Two Three.

The show that made Nashville famous, the *Grand Ole Opry,* 2804 Opryland Dr.
(© **800/SEE-OPRY** [733-6779] or 675/871-OPRY [871-6779]; www.opry.com), is the
country's longest continuously running radio show and airs every weekend from this
theater next to the Opryland Hotel. Over the decades, the Opry has featured nearly all
the greats of country music. There's no telling who you might see, but the show's membership roster includes Vince Gill, Martina McBride, Garth Brooks, Loretta Lynn, Porter
Wagoner, Ricky Skaggs, and many others. Nearly all performances sell out, and though
it's often possible to get last-minute tickets, you should try to order tickets as far in
advance of your trip as possible.

Once the home of the Grand Ole Opry, **Ryman Auditorium,** 116 5th Ave. N.
(© **615/254-1445** or 889-6611; www.ryman.com), was renovated a few years back and
is once again hosting performances with a country-music slant. The schedule at the
Ryman also usually includes a weekly bluegrass night in the summer and occasional
Sunday-night gospel/Christian contemporary shows. You can also catch pop, rock, and
classical concerts.

The **Texas Troubadour Theatre/Cowboy Church,** Music Valley Village, 2416 Music
Valley Dr. (© **615/889-2474**), is home to the Ernest Tubb Midnight Jamboree (www.
etrecordshop.com) and the Sunday morning Cowboy Church (www.nashvillecowboy
church.org).

The **Nashville Palace,** 2400 Music Valley Dr. (© **615/884-3004;** www.nashville
palace.net), is open nightly with live country-and-western music, a dance floor, and a full
restaurant. This is where Randy Travis got his start. There's a $5 cover.

The **Wildhorse Saloon,** 120 2nd Ave. N. (© **615/251-1000;** www.wildhorsesaloon.
com), is a massive dance hall that's the hot spot for boot scooters, attracting everyone
from country-music stars to line-dancing senior groups. Free line-dance lessons are available every hour.

The **Bluebird Café,** 4104 Hillsboro Rd. (© **615/383-1461;** www.bluebirdcafe.com),
is Nashville's premier venue for both up-and-coming and established songwriters.
Between 6 and 7pm, there is frequently music in the round, during which four singer-
songwriters play some of their latest works. After 9pm, when more established acts take

the stage, there's a cover charge. Reservations are recommended. The Bluebird's main competition is the **Douglas Corner Café,** 2106 8th Ave. S. (© **615/298-1688;** www. douglascorner.com). Though it has the look and feel of a neighborhood bar, this is one of Nashville's top places for songwriters trying to break into the big time. The club also has occasional shows by performers already established. It's located a few minutes south of downtown.

Tootsie's Orchid Lounge, 422 Broadway (© **615/726-0463;** www.tootsies.net), has been a Nashville tradition for decades and still offers free live country music from 10am to 3am daily.

SIDE TRIPS FROM NASHVILLE

To visit both the battlefield and the distillery described below, head south from Nashville on I-24.

On New Year's Eve 1862, what would become the bloodiest Civil War battle west of the Appalachian Mountains began just north of Murfreesboro along the Stones River. By the end of the first day of fighting, the Confederates thought they were assured a victory, but Union reinforcements turned the tide against the Rebels. By January 3, the Confederates were in retreat and 23,000 soldiers lay dead or injured on the battlefield. Today 351 acres of the site of the conflict are preserved in the **Stones River National Battlefield,** 3501 Old Nashville Hwy., Murfreesboro (© **615/893-9501;** www.nps.gov/stri). The site includes a national cemetery and the Hazen Brigade Monument, which was erected in 1863 and is believed to be the oldest Civil War memorial in the United States. In the visitor center, you'll find a museum full of artifacts and details of the battle. Free admission; open daily from 8am to 5pm.

Old Jack Daniel (or Mr. Jack, as he was known hereabout) didn't waste any time setting up his whiskey distillery after the Civil War came to an end. Founded in 1866, the **Jack Daniel's Distillery,** Tenn. 55, Lynchburg (© **931/759-4221;** www.jackdaniels. com), is the oldest registered distillery in the United States and is on the National Register of Historic Places. After touring the distillery, you can glance into the office used by Mr. Jack and see the safe that did him in. Old Mr. Jack kicked that safe one day in a fit of anger and wound up getting gangrene for his troubles. If you want to take home a special bottle of Jack Daniel's, it can be purchased here at the distillery but nowhere else in this county, which is another of Tennessee's dry counties. Free admission. It's open to the public daily except major holidays from 8am to 4:30pm, with tours at regular intervals throughout the day. No reservations.

19 MEMPHIS

A trip to Memphis is a pilgrimage for Elvis fans and for music fans drawn to the birthplace of the most important musical styles of the 20th century—blues, soul, and rock 'n' roll. Memphis is where W. C. Handy put down on paper the first written blues music, where the King made his first recording, and where Otis Redding and Al Green expressed the music in their souls.

At the far western end of Tennessee, Memphis sits on a bluff overlooking the Mississippi River, Arkansas, and, a few miles to the south, Mississippi. With a metropolitan area of one million, it is a sprawling city, with high-rises sprouting in suburban neighborhoods. The wealthy live, do business, and shop in East Memphis, but in recent years,

Midtown, with its old homes and tree-lined streets, has been rediscovered and now blossoms with hip restaurants, boutiques, and nightlife.

But it was the renovation of Beale Street that succeeded in bringing business and people back downtown in the '90s. Beale Street was home to W. C. Handy, B. B. King, Muddy Waters, and others who merged the gospel singing and cotton-field word songs of the Mississippi Delta into music called the blues.

ESSENTIALS

GETTING THERE   By Plane   The **Memphis International Airport** (© 901/922-8000) is located approximately 11 miles south of downtown Memphis and 9 miles from East Memphis, both off I-240. Generally, allow about 20 minutes for the trip between the airport and downtown, and 15 minutes between the airport and East Memphis—more during rush hour. A taxi from the airport to downtown Memphis will cost about $25; to East Memphis, it will cost about $20.

By Train   Amtrak (© 800/872-7245) serves Memphis with a route that goes from Chicago through Memphis to New Orleans on the *City of New Orleans,* stopping in Memphis at **Central Station,** 545 S. Main St., near Calhoun Street (© 901/526-0052).

By Car   The main routes into Memphis include **I-40** from the east (Nashville) and west (Little Rock/Oklahoma City), **I-55** from the north (St. Louis/Chicago) and south (New Orleans).

VISITOR INFORMATION   For information on Memphis, contact the **Memphis Convention & Visitors Bureau,** 47 Union Ave., Memphis, TN 38103 (© 800/8-MEM-PHIS [863-6744] or 901/543-5300). You can also get information online at **www.memphistravel.com**. The city's main visitor information center, located downtown at the base of Jefferson Street, is the **Tennessee State Welcome Center,** 119 N. Riverside Dr. (© 901/543-6757). It's open daily 24 hours but staffed only between 8am and 7pm (until 8pm in the summer months). Inside this large information center, you'll find soaring statues of both Elvis and B. B. King.

GETTING AROUND   A car is nearly indispensable for traveling between downtown and East Memphis, yet traffic can make this trip take up to 45 minutes. East-west avenues and almost any road in East Memphis at rush hour are the most congested. When driving between downtown and East Memphis, you'll usually do better to take the interstate.

If you want to take the bus, the best bet is to contact **Memphis Area Transit Authority (MATA;** © 901/274-6282) or ask a bus driver for the latest schedule information. The standard fare is $1.50, and exact change is required.

The **Main Street Trolley** (© 901/577-2640) operates renovated 1920s trolley cars (and modern reproductions) on a circular route that includes Main Street from the Pyramid to the National Civil Rights Museum and Central Station, and then follows Riverside Drive, passing the Tennessee State Visitors Center. It's a unique way to get around the downtown area. The fare is $1 each way, with a special lunch-hour rate of 50¢ between 11am and 1:30pm. An all-day pass is $3.50; exact change is required, and passengers may board at any of the 20 stations along Main Street. Trolleys are wheelchair accessible.

For quick cab service, call **Checker/Yellow Cab** (© 901/577-7777) or **City Wide Cab Company** (© 901/324-4202), or have your hotel or motel call one for you. The first mile is $3; after that, it's $1.80 per mile. Each additional passenger is $1 extra.

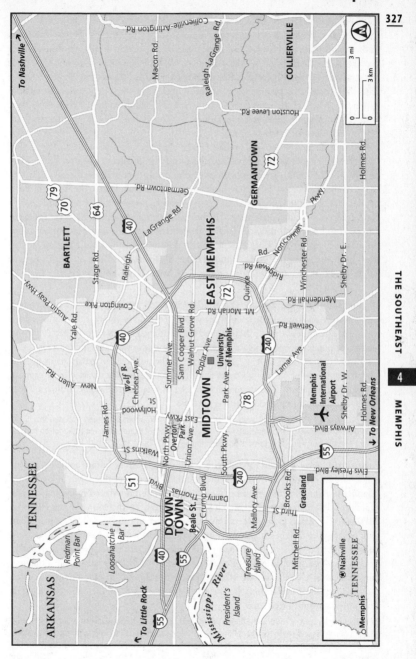

To blues fans, **Beale Street** is the most important street in America. The musical form known as the blues—with roots that stretch back to the African musical heritage of slaves brought to the United States—was born here. W. C. Handy was performing on Beale Street when he penned "Memphis Blues," the first published blues song. Shortly after the Civil War, Beale Street became one of the most important streets in the South for African Americans. Many of the most famous musicians in the blues world got their starts here; besides W. C. Handy, other greats include B. B. King, Furry Lewis, Rufus Thomas, Isaac Hayes, and Alberta Hunter.

Today Beale Street continues to draw fans of blues and popular music, and nightclubs line the blocks between Second and Fourth streets. The **Orpheum Theatre,** 203 S. Main St. (© **901/525-3000;** www.orpheum-memphis.com), once a vaudeville palace, is now the performance hall for Broadway roadshows; and the **New Daisy Theatre,** 330 Beale St. (© **901/525-8981;** www.newdaisy.com), features performances by up-and-coming bands and once-famous performers. Historic markers up and down the street relate the area's colorful past, and two statues commemorate the city's two most important musicians: W. C. Handy and Elvis Presley. In addition to the many clubs featuring nightly live music, check out the **W. C. Handy House Museum,** 352 Beale St., at 4th Avenue (© **901/527-3427**), and the museum-like **A. Schwab Dry Goods Store,** 163 Beale St. (© **901/523-9782**).

Dixon Gallery & Gardens   The South's finest collection of French and American Impressionist and post-Impressionist artworks is the highlight of this exquisite little museum. The museum, art collection, and surrounding 17 acres of formal and informal gardens once belonged to Margaret and Hugo Dixon, who were avid art collectors. After the deaths of the Dixons, their estate opened to the public as an art museum and has since become one of Memphis's most important museums. With strong local support, the museum frequently hosts temporary exhibits of international caliber. Allow an hour for the museum and more time for the gardens.

4339 Park Ave. © **901/761-5250.** www.dixon.org. Admission $7 adults, $5 seniors and students, $3 for children 7–17. Tues–Fri 10am–4pm; Sat 10am–5pm; Sun 1–5pm. Located adjacent to Audubon Park, off of Park Ave. at Cherry Rd. (btw. Getwell and Perkins roads).

Graceland (Kids)   It seems hard to believe, but Graceland, the former home of rock-'n'-roll legend Elvis Presley and annually the destination of tens of thousands of love-struck pilgrims searching for the ghost of Elvis, is the second-most-visited home in America. Only the White House receives more visitors each year. Purchased in the late 1950s for $100,000, Graceland today is Memphis's biggest attraction and resembles a small theme park or shopping mall in scope and design. There are his two personal jets (the *Lisa Marie* and the *Hound Dog II*), the Elvis Presley Automobile Museum, the Sincerely Elvis collection of Elvis's personal belongings, the *Walk a Mile in My Shoes* video, and, of course, guided tours of Graceland itself. If your time here is limited to only one thing, by all means, go for the mansion tour. It's the essence of the Big E. All the rest is just icing on Elvis's buttercream-frosted cake.

3734 Elvis Presley Blvd. © **800/238-2000** or 901/332-3322. www.elvis.com. Graceland Mansion Tour $27 adults; $24 seniors and students; $10 children 7–12. The Platinum Tour (includes admission to all Graceland attractions, including Elvis's Automobile Museum, tours of Elvis's custom jets [the *Lisa Marie* and *Hound Dog II*], and *Sincerely Elvis* film presentation) $32 adults, $29 seniors, $15 children 7–12. Graceland Elvis Entourage VIP Tour (includes the "Elvis After Dark" exhibit) $68 for all ages. Tour reservations can be made 24 hr. in advance and are recommended if you have a tight schedule. Mar–Oct Mon–Sat 9am–5pm,

Sun 10am–4pm; Nov–Feb 10am–4pm daily. (Dec–Feb mansion tour does not operate Tues). Closed **329**
Thanksgiving, Christmas, and New Year's Day. Take Bellevue S. (which turns into Elvis Presley Blvd.) south
a few miles of downtown, past Winchester Ave. Graceland is on the left.

National Civil Rights Museum (Best)   On April 4, 1968, Dr. Martin Luther King
stepped out onto the balcony outside his Lorraine Motel room and was shot dead by James
Earl Ray. The assassination of King struck a horrible blow to the American civil rights
movement and incited riots in cities across the country. Saved from demolition, the Lorraine Motel was remodeled and today serves as the nation's memorial to the civil rights
movement. In evocative displays, the museum chronicles the struggle of African Americans
from the time of slavery to the present: a public bus like the one Rosa Parks was riding
when she refused to move to the back of the bus; a Greensboro, North Carolina, lunch
counter; and the burned shell of a freedom-ride Greyhound bus. Allow 2 to 3 hours.

450 Mulberry St. (at Huling Ave.). $\textcircled{C}$ **901/521-9699.** www.civilrightsmuseum.org. Admission $12 adults,
$10 seniors and students, $8.50 children 4–17, free for children 3 and under. Wed–Mon 9am–5pm. Closed
Tuesday.

Sun Studio   Owner and recording engineer Sam Phillips first recorded, in the early
1950s, such local artists as Elvis Presley, Jerry Lee Lewis, Roy Orbison, and Carl Perkins,
who together created a sound that would shortly become known as rock 'n' roll. Over the
years, Phillips also helped start the recording careers of the blues greats B. B. King and
Howlin' Wolf, and country giant Johnny Cash. By night, Sun Studio is still an active
recording studio and has been used by such artists as U2, Spin Doctors, the Tractors, and
Bonnie Raitt. The place has great vibes, and for those who know their music history,
touching Elvis's microphone will be a thrill beyond measure. Allow an hour.

706 Union Ave. (at Marshall Ave.). $\textcircled{C}$ **800/441-6249** or 901/521-0664. www.sunstudio.com. Admission
$10 adults, free for children 11 and under accompanied by parent. Daily 10am–6pm (studio tours con-
ducted on the hour 10:30am–5:30pm). Closed some holidays.

WHERE TO STAY

National and regional motel chains in the area include the following (see also appendix
D for toll-free telephone numbers): **Hyatt Place,** 1220 Primacy Pkwy. ($\textcircled{C}$ **901/680-
9700**), charging $109 to $149 double; and **La Quinta Inn & Suites,** 1236 Primacy
Pkwy. ($\textcircled{C}$ **901/374-0330**), charging $69 to $99 double.

Elvis Presley's Heartbreak Hotel–Graceland   If your visit to Memphis is a pilgrimage to Graceland, there should be no question as to where to stay. This hotel has a
gate right into the Graceland parking lot. In the lobby, you'll find two big portraits of the
King and Graceland-esque decor. In the back courtyard, there's a smallish, heart-shaped
outdoor pool. Indoors, four themed suites include the irresistibly named "*Burning Love*
Suite." If you don't want to shell out big bucks for the entire suite, ask to split it and just
rent a portion (or one room) of the suite. Many guests do this, we're told. If this place
has one drawback, it's that there's no in-room Internet access (though it's available in the
lobby).

3677 Elvis Presley Blvd., Memphis, TN 38116. $\textcircled{C}$ **877/777-0606** or 901/332-1000. Fax 901/332-1636.
www.elvis.com. 128 units. $110–$135 regular suite; $520 themed suite. AE, DC, DISC, MC, V. Free parking.
Amenities: Pool.

French Quarter Suites Hotel   Its perch in the heart of Overton Square used to be
a big plus, but just as this fledgling midtown entertainment district has been upstaged by
a newly revitalized downtown, so have the few hotels here. Though this hotel looks

charming enough with its French Quarter–style courtyards and balconies, the guest rooms and public areas suggest that the hotel has not been as well maintained as others in town.

2144 Madison Ave., Memphis, TN 38104. (©) **800/843-0353** or 901/728-4000. Fax 901/278-1262. www. memphisfrenchquarter.com. 103 units. $139–$159 double. AE, DC, DISC, MC, V. Free parking. **Amenities:** Pool; exercise room. *In room:* Fridge.

Homewood Suites (Kids) Homewood Suites offers some of the most attractive and spacious accommodations in Memphis. The suites, which are arranged around an attractively landscaped central courtyard with a swimming pool and basketball court, resemble an apartment complex rather than a hotel. The lobby has the feel of a mountain lodge and features pine furnishings, lots of natural-wood trim, and attractive decorations and artwork. Early American styling, with pine furnishings, sets the tone in the suites, many of which have wood-burning fireplaces and contemporary wrought-iron beds. There are two televisions (and a VCR) in every suite, as well as full kitchens and big bathrooms with plenty of counter space.

5811 Poplar Ave. (just off I-240), Memphis, TN 38119. (©) **800/CALL-HOME** (225-5466) or 901/763-0500. Fax 901/763-0132. www.homewood-suites.com. 140 units. $169–$209 double. Rates include cooked breakfast. AE, DC, DISC, MC, V. Free parking. **Amenities:** Pool; exercise room. *In room:* Kitchen.

Madison Hotel (Best) A member of the prestigious Small Luxury Hotels of the World, this sleek new hotel occupies the site of a former bank building. The graceful Beaux Arts architecture belies the bold, contemporary furnishings inside. From the elegant lobby, with its grand piano and musical instrument motif, to the rich, solid colors in the guest rooms, the Madison is a contrast between classic and modern. Whirlpool or jet tubs are available in many rooms. Nightly turndown and twice-daily housekeeping service keep guests feeling pampered. Take the elevator to the outdoor rooftop for breathtaking views of the Mississippi River and surrounding downtown.

79 Madison Ave., Memphis, TN 38103. (©) **866/44-MEMPHIS** (446-6744) or 901/333-1200. Fax 901/333-1297. www.madisonhotelmemphis.com. 110 units. $220–$260 double; $330 and up for suite. AE, DC, DISC, MC, V. Valet parking $15. **Amenities:** Restaurant; indoor pool; fitness center. *In room:* Minibar.

The Peabody Memphis For years, the Peabody enjoyed a reputation as one of the finest hotels in the South. A recent renovation has spiffed up rooms and public spaces, which exude genteel elegance. Marble columns, gilded mezzanine railings, hand-carved and burnished woodwork, and ornate gilded plasterwork on the ceiling give the lobby the air of a palace. The lobby's most prominent feature is its Romanesque fountain. Here the famous Peabody ducks, one of Memphis's biggest attractions, while away each day.

149 Union Ave., Memphis, TN 38103. (©) **800/PEABODY** (732-2639) or 901/529-4000. Fax 901/529-3677. www.peabodymemphis.com. 468 units. $280–$295 double; $670 and up for suite. AE, DC, DISC, MC, V. Valet parking $21; self-parking $16. **Amenities:** 2 restaurants; athletic facility w/small pool.

Talbot Heirs Guesthouse (Value) Trendy, contemporary styling is not something you often associate with the tradition-oriented South, which is what makes this upscale downtown B&B so unique. Each of the rooms is boldly decorated in a wide variety of styles. One room is done in bright solid colors (yellow walls and a fire engine–red tool chest for a bedside stand), while another is done in rich, subtle colors and has a neo-Victorian daybed. The rooms vary in size from large to huge; all have full kitchens—including a refrigerator stocked with milk, juice, and breakfast items.

The Peabody Ducks

It isn't often that you find live ducks in the lobby of a luxury hotel. However, ducks are a fixture at the **Peabody Memphis.** Each morning at 11am, the Peabody ducks, led by a duck-master, take the elevator down from their penthouse home, waddle down a red carpet, and hop into the hotel's Romanesque travertine-marble fountain. And each evening at 5pm they waddle back down the red carpet and take the elevator back up to the penthouse. During their entry and exit, the ducks waddle to John Philip Sousa tunes and attract large crowds of curious onlookers that press in on the fountain and red carpet from every side.

The Peabody ducks first took up residence in the lobby in the 1930s when Frank Schutt, the hotel's general manager, and friend Chip Barwick, after one too many swigs of Tennessee sippin' whiskey, put some of his live duck decoys in the hotel's fountain as a joke (such live decoys were legal at the time but have since been outlawed as unsportsmanlike). Guests at the time thought the ducks were a delightfully offbeat touch for such a staid and traditional establishment, and since then ducks have become a beloved fixture at the Peabody.

99 S. 2nd St., Memphis, TN 38103. ℂ **800/955-3956** or 901/527-9772. Fax 901/527-3700. www.talbot house.com. 8 units. $130–$275 double. Rates include continental breakfast. AE, DC, DISC, MC, V. Self-parking $10. *In room:* Kitchen.

WHERE TO DINE

Automatic Slim's Tonga Club NEW AMERICAN   For relaxed artiness and creative food in downtown Memphis, try Automatic Slim's. The name "Automatic Slim" comes from an old blues song, and the Tonga Club was a local teen hangout popular in the early 1960s. Artists from New York and Memphis created the decor (they're credited on the menu), including zebra-print upholstered banquettes, slag-glass wall sconces, and colorfully upholstered bar stools. Be sure to try a cocktail with some of the vodka-soaked fruit. The food here is as creative as the atmosphere.

83 S. Second St. ℂ **901/525-7948.** Reservations recommended. Main courses $16–$25. AE, DC, MC, V. Mon–Fri 11am–2pm; Mon–Thurs 5–10pm; Fri–Sat 5–11pm.

Chez Philippe FRENCH/NEW SOUTHERN   Still the most opulent dining room in Memphis (though the Peabody's palatial flagship restaurant has lost a bit of its cache in recent years), Chez Philippe still enthralls affluent gourmands who relish its Old South splendor. On the menu, Cuban-born, French-trained chef Reinaldo Alfonso exploits Asian influences in dishes such as seaweed salad with soba noodles, cucumbers, and daikon radishes in a sugar-cane-sesame vinaigrette; and wild salmon slathered in citrus-soy barbecue sauce with a crispy sushi-rice cake and carrot-ginger purée. Prices are the steepest in town, but expect to be pampered.

The Peabody Memphis hotel, 149 Union Ave. ℂ **901/529-4188.** www.peabodymemphis.com. Reservations recommended. Main courses $65–$70. AE, DC, DISC, MC, V. Tues–Sat 6–10pm.

Corky's BARBECUE   Corky's is good-natured and boisterous, with rock-'n'-roll tunes both indoors and out. Aromatic barbecue permeates the air. An argument over which is the best barbecue restaurant in Memphis persists, but this one pretty much leads the pack when it comes to pulled pork shoulder barbecue, topped with tangy coleslaw. Photographs and letters from satisfied customers line the rough-paneled lobby, where you always have to wait for a table. Corky's even has a toll-free number (© **800/9-CORKYS** [926-7597]) to get their delicious ribs shipped "anywhere." A downtown location at 175 Peabody Place (© **901/529-9191**) is around the corner from Beale Street. There's also a Corky's at Dexter Road in Cordova (© **901/737-1988**).

5259 Poplar Ave. © **901/685-9744.** www.corkysbbq.com. Reservations not accepted. Main courses $4–$20. AE, DC, DISC, MC, V. Sun–Thurs 10:45am–9:30pm; Fri–Sat 10:45am–10pm.

Huey's AMERICAN   Ask Memphians where to get the best burger in town, and you'll invariably be directed to Huey's. This good-times tavern also has one of the most extensive beer selections in town. The original Huey's, at 1927 Madison Ave. (© **901/726-4372**), in the Overton Square area, is still in business. In recent years, suburban locations have also sprouted up in East Memphis and beyond.

77 S. Second St. © **901/527-2700.** www.hueyburger.com. Reservations not accepted. Main courses $5–$10. AE, DISC, MC, V. Daily 11am–2am.

The Rendezvous Restaurant BARBECUE   Rendezvous has been a Memphis institution since 1948, and it has a well-deserved reputation for serving the best ribs in town. You can see the food being prepared in an old open kitchen as you walk in, but more important, your sense of smell will immediately perk up as the fragrance of hickory-smoked pork wafts past. You'll also likely be intrigued by all manner of strange objects displayed in this huge but cozy cellar. And when the waiter comes to take your order, there's no messin' around; you're expected to know what you want when you come in—an order of ribs. This Memphis landmark is tucked along General Washburn Alley, across from the Peabody Hotel. Upstairs, you'll find a large bar.

52 S. Second St. © **901/523-2746.** www.hogsfly.com. Main plates $6.50–$18. AE, DC, DISC, MC, V. Tues–Thurs 4:30–10:30pm; Fri 11:30am–11pm; Sat noon–11pm.

MEMPHIS AFTER DARK

To find out about what's happening in the entertainment scene while you're in town, pick up a copy of the *Memphis Flyer,* Memphis's free arts-and-entertainment weekly, which comes out on Thursday. You'll find it in convenience, grocery, and music stores; some restaurants; and nightclubs. You could also pick up the Friday edition of the *Commercial Appeal,* Memphis's morning daily newspaper. The "Playbook" section of the paper has very thorough events listings.

BEALE STREET   This is the epicenter of Memphis's nightclub scene. This street, where the blues gained widespread recognition, is now the site of more than half a dozen nightclubs, plus a few other bars, restaurants, and theaters. For links to various clubs and other big businesses along Beale, click on **www.bealestreet.com**.

The "King of the Blues" does play occasionally, though not regularly, at **B. B. King's Blues Club,** 147 Beale St. (© **800/443-0972** or 901/524-5464). However, any night of the week you can catch blazing blues played by one of the best house bands in town here. Across the street, the **Blues City Café,** 138–140 Beale St. (© **901/526-3637**), takes up two old storefronts, with live blues wailing in one room (called the Band Box) and a restaurant serving steaks and barbecue in the other.

Dozens of autographed guitars, including ones signed by Cal Perkins, Stevie Ray Vaughan, Billie Gibbons of ZZ Top, Joe Walsh, George Thorogood, Albert Collins, and other rock and blues guitar wizards, hang from the ceiling at the **Rum Boogie Café & Mr. Handy's Blues Hall,** 182 Beale St. (© **901/528-0150**). There's live music nightly, with guest artists alternating with the house band, which plays everything from blues to country. Though actually 4 blocks south of Beale Street, **Earnestine & Hazel's,** 531 S. Main St. (© **901/523-9754**), is a downtown dive that has become one of Memphis's hottest nightspots. Things don't really get cookin' here until after midnight. The music is a mix of blues, R&B, and rock, and the clientele is equally mixed.

MORE MUSIC & DANCING   Retro coffeehouse **Java Cabana,** 2170 Young St. (© **901/272-7210**), has poetry readings and live acoustic music on different nights of the week. Although you can't get alcohol here, you can order an espresso.

Club 152, 152 Beale St. (© **901/544-7011;** www.bealestreet.com), is Beale Street's best dance club and is a favorite with energetic young adults who dance the night away on three floors. DJs such as Dave the Worm crank up techno, house, and alternative dance music for revelers who usually party until the early morning hours.

GAMBLING ON THE MISSISSIPPI   A few miles south of Memphis, across the Mississippi state line, casinos are sprouting like cotton plants in the spring. Off U.S. 61 near the town of Robinsonville, you'll find **Goldstrike Casino,** 1010 Casino Center Dr. (© **888/24K-PLAY** or 866/245-7511), and **Sheraton Casino,** 1107 Casino Center Dr. (© **800/391-3777** or 662/363-4900). Continuing south on U.S. 61 and then west on Miss. 304, you come to **Sam's Town Hotel and Gambling Hall,** 1477 Casino Strip Blvd. (© **800/456-0711** or 662/363-0711); **Fitzgerald's Casino,** 711 Lucky Lane (© **800/766-LUCK** [766-5825] or 662/363-5825); **Hollywood Casino,** 1150 Commerce Landing (© **800/871-0711** or 662/357-7700); and **Harrah's,** 1100 Casino Strip Blvd. (© **800/HARRAHS** [427-7247] or 662/363-7777). Continuing south on U.S. 61 to Tunica and then west on either Mhoon Landing Road or Miss. 4, you'll come to **Bally's Saloon and Gambling Hall,** 1450 Bally's Blvd. (© **800/38-BALLY** [382-2559]).

Florida

Florida is the most popular year-round family vacation destination in
the United States. Every year millions escape bleak northern winters to bask in Florida's
warmth, lured to the Sunshine State by the promise of clear skies and 800 miles of spectacular sandy beaches. And for those with children, there's the added bonus of numerous
theme parks and kid-pleasers, from Busch Gardens to Walt Disney World, to add a dash
of magic to your trip. We outline the major visitor highlights of Florida here, but for the
works, we suggest getting a comprehensive guidebook such as *Frommer's Florida* or (if
you're off to the theme parks) *Frommer's Walt Disney World & Orlando*.

For general information, contact **Visit Florida,** P.O. Box 1100, Tallahassee, FL
32302-1100 (© **888/7-FLA-USA** [735-2872]; www.flausa.com). You can request a
visitors' guide in English, Spanish, German, or Portuguese, or browse the guides online.

1 WALT DISNEY WORLD & ORLANDO

When Disney opened the Magic Kingdom in 1971, few imagined what Central Florida
would be like nearly 4 decades later. Today it's bursting (and, in some cases, imploding)
with newer, bigger, and better things to do. **Walt Disney World (WDW)** has four theme
parks, dozens of smaller attractions, tens of thousands of hotel rooms, scores of restaurants, a ton of bars and clubs, and two cruise ships. Toss in **Universal Orlando**'s two
theme parks, **SeaWorld**'s three, and the marginal players, and, well, you really won't have
a problem finding something to do.

GETTING THERE   By Plane   More than 50 scheduled airlines and several more
charter companies serve more than 37 million Orlando-bound passengers who arrive at
the **Orlando International Airport** (© **407/825-2001;** www.orlandoairports.net) each
year. The best travel fares to Orlando are often available during the months of November,
December, and January, excluding holidays (when fares go way up).

If you're not renting a car, **Mears Transportation** (© **407/423-5566;** www.
mearstransportation.com) provides town car and shuttle service to and from the airport;
vans run 24 hours a day and depart every 15 to 25 minutes. Round-trip fares are $27 to
$32 for adults and $21 to $24 for children ages 4 to 11 (actual price depends on your
destination); children 3 and under ride free.

By Train   **Amtrak** trains (© **800/872-7245;** www.amtrak.com) pull into stations in
Downtown Orlando (23 miles from WDW) and Kissimmee (15 miles from WDW).
Winter Park (10 miles north of downtown) and Sanford (23 miles northeast of Down-
town Orlando) also have stations. Amtrak's **Auto Train** provides daily service from Lor-
ton, Virginia, outside Washington, D.C., to Sanford, Florida, 23 miles northeast of
Orlando (17 hr.).

By Car   From Atlanta, take **I-75 South** to the Florida Turnpike to **I-4 West.** From the
northeast, take **I-95 South** to I-4 West. From Chicago, take **I-65 South** to Nashville,
then **I-24 South** to **I-75,** then go south to the Florida Turnpike to I-4 West. From

Dallas, take **I-20 East** to **I-49 South,** then head south to **I-10,** east to I-75, and south to the Florida Turnpike to I-4 West.

VISITOR INFORMATION The **Orlando/Orange County Convention & Visitors Bureau,** 8723 International Dr., Ste. 101, Orlando, FL 32819 (© **800/972-3304** or 407/363-5872; www.orlandoinfo.com), can answer questions and will send you an array of maps and brochures, including the *Official Vacation Guide.* The packet includes the "Orlando Magicard," good for up to $500 in discounts on rooms, car rentals, attractions, and more. You can also order it by calling © **800/643-9492.** For information about **Walt Disney World**—including vacation brochures, CDs and DVDs—contact Walt Disney World, Box 10000, Lake Buena Vista, FL 32830-1000 (© **407/934-7639** or 939-6244; www.disneyworld.com). The website is easy to navigate and provides detailed information and photos. A comprehensive unofficial website is **www.allearsnet.com**. Another site covering the entire Orlando and Central Florida area is **www.travel-insights.com**. For information about **Universal Orlando,** call © **800/837-2273** or 407/363-8000; click on **www.universalorlando.com**; or write Universal Orlando, 1000 Universal Studios Plaza, Orlando, FL 32819. You can obtain **SeaWorld** information at **www.seaworld.com** or by calling © **407/351-3600.**

GETTING AROUND Although you can manage without a car, if you want to see attractions outside Walt Disney World or are staying at some of the outlying Disney resorts, a car is almost a must.

A thorough, free transportation network runs throughout the WDW complex. Disney resorts and official hotels offer unlimited free transportation via bus, monorail, ferry, or water taxi to all WDW parks and properties 14 to 18 hours a day. You can get to Universal and other attractions, too, but you'll have to pay extra. *The pluses:* The system is free; you can save on a rental car, insurance, and gas; and you don't have to pay for theme-park parking. *The minuses:* You're at the mercy of the system, which is often slow and *very* indirect.

Mears Transportation (© **407/423-5566;** www.mearstransportation.com) operates town cars, vans, and buses that go to all of the theme parks, as well as the Kennedy Space Center and Busch Gardens Africa (yes, in Tampa), among others.

Taxis gather at the major resorts, and smaller properties will be happy to call a cab for you. **Yellow Cab** (© **407/699-9999**) and **Ace Metro** (© **407/855-0564**) are both good choices, but keep in mind that taxis are expensive and charges may run as high as $3.25 for the first mile and $1.75 or more per mile thereafter.

FAST FACTS There are first-aid centers in all the major parks. **Doctors on Call Service** (© **407/399-3627**) makes house calls in most of the Orlando area (including the Disney resorts). **Walgreens** has a 24-hour drive-through pharmacy at 5935 W. Irlo Bronson Memorial Hwy. (U.S. 192; © **407/396-2002**). A 6% to 7.5% sales tax (depending on which county you are in) is charged on all goods, with the exception of most edible grocery-store items and medicines. Hotels add an additional 2% to 5% in resort taxes to your bill, so the total tax on accommodations can run up to 12%.

TIPS FOR VISITING WALT DISNEY WORLD ATTRACTIONS

Walt Disney World, home to the four major theme parks of Magic Kingdom, Epcot, Disney's Hollywood Studios, and Animal Kingdom, welcomes around 50 million guests in a typical year.

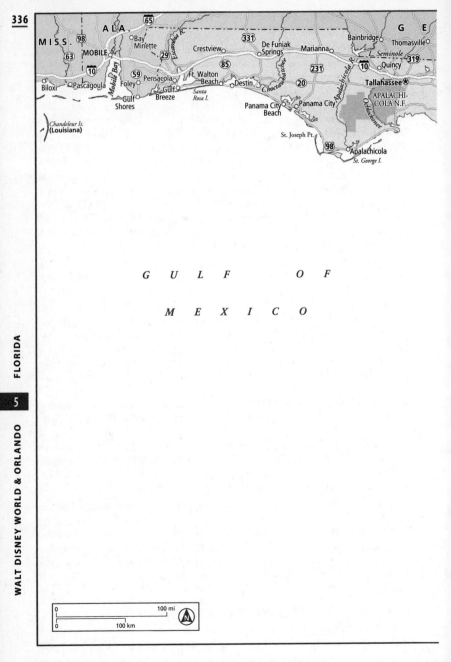

A Note on Area Codes

If you're making a local call in Orlando, you must dial the 407 area code followed by the number you wish to call, for a total of 10 digits.

Besides its larger theme parks, Disney has an assortment of other venues, including Downtown Disney (Cirque du Soleil, DisneyQuest, Pleasure Island, West Side, and the Marketplace), Blizzard Beach, and Typhoon Lagoon, just to name a few.

AVOIDING THE CROWDS   There isn't really an off season in Orlando, but crowds are usually thinner from early January to mid-March and from mid-September until the week before Thanksgiving. The busiest days are generally Saturday and Sunday, when the locals visit. Major holidays attract scores of visitors: Christmas to New Year's is by far the busiest time of year, with the weeks preceding and following Easter a close second. *Note:* Summer, though one of the least expensive times to visit, can also be the worst. The crowds are heavy with locals, and the heat and humidity can be intolerable.

ARRIVE EARLY   Always arrive a good 30 to 45 minutes before opening time, thus avoiding a traffic jam entering the park and a long line at the gate. Grab a park guide. It not only tells you where the fun is (including current ride-restriction and FASTPASS information), but when and where to eat and shop. Pick up a copy of the "Times Guide," too—it includes a schedule for the parks' daily shows and parades. Arrive early (usually about 20–30 min., depending on the season) to get a good seat.

PARKING   Cars, light trucks, and vans pay $12. Visitors with disabilities can park in special areas near the entrances; ask the attendants or call ✆ **407/824-4321.** *Don't forget* to write down where you parked (area and row number); after a long day at the parks, Minnie, Mickey, Goofy, and Donald all start to look and sound alike.

OPERATING HOURS   Park hours vary and are influenced by special events as well as the economy. Don't just assume that a park is open; check the schedule by calling or by visiting **www.disneyworld.com** ahead of time and when you arrive. Hours will vary from park to park as well as from week to week and even day to day.

   Tip: If you are a WDW Resort guest (or are staying at the WDW Hilton, WDW Swan, or WDW Dolphin), you can take advantage of the **Extra Magic Hour** program. This allows WDW Resort guests early entry (or extended evening hours) at select theme parks on select days. Check with your resort on arrival for the latest information.

TICKETS   Disney's ticketing structure (called **Magic Your Way**) gives visitors who stay for a few days far better deals than those who come for just a day. The system allows guests to purchase a base ticket for a set fee and then purchase add-ons, including a Park-Hopper option, and admission to some of Disney's smaller venues. The prices listed below don't include 6.5% sales tax unless noted. *Note:* Price hikes are frequent, so call (✆ **407/824-4321**) or check the website (**www.disneyworld.com**) for the most up-to-the-minute pricing. Note that some tickets can now be purchased in advance on the Web at a small discount

   Ticket durations can vary from a single day to 10 days. Do note that, unlike years past, unless you purchase a no-expiration add-on, it will expire within 14 days of the first day of use. (You don't, however, have to use your tickets on consecutive days.)

One-day/one-park tickets, for admission to the Magic Kingdom, Epcot, Animal Kingdom, or Disney's Hollywood Studios, are $75 for adults, $63 for children 3 to 9. Multiday tickets allow you to visit *one park per day.* A 7-day ticket costs $228 for adults, $193 for kids. A Park-Hopper add-on ($50 *per ticket,* per person) allows visitors unlimited admission to the Magic Kingdom, Epcot, Animal Kingdom, and Disney's Hollywood Studios for the length of their ticket. A 1-day adult Park-Hopper ticket costs $125, while the 7-day version costs $278.

Water Park Fun & More tickets also allow visitors their choice of three to six admissions (the number depends on the length of your pass) to Typhoon Lagoon, Blizzard Beach, DisneyQuest, or Disney's Wide World of Sports. Prices range from $125 for a 1-day adult pass to $278 for a 7-day pass. A 1-day ticket to Typhoon Lagoon or Blizzard Beach is $40 for adults, $34 for children, while a 1-day ticket to DisneyQuest will cost $40 for adults and $34 for children.

THE MAGIC KINGDOM

The most enchanting theme park in Orlando, the Magic Kingdom offers a plethora of attractions, restaurants, and shops in a 107-acre package. Its symbol, Cinderella Castle, forms the hub of a wheel whose spokes reach to seven "lands."

MAIN STREET, USA   The gateway to the Kingdom, Main Street is designed to resemble a turn-of-the-20th-century American street. As soon as you arrive, you can board the Walt Disney World Railroad, an authentic 1928 steam-powered train, for a 20-minute trip around the perimeter of the park. It's a good way to travel if you're headed to one of its three stations—the park entrance, Frontierland, or Mickey's Toontown Fair—or if you want to go for a relaxing ride that has shorter lines. At the end of Main Street, in the center of the park, you'll come to Cinderella Castle, 185 feet high, housing a restaurant and shops. Cinderella herself, dressed for the ball, often makes appearances in the lobby.

ADVENTURELAND   Cross a bridge and stroll through an exotic jungle of foliage, thatched roofs, and totems. On the Jungle Cruise, you sail through an African veldt, an

Go to the Head of the Line with FASTPASS

Don't like standing in long lines? Use the FASTPASS system. Here's the drill:

Hang on to your ticket stub when you enter, and head to the hottest ride of your choosing. If it's a FASTPASS attraction (they're noted in the park guide) and there's a line, feed your ticket stub into the FASTPASS ticket taker. Retrieve both your ticket stub and the FASTPASS stub that comes with it. Two times will be stamped on the FASTPASS—come back during that 1-hour window, and head straight for the FASTPASS entrance where you'll have little or almost no wait.

Note: Early in the day, your window may begin as soon as 40 minutes after you feed the FASTPASS machine, but later in the day it could be hours. Initially, Disney allowed you to do this on only one ride at a time; now you can get a pass for a second attraction 2 hours after your first assigned time. The system can max out, so head to the rides most important to you earliest in the day.

Amazon rainforest, and the Nile River, among other locales. Dozens of animatronic creatures inhabit the hanging vines, cascading waterfalls, and tropical foliage. The **Magic Carpets of Aladdin** delights wee ones with carpets circling a giant genie's bottle while the camels spit water at the passengers and passersby. In the classic **Pirates of the Caribbean,** pillaging pirates wreak havoc upon a small Caribbean town as your boat passes by. Spurred by the popularity of the movie *Pirates of the Caribbean* and its sequels, Jack Sparrow, Barbossa, and Davy Jones have signed on as part of the crew. A tweak in the story line to better mirror the movies, and a mix of new, updated special effects have been added. **Captain Jack's Pirate Tutorial** allows pint-size pirates (pulled from the audience) to train alongside Captain Jack himself. The **Enchanted Tiki Room Under New Management** is a very upbeat and enchanting show featuring a slew of tropical birds singing and telling jokes.

FRONTIERLAND The **Big Thunder Mountain Railroad** roller coaster, on a 200-foot-high red-stone mountain, has tight turns and dark descents rather than sudden, steep drops. It's tailor-made for kids and grown-ups who want a thrill but aren't quite up to tackling the big coasters. The **Country Bear Jamboree** is a hoot, featuring audio-animatronic bears belting out rollicking country tunes and crooning plaintive love songs. Based on Disney's 1946 film *Song of the South,* **Splash Mountain** takes you flume style past 26 colorful scenes that include swamps, bayous, caves, and waterfalls. The ride leads to a 52-foot-long, 40-mph splashdown in a briar-filled pond.

LIBERTY SQUARE Thirteen lanterns, symbolizing the colonies, hang from the Liberty Tree, an immense live oak in the center of the courtyard. Every American president is represented by a lifelike audio-animatronic figure in the **Hall of Presidents.** In the **Haunted Mansion,** darkness, spooky music, howling, and screams enhance the ambience. It's a classic that's more amusing than terrifying for anyone older than 5. A refurbishment has enhanced its unearthly effects and spectral silliness.

FANTASYLAND The attractions in this happy land are themed after classics such as *Snow White, Peter Pan,* and *Dumbo.* If your kids are 8 and under, you may want to make this and Mickey's Toontown your primary stops in the Magic Kingdom.

Cinderella Castle is the Magic Kingdom's icon. Mickey, along with a slew of Disney characters, appears daily. **Cinderella's Golden Carousel** was constructed by Italian carvers in 1917 and refurbished by Disney artists. **Dumbo the Flying Elephant** is a very tame kids' ride, in which the Dumbos go around in a circle, gently rising and dipping. Built for the 1964 New York World's Fair, **"it's a small world"** takes you to countries inhabited by appropriately costumed audio-animatronic dolls singing "It's a small world after all," in tiny doll voices. **Mad Tea Party** is a traditional amusement park ride with an *Alice in Wonderland* theme that's always a hit with the younger set. **Mickey's Philhar-Magic** is an amazing 3-D film. The production's special and sensory effects are incredible. Many of Disney's most beloved characters make an appearance. On **Peter Pan's Flight** you'll ride in airborne versions of Captain Hook's ship. Be prepared for one of the longest waits in the park. A bit too scary for kids 4 and under, **Snow White's Scary Adventure** is as scary as the name implies. The heroine does, however, appear in a few pleasant scenes as she rides off to live happily ever after.

MICKEY'S TOONTOWN FAIR Head off those cries of "Where's Mickey?" by taking the kids to this 2-acre area where they can meet their favorite characters. Everything is brightly colored and kid friendly; there is a kid-size roller coaster, the **Barnstormer at Goofy's Wiseacre Farm. Donald's Boat (S.S.** *Miss Daisy***)** offers a lot of interactive fun,

and the "waters" around it feature lots of fun things. Bring extra clothes or a swimsuit.
Mickey's & Minnie's Country Houses are separate cottages that offer a lot of visual fun and some interactive areas for youngsters.

TOMORROWLAND The cute **Stitch's Great Escape** recruits riders to help capture "experiment 626." On **Buzz Lightyear's Space Ranger Spin,** try to save the universe while flying your cruiser through a world you'll recognize from the *Toy Story* movie. **Space Mountain** usually has *long* lines (if you don't use FASTPASS), even though it's years past its prime. The **Monsters, Inc. Laugh Floor** takes its cue from the hit Disney/Pixar flick as Mike, along with an entire cast of monster comedians, pokes fun at audience members. It is live and unscripted, using real-time animation, digital projection, sophisticated voice-activated animation, and a tremendous cast of talented improv comedians. Younger kids love **Tomorrowland Indy Speedway.**

PARADES, FIREWORKS & MORE For up-to-the-moment information, see the entertainment schedule in the park guide map, as well as the *Times Guide & New Information* card that you can (and should) pick up when entering the park. The Magic Kingdom's first new fireworks display in a little more than 30 years, **Wishes** debuted in October 2003 to lots of acclaim. Its precise mix of choreographed bursts, music, and story is amazing. This is absolutely the best way to end your day in the Magic Kingdom. The fireworks go off nightly during peak periods, but only on selected nights the rest of the year. A 20-minute after-dark display, **SpectroMagic,** combines fiber optics, holographic images, old-fashioned twinkling lights, and a soundtrack featuring classic Disney tunes. The parade runs on a *very limited basis.*

EPCOT

Epcot is an acronym for Experimental Prototype Community of Tomorrow, and it was Walt Disney's dream for a planned residential community. But after his death, it opened in 1982 as Central Florida's second theme park.

The 260-acre park has two sections: **Future World** and **World Showcase.** It's so large that hiking World Showcase from tip to tip (1^1/$_3$ miles) can be exhausting. Depending on how long you intend to linger at the 11 countries in World Showcase, this park can be seen in 1 day, but it's better to do it in 2 days to take it all in properly.

FUTURE WORLD Future World is centered on Epcot's icon, a giant geosphere known as Spaceship Earth. Here are the headliners:

The fountains at the **Imagination** pavilion fire "water snakes" that arch in the air and dare kids to avoid their "bite." The 3-D *Honey, I Shrunk the Audience* show shrinks you, then terrorizes you with giant mice, a cat, and a 5-year-old. **Journey into Your Imagination** features a park favorite, Figment the dragon. **Innoventions** is divided into two sections (both constantly updated). House of Innoventions in **Innoventions East** heralds a smart house equipped with a refrigerator that can make your grocery list, and a picture frame that can send photos to other smart frames. The exhibits in **Innoventions West** are led by Sega's Video Games of Tomorrow.

The largest of Future World's pavilions, the **Land** looks at human relationships with food and nature. **Living with the Land** is a 13-minute boat ride through a rainforest, an African desert, and the windswept American plains. **Circle of Life** blends live-action footage with animation in a 15-minute movie based on *The Lion King.* Soarin' allows guests a bird's-eye view of the diverse California landscape. With feet freely dangling 40 feet above the ground, you'll soar above spectacular scenery projected onto the gigantic domed screen. The **Seas with Nemo & Friends** pavilion has been completely renovated, save the 5.7-million-gallon aquarium that holds a reef and more than 4,000 sea creatures, including, among other aquatic creatures, sharks, barracudas, parrotfish, rays, and dolphins. Also inside is a family-friendly "clamobile" ride that slowly moves you along several stunning undersea scenes; using new animation technology, the characters seemingly swim right along with the live inhabitants in the aquarium. Kids will get a kick out of **Turtle Talk with Crush,** as Crush, the turtle from *Finding Nemo,* engages them in a real-time conversation.

Blast off to Mars on **Mission: SPACE.** Sophisticated simulator technology launches you on an amazing ride through space that feels like the real deal (so some NASA astronauts have claimed, anyway). The original, or orange, version is not for the faint at heart—the green version is far less intense, allowing astronauts-in-training a chance to experience space travel. **Spaceship Earth** is a giant geosphere with an audiovisual adventure inside. Slow-moving cars take you on a journey through the history of communications, which, thanks to recent updates, has improved the experience somewhat. The addition of touch screens enables guests to create their own idea of what the future will look like. An all-new interactive exhibit area where guests can test their skills in the areas of medicine, transportation, and energy management through interactive games and displays has been added as well.

In **Test Track,** you're in your six-passenger convertible that follows what looks like a real highway and includes a brake test, a climb, and tight S-curves. There's also a 12-second burst of speed that reaches 65 mph on the straightaway. The **Universe of Energy** pavilion is home to **Ellen's Energy Adventure,** which features Ellen DeGeneres being tutored by Bill Nye the Science Guy to be a *Jeopardy!* contestant.

WORLD SHOWCASE   Surrounding the lagoon at the north end of the park is a community of 11 miniaturized nations, featuring indigenous architecture, landscaping, restaurants, and shops. The nations' cultural facets are explored in art, dance and live performances, or films. The cast members working at each pavilion are natives of that country. The World Showcase opens at 11am and remains open generally up to 2 hours after Future World closes, so plan on heading there after Future World.

The highlight of **Canada** is *O Canada!,* a 360-degree CircleVision film that shows Canada's scenic splendor, from a dog-sled race to the thundering flight of thousands of snow geese. Bounded by a serpentine wall, the **China** pavilion is entered via a triple-arched ceremonial gate inspired by the Temple of Heaven in Beijing. Outside, the **Dragon Legend Acrobats** provide live thrills. The **France** pavilion is entered via a replica of the Pont des Arts footbridge over the Seine and leads to a $^1/_{10}$-scale model of the Eiffel Tower. Enclosed by castle walls and towers, the **Germany** pavilion is centered on a cobblestone square. The clock tower's glockenspiel figures herald each hour with quaint

A Grand Nightcap

IllumiNations is a blend of fireworks, lasers, and fountains in a display that's signature Disney. The show is worth the crowds that flock to the parking lot when it's over—don't miss it! *Tip:* Stake your claim to the best viewing areas a half-hour before showtime (listed in your *Times Guide*). The ones near Showcase Plaza have a head start for the exits. The Rose & Crown Pub in the U.K. pavilion offers a great view of the proceedings.

melodies. One of the prettiest pavilions, **Italy,** brings visitors over an arched footbridge to a replica of Venice's Doge's Palace.

At **Japan,** a flaming-red *torii* (gate of honor) leads the way to the Goju No to pagoda. The drums of **Matsuriza**—one of the best performances in the World Showcase— entertain guests daily. You'll hear marimbas and mariachi bands as you approach the festive **Mexico** showcase. The newly refurbished **Gran Fiesta Tour Starring the Three Caballeros** offers a cruise through Mexico with a new story line and an overlay of anima- tion staring Donald Duck, Jose, and Carioca. In **Morocco,** the **Medina (Old City)** is entered via a replica of an arched gateway in Fez, leading to Fez House and the narrow, winding streets of the *souk,* a bustling marketplace where all manner of authentic hand- crafted merchandise is on display.

Inside **Norway,** a *stavekirke* (stave church), styled after the 13th-century Gol Church of Hallingdal, features changing exhibits. **Maelstrom,** a ride in a dragon-headed Viking vessel, traverses fiords before you crash through a gorge into the North Sea, where you're hit by a storm (albeit a relatively calm one). The **United Kingdom** pavilion beckons you with **Britannia Square,** a formal London-style park. *Tip:* Don't miss the **British Inva- sion,** a group that impersonates the Beatles daily except Sunday.

U.S.A.—The American Adventure is a dramatization of U.S. history using video, music, and a cast of audio-animatronic figures, including Mark Twain and Ben Franklin. Entertainment includes the **Spirit of America Fife & Drum Corps.**

DISNEY'S HOLLYWOOD STUDIOS

Disney bills this park as "the Hollywood that never was and always will be." Hollywood's Golden Era, around 1940 or so, and done up a la Disney, surrounds you with Art Deco– style buildings accented with pastel colors and neon lights. You'd be hard-pressed to miss Mickey's giant sorcerer's hat looming ahead on Hollywood Boulevard, or the Tower of Terror and the Earful Tower rising above the landscape.

The 35-minute **Hollywood Studios Backlot Tour** takes you behind the scenes via tram for a look at the vehicles, props, costumes, sets, and special effects used in movies and TV shows. In **Catastrophe Canyon,** an earthquake causes canyon walls to rumble. A raging oil fire, massive explosions, torrents of rain, and flash floods threaten you and other riders before you're taken behind the scenes to see how it's done. Over at sound- stage 4, visitors to **Journey Into Narnia** can explore Aslan's stone table chamber and meet Prince Caspian. In the small gallery just beyond the set are elaborate creatures, actual costumes, armory, artwork, and props used in the latest film. Producers adapted *Beauty and the Beast Live on Stage* from the movie.

On the **Great Movie Ride,** film footage, audio-animatronic movie stars, and minia- ture movie sets re-create some of the most famous scenes in film, including clips from *Casablanca, Mary Poppins,* and *Alien.* Peek into the world of movie stunts at the **Indiana Jones Epic Stunt Spectacular.** Arrive early and sit near the stage for your shot at being an audience participant. Kermit and Miss Piggy star in *Jim Henson's Muppet*Vision 3D,* a film that marries Jim Henson's puppets with Disney audio-animatronics, special effects, 70-millimeter film, and 3-D technology.

Younger kids will like the Honey, I Shrunk the Kids Movie Set Adventure, as they can crawl and climb their way through the larger-than-life set. The **Magic of Disney Anima- tion** begins with a presentation co-hosted by Mushu the dragon (from Disney's *Mulan*). Guests can then draw their own Disney characters under the supervision of a working animator. You'll also get the chance to meet a variety of Disney characters.

A Nighttime Spectacle

The fireworks, laser lights, and choreography of **Fantasmic!** make it a spectacular end-of-day experience. The extravaganza features shooting stars, fireballs, animated fountains, a cast of 50, a giant dragon, a king cobra, and 1 million gallons of water. Everything is orchestrated by a familiar sorcerer mouse, accompanied by music and characters from Disney classics.

Younger audiences (ages 2–5) love the 20-minute *Playhouse Disney—Live on Stage!* where they meet characters from *Mickey Mouse Clubhouse, Little Einsteins,* and *Handy Manny,* and dance, sing, and play along with the cast.

The best thrill ride at WDW is the **Rock 'n' Roller Coaster.** Sitting in a 24-passenger "stretch limo" with speakers blaring Aerosmith tunes, you'll blast from 0 to 60 mph in 2.8 seconds, then fly into the first gut-tightening inversion at 5Gs. **Star Tours,** based on the original *Star Wars* trilogy, is a couple of rungs below the latest technology, but still fun. After boarding a 40-seat "spacecraft," you're off in a whoosh on a journey that takes you through some of the more famous *Star Wars* scenes. Next door, pint-size padawans can train with Jedi masters at the **Jedi Training Academy.**

The **Twilight Zone Tower of Terror** is one of the most exciting rides at WDW. As legend has it, during a storm on Halloween 1939, lightning struck the Hollywood Tower Hotel, causing an entire wing and an elevator full of people to disappear—and you're about to meet them in a special episode of *The Twilight Zone.* The ride features random drop sequences. New visual, audio, and olfactory effects have been added. Because it offers a different experience every time, it's the best attraction of its kind.

In a reef-walled theater is the charming musical *Voyage of the Little Mermaid,* which combines live performers with puppets, film clips, and more. Lights, Motors, Action! Extreme Stunt Show features high-speed movie stunts full of pyrotechnic effects and more. Toy Story Mania made its debut in the summer of 2008. Donning 3-D glasses, guests shrink to the size of a toy, hop into fanciful vehicles, then travel and twist along a colorful midway-themed route. American Idol, also debuting in 2008, follows in the footsteps of the hit TV show. Guests can audition, compete—and be judged live on stage. Block Party Bash, an all-new dance party parade, takes to the streets each afternoon. Debuting in 2008, this lively celebration has guests singing and dancing along as acrobats and favorites from Disney-Pixar flicks like Finding Nemo; Toy Story 2; Monsters, Inc.; The Incredibles; A Bug's Life; and others join in.

ANIMAL KINGDOM

Disney's fourth major park combines the elaborate and impressive landscapes of Asia and Africa, including their exotic (and real!) creatures, with the prehistoric lands of the dinosaur. It is as much a conservation venue as much as an attraction, so you won't find the animals blatantly displayed; instead, their habitats blend into the spectacular surroundings.

DISCOVERY ISLAND   The 14-story **Tree of Life** is Discovery Island's central landmark. The tree itself has 8,000 limbs, 103,000 leaves, and 325 mammals, reptiles, amphibians, bugs, birds, Mickeys, and dinosaurs carved into its trunk, limbs, and roots. *It's Tough to Be a Bug!* is a fun 3-D movie with impressive special effects.

DINOLAND U.S.A. Enter beneath "Olden Gate Bridge," a 40-foot Brachiosaurus reassembled from fossils. Slip, slither, slide, and slink through the **Boneyard,** a giant playground with the realistic-looking remains of Triceratops, T-Rex, and other vanished giants. **Dinosaur** hurls you through the darkness in a CTX Rover "time machine" to the time when dinosaurs ruled the earth. **Primeval Whirl** is a spinning, freestyle twin roller coaster, where you control the action through its wacky maze of curves, peaks, and dip-pity-do-dahs. In **TriceraTop Spin,** friendly-looking dinosaur "cars" circle a hub while moving up and down and all around. *Finding Nemo–The Musical,* Disney's new stage production, sees Nemo, Marlin, Dory, Crush, and Bruce (among others) come to life, as live actors in creatively designed, puppetlike costumes work together to re-create the undersea adventure made popular by the hit film.

CAMP MINNIE-MICKEY A character meet-and-greet zone and one of the best theme-park shows in town are the main attractions. The **Character Greeting Trails** should be your first stop (though lines can get quite long). Everyone in the audience comes alive when the music starts at the rousing *Festival of the Lion King,* which celebrates nature's diversity with a troupe of singers, dancers, and life-size critters.

AFRICA Enter through Harambe, a re-creation of an African coastal village at the edge of the 21st century. The **Kilimanjaro Safaris** is one of the most popular rides. As you bump along through a simulated African savanna, you may spot black rhinos, hippos, crocodiles, antelopes, wildebeests, zebras, giraffes, and lions. The downside: If the animals aren't feeling cooperative at the time you're riding, you may not see much. *Ride this one as close to the park's opening or closing as you can.* Hippos, tapirs, mole rats, and other critters are often on the **Pangani Forest Exploration Trail,** but the real prize is getting a look at the gorillas. Don't expect full cooperation, because in hot weather, they spend most of the day in shady areas and out of view.

ASIA Disney's Imagineers did an amazing job of creating the kingdom of **Anandapur. Kali River Rapids** is a good raft ride. Its churning waters and optical illusions will have you wondering if you're about to drop over the falls. You *will* most likely get wet. The **Maharajah Jungle Trek** is an often-overlooked jewel. You may see Bengal tigers through thick glass, while nothing but air divides you from giant fruit bats (with wingspans up to 6 ft.) and smaller inhabitants. **Expedition Everest,** the newest, most impressive attraction in the park, transports guests to the Himalayan village of Serka Zong. Guests board the Anadapur Rail Service train. After passing through bamboo forests and waterfalls, diving through fields of glaciers, and climbing to the snowcapped peaks, the train veers "out of control." A close encounter with a legendary Yeti will have your hair standing on end before it's over.

UNIVERSAL ORLANDO

Universal Orlando encompasses Universal Studios Florida (USF) park; its high-tech theme park, Islands of Adventure (IOA); the entertainment district CityWalk; and three resort hotels.

TICKETS A **1-day, one-park ticket** costs $75 for adults, $63 for children 3 to 9. A two-park unlimited admission ticket, good for 7 consecutive days, runs $90 for adults and children alike. At press time, Universal was also offering a **1-day/two-park** pass for $84 (adults) and $74 (kids ages 3–9), as well as a **3-Park Unlimited Admission ticket** good for unlimited admission to USF, IOA, and **Wet 'n Wild** with park-hopping privileges for 7 consecutive days ($100 for all ages—the best bargain by far), among others. You can save money by purchasing online. You can pick up your tickets at either park or have them sent (for a delivery charge) to your home.

THE FLEX TICKET   The least expensive way to see Universal, SeaWorld, Aquatica, *and* Wet 'n Wild is with a **Flex Ticket,** which lets you pay one price for unlimited admission to participating parks during a 14-day period. The Orlando Flex Ticket, which includes Universal Studios Florida, Islands of Adventure, Wet 'n Wild, SeaWorld, and Aquatica, is $235 for adults and $195 for children 3 to 9. The Orlando Flex Ticket Plus, which adds Busch Gardens Africa in Tampa Bay, is $280 for adults and $234 for kids. FlexTickets can be ordered through Universal (© **800/711-0080** or 407/363-8000; www.universalorlando.com) and the other participating parks. Shuttle service between the parks, even Busch Gardens Africa, is included.

PARKING   Parking is $12 for cars, light trucks, and vans. Valet parking is $18.

Universal Studios Florida

Universal Studios Florida (© **800/711-0080** or 407/363-8000; www.universalorlando. com) features a host of grown-up rides and fun moments for kids. And it's a working motion-picture and TV studio, so occasionally there's filming being done at Nickelode-on's sound stages or elsewhere in the park.

The park is open 365 days a year, usually from 9am to 6pm, though it's open as late as 8 or 9pm in summer and around holidays. Sometimes the park also closes early for special events, so call before you go so that you're not caught by surprise.

Major Attractions

A Day in the Park with Barney stars that big purple dinosaur, Baby Bop, and BJ. It uses song, dance, interactive play, and unique special effects to entertain younger guests. It's a must for preschoolers. Not long after you climb on a San Francisco BART train at **Disaster,** there's an 8.3 earthquake! Concrete slabs collapse, a propane truck bursts into flames, a runaway train hurtles your way, and the station begins to flood. Revenge of the Mummy is a high-speed twisting, turning, adventure through Egyptian tombs, with skeletal warriors in hot pursuit. There are pyrotechnic effects, a state-of-the-art propulsion system, and hair-raising robotic creatures.

Soar with E.T. on a mission to save his planet at **E.T. Adventure;** you'll pass through a forest and glide into space aboard a bicycle. **Jaws** begins calmly enough with a boat ride through New England coastal waters, when suddenly a 3-ton, 32-foot-long great white shark is spotted. You can figure out what happens next. There are plenty of special effects, including a rather heated wall of flame that surrounds your boat.

Buckle up for **Jimmy Neutron's Nicktoon Blast,** as Jimmy's Rocket Pod hurtles you through hyperspace. The attraction also features other popular characters, including SpongeBob SquarePants and Rugrats. In **Men in Black Alien Attack,** you board a six-passenger cruiser, buzz the streets of New York, and use your "zapper" to splatter up to 120 bug-eyed targets. Your laser tag–style gun fires infrared bullets.

Rockit, Universal Studios' newest (and Central Florida's tallest) coaster to date, is slated to debut in 2009. Located between Jimmy Neutron's Nicktoon Blast and the AQUOS Theater (home to the Blue Man Group), on a track spilling out beyond the boundaries of the park, twisting high above Citywalk, riders will be sent careening through corkscrews, tight turns, and dramatic drops—and a record-breaking loop.

Shrek 4-D is a show that can be seen, heard, felt, and smelled, thanks to motion-simulator technology, OgreVision glasses, and special sensory effects. The **Simpsons**

Ride, which made its debut in the summer of 2008, sends guests on an amusing adventure through a side of Springfield that has yet to be explored.

James Cameron supervised the ***Terminator 2: 3-D Battle Across Time,*** featuring original cast members (on film). It combines three huge screens with technical effects and live action on stage, including a custom-built Harley and 8-foot-tall cyberbots. The 3-D effects are among the best in any Orlando park (and rated PG-13). Two million cubic feet of air create a funnel cloud five stories tall at ***Twister . . . Ride It Out.*** Crowds applaud the (PG-13-rated) show when it's all over. **Woody Woodpecker's Nuthouse Coaster** is a kiddie coaster that will thrill some moms and dads, too.

For a good dose of reality TV, catch ***Fear Factor Live.*** Audience members can sign up to participate, but be prepared—the stunts, while toned down, are just as disgusting as on the real show, so be sure you're up for the task before volunteering. ***The Blue Man Group,*** a visually exciting and unique stage show, can be seen daily at the Sharp AQUOS Theater. Show-only tickets start at $59 for adults, $49 for children ages 3 to 9, with combination tickets starting at $112 for adults and $101 for children ages 3 to 9.

Islands of Adventure

This is, bar none, *the* Orlando theme park for thrill-ride junkies. Note that *9 of the park's 14 major rides have height restrictions,* and many rides may not be suitable for those who are tall enough but who are pregnant or have health problems.

Major Attractions

Port of Entry is a towering lighthouse that is the gateway to the five themed "islands." Guest Services is near the gates; the remaining area is filled with shops and restaurants.

At **Seuss Landing,** you'll feel as if you have jumped into the pages of a Dr. Seuss classic. The cat's candy-striped hat marks the entrance to the **Cat in the Hat,** where guests follow the famous story from beginning to end. This chaotic ride has a few swirls and whirls along the way. The High in the Sky Seuss Trolley Train Ride is a whimsical ride that runs along two separate tracks suspended high above Seuss Landing. Traveling in individual "cars," you'll pass by classic Seussian scenes and colorful characters. **One Fish, Two Fish, Red Fish, Blue Fish** is a family favorite where controls let you move your funky fish up or down as you circle a central hub. Watch out for "squirt posts," which spray unsuspecting riders.

Hop on **Caro-Seuss-El.** The not-so-normal carousel gives you a chance to ride characters from Dr. Seuss, including Cowfish, elephant birds, and Mulligatawnies. The outdoor interactive play area, **If I Ran the Zoo,** features flying water snakes and a chance to tickle the toes of a Seussian animal. Kids can also spin wheels, explore caves, fire water cannons, climb, slide, and otherwise burn off excited energy. Be prepared with extra clothes or a swimsuit.

Adrenaline junkies and thrill-seekers thrive on the rides found on **Marvel Super Hero Island.** The original Web master is the star of the **Amazing Adventures of Spider-Man.** Passengers wearing 3-D glasses squeal as their 12-passenger cars twist and spin, plunge, and soar through a comic-book universe. A simulated 400-foot drop feels like the real thing. Look! Up in the sky! It's a bird, it's a plane . . . uh, it's you falling 150 feet, on **Doctor Doom's Fearfall.** The screams that can be heard far from the ride's entrance add to the anticipation. You're fired to the top, with feet dangling, and dropped in intervals, leaving your stomach at several levels. On the **Incredible Hulk Coaster,** you're launched from a dark tunnel and hurtled into the lower ozone while accelerating from 0 to 40 mph in 2 seconds. You will spin upside down 128 feet from the ground, feel weightless, and careen through the center of the park.

More than 150 life-size cartoon images in **Toon Lagoon** let you know you've entered an island dedicated to your favorites from the Sunday funnies. **Dudley Do-Right's Ripsaw Falls** has a lot more speed and drop than onlookers think. Six-passenger logs launch you into a 75-foot dip at 50 mph. You *will* get wet. The three-story boat *Me Ship, The Olive,* is family friendly from bow to stern. Kids can toot whistles, clang bells, or play the organ. Adults and kids 6 and over love Cargo Crane, which lets you drench riders on **Popeye & Bluto's Bilge-Rat Barges,** which are fast, bouncy rafts. The rafts bump and dip 14 feet at one point, as you travel a *c-c-cold* white-water course. You will get *soaked!*

All the basics and some of the high-tech wizardry from Steven Spielberg's successful films are incorporated in **Jurassic Park. Camp Jurassic** play area has everything from lava pits with dino bones to a rainforest. Watch out for the spitters that lurk in dark caves. The multilevel play area has plenty of places for kids to crawl, explore, and expend energy on. **Jurassic Park Discovery Center,** a replica of the lab from the movie, is an amusing pit stop that offers dinosaur replicas and interactive games. The highlight is watching a Velociraptor "hatch." On the **Jurassic Park River Adventure,** a T-Rex thinks you look like a tasty morsel, with spitters launching "venom" your way. The only way out: an 85-foot, almost vertical plunge in your log-style raft. It's steep enough to lift your fanny out of the seat. Expect to get wet.

The **Lost Continent** is a blend of the mysterious and the mythical. The biggest thrill here is **Dueling Dragons,** an intertwined set of two leg-dangling racing roller coasters that send you soaring 125 feet, invert five times, and miss each other by a mere 12 inches. There's a special (longer!) line for the front seat. The **Flying Unicorn** is a smaller coaster that travels through a mythical forest with a fast corkscrew run sure to earn squeals. Those who notice it have fun at the **Mystic Fountain,** a "smart" fountain. It can "see," "hear," and "talk," leading to a lot of kibitzing with those who stand before it and take the time to kibitz back. But be careful: It can squirt you.

The show *Poseidon's Fury* revolves around a battle between Poseidon, god of the sea, and Darkenon, an evil sorcerer. The most impressive effect occurs as you pass through a vortex, where 17,500 gallons of water swirl around.

The much-anticipated **Wizarding World of Harry Potter** is set to debut in 2009.

SEAWORLD

This 200-acre park explores the mysteries of the deep by combining conservation awareness with entertainment. Through the years it has expanded, adding a handful of rides, a shopping and dining area, additional entertainment, and more wildlife. While not as large as its neighbors (Universal and Disney), it won't leave you as exhausted, or exasperated by crowds. The combination of its animal life, calmer atmosphere, beautifully landscaped grounds, shows, and sprinkling of rides makes it a must-see.

TICKET PRICES   A **1-day ticket** costs $70 for ages 10 and over, $60 for children 3 to 9, plus 6.5% sales tax. If you purchase tickets online (at home only) at least 7 days in advance, you can save $10 off the price of an adult ticket and, in addition, each ticket holder (child or adult) will get a second day free.

PARKING   Parking is $10 for cars, light trucks, and vans. For $15, you can park close to the entrance in a specially designated section.

Everyone comes to SeaWorld to see Shamu and his friends—the stars of the new show *Believe.* A new set, spectacular special effects, and an excellent score combine to produce a great show. Those sitting in the first 14 rows are sure to get soaked. *Blue Horizons,* the new dolphin show, features aerial acrobatics, exotic birds, and dolphins. A lovable sea lion and otter, with a supporting cast of walruses and harbor seals, appear in *Clyde & Seamore Take Pirate Island.* It's corny but fun.

SeaWorld's water coaster is **Journey to Atlantis,** which offers a wild plunge from 60 feet with lugelike curves. **Kraken** is a floorless, open-sided coaster where 32-passenger trains place you on a pedestal, feet dangling. You'll climb 151 feet, only to fall 144 feet at speeds of up to 65 mph seconds later, passing underground a total of three times. It's actually higher and faster than any coaster at Universal.

In **Manatee Rescue,** underwater viewing stations and interactive displays combine for a tribute to these gentle marine mammals. You are transported by moving sidewalk through arctic and Antarctic displays at **Penguin Encounter.** You'll get a glimpse of penguins as they preen, socialize, and swim.

The 4-acre **Shamu's Happy Harbor** play area has a four-story net tower with a 35-foot-high crow's nest, water cannons, remote-controlled vehicles, nine slides, a submarine, a water maze, and six new kid-friendly rides, including a cool little coaster.

SeaWorld has added 220 species to its **Shark Encounter.** The pools out front contain small sharks and rays. The interior aquariums have eels, lionfish, barracudas, puffer fish, and larger and more menacing sharks. Enveloping guests in the beauty, exhilaration, and danger of a polar expedition, **Wild Arctic** combines an adventure film with flight-simulator technology to display breathtaking arctic panoramas. Visitors emerge into an exhibit where you can see a polar bear, beluga whales, and walruses.

The **Waterfront,** SeaWorld's most recent expansion, is a wonderfully themed 5-acre Mediterranean seaport village with shops, restaurants (each offering a different atmosphere and menu), and formal shows and street performances.

DISCOVERY COVE: A DOLPHIN ENCOUNTER

Discovery Cove is SeaWorld's newer sister park. Prices vary seasonally but range from $269 to $289 per person (plus 6.5% sales tax) for ages 6 and up if you want to swim with the dolphins, and $169 to $189 if you forego the experience. Double-check prices when you make your reservations (required to enter the park).

The **dolphin encounter** allows guests the opportunity to swim, touch, play, and interact with these intelligent creatures. They can even take a brief, albeit thrilling ride with one. The experience lasts 90 minutes, 35 to 40 minutes of which are spent in the lagoon with a dolphin. The rest is a classroom experience.

Here's what you get for your money, with or without the dolphin encounter: A limit of *no more than 1,000 other guests a day;* continental breakfast, lunch, snacks and drinks, a towel, a locker, sunscreen, snorkeling gear, a souvenir photo, and free parking. Other activities include a chance to swim near (on the other side of Plexiglas) **barracudas** and **blacktip sharks,** and 7 consecutive days of **unlimited admission** to either SeaWorld, Busch Gardens Africa, *or* Aquatica. For an additional $30 per person, you can upgrade to 14 days of unlimited admission to two additional parks (choose from SeaWorld, Busch Gardens Africa, and Aquatica), or for an additional $50 per person you can upgrade to 14 days of unlimited admission to all three.

FLORIDA

5

WALT DISNEY WORLD & ORLANDO

For more information, call ℂ **877/434-7268,** or go to **www.discoverycove.com**. Reserve as far in advance as possible, as it reaches its capacity almost every day.

AQUATICA: SEAWORLD'S WATERPARK

SeaWorld's latest park made its debut as this book went to print. The 59-acre eco-themed waterpark blends up-close animal encounters with high-energy thrills (including racing tunnels and raft rides, slides, and more), a plethora of pools, lagoons, winding rivers, and stretches of sandy beaches. For information, call ℂ **888/800-5447** or go to www. aquaticabyseaworld.com. Admission runs $45 for adults, $39 for kids ages 3 to 9. You can also purchase multiday and multipark passes.

WHERE TO STAY

There are more than 115,000 rooms in the Orlando area, with more added each year. Occupancy can be high much of the time, so always try to book your room as far ahead as possible, especially during peak season, around the holidays and in the summer. The lowest rates are usually available September through early December (excluding Thanksgiving week) and January through April (excluding spring break). In addition to the accommodations here, there are scores of chain hotels and motels. See appendix D at the end of this book for toll-free numbers and websites.

WALT DISNEY WORLD CENTRAL RESERVATIONS OFFICE   To reserve a room or book packages at Disney's resorts, villas, campgrounds, and official hotels, contact **Central Reservation Operations (CRO),** P.O. Box 10000, Lake Buena Vista, FL 32830-1000 (ℂ **407/934-7639** or 939-6244; www.disneyworld.com). They can recommend accommodations suited to your price range and needs. Though the staff can be helpful and knowledgeable, they won't volunteer information about a better deal or a special, so be sure to ask.

Comfort Suites Maingate East (Value   Set back from the main drag, this welcoming hotel is one of the nicest in the area. The lobby and accommodations—consisting of studio and one-bedroom suites—are bright and inviting. Nonsmoking suites are available upon request. The main pool and the children's pool, with an umbrella fountain to keep everyone cool, are open round-the-clock. Entertainment is a stone's throw away: Old Town (a small-scale shopping, dining, and entertainment complex) is just next door, and a great miniature-golf course is located in front of the property.

2775 Florida Plaza Blvd., Kissimmee, FL 34746. ℂ **888/782-9772** or 407/397-7848. Fax 407/396-7045. www.comfortsuitesfl.com. 198 units. $79–$175 double. Extra person $10. Rates include continental breakfast. Children 17 and under stay free in parent's room. AE, DC, DISC, MC, V. Self-parking free. From I-4 take the U.S. 192 E. exit; continue 1¾ miles, then turn right on Florida Plaza Blvd. **Amenities:** Outdoor heated pool; kids' pool; fitness center; free shuttle to Disney, Universal, and SeaWorld. *In room:* Fridge.

Disney's Grand Floridian Resort & Spa   As an orchestra plays in the background, the elegance of this turn-of-the-20th-century Victorian resort transports guests back in time. The crystal chandeliers that hang above the grand five-story domed lobby are just one of the opulent touches you'll find throughout. High tea is served in the afternoon. If you prefer, you can spend the day luxuriating at the spa, the best in WDW. The Grand Floridian is one of the most romantic resorts for couples, especially honeymooners, though families will appreciate the children's programs and recreational facilities. The Victorian-style rooms sleep at least four; almost all overlook a garden, a pool, a courtyard, or the Seven Seas Lagoon. Located directly on the monorail system, the resort makes for a quick trip to the Magic Kingdom or Epcot.

4401 Floridian Way (P.O. Box 10000), Lake Buena Vista, FL 32830-1000. ℂ **407/934-7639** or 824-3000. Fax 407/824-3186. www.disneyworld.com. 900 units. $385–$710 double; $490–$2,795 concierge level; $670–$2,795 suite. Extra person $25. Children 17 and under stay free in parent's room. AE, DC, DISC, MC, V. Valet parking $10; self-parking free. Pets $13 per night. Take I-4 to the Hwy. 536/Epcot Center Dr. exit and follow the signs. **Amenities:** 5 restaurants; grill; character meals; heated outdoor pool; kids' pool; beach; 2 lighted tennis courts; health club; spa; WDW Transportation System; transport to non-Disney parks for a fee. *In room:* Fridge.

Disney's Pop Century Resort ⓥ Value   Gigantic memorabilia from decades past—remember the eight-track and Rubik's Cube?—mark the exteriors at Disney's newest value resort. While there might not be a lot of frills, the price is right for families on a budget who want to bunk with Mickey. The guest rooms and bathrooms—just like those at Disney's All-Star properties—are tiny but will work for a family of four with a bit of concerted effort. The resort is closest to the Wide World of Sports Complex.

1050 Century Dr. (off Osceola Pkwy.; P.O. Box 10000), Lake Buena Vista, FL 32830-1000. ℂ **407/938-4000** or 939-6000. Fax 407/938-4040. www.disneyworld.com. 2,880 units. $82–$141 double. Extra person $10. Children 17 and under stay free in parent's room. AE, DC, DISC, MC, V. Free parking. Take I-4 to exit 65; make a right on Victory Way followed by a right onto Century Dr., which takes you to the resort. Pets $13 per night. **Amenities:** Food court; 2 heated outdoor pools; kids' pool; WDW Transportation System; transport to non-Disney parks for a fee. *In room:* Fridge (upon request for a fee).

Disney's Port Orleans Resort ⓥ Value   Made up of two sections, each with a Southern theme, Port Orleans has the best landscaping and coziest atmosphere of Disney's moderate resorts. The **French Quarter** reflects the charm of New Orleans at the turn of the 20th century, with accents of Mardi Gras; **Riverside,** filled with grand mansions and back bayous, is reflective of the Old South. The dragon-themed Doubloon Lagoon pool, the Ol' Man Island swimming hole, and a playground are a hit with kids. Guest rooms are large enough for four, but it'll be a tight fit. (Bayou Rooms have a trundle bed, offering room for an extra child.) Its central location is just east of Epcot and Disney's Hollywood Studios; there's boat service to Downtown Disney.

2201 Orleans Dr. (off Bonnet Creek Pkwy.; P.O. Box 10000), Lake Buena Vista, FL 32830-1000. ℂ **407/934-7639** or 934-5000. Fax 407/934-5353. www.disneyworld.com. 3,056 units. $149–$230 double. Extra person $15. Children 17 and under stay free in parent's room. AE, DC, DISC, MC, V. Free parking. Take I-4 to the Hwy. 536/Epcot Center Dr. exit and follow the signs. Pets $13 per night. **Amenities:** 2 restaurants; grill/food court; 6 heated outdoor pools; 2 kids' pools; WDW Transportation System; transport to non-Disney parks for a fee. *In room:* Fridge.

Disney's Wilderness Lodge & Villas   The Wilderness Lodge is surrounded by a forest of towering pines, cypress, and oaks. Beyond the "spring fed" pool, set amid the rocky landscape, a spouting geyser erupts periodically. The grand log-framed lobby is adorned by a stone hearth, two gigantic totem poles, and four tepee chandeliers, giving the resort an old-time national park feel. Standard rooms at the lodge sleep 4, while the villas next door can accommodate up to 12. The decor is among Disney's best, and the restaurants have some of the most spectacular views in WDW.

901 W. Timberline Dr. (on the southwest shore of Bay Lake just east of the Magic Kingdom; P.O. Box 10000), Lake Buena Vista, FL 32830-1000. ℂ **407/934-7639** or 938-4300. Fax 407/824-3232. www.disneyworld.com. 909 units. $225–$710 lodge; $385–$1,330 concierge level; $405–$1,330 suite; $305–$1,075 villa. Extra person $25. Children 17 and under stay free in parent's room. AE, DC, DISC, MC, V. Valet parking $10; self-parking free. Take I-4 to the Hwy. 536/Epcot Center Dr. exit and follow the signs. Pets $13 per night. **Amenities:** 2 restaurants; heated outdoor pool; kids' pool; WDW Transportation System; transport to non-Disney parks for a fee. *In room:* Full kitchen (in villas), kitchenette (in villa studios), fridge.

Disney's Yacht Club Resort   The upscale, nautically themed Yacht Club shares its extensive recreational facilities with the Beach Club, just next door. White sandy beaches and an immense, beautifully landscaped swimming area (with sand-bottom pools, water slides, and a shipwreck to explore) line the lagoon side of the resort. The atmosphere is geared more toward adults and families with older children. The turn-of-the-20th-century New England theme can be felt throughout. Rooms have space for up to five people, and most have balconies. Epcot is just a short walk away.

1700 Epcot Resorts Blvd. (off Buena Vista Dr.; P.O. Box 10000), Lake Buena Vista, FL 32830-1000. © **407/ 934-7639** or 934-7000. Fax 407/924-3450. www.disneyworld.com. 630 units. $325–$560 double; $445– $2,385 concierge level; $590–$2,385 suite. Extra person $25. Children 17 and under stay free in parent's room. AE, DC, DISC, MC, V. Valet parking $10; self-parking free. Take I-4 to the Hwy. 536/Epcot Center Dr. exit and follow the signs. Pets $13 per night. **Amenities:** 3 restaurants; grill; 2 heated outdoor pools; kids' pool; 2 lighted tennis courts; WDW Transportation System; transport to non-Disney parks for a fee; all rooms nonsmoking. *In room:* Fridge.

Fairfield Inn and Suites International Drive ⓥ**alue**   If you're looking for I-Drive's best value, it's hard to beat the Fairfield. It has a quiet location off the main drag; earthly rates; and clean, comfortable motel rooms in one package. Some of the shops, restaurants, and smaller attractions that line I-Drive are within walking distance.

7495 Canada Ave. (off International Dr. near Sand Lake Rd.), Orlando, FL 32819. © **407/351-7000.** Fax 407/351-0052. www.fairfieldinn.com. 200 units. $98–$120 for up to 4. Rates include continental breakfast. AE, DC, DISC, MC, V. Self-parking free. From I-4, take the Sand Lake Rd./Hwy. 482 exit east, then turn east onto Canada Ave. **Amenities:** Outdoor heated pool; transportation to the parks for a fee. *In room:* Fridge (in some), microwave (in some).

Hyatt Regency Grand Cypress Resort   Long a favorite of honeymooners, this upscale resort offers plenty for families, too. The lobby invites you in with its lush foliage, walkways, and soft music. The 18-story atrium has inner and outer glass elevators and a skylight. The rooms, decorated with a Laura Ashley flair, are large enough to sleep four. Major renovations are planned for 2009 and include the addition of a full-service spa, a complete overhaul of the guest rooms and suites, the addition of new restaurants, and more. The Hyatt shares a golf club, racquet club, and equestrian center with the Villas of Grand Cypress; both offer packages aimed at the sports set. The Hyatt's half-acre, 800,000-gallon pool is one of the best in Orlando and features caves, grottoes, waterfalls, rope bridges, and a 45-foot water slide.

1 N. Jacaranda (off Hwy. 535), Orlando, FL 32836. © **800/233-1234** or 407/239-1234. Fax 407/239-3800. www.grandcypress.com. 750 units. $219–$529 double; $599–$5,750 suite. Optional daily resort fee $13. Extra person $25. Children 17 and under stay free in parent's room. AE, DC, DISC, MC, V. Valet parking $19; self-parking free. Take I-4 to the Hwy. 535/Apopka-Vineland Rd. exit and go north; then turn left at the 2nd light (after the ramp light) onto Hwy. 535. **Amenities:** 4 restaurants; large heated outdoor pool; 45 holes of golf; 12 tennis courts (5 lighted); health club; spa; free Disney shuttle; transportation to non-Disney parks for a fee.

Marriott's Orlando World Center   Golf, tennis, and spa lovers will find plenty to do at this 230-acre upscale resort, thanks to the array of activities it offers. The largest of its five pools has water slides and waterfalls surrounded by plenty of space to relax among the palm trees and tropical landscaping. The location, set back from the main thoroughfare, 2 miles from the Disney parks, is a plus. The large, comfortable, and beautifully decorated rooms sleep four, and the higher poolside floors have views of Disney. Discounts and special packages are often offered throughout the year.

8701 World Center Dr. (on Hwy. 536 btw. I-4 and Hwy. 535), Orlando, FL 32821. © **800/621-0638** or 407/239-4200. Fax 407/238-8777. www.marriottworldcenter.com. 2,111 units. $340–$406 for up to 5;

$750–$1,600 suite. Children 17 and under stay free in parent's room. AE, DC, DISC, MC, V. Valet parking $19; self-parking $11. Take I-4 to the Hwy. 535/Apopka-Vineland Rd. exit, go south 1½ miles, proceed right/west on Hwy. 536, and continue ¼ mile. **Amenities:** 4 restaurants; 3 heated outdoor pools; heated indoor pool; kids' pool; 18-hole golf course; 8 lighted tennis courts; health club; spa; transportation to all theme parks for a fee.

Nickelodeon Family Suites Ⓚⁱᵈˢ This all-suite property is the first Nickelodeon-branded resort and one of the best in the Orlando area for families. Its brightly colored Kid Suites feature a separate bedroom for the kids (with either bunks or twin beds, TV, video game system, and more), mini-kitchens, and pullout sofas in the living areas. Three-bedroom suites include a second bathroom and a full kitchen. The lobby and Mall area are filled with casual restaurants, an arcade, shops, and nightly entertainment venues. The resort's two pool areas have extensive multilevel water slides, flumes, climbing nets, and water jets. "Nick After Dark," an evening supervised activity program for kids ages 5 to 12, allows weary parents a night off. Up to four kids can eat for free per paying adult at the breakfast buffet (not including the character breakfast).

14500 Continental Gateway (off Hwy. 536), Lake Buena Vista, FL 32821. Ⓒ **877/387-5437,** 407/387-5437, or 866/GO2-NICK (462-6425). Fax 407/387-1489. www.nickhotel.com. 789 units. $179–$1,050 suite. AE, DC, DISC, MC, V. Self-parking free. From I-4, take the Hwy. 536/International Dr. exit east 1 mile to the resort. **Amenities:** Restaurant; fast-food counters; kids-eat-free program; character breakfast; kids' spa; 2 waterpark pools; minigolf course; fitness center; complimentary recreation center for ages 4–12; free shuttle to Disney, Universal Orlando, and SeaWorld parks. *In room:* Full kitchen (in some suites), fridge.

Peabody Orlando The five mallards that march into a lobby fountain every morning at 11am are just part of the appeal of this upscale, service-oriented hotel. Primarily a business and convention destination, the Peabody also appeals to adults looking for a hotel that provides top-of-the-line amenities and atmosphere. Rooms sleep up to five and are well appointed. Those on the west side (sixth floor and higher) offer distant views of Disney. As we went to press, a second tower was under construction, adding 750 additional rooms, a full-service spa, and a grotto-style pool.

9801 International Dr. (btw. Beach Line Expwy. and Sand Lake Rd.), Orlando, FL 32819. Ⓒ **800/732-2639** or 407/352-4000. Fax 407/354-1424. www.peabodyorlando.com. 891 units. $336–$395 standard room for up to 3; $550–$1,775 suite. Extra person $25. Children 17 and under stay free in parent's room. AE, DC, DISC, MC, V. Valet parking $18; self-parking free. From I-4, take the Sand Lake Rd./Hwy. 482 exit east to International Dr., then go south. Hotel is on the left across from the Convention Center. **Amenities:** 4 restaurants; outdoor heated pool; kids' pool; 4 lighted tennis courts; fitness center; spa; shuttle to WDW and other parks for a fee.

Royal Pacific Resort Ⓚⁱᵈˢ This Universal Orlando resort features a spectacular beachfront lagoon-style pool. It's lined with palm trees, walkways, waterfalls, and an orchid garden, giving it a remote island feel. The rooms are decorated with wooden carvings and accents. Recent renovations include the addition of Jurassic Park kids' suites—they feature a separate bedroom for the kids complete with a flatscreen TV, twin beds, and dino-themed decor. The public areas are well worth exploring. The addition of the Wantilan Luau Pavilion ensures the weekly luau is held rain or shine. If you're traveling with young children, the Royal Pacific is the best choice at Universal.

6300 Hollywood Way, Orlando, FL 32819. Ⓒ **800/232-7827** or 407/503-3000. Fax 407/503-3202. www.loewshotels.com/hotels/Orlando or www.universalorlando.com. 1,000 units. $219–$429 double; $339–$1,950 suite. Extra person $25. Children 17 and under stay free in parent's room. AE, DC, DISC, MC, V. Valet parking $20; self-parking $14. From I-4, take exit 75B, Kirkman Rd./Hwy. 435 and follow the signs to Universal. Small pets $25. **Amenities:** 2 restaurants; outdoor heated pool; kids' pool; free water taxi and bus transportation to Universal Studios, Islands of Adventure, and CityWalk; free shuttle to SeaWorld; transportation for a fee to WDW parks. *In room:* Fridge.

Staybridge Suites Lake Buena Vista   This member of the Staybridge Suites chain is just off Apopka-Vineland, close to the action of Downtown Disney and the theme parks, as well as many restaurants, shops, and smaller venues along Route 535. One- and two-bedroom suites come with full kitchens and all the comforts of home. The suites' separate living areas are larger and more comfortable than similar ones at other all-suite hotels. A landscaped inner courtyard is where you'll find the resort's pool.

8751 Suiteside Dr., Orlando FL 32836. ✆ **800/866-4549** or 407/238-0777. Fax 407/238-2640. www. sborlando.com. 150 units. $139–$299 2-bedroom suite (up to 8 people). Rates include continental breakfast, evening reception, and high-speed Internet access. AE, DC, DISC, MC, V. Self-parking free. From I-4, take the 535 exit no. 68 and turn right. Follow the road to Vinings Way Rd. and turn right. The hotel is located on the left. **Amenities:** Outdoor heated pool; children's pool; exercise room; free shuttle to Disney parks. *In room:* Kitchen.

WHERE TO DINE

Artist Point SEAFOOD/STEAK   Enjoy a view of Disney's Wilderness Lodge in this rustically elegant establishment. Hand-painted murals of Southwestern scenery adorn the raised center ceiling, and ornate lanterns hang from timber columns. Select from a seasonal menu that might include grilled buffalo sirloin with a sweet potato and hazelnut gratin. Kids will have more fun at the **Whispering Canyon Café** next door.

901 W. Timberline Dr., in Disney's Wilderness Lodge. ✆ **407/939-3463** or 824-1081. www.disneyworld. com. Advanced Reservations recommended. Main courses $21–$32; fixed price $46. AE, DC, DISC, MC, V. Daily 5:30–10pm. Valet and self-parking free.

Boma INTERNATIONAL   At the Animal Kingdom Lodge, Boma offers a diversion from the usual Disney fare and a warm atmosphere in a setting that evokes an African marketplace. In front of the open kitchens is a buffet of international cuisine featuring African dishes alongside a few familiar favorites—including dishes especially for kids. Chefs can answer questions and make suggestions throughout the various stations. A specialty is the delicious watermelon rind.

2901 Osceola Pkwy., at Disney's Animal Kingdom Lodge. ✆ **407/938-3000.** www.disneyworld.com. Advanced Reservations recommended. All-you-can-eat buffet $17–$26 adults, $10–$12 children 3–9. AE, DC, DISC, MC, V. Daily 7:30–11am and 5:30–10pm. Self-parking free.

California Grill CALIFORNIA   On the 15th floor of the Contemporary Resort, you'll enjoy views of the Magic Kingdom—and its fireworks. Entrees usually include Atlantic salmon, and grilled pork tenderloin with creamy goat-cheese polenta, cremini mushrooms, and a zinfandel glaze. A vegetarian selection is available. The Grill also

How to Arrange Advanced Reservations at Disney Restaurants

"Advanced Reservations" *aren't* really reservations. They are a way of claiming the first table that becomes available (and can accommodate your party) close to the time of your choosing. You'll be given priority over any walk-in diners. There may still be a wait (usually 10–20 min.), but it will be much shorter than it would be if you simply walked in. If you don't make Advanced Reservations, especially for the most popular restaurants, you may miss out altogether, as they're usually booked well in advance. To make Advanced Reservations at any WDW restaurant, call ✆ **407/939-3463.** You can book as far as 180 days in advance of your arrival for most restaurants.

ⓥ Value Bring On the BBQ

Come to **Bubbalou's Bodacious BBQ,** 5818 Conroy Rd., Orlando (② **407/423-1212;** www.bubbalous.com), for the best barbecue in Florida. Go for the full pork platter that comes with a heaping helping and all the fixin's. The uninitiated should stay away from the "Killer" sauce if you value your taste buds. Main courses run $4 to $13. Hours are Monday through Saturday from 10am to 9pm. To get here, take exit 75B off of I-4, follow Kirkman, then make a left onto Conroy and follow your nose; Bubbalou's is on the left.

features a sushi and sashimi menu. The upbeat and charged atmosphere is enhanced by the contemporary yet colorfully artistic decor. Reservations are required to ride the elevator to the restaurant, so make arrangements well ahead of time.

4600 N. World Dr., at Disney's Contemporary Resort. ② **407/939-3463** or 824-1576. www.disneyworld.com. Reservations required. Main courses $24–$38; sushi and sashimi $13–$24. AE, DC, DISC, MC, V. Daily 5:30–10pm. Self-parking free.

Emeril's NEW ORLEANS   Reserve as far in advance as you can; short-term reservations are near impossible to get. When you finally get one, the dynamic, Creole-inspired cuisine is worth the struggle. Best bets are the andouille-crusted Texas redfish with roasted vegetable relish and Creole meunière sauce and toasted pecans; and the pan-seared filet mignon served with garlic creamed mashed potatoes, red-wine reduction, horseradish-herb compound butter, asparagus, and yellow pea shoots. There's a 12,000-bottle aboveground wine cellar. If you want a show, we recommend one of eight counter seats, where you can watch chefs work their magic. *Note:* Lunch costs much less than dinner, and the menu and portions are almost the same.

6000 Universal Studios Blvd., in CityWalk. ② **407/224-2424.** www.emerils.com/restaurants. Reservations necessary. Main courses $19–$28 lunch, $25–$40 dinner. Sun–Thurs 11:30am–2pm and 5:30–10pm; Fri–Sat 11:30am–2pm and 5:30–11pm. AE, DISC, MC, V. Self-parking $10 (free after 6pm). From I-4, take the Kirkman Rd./Hwy. 435 exit and follow the signs to Universal.

Ming Court CHINESE   Its diverse menu and tasty dishes make this one of Orlando's most popular Chinese restaurants. The lightly battered, deep-fried chicken breast gets zip from a lemon-tangerine sauce. Portions are sufficient and the service is excellent. The ornately carved dragons that greet you at the entrance are a hint at what awaits inside. There's a kids' menu with an Asian flair.

9188 International Dr. (btw. Sand Lake Rd. and Bee Line Expwy.). ② **407/351-9988.** www.ming-court.com. Reservations recommended. Main courses $7–$14 lunch, $13–$36 dinner; dim sum mostly $3–$6. AE, DC, DISC, MC, V. Daily 11am–2:30pm and 4:30–11:30pm. Self-parking free. From I-4, take the Sand Lake Rd./Hwy. 528 exit east to International Dr., then south. Ming Court is on the right opposite Pointe Orlando.

Pastamore Ristorante SOUTHERN ITALIAN   The *antipasto amore* here is a meal unto itself and includes bruschetta, melon with prosciutto, grilled portobello mushrooms, sliced Italian meats, marinated olives, tomato caprese, and mozzarella. This casual family eatery has a menu of Italian classics, seafood, pastas, and grilled specialties. An open kitchen allows diners a view of the chefs at work. You can also eat in a cafe where lighter fare—breakfast and sandwiches—is served from 8am to 2am.

1000 Universal Studios Plaza, in CityWalk. ℂ **407/363-8000.** www.universalorlando.com. Reservations accepted. Main courses $13–$28. AE, DISC, MC, V. Daily 5pm–midnight. Self-parking $10 (free after 6pm). From I-4, take the Kirkman Rd./Hwy. 435 exit and follow the signs to Universal.

Tchoup Chop PACIFIC RIM   Culinary perfection is pronounced "chop chop." Emeril Lagasse's second restaurant in Orlando is named for Tchoupitoulas Street in New Orleans. It's chic, contemporary, and impressive. Service is impeccable, and the atmosphere, decor, and food ensure that the experience is worth the price. Some of the Polynesian- and Asian-influenced dishes include macadamia nut–crusted Atlantic salmon and Hawaiian-style rotisserie chicken.

6300 Hollywood Way, in Universal's Royal Pacific Hotel. ℂ **407/503-2467.** www.emerils.com/ restaurants. Reservations strongly recommended. Main courses $13–$34. AE, DISC, MC, V. Sun–Thurs 11:30am–2pm and 5:30–10pm; Fri–Sat 11:30am–2pm and 5:30–11pm. Valet parking $5. From I-4, take the Kirkman Rd./Hwy. 435 exit and follow the signs to Universal.

Todd English's bluezoo SEAFOOD   The hippest, hottest place in town, with a sophisticated marine-themed decor, an impressive open kitchen, and an intimate lounge. Celeb chef Todd English has created an amazing menu of fresh seafood and coastal dishes served with creative flair. Entrees include lobster Bolognese and fresh grilled fish with a choice of three sauces. Portions are large, but side dishes will run you an extra $5 to $7. Dress is casual, but the upscale atmosphere is chic and adult.

1500 Epcot Resort Blvd., at the WDW Dolphin. ℂ **407/934-1111.** www.swandolphin.com/bluezoo. Advanced Reservations recommended. Main courses $20–$52. AE, DISC, MC, V. Daily 5–11pm. Validated valet and self-parking free.

Victoria & Albert's (Best) INTERNATIONAL   It's not often that dinner can be described as "an event," but Disney's most elegant restaurant earns that distinction. Dinner is next to perfect—if the portions seem small, it's so you can better enjoy all seven courses. The setting is romantic; a violinist or harpist often plays softly. The fare changes nightly, but you might find main events such as lamb seared with foie gras over brioche with imported Fuji apples, or Colorado lamb with corn risotto. The dining room is crowned by a domed, chapel-style ceiling; 20 exquisitely appointed tables are lit by Victorian lamps; and your waitstaff (always named Victoria and Albert) provide superb service.

4401 Floridian Way, in Disney's Grand Floridian Resort & Spa. ℂ **407/939-3463.** www.disneyworld.com. Reservations required. Jackets required for men. Not recommended for children. Prix fixe $125 per person, $185 with wine pairing. AE, DC, DISC, MC, V. 2 dinner seatings daily Sept–June, 5:45–6:30pm and 9–9:45pm; 1 seating July–Aug, 6:45–8pm. Chef's Table 6pm only. Valet parking $10.

The Chef's Table: Best Seat in the World

There's a special dining option at **Victoria & Albert's.** Reserve the **Chef's Table** (far, *far* in advance) and dine in an alcove at a candlelit table in the kitchen! Begin by sipping bubbly with the chef while discussing the menu (up to 13 courses) created for you. Diners get to tour the kitchen and observe the chefs at work. The Chef's Table can accommodate up to 10 people a night. It's a leisurely affair, lasting 3 or 4 hours. The price is $185 per person without wine, $245 including five wines. Advance Reservations are a must.

WORLD SHOWCASE   The World Showcase has the best dining options inside the WDW theme parks, thanks to the cuisine of its 11 nation pavilions. These are our favorites of the many choices.

Le Cellier Steakhouse, in **Canada,** has a castlelike ambience accentuated by vaulted stone arches. Red-meat main events include the usual range of cuts—filet, porterhouse, prime rib, sirloin, and so on. Try one of the Canadian Ice Wines for a very sweet after-dinner treat. Lunch runs $12 to $22; dinner is $20 to $28.

The **Rose & Crown** in the **United Kingdom** is an English pub where folk music and saucy servers entertain as you dine. The menu has traditional British favorites, including fish and chips, bangers and mash, and warm bread pudding. Head over in the evening for a pint of Bass or Guinness, as the patio is one of the best places to see the IllumiNations fireworks. Lunch is $13 to $18; dinner is $16 to $24.

Les Chefs de France has a pretty glass exterior. The interior is agleam with mirrors and brass chandeliers. Three renowned French chefs can take credit for the menu, which includes such entrees as roasted perch with lobster mousse, and potato scales on sautéed fennel with a lobster reduction. Lunch is $12 to $19; dinner is $18 to $29.

Of the Epcot restaurants, **Marrakesh** best exemplifies the spirit of the park. The setting is grand; the interior is filled with tile mosaics, carpets, and brass chandeliers. Belly dancers and Moroccan music often entertain guests as they feast on dishes like roast lamb, marinated beef, or chicken shish kabobs. The combination appetizer (for two) is a great starter—allowing you to sample a variety of Moroccan flavors. Couscous accompanies most entrees. Lunch costs $16 to $22; dinner is $20 to $32.

In **Japan, Tokyo Dining** features a menu of traditional Japanese cuisine with an emphasis on sushi. The adjoining **Yakitori House** features such fare as teriyaki chicken and sushi rolls. Meals here are generally less than $8.

Tutto Italia, inside one of the most beautiful of the pavilions, is one of Epcot's most popular restaurants. This elegant establishment features a menu filled with traditional pastas, fish, chicken, and pork. Lunch costs $12 to $25; dinner runs $24 to $34. Another restaurant is slated to replace Tutto Italia in late 2009.

Akershus in **Norway** has an impressive smorgasbord. A variety of traditional Norwegian fare, including cured salmon with spicy mustard, and poached cod, are among the choices during the Storybook lunch and dinner. Several Disney princesses (excluding Cinderella) make their way around the hall, stopping at each table. Storybook Breakfast costs $23 for adults, $13 for kids 4 to 9; Storybook Lunch costs $25 for adults, $14 for kids; and Storybook Dinner costs $30 for adults, $15 for kids.

In **Mexico,** it's always night at the **San Angel Inn,** where candlelit tables set a romantic mood under a faux star-lit sky. Reasonably authentic food is on the menu. Lunch runs $14 to $20, and dinners $20 to $28. The **Cantina de San Angel,** a cafeteria with outdoor seating, offers soft tacos, churros, and other items less than $8. Look for a new tequila bar (inside the pavilion) and a new menu at the Cantina (outside) in 2009.

FUTURE WORLD   Inside the Living Seas pavilion, the **Coral Reef** features tables scattered around a 5.6-million-gallon aquarium filled with tropical fish. The menu features mainly fresh seafood. Lunch is $12 to $22; dinner is $21 to $32. The **Sunshine Season Food Faire,** an upscale food court inside the Land pavilion, has six separate eateries, offering a variety of items, including Asian dishes; salads; chicken, fish, and beef entrees; sandwiches; and desserts. Most items cost $4 to $12.

FLORIDA

5

WALT DISNEY WORLD & ORLANDO

There are plenty of fast-food outlets throughout the park, of which **Pecos Bill Cafe, Cosmic Ray's Starlight Cafe,** and the **Columbia Harbour House** are your best choices. That said, you may find that a quiet, sit-down meal is an essential, if brief, getaway from the day's activities, even if the adults can't have an alcoholic beverage.

Romantics may find it hard to beat the ambience of eating at **Cinderella's Royal Castle.** Stained-glass windows line the stone walls, and servers treat you like a lord or lady as Disney princesses visit your table. Breakfast is $23 to $34; lunch $24 to $36; dinner is $28 to $45. Advanced Reservations are a must.

The **Crystal Palace,** named for its glass exterior, is a favorite with families because of its all-you-can-eat character buffets. Breakfast costs $19 for adults and $11 for children ages 3 to 9. Lunch is $21 for adults, $12 for children 3 to 9. Dinner is $28 for adults, $13 for children 3 to 9. Advanced Reservations are strongly suggested.

At Disney's Hollywood Studios

There are a lot of places to refuel here. The ones listed below are the best of the bunch. Again, Advanced Reservations are a must.

The **Hollywood Brown Derby** re-creates the atmosphere of a 1930s supper club. Caricatures of Hollywood's most famous celebrities line the walls. Highlights include the Cobb salad and spiced pan-roasted pork; the Derby's signature dessert is grapefruit cake with cream-cheese icing. Entrees go for $14 to $23 at lunch, $18 to $32 at dinner.

At the **50's Prime Time Café,** black-and-white TV sets show *My Little Margie* and servers threaten to withhold dessert if you don't eat your veggies. The mainstays are the meatloaf and pot roast. Kids will get a kick out of the neon ice cubes in their drinks. Lunch costs $12 to $16; dinner costs $13 to $20. Advanced Reservations are a must.

The best bets at **Mama Melrose's Ristorante Italiano** are the wood-fired and brick-baked specialties, including the flatbreads (pepperoni, portobello mushroom, and four cheeses). The welcoming atmosphere makes you feel like you're at your local mom-and-pop restaurant. Lunch costs $12 to $18; dinner costs $12 to $23.

At the **Sci-Fi Dine-In Theater Restaurant,** diners sit in colorful chrome-plated convertibles with the Hollywood Hills as a backdrop and are treated to newsreels, cartoons, and "B" horror flicks. Sandwiches, burgers, and salads make up the lunch menu; dinner features heartier fare such as steak, pasta, ribs, and chicken. Lunches run $11 to $20; dinners are $13 to $22. Advanced Reservations are a must.

In the Animal Kingdom

Here most of the options are fast-food style (of these, the **Flame Tree BBQ** is the best). Nevertheless, there are three spots where you can sit yourself down for a spell.

Most people come for the junglelike atmosphere at the **Rainforest Cafe.** Expect California fare with an island spin. Menu offerings tend to be tasty and somewhat creative. Lunch and dinner run anywhere from $9 to $40.

The thatched-roof **Tusker House** in Harambe village features a buffet. The patio out back allows you to relax and enjoy your meal away from the crowds. Out front, the pavilion provides shade and, if timed right, a view of the live entertainment. Options include a variety of salads, vegetarian dishes, and meats. There's a kids' menu as well. Prices run $20 for kids, $27 for adults. A character meal is available at breakfast.

Yak & Yeti, a Pan-Asian eatery, offers both sit-down and counter service dining in a setting that blends seamlessly into the Himalayan village surrounding it. The menu features specialties including crispy wok-fried green beans and lettuce cups filled with

> ## No Smoking!
>
> Under Florida law, smoking in restaurants is prohibited, so forget about lighting up with your meal.

minced chicken, chopped veggies, and a yummy maple tamarind sauce. Leave room for dessert—the mango pie and fried wontons are delish. Entrees run between $15 and $24 (the same for lunch and dinner), while kids' meals cost just under $8.

DINING WITH DISNEY CHARACTERS

Only in Orlando: The characters will greet you, sign autographs, pose for photos, and interact with the family. These are *extremely* popular, so make Advanced Reservations (*©* 407/939-3463) early (up to 180 days in advance), and call for schedules. Prices vary, but expect breakfast to be $19 to $33 for adults, $11 to $23 for kids 3 to 9. Restaurants that serve dinner charge $28 to $45 for adults and $13 to $26 for kids.

Character meals are offered at **Cape May Café** (in Disney's Beach Club Resort), **Chef Mickey's** (at Disney's Contemporary Resort), **Cinderella's Royal Table** (in Cinderella Castle, Magic Kingdom), **Crystal Palace Buffet** (at the Crystal Palace, Magic Kingdom), **Donald's Safari Breakfast at the Tusker House** (in Africa, Animal Kingdom), **Garden Grill** (in the Land Pavilion, Epcot), **Liberty Tree Tavern** (in Liberty Square, Magic Kingdom), **'Ohana** (at Disney's Polynesian Resort), **Akershus Royal Banquet Hall** (in Epcot's Norway Pavilion), **Hollywood & Vine** (at Disney–MGM Studios), **1900 Park Fare** (at Disney's Grand Floridian Resort & Spa), and the **Garden Grove Café** and **Gulliver's Grill** (at the WDW Swan).

ORLANDO AFTER DARK

The easiest way to find nighttime fun is to head for **Pleasure Island, Disney's West Side** (both part of the Downtown Disney district), and **CityWalk.**

In September 2008, the clubs at the 6-acre entertainment district of **Pleasure Island** (*©* 407/939-2648) were closed while Disney "re-imagines" the space. No word on the final design, but check Disney's website to see if anything is up and running when you are there. Shops and restaurants in the district remain open.

Down the block is **Disney's West Side.** It includes the 1,500-seat **House of Blues,** a concert hall that books big-name acts. You'll also find **Cirque du Soleil** (*©* 407/939-7600;* www.cirquedusoleil.com). The international theater company known for combining acrobatics and avant-garde theatrics into a stage production has a permanent venue here. Seats for the show, dubbed *La Nouba,* range from $63 to $112 for adults and $50 to $90 for kids 3 to 9 (including tax).

Universal's answer to Pleasure Island and Disney's West Side is the 30-acre complex **City-Walk** (*©* 407/363-8000;* www.citywalk.com). Alcohol is prominently featured here, so an adult should accompany teens and children. You can wander the area for free, but some clubs charge a cover. CityWalk offers a **party pass** that includes access to all the clubs for $12 plus tax. Visitors can shake their booties at **the groove** or listen to live reggae at **Bob Marley—A Tribute to Freedom.** Parrot-heads can make their way to **Jimmy Buffet's Margaritaville.** Or you can channel your inner American Idol at **Rising Star,** a karaoke club.

Note: Daytime parking in the Universal Orlando garages costs $12 but is free after 6pm. Universal offers free club access with 2- and 3-day theme-park tickets.

FLORIDA

5

WALT DISNEY WORLD & ORLANDO

COCOA BEACH, CAPE CANAVERAL & THE KENNEDY SPACE CENTER

The "Space Coast" was once a sleepy place where city dwellers escaped the urban pace of Miami and Jacksonville. Then came NASA. Today visitors from all over come for the Kennedy Space Center, the 72 miles of beaches, and fishing, surfing, and golfing.

Essentials

GETTING THERE   The nearest airport is **Melbourne International Airport** (© 321/ 723-6227; www.mlbair.com), 22 miles south of Cocoa Beach. However, **Orlando International Airport,** about 35 miles to the west, is a much larger hub with more flight options and generally less expensive fares. A car is essential in this area, so rent one at whatever airport you arrive in, and hit the roads. By car, major routes into Cocoa Beach are **I-95** from the north (Daytona Beach and Jacksonville) and south (Miami), and **Fla. 528** (Bee Line Expwy.) from the west (Orlando).

VISITOR INFORMATION   Contact the **Florida Space Coast Office of Tourism/ Brevard County Tourist Development Council,** 8810 Astronaut Blvd., Ste. 102, Cape Canaveral, FL 32920 (© **800/872-1969** or 321/868-1126; www.space-coast.com). The office is in the Sheldon Cove building, on Fla. A1A a block north of Central Boulevard, and is open Monday through Friday from 8am to 5pm. It also operates a booth at the Kennedy Space Center Visitor Complex.

Exploring the Area

The **Kennedy Space Center Visitor Complex,** on NASA Parkway (© **321/449-4444;** www.KennedySpaceCenter.com), is the top attraction here. Begin your visit at the **Kennedy Space Center Visitor Complex.** The complex has received a $130-million renovation and expansion, so check beforehand to see if tours and exhibits have changed since press time. Call ahead to see what's happening the day you will visit, and arrive early. You'll need at least 2 hours to see the center's highlights on the bus tour, more if you linger at the stops. Buy a copy of the *Official Tour Book.* Along with information on what you're seeing, it's a great souvenir.

The complex has NASA rockets and the Mercury Mission Control Room. Exhibits portray space exploration in its early days and where it's going. There are hands-on activities, a daily "Encounter" with a real astronaut, dining venues, and a souvenir shop. Informative IMAX movies are shown on $5^1/_2$-story-high screens.

You could spend an whole day at the complex, but if you want to see the actual space center, you have to take a **KSC Tour.** Buses depart every 10 minutes or so. They stop at the LC-39 Observation Gantry, with a 360-degree view over launchpads; the International Space Station Center, where scientists and engineers prepare additions to the space station now in orbit; and the Apollo/Saturn V Center.

Don't miss the **Astronaut Memorial,** a moving black-granite monument that bears the names of the U.S. astronauts who died on missions or while in training.

On launch days, the center is closed at least part of the day. These aren't good days to see the center, but they're great to observe history in the making. For $38 per adult and $28 per child ages 3 through 11, you get a **combined ticket** that entitles you to admission to the center, plus at least a 2-hour excursion to NASA Parkway to see the liftoff. You must pick up tickets, available 5 days before the launch, on-site.

For an out-of-this-world experience, do lunch with an astronaut, a once-in-a-lifetime opportunity available every day ($23 adults, $16 kids 3–11, in addition to space center admission). Seating is limited; call *C* **321/449-4400** to make a reservation.

New at the Space Center is the **Astronaut Training Experience,** a combination of hands-on training and preparation for the rigors of spaceflight. You'll hear firsthand from veteran NASA astronauts as you progress through an authentic day of mission simulation and exploration. It's pricey, though, at $250 per person.

Note: Kennedy Space Center acquired many of the exhibits from the **Astronaut Hall of Fame** and added them as a separate attraction at the KSC visitor center ($17 adults, $13 kids 3–11; or $38 adults and $28 kids for a 2-day Maximum Access Admission to the Center and the Hall of Fame). The attraction includes exhibits and tributes to the heroes of the Mercury, Gemini, and Apollo space programs. In "Simulator Station," guests can experience four times the force of gravity, ride a Rover across Mars, and land a space shuttle.

To the north of the Kennedy Space Center, **Canaveral National Seashore** is a 13-mile stretch of barrier-island beach backed by cabbage palms, sea grapes, palmettos, marshes, and Mosquito Lagoon. This is a great area for watching all kinds of birds. You might also glimpse dolphins and manatees in Mosquito Lagoon. The main **visitor center** is at 7611 S. Atlantic Ave., New Smyrna Beach, FL 32169 (*C* **321/867-4077;** www.nps.gov/cana), on Apollo Beach, at the north end of the island. The southern access gate to the island is 8 miles east of Titusville on Fla. 402, just east of Fla. 3. A paved road leads from the gate to undeveloped **Playalinda Beach,** one of Florida's most beautiful. The beach has toilets but no running water or other amenities, so bring everything you'll need. The seashore is open daily from 6am to 8pm during daylight saving time, daily from 6am to 6pm during standard time. Entry fees are $7 per person. Backcountry camping permits cost $10 for up to six people and must be obtained from the New Smyrna Beach visitor center.

Canaveral National Seashore's neighbor to the south and west is the 140,000-acre **Merritt Island National Wildlife Refuge.** Pick up a map and other information at the visitor center, on Fla. 402 about 4 miles east of Titusville. The center has a quarter-mile boardwalk along the edge of the marsh. Displays show the animals you may spot from 6-mile Black Point Wildlife Drive or from one of the nature trails through the hammocks and marshes. The visitor center is open Monday through Friday from 8am to 4:30pm, Saturday and Sunday from 9am to 5pm (closed Sun Apr–Oct). Entry is free. For more information and a schedule of programs, contact the refuge at P.O. Box 6504, Titusville, FL 32782 (*C* **321/861-0667;** www.nbbd.com/godo/minwr).

Note: Parts of the national seashore near the Kennedy Space Center and all of the refuge close 4 days before a shuttle launch and usually reopen the day after.

The beach at **Cocoa Beach Pier,** on Meade Avenue east of Fla. A1A (*C* **321/783-7549**), is a popular spot with surfers. The rustic pier was built in 1962 and has 842 feet of fishing, shopping, and dining overlooking a wide, sandy beach.

Head to **Port Canaveral** for catches such as snapper and grouper. The south bank of the port is lined with charter boats. Try deep-sea fishing on *Miss Cape Canaveral* (*C* **321/783-5274,** or 648-2211 in Orlando; www.misscape.com), one of the party boats.

Where to Stay & Dine

The **DoubleTree Cocoa Beach Oceanfront Hotel,** 2080 N. Atlantic Ave. (*C* **800/552-3224** or 321/783-9222; www.cocoabeachdoubletree.com), is the pick of the beachfront properties; all rooms have balconies with ocean views. Rates $99 to $129 double. The **Inn at Cocoa Beach,** 4300 Ocean Blvd. (© **800/343-5307** or 321/799-3460; www.theinnatcocoabeach.com), is romantic and draws many couples with its well-furnished rooms. Rates ($125–$325 double) include breakfast and afternoon tea.

Two good motels are the **Hampton Inn Cocoa Beach,** 3425 Atlantic Blvd. (© **877/492-3224** or 321/799-4099; www.hamptoninncocoabeach.com), and **Courtyard by Marriott,** 3435 Atlantic Blvd. (© **800/321-2211** or 321/784-4800; www.marriott.com). They have beach access via a pathway through a condo complex.

On the **Cocoa Beach Pier** (www.cocoabeachpier.com), at the beach end of Meade Avenue, you'll get a fine view down the coast to accompany the seafood offerings at **Atlantic Ocean Grill** (© 321/783-7549); also on the pier is the outdoor, tin-roofed **Boardwalk,** a prime spot to have a cold one while watching the surfers or a sunset. At **Bernard's Surf/Fischer's Seafood Bar & Grill** (2 S. Atlantic Ave. at Minuteman Causeway Rd. (© **321/783-2401**), photos on the walls testify that many astronauts come to these adjoining establishments to celebrate their landings. At the **Mango Tree,** 118 N. Atlantic Ave., Fla. A1A, between North 1st and North 2nd streets (© **321/799-0513;** http://themangotreerestaurant.com), gourmet seafood, pastas, and chicken are served in a plantation-home atmosphere with elegant furnishings in this stucco house.

DAYTONA BEACH

Daytona Beach is the self-proclaimed "World's Most Famous Beach" and "World Center of Racing," a mecca for motorcyclists and spring-breakers. Hundreds of thousands of race enthusiasts come to see the Daytona 500, the Pepsi 400, and other races, and to visit Daytona USA, a state-of-the-art motorsports entertainment attraction.

Essentials

GETTING THERE Fly into **Daytona Beach International Airport** (© **386/248-8030;** http://flydaytonafirst.com), 4 miles inland on International Speedway Boulevard (U.S. 92), or into **Orlando International Airport,** about an hour's drive away. **Daytona-Orlando Transit Service** (**DOTS;** © **800/231-1965** or 386/257-5411; www.dots-daytonabeach.com) provides van transportation to and from Orlando Airport. One-way fares are about $35 for adults, $18 for children ages 11 and under.

If you fly into the Daytona Airport, rates into town for the **Daytona Shuttle** (© **386/255-2294**) run up to $15 per person, $18 per couple, and $9 per person for parties of three or more. The major car-rental agencies have desks here (and Daytona is a driver's town anyway, so it's best to rent a car). By car, the major route into Daytona Beach is **I-95** from the north and south, and **I-4** from the southwest (Orlando).

VISITOR INFORMATION The **Daytona Beach Area Convention & Visitors Bureau,** 126 E. Orange Ave. (P.O. Box 910), Daytona Beach, FL 32115 (© **800/544-0415** or 386/255-0415; www.daytonabeach.com), can help you with information on attractions, accommodations, dining, and events. The office is on the mainland just west of the Memorial Bridge. The information area of the lobby is open daily from 9am to 5pm. The bureau also maintains a branch at DAYTONA USA, 1801 W. International Speedway Blvd. (daily 9am–7pm), as well as a kiosk at the airport.

What to See & Do

You don't have to be a racing fan to enjoy a visit to the **Daytona International Speedway complex,** 1801 W. International Speedway Blvd. (© **386/253-7223** for race tickets and information; www.daytonaintlspeedway.com). Entertaining 30-minute guided tram tours ($7.50) of the facility (garage area, pit road, and so on) depart from the visitor center and are well worth taking. The visitor center houses the popular **Daytona USA** (© **386/947-6800;** www.daytonausa.com), a state-of-the-art interactive attraction that costs $24 adults, $19 seniors, $19 children 6 to 12, free for children 5 and under. You can participate in a pit stop on a NASCAR Winston Cup stock car, see the winning Daytona 500 car, talk via video with favorite competitors, and play radio or television announcer by calling the finish of a race. An action-packed IMAX film will put you in the winner's seat of a Daytona 500 race.

You can actually make (for $134) three laps around the track in a stock car from May to October with the **Richard Petty Driving Experience Ride-Along Program** (© **800/ 237-3889;** www.1800bepetty.com). Professional drivers are at the wheel as you see and feel what it's like to travel an average 115 mph.

The hub of beach activity is the **Main Street Pier.** You can drive and park on the sand along most of the beach, but watch for signs warning of sea turtles nesting. *And watch out for the tides.* If you park on an incoming tide and lose track of time, your vehicle may become an artificial reef! There's a $5 vehicle-access fee in most areas.

There are more than 25 **golf courses** within 30 minutes, and most hotels can arrange tee times for you. **Golf Daytona Beach,** 126 E. Orange Ave., Daytona Beach, FL 32114 (© **800/881-7065** or 386/239-7065; fax 386/239-0064), publishes a brochure describing the major courses. It's available at the tourist information offices.

Where to Stay

After $70 million in renovations, the **Plaza Resort & Spa,** 600 N. Atlantic Ave. (© **800/ 874-7420** or 386/255-4471; www.plazaresortandspa.com), features some of Daytona Beach's best rooms. The choice units are the corner suites, which have balconies overlooking the Atlantic; some even have a Jacuzzi. All units have balconies and microwaves. Rates run $119 to $199 double.

The **Shoreline All Suites Inn & Cabana Colony Cottages,** 2435 S. Atlantic Ave. (© **800/293-0653** or 386/252-1692; www.daytonashoreline.com), has both spacious suites and small beachside cottages. Rates run $69 to $299 for suites and cottages, including continental breakfast.

Thousands of rental condominiums line the beach. Among the most luxurious is the 150-unit **Ocean Walk Resort,** 300 N. Atlantic Ave., Daytona Beach, FL 32118 (© **800/ 649-3566** or 386/323-4800; www.oceanwalk.com). Near the Main Street Pier, it's in the center of the action and has one- and two-bedroom apartments with full kitchens, washers and dryers, and all of the usual hotel amenities, plus a computer-golf simulator, a "lazy river" in the outdoor pool, an island putting green, and the gaudiest lobby I've ever seen. Rates are $100 to $299 in winter and $130 to $350 in summer.

JACKSONVILLE

The metropolis of Jacksonville—residents call it "Jax"—is one of the South's insurance and banking capitals. Downtown Jacksonville is a vibrant center of activity during weekdays, and on weekends, locals head to the restaurants and bars of Jacksonville Landing and Southbank Riverwalk. And, of course, the beaches.

Essentials

GETTING THERE By Plane   Several airlines fly into **Jacksonville International Airport,** on the city's north side about 12 miles from downtown (© **904/741-2000;** www.jaxairports.org). The major car-rental firms have booths here. **Gator City Taxi**

(© **904/741-0008** at the airport, or 355-8294 elsewhere) and **Express Shuttle** (© **904/353-8880**) provide service to and from hotels and resorts.

By Car   Major routes into Jacksonville are **I-95** from the north (Savannah) and south (Miami), and **I-10** from the west (Tallahassee).

VISITOR INFORMATION   Contact the **Jacksonville and the Beaches Convention & Visitors Bureau,** 201 E. Adams St., Jacksonville, FL 32202 (© **800/733-2668** or 904/798-9111; fax 904/789-9103; www.jaxcvb.com). The bureau is open Monday through Friday from 8am to 5pm. It operates an information booth in the upstairs food court of **Jacksonville Landing,** open Monday through Saturday from 10am to 7pm, and Sunday from 12:30 to 5:30pm, as well as a walk-in office in **Jacksonville Beach,** at 403 Beach Blvd., between 3rd and 4th streets (© **904/242-0024**), open Monday through Saturday from 10am to 6pm.

What to See & Do

Spanning the broad, curving St. Johns River, downtown Jacksonville is a hub of activity during weekdays and on weekends, when many locals head to **Jacksonville Landing** (www.jacksonvillelanding.com) and **Southbank Riverwalk,** two dining-and-entertainment complexes facing each other across the river.

Also worth seeing here are the small but outstanding **Cummer Museum of Art & Gardens,** 829 Riverside Ave. (© **904/356-6857;** www.cummer.org), especially for its American Impressionist paintings; the **Jacksonville Zoo and Gardens,** 8605 Zoo Rd. (© **904/757-4462** or 757-4463; www.jaxzoo.org), whose main exhibits center on an extensive collection of African wildlife; and the **Fort Caroline National Memorial,** on Fort Caroline Road (© **904/641-7155;** www.nps.gov/timu), a replica of a 16th-century fort built by French Huguenots. The fort serves as the main visitor center for the **Timucuan Ecological and Historic Preserve,** a national park that includes natural preserves as well as historic sites.

You can fish, swim, snorkel, sail, sunbathe, or stroll on the sand dunes—at least from March to November. All of these activities are just a 20- to 30-minute drive east of downtown at Jacksonville's four beach communities.

Atlantic Boulevard (Fla. 10) will take you to **Atlantic Beach** and **Neptune Beach.** The boulevard divides the two towns, and where it meets the ocean, you'll come to **Town Center,** a community with shops, restaurants, pubs, and a few inns. Beach Boulevard (U.S. 90) ends at **Jacksonville Beach,** where you'll find concessions, rental shops, and a fishing pier. To the south, J. Turner Butler Boulevard (Fla. 202) leads to **Ponte Vedra Beach.**

Where to Stay & Dine

Prudential Drive in the Southbank Riverwalk area is home to the **Wyndham Jacksonville Riverwalk Hotel** (© **800/996-3426** or 904/396-5100), the **Hampton Inn Central** (© **800/426-7866** or 904/396-7770), and the all-suites **Extended Stay America Downtown** (© **800/398-7829** or 904/396-1777; www.extendedstay.com).

A dozen modest chain hotels line Jacksonville Beach, including the **Comfort Inn Oceanfront,** 1515 N. 1st St., 2 blocks east of Fla. A1A (© **800/654-8776** or 904/241-2311; www.comfortinnjaxbeach.com), one of the best-priced beachfront options. One of the anchors of Town Center, the inexpensive **Sea Horse Oceanfront Inn,** 120 Atlantic Blvd. (© **800/881-2330** or 904/246-2175; www.seahorseoceanfrontinn.com), offers clean rooms with ocean views. Also worth checking out in Town Center is the **Sea Turtle** **Inn,** 1 Ocean Blvd. (© **800/874-6000** or 904/249-7402), an older property with a lovely interior.

In Ponte Vedra Beach, the upscale **Sawgrass Marriott Resort & Beach Club,** 1000 PGA Tour Blvd. (© **800/228-9290** or 904/285-7777; www.sawgrassmarriott.com), and **Ponte Vedra Inn & Club,** 200 Ponte Vedra Blvd. (© **800/234-7842** or 904/285-1111; www.pvresorts.com), are built around championship golf courses and offer a variety of accommodations, from hotel rooms to condos. Smaller and more intimate, the **Lodge & Club at Ponte Vedra Beach,** 607 Ponte Vedra Blvd. (© **800/243-4304** or 904/273-9500; www.pvresorts.com), is one of Florida's more romantic hotels.

In downtown Jacksonville, **Southbank Riverwalk** is the city's mecca for eating out. In addition to the bistro **B.B.'s,** 1019 Hendricks Ave., between Prudential Drive and Home Street (© **904/306-0100**), and the **River City Brewing Company,** 835 Museum Circle (© **904/398-2299;** www.rivercitybrew.com), the area has a branch of **Ruth's Chris Steak House,** in the Crowne Plaza Jacksonville Riverfront, 1201 Riverplace Blvd. (© **904/396-6200**); and the **Wine Cellar,** 1314 Prudential Dr. (© **904/398-8989**), which offers very good continental fare and has a wine list to justify its name.

At the beach, head for **Ragtime Tavern & Taproom,** 207 Atlantic Blvd. at 1st Avenue, Atlantic Beach (© **904/241-7877;** www.ragtimetavern.com). You'll also find several dining (and drinking) choices in the brick storefronts of **Town Center.** Among the best is the oceanfront **Plantains,** in the Sea Turtle Inn.

ST. AUGUSTINE

With its 17th-century fort, old city gates, horse-drawn carriages clip-clopping along narrow streets, historic buildings, and reconstructed 18th-century Spanish Quarter, St. Augustine seems more like a European village than a modern Floridian city. This is, after all, the oldest continuous European settlement in the United States, originally established as a colony by Spain in 1562. Tourism is St. Augustine's main industry, but despite the daily invasion, it's an exceptionally charming town, with good restaurants, a small-town nightlife, and shopping bargains.

Essentials

GETTING THERE The **Daytona Beach** airport (p. 362) is about an hour's drive south of St. Augustine, but services are more frequent—and fares usually lower—at **Jacksonville's International Airport** (see above), about the same distance north.

VISITOR INFORMATION Before you go, contact the **St. Augustine, Ponte Vedra & The Beaches Visitors and Convention Bureau,** 88 Riberia St., Ste. 400, St. Augustine, FL 32084 (© **800/653-2489** or 904/829-1711; www.visitoldcity.com). Request the *Visitor's Guide.* The **St. Augustine Visitor Information Center** is at 10 Castillo Dr., at San Marco Avenue, opposite the Castillo de San Marcos National Monument (© **904/ 825-1000**). Check out the free 22-minute orientation video. You can also buy tickets for the sightseeing trains and trolleys, which include discounted admissions to the attractions. The center is open daily from 8:30am to 5:30pm.

What to See & Do

Tip: Yes, the city is famed for being the supposed site of the Fountain of Youth, but that tourist trap is such a waste of time, we don't even bother covering it.

Parking is nonexistent in the historic district—where many of the best sights are located—which makes a decision to take one of the hop-on/hop-off trolley tours of the area that much easier. **Old Town Trolley Tours** (© 904/829-3800; www.staugustine.com) takes you on an hour tour with more than 20 stops. Tickets include admission to the Florida Heritage Museum and the St. Augustine Beach Bus. The tour costs $20 for adults, $7 for kids 6 to 12. **St. Augustine Sightseeing Trains** (© 800/226-6545 or 904/829-6545; www.redtrains.com) cover all the main sights except the Authentic Old Jail and the Florida Heritage Museum at the Authentic Old Jail, but its red open-air trains are small enough to go down more of the narrow historic-district streets. Tickets are $20 for adults, $6 for kids 7 and up. **St. Augustine Transfer Company** (© 904/829-2391; www.st augustinetransfer.com) has been showing people around town by horse-drawn carriage since 1877. Slow-paced, entertaining, driver-narrated 45-minute to 1-hour rides past major landmarks and attractions are offered from 8am to midnight. Carriage tours cost $20 for adults, $10 for kids 5 to 11.

Do not think of leaving town without checking out the magnificent **Lightner Museum,** 75 King St. (© 904/824-2874; www.lightnermuseum.org). Henry Flagler's opulent Spanish Renaissance–style Alcazar Hotel, built in 1889, closed during the Depression and stayed vacant until Chicago publishing magnate Otto C. Lightner bought the building in 1948 to house his vast collection of Victoriana. Both the building and the varied collection are must-sees (admission $8 adults, $2 students with ID, free for children 11 and under with adult). The imposing building across King Street was the Ponce de León Hotel. It now houses **Flagler College,** which runs don't-miss-it 45-minute tours daily (at 10am and 2pm) of its Tiffany stained-glass windows, ornate Spanish Renaissance architecture, and gold-leafed Maynard murals ($5 adults, $1 kids 11 and under; call © 904/823-3378 or visit http://legacy.flagler.edu/Tours-sp8.html for information).

America's oldest and best-preserved masonry fortification, **Castillo de San Marcos National Monument,** East Castillo Drive (© 904/829-6506; www.nps.gov/casa; admission $7 adults), is pretty cool. Today the old bombproof storerooms surrounding the central plaza house exhibits documenting the history of the fort. You can tour the vaulted powder magazine, a prison cell (supposedly haunted), the chapel, and guard rooms. The **Colonial Spanish Quarter and Spanish Quarter Museum,** 33 St. George St. (© 904/825-6830; www.historicstaugustine.com), is a re-created colonial Spanish village, with costumed folk doing things they used to do back in the 1700s. Watch as the blacksmiths, carpenters, leatherworkers, and homemakers demonstrate their skills. Admission is $7 adults, $6 seniors, $4.25 students 6 to 18, $13 per family.

For something a bit less historical, head out to the century-old **St. Augustine Alligator Farm and Zoological Park,** 999 Anastasia Blvd. (© 904/824-3337; www.alligatorfarm.com), where more than 2,700 gators and crocodiles—including some rare white ones—are on display. It houses the world's only complete collection of all 22 species of crocodilians, a category that includes alligators, crocodiles, caimans, and gavials. Admission is $20 adults, $18 seniors, $11 children 3 to 10.

Golf fans can spend a day at the **World Golf Hall of Fame,** at exit 95a off I-95 (© 904/940-4123; www.wgv.com), a state-of-the-art museum honoring pro golf, its great players, and the sport's famous supporters (including comedian Bob Hope and singer Dinah Shore). Admission is $17 for adults, $15 for seniors and students, and $8.50 for children 4 to 12. It's the centerpiece of **World Golf Village,** 21 World Golf

Place (© **904/940-4000;** www.wgv.com), a complex of hotels, shops, and 18-hole golf **367** courses. There's an IMAX screen next door (with a separate admission charge).

Where to Stay

There are plenty of moderate and inexpensive motels and hotels. Most convenient to the historic district is the 40-room **Best Western Spanish Quarter Inn,** 6 Castillo Dr. (© **800/528-1234** or 904/824-4457; www.staugustinebestwestern.com), directly across the street from the visitor center.

St. Augustine also has many bed-and-breakfasts in restored historic homes. Contact **St. Augustine Historic Inns,** P.O. Box 5268, St. Augustine, FL 33085-5268 (www.staugustineinns.com), for descriptions of its member properties.

Built in 1888, the Moorish-style **Casa Monica Hotel** (rates $159–$299 double), 95 Cordova St. (© **800/648-1888** or 904/827-1888; www.casamonica.com), is the best in town, with top-notch services and accommodations. Also built in 1888, the **Alexander Homestead,** 14 Sevilla St. (© **888/292-4147** or 904/826-4147; www.alexander homestead.com), is a Victorian beauty with antiques-laden rooms that offers a romantic stay. Rates ($159–$209 double) include full breakfast.

The 1897 **Victorian House,** 11 Cadiz St. (© **877/703-0432** or 904/824-5214; www.victorianhousebnb.com), accepts kids in its annex building (a former general store). Rooms in the main building offer more character, though children aren't permitted to stay in it. There are no telephones or TVs. Rates ($119–$299 double) include full breakfast.

3 FORT LAUDERDALE & PALM BEACH

FORT LAUDERDALE

Fort Lauderdale, with its well-known strip of beaches, restaurants, bars, and souvenir shops, has undergone a major transformation. Once infamous for the annual mayhem of spring break, this area now attracts a more affluent, better-behaved boating crowd. In addition to beautiful wide beaches, the city includes more than 300 miles of navigable waterways and canals that permit thousands of residents to anchor boats in their backyards. Boating is not just a hobby here; it's a lifestyle. Huge cruise ships also take advantage of Florida's deepest harbor, Port Everglades. It is the second-busiest cruise-ship base in Florida (after Miami) and one of the top five in the world.

Essentials

GETTING THERE If you're driving from Miami, it's a straight shot north. Visitors on their way to or from Orlando should take the **Florida Turnpike** to exits 53, 54, 58, or 62. The **Fort Lauderdale–Hollywood International Airport** is small, easy to negotiate, and 15 minutes from the downtown areas. However, due to its popularity, the airport is undergoing a $650-million expansion and renovation that often renders it just as maddening as any other major metropolitan airport. All the major car-rental outfits have desks here.

Amtrak (© **800/USA-RAIL** [872-7245]; www.amtrak.com) stations are at 200 SW 21st Terrace (Broward Blvd. and I-95), Fort Lauderdale (© **954/587-6692**), and at 3001 Hollywood Blvd., Hollywood (© **954/921-4517**).

The **Greater Fort Lauderdale Convention & Visitors Bureau,** 1850 Eller Dr., Ste. 303 (off I-95 and I-595 E.), Fort Lauderdale, FL 33316 (© **954/765-4466;** fax 954/765-4467; www.sunny.org), is an excellent resource for area information in English, Spanish, and French. Call to request a free guide covering events, accommodations, and sightseeing in Broward County.

Fun On & Off the Beach

The **Fort Lauderdale Beach Promenade** underwent a $26-million renovation and looks fantastic. It's especially peaceful in the mornings, when there's just a smattering of joggers and walkers, but even at its most crowded on weekends, the promenade provides room for everyone. The beach is across the street from an uninterrupted stretch of hotels, bars, and retail outlets. But the waters are clear and under the careful watch of lifeguards. Freshen up in any of the clean showers and restrooms along the strip. Nearby, on Fla. A1A, midway between Las Olas and Sunrise boulevards, is **Beach Place,** a retail and dining complex, undergoing its own spiffing-up.

Fort Lauderdale provides ample opportunity for visitors to get on the water, either along the Intracoastal Waterway or out on the open ocean. **Aloha Watersports,** Marriott's Harbor Beach Resort, 3030 Holiday Dr., Fort Lauderdale (© **954/462-7245**), can outfit you with a variety of watercraft.

The **IGFA World Fishing Center,** at 300 Gulf Stream Way (© **954/922-4212;** www. igfa.org) in Dania Beach, is an angler's paradise. One of the highlights of this museum, library, and park is the virtual-reality fishing simulator, which allows visitors to reel in their own computer-generated catch. To get a list of local captains and guides, call IGFA headquarters and ask for the librarian (© **954/927-2628**). Admission is $6 for adults, $5 for children between 3 and 16. On the grounds is also **Bass Pro Outdoor World Store,** a huge multifloor retail complex situated on a 3-acre lake.

More than 50 golf courses in all price ranges compete for players. Some of the best include **Emerald Hills,** at 4100 N. Hills Dr., Hollywood, west of I-95 between Sterling Road and Sheridan Street (**www.theclubatemeraldhills.com**). This beauty consistently lands on "best of" lists. Weekends, greens fees start at $150 for tee times after 1pm, and $175 before noon during high season; Monday through Friday, the fees are $125 before noon and $110 after 1pm. Call © **954/961-4000** for tee times. For one of Broward's best municipal challenges, try the **Orangebrook Golf Course,** 400 Entrada Dr., Hollywood (© **954/967-GOLF** [967-4653]). Built in 1937, this is one of the state's oldest courses and a bargain, to boot. Morning and noon rates are $17 to $23. After 3pm, you can play for about $13, including a cart.

Plan to spend some time cruising Fort Lauderdale's waterways. The **Water Bus of Fort Lauderdale** (© **954/467-6677;** www.watertaxi.com) is a fleet of old-port boats that serve the dual purpose of transporting and entertaining visitors. Taxis operate on demand and along a fairly regular route, and carry up to 48 passengers. Choose a hotel on the route so that you can take advantage of this system. You can be picked up at your hotel, usually within 15 minutes of calling, and then be shuttled to any of the dozens of restaurants, bars, and attractions on or near the waterfront. Starting daily at 8am, boats run until midnight 7 days a week, depending on the weather. The cost is $11 for an all-day pass with unlimited stops on and off. If you want to go to South Beach, it's $19. Tickets are available on board; no credit cards are accepted.

If you are looking for unusual boutiques, especially art galleries, head to **Las Olas Boulevard,** where there are hundreds of shops with alluring window displays and intriguing merchandise.

The Fort Lauderdale beach has a hotel or motel on nearly every block, and they range from the run-down to the luxurious. Both the **Howard Johnson,** 700 N. Atlantic Blvd., on Fla. A1A south of Sunrise Boulevard (© **800/327-8578** or 954/563-2451); and the **Fort Lauderdale Beach Resort Hotel and Suites,** 4221 N. Ocean Blvd. (© **800/329-7466** or 954/563-2521), have clean oceanside rooms starting at about $60. For a cushier stay, look into the **St. Regis** resort (© **954/465-2300**), featuring 183 suites, a gourmet restaurant, and a spa.

The **Lago Mar Resort and Club,** 1700 S. Ocean Lane, Fort Lauderdale (© **800/524-6627** or 954/523-6511; www.lagomar.com), is a casually elegant resort that occupies its own island between Lake Mayan and the Atlantic. It's great for families, as most accommodations are suites with kitchenettes, and there are sports and facilities galore. Rates run from $295 double in high season.

Another find is the **Courtyard Villa on the Ocean,** 4312 El Mar Dr., Lauderdale-by-the-Sea (© **800/291-3560** or 954/776-1164; www.courtyardvilla.com), an eight-room historic hotel offering a romantic getaway on the beach. It features oceanfront efficiencies with balconies, suites overlooking the pool, and two-bedroom apartments. Rooms are plush, with four-poster beds, fully equipped kitchenettes, and tiled bathrooms. Relax in the hotel's heated pool/spa or on the sun deck. Rates run from $249 double, including full breakfast in high season.

PALM BEACH & WEST PALM BEACH

Palm Beach has been the traditional winter home of America's aristocracy—the Kennedys, the Rockefellers, the Pulitzers, the Trumps. By contrast, West Palm Beach is a more workaday city. Recent renovations have made the metropolitan area a lively and affordable place to dine, shop, and hang out. In addition to good beaches, boating, and diving, you'll find great golf and tennis throughout the county.

Essentials

GETTING THERE If you're driving up or down the coast, you'll probably reach Palm Beach by way of **I-95.** Exit at Belvedere Road or Okeechobee Boulevard.

Visitors on their way to or from Orlando or Miami should take the **Florida Turnpike,** a toll road. If you're coming from Florida's west coast, you can take **S.R. 70,** which runs north of Lake Okeechobee to Fort Pierce, or **S.R. 80,** which runs south of the lake to Palm Beach. All major airlines fly to the **Palm Beach International Airport,** at Congress Avenue and Belvedere Road (© **561/471-7400**). **Amtrak** (© **800/USA-RAIL** [872-7245]; www.amtrak.com) has a terminal in West Palm Beach, at 201 S. Tamarind Ave. (© **561/832-6169**).

VISITOR INFORMATION The **Palm Beach County Convention and Visitors Bureau,** 1555 Palm Beach Lakes Blvd., Ste. 204, West Palm Beach, FL 33401 (© **800/554-PALM** [554-7256] or 561/471-3995; www.palmbeachfl.com), distributes a brochure and answers questions about visiting the Palm Beaches. Ask for the *Arts and Attractions Calendar,* a day-to-day guide to art, music, stage, and other events.

Fun On & Off the Beach

Most of the island's best **beaches** are fronted by private estates and inaccessible to the general public. However, there are a few exceptions, including **Midtown Beach,** east of Worth Avenue, on Ocean Boulevard between Royal Palm Way and Gulfstream Road, which boasts more than 100 feet of undeveloped sand. This newly widened coast is a centerpiece and a natural oasis in a town dominated by glitz. There are no restrooms or concessions here, though a lifeguard is on duty until sundown. At the south end of Palm Beach, there's a less popular but better-equipped beach at **Phipps Ocean Park.** On Ocean Boulevard, between the Southern Boulevard and Lake Avenue causeways, there's a lively public beach encompassing more than 1,300 feet of groomed oceanfront. With picnic and recreation areas and plenty of parking, the area is especially good for families.

There's good **golfing** in the Palm Beaches, but many courses are private. Ask at your hotel or contact the **Palm Beach County Convention and Visitors Bureau** (© 561/471-3995) for information on which clubs are available for play. In the off season, some courses open to visitors staying in Palm Beach County hotels. This "Golf-A-Round" program offers free greens fees; reservations can be made through most major hotels. The **Palm Beach Public Golf Course,** 2345 S. Ocean Blvd. (© 561/547-0598), a popular 18-hole course, is a par-54. The course opens at 8am on a first-come, first-served basis. Club rentals are available. Greens fees start at $17 to $47 per person.

The annual ritual of the ponies is played out each season at the **Palm Beach Polo and Country Club.** It is one of the world's premier polo grounds. Matches are open to the public and are surprisingly affordable. Unless it is an opening game or some other special event, dress is casual. A navy or tweed blazer over jeans or khakis is a standard for men, while neat-looking jeans or a pantsuit is the norm for women. On warmer days, shorts and, of course, a polo shirt are fine, too. General admission is $15 to $45. Matches are held throughout the week. The big names usually compete on Sunday at 3:30pm January through April. The fields are at 11809 Polo Club Rd., Wellington, 10 miles west of the Forest Hill Boulevard exit of I-95. Call © **561/793-1440** or visit **www.palmbeachpolo. com** for more information.

The **Flagler Museum,** 1 Whitehall Way (at Cocoanut Row), Palm Beach (© 561/655-2833; www.flaglermuseum.us), is a luxurious mansion commissioned by Henry Flagler, a co-founder of the Standard Oil Company. The classically columned Edwardian-style mansion contains 55 rooms that include a Louis XIV music room and art gallery, a Louis XV ballroom, and 14 guest suites outfitted with original antique European furnishings. Admission is $15 adults, $8 ages 13 to 18, $3 children 6 to 12. The **Norton Museum of Art,** 1451 S. Olive Ave., West Palm Beach (© **561/832-5196;** www.norton. org), is famous for its prestigious collection, which includes works by American artists such as Georgia O'Keeffe and Jackson Pollock; works by French artists such as Monet, Picasso, and Renoir; and a number of Chinese bronzes, jades, and ceramics. Admission is $8 adults, $3 ages 13 to 21.

Lion Country Safari, Southern Boulevard West at S.R. 80, West Palm Beach (© 561/793-1084; www.lioncountrysafari.com), has more than 1,300 animals on its 500-acre preserve. The animals—lions, elephants, buffalo, watusi, pink flamingos, and more—wander the grassy landscape while visitors remain in their cars. Also on the premises are an amusement park, a carousel, and an animal nursery. Picnics are encouraged. Admission is $22 adults, $20 seniors, $17 children 3 to 9. Van rental is $8 per hour. Cool for little kids is the 17,000-square-foot **Playmobil Fun Park,** 8031 N. Military Trail, Palm Beach Gardens (© **800/351-8697** or 561/691-9880; www.playmobil.com), housed in a replica castle and loaded with themed areas: a medieval village, a Western town, a fantasy dollhouse, and more. Admission is $1.

Known as "the Rodeo Drive of the South," **Worth Avenue** is a window-shopper's dream. No matter what your budget, don't miss the Worth Avenue experience. The 4 blocks between South Ocean Boulevard and Cocoanut Row—a stretch of more than 200 boutiques, posh shops, art galleries, and upscale restaurants—are home to Gucci, Chanel, Armani, Hermès, and Louis Vuitton, among others.

City Place, Okeechobee Road, at 1-95, West Palm Beach (© **561/820-9716**), is a $550-million, Mediterranean-style shopping, dining, and entertainment complex that's responsible for revitalizing what was once a lifeless downtown West Palm Beach.

Where to Stay & Dine

The **Breakers,** 1 S. County Rd., Palm Beach (© **800/833-3141,** 888/BREAKERS [273-2537], or 561/655-6611; www.thebreakers.com), is what Palm Beach is all about. Elaborate, stately, and resplendent in all its Italian Renaissance–style glory, it's where old money mixes with new money, and the Old World gives way, albeit reluctantly, to a bit of modernity. The lush 140-acre grounds also sport Florida's oldest (though newly revamped) 18-hole golf course, a magnificent spa, a huge family entertainment center, and numerous top-notch restaurants. Doubles run $470 to $685 in high season.

For over-the-top pampering in a perfect location, the elegant **Four Seasons Resort Palm Beach,** 2800 S. Ocean Blvd., Palm Beach (© **800/432-2335** or 561/582-2800; www.fourseasons.com), is a favorite. The marble lobby is replete with hand-carved European furnishings, oil paintings, tapestries, and flower arrangements. In addition to a host of services and sports facilities, there's a 6,000-square-foot spa and health club. Rates run $429 to $745 double in winter. For a more intimate experience, try the **Chesterfield Palm Beach,** 363 Cocoanut Row, Palm Beach (© **800/243-7871** or 561/659-5800; www.redcarnationhotels.com), 3 blocks from the beach. Reminiscent of an English country manor, it is a magnificent, charming hotel with lovely rooms and exceptional service. Rates run $395 to $570 double in winter.

Looking for a bargain? A special find is **Hibiscus House,** 501 30th St., West Palm Beach (© **800/203-4927** or 561/863-5633; www.hibiscushouse.com), a 1920s-era B&B filled with handsome antiques. Every room here has its own private terrace or balcony. Rates run $125 to $210 double in high season and include breakfast.

Palm Beach has some very chic restaurants, including **Café Boulud** (in the Brazilian Court, 301 Australian Ave.; © **561/655-6060;** www.danielnyc.com), from celebrity chef Daniel Boulud, and **Echo,** 230 Sunrise Ave. (© **561/802-4222;** www.echopalmbeach.com), a hyperstylish eatery that's the Breakers hotel's homage to young and hip. Thanks to the development of downtown West Palm Beach, there is a great selection of trendier, less expensive spots like the popular **City Cellar** (700 S. Rosemary Ave., West Palm Beach (© **561/659-1853**), and **Tom's Place for Ribs,** 1225 Palm Beach Lakes Blvd., West Palm Beach (© **561/832-8774**).

4 MIAMI

There's much more to South Florida than the neon-hued nostalgia of *Miami Vice* and pink flamingos. Beyond the glitzy, *Access-Hollywood*-meets-beach-blanket-bacchanalia-as-seen-on-TV, Miami has an endless number of sporting, cultural, and recreational activities. Its sparkling beaches are beyond compare. Plus, there's excellent shopping and other nightlife activities that include ballet, theater, and opera.

GETTING THERE   **Miami International Airport (MIA)** ranks 10th in the world for total passengers. Despite the heavy traffic, the airport is user-friendly and not as much of a hassle as you'd think. Visitor information is available 24 hours a day at the **Miami International Airport Main Visitor Counter,** Concourse E, second level (© **305/876-7000**). Information is also available at **www.miami-airport.com**. The airport is about 6 miles west of downtown and about 10 miles from the beaches, so it's likely you can get from the plane to your hotel room in less than half an hour.

Note: Because MIA is the busiest airport in South Florida, travelers may want to consider flying into **Fort Lauderdale–Hollywood International Airport (FLL)** (© **954/359-1200**), which is closer to north Miami than MIA, or the **Palm Beach International Airport (PBI;** © **561/471-7420**), about 1½ hours from Miami.

All the major car-rental firms operate off-site branches reached via shuttle from the terminals, and we *strongly recommend that you rent a car.* **SuperShuttle** (© **305/871-2000;** www.supershuttle.com) is one of the largest airport operators, charging between $10 and $40 per person for a ride within the county. Its vans operate 24 hours a day and accept American Express, MasterCard, and Visa.

If you're driving to Miami, no matter where you start your journey, chances are, you'll reach it by way of **I-95.** This north-south interstate is the city's lifeline, connecting all of Miami's different neighborhoods, the airport, and the beach, and it connects all of South Florida to the rest of America.

VISITOR INFORMATION   The most up-to-date information is provided by the **Greater Miami Convention and Visitor's Bureau,** 701 Brickell Ave., Ste. 700, Miami, FL 33131 (© **800/933-8448** or 305/539-3000; fax 305/530-3113). Information on everything from dining to entertainment is available on the Net at www.miami.citysearch.com, www.miaminewtimes.com, and www.herald.com.

GETTING AROUND   If you're counting on exploring the city, even to a modest degree, a car is essential. You can manage to get by without one only if you are spending your entire vacation at a resort or if you are here for a short stay centered in one area of the city, such as South Beach. Every major rental-car agency is represented in the city and at the airport. A minimum age, generally 25, is usually required of renters, while some rental agencies have also set maximum ages.

FAST FACTS   The Dade County Medical Association sponsors a **Physician Referral Service** (© **305/324-8717**), weekdays from 9am to 5pm. **Health South Doctors' Hospital,** 5000 University Dr., Coral Gables (© **305/666-2111**), is a 285-bed acute-care hospital with a 24-hour physician-staffed emergency department. **Walgreens Pharmacy** (**www.walgreens.com**) has locations all over town. The branch at 5731 Bird Rd., at SW 40th Street (© **305/666-0757**), is open 24 hours.

A 6.5% **sales tax** is added on at the register for all goods and services purchased in Miami. In addition, most municipalities levy **special taxes on restaurants and hotels.** In Miami Beach (including South Beach), it's 11.5%, and in the rest of Dade County, it's a whopping 12.5%.

SPECIAL EVENTS   New Year's Day is the date of the **Orange Bowl,** in which two of the year's top college football teams do battle at Pro Player Stadium. (Tickets to the game are available starting Mar 1 of the previous year through the Orange Bowl Committee at © **305/371-4600.**)

Perhaps Miami's most popular attraction is its incredible 35-mile stretch of beachfront, which runs from the tip of South Beach north to Sunny Isles and circles Key Biscayne and the numerous other pristine islands dotting the Atlantic. Whatever type of beach vacation you're looking for, you'll find it in one of Miami's two distinct beach areas: Miami Beach and Key Biscayne.

IN MIAMI BEACH Collins Avenue fronts more than a dozen miles of white-sand beach and blue-green waters from 1st to 192nd streets. Although most of this stretch is lined with a wall of hotels and condos, beach access is plentiful. There are lots of well-maintained public beaches here, with lifeguards, restroom facilities, concession stands, and metered parking (bring lots of quarters). Except for a thin strip close to the water, most of the sand is hard packed—the result of a $10-million Army Corps of Engineers Beach Rebuilding Project meant to protect buildings from the effects of eroding sand.

In general, the beaches on this barrier island (all on the eastern, ocean side of the island) become less crowded the farther north you go. A wooden boardwalk runs along the hotel side of the beach from 21st to 46th streets—about 1½ miles—offering a terrific sun-and-surf experience without getting sand in your shoes. Miami's lifeguard-protected public beaches include 21st Street, at the beginning of the boardwalk; 35th Street, popular with an older crowd; 46th Street, next to the Fontainebleau Hilton; 53rd Street, a narrower, more sedate beach; 64th Street, one of the quietest strips around; and 72nd Street, a local old-timers' spot.

KEY BISCAYNE'S BEACHES If Miami Beach doesn't provide the privacy you're looking for, try Virginia Key and Key Biscayne. Crossing the Rickenbacker Causeway ($1 toll) can be a lengthy process, especially on weekends, when beach bums and tan-o-rexics flock to the Key. The 5 miles of public beach there are blessed with softer sand and are less developed and more laid-back than the hotel-laden strips.

ACTIVE PURSUITS

BIKING The cement promenade on the southern tip of South Beach is a great place to ride. Biking up the beach is great for surf, sun, sand, exercise, and people-watching. Most of the big hotels rent bicycles, as does the **Miami Beach Bicycle Center,** 601 5th St., South Beach (© **305/674-0150;** www.bikemiamibeach.com), which charges $8 per hour or $24 for up to 24 hours. It's open Monday through Saturday from 10am to 7pm, Sunday from 10am to 5pm. Bikers can also enjoy more than 130 miles of paved paths throughout Miami. The beautiful, quiet streets of Coral Gables and Coconut Grove are great for bicyclists, where old trees form canopies over wide, flat roads lined with grand homes and quaint street markers. For a decent list of trails throughout South Florida, visit www.geocities.com/floutdoorzone/bike.html.

BOATING & SAILING Private rental outfits include **Boat Rental Plus,** 2400 Collins Ave., Miami Beach (© **305/534-4307**), where 50-horsepower, 18-foot powerboats rent for some of the best prices on the beach. There's a 2-hour minimum, and rates go from $100 to $500, including taxes and gas. They also have great specials on Sunday. Cruising is permitted only in and around Biscayne Bay, and renters must be 21 or older to rent a boat. The rental office is at 23rd Street, on the inland waterway in Miami Beach. It's open daily from 10am to sunset. If you want a specific type of boat, call ahead to reserve. Otherwise, show up and take what's available.

FLORIDA

5

MIAMI

Aquatic Rental Center, in the Pelican Harbor Marina, in Biscayne Bay, 1275 NE 79th St. (© 305/751-7514 days, 279-7424 evenings; www.arcmiami.com), can rent you a 22-foot sailboat for $80 for 2 hours, $135 for a half-day, and $195 for a full day. A Sunfish sailboat for two people rents at $30 per hour. They also offer a 10-hour course over 5 days for $350 for one person, or $450 for you and a buddy.

GOLF There are more than 50 private and public golf courses in the Miami area. Contact the **Greater Miami Convention and Visitor's Bureau** (© 800/933-8448; www.miamiandbeaches.com) for a list of courses and costs.

Some of the area's best and most expensive are at the big resorts, many of which allow nonguests to play. Otherwise, the following represent some of the area's best public courses. **Crandon Park Golf Course,** 6700 Crandon Blvd., Key Biscayne (© 305/361-9129), is the number-one municipal course in the state and one of the top five in the country. The park is on 200 bayfront acres and offers a pro shop, rentals, lessons, carts, and a lighted driving range. The course is open daily from dawn to dusk; greens fees (including cart) are $57 for nonresidents. Special twilight rates are also available.

One of the most popular courses among real enthusiasts is the **Doral Park Golf and Country Club,** 5001 NW 104th Ave., West Miami (© 305/591-8800); it's not related to the Doral Hotel or spa. Call to book in advance, since this challenging, semiprivate 18-holer is extremely popular with locals. The course is open from 6:30am to 6pm during the winter and until 7pm during the summer. Cart and greens fees vary, so call © 305/592-2000, ext. 2104, for information.

One of the best in the city, the **Country Club of Miami,** 6801 Miami Gardens Dr., at NW 68th Avenue, North Miami (© 305/829-8456; www.golfmiamicc.com), has three 18-hole courses of varying degrees of difficulty. You'll encounter lush fairways, rolling greens, and some history. The west course, designed in 1961 by Robert Trent Jones, Sr., and updated in the 1990s by the PGA, was where Jack Nicklaus played his first professional tournament and Lee Trevino won his first professional championship. The course is open daily from 7am to sunset. Cart and greens fees are $13 to $38, depending on season and tee times. Special twilight rates are available.

SNORKELING & SCUBA DIVING **Diver's Paradise** of Key Biscayne, 4000 Crandon Blvd. (© 305/361-3483; www.keydivers.com), offers one dive expedition per day during the week and two per day on the weekends to the more than 30 wrecks and artificial reefs off the coast of Miami Beach and Key Biscayne. You can take a 3-day certification course for $499, which includes all the dives and gear. If you already have your C-card, a dive trip costs about $100 if you need equipment and $55 if you bring your own gear. It's open Tuesday through Friday from 10am to 6pm and Saturday and Sunday from 8am to 6pm. Call ahead for times and locations of dives. For snorkeling, they will set you up with equipment and maps on where to see the best underwater sights. Rental for mask, fins, and snorkel is $50.

WHAT TO SEE & DO

In South Beach, the **Art Deco District** is a whole community made up of outrageous and fanciful 1920s and 1930s architecture. The district is roughly bounded by the Atlantic Ocean on the east, Alton Road on the west, 6th Street to the south, and Dade Boulevard (along the Collins Canal) to the north. Most of the finest examples of the Art Deco style are concentrated along three parallel streets—Ocean Drive, Collins Avenue, and Washington Avenue—from about 6th to 23rd streets. Hundreds of new hotels,

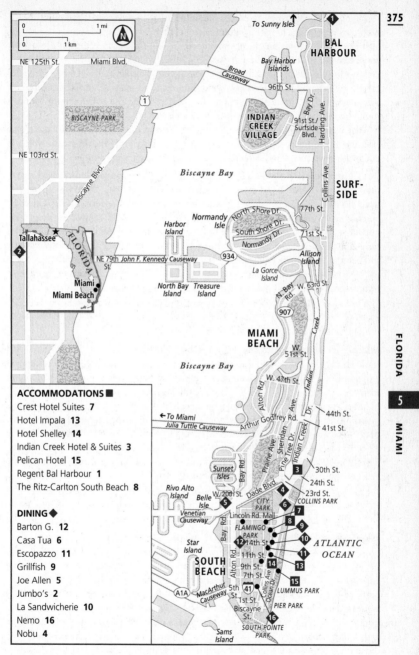

ACCOMMODATIONS ■

Crest Hotel Suites **7**

Hotel Impala **13**

Hotel Shelley **14**

Indian Creek Hotel & Suites **3**

Pelican Hotel **15**

Regent Bal Harbour **1**

The Ritz-Carlton South Beach **8**

DINING ◆

Barton G. **12**

Casa Tua **6**

Escopazzo **11**

Grillfish **9**

Joe Allen **5**

Jumbo's **2**

La Sandwicherie **10**

Nemo **16**

Nobu **4**

restaurants, and nightclubs have been renovated or are in the process, and South Beach is on the cutting edge of Miami's cultural and nightlife scene.

If you're touring this unique neighborhood on your own, start at the **Art Deco Welcome Center,** 1001 Ocean Dr. (© **305/531-3484**), which is run by the Miami Design Preservation League. This is the only beachside building across from the Clevelander Hotel and Bar, and they give away lots of informational material, including maps and pamphlets, and run guided tours about the neighborhood. The center is open Monday through Saturday from 9am to 6pm, sometimes later.

Take a stroll along **Ocean Drive** for the best view of cafes, bars, colorful hotels, and even more colorful people. Another great place for a walk is **Lincoln Road,** which is lined with boutiques, large chain stores, cafes, and funky art and antiques stores.

Bass Museum of Art   The Bass Museum of Art has expanded and received a dramatically new look. World-renowned Japanese architect Arata Isozaki designed the magnificent new facility, which has triple the former exhibition space, and added an outdoor sculpture terrace, a museum cafe and courtyard, and a museum shop. The museum's permanent collection includes European paintings from the 15th through the early 20th centuries, with special emphasis on northern European art of the Renaissance and baroque periods, including Dutch and Flemish masters. The museum also has a lab, the New Information Workshop, making it possible for all aspiring artists to create their own masterpieces on computers for free or a nominal charge.

2121 Park Ave. (1 block west of Collins Ave.), South Beach. © **305/673-7530.** www.bassmuseum.org. Admission $8 adults, $6 students and seniors, free for children 6 and under. Free 2nd Thurs of the month 6–9pm. Tues–Wed and Fri–Sat 10am–5pm; Thurs 10am–9pm; Sun 11am–5pm.

Miami Art Museum at the Miami-Dade Cultural Center   The Miami Art Museum (MAM) features an eclectic mix of modern and contemporary works by such artists as Eric Fischl, Max Beckmann, Jim Dine, and Stuart Davis. Rotating exhibitions span ages and styles, and often focus on Latin American or Caribbean artists. JAM at MAM is the museum's popular happy hour, which takes place the third Thursday of the month. Almost as artistic as the works inside the museum is the composite sketch of the people—young and old—who attend these events. Work has begun on Museum Park, a 29-acre property on the bay in downtown Miami that will become MAM's new home. The 125,000-square-foot Museum Park will include a sculpture garden and spacious galleries. Estimated completion is sometime in 2009.

101 W. Flagler St., Miami. © **305/375-3000.** www.miamiartmuseum.org. Admission $5 adults, $2.50 seniors and students, free for children 11 and under. Tues–Fri 10am–5pm (3rd Thurs of each month 10am–9pm); Sat–Sun noon–5pm. Closed major holidays.

Miami Metrozoo (Kids)   This 290-acre complex is never really crowded and it's completely cageless—animals are kept at bay by cleverly designed moats. There's a wonderful petting zoo and play area, and the zoo offers several daily programs designed to educate and entertain. Other highlights include two rare white Bengal tigers, a Komodo dragon, koala bears, a number of kangaroos, an African meerkat, a monorail tour, and an impressive aviary. Scheduled to open in late 2008, **Tropical America** will feature jaguars, anacondas, giant river otters, harpy eagles, stingray touch tanks, and a unique display of a forest before and during flood times. At 27 acres and $35 million, the exhibit is massive. *Note:* The distance between animal habitats can be great, so you'll be doing *a lot* of walking here.

12400 SW 152nd St., South Miami. © **305/251-0400.** www.miamimetrozoo.com. Admission $14 adults, $13 seniors, $10 children 3–12. Daily 9:30am–5:30pm (ticket booth closes at 4pm). Free parking.

Museum of Contemporary Art (MOCA) MOCA boasts an impressive collection of internationally acclaimed art with a local flavor. It is also known for its forward thinking and ability to discover and highlight new artists. A high-tech screening facility allows for film presentations to complement the exhibitions. You can see works by Jasper Johns, Roy Lichtenstein, Larry Rivers, Duane Michaels, and Claes Oldenberg, plus there are special exhibitions by such artists as Yoko Ono, Sigmar Polke, John Baldessari, and Goya. The MOCA Annex at the Goldman Warehouse in the gritty yet burgeoning Wynwood Arts District, 404 NW 26th St., is used to exhibit portions of the museum's permanent collection and projects by emerging artists.

770 NE 125th St., North Miami. ✆ **305/893-6211.** Fax 305/891-1472. www.mocanomi.org. Admission $5 adults, $3 seniors and students with ID, free for children 12 and under. Tues by donation. Tues–Sat 11am–5pm; Sun noon–5pm. Closed major holidays.

Spanish Monastery Cloisters Did you know that the allegedly oldest building in the Western Hemisphere dates from 1133 and is in Miami? The Spanish Monastery Cloisters were first erected in Segovia, Spain. Centuries later, newspaper magnate William Randolph Hearst purchased and brought them to America in pieces. The carefully numbered stones were quarantined for years until they were reassembled on the present site in 1954. It has often been used as a backdrop for weddings, movies, and commercials, and is a very popular tourist attraction.

16711 W. Dixie Hwy. (at NE 167th St.), North Miami Beach. ✆ **305/945-1461.** www.spanishmonastery. com. Admission $5 adults, $2.50 seniors and students with ID, $1 children 3–12. Mon–Fri 10am–4pm; Sun 1–5pm. Call ahead because the monastery closes for special events.

Venetian Pool (Kids) Miami's most beautiful and unusual swimming pool, dating from 1924, is hidden behind pastel stucco walls and is honored with a listing in the National Register of Historic Places. Underground artesian wells feed the free-form lagoon, which is shaded by three-story Spanish porticos and has both fountains and waterfalls. It can be cold in the winter months. During summer, the pool's 800,000 gallons of water are drained and refilled nightly, thanks to an underground aquifer, ensuring a cool, *clean* swim. Visitors are free to swim and sunbathe, just as Esther Williams and Johnny Weissmuller did decades ago.

2701 DeSoto Blvd. (at Toledo St.), Coral Gables. ✆ **305/460-5356.** www.venetianpool.com. Admission Nov–Mar $5.50 for those 13 and older, $3.50 for children 12 and under; Apr–Oct $10 for those 13 and older, $6.75 for children 12 and under. Children must be at least 3 years old and provide proof of age with birth certificate, or 38 in. tall to enter. Daily hours are at least 11am–4:30pm but are often longer. Call for more information.

The Vizcaya Museum and Gardens (Best) Sometimes referred to as the "Hearst Castle of the East," this magnificent villa was built in 1916 as a winter retreat for James Deering, co-founder of International Harvester. The industrialist was fascinated by 16th-century art and architecture; his ornate mansion, which took 1,000 artisans 5 years to build, became a celebration of that period. Most of the original furnishings, including dishes and paintings, are still intact. A free guided tour of the 34 furnished rooms on the first floor takes about 45 minutes. The second floor is open to tour on your own. Outside, lush formal gardens, accented with statuary, balustrades, and decorative urns, front an enormous swath of Biscayne Bay. Definitely take the villa tour, but immediately thereafter, wander and get lost in the resplendent gardens.

3251 S. Miami Ave. (just south of Rickenbacker Causeway), North Coconut Grove. ✆ **305/250-9133.** www.vizcayamuseum.com. Admission $12 adults, $5 children 6–12, free for children 5 and under. Villa daily 9:30am–5pm (ticket booth closes at 4:30pm); gardens daily 9:30am–5:30pm.

Wolfsonian-Florida International University Mitchell Wolfson, Jr., an eccentric millionaire, was the ultimate packrat. A premier collector of propaganda and advertising art, Wolfson bought a warehouse to house 70,000 of his items, from Nazi propaganda to King Farouk of Egypt's match collection. Thrown in the mix are zany works from great modernists such as Charles Eames and Marcel Duchamp. He gave his incredibly diverse collection to Florida International University. The former 1927 storage facility has been transformed into a museum that is unquestionably fascinating and hosts lectures and rather swinging events surrounding particular exhibits.

1001 Washington Ave., South Beach. © **305/531-1001.** www.wolfsonian.org. Admission $7 adults, $5 seniors, students with ID, and children 6–12. Mon–Tues and Fri–Sat 11am–6pm; Thurs 11am–9pm; Sun noon–5pm.

PRIME SHOPPING AREAS

Miami has earned a worldwide reputation as a shopping capital, especially among visitors from Latin America and the Caribbean. Take a quick glance around the airport, and you'll see departing passengers lugging refrigerator-size cardboard boxes and bulging suitcases. From tropical fruits to high-tech electronics, fine art and Art Deco collectibles, Latin music and hand-rolled cigars, Miami has something for everyone.

You may want to order the Greater Miami Convention and Visitors Bureau's *Shop Miami: A Guide to a Tropical Shopping Adventure.* Although it is limited to details on the bureau's paying members, it provides some good advice and otherwise unpublished discount offers. The glossy little pamphlet is printed in English, Spanish, and Portuguese, and provides information on transportation from hotels, translation services, and shipping. Call © **800/283-2707** or 305/539-3000 for more information.

AVENTURA On Biscayne Boulevard between Miami Gardens Drive and the county line at Hallandale Beach Boulevard is a 2-mile stretch of major retail stores, including Best Buy, Borders, DSW, Bed, Bath and Beyond, Loehmann's, Circuit City, Linens 'n Things, Marshalls, Sports Authority, and more. Also here is the mammoth Aventura Mall, housing a fabulous collection of shops and restaurants.

CALLE OCHO For a taste of Little Havana, take a walk down 8th Street between SW 27th Avenue and SW 12th Avenue, where you'll find some lively streetlife and many shops selling cigars, baked goods, shoes, and furniture, and record stores specializing in Latin music. For help, take your Spanish dictionary.

COCONUT GROVE Downtown Coconut Grove, centered on Main Highway and Grand Avenue, and branching onto the adjoining streets, is one of Miami's most pedestrian-friendly zones. The wide sidewalks, lined with cafes and boutiques, can provide hours of browsing. Coconut Grove is best known for its chain stores (Gap, Banana Republic) and some funky holdovers from the days when the Grove was a bit more bohemian, plus sidewalk cafes centered on CocoWalk and the Streets of Mayfair.

MIRACLE MILE (CORAL GABLES) Only a half-mile long, this central shopping street was an integral part of the original city plan. Today the strip still enjoys popularity, especially for its bridal stores, ladies' shops, haberdashers, and gift shops. Recently, newer chain stores, such as Barnes & Noble, Old Navy, and Starbucks, have been appearing. The upscale **Village of Merrick Park,** a mammoth, 850,000-square-foot outdoor shopping complex between Ponce de León Boulevard and Le Jeune Road, houses Neiman Marcus, Armani, Gucci, and Yves St. Laurent, to name a few.

DOWNTOWN MIAMI   If you're looking for discounts on all types of goods—especially watches, fabric, buttons, lace, shoes, luggage, and leather—**Flagler Street**, just west of Biscayne Boulevard, is the place to start. I wouldn't necessarily recommend buying expensive items here, as many stores seem to be on the shady side. However, you can still have fun as long as you are a savvy shopper and don't mind haggling. Most signs are printed in English, Spanish, and Portuguese; however, many shopkeepers may not be entirely fluent in English. **Mary Brickell Village** is a 192,000-square-foot urban entertainment center west of Brickell Avenue and straddling South Miami Avenue between 9th and 10th streets downtown. The $80-million complex will eventually consist of a slew of trendy restaurants, boutiques, and the requisite Starbucks—a sure sign that a neighborhood has been revitalized.

SOUTH BEACH   While the requisite stores such as Gap and Banana Republic are here, several higher-end stores have opened on the southern blocks of Collins Avenue, which has become the Madison Avenue of Miami. For the hippest boutiques (including Armani Exchange, Ralph Lauren, Versace, Benetton, Levi's, Barneys Co-Op, and Nicole Miller), stroll along this strip of the Art Deco District.

For those who are interested in a little more fun with their shopping, consider South Beach's legendary Lincoln Road. This pedestrian mall, originally designed in 1957 by Morris Lapidus, recently underwent a multimillion-dollar renovation, restoring it to its former glory. Here shoppers find an array of clothing, books, tchotchkes, and art, as well as a menagerie of sidewalk cafes flanked on one end by a multiplex movie theater and, at the other, by the Atlantic Ocean.

WHERE TO STAY

Central Reservation Service (© **800/950-0232** or 305/274-6832; www.reservation-services.com) works with many of Miami's hotels and can often secure discounts of up to 40%. It also gives advice on specific locales, especially in Miami Beach and downtown. During holiday time, there may be a 3-to-5-day minimum stay required to use their services. Call for more information.

For bed-and-breakfast information, contact **Florida Bed and Breakfast Inns** (© **800/524-1880**; www.florida-inns.com). For boutique hotels, check out the Greater Miami Convention and Visitor's Bureau's website, **www.miamiboutiquehotels.com**.

South Florida's tourist season is well defined, beginning in mid-November and lasting until Easter. Hotel prices escalate until about March, after which they begin to decline. Off-season hotel rates are typically 30% to 50% lower than their winter highs.

The Biltmore   A romantic sense of old-world glamour combined with a rich history permeates the Biltmore as much as the pricey perfume of the guests who stay here. Built in 1926, it's the oldest Coral Gables hotel and is a National Historic Landmark—one of only two operating hotels in Florida to receive that designation. Rising above the Spanish-style estate is a majestic 300-foot copper-clad tower, modeled after the Giralda bell tower in Seville and visible throughout the city. Large Moorish-style rooms are decorated with tasteful decor, European feather beds, Egyptian cotton duvets, writing desks, and some high-tech amenities. The landmark 23,000-square-foot, winding pool now has the requisite hipster accessories—the private cabana, alfresco bar, and restaurant. Always a popular destination for golfers, including former president Clinton (who stays in the **Al Capone suite**), the Biltmore is situated on a lush, rolling, 18-hole

(Best) Five Fabulous Historic Hotels

The U.S. is loaded with notable historic lodging (how many places can George Washington really have slept in?), but we've picked five that we are especially fond of from across the nation for those who like their accommodations to have a little history (or a lot). All these National Historic Landmarks offer some unique features or a noteworthy background. For more information on these hotels and other historic properties, consult the **Historic Hotels of America** database (**www.historichotels.org**) maintained by the National Trust for Historic Preservation, or call (C) **800/678-8946.** And for info on two more beloved historic properties—the **Greenbrier** and the **Eldridge**—check out p. 1036 and 1029).

1. **Hotel Del Coronado** (San Diego, California; p. 916): When the Del opened in 1888, it was the largest electrically lit building outside of New York City. In its 116-year history, it's hosted 10 U.S. presidents (starting with Benjamin Harrison in 1891) and numerous foreign dignitaries (reportedly the Duke of Windsor met Wallis Simpson here). The property has been thoroughly modernized but still retains its Victorian charm, and is considered one of the loveliest resorts in the country.

2. **The Biltmore** (Miami, Florida; p. 379): This Mediterranean Revival masterpiece, with its signature tower modeled on Seville's La Giralda, debuted in 1926 and became *the* place to see and be seen in the 1930s. Everyone from Bing Crosby to Al Capone stayed here. Olympic swimmer (and future *Tarzan* star) Johnny Weissmuller once broke the world record in the hotel's exceptional 700,000-gallon pool. World War II saw the hotel transformed into an army hospital, which it remained until a $60-million restoration returned it to its place as one of the country's most elegant and upscale resorts in the late 1980s.

Donald Ross course that is as challenging as it is beautiful. Sunday brunch is an equal feat—book early.

1200 Anastasia Ave., Coral Gables, FL 33134. (C) **800/727-1926** or 305/445-1926. Fax 305/442-9496. www.biltmorehotel.com. 276 units. Winter $395–$895 double; off season $229–$499 double; year-round $659–$6,500 specialty suites. Additional person $20. Special packages available. AE, DC, DISC, MC, V. Overnight valet parking $16; free self-parking. **Amenities:** 4 restaurants; pool; 18-hole golf course; 10 lighted tennis courts; state-of-the-art health club; spa. *In room:* Kitchenette (in tower suites only).

Crest Hotel Suites (Value)   One of South Beach's best-kept secrets, the Crest Hotel has a quietly fashionable, relaxed atmosphere with friendly service. Built in 1939, the Crest was restored to preserve its Art Deco architecture, but the interior is thoroughly modern, with rooms resembling cosmopolitan apartments. All suites have a living room/dining room area, kitchenette, and executive work space. An indoor/outdoor cafe with terrace and poolside dining isn't besieged with trendy locals, but does attract a younger crowd. Around the corner from the hotel is Lincoln Road, with its sidewalk cafes, gourmet restaurants, theaters, and galleries.

3. **The Menger Hotel** (San Antonio, Texas; p. 647). Opened on the site of Texas's first brewery in 1859, the Menger was billed as "the finest hotel west of the Mississippi River," and many famous names have stayed here (from Robert E. Lee and Sam Houston to Babe Ruth and Sarah Bernhardt). Teddy Roosevelt recruited a bunch of his famed Rough Riders in the hotel's Menger Bar. Though it's been enlarged and modernized since its birth, the Menger still retains an atmosphere of period elegance, its original wrought iron balconies remain intact, and the ghost of a 19th-century chambermaid is rumored to haunt its halls.

4. **Colonial Houses** (Colonial Williamsburg, Virginia; p. 227). For an authentic historical experience, this is the top place to stay in the country. Accommodations are set in 28 restored Colonial-era buildings (modernized plumbing, but forget high-tech) of various sizes and layouts (some as large as 16 rooms). Thomas Jefferson lived in the Market Square Tavern as a law student, and John Tyler owned the Nicholas-Tyler Office, where, as vice president, he received the news he'd become America's 10th president upon the death of William Henry Harrison.

5. **Brown Palace Hotel** (Denver, Colorado; p. 669). Businessman Henry Cordes Brown commissioned architect Frank E. Edbrooke to design an "unprecedented" hotel in the Italian Renaissance style, and Edbrooke came through—in spades. Still the best hotel in Denver (and among the best in the world), the Brown Palace opened its doors in 1892 as a triangular mass of red sandstone and granite, with an exquisite eight-story stained-glass atrium lobby. The hotel has sheltered more than its fair share of famous guests: It was a favorite of Harry Truman, and Dwight D. Eisenhower used the hotel as his summer headquarters during his presidency.

FLORIDA

5

MIAMI

1670 James Ave., Miami Beach, FL 33139. ℂ **800/531-3880** or 305/531-0321. Fax 305/531-8180. www. crestgrouphotels.com/cresthotelsuites.htm. 64 units. Winter $120–$165 double, $211 suite; off season $115 double, $175 suite. Packages available and 10% discount offered if booked on website. AE, MC, V. **Amenities:** 2 restaurants; pool. *In room:* Kitchenette (select units).

Fairmont Turnberry Isle Resort & Club   One of Miami's classiest—and priciest—resorts, this gorgeous 300-acre compound has every possible facility for active guests, particularly golfers. You'll pay a lot to stay here, thanks to a $100-million renovation of all guest rooms, suites, golf courses, the spa, pool, fitness center, and beach club. The main attractions are two Raymond Floyd courses, available only to members and guests of the hotel, and Bourbon Steak, a restaurant by star chef Michael Mina. A new, seven-story Mediterranean-style wing is surrounded by tropical gardens that are joined by covered marble walkways. The **Willow Stream Spa** offers an unabridged menu of treatments. A location in the well-manicured residential and shopping area of Aventura appeals to those who want peace, quiet, and a great mall. The only drawback to this hotel is that you'll need to take a shuttle to the beach.

19999 W. Country Club Dr., Aventura, FL 33180. ✆ **800/327-7028** or 305/936-2929. Fax 305/933-6560. www.turnberryisle.com. 392 units. Winter $699–$809 double, $1,999–$4,000 suite; off season $299–$399 double, $599–$1,700 suite; year-round $4,000 grand presidential suite. AE, DC, DISC, MC, V. Valet parking $12; self-parking free. **Amenities:** 6 restaurants; 2 outdoor pools; 2 golf courses; 2 tennis complexes; state-of-the-art spa. *In room:* Fridge (upon request).

Hotel Impala   This charming Mediterranean hideaway is one of the area's best, and it's beautiful, from the Greco-Roman frescoes and friezes to an intimate garden perfumed with the scents of hanging lilies and gardenias. Rooms have super-cushy sleigh beds, sisal floors, wrought-iron fixtures, imported Belgian cotton linens, wood furniture, and fabulous-looking, but also incredibly small, bathrooms done up in stainless steel and coral rock. The two smallest are nos. 102 and 206; otherwise, the rooms are roomy and cushy. Adjacent to the hotel is **Spiga**, an intimate, excellent Italian restaurant that is reasonably priced. Enclaves like this are rare on South Beach. Rates include complimentary continental breakfast and access to Nikki Beach Club.

1228 Collins Ave., South Beach, FL 33139. ✆ **800/646-7252** or 305/673-2021. Fax 305/673-5984. www. hotelimpalamiamibeach.com. 17 units. Winter $195–$225 double, $325–$425 suite; off season $145–$195 double, $250–$325 suite. Rates include continental breakfast. AE, DC, MC, V. Valet parking $20. Small pets permitted. **Amenities:** Restaurant.

Hotel St. Michel   This European-style hotel, in the heart of Coral Gables, is one of the city's most romantic options. The accommodations and hospitality are straight out of old-world Europe, complete with dark-wood-paneled walls, cozy beds, beautiful antiques, and a quiet elegance that seems out of place in trendy Miami. Everything here is charming—from the brass elevator and parquet floors to the paddle fans. One-of-a-kind furnishings make each room special. Bathrooms are on the smaller side. All have tub/showers except for two, which have one or the other. Guests are treated to fresh fruit upon arrival and enjoy perfect service throughout their stay. The exceptional **Restaurant St. Michel** is a romantic dining choice. *Tip:* Ask for the hotel's stay-and-dine specials, in which dinner is included in the rate.

162 Alcazar Ave., Coral Gables, FL 33134. ✆ **800/848-HOTEL** (848-4683) or 305/444-1666. Fax 305/529-0074. www.hotelstmichel.com. 27 units. Winter $200 double, $250 suite; off season $125 double, $155 suite. Additional person $10. Rates include continental breakfast and fruit basket upon arrival. AE, DC, MC, V. Self-parking $7. **Amenities:** Restaurant; access to nearby health club.

Hotel Shelley Ⓥ**alue**   The Hotel Shelley has a laid-back beach atmosphere, yet cutting-edge style. The architecturally sound boutique hotel, built in 1931 in the heart of the Art Deco district, has reinvented itself with a $1.5-million renovation of its 49 guest rooms. Complete with Mascioni 300-thread-count linens, goose-down pillows and comforters, flatscreen TVs, and custom-built cabinetry, the guest rooms at the Shelley allow you to chill out after a long day at the beach or rock out before a big night of partying. The subtle purple hues in the rooms and public areas are in true Art Deco style. The bar in the lobby offers free drinks from 7 to 8pm every night and VIP passes to area nightclubs. Located on Collins and 1 block from Ocean Drive, this hotel allows you to reach beach, shopping, or nightlife within a few minutes' walk.

844 Collins Ave., Miami Beach, FL 33139. ✆ **305/531-3341.** Fax 305/535-9665. www.hotelshelley.com. 49 units. Winter $145–$225 double, $165–$245 king, $165–$300 minisuite; off season $75–$125 double, $95–$145 king, $115–$165 minisuite. During special events and holidays, rates are subject to change. Rates include free cocktails in the lobby. AE, DC, MC, V. Parking $30.

Indian Creek Hotel & Suites Off the beaten path, the Indian Creek Hotel is a
meticulously restored 1936 building with one of the first operating elevators in Miami
Beach. Because of its location facing the Indian Creek waterway and its lush landscaping,
this place feels like an old-fashioned Key West bed-and-breakfast. The revamped rooms
are outfitted in Art Deco furnishings, such as antique writing desks, tropical prints, and
small but spotless bathrooms. Just 1 block from a good stretch of sand, the hotel also has
a landscaped pool area in the back garden. The hotel's restaurant, **Creek 28,** is one of
Miami's best-kept secrets.

2727 Indian Creek Dr. (1 block west of Collins Ave. and the ocean), Miami Beach, FL 33140. ✆ **800/491-
2772** or 305/531-2727. Fax 305/531-5651. www.indiancreekhotel.com. 61 units. Winter $149–$199 double, $269–$289 suite; off season $69–$199 double, $179–$249 suite. Additional person $25. Packages
and summer specials available. AE, DC, DISC, MC, V. **Amenities:** Restaurant; pool. *In room:* Fridge (in
suites).

Mandarin Oriental, Miami (Best)   Corporate big shots and celebrities not in the
mood for the South Beach spotlight have a high-end luxury hotel to stay in while wheel-
ing and dealing their way through Miami. Catering to business travelers, big-time celebrities (J.Lo, Will Smith, and so on), and the leisure traveler who doesn't mind spending
big bucks, the Mandarin Oriental features a waterfront location, residential-style rooms
with Asian touches (most with balconies), and upscale dining. The waterfront view of the
city is the hotel's best asset. The hotel's two restaurants, the high-end **Azul** and the more
casual **Café Sambal,** are two of Miami's best, as is the 15,000-square-foot spa, which
offers traditional Thai massages and Ayurvedic treatments. The hotel is home to a
20,000-foot white-sand beach club with a fabulous Friday-night happy hour, beach
butlers, and beachside cabana treatments, which is nice, considering that the hotel is 15
minutes from the beach.

500 Brickell Key Dr., Miami, FL 33131. ✆ **305/913-8383.** Fax 305/913-8300. www.mandarinoriental.com.
326 units. $435–$900 double; $1,300–$6,500 suite. AE, DC, DISC, MC, V. Valet parking $24 plus tax. **Ameni-
ties:** 2 restaurants; beach club; infinity pool; nearby tennis and golf; state-of-the-art fitness center; spa.

Pelican Hotel   Owned by the same creative folks behind the Diesel Jeans company,
the Pelican is South Beach's only self-professed "toy-hotel," in which each of its 30 rooms
and suites is decorated as outrageously as some of the area's more colorful drag queens.
Each room has been designed daringly and rather wittily by Swedish interior decorator
Magnus Ehrland. Countless trips to antiques markets, combined with his wild imagination, have turned room no. 309, for instance, into the "Psychedelic(ate) Girl," room no.
201 into the "Executive Fifties" suite, and no. 209 into the "Love, Peace, and Leafforest"
room. But the most popular room is the tough-to-score no. 215, or the "Best Whore-
house." The Ocean Drive location and the hotel's cafe make the Pelican a very popular
people-watching spot.

826 Ocean Dr., Miami Beach, FL 33139. ✆ **800/7-PELICAN** (773-5422) or 305/673-3373. Fax 305/673-
3255. www.pelicanhotel.com. 30 units. Winter $240–$350 double, $480–$800 oceanfront suite; off season $165–$220 double, $330–$540 oceanfront suite. AE, DC, MC, V. Valet parking $22. **Amenities:**
Restaurant; access to area gyms. *In room:* Fridge.

Regent Bal Harbour   Proving too swanky for South Beach, the regal Regent packed
its bags and moved uptown—to a more fitting locale in the chichi shopping hamlet of
Bal Harbour. Until the St. Regis finishes completion in the former Sheraton Bal Harbour, this is the only oceanfront resort in the area. The ultimate in luxury, Regent suites
are resplendent in mahogany floors, with leather walls, panoramic views, bathrooms with

10-foot floor-to-ceiling windows, and a free-standing tub overlooking the ocean. Elevators take you directly into your suite. A Guerlain spa, butler service, spectacular pool and beach area, and world-class dining will cost you, but if you're looking to be doted on without lifting a finger—this is the place.

10295 Collins Ave., Bal Harbour, FL 33154. (© **800/545-4000** or 305/866-2121. Fax 305/866-2419. www. regenthotels.com/balharbour. 124 units. Winter $750–$900 deluxe, $1,000–$2,500 suite; off season $450–$600 deluxe, $780–$1,550 suite; $8,500 presidential suite. AE, MC, V. Valet parking. **Amenities:** Restaurant; outdoor pool; spa.

Ritz-Carlton Key Biscayne (Kids) The Ritz-Carlton in Key Biscayne offers 44 acres of tropical gardens, a 20,000-square-foot European-style spa, and a world-class tennis center under the direction of Cliff Drysdale. Decorated in British colonial style, the Ritz-Carlton is straight out of Bermuda, with its flower-laden landscaping. The Ritz Kids programs provide children ages 5 to 12 with fantastic activities, and the 1,200-foot beachfront offers everything from pure relaxation to fishing, boating, or windsurfing. Spacious, luxuriously appointed rooms are elegantly Floridian, featuring large balconies overlooking the ocean or gardens. The oceanfront Italian restaurant **Cioppino** is excellent for formal dining, or if you prefer casual dining, the oceanfront **Cantina Beach** serves Mexican food and even a "Tequlier"—a sommelier for tequila and a brand-new **Rum Bar.** The hotel's remote location—just a 10-minute drive from the hustle and bustle—makes it a favorite for those who want to avoid the hubbub.

455 Grand Bay Dr., Key Biscayne, FL 33149. (© **800/241-3333** or 305/365-4500. Fax 305/365-4501. www. ritzcarlton.com. 402 units. Winter $669 double, $954 suite; off season $289 double, $499 suite. AE, DC, DISC, MC, V. Valet parking (call for fees). **Amenities:** 3 restaurants; 2 outdoor heated pools; tennis center w/lessons available; fitness center; spa.

Ritz-Carlton South Beach (Kids) Far from ostentatious, the Ritz-Carlton South Beach moves away from gilded opulence in favor of the more soothing pastel-washed touches of Deco. Though South Beach is better known for its boutique hotels, the Ritz-Carlton provides comfort to those who might prefer 100% cotton Frette sheets and goose-down pillows to high-style minimalism. The best rooms are the 72 poolside and oceanview lanai rooms. There's also a tanning butler who will spritz you with SPF and water whenever you want. With its impeccable service, an elevated pool with unobstructed views of the Atlantic and a weekend DJ, an impressive stretch of sand with a beach club, and a 13,000-square-foot spa and wellness center, the Ritz-Carlton kicks sand in the faces of some smaller hotels that think they're doing *you* a favor by allowing you to sleep there. Parents love the Ritz Kids program for kids ages 5 through 12, and for gourmands there's the Ritz's amazing Sunday champagne brunch.

1 Lincoln Rd., South Beach, FL 33139. (© **800/241-3333** or 786/276-4000. Fax 786/276-4001. www. ritzcarlton.com. 375 units. Winter $739 double, $1,009 suite; off season $359 double, $479 suite. AE, DISC, MC, V. Valet parking $30. **Amenities:** 3 restaurants; outdoor heated pool; health club; spa.

WHERE TO DINE

With more than 6,000 restaurants to choose from, dining out in Miami has become a passionate pastime for locals and visitors alike. Our star chefs have fused Californian-Asian with Caribbean and Latin elements to create a world-class flavor all its own: *Floribbean.* Thanks to a thriving cafe society in South Beach and Coconut Grove, you can enjoy a moderately priced meal and linger without having a waiter hover over you. Whatever you're craving, Miami's got it—with the exception of decent Chinese food and a

New York–style slice of pizza. The biggest complaint when it comes to Miami dining isn't the haughtiness, but the dearth of truly moderately priced restaurants.

Barton G. The Restaurant AMERICAN   Barton G. The Restaurant is an homage to gourmet kitsch. It's a place that looks like a trendy restaurant but eats like a show. Take the popcorn shrimp appetizer. Served on a plateful of, yes, popcorn, with field greens and the plump, crispy rock shrimp stuffed into an actual popcorn box, this dish is one of many awe-inspiring—and tasty—menu items in the most unique restaurant in Miami. A grilled sea bass is served in a brown paper bag with laundry clips keeping the steam in until your server unclips them. Desserts are equally outrageous, including the Chocolate Fun-Do, a mini chocolate fountain overflowing with 4 pounds of Belgian chocolate and tons of dipping delicacies. A giant plume of cotton candy reminiscent of Dame Edna's hair is surrounded by white-, dark-, and milk-chocolate-covered popcorn balls that, when cracked, reveal a chocolate truffle inside. An elegant, well-lit indoor dining room is popular with members of the socialite set, while the bar area and outdoor courtyard is the place to be for younger trend-seekers.

1427 West Ave., South Beach. ✆ **305/672-8881.** www.bartong.com. Reservations suggested. Main courses $10–$50. AE, DC, DISC, MC, V. Daily 6pm–midnight.

Bayside Seafood Hut SEAFOOD   Known as "the Hut," this ramshackle restaurant and bar is a laid-back outdoor Tiki hut and terrace that serves good sandwiches and fish platters on paper plates. A blackboard lists the latest catches, which can be prepared blackened, fried, broiled, or in a garlic sauce. Local fishers and yachties share this rustic outpost with equal enthusiasm and loyalty. A new, air-conditioned area is a welcome addition, as is the new deck and the spruced-up decor. But behind it all, it's nothing fancier than a hut—if it were anything else, it wouldn't be as appealing.

3501 Rickenbacker Causeway, Key Biscayne. ✆ **305/361-0808.** Reservations accepted for parties of 15 or more. Appetizers, salads, and sandwiches $5–$15; platters $7–$13. AE, MC, V. Daily 10am–closing (which varies).

Casa Tua ITALIAN   The stunning Casa Tua is a sleek and chic, country Italian–style establishment set in a 1925 Mediterranean-style house-cum-hotel. It has several dining areas, including an outdoor garden, a Ralph Lauren–esque living room, and a communal eat-in kitchen. The lamb chops are stratospheric in price ($42) but sublime in taste and a bargain compared to the $50 milk-fed veal chop. Service is, as always with South Beach eateries, inconsistent, ranging from ultraprofessional to absurdly lackadaisical. For these prices, they should be wiping our mouths for us.

1700 James Ave., South Beach. ✆ **305/673-1010.** Reservations required. Main courses $24–$100. AE, DC, MC, V. Mon–Sat 7pm–midnight.

Chef Allen's NEW WORLD   Winner of the James Beard Award for Best American Chef in the Southeast, Chef Allen Susser is royalty around here. Here he offers New World Cuisine and the harmony of exotic tropical fruits, spices, and vegetables. Under Chef Allen's touch, Key limes and mangoes reappear in the forms of succulent salsas and sauces. A traditional antipasto is transformed into a Caribbean one, with papaya-pineapple barbecued shrimp, jerk calamari, and charred rare tuna. Unlike other restaurants where location is key, Chef Allen's, at the rear of a strip mall, could be in the desert and hordes of people would still make the trek.

19088 NE 29th Ave. (at Biscayne Blvd.), North Miami Beach. ✆ **305/935-2900.** Reservations recommended. Main courses $25–$45. AE, DC, MC, V. Sun–Thurs 6–10pm; Fri–Sat 6–11pm.

Escopazzo ITALIAN *Escopazzo* means "I'm going crazy" in Italian, but the only sign of insanity in this primo Northern Italian eatery is the fact that it seats only 90 and it's one of the best restaurants in town. The wine bottles have it better—the restaurant's cellar holds 1,000 bottles. In 2007, Escopazzo added "Organic Italian Restaurant" to its title. If you score a table at this romantic favorite (choose one in the back dining room that's reminiscent of an Italian courtyard, complete with fountain and faux windows), you'll have trouble deciding between dishes like milk and basil dough pasta with baby calamari, chickpeas, tomatoes, and arugula, or grass-fed hanger steak with roasted baby organic veggies in a truffle sauce. The hand-rolled pastas and risotto are near perfection. The service is excellent, and nobody's happy until you are blissfully full.

1311 Washington Ave., South Beach. ✆ **305/674-9450.** www.escopazzo.com. Reservations required. Main courses $14–$34. AE, MC, V. Mon–Fri 6pm–midnight; Sat 6pm–1am; Sun 6–11pm.

Grillfish SEAFOOD   From the Byzantine-style mural and the gleaming oak bar, you'd think you were eating in a much more expensive restaurant, but Grillfish manages to pay the exorbitant South Beach rent with the help of a loyal following who come for fresh, simple seafood in a relaxed, upscale atmosphere. The barroom seafood chowder is full of chunks of shellfish, as well as some fresh whitefish filets in a tomato broth. The small ear of corn included with each entree is about as close as you'll get to any type of vegetable, besides the pedestrian salad. Still, at these prices, it's worth a visit to try some local fare, including mako shark, swordfish, tuna, marlin, and wahoo. Most recently, they opened up a pizza restaurant next door called Crust.

1444 Collins Ave. (corner of Española Way), South Beach. ✆ **305/538-9908.** www.grillfish.com. Reservations accepted for parties of 6 or more only. Main courses $9–$26. AE, DC, DISC, MC, V. Daily 11:30am–4pm and 5:30pm–midnight.

Joe Allen AMERICAN   It's hard to compete in a city with haute spots everywhere, but Joe Allen has proven itself in both New York and London, and now has established itself off the beaten path in possibly the only area of South Beach that has remained impervious to trendiness. On the bay side of the beach, Joe Allen is devoid of neon lights, valet parkers, and fashionable pedestrians. Inside, one discovers a hidden jewel: a stark yet elegant interior and no-nonsense, fairly priced, ample-portioned dishes such as meatloaf, pizza, fresh fish, and salads. The scene has a homey feel favored by locals looking to escape the hype without compromising quality.

1787 Purdy Ave./Sunset Harbor Dr. (3 blocks west of Alton Rd.), South Beach. ✆ **305/531-7007.** Reservations recommended, especially on weekends. Main courses $15–$25. MC, V. Daily 11:30am–11:30pm.

Jumbo's SOUL FOOD   Open 24 hours, this Miami institution is the kind of place where you'll see everyone from Rastafarian musicians and cabdrivers to Lenny Kravitz. It's in a shady neighborhood—Carol City—so if you go there, you're going for only one reason—Jumbo's. Family owned for more than 50 years, Jumbo's is known for its fried shrimp, fried chicken, catfish fingers, and collard greens. Their motto—"Life is to be enjoyed, not to be endured . . . Making friends is our business" is spot on. The service is friendly and fun. Jumbo's was the first restaurant in Miami to integrate (in 1966) and the first to hire African-American employees (in 1967).

7501 NW 7th Ave., Miami. ✆ **305/751-1127.** Main courses $5–$15. AE, DC, MC, V. Daily 24 hr.

La Sandwicherie SANDWICHES   You can get mustard, mayo, or oil and vinegar on sandwiches elsewhere, but you'd be missing out on the local flavor. This gourmet

sandwich bar, open until the crack of dawn, caters to club kids, biker types, and the body
artists who work in the tattoo parlor next door. For many people, in fact, no night of
clubbing is complete without capping it off with a turkey sub from La Sandwicherie.

229 14th St. (behind the Amoco station), South Beach. ℂ **305/532-8934.** Sandwiches and salads
$6–$12. AE, MC, V. Daily 9am–5am. Delivery 9:30am–11pm.

Michael Mina's Bourbon Steak STEAKHOUSE Everything here is massive—
from the all-glass wine cellar that takes up an entire wall, to the size of the place at 7,600
square feet. If you don't mind splurging, a meal at the star chef's first and only South
Florida location is worth it. Start off with oysters on the half shell—East Coast or West
Coast—then continue with the all-natural farm-raised angus beef, American Kobe beef,
or actual Japanese Kobe beef—where a 6-ounce rib-eye will set you back $170! Side
dishes are delicious—including jalapeño creamed corn ($9), truffled mac and cheese
($12), and a Bourbon Steak trio of Duck Fat Fries ($8). A scene of well-heeled Aventura
residents and elegantly dressed hotel guests compose the rich crowd.

1999 W. Country Club Dr. (in the Fairmont Turnberry Isle Resort & Club), Aventura. ℂ **786/279-6600.**
Reservations recommended. Main courses $29–$190. AE, DC, DISC, MC, V. Mon–Thurs 5–10:30pm; Fri–Sat
5–11:30pm.

Nemo PAN-ASIAN In the chic South Beach area known as SoFi ("South of Fifth
St."), Nemo is a funky, high-style eatery with an open kitchen and an outdoor courtyard
canopied by trees and lined with an eclectic mix of model types and foodies. Among the
reasons to eat in this restaurant, whose name is actually *omen* spelled backward: grilled
Indian-spiced pork chop; grilled local mahimahi with citrus and grilled sweet-onion
salad, kimchi glaze, basil, and crispy potatoes; and an inspired dessert menu. Seating
inside is comfy-cozy but borders on cramped. On Sunday mornings, the open kitchen is
converted into a buffet counter for an unparalleled brunch. Be prepared for a wait, however, and the line tends to spill out onto the street.

100 Collins Ave., South Beach. ℂ **305/532-4550.** www.nemorestaurant.com. Reservations recommended. Main courses $29–$75; Sun brunch $29. AE, MC, V. Mon–Sat noon–3pm and 6:30pm–midnight;
Sun 11am–3pm and 6pm–midnight. Valet parking $10, or $20 for curbside.

Nobu SUSHI When Justin Timberlake and Cameron Diaz canoodled here, no one
noticed, because the real star at Nobu is the sushi. Nobu has been hailed as one of the
best sushi restaurants in the world, with always-packed eateries in New York, London,
and Los Angeles. The Omakase, or Chef's Choice—a multicourse menu up to the chef
for $70 per person and up—gets raves. Although you won't wait long for your food to
be cooked, you will wait forever to score a table.

At the Shore Club Hotel, 1901 Collins Ave., South Beach. ℂ **305/695-3232.** Reservations only for parties
of 6 or more. Main courses $26 and above. AE, MC, V. Sun 7–11pm; Mon–Thurs 7pm–midnight; Fri–Sat
7pm–1am.

Versailles CUBAN Versailles is the meeting place of Miami's Cuban power brokers,
who meet over *café con leche* to discuss the future of the exiles' fate. A glorified diner, the
place sparkles with glass, chandeliers, murals, and mirrors meant to evoke the French
palace. There's nothing fancy—nothing French, either—just straightforward food from
the home country. The menu is a survey of Cuban cooking and includes specialties such
as Moors and Christians (flavorful black beans with white rice), *ropa vieja* (shredded beef
stew), and fried whole fish. Versailles is the place to come for *mucho* helpings of Cuban

kitsch. With its late hours, it's also the perfect place to come after spending your night in Little Havana.

3555 SW 8th St., Little Havana. ✆ **305/444-0240.** Main courses $5–$20; soup and salad $2–$10. DC, DISC, MC, V. Mon–Thurs 8am–2am; Fri 8am–3am; Sat 8am–4:30am; Sun 9am–1am.

MIAMI AFTER DARK

For up-to-date listing information, and to make sure the club of the moment hasn't expired, check the *Miami Herald*'s "Weekend" section, which runs on Friday, or the more comprehensive listings in *New Times,* Miami's free alternative weekly, available each Wednesday; or visit **www.miami.citysearch.com online**.

THE PERFORMING ARTS   The **Concert Association of Florida** (**CAF;** ✆ **877/433-3200**) produces one of the most important and longest-running series. CAF arranges the best "serious" music concerts for the city. Season after season, the schedules are punctuated by world-renowned dance companies and virtuosi such as Itzhak Perlman, Andre Watts, and Kathleen Battle. Performances are usually in the Miami-Dade County Auditorium or the Jackie Gleason Theater of the Performing Arts. The season lasts October through April, and ticket prices range from $20 to $70.

The artistically acclaimed and innovative **Miami City Ballet** (✆ **305/929-7000** or 929-7010) is directed by Edward Villella and features a repertoire of more than 60 ballets. The company's headquarters are located at the Ophelia and Juan, Jr., Roca Center at the Collins Park Cultural Center in Miami Beach. For a taste of local Latin flavor, see the **Ballet Flamenco La Rosa** (✆ **305/899-7729**) perform impressive flamenco and other styles of dance on various Miami stages.

South Florida's premier symphony orchestra, under the direction of James Judd, the **Florida Philharmonic Orchestra** (✆ **800/226-1812**) presents a full season of classical and pops programs interspersed with several children's and contemporary popular-music dates. The Philharmonic performs Downtown in the Gusman Center for the Performing Arts and at the Dade County Auditorium.

Over 60 years old, the **Florida Grand Opera** (✆ **800/741-1010;** www.fgo.org) regularly features singers from top houses in America and Europe. All productions are sung in their original language and staged with English supertitles. The opera's season runs roughly from November to April, with five performances each week. In 2007, the opera moved into more upscale headquarters in the Sanford and Dolores Ziff Ballet Opera House at the Arsht (formerly Carnival Center) Center for the Performing Arts.

LIVE MUSIC   **Tobacco Road,** 626 S. Miami Ave., over the Miami Avenue Bridge near Brickell Avenue (✆ **305/374-1198**), is an institution that's been around since 1912 (Al Capone hung out here when it was a speak-easy). These days, you'll find locals flocking here to see local bands (and a few national acts). It's small and gritty, and meant to be that way. Cover is usually $5 to $10.

Jazid, 1342 Washington Ave., South Beach (✆ **305/673-9372**), is smoky, sultry, and illuminated by flickering candelabras. Music consists of live jazz (sometimes on acid), soul, and funk. There's a $10 cover.

In Miami Beach, the elegant **Upstairs at the Van Dyke Cafe,** 846 Lincoln Rd. (✆ **305/534-3600**), has live jazz 7 nights a week until midnight. There's a $10 cover for a seat, no charge if you sit at the bar.

DANCE CLUBS   Clubs are as much a cottage industry in Miami as is, say, cheese in Wisconsin. Clubland is not just a nocturnal theme park, but a way of life for some. Ask your hotel's concierge to get you on a club's guest list; you'll still have to wait to get in, but you won't need to fork over a ridiculous $20 or more to walk past the ropes. This is a fickle scene, but at press time, some of the hottest spots included **Cameo,** in the space formerly occupied by crobar, 1445 Washington Ave., South Beach (© **305/531-8225; www.crobarmiami.com); Mansion,** 1235 Washington Ave., South Beach (© **305/531-5535); Club Space,** 34 NE 11th St., downtown (© **305/372-9378); Opium Garden,** 136 Collins Ave., South Beach (© **305/531-5535);** and **Bongo's Cuban Café,** 601 Biscayne Blvd., attached to the American Airlines Arena in downtown Miami (© **786/ 777-2100).**

Tip: The club scene generally doesn't get started in Miami before 11pm.

LATIN CLUBS **Casa Panza,** 1620 SW 8th St. (Calle Ocho), Miami (© **305/643-5343),** is one of Little Havana's most happening nightspots. Its Thursday night party, **Fuacata** (slang for "Pow!"), is a magnet for Latin hipsters, featuring classic Cuban music mixed in with modern DJ-spun sound effects.

Also check out **Mango's Tropical Café,** 900 Ocean Dr., South Beach (© **305/673-4422).** Mango's is *Cabaret,* Latin style. Nightly live Brazilian and other Latin music, not to mention scantily clad male and female dancers, draws huge gawking crowds in from the sidewalk. The hottest Latin joint in the city is **La Covacha,** 10730 NW 25th St., at NW 107th Avenue, West Miami (© **305/594-3717).** It's a hut in the middle of nowhere, but the shack is really jumping on weekend nights, when the place is open until 5am. Do not wear silk here, as you *will* sweat.

THE BAR SCENE On the beach, walk along Ocean Drive and Washington Avenue to see what's hot. Hold on to your bags—it's not dangerous, but shady types occasionally manage to slip in. *Also: Never put your drink down out of your sight*—there have been incidents in which drinks have been spiked with illegal chemical substances. For a less hard-core, more collegiate nightlife, head to Coconut Grove.

The **Clevelander,** 1020 Ocean Dr., South Beach (© **305/531-3485),** is an old standby that's always crowded. It attracts a lively, sporty, adults-only crowd who have no interest in being part of a scene but are interested in the very revealing scenery (wet-T-shirt contests). The **Rose Bar at the Delano,** 1685 Collins Ave., South Beach (© **305/ 672-2000),** is for amazing people-watching. The crowd here is full of glitterati, fabulatti, and other assorted poseurs who view life through (Italian-made) rose-colored glasses and down excruciatingly high-priced cocktails.

Standing on its own amid an oasis of trendiness, **Mac's Club Deuce,** 222 14th St., South Beach (© **305/673-9537),** is the quintessential dive bar, with cheap drinks and a cast of characters ranging from your typical barfly to your typical drag queen. It's got a well-stocked jukebox, friendly bartenders, a pool table, and, it's open daily from 8am to 5am. **Automatic Slim's,** 1216 Washington Ave., South Beach (© **305/695-0795),** is *the* bar where Ozzie and Harriet types become more like Ozzy and Sharon. Automatic Slim's packs people in thanks to an exhaustive list of cheap(er) drinks, lack of attitude, great rock music, and a decor that can only be described as white trash chic.

THE GAY & LESBIAN SCENE The gay scene in Miami is outrageous, especially on South Beach. Still, most of the gay clubs welcome hetero visitors, too. And many of the "straight" clubs also have gay nights. Miami Beach is one of the major stops for circuit parties, though ever since South Beach got bit by the hip-hop bug, many of Miami's gays have been crossing county lines into Fort Lauderdale, where there are, surprisingly, many more gay establishments.

There's a reason it's called **Score,** 727 Lincoln Rd., South Beach (© **305/535-1111**): It's a huge pickup scene with a multitude of bars, dance floors, loungelike areas, and outdoor tables. **Twist,** 1057 Washington Ave. (© **305/53-TWIST** [538-9478]) claims to be the longest-running gay club in South Beach, going strong for 15 years. **O-Zone,** 6620 SW 57th Ave. (Red Rd.), South Miami (© **305/667-2888**), is one of the most popular bars (and hideaways) on South Beach. It has a casual yet lively atmosphere.

5 EVERGLADES NATIONAL PARK

There's no better reality show than the one that exists in the Everglades. Up-close-and-personal views of alligators, crocodiles, and bona fide wildlife make for an interesting, photo-opportunistic experience that's worthy of a show on Animal Planet. Visitors shouldn't leave the area without taking time to see some of the wild plant and animal life in the swampy Everglades. Although they may seem overwhelmingly large, it's easy to get to the park's two main areas—the northern section, accessible via Shark Valley and Everglades City, or the southern section, accessible through the Ernest F. Coe Visitor Center, near Homestead and Florida City.

Shark Valley, a 15-mile paved loop road (with an observation tower) overlooking the heart of the Everglades, is the easiest and most scenic way to explore. Just 25 miles west of the Florida Turnpike, Shark Valley is best reached via the Tamiami Trail, the two-lane road that cuts across the park's northern border. Roadside attractions (boat rides and alligator farms) along the Tamiami Trail are operated by the Miccosukee Indian Village and are worth a stop. An excellent **tram tour** (leaving from the Shark Valley Visitor Center) goes deep into the park along a trail that's also terrific for biking. Shark Valley is about an hour's drive from Miami.

If you're in a rush to hit the 'glades, the southern route is your best bet. Just southeast of Homestead and Florida City, off State Road 9336, the southern access to the park will bring you to the **Ernest F. Coe Visitor Center.** In addition to details on tours and boat rentals, and free brochures outlining trails, wildlife, and activities, you will find educational displays, films, and exhibits. A gift shop sells postcards, film, an impressive selection of books, unusual gift items, and a supply of your most important gear: insect repellent. The shop is open daily from 8am to 5pm. From Miami to the southern entrance: Go west on I-395 to State Road 821 South (Florida Tpk.). The Turnpike will end in Florida City. Take your first right turn through the center of town (you can't miss it) and follow the signs to the park entrance on State Road 9336. The Ernest F. Coe Visitor Center is about $1^1/2$ hours from Miami.

The **Royal Palm Visitor Center,** a small nature museum located 3 miles past the park's main entrance, is a smaller information center. The museum is not great, but the center is the departure point for the popular Anhinga and Gumbo–Limbo trails (see below). Open daily from 8am to 4pm.

The **Flamingo Lodge, Marina, and Outpost Resort,** 1 Flamingo Lodge Hwy., Flamingo (© **800/600-3813** or 941/695-3101; www.flamingolodge.com), is the one-stop clearinghouse—and the only option—for in-park accommodations, equipment rentals, and tours. If you want to stay overnight, this is the number to call.

General inquiries and specific questions should be directed to **Everglades National Park Headquarters,** 40001 S.R. 9336, Homestead, FL 33034 (© **305/242-7700;** www. nps.gov/ever). Ask for a copy of *Parks and Preserves,* a free newspaper that's filled with

to 4:30pm. You can also try www.nps.gov.

Permits and passes can be purchased only at the main park or Shark Valley entrance station. Even if you are just visiting for an afternoon, you'll need to buy a 7-day permit, which costs $10 per vehicle. Pedestrians and cyclists pay $5 each. An **Everglades Park Pass,** valid for a year's worth of unlimited admissions, is available for $25.

There are two distinct seasons in the Everglades: high season and mosquito season. High season is also dry season and lasts from late November to May. This is the best time to visit because low water levels attract the largest variety of wading birds and their predators. As the dry season wanes, wildlife follows the receding water; by the end of May, the only living things you are sure to spot will make you itch. If you choose to visit during the buggy season, be vigilant in applying bug spray. Also, many establishments and operators either close or curtail offerings in summer.

SEEING THE HIGHLIGHTS

For a quick overview, consider a tram tour. Tours run December through April daily on the hour between 9am and 4pm, and May through November at 9:30am, 11am, 1pm, and 3pm. Reservations are recommended from December to March. The tour costs $15 for adults, $14 for seniors, and $8.75 for children 12 and under. For information, contact **Shark Valley Tram Tours** (© 305/221-8455; www.sharkvalleytramtours.com).

If you'd like to explore on foot, the **Anhinga and Gumbo–Limbo trails,** which start next to one another, 3 miles from the park's main entrance provide a thorough introduction to Everglades flora and fauna, and are recommended to first-time visitors. Alligators, turtles, river otters, herons, egrets, and other animals abound, making it one of the best trails for seeing wildlife. Take your time. If you treat the trails and modern boardwalk as pathways to get through quickly rather than destinations to experience, you'll miss out on the still beauty and hidden treasures that await.

Also, it's worth climbing the observation tower at the end of the quarter-mile-long **Pa-hay-okee Trail.** The panoramic view of undulating grass and seemingly endless vistas gives the impression of a semiaquatic Serengeti. Flocks of tropical and semitropical birds traverse the landscape, alligators and fish stir the surface of the water, and grottoes of trees thrust up from the sea of grass marking higher ground.

If you want to get closer to nature, a few hours in a **canoe** allows paddlers the chance to sense the park's fluid motion. You'll get a closer look into the park's shallow estuaries where water birds, sea turtles, and manatees make their homes. Everglades National Park's longest "trails" are designed for boat and canoe travel, and many are marked as clearly as walking trails. Park rangers can recommend trails that suit your abilities, time limitations, and interests. You can rent a canoe at **Everglades Adventures** (© 239/695-3299; www.evergladesadventures.com) for $50 for 24 hours, $35 per full day (any 8-hr. period), or $25 per half-day (1–5pm only). The concessionaire will shuttle your party to the trail head of your choice and pick you up afterward.

Shark Valley offers South Florida's most scenic **bicycle trail.** You can ride the 17-mile loop with no other traffic in sight. Instead, you'll share the flat paved road with other bikers and a menagerie of wildlife. Don't be surprised to see a 'gator lounging in the sun or a deer munching on some grass. Otters, turtles, alligators, and snakes are common companions in the Shark Valley area. You can rent bikes at the Flamingo Lodge, at Marina and Outpost Resort, or at **Shark Valley Tram Tours,** at the park's Shark Valley entrance (© 305/221-8455).

FLORIDA

5

EVERGLADES NATIONAL PARK

RANGER PROGRAMS   More than 50 ranger programs, free with entry, are offered each month during high season. Ranger-led walks and talks are offered year-round from Royal Palm Visitor Center and at the Flamingo and Gulf Coast visitor centers, as well as Shark Valley Visitor Center during winter months. Park rangers tend to be helpful, well informed, and good humored. Some programs occur regularly, such as Royal Palm Visitor Center's **Glade Glimpses,** a walking tour on which rangers point out flora and fauna, and discuss issues affecting the Everglades' survival. Tours are scheduled at 1:30pm daily. The **Anhinga Amble,** on the Anhinga Trail, starts at 10:30am daily. Times, programs, and locations can vary, so check the schedule, available at any of the visitor centers.

6 THE KEYS & KEY WEST

The islands of the Keys are strung out across the southern waters of Florida like cultured pearls, and each of the more than 400 islands in this 150-mile chain has a distinctive character. Some are crammed with strip malls and shell shops, but most are filled with unusual species of tropical plants, birds, and reptiles. All are surrounded by calm blue waters, populated by stunning sea life, and graced by year-round warmth. This vibrant underwater habitat thrives on one of only two living tropical reefs in the North American continent (the other is off the coast of Belize). As a result, anglers, divers, snorkelers, and watersports enthusiasts of all kinds come to explore. The heavy traffic has taken its toll on this fragile ecoscape, but efforts are underway to protect it.

THE UPPER & MIDDLE KEYS: KEY LARGO TO MARATHON

This is the fishing and diving capital of America, and the swarms of outfitters and billboards never let you forget it. From Miami International Airport, take Le Jeune Road (NW 42nd Ave.) to **Route 836 West.** Follow signs to the Florida Turnpike south (about 7 miles). The turnpike extension connects with **U.S. 1** in Florida City. Continue south on U.S. 1.

Make sure you get your information from an official not-for-profit center. The **Key Largo Chamber of Commerce,** U.S. 1 at MM 106, Key Largo, FL 33037 (© **800/822-1088** or 305/451-1414; fax 305/451-4726; www.keylargo.org), runs an excellent facility, with free direct-dial phones and plenty of brochures. Headquartered in a handsome clapboard house, the chamber operates as an information clearinghouse for all of the Keys and is open daily from 9am to 6pm.

Key Largo is the largest Key and is more developed than its neighbors to the south. Dozens of chain hotels, restaurants, and tourist information centers service the many water enthusiasts who come to explore the nation's first underwater state park, **John Pennekamp Coral Reef State Park,** on U.S. 1 at MM 102.5 (© **305/451-1202;** www.pennekamppark.com). It's a sanctuary for part of the only living coral reef in the continental United States. Because the water is extremely shallow, the 40 species of corals and more than 650 species of fish here are particularly accessible to divers, snorkelers, and glass-bottomed-boat passengers. Your first stop should be the visitor center, which is full of fish tanks and a 30,000-gallon saltwater aquarium that re-creates a reef ecosystem. At the adjacent dive shop, you can rent snorkeling and diving equipment and join one of the boat trips that depart for the reef throughout the day. Visitors can also rent motorboats, sailboats, windsurfers, and canoes. Glass-bottom boat tours cost $22 for adults and

$15 for children 11 and under. Snorkeling tours are $29 for adults and $24 for children 17 and under, including equipment. Park admission is $3.50 per vehicle for one occupant; for two or more, it's $6 per vehicle, plus 50¢ per passenger. Pedestrians and bicyclists pay $1.50 each.

The **Florida Keys Dive Center,** on U.S. 1 at MM 90.5, Tavernier (© **305/852-4599;** www.floridakeysdivectr.com), takes snorkelers and divers to the reefs of John Pennekamp Coral Reef State Park and environs every day. PADI (Professional Association of Diving Instructors) training courses are also available for the uninitiated. Tours leave at 8am and 12:30pm; the cost is $35 per person to snorkel (plus $10 rental fee for mask, snorkel, and fins) and $50 per person to dive (plus an extra $24 if you need to rent all the gear).

Islamorada, the unofficial capital of the Upper Keys, offers the area's best atmosphere, food, fishing, entertainment, and lodging. In these "purple isles," nature lovers can enjoy nature trails, historical explorations, and big-purse fishing tournaments. At **Robbie's Pier,** U.S. 1 at MM 77.5, Islamorada (© **305/664-9814;** www.robbies.com), the fierce steely tarpons have been gathering for the past 20 years. You may recognize these prehistoric-looking giants that grow up to 200 pounds; many are displayed as trophies and mounted on local restaurant walls. At Robbie's Pier, tens and sometimes hundreds of these behemoths circle the shallow waters waiting for you to feed them a bucket of fish (admission $1, bucket of fish $2). **Robbie's Partyboats & Charters,** on U.S. 1 at MM 84.5, Islamorada (© **305/664-8070** or 664-4196), at Robbie's Marina on Lower Matecumbe Key, offers day and night deep-sea and reef-fishing trips aboard a 65-foot party boat. Big-game fishing charters are also available, and "splits" are arranged for solo fishers. Phone for information and reservations. No trip is complete without a stop at the **Tiki Bar at the Holiday Isle Resort,** U.S. 1 at MM 84, Islamorada (© **800/327-7070** or 305/664-2321). It claims to have invented the rum runner, and we have no reason to doubt that. Hundreds of revelers visit this ocean-side spot for drinks and dancing any time, but the live music starts at 8:30pm.

Marathon, smack in the middle of the chain of islands, is one of the most populated Keys. It is part fishing village, part tourist center, and part nature preserve. This area's highly developed infrastructure includes resort hotels, a commercial airport, and a highway that expands to four lanes. The best beach in the area is **Sombrero Beach,** in Marathon at the end of Sombrero Beach Road (near MM 50). More than 90 feet of sand is dotted with palms, Australian pines, and royal poincianas, as well as with barbecue grills, clean bathrooms, and some Tiki huts for relaxing in the shade. Admission and parking at this little-known gem are free.

A stop at the **Seven-Mile Bridge,** between MM 40 and MM 47 on U.S. 1, is a relaxing break from the drive south. Built alongside the ruins of oil magnate Henry Flagler's Overseas Railroad, the "new" bridge (btw. MM 40 and MM 47) is still considered an architectural feat. The wide arched span, completed in 1982, is impressive, its apex being the highest point in the Keys. The new bridge and its now-defunct neighbor provide excellent vantage points to view the waters of the Keys.

Where to Stay

U.S. 1 is lined with chain hotels in all price ranges. In the Upper Keys, the best moderately priced option is the **Key Largo Ramada,** off U.S. 1 at MM 100, Key Largo (© **800/THE-KEYS** [843-5397] or 305/451-3939), which has three pools and a casino boat, and is 3 miles from John Pennekamp Coral Reef State Park. Another good Upper Keys option is **Days Inn Oceanfront Resort,** U.S. 1 at MM 82.5 (© **800/DAYS-INN** [329-7466] or 305/664-3681). In the Middle Keys, the **Wellesley Inn,** 13351 Overseas

Hwy., MM 54 in Marathon (© **305/743-8550**), offers reasonably priced ocean-side rooms.

If you want moderate prices but not a standard chain hotel, try **Conch Key Cottages,** near U.S. 1 at MM 62.3, Marathon (© **800/330-1577** or 305/289-1377; www.conch keycottages.com), or the **Kona Kai Resort & Gallery,** U.S. 1 at MM 97.8, Key Largo (© **800/365-7829** or 305/852-7200; www.konakairesort.com).

More luxurious choices include the recently renovated **Hawk's Cay Resort,** U.S. 1 at MM 61, Duck Key (© **888/814-9104** or 305/743-7000; www.hawkscay.com), which is on its own 60-acre island just outside Marathon; it's an impressive resort encompassing a marina and a saltwater lagoon that's home to a half-dozen dolphins. The **Moorings,** 123 Beach Rd. near MM 81.5 on the ocean side, Islamorada (© **305/664-4708;** www. themooringsvillage.com), offers romantic whitewashed houses and a sense that you've gotten away from it all, as you lounge on the 1,000-foot beach.

THE LOWER KEYS: BIG PINE KEY TO COPPITT KEY

The Lower Keys (farther south on U.S. 1, below the Seven-Mile Bridge) are less developed and more tranquil than the Upper Keys. They're not for haute cuisine and happening nightlife. But if you want to commune with nature or adventure in solitude, you've come to the right place.

Big Pine and Lower Keys Chamber of Commerce, ocean side of U.S. 1 at MM 31 (P.O. Box 430511), Big Pine Key, FL 33043 (© **800/872-3722** or 305/872-2411; fax 305/872-0752; www.lowerkeyschamber.com), is open Monday through Friday from 9am to 5pm, and Saturday from 9am to 3pm. The pleasant staff will help with anything a traveler may need. Call, write, or stop in for a comprehensive, detailed information packet.

Bahia Honda State Park, U.S. 1 at MM 37.5, Big Pine Key (© **305/872-2353;** www.bahiahondapark.com), has one of the most beautiful coastlines in South Florida. Bahia Honda (pronounced *Bah*-ya) is a great place for hiking, bird-watching, swimming, snorkeling, and fishing. The 524-acre park encompasses a wide variety of ecosystems, including coastal mangroves, beach dunes, and tropical hammocks. There are miles of trails packed with unusual plants and animals, and a small white beach. Shaded seaside picnic areas are fitted with tables and grills. Although the beach is never wider than 5 feet even at low tide, this is the Lower Keys' best beach area. The park has relatively deep waters close to shore that are perfect for snorkeling and diving, with beautiful vibrant fish and coral. Entry to the park is $5 per vehicle (plus 50¢ per person), $1.50 per pedestrian or bicyclist, free for children 5 and under. If you're alone in a car, you'll pay only $2.50. Open daily from 8am to sunset.

The most famous residents of the Lower Keys are the tiny Key deer. Of the estimated 300 left, two-thirds live on Big Pine Key's **National Key Deer Refuge.** Stop by the rangers' office at the Winn-Dixie Shopping Plaza, near MM 30.5 off U.S. 1. They'll give you an informative brochure and map. The refuge is open Monday through Friday from 8am to 5pm.

A stopping point for migratory birds on the Eastern Flyway, the Lower Keys are populated with many West Indian bird species, especially during spring and fall. The small vegetated islands of the Keys are the only nesting sites in the United States for the **great white heron** and the **white-crowned pigeon.** They're also some of the very few breeding places for the reddish egret, the roseate spoonbill, the mangrove cuckoo, and

ⓑest Under the Sea

Snorkelers and divers should not miss the Keys' most dramatic reefs at **Looe Key National Marine Sanctuary.** Here you'll see more than 150 varieties of hard and soft coral—some centuries old—as well as every type of tropical fish, including gold and blue parrotfish, moray eels, barracudas, French angels, and tarpon. **Looe Key Dive Center,** U.S. 1 at MM 27.5, Ramrod Key (ⓒ **305/872-2215;** www. diveflakeys.com), offers a 5-hour tour aboard a 45-foot catamaran with two shallow 1-hour dives for snorkelers and scuba divers. Snorkelers pay $40; divers pay $80. Equipment is available for rental for $10. On Wednesday and Saturday, you can do a fascinating dive to the *Adolphus Busch, Sr.,* a shipwreck off Looe Key in 100 feet of water, for $80.

the black-whiskered vireo. Look for them on Bahia Honda and the many uninhabited islands nearby.

The Overseas Highway (U.S. 1) touches on only a few dozen of the hundreds of islands of the Keys. To really see the Lower Keys, rent a kayak or canoe. **Reflections Kayak Nature Tours,** at Old Wooden Bridge Fishing Camp, 1791 Bogie Dr., mile marker 30, Big Pine Key (ⓒ **305/872-4668;** www.floridakeyskayaktours.com), offers backcountry wildlife tours, on your own or with an expert. The expert, U.S.C.G.-licensed Capt. Bill Keogh, wrote the book on the subject. His *The Florida Keys Paddling Guide* covers all the unique ecosystems and inhabitants, as well as launches and favorite routes from Key Biscayne to the Dry Tortugas National Park. The 3-hour kayak tours cost $50 per person. Reservations required.

Where to Stay

Exclusive **Little Palm Island Resort & Spa,** reached by launch at the ocean side of U.S. 1 at MM 28.5, Little Torch Key (ⓒ **800/343-8567** or 305/872-2524; www.littlepalm island.com), offers pricey and posh thatch-roof bungalows on a private 5-acre island. Many villas have ocean views and private sun decks with rope hammocks. On the other end of the price scale is **Parmer's Resort,** near MM 28.5, Little Torch Key (ⓒ **305/872-2157;** www.palmersresort.com), offering 45 modest but comfortable cottages. Some are waterfront, many have kitchenettes, and others are just a bedroom. Parmer's, a fixture here for more than 20 years, is well known for its charming hospitality and helpful staff.

KEY WEST

There are two schools of thought on Key West—one is that it has become way too commercial, and the other is that it's still a place where you can go and not worry about being prim, proper, or even well groomed. It's probably a bizarre fusion of both—a fascinating look at small-town America in which people truly live by the (off)beat of their own drum, albeit one with a Banana Republic and Starbucks. The locals, or "conchs" (pronounced *conks*), and the developers here have been at odds for years. This once low-key island has been thoroughly commercialized—there's a Hard Rock Cafe in the middle of Duval Street, and thousands of cruise-ship passengers descend on Mallory Square each day. It's definitely not the seedy town Hemingway and his cronies once called their own. Or is it?

The heart of town offers party people a good time. Here you'll find good restaurants, fun bars, live music, rickshaw rides, and lots of shopping. Don't bother with a watch or tie—this is the home of the perennial vacation.

Essentials

GETTING THERE   If you're driving, continue south on **U.S. 1.** When entering Key West, stay in the far-right lane onto North Roosevelt Boulevard, which becomes Truman Avenue in Old Town. Continue for a few blocks, and you will find yourself on Duval Street, in the heart of the city.

Several regional airlines fly nonstop (about 55 min.) from Miami; fares are about $120 to $300 round-trip. Planes land at **Key West International Airport,** South Roosevelt Boulevard (© 305/296-5439), on the southeastern corner of the island.

VISITOR INFORMATION   The **Key West Chamber of Commerce,** 402 Wall St., Key West, FL 33040 (© **800/527-8539** or 305/294-2587; www.keywestchamber.com), provides general and specialized information. The lobby is open daily from 8:30am to 6pm; phones are answered from 8am to 8pm. The **Key West Visitor Center** (© **800/ LAST-KEY** [527-8539]) is the area's best for info on accommodations, goings-on, and restaurants; it's open Monday through Friday from 8am to 5:30pm, Saturday and Sunday 8:30am to 5pm. Gay travelers can call the **Key West Business Guild** (© **305/294-4603**), which represents over 50 guesthouses and B&Bs, as well as many gay-owned businesses (ask for their brochure).

GETTING AROUND   With limited parking, narrow streets, and congested traffic, driving in Old Town Key West is more of a pain than a convenience. Unless you're staying in one of the more remote accommodations, consider trading in the car for a bicycle. Rates for simple one-speed cruisers start at about $10 per day. The best shops include the **Bicycle Center,** 523 Truman Ave. (© **305/294-4556**), and **Tropical Bicycles & Scooter Rentals,** 1300 Duval St. (© **305/294-8136**).

What to See & Do

The city's whole story is packed into a neat 90-minute package on the **Conch Tour Train** (© 305/294-5161; www.conchtourtrain.com), which covers the island and all its rich, raunchy history. Tours depart from both Mallory Square and the Welcome Center, near where U.S. 1 becomes North Roosevelt Boulevard, on the other side of the island. The cost is $25 for adults, $12 for children 4 to 12, and free for children 3 and under. Daily departures are every half-hour from 9am to 4:30pm.

The **Old Town Trolley** (© 305/296-6688) is the choice in bad weather or if you are staying at one of the many hotels on its route. Humorous drivers maintain a running commentary as the enclosed tram loops around the island's streets past all the major sights. Trolleys depart from Mallory Square and other points around the island, including many area hotels. Tours are $27 for adults, $13 for children 4 to 12. Tickets are cheaper on the website. Departures are daily every half-hour (though not always on the half-hour) from 9am to 4:30pm.

Dating from the early 19th century, the **Audubon House & Tropical Gardens,** 205 Whitehead St., between Greene and Caroline streets (© 305/294-2116; www.audubon-house.com), is a prime example of early Key West architecture. Named after the renowned painter and bird expert John James Audubon, who was said to have visited the house in 1832, the graceful two-story home is a peaceful retreat from the bustle of Old Town. See rare Audubon prints, gorgeous antiques, historical photos, and lush tropical

> ## (Best) Going, Going, Gone . . . Sunset in Key West
>
> A daily tradition in Key West, the Sunset Celebration is the best example of local flavor and the Jimmy Buffett–inspired attitude that prevails throughout the Keys. Every evening, locals and visitors alike gather at the docks behind Mallory Square (at the western end of Whitehead St.) to celebrate the day gone by. Secure a spot on the docks about an hour before sundown for the full effect, complete with portrait artists, acrobats, food vendors, and animal acts.
>
> If crowds aren't your thing, grab a seat at the Westin's **Sunset Deck,** at the intersection of Front and Greene streets (© **305/294-4000**). From the calm of the bar, you can relax with a drink and look down on the mayhem. For the best cocktails and great bar food on an outside patio or enclosed lounge, try **Pier House Resort and Caribbean Spa's Havana Docks,** at 1 Duval St. (© **305/296-4600**). There's usually live music and a lively gathering. The bar is right on the water and is a prime sunset-viewing spot.

gardens. Admission is $11 adults, $5 children 6 to 12, $6.50 children 13 to 17. Daily 9:30am to 5pm (last entry at 4:30pm).

Hemingway's particularly handsome stone Spanish colonial house, now preserved as the **Ernest Hemingway Home and Museum,** 907 Whitehead St., between Truman Avenue and Olivia Street (© **305/294-1136;** www.hemingwayhome.com), was built in 1851. The author lived here from 1928 until 1940, along with about 50 cats, whose descendants still roam the premises. It was during those years that the Nobel Prize winner wrote *For Whom the Bell Tolls, A Farewell to Arms,* and *The Snows of Kilimanjaro.* Guided tours are given every 15 minutes and are included in the price of admission, which is $11 for adults, $6 for children. It's open daily from 9am to 5pm.

Funky, picturesque **Key West Cemetery,** entrance at Margaret and Angela streets, captures the quintessential Key West attitude. Many tombs are stacked several high, condominium style—the rocky soil made digging 6 feet under nearly impossible for early settlers. I TOLD YOU I WAS SICK is one of the more famous epitaphs, as is the tongue-in-cheek widow's inscription AT LEAST I KNOW WHERE HE'S SLEEPING TONIGHT. Admission is free and it's open dawn to dusk.

The **Mel Fisher Maritime Heritage Museum,** 200 Greene St. (© **305/294-2633;** www.melfisher.org), honors local hero Mel Fisher, whose death in 1998 was mourned throughout South Florida and who found a multimillion-dollar treasure-trove in 1985 aboard the wreck of the Spanish galleon *Nuestra Señora de Atocha.* The admission price is somewhat steep, but if you're into diving, pirates, and the mystery of sunken treasures, check out this small informative museum, full of doubloons, pieces of eight, emeralds, and solid-gold bars. Admission is $11 for adults, $6 for children ages 6 to 12. Open daily from 9:30am to 5pm.

Unlike the rest of the Keys, Key West has a few small beaches, although they don't compare to the state's wide natural wonders up the coast. Here are your options: **Smathers Beach,** off South Roosevelt Boulevard west of the airport; **Higgs Beach,** along Atlantic Boulevard between White Street and Reynolds Road; and **Fort Zachary Beach,** off the western end of Southard Boulevard. Although there is an entrance fee ($3 per car, plus more for each passenger), we recommend Fort Zachary, since it includes a great

FLORIDA

5

THE KEYS & KEY WEST

historical fort, a Civil War museum, shade trees, and a large picnic area with tables, barbecue grills, restrooms, and showers.

One of the area's largest scuba schools, **Dive Key West, Inc.,** 3128 N. Roosevelt Blvd. (© **800/426-0707** or 305/296-3823; www.divekeywest.com), offers instruction at all levels; its dive boats take participants to scuba and snorkel sites on nearby reefs. Wreck dives and night dives are two of the special offerings of **Lost Reef Adventures,** 261 Margaret St. (© **800/952-2749** or 305/296-9737).

Key West Marine Park (© **305/294-3100**), the newest dive park along the island's Atlantic shore, incorporates no-motor "swim-only" lanes marked by buoys, providing swimmers and snorkelers with a safe way to explore the waters around Key West. The park's boundaries stretch from the foot of Duval Street to Higgs Beach.

As any angler will tell you, there's no fishing like Keys fishing. Key West has it all: bonefish, tarpon, dolphin, tuna, grouper, cobia, and more. You'll find plenty of competition among the charter fishing boats in and around Mallory Square. However, you should know the bookers from the kiosks in town generally take 20% of a captain's fee in addition to an extra monthly fee. So you can save yourself money by booking directly with a captain or going straight to one of the docks. You can negotiate a good deal at **Charter Boat Row,** 1801 N. Roosevelt Ave. (across from the Shell station), home to more than 30 charter-fishing and party boats. Just show up to arrange your outing, or call **Garrison Bight Marina** (© **305/292-8167**) for details.

Serious anglers should consider the light-tackle boats that leave from **Oceanside Marina,** on Stock Island at 5950 Peninsula Ave., 1¹/₂ miles off U.S. 1 (© **305/294-4676**). It's a 20-minute drive from Old Town on the Atlantic side. There are more than 30 light-tackle guides, which range from flatbed, backcountry skiffs to 28-foot open boats. There are also a few larger charters and a party boat that goes to the Dry Tortugas. Call for details. For a light-tackle outing with a colorful Key West flair, call **Capt. Bruce Cronin** (© **305/294-4929;** www.fishbruce.com) or **Capt. Kenny Harris** (© **305/294-8843**), two of the more famous (and pricey) captains working these docks for more than 20 years. You'll pay from $750 for a full day, usually about 8am to 4pm, and from $500 for a half-day.

Once the main industry of Key West, cigar making is enjoying renewed success at the handful of factories that survived the slow years. Stroll through **"Cigar Alley,"** between Front and Greene streets, where you will find *viejitos* (little old men) rolling fat stogies as they used to in their homeland across the Florida Straits. Stop at the **Conch Republic Cigar Factory,** at 512 Greene St. (© **305/295-9036**), for a selection of imported and locally rolled smokes, including the famous El Hemingway.

Where to Stay

Once a private residence, the **Gardens Hotel,** 526 Angela St. (© **800/526-2664** or 305/294-2661; www.gardenshotel.com), offers the best lodging in town and is hidden amid the exotic Peggy Mills tropical botanical gardens. It's a luxurious and romantic Bahamian-style hideaway featuring 17 luxuriously appointed accommodations in several buildings (the main one is a National Historic Landmark). The rooms are resplendent, with Aveda products, Jacuzzi bathtubs, hardwood floors, brass and iron beds, marble bathrooms, and a sense of serenity that words can't describe. Winter rates are $300 to $415 double, $495 to $620 suite, including continental breakfast.

The **Westin Key West Resort and Marina,** 245 Front St., at the end of Duval Street (© **800/221-2424** or 305/294-4000; www.keywestresort.hilton.com), is a prime spot from which to enjoy sunsets, as well as that hard-to-find, quietly elegant ambience that's so lacking in most big resorts here. The sparkling rooms are large and well appointed. Winter rates are $389 to $550 double, $469 to $1,149 suite. Another upscale resort is the **Pier House Resort and Caribbean Spa,** 1 Duval St., near Mallory Docks (© **800/ 327-8340** or 305/296-4600; www.pierhouse.com), an oasis of calm offering luxurious rooms, top-notch service, and a full-service spa. Its excellent location—at the foot of Duval Street and just steps from Mallory Docks—is the envy of every hotel on the island. Winter rates are $309 to $529 double, $479 to $3,000 suite.

One of our favorites, the **Marquesa Hotel,** 600 Fleming St., at Simonton Street (© **800/869-4631** or 305/292-1919; www.marquesa.com), offers all the charm of a small historic hotel with the amenities of a large resort. It encompasses four different buildings, two adjacent swimming pools, and a three-stage waterfall that cascades into a lily pond. Rooms have stunning plush decor. Winter rates are $250 to $340 double, $400 to $450 suite. The **Grand,** 1116 Grinnell St., between Virginia and Catherine streets (© **888/947-2630** or 305/294-0590; www.thegrandguesthouse.com), is an exceptionally run guesthouse with almost anything you could want, including a moderate price tag. It's the best bargain in town. Winter $158 to $268 double, including an "expanded" continental breakfast and free parking.

If you're having trouble finding a room, contact **Vacation Key West** (© **800/595-5397** or 305/295-9500; www.vacationkw.com), a wholesaler that offers discounts of 20% to 30% and is skilled at finding last-minute deals. It represents mostly larger properties but can also place visitors in guesthouses. The phones are answered Monday through Friday from 9am to 6pm, and Saturday from 11am to 2pm. **Key West Innkeepers Association** (© **800/492-1911** or 305/292-3600) can also help you find lodging in any price range from among its members and affiliates.

Gay travelers may want to call the **Key West Business Guild** (© **305/294-4603**), which represents more than 50 guesthouses and B&Bs in town, as well as many other gay-owned businesses. Most gay guesthouses have a clothing-optional policy. One of the most elegant and popular is **Big Ruby's,** 409 Applerouth Lane (© **800/477-7829** or 305/296-2323; www.bigrubys.com), on a little alley just off Duval Street. Rates start at $171 double in peak season and $119 off season. A low cluster of buildings surrounds a lush courtyard where a hearty breakfast is served each morning and wine is poured at dusk. The all-male guests hang out by the pool, tanning in the buff.

For women only, **Pearl's Rainbow,** 525 United St. (© **800/74-WOMYN** [749-6636] or 305/292-1450; www.pearlsrainbow.com), is a large, fairly well-maintained guesthouse with lots of privacy and amenities, including two pools and two hot tubs. Rates range from $99 to $379.

Key West After Dark

Duval Street is the Bourbon Street of Florida. Amid the T-shirt shops and clothing boutiques, you'll find bar after bar serving neon-colored frozen drinks to revelers who bounce from one to the next from noon until dawn. Your best bet is to start at Truman Avenue and head up Duval to check them out for yourself. Cover charges are rare except in gay clubs, so stop into a dozen and see which you like.

Just around the corner from Duval's beaten path, **Captain Tony's Saloon,** 428 Greene St. (© **305/294-1838**), is a smoky old wooden bar, about as authentic as you'll find. **Durty Harry's,** 208 Duval St. (© **305/296-4890**), is a large entertainment complex that features live rock bands almost every night. You can wander to one of the many outdoor bars or head to **Upstairs at Rick's,** an indoor/outdoor dance club that gets going late.

For the more racy singles or couples, there is also the **Red Garter,** a pocket-size strip club.

You'll have to stop into **Sloppy Joe's,** 201 Duval St. (© **305/294-5717;** www.sloppy joes.com), just to say you did. Scholars and drunks debate whether this is the same Sloppy Joe's that Hemingway wrote about, but there's no argument that this classic bar's turn-of-the-20th-century wooden ceiling and cracked tile floors are Key West originals. There's live music most days and nights.

The best music and dancing can be found at the predominantly gay clubs. None of the spots mentioned here discriminate—anyone open-minded and fun is welcome. Cover varies but is rarely more than $10. Two adjacent popular late-night spots are the **801 Bourbon Bar/Number One Saloon,** 801 Duval St. and 514 Petronia St. (© **305/294-9349** for both), featuring great drag and lots more disco. A mostly male clientele frequents this hot spot from 9pm until 4am. Another Duval Street favorite is **Aqua,** at 711 Duval St. (© **305/292-8500**), where you might catch drag queens belting out torch songs or judges voting on the best package in the wet jockey shorts contest. Better known around town as La-Te-Da, **La Terraza de Martí,** the former Key West home of Cuban exile José Martí, at 1125 Duval St. (© **305/296-6706**), is a great spot to gather poolside for the best martini in town—don't bother with the food.

7 TAMPA & ST. PETERSBURG

Sitting on a large estuary midway down Florida's west coast, the city of Tampa is known as the home of Busch Gardens Africa, but there's much more to it. You can also see the sea life at the Florida Aquarium; stroll through the ornate, Moorish-style Henry B. Plant Museum; and experience exciting dining and nightlife in Ybor City, Tampa's historic Cuban enclave. Across the bay, St. Petersburg has one of the most picturesque and pleasant downtowns of any city in Florida, with a waterfront promenade, a famous pyramid-shaped pier, quality museums, interesting shops, and good restaurants. You'll find plenty of sun and sand on the 28 miles of slim barrier islands that skirt the gulf shore here. St. Pete Beach and Clearwater Beach are typical beach resort towns, with towering hotels and condos, but this area also has protected some of the nation's finest beaches from development. From here, you can take a side trip south across the bay to affluent Sarasota, one of Florida's cultural centers.

Tampa, St. Petersburg, and the beaches are about 30- to 45-minute drives apart (longer in rush-hour traffic), so unless you're on business and need quick access to Tampa or downtown St. Pete, you may want to stay at the beaches.

ESSENTIALS

GETTING THERE   By Plane   Tampa International Airport (© **813/870-8770;** www.tampaairport.com), 5 miles northwest of downtown, is serviced by most major airlines. **St. Petersburg–Clearwater International Airport** (© **727/453-7800;** www.fly2pie.com), on the western side of the bay, offers limited service. The **Limo/Super-Shuttle** (© **800/282-6817** or 727/527-1111; www.supershuttle.com) operates van service between the airport and hotels throughout the area. Fares for one person range from $36 to $50 round-trip, depending on your destination. In a **taxi,** the ride to downtown Tampa takes about 15 minutes and costs $20 to $22.

By Train Amtrak trains arrive downtown at the **Tampa Amtrak Station,** 601 Nebraska Ave. N. (© **800/USA-RAIL** [872-7245]; www.amtrak.com).

By Car Major routes into Tampa are **I-75** from the north (Atlanta) and south (Fort Myers and Miami), and **I-4** from the east (Orlando).

VISITOR INFORMATION Contact the **Tampa Bay Convention & Visitors Bureau,** 400 N. Tampa St., Tampa, FL 33602-4706 (© **800/448-2672,** 800/368-2672, or 813/223-2752; www.visittampabay.com), for information. Downtown, there's a **visitor information center** at 400 N. Tampa St. (Channelside), Ste. 2800 (© **813/223-1111**), open Monday through Saturday from 9:30am to 5:30pm.

For advance information about St. Petersburg and the beaches, contact the **St. Petersburg/Clearwater Area Convention & Visitors Bureau,** 14450 46th St. N., Clearwater, FL 34622 (© **800/345-6710,** or 727/464-7200 for hotel reservations; www.floridasbeach.com for information specific to the beaches). After you arrive, the **St. Petersburg Area Chamber of Commerce,** 100 2nd Ave. N. (at 1st St.), St. Petersburg (© **727/821-4069;** fax 727/895-6326; www.stpete.com), has a visitor center that is open Monday through Friday from 8am to 5pm, Saturday from 10am to 4pm, and Sunday from noon to 4pm.

Also downtown, you'll find walk-in **information centers** on the first level of the Pier and in the lobby of the Florida International Museum. The chamber also operates the **Suncoast Welcome Center** (© **727/573-1449**), on Ulmerton Road at exit 31B southbound off I-275 (there's no exit here for northbound traffic). The center is open daily from 9am to 5pm except New Year's Day, Easter, Thanksgiving, and Christmas.

GETTING AROUND You really need a car here. All major rental agencies have desks at the Tampa airport.

FAST FACTS **Tampa General Hospital,** 2 Columbia Dr. (© **813/251-7000;** www.tgh.org), offers 24-hour emergency service.

SPECIAL EVENTS & FESTIVALS In early February, hundreds of boats and rowdy "pirates" invade downtown Tampa during the **Gasparilla Pirate Fest** (© **813/353-8108;** www.gasparillapiratefest.com). In mid-February, the **Florida State Fair** in Tampa displays the best of the state's agriculture and crafts (© **800/345-FAIR** [345-3247]; www.floridastatefair.com). Held on the last Saturday in October, Ybor City's Latin-style Halloween celebration **Guavaween** begins with the "Mama Guava Stumble," a wacky costume parade (© **813/248-0721;** www.ybor.org).

WHAT TO SEE & DO

Busch Gardens Africa (Best) (Kids) Although its heart-stopping thrill rides get much of the ink, this venerable theme park (it predates Disney World) ranks among the largest zoos in the country. It's a don't-miss attraction for children and adults, who can see, in person, all those wild beasts they've watched on *Animal Planet*—and they'll get better views of them here than at Disney's Animal Kingdom in Orlando (p. 344). Busch Gardens has several thousand animals living in naturalistic environments that help carry out the park's overall African theme. Most authentic is the 80-acre plain, strongly reminiscent of the real Serengeti of Tanzania and Kenya, upon which zebras, giraffes, and other animals graze. Unlike the animals on the real Serengeti, however, the grazing animals have nothing to fear from lions, hyenas, crocodiles, and other predators, which are confined to enclosures—as are hippos and elephants. The park's sixth roller coaster, SheiKra, is the

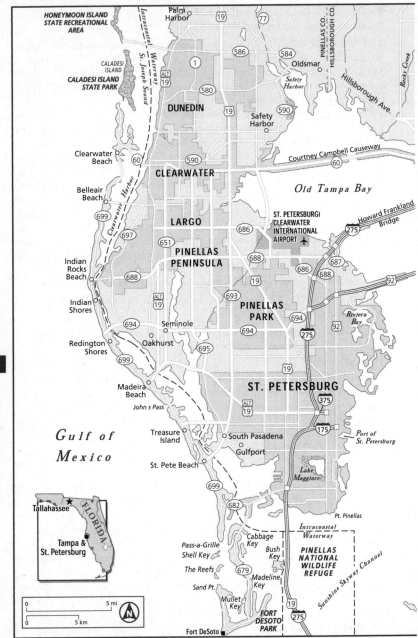

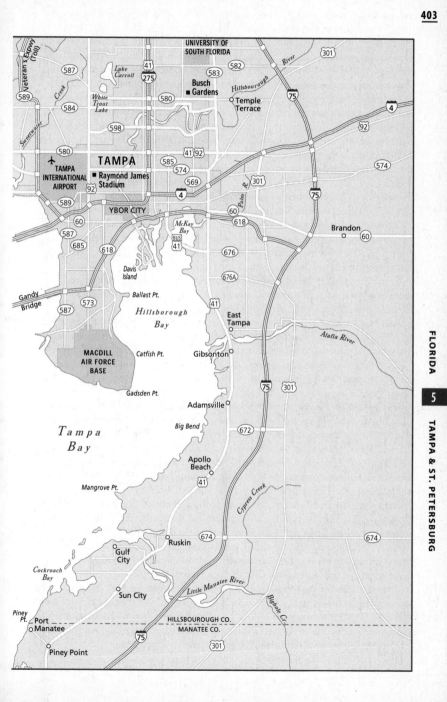

nation's first dive coaster that carries riders up 200 feet at 45 degrees and then hurtles them 70 mph back at a 45-degree angle. Yikes.

The park has eight areas, each with its own theme, animals, live entertainment, thrill rides, kiddie attractions, dining, and shopping. A Skyride cable car soars over the park, offering a bird's-eye view. Turn left after the main gate and head to **Morocco,** a walled city with exotic architecture, crafts demonstrations, a sultan's tent with snake charmers, and an exhibit featuring alligators and turtles. The Moorish-style Moroccan Palace Theater features an ice show that many consider to be the park's best entertainment for both adults and children. You can also attend a song-and-dance show in the Marrakech Theater. Overlooking it all is the Crown Colony Restaurant, the park's largest.

Walk east past Anheuser-Busch's fabled Clydesdale horses to **Egypt,** where you can visit King Tut's tomb with its replicas of the real treasures and listen to comedian Martin Short narrate "Akbar's Adventure Tours," a wacky simulator that "transports" one and all across Egypt via camel, biplane, and mine car. The whole room moves on this ride, which lasts only 5 minutes—much less time than the usual wait to get inside. Youngsters can dig for their own ancient treasures in a sand area. Adults and kids 54 inches or taller can ride Montu, the tallest and longest inverted roller coaster in the world, with seven upside-down loops. Your feet dangle loose on Montu, so make sure your shoes are tied tightly and your lunch has had time to digest.

From Egypt, walk to the **Edge of Africa,** the most unique of the park's eight areas, and home to most of the large animals. Go immediately to the Expedition Africa Gift Shop and see if you can get on one of the park's zoologist-led wildlife tours.

Next stop is **Nairobi,** the most beautiful part of the park, where you can see gorillas and chimpanzees in their lush rainforest habitat in the Myombe Reserve. Nairobi also has a baby-animal nursery, a petting zoo, turtle and reptile displays, an elephant exhibit, and Curiosity Caverns, where bats, reptiles, and small mammals that are active in the dark are kept in cages (it's the most traditional zoolike area here). The entry to Rhino Rally, the park's safari adventure, is at the western end of Nairobi.

Now head to the **Congo,** where the highlights are the white Bengal tigers that live on Claw Island. The Congo is also home to two roller coasters: Kumba, the largest and fastest coaster in the southeastern United States (54-in. minimum height for riders), and the Python (48-in. minimum), which twists and turns for 1,200 feet. You will get drenched—and refreshed on a hot day—by riding the Congo River Rapids, where you're turned loose in round boats that float down the swiftly flowing "river" (42-in. minimum). Bumper cars and kiddie rides can be found here, too.

From the Congo, walk south into **Stanleyville,** a prototype African village, with a shopping bazaar, orangutans living on an island, and the Stanleyville Theater, featuring shows for children. Two more water rides here are the Tanganyika Tidal Wave (48-in. minimum height for riders), where you'll come to a very damp end, and the Stanley Falls Flume (an aquatic version of a roller coaster). Also, the picnic-style Stanleyville Smokehouse serves ribs and chicken—some of the best chow in the park.

Up next is **Land of the Dragons,** the most entertaining area for small children. They can spend the day enjoying a variety of entertainment in a fairy-tale setting, plus just-for-kids rides. The area is dominated by Dumphrey, a whimsical dragon who interacts with visitors and guides children around a three-story treehouse with winding stairways, tall towers, steppingstones, illuminated water geysers, and an echo chamber.

The next stop is **Bird Gardens,** the park's original core, offering rich foliage, lagoons, and a free-flight aviary for hundreds of exotic birds, including golden and American bald eagles. Be sure to see the Florida flamingos and Australian koalas while you're here.

Then you're off to take a break at the **Hospitality House,** which offers piano entertainment and free samples of Anheuser-Busch's famous beers. You must be 21 to imbibe (there's a limit of two free mugs per seating); soft drinks are also available.

If your stomach can take another hair-raising ride, try **Gwazi** (48-in. minimum for riders), an adrenaline-pumping attraction in which a pair of old-fashioned wooden roller coasters (named the Lion and the Tiger) start simultaneously and whiz within a few feet of each other six times as they roar along at 50 mph and rise to 90 feet. If you want to experience the park's fifth roller coaster, head to **Timbuktu** and climb aboard the **Scorpion,** a high-speed number with a 60-foot drop and 360-degree loop (42-in. height minimum). Or if you're really crazy, check out the floorless **Sheikra,** where for 200 feet up and 90 degrees straight down, you can view the world—from a floorless perspective. For visual amusement, there's *Pirates 4-D,* an animated 4-D special-effects movie and theater production starring actor Leslie Nielsen. Set to open in 2008 is **Jungala,** a 4-acre attraction in the Congo area, featuring exotic creatures, animal interactions, multistory family play areas, rides, and live entertainment.

Added attractions are a $350, 6-hour zookeeper-for-a-day program and a 4-D multisensory R. L. Stine film. You can exchange foreign currency in the park, and interpreters are available. *Note:* You can get to Busch Gardens from Orlando via shuttle buses, which pick up at area hotels between 8 and 10:15am for the 1½- to 2-hour ride, with return trips starting at 5pm and continuing until the park closes. Round-trip fares are $10 per person. Call C 800/511-2450 for schedules, pickup locations, and reservations.

3000 E. Busch Blvd. (at McKinley Dr./N. 40th St.). C 888/800-5447 or 813/987-5283. www.buschgardens. com. **Note:** Admission and hours vary, with combination tickets and discounts offered for online purchase, so call ahead, check website, or get brochure at visitor centers. At press time, a Busch Gardens–only admission for a 1 day was $68 adults, $58 children ($10 less when purchased online). Adventure Islands 1-day ticket was $38 adults, $35 children. Daily 10am–6pm (to 7 and 8pm in summer and on holidays). Parking $9 for cars, $10 for trucks and campers. Take I-275 north of downtown to Busch Blvd. (exit 50) and go east 2 miles. From I-75, take Fowler Ave. (exit 54) and follow the signs west.

Florida Aquarium (Kids)   See the more than 5,000 aquatic animals and plants that call Florida home at this entertaining attraction. The exhibits follow a drop of water from the springs of the Florida Wetlands Gallery, through a mangrove forest in the Bays and Beaches Gallery, and out onto the Coral Reefs, where an impressive 43-foot-wide, 14-foot-tall panoramic window lets you look out at schools of fish and lots of sharks and stingrays. You can look for birds and sea life on 90-minute Eco Tour cruises in the *Bay Spirit,* a 64-foot catamaran. The aquarium also offers a **Dive with the Sharks** program (C 813/367-4005) that gives certified divers the chance to swim with blacktip, sand tiger, and nurse sharks for 30 minutes. The $150 price tag includes a souvenir photo and T-shirt.

701 Channelside Dr. C 813/273-4000. www.flaquarium.org. Admission $18 adults, $15 seniors, $12 children 3–11, free for children 2 and under. Eco Tour $20 adults, $19 seniors, $15 children 3–11, free for children 2 and under. Combination aquarium admission and Eco Tour $33 adults, $30 seniors, $23 children 3–11, free for children 2 and under. Website sometimes offers discounts. Parking $5. Daily 9:30am–5pm. Dolphin Quest Mon–Fri 2pm; Sat–Sun 1 and 3pm. Eco Tour Sun–Fri 2 and 4pm; Sat noon, 2, and 4pm. Closed Thanksgiving and Christmas.

Plant Museum Built in 1891 by railroad tycoon Henry B. Plant as the Bay Hotel, this ornate building is worth a short trip from downtown. Its 13 silver minarets and Moorish architecture, modeled after the Alhambra in Spain, make this National Historic Landmark a focal point of the Tampa skyline. Although the building is the highlight of a visit, don't skip its contents: art and furnishings from Europe and Asia, plus exhibits that explain the history of the original railroad resort and Florida's early tourist industry.

401 W. Kennedy Blvd. (btw. Hyde Park and Magnolia aves.). © 813/254-1891. www.plantmuseum.com. Free admission; suggested donation $5 adults, $2 children 12 and under. Tues–Sat 10am–4pm; Sun noon–4pm. Closed Thanksgiving, Christmas Eve, and Christmas. Take Kennedy Blvd. (Fla. 60) across the Hillsborough River.

MOSI (Museum of Science and Industry) (Kids) MOSI is the largest science center in the Southeast, with more than 450 interactive exhibits. Step into the Gulf Hurricane to experience 74 mph winds, explore the human body in "The Amazing You," and, if your heart is up to it, ride a bicycle across a 98-foot-long cable suspended 30 feet above the lobby. You can also watch movies in the IMAX dome theater. Outside, trails wind through a nature preserve with a butterfly garden. The museum is one of very few in the world to feature the articulated remains of a Sauropod dinosaur.

4801 E. Fowler Ave. (at N. 50th St.). © 813/987-6100. www.mosi.org. Admission $21 adults, $20 seniors, $17 children 2–12, free for children 1 and under. Admission includes IMAX movies. Daily 9am–5pm or later. From downtown, take I-275 N. to the Fowler Ave. E. exit (no. 51). Take this 2 miles east to museum on right.

Museum of Fine Arts Resembling a Mediterranean villa on the waterfront, this museum houses an excellent collection of European, American, pre-Columbian, and Far Eastern art, with works by such artists as Fragonard, Monet, Renoir, Cézanne, and Gauguin. Other highlights include period rooms with antique furnishings, plus a gallery of Steuben crystal, a new decorative-arts gallery, and world-class rotating exhibits. The best way to see it all is on a guided tour, which takes about 1 hour. Ask about classical-music performances from October to April.

255 Beach Dr. NE (at 3rd Ave. N.). © 727/896-2667. www.fine-arts.org. Admission $8 adults, $7 seniors 65 and over, $4 students with ID, free for children 5 and under (special exhibits cost extra). Admission includes guided tour. Tues–Sat 10am–5pm; Sun 1–5pm. Guided tours Tues–Sat 11am and 1, 2, and 3pm; Sun 1 and 2pm. Closed New Year's Day, Martin Luther King Day, Thanksgiving, and Christmas.

The Pier (Kids) The Pier is a festive waterfront dining-and-shopping complex overlooking Tampa Bay. Originally built as a railroad pier in 1889, today it's capped by a spaceshiplike inverted pyramid offering five levels of shops, three restaurants, a tourist information desk, an observation deck, catwalks for fishing, boat docks, miniature golf, boat and watersports rentals, sightseeing boats, a food court, plus an aquarium. Cruise boats often operate from the Pier during the winter months, and you can rent fishing gear and drop your line into the bay year-round. There's valet parking at the end of the Pier, or you can park on land and ride a free trolley out to the complex.

800 2nd Ave. NE. © 727/821-6443. www.stpete-pier.com. Free admission to all public areas and decks; donations welcome at the Pier Aquarium. Valet parking $4; self-parking $3. Pier Mon–Thurs 10am–9pm; Fri–Sat 10am–10pm; Sun 11am–7pm. Aquarium Mon–Sat 10am–8pm; Sun 11am–6pm.

Salvador Dalí Museum This starkly modern museum houses the world's most comprehensive collection of works by the Spanish surrealist—and, for art lovers, is reason enough to visit downtown St. Petersburg. Housing six of the artist's masterworks, the museum was given three stars by the Michelin Guide—the highest-ranked museum in the South. It includes oil paintings, watercolors, drawings, and more than 1,000 graphics, plus posters, photos, sculptures, objets d'art, and a 5,000-volume library on Dalí and surrealism. Take one of the free docent-led tours.

1000 3rd St. S. (near 11th Ave. S.). © 727/823-3767. www.salvadordalimuseum.org. Admission $15 adults, $14 seniors, $10 students, $4 children 5–9, free for children 4 and under; $5 for all Thurs 5–8pm. Mon–Wed and Fri–Sat 9:30am–5:30pm; Thurs 9:30am–8pm; Sun noon–5:30pm. Closed Thanksgiving and Christmas.

FUN ON & OFF THE BEACH

This entire stretch of coast is one long beach, but since hotels, condos, and private homes line much of it, you may want to sun and swim at one of the area's public parks. On a 3¹/₂-mile-long island north of Clearwater Beach, **Caladesi Island State Park** boasts one of Florida's top beaches—a lovely, relatively secluded stretch with fine, soft sand edged in sea grass and palmettos. In the park itself is a nature trail where you might see rattlesnakes, raccoons, armadillos, or rabbits. A concession stand, a ranger station, and bathhouses are available. Caladesi Island is accessible only by ferry from **Honeymoon Island State Recreation Area,** which is connected by Causeway Boulevard (Fla. 586) to Dunedin, north of Clearwater. You'll first have to pay the admission to Honeymoon Island: $5 per vehicle with two to eight occupants, $2 per single-occupant vehicle, $1 for a pedestrian or bicyclist. Beginning daily at 10am, the ferry (© 727/734-5263) departs Honeymoon Island every hour. Round-trip rides cost $9 for adults, $5.50 for kids ages 4 to 12. The parks are open daily from 8am to sunset and are administered by **Gulf Islands Geopark** (© 727/469-5918; www.floridastateparks.org/caladesiisland and www.florida stateparks.org/honeymoonisland).

At the mouth of Tampa Bay, **Fort DeSoto Park** (© 727/582-2267; www.fortdesoto. com) has a white-sugar sand beach, a Spanish-American War–era fort, great fishing from piers, playgrounds for kids, and 4 miles of trails through the park for in-line skaters, bicyclists, and joggers. The park's 230 bayside campsites usually are sold out, especially on weekends. Entry to the park is free. It's open daily from 8am to dusk, although campers and persons fishing from the piers can stay later.

You can go parasailing, boating, deep-sea fishing, wave running, sightseeing, dolphin-watching, water-skiing, and just about any other waterborne diversion in the St. Pete and Clearwater beaches area. Just head to one of two beach locations: **Hubbard's Marina,** at John's Pass Village and Boardwalk (© 800/755-0677 or 727/393-1947; www.hubbards-marina.com), in Madeira Beach on the southern tip of Sand Key; or **Clearwater Beach Marina,** at Coronado Drive and Causeway Boulevard (© 800/772-4479 or 727/461-3133), which is at the beach end of the causeway leading to downtown Clearwater. Agents in booths will give you the schedules and prices (expect to pay $35–$50 for a half-day of fishing on a large party boat, $65–$80 for a full day), answer your questions, and make reservations. You can dive on reefs and wrecks with **Dive Clearwater** (© 800/875-3483 or 727/443-6731; www.divingclearwater.com), which also operates the live-aboard boat *Plunger V.* Call for schedules and prices.

The Tampa Bay area has a wide range of golf courses, with greens fees ranging from about $30 to more than $100. Contact the tourist information offices for complete lists (see "Visitor Information," earlier in this chapter). Call **Tee Times USA** (© 800/374-8633; www.teetimesusa.com) to reserve times at all area courses. The **Innisbrook Resort and Golf Club,** 36750 U.S. 19 (P.O. Box 1088), Tarpon Springs, FL 34688 (© 877/752-1480 or 727/942-2000; www.innisbrookgolfresort.com), is one of the country's best

FLORIDA

5

TAMPA & ST. PETERSBURG

places to play (some golf magazines rank its Copperhead course, former home of the annual JCPenney Classic, as number one in Florida). St. Petersburg's **Mangrove Bay Golf Course,** 875 62nd Ave. NE (© 727/893-7800), is one of the nation's top 50 municipal courses. To learn or sharpen your game, the **Arnold Palmer Golf Academy World Headquarters** is at Saddlebrook Resort, 5700 Saddlebrook Way, Wesley Chapel, 12 miles north of Tampa (© 800/729-8383 or 813/973-1111; www.saddlebrookresort. com), though you'll have to stay at the resort in order to play.

SHOPPING

A terrific alternative to cookie-cutter suburban malls, Tampa's **Old Hyde Park Village,** 1507 W. Swann Ave., at South Dakota Avenue (© 813/251-3500; www.oldhydepark village.com), in a picturesque Victorian neighborhood, is a cluster of 50 upscale shops and boutiques, including some of the mall regulars. Tampa's Ybor City no longer is a major producer of hand-rolled cigars, but you can watch artisans making stogies at the **Gonzales y Martinez Cigar Factory,** 2025 7th Ave. (© 813/247-2469; www.gonzalezy martinez.com), in the Columbia restaurant building. Gonzalez and Martinez don't speak English, but the staff does at the adjoining **Columbia Cigar Store** (it's best to enter here). Rollers are on duty Monday through Saturday from 10am to 6pm.

In St. Petersburg, **Beach Drive** along the waterfront is the most fashionable downtown strolling and shopping venue. Be sure to check out the **Glass Canvas Gallery,** at 4th Avenue NE (© 727/821-6767), and **Red Cloud** (© 727/821-5824), an oasis for Native American crafts. Central Avenue is another shopping area, featuring the **Gas Plant Antique Arcade,** between 12th and 13th streets (© 727/895-0368), with more than 100 dealers displaying their wares.

WHERE TO STAY

Most vacationers elect to stay at the beaches and drive into Tampa and St. Petersburg to see the sights. The nearest chain motel is the **Rodeway Inn,** 4139 E. Busch Blvd. (© 813/386-1000), 1¹/₂ blocks east of the main entrance. Doubles start at $50 in winter, including continental breakfast. The 500-room **Embassy Suites Hotel and Conference Center,** 3705 Spectrum Blvd., facing Fowler Avenue (© 800/362-2779 or 813/977-7066), is the plushest establishment near the park, with doubles starting at $120, and packages including park admission available. Almost across the avenue stands **LaQuinta Inn & Suites,** 3701 E. Fowler Ave. (© 800/687-6667 or 813/910-7500). Just south of Fowler Avenue are side-by-side branches of **AmeriSuites,** 11408 N. 30th St. (© 800/833-1516 or 813/979-1922), and **DoubleTree Guest Suites,** 11310 N. 30th St. (© 800/222-8733 or 813/971-7690).

In downtown Tampa, the **Hyatt Regency Tampa,** 2 Tampa City Center (© 800/233-1234 or 813/225-1234; www.hyatt.com); the **Sheraton Tampa Riverwalk Hotel,** 200 N. Ashley St. (© 800/333-3333 or 813/223-2222; www.tampariverwalkhotel.com); and the **Tampa Marriott Waterside Hotel & Marina,** 710 N. Florida Ave. (© 800/228-9290 or 813/221-4900; www.marriott.com), all cater primarily to the corporate crowd.

St. Pete Beach and Clearwater Beach have national chain hotels and motels of every name and description. The **St. Petersburg/Clearwater Area Convention & Visitors Bureau** operates a free **reservations service** (© 800/345-6710), through which you can book rooms at most hotels and motels in St. Petersburg and at the beaches.

Best Western All Suites Hotel (Value)   This three-story all-suite hotel is the most beachlike vacation venue you'll find close to the park. Whimsical signs lead you around a lush courtyard with a heated pool, hot tub, and lively Tiki bar. Bathrooms were renovated in 2007. The bar can get noisy before closing at 9pm, and ground-level units are musty, so ask for an upstairs suite away from the action. Suite living rooms are well equipped; the separate bedrooms have narrow screened patios or balconies.

Behind Busch Gardens, 3001 University Center Dr. (faces N. 30th St. btw. Busch Blvd. and Fowler Ave.), Tampa, FL 33612. ✆ 800/786-7446 or 813/971-8930. Fax 813/971-8935. www.bestwestern.com. 150 units. Winter $99–$189 suite for 2; off season $99–$109 suite for 2. Rates include hot and cold breakfast buffet. AE, DC, DISC, MC, V. **Amenities:** Restaurant; heated pool; access to nearby health club. *In room:* Fridge.

Don CeSar Beach Resort, A Loews Hotel (Kids)   This Moorish-style "Pink Palace" on the National Register of Historic Places has a rich history and appeals to groups, families, and couples. Sitting on 7½ acres of beachfront, this landmark sports a lobby of classic high windows and archways, crystal chandeliers, marble floors, and original artwork. Some of the 275 rooms under the minarets of the original building may seem small, but they have high windows and offer views of the Gulf or Boca Ciega Bay. Some have balconies. If you want more space but less charm, go for one of the 70 luxury condominiums in the Don CeSar Beach House, a mid-rise building ¾ mile to the north (there's 24-hr. complimentary transportation btw. the two). An excellent kids' program features supervised activities, including etiquette classes, instructing kids *and* adults on which fork to use. A new spa debuted in 2007.

3400 Gulf Blvd. (at 34th Ave./Pinellas Byway), St. Pete Beach, FL 33706. ✆ 866/728-2206 or 727/360-1881. Fax 727/367-6952. www.doncesar.com. 347 units. Winter $279–$541 double, $393–$3,000 suite; off season $189–$429 double, $299–$2,000 suite. $10 per person per day resort fee. Packages available. AE, DC, DISC, MC, V. Valet parking $20 overnight; $13–$18 day; self-parking free. **Amenities:** 4 restaurants; 2 heated outdoor pools; exercise room; spa.

The Heritage Holiday Inn   When it comes to Holiday Inns, most people complain about the old, musty decor. This hotel has that feel, but it also has atypical qualities that may appeal to some (though the rooms are still pretty basic). No ordinary Holiday Inn, the Heritage dates from the early 1920s, and although significantly updated, it retains the ambience of an old-fashioned hotel, with tall double-hung windows and hardwood floors in the long central hallway. A lovely sweeping veranda, French doors, and a tropical courtyard help attract an eclectic clientele, from business travelers to seniors.

234 3rd Ave. N. (btw. 2nd and 3rd sts.), St. Petersburg, FL 33701. ✆ 800/283-7829 or 727/822-4814. Fax 727/823-1644. www.theheritagehi.com. 71 units. $134–$152 double. AE, DC, DISC, MC, V. **Amenities:** Restaurant; heated outdoor pool.

Hilton Garden Inn   This modern four-story hotel stands 2 blocks north of Ybor City's dining and entertainment district. A one-story brick structure in front houses the lobby, a comfy relaxation area with a fireplace, a dining area providing cooked and continental breakfasts, and a 24-hour pantry selling beer, wine, soft drinks, and frozen dinners. You can heat up the dinners in your room's microwave or store them in your fridge. Since Hilton's Garden hotels are aimed primarily at business travelers, your room will also have a large desk and two phones. If you opt for a suite, you'll get a separate living room and a larger bathroom.

1700 E. 9th Ave. (btw. 17th and 18th sts.), Tampa, FL 33605. ✆ 800/445-8667 or 813/769-9267. Fax 813/769-3299. www.hiltongardeninn.com. 95 units. $129–$299 double. AE, DC, DISC, MC, V. **Amenities:** Restaurant (breakfast only); heated outdoor pool; exercise room. *In room:* Fridge, microwave.

Innisbrook Resort and Golf Club   *Golf Digest, Golf,* and others pick this as one of the country's best places to play golf. Situated between Palm Harbor and Tarpon Springs, this 1,000-acre, all-condominium resort has 90 holes on championship courses more like the rolling links of the Carolinas than the usually flat courses in Florida. Some pros think the **Copperhead Course** is number one in Florida. If you want to learn, Innisbrook has the largest resort-owned and -operated golf school in North America. In addition, it boasts a tennis center with instruction. It's similar to the sports-oriented Saddlebrook Resort near Tampa, except that the courses are more challenging and you're much closer to the beach. A free shuttle runs around the property, and another goes to the beach three times a day. Ranging in size from suites to two-bedroom models, the quarters are privately owned condos spread all over the premises.

36750 U.S. 19 N., Palm Harbor, FL 34684. (C) **877/752-1480** or 727/942-2000. Fax 727/942-5576. www. innisbrookgolfresort.com. 700 units. Winter $229–$485 suite; off season $155–$289 suite. Golf packages available. AE, DC, DISC, MC, V. **Amenities:** 7 restaurants; heated outdoor pools; 4 golf courses; 15 tennis courts; health club. *In room:* Kitchen.

Island's End Resort (Value)   A wonderful respite and a great bargain, this all-cottage hideaway sits on the southern tip of St. Pete Beach, on Pass-a-Grille, where the Gulf of Mexico meets Tampa Bay. Since the island curves sharply here, nothing will block your view of the bay. You can safely swim in the Gulf or grab a brilliant sunset at the Pass-a-Grille's public beach, one door down. Linked to one another by boardwalks, the one- and three-bedroom cottages have dining areas, living rooms, VCRs and DVDs, and fully equipped kitchens.

1 Pass-a-Grille Way (at 1st Ave.), St. Pete Beach, FL 33706. (C) **727/360-5023.** Fax 727/367-7890. www. islandsend.com. 6 units. Winter $175–$325 cottage; off season $145–$325 cottage. Weekly rates available. Complimentary breakfast served Tues, Thurs, and Sat. MC, V. *In room:* Kitchen.

Renaissance Vinoy Resort and Golf Club (Best)   For the swankiest digs in the area, the Renaissance Vinoy is it. Built as the grand Vinoy Park in 1925, this elegant Spanish-style establishment has hosted everyone from Jimmy Stewart to Bill Clinton; it reopened in 1992 and landed on the National Register of Historic Places after a meticulous $93-million restoration that has made it the city's finest hotel. All the guest rooms, many of which enjoy lovely views of the bayfront, offer the utmost in comfort and elegance. Some rooms in the original building have standing-room-only balconies, so if you need enough room to sit outside, request a balconied unit in the new Tower wing (some of these have whirlpool tubs, too). The Vinoy also has 12 tennis courts and an 18-hole golf course. The hotel is nonsmoking.

501 5th Ave. NE (at Beach Dr.), St. Petersburg, FL 33701. (C) **800/468-3571** or 727/894-1000. Fax 727/822-2785. www.renaissancehotels.com. 360 units. Winter $319–$525 double; off season $199–$329 double. Packages available. AE, DC, DISC, MC, V. Valet parking $13; self-parking $9. **Amenities:** 4 restaurants; 2 heated outdoor pools; golf course; 12 tennis courts; health club; spa.

Saddlebrook Resort—Tampa (Kids)   Set on 480 rolling acres of countryside, Saddlebrook is a landlocked condominium development off the beaten path (30 min. north of Tampa International Airport). But if you're interested in spas, tennis, or golf, we recommend this resort, which offers complete spa treatments, the Hopman Tennis Program (with Jennifer Capriati), and the Arnold Palmer Golf Academy. Guests are housed in hotel rooms with Tommy Bahama–esque decor, or one-, two-, or three-bedroom suites. Much more appealing than the rooms, the suites come with a kitchen and either a patio or balcony overlooking lagoons, cypress and palm trees, and the resort's two 18-hole championship golf courses. There are shops, restaurants, a stunning pool, and a kids' club **411** with supervised activities.

5700 Saddlebrook Way, Wesley Chapel, FL 33543. ⓒ **800/729-8383** or 813/973-1111. Fax 813/973-4504. www.saddlebrookresort.com. 800 units. Winter $275–$420 suite; off season $135–$230 suite. Packages available. AE, DC, DISC, MC, V. Valet parking $10 overnight. **Amenities:** 4 restaurants; heated outdoor pool; 2 golf courses; 45 grass, clay, and hard tennis courts; health club; spa. *In room:* Kitchen (suites only), fridge.

Safety Harbor Resort and Spa (Value)   Hernando de Soto thought he found the fabled Fountain of Youth when, in 1539, he happened upon five mineral springs in what is now Safety Harbor on the western shore of Old Tampa Bay. You may not recover your youth at this venerable 50,000-square-foot Aveda Concept Spa, the recipient of a multi-million-dollar renovation, but you will be rejuvenated. The healing mineral springs are the site of acclaimed water-fitness programs. There's also a tennis academy. The complex of beige-stucco buildings with Spanish-tile roofs offers upgraded rooms with new furniture and understated, yet crisp, new decor with a beige-and-cream motif. It sits on 22 waterfront acres in the sleepy town of Safety Harbor, north of St. Petersburg, with a number of shops and restaurants just steps away.

105 N. Bayshore Dr., Safety Harbor, FL 34695. ⓒ **888/237-8772** or 727/726-1161. Fax 727/724-7749. www.safetyharborresort.com 175 units. Winter $169–$359 double; off season $149–$259 double; year-round from $345 suite. Packages available. AE, DC, DISC, MC, V. Valet parking $12; self-parking free. No pets. **Amenities:** Restaurant; indoor/outdoor pools; tennis courts; fitness center; spa.

Sheraton Sand Key Resort   Set on 10 acres next to Sand Key Park, away from the honky-tonk of Clearwater, this nine-story Spanish-style hotel is a favorite with groups and watersports enthusiasts. It's only a 450-foot walk across the broad beach in front of the hotel to the water's edge. The guest rooms here have traditional dark-wood furniture and balconies or patios with views of the Gulf or the bay. The exercise room is on the top floor, affording great workout views.

1160 Gulf Blvd., Clearwater Beach, FL 33767. ⓒ **800/325-3535** or 727/595-1611. Fax 727/596-1117. www.sheratonsandkey.com. 390 units. Winter $175–$356 double; off season $155–$269 double. AE, DC, DISC, MC, V. **Amenities:** 2 restaurants; heated outdoor pool; 3 tennis courts; exercise room.

WHERE TO DINE

Don't overlook the food court at St. Petersburg's the **Pier,** where the inexpensive chow is accompanied by a rich, but free, view of the bay. You can take a shopping break at **Old Hyde Park Village**'s trendy sidewalk bistros.

Bella's Italian Cafe (Value) ITALIAN   While trendy restaurants come and go, Bella's has been around for over 20 years, and for good reason. A casual, rustic ambience with a wood-fired oven and indoor and outdoor seating attract a sophisticated crowd. The Italian fare is delicious, from the paper-thin carpaccio with garlic, olives, capers, and basil, to old-fashioned spaghetti and meatballs. You can also create your own combination of pasta and sauce, choosing from a large list of options, or just order a pizza cooked in the oak-burning oven. Executive chef and co-owner Joanie Corneil studied cooking in Italy. For those who like a strong drink with their dinner, the Bellarita is a popular potion of Conmemorativo tequila and Grand Marnier.

1413 S. Howard Ave. ⓒ **813/254-3355.** www.bellasitaliancafe.com. Reservations recommended. Main courses $13–$20; pizza $8–$12. AE, DC, DISC, MC, V. Mon–Wed 11:30am–11:30pm; Thurs 11:30am–12:30am; Fri 11:30am–1:30am; Sat 4pm–1:30am; Sun 4–11:30pm.

Bern's Steak House STEAKHOUSE   This famous steakhouse has eight ornate dining rooms with themes such as Rhone, Burgundy, and Irish Rebellion. They set an appropriately dark atmosphere for huge charcoal-grilled steaks (beef or buffalo). The phone book–size wine list offers more than 7,000 selections, many available by the glass. In the dessert quarters upstairs, 50 romantic booths can seat from 2 to 12 guests, who can select from a dessert menu offering almost 100 selections and 1,400 after-dinner drinks. Here's a tip: Steak sandwiches are available at the bar but are not mentioned on the menu. Smaller versions of the chargrilled steaks are served in the dining rooms; they come with a choice of fries or onion rings. Add a salad, and you have a terrific meal for about half the price of the least-expensive main course. In 2007, Bern's announced it is building the **Epicurean Hotel**, a 75-room boutique condo/hotel with a new restaurant, wine shop, culinary school, and day spa, next to the original restaurant. Completion was expected by the end of 2008.

1208 S. Howard Ave. (at Marjory Ave.). © **813/251-2421.** www.bernssteakhouse.com. Reservations recommended. Main courses $17–$60; sandwiches $9–$15. AE, DC, DISC, MC, V. Daily 5–11pm. Closed Christmas. Valet parking $5.

Carmine's Restaurant & Bar CUBAN/ITALIAN/AMERICAN   Bright blue poles hold up a pressed-tin ceiling above this noisy corner cafe. It's not the cleanest joint in town, but a variety of loyal patrons gather for genuine Cuban sandwiches—smoked ham, roast pork, Genoa salami, Swiss cheese, pickles, salad dressing, mustard, lettuce, and tomato on crispy Cuban bread. The combination of a half-sandwich and choice of black beans and rice or a bowl of Spanish soup made with sausages, potatoes, and garbanzo beans is a filling meal by itself. Main courses are led by Cuban-style roast pork, and spaghetti with a blue-crab tomato sauce.

1802 E. 7th Ave. (at 18th St.). © **813/248-3834.** Reservations not accepted. Main courses $10–$20; sandwiches $5–$10. AE, MC, V. Mon–Tues 11am–11pm; Wed–Thurs 11am–1am; Fri–Sat 11am–3am; Sun 11am–6pm.

Chateau France CLASSICAL FRENCH   Chef Antoine Louro provides St. Petersburg's most romantic setting in this cozy, charming Victorian house built in 1910. He specializes in French classics such as homemade pâté, Dover sole meunière, filet mignon au poivre, coq au vin, and rich seafood bouillabaisse. The wine list is excellent, as are the bananas flambé and crêpes suzette.

136 4th Ave. N. (btw. Bayshore Dr. and 1st St. N.). © **727/894-7163.** www.chateaufrancecuisine.com. Reservations recommended. Main courses $22–$38. AE, DC, DISC, MC, V. Daily 5–11pm.

Columbia ⓑest SPANISH   Columbia celebrated 100 years in 2005. Its tile building occupies a city block in the heart of Ybor City. Tourists flock here to soak up the ambience, and so do the locals because it's so much fun to clap along during the Spanish flamenco floor shows Monday through Saturday evenings ($6 per person additional charge). Try the famous Spanish bean soup and "1905" salad. Entrees come with a crispy hunk of Cuban bread with butter. Lighter appetites can choose from a limited menu of tapas. The decor throughout is graced with hand-painted tiles, wrought-iron chandeliers, dark woods, rich red fabrics, and stained-glass windows.

2117 E. 7th Ave. (btw. 21st and 22nd sts.). © **813/248-4961.** www.columbiarestaurant.com. Reservations recommended especially for flamenco shows. Main courses $14–$30. AE, DC, DISC, MC, V. Mon–Thurs 11am–10pm; Fri–Sat 11am–11pm; Sun noon–9pm.

Fourth Street Shrimp Store (Value) SEAFOOD If you're anywhere in the area, don't miss at least driving by to see the colorful, cartoonlike mural on the outside of this eclectic establishment just north of downtown. Inside you'll pass a seafood market counter when you enter, from which comes the fresh namesake shrimp, the star here. You can also pick from grouper, clam strips, catfish, or oysters fried, broiled, or steamed, all served in heaping portions. This is the best and certainly the most interesting bargain in town.

1006 4th St. N. (at 10th Ave. N.). (C) 727/822-0325. Main courses $5–$15; sandwiches $4–$10. MC, V. Daily 11am–9pm.

Mise en Place ECLECTIC Chef Marty Blitz and his wife, Maryann, have been among the culinary darlings of Tampa since 1986. They present the freshest of ingredients in a creative, award-winning menu that changes weekly. Main courses often include choices such as ancho spice pan-seared venison rack with pork belly, mushroom ragout, and avocado lime butter. The tasting menu, with wine, is listed on the menu under "Get Blitzed."

In Grand Central Place, 442 W. Kennedy Blvd. (at S. Magnolia Ave., opposite the University of Tampa). (C) 813/254-5373. www.miseonline.com. Reservations recommended. Main courses $18–$35; tasting menu $65 with wine, $45 without. AE, DC, DISC, MC, V. Tues–Thurs 11:30am–2:30pm and 5:30–10pm; Fri 11:30am–2:30pm and 5:30–11pm; Sat 5–11pm.

The Salt Rock Grill SEAFOOD/STEAKS Affluent professionals and the so-called beautiful people pack this waterfront restaurant. The big dining room is built on three levels, thus affording every table a view over the waterway out back. In fair weather, you can dine out by the dock or slake your thirst at the Tiki bar (bands play Sat–Sun during the summer). Thick, aged steaks are the house specialties. Pan-seared peppered tuna and salmon cooked on a cedar board lead the seafood. Save money by showing up for the early-bird specials or by ordering the meatloaf topped with mashed potatoes and onion straws ($9.90), or the half-pound sirloin steak ($13).

19325 Gulf Blvd. (north of 193rd Ave.), Indian Shores. (C) 727/593-7625. www.saltrockgrill.com. Reservations strongly advised. Main courses $8–$40; early-bird specials $8–$10. AE, DC, DISC, MC, V. Sun–Thurs 4–10pm; Fri–Sat 4–11pm; early-bird specials daily 4–5:30pm. Tiki bar Sat 2pm–midnight (or later); Sun 2–10pm.

Ted Peters' Famous Smoked Fish (Value) SEAFOOD This open-air eatery is an institution in these parts: Ted's has been around since the '50s. Some folks bring their catches for the staff to smoke, while others figure fishing is a waste of time and come right to Ted's for mullet, mackerel, salmon, and other fish slowly cooked over red oak. Enjoy the aroma and sip a cold one while you wait for your order.

1530 Pasadena Ave. (just across St. Pete Beach Causeway), Pasadena. (C) 727/381-7931. Main courses $8–$20. No credit cards. Wed–Mon 11:30am–7:30pm.

Wine Exchange MEDITERRANEAN This hot spot is an oenophile's dream, in which each dish is paired with a particular wine. The menu is simple, featuring pizzas, pastas, salads, and sandwiches, but daily specials are more elaborate, including grilled Delmonico steak, blackened pork tenderloin, or Dijon-crusted salmon. The outdoor patio is a great place to sit. There's almost always a wait at this buzz-worthy eatery.

1611 W. Swan Ave. (C) 813/254-9463. Reservations not accepted. Main courses $10–$22. AE, DC, DISC, MC, V. Mon–Fri 11:30am–10pm; Sat 11am–11pm; Sun 11am–9pm; brunch Sat–Sun 11am–3pm.

FLORIDA

5

TAMPA & ST. PETERSBURG

The Tampa/Hillsborough Arts Council maintains an **Artsline** (© **813/229-2787**), a 24-hour information service providing the latest on cultural events. You'll find *Creative Loafing Tampa* (**www.tampa.creativeloafing.com**) in many bars and restaurants. *Focus* (**www.focusmag.net**) and *Accent on Tampa Bay* (**www.ampubs.com**) detail what's going on in the entire bay area. You can check the "BayLife" and "Friday Extra" sections of the *Tampa Tribune* (**www.tampatrib.com**), and the Thursday "Weekend" section of the *St. Petersburg Times* (**www.sptimes.com**).

THE PERFORMING ARTS   The **Tampa Bay Performing Arts Center,** 1010 N. MacInnes Place (© **800/955-1045** or 813/229-7827; www.tampacenter.com), is the largest performing-arts venue south of the Kennedy Center. This four-theater complex is the focal point of Tampa's performing-arts scene, presenting a range of Broadway plays, classical and pop concerts, operas, improvisation, and special events.

The restored **Tampa Theatre,** 711 Franklin St., between Zack and Polk streets (© **813/274-8286;** www.tampatheatre.org), dates from 1926 and is on the National Register of Historic Places. It presents a varied program of classic, foreign, and alternative films, as well as concerts and special events (and it's said to be haunted!).

THE CLUB & BAR SCENE   **Ybor City** is Tampa's favorite nighttime venue. Stroll along 7th Avenue East between 15th and 20th streets to find a club or bar you like. The avenue is packed with people, a majority of them high schoolers and early-20-somethings, on Friday and Saturday from 9pm to 3am, but you'll find something going on from Tuesday to Thursday and even on Sunday. With all of the sidewalk seating, it's easy to judge what the clientele is like and make your choice from there.

In St. Petersburg, the Moorish-style **Coliseum Ballroom,** 535 4th Ave. N. (© **727/892-5202;** www.stpete.org/coliseum), has been hosting dancing, big bands, boxing, and other events since 1924. Call for schedule and prices. The heart of downtown's nighttime scene is **BayWalk** (© **727/895-9277;** www.yourbaywalk.com), an open-air shopping, dining, and entertainment complex bordered by 1st and 2nd streets and 2nd and 3rd avenues North.

At the beaches, the restored fishing community of **John's Pass Village and Boardwalk,** on Gulf Boulevard at John's Pass in Madeira Beach, has a handful of restaurants, bars, and shops. In Pass-a-Grille, there's the lively lounge in **Hurricane,** 807 Gulf Way, at 9th Avenue (© **727/360-9558**). In Clearwater Beach, the **Palm Pavilion Grill & Bar,** on the beach at 18 Bay Esplanade (© **727/446-2742**), has live music Tuesday through Sunday nights during winter and on weekends in the off season. **Frenchy's Rockaway Grill,** at 7 Rockaway St. (© **727/446-4844**), is another popular hangout.

The Gulf South

In the popular mind, some parts of the South are still the "Old South," a land of magnolias and Spanish moss, of plantations, of racial tension, and the Civil War. But unlike their stereotypical image, the Gulf South states are much more modern, and a good deal more ethnically diverse, ranging from the Cajuns and Catholics of Louisiana to the African-American descendants of slaves in Mississippi and Alabama.

Yes, you can find many remnants of the Old South in many places, especially in historic cities such as Natchez, Mississippi, where plantation homes are plentiful and blooming gardens abound. But though economic gaps still exist between whites and blacks, desegregation and the civil rights movement have made long strides in alleviating the racial tension that has marked the area for so long. And the states in the region have taken pains to document all of the struggles and preserve the historic moments. This is the land of the Civil Rights Trail, the place where jazz and the blues were birthed, where battles between North and South hallowed many a field, and where literary giants (Faulkner and Welty, among others) penned their first works.

We'll take you from the pizazz of the French Quarter to the long stretches of the Mississippi Delta, making sure to stop off for the region's best music (from country to the blues to jazz to zydeco) and dining (from home-style barbecue and fried green tomatoes in Alabama to the decadent Creole cuisine of New Orleans).

Note: After struggling back to its feet following the devastation of Hurricane Katrina in 2005, the region took another hit, though not nearly as damaging, in the fall of 2008 with Hurricane Gustav. The long-term effects of the terrible storms on the Gulf South are still in evidence in many places. They've caused some places to completely revamp and renovate, and other places, sadly, to close their doors.

Tip: For information on Arkansas, please see "Appendix A: The Best of the Rest."

1 BIRMINGHAM

Birmingham has come a long way since the 1960s, when the civil rights struggles erupted in bombings, riots, and arrests that drew international attention to this city in north-central Alabama. The pioneer farm settlement of the mid-1850s expanded with the advent of railroads and influence of land barons that helped establish Birmingham as a city in 1871. Fueled by the area's coal, iron ore, and limestone resources, the city earned the nickname the "Magic City" for the rapidity with which Birmingham grew and prospered. Its fortunes waned with the Great Depression in the 1930s, even though the city was largely ruled by wealthy Northern industrialists.

Racial tensions exploded throughout the South during the 1955 Montgomery Bus Boycott. In Birmingham, when the Ku Klux Klan bombed the Sixteenth Street Baptist Church on September 15, 1963, killing four innocent black girls, the city's reputation changed, earning it the derogatory nickname "Bombingham."

Today the city has preserved the painful lessons of the past in many attractions and landmarks that offer the opportunity for reconciliation and reflection. In addition to important civil rights sites, this lovely city that hugs the foothills of the Appalachian Mountains boasts both a nationally renowned art museum and a motorsports park that racing enthusiasts revere as one of the best in the country.

ESSENTIALS

GETTING THERE By Plane Birmingham International Airport (© 205/595-0533; www.flybirmingham.com) is about 5 miles east of downtown. Major car-rental companies are housed at ground level on Concourse B, near baggage claim. It's an easy 10-minute drive into the city; take I-20/59 west into downtown.

If you're not renting a car, you can take the **E-Shuttle** (© 205/702-4566), which offers town car service between the airport and area hotels and motels. Rates start at $45 per person one-way. The **Birmingham Door-to-Door Shuttle Service** (© 205/591-5550) provides van service between the airport and points throughout Alabama. Reservations are required.

Taxis are available outside baggage claim; it will cost about $25 to get downtown.

By Train Amtrak (© 800/USA-RAIL [872-7245]; www.amtrak.com) runs trains from New York (trip time: 23 hr.) through Washington, D.C. (18 hr.), and Atlanta (4 hr.) to Birmingham's station at 1819 Morris Ave. (© 205/324-3033).

By Car The principal highway routes into Birmingham are I-65 from the north (Nashville), I-20 from the east (Atlanta), I-59 from the northeast (Chattanooga, Tenn.), I-20/59 from the southwest (Jackson, Miss.), and I-65 from the south (Montgomery, Ala.).

VISITOR INFORMATION To receive visitor information on the Birmingham area before your arrival, contact the **Greater Birmingham Convention and Visitors Bureau,** 2200 Ninth Ave. N., Birmingham, AL 35203-1100 (© 800/458-8085 or 205/458-8000; www.birminghamal.org). Another useful resource is the **Alabama Bureau of Tourism and Travel** (© 800/ALABAMA [252-2262]; www.alabama.travel). In addition to its downtown location, the Greater Birmingham CVB has a satellite location at Birmingham International Airport, lower level (© 205/458-8002).

GETTING AROUND For a taxi, call the **Yellow Cab Company of Greater Birmingham** (© 205/328-4444); the meter starts at $4.50 and runs $2 per mile.

FAST FACTS Emergency and urgent-care services are available at **University of Alabama Birmingham Hospital,** 619 19th St. S. (© 205/934-4011; www.health.uab.edu). A 24-hour **CVS Pharmacy** (© 205/942-7503) is located at 418 W. Valley Ave., in the suburb of Homewood. Sales tax is 10%; hotel tax is 14%.

WHAT TO SEE & DO

Many of Birmingham's major attractions are **Downtown,** where you'll find a handful of hotels, government buildings, and corporate headquarters, as well as all of the noted attractions in the Civil Rights District. The **Five Points South** area, just south of downtown, is a vibrant neighborhood that encompasses the University of Alabama at Birmingham and blocks teeming with upscale restaurants, boutiques, and apartments.

Inside the Civil Rights District

The **Civil Rights District** is the heart and soul of Birmingham. Visitors from throughout the world travel here to remember the violent struggles for racial equality that shocked the nation in the 1950s and 1960s.

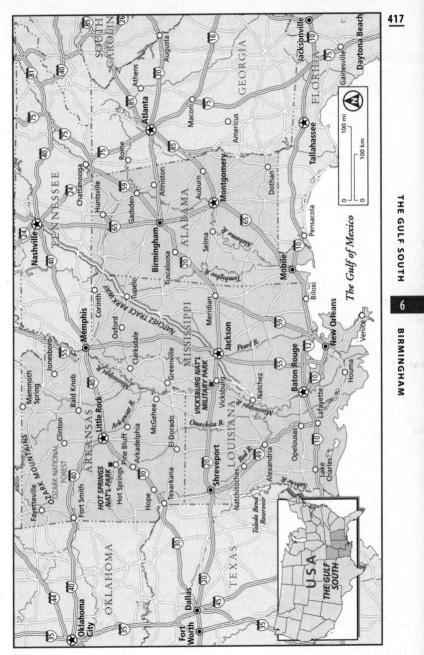

A good place to start exploring this period in American history is at the **Birmingham Civil Rights Institute,** 520 16th St. N. (*©* **205/328-9696;** www.bcri.org). Allow at least half a day to tour this emotionally wrenching museum that takes visitors through the riots that erupted in Birmingham and throughout the South in the 1950s and 1960s. Deeply moving and ultimately inspiring, the museum's displays take the viewer back to a harrowing place and time in our nation's history. With the joyfulness of gospel choirs singing in the background, the museum journey culminates with a room-size mural that re-creates the March on Washington, D.C., when the Rev. Martin Luther King, Jr., delivered his "I Have a Dream" speech. Visitors are transfixed by the video of King's historic address, with many children reciting the pledge along with the slain civil rights leader. Other galleries address human rights issues throughout the world. In addition, the institute offers ongoing educational programs and houses a state-of-the-art library and research center. Admission costs $10 adults, $5 seniors, $4 college students, and is free to kids 17 and under. Admission is free on Sunday. The institute is closed on Monday (except from Martin Luther King Day in Jan through the end of Feb) and national holidays.

Kelly Ingram Park, across the street from the Birmingham Civil Rights Institute and cater-cornered from the landmark 16th Street Baptist Church, has often been referred to as being at the threshold of the civil rights movement. Within the park, a paved Freedom Path features sculptures commemorating the riots that occurred here in the 1960s, when police turned attack dogs and fire hoses on men, women, and children protesting segregation. There are plaques recounting the importance of clergy in the movement, as well as an emotionally charged statue of children standing defiantly behind bars, in remembrance of those who went to jail for the cause of freedom. A placid water fountain flows in the center of the park, providing a shady spot for quiet reflection and contemplation. Hand-held electronic devices that provide audio tours of the park are available across the street at the Civil Rights Institute ticket office for a nominal fee. Using narrative and eyewitness accounts, the audio tours provide context and background for what visitors are seeing as they walk through the park.

From the park, walk back across the street to tour the **16th Street Baptist Church,** 1530 6th Ave. N. (*©* **205/251-9402**), where the infamous 1963 Klan bombing killed four adolescent girls—Cynthia Wesley, Addie Mae Collins, Carole Robertson, and Denise McNair—as they got ready for a Sunday School program. Tours begin in the resplendent sanctuary, where guides give an overview of the church's history before showing an interesting film tracing the devastating impact of the notorious hate crime, and the ensuing decades-long legal trials that eventually brought the perpetrators to justice. In the church's basement and fellowship hall, a memorial to the girls contains enlarged black-and-white photographs of the chaos and aftermath of the bombing. Most chilling is the well-known photograph of the stained-glass window that remained undamaged except for the face of Jesus, which was blown away by the blast. Take a moment to reflect on the wall clock that is frozen at the time the bombings occurred, 10:22am, and which remains a symbol of the church's defining moment. Allow at least 2 hours to see the church, where admission is by a suggested donation of $3.

In 2006 the church was designated as a national historic landmark. It is still an ongoing, active congregation of some 600 members. Worship services usually begin at 11am on Sunday. Visiting tourists are warmly welcomed to participate.

Families have various options for keeping the kids entertained. The **Birmingham Zoo,** 2630 Cahaba Rd. (© **205/879-0409;** www.birminghamzoo.com), is home to more than 800 animals, including bald eagles and Bengal tigers, red pandas and ring-tailed lemurs. A Children's Zoo area offers such other draws as a train ride and picnic areas. Admission is $12 adults, $7 children and seniors. Educational fun awaits at the hands-on **McWane Center,** 200 19th Street N. (© **205/714-8300;** www.mcwane.org), which features hands-on displays, discovery areas, and an IMAX theater. Admission to the exhibit halls and the IMAX theater is $16 adults, $12 kids 2 to 12.

Alabama Adventure (formerly known as Visionland), 4599 Alabama Adventure Pkwy., Bessemer (© **205/481-4750;** www.alabamaadventure.com), is the area's amusement park, about 15 miles southwest of town. The park is home to Magic City USA Theme Park and its signature wooden roller coaster, the Rampage. Alabama Adventure also has a 600,000-gallon wave pool with sand beach at Splash Beach Water Park. Admission to both the theme park and waterpark costs $34 adults, $24 kids under 48 inches tall.

Museums

In downtown, the best cultural value around can be found at the brilliant **Birmingham Museum of Art,** 2000 Eighth Ave. N. (© **205/254-2565;** www.artsbma.org), regarded as one of the finest in the South. Besides its free admission, what makes this modern facility so outstanding is its impressive permanent collection of more than 21,000 works of art dating from antiquity to the present day, including a sculpture garden, the Kress Collection of Renaissance Art, and 18th-century French paintings and decorative arts. In addition to masterpieces by Claude Monet, John Singer Sargent, and many others, the museum has a popular children's gallery.

Music lovers should not miss a chance to visit the **Alabama Jazz Music Hall of Fame Museum,** 1631 Fourth Ave. N. (© **205/254-2731;** www.jazzhall.com), which pays homage to musicians such as W. C. Handy, who was born in this state, and Erskine Hawkins, a noted local music educator who wrote Big Band leader Glenn Miller's hit song *Tuxedo Junction.* An entertaining, if rather outdated, film shown in the historic movie theater, now known as the Carver Center for the Performing Arts, begins the self-guided tour. In it, interviews and historical photos and voiceovers detail the state's contributions to the art form of jazz music. The bi-level museum exhibits costumes, musical instruments, records, and playbills recalling the glory days of jazz, primarily in the early part of the last century. Look for the display case devoted to Ella Fitzgerald (who had no other ties to Alabama other than once being hospitalized here for a brief illness), where the scat-singing diva's sequined dress is displayed along with her well-worn Neiman Marcus credit card. It's closed on Sunday and Monday. Admission is $3 for a guided tour or $2 for a self-guided tour.

Paying homage to pioneers of aviation is the **Southern Museum of Flight,** 4343 73rd St. N. (© **205/833-8226;** www.southernmuseumofflight.org), located 2 blocks east of Birmingham International Airport. More than 8 decades of aviation history are detailed in display and restoration projects being undertaken at the hangars. World War II bombers, biplanes, and an F14-Tomcat are among the vintage as well as experimental aircraft on display, along with ultralights and glider planes. Among aircraft from the Vietnam era are an A-12 Blackbird, a Huey UH-1 helicopter, and an F-4 Phantom jet fighter. A detailed history of the courageous Tuskegee Airmen is chronicled as part of the Alabama Aviation Hall of Fame gallery. The museum is closed Monday. Admission is $5 for adults and $4 for seniors and students.

If you long to stretch your legs and let the kids run and explore, there's no better tourist attraction than **Vulcan Park,** 1701 Valley View Dr. (© **205/933-1409;** www.vulcanpark. org), site of the largest cast-iron statue in the world. Created for the 1904 World's Fair in St. Louis, the imposing statue depicts Vulcan, the god of forge. After a recent restoration, the statue once again dominates a 10-acre park atop Red Mountain. The grounds offer unparalleled views of the Birmingham skyline—not to mention free Wi-Fi. A visitor center includes exhibits and displays showcasing the city's rise as an iron-producing center at the turn of the 20th century, and traces the decline of the industry during the Great Depression of the 1930s and beyond.

    Tannehill Ironworks Historical State Park, 12632 Confederate Pkwy., McCalla (© **205/477-5711;** www.tannehill.org), is a 1,500-acre haven for hiking, camping, horseback riding, and other recreation. Artisans such as a blacksmith and miller ply their trades outside restored 19th-century pioneer cabins to create a vision of a village from long ago. The ironworks give visitors a glimpse into life in the 1800s. The festive Tannehill Trade Days take place every third Saturday March through November. To reach the park from Birmingham, take I-59 south to exit 100 and follow the signs.

    Among other family-friendly options are spectator sports, including minor league baseball's **Birmingham Barons,** 100 Ben Chapman Dr. (© **205/988-3200;** http://barons. com). The team, an AA Southern Class affiliate of the Chicago White Sox, plays at Regions Park, 100 Ben Chapman Dr. Tickets range from $6 to $12.

Attractions near Birmingham

Those in search of more testosterone-tested attractions should hit the road and head out to the rolling, wooded hills that surround the **Barber Vintage Motorsports Museum,** 6030 Barber Motorsports Pkwy. (© **205/699-7275;** www.barbermuseum.org). This one-of-a-kind museum, founded by a Birmingham businessman, showcases more than 1,100 motorcycles representing nearly 140 manufacturers. The 80,000-square-foot venue's most-photographed chopper? The star-spangled replica of the Harley-Davidson Peter Fonda and Jack Nicholson rode in the film *Easy Rider.* The massive glass-and-concrete building reaches several stories, with seamless displays that trace the evolution of motorized two-wheelers from the early 1900s to today's ultramodern machines. Mechanically inclined visitors may want to visit the in-house restoration shop in the basement to watch as workers spiff up, shine, and fine-tune the antique cycles. Every bike in the museum is in working condition. Admission is $10 adults, $6 children. They're road-tested outside, along the awe-inspiring **Barber Motorsports Park,** a 2½-mile road course considered to be among the best in the U.S. Porsches also whiz along this winding ribbon of road during the **Porsche Sport Driving School,** where, for a hefty fee, VIPs with advance reservations embark on a multiday training course to learn to drive these quintessential sports cars. For more information on the school, call © **888/204-7474** or 205/699-2657 (www.porschedriving.com).

    And, of course, if you're in Birmingham, you can't be this close to Talladega and not take a day trip to see what NASCAR fanatics have labeled the world's biggest, fastest, and most competitive motorsports facility in the world. A short drive east of Birmingham, the **Talladega Superspeedway,** off I-20 on Speedway Boulevard (© **800/G0-2-DEGA** [402-3342] or 256/362-9064; www.talladegasuperspeedway.com), is a shrine to speed that covers more than 2,000 acres and offers stadium seating capacity for more than 143,000 spectators. Tours of the 2¾-mile track are offered daily, except on race days. To attend an actual racing event, call well in advance to inquire about ticket availability.

Swinging Into Birmingham

Alabama has been called a golfer's paradise, and the **Robert Trent Jones Golf Trail** that spans the state has become one of its top attractions. When visiting the Birmingham area, golfers will find a challenging scenic course at the **Oxmoor Valley Golf Club,** 100 Sunbelt Pkwy. (© **800/949-4444** or 205/942-1177; www. rtjgolf.com). The public 54-hole course (greens fees $43–$64) is one of the trail's 11 golf sites. It's only a few miles from downtown.

Next door to the track is the **International Motorsports Hall of Fame and Museum** (www.motorsportshalloffame.com), a must for racing fans of all ages. Admission to the museum costs $10 adults, $5 kids 7 to 17. Combination tickets that include guided bus tours of the racetrack cost $12 for adults and $8 for kids. It's open daily, but the track is closed during and after racing events.

WHERE TO STAY

Downtown has several distinctive choices for travelers. The **Historic Redmont,** 2101 Fifth Ave. N. (© **877/536-2085** or 205/324-2101; www.theredmont.com), is a modern high-rise. The rooms offer the usual business amenities. Doubles run about $139. With its ideal location in the heart of downtown, the historic **Tutwiler,** 2021 Park Place N. (© **205/322-2100;** www.thetutwilerhotel.com), offers spacious rooms and turn-of-the-20th-century decor. The property had become a bit ragged until 2007, when it was acquired and renovated by the Hilton chain as a Hampton Inn & Suites. New in-room amenities include 32-inch flatscreen, high-definition TVs, and wooden lap desks. Rates average $199 double.

The upscale and thoroughly modern **Birmingham Marriott,** 3590 Grandview Pkwy. (© **800/228-9290** or 205/968-3775; www.marriott.com), is an attractive alternative in which all rooms have large work desks and ottomans. Suites sport two bathrooms, including one with a Jacuzzi. In addition, the hotel offers an indoor pool and a health club. Rates run $129 to $189 double.

If you don't mind traveling along the interstate to the outskirts of town, and if you love to shop, there's no better place to stay than the luxurious **Wynfrey Hotel,** 1000 Riverchase Galleria (© **800/996-3739** or 205/987-1600; www.wynfrey.com). Package specials make weekend or shopping getaways to the Wynfrey surprisingly affordable. The gleaming Italian-marble lobby is accented with fresh floral arrangements and French chandeliers. In each of the 15-story high-rise's 329 spacious rooms (including 12 suites), you'll find amenities such as beds with pillow-top mattresses and down comforters. All guest bathrooms were recently upgraded with Italian marble floors and fixtures. The Wynfrey has direct access into the massive Riverchase Galleria, a shopping paradise with hundreds of shops, restaurants, and one of the largest skylight-covered courtyards in the country. Doubles run $189 to $289.

WHERE TO DINE

Bottega Restaurant and Cafe, 2242 Highland Ave. S. (© **205/939-1000;** www.bottegarestaurant.com), is an upscale Mediterranean- and Tuscan-style restaurant featuring a mixture of North African, Greek, and Italian cuisines. Noted local chef/restaurateur Frank Stitt's appetizers run the gamut from traditional carpaccio to exotic Spanish octopus. Varied preparations of monkfish, grouper, pastas, and veal dominate the menu. Pizzas and sandwiches also are available for takeout at the cafe next door, which is open daily except Sunday. Main courses cost $11 to $39.

Another local favorite is **Café Dupont,** 113 20th St. N. ((*C*) **205/322-1282;** www. cafedupont.com). Chef/owner Chris Dupont draws raves as one of Birmingham's newest culinary stars. This casually elegant bistro makes a great place for a business lunch or a romantic dinner with its New Orleans–influenced menu. Start with a bowl of gumbo and then try the chorizo and crabmeat tart. Yes, just like the similarly named Café du Monde in the Big Easy (p. 449), beignets are on the dessert menu. Main courses cost $19 to $23. **Hot and Hot Fish Club,** 2180 11th Court S. ((*C*) **205/933-5474;** www.hotand hotfishclub.com), is up-and-coming chef Christopher Hastings's trendy eatery, housed in a former creamery turned '50s burger joint. Noted artisans have designed all the artwork, from paintings and sculptural details to the handmade pottery in which meals are served. The menu includes shrimp and grits with country ham, and barbecued beef short ribs with sweet-corn succotash, coleslaw, and cracklin' corn bread. For dessert, try the buttermilk panna cotta with local blueberries. Main courses cost $24 to $36.

Highlands Bar and Grill, 2011 11th Ave. S. ((*C*) **205/939-1400;** www.highlands barandgrill.com), is the darling of the Birmingham culinary scene. With raves from major food magazines and consistently good food and service, it's sometimes difficult to snare a reservation at this popular place that combines the homey ambience of a French bistro with the familiarity of an American bar. The upscale crowd favors signature dishes such as fluffy baked grits with country ham and wild mushrooms. The seared tuna is succulent and flavorful, served rare over a bed of steamed vegetables. The trio of homemade ice creams—butter pecan, coconut, and caramel—is sublime. Main courses cost $28 to $40.

A must for fans of the movie *Fried Green Tomatoes*—or for the batter-fried dish itself—is just a short ride out of town. The **Irondale Café,** 1906 1st Ave. N., Irondale ((*C*) **205/956-5258;** www.irondalecafe.com), is the nostalgic diner that served as the inspiration for Alabama novelist Fannie Flagg's *Fried Green Tomatoes at the Whistle Stop Café*. Diners eat at red-and-white-checked tablecloths. Old-fashioned Southern vegetables such as okra, sweet potatoes, and turnip greens accompany entrees of fried chicken, dumplings, and a multitude of other dishes that change daily. Don't miss the crispy, batter-fried green tomatoes or the rich macaroni and cheese. Peach cobbler and chocolate cream pie are dessert favorites. Entrees cost $5.50 to $11.

Another home-cooking restaurant that's a bit out of the way but worth the trip is **Niki's West,** 233 Finley Ave. W. ((*C*) **205/252-5751**). Though the restaurant bills itself as a steak and seafood place, locals swarm here to stand in the cafeteria line for the knee-weakening array of old-fashioned meatloaf, fried fish, and chicken, and a rainbow of seasoned Southern vegetables. Try the greens or macaroni and cheese, and don't miss the gooey, ultrasweet banana pudding for dessert. A platter of meat and three vegetables, plus drink and tax, costs about $10.

When you tire of Southern fried foods, opt for the **Purple Onion Deli and Grill,** 1717 10th Ave. S. ((*C*) **205/933-2424**), a casual, locally owned chain restaurant that serves fresh sandwiches, salads, and side dishes in a fast-food-style atmosphere. Try the kabobs with charred chicken, lamb, and juicy vegetables. There are several locations scattered throughout the metropolitan Birmingham area. Entrees average $9 to $11 with all of the trimmings (rice, salad, and so on).

Tickets for many local events are sold through **Ticketmaster** (© **205/715-6000;** www. ticketmaster.com).

THE PERFORMING ARTS   The **Alabama Ballet** (© **205/322-4300;** www.alabama ballet.org) performs a handful of programs each season, including a traditional holiday *Nutcracker* as well as performances featuring the classics and a more contemporary repertoire. Now in its 10th season, the **Alabama Symphony Orchestra** (© **205/251-7727;** http://alabamasymphony.org) offers a variety of classical, pops, and family programs at concert halls and outdoor venues such as the Birmingham Zoo. **Opera Birmingham** (© **205/975-2787;** www.operabirmingham.org) stages fall and spring productions, offering classics such as Puccini's *Madame Butterfly* and Verdi's *Rigoletto.* In addition, the company promotes up-and-coming vocal talents through competitions and recitals. One of the primary performing arts venues is the **Alys Robinson Stephens Performing Arts Center,** 1200 10th Ave. S. (© **877/ART-TIKS** [278-8457] or 205/975-ARTS [975-2787]; www.alysstephens.org), a multiple-theater complex on the campus of the University of Alabama Birmingham. In addition to performances by local performing-arts organizations, the venue attracts top-name entertainers and touring productions.

THE BAR & CLUB SCENE   To find out what's on, pick up a copy of the *Birmingham News,* or check its website at **www.al.com.** There's always a big-name act coming to the **Verizon Wireless Music Center** (© **800/277-1700** or 205/985-4900; www.livenation. com) in the town of Pelham, a short drive south on I-65. Recent headliners have included John Fogerty, Willie Nelson, Bela Fleck, and Rascal Flatts.

Jazz lovers are on a first-name basis with **Ona's Music Room,** 423 20th St. S. (© **205/ 322-4662;** www.onasmusicroom.com), where swing, rhythm and blues, and contemporary jazz performances are held Thursday through Saturday nights. Another favored hangout is the **22nd Street Jazz and Blues Café,** 710 22nd St. S. (© **205/252-0407**). In the Five Points South area, the **Nick,** 2510 10th Ave. S. (© **205/252-3831;** www. thenickrocks.com), is the preeminent alternative rock venue, drawing heavily from the college crowd at nearby University of Alabama Birmingham.

---

2 MONTGOMERY

GETTING THERE   **By Plane**   Most tourists flying into Montgomery do so via Birmingham (see p. 416 for airport information). By car, it is about 90 miles south along Interstate 65 from Birmingham to Montgomery. However, three carriers serve **Montgomery Regional Airport,** 4445 Selma Hwy. (© **334/281-5040;** www.montgomeryairport.org), located 15 minutes from downtown on U.S. Hwy. 80 West. **Northwest Airlink** (© **800/225-2525**) offers daily flights to Memphis; **Atlantic Southeast** (© **800/221-1212**) to Atlanta and Dallas/Fort Worth; and **US Airways Express** (© **800/428-4322**) to Charlotte, North Carolina.

By Car   The major routes into Montgomery are I-65 from the north (Birmingham) and southwest (Mobile), and I-85 from the northeast (Atlanta).

VISITOR INFORMATION   Contact the **Montgomery Area Visitor Center,** 300 Water St., Montgomery, AL 36104 (© **800/240-9452** or 334/262-0013; www.visiting montgomery.com).

THE GULF SOUTH

6

MONTGOMERY

GETTING AROUND   The nation's first electric streetcar system began in Montgomery in 1886. Motorized replicas of those cars (they're actually buses) make up the fleet of the **Lightning Route Trolley** (© **334/262-0013**; www.montgomerytransit.com), which provides daily service from the visitor center in Historic Union Station to major downtown points of interest, including Old Alabama Town, the Civil Rights Memorial, and the Rosa Parks Museum. One-way fares start at $1. For exact hours, call the visitor center (see above).

If you want to explore outlying areas, such as the Alabama Shakespeare Festival or Montgomery Museum of Fine Arts, you will need a car.

FAST FACTS   A major local hospital is **Jackson Hospital,** 1725 Pine St. (© **334/293-8000**). Although there are no drugstores with 24-hour pharmacies in the metro area, there's a **CVS** pharmacy at 1525 Forest Ave. (© **334/263-9272**). In downtown, you'll find **Adams Drug,** 934 Adams Ave. (© **334/264-3496**). Sales tax is 10%; hotel tax is 12.5%.

SPECIAL EVENTS & FESTIVALS   The city's premier music festival, **Jubilee CityFest** (© **334/834-7220;** www.jubileecityfest.org), features nationally known entertainers on several stages throughout the downtown area Memorial Day weekend.

WHAT TO SEE & DO

Montgomery is in the flat south-central part of Alabama, perched along the banks of the Alabama River. All of the city's civil rights sites are downtown. To see more of the area's cultural attractions, drive to Blount Cultural Park, off I-85 North at exit 6 (follow the signs). Old Cloverdale features popular restaurants and boutiques. To get there, take Hull Street south out of downtown. It will take you straight into the district.

Civil Rights Sites

If there is a single don't-miss attraction in Montgomery, it is the wonderful **Rosa Parks Library and Museum,** 252 Montgomery St. (© **334/241-8615;** http://montgomery. troy.edu/rosaparks/museum), at Troy State University. Through a series of galleries, interactive displays help viewers empathize with the black seamstress Rosa Parks, who sparked the Montgomery Bus Boycott in 1955 by refusing to give her seat on the bus to a white man. Her subsequent arrest made international headlines and led to a citywide boycott of public transportation, led by the Rev. Martin Luther King, Jr. An emotional highlight of the museum is the gallery that re-creates a 1955 street scene with a replica of the bus on which Parks rode. In a multimedia tableau, actors' dialogue is played over video images to bring alive that fateful encounter that sparked a long ride to freedom for the city's black population. There's now a children's wing, which provides computer stations where visitors may research historical documents and hear testimonials from those associated with the Montgomery Bus Boycott. Admission is $5.50 for those 13 and older, and $3.50 for kids 12 and under. The museum is closed Sunday and holidays.

In keeping with the civil rights theme in Montgomery, we highly recommend a visit to **Dexter Avenue King Memorial Baptist Church,** 454 Dexter Ave. (© **334/263-3970;** www.dexterkingmemorial.org). This National Historic Landmark is where the Rev. Martin Luther King, Jr., first preached as a young pastor, and it was from this pulpit that he rose to the challenge of leading the Montgomery bus boycott. In the basement of the church, a large mural depicts King's civil rights crusade, which took him from Montgomery to Selma and, ultimately, to Memphis, where he was assassinated. Guided tours ($2 adults, $1 children) of the church are offered Monday and Thursday at 10am and 2pm. Self-guided walk-through tours are available on Friday; Saturday tours are by

The Civil Rights Trail

The picturesque small town of Selma, Alabama, a leisurely hour's drive south-west of Montgomery, makes a good day trip for those who want to explore more civil rights history. The **National Voting Rights Museum**, 1012 Water Ave. (© **334/418-0800**), is a simple but moving collection of galleries and artifacts that detail the fight by black residents to obtain rights to vote.

Selma is best known for the aborted March 7, 1965, voting rights march, "Bloody Sunday," when civil rights protestors trying to march from Selma to Montgomery were brutalized by tear gas, cattle prods, and clubs at the hands of police, state troopers, and local vigilantes. The bloody riot took place on the Edmund Pettus Bridge, named for a Confederate hero who, after the Civil War, lost his seat in the state legislature to a black man. For a free *Black Heritage Guide* that includes information about prominent civil rights sites in various Alabama cities and towns, contact the **Alabama Bureau of Tourism and Travel** (© **800/ALABAMA** [252-2262]; www.800alabama.com).

appointment only. Sunday tours are not conducted, but visitors are welcome to attend the worship service that usually begins at 10:30am.

In conjunction with a visit to Dr. King's church, Montgomery has opened another site that explores the personal side of the slain civil rights leader. The newly restored **Dexter Parsonage Museum,** 309 S. Jackson St. (© **334/261-3270;** www.dakmf.org), is a few blocks from the center of downtown. King lived in the parsonage from 1954 to 1960 while leading the Montgomery Bus Boycott. The bungalow with the wide front porch was built in the 1920s, but the interior has been restored to the style of the mid-1950s, when King lived here with his new bride, Coretta Scott King, while he served as minister of Dexter Avenue Baptist Church. Tourists may enter the study where King read, studied, and typed his sermons, often while listening to music. Kids are usually amazed to see the small 1950s-era kitchen, which includes a tub-style washing machine and a Frigidaire "icebox." Furniture and furnishings used by the King family fill the home, including the dining room where the Kings entertained fellow church members and conducted business meetings. In chilling detail, a tour guide recounts the day when a bomb exploded in the parsonage's front window and destroyed much of the home, though the King family escaped injury. Admission costs $3 adults, $2 children 11 and under. *Note:* The Dexter church and parsonage are not within easy walking distance of each other; be prepared to drive.

Outside the offices of the Southern Poverty Law Center downtown lies the city's most impressive monument. Designed by renowned architect Maya Lin (whose best-known work is the Vietnam Veterans Memorial in the nation's capital; p. 202), the **Civil Rights Memorial and Center,** 400 Washington Ave. (© **334/956-8200;** www.splcenter.org), is a simple yet stunning touchstone for absorbing the impact and meaning of the civil rights movement that tore apart this city and so much of the nation. The names of some of those who died during the struggle are inscribed in a circular black granite table over which a gentle stream of water flows. Adjacent to the Memorial, the new **Civil Rights Memorial Center** provides an in-depth look at civil rights martyrs. Educational exhibits, a 69-seat theater, and a Wall of Tolerance are among the displays. Admission is $2 for adults and free to children 17 and under. The Center is closed Sunday. Civil War buffs should not miss the **First White House of the Confederacy,** 644 Washington Ave. (© **334/242-1861**), where Jefferson Davis and his family once lived. The Confederate White House contains period furnishings and many of Davis's personal belongings. It was here that Confederate President Davis gave the order to fire on Fort Sumter. Closed weekends; admission is free.

More Things to See & Do

The **Hank Williams Museum,** 118 Commerce St. (© **334/262-3600;** www.thehank williamsmuseum.com), is a labor of love for the venue's founder, who was a friend and a fan of the beloved country music singer/songwriter who shot to fame in the 1940s. The centerpiece of the museum is the baby-blue 1952 Cadillac in which Williams was riding when he collapsed and died. Other galleries overflow with vinyl 78 records; many of Williams's belongings, costumes, and guitars; and an antique jukebox on which visitors can hear such classics as "Hey Good Lookin'" and "I'm So Lonesome I Could Cry." Williams is buried in Oakwood Cemetery Annex, 1304 Upper Wetumpka Rd., and there's a bronze statue of the lanky entertainer in the heart of downtown. If you're interested in seeing these, the museum offers directions on how to get to both sites. Admission is $8 adults, $3 children 11 and under.

Another fun-filled attraction in the downtown area is **Old Alabama Town,** 301 Columbus St. (© **888/240-1850** or 334/240-4500; www.oldalabamatown.com), a reconstruction of an Alabama village in the 19th and early 20th centuries. Among the more than 40 restored structures are homes from the era, along with a tavern, drugstore, doctor's office, schoolhouse, cotton gin, and grocery. Self-guided walking tours are offered daily. Admission costs $8 adults, $4 children ages 6 to 18. Closed Sunday.

Set amid the verdant **Blount Cultural Park** just outside of downtown lies the **Montgomery Museum of Fine Arts,** 1 Museum Dr. (© **334/244-5700;** www.mmfa.org). The free museum features Southern regional art as well as paintings and prints by the old masters. If the museum has a signature artwork, it is Edward Hicks's well-known *The Peaceable Kingdom* (ca. 1830). This magnificent building also houses Alabama's first interactive fine arts gallery for children, ARTWORKS. All activities are hands-on, giving children ample opportunity for creative exploration.

Literary enthusiasts should seek out the **F. Scott and Zelda Fitzgerald Museum,** 919 Felder Ave. (© **334/264-4222;** www.fitzgerald-museum.com). Fitzgerald, author of such 20th-century classic novels as *The Great Gatsby* and *Tender Is the Night,* lived here off and on during the early years of the couple's tempestuous relationship. F. Scott met Montgomery native Zelda while he was stationed in the city during World War I. After their marriage, the couple lived in this rambling old home that now houses a modest museum. Although it's not a heavily attended tourist attraction, it is the only museum in the world devoted to the author. After watching a video about the Fitzgeralds, guests may peruse handwritten love letters Zelda wrote to her husband and admire her cigarette holder, a few pieces of jewelry, and other belongings, along with books and historical archives. Zelda's self-portraits and other paintings and drawings also fill the space, lending poignancy to the telling of her life story, in which she teetered in and out of madness for most of her adult life. Admission is free, but donations of $5 for adults are accepted. The museum is open Wednesday through Friday from 10am to 2pm, Saturday and Sunday 1 to 5pm.

The city's minor league baseball team, lovingly named the **Montgomery Biscuits,** 200 Coosa St. (© **334/323-2255;** www.biscuitsbaseball.com), is an affiliate of the Tampa

Bay Rays. The team plays at downtown's Riverwalk Stadium, at the corner of Coosa and Tallapoosa streets. Stadium seats have excellent sightlines, and a picnic area makes a great place for families to spread out and enjoy a game. Concessions sold on-site include all the traditional game-day fare, as well as the eponymous Southern biscuits and honey. There's also a playground, as well as lots of activities designed to appeal to all ages. Tickets range from $6 to $12.

Riverfront Amphitheater, 355 Coosa St. (© **334/240-4092;** www.funontheriver. net), is the latest addition to the ongoing Riverwalk development. This outdoor venue, with a white-columned pergola, overlooks the Alabama River in this shady setting for picnics, concerts, movies, and plays. A "splash pad" water feature cools off the kids. The park is free and open to the public year-round, though admission fees are charged for some amphitheater events.

WHERE TO STAY

Lodging choices are somewhat limited in downtown Montgomery, which has only a few reputable hotels and one excellent bed-and-breakfast, but all the familiar hotel-motel chains can be found near the interstate exits.

There is only one bed-and-breakfast in town, but we can heartily recommend it. **Red Bluff Cottage Bed and Breakfast,** 551 Clay St. (© **888/551-2529** or 334/264-0056; www.redbluffcottage.com), is an immaculate and cozy retreat for travelers who appreciate being pampered in homey surroundings. Four spacious guest rooms are beautifully furnished with quilts, antiques, and overstuffed furniture—as well as wireless Internet access. From the front porch, there are lovely views of the State Capitol and Alabama River. In the quiet Cottage Hill residential neighborhood, Red Bluff has easy interstate access and is just a few blocks from downtown attractions. Children are welcome. Doubles run from $110 to $155.

Downtown's newest and best full-service hotel is the **Embassy Suites Hotel Montgomery–Conference Center,** 300 Tallapoosa St. (© **334/269-5055;** www.embassy suites.com). Across the street from the visitor center and trolley stop, the all-suite hotel offers kitchenette-equipped suites, an indoor pool, and a fitness center. Rates ($119–$149) include breakfast. Despite its outdated exterior, the **Capitol Inn,** 205 N. Goldthwaite St. (© **866/471-9028** or 334/265-3844; www.capitolinnhotel.com), in the heart of downtown, is an excellent bargain. Rates are about $75 double. Rooms are tidy and basic, but the friendly staff and caring service create a welcoming atmosphere. There's also an outdoor pool. Foodies, take note: Locals and in-the-know travelers alike storm the motel's restaurant at breakfast and lunch for old-fashioned Southern cooking that locals brag is the best in town. If you're taking in a few plays at the Alabama Shakespeare Festival, the attractive, budget-priced **Fairfield Inn Montgomery,** 5601 Carmichael Rd. (© **334/270-0007;** www.marriott.com), located a mile from the theater, is convenient and comfortable. Free local calls and an outdoor pool are other perks. Fridges and microwaves are available in some rooms. Rates run $64, plus tax, double.

WHERE TO DINE

Montgomery has no shortage of good restaurants, many of which specialize in Southern cooking. Since the 1940s, **Martin's Restaurant,** 1796 Carter Hill Rd. (© **334/265-1767**), has been serving home-style cooking at various locations around town. Today Martin's sits in a modern shopping center near the local country club. The food is unpretentious, plentiful, and inexpensive. Did somebody say pies? They're legendary! Our weakness is the creamy coconut, piled with golden meringue. You may want to steer clear of Martin's on Sunday after church, when the place can become very crowded. Main courses range from $5 to $7. Downtown's newest restaurant, **Nobles,** 129 Montgomery St. (© 334/262-3326; www.noblesandoliveroom.com), is a casually sophisticated lunch spot serving generous salads, seafood entrees, and Southern staples such as fried pork chops. Sweet iced tea is the perfect accompaniment. The restaurant also has a full bar. Main courses cost $12 to $16.

One of the newest fine-dining restaurants in Montgomery is **Garrett's,** 7780 Atlanta Hwy. (© 334/396-9950). Locally owned and operated by chef Gary Garner, the upscale eatery features Art Deco decor and a menu specializing in steaks and seafood. Reservations are recommended. Open for dinner only Tuesday to Saturday.

In the Old Cloverdale district, there are a couple of tempting dining options. Scores of young professionals dominate happy hour at **Sinclair's,** 1051 E. Fairview Ave. (© 334/834-7462; www.sinclairsrestaurants.com), a locally owned bar and grill. The menu is varied, running from spaghetti pie made with lean turkey to Buffalo chicken wings, specialty burgers, and seafood. There's also a decent wine list. Service is unassuming and efficient. There are two other area Sinclair's locations, including one at 7847 Vaughn Rd. (© 334/271-7654). Main courses cost $10 to $23.

MONTGOMERY AFTER DARK

THE PERFORMING ARTS   The city's cultural pride and joy, the **Alabama Shakespeare Festival (ASF),** 1 Festival Dr. (© 800/841-4-ASF [841-4273] or 334/271-5353; www.asf. net), is renowned throughout the nation for its high-caliber performances and ambitious programming. Performances are staged in two theaters within the $22-million Carolyn Blount Theatre complex. The ASU operates year-round, producing 14 world-class

Cruise Through Mobile

The gateway to southern Alabama's pristine beaches on the Gulf of Mexico is the bayside city of **Mobile.** Since 2004 (with a temporary interruption following Hurricane Katrina), Mobile became a cruise port, when Carnival Cruise Lines' *Holiday* began launching 4- and 5-day cruises to Cozumel and the Yucatán out of the city's harbor. Pre- and post-cruise hotel options include the **Battle House Hotel: A Renaissance Hotel Home,** 26 N. Royal St. (© 866/316-5957 or 251/338-2000; www.marriott.com), which opened in May 2007 following a $200-million renovation. The historic 1852 property has a rich roster of past guests, including Ulysses S. Grant and Babe Ruth. Rates range from $170 to $194 double. A luxury spa was slated to open in fall 2008.

Attractions close to the port include the **Museum of Mobile,** 111 S. Royal St. (© 251/208-7569; www.museumofmobile.com), an interesting spot detailing the city's 300-year-history. Admission is $5 adults, $4 seniors, and $3 students. When you've worked up an appetite, great seafood awaits you at **Wintzell's Oyster House,** 605 Dauphin St. (© 251/432-4605; www.wintzellsoyster house.com). For more information on the city, contact the **Mobile Bay Convention & Visitors Bureau,** 1 S. Water St. (© 800/5-MOBILE [566-2453] or 251/208-2000; www.mobile.org).

productions annually, including 3 works of William Shakespeare, as well as classics by such playwrights as George Bernard Shaw, Anton Chekhov, and Tennessee Williams. The ASF also commissions new works.

The city boasts two ballet companies, the professional **Montgomery Ballet** (© 334/409-0522; www.montgomeryballet.com) and **Alabama Dance Theatre** (© 334/241-2590; www.alabamadancetheatre.com), which stages traditional and contemporary works in two major performances annually. The 75-piece **Montgomery Symphony** (© 334/240-4004; www.montgomerysymphony.org) performs 10 concerts a year. Its primary venue is the **Davis Theater for the Performing Arts,** 251 Montgomery St., at Troy State University. Built in 1941, the **Capri Theatre,** 1045 E. Fairview Ave. (© 334/262-4858; www.capritheatre.org), was the city's first movie palace. Since being purchased by a community group in 1983, the venue has operated as a nonprofit cinema specializing in independent films. Call for features and showtimes. One of the newest entertainment venues in Montgomery is **Faulkner University Dinner Theatre,** 5345 Atlanta Hwy. (© 334/386-7190; www.faulkner.edu/campuslife/dinnertheatre.asp), where Broadway-style family entertainment is offered in a Christian-based atmosphere.

3 HIGHLIGHTS OF MISSISSIPPI

CLARKSDALE

An unmistakable vibe pervades the languid Mississippi Delta town of Clarksdale, about an hour's drive south of Memphis, Tennessee. It's by turns eerie and endearing, a flat landscape where fertile fields, endless railroad tracks, and run-down shacks are giving way to pockets of progress—an upscale restaurant, a strip mall full of dollar stores and fast-food drive-throughs, a museum celebrating the blues music that took root here in the early 20th century and changed the course of popular music.

This is a good place to begin a driving tour of legendary **Hwy. 61 (U.S. 61),** the two-lane road that took blues legends such as Muddy Waters, Robert Johnson, and B. B. King north from the impoverished cotton plantations of the South to the cities of Memphis and Chicago to the north. The long drive south will take you through the proverbial dusty Delta towns, and cities such as Greenville, Vicksburg, and, finally, where Mississippi meets Louisiana in the southwest part of the state, historic Natchez.

Essentials

GETTING THERE   By Plane   Major airlines fly into Memphis International Airport (see p. 325, "Memphis" in chapter 4). Rent a car and head south on Hwy. 61, past the casinos in Tunica and on into Clarksdale.

By Car   The major route into Clarksdale is **Hwy. 61,** from Memphis, to the north.

VISITOR INFORMATION   Contact the **Clarksdale/Coahoma County Chamber of Commerce,** 1540 Desoto Ave., Clarksdale, MS 39614 (© 800/626-3764 or 662/627-7337; www.clarksdale.com).

What to See & Do

As you ease into town, your first stop should be at the **Crossroads,** at the intersection of highways 49 and 61. The site is legendary as the place where bluesman Robert Johnson is said to have sold his soul to the devil in exchange for the guitar prowess that has made him one of the most revered musicians of the past century. A guitar statue marks the spot.

From here, your next stop should be the **Delta Blues Museum,** 1 Blues Alley (© 662/672-6820; www.deltabluesmuseum.org). Housed in a renovated train depot built in 1918, it includes a treasure-trove of old blues memorabilia, including the log cabin where Muddy Waters grew up, on a cotton plantation not far from here. There are displays, musical instruments, and costumes of some of the Mississippi-born greats, such as Albert King, James Cotton, and Son House. Admission is $6 adults, $3 children 6 to 12; it is open daily except Sunday. Bessie Smith fans can do a drive-by tour of the **Riverside Hotel,** 615 Sunflower Ave. (© 662/624-9163), the former blacks-only hospital where the great blues singer died after a car crash in 1937. Blues legends Sonny Boy Williamson II, Ike Turner, Robert Nighthawk, and even politician Robert F. Kennedy once stayed here. Today it still operates as a motel, but most visitors see it only from their windshields.

While downtown, don't miss **Cathead Delta Blues & Folk Art,** 252 Delta Ave. (© 662/624-5992; www.cathead.biz). The store sells new blues CDs, DVDs, and books, as well as eye-catching—and affordable—folk and outsider art. The hepcat-cool hot spot also serves as a clearinghouse for what's going on around town. Check Cathead's chalkboard that tells of weekly music events and updates. The store also occasionally has book signings and special events. You'll likely find the owner chatting up tourists who've made the pilgrimage for some serious blues sightseeing.

Where to Stay & Dine

There's a pitiful lack of decent hotels in Clarksdale. Your best bet is to grab one of the inexpensive to moderately priced chain properties along State Street. Equally amenable are the **Comfort Inn,** 818 S. State St. (© 662/627-5122), and the nearby **Best Western,** 710 S. State St. (© 662/627-9292).

The best restaurant in town is **Madidi,** 164 Delta Ave. (© 662/627-7770; www.madidires.com), the upscale eatery and bar opened in 2001 by actor Morgan Freeman, who grew up in the area and is still seen around town from time to time. (He is also a partner in **Ground Zero Blues Club,** reminiscent of an old juke joint, in downtown.) Other popular venues are **Abe's Bar-B-Que,** 616 State St. (© 662/624-9947), and **Sarah's Kitchen,** 203 Sunflower Ave. (© 662/627-3239), which serves Southern cooking.

Shacking Up

In the lodging category of "too creepy for anyone but the most die-hard blues fan," there's the **Shack Up Inn,** 1 Commissary Circle (© 662/624-8329; www.shackupinn.com), on old Hwy. 49 south of Clarksdale. Billed as Mississippi's oldest B&B (Bed and Beer), the property is on the site of a weedy cotton gin littered with rusting farming implements, old road signs, and crumbling sharecropper shacks that have been modernized enough to accommodate easy-to-please travelers in search of a place to crash—and great music at the on-premises Commissary Club. Some shacks have kitchenettes. Rates range from $50 to $75 per room. There's a $5 additional fee per person, but, hey—rates include tax *and* a Moon Pie on your pillow.

Essentials

GETTING THERE   Vicksburg is near the midpoint along Mississippi's fabled Hwy. 61, just north of Natchez and a few hours' drive south of Clarksdale.

VISITOR INFORMATION   Contact the **Vicksburg Convention and Visitors Bureau,** P.O. Box 110, Vicksburg, MS 39181 (© **800/221-3536** or 601/636-9421; www.visit vicksburg.com).

Civil War Sites

Vicksburg National Military Park, 3201 Clay St. (© **601/636-0583;** www.nps.gov/ vick), the city's best-known tourist attraction, operates under the auspices of the National Park Service. One of the oldest national parks in the country, it was established in 1899 and today draws more than one million visitors annually. Tours begin at the Visitors Center, where Confederate swords, uniforms, and other artifacts from the Siege of Vicksburg are on display. A tedious 18-minute film may stir history buffs but will bore children. It does, however, set the stage for a driving tour of the park. Get in your vehicle and go on the 16-mile self-guided trail that follows Union and Confederate siege lines. Tombstones and markers convey sobering statistics about the soldiers who suffered in the Civil War. The newest addition to the park is the **Mississippi African American Monument,** to honor the black soldiers who served during the Vicksburg Campaign. Aside from its rich history, the vast park is popular for such outdoor pastimes as bird-watching, hiking, and bicycling. The Visitors Center is open daily from 8am to 5pm. Admission is $8 per car.

The **Old Court House Museum–Eva W. Davis Memorial,** 1008 Cherry St. (© **601/ 636-0741;** www.oldcourthouse.org), is a National Historic Landmark. Built by slaves in 1858, the home has seen such figures as Ulysses S. Grant, Jefferson Davis, Booker T. Washington, and Theodore Roosevelt pass through its doors. Admission costs $5 adults, $3 children. In the historic downtown district, the **Biedenharn Museum of Coca-Cola Memorabilia,** 1107 Washington St. (© **601/638-6514**), is a gaudy red-and-white shrine to all things Coke. It's in the building where Coke was first bottled in 1894. From billboards of Santa Claus sipping from ice-cold bottles to the ad-related merchandise of today, the soda shop is worth a quick peek. Admission costs $2.75 adults, $1.75 children 11 and under.

Shopping

Shopping enthusiasts, or those who aren't interested in historic homes or Civil War sites, will be thrilled with the factory outlet mall. **Vicksburg Factory Outlets,** 4000 S. Frontage Rd. (© **601/636-7434;** www.vicksburgfactoryoutlet.com), offers bargains on name-brand goods by Bass, Claire's, Gap, Lane Bryant, and Reebok, among others.

Where to Stay & Dine

Sure, there are newer chain hotels on the interstates leading into Vicksburg, but to experience the true flavor of gracious Southern living, consider staying in one of the city's many historic homes that also double as bed-and-breakfast properties.

The eight-room **Anchuca,** 1010 First East St. (© **888/686-0111** or 601/661-0111; www.anchuca.com), a peach-colored Greek Revival mansion built in 1830, features a year-round swimming pool. The inn's rooms are furnished with period antiques and fine linens; many sport canopy beds. Rates run from $180 to $210. Four guest rooms in the Carriage House next door have rates of $125 to $135 double. Children 14 and under are not permitted.

Built in 1840, **Cedar Grove Mansion Inn,** 2200 Oak St. (© **800/862-1300** or 601/636-1000; www.cedargroveinn.com), sits on 4 acres overlooking the Mississippi River. There are 33 rooms $120 to $260 double, all with private bathrooms; some units sport Jacuzzi tubs, fireplaces, or canopy beds (Ulysses S. Grant once slept in one of them). **Annabelle,** 501 Speed St. (© **800/791-2000** or 601/638-2000; www.annabellebnb.com), is a Victorian Italianate home that dates back to 1868. The eight rooms, including a suite with a kitchen, are housed in the main mansion and an adjoining two-story building that overlooks an outdoor pool—a definite advantage during the hot summers. Rooms ($93–$115 double, $125–$160 suite) feature high ceilings, private bathrooms (one with a Jacuzzi), and period antiques.

Back out on the highways, there are several decent chain hotels and motels. Try the **Jameson Inn,** 3975 S. Frontage Rd. (© **800/526-3766** or 601/619-7799; www.jamesoninns.com); **Hampton Inn,** 3332 Clay St. (© **800/568-4044** or 601/636-6100; www.hamptoninn.com); or the aging but popular **Battlefield Inn,** 4137 I-20 Frontage Rd. (© **800/359-9363** or 601/638-5811; www.bestwesternbattlefieldinn.com). Rooms at any of these spots range from $85 to $154 double.

If you have time to sample only one meal in Vicksburg, make it **Walnut Hills Restaurant,** 1214 Adams St. (© **601/638-4910;** www.walnuthillsms.net). It looks like any other common, turn-of-the-20th-century house on the street of this residential neighborhood—except for the long lines of families that curl across the wide front porch. Walnut Hills is a longtime local institution that serves sensational Southern cooking family style. Fried chicken, shrimp, casseroles, green beans, mashed potatoes, and plenty of corn bread and sweet iced tea are always on tap. Main courses cost $10 to $20. Closed Saturday. The city's best locally owned seafood restaurant is **Rowdy's Family Catfish Shack,** at the intersection of highways 27 and 80, I-20 exit 5B (© **601/638-2375**). Order the platter, with coleslaw, fries, and hush puppies. Main courses cost $6 to $16. Another beloved eatery is **Goldie's Trail Bar-B-Que,** 4127 S. Washington St. (© **601/636-9839**), an informal place for pork and beef ribs, chicken, and all the trimmings. Main courses cost $5 to $15. Closed Sunday.

NATCHEZ

Boasting more antebellum homes than anywhere in the U.S., this charming town on a bluff overlooking the Mississippi River is best visited in the spring and fall, when pilgrimages to historic houses are in full swing. With its semitropical climate, however, the city is pleasant year-round, though it can get muggy during the summer months.

Essentials

GETTING THERE   Fly into Jackson, Mississippi (see "Visiting Jackson," p. 434), and drive along U.S. 155 S. to Brookhaven (U.S. 94). Take U.S. 84 straight into Natchez. If you're driving in from New Orleans (trip time: 3¹⁄₂ hr.) in neighboring Louisiana, take I-10 West to I-55 North. Follow I-55 North to Hwy. 84 West and take the third McComb exit, which leads to Hwy. 61 and into Natchez.

VISITOR INFORMATION   One of the most attractive welcome centers in the South awaits travelers in the spacious **Natchez Visitor Reception Center,** 640 S. Canal St. (© **800/647-6724;** www.visitnatchez.com). An introductory film about the city's history provides an excellent overview for tourists about to embark on the area's Civil War–era attractions. Elsewhere in the visitor center, you'll find interactive exhibits, displays, and oversize maps, as well as brochures, a gift shop, and a helpful staff.

In addition, advance information is available by contacting the **Natchez Convention and Visitors Bureau,** 211 Main St., Natchez, MS 39120 (© 800/647-6724 or 601/442-5880; www.visitnatchez.com). The staff is especially helpful to travelers looking for suggested itineraries or other tourist recommendations.

What to See & Do

Antebellum homes are everywhere in Natchez, the oldest permanent settlement on the Mississippi River. The **Natchez Spring Pilgrimage** (© 800/647-6742; www.natchez pilgrimage.com), which occurs annually mid-March through mid-April, is an opportunity to visit all 32 of the city's antebellum homes, hosted by Southern belles in hoop skirts and other period dress.

You will need several days to see all the homes, or you can pick and choose a few. Representative of most is **Rosalie,** 100 Orleans St. (© 601/446-5676), which was built in the early 1820s and later purchased by the Daughters of the American Revolution, who operate it as a museum. The Federal-style mansion overlooks the Mississippi River, and its 4-acre gardens delight the senses with winding brick pathways and wrought-iron benches. Admission is $8 for adults and $4 for students. Atypical of the area's plantation homes is **Longwood,** 140 Lower Woodville Rd. (© 601/442-5193), one of the most unusual mansions of Natchez. Designated as both a National Historic Landmark and a site on the Civil War Discovery Trail, it is a lavish octagonal home (the largest of its kind in the country) dating from 1859. The 32-room home has four floors and a solarium and observatory. It is crowned with a Byzantine dome. Construction on the interior of the home stopped during the Civil War and was never completed, but Longwood is nevertheless a sight to behold. Admission is $10 for adults (including teens) and $8 for youth ages 3 to 12.

Aside from mansions, there are other sites of historical importance in Natchez. Drive by **Holy Family Catholic Church,** 28 St. Catherine St. (© 601/445-5700), the state's first African-American Catholic church. Built in 1894, the sanctuary is a beautifully preserved landmark where Masses are still held. Tours are available by appointment only. Established in 1821, the **Natchez City Cemetery,** 2 Cemetery Rd. (© 601/445-4981), is a hauntingly beautiful green space dotted with tree-shaded graves dating back to the 1700s. Guests may drive through these hilly bluffs, which overlook the Mississippi River. If you'd like to know more about the cemetery, pick up a brochure at the Visitors Reception Area. It's open dawn to dusk.

Where to Stay

If you want to live like a Southern plantation owner, book a room at one of the area's plantation inns. **Dunleith Historic Inn,** 84 Homochitto St. (© 800/433-2445 or 601/446-8500; www.dunleith.com), is an august 1856 Greek Revival mansion that dominates a 40-acre spread. The 26 rooms are decorated in period style and offer high ceilings and bathrobes, along with amenities such as an outdoor swimming pool. Rates range from $135 to $240 double and include full breakfast; children 13 and under are not accepted. The much-acclaimed (and nonsmoking) **Monmouth Plantation,** 36 Melrose Ave. (© 800/828-4531 or 601/442-5852; www.monmouthplantation.com), has 30 lavish rooms in its 1818 mansion and modern, antiques-packed cottages nestled throughout the property's wooded and meticulously landscaped 26 acres. Several rooms offer canopy beds and/or Jacuzzi tubs. Rates range from $195 to $395 double and include full breakfast and evening canapés. Children 13 and under are not accepted.

Visiting Jackson

If you're driving through Mississippi, the capital city of Jackson—a pleasant if not particularly picturesque city of 184,000 people—makes a good home base for exploring sites in the southern half of the state. It's also your best alternative to flying into Memphis, Tennessee (p. 325), which is just a few miles over the border from the northwest corner of Mississippi.

Jackson is near the intersection of **Interstate 55,** which runs north and south, and **Interstate 20,** which runs east and west. Several major air carriers about 40 daily flights to **Jackson International Airport** (© **601/939-5631;** www.jmaa.com) from such cities as Detroit, Baltimore/Washington, D.C., Atlanta, and Houston. All major car-rental agencies are located at the airport. **Amtrak,** 300 W. Capitol St. (© **800/872-7245** or 601/355-6350; www.amtrak. com), offers daily passenger rail service to New Orleans and Chicago.

The **Mississippi Museum of Art,** 201 E. Pascagoula St. (© **601/960-1515;** www.msmuseumart.org), includes everything from folk art and photography to pre-Columbian art and American landscapes.

Elsewhere in Jackson, a visit to the **Eudora Welty House and Garden,** 119 Pinehurst St. (© 601/353-7762; www.mdah.state.ms.us/welty/index.html), is a must for literary fans. The late Eudora Welty (1909–2001) was one of Mississippi's most beloved writers and photographers. The Pulitzer Prize winner and her mother, Chestina, lived in the historic Belhaven neighborhood, where they cultivated a backyard flower garden bursting with camellias, roses, iris, jonquils, hyacinths, day lilies, and other perennials. The house is open for tours by reservation only Wednesday through Friday at 9 and 11am and 1 and 3pm. The

More modest in scope but still elegant is the **Natchez Eola Hotel,** 110 N. Pearl (© **866/445-3652** or 601/445-6000; www.natchezeola.com), a four-story red-brick hotel built in 1927. Located in the heart of downtown, the property has a grand but dark lobby dominated by marble, chandeliers, and oversize floral arrangements. There's also a pleasant lounge and outdoor courtyard reminiscent of old New Orleans. Guest rooms are a bit more bright and cheerful, and contain all the basics travelers have come to expect. *A bonus:* All rooms have ceiling fans, important in the sweltering summer months, even on an air-conditioned property. Rates start at $121 double per night.

Natchez also has a wealth of wonderful bed-and-breakfast properties. Most are located in historic homes or bungalows and offer comfortable rooms and home-cooked breakfasts at reasonable rates. The inn owners are almost universally warm and gracious, eager to extend old-fashioned Southern hospitality to the thousands of tourists that are the backbone of Natchez's economy.

Where to Dine

On the lush grounds of Stanton Hall, the **Carriage House Restaurant,** 401 High St. (© **601/445-5151**), open since 1926, serves lunch daily and dinner only during pilgrimage tours. Sip a mint julep in the dining room, where polished, pale-wood furnishings

house itself, listed on the National Register of Historic Places, is a two-story Tudor Revival–style residence built in 1924. For more information, call ✆ **601/353-7762** or e-mail weltytours@mdah.state.ms.us.

History buffs will want to see some of the city's old buildings downtown. The **Mississippi State Capitol,** 400 High St., is a Beaux Arts beauty that resembles the nation's capitol in Washington, D.C. Free tours are conducted weekdays. Nearby, the **Mississippi Governor's Mansion,** 300 E. Capitol St. (✆ **601/359-6421**), is a fine example of Greek Revival architecture dating from 1841. Free tours are held Tuesday through Friday mornings.

For antiques shopping, gallery hopping, and myriad drinking and dining options, take State Street north from Woodrow Wilson to Meadowbrook Road to the **Fondren District,** 3318 N. State St. (✆ **601/981-9606;** www.fondren.org).

Hotels and motels in Jackson cater to a range of tastes and budgets. One of the nicest is the **Fairview Inn,** 734 Fairview St., Jackson, MS 39202 (✆ **601/948-3429;** www.fairviewinn.com), a white mansion with 18 luxurious rooms and formal gardens shaded by ancient magnolias. To reach the Fairview, which is in a lovely residential neighborhood, take I-55 to exit 98A. Rates are from $144 to $314 double. Dating from the 1920s, downtown's standby is the venerable **Edison Walthall Hotel,** 225 E. Capitol St. (✆ **601/948-6161;** www.edisonwalthallhotel.com), which is within a few blocks of the art museum and other downtown sites. From I-55, take the Pearl Street exit.

For more info, contact the **Jackson Convention & Visitors Bureau,** 921 N. President St. (✆ **800/354-7695** or 601/960-1891; www.visitjackson.com).

are illuminated by lots of natural light. The menu features burgers, salads, sandwiches, and Southern staples such as fried chicken. Main courses run about $12.

Check your political correctness at the door if you want a peek at **Mammy's Cupboard,** 555 Hwy. 61 S. (✆ **601/445-8957**), an eye-popping, lunchtime-only landmark known as much for its food (try the chicken salad, or chocolate "mud" pie for dessert) as for the unusual shape of its building. It's essentially a statue several stories high depicting the stereotypical Old South black "Mammy" figure; her hoop skirt forms a dome that houses the restaurant. This is one of those quirky places that you have to see to believe. Entrees run $6 to $8. For a potent combination of tangy, "knock-you-naked" margaritas and spicy tamales, head to another maternalistic favorite, **Fat Mama's Tamales,** 500 S. Canal St. (✆ **601/442-4548**). Look for the cactus-bedecked log cabin aglow with orange neon. Nachos, chili, homemade sweet pickles, and Snickers pie round out the short menu. Nothing here costs over $8. In the downtown area, there are several notable diners, including **Pearl Street Pasta,** 104 A. Pearl St. (✆ **601/442-9284**), and even the unexpected, new **Thai Planet,** 112 N. Commerce St. (✆ **601/442-4220**).

In the area along the river known as Natchez-Under-the-Hill, you'll find **Bowie's Tavern,** 100 Main St. (✆ **601/445-6627;** www.bowiestavern.com). Spirits and pub grub are dished out at this convivial nightspot that's part sports bar and part Old English–style

---

Pull Over & Into the Past

If you're driving the lonely stretch of Hwy. 61 between Natchez and Vicksburg, take a break at the **Old Country Store** in the tiny burg of Lorman. The weathered wooden building used to be a general store and gas station. Today it's a run-down but atmospheric flea market and souvenir shop that also offers a limited selection of hot soul food dishes prepared on the premises.

---

tavern. Televisions carry live sporting events, and there's also occasional live music. Main courses run $9 to $14.

OXFORD

Home to the University of Mississippi, "Ole Miss," Oxford is a quaint small town where daily life revolves around its 150-year-old Court Square. A popular weekend destination for out-of-towners and visiting alumni, Oxford offers an array of great art galleries, bookstores, restaurants, and historic homes. Its proximity to Memphis (about 70 miles) makes it a doable day-trip, but Oxford's offbeat charms might entice you to stay a day or two.

Essentials

GETTING THERE By Car   The major route into Oxford is **I-55** from both the north (Memphis) and south (Jackson). It's about a 90-minute drive.

VISITOR INFORMATION   Contact the **Oxford Tourism Council,** 107 Courthouse Sq., Ste. 1, Oxford, MS 38655 (© **800/758-9177** or 662/234-4680; www.touroxfordms.com).

Exploring the Area

Oxford's favorite son is Nobel Prize–winning author William Faulkner, whose residence from 1930 until his death in 1963 was his beloved home, **Rowan Oak,** Old Taylor Road (© **662/234-3284**). A tour of the grounds, with its graceful magnolias and old farm buildings, is a trip back in time. Inside, literary enthusiasts can still marvel at the author's old manual typewriter and read his handwritten outline for a *Fable,* which is scrawled on the wall of his study. It's closed Monday and major holidays.

The most popular pastime in Oxford is simply strolling the **Square,** where travelers might spot former local residents such as John Grisham. **Square Books,** 160 Courthouse Sq. (© **662/236-2262;** www.squarebooks.com), in business since 1870, is regarded as one of the best independent bookstores in the country. Down the street is its bargain-priced annex, **Off Square Books,** 129 Courthouse Sq. (© **662/236-2828**). Thousands of discounted and remaindered books cram shelves and bins. It's also the site of Square Books' author signings and readings, as well as *Thacker Mountain Radio,* Oxford's original music and literature radio show. Best-selling authors such as Robert Olen Butler, Elmore Leonard, and Ray Blount, Jr., have read their works on the live show. Musical guests have run the gamut from Elvis Costello and Marty Stuart to the Del McCoury band and the North Mississippi Allstars. The show is recorded live from 5:30 to 6:30pm Thursday.

Next door, **Southside Gallery,** 150 Courthouse Sq. (© **662/234-9090**), is an always-interesting place that showcases everything from photography, painting, and sculpture to outsider art by the likes of Howard Finster.

There are only a handful of hotels and motels, most of them chains on the outskirts of town that cater to the parents of college kids and other travelers to the university.

Among the cleanest and most modern are the **Comfort Inn,** 1808 Jackson Ave. S. (© 662/234-6000), which has an outdoor pool ($80 plus tax); the **Days Inn,** 1101 Frontage Rd. (© 662/234-9500; $70 plus tax); and **Holiday Inn Express and Suites,** 112 Heritage Rd. (© 800/465-4329 or 662/236-2500). Rates run about $99 double.

Call ahead and book early if you want to reserve a room at one of the city's bed-and-breakfast properties, which are often booked during weekends when Ole Miss has home football games or other major events. You won't see it advertised much because the place is always full, but try to book a stay at **Puddin' Place,** 1008 University Ave. (© 662/234-1250), a spotless, cheerfully decorated 1892 house that has two large suites with private bathrooms. The owner is in the process of adding a private cottage in the tree-shaded backyard. Gourmet breakfasts are included in the room rates, which usually run $115 double (during Ole Miss football season it's $350 for the 2-night-minimum weekend stay, and the hotel sells out these weekends months in advance).

For guests who don't mind rather simple furnishings and a lack of pizazz, try the **Oliver-Britt House Inn,** 512 Van Buren Ave. (© 662/234-8043). The white-columned, red-brick structure has a front porch packed with potted plants and flowers. There are five guest rooms, all with private bathroom but no phone. Rates run $105 to $150 double; continental breakfast is available weekdays, and a full breakfast is served on weekends.

City Grocery, 152 Courthouse Sq. (© 662/232-8080; www.citygroceryoxford.com), is one of the best restaurants in Mississippi. New Orleans–born chef John Currence finesses spicy cheese grits topped with plump shrimp, mushrooms, and smoked bacon, while offering an array of gourmet salads, soups, and Cajun delicacies. Main courses cost $20 to $25. Reservations are recommended. **Bottletree Bakery,** 923 Van Buren Ave. (© 662/236-5000), is a must if you crave caffeine and the aroma of warm muffins being pulled from the oven. The cheery nook serves pastries and freshly baked breads as well as fine coffees, sandwiches, and salads. Oxford's favorite dive bar is **Proud Larry's,** 211 S. Lamar Blvd. (© 662/236-0050), where live music and drink specials augment a simple menu of burgers, pasta, salads, and hand-tossed pizzas.

---

4 NEW ORLEANS

It may sound clichéd to call New Orleans magical and seductive, but it's the truth. Every one of your senses is engaged from the moment you arrive. Visually, the city is superb, from the lacy ironwork wrapped around the buildings of the French Quarter, to the stately, graceful old homes of the Garden District, to the giant oaks that drip with ghostly Spanish moss in City Park. But one cannot picture New Orleans anymore without recalling a storm named Katrina. On August 29, 2005, New Orleans changed forever. In the wake of Hurricane Katrina, at least three of the levees designed to keep the below-sea-level city safe from the waters of Lake Pontchartrain either broke or were breached. Eighty percent of one of the most historic and culturally rich cities in America was underwater. The water remained for weeks, months in certain places, and by the time it was gone, the landscape of New Orleans was permanently altered. For a few days in the fall of 2008, the nation looked on in horror as Hurricane Gustav threatened to make an anniversary visit to the Big Easy, but despite wreaking some havoc on the Gulf Coast, that storm struck only a glancing, nonfatal blow.

Today recovery is ongoing, and the fate of many citizens and establishments remains in question. Which prompts a question of your own, probably: Should I go?

Oh, yes.

Go, because everything in life is fragile and precarious, and we can take nothing for granted, and someday it really will all be gone. Go, because it's not gone, not at all. Go, because the things you wanted—the beautiful architecture, the majestic oaks, the river wind, the quality of light that makes even the most mundane just a little bit magical—all remain. Go, because people are there, and as long as they are, there will be music and food, and it will be some of the best of your life. Go, because perhaps you've wanted to help in any way you can, and now the best way you can is to help a historic city regain its economic feet. Go, because every brick in the French Quarter has a story to tell, and so does the damaged ground of the 9th Ward, and you should bear witness. Go, because there is much to celebrate, and this is still the best place there is to do so.

"I want to be in that number," goes the song. I do indeed. I hope you do, too.

ESSENTIALS

GETTING THERE   By Plane   The city's **Louis Armstrong New Orleans International Airport** (www.flymsy.com) is served by most domestic major airlines. You'll find information booths scattered around the airport and in the baggage claim area, as well as a branch of the **Travelers Aid Society** (© 504/464-3522).

From the airport, you can reach the Central Business District by bus for $1.50 (exact change required). Buses run from 6am to 6:30pm. For more information, call the **Regional Transit Authority** (© 504/827-2600; www.norta.com). From the airport, you can get to your hotel on the **Airport Shuttle** (© 504/522-3500). For $13 per person (one-way), the van will take you directly to your hotel. There are Airport Shuttle information desks (staffed 24 hr.) in the airport. If you plan to take the Airport Shuttle *to* the airport when you depart, you must call a day in advance and let them know what time your flight is leaving.

A **taxi** from the airport to most hotels will cost about $29 for one to two persons; if there are three or more passengers, the fare is $12 per person plus a $1 gas surcharge.

By Train   Amtrak (© 800/USA-RAIL [872-7245] or 504/528-1610; www.amtrak.com) provides service to **Union Passenger Terminal,** 1001 Loyola Ave., in the Central Business District.

By Car   You can drive to New Orleans via **I-10, I-55, U.S. 90, U.S. 61,** or across the Lake Pontchartrain Causeway on **La. 25.** For the best roadside views, take U.S. 61 or La. 25, but only if you have time to spare. The larger roads are considerably faster.

VISITOR INFORMATION   Contact the friendly, helpful **New Orleans Metropolitan Convention and Visitors Bureau,** 2020 St. Charles Ave., New Orleans, LA 70130 (© 800/672-6124 or 504/566-5011; www.neworleanscvb.com). **NOLA.com** is an excellent resource, offering online versions of the *Times-Picayune,* information about nightlife and festivals, good links, and, of course, Bourbo-cam (a webcam aimed 24/7 at a certain corner of Bourbon Street).

SPECIAL EVENTS & FESTIVALS   Details on Mardi Gras and Jazz Fest, the city's two premier events, are found below.

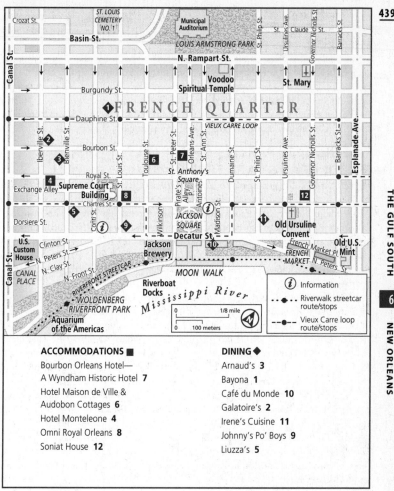

ACCOMMODATIONS ■

Bourbon Orleans Hotel—
A Wyndham Historic Hotel **7**

Hotel Maison de Ville &
Audobon Cottages **6**

Hotel Monteleone **4**

Omni Royal Orleans **8**

Soniat House **12**

DINING ◆

Arnaud's **3**

Bayona **1**

Café du Monde **10**

Galatoire's **2**

Irene's Cuisine **11**

Johnny's Po' Boys **9**

Liuzza's **5**

From late March to early April is **Spring Fiesta,** with tours of many of the city's private homes, courtyards, and plantations. For the schedule, call the **Spring Fiesta Association** (© **504/581-1367**). The mid-April **French Quarter Festival** kicks off with a parade down Bourbon Street. You can join people dancing in the streets, learn the history of jazz, visit historic homes, and take a ride on a riverboat. Many local restaurants set up booths in Jackson Square. For information, contact **French Quarter Festivals** (© **504/522-5730;** www.frenchquarterfestivals.org).

Halloween is celebrated citywide with events including Boo-at-the-Zoo for children, costume parties (including a Monster Bash), haunted houses (the best is in City Park), and the Moonlight Witches Run.

FAST FACTS If you need immediate medical assistance, go to the emergency room at **Ochsner Medical Institutions,** 1516 Jefferson Hwy. (© **504/842-3460**), or the **Tulane**

University Medical Center, 1415 Tulane Ave. (© **504/588-5800**). The 24-hour pharmacy closest to the French Quarter is **Walgreens,** 1801 St. Charles Ave. (© **504/561-8458**).

You're allowed to drink on the street, but not from a glass or a bottle. Don't walk alone at night, and don't go into the cemeteries alone at any time during the day or night. Ask around locally about safety before you go anywhere. People will tell you if you should take a cab instead of walking or using public transportation.

The **sales tax** in New Orleans is 9%. An additional 4% tax is added to hotel bills. There is also a nightly tax of 50¢ to $2 based on the number of rooms a hotel has.

THE BIGGEST PARTIES OF 'EM ALL: MARDI GRAS & JAZZ FEST

MARDI GRAS   The granddaddy of all New Orleans celebrations is Mardi Gras (French for "Fat Tuesday," the day before Ash Wednesday, when Lent begins). Two or 3 weeks before Mardi Gras itself, parades begin chugging through the streets with increasing frequency. If you want to experience Mardi Gras but don't want to face the full force of craziness, consider coming for the weekend 10 days before Fat Tuesday (the season officially begins the Fri of this weekend). You can count on 10 to 15 parades during the weekend by lesser-known krewes (sort of a social club) such as Cleopatra, Pontchartrain, Sparta, and Camelot.

Mardi Gras krewe Rex's King of Carnival arrives downtown from the Mississippi River on **Lundi Gras** the Monday night before Fat Tuesday. Festivities at the riverfront begin in the afternoon, with lots of drinking and live music leading up to the king's arrival around 6pm. Down the levee a few hundred feet, at Wolfenberg Park, the Zulu krewe has its own Lundi Gras celebration, with the king arriving around 5pm. That night, the Krewe of Orpheus holds their parade, with spectacular floats and a generous amount of trinkets and beads for parade-watchers.

The actual day of Mardi Gras starts with the two biggest parades, Zulu and Rex, which run back to back. Zulu starts near the Central Business District (CBD) at 8:30am; Rex starts Uptown at 10am. It will be early afternoon when Rex spills into the CBD. Nearby, at about this time, you can find some of the most elusive New Orleans figures, the Mardi Gras Indians, small communities of African Americans, and Creoles (some of whom have Native American ancestors), mostly from the inner city, decked out in elaborate beaded and feathered costumes.

After the parades, the action picks up in the French Quarter. The frat-party action is largely confined to Bourbon Street. The more interesting activity is in the lower Quarter and the Frenchmen section of the Faubourg Marigny.

Tips: Accommodations in the city and the nearby suburbs are booked solid during Mardi Gras, *so make your plans well ahead and book a room as early as possible.* Many people plan a year or more in advance. Prices are *much* higher during Mardi Gras, and most hotels and guesthouses impose minimum-stay requirements. Many, many cops are out, making the walk from Uptown to Downtown safer than at other times of year, but, not surprisingly, the streets of New Orleans are a haven for pickpockets. Take precautions.

JAZZ FEST   The New Orleans Jazz & Heritage Festival, or simply Jazz Fest, is one of the best-attended, most-respected, and most musically comprehensive festivals in the world. Stand in the right place and, depending on which way the wind's blowing, you

can catch as many as 10 musical styles from several continents and smell the tantalizing **441**
aromas of a dozen different food offerings.

Serious Jazz Fest aficionados eschew the big headliners and savor the lesser-known acts. They range from Mardi Gras Indians to old-time bluesmen who have never played outside the Delta, from Dixieland to avant-garde, from African artists making rare U.S. appearances to the top names in Cajun, zydeco, and, of course, jazz.

You must book hotels and flights months in advance, so you may have to schedule your visit around your own availability, not an appearance by a particular band. Just about every day at Jazz Fest is a good day, so this is not a hardship.

Try to purchase tickets as early as February. They're available by mail through **Ticket-master** (© **504/522-5555;** www.ticketmaster.com). To order tickets by phone, or to get ticket information, call **New Orleans Jazz & Heritage Festival** (© **800/488-5252** or 504/522-4786; www.nojazzfest.com). Admission for adults is $30 to $40, depending on when you buy them in advance (Ticketmaster charges a large per-ticket handling fee) and $40 or $50 at the gate depending on the date; $5 for children. Evening events and concerts (order tickets in advance for these events as well) may be attended at an additional cost.

Parking at the Fair Grounds is next to impossible. Take public transportation or one of the shuttles. The **Regional Transit Authority** operates buses to the Fair Grounds. For schedules, contact © **504/827-7802** (www.norta.com).

WHAT TO SEE & DO

Audubon Aquarium of the Americas (Kids) Enough time has passed that this is once again a world-class aquarium, highly entertaining and painlessly educational, with beautifully constructed exhibits. Kids love it, even those too impatient to read the graphics, but adults shouldn't overlook it, if for no other reason than it's a handy refuge from the heat or rain. Five major exhibit areas and dozens of smaller aquariums hold a veritable ocean of aquatic life native to the region and to the Americas. You can walk through the underwater tunnel in the Caribbean Reef exhibit, view a shark-filled re-creation of the Gulf of Mexico, or drop in to see the penguin exhibit. We particularly like the walk-through Waters of the Americas, where you wander in rainforests (complete with birds and piranhas) and see what goes on below the surface of swamps. The **IMAX theater** shows two or three films at regular intervals. Look for an astonishing Katrina documentary, "Hurricane on the Bayou," showing the flooding and the rest of the devastation.

1 Canal St., at the river. © **800/774-7394** or 504/581-4629. www.audoboninstitute.org. Aquarium $18 adults, $14 seniors, $11 children 2–12. IMAX $8.50 adults, $7.50 seniors, $5.50 children. Combination aquarium/IMAX tickets $31 adults, $22 seniors, $21 children. Aquarium Tues–Sun 10am–5pm. IMAX Tues–Sun 10am–5pm. Call for showtimes; advance tickets recommended. Closed Mardi Gras and Christmas.

Audubon Insectarium (Kids) This long-anticipated museum is dedicated to all things bug (okay, and arachnid—don't get picky), specifically 900,000 species of critters that creep, crawl, and flutter. Located in the old U.S. Customs House, it's the largest free-standing museum in the world dedicated to its multilegged, winged subjects. Don't like insects? You might well be surprised; this latest addition to the Audubon Group has all the elements of a great adventure: surprise, humor, special effects, beauty, and intrigue—and by the time all that's been applied to the main topic at hand, you might not only find your attitude changed considerably, you may even muster the courage to "pet" an Australian Prickly Stick bug or a giant beetle. In the Tiny Termite Café, each glass-topped table has an insect colony living in it (watch silkworms spin their fibers

THE GULF SOUTH

6

NEW ORLEANS

while you dine). The Japanese-inspired butterfly gallery, full of living, fluttering beauty, is a peaceful departure from the hustle of Canal Street.

423 Canal St. ✆ **800/774-7394** or 504/581-4629. www.auduboninstitute.org. Tues–Sun 10am–6pm (last entry at 5pm). $15 adults, $12 seniors, $10 children 2–12. Insectarium, aquarium, and IMAX tickets $34 adults, $25 seniors, $20 children.

Audubon Zoo (Kids)

This is one of the country's best zoos. What's more, nearly perfectly planned and executed hurricane preparation meant the zoo virtually sailed through the catastrophe, with almost zero animal loss. Here, in a setting of subtropical plants, waterfalls, and lagoons, some 1,800 animals (including rare and endangered species) live in natural habitats rather than cages. Don't miss the replica of a Louisiana swamp (complete with a rare white gator). Keep your eyes peeled for wry, post-disaster additions like a few Katrina-victim fridges! During your visit to the zoo, look for the bronze statue of naturalist John James Audubon standing in a grove of trees with a notebook and pencil in hand.

6500 Magazine St. ✆ **504/581-4629.** www.auduboninstitute.org. Admission $13 adults, $9.50 seniors (65 and over), $7.50 children 2–12. Tues–Sun 10am–5pm. Last ticket sold 1 hr. before closing. Closed Mardi Gras Day, Thanksgiving Day, and Christmas.

The Cabildo

Constructed from 1795 to 1799 as the Spanish government seat in New Orleans, the Cabildo was the site of the signing of the Louisiana Purchase transfer. It is now the center of the Louisiana State Museum's facilities in the French Quarter. A multiroom exhibition informatively, entertainingly, and exhaustively traces the history of Louisiana from exploration through Reconstruction. Topics include antebellum music, mourning and burial customs, immigrants and how they fared here, and the changing roles of women in the South. Throughout are fabulous artifacts, including Napoleon's death mask.

701 Chartres St. ✆ **800/568-6968** or 504/568-6968. Fax 504/568-4995. http://lsm.crt.state.la.us/cabildo/cabildo.htm. Admission $6 adults, $5 students and seniors, free for children 11 and under. Tues–Sun 9am–5pm.

Historic New Orleans Collection—Museum/Research Center

This museum of local and regional history is almost hidden away within a complex of historic French Quarter buildings. The oldest, constructed in the late 18th century, was one of the few structures to escape the disastrous fire of 1794. These buildings were owned by the collection's founders, Gen. and Mrs. L. Kemper Williams. Their former residence is open to the public for tours. There are also excellent tours of the Louisiana history galleries, with expertly preserved and displayed art, maps, and original documents like the transfer papers for the Louisiana Purchase of 1803. The Williams Gallery, also on the site, is free to the public and presents changing exhibitions that focus on Louisiana's history and culture, including a terrific Katrina-related one.

533 Royal St. (btw. St. Louis and Toulouse sts.). ✆ **504/523-4662.** Fax 504/598-7108. www.hnoc.org. Free admission; tours $5. Tues–Sat 9:30am–4:30pm, Sun 10:30am–4:30pm; tours Tues–Sat 10 and 11am and 2 and 3pm. Closed major holidays and Mardi Gras.

National World War II Museum

Created by best-selling author (and *Saving Private Ryan* consultant) Stephen Ambrose, this unique museum tells the story of all 19 U.S. amphibious operations worldwide on that fateful day of June 6, 1944. A rich collection of artifacts (including some British Spitfire airplanes), plus top-of-the-line educational materials, make this museum one of the highlights of New Orleans. An expansion to be completed in 2009 will triple the museum's size and cover all the theaters and services in

World War II, turning this already world-class facility into one of the major WWII museums.

945 Magazine St., in the Historic Warehouse District. (✆ **504/527-6012.** www.ddaymuseum.org. Admission $14 adults, $8 seniors, $6 active or retired military with ID and children 5–17, free for military in uniform and children 4 and under. Tues–Sun 9am–5pm. Closed holidays.

New Orleans Museum of Art   NOMA, located in an idyllic section of City Park, is home to a 40,000-piece collection that includes pre-Columbian and Native American ethnographic art; 16th- to 20th-century European paintings, drawings, sculptures, and prints; Early American art; Asian art; and one of the largest decorative glass collections in the United States. Be sure to pick up a guide pamphlet from the information desk at the entrance. A great addition to the city's artistic offerings is the **Besthoff Sculpture Garden,** 5 acres of gardens, grass, and walkways that spotlight 50 modern sculptures. The garden has quickly become a New Orleans cultural highlight and is open Wednesday to Sunday 10am to 5pm, with free admission.

1 Collins Diboll Circle, at City Park and Esplanade. (✆ **504/658-4100.** www.noma.org. Admission $8 adults, $7 seniors (65 and over) and students, $4 children 3–17, free to Louisiana residents. Wed–Sun 10am–4:30pm. Closed most major holidays.

The Ogden Museum of Southern Art   This museum may well be the premier collection of Southern art in the United States. The new dramatic interior is a tad too short on space for art, and the fear is that certain exhibits may get short shrift, and the breadth and range of Southern artistry may be limited to outsider folk artists or photographers who specialize in old bluesmen (two of our favorite genres, we must admit). But we must also admit that the facility is wonderful, the artists are impressive, and the graphics are well designed. Consider dropping by on Thursday for their delightful **Ogden After Hours,** which includes a live band (anything from 1930s country to the New Orleans Klezmer All-Stars) playing in the atrium.

925 Camp St. (✆ **504/539-9600.** www.ogdenmuseum.org. Admission $10 adults, $8 seniors and students, $5 children 5–17. Wed–Sun 11am–4pm, plus Thurs 6–8pm for evening shows.

The Presbytère   The Presbytère, part of the Louisiana State Museum, has turned the entire building into a smashing Mardi Gras museum. Five major themes (History, Masking, Parades, Balls, and the Courir du Mardi Gras) trace the history of this high-profile but, frankly, little-understood (outside of New Orleans) annual event. A re-creation of a float allows you to pretend you are throwing beads to a crowd on a screen in front of you. Heck, even some of the restrooms masquerade (appropriately) as the ubiquitous Fat Tuesday Porta Pottis! Allow a couple of hours to see it all.

751 Chartres St., Jackson Sq. (✆ **800/568-6968** or 504/568-6968. http://lsm.crt.state.la.us. Admission $6 adults, $5 seniors and students, free for children 12 and under. Tues–Sun 9am–5pm.

Southern Food and Beverage Museum and Museum of the American Cocktail   Local restaurateur Dickie Brennan, Liz Williams, and a host of other NOLA foodies have opened the South's first food and beverage museum. It's an impressive assemblage of Southern food and drink history, from farmers to cooks and all between. The location in the Riverwalk Marketplace offers stunning panoramic views of the Mississippi River. The main hall houses a comprehensive collection of artifacts illustrating how different ethnic groups, geography, and time have contributed to the local cuisine. In addition to the expected museum fare, free samples of local chicory-roasted coffee and sweet tea are available to patrons. As if your appetite wasn't whetted enough, get a load of those delicious smells from the food court—a little l'eau de red beans 'n' rice and crawfish étouffée adds to the atmosphere. Included in your admission fee is the Museum of the American Cocktail. It's a fascinating walk through 200 years of cocktail history and New Orleans's own vital role in same. Historic artifacts include bottles from defunct products, menus, and photos with displays on subjects such as Prohibition and what it did to the cocktail.

1 Poydras St. (in the Riverwalk Marketplace Mall). (© **504/569-0405.** www.southernfood.org and www. museumoftheamericancocktail.org. Admission $10 adults, $5 seniors and students with ID. Mon–Sat 10am–7pm; Sun noon–6pm.

ORGANIZED TOURS

Historic New Orleans Tours (© **504/947-2120;** www.tourneworleans.com) is the place to go for authenticity. Here the tour guides are chosen for their combination of knowledge and entertaining manner, and we cannot recommend the guides or the tours highly enough. The French Quarter tours are the best straightforward, nonspecialized walking tours of this neighborhood. They also offer a Voodoo tour, a Haunted tour, and a Garden District tour. All of their tours are $15 for adults, while students and seniors with ID receive $2 off; children 6 to 12 are $7, and those 5 and under are free.

Dr. Wagner's Honey Island Swamp Tours (© **985/641-1769** or 504/242-5877; www.honeyislandswamp.com), at 41490 Crawford Landing Rd. in Slidell, about 30 miles outside of New Orleans, takes you by boat into the interior of Honey Island Swamp to view wildlife with naturalist guides. The tour guides provide a solid educational experience to go with the swamp excitement. Tours last approximately 2 hours. Prices are $23 for adults, $15 for children 11 and under, from the launch site; the rates are $45 for adults and $32 for children if you want hotel pickup.

SHOPPING

Among the hunting grounds you may want to explore is the **Historic French Market.**

Just across from Jackson Square at 600–620 Decatur St., the old **Jackson Brewery** building has been transformed into a jumble of shops (Cajun-Creole foodstuffs, souvenirs, fashion), cafes, and entertainment venues. For the best gallery-hopping, head straight to **Julia Street. Magazine Street** is the Garden District's premier shopping street. More than 140 shops (antiques, art galleries, boutiques, crafts, dolls) line the street in 19th-century brick storefronts and quaint cottagelike buildings. At the foot of Canal Street (365 Canal St.), where the street reaches the Mississippi River, **Canal Place** shopping center holds more than 50 shops, many of them branches of some of this country's most elegant retailers.

If you need a Mardi Gras costume, head for the **Uptown Costume & Dance Company,** 4326 Magazine St. (© **504/895-7969**). The shop designs party uniforms for a number of Mardi Gras krewe members. Owner Cheryll Berlier also creates a limited number of wacky Mardi Gras tuxedo jackets, which get gobbled up quickly. The **Louisiana Music Factory,** 210 Decatur St. (© **504/586-1094;** www.louisianamusicfactory. com), carries a large selection of regional music. It also has frequent live music and beer bashes—shop while you bop!

WHERE TO STAY

Ashton's Bed & Breakfast This charming guesthouse represents one of the gutsiest ventures in the city; post-Katrina, their chimney collapsed and 5,000 bricks tore a gaping hole in their top story. Now it's fully restored and is a fine and worthy alternative to some

A Side Trip to a Plantation

About 60 miles away from New Orleans, **Houmas House Plantation & Gardens** is a different sort of plantation house, in that it is actually two houses joined together. The original structure was four rooms built in 1775. In 1828, a larger, Greek Revival–style house was built next to it, and then a roof was put over both, joining them together. The property, a former sugar plantation, has had multiple owners. The late Dr. George Crozat of New Orleans restored it, bringing in authentic period furnishings. Current owner Kevin Kelly now lives there, and the place reflects the feel of both an active home and a historic property.

Live oaks, magnolias, and beautifully landscaped gardens frame Houmas House (once called "The Sugar Palace") in a way that is precisely what comes to mind when most of us think "plantation house." You might recognize the exterior from the film *Hush...Hush, Sweet Charlotte*. The inside has been lovingly brought back to early 1800s detail, including period touches such as accurate paint colors, 19th-century paintings, antique rugs, and several unexpected exquisite touches. Excellent, informative costumed guides deliver stories from the house's busy past. Because scenes from *All My Children* were shot here, be sure to ask for those Susan Lucci stories (they've got 'em). There is also a cafe, and a restaurant, **Latil's Landing,** touted by *Esquire* as one of the best in the country.

Houmas House & Plantation is at 40136 La. 942, Burnside (mailing address: 40136 Hwy. 942, Darrow, LA 70725; ☎ **888/323-8314** or 225/473-9830; www.houmashouse.com). Admission (including guided tour) is $20 adults, $15 children ages 13 to 18, $10 children ages 6 to 12, free for children 5 and under; gardens and grounds only $10. It's open year-round Monday to Wednesday 9am to 5pm, Thursday to Sunday 9am to 8pm. Take I-10 from New Orleans or Baton Rouge. Exit on La. 44 to Burnside and turn right on La. 942.

of its more costly compatriots. There are pretty custom paint treatments like shadow striping, on top of new molding and chandeliers, and other careful attention to detail. One room has a most inviting fluffy white bed, but its bathroom is contained in a curtained-off corner. Those with personal space and privacy issues might want to head to room no. 3, with a four-poster bed and the nicest bathroom in the guesthouse, complete with a claw-foot tub. A full breakfast is served, featuring such fun as bananas Foster waffles and sweet-potato-stuffed French toast.

2023 Esplanade Ave., New Orleans, LA 70116. ☎ **800/725-4131** or 504/942-7048. Fax 504/947-9382. www.ashtonsbb.com. 8 units. $115–$160 double; $170–$195 for Mardi Gras and special events; $215–$240 during Jazz Fest; call for off-season specials. Rates include full breakfast. AE, DISC, MC, V. Free secure parking. **Amenities:** Complimentary soft drinks.

Bourbon Orleans Hotel—A Wyndham Historic Hotel This hotel occupies three historic buildings. Beds are too firm, while bathrooms are long and narrow, with a natty use of stripes and brocades (they feature Golden Door Spa toiletries). Small rooms are cozy but not unbearable, though if occupied by two people, they had better like each other. The rooms for the mobility-impaired are well designed. Some rooms have only armoires, no closets, and some have balconies. Rooms in the no. 17s have views up

Bourbon Street, but if you want to escape street noise, ask for an interior room. We are fond of the two-story town-house rooms, with exposed brickwork on the walls, and the beds upstairs in a loft. It's classy sexy, good for a multiple-day stay.

717 Orleans St., New Orleans, LA 70116. ✆ **504/523-2222.** Fax 504/525-8166. www.bourbonorleans. com. 220 units. $139–$199 petite queen or twin; $189–$329 deluxe king or double; $239–$489 junior suite; $299–$599 town-house suite; $272–$482 town-house suite with balcony. Extra person $30. AE, DC, DISC, MC, V. Valet parking $30. **Amenities:** Restaurant; outdoor pool.

Chimes B&B   This is a real hidden gem. Jill and Charles Abbyad have run this B&B for over 20 years, and their experience shows. The Chimes opened days after Katrina as the home base for Reuters, who are still a presence. Rooms vary in size from a generous L-shape to a two-story loft type (with a very small bathroom) to some that are downright cozy. All have antiques but are so tastefully underdecorated, particularly in contrast to other B&Bs, that they are positively Zen. An ambitious continental breakfast is served in the hosts' house. The Chimes has made improvements designed for the business traveler, and all we need to say is laptop + courtyard = working bliss.

1146 Constantinople St., New Orleans, LA 70115. ✆ **504/899-2621** or 453-2183 (owner's cell). Fax 504/ 899-9858. www.chimesneworleans.com. 5 units. $130–$155 double in season; $86–$140 off season; rates can go higher during special events. Rates include breakfast. Look for rates, availability, and featured specials online. AE, MC, V. Limited off-street free parking. Well-behaved pets accepted.

The 1896 O'Malley House   One of the most smashing B&Bs in the city, just a treasure inside, full of gorgeous antiques and repro furniture. Many of the original details, including marvelous tile on the various fireplaces, are still intact. The handsome rooms are each meticulously decorated, using clever touches such as vintage (at least, appearing) oil paintings, Bali puppets, and European art. Second-floor rooms are larger, and most have Jacuzzi tubs. The third floor is a clever use of design and space, with formerly dull wood walls turned most striking by pickling the wood to a lighter color (ask to see the photos of the mysterious science equations found scrawled on one wall). These rooms are smaller and more garretlike, though they pale in desirability only if you really, *really* want that classic high-ceilinged look.

120 S. Pierce St., New Orleans, LA 70119. ✆ **866/226-1896** or 504/488-5896. www.1896omalleyhouse. com. 9 units. $135–$155 double; $200 special events such as Mardi Gras and Jazz Fest; call for special summer rates. Rates include breakfast. AE, MC, V.

Harrah's New Orleans   New Orleans doesn't lack for grand hotels, but there is something so . . . *big* . . . about the Harrah's lobby that it passes right through grand and into something almost too immense to be truly elegant. Which isn't to knock the place; everyone did a good job. The rooms are sharp, with photos by local artist Richard Sexton and splashes of Mardi Gras purple and gold. There is an airy gym with a tall ceiling and windows, well stocked with a good mix of aerobic and weight machines. Naturally, it's right across from the casino. *Tip:* Since this is a casino property, special deals are offered to players club members. The on-site restaurant is **Ruth's Chris,** and there's an underground walkway to the casino, which offers six more dining options, ranging from a buffet to an Asian/sushi place (**Bambu**) to a microbrewery (**Gordon Biersch**) and another high-end steakhouse (**Besh's**). Player-club members are also eligible for discounts to many of the city's top restaurants.

228 Poydras St. ✆ **800/VIP-JAZZ** (847-5299) or 504/533-6000. www.harrahsneworleans.com. 450 units. $149–$449 double. $30 additional person. AE, DC, DISC, MC, V. Valet and self-parking $30. **Amenities:** Restaurant; gym. *In room:* Fridge.

Hotel Maison de Ville & Audubon Cottages   A member of the Small Luxury Hotels of the World, the Maison de Ville is not quite as sterling as it has been, despite sweet rooms with feather beds and an outside atmosphere that can't be beat. Still, this was the hotel where Tennessee Williams was a regular guest in room no. 9. Most of the rooms surround a charming courtyard (complete with fountain and banana trees). Rooms vary dramatically in size, however; some can be downright tiny, so ask when you reserve, noting that rooms are priced by bed size, not the size of the room itself. Be careful you don't get a room overlooking the street—Bourbon (and its noise) is less than half a block away. The far more spacious **Audubon Cottages** (larger than many apartments, some with their own private courtyards), a few blocks away and including a small, inviting pool, can go for less than the cramped queen rooms in the main hotel. Overall, it's a romantic getaway—we just wish it wasn't so expensive.

727 Toulouse St., New Orleans, LA 70130. ⓒ **800/634-1600** or 504/561-5858. Fax 504/528-9939. www.maisondeville.com. 16 units, 7 cottages. $179–$239 double and queen; $219–$259 king; $329–$399 suite; $239–$329 1-bedroom cottage; $599–$699 2-bedroom cottage; $770–$960 3-bedroom cottage. Rates include continental breakfast. DISC, MC, V. Valet parking $30. **Amenities:** Restaurant; outdoor pool.

Hotel Monteleone   Opened in 1886, the Monteleone is the largest hotel in the French Quarter. Everyone who stays here loves it, probably because it's a family hotel whose approach to business is reflected by the staff, among the most helpful in town. Rooms in the no. 60s are near the ice machine; rooms from nos. 56 to 59 are slightly bigger, with old, high ceilings; rooms in the no. 27s have no windows. Executive suites are just big rooms but have the nicest new furniture, including four-poster beds and Jacuzzis. The glass fitness room overlooking the city got nailed by the storm, but to its benefit, it's now well stocked with the latest elliptical machines. One of the city's best-kept secrets is the renovated rooftop pool; on a recent visit, we were among a handful of folks lounging on the deck high above the street noise, with unencumbered views of the city and beyond. It's quite a scene, with snacks served there in the evening.

214 Royal St., New Orleans, LA 70130. ⓒ **800/535-9595** or 504/523-3341. Fax 504/561-5803. www.hotelmonteleone.com. 570 units. $199–$309 double; $360–$2,500 suite. Extra person $25. Children 17 and under stay free in parent's room. Package rates available. AE, DC, DISC, MC, V. Valet parking $30 car, $35 small SUV and trucks. Pets allowed on the 3rd floor only, for a fee and deposit. **Amenities:** 3 restaurants; heated rooftop swimming pool (open year-round); fitness center.

International House   The International House sets the local standard for modern hotels with its creative design and meticulous attention to detail. Here a wonderful old Beaux Arts bank building has been transformed into a modern space that still pays tribute to its locale. Interiors are the embodiment of minimalist chic. Rooms are simple, with muted, monochromatic (okay, beige) tones, tall ceilings and ceiling fans, up-to-the-minute bathroom fixtures, and black-and-white photos of local musicians and characters, books about the city, and other clever decorating touches that anchor the room in its New Orleans setting. The big bathrooms boast large tubs or space-age glassed-in showers. As of this writing, there is no room service, as they wait for the new restaurant to open, but it should be back by the time you read this.

221 Camp St., New Orleans, LA 70130. ⓒ **800/633-5770** or 504/553-9550. Fax 504/553-9560. www.ihhotel.com. 117 units. $149–$379 double; $369–$1,799 suite. Rates include continental breakfast. Look for special deals online. AE, DC, DISC, MC, V. Valet parking $30 for cars, $38 for SUV. Hotel is entirely non-smoking. **Amenities:** Restaurant.

The McKendrick-Breaux House   This is one of the best B&Bs in town. The rooms are done in impeccable good taste, with high-quality mattresses and pillows, and each has its own style; the ones in the main house have claw-foot tubs. Room no. 36 is the largest but also has the most traffic noise. Third-floor rooms (reached by a steep, narrow staircase) evoke classic garret quarters, with exposed brick walls and less of that traffic noise. Rooms in the second building are somewhat larger. A full breakfast has been added, and the staff offers great suggestions for how to spend your time here.

1474 Magazine St., New Orleans, LA 70130. ✆ **888/570-1700** or 504/586-1700. Fax 504/522-7134. www. mckendrick-breaux.com. 9 units. $145–$235 double. Rates include tax and breakfast. AE, DC, DISC, MC, V. Limited free off-street parking.

Omni Royal Orleans (Kids)   This is an elegant hotel that escapes a generic "chain" feel. This is only proper, given that it is on the former site of the venerable 1836 St. Louis Exchange Hotel, one of the country's premier hostelries and a center of New Orleans social life until the final years of the Civil War. The original building was destroyed by a 1915 hurricane (it suffered no damage from Katrina), but the Omni is a worthy successor, enjoying a prime location in the center of the Quarter. Truman Capote and William Styron have stayed here, and there is a Tennessee Williams suite. Furnishings in the guest rooms have grave good taste, full of muted tones and plush furniture, with windows that let you look dreamily out over the Quarter. Suites are vast, making this a good choice for families. Service is swift and conscientious, and there are more amenities available than in comparable properties.

621 St. Louis St., New Orleans, LA 70140. ✆ **800/THE-OMNI** (843-6664) in the U.S. and Canada, or 504/529-5333. Fax 504/529-7089. www.omniroyalorleans.com. 346 units. $169–$339 double; $339–$850 suite; $1,200–$1,600 penthouse. Children 17 and under stay free in parent's room. AE, DC, DISC, MC, V. Valet parking $28. **Amenities:** Restaurant; heated outdoor pool; health club.

Soniat House   The recipient of endless tributes, the wonderful and romantic Soniat House lives up to the hype, though the prices are daunting. Inside the unassuming plain Creole exterior is an oasis of calm that seems impossible in the Quarter. The beyond-efficient staff spoils guests, and the sweet courtyards, candlelit at night, soothes them.

Rooms do vary, if not in quality, then at least in distinction. All have antiques, but if you want, say, high ceilings and really grand furniture, you are better off in the main house or the suite-filled annex across the street. On the main property, bathrooms are small, though some rooms have their own private balconies. Our only real complaint is the extra charge ($13) for the delicious but small breakfast—it seems petty, given the already high prices and lack of room service.

1133 Chartres St., New Orleans, LA 70116. ✆ **800/544-8808** or 504/522-0570. Fax 504/522-7208. www. soniathouse.com. 33 units. $265–$325 double; $395–$695 suite. AE, MC, V. Valet parking $25. No children 11 and under. **Amenities:** Access to nearby health club (for additional charge).

Windsor Court   Pre-Katrina, *Condé Nast Traveler* voted the Windsor Court the Best Hotel in North America. And post-Katrina? It's still mighty fine. There's a reason this remains the center of high New Orleans society, from traditional afternoon tea to fancy dinners before or after some society function. Two corridors downstairs are mini galleries that display original 17th-, 18th-, and 19th-century art. Everything is very traditional and serene, though not unwarm. The accommodations, admittedly showing a touch of wear, are spacious, with classy, not flashy, decor. Almost all are suites (either big or huge) featuring large bay windows or a private balcony overlooking the river (get a river view, if at all possible) or the city, a private foyer, a large living room, a bedroom with French doors, a large marble bathroom with particularly *luxe* amenities, two dressing rooms, and a "petite kitchen."

300 Gravier St., New Orleans, LA 70130. ℂ **800/262-2662** or 504/523-6000. Fax 504/596-4749. www. windsorcourthotel.com. 324 units. $149–$520 standard double; $199–$550 junior suite; $199–$600 full suite. Children 11 and under stay free in parent's room. Packages available. AE, DC, DISC, MC, V. Valet parking $28. **Amenities:** Restaurant; large pool; health club.

WHERE TO DINE

Arnaud's CREOLE Arnaud's seems to have the lowest profile of all the classic old New Orleans restaurants, but undeservedly so, since it tops them in quality. Apart from the signature appetizer, shrimp Arnaud (boiled shrimp topped with a spicy rémoulade sauce), we love the crabmeat Ravigotte (generous amounts of sweet lump crabmeat tossed with a Creole mustard–based sauce, hearts of palm, and other veggies), and the char-broiled oysters, all smoky and buttery flavor. Delicious fish dishes include snapper or trout Pontchartrain (topped with crabmeat), the spicy pompano Duarte, and the pompano David and tuna Napoleon. Any filet mignon entree is superb. For dessert, the bananas Foster is spot on.

813 Bienville St. ℂ **866/230-8892** or 504/523-5433. www.arnauds.com. Reservations requested. Business casual. Main courses $23–$50. AE, DC, DISC, MC, V. Sun–Thurs 6–10pm; Fri–Sat 6–10:30pm; Sun brunch 10am–2:30pm.

Bayona INTERNATIONAL A dedicated chef-owner, Susan Spicer, who is a local treasure, superior food, and one of the loveliest courtyards in the restaurant scene—all reasons to eat at Bayona. Begin with the outstanding cream of garlic soup. Appetizers include grilled shrimp with cilantro sauce and black-bean cakes. Knockout entrees have included medallions of lamb loin with a lavender honey aioli (a mayonnaise-based sauce) and a zinfandel demi-glace. Entrees come with a well-balanced selection of sides such as gnocchi, puréed butternut squash, or fresh sweet corn. And lunch brings a smoked-duck (with cashew butter and pepper jelly) sandwich that has been boxed to go on many a plane flight! A light lunch on Saturday features three courses of tapaslike plates you can mix and match for $20.

430 Dauphine St. ℂ **504/525-4455.** www.bayona.com. Reservations required at dinner, recommended at lunch. Main courses $10–$15 lunch, $24–$29 dinner. AE, DC, DISC, MC, V. Tues–Thurs 6–9:30pm; Fri–Sat 6–10pm; Wed–Sat 11:30am–2pm.

Brigtsen's CAJUN/CREOLE In a converted 19th-century house at the Riverbend, Brigtsen's is warm, intimate, and romantic. The menu changes daily. Generous portions make appetizers superfluous, but their seasonal salads are so good and the BBQ shrimp with shrimp calas hard to pass up. Brigtsen has a special touch with rabbit. You can't miss with any of the soups, especially the lovely butternut squash shrimp bisque. A broiled Gulf fish with crabmeat Parmesan crust and béarnaise sauce is a great piece of seafood.

723 Dante St. ℂ **504/861-7610.** www.brigtsens.com. Reservations recommended. Main courses $24–$38. AE, DC, DISC, MC, V. Tues–Sat 5:30–10pm.

Café du Monde COFFEE Since 1862 Café du Monde has been selling café au lait and beignets (and nothing but) on the edge of Jackson Square. A New Orleans landmark, it's *the* place for people-watching. Not only is it a must-stop, you may find yourself wandering back several times a day. What's a beignet? (Say ben-*yay*, by the way.) A square French doughnut–type object, hot and covered in powdered sugar. You might be tempted to shake off some of the sugar. Don't. Trust us. Pour more on, even. You'll be glad you did. Wash them down with chicory coffee.

In the French Market, 800 Decatur St. ℂ **504/525-4544.** www.cafedumonde.com. 3 beignets for $2. No credit cards. Daily 24 hr. Closed Christmas. Additional location at Riverwalk Mall.

Whole Lotta Muffuletta Goin' On

Muffulettas are almost mythological, enormous concoctions of round Italian bread, Italian cold cuts and cheeses, and olive salad. One person cannot eat a whole one—at least, not in one sitting. Instead, share; a half makes a good meal. Judging from the line that forms at lunchtime, many others agree with us that **Central Grocery,** 923 Decatur St. (𝒞 **504/523-1620**), makes the best muffuletta there is (about $14 for a whole sandwich).

The Cake Café SANDWICHES/DESSERT   If you are looking for something interesting but not overwhelming, this sweet cafe (about a 10-min. walk from the Esplanade end of the Quarter) should suit the bill. Breakfast and lunch are served all day, with breads, enormous biscuits (with homemade jam), and bagels baked on-site. There are sandwiches such as grilled crabmeat with brie, big salads, and of course, cake—coconut, red velvet, pineapple upside-down, all the down-home flavors. A buck gets you a cupcake with your lunch, and there are other specials as well.

2440 Chartres St. 𝒞 **504/943-0010.** Everything under $10. AE, DC, DISC, MC, V. Tues–Sun 7am–3pm.

Commander's Palace CREOLE   The much-beloved Commander's is perhaps *the* symbol of the New Orleans dining scene. The building has been a restaurant for a century, it's at the top of the Brennan family restaurant tree, and its chefs have gone on to their own fame and household-name status (Prudhomme and Emeril ring any bells?). The many months it spent shuttered after Katrina were a frustrating symbol of the pace of city recovery. But now it's back, gleaming on the outside and amusing on the inside with new, subtly eccentric decor. Such a relief. The current menu reflects Chef Tory McPhail's constantly working imagination. Favorites like the pecan-crusted gulf fish and the tasso shrimp in pepper jelly appetizer remain, but new dishes reveal all sorts of culinary fun. A standout appetizer is the molasses and black pepper–cured pork belly. It's slow cooked over a couple of days and it falls apart at the touch, releasing a waft of brandy–black truffle and goat cheese grits, a smell so luscious it can make one weak in the knees. The three-course dinner (appetizer, entree, dessert) for no more than $39 remains a good deal. For dessert, we remain torn over such choices as the bread pudding soufflé your waiter will (justly) press upon you, the seasonal strawberry shortcake, the signature crème brûlée, and the Creole cream cheesecake.

1403 Washington Ave. 𝒞 **504/899-8221.** www.commanderspalace.com. Main courses $30–$42. AE, DISC, MC, V. Mon–Fri 11:30am–1:30pm; daily 6–9:30pm; brunch Sat 11:30am–1pm and Sun 10:30am–1:30pm. Closed Christmas and Mardi Gras Day.

Cuvée CONTEMPORARY CREOLE   Cuvée is certainly the most innovative and interesting restaurant in town. Join local raving foodies in a romantic and cozy brick-lined room where you might get to sample the foie gras daily special (such as a foie grase mousse with brandy-soaked cherries). Entrees could be sea bass wrapped in parma ham, or a deconstructed *osso buco* with the "bone" made of potato with the marrow whipped into more potato filling the interior. Desserts are equally witty. (Look for their take on the moon pie with Dreamsicle ice cream.)

322 Magazine St. 𝒞 **504/587-9001.** www.restaurantcuvee.com. Reservations highly recommended. Main courses $20–$30 dinner. AE, DC, MC, V. Mon–Thurs 6–9:30pm, Fri–Sat. 6–10:30pm Lunch Wed–Thurs 11:30am–2pm.

Dooky Chase SOUL FOOD/CREOLE   For decades, Leah and husband Dooky Chase have served prominent African-American politicians, musicians, and businesspeople Chef Leah's classic soul food, as gloriously influenced by the city's French, Sicilian, and Italian traditions. The restaurant had 2 feet of flooding, and mold issues, and rebuilding has come along slowly, despite benefits held for the Chases both here and in other cities. (Ms. Leah is pleased she got a new stove out of the deal, though, since she's wanted one for so long. An octogenarian, she says she has to keep going long enough to cook on it!) At the end of 2008, they had finally been able to return to regular service. The Chases lived for over a year in a FEMA trailer outside their restaurant, and they are as wonderful as their cooking. They are everything that is New Orleans. Long may they cook.

2301 Orleans Ave. (©) **504/821-0600.** Main courses $9–$20; lower for takeout, slightly higher for dine-in. MC, V. Tues–Fri takeout 11am–7pm. Dine-in only if staff is available Tues–Fri 11am–2pm, so call ahead.

Elizabeth's CREOLE   The average tourist may not head over to the Bywater because, well, it's not the Quarter. That's too bad—not only will they miss a true N'Awlins neighbahood, but they will also miss experiences like Elizabeth's. Here you eat, as they say, "Real Food, Done Real Good." Food such as Creole rice calas (sweet rice fritters), a classic breakfast dish that is nearly extinct from menus around town. The food is both delicious *and* calls for health advisories, with dishes such as the praline bacon (topped with sugar and pecans—"pork candy" the shameless chef calls it—or stuffed French toast (*pain perdu* piled high with cream cheese flavored with strawberries). They are now open for dinner, featuring nightly specials like pan-seared salmon with Dijon beurre blanc sauce, and Southern fried chicken livers with pepper jelly. Out-of-the-way or not, this is one of the city's best restaurants.

601 Gallier St. (©) **504/944-9272.** www.elizabeths-restaurant.com. Breakfast and lunch, everything under $10; dinner $8.50–$17. MC, V. Wed–Fri 11am–2:30pm; Sat–Sun 8am–2:30pm; Wed–Sat 6–10pm.

Emeril's CREOLE/NEW AMERICAN   Although it may no longer be trendsetting, Emeril's isn't resting on its laurels in terms of quality, a remarkable feat given how long the place has been around. What's more, there is all kinds of interesting chef action in the kitchen. The menu will change according to the chef, but you should try the barbecued shrimp, which comes with a heavier sauce than the classic versions of this local dish and is paired with little rosemary biscuits. The "salad" of Abita root beer–glazed pork belly consists mostly of large slabs of the soft rich meat and is a must for carnivores in the crowd. Entree standouts include oyster dressing–crusted salmon with tuna "bacon" and andouille-crusted redfish. Try to save part of your generously portioned meal for leftovers so that you have room for the notable banana cream pie or some delicate homemade sorbets.

800 Tchoupitoulas St. (©) **504/528-9393.** www.emerils.com. Reservations highly recommended at dinner. Main courses dinner $26–$39, lunch $19–$25; menu degustation (tasting menu) $65, only on weekends. AE, DC, DISC, MC, V. Dinner daily 6–10pm; lunch Mon–Fri 11:30am–2pm.

Galatoire's FRENCH   Is this the best restaurant in New Orleans or past its prime? This conversation was rendered irrelevant when it reopened after Katrina. Walking into its classic green-wallpaper interior, exactly as it used to be, complete with favorite waiter John, at his post for 35 years and counting, despite the loss of his home to flooding, was such a relief, such a return to normalcy that any gastronomic inadequacies are easy to overlook. Or even welcomed—you don't come to Galatoire's for cutting-edge cuisine. You come here to eat a nice piece of fish, perfectly sautéed or broiled, topped with fresh crabmeat. It was Tennessee Williams's favorite restaurant. Galatoire's has been run by the same family since 1905, and its traditions remain intact. It is New Orleans tradition and a symbol of everything else we could have lost, and that alone makes it worth the trip.

209 Bourbon St. © 504/525-2021. www.galatoires.com. Reservations accepted for upstairs. Jackets required after 5pm and all day Sun. Main courses $19–$34. AE, DC, DISC, MC, V. Tues–Sat 11:30am–10pm; Sun noon–10pm. Closed Memorial Day, July 4th, Thanksgiving, and Christmas.

Irene's Cuisine FRENCH/ITALIAN   Waiting upward of 90 minutes for a table at Irene's is something you can count on. But those same locals feel the French Provincial and Italian food is worth it. Once you do enter, after being lured in from a block away by the smell of garlic, you will find a dark, cluttered tavern, not unromantic, with ultra-friendly waiters who seem delighted you came and who keep the crowds happy with prompt service. The menu is heavier on meats and fish than pasta; salads come with a tangy balsamic dressing; and soups can be intriguing combinations, such as the sweet potato–andouille sausage concoction. The panned oysters and grilled shrimp appetizer can be magnificent, and don't forget the *pollo rosemarino*—five pieces of chicken marinated, partly cooked, marinated again, and then cooked a final time. Irene's longtime partner, Tommy, opened up his own place, which is more or less Irene's all over again, with one crucial detail: It takes reservations. **Tommy's** is at 746 Tchoupitoulas St. (© **504/581-1103**; www.tommyscuisine.com).

539 St. Philip St. © **504/529-8811.** Limited reservations accepted if space is available. Main courses $17–$28. AE, MC, V. Mon–Sat 5:30–10pm. Closed New Year's Day, July 4th, the week before and including Labor Day (to honor the loss caused by Katrina), Thanksgiving, and Christmas.

Johnny's Po' Boys SANDWICHES   For location (near a busy part of the Quarter) and menu simplicity (po' boys and more po' boys), you can't ask for much more than Johnny's. They put anything you could possibly imagine on huge hunks of French bread, including the archetypal fried seafood (add some Tabasco), deli meats, ham and eggs, and the starch-o-rama that is a french-fry po' boy. You need to try it. *Really.* Johnny boasts that "even my failures are edible," and that says it all. And they deliver!

511 St. Louis St. © **504/524-8129.** Everything under $13. No credit cards. Mon–Fri 9am–3pm; Sat–Sun 8am–4pm.

Liuzza's CREOLE/ITALIAN   Yep, this is a neighborhood institution (since 1947), and when the waitress talks, you betcha you listen. You can only imagine the sorrow regulars felt seeing photos of Liuzza's under 8 feet of water (that's over Shaquille O'Neal's head, the owners pointed out) and the joy they felt when, against so many odds, it reopened, looking the same as always, if cleaner and newer. Everything is back, all that hearty Italian and other comfort food, including the famous deep-fried dill pickle slices and po' boys. Don't miss having a beer in the massive frosted mugs that rode out Katrina safely in the fridge!

3636 Bienville St. © **504/482-9120.** www.liuzzas.com. Main courses $9.50–$20. Cash only. Tues–Thurs 11am–9pm; Fri–Sat 11am–10pm.

Mandina's CREOLE/ITALIAN   In a city renowned for its small, funky local joints as well as its fine-dining establishments, "dis is da ultimate neighbahood N'Awlins restaurant." Tommy Mandina's family has owned and operated this restaurant and bar since the late 1800s, and the menu hasn't changed much in the last 50 years or so. This is a good thing. Standouts among the appetizers are the greasy but yummy fried onion rings, the excellent tangy shrimp rémoulade, and the crawfish cakes. Soups are always fine as well, especially seafood gumbo and turtle soup au sherry. Then go for the wonderful red beans **453** and rice with Italian sausage, the trout meunière, or the grilled trout.

3800 Canal St. © **504/482-9179.** www.mandinasrestaurant.com. Main courses $10–$25. AE, MC, V. Mon–Thurs 11am–9:30pm; Fri–Sat 11am–10:30pm; Sun noon–9pm.

Mother's SANDWICHES/CREOLE   Perhaps the proudest of all restaurants when New Orleans was named Fattest City in the U.S. was Mother's, whose overstuffed, mountain-size po' boys absolutely helped contribute to the results. It has long lines and zero atmosphere, but who cares when faced with a Famous Ferdi Special—a giant roll filled with baked ham (the homemade house specialty), roast beef, gravy, and debris (the bits of beef that fall off when the roast is carved)? There's other food, including one of the best breakfasts in the city.

401 Poydras St. © **504/523-9656.** www.mothersrestaurant.net. Menu items $2.50–$20. AE, MC, V. Mon–Sat 7:30am–8pm.

Patois CONTEMPORARY CREOLE   A sweet setting, in an old house on an otherwise residential street, and equally sweet, if not culinarily thrilling, food makes this a fine choice for a low-key but pleasurable uptown meal. For brunch, it's delightful. Braised pork belly comes as toad in the hole, while tuna carpaccio is topped with ginger and orange blossom vinaigrette. The grilled hanger steak, with a rich red wine bone marrow reduction, is really quite excellent, while the roasted duck breast with a bacon potato apple hash is precisely done. Desserts show an interest of working with twists on standard local offerings; sample one, for sure.

6078 Laurel St. © **504/895-9441.** www.patoisnola.com. Main courses $21–$27. AE, MC, V. Wed–Thurs 5:30–10pm; Fri 11:30am–2pm and 5:30–10:30pm; Sat 5:30–10:30pm; Sun 10:30am–2:30pm.

NEW ORLEANS AFTER DARK

JAZZ & BLUES CLUBS   Donna's, 800 N. Rampart St. (© **504/596-6914;** www. donnasbarandgrill.com), a corner bar at the northern edge of the Quarter, has become one of the top spots for great local music, including the revival of the brass-band experience and a variety of jazz and blues traditions. It doesn't get any more authentic than the jazz at **Preservation Hall,** 726 St. Peter St. (© **888/946-JAZZ** [946-5299] or 504/522-2841). With no seats, terrible sightlines, and constant crowds, you won't be able to see much, but you won't care because you will be having too fun and cheerfully sweaty a time. Even if you don't consider yourself interested in jazz, there is a seriously good time to be had; you probably will come away with a new appreciation for the music.

If your idea of jazz extends beyond Dixieland and you prefer a concert-type setting over a messy nightclub, head for **Snug Harbor,** 626 Frenchmen St. (© **504/949-0696**). On the fringes of the French Quarter (1 block beyond Esplanade Ave.), Snug Harbor is the city's premier showcase for contemporary jazz, with a few blues and R&B combos thrown in for good measure.

ZYDECO   Mid City Lanes Rock 'n' Bowl, 4133 S. Carrollton Ave. (© **504/482-3133;** www.rockandbowl.com), is set in the middle of a bowling alley, in the middle of a strip mall. Mid City bowling is nothing to write home about unless you like lanes that slope. But as a club, it's one of the finest and best experiences in New Orleans. Certainly, it's the best place for zydeco. Mid City is not limited to just zydeco: It also features top New Orleans rock and R&B groups and some touring acts.

The **Spotted Cat Cocktail Lounge,** 623 Frenchmen St. (© **504/943-3887**), is our favorite live-music venue in New Orleans, but that's because of our particular New Orleans aesthetic bent: We are partial to cramped rooms where the band plays without much (if any) amplification, and what they play is usually fresh takes on classic and big-band jazz. **House of Blues,** 225 Decatur St. (© **504/529-2583**), is a little too Disney for New Orleans, but give them credit for adequate sightlines, good sound, and first-rate bookings, from local legends such as the Neville Brothers to such ace out-of-towners as Los Lobos, Marcia Ball, and Nanci Griffith.

The **Maple Leaf Bar,** 8316 Oak St. (© **504/866-9359**), is what a New Orleans club is all about, and its reputation was only furthered when it became the very first live music venue to reopen, just weeks after Katrina, with an emotional, generator-powered performance by Walter "Wolfman" Washington. More often than not, the crowd spills onto the sidewalk and into the street to dance and drink. A good bar and a rather pretty patio out back make the Maple Leaf worth hanging out at.

THE BAR SCENE At the **Carousel Bar & Lounge** in the Monteleone Hotel, 214 Royal St. (© **504/523-3341**), the real attraction is the bar itself—it really is a carousel, and it really does revolve. **Feelings Café,** 2600 Chartres St. (© **504/945-2222**), is a funky, low-key neighborhood restaurant and hangout, set around a classic New Orleans courtyard. **Pat O'Brien's,** 718 St. Peter St. (© **504/525-4823;** www.patobriens.com), is a reliable, rowdy, and friendly introduction to New Orleans, though the wait to get in can be long. It's world famous for its gigantic rum-based **hurricane** drink, served in signature 29-ounce glasses.

Lafitte's Blacksmith Shop, 941 Bourbon St. (© **504/593-9761**), dating from the 1770s, is the oldest building in the Quarter. In other towns, this would be a tourist trap. Here it feels authentic and is totally worth a stop, even if you don't drink.

Outside the Quarter, **Circle Bar,** 1032 St. Charles Ave. (© **504/588-2616**), is a happening place, with a quirky mood. **Ray's Boom Boom Room,** 508 Frenchmen St. (© **504/309-7137**), is the epitome of New Orleans style and is partly owned by local music fave and staunch supporter Kermit Ruffins. Expect nightly music on two stages.

7

The Midwest

The Midwestern states are where traditional small-town America is going strong: You can still find small towns centered around a Main Street; family farms; as well as modern urban metropolises, offering top lodging, dining, and culture.

This chapter concentrates on an area you could call "The Heart of the Heartland": Illinois, Indiana, Michigan, Minnesota, Ohio, and Wisconsin, as well as Missouri. America's richest farmland is found here, as well as some of America's most important big cities, including the great metropolis of Chicago.

The ideal small town still exists, and as you travel through the region, you'll find that people often seem more open, friendly, and down-to-earth—even the cities have a sense of community. Sports are a way of life here, from rooting for your baseball or basketball team—national or local—to hiking, boating, or biking in gently rolling landscape or rugged terrain. And history is everywhere, reflecting the Midwest's Native American legacy and its immigrant heritage, the pioneers of every nationality who first came to settle this land.

1 CHICAGO

Like any great city, Chicago's got something for everyone, whether your tastes run toward world-famous museums and blow-your-budget luxury hotels or family-friendly lodgings and low-key neighborhood restaurants. Like other major American cities, Chicago has benefited from a renewed interest in urban living during the last 10 years. Relatively affordable compared to New York, Chicago is a destination for ambitious young people from throughout the Midwest. The stockyards that built the city's fortune have disappeared; the industrial factories that pumped smoke into the sky south of the city now sit vacant. And yet, a certain brashness remains.

ESSENTIALS

GETTING THERE **By Plane** **O'Hare International Airport** (© **773/686-2200;** www.flychicago.com, online airport code ORD) has long battled with Atlanta's Hartsfield for the title of the world's busiest airport and is served by most domestic carriers and many international airlines. It's northwest of the city proper, about a 30-minute to an hour's drive from downtown; a cab costs about $35. From the airport, the "El" (elevated train) takes you to the Loop for $2 (30- to 40-min. ride).

On the southwest side of the city is Chicago's other major airport, **Midway** (© **773/ 838-0600;** www.flychicago.com, online airport code MDW), smaller than O'Hare and served by fewer airlines (but many of them are discount airlines, so fares into Midway can be cheaper). The El can take you to the Loop in about half an hour. A taxi into town will cost about $30.

GO Airport Express (© **888/2-THEVAN** [284-3826]; www.airportexpress.com) serves most hotels in Chicago with its green-and-white vans; ticket counters are at both airports near baggage claim. The cost is $27 one-way ($49 round-trip) to or from

O'Hare, and $22 one-way ($37 round-trip) to or from Midway. Children ages 6 to 12 ride for half-price. The shuttles operate from 4am to 11:30pm.

By Train   Amtrak (© 800/USA-RAIL [872-7245]; www.amtrak.com) pulls into **Union Station,** 210 S. Canal St., between Adams and Jackson streets (© **312/655-2385;** subway/El: Clinton or Quincy; bus: 1, 60, 151, or 156). There's frequent service from Milwaukee (trip time: 1½ hr.) and Cleveland (6½ hr.); daily service from Detroit (6 hr.), Indianapolis (5½ hr.), St. Louis (5½ hr.), Kansas City (8 hr.), New York (20 hr.), Washington, D.C. (19 hr.), New Orleans (19½ hr.), Los Angeles (30 hr.), San Francisco (53 hr.), and Seattle (46 hr.).

By Car   The major routes into Chicago are **I-80/I-90** from the east (Cleveland), **I-80** and **I-88** from the west (Des Moines), **I-94** from the east (Detroit) and north (Milwaukee), **I-65** from the southeast (Indianapolis), and **I-55** from the southwest (Springfield, St. Louis). I-294 loops around the outer suburbs.

VISITOR INFORMATION   Before your trip, visit the website of the **Chicago Office of Tourism,** Chicago Cultural Center, 78 E. Washington St., Chicago, IL 60602 (© **877/ CHICAGO** [244-2246] or TTY 866/710-0294; www.choosechicago.com), to find out about upcoming events and attractions (they'll also mail you a packet of materials, if you want). Click the "Maps & Transportation" link at the top of the home page for links to maps of Chicago neighborhoods. You can even create your own personalized map of sights you'd like to visit. The **Illinois Bureau of Tourism** (© **800/2CONNECT** [226-6632] or TTY 800/406-6418; www.enjoyillinois.com) will also send you information about Chicago and other Illinois destinations.

GETTING AROUND   By Public Transportation   The **CTA** (Chicago Transit Authority) operates a useful information service (© **836-7000,** or 836-4949 TTY from any area code in the city and suburbs; www.transitchicago.com) that functions daily from 5am to 1am. Excellent CTA maps are usually available at subway or El stations, or by calling the CTA.

Fares for the bus, subway, and El are $2, with an additional 25¢ for a transfer that allows CTA riders to make two transfers on the bus or El within 2 hours of receipt. Children 6 and under ride free, and those between the ages of 7 and 11 pay $1. Seniors can also receive the reduced fare if they have the appropriate reduced-fare permit (call © 312/836-7000 for details on how to obtain one, although this is probably not a realistic option for a short-term visitor).

The CTA uses credit card–size farecards that automatically deduct the exact fare each time you take a ride. The reusable cards can be purchased with a preset value already stored, or riders can obtain cards at vending machines located at all CTA train stations and charge them with whatever amount they choose (a minimum of $2 and up to $100). If within 2 hours of your first ride you transfer to a bus or the El, the turnstiles at the El stations and the fare boxes on buses will automatically deduct from your card just the cost of a transfer (25¢). If you make a second transfer within 2 hours, it's free. The same card can be recharged continuously. Farecards can be used on buses, but you can't buy a card on the bus. If you get on the bus without a farecard, you'll have to pay $2 cash (either in coins or in dollar bills); the bus drivers cannot make change, so make sure that you've got the right amount before hopping on board.

By "El"/Subway   The rapid transit system operates five major lines. The "El" (elevated train) runs partly aboveground and partly below ground, so it's known as both the "El" and the subway. While most trains run every 5 to 20 minutes, decreasing in

frequency in the off-peak and overnight hours, some stations close after work hours (as early as 8:30pm) and remain closed on Saturday, Sunday, and holidays.

By Bus   A few buses that are particularly handy for many visitors are the **no. 146 Marine/Michigan,** an express bus from Belmont Avenue on the North Side that cruises down North Lake Shore Drive (and through Lincoln Park during nonpeak times) to North Michigan Avenue, State Street, and the Grant Park museum campus; the **no. 151 Sheridan,** which passes through Lincoln Park en route to inner Lake Shore Drive and then travels along Michigan Avenue as far south as Adams Street, where it turns west into the Loop (and stops at Union Station); and the **no. 156 LaSalle,** which goes through Lincoln Park and then into the Loop's financial district on LaSalle Street. To locate bus stops, look for the **blue-and-white signs** spaced about 2 blocks apart.

By Metra   The Metra commuter railroad (© **312/322-6777,** or 312/322-6774 TTY Mon–Fri 8am–5pm; www.metrarail.com) serves the six-county suburban area around Chicago with 12 train lines. Several terminals are located downtown, including **Union Station** at Adams and Canal streets, **LaSalle Street Station** at LaSalle and Van Buren streets, **North Western Station** at Madison and Canal streets, and **Randolph Street Station** at Randolph Street and Michigan Avenue. Commuter trains have graduated fare schedules based on the distance you ride.

Free Ride on the Trolley

During the summer, the city of Chicago operates **free trolleys** daily between Michigan Avenue and the Museum Campus (site of the Adler Planetarium, the Field Museum of Natural History, and the Shedd Aquarium); the trolleys run on weekends in the fall and spring. Free trolleys also run year-round between Navy Pier and the Grand/State El station on the Red Line. While the trolleys are supposed to make stops every 30 minutes, waits can be longer during peak tourist season—and they aren't air-conditioned. If you get tired of waiting, CTA public buses travel the same routes for only $2 per person.

By Taxi The meter in Chicago cabs currently starts at $2.25 for the first mile and costs $1.80 for each additional mile, with a $1 surcharge for the first additional rider and 50¢ for each person after that. Due to recent high gas prices, you'll also have to pay an additional $1 fuel surcharge whenever gas prices are above $3 per gallon. Taxis are easy to hail in the Loop, on the Magnificent Mile and the Gold Coast, in River North, and in Lincoln Park, but if you go far beyond these key areas, you might need to call. Cab companies include **Flash Cab** (© 773/561-4444), **Yellow Cab** (© 312/TAXI-CAB [829-4222]), and **Checker Cab** (© 312/CHECKER [243-2537]).

FAST FACTS The best hospital emergency room in Chicago is **Northwestern Memorial Hospital,** 251 E. Huron St. (© 312/926-2000; www.nmh.org), with a right off North Michigan Avenue. The emergency department is located at 240 E. Erie St., near Fairbanks Court (© 312/926-5188, or 312/944-2358 TTY). The hospital's **Physician Referral Service** can be reached at © 877/926-4664. Chicago's 10.25% sales tax is the highest in the country, and the hotel room tax is a steep 14.9%.

SPECIAL EVENTS & FESTIVALS The **Mayor's Office of Special Events** operates a recorded hot line (© 312/744-3370) listing current special events, festivals, and parades occurring throughout the city. The city of Chicago also maintains a 24-hour information line for those with hearing impairments; call © 312/744-8599.

During the second week of June, you can catch the free **Chicago Blues Festival** at the Petrillo Music Shell, at Jackson and Columbus drives in Grant Park (© 312/744-3315), with dozens of acts performing over 4 days. In late June/early July, the **Taste of Chicago** (© 312/744-3315) brings more than 10 days of feasting in the streets, when scores of Chicago restaurants cart their fare to food stands set up throughout Grant Park. Admission is free. The **Chicago Air & Water Show** (© 312/744-3315), at North Avenue Beach, is a hugely popular aquatic and aerial spectacular. It takes place mid-August. On the Saturday before Thanksgiving, at the **Magnificent Mile Lights Festival** (© 312/642-3570), a colorful parade of Disney characters makes its way south along Michigan Avenue, from Oak Street to the Chicago River, with lights being illuminated block by block as the procession passes.

WHAT TO SEE & DO
The Top Attractions

Unless you have a lot of time and a ton of patience, we recommend skipping the view from Chicago's tallest landmark, the famed Sears Tower (no longer owned by Sears nor the tallest building in the world). The view from the 103rd-floor **Sears Tower Skydeck,**

233 S. Wacker Dr. (© **312/875-9696;** www.the-skydeck.com), is everything you'd expect it to be—once you get there. Unfortunately, you're usually stuck in a *very long, very noisy* line, so by the time you make it to the top (sometimes in 2 hr.), your patience could be as thin as the atmosphere up there. And the $13 admission price doesn't make it any more attractive.

Adler Planetarium and Astronomy Museum   The building—a zodiacal 12-sided structure at the end of ornamental Solidarity Drive—is historic, but some of the attractions here will captivate the most jaded video-game addict. The exhibit galleries feature a variety of displays and interactive activities designed to foster understanding of our solar system and more. The 60,000-square-foot **Sky Pavilion** features the must-do **Star-Rider Theater,** which takes you on a mind-blowing interactive virtual-reality trip through the Milky Way and into deep space. The planetarium's signature exhibit, *From the Night Sky to the Big Bang,* traces changing views of the cosmos over 1,000 years and features artifacts from the planetarium's extensive collection of historical astronomical instruments. On the first Friday evening of the month, visitors can view dramatic close-ups of the moon, the planets, and distant galaxies through a closed-circuit monitor connected to the planetarium's Doane Observatory telescope. Allow 2 hours, more if you want to see more than one show.

1300 S. Lake Shore Dr. © **312/922-STAR** (922-7827). www.adlerplanetarium.org. Admission $10 adults, $8 seniors, $6 children 4–17, free for children 3 and under; admission including 1 show and audio tour $19 adults, $17 seniors, $15 children. Free admission Mon–Tues Oct–Nov and Jan–Feb. Memorial Day to Labor Day daily 9:30am–6pm; early Sept to late May daily 9:30am–4:30pm; 1st Fri of every month until 10pm. StarRider Theater and Sky Shows run throughout the day; call main number for current times. Bus: 12 or 146.

Art Institute of Chicago (Kids)   You can't (and shouldn't) miss the Art Institute, which features one of the world's major collections: Japanese *ukiyo-e* prints, ancient Egyptian bronzes and Greek vases, 19th-century British photography, masterpieces by most of the greatest names in 20th-century sculpture, and modern American textiles. Especially notable is the popular Impressionist collection (including one of the world's largest collections of Monet paintings), which boasts George Seurat's pointillist masterpiece *Sunday Afternoon on the Island of La Grande Jette.* Also worth seeing are the galleries of European and American contemporary art, ranging from paintings, sculptures, and mixed-media works by artists from Pablo Picasso and Salvador Dalí to Jackson Pollock and Andy Warhol. Don't miss Marc Chagall's stunning stained-glass windows. Allow 3 hours. The museum has a cafeteria and an elegant full-service restaurant, a courtyard cafe (open June–Sept), and a large shop. It offers a busy schedule of lectures, films, and other special presentations, as well as guided tours.

111 S. Michigan Ave. (at Adams St.). © **312/443-3600.** www.artic.edu. Admission $12 adults, $7 seniors and students with ID, free for children 11 and under. Additional cost for special exhibitions. Free admission Thurs 5–8pm. Mon–Fri 10:30am–5pm (Thurs until 8pm, until 9pm Thurs–Fri Memorial Day to Labor Day); Sat–Sun 10am–5pm. Closed Thanksgiving, Christmas, and New Year's Day. Bus: 3, 4, 60, 145, 147, or 151. Subway/El: Green, Brown, Purple, or Orange line to Adams, or Red Line to Monroe/State or Jackson/State.

Chicago Children's Museum (Kids)   This popular museum has areas especially for preschoolers, as well as for children up to age 10, and several permanent exhibits allow kids a maximum of hands-on fun. There are always creative temporary exhibitions on tap as well: A recent show on games included a larger-than-life chess set. Other exhibits explore such diverse topics as dinosaurs, water resources, prejudice, and more. There's also an **arts-and-crafts area** where visitors can create original artwork to take home. Allow 2 to 3 hours.

Navy Pier, 700 E. Grand Ave. ✆ 312/527-1000. www.chichildrensmuseum.org. Admission $9 adults and children, $8 seniors. Free admission Thurs 5–8pm; free for ages 15 and under 1st Mon of every month. Mon–Fri 10am–5pm (Thurs until 8pm); Sat 10am–8pm; Sun 10am–5pm. Closed Thanksgiving and Christmas. Bus: 29, 65, or 66. Subway/El: Red Line to Grand; transfer to city bus or Navy Pier's free trolley bus.

Field Museum of Natural History (Best) (Kids) You may recognize the museum as the very suitable home turf of the intrepid archaeologist and adventurer hero of the *Indiana Jones* movies. Spread over the museum's 9 acres of floor space are scores of permanent and temporary exhibitions—some interactive, but most requiring the old-fashioned skills of observation and imagination. Highlights include the largest, most complete *Tyrannosaurus rex* fossil ever unearthed—named **"Sue"** for the paleontologist who found it in 1990—an exhibit on ancient Egypt, including 23 mummies. The already kid-friendly place has become even more family friendly with the opening of the **Crown Family PlayLab.** Geared toward children 7 and under, it's filled with hands-on activities for little ones, including an art room, a mini dinosaur dig, and a percussion room filled with drums and other loud instruments.

Roosevelt Rd. and Lake Shore Dr. ✆ 312/922-9410. www.fieldmuseum.org. Admission $14 adults, $11 seniors and students with ID, $9 children 4–11, free for children 3 and under. Free admission the 2nd Mon of every month and daily during Feb. Daily 9am–5pm. Closed Christmas. Bus: 6, 12, or 146.

John G. Shedd Aquarium The Shedd is a city treasure and well deserving of its title as world's largest indoor aquarium, though we wish the admission price to all of the exhibits weren't so steep (though you really should pony up for all of them to truly experience the best the aquarium has to offer). The first thing you'll see as you enter is the **Caribbean Coral Reef** exhibit. This 90,000-gallon circular tank occupies the Beaux Arts–style central rotunda, entertaining spectators who press up against the glass to ogle divers feeding nurse sharks, barracudas, stingrays, and a hawksbill sea turtle. The 3-million-gallon saltwater **Oceanarium** is an indoor marine mammal pavilion that re-creates a Pacific Northwest coastal environment. (*Note:* The Oceanarium will be closed for structural maintenance from Sept 2008 until early June 2009.) As you follow a winding nature trail, you'll encounter beluga whales, white-sided dolphins, Alaskan sea otters, and harbor seals along the way. On a fixed performance schedule in a large pool flanked by an amphitheater, a crew of friendly trainers puts dolphins through their paces of leaping dives, breaches, and tail walking. The newest signature exhibit is *Wild Reef—Sharks at Shedd,* a series of 26 interconnected habitats that house a Philippine coral reef patrolled by sharks and other predators. The floor-to-ceiling windows bring those toothy swimmers up close and personal. Allow 2 to 3 hours.

1200 S. Lake Shore Dr. ✆ 312/939-2438. www.sheddaquarium.org. Day Pass (for all exhibits) $25 adults, $21 seniors and children 3–11, free for children 2 and under; aquarium only $8 adults, $6 seniors and children. Free admission to aquarium only Mon–Tues mid-Sept to Nov and Jan–Feb. Memorial Day to Labor Day daily 9am–6pm; early Sept to late May Mon–Fri 9am–5pm, Sat–Sun 9am–6pm. Bus: 6 or 146.

Lincoln Park Zoo (Value) (Kids) One of Chicago's don't-miss attractions; and because it's free, it's worth at least a quick stop during a stroll through Lincoln Park. The term "zoological gardens" truly fits here: Landmark Georgian Revival brick buildings and modern structures sit among gently rolling pathways, verdant lawns, and a kaleidoscopic profusion of flower gardens. The zoo has taken on an ambitious modernization campaign, and exhibits have been renovated and expanded to reflect natural habitats. The star attraction is the **Regenstein Center for African Apes,** which was completely rebuilt in 2004. **Regenstein African Journey** is home to elephants, giraffes, rhinos, and other large mammals; large glass-enclosed tanks allow visitors to go face-to-face with swimming pygmy hippos and Madagascar hissing cockroaches. The **Small Mammal–Reptile House** is a state-of-the-art facility, housing 200 species in a glass-enclosed walk-through ecosystems simulating river, savanna, and forest habitats. The popular **Sea Lion Pool** is home to harbor seals, gray seals, and California sea lions. The adjoining kids' zoo is very popular with little ones. Allow 2 to 3 hours.

2200 N. Cannon Dr. (at Fullerton Pkwy.). ✆ **312/742-2000.** www.lpzoo.com. Free admission. Buildings daily 10am–5pm (Memorial Day to Labor Day until 6:30pm Sat–Sun). Grounds Memorial Day to Labor Day daily 9am–7pm; Apr–late May and early Sept–Oct daily 9am–6pm; Nov–Mar daily 9am–5pm. Parking $14 for up to 3 hours in on-site lot. Bus: 77, 151, or 156.

McCormick Tribune Bridgehouse & Chicago River Museum

Chicago has more moveable bridges than any other city in the world, and this modest museum provides a glimpse into the machinery that operates them. Although it's located on one of the busiest corners in town, the entrance is easy to miss (you have to walk down a flight of stone steps to river level). Inside, as you walk up the bridgehouse's five floors, historic engravings and photos trace the history of the city as it relates to the river (including the engineering feat that reversed the river's flow). The coolest part is the observation deck directly under the bridge, where you can gawk at the massive gears while listening to the pounding of traffic overhead. To see the gears in action, reserve a spot during one of the scheduled bridge lifts, which take place about six times a month; admission is $10 per person (check the museum's website for dates).

376 N. Michigan Ave. (at the Chicago River). ✆ **312/977-0227.** http://bridgehousemuseum.org/home. Admission $3; free for children 4 and under. May–Oct Thurs–Mon 10am–5pm. Bus: 3, 4, 20, 56, 145, 146, 147, 151, or 157. Subway/El: Brown, Green, Orange, or Purple line to Randolph, or Red Line to Washington/State.

Museum of Contemporary Art (MCA)

The MCA claims to be the largest contemporary art museum in the country, emphasizing experimentation in a variety of mediums—painting, sculpture, photography, video and film, dance, music, and performance. You can see the MCA's highlights in about an hour, although art lovers will want more time to wander (especially if a high-profile exhibit is in town). The permanent collection highlights works created since 1945 by such artists as Alexander Calder, Sol LeWitt, and Bruce Nauman. For visitors who'd like a little guidance about the rather challenging works found here, there is an audio tour for rent as well as a free tour (1 and 6pm Tues; 1pm Wed–Fri; 11am, noon, 1, and 2pm Sat–Sun).

220 E. Chicago Ave. (1 block east of Michigan Ave.). ✆ **312/280-2660.** www.mcachicago.org. Admission $10 adults, $6 seniors and students with ID, free for children 12 and under. Free admission Tues. Tues 10am–8pm; Wed–Sun 10am–5pm. Closed Thanksgiving, Christmas, and New Year's Day. Bus: 3, 10, 66, 145, 146, or 151. Subway/El: Red Line to Chicago.

Museum of Science and Industry (Kids)

The massive Museum of Science and Industry is the granddaddy of interactive museums, with some 2,000 exhibits spread over 14 acres in 75 exhibition halls. A headline attraction is the **Henry Crown Space Center,** where the story of space exploration is documented. A favorite is the descent into a full-scale replica of an Illinois **coal mine.** From historic railroad trains to submarines (a real U-505 German World War II sub!) to space capsules, and from special effects to the mysteries of the human immune system, you'll find the object of your curiosity somewhere in this amazing place. The five-story OMNIMAX Theater offers double features

Value   Museums for Less

If you're planning on visiting lots of Chicago museums, you should invest in a **CityPass,** a prepaid ticket that gets you into the biggest attractions (the Art Institute, Field Museum of Natural History, Shedd Aquarium, Adler Planetarium, Museum of Science and Industry, and Hancock Observatory). The cost at press time was $59 for adults and $49 for children, which is about 50% cheaper than paying all the museums' individual admission fees. You can buy a CityPass at any of the museums listed above or purchase one online before you get to town (**www.citypass.net**).

on weekends (call for times). Although it's a distance from the rest of Chicago's tourist attractions, the museum is easy to reach without a car; take the no. 6 Jeffrey Express bus and the Metra Electric train from downtown (the no. 10 bus runs from downtown to the museum's front entrance during the summer).

57th St. and Lake Shore Dr. (2) **800/468-6674** outside the Chicago area, 773/684-1414, or TTY 773/684-3323. www.msichicago.org. Admission to museum only: $13 adults, $12 seniors, $9 children 3–11, free for children 2 and under. Free admission weekdays in Sept and daily in Jan. Combination museum and OMNIMAX Theater: $20 adults, $19 seniors, $14 children 3–11, free for children 2 and under on an adult's lap. Memorial Day to Labor Day Mon–Sat 9:30am–5:30pm, Sun 11am–5:30pm; early Sept to late May Mon–Sat 9:30am–4pm, Sun 11am–4pm. Closed Christmas. Bus: 6 or Metra Electric train to 57th St. and Lake Park Ave.

Navy Pier (Kids)   Built during World War I, this 3,000-foot-long pier has been transformed into Chicago's top attraction, with eight million visitors each year. A combination of carnival, food court, and boat dock, the pier makes a fun place to stroll (if you don't mind crowds), but you'll have to walk all the way to the end to get the best views back to the city. There's a winter garden, a 3-D IMAX theater, a concert stage, a space that holds an ice rink in winter and a merry-go-round in summer, and a giant 15-story Ferris wheel. Decorative arts fans shouldn't miss the free **Smith Museum of Stained Glass Windows** on the pier's ground floor. The pier is also home to many bland shops and several decent restaurants. During the summer there are fireworks on Wednesday and Saturday. Allow 1 hour.

600 E. Grand Ave. (at Lake Michigan). (2) **800/595-PIER** (595-7437; outside 312 area code) or 312/595-PIER (595-7437). www.navypier.com. Free admission. Summer Sun–Thurs 10am–10pm, Fri–Sat 10am–midnight; fall–spring Mon–Thurs 10am–8pm, Fri–Sat 10am–10pm, Sun 10am–7pm. Parking $19 per day Mon–Thurs; $23 per day Fri–Sun (lots fill quickly). Bus: 29, 65, 66, 120, or 121. Subway/El: Red Line to Grand/State; transfer to city bus or board a free pier trolley bus.

Robie House   One of Frank Lloyd Wright's finest creations, Robie House is one of the great works of 20th-century American architecture. The open layout, linear geometry of form, and craftsmanship are typical of Wright's Prairie School design. Completed in 1909, the home is also notable for its exquisite leaded- and stained-glass doors and windows. The house is undergoing a massive, 10-year restoration, and though it will be open throughout the process, your photos may include plenty of scaffolding. Recommended visiting time: 2 hours.

5757 S. Woodlawn Ave. (at 58th St.). (2) **773/834-1847.** www.wrightplus.org. Admission $12 adults, $10 seniors and children 7–18, free for children 6 and under. Mon–Fri tours at 11am, 1, and 3pm; Sat–Sun

The Wright Stuff in Oak Park

The suburb of Oak Park has the highest concentration of houses or buildings anywhere designed and built by Frank Lloyd Wright, the dean of American architecture.

Oak Park is 10 miles west of downtown Chicago. By car, take the Eisenhower Expressway west (I-290) to Harlem Avenue (Ill. 43) and exit north. Continue on Harlem north to Lake Street. Take a right on Lake and continue to Forest Avenue. Turn left here, and immediately on your right you'll see the **Oak Park Visitor Center,** 158 Forest Ave. (© **888/ OAK-PARK** [625-7275]; www.visitoakpark.com), open daily from 10am to 5pm April through October and from 10am to 4pm November through March. Stop in for orientation, maps, and guidebooks. There's a parking lot next door. From here it's only a few blocks to the heart of the historic district and the Frank Lloyd Wright Home and Studio.

By public transportation, take the Green Line west to Harlem, roughly a 25-minute ride from downtown. Exit the station onto Harlem Avenue, and proceed north to Lake Street. Take a right on Lake to Forest Avenue, and then turn left.

Oak Park has, in all, 25 homes and buildings by Wright, constructed between the years 1892 and 1913, which constitute the core output of his Prairie School period. An extensive tour of Oak Park's historic district leaves from the **Ginkgo Tree Bookshop,** 951 Chicago Ave., on weekends from 11am to 4pm on the hour (tour times are noon, 1pm, and 2pm Nov–Feb). The tour lasts 1 hour and costs $12 for adults, $10 for seniors and students ages 11 to 18, and $5 for children 4 to 10. There's also a self-guided map and audiocassette tour of the historic district for the same price; the audio tour is available at the Ginkgo Tree Bookshop from 10am to 3:30pm. In addition to homes designed by Wright, you will see work by several of his disciples, as well as some charming examples of the Victorian styling that he so disdained.

Frank Lloyd Wright Home and Studio   For the first 20 years of Wright's career, this complex served as the sanctuary from which Wright was to design and execute more than 130 of an extraordinary output of 430 completed buildings. The home began as a cottage that Wright built for his bride in 1889, but it became a work in progress, as Wright remodeled it constantly until 1911 (he left there in 1909). The place has a certain whimsy even if it's not a masterpiece, and you should savor every room as an insight into the workings of a remarkable mind. Tours cannot be booked in advance by phone, but a select number of tickets for each day can be reserved online. Allow 1 hour for the tour, more if you want to browse in the bookshop.

951 Chicago Ave. © **708/848-1976.** www.wrightplus.org. Admission $12 adults, $10 seniors and students 11–18, $5 children 4–10; combined admission for Home and Studio tour and guided or self-guided historic district tour $20 adults, $10 seniors and students 11–18, $5 children 4–10. Admission to home and studio is by guided tour only; tours depart from bookshop Mon–Fri 11am, 1, and 3pm; Sat–Sun every 20 min. 11am–3:30pm. Closed last week in Jan, Thanksgiving, Christmas, and New Year's Day. Facilities for people with disabilities are limited; please call in advance.

Unity Temple   In 1871, a community of Unitarian/Universalists settled near here and built a timber-framed house of worship typical of their native New England. Fire destroyed it around the turn of the 20th century. The congregation asked Frank Lloyd Wright, who was a member, to design an affordable replacement. Using poured concrete with metal reinforcements—a necessity owing to the project's small budget of $40,000—Wright created a building that seems as forbidding as a mausoleum on the outside. But inside, its details capture the tenets of the Prairie School that has made

Wright's name immortal. His use of wood for trim and other decorative touches is exciting to behold; his sensitivity to grain and tone and placement was akin to that of an exceptionally gifted woodworker. Wright's stunning, almost minimalist use of form is what still sets him apart as a relevant and brilliant artist. Allow a half-hour.

875 Lake St. (C) **708/383-8873.** http://unitytemple-utrf.org. Self-guided tours $8 adults; $6 seniors, children 6–12, and students with ID; free for children 5 and under. Free guided tours weekends at 1, 2 and 3pm. Mon–Fri 10:30am–4:30pm; Sat–Sun 1–4pm. Church events can alter schedule; call in advance.

Organized Sightseeing Tours

The **Chicago Trolley Company** (C 773/648-5000; www.chicagotrolley.com) offers guided tours on a fleet of rubber-wheeled "San Francisco–style" trolleys that stop at a number of popular spots around the city. An all-day hop-on, hop-off pass costs $29 adults, $24 seniors, and $15 children 3 to 11.

Chicago is the first city of architecture, and the **Chicago Architecture Foundation (CAF),** 224 S. Michigan Ave. (C **312/922-3432,** or 922-TOUR [922-8687] for recorded information; www.architecture.org), offers first-rate guided programs, led by nearly 400 trained and enthusiastic docents. The foundation offers walking, bike, boat, and bus tours to more than 60 architectural sites and environments in and around Chicago.

We recommend CAF's popular $1^{1}/_{2}$-hour **Architecture River Cruise,** which offers a unique perspective on some of Chicago's top buildings. The docents generally do a good job of making the cruise enjoyable for visitors with all levels of architectural knowledge. Tickets are $28 per person weekdays, $30 on weekends and holidays, and are scheduled hourly every day June through October. The trips are extremely popular, so purchase tickets in advance through **Ticketmaster** (C **312/902-1500;** www.ticketmaster.com/ Illinois), or avoid the service charge and buy your tickets at one of the foundation's tour centers, 224 S. Michigan Ave., or the John Hancock Center, or from the boat launch on the southeast corner of Michigan Avenue and Wacker Drive.

SHOPPING

The **Magnificent Mile** refers to the roughly mile-long stretch of North Michigan Avenue between Oak Street and the Chicago River. The density of first-rate shopping is unmatched anywhere. Whether your passion is Tiffany diamonds, Chanel suits, or Gap jeans, you'll find it on this stretch of concrete. **American Girl Place,** on the ground floor of the Water Tower Place mall, 835 N. Michigan Ave. (C **877/AG-PLACE** [247-5223]) is one of the most-visited attractions in town, thanks to the popularity of the company's historical character dolls. A stage show brings stories from the American Girl books to life. At the intersection of Michigan Avenue and Erie Street is a Chicago retail institution, the barrel-shaped flagship store of **Crate & Barrel,** 646 N. Michigan Ave. (C **312/787-5900**). Chicago's first—and still busiest—vertical mall is **Water Tower Place,** a block-size marble-sheathed building at 835 N. Michigan Ave., between East Pearson and East Chestnut streets (C **312/440-3165**).

In the State Street area, **Macy's at State Street** (formerly Marshall Field's), 111 N. State St., at Randolph (C **312/781-1000**), remains one of the world's largest department stores, occupying an entire city block and featuring the largest Tiffany glass mosaic dome in the United States. Aside from Macy's, State Street has become a hot destination for bargain hunters in recent years, thanks to the opening of discount stores such as **Loehmann's,** 151 N. State St. (C **312/705-3810**); **Nordstrom Rack,** 24 N. State St. (C **312/377-5500**); **T.J. Maxx,** 11 N. State St. (C **312/553-0515**); and **Filene's Basement,** 1 N. State St. (C **312/553-1055**).

It's a Beautiful Day, So Let's Play Two

Forget about all these new old-style ballparks. **Wrigley Field** (© **773/404-CUBS** [404-2827]; www.cubs.mlb.com), the home of the Cubs—with its ivy-covered outfield walls, its hand-operated scoreboard, and its "W" or "L" flag announcing the outcome of the game to the unfortunates who couldn't attend—is the real McCoy. To get here, take the Red Line to Addison. To buy tickets in person, stop by the ticket windows Monday through Friday from 9am to 6pm, Saturday from 9am to 4pm, and game days. Or call © **800/THE-CUBS** [843-2827] for tickets through **Tickets.com** (© **866/652-2827** outside of Illinois).

Along with becoming Chicago's primary art gallery district, **River North**—the area west of the Magnificent Mile and north of the Chicago River—has attracted many interesting shops, concentrated on Wells Street from Kinzie Street to Chicago Avenue. **Manifesto,** 755 N. Wells St., at Chicago Avenue (© **312/664-0733**), offers custom-designed furniture, as well as imports from Italy and elsewhere in Europe; **Mig & Tig,** 540 N. Wells St., at Ohio Street (© **312/644-8277**), carries charming furniture and decorative accessories; and **Lightology,** 215 W. Chicago Ave., at Wells Street (© **312/944-1000**), boasts a mind-boggling array of lighting from more than 400 manufacturers.

The North Side neighborhood of **Lincoln Park** has a variety of unique specialty shops that make it easy to browse your way through this leafy, picturesque community. One constant in the ever-changing youth culture has been the **Alley,** 3228 N. Clark St., at Belmont Avenue (© **773/883-1800**), an "alternative shopping complex" selling everything from plaster gargoyles to racks of leather jackets. It has separate shops specializing in condoms, cigars, and bondage wear.

WHERE TO STAY

Discounted rooms at more than 30 downtown hotels are available through **Hot Rooms** (© **800/468-3500** or 773/468-7666; www.hotrooms.com). The 24-hour service is free, but if you cancel a reservation, you're assessed a $25 fee. A centralized B&B reservations service called **At Home Inn Chicago** (© **800/375-7084** or 312/640-1050; www.athomeinnchicago.com) lists more than 70 accommodations in Chicago. Options range from high-rise and loft apartments to guest rooms carved from a former private club on the 40th floor of a Loop office building.

The Blackstone, A Renaissance Hotel   The Blackstone was once one of Chicago's top hotels; in 1920, Republican leaders gathered there to pick Warren Harding as their presidential candidate. Following a renovation, the place reopened in 2008, and guests can get a glimpse of the hotel's original glamour in the wood-lined lobby. The rooms, decorated in understated cream, red, and wood tones, are quite spacious, and the large modern bathrooms have marble vanities and glass-enclosed shower stalls. For a great view, book a (more expensive) lakefront room; the well-stocked fitness room also looks out over Lake Michigan. When you've worked up an appetite, head for the Starbucks off the lobby or grab dinner at **Mercat a la Planxa,** a bright, airy tapas restaurant.

636 S. Michigan Ave. (at Balbo St.), Chicago, IL 60605. © **800/468-3571** or 312/447-0955. Fax 312/765-0545. www.blackstonerenaissance.com. 332 units. $229–$509 double; $3,000 suite. AE, DC, DISC, MC, V. Valet parking $45 with in/out privileges. Subway/El: Red Line to Harrison. **Amenities:** Restaurant; fitness room.

The Drake Hotel Fronting East Lake Shore Drive, this 1920 landmark building is more old-time glamour than glitz, but a $100-million renovation has streamlined its design and modernized the guest rooms. The typical room is spacious and furnished comfortably with a separate sitting area; some have two bathrooms. The lake-view rooms are lovely, though you'll pay more for them. All rooms have bathrobes. The **Coq d'Or is** one of Chicago's most atmospheric piano bars.

140 E. Walton Place (at Michigan Ave.), Chicago, IL 60611. (𝐶) **800/55-DRAKE** (553-7253) or 312/787-2200. Fax 312/787-1431. www.thedrakehotel.com. 535 units. $199–$425 double; $279–$495 executive floor; from $545 suite. AE, DC, DISC, MC, V. Valet parking $41 with in/out privileges. Subway/El: Red Line to Chicago. **Amenities:** 3 restaurants; fitness center.

Four Seasons Hotel (Best) (Kids) The Four Seasons—occupying a rarefied aerie between the 30th and 46th floors above the Mag Mile's most upscale vertical mall— offers an understated luxury that appeals to publicity-shy Hollywood stars and wealthy families. The beautiful rooms have English furnishings, custom-woven carpets and tapestries, and dark-wood armoires. Each has a VCR and windows that open to let in the fresh air. Bathrooms boast such indulgences as a lighted makeup mirror, oversize towels and robes, scales, and Bulgari toiletries. Kid-friendly services include little robes, balloon animals, Nintendo, and milk and cookies. The hotel's elegant fitness center and spa exude the same upscale, old-money feel as the rest of the public areas.

120 E. Delaware Place (at Michigan Ave.), Chicago, IL 60611. (𝐶) **800/332-3442** or 312/280-8800. Fax 312/280-1748. www.fourseasons.com. 343 units. $495–$695 double; $735–$3,700 suite; weekend rates from $385. AE, DC, DISC, MC, V. Valet parking $36 with in/out privileges; self-parking $30. Subway/El: Red Line to Chicago. Pets accepted. **Amenities:** 2 restaurants; indoor pool; fitness center; spa.

Hotel Allegro Chicago (Value) The Allegro has a more laid-back vibe than other Loop hotels. That makes it a good bet for families, as long as you don't need to spread out (the rooms don't have much space beyond the bed, an armoire, and an armchair). Still, the white-and-blue color scheme is cheery, and the compact bathrooms have built-in marble shelves. Befitting a place where the doorman hums along to the tunes playing on speakers out front, the Allegro appeals to younger travelers. **Encore,** the in-house lounge, serves cocktails late into the night, and the hotel's restaurant, **312 Chicago,** attracts nonguests in search of excellent Italian cuisine. *A note to theater fans:* The Allegro has access to exclusive seats for many high-profile downtown shows and often promotes special theater packages.

171 W. Randolph St. (at LaSalle St.), Chicago, IL 60601. (𝐶) **800/643-1500** or 312/236-0123. Fax 312/236-0917. www.allegrochicago.com. 483 units. $149–$299 double; $225–$399 suite. AE, DC, DISC, MC, V. Valet parking $40 with in/out privileges. Subway/El: All lines to Washington. Pets allowed. **Amenities:** Restaurant; exercise room (and access to nearby health club w/indoor pool for $10 per day).

Hotel Cass, A Holiday Inn Express A hidden gem, the Hotel Cass is tucked just 2 blocks off the Magnificent Mile, within walking distance of shopping, restaurants, and far more expensive luxury hotels. Space may be at a premium—the check-in area and lobby-lounge are compact—but everything is bright and stylish. The rooms are small (in some, there's barely room for the flatscreen TVs, which are mounted on mechanical arms that reach over the bed). But the beds are soft and comfortable, with masses of pillows, and bathrooms tuck stylish amenities like rectangular sinks into a compact space. A bonus for budget-conscious travelers: the complimentary buffet breakfast, which includes eggs, bacon, and decadently delicious cinnamon rolls.

Chicago

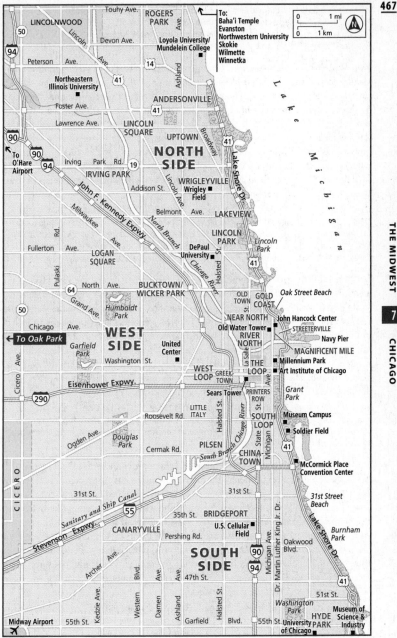

640 N. Wabash Ave. (btw. Erie and Ontario sts.), Chicago, IL 60611. ℂ **800/799-4030** or 312/787-4030. Fax 312/787-8544. www.casshotel.com. 175 units. $99–$189 double. AE, DC, DISC, MC, V. Valet parking $42 with in/out privileges; self-parking $32 with no in/out privileges. Subway/El: Red Line to Grand. Small pets accepted for a $25 fee. **Amenities:** Access to nearby health club for $10 per day.

Majestic Hotel   Located on a charming tree-lined street (but convenient to the many restaurants and shops of Lincoln Park), this is a good choice for anyone who wants a quiet, bed-and-breakfast type of hotel stay. Some of the larger suites—the most appealing are those with sun porches—offer butlers' pantries with fridge, microwave, and wet bar. Avoid the claustrophobic single rooms with alley views. Guests receive a complimentary continental breakfast and afternoon tea in the lobby. Some of the larger suites—the most appealing are those with sun porches—offer butler's pantries with a fridge, microwave, and wet bar. *Tip:* The owners of this property also run the nearby **City Suites Hotel,** 933 W. Belmont Ave. at Sheffield Avenue (ℂ **800/248-9108**), which offers excellent value in a somewhat noisy location.

528 W. Brompton St. (at Lake Shore Dr.), Chicago, IL 60657. ℂ **800/727-5108** or 773/404-3499. Fax 773/404-3495. www.cityinns.com. 52 units. $99–$179 double; $129–$219 suite. Rates include continental breakfast. AE, DC, DISC, MC, V. Self-parking $22 in nearby garage with no in/out privileges. Subway/El: Red Line to Addison; walk several blocks east to Lake Shore Dr. and then 1 block south. **Amenities:** Free passes to nearby Bally's health club. *In room:* Fridge and microwave (some suites only).

Park Hyatt Chicago   For those in search of chic modern luxury, the Park Hyatt is the coolest hotel in town. The property's best rooms are those that face east, overlooking the bustle of the Mag Mile and the lake in the distance. Luxury might be the watchword here, but the look is anything but stuffy: The lobby feels like a sleek modern art gallery and rooms feature Eames and Mies van der Rohe reproduction furniture and window banquettes with stunning city views (the windows actually open). The spalike bathrooms are especially wonderful: Slide back the cherrywood wall for views of the city while you soak in the tub. The comfortable beds are well appointed with several plush pillows, and all rooms offer DVD players, CD players, and flatscreen TVs.

800 N. Michigan Ave., Chicago, IL 60611. ℂ **800/233-1234** or 312/335-1234. Fax 312/239-4000. http://park.hyatt.com. 203 units. $385–$525 double; $695–$3,000 suite. AE, DC, DISC, MC, V. Valet parking $42 with in/out privileges. Subway/El: Red Line to Chicago. **Amenities:** Restaurant; indoor pool; health club; spa.

The Peninsula Chicago   The Peninsula Chicago mixes an Art Deco sensibility with top-of-the-line amenities. Although the lobby is grand, rooms are average in size. But the technology is cutting edge: A "command station" by every bed allows guests to control all the lights, the TV, and room temperature without getting out from under the covers. The marble-filled bathrooms have separate shower stalls and tubs, vanities with plenty of room to sit, and another "command station" by the bathtub. Add in the flatscreen TVs, and you have a classic hotel that's very much attuned to the present. The hotel bar is one of the city's top spots for romantic assignations (or confidential late-night business negotiations). The sleek, light-filled spa and fitness center are among the city's best and make a lovely retreat (especially the outdoor deck).

108 E. Superior St. (at Michigan Ave.), Chicago, IL 60611. ℂ **866/288-8889** or 312/337-2888. Fax 312/751-2888. http://chicago.peninsula.com. 339 units. $525–$650 double; $795–$7,500 suite. AE, DC, DISC, MC, V. Valet parking $45 with in/out privileges. Subway/El: Red Line to Chicago. Pets accepted. **Amenities:** 4 restaurants; indoor pool w/outdoor deck; fitness center; spa. *In room:* Fridge (upon request).

Ritz-Carlton Chicago (Kids) Top-notch service and a bright, airy setting make this one of Chicago's most welcoming hotels. High atop the Water Tower Place mall, the Ritz-Carlton's lobby is on the 12th floor, with a large bank of windows to admire the city below. The quality of the accommodations is of the highest caliber, although the standard rooms aren't large. Lake views cost more but are spectacular. Families will find this luxury crash pad quite welcoming: Kids can borrow toys and games from a stash kept by the concierge, and family-friendly food is available from room service 24 hours a day. The hotel's excellent Sunday brunch includes a special buffet for children replete with M&Ms, macaroni and cheese, and pizza.

160 E. Pearson St., Chicago, IL 60611. (©) **800/621-6906** or 312/266-1000. Fax 312/266-1194. www. fourseasons.com. 435 units. $495–$635 double; $710–$4,000 suite; weekend rates from $385. AE, DC, DISC, MC, V. Valet parking $40 with in/out privileges; self-parking $32 with no in/out privileges. Subway/ El: Red Line to Chicago. Pets accepted. **Amenities:** 2 restaurants; indoor pool; health club w/spa.

The Silversmith Hotel & Suites (Value) This landmark building was built in 1897 to serve the jewelry and silver trade on Wabash Avenue, still known as Jeweler's Row. Rooms come in varying configurations, with 12-foot-high ceilings, 10-foot picture windows, Frank Lloyd Wright–inspired wrought-iron fixtures, armoires, and homey bedding; bathrooms are generously sized and some have whirlpool tubs. Natural light is limited in the rooms; those along the hotel's main corridor tend to be dark. And though windows are extra thick to muffle the noise of nearby El trains, you'll want to avoid the lower-level floors if you like things quiet; request a Wabash Avenue room on the 9th or 10th floor. Rooms don't book up as quickly as at other, hotter spots, so this is one place thrifty travelers can look for a good deal.

10 S. Wabash Ave. (at Madison St.), Chicago, IL 60603. (©) **800/2-CROWNE** (227-6963) or 312/372-7696. Fax 312/372-7320. www.crowneplaza.com/silversmith. 143 units. $179–$359 double; from $289 suite; weekend rates available. AE, DC, DISC, MC, V. Valet parking $30 with in/out privileges. Subway/El: Brown, Green, or Orange line to Madison, or Red Line to Washington. **Amenities:** Restaurant (deli); fitness room (w/access to nearby health club for $10 per day). *In room:* Fridge.

Sofitel Chicago Water Tower Architect Jean-Paul Viguier created a building that's impossible to pass without taking a second look: a soaring, triangular white tower that sparkles in the sun. But the place doesn't take itself too seriously, as you'll see when you walk in the airy lobby and check out the luminescent floor tiles that change color in a never-ending light show. The overall feel is European modern; you'll hear French accents from some of the front desk staff. Guest rooms feature contemporary decor with natural beechwood walls and chrome hardware. All the rooms enjoy good views of the city (but the privacy-conscious will want to stay on the upper floors, where they won't be as close to surrounding apartment buildings). The standard doubles are fairly compact—but thanks to large picture windows, the spaces don't feel cramped, and the luxurious marble bathrooms are quite spacious.

20 E. Chestnut St. (at Wabash St.), Chicago, IL 60611. (©) **800/SOFITEL** (763-4835) or 312/324-4000. Fax 312/324-4026. www.sofitel.com. 415 units. $240–$555 double; $370–$685 suite. AE, DC, DISC, MC, V. Valet parking $40. Subway/El: Red Line to Chicago. Small pets accepted. **Amenities:** Restaurant; fitness center.

Talbott Hotel The Talbott's cozy atmosphere and personal level of service appeal to visitors who don't mind forgoing extensive amenities in exchange for a hotel with the intimacy and atmosphere of a bed-and-breakfast. The wood-paneled lobby, decorated with leather sofas and velvety armchairs, two working fireplaces, tapestries, and numerous French horns used for fox hunts, is intimate and inviting. Although comfortable, the rooms aren't quite as distinctive; they also vary in size, so ask when making reservations. Suites and the hotel's "executive king" rooms have Jacuzzi tubs; suites also have separate sitting areas with sofa beds and dining tables.

20 E. Delaware Place (btw. Rush and State sts.), Chicago, IL 60611. © **800/TALBOTT** (825-2688) or 312/944-4970. Fax 312/944-7241. www.talbotthotel.com. 149 units. $169–$449 standard kings; $260–$671 suites. AE, DC, DISC, MC, V. Valet parking $40 with in/out privileges; self-parking $30. Subway/El: Red Line to Chicago. **Amenities:** Complimentary access to nearby health club.

W Chicago Lakeshore   The only hotel in Chicago with a location on the lake, this property prides itself on being a hip boutique hotel—but sophisticated travelers may feel like it's trying way too hard with dance music playing in the lobby and black-clad staff members doing their best to be eye candy. The compact rooms are decorated in deep red, black, and gray—a scheme that strikes some travelers as gloomy—and sport such high-tech amenities as VCRs and CD players. The Asian-inspired bathrooms are stylish, but the wooden shades that separate them from the bedroom don't make for much privacy. In W-speak, rooms and suites are "wonderful" (meaning standard, with a city view), which we prefer, or "spectacular" (meaning a lake view, for which you'll pay more). Unwind at the hotel's outpost of New York's popular Bliss Spa.

644 N. Lake Shore Dr. (at Ontario St.), Chicago, IL 60611. © **877/W-HOTELS** (946-8357) or 312/943-9200. Fax 312/255-4411. www.whotels.com. 520 units. $219–$429 double; from $399 suite. AE, DC, DISC, MC, V. Valet parking $44 with in/out privileges. Subway/El: Red Line to Grand. Pets accepted. **Amenities:** Restaurant; pool; exercise room; spa.

WHERE TO DINE

Ann Sather SWEDISH/AMERICAN   This is a Chicago institution where you can enjoy Swedish meatballs with noodles and brown gravy, or the Swedish sampler of duck breast with lingonberry glaze, meatball, potato-sausage dumpling, sauerkraut, and brown beans. All meals are full dinners, including appetizer, main course, vegetable, potato, and dessert. It's the sticky cinnamon rolls, though, that make addicts out of diners. Weekend brunch here can get frenzied, but the people-watching is priceless: a cross section of gay and straight, young and old, from club kids to elderly couples.

929 W. Belmont Ave. (btw. Clark St. and Sheffield Ave.). © **773/348-2378.** www.annsather.com. Reservations accepted for parties of 6 or more. Main courses $6–$12. AE, DC, MC, V. Mon–Fri 7am–3pm; Sat–Sun 7am–4pm. Free parking with validation. Subway/El: Brown or Red line to Belmont.

Bistrot Margot FRENCH BISTRO   Bistrot Margot is not only one of the best restaurants in Old Town—it's also one of the city's better French bistros. It can get very busy and loud, and the tables are quite close together, but for many, that only adds to its charm. Start with out-of-this-world mussels in white wine with fresh herbs, then try one of the specials for the main course. The usual suspects (roasted chicken with garlic, lemon, herbs, and french fries or a terrific steak frites) are proof that, when done right, it's hard to beat classic French cuisine. On warm summer nights, the restaurant sets about half a dozen tables on the sidewalk, which, on this colorful stretch of Wells Street, makes for a truly memorable meal.

1437 N. Wells St. (at W. Schiller St.). © **312/587-3660.** www.bistrotmargot.com. Reservations recommended. Main courses $16–$26. AE, DC, MC, V. Mon 11:30am–9pm; Tues–Thurs 11:30am–10pm; Fri 11:30am–11pm; Sat 10:30am–11pm; Sun 10:30am–9pm. Subway/El: Red Line to Clark/Division, or Brown Line to Sedgwick.

Carson's Value AMERICAN/BARBECUE   A true Chicago institution, Carson's calls itself "The Place for Ribs," and, boy, is it ever. The barbecue sauce is sweet and tangy, and the ribs are meaty. Included in the $22 price for a full slab of baby backs are coleslaw and one of four types of potatoes (the most decadent are au gratin), plus right-out-of-the-oven rolls. When you're seated at your table, tie on your plastic bib—and indulge. There are some selections for noncarnivores, but let's be honest, you don't go to a rib joint to have seafood. If by some remarkable feat you have room left after dinner, the candy-bar sundaes are a scrumptious finale to the meal. *Note:* There's often a wait for a table at dinnertime.

612 N. Wells St. (at Ontario St.). ✆ 312/280-9200. www.ribs.com. Reservations accepted for groups of 6 or more. Main courses $13–$34. AE, DC, DISC, MC, V. Mon–Thurs 11:30am–10:30pm; Fri 11:30am–11:30pm; Sat noon–11:30pm; Sun noon–10:30pm. Subway/El: Red Line to Grand.

Charlie Trotter's (Best) ECLECTIC   Foodies flock to the namesake restaurant of celebrity chef Charlie Trotter. There is no a la carte menu, so this is not the place to come if you're a picky eater. Your choice of the vegetable ($135) or grand ($155) menu degustation (the extensive nonmeat choices make this an excellent spot for vegetarians) will feature an ever-changing lineup of exceptional dishes made with organic or free-range products. Recent menus featured ragout of leek confit, braised carrots, salsify, and cauliflower with Perigord black truffle emulsion; and black buck venison with Japanese kumai jasmine rice cake and red-wine Kalamata olive emulsion. The dining room is relatively formal, the staff highly professional but not intimidating. The wine list is extensive, and a sommelier will help match wines with each course. The entire restaurant is nonsmoking. For a taste of Trotter's gourmet fare without the high price tag, check out **Trotter's to Go,** his gourmet food store in Lincoln Park at 1337 W. Fullerton Ave., between Lakewood and Wayne avenues (✆ 773/868-6510).

816 W. Armitage Ave. (at Halsted St.). ✆ 773/248-6228. www.charlietrotters.com. Reservations required. Jackets required, ties requested. Fixed-price menus $135 and $155. AE, DC, DISC, MC, V. Seatings Tues–Thurs at 6 and 9pm; Fri–Sat at 5:30 and 9pm. Subway/El: Brown Line to Armitage.

Crofton on Wells CONTEMPORARY AMERICAN   Chef-owner Suzy Crofton has devoted herself to this acclaimed restaurant, a 70-seat River North storefront with a loyal following. Crofton's food is simply sophisticated and decidedly American, and the spare dining room fits in with her no-attitude, Midwestern aesthetic. The menu is based on seasonally available ingredients: You might start with a chilled cucumber and Vidalia onion soup with shrimp, melon, and avocado; then move on to grilled venison medallions, soaked in a red-wine sauce with cabbage, huckleberries, and arugula pesto. Entree selections always include a vegan choice. Close with a Granny Smith apple tart or bittersweet chocolate cake with espresso ice cream and black-peppercorn caramel sauce. A four-course prix-fixe meal is available Monday through Saturday from 5 to 6:30pm for $45 ($65 with wine).

535 N. Wells St. (btw. Grand Ave. and Ohio St.). ✆ 312/755-1790. www.croftononwells.com. Reservations recommended. Main courses $26–$34. AE, DC, MC, V. Mon–Sat 5–10pm. Subway/El: Brown Line to Merchandise Mart.

Everest ALSATIAN/FRENCH   Forty stories above the Chicago Stock Exchange, the refined Everest features the best views of any restaurant in the city and four-star fine dining. Its windows overlook the nightscape of downtown Chicago, and its culinary experience is one of the finest in town. Refined sensibilities, culinary imagination, and a focus on "noble" and "simple" ingredients enhance chef Jean Joho's appreciation of the cookery of his native Alsace. While the menu changes frequently, you might find a starter of salmon soufflé followed by an entree of poached tenderloin of beef cooked *pot-au-feu* style and served with horseradish cream. Desserts are sumptuous and the wine list offers wonderful American and Alsatian selections.

440 S. LaSalle St., 40th floor (at Congress Pkwy.). ✆ **312/663-8920.** www.everestrestaurant.com. Reservations required. Main courses $27–$46; menu degustation $89; 3-course pretheater dinner $49. AE, DC, DISC, MC, V. Tues–Thurs 5:30–9pm; Fri 5:30–9:30pm; Sat 5–10pm. Complimentary valet parking. Subway/El: Brown Line to LaSalle/Van Buren, or Red Line to Adams.

The Gage IRISH/AMERICAN Downtown's first gastropub feels as if it's been here forever, thanks to an impeccable remodeling of a historic space. With the Gage they have created a place where the food deserves equal billing with the drinks. (This is also one of the few places in the Loop that serves decent food late, even on weeknights.) The menu has headings listed simply "First," "Second," "Third," and "Fourth"; the result is an emphasis on appetizer-size portions, which you can order in any combination. Choices run the gamut from basic (homemade chicken noodle soup; burgers; roasted Amish chicken) to exotic (the roast saddle of elk, for which you'll pay an eye-popping $38). On weekends, they serve brunch, including a traditional Irish breakfast of eggs, rashers, black and white puddings, sausages, and beans on toast.

24 S. Michigan Ave. (btw. Madison and Monroe sts.). ✆ **312/372-4243.** www.thegagechicago.com. Reservations recommended on weekends. Main courses $12–$18 lunch, $20–$38 dinner. AE, DC, MC, V. Mon–Fri 11am–2am; Sat 10am–3am; Sun 10am–midnight. Subway/El: Red Line to Monroe, or Brown or Orange line to Madison.

Gino's East PIZZA Gino's East was once the only Chicago restaurant where patrons would wait outside nightly—even in the winter—for pizza. Now that the restaurant has moved into new digs, there are no more lines out front, though diners still sit in dark-stained booths, surrounded by paneled walls covered with graffiti. Many Chicagoans consider Gino's *the* quintessential deep-dish Chicago-style pizza. True to its reputation, the pizza is heavy (a small cheese pizza is enough for two), so work up an appetite before chowing down. Specialty pizzas include the supreme, with layers of cheese, sausage, onions, green pepper, and mushrooms; and the vegetarian, with cheese, onions, peppers, asparagus, summer squash, zucchini, and eggplant.

633 N. Wells St. (at Ontario St.). ✆ **312/943-1124.** www.ginoseast.com. Reservations not accepted. Pizza $12–$29. AE, DC, DISC, MC, V. Mon–Thurs 11am–10pm; Fri–Sat 11am–11pm; Sun noon–9pm. Subway/El: Red Line to Grand.

Hot Chocolate AMERICAN Mindy Segal's desserts got raves when she worked at the restaurant mk, so when she opened her own place—with a dessert theme, no less—there were lines almost immediately. Stop by for a brioche and coffee in the morning, a Kobe beefsteak sandwich at lunch, or a plate of glazed pork tenderloin in the evening. Don't leave without having dessert. Many, including the apple-cider potpie and the banana napoleon, with layers of caramelized bananas, banana coffeecake, graham crackers, and a topping of banana ice cream, use seasonal fruit, but chocoholics can get their fill, too, with dishes such as the rich chocolate soufflé with caramel ice cream or a flight of mini hot chocolates served with homemade marshmallows. Come on a weekday (for a late lunch or early dinner) to avoid a wait.

1747 N. Damen Ave. (at Willow St.). ✆ **773/489-1747.** Reservations not accepted. www.hotchocolate chicago.com. Main courses $10–$13 lunch, $12–$23 dinner. AE, MC, V. Tues–Fri 11am–3pm; Tues–Wed 5:30–10pm; Thurs 5:30–11pm; Fri 5:30pm–midnight; Sat 10am–2pm and 5:30pm–midnight; Sun 10am–2pm and 5:30–10pm. Subway/El: Blue Line to Damen.

Morton's STEAK   The well-known Morton's chain is Chicago born and bred, and the original is still the king of the Chicago-style steakhouses. It holds its own against an onslaught of steakhouse competition with gargantuan portions of prime, wet-aged steaks, football-size baking potatoes, and trees of broccoli rolled out on a presentation cart. The restaurant is somewhat hidden in an undistinguished high-rise, and the decor hasn't changed in years. Neither has the menu: House specialties include the double filet mignon with sauce béarnaise, and classic cuts of porterhouse, New York strip, and rib-eye. This is a great place for a slice of carnivorous Chicago power dining—and a slice of Key lime pie or New York cheesecake.

1050 N. State St. (at Rush St.). ℂ **312/266-4820.** www.mortons.com. Reservations recommended. Main courses $26–$44. AE, DC, DISC, MC, V. Mon–Sat 5:30–11pm; Sun 5–10pm. Subway/El: Red Line to Chicago.

North Pond AMERICAN   Tucked away in Lincoln Park, North Pond is a hidden treasure. The restaurant's Arts and Crafts–inspired interior blends perfectly with the park outside, and a recently added glass-enclosed addition lets you dine "outside" year-round. Chef Bruce Sherman emphasizes organic, locally grown ingredients and favors simple preparations—although the overall result is definitely upscale. One of the seasonal menu items might be grilled sea scallops with orange-Parmesan grain salad, glazed organic baby carrots, and spiced lobster sauce. For dessert, try mango "soup" with banana mousse and candied hazelnuts. To enjoy the restaurant's setting with a slightly lower price tag, try the fixed-price Sunday brunch ($32). The all-American wine list of 100 or so selections focuses on boutique vintners.

2610 N. Cannon Dr. (south of Diversey Pkwy.). ℂ **773/477-5845.** www.northpondrestaurant.com. Reservations recommended. Main courses $29–$37. AE, DC, MC, V. Tues–Sat 5:30–10pm; Sun 10:30am– 1:30pm and 5:30–10pm. Lunch served June–Sept Tues–Fri 11:30am–2pm. Bus: 151.

RoseAngelis ⓥalue NORTHERN ITALIAN   This is neighborhood dining at its best, a place with reliably good food and very reasonable prices. Tucked in a residential side street in Lincoln Park, the restaurant fills the ground floor of a former private home, with a charming series of cozy rooms and a garden patio. The menu emphasizes pasta (the rich lasagna is a favorite). RoseAngelis is vegetarian friendly; there's no red meat on the menu, and many of the pastas are served with vegetables. Finish up with the deli-ciously decadent bread pudding with warm caramel sauce (it's big enough to share). Weeknights are your best bet; on weekends you'll wait up to 2 hours for a table.

1314 W. Wrightwood Ave. (at Lakewood Ave.). ℂ **773/296-0081.** www.roseangelis.com. Reservations accepted for parties of 8 or more. Main courses $10–$16. DISC, MC, V. Tues–Thurs 5–10pm; Fri–Sat 5–11pm; Sun 4:30–9pm. Subway/El: Brown or Red line to Fullerton.

Spiaggia ITALIAN   Spiaggia is the best fine-dining Italian restaurant in the city. The dining room is bright, airy, and sophisticated (wear your jackets, gentlemen). Linger over long lunches, have romantic interludes, and celebrate that big merger. You can order a la carte or try a seven-course degustation menu; entree choices change often and emphasize seasonal ingredients. For your starter, consider carpaccio of smoked Sicilian swordfish. The pasta roster tempts with pheasant-stuffed ravioli, and gnocchi with wild mush-rooms. Entrees include classic zuppa di pesce, and grilled squab over lentils with foie gras. For dessert, the chilled mascarpone cheese torte with rich chocolate gelato and espresso sauce is a high point. Adjacent to the restaurant is the more informal **Café Spiaggia** (ℂ **312/280-2755**), which has the same dinner hours as the main restaurant but is also open for lunch every day. Although prices are lower than at the main restaurant, I wouldn't consider them cheap; lunch entrees (which run $15–$25) include pastas, fish, and pizzas rather than sandwiches.

980 N. Michigan Ave. (at Oak St.). © **312/280-2750.** www.levyrestaurants.com. Reservations strongly suggested on weekends. Main courses $34–$41; menu degustation $165. AE, DC, DISC, MC, V. Sun–Thurs 6–9:30pm; Fri–Sat 5:30–10:30pm. Subway/El: Red Line to Chicago.

Tru AMERICAN   Chefs Rick Tramonto and Gale Gand have made Tru a top dining destination, thanks to its sophisticated-but-not-snobbish cuisine and atmosphere. If your wallet and stomach permit, go for the nine-course Chef Tramonto's Market Collection ($145), featuring selections inspired by what was available at that day's markets. For a conspicuous splurge, order the visually sensational caviar staircase (caviars and fixin's climbing a glass spiral staircase), which goes for $250. Gand is one of the city's best pastry chefs, and her desserts perfectly echo Tramonto's savory menus. For a taste of Gand's talent, a three-course dessert tasting menu is available in the restaurant's lounge for $35 per person. Service is generally polished but not pompous. The expansive wine list is a treat for oenophiles, with 1,200 selections.

676 N. St. Clair St. (at Huron St.). © **312/202-0001.** www.trurestaurant.com. Reservations required. Prix-fixe menu $95–$145. AE, DC, DISC, MC, V. Mon–Thurs 5:30–10pm; Fri–Sat 5–11pm. Subway/El: Red Line to Chicago.

Wishbone ⓥalue ⓚids SOUTHERN   Wishbone is a down-home, casual family spot that inspires intense loyalty (even if the food is only good rather than outstanding). Known for Southern food and big breakfasts, Wishbone's extensive, reasonably priced menu blends hearty, home-style choices with healthful and vegetarian items. Brunch is the 'bone's claim to fame, when an eclectic crowd packs in for the plump and tasty salmon cakes and omelets. For a main course, try the "yardbird," a charbroiled chicken with sweet red-pepper sauce. The tart Key lime pie is one of the best desserts in the city. There's a newer location on the North Side, at 3300 N. Lincoln Ave. (at W. School St.; © **773/549-2663**), but the original location has more character.

1001 Washington St. (at Morgan St.). © **312/850-2663.** www.wishbonechicago.com. Reservations accepted, except for weekend brunch. Main courses $5–$10 breakfast and lunch, $8–$15 dinner. AE, DC, DISC, MC, V. Mon 7am–3pm; Tues–Thurs 7am–3pm and 5–9pm; Fri 7am–3pm and 5–10pm; Sat 8am–3pm and 5–10pm; Sun 8am–3pm.

ZED 451 ECLECTIC   Pay a set price ($49 per person), and you get unlimited trips to the "Harvest Table," a trendy take on the salad bar, with offerings such as roasted cauliflower with balsamic vinegar glaze, wine-poached pears topped with crumbled goat cheese, and homemade soups. Then head back to your table, where the main course comes to you: Chefs stroll throughout the restaurant, offering appetizer-size portions of the day's specialties, which could be anything from glazed pork ribs to lamb chops to duck. The restaurant itself is gorgeous, with soaring ceilings and sexy lighting; the extensive use of natural materials (from the stone pillars to the bar's rock garden) give this distinctly urban environment a warm, sultry vibe.

739 N. Clark St. (1 block south of Chicago Ave.). © **888/493-3451.** www.zed451.com. Prix-fixe meal $49 per person. AE, DC, DISC, MC, V. Mon–Fri 11:30am–2pm and 5–10pm; Sat 4:30–10pm; Sun noon–8pm. Subway/El: Brown or Red line to Chicago.

CHICAGO AFTER DARK

For up-to-date entertainment listings, check the local newspapers and magazines, particularly the "Friday" and "Weekend Plus" sections of the two dailies, the *Chicago Tribune*

and the *Chicago Sun-Times;* the *Chicago Reader* or *New City,* two free weekly tabloids
with extensive listings; and the monthly *Chicago* magazine. The *Tribune's* entertainment-
oriented website, **www.metromix.com**; the *Reader's* website, **www.chireader.com**; and
the Citysearch website, **http://chicago.citysearch.com**, are also excellent sources of
information, with lots of opinionated reviews. For current listings of classical music
concerts and opera, call the **Chicago Dance and Music Alliance** (© **312/987-1123;**
www.chicagoperformances.org).

THE PERFORMING ARTS   The world-class **Chicago Symphony Orchestra,** Orchestra Hall, Symphony Center, 220 S. Michigan Ave. (© **312/294-3000;** www.cso.org),
celebrates the appointment of superstar conductor Riccardo Muti as musical director
(starting in 2010). Summertime visitors have an opportunity to hear a CSO performance
at the delightful **Ravinia Festival** (© **847/266-5100**) in suburban Highland Park. It's
also a tranquil setting for chamber music, world music, jazz and pop concerts, dance, and
music study.

The **Lyric Opera of Chicago,** Civic Opera House, Madison Street and Wacker Drive
(© **312/332-2244;** www.lyricopera.org), performs in the handsome 3,563-seat 1929 Art
Deco Civic Opera House, the second-largest opera house in the country. It attracts top-
notch singers from all over the world and has a strong commitment to new American
works.

If you're going to see just one dance performance while you're in town, make it **Hubbard Street Dance Chicago** (© **312/850-9744;** www.hubbardstreetdance.com), which
combines elements of jazz, modern, ballet, and theater dance. The **Joffrey Ballet of
Chicago** (© **312/739-0120;** www.joffrey.com) has a repertoire that extends from the
ballets of founder Robert Joffrey, George Balanchine, and Jerome Robbins to the cutting-
edge works of Alonzo King and Chicago choreographer Randy Duncan. The Joffrey and
other noted dance and musical performers and touring Broadway shows take the stage at
the landmark **Auditorium Theatre,** 50 E. Congress Pkwy., between Michigan and
Wabash avenues (© **312/922-2110;** www.auditoriumtheatre.org).

THE THEATER SCENE   With more than 200 theaters, Chicago may have dozens of
productions playing on any given weekend. It's one of the best theater cities in the country. To order tickets for many plays and events, call **Ticketmaster Arts Line** (© **312/
902-1500**), a centralized phone-reservation system that allows you to charge full-price
tickets (with an additional service charge) for productions at more than 50 Chicago
theaters. For half-price tickets on the day of the show (on Fri you can also purchase
tickets for weekend performances), drop by one of the **Hot Tix** ticket centers (© **312/
977-1755;** www.hottix.org), located in the Loop at 72 E. Randolph St. (btw. Wabash
and Michigan aves.); at the Water Works Visitor Center, 163 E. Pearson St.; and in
Lincoln Park at Tower Records, 2301 N. Clark St. Tickets are not sold over the phone.
The website lists what's on sale for that day beginning at 10am.

The dean of legitimate theaters in Chicago is the **Goodman,** Dearborn Street,
between Randolph and Lake streets (© **312/443-3800;** www.goodman-theatre.org).
You may not see anything revolutionary, but you'll get some of the best actors in the city
and top-notch production values. The **Steppenwolf Theater Company,** 1650 N. Halsted St., at North Avenue (© **312/335-1650;** www.steppenwolf.org), is famous for
launching the careers of luminaries such as John Malkovich and Gary Sinise. Unfortunately, it may be a victim of its own success. Though the acting is always high caliber,
shows can be hit-or-miss, and unlike in the early days, you're certainly not guaranteed a
thrilling theatrical experience. The home of the **Chicago Shakespeare Theatre** on Navy

Pier, 800 E. Grand Ave. (© **312/595-5600;** www.chicagoshakes.com), is a glittering glass-box complex that rises seven stories. It features a 525-seat courtyard-style theater patterned loosely on the Swan Theatre in Stratford-upon-Avon. The main theater presents three Shakespeare plays a year; founder and artistic director Barbara Gaines usually directs one show. What keeps subscribers coming back is the talented company of actors, including some of the finest Shakespearean performers in the country.

COMEDY & IMPROV   Chicago continues to nurture young comics, drawn to Chicago for the chance to hone their improvisational skills. The **iO** improv troupe (formerly known as ImprovOlympic), 3541 N. Clark St., at Addison Street (© **773/880-0199;** www.iochicago.net), offers a nightclub setting for a variety of unscripted nightly performances, from free-form shows to shows loosely based on concepts such as *Star Trek* or dating. **Second City,** 1616 N. Wells St., in the Pipers Alley complex at North Avenue (© **312/337-3992;** www.secondcity.com), remains the top comedy club in Chicago. You'll rarely see a weak or unfunny show—these actors are magicians at salvaging material that bombs with audiences.

LIVE MUSIC   Born in the Storyville section of New Orleans, **jazz** moved upriver to Chicago some 75 years ago, and it still has a home here. The **Green Mill,** 4802 N. Broadway, off Lawrence (© **773/878-5552;** subway/El: Red Line to Lawrence), is a Chicago treasure; get there early to claim one of the plush velvet booths. Still retaining its speak-easy flavor, it was a popular watering hole during the '20s and '30s, when Al Capone was a regular and the headliners included Sophie Tucker and Al Jolson. The **Back Room,** 1007 N. Rush St., between Oak Street and Bellevue Place (© **312/751-2433;** www.backroomchicago.com), is a vestige of the celebrated old Rush Street, packing a well-dressed crowd into an intimate spot at the back of a long gangway.

The Bucktown/Wicker Park neighborhood is the center of the alternative rock movement. Scan the *Reader* or *New City* to see who's playing where. **Martyrs',** 3855 N. Lincoln Ave., between Berenice Avenue and Irving Park Road (© **773/404-9494;** www.martyrslive.com; subway/El: Brown Line to Addison), presents a variety of local bands and the occasional performance by national touring acts. The low tables, high ceiling, and huge windows make Martyrs' one of the best places to catch a rock-'n'-roll show. **Metro,** 3730 N. Clark St., at Racine Avenue (© **773/549-0203;** www.metrochicago. com; subway/El: Red Line to Sheridan), in an old auditorium, is Chicago's premier venue for live alternative/rock acts on the verge of breaking into the big time. Everybody who is anybody has played here over the years, from REM to such local heroes as Smashing Pumpkins.

The **House of Blues,** 329 N. Dearborn St., at Kinzie Street (© **312/923-2000;** www. hob.com; subway/El: Red Line to Grand), is a massive complex, extravagantly decorated with 600 pieces of Mississippi Delta folk art. It isn't really a blues club as much as a showcase for rock, R&B, zydeco, reggae, and more, consistently booking top national acts. The popular Sunday gospel brunch, offering a Southern-style buffet, brings a different Chicago gospel choir to the stage each week; get tickets in advance.

Country, folk, bluegrass, Latin, and Celtic—the **Old Town School of Folk Music** has it: 4544 N. Lincoln Ave., between Wilson and Montrose avenues (© **773/728-6000;** www.oldtownschool.org; subway/El: Brown Line to Western). The school has hosted everyone from Pete Seeger to bluegrass phenom Alison Krauss. Its pristine 425-seat concert hall in a former 1930s library in Lincoln Square is the world's largest facility dedicated to presenting traditional and contemporary folk music.

I Got the Blues

With a few notable exceptions, Chicago's best and most popular blues showcases are located in the entertainment districts of the Near North Side. **B.L.U.E.S,** 2519 N. Halsted St., between Wrightwood and Fullerton avenues (✆ **773/528-1012;** www.chicagobluesbar.com; subway/El: Red/Brown lines to Fullerton), is a small joint for the serious blues aficionado—you won't miss a single move of the musicians standing on stage only yards away. Nearby, at 2548 N. Halsted St., between Wrightwood and Fullerton avenues, is **Kingston Mines** (✆ **773/477-4646;** www.kingstonmines.com; subway/El: Red/Brown lines to Fullerton), one of Chicago's premier blues bars, which celebrated its 40th anniversary in 2008. Kingston Mines is where musicians congregate after their own gigs to jam together and to socialize. There's also a kitchen open late serving up burgers and ribs.

THE CLUB SCENE   Chicago is the hallowed ground where house music was hatched in the 1980s, so it's no surprise to find a few big dance clubs pounding away the big beat. The **Funky Buddha Lounge,** 728 W. Grand Ave. (✆ 312/666-1695; www.funkybuddha.com; subway/El: Blue Line to Grand), is one of the coolest temples of nightlife in the city, located west of the River North gallery district. The DJs flood the nice-size dance floor with a disco-tech mix infused with salsa, hip-hop, and soul. At **Le Passage,** One Oak Place, between Rush and State streets (✆ 312/255-0022; www.lepassage.tv; subway/El: Red Line to Chicago), the beautiful, the rich, and the designer-suited are attracted by the lush loungey aesthetic; cool blend of house, dance, R&B, soul, and acid jazz music; and a stellar French/international fusion menu.

  Rednofive, 440 N. Halsted St. (✆ 312/733-6699; www.rednofive.com; subway/El: Green Line to Clinton), has a sleek design and a tight lineup of local DJs spinning progressive and abstract house music, hip-hop, and pop, often accompanied by a percussionist. **Transit,** 1431 W. Lake St. (✆ 312/491-8600; www.transitnightclubchicago.com; subway/El: Green Line to Ashland), is a no-nonsense dance club carved out of a warehouse space beneath the elevated train tracks just west of the hip Randolph Street restaurant row.

THE BAR SCENE   The **Near North Side** has a few entertainment zones saturated with bright, upscale neighborhood bars. Around **Rush and Division streets** (subway/El: Red Line to Clark/Division) are what a bygone era called singles bars—attracting primarily a college-aged contingent.

  Near the Magnificent Mile, the **Billy Goat Tavern,** 430 N. Michigan Ave. (✆ 312/222-1525; subway/El: Red Line to Grand/State), has been a longtime hangout for newspaper reporters over the years, but it's the "cheezeborgers, cheezeborgers" served at the grill that gave inspiration to the famous *Saturday Night Live* sketch. In the Old Town 'hood, the family-run **Corcoran's,** 1615 N. Wells St. (✆ 312/440-0885; subway/El: Brown Line to Sedgwick), is a cozy local hangout. At the top of any self-respecting Lincoln Park yuppie's list of meeting places is **Glascott's Groggery,** 2158 N. Halsted St., at Webster Avenue (✆ 773/281-1205; subway/El: Brown Lines to Armitage), an Irish pub that's been in the same family since it opened in 1937.

  In Wicker Park, hundreds of travel books and guides line the shelves of the **Map Room,** 1949 N. Hoyne Ave., at Armitage Avenue (✆ 773/252-7636; subway/El: Blue

Line to Damen). Peruse that tome on Fuji or Antarctica while sipping a pint of one of the 20-odd draft beers available. At **Marie's Riptide Lounge,** 1745 W. Armitage Ave., at Hermitage Avenue (© 773/278-7317; subway/El: Blue Line to Damen), nothing looks as though it has been updated since the 1960s, but personal touches and the retro cool of the place have made it a hip stop on the late-night circuit. The owner takes great pains to decorate the interior of the little bar for each holiday season (the wintertime "snow-covered" bar is not to be missed.)

THE GAY & LESBIAN SCENE Most of Chicago's gay bars are conveniently clustered on a stretch of North Halsted Street in Lakeview, making it easy to sample many of them in a breezy walk. To find out what's happening, check out the weekly *Nightlines* and *Gab.*

Step into **Berlin,** 954 W. Belmont Ave., east of Sheffield Avenue (© 773/348-4975; subway/El: Red/Brown lines to Belmont), where the disco tunes pulse, the clubby crowd chatters, and the lighting bathes everyone in a cool reddish glow. **Sidetrack,** 3349 N. Halsted St., at Roscoe Street (© 773/477-9189), is a sleek video bar where TV monitors are never out of your field of vision, nor are the preppy professional patrons.

2 CLEVELAND

More than nine million people a year visit this plucky city perched along the Lake Erie shoreline in northeastern Ohio. What's the draw? Professional sports, cutting-edge medical care, and world-class cultural institutions are part of the appeal. Perhaps less well known to outsiders are the array of charming neighborhoods—Coventry Village, Little Italy, Tremont, and Shaker Heights—filled with boutiques, galleries, and coffee shops. This underrated city's abundance of locally owned restaurants is also helping Cleveland burnish its reputation as the "epicenter of the Midwest food scene," in the words of the *Chicago Tribune.*

Cleveland has a rich history. George Washington once said that a great city would stand in the blessed spot where the Cuyahoga River met Lake Erie. Industrial success infused the city with money early on, as steel and oil barons built a monumental downtown and a cultural legacy that includes the world-renowned Cleveland Museum of Art, Case Western Reserve University, and the Cleveland Orchestra. These institutions provided a solid foundation for postindustrial urban development, which took a giant step forward in 1994 with the opening of Jacobs (now Progressive) Field, the first of the nation's new wave of retro-modern Major League ballparks. A year later came I. M. Pei's splendid Rock & Roll Hall of Fame, which mirrors Pei's own Louvre expansion with its playful pyramid-shaped design.

Although Cleveland's industrial foundation is very much in evidence, downtown's steel warehouses and tool-and-die factories now house clubs and restaurants, and its many bridges lead to gentrified neighborhoods. The city still has some rough edges and bleak areas of poverty, but these days is striving for global recognition and focusing on spreading the word to attract both American and international visitors.

ESSENTIALS

GETTING THERE   By Plane   Cleveland Hopkins International Airport (© 216/265-6030; www.clevelandairport.com) is 10 miles south of downtown. Major car-rental companies are housed at a central off-site lot; pick up the free shared shuttle bus, which

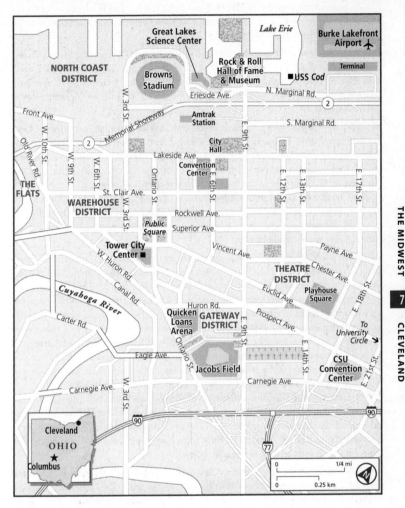

stops just outside baggage claim. It's an easy 20-minute drive into the city; take I-480 to I-71 north to I-90 into downtown.

If you're not renting, the most convenient way to reach downtown from the airport is via the **RTA Red Line.** For $1.50 per person, the 20-minute ride will deliver you at Tower City Center, in the heart of downtown. For more information, see "Getting Around," below. **Taxis** are available outside baggage claim exit 2; expect the fare to run about $40 (plus tip) to downtown. More than 30 **limousine services** run between downtown hotels; with **Hopkins Airport Limousine Service** (© **800/543-9912** or 216/267-8282; www.gohopkins.com), the per-person, one-way fare runs about $65.

By Train Amtrak (© 800/USA-RAIL [872-7245]; www.amtrak.com) provides daily service from Chicago (trip time: 7 hr.), New York (12 hr.), and Washington, D.C. (11 hr.), to its downtown station, 200 Cleveland Memorial Shoreway, across from the Great Lakes Science Center (© **216/696-5115**).

By Car The principal highway routes into Cleveland are **I-77** from the south (Akron), **I-80** or **I-76** from the east (Youngstown and Pittsburgh, both connecting with I-77 north near Akron), **I-90** from the northeast (Buffalo), **I-71** from the southwest (Columbus), and I-80/90 from the west (Toledo). Both I-77 and I-90 will take you right into downtown Cleveland.

VISITOR INFORMATION   Contact **Positively Cleveland,** the new name for the Convention and Visitors Bureau of Greater Cleveland, in the historic Higbee Building, 100 Public Square, Ste. 100, Cleveland, Ohio 44113 (© **216/875-6600**). The staff will answer your questions and can sell you discount tickets to the city's main attractions. You can even get iPod-friendly guides to the city (**www.cityprowl.com**).

The **Cleveland + (Plus) information hot line** (© **888/323-2787**) is helpful, as is the hot line for hotel reservations and information (© **800/321-1004**). Another useful site, especially for news and the latest sports and entertainment coverage, is the *Cleveland Plain Dealer's* **www.cleveland.com**.

ORIENTATION   Cleveland's major attractions are concentrated in two areas. **Downtown** is where you'll find most hotels, government buildings and corporate headquarters, the major sports arenas, and attractions such as the Rock & Roll Hall of Fame and Playhouse Square Center. **University Circle** is about 4^1/$_2$ miles east via Euclid Avenue; this leafy district is home to Case Western University (hence the name) and most of the city's major cultural institutions. Plans are underway to link the two enclaves via a redeveloped Euclid Avenue Corridor. Public transportation (with new hybrid-electric buses), tree-lined sidewalks, retail developments, and apartments are going up as part of this $325-million urban renewal project, which celebrated the conclusion of the first phase with the completion of the "Health Line" bus route down Euclid Avenue in October 2008.

The **Gateway** and **Warehouse districts** are an easy walk from Public Square. You can also walk to **North Coast Harbor** and down to the east bank of the **Flats** (as long as you don't mind the steep slope), or take the RTA rail's Waterfront Line. You'll want to drive or take a taxi to the west bank of the Flats. Ohio City has its own RTA stop on the Red Line. (For RTA information, see directly below.)

GETTING AROUND   The **Greater Cleveland Rapid Transit Authority (RTA) rail system** is not extensive. Visitors usually stick to the main Red Line, which travels between the airport and University Circle, with stops at downtown's Tower City Center and Ohio City, and the Waterfront Line, which connects Tower City with the Flats and North Coast Harbor. In addition, **RTA buses** cover five downtown loop routes from Public Square. For complete information, call the **RTA Answerline** at © **216/621-9500,** or check out its website at www.gcrta.org.

You don't need a car downtown, but it's convenient to have one if you'd like to really explore. The cost of taxis will negate what you save by not renting, and a 20- or 30-minute wait for a summoned cab is common, especially on evenings and weekends. Driving is also easier than using the RTA rail system to travel between downtown and University Circle. (See "Getting There," above, for car-rental information.)

If you still want to use a cab, try **Yellow Cab Company of Cleveland** (© 216/623-1500) or **Ace Taxi Service** (© 216/361-4700). The flag drops at $2.25 for the first ¹⁄₆ of a mile, and $2 for each additional mile.

FAST FACTS Emergency and urgent-care services are available at **Metro Health Medical Center,** 2500 MetroHealth Dr. (© 216/778-7700; www.metrohealth.org). The closest 24-hour pharmacy to the downtown area is the **Walgreens** at 117th Street and Detroit Avenue (© 216/227-0819), a few miles south in suburban Lakewood. Sales tax is 7.75% and hotel tax is 15.25%.

WHAT TO SEE & DO

Lolly the Trolley (© 800/848-0173 or 216/771-4484; www.lollytrolley.com) offers excellent 1- and 2-hour narrated tours aboard a fleet of replica trolley cars; the 1-hour version concentrates on downtown, skipping University Circle and the Lake Erie shoreline. Tours, which leave from the Plain Dealer Pavilion at Nautica on the west bank of the Flats, are offered daily from May to October, on Friday and Saturday only the rest of the year. The fare is $11 or $17 adults, $10 or $16 seniors, and $8 or $12 kids 2 to 17; reservations are required.

Cleveland Botanical Garden In spring and summer, 7 acres of lush blossoms and greenery abound at this oasis of nature at University Circle. Year-round, visitors are drawn to the tropical ecosystems housed in the stunning new Eleanor Armstrong Smith Glasshouse and Environmental Education Center. The crystal-like conservatory is home to hundreds of species of butterflies, birds, animals, and plant life of both Madagascar and a Costa Rican cloud forest. Although the Hershey Children's Garden closes for the winter on November 1, all other gardens remain open year-round.

11030 East Blvd., University Circle. © **888/853-7091** or 216/721-1600. www.cbgarden.com. Admission $7.50 adults, $5.50 seniors, $3 children 3–12. On-site parking rates start at $5 ($10 maximum). Apr 1–Nov Mon–Sat 10am–5pm (until 9pm Wed); Sun noon–5pm. Closed Mon Nov–Mar; closed Thanksgiving, Christmas, and Jan. 1.

Cleveland Metroparks Zoo and RainForest This well-maintained and well-organized zoo is a great place to spend half a day, especially if you're traveling with kids. The must-see is the $30-million multilevel **RainForest,** which offers gentle thunderstorms inside its simulated biosphere, along with more than 600 animals and insects from all seven continents. Elsewhere, in the **Wolf Wilderness** area, you will encounter gray wolves, beavers, and bald eagles. Meanwhile, the 8-acre interactive kids section of the zoo has an Australian theme.

3900 Wildlife Way, off I-71, btw. W. 25th St. and Fulton Rd. © **216/661-6500.** www.clemetzoo.com. Admission Apr–Oct $10 adults, $6 children 2–11; Nov–Mar $7 adults, $5 children. Daily 10am–5pm (summer Sat–Sun to 7pm). Closed Christmas and New Year's Day.

Cleveland Museum of Art (Value) Works by Titian, Picasso, and Monet are among the masterpieces in the museum's permanent collection, but you won't be able to see them until 2011. The CMA is midway through a 6-year, $258-million expansion, designed by internationally renowned architect Rafael Vinoly. Some special exhibitions and events are still being held on-site, so call for current updates.

11150 East Blvd., University Circle. © **216/421-7350,** or 888/CMA-0033 (262-0033) for advance exhibition tickets. www.clevelandart.org. Call for hours and special events.

Cleveland Museum of Natural History   Another fine University Circle museum, this one includes the state-of-the-art, sphere-shaped Shafran Planetarium. Among the museum's other draws are *Happlocanthosaurus,* a 70-foot-long plant-eating dinosaur; an excellent gem and jewels collection; a fascinating array of fossils and geological specimens, with a special emphasis on prehistoric Ohio; and a hands-on natural sciences Discovery Center for the little ones.

1 Wade Oval Dr., University Circle. (C) 800/317-9155 or 216/231-4600. www.cmnh.org. Admission $9 adults; $7 seniors, college students, and children 7–18; $6 children 3–6. Planetarium admission $4 with general admission. Mon–Sat 10am–5pm; Sun noon–5pm; observatory hours Sept–May Wed 8–10pm. Closed major holidays.

Great Lakes Science Center (Kids)   More than 400 hands-on exhibits let kids and adults build their brain power. Daily live demonstrations are offered at the museum, which includes a 3,000-square-foot interactive Great Lakes Environment and new exhibits on solar energy. The six-story **Cleveland Clinic OMNIMAX Theater** shows larger-than-life features. The 1925 freight steamship *William G. Mather,* which was previously a separate tourist attraction, is now under the GLSC umbrella. It's a fully restored former iron-carrying cargo ship and floating maritime museum on Lake Erie.

601 Erieside Ave., at North Coast Harbor btw. the Cleveland Browns Stadium and the Rock & Roll Hall of Fame & Museum. (C) 216/694-2000. www.GreatScience.com. Exhibits only $9.50 adults, $8.50 seniors, $7.50 children 3–17. Combination ticket (with OMNIMAX movie) $15 adults, $12 seniors, $9.95 children. Daily 10am–5pm; call for Omnimax showtimes.

Rock & Roll Hall of Fame & Museum (Best)   If any one thing is most responsible for Cleveland's rebirth, this glass-and-porcelain pyramid is it. Designed by I. M. Pei, this temple to rock music is a high-concept, multimedia collection of exhibits, archives, and films that tell the story of rock from its bluesy roots through its post-grunge days. Fun for all ages, the museum offers the coolest collection of pop-culture memorabilia around. For an electrifying experience, check out the **Jimi Hendrix Surround Sound Theater and Exhibit,** where fans can revel in jaw-dropping videotaped performances and then peruse the legend's guitars, costumes, handwritten lyrics, and watercolor landscapes. The museum will remain open through a planned renovation set to begin in 2009. That's the same year that the venue will take back the televised Rock 'n' Roll Hall of Fame induction awards ceremony from New York City. Cleveland will then host the live show every 3 years.

1100 Rock 'n' Roll Blvd., downtown. (C) 888/764-ROCK (764-7625) or 216/781-7625. www.rockhall.com. Admission $22 adults, $17 seniors, $13 children 9–11, free for children 8 and under with purchase of adult admission. Daily 10am–5:30pm (Wed until 9pm, extended evening hours Memorial Day to Labor Day Sat 10am–9pm). Closed Thanksgiving and Christmas.

World War II Submarine USS Cod   This World War II–fleet sub is credited with sinking more than 30,000 tons of Japanese shipping vessels. Completely intact and a designated National Historic Landmark, the *Cod* is particularly enlightening to tour because it has not been adapted for civilian access—visitors use the same vertical ladders and hatches that were used by the wartime crew.

1089 E. 9th St. (east of the Rock & Roll Hall of Fame). (C) 216/566-8770. www.usscod.org. Admission $6 adults, $5 seniors and college students with ID, $3 students 5–12. May–Sept daily 10am–5pm (last admission at 4:30pm).

More Attractions

MUSEUMS   Paying homage to Holocaust victims and recognizing the achievements of the area's Jewish population is the **Milton and Tamar Maltz Jewish Heritage Museum,**

In the Grandstands

Cleveland is a die-hard **sports** town. All the city's pro teams play in fairly new venues within walking distance of one another in the heart of the city. When a game is on, downtown becomes electric with excitement (especially when the home team is winning).

Popularly known as "the Tribe," the Cleveland Indians play at state-of-the-art, 42,000-seat **Progressive Field,** at Ontario Street and Carnegie Avenue ((C) **216/ 420-4636;** www.indians.com), a retro-modern ballpark that's won many fans. Take the kids, and be sure to order your hot dogs with the city's famous Bertman's Original Ballpark Mustard.

Next door is **Quicken Loans Arena** at Ontario Street and Huron Road ((C) **216/ 420-2200;** www.theqarena.com), home to the NBA's Cleveland Cavaliers ((C) **800/ 332-CAVS** [332-2287] or 216/420-CAVS [420-2287]; www.nba.com/cavs). *Tip:* If you want to fit in with the locals, call the venue "the Q" or "King James" Court, in honor of the Cav's star player, Akron-born LeBron James. Also at the Q, the American Hockey League entry has a killer name, the Lake Erie Monsters ((C) **866/99-PUCKS** [997-8257] or 216/420-2000; www.lakeeriemonsters.com).

The NFL's Cleveland Browns play at **Cleveland Browns Stadium,** lakefront on Erieside Avenue ((C) **440/891-5050;** www.clevelandbrowns.com). The newest pro sports entry in town, the **Cleveland Gladiators,** formerly of Las Vegas, is the city's new arena football team. They, too, play at the Q.

THE MIDWEST

7

CLEVELAND

2929 Richmond Rd., Beachwood ((C) **216/593-0575;** www.maltzjewishmuseum.org). The museum includes interactive exhibits and other displays, as well as traveling exhibitions. It is located next to the Temple-Tifereth Israel, 26000 Shaker Blvd., about a 30-minute drive from downtown Cleveland.

PARKS In the University Circle section of the city is **Rockefeller Park,** a 296-acre oasis between Lake Erie and Case Western Reserve University. Take 105th Street, Martin Luther King Jr. Drive, or East Boulevard for easiest park access. In adjoining **Wade Park** are the Cleveland Museum of Art, the Museum of Natural History, and the Cleveland Botanical Garden.

History buffs will enjoy a stroll or drive through the lovely gardens of **Lake View Cemetery,** 12316 Euclid Ave. ((C) **216/421-2665;** www.lakeviewcemetery.com), where famous sons such as Eliot Ness, John D. Rockefeller, and President James A. Garfield are laid to rest. Nicknamed "Lawnfield," the 225-acre arboretum and still-in-operation cemetery was founded in the 1880s. A focal point of the 1901 Wade Chapel is the glorious Tiffany-designed leaded-glass window "The Flight of Souls."

West of downtown is **Edgewater Park,** 6700 Memorial Shoreway, at West Boulevard ((C) **216/881-8141**), one of the city's best swimming beaches, with bathhouses, concessions, fishing piers, and more. Beach access is free.

CRUISES Cleveland's largest sightseeing boat is the *Goodtime III* ((C) **888/916-7447** or 216/861-5110; www.goodtimeiii.com), offering daily trips with buffet meals and live entertainment. The four-deck, 1,000-person luxury ship operates from Cleveland's North Coast Inner Harbor at the East 9th Street Pier, next to the Rock & Roll Hall of

Fame and the Great Lakes Science Center. Tickets are $15 for adults, $14 for seniors, and $9 for children for the 2-hour, narrated Lake Erie and Cuyahoga River tour. Sunday Brunch cruises start at $32 for adults, while the Saturday-night (adults-only) dinner and dancing cruises start at $49 per person. Other party ships also cruise the harbor, including the *Nautica Queen* (© **800/837-0604** or 216/696-8888; www.nauticaqueen.com). Call for more information—and plan to book ahead, as these hugely popular cruises regularly sell out in advance.

ATTRACTIONS NEAR CLEVELAND

Cedar Point Amusement Park   Lakefront Cedar Point boasts the world's biggest collection of rides (75) and more roller coasters (17) than any other park. Thrill-seekers love the **Top Thrill Dragster,** which reaches speeds of 120 mph in under 4 seconds. New in 2008 were the park's fourth designated children's area, **Planet Snoopy,** which includes a railroad and other new rides. Grown-ups still thrill to Cedar Point's Skyhawk, the tallest ride of its kind in the world. **Splash Zone,** a multistory interactive play area with more than 100 water gadgets, is located inside the 18-acre **Soak City** waterpark. **Castaway Bay** is a massive indoor waterpark resort that includes a wave pool and wave coaster, as well as day-care and spa facilities.

1 Cedar Point Dr. (U.S. 250), Sandusky. © **419/627-2350.** www.cedarpoint.com. Full-day admission $43 for ages 3–61 and those 48 in. or taller, $16 for those under 48 in. tall; free for those 2 and under; Starlight admission (4pm–close on days when the park closes at 10pm, 5pm–close on days when the park is open past 10pm) $26. Additional admission charges for Soak City and selected rides apply. Multiple-day passes are also available. Daily May to Labor Day; weekends Sept–Oct. Call for exact operating schedule, which often changes. Cedar Point is 61 miles, or a 1¼-hr. drive, from Cleveland. Follow I-90 to I-71 south to I-480 west to I-80 west to exit 118 (Sandusky); turn right onto U.S. 250. Parking $10–$15.

Geauga Lake's Wildwater Kingdom   The $24-million waterpark is about a 40-minute drive east of downtown Cleveland. Owned by the same company that runs Cedar Point, Geauga Lake formerly operated as an amusement park but is now exclusively a water-based attraction. Visitors can play wet basketball in the **Coral Cove** activity pool, surf in the 30,000-square-foot **Tidal Wave Bay,** climb the four-story, interactive **Splash Landing,** or bob along in an inner tube on **Riptide Run.**

1100 Squires Rd., Aurora. © **330/562-8303.** www.wildwaterfun.com. Admission $24 for those 48 in. and taller, $12 those under 48 in. Parking $5.

WHERE TO STAY

All of downtown's hotels also offer discounted weekend rates, and some feature attractive packages that can include such additional premiums as admission to the Rock & Roll Hall of Fame or weekend brunch.

Cleveland Marriott Downtown at Key Center   One of downtown's top moderately priced choices, this 25-story high-rise has better in-room decor than the often pricier Renaissance (see below). Request a room with lake and Rock & Roll Hall of Fame views at no extra cost. The hotel's 14 suites, or "lofts," each have a 42-inch HDTV in the living rooms.

127 Public Sq., Cleveland, OH 44114. © **800/228-9290** or 216/696-9200. Fax 216/696-0966. www.marriott.com. 410 units. $120–$199 double. Children 17 and under stay free in parent's room. Weekend rates as low as $119. AE, DC, DISC, MC, V. Valet parking $20; self-parking on weekends $10. **Amenities:** Restaurant; indoor pool. *In room:* Fridge.

Doubletree Cleveland Downtown Lakeside   At press time, this former Holiday
Inn Select property was undergoing a $15-million renovation and transformation by the
Hilton chain. Scheduled to reopen in 2009, the 17-story property was being refurnished
with new furniture, mattress, fixtures, flatscreen TVs, and Wi-Fi access in all 379 units.
A new fitness room and an off-the-lobby Starbucks are other additions. Located within
walking distance of Paul Brown Stadium and the Rock & Roll Hall of Fame, the property
hugs Lake Erie. For the best views, book a room on the sixth floor or higher.

1111 Lakeside Ave. (at E. 9th St.), Cleveland, OH 44114. (**C**) **888/425-3835** or 216/241-5100. Fax 216/241-
7437. www.doubletree.com. 379 units, including 3 suites. $129–$179 double. Children 17 and under stay
free in parent's room. AE, DC, DISC, MC, V. Self-parking $16. **Amenities:** Restaurant and coffee shop;
indoor pool; fitness room.

Glidden House   Cleveland's best full-service boutique hotel (formerly a bed-and-
breakfast) is in an elegant 1910 French Gothic mansion. After a $2-million renovation,
the rooms and suites feature vibrant primary colors and such technological upgrades as
plasma televisions and in-room Wi-Fi access. Situated in the leafy heart of University
Circle, the location is tops for culture vultures. The cozy inn is within walking distance
of all the area's parks and gardens.

1901 Ford Dr., Cleveland, OH 44106. (**C**) **800/759-8358** or 216/231-8900. Fax 216/231-2130. www.glidden
house.com. 60 units, including 2 suites. $139–$179 double; $199–$229 suites. Rates include free local calls
and complimentary continental breakfast. AE, DC, DISC, MC, V. Free parking. **Amenities:** Restaurant.

Hampton Inn Cleveland—Downtown (**Value**)   Here's Cleveland's best budget
hotel. Rooms have a fresh, new feel and come with the kinds of amenities that usually
cost more: coffeemakers, hair dryers, and irons and boards, plus sofas in some king
rooms. Same-day valet service is available. The location is excellent, on a nice downtown
block within walking distance of all major attractions.

1460 E. 9th St. (at Superior Ave.), Cleveland, OH 44114. (**C**) **800/HAMPTON** (426-7866) or 216/241-6600.
Fax 216/241-8811. www.hampton-inn.com. 194 units. $99–$209 double. Children 17 and under stay free
in parent's room. Rates include hot breakfast. AE, DC, DISC, MC, V. Valet parking $18; self-parking $15.
Amenities: Small fitness center.

InterContinental Hotel & Conference Center Cleveland (**Best**)   Ohio's only
five-star hotel is on the campus of the Cleveland Clinic and close to downtown museums
and shopping. The modern, smoke-free facility features luxurious, elegant decor in public spaces, including the lobby with fireplaces and a grand staircase. Accommodations are
designed for business travelers and equipped with such extras as bathrobes, scales, multiple telephones, Wi-Fi, and Web TV. The hotel's top two floors offer club-level access,
where breakfast, afternoon tea, and evening appetizers and drinks are served. There's also
a conference room with free computer access.

9801 Carnegie Ave., Cleveland, OH 44106. (**C**) **216/707-4100** or 877/707-8999. Fax 216/707-4101. www.
cleveland.intercontinental.com. 323 units. $149–$249 double. AE, DC, DISC, MC, V. Valet parking $24.
Amenities: 2 restaurants.

Radisson Hotel Cleveland–Gateway   This terrific, moderately priced hotel is
perfect for sports fans, as both Progressive Field and Quicken Loans (Q) Arena are just a
block away (you may even see the visiting team in the halls). The plush, pretty Shaker-
style rooms feature all the extras, plus video games and free wireless Internet access.
Complimentary cookies are served in the lobby every evening.

651 Huron Rd. (across from Progressive Field/Quicken Loans Arena), Cleveland, OH 44115. ✆ **800/333-3333** or 216/377-9000. Fax 216/377-9001. www.radisson.com. 142 units. $119–$179 double; from $175 suite. Extra person $15. Children 17 and under stay free in parent's room. AE, DC, DISC, MC, V. Valet parking $18. **Amenities:** Restaurant.

Renaissance Cleveland Hotel Attached to Tower City Center, this property, a member of Historic Hotels of America, looks more formal than it actually is. Don't be intimidated. The opulent lobby, with its marble floors and oversize floral arrangements, makes a dramatic backdrop for an evening cocktail or special-occasion photo op. The Americana-style rooms are smaller than most in town due to the building's age, though suites are spacious and comfortable. Service is especially friendly and welcoming.

At Tower City Center, 24 Public Sq., Cleveland, OH 44113. ✆ **800/696-6898** or 216/696-5600. Fax 216/696-0432. www.renaissancehotels.com. 491 units. $169–$249 double; from $269 suite. Extra person $20. AE, DC, DISC, MC, V. Valet parking $30; self-parking $23. **Amenities:** 2 restaurants; indoor pool; fitness center.

The Ritz-Carlton, Cleveland Elegant and stylish, the city's only Mobil four-star and AAA four-diamond winner is on the upper floors of the Tower City shopping center downtown. Perfect for a romantic getaway, the hotel offers exceptional service in beautiful surroundings. In-room extras include oversize desks, European toiletries, bathroom scales, and plush terry or lightweight robes in every room. The fitness center and pool are free to guests and open 24 hours a day.

At Tower City Center, 1515 W. 3rd St., Cleveland, OH 44113. ✆ **800/241-3333** or 216/623-1300. Fax 216/623-1491. www.ritz-carlton.com. 206 units. $279–$429 double; $359–$459 suite. Children 17 and under stay free in parent's room. AE, DC, DISC, MC, V. Valet parking $22. **Amenities:** Restaurant; indoor rooftop pool; fitness center.

Wyndham Cleveland Hotel at Playhouse Square This modern hotel, just a stone's throw from Progressive Field and Playhouse Square, caters to both the business and leisure crowds. For theatergoers, the location is great, and guests staying here are quick to commend the friendly service. The welcoming public spaces lead to rooms that are large, comfortable, and outfitted with all the extras. Note that all rooms are set to be renovated beginning in late 2008.

1260 Euclid Ave. (at Huron Rd.), Cleveland, OH 44115. ✆ **800/WYNDHAM** (996-3426) or 216/615-7500. Fax 216/615-3355. www.wyndham.com. 205 units. $169–$209 double. Children 17 and under stay free in parent's room. Inquire about packages. AE, DC, DISC, MC, V. Valet parking $22. **Amenities:** Restaurant; indoor pool.

WHERE TO DINE

Cleveland is a food-lover's delight, a city where independent bistros, brewpubs, and ethnic eateries in charming neighborhoods outnumber generic chain restaurants.

Blue Point Grille SEAFOOD This Warehouse District spot is Cleveland's premier seafood restaurant, hailed by the *New York Times* and frequented by local sports heroes and other stylish patrons. The kitchen excels at both creative and straightforward preparations of flown-in-daily fish, which can range from a masala-spiced sea bass to a simple seared sushi-grade ahi. The oysters are top grade, and steaks are on hand for non–fish eaters.

700 W. St. Clair Ave. (at W. 6th St.). ✆ **216/875-7827.** www.bluepointgrille.com. Reservations highly recommended. Main courses $18–$39. AE, DC, DISC, MC, V. Mon–Fri 11:30am–3pm and 5–10:30pm; Fri 11:30am–3pm and 4–11:30pm; Sat 4–11:30pm; Sun 5–10pm.

CROP Bistro and Bar (Best) AMERICAN Since opening in 2007, Steve Schimoler's inventive Warehouse District eatery has been a big hit. Locally grown produce and farm products form the basis of the cuisine here. It's a warm and friendly, boisterous dining room with an open kitchen and exceptionally attentive staff. Menus change almost daily, which is to be expected. Schimoler is a corporate test chef by day and restaurateur/chef at night. Steak, seafood, poultry, and pasta—such as the "Big Pile of Crop Pasta," all place emphasis on freshness and flavor. Diners are delighted by such unexpected appetizers as fresh popcorn and bell peppers drizzled with balsamic dressing and desserts such as the blood-orange flan or the French Kiss—a luscious, lavender-lemon ice-cream sandwich with a vanilla cream soda.

1400 W. 6th St. (C) 216/696-CROP (696-2767). www.cropbistro.com. Reservations recommended. Main courses $16–$28. AE, DC, DISC, MC, V. Tues–Fri 11am–2pm; Tues–Sat 5–10:30pm; Sun 5–9pm.

Lola AMERICAN/BISTRO   Chef/owner Michael Symon, of Food Network's *Iron Chef* fame, is one of Cleveland's most beloved in a growing list of celebrity chefs. *Sophisticated* and *sexy* are adjectives often used to describe the atmosphere at Lola, his popular downtown restaurant. The menu is similarly chic, with a few jarring twists: You can get crispy sweetbreads with leeks and blue cheese for dinner, or a fried bologna sandwich with pickles at lunch. Fresh fish, steaks, and ribs ensure there's something for everyone, while desserts include such surprises as French toast with maple-bacon syrup and caramelized apples. Symon's Greek-inspired **Lolita** serves urban comfort food in the suburb of Tremont (900 Literary Rd.; (C) 216/771-5652).

2058 E. 4th St. (C) 216/621-5652. www.lolabistro.com. Reservations suggested. Main courses $25–$34. AE, DC, DISC, MC, V. Mon–Fri 11:30am–2:30pm; Mon–Thurs 5–10pm; Fri–Sat 5–11pm.

Maxi's (Kids) PIZZA   Close to University Circle's museums is this Little Italy bar and restaurant, which serves up excellent pizzas made from scratch with fresh ingredients, including whole-clove garlic and mushrooms. Other Italian dishes, along with burgers, steaks, and seafood, round out the menu. Service is as friendly as can be. Down the street is **Mama Santa,** 12305 Mayfield Rd. ((C) 216/231-9567), another inexpensive, family-friendly favorite that bakes a top-notch pie.

12113 Mayfield Rd. (C) 216/421-1500. www.maxisinlittleitaly.com. Reservations recommended. Pizzas $14–$18; pastas $14–$19. AE, DISC, MC, V. Mon–Thurs 11am–11pm; Fri 11am–midnight; Sat 5pm–midnight; Sun 5–10pm.

Sans Souci FRENCH/MEDITERRANEAN   Cleveland's finest Continental restaurant, this French-country dining room in the Renaissance Cleveland hotel is ideal for a special occasion. Sunny Provençal decor and a stone hearth provide a setting for enjoying such classics as *osso buco* and roasted veal chops, as well as a selection of Mediterranean-style pastas. Save room to savor the luscious dessert-cart choices, or opt for a simple plate of ripe cherries, dates, and grapes.

In the Renaissance Cleveland Hotel, 24 Public Sq. (C) 216/902-4095. www.sanssoucicleveland.com. Reservations recommended. Main courses $12–$18 lunch, $20–$30 dinner. AE, DC, DISC, MC, V. Mon–Fri 11:30am–2:30pm; daily 5:30–10pm.

Sarava (Best) BRAZILIAN   Craving a lime-spiked *caipirinha* cocktail or a bowl of meaty black-bean feijoada while you're in Cleveland? Brazilian chef/restaurateur Sergio Abramof has got you covered. In addition to his eponymous restaurant in University Circle, Sergio has expanded his empire to the picturesque suburb of Shaker Heights with Sarava. The rhythms and flavors of Brazil mesh harmoniously in this upscale bar and eatery. Small plates are a specialty. *Salgadinhos,* or Brazilian bar snacks, vary daily but are a bargain during happy hour at 3 for $12. Beef eaters should be sure to order the signature churrasco–skewers of barbecued meat. I also recommend the sublime artichoke fritters with lemon-thyme dipping sauce; *pao de queijo* (chewy Brazilian cheese bread puffs); and the grilled cornmeal cakes topped with guacamole, sour cream, tomato carioca relish, and ancho sauce.

13225 Shaker Sq. © **216/295-1200.** www.sergioscleveland.com. Reservations recommended. Main courses $17–$27. AE, DC, DISC, MC, V. Mon–Thurs 5–10pm; Fri–Sat 5pm–midnight; Sun 5–9pm.

Slyman's (Value) DELI   Patty melts, pierogies, Reubens, and salami sandwiches are on the menu, but this legendary deli is best known for its corned beef. The slivers of meat are piled between fresh bread and served with a pickle spear. No frills needed. Its location is a bit off of Downtown's beaten path, but worth the hunt. You can smell the enticing aromas before you spot the tiny hole in the wall.

3016 St. Clair Ave. © **216/621-3760.** www.slymans.com. Sandwiches $2.95–$8.50. MC, V. Mon–Fri 6am–2:30pm.

Table 45 FUSION   Chef Zack Bruell has been garnering rave reviews for his new minimalist restaurant that showcases global fusion cuisine with bistro flavors. From Chinese steamed mussels with ginger and black-bean sauce to oven-warm *naan* with three dipping sauces, including goat-cheese hummus and pickled lime aioli, appetizers are varied and adventurous. Bruell's intimate chef's tables inside the kitchen have become a culinary hot ticket, where diners feast on such specialties as grilled chicken with watercress and rosemary *pommes frites* with beurre blanc; and crispy, seared duck breast with mashed cauliflower and a sherry vinegar sauce.

9801 Carnegie Ave., in the InterContinental Hotel and Conference Center. © **216/707-4045.** www.tbl45.com. Reservations recommended. Main courses $26–$30. AE, DC, DISC, MC, V. Daily 11am–11pm.

XO Prime Steaks NEW AMERICAN   The chic steakhouse (formerly XO Restaurant and Bar) in the Warehouse District is awash in candlelight, white fabrics, and pale pink accents. Lobster, veal and lamb chops, salads, and soups are on the menu, but this is primarily a steakhouse. A choice of six house-made sauces (such as horseradish cream truffle or Hollandaise blue cheese) awaits your T-bones, rib-eyes, sirloins, filets, and New York strips. Sides include potatoes—and such unexpected options as three-cheese truffle macaroni with peas and prosciutto.

500 W. St. Clair Ave. (at W. 6th St.). © **216/861-1919.** www.xoprimesteaks.com. Reservations recommended. Main courses $20–$40. AE, MC, V. Mon–Thurs 11am–3pm and 5–11pm; Fri 11am–3pm and 4pm–midnight; Sat 4pm–midnight; Sun 4–9pm.

CLEVELAND AFTER DARK

Tickets for many events are sold through **Ticketmaster** (© **216/241-5555;** www.ticketmaster.com). **Tickets.com** (© **800/766-6048** or 216/241-6000; www.tickets.com) sells tickets to events at Playhouse Square Center. Another great option is the online-only **Ctix** outlet (**www.ctix.org**), where budget culture vultures may purchase half-price, day-of-show theater tickets and discounted movie tickets.

THE PERFORMING ARTS   Considered by many to be one of the top orchestras in the U.S., the world-renowned **Cleveland Orchestra** (© **800/686-1141** or 216/231-1111; www.clevelandorch.com), under the leadership of music director Franz Welser-Most, performs at **Severance Hall,** 11001 Euclid Ave., at East Boulevard, in University Circle. The stately 1931 concert hall was greeted by rave reviews when it emerged from a massive renovation in early 2000. In summer, the orchestra takes up residence at the open-air

Blossom Music Center. Blossom Music Center is located in Cuyahoga Falls, 34 miles south of the city off I-77.

The nation's second-largest performing arts center (after New York City's Lincoln Center) is **Playhouse Square Center,** 1501 Euclid Ave. (© 216/771-4444; www. playhousesquare.com), a symbol of Cleveland's cultural renaissance. Four restored theaters present theatrical and musical performances, including touring productions of Broadway shows. It's also home to such resident companies as the **Ohio Ballet** (www. ohioballet.org) and **DanceCleveland** (www.dancecleveland.org), which presents such renowned modern companies as Alvin Ailey Trinity Irish Dance Company; and the **Cleveland Opera** (www.clevelandopera.org), among others.

THE BAR & CLUB SCENE To find out what's happening, pick up one of the free weeklies, the **Cleveland Free Times** and the **Cleveland Scene,** available all over town.

Downtown's **House of Blues,** 308 Euclid Ave. (© 216/523-2583; www.hob.com), books the best in live blues music (as well as other genres) and serves up a soul-stirring Sunday gospel brunch. Don't miss this all-ages feast, which is part church service and part all-you-can-eat Southern soul-food buffet. Sip a mimosa with your fried chicken and grits, country ham and biscuits, and crawfish cakes—but be sure to save room for a spoonful of white chocolate banana bread pudding.

Another fun evening option is **Pickwick & Frolic Restaurant and Club,** 2035 E. 4th St. (© 216/241-7425; www.pickwickandfrolic.com), a swanky, multilevel venue with a restaurant and cabaret theater, an ultramodern downstairs martini bar, as well as Hilarities 4th Street Theatre, which draws nationally known comedy acts.

The Fourth Street area abounds with new restaurants, pubs, and bars. Take **Corner Alley,** 402 Euclid Ave. (© 216/298-4070; thecorneralley.com), a combination martini bar, American diner, and bowling alley where you can score strikes and spares while throwing back Tootsie Roll Martinis and munching on meatloaf or four-cheese macaroni.

On the west bank of the Flats, at Main Avenue and the river, is the waterfront **Nautica Entertainment Complex** (www.nauticaflats.com), where century-old smokestacks top the four-story warehouse now known as the **Plain Dealer Pavilion.** Among the complex's other after-dark attractions are the waterfront **Shooters** (© 216/861-6900; www. shootersflats.com), a hulking behemoth of a restaurant and dance club that caters to young adults on the prowl and other revelers; and the **Improv Comedy Club** (© 216/ 696-4677; www.improvupcoming.com), featuring up-and-coming stand-up talent.

A somewhat more sophisticated crowd gathers in the **Warehouse District,** mainly along West 6th Street between Superior and Lakeside avenues. Young hipsters meet to relax in comfy chairs and play board games at lively **Liquid/Fusion,** 1212 W. 6th St. (© 216/479-7717; www.liquidliving.com). **Velvet Dog,** 1280 W. 6th St. (© 216/664-1116; velvetdogcleveland.com), is a high-style, three-story dance club and lounge. Other trendy options for energetic barhoppers include the eclectic **Blind Pig,** 1228 W. 6th St. (© 216/621-0001; www.theblindpig.com).

In **Coventry Village,** a lovely, hip neighborhood not far from downtown and University Circle, look for Lucy, a real-life reptile in a glass cage, at the **Winking Lizard,** 1852 Coventry (© 216/397-8380), a chain of local taverns with a great beer selection and laid-back vibe. Nearby, check out the coolest toy store you've probably ever seen, the offbeat yet old-timey **Big Fun,** 1814 Coventry (© 216/371-4386).

Farther afield, northeast of downtown, Cleveland's undisputed best live music venue is the venerable **Beachland Ballroom and Tavern,** 15711 Waterloo Rd. (© 216/383-1124). Sensitive singer-songwriters, Elvis impersonators, punks, and rock's best-known acts all play at this classic dive. The bar serves decent pub grub (even breakfast), and *Blender* magazine dubbed its 1966-era jukebox the best in the USA.

In Cleveland Heights, **Nighttown,** 12387 Cedar Rd. (© **216/795-0550**), offers a full restaurant menu and bar along with live jazz and world music. The influential magazine *Down Beat* recently named it one of the world's best jazz clubs.

Ohio City is great for those looking for an easygoing night on the town. **Great Lakes Brewing Company** is arguably the most popular bar chain in Cleveland. For beer connoisseurs, it's heaven. During the daytime, book a guided tour of the brewery, during which you'll learn not only how their beer is crafted, but about their impressive, eco-friendly business practices as well.

While you're in the area, another great local favorite is the Vietnamese restaurant **Phnom Penh,** 1929 W. 25th St. (© **216/357-2951**). And around the corner is the **West Side Market,** where you can load up on all sorts of locally grown produce, fresh meats, spices, and pastries.

3 CINCINNATI

Along the banks of the Ohio River and tucked amid rolling hills that are home to its historic and eclectic neighborhoods, Cincinnati is a major Midwestern hub of commerce, art, family attractions, and entertainment. When it became an important rail and river hub, Henry Wadsworth Longfellow pronounced it the "Queen City of the West." Settled primarily by Germans in the 19th century, Cincinnati today remains a clean, attractive, and dynamic urban center, where life proceeds at an unhurried pace.

ESSENTIALS

GETTING THERE   By Plane   Major airlines fly into **Cincinnati/Northern Kentucky International Airport** (© **859/767-3144;** www.cvgairport.com), one of the fastest-growing airports in the world, which also serves as a gateway to northern Kentucky (p. 307). The airport (its code is CVG) is 13 miles south of downtown in northern Kentucky. Cincinnati taxis cannot pick up passengers in Kentucky, and Kentucky taxi companies cannot pick up passengers in Ohio. However, taxi companies with licenses, including Yellow Community Cab Co. (see below) can pick up at the airport. For more information, go to the tax desk in the airport's Terminal 3 baggage claim area or use the courtesy phone near the exit of Terminal 2 (dial 3260) to make arrangements.

Look for the 14 Art Deco murals from Union Station before you leave the airport. **Executive Transportation** (© **859/261-8841;** www.executivetransportation.org) provides regular service to downtown hotels for $15 one-way, $25 round-trip. Cab fare is $25 for four people.

By Train   Amtrak (© **800/USA-RAIL** [872-7245]; www.amtrak.com) serves Union Station, 1301 Western Ave. There's service 3 days a week to Chicago (trip time: 9 hr.), Indianapolis (3½ hr.), and Washington, D.C. (16 hr.).

By Car   The major routes into Cincinnati are **I-75** from the north (Dayton) and south (Lexington); **I-71** from the northeast (Columbus) and southwest (Louisville); and I-74 from the northwest (Indianapolis).

VISITOR INFORMATION   Contact the **Cincinnati USA Convention & Visitor Bureau,** 525 Vine St., Ste. 1500, Cincinnati, OH 45202 (© **800/543-2613** or 513/ 621-2142; www.cincyusa.com).

GETTING AROUND   The Southwest Ohio Regional Transit Authority (SORTA), better known as the Metro, provides inexpensive bus service (© **513/621-4455;** www.sorta.com). Exact change or token is required. Within the city, base fare is $1.50; transfers cost 25¢.

A city ordinance does not allow cabs to cruise downtown for fares; they must park at taxi stands and wait for passengers. Cabs can usually be found on the west end of Fifth Street, where the convention center and many hotels are located. You can also call a cab. **Yellow Community Cab** (© **859/727-2900**) charges $3.60 plus $1.60 per mile.

FAST FACTS   A major local hospital is **University Hospital,** 234 Goodman St., Clifton (© **513/584-1000;** www.medcenter.uc.edu). There's a 24-hour **CVS** pharmacy at 2520 Vine St. (© **513/569-4301;** www.cvs.com). Sales tax is 6.5% and hotel tax is a whopping 17%.

SPECIAL EVENTS & FESTIVALS   Fans of choral music fill Music Hall for the internationally renowned **May Festival** (© **513/381-3300;** www.mayfestival.com), an annual event since 1875. Summer officially kicks off downtown Memorial Day weekend with the **Taste of Cincinnati,** when dozens of area restaurants sell small but tasty portions of their best dishes. Summer closes with Labor Day weekend's **Riverfest,** featuring fireworks, entertainment, and food throughout the city's waterfront parks. In mid-September, Fountain Square becomes a German *biergarten* for **Oktoberfest-Zinzinnati,** with German music, dancing, food, and lots of beer.

WHAT TO SEE & DO

Cincinnati is built on hills overlooking the Ohio River. Take time to walk around the city's colorful and historic neighborhoods. The **Over-the-Rhine** district just north of downtown has the largest collection of 19th-century civic, religious, and residential architecture in the U.S. It's home to Music Hall and historic **Findlay Market,** a year-round, open-air fresh foods market that was recently expanded and renovated. The narrow, winding streets of **Mount Adams** reveal stunning views of downtown and the Ohio River. For attractions across the Ohio, see "Northern Kentucky," on p. 307.

Cincinnati Art Museum   Perched atop a hill in a 19th-century park, Cincinnati's Art Museum houses a rich collection of sculpture, photography, African and Native American art, and decorative objects. A cobalt chandelier by superstar glass artist Dale Chihuly glimmers in the museum's entryway. Paintings from Botticelli and Titian to Mary Cassatt, John Singer Sargent, Picasso, and Andy Warhol adorn the galleries.

953 Eden Park Dr. © **513/721-5204.** www.cincinnatiartmuseum.org. Free admission (special exhibition fees may apply). Tues–Sun 11am–5pm (Wed until 9pm). Closed Thanksgiving, Christmas, Jan. 1 and July 4.

Cincinnati Museum Center (Kids)   The Cincinnati Museum Center is in Union Terminal, built in 1931 and recently restored to its original Art Deco grandeur. Inside you'll find three museums and the OMNIMAX Theater. In the Museum of Natural History and Science, exhibits immerse you in different Ohio Valley environments. The Cincinnati History Museum has one of the largest regional collections in the U.S. At the Duke Energy Children's Museum, you'll find nine interactive exhibits, including Little Sprouts Farm and Kids Town.

1300 Western Ave. © **800/733-2077** or 513/287-7000. www.cincymuseum.org. Single-attraction tickets $7.25 adults, $6.25 seniors, $5.25 children 3–12. Multiple-discount ticket combinations are also available. Mon–Sat 10am–5pm; Sun 11am–6pm. Closed Thanksgiving and Christmas. Parking $3.

Cincinnati Zoo & Botanical Garden   More than 125 years old, this 75-acre zoo is America's second oldest and one of its best. More than one million people visit the museum each year to see more than 500 animal and 3,000 plant species. Favorites include the exotic collection of felines (including some white lions); the creatures of the zoo's 75 acres include elephants, manatees, polar bears, and a children's zoo. New in 2008 were unusual red-crowned cranes and an adorable baby bearcat named Lucy.

3400 Vine St. (© **800/94-HIPPO** (944-4776) or 513/281-4700. www.cincinnatizoo.org. Admission $13 adults, $11 seniors, $8 children 2–12, free for children 1 and under. Memorial Day to Labor Day gates daily 9am–6pm, grounds until 8pm; other times gates daily 9am–6pm, grounds to dusk. Parking $6.50.

Contemporary Arts Center (Kids)   At the cutting edge of modern art for decades, this museum was one of the first in America to exhibit Picasso's savage *Guernica* in the 1940s and the controversial nude photographs of Robert Mapplethorpe in 1990. A noncollecting museum, the center showcases special exhibitions at its digs in the $28-million Lois and Richard Rosenthal Contemporary Arts Center. Opened in 2003, it was the first U.S. art museum designed by a woman, London-based Zaha Hadid, who won the prestigious Pritzker Prize for her work. The sixth floor of the museum, called the **UnMuseum,** is devoted to hands-on, interactive art experiences for children, families, and art lovers of all ages. Admission is free on Monday after 5pm.

44 E. Sixth St. (© **513/345-8400.** www.contemporaryartscenter.org. Admission $7.50 adults, $6.50 seniors, $5.50 students, $4.50 children 3–13. Mon 10am–9pm; Wed–Fri 10am–6pm; Sat–Sun 11am–6pm.

National Underground Railroad Freedom Center (Best)   Costumed storytellers bring their triumphant stories alive for the continuous flow of schoolchildren who tour this don't-miss museum. Adults appreciate it, too. On the banks of the Ohio River downtown, the $110-million center traces 500 years of oppression and focuses on slavery that exists today in various parts of the world. The history of American slavery focuses on Africans' arrival in the New World through Colonial times and the Civil War, and the bravery of abolitionists involved in the underground railroad. Interactive displays in three pavilions include educational activities and gripping films—including one narrated by Oprah Winfrey. The modern Italian-marble and copper-sheathed building's most sobering site is the old log-cabin-like slave pen that was recovered from nearby Kentucky and carefully reconstructed on-site.

50 E. Freedom Way. (© **877/648-4838** or 513/333-7500. www.freedomcenter.org. Admission $12 adults, $10 seniors, $8 children 6–12, children 5 and under free. Free admission for all active Armed Forces and Guard/Reserves personnel, and discounts for their immediate families. Tues–Sun 11am–5pm. Closed major holidays.

Taft Museum   The 1820 Federal-style mansion is a true gem. The museum reopened in 2004 after a $23-million expansion and renovation. Furnished with period antiques and filled with paintings by Rembrandt, Hals, Turner, and Gainsborough, it also boasts a Limoges porcelain and enamel collection that is among the best on the planet. If you're taking the kids (strollers are allowed), pick or download in advance one of the many self-guided family tours geared toward those with children as young as 3. In the heart of downtown, the museum serves sandwiches, soups, and desserts in its Tea Room. The Taft's underground parking garage is free to visitors.

316 Pike St. (© **513/241-0343.** www.taftmuseum.org. Admission $8 adults, $6 seniors and students over 18, free for students 18 and under, free to all on Wed. Tues–Sun 11am–5pm.

More Attractions

Professional sports dominate the new developments on Cincinnati's famed downtown riverfront. Of course, baseball has been a favorite spring and summer pastime in Cincinnati since 1869. The **Cincinnati Reds,** featuring future Hall of Famer (and native son) Ken Griffey, Jr., play at the **Great American Ballpark,** a nostalgic but modern facility overlooking the Ohio River. Tickets range from $7 to $67. Call Ticketmaster at ☎ **800/877-REDS** (877-7337) or 513/421-REDS (421-7337), or go online to www.cincinnatireds.com.

The NFL's **Cincinnati Bengals** (☎ **513/621-8383;** www.bengals.com) battle their opponents at the $400-million **Paul Brown Stadium,** another waterfront gem. Single ticket rates start at around $50.

Kings Island (☎ **800/288-0808** or 513/754-5600; www.visitkingsisland.com), formerly known as Paramount King's Island—and now operated by the same company that owns Cedar Point in Sandusky (p. 484)—is located off exits 24 and 25 on I-71 north of Cincinnati in Mason, Ohio. With its pedestrian walkways and Eiffel Tower replicas, the park is a family-oriented destination that boasts more than 80 rides, including 14 world-class roller coasters. The **Beast** is billed as the world's longest wooden roller coaster, while **Son of Beast** is touted as the world's tallest and fastest wooden coaster. Kids can meet cartoon heroes such as Dora the Explorer and SpongeBob SquarePants at the **Nickelodeon Universe. Boomerang Bay,** an Australian-themed, 15-acre waterpark with 30 water slides, is free with park admission. Single-day passes start at $46 ages 3 to 61 and 48 inches and taller; $30 ages 3 and up, under 48 inches tall, and ages 62 and up; free for children 2 and under. Discounted tickets of $30 are available to active military. Parking is $10. Multiday passes also are available. Kings Island is open daily from Memorial Day to late August at 10am; closing times vary. Also open some weekends in April, May, September, and October.

Riverboat excursions on the Ohio, especially popular at night, leave from Covington, Kentucky, just across the river from downtown Cincinnati (see "Northern Kentucky," on p. 307).

WHERE TO STAY

Ask about weekend packages that include Reds games or discount tickets to sights. For accommodations across the Ohio River, see "Northern Kentucky," p. 307.

Cincinnatian Hotel The grande dame of the city's hotels is the elegant Cincinnatian, a AAA four-diamond winner. Built in 1882 and on the National Register of Historic Places, it offers award-winning, round-the-clock service. Rooms have oversize tubs, dual-head showers, and bathrobes; some have whirlpools and fireplaces. In addition to the excellent **Palace** restaurant, the **Cricket Lounge** offers lighter fare, including afternoon tea.

601 Vine St., Cincinnati, OH 45202. ☎ **800/942-9000** or 513/381-3000. www.cincinnatianhotel.com. 146 units. $165–$425. Children 17 and under stay free in parent's room. AE, DC, DISC, MC, V. Valet parking $28. **Amenities:** Restaurant; fitness center.

Hilton Cincinnati Netherland Plaza (Best) Travelers looking for a splendid property downtown should head here; the Hilton Cincinnati Netherland Plaza has drawn raves for its French Art Deco styling since 1931. Listed on the National Register of Historic Places, the hotel is connected via skywalk to Tower Place, a four-story complex with shopping and restaurants. Tastefully decorated in dove grays, soft whites, and charcoal colors, the luxurious guest rooms have soft beds with down comforters and large work desks. Ask about upgrading your room to gain access to the Belvedere Club, the hotel's 16th-floor lounge that offers free breakfast and evening appetizers and free Wi-Fi. The club's wraparound outdoor terrace offers sweeping views of the Ohio River and surrounding city skyline.

35 W. 5th St., Cincinnati, OH 45202. ☎ **800/445-8667** or 513/421-9100. www.hilton.com. 561 units. $159–$249 double. Children 17 and under stay free in parent's room. AE, DC, DISC, MC, V. Valet parking $21. **Amenities:** 2 restaurants; health club w/indoor pool.

Millennium Hotel Cincinnati   Business travelers favor the Millennium, in the city's business district just west of Fountain Square and connected by skywalk to the convention center. Club Level rooms on the hotel's upper floors include complimentary continental breakfast, as well as bathrobes and upgraded room amenities. During sweltering summer weather, the outdoor rooftop pool and sun deck make a nice place to cool off. There's also a 24-hour business center.

150 W. 5th St., Cincinnati, OH 45202. ✆ **800/876-2100** or 513/352-2100. www.millennium-hotels.com. 872 units. $159–$259 double. Children 17 and under stay free in parent's room. AE, DC, DISC, MC, V. Valet parking $20. **Amenities:** Restaurant; outdoor pool; fitness room.

Westin Cincinnati   Business and leisure travelers like the upscale Westin, a high-rise overlooking the Ohio River. A chic yet unpretentious property that draws an eclectic mix of families and business travelers, the hotel is a good choice for sports and culture fans. The city's major performing arts center, along with its baseball and football fields, are all within a few blocks' walking distance. The comfortable guest rooms have all the amenities associated with a hotel of this class, including heavenly soft beds and sumptuous linens. Trendy **McCormick & Schmick's** seafood restaurant adjoins the hotel; you can charge meals to your room.

21 E. 5th St., Cincinnati, OH 45202. ✆ **800/937-8461,** 888/627-8071, or 513/621-7700. www.westin.com/cincinnati. 456 units. $309–$349 double; $600–$1,200 suite. Children 17 and under stay free in parent's room. AE, MC, V. Valet parking $24; self-parking $15. **Amenities:** 2 restaurants; indoor pool; fitness center.

WHERE TO DINE

For cheap eats, **Skyline Chili** has dozens of franchises in the city. Be forewarned, this "chili" may look more like spaghetti than chili to novices. For dining with a view of the downtown skyline from across the Ohio River, see "Northern Kentucky," p. 307.

JeanRo Bistro (Best)   FRENCH   Full-bodied coffee, patisserie-style desserts, and polished service help make this my favorite restaurant in Cincinnati. I'm not alone. Boisterous gourmands pack the narrow room with its sunny yellow walls and butcher-paper-covered tables at this Parisian bistro to sip wine and sample such quintessential dishes as chicken coq au vin or seared steak and *pommes frites*. In the past few years, its noted chef, Jean-Robert de Cavel, has opened several hot spots, including the fine-dining establishment **Jean-Robert at Pigall's,** 127 W. Fourth St. (✆ **513/721-1345**); a hip wine bar known as the **Lavomatic Café,** 1211 Vine St. in Over-the-Rhine (✆ **513/621-1999**); and a cafe or two across the river in Covington.

413 Vine St. ✆ **513/621-1465.** www.bistrojeanro.com. Reservations recommended. Lunch sandwiches about $9; entrees $10–$20; dinner main courses $16–$31; side dishes are a la carte. AE, DC, DISC, MC, V. Mon–Sat 11:30am–3:30pm for lunch; nightly from 5:30pm for dinner.

Orchids at Palm Court   AMERICAN/CONTINENTAL   Art Deco elegance and gourmet food make Orchids downtown's top choice for fine American/Continental cuisine. Located in the splendid 1930s-era lobby of the Hilton–Cincinnati Netherland Hotel, the atmosphere is a showstopper. Expensive but worth it, the menu offers everything from foie gras to Kobe beef with Yorkshire pudding, and yellowtail snapper "En Papillote." There's also complimentary valet parking, giving you no excuse not to splurge downtown's most lavish culinary indulgence.

In the Hilton-Cincinnati Netherland Plaza, 35 W. 5th St. ✆ **513/564-6465.** www.orchidsatpalmcourt. com. Reservations recommended. Main courses $32–$57. AE, DC, DISC, MC, V. Tues–Thurs 5:30–9:30pm; Fri–Sat 5:30–10pm.

CINCINNATI AFTER DARK 495

THE PERFORMING ARTS Music Hall, 1241 Elm St. (© 513/721-8222), is home of the **Cincinnati Symphony Orchestra** (© 513/381-3300; www.cincinnatisymphony. org), and the **Cincinnati Opera** (© 513/241-2742; www.cincinnatiopera.com). The **Cincinnati Ballet** (© 513/621-5219; www.cincinnatiballet.com) performs at the Aronoff Center, 6th and Walnut (© 513/621-2787). Modern and classic plays and musicals are presented at **Playhouse in the Park,** Eden Park (© 513/345-2242; www. cincyplay.com), which won regional Tony Awards in 2004 and 2007.

THE BAR SCENE Arnold's Bar and Grill, 210 E. 8th St., downtown between Main and Sycamore (© 513/421-6234; www.arnoldsbarandgrill.com), is Cincinnati's oldest tavern, with live Celtic, bluegrass, jazz, and swing music.

In the **Over-the-Rhine** district, along Main Street beyond Central Parkway, you'll find many bars, cafes, and microbreweries that offer entertainment. Along cobblestone streets with excellent city views, **Mount Adams** has many bars that also offer entertainment. The **Incline Lounge** at the fine-dining restaurant Celestial Steakhouse, 1071 Celestial St., Mount Adams (© 513/241-4455; www.thecelestial.com), is a favorite of locals for weekend jazz (Fri–Sat starting at 8:30pm).

4 INDIANAPOLIS

Indianapolis is a *serious* sports town. The Indianapolis 500 and the Allstate 400 at the Brickyard attract hundreds of thousands of visitors to each event. The city also justifiably bills itself as the "Amateur Sports Capital of the World" and boasts world-class sports facilities (including the brand-new home of the Indianapolis Colts, the Lucas Oil Stadium). Indy natives rally behind the city's pro franchises—the NBA's Pacers, the WNBA's Fever, the NFL's Colts, and the Indianapolis Indians.

In its passion for sports, however, the city does not neglect the arts. In addition to a few notable art museums and galleries, the city boasts a number of theater companies. Indianapolis also has neighborhoods worth exploring: the Lockerbie Square district with renovated Victorian homes on cobblestone streets; the shops, restaurants, and art galleries along Massachusetts Avenue downtown; and Broad Ripple Village, a canal-side neighborhood with boutiques, restaurants, and nightlife.

ESSENTIALS

GETTING THERE By Plane Flights arrive at **Indianapolis International Airport** (© 317/487-9594; www.indianapolisairport.com). Most major domestic airlines can get you there. **IndyGo**'s (© 317/635-3344; www.indygo.net) Green Line Express provides nonstop service from the airport to downtown daily 5am to 9pm, departing every 20 minutes or so, for $7. Taxis average $25 to downtown and $45 and up for trips to the north side. Share-a-ride car service through **Carey Indiana** (© 800/888-INDY [888-4639] or 317/241-6700; www.careyindiana.com) costs $13 to downtown and around $40 to the north side. All major national car-rental agencies are represented at the airport. (Phone numbers and websites for all the major U.S. airlines and car-rental agencies can be found in appendix D.)

By Train Amtrak (© 800/USA-RAIL [872-7245]; www.amtrak.com) has a station at 350 S. Illinois St. (© 317/263-0550), with trains arriving from Chicago (trip time: 5½ hr.), Cincinnati (3¹/₂ hr.), and Washington, D.C. (18¹/₂ hr.). *Note:* Amtrak service to Indianapolis is spotty and often includes some time on a bus.

By Bus   Greyhound (© **800/231-2222;** www.greyhound.com) has a station downtown at 350 S. Illinois Street. The discount carrier **Megabus** (© **877/462-6342;** www. megabus.com), with drop-offs and pickups downtown (no station), connects Indy with Chicago, Cincinnati, and Columbus. If you're willing to detour through the Windy City, you might be able to save a bundle (early bookers can snag seats on some routes for as little as $1, though $15–$30 is more common).

By Car   Major routes into Indianapolis are I-65 from the northwest (Chicago) and south (Louisville), I-69 from the northeast (Detroit), I-70 from the west (St. Louis) and east (Columbus, Ohio), and I-74 from the southeast (Cincinnati).

VISITOR INFORMATION   The **Indianapolis Convention & Visitor Bureau** is at 30 S. Meridian St., Ste. 410 (© **800/323-INDY** [323-4639] or 317/639-4282; www.indy. org); its website offers video podcasts of what to see and do in the city and a variety of printable maps. The **Indiana Tourism Hotline** is © **800/556-INDY** (556-4639). Find local events online at www.indydt.com and www.indyarts.org. Indy's free alternative paper, *Nuvo,* covers the local dining and entertainment scene, and is available at locations around the city, or you can check it out online at www.nuvo.net.

GETTING AROUND   IndyGo buses (© **317/635-3344;** www.indygo.net) run on heavily traveled routes; fares are $1.50 (or $3.50 for a day pass). The Red Line Circulator buses are free and run a continuous path circling downtown and around the IUPUI campus (Mon–Sat 7am–10pm). But you can't rely on public transportation to get everywhere you want to go, so you'll really need a car. Based on a grid system, the city is easy to negotiate, and parking is generally easy to come by. The Circle Centre mall lots are usually a good parking bet downtown, and it's only $1.50 for up to 3 hours; you can park there all day (6–12 hr.) for $12 (higher during special events).

Cabs usually line up at downtown hotels, or you can call a radio-dispatched taxi. Try **Yellow Cab** (© **317/487-7777**).

FAST FACTS   If you need a **doctor,** call **Methodist Hospital,** at I-65 and 21st Street (© **317/916-3525**), for a referral. **Riley Children's Hospital,** 702 Barnhill Dr. (© **317/ 274-5000**), is a top-notch children's hospital.

A growing number of Walgreens and CVS locations have **24-hour pharmacies.** If you're staying downtown, the Walgreens at 1530 N. Meridian St. (© **317/261-1753**) is convenient; otherwise, check the Yellow Pages.

Indianapolis is fairly safe, but do exercise standard precautions as you would in any city. Stick to well-lit/well-traveled areas when walking around (especially at night), and be careful walking alone to your car in large outdoor parking lots.

SPECIAL EVENTS   Seats for both the **Indianapolis 500** (run the day before Memorial Day) and the **Allstate 400 at the Brickyard** (late July) sell out very early, though you may be able to get tickets at the last minute. Call the Indianapolis Motor Speedway ticket office at © **317/484-6700** at least 10 to 12 months in advance.

For a particularly smashing time, crash the **Indy Tennis Championships,** held in mid- to late July. Past champs include Pete Sampras and Andy Roddick, and the stadium court also grants a great view of the downtown skyline. Call © **800/622-LOVE** (622-5683), or check out www.tennisindy.com for further details and tickets.

The **Indy Jazz Fest** (www.indyjazzfest.net) runs for a long weekend each June, and the Indiana Black Expo (© 317/925-2702; www.indianablackexpo.com) spans a full 10 days in July featuring speakers, live music, and more.

For 10 days in late August/early September, downtown plays host to the **Indianapolis Theatre Fringe Festival** (© 317/223-8616; www.indyfringe.org), which showcases local, national, and international theater, dance, music, and more.

WHAT TO SEE & DO

The center of downtown Indianapolis is **Monument Circle,** with the 284-foot-tall Soldiers' and Sailors' Monument at its core, crowned by a statue of Victory, known as *Miss Indiana*. An observation deck offers a panoramic view. Lights strung from the top of the monument during the holidays make it the "world's largest Christmas tree."

About a half-mile north of Monument Circle, bordered by Meridian Street on the west and Pennsylvania Street on the east, is the 24-acre **Indiana War Memorial Plaza Historic District** (www.in.gov/iwm), composed of sculptures, landscaped open spaces, and the neoclassical War Memorial Museum.

The beautifully restored **Lockerbie Square** area, about a mile northeast of Monument Circle, is Indianapolis's oldest surviving neighborhood, and the first district in the city to be placed on the National Register of Historic Places. Visit the website of the Lockerbie Square People's Club (www.lockerbiesquare.org) for more information and to download a walking tour of the neighborhood.

Eagle Creek Park, 7840 W. 56th St. (© 317/327-7110; www.indyparks.org), is one of the largest municipal parks in the country, with 4,000 acres of wooded terrain for hiking, biking, and cross-country skiing, and a 1,300-acre reservoir. The main attraction of the 128-acre **Garfield Park Conservatory,** 2450 Shelby St. (© 317/327-7184; www.garfieldgardensconservatory.org), is a tropical greenhouse—complete with parrots and macaws, and waterfall-fed pools—planted with flora from around the world. Admission to the conservatory is free (donations welcome), though entrance to the park is $5 per vehicle; open daily from 10am to 5pm.

Children's Museum of Indianapolis (Kids)

This is one of the largest children's museums in the world, with interactive exhibits covering everything from archaeology to world cultures to biotechnology, plus extensive toy and dollhouse displays, a working antique carousel ($1 per ride), and a planetarium. Recent additions include **Dinosphere,** a multisensory exhibit that combines serious science with kid-friendly interactive exhibits, and *Fireworks of Glass,* a 43-foot-tall blown-glass sculpture by Dale Chihuly. If you have kids, this is the place to take them.

3000 N. Meridian St. © 317/334-3322. www.childrensmuseum.org. Admission $14 adults, $13 seniors, $8.50 children ages 2–17, free for children 1 and under. Mar to early Sept daily 10am–5pm; early Sept to Feb Tues–Sun 10am–5pm.

Conner Prairie Pioneer Settlement (Kids)

Located 30 miles northeast of downtown, this restored 19th-century village faithfully reproduces pioneer life between 1820 and 1840. In summer, you can pack a picnic and listen to a concert under the stars as part of the Indianapolis Symphony Orchestra's "Symphony on the Prairie" series.

13400 Allisonville Rd., Fishers. © 800/966-1836 or 317/776-6000. www.connerprairie.org. Admission $11 adults, $10 seniors, $7 children ages 5–12, free for children 4 and under. May–Sept Tues–Sat 10am–5pm, Sun 11am–5pm; reduced hours off season.

Indianapolis Motor Speedway (Best)   Built in 1909, this is one of the most celebrated auto raceways in the world. Each May, more than 400,000 spectators throng to the 2.5-mile oval course to watch the Indianapolis 500, the largest single-day sporting event in the world, boasting the largest purse in motor racing.

The **Indianapolis Motor Speedway Hall of Fame Museum** (open daily 9am–5pm; $3 adults, $1 children 6–15) is within the track's oval. The speedway also features **Brickyard Crossing,** an acclaimed golf course with 4 of its 18 holes inside the track.

4790 W. 16th St. ✆ 317/481-8500, 800/822-4639, or 317/484-6700 to charge tickets to events. www.brickyard.com. Daily 9am–5pm.

Indianapolis Museum of Art (Value)   This world-class museum has paintings by El Greco, Rubens, American Impressionists, and European neo-Impressionists. Other strengths include African art, Japanese Edo-period paintings, American furniture, textiles, costumes, and a superb collection of Turner works on paper. The museum's contemporary art collection includes Robert Indiana's famed *LOVE.* In summer, the museum hosts the Summer Nights concert and film series. Also on the grounds is the **Oldfields-Lilly House,** a historic 22-room mansion open to the public.

4000 Michigan Rd. (at 38th St.). ✆ **317/923-1331.** www.ima-art.org. General admission to the museum and Lilly House free; admission to the special exhibition gallery varies. Tues–Sat 11am–5pm (until 9pm Thurs–Fri); Sun noon–5pm.

White River State Park (Best)   White River State Park (and the adjacent Central Canal area), located in the heart of downtown, has something for just about everyone. Like many parks, it contains trails, greenery, and waterways, but it's also home to a number of museums and attractions (see below), as well as an open-air concert venue and a sculpture program that showcases local artists. **Bicycle rentals** (✆ **317/767-5072;** www.wheelfunrentals.com), **Segway tours** (✆ **317/569-0879;** www.segwayofindiana.com), **pedal boat and kayak rentals** (Ohio and West sts. beneath fire station #13), and **gondola rides** (✆ **317/491-4835;** www.4gondola.com) along the canal—complete with Italian serenade—are available.

The 64-acre **Indianapolis Zoo** (✆ **317/630-2001;** www.indyzoo.com) features 2,000 animals roaming through simulated environments. Admission is $14 adults, $8.50 seniors and children 2 to 12 ($8.50 and $6.50 in the winter). The zoo generally opens at 9am and closes at 4pm on weekdays and 5 or 6pm on weekends, but hours vary considerably throughout the year; call ahead or visit the website.

The **White River Botanical Gardens,** located on the zoo grounds and included with your zoo ticket, is a botanical showcase, with more than 1,000 types of plants on display and special exhibits throughout the year.

Victory Field (www.indyindians.com), home of the Indianapolis Indians, was named the "Best Minor League Ballpark in America" by *Baseball America* and *Sports Illustrated.* Enjoy a game of baseball and a fantastic view of the downtown skyline.

The **Eiteljorg Museum of American Indian and Western Art,** 500 W. Washington St. (✆ **317 636-9378;** www.eiteljorg.org), houses the country's most notable collection of Native American and Western art. The "Art of the American West" collection includes works by Frederic Remington and Georgia O'Keeffe. The Native American artifacts include clothing, beadwork, and pottery from all over North America, as well as a special section focusing on the three main tribes of Indiana. The museum is open Monday to Saturday 10am to 5pm, Sunday noon to 5pm. Admission is $8 adults, $7 seniors, and $5 students and children 5 to 17.

The **Indiana State Museum,** 650 W. Washington St. (© **317/232-1637;** www.indiana museum.org), documents the history of Indiana since the pioneer era. Admission is $7 adults, $6.50 seniors, and $4 for children 3 to 12 (IMAX films are extra). It's open Monday through Saturday 9am to 5pm and Sunday 11am to 5pm.

Sports fanatics might want to check out the **NCAA Hall of Champions,** 700 W. Washington St. (© **800/735-NCAA** [735-6222]; www.ncaahallofchampions.org). Past collegiate sports highlights are displayed on video monitors, and you can listen to university school songs on a push-and-play display. A 1920s gymnasium keeps the kids busy when it's not in use for educational programs. Admission is $3 adults, $2 students (free for children 5 and under); it's open from 10am to 5pm Tuesday through Saturday, noon to 5pm Sunday.

For more information, as well as a list of concerts and scheduled events, check out www.discovercanal.com.

801 W. Washington St. © **317/233-2434.** www.in.gov/whiteriver.

SHOPPING

The cornerstone of Indy's downtown shopping scene is **Circle Centre,** 49 W. Maryland St. (© **317/681-8000;** www.circlecentre.com), with anchor stores Nordstrom and Carson Pirie Scott, 100 specialty shops, restaurants, nightclubs, a cinema, and the Artsgarden (a performance space suspended over a busy intersection and covered by a glass dome).

The **Fashion Mall at Keystone,** 86th Street and Keystone Avenue (© **317/574-4000;** www.fashionmallatkeystone.com), is the city's other leading mall, with anchor stores Saks Fifth Avenue and Nordstrom, a number of national chain stores, and numerous specialty and designer boutiques. The mall also features the **Keystone Art Cinema and Indie Lounge** (© 317/577-3009), with a full-service bar (and live music on weekends) where you can stop before or after taking in the latest indie flick.

The **Castleton Square Mall,** 82nd Street just east of Allisonville Road (© **317/849-9993;** www.shopcastletonsquare.com), is larger than Keystone and has more choices for shoppers on a budget (such as JCPenney and Sears). Other department stores include Von Maur, plus plenty of national chain stores, as well as a new multiplex movie theater.

For something different, head to **Broad Ripple,** a charming neighborhood 15 minutes north of downtown filled with unique shops such as **Girly Chic Boutique,** 841 E. Westfield Blvd. (© **317/217-1525;** www.girlychicboutique.com), and local independent chain **LUNA music,** 5202 N. College Ave. (© **317/283-5862;** www.lunamusic.net), which sells CDs, vinyl, and posters, and hosts in-store live performances. (LUNA also has a store downtown at 431 Massachusetts Ave.) For a directory of Broad Ripple's shops, galleries, and restaurants, visit www.discoverbroadripplevillage.com.

WHERE TO STAY

The more expensive hotels are downtown, but many moderate and budget hotels are in the surrounding area. Most downtown hotels offer weekend or theme packages. Throughout the city, chains dominate. In addition to the choices below, we recommend the **Embassy Suites** (© **800/EMBASSY** [362-2779]; www.embassysuites.com) downtown location, with a sky bridge connection to Circle Centre Mall, 110 W. Washington St. (© **317/236-1800**), which features suites with coffeemakers, wet bars, refrigerators, and microwaves. The **Westin Indianapolis,** 50 S. Capitol Ave. (© **800/228-3000** or 317/262-8100; www.starwood.com), also connects to Circle Centre. For a moderately priced downtown hotel, try **Hampton Inn Indianapolis–Downtown,** 105 S. Meridian St. (© **800/426-7866** or 317/261-1200). Housed in a 1920s National Historic Landmark building, this hotel offers two-room suites and king rooms with whirlpool tubs in addition to the usual doubles. The **Indianapolis Marriott Downtown,** 501 W. Washington St. (© **800/321-2211** or 317/635-4443; www.marriott.com), on the edge of White River State Park, is another solid choice.

If you'll be spending a lot of time at the Speedway, the **Brickyard Crossing Golf Resort & Inn,** 4400 W. 16th St. (© **317/241-2500;** www.brickyardcrossing.com), is worth checking out. It's a convention motel, and its location is really the only reason to stay here, but the rates are reasonable and it offers free outdoor parking, as well as a golf course (with 4 holes inside the Speedway).

For a bed-and-breakfast alternative that's near downtown but sports a local charm, check into the **Villa Inn,** 1456 N. Delaware St. (© **866/626-8500** or 317/916-8500; www.thevillainn.com). The property offers six rooms, a full spa, and a restaurant.

Near the airport, **Days Inn,** 5860 Fortune Circle W. (© **800/DAYS-INN** [329-7466] or 317/248-0621), is your standard budget motel, with a restaurant, bar, small workout room, and outdoor pool. Another good airport choice is the **Holiday Inn,** 2501 S. High School Rd. (© **800/465-4329** or 317/244-6861), right on the airport grounds and 10 minutes from downtown.

The Canterbury (Best) This charming European-style hotel, with direct access into Circle Centre Mall, sports "a bit of England" and is a registered historic landmark. This is where most celebrities stay when they're in Indianapolis, and it's still the best in town. Rooms are large, with four-poster beds, armoires, bathroom telephones, and refrigerators. Tea is served daily.

123 S. Illinois St. (north end of Circle Centre), Indianapolis, IN 46225. © **800/538-8186** or 317/634-3000. Fax 317/685-2519. www.canterburyhotel.com. 99 units. $169–$299 double; $399–$1,599 suite (lower rates on weekends). Extra person $25. Children stay free in parent's room. AE, DC, DISC, MC, V. Valet parking $20. **Amenities:** Restaurant; health club.

The Conrad Only the fourth American branch of the global luxury chain, the Conrad commands a prime corner across from Circle Centre (it offers private access to guests) and lends a much-needed touch of swank to the downtown scene. Decor is simultaneously grand and subdued. Luxury is the keyword, with attention to details such as fresh flowers in every space. Biz travelers are indulged with in-room Wi-Fi and multiroomed suites for added privacy.

50 W. Washington St., Indianapolis, IN 46204. © **800/CONRADS** (266-7237) or 317/713-5000. Fax 317/638-3687. www.conradindianapolis.com. 243 units. $229–$499 double; $699 suite (lower rates on weekends). Extra person $30. AE, DC, DISC, MC, V. Valet parking $30. **Amenities:** 3 restaurants; indoor pool; health club; spa.

Hotel Indigo This visually inviting hotel injects much-needed boutique charm to the scene. Opened in February 2008, it's tucked into Indy's Northside with hardwood-floor appeal and a business center for work gatherings. A communal outlook has Indigo decorating with local artists' work and tending to Fibi, a yorkie mix and the resident pup. (Pets are "family" here; Indigo has no size restrictions.) These features lend the hotel a B&B feel as it maintains all the amenities of a spalike stay. It's spacious, serene, smoke free—and completely Wi-Fi ready, including in the sleek lounge. Each morning the **Golden Bean Café** serves Starbucks coffee and scones before turning into the health-minded PHI restaurant and bar after 5pm. Seven rooms are specially equipped for travelers with limited mobility.

9791 North by Northeast Blvd., Fishers, IN 46037. © **800/496-7621** or 317/558-4100. Fax 317/558-4111. www.hotelindigo.com. 115 units. $149–$169 double; $179–$199 suite (lower rates on weekends). Extra person stays free. Children 17 and under stay free in parent's room. AE, DISC, MC, V. Free parking. Pets $25. **Amenities:** Restaurant; indoor pool; fitness center.

University Place Conference Center and Hotel (Kids) Located on the campus of Indiana University/Purdue University Indianapolis (IUPUI), this hotel offers well-furnished and functional rooms with refrigerators, coffeemakers, flat-panel TVs, and hair dryers. The hotel features a fitness center and complimentary Wi-Fi throughout the building.

850 W. Michigan St., Indianapolis, IN 46202. © **800/627-2700** or 317/269-9000. Fax 317/231-5168. www. universityplace.iupui.edu. 278 units. $149–$249 double; $249–$799 suite. Extra person (in doubles) $20. Children 17 and under stay free in parent's room. AE, DISC, MC, V. Indoor parking $14. **Amenities:** 2 restaurants; fitness center. *In room:* Fridge.

WHERE TO DINE

In addition to the places listed below, you'll find many dining options in the Circle Centre Mall. Chains such as **Palomino Euro Bistro** and the **Alcatraz Brewing Co.** are consistent with most of what you'll find in the downtown area. The old **City Market,** 222 E. Market St. (© **317/634-9266**), has been revitalized with many new restaurants and food stands opening. It's a good place to grab a bite if you're downtown. An outdoor farmers' market is open Wednesday (10am–1:30pm).

And while chain restaurants and your typical American fare make up the bulk of the Indy dining scene, the city does have a fair selection of world cuisine. In Broad Ripple, check out Indy's Indian food outpost, **Shalimar,** 1043 Broad Ripple Ave. (© **317/465-1100;** www.shalimarindianapolis.com), or **Thai Café,** 1041 Broad Ripple Ave. (© **317/722-1008;** www.indythaicafe.com). If you're up for a bit of a drive to the northeast side, **Ma Ma's Restaurant,** 8867 Pendleton Pike (© **317/897-0808**), serves great Korean food. **Taj of India,** 5929 E. 82nd St. (© **317/578-4400**), on the north side, is the perfect place to grab a fantastic meal after a day wandering the Castleton Square mall. On the northwest side, try **Udupi Café,** 4225 Lafayette Rd. (© **317/299-2127**), tucked away down a long hall in a strip mall, and nearby **Abyssinia,** 5352 W. 38th St. (© **317/299-0608;** www.abyssiniarestaurant.com), serving Indian (all vegetarian) and Ethiopian, respectively; both are located just a bit west of the Museum of Art. For sushi, try **H2O Sushi,** 1912 Broad Ripple Ave. (© **317/254-0677;** www.h2osushibar.com), or **Forty-Five°,** 765 Massachusetts Ave. (© **317/634-4545;** www.fortyfiveindy.com).

Also recommended are **Bazbeaux Pizza,** 811 E. Westfield Blvd. (© **317/255-5711;** www.bazbeaux.com) and 334 Massachusetts Ave., downtown (© **317/636-7662**), for gourmet pizza; **Mama Carolla's,** 1031 E. 54th St. (© **317/259-9412;** www.mama carollas.com), for neighborhood Italian in a renovated house; or **Yat's,** 5363 N. College Ave. (© **317/253-8817;** www.yatscajuncreole.com), 659 Massachusetts Ave., downtown (© **317/686-6380**), and 8352 E. 96th St. (© **317/585-1792**), for a heaping plate of cheap ($5–$6) Cajun food.

Café Patachou (Kids) NEW AMERICAN/FRENCH This lunch and breakfast cafe maintains its popularity due to Bruce Steckler's consistent menu and owner Martha

Hoover's keen sense of keeping the clients happy. Expect to pay New York prices ($2.75 for a cup of coffee that's, frankly, weak, at best—for decent java, run across the street to local fave **Hubbard and Cravens**), but the food is truly worth it. There are three other locations throughout Indy.

4911 N. Pennsylvania. (*✆*) **317/925-2823.** www.cafepatachou.com. Omelets and sandwiches from $8.95. AE, MC, V. Mon–Fri 7am–3pm; Sat–Sun 8am–2pm.

Elements REGIONAL AMERICAN   Dropping in for dinner here is always a surprise because the menu changes daily. Chef Greg Hardesty keeps it fresh both figuratively and literally by structuring the offerings around whatever is currently in season. In summer, enjoy organically grown heirloom tomato salads, perhaps, with Hoosier melons and a dash of pine nuts and cheese. Ask the capable staff for a suggested pairing from the manageable and well-selected wine list.

415 N. Alabama. (*✆*) **317/634-8888.** www.elementsindy.com. Reservations recommended. Main courses $27–$32. AE, DC, MC, V. Tues–Thurs 5–9:30pm; Fri–Sat 5–10:30pm.

Meridian NEW AMERICAN   The cozy but sophisticated lodgelike interior of Meridian incorporates logs from the 1880s cabin that once stood on this site. It's a fitting backdrop for the cuisine, which similarly updates and refines classic comfort foods. Our favorite: grilled lamb loin with splashes of puréed eggplant and *tzatziki* sauce painting the plate, served with a chickpea cake. Other options include pork loin with sweet-potato hash and chorizo and lobster carbonara. The tangy, meltingly tender tuna poke appetizer is the perfect starter, or try Meridian's take on oysters Rockefeller (lightly breaded and fried, served on creamed spinach with Hollandaise). Finish up with the signature dessert: warm mini doughnuts with thick, coffee-flavored sauce for dipping, or the sinfully rich (and huge) chocolate torte with walnut crust.

5694 N. Meridian St. (*✆*) **317/466-1111.** www.meridianonmeridian.com. Reservations recommended. Main courses $22–$32. AE, DISC, MC, V. Mon–Thurs 11am–2:30pm and 5–9:30pm; Fri–Sat 11am–2:30pm and 5–10:30pm; Sun brunch 10am–1:30pm.

R bistro CONTEMPORARY AMERICAN   This casual but chic restaurant snuck onto the dining scene quietly but has gained a local following. The airy atmosphere and fresh cuisine make it popular with the young and fashionable crowd. The chef generally sticks to fresh local produce, so the dinner menu changes weekly and the lunchtime menu changes seasonally.

888 Massachusetts Ave. (*✆*) **317/423-0312.** www.rbistro.com. Reservations suggested. Entrees $10–$15 lunch, $17–$25 dinner. AE, DC, DISC, MC, V. Mon–Fri 11am–2:30pm; Wed–Sat 5–10pm.

Scholar's Inn Restaurant & Lounge ECLECTIC   Though the name may conjure up images of exposed beams and rustic charm, there's nothing folksy about this downtown restaurant. The ambience is aggressively hip, with liberal use of floor-to-ceiling curtains as dividers, multihued concealed lighting, house/techno music in the background, and other funky touches. The award-winning food is some of the best in the city, and the diverse menu includes two vegetarian selections. It's all so good you really can't make a bad selection, but notable entrees include the braised beef short rib with Hoisin barbecue sauce, served with soba noodles, and the duck breast with curry peach purée, parsnip mushroom croquettes, and cranberry rhubarb compote. *Tip:* Seasonal half-price specials (bottles of wine on Mon, starters on Tues, and so on) can help keep costs down; call or check the website to see what's on offer.

725 Massachusetts Ave. ⓒ **317/536-0707.** www.scholarsinn.com. Reservations recommended. Lunch entrees $8–$15; dinner entrees $17–$32. AE, DISC, MC, V. Lunch Mon–Fri 11am–2pm; dinner Mon–Sat 5–10pm; brunch Sun 10am–2pm.

St. Elmo Steak House ⒷestⒷ AMERICAN/STEAK   Popular with celebrities and politicians, this atmospheric National Historic Landmark is the city's premier steakhouse, and has been for the last 103 years. The restaurant's original tiger-oak back bar is still in operation, and the decor is straight out of 1940s Chicago, with mahogany paneling and a tin ceiling; the ultraprofessional waiters even wear tuxedos. Start with the shrimp cocktail, and then wash down your juicy prime rib or filet mignon with a selection from the award-winning 20,000-bottle wine cellar. *Note:* The congenial atmosphere is really too boisterous for a romantic meal.

127 S. Illinois St. (at the south edge of Circle Centre). ⓒ **317/635-0636.** www.stelmos.com. Reservations recommended. Main courses $24–$49. AE, DC, DISC, MC, V. Mon–Sat 4–11pm; Sun 4–10pm.

Taste Café & Marketplace NEW AMERICAN/DELI   After heading the kitchen at L.A.'s Standard Hotel, chef Marc Urwand and partners set up shop here between downtown and Broad Ripple. Nearly everything on the premises is made fresh each day, and the fluffy overstuffed omelets, seasonal soups, and dense flaky cheddar biscuits stand out. If you can't dine in, check out the counter, where you can order breads, cheeses, pastries, jams, and more—all perfect for a picnic.

5164 N. College Ave. ⓒ **317/925-2233.** www.tastecafeandmarketplace.com. Omelets from $6.75; lunch entrees from $5.50. AE, DC, DISC, MC, V. Tues–Sat 7am–3pm; Sun–Mon 8am–2pm.

INDIANAPOLIS AFTER DARK

THE PERFORMING ARTS   The **Indianapolis Symphony Orchestra** (ⓒ **800/366-8457** or 317/639-4300; www.indyorch.org) has its home in the Hilbert Circle Theater, a vintage 1916 film palace on Monument Circle. **Clowes Memorial Hall,** 4600 Sunset Ave. (ⓒ **800/732-0804,** 317/940-6444, or 940-9696; www.cloweshall.org), a performing arts center on the campus of Butler University, is home to the **Indianapolis Opera, Butler Ballet,** and **Indianapolis Chamber Orchestra.** The professional **Indiana Repertory Theatre,** 140 W. Washington St. (ⓒ **317/635-5277;** www.indianarep.org), offers a September-to-May season, including classics such as *A Christmas Carol.* **Theatre on the Square,** 627 Massachusetts Ave. (ⓒ **317/685-8687;** www.tots.org), and the **Phoenix Theatre,** 749 N. Park Ave. (ⓒ **317/635-7529;** www.phoenixtheatre.org), tend to produce more irreverent and cutting-edge shows.

The **Madame Walker Theatre Center,** 617 Indiana Ave. (ⓒ **317/236-2099** for information and tickets; www.walkertheatre.com), is an ornate 1927 Art Deco theater offering jazz, gospel, drama, and dance performances. Every other Friday from 6 to 10pm, "Jazz on the Avenue" showcases local, regional, and national talent.

THE CLUB & BAR SCENE   Indianapolis's nightlife is primarily located in the downtown area and in Broad Ripple Village, an artsy enclave of boutiques, bistros, and bungalows 15 minutes north of downtown.

For live jazz every night except Sunday, downtowners head to the cozy **Chatterbox Tavern,** 435 Massachusetts Ave. (ⓒ **317/636-0584;** www.chatterboxjazz.com), where big-name acts playing in town sometimes stop by. (Mick Jagger once dropped in after a Stones concert.) Another downtown top spot for live music is the **Slippery Noodle Inn,** 372 S. Meridian St. (ⓒ **317/631-6974;** www.slipperynoodle.com), Indiana's oldest standing bar (established 1850; rumor has it that Hoosier hoodlum John Dillinger used

7

the club's back wall for target practice) and *the* place in the city for blues. You can also check out the local scene at the friendly **Old Point Tavern,** 401 Massachusetts Ave. (© 317/634-8943); in warm weather, the action spills onto an outside patio. To hear talented DJs (local and touring) spinning the latest techno/trance beats, head to **Therapy,** 605 E. Market St. (© 317/632-0325).

For dancing (or cruising), gay travelers shoot for **Greg's Indianapolis,** 231 E. 16th St. (© 317/638-8138; www.gregsindiana.com); the **Metro Nightclub,** 707 Massachusetts Ave. (© 317/639-6022; www-metro-indy.com); or **Talbott Street,** 2145 N. Talbott St. (© 317/931-1343; www.talbottstreet.com). Lesbians can hop over to mostly female dance club the **Ten,** 1218 N. Pennsylvania (© 317/638-5802); the neighborhood is on the dodgy side, but the crowd inside is generally welcoming and very diverse.

If you're not sure what you're in the mood for, check out **Jillian's,** 141 S. Meridian St. (© 317/822-9300), a multistory complex that includes two restaurants, a game room, billiards, a dance club, and "multimedia" bowling (neon lanes, glow-in-the dark balls, and video walls).

Broad Ripple Village, an easy drive north of downtown straight up Meridian Street, is where the local yuppies, college students, *and* high school cool kids go for weekend fun. At the **Vogue,** 6259 N. College Ave. (© 317/259-7029; www.thevogue.ws), local bands and big names perform in a renovated movie theater; when nobody's playing, it's a hot dance club. Other good bets are the casual **Broad Ripple Brew Pub,** 840 E. 65th St. (© 317/253-2739; www.broadripplebrewpub.com); the cigar/martini bar on the second floor of the **Broad Ripple Steak House,** 929 E. Westfield Blvd. (© 317/253-8101; www.broadripplesteakhouse.com); and the **Alley Cat Lounge,** 6267 Carrollton Ave. (© 317/257-4036), considered by most locals to be the best dive bar in town. For a DJ and dancing with a younger crowd, head to **Rock Lobster,** 820 Broad Ripple Ave. (© 317/253-5844; www.rocklobster.ws). Mature audiences head to the **Jazz Kitchen,** 5377 N. College Ave. (© 317/253-4900; www.thejazzkitchen.com), for live jazz Friday and Saturday.

5 DETROIT & HIGHLIGHTS OF MICHIGAN

DETROIT

They don't call Detroit the "Motor City" for nothing. The American automobile made Detroit what it is, and the city's modern attractions still revolve around cars: The Henry Ford Museum; factory tours at Ford's Rouge Plant; historic mansions owned by the Ford family; and the annual August automotive pageant, the Woodward Dream Cruise. But Detroiters take special pride in all that's new in their hometown, from the open-air concerts at Campus Martius Park to the recently renovated Detroit Institute of Arts and the city's plethora of new downtown restaurants, casinos, and sports arenas.

Essentials

GETTING THERE   By Plane   The **Detroit Metropolitan Airport** (www.metro airport.com), 35 miles southwest of downtown, is a hub for **Northwest Airlines** (© 800/225-2525). Cab service to downtown costs $41.

By Train   Amtrak (© 800/USA-RAIL [872-7245]; www.amtrak.com) provides daily service from Chicago (trip time: 5^1/$_2$ hr.) and Ann Arbor (1 hr.) to its station at 11 W.

Baltimore St. at Woodward Avenue. Trains also stop at stations in Dearborn, 16121 Michigan Ave.; Greenfield Village, 20900 Oakwood Blvd.; Royal Oak, 202 S. Sherman Dr.; Birmingham, Villa Road at Lewis Street; and Pontiac, 51000 Woodward Ave.

By Car   Major routes into Detroit are **I-75** from the south (Toledo) and north (Flint), **I-94** from the west (Chicago), and **Route 401** from the east (Toronto).

VISITOR INFORMATION   Contact the **Detroit Metro Convention & Visitors Bureau,** 211 W. Fort St., Ste. 1000, Detroit, MI 48226 (© **800/DETROIT** [338-7648]; www.visitdetroit.com).

GETTING AROUND   Detroit is a city built for cars—expect little public transportation. The exception is the **People Mover** train that loops around downtown, a convenient way of visiting downtown tourist sites and Cobo Hall Convention Center for 50¢ per ride. But unless you remain downtown, you'll need a car.

FAST FACTS   To find a physician, contact the **Detroit Medical Center** (© 888/ **DMC-2500** [362-2500]; www.dmc.org). Medical assistance is available at **Detroit Receiving Hospital,** 4201 St. Antoine Blvd. (© **313/745-3000;** www.drhuhc.org). Sales tax in Michigan is 6%; hotel taxes in Detroit range between 13% and 15%, depending on the county.

SPECIAL EVENTS & FESTIVALS   The Motor City displays her best and newest at the annual **North American International Auto Show** (www.naias.com) in mid-January. In mid-August, '50s- and '60s-era muscle cars and street rods rule at the annual **Woodward Dream Cruise** (www.woodwarddreamcruise.com), a 16-mile parade of 40,000 vehicles along Woodward Avenue, the largest single-day car event in the world. The weeklong Windsor-Detroit **International Freedom Festival** celebrates Canada Day (July 1) and American Independence Day, ending with fireworks over the Ambassador Bridge.

What to See & Do

Detroit's rich cultural history comes alive in the **Cultural Center,** an area flanking Woodward Avenue 3 blocks south of I-94. Here you'll find a celebration of history, culture, and music at the Detroit Institute of Arts, the Detroit Historical Museum, the Charles H. Wright Museum of African American History, and the Detroit Science Center. The Detroit Public Library and Wayne State University also call the area home.

Further explore Detroit culture at one of the city's fine galleries or on a downtown walking tour of public art. **Plum Tree Pottery,** 30435 W. 10-Mile Rd. (© **248/476-4875;** www.plumtreepottery.com), in Farmington Hills, sells the creations of master ceramist John Glick. The **Sherry Washington Gallery,** 1274 Library St. (© **313/961-4500;** www.sherrywashingtongallery.com), and **G. R. N'Namdi Gallery,** 1435 Randolph St. (© **313/831-8700;** www.grnnamdigallery.com), feature works by some of the nation's preeminent African-American artists. Public art is easy to find on the **People Mover.** Each station along this landmark Detroit monorail features original paintings, mosaics, tilework, and sculptures. Other famous public artworks include **"Spirit of Detroit," "Monument to Joe Louis"** (often called "The Fist"), and the **"Pylon"** tower—all near the intersection of Woodward and Jefferson avenues.

Arab American National Museum   America's first and only Arab-American museum is located in Dearborn. Permanent exhibits highlight Arab civilizations' contributions to mathematics, science, medicine, architecture, and the decorative arts; the history and diversity of Arab immigrants in the U.S.; and the impact that Arab Americans have had on American society and culture. Allow 1 to 2 hours.

13624 Michigan Ave., Dearborn. ✆ **313/582-2266.** www.arabamericanmuseum.org. Admission $6 adults, $3 seniors and students, free for children 5 and under. Wed–Sat 10am–6pm (Thurs until 8pm Oct–Apr); Sun noon–5pm.

Detroit Historical Museum   Begin your exploration of Detroit with this repository of the city's history. You can walk a re-created cobblestone and brick street lined with 19th-century shops, and check out the two-story assembly line in the Motor City exhibit. Interactive displays entertain children of all ages. Allow 1 to 2 hours.

5401 Woodward Ave. ✆ **313/833-1805.** www.detroithistorical.org. Admission $6 adults, $4 seniors and students 5–17, free for children 4 and under. Wed–Fri 9:30am–3pm; Sat 10am–5pm; Sun noon–5pm.

Detroit Institute of Arts   The DIA completed a 6-year expansion in late 2007, providing more space for a collection renowned for its diversity. Expect works by the masters, including Rembrandt, Rubens, and Whistler; works from Egypt, Africa, Asia, and Native America; and an impressive African-American collection. The DIA is best known for its Diego Rivera murals, *Detroit Industry*, considered Rivera's most important work in the United States, and its van Gogh *Self Portrait*, the first van Gogh painting to enter an American museum collection. Allow 2 to 3 hours.

5200 Woodward Ave. ✆ **313/833-7900.** www.dia.org. $8 adults, $6 seniors, $4 students, 5 and under free. Wed–Thurs 10am–5pm; Fri 10am–10pm; Sat–Sun 10am–6pm.

Detroit Zoo (Kids)   The Detroit Zoo is one of the finest in the nation, with all of the expected animals—elephants, giraffes, bears, lions, and more. The **Arctic Ring of Life** features the world's largest polar bear display. Visitors watch bears and seals from outside or through a 70-foot-long underwater Polar Passage. Other highlights include a butterfly and hummingbird garden, a free-flight aviary, and a great apes exhibit. Allow 3 hours.

8450 W. 10-Mile Rd., Royal Oak. ✆ **248/541-5717.** www.detroitzoo.org. Admission $11 adults, $9 seniors, $7 children 2–12, free for children 1 and under. Daily 10am–5pm (opens 9:30am in summer, closes 4pm in winter).

Henry Ford Museum & Greenfield Village (Best)   The **Henry Ford Museum,** a 12-acre repository of Americana, holds something of interest for everyone. "Heroes of the Sky" features dozens of historic airplanes: Byrd's Arctic Fokker, a Sikorsky helicopter, and early commercial and barnstorming planes. But the museum's highlight is, not surprisingly, "The Automobile in American Life," exploring our nation's infatuation with cars. Look for the Rosa Parks Bus as well as Ford's 1901 Model-T, the Oscar Meyer Wienermobile, and a host of presidential cars, including the limousine in which Kennedy was shot. Facilities also include an IMAX theater. Allow 3 hours.

Greenfield Village encapsulates Ford's infatuation with history and the world's innovators. A hundred genuine 17th-, 18th-, and 19th-century homes were transported from throughout the U.S. and Europe to bring history to Detroit. The Wright brothers' bicycle shop, Edison's laboratory, and a collection of slave quarters are highlights. *Note:* The village is closed January through mid-April. Allow 2 hours.

The Henry Ford's newest addition is the **Ford Rouge Factory Tour.** Visitors view the production of Ford's most popular truck, the F-150, through the magic of virtual reality and an assembly plant walking tour. Tours begin in front of the Henry Ford Museum; reservations are strongly recommended. Allow 2 hours.

20900 Oakwood Blvd., Dearborn. © **800/835-5237.** www.hfmgv.org. Museum $14 adults, $13 seniors, $10 children 5–12, free for children 4 and under. Village $20 adults, $19 seniors, $14 children 5–12, free for children 4 and under. Factory tour $14 adults, $13 seniors, $10 children 3–12, free for children 2 and under. IMAX $10 adults, $9 seniors, $8.50 children 12 and under. Combination tickets available. Daily 9:30am–5pm; Village Fri–Sun only Nov–Dec, closed Jan to mid-Apr; Factory tours Mon–Sat 9:30am–5pm.

Motown Historical Museum   The Motown sound was born in two simple houses under the sign HITSVILLE U.S.A., and American music has never been the same. See the original control room and studio (with linoleum worn through by tapping feet) where the Supremes, the Temptations, Stevie Wonder, the Jackson 5, and many others made gold records from 1959 to 1972. Also on display are costumes worn by the famous performers and Berry Gordy's apartment, left just the way it was in the 1960s when artists packed their records for shipment throughout the country. Allow 1 hour.

2648 W. Grand Blvd. © **313/875-2264.** www.motownmuseum.com. Admission $10 adults, $8 seniors and children 12 and under. Tues–Sat 10am–6pm; Mon–Sat 10am–6pm in summer.

Where to Stay

Best Western Sterling Inn (Kids)   The Sterling Inn offers great value for families— clean, comfortable rooms; a kid-friendly staff; and the hotel's chief draw: an indoor waterpark including a 5,000-square-foot pool, a three-story water slide, a lazy river, two large whirlpools, lots of squirting contraptions, and several lifeguards. More adult activities include an indoor running track and a good fitness center.

34911 Van Dyke Ave., Sterling Heights, MI 48312. © **800/953-1400** or 586/979-1400. Fax 586/979-0430. www.bestwestern.com. 240 units. $100–$180 double. Children 17 and under stay free in parent's room. AE, DC, DISC, MC, V. **Amenities:** Restaurant; indoor pool; fitness center.

The Dearborn Inn   The Dearborn Inn opened its doors in 1931 as the world's first airport hotel, located right across the street from Ford Airport. The airport has long since closed, but this historic inn remains popular, known for its Georgian elegance, first-class service, and business amenities. Twenty-three acres of meticulously landscaped grounds and gardens make this hotel feel worlds away from the big city. The Henry Ford Museum complex is within walking distance.

20301 Oakwood Blvd., Dearborn, MI 48124. © **800/228-9290** or 313/271-2700. Fax 313/271-7464. www.marriotthotels.com. 228 units. $140–$290 double. AE, DC, DISC, MC, V. Valet parking $17; free self-parking. **Amenities:** 3 restaurants; pool; fitness center.

Detroit Marriott at the Renaissance Center   Since the 1970s, the Renaissance Center has served as General Motors' corporate headquarters, and the building recalls its automotive history in a ground-floor classic car museum. The Marriott is popular with business travelers, but leisure guests love the downtown location; its People Mover station; proximity to the Joe Louis, Comerica Park, and Ford Field stadiums; and frequent leisure package deals. The hotel's Wintergarden—a glass atrium meeting and retail center—is just the spot for casual dining, shopping, and riverfront views. Book an upper-floor room for great views of the Detroit River and Windsor.

Renaissance Center (Jefferson Ave., btw. Brush St. and Beaubien), Detroit, MI 48243. © **800/228-9290** or 313/568-8000. Fax 313/568-8146. www.marriott.com. 1,298 units. $140–$300 double. AE, DC, DISC, MC, V. Valet parking $20; self-parking $12. Adjacent to "Renaissance Center" People Mover station. **Amenities:** 4 restaurants; health club.

The Inn on Ferry Street The Inn on Ferry Street is actually a collection of four large 19th-century homes and their carriage houses. Once slated for demolition, the buildings were rescued and converted into a charming B&B complex, each with its own parlor with fireplace. The individually decorated rooms have the usual array of modern amenities and up-to-date private bathrooms. The inn is located in the heart of the Cultural Center, within easy walking distance of museums. Complimentary shuttle service is provided within a 5-mile radius.

84 E. Ferry St. (at Woodward Ave.), Detroit, MI 48202. ✆ **313/871-6000.** Fax 313/871-1473. http://inn onferrystreet.com. 40 units. $134–$170 double; $170–$270 suite. Rates include deluxe continental breakfast. AE, DC, DISC, MC, V. Free parking.

The Townsend Hotel (Best) The gorgeous Townsend is one of Michigan's finest hotels, although it's about a 30-minute drive from downtown Detroit in Birmingham. You'll feel like a celebrity, and you just might see one—Hollywood's elite stay at the Townsend when they're in town. Rooms feature English-style decor and have Egyptian cotton linens, down comforters and pillows, and deep marble tubs and terry robes. Suites sport full kitchens. The Rugby Grille serves award-winning Continental cuisine, and you can work off your meal in the hotel's state-of-the-art fitness center.

100 Townsend St., Birmingham, MI 48009. ✆ **248/642-7900.** Fax 248/645-9061. www.townsendhotel. com. 150 units. $270–$365 double; $290–$2,000 suite. Children 18 and under stay free in parent's room. AE, DC, DISC, MC, V. Valet parking $24; self-parking $13. **Amenities:** 2 restaurants; fitness center. *In room:* Kitchen (suites only).

Where to Dine

Detroit Beer Co. MICROBREWERY This downtown Motor City brewpub lures beer lovers with its gleaming copper fermentation tanks and a selection of half a dozen varieties, from red and amber ales to IPAs, stouts, and seasonal beers. But the Detroit Beer Co. also serves up better-than-average pub food—brick oven pizzas, ribs, catfish, sandwiches, and salads. The restaurant's warm interior features exposed brick walls and ductwork, tin ceilings, and broadcasts of Detroit sports events.

1529 Broadway. ✆ **313/962-1529.** www.detroitbeerco.com. Entrees $9–$15. AE, DC, DISC, MC, V. Daily 11am–midnight.

Detroit's Breakfast House & Grill SOUTHERN An orange, green, and white decor and east-facing windows give Detroit's Breakfast House the feeling of morning sunshine even on dismal winter days. This restaurant is the hip place to see and be seen, and its food won't disappoint, either. Breakfast is the most popular meal, featuring bananas foster French toast, bacon pancakes, smoked salmon Benedict, and New Orleans frittatas. Lunchtime specials include a fried chicken and waffle club sandwich, barbecued tuna salad, and catfish filets. Expect a wait, especially on weekends.

1241 Woodward Ave. ✆ **313/961-1115.** www.detroitbreakfasthouse.com. Main courses $8–$14. AE, DISC, MC, V. Mon–Thurs 7:30am–3pm; Fri 7:30am–4pm; Sat 8am–5pm; Sun 8am–4pm.

The Lark (Best) CONTINENTAL Considered one of the finest restaurants in greater Detroit, the restaurant's decor is reminiscent of a southern European country inn. Beautiful gardens, fountains, and grape trellises adorn the grounds. The Lark's menu features a wide selection of seafood, ranging from fresh Maine lobster to roast halibut, as well as mouthwatering steaks, poultry, and vegetarian offerings. More than 1,000 varietals fill the wine list.

6430 Farmington Rd., West Bloomfield. ✆ **248/661-4466.** www.thelark.com. Reservations required. Main courses $43–$60; prix-fixe menu $65–$85. AE, DC, DISC, MC, V. Tues–Sat 5:30–9:30pm.

Pegasus Taverna GREEK Pegasus Taverna serves up hearty portions of all the requisite Greek dishes—moussaka, stuffed grape leaves, and gyros—including a nice selection of vegetarian offerings and Greek beers and wines. You'll also find a few American favorites, such as steaks and BBQ chicken. Classical Greek art reproductions adorn the walls, and faux grape arbors lend the large restaurant some intimacy. Expect big crowds—and noise—on weekends. Late hours and proximity make this restaurant a favorite after a night at the Greektown Casino.

558 Monroe St. (℃ **313/964-6800.** Reservations accepted. Main courses $8–$27. AE, DC, DISC, MC, V. Mon–Thurs 11am–1am; Fri–Sat 11am–3am; Sun 11am–midnight.

Seldom Blues AMERICAN Steaks and seafood dominate the menu at this hip fine-dining and jazz restaurant located in Detroit's landmark Renaissance Center. Try the Blue-B-Q Bass on fresh thyme Vidalia onion hash; the Lobster Pontchartrain, two lobster tails dusted, baked, and finished with shrimp, lump crabmeat, and mushrooms; or the Michigan mixed grill, with cranberry-stuffed quail, game sausage, and venison medallions. Live music is a mainstay at this restaurant. Expect blues, jazz, and maybe a little big band from local and national acts every night of the week.

400 Renaissance Center. (℃ **313/567-7301.** www.seldomblues.com. Reservations accepted. Main courses $23–$46. AE, DISC, MC, V. Mon–Thurs 11:30am–10pm; Fri 11:30am–midnight; Sat 5pm–midnight; Sun 11:30am–4pm.

Detroit After Dark

PERFORMING ARTS The renowned **Detroit Symphony Orchestra** (℃ **313/576-5111;** www.detroitsymphony.com) performs at Max M. Fisher Hall, 3711 Woodward Ave. **Michigan Opera Theatre** (℃ **313/961-3500;** www.motopera.org) performs at the Detroit Opera House, 1526 Broadway. Touring Broadway shows play at the **Fox Theatre,** 2211 Woodward Ave. (℃ **313/471-3200;** www.olympiaentertainment.com); the **Fisher Theatre,** 3011 W. Grand Blvd. (℃ **313/872-1000;** www.nederlanderdetroit.com); or the **Masonic Temple,** 500 Temple St. (℃ **313/832-7100;** http://themasonic.com).

THE BAR & CLUB SCENE For more than 70 years, Detroiters have whiled away their evenings at **Baker's Keyboard Lounge,** 20510 Livernois (℃ **313/345-6300;** www.bakerskeyboardlounge.com). Billing themselves as the "world's oldest jazz club," Baker's treats guests to the city's coolest live jazz and drinks every night but Monday. Downtown, the Majestic Theater building, 4120 Woodward Ave. (℃ **313/833-9700;** www.majesticdetroit.com), is home to two favorite music venues: **Garden Bowl,** a 16-lane glow-in-the-dark bowling alley accompanied by Detroit's hottest DJs; and the **Magic Stick** upstairs, a bar and billiards establishment widely known as the city's finest live music venue (the White Stripes got their start here).

Detroit is crazy for its sports, and one of its favorite sports bars is **Nemo's,** 1384 Michigan Ave. (℃ **313/965-3180;** www.nemosdetroit.com). Fun, friendly, and full of Detroit sports fans, the bar ranked number three on *Sports Illustrated*'s list of the "25 Best Sports Bars in America." Likewise, the **Post Bar,** 408 W. Congress (℃ **313/962-1293;** www.postbars.com), is the place to be after Tigers and Red Wings games. No less fun—but certainly more upscale—is **Hockeytown Café,** 2301 Woodward Ave. (℃ **313/965-9500;** www.hockeytowncafe.com). An ice-rink bar keeps drinks cold while Red Wings fans talk about the game; Red Wings paraphernalia covers the walls.

CASINOS In 1999, casino gambling came to Detroit with the **MGM Grand Detroit,** 1777 Third St. (℃ **877/888-2121;** www.mgmgranddetroit.com); the **MotorCity Casino,** 2901 Grand River Ave. (℃ **877/777-0711;** www.motorcitycasino.com); and

THE MIDWEST

7

DETROIT & HIGHLIGHTS OF MICHIGAN

Greektown Casino, 555 E. Lafayette (© **888/771-4386;** www.greektowncasino.com). All casinos are open 24 hours and have slots, table games, restaurants, entertainment, and parking. You must be 21 to enter.

WEST MICHIGAN BEACHES

Strung along the entire West Michigan shoreline, from Mackinaw City in the north to the Warren Dunes in the south, is a solid strip of sandy white beaches, the finest in the Midwest. A quick glance at any Michigan map reveals scores of sunning and swimming options. **State parks** provide inexpensive access ($6 per day, $24 per year for state residents; $8 per day, $29 per year for nonresidents). And the parks often feature great campgrounds. (Reserve your site *early*—a year in advance, if possible.) You can get more information by calling © **800/44-PARKS** (447-2757) or checking online at **www. michigandnr.com/parksandtrails**.

Traverse City

Traverse City, in Michigan's northwestern Lower Peninsula, is known for boutique shopping, wineries, and a vibrant arts scene, as well as its beaches. **Traverse City State Park,** 1132 U.S. 31 N. (© **231/922-5270**), and **Bayside Park,** U.S. 31 North, 8 miles east in Acme, both offer great beaches, swimming, and picnicking. Twenty-five miles east, near Empire on M-22, **Sleeping Bear Dunes National Lakeshore** (© **231/326-5134;** www. nps.gov/slbe) boasts some of the best beaches and dunes in the state. Contact the **Traverse City Convention & Visitors Bureau** (© **800/TRAVERSE** [872-8377]; www. visittraversecity.com) for information.

WHERE TO STAY & DINE   The Victorian-style **Bayshore Resort,** 833 E. Front St. (© **800/634-4401** or 231/935-4400; www.bayshore-resort.com), has doubles beginning at $176. The **Grand Beach Resort Hotel,** 1683 U.S. 31 N. (© **800/968-1992** or 231/938-4455; www.grandbeach.com), is a great family choice, with doubles starting at $169. Both hotels include continental breakfast and are right on the beach. The **Grand Traverse Resort & Spa,** 100 Grand Traverse Village Blvd., Acme (off U.S. 31 N; © **800/ 236-1577;** www.grandtraverseresort.com), is the place to go for pampering. The property recently received a $15-million renovation and offers a trio of 18-hole golf courses, shopping, dining, and a spa. Doubles begin at $146.

For dining out, head to Traverse City's Front Street downtown, with a wide array of choices. For a special evening out, try the contemporary Italian **Trattoria Stella,** 1200 W. 11th St. (© **231/929-8989;** www.stellatc.com), a beautiful brick turn-of-the-20th-century manse on the wooded grounds of Grand Traverse Commons. Expect an extensive wine list and a changing menu based on the availability of local ingredients and Atlantic and Pacific seafood.

Ludington

It's worth a trip just to experience the pristine 8-mile dune drive along **Ludington's** shoreline. Wild dune vistas and superb swimming beaches are dotted with free parking, both in **Ludington City Park** (Lakeshore Dr.) and en route to **Ludington State Park** (© **231/843-2423**) on M-116. Both parks offer sugar-sand beaches and "Big Lake" boating; the latter includes massive dunes, a lighthouse, and Hamlin Lake, a calmer (and warmer) inland option. For more information, contact the **Ludington Convention and Visitors Bureau** (© **877/420-6618;** www.ludingtoncvb.com).

WHERE TO STAY & DINE   You'll find many chain hotels on U.S. 10 between U.S. 31 and Ludington. If you want to be near the beach, head for **Snyder's Shoreline Inn,** 903

W. Ludington Ave. (© **231/845-1261;** www.snydersshoreinn.com), across the street from the city beach. Doubles begin at $109. Favorite Ludington B&Bs include the **Lamplighter,** 602 E. Ludington Ave. (© **800/301-9792;** www.ludington-michigan. com), with doubles for $125 to $170 (no children); and the **Inn at Ludington,** 701 E. Ludington Ave. (© **800/845-9170** or 231/845-7055; www.inn-ludington.com), with doubles from $100 to $195 (children 9 and under stay free). Both properties include full breakfast and are within walking distance of Lake Michigan. Outdoor lovers should consider **Ludington State Park,** with three popular, well-maintained campgrounds.

Most restaurants are clustered along Ludington Avenue, and an additional couple of good choices are **P. M. Steamers,** 502 W. Loomis St. (© **231/843-9555;** www.pm steamers.com), featuring American fare and waterfront views; and **Scotty's,** 5910 E. Ludington Ave. (© **231/843-4033;** www.scottysrestaurant.com), famous for prime rib and seafood.

Holland

The **Holland** area enjoys four great beaches: **Holland State Park,** 2215 Ottawa Beach Rd. (© **616/399-9390**); **Oval Beach,** Oval Drive just off Perryman Street, Saugatuck; **Dunes State Park,** western end of 138th Avenue, Saugatuck (© **616/637-2788**); and **Tunnel Park,** 66 Lakeshore Dr. (© **616/738-4810**), named for its unique tunnel through a sand dune. All four have picnic and playground facilities, but it's the huge sugar-sand beaches that attract thousands every year. For details, contact the **Holland Convention and Visitors Bureau** (© **800/506-1299;** http://holland.org).

WHERE TO STAY & DINE   Holland's chain hotels cluster along U.S. 31. For a unique downtown stay, try the new **City Flats,** 61 E. 7th St. (© **866/609-2489** or 616/796-2100; www.cityflatshotel.com), one of the first LEED-certified hotels in the nation, with doubles starting at $140. Also downtown is the **Haworth Inn,** 225 College Ave. (© **800/903-9142** or 616/395-7200; www.haworthinn.com), with doubles starting at $110, including continental breakfast.

In downtown Holland, numerous restaurants lie on or near 8th Street. Try **Alpenrose,** 4 E. 8th St. (© **616/393-2111;** www.alpenroserestaurant.com), featuring German and Austrian fare; **Butch's,** 44 E. 8th St. (© **616/396-8227;** www.butchs.net), a deli and wine shop by day and fine-dining restaurant by night; or the **New Holland Brewing Co.,** 66 E. 8th St. (© **616/355-6422;** http://newhollandbrew.com).

MACKINAC ISLAND

Set in the waters separating Michigan's upper and lower peninsulas, Mackinac (pronounced *Mack*-i-naw) Island is one of Michigan's most popular and romantic destinations. Cars are strictly prohibited; visitors get around the island on foot, bicycles, and horse-drawn carriages. The lack of modern transportation cultivates the sense of 19th-century nostalgia pervading the island, a veritable storehouse of beautifully restored Victorian homes. **Mackinac Island State Park** (© **906/847-3328;** www.mackinacparks. com) constitutes 80% of the island. For more information, contact the **Mackinac Island Tourism Bureau** (© **877/847-0086;** www.mackinacisland.org).

GETTING THERE   The major route to Mackinac Island is **I-75** from the south. From the lower peninsula, ferries depart from **Mackinaw City;** from the upper peninsula, ferries sail from **St. Ignace. Arnold Transit Co.** (© **800/542-8528;** www.arnoldline.com), **Shepler's Ferry** (© **800/828-6157;** www.sheplersferry.com), and **Star Line Ferry** (© **800/638-9892;** www.mackinacferry.com) all service the island from both cities and charge $25 adults and $12 children 5 to 12 for round-trip tickets. Children 4 and under are free; bike transport is $7.50. You can also travel by plane from St. Ignace on **Great Lakes Air** (© 906/643-7165; www.greatlakesair.net).

The oldest structure in Michigan, and one of the nation's few remaining Revolutionary War–era ruins, **Fort Mackinac** (© 906/847-3328; www.mackinacparks.com) looms high on a bluff overlooking the Straits of Mackinac. Originally a British outpost, Fort Mackinac was conquered by American soldiers 20 years after the Revolution. In addition to housing historic ruins, the Fort hosts Victorian children's games; bagpipe, bugle, and drum corps music; hourly rifle and cannon firings; and military reenactments performed by costumed interpreters.

Another prime vantage on the straits can be had from the porch at the **Grand Hotel** (© 800/33-GRAND [334-7263] or 906/847-3331; www.grandhotel.com), a National Historic Landmark. The veranda exudes romance and is a focal point of this wood-frame summer hotel, built in 1887. For $15, take a self-guided tour of this lovely landmark (see below) and enjoy the view from a rocking chair on the world's longest front porch. The price of the tour can be deducted from the cost of a meal.

If you like to bike, take a spin around the island following an 8-mile circuit on **M-185 (Lake Shore Rd.).** The view of the straits is spellbinding from here, and you can rubberneck without fear, given the prohibition on motorized vehicles. Bike rentals ($4–$8 per hour, depending upon the model) are available downtown. Ask about day rates and children's seats.

For an easier tour of the island, travel via horse and buggy with **Mackinac Island Carriage Tours** (© 906/847-3307; www.mict.com; $24 adults, $9 children 5–12). Two-hour trips begin near the boat docks in the shopping district and take in the Governor's Mansion, the Grand Hotel, Fort Mackinac, and Arch Rock, a limestone formation that is among the island's most popular natural attractions.

View natural attractions of a different sort at the **Mackinac Island Butterfly House,** 1308 McGulpin St. (© 906/847-3972; www.originalbutterflyhouse.com; $7.50 adults, $4 children 5–12); and the **Wings of Mackinac** butterfly house on Carriage Road (© 906/847-WING [847-9464]; www.wingsofmackinac.com; $5.50 adults, $2.50 children 5–12). Downtown, a smattering of shops and galleries are worth a stroll. Don't leave the island without sampling its famous fudge. Many downtown shops sell the island's favorite confection to tourists, who are affectionately known as "fudgies."

WHERE TO STAY & DINE Everyone should experience fine living at the 19th-century **Grand Hotel** (© 800/33-GRAND [334-7263] or 906/847-3331; www.grandhotel. com) at least once. Comfortable rooms in the world's largest summer hotel are individually decorated in bold tones, some with balconies and lake views. The suites are exceptionally luxurious, many named after famous figures, including six First Ladies. Resort grounds include tennis courts, an outdoor pool, an 18-hole golf course, and formal gardens. Doubles start at $225 per person, including elaborate daily breakfast and dinner and all tips. More moderately priced choices include the family-run **Hotel Iroquois,** Main Street (© 906/847-3321; www.iroquoishotel.com), a 100-year-old thoroughly modernized inn. Doubles start at $205. Suites at the **Lilac Tree Hotel,** Main Street (© 866/847-6575 or 906/847-6575; www.lilactree.com), include a fridge and microwave and start at $130.

For fine dining, nothing surpasses the **Grand Hotel's Salle à Manger** (© 800/33-GRAND [334-7263] or 906/847-3331; www.grandhotel.com), known for its French-inspired entrees, pecan ball dessert, and service fit for royalty. The hotel's **Jockey Club** and **Woods** restaurants offer casual meals—pasta, chicken, and steaks—at lower prices. The **Carriage House,** Main Street (© 906/847-3321; www.iroquoishotel.com), in the Hotel Iroquois, features local specialties such as broiled Great Lakes whitefish. A nice casual spot downtown is **Patrick Sinclair's Irish Pub** (© 906/847-8255; www.patrick sinclairs.com), with Irish and American favorites.

PICTURED ROCKS NATIONAL LAKESHORE

On the north coast of Michigan's upper peninsula, rain, wind, and waves have sculpted 17 miles of multicolored sandstone cliffs into **Pictured Rocks,** one of the state's most scenic shores. The most spectacular cliffs extend from Munising to Grand Marais and soar to a height of 200 feet, varying from caves and arches to narrow columns and overlooks. Lodging, restaurants, information, and camping supplies can be found in Munising on Route 28 and in Grand Marais on Route 77. For information, contact **Grand Marais Chamber of Commerce** (© 906/494-2447; www.grandmaraismi.com) or park headquarters (© 906/387-2607; www.nps.gov/piro).

There are miles of hiking trails and roads, which yield close-up views of the Pictured Rocks, including the **North Country Trail.** Many visitors prefer to see the multicolored shore via 2-hour cruise. Boats dock at the **Munising City Pier,** Mich. 28 and Elm Avenue (© 800/650-2379 or 906/387-2379; www.picturedrocks.com). Adults pay $33, children 6 to 12 $10, and children 5 and under ride free.

In the summer, lakeshore pastimes include hiking, picnicking, and swimming (if you can brave Lake Superior's frigid waters). In the winter, visitors enjoy snowshoeing, snowmobiling, or cross-country skiing on 21 miles of trails.

Near **Grand Marais,** the cliffs ease into **giant sand dunes,** which lumberjacks used as chutes to send forested timber into the lake below. Inland, you'll find waterfalls, forests, abundant wildlife, and fish swarming in lakes, ponds, and streams. At the base of the cliffs, a sand beach stretches for 12 miles.

After a rigorous day in the outdoors, replenish your energy without depleting your funds at **Sydney's,** 400 Cedar St., Munising (© 906/387-4067). Grilled steaks or fresh Great Lakes whitefish are the specialties. Dine in or take out.

There are three drive-in campsites in the 40-mile Pictured Rocks National Lakeshore between Munising and Grand Marais. You can also hike into primitive campgrounds along the water. In Grand Marais, **North Shore Lodge,** 22020 Coast Guard Pt., 1 mile east of Route 77 (© 906/494-2361), offers humble, affordable lodging on a stretch of private beach, with an indoor pool and a kids' play area.

GETTING THERE   To reach Pictured Rocks from the Mackinac Bridge (I-75), take **U.S. 2 west** immediately after the bridge, then M-77 north to Grand Marais. For Munising, turn west on **M-28** at Seney.

ISLE ROYALE NATIONAL PARK

It's tough to get to **Isle Royale National Park** (© 906/482-0984; www.nps.gov/isro), which is precisely its appeal. The remote, craggy islands are populated with hardwood forests, wildlife, lakes, and streams rather than loads of tourists and RVs. Cars are prohibited in this northern oasis, accessible only by boat and floatplane, 50 miles from Michigan's northwest coast and surrounded by icy Lake Superior. The main island is the largest (45 miles wide×8 miles long) and most visited, but 400 smaller islands pepper the surrounding waters. It's likely you'll have one all to yourself, provided you can paddle there. And you can do so only mid-April through October; the park is closed to visitors the rest of the year.

A trip to Isle Royale takes careful planning. Ferries to the island return just a few hours after they dock; don't waste your time and money on the long voyage unless you plan to stay overnight. If you're traveling midsummer, it's wise to reserve ferry space in advance. The one-way, 2½-hour cruise from Grand Portage, Minnesota (on Hwy. 61 near Ontario) on *Voyageur II* (© 218/475-0024 summer, 651/653-5872 off season; www.grand-isle-royale.com) costs $59 adults, $39 children 11 and under to Windigo; $69 adults and $46 children to Rock Harbor. The 3-hour, one-way trip from Copper Harbor, Michigan (on U.S. 41, on the Keweenaw Peninsula) on the *Isle Royale Queen IV* (© 906/289-4437; www.isleroyale.com) costs $62 adults, $31 children 11 and under. And the 6-hour trip from Houghton, Michigan (on U.S. 41, on the Keweenaw Peninsula) on *Ranger III* (© 906/482-0984; www.nps.gov/isro) costs $60 adults, $20 children 11 and under. The *Ranger III* is the only ferry large enough to transport boats; fees vary according to boat size. From Houghton you can also catch a **seaplane** (© 877/359-4753; www.royaleairservice.com) for $269 per person, round-trip. Visitors also need to pay a user fee of $4 per day for every person age 12 and over.

You'll encounter Isle Royale's sole inhabitants—200 bird species, foxes, beavers, wolves, and about 700 moose—along the park's 165 miles of foot trails. **Greenstone Ridge Trail,** the main artery, is strenuous, running east-west along the island—a 4- or 5-day trek even for fit hikers. Easier routes include the treks along the rugged bluffs of **Stoll Trail** and along **Tobin Harbor Trail** to Suzy's Cave; and up 880 feet to **Lookout Louise,** a more difficult climb that rewards with unsurpassed views. Even inexperienced paddlers can manage a canoe trip across **Hidden Lake,** where a natural salt lick attracts the local moose population.

Rock Harbor Lodge, Rock Harbor (© 906/337-4993 summer, 866/644-2003 off season; www.isleroyaleresort.com; open Memorial Day to Labor Day), provides lodging and meals to those who need more comfort than a tent. Doubles begin at $230 per night without meals or $360 per night with three meals. The lodge's surprisingly good dining room is open to all, or you can bring your own food (there are no grocery stores on Isle Royale) and rent a cottage with kitchenette beginning at $223 a night. All lodging includes a half-day canoe rental. Sightseeing cruises depart Rock Harbor for a variety of island destinations, beginning at $36 adults, $18 children 11 and under. Water Bus service to points along Isle Royale's shore is a popular means of exploring distant trails without the lengthy hike out. Rates begin at $15 per person.

The campgrounds near Rock Harbor have three-sided wooden shelters, but they fill up fast because of their proximity to the island's entry point. **Three Mile** and **Daisy Farm** are within a day's hike of Rock Harbor, west along the southern shore. The popular **West Chickenbone** campground lies a 2- to 3-day hike from Rock Harbor, along the Greenstone Ridge Trail.

For more information, call **Park Headquarters** at © 906/482-0984. **Ranger stations** are at Windigo, Rock Harbor, Malone Bay, and Amygdaloid.

6 MILWAUKEE & HIGHLIGHTS OF WISCONSIN

MILWAUKEE

Milwaukee celebrated 2008 with the opening of the new Harley-Davidson Museum. But while the museum deserves all the attention it received, there's much more to Milwaukee than motorcycles. This Great Lakes city has considered itself the authority on beer since

beverage needs. Summertime is packed with ethnic and music festivals on Lake Michigan. And Milwaukee is home to a number of impressive arts offerings, including the spectacular Santiago Calatrava–designed Milwaukee Art Museum.

Essentials

GETTING THERE By Plane The **General Mitchell International Airport** (© 414/747-5300; www.mitchellairport.com) is 6 miles south of downtown, a 15-minute drive on I-94 West to I-794 East. One-way transportation to downtown costs $13 via **Airport Connection** shuttle service (© 800/236-5450; reservations recommended); $2 via the local Transit System (Rte. 80 serves the airport); $7 via Amtrak to its station at 433 W. St. Paul Ave.; and $30 via taxi.

By Train Amtrak (© 800/USA-RAIL [872-7245]; www.amtrak.com) provides service from Chicago (trip time: $1^1/_2$ hr.) and Minneapolis/St. Paul ($6^1/_4$ hr.) to its station at 433 W. St. Paul Ave.

By Car Milwaukee is 90 miles from Chicago, a $1^1/_2$-hour drive, and 80 miles from Madison, also a $1^1/_2$-hour drive. Both cities are reached via **I-94.**

By Ferry The **Lake Express Ferry** (© 866/914-1010; www.lake-express.com) offers high-speed car and passenger service from Muskegon, Michigan (trip time: $2^1/_2$ hr.). One-way fares are $70 for adults, $40 for children, $80 for autos.

VISITOR INFORMATION The **Milwaukee Convention and Visitors Bureau** has an office inside the Midwest Airlines Center at 400 W. Wisconsin Ave., Milwaukee, 53203 (© 800/554-1448 or 414/273-7222; www.visitmilwaukee.org).

GETTING AROUND The **Milwaukee County Transit System** (© 414/344-6711; www.ridemcts.com) offers service downtown and into the suburbs for $2. From early June through mid-August, the MCTS operates a free **Trolley** on a downtown Milwaukee loop, hitting all the big attractions and popular shopping, dining, and lodging locations. During lakeside festivals like Summerfest, MCTS provides downtown **Shuttle** service between events, hotels, and city parking lots for $3 round-trip. If you plan to venture outside the immediate downtown, it's best to drive.

SPECIAL EVENTS & FESTIVALS There are dozens of festivals held throughout the year. The biggest and best include **Summerfest** (© 800/273-FEST [273-3378]; www.summerfest.com), with over 700 bands on 11 waterfront stages for nearly 2 weeks in late June and early July; and **Irish Fest** (© 414/476-3378; www.irishfest.com), in mid-August, the world's largest Irish cultural festival. In early August, the **Wisconsin State Fair** (© 800/884-FAIR [884-3247]; www.wistatefair.com) features entertainment, auto races, exhibits, fireworks, and more.

What to See & Do

The **Harley-Davidson Museum** displays over 400 classic motorcycles and memorabilia, including the original 1903 Serial No. 1 and Elvis Presley's orange-and-white 1956 motorcycle. Reconstructed board tracks and photo exhibits recall the lives of early Harley enthusiasts, and a park, cafe, restaurant, and retail shop complete the experience at 6th and Canal streets (© 414/343-4235; www.h-dmuseum.com). Tickets cost $16 for adults, $10 children, 4 and under free. Motorcycle lovers will also enjoy the **Harley-Davidson Tour Center**, 11700 W. Capitol Dr., Wauwatosa (© 877/883-1450 or

414/343-7850; www.harley-davidson.com), with free hour-long tours showcasing the plant's powertrain production. No children 11 and under.

Miller Brewing Company, 4251 W. State St. (© **800/944-LITE** [944-5483] or 414/931-BEER [931-2337]; www.millerbrewing.com), operates one of the world's largest breweries. After a free 1-hour tour, visitors sample the product in the city's last remaining outdoor *biergarten,* weather permitting—in the 19th-century Miller Inn the rest of the year.

Enjoy hands-on science-and-technology exhibits at **Discovery World at Pier Wisconsin,** 500 N. Harbor Dr. (© **414/765-9966;** www.discoveryworld.org), reopened in 2006 in a new lakeshore location. Highlights include an aquarium and the tall ship *S/V Denis Sullivan,* a re-creation of a 19th-century Great Lakes schooner. Admission is $17 adults, $13 children, and free for children 2 and under. Ship tours cost $5; 2-hour public sails cost $50 for adults, $25 for children.

Downtown, the **Milwaukee Public Museum,** 800 W. Wells St. (© **888/700-9069** or 414/278-2702; www.mpm.edu), is home to a staggering array of re-created international villages, a live butterfly garden, dinosaur skeletons, a simulated rainforest, a planetarium, and an IMAX theater. Museum admission is $11 adults, $7 children 3 to 15, 2 and under free; planetarium and IMAX films each cost $8 adults, $6 children.

A favorite for the kids is the **Milwaukee County Zoo,** 10001 W. Blue Mound Rd. (© **414/256-5412;** www.milwaukeezoo.org). All the favorites are on hand, including elephants, bears, zebras, gorillas, and the big cats, but you'll also see raptor and sea lion shows and you can take a ride on a camel. Admission fees vary seasonally but are generally $11 adults, $8 children 3 to 12.

Santiago Calatrava's redesign of the **Milwaukee Art Museum,** 700 N. Art Museum Dr. (at Michigan St. and Lincoln Memorial Dr.; © **414/224-3200;** www.mam.org), renders the museum building as stunning as any of the works on display inside. The Burke Brise Soleil sunscreen on the roof opens and closes to resemble a large white gull. Inside, artworks range from ancient Greek to modern American, Asian, and African pieces, including Renoir, Monet, Kandinsky, and Miró. Admission is $8 for adults, $4 for students, and free for children 12 and under.

Where to Stay & Dine

The new, motorcycle-friendly **Iron Horse Hotel** (© **888/543-IRON** [543-4766]; www.theironhorsehotel.com), at 500 W. Florida St., sits just across the canal from the Harley-Davidson Museum and offers amenities like in-room boot and leather storage, indoor motorcycle parking, and a bike wash. The boutique hotel also includes amenities to make business and leisure travelers feel at home. Doubles begin at $163. The **Hilton City Center,** 509 W. Wisconsin Ave. (© **800/HILTONS** [445-8667] or 414/271-7250; www.hiltonmilwaukee.com), is convenient to downtown and features the nation's first urban indoor waterpark, "Paradise Landing." Doubles begin at $119. Milwaukee's most historic hotel, the **Pfister,** 424 E. Wisconsin Ave. (© **800/472-4403** or 414/273-8222; www.thepfisterhotel.com), was built in 1893. The hotel exudes old-style European elegance; doubles begin at $209 and go way up.

Enjoy fish, poultry, and produce from the world's great coastal regions (including the Great Lakes) at **Coast,** 931 E. Wisconsin Ave. (© **414/727-5555;** www.coastrestaurant.com). **Il Mito,** at 6913 W. North Ave. (© **414/443-1414;** www.ilmito.com), combines inventive Mediterranean flavors in a relaxed atmosphere. The **Milwaukee Ale House,** 233 N. Water St. (© **414/226-BEER** [226-2337]; www.ale-house.com), in the historic

Third Ward, was founded by home-brewers. Try their craft beers and better-than-average pub grub.

A Side Trip to Kohler & the American Club

One hour north of Milwaukee is the planned garden community of Kohler, its centerpiece the luxurious **American Club,** Highland Drive (© **800/344-2838;** www.destination kohler.com). Built in 1918 to house employees of the Kohler plumbing factory, the grand Tudor-style American Club was converted into a hotel in 1981. It is now the Midwest's premier resort hotel, offering 236 luxurious guest rooms, each outfitted with fabulous bathroom fixtures. Also on-site is Kohler's **Inn on Woodlake,** a 121-room Arts and Crafts–style inn. The resort's extensive facilities include four Pete Dye–designed golf courses, a 500-acre wilderness preserve, a salon and day spa, health and racquet facilities, upscale boutiques, and the Kohler Design Center. Golf is the star attraction, though, and guests are encouraged to reserve tee times when they book their room—greens fees begin at $155. Double rooms at the American Club begin at $195; doubles at the Inn begin at $123.

MADISON

For a small city, Madison has a lot of flair. Credit the presence of 41,000 university students, or perhaps the city's designation as Wisconsin's state capitol, or maybe its location between two scenic lakes. Whatever the reason, Madison boasts inexpensive entertainment, city parks, and streets enlivened by bookstores, cafes, and funky boutiques. Madison's most bustling thoroughfare, **State Street,** and the downtown area, **Capitol Square,** are great places to shop and dine. And late April through early November, Capitol Square hosts the vibrant, open-air **Dane County Farmer's Market** (www.dcfm.org) on Saturday and Wednesday, with local produce and cheese, arts and crafts booths, musicians, and more than a few speakers on soapboxes.

VISITOR INFORMATION For more information, contact the **Greater Madison Convention and Visitors Bureau,** 615 E. Washington Ave. (© **800/373-6376** or 608/255-2537; www.visitmadison.com).

What to See & Do

Madison's 100-year-old **State Capitol** (© **608/266-0382**) dominates the city center, topped by Daniel Chester French's gilded bronze statue *Wisconsin.* Hour-long tours are offered daily here and at **Monona Terrace,** 2 blocks away, 1 John Nolen Dr. (© **608/261-4000;** www.mononaterrace.com). Monona Terrace community and convention center was designed by Frank Lloyd Wright, whose presence is richly felt in Madison and nearby Taliesin (see below). Tours examine building highlights and Wright's design philosophy. Enjoy superb lake and city views from the building's rooftop garden, a popular stop for lunchtime picnickers.

For more examples of Wright's Prairie School architecture, visit **First Unitarian Society,** 900 University Bay Dr. (© **608/233-9774**), which is open to the public, or drive past these private residences: **Airplane House** (1908), 120 Ely Place; **Dr. Arnold Jackson House** (1957), 3515 W. Beltline Hwy.; **Lamp House** (1899), 22 N. Butler St.; **J. C. Pew House** (1939), 3650 Lake Mendota Dr.; **Louis Sullivan Bradley's House,** 106 N. Prospect; and **"Jackobs I" House** (1937), 441 Toepfer Ave.

Madison enjoys more than its fair share of public green spaces, settled as it is on an isthmus between lakes Mendota and Monona. Of the city's more than 150 public parks, one of the most popular is the free **Henry Vilas Park Zoo,** 702 S. Randall Ave. (© **608/266-4733;** www.vilaszoo.org), where locals gather to picnic, feed ducks, and view more than 600 animals. **Olbrich Botanical Gardens,** 3330 Atwood Ave. (© 608/246-4550; www.olbrich.org), boasts 14 acres of outdoor flowering plants and a conservatory. **Olbrich Park,** across the street, sits on the northeastern shore of Lake Monona, with picnic tables and a swimming beach.

Where to Stay & Dine

Head to the **Arbor House,** 3402 Monroe St. (© 608/238-2981; www.arbor-house. com), for a luxurious stay in a green inn, with organic cotton sheets, biodegradable cleaning supplies, and native landscaping. Doubles start at $110 and include organic, homemade breakfast and the free use of mountain bikes. The **Hilton Madison Monona Terrace,** 9 E. Wilson St. (© 608/255-5100; www.hiltonmadison.com), is ideally located in central Madison, within a few blocks of the capitol and the university, and adjacent to Lake Monona and the Monona Terrace Convention Center. Doubles begin at $189. The **Edgewater,** 666 Wisconsin Ave. (© 800/922-5512 or 608/256-9071; www.the edgewater.com), on Lake Mendota, boasts beautiful lakeside sunsets and a fine restaurant. Doubles begin at $129.

For a casual meal out, you can't beat the atmosphere and food at **Great Dane Pub & Brewing Co.,** 123 E. Doty St. (© 608/284-0000; www.greatdanepub.com), serving up a dozen craft beers alongside sandwiches, burgers, and dinners. Updated Wisconsin comfort food comprises the menu at the **Old Fashioned,** 23 N. Pinckney St. (© 608/310-4545; www.theoldfashioned.com); expect mac-n-cheese, walleye, and burgers in an upscale tavern. Visit the 19th-century stone house that is **Quivey's Grove,** 6261 Nesbitt Rd. (© 608/273-4900; www.quiveysgrove.com), for steaks, chicken, vegetables, and pies like Grandma used to make.

SPRING GREEN & TALIESIN

Frank Lloyd Wright's former home, which he built and perfected over the course of 40 years, **Taliesin** (tally-*es*-in), intersection of Hwy. 23 and County Hwy. C (© 877/588-7900 or 608/588-7900; www.taliesinpreservation.org), has been called the architect's "autobiography in wood and stone." Taliesin was also the architect's studio and laboratory. Located in south-central Wisconsin (an hour's drive west of Madison), the 600-acre National Historic Landmark is now a studio, farm, and architectural school for 40 undergraduates.

Welsh for "shining brow," Taliesin is built on the crest of a hill facing the Wisconsin River on land Wright's grandfather settled after immigrating from Wales. Wright built each of the grounds' five buildings during consecutive decades of his 50-year career. Visitors can purchase tickets to one of six Taliesin tours, the most popular being the **Hillside Studio Tour** (1 hr.; $16, children free); the **Shuttle/Walking Tour** of the grounds (2 hr.; $20, children $10); and the **Highlights Tour** (2 hr.; $52). The regular season runs May through October, but tour dates, hours, and prices vary widely. Reservations are strongly recommended; children are not permitted on certain tours.

South of town, the multilevel **House on the Rock,** Hwy. 23 (© 608/935-3639; www.thehouseontherock.com), sits atop a 450-foot rock chimney. Built by Alexander Jordan, the stone house is an architectural curiosity, with massive fireplaces, trees, and pools of running water throughout the building. Views of the surrounding landscape are equally spectacular and easily visible through the house's 3,264 windows.

You can stay at **House on the Rock Resort,** 400 Springs Dr. (© 608/334-5275; www.thehouseontherock.com), just a few miles from its famous namesake. The all-suite resort features private patios and balconies, as well as a fine restaurant and 27 holes of championship golf. Doubles begin at $128.

For more information, contact the **Spring Green Chamber of Commerce,** 259 E. Jefferson St., Spring Green (© **800/588-2042** or 608/588-2054; www.springgreen.com).

THE WISCONSIN DELLS

The Wisconsin Dells draw thousands of tourists every year, claiming the title "The Waterpark Capital of the World." But it was the region's natural beauty that first drew visitors to its 15 miles of weathered sandstone cliffs and cool, wooded gullies. Ironically, few visitors to this popular attraction ever see the Dells themselves.

You can observe the region's natural beauty from April to October on **Dells Boat Tours** (© **608/254-8555;** www.dellsboats.com) or aboard World War II amphibious "ducks" at **Original Wisconsin Ducks** (© **608/254-8751;** www.wisconsinducktours. com). Both offer 2-hour tours of the sandstone gorges for $21 adults, $11 children (age 5 and under free). During the warm months, you can also explore the gorgeous landscape on horseback with a guide at the **Beaver Springs Fishing Park, Riding Stables and Aquarium,** 600 Trout Rd. (© **608/254-2707;** www.beaverspringsfun.com). An hour's ride costs $25 adults, $8.50 children 5 and under sharing a horse with an adult. Fifty-foot cliffs form the lakeshore of **Mirror Lake State Park,** Fern Dell Road (© **608/254-2333;** www.mirrorlakewisconsin.com). A popular boating spot, the lake is surrounded by pine and oak woods where visitors can picnic and camp.

But there's no denying the appeal of the Wisconsin Dells' man-made attractions. **Noah's Ark Waterpark,** 1410 Wisconsin Dells Pkwy. (© **608/254-6351;** www.noahs arkwaterpark.com), which claims to be the nation's largest, offers 47 water slides, two wave pools, two endless rivers, 4 children's water play areas, minigolf, and 12 restaurants and lounges. The park's newest addition is a 4D Dive-In Theatre that incorporates watery special affects throughout the movie. A day pass costs $33 adults, $26 children under 47 inches, age 2 and under free.

The popularity—and plethora—of indoor waterparks in the Dells has made the area a year-round family destination. Parks combine water slides, wave pools, and squirting toys with resort-style accommodations (and sometimes golf and spa facilities) under one roof at an affordable price. **Great Wolf Lodge,** 1400 Great Wolf Dr. (© **800/559-WOLF** [559-9653]; www.greatwolflodge.com), follows a North Woods log cabin theme and offers lots of children's activities. Rates begin at $129 for a family of four. **Kalahari Resort,** 1305 Kalahari Dr. (© **877/525-2427;** www.kalahariresort.com), also has a day spa on-site. Rates begin at $129. One of the Dells' largest waterpark resorts, which also claims to be the nation's largest, is **Wilderness Lodge,** 511 E. Adams St. (© **800/867-WILD** [867-9453]; www.wildernessresort.com), with over 12 football fields' worth of indoor and outdoor waterpark fun, as well as dry parks, nearly 450 hotel rooms, cabins, condos, 9-hole and 18-hole golf courses, and a spa. Room rates begin at $99. *Note:* Rates for all of the above resorts include waterpark entry and lodging for up to four guests.

Wally's House of Embers, 935 Wisconsin Dells Pkwy., Lake Delton (© **608/253-6411;** www.houseofembers.com), has been a Dells institution since 1959. The family-owned restaurant specializes in ribs but also serves fresh seafood and steaks. The romantic themed rooms are worth reserving for a special night out. For great burgers, sandwiches, and salads, check out **Monks Bar & Grill,** 220 Broadway (© **608/254-2955;** www.monksbarandgrill.com), a local fixture with a friendly staff.

The Dells—both the town and the geologic wonder—are 55 miles north of Madison off I-90/94. For information, contact the **Wisconsin Dells Visitor and Convention Bureau,** 701 Superior St., Wisconsin Dells (© **800/223-3557;** www.wisdells.com).

DOOR COUNTY

Door County's rugged Lake Michigan coast, fishing villages (now converted into resort towns), and laid-back atmosphere draw scores of visitors looking for family and romantic getaways. With Green Bay to the west and Lake Michigan on three sides, Door County is a 75-mile-long strip of cliffs and unsullied beaches with 250 miles of limestone or dune coastline. No matter where you are on the peninsula, you're never more than 10 minutes from a water view.

Routes 57 and 42 circle the peninsula, passing through splendid natural scenery and inviting towns like the bayside villages of **Fish Creek, Sister Bay,** and **Ephraim,** each one charmingly different from the next. Tidy dairy farms and fruit orchards with ubiquitous red barns dot the landscape. Contact the **Door County Chamber of Commerce,** 1015 Green Bay Rd., Sturgeon Bay (© **800/52-RELAX** [527-3529] or 920/743-4456; www.doorcounty.com), for detailed information.

Door County is home to several lovely state parks, each with miles of hiking and biking trails, fishing, sailing, camping, and swimming in the summer; beautiful fall leaf-peeping in the fall; and cross-country skiing and snowmobiling in the winter. **Peninsula State Park,** near Fish Creek (© **920/868-3258**), has all of that, a picturesque lighthouse, 18 holes of championship golf, and the American Folklore Theatre. Ninety-foot dunes, jagged cliffs, and surf-carved caves lure visitors to **Whitefish Dunes State Park,** near Jacksonport (© **920/823-2400**). **Potawatomi State Park,** near Sturgeon Bay (© **920/746-2890**), has a nice observation tower offering sweeping views of Green Bay. State park campgrounds are popular—be sure to reserve a site early (© **888/947-2757**). An annual pass to any Wisconsin state park costs $25 for state residents, $35 for others; a day pass costs $7 for Wisconsin residents, $10 for others. Camping fees run $12 to $17. For online info on Wisconsin's state parks, see **www.dnr.state.wi.us/org/land/parks**.

Art galleries and crafts boutiques are located throughout Door County. Fish Creek, Egg Harbor, Sister Bay, and Ephraim have the best assortment. **Edgewood Orchard Galleries,** 4140 Peninsula Players Rd., Fish Creek (© **920/868-3579;** www.edgewoodorchard.com), exhibit oil paintings, jewelry, metal, and glass works, most of which are created by Wisconsin artists. **Dovetail Gallery,** 7901 Hwy. 42, Egg Harbor (© **920/868-3987;** www.dovetailgallery.com), displays jewelry, Fimo clay, glass, and copper works, but is best known for its plethora of works crafted locally from eggshells. And **Popelka Trenchard,** 64 S. 2nd Ave. (© **920/743-7287;** www.popelkaglass.com), creates vibrant glass art in a studio/gallery in Sturgeon Bay.

French and Scandinavian fishermen settled the Door in the 17th century, and the surrounding waters are still home to a mother lode of walleye, pike, trout, and salmon. **Fish boils** are the stuff of ceremonial ritual here: Fresh whitefish, onions, and potatoes are tossed into a boiling cauldron, then finished off when a pint of kerosene is splashed onto the wood fire. This quintessential Door County dinner is available throughout the peninsula, with most restaurants charging about $20 per adult, $12 per child, including Door County cherry pie. The **White Gull Inn,** 4225 Main St., Fish Creek (© **920/868-3517;** www.whitegullinn.com), claims to have been boiling fish longer than anyone else on the peninsula. The **Square Rigger,** 6332 Hwy. 57, Jacksonport (© **877/347-4264;** www.squareriggerlodge.com), serves their fish boil in their dining room rather than from a buffet line.

For an authentic Swedish breakfast of pancakes with lingonberry sauce, everyone heads to **Al Johnson's Swedish Restaurant,** 10698 N. Bayshore Dr., Sister Bay (© **800/ 241-9914;** www.aljohnsons.com). You'll recognize the building from its sod-covered roof (where you might see a grazing goat or two keeping the grass trimmed). **Wilson's Restaurant and Ice Cream Parlor,** Route 42, Ephraim (© **920/854-2041**), has been serving sundaes, chocolate sodas, and burgers under its red-and-white awning since 1906. Enjoy fine dining at the **Mission Grille,** Hwys. 42 and 57, Sister Bay (© **920/854-9070;** www.missiongrille.com), a remodeled turn-of-the-20th-century church incorporating local Wisconsin ingredients and serving an outstanding wine list.

Door County is known for its romantic B&Bs. The **Whistling Swan,** 4192 Main St., Fish Creek (© **77-4289** or 920/868-3442; www.whistlingswan.com), was built on mainland Wisconsin in 1887 and moved across the frozen Green Bay 20 years later to serve as an inn. It remains a charming B&B, furnished with antiques. Doubles start at $100 and include continental breakfast. Across the street is the elegant **White Gull Inn,** 4225 Main St. (© **888/364-9542** or 920/868-3517; www.whitegullinn.com). Doubles begin at $150 and include a full breakfast. **Edgewater Resort,** 10040 Water St., Ephraim (© **800/603-5331** or 920/854-2734; www.edge-waterresort.com), features spacious accommodations, most with water views and balconies, some with double whirlpool tubs and kitchens. Doubles begin at $80.

7 MINNEAPOLIS & ST. PAUL

Fertile prairie land and the Mississippi River put the Twin Cities on the map in the 19th century, producing tons of grain, milling it, and then transporting it to the nation. These days Minneapolis and St. Paul are more closely associated with arts and culture than gristmills. First-time visitors are often overwhelmed by the wealth of first-class museums and theaters in the Twin Cities. Minneapolis has also become a hot spot for architectural gems, including the Weisman Art Museum, the Walker Art Center, and the Guthrie Theatre. And lest Minnesota's reputation for harsh weather trouble you, both cities incorporate miles of climate-controlled skyways enabling residents and visitors to work, shop, and dine without ever stepping outdoors.

ESSENTIALS

GETTING THERE   By Plane   Minneapolis/St. Paul International Airport (www. mspairport.com), located between the cities, is 16 and 12 miles south of each downtown, respectively, and is a hub for Northwest Airlines. The **Metropolitan Transit Commission** runs buses to both cities (© **612/373-3333;** www.metrotransit.org), and light-rail service to Minneapolis for $2 in off-peak hours and $2.75 during rush hour. **Super-Shuttle** (© **612/827-7777;** www.supershuttle.com) vans run to downtown Minneapolis or St. Paul hotels for $16; other metro areas vary in price. Taxi fares to downtown Minneapolis begin at $32; the trip to downtown St. Paul begins at $26.

By Train   Amtrak (© **800/USA-RAIL** [872-7245]; www.amtrak.com) provides service from Chicago (trip time: 8 hr.) and Milwaukee (6¹/₂ hr.) to its station at 730 Transfer Rd., St. Paul (© **651/644-6012**).

By Car   Major routes into the Twin Cities are **I-94** from the east (Milwaukee and Chicago) and west (Fargo), and **I-35** from the south (Des Moines) and north (Duluth).

VISITOR INFORMATION   The **Minneapolis Convention & Visitors Bureau** is at 250 Marquette Ave. S., Ste. 1300, Minneapolis, MN 55401 (© **888/676-MPLS** [676-6757]; www.minneapolis.org). The **St. Paul Convention & Visitors Bureau** is at 175 W. Kellogg Blvd., Ste. 502, St. Paul, MN 55102 (© **800/627-6101;** www.stpaulcvb.org).

GETTING AROUND   The **Metropolitan Transit Commission** (© **612/373-3333;** www.metrotransit.org) operates buses between the Twin Cities. The **Hiawatha Light Rail** runs along Hiawatha Avenue from Minneapolis's Warehouse District to the Minneapolis/St. Paul Airport and the Mall of America with a dozen stops in between. Fares for the bus or train system are the same: Rush-hour fare is $2.75; off-peak fare is $2. A day pass good for both buses and trains costs $6.

Both Minneapolis and St. Paul have an extensive skyway system (a godsend during below-zero winters) that makes it easy to explore downtown areas on foot. Visitors will need a car to reach attractions outside downtown and in the suburbs.

FAST FACTS   There's an emergency room at the **University of Minnesota Medical Center, Fairview,** 500 Harvard St., Minneapolis (© **612/273-3000**). **St. Joseph's Hospital** operates an emergency room at 69 W. Exchange St., in St. Paul (© **651/232-3000**).

There is no sales tax on clothing or shoes in Minnesota. Both Minneapolis and St. Paul are among the safest large cities in the country, and crime rates are low. Exercise the same caution you would in any other major city, and you should have no problems.

WHAT TO SEE & DO
In Minneapolis

Frederick R. Weisman Art Museum   Set on a bluff overlooking the Mississippi River, the Weisman Art Museum is part of the University of Minnesota campus. You won't miss the trademark Frank Gehry–designed building; its fluid form defies conventional architectural lines, and its metallic finish gleams in the sunlight. The permanent collection is especially strong in American modernist paintings, ceramics, Mimbres pottery, and Korean furniture. Allow 1 hour.

333 E. River Rd. © **612/625-9494.** www.weisman.umn.edu. Free admission. Tues–Wed and Fri 10am–5pm; Thurs 10am–8pm; Sat–Sun 11am–5pm. Head southeast on Washington Ave. and take the "Washington Ave. SE" ramp downhill and across the Mississippi. E. River Rd. is immediately to your right.

Mill City Museum   Minneapolis's Mill City Museum recounts the history of the flour industry that earned the city the nickname "Mill City" in the late 19th century. Set in the ruins of what was once the world's largest flour mill, and one of over two dozen such Minneapolis mills, the museum re-creates old milling techniques with period equipment, railroad cars, and interactive exhibits. Visitors also learn the impact of the nation's first high-quality, finely milled flour on the gastronomy of the Twin Cities and the country. Allow 1 hour.

704 S. 2nd St. © **612/341-7555.** www.millcitymuseum.org. Admission $10 adults, $5 children 6–17, free for children 5 and under. Tues–Wed and Fri–Sat 10am–5pm; Thurs 10am–9pm; Sun noon–5pm. Closed Mon except select holidays: Martin Luther King, Jr., Day, Presidents' Day, Memorial Day, July 4, and Labor Day.

Minneapolis Institute of Arts (Best)   More than 5,000 years and 80,000 pieces of fine and decorative arts comprise the permanent collection at the MIA, including a 2,000-year-old mummy, European masters (Rembrandt, Titian, and Monet, among others), architectural and decorative arts, and a comprehensive photography exhibit. If

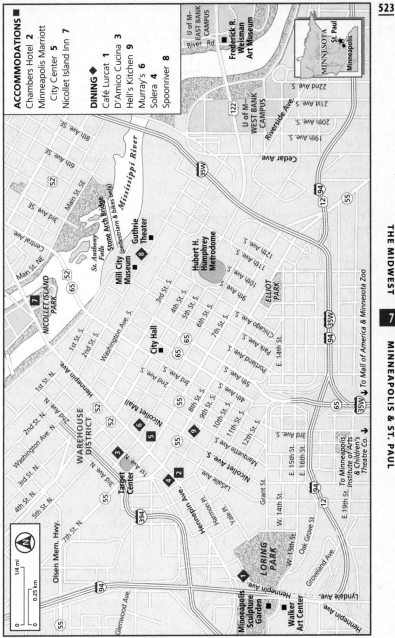

ACCOMMODATIONS ■

Chambers Hotel **2**
Minneapolis Marriott
City Center **5**
Nicollet Island Inn **7**

DINING ◆

Café Lurcat **1**
D'Amico Cucina **3**
Hell's Kitchen **9**
Murray's **6**
Solera **4**
Spoonriver **8**

you're short on time, ask for the "Highlights" brochure to make sure you don't miss the museum's best. Allow 2 hours.

2400 S. 3rd Ave. (𝑪) **888/MIA-ARTS** (642-2787). www.artsmia.org. Free admission (excludes select special exhibits). Tues–Wed and Fri–Sat 10am–5pm; Thurs 10am–9pm; Sun 11am–5pm.

Minnesota Zoo (Kids) "Russia's Grizzly Coast" became the Minnesota Zoo's newest exhibit in 2008, highlighting animals and habitats of Russia's eastern wilderness. Other favorites at this 485-acre zoo include an array of North American animals—wolves, bison, pumas, and wolverines—as well as exotic mainstays like tigers, camels, dolphins, and monkeys. The Minnesota Zoo also includes an IMAX theater and a monorail for easy navigation of the grounds. Allow 2 hours.

13000 Zoo Blvd., Apple Valley. (𝑪) **800/366-7811** or 952/431-9200. www.mnzoo.com. Admission to zoo $13 adults, $8 children 3–12. Zoo/IMAX combo $21 adults, $14 children 3–12. Monorail $4. Always free for children 2 and under. Parking $5. Memorial Day to Labor Day daily 9am–6pm; May and Sept Mon–Fri 9am–4pm, Sat–Sun 9am–6pm; Oct–Apr daily 9am–4pm.

University of Minnesota One of the Midwest's oldest (1851) and most important universities, with 50,000 students on the Twin Cities campus, the UMN offers three significant museums—the **James Ford Bell Museum of Natural History, the University Art Gallery,** and the **Frederick R. Weisman Art Museum** (see above). The 4,800-seat Northrop Auditorium has been a home for distinguished performances since 1929, and the University Theatre has four separate stages.

Located btw. Mississippi and University aves. and 10th Ave. and Oak St. SE (𝑪) **612/625-5000.** www. umn.edu.

Walker Art Center/Minneapolis Sculpture Garden The Walker Art Center is as well known for its striking architectural features as for the edgy, contemporary art inside: paintings, sculptures, drawings, photographs, and multimedia installations. A fine-dining restaurant and cafe, both by Wolfgang Puck, and gift shop are also new. Across the street is the **Minneapolis Sculpture Garden,** the largest urban sculpture garden in the country. A variety of 20th-century sculpture shares space with horticultural plantings, including the famous "Spoonbridge and Cherry" sculpture. Allow 2 hours for both.

1750 Hennepin. (𝑪) **612/375-7600.** www.walkerart.org. Admission to museum $10 adults, $6 seniors and students, free for children under 12, free to all Thurs 5–9pm and 1st Sat of every month. Free admission to sculpture garden. Museum Tues–Wed and Fri–Sun 11am–5pm; Thurs 11am–9pm. Sculpture garden daily 6am–midnight.

In St. Paul

Cathedral of St. Paul Built in 1915 on the highest point in the city, this cathedral is one of the largest in the country. A replica of St. Peter's in Rome, the building boasts a newly restored 175-foot-high copper dome, a massive rose window, and granite-and-travertine construction. Allow 30 minutes.

239 Selby Ave. (𝑪) **651/228-1766.** www.cathedralsp.org. Free admission, donations welcome. Mon–Thurs 7:30am–6pm; Fri 7:30am–4pm; Sat 8am–8pm; Sun 8am–6pm. Guided tours Mon, Wed, and Fri 1pm.

Historic Fort Snelling This living history museum commemorates the establishment of a fort here in the wilderness in 1819 by Col. Josiah Snelling and his troops, who opened the area for homesteaders. Costumed guides are the focus of a living history reenactment during the summer months, re-creating the activities of everyday army life during the 1820s. Allow 1 to 2 hours.

Highways 5 and 55 ⓒ **612/726-1171.** www.mnhs.org/fortsnelling. Admission $10 adults, $8 seniors, $5
children 6–17, free for children 5 and under. Memorial Day to Labor Day Mon–Sat 10am–5pm, Sun noon–
5pm; May and Sept–Oct Sat 10am–5pm, Sun noon–5pm. Open Mon holidays 10am–5pm. Closed
Nov–Apr.

Minnesota History Center (Kids)

An impressive array of artifacts is housed in this
three-story museum, including photographs, music, and videos, all of it celebrating Minnesota history. Kids enjoy sitting in the re-created basement of a Minnesota farmhouse
while a simulated tornado passes overhead. Adults enjoy listening to recordings of Minnesota musicians, including Bob Dylan, Steven Greenberg, and Prince. Allow $1^1/_2$ hours.

345 Kellogg Blvd. W. ⓒ **800/657-3773** or 651/259-3000. www.minnesotahistorycenter.org. Admission
$10 adults, $8 seniors, $5 children 6–17, free for children 5 and under. On all Mon holidays and from
Memorial Day to Labor Day 10am–5pm; Tues 10am–8pm; Wed–Sat 10am–5pm; Sun noon–5pm.

Minnesota Museum of American Art

Temporary exhibits are the rule at the
Minnesota Museum of American Art, which overlooks the Mississippi River. Expect
edgy, contemporary installation pieces, as well as paintings, fiber art, ceramics, works on
paper, and works created from found objects. Allow 30 minutes.

50 Kellogg Blvd. W. (at Market St.) ⓒ **651/266-1030.** www.mmaa.org. Free admission, suggested $2
donation. Tues–Wed and Fri–Sat 11am–4pm; Thurs 11am–8pm; Sun 1–5pm.

Minnesota State Capitol

Built in 1905 on a hill overlooking downtown St. Paul,
the capitol is crowned by the world's largest unsupported marble dome (modeled after
the one Michelangelo created for St. Peter's Basilica in Rome). The interior is equally
impressive, with its marble stairways, chambers, and halls, as well as its oil paintings.
Allow 1 hour.

75 Rev. Dr. Martin Luther King, Jr., Blvd. ⓒ **651/296-2881.** www.mnhs.org/statecapitol. Free admission.
Mon–Fri 9am–4pm; Sat 10am–3pm; Sun 1–4pm. Guided tours offered on the hour, last tour departs 1 hr.
before closing.

Mississippi River Visitor Center

Located inside the entrance to the Science
Museum of Minnesota (see below), the Mississippi River Visitor Center is operated by
the National Park Service and designed to educate visitors about the Mississippi National
River & Recreation Area. Park rangers can assist travelers with planning outdoor excursions, including canoe and riverboat trips, hiking, biking, and birding. If you're at all
outdoorsy, it's worth a stop.

120 W. Kellogg Blvd. ⓒ **651/293-0200.** Free admission. Mon–Wed 9:30am–5pm; Thurs–Sat 9:30am–
9pm; Sun noon–5pm. Extended hours during the summer.

Science Museum of Minnesota (Best)

Hands-on exhibits introduce visitors to
natural history, science, and technology in this massive museum. Highlights include the
Human Body Gallery, navigating a virtual towboat down the Mississippi River, and the
dinosaur lab in the Hall of Paleontology. In warm months check out EarthScapes Mini
Golf, a new activity designed to teach earth surface dynamics. There's also an Omnithe-
ater. Allow 2 to 3 hours.

120 W. Kellogg Blvd. ⓒ **800/221-9444** or 651/221-9444. www.smm.org. Admission to exhibits $11
adults, $8.50 children; Omnitheater $7.50 adults, $6.50 children; combination tickets $16 adults, $13
children. All tickets free for children 3 and under. Mon–Wed 9:30am–5pm; Thurs–Sat 9:30am–9pm; Sun
noon–5pm. Extended hours in summer.

MINNEAPOLIS & ST. PAUL

ARCHITECTURAL HIGHLIGHTS   Minneapolis is quickly developing a reputation for attracting some of the most interesting architecture in the country. Jean Nouvel's **Guthrie Theater,** 818 S. 2nd St., is a 2006 addition; its dark-blue steel exterior is illuminated with visions of past productions. Other gems include Herzog and de Meuron's **Walker Art Center,** 1750 Hennepin; Cesar Pelli's **Minneapolis Central Library,** 300 Nicollet Mall; and Frank Gehry's **Frederick R. Weisman Art Museum,** 333 E. River Rd.

In St. Paul, don't miss a stroll down **Summit Avenue,** just west of St. Paul Cathedral, one of the finest collections of Victorian residential architecture in the nation. The area has been home to such authors as F. Scott Fitzgerald, Sinclair Lewis, and Garrison Keillor. Stroll on your own or join a guided weekend walking tour. Tours depart from the James J. Hill House, 240 Summit Ave. (© **651/297-2555**).

PARKS   **Lake Calhoun** is one of 22 Minneapolis city lakes, a favorite for year-round sports like fishing, swimming, bicycling, and Nordic skiing. Located at 3000 Calhoun Parkway in Uptown (© **612/230-6400**), the park is open daily from 6am to 10pm. **Minnehaha Park,** Minnehaha Parkway at Hiawatha Avenue (© **612/230-6400**), on the Mississippi, is the site of the famed Minnehaha Falls, the "laughing water" Longfellow celebrated in his poem *Song of Hiawatha.* Other attractions include 15 miles of jogging and bicycle trails and picnic facilities. The park is open daily from 6am to 10pm. Information on both parks, as well as dozens of others, is available online at **www.minneapolis parks.org**.

St. Paul's **Como Park,** 1250 Kaufman Dr. (© **651/487-8200;** www.comozooconservatory.org), is one of the busiest and most beautiful parks in the Twin Cities, best known for its free zoo and conservatory with a half-acre domed botanical garden. There's also a golf course, ski trails, footpaths, paddle boats, canoes, bikes, and skates for rent. Hours are daily from 10am to 6pm April through September, from 10am to 4pm off season. St. Paul's **Landmark Plaza,** adjacent to the Landmark Center at 5th and Washington streets, is home to four bronze statues of the *Peanuts* comic book characters. The statues pay homage to hometown artist Charles Schulz.

BEST BETS FOR KIDS   **In Minneapolis**   The **Minnesota Zoo** (see above; © **800/366-7811** or 952/431-9200; www.mnzoo.com), in Apple Valley, houses more than 2,300 animals. The **Children's Theater Company,** 2400 3rd Ave. S. (© **612/874-0400;** www.childrenstheatre.org), presents plays for all age groups in one of America's best regional theaters. The **Mall of America** (© **952/883-8800;** www.mallofamerica.com) houses the indoor amusement park Nickelodeon Universe, Underwater Adventures Aquarium, and NASCAR, an indoor race-car simulator, among other attractions.

IN ST. PAUL   The **Minnesota Children's Museum,** 10 W. 7th St. (© **651/225-6000;** www.mcm.org), offers features such as papermaking, a music studio, and a Rooftop ArtPark. **Como Zoo,** 1250 Kaufman Dr. (© **651/487-8200;** www.comozooconservatory. org), inside Como Park, is Minnesota's only free zoo.

SHOPPING

Nicollet Mall, a pedestrian avenue in downtown Minneapolis, is home to Neiman Marcus, Macy's, and two malls, upscale **Gaviidae Common** and **City Center.** Funky galleries and boutique stores abound in **Uptown,** near Hennepin and Lake streets. And **50th and France** offers distinctive shops in a traditional village shopping square. In St. Paul,

don't miss **Grand Avenue,** just west of the downtown. The boutique shops along here are
housed in former residences, and 95% remain independently owned.

WHERE TO STAY

In addition to the choices listed below, you'll find many chain hotels near shopping malls (especially the Mall of America) and along I-494 in the suburbs.

Near the airport, the **Hilton Minneapolis/St. Paul Airport** (✆ **800/HILTONS** [445-8667] or 952/854-2100; www.hilton.com) offers extensive facilities and services, including free shuttle service to the airport, the Mall of America, and the Mall of America light rail station. Doubles begin at $100. Also near the airport are the **Courtyard Minneapolis Bloomington** (✆ **800/321-2211** or 952/876-0100; www.courtyard. com), with doubles from $99; and the **Embassy Suites Airport** (✆ **800/EMBASSY** [362-2779] or 952/854-1000; www.embassysuites.com), with doubles from $129.

In Minneapolis

Chambers Hotel (**Best**)   The Chambers is widely considered the sexiest, most sophisticated hotel in Minneapolis. As much a contemporary art museum as lodging, the luxury hotel's spare white walls and minimalist design showcase 250 original modern paintings, sculpture, and video installations. Other amenities include flatscreen TVs and iPod docking stations. Check out the Ice Bar in winter, a giant cube of a bar comprised of 6 tons of crystal-clear ice. The hotel is in the heart of the Warehouse District, within easy walking distance of the historic theaters and the Target Center.

901 Hennepin Ave., Minneapolis, MN 55403. ✆ **877/767-6990** or 612/767-6900. Fax 612/767-6801. www.chambersminneapolis.com. 60 units. $225–$405 double; $480–$1,000 suite. AE, DC, DISC, MC, V. Valet parking $24; self-parking varies with local garage. **Amenities:** Restaurant; fitness center.

Doubletree Park Place   Located $3^1/_2$ miles west of downtown, this hotel boasts a five-story pool atrium and reasonable rates outside the hubbub of the busy downtown area. The spacious guest rooms were designed with business travelers in mind but are perfectly comfortable for leisure travelers as well. Deluxe-level accommodations include complimentary breakfast and high-speed Internet access.

1500 Park Place Blvd., Minneapolis, MN 55416. ✆ **800/222-TREE** (222-8733) or 952/542-8600. Fax 612/ 542-8063. www.doubletree.com. 297 units. $93–$219 double; $109–$304 suite. Children 17 and under stay free in parent's room. AE, DC, DISC, MC, V. Free parking. Pets permitted with refundable $15 deposit. **Amenities:** Restaurants; indoor pool; fitness center.

Minneapolis Marriott City Center   In the heart of downtown, this facility adjoins the three-story City Center shopping mall and is within walking distance of the Target Center and much of the city's nightlife. The hotel caters to the convention crowds, and the rooms are standard business-hotel issue, with a friendly and attentive staff.

30 S. 7th St., Minneapolis, MN 55402. ✆ **800/228-9290** or 612/349-4000. Fax 612/332-7165. www. marriott.com. 583 units. $119–$274 double; $159–$399 suite. Children 17 and under stay free in parent's room. AE, DC, DISC, MC, V. Valet parking $25; self-parking $19. Pets permitted with refundable $100 deposit. **Amenities:** Restaurant; health club.

Nicollet Island Inn   Just across from the Mississippi River, this lovely inn was once an 1893 window-shade and blind company. The individually, classically decorated rooms are furnished with lots of modern amenities, including plasma TVs, free Wi-Fi, and some Jacuzzis. The Nicollet Island Inn Restaurant is highly recommended (make a reservation), featuring contemporary American cuisine and a selection of over 350 wines; it also serves an excellent Sunday brunch ($30 adults, $12 children ages 6–12, free for children 5 and under). Ask about weekend B&B packages.

95 Merriam St., Minneapolis, MN 55401. ✆ **612/331-1800.** Fax 612/331-6528. www.nicolletislandinn. com. 24 units. $209–$259 double. Children stay free in parent's room; rollaway beds $25. AE, DC, DISC, MC, V. Free parking. **Amenities:** Restaurant; smoking not permitted.

In St. Paul

Best Western Kelly Inn (Value) (Kids) This older, plain facility is a good bet for families on a tight budget—the affordable inn features basic but comfortable accommodations. All of the city's downtown attractions are less than a mile away, and an indoor pool means there's always something fun to do, whatever the weather. Some rooms offer scenic views and some units have whirlpools.

161 St. Anthony Ave., St. Paul, MN 55103. ✆ **800/780-7234** or 651/227-8711. Fax 651/227-1698. www. bestwestern.com. 126 units. $107–$119 double. Children 17 and under stay free in parent's room. AE, DC, DISC, MC, V. Free parking. Pets permitted. **Amenities:** Restaurant; indoor pool; health club.

Crowne Plaza St. Paul Riverfront Hotel Formerly the Radisson Riverfront, a $9.2-million renovation has spruced up this hotel considerably. Its terrific downtown location, views over the Mississippi River, and the Twin Cities' only revolving restaurant remain unchanged. The St. Paul RiverCentre convention center adjoins the hotel, making it popular with business travelers and conventions. It's also an easy walk to the Science Museum of Minnesota and the Mississippi River Visitor Center, for those more interested in leisure pursuits.

11 E. Kellogg Blvd., St. Paul, MN 55101. ✆ **800/593-5708** or 651/292-1900. Fax 651/605-0189. www. ichotelsgroup.com. 470 units. $144–$219 double; $255–$299 suite. Children 17 and under stay free in parent's room. AE, DC, DISC, MC, V. Valet parking $18; self-parking $14. **Amenities:** 2 restaurants; indoor pool; fitness center.

Saint Paul Hotel (Best) This beautiful, exquisitely decorated hotel, housed in a landmark 1910 building, makes for a great romantic getaway. The historic property has welcomed many a famous guest over the years, including Calvin Coolidge and Ma Barker. A number of rooms offer great views; all are decorated in elegant European style and feature Aveda toiletries. The hotel is famous for its afternoon tea and the landmark St. Paul Grill (see "Where to Dine," below).

350 Market St. (at 5th St.), St. Paul, MN 55102. ✆ **800/292-9292** or 651/292-9292. Fax 651/228-9506. www.stpaulhotel.com. 254 units. $159–$359 double; $369–$449 suite. AE, DC, DISC, MC, V. Parking $18. **Amenities:** 2 restaurants; fitness center.

WHERE TO DINE
In Minneapolis

Barbette FRENCH BISTRO Expect inventive food combinations, French inspiration, and lots of local, seasonal, organic ingredients at Barbette in Minneapolis's Uptown district. A casual and eclectic interior of stained glass, blond wood, and lots of natural sunlight, this bistro begins each day serving homemade pastries and granola. Lunch may include a quiche of the day, a *tartare* of the day, steak frites, or a heaping platter of steamed mussels. Late-night Barbette transforms itself into a vibrant wine and coffee bar. Many dishes can be altered for vegetarian or vegan preferences. A pleasant patio welcomes guests in the summer.

1600 W. Lake St. ✆ **612/827-5710.** www.barbette.com. Reservations recommended. Main courses $15–$33. AE, DC, DISC, MC, V. Sun–Thurs 8am–1am; Fri–Sat 8am–2am.

Café Lurcat AMERICAN   Café Lurcat makes its home in a restored urban building just off Loring Park. A hip crowd dines and passes the time here, often just before or after events at the nearby Walker Art Center. A simple but vogue decor pairs beautifully with the restaurant's simple but sophisticated menu: apple, cheese and chive salad; foie gras with prosciutto and roasted pears; prime rib with béarnaise; sea bass marinated in miso. The adjoining Bar Lurcat offers a variety of small plates and a 200-bottle wine list with 40 wines by the glass.

1624 Harmon Place on Loring Park ⓒ **612/486-5500**. www.cafelurcat.com. Reservations recommended. Main courses $20–$35. AE, DISC, MC, V. Cafe Mon–Thurs 5–10pm; Fri–Sat 5–11pm; Sun 5–9pm. Bar Fri–Sat until 1am.

Chino Latino ASIAN/LATIN   If it's hot, Chino Latino serves it. This Uptown restaurant's menu spotlights the spicy cuisines of the world, from Thai coconut shrimp curry to Montego Bay jerked chicken to Argentine tenderloin steaks. You'll also find small-plate servings and sizable sushi, taco, and satay selections. Cool your palate with one of three dozen tequilas; a creative martini; sake; or a "hot zone" beer from Cuba, Kenya, India, or Thailand.

2916 Hennepin Ave. S. ⓒ **612/824-7878**. www.chinolatino.com. Reservations recommended. Main courses $18–$45. AE, DC, DISC, MC, V. Sun–Thurs 4:30pm–1am; Fri–Sat 4:30pm–2am.

D'Amico Cucina ITALIAN   The perfect restaurant for a romantic dinner out, this beautifully appointed restaurant has a distinctive atmosphere, enhanced by warm golden hues, whitewashed wood beams, and French doors. One hundred fifty Italian wines complement the menu's Italian dishes, including house-made ravioli with black truffle butter, and pancetta-wrapped pork tenderloin served with mustard greens alla Genovese and balsamic red onion sauce.

100 N. 6th St. (in Butler Sq.) ⓒ **612/338-2401**. www.damico.com. Reservations recommended. Main courses $24–$36. AE, DC, DISC, MC, V. Mon–Thurs 5:30–9pm; Fri–Sat 5:30–10pm.

Hell's Kitchen AMERICAN   Inventive breakfast and lunch entrees make for very long lines at this popular downtown restaurant. The restaurant's signature breakfast dishes include lemon ricotta hotcakes and Minnesota wild rice porridge with dried blueberries, cranberries, and hazelnuts. Lighter offerings include homemade lemon yogurt with fresh berries and breakfast bruschetta, topped with homemade lemon oil, mascarpone cheese, and berries. Breakfast is served up until closing time, as are lunchtime sandwiches, soups, and salads. Hell's Kitchen is locally famous for its homemade peanut butter; buy a jar to take home.

89 S. 10th St. (just off Nicollet Mall). ⓒ **612/332-4700**. www.HellsKitchenInc.com. Reservations recommended Sat–Sun. Main courses $10–$17. MC, V. Mon–Fri 6:30am–2pm; Sat–Sun 8am–2pm.

Murray's STEAKHOUSE   Since 1946, this classy downtown establishment has delighted guests with steaks so tender they won the "Silver Butter Knife" award. Murray's is still famous for its steaks, but you'll also find an assortment of seafood and pasta dishes and a wine list with over 500 labels. With its strolling violinist, Murray's remains a favorite for a romantic dinner. Look for the old neon sign hanging out front.

26 S. 6th St. ⓒ **612/339-0909**. www.murraysrestaurant.com. Reservations required Fri–Sat. Main courses $20–$50. AE, DC, DISC, MC, V. Mon–Fri 11am–2pm and 5–10:30pm; Sat–Sun 5–10:30pm.

Solera ⓑest SPANISH   This chic Spanish-inspired restaurant offers over 40 hot and cold tapas—small, savory samplings that encourage experimentation and sharing—and one of the largest sherry menus you've ever seen. Located in the heart of the Theater

District, the restaurant features an interior as appealing as its food, with bright mosaic tiles and colorful art glass fixtures.

900 Hennepin Ave. ✆ 612/338-0062. www.solera-restaurant.com. Tapas $2.50–$9.75. AE, MC, V. Dining room Sun–Thurs 5–10pm; Fri–Sat 5–11pm. Tapas bar Sun 5–11pm; Mon–Thurs 4pm–1am; Fri 4pm–2am; Sat 5pm–2am.

Spoonriver AMERICAN   Right across the street from Minneapolis's beloved Guthrie Theater, Spoonriver is a favorite among theatergoers. But the warm, orange-hued interior is packed with gourmands even when the stage is dark. Award-winning restaurateur Brenda Langton has long championed organic eating in the Twin Cities, and her own restaurant proves the results are delicious. The house-made chèvre and ricotta ravioli melt in your mouth, grass-fed steaks are tender as can be, and the kitchen can accommodate any food preference or allergy—just ask.

750 S 2nd St. ✆ 612/436-2236. www.spoonriverrestaurant.com. Reservations recommended. Main courses $16–$29. AE, MC, V. Lunch Tues–Fri 11:30am–2pm. Dinner Tues–Sun 5:30–10pm. Brunch Sat–Sun 10am–2pm (open Sat at 8am in summer).

In St. Paul

Café Latté CAFETERIA   Put aside all previous notions of what cafeteria food is like. The contemporary Café Latté serves a little of everything, all made with the freshest local ingredients, at stations throughout its restaurant space: soups and breads, make-your-own salads and sandwiches, decadent desserts, and box lunches to go. There's also a pizza wine bar with an extensive selection of wines by the glass. Seating is located on two floors, all within easy view of large plate-glass windows for people-watching on St. Paul's Grand Avenue below.

850 Grand Ave. ✆ 651/224-5687. www.cafelatte.com. Main courses $5–$11. MC, V. Sun–Wed 9am–10pm; Thurs 9am–11pm; Fri–Sat 9am–midnight.

Great Waters Brewing Co. AMERICAN   This restaurant is known for its beers, of course, including cask-conditioned ales (common in Britain, rare in the U.S.), as well as the standard pilsners and IPAs. Five homemade beer selections are offered daily. Great Waters' menu gives reason to visit for more than just a drink. In addition to the traditional pub fare, you'll find interesting sandwiches (try the brie and green apple–grilled chicken) and dinners, such as the London broil or pasta.

426 St. Peter St. ✆ 651/224-2739. www.greatwatersbc.com. Main courses $13–$24. MC, V. Mon–Sat 11am–2am; Sun noon–midnight.

Pazzaluna ITALIAN   This upscale restaurant in the heart of downtown St. Paul serves authentic Italian dishes in a sophisticated urban setting. The interior is one of rich earth tones, revamped Roman columns, and a vivid mural here and there, while little nooks and high-backed booths allow for quiet conversations. Mix and match pasta or gnocchi with half a dozen sauces, or try the lobster ravioli, scallops with hazelnut vinaigrette, or grilled tuna with sweet-and-sour sauce and pistachios. Pazzaluna also offers one of St. Paul's favorite happy hours, popular with urban professionals.

360 St. Peter St. ✆ 651/223-7000. www.pazzaluna.com. Reservations recommended. Main courses $14–$35. AE, MC, V. Daily 5–10pm. Bar opens at 4pm.

St. Clair Broiler AMERICAN   Since 1956, the St. Clair Broiler, one of the first in the nation to grill food over an open flame, has served up all-American food—hand-dipped malts and shakes, tuna salad and grilled cheese sandwiches, cheeseburgers and fish and chips. There's nothing gimmicky about this restaurant—no red-and-white-checked tablecloths or mouthy waiters—just a pleasant, contemporary interior of sage green, gleaming chrome, and really good food. The restaurant's terrific breakfast entrees, including omelets, pancakes, and French toast, are served all day.

1580 St. Clair Ave. (℃ **651/698-7055.** www.stclairbroiler.com. Main courses $11–$20. AE, DC, DISC, MC, V. Mon–Thurs 6:30am–10pm; Fri 7am–10pm; Sun 8am–9pm.

St. Paul Grill (Best) AMERICAN   This multiple award–winner is popular with pretheater diners and is the top choice in town for adults seeking an upscale night out. The elegant interior is enhanced by views of the hotel's lovely English garden and nearby Rice Park; the atmosphere is sophisticated but not stuffy. Juicy steaks, bourbon grilled pork chops, and excellent pastas top a stellar menu. The award-winning bar features a huge collection of single-malt scotches and martinis, as well as a *Wine Spectator*–honored wine list.

Saint Paul Hotel, 350 Market St. (℃ **651/224-7455.** www.stpaulgrill.com. Reservations recommended. Main courses $16–$80. MC, V. Daily 11am–2pm; Sun–Mon 5–10pm; Tues–Sat 5–11pm.

THE TWIN CITIES AFTER DARK

The best place to find out what's happening in the Twin Cities is the free newsweekly *City Pages*, which lists all events. Other good sources of information are the local papers (*Star Tribune* and *St. Paul Pioneer Press*), the calendar in *Minneapolis–St. Paul* magazine, and the monthly *Twin Cities Directory*. On the Web, check out **www.minneapolis.org** or **www.stpaulcvb.org** for the most up-to-date information.

THE PERFORMING ARTS   There are more theater seats per capita in Minneapolis than anywhere outside New York City. The famous **Guthrie Theater,** 818 S. 2nd St. (℃ **877/44-STAGE** [447-8243] or 612/377-2224; www.guthrietheater.org), is one of the nation's premier classical repertory companies, set in an architecturally stunning venue overlooking the Mississippi. Three historic, renovated theaters, the **State** (805 Hennepin Ave.), **Orpheum** (910 Hennepin Ave.), and **Pantages** (710 Hennepin Ave.), feature a variety of entertainment, from pop music to comedy, to adult and children's theater. Get information about all three theaters from the central Hennepin Theatre District office (℃ **612/373-5600;** www.hennepintheatredistrict.org). The **Children's Theater Company,** 2400 3rd Ave. S. (℃ **612/874-0400;** www.childrenstheatre.org), presents plays for all age groups in one of America's best regional theaters.

For more than 20 years, **Orchestra Hall,** 1111 Nicollet Mall (℃ **800/292-4141** or 612/371-5656; www.minnesotaorchestra.org), has been home to the internationally acclaimed **Minnesota Orchestra.**

In St. Paul, Minnesota Public Radio's **Fitzgerald Theater,** 10 E. Exchange St. (℃ **651/ 290-1221;** http://fitzgeraldtheater.publicradio.org), is home to Garrison Keillor's popular radio show, *A Prairie Home Companion.* Touring companies also perform in this restored historic building. The **St. Paul Chamber Orchestra** (℃ **651/291-1144;** www. thespco.org) makes its home in the **Ordway Center for the Performing Arts,** 345 Washington St. (℃ **651/224-4222;** www.ordway.org). **Minnesota Opera** recitals, pop and classical concerts, and dance are also presented at Ordway Center. The **Schubert Club,** 302 Landmark Center (℃ **651/292-3267;** www.schubert.org), brings celebrated artists to perform, provides music lessons, and commissions new works.

THE BAR & MUSIC SCENE   The **Warehouse District** has always been considered the heart of Minneapolis nightlife, but **Block E,** bordered by 6th and 7th streets and by Hennepin and 1st avenues, has its fair share of dining and dancing. **First Avenue,** 701 1st Ave. N. (℃ **612/332-1775;** www.first-avenue.com), is where Prince got his start

(*Purple Rain* was filmed here). Connected to it is the **Entry,** a small, loud venue for local music.

For interesting music and great food visit the **Dakota Jazz Club,** 1010 Nicollet (© **612/332-1010;** www.dakotacooks.com). The intimate downtown club is known for its internationally acclaimed jazz musicians, as well as Minneapolis talent. **Babalú,** 800 Washington Ave. N. (© **612/746-3158;** www.babalu.us), serves up Latin American and Spanish music (bossa nova, Afro-Cuban jazz, flamenco) and food in a classy, pre-Castro Cuban decor. Cuban entrees are available, as are over 70 rums.

Sports fans prefer the digs at **NBA City,** 600 1st Ave. N. (© **612/767-2960;** www.nba.com/nbacity). The restaurant and bar adjoins the Target Center, home of the Minnesota Timberwolves and the WNBA's Minnesota Lynx. "Friendly" and "casual" is how regulars describe **19 Bar,** 19 W. 15th St. (© **612/871-5553**), the city's oldest gay bar, which offers food, a pool table, and dartboards.

In St. Paul, visit the **Spot,** 859 Randolph Ave. (© **651/224-7433**), the city's oldest bar, said to be in business at this location since 1885. Locals frequent the modest pub, which entertains with sporting events on TV. Two popular gay bars are **Innuendo & Rumours,** 213 4th St. E. (© **651/225-GLBT** [225-4528]; www.rumours-stpaul.com), and **Camp,** 490 N. Robert St. (© **651/292-1844;** www.camp-bar.com). Both clubs feature live music and dancing and a large gay crowd, but all are welcome.

8 KANSAS CITY

Established as a trading post in 1821, Kansas City served as the starting point for wagon trains heading over the Santa Fe, California, and Oregon trails, and later emerged as the nation's center for cattle stockyards and slaughterhouses. Today greater Kansas City is a sprawling metropolis of 1.9 million straddling the Kansas-Missouri state line. Downtown Kansas City, a blend of Art Deco buildings, brick warehouses dating from the 1880s, and modern skyscrapers, is also home to the new **Power & Light District,** an 8-block development of dining-and-entertainment venues. Yet the metropolitan area retains something of a small-town atmosphere, with tree-lined boulevards, bubbling fountains, and a large number of parks spread over gently rolling hills. Need further incentive to visit? Kansas City is famous for its steaks, barbecue, jazz, rich frontier history, and unique attractions found nowhere else.

ESSENTIALS

GETTING THERE   By Plane   Kansas City International Airport (© **816/243-5237;** www.flykci.com) is 25 minutes northwest of downtown. **SuperShuttle buses** (© **800/258-3826;** www.kctg.com) service more than 90 hotels, with fares to downtown costing $17 one-way. The average taxi fare to downtown is $45. The **Metro bus no. 129** travels weekdays between the airport's Terminal C and downtown (10th & Main Transit Plaza) for $1.25 (© **816/221-0660;** www.kcata.org).

By Train   Amtrak (© **800/USA-RAIL** [872-7245]; www.amtrak.com) provides daily service from Chicago (trip time: 8 hr.) and St. Louis (trip time: 5¹/₂ hr.) to Kansas City's historic Union Station at 30 W. Pershing Rd. (© **816/842-4409**).

By Car   Major routes into Kansas City are **I-70** from the east (St. Louis) and west (Denver); **I-35** from the north (Des Moines) and southwest (Wichita); and **I-29** from the northwest (Omaha).

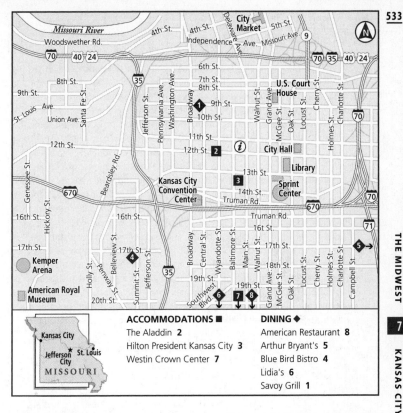

ACCOMMODATIONS ■

The Aladdin **2**

Hilton President Kansas City **3**

Westin Crown Center **7**

DINING ◆

American Restaurant **8**

Arthur Bryant's **5**

Blue Bird Bistro **4**

Lidia's **6**

Savoy Grill **1**

VISITOR INFORMATION The **Kansas City Convention and Visitors Association** is downtown at City Center Square, 1100 Main St., Ste. 2200, Kansas City, MO 64105 (© **800/767-7700** or 816/221-5242; www.visitkc.com), open Monday through Friday from 8:30am to 5pm. More convenient is the Visitor Information Center at Country Club Plaza, 4709 Central, open Monday through Saturday from 10am to 6pm and Sunday from noon to 5pm. The **Missouri State Tourism Welcome Center**, east of downtown off I-70 at exit 9, 4010 Blue Ridge Cutoff (© **800/519-2300** or 816/889-3330), is open daily 8am to 5pm, with information on Kansas City, as well as St. Louis, Branson, and other destinations.

GETTING AROUND A car is extremely useful in Kansas City; although the downtown is compact, attractions are located throughout the city. Main Street connects to many city attractions. Despite its name, the **Metro** (© **816/221-0660;** www.kcata.org) is the city's public bus system, with many buses departing from downtown's 10th & Main Transit Plaza. Most convenient for sightseeing is the **MAX** (Metro Area Express), which runs daily about 5am to midnight and connects City Market with Country Club Plaza, with stops at downtown, the Crossroads Arts District, Union Station, Crown Center, and Westport. Fares start at $1.25; a day pass costs $3.

(Kids) Best Bets for Kids

Kansas City's most centrally located attraction for kids is **Science City,** in the restored 1914 Union Station, cater-cornered from Crown Center at 30 Pershing Rd. ((C) **816/460-2020;** www.sciencecity.com). At this multilevel, interactive museum, open daily, kids can create a personal newspaper front page, anchor a TV news program, bicycle across a tightrope, train as an astronaut, solve a crime, play miniature golf, take a tour through the human body, dig for fossils, explore Kansas City's history, view the stars at a planetarium, catch a movie in a five-story theater, climb aboard vintage trains at the KC Rail Experience exhibit, and more. Admission to everything is $20 (children 3 and under are free).

For outdoor fun, there's the 175-acre theme park **Worlds of Fun,** I-435 and Parvin Road ((C) **816/454-4545;** www.worldsoffun.com), open daily in summer and weekends in April, May, September, and October, with six roller coasters, including the Patriot, the longest, tallest, and fastest full-circuit inverted roller coaster in the Midwest; dozens of other thrill rides, like the tumble-and-spin Thunderhawk; and Camp Snoopy for younger kids, featuring attractions based on the comic strip. Admission is $39 adults, $15 children under 48 inches and seniors. Next door is Worlds of Fun's water-themed counterpart, the 60-acre **Oceans of Fun** (same contact information as Worlds of Fun, above), open June through August and featuring 18 water slides and various pools (including a wave pool). Admission costs $28 adults, $15 children under 48 inches and seniors. Discounts are provided for combined passes and evening admission.

The revitalized **Kansas City Zoo,** at I-435 and 63rd St. in Swope Park ((C) **816/513-5700;** www.kansascityzoo.org), is open daily 9am to 5pm and features animals of Australia, Africa, and more in their natural habitats. Admission is $11 adults, $9.50 seniors, and $7 children 3 to 11; on Tuesday, prices are $8, $7, and $6 respectively.

FAST FACTS A major hospital is **Saint Luke's Hospital,** 4400 Wornall Rd. ((C) **816/932-2000**). **Walgreens** is a 24-hour pharmacy located at 39th Street and Broadway ((C) **816/561-7620**). Sales tax is 7.85%; the hotel tax is 7.5%.

SPECIAL EVENTS Around since 1899, the **American Royal** celebration in October or November ((C) **816/221-9800;** www.americanroyal.com) features a livestock show, parades, horse shows, a rodeo, big-name entertainment, and the world's largest barbecue competition. The **Kansas Speedway** ((C) **866/460-RACE** [460-7223]; www.kansas speedway.com) attracts NASCAR fans with races several times a year.

WHAT TO SEE & DO

In addition to the attractions listed in this section, baseball fans will be treated to one of the world's largest video boards if the home team **Kansas City Royals** are playing at Kauffman Stadium, I-70 and Blue Ridge Cut-off ((C) **816/921-8000;** www.kcroyals.com).

Arabia Steamboat Museum This cargo steamboat, laden with 220 tons of merchandise destined for settlers out west, sank in the Missouri River in 1856, where it

remained preserved in cold mud until it was excavated in the 1980s. A virtual time cap-
sule of the 1850s and one of the best collections of pre–Civil War artifacts in the world,
the museum provides a fascinating look at frontier life, with displays of the steamboat's
cargo, from china and hardware to jewelry and leather boots (900 shoes and boots alone
are on display). Tours begin with a film of the excavation and restoration of parts of the
boat (which are now on display); plan on 1¹/₂ hours here.

400 Grand Ave., City Market. ✆ **816/471-4030.** www.1856.com. Admission $13 adults, $12 seniors,
$4.75 children 4–12. Mon–Sat 10am–4pm (last tour); Sun noon–3:30pm (last tour).

College Basketball Experience (Kids)
Located in the downtown Power & Light
District, this hands-on attraction is a great place for kids of all ages. Operated by the
National Association of Basketball Coaches (headquartered in Kansas City), it has a full-
size court for free play, a 3-on-3 court, a small kids' court, a broadcasting station where
kids can try their hand at sportscasting a live event, and various shooting, rebounding,
and passing games along with tips on strategy. There's also a timeline of college basketball, a film highlighting the sport, information on college coaches, and a collegiate basketball hall of fame. Basketball fans can easily spend 2 hours here.

Sprint Center, 1401 Grand Blvd. ✆ **816/949-7500.** www.collegebasketballexperience.com. Admission
$10 adults, $7 children 6–17. Wed–Sat 10am–6pm; Sun 11am–6pm.

National World War I Museum
The nation's only public museum and memorial
dedicated to World War I features the 217-foot-tall Memorial Tower, which opened in
1926 and offers views of downtown Kansas City from its top (which you can skip), and
a fascinating underground museum documenting the history of the "Great War" (36
nations were involved) with touch screens, films providing an overview of the war and
America's entry into the conflict, and the largest collection of World War I artifacts in the
United States, much of it donated. Exhibits include photographs, uniforms, letters from
the field, weaponry (like the world's only remaining Bavarian Howlitzer and a French
Renault FT17 tank), and displays that give a human dimension to the conflict, including
life-size trenches that defined the Western Front. Most people spend 2 to 3 hours here,
but you could easily stay the entire day.

Liberty Memorial, 100 W. 26th St. ✆ **816/784-1918.** www.nww1.org. Admission $8 adults, $7 seniors, $4
children 6–11. Tues–Sun 10am–5pm.

Negro Leagues Baseball Museum/American Jazz Museum
These two unique
museums, housed under one roof, are in the historic 18th and Vine Jazz District. The
Negro Leagues Baseball Museum tells the compelling story of segregated baseball, from the
founding of the Negro National League just a few blocks away in 1920, until Jackie Robinson, who played for the Kansas City Monarchs, signed with the Brooklyn Dodgers in
1947. The Jazz Museum pays tribute to jazz greats ranging from Louis Armstrong and
Duke Ellington to Ella Fitzgerald and Charlie Parker, with listening stations throughout.
Be sure to see the gallery with changing exhibits relating to jazz, baseball, and African-
American life, as well as the film in the visitor center highlighting the golden days of the
1930s, when this very district boasted more than 60 jazz clubs and served as the commercial heart of Kansas City's African-American community. The Blue Room, attached to the
complex, stages jazz concerts with local musicians 4 nights a week. Plan on 2 hours here.

18th and Vine. ✆ **816/221-1920** and www.nlbm.com for Baseball Museum; ✆ **816/474-8463**
and www.americanjazzmuseum.org for Jazz Museum. Admission to either $6 adults, $2.50 children 11
and under; combination ticket to both $8 adults, $4 children. Both museums Tues–Sat 9am–6pm; Sun
noon–6pm.

Nelson-Atkins Museum of Art (Best) Kansas City's premier museum, occupying an impressive 1933 neoclassical building and a strikingly modern addition, boasts a collection spanning 5,000 years. It's especially noted for Asian art, including Tang dynasty bowls and Ming dynasty furniture; a 22-acre outdoor sculpture garden with the largest U.S. collection of bronzes by Henry Moore; the largest public collection of works by Missouri native Thomas Hart Benton; and one of the country's largest collections of American photography. It also has European paintings, from Romanesque and baroque to Impressionist, along with more contemporary works from expressionism to pop art. The museum includes works by Caravaggio (his *Saint John the Baptist in the Wilderness* is a museum treasure), Rubens, Rembrandt, Renoir, Monet, Picasso, van Gogh, Kandinsky, Willem de Kooning, Jackson Pollock, and Andy Warhol. The Rozelle Court Restaurant, in the style of a 15th-century courtyard, has extended dinner hours on Friday. Plan on 2 to 3 hours here.

4525 Oak St. (just east of Country Club Plaza). (C) **816/751-1278.** www.nelson-atkins.org. Free admission (special exhibitions cost extra). Tues–Wed 10am–4pm; Thurs–Fri 10am–9pm; Sat 10am–5pm; Sun noon–5pm.

SHOPPING

Kansas City's premier shopping district (and the country's first suburban shopping center) is **Country Club Plaza,** centered around 47th Street and Ward Parkway ((C) **816/753-0100;** www.countryclubplaza.com). Built in 1922 to resemble a Spanish town, it's a tree-lined, 15-square-block area with more than 150 shops, restaurants, and nightspots. **Crown Center,** 2450 Grand Ave. ((C) **816/274-8444;** www.crowncenter.com), is an 85-acre business and residential complex owned by the world's largest greeting-card company, Hallmark. It contains specialty shops, restaurants, hotels, theaters, and the free Hallmark Visitor Center (closed Sun–Mon), which chronicles 98 years of history with displays of Keepsake Ornaments and other Hallmark products and memorabilia, and excerpts from Hallmark Hall of Fame television movies. Just northwest of Crown Center is the **Crossroads Arts District** (www.kccrossroads.org), where First Friday lures an artsy crowd to restaurants, bars, and more than 60 galleries and shops the first Friday evening of every month.

City Market, at 5th and Main streets north of downtown and I-70 ((C) **816/842-1271;** www.kc-citymarket.com), is an outdoor market in operation since the 1850s. It's busiest on Saturday, when 150 vendors offer everything from vegetables and flowers to live chickens and T-shirts, but there are also permanent indoor specialty shops, international groceries, and restaurants occupying an Art Deco building. Just west of Kansas City, at the intersection of interstates 70 and 435, is **Village West,** a new leisure destination with hotels, restaurants, and shops, including the Kansas Speedway; Great Wolf Lodge; Cabela's (Kansas's top shopping attraction for its eye-popping wildlife displays and massive showrooms of outdoor equipment); Nebraska Furniture Mart; and the Legends ((C) **913/788-3700**), an outdoor shopping and dining center.

WHERE TO STAY

In addition to the choices below, consider **Embassy Suites,** conveniently located between Westport and Country Club Plaza at 220 W. 43rd St. ((C) **800/EMBASSY** [362-2779] or 816/756-1720; http://embassysuites.hilton.com). A hit with families, it offers two-room suites with kitchenette, free breakfasts, a nightly cocktail hour, and an indoor pool.

The Aladdin Built in 1925 as Kansas City's tallest hotel, the 16-story Aladdin retains its yesteryear charm (it's on the National Register of Historic Places; check out the old-fashioned mail drop by the elevator) but adds a hip, quirky twist, with Art Deco trimmings accented by Day-Glo-colored decor. Rooms are small but contemporary, with lime-green and red furnishings, 32-inch HDTVs with DVD players (and free DVDs), pullout desktops for more work space, free Wi-Fi, and queen- or king-size beds. And what's not to love about a boutique hotel that serves champagne at check-in?

1215 Wyandotte, MO 64105. © **800/HOLIDAY** (465-4329) or 816/421-8888. Fax 816/421-8889. www. hialaddin.com. 193 units. $136 double; $190 suite. Children 17 and under stay free in parent's room. AE, DC, DISC, V. Valet parking $15; self-parking $13. **Amenities:** Restaurant; exercise room; spa.

The Elms Resort & Spa (Value) The Kansas City area's only full-service resort and spa occupies a historic 1912 limestone hotel situated on 16 landscaped acres, about a 30-minute drive from downtown and the airport. Its holistic spa and wellness center offers body and beauty treatments, including Vichy massage showers, mud and aloe body wraps, mineral baths, hydrotherapy, massage (including hot stone and couples massage), and more. Rooms are basic, but the historic lobby, extensive recreational offerings (including an indoor swim track, landscaped outdoor pool, banked jogging track, hiking and biking trails, badminton, horseshoes, and volleyball), its parklike setting, and rustic grandeur make this a top-choice restorative getaway.

401 Regent St., Excelsior Springs, MO 64024. © **800/843-3567** or 816/630-5500. Fax 816/630-5380. www.elmsresort.com. 153 units. $99–$109 double; $139–$239 suite. Extra person $10. Children 17 and under stay free in parent's room. Spa packages available. AE, DC, DISC, MC, V. Free outdoor parking. Pets permitted for $10 fee. **Amenities:** 2 restaurants; 2 pools (1 indoor); health club; spa. *In room:* Fridge.

Great Wolf Lodge (Kids) Geared toward families with its massive indoor/outdoor waterpark (free for hotel guests), huge game arcade, children's activity room, interactive game quest that involves tracking down clues throughout the hotel (fee charged), and laundry facilities, this woods-themed lodge combines the adventure of a rustic retreat with the comfort of an upscale hotel. From the moment guests walk into the four-story grand lobby with its overstuffed sofas, huge stone fireplace, stuffed wolves, and animated clock tower that captivates wee ones, this hotel aims for the "wow" factor. Seven styles of suites, all with patio or balcony and sleeping four to eight persons, are available, including KidCabin Suites that feature a "log cabin" complete with bunk beds. Some suites also have fireplaces and whirlpools.

10401 Cabela Dr. (in Village West at interstates 70 and 435), Kansas City, KS 66111. © **800/608-9653** or 913/299-7001. Fax 913/299-7002. www.greatwolflodge.com. 281 units. $297–$399 suite. Rates include admission to waterpark. Off-season rates available. AE, DC, DISC, MC, V. Free outdoor parking. **Amenities:** Restaurant; exercise room; spa; smoking not permitted. *In room:* Fridge, microwave.

Hilton President Kansas City (Best) Houdini stayed at the President; Frank Sinatra, Benny Goodman, and Patsy Kline all performed here. But then the 1926 historic landmark shut down and remained empty for 25 years, reopening in 2006 in a prime spot next to the Power & Light District. It's been restored to its former grandeur, with a stately lobby that closely matches its 1941 former self; the impressive, high-ceilinged Walnut Room offering fine dining; the historic Drum Room offering dinner and entertainment; and comfortable guest rooms adorned with black-and-white photographs of Kansas City. With its history-evoking setting, great location, and lively past, it's a good choice for celebratory occasions.

1329 Baltimore, Kansas City, MO 64105. © **800/433-1426** or 816/221-9490. Fax 816/221-9422. www. presidentkansascity.hilton.com. 213 units. $209 double; $259–$369 suite. Children 17 and under stay free in parent's room. AE, DC, DISC, MC, V. Valet parking $16; self-parking $13. **Amenities:** 2 restaurants; fitness room; smoking not permitted.

Q Hotel & Spa (Value) Near Westport's nightlife but far enough away for a good night's sleep, this locally owned hotel is way ahead of the game when it comes to being green. Recently renovated with almost entirely recycled materials, it uses energy-saving light bulbs and water devices, chemical-free cleaning agents, and recycled products for almost all its needs (from toilet paper to office printing paper); takes all glass, paper, and other waste (including that generated by guests) to a recycling center; employs bulk dispensers for shampoo in guest bathrooms; and offers bikes and free shuttle to area attractions in a hybrid car. Yet the hotel doesn't scrimp on amenities, providing free breakfast and evening cocktails, free Wi-Fi and local calls, and soothing, unfussy rooms. Perhaps someday all hotels will be as environmentally friendly as this.

560 Westport Rd., Kansas City, MO 64111. (☎) **800/942-4233** or 816/931-0001. Fax 816/931-8891. www. quarteragehotel.com. 123 units. $129 double; $209 suite. Children 16 and under stay free in parent's room. Rates include buffet breakfast. Pets under 25 lb. for $50 fee. AE, DC, DISC, MC, V. Free outdoor parking. **Amenities:** Free access to local gym; spa; smoking not permitted.

The Raphael Overlooking Country Club Plaza with its many shops and restaurants, this intimate, European-style hotel occupies a converted 1927 brick apartment house. Though not as grand as Kansas City's downtown historic hotels, it has a cozy ambience that attracts many repeat guests. Standard rooms, with free Wi-Fi, vary in size; those facing the back are larger, but preferable are the suites or one of the smaller rooms with views of the plaza.

325 Ward Pkwy., Kansas City, MO 64112. (☎) **800/821-5343** or 816/756-3800. Fax 816/802-2131. www. raphaelkc.com. 123 units. $149–$169 double; $199–$279 suite. Extra person $20. Children 17 and under stay free in parent's room. Weekend packages available. AE, DC, MC, V. Free valet parking. **Amenities:** Restaurant. *In room:* Fridge.

Southmoreland on the Plaza This is a gem of a bed-and-breakfast, located in a 1913 Colonial Revival mansion in a peaceful residential area near the Nelson-Atkins Museum of Art and Country Club Plaza. The B&B offers well-appointed, themed rooms named after famous Kansas Citians, equipped with free Wi-Fi and one of three extras: a fireplace, Jacuzzi, or outdoor deck—a suite in a carriage house has all three. Rates include late-afternoon complimentary wine and appetizers, evening hot beverages and sweets, and gourmet breakfast served in an enclosed veranda or on an outdoor deck. Televisions are available in rooms during the week but are removed on weekends (except for single occupancy).

116 E. 46th St., Kansas City, MO 64112. (☎) **816/531-7979.** Fax 816/531-2407. www.southmoreland.com. 13 units. $135–$250 double. Rates include breakfast. AE, MC, V. Free outdoor parking. No children 12 and under. **Amenities:** Free access to 2 nearby fitness centers; smoking not permitted. *In room:* No TV on weekends.

Westin Crown Center Connected to Crown Center with its many shops and restaurants and via walkway to Union Station with its Science City, the Westin incorporates a limestone bluff with a rock garden and 60-foot waterfall in its multilevel lobby. Rooms are endowed with all the comforts, including the Westin's trademark Heavenly Beds, Wi-Fi, tiny balconies, and, on the north side, great views of downtown. The hotel's central location, facilities that include a jogging track and basketball court, and special Heavenly Dog Beds complete with dog dishes make this a popular choice for families, dog owners, and groups.

One Pershing Rd., Kansas City, MO 64108. (☎) **800/WESTIN-1** (937-8461) or 816/474-4400. Fax 816/391-4438. www.westin.com/crowncenter. 729 units. $329 double; from $403 suite. Extra person $25. Children

15 and under stay free in parent's room. Packages available. AE, DC, DISC, MC, V. Valet parking $17; self-parking $14. Dogs (only under 40 lb.) stay free. **Amenities:** 2 restaurants; heated outdoor pool; 2 lighted outdoor tennis courts; health club ($5 usage fee). *In room:* Fridge.

WHERE TO DINE

Kansas City is known for steak and barbecue, but there are plenty of other cuisine possibilities downtown, in Country Club Plaza, and in Westport. Kansas City's restaurants are all smoke free.

American Restaurant (Best) NEW AMERICAN   One of Kansas City's top fine-dining establishments for more than 35 years, this contemporary, high-ceilinged, glass-enclosed restaurant features the best in regional fare (recipes are shared on its website), offers one of the city's most extensive wine lists, and has good views of the downtown skyline. The changing dinner menu offers fixed-price meals with entrees such as Wagyu beef with potato cake and green-bean casserole, or soft-shell crab with shrimp sausage and fiddlehead fern gumbo. With its gorgeous setting, polished staff, and beautifully presented cuisine, this is a great choice for a celebration.

In Crown Center, 25th and Grand Blvd. ✆ 816/545-8000. www.theamericanrestaurantkc.com. Reservations recommended. Fixed-price dinners $50–$83; fixed-price lunch $24. AE, DC, DISC, MC, V. Mon–Fri 11:30am–2pm; Mon–Thurs 6–9:30pm; Fri–Sat 5:45–10pm.

Arthur Bryant's BARBECUE   A few blocks east of 18th and Vine, this unpretentious self-serve restaurant, with origins stretching back to the early 1920s, is the most famous—and, some swear, the best—barbecue joint in town. White bread smothered with tender barbecued meat and barbecued ribs are the specialties, along with Bryant's signature gritty sauce and lard-fried fries.

1727 Brooklyn. ✆ 816/231-1123. www.arthurbryantsbbq.com. Main courses $7.95–$11. AE, MC, V. Mon–Thurs 10am–9:30pm; Fri–Sat 10am–10pm; Sun 11am–8pm.

Blue Bird Bistro LOCAL ORGANIC/VEGETARIAN   This restaurant, housed in a historic 1890s building with its original pressed-tin ceiling, imparts an earthy yet chic atmosphere, just what you'd expect from a restaurant that prides itself on purchasing fresh produce, all-natural meats, range-free chickens, and other organic ingredients from local farmers for its health-oriented cuisine. Entrees range from bison or black-bean burgers to vegetarian green curry, brisket, and salmon.

1700 Summit St. ✆ 816/221-7559. www.kansascitymenus.com/bluebirdbistro. Main courses $8–$26. AE, DISC, MC, V. Mon–Thurs 7am–9pm; Fri–Sat 7am–10pm; Sun 10am–2pm.

Lidia's ITALIAN   Located in a renovated railway freight house in the Crossroads Art District and sporting exposed ceiling beams, brick walls, and an outdoor patio, this very popular restaurant (owned by TV culinary star Lidia Bastianich) specializes in excellent yet affordable Northern Italian cuisine. Try the three-pasta sampler, delivered to your plate straight from the kitchen via a frying pan (you can have as much as you wish) or the very popular veal shanks. There are two wine lists, one with about 30 choices of bottles all priced at $25.

101 W. 22nd St. ✆ 816/221-3722. www.lidias-kc.com. Reservations recommended. Main courses $16–$32; Sat–Sun brunch $22. AE, DC, MC, V. Daily 11am–2pm; Sun–Thurs 5:30–9pm; Fri–Sat 5–10pm.

Plaza III STEAKS   Open since 1963 and an icon in Country Club Plaza, this steakhouse is renowned for its USDA prime cuts of Midwestern beef, aged in specially designed, temperature-controlled lockers for up to 28 days, as well as its extensive wine list. Lobster and fresh fish are also available, and lunch offers sandwiches and lighter fare in addition to steaks. The dining areas impart a clubby atmosphere, with pictures of cowboys and cattle on the walls and one room devoted to the American Royal. On weekends, you can opt to dine downstairs in the basement, listening to live music ranging from jazz to R&B.

4749 Pennsylvania St. ✆ 816/753-0000. www.plazaiiisteakhouse.com. Reservations recommended. Main dishes $22–$60. AE, DC, DISC, MC, V. Mon–Sat 11am–3pm; Mon–Fri 5–10pm; Sat 5–11pm; Sun 5–9pm.

Savoy Grill AMERICAN   Located in downtown's historic Hotel Savoy and established in 1903, this well-known landmark exudes turn-of-the-20th-century Kansas City with Art Deco stained-glass windows, dark wainscoting, murals depicting the Santa Fe Trail, and white-coated waiters with black bow ties. The menu, which has hardly changed over the decades, is unabashedly straightforward American cuisine, primarily steaks and seafood. Although some dishes fall short of the venue, you can't go wrong with the steaks or lobster. In any case, you're dining here mainly for the old-fashioned ambience, so make reservations for a booth in the main dining room.

In the Hotel Savoy, 219 W. 9th St. ✆ 816/842-3890. www.savoygrill.net. Main courses $22–$50. AE, DC, DISC, MC, V. Mon–Thurs 11am–11pm; Fri–Sat 11am–midnight; Sun 4–10pm.

Stroud's Oak Ridge Manor CHICKEN   In northeast Kansas City, not far from Worlds of Fun, this casual family restaurant is located in an expanded 1829 log cabin and farmhouse. It specializes in pan-fried chicken served with all the trimmings, but it also offers steaks, catfish, and sandwiches. There's a children's menu, a piano player obliges with old-time favorites, and portions are so hearty that few leave without doggie bags. Expect a long wait on weekends.

5410 NE Oak Ridge Rd. (take the Brighton or Vivion exit off I-35). Reservations not accepted. ✆ 816/454-9600. www.stroudsrestaurant.com. Meals $14–$26. AE, MC, V. Mon–Thurs 5–9:30pm; Fri 11am–10:30pm; Sat 2–10:30pm; Sun 11am–9:30pm.

T-Rex (Kids) AMERICAN   Look for the Tyrannosaurus Rex at the entrance to this restaurant in the Legends, where inside it's a Disney-esque fantasyland of more animatronic dinosaurs, brightly colored planets hanging from the ceiling, a shark tank, and a "meteor shower" every 30 minutes. But while the decor is prehistoric, the eclectic menu is anything but, with pizzas, pastas, sandwiches, seafood, fire-roasted rotisserie chicken, steaks, and other dishes sure to please human carnivores, along with a children's menu.

The Legends at Village West (off I-435 and I-70). ✆ 913/334-8888. Main dishes $9–$23. AE, DC, DISC, MC, V. Mon–Thurs 11am–9pm; Fri–Sat 11am–10pm; Sun 11am–8pm.

Winstead's (Kids) DINER   Just east of Country Club Plaza, this Art Deco–style diner has been going strong since 1940 and now has almost a dozen branches. Hamburgers made from steak (ground daily on the premises) are served in tissue paper, the jukebox plays oldies, there's a kids' menu, and the milkshakes are the best in town.

101 Cleaver Blvd. ✆ 816/753-2244. Sandwiches $2.05–$4.05. AE, DC, DISC, MC, V. Sun–Thurs 6:30am–midnight; Fri–Sat 6:30am–1am.

KANSAS CITY AFTER DARK

Much of the city's nightlife can be found downtown (especially in the Power & Light District), in Westport, and at Country Club Plaza. For information about what's going on, pick up the free weekly *Pitch*. For tickets to main events, call **Ticketmaster** (✆ 816/931-3330; www.ticketmaster.com).

Lyric Opera of Kansas City (© 816/471-7344; www.kcopera.org), which presents four
productions yearly in the original language with projected translations; the **Kansas City
Symphony** (© 816/471-0400; www.kcsymphony.org); and most performances by the
Kansas City Ballet (© 816/931-2232; www.kcballet.org). The Lyric Opera, Kansas
City Symphony, and Kansas City Ballet will have a new home when the Kauffmann
Center for the Performing Arts opens downtown in December 2009. The turn-of-the-
20th-century **Folly Theater,** 300 W. 12th St. (© 816/474-4444; www.follytheater.
com), is known for its Jazz and Children's series. In summer, open-air **Starlight Theatre**
in Swope Park (© 816/363-7827; www.kcstarlight.com) has presented Broadway musicals and concerts for almost 60 years.

THE CLUB & BAR SCENE **Majestic Steakhouse,** 931 Broadway (© 816/471-8484;
www.magesticsteakhouse.com), offers dining and jazz nightly in a historic setting, while
Jardine's Restaurant & Jazz Club, 45436 Main St., near Country Club Plaza (© 816/
561-6480; www.jardines4jazz.com), offers live jazz nightly and New American regional
cuisine. **Raglan Road,** in the Power & Light District at 170 E. 14th St. (© 816/944-
9700; www.raglanroadirishpub.com), looks like it was airlifted straight from Dublin and
offers live Irish music and tabletop Irish step dancing Tuesday through Saturday nights,
along with high-end pub food.

In the historic 18th and Vine District, the best spots offering live blues and jazz
include the **Blue Room,** 1600 E. 18th St. (© 816/474-8463; www.americanjazz
museum.com), featuring jazz on Monday, Thursday, Friday, and Saturday; and the
Mutual Musicians Foundation, 1823 Highland Ave. (© 816/471-5212), a National
Historic Landmark where musicians have been meeting for decades to jam after
midnight—Fridays it's blues, Saturdays it's jazz.

In Westport, **Blayney's,** 415 Westport Rd. (© 816/561-3747; www.blayneys.com),
offers mainly blues Monday to Saturday in a pub setting, while farther south, barbecue
meets the blues at the casual **B. B.'s Lawn Side Bar-B-Que,** at 1205 E. 85th St. east of
Troost (© 816/822-7427; www.bbslawnsidebbq.com), with live blues Wednesday to
Sunday nights.

RIVERBOAT GAMBLING Riverboat gambling takes place on noncruising boats along
the banks of the Missouri River, including **Harrah's Casino,** U.S. 210 and Chouteau
Trafficway, North Kansas City (© 816/472-7777; www.harrahsnkc.com); **Ameristar
Casino,** I-435 and Route 210 (© 816/414-7000; www.ameristarcasinos.com); and
Argosy, I-635 and Hwy. 9 (© 816/746-3100; www.stayargosy.com).

9 ST. LOUIS

Established as a French trading post in 1764, St. Louis served as a gateway to the west
after the Louisiana Purchase and as a major port for steamboats traveling the Mississippi.
Today the city's landmark is the soaring, shining steel **Gateway Arch,** designed by Eero
Saarinen in 1966 to commemorate Thomas Jefferson's vision of westward expansion.
Though visitors often make it their first stop, there's plenty more beckoning, including
expansive Forest Park with its first-rate museums, one of the nation's top botanical gar-
dens, and numerous attractions geared toward children, many of them free, making St.
Louis a prime family destination.

GETTING THERE   **By Plane**   Flights arrive at **Lambert–St. Louis International Airport** (© 314/426-8000; www.lambert-stlouis.com), about 20 minutes northwest of downtown. The **MetroLink** light rail (© 314/231-2345) connects the airport with downtown for $3.50. **Taxis** cost about $36 to downtown.

By Train   **Amtrak** (© 800/USA-RAIL [872-7245]; www.amtrak.com) provides daily service from Chicago and Kansas City (trip time for both: 5^1/$_2$ hr.) to its station at 551 S. 16th St., 2 blocks southeast of Union Station (© 314/331-3304).

By Car   The major routes into St. Louis are **I-70** from the east (Indianapolis) and west (Kansas City), **I-55** from the north (Chicago) and south (Memphis), **I-64** from the southeast (Louisville), and **I-44** from the southwest (Springfield).

VISITOR INFORMATION   **St. Louis Visitor Information Centers** are located at America's Center, 7th Street and Washington Avenue (open Mon–Fri 8:30am–5pm, Sat 9am–5pm, Sun 11am–4pm; MetroLink: Convention Center); at Kiener Plaza, 6th and Chestnut streets behind the Old Courthouse (open Mon–Fri 9am–4pm; closed Jan–Feb; MetroLink: 8th St. and Pine); and Forest Park (open daily 10am–5pm; MetroLink: Forest Park–DeBaliviere). There's also a **Visitor Information Center** at the airport's main terminal (open Mon–Fri 10am–6pm, Sat–Sun 1–5pm) and its east terminal (open Mon–Fri 10am–3pm, Sat–Sun 1–5pm). The **Fun Phone** (© 314/421-2100) is a recording of special events. For more information, call © 800/916-0092 or check www.explorestlouis.com.

GETTING AROUND   **MetroLink** (© 314/231-2345; www.metrostlouis.org) travels from the airport (with a branch at Shrewsbury) through St. Louis into Illinois, with stops at Delmar Loop, Forest Park–DeBaliviere, Central West End, Union Station, Busch Stadium, downtown (at 8th and Pine and Convention Center), Laclede's Landing, and other neighborhoods. A one-way ticket costs $1.75 for the entire zone (except for the airport, which costs $3.50); a day pass costs $4.50 (discounts given for seniors and children). Travel is free weekdays from 11:30am to 1:30pm in the downtown area between Union Station and Laclede's Landing. In Forest Park, where many of St. Louis's top sights are located, the Forest Park Shuttle travels from the Forest Park–DeBaliviere MetroLink Station through the park from Memorial Day weekend to Labor Day and is included in the $4.50 MetroLink day pass.

If you're driving a car, be aware that parking is costly. Most hotels and upper-end restaurants offer valet parking. Hotels almost always charge a fee for this service and restaurants sometimes charge as well, though occasionally only a tip is expected.

FAST FACTS   A major hospital is **Saint Louis University Hospital,** 3635 Vista Ave., at Grand Avenue (© 314/577-8000). **Walgreens** is open 24 hours at 4140 S. Broadway (© 314/832-4995). Sales tax is 7.6% and the hotel tax is 7.25%.

WHAT TO SEE & DO

Many of St. Louis's top attractions are spread in or around expansive Forest Park, site of the 1904 World's Fair and one of the nation's largest parks (it beats New York City's Central Park by 500 acres).

WHAT TO SEE & DO

Anheuser-Busch Brewery   Anheuser-Busch, one of the world's largest beer brewers, was established at this site in the 1860s, and many architectural gems from that time period remain. Tours of the brewing process take in the 1885 Clydesdale stable, the

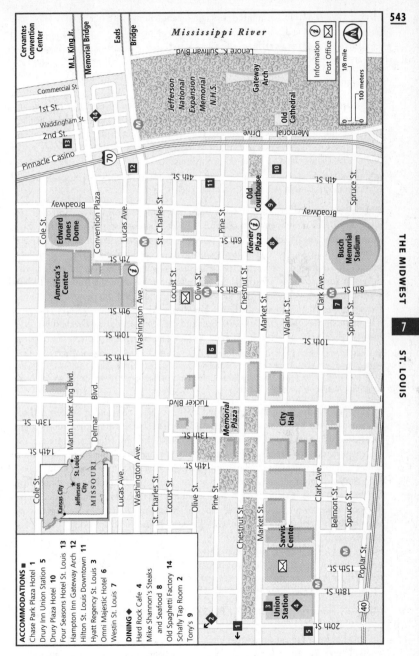

Mississippi River

Lenore K. Sullivan Blvd.

Cervantes Convention Center

M.L. King Jr.

Memorial Bridge

Eads Bridge

Jefferson National Expansion Memorial N.H.S.

Gateway Arch

Old Cathedral

Memorial Drive

Commercial St.

1st St.

Waddingham St.

2nd St.

Pinnacle Casino

70

Cole St.

Broadway

Convention Plaza

Edward Jones Dome

Lucas Ave.

St. Charles St.

4th St.

Pine St.

6th St.

Old Courthouse

Kiener Plaza

4th St.

Spruce St.

Broadway

Busch Memorial Stadium

America's Center

7th St.

Washington Ave.

9th St.

Locust St.

Olive St.

8th St.

Chestnut St.

Market St.

Walnut St.

Clark Ave.

8th St.

Spruce St.

10th St.

11th St.

10th St.

Martin Luther King Blvd.

Delmar Blvd.

13th St.

14th St.

Cole St.

Kansas City

St. Louis

Jefferson City

MISSOURI

Washington Ave.

Lucas Ave.

St. Charles St.

Locust St.

Olive St.

Pine St.

Chestnut St.

Market St.

Tucker Blvd.

Memorial Plaza

13th St.

14th St.

City Hall

Clark Ave.

Belmont St.

Spruce St.

Savvis Center

Union Station

15th St.

18th St.

Poplar St.

20th St.

40

Information

Post Office

1/8 mile

100 meters

0

0

ACCOMMODATIONS ■
Chase Park Plaza Hotel **1**
Drury Inn Union Station **5**
Drury Plaza Hotel **10**
Four Seasons Hotel St. Louis **13**
Hampton Inn Gateway Arch **12**
Hilton St. Louis Downtown **11**
Hyatt Regency St. Louis **3**
Omni Majestic Hotel **6**
Westin St. Louis **7**

DINING ◆
Hard Rock Cafe **4**
Mike Shannon's Steaks
   and Seafood **8**
Old Spaghetti Factory **14**
Schafly Tap Room **2**
Tony's **9**

historic 1892 Brew House, and the packaging plant, ending with free drinks. Allow 1¹/₂ hours. Tours begin at 12th and Lynch streets (I-55 at Arsenal).

12th and Lynch sts. ✆ **314/577-2626.** www.budweisertours.com. Free admission. June–Aug Mon–Sat 9am–5pm, Sun 11:30am–5pm; Sept–May Mon–Sat 9am–4pm (Nov–Feb from 10am), Sun 11:30am–4pm. Tours run several times an hour on first-come, first-served basis. Frequency depends on demand (as often as every 10 min. in summer and about every 30 min. in winter).

Cathedral Basilica of Saint Louis Built after the turn of the 20th century and something of a curiosity, this cathedral combines a Romanesque exterior with a brilliant Byzantine interior and boasts the largest collection of mosaics in the world—42 million pieces of glass used in 83,000 square feet of mosaic art, created by 20 artists over a span of 75 years. Plan at least 15 minutes for this must-see.

4431 Lindell Blvd. (at Newstead Ave.), in Central West End. ✆ **314/373-8240.** www.cathedralstl.org. Free admission. Daily 6am–5pm. MetroLink: Central West End.

Gateway Arch/Jefferson National Expansion Memorial ⟨Best⟩ America's tallest national park monument, this graceful rainbow of shining steel soars 630 feet above downtown and the Mississippi River, commemorating westward expansion in the 1800s. Tram rides to the top (with great views on clear days) can involve lengthy waits in summer and on weekends; come first thing in the morning to purchase tickets (or order tickets in advance for an additional $3 fee online), then take in the **Museum of Westward Expansion,** which traces the journey of Lewis and Clark and those who followed. Extra fees are charged for both the Arch Odyssey Theatre, which features changing, 45-minute movies on a giant IMAX screen; and the *Monument to the Dream* film, documenting the Arch's construction. Plan on spending at least 2 hours here.

St. Louis Riverfront (btw. Memorial Dr. and Lenore K. Sullivan Blvd., on the riverfront). ✆ **877/982-1410.** www.gatewayarch.com. Admission for tram and 1 movie $14 adults, $11 children 13–15, $5.50 children 3–12. Memorial Day to Labor Day daily 8am–10pm (tram until 9pm); rest of year daily 9am–6pm (tram until 5pm). MetroLink: Laclede's Landing.

Missouri Botanical Garden Opened in 1859, this is the country's oldest and one of the world's top-rated botanical gardens: a 79-acre delight featuring the nation's largest Japanese strolling garden, a Chinese garden, the world's first geodesic-domed greenhouse, a scented garden for the visually impaired, a hedge maze, a home-gardening resource center, and themed gardens ranging from a Turkish Ottoman garden to an English woodland garden. A must-see for gardeners, who can easily spend 2 or 3 hours of bliss here, but for families there's also the Children's Garden, designed to resemble a mid-1800s Missouri river town and combining fun and education, with paths leading through woodlands and over streams to a pioneer village, treehouse, fort, rope bridge, cave, splash area, Osage Indian camp, and more.

4344 Shaw Blvd. (Vandeventer exit off I-44). ✆ **314/577-9400.** www.mobot.org. Admission $8 adults, free for children 12 and under (Children's Garden free for adults, $3 for children). Daily 9am–5pm (Memorial Day to Labor Day grounds close Wed 8pm and are open Wed and Sat 7–9am for walkers; Children's Garden closed Nov–Mar). MetroLink: Central West End, then bus no. 59, 92, 93, or 95.

Missouri History Museum St. Louis's history is presented through photographs, memorabilia, first-person narratives, portraits, and more, with displays featuring the city's role in westward expansion, the Dred Scott case (which upheld slavery), famous St. Louisans such as Chuck Berry and Tennessee Williams, the 1904 World's Fair held at Forest Park, a replica of Charles Lindbergh's *Spirit of St. Louis* plane and other items

relating to his life and solo transatlantic flight, and exhibits of the city's past. Allow 1
hour for the permanent exhibits, more for special exhibits.

Jefferson Memorial Building, Forest Park (at Lindell and DeBaliviere). (© **314/746-4599.** www.mohistory.
org. Free admission; special exhibitions cost extra (but are free on Tues). Tues 10am–8pm; Wed–Mon
10am–5pm. MetroLink: Forest Park–DeBaliviere.

Museum of Transportation   Founded in 1944 but only now getting the attention
it deserves with newly expanded grounds, this unique museum "houses one of the largest
and best collections of transportation vehicles in the world" (according to the Smithsonian). Certainly, with more than 70 locomotives, the museum boasts one of the most
complete collections of American rail power anywhere, including an 1858 wood-burning
locomotive, a Big Boy (the world's largest steam locomotive), and a 1920s Pullman sleeping car. Automobiles on display range from a 1915 Ford Model T to Bobby Darin's 1960
dream car. Other highlights include a miniature passenger train and a trolley circulating
the museum's 129 acres. Allot at least 2 hours to explore.

3015 Barrett Station Rd. (west of I-270, at the Dougherty Ferry Rd. exit). (© **314/965-7998.** http://transport
museumassociation.org. Admission $6 adults, $5 seniors and children 5–12. Summer (May 1 to Labor
Day) Mon–Sat 9am–5pm, Sun 11am–5pm; winter Tues–Sat 9am–4pm, Sun 11am–4pm.

Saint Louis Art Museum   Housed in a Beaux Arts–style building constructed for
the 1904 World's Fair, this great museum is a buffet of the arts, where visitors can sample
as much as they like of the displays from around the globe and from virtually all time
periods. It contains works ranging from ancient and medieval art to European old masters, French Impressionists, American art from 1800 to 1945, and contemporary art. Its
pre-Columbian, Asian, and German expressionist collections are ranked among the best
in the world (it owns more paintings by Max Beckmann than any museum on the
planet). Other galleries feature Islamic and ancient art; an Egyptian collection (including
three mummies); arms and armor; media art; and art from Africa, Oceania, and the
Americas. There are also displays of Chinese, European, and American decorative arts.
You should spend at least 2 hours here.

Fine Arts Dr., Forest Park. (© **314/721-0072.** http://saintlouis.art.museum. Free admission; special exhibitions cost extra (but are free on Fri). Tues–Sun 10am–5pm (Fri to 9pm). MetroLink: Forest Park-DeBaliviere,
then Forest Park Shuttle (summer only) or Hampton no. 90 Metrobus.

More Highlights

HISTORIC HOMES   The **Campbell House Museum,** 1508 Locust St. (© **314/421-
0325;** www.campbellhousemuseum.org; open Wed–Sun), is an elegant, 10,000-square-
foot 1851 Victorian mansion, with most of its original family furnishings remarkably
intact. Tours cost $6. The Romanesque Revival–style 1889 **Samuel Cupples House,**
3673 W. Pine Blvd. (© **314/977-3575;** http://cupples.slu.edu; open Tues–Sat), is a gem
of the Gilded Age on the campus of Saint Louis University, containing 42 rooms, a glass
collection, and other fine and decorative arts. Tours cost $5. The **Chatillon-DeMenil
Mansion,** 3352 DeMenil Place (© **314/771-5828;** www.demenil.org; open Tues–Sat),
built as a 4-room farmhouse in 1848 and later expanded to 14 rooms in the Greek
Revival style, contains period furnishings, a collection of 1904 World's Fair memorabilia,
and two paintings by Missouri artist George Caleb Bingham. Admission here is $4.

From 1900 to 1903, the **Scott Joplin House State Historic Site,** 2658A Delmar
Blvd. (© **314/340-5790;** www.mostateparks.com/scottjoplin.htm; open Mar–Oct
Tues–Sun, Nov–Feb Tues–Sat), was the modest four-family antebellum home of the
musician and composer known as the "King of Ragtime." Now a National Historic

Landmark, it offers guided tours for $2.50 that include Joplin's second-floor apartment with furnishings representative of the times and a player piano that rags out renditions of Joplin's best-known tunes, including "The Entertainer."

MAJOR LEAGUE FUN   Watch the **St. Louis Cardinals** hit some homers at the new downtown Busch Stadium, Broadway and Clark streets (📞 **314/345-9000;** www. stlcardinals.com).

BEST BETS FOR KIDS   St. Louis is a children's town, with more than enough to keep them amused, much of it absolutely free (though there is generally a charge for parking). The top-rated **St. Louis Zoo,** Forest Park (📞 **314/781-0900;** www.stlzoo.org), with its Big Cat Country, Fragile Forest for the zoo's great apes, River's Edge with elephants and hippos, Penguin and Puffin Coast, and fascinating Insectarium with everything from giant cockroaches to a butterfly house, is free (fees charged for some attractions, like the animal-contact Children's Zoo). Another freebie is the **St. Louis Science Center,** 5050 Oakland Ave. (📞 **800/456-7572** or 314/289-4400; www.slsc.org), with full-size, animated dinosaurs and 750 hands-on exhibits covering DNA and genetics, health, aviation, the environment, and more (admission charged for special exhibitions, planetarium, and OMNIMAX Theater). Another free attraction is **Grant's Farm,** 10501 Gravois (📞 **314/843-1700;** www.grantsfarm.com), once farmed by Ulysses S. Grant and now part of the Busch family estate, open mid-April through October and featuring a tram ride through an exotic game preserve, a small zoo, animal shows, a Clydesdale stable, a carriage collection, and a free glass of Anheuser-Busch beer.

Older kids—and adults—love the whimsical, one-of-a-kind **City Museum,** 701 N. 15th St. (📞 **314/231-2489;** www.citymuseum.org), created by artists and housed in a former shoe factory. The adventure land features a huge indoor play area filled with imaginative caves, slides, and crawling tubes; a circus performance; train rides; art workshops; a collection of oddities; a funky aquarium; and a five-story outdoor climbing contraption called MonstroCity. With a school bus teetering on its roof, this fun house is like no other. Admission is $12, plus $6 for the aquarium. At the education-oriented **Magic House** children's museum, 516 S. Kirkwood Rd. (📞 **314/822-8900;** www. magichouse.org), children 10 and under have a blast experimenting with magnets, water, and tools; testing their fitness; role-playing in a kid-size village; zooming down a three-story slide; and watching their hair stand on end as they touch an electrically charged ball. Special sections are geared toward younger children and toddlers. Admission is $7.50.

The biggest attraction for kids is the huge amusement park, **Six Flags St. Louis,** 30 miles west of St. Louis on I-44 (📞 **636/938-4800;** www.sixflags.com), with thrill rides such as Xcalibur (a slinging, rotating catapult) and the Evel Knievel Coaster, plus Looney Tunes Town for younger visitors, live entertainment, and even a waterpark with a wave pool, slides, and more. Admission is $45 adults, $30 kids under 48 inches tall; 2 years and younger are free. Discount tickets are often available on the park's website. It's open weekends April, May, September, and October, and daily in summer.

WHERE TO STAY

Downtown St. Louis has an impressive number of hotel chains ensconced in renovated historic buildings. In addition to the choices below, consider the **Westin St. Louis,** next to Busch Stadium at 811 Spruce St. (📞 **314/621-2000;** www.westin.com/stlouis), which gave new life to a group of former 19th-century railroad warehouses with a gorgeous, contemporary interior; and the upscale **Hilton St. Louis Downtown,** 400 Olive St. (📞 **314/436-0002;** www.stlouisdowntown.hilton.com), in the historic Merchants-Laclede building, with many of its original features intact (a former vault is now a gift shop). The most elegant modern newcomer is unquestionably **Four Seasons Hotel St. Louis,** 999 N. 2nd St. (© **314/881-5800;** www.fourseasons.com/stlouis), located next to Laclede's Landing and the riverfront, with great views, a spa, outdoor pool, and Lumiere Place Casino.

Chase Park Plaza Hotel (Best) Located across from Forest Park in the elegant Central West End, with its antiques shops, sidewalk cafes, and sophisticated restaurants, this restored 1920s historic hotel is one of the city's poshest, offering luxuriously appointed rooms and one- and two-bedroom suites, the latter two featuring minikitchens with microwaves, two-burner stoves, and small fridges. The hotel's many facilities, including a five-screen movie complex, and its proximity to the attractions of Forest Park make it a winner with the business and leisure set.

212–232 N. Kingshighway (at Lindell Blvd.), St. Louis, MO 63108. © **877/587-2427** or 314/633-3000. Fax 314/633-1144. www.chaseparkplaza.com. 290 units. $269–$309 double; from $289 suite. No charge for additional room occupants. AE, DC, DISC, MC, V. Valet parking $22; self-parking $14. **Amenities:** 4 restaurants; outdoor heated pool; state-of-the-art health club. *In room:* Kitchen (suites only).

Drury Plaza Hotel Here's a great location for both business and leisure travelers. Part of a St. Louis–based chain but more upscale than sister Drury Inns, this downtown hotel, situated just minutes from the Arch, occupies three renovated buildings, including the 1919 Fur Exchange Building. Rooms with the best views face the Arch and river. A less expensive choice is **Drury Inn Union Station,** across from Union Station at 201 S. 20th St. (© **314/231-3900**), housed in a restored former YMCA built in 1907. With its indoor pool, exercise room, free parking, and laundry facilities, it's a great choice for families. Like all Drury properties, both offer free breakfasts, free local calls and 60 minutes of long-distance calls, free evening beverages and snacks, and free Internet access.

4th and Market sts., St. Louis, MO 63102. © **800/378-7946** or 314/231-3003. Fax 314/231-2952. www.druryhotels.com. 367 units. $129–$142 double; from $168 suite. Children 17 and under stay free in parent's room. Rates include hot breakfast buffet. AE, DC, DISC, MC, V. Parking $15. MetroLink: 8th and Pine. Pets permitted free. **Amenities:** 2 restaurants; indoor pool; exercise room. *In room:* Fridge, microwave.

Hampton Inn St. Louis Downtown at the Arch (Value) This property boasts better-than-average service for its price range, a great downtown location near Laclede's Landing and the Arch, laundry facilities, a game room, free local calls, and free Internet access in its business center and rooms, some of which boast views of the Arch and all of which have recliners and queen- or king-size beds.

333 Washington Ave., St. Louis, MO 63102. © **800/HAMPTON** (426-7866) or 314/621-7900. Fax 314/421-6468. www.hamptoninnstlouis.com. 190 units. $109–$179 double. Extra person $10. Children 17 and under stay free in parent's room. Rates include free breakfast. AE, DC, DISC, MC, V. Parking $10. MetroLink: Laclede's Landing or Convention Center. **Amenities:** Restaurant; indoor pool; exercise room. *In room:* Fridge.

Hyatt Regency St. Louis Located in restored Union Station, with its many shops and restaurants, this hotel boasts Missouri's most spectacular lobby—the station's former Grand Hall, with a six-story vaulted ceiling and gold-leaf frescoes. Most of the spacious (and quiet) rooms are in a modern addition beneath the trusses of the former train shed and feature such luxuries as bathroom TVs. For more pampering, stay in the Regency Club in the historic part of the station, which has the added perks of its own lounge and complimentary breakfast and evening appetizers. Everyone from business travelers to families stays here.

One St. Louis Union Station (18th and Market sts.), St. Louis, MO 63103. © **800/233-1234** or 314/231-1234. Fax 314/923-3970. www.stlouis.hyatt.com. 539 units. $179–$319 double. Children 17 and under stay free in parent's room. Packages available. AE, DC, DISC, MC, V. Valet parking $24; self-parking $14. MetroLink: Union Station. **Amenities:** 2 restaurants; outdoor pool; 24-hr. health club.

Omni Majestic Hotel   Built in 1914, this National Historic Landmark and boutique hotel appeals to business travelers and celebrities alike with its old-world charm, downtown location, complimentary downtown shuttle, and excellent service. Comfortable rooms have more character than most and are equipped with free Wi-Fi and also bathrobes. The **Get Fit rooms** sport treadmills.

1019 Pine St., St. Louis, MO 63101. (©) **800/THE-OMNI** (843-6664) or 314/436-2355. Fax 314/436-0223. www.omnihotels.com. 91 units. $149–$219 double. Extra person $10. Children 18 and under stay free in parent's room. Rates include free breakfast. AE, DC, DISC, MC, V. Valet parking $24. MetroLink: 8th and Pine. Pets up to 25 lb. accepted with security deposit. **Amenities:** Restaurant; 24-hr. health club. *In room:* Fridge.

WHERE TO DINE

Dining in one of St. Louis's distinctive neighborhoods ranks high on a short list of must-dos. Clustered around Forest Park are trendy **Central West End,** with its grand residences, antiques stores, and fashionable eateries (many with sidewalk seating); the **Loop,** named after an old streetcar turnaround and home to funky shops, art galleries, ethnic restaurants, and the St. Louis Walk of Fame; and the **Hill,** an Italian district famous for its many Italian restaurants (a perennial favorite is **Charlie Gitto's,** 5226 Shaw Ave.; (©) **314/772-8898;** www.charliegittos.com).

For children, good bets include the **Old Spaghetti Factory,** housed in an old warehouse in Laclede's Landing at 727 N. 1st St. ((©) **314/621-0276;** www.osf.com); and **Hard Rock Cafe** ((©) **314/621-7625;** www.hardrockcafe.com), in Union Station, which also has a food court.

It's a St. Louis tradition to drop by **Ted Drewes Frozen Custard,** 6726 Chippewa ((©) **314/481-2652;** www.teddrewes.com), after a night on the town. Founded almost 80 years ago and open daily except January, this roadside stand and Route 66 attraction specializes in frozen custards, including the Concrete, available in a range of flavors and so thick that it's served upside down. An additional location is open summers only at 4224 S. Grand ((©) **314/352-7376**).

Blueberry Hill (Kids) SANDWICHES/BURGERS   In the lively Loop, this St. Louis institution is a treasure-trove of pop-culture memorabilia, including vintage posters and more Chuck Berry memorabilia than you can shake a dingaling at. The digital jukebox is one of the best in the country, and the hamburgers are among the best in town. There's live music in the Elvis Room and Duck Room several nights a week (Chuck Berry still performs here), and outside on the sidewalk is the St. Louis Walk of Fame honoring famous St. Louisans, including Chuck Berry, Josephine Baker, Tennessee Williams, Ulysses S. Grant, and Tina Turner.

6504 Delmar. (©) **314/727-4444.** www.blueberryhill.com. Main courses $5.50–$8.75. AE, DC, DISC, MC, V. Mon–Sat 11am–1:30am; Sun 11am–midnight. MetroLink: Delmar, then bus 97.

Chez Léon (Value) FRENCH   One of the hip Central West End's friendliest restaurants, this neighborhood bistro has a relaxed atmosphere, sidewalk seating, a staff that aims to please, and standard French fare served in hearty portions. Its 3 Plats dinner for $38 is a popular choice, giving diners a choice of entree (like grilled salmon with tarragon cream sauce, or roasted free-range chicken with truffle sauce) and two other dishes from the regular menu.

4580 Laclede Ave. (at Euclid). (©) **314/361-1589.** www.chezleon.com. Main courses $25–$48. AE, DC, MC, V. Tues–Thurs 5:30–10pm; Fri–Sat 5:30–11pm; Sun 5–9pm. MetroLink: Central West End.

Meriwether's NEW AMERICAN On the second floor of the Missouri History Museum, this light and airy casual restaurant overlooking Forest Park offers salads, sandwiches (like a bison burger), quiche, and main dishes (grilled salmon topped with a sauce of tomatoes, olives, white wine, garlic, and herbs), as well as a children's menu. It's a good place for lunch if you're visiting the many sights in Forest Park, but more recommendations include the casual **Boathouse,** with its sandwiches, pizzas, and rental paddle boats (© **314/367-2224;** www.boathouseforestpark.com); and **Puck's,** in the Saint Louis Art Museum (© **314/655-5490;** www.wolfgangpuck.com), with its innovative American cuisine and popular Sunday brunch.

Missouri History Museum, Forest Park. © **314/361-7313.** Main courses $8–$11. Sun brunch $20. AE, MC, V. Mon–Sat 11am–2pm; Sun 10am–2pm. MetroLink: Forest Park.

Mike Shannon's Steaks and Seafood STEAKS/SEAFOOD Owned by a former Cardinals baseball great and current sportscaster (his radio show is broadcast live from a table in the restaurant after Fri evening home games), this downtown fine-dining venue is formal yet relaxed, with white tablecloths in a glass-enclosed dining room, an adjoining sports bar, and displays of sports memorabilia. It caters to a business crowd with a menu that concentrates on aged steaks and fresh seafood, plus sandwiches for lunch. With Busch Stadium just a couple minutes' walk away, it's so popular for a meal before or after a Cardinals game that it opens early for weekend games.

620 Market St. © **314/421-1540.** www.shannonsteak.com. Reservations recommended. Main courses $20–$48. AE, DC, DISC, MC, V. Mon–Fri 11am–10pm; Sat 5–11pm; Sun 5–10pm. MetroLink: 8th and Pine.

The Schlafly Tap Room AMERICAN A few blocks north of Union Station, in a 1904 brick building that used to house a printing company, this microbrewery brews more than 30 kinds of Schlafly brand beer on the premises (eight or so are usually on offer) and serves a variety of sandwiches and entrees, many of which include beer in their recipes, including Oatmeal Stout steak-and-mushroom pie, and beer-and-cheddar soup. An upstairs bar offers live music every Friday, Saturday, and Sunday evening.

2100 Locust St. © **314/241-2337.** www.schlafly.com. Main courses $7–$17. AE, DC, DISC, MC, V. Mon–Thurs 11am–10pm; Fri–Sat 11am–midnight; Sun noon–9pm.

Tony's Best ITALIAN If you want to splurge on one meal in St. Louis, do it here. Most agree that Tony's is the finest restaurant in the city. Open since 1946, it offers impeccable service, sublime Italian cuisine, an extensive wine selection, one of the cleanest and quietest kitchens on earth, and sophisticated, elegant dining. Star entrees include the lobster Albanello (served in a heavy, white-wine cream sauce with mushrooms and shallots) and various veal dishes, but everything is fabulous.

410 Market St. © **314/231-7007.** www.tonysstlouis.com. Reservations recommended. Jackets required for men. Main courses $20–$41. AE, DC, DISC, MC, V. Mon–Thurs 5–11pm (last order); Fri–Sat 5–11:30pm. MetroLink: 8th and Pine.

ST. LOUIS AFTER DARK

To find out what's on, look for the free weekly *Riverfront Times* at restaurants, bars, and venues around town; buy the Thursday edition of the *St. Louis Post-Dispatch* for its entertainment section; or check the constantly updated *St. Louis Calendar of Events* online at **www.explorestlouis.com** or the Regional Arts Commission's **www. artszipper.com.**

THE PERFORMING ARTS Grand Center (MetroLink: Grand) is the premier performing arts district, with the 1920s-era **Powell Symphony Hall,** 718 N. Grand Blvd.

(© **314/534-1700**), home of the **St. Louis Symphony Orchestra** (www.slso.org), founded in 1880 and America's second-oldest symphony orchestra. The **Fabulous Fox Theatre,** 527 N. Grand Blvd. (© **314/534-1111;** www.fabulousfox.com), is a lavish, 1929 Byzantine venue for musicals, dance, and concerts. The **Grandel Theater,** 3610 Grandel Sq. (© **314/534-3810;** www.theblackrep.org), is home of the Black Rep, which stages contemporary works by African-American playwrights and is the nation's largest African-American theater company. The **Muny,** in Forest Park (© **314/361-1900;** www. muny.org), which opened in 1916 and is the nation's oldest and largest outdoor musical theater, features Broadway musicals in summer.

THE CLUB & CASINO SCENE St. Louis's nightlife is concentrated around Laclede's Landing, the Loop, and in Soulard on the south edge of downtown. Good bets for live music virtually every night of the week include **BB's Jazz, Blues & Soups,** near Busch Stadium at 700 S. Broadway (© **314/436-5222;** www.bbsjazzbluessoups.com), and the **Broadway Oyster Bar**, 736 S. Broadway (© **314/621-8811;** www.broadwayoysterbar. com), home to live blues and R&B and Cajun/Creole cuisine. The **Big Bang,** featuring dueling piano players who lead the audience in high-energy singalongs Tuesdays through Saturdays, is a popular hangout in Laclede's Landing at 807 N. 2nd St. (© **314/241-2264;** www.thebigbangbar.com), while in Soulard, the **1860 Hard Shell Cafe & Saloon,** 1860 S. 9th St. (© **314/231-1860;** www.soularddining.com), offers blues, R&B, rock, and more nightly. In the Loop, 1,500-seat the **Pageant,** 6161 Delmar (© **314/726-6161;** www.thepageant.com), and **Blueberry Hill,** 6504 Delmar (© **314/727-0880;** www.blueberryhill.com), bring in the hottest national acts. Among several places to gamble, most convenient are the **President Casino,** docked at Laclede's Landing (© **800/772-3647;** www.presidentcasino.com) and **Lumiere Place,** just north of Laclede's Landing at 999 N. 2nd St. (© **877/450-7711;** lumiereplace.com).

10 BRANSON & THE OZARKS

With a population of about 7,000 and a quaint, historic downtown, Branson attracts more than eight million visitors a year, primarily retirees, families, and RVers drawn by the irresistible lure—and improbable pairing—of outdoor recreation and big-time entertainment. Surrounded by three pristine lakes in the scenic, wooded, mountainous region of the Ozarks in southern Missouri, Branson offers fishing, swimming, golfing, and boating, and is also home to big-name entertainers who present everything from country music to comedy and magic acts in more than 100 live shows daily. Branson also boasts theme parks such as Silver Dollar City, unique museums, and Branson Landing, a shopping-and-dining complex on the shores of Lake Taneycomo.

ESSENTIALS

GETTING THERE & GETTING AROUND The nearest airport is **Springfield-Branson Regional Airport** (© **417/869-0300;** www.sgf-branson-airport.com), in Springfield, 43 miles to the north, though that will change when Branson Airport opens in May 2009 (www.bransonair.net). You need a car when visiting Branson, and all the major car-rental agencies have desks at the airport. The major highway into Branson, which is 3¹/₂ hours from Kansas City and 4 hours from St. Louis, is U.S. 65 from the north, where it intersects with I-44 at Springfield. Be forewarned that traffic on "the

Strip," or "76 Country Boulevard" (W. Hwy. 76), in Branson is notorious for traffic jams, but a number of color-coded relief roads help.

VISITOR INFORMATION Contact the **Branson/Lakes Area Chamber of Commerce** (© 800/214-3661 or 417/334-4084; www.explorebranson.com) or stop by one of two Welcome Centers for brochures, maps, and coupon books offering discounts: north of Branson at the junction of highways 65 and 160, and in town at the junction of highways 65 and 248. Both are open Monday through Saturday from 8am to 5pm (to 6pm in summer) and Sunday from 10am to 4pm.

WHAT TO SEE & DO

Look for free tourist tabloids and booklets throughout town offering discount coupons for many Branson shows, sights, and attractions. Prices below do not include tax.

The Shows

It all started in 1959 with the **Baldknobbers Jamboree** (© 417/334-4528; www. baldknobbers.com), when four brothers began performing twice a week in a converted building by Lake Taneycomo. In 1968, the **Presleys' Country Jubilee** (© 417/334-4874; www.presleys.com) opened the first theater on West Hwy. 76, after years of performing to sellout crowds in cool underground venues—Ozark caves. Both are still going strong, offering family-oriented music, dancing, and comedy.

They're joined by 50 other theaters, most with performances from mid-March or April to December. Ticket prices average $25 to $40 for adults (more for dinner shows) and are half-price or free for children; family tickets are also often available. It's a Branson tradition for many performers to sign autographs after the show.

Branson had a run as *the* place for live country music. Although **Roy Clark, Mel Tillis,** the **Oak Ridge Boys,** and other country greats still return for engagements at Branson theaters, the past 10 years have witnessed an explosion in Las Vegas–style production shows. **Andy Williams** was the first major noncountry star to build a venue here, the **Moon River Theatre** (© 417/334-4500; www.andywilliams.com), in 1994. Nowadays, entertainment includes everything from magic shows such as the **Kirby & Bambi VanBurch Show** (© 417/334-7140; www.kirbyvanburch.com) to nostalgia-inducing shows like **#1 Hits of the 60s** (© 417/339-1960; www.1hitsofthe60s.com) and **Legends in Concert** (© 417/339-3003; www.legendsinconcert.com), with music by Johnny Cash, Buddy Holly, Elvis, and other greats. For comedy, **Yakov Smirnoff** (© 800/728-4546 or 417/332-1234; www.yakov.com) leads the pack with his unique insights into the quirks of everyday life and relationships between men and women.

One of the hottest shows in town is that provided by violinist **Shoji Tabuchi** (© 417/334-7469; www.shoji.com), whose repertoire ranges from country and jazz to classical and Broadway, and whose shows include elaborate production numbers, lasers and other stunning visual effects, an 18-piece orchestra, and gorgeous costumes. Another high-powered act is **Six** (© 417/334-0076; www.thesixshow.com), featuring six vocalist brothers who are so adept at harmonies and creating drum sounds using only their voices that they sound like a complete band.

A great hit with families is the **Incredible Acrobats of China** (© 417/336-8888; www.acrobatsofchina.com), with their gravity-defying performances. **Sight & Sound Theatres** (© 800/377-1277; www.sight-sound.com) is a faith-based theater company with lavish Bible-related productions (*Noah,* which runs through Oct 2009, features 100 live animals and 200 animatronic animals).

Branson's oldest and most widely beloved theater is the **Shepherd of the Hills Homestead and Outdoor Theater** (© 800/653-6288 or 417/334-4191; www.oldmatt.com), an outdoor amphitheater which for more than 45 years has presented evening reenactments of Harold Bell Wright's 1907 novel *The Shepherd of the Hills,* which introduced the Ozarks to the world. The mystery/love drama unfolds on a football-field-size dirt stage with 90 performers, 40 horses, a fire, a shootout, a hoedown, comedy, and, essentially, entertainment for the whole family. During the day, the grounds are open for homestead tours of Old Matt's Cabin (the original home of the main characters in the book), a trip up Inspiration Tower for fine views of the Ozarks, and horseback trail rides.

Theme Parks

Celebration City (Kids)
Branson's biggest nighttime attraction centers on the top events and eras of 20th-century America, with areas based on such themes as historic Route 66 and a boardwalk harking back to the days of arcades and amusement rides. Mostly, however, it's a place for evening family fun, with more than 30 rides and attractions (including a water ride with a five-story drop) and a nightly must-see outdoor laser and fireworks display that takes viewers on a visual tour of important events of the 20th century.

Hwy. 376. © **800/831-4FUN** (831-4386) or 417/336-7171. www.celebrationcity.com. Admission $26 adults, $21 seniors and children 4–11. Weekends May and Sept–Oct and daily June–Aug, 3–10pm.

Silver Dollar City (Best) (Kids)
About 5 miles west of Branson, this is the biggest and best of the area's theme parks, featuring more than 30 thrill rides (such as the Powderkeg, which accelerates from 0 to 53 mph in 2.8 seconds), imaginative playgrounds, 40 live shows daily at a dozen arenas (from gospel to country and bluegrass), restaurants featuring traditional cuisine, about 60 specialty shops, and resident craftspeople practicing their trades, all in a wooded, 1880s mountain-town setting. **Marvel Cave,** the site's original attraction, can be explored on a 1-hour guided walking tour (included in the park's admission price). Plan on arriving first thing in the morning to avoid traffic jams, and spend all day here. Kids of all ages love this place.

W. Hwy. 76. © **800/831-4FUN** (831-4386) or 417/336-7171. www.bransonsilverdollarcity.com. Admission $48 adults, $46 seniors, $38 children 4–11. Mid-May to mid-Aug daily 9:30am–7pm; Sept–Dec and Apr Wed–Sun varying hours.

White Waterpark (Kids)
This 12-acre waterpark features a half-dozen rides and slides (including a seven-story, six-slide thrill ride), a float down Lazy River, a wave pool, lots of water blasters, geysers, and shower shooters at Raintree Island. For little ones, there's Little Squirts Water Works slides, nozzles, and sprays.

3501 W. Hwy. 76. © **800/475-9370** or 417/336-7171. www.bransonwhitewater.com. Admission $35 adults, $30 children 4–11. End of May to mid-June and last half of Aug daily 10am–6pm; mid-June to mid-Aug daily 10am–8pm.

> ## (Value) For Theme Park Fanatics
>
> Those who plan on visiting all three parks—Silver Dollar City, Celebration City, and White Water—can save money with a **CityHopper Pass** costing $99 for adults and $89 for children. You can buy the pass at any of the three parks (it's good for 4 days), order it online at **www.silverdollarcity.com**, or call © **800/ 475-9370.** Three-day, two-park passes are also available.

MUSEUMS   Branson bills itself as a year-round home for America's veterans, and nowhere is the city's commitment to veterans more apparent than at the **Veterans Memorial Museum,** 1250 W. Hwy. 76 (© **417/336-2300;** www.veteransmemorialbranson. com), which honors those who served in both world wars, Korea, Vietnam, and the Persian Gulf. Uniforms, personal histories, weapons, photographs, and thousands of memorabilia ranging from Adolf Hitler's World War I dog tag to a bicycle used on the Ho Chi Minh Trail are on display. Those who remember one of America's most beloved couples might want to pay their respects at the **Roy Rogers–Dale Evans Museum,** Hwy. 376 and Green Mountain Drive (© **417/339-1900;** www.royrogers.com), packed with photographs and the couple's collection of memorabilia and personal effects, including guns, cowboy clothing and boots, cars, and guitars. Trigger and Buttermilk are preserved here, two films document the stars' lives and careers, and Roy "Dusty" Rogers, Jr., and grandson Dustin Rogers perform Tuesday to Saturday at the adjoining Happy Trails Theater.

Visitors to *Titanic:* **The World's Largest Titanic Museum Attraction,** 3235 W. Hwy. 76 (© **417/334-9500;** www.titanicbranson.com), can walk a replica of the ship's grand staircase, see the difference between first- and third-class staterooms, touch an iceberg, view 400 artifacts (each with a personal story and donated by those on the ship or their relatives), and learn about the fateful last hours of the doomed journey; audio guides include accounts by actual *Titanic* survivors. Kids are drawn to **Ripley's Believe It or Not!,** 3325 W. Hwy. 76 (© **417/337-5300;** www.ripleysbranson.com), like moths to a flame for its collection of oddities from around the world, optical illusions, TV shows (both old and new), and world records, while kids of all ages can enjoy the **World's Largest Toy Museum,** 3609 W. Hwy. 76 (© **417/332-1499;** www.worldslargesttoymuseum. com), packed with dolls, pedal cars, windups, and other toys from the 1800s to today. The **Ralph Foster Museum,** 2 miles south of Branson in the College of the Ozarks (© **417/334-6411,** ext. 3407; www.rfostermuseum.com), celebrates Ozark history with an amazing, eclectic collection of items relating to Ozark history and folklore, including handmade dolls, antiques, paintings, musical instruments, farm tools, a huge display of firearms, quilts, stuffed animals, Native American artifacts, and much, much more, including the original truck from *The Beverly Hillbillies* TV show.

TRAIN & BOAT TRIPS   Departing from downtown Branson's century-old depot March to early December, the **Branson Scenic Railway,** 206 E. Main (© **417/334-6110;** www.bransontrain.com), revives the romance of classic rail travel with 40-mile round-trips through the wooded Ozark hills aboard restored vintage 1940s and 1950s dome and passenger cars. These trips appeal to a mostly older crowd, especially for the Saturday night dinner ride. For a lunch or dinner cruise on Table Rock Lake, board the *Showboat Branson Belle,* 4800 Mo. 165 (© **800/775-BOAT** [775-2628] or 417/336-7171; www.showboatbransonbelle.com), a luxury paddle-wheeler boat offering 2-hour cruises with dining, music, comedy, and entertainment mid-March through December. For a land and water tour, **Ride the Ducks,** 2320 W. Hwy. 76 (© **877/88-QUACK** [887-8225]; www.bransonducks.com), is a wacky 70-minute tour aboard World War II amphibious military assault vehicles that appeals to kids with corny jokes and a cruise of either Table Rock Lake or Lake Taneycomo March through December.

OUTDOOR ACTIVITIES   Fisherfolk favor Table Rock Lake for bass and Lake Taneycomo for trout. **State Park Marina,** on Hwy. 165 inside Table Rock State Park (© **417/334-BOAT** [334-2628]; www.stateparkmarina.com), is Branson's closest marina and offers everything from pontoons and WaveRunners to ski or fishing boats, as well as activities like parasailing and scuba diving. Table Rock Lake also has several public swimming areas and the 2.2-mile Table-Rock Lakeshore Trail. Outdoor enthusiasts should also head to **Dogwood Canyon Nature Park** (© 417/779-5983; www.dogwoodcanyon.org), a beautiful 2,200-acre wooded wilderness 35 miles south of Branson with spring-fed streams and waterfalls, accessible via a 6.5-mile hiking and biking path (rental bikes are available) and 2-hour wildlife tram tours that also take in a refuge for elk, bison, Texas longhorns, and other wildlife. Horseback rides and trout fishing are also available (fees charged for each activity). Several of the Branson area's dozen golf courses, open to the public year-round, are described in the brochure "Golf Branson," available at the Welcome Center. A favorite is the 9-hole, par-3 **Top of the Rock,** 150 Top of the Rock Rd. (© 417/339-5312). It's owned by Big Cedar Lodge (which does everything to perfection), was designed by Jack Nicklaus, has great views of Table Rock Lake, and includes an Arnold Palmer–designed practice facility. Eighteen-hole **Branson Creek Golf Club** (© 417/339-4653; www.bransoncreekgolf.com) is one of Missouri's top public courses.

SHOPPING   Branson Landing (www.bransonlanding.com), a pedestrian waterfront development stretching 1.5 miles on Lake Taneycomo with free trolley service, features more than 100 restaurants and shops (including a Bass Pro Shop and Belk department store) and a town square with a synchronized fountain and fire show. Outlet malls include **Factory Merchant's Branson,** 1000 Pat Nash Dr. (© 417/335-6686), and **Tanger Outlet Center,** 300 Tanger Blvd. (© 417/337-9328), while **Apple Tree Mall,** 1830 W. Hwy. 76 (© 417/335-2133), is Branson's largest antique flea market with more than 300 vendors.

WHERE TO STAY

Branson offers resorts, countless motels and hotels, and many camping facilities. For something unique, stay in a houseboat; contact **Tri-Lakes Houseboat Rentals** (© 800/982-2628; www.tri-lakeshouseboat.com) on Table Rock Lake.

Unless otherwise noted, hotels below offer free outdoor parking.

Big Cedar Lodge (Best)   Spread over 800 beautifully cultivated acres on a hill overlooking Table Rock Lake and owned by Bass Pro Shop, Branson's most impressive and classiest resort is a lovely refuge from Branson's congested Strip and is great for families, reunions, and romantic getaways. It offers a wide range of accommodations, from rooms in a rustic and majestic Northwest-style lodge to luxurious log cabins that sleep two to six adults and come with wood-burning fireplace, outdoor gas grill, kitchen, DVD (free DVDs available), and Jacuzzi; all have Internet access. Facilities are extensive and first class, including a spring-fed pool, outdoor hot tub, jogging and hiking trails, a children's center (ages 4–12), miniature golf, boat rentals, horseback riding, a playground, and laundry facilities.

612 Devil's Pool Rd. (10 miles south of Branson at Table Rock Lake), Ridgedale, MO 65739. © 800/225-6343 or 417/335-2777. Fax 417/335-2340. www.bigcedar.com. 247 units, 61 cottages and cabins. $159–$362 double; $189–$749 cottage/cabin. Children 11 and under stay free in parent's room. 3-night minimum stay holiday weekends. Off-season rates and packages available. AE, DC, DISC, MC, V. **Amenities:** 4 restaurants; 3 pools (1 indoor) and 2 children's pools; 9-hole golf course; 2 outdoor lighted tennis courts; health club; spa.

Grand Country Inn (Kids)   Families that want to be in the thick of 76 Country Boulevard's never-ending string of theaters, go-cart tracks, restaurants, shops, and motels will find this property to their liking. It includes **Splash Country Indoors,** a large indoor/outdoor waterpark free to hotel guests, as well as two buffet restaurants, a theater with a variety of music shows throughout the day, game arcade, and indoor minigolf. There's so much to do, most guests don't care that rooms are rather basic and ordinary, with free local telephone calls. To find it, look for the world's largest banjo.

Grand Country Sq., 1945 W. Hwy. 76, Branson, MO 65616. © **800/828-9068** or 417/335-3535. Fax 417/334-1647. www.grandcountry.com. 319 units. $80–$100 double. Children 17 and under stay free in parent's room. Packages available. AE, DC, DISC, MC, V. **Amenities:** 3 restaurants; 3 pools (1 indoor).

Hilton Promenade at Branson Landing

This is actually one of two Hilton properties at Branson Landing, both boasting downtown Branson's most posh accommodations. While the other Hilton with its large convention facilities attracts mostly business travelers, the Hilton Promenade at Branson Landing offers a cozier, boutique-hotel-like atmosphere, with one-bedroom condos complete with balconies and full kitchens in addition to well-appointed standard rooms. Many shops and restaurants are right outside hotel doors, and downtown is just a short walk away.

3 Branson Landing Blvd., Branson, MO 65616. © **800/HILTONS** (445-8667) or 417/336-5500. Fax 417/336-5513. www.promenadebransonlanding.hilton.com. 242 units. $179–$229 double; $279 condo. Children 17 and under stay free in parent's room. Valet parking $12; self-parking $8. AE, DC, DISC, MC, V. **Amenities:** Restaurant; indoor pool (access also to sister Hilton's outdoor pool); fitness room. *In room:* Fridge.

Indian Point Resorts (Value)

On a wooded point on Table Rock Lake 2¹/₂ miles from Silver Dollar City and 6 miles from Branson, this casual, low-key lakefront resort appeals mainly to families with its recreational facilities (playgrounds; volleyball and badminton; shuffleboard; game room; free paddle boats; and marina with rentals for fishing and ski boats, pontoons, and WaveRunners) and wide range of accommodations, all equipped with stocked kitchens and barbecue grills. These include comfortable, if rather standard, lodge units, ranging from one-room efficiencies for two people to four-bedroom units that sleep 18, free-standing cottages, and log cabins of various sizes with fireplaces and decks. Slightly more upscale condos offer the additional luxuries of laundry facilities, dishwashers, fireplaces, Jacuzzis, and decks overlooking the lake. An RV park is also here, with rental RVs.

Indian Point Rd., Branson, MO 65616. © **800/888-1891** or 417/338-2250. Fax 417/338-3507. www.indianpoint.com. 142 units, 32 cottages and cabins. $72–$112 double; $62–$102 cottages for 2 people; $95–$135 cabins for 2 people; $99–$169 condo double. Off-season rates and packages available. AE, DC, DISC, MC, V. **Amenities:** 3 heated outdoor pools (open Mar–Dec); 3 children's pools. *In room:* Kitchen.

WHERE TO DINE

In addition to the choices below, there are many restaurants in Branson Landing, including the **White River Fish House** (© **417/243-5100**), a floating restaurant offering sandwiches, steak, and seafood.

Branson Café (Value) AMERICAN

This casual, busy, friendly diner in downtown Branson—a real regulars' hangout—has been the place to go since 1910 for down-home country cooking, including hearty breakfasts, fried chicken, catfish, and sandwiches. Leave room for one of the famous pies.

120 W. Main St. © **417/334-3021.** Reservations accepted. Main courses $6–$12. MC, V. Sun–Fri 8am–3pm; Sat 8am–8pm.

BT Bones Steakhouse AMERICAN/STEAKS

Popular with an older crowd and also welcoming families, this dimly lit restaurant/bar is one of the few places offering free live country music nightly from 5pm. You can chow down on dinner as you listen, with choices ranging from sandwiches and wraps to steaks, prime rib, chicken, and barbecue ribs. There's also a children's menu and a cheaper lunch menu until 4pm.

2280 Shepherd of the Hills Expwy. (at Roark Valley Rd.). © **417/335-2002.** www.btbones.com. Reservations not accepted. Main courses $7.65–$29. AE, DISC, MC, V. Sun–Thurs 11am–10pm; Fri–Sat 11am–11pm.

Candlestick Inn (Best) STEAKS/SEAFOOD   On the other side of Lake Taneycomo, on a bluff with fine views over downtown Branson, this upscale restaurant with an outdoor deck is perfect for romantic dining or a special occasion. In business since 1962, it specializes in chateaubriand and fresh seafood like sautéed scallops, but other great choices include the Truite Provencal (trout cooked with garlic, onion, tomatoes, fresh peppers, mushrooms, and olive oil) and beef Wellington.

127 Taney St. (© **417/334-3633.** www.candlestickinn.com. Reservations recommended. Main courses $24–$39. AE, DISC, MC, V. Wed–Sat 5–9pm.

McFarlain's OZARK SPECIALTIES/AMERICAN   Its location in a commercial complex housing souvenir shops, a food court, and IMAX theater may not sound promising, but this antiques-filled restaurant garners high marks for its home-cooked food, with standouts including the Ozark Mountain Skillet for breakfast (eggs scrambled with ham, bacon, sausage, and cheese, topped with sausage gravy and served over hash browns), fried green tomatoes, honey corn bread, and Pioneer Pot Roast. For some good-natured fun, a few hydraulic-powered tables slowly rise to chin height, with everyone except those seated at the trick table in on the joke (you can also reserve one, to fool an unsuspecting table mate).

3562 Shepherd of the Hills Expwy. (© **417/336-4680.** Main courses $8–$15. AE, DC, DISC, MC, V. Sun–Thurs 7:30am–8:30pm; Fri–Sat 7:30am–9:15pm.

A SIDE TRIP TO EUREKA SPRINGS

Named one of America's Dozen Distinctive Destinations by the National Trust for Historic Preservation, **Eureka Springs** first drew interest because of its natural springs with purported healing powers. It was settled in the late 1800s as a spa destination, and today its entire downtown district is on the National Register of Historic Places. While baths and spa treatments are still available, the city is now nationally renowned for its art and well-preserved Victorian-era architecture. It's actually a charming Victorian hillside village with historic homes, winding roads, and antiques and crafts shops. For information, contact the **Eureka Springs Chamber of Commerce,** 137 W. Van Buren (© **866/566-9387;** www.eurekasprings.org). *Tip:* For more information on Arkansas, check out appendix A, "The Best of the Rest," on p. 1021.

GETTING THERE   Eureka Springs is a scenic drive across the Missouri border to Arkansas. From Branson, take U.S. 65 south 30 miles to Bear Creek Springs, then U.S. 62 west 37 miles to Route 23.

What to See & Do

Eureka Springs' biggest attraction is the **Great Passion Play,** U.S. 62 East (© **866/882-7529** or 479/253-9200; www.greatpassionplay.com), a religious extravaganza about the life of Jesus that takes place May to October in an outdoor theater with a cast of 250 people and live animals. Also offered are the New Holy Land Tour, a 2¹/₂-hour tour past 38 reproductions of structures referred to in the Bible, and the Museum of Earth History, which presents earth's history (and dinosaurs) from a biblical view.

Other attractions worth seeking out are the **Abundant Memories Heritage Village,** 2¹/₂ miles north of Branson at 2434 Hwy. 23 N. (© **479/253-6764;** www.abundant memories.com), with 25 village buildings packed with artifacts of yesteryear; and the **Eureka Springs and North Arkansas Railway,** 299 N. Main St. (© **479/253-9623;** www.esnarailway.com), a restored 1906 steam passenger train that takes a scenic route through the Ozark Hills.

The Northern Rockies & Great Plains

Welcome to Middle America, stretching from the grassy plains of Oklahoma and Nebraska to the wild mountains of the Rockies and the desolation of the Badlands. Montana, Wyoming, and South Dakota proudly stand with one cocksure foot rooted in their Wild West past and the other firmly fixed in a setting of unparalleled splendor and majesty. Whether you come to this region to play cowboy on a guest ranch or to stay in one of the classic lodges in the region's national parks, you'll experience firsthand nature's magnanimity: Yellowstone's wild abundance, the less traveled vastness of Glacier National Park, the towering peaks of the Grand Tetons, the eerie desolation of the Badlands. Few ski buffs have to be told twice about the allure of the mountains in Idaho's famous Sun Valley. Opt for the prairies and the grasslands of Nebraska and Oklahoma, and you'll be treated to loads of historical sites, top-flight museums, and scenic routes that are among the most storied in the nation. (Route 66, anyone?)

But that's not all. People come here to experience the area's back-to-basics way of life, an attitude that makes these states so endearing to visitors and enduring to residents. The residents of these states are self-reliant, hardy folks who are still America's pioneers. They like to fish with flies, hike with bears, and ride horses that buck. They've tried mining, logging, farming, and ranching, and still believe that no matter what they have to do to live here, the land here makes it all worthwhile.

Tip: For information on Iowa and North Dakota, two other states in the Great Plains, see "Appendix A: The Best of the Rest," on p. 1021.

1 FLATHEAD & MONTANA'S NORTHWEST CORNER

If it's mountains, lakes, and streams you've come for, you'll find them in northwestern Montana. The area, almost empty in the spring and fall, encompasses Flathead Lake, majestic Glacier National Park (see later in this chapter), and Missoula.

ESSENTIALS

GETTING THERE   A number of major airlines offer flights to the **Missoula International Airport** (© **406/728-4381;** www.flymissoula.com), northwest of downtown Missoula on U.S. 93.

I-90 leads into Missoula from the west (Washington State and Idaho) and the east (Billings and Bozeman). Two major roads will get you around this area: **U.S. 93** runs north to south (from the Bitterroot Valley south of Missoula to the state's nether regions), and **U.S. 2** runs east to west. **Mont. 200** follows the Clark Fork, Blackfoot, and Flathead rivers, and is one of the state's most scenic highways.

  The **Missoula Convention and Visitors Bureau,** 1121 E. Broadway, Ste. 103, Missoula, MT 59802 (© **800/526-3465** or 406/532-3250; www. missoulacvb.org), has brochures, city maps, and area maps for outdoor activities, shopping, dining, and tours for most of northwestern Montana.

MISSOULA

Missoula has been growing by leaps and bounds for a decade, and the reason is clear: The city is in a beautiful valley along the Clark Fork River, with a relatively mild climate more influenced by the Pacific Northwest than the high Rockies. You could say the same about the local culture.

Since this is the home of the University of Montana, the crowds in Missoula's vibrant downtown are more often young and Birkenstocked than grizzled and cowboy-booted. The **Fair Trade Store,** 519 S. Higgins Ave. (© 406/543-3955), is a project of the Jeannette Rankin Peace Resource Center, selling jewelry, clothing, and musical items from communities around the world. **Butterfly Herbs,** 232 N. Higgins Ave. (© **406/728-8780**), features an eclectic collection of items, including fresh herbs, jewelry, coffee mugs, teapots, and handmade paper and candles. If you begin to feel the bohemian spirit and suddenly want your own pair of Birkenstocks, just go next door to **Hide & Sole,** 236 N. Higgins Ave. (© **406/549-0666**), for reshodding.

Missoula is home to an impressive literary community, and the city's bookstores are among the state's best, including **Fact and Fiction,** 220 N. Higgins Ave. (© **406/721-2881**). Vintage, rare, and first-edition books are available from **Bird's Nest Books** at 219 N. Higgins Ave. (© **406/721-1125**).

The great outdoors—be it fly-fishing on Rock Creek, skiing at Snowbowl, hiking in the Selway-Bitterroot, or cross-country skiing on Lolo Pass—is probably what most attracts these types to the area. **Pipestone Mountaineering,** 129 W. Front St. (© **406/721-1670**), has an excellent range of outdoor gear for serious climbers, river runners, and campers. **The Trail Head,** 221 E. Front St. (© **406/543-6966;** www.trailheadmontana. net), is another good outdoors store, with gear for snowshoers, kayakers, and everybody in between. The outdoors figures heavily in Missoula-area politics as well. There is a strong pro-environment sentiment among the populace.

Where to Stay & Dine

You won't find a whole lot of lodging variety within Missoula's city limits. For a distinctive night's sleep, try roughing it in a historic cabin. Information on rental of **old-fashioned miner's cabins** at the ghost town of Garnet is available by contacting the **Garnet Preservation Association,** 3255 Fort Missoula Rd., Missoula, MT 59804 (© **406/329-3883;** www.garnetghosttown.net). The cabins are available for $30 to $40 a night from December through April, when they are typically accessible only on skis, snowshoes, or snowmobiles.

Among the list of mostly chain lodgings, there are a couple of standouts. The beautiful 1911 brick home known as **Goldsmith's Inn** (© **866/666-9945;** www.goldsmithsinn. com) is Missoula's only riverside B&B, right on the Clark Fork River just across from the University of Montana. The Goldsmith's fabulous ice cream is a Missoula favorite, and you can get some right next door at Goldsmith's Waterfront Pasta House. Rates from $89 to $139 double, including full breakfast. **Fort Lolo Hot Springs and Lolo Trail Center** (© **406/273-2201;** www.lolotrailcenter.com), 25 miles west of Lolo, provides a stunning resort setting for the rejuvenating powers of the hot springs. Doubles range from $79 to $139.

Thanks to the university and a relatively cultured populace, Missoula is blessed with an excellent variety of restaurants, ranging from organic vegetarian to full-blown carnivorous. In addition to perennial favorites like the **Red Bird** (© **406/549-2906**) and **Bernice's Bakery** (© **406/728-1358**), we suggest **Scotty's Table,** 529 S. Higgins Ave. (© **406/549-2790**), a chic, upscale bistro that uses organic and local ingredients in large part in its menu, which is the perfect balance of Montana and Mediterranean cuisine. Even if you don't eat at the **Oxford Cafe** (also known as the Ox) at 337 N. Higgins Ave. (© **406/549-0117;** www.the-oxford.com), you really should go in and look around. Established in 1883, this is a Missoula institution, adorned with beer signs, a long bar, a breakfast counter, a bison head, and an endless stream of eccentrics, cowboys, and bikers. It's open 24/7/365.

SIDE TRIPS FROM MISSOULA

Founded in the early 1850s by Jesuit priests, the town of **St. Ignatius** (32 miles north of Missoula on U.S. 93), nestled in the heart of the Mission Valley, has one of Montana's most prized architectural treasures, the **St. Ignatius Mission,** P.O. Box 667, St. Ignatius, MT 59865 (© **406/745-2768**). Established in 1854, the mission contains 58 unique murals by Brother Josephy Carignano on its walls and ceilings.

The **Ninepipe National Wildlife Refuge** (© 406/644-2211; www.fws.gov/bison range/ninepipe), just off U.S. 93 about 10 miles north of St. Ignatius, is home to a huge waterfowl population. Southwest off U.S. 93 on County Road 212 is the **National Bison Range** (www.fws.gov/bisonrange/nbr), a protected open range for buffalo, deer, bighorn sheep, and pronghorn located on reservation land.

FLATHEAD LAKE

This is one of the most beautiful areas in Montana. Towering peaks rise from the valley floor on the east, and the mountains of the Flathead National Forest define the edge of the valley to the west. This is a land of forests, cattle, and alfalfa—with a velvet-green valley floor, green and granite mountains, and, on a sunny day, a dramatic deep-blue ceiling.

This part of Montana seems to offer something for everyone, whether your interests lie indoors or out. There are watersports on the lake and hikes that lead to sparkling mountain streams with views. But if you want to shop or see a play, you can easily spend your day inside the boutiques, galleries, and theater of Bigfork.

With much of this area lying within tribal lands, there is also a long-standing American Indian heritage. The Confederated Salish and Kootenai Tribes make their home on the Flathead Indian Reservation, with tribal headquarters for the 1.2-million-acre reservation in Pablo.

Your best bet for information on the south end of the lake is the **Polson Chamber of Commerce,** 418 Main St., Polson, MT 59860 (© 406/883-5969; www.polsonchamber. com). For goings-on north, contact the **Bigfork Chamber of Commerce,** P.O. Box 237, Bigfork, MT 59911 (© 406/837-5888; www.bigfork.org). The **Flathead Convention and Visitor Bureau** (© 406/756-9091; www.fcvb.org), **Travel Montana** (© 800/847-4868), and **Glacier Country** (© 800/338-5072; www.glaciermt.com) can supplement this information.

The Flathead is one of those rare places where you see the serious golfer and the serious backpacker in the same spot, sometimes in the same body. The golfing is excellent on several courses, and the backpacking, hiking, and fishing are even better. Fishing, boating, and "yachting" are popular sports for those who can afford to practice them. If your plans take you to one of the lakes or trails on the Salish-Kootenai Reservation, don't forget to buy a tribal permit.

Boat rentals are available at the **Bigfork Marina and Boat Center** (© 406/837-5556), **Kwa Taq Nuk Resort** (© 800/882-6363), **Bayview Resort and Marina** (© 406/837-4843), and **Marina Cay Resort** (© 406/837-5861).

Fishing the southern half of Flathead Lake requires a Salish-Kootenai tribal permit, which you can purchase at stores in Polson or at the tribal headquarters in Pablo. The brochure *Fishing the Flathead* is available from the **Flathead Convention and Visitor Bureau** (© 406/756-9091). It provides information on 14 different fishing opportunities, as well as an outline of the licensing and catch-and-release regulations. This brochure includes information on Whitefish, Flathead, and Swan lakes, and several lesser-known lakes. To increase your odds of snagging something besides a log, contact **Glacier Fishing Charters** (© 406/892-2377). Also, "Shorty" George's **A-Able Fishing** (© 800/231-5214 or 406/257-5214; www.aablefishing.com) will outfit a fishing trip with guides who know the area.

Eagle Bend Golf Club (© 406/837-7300; www.golfmt.com), a challenging Jack Nicklaus–designed track with views of Flathead Lake and the surrounding mountains, is in Bigfork just off the highway on Holt Drive. The 18-hole course is only 6,300 yards from the white tees, but it's harder than Chinese arithmetic. Greens fees range from $50 **561** to $85 for 18 holes.

Hikers, welcome to bear country. With a little effort, avoiding grizzly confrontations is as easy as making noise and being watchful. Like your mama said, don't surprise them and they won't surprise you. Besides strolling by the lake at one of the marinas or state parks, the best bet for trekking is in the **Jewel Basin,** a designated hiking area north of Bigfork. More than 30 miles of trails make it a great place for day hiking as well as overnights.

Where to Stay & Dine

There are five campgrounds in **Flathead Lake state parks,** each located at a different point around the lake: Big Arm (© 406/849-5255) and West Shore (© 406/844-3066) on the west side of the lake; and Finley Point (© 406/887-2715), Yellow Bay (© 406/752-5501), and Wayfarers (© 406/837-4196) on the east shore. The phone numbers are operational only in summer. You can also call © 406/752-5501 for information on any of these state park campgrounds, which are open May through September and charge $15 per night.

Accommodations on and near the lake include guest ranches, water-oriented resorts with the gamut of recreational opportunities, and basic motels that offer clean but modest rooms. For an all-around vacation experience, **Averill's Flathead Lake Lodge,** P.O. Box 248, Bigfork, MT 59911 (© 406/837-4397; www.averills.com), is the best on the lake. A beautiful log lodge surrounded by thousands of acres of forest serves as your home base for all activities, which include horseback riding, boating, and fishing. Rates start at $3,143 per adult per week.

Tucked away on 10 acres of pine forest at the foot of the Swan Mountains, the **Candlewycke Inn,** 311 Aero Lane, Bigfork, MT 59911 (© 888/617-8805 or 406/837-6406; www.candlewyckeinn.com), is a luxurious modern home that innkeepers Megan and Steve Ward converted into a first-rate inn. There's a trail system on the property, an immaculate lawn, and all sorts of little touches (such as antlers converted to back scratchers). The breakfasts are tailored to the tastes of guests. Rates from $135 to $185 double, including full breakfast.

La Provence, 408 Bridge St., Bigfork (© 406/837-2923; www.bigforklaprovence.com), is one of the best restaurants in the area, serving French-Mediterranean cuisine. In Somers, the locals like **Tiebuckers Pub and Eatery,** 75 Somers Rd. (© 406/857-3335), for the fresh fish and steamed clams, but they also offer beef, pasta, chicken, and ribs.

WHITEFISH: A GATEWAY TO GLACIER

Whitefish has boomed as a resort community, attracting people from all over the country and making it Montana's fastest-growing area. Longtime residents have feared it will become another Aspen or Jackson Hole, but that hasn't quite happened yet. In fact, Whitefish is still relatively sedate.

Whitefish is almost two different towns—the town itself and the Big Mountain ski area. The busy season in town is the summer, and room rates are higher there during warm weather. This may seem odd for a ski town, but Glacier National Park attracts about 2 million visitors a year, while the ski area brings in only about 300,000.

Up on the mountain, however, the peak season is winter, especially during Christmas vacation. So if you don't mind the winding 5-mile drive up (or down) the Big Mountain road, you can find slightly less expensive accommodations in the appropriate season.

Whitefish is extremely accessible. It's easier to get to than virtually any other Montana vacation town. It's a quick drive up U.S. 93 from Kalispell.

The **Whitefish Chamber of Commerce** is at 520 E. 2nd St. (© **877/862-3548** or 406/862-3501; www.whitefishchamber.com). Here you'll find just about everything you need in the way of brochures, area maps, and travel information.

Whitefish is a paradise for outdoors enthusiasts, with ski slopes, hiking trails, watersports opportunities, and Glacier National Park down the road. For outdoor equipment or apparel, check out **Sportsman & Ski Haus** at the Mountain Mall (© **406/862-3111**) or **Mountain Sports Cycle and Ski,** 242 Central Ave. (© **406/863-9022**). The **Wave,** 1250 Baker Ave. (© **406/862-2444;** www.whitefishwave.com), is a first-rate new aquatic-and-fitness facility, with several pools, weight machines and free weights, massage therapists, and much more.

Just 12 miles north of Whitefish is one of the best-kept ski resort secrets in the country. **Whitefish Mountain Resort** (© **800/858-5439** or 406/862-2900; www.ski whitefish.com) offers lots of powder, lots of skiing in the trees, and plenty of runs for every level of skier. With an annual snowfall of 300 inches, lower night-skiing rates (Fri– Sat mid-Dec to mid-Mar), a vertical drop of 2,500 feet, and virtually no lines, the Big Mountain is one of the best resorts in the northwestern United States. More than half the mountain is geared to the intermediate skier, but there is plenty of terrain for experts and beginners. The expert runs are pretty steep. There are never any crowds, even in the holiday seasons, so although the prices have gone up over the years, at least you can spend your time skiing rather than waiting in lift lines.

During the summer months, bikes are nearly as prevalent as cars in the north part of the Flathead Valley. Another Whitefish operation shares the expertise for mountain bikers seeking adventure on seemingly undiscovered paths. **Glacier Cyclery and Fitness,** 326 E. 2nd St. (© **406/862-6446**), provides excellent service and maintenance, as well as rentals, area maps, and up-to-date information for the serious mountain biker. This outfit has been ranked among the 100 best cycle shops in a pool of 6,800 independent dealers. For a less challenging ride, you can make the 20-mile round-trip on paved roads from downtown Whitefish to the head of Whitefish Lake.

It's not the Madison Valley, but Whitefish does have some hot spots for anglers wanting to try their hand. **Tally Lake** is a deep hole located north of Whitefish off U.S. 93. Five miles north of town, turn left onto the Tally Lake Road (signs will direct you). You can expect cutthroat, rainbow, kokanee, brook trout, and whitefish. In town, across the viaduct toward the Big Mountain, lies **Whitefish Lake.** If you can handle all the recreationists hovering about like flies, the lake offers some pretty good lake trout. Northern pike can be found here, and rainbow and cutthroat can be nabbed on dry flies in the evening. The **Lakestream Flyshop,** 334 Central Ave. (© **406/862-1298;** www.lakestream.com), is the best resource in town for information about fly-fishing the Flathead River and local streams.

The **Whitefish Lake Golf Club,** U.S. 93 North (© **406/862-4000;** www.golfwhite fish.com), is the only 36-hole golf course in the state. Built in the 1930s, the golf club's trees have grown up considerably in the time since. While not especially long, the course offers a wide variety of shots that will require you to use all the clubs in your bag (and maybe some you forgot). Almost all the fairways are lined with trees. There are few fairway bunkers, but they are strategically placed around the greens. Both 18-hole setups measure a little more than 6,500 yards from the tips. There is also a driving range and putting green. Greens fees are $25 to $46.

Where to Stay & Dine

Whitefish might have the best range of accommodations in Montana, with everything from mom-and-pop motels to graceful inns to slope-side condos. There's a **Super 8,** 800

Spokane Ave. (© **800/800-8000** or 406/862-8255), with doubles for $65 to $100 nightly. The **Pine Lodge,** 920 Spokane Ave. (© **800/305-7463** or 406/862-7600; www. thepinelodge.com), is a good independent option, with doubles for $140 to $225 in the summer.

While it's right on the main Whitefish drag, the **Garden Wall Inn,** 504 Spokane Ave. (© **888/530-1700** or 406/862-3440; www.gardenwallinn.com), is a world of its own. The owners clearly take pride in providing all of the little luxurious extras. Every detail is just about perfect, right down to the towels, which are large and fluffy enough to dry two adults. Rates from $135 to $185 double, including full breakfast.

Grouse Mountain Lodge, 2 Fairway Dr., Whitefish (© **800/321-8822** or 406/862-3000; www.grousemountainlodge.com), is one of Montana's premier vacation lodge properties, with a variety of rooms from standard hotel-like rooms—called the executive rooms—to loft rooms with kitchens. The lodge has two outdoor Jacuzzis and three places to eat: a casual grill, an outdoor patio, and the fine-dining **Wine Room.** Rates from **$205** to $235 double.

The **Lodge at Whitefish Lake,** 1399 Wisconsin Ave. (© **800/735-8869**), opened in late 2006 after several years of delays. The wait was worth it: It's the ritziest lakeside resort in Whitefish. Rates from $220 to $285 double.

The Big Mountain provides a wide variety of accommodations to fit almost every budget. You can reach a **central reservations line** that books a number of local lodgings at © **800/858-5439.**

A good cup of organic coffee and baked goods are available at the **Montana Coffee Traders,** located at 110 Central Ave. (© **406/862-7667**), which also houses a nifty used bookstore and a nice place to sprawl on a couch and read a book. **Loula's Café,** located downstairs at 300 E. 2nd St. (© **406/862-5614**), serves traditional American breakfasts and salads and sandwiches for lunch in an attractive setting. The **Buffalo Cafe,** 514 3rd St. (© **406/862-2833**), is Whitefish's best breakfast spot—try their legendary bacon-and-egg-filled pies. And for plump subs, try **Quickee,** 28 Lupfer Ave. (© **406/862-9866**)—just look for the house with the gas pump above the door.

If it's a dressy night out that you're after, the **Whitefish Lake Restaurant,** U.S. 93 North at the Whitefish Golf Club (© **406/862-5285**), is known as "the best restaurant in the state" to many locals. The **Red Caboose,** 101 Central Ave. (© **406/863-4563**; www.redcaboosediner.com), is a new eatery that caters to rail travelers with its always-open hours and railroad-themed decor. The menu offers a creative spin on traditional diner fare. **Cafe Kandahar,** 3824 Big Mountain Rd. (© **406/862-6247**) has emerged as a dining standout under the direction of Chef Andy Blanton. Inspired by French and Creole traditions but willing to experiment, Blanton uses as much local produce and meats as he can in such creations as seared elk roulade with forest mushrooms.

2 GLACIER NATIONAL PARK

ESSENTIALS

GETTING THERE   The closest cities to the park with airline service are **Kalispell,** 29 miles southwest of the park; **Missoula,** 150 miles south; and **Great Falls,** 143 miles southeast. If you're driving, you can reach the park from U.S. highways 2 and 89. **Amtrak's Empire Builder** (© **800/872-7245;** www.amtrak.com), a Chicago-Seattle round-trip route, makes daily stops at West Glacier and Essex year-round and East Glacier from May 1 to October 1.

ACCESS/ENTRY POINTS   There are six paved entrances that provide vehicular access to Glacier National Park, but if you are traveling by car, you will most likely use **West Glacier** and **St. Mary.** These entrances are located at either end of Going-to-the-Sun Road, with West Glacier on the southwest side and St. Mary on the east. Visitor entrances passes are sold only at these two entrances. The four other entrances are Camas Creek and Polebridge on the west, and Many Glacier and Two Medicine on the east. *Caution:* Entrance to the park is severely restricted during winter months when the Alpine section of Going-to-the-Sun Road is closed.

VISITOR INFORMATION   For information about the park before your trip, contact **Glacier National Park,** West Glacier, MT 59936 (© **406/888-7800;** www.nps.gov/glac). For up-to-date information on park activities once you arrive, check in at visitor centers located at **Apgar** (open May–Oct and weekends during the winter), **Logan Pass** (open mid-June to late Sept), and **St. Mary** (from mid-May to mid-Oct). Park information may also be obtained from the **Many Glacier Ranger Station** or park headquarters in **West Glacier.**

FEES   Admission to the park for up to 7 days costs $25 per vehicle, $20 per motorcycle, or $12 per person for those on foot, bicycles, and motorcycles ($10 in winter). A season pass costs $30 and allows unlimited entry to Glacier National Park for 1 year. The America the Beautiful interagency passes are also honored. A separate entrance fee is charged for visitors to Waterton Lakes National Park.

SEASONS   In winter, Glacier shuts itself off from the motorized world: Even snowmobiles are forbidden. All unplowed roads—and very little is plowed—become trails for snowshoers and cross-country skiers, who rave about the vast powdered wonderland. Guided trips into the backcountry are a great way to experience the park in winter.

TOURS   From mid-June to mid-September, **Glacier Park Boat Company,** P.O. Box 5262, Kalispell, MT 59903 (© **406/257-2426;** www.glacierparkboats.com), offers daily **narrated boat tours,** often including hikes and picnics, from Lake McDonald, St. Mary, Two Medicine, and Many Glacier. Fees run no more than $17, and kids 4 to 12 are half-price.

GOING-TO-THE-SUN ROAD

One of the most important Glacier things to do is to drive **Going-to-the-Sun Road,** the 50-mile road that bisects the park between West Glacier and St. Mary. Points of interest are clearly marked along this road and correspond to the park brochure, which is available at visitor centers. Bring plenty of film.

A 2006 thunderstorm washed out a chunk of the road, which is in the midst of a multidecade restoration project. The washout was replaced by a temporary bridge. However, expect to see some delays, late openings, and early closures in coming years.

The road gains more than 3,400 feet in 32 miles and is very narrow in places. Visitors with a fear of heights should take a van tour or shuttle. Because of the road's narrowness, oversize vehicles and trailers must use U.S. 2.

As you begin the drive from the West Glacier entrance, you'll pass the largest of the 653 lakes in Glacier—**Lake McDonald.** Numerous turnouts along the way present opportunities to photograph the panoramic views of the lake with its mountainous backdrop. You can see **Sacred Dancing Cascade** and **Johns Lake** after an easy, half-mile hike from the roadside through a hemlock and red cedar forest. The trail head for this hike is 2 miles north of the Lake McDonald Lodge along Going-to-the-Sun Road.

The **Trail of the Cedars** is a short, wheelchair-accessible boardwalk trail through terrain thickly carpeted in vibrant, verdant hues. This is also the beginning of the Avalanche Lake Trail, a 2.1-mile hike (one-way) to the foot of Avalanche Lake, one of the most popular day hikes in the park. The trail head is about 5^1/$_2$ miles north of Lake McDonald Lodge, just past the Avalanche Creek Campground.

Almost exactly halfway along Going-to-the-Sun is the overlook for Heaven's Peak, the snow-covered mountain to the south that you've just driven around. This is also the jumping-off point for the **Loop Trail,** which can take you to the Granite Park Chalet. Just 2 miles farther is the **Bird Woman Falls Overlook.** Bird Woman Falls drops in a bounty of water from a hanging valley above the road. Next along the road is the oft-photographed **Weeping Wall,** which is a wall of rock with water pouring forth.

At the 32-mile mark from West Glacier is **Logan Pass,** one of the park's busiest areas and the starting point for the hike to **Hidden Lake,** likely the park's most popular trail. There's a visitor center here atop the Continental Divide, with a bookstore and a small display about the wildlife, flora, and geology of the area.

As you continue the drive downhill, you'll reach the turnout for **Jackson Glacier,** the most recognizable glacier in the entire park, followed by **Sunrift Gorge** and **Sun Point,** which are accessible via two short trails rife with wildlife.

Outdoor Activities

FISHING   Glacier's streams and lakes are habitat for whitefish, kokanee salmon, arctic grayling, and five kinds of trout. Try the North Fork of the Flathead to fish for cutthroat and bull trout, and any of the park's three larger lakes (Bowman, St. Mary, and McDonald) for rainbow, brook trout, and whitefish. State of Montana fishing licenses are generally not required within the park's boundaries, although you will need one on the North Fork and Middle Fork of the Flathead River. Also, keep in mind that since the eastern boundary of the park abuts the Blackfeet Indian Reservation, you may find yourself fishing in their territorial waters. To avoid a problem, purchase a $10 use permit from businesses in the gateway towns; the permit covers fishing, hiking, and biking in the reservation. Fishing outside the park in Montana waters requires a state license; check in at a local fishing shop to make certain you're within the law.

HIKING   Glacier is a park that is best seen on foot. Its 1,600 square miles have more than 150 trails, totaling more than 750 miles. You can hike more than 100 miles along the Continental Divide alone. **Trail maps** are available at outdoor stores in Whitefish and Kalispell, as well as at the visitor centers and ranger stations in the park. Before heading off, however, check with the nearest ranger station to determine the accessibility of your destination, trail conditions, and recent bear sightings.

Among the park's shorter and easier trails is the **Trail of the Cedars Nature Trail** (.25 mile round-trip; access is across from the Avalanche Campground Ranger Station), an easy, level trail that's wheelchair accessible. It has interpretive signs along the way. The **Hidden Lake Nature Trail** (3 miles round-trip; accessed from the Logan Pass Visitor Center) is an easy-to-moderate interpretive trail that climbs 460 feet to an overlook of Hidden Lake. It's a popular trail, but by hiking all the way to the overlook, you'll avoid some of the crowds, and you might even see a mountain goat.

The **Loop** (8 miles round-trip; access is on Going-to-the-Sun Rd., about halfway btw. Avalanche Campground and Logan Pass Visitor Center) offers a moderate hike that climbs to Granite Park Chalet and back. Many people use it as a continuation of the Highline Trail, but this is the section to do if you're not quite so adventurous (the Highline Trail is almost 8 miles long). If you want to spend the night in the chalet, contact **Belton Chalets** for reservations (© 888/345-2649).

The easy **Running Eagle Falls Trail** (.6 mile round-trip; access is 1 mile west of the Two Medicine entrance) winds through a heavily forested area to a large, noisy waterfall. The popular **Twin Falls Trail** (7.6 miles round-trip; accessed from Two Medicine Campground) is an easy hike to Twin Falls. Hikers can walk the entire distance on a clearly identified trail, or boat across Two Medicine Lake to the foot of the trail head and hike the last mile. The **St. Mary Falls Trail** (1.6 miles round-trip; accessed from Jackson Glacier Overlook) is a fairly easy walk that takes you to rushing falls of the St. Mary River. The roar of the cascade is prodigious and satisfying.

HORSEBACK RIDING **Swan Mountain Outfitters** (© 406/888-5121 or 732-4203; www.swanmountainoutfitters.com) provides horseback riding at Lake McDonald, Apgar Village, and Many Glacier. The company offers hourly ($32) and full-day rides ($135) into the nearby wilderness.

RAFTING **Glacier Raft Company,** P.O. Box 210, West Glacier, MT 59936 (© 800/235-6781 or 406/888-5454; www.glacierraftco.com), is Montana's oldest raft company. Offerings include half-day trips ($44 per person), full-day excursions ($76 per person), 2-day trips ($315 per person), and 3-day outings ($435 per person). Prices include all equipment and food. The company also offers scenic trips, inflatable-kayak rentals, and a number of other services.

WHERE TO CAMP & STAY

There are a variety of camping opportunities. Campgrounds accessible by paved roads include **Apgar,** near the West Glacier entrance; **Avalanche Creek,** just up from the head of Lake McDonald; **Fish Creek,** on the west side of Lake McDonald; **Many Glacier,** in the northeast part of the park; **Rising Sun,** on the north side of St. Mary Lake; **St. Mary,** on the east side of the park; and **Two Medicine,** in the southeast part of the park near East Glacier. **Sprague Creek,** near the West Glacier entrance, offers a paved road but does not allow towed vehicles. There are also five campgrounds accessed by narrow dirt roads. Though utility connections are not provided at these sites, fireplaces, picnic tables, washrooms (with sinks and flush toilets), and cold running water are at each campground. Campsites are available on a first-come, first-served basis, payable by cash or check, except for Fish Creek and St. Mary campgrounds, where sites can be reserved by credit card through the **National Park Service Reservation System** (© 877/444-6777; www.recreation.gov).

Glacier Park Inc. (GPI), P.O. Box 2025, Columbia Falls, MT 59912 (© 406/892-2525; fax 406/892-1375; www.glacierparkinc.com), operates the hostelries in Glacier National Park. **Lake McDonald Lodge, Glacier Park Lodge,** and **Many Glacier Hotel** are first-tier properties that have been popular destinations since early in the 20th century. **Swiftcurrent Motor Inn** is typical of the casual motel-style properties at the other end of the spectrum, providing decent but undistinguished accommodations for less money. Although the lodges have a considerable charm, they don't have spas, air-conditioning, or in-room televisions. Reserve well in advance.

Originally housing railway workers, the historic, moderately priced **Izaak Walton Inn,** 290 Izaak Walton Inn Rd., Essex, MT (© 406/888-5700; www.izaakwaltoninn. com), maintains a railroad ambience. Situated at the end of Going-to-the-Sun Road, **St.**

motel-style units with two single beds or a queen-size, but the nicest units are the cabins, with living areas, kitchenettes, and separate sleeping areas. The **Vista Motel** in West Glacier (© **406/888-5311**) boasts tremendous views of the mountains.

3 BOZEMAN & SOUTH-CENTRAL MONTANA

Relatively unspoiled, yet one of the most heavily touristed areas in the state, south-central Montana is a world-class playground for the outdoor recreational enthusiast. Its biggest draws are the surrounding mountains that are a haven for hikers and campers, and, without a doubt, the fly-fishing waters of the four major rivers that flow through its valleys (the Madison, Jefferson, Gallatin, and Yellowstone), all of which double as recreation areas for rafting, kayaking, and canoeing.

Bozeman, home of Montana State University, provides the hip, intellectual charm and culture of a college town—good bookstores and restaurants, charming shops—as well as cultural events that appeal to both the cosmopolitan and cowboy cultures.

BOZEMAN

A college town and tourism hot spot with a friendly, semi-bohemian vibe, Bozeman was first settled in the 1860s as a ranching hub. Today its cowboy edge has been mostly chipped away, revealing a sophisticated Western chic. The vibrant downtown strip is filled with independent shops and restaurants. The area bustles year-round—whatever the season, the locals always seem to be out and about.

Bozeman has experienced its greatest growth since 1990, and it shows little sign of slacking off. (In fact, longtime residents worry that the town may be getting a little too hip.) The city probably has more nice restaurants per capita than any other town in Montana. The university is a good one, and the students gravitate here for the excellent downhill skiing at nearby Bridger Bowl. The fact that Bozeman is less than 100 miles from Yellowstone National Park certainly hasn't hurt its popularity, either.

Essentials

GETTING THERE Bozeman's **Gallatin Field Airport** (© 406/388-8321; www.gallatin field.com) serves a wide region in this part of the state. Daily service is available from **Delta** (© 800/221-1212), **Northwest** (© 800/225-2525), **Alaska/Horizon** (© 800/547-9308), and **United Express** (© 800/864-8331); **Big Sky Airlines** (© 800/237-7788) offers seasonal service.

By car, **Interstate 90** handles most of the traffic. It is 140 miles along I-90 from Billings to the east and 202 miles from Missoula to the west.

VISITOR INFORMATION The **Bozeman Area Chamber of Commerce** is at 2000 Commerce Way (© 800/228-4224 or 406/586-5421; www.bozemanchamber.com). There's also information from Memorial Day to Labor Day at 1001 N. 7th Ave., and year-round at the **Downtown Bozeman Visitor Center** (© 406/586-4008; www.historic bozeman.com), at 224 E. Main. The chamber publishes an extensive visitors guide.

What to See & Do

Many of the outdoor activities discussed in this section take place in the **Gallatin National Forest.** For additional information, including current road and trail conditions,

THE NORTHERN ROCKIES & GREAT PLAINS

8

BOZEMAN & SOUTH-CENTRAL MONTANA

contact the Bozeman Ranger District, 3710 Fallon St., Ste. C, Bozeman, MT 59718 (© **406/522-2520** or 587-6701; www.fs.fed.us/r1/gallatin).

Ski enthusiasts will find **Bridger Bowl** 16 miles north of town, on Mont. 86 (15795 Bridger Canyon Rd., Bozeman; © **800/223-9609** or 406/587-2111; www.bridgerbowl. com). Although not as steep as Teton Village in Jackson Hole, Bridger Bowl is plenty steep for most of us. With 20 feet of snowfall annually, Bridger sees a lot of powder days. It's usually open from the second Friday in December to mid-April daily from 9am to 4pm. Oh, and there are seldom any lift lines.

The **River's Edge,** 2012 N. 7th Ave. (© **406/586-5373;** www.theriversedge.com), is a highly professional fly-fishing specialty shop "in the heart of Montana's blue-ribbon trout streams." They offer guided fishing trips year-round—including float fishing and walking or wading trips, plus equipment rental and shuttle service. Two outfitters offer anglers memorable, albeit expensive, **fly-fishing** outings. A full-line Orvis shop, **Montana Troutfitters,** 1716 W. Main St. (© **800/646-7847** or 406/587-4707; www. troutfitters.com), has been operating guide services since 1978. The **Bozeman Angler,** 23 E. Main St. (© **800/886-9111** or 406/587-9111; www.bozemanangler.com), provides guided trips in the Madison, Gallatin, Yellowstone, Jefferson, and Missouri rivers plus numerous creeks, reservoirs, and lakes. Anglers can choose float trips in hard-sided drift boats, walk and wade, or backcountry fishing trips. From all three, full-day guided trips typically run $350 to $450 for two people, a price that includes lunch.

There's a beautiful and popular hiking area near Bozeman, known as the **Hyalite drainage,** in the Gallatin National Forest. The area includes Hyalite Canyon and reservoir, Palisades Falls Trail, and many trail heads for access to the national forest. A lot of the trails here are steep and difficult, though. An excellent introductory hike to get the lay of the land is the half-mile **Palisades Falls National Recreational Trail.**

Hyalite Reservoir is a wonderful place to hike, scale small peaks, and take in some of the Bozeman area's scenic wealth. The **Grotto Falls Trail** is a "difficult" 1.25-mile graveled trail to Grotto Falls located 13 miles up the West Fork Road in Hyalite Canyon. For a longer hike, go the 7.25 miles up the **Hyalite Peak Trail** to the peak. There is a 3,300-foot elevation gain on this hike.

As well as being a center for outdoor activities, Bozeman offers a surprising number of indoor education experiences for the whole family. The unique **American Computer Museum,** 2304 N. 7th Ave., Ste. B, in the Bridger Park Mall (© **406/582-1288;** www. compuseum.org), traces the history of computing technologies from the abacus to the Apple. Admission is $4 adults, $2 children. The **Emerson Center for the Arts and Culture,** 111 S. Grand Ave. (© **406/587-9797;** www.theemerson.org), is the home base for Bozeman's art scene, with gallery space and studios for more than 80 artists. Admission is free. The **Gallatin County Pioneer Museum,** 317 W. Main St. (© **406/522-8122;** www. pioneermuseum.org), gives an excellent perspective on early pioneer life in Montana, from its home in an old jail building—a murderer was hanged here in 1924—to the authentic homestead cabin on the premises. Admission is $3 adults, free for 12 and under.

The **Museum of the Rockies,** 600 W. Kagy Blvd. (© **406/994-2251;** www.museum oftherockies.org), on the campus of Montana State University, underwent a makeover from 2005 to 2007 that made the facility one of the best dinosaur museums in the country, with cutting-edge exhibits in the **Hall of Horns and Teeth,** the **Mesozoic Media Center,** and the **Hall of Giants,** populated with realistic life-size dinosaur models. Also on the premises is the **Taylor Planetarium,** a state-of-the-art, 40-foot domed multimedia theater.

Main Street offers an Old West feel and New West selection, starting at about 7th Avenue and running out to I-90. Among our favorite stops here are **Vargo's Jazz City and Books,** 6 W. Main (© **406/587-5383**), which sells an eclectic mass of new, used, and out-of-print books, CDs, and LPs (or the elusive, vanishing vinyl); **Schnee's Powder Horn Outfitters,** 35 E. Main St. (© **406/587-7373**), which sells high-end Western wear and all sorts of outdoor gear; the **Montana Gift Corral,** 237 E. Main (© **406/585-8625**), which offers a wide selection of made-in-Montana gifts, in case you need a moose clock to take home; **Thomas Nygard Gallery,** 135 E. Main (© **406/586-3636**), which specializes in pre-1950 artwork from the Northern Plains; and the **Country Bookshelf,** 28 W. Main (© **406/587-0166**), a terrific bookstore.

Where to Stay & Dine

Bozeman has a full complement of chain motels, most just off I-90. In addition to the places listed below, you can stay at the **Best Western GranTree Inn,** 1325 N. 7th Ave., Bozeman, MT 59715 (© **800/624-5865** or 406/587-5261); the **Fairfield Inn,** 828 Wheat Dr., Bozeman, MT 59715 (© **406/587-2222**); and the **Hampton Inn,** 75 Baxter Lane, Bozeman, MT 59715 (© **406/522-8000**). The above are all at I-90 exit 306 and have rates for two in the $80-to-$140 range. Newer is the **Hilton Garden Inn,** 2023 Commerce Way (© **877/782-9444** or 406/582-9900), south of I-90, exit 305, with double rates of $99 to $169.

In addition, consider checking out **Lehrkind Mansion,** 719 N. Wallace Ave. (© **800/992-6932** or 406/585-6932; www.bozemanbedandbreakfast.com), the former home of Julius Lehrkind, a Swiss-born brewer who wanted to live next door to his brewery. Ninety-nine years later, the 1897 Queen Anne mansion was turned into a bed-and-breakfast by former national park rangers, who have done a remarkable job of capturing the house in 1890s amber: Everything, from the rare 1897 Regina music box in the parlor to the many original fixtures in the bathrooms to the amazingly preserved original carpet in the Muir Room, is from Lehrkind's day—with the exception of the hot tub out back. Rates from $129 to $169 double, including full breakfast.

A popular local favorite is **John Bozeman's Bistro,** 125 W. Main St. (© **406/587-4100**), with buffalo, beef, and chicken plus vegetarian dishes. Beyond these restaurants, we're firm believers in the restorative powers of the breakfast burritos at **Soby's,** in the Bozeman Hotel at 321 E. Main St. (© **406/587-8857**), a favorite student haunt for breakfast and lunch. For a burger and a beer on an outdoor deck, you can't beat the **Garage,** 451 E. Main St. (© **406/585-8558**). In the winter, the town compensates for the cold weather with the **Soup Shack,** serving seven hot soups and an array of toppings, from a space that houses the ice-cream-oriented **Scoop Shack** in summer. **Over the Tapas,** 19 S. Willson Ave. (© **406/556-8282**), is a new entry on the scene, a tapas bar with a good midpriced menu. For a great cheap lunch, head to **La Tinga,** 12 E. Main St. (no phone) for terrific (and very spicy) Mexican fare.

THE MADISON RIVER VALLEY

The Madison Valley is an almost mythical place surrounded by spectacular mountain scenery where anglers from all over gather to fish. The main attraction is the Madison River, which flows through the valley at the base of the Madison Range, a stretch of peaks that runs toward Yellowstone Park.

Besides the phenomenal fishing, the Madison Valley has tourist-worthy historical sites. The **Missouri Headwaters State Park** is at the confluence of the Jefferson, Madison, and Gallatin rivers, where Lewis and Clark paused to take shelter; **Lewis and Clark Caverns** with its spectacular underground peaks, is just up the road; and **Madison Buffalo Jump State Park** is nearby.

Contact the **Three Forks Chamber of Commerce,** P.O. Box 1103, Three Forks, MT 59752 (© **406/285-4753;** www.threeforksmontana.com), or the **Ennis Chamber of Commerce,** P.O. Box 291, Ennis, MT 59729 (© **406/682-4388;** www.ennischamber. com). **Yellowstone Country** (© **800/736-5276;** www.yellowstonecountry.net) is the Travel Montana tourism office for the region.

World-Class Fishing

There is plenty of fishing water along the road from Three Forks to Quake and Hebgen lakes along U.S. 287. The first fishing access is **Cobblestone,** just a few miles south of Three Forks on the right side of U.S. 287. If you plan to base yourself in Ennis, the **Valley Garden, Ennis Bridge, Burnt Tree,** and **Varney Bridge** fishing accesses are within minutes of town along U.S. 287. Between Ennis and Quake Lake, the accesses begin popping up frequently. **McAtee Bridge, Wolf Creek, West Fork,** and **Reynolds Pass** are all accessible from the roadside. Hebgen Lake, just south of the dam, and Quake Lake are also great fishing spots.

On Ennis's Main Street, it seems that every second door houses a fly-fishing outfitter. The **Madison River Fishing Company,** 109 Main St. (© **800/227-7127** or 406/682-4293; www.mrfc.com), has a good stock of fishing supplies and a guide service. Guided trips, for one or two people, cost $275 for a half-day and $375 for a full day; full-day trips include lunch. They also offer a free brochure that contains a map of fishing spots and various facilities along the way. Other guide services, with similar rates, include **Clark's Guide Service** (© **406/682-7474**); **Howard Outfitters** (© **406/682-4834**); and the **Tackle Shop Outfitters,** 127 Main St. (© **800/808-2832** or 406/682-4263; www.thetackleshop.com).

What to See & Do

The lovely limestone **Lewis & Clark Caverns,** located 19 miles west of Three Forks (midway btw. Butte and Bozeman) on Mont. 2 (© **406/287-3541;** www.fwp.state. mt.us), are named for the famous explorers, but there is no evidence that their party ever saw or visited them. Discovered in the late 19th century, these caverns are a succession of vaulted chambers and passageways, thickly decorated with stalactites and stalagmites, as well as other underground formations such as massive, gleaming organ pipes; silky, delicate soda straws; intricate filigrees; and weirdly hung draperies. Plan at least 2 hours for the 2-mile guided tour through the caverns, and aboveground there are hiking trails, several picnic areas, and a large campground. A Christmas candlelight tour is held on 2 weekends in December. Reservations should be made in early December for one of the 200 or so spots available. There are three cabins on the premises with electric heat; rates are $40 in summer.

You can easily spend an hour exploring the interpretive signage at **Missouri Headwaters State Park,** 4 miles northeast of Three Forks (© **406/994-4042;** www.fwp.state. mt.us). Begin by following the Missouri River out from Three Forks. The headwaters themselves are no great shakes—just another river—but the sunsets from the bank of the river are breathtaking. From the headwaters, drive back toward Three Forks, where, on the opposite side of the road, you'll see a parking area with interpretive markers. Allow plenty of time to read about Lewis and Clark and the young Shoshone guide Sakakawea (which is the correct spelling of her Hidatsa name), as well as early American Indians,

trappers, traders, and settlers. Camping and RV sites are available, as well as access to 571 **571**
hiking, boating, and fishing.

Where to Stay & Dine

Anglers should head for **Bud Lilly's Anglers Retreat,** 16 W. Birch St., P.O. Box 983, Three Forks, MT 59752 (© **406/285-6690;** fax 406/284-9945). Having Bud master-mind your fishing itinerary is reason enough to stay here, but it's by no means the only reason. The Anglers Retreat has been refurbished and is now a cozy lodge. Every reserva-tion includes a personalized, detailed itinerary of where to fish locally, based on your preferences and length of stay. Doubles from $65; $135 to $176 suite.

El Western Cabins & Lodges, 4787 U.S. 287 N. (© **800/831-2773** or 406/682-4217; www.elwestern.com), has some log duplex-style cabins, as well as large, expensive two- and three-bedroom lodges. Doubles from $80 to $105, cabins from $135 to $285, $275 to $475 lodge.

The **Willow Creek Café and Saloon** (© **406/285-3698**) is a find, if you can find it—it's 7 miles southwest of Three Forks on the Old Yellowstone Trail. It's worth the search, though, because Willow Creek is the best restaurant in the area (don't let the bul-let holes in the ceiling scare you off).

THE GALLATIN VALLEY

According to legend, the Sioux and Nez Perce once engaged in a bloody battle in the lower Gallatin Valley. On the third day of fighting, the sun was blotted out and a boom-ing voice told the warriors to forget old wrongs and stop fighting, because they were in the Valley of Peace and Flowers.

Since those days, the sun still mostly shines around here, but the only booming voices heard are those calling you for your tee time or your dinner reservation. The transition of Big Sky from peace and flowers to year-round resort was not entirely without dissen-sion, however. When legendary NBC newsman Chet Huntley—a Montana native—proposed the Big Sky ski resort, there was an outcry from the budding environmental movement. But Huntley's dream was realized in 1973, and the resort has blossomed into a world-class facility.

Big Sky Resort, P.O. Box 160001, Big Sky, MT 59716 (© **800/548-4486** or 406/995-5000; www.bigskyresort.com), handles a wide variety of lodgings—from economy to full-fledged luxury scattered among nearly 70 properties. The three-story **Huntley Lodge,** with 205 units, was the beginning of Chet Huntley's original vision for Big Sky. It offers rooms that can sleep up to four and loft rooms that can accommodate six. The 97-unit **Shoshone Condominium Hotel** combines the living quarters of a condo with the amenities and services of a hotel, with sleeping for four to six. Weight-training cen-ters, saunas, an outdoor pool, gift shops, and ski storage are included at both. The **Sum-mit at Big Sky,** with 213 condominiums, offers European sophistication in a Western style. All lodgings offer ski-in/ski-out convenience. Winter rates start around $160 a night double and top out at more than $1,000.

Moonlight Basin, P.O. Box 160040, Big Sky, MT 59716 (© **877/822-0430** or 406/993-6000; www.moonlightbasin.com), offers properties ranging from condos to private residences to luxurious penthouses. The **Moonlight Lodge and Spa** (© **800/845-4428**) is a magnificent lodge offering penthouse suites and secluded midmountain cabins, plus a sophisticated yet down-home restaurant, a relaxed-atmosphere bar, and a deli. There's also a full-service spa with treatment rooms, fitness center, steam rooms, heated pool, and a cascading waterfall hot tub; a concierge ready and able to organize

THE NORTHERN ROCKIES & GREAT PLAINS

BOZEMAN & SOUTH-CENTRAL MONTANA

everything from fly-fishing trips, to backcountry skiing, to dog-sled adventures; and even an ice-skating rink just outside in winter. Winter rates start at around $200 a night double during the ski season and top out well over $1,000.

4 LITTLE BIGHORN BATTLEFIELD

Perhaps there is no phrase in the English language that serves as a better metaphor for an untimely demise than "Custer's Last Stand." It was on this battlefield, on the dry, sloping prairies of southeastern Montana, that George Armstrong Custer met his end. Though the details of the battle that took place on June 25, 1876, are sketchy, at best, much remains for the visitor to explore and ponder in this mysterious place. The **Little Bighorn Battlefield National Monument** chronicles the history of this world-famous engagement, offering a coherent look at how the battle developed, where the members of Custer's contingent died, and how it might have looked to the swarming warriors.

ESSENTIALS

GETTING THERE   The monument is located 56 miles east of Billings. Take I-94 East to I-90 South; just past Crow Agency, take exit 510 for U.S. 212. The battlefield is located a few hundred yards east.

ADMISSION & HOURS   The park and visitor center are open daily 8am to 9pm from Memorial Day to Labor Day, 8am to 6pm in spring and fall, and 8am to 4:30pm in winter. The visitor center is closed on Christmas, New Year's Day, and Thanksgiving. Admission costs $10 per vehicle or $5 for those on foot or motorcycle.

VISITOR INFORMATION   At the **Visitor Center** (© **406/638-2224**) just inside the park entrance, you'll see actual uniforms worn by Custer, read about his life, and view an eerie reenactment of the battles on a small-scale replica of the battlefield. For information, contact the Superintendent, Little Bighorn Battlefield National Monument, P.O. Box 39, Crow Agency, MT 59022 (© **406/638-3204;** www.nps.gov/libi).

TOURING THE MONUMENT   It's possible to view the site in less than a half-hour, but you'll shortchange yourself with that approach. Instead, plan to spend enough time to explore the visitor center, listen to interpretive historical talks presented by rangers there, and then tour the site. You'll leave with a greater appreciation for the monument and an understanding of the history that led up to the battle.

After stopping at the **visitor center,** drive 4^1/$_2$ miles to the **Reno-Benteen Monument Entrenchment Trail,** at the end of the monument road, and double back. Interpretive signs at the top of this bluff show the route followed by the companies under Custer, Benteen, and Reno as they approached the area from the south, and the positions from which they defended themselves from their Indian attackers.

As you proceed north along the ridge, you'll pass **Custer's Lookout,** the spot from which the general first viewed the Indian village. This was the spot at which Custer sent for reinforcements, though he continued marching north.

Capt. Thomas Weir led his troops to **Weir Point** in hopes of assisting Custer but was discovered by the Indian warriors and forced to retreat to the spot held by Reno.

The **Medicine Trail Ford,** on the ridge, overlooks a spot below the bluffs in the Medicine Trail Coulee on the Little Bighorn River, where hundreds of warriors who had been sent from the Reno battle pushed across in pursuit of Custer and his army.

Farther north, the Cheyenne warrior Lame White Man led an attack up **Calhoun**
Ridge against a company of the Seventh Cavalry that had charged downhill into the coulee. When Indian resistance overwhelmed the army, troops retreated back up the hill, where they were killed.

As you proceed to the north, you will find detailed descriptions of the events that occurred on the northernmost edges of the ridge, as well as white markers that indicate the places where army troops fell in battle. The bodies of Custer, his brothers Tom and Boston, and nephew Autie Reed were found on Custer Hill.

Indian casualties during the rout are estimated at 60 to 100 warriors. Following the battle, which some say began early in the morning and ended within 2 hours, the Indians broke camp in haste and scattered to the north and south. Within a few short years, they were all confined to reservations.

The survivors of the Reno and Benteen armies buried the bodies of Custer and his slain army where they fell. In 1881, the graves that could be located were reopened, and the bones reinterred at the base of a memorial shaft overlooking the battlefield. Custer's remains were eventually reburied at the U.S. Military Academy at West Point in 1877.

The adjacent **National Cemetery,** established in 1879, incorporates a self-guided tour to some of the more significant figures buried there. In 2003, there was a dedication for a new Indian memorial, a sculpture garden dubbed "Peace Through Unity." There are also three **walking trails** within the monument for visitors wishing to explore the battle in greater depth.

A SPECIAL EVENT   The **Hardin Area Chamber of Commerce** (I-90 exits 497 and 503) sponsors **Little Bighorn Days,** around June 25 each year, but not at the monument. The events include a reenactment, parade, symposiums, and, of course, food. For information, call ✆ **406/665-1672.**

5 JACKSON HOLE & THE GRAND TETONS

Grand Teton National Park may be smaller than Yellowstone, but in many ways it's no less spectacular—and it's far less crowded. The park encompasses towering mountain spires reaching almost 14,000 feet and the picturesque, glacier-fed waters of Jackson Lake and the Snake River. Jackson Hole, close to the end of the Grand Teton National Park and within an easy drive of Yellowstone, is one of the nation's premier ski resorts and offers many other kinds of outdoor recreation year-round.

JACKSON HOLE

Of the few communities in the Rockies that have successfully toed the line between promoting themselves as resort towns and retaining some semblance of indigenous character, Jackson is a standout. The million-dollar homes are sprouting all over the valley, but there is still open space, a memory of the cowboy past, and some resistance to letting in too much commercial glitz.

The remaining open spaces allow visitors to imagine what it was like in the 19th century, when fur trappers camped here. They were followed by ranchers, who soon became *dude* ranchers. Today the community holds an eclectic mixture of ski bums, blue bloods, nouveau riche, avid outdoor types, and even a few old-time cowboys. The cosmopolitans of this motley crew came not just with a hunger for scenery, but also with a taste for music, art, and good restaurants, and the selection here is unrivaled in

Wyoming. The big ski hill lures a younger crowd, with the final ingredient for resort status—celebrities—supplied by transplants such as Harrison Ford.

Essentials

GETTING THERE   The **Jackson Airport** (© **307/733-7682;** www.jacksonholeairport. com) is north of town at the southern end of Grand Teton National Park. If you're getting here by car, come north from I-80 at Rock Springs on U.S. 189/191; or come east from I-15 at Idaho Falls on U.S. 26 and either come through Snake River Canyon on that highway or veer north over Teton Pass on Wyo. 32. If you are coming south from Yellowstone National Park, you can stay on U.S. 89, which runs north and south through both parks and into town.

VISITOR INFORMATION   The **Jackson Hole Chamber of Commerce** has information on just about everything in and around Jackson. Along with the U.S. Forest Service and National Park Service, representatives of the chamber can be found at the informative **Visitors Center,** 532 N. Cache, about 3 blocks north of Town Square with a view of the National Elk Refuge. For information on lodging, events, and activities, contact the chamber at P.O. Box 550, Jackson, WY 83001 (© **307/733-3316;** www.jackson holechamber.com).

What to See & Do

Beyond its role as a staging area for explorations of Grand Teton and Yellowstone national parks, Jackson is a place to relax, shop, golf, or simply check out the sights.

The **National Museum of Wildlife Art,** 2820 Rungius Rd. (© **307/733-5771;** www. wildlifeart.org), is a 50,000-square-foot castle that houses some of the best wildlife art in the country. Admission is $10 adults, $9 students and seniors, free for children 17 and younger when accompanied by an adult.

If you don't have the time, money, or inclination for the full guest ranch experience, a fun alternative is to make a beeline for the nearest guest ranch around mealtime to enjoy Western cuisine served up to the strains of yodelin' cowpokes. The **Bar-T-5 Covered Wagon Cookout and Wild West Show,** 790 E. Cache Creek Dr., Jackson (© **800/ 772-5386** or 307/733-5386; www.bart5.com), offers a covered-wagon ride through Cache Creek Canyon to the "dining room" for an evening of Western victuals and after-dinner songs from the Bar-T-5's singing cowboys. The covered-wagon dinner runs around $42 for adults, $35 for youngsters 5 to 12; children 4 and under enjoy the night free. Reservations are recommended.

There are more than 20 **galleries** in downtown Jackson alone, with, of course, an excellent representation of Western art, although a growing number of galleries are showing a variety of styles.

SUMMER ACTIVITIES   Grand Teton National Park has incredible fishing. The Snake River, which flows through the park, is beaten to a froth every summer by hordes of fly-fishermen. **High Country Flies,** 185 N. Center St. (© **877/732-7210** or 307/733-7210; www.highcountryflies.com), has all the goods and offers guided fishing trips and schools, as well as the best in angling fashion. The most renowned fishing experts assemble at the **Jack Dennis Outdoor Shop** on the Town Square at 50 E. Broadway (© **800/570-3270** or 307/733-3270; www.jackdennis.com). The going rate for guided fishing is about $450 for a full day for two people.

Adventure Sports, at Dornan's in the town of Moose (© **307/733-3307**), has a small selection of mountain bike, kayak, and canoe rentals, and advice on where to go with the

gear. When snowboards are put away for the summer, the **Boardroom** switches to BMX
bikes and skateboards, at 225 W. Broadway (© 307/733-8327).

Some hotels, including those in Grand Teton National Park, have stables and operate
trail rides for their guests. Contact **Jackson Hole Outfitters** (© 307/654-7008; www.
jacksonholetrailrides.com), **Spring Creek Ranch Riding Stables** (© 800/443-6139;
www.springcreekranch.com), or the **Mill Iron Ranch** (© 307/733-6390; www.milliron
ranch.net). Rides typically cost around $50 for 2 hours or $125 for a day.

The **Jackson Hole Golf and Tennis Club,** north of Jackson off U.S. 89 (© 800/628-
9988 or 307/733-3111), has an 18-hole course that's been rated one of the nation's top
resort courses, and it underwent a major renovation and saw a new clubhouse open in
2007. Seasonal greens fees range from $65 to $195 for 18 holes, cart included. The
Teton Pines Resort and Country Club, 3450 N. Clubhouse Dr. (© 800/238-2223 or
307/733-1005; www.tetonpines.com), designed by Arnold Palmer and Ed Seay, is a challenging course and prime real estate; greens fees are $85 to $160 for 18 holes. Both
courses are open to the public.

There are two parts to the Snake River—the smooth water north of Jackson, and the
white water of the canyon, to the south and west. A rafting trip down the upper Snake,
usually from Jackson Lake Dam or Pacific Creek to Moose, is not about wild water but
about wildlife: Moose, bald eagles, osprey, and other creatures come to the water just like
we do. Several operators provide scenic float trips. Contact **Barker-Ewing** (© 800/448-
4202; www.barker-ewing.com) or **Charlie Sands Wildwater** (© 800/358-8184; www.
sandswhitewater.com). Generally, a full-day trip runs around $70 to $90, lunch included,
and a half-day trip costs about $40 to $60.

WINTER ACTIVITIES   This is one of the premier destinations for skiers in the entire
country. **Jackson Hole Mountain Resort,** 3395 W. Village Dr., Teton Village (© 888/
DEEP-SNO** [333-7766] or 307/733-2292, 733-2291 for snow conditions, 800/443-
6931 for central reservations; www.jacksonhole.com), has one of the best hills in North
America and is constantly upgrading its facilities. Here's the trade-off: Prices are
approaching those of Colorado resorts, although aficionados of the sport keep coming
back for more. *Note:* The resort's tram was shut down in 2006; a new $25-million,
100-passenger tram was under construction at press time and slated to open in December
2008. Cross-country skiers should contact the attached **Jackson Hole Nordic Center,**
7658 Teewinot, Teton Village (© 307/733-2629), or **Teton Pines Cross Country Skiing Center** (© 307/733-1005).

If you want to try your hand at dog-sledding, **Jackson Hole Iditarod Sled Dog
Tours,** P.O. Box 1940, Jackson (© 800/554-7388 or 307/733-7388; www.jhsleddog.
com), offers both half- and full-day trips in five-person sleds (the fifth companion is your
guide) and you can take a turn in the driver's stand. The half-day ride costs around $190
per person, gives the dogs an 11-mile workout, and includes a lunch of hot soup and
cocoa before you head back to the kennels.

Where to Stay

Jackson lodgings these days come with palatial trappings and, in some cases, prices that
start at $500 a night. Prices are generally discounted in the off season (spring/fall), but
not during ski season. For lodging information and reservations, call **Jackson Hole
Central Reservations** (© 888/838-6606; www.jacksonholewy.com).

Amangani (Best)   Cut into the side of East Gros Ventre Butte, Amangani's rough rock
exterior blends incredibly well so that the lights from its windows and pool appear at

night to glow from within the mountain. Understated and rustic, all details are done with high contemporary style. From the high-ceilinged corridors to the outdoor pool, this place is all about class and privacy, not to mention superlative views. Hotelier Adrian Zecha has resorts like this around the world, from Bali to Bora Bora, and while the designs are tailored to the landscape, the approach is the same: personal service, luxury, and all the little touches. There are iPod cradles in every bedroom, cashmere throws on the daybeds, and stunning slate and redwood interiors.

1535 NE Butte Rd., Jackson, WY 83002 (on top of East Gros Ventre Butte). *C* **877/734-7333** or 307/734-7333. www.amanresorts.com. 40 units. $565–$1,400 double. AE, DC, DISC, MC, V. **Amenities:** Restaurant; year-round outdoor pool; health club; spa.

Bentwood Inn   This B&B is an architectural marvel. Built from 200-year-old timber cleared from Yellowstone, the inn is a 6,000-square-foot log mansion with 43 corners. The parlor, centered about a three-story river-rock fireplace, is an ideal place to while away a thunderstorm, but the real beauty here is outside, situated just west of the Snake River and south of Teton Village on 3 acres of cottonwood and pine forest with a breezy deck and back lawn. The rooms, all with remote-controlled gas fireplaces, private balconies, and Jacuzzi tubs, are extensions of the innovative design, with touches both urban and rural, from ornate tile work to longhorn skulls above the bed. The breakfasts are hearty and gourmet, and the fridge is always stocked with a range of soft drinks and libations. One room is pet friendly (10% charge per night).

4 miles west of Jackson on Teton Village Rd., P.O. Box 561, Jackson Hole, WY 83001. *C* **307/739-1411.** Fax 307/739-2453. www.bentwoodinn.com. 5 units. $195–$295 double; $245–$325 suite. Rates include complimentary full breakfast and evening wine and cheese. AE, DISC, MC, V.

Four Seasons Resort Jackson Hole   The newest and most deluxe lodging option in Teton Village, the ultrastylish Four Seasons set a new standard for ski-in, ski-out luxury. From a year-round pool landscaped to resemble a mountain creek to the cowboy-hatted doorman, to the rooms—stately, luxurious, and Western—this is one of the top slope-side properties in the country. The range of rooms starts at the high end and goes up from there, but even the standard kings are large and plush, and most units have a balcony or a fireplace. One notable perk: the hotel's "Base Camp," a full-service outdoor-activity concierge who can arrange mountain biking, hiking, fishing, and ballooning excursions, and who will outfit you in style. In winter, the service transforms into a first-rate ski concierge, and s'mores and hot chocolate are served outside, where heated towels are distributed at the pool. The eating and drinking facilities range from casually hip to extraordinarily extravagant.

7680 Granite Loop (P.O. Box 544), Teton Village, WY 83025. *C* **307/732-5000.** Fax 307/732-5001. www.fourseasons.com. 124 units, 18 suites, 27 condos. $400–$750 double; $700–$4,000 condo or suite. Lower rates spring and fall. AE, DC, DISC, MC, V. Valet parking $20 daily. **Amenities:** 2 restaurants; year-round outdoor pool; health club; spa. *In room:* Kitchen.

Rusty Parrot Lodge and Spa   The name sounds like an out-of-tune jungle bird, but the Rusty Parrot demonstrates excellent pitch, cultivating a country lodge and spa in the heart of Jackson. Across from Miller Park, the Parrot is decorated in the nouveau Western style of peeled log, with an interior appointed with elegant furnishings and river-rock fireplaces. One very attractive lure is the **Body Sage Spa**, where you can get yourself treated to all sorts of scrubs, wraps, massages, and facials. Another is the excellent restaurant, the **Wild Sage.** Breakfast includes omelets, fresh pastries, fruits, cereals, and freshly ground coffee; food also appears later in the day, but the lodge likes to make that a surprise. Rooms are gigantic, and several have private balconies.

175 N. Jackson St. (P.O. Box 1657), Jackson, WY 83001. (𝄐 **800/458-2004** or 307/733-2000. www.rusty parrot.com. 31 units. $290–$425 double; $625–$750 suite. Rates include full breakfast. AE, DC, DISC, MC, V. **Amenities:** Restaurant.

Spring Creek Ranch Perched atop East Gros Ventre Butte, 1,000 feet above the Snake River and minutes from both the airport and downtown Jackson, this resort commands a panoramic view of the Grand Tetons and 1,000 acres of land populated by deer, moose, and the horses at its riding facility. The rooms, divided among nine buildings with cabinlike exteriors, all have wood-burning fireplaces, Native American floor and wall coverings, and balconies with views of the Tetons. Most rooms have a king- or two queen-size beds, and the studio units boast kitchenettes. In addition to its own rooms, the resort arranges accommodations in the privately owned condominiums and vacation homes that dot the butte—large, lavishly furnished, and featuring completely equipped kitchens. The resort also has an **"Adventure Spa,"** offering a combination of guide service and post-outing treatments, and in-house naturalists who lead guests on "Wildlife Safaris" into the parks.

1800 Spirit Dance Rd. (on top of the East Gros Ventre Butte), Jackson, WY 83001. (𝄐 **800/443-6139** or 307/733-8833. www.springcreekranch.com. 126 units. $300–$500 double; $375–$2,200 condo or home. Lower rates in spring and fall. AE, MC, V. **Amenities:** Restaurant; outdoor pool; tennis court; spa. *In room:* Kitchenette.

Trapper Inn Just 2 short blocks from Town Square, the Trapper Inn was reborn as a slick hotel when it opened 36 new rooms in a pair of attractive "mountain contemporary" buildings in 2006. The rooms are stylish and spacious—the newest are all suites that adjoin, with a kitchen in every other unit—and the employees here are some of the most helpful you'll find in Jackson.

235 N. Cache St., Jackson, WY 83001. (𝄐 **888/771-2648,** or 307/733-2648 for reservations. www.trapper inn.com. 90 units. $170–$189 double; $239–$249 suite. Rates include expanded continental breakfast. AE, MC, V. **Amenities:** Indoor pool. *In room:* Kitchen.

Virginian Lodge (Value) It's not brand-new. It's not a resort, it doesn't have a golf course, and the highway is right outside the door. However, the Virginian is one of the better motels in Jackson: The prices remain reasonable, the interior courtyard (with a large grassy play area and central pool) is a world away from the Broadway-facing exterior, and it's a busy, cheerful place to stay. You can get a room with a private Jacuzzi or a kitchenette, and many have "dry" bars and sofa sleepers.

750 W. Broadway, Jackson, WY 83001. (𝄐 **800/262-4999** or 307/733-2792. Fax 307/733-4063. www. virginianlodge.com. 170 units. $108 double; $138–$218 suite. AE, DC, DISC, MC, V. **Amenities:** Restaurant; outdoor pool. *In room:* Kitchenette.

Wort Hotel On Broadway, just off the Town Square, the Wort stands like an old tree. Opened in the 1940s by the sons of Charles Wort, an early-20th-century homesteader, the Tudor-style two-story building was largely rebuilt after a 1980 fire. Nowadays, it has an old-fashioned style, in the relaxed **Silver Dollar Bar** (distinctively graced with 2,032 silver dollars) and in the quiet, formal dining room. The lobby is graced by a warm, romantic fireplace; another fireplace and a huge hand-carved mural accent a mezzanine sitting area, providing a second hideaway. The rooms aren't Tudor at all—the Wort labels them "New West." Brass number plates and doorknobs welcome you into comfortable, air-conditioned guest rooms with modern decor, thick carpeting, and armoires.

50 N. Glenwood St., Jackson, WY 83001. © 307/733-2190. www.worthotel.com. 59 units. $165–$289 double; $399–$699 suite. AE, DISC, MC, V. Valet parking $10 daily. **Amenities:** Restaurant; health club.

Where to Dine
The Blue Lion (Best) ECLECTIC
In the fast-moving, high-rent world of Jackson dining, the Blue Lion stays in the forefront by staying the same. Owned and operated by Ned Brown since 1978, the restaurant is in a two-story blue clapboard building across from a park that looks like a family home. Inside, in intimate rooms accented with soft lighting or outside on a patio, diners enjoy slow-paced and elegant meals. The menu features rack of lamb and wild-game specialties, such as grilled elk loin in a peppercorn sauce. Fresh fish is flown in daily for dishes such as the nori-crusted ahi.

160 N. Millward St. © 307/733-3912. www.bluelionrestaurant.com. Reservations recommended. Main courses $15–$33. AE, DC, DISC, MC, V. Summer daily 5:30–10pm; winter daily 6–10pm.

43° North STEAK/SEAFOOD/GAME
A former radio station at the foot of Snow King Mountain is now a top-notch eatery and nightspot, capped with a popular rooftop deck. The lunch menu includes Angus buffalo, veggie, and beef burgers alongside fish tacos and barbecue pork. (I especially enjoy the sweet-potato fries.) Dinners are more upscale: Think pan-seared elk chops, pecan-crusted salmon, and an excellent Wyoming rib-eye. After the kitchen closes, the throngs arrive in force for live music (Wed–Sat) and drinks from the 180-year-old restored Irish bar.

645 S. Cache St. © 307/733-0043. Reservations accepted for dinner. Main courses $9–$13 lunch, $20–$36 dinner. AE, DISC, MC, V. Daily 11:30am–9:30pm (from 10:30am Sun). Bar open later.

Jedediah's House of Sourdough (Kids) AMERICAN
You feel like you've walked into the kitchen of some sodbuster's log cabin when you enter Jedediah's—the structure built in 1910 is on the National Register of Historic Places. Bring a big appetite for breakfast and a little patience—you might have to wait for a table, and then you might have to wait for food while you stare at the interesting old photos on the wall. But it's worth it, especially for the rich flavor of the sourjacks (sourdough pancakes) served with blueberries. Lunches include soups, salads, and burgers and sandwiches. The sourdough starter here is also historic: It dates from the 1870s.

135 E. Broadway. © 307/733-5671. Reservations not accepted. Breakfast $6–$12; lunch $7–$11. AE, DC, DISC, MC, V. Daily 7am–2pm.

Nani's Genuine Pasta House ITALIAN
The food is extraordinary at Nani's. You are handed two menus when you are seated: a "Carta Classico" featuring pasta favorites such as *amitriciana* (tomato, onion, guanciale [a kind of bacon], and freshly ground black pepper) and fresh mussels in wine broth, and a list of specialties from a different featured region of Italy. It might be Sicily, where Head Chef Camille Parker's family has its roots, or Emilia-Romagna, where prosciutto, Parmesan, and balsamic vinegar are culinary staples. Parker ventures to Italy annually for research. Almost hidden behind a relic of a motel, it is worth seeking out.

242 N. Glenwood St. © 307/733-3888. www.nanis.com. Reservations recommended. Main courses $13–$33. MC, V. Daily 5–10pm. Bar open later.

Snake River Grill CONTEMPORARY AMERICAN
This is a popular drop-in spot for locals, including some of the glitterati who sojourn in the area—Harrison Ford and

Calista Flockhart, to name two. The front-room dining area overlooks Town Square, but there's a more private, romantic room in the back. It's an award-winning restaurant for both the wine list and menu, which features regular fresh-fish dishes (ahi tuna is a favorite), crispy pork shank, and some game-meat entrees such as venison chops and Idaho trout. The pizzas—cooked in a wood-burning oven—are topped with exotic ingredients such as duck sausage or eggplant with portobello mushrooms.

84 East Broadway, on the Town Square. (© **307/733-0557.** www.snakerivergrill.com. Reservations recommended. Main courses $20–$40. AE, MC, V. Summer daily 5:30–10pm; winter daily 6–10pm. Closed Nov and Apr.

Trio CONTEMPORARY AMERICAN   Opened by a trio of owner-chefs, this local favorite offers a winning combination of inviting atmosphere and remarkable food. Served in a dimly lit, social room with a fossil-rock bar and semi-open kitchen, the seasonal menu might include appetizers such as sautéed shrimp with Szechuan peppercorns and wonton crisps and entrees including a killer Idaho rainbow trout on a bed of blackened corn and avocado. Lunch is mostly gourmet salads, pizzas, and sandwiches. Both lunch and dinner bring killer fries—made of either sweet potatoes with black pepper aioli or russets with addictive blue cheese fondue.

45 S. Glenwood St. (© **307/734-8038.** www.bistrotrio.com. Reservations recommended. Main courses $8–$15 lunch, $14–$30 dinner. AE, MC, V. Mon–Fri 11am–2pm; daily 5:30pm–close (usually 9–10pm).

After Dark

Head down to the **Silver Dollar Bar,** 50 N. Glenwood, in the Wort Hotel (© **307/733-2190**), for a drink with one of the real or wannabe cowpokes at the bar. And, yes, those 1921 silver dollars are authentic. At the famous **Million Dollar Cowboy Bar** on the Town Square, 25 N. Cache St. (© **307/733-2207**), you can dance the two-step to live bands. If you want some high-octane dancing fun led by talented local hoofers, head west to Wilson and the **Stagecoach Bar** (© **307/733-4407**), on Wyo. 22, on a Sunday night. It's the only night there's live music in this scruffy bar and hamburger joint, and the place is jammed wall-to-wall.

GRAND TETON NATIONAL PARK

Yellowstone may have its geysers, but only this park can boast the bare, towering spires of the Cathedral Group, "Le Trois Tetons" (or "the three breasts," as cheeky French trappers named them). The Grand Teton, the largest of the three (known as "The Grand" by locals), is a mountaineer's dream, and hiking throughout the park draws hundreds of thousands each year. In addition to unparalleled mountain views, wildlife-watching is immensely popular; elk, bison, bald eagles, moose, and beavers are just some of the critters with whom you'll be sharing parkland.

Essentials

ACCESS/ENTRY POINTS   There are really only three ways to enter the park. From the **north,** you can enter the park from Yellowstone National Park, which is connected to Grand Teton by a wilderness corridor called the **John D. Rockefeller Jr. Memorial Parkway** through which U.S. 89/191/287 runs for 8 miles. You can also approach the park from the **east,** via U.S. 26/287. This route comes from Dubois, 55 miles east on the other side of the Absaroka and Wind River mountains, and crosses **Togwotee Pass,** where you'll get your first—and one of the best—views of the Tetons towering above the valley. Finally, you can enter Grand Teton from Jackson in the **south,** driving about 13 miles north on U.S. 26/89/191 to the Moose turnoff and the park's south entrance. Here you'll find the park headquarters, a visitor center, and a small community that includes dining, rental cabins, and shops.

VISITOR INFORMATION There are three visitor centers in Grand Teton National Park. Opened in August 2007, the dazzling $22-million **Craig Thomas Discovery and Visitor Center** (© 307/739-3399) is a half-mile west of Moose Junction at the southern end of the park; it's open 8am to 7pm daily from June through Labor Day and 8am to 5pm the rest of the year. The **Colter Bay Visitor Center** (© 307/739-3594), the northernmost of the park's visitor centers, is open 8am to 8pm from early June through Labor Day, and from 8am to 5pm after Labor Day through early October. There is also **Jenny Lake Visitor Center** (© 307/739-3392), open 8am to 7pm daily from early June through Labor Day, and 8am to 5pm after Labor Day through early October. Maps and ranger assistance are available at all three centers, and there are bookstores and exhibits at Moose and Colter Bay. Finally, there is an information station at the **Flagg Ranch** complex (© 307/543-2861), which is located approximately 5 miles north of the park's northern boundary.

FEES & BACKCOUNTRY PERMITS There are no park gates on U.S. Hwy. 26/89/191, so you can get a free ride through the park on that route; to get off the highway and explore, you'll pay $25 per automobile for a 7-day pass (admission is good for Yellowstone or Grand Teton). If you expect to visit the parks more than once in a year, buy an annual pass for $50, but I consider the various interagency passes, which are also honored here, to be a better deal.

   Backcountry permits are required from the Park Service for overnight use of backcountry campsites. The permits are free, but they can be reserved only from January 1 to May 15 (and the reservation itself costs $25); thereafter, all backcountry permits are issued on a first-come, first-served basis up to 24 hours before your first night out. Reservations may be made by writing the **Permits Office,** Grand Teton National Park, P.O. Drawer 170, Moose, WY 83012, or faxing 307/739-3438. Reservations can also be made online at **www.nps.gov/grte**.

SEEING THE GRAND TETON HIGHLIGHTS

Just viewing the spectacularly beautiful peaks is one of the main reasons to visit. Grand Teton National Park is famous for its mountains, and rightly so. The Cathedral Group is composed of **Grand Teton** (elevation 13,770 ft.), **Teewinot** (elevation 12,325 ft.), and **Mount Owen** (elevation 12,928 ft.). Nearby, almost as impressive, are **South Teton** (elevation 12,514 ft.) and **Middle Teton** (elevation 12,804 ft.). The best views of the Cathedral Group are along the trails and roads that ring **Jenny Lake.**

COLTER BAY **Colter Bay** is a busy outpost of Park Services where you can get groceries, postcards and stamps, T-shirts, and advice. If this is your first stop in the park, get maps and information at the **Colter Bay Visitor Center.** Here you can view park and wildlife videotapes and attend a park-orientation slide program throughout the day. Ranger-led activities include museum tours, park orientation talks, natural history hikes, and evening amphitheater programs. Colter Bay has lots of overnight options, from its cabins to its old-fashioned tent camps to its trailer park and campground. There are also a general store and laundromat, two restaurants, a boat launch and boat rentals, and tours. You can take pleasant short hikes in this area, including a walk around the bay or out to **Hermitage Point.**

DORNAN'S This is a small village area just south of the visitor center on some private land owned by one of the area's earliest homesteading families. There are a few shops and a semigourmet grocery store, a post office, a bar where there is sometimes live music, and, surprisingly, a first-rate wine shop.

JACKSON LAKE The north end of the park is dominated by **Jackson Lake,** a huge expanse of water that fills a gorge left 10,000 years ago by retreating glaciers. Though it empties east into the Snake River, curving around in the languid **Oxbow Bend**—a favorite wildlife-viewing float for canoeists—the water from Jackson Lake eventually turns south, then west through Snake River Canyon and into Idaho.

JENNY LAKE Along Teton Park Road, you move into the park's southern half, where the tallest peaks rise abruptly above a string of smaller lakes strung together in the foothills—**Leigh Lake, String Lake,** and **Jenny Lake,** which is the favorite of many park visitors. At North Jenny Lake Junction, you can take a turnoff west to **Jenny Lake Lodge**—the road then continues as a one-way scenic loop along the lakeshore before rejoining Teton Park Road about 4 miles later.

SIGNAL MOUNTAIN If you're here to enjoy the park, you'd probably turn west on **Teton Park Road** at Jackson Lake Junction, and arrive after only 5 miles at **Signal Mountain.** Like its counterpart at Colter Bay, this developed recreation area, on Jackson Lake's southeast shore, offers camping sites, accommodations in cabins and multiplex units, two restaurants, and a lounge with one of the few live televisions in the park. This is also the place to fill up on gasoline and provisions from the small convenience store. Boat rentals and scenic cruises of the lake also originate here.

Sports & Outdoor Activities

For lovers of outdoor recreation, Grand Teton National Park offers one of the most accessible play lands of rock and water in the Lower 48. In addition to hiking, mountaineers and technical climbers can attack the highest hills; paddlers glide across the smooth waters of the lakes or splash along the livelier flow of the Snake River; and there are also waters open to motorized vessels and sailboats.

Where to Camp & Stay

Since Grand Teton is so much smaller than its counterpart to the north, the mileage between campgrounds is much shorter. As a consequence, selecting a site in one of the five National Park Service campgrounds within the park becomes a matter of preference (rather than geography) and availability. Fees in all campgrounds are $15 per night, and all have modern comfort stations. Campgrounds operate on a first-come, first-served basis, but reservations are available to groups of 10 or more by contacting the **Grand Teton Lodge Co.,** P.O. Box 240, Moran, WY 83013 (© **307/543-3100**). You can get recorded information on site availability by calling © **307/739-3603.**

All the campgrounds but Jenny Lake can accommodate tents, RVs, and trailers, but there are no utility hookups. **Jenny Lake Campground,** a tents-only area with 51 sites, is in a quiet, wooded area near the lake. You have to be here first thing in the morning to get a site. The largest campground, **Gros Ventre,** is the last to fill, probably because it's on the east side of the park, a few miles from Kelly on the Gros Ventre River Road. It has 265 sites, a trailer dump station, a tents-only section, and no showers. If you arrive late in the day and you have no place to stay, go here first. **Signal Mountain Campground,** with views of the lake and access to the beach, is another popular spot that fills first thing in the morning. It has 81 sites overlooking Jackson Lake and Mount Moran, as well as a pleasant picnic area and boat launch. No showers or laundry, but there's a store and service station nearby. **Colter Bay Campground and Trailer Village** has 350 sites (some with RV hookups), a general store, showers, and a laundromat. The area has access to the lake but is far enough from the hubbub of the village to offer a modicum of solitude; spaces are usually gone by noon. **Lizard Creek Campground,** at the north end of Grand Teton National Park near Jackson Lake, offers an aesthetically pleasing wooded area near the lake. It's only 8 miles from facilities at Colter Bay and has 60 sites that usually fill by 2pm.

For those who don't want to camp, the premier destination is pricey (from $525 double) **Jenny Lake Lodge** (© **800/628-9988** or 307/543-3100; www.gtlc.com), offering seclusion, award-winning food, and the individual attentions that come with a cabin resort kept intentionally small. Another top choice is **Jackson Lake Lodge** (© **800/628-9988** or 307/543-3100; www.gtlc.com), which is to Grand Teton what Old Faithful is to Yellowstone ($189–$269 double). The moderately priced ($151 double) **Signal Mountain Lodge** (© **307/543-2831;** www.signalmountainlodge.com) is the only resort on the shores of Jackson Lake inside the park.

6 YELLOWSTONE NATIONAL PARK

What other national park boasts such an assortment of thermal geysers and hot springs that their total exceeds the number found on the rest of the planet? On top of that, there's a waterfall twice as tall as Niagara Falls. Not to mention a canyon deep and colorful enough to fall into the "grand" category.

Wildlife? Ever focus your telephoto lens on a wild grizzly bear? Or a bald eagle? What about a wolf? Thousands of visitors have these experiences here every year.

ESSENTIALS

GETTING THERE If interstate highways and international airports are the measure of accessibility, then Yellowstone is as remote as Alaska's Denali National Park or the Serengeti Plains of Africa. But three million people make it here every year, on tour buses, in family vans, on bicycles, and astride snowmobiles.

The closest airport is in **West Yellowstone,** Montana, which sits just outside the park's west entrance. Also, visitors can reach the park from the south by flying into **Jackson,** Wyoming (14 miles from the southern entrance to Grand Teton), then driving 56 miles through Grand Teton to the southern entrance of Yellowstone.

To the north, **Bozeman,** Montana, is 87 miles from the West Yellowstone entrance on U.S. 191. Or you can drive east from Bozeman to Livingston, a 20-mile journey on Interstate 90, and then south 53 miles on U.S. 89 to the northern entrance at Gardiner. Bozeman's airport, **Gallatin Field** (© **406/388-8321**), provides daily service through both national and regional carriers. If you're driving to West Yellowstone from Bozeman, take U.S. 191 south to U.S. 287 and continue south into town.

Also to the north, **Billings,** Montana, is 129 miles from the Cooke City entrance. Billings is home to Montana's busiest airport, **Logan International** (© **406/247-8609**), 2 miles north of downtown. Several major carriers serve Billings. From there, it's a 65-mile drive south on U.S. 212 to Red Lodge, then 30 miles on the Beartooth Highway to the northeast entrance to the park. Keep in mind that the Beartooth Highway (U.S. 212), which takes you on a high, twisting journey over a spectacular pass, is open only from Memorial Day weekend until late October.

VISITOR CENTERS & INFORMATION There are five major visitor and information centers in the park, and each has something different to offer. Unless otherwise indicated, summer hours are from 8am to 7pm.

The **Albright Visitor Center** (© 307/344-2263), at Mammoth Hot Springs, is the largest and is open year-round. It provides visitor information and publications about the park, has exhibits depicting park history from prehistory through the creation of the National Park Service, and houses a wildlife display on the second floor.

The **Old Faithful Visitor Center** (© 307/545-2750) is in a temporary facility until the Park Service opens a new, state-of-the-art building in 2009. A film on Yellowstone's thermal features is shown throughout the day. Rangers dispense various park publications and post projected geyser-eruption times here.

The **Canyon Visitor Center** (© 307/242-2550), in Canyon Village, reopened in 2007 after a renovation and is the place to go for books and an informative display about the park's geology, with a focus on the underlying volcanism. It's staffed with friendly rangers used to dealing with crowds.

The **Fishing Bridge Visitor Center** (© 307/242-2450), near Fishing Bridge on the north shore of Yellowstone Lake, has an excellent display that focuses on the park's bird life. You can get information and publications here as well.

The **Grant Village Visitor Center** (© 307/242-2650) has information, publications, a video program, and a fascinating exhibit that examines the role of fire in Yellowstone.

Helpful staff and park literature can also be found at several small information stations: the **Madison Information Station** (© 307/344-2821); the **Museum of the National Park Ranger** (no phone; daily in summer 9am–5pm) and the **Norris Geyser Basin Museum and Information Station** (© 307/344-2812; daily in summer 10am–5pm), both at Norris; the **West Thumb Information Station** (no phone; daily in summer 9am–5pm); and the **Public Lands Desk** at the West Yellowstone Visitors Information Center, 100 Yellowstone Ave. (© 406/646-4403; daily in summer 8am–8pm, limited hours the rest of the year).

FEES & PERMITS Entrance for up to 7 days costs $25 per vehicle and covers both Yellowstone and Grand Teton national parks. A snowmobile or motorcycle pays $20 for 7 days, and visitors on bicycles, skis, or on foot pay $12. You can buy an **annual permit** for $40, but the various national park passes are the best deal.

Backcountry permits are free, but you have to have one for any overnight trip, on foot, on horseback, or by boat. Camping is allowed only in designated campsites, many of which are equipped with food-storage poles to keep wildlife away. These sites are primitive and well situated, and you won't feel at all like you're in a campground. If designated campsites in a particular area have already been reserved, you're out of luck. So while you can make a reservation as few as 48 hours before beginning a trip, you would be wise during peak season to make a reservation well in advance (you can contact the park for reservations for the upcoming year beginning Apr 1), although it costs $20. The **Yellowstone Backcountry Office** (P.O. Box 168, Yellowstone National Park, WY 82190) will send you a useful *Backcountry Trip Planner* with a detailed map showing where the campsites are. Call the office for more information at © 307/344-2160.

EXPLORING THE PARK

MAMMOTH HOT SPRINGS At the park's north entrance, 5 miles south of Gardiner, Mammoth Hot Springs is home to spectacular limestone terraces, historic park buildings, and the Mammoth Hot Springs Hotel. It's one of the older park settlements, with stone buildings dating from the late 19th century, when the army was stationed here at Fort Yellowstone.

There are no geysers at **Mammoth Hot Springs Terraces,** but this cascading staircase of hillside hot pools offers a boardwalk tour of gorgeous pastels in shades of white, yellow, orange, and green, the unintentionally artistic work of microscopic bacteria in the sediments. The mineral-rich springs constantly bubble to the surface, depositing travertine as the water cools in contact with the air. It's a vivid illustration of the park's unusual geological situation: a rare geologic hot spot of seismic activity in the middle of the continent, where molten rock nearly makes it to earth's surface.

Whether or not you spend the night at the **Mammoth Hot Springs Hotel**—not the most distinguished lodging in the park, but it has historical character—you should drop by the **Albright Visitor Center.** This building once housed Fort Yellowstone's bachelor officers; today you'll find displays on park history, wildlife and photography exhibits, rangers dispensing advice, and park publications and maps. Films on the park's origin and the art it inspired are shown throughout the day. A special treat for international visitors is the opportunity to get their visas stamped with the official Yellowstone National Park document stamp. For information, call © **307/344-2263.**

TOWER-ROOSEVELT AREA   East of Mammoth Hot Springs, you enter a delicious mix of high plains, deep forest, and twisting rivers. Toward the northeast corner lies one of the most beautifully serene valleys in the Rockies, the **Lamar Valley.** This glacier-carved swath of grassy bottom and forested flanks sits apart from the vehicular chaos at the center of the park, a good thing because the traffic here is not automobiles, but the bison, bears, wolves, and elk whose presence has earned the valley the nickname "The Serengeti of the United States." If you continue east and leave Yellowstone via the park's northeast entrance, you'll be heading up to the spectacular views of the **Beartooth Highway.**

The area around the Tower-Roosevelt Junction was once a favorite spot of U.S. president Theodore Roosevelt. At **Roosevelt Lodge,** visitors can enjoy the kind of simple accommodations that fit the tastes of the Bull Moose himself: those with the rustic flavor of the Old West. This is the most relaxed of the park's villages, and a great place to take a break from the more crowded attractions. Get into the cowboy spirit by taking a **guided trail ride, stagecoach ride,** or **wagon ride.** You can skip the dining room and ride out for an **Old West cookout,** served from a chuck wagon to patrons who arrive by either horseback or wagon. The nearby 132-foot **Tower Falls** is named for the looming volcanic pinnacles at its brink and provides an excellent photo opportunity. While in the area, take time to view the petrified forests on **Specimen Ridge,** where a wide variety of fossilized plants and trees date back millions of years. All things considered, Roosevelt is a great place to escape the hordes.

Farther south, **Pelican and Hayden valleys** are the two most prominent remnants of ancient lakebeds in the park. They are now sub-Alpine meadows, thriving with plant life that provides feed for the bison and elk populations. You might see a bear, too.

THE GRAND CANYON OF YELLOWSTONE   Hayden Valley flanks the featured attraction of the park's center: the **Grand Canyon of the Yellowstone River,** a 1,000-foot-deep, 24-mile-long gorge that some can't resist comparing to its counterpart in Arizona. Okay, then: This canyon is greener, the water clearer, the air cooler, and it has two dramatic waterfalls. As it drops through this gorge, the Yellowstone River in some places moves at 64,000 cubic feet of water per second.

Volcanic explosions and glaciers surging and receding shaped the canyon. The geological story is told in the canyon itself, where hard lava flows formed the lip of the falls next to softer quartz-rich rock that gave way, allowing the river to cut deeply through the layers of red, orange, tan, and brown hue. Plumes of steam pinpoint vents along the canyon's rock spires, where viewing opportunities are extensive and varied. There are many hikes along and down into the canyon, which is 24 miles long and up to 1,200 feet deep, and you'll be surprised at how few people you encounter away from the parking areas. Many do trek down to a view of the Lower Falls on **Uncle Tom's Trail** from the South Rim, and a short path from a parking area for Upper Falls View also offers breathtaking views. Two other favorite trails are **Inspiration Point** and **Artist Point;** both are wheelchair accessible.

Canyon Village has a sprawling 1950s look, which puts off some visitors. It's usually crowded, but you can find many useful services there, and some of the newer lodging is an improvement.

NORRIS GEYSER BASIN   If you travel south from Mammoth on the west side of the park, you pass some interesting rock formations, **Obsidian Cliff** and **Roaring Mountain,** before coming to **Norris Geyser Basin.** Norris is not nearly as famous as the Mammoth terraces or the crowd of geysers around Old Faithful, but there's a lot going on here, from the steaming pools of the **Porcelain Basin** to the eruptions of **Echinus Geyser.** If you're the patient type, you can sit by the blowhole of **Steamboat Geyser** and hope that this, the largest of park geysers with a maximum height of 400 feet, will erupt. But be prepared to wait: Although it erupted six times between 2000 and late 2005, it only blew twice during the preceding 12 years. This is one of the hottest, most active thermal areas on the plateau, at the intersection of three faults in earth's crust; when they shift, new geysers pop up and old ones disappear. The **Norris Geyser Basin Museum** explains geothermal features, and the nearby **Museum of the National Park Ranger** tracks the history of the park's stewards.

OLD FAITHFUL   About a quarter of the world's geysers are crowded into hills, valleys, and riverbanks around **Old Faithful,** where the hot pools and spouts are divided into three areas: the **Lower, Midway,** and **Upper geyser basins.** Here you'll find burbling mud pots, radiant pools like **Chromatic Spring,** and geysers with a variety of tricks, from the angled shots of **Daisy Geyser** to the witches' cauldron of **Crested Pool.**

But the grande dame of geysers, the star of the show, is **Old Faithful.** Over the past 100 years, its eruptions have been remarkably consistent, blowing 15 to 23 times daily with a column averaging about 134 feet and a duration of about 40 seconds. Recent seismic activity has elongated the intervals (to about 92 min.) between eruptions a tad, but it's still the most predictable geyser in the world. Estimates posted at the visitor centers are give-or-take 10 minutes; if the last eruption was a long one, you might have to wait 2 hours for the next burst. (No big deal—there's plenty else to see here.)

Since the geyser is one of the key park attractions, the **Old Faithful Visitor Center** (© **307/545-2750**) is larger than most of its counterparts. An excellent film describing the geysers and their microscopic inhabitants is shown throughout the day in an air-conditioned auditorium—a relief on hot July afternoons! At press time, the visitor center was housed in a temporary structure near Old Faithful Lodge with construction underway on a new, cutting-edge facility; park officials hope to open the new building in 2009.

A National Historic Landmark, the shingled, steep-roofed **Old Faithful Inn** was built of local stone and hand-hewn timber, including a pair of interior balconies above the lobby floor.

YELLOWSTONE LAKE

West of Old Faithful, over Craig Pass, or south of Canyon, through the wildlife-rich **Hayden Valley,** is **Yellowstone Lake,** another natural wonder unique to Yellowstone. At

20 miles long, 14 miles wide, and more than 300 feet deep in places, it's the largest lake in the world above 7,000 feet in elevation. If you took a dip in the frigid water (not recommended), you could hardly guess that the caldera under the lake is filling with hot liquid magma, actually tilting the lake northward at a measurable pace. The caldera is the sunken remainder of a huge volcanic blast 600,000 years ago, and another about 700,000 years before that. Experts believe it's due to blow again sometime in the next 100,000 years—any day now, at least in geologic time. Volcanic underpinnings aside, grizzlies work the tributary streams in the spring when fish spawn (some campgrounds are closed), and lots of other wildlife congregate here, including moose and osprey.

The lake has long been a favorite fishing spot, but recent regulations have made cutthroat trout a catch-and-release species park-wide. This is part of a desperate attempt by park biologists to help the cutthroat come back against the planted Mackinaw or lake trout, which dine on small cutthroat and, therefore, are not to be released alive. You'll see some big sailboats braving the quirky winds of the lake, and experienced paddlers may want to **kayak** or **canoe** into the south and southeast arms of the lake, which are closed to motorboats. These deep bays are true wilderness, and great areas to fish and view wildlife. When you pick up a boating permit, you'll also get a stern warning from rangers to watch out for the changeable weather if you get out on the lake's open water. They're right to urge caution; even the best paddlers risk their lives in a sudden afternoon storm.

Lake Village, on the north shore of the lake, offers a large range of amenities, including fine restaurants at either the rustic cabins at **Lake Lodge** or the majestic 100-year-old **Lake Yellowstone Hotel.** This hotel has Greek columns and a spacious solarium overlooking the lake, the best place for a cocktail or a romantic dinner within park boundaries. It's very different from the Old Faithful Inn, but a rival for its beauty and history. Just south of Lake Village is **Bridge Bay Marina,** the park's water-activity center. Here you can obtain guided fishing trips, small-boat rentals, and dock rentals; there's also a store and tackle shop.

WEST THUMB & GRANT VILLAGE   On the south end of the lake, at **West Thumb,** the boiling thermal features extend into the lake. You can see steaming cones and churning water created by the action of the underwater hot springs. **Fishing Cone** is rumored to be the place where fishermen once used the "hook and cook" method, immediately tossing their catch into a hot pot for instant meal preparation. Don't try it—it's illegal to drop anything into a thermal feature, and the geyser water has traces of mercury and arsenic. You can walk among the lakeshore pools at the **Central Basin** and look at the colorful, thick fudge of the **Thumb Paint Pots.**

Grant Village, named for President Ulysses S. Grant, was completed in 1984 and is the newest of Yellowstone's villages. It has some of the most modern facilities in the park, but it's also the least inspired. On the plus side, this area is a great vantage point for watching sunrises and afternoon squalls move across the lake, and you may see **river otters** and **cutthroat trout** in the old marina's waters. (Come wintertime, the otters like to use holes melted by the underwater thermal features as base camps for ice-fishing escapades.) The **Grant Visitor Center** plays a video that explores the role of fire in the Yellowstone ecosystem.

Sports & Outdoor Activities

HIKING   If you have time for only one hike, hit the **Mount Washburn Trail** (trail heads are at the end of Old Chittenden Rd. and at Dunraven Pass). The rises are fairly gradual, and they're interspersed with long, fairly level stretches. The views are of the

Absaroka Mountains, Yellowstone Lake to the south, and the Gallatin Mountains to the west. You might even see mountain sheep. The hike to the summit is an easy 90-minute walk at a steady pace, or 2 hours with breaks. Bring several layers of clothing—it can get cold at the top.

The **Lonestar Geyser Trail** (start at the parking lot opposite Kepler Cascades) is another great walk; it's an easy 5-mile outing, and its popularity is its only disadvantage. From the trail head you'll wend your way through a forested area along a trail that parallels the Firehole River. The payoff for your effort is the arrival at the geyser—a vanilla-chocolate ice-cream cone near the middle of a vast meadow partially covered by grass and tress, exposed rock, gravel, and volcanic debris. Surrounding it are small, bubbling geysers and steam vents.

SUMMER SPORTS & ACTIVITIES   The best place to enjoy **boating** in Yellowstone is on **Yellowstone Lake,** which has easy access and panoramic views. The lake is one of the few areas where powerboats are allowed; you can rent rowboats and outboards at **Bridge Bay Marina** ((C) **307/242-3876**). Motorboats, canoes, and kayaks can be used on Lewis Lake (about 15 miles north of the south entrance) also.

In June, one of the best **fishing** spots is on the **Yellowstone River** downstream from Yellowstone Lake, where the cutthroat trout spawn. Anglers head to **Madison River** near the west entrance in July and then again in late fall for rainbow and some brown trout; in late summer, the **Lamar River** and **Soda Butte Creek** in the park's beautiful northeast corner are popular spots to hook cutthroats. You'll find more isolation at **Trout Lake,** a small backcountry lake about 10 miles west of the northeast entrance. The **required Yellowstone fishing permit** is available at any ranger station, visitor center, or Yellowstone General Store in the park. Anyone 16 and older needs a fishing permit, which costs $15 for 3 days, $20 for 7 days, and $35 for the season. Fishers ages 12 to 15 also need a permit, but it's free. Casters 11 and under can fish without a permit when supervised by an adult.

People who want to pack their gear on a **horse,** llama, or mule must get permits to enter the Yellowstone backcountry, or hire an outfitter with a permit. **Xanterra Parks and Resorts** ((C) **307/344-7311;** www.travelyellowstone.com) offers 1- and 2-hour guided trail rides daily aboard well-broken, tame animals. Stables are at Canyon Village, Roosevelt Lodge, and Mammoth Hot Springs. If you're looking for a longer, overnight horse-packing experience, contact the park and request a list of approved concessionaires that lead backcountry expeditions.

WINTER SPORTS & ACTIVITIES   In winter, Yellowstone is transformed into a surreal wonderland of snow and ice. The geyser basins take on a more dominant role, with the air's temperature in stark contrast to their steaming waters. Nearby trees are transformed into "snow ghosts" by frozen thermal vapors.

Transportation into the park is mainly by snowmobiles and tracked vehicles called snow coaches. **Old Faithful Snow Lodge** and the **Mammoth Hot Springs Hotel,** the park's two winter lodging options, are open December through March. The only road that's open for cars is the **Mammoth Hot Springs–Cooke City Road.**

The best **cross-country** trails in Yellowstone are the **Lonestar Geyser Trail,** a level 5-mile round-trip through a remote setting, starting at the Old Faithful Snow Lodge; and the **Fern Cascades Trail,** which begins in the Old Faithful housing area on the south side of the road and winds for 3 miles through a rolling wooded landscape. Skiers can tackle the 12-mile **Mallard Lake Trail,** though it may take them all day—it departs north of the Old Faithful Lodge area along the north side of the Upper Geyser Basin, then loops north and east to Mallard Lake and back to Old Faithful.

Equipment rentals, ski instruction, ski shuttles to various locations, and guided ski tours are all available at the park's two winter lodgings. Discounts are available for multiday rentals of skis or snowshoes. Ski instruction costs around $25 per person for a 2-hour group lesson; a full-day guided excursion costs $65 to $115 per person (lunch may or may not be included).

The **Mammoth Hot Springs outdoor ice rink** is behind the old Mammoth Hot Springs Recreation Center. On a winter's night, you can rent a pair of skates ($1 an hour, $4 per day) and glide across the ice while seasonal melodies are broadcast over the PA system. It's cold out there, but there's a warming fire at the rink's edge.

Roads that are jammed with cars during the summer fill up with **snowmobiles** (at least right now; the number of machines permitted has been limited in number in the last few years, and they may eventually be banned) and bison during the winter. In deference to the shaggier road warriors, moderate speed limits are strictly enforced, but this is still an excellent way to sightsee at your own pace. A driver's license is required for rental ($215 for a single rider or $235 double). A helmet is included with the snowmobile, and you can rent a clothing package for protection against the bitter cold. For additional information on winter activities and accommodations, as well as snow coach transportation and equipment rentals, contact **Xanterra Parks and Resorts** (© 307/344-7311).

Where to Camp & Stay in the Park

The National Park Service has shifted management of five major campgrounds to Xanterra Parks & Resorts, the park concessionaire, which means you can make reservations ahead of arrival. The other seven campgrounds still managed by the park are available only on a first-come, first-served basis. These lower-cost campgrounds ($12–$14 per night) are located at Indian Creek, Lewis Lake, Mammoth, Norris, Pebble Creek, Slough Creek, and Tower Fall. We like Lewis Lake and Indian Creek, which tend to be available when others are full. Check with rangers about campsite availability when you enter the park; some campgrounds fill up as early as 8am.

Xanterra Parks & Resorts operates the campgrounds at Bridge Bay, Canyon, Grant Village, Madison, and Fishing Bridge, where the fees are $17 per night. The **Fishing Bridge RV Park** is the only campground equipped with water, sewer, and hookups for RVs and trailers, though it accepts hard-sided vehicles only (no tents or tent trailers), and the fees are $35 per night. The **Madison campground** is the first to open in May, while **Grant Village** is closed until mid-June to avoid bear conflicts during trout-spawning season. These campgrounds are usually busier, and some are rather barren of trees unless you get a site on the fringes. Most campgrounds close in September, but Madison is open until mid-October, and Mammoth is year-round. To book a campsite or a room within any Yellowstone lodging, you also need to contact **Xanterra Parks and Resorts** (see above). It bears repeating: If you plan to travel in July or August, *make your reservations 6 months ahead of time.*

The crown jewel of the park's hotels, the **Old Faithful Inn** is 30 miles from West Yellowstone and 39 miles from the South Entrance. The lazy geyser-watcher can avoid the crowds by watching the show from a comfortable second-floor terrace with excellent views of eruptions. The original rooms are well appointed but may not have private bathrooms, while the new-wing rooms offer better facilities and more privacy. Doubles with private bathrooms from $117 to $198.

Old Faithful Snow Lodge and Cabins offers modern rooms that are spacious and comfortable, and there's also the usual selection of cabins. This is only one of two facilities in the park open during winter months. From $184 double, $91 to $133 cabin.

Do You Have Reservations?

Yellowstone accommodations are normally open from May to mid-October. Rooms are typically fully booked during the peak season in July and August, so **reservations should be made up to 6 months in advance.** For information or reservations at any of the locations within the park, contact **Xanterra Parks & Resorts** at P.O. Box 165, Yellowstone National Park, WY 82190 (© **866/439-7375** or 307/344-7311; www.travelyellowstone.com).

In the Mammoth Hot Springs area, on the site of old Fort Yellowstone, 5 miles from the north entrance, is the **Mammoth Hot Springs Hotel and Cabins** (at Mammoth Hot Springs). This is one of two hotels that are open during both summer and winter seasons. Suites measure up to those at the Old Faithful Inn and Lake Yellowstone Hotel. Standard rooms and cabins offer adequate appointments. Some of the cottage-style cabins have private hot tubs and sun decks. There are also a formal dining room and a fast-food restaurant. From $82 to $110 double, $72 to $104 cabin.

In the Canyon Village area, the **Canyon Lodge and Cabins** is a half-mile from the Grand Canyon of Yellowstone and Inspiration Point, one of the busiest spots in the park. The lodge offers tastefully appointed but ordinary motel-style accommodations in the three-story lodge building and in cabins. From $155 double, $66 to $142 cabin.

The **Roosevelt Lodge Cabins** were built in the wake of one of Teddy Roosevelt's legendary treks west, although he didn't sleep here. It is a rugged but charming stone edifice with a building-long porch. Stagecoach rides, horseback trips, and cookouts give this place a cowboy flavor, and it's a less hectic scene than the other park villages.

The bare-bone cabins, called **Roughriders,** are aptly named, with showers nearby. More-attractive Frontier cabins have showers. From $64 to $104 cabin.

At the affordable **Lake Lodge Cabins** (on Lake Yellowstone), the cabins are most suitable for outdoor types. The lodge is an old Western longhouse fronted by a porch and rockers that invite visitors to sit and gaze out across the waters. From $65 Pioneer cabin, $132 Western cabin. **Lake Yellowstone Hotel & Cabins** (Grand Loop Rd., on the north side of the lake) is one of the most attractive hotels in the park. Accommodations are in the hotel, in a motel-style annex, and in cabins. Opt for one of the cabins decorated with knotty-pine paneling. Request a single cabin rather than a duplex, because the walls are paper thin. Doubles from $139 to $211, $111 cabin.

Where to Stay & Dine in the Gateway Towns

COOKE CITY   Lodging here will be less expensive than in other gateway towns, ranging from $60 to $90 a night. The **Soda Butte Lodge,** 209 Main St. (© **800/527-6462** or 406/838-2251; www.cookecity.com), is the biggest motel in Cooke City, and it includes the **Prospector Restaurant** and a small casino; or you can go to the cheaper, bare-bones **Alpine Motel,** 105 Main St. (© **406/838-2262;** www.ccalpinemotel.com). For a bite to eat and a great selection of beers, try the funky **Beartooth Cafe** (© **406/838-2475**), also on Main Street.

GARDINER   Dinky, personable, and a bit eccentric, Gardiner has long had ultra-friendly lodging—places where, if you show up late, they've gone to bed and left a key in the door. Inexpensive motels are moving in and filling up during the summer months:

The **Yellowstone Park Travelodge,** 109 Hellroaring Rd. (© **406/848-7520**), and **Super 8,** 702 U.S. Hwy. 89 (© **800/800-8000** or 406/848-7401), are open year-round with rates during the high season between $90 and $105 for a double. The **Best Western by Mammoth Hot Springs,** on U.S. Hwy. 89 (© **800/828-9080** or 406/848-7311), is another option, with doubles for $119 to $129 in the summer. **Absaroka Lodge** (© **800/755-7414** or 406/848-7414; www.yellowstonemotel.com) offers well-appointed rooms with private balconies offering views into Yellowstone Park. From $95 to $105 double in summer.

An indication that Gardiner has kept in touch with its mining-town roots is the relative dearth of fancy restaurants—you'll find mostly steakhouse fare, hearty breakfasts, and travelers' food. A few upscale eateries have shown up in recent years, but the dish-clattering local color of the park-side coffee shops is hard to beat. My favorite Gardiner lunch spot is the **Sawtooth Deli,** 270 W. Park St. (© **406/848-7600**), serving up over-stuffed, New York–style subs and eclectic specials.

WEST YELLOWSTONE   West Yellowstone **Central Reservations** handles booking for many of the hotels (© **888/646-7077**). You'll find chains like the **ClubHouse Inn** (© **406/646-4892**), at 105 S. Electric St., with summertime doubles for $119 to $169; and the **Days Inn** (© **800/548-9551**), at 301 Madison Ave., with rates of $115 to $165 for a double. There are three **Best Western** affiliates, ranging from about $100 to $150 a night for a double during the summer. Call © **800/528-1234,** or go online to **www. bestwestern.com** for information and reservations.

The **One Horse Motel,** 216 N. Dunraven St. (© **800/488-2750** or 406/646-7677; www.onehorsemotel.com), is a top-notch independent across the street from City Park, with doubles for $82 to $92 a night. Another good inexpensive option (with more character than the chains, to boot), the 1912 **Madison Hotel,** 139 Yellowstone Ave. (© **800/ 838-7745** or 406/646-7745; www.madisonhotelmotel.com), has historic rooms for $41 to $75 for a double and newer motel doubles for $70 to $130. There is no finer hotel in the area than the **Holiday Inn SunSpree Resort,** 315 Yellowstone Ave. (© **800/ HOLIDAY** [465-4329] or 406/646-7365; www.doyellowstone.com). This resort is first-rate. A heated indoor pool, exercise room, sauna, children's program, and activities desk round out the amenities. From $99 to $175 double.

Just as the chain motels have arrived, so have garden-variety fast-food joints; West Yellowstone is a good place to stop for a quick bite on your way into the park. **Uncle Laurie's Riverside Café,** 237 U.S. Hwy. 20 (© **406/646-7040**), is a small but excellent alternative to steak-and-eggs breakfast joints. The menu migrates from breakfast calzones and huckleberry cinnamon rolls in the morning to a lunch menu of cold sandwiches, wraps, and "stinky burgers," so named for their garlic content. For the best variety of coffee drinks and baked goods, visit the espresso bar at the excellent **Book Peddler** in Canyon Square (© **406/646-9358**). **Beartooth Barbecue,** 111 Canyon St. (© **406/ 646-0227**), is a fun place with a nice selection of local microbrews and top-notch slow-smoked ribs. Locals snowmobile out from West Yellowstone to **Eino's Tavern** (there's a trail that follows U.S. Hwy. 191), 155 Eino's Loop (© **406/646-9344**), to become their own chefs. After placing your order, you're handed an uncooked piece of meat. Go to the grill, slap it on, and stand around, drink in hand, shooting the breeze with other patrons until your food is done.

7 BLACK HILLS & BADLANDS
OF SOUTH DAKOTA

The **Black Hills** area, with its wooded mountains, waterfalls, and rushing streams, is a natural delight. This is where you'll find Wind Cave, one of the country's most beautiful natural caverns; Custer State Park, with its herds of bison, elk, and deer; the imposing visages carved on Mount Rushmore; and the dramatic and still-developing **Crazy Horse Memorial.**

To the east of the Black Hills lie the **Badlands,** a strange and mysterious place. From the ragged ridges and saw-toothed spires to the wind-ravaged desolation of Sage Creek Wilderness Area, Badlands National Park is an awe-inspiring sight and an unsettling experience. Few leave here unaffected by the vastness of this geologic anomaly, spread across 381 square miles in western South Dakota. Steep canyons, towering spires, and flat-topped tables are all found among Badlands buttes.

AREA ESSENTIALS

GETTING THERE   The gateway to this area is the **Rapid City Regional Airport** (© **605/393-9924;** www.rcgov.org/Airport/pages), 10 miles southeast of Rapid City on U.S. 44. Northwest Airlines and United from Minneapolis; Delta SkyWest United and US Airways from Salt Lake City; and United, Frontier, and Delta from Denver serve the airport with daily flights that connect to every major U.S. city. Rental cars from the major chains are available at the airport.

VISITOR INFORMATION   For information about the area, call or write **South Dakota Tourism,** 711 E. Wells Ave., Pierre, SD 57501-3369 (© **800/S-DAKOTA** [732-5682] for brochures or 605/773-3301; www.TravelSD.com).

MOUNT RUSHMORE NATIONAL MEMORIAL

Widely regarded as one of the man-made wonders of the world, Mount Rushmore is as much a work of art as it is an engineering marvel. The faces of Washington, Jefferson, Lincoln, and Theodore Roosevelt carved into granite make up one of America's most enduring icons.

To get to Mount Rushmore, take I-90 to exit 57 at Rapid City, and then take U.S. 16 (Mt. Rushmore Rd.) southwest to **Keystone,** then Hwy. 244 to the entrance. For information, contact **Mount Rushmore National Memorial,** P.O. Box 268, Keystone, SD 57751-0268 (© **605/574-2523;** www.nps.gpve/moru). The **visitor center,** just inside the entrance to the memorial, is open every day of the year (except Christmas) from 8am to 5pm in winter and 8am to 10pm in summer. Mount Rushmore has no admission charge, but there's a $10 fee for parking. Limited free parking is available across from the main parking lot as you arrive at Rushmore from Keystone.

You really need only 2 to 3 hours to see everything. Particularly in summer, try to come at the very beginning or end of your day. Excellent light at daybreak, coupled with its scenic setting and great breakfasts in the **Carver's Cafe,** make Mount Rushmore hard to beat for the first stop of the day. The patriotic ranger program and dramatic lighting ceremony, held nightly at 9pm mid-May through September, also make the memorial memorable at night.

While Mount Rushmore is best enjoyed on foot, many visitors overlook an impressive view of the sculpture that can be reached by car. After leaving the park's parking lot, turn right on S. Dak. 244 and proceed west, then northwest, around the memorial. Less than a mile from the parking lot, you'll discover the proud profile of George Washington in the upper-right corner of your windshield. While surveying the scene, keep an eye out for Rocky Mountain goats that frequent the memorial and the Black Elk Wilderness Area to the west.

Note: Though it's an American icon, some Native Americans consider the monument an intrusion on sacred landscapes that were swiped from them. We know a member of the Illini tribe who calls the monument "the Ugly Faces." She's not alone.

CUSTER STATE PARK

There's little doubt that, had not thoughtful state leaders preserved 83 square miles of the Black Hills as Custer State Park, the area would have become a national park. Its natural attractions are that outstanding. Perhaps the park's main draw is its 1,500-head herd of bison, along with its many elk, deer, and antelope.

The park is between Mount Rushmore and Wind Cave. It's accessible via S. Dak. 79 and S. Dak. 36 from the east, U.S. 16A from the north and west, and S. Dak. 87 from the north and south. For information, contact the park directly at HC83, Box 70, Custer, SD 57730-9705 (© **605/255-4515;** www.sdgfp.info/parks/Regions/Custer/Index.htm). Once in the park, head to the **Peter Norbeck Visitor Center,** 13329 U.S. Hwy. 16A, Custer, SD 57730, between the State Game Lodge and the Coolidge Inn Store on U.S. 16A; it offers informational brochures, exhibits, and a variety of displays. Also, the **Wildlife Station Visitor Center,** on the southeast part of the Wildlife Loop, offers shade, information, and exhibits. An annual park pass is $23; a temporary license (valid for 7 days) is $5 per person or $12 per vehicle. For memorable sightseeing, pick any of the park's three scenic drives: the Needles Highway, the Wildlife Loop Road, or the Iron Mountain Road. Each of these winding drives is enjoyed at a slower pace—25 mph or slower.

The **Needles Highway** is a mesmerizing 14-mile journey through pine and spruce forests, meadows surrounded by birch and quaking aspen, and giant granite spires that reach to the sky. Visitors pass the picturesque waters of Sylvan Lake, walk through tunnels, and pass a unique rock formation called the "Needle's Eye."

The **Wildlife Loop Road** is an 18-mile drive through open grasslands and pine-clad hills—an area that is home to most of the park's wildlife. Count pronghorn, bison, white-tailed and mule deer, elk, coyote, begging burros, prairie dogs, eagles, hawks, and other birds. The best wildlife-viewing time is early morning and evening, when animals are most active. Stop by the Wildlife Station Visitor Center on the southeast part of the loop for information and interesting exhibits.

Although only a portion of the scenic **Iron Mountain Road** rests in Custer State Park, it ranks as a must-see on any South Dakota visit. The winding road runs between Mount Rushmore and the junction of U.S. 16A and S. Dak. 36. Along the route are wildfire exhibits, wooden pig-tail bridges, pullouts with wonderful views, and tunnels that frame the four presidents at Mount Rushmore. Some of the tunnels have vehicle height and width limits, so RV drivers should check restrictions ahead of time.

Custer State Park is home to a wide variety of **hiking** experiences, ranging from short nature walks to backcountry treks through some of the grandest scenery anywhere. A 22-mile segment of the South Dakota Centennial Trail, the **Harney Peak Summit Trail,**

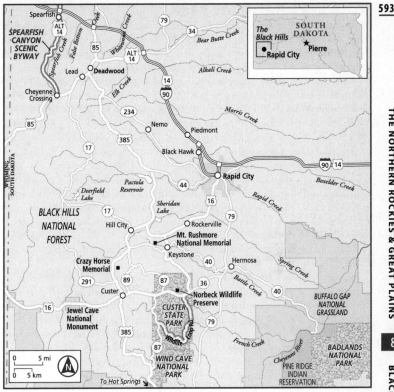

extends through Custer State Park. The **Cathedral Spires Trail** is also a popular choice. Most trails are open to mountain bikers, too.

CRAZY HORSE MEMORIAL

The world's largest mountain carving is so big that all four heads on Mount Rushmore would fit inside the chief's head. Begun in 1947 by the late Polish-American sculptor Korczak Ziolkowski in response to a request from Lakota chief Henry Standing Bear, the monument is being carried on by Korczak's large family with donations and private funding (the sculptor refused to accept federal funding, and all admission fees get funneled into the project). The finished sculpture will be 641 feet long and 563 feet high. The carving is in Crazy Horse, north of Custer on U.S. 385.

At the base of the mountain, the **Indian Museum of North America** features exhibits focusing on the history and tribal life of many Native American cultures. Lectures, concerts, and other special events are held here in summer. The building itself—a wonder of natural wood and light—is worth a look; it was designed by Korczak himself to fit in with the landscape. The museum and memorial are open year-round from 8am to 5pm in winter, in summer 8am to 10pm with a laser light show beginning when dark. Admission is $10 adults and children or $27 per carload. Children 5 and under are admitted free. For more information, call © 605/673-4681, or go online to **www.crazyhorse.org**.

The rolling prairies of western South Dakota run smack into the ponderosa pine forests of the Black Hills in Wind Cave National Park. The park is home to prairie dog towns, large herds of elk and pronghorn antelope, and more than 300 bison—and that's just aboveground. Below lies the eighth-longest cave in the world.

Wind Cave is about an hour's drive south of Mount Rushmore on Route 87. From points south or west, you can also take U.S. 385. For advance information, contact **Wind Cave National Park,** R.R. 1, P.O. Box 190, Hot Springs, SD 57747-9430 (© **605/745-4600;** www.nps.gov/wica). The **visitor center** (right off U.S. 385) is open year-round from 8am to 4:30pm (except Thanksgiving and Christmas) and has books, brochures, exhibits, and slide programs about the cave and other park resources. It also has tickets for cave tours and a posted schedule of activities, including talks and nature walks. Wind Cave National Park has no entrance fee, but it does charge for cave tours, ranging from $7 adults and $3.50 ages 6 to 16 (half-price with a Golden Age Passport) for a simple guided tour to $23 for a 4-hour introduction to basic caving techniques; most tours are $9. The park's highways and backcountry roads provide the scenic backdrop for some of the best **wildlife-viewing** opportunities in the region. Wildlife abounds in this rugged preserve, and you may be able to see some of it as you drive down through Custer State Park on S. Dak. 87 to Wind Cave.

No visitor should leave the park without taking a **cave tour.** Five are offered in the summer (fewer in the off season); call ahead for departure times, as they vary. They range from the easy 1-hour the **Garden of Eden Tour** ($7 adults) to the **Candlelight Tour** ($9 adults), one of the most popular, in which participants trek through a less developed, unlighted part of the cave to experience the cave by candlelight. This strenuous tour covers 1 mile of rugged trail and lasts 2 hours. Reservations, available up to 1 month beforehand, are strongly advised. Most tours, even the easiest, involve climbing lots of steps, but all give you an excellent perspective on a unique underground world.

Visitors with more time should get out on the trail. The park hosts a 6-mile stretch of the **Centennial Trail,** which goes through the heart of the Black Hills and offers a taste of everything the area has to offer. There's also usually a ranger-led **prairie hike** in summer mornings at 9am.

WHERE TO STAY IN RAPID CITY & THE BLACK HILLS

Hotels in Rapid City include the **Alex Johnson Hotel,** 523 Sixth St. (© **800/888-2539** or 605/342-1210; www.alexjohnson.com), a restored hotel with moderate prices listed on the National Historic Register; and the **Econo Lodge,** 625 E. Disk Dr. on I-90 at exit 59 (© **800/214-1971** or 605/342-6400; www.choicehotels.com/hotel/sd010), with an indoor water slide, cable TV, Jacuzzi suites, and guest laundry facilities.

Custer State Park has five mountain resorts and seven campgrounds. The **State Game Lodge,** 13389 U.S. 16A near the park's main visitor center (© **605/255-4541**), features historic decor and pine-shaded cabins. A new addition is **Creekside Lodge,** with 30 large rooms and meeting room (© **605/255-4541**). The **Sylvan Lake Lodge,** on S. Dak. 87 at its junction with S. Dak. 89 in the northeast corner of Custer State Park (© **605/574-2561**), overlooking Sylvan Lake and the Harney Range, provides cozy lodge rooms and rustic family cabins. The **Blue Bell Lodge & Resort,** on S. Dak. 87 just before the turnoff for the Wildlife Loop Road (if you're traveling south; © **605/255-4772**), offers handcrafted log cabins as well as lodge rooms, the Buffalo Willow Lounge, and hayrides and chuck-wagon cookouts. The **Legion Lake Resort** (© **605/255-4521**), near the

tures 25 cottages nestled in the pines on the lakeshore. Rates at these lodges range from
around $95 for a sleeping cabin at Legion Lake to $410 for a four-bedroom cabin at the
State Game Resort. All are near outdoor activities such as fishing, hiking, and animal
watching; some offer excursions into the backcountry. For more information or to make
reservations at any of Custer State Park's resorts, call ✆ **605/255-4772,** or surf over to
www.custerresorts.com.

WHERE TO DINE IN RAPID CITY & THE BLACK HILLS

Dining in the Black Hills tends to be casual, but the selection can be wide, ranging from
homemade pies and ranch-raised buffalo to hearty steaks and local pheasant.

The **Carver's Cafe,** at Mount Rushmore National Memorial (✆ **605/574-2515),**
open daily 8am to 4:30pm, offers a "Monumental" breakfast buffet with eggs, French
toast, ham, bacon, and more from 8 to 11am for $4.95. Lunch is also served. Near
Mount Rushmore, in Keystone, you'll find the **Ruby House Restaurant,** Main Street
(✆ **605/666-4404**), which offers steaks, seafood, and other specialties in a richly
appointed Victorian dining room. Open daily 11am to 9pm. It's closed in winter.

There's no dining at Wind Cave National Park; in Custer State Park, the **Pleasant
Pheasant Dining Room** in the State Game Lodge serves great breakfasts, such as buffalo
sausages with hot biscuits. In summer, a lunch buffet and dinners are served.

In Rapid City, try the **1915 Firehouse Brewing Co.,** 610 Main St. (✆ **605/348-
1915**), where brats, burgers, buffalo, and chicken wings accompany the hearty microbrews on tap. Open 11am to 10pm every day except Sunday, when it opens at 4pm. The
Fireside Inn, 7 miles west of Rapid City on U.S. 44 (✆ **605/342-3900**), with prime rib
and an intimate fireside (and nonsmoking) setting, makes a romantic choice for dinner.
Open daily 5 to 9pm for dinner only.

BADLANDS NATIONAL PARK

The Badlands offers not only an unforgettably eerie landscape, but also a wealth of plant
and animal life. You'll find 56 different types of grasses here—and almost no trees. Wildflowers abound in a good year. As for animals, you're likely to see bison and Rocky
Mountain bighorn sheep (the native Audubon's bighorn is now extinct), as well as prong-
horns and mule deer, if you travel at dawn and dusk. You can also see desert and eastern
cottontail rabbits darting in and out of the grass. And prairie dogs thrive; there's a prairie
dog town just beyond the end of the Badlands Loop Road.

Essentials

GETTING THERE Badlands National Park is easily accessed by car either on U.S. 44
east of Rapid City or off I-90 at Wall or Cactus Flat. Westbound I-90 travelers take exit
131 south (Cactus Flat) onto S. Dak. 240, which leads to the park boundary and the Ben
Reifel Visitor Center at Cedar Pass. This roadway becomes Badlands Loop Road, the
park's primary scenic roadway. After passing through the park, S. Dak. 240 rejoins I-90
at exit 110 at Wall.

VISITOR INFORMATION For information in advance, write to 25216 Ben Reifel Rd.,
P.O. Box 6, Interior, SD 57750, call ✆ **605/433-5361,** or check out the park's website at
www.nps.gov/badl. Once you're in the park, head to the visitor center at Cedar Pass or
White River. The **Ben Reifel Visitor Center** at Cedar Pass is open daily year-round (7am–
8pm June 10–Aug 15, and 9am–4pm the rest of the year) and features exhibits on the
park's natural and cultural history. The nearby Cedar Pass Lodge has cabins, a gift shop,

and a restaurant; there's a campground (first-come, first-served, $10; no hookups and 14-day limit) here as well. The **White River Visitor Center** (📞 605/455-2878) is open during the summer season only and houses exhibits about Oglala Sioux history.

ENTRANCE FEES   There is an entrance fee of $15 per passenger vehicle, which allows admission for up to 7 days. The single-person entry fee is $10 per motorcycle, bicycle, or person on foot, plus $7 for each additional passenger.

Seeing the Highlights

It's relatively easy to see the highlights of the North Unit of Badlands National Park in a day. A few miles south of the park's northeast entrance (on S. Dak. 240, the closest entrance to I-90) is the **park headquarters,** open year-round, which includes the Ben Reifel Visitor Center, Cedar Pass Lodge, a campground, an amphitheater, and a dump station. After stopping at the visitor center, which has a bookstore, information desk, and restrooms, and an orientation video (recommended), it's time to hit the trail.

The visitor center is within 5 miles of several trail heads, scenic overlooks, and three self-guided nature trails. Each of the trails offers an opportunity to view some of the formations for which the Badlands is famous. The **Fossil Exhibit Trail** is wheelchair accessible. The **Cliff Shelf Nature Trail** and the **Door Trail** are moderately strenuous and provide impressive glimpses of Badlands formations. But none is longer than a mile, and any one of them can be hiked comfortably in less than an hour.

Leading from the visitor center is the 30-mile-long **Badlands Loop Road,** the park's most popular scenic roadway. Angling northwest toward the town of Wall, this road passes numerous overlooks and trail heads, each of which commands inspiring views of the Badlands and the prairies of the Buffalo Gap National Grassland. Binoculars will increase your chances of spotting bison, pronghorn, bighorn sheep, or coyote. The paved portion of the Loop Road ends at the turnoff for the **Pinnacles Entrance.** Beyond this point, the pavement ends and the road becomes the Sage Creek Rim Road, a 30-mile gravel road, at the end of which is the **Sage Creek Campground,** although this one is primitive and does not offer drinking water. Five miles west of the end of the pavement, a visit to the **Roberts Prairie Dog Town** gives you a chance to watch black-tailed prairie dogs "barking" their warnings and protecting their "town." The Sage Creek Basin is the best spot to see bison and bighorn sheep.

Warnings in the Badlands

Water in the Badlands is too full of silt for humans to drink and will quickly clog a water filter. When hiking or traveling in the park, always carry an adequate supply of water. Drinking water is available only at the Cedar Pass area, the White River Visitor Center, and the Pinnacles Ranger Station.

Climbing Badlands buttes and rock formations is allowed but can be extremely dangerous due to loose, crumbly rock. Watch for rattlesnakes and cacti hidden in the prairie grass.

Finally, Badlands **weather** is often unpredictable. Heavy rain, hail, and high, often damaging winds are possible, particularly during spring and summer. Lightning strikes are also common. And winters are simply brutal. But what were you expecting from a place called the Badlands?

(© **605/455-2878**), open from late May to August. The visitor center has drinking water, restrooms, information, Lakota exhibits, and a video program.

Where to Stay & Dine in the Badlands

The night sky in the Badlands is an unforgettable sight, so we recommend staying overnight if you have time. **Camping** is available inside Badlands National Park at either the Cedar Pass Campground or the Sage Creek Primitive Campground (no reservations). Camping in pullouts, parking areas, or picnic grounds is not permitted. The park also provides free permits for backcountry camping.

The only other accommodations in the park are adjacent to the Ben Reifel Visitor Center, with 25 cabins, at **Cedar Pass Lodge Cabins,** P.O. Box 5, Interior, SD 57750 (© **605/433-5460;** fax 605/433-5560). The lodge also has an inexpensive restaurant, whose menu includes buffalo burgers, Indian tacos, and trout, as well as ice-cold soft drinks, beer, and wine.

You'll find a few more restaurants and two motels a few miles north of the park in the small town of Wall, home of the world-famous **Wall Drug Store,** 510 Main St. (© **605/ 279-2175;** www.walldrug.com). The **Super 8 Motel,** 711 Glenn St., 2 blocks north of I-90 at exit 110 (© **800/800-8000** or 605/279-2688), has clean rooms at reasonable rates and is open year-round. The **Best Western Plains Motel,** 712 Glenn St., 2 blocks north of I-90 at exit 110 (© **800/528-1234** or 605/279-2145; www.bestwesternplains. com), is another reliable choice.

A SIDE TRIP TO DEADWOOD

Deadwood was once known as the wildest, wickedest, woolliest town in the West, where Wild Bill Hickok was gunned down and where Calamity Jane claimed she could out-drink, out-swear, and out-spit any man. Its colorful history inspired the eponymous, award-winning HBO series (which was actually filmed in California). At the same time, the city's merchants, bankers, and saloonkeepers invested their money in beautiful Victorian buildings and residences that still stand as solid testaments to civic pride.

Today legalized gambling has revitalized the old town, with more than 80 casinos. Plan to park in one of the edge-of-town lots and take a trolley shuttle into town.

Deadwood is northwest of Rapid City off I-90 and U.S. 14. For more information on accommodations, walking tours, museums, attractions, special events, and gaming packages, contact the **Deadwood Chamber of Commerce & Visitor Bureau,** 735 Main St. (© **800/999-1876;** www.deadwood.org), or stop by the **History and Information Center** in the classic train depot at 3 Siever St.

The **Adams Museum,** 54 Sherman St. (© **605/578-1714;** www.adamsmuseum andhouse.org), is a repository of local history and memorabilia, including a stuffed two-headed calf. The **Broken Boot Gold Mine** (© **605/578-1876**) has guided tours of a gold mine and offers gold-panning. Wild Bill Hickok, Calamity Jane, and other notorious residents are buried in **Mount Moriah Cemetery.**

Deadwood restaurants are more upscale than what you'll find in the rest of the area. **Jakes,** upstairs from the casual dining room, **Midnight Star,** 677 Main St. (© **800/999-6482** or 605/578-1555), owned by Kevin Costner and his brother Dan, offers a menu ranging from pheasant quesadillas to buffalo carpaccio. Locals consider it the best dining in the region. If you're not hungry, drop in to peruse the displays of movie costumes and props from *Dances with Wolves* at Diamond Lil's bar, below Jakes.

In nearby Lead (pronounced Leed), **Homestake** is the oldest gold mine in continuous operation in the Western Hemisphere, with a visitor center open year-round at 160 W. Main St. (© **888/701-0164** or 605/584-3110; www.homestakevisitorcenter.com).

8 IDAHO

Think Idaho and imagine a state bursting with natural beauty. Within its borders you will find vast stretches of sage-covered high desert, white-water rivers rolling and roaring through Rocky Mountain canyons, eerie volcanic landscapes, jagged snowy mountain peaks, glacier lakes, and green pine woods. Most of all, Idaho is home to welcoming and friendly people who will help make your visit a memorable one. For information on the state, call © **800/VISIT-ID** (847-4843), or go to **www.visitidaho.org**.

BOISE

Boise is one of the nation's fastest-growing metropolitan areas. A remarkably sophisticated and culturally active city of 210,000, Boise offers a variety of scenery, indoor and outdoor activities, and great restaurants. The modern cityscape is nestled against mainly undeveloped foothills and offers a moderate four-season climate with easy access to year-round activities.

Essentials

GETTING THERE   By Plane   Boise Airport (© **208/383-3110;** www.cityofboise. org/departments/airport), 3 miles south of the city center, serves much of southern Idaho with service from most western and some Midwestern hubs.

By Car   The major route into Boise is **I-84** from the southeast (Salt Lake City) and northwest (Portland and Seattle). Twenty-four-hour road conditions are available at © **208/336-6600.**

VISITOR INFORMATION   For advance information, contact the **Boise Convention and Visitors Bureau,** 312 S. 9th St., Ste. 100, Boise, ID 83702 (© **800/635-5240** or 208/344-7777; www.boise.org). **Visitor Information Centers** are located in the Boise Centre on the Grove, 850 W. Front St. (© **208/344-5338**), and near the airport at 2676 Airport Way, near I-84 at the Vista Avenue exit (© **208/385-0362**). Hours at both centers vary seasonally, so call before you go.

Getting Outside

Boise offers a huge variety of outside activities. Whether you ski, bike, swim, jog, or just like to enjoy the out-of-doors from your favorite sidewalk cafe table, you will find something year-round here.

Twenty-five miles of Greenbelt, mostly paved, have been established along the Boise River and provide recreation for Boiseans and visitors of all ages. The Greenbelt connects most of the city's large downtown parks as well. You can access the Greenbelt from anywhere downtown—just head for the river.

For slightly more strenuous hiking or biking activity, check out the **Ridge to Rivers Trail System** (**www.ridgetorivers.org**) in the foothills above Boise. This 125-mile system has been established by connecting public land and right of ways through private property to provide several multiuse nonmotorized trails around the foothills.

While not a big spot for watersports, a Boise tradition is floating the Boise River. You can float on almost anything, and rafts and tubes can be rented at **Barber Park** (© 208/343-6564). The Boise River is also a great place to fish. For fishing information, pick up the **Idaho Department of Fish & Game**'s *Official Guide to Fishing in Idaho* and *General Fishing Seasons and Rules* in local shops, or contact the department at 600 S. Walnut St., P.O. Box 25, Boise, ID 83707 (© **208/334-3700;** http://fishandgame. idaho.gov).

Though it doesn't quite have the reputation of other ski areas in the state, **Bogus Basin** (© **800/367-4397** or 208/332-5100; www.bogusbasin.com) is about a 45-minute drive (16 miles north) from Boise. With 2,600 acres of skiable terrain, 52 runs, and 23 miles of Nordic trails, Bogus offers deep powder, short lift lines, and great night skiing. It's open, on average, for 140 days beginning Thanksgiving Day. From mid-June through October, the ski area remains open to mountain bikers along the Shafer Butte Trail System, a 52-mile bike trail that eventually links up with the Ridge to Rivers Trail system.

What to See & Do

Boise is home to more people of Basque ancestry than anywhere outside the Basque Country in Europe. You can learn more by visiting the **Basque Museum and Cultural Center,** 611 Grove St. (© **208/343-2671;** www.basquemuseum.com). Just a few blocks away, you can wander riverfront Julia Davis Park, which houses the **Idaho Historical Museum** (© 208/334-2120; www.idahohistory.net/museum.html), the **Boise Art Museum** (© 208/345-8330; www.boiseartmuseum.org), **Zoo Boise** (© 208/384-4260; www.zooboise.org), and the **Discovery Center of Idaho** (© 208/343-9895; www.scidaho.org), a family-oriented science-and-activities center. The park's newest addition is the **Idaho Anne Frank Human Rights Memorial,** across from the art museum. The memorial is part of an educational park dedicated to promoting respect for human dignity and diversity.

The unofficial center of Boise (or "BoDo," for Boise Downtown) is the **Grove,** a public square at 8th Street and Grove Street, with a large fountain, summer concerts, sunbathing, and great people-watching. On Saturdays from mid-April through October, the open-air **Capitol City Public Market** takes over 8th Street just north of the Grove, with an excellent selection of local produce, crafts, and fresh food carts.

Head up to the **Idaho State Capitol** (© 208/334-5174), the nation's only state capitol building heated with geothermal water. Travel east of town on Warm Springs Avenue and take a tour of the **Old Idaho Penitentiary** (© 208/334-2844; www.idahohistory.net/oldpen.html), built in territorial times and holding prisoners until 1973. Also part of the Old Pen complex are the History of Electricity in Idaho Museum, the Idaho Transportation Museum, and the Museum of Mining & Geology.

Farther out, 6 miles south of I-84 exit 50, don't miss the **World Center for Birds of Prey** (© 208/362-3716; www.peregrinefund.org), with a visitor center and injured-bird recovery area that serves as an introduction to the 500,000-acre **Snake River Birds of Prey National Conservation Area** (© 208/384-3300; www.birdsofprey.blm.gov), home to one of the nation's densest concentrations of nesting raptors, along with more than 250 other wildlife species.

Where to Stay

For the best digs in town, try the **Grove Hotel,** 245 S. Capitol Blvd. (© **800/716-6199** or 208/333-8000; www.grovehotelboise.com), which has all the amenities you could want and high-season doubles starting at $149—plus, it's connected to Qwest Arena, a sports and entertainment complex. Downtown's historic hotel is the lovingly refurbished **Owyhee Plaza,** 1109 Main St. (© 800/233-4611 or 208/343-4611; www.owyheeplaza.com), with doubles starting at $99. **Hotel 43,** 981 Grove St. (© 208/342-4622; www.hotel43.com), is stylishly remodeled and near the convention center; double rooms start at $179. Nearby, the **Courtyard by Marriott,** 222 S. Broadway (© 800/321-2211 or 208/331-2700), offers doubles starting at $129. The airport area, only 3 miles from downtown, offers a large number of moderately priced hotels, with doubles from $65 to $75. Try the **Inn America** (© 800/469-4667 or 208/389-9800; www.innamerica.com), the Comfort Inn Airport (© 800/228-5150 or 208/336-0077; www.comfortinn.com/hotel/id011), and **Extended Stay America** (© 800/398-7829 or 208/363-9040; www.extendedstayhotels.com).

Where to Dine

At the following fine-dining restaurants, entrees range between $18 and $30. For a unique dining experience, try **Mortimer's Idaho Cuisine,** 110 S. 5th St. (© 208/338-6550), featuring inventive regional cuisine based on locally sourced produce and meats. One of Boise's favorites and right on the Greenway, **Cottonwood Grille,** 913 W. River St. (© 208/333-9800), offers French via Northwest cuisine in a lodgelike dining room dominated by a massive stone fireplace. **Barbacoa,** 276 Bobwhite Court (© 208/338-5000), offers upscale Latin cuisine in a wildly decorated dining room. For old-fashioned elegance and fine service, try the **Gamekeeper,** in the Owyhee Plaza Hotel (© 208/343-4611), or **Chandler's** (© 208/383-3479), the swank dining room and martini bar in Hotel 43. In a city known for steaks, try **Lock, Stock and Barrel,** 205 N. 10th St. (© 208/343-4334), for hand-cut steaks and old-fashioned atmosphere. To experience Basque cooking, drive a dozen miles west of Boise to the town of Meridian, where cozy family-oriented **Epi's Basque Restaurant,** 1115 N. Main St., Meridian (© 208/884-0142), serves fantastic northern Spanish country-style cooking that many consider the best Basque cooking outside of Europe.

Boise's pubs and wine bars are popular for lunch and inexpensive dinners ($8–$12) and locally produced beverages. **TableRock Brew Pub,** 705 Fulton St. (© 208/342-0944), has excellent ales and classic pub fare, while the **8th St. Wine Café,** 405 S. 8th St. (© 208/426-9463), offers casual fine dining with a selection of local wines. **Gernika Basque Pub & Eatery,** 202 S. Capitol Blvd. (© 208/344-2175), features Basque cooking in addition to traditional soup and sandwiches, and **Ha'Penny Bridge Pub,** 855 Broad St. (© 208/343-5568), is the local Irish pub. For a unique experience, try **Bardenay,** 610 Grove (© 208/426-0538), the first "distillery-pub" in the United States, featuring its own rum, vodka, and gin in addition to deli-style food. For Boise's favorite breakfast spot, don't miss **Goldy's,** 108 S. Capitol Blvd. (© 208/345-4100).

SUN VALLEY & KETCHUM

The nation's first destination ski resort, Sun Valley was developed near the small town of Ketchum in 1936 by Averell Harriman and immediately attracted the Hollywood set. Still a hangout for the stars, it has been named the number-one ski resort by *Condé Nast Traveler, Ski Magazine,* and *Gourmet Magazine.* It has received numerous other honors as one of the top resorts in the nation.

Essentials

GETTING THERE   By Plane   The closest airport to Sun Valley is **Friedman Memorial Airport** (© 208/788-4956), 12 miles south in Hailey. There are direct flights from

Salt Lake City, Los Angeles, and Seattle. You can also fly into Boise and take a **Sun Valley**
Express bus (© **877/622-8267;** www.sunvalleyexpress.com). Be sure to check availability ahead of time and book your bus ticket in advance.

By Car The major route into Sun Valley is **Hwy. 75,** which runs south from **I-90** at Missoula, Montana, and north from **I-84** at Twin Falls.

VISITOR INFORMATION You can get a vacation planner and free lodging reservation service from the **Sun Valley–Ketchum Chamber of Commerce,** P.O. Box 2420, Sun Valley, ID 83353 (© **866/305-0408;** www.visitsunvalley.com). A **Visitor Information Center** for the area is located on the corner of 4th and Main in Ketchum. You can also check out the seasonally updated *Official Sun Valley Guide* at **www.sunvalley central.com.**

Getting Outside

Sun Valley's claim to fame is its world-class ski resort (© **800/786-8259** or 208/622-2151; www.sunvalley.com). You can choose from two mountains with more than 2,000 skiable acres with 75 ski runs (the longest 3 miles), 25 miles of groomed cross-country trails, and 21 chairlifts. High-season lift tickets are $80 adult. For backcountry skiing, try **Sun Valley Trekking Company** (© **208/788-1966;** www.svtrek.com). In summer, they offer day hikes and guided mountain-biking trips. For sleigh rides, try the **Sun Valley Horsemen's Center** (© **208/622-2387**). You can enjoy ice-skating year-round at the Sun Valley Resort Lodge's two rinks. Saturday nights during the summer, Olympic skaters perform on the outdoor ice rink adjoining the lodge (© **208/622-2135** for reservations).

In addition to the resort's trails, cross-country skiers and snowshoers can explore the 75-mile North Valley Trails system, which meanders through the Big Wood River Valley north of town and leads to the gold-rush ghost town of Galena, where the rustic **Galena Lodge** (© **208/726-4010**) serves up meals to skiers and other passersby.

Summer in Sun Valley brings even more outdoor adventure. Almost anything you could ask for is available—from paragliding to white-water rafting to skeet shooting. Ketchum is filled with outfitters, and you'll have no trouble lining up activities even at the last minute. Trail systems around Ketchum offer miles of paved and unpaved trails for biking, hiking, skating, or walking. Information is available from the **Blaine County Recreation District** (© **208/788-2117;** www.bcrd.org) or at the Ketchum Visitor Center. In summer, you can ride the Sun Valley Resort **chairlift** (© **208/622-6136**) to the top of Bald Mountain and hike in wildflower meadows, or bring along a mountain bike and ride down the slopes on two wheels. If you want to really get away, try a llama trek with **Venture Outdoors** (© **800/528-5262;** www.venout.com); hiking, mountain biking, and kayaking adventures are also offered.

The **Sun Valley Resort Golf Course** (© **208/622-2251**) offers an 18-hole Robert Trent Jones, Jr.–designed course, rated the number-one course in Idaho by *Golf Digest.* The 9-hole **Bigwood Golf Course** (© **208/726-4024;** www.bigwoodgolf.com) is a challenging public course.

Other activities include tennis at the **Sun Valley Resort Tennis Club** (© **208/622-2156**), horseback riding at **Sun Valley Resort Horsemen's Center** (© **208/622-2387**), white-water rafting trips with **White Otter Outdoor Adventures** (© **208/726-4331;** www.whiteotter.com), and fishing. A guide to area fishing is available at the Ketchum visitor center.

Take a drive north of Ketchum to the **Sawtooth National Recreation Area** (© 208/727-5013; www.fs.fed.us/r4/sawtooth) to view spectacular jagged peaks. The headquarters is located 8 miles north of Ketchum on Hwy. 75.

Southeast of Ketchum you will find the **Craters of the Moon National Monument,** a relatively recent (only 2,000 years old) lava bed. This eerie landscape will make you feel as if you've landed on the moon. There is a **visitor center** off Hwy. 20/26/93 (© 208/527-3257), which has maps of the area.

Closer to Ketchum you can visit **Ernest Hemingway's grave** in the Ketchum Cemetery on Route 75 North at 10th Street East, or the **Ernest Hemingway Memorial** alongside Trail Creek just north of Sun Valley Lodge. Check out the **Heritage and Ski Museum** in Ketchum to see artifacts from Idaho's ski history (© 208/726-8118). For a history of Sun Valley and its famous visitors, check out the Sun Valley Lodge lobby to see dozens of photos dating from the 1930s picturing visitors from the Shah of Iran to Lucille Ball.

Where to Stay

The **Sun Valley Resort** (© 800/786-8259 or 208/622-2151; www.sunvalley.com) offers more than 500 rooms, ranging from the original lodge and inn to more than 100 apartments and condominiums. High-season rates in winter are higher on weekends and much higher over the holidays; a basic hotel double starts around $239 and goes up quickly. Minimum stays may apply. Off-season rates (spring and fall) are about 25% less. There are not many bargain rates in the Sun Valley area, but a couple of lower-priced hotels offer high-season rooms between $140 and $160, and discounted off-season rates. **Best Western Kentwood Lodge,** 180 S. Main St. (© 800/805-1001 or 208/726-4114; www.bestwestern.com/kentwoodlodge), is in the heart of Ketchum, and the **Best Western Tyrolean Lodge,** 260 Cottonwood St. (© 800/333-7912 or 208/726-5336; www.bestwestern.com), is by the River Run chairlift.

Where to Dine

Sun Valley and Ketchum offer a huge variety of restaurants for a community their size. Top-end choices for fine dining include two Continental restaurants, the **Lodge Dining Room** at the Sun Valley Lodge (© 208/622-2150) and **Michel's Christiania Restaurant,** 309 Walnut Ave. N. (© 208/726-3388), where dinner for two will easily top $120. The **Sawtooth Club,** 231 Main St. N. (© 208/726-5233), and the vintage **Pioneer Saloon,** 308 N. Main St. (© 208/726-3139), are favorites for steaks and seafood in the $18-to-$30 range. An excellent spot for casual fine dining is the **Ketchum Grill,** 520 East Ave. (© 208/726-4660). **Whiskey Jacques,** 251 N. Main St. (© 208/726-5297), and the **Roosevelt Tavern,** 280 N. Main St. (© 208/726-0051), both offer live music and bistro-style dining. The **Kneadery,** 260 Leadville Ave. N. (© 208/726-9462), is a local favorite for breakfast. For a funky Old West bar, check out the **Casino Club,** 220 N. Main St. (© 208/726-9901), one of Hemingway's favorite watering holes.

COEUR D'ALENE

Idaho's northern resort town, Coeur d'Alene, sits amid lakes and green pines, and offers year-round recreation and one of the world's top resort hotels and golf courses.

Essentials

GETTING THERE The closest major airport is **Spokane International Airport** (© 509/455-6455; www.spokaneairports.net) in Spokane, Washington, 40 miles west.

Major highways into Coeur d'Alene are **I-90** from the west (Spokane) and east (Missoula, Montana), and **Hwy. 95** from the south (Boise).

VISITOR INFORMATION Contact the **Coeur d'Alene Visitor and Convention Services,** P.O. Box 850, Coeur d'Alene, ID 83816 (© **877/782-9232;** www.coeurdalene. org).

Getting Outside

Coeur d'Alene is an outdoor playground. Twenty-five miles long, glacier-dug **Lake Coeur d'Alene** is the center of activities. Boating, sailing, jet-skiing, water-skiing, fishing, and anything else you can do on water are available. The world's first water skis were used on Lake Coeur d'Alene in the 1920s. Today you can jet-ski, take a seaplane tour with **Brooks Seaplane Service** (© **208/664-2842**), or parasail with **Coeur d'Alene Parasail** (© **208/765-5367**). **Lake Coeur d'Alene Cruises** offers a variety of cruises, including a sunset dinner cruise (© **800/365-8338**).

A summer visit means you can tee up on the **Coeur d'Alene Golf Course** (© **800/ 688-5253;** www.cdaresort.com/golf), one of only 16 golf resorts in America to receive the "five-star" designation by *Golf Digest* (which also named it "America's most beautiful resort course"), and one of 20 with a *Golf Magazine* Gold Medal. The course is known for its famous **Floating Green,** anchored to the lake bottom and reachable only by boat.

Winter in northern Idaho means skiing. A 30-mile drive east of Coeur d'Alene brings you to **Silver Mountain Ski Resort,** near Kellogg (© **800/204-6428** or 208/783-1111; www.silvermt.com), with the world's longest gondola operating year-round. Summer concerts are held at Silver Mountain; an indoor waterpark operates year-round. **Schweitzer Mountain Resort** (© **800/831-8810;** www.schweitzer.com), 44 miles north in Sandpoint, offers stunning views of Lake Pend Oreille. Summer brings horseback riding, biking, and adventure camps.

What to See & Do

Coeur d'Alene has a variety of historical and natural sites for the visitor. The **Museum of North Idaho** (© **208/664-3448;** www.museumni.org) covers the history of the area with exhibits and photos. Part of that history goes back to the **Cataldo Mission,** 28 miles east on I-90 (© **208/682-3814**), built in 1842 and the oldest-standing building in Idaho. Climb **Tubbs Hill** in town for a view of the area. For family fun, check out **Silverwood Theme Park** (© **208/683-3400;** www.silverwoodthemepark.com), 15 minutes north on Hwy. 95, with 65 rides and a waterpark. In town, **Wild Waters,** 2119 N. Government Way (© **208/667-6491;** www.wildwaterswaterpark), offers a towering water slide and other aqua activities.

Where to Stay

Dominating the shoreline in Coeur d'Alene is the **Coeur d'Alene Resort** (© **800/688-5253** or 208/765-4000; www.cdaresort.com), at the western edge of downtown, named by the readers of *Condé Nast Traveler* as America's number-one mainland resort. High-season summer rates begin at $229 double. Find cheaper rates ($130–$180), but no lake views, at **La Quinta Inn & Suites,** 2209 E. Sherman Ave. (© **800/531-5900** or 208/667-6777); the **Best Western Coeur d'Alene Inn,** 414 W. Appleway (© **800/523-2464;** www.cdainn.com); and **Holiday Inn Express & Suites,** 2300 West Seltice Way (© **877/270-6397** or 208/667-3100).

Downtown, check out **Coeur d'Alene Brewing,** 209 Lakeside Ave. (© **208/664-2739**), with good pub fare; the **Wine Cellar,** 313 Sherman Ave. (© **208/664-9463**), with Mediterranean bistro dining and nightly jazz; and **Brix,** 317 Sherman Ave. (© **208/665-7407**), an upscale dining room featuring New American Cuisine, with main dishes costing $17 to $27 and the option of chef's tasting menus, starting at three courses for $35. Eight miles east on East Frontage Road is the locals' favorite for steak and prime rib, the **Wolf Lodge Steakhouse** (© **208/664-6665**). For elegant dining, dress up and make reservations at award-winning **Beverly's** (© **208/765-4000**) in the Coeur d'Alene Resort, with great views, refined service, and Northwest regional cuisine. Main dishes range from $24 to $54, with a six-course tasting menu at $75.

9 OKLAHOMA CITY

Oklahoma City was born in a single day, when the Great Land Run of April 22, 1889, allowed tens of thousands of people to race across the border on foot, horseback, wagon, and even bicycle to settle unclaimed land: What was just a solitary railroad station grew to a tent city of 10,000 residents overnight. In 1907, Oklahoma became a state, and 3 years later, Oklahoma City became its capital. But it was a tragic event—the April 1995 bombing of a federal building that claimed 168 lives—that catapulted the city to headline status on the international news front. Since then, Oklahoma City, with a population of more than 500,000 people, has reinvented itself with ongoing revitalization projects (such as the Bricktown entertainment district) that have transformed it into one of the state's most exciting destinations. Yet despite its push to modernity, its frontier heritage remains evident in attractions such as the must-see National Cowboy & Western Heritage Museum and the Oklahoma History Center, and in annual events such as Red Earth, the largest Native American festival in the world.

ESSENTIALS

GETTING THERE   By Plane   Will Rogers World Airport (© 405/680-3200; www.flyokc.com) is 10 miles southwest of downtown. The **Airport Express** (© 405/681-3311; www.taxivan.com) charges $20 for one to two passengers to downtown hotels (three or more passengers pay $7 a head), though many hotels provide free airport shuttles. A cab ride downtown costs about $20.

By Train   Amtrak (© 800/USA-RAIL [872-7245] or 405/297-0236; www.amtrak. com) provides daily service from Fort Worth, Texas (trip time: 4 hr.), to the historic downtown Santa Fe Depot at 100 E. K. Gaylord.

By Car   Major routes into Oklahoma City are **I-35** from the northeast (Kansas City, 353 miles) and south (Dallas, 205 miles); **I-40** from the east (Little Rock, 344 miles) and west (Albuquerque, 540 miles); and **I-44** from the northeast (St. Louis, 500 miles).

VISITOR INFORMATION   The **Oklahoma City Convention & Visitors Bureau** is located downtown at 189 W. Sheridan (© **800/225-5652** or 405/297-8912; www.visit okc.com) and is open Monday through Friday from 8:30am to 5pm. The state operates the **Oklahoma Welcome Center** in the city's northeastern end near Frontier City amusement park, 12229 N. I-35 Service Rd., open daily 8:30am to 5pm.

org) operates bus service to most Oklahoma City destinations Monday through Saturday; bus no. 22 is useful for traveling between downtown and the Oklahoma City Zoo
and National Cowboy & Western Heritage Museum. The fare is $1.25. Otherwise, the
best option for tourists is Metro Transit's rubber-tire **Spirit Trolleys**, with two routes (the
Blue and Red lines) circling through the downtown area and a third (the Orange Line)
making runs between downtown and hotels along Meridian to Stockyards City. Fares are
25¢ for the Red and Blue lines and $1 for the Orange, and require exact change. A pass
for all trolley lines is $2 for 1 day or $3 for 3.

SPECIAL EVENTS   Red Earth ((C) 405/427-5228; www.redearth.org), a celebration
of Native American cultures and traditions held every June, features a parade, juried art
competitions, an art market, and performing arts. From April to December, Oklahoma
hosts nine major **horse shows,** more than any other city (contact the Oklahoma City
Convention & Visitors Bureau, above, for more information).

WHAT TO SEE & DO
In the past decade, Oklahoma City's downtown has blossomed into a prime vacation
destination with new hotels, lively restaurants, the Bricktown entertainment district with
a river canal and boat rides, and several worthy attractions. One of downtown's oldest
attractions is the lovely **Myriad Botanical Gardens,** at Reno and Robinson avenues
((C) 405/297-3995; www.myriadgardens.com), a 17-acre landscaped oasis centered on a
sunken lake. Spanning the lake—and the centerpiece of the gardens—is Crystal Bridge,
a seven-story, 224-foot-long cylindrical conservatory filled with exotic plants ranging
from tropical to desert and set in a wonderland of cliffs, waterfalls, and ponds. Lizards,
fish, and butterflies also call the Crystal Bridge home. Crystal Bridge is open Monday to
Saturday 9am to 6pm and Sunday noon to 6pm. Admission costs $6 adults; $5 seniors,
children ages 13 to 18, and students; and $3 children ages 4 to 12.

Nearby is the **Oklahoma City Museum of Art,** 415 Couch Dr. ((C) 405/236-3100;
www.okcmoa.com), which boasts one of the most stunning collections you'll see anywhere:
18 installations and ensembles created by Dale Chihuly, representing 3 decades of the glass
master's whimsical and color-saturated works. It's worth visiting the museum for the Chihuly exhibition alone, though visitors will also want to take a spin through galleries featuring European and American art. A theater screens independent, foreign, and classic films
Thursday through Sunday, while a rooftop outdoor lounge is open for cocktails Thursday
evenings. The museum is open Tuesday to Saturday 10am to 5pm (Thurs to 9pm) and
Sunday noon to 5pm. Admission costs $9 adults; $7 children, students, and seniors.

A few blocks to the northeast is the **Oklahoma City National Memorial and
Museum,** 620 N. Harvey Ave. ((C) 405/235-3313; www.oklahomacitynationalmemorial.
org), which honors the victims, survivors, and rescuers of the April 19, 1995, bomb that
destroyed the Alfred P. Murrah Federal Building and took 168 lives. The museum
recounts that fateful day and the days, weeks, and years that followed with eyewitness
accounts, news footage, and exhibitions that document everything from rescue missions
to how the explosion affected families and the city. The most moving room is filled with
photographs of the 168 victims, who are also honored in an outside memorial by 168
empty chairs lined in rows; smaller chairs represent the 19 children who died in the blast.
A fence on the west perimeter of the memorial gives visitors a place to leave tokens of
remembrance. The museum is open Monday to Saturday 9am to 6pm and Sunday 1 to
6pm (you must purchase tickets 1 hr. before closing), while the outdoor memorial is

(Best) **Ride 'em Cowboy**

Oklahoma City's top attraction is the outstanding **National Cowboy & Western Heritage Museum,** 1700 NE 63rd St. (© **405/478-2250;** www.national cowboymuseum.org), which celebrates the life of the cowboy and the Old West with historic artifacts and one of the country's finest collections of Western art. Works by Charles Russell, Frederick Remington, and contemporary artists who have won top prize in the museum's annual Prix de West invitational exhibition (held every June) are on display, along with a Western Performers Gallery that honors Gene Autry, John Wayne, Gary Cooper, and others who contributed to the myths and legends of the West.

Other features include a lifelike rodeo arena with displays on bull riding, calf roping, and other activities; and a re-created cattle town complete with livery stable, saddle maker, saloon, and other buildings. More exhibits display Native American crafts, saddles, guns, boots, and hats, as well as explore related subjects such as the U.S. cavalry and trail drives. The museum is open daily 9am to 5pm; plan on spending at least 2 hours here. Admission costs $10 adults, $8.50 seniors and students, and $4.50 children ages 6 to 12.

open free 24 hours a day. Admission is $10 adults, $8 seniors, and $6 children and students.

A 5-minute drive northeast of downtown is the state capitol, as well as the **Oklahoma History Center,** 2401 N. Laird Ave. (© **405/522-5248;** www.oklahomahistorycenter. org), which explores Oklahoma's history through interactive and visual exhibits that include firsthand accounts, photographs, and artifacts. Memorable events, such as the 1889 Land Run, Wild West shows, and horrific droughts and resultant Dust Bowl of the 1930s are covered, while other displays chronicle the history and traditions of Oklahoma's African Americans and 39 American Indian tribes. Visitors can listen to American Indian languages, view a map depicting Oklahoma's former All-Black Towns (founded from the mid–19th c. to 1920 and numbering more than 50, more than any other region in the U.S.), watch movies filmed in or about Oklahoma, and learn about such Oklahoma greats as Mickey Mantle, Olympic gold medalist Jim Thorpe, and musicians Woody Guthrie and Gene Autry. It's open Monday to Saturday 9am to 5pm and Sunday noon to 5pm. Admission is $5 adults, $4 seniors, and $3 children.

Two miles west of downtown is Oklahoma City's most authentic signpost of its cowboy past: **Stockyards City** (© **405/235-7267;** stockyardscity.org), founded in 1910, is listed on the National Historic Register and is centered on Agnew and Exchange streets. Popular for its restaurants and shops specializing in Western wear, custom-made boots, and saddles, it's next to the **Oklahoma National Stockyards,** which claims to be the largest live cattle market in the world. Cattle auctions, open to the public, are held all day Monday and Tuesday starting at 9am.

The rolling hills of northeast Oklahoma City, nicknamed the Adventure District and easily accessible via I-35 and I-44, are home to several of Oklahoma's top attractions, including the National Cowboy & Western Heritage Museum (see "Ride 'em Cowboy," above). For families, nothing beats a trip to the **Oklahoma City Zoo,** east of Martin

which celebrated its 100th anniversary in 2004. Consistently ranked one of the nation's best zoos (it's accredited as a zoo and a botanical garden), it houses more than 1,500 animals, including more than 50 endangered or threatened species, in innovative habitats such as the Great EscApe with its lowland gorilla troops, orangutans, and chimpanzees; Cat Forest/Lion Overlook; and Oklahoma Trails featuring native animals. A kid's-dream playground, aquarium, and all the usual exotic animals—including orphaned grizzly cubs from Alaska—make this one of the city's hottest attractions. Tickets ($7 adults, $4 children 3–11 and seniors) go on sale daily at 9am until 6pm Memorial Day to Labor Day (grounds stay open until 8pm) and until 5pm the rest of the year (grounds close at dusk).

Next to the zoo is **Omniplex,** 2100 NE 52nd St. (© **405/602-OMNI** [602-6664]; www.omniplex.org), a hangarlike building housing hands-on science exhibits that appeal to children ages 12 and younger, a space gallery, vintage aircraft, a toy train collection, the Red Earth Museum with its impressive collection of Native American cradleboards, a planetarium, and a dome-shaped theater. Although newer, more technically advanced museums make this one seem rather old-fashioned (plans call for a gradual overhaul), there's plenty to warrant a 2- or 3-hour visit here, especially in inclement weather. It's open Monday to Friday 9am to 5pm, Saturday 9am to 6pm, and Sunday 11am to 6pm. Admission is $9.95 adults; $8.75 seniors and children 3 to 12. The planetarium and Omnidome theater cost extra.

Also for children, two popular seasonal attractions are **Frontier City,** located in northeast Oklahoma City just off I-35 at the NE 122nd Street exit (© **405/478-2140;** www. frontiercity.com; $28 adults, $20 seniors and children), an Old West theme park with 50 thrill rides (its 250-ft. free-fall Eruption is Oklahoma's tallest ride), attractions, and action-packed shows set against a colorful backdrop of log cabins and Wild West storefronts; and **White Water Bay,** a waterpark with raft rides, a wave pool, slides, and more, located west of downtown just off I-40 (take the Meridian Ave. exit) at 3908 W. Reno (© **405/943-9687;** www.whitewaterbay.com; $25 adults, $21 children).

SHOPPING   Wranglers and would-be cowboys should head to **Sheplers,** 812 S. Meridian Ave. (© **405/947-6831;** www.sheplers.com), and **Langston's,** in Stockyards City at 2224 Exchange Ave. (© **405/235-9536;** www.langstons.com), for the city's largest selection in Western wear, hats, and boots. **Bass Pro Shop,** in Bricktown at 200 Bass Pro Dr. (© **405/218-5200;** www.basspro.com), is an outdoor enthusiast's paradise with departments devoted to camping, fishing, hunting, and more.

WHERE TO STAY

A top choice downtown for both business and leisure travelers is the **Renaissance Oklahoma City Hotel,** located on the edge of Bricktown at 10 N. Broadway (© **888/236-2427** or 405/228-8000; www.marriott.com). With a dramatic, 15-story glass-topped atrium lobby complete with waterfalls, ponds, and plants, it offers a 24-hour fitness room, indoor pool, full-service spa, and 311 rooms ($199–$249 double) that face Bricktown or downtown (many with balcony), including club-level rooms with extra privileges. Those with more limited expense accounts can try the nearby **Courtyard by Marriott,** 2 W. Reno Ave. (© **888/236-2427** or 405/232-2290; www.courtyard.com/okcdt), a smart-looking property decorated in bright contemporary colors and offering a 24-hour exercise room, indoor pool, and chic rooms ($149–$179 double) that rise above the ordinary in decor and comfort.

Couples searching for a romantic getaway might consider the **Grandison Inn at Maney Park,** just a few minutes' drive from downtown at 1200 N. Shartel (© **888/799-4667** or 405/232-8778; www.grandisoninn.com). Built in 1904, this Victorian bed-and-breakfast with a wraparound porch and original woodwork retains all its turn-of-the-20th-century charm and offers nine rooms ($129–$169 double), each one different but decorated with antiques and with private bathroom (most have whirlpool tubs as well). Travelers on a budget can try **Best Western Saddleback Inn,** 4300 SW 3rd St. (© **800/228-3903** or 405/947-7000; www.bestwestern.com/saddlebackinn), one of many motels on or near Meridian Avenue west of downtown with easy access to I-40. Built by the owner's father more than 20 years ago, it's decorated in a Native American/Western theme and has more character than most hotels. It targets business travelers, but families, too, appreciate the rooms ($120 double) or the extralarge suites ($149), both with fridge and microwave, as well as the free buffet breakfast, full-service restaurant, outdoor pool, exercise room, hot tub, sauna, free cocktail hour Monday through Thursday, and free shuttle service to the airport and within a 3-mile radius of the hotel, including nearby White Water Bay. The Orange Line trolley to downtown stops in front of the hotel.

WHERE TO DINE

Oklahoma City's most famous restaurant is **Cattlemen's Steakhouse,** located in Stock-yards City at 1309 S. Agnew (© **405/236-0416;** www.cattlemensrestaurant.com). Established in 1910 and catering to tourists and cowboys alike, it serves steaks hand-cut and aged on the premises, then broiled to perfection and served with a salad, baked potato, and rolls for $16 to $26. Popular also for its hearty breakfasts, it opens daily at 6am. No reservations are accepted.

Western Avenue, a short drive west of the many attractions in the Adventure District, is lined with restaurants, bars, and one-of-a-kind shops. For a romantic splurge or cele-bratory meal, the **Metro Wine Bar & Grill,** 6418 N. Western Ave. (© **405/840-9463;** www.metrowinebar.com), fits the bill with its drawing-room ambience, subdued light-ing, and eclectic cuisine that blends American fare with French and Asian influences, with most dishes priced between $16 and $30. True to its name, it also offers more than 400 bottles of wine, including half-bottles and more than 20 choices of wine by the glass. For families, a popular neighborhood choice is the **Hideaway,** 6616 N. Western Ave. (© **405/840-4777;** www.hideawaypizza.com), known for its build-your-own pizzas made with fresh dough and signature thick, slightly sweet tomato sauce. Medium-size pizzas (eight slices) start at around $14.

OKLAHOMA CITY AFTER DARK

Bricktown, a renovated warehouse district a stone's throw east of downtown, is the city's premier nightlife district. Its focal point is a mile-long canal, with **Water Taxi** boat tours (© **405/234-8294;** www.bricktownwatertaxi.com) offering the most entertaining intro-duction to the area's history. Alongside the canal are restaurants and larger-than-life-size bronze statues commemorating the 1889 Land Run.

Feeding the Meter

The eternal quest for change to feed parking meters started in, of all places, Oklahoma, when the first meter in the U.S. was installed here in 1935.

A good watering hole is **Bricktown Brewery,** 1 N. Oklahoma Ave. (© **405/232-**
2739; www.bricktownbrewery.com), a microbrewery famous for its barbecued meats and
live music on weekends. Down the street is **Citywalk,** 70 N. Oklahoma (© **405/232-**
9255; www.citybrickwalk.com), which offers seven clubs and bars under one roof Friday
through Sunday nights. On Western Avenue, a good choice for live music on weekends
is **VZD's,** 4200 N. Western Ave. (© **405/524-4203;** www.vzds.com), which offers rock,
country, reggae, and other kinds of music in addition to salads, soups, and burgers. For
families, **Rodeo Opry,** in Stockyards City at Agnew and Exchange avenues (© **405/297-**
9773; www.ohfo.org), showcases up-and-coming country-and-western entertainers every
Saturday evening.

10 OMAHA

Located on the western bank of the Missouri River, Omaha was founded in 1854 to
outfit those traveling the Oregon and Mormon trails. It wasn't until 1863, when President Lincoln made Omaha the eastern terminus of the first transcontinental railroad,
that the city began to grow. Today Nebraska's largest city, with a population approaching
a half-million, comes as something of a surprise to first-time visitors or those returning
after many years. While its **zoo**—one of the nation's most unique—has long been a top
draw as Nebraska's number-one tourist attraction, Omaha boasts several other outstanding attractions, too, including a drive-through wildlife park, a museum devoted to U.S.
military aircraft and missiles, and Boys Town, made famous in a 1938 film starring
Spencer Tracy and Mickey Rooney.

In recent years, Omaha's riverfront has enjoyed a renaissance, with footpaths, parks, and
pedestrian bridges linking it to Iowa across the Missouri River and to the downtown Old
Market district, 12 square blocks of former warehouses now enjoying new life as restaurants
and shops. Omaha is the Midwest at its best: friendly, casual, and unpretentious. Apparently,
those traits are a perfect match for one of the world's richest men; the so-called "Oracle of
Omaha," investor Warren Buffett, was raised in Omaha and continues to call it home.

ESSENTIALS
GETTING THERE By Plane Eppley Airfield, 4501 Abbott Dr. (© **402/422-**
6817; www.eppleyairfield.com), is 5 miles northeast of downtown. Most hotels provide
free shuttle service from the airport.

By Train Amtrak (© **800/USA-RAIL** [872-7245] or 402/342-1501; www.amtrak.
com) provides daily service from Chicago and Denver ($8^1/_2$ hr. from both destinations)
to its station at South 9th and Pacific streets.

By Car Major routes into Omaha are **I-29** from the south (Kansas City, 190 miles)
and **I-80** from the east (Des Moines, 130 miles) and west (Denver, 540 miles).

VISITOR INFORMATION The **Omaha Convention & Visitors Bureau,** in the Old
Market at 1001 Farnam St. (© **866/937-6624** or 402/444-4660; www.visitomaha.
com), is open Monday to Saturday 9am to 4:30pm and Sunday 1 to 4:30pm. At Eppley
Airfield, visitor booths are open Monday to Friday 9am to 5pm.

GETTING AROUND Metro Area Transit (© **402/341-0800;** www.metroareatransit.
com) operates bus service Monday through Saturday; bus no. 13 is useful for traveling
between downtown and the zoo. The fare is $1.25.

SPECIAL EVENTS Every June, fans from across the nation converge at Rosenblatt Stadium to watch collegiate baseball teams vie to win the **NCAA College World Series** (© 402/554-4404). In September, **River City Roundup** (© 402/554-9610; www. rivercityroundup.org) features rodeos, concerts, and a parade.

WHAT TO SEE & DO

First on a tour of Omaha should be the **Durham Museum,** 801 S. 10th St. (© 402/444-5071; www.durhammuseum.org), an easy walk from the Old Market. Housed in a restored 1931 Union Station, this Art Deco landmark (and Smithsonian Institute affiliate) chronicles regional history, displays train cars (kids love the caboose), boasts an authentic soda fountain overlooking the elaborately decorated Main Waiting Room, and hosts nationally acclaimed touring exhibitions. It's open Tuesday 10am to 8pm, Wednesday to Saturday 10am to 5pm, and Sunday 1 to 5pm. Admission is $7 adults, $6 seniors, and $5 children. Just west of downtown is another Art Deco gem, the **Joslyn Art Museum,** 2200 Dodge St. (© 402/342-3300; www.joslyn.org). Although its collection concentrates on 19th- and 20th-century art from Europe and America, it's noted for its art of the American West, including Swiss artist Karl Bodmer's watercolors and prints documenting his journeys in the 1830s across North America and up the Missouri River, American Indian art, and works by Catlin, Remington, and Russell. Check the museum's website for information on free entertainment, such as its outdoor Jazz on the Green in summer. It's open Tuesday to Saturday 10am to 4pm and Sunday noon to 4pm. Admission is $7 adults, $5 seniors and students, and $4 children.

A must for gardeners is the 100-acre **Lauritzen Gardens,** near Henry Doorly Zoo at 100 Bancroft (© 402/346-4002; www.omahabotanicalgardens.org), with 3 miles of trails through Victorian, rose, herb, hosta, peony, and wildflower gardens. It's open daily 9am to 5pm; admission is $7 for adults and $3 for children.

Unique to Omaha is **Boys Town,** on the west end of town at 137th Street and West Dodge Road (© 402/498-1140; www.visitboystown.org). Founded in 1917 by Irish-born immigrant Father Flanagan, Boys Town today is a well-tended 900-acre village housing more than 700 at-risk boys and girls between the ages of 9 and 18, most of whom stay an average of 18 to 24 months (girls have been accepted since 1979 and now make up half of the residents). Stop by the visitor center to pick up a map and audio guide for a self-guided tour of the campus; in the afternoon, resident children are available as tour guides. Must-sees include Father Flanagan's 1920s home, Protestant and Catholic chapels, and the Hall of History, which displays such artifacts as the Oscar that Spencer Tracy won for his performance in *Boys Town.* Admission to Boys Town is free (donations are appreciated); it's open daily.

About 40 minutes southwest of downtown, just off I-80 at exit 426, is the **Strategic Air & Space Museum** (© 402/827-3100; www.strategicairandspace.com), which displays more than 40 military aircraft, missiles, and spacecraft in two massive hangars, including bombers, cargo and troop transporters, jet fighters, and helicopters. Standouts include an SR-71 Blackbird (the world's fastest and highest-flying plane, capable of flying from New York to London in 1 hr. and 55 min.), a B-52 (the principal Air Force bomber), a B-25 (similar to the one used in the Doolittle bombing raid over Tokyo), and the Apollo 9, launched in 1966. The museum is open daily 9am to 5pm. Admission is $7 for adults, $6 for seniors, and $3 for children ages 5 to 12.

SHOPPING In addition to **Old Market's** specialty stores, antiques shops, and Farmer's Market held Saturday mornings May to mid-October, Omaha boasts two originals:

(Best) It's All Happening at the Zoo

Most zoos nowadays give animals free reign of the outdoors, and **Omaha's Henry Doorly Zoo,** 3701 S. 10th St. ((℃) **402/733-8401;** www.omahazoo.com), is no exception. What sets this zoo apart is its indoor habitats, for this is truly a fantasyland of interiors, making it a great destination year-round. (*Reader's Digest* named it the best zoo in America in 2004.)

The zoo's **Desert Dome,** the world's largest geodesic dome, is a journey of discovery through changing vistas of desert plants and animals, culminating in an underground exploration of caves (lots of bats) and other nocturnal habitats, including the world's largest indoor swamp, filled with alligators and other creatures of the night. The **Lied Jungle** houses the world's largest indoor rainforest, with footpaths leading past waterfalls, ponds, and vegetation that provide home to monkeys, tapirs, and other animals, while the **Scott Aquarium** provides views of sharks through its underwater tunnel. Other highlights include the **Hubbard Gorilla Valley,** where the animals roam free while humans are confined to indoor passageways and bubble windows; **Hubbard Orangutan Forest,** an outdoor habitat where primates hang out in 65-foot-high concrete trees and swing on man-made vines; a huge free-flight aviary that encompasses natural woods; and a butterfly and insect pavilion with 1,500 free-flying butterflies.

Plan on spending 5 hours here, more if you wish to include a show at the zoo's IMAX 3-D theater ($8.25 adults, $6.25 children 3–11). Ticket windows open daily 9:30am to 5pm (8:30am–5pm weekends in summer), with zoo grounds closing 1 hour later. Zoo admission is $11 adults and $7.25 children ages 3 to 11; discount zoo/IMAX tickets are available.

THE NORTHERN ROCKIES & GREAT PLAINS

8

OMAHA

Borsheim's, 120 Regency Pkwy. ((℃) **402/391-0400;** www.borsheims.com), founded in 1870 and today the country's largest single jewelry store under one roof; and **Nebraska Furniture Mart,** 700 S. 72nd St. ((℃) **402/255-6327;** www.nfm.com), the world's largest furniture store. Both are owned by Berkshire Hathaway, which is headed by Warren Buffett.

WHERE TO STAY

Omaha's most historic hotel is the **Magnolia,** 1615 Howard St. ((℃) **888/915-1110** or 402/341-2500; www.magnoliahotels.com), built in 1923 in a Renaissance Revival style that imitates a Florentine palace. Its 145 rooms ($129–$199 double), decorated in rich, warm colors, offer all the amenities you'd expect, complemented by free guest services such as breakfast in the morning, wine and beer at an evening reception, and cookies and milk before bed; and a 24-hour fitness center. Another good downtown choice is **Embassy Suites,** across from Old Market at 555 S. 10th St. ((℃) **800/EMBASSY** [362-2779] or 402/346-9000; www.embassysuitesomaha.com). Its seven-story, glass-topped atrium, filled with plants, waterfalls, and streams full of *koi,* is surrounded by 249 two-room suites ($149–$219, including breakfast) with fridge and microwave, making them a hit with families, who also like the indoor pool and fitness room.

(Kids) Best Bets for Kids

Omaha's Henry Doorly Zoo, the city's top attraction, maintains **Wildlife Safari** (© **402/944-WILD** [944-9453]; www.omahazoo.com), near the Strategic Air & Space Museum off I-80 at exit 426. This 4-mile drive-through park of prairie, woods, and wetlands takes visitors past herds of buffalo, elk, pronghorn, deer, wolves, and cranes. It's open daily end of March to early November 9:30am to 5pm ($5 adults, $4 seniors, $3 children 5–11).

The **Omaha Children's Museum,** at 500 S. 20th St. (© **402/342-6164;** www.ocm.org), is great for kids 10 and younger, with its colorful toddler room; make-believe town with a kid-size grocery store, fire station, farm, and other areas; a creative center where children can make art and stage puppet shows; a science and technology center with hands-on activities; and a seasonal splash garden. It's open Tuesday to Sunday, and admission is $7.

Fun-Plex, farther south of downtown at 70th and Q streets (© **402/331-8436;** www.fun-plex.com), is a small waterpark that is reminiscent of county fairs with its handful of old-fashioned thrill rides, bumper cars, go-carts, and minigolf, in addition to its wave pool, slides, and other pools. It's open Memorial Day to Labor Day. Admission options vary; call or check the website before you go.

Another good bet for families is **Regency Lodge,** west of downtown at 909 S. 107th St. (© **800/617-8310** or 402/397-8000; www.regencylodge.com). Decorated with natural stone, fixtures reminiscent of Frank Lloyd Wright, and nature photography, it evokes the atmosphere of a mountain lodge but with all the creature comforts, including an indoor pool, fitness room, game room, laundry, and restaurant. In addition to standard rooms ($119–$159 double, including breakfast), all with fridge and microwave, there are suites ($200–$275) that boast a full kitchen and gas fireplace (some also with whirlpool tubs). Travelers on a budget can try **Comfort Inn at the Zoo,** 2920 S. 13th Court (© **877/395-3253** or 402/342-8000; www.comfortinn.com), 2 miles from downtown near the zoo, which offers an indoor pool, fitness room, and 79 rooms ($80–$150 double, including breakfast) with fridge, microwave, and free Wi-Fi.

Couples searching for a romantic getaway might consider the **Cornerstone Mansion,** west of downtown at 140 N. 39th St. (© **888/883-7745** or 402/558-7600; www.cornerstonemansion.com). Built in 1894 and on the National Register of Historic Places, this B&B offers seven rooms ($85–$150 double), individually decorated with antiques and with private bathroom. There's also a sitting room with a piano, a library, and a pleasant patio lined with flowers.

WHERE TO DINE

All Omaha restaurants are smoke free. The most atmospheric place to dine is undoubtedly **Rick's Café Boatyard,** located beside the Missouri River at 345 Riverfront Dr. (© **402/345-4545;** www.rickscafeboatyard.com). A bustling, airy restaurant seating 1,000 diners both inside and on a huge deck overlooking the river, it's known for its live music in summer (Thurs–Sat) and fresh seafood, but also offers burgers, steaks, and pasta, all priced between $12 and $45. In the Old Market, **M's Pub,** 422 S. 11th St. (© **402/342-2550;** www.mspubomaha.com), has a bistro atmosphere with its sidewalk seating and open kitchen. It serves a wide range of salads, sandwiches, *lahvosh* (pizza on Armenian crackers), and satays, priced from $8 to $36.

For a taste of Omaha's famous steaks, head to **Gorat's,** 4917 Center St. (© **402/551-3733**). This family-owned Omaha institution has been serving steaks hand-cut and aged on the premises since 1944 and is a popular hangout of investor Warren Buffet. Seafood, pastas, daily specials, and a children's menu round out the offerings, with steaks and all the trimmings ranging from $17 to $26. Another popular choice is **Dundee Dell,** in the quaint Dundee neighborhood west of downtown at 5007 Underwood (© **402/533-9501;** www.dundeedell.com). Established in 1934, it's famous for its fish and chips and large assortment of sandwiches, all priced below $10, but also available are a children's menu and the world's largest selection of single-malt Scotch. The **Amazing Pizza Machine,** on the western edge of the city off I-80 at 139th and Millard Ave. (© **402/829-1777;** www.amazingpizzamachine.com), offers a buffet (dinner $11 for adults, $5.50–$6.50 for children) and a huge game arcade.

OMAHA AFTER DARK

Omaha is home to the nation's largest community theater, the **Omaha Community Playhouse,** 6915 Cass St. (© **402/553-0800;** www.omahaplayhouse.com), founded in 1925 with the help of Marlon Brando's mother and where Henry Fonda made his acting debut. It's also home to one of the nation's oldest children's theater companies, the **Omaha Theater Company for Young People,** 2001 Farnam St. (© **402/345-4849;** www.rosetheater.org), founded in 1949. The 1927 **Orpheum Theater,** 409 S. 16th St. (© **402/345-0606;** www.omahaperformingarts.org), restored to its French Renaissance splendor, is home to touring shows and concerts, while the **Holland Performing Arts Center,** 13th and Douglas streets (© **402/345-0606;** www.omahaperformingarts.org), hosts the **Omaha Symphony** (© **402/342-3560;** www.omahasymphony.org) and other musical events.

Old Market, a renovated downtown warehouse district, is a good place for a nighttime stroll. The **Upstream Brewing Company,** 11th and Jackson (© **402/344-0200;** www.upstreambrewing.com), housed in a turn-of-the-20th-century firehouse and with outdoor seating, offers handcrafted beers and root beer on tap, as well as New American pub fare ranging from steaks and sandwiches to pizzas. A good place to hear music is **Sokol Underground,** 13th and Martha streets (© **402/346-9802;** www.sokolunderground.com), where many Omaha bands get their start, while **Slowdown,** 729 N. 14th St. (© **402/345-7575;** www.theslowdown.com), is the place to hear nationally touring indie bands.

Texas

Texas has an identity and mystique that no other state can match. It fought its own war for independence and remained an independent country for several years. Its history is full of stories of wild characters and unlikely events: the Alamo and its courageous defenders, such as Davy Crockett and James Bowie; reckless and gritty Texas Rangers, such as John Coffee Hayes; empire-building ranchers such as Richard King; flamboyant wildcatters such as Glen McCarthy; and plenty of desperadoes such as Sam Bass or Bonnie and Clyde. Today Texas is as much a land of modern cities and high-tech industries as of small towns and open prairies. But both places share a lot in common: Pickup trucks and cowboy boots abound, the menu favorites are the same—steaks, chili con carne, fajitas, barbecue, and Tex-Mex enchiladas (beef being the common denominator)—and a good honky-tonk is an agreeable way to pass the evening. And, of course, Texas is *big*. Driving through the state can be taxing; it's more than 800 miles from the Louisiana border in the east to El Paso in the west, and the same going north to south. But if you're not in a hurry, you can enjoy one more thing Texas is famous for—its hospitality.

1 DALLAS

Dallas is in the northeast part of the state, where the Trinity River cuts through a gently undulating prairie. The city was born in the 1840s and became the commercial and financial center for the region. First cotton was king, and then oil. Now it's a mix of high-tech, financial, and service industries. Dallas is the ninth-largest city in the United States. A modern, attractive city, it offers visitors fine restaurants, fashionable stores and boutiques, and a wide range of entertainment, from concerts, plays and club acts, to golf and many other sporting events.

ESSENTIALS

GETTING THERE   By Plane   Dallas–Fort Worth International Airport (DFW; © 972/574-8888; www.dfwairport.com) is a 40-minute drive from downtown Dallas. It is a hub for American Airlines. From DFW, a cheap and quick way to get to downtown Dallas or Fort Worth is to catch the free shuttle to the CentrePort station of the **Trinity Railway Express** (© 214/979-1111; www.trinityrailwayexpress.org). The trains are frequent but don't run after midnight or on Sunday; the fare is $1.50 to $2.50. **Super-Shuttle** (© 800/258-3826 or 817/329-2000; www.supershuttle.com) offers van service to anywhere in town. Rates vary with length of trip; for downtown the fare is from $17 to $25 for one person. A taxi into central Dallas will cost around $45. **Love Field (DAL;** © 214/670-6073; www.dallas-lovefield.com) is closer to the center of town and is a hub for Southwest Airlines. It is a $25 taxi ride from downtown. A few other airlines offer limited service from Love Field. SuperShuttle offers van service from Love Field at rates slightly lower than from DFW for downtown destinations.

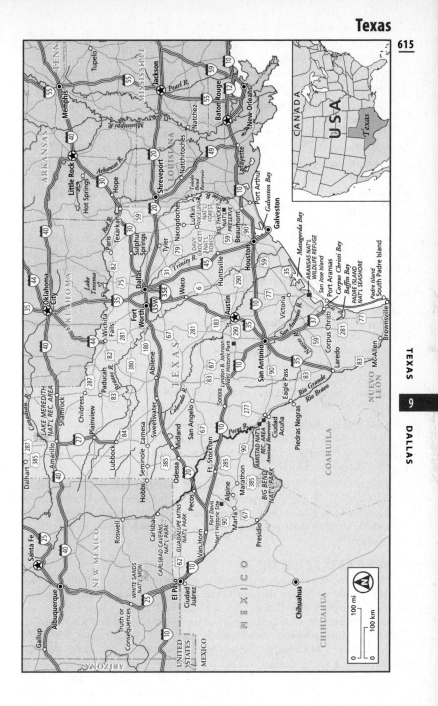

By Train The **Trinity Railway Express** (see above) has several trains per day to and from Fort Worth. **Amtrak** (© **800/USA-RAIL** [872-7245] or 214/653-1101; www. amtrak.com) serves **Union Station,** 400 S. Houston St., with daily trains from Austin (trip time: 6¼ hr.), San Antonio (9½ hr.), St. Louis (15 hr.), and Chicago (21 hr.).

By Car The principal routes into Dallas are **I-35E** from the north (Oklahoma City) and southwest (Austin and San Antonio), **I-30** from the northeast (Little Rock) and west (Fort Worth), **I-20** from the east (Shreveport) and west (Abilene), and **I-45** from the south (Houston). The **I-635** ring road (**LBJ Fwy.**) circles most of the city.

VISITOR INFORMATION Contact the **Dallas Convention and Visitors Bureau** (© **800/232-5527**; www.visitdallas.com). Go to the **Dallas Tourist Information Center,** in the Old Red Courthouse, 100 S. Houston St. (© **214/571-1300**), in the West End Historic District. You'll find touch-screen computer kiosks, Internet access, brochures and coupons, and a helpful staff. It's open daily from 9am to 5pm.

GETTING AROUND Public transportation in Dallas is good (for Texas), but having a car helps a lot. The **Dallas Area Regional Transit (DART;** © **214/979-1111;** www.dart. org) operates a light-rail system and citywide bus service. A local day pass is $3 for an adult; $1.50 for seniors, persons with disabilities, and children 5 to 14. This is good for both buses and the light rail. Single-trip fares are half-price but are good for only the bus or the train, but not both. Tickets can be purchased at vending machines at each light-rail station. The restored **McKinney Avenue Trolley** (© **214/855-0006;** www.mata.org) runs 3½ miles from the downtown Arts District up through lower McKinney Avenue. This is a genuine old streetcar operated by volunteers. The trolley runs every 20 minutes during the day, with slightly reduced hours on the weekends. The ride is free.

It's almost impossible to hail a cab on the street; call the dispatch, or look for a hotel cabstand. Call **Yellow Checker Cab Co.** (© **817/534-5555** or 214/426-6262). The fare is $2.25 plus $2 per additional passenger plus $1.80 per mile plus fuel surcharge.

FAST FACTS **Baylor University Medical Center,** 3500 Gaston Ave. (© **214/820-0111**), provides world-class healthcare. Dallas has three **area codes**—214, 972, and 469—with 10-digit dialing (1+ the number) for all local numbers. The local hotel tax is 15%; the sales tax is 8.25%.

SPECIAL EVENTS The **State Fair of Texas** (© **214/565-9931;** www.bigtex.com), the largest state fair in the nation, takes place from late September to mid-October in Fair Park. The **Cotton Bowl Classic Football Game** (Jan 1) and **Parade** (Dec 31; © **888/792-BOWL** [792-2695] or 214/634-7764; www.attcottonbowl.com) get a lot of local attention.

WHAT TO SEE & DO

Downtown Dallas is clean and attractive. Its two biggest draws are the **6th Floor Museum** and the **Nasher Sculpture Center.** To the east is **Deep Ellum;** to the north is the **McKinney Avenue District** (also called Uptown). These are both restaurant-and-club districts where the visitor can find food and nightlife. Deep Ellum is bohemian and has been growing shabbier, while McKinney Avenue is society and pretty glitzy. East of Deep Ellum is **Fair Park,** an enclosed area of several blocks (see below), which is a popular attraction for families. Also popular with families is the city of Arlington, to the west between Dallas and Fort Worth, which is home to the **Six Flags** amusement park; its sister waterpark, **Hurricane Harbor;** and the **Ballpark in Arlington,** home of the Texas Rangers baseball team.

Sporting Options

Dallas is a sports town. Golfers can contact **Golf Guys** (📞 **800/470-9634;** www. golfguys.net) to schedule a round at one of the city's local clubs. The company works with several courses. You should schedule in advance. Professional team sports include the NFL **Dallas Cowboys** football team (📞 **972/785-5000**), the NBA **Mavericks** basketball team (📞 **214/747-6287**), the MLB **Texas Rangers** baseball team (📞 **817/273-5100**), and the NHL **Stars** hockey team (📞 **214/ GO-STARS** [467-8277]). Other sporting events include horse racing at **Lone Star Park** (📞 **972/263-7669**) and auto racing at **Texas Motor Speedway** (in Fort Worth; 📞 **817/215-8500**).

Dallas Arboretum & Botanical Garden   Bordering the eastern shore of White Rock Lake, 10 minutes from downtown, are 66 acres of gardens, woods, and trails. It's the best urban green space in Texas. In springtime the 2,000 varieties of azaleas explode in gaudy colors, while the rest of the year there's always something blooming. You'll find lots of trails, including the wildflower trail and an 11-mile path around the lake. Seeing just the park without lollygagging takes about an hour (but why rush?).

8525 Garland Rd. (east Dallas). 📞 **214/515-6500.** www.dallasarboretum.org. Admission $8 adults, $7 seniors, $5 children 3–12. Parking $5. Daily 9am–5pm.

Dallas World Aquarium   Of the downtown attractions, this is the one most likely to keep children entertained. In addition to the aquariums (one of which has a walk-through tunnel), there are exhibits of the fauna and habitat of a South American rainforest, the southernmost tip of South Africa, and the Yucatán peninsula. A leisurely visit will take 2 hours.

1801 N. Griffin St. (downtown). 📞 **214/720-2224.** www.dwazoo.com. Admission $19 adults, $15 seniors, $11 children 3–12. Daily 10am–5pm.

Fair Park (Kids)   This is an enclosed area of several blocks that holds nine museums, the Cotton Bowl, and two concert halls. Built in 1936, the grand pavilion and several of the museums are bold examples of Art Deco architecture. Each fall the Texas State Fair is held here. During the rest of the year, Fair Park attracts lots of families. Of the nine museums, the highlights are: The **Women's Museum** (📞 **214/915-0860;** www.thewomensmuseum. org) honors American women and their achievements with a panoply of high-tech, visually striking exhibits. The **Museum of Science & Nature** (📞 **214/428-5555;** www. natureandscience.org) is an especially good museum for kids because it offers plenty of interactive exhibits that demonstrate principles of physics, electricity, space, and ecology in imaginative ways. It also has a planetarium and an IMAX theater. The **African-American Museum** (📞 **214/565-9026;** www.aamdallas.org) is one of few museums in the country to present aspects of the African-American experience in the U.S., which it does in part through exhibitions of folk art (with a fascinating look at connections with African art) and fine art.

3809 Grand Ave. 📞 **214/670-8400.** www.fairpark.org. **Women's Museum** Tues–Sun noon–5pm; **Museum of Science & Nature** Mon–Sat 10am–5pm, Sun noon–5pm; **African-American Museum** Tues–Fri noon–5pm, Sat 10am–5pm, Sun 1–5pm. Admission fees vary.

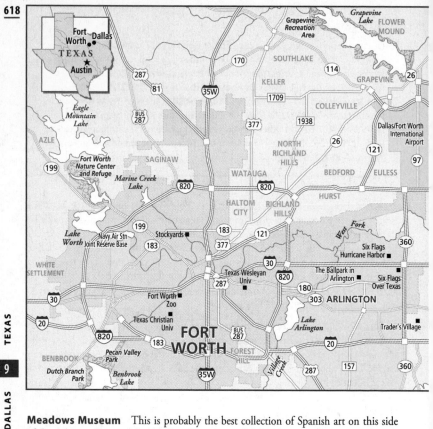

Meadows Museum   This is probably the best collection of Spanish art on this side of the Atlantic. Paintings by the Spanish masters of the 16th, 17th, and 18th centuries, as well as works by more modern artists from Goya to Picasso to Miró, are all on display in serene and spacious surroundings. Classic Spanish painting, as represented by Velázquez, Murillo, and others, is inventive in style and intriguing in subject matter. Many of the works displayed here are breathtaking.

5900 Bishop Blvd. at Mockingbird Lane (SMU campus). ✆ **214/768-2516.** www.meadowsmuseumdallas. org. Admission $8 (free after 5pm Thurs). Tues–Sat 10am–5pm (until 8pm Thurs); Sun noon–5pm.

Nasher Sculpture Center (Best)   Now the centerpiece of Dallas's "Arts District," the Nasher Sculpture Center opened in 2003 to wide acclaim. Raymond Nasher, a rich local developer, has collected modern sculpture for decades, assembling, according to some, the finest collection in the world. Renzo Piano was chosen to create the space for viewing these pieces, and he's done an admirable job of situating the building and garden within the downtown skyline, at the same time creating a feel of separation.

Note: Across Harwood Street from the Nasher—and with the same admission charges and hours—is the **Dallas Museum of Art,** 1717 N. Harwood St. (✆ **214/922-1200;** www.dm-art.org). The building, designed by Edward Larrabee Barnes, upstages the collection, which is small but has in recent years received three large private collections adding greatly to the collection. And across Flora Street is the small but lovely **Crow Collection of Asian Art,** 2010 Flora St. (© **214/979-6430;** www.crow collection.org). Hours are identical to those at Nasher and the Museum of Art, but admission here is free.

2001 Flora St. (downtown). © **214/242-5100.** www.nashersculpturecenter.org. Admission $10 adults, $7 seniors, $5 students, free for children 11 and under. Tues–Sun 11am–5pm (until 9pm Thurs).

Six Flags Over Texas (Kids) In Arlington, halfway between Dallas and Fort Worth, is this large amusement park with lots of roller coasters and thrill rides. It is one of the largest parks in the country and the most-visited attraction in Texas. Nearby is its sister park, **Hurricane Harbor,** 1800 E. Lamar Blvd. (© **817/265-3356;** www.sixflags.com), a waterpark with pretty much the same thing in mind. In addition there are shows, theme rides, and other amusements.

I-30 at Hwy. 360 (Arlington). © **817/607-6150.** www.sixflags.com. Admission to Six Flags $47 adults, $30 children under 4 ft. and seniors, free for children 2 years and under; Hurricane Harbor $25 adults, $20 children under 4 ft., free for children 2 years and under. Online discounts often available for both parks. Daily mid-May to Aug; weekends only in late spring and early fall. Parking $15.

Sixth Floor Museum The museum is in the old Texas School Book Depository. Does this ring a bell? It was from here that Lee Harvey Oswald assassinated JFK (or did he?). This and many issues surrounding the Kennedy presidency and the events leading up to that fateful day are effectively portrayed through the use of film, photographs, artifacts, and displays. The corner window from which Oswald is said to have fired the fatal shots is part of the exhibit. The museum does a good job of presenting the different findings on the assassination and lets visitors draw their own conclusions. If you're interested in modern history, you can spend 2 hours here.

411 Elm St. (West End). © **214/747-6660.** www.jfk.org. Admission $14 adults, $13 seniors and kids 6–18. Admission includes audio guide. Tues–Sun 10am–6pm; Mon noon–6pm.

SHOPPING

Shopping has been called Dallas's number-one indoor sport. Most of the city's shopping malls are north of downtown. **Highland Park Village** (www.hpvillage.com), opened in 1931, was the first mall built in Dallas and is still one of *the* fashionable shopping centers, with many boutiques and small shops catering to its well-heeled clientele. It's not far from downtown, in a lovely part of the city. **NorthPark Center** (www.northparkcenter. com), anchored by a Neiman Marcus, is notable because developer Raymond Nasher displays pieces from his famous modern art collection throughout. You can get there by taking the light rail's Red Line to the Park Lane station, where you can catch a free shuttle to the mall. The **Galleria,** LBJ Freeway and Dallas North Tollway (www.galleria dallas.com), is one of Dallas's largest upscale malls, with more than 200 shops—including Nordstrom, Tiffany, and Saks Fifth Avenue. It has the advantage of activities to amuse those not interested in shopping, including a skating rink, race car simulators, and high-tech arcades.

Many shoppers frequent the **uptown** area, just north of downtown. A mixed-use development here, called **West Village** (McKinney Ave. at Lemmon Ave.), is all the rage. It offers 4 square blocks of shops, boutiques, restaurants, and bars. If you're **downtown** (or even if you're not), you might want to visit the original **Neiman Marcus,** a popular destination for many visitors to Dallas.

WHERE TO STAY

Convenient to DFW Airport is the **Hyatt Regency DFW Airport,** International Parkway, at terminal C inside the airport (© **888/591-1234** or 972/453-1234). Easier on the budget is the **Embassy Guest Suites,** 4650 W. Airport Fwy., Irving (© **800/362-2779** or 972/790-0093), near the south entrance to DFW.

For a hotel in Arlington, close to Six Flags and Hurricane Harbor, you have 50 choices representing just about every chain in America. Many of these properties pay for shuttle service to and from their hotel and the amusement parks and the ballpark. This will save you a little money on parking and is a real convenience; ask about it when making reservations. Lodging options in the area include the **Wingate by Wyndham,** 1024 Brook-hollow Plaza Dr. (© **817/640-8686**), which is located close by both Six Flags and the ballpark. We also like the **Courtyard Marriott,** 1500 Nolan Ryan Expwy. (© **800/321-2211**), for its location and rooms.

Fairmont Dallas Combine elegance and comfort with a great location (downtown btw. the Arts District and the West End), and the result is the Fairmont. The hotel occupies two towers with a terrace pool and patio in between. Rooms, thoughtfully furnished to make them suitable for business or pleasure, are large and attractive in a modern style, with a few flourishes such as granite tabletops. All beds are extra long.

1717 N. Akard St., Dallas, TX 75201 (downtown). ✆ **800/527-4727** or 214/720-2020. Fax 214/720-7403. www. fairmont.com/dallas. 551 units. $179–$279 double; $279–$550 suite. AE, DC, DISC, MC, V. Valet parking $23. Children not permitted. Small pets allowed for $25 fee. **Amenities:** Restaurant; outdoor pool; health club.

Four Seasons Resort and Club
Attention to detail and an amazing array of recreational facilities highlight this impressive resort. The main golf course is considered to be the best in the Dallas area, while the European spa wins high praise from guests. In addition, the resort offers racquetball courts, 40 exercise classes per week, and lovely settings for relaxing. Rooms are spacious and well furnished. Bathrooms are large, especially in the deluxe rooms and villas, which come with a large soaking tub and separate shower.

4150 N. McArthur Blvd., Irving, TX 75038 (west of Dallas off Hwy. 114). ✆ **800/332-3442** or 972/717-0700. Fax 972/717-2550. www.fourseasons.com/dallas. 357 units. $350–$480 double; $505 villa; $750 and up suite. Children 17 and under stay free in parent's room. Golf packages available. AE, DC, DISC, MC, V. Valet parking $22; free self-parking. Pets 15 lb. and under accepted. **Amenities:** 3 restaurants; 4 pools (1 indoor); 2 18-hole golf courses; 12 tennis courts (4 indoor); health club; spa.

Hotel Adolphus (Best)
The Adolphus is Dallas's original grand hotel—a classic skyscraper, built in 1912 in the Beaux Arts style by beer mogul Adolphus Busch. The lobby holds a collection of furniture, tapestries, and paintings plundered from Europe during a shopping trip by the owner's wife. Large guest rooms offer separate sitting areas, fresh flowers, and understated furnishings with large marble bathrooms. The level of service could not be better. If you stay here, or even if you don't, try the hotel's restaurant, the French Room, which is one of the best restaurants in Dallas.

1321 Commerce St., Dallas, TX 75202. ✆ **800/221-9083** or 214/742-8200. Fax 214/651-3588. www. hoteladolphus.com. 428 units. $175–$325 double; $279–$369 junior suite; $700 and up suite. Children 11 and under stay free in parent's room. AE, DC, DISC, MC, V. Valet parking $21. **Amenities:** 3 restaurants; health club.

Hotel ZaZa
This is Dallas's hot property, and it's easy to see why—it's the guest rooms. Instead of taking the bland-but-safe approach, the designers took chances—lots of color, texture, dramatic furniture arrangements, and accent lighting. This is especially true of the suites, which come in several motifs that provide the perfect *mise-en-scène* for a weekend getaway, or for the executive who wants to feel like there's more to travel than business. All rooms feature marble bathrooms with bathrobes, CD players, and flatscreen TVs; some rooms offer balconies. The hotel's restaurant and courtyard are "in" with the Uptown crowd.

2332 Leonard St., Dallas, TX 75201. ✆ **800/597-8399** or 214/468-8399. Fax 214/468-8397. www.hotel zaza.com. 153 units. $259–$329 deluxe; $515 and up suite. AE, DC, DISC, MC, V. Valet parking $18. **Amenities:** Restaurant; pool; fitness center; spa.

The Mansion on Turtle Creek
This is the hotel of choice for moguls, celebrities, and CEOs. Its flawless accommodations and world-class pampering get it regularly named as one of the top hotels in the country. The large, plush rooms exude comfort and coolness, and the bathrooms are large, with double sinks and/or separate shower and tub. The original mansion (built by a cotton baron in 1925) is the most visually striking part of the property, but what impresses us most about this hotel is the service.

2821 Turtle Creek Blvd., Dallas, TX 75219. ✆ **800/767-3966** or 214/559-2100. Fax 214/528-4187. www. mansiononturtlecreek.com. 143 units. $415–$560 double; $695 and up suite. AE, DC, DISC, MC, V. Valet parking $25. Pets accepted for a $100 fee. **Amenities:** Restaurant; heated outdoor pool; health club.

Stoneleigh Hotel   This 1923 hotel in the McKinney Avenue area near downtown is a national historic landmark and offers large, well-furnished rooms at good prices. Bathrooms are medium to large and attractively furnished. Some suites come with kitchens. Dallas never looks as good as it does from the hotel's penthouse bar at sunset. We've seen big discounts for rooms at this hotel on the Internet reservation sites. Get a room facing away from the street.

2927 Maple Ave., Dallas, TX 75201. ✆ **800/255-9299** or 214/871-7111. Fax 214/871-9379. www. stoneleighhotel.com. 153 units. $149–$189 double; $200–$330 suite. Children 17 and under stay free in parent's room. AE, DC, DISC, MC, V. Valet parking $22. **Amenities:** Restaurant. *In room:* Kitchen (some suites only).

Westin Hotel Galleria Dallas (**Kids**)   If you're the type to shop until you drop, think about dropping in here. It's part of the Galleria complex, so you're only a short elevator ride from the mall. And the hotel has more to offer than just its location: Rooms are large and attractive, with big windows and little extra touches; the beds' thick, plush mattresses will certainly get you rested for another day's grueling shopping. Bathrooms are fine but nothing special.

13340 Dallas Pkwy., Dallas, TX 75240. ✆ **800/228-3000** or 972/934-9494. Fax 972/851-2869. www. westin.com/dallas. 432 units. $169–$309 double; $480–$1,275 suite. AE, DC, DISC, MC, V. Valet parking $20; free outdoor parking at connected Galleria shopping mall. Pets allowed (ask about the "Heavenly Pet" package). **Amenities:** Restaurant; outdoor pool.

WHERE TO DINE

Bob's Steak & Chop House STEAKS   In Dallas, a great steak is mightily appreciated. Here, they are served in a classic steakhouse dining room—lots of dark wood and crisp white tablecloths. Bob's is known for its perfectly aged and beautifully grilled, corn-fed, prime beef, and for its hearty side dishes. Good salads, too.

4300 Lemmon Ave. ✆ **214/528-9446.** www.bobs-steakandchop.com. Reservations recommended. Main courses $23–$50. AE, DC, DISC, MC, V. Mon–Thurs 5–10pm; Fri–Sat 5–11pm.

The French Room FRENCH   This downtown restaurant consistently wins top honors in Dallas for food, ambience, and service. The surroundings are extravagant in an old-world style, with painted ceilings and lots of white linen. The cooking is French but not strictly so. The executive chef, Jason Weaver, has adapted it to the local surroundings and inserted his own touch. The combinations of ingredients are original and well thought out. If you are seeking to impress someone, take them here.

1321 Commerce St. (inside the Adolphus Hotel). ✆ **214/742-8200.** Reservations recommended. Main courses $25–$50; tasting menus $95 and up. AE, DC, DISC, MC, V. Tues–Sat 6–10pm.

The Mansion on Turtle Creek (**Best**)   NEW AMERICAN   If you want to splurge while in Dallas, this restaurant in the dining room of the original 1920s mansion is the place. It has captured attention for its inventive menu of contemporary American food that emphasizes local produce. The chef, John Tesar, comes to the hotel by way of New York, where he owned or managed several acclaimed restaurants. The dining room is an opulent fantasy full of carved stone and Italian marble and can be enjoyed for less money by going for lunch instead of dinner. In addition to the main restaurant there is the **Chef's Room,** an intimate space offering a prix-fixe dinner.

2821 Turtle Creek Blvd. ✆ **214/443-4747.** www.mansiononturtlecreek.com. Reservations recommended. Jacket required for men. Main courses $35–$55. AE, DC, DISC, MC, V. Mon–Sat 11:30am–2pm; Mon–Thurs 6–10pm; Fri–Sat 6–11pm; Sun 6–9:30pm; brunch Sun 11am–2pm.

Mi Cocina MEXICAN/TEX-MEX   Don't pass through Texas without trying the local version of Mexican food. This restaurant is an excellent source for the real thing. Choose from several combination dinners for the sake of variety or go with one of special fajita plates. The dining area is modern and roomy, with high ceilings and comfortable furniture. There are also tables outside on the sidewalk.

3699 McKinney Ave. (West Village). ✆ **469/533-5633.** Main courses $8–$19. AE, MC, V. Sun–Thurs 11am–10pm; Fri–Sat 11am–11pm.

Monica's Aca y Alla MEXICAN   The contemporary decor doesn't attempt to hide the warehouse origins of this restaurant's dining room, which is perfectly appropriate for Deep Ellum. So is the menu. Alongside Mexican and Tex-Mex standards such as green enchiladas and chili con queso, you have unlikely hybrids such as the green pasta with chicken and black beans, pumpkin ravioli, and Mexican lasagna. It's always popular and sometimes noisy. Thursdays and weekends, you can dine to the sounds of live flamenco, and occasionally there will be some salsa and mambo, too.

2914 Main St. ✆ **214/748-7140.** www.monicas.com. Reservations accepted for parties of 5 or more. Main courses $8–$20. AE, DISC, MC, V. Mon–Fri 11am–2pm; Tues–Thurs 5–10pm; Fri–Sat 5pm–midnight; Sun 11am–11pm; Sat–Sun brunch 11am–3pm.

Sonny Bryan's Smokehouse (Kids) BARBECUE   This chain is the first place people think of for barbecue in Dallas. There are several locations. A lot of people consider the original site, at 2202 Inwood Rd. (✆ **214/357-7120**), special, but we found the food as good at other locations, like this one in the West End. Sonny Bryan's is known for its brisket, but the ribs and sausage are also good, as are the classic sides of potato salad and coleslaw. The surroundings are simple and the service is friendly.

302 N. Market. ✆ **214/744-1610.** www.sonnybryans.com. Sandwiches $4–$5; plates $11–$15. AE, DC, MC, V. Sun–Thurs 11am–9pm; Fri–Sat 11am–10pm.

Stephen Pyles SOUTHWESTERN   In the Arts District, this eye-catching restaurant is the latest endeavor by local celebrity chef Stephen Pyles, who gained popularity with his Star Canyon restaurant. The menu he has created for this restaurant draws from several Latin and Mediterranean traditions. Representative dishes include a *poblano-asiago* (poblano chilies and asiago cheese) soup, seared red snapper with a crab *ceviche* (marinated in lime juice), and beef tenderloin with sweet potato *chilaquiles* (cooked in a tomato and chili sauce).

1807 Ross Ave. (downtown). ✆ **214/580-7000.** Reservations recommended. Main courses $26–$43. AE, DC, DISC, MC, V. Mon–Fri 11am–2:30pm and 6–10:30pm; Sat 6–11pm.

Tom Tom Asian Grille NOODLE HOUSE/SUSHI   This is a small, modern eatery tucked away in the trendy West Village in the Uptown district. It offers a wide range of light Pan-Asian dishes at moderate prices. The noodle dishes are quite good, the sushi is well presented, and the curries are great. You can eat in the minimalist, Zen-inspired dining area or outdoors on the patio where you can watch the street scene.

3699 McKinney Ave., Ste. C319 (West Village). ✆ **214/522-9886.** www.tomtomasiangrill.com. Main courses $8–$16. AE, DC, DISC, MC, V. Daily 11am–10pm.

DALLAS AFTER DARK

THE PERFORMING ARTS   The **Dallas Symphony Orchestra** (✆ **214/692-0203**; www.dallassymphony.com) performs at the beautiful Meyerson Symphony Center, 2301 Flora St. (✆ **214/670-3600**), designed by I. M. Pei. The **Texas Ballet Theater** (✆ **214/**

369-5200; www.texasballettheater.org) performs in Fort Worth and Dallas. If you want to see a play, the **Dallas Theater Center,** 3636 Turtle Creek Blvd. (© **214/522-8499;** www.dallastheatercenter.org), designed by Frank Lloyd Wright, has a 7-month season ranging from Shakespeare to contemporary works.

THE CLUB & BAR SCENE   Deep Ellum was once the city's blues and jazz center. It became popular again in the '80s but has declined in recent years. Many of the clubs have shut down, and patrons have been heading to upscale bars in the Uptown area. Indicative of what you'll find is **Gypsy Tea Room,** 2548 Elm St. (© **214/744-9779**), which gets a lot of touring acts playing alternative and roots rock; **Trees,** 2709 Elm St. (© **214/748-5009**), a cavernous club that hosts the larger alternative rock touring acts; and **Sons of Hermann Hall,** 3414 Elm St. (© **214/747-4422**), a dance hall (and real fraternal organization) that has live country music on weekends—often Texas pickers—and attracts everyone from straight-ahead country types to alternative club dabblers.

In the Uptown area along McKinney Avenue you can find a lot of bars that attract the fashionable crowd. For live music over drinks and good food, try **Sambuca,** at 2120 McKinney Ave. (© **214/744-0820**). It offers some great jazz, blues, and other acts in a stylish club/restaurant (good menu and wine list). It's popular, so make reservations. Also, the restaurant and bar at **Hotel ZaZa** (see above) packs the same crowd in for drinks and dinner. Just a bit farther up McKinney, at 2601, is a **Hard Rock Cafe** (© **214/855-0007**). And then there's the **West Village** development, which occupies a few blocks of McKinney between Lemmon Avenue and Blackburn. It has a popular bar and restaurant zone that's pedestrian friendly. There you'll find a modern, comfortable wine bar, **Cru** (© **214/256-9463**), and a stylish cocktail bar attached to the **Magnolia Theatre** (© **214/520-3939**).

2 FORT WORTH

Fort Worth is a city of two tales. One is that of the cattle business, which drove herds from south Texas up to Fort Worth's stockyards to be shipped back East. The cowboys who drove these herds were only too happy to celebrate the end of their trail ride, so a number of saloons and other establishments sprang up to cater to their wants. This made Fort Worth a rough-and-tumble place and earned it the nickname "Cowtown." Today you can visit the historic stockyards district and see saloons, boardinghouses, Western-wear stores, a small cattle drive, and the biggest honky-tonk bar in the world.

The other tale is the story of rich philanthropists who have made their city a delightful place to visit, preserving many of the Art Deco buildings downtown and funding some great museums that belie the town's nickname. Fort Worth is fun to visit, possessing all the cosmopolitan pleasures of a bigger city with none of the drawbacks.

ESSENTIALS

GETTING THERE   By Plane   Flights to Fort Worth arrive at the **Dallas–Fort Worth International Airport (DFW);** see "Essentials" under "Dallas," earlier in this chapter, for details. The **Trinity Railway Express** (© **817/215-8600;** www.trinityrailwayexpress. org) can get you to the downtown area for $1.50, but it doesn't run on Sunday or late at night. **SuperShuttle** (© **800/258-3826** or 817/329-2000; www.supershuttle.com) offers 24-hour service to downtown for $18 to $30.

By Train The Trinity Railway Express offers several trains to and from Dallas Monday through Saturday. **Amtrak** (© **800/USA-RAIL** [872-7245] or 817/332-2931; www. amtrak.com) serves the old **Santa Fe Depot,** 1501 Jones St., with daily trains to and from Oklahoma City (trip time: 4 hr.), Austin (4 hr.), San Antonio (7 hr.), St. Louis (16 hr.), and Chicago (22 hr.).

By Car The principal routes into Fort Worth are **I-35W** from the north (Oklahoma City) and southwest (Austin and San Antonio), **I-30** from the east (Dallas) and west (Abilene), and **I-45** from the south (Houston).

VISITOR INFORMATION The **Fort Worth Convention and Visitors Bureau** has its main office at 415 Throckmorton St., Fort Worth, TX 76102 (© **800/433-5747** or 817/336-8791; www.fortworth.com), open Monday through Friday from 8:30am to 5pm, Saturday from 10am to 4pm. There are also **visitor information centers** at the Stockyards National Historic District, 130 E. Exchange Ave. (© **817/624-4741**), open Monday through Saturday from 9am to 6pm, Sunday from noon to 5pm; and in the Cultural District/Zoo at 3401 W. Lancaster Ave. (© **817/882-8588**), open Monday through Saturday from 10am to 5pm.

GETTING AROUND Many people find Fort Worth a more manageable city to visit than Dallas because it's smaller and most of its attractions are located in three places (downtown, the Stockyards Historic District, and the Cultural District). **Taxi** service is by dispatch or hotel stand only (© **817/534-5555**). The initial charge is $2.25 plus $2 per additional passenger plus $1.80 per mile plus fuel surcharge.

FAST FACTS **John Peter Smith Hospital** (© **817/921-3431**) provides 24-hour emergency services at 1500 S. Main St. The downtown area, especially around Sundance Square, has a lot of officers on bikes and is safe at all times. The local hotel tax is 15%; the local sales tax is 8.25%.

SPECIAL EVENTS & FESTIVALS The Stockyards District holds all kinds of special events, from cowboy gatherings to rodeos. Information on all of these can be found on the Fort Worth CVB's comprehensive website at **www.fortworth.com**.

EXPLORING THE CITY

Fort Worth's **downtown** has shopping, dining, and a fun and relaxed nightlife. Most of the restaurants, shops, clubs, and the Bass Concert Hall are in the **Sundance Square** section, which occupies 16 blocks. It's a lively scene with crowds of pedestrians.

The **Stockyards National Historic District** (www.fortworthstockyards.org) is 2 miles northwest of downtown, across the Trinity River. The old stockyards and surrounding buildings bring to mind the days of the Old West. Several stores sell Western wear. For high-quality boots, try **M. L. Leddy's Boot and Saddlery,** 2455 Main St. (© **817/624-3149**). In memory of the cattle drives of yore, each morning professional cowboys drive 12 longhorns from the stockyards to the nearby Trinity River to graze, and return them in the midafternoon to coincide with the arrival of an excursion train. The **Grapevine Vintage Railroad** (© **817/410-3123;** www.grapevinesteamrailroad.com) offers steam-engine train rides from the Stockyards Station to 8th Avenue and back most of the year Thursday through Sunday. Fares are $10 adults, $9 seniors, and $6 children. The same company offers a longer train ride that goes round-trip from the town of Grapevine to the Stockyards Station, but to take this train, you must start and finish in Grapevine.

The **Cultural District** is home to the Amon Carter Museum, the Kimbell Art Museum, the Modern Art Museum of Fort Worth, and a few others. The district also holds the Fort Worth zoo and the botanical garden. Any of these are worth the short trip from downtown or the stockyards area. For attractions in nearby Dallas and Arlington, see the "Dallas" section, earlier in this chapter.

Amon Carter Museum (Value) With its large collection of American and Western art, this museum ranks among the premier museums in the state. Holdings include 19th- and early-20th-century American paintings, sculpture, and prints from artists such as Frederic Remington, Charles M. Russell, Georgia O'Keeffe, and Winslow Homer. There is also an impressive collection of photographs from the likes of Ansel Adams and Eliot Porter.

3501 Camp Bowie Blvd. (Museum District). © 817/738-1933. http://cartermuseum.org. Free admission to permanent collection. Audio tour $4 adults, $2 seniors and kids 11 and under. Free docent-guided tour Thurs–Sun at 2pm. Tues–Sat 10am–5pm (Thurs until 8pm); Sun noon–5pm.

Fort Worth Botanic Garden The gardens showcase 150,000 plants representing 2,500 species, displayed in formal and natural settings. A 10,000-square-foot glass conservatory houses more than 2,500 tropical plants native to Central and South America. Especially lovely is the Japanese Garden. A leisurely tour of the grounds and conservatory requires 2 hours.

3220 Botanic Garden Blvd. (Cultural District). © 817/871-7686. www.fwbg.org. Japanese Garden $3.50 adults, $2.50 children; conservatory $1 adults, 50¢ children. Japanese garden daily 9am–6pm. Conservatory Mon–Sat 10am–4pm; Sun 1–6pm.

Fort Worth Museum of Science and History (Kids) This museum has a lot to keep kids interested. Most of the museum is closed to allow for construction of a new building designed by Ricardo Legorreta. The new building is set to open in 2009. Until then the major exhibits have been moved to the nearby **National Cowgirl Museum** (www.cowgirl.net).

1501 Montgomery St. (Cultural District). © 817/255-9300. www.fwmuseum.org. Museum $8 adults, $7 seniors and children 3–12; Omni theater $7 adults, $6 seniors and children 3–12; planetarium $3.50 for all; combination tickets available. Mon–Thurs 9am–5:30pm; Fri–Sat 9am–8pm; Sun noon–5:30pm.

Kimbell Art Museum (Best) A small but nationally acclaimed museum, the Kimbell thrills visitors with a collection of masterpieces ranging from Fra Angelico and El Greco to Matisse and Mondrian. The collection includes some beautiful works from the ancient world. The museum also attracts many fine traveling exhibitions; make a point of finding out what will be on when you are in town. Allow 2 hours.

3333 Camp Bowie Blvd. (Cultural District). © 817/332-8451. www.kimbellart.org. Free admission. Tues–Thurs 10am–5pm; Fri noon–8pm; Sat 10am–5pm; Sun noon–5pm.

Modern Art Museum of Fort Worth This museum is in an eye-catching 2002 creation of Japanese architect Tadao Ando. The building, constructed mostly of concrete and glass, is light, airy, and serene. It has greatly increased the museum's exhibition space, allowing more of the permanent collection to be displayed, including works from such artists as Picasso and Rothko. The majority of the collection dates from no earlier than the '40s.

3200 Darnell St. (Cultural District). © 866/824-5566. www.themodern.org. $10 adults, $4 seniors and students. Tues–Sat 10am–5pm (until 8pm on the 1st Fri of every month); Sun 11am–5pm.

See the "Dallas" section, earlier in this chapter, for hotels near the DFW Airport. Of the chain hotels in Fort Worth, Marriott (and its affiliate brands) has the most properties.

The Ashton Hotel (Best)   Inside two national landmark buildings, the Ashton offers spacious, distinctive guest rooms with lots of comforts such as plush mattresses, refrigerators, and large bathrooms. Rooms and suites vary quite a bit. Some come with Jacuzzis; others come with large sitting areas or larger bathrooms with separate shower and tub, such as the L-shaped "Signature Executive King" rooms, which are quite attractive. The service is excellent, and so is the location.

610 Main St., Fort Worth, TX 76102 (downtown). © 866/327-4866 or 817/332-0100. Fax 817/332-0110. www.theashtonhotel.com. 39 units. $280–$370 double; $350–$420 junior suite. AE, DC, DISC, MC, V. Valet parking $15. Small pets with $100 deposit. **Amenities:** Restaurant; exercise room; smoking not permitted. *In room:* Fridge.

Courtyard by Marriott Downtown—Blackstone   Opened in 1929 as the Blackstone, this 20-story hotel offers comfortable rooms. It's next to the entertainment district and within easy walking distance of everything. Rooms are large (corner rooms are larger still and go for the same price) and the bathrooms are medium to large, with separate vanities. Four rooms on the 16th floor include balconies where guests can take in the view of downtown. It's a popular hotel, so make reservations in advance.

601 Main St., Fort Worth, TX 76102 (downtown). © 800/321-2211 or 817/885-8700. Fax 817/885-8303. www.marriott.com/dfwms. 203 units. $179–$209 double; $229–$299 suite. AE, DC, DISC, MC, V. Valet parking $12. **Amenities:** Heated outdoor pool; exercise room.

Etta's Place   Named for Etta Place, the Sundance Kid's girlfriend, this B&B offers comfortable lodging and feels more like a small hotel than a B&B. The common areas are large and attractive and mostly modern. Guest rooms are comfortable and come with period furniture and either one king- or one queen-size bed. Service is good and the staff is helpful.

200 W. Third St., Fort Worth, TX 76102 (downtown). © 866/355-5760 or 817/255-5760. Fax 817/878-2560. www.ettas-place.com. 10 units. $150–$185 double; $185–$200 suite. Rates include full breakfast. AE, DC, DISC, MC, V. Self-parking $8. Children 9 and under not accepted. Pets under 25 lb. accepted for $20 fee per night, restrictions apply. **Amenities:** Smoking not permitted. *In room:* Kitchen (in suites only).

Hotel Texas (Value)   A comfortable, no-frills hotel with a good location in the Stockyards District, this retains a good bit of the feel of an old "Cowtown" hotel. This is a better choice than the chain hotels in this price range. Rooms are medium in size, with plain, standard-size bathrooms.

2415 Ellis Ave., Fort Worth, TX 76106 (Stockyards District). © 817/624-2224. Fax 817/624-7177. 20 units. Weekends $79–$149 double; weekdays $69–$99 double. AE, DC, DISC, MC, V.

Miss Molly's   Charming and different, Miss Molly's has preserved the floor plan of the original second-story boardinghouse/bordello built in 1910. Stairs lead from the street up to a common room around which all the guest rooms are situated. Rooms are decorated in period furniture. Each depicts a different aspect of turn-of-the-20th-century Fort Worth society. All except one share the three bathrooms in back, and robes are provided for guests.

109½ W. Exchange Ave., Fort Worth, TX 76106 (Stockyards District). © 817/626-1522. Fax 817/626-2589. www.missmollyshotel.com. 7 units. $125–$140 with shared bathroom; $200 with private bathroom. Rates include breakfast. AE, DC, DISC, MC, V. Free parking. **Amenities:** Smoking not permitted. *In room:* No TV.

Stockyards Hotel (Kids)   This historic hotel (Bonnie and Clyde once hid out in room no. 305) has medium-size rooms decorated in several styles, all of which take their inspiration from the Old West. If cowhide chairs and mounted longhorn heads are your thing, you'll like it. A saloon-style restaurant serves breakfast, lunch, and dinner.

109 E. Exchange Ave., Fort Worth, TX 76106 (Stockyards District). ☎ **800/423-8471** or 817/625-6427. Fax 817/624-2571. www.stockyardshotel.com. 52 units. $169–$199 double; $235–$425 suite. AE, DC, DISC, MC, V. Valet parking $10. Pets accepted for a $50 fee. **Amenities:** Restaurant.

WHERE TO DINE

Angelo's Barbecue BARBECUE   The emphasis at Angelo's is on the food, not the decor. Step inside and you'll find a dimly lit large room with concrete floor, cheap tables and chairs, and lazy ceiling fans. But the barbecue is cooked to perfection and the beer is as cold as it can be. The ribs and the brisket are especially noteworthy.

2533 White Settlement Rd. (btw. Henderson and University, near downtown). ☎ **817/332-0357.** Reservations not accepted. Barbecue plates $8–$12; sandwiches $4–$6. No credit cards. Mon–Sat 11am–10pm.

Cattlemen's Steak House (Kids) STEAK   This old-style steakhouse is a Fort Worth institution. It has the cowboy feel of many of the establishments of the Stockyards District but seems less self-conscious about it. There's a lot of rough-cut wood paneling, plain wood furniture, and vivid cowboy murals to brighten the place. The steaks are great, and this place is known for the Texas delicacy, chicken-fried steak.

2458 N. Main St. (Stockyards District). ☎ **817/624-3945.** www.cattlemenssteakhouse.com. Reservations accepted. Main courses $14–$36. AE, DC, DISC, MC, V. Mon–Thurs 11am–10:30pm; Fri–Sat 11am–11pm; Sun 1–9pm.

Joe T. Garcia's MEXICAN   Behind the nondescript entrance of this 70-year-old restaurant is a patio that seats 300 people amid fountains, a swimming pool, and a small garden. Seating is also available indoors, but it's not quite the same. The friendly and casual service remains unaffected by celebrity patrons. The menu is simple: beef or chicken fajitas, or a Tex-Mex enchilada dinner. The margaritas are renowned.

2201 N. Commerce St. (Stockyards District). ☎ **817/626-4356.** www.joets.com. Reservations accepted for groups of 20 or more. Main courses $11–$18. No credit cards. Mon–Thurs 11am–2:30pm and 5–10pm; Fri–Sat 11am–11pm; Sun 11am–10pm.

Lonesome Dove Western Bistro (Best) SOUTHWESTERN   For fine dining in Fort Worth, this small restaurant in the Stockyards District is the place. The dining room is comfortable and attractive, with solid-looking furniture and white tablecloths. A bar runs the length of the room, adding to the Western flavor. The intriguing menu includes ingredients from all over the world in bold combinations that tell of "New Cuisine" influences and often include a Mexican touch. The wine list has racked up numerous awards. For lunch, the bargain is the **Stockyards Special;** it changes every day but costs just $7.

2406 N. Main St. (Stockyards District). ☎ **817/740-8810.** www.lonesomedovebistro.com. Reservations recommended. Main courses $7–$17 lunch, $22–$34 dinner. AE, DISC, MC, V. Tues–Sat 11:30am–2:30pm and 5–10pm.

Reata WESTERN   The plucky menu characterizes the food here as Texas cowboy cuisine, which is a tad misleading. Certainly the chicken-fried steak and the rib-eye topped with a pat of butter qualify, and perhaps even the smoked shrimp enchiladas, but what about the pecan-crusted chicken breast with a tomato and raspberry sauce? Or the angel-hair pasta with Gulf shrimp? The food is excellently prepared, and the margaritas are outstanding. There's a large main dining room, a rooftop section, and a quieter basement room.

310 Houston St. (downtown). © **817/336-1009**. www.reata.net. Reservations recommended. Main courses $16–$41. AE, DISC, MC, V. Daily 11am–2:30pm and 5–10:30pm.

FORT WORTH AFTER DARK

The **Sundance Square Downtown Entertainment District** is grabbing the lion's share of city nightlife these days. Dozens of dining and entertainment options abound. The most spectacular venue is the **Bass Performance Hall** (© 817/212-4325), the 2,056-seat, acoustically amazing theater designed by David M. Schwartz, which serves as home for the **Fort Worth Symphony** (© 817/665-6000; www.fwsymphony.org), **Texas Ballet Theater** (© 877/212-4280; www.texasballettheater.org), and **Fort Worth Opera** (© 817/731-0726; www.fwopera.org).

Sundance Square's other options include the **Circle Theatre** (© 817/877-3040) and the **Jubilee Theatre** (© 817/338-4411), as well as two multicinemas. For bars and clubs, you have quite a few to choose from and might do well just to walk through the area until you find one to your taste. For dancing, the main venue is **City Streets** (© 817/335-5400), a collection of four clubs at 425 Commerce St. offering pop music and tunes from the '70s and '80s. the **Flying Saucer Beer Emporium** (© 817/336-7468) offers a variety of music and libations. Also very popular is the **Fox & Hound** at 604 Main St. (© 817/338-9200), a large, lively, publike bar.

For cowboy entertainment, go to the **Stockyards District.** There you'll find one of Fort Worth's most popular attractions, the 127,000-square-foot **Billy Bob's Texas,** 2520 Rodeo Plaza (© 817/624-7117; www.billybobstexas.com), which bills itself as "the world's largest honky-tonk." But before going to Billy Bob's, try the **Cowtown Coliseum,** 121 E. Exchange Ave. (© 817/625-1025), which has a small rodeo on Friday and Saturday nights, usually starting at 8pm.

3 HOUSTON

Situated on a flat, nearly featureless Gulf Coast plain, Houston spreads out from its center in vast tracts of subdivisions, freeways, and shopping malls covering an area larger than half the state of Rhode Island. It is the largest, most cosmopolitan city in Texas, and like its terrain, Houston is wide open economically and socially. This has made it the land of opportunity for many who have come here, which includes a large and varied immigrant population. Houston is also a seaport, the second busiest in the country, thanks to a ship channel that cuts inland from Galveston Bay.

A few years back, residential construction shifted away from the suburbs and toward the downtown and inner-city areas as many Houstonians returned from the suburbs. Some were lured in by the performing arts and cultural scene, including an excellent symphony orchestra, highly respected ballet and opera companies, a dynamic theater scene that few cities can equal, and some tiptop museums. Always the most popular attraction for visitors is NASA's Johnson Space Center, which teamed up with Disney to create Space Center Houston. Aside from NASA, Houston is best known for its oil industry and for the Texas Medical Center, one of the best in the country.

GETTING THERE   By Plane George Bush Intercontinental/Houston Airport **(IAH)** is 45 minutes north of downtown, with taxi fare around $50. It is a hub for Continental Airlines. **Hobby Airport (HOU)** is closer to downtown, 30 minutes to the southeast; taxi fare is about $30. Fares to hotels in the Galleria shopping area run $55 from IAH and $50 from Hobby. Information on both airports is available online at **www.fly2houston.com.**

Shuttle service from either airport to different parts of the city is operated by **Super-Shuttle** (✆ **713/523-8888;** www.supershuttle.com). The fare between downtown and Houston Intercontinental Airport costs $22. C**ity bus service** (✆ **713/635-4000**) from IAH (terminal C) to downtown costs $1.50 (route 102). It runs daily until midnight.

By Train   Amtrak (✆ **800/USA-RAIL** [872-7245]; www.amtrak.com) serves the **Southern Pacific Station,** 902 Washington Ave. (✆ **713/224-1577**), with trains from San Antonio (trip time: 4 hr.) and New Orleans (9 hr.).

By Car   The principal routes into Houston are **I-45** from the north (Dallas) and southeast (Galveston), and **I-10** from the east (New Orleans) and west (San Antonio and El Paso). The outermost loop, known as Beltway 8 (**Sam Houston Pkwy.**), circles the outer city. **Loop 610** circles the central city.

VISITOR INFORMATION   The **Greater Houston Convention and Visitors Bureau** (✆ **800/4-HOUSTON** [446-8786]; www.visithoustontexas.com) has a **Visitors Center** at City Hall, 901 Bagby St., Houston, TX 77002 (✆ **713/437-5556**), open Monday to Saturday from 9am to 4pm. While you're there, make sure to see the Art Deco lobby of the city hall proper.

GETTING AROUND   The **Metropolitan Transportation Authority (MTA;** ✆ **713/635-4000;** www.ridemetro.org) offers a **light-rail train service,** which connects downtown with the Museum District, the Medical Center, and the Reliant Stadium complex. This route is handy for the visitor. Tickets can be purchased at vending machines at every station. A day pass is $2 and is good for bus service, too. Citywide bus service costs $1 for most fares; express service costs $1.50. Seniors and riders with disabilities pay 40¢; children 3 and under ride free.

Taxis are plentiful in the city, but trying to hail one on the street can be an exercise in frustration. Call ahead or use hotel taxi stands. The principal companies are **Yellow Cab** (✆ **713/236-1111;** www.yellowcabhouston.com), **Fiesta Cab** (✆ **713/225-2666**), **Liberty Cab** (✆ **713/695-6700**), and **United Cab** (✆ **713/699-0000**). Cabs run $4 for the first mile and $1.85 for each mile thereafter plus a fuel surcharge.

FAST FACTS   Ben Taub General Hospital, 1502 Taub Loop (✆ **713/793-2000**), is a nationally recognized emergency center. The local hotel tax is 17%; the local sales tax is 8.25%. Houston has three area codes: **713, 281,** and **832.** Local calls require dialing the 10-digit number.

SPECIAL EVENTS & FESTIVALS   The **Houston Livestock Show and Rodeo** (✆ **713/791-9000;** www.rodeohouston.com), which runs from late February to mid-March, is the largest rodeo in the world. In April the city celebrates the **Houston International Festival** (✆ **713/654-8808;** www.ifest.org), which highlights a particular country each year. It takes place downtown over 2 weekends and gets more than a million celebrants. Houston is also famous for its **Art Car Parade** (www.orangeshow.org/artcar. html), usually held the second weekend in May.

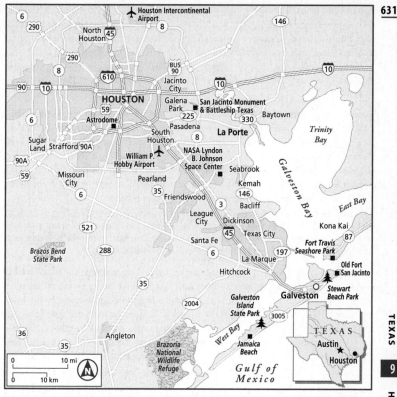

EXPLORING THE CITY
The Top Attractions

Battleship *Texas* & San Jacinto Monument and Museum   It was here, in 1836, that Sam Houston and his Texas army attacked and defeated the Mexican army and won Texas its independence. The site is marked by an obelisk the size of the Washington Monument but topped with a lone star. You can take the elevator up to the observation room, but the view is mostly of the Houston Ship Channel. In the base of the obelisk is an interesting museum and a movie theater with shows describing the battle. Next to the battlefield is the USS *Texas*. Built in 1914, it's the world's last remaining dreadnought battleship. You can clamber up to its small-caliber guns or onto the navigation bridge, inspect the crew's quarters, or check out the engine room. It can take as much as 3 hours to see both museum and battleship.

3527 Battleground Rd. (La Porte, off Hwy. 225). (⌀ **281/479-2421.** www.sanjacinto-museum.org. Admission to park $1 for adults and kids 13 and over. For battleship $10 adults, $5 seniors, free for kids 12 and under. Monument and museum free admission; observation room $4 adults, $3.50 seniors, $3 children; movie $4.50 adults, $4 seniors, $3.50 children. Daily 9am–6pm (for battleship 10am–5pm).

Bayou Bend Collection & Gardens   Twenty-eight rooms of the mansion built for Ima Hogg, daughter of a former governor of Texas, who obviously had a cruel sense of humor when he named his offspring, hold an important collection of American furniture and paintings from the 17th, 18th, and 19th centuries. These are seen by guided or audio tour. Fourteen acres of gardens surrounding the estate can be viewed without a guide; children 9 and under are not admitted. Allow 2^1/$_2$ hours.

1 Westcott St. (off Memorial Dr.). ✆ **713/639-7750.** www.mfah.org/bayoubend. Admission $10 adults, $8.50 seniors, $5 ages 10–18. Tues–Fri 10–11:30am and 1–2:45pm; Sat 10–11:15am. Reservations required.

Houston Museum of Natural Science (Kids) Much better than your average natural history museum, this one has had success attracting important traveling exhibitions. The permanent collection is large and impressive. A special attraction is the **Cockrell Butterfly Center,** which houses 2,000 butterflies flying freely in a six-story glass cone. (Next to it is the "bug zoo," with live specimens of enormous insects from the world's tropical forests.) There is also a planetarium and an IMAX theater. A stroll through the permanent exhibition and the butterfly center can take 3 hours.

1 Hermann Circle Dr. (in Hermann Park). ✆ **713/639-4629.** www.hmns.org. Admission $10 adults, $7 seniors and children 3–11; Butterfly Center $8 adults, $6 seniors and children; IMAX tickets $10 adults, $8 seniors and children. Multivenue ticket packages available. General hours Mon–Sat 9am–5pm (until 8pm Tues); Sun 11am–5pm; hours for planetarium and IMAX can differ. Parking $8.

Menil Collection (Value) The collections of this private museum, one of the world's most highly regarded, break down roughly into four sections: antiquity, Byzantine, tribal art, and the 20th century. This last section, with its large holdings of works by the modern masters, is what garners most of the attention. Besides the main building (designed by Renzo Piano), there are satellite galleries holding works by Mark Rothko, Cy Twombly, and a Byzantine fresco ransomed from art thieves. Because it's free and has easy access, it's perfect for a quick stop, but you could also spend hours here.

1515 Sul Ross St. (Montrose). ✆ **713/525-9400.** www.menil.org. Free admission. Wed–Sun 11am–7pm.

Museum of Fine Arts Houston (Best) This is the best and biggest public art museum in Texas. It occupies two large buildings connected by a tunnel (make a point of seeing it): an earlier building largely designed by Mies van der Rohe, and a newer, more conservative building by Spanish architect Rafael Moneo. The museum's collection of over 40,000 pieces is wide and varied, but it is perhaps strongest in the areas of Impressionist and post-Impressionist works, baroque and Renaissance art, and 19th- and 20th-century American art. The museum attracts important traveling exhibits, so look for them.

1001 Bissonnet St. (at the intersection of S. Main and Montrose Blvd.). ✆ **713/639-7300.** www.mfah.org. Admission $7 adults, $3.50 seniors and children 6–18; free general admission Thurs. Tues–Wed 10am–5pm; Thurs 10am–9pm; Fri–Sat 10am–7pm; Sun 12:15–7pm.

The Orange Show (Kids) Former postman Jeff Mckissack spent 25 years assembling a collection of found objects and mundane artifacts to "encourage people to eat oranges, drink oranges, and be highly amused." The fruits of his labor form a unique urban folk-art park, preserved by the Orange Show Foundation. Great for kids and anyone who enjoys seeing a little outlandishness—the place can easily be seen in an hour and is on the way to the space center from central Houston. *Note:* For the last couple of years, the Orange Show has closed for restoration during the month of August—this might become a yearly practice.

2402 Munger St. (off the Gulf Fwy., exit Telephone Rd.). ✆ **713/926-6368.** www.orangeshow.org. Admission $1 adults, free for children 11 and under. Memorial Day to Labor Day Wed–Fri 9am–1pm; Sat–Sun noon–5pm. Open only on weekends rest of the year.

... But It's a Wet Heat

Hot and humid, Houston has earned the unofficial title of "Air-Conditioning Capital of the World." If you are unaccustomed to high humidity and its consequences (profuse sweating, bad-hair days), you might want to take it easy at first and work on acquiring some degree of philosophical acceptance. One more thing—bopping around Houston in summertime means jumping from the frying pan into the freezer (to mangle yet another cliché). You'll be going from steamy outdoors into super-chilled shops, restaurants, and so on.

Space Center Houston (Kids)   Space Center Houston is the product of the joint efforts of NASA and Disney Imagineering. It is the most popular attraction in Houston, and there's nothing like it anywhere else in this sector of the galaxy. It's heavy on interactive displays and simulations, as well as actual access to the real thing. For instance, the **Feel of Space** gallery simulates working in the frictionless environment of space by using an air-bearing floor (something like a giant air hockey table). Another simulator shows what it's like to land the lunar orbiter. For a direct experience of NASA, the $1^1/_2$-hour tram tour takes you to the International Space Station Assembly Building and NASA control center. A visit lasts an average of 4 hours.

Johnson Space Center, 1601 NASA Rd. 1 (in Clear Lake, 20 miles south of downtown, off Gulf Fwy.). ✆ **281/244-2100.** www.spacecenter.org. Admission (including tours and IMAX theater) $19 adults, $18 seniors, $15 children 4–11. Daily 10am–7pm in summer; otherwise Mon–Fri 10am–5pm, Sat–Sun 10am–6pm. Parking $5.

More to See & Do

SPORTS   In recent years, Houston has built modern venues for each of its big three sports teams. The MLB **Astros** (✆ 877/9-ASTROS [927-8767]; www.astros.com) are enjoying their downtown ballpark with retractable roof, Minute Maid Field (formerly Enron Field). The NFL **Texans** (✆ 866/GO-TEXANS [468-3926]; www.houstontexans.com) have Reliant Stadium, also with a retractable roof. It's located in south Houston on the light rail line. And the NBA **Rockets** (✆ 877/622-7625; www.nba.com/rockets) perform at the Toyota Center downtown. The WNBA's **Comets** (✆ 713/627-9622; www.wnba.com/comets) play at Reliant Arena.

The easiest way to play a round of golf is to call **Golf Guys** (✆ 800/470-9634; www.golfguys.net). You can consult with the people there about local courses and reserve tee times.

PARKS & ZOOS   The city's playground is **Hermann Park,** a 545-acre park minutes from downtown. It has an 18-hole golf course, picnic areas, the Garden Center, the Miller Outdoor Theater, and many other recreational facilities. It is also home to the **Houston Zoo,** 1513 N. MacGregor (✆ 713/523-5888; www.houstonzoo.org), open daily 9am to 6pm March through September, 9am to 5pm daily October to February. This 50-acre zoo features a gorilla habitat, rare albino reptiles, a cat facility, a huge aquarium, and vampire bats that eat lunch every day at 2:30pm. Admission to the zoo is $8.50 adults, $5 seniors, $4 children 2 to 11.

ESPECIALLY FOR KIDS   The **Children's Museum of Houston,** 1500 Binz (✆ 713/522-1138; www.cmhouston.org), does a wonderful job of grabbing the attention and engaging the imaginations of children up to 12 years old. It blurs the distinction between museum and playhouse, and there always seems to be something special going on here. It's open Tuesday to Saturday 9am to 5pm, and Sunday noon to 5pm; during summer, it's also open Monday 9am to 5pm. Admission is $5.

Houston is home to **SplashTown** (© 281/355-3300; www.splashtownpark.com), 40 minutes north of downtown off I-45 (exit 70A), a waterpark with rides. General admission is $33 (often $2 cheaper if purchased online); children under 48 inches are $25. The park is open during the summer and on some weekends in fall.

SHOPPING

The main shopping area in Houston is called Uptown, which includes the **Galleria** (www.simon.com), home to 320 shops, and a few nearby shopping centers, along Post Oak Boulevard and Westheimer Road. Also worth visiting are the stores in the **River Oaks Shopping Center** (www.riveroaksshoppingcenter.com), Houston's first shopping strip, at Shepherd Drive and Gray Street. And in the **Village,** near Rice University (www.ricevillageonline.com), you'll find several blocks of mixed retail/restaurant space, including a number of boutiques and small shops. The **Parks Shops in Houston Center,** 1200 McKinney St., is the only downtown mall. The **Montrose** area, along Westheimer from Woodward Street to Mandell Street, is a jumble of dealers hawking antiques. Let the buyer beware.

WHERE TO STAY

A number of good hotels are at or near IAH, including the **Houston Airport Marriott,** 18700 John F. Kennedy Blvd. (© 800/228-9290 or 281/443-2310), between terminals B and C. Near Hobby Airport there is a **Days Inn Hobby Airport,** 1505 College Ave. (© 800/DAYS-INN [329-7466] or 713/946-5900), which is also close to the Astrodome and the Texas Medical Center.

Best Western Downtown Inn and Suites   Located in the shadow of downtown's skyline, this hotel offers convenient location and extra-large rooms with one king-size or two queen-size beds. On the downside, style takes a back seat to comfort and convenience, and there's no restaurant or room service. The greatest savings are had during the week; for a weekend, consider paying a bit extra to stay at one of the fancy hotels, which offer deeper discounts.

915 W. Dallas St., Houston, TX 77019. © 800/528-1234 or 713/571-7733. Fax 713/571-6680. www. bestwestern.com. 77 units. $169–$209 double; $189–$229 suite. Rates include continental breakfast. AE, DC, DISC, MC, V. Free guarded parking. **Amenities:** Covered outdoor pool; fitness room. *In room:* Fridge, microwave.

Four Seasons Hotel Houston (Best)   This hotel has lots of space so that you can stretch out in the oversize guest rooms and large health club, and offers excellent service so you don't have to stretch too far. It's close to the city's theater and entertainment district, and closer to the ballpark and basketball arena. Rooms are beautifully furnished, and those facing west have great views.

1300 Lamar St., Houston, TX 77010 (downtown). © 800/332-3442 or 713/650-1300. Fax 713/652-6220. www.fourseasons.com/houston. 406 units. $355–$415 double; $470 and up suite. Children 17 and under stay free in parent's room. AE, DC, DISC, MC, V. Valet parking $27. Pets accepted. **Amenities:** Restaurant; pool; health club; spa.

Hilton University of Houston   Part of the Conrad Hilton College of Hotel and Restaurant Management, this hotel is staffed by professional full-timers, as well as students performing their course work. It deserves consideration because its rates often drop very low. The location between downtown and the attractions on Houston's southeast side is excellent. Rooms have large L-shaped layouts with modern furnishings. The University Center next door has a health club, and a large pool that guests have access to. Note that the parking garage has a low ceiling and cannot accommodate vehicles such as large SUVs and pickup trucks.

4800 Calhoun Rd., Houston, TX 77004. © **800/HOTEL-UH** (468-3584) or 713/741-2447. Fax 713/743-2498. www.hilton.com. 86 units. $99–$180 double. AE, DC, DISC, MC, V. Parking $8. **Amenities:** Restaurant.

Hotel Derek This modern hotel's namesake, Derek, is a fictitious aging rock star and owner of the hotel. Given the premise, it would have been easy to lapse into cliché and stereotype, but it doesn't. There are nods to the 1960s, but these are blended with unexpected touches and the playful mix of materials new and old into a thoughtful design. Guest rooms are functional but with the feel of a "pad." Beds, mostly king-size, are on platforms, and the sitting area is a wonderful mohair velvet built-in sofa stretching the width of the room.

2525 W. Loop S., Houston, TX 77027. © **866/292-4100** or 713/961-3000. Fax 713/297-4392. www.hotel derek.com. 314 units. $280 standard; $310 studio; $375 and up suite. AE, DC, DISC, MC, V. Valet parking $14. Pets allowed for a $50 fee. **Amenities:** Restaurant; fitness center.

Hotel Icon Lots of texture, ornament, and a definite boudoir feel to the rooms makes staying at this downtown hotel a lot of fun. In renovating the old Union National Bank Building (1911), the designers sought to capture something of the feel of that golden age of refinement and exuberance. The most fun is to be had in the suites on the top floor, each named after a glorious old hotel. These are extra large and extra plush, and touched by a bit of idiosyncrasy. Location is excellent.

220 Main St., Houston, TX 77002. © **800/323-7500** or 713/224-4266. Fax 713/223-3223. www.hotelicon. com. 135 units. $199–$349 double; $359 and up suite. Look for weekend discounts and Internet packages. AE, DC, DISC, MC, V. Valet parking $25. **Amenities:** Restaurant; spa; fitness center.

Hotel ZaZa This new property, set in what once was the Warwick Hotel, enjoys a great location in the Museum District, close by Hermann Park and Rice University—the greenest part of the city. Rooms are done up with flair, and the more expensive the room, the more the flair. At top of the building and the room rate chart are the expensive "concept suites," which are definitely for the party set and put you right into vacation mode. Common space includes a comfortable pool area and terrace.

5701 Main St., Houston, TX 77005. © **713/526-1991.** Fax 713/526-0359. www.hotelzazahouston.com. 315 units. $235–$255 double; $385 and up suites. AE, DISC, MC, V. Free valet parking. Small pets allowed with $150 deposit. **Amenities:** Restaurant; pool; fitness room; spa.

Lancaster Hotel For those who enjoy the performing arts and nightlife in general, there is no better place to stay. Within 1 block you have the symphony, the ballet, the opera, and the theater, and, when reserving a room, you can have the concierge buy tickets for performances at any of these venues. The hotel occupies a 12-story landmark building that dates from the 1920s. Rooms are smaller than their counterparts at other downtown hotels but have character and a host of amenities (Frette bathrobes, VCRs, and so on). Service is excellent and includes lots of personal touches.

701 Texas Ave., Houston, TX 77002 (downtown). © **800/231-0336** or 713/228-9500. Fax 713/223-4528. www.thelancasterhouston.com. 93 units. $250–$350 double; $350 and up suite. AE, DC, DISC, MC, V. Valet parking $30. **Amenities:** Restaurant.

Lovett Inn (Value) Located 1 block off Westheimer and 3 blocks from Montrose Boulevard, the Lovett Inn is on a quiet street in the middle of the restaurant and club district of the Montrose Area. The house dates from the early 1900s. Most rooms are large (well above the usual size for B&Bs). The four rooms in the main house and two in the carriage house are attractive and well furnished with period pieces, wood floors, and area rugs, yet without the cutesiness that so many B&Bs feel obliged to deliver. Almost all have private balconies. There are also six town-house units around the corner (two per house), which have separate entrances and greater privacy. These are comfortable but modern.

501 Lovett Blvd., Houston, TX 77006. ℂ 800/779-5224 or 713/522-5224. Fax 713/528-6708. www.lovett inn.com. 12 units. $115–$175 traditional doubles; $99–$130 town-house doubles. Rates include continental breakfast. AE, DC, DISC, MC, V. Free parking. **Amenities:** Outdoor pool.

WHERE TO DINE

Brennan's SOUTHERN/CREOLE   Fine dining New Orleans style, Brennan's is a perennial favorite of Houstonians. The dining rooms are elegant, perhaps the most elegant in Houston, and the service is superb. The selection of dishes varies daily, but a few classic Creole specialties such as a roux-less seafood gumbo or its well-known turtle soup are always on the menu.

3300 Smith St. ℂ 713/522-9711. www.brennanshouston.com. Reservations recommended. Main courses $27–$44. AE, DISC, MC, V. Mon–Fri 11:30am–1:30pm; Sun–Thurs 5:45–9pm; Fri–Sat 5:45–9:30pm; brunch Sat 11am–2pm, Sun 10am–2pm.

Cafe Annie (Best) SOUTHWESTERN   No restaurant in Houston has received more coverage, more acclaim, or more awards. The softly lit dining room has lots of dark woodwork and a quiet atmosphere. Dinner is expensive, but you can save money by going for lunch or ordering from the *botanitas* menu (tapas), served at the bar. One of the restaurant's signature dishes, the crabmeat tostadas, is available on the dinner, lunch, and *botanitas* menus. Also notable is the risotto of Maine lobster and Gulf shrimp in a broth lightly flavored with *chile cascabel* and cream.

1728 Post Oak Blvd. (just south of San Felipe). ℂ 713/840-1111. www.cafe-annie.com. Reservations recommended. Main courses $28–$50. AE, DC, DISC, MC, V. Tues–Fri 11:30am–2pm; Mon–Fri 6:30–10pm; Sat 6:30–10:30pm.

Churrascos SOUTH AMERICAN/STEAKS   The signature dish at this elegant dining spot is the beef tenderloin butterflied and served with *chimichurri* sauce, the Argentine condiment that accompanies steak. Popular, too, are the fried plantain chips served at every table, the Cuban-style black-bean soup, and the Peruvian-style seviche. Grilled vegetables come "family style" with every entree. Tables are well separated and the decor is in the simple style of an Argentine *estancia*.

2055 Westheimer. ℂ 713/527-8300. www.churrascos.com. Reservations recommended. Main courses $16–$25; lunch $10–$13. AE, DC, DISC, MC, V. Mon–Thurs 11am–10pm; Fri 11am–11pm; Sat 5–11pm; Sun 11am–9pm.

Goode Company Texas Barbeque (Kids) BARBECUE   Buffalo trophies, snake skins, and stuffed armadillos adorn this popular cowboy barbecue joint—a prime destination for those who love good, honest barbecue. Jim Goode's crew smokes delicious duck, chicken, links, and ribs. Try the brisket sandwich on jalapeño bread and see if you don't think you're on to something special. The pecan pie is a must for dessert. ***Note:*** An additional location is at 8911 Katy Fwy. (ℂ 713/464-1901).

5109 Kirby Dr. (near the Village shopping center). ℂ 713/522-2530. www.goodecompany.com. Barbecue plates $8–$13. AE, DC, DISC, MC, V. Daily 11am–10pm.

Hugo's MEXICAN   Serving the best interior Mexican food in Houston, this restau- rant enjoys a strong local following. Main courses include duck in a *mole poblano* (the classic dark red, bittersweet sauce of the Mexican highlands) and a *chile relleno* with roasted chicken smothered in a *pipián* (a spicy sauce in a base of ground roasted pumpkin seeds). Keep an eye out for daily specials; the chef/owner, Hugo Ortega, enjoys seasonal cooking. The dining room is large and airy, owing to a very high ceiling—the building dates from 1935 and was once a drugstore.

1602 Westheimer Rd. (at Mandell St.). © **713/524-7744.** www.hugosrestaurant.net. Reservations recommended. Main courses $15–$30. AE, DC, DISC, MC, V. Sun–Thurs 11am–10pm; Fri–Sat 11am–11pm.

La Mexicana Restaurant MEXICAN   Once a little Mexican grocery store, La Mexicana started serving tacos and such before gradually turning exclusively to the restaurant business. It's known for delicious Mexican breakfasts and classic enchilada plates (red or green are good choices). There is an extensive menu of tacos a la carte, and good fajitas as well. Service is good, and there's a choice of dining outside or in.

1018 Fairview (at Montrose). © **713/521-0963.** www.lamexicanarestaurant.com. Reservations not accepted. Main courses $7–$13. AE, DC, DISC, MC, V. Daily 7am–11pm.

Mark's American Cuisine NEW AMERICAN   Formerly chef at the renowned Tony's, Mark Cox now sets a formidable table inside a refurbished former church. The ever-changing menu keeps regulars delighted; selections might include lamb in a basil sauce with white cheddar potatoes or bourbon-glazed pork with yams and an apple compote. Many dishes are elegant variations of American classics that can be satisfying while at the same time providing a sensation of newness.

1658 Westheimer (in the Montrose area). © **713/523-3800.** www.marks1658.com. Reservations recommended. Main courses $15–$32. AE, DC, DISC, MC, V. Mon–Fri 11am–2pm; Mon–Thurs 6–11pm; Fri–Sat 5pm–midnight; Sun 5–10pm.

Thai Bistro THAI   Houston is rich in Thai restaurants, having more than 70. This one, in a strip center along the Southwest Freeway, is particularly good. If you have an appetite, do yourself a favor and order the assorted appetizer platter. From there you can go in any number of directions: healthy (barbecued lemon-grass tofu or lettuce wraps), spicy (tiger cries or blazing noodles), classic (pad Thai), or curry (Panang).

3241 Southwest Fwy. © **713/669-9375.** Reservations not accepted. Main courses $7–$16. AE, DC, DISC, MC, V. Mon–Fri 11am–3pm and 5–10pm; Sat 11am–10:30pm; Sun 11am–9pm.

Treebeards ⟨Value⟩ CAJUN/CREOLE   A downtown tradition for lunch that's both good and economical. Try out red beans and rice, jambalaya, étouffée, and chicken and shrimp gumbo that'll fly with the best of them. Service is cafeteria style. Go early or late to beat the rush of office workers. Other downtown locations include 1100 Louisiana and 1117 Texas, next to the Christ Church Cathedral.

315 Travis St. © **713/228-2622.** www.treebeardsrestaurant.com. Reservations not accepted. Main courses $5–$9. AE, DC, MC, V. Mon–Fri 11am–2pm.

HOUSTON AFTER DARK

THE PERFORMING ARTS   The performing arts venues listed here are within a small area of a few blocks in the northwest part of downtown. This is quite a convenience for visitors. **Jesse H. Jones Hall for the Performing Arts,** 615 Louisiana St., is the home of the **Houston Symphony Orchestra** (© **713/224-7575;** www.houstonsymphony. org). The **Wortham Theater Center,** 510 Preston (www.worthamtheaterhouston.com), is home to the innovative **Houston Grand Opera** (© 713/228-6737; www.houston grandopera.org), whose season runs October through May. The **Houston Ballet** (© 800/828-ARTS [828-2787]; www.houstonballet.org) also performs here. The **Society for the Performing Arts (SPA),** 615 Louisiana St. (© 713/632-8100; www.spa houston.org), sponsors distinguished artists and productions from all areas of the performing arts. The nationally recognized **Alley Theatre,** 615 Texas Ave. (© 713/228-8421; www.alleytheatre.org), is at home in a futuristic theater complex, designed by Ulrich Fransen. The Alley presents about 10 different productions a year, both modern plays and the classics.

THE CLUB & MUSIC SCENE   Downtown is the hottest place to be. **Bayou Place,** 530 Texas Ave., is a large multivenue nightclub-and-restaurant complex in the heart of the Theater District, with live music spots, a movie theater, and **Verizon Wireless Theater** (© 713/230-1666), a good concert hall that gets a variety of acts. A few blocks away, in the city's oldest commercial building, **La Carafe,** 813 Congress Ave. (© 713/229-9399), is one of the city's most interesting bars, a place to drink and relax and chat with some of the regulars. Also a couple of blocks away are a few jazz clubs: **Red Cat Jazz Café** is at 924 Congress (© 713/226-7870), and **Sambuca Jazz Café** is at 909 Texas Ave. (© 713/224-5299). A number of clubs are springing up in this area, so you might want to take a spin around this part of downtown.

Outside of downtown, you can go to an old Houston institution known as **Fitzgerald's,** 2706 White Oak (© 713/862-3838). It occupies an old Polish dance hall near the Heights neighborhood and gets talented local and touring bands, mostly rock acts. For country, the best place to go is **Blanco's** (© 713/439-0072), a Texas-style honky-tonk that packs [']em in Mondays through Fridays, attracting all sorts, from yuppies to tool pushers. Lots of good Texas bands like to play here, so it's a good opportunity to see a well-known local band in a small venue. There's a midsize dance floor. Monday through Wednesday is open-mic night, usually with one or another local band. Thursday and Friday offer live music, and the club is closed on Saturdays for private parties. It's located at 3406 W. Alabama, between Kirby Drive and Buffalo Speedway. When there's live music, the cover ranges from $5 to $15.

4 GALVESTON

Galveston is on the barrier island directly across from the mainland coast closest to Houston. Older than Houston, it was a prosperous port throughout most of the 19th century and is once again being used as a home port by the cruise industry. One of its main attractions is the downtown historic district, with its Victorian commercial buildings and houses. Another attraction—the beaches—draws Houstonians and other Texans down in droves. Its leading claim to historical fame, however, lies in tragedy: Galveston was the site of the worst natural disaster ever to strike the United States—the 1900 Galveston Storm, which killed 6,000 people.

In September 2008 another killer storm, Hurricane Ike, made a direct hit on Galveston, but the seawall did its job, bearing the brunt of the storm's surge, though leaving behind millions, if not billions, of dollars' worth of damage. On the east and west ends of the island, beyond the seawall, the storm caused greater damage. Most of the construction in these areas was vacation houses and rentals. These parts will be a long time coming back—the amount of debris, the erosion of the beaches, and the tangle of legal issues will

slow recovery. As purely a beach destination, Galveston won't be regaining its old form
anytime soon. But we are estimating that by summer 2009, almost all the hotels, restaurants, and attractions will be open, and some of the city's beaches (not the ones farther out) will be back in business. The city of Galveston, with its attractions—the Historic East End, the Strand, and the harbor area, as well as the amusement park, Schlitterbahn, and Moody Gardens—should be up and running.

ESSENTIALS

GETTING THERE   Most visitors arrive here via Houston (50 miles away). The **Gulf Freeway** (I-45) leads directly into Galveston. Houston's Hobby Airport, just off this freeway, is the most convenient airport, though the island does have its own small airport, called Scholes Field.

VISITOR INFORMATION   If you're planning a trip, contact the **Galveston Convention and Visitors Bureau** (© **888/GAL-ISLE** [425-4753]; www.galveston.com). If you're in town already, check out their **Visitor Information Center,** 2027 61st St., open daily from 8:30am to 5pm during the summer.

GETTING AROUND   After entering Galveston, I-45 becomes Broadway, Galveston's principal street. Instead of crossing straight to the water, it cuts across the island diagonally, heading eastward until it comes to the coastline at Stewart Beach. Streets crossing Broadway are numbered; those parallel to Broadway have letters, and many have names as well. The East End Historic District and the historic Strand District are north of Broadway between 25th and 9th streets. Galveston has a restored **trolley line** that loops through the Strand District before heading down 25th Street to the beach and the sea wall. After the 1900 storm, Galveston built miles of sea wall along its seaward shore; here you'll find many of Galveston's hotels, motels, and restaurants. **Taxis** are not commonly seen; if you need one, call **Yellow Cab** (© **409/763-3333**). Rates run $4 for the first mile, $1.85 for each additional mile.

FAST FACTS   Galveston's hospital is the **University of Texas Medical Branch** (© **409/ 772-1011**). The physician referral line is © **409/763-4111.** Sales tax is 8.25% and hotel tax is 13%.

SPECIAL EVENTS & FESTIVALS   In February/March, Galveston holds a popular 12-day **Mardi Gras** (www.mardigrasgalveston.com) with parades, masked balls, and a live entertainment district. The first weekend in June is the annual **American Institute of Architects Sandcastle Competition** (www.aiasandcastle.com), on East Beach. About 60 architectural firms take the building of sandcastles and sand sculptures to a new level. There are a lot of food and drink stalls, and everybody has a good time. The first weekend in December, Galveston hosts **Dickens on The Strand** (© **409/765-7834;** www. dickensonthestrand.org), a street party in the historic district to celebrate the Victorian age (Galveston's heyday) and the Christmas holidays with parades, entertainers, lots of the locals in Victorian costume, and street vendors.

WHAT TO SEE & DO

Popular activities among visitors and locals alike are to walk, skate, or ride a bike atop the **sea wall,** which extends 10 miles along the coast. The **beaches** are always Galveston's most popular attraction. They may not measure up to those of the most popular beach destinations; the sand is a light tan color instead of white (but it's pure sand without rocks), and the water isn't turquoise (but it's a wonderful temperature). **East Beach** and

Stewart Beach, operated by the city, have pavilions with dressing rooms, showers, and restrooms, ideal for day-trippers. There's a $5-per-vehicle entrance fee. Most other beaches are free.

Many tours are offered on the island: **Galveston Harbour Tours** (© **409/765-1700**) offers a Saturday-morning dolphin-watch tour and a frequent harbor tour; **Duck Tours** (© **409/621-4771**) offers tours of the island in their amphibious buses; **Ghost Tours** (© **409/949-2027**) offers a walking tour of the Strand District. On Broadway there are a few massive 19th-century mansions that offer tours: **Ashton Villa,** 2328 Broadway (© **409/762-3933**); the **Bishop's Palace,** 1402 Broadway (© **409/762-2475**); and the **Moody Mansion,** 2618 Broadway (© **409/762-7668**).

MUSEUMS Except for Moody Gardens and its neighbor, the Lone Star Flight Museum (see below), all of Galveston's museums are in and around the Strand (the old commercial center). These include the **Pier 21 Theater** (© **409/763-8808**), which shows short films: one about the 1900 storm that devastated the town, and another about a one-time Galveston resident, the pirate Jean Laffite. On the same pier are the **Texas Seaport Museum** (© **409/763-1877;** www.tsm-elissa.org) and the *Elissa,* a restored tall ship. Admission to both attractions is $6 adults, $4 children.

Next door, at Pier 19, is a one-of-a-kind museum about offshore drilling rigs. These mammoth constructions often come to the Port of Galveston to be reconditioned. Since they spend most of their time far offshore, you don't see them often, but here in Galveston you have an opportunity to get up close to one, the **Ocean Star** (© **409/766-STAR** [766-7827]; www.oceanstaroec.com), a rig converted into a museum. Through a short film, scale models, actual drilling equipment, and interactive displays, every aspect of the drilling process is explored, including the many rather daunting engineering challenges. Hours for this and the other museums around the Strand are roughly the same: daily from 10am to 4pm (to 5pm in summer). Admission is $6 adults, $5 seniors, $4 students ages 7 to 18.

The **Texas Aviation Hall of Fame and the Lone Star Flight Museum,** 2002 Terminal Dr. (© **888/354-4488;** www.lsfm.org), just down the road from the Moody Gardens (see below), features restored historical aircraft. Admission is $6 adults, $5 students ages 13 to 17, $4 children ages 5 to 12.

Moody Gardens (© **800/582-4673;** www.moodygardens.com) is across from the aviation museum. It is a large complex, set off by its three big glass pyramids, which hold a rainforest habitat, an ocean habitat, and an exhibition on space exploration. It also has a couple of IMAX theaters (one is 3-D and the other is a Ridefilm), a pool, a white-sand beach, and an old paddle-wheel boat that journeys out into the bay. Admission prices for the individual attractions run from $10 to $18 adults, $6 to $10 kids ages 4 to 12; they are a bit overpriced.

WHERE TO STAY

All the economical hotel/motel chains have properties in Galveston, with higher prices for lodgings along the sea wall. Of the big chains, **La Quinta Galveston,** at 1402 Seawall Blvd. (© **800/531-5900**), ranks highly. Galveston also has a dozen B&Bs, most in Victorian-era houses. For a dependable B&B, go to the **Galveston Bed and Breakfast Association** website at **www.galvestonbedandbreakfast.com.**

Harbor House A different hotel for Galveston, the Harbor House is built on a pier overlooking the harbor instead of a beach. It's an excellent location. Rooms are large and well appointed in the modern taste without a lot of clutter. Bleached wood floors, Berber carpets, and exposed wood and steel superstructure are design highlights. There's no restaurant, but there are many restaurants within 2 blocks of the hotel.

No. 28, Pier 21, Galveston, TX 77550. © **800/874-3721** or 409/763-3321. Fax 409/765-6421. www.harbor housePier21.com. 42 units. Weekdays $115–$185 double; weekends $135–$195 double. Rates include continental breakfast. AE, DC, DISC, MC, V. Self-parking $10.

Hotel Galvez (Best) Galveston's historic grand hotel (it opened in 1911 and has hosted such luminaries as Theodore Roosevelt and Frank Sinatra), the Hotel Galvez is located on the sea wall and has been thoroughly renovated. The spacious, well-furnished, and conservatively decorated rooms come with marble bathrooms with bathrobes and lots of amenities. You have a choice of "gulf view" (about $30 extra) or "city view" rooms. Prices fluctuate a lot depending on the season.

2024 Seawall Blvd., Galveston, TX 77550. © **800/WYNDHAM** (996-3426) or 409/765-7721. Fax 409/765-5780. www.wyndham.com. 231 units. $119–$245 double. AE, DC, DISC, MC, V. Valet parking $9; free self-parking. **Amenities:** Restaurant; outdoor pool.

WHERE TO DINE

Seafood is what people come to Galveston for. For the best of Galveston's seafood, try one of the places listed below. If you hanker after steak, the best in town is the **Steakhouse** in the San Luis Resort, 5222 Seawall Blvd. (© **409/744-1500**).

Gaido's (Best) SEAFOOD This is a Galveston tradition, owned and operated by the Gaido family for four generations. The Gaidos have maintained quality by staying personally involved in all the aspects of the restaurant; the seafood is fresh and the service attentive. The soups and side dishes are traditional recipes cooked Southern style and have become comfort food for the longtime customers. The seasonally changing menu includes a few chicken, pork, and beef items, but seafood rules here.

3800 Seawall Blvd. © **409/762-9625.** Reservations not accepted. Main courses $15–$38; complete dinners $19–$29. AE, DISC, MC, V. Daily 11:45am–10:30pm. Closes 1–2 hr. earlier during low season.

Saltwater Grill SEAFOOD The restaurant's seafood is fresh, and the preparation shows a light touch. The menu is printed up daily and generally includes some inventive seafood pasta dishes, perhaps a Gulf red snapper pan-sautéed and topped with lump crabmeat, a fish dish with an Asian bent, gumbo or bouillabaisse, and a few nonseafood options. Situated in an old building on Post Office Street (near the Strand), the dining room offers a pleasant mix of past and present, formal and informal.

2017 Post Office St. © **409/762-FISH** (762-3474). www.galveston.com/saltwatergrill. Reservations recommended. Main courses $14–$35. AE, MC, V. Mon–Fri 11am–2pm and 5–10pm; Sat 5–11pm; Sun 5–9pm. Parking in rear.

GALVESTON AFTER DARK

This city isn't known for its nightlife. Your best bet is the so-called **Post Office Street Arts and Entertainment District,** the area around Post Office Street between 25th and 19th streets. For concerts, musicals, and plays, check out the 200-seat **Strand Theatre,** 2317 Ship's Mechanic Row (© **877/787-2639;** www.strandtheatregalveston.org), in the heart of the historic district, or the **Grand 1894 Opera House,** 2020 Postoffice St. (© **800/821-1894;** www.thegrand.com), for Broadway-style productions, orchestral performances, country music, and more.

Remember the Alamo? Have you heard about the River Walk or the Mission Trail? Or SeaWorld? There's a lot to see and do in San Antonio. Even without the attractions, you would still be left with a city fascinating in its own right. It was settled in the early 1700s by Canary Islanders, sent there by the king of Spain and at the invitation of the local Indians who were feeling the depredations of the Apache. The city lies on the edge of south Texas, with Laredo and the Mexican border a scant 3 hours away, and has always been linked to the Mexican world. But it is also on the edge of Texas Hill Country, which ties it to the frontier culture and to the culture of the German settlers who migrated in the mid–19th century. San Antonio is Texas through and through, all of which makes it an intriguing, multifaceted city that surprises and delights.

ESSENTIALS

GETTING THERE   By Plane   The two-terminal **San Antonio International Airport** (© 210/207-3411; www.sanantonio.gov/aviation) sits about 7 miles north of downtown. Among the many carriers serving the city, **Southwest Airlines** (© 800/435-9792) offers direct flights from a number of cities.

If you're renting a car, it should take about 15 to 20 minutes to drive downtown via U.S. 281 South. VIA Metropolitan Transit's bus no. 2 is the cheapest ($1) way to get downtown but takes 40 to 45 minutes. A taxi should cost about $30 to get downtown.

By Train   Amtrak (© 800/USA-RAIL [872-7245] or 210/233-3226; www.amtrak. com) provides daily service to its station at 250 Hoefgen St. from Austin (trip time: 2 hr.), Fort Worth (7 hr.), Dallas (9 hr.), and Chicago (30 hr.); there is less frequent service from New Orleans (14 hr.) and Los Angeles (29 hr.).

By Car   Major routes into San Antonio are **I-35** from the north (Austin) and south (Laredo), and **I-10** from the east (Houston) and west (El Paso).

VISITOR INFORMATION   Contact the **San Antonio Convention and Visitors Bureau (SACVB),** P.O. Box 2277, San Antonio, TX 78298 (© 800/447-3372; www. sanantoniovisit.com), for an information packet. The **City of San Antonio Visitor Information Center,** 317 Alamo Plaza, across the street from the Alamo, is open daily from 9am to 5pm. There are two unstaffed satellite offices at the airport.

GETTING AROUND   The **VIA Metropolitan Transit Service** (© 210/362-2020; www.viainfo.net) has bus routes that cost $1 for regular lines and $2 for express lines (15¢ for transfers). You'll need exact change. VIA also offers four convenient downtown streetcar routes that cover all the most popular tourist stops.

Taxis are next to impossible to hail on the street; call **Yellow Checker Cab** (© 210/222-2222). The base charge is $2; add $2.15 per mile, plus fuel surcharge.

FAST FACTS   For a doctor referral, contact the **Bexar County Medical Society** at 202 W. French Place (© 210/301-4368). The main downtown hospital is **Baptist Medical Center,** 111 Dallas St. (© 210/297-7000). Sales tax is 8.25%; the city surcharge on hotel rooms is 17%.

SPECIAL EVENTS & FESTIVALS   The third week of April brings **Fiesta San Antonio** (© 210/227-5191; www.fiesta-sa.org), a celebration marking Texas independence with an elaborately costumed royal court presiding over 10 days of revelry: parades, balls, food fests, sports, concerts, and art shows all over town.

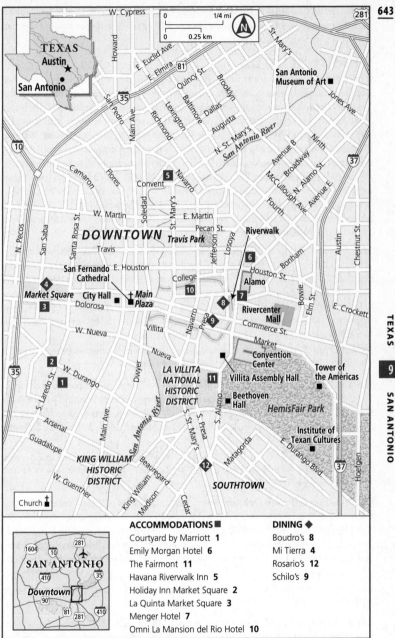

TEXAS
Austin ★
San Antonio

DOWNTOWN

San Antonio
Museum of Art ■

Travis Park

Riverwalk

San Fernando
Cathedral

Market Square City Hall
Main Plaza

Alamo

Rivercenter
Mall

Convention
Center

LA VILLITA
NATIONAL
HISTORIC
DISTRICT

Villita Assembly Hall

Beethoven
Hall

Tower of
the Americas

HemisFair Park

KING WILLIAM
HISTORIC
DISTRICT

Institute of
Texan Cultures

SOUTHTOWN

Church ✝

SAN ANTONIO

Downtown

TEXAS

9

SAN ANTONIO

ACCOMMODATIONS ■

Courtyard by Marriott **1**
Emily Morgan Hotel **6**
The Fairmont **11**
Havana Riverwalk Inn **5**
Holiday Inn Market Square **2**
La Quinta Market Square **3**
Menger Hotel **7**
Omni La Mansion del Rio Hotel **10**

DINING ◆

Boudro's **8**
Mi Tierra **4**
Rosario's **12**
Schilo's **9**

The **Tejano Conjunto Festival,** at Rosedale Park and Guadalupe Theater, is an annual festival in mid-May that celebrates the lively and unique blend of Mexican and German music born in South Texas.

WHAT TO SEE & DO

It goes without saying that the River Walk (see below) is the place to take a stroll in San Antonio, but if you want to see a little more of town, stroll through **La Villita National Historic District,** bounded by Durango, Navarro, and Alamo streets and the River Walk. Boutiques, crafts shops, and restaurants occupy this historic district, which resembles a Spanish-Mexican village. Another good walking area is the **King William Historic District,** on the east bank of the river just south of downtown (within walking distance of the convention center). It has beautifully landscaped lawns and mansions.

The river tours offered by **Rio San Antonio Cruises** (✆ **210/244-5700;** www.riosan antonio.com) go more than 2 miles down the most built-up sections of the Paseo del Rio. You can buy a ticket and catch a boat under the Market Street bridge. The cost is $7.75 general admission, $5 seniors, $2 for children 1 to 5. Boats leave every half-hour from 10am for the 40-minute cruise.

The Alamo Inevitably, the first thing visitors think when they see the Alamo is "Hmmm, I thought it would be bigger." Such a reaction only underscores the heroic and desperate actions of the Alamo's defenders who in 1836 held off their attackers for 13 days against overwhelming odds. More shrine than museum, the Alamo doesn't do the best job of explaining the battle. If you want to understand more, see the IMAX show *Alamo . . . The Price of Freedom,* at the IMAX theater around the corner from the Alamo in the Rivercenter Mall (✆ **210/247-4629;** www.imax-sa.com).

300 Alamo Plaza. ✆ **210/281-0710.** www.thealamo.org. Free admission (donations welcome). Mon–Sat 9am–5:30pm; Sun 10am–5:30pm. Streetcar: Red, Brown, and Blue lines.

Market Square Market Square will transport you south of the border. Stalls in El Mercado sell everything from onyx chess sets and cheap serapes to beautifully made crafts from the interior of Mexico. Every weekend food stalls hawk specialties such as *gorditas* (thick tortillas topped with a variety of goodies) and funnel cakes. Some of the buildings date from the late 1800s.

Btw. Dolorosa and Commerce sts. ✆ **210/207-8600.** Free admission. El Mercado and Farmer's Market Plaza June–Aug daily 10am–8pm; Sept–May daily 10am–6pm. Restaurants and some of the shops open later. Streetcar: Red and Yellow lines.

The River Walk/Paseo Del Rio (Best) The quieter areas of these 4 miles of winding riverbank, shaded by cypresses, oaks, and willows, exude a tropical, exotic aura; the Big Bend section, filled with sidewalk cafes, popular restaurants and bars, high-rise hotels, and even a shopping mall, has a festive, sometimes frenetic feel. Tour boats, water taxis, and floating picnic barges regularly ply the river, and local parades and festivals fill its banks with revelers.

Downtown from the Municipal Auditorium on the north end, to the King William Historic District on the south end. All streetcar lines.

San Antonio Missions National Historical Park The Alamo was originally the first of five missions established by the Franciscans along the San Antonio River. The four missions that now fall under the aegis of the National Park Service are still active parishes, run in cooperation with the Archdiocese of San Antonio. **Concepción,** 807 Mission Rd. at Felisa, is the oldest unrestored Texas mission, and looks much as it did 200 years ago.

For Art Lovers

Art aficionados should check out the **Marion Koogler McNay Art Museum,** 6000 N. New Braunfels Ave. ((*C* **210/824-5368;** www.mcnayart.org), a gem of a museum, which has just completed an expansion to allow it to display more of its collection. It is particularly strong in French post-Impressionist and early-20th-century European painting, and the building and grounds are lovely. Admission is $8. The **San Antonio Museum of Art,** 200 W. Jones Ave. (*C* **210/978-8100;** www.samuseum.org), houses the Rockefeller Center for Latin American Art. It exhibits pre-Columbian, colonial, folk, and contemporary works from all over Latin America. Admission is $8 adults, $7 seniors, $5 students, and $3 children 4 to 11.

San José, 6707 Roosevelt Ave., established in 1720, was the largest, best known, and most beautiful. It has been reconstructed. Moved from an earlier site in east Texas to its present location in 1731, **San Juan Capistrano,** 9102 Graf at Ashley, doesn't have the grandeur of the missions to the north. **San Francisco de la Espada,** 10040 Espada Rd., also has an ancient, isolated feel, although the beautifully kept-up church shows just how vital it still is to the local community.

Headquarters: 2202 Roosevelt Ave. *C* **210/534-8833.** Visitor center: 6707 Roosevelt Ave. *C* **210/932-1001.** www.nps.gov/saan. Free admission; donations accepted. All the missions are open daily 9am–5pm.

SeaWorld San Antonio (Kids) At 250 acres, this is the largest marine theme park in the world. The walk-through habitats where you can watch penguins, sea lions, sharks, tropical fish, and flamingos do their thing are endlessly fascinating, but the aquatic acrobatics at the stadium shows are even more fun. The **Lost Lagoon** has a huge wave pool, and there are water slides aplenty.

10500 SeaWorld Dr. (16 miles northwest of downtown San Antonio at Ellison Dr. and Westover Hills Blvd.). *C* **210/523-3611.** www.seaworld.com. $53 adults, $45 children ages 3–9, free for children 2 and under. Schedule varies with season; generally open weekends and some weekdays in spring and fall, daily during summer (through mid-Aug) 10am–9pm. Parking $10.

Six Flags Fiesta Texas An amusement park with a San Antonio motif, it has all the roller coasters and rides, plus cartoon characters, shops, and more. The attractions are organized into four local themes: Mexican fiesta, German village, country and western, and vintage rock 'n' roll (remember, Buddy Holly was from Texas).

17000 I-10 W. (corner of I-10 W. and Loop 1604; about 15 min. from downtown). *C* **210/697-5050.** www.sixflags.com. Admission $47 adults, $32 children under 48 in., free for children 2 and under. Prices do not include tax. The park is generally open daily late May to late Aug, Fri–Sun Mar–May and Sept–Dec, closed Jan–Feb. It opens at 8 or 10am, depending on the season, and closes at 10pm. Call ahead or check the website, since times often vary. Parking $10.

Witte Museum The Witte focuses on Texas history, natural science, and anthropology, but often ranges as far afield as the Berlin Wall or the history of bridal gowns in the United States. An **EcoLab** is home to live Texas critters ranging from tarantulas to tortoises; the wonderful **HEB Science Treehouse** is a science center with hands-on activities for all ages. Outside are a butterfly and hummingbird garden, as well as three restored historic homes.

3801 Broadway (at the edge of Brackenridge Park). *C* **210/357-1900.** www.wittemuseum.org. $7 adults, $6 seniors, $5 children 4–11, free for children 3 and under. Mon 10am–5pm; Tues 10am–8pm; Wed–Sat 10am–5pm; Sun noon–5pm.

TEXAS

9

SAN ANTONIO

Pro Hoops, Texas Style

San Antonio is home to two pro basketball teams: the NBA's **Spurs** (© 210/444-5000; www.nba.com/spurs), who won the championship in 2005 and 2007, and the WNBA's **Silver Stars** (© 210/410-5050; www.wnba.com/silverstars), who went to the league finals in 2008. Both teams play at AT&T Center.

Golf

As San Antonio has cemented its reputation as a vacation destination, golf has acquired a bigger presence, and more visitors are deciding to shoot a round or two. The easiest way to play a round is to call **Golf Guys** (© 800/470-9634; www.golfguys.net). You can consult with them about local courses and reserve tee times. You don't pay any more for this service than you would if you were to reserve your own tee times.

SHOPPING

Most out-of-town shoppers will find all they need downtown, between the large **Rivercenter Mall** (www.shoprivercenter.com); the boutiques and crafts shops of **La Villita** (www.lavillita.com); **Market Square,** with its colorful Mexican wares; and assorted souvenir retailers and galleries on and around **Alamo Plaza.**

In the Southtown section near King William, the **Blue Star Arts Complex,** 1400 S. Alamo St. (© 210/227-6960; www.bluestarcomplex.com), is the up-and-coming place to buy art. More and more galleries are opening downtown as well. You'll find a slew of **antiques shops** on Hildebrand between Blanco and San Pedro, and McCullough between Hildebrand and Basse.

Many of San Antonio's countless small *botánicas* specialize in articles used in the practice of *curandería,* a Latin American fusion of African and Native American magical practices. **Papa Jim's,** 5630 S. Flores St. (© 210/922-6665; www.papajimsbotanica. com), is the best known of all the *botánicas.*

WHERE TO STAY

For information about bed-and-breakfasts around the city, contact the **San Antonio Bed & Breakfast Association** (www.sanantoniobb.org). It includes several moderately priced lodging options. There are no bargain hotels around the River Walk. Several moderate and affordable chain properties are near Market Square, on the west side of downtown, about 6 blocks from the river and easily accessible to it via the trolley. One is **La Quinta Market Square,** 900 Dolorosa (© 866/725-1661 or 210/271-0001), offering a swimming pool. A little farther south, but equipped with restaurant, pool, exercise room, and room service, are the **Holiday Inn Market Square,** 318 W. Durango (© 800/ HOLIDAY [465-4329] or 210/225-3211), and **Courtyard by Marriott,** 600 S. Santa Rosa (© 800/648-4462 or 210/229-9449).

Emily Morgan Hotel   Right next to the Alamo, this hotel is set in a beautiful 1926 Gothic Revival skyscraper. Rooms are modern, bright, and immaculate. Corner rooms are called plaza suites and come with a separate sitting area, a minifridge, a CD player, a view overlooking the Alamo, and an oversize Jacuzzi. All rooms offer such *luxe* amenities as Aveda toiletries, feather-topped beds, and bathrobes; many standard rooms also have Jacuzzis, and some offer Alamo views.

705 E. Houston St., San Antonio, TX 78205. ✆ **800/824-6674** or 210/225-5100. Fax 210/225-7227. www. emilymorganhotel.com. 177 units. $169–$200 standard; $309 suite. AE, DC, DISC, MC, V. Valet parking $24. **Amenities:** Restaurant; pool; fitness center.

The Fairmount   If you're looking for a small hotel with attentive service, this Victorian-era downtown hotel is your place. Rooms are decorated in a predominantly European style, with rich wood furniture, lots of textured fabrics, antiques, and some great detail work. Many rooms have balconies. The bathrooms are large and come with lots of amenities. The downtown location is excellent.

401 S. Alamo St., San Antonio, TX 78205. ✆ **877/365-0500** or 210/224-8800. Fax 210/475-0082. www. thefairmounthotel-sanantonio.com. 37 units. $159–$229 double; $229–$249 suite. AE, DISC, MC, V. Valet parking $18. **Amenities:** Restaurant; pool; fitness center.

Havana Riverwalk Inn   This small inn, built in 1914 in a Mediterranean Revival style, avoids all the standard hotel room appointments and is the hippest place to stay on the river. Lots of dark-wood trim and window shutters in the guest rooms provide soft lighting and soften the harsh Texas sunlight. Worn wood floors, antique furnishings, and objects usually referred to as "conversation pieces" make staying here fun, and touches such as fresh flowers and free bottled water add to the charm. But all this character and charm come at a price—the standard rooms don't have closets.

1015 Navarro, San Antonio, TX 78205. ✆ **888/224-2008** or 210/222-2008. Fax 210/222-2717. www. havanariverwalkinn.com. 27 units. $159–$209 double; $199–$209 deluxe; $249–$599 suite. AE, DC, DISC, MC, V. Self-parking $10. **Amenities:** Restaurant.

Hyatt Regency Hill Country Resort (Kids)   Okay, perhaps the hotel does look as if it had been designed by Albert Speer in Texas vernacular. Still, there's no place in San Antonio with such lovely grounds: 200 acres of rolling ranchland complete with a stream for tubing. There are lots of facilities for being active (and quite a few for being lazy, too—the spa is first rate). Rooms are cheerfully decorated in a modern country style. *A plus:* SeaWorld's just a hop, skip, and a jump away.

9800 Hyatt Resort Dr., San Antonio, TX 78251. ✆ **210/223-1234** or 647-1234. Fax 210/681-9681. www. hyatt.com. 500 units. $285–$400 double; $450 and up suite. Special family packages available. AE, DC, DISC, MC, V. Valet parking $15; free self-parking. **Amenities:** 4 restaurants; pool; golf course; 3 tennis courts; health club; spa. *In room:* Fridge.

Menger Hotel   Its location, between the Alamo and the Rivercenter Mall, a block from the River Walk, is perfect. Its history—it was built in 1859—is fascinating. A self-guided tour pamphlet will take you to halls, ballrooms, and gardens through which Ulysses S. Grant, Sarah Bernhardt, and Oscar Wilde have walked. Its guest rooms are charming, ranging in decor from ornate 19th-century style to modern but with character. The rooms that are not part of the original building go for significantly less. Some rooms offer kitchenettes and balconies. The **Menger Bar** is one of San Antonio's great historic taverns.

204 Alamo Plaza, San Antonio, TX 78205. ✆ **800/345-9285** or 210/223-4361. Fax 210/228-0022. www.mengerhotel.com. 316 units. $215 double; $345–$439 suite. AE, DC, DISC, MC, V. Valet parking $25. **Amenities:** Restaurant; pool; spa. *In room:* Kitchenettes (some rooms only).

Omni La Mansión del Rio (Best)   This place is pure San Antonio and is the favorite choice of visiting Texans. The building, built in 1852, was once a seminary and has been meticulously renovated over the years. Rooms have more character than at the Hyatt, and many feature Mexican tile floors, beamed ceilings, and wrought-iron balconies. Unlike the city's other big hotels, this one is not a skyscraper (six floors). Rooms with a river view are level with the tall cypress trees, and the hotel's location on a central yet relatively quiet section of the River Walk is perfect. Guests can use the health club and spa at the hotel's sister property, the Watermark Hotel.

112 College St., San Antonio, TX 78205. ☏ **888/444-6664** or 210/518-1000. Fax 210/226-0389. www.lamansion.com. 337 units. $249–$429 double; $1,000 and up suite. AE, DC, DISC, MC, V. Children 17 and under stay free in parent's room. Valet parking $21. Small pets accepted. **Amenities:** Restaurant; pool.

WHERE TO DINE

Boudro's NEW AMERICAN   Locals tend to look down their noses on River Walk restaurants, but Boudro's has won their respect. The kitchen uses fresh local ingredients—Gulf Coast seafood, Texas beef, Hill Country produce—and the preparations and presentations do them justice. The setting is also out of the ordinary: If you've entered from the river, turn around and look inside the turn-of-the-20th-century limestone building to see its hardwood floors and handmade mesquite bar.

421 E. Commerce St./River Walk. ☏ **210/224-8484.** www.boudros.com. Reservations strongly recommended. Main courses $15–$32. AE, DC, DISC, MC, V. Sun–Thurs 11am–11pm; Fri–Sat 11am–midnight.

La Calesa (Value) REGIONAL MEXICAN   Tucked away in a small house off Broadway—look for Earl Abel's sign across the street—this family-run restaurant features several dishes from the southern Yucatán, as well as those from the northern areas that influenced the Tex-Mex style. The difference is mainly in the sauces, and they're done to perfection. The mole, for example, strikes a fine balance between its rich chocolate base and the picante spices. The *conchinita pibil,* a classic pork dish, has a marvelous texture and taste. A separate margarita menu adds even more zest.

2103 E. Hildebrand St. (just off Broadway). ☏ **210/822-4475.** Reservations not accepted. Main courses $8–$16. AE, DC, DISC, MC, V. Mon–Thurs 11am–9:30pm; Fri 11am–10:30pm; Sat 11:30am–10:30pm; Sun 11:30am–8pm.

Liberty Bar AMERICAN/SOUTHERN/MEXICAN   You'd be hard-pressed to guess from the outside that this ramshackle former brothel (opened in 1890) near the Hwy. 281 underpass hosts one of the hippest haunts in San Antonio. But as every foodie in town can tell you, it's bright and inviting inside, and you'll find everything here from comfort food (pot roast, say, or a ham-and-Swiss sandwich) to regional Mexican cuisine (the *chiles rellenos en nogada* are super).

328 E. Josephine St. ☏ **210/227-1187.** www.liberty-bar.com. Reservations accepted. Main courses $8–$19. AE, MC, V. Sun–Thurs 11:30am–10:30pm; Fri–Sat 11:30am–midnight; Sun brunch 10:30am–2pm. Bar open until midnight Sun–Thurs, until 2am Fri–Sat.

Mi Tierra MEXICAN   This Market Square restaurant has been open since 1946. Much expanded and gussied up since then, it still draws a faithful clientele of Latino families and businesspeople along with busloads of tourists. Where else can you come at 2am and order anything from chorizo and eggs to an 8-ounce charbroiled rib-eye—and be serenaded by mariachis? Mi Tierra is justly renowned for its *panadería* (bakery) and its wide variety of margaritas.

218 Produce Row. ☏ **210/225-1262.** www.mitierracafe.com. Reservations accepted for large groups only. Main courses $6.95–$15. AE, MC, V. Open 24 hr.

Rosario's MEXICAN   Modern and colorful, with lots of neon, glass blocks, and a concrete/metal bar that mixes killer margaritas, this restaurant draws a crowd intent on having a good time. Main courses such as the pork *carnitas* in cascabel pepper sauce or the excellent mole enchiladas are favorites. The bargain weekday lunch specials draw a sizable local crowd. Evenings, especially on weekends, the place can be a little noisy.

910 S. Alamo. ✆ **210/223-1806.** Reservations not accepted. Main courses $8–$16. AE, DC, DISC, MC, V. Mon 11am–3pm; Tues–Thurs 11am–10pm; Fri–Sat 11am–11pm.

Schilo's (Kids) GERMAN/DELI   You can't leave town without stopping at this San Antonio institution, if only for a hearty bowl of split-pea soup or a piece of the cherry cheesecake. The large, open room with its wooden booths is evidence of the city's German past. An oompah band plays on Saturday from 5 to 8pm. It's a great place to come for refueling when you're sightseeing near Alamo Plaza; for under $5, a good Reuben sandwich or a bratwurst plate should keep you going for the rest of the day.

424 E. Commerce St. ✆ **210/223-6692.** Reservations not accepted. Sandwiches $4–$7; hot or cold plates $6–$9; main dishes (served after 5pm) $9–$11. AE, DC, DISC, MC, V. Mon–Sat 7am–8:30pm.

Silo NEW AMERICAN   Silo is regularly top-listed by San Antonio foodies, and deservedly so. More than the other chic restaurants in town, it has concentrated on food rather than on attitude, consistently presenting a small but well-balanced menu using fresh ingredients in fresh combinations. Starters such as the spicy Angus beef tenderloin lettuce wrap with chili and mint or a salad of roasted figs, spicy pecans, and goat cheese get the mix of textures and tastes just right, as do entrees such as seared yellowfin tuna au poivre with soba noodle salad or chipotle marinated pork tenderloin on white cheddar andouille grits.

1133 Austin Hwy. ✆ **210/824-8686.** www.siloelevatedcuisine.com. Reservations recommended. Main courses $17–$35. AE, DC, DISC, MC, V. Daily 11am–2:30pm; Sun–Thurs 5:30–10pm; Fri–Sat 5:30–11pm.

SAN ANTONIO AFTER DARK

A Latin flavor lends spice to some of the best local nightlife in San Antonio—this is America's capital for Tejano music, a unique blend of German polka and northern Mexico ranchero sounds, with a dose of pop for good measure. **Southtown,** with its many Hispanic-oriented shops and galleries, celebrates its art scene with the monthly First Friday, a kind of extended block party.

For the most complete listings of what's happening, pick up a free copy of the weekly alternative newspaper, the *Current,* or the Friday "Weekender" section of the *San Antonio Express-News.* You can also call the **San Antonio Arts Hotline** (✆ **210/222-ARTS** [222-2787]).

If you're visiting in the summer, try seeing something at the **Arneson River Theatre,** 418 La Villita, on the River Walk (✆ **210/207-8610**), which stages shows on one side of the river while the audience watches from an amphitheater on the other.

The closest San Antonio comes to having a club district is the stretch of North St. Mary's between Josephine and Magnolia—just north of downtown and south of Brackenridge Park—known as the **Strip.**

Boots, hats, and antique farm equipment hang from the ceiling of the typical Texas roadhouse known as **Floore Country Store,** 14664 Bandera Rd./Hwy. 16, Helotes, 2 miles north of Loop 1604 (✆ **210/695-8827**), where there's always live music on weekends.

The history at the **Menger Bar,** at the Menger Hotel, 204 Alamo Plaza (✆ **210/223-4361**), dates from more than 100 years ago, when Theodore Roosevelt recruited men for his Rough Riders unit at this dark, wooded bar. It moved to its current location in 1956, but 90% of its historic furnishings remain intact. Just below the observation deck level, the **Tower of the Americas Restaurant bar,** 600 HemisFair Park (✆ **210/223-3101**), affords dazzling views of the city at night.

6 AUSTIN

Austin, the state's capital, lies in an area of hills and lakes in the middle of Texas. It has a comfortable mix of cyberpunks and honky-tonkers, environmentalists and hedonists. With its leafy intellectual enclave and large university community, Austin is often compared to Berkeley or Seattle, but its Texas flavor belies such comparisons. The city has now passed the half-million population mark and is feeling its growing pains, but society here retains a leisurely, small-town quality.

ESSENTIALS

GETTING THERE   By Plane   Austin-Bergstrom International Airport (© **512/ 530-ABIA** [530-2242]; www.ci.austin.tx.us/austinairport) is just off Hwy. 71, some 8 miles southwest of the center of town. Many hotels offer complimentary shuttle service from the airport. The taxi ride between the airport and downtown generally costs $25. **SuperShuttle** (© **800/258-3826;** www.supershuttle.com) charges $10 to $14. A city bus called the Airport Flyer (Rte. 100) runs every day and costs 50¢.

By Train   Amtrak (© **800/USA-RAIL** [872-7245]; www.amtrak.com) provides daily service from Fort Worth (trip time: 4 hr.), Dallas (6 hr.), and San Antonio (2 hr.) to its station at 250 N. Lamar Blvd.

By Car   Major routes into Austin are **I-35** from the southwest (San Antonio) and northeast (Dallas–Fort Worth), and **Hwy. 71** (Ben White Blvd.) from the southeast (Houston).

VISITOR INFORMATION   Contact the **Austin Convention and Visitors Bureau,** 201 E. Second St., Austin, TX 78701 (© **866/GO-AUSTIN** [462-8784] or 512/478-0098; www.austintexas.org), located down the street from the convention center downtown; or stop by Monday through Friday from 9am to 5pm, Saturday and Sunday from 9am to 6pm. Or try the **Austin-Bergstrom International Airport Visitors Center** (© **512/530-6810**), on the baggage claim level.

GETTING AROUND   There are two north-south freeways: I-35 on the east and Mo-Pac on the west. The east-west freeways are Ben White Boulevard (Hwy. 71) in the south and Hwy. 183 in the north. The central city is bicycle friendly—many streets have separate bicycle lanes.

Capital Metro (© **512/474-1200;** www.capmetro.org) provides bus service throughout the Austin area. A day pass is $1. Free 'Dillo trolley buses circulate through downtown, the Capitol Complex, and the University of Texas campus; the orange 'Dillo is a good choice for seeing the sights of central Austin.

Among the major cab companies are **Austin Cab** (© **512/478-2222**) and **Roy's Taxi** (© **512/482-0000**). The flag drops at $2.05 and it's $2.10 per additional mile. A fuel surcharge of 10¢ per mile is tacked on when gas is over $3.50.

FAST FACTS   Brackenridge Hospital, 601 E. 15th St. (© **512/324-7000**), has emergency-care facilities. **Walgreens** at Capitol Plaza, I-35 and Cameron Road (© **512/ 452-9452**), is open 24 hours. The tax on hotel rooms is 15%. Sales tax, added to restaurant bills as well as to other purchases, is 8.25%.

SPECIAL EVENTS & FESTIVALS   Around the third week of March, the Austin Music Awards kick off the acclaimed **South by Southwest (SXSW) Music & Media Conference**

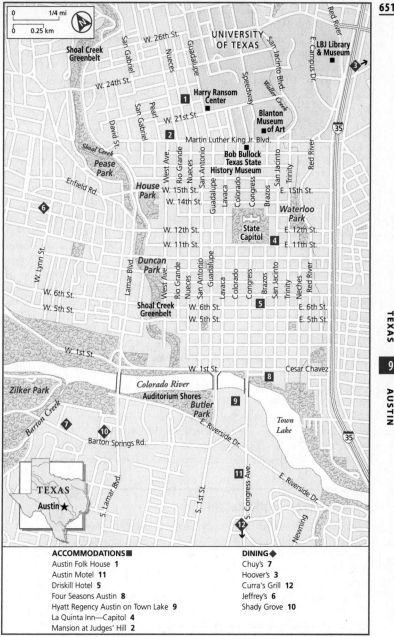

ACCOMMODATIONS ■

Austin Folk House **1**
Austin Motel **11**
Driskill Hotel **5**
Four Seasons Austin **8**
Hyatt Regency Austin on Town Lake **9**
La Quinta Inn—Capitol **4**
Mansion at Judges' Hill **2**

DINING ◆

Chuy's **7**
Hoover's **3**
Curra's Grill **12**
Jeffrey's **6**
Shady Grove **10**

(© 512/467-7979; www.sxsw.com). The event schedules dozens of concerts at a variety of venues—all in a 5-day period.

Around June 19, Austin celebrates the **Juneteenth Freedom Festival,** a celebration of African-American emancipation featuring parades, a jazz and blues festival, gospel singing, a rap competition, and a children's rodeo and carnival.

Mariachis and folk dancers, Tex-Mex *conjunto* and Tejano music, as well as fajitas, piñatas, and clowns help celebrate **Mexican Independence Day** at the Fiesta Gardens on the 4 days around September 16.

WHAT TO SEE & DO

A lot of Austin life revolves around the campus of the **University of Texas,** roughly bounded by Guadalupe; I-35; Martin Luther King, Jr., Boulevard; and 26th Street (© 512/471-3434; www.utexas.edu). With 50,000 students, it is the largest university in the country. The special collections of the **Harry Ransom Center (HRC),** on 21st and Guadalupe streets (© 512/471-8944), contain approximately a million rare books, 36 million manuscripts, 5 million photographs, and more than 100,000 works of art, including a Gutenberg Bible, paintings by Diego Rivera and Frida Kahlo, and the original manuscript of *Death of a Salesman.* Another museum worth visiting is the **Blanton Museum of Art,** at the corner of Martin Luther King, Jr., Boulevard and Congress Avenue (© 512/471-7324; www.blantonmuseum.org), right across the street from the Bob Bullock Texas State History Museum (see below). It is one of the best university art museums in the United States, with an especially good Latin American collection. Another thing to do on campus is to take in the sights from atop the University of Texas Tower. The only way to do so is by guided tour, which costs $3. Hours for the tour are irregular; call © 877/475-6633 to book the tour in advance.

PBS's longest-running show, *Austin City Limits,* has showcased major country-and-western talent. It's taped live August through February at KLRU-TV (© 512/475-9077; www.pbs.org/klru/austin). Free tickets are distributed on a first-come, first-served basis, on the day of the taping.

Barton Springs Pool   The Native Americans who settled near here believed these waters had spiritual powers, and today's residents still place their faith in them. Each day approximately 32 million gallons of water from the underground Edwards Aquifer flow to the surface. Although the original limestone bottom remains, concrete was added to

Hanging Out at the Bat Bridge

In the evening hours between March and November, you're likely to see crowds of people standing on or under the Congress Avenue Bridge waiting for one of the city's star attractions to begin. At some point in the 1980s, a Mexican freetail bat discovered that the underside of the bridge made a good resting place during daylight hours. He invited a million of his closest friends and—*voilà!*—an instant tourist attraction, as well as an easy way of keeping the local mosquito population under control. The bats time their flights according to weather and feeding conditions. Call the **Bat Hotline** (© 512/416-5700, ext. 3636) for their projected departure time.

the banks to form uniform sides to what is now a swimming pool of about 1,000 feet by
125 feet. A large bathhouse offers changing facilities.

Zilker Park, 2201 Barton Springs Rd. (C) **512/476-9044.** www.ci.austin.tx.us/parks/bartonsprings.htm. Admission $3 adults, $2 teens 12–17, $1 children and seniors. Free to all Nov to mid-Mar. Daily 5am–10pm except during pool maintenance (mid-Mar to Oct Mon and Thurs from 7:30pm; Nov to mid-Mar Mon 10am–5pm). Lifeguard on duty Sept–May 9am–dusk; June–Aug 9am–10pm.

The Bob Bullock Texas State History Museum (Kids)   To enjoy this museum, you must make allowances for Texas chauvinism. The building looks grandiose for a history museum—with lots of polished granite, a mammoth lone star of bronze in front, and a dramatic domed entrance chamber. Yet another act of self-aggrandizement of the state? No. Actually, the collection (all three floors of it) is thoughtfully put together and focuses on social history rather than the spinning of myths and the worship of heroes. Also in the museum are a 3-D IMAX theater and a special effects theater called the Texas Spirit Theater.

1800 N. Congress Ave. (C) **512/936-4649.** www.thestoryoftexas.com. Admission to exhibits: $7 adults, $6 seniors, $4 youths 5–18. IMAX: $7 adults, $6 seniors, $5 youths 18 and under. Texas Spirit Theater: $5 adults, $4 seniors, $4 youths 18 and under. Combination ticket to all 3 attractions $15 adults, $12 seniors, $10 youths 18 and under. Mon–Sat 9am–6pm; Sun noon–6pm. Check website for IMAX showtimes.

Lady Bird Johnson Wildflower Center   Founded by Lady Bird Johnson in 1982, the center is dedicated to the study and preservation of native plants. The main attractions are, naturally, the display gardens—including one designed to attract butterflies—and the wildflower-filled meadow, but the native stone architecture of the visitor center and observation tower is attention grabbing, too.

4801 La Crosse Ave. (C) **512/292-4100.** www.wildflower.org. Admission $7 adults, $6 seniors 60 and older and students, $3 children 5–12. Tues–Sat 9am–5:30pm; Sun noon–5:30pm. Take Loop 1 (Mo-Pac) south to Slaughter Lane; drive ¾ mile to La Crosse Ave.

LBJ Library and Museum (Value)   Set on a hilltop commanding an impressive campus view, the LBJ Library contains some 45 million documents relating to the 36th president, along with gifts, memorabilia, and other historical objects. Johnson's large cartoon collection (even with him as the target) is one of the museum's most interesting rotating exhibits. Adults and kids alike are riveted by an animatronic version of LBJ, which looks eerily alive from afar.

University of Texas, 2313 Red River. (C) **512/721-0200.** www.lbjlib.utexas.edu. Free admission. Daily 9am–5pm.

State Capitol (Best)   Constructed of pink granite in the usual Renaissance Revival style, this is the largest state capitol building in the country. It has an impressive dome that, though smaller than the U.S. Capitol's dome, is still a few feet taller. A striking underground annex, which connects the capitol and four other state buildings by tunnels, was added in the mid-1990s. Take the tour, which is engaging for some of the oddities and tidbits you learn.

11th and Congress sts. (C) **512/463-0063.** www.capitol.state.tx.us. Free admission. Mon–Fri 7am–10pm; Sat–Sun 9am–8pm. Free 45-min. guided tours every 15 min. on weekdays, every 30 min. on weekends.

SHOPPING

Specialty shops and art galleries are filtering back to the renovated 19th-century buildings along **Sixth Street** and **Congress Avenue.** Little enclaves offering more intimate retail experiences can be found in the **West End** on Sixth Street west of Lamar and, nearby, north of 12th Street and West Lynn. Below Town Lake, **South Congress Avenue,** from Riverside south to Annie Street, has long been a fun place to seek vintage clothing and antiques. Bargain hunters head for two factory-outlet malls in **San Marcos** (26 miles south of Austin, exit 200 on I-35) and **New Braunfels** (16 miles south of San Marcos).

WHERE TO STAY

Favorite affordable chain hotel deals in town include **La Quinta Inn—Capitol,** 300 E. 11th St. (© **800/NU-ROOMS** [687-6667] or 512/476-1166), practically on the grounds of the state capitol.

Austin Folk House (Value   In the West Campus part of town, this B&B offers attractive, comfortable, slightly offbeat rooms for a good price. As you might imagine, there are folk art pieces scattered throughout the house. This adds a light, playful feel to the place. Room size varies, but none of them are cramped; all have plush mattresses, bathrobes, and VCRs. The owner-manager is helpful and obliging. She and her husband also run a B&B, the **Star of Texas Inn** (http://staroftexasinn.com), which is along more normal lines and is located a block from this one.

506 W. 22nd St., Austin, TX 78705. © **866/472-6700** or 512/472-6700. www.austinfolkhouse.com. 9 units. $110–$195 double. Rates include full breakfast. AE, DISC, MC, V. Free parking. Smoking is not permitted.

Austin Motel (Value   A convenient (but not quiet) location in the hip area just south of downtown, along with reasonable rates, are two good reasons to stay at this motel, which has been run by the same family for more than 5 decades. Others are a classic kidney-shaped pool, a coin-op laundromat, free coffee in the lobby (doughnuts, too, on Sun), and **El Sol y La Luna,** a good Mexican restaurant that's popular on weekend mornings. Ask to see the rooms—all are different and some are in better shape than others; some suites have Jacuzzis.

1220 S. Congress Ave., Austin, TX 78704. ©/fax **512/441-1157.** www.austinmotel.com. 41 units. $80–$130 double; $135–$150 suite. AE, DC, DISC, MC, V. Free parking. Pets accepted for a $15 fee. **Amenities:** Restaurant; pool. *In room:* Fridge (suites), microwave (some suites).

Driskill Hotel   Austin's original grand hotel, the Driskill is a national historic landmark (Lady Bird and Lyndon Johnson had their first date in the hotel dining room) that has been renovated with a loving touch and is easily the most eye-catching hotel in town. It offers guests a choice between rooms in the original 1886 building (labeled "historic") and in the 1928 addition ("traditional"); the latter are the better deal, especially those on the 12th floor, which have higher ceilings. Rooms are well lit, distinctively decorated, and furnished with period pieces. Bathrooms in both buildings are attractive and come with several amenities, including plush bathrobes. This hotel is on Austin's lively Sixth Street, and some of the rooms with balconies can be noisy.

604 Brazos St., Austin, TX 78701. © **800/252-9367** or 512/474-5911. Fax 512/474-2214. www.driskillhotel. com. 188 units. $300–$320 double; $320–$340 deluxe; $480 and up suite. AE, DC, DISC, MC, V. Valet parking $20. Pets accepted for $50 fee. **Amenities:** 2 restaurants; health club.

Four Seasons Austin (Best   Polished sandstone floors, a cowhide sofa, horn lamps, and an elk head hanging over the fireplace in the lobby remind you you're in Texas, but airy, well-equipped rooms look European country elegant, with amenities such as CD players, terry bathrobes, and DVD players on request. Some rooms offer balconies. You can gaze out at the lake over cocktails in the **Lobby Lounge,** which serves hors d'oeuvres from midday until the wee hours. Some of the best bat-watching in the city draws diners to vie for seating at dusk. Work off your meals at one of the best health clubs in town.

98 San Jacinto Blvd., Austin, TX 78701. ✆ **800/332-3442** or 512/478-4500. Fax 512/478-3117. www.fourseasons.com/austin. 291 units. $360–$455 double; $578 and up suite. AE, DC, DISC, MC, V. Valet parking $25. Small pets accepted. **Amenities:** Restaurant; pool; health club; spa.

Hyatt Regency Austin on Town Lake (Kids) You'll enjoy lake views with city backdrops at this choice on Town Lake's south shore, but it's the outdoor recreation that makes the hotel tick. Bat tours and other Town Lake excursions depart from the hotel's dock, which also rents canoes; guests can rent mountain bikes for the hike-and-bike trail, right outside the door. Guest rooms are large and modern, with medium-size bathrooms; the most sought-after rooms are on the upper floors facing the lake.

208 Barton Springs Rd., Austin, TX 78704. ✆ **800/233-1234** or 512/477-1234. Fax 512/480-2069. www.hyatt.com. 447 units. $185–$230 double; $345 and up suite. AE, DC, DISC, MC, V. Valet parking $17; self-parking $11. Pets accepted for a $25 fee. **Amenities:** Restaurant; pool; health club.

Mansion at Judges' Hill All the rooms in this boutique hotel are furnished and decorated with much more character than you'll find at any of the local chain hotels. This is as true of the modern rooms in the north building as it is for the ones in the mansion. The rooms that are the most fun are the second-story signature rooms, which all open onto a sweeping upstairs porch and have tall ceilings and large bathrooms with special amenities (including L'Occitane toiletries and bathrobes). Beds have particularly good mattresses and linens. The West Campus location is convenient to the university and to downtown.

1900 Rio Grande., Austin, TX 78705. ✆ **800/311-1619** or 512/495-1800. Fax 512/495-1869. www.judgeshill.com. 48 units. $139–$199 standard in north wing; $169 3rd-floor standard in mansion; $299 signature rooms in mansion. Children 11 and under stay free in parent's room. AE, DC, DISC, MC, V. Free covered parking. Pets allowed with $50 fee. Smoking is not permitted. **Amenities:** Restaurant.

WHERE TO DINE

Chuy's MEXICAN This Tex-Mex joint is a bit loud and boisterous but serves good food that keeps the locals coming back. The eclectic decor is funky, with a lot of references to Elvis. Try the special enchiladas or any of the combo plates, and you'll see why it's so popular.

1728 Barton Springs Rd. ✆ **512/474-4452.** www.chuys.com. Reservations not accepted. Main courses $7–$12. AE, DC, MC, V. Sun–Thurs 11am–10:30pm; Fri–Sat 11am–11pm.

Curra's Grill (Value) INTERIOR MEXICAN This crowded restaurant serves up the best regional Mexican food in south Austin. A couple of breakfast tacos and a cup of Mexican dark roast coffee are a great way to jump-start your day. The chilies rellenos topped with cream pecan sauce make a super entree; for something lighter, try one of the fish dishes. The tamales are excellent here, and the margaritas are tops.

614 E. Oltorf. ✆ **512/444-0012.** www.lascurras.com. Reservations not accepted. Main courses $7–$15. AE, DC, DISC, MC, V. Sun–Thurs 7am–10pm; Fri–Sat 7am–11pm.

Fonda San Miguel MEXICAN This restaurant's beautifully lit dining room, with its carved wooden doors, bold paintings, and soft light, is a gorgeous backdrop to the food. The kitchen turns out several styles of regional Mexican cooking. For appetizers you might try the Veracruz-style seviche. For an entree, the *conchinita pibil,* a Yucatán dish of

9

AUSTIN

pork baked in banana leaves, is very good. The restaurant is famous for its mammoth Sunday brunches.

2330 W. North Loop. ✆ **512/459-4121.** www.fondasanmiguel.com. Reservations recommended. Main courses $18–$40. AE, DC, DISC, MC, V. Mon–Thurs 5–9:30pm; Fri–Sat 5–10:30pm. Sun brunch 11am–2pm.

Hoover's COMFORT FOOD   This popular restaurant in East Austin dishes up Texas classics like chicken-fried steak in cream gravy and cornmeal-battered fried catfish. It's owned by a local man, Alexander Hoover, who has always had the knack for cooking. The sandwiches, such as the New Orleans muffuletta are all filling. Plates come with one or two sides, including a tasty creamed spinach. Cream pies are the favorites for dessert. The salads, especially the spinach salad, are great. On weekends this place serves a righteous breakfast.

2002 Manor Rd. ✆ **512/479-5006.** www.hooverscooking.com. Reservations not accepted. Main courses $7–$12; lunch $7–$10. DISC, MC, V. Mon–Fri 11am–10pm; Sat 8am–10pm.

Jeffrey's (Best) NEW AMERICAN   In a setting of soft tones and soft lighting, executive chef David Garrido creates dishes known for their creative combinations of flavors and textures. Among the appetizers are his signature crisp oysters and crunchy yucca chips topped with habanero honey aioli—a must. The main courses are along the same vein, combining disparate ingredients in the search for original tastes.

1204 W. Lynn. ✆ **512/477-5584.** www.jeffreysofaustin.com. Reservations recommended. Main courses $26–$40. AE, DC, DISC, MC, V. Mon–Thurs 6–10pm; Fri–Sat 5:30–10:30pm; Sun 5–9:30pm.

The Salt Lick BARBECUE   Driftwood is just a wide spot on the road outside of Austin, but it attracts barbecue aficionados from far and wide. Moist spareribs, brisket, sausage, and chicken, as well as terrific homemade pickles, make for a glorious meal. Bring a cooler and your own drinks. In warm weather, seating is outside at picnic tables under live oak trees; in winter, fireplaces blaze in a series of large, rustic rooms. The Salt Lick prides itself on its sauce, which has a sweet-and-sour tang.

18300 FM 1826, Driftwood. ✆ **512/858-4959,** or 888/SALT-LICK (725-8542) (mail order). Reservations not accepted. Main courses $15 for the all-you-can-eat "family style"; $10 for barbecue plates. No credit cards. Daily 11am–10pm.

Shady Grove (Kids) TEX-AMERICAN   When you crave something spicy, Shady Grove's Airstream chili might be just the thing. Try a Frito pie (chili in a corn-chip bowl), a burger, or the tortilla-fried queso catfish. Large salads—among them noodles with Asian vegetables—or the hippie sandwich (grilled eggplant, veggies, and cheese) will satisfy less hearty appetites. The inside dining area, with its Texas kitsch roadhouse decor and cushy booths, is plenty comfortable, but most people head for the large, tree-shaded patio when the weather permits.

1624 Barton Springs Rd. ✆ **512/474-9991.** www.theshadygrove.com. Reservations not accepted. Main courses $7–$12. AE, DC, DISC, MC, V. Sun–Thurs 11am–10:30pm; Fri–Sat 11am–11pm.

AUSTIN AFTER DARK

Austin enjoys lots of live venues with low cover charges. The best sources for what's happening are the *Austin Chronicle* and *XLent,* the entertainment supplement of the *Austin-American Statesman;* both are free and available in hundreds of outlets every Thursday. If all you want to do is explore the nightlife, you should try two places: **Sixth Street,** which attracts patrons of all ages to bars and clubs with all kinds of music; and, across Congress a couple of blocks south, the **Warehouse District,** where you'll find numbers of young professionals and an eclectic collection of bars.

The **Ticketmaster** number for the University of Texas, the locus for most of the city's performing-arts events, is ☎ 512/477-6060. The **Box Office** (☎ **512/454-8497;** www. austix.com) handles phone charges for many of the smaller theaters in Austin, as well as half-price ticket sales (☎ **512/454-4253**).

The **Continental Club,** 1315 S. Congress Ave. (☎ **512/441-2444;** www.continental club.com), is a not-to-be-missed Austin classic. Although Willie Nelson and crossover C&W bands such as the Austin Lounge Lizards have been known to turn up at **Antone's,** 213 W. Fifth St. (☎ **512/474-5314;** www.antones.net), the club owner's name has always been synonymous with the blues. The **Broken Spoke,** 3201 S. Lamar Blvd. (☎ **512/442-6189;** www.brokenspokeaustintx.com), is the genuine item, a Western honky-tonk with a wood-plank floor and a cowboy-hatted, two-steppin' crowd.

A terrific sound system and a casual country atmosphere make the **Backyard,** on Hwy. 71 West at R.R. 620, Bee Cave (☎ **512/263-4146,** or 469-SHOW [469-7469] for tickets; www.thebackyard.net), a hot venue, attracting acts that range from John Fogerty to Heart to Norah Jones. Come early and enjoy some barbecue. Another Austin classic, **La Zona Rosa,** 612 W. Fourth St. (☎ **512/263-4146;** www.lazonarosa.com), mixes a Tex-Mex menu with high-quality music, from Latino and alternative country to punk rock.

Since 1866, when councilman August Scholz first opened his tavern near the state capitol, every Texas governor has visited Texas's oldest operating *biergarten,* **Scholz Garten,** 1607 San Jacinto Blvd. (☎ **512/474-1958**). Chow down on some barbecue while a state-of-the-art sound system cranks out the polka tunes; patio tables as well as a few strategically placed TV sets help Longhorn fans cheer on their team.

7 THE HILL COUNTRY

The highway that runs between San Antonio and Austin parallels a geological feature called the Balcones Escarpment, a fault zone that divides the coastal plains from the Hill Country, which was produced when the Edwards Plateau was pushed up about 1,500 feet above the plains. This plateau is a thick shelf of limestone that extends for hundreds of miles north and west of San Antonio and Austin, but the part closest to these cities is called the Hill Country. The extra elevation makes the climate a little milder, and the water pouring through the limestone creates an abundance of natural springs (and lots of caverns and caves, too).

These features attracted many German and Czech settlers in the mid–19th century, who were fleeing the social upheavals in Europe. They established small towns that now dot the area and add a little contrast to the prevailing cowboy culture. The mild climate, rolling hills, and abundant springs continue to attract visitors, with summer camps, guest ranches, and resorts serving a public that comes to enjoy the outdoors.

NEW BRAUNFELS & GRUENE

New Braunfels, a town of 40,000, and the attached village of Gruene (pronounced *Green*) are off I-35 between Austin and San Antonio. They mostly attract visitors seeking fun in the water. Many head for the popular **Schlitterbahn** waterpark, 305 W. Austin St. (☎ **830/625-2351;** www.schlitterbahn.com). It is Texas's largest waterpark, and the *Travel Channel* recently rated it tops in the country.

A much mellower option is what the locals call "tubing," floating down the Guadalupe River in an inner tube. This is a popular and enjoyable activity. There are a number of companies that will rent you a tube, haul you to a drop-off point, and then pick you up downstream. The quality of the experience depends on the amount of water that is being released from the dam upstream. Two organizers of this activity are **Rockin "R" River Rides** (© 800/553-5628) and **Gruene River Raft Company** (© 830/625-2800), both on Gruene Road just south of the bridge. An even simpler option, if you're just passing through, is to go for a swim at the city's **Landa Park** (© 830/608-2160), which has the second-largest spring-fed pool in Texas.

Other activities include shopping for antiques in the New Braunfels historic downtown or taking in some country music at the landmark **Gruene Hall** (© 830/606-1281; www.gruenehall.com), the state's oldest dance hall.

CASTROVILLE

West of San Antonio, on U.S. 90, is the quaint town of **Castroville** (www.castroville. com), originally settled by the Alsatians. It has conserved much of its early small-town feel. If you want to find everything open, come on Thursday, Friday, or Saturday. Almost 100 of the original settlers' uneven slope-roofed houses remain in Castroville. The oldest standing structure, the **First St. Louis Catholic Church,** went up in 1846 on the corner of Angelo and Moy. A gristmill and wood-and-stone dam are among the interesting artifacts at the **Landmark Inn State Historical Park,** 402 Florence St. (© 830/931-2133).

Get a delicious taste of the past at **Haby's Alsatian Bakery,** 207 U.S. 90 East (© 830/931-2118), which offers apple fritters, strudels, breads, and coffeecakes. Among the specialties of the **Alsatian Restaurant,** 403 Angelo St. (© 830/931-3260), set in a 19th-century house, is the boneless Strasbourg chicken seasoned with curry.

BANDERA

North of Castroville, on Hwy. 16, you'll find the town of Bandera. Here you can get some of the feel of the Old West. Pick up a self-guided tour brochure and information about roping and rodeos at the **Bandera County Convention and Visitors Bureau,** 1808 Hwy. 16 South (© 800/364-3833 or 830/796-3045; www.banderacowboycapital. com). Most people take advantage of the town's living traditions by strolling along Main Street, where craftspeople work in the careful, hand-hewn styles of yesteryear.

You and your horse can canter through the **Hill Country State Natural Area,** 10 miles southwest of Bandera (© 830/796-4413), the largest state park in Texas allowing horseback riding. The nearest outfitter is the helpful and reliable **Running-R Ranch,** Route 1 (© 830/796-3984; www.rrranch.com).

Tubing on the Medina River and swimming in an Olympic-size pool are among the things you can do at the moderately priced **Mayan Ranch** (© 830/796-3312 or 460-3036; www.mayanranch.com). Rates at both ranches (about $800 per adult per week) include three home-cooked meals, two trail rides, and other activities.

Main Street's **O.S.T.** (© 830/796-3836) serves down-home Texas and Tex-Mex fare. For a more upscale setting but similarly down-home cooking, head to **Billy Gene's,** 1105 Main St. (© 830/460-3200). **Arkey Blue & The Silver Dollar Bar** (© 830/796-8826) is a genuine spit-and-sawdust cowboy honky-tonk on Main Street.

LYNDON B. JOHNSON COUNTRY

Welcome to Johnson territory, where the forebears of the 36th president settled almost 150 years ago. Try to make a day out of a visit to LBJ's boyhood home and the sprawling ranch that became known as the Texas White House.

Take U.S. 290 west of Austin. Before arriving at Johnson City, you'll see a sign for **Pedernales State Park** on Ranch Road 3232. This is a beautiful state park, with lots of

park continues on to Johnson City by a scenic back route. **Johnson City** is a pleasant agricultural town named for founder James Polk Johnson, LBJ's first cousin once removed. The **Boyhood Home**—the house on Elm Street where Lyndon was raised after age 5—is the centerpiece of this unit of the National Historic Park. To get to the visitor center, take F Street to Lady Bird Lane and you'll see the signs.

The **Lyndon B. Johnson State and National Historical Parks at LBJ Ranch** (© 830/868-7128 or 644-2252; www.tpwd.state.tx.us) is 14 miles west of Johnson City. Tour buses depart regularly from the visitor center to the still-operating Johnson Ranch. A reconstructed version of the former president's modest birthplace lies close to his final resting place, shared with five generations of Johnsons. On the side of the river sits the **Sauer-Beckmann Living History Farm,** which gives visitors a look at typical Texas-German farm life at the turn of the 20th century. Farm animals roam freely or in large pens, while family members go about their chores. Nearby are nature trails, a swimming pool (open only in summer), and lots of picnic spots. Admission is $3 per person for bus tours; all other areas are free.

FREDERICKSBURG

Farther west on U.S. 290 lie the towns of Stonewall and Fredericksburg. This area produces delicious peaches and, during the season from May to July, you'll see lots of roadside stands selling fresh peaches. Fredericksburg offers good shopping, lots of historic sites, and some of the most unusual accommodations around, all in a pretty rural setting. Many homes were built in the Hill Country version of the German *fachwerk* design, made out of limestone with diagonal wood supports. Fredericksburg became and remains the seat of Gillespie County. The **Visitor Information Center** is on 302 E. Austin, Fredericksburg, TX 78624 (© 888/997-3600 or 830/997-6523).

More than 100 specialty shops, many of them in mid-19th-century houses, feature work by Hill Country artisans. A one-of-a-kind chocolate shop is at 330 W. Main St.—**Chocolat** (© 830/990-9382; www.chocolat-tx.us) makes liqueur-filled chocolates using an old-world technique practiced nowhere else in the U.S. and in few places in Europe. The family-run **Fredericksburg Winery,** 247 W. Main St. (© 830/990-8747; www.fbgwinery.com), sells its own hand-bottled, hand-corked, and hand-labeled wines. Becoming increasingly well known via its mail-order business is the **Fredericksburg Herb Farm,** 402 Whitney St. (© 800/259-HERB [259-4372] or 830/997-8615; www.fredericksburgherbfarm.com). It's on the south side, where you can visit the flower beds that produce salad dressings, teas, fragrances, and air fresheners.

If you get hungry while you're in Fredericksburg, try **Rather Sweet Bakery and Café,** at 249 W. Main St. (© 830/990-0498; www.rathersweet.com). It is open for breakfast and lunch and serves delicious sandwiches, salads, and a famous chicken potpie, not to mention all the baked goods. Owner Rebecca Rather is an accomplished cookbook author, well known in these parts and beyond. The **Hilltop Café** (© 830/997-8922; www.hilltopcafe.com) is 10 miles northwest of town on the road to Mason. Being a restored old gas station right on the highway, it's easy to find. One of the owners was a member of the Austin band Asleep at the Wheel. He provides entertainment on weekend nights. The cooking is great without being pretentious.

Lots of well-known performers turn up in the dance hall of **Luckenbach** (11 miles southeast on R.R. 1376), immortalized in song by Waylon Jennings and Willie Nelson. It's a great place to hang out on a weekend afternoon, when someone's almost always strumming the guitar.

Fredericksburg is known for its *gastehauses* (guest cottages). Many historic homes have been converted into romantic havens replete with robes, fireplaces, and even spas. To get a booklet detailing some of the most interesting *gastehauses,* contact **Gastehaus Schmidt,** 231 W. Main St. (© **830/997-5612;** www.ktc.com/GSchmidt). For something more up-to-date, try the stylish **Roadrunner Inn** (© **830/997-1844;** www.theroadrunnerinn. com), at 306B E. Main St. Rooms are large, with large bathrooms, and are done up with a mix of [']50s and industrial furniture.

8 THE TRANS-PECOS

As you drive west from Bandera or Fredericksburg, you start leaving the Hill Country behind. By small degrees, the roads become few, vegetation thins out, the vistas become wide and distant, and the rounded hills are replaced by flat-topped buttes and mesas. You are now entering the "West," which in the U.S. is simultaneously a place and an idea. And being both, it charges what we view with mythic significance. Or, to put it another way, we cannot help but see the land with both our eyes and our imaginations.

Whether coming from Austin or San Antonio, by the time you get to the town of **Junction,** you'll be traveling on I-10. When you get to Sonora, make a point of seeing the famous **Sonora Caverns** (www.cavernsofsonora.com), which are close by the highway (billboards point the way). These caverns are famous among speleologists for their wealth of crystalline formations, a few of which defy explanation. The chambers do not impress with their size, in the manner of **Carlsbad Caverns** (p. 802), but with their beauty. There is so much living rock that some rooms look like jewel boxes.

Farther west, after you pass the town of Ozona, you'll see lots of spinning propellers of giant windmills as they convert the West Texas wind into electricity for Austin and other cities to the east. Once you reach the town of Fort Stockton, you will have entered the Trans-Pecos, home to Texas's tallest mountain ranges and best views.

DAVIS MOUNTAINS

Viewed as they usually are, against the clear blue sky of the desert, these mountains, with their stark lines and sculpted palisades, offer some of the most dramatic landscapes in Texas. Things to do in this part of the world include stargazing at the University of Texas's **McDonald Observatory** (© **432/426-3640;** www.mcdonaldobservatory.org). The observatory sits on Mount Locke at an elevation of 6,791 feet. The visitor center arranges solar viewing sessions twice a day and star parties 3 nights a week. Also in the area is **Balmorhea** (bal-mo-*ray*) **State Park** (© **432/375-2370**), which is a veritable oasis in the West Texas desert and home to the largest spring-fed pool in the state. Swimming in the crystal-clear water is like swimming in an aquarium full of fish.

If you want to do some hiking, the **Davis Mountains State Park** (© **432/426-3337**) has several trails. The longest goes from the park to the historic Fort Davis and is 7.5 miles round-trip. Should you want a little mystery in your vacation, try viewing the **"Marfa mystery lights,"** which can be seen most nights from the official Texas Department of Transportation viewing area, on U.S. 90, 9 miles out of Marfa in the direction of Alpine. These lights appear along the horizon. They move around and can be of different hues, but are mostly white. They have been observed since the 19th century but have yet to be explained.

Marfa has another claim to fame. It attracted minimalist artist Donald Judd as a permanent resident for the last 2 decades of his life. He was looking for someplace beautiful and desolate, and he found it here. He also established the **Chinati Foundation**

Bad Food Next 100 Miles

If, for any segment of your trip, you were considering economizing on food costs by packing sandwiches, this part of Texas would be the perfect place to do so. West Texas does not have a food culture. What you are served here runs the gamut from horrid to a notch below mediocre. Of course, there are exceptions—the work of non-natives. Otherwise, keep to simple dishes—something grilled, for instance. In Alpine there is **Reata** (© **432/837-9232;** www.reata.net), the sister restaurant to the one in Fort Worth. In Marfa, try the **Food Shark** (no phone; www.foodsharkmarfa.com), which is a lunch truck that sets up Tuesday to Friday from 11:30am to 3pm under the big metal roof next to the Marfa bookstore. It serves delicious and healthy Mediterranean and Middle Eastern food. A more conventional eatery is the new **Cochineal** (© **432/729-3300**), a sharp-looking restaurant serving New American Cuisine at 107 W. San Antonio St. It's small, so definitely call ahead for reservations.

(© **432/729-4362;** www.chinati.org), which displays hundreds of works, including Judd's and those of fellow minimalist Dan Flavin.

There are three small towns in the area that can provide food and lodging: Alpine, Fort Davis, and Marfa. But if you're coming to these parts to get away from civilization (but aren't enamored of camping), your first choice for a hotel should be the **Indian Lodge** inside the Davis Mountains State Park. It was built during the Depression as a works project. The construction makes use of local materials and Pueblo Indian designs, with adobe walls covered in stucco. You should make reservations as far in advance as possible by calling © **432/426-3254.** Rates range from $95 to $135 and include the admission fee to the state park. The historic rooms are comfortable and attractive. Another option is the **Prude Guest Ranch** (© **800/458-6232;** www.prude-ranch.com). It's near the park, at least 6 miles outside of town. Rates run from $80 to $100 a night. You also have the option of camping in the Davis Mountains State Park—first-come, first-served.

BIG BEND NATIONAL PARK

Big Bend National Park (© **432/477-2251;** www.nps.gov/bibe), among the greatest of the national parks, is beautiful, dramatic, and rugged. Do not consider it for a quick day's side trip. It's too far away from everything else and too vast (more than a million acres) to enjoy in anything less than 2 days.

The park gets its name from the Rio Grande, which divides Texas from Mexico. The river flows southeast toward the Gulf above the park, but then makes a big turn northeast, forming the distinctive notch on Texas's southern border. Big Bend Park is in the hollow of the turn. The water, in its course through the mountains, has carved out rugged, spectacular canyons that can be viewed while rafting down the river.

If you come from either Alpine or Marfa, you will arrive at the western side of the park, where the rafting trips begin.

Just west of the park are three settlements (they're too small to call towns): **Lajitas** (rhymes with *fajitas*), an old trading post that is now an overpriced development being marketed to rich Texans; **Terlingua** (www.terlinguatx.com), a ghost town that in its heyday was one of the largest mines for cinnabar (mercury) in the world; and **Study Butte** (*Study* rhymes with *Judy*). There are several river outfitters here. You need to contact

Don't Get Sidetracked

Coming from the west, you'll see signs for Big Bend Ranch State Park. Though large, too, and interesting for a couple of reasons, this park doesn't have the variety and grandeur or the visitor infrastructure that the national park enjoys. Keep right on going.

them ahead of time. Two I can recommend are **Far Flung Adventures** (© 800/359-2627; www.farflung.com) and **Big Bend River Tours** (© 800/545-4240; www.bigbendrivertours.com). There is lodging here, too: **Big Bend Motor Inn** (© 800/848-2363) and **Chisos Mining Co. Motel** (© 432/371-2254; www.cmcm.cc). You should avoid this area in November when around 7,000 crazy Texans gather here for the annual **Terlingua Chili Cook-off** and lodging becomes impossible to find.

By far the most dramatic sight on the western side of the park is the Santa Elena Canyon and the Sierra Ponce. Viewed from the Santa Elena overlook, the Sierra Ponce mountain range looks like a wall rising straight up from the desert floor. It would be one continuous wall if not for a sharp and deep cleft that is the Santa Elena Canyon. A hiking path leads into the canyon above the river.

The other entrance to the park is from the north, passing through the town of **Marathon** (rhymes with *paraffin*). Here is the closest lodging north of the park. There is a grand old hotel that is beautifully kept, called the **Gage Hotel** (© 800/884-4243; www.gagehotel.com). It's moderately priced, and one of a kind, and has a good restaurant. From this town, it's still about 60 miles to the park, but it's a straight shot from there to the park's main attraction—the rugged **Chisos Mountains,** where the park has lodging and camping sites at a refreshing 5,400-foot elevation. Call © 432/477-2291 for reservations. There are three categories of lodging: motel, lodge, and stone cottages, with the last being the favorite. Rates run from $111 to $150 for two people. There is also a **campground** with 65 lots that go for $20 per night and should be reserved ahead of time during the park's busy season (Nov 15–Apr 15), but for the rest of the year are had on a first-come, first-served basis. To reserve a camping space, call © 877/444-6777 or go to **www.recreation.gov**. In the Chisos there are several beautiful trails that vary in length from 1.5 to 15 miles.

Entrance fees to the park are $20 per vehicle. For advance information, contact the **Big Bend Travel Association** (© 432/477-2236; www.visitbigbend.com).

GUADALUPE MOUNTAINS NATIONAL PARK

The Guadalupe Mountain Range is the highest in Texas. Its most distinctive peak is El Capitan, with its massive white south face, the remains of ancient coral reef. **Guadalupe Mountains National Park** isn't as big as Big Bend, but it is still quite large. The National Park Service has kept development in this park to a minimum. Hence, it is a favorite place for those who enjoy primitive camping. The park is on the New Mexico border, only about 35 miles from Carlsbad Caverns. From I-10, take Hwy. 54 north from the town of Van Horn. It's a pretty road, as it runs between two ranges, the Diablo and the Delaware mountains. From quite a long distance, you'll see the white cliffs of El Capitan. The road leads straight to the visitor center, which offers a limited number of camping sites but no lodging inside the park. The closest lodging is on the New Mexico side by the caverns (p. 802). Entrance fees for the park are $5 per person and are good for several days. For more information, call © 915/828-3251 or see **www.nps.gov/gumo**.

10

Colorado & Utah

These two states contain some of the most gorgeous scenery in the West, from the glorious peaks of the Rockies to the spectacular red-rock formations of Zion, Bryce Canyon, Capitol Reef, and Arches national parks. If you're interested in skiing, rafting, mountain biking, hiking, or wildlife viewing—or experiencing something with the flavor of the Old West—this area is for you.

1 DENVER

Denver is the biggest city between the Great Plains and the Pacific, with about 600,000 residents in the city itself and over 3 million in the metro area. Today it's a sprawling city, extending from the Rocky Mountain foothills in the west, far into the plains to the south and east. It's also a major destination for both tourists and business travelers. Denver is noted for its dozens of tree-lined boulevards; 200 city parks comprising more than 20,000 acres; and its architecture, which ranges from Victorian to sleek contemporary.

ESSENTIALS

GETTING THERE By Plane   **Denver International Airport** (© 800/AIR-2-DEN [247-2336] or 303/342-2000; www.flydenver.com) is 23 miles northeast of downtown, usually a 35- to 45-minute drive. A city bus ride can take you downtown for $9. The **SuperShuttle** (© 800/525-3177 or 303/370-1300; www.supershuttle.com) has frequent scheduled service between the airport and downtown hotels for $19 one-way; door-to-door service is also available. Expect to spend anywhere from $30 to $50 if you take a taxi downtown, and you can often share a cab and split the fare by calling the cab company ahead of time. **Yellow Cab** (© 303/777-7777) will take up to five people from DIA to most downtown hotels for a flat rate of $45. **Metro Taxi** (© 303/333-3333) is the other service in Denver. All major car-rental agencies have desks at the airport.

By Train   **Amtrak** serves Union Station, 17th and Wynkoop streets (© 800/USA-RAIL [872-7245] or 303/825-2583; www.amtrak.com), in the lower downtown historic district. Denver is a stop for **California Zephyr.**

By Car   The principal highway routes into Denver are **I-25** from the north (Fort Collins and Wyoming) and south (Colorado Springs and New Mexico), **I-70** from the east (Burlington and Kansas) and west (Grand Junction and Utah), and **I-76** from the northeast (Nebraska). If you're driving into Denver from Boulder, take **U.S. 36;** from Salida and the Southwest, **U.S. 285.**

VISITOR INFORMATION   The **Denver Metro Convention and Visitors Bureau** operates a visitor center on the 16th Street Mall at 1600 California St. (© 303/892-1505). It's open Monday through Friday from 9am to 5pm. In summer, it is open until 6pm on weekdays, as well as on Saturday from 9am to 5pm and Sunday from 11am to 3pm. Visitor information is also available at Denver International Airport. Ask for the

Official Visitors Guide, a 150-plus-page full-color booklet with a comprehensive listing of accommodations, restaurants, and other visitor services in Denver and surrounding areas.

GETTING AROUND   The **Regional Transportation District,** or **RTD** (© **800/366-7433,** 303/299-6000, or TDD 303/299-6089 for route and schedule information; 299-6700 for other business; www.rtd-denver.com), calls itself "The Ride." It operates bus routes and a light-rail system. It provides good service within Denver and its suburbs and outlying communities, as well as free parking at 65 Park-n-Ride locations throughout the Denver-Boulder metropolitan area. The light-rail service is designed to get buses and cars out of congested downtown Denver; many of the bus routes from outlying areas deliver passengers to light-rail stations rather than downtown. The local one-way fare is $1.75; seniors and passengers with disabilities pay 85¢, and children age 5 and under travel free. Regional bus fares vary (for example, Denver to Boulder costs $4). Exact change is required for buses, and train tickets can be purchased at vending machines beneath light-rail station awnings.

Depending on the route, the departure time of the last bus or train varies from 9pm to 2am. Maps for all routes are available at any time at the RTD **Civic Center Station,** 16th Street and Broadway, and the **Market Street Station,** Market and 16th streets. RTD also provides special service to Colorado Rockies (baseball) and Denver Broncos (football) games. All RTD buses and trains are completely wheelchair accessible.

Free buses run up and down the 16th Street Mall between the Civic Center and Market Street, daily from 6am to 1am.

The **C Line** on the light rail stops at Invesco Field at Mile High, the Pepsi Center, and Elitch Gardens before chugging into Union Station at 17th and Wynkoop streets in lower downtown. The open-air **Platte Valley Trolley** (© **303/458-6255;** www.denver trolley.org) operates year-round. From April to October between 12:30 and 4pm Friday through Sunday, there's a 25-minute "Riverfront Ride" ($3 adults, $2 seniors and children), which operates from 15th Street at Confluence Park, south to the Denver Children's Museum along the west bank of the Platte River.

The main taxi companies are **Yellow Cab** (© **303/777-7777**) and **Metro Taxi** (© **303/333-3333**). Taxis can be hailed on the street, though it's preferable to telephone for a taxi or wait for one at a taxi stand outside a major hotel.

Because cars are not necessary downtown, visitors can save money by staying downtown while in Denver, then renting a car to leave the area.

FAST FACTS   Doctor and dentist referrals are available by calling © **800/DoctorS** (362-8677). Among Denver-area hospitals are **St. Joseph Hospital,** 1835 Franklin St. (© **303/837-7111**), just east of downtown; and **Children's Hospital,** 1056 E. 19th Ave. (© **303/861-8888**), which expects to move east to the Fitzsimons area by year's end 2007. **Walgreens,** at 2000 E. Colfax Ave. (© **303/331-0917**), is open 24 hours a day. State and local **sales tax** in Denver is about 7.75% (it varies slightly in neighboring counties and suburbs). The **hotel tax** is about 10.75%, bringing the total tax on accommodations to nearly 18.5%.

SPECIAL EVENTS & FESTIVALS   The second and third weeks of January bring the **National Western Stock Show and Rodeo** (© **303/297-1166;** www.nationalwestern. com), the world's largest livestock show and indoor rodeo. In mid-March, more than 1,500 American Indians, representing some 85 tribes, perform traditional music and dances in the **Pow Wow** (© **303/934-8045;** www.denvermarchpowwow.org). Early

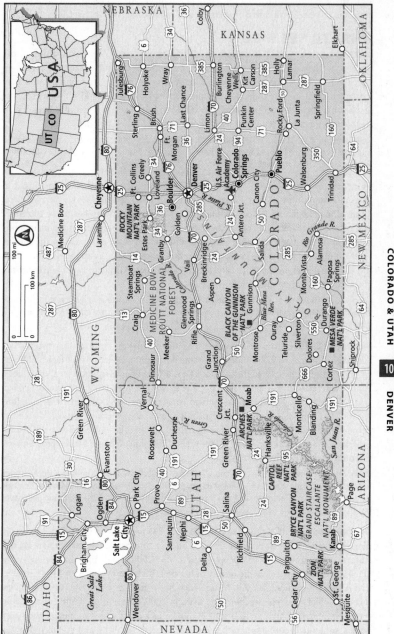

October brings the **Great American Beer Festival** (© **303/447-0816;** www.beertown. org), where hundreds of American beers are available for sampling, and seminars are presented at what is considered the largest and most prestigious beer event in the U.S.

WHAT TO SEE & DO

Black American West Museum & Heritage Center   Nearly one-third of the cowboys in the Old West were black, and this museum chronicles their history, along with those of black doctors, teachers, miners, farmers, newspaper reporters, and state legislators. The extensive collection occupies the Victorian home of Dr. Justina Ford, the first black woman licensed to practice medicine in Denver. The museum is loaded with artifacts, memorabilia, photographs, and oral histories. Allow 1 hour.

3091 California St. (at 31st St.). © **303/482-2242.** www.blackamericanwestmuseum.com. Admission $8 adults, $7 seniors, $6 children 12 and under. June–Aug Tues–Sat 10am–5pm; Sept–May Tues–Sat 10am–2pm. Light rail: 30th and Downing.

Colorado State Capitol   Built to last 1,000 years, the capitol was constructed in 1886 of granite from a Colorado quarry; its dome, rising 272 feet above the ground, is sheathed in gold. The first-floor rotunda offers a splendid view upward to the underside of the dome, the west lobby offers changing exhibits, and to the west of the main lobby is the governor's reception room. The second floor has main entrances to the House, Senate, and old Supreme Court chambers, and the third floor has entrances to the public and visitor galleries for the House and Senate. The Colorado Hall of Fame is near the top of the dome. Allow about an hour.

Lincoln St. and Colfax Ave. © **303/866-2604.** Free admission. 45-min. tours offered year-round (more frequently in summer) Memorial Day to Labor Day Mon–Fri 9am–3:30pm; rest of year Mon–Fri 9:15am–2:30pm. Bus: 0, 2, 7, 12, 15, or 50.

Denver Art Museum   Founded in 1893, this seven-story museum has two distinct buildings. The main 1972 building is wrapped by a thin, 28-sided wall faced with one million sparkling tiles, while the second, a jagged, avant-garde addition by Daniel Libeskind, was finished in fall 2006, doubling the size of the museum. The museum's collection of Western and regional works is its cornerstone. Included are Frederic Remington's bronze *The Cheyenne,* Charles Russell's painting *In the Enemy's Country,* and 19th-century photography and historical pieces. The American Indian collection represents 150 North American tribes, spanning nearly 2,000 years. Child-oriented and family programs are scheduled regularly. Allow 2 to 3 hours.

100 W. 14th Ave. Pkwy. (at Civic Center Park). © **720/865-5000.** www.denverartmuseum.org. Admission $13 adults, $10 college students and seniors 65 and over, free for children 5 and under; free for Colorado residents the 1st Sat of each month. Tues–Thurs and Sat 10am–5pm; Fri 10am–10pm; Sun noon–5pm. Bus: 0, 2, 7, 12, 15, or 50.

Denver Museum of Nature & Science (Best) (Kids)   Exquisitely fashioned figures in dioramas depict the history of life on earth on four continents. Displays explore ancient cultures, prehistoric American peoples, Colorado wildlife, and Australian ecology. The "Prehistoric Journey" traces the history of life over 3.5 billion years, with fossils, interactive exhibits, and dioramas. At "Space Odyssey," visitors experience a carefully crafted mix of exhibits about space exploration. New in 2009, "Expedition Health" is a state-of-the-art exhibit that allows visitors an eye-opening look at the workings of their own bodies, gathering information as they move through the exhibits, and getting a printout about their own physical condition at the end. The state-of-the-art Gates Planetarium

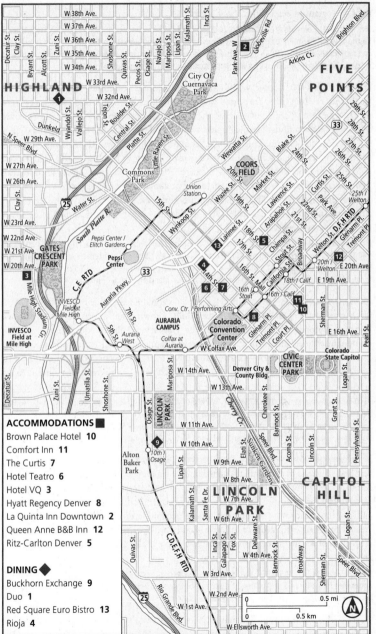

ACCOMMODATIONS ■

Brown Palace Hotel **10**

Comfort Inn **11**

The Curtis **7**

Hotel Teatro **6**

Hotel VQ **3**

Hyatt Regency Denver **8**

La Quinta Inn Downtown **2**

Queen Anne B&B Inn **12**

Ritz-Carlton Denver **5**

DINING ◆

Buckhorn Exchange **9**

Duo **1**

Red Square Euro Bistro **13**

Rioja **4**

has an advanced computer graphics and video system unlike any other in the world. The **IMAX Theater** (✆ **303/322-7009**) presents science, nature, or technology-oriented films on a giant screen. Allow 2 to 4 hours.

City Park, 2001 Colorado Blvd. ✆ **800/925-2250** outside Metro Denver, or 303/322-7009; 303/370-8257 for those with hearing impairment. www.dmns.org. Admission to museum $11 adults, $6 children 3–18 and seniors 65 and older; IMAX $8 adults, $6 children and seniors; planetarium $5 subsequent adults, $4 subsequent children and seniors. Daily 9am–5pm. Closed Christmas. Bus: 32 or 40.

Denver Zoo (Kids) Some 4,000 animals representing more than 700 species call the zoo home. Feeding times are posted near the entrance. "Northern Shores" allows you to see polar bears and sea lions underwater, while "Tropical Discovery" re-creates an entire tropical ecosystem under glass, complete with crocodiles, piranhas, and king cobras, plus the rare Komodo dragon. The "Primate Panorama" is a 7-acre world-class primate exhibit with 29 species, ranging from a 6-ounce marmoset to a 581-pound gorilla. The newest (and most ambitious) habitat here is "Predator Ridge," a re-created African savanna with lions, hyenas, and other African predators. The zoo is home to the nation's first natural gas–powered train ($2). The electric Safari Shuttle ($2.50 adults, $1.50 children) tours all zoo paths spring through fall. Kids can ride the Conversation Carousel ($2). Allow from 2 hours to a whole day.

City Park, 2300 Steele St. (main entrance btw. Colorado Blvd. and York St. on 23rd Ave.). ✆ **303/376-4800**. www.denverzoo.org. Admission $12 adults summer, $9 adults winter; $9 seniors 62 and over summer, $7 seniors winter; $7 children 3–12 (accompanied by an adult) summer, $5 children winter; free for children 2 and under. Apr–Sept daily 9am–5pm; Oct–Mar daily 10am–4pm. Bus: 24 or 32.

Molly Brown House Museum This is a neat, old house, which from 1894 to 1932 was the residence of James and Margaret (Molly) Brown. The "unsinkable" Molly Brown became a national heroine in 1912 when the *Titanic* sank: She took charge of a group of immigrant women in a lifeboat and later raised money for their benefit. Restored to its 1910 appearance, the Molly Brown House has a large collection of turn-of-the-20th-century furnishings and art objects, many of which belonged to the Brown family. Allow 1 hour.

1340 Pennsylvania St. ✆ **303/832-4092**. www.mollybrown.org. Guided tour $6.50 adults, $5 seniors over 65, $3 children 6–12, free for children 5 and under. June–Aug Mon–Sat 10am–4pm, Sun noon–4pm; Sept–May Tues–Sat 10am–4pm, Sun noon–4pm. Guided tours every 30 min.; last tour of the day begins at 3:30pm. Closed major holidays. Bus: 2 on Logan St. to E. 13th, and then 1 block east to Pennsylvania.

Museum of Contemporary Art Denver Moving into a translucent new LEED-certified structure in LoDo that is actually three buildings wrapped in glass in 2007, this is a stark canvas for the artists who are on center stage here. There are five galleries dedicated to five different disciplines (photography, paper works, large works, new mediums, and projects), and only one artist at a time occupies a given gallery; most works were created for their exhibition or are a year or two old. An interesting library showcases influences of the artists currently on display. There is also a small gift shop full of books and oddball knickknacks. Allow 1 hour.

1485 Delgany St. ✆ **303/298-7554**. www.mcadenver.org. Admission $10 adults, $5 seniors and students, free for children 5 and under. $1 discount for those who come via public transportation, foot, or bike. Tues–Sun 10am–6pm; Sun noon–5:30pm.

U.S. Mint The Denver Mint stamps 10 billion coins a year, and each has a small *D* on it. Video monitors along the visitors' gallery through the mint provide a close view of the actual coin-minting process. Although visitors today don't get as close as they once did, a self-guided tour provides a good look at the process, with a bird's-eye view from the mezzanine of the actual coin-minting process. A variety of displays help explain the minting process, and an adjacent **gift shop** on Cherokee Street (© **303/572-9500**) offers a variety of souvenirs. Allow 1 hour.

320 W. Colfax Ave. (btw. Cherokee and Delaware sts.). © **303/405-4757** or 405-4761; 572-9500 for gift shop. www.usmint.gov. Free admission. Tours Mon–Fri 8am–2pm. Gift shop 8am–3:30pm. Reservations recommended; online reservations available. Closed 1–2 weeks in summer for audit; call for exact date. Bus: 7.

SHOPPING

Most visitors do their shopping along the **16th Street Mall** (the mile-long pedestrian walkway btw. Market St. and Tremont Place) and adjacent areas, including **Larimer Square,** the **Shops at Tabor Center, Writer Square,** and the newest retail development downtown, **Denver Pavilions.**

Outside the downtown area there are more options, primarily the huge **Cherry Creek Shopping Center**—a shopper's dream—south of downtown.

Denver claims the world's largest sporting-goods store: the five-story **Sports Authority Sportscastle,** 1000 Broadway (© **303/861-1122;** www.sportsauthority.com). The rental department at the **REI** Flagship store, 1416 Platte St. (© **303/756-3100**), is stocked with tents, stoves, kayaks, and other gear. A good source for area maps and hiking guides is **Mapsco Map and Travel Center,** 800 Lincoln St., Denver (© **303/623-4299**).

WHERE TO STAY

Denver is home to a host of chain properties. Reliable (and relatively inexpensive hotels) downtown choices include **Comfort Inn,** 401 17th St., Denver, CO 80202 (© **800/228-5150** or 303/296-0400), with a convenient location and rates of $149 double and $189 to $329 suite; **La Quinta Inn Downtown,** 3500 Park Ave. W. (at I-25, exit 213), Denver, CO 80216 (© **800/531-5900** or 303/458-1222), charging $99 for a double; and **Hotel VQ,** 1975 Mile High Stadium Circle (at I-25, exit 210B), Denver, CO 80204 (© **800/388-5381** or 303/433-8331), with rates of $89 to $129 double.

Brown Palace Hotel (Best)   For more than 100 years, this National Historic Landmark has been *the* place to stay in Denver—if you're looking to celebrate a special occasion in relaxed elegance, then look no further. Designed in an odd triangular shape, it was built of Colorado red granite and Arizona sandstone. Elaborate cast-iron grillwork surrounds six tiers of balconies up to the stained-glass ceiling high above the lobby. Rooms are either Victorian or Art Deco style and have all the amenities of a modern luxury hotel. The staterooms on the ninth floor are especially enticing, with cordless phones, big-screen TVs, fridges, fax/printers, and safes. The water's great here: The Brown Palace has its own artesian wells!

321 17th St., Denver, CO 80202. © **800/321-2599** or 303/297-3111. Fax 303/312-5900. www.brown palace.com. 241 units. $210–$385 double; $360–$535 suite. Lower weekend rates. AE, DC, DISC, MC, V. Valet parking $24 overnight. Pets up to 20 lb. accepted. **Amenities:** 3 restaurants; exercise room. *In room:* Fridge (in some rooms only).

The Curtis   A convention center lodging reimagined as a pop-culture-themed hotel, the Curtis reopened in 2007, with nostalgic board games in the lobby, floors with various themes (from "The Big Hair Floor" with art of oversize hairdos to "The 13th Floor," the hallway graced by Jack Nicholson's leering mug from *The Shining*) and wake-up calls by Darth Vader and Austin Powers sound-alikes. The rooms are modern and outfitted with techie perks like iPod-friendly speaker systems and flatscreen TVs. There is a "5 & Dime" store selling toys and candy in the lobby. Corner rooms have fridges and great downtown views.

1405 Curtis St., Denver, CO 80202. ✆ **800/525-6651** or 303/572-3300. Fax 303/825-4301. www.thecurtis. com. 336 units, including 2 suites. $229–$425 double; suites from $450. AE, DC, DISC, MC, V. Valet parking $24; self-parking $15. **Amenities:** Restaurant; indoor heated pool; exercise room.

Hotel Teatro   One of Denver's most luxurious hotels, Hotel Teatro is also the most dramatic: The Denver Center for the Performing Arts (across the street) inspired the decor, which features masks, playbills, and wardrobe from past productions. The exquisitely furnished guest rooms feature Indonesian marble, cherrywood furnishings, Frette linens, and Aveda toiletries. The nine-story building is a historic landmark, constructed as the Denver Tramway Building in 1911. Cutting-edge perks include iPod docking stations and 36-inch plasma-screen TVs in each room. All rooms also feature Aveda amenities and a rainforest shower head. Kevin Taylor, one of Denver's best-known chefs, runs both restaurants and the room service.

1100 14th St. (at Arapahoe St.), Denver, CO 80202. ✆ **303/228-1100.** Fax 303/228-1101. www.hotel teatro.com. 111 units. $269–$399 double; $469–$1,500 suite. AE, DC, DISC, MC, V. Valet parking $24 overnight. Pets accepted. **Amenities:** 2 restaurants. *In room:* Fridge.

Hyatt Regency Denver   The 37-story Hyatt Regency is one of the biggest and best such properties in the Rockies and the first skyscraper to rise in downtown Denver since the early 1980s. With an ideal location—adjacent to the Colorado Convention Center and its trademark "Blue Bear" sculpture—and a thorough list of amenities, the Hyatt immediately emerged as the top convention hotel in the Rockies. The sleek lobby features automated check-in kiosks and the Strata bar. On the 27th floor, another bar, Peaks Lounge, offers the best views downtown. The guest rooms are contemporary but comfortable, with plush furnishings and an ergonomic workstation.

650 15th St., Denver, CO 80202. ✆ **800/233-1234** or 303/436-1234. Fax 303/436-9102. www.denver regency.hyatt.com. 1,100 units, including 60 suites. $125–$429 double; $550–$5,000 suite. AE, DC, DISC, MC, V. Underground valet parking $24; self-parking $20. **Amenities:** Restaurant; heated indoor pool; health club; spa.

Queen Anne Bed & Breakfast Inn   A favorite of both business travelers and couples, the Queen Anne might be considered the perfect bed-and-breakfast in the perfect home (actually, the B&B encompasses two Victorian homes). Each of the four two-room suites in the adjacent 1886 Roberts house is dedicated to a famous artist (Norman Rockwell, Frederic Remington, John Audubon, and Alexander Calder). Each of the 10 double rooms in the 1879 Pierce House is unique, decorated with period antiques (three of the rooms boast original murals). The entire property is nonsmoking.

2147–51 Tremont Place, Denver, CO 80205. ✆ **800/432-4667** or 303/296-6666. Fax 303/296-2151. www. queenannebnb.com. 14 units. $135–$185 double; $215 suite. Rates include hot breakfast and Colorado wine each evening. AE, DC, DISC, MC, V. Free off-street parking.

Ritz-Carlton, Denver   Opening in early 2008, the Ritz-Carlton is downtown Denver's only household-name luxury hotel, at least until the Four Seasons opens in late 2009. The former Embassy Suites was gutted and rebuilt to Ritz-Carlton's exacting standards and now has a distinctive sense of style and a long list of perks for guests. The plush rooms—at 550 square feet, the largest in the city—feature such amenities as steam-free mirrors, iPod-ready clock radios, down comforters, and combination coffee/tea/cappuccino makers. Beyond the rooms, the lavish common areas lead the way to **Elway's,** the down- town sibling to the Denver quarterbacking legend's Cherry Creek steakhouse, a spa, and a fully equipped business center.

1881 Curtis St., Denver, CO 80202. ✆ **303/312-3800.** Fax 303/312-3801. www.ritzcarlton.com. 202 units, including 48 suites. $309–$429 double; $409–$1,200 suite. Weekend rates from $209. AE, DC, DISC, MC, V. Underground valet parking $26; self-parking $15. **Amenities:** Restaurant; heated indoor lap pool; health club; spa. *In room:* Fridge.

WHERE TO DINE

Buckhorn Exchange Best ROCKY MOUNTAIN   In the same rickety premises where it was established in 1893, this landmark restaurant displays its Colorado Liquor License No. 1 above the 140-year-old bar in the upstairs saloon. On the first level, the densely decorated dining room dishes out the best game dishes (slow-roasted buffalo prime rib, lean and served medium rare; elk; pheasant; and quail) in the city. The beef-steaks, ranging from 8-ounce tenderloins to 64-ounce table steaks for five, are also quite good. Portions are large. A mile southwest of the State Capitol, the Buckhorn sits adja-cent to a light-rail stop, making it an easy trip from downtown.

1000 Osage St. (at W. 10th Ave.). ✆ **303/534-9505.** www.buckhorn.com. Reservations recommended. Main courses $8–$16 lunch, $18–$44 dinner. AE, DC, DISC, MC, V. Mon–Fri 11am–2pm; Mon–Thurs 5:30–9pm; Fri–Sat 5–10pm; Sun 5–9pm. Bar open all day. Light rail: Osage.

Casa Bonita Kids MEXICAN/AMERICAN   A west Denver landmark, Casa Bonita is more theme park than restaurant. The 52,000-square-foot restaurant is said to be the largest in the Western Hemisphere. A pink Spanish cathedral–type bell tower greets visi-tors, and inside are divers plummeting into a pool beside a 30-foot waterfall, puppet shows, a video arcade, and strolling mariachi bands. Food—enchiladas, tacos, fajitas, country-fried steak, and fried chicken—is served cafeteria style. Hot *sopaipillas* (deep-fried sweet dough) served with honey are included with each meal.

In the JCRS Shopping Center, 6715 W. Colfax Ave., Lakewood. ✆ **303/232-5115.** www.casabonitadenver. com. Reservations not accepted. All-you-can-eat dinners $10–$20; children's meals around $4. DISC, MC, V. Mon–Thurs 11am–9:30pm; Fri–Sat 11am–10pm.

Duo CONTEMPORARY AMERICAN   Nestled in the back of a homey and warm room with brick, worn wood, and a wall of suspended old window frames, Duo's open kitchen plates up a variety of dishes that start with tradition but exude creativity in terms of both presentation and flavor. The menu changes seasonally, but you might find expertly grilled pork chops, buttermilk-fried chicken, or an artful tower of vegetarian gratin. Appetizers are similarly remarkable, my favorite being the leek tart, topped with the transcendental contrast of creamy goat cheese and salty pancetta.

2413 W. 32nd Ave. ✆ **303/477-4141.** www.duodenver.com. Reservations recommended. Main courses $17–$25 dinner, $8–$12 brunch. AE, DISC, MC, V. Mon–Sat 5–10pm; Sun 5–9pm; Sat–Sun 10am–2pm.

Elway's STEAKS/SEAFOOD   Owned by retired Denver Broncos QB John Elway, this Cherry Creek eatery—unlike many celebrity restaurants—is no flash in the pan. Dim but lively, the restaurant is a model of "New West" design, with a menu that melds swank and comfortable. On the swank side: hand-cut USDA prime steaks, bone-in swordfish chops, and veggies served a la carte. And the comfy: creamed corn, steak loaf, and a dessert menu that includes Ding Dongs and warm chocolate-chip cookies and cold milk. But it's the little details, such as buttonholes in the napkins, milk bottles full of water, and tiramisu cones, that won us over in the end. Service is smooth and business is brisk. If you're lucky, you might bump into Elway himself here—he's not just the owner, but a regular, too.

2500 E. 1st Ave. (immediately west of the Cherry Creek Shopping Center). ℂ **303/399-5353.** www. elways.com. Reservations recommended. Main courses $10–$33 lunch and brunch, $16–$50 dinner. AE, DC, DISC, MC, V. Mon–Thurs 11am–10pm; Fri–Sat 11am–11pm; Sun 11am–9pm.

Encore CONTEMPORARY MEDITERRANEAN   This smart and hip eatery adjoins the Tattered Cover bookstore and an art cinema, and is a good pick for lunch or dinner east of downtown. With black-and-white tiled floors, great happy hour deals, and excellent service, the long and narrow room is a nice fit for a variety of options, from vegetarian (falafel burgers) to carnivorous (black-pepper crusted rib-eye). In between are great appetizers, wood-fired pizzas, mussels, pastas, and big salads. To finish, the house take on carrot cake is a delectable dessert in a pumpkin-pie-like guise.

2250 E. Colfax Ave. ℂ **303/355-1112.** www.encoreoncolfax.com. Reservations accepted. Main courses $9–$27. AE, DISC, MC, V. Daily 11am–10pm. Bar open later.

Red Square Euro Bistro RUSSIAN/CONTEMPORARY   This restaurant has a rich red interior, contemporary Russian art, and a vodka bar stocked with infusions made in-house (ranging from raspberry to garlic) and about 100 brands from 17 countries. Chef Maxim Ionikh's excellent entrees are not purely Russian: The steak stroganoff has a salmon counterpart, but there is cold borscht and *golubtsi* (a meat-filled cabbage roll), and vodka. Lots and lots of vodka.

1512 Larimer St. at Writer Sq. ℂ **303/595-8600.** www.redsquarebistro.com. Main courses $16–$23. AE, DC, DISC, MC, V. Daily 5–10pm. Bar open later.

Rioja CONTEMPORARY MEDITERRANEAN   Chef-owner Jennifer Jasinski emerged as Denver's most creatively inspired restaurateur since opening Rioja in 2004. In the time since, the slick Larimer Square eatery has emerged as a national standout, a critical darling, and our pick for dinner in downtown Denver. With a copper-topped bar and an atmosphere that's formal without being stuffy, Rioja is the perfect vehicle for Jasinski's menu of contrasting flavors and textures. Offerings range from fresh bacon and cardamom-spiced pork belly to curried cauliflower soup served with fresh apple salad. Jasinski keeps the menu fresh, but you'll always get a selection of her delectable handmade pastas for dinner, and transcendent beignets for dessert.

1431 Larimer Sq. ℂ **303/820-2282.** www.riojadenver.com. Reservations recommended. Main courses $10–$20 brunch and lunch, $16–$30 dinner. AE, DISC, MC, V. Wed–Fri 11:30am–2:30pm; Sat–Sun 10am–2:30pm; Sun–Thurs 5–10pm; Fri–Sat Sat 5–11pm.

DENVER AFTER DARK

Current entertainment listings appear in special Friday morning sections of the two daily newspapers, the *Denver Post* and *Rocky Mountain News. Westword,* a weekly newspaper distributed free throughout the city every Wednesday, has perhaps the best listings: It focuses on the arts, entertainment, and local politics.

You can get tickets for nearly all major entertainment and sporting events from **Ticketmaster** (ℂ **303/830-TIXS** [830-8497]), which has several outlets in the Denver area.

THE PERFORMING ARTS   Denver's performing arts scene is anchored by the 4-square-block **Denver Center for the Performing Arts** downtown, just a few blocks from major hotels at 14th and Curtis streets (ℂ **800/641-1222** or 303/893-4100; www. denvercenter.org). The complex houses nine theaters, a concert hall, and what may be the nation's first symphony hall in the round. It's home to the **Colorado Symphony**

Orchestra (© 303/623-7876; www.coloradosymphony.org), **Colorado Ballet** (© 303/
837-8888; www.coloradoballet.org), **Opera Colorado** (© 877/475-4833 for tickets, or
303/468-2030; www.operacolorado.org), and more.

Quite possibly the country's best and most beautiful venue for top-name outdoor
summer concerts, **Red Rocks Amphitheatre,** I-70 exit 259 South, 16351 County Rd.
93, Morrison (© **303/295-4444;** www.redrocksonline.com), is set in the foothills of the
Rocky Mountains, 15 miles west of the city. Four-hundred-foot-high red sandstone rocks
flank the 9,000-seat amphitheater, a product of the Civilian Conservation Corps; at
night, with the lights of Denver spread across the horizon, the atmosphere is magical.

THE BAR SCENE   More beer is brewed in Denver than in any other city in the country,
so finding a bar won't be a problem. The hip place for barhopping is **LoDo,** which
attracts all manner of Gen-Xers and yuppies. Its trendy nightspots are often noisy and
crowded, but if you're looking for action, this is where to find it, in spots like **Falling
Rock Tap House,** 1919 Blake St. (© **303/293-8338**), which has the best selection of
beers in Denver, darts and pool, and occasional live music.

Owned by Denver mayor John Hickenlooper, Denver's first modern microbrewery,
the **Wynkoop Brewing Co.,** 1634 18th St., at Wynkoop Street (© **303/297-2700**),
offers tours Saturday from 1 to 5pm. Housed in the renovated 1898 J. S. Brown Mercantile Building across from Union Station, the Wynkoop is also a popular restaurant.
Among its most interesting offerings are India pale ale, chili beer, and Scotch ale. On the
second floor is a pool hall with billiards, snooker, and darts.

You'll find an excellent selection of fine cigars, single-malt Scotches, and after-dinner
drinks at the refined **Churchill Bar,** 321 17th St., in the Brown Palace Hotel (© **303/
297-3111**).

THE CLUB & MUSIC SCENE   The historic **Bluebird Theater,** 3317 E. Colfax Ave. (at
Adams St.; © **303/322-2308;** www.nipp.com), built in 1913 to show silent movies, has
been restored and now offers a diverse selection of jazz, rock, alternative, and other live
music, as well as films. The **Mercury Cafe,** 2199 California St., at 22nd Street (© **303/
294-9281;** www.mercurycafe.com), has a wide array of live offerings, from avant-garde
jazz to progressive rock.

The **Grizzly Rose,** 5450 N. Valley Hwy., at I-25 exit 215 (© **303/295-1330** or 295-
2353; www.grizzlyrose.com), has a 5,000-square-foot dance floor and draws nationally
known country performers, offering live music every night.

2 BOULDER

Set at the foot of the Flatirons of the Rocky Mountains, just 30 miles northwest of downtown Denver, Boulder is a college town. With nearly 30,000 students, the University of
Colorado (C.U.) dominates the city. Sophisticated and artsy, Boulder is home to numerous high-tech companies; it has also attracted many outdoor enthusiasts who have been
drawn by the delightful climate, vast open spaces, and proximity to Rocky Mountain
National Park. Boulder has 30,000 acres of open space within its city limits, 56 parks, and
200 miles of trails—on any given day, most of the population is outside making great use
of this land, frequently from the vantage point of a bicycle seat. There are about 100,000
bicycles in Boulder, one for each of the city's residents. The National Trust for Historic
Preservation has named Boulder one of the nation's "dozen distinctive destinations" for
preserving historic sites, managing growth, and maintaining a vibrant downtown.

GETTING THERE   By Plane   Air travelers fly into **Denver International Airport,** then make ground connections to Boulder. Buses operated by the **Regional Transportation District,** known locally as **RTD** (© 800/366-7433 or 303/299-6000, or 303/299-6089 TTY; www.rtd-denver.com), charge $11 for a one-way trip to the airport (exact change required). Buses leave from and return to the main terminal at 14th and Walnut streets daily every hour from before 4am to after midnight.

By Car   The Boulder Turnpike (**U.S. 36**) branches off **I-25** north of Denver and passes through several suburbs before reaching Boulder. The trip takes about 30 minutes. If you are coming from Denver International Airport, **E-470 West** to **I-25 South** is the best route to U.S. 36.

VISITOR INFORMATION   The **Boulder Convention and Visitors Bureau,** 2440 Pearl St. (at Folsom St.), Boulder, CO 80302 (© 800/444-0447 or 303/442-2911; www.bouldercoloradousa.com), is open Monday through Friday from 8:30am to 5pm and can provide excellent maps, brochures, and general information on the city.

SPECIAL EVENTS & FESTIVALS   In the wacky, crowd-pleasing **Kinetic Conveyance Race** (© 303/444-5600), held in early May at Boulder Reservoir, some 70 teams race over land and water in a variety of imaginative human-powered, handmade machines.

One of the best in the country, the annual **Colorado Shakespeare Festival** (© 303/492-0554; www.coloradoshakes.org) takes place from late June to late August, with more than a dozen performances each of four Shakespeare plays. Tickets run $5 to $52 for single performances and previews, with series packages available.

EXPLORING THE AREA

The tree-lined, pedestrian-only **Pearl Street Mall,** along Pearl Street from 11th to 15th streets, is the city's hub for dining, shopping, strolling, and people-watching. Musicians, mimes, jugglers, and other street entertainers hold court on the landscaped mall day and night, year-round.

Boulder maintains more than 200 miles of hiking trails and long stretches of bike paths. Several canyons lead down from the Rockies directly into Boulder, attracting mountaineers and rock climbers. Families enjoy picnicking and camping in the beautiful surroundings. Everywhere you look, people of all ages are running, walking, biking, skiing, or engaging in other active sports.

On some days, you can see more bikes than cars in Boulder. For current information on biking events, tips on the best places to ride, and equipment sales and repairs, check with **University Bicycles,** 839 Pearl St., about 2 blocks west of the Pearl Street Mall (© 303/444-4196; www.ubikes.com); and with **Full Cycle,** 1211 13th St., near the campus (© 303/440-7771; www.fullcycleboulder.com).

The **Boulder Creek Path,** 55th Street and Pearl Parkway to the mouth of Boulder Canyon (© 303/413-7200), provides a 16-mile-long oasis and recreation area through the city and west into the mountains. The C.U. campus and several city parks are linked by the path. Near the east end, watch for deer, prairie dog colonies, Canada geese, spotted sandpipers, owls, and woodpeckers.

I. M. Pei designed the striking pink-sandstone building that houses the **National Center for Atmospheric Research,** 1850 Table Mesa Dr. (© 303/497-1174; www.ncar.ucar.edu), high atop Table Mesa in the southwestern foothills. Here scientists study the greenhouse effect, wind shear, and ozone depletion. Among the technological tools on display are satellites, weather balloons, robots, and supercomputers that can simulate the world's climate. There are also hands-on, weather-oriented exhibits and the outdoor, interpretive Walter Orr Roberts Nature and Weather Trail (.4 mile long and wheelchair accessible). Admission is free.

Celestial Seasonings, 4600 Sleepytime Dr., off Spine Road at Colo. 119, Longmont Diagonal (© **303/581-1202;** www.celestialseasonings.com), the nation's leading producer of herbal teas, offers free 45-minute tours (and some sample tastings) on the hour every day.

WHERE TO STAY

Major chains and franchises that provide reasonably priced lodging include **Best Western Boulder Inn,** 770 28th St., Boulder, CO 80303 (© **800/780-7234** or 303/449-3800), with rates of $89 to $149 double; and **Days Inn,** 5397 S. Boulder Rd., Boulder, CO 80303 (© **800/329-7466** or 303/499-4422), with rates of $89 to $129 double.

We also recommend the **Alps,** a beautiful B&B housed in a historic log lodge, 38619 Boulder Canyon Dr. (© **800/414-2577** or 303/444-5445; www.alpsinn.com; $149–$269 double), and the series of pleasant log cabins near the east gate of Boulder Canyon at **Foot of the Mountain Motel,** 200 Arapahoe Ave. (© **866/773-5489** or 303/442-5688; www.footofthemountainmotel.com; $90 double).

At the top of the class of hotels in Boulder is the elegant and historic **Hotel Boulderado,** 2115 13th St. (© **800/433-4344** or 303/442-4344; www.boulderado.com), which boasts a cantilevered, cherrywood staircase and rich woodwork. The original five-story hotel, just a block off the Pearl Street Mall, has 42 bright and cozy rooms, all with a Victorian flavor. The newer North Wing rooms also capture the turn-of-the-20th-century feel with reproduction antiques. Some rooms have refrigerators and a few have jetted tubs. Rates run $174 to $304 double.

The posh $24-million **St. Julien,** 900 Walnut St. (© **877/303-0900** or 720/406-9696; www.stjulien.com), raised the bar for lodging in Boulder when it opened in 2005. The flagstone and Norman brick exterior sheaths a sumptuous lobby and exquisite guest rooms, averaging a healthy 400 square feet each. Everything from the luxurious linens to the premium bath amenities is first-rate. Honeyed tones and French doors accent the guest rooms, which feature either one California king or two queens. The bathrooms are the best in town; there are separate tubs and showers in every granite-laden one. Perks include live music Tuesday through Saturday in the lobby or back terrace, a two-lane lap pool, complimentary yoga classes on summer weekend mornings, and a spa that offers "indigenous therapies" using local minerals and plants. Expect to be wowed. Rooms $239 to $329 double.

WHERE TO DINE

Note: A Boulder city ordinance prohibits smoking inside restaurants.

Frasca, 1738 Pearl St. (© **303/442-6966;** www.frascafoodandwine.com), is the critical darling in Boulder for its impeccable service and peerless cuisine, drawn exclusively from the culinary traditions of Friuli-Venezia Giulia, a sub-Alpine region in northeastern Italy. The **Kitchen,** 1039 Pearl St. (© **303/544-5973;** www.thekitchencafe.com), has also emerged as a standout with its fresh, often organic food; expert service; and casual atmosphere.

Head to the **Flagstaff House Restaurant,** 1138 Flagstaff Rd. (© **303/442-4640;** www.flagstaffhouse.com), for excellent American cuisine and a spectacular nighttime view of the lights of Boulder, spread out 1,000 feet below. This family-owned and -operated restaurant has an elegant, candlelit dining room with glass walls to maximize the view. The menu, which changes daily, offers an excellent selection of seafood and Rocky Mountain game prepared with a creative flair, plus the state's best wine cellar. Main courses run $32 to $56.

At the far east end of the Pearl Street Mall, **Illegal Pete's,** 1447 Pearl St. (© **303/440-3955;** www.illegalpetes.com), is renowned locally for its creative, healthy burritos, packed with chicken, steak, veggies, or fish. The menu also includes a similar range of tacos, as well as salads, quesadillas, and chili. Menu items run $5 to $7.

One of the smallest restaurants in Boulder, the **Black Cat,** 1964 13th St. (© **303/444-5500;** www.blackcatboulder.com), is also one of the best. Owner-chef Eric Skokan changes the menu nightly, using herbs and vegetables he personally harvests from his own half-acre garden. The menu might include starters like warm mozzarella with rosemary coulis, inventively prepared seafood, garlic-polenta gratin, and anything else that is in season or strikes the kitchen staff's fancy. For a special evening, the Black Cat offers a tasting menu for $62 for five courses, $99 with wine pairings.

BOULDER AFTER DARK

The **Catacombs,** in the basement of the Hotel Boulderado, 13th and Spruce streets (© 303/443-0486), offers live blues and jazz by local and regional performers. The **West End Tavern,** 926 Pearl St. (© 303/444-3535), is a great neighborhood bar offering 48 bourbons and a different specialty burger every day, barbecue, and more upscale items. Boulder's leading sports bar is the **Lazy Dog,** 1346 Pearl St. (© **303/440-3355;** www.thelazydog.com), with a great rooftop deck and a plethora of TVs tuned into games of all kinds.

The best local brewpub is the **Walnut Brewery,** 1123 Walnut St., near Broadway (© 303/447-1345), in a historic brick warehouse a block from the Pearl Street Mall. The spacey wall murals make the **Sink,** 1165 13th St. (© **303/444-SINK** [444-7465]; www.thesink.com), one of Boulder's funniest nightspots. There's a full bar with more than a dozen regional microbrews, live music, and light fare.

3 ROCKY MOUNTAIN NATIONAL PARK

ESTES PARK: THE GATEWAY

Estes Park is the eastern gateway to Rocky Mountain National Park, and Grand Lake is the closest town to the park's western entrance. Of the two, Estes Park is more developed, with more lodging and dining choices, lots of galleries, and shopping. If you're driving to Rocky Mountain National Park via Boulder or Denver, you'll want to make Estes Park your base camp. (The town of Grand Lake is more rustic, with plenty of spots to camp, a number of motels, and a few guest ranches. If you're coming from Steamboat Springs or Glenwood Springs, Grand Lake is a more convenient base.)

Essentials

GETTING THERE The most direct route is **U.S. 36** from Denver and Boulder. At Estes Park, U.S. 36 joins **U.S. 34,** which runs up the Big Thompson Canyon from **I-25** and Loveland, and continues through Rocky Mountain National Park to Grand Lake and Granby.

VISITOR INFORMATION   The **Estes Park Convention and Visitors Bureau** (© 800/ 443-7837; www.estesparkcvb.com) has a visitor center on U.S. 34, just east of its junction with U.S. 36, with access from both highways.

GETTING AROUND   In summer, a free national park **shuttle bus** runs from Moraine Park Campground, Moraine Park Museum, and the Glacier Basin parking area to Bear Lake, with departures every 10 to 20 minutes.

Where to Stay

The highest rates here, sometimes dramatically higher, are in summer. For help in finding accommodations, call the **Estes Park Convention and Visitors Bureau** (© 800/443-7837; www.estesparkcvb.com). National chains here include **Best Western Silver Saddle**, 1260 Big Thompson Ave. (U.S. 34), Estes Park, CO 80517 (© 800/WESTERN [937-8376] or 970/586-4476), with rates of $79 to $259 double from June to mid-September, $79 to $199 double during the rest of the year; and **Super 8,** 1040 Big Thompson Ave., Estes Park, CO 80517 (© 800/800-8000 or 970/586-5338), charging $99 to $119 double in summer, $59 to $89 double during the rest of the year.

Elk Meadows Lodge & RV Park (© 800/582-5342 or 970/586-5342; www.elk meadowrv.com) is close to the national park's Beaver Meadows entrance, with 30 open and wooded acres, grand views, and sites that can handle "big rigs." There are several historic cabins, a swimming pool, convenience store, laundry, playgrounds, a dump station, and a recreation room. There are also a number of tepees for rent. Rates for two adults $43 to $48 RV, $25 to $28 tent, $34 tepee, $90 to $250 cabin.

Alpine Trail Ridge Inn (Value)   This top-notch independent motel, right next to the entrance to Rocky Mountain National Park, offers nicely maintained rooms, many with private balconies, with basic Western decor and plenty of functionality. There are rooms with kings and queens and two doubles, as well as a few two-room family units.

927 Moraine Ave., Estes Park, CO 80517. © **800/233-5023** or 970/586-4585. Fax 970/586-6249. www. alpinetrailridgeinn.com. 48 units. Summer $80–$139 double. AE, DC, DISC, MC, V. Closed mid-Oct to Apr. **Amenities:** Restaurant; outdoor heated pool. *In room:* Fridge.

Baldpate Inn   Located 7 miles south of Estes Park, the Baldpate was built in 1917 and named for the novel *Seven Keys to Baldpate,* a murder mystery in which seven visitors believe each possesses the only key to the hotel (guests today can contribute to the hotel's collection of more than 30,000 keys). Each of the early-20th-century-style rooms is unique, with handmade quilts on the beds. Several rooms are a bit small, and although most of the lodge rooms share bathrooms (five bathrooms for nine units), each room does have its own sink. Among our favorites are the Mae West Room (yes, she was a guest here), with a red claw-foot tub and wonderful views of the valley; and the Pinetop Cabin, with a whirlpool tub, canopy bed, and gas fireplace.

4900 S. Colo. 7 (P.O. Box 700), Estes Park, CO 80517. © **866/577-5397** or 970/586-6151. www.baldpateinn. com. 12 units (5 with private bathroom), 4 cabins. $110 double with shared bathroom; $135 double with private bathroom. Rates include full breakfast. DISC, MC, V. Closed Nov–Apr. **Amenities:** Restaurant. *In room:* No phone.

Taharaa Mountain Lodge   A luxurious mountain lodge, Taharaa is named for the French Polynesian word for "beautiful view." There are jaw-dropping views of the Mummy Range. Built in 1997 and expanded in 2005 by Diane and Ken Harlan, Taharaa melds upscale hotel amenities and service with the intimacy of a B&B. With a contemporary

"New West" feel, the sumptuous interiors are a good match with the sublime panoramas. All rooms have gas fireplaces and private balconies. The property has a guest library with Internet access and a Great Room, with a 30-foot ceiling and fireplace, a wrought-iron chandelier, and picture windows framing the stunning view.

3110 Colo. 7 (P.O. Box 2586), Longs Peak Route, Estes Park, CO 80517. ⓒ **800/597-0098** or 970/577-0098. Fax 970/577-0819. www.taharaa.com. 18 units, including 2 suites. May to mid-Oct $185–$255 double, $305–$345 suite; mid-Oct to Apr $155–$225 double, $245–$285 suite. Rates include full breakfast and happy hour. AE, DISC, MC, V. **Amenities:** Exercise room.

ROCKY MOUNTAIN NATIONAL PARK

One of the most beautiful spots in America, Rocky Mountain National Park should top your list for your trip to Colorado. The scenery is stupendous: Snow-covered peaks—17 mountains above 13,000 feet—stand over lush valleys and shimmering Alpine lakes in the 415 square miles (265,727 acres) that comprise the park.

In relatively low areas, from about 7,500 to 9,000 feet, a lush forest of ponderosa pine and juniper cloaks the sunny southern slopes, with Douglas fir on the cooler northern slopes. Thirstier blue spruce and lodgepole pine cling to stream sides, with occasional groves of aspen. Elk and mule deer thrive. On higher slopes, a sub-Alpine ecosystem exists, dominated by forests of Engelmann spruce and sub-Alpine fir, but interspersed with wide meadows alive with wildflowers during spring and summer. This is also home to bighorn sheep, which have become unofficial symbols of the park. Above 11,500 feet, the trees become increasingly gnarled and stunted, until they disappear altogether and Alpine tundra predominates.

Trail Ridge Road, the park's primary east-west roadway, is one of America's great Alpine highways. It cuts west through the middle of the park from Estes Park, then south down its western boundary to Grand Lake. Climbing to 12,183 feet near Fall River Pass, it's the highest continuous paved highway in the United States. The road is usually open from sometime in May into October, depending on the snowfall. The 48-mile scenic drive from Estes Park to Grand Lake takes about 3 hours, allowing for stops at numerous scenic outlooks. Exhibits at the **Alpine Visitor Center** at Fall River Pass, 11,796 feet above sea level, explain life on the Alpine tundra.

Fall River Road, the original park road, leads to Fall River Pass from Estes Park via Horseshoe Park Junction. West of the Endovalley picnic area, the road is one-way uphill, and closed to trailers and motor homes. As you negotiate its gravelly switchbacks, you get a clear idea of what early auto travel was like in the West. This road, too, is closed in winter.

One of the few paved roads in the Rockies that leads into a high mountain basin is **Bear Lake Road;** it's kept open year-round, with occasional half-day closings to clear snow. Numerous trails converge at Bear Lake, southwest of the park headquarters/visitor center, via Moraine Park.

Park Essentials

ENTRY POINTS   Entry into the park is from the east (through Estes Park) or the west (through Grand Lake). **Trail Ridge Road** connects the two sides. Most visitors enter the park from the Estes Park side. The **Beaver Meadows entrance,** west of Estes Park on U.S. 36, is the national park's main entrance. U.S. 34 west from Estes Park takes you to the **Fall River entrance** (north of the Beaver Meadows entrance). Those entering the park from the west side should take U.S. 40 to Granby, then follow U.S. 34 north to the **Grand Lake entrance.**

Park admission for up to a week costs $20 per vehicle or $10 per person for motor- **679** cyclists, bicyclists, and pedestrians.

VISITOR CENTERS & INFORMATION   Entering the park on U.S. 36 from Estes Park, the **Beaver Meadows Visitor Center** (© **970/586-1206**) has knowledgeable people to answer questions, a wide choice of books and maps for sale, interpretive exhibits, and an audiovisual program. It's open daily from 8am to 9pm in summer and from 8am to 5pm the rest of the year.

Just outside the park, on U.S. 34 and just east of the Fall River entrance, is the **Fall River Visitor Center** (© **970/586-1206**). Located in a mountain lodge–style building, it is staffed by park rangers and volunteers from the Rocky Mountain Nature Association. It contains exhibits on park wildlife, including some spectacular full-size bronzes of elk and other animals, plus information and a bookstore. Next door is a large (but somewhat pricey) souvenir and clothing shop plus a cafeteria-style restaurant. Hours are from 9am to 6pm in summer and 9am to 5pm in spring and fall.

Near the park's west side entrance is the **Kawuneeche Visitor Center** (© **970/586-1513**), open daily from 8am to 6pm in summer, 8am to 5pm in late spring, and 8am to 4:30pm in fall and winter. High in the mountains (11,796 ft. above sea level) is the **Alpine Visitor Center** (© **970/586-1206**), at Fall River Pass, open from late June to early October, daily from 10:30am to 4:30pm, with shorter hours toward the end of the season; exhibits here explain life on the Alpine tundra. Visitor facilities are also available at the **Moraine Park Museum** (© **970/586-1206**) on Bear Lake Road on the east side of the park, open from mid-April to mid-October, daily from 9am to 4:30pm.

For more specifics on planning a trip, contact **Rocky Mountain National Park,** 1000 U.S. 36, Estes Park, CO 80517-8397 (© **970/586-1206** or 586-1333 for recorded information; www.nps.gov/romo). You can also get information from the **Rocky Mountain Nature Association,** P.O. Box 3100, Estes Park, CO 80517 (© **970/586-0108;** www.rmna.org), which sells maps, guides, books, and videos.

WHEN TO GO   Because large portions of the park are closed half the year due to snowfall, practically everyone visits in spring and summer. The busiest period is from mid-June to mid-August (during school vacations). To avoid the largest crowds, try to visit just before or just after that period. For those who don't mind chilly evenings, late September and early October are less crowded and can be beautiful, although there's always the chance of an early winter storm. Regardless of when you visit, the best way to avoid crowds is by putting on a backpack or climbing onto a horse. Rocky Mountain has almost 350 miles of trails leading into all corners of the park.

GETTING AROUND   In summer, a free national park **shuttle bus** runs from Moraine Park Campground, Moraine Park Museum, and the Glacier Basin parking area to Bear Lake, with departures every 10 to 20 minutes. Shuttle buses also began operating in 2006 throughout the business district of Estes Park and from Estes Park into Rocky Mountain National Park. The buses run daily from July through Labor Day; schedules are available at the Estes Park Visitor Center.

Sports & Outdoor Activities
HIKING & BACKPACKING   Park bookstores sell topographic maps and guidebooks, and rangers can direct you to lesser-used trails.

One particularly easy park hike is the **Alberta Falls Trail** from the Glacier Gorge Parking Area (.6 mile one-way), which rises in elevation only 160 feet as it follows Glacier Creek to pretty Alberta Falls.

A slightly more difficult option is the **Bierstadt Lake Trail,** accessible from the north side of Bear Lake Road about 6.4 miles from Beaver Meadows. This 1.4-mile (one-way) trail climbs 566 feet through an aspen forest to Bierstadt Lake, where you'll find excellent views of Longs Peak.

Starting at Bear Lake, the trail up to **Emerald Lake** offers spectacular scenery en route, past Nymph and Dream lakes. The .5-mile hike to Nymph Lake is easy, climbing 225 feet; from there the trail is rated moderate to Dream Lake (another .6 mile) and then on to Emerald Lake (another .7 mile), which is 605 feet higher than the starting point at Bear Lake. Another moderate hike is the relatively uncrowded **Ouzel Falls Trail,** which leaves from Wild Basin Ranger Station and climbs about 950 feet to a picture-perfect waterfall. The distance one-way is 2.7 miles.

Among our favorite moderate hikes is the **Mills Lake Trail,** a 2.5-mile (one-way) hike, with a rise in elevation of about 700 feet. Starting from Glacier Gorge Junction, the trail goes up to a picturesque mountain lake, nestled in a valley among towering mountain peaks. This lake is an excellent spot for photographing dramatic Longs Peak, especially in late afternoon or early evening, and it's the perfect place for a picnic.

Backcountry permits (required for all overnight hikes) can be obtained ($20 May–Oct, free Nov–Apr) at park headquarters and ranger stations (in summer); for information, call ✆ **970/586-1242.** There is a 7-night backcountry camping limit from June to September, with no more than 3 nights at any one spot.

HORSEBACK RIDING   Many of the national park's trails are open to horseback riders. Several outfitters provide guided rides inside and outside the park, including a 1-hour ride (about $35) and popular 2-hour rides (about $50). There are also all-day rides ($120–$130, bring your own lunch) plus breakfast and dinner rides and multiday pack trips. **SK Horses** (www.cowpokecornercorral.com) operates **National Park Gateway Stables,** at the Fall River entrance of the national park on U.S. 34 (✆ **970/586-5269**). **Sombrero Ranches** (✆ **970/586-4577;** www.sombrero.com) operates two stables inside park boundaries, **Moraine Park Stables** (✆ **970/586-2327**) and **Glacier Creek Stables** (✆ **970/586-3244**), and stables in Estes Park, Grand Lake, and Allenspark.

WILDLIFE VIEWING & BIRD-WATCHING   Rocky Mountain National Park is a premier wildlife-viewing area. Fall, winter, and spring are the best times. Large herds of elk and bighorn sheep can often be seen in the meadows and on mountainsides. In addition, you may spot mule deer, beavers, coyotes, and river otters. Watch for moose among the willows on the west side of the park. In the forests are lots of songbirds and small mammals; particularly plentiful are gray and Steller's jays, Clark's nutcrackers, chipmunks, and golden-mantled ground squirrels. There's a good chance of seeing bighorn sheep, marmots, pikas, and ptarmigan along Trail Ridge Road. For current wildlife-viewing information, stop by one of the park's visitor centers and check on the many interpretive programs, including bird walks.

Where to Camp

The park has five campgrounds, with a total of almost 600 sites. Nearly half are at **Moraine Park;** another 150 are at **Glacier Basin.** Moraine Park, **Timber Creek** (98 sites), and **Longs Peak** (26 tent sites) are open year-round; Glacier Basin and **Aspenglen** (54 sites) are seasonal. Camping in summer is limited to 3 days at Longs Peak and 7 days at other campgrounds; the limit is 14 days at all the park's campgrounds in winter. Arrive early in summer if you hope to snare one of these first-come, first-served campsites. Reservations for Moraine Park and Glacier Basin are accepted from Memorial Day through early September and are usually booked well in advance. However, any sites not reserved—as well as sites at Timber Creek, Longs Peak, and Aspenglen—are available on a first-come, first-served basis. Make reservations with the **National Park Reservation Service** (© 800/365-2267; www.recreation.gov). Campsites cost $20 per night during the summer, $14 in the off season when water is turned off. No showers or RV hookups are available.

4 NORTHERN COLORADO ROCKIES HIGHLIGHTS

The northern Rockies begin just outside Denver and extend on either side of the meandering Continental Divide, down saw-toothed ridgelines, through precipitous river canyons, and across broad Alpine plains. Here snowfall is measured in feet, not inches. And when spring's sun finally melts away the walls of white, a whole new world opens up amid the brilliantly colored Alpine wildflowers. Skis are replaced by mountain bikes, and summer festivals fill the mountains with music.

STEAMBOAT SPRINGS

In this state-of-the-art ski resort town, ranchers still go about their business in cowboy boots and Stetsons, seemingly unaware of the fashion statement they're making to city-slicker visitors.

Essentials

GETTING THERE **By Plane** The **Yampa Valley Regional Airport,** 22 miles west of Steamboat Springs (© 970/276-5004; www.co.routt.co.us), is served by several major airlines, with the most flights in winter. Car rentals are available at the airport.

By Car The most direct route to Steamboat Springs from Denver is via **I-70** west 68 miles to Silverthorne, **Colo. 9** north 38 miles to Kremmling, and **U.S. 40** west 52 miles to Steamboat. For statewide **road-condition reports,** call © 303/639-1111.

VISITOR INFORMATION The **Steamboat Springs Chamber Resort Association,** 1255 S. Lincoln Ave. (P.O. Box 774408), Steamboat Springs, CO 80477 (© 970/879-0880; www.steamboat-chamber.com or www.steamboatsummer.com), operates a visitor center, open in summer from 8am to 6pm Monday through Saturday and from 10am to 4pm Saturday, and shorter hours the rest of the year.

SPECIAL EVENTS & FESTIVALS The first full week in February brings the **Steamboat Springs Winter Carnival** (© 970/879-0695), with races, jumping, broomball, and skijoring street events. Mid-June through August, you'll hear top-notch classical, jazz, country, and pop musicians perform at the **Strings in the Mountains Festival of Music** (© 970/879-5056; www.stringsinthemountains.org).

Skiing & Other Winter Activities

When devoted skiers describe Steamboat, they practically invent adjectives to describe its incredibly light powder. Six peaks make up the ski area (mounts Werner, Christie, Storm, Sunshine, Pioneer Ridge, and Thunderhead) and provide slopes for skiers of all ability levels. The 3,668-foot vertical drop here is among the highest in Colorado. There are 143 trails, served by 20 lifts, and it's also a great mountain for snowboarders.

Steamboat is usually open from the third week in November through mid-April daily from 8:30am to 4pm. For information, contact **Steamboat Ski & Resort Corporation,** 2305 Mt. Werner Circle, Steamboat Springs, CO 80487 (© **877/237-2628** or 970/879-0740 for reservations, 879-6111 for info; www.steamboat.com). For daily **ski reports,** check the website or call © **970/879-7300.**

Seasoned cross-country skiers swear by **Steamboat Ski Touring Center** at the Sheraton Steamboat Resort (© **970/879-8180;** www.nordicski.net). Some 19 miles of groomed cross-country trails are set beside Fish Creek, near the foot of the mountain; there are also 6 miles of snowshoe trails.

One of the best snowmobile trails in the Rockies is the **Continental Divide Trail,** which runs more than 50 miles from Buffalo Pass north of Steamboat to Gore Pass, west of Kremmling. Among those offering guided snowmobile tours is **High Mountain Tours,** P.O. Box 749, Clark, CO 80428 (© **877/879-6500** or 970/879-6500; www. steamboatsnowmobile.com).

Warm-Weather & Year-Round Activities

Most outdoor recreation is enjoyed in 1.1-million-acre Routt National Forest, which virtually surrounds Steamboat Springs and offers opportunities for camping, hiking, backpacking, mountain biking, horseback riding, fishing, and hunting. For trail maps and information, contact **Medicine Bow–Routt National Forest,** Hahns Peak/Bears Ears Ranger Station, 925 Weiss Dr., Steamboat Springs, CO 80477 (© **970/879-1870;** www.fs.fed.us/r2).

BIKING & MOUNTAIN BIKING   The 5-mile, dual-surface **Yampa River Trail** connects downtown Steamboat Springs with Steamboat Village, and links area parks and

Hitting Colorado's Slopes

For current ski conditions and general information, contact **Colorado Ski Country USA** (© **303/837-0793** or 825-7669 for snow conditions).

Most skiers buy packages that include lift tickets for a given number of days and may also include transportation, rental equipment, lessons, lodging, meals, and lift tickets for nearby ski areas. There are also season passes that can be worthwhile for skiers who plan lengthy stays or several trips to the same resort. And for high rollers, Colorado Ski Country USA (see above) sells a coveted Gold Pass good at almost all of the state's resorts any day they're open. The possibilities are almost endless.

Some resorts charge more for lift tickets at busy times and offer discounts at slow times, so it's impossible for us to guarantee the accuracy of even the daily lift-ticket prices. Certainly, the most expensive time to ski is between December 20 and January 1, as well as the Martin Luther King, Jr., and Presidents' Day weekends. February through March is next, nonholiday times in January are generally cheaper, and the least expensive time is from Thanksgiving until mid-December and April until ski areas close. We generally prefer the last few weeks of the season—the snow's still great, the weather's nice, and the slopes are less crowded because many skiers are turning their thoughts to golf and tennis.

numerous slopes open to mountain bikers in summer. **Spring Creek Trail** climbs from Yampa River Park into Routt National Forest. Touring enthusiasts can try their road bikes on the 110-mile loop over Rabbit Ears and Gore passes, rated 1 of the 10 most scenic rides in America by *Bicycling* magazine.

Rent bikes from **Ski Haus,** 1457 Pine Grove Rd. (© **800/932-3019** or 970/879-0385). Basic mountain bikes cost about $35 for a half-day and $50 for a full day. Town cruisers and road bikes are also available, as are repairs, gear, and advice.

HOT SPRINGS   There are more than 150 mineral springs in and around the Steamboat Springs area. Heart Spring had a log bathhouse built over it in 1884. Today Heart Spring is part of the **Old Town Hot Springs,** 136 Lincoln Ave. (© **970/879-1828;** www.steamboathotsprings.org), in downtown Steamboat Springs. In addition to the man-made pools into which the spring's waters flow, you'll find tennis courts, a lap pool, water slide, spa, whirlpool, fitness center, and massage therapy. The **Strawberry Park Hot Springs,** 44200 C.R. 36 (© **970/879-0342;** www.strawberryhotsprings.com), are 7 miles north of downtown. Spend a moonlit evening in a sandy-bottomed, rock-lined soaking pool, kept between 101° and 106°F (38°C–41°C), with snow piled high around you.

More to See & Do

You can learn about Steamboat's history at **Tread of Pioneers Museum,** 800 Oak St. (© **970/879-2214**), a restored Victorian home that features exhibits on pioneer ranch life, the Utes, and 100 years of skiing history. Admission is $5 adults, $4 seniors 62 and older, and $1 children 11 and under. The museum is open Tuesday through Saturday from 10am to 5pm (opens at 11am Oct–Apr).

Just 4 miles from downtown in Routt National Forest is **Fish Creek Falls** (© **970/879-1870**). A footpath leads to a historic bridge at the base of this 283-foot waterfall. There's also an overlook with a short .13-mile trail and ramp designed for those with disabilities, as well as a picnic area and hiking trails. Turn right off Lincoln Avenue onto Third Street, go 1 block, and turn right again onto Fish Creek Falls Road.

Where to Stay

Steamboat Central Reservations (© **877/237-2628** or 970/879-0740; www.steamboat.com) can book your lodging and make your travel arrangements. Be sure to ask about special packages and programs. **Resort Quest Steamboat** (© **800/228-2458** or 970/879-8811; www.resortqueststeamboat.com) and **Steamboat Resorts** (© **800/525-5502** or 970/879-8000; www.steamboatresorts.com) rent everything from ski-in/ski-out con-dos and town houses to lodge rooms.

Our favorite lodging choices include the **Sheraton Steamboat Resort,** 2200 Village Inn Court (© **800/848-8878** or 970/879-2220; www.sheraton.com/steamboat; $119–$399 double), offering a host of facilities; the **Hotel Bristol,** 917 Lincoln Ave. (© **800/851-0872** or 970/879-3083) offering lodging with character in a 1940s-era hotel ($109–$139 double); and the relatively affordable **Rabbit Ears Motel,** 201 Lincoln Ave. (© **800/828-7702** or 970/879-1150; www.rabbitearsmotel.com; $99–$179 double).

BRECKENRIDGE & SUMMIT COUNTY

Summit County is a major recreational sports center, with skiing in winter and fishing, hiking, and mountain biking in summer. Breckenridge is a good place to base yourself, as the entire Victorian core of this 19th-century mining town has been carefully preserved, with colorfully painted shops and restaurants occupying the old buildings, most dating from the 1880s and 1890s.

Essentials

GETTING THERE   By Plane   Most visitors fly into Denver International or Colorado Springs and continue to Breckenridge via shuttle. **Colorado Mountain Express** (© 800/525-6363 or 970/926-9800; www.cmex.com) offers shuttles; the cost from Denver starts at about $80 per person, one-way.

By Car   I-70 runs through the middle of Summit County. For Keystone, exit on U.S. 6 at Dillon; the resort is 6 miles east of the interchange. For Breckenridge, exit on **Colo. 9** at Frisco and head south 9 miles to the resort. Copper Mountain is right on I-70 at the **Colo. 91** interchange.

VISITOR INFORMATION   The **Breckenridge Resort Chamber** has a new welcome center at 203 S. Main St. (open daily 9am–9pm summer and winter, with shorter hours in spring and fall), and administrative offices at 311 S. Ridge St., Breckenridge, CO 80424 (© **800/221-1091** or 970/453-2913; www.gobreck.com). A source of visitor information for the entire region is the **Summit County Chamber of Commerce,** P.O. Box 2010, Frisco, CO 80443 (© **800/530-3099** or 970/668-2051; www.experiencethe summit.com).

SPECIAL EVENTS & FESTIVALS   The **Breckenridge Music Festival** (© **970/453-9142** or 547-3100; www.breckenridgemusicfestival.com) presents dozens of classical and nonclassical music performances mid-June through mid-August. The **Breckenridge Festival of Film** (© **970/453-6200;** www.breckfilmfest.com), held in mid-September, attracts Hollywood directors and actors to town to discuss some two dozen films representing all genres.

Skiing & Other Winter Activities

Arapahoe Basin, 28194 U.S. 6, between Keystone and Loveland Pass (© **888/272-7246** or 970/496-0718; www.arapahoebasin.com), is one of Colorado's oldest ski areas. Most of its 490 skiable acres are intermediate and expert terrain, and it's often the last Colorado ski area to close for the season—sometimes not until mid-June.

Spread across four large mountains on the west side of the town, **Breckenridge** ranks third in size among Colorado's ski resorts. Once known for its wealth of open, groomed beginner and intermediate slopes, Breckenridge has, in recent years, expanded its acreage for expert skiers as well. The resort has 146 trails served by 28 lifts. Contact **Breckenridge Ski Resort** (© **800/789-7669** or 970/453-5000, or 453-6118 for snow conditions; http://breckenridge.snow.com).

Other notable ski areas in Summit County include **Copper Mountain** (© **866/841-2481;** www.coppercolorado.com); **Keystone,** a superb mountain for intermediate skiers, but also one of the best spots for night skiing in America (© **800/468-5004** or 970/496-4386; www.keystone.snow.com); and **Loveland Ski Area** (© **800/736-3754** or 303/571-5580; www.skiloveland.com).

Frisco Nordic Center, on Colo. 9 south of Frisco (© **970/668-0866;** www.brecken ridgenordic.com), sits on the shores of Dillon Reservoir. Its trail network includes 43km of set tracks and groomed skating lanes, and access to backcountry trails. From the Frisco Nordic Center you can ski to the **Breckenridge Nordic Center,** on Willow Lane near the foot of Peak 8 (© **970/453-6855;** www.breckenridgenordic.com), with its own

30km of groomed trails. The **Gold Run Nordic Center** (© 970/547-7889), at Breckenridge Golf Club, offers more than 20km of groomed trails.

Snowboarding is permitted at all local resorts.

Warm-Weather & Year-Round Activities

Two national forests—**Arapahoe** and **White River**—overlap the boundaries of Summit
County. These recreational playgrounds offer opportunities not only for downhill and
cross-country skiing and snowmobiling in winter, but also for hiking and backpacking,
horseback riding, boating, fishing, hunting, and bicycling in summer.

The **U.S. Forest Service's Dillon Ranger District,** in the town of Silverthorne at 680
Blue River Pkwy., just north of I-70 exit 205 (© 970/468-5400; www.fs.fed.us/r2), has
unusually good information on outdoor recreation, including maps and guides. You can
also get information on a wide variety of outdoor activities from the **Breckenridge
Resort Chamber Welcome Center,** 203 S. Main St. (© 877/864-0868).

BIKING   There are more than 40 miles of paved bicycle paths in the county, including
a path from Breckenridge (with a spur from Keystone) to Frisco and Copper Mountain,
continuing across Vail Pass to Vail. This spectacularly beautiful two-lane path is off-
limits to motorized vehicles of any kind.

BOATING   Dillon Reservoir, a beautiful mountain lake along I-70 between Dillon and
Frisco, is the place to go. At 9,017 feet in elevation, it claims to have America's highest-
altitude yacht club and holds colorful regattas most summer weekends. No swimming.
The full-service **Dillon Marina,** 150 Marina Dr. (© 970/468-5100; www.dillonmarina.
com), is open late May to late October.

FISHING   Major fishing rivers within an hour of Breckenridge include the South
Platte, Arkansas, Eagle, Colorado, and Blue rivers. For lake fishing, try Dillon Reservoir
and Spinney Mountain Reservoir. The Blue River, from Lake Dillon Dam to its confluence with the Colorado River at Kremmling, is rated a gold-medal fishing stream. For
tips on where they're biting, as well as supplies, fishing licenses, and all the rest, stop at
Mountain Angler, 311 S. Main St., in the Main Street Mall (© 800/453-4669 or
970/453-4665; www.mountainangler.com).

MOUNTAIN BIKING   Numerous trails beckon mountain bikers as they wind through
the mountains, often following 19th-century mining roads and burro trails and ending
at ghost towns. Energetic fat-tire fans can try the **Devil's Triangle,** a difficult 80-mile
loop that begins and ends in Frisco after climbing four mountain passes (including
11,318-ft. Fremont Pass). Check with the U.S. Forest Service or Activity Center for
directions and tips on other trails. For mountain bikers who prefer not to work so hard,
check with the Activity Center on times and costs for taking your bike up the mountain
on the Breckenridge chairlift.

Where to Stay

Throughout Summit County, condominiums prevail. While they often offer the best
value, they're sometimes short on charm. If you're planning to spend much time in one,
it pays to ask about views and fireplaces before booking. Local reservation services
include **Wildernest Lodging** (© 800/554-2212; www.skierlodging.com), **Breckenridge Central Reservations** (© 877/593-5260; www.gobreck.com), and, in Keystone,
Key to the Rockies (© 800/248-1942; www.keytotherockies.com). Our favorite B&B
is **Allaire Timbers Inn Bed & Breakfast,** 9511 Colo. 9, Breckenridge (© 800/624-
4904 or 970/453-7530; www.allairetimbers.com; $149–$275 double).

Vail is the *big one*. In fact, it's hard to imagine a more celebrated spot to schuss. Off the slopes, Vail is an incredibly compact Tyrolean village, frequented by almost as many Europeans as Americans, a situation that lends its restaurants, lodgings, and trendy shops a more cosmopolitan feel than other Colorado resorts. But the mountain's size and its exciting trails are still what draw the faithful.

Essentials

GETTING THERE   By Plane   Visitors can fly into **Denver International Airport** or directly into **Eagle County Regional Airport,** 35 miles west of Vail between I-70 exits 140 and 147 (© 970/524-9490; www.eaglecounty.us/airport), on major national carriers. **Colorado Mountain Express** (© 800/525-6363 or 970/926-9800; www.cmex.com) offers shuttles from Denver and Eagle for about $89 a person.

By Car   Vail is right on the **I-70** corridor, so it's easy to find. Just take exit 176, whether you're coming from the east (Denver) or the west (Grand Junction). A more direct route from the south may be **U.S. 24** through Leadville; this Tennessee Pass road joins I-70 5 miles west of Vail.

VISITOR INFORMATION   For information or reservations in the Vail Valley, contact the **Vail Valley Partnership,** 113 Fawcett Rd., Ste. 201, in Avon (P.O. Box 1130, Vail, CO 81658; © 970/476-1000; www.visitvailvalley.com); **Vail Mountain Resort,** P.O. Box 7, Vail, CO 81658 (© 877/204-7881 or 970/476-5601; www.vail.com); or **Beaver Creek Resort** (© 970/845-9090; www.beavercreek.com). For information on year-round activities, call the **Resort Information and Activities Center** (© 970/476-9090). Information centers are at the parking structures in Vail and the Lionshead area on South Frontage Road.

GETTING AROUND   Vail is one of only a few Colorado communities where you really don't need a car. The Town of Vail runs a free **shuttle bus** service daily from 6am to 2am.

SPECIAL EVENTS & FESTIVALS   The summer season's big cultural event is the **Bravo! Vail Valley Music Festival** (© 877/812-5700 or 970/827-5700; www.vailmusic festival.org), from late June to early August, featuring everything from classical orchestra and chamber music to baroque and jazz. The **Vail International Dance Festival** features both classes and performances. The World Masters Ballet Academy at Vail teaches the Russian style of artistic expression and other techniques, and presents a series of performances each summer. For information, contact the **Vail Valley Foundation** (© 888/883-8245 or 970/949-1999; www.vvf.org).

Skiing & Other Winter Activities

Vail is a place that all serious skiers must experience at least once. You can arrive at the base village, unload and park your car, and not have to drive again until it's time to go. You'll find all the shops, restaurants, and nightlife you could want within a short walk of your hotel or condominium.

Ski area boundaries stretch 7 miles from east to west along the ridge-top, from Outer Mongolia to Game Creek Bowl, and the skiable terrain is measured at 5,289 acres. Virtually every lift on the front (north-facing) side of the mountain has runs for every level of skier, with a predominance of novice and intermediate terrain. The world-famous Back Bowls are decidedly not for beginners, and there are few options for intermediates. All told, there are 193 conventional trails served by 34 lifts. Vail also has a highly respected children's program. For further information, contact **Vail Mountain,** P.O. Box 7, Vail, CO 81658 (© **800/404-3535** or 970/476-5601; 476-4888 for snow report; www.vail.com).

Vail Resorts, Inc., also owns nearby **Beaver Creek Resort** (© **800/404-3535** or 970/845-9090, or 800/427-8308 for snow reports; www.beavercreek.com), an outstanding resort in its own right, with a more secluded atmosphere. Located in a valley 1¹/₂ miles off the I-70 corridor, Beaver Creek combines European château-style elegance in its base village, with expansive slopes for novice and intermediate skiers. The big news here is the Stone Creek Chutes, an expert terrain area with chutes up to 550 vertical feet long, with pitches up to 44 degrees. The 2007–08 season saw a new gondola from Avon, connecting the Westin with the Lower Beaver Creek lift.

The Grouse Mountain Express lift reaches expert terrain. Currently, 16 lifts serve 162 trails. Snowboarding is permitted, and there is a snowboarding park with a half-pipe located off the Moonshine Trail. There are seven mountain restaurants, including the highly praised **Beano's Cabin.**

Paragon Guides (© **877/926-5299** or 970/926-5299; www.paragonguides.com) is one of the country's premier winter guide services, offering backcountry ski trips on the Tenth Mountain Trail and Hut System between Vail and Aspen. A variety of trips are available, lasting from 3 to 6 days. Costs start around $400 for two people for the day trip and $1,000 per person for a 3-day expedition.

Cross-country skiers won't feel left out here, with trails at both resorts as well as a system of trails through the surrounding mountains. **Vail's Nordic Center** (© **970/476-8366**) has 33km of trails and offers guided tours, lessons, and snowshoeing. The **Beaver Creek Nordic Center** (© **970/845-5313**) has a 32km mountaintop track system with a skating lane in 9,840-foot McCoy Park. Most of the high-altitude terrain here is intermediate. For general information on backcountry trails, contact the **Holy Cross Ranger District Office** (© **970/827-5715;** www.fs.fed.us/r2). Of particular note is the system of trails known as the **10th Mountain Division Hut System** (© **970/925-5775;** www.huts.org). Generally following the World War II training network of the Camp Hale militia, the trails cover 300 miles and link Vail with Leadville and Aspen. There are a number of overnight cabins ($20–$40 per person per night), and hikers and mountain bikers also use this trail.

Warm-Weather & Other Year-Round Activities

Nova Guides (© **888/949-6682** or 719/486-2656; www.novaguides.com) offers guided fishing, mountain-bike and off-road tours, and white-water rafting.

FISHING   The streams and mountain lakes surrounding Vail are rich with trout. Gore Creek through the town of Vail is a popular anglers' venue, especially toward evening from its banks along the Vail Golf Course. Also good are the Eagle River, joined by Gore Creek 5 miles downstream near Minturn; the Black Lakes near the summit of Vail Pass; and 60-acre Piney Lake. The **Lazy J Ranch** in Wolcott (© **970/926-3472;** www.lazyjranch.net) offers guided fly-fishing trips on 4 miles of private Eagle River frontage and to stocked lakes. For fishing supplies plus guided trips, contact **Fly Fishing Outfitters, Inc.** (© **800/595-8090** or 970/476-3474; www.flyfishingoutfitters.net).

HIKING & BACKPACKING   The surrounding White River National Forest has a plethora of trails leading to pristine lakes and spectacular panoramic views. The Holy Cross Wilderness Area, southwest of Vail, encompasses 14,005-foot Mount of the Holy Cross and is an awesome region with more than 100 miles of trails. Eagle's Nest Wilderness Area lies to the north, in the impressive Gore Range. For information on these and other hiking areas, consult the **Holy Cross Ranger District Office** (see "Skiing & Other Winter Activities," above).

MOUNTAIN BIKING   Summer visitors can take their bikes up the Eagle Bahn Gondola to Adventure Ridge on Vail Mountain and cruise downhill on a series of trails. There are many other choices for avid bikers, on both backcountry trails and road tours. A popular trip is the 13-mile Lost Lake Trail along Red Sandstone Road to Piney Lake. The 30-mile Vail Pass Bikeway goes to Frisco, with a climb from 8,460 feet up to 10,600 feet. Pick up a trail list (with map) at an information center.

Mountain bike repairs and rentals are available at a number of shops, including **Vail Bike Tech,** 555 E. Lionshead Circle, Vail (© 800/525-5995 or 970/476-5995; www.vailbiketech.com), which also offers guided tours; and **Wheel Base,** 610 W. Lionshead Circle (© **970/476-5799**).

Where to Stay

Like most of Colorado's ski resorts, Vail has an abundance of condominiums, and it seems that more are built every day. Contact the **Vail Valley Partnership** (p. 686), which can provide additional lodging information or make your reservations for you, as well as provide information on skiing and other activities.

Our favorite luxury resorts are the posh **Vail Cascade Resort & Spa,** 1300 Westhaven Dr., Vail (© 800/420-2424 or 970/476-7111; www.vailcascade.com; $259–$619 double), which seems to get better every time we visit; and the **Park Hyatt Regency Beaver Creek Resort and Spa,** 50 W. Thomas Place, Avon (© 800/55-HYATT [554-9288] or 970/949-1234; www.beavercreek.hyatt.com; $479–$1,179 double), an architecturally unique hotel at the foot of the Beaver Creek lifts. Other deluxe options include the **Charter at Beaver Creek,** 120 Offerson Rd., Beaver Creek (© 800/525-6660 or 970/949-6660; www.thecharter.com; $119–$500 double); and the **Ritz-Carlton, Bachelor Gulch** (© 800/241-3333 or 970/748-6200; www.ritzcarlton.com; $400–$1,800 double), modeled after the grand national park lodges, with its own branch of Wolfgang Puck's Spago.

More-affordable options include the **Inn & Suites at Riverwalk,** 27 Main St., Edwards (© 888/926-0606 or 970/926-0606; www.innandsuitesatriverwalk.com; $140–$240 double).

ASPEN

Aspen's glitzy, celebrity-studded reputation precedes it. But if you dig beneath the hype, you'll find a real town with a fascinating history, some great old buildings, and spectacular mountain scenery. If you're a serious skier, you owe yourself at least a few days of hitting the slopes. However, if you've never strapped on boards and you're thinking of visiting in summer, you'll be doubly pleased: Prices are significantly lower, and the crowds thin out. The surrounding forests teem with great trails for hiking, biking, and horseback riding, and Aspen becomes one of the best destinations in the country for summer festivals.

Essentials

GETTING THERE   By Plane   Visitors can fly direct to **Aspen/Pitkin County Airport,** 5 miles northwest of Aspen on Colo. 82 (© **970/920-5384;** www.aspenairport.com). **Colorado Mountain Express** (© 800/525-6363 or 970/926-9800; www.cmex.com) offers shuttle service from Denver International Airport, starting at $104 per person, one-way.

By Car Aspen is on **Colo. 82,** halfway between **I-70** at Glenwood Springs (42 miles northwest) and **U.S. 24** south of Leadville (44 miles east). In summer, it's a scenic 3¹/₂-hour drive from Denver: Leave I-70 west at exit 195 (Copper Mountain); follow **Colo. 91** south to Leadville, where you pick up U.S. 24; turn west on Colo. 82 through Twin Lakes and over 12,095-foot Independence Pass. In winter, the Independence Pass road is closed, so you'll have to take I-70 to Glenwood Springs and head east on Colo. 82. In optimal winter driving conditions, it takes about 4 hours from Denver.

VISITOR INFORMATION Contact the **Aspen Chamber of Commerce and Resort Association,** 425 Rio Grande Place, Aspen, CO 81611 (𝄒 **800/670-0792** or 970/925-1940; www.aspenchamber.org), which also offers a **visitor center** at its offices (open Mon–Fri 8:30am–5pm), and another at the Wheeler Opera House, at Hyman Avenue and Mill Street (usually open daily 10am–6pm), as well as at the Aspen/Pitkin County Airport and on the Cooper Avenue Mall. You can also get information from the **Snowmass Village Resort Association,** 130 Kearns Rd. (P.O. Box 5010), Snowmass Village, CO 81615 (𝄒 **800/766-9627;** www.snowmassvillage.com).

SPECIAL EVENTS & FESTIVALS The **Aspen Music Festival and School** (𝄒 **970/925-9042;** www.aspenmusicfestival.com) originated in 1949. Lasting 9 weeks from mid-June to late August, it offers more than 350 events, including symphonic and chamber music, opera, choral, and children's programs. **Jazz Aspen at Snowmass** (𝄒 **970/920-4996;** www.jazzaspen.com) takes place at Snowmass Village in late June, and again on Labor Day weekend.

Skiing & Other Winter Activities

Skiing Aspen really means skiing the four Aspen-area resorts—Aspen Mountain, Aspen Highlands, Buttermilk, and Snowmass. All are managed by the Aspen Skiing Company, and one ticket gives access to all. For further information, contact the **Aspen Skiing Company** (𝄒 **800/525-6200** or 970/925-1220; www.aspensnowmass.com).

Aspen Mountain is not for the timid. It's the American West's original hard-core ski mountain, with no fewer than 23 of its named runs double diamond—for experts only. There are mountain-long runs for intermediate as well as advanced skiers, but beginners should look to one of the other Aspen areas.

Aspen Highlands has the most balanced skiable terrain—novice to expert, with lots of intermediate slopes—in the Aspen area. Freestyle Friday, a tradition at Highlands for almost 3 decades, boasts some of the best freestyle bump and big air competitors in the state of Colorado every Friday from early January to mid-April.

Buttermilk is a premier beginners' mountain that's also home of the ESPN Winter X Games. But there's plenty of intermediate and ample advanced terrain as well. Special features include the ski and snowboard school's Powder Pandas program for 3- to 6-year-olds, and a snowboard park with a 23% grade.

A huge intermediate mountain with something for everyone, **Snowmass** has 33% more skiable acreage than the other three Aspen areas combined. It's actually four distinct self-contained areas, each with its own lift system and restaurant, and its terrain varies from easy beginner runs to the pitches of the Cirque and the Hanging Valley Wall, the steepest in the Aspen area. The renowned Snowmass ski school has hundreds of instructors, as well as Snow Cubs and Big Burn Bears programs for children 18 months and older. The area also caters to snowboarders with three terrain parks, one super pipe, and a rail yard.

The **Aspen/Snowmass Nordic Council** operates a free Nordic trail system with nearly 60km of groomed double track extending throughout the Aspen-Snowmass area and incorporating summer bicycle paths. Instruction and rentals are offered along the trail at the **Aspen Cross-Country Center,** Colo. 82 between Aspen and Buttermilk (© 970/925-2145; www.utemountaineer.com), and the **Snowmass Cross Country Center,** Snowmass Village (© 970/923-9180), both of which provide daily condition reports and information on the entire trail system.

Warm-Weather & Year-Round Activities

Your best source of information on a wide variety of outdoor activities in the mountains around Aspen is the **White River National Forest,** 806 W. Hallam St. (© 970/925-3445; www.fs.fed.us/r2).

Among the best one-stop outfitters is **Blazing Adventures,** Snowmass Village (© 800/282-7238 or 970/923-4544; www.blazingadventures.com), which offers river rafting, mountain biking, four-wheeling, and horseback riding.

FISHING   Perhaps the best trout fishing is in the Roaring Fork and Frying Pan rivers, both considered gold-medal streams. The Roaring Fork follows Colo. 82 through Aspen from Independence Pass; the Frying Pan starts near Tennessee Pass, northeast of Aspen, and joins the Roaring Fork at Basalt. Stop at **Aspen Fly Fishing** in the Gondola Plaza at 601 E. Dean St. (© 970/920-6886; www.aspenflyfishing.com), for a guided fishing trip; two people wading for a half-day is $350.

HORSEBACK RIDING   Several stables in the Aspen valley offer a variety of rides, and some outfitters even package gourmet meals and country-and-western serenades with their expeditions. A wide variety of adventures are offered; rates for day trips usually run about $70 to $100 per person for a 2-hour ride or $150 to $200 for a half-day. Inquire at **Aspen Wilderness Outfitters** (© 970/963-0211; www.aspenwilderness.com) and **OutWest Guides** (© 970/963-5525; www.outwestguides.net).

MOUNTAIN BIKING   There are hundreds of miles of trails through the White River National Forest that are perfect for mountain bikers, offering splendid views of the mountains, meadows, and valleys. Check with the Forest Service and local bike shops for tips on the best trails. Among full-service bike shops offering rentals are **Aspen Velo Bike Shop,** 465 N. Mill St. (© 970/925-1495; www.aspenvelo.com), and **Durrance Sports,** 414 E. Cooper Ave. (© 970/429-0101; www.durrancesports.com). A full-day rental is typically $40 to $60.

RIVER RAFTING   Rafting trips are offered on the Roaring Fork, Arkansas, and Colorado rivers with several companies, including **Colorado Riff Raft** (© 800/282-7238 or 970/923-4544; www.riffraft.com), **Up Tha Creek Expeditions** (© 877/982-7335 or 970/947-0030; www.upthacreek.com), and **Blazing Adventures** (see above). Rates are usually about $65 to $95 for a half-day.

Where to Stay

It's essential to make reservations as early as possible. The easiest way to book your lodgings is to call **Stay Aspen Snowmass** central reservations (© 888/649-5982; www.stayaspensnowmass.com). You can also find lodging through **Aspen Resort Accommodations** (© 800/727-7369; www.aspenreservations.net).

Our favorite choice for luxury accommodations is the historic **Hotel Jerome,** 330 E. Main St. (© 800/331-7213 or 970/920-1000; www.hoteljerome.com; $495–$675 double), with its period antiques and lovingly preserved Eastlake Victorian architecture. A very worthy alternative is the **St. Regis Resort, Aspen,** 315 E. Dean St. (© 888/454-9005 or 970/920-3300; www.stregisaspen.com; $900–$1,500 double). A bit more

affordable is the **Hotel Lenado,** 200 S. Aspen St. (© **800/321-3457** or 970/925-6246;
www.hotellenado.com; $285–$499 double); torn down in 2006 but rebuilt in 2008 is the **Limelite Lodge,** 228 E. Cooper Ave. (© **800/433-0832** or 970/925-3025; www.limelite-lodge.com; $200–$350 double).

5 COLORADO SPRINGS

Colorado Springs is a city of about 400,000, with more than 600,000 in the metro area. The majority of its residents are conservative, and the city is also home to some of the country's largest nondenominational churches and conservative groups. To many visitors, the city retains the feel and mood of a small Western town. Most tourists come to see the Air Force Academy, marvel at the scenery at Garden of the Gods and Pikes Peak, and explore the history of America's West. We're pleased to report that Colorado Springs also has some of the best lodging and dining in the state.

ESSENTIALS

GETTING THERE   By Plane   Major airlines offer nearly 100 daily flights to **Colorado Springs Airport** (© 719/550-1972; www.flycos.com). Call © **719/550-1930** for information on ground transportation from the airport to local hotels and Denver. We recommend you rent a vehicle; all major rental-car agencies have desks at the airport.

By Car   The principal artery to and from the north (Denver: 70 miles) and south (Pueblo: 42 miles), **I-25** bisects Colorado Springs. **U.S. 24** is the principal east-west route through the city. Visitors arriving via **I-70** from the east can take exit 359 at Limon and follow U.S. 24 into the Springs. If you arrive on I-70 from the west, the most direct route is exit 201 at Frisco, then **Colo. 9** through Breckenridge 53 miles to U.S. 24 (at Hartsel), and then east 66 miles to Colorado Springs. This route is mountainous, so check road conditions before setting out in winter (© 303/639-1111; www.cotrip.org).

VISITOR INFORMATION   The **Experience Colorado Springs at Pikes Peak Convention and Visitors Bureau** is at 515 S. Cascade Ave., Colorado Springs, CO 80903 (© **800/888-4748** or 719/635-7506; fax 719/635-4968; www.experiencecolorado springs.com). Ask for the free *Official Visitor Guide to Colorado Springs and the Pikes Peak Region,* which has a comprehensive listing of accommodations, restaurants, and other area visitor services, as well as a basic but efficient map. The **Visitor Information Center,** at the southeast corner of Cascade Avenue and Cimarron Street, is open from 8:30am to 5pm daily in summer, Monday through Friday in winter.

EXPLORING THE AREA

The **Colorado Springs Pioneers Museum,** 215 S. Tejon St. (© **719/385-5990;** www.cspm.org), is an excellent place to begin your visit (and admission is free). Exhibits depict the community's history, including its beginning as a fashionable resort, the railroad and mining eras, and its growth and development into the present.

One of the West's unique geological sites, the **Garden of the Gods,** 1805 N. 30th St. (I-25 exit 146; © **719/634-6666;** www.gardenofgods.com), is a beautiful giant rock garden, composed of spectacular red-sandstone formations sculpted by rain and wind over millions of years. Located where several life zones and ecosystems converge, the city-run park harbors a variety of plant and animal communities. Hiking maps for the 1,300-acre park are available at the visitor center. Admission is free; a 12-minute multimedia theater presentation, *How Did Those Red Rocks Get There?* ($5 adults, $2 children 5–12), newly remade by local filmmaker John Bourbonais in 2008 in high definition, is an excellent introduction to the geologic history of the area.

Colorado Springs's pride and joy, the **United States Air Force Academy,** off I-25 exit 156B (© 719/333-8723; www.usafa.af.mil), is open to the public daily. Soon after entering the grounds, you'll see an outdoor B-52 bomber display. After another mile or so, look to your left to see the Parade Ground, where cadets can sometimes be spotted marching. Six miles from the entrance, signs mark the turnoff to the visitor center. Nearby is the Cadet Chapel, whose 17 gleaming spires soar 150 feet skyward. After leaving the visitor center, you will pass Falcon Stadium and then Thunderbird Airmanship Overlook, where you might be lucky enough to see cadets parachuting, soaring, and practicing takeoffs and landings in U.S. Air Force Thunderbirds.

There is perhaps no view in Colorado equal to the 360-degree panorama from the 14,110-foot summit of Pikes Peak (but it's not for anyone with heart or breathing problems or a fear of heights). One way to get there is by taking a ride on the **Pikes Peak Cog Railway,** 515 Ruxton Ave., Manitou Springs (© 719/685-5401; www.cograilway.com), after you've acclimated to the high elevations. The 9-mile route, with grades up to 25%, takes 75 minutes to reach the top of Pikes Peak, and the round-trip requires 3 hours and 10 minutes (including a 40-min. stopover at the top). Take a jacket or sweater—it can be cold and windy on top, even on warm summer days. It's $31 to $33 adults, $17 to $18 children 11 and under (those 2 and under held on an adult's lap ride free). There are several departures daily, and reservations are required.

Another way to take in this spectacular view is to drive the **Pikes Peak Highway,** off U.S. 24 at Cascade; take I-25 exit 141 west on U.S. 24 about 10 miles (© 800/318-9505 or 719/385-7325; www.pikespeakcolorado.com). This 19-mile road (paved for 7 miles, graded gravel thereafter) starts at 7,400 feet, some 4 miles west of Manitou Springs, with numerous photo stops as you head up the mountain. There's a toll of $10 per person, $5 for kids ages 6 to 15, or $35 per car.

The **United States Olympic Complex,** 1 Olympic Plaza, at the corner of Boulder Street (entrance) and Union Boulevard (© 888/659-8687 or 719/866-4618; www.usolympicteam.com), houses a sophisticated training center for many U.S. Olympic sports. Free guided tours, available daily, show off the center's state-of-the-art facilities, where you may see athletes sharpening their skills. The visitor center includes the U.S. Olympic Hall of Fame, interactive kiosks on Olympic subjects, various other displays, and a gift shop that sells Olympic-logo merchandise.

WHERE TO STAY

In addition to the listings below, we highly recommend the **Cliff House at Pikes Peak,** 306 Cañon Ave., Manitou Springs (© 888/212-7000 or 719/685-3000; www.thecliffhouse.com; $145–$200 double), a beautifully restored historic hotel with an outstanding restaurant. Our favorite B&Bs are the **Old Town GuestHouse,** 115 S. 26th St. (© 888/375-4210 or 719/632-9194; www.oldtown-guesthouse.com); the **Holden House 1902 Bed & Breakfast Inn,** 1102 W. Pikes Peak Ave. (© 888/565-3980 or 719/471-3980; www.holdenhouse.com; $99–$210 double); and the **Two Sisters Inn,** 10 Otoe Place, Manitou Springs (© 800/2-SIS-INN [274-7466] or 719/685-9684; www.twosisinn.com; $94–$188 double). Bargain hunters should try the simple, well-maintained rooms at the **Travel Inn,** 512 S. Nevada Ave. (© 719/636-3986; $49–$89 double). There are also numerous chain options available in the area.

The Broadmoor (Best) (Kids) The best of the best, the Broadmoor is a sprawling, family-friendly resort complex of historic pink Italian Renaissance–style buildings, built in 1918 upon magnificently landscaped 3,000-acre grounds at the foot of Cheyenne Mountain. The hotel's marble staircase, chandeliers, Italian tile, carved-marble fountain, and art collection are quite a spectacle. The spacious and luxurious rooms are beautifully decorated in European style, with Italian fabrics, rich wood, and original works of art. Most units hold two double beds or one king-size bed, desks and tables, plush seating, two-line portable phones, and wireless Internet access. Service is impeccable. There's an array of bars and restaurants of every level of formality, including the outstanding Charles Court, plus, the number of recreational activities, from horseback riding to fly-fishing, is extensive.

Lake Circle, at Lake Ave. (P.O. Box 1439), Colorado Springs, CO 80901. (C) **800/634-7711** or 719/634-7711. Fax 719/577-5700. www.broadmoor.com. 700 units. May–Oct $420–$565 double, $625–$1,000 standard suite; Nov–Apr $300–$420 double, $425–$850 standard suite; year-round up to $3,400 large suite. AE, DC, DISC, MC, V. Self-parking $14; valet $16. **Amenities:** 12 restaurants; 3 swimming pools (1 indoor); 3 18-hole golf courses; 9 all-weather tennis courts; state-of-the-art fitness center; full-service spa.

Eastholme in the Rockies Nestled in the quaint Pikes Peak mountain village of Cascade, 10 miles west of downtown Colorado Springs, this Victorian B&B gives guests an opportunity to see the city and get away from it all in the same day. Originally built in 1885 as a resort hotel, this property has a storied history that includes a stint as a boardinghouse before becoming a guest inn in 1988. Most of the inn's large rooms feature 10-foot ceilings, and all provide plush quilts and remarkable views. The Marriott and Eisenhower suites feature original furnishings and a plethora of antiques, and the cottages offer DVD players, fireplaces, and spacious bathrooms with whirlpool tubs. Breakfasts include freshly baked breads, pastries, and soufflés or frittatas; gourmet dinners are available with advance reservations. Guest amenities include a wedding gazebo, shared kitchen, and library. Smoking is not permitted.

4445 Hagerman Ave. (P.O. Box 98), Cascade, CO 80809. (C) **800/672-9901** or 719/684-9901. www.eastholme.com. 8 units (6 with bathroom), including 2 cottages. $95–$135 double; $135 suite; $150 cottage. Rates include full breakfast. DISC, MC, V. 10 miles west of I-25, about 1 mile off U.S. 24. **Amenities:** Outdoor hot tub. *In room:* Fridge.

WHERE TO DINE

In addition to the listings below, we recommend any of the restaurants at the **Broadmoor** or the **Cliff House at Pikes Peak.**

Craftwood Inn (Best) COLORADO CUISINE Ensconced in an English Tudor building with beamed ceilings, stained-glass windows, and a copper-hooded fireplace, the Craftwood Inn specializes in regional game, including antelope and wild boar, plus seafood, steak, chicken, and vegetarian dishes. Save room for one of the superb desserts. The outdoor patio provides wonderful views of Pikes Peak.

404 El Paso Blvd., Manitou Springs. (C) **719/685-9000.** www.craftwood.com. Reservations recommended. Main courses $24–$38. AE, DC, DISC, MC, V. Daily 5:30–8:30pm. Turn north off Manitou Ave. onto Mayfair Ave., go uphill 1 block, and turn left onto El Paso Blvd.; the Craftwood is on your right.

Margarita at PineCreek ECLECTIC This delightful restaurant, with a tree-shaded outdoor patio and simply decorated dining room, offers the perfect spot to sit and watch the sun setting over Pikes Peak. Six-course dinners offer three choices of entrees, often including a seafood selection, with an emphasis on fresh ingredients. The food is top-notch.

Saturday evenings bring live harpsichord music in the dining room, and Friday nights often feature live acoustic music—bluegrass to Celtic.

7350 Pine Creek Rd. (C) **719/598-8667.** Reservations recommended. Fixed-price lunch $10–$11; fixed-price dinner $30–$38; brunch $10–$15. AE, DISC, MC, V. Tues–Fri 11:30am–2pm; Tues–Sat 5:30–9pm; Sun 10:30am–2pm.

Phantom Canyon Brewing Co. AMERICAN   This popular brewpub is in the Cheyenne Building, home to the Chicago, Rock Island & Pacific Railroad from 1902 to 1909. On any given day, 8 to 10 of Phantom Canyon's specialty beers are on tap, including their homemade root beer. Selections here are typical brewpub at lunch, when you might get wood-fired pizzas, salads, burgers, and fish and chips. The dinner menu is varied and more innovative, with choices such as roasted chicken and hot bacon salad, Queen's Blonde Ale soup, steak, and trout.

2 E. Pikes Peak Ave. (C) **719/635-2800.** Main courses $8–$13 lunch, $9–$25 dinner. AE, DC, DISC, MC, V. Mon–Thurs 11am–10pm; Fri–Sat 11am–midnight; Sun 10am–10pm. Bar open later.

COLORADO SPRINGS AFTER DARK

Current weekly entertainment schedules can be found in the Friday *Gazette.* Also check the listings in the *Independent* (a free weekly). A good online resource for events and nightlife, as well as restaurants, is **www.sceneinthesprings.com.** Tickets for many major entertainment and sporting events can be obtained from **Ticketmaster** ((C) **719/520-9090;** www.ticketmaster.com).

THE PERFORMING ARTS   Pikes Peak Center, the Colorado Springs Fine Arts Center, City Auditorium, Colorado College, and the various facilities at the U.S. Air Force Academy are all venues for the performing arts. The city's newest facility is the 8,000-seat **Colorado Springs World Arena,** 3185 Venetucci Blvd., at I-25 exit 138 ((C) **719/477-2100;** www.worldarena.com), which hosts big-name country and rock concerts as well as a variety of sporting events.

THE BAR & CLUB SCENE   Two-steppers and country-western music lovers flock to **Cowboys** (25 N. Tejon St.; (C) **719/596-1212;** www.cowboyscs.com), which offers dance lessons and live music. There's an eclectic offering of live music at **Poor Richard's Restaurant,** 324¹/₂ N. Tejon St. ((C) **719/632-7721**). Bijou Bar and Grill, 2510 W. Bijou Ave. ((C) **719/473-5718**), is Southern Colorado's longest-standing gay and lesbian bar. **15C,** located just off Bijou Street in the alley between Cascade Avenue and Tejon Street ((C) **719/635-8303**), is a slick martini and cigar bar with an upscale ambience accented by dim lighting and leather couches.

6 SOUTHWESTERN COLORADO

A land apart from the rest of the state, southwestern Colorado is set off by the spectacular mountain wall of the San Juan Range. The Ancestral Puebloans (also called Anasazi) who once lived here created spectacular cliff dwellings, which you can see at Mesa Verde National Park.

This area is also John Wayne country, where the Duke slugged it out and shot it out as he tamed the West on movie screens from the late 1920s through the 1970s. It was also the location shoot for *Butch Cassidy and the Sundance Kid,* and for *City Slickers,* with Billy Crystal as a hapless city dweller on an Old West–style cattle drive.

Born as a railroad town more than a century ago, Durango remains a railroad town to this day, as thousands of visitors take a journey back in time aboard the Durango & Silverton Narrow Gauge Railroad.

Essentials

GETTING THERE   Durango is at the crossroads of east-west U.S. 160 and north-south U.S. 550. By plane, there's frequent service from several major airlines to **Durango/La Plata County Airport,** 14 miles southeast of Durango off Colo. 172 (© **970/247-8143;** www.flydurango.com).

VISITOR INFORMATION   Contact the **Durango Area Tourism Office,** 111 S. Camino del Rio, Durango, CO 81302 (© **800/463-8726;** www.durango.org). The **Durango Visitor Center** is just south of downtown, on U.S. 160/550. June through October, it's open Monday through Saturday from 8am to 5pm, and Sunday from 10am to 4pm; the rest of the year, hours are from 8am to 5pm Monday through Friday.

SPECIAL EVENTS & FESTIVALS   Mid-July through the first week of August, the **Music in the Mountains** classical music festival (© **970/385-6820;** www.musicinthe mountains.com) takes place at locations in and around Durango.

Exploring the Area

Colorado's most famous train (and Durango's best attraction), the **Durango & Silverton Narrow Gauge Railroad,** 479 Main Ave. (© **888/872-4607** or 970/247-2733; www. durangotrain.com), has been in operation since 1881. In all that time, its route has never varied: up the Rio de las Animas Perdidas (River of Lost Souls), through 45 miles of mountains and San Juan National Forest wilderness to the historic mining town of Silverton, and back. The coal-fired steam locomotives pull strings of gold-colored Victorian coaches on the 3,000-foot climb, past relics of mining and railroad activity from the last century. In summer, the trip takes $3^{1}/_{4}$ hours each way, with a 2-hour stopover in Silverton before the return trip. Summer round-trip fare starts at $75 adults, $45 children 5 to 11. Parking is $7 per day per car.

The **Durango & Silverton Narrow Gauge Railroad Museum,** 479 Main Ave. (© **970/247-2733**), contains exhibits on steam trains, historical photos, and railroad art. It also has restored railroad cars and a locomotive that can be entered. Hours correspond to the train depot hours, and museum admission is included with train excursion tickets. Admission to the museum only is $5 adults, $2.50 children 11 and under.

Those interested in a close-up view of Durango's numerous historic buildings can pick up free walking-tour brochures from the visitor center. There are particularly interesting banks, saloons, churches, and fine homes along Main and Third avenues.

Outdoor Activities

The varied terrain and myriad trails of **San Juan National Forest** have made Durango a nationally known mountain-biking center. The Colorado Trail, Hermosa Creek Trail (beginning 11 miles north of Durango off U.S. 550), and La Plata Canyon Road (beginning 11 miles west of Durango off U.S. 160) are favorite jaunts. You can also get information and rent mountain bikes at **Hassle Free Sports,** 2615 Main Ave. (© **800/835-3800** or 970/259-3874; www.hasslefreesports.com), which rents full-suspension mountain bikes for $35 per half-day or $45 for a full day.

The three stages of the Animas River provide excitement for rafters of all experience and ability levels. Most outfitters in Durango offer a wide variety of rafting excursions, such as 2- to 4-hour raft trips that cost $25 to $45 for adults and $20 to $35 for kids; and full-day river trips, which include lunch, costing $75 for adults and $65 for kids. Among our favorite companies are **Durango Rivertrippers** (© **800/292-2885** or 970/259-0289; www.durangorivertrippers.com), **Mild to Wild Rafting** (© **800/567-6745** or 970/247-4789; www.mild2wildrafting.com), and **Mountain Waters Rafting** (© **800/585-8243** or 970/259-4191; www.durangorafting.com).

Some 25 miles north of Durango on U.S. 550, **Durango Mountain Resort,** 1 Skier Place, Durango, CO 81301 (© **800/982-6103** or 970/247-9000; www.durangomountain resort.com), has a reputation of getting more sunshine than any other Colorado ski area, although the average annual snowfall is 260 inches. There are 85 trails for all levels, served by 11 lifts. Snowboarders are welcome on all lifts and trails, and a snowboard park offers jumps, slides, and a quarter-pipe. The Durango Nordic Center has 16km of trails for Nordic skiers for both classic and skate skiing.

Where to Stay

An easy way to book accommodations is to contact **Durango Central Reservations** (© **866/294-5187;** www.durangoreservations.org). Room taxes add 9.4% to lodging bills.

Durango's most famous lodging is the 1887 **Strater Hotel,** 699 Main Ave. (© **800/247-4431** or 970/247-4431; www.strater.com), a wonderful place to relax and soak up the ambience of the real Old West (at least, the real Old West for those who had money). It's an exceptional example of American Victorian architecture, with one of the world's largest collections of American Victorian walnut antiques, and home to a superb restaurant plus the Diamond Belle Saloon, where author Louis L'Amour gave life to his Western heroes. Service is superb. Doubles run $175 to $265 in high season.

Another National Historic Landmark, the 1892 **Rochester Hotel,** 726 E. Second Ave. (© **800/664-1920** or 970/385-1920; www.rochesterhotel.com), also captures the feel of the Old West and is among our favorite places to stay in Durango. Rates run $129 to $219 double.

The **Wit's End Guest Ranch & Resort,** 254 C.R. 500, Bayfield (© **800/236-9483** or 970/884-4113; www.witsendranch.com), is a delightful, if pricey, dude ranch encompassing 550 acres on Vallecito Lake, surrounded by the peaks of the Weminuche Wilderness; it's a unique combination of rustic outdoors and sophisticated luxury. Rates start at $2,549 per guest per week per cabin.

THE SAN JUAN SKYWAY

The San Juan Skyway, a 233-mile circuit that crosses five mountain passes, takes in the magnificent San Juan Mountains, as well as the cities and towns of the region. It can be accomplished in a single all-day drive from Durango or divided into several days, incorporating stops in Cortez, Telluride, and Ouray. Check for closed passes in winter and early spring. The route can be driven either clockwise (heading west from Durango on U.S. 160) or counterclockwise (heading north from Durango on U.S. 550). We'll describe the clockwise route.

Leaving Durango, 11 miles west you'll pass through the village of Hesperus, from which a county road runs 10 miles north into **La Plata Canyon,** with its mining ruins and ghost towns.

Farther west, U.S. 160 passes the entrance road to **Mesa Verde National Park.** About 45 miles west of Durango, just before Cortez, turn north on Colo. 145, which traverses the historic town of Dolores, site of the **Anasazi Heritage Center and Museum,** then proceed up the Dolores River Valley, a favorite of trout fishermen.

Sixty miles from Cortez, the route crosses 10,222-foot **Lizard Head Pass,** named for a rock spire looming above the roadside Alpine meadows. It then descends 13 miles to the town of **Telluride,** set in a beautiful box canyon 4 miles off the main road.

Follow Colo. 145 west from Telluride down the San Miguel River valley to Placerville, then turn north on Colo. 62, across 8,970-foot Dallas Divide, to Ridgway, a historic railroad town and home of **Ridgway State Park** (© **970/626-5822;** www.parks.state. co.us), with a sparkling mountain reservoir.

From Ridgway, turn south, and follow U.S. 550 to the scenic and historic town of Ouray. Here begins the remarkable **Million Dollar Highway,** so named for all the mineral wealth that passed over it.

The 23 miles from Ouray over 11,008-foot **Red Mountain Pass** to Silverton is an unforgettable drive. The drive shimmies up the sheer sides of the Uncompahgre Gorge, goes through tunnels and past cascading waterfalls, then follows a historic toll road built in the 19th century. Mining equipment and log cabins are in evidence on the slopes of the iron-colored mountains, many of them more than 14,000 feet in elevation. Along this route you'll pass a monument to the snowplow operators who died trying to keep the road open during winter storms.

From Silverton, U.S. 550 climbs over the **Molas Divide** (elevation 10,910 ft.), then more or less parallels the track of the Durango & Silverton Narrow Gauge Railroad as it follows the Animas River south to Durango, passing en route the Durango Mountain Resort ski area (see above).

CORTEZ: GATEWAY TO THE ARCHAEOLOGICAL SITES OF THE FOUR CORNERS REGION

Cortez is surrounded by a vast complex of ancient villages that dominated the Four Corners region—where Colorado, New Mexico, Arizona, and Utah meet—1,000 years ago. The inhabitants of those ancient villages, called Ancestral Puebloans, have long been known as the Anasazi, but that Navajo word, considered offensive to some modern Pueblo peoples, is being phased out.

Essentials

GETTING THERE   By Plane   Cortez Airport, off U.S. 160 and 491, southwest of town (© **970/565-7458;** www.cityofcortez.com), is served by **Great Lakes Airlines** (© **800/554-5111** or 970/565-9510), with direct flights to Denver.

By Car   Cortez is at the junction of north-south **U.S. 666** and east-west **U.S. 160,** 45 miles west of Durango. As it enters Cortez from the east, **U.S. 160** crosses Dolores Road (Colo. 145, which goes north to Telluride and Grand Junction), then runs due west through town for about 2 miles as Main Street. The city's main thoroughfare, Main Street, eventually intersects U.S. 666 (Broadway) at the west end of town.

VISITOR INFORMATION   Stop at the **Colorado Welcome Center at Cortez/Cortez Area Chamber of Commerce,** 928 E. Main St. (© **970/565-4048** or 565-3414; www. cortezchamber.org), open daily from 8am to 6pm in summer and from 8am to 5pm the rest of the year; or contact the **Mesa Verde Country Visitor Information Bureau** (© **800/253-1616;** www.mesaverdecountry.com).

The Major Archaeological Sites

MESA VERDE NATIONAL PARK   The largest archaeological preserve in the United States, Mesa Verde National Park, located about 10 miles east of Cortez, has some 4,000 known sites dating from A.D. 300 to 1300, including the most impressive cliff dwellings in the Southwest.

The earliest known inhabitants of Mesa Verde (Spanish for "green table") built subterranean pit houses on the mesa tops. During the 13th century they moved into shallow caves and constructed complex cliff dwellings. Although a massive construction project, these homes were occupied for only about a century; their residents left around 1300 for unknown reasons.

The **Cliff Palace,** the park's largest and best-known site, is a four-story apartment complex with stepped-back roofs forming porches for the dwellings above. Accessible by guided tour only, it is reached by a quarter-mile downhill path. Its towers, walls, and kivas (large circular rooms used for ceremonies) are all set back beneath the rim of a cliff. Another ranger-led tour takes visitors up a 32-foot ladder to explore the interior of **Balcony House.** Each tour is given only in summer and into fall (call for exact dates).

Two more important sites—**Step House** and **Long House,** both on Wetherill Mesa— can be visited in summer only. Rangers lead tours to **Spruce Tree House,** another of the major cliff-dwelling complexes, only in winter, when other park facilities are closed. Visitors can also explore Spruce Tree House on their own at any time. Three-hour and 6-hour guided park tours are offered from Far View Lodge (see below) during the summer.

For those who want to avoid hiking and climbing, the 12-mile **Mesa Top Road** makes a number of pit houses and cliff-side overlooks easily accessible by car.

Chapin Mesa, site of the park headquarters, museum, and a post office, is 20 miles from the park entrance on U.S. 160. The **Far View Visitor Center,** site of Far View Lodge, a restaurant, gift shop, and other facilities, is 15 miles off U.S. 160. For a park brochure, contact Mesa Verde National Park, P.O. Box 8, Mesa Verde, CO 81330 (© **970/ 529-4465;** www.nps.gov/meve).

Open from mid-April to mid-October, **Morefield Campground** (© **800/449-2288** or 970/529-4421; www.visitmesaverde.com), 4 miles south of the park entrance, has 435 sites, including 15 with full RV hookups.

Admission to the park for up to 1 week costs $15 per vehicle in summer, $10 spring to fall. Tours of Cliff Palace, Balcony House, and Long House are $3; ranger-guided tours of other areas are free.

UTE MOUNTAIN TRIBAL PARK If you liked Mesa Verde but would have enjoyed it more without the crowds, you'll love the **Ute Mountain Tribal Park,** in Towaoc (© **800/847-5485** or 970/565-3751, ext. 330; www.utemountainute.com/tribalpark. htm). Set aside by the Ute Mountain tribe to preserve its heritage, the 125,000-acre park—which abuts Mesa Verde National Park—includes wall paintings, ancient petroglyphs, and hundreds of surface sites and cliff dwellings that compare in size and complexity with those in Mesa Verde.

Access to the park is strictly limited to guided tours. Full- and half-day tours begin at the Ute Mountain Museum and Visitor Center at the junction of U.S. 491 and U.S. 160, 20 miles south of Cortez. Mountain-biking and backpacking trips are also offered. No food, water, lodging, gasoline, or other services are available within the park. Some climbing of ladders is necessary on the full-day tour. There's one primitive **campground** ($12 per vehicle; reservations required). Charges for tours in your vehicle start at $24 per person for a half-day, $44 for a full day; it's $9 per person extra to go in the tour guide's vehicle, and reservations are required.

Among the chains providing comfortable, reasonably priced lodging in Cortez are **Best Western Turquoise Inn & Suites,** 535 E. Main St. (© 800/547-3376 or 970/565-3778), with rates for two from $79 to $159; **Econo Lodge,** 2020 E. Main St. (© 800/553-2666 or 970/565-3474), with double rates of $59 to $139 in peak season and $39 to $89 the rest of the year; and **Holiday Inn Express,** 2121 E. Main St. (© 888/465-4329 or 970/565-6000), with double rates from $99 to $159. Room tax adds about 8%.

TELLURIDE

This was one seriously rowdy town a century ago—in fact, this is where Butch Cassidy robbed his first bank, in 1889. Telluride became a National Historic District in 1964, and in 1968 entrepreneur Joe Zoline set to work on a "winter recreation area second to none." Today Telluride is a year-round outdoor recreation destination and hosts world-renowned film and music festivals.

Essentials

GETTING THERE   By Car   From Cortez, follow **Colo. 145** northeast for 73 miles. From the north (Montrose), turn west off **U.S. 550** at Ridgway, onto **Colo. 62.** Proceed 25 miles to Placerville and turn left (southeast) onto **Colo. 145.** Thirteen miles ahead is a junction—a right turn will take you to Cortez, but for Telluride, continue straight ahead 4 miles to the end of a box canyon. From Durango, in summer take U.S. 550 north to Colo. 62 and follow the directions above; in winter it's best to take the route through Cortez and avoid Red Mountain Pass above Silverton.

By Plane   Telluride Regional Airport (© **970/728-5313;** www.tellurideairport.com) is served year-round by **Great Lakes Airline** (© 800/554-5111) from Denver. During ski season, flights from various cities are available from **Frontier** (© 800/432-1359), **US Airways** (© 800/428-4322), and **United** (© 800/241-6522).

VISITOR INFORMATION   Contact **Telluride Tourism Board,** 630 W. Colorado Ave. (P.O. Box 1009), Telluride, CO 81435 (© **888/605-2578;** www.visittelluride.com). The **Telluride Visitor Information Center,** open daily from 9am to 6pm, is at the corner of West Colorado Avenue and Davis Street.

SPECIAL EVENTS & FESTIVALS   The **Telluride Film Festival** (© **970/728-4640;** www.telluridefilmfestival.com), an influential event that takes place over Labor Day weekend, has premiered award-winners such as *Brokeback Mountain* and *Juno.* What truly sets it apart, however, is the casual interaction between stars and attendees. Open-air films and seminars are free. The **Telluride Bluegrass Festival** (© **800/624-2422;** www.bluegrass.com) is one of the most renowned bluegrass, folk, and country jam sessions in the U.S. It's held over 4 days in late June.

What to See

To get a glimpse of Telluride's wild and wicked past, stop at the **Telluride Historical Museum,** 201 W. Gregory Ave. (© **970/728-3344;** www.telluridemuseum.com). It was built in 1888 as the community hospital. The museum houses artifacts, historical photos, and exhibits that show what Telluride was like in its Wild West days, when the likes of Butch Cassidy stalked the streets. There are also exhibits on the area's Indian heritage, mining, and even Telluride's ski boom of the 1970s. Admission is $5 adults, $3 seniors and students 6 to 17; the museum is open Tuesday through Saturday from 11am to 5pm, Sunday 1 to 5pm (closed Sun Sept–May).

The best way to see the Telluride National Historic District and get a feel for the West of the late 1800s is to take to the streets, following the excellent **walking tour** described in the *Telluride Visitor's Guide,* available at the Telluride Visitor Information Center (see "Visitor Information," above).

Outdoor Activities

The elegant European-style Mountain Village offers a fascinating contrast to the laid-back community of artists, shopkeepers, and dropouts in the 1870s Victorian mining town of Telluride below. Located midmountain at an elevation of 9,450 feet, the Mountain Village offers ski-in/ski-out accommodations; eight slope-side restaurants, including Gorrono Ranch, a historic homestead; spectacular scenery; and, of course, great skiing for all ability levels. There are 84 trails served by 16 lifts. For snow reports and additional information, contact **Telluride Ski and Golf Company** (© 800/801-4832 or 970/728-6900; www.tellurideskiresort.com).

The Mountain Village at Telluride Ski Resort (see above) has 30km of **Nordic trails,** which connect with 20km of groomed trails at Town Park and River Corridor Trail, giving cross-country skiers a total of 50km. Telluride also has one of the top **snowboarding parks** in Colorado, offering more than 13 acres of terrain.

In addition to splendid skiing and snowboarding, there are numerous outdoor recreation opportunities year-round. The major outfitter and arranger of summertime outdoor activities here is the versatile and dependable **Telluride Outside,** 121 W. Colorado Ave. (© 800/831-6230 or 970/728-3895; www.tellurideoutside.com).

Town Park, at the east end of town (© 970/728-3071; www.town.telluride.co.us), is home to the community's various festivals. It also has a public outdoor pool, open in summer, plus tennis courts, sand volleyball courts, a small outdoor basketball court, a skateboarding ramp, playing fields, a picnic area, and a fishing pond.

There's excellent **fishing** in the San Miguel River through Telluride, but it's even better in nearby Alpine lakes, including Silver Lake, reached by foot in Bridal Veil Basin, and Trout and Priest lakes, about 12 miles south via Colo. 145.

Telluride is a major **mountain-biking** center. The **San Juan Hut System** (© 970/626-3033; www.sanjuanhuts.com) links Telluride with Moab, Utah, via a 206-mile-long network of backcountry dirt roads. Every 35 miles is a primitive cabin, with bunks, a woodstove, a propane cooking stove, and cooking gear. The route is appropriate for intermediate-level riders in good physical condition. Cost for riders who plan to make the whole trip is about $750, which includes use of the six huts, three meals daily, sleeping bags at each hut, and maps and trail descriptions.

Where to Stay

A good way to book lodging is with **ResortQuest Telluride** (© 866/538-7731; www.resortquesttelluride.com). The best way to book lodging, however, is with the **Telluride & Mountain Village Convention & Visitors Bureau** (© 888/605-2578; www.visit telluride.com). Room tax adds a bit over 12%.

Among the top luxury choices is the **Camel's Garden Resort Hotel,** 250 W. San Juan Ave. (© 888/772-2635 or 970/728-9300; www.camelsgarden.com), which has a perfect location—it's ski-in/ski-out and only steps from the town gondola, and also within 2 short blocks of the main shopping-and-dining section of historic Telluride. Doubles run $375 to $675 in high season.

More moderately priced is the **Hotel Telluride,** 199 N. Cornet St., Telluride, CO 81435 (© 970/369-1188; www.thehoteltelluride.com; $219–$259 double), a thoroughly

modern luxury hotel. The **Victorian Inn,** 401 W. Pacific Ave. (𝒞 **800/611-9893** or
970/728-6601; www.tellurideinn.com), is an affordable B&B-style alternative to renting
a condo. Rates run $159 to $249 double in high season.

7 SALT LAKE CITY

Between the Wasatch Mountains on the east and the Great Salt Lake on the west, at an
elevation of 4,330 feet, lies Salt Lake City. Utah's capital is relatively small, with a population of around 180,000. But travelers come from around the world to visit magnificent
Temple Square, world headquarters of the Church of Jesus Christ of Latter-Day Saints
(LDS), and to hear the Mormon Tabernacle Choir.

Exhilarating outdoor recreation possibilities are only about an hour's drive from the
city and include some of the country's best ski resorts; miles of terrific mountain trails
for hiking, biking, and horseback riding; and the intriguing Great Salt Lake.

ESSENTIALS

GETTING THERE   By Plane   Direct flights connect Salt Lake City to almost 70 cities in the United States and Canada. **Salt Lake City International Airport** (𝒞 **800/595-
2442** or 801/575-2400; www.slcairport.com) is located just north of I-80 at exit 115, on
the west side of the city.

By Train   Amtrak has several trains arriving daily from both coasts. The station is at
340 S. 600 W. (𝒞 **800/872-7245;** www.amtrak.com).

By Car   Salt Lake City is 303 miles north of St. George, 238 miles northwest of Moab,
45 miles north of Provo, and 35 miles south of Ogden. You can reach it via **I-80** from
the east (Cheyenne) or west (Reno), or from the north (Pocatello) or south (Las Vegas)
via **I-15.**

VISITOR INFORMATION   The **Salt Lake Convention and Visitors Bureau** has an
information center downtown in the Salt Palace Convention Center, 90 S. West Temple
(𝒞 **800/541-4955** or 801/521-2822; www.visitsaltlake.com). It's open Monday through
Friday from 8:30am to 5pm (until 6pm from Memorial Day to Labor Day), Saturday
and Sunday from 9am to 5pm, and sells the **Connect Pass** ($18 adults, $14 children for
a 1-day pass; 2- and 3-day passes are also available), which covers admission at a dozen
local attractions. Additional information centers, staffed 9am to 9pm daily, can be found
at Salt Lake City International Airport Terminals I and II.

GETTING AROUND   Salt Lake is a fairly easy city in which to drive, with wide streets
and abundant parking. There are many public parking lots in the downtown area, costing
from $1 to $7 per day. Parking on streets downtown is metered, costing 25¢ per half-
hour, and usually limited to 130 minutes or 2 hours.

The **Utah Transit Authority** (𝒞 **888/743-3882** or 801/743-3882; www.utabus.com)
provides **bus service,** with a "free fare zone" in the downtown area. You can ride free
within this zone, getting on and off as many times as you'd like. The fee for traveling in
the other zones is $1.60 per person, 80¢ for seniors and those with disabilities, or $4.25
for a day pass. Some buses are wheelchair accessible, and all have bicycle carriers. **Trax,** a
light-rail system also operated by the Utah Transit Authority, with the same contact
information and same rates as the Utah Transit Authority's bus service (albeit free in the
downtown area), runs 15 miles from the Sandy Civic Center in the Salt Lake City suburb

of Sandy north to EnergySolutions Arena downtown, with another line running east to the University of Utah. The trains are wheelchair accessible and bicycles are permitted. Route schedules and maps for both the buses and light rail are available at malls, libraries, and visitor centers.

For a taxi, contact **City Cab** (𝄞 **801/363-5550**), **Yellow Cab** (𝄞 **801/521-2100**), or **Ute Cab** (𝄞 **801/359-7788**), all available 24 hours a day.

FAST FACTS   For physician referrals, contact the **Utah Medical Association** (𝄞 **801/ 355-7477**) during normal business hours. Hospitals include **LDS Hospital,** 8th Avenue and C Street (𝄞 **801/408-1100**), and **Salt Lake Regional Medical Center,** 1050 E. South Temple (𝄞 **801/350-4111**); both have 24-hour emergency rooms. **Sales tax** is 6.9%, and **lodging taxes** total 11.5%.

EXPLORING TEMPLE SQUARE

This is sacred ground for members of the Church of Jesus Christ of Latter-Day Saints (LDS), also known as Mormons. The 10-acre **Temple Square** is enclosed by 15-foot walls, with a gate in the center of each. In addition to the church buildings, the square houses lovely gardens and statuary, and the North and South Visitor Centers, which have exhibits on the church's history and beliefs, interactive videos, and films. Also in the North Center is an 11-foot-tall replica of the awe-inspiring sculpture *Christus,* a statue of Christ by Danish artist Bertel Thorvaldsen.

The **Temple** is used only for the Mormons' most sacred services and is not open to the public. Early church leader Brigham Young chose the site within 4 days of entering the valley, and work was begun on the six-spired granite structure in 1853. It took 40 years to complete.

The oval **Tabernacle** seats 6,500 people and has one of the West's largest unsupported domed roofs. Boasting unbelievable acoustics, it has served as the city's cultural center for over a century.

On Thursday evenings at 8pm, you can listen to the **Mormon Tabernacle Choir** rehearse (except when they're on tour; call 𝄞 **801/240-3221** or visit www.mormon tabernaclechoir.org for schedules), and on Sunday mornings you can attend their broadcast from 9:30 to 10am (you must be seated by 9:15am). The choir, composed entirely of volunteers, was formed shortly after the first pioneers arrived; many families participate, sometimes over several generations. Half-hour organ recitals take place year-round Monday through Saturday at noon, Sunday at 2pm. At peak times, an additional 2pm recital is often scheduled Monday through Saturday. Admission to these performances is free.

The Gothic-style **Assembly Hall** was constructed in 1880 from leftover granite from the Temple and is often the site of concerts and lectures. Inquire at one of the visitor centers for schedules. Two monuments stand in front of the Assembly Hall: One depicts a pioneer family arriving with a handcart filled with their belongings, and the second commemorates the salvaging of the first crops from a plague of crickets (seagulls swooped down and ate the insects).

Guided tours of the square, lasting approximately 45 minutes and available in 30 languages, leave every few minutes from the flagpole in front of the Tabernacle; personnel in the visitor center can direct you. Tour guides provide a general history of the church (touching upon the church's doctrine) and take you around the square, briefly explaining what you are seeing. Our favorite part of the tour is in the Tabernacle: To demonstrate the incredible acoustics, the group is ushered to the back of the seats while someone stands at the podium and drops three pins—the sound is as clear as a bell!

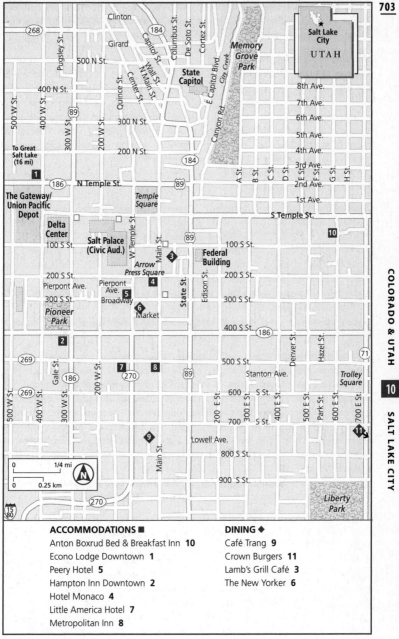

Downtown Salt Lake City map showing streets including Clinton, Girard, 500 N St., 400 N St., 300 N St., 200 N St., N Temple St., 100 S St., 200 S St., 300 S St., 400 S St., 500 S St., Stanton Ave., Lowell Ave., 800 S St., 900 S St., and numbered avenues (1st Ave.–8th Ave.). Landmarks include State Capitol, Memory Grove Park, The Gateway/Union Pacific Depot, Delta Center, Salt Palace (Civic Aud.), Arrow Press Square, Federal Building, Pioneer Park, Temple Square, Trolley Square, and Liberty Park.

ACCOMMODATIONS ■

Anton Boxrud Bed & Breakfast Inn **10**
Econo Lodge Downtown **1**
Peery Hotel **5**
Hampton Inn Downtown **2**
Hotel Monaco **4**
Little America Hotel **7**
Metropolitan Inn **8**

DINING ◆

Café Trang **9**
Crown Burgers **11**
Lamb's Grill Café **3**
The New Yorker **6**

The square is bounded by Main Street on the east, and by North, South, and West Temple streets. Tours are given daily from 9am to 8pm. Call © **800/537-9703** or 801/240-4872 for information, or browse www.visittemplesquare.com or www.lds.org.

MORE ATTRACTIONS

Beehive House   Brigham Young built this house in 1854 as his family home, but he also kept an office and entertained church and government leaders here. Young, who loved New England architecture, used much of that style, even including a widow's walk for keeping an eye on the surrounding desert. Today visitors can get a glimpse of the lifestyle of this famous Mormon leader by taking a guided half-hour tour of the house. It has been decorated with period furniture (many pieces original to the home) to resemble its appearance when Young lived here. Allow 1 hour.

67 E. South Temple. © **801/240-2671.** www.lds.org/placestovisit. Free admission. Mon–Sat 9am–9pm. Trax: Temple Sq.; walk a half-block east.

Capitol Building   Built between 1912 and 1915 (and restored and earthquake-proofed from 2004–08) of unpolished Utah granite and Georgia marble, the capitol rests on a hill in a beautifully landscaped 40-acre park. The state symbol, the beehive (representing industry and cooperation), is a recurring motif both inside and out. The Rotunda, which stretches upward 165 feet, is decorated with WPA murals and houses several busts of prominent historical figures, including Brigham Young and Philo T. Farnsworth, the man who brought us television. The chandelier is astounding—it weighs 6,000 pounds and hangs from a 7,000-pound chain. Allow 1 to 2 hours.

Capitol Hill, at the north end of State St. © **801/538-3000.** www.utahstatecapitol.utah.gov. Free admission and tours. Building daily 8am–8pm; guided tours Mon–Fri 9am–4pm. Bus: 23 up Main St.

Family History Library   This incredible facility contains what is probably the world's largest collection of genealogical records under one roof. Most date from 1550 to 1920 and are from governments, churches, other organizations, and individuals. The collection is composed of a substantial number of records from around the United States, fairly comprehensive data from Scotland and England, and information from many other countries. When you enter the library, you'll find people ready to assist with your research. They'll offer forms you can fill out with any and all data you already know (so come prepared with copies of whatever you have), and can direct you from there. Allow at least 2 hours.

35 N. West Temple. © **866/406-1830** or 801/240-2584. www.familysearch.org. Free admission. Mon 8am–5pm; Tues–Sat 8am–9pm. Closed major holidays and July 24. Trax: Temple Sq.

This Is the Place Heritage Park   Brigham Young and the first group of pioneers got their first glimpse of the Salt Lake Valley here. A tall granite and bronze sculpture was erected in 1947 to commemorate the centennial of their arrival. Old Deseret is a village made up of original pioneer buildings from across the state. In the summer, it becomes a living history museum of the years 1847 to 1869, featuring people in period garb living and working the way their forefathers did. Pioneer events and demonstrations are offered throughout the year. The 1,600-acre park also offers hiking along part of the trail used by the pioneers, plus picnicking, bird-watching, and cross-country skiing. Allow 1 to 3 hours.

2601 E. Sunnyside Ave. © **801/582-1847.** www.thisistheplace.org. Free admission to park and visitor center. Admission to Heritage Village $8 adults, $6 children 3–11 and seniors 62 and over ($2 less on Sun). Park daily dawn–dusk; visitor center Mon–Sat 9am–6pm; Heritage Village summer daily 9am–5pm, call for off-season hours.

In addition to the properties discussed below, we recommend the **Hotel Monaco,** 105 W. 200 S. (© **800/294-9710** or 801/595-0000; www.monaco-saltlakecity.com; $139–$209 double), in the 14-story former Continental Bank Building. The lobby and rooms are a mix of classic and contemporary, pets are welcome (the pet-less are provided with goldfish), and Sweet Tarts replace the usual pillow mints. The Monaco also has an excellent restaurant, **Bambara,** and complimentary Wi-Fi throughout the building. The **Little America Hotel,** 500 S. Main St. (© **800/453-9450** or 801/363-6781; www.littleamerica. com/slc; $99–$209 double), is among Salt Lake City's best hotels, offering a wide variety of rooms, all individually decorated, that range from standard courtside rooms in the two-story motel-like buildings to extra-large deluxe tower suites in the 17-story high-rise.

Affordable and comfortable, the **Metropolitan Inn,** 524 S. West Temple (© **801/531-7100;** www.metropolitaninn.com; $67–$99 double), is a former chain hotel turned first-rate independent. Or try the **Econo Lodge,** 715 W. North Temple (© **877/233-2666** or 801/363-0062), or the **Hampton Inn Downtown,** 425 S. 300 W. (© **800/426-7866** or 801/741-1110).

The huge **Salt Lake KOA/VIP,** 1400 W. North Temple (© **800/562-9510** or 801/355-1214; www.slckoa.com), is the closest camping and RV facility to downtown Salt Lake City. Sites are $28 to $50, cabins $49 to $54.

Anton Boxrud Bed & Breakfast Inn This former boardinghouse, built in 1901, is a lovely, comfortable bed-and-breakfast inn. Each room is individually decorated with a mix of antiques and reproductions; all have queen-size beds with down comforters. Pocket doors and stained-glass windows grace the sitting room, where guests gather to enjoy evening refreshments. The homemade full breakfast includes a hot dish, and a continental breakfast is available for early risers. The entire property is nonsmoking.

57 S. 600 E., Salt Lake City, UT 84102. © **800/524-5511** or 801/363-8035. Fax 801/596-1316. www.anton boxrud.com. 7 units, 2 single rooms with shared bathroom. $85–$160 double. Rates include full breakfast. AE, DC, DISC, MC, V. *In room:* No phone.

Peery Hotel (Best) The 1910 Peery is the only truly historic hotel in downtown Salt Lake City. It has been fully renovated and restored to its former understated European elegance, offering comfortable, tastefully decorated accommodations. Each unique, handsomely appointed room contains period furnishings and pedestal sinks with antique brass fixtures in the bathroom. Wi-Fi is complimentary, some units have fridges, and a few suites have jetted tubs. The entire hotel is nonsmoking.

110 W. 300 S. (Broadway), Salt Lake City, UT 84101. © **800/331-0073** or 801/521-4300. Fax 801/575-5014. www.peeryhotel.com. 73 units. $99–$159 double; $169 and up suite. AE, DC, DISC, MC, V. Parking fee $9 per day self or valet. **Amenities:** 2 restaurants; exercise room. *In room:* Fridge in some.

WHERE TO DINE

In-the-know locals say that **Crown Burgers,** 3190 S. Highland Dr. (© **801/467-6633**), serves the best fast-food burger in town. The upscale European hunting lodge decor sets it apart from your average hamburger joint. Additional locations include 377 E. 200 S. (© **801/532-1155**) and 118 N. 300 W. (© **801/532-5300**).

Café Trang VIETNAMESE/CHINESE Serving the best Vietnamese food in the state, this family-run restaurant also serves Cantonese dishes with some Vietnamese influences. A popular vegetarian specialty is the fried bean curd with grilled onions and crushed peanuts, served with rice papers, a vegetable platter, and peanut sauce. The dining room is decorated with Vietnamese paintings, and two large aquariums give you something to watch while waiting for your food.

818 S. Main St. ⓒ **801/539-1638.** www.cafetrangutah.com. Reservations recommended in winter. Main courses $8–$14. AE, DISC, MC, V. Mon–Thurs 11:30am–9:30pm; Fri–Sat 11:30am–10pm; Sun 4:30–9:30pm.

Lamb's Grill Cafe AMERICAN/CONTINENTAL   Lamb's has been here since 1939, offering very good food at reasonable prices, with friendly, efficient service. Decorated with antiques and furnishings from the 1920s and 1930s, Lamb's is comfortable and unpretentious. The extensive menu offers mostly basic American and Continental fare, although the restaurant's Greek origins are also evident. Several lamb dishes appear on the menu, including broiled French-style lamb chops and barbecued lamb shank. You'll also find a good selection of sandwiches and salads, daily pasta and salad specials, and a variety of desserts, including an extra-special rice pudding. Full liquor service is available.

169 S. Main St. ⓒ **801/364-7166.** http://lambsgrill.com. Main courses $5–$21. AE, DC, DISC, MC, V. Mon–Fri 7am–9pm; Sat 8am–9pm.

The New Yorker (Best) AMERICAN   Among Salt Lake's finest restaurants, the elegant New Yorker is noted for quiet sophistication, excellent food, and impeccable service. As it's technically a private club (and thus able to offer complete liquor service even without a food purchase), you'll have to buy a membership to enter (a well-spent $4). Sit either in the dining room or in the less formal cafe, where you'll dine under the original stained-glass ceiling from the old Hotel Utah. From the dining-room dinner menu, you might choose the superb Dungeness crab cakes or the roasted rack of American lamb with rosemary cream sauce. The cafe menu offers lighter choices.

60 W. Market St. ⓒ **801/363-0166.** www.newyorkerslc.com. Reservations recommended. Dining room main courses $10–$20 lunch, $22–$35 dinner; cafe main courses $10–$20. AE, DC, DISC, MC, V. Dining room Mon–Thurs 11:30am–2:30pm and 5:30–10pm; Fri 11:30am–2:30pm and 5:30–10:30pm; Sat 5:30–10:30pm. Cafe Mon–Thurs 11:30am–2:30pm and 4:30–10:30pm; Fri 11:30am–2:30pm and 4:30–11pm; Sat 5:30–11pm.

SALT LAKE CITY AFTER DARK

THE PERFORMING ARTS   The historic **Capitol Theatre,** 50 W. 200 S. (ⓒ **801/355-2787**), is home to several local performing arts companies. It's the place to go for dance, theater, and musical productions. The **Utah Symphony & Opera** (ⓒ **801/533-6683;** www.utahsymphonyopera.org) combines one of the country's top symphony orchestras and the well-respected Utah Opera Company. They present four operas a year plus a year-round symphony season at Abravanel Hall, 123 W. South Temple, an elegant 2,800-seat venue known for its excellent acoustics.

The **Pioneer Theatre Company,** 300 S. 1400 E., Room 325 (ⓒ **801/581-6961;** www.pioneerthatre.org), is Utah's resident professional theater. Its repertoire ranges from classical to contemporary plays and musicals.

Tickets for performances at a variety of venues can be obtained from **Art-Tix** (ⓒ **888/451-2787** or 801/355-2787; www.arttix.org).

THE CLUB & BAR SCENE   One of the city's more with-it and cosmopolitan nightspots is **Mynt Lounge,** 63 W. 100 S. (ⓒ **801/355-6968**), an upscale bar with an extensive martini menu. This place attracts one of Salt Lake City's hippest crowds. Established in 1965, the **Dead Goat Saloon,** 119 S. West Temple, in Arrow Press Square (ⓒ **801/328-4628;** www.deadgoat.com), is a fun, funky bar featuring live blues bands. **Squatter's Pub Brewery,** 147 W. Broadway (ⓒ **801/305-2739**), brews top-notch suds and thumbs its nose at local conservatism with such beer names as Provo Girl and Chasing Tail.

You say you want snow? Here it is, some 500 inches of it every year, just waiting for powder-hungry skiers to make that short drive from Salt Lake City. You'll find Brighton and Solitude ski resorts in Big Cottonwood Canyon, and Alta and Snowbird in its sister canyon, known as Little Cottonwood.

If you're on a budget, you might want to stay in Salt Lake City, where lodging is much cheaper, rather than at the resorts themselves. The resorts are so close—less than an hour's drive—that city dwellers sometimes hit the slopes after a hard day at the office. Full-day adult lift ticket prices at these resorts range from $53 during the day to around $30 at night, with Alta and Brighton offering the best bargains.

But this area is more than just a winter playground. Big Cottonwood Canyon, cut by ancient rivers over centuries, is a spectacular setting for warm-weather picnicking, camping, mountain-biking, and hiking. Rugged, glacier-carved Little Cottonwood Canyon is filled with lush fields of wildflowers in the summer; that rainbow of color later takes a back seat to the brilliant hues of autumn.

Brighton Ski Resort (© **800/873-5512** or 801/532-4731; www.brightonresort.com) is a low-key, family-friendly resort. The ski school is highly regarded, children 10 and under stay and ski free with their parents, and teens enjoy the bumps of Lost Maid Trail as it winds through the woods. Brighton's slopes are graced with a full range of terrain, all the powder you can ski, and virtually no crowds. Brighton is also one of the best snowboarding destinations in the state.

Solitude (© **800/748-4754** or 801/534-1400; www.skisolitude.com) is another friendly, family-oriented ski area that hasn't been "discovered" yet, so lift lines are virtually nonexistent. Solitude enjoys excellent powder. Its 1,200-plus acres of skiable terrain range from well-groomed, sunny beginner and intermediate trails to gently pitched bowls and glades. Intermediates also have several excellent forest runs and some great bumpy stretches on which to hone their mogul skills. Advanced skiers will also find plenty to keep them happy. Solitude boasts a world-class Nordic center, which connects to Brighton Ski Resort.

Alta (© **801/359-1078**; www.alta.com) is famous for its snow—over 500 inches annually of some of the lightest powder in the world—and its lift tickets are one of the best skiing bargains in the country (around $60 a day). This is an excellent choice for serious skiers of all levels. Intermediates will find plenty of open cruising ground, forested areas, and long arcing chutes to glide through; experts will find an abundance of the Cottonwood Canyons' famous powder and spectacular runs, like steep, long Alf's High Rustler. Alta has chosen to limit its uphill capacity by not installing high-speed quads, and people are turned away on those occasions when the ski gods determine there are already enough skiers on the mountain. There's a highly regarded ski school here, too. Snowboarding is not permitted.

Snowbird Ski & Summer Resort (© **800/232-9542** or 801/742-2222; www.snowbird. com) offers super skiing and super facilities. Consistently rated among America's top-10 ski resorts, Snowbird has been called Alta's "younger, slicker sister." You'll find the same wonderful snow here, but with a wider range of amenities, including Snowbird's extremely popular spa and salon—worth the trip even if you don't ski. Some, however, find its dense, modern village and resort atmosphere cold compared to Alta's historic, European-style lodges and ruggedly Western attitude. Snowbird gives over almost half of its skiable terrain to the expert skier. There's not a lot for beginners and intermediates, but enough to keep them happy—what is here is top-notch. The entire mountain is open to snowboarders.

GETTING THERE   From Salt Lake City, take I-215 south to exit 7; follow Utah 210 south. Turn east onto Utah 190 to reach Solitude and Brighton in Big Cottonwood Canyon; continue on Utah 210 south and east to Snowbird and Alta in Little Cottonwood Canyon. From Salt Lake City International Airport, it'll take about an hour to reach any of the four ski areas.

8 PARK CITY: UTAH'S PREMIER RESORT TOWN

Park City reminds us of Aspen, Colorado, a historic Western town that has made the most of excellent ski terrain, evolving into a popular year-round vacation destination, offering a casual Western atmosphere with a touch of elegance—for those willing to pay for it. Today's visitors will find three separate ski areas, lodgings that range from basic to luxurious, some of the state's most innovative restaurants and best shops, an abundance of fine performing arts events, many of Utah's liveliest nightspots, and plenty of hiking, mountain biking, fishing, and other outdoor opportunities.

ESSENTIALS

GETTING THERE   Park City is 32 miles east of Salt Lake City via I-80. At exit 145, take Utah 224 into Park City. Driving time from Salt Lake City International Airport is about 35 minutes.

VISITOR INFORMATION   The **Park City Chamber of Commerce/Convention and Visitors Bureau,** 1910 Prospector Ave. (P.O. Box 1630), Park City, UT 84060 (© 800/453-1360 or 435/649-6100; www.parkcityinfo.com), is open Monday through Friday from 8am to 5pm. It operates a visitor information center at 1826 W. Olympic Pkwy. near I-80, open daily from 9am to 6pm; and another center in the Park City Historical Society Museum, 518 Main St., open Monday through Saturday from 10am to 7pm and Sunday from noon to 6pm.

GETTING AROUND   Parking in Park City is tough, especially in the historic Main Street area. The best plan is to park your car and ride the free city bus. Park City's efficient transit system connects Deer Valley, Main Street, the Canyons, the factory store area, and the Park City Mountain Resort. The **Main Street Trolley** links Main Street and Park City Mountain Resort, and **public buses** travel to the outlying areas. Pick up the *Transit System Guide* brochure for a good route map and specific schedules. *This Week in Park City* contains helpful info plus area maps, including one of Main Street. Both are available at the visitor centers and many lodgings.

SPECIAL EVENTS & FESTIVALS   Throughout the summer, free concerts are presented each Wednesday evening from 6 to 8pm at City Park. One week you might hear bluegrass; the next, classical; and yet another it might be rock or jazz.

The **Deer Valley Music Festival** (© 801/533-6683; www.deervalleymusicfestival.org) is in July and August. The program includes classical masterpieces, plus jazz and popular works by composers such as Gilbert and Sullivan and John Philip Sousa. There are also concerts by acts such as Air Supply and the Gatlin Brothers. The stage faces the mountainside; bring a chair or blanket and relax under the stars.

The **Park City International Music Festival** (© 435/649-5309; www.pcmusicfestival.com) presents classical performances year-round and goes all out for its summer concert series from early July to early August. Musicians from around the world attend, **709** and programs feature soloists, chamber music, and orchestras.

In January, the **Sundance Film Festival** takes place, with numerous film showings in Park City (see "Sundance," later in this chapter).

SKIING THE PARK CITY AREA RESORTS

The three area ski resorts, all within a few minutes' drive of Park City, are vastly different. Many skiers try all three resorts, and if you're going to do so, it will pay to do a bit of advance planning. The resorts offer a **"Silver Passport,"** a discounted multiday package for use at all three resorts. There are various restrictions, though, including that it *must* be purchased before your arrival in Park City, and that it must be purchased in conjunction with lodging. Contact the Park City Chamber of Commerce for details.

Utah's most elegant and sophisticated ski area, **Deer Valley** (© 800/424-3337 or 435/649-1000; www.deervalley.com) offers perfectly manicured slopes, ski valet service, heated sidewalks, and some of the state's finest dining and lodging. Along with all this, you get great skiing—especially if you crave long, smooth, perfectly groomed cruising runs that let you enjoy the spectacular mountain scenery around you.

Park City Mountain Resort (© 800/222-7275 or 435/649-8111; www.parkcity mountain.com), one of Utah's largest and liveliest resorts, is where the U.S. Olympic ski team comes to train. What brings them here? Plenty of dependable, powdery snow and a variety of terrain and runs that offer something for everyone. Surveys continually rank Park City among the country's top resorts for both its terrain and its challenging runs. There's a triple-chair access lift directly from the Old Town onto the mountain, as well as two runs that lead back into town, so those staying in Park City proper don't have to ride back and forth to the base resort every day. Snowboarding is allowed.

The **Canyons Resort** (© 888/CANYONS [226-9667] or 435/649-5400; www. thecanyons.com), America's fifth-largest ski area, offers a wide variety of terrain on eight distinct mountains, with an excellent people-moving system to get you to the runs that you want to ski quickly and efficiently. In the past few years, intermediate and expert terrains have been greatly expanded.

White Pine Touring Center (© 435/649-8701 or 615-5858; www.whitepinetouring. com), Park City's cross-country ski center, has 12 miles of groomed trails on the Park City Golf Course.

WARM-WEATHER ACTIVITIES IN & AROUND PARK CITY

Getting into the mountains above Park City in summer couldn't be easier for hikers and bikers, thanks to the chairlifts at two resorts. **Deer Valley Resort** offers more than 50 miles of trails, and **Park City Mountain Resort**'s chairlifts provide access to more than 30 miles of trails. As you might expect, the terrain is steep but beautiful.

FLY-FISHING   Anglers have plenty of opportunities for fishing in the streams in the mountains around Park City, either on their own or with local guides. For tips on where they're biting, as well as equipment and information on guided trips, check with **Jans Mountain Outfitters,** 1600 Park Ave. (© 800/745-1020 or 435/649-4949; www.jans. com), or **Park City Fly Shop,** 2065 Sidewinder Dr., Prospector Square (© 435/645-8382; www.pcflyshop.com).

HIKING & MOUNTAIN BIKING   With more than 350 miles of trails crisscrossing the mountains around Park City, opportunities abound for hiking and mountain biking. For

COLORADO & UTAH

10

PARK CITY: UTAH'S PREMIER RESORT TOWN

a short hike with a variety of terrain and good views of both mountains and town, try the 1.5-mile **Sweeny Switchbacks Trail,** accessible from the base of the town lift.

The 30-mile **Historic Union Pacific Rail Trail State Park** hiking and biking path follows the old Union Pacific railroad bed from Park City to Echo Reservoir. It offers wonderful views of meadows, the volcanic crags of Silver Creek Canyon, the Weber River, Echo Reservoir, and the steep walls of Echo Canyon. You might spot deer, elk, moose, and bald eagles along the trail. An end-of-the-trail pickup service is available from **Daytrips** (© 888/649-8294; www.daytrips.com).

More than 30 miles of dirt roads and single-track trails at **Park City Mountain Resort** (p. 709) are open to hikers and mountain bikers, who can ride the PayDay chairlift up and then bike or hike down. Tickets cost $11 for a single ride or $18 for an all-day pass; bike rentals are $32 daily. **Deer Valley Resort** (p. 709) offers more than 50 miles of panoramic trails for both hikers and bikers, with chairlift access in summer ($13 a ride or $24 a day). As you might expect, the terrain is steep and beautiful.

For a good description of several other area trails, pick up a copy of the free *Park City Hiking & Biking Trail Map* at either visitor center and at sporting goods shops.

WHERE TO STAY

Rates are almost always higher—sometimes dramatically so—during ski season, and rates during Christmas week can be absurd. You'll find the best bargains in spring and fall. Sales and lodging taxes in Park City total just over 10%.

Although it's possible to book reservations directly with individual lodges, many people find it more convenient to go the one-stop-shopping route, making all their arrangements directly with one of the resorts. **Deer Valley Resort** (© 800/424-3337 or 435/649-1000; www.deervalley.com) and **Park City Mountain Resort** (© 800/222-7275 or 435/649-8111; www.parkcitymountain.com) both have central reservation offices that can reserve lodging for you at a nearby condo or lodge, and can also make airline, car rental, and lift-ticket reservations.

Goldener Hirsch Inn   This château-style inn combines warm hospitality with European charm. Austrian antiques dot the common areas and decorate the walls. The spacious rooms are elegantly furnished with hand-painted and hand-carved furniture from Austria and king-size beds with down comforters. Suites have wood-burning fireplaces and small private balconies. The excellent restaurant is Austrian in decor and features international cuisine.

7570 Royal St. E., Silver Lake Village, Deer Valley (P.O. Box 859), Park City, UT 84060. © **800/252-3373** or 435/649-7770. Fax 435/649-7901. www.goldenerhirschinn.com. 20 units. Winter (including continental breakfast) $279–$1,239 double; summer $155–$300 double. AE, MC, V. Closed mid-Apr to mid-June and Oct–Nov. **Amenities:** Restaurant.

Hotel Park City   This all-suite hotel is one of the most posh places to hang your hat in the area, if not the entire state. Drawing inspiration from the grand lodges of the national park system, the brain trust behind Hotel Park City spared no expense, from the masculine guest rooms, all with sublime mountain views, to the year-round pool in the central courtyard. The rooms all feature king-size beds, two TVs, kitchenettes, washers and dryers, and Western decor; the bathrooms are superb, with big jetted tubs and separate three-headed showers. The on-site spa is top rate.

2001 Park Ave. (P.O. Box 683120), Park City, UT 84068. © **435/200-2000.** Fax 435/940-5001. www.hotel parkcity.com. 100 suites. Winter $299–$3,000; summer $229–$1,500. AE, DC, DISC, MC, V. **Amenities:** Restaurant; outdoor heated pool; spa. *In room:* Kitchenette.

Old Town Guest House This cozy little B&B is perfect for outdoor enthusiasts— the innkeeper is a backcountry ski guide in winter and avid hiker and biker in summer. The inn is within easy walking distance of both the Park City Mountain Resort and Main Street. The delightfully homey living room retains its original 1910 fireplace. The decor is country, with lodgepole pine furniture and hardwood floors throughout, but as with most historic bed-and-breakfasts, each guest room is unique. The hearty breakfasts will sustain your energy throughout a day of hiking, biking, or skiing.

1011 Empire Ave. (P.O. Box 162), Park City, UT 84060. © 800/290-6423, ext. 3710, or 435/649-2642. Fax 435/649-3320. www.oldtownguesthouse.com. 4 units. Winter (including breakfast) $159–$250 double; summer $79–$119 double. AE, MC, V. *In room:* No phone in some rooms.

Stein Eriksen Lodge (Best) This luxurious full-service lodge features a warm, friendly atmosphere and Scandinavian decor and charm. The lobby is impressive, with a three-story stone fireplace. There are 13 rooms in the main lodge, with the remaining units in nearby buildings. The connecting sidewalks are heated, and the grounds are beautifully landscaped with aspen trees, manicured lawns, and flowers cascading over rock gardens and retaining walls. The spacious deluxe rooms, each individually decorated, contain a king- or queen-size bed, plenty of closet space, a whirlpool tub, vaulted ceiling, and tasteful, solid wood furniture; suites have full kitchens.

Stein Way (P.O. Box 3177), Park City, UT 84060. © 800/453-1302 or 435/649-3700. Fax 435/649-5825. www.steinlodge.com. 180 units. Winter (including buffet breakfast) $735–$1,130 double, from $1,350 suite; mid-Apr to late Nov $220–$260 double, from $295 suite. AE, DC, DISC, MC, V. **Amenities:** 2 restaurants; outdoor heated pool; exercise room; full-service spa.

Washington School Inn Housed in an 1889 limestone schoolhouse nestled against the Wasatch Mountains, this lovely country inn has preserved its original charm even through modernization. Rooms are individually decorated, many in country style, with antiques and reproductions. Two suites have wood-burning fireplaces. Though the inn has no televisions or air-conditioning, there are ski lockers, a sauna, and a whirlpool area. The inn provides a full breakfast buffet each morning, afternoon tea in the summer, and hearty après-ski refreshments in the winter.

543 Park Ave. (P.O. Box 536), Park City, UT 84060. © 800/824-1672 or 435/649-3808. Fax 435/649-3802. www.washingtonschoolinn.com. 15 units. Winter $195–$345 double, $295–$650 suite; summer $140–$150 double, $220–$240 suite. Rates include full breakfast. AE, DISC, MC, V.

WHERE TO DINE

The Eating Establishment AMERICAN The Eating Establishment, probably the oldest continuously operating restaurant on Park City's Main Street (since 1972), is casual and comfortable, a great choice for families or anyone who wants a heaping serving of comfort food at reasonable prices. The dining room is brick and light-colored wood, with several fireplaces. The menu offers a variety of salads, barbecued baby back ribs, a Black Angus Kansas City strip steak (charbroiled and served with sautéed whole mushrooms), and several pasta selections. There's full liquor service.

317 Main St. © 435/649-8284. www.theeatingestablishment.net. Main courses $6–$11 breakfast and lunch; $8–$23 dinner. AE, DISC, MC, V. Daily 8am–10pm. Closed 3–5pm Mon–Thurs spring-fall. Main St. Trolley.

Glitretind Restaurant (Best) CONTEMPORARY INTERNATIONAL In the elegant Stein Eriksen Lodge, this equally stylish restaurant is a top pick for the best dining in the Park City area, and possibly the entire state. The Glitretind serves innovative, impeccably prepared meals in a modern, airy dining room with views of the spectacular

Wasatch Mountains. The menu changes with the seasons and reflects the New American style of executive chef Zane Holmquist. Breakfast offerings include French toast, pancakes, a fruit plate, and omelets; for lunch, choose a soup, salad, sandwich, or full meal. At lunch and dinner, Stein's Wild Game Chili, with wild boar, buffalo, and elk, is a stalwart on the ever-changing menu. The restaurant has an excellent wine list and also offers full liquor service.

Stein Eriksen Lodge (p. 711), Deer Valley. ☎ **435/649-3700.** www.steinlodge.com. Reservations requested. Main courses $10–$20 breakfast, $8–$18 lunch, $22–$47 dinner. AE, DC, DISC, MC, V. Mon–Sat 7–10am and 11:30am–2:30pm; brunch Sun 10:30am–2:30pm; daily 6–9pm. Bus: Deer Valley Loop.

Jean Louis CONTEMPORARY/ECLECTIC   After guiding the restaurant at the Goldener Hirsch Inn at Deer Valley, Jean Louis Montecot opened his own place in downtown Park City, and the results are electrifying. Centered on an amber onyx bar, the casual, contemporary space is dimly lit and attractive to the barhopping crowd, but it prides itself on providing a fine-dining experience at the same time. The diverse menu ranges from gourmet pizza to seared Peruvian trout to fish tacos to rack of New Zealand lamb. With side dishes of such comfort foods as onion rings and corn mashed potatoes, the results are reliably dazzling. Full liquor service is available.

136 Heber Ave. ☎ **435/200-0260.** www.jeanlouisrestaurant.com. Main courses $19–$40. AE, DISC, MC, V. Daily 5–11pm (10pm in summer/off season). Bar open later.

Wahso—An Asian Grill ASIAN   This distinctively elegant restaurant boasts an Art Deco and Victorian interior furnished with authentic Asian screens, an ebony fireplace, and carvings and pictures from around the world. The food is equally unique, an amalgamation of traditional Asian ingredients with French cooking style, which gives rise to deliciously light and healthy offerings. Entrees change frequently but might include specialties such as Szechuan-style grilled filet mignon, soy- and ginger-glazed sea bass, and spicy Balinese stir-fry of shrimp. Be sure to save room for the dessert specialty—crème brûlée in a coconut shell. Premium sake, imported beer, and an extensive wine list are available.

577 Main St. ☎ **435/615-0300.** www.wahso.com. Main courses $24–$35. AE, DISC, MC, V. Winter daily 5–10pm; spring–fall Sun–Thurs 6–9pm, Fri–Sat 6–10pm. Main St. Trolley.

PARK CITY AFTER DARK: THE CLUB SCENE

Park City probably has the best nightlife in the state. If you're looking for drinking and dancing, join a private club (memberships are available on a short-term basis, usually for $4, and membership entitles you to bring several guests). The following are busiest during ski season and generally have fewer nights of live music at other times.

The **Spur,** 350¹/₂ Main St. (☎ **435/615-1618**), is a contemporary Western joint that's smoke free and has regular live music. **Cisero's,** downstairs at 306 Main St. (☎ **435/649-6800;** www.ciseros.com), with a large dance floor, hosts good bands. **J.B. Mulligan's Club & Pub,** 804 Main St. (☎ **435/658-0717**), also has live music, including a variety of jazz, reggae, bluegrass, and funk; and you can also order food—try their peppercorn burger—between 5 and 10pm. The **No Name Saloon,** 447 Main St. (☎ **435/649-6667;** www.nonamesaloon.net), another fun place to drink, is old and oddly furnished. **Harry O's,** 427 Main St. (☎ **435/647-9494**), is very popular, with a huge dance floor and live band or DJ nightly. Romantic and dimly lit, **Bacchus Wine Bar,** 442 Main St. (☎ **435/940-9463**), pours 100 different wines by the glass and serves a scrumptious menu of light fare.

Situated in beautiful Provo Canyon, at the base of 12,000-foot Mount Timpanogos, Sundance is a year-round resort that emphasizes its arts programs as much as its skiing and other outdoor activities. That should come as no surprise—it's owned by actor/director Robert Redford, who bought the property in 1969 and named it after his character in the classic film *Butch Cassidy and the Sundance Kid.* You might recognize the area: Redford's 1972 film *Jeremiah Johnson* was set here.

The goal for Sundance was to create a place where the outdoors and the arts could come together in a truly unique mountain community, and it seems to be a success. The rustic yet elegant, environmentally friendly retreat is a full-service ski resort in winter. During the summer, you'll find great hiking trails and other outdoor activities, as well as the Sundance Institute, which Redford founded in 1980 to support and encourage independent American filmmaking and playwriting.

For information on all facilities and activities, plus lodging reservations, contact **Sundance Resort,** R.R. 3, Box A-1, Sundance, UT 84604 (© **800/892-1600** or 801/225-4100; fax 801/226-1937; www.sundanceresort.com).

Outdoor Activities

Sundance is known for its quiet, intimate setting and lack of lift lines. It offers runs for all levels—some quite challenging—including several delightfully long cruising trails for novices. The area is gaining a reputation as a good place to learn to ski or snowboard. The two levels of skiing are pretty well separated from each other: The beginner and some of the intermediate terrain are on the front mountain, whereas the prime blue runs and all of the expert slopes are on the back mountain. The expert crowd will be pleased with the steep glades, precipitous bump runs (due to the general lack of traffic, the mountain never really bumps up too high, though), and untracked snow on the back mountain, where you'll have to work at it to run into another skier.

The terrain is rated 20% beginner, 40% intermediate, and 40% advanced, with a total of 41 runs over 450 skiable acres. One quad and two triple chairlifts, plus a handle tow, serve the mountain, which has a vertical drop of 2,150 feet, from a base elevation of 6,100 feet to the top at 8,250 feet. Sundance is usually open from mid-December to early April and has state-of-the-art snow-making equipment on the entire front mountain. Lifts operate daily from 9am to 4:30pm.

Bearclaw's Cabin, the only mountaintop day lodge in Utah, offers snacks, hot drinks, and stupendous views. **Creekside** day lodge, at the base of the ski area, serves excellent quick lunches during ski season. Equipment rental and sales are available.

The Provo River provides great **fly-fishing** just 10 minutes away. Sundance offers guided fishing trips, including equipment rentals. Rates start at $155 for group, $195 for private half-day fly-fishing trips.

The Festival, Film & Performing Arts Scene

For more than 20 years, the hottest independent films have been discovered at this **Sundance Film Festival,** a weeklong January event, hosted by Robert Redford's Sundance Institute. (The festival itself is actually held in Park City.)

Admission to the festival is nonexclusive, so you can rub shoulders with the rich and famous and the up-and-coming. To receive a free guide, or to reserve tickets, contact the **Sundance Institute** (© **877/733-7829** or 801/924-0882 for tickets; www.sundance.org).

Past **Sundance films** are screened in City Park on summer Friday nights. The **Park City Film Series** (www.parkcityfilmseries.com) screens a different independent movie every weekend at the Park City Library for $6.

Where to Stay

Sundance offers standard rooms, studios, and cottage suites that range from $250 to $591 per night, as well as larger mountain suites and several luxury mountain homes that cost from $337 to over $1,000 per night. Each suite is outfitted with well-crafted hand-made furnishings that match the rustic luxury of the entire resort, as well as American Indian crafts, stone fireplaces, and outdoor decks; most have fully equipped kitchens. All accommodations come with Sundance's own natural bath products. Contact the **Sundance Resort,** R.R. 3, Box A-1, Sundance, UT 84604 (© **800/892-1600** or 801/225-4100; www.sundanceresort.com), for information and reservations.

9 ZION NATIONAL PARK

Early Mormon settler Isaac Behunin is credited with naming his homestead "Little Zion" because it seemed to be a bit of heaven on earth. Today, 150 years later, Zion National Park will cast a spell over you as you gaze upon its sheer multicolored walls of sandstone, explore its narrow canyons, hunt for hanging gardens of wildflowers, or listen to the roar of the churning, tumbling Virgin River.

Because of its extremes of elevation (3,666 to almost 9,000 ft.) and climate (temperatures soar over 100°F/38°C in summer, and the landscape is carpeted in snow in winter), Zion harbors a vast array of plants and animals. About 800 native species of plants have been found: cactus, yucca, and mesquite in the hot, dry desert areas; ponderosa pine trees on the high plateaus; and cottonwoods and box elders along the rivers and streams. And Zion is a veritable zoo, with mammals ranging from pocket gophers to mountain lions, hundreds of birds, and lizards of all shapes and sizes.

ESSENTIALS

Zion National Park has three sections: Zion Canyon, the main part of the park, where everyone goes, and the less-visited Kolob Terrace and Kolob Canyons. The main east-west road through Zion Canyon is the park-owned extension of Utah 9, from which you can access a 14-mile round-trip scenic drive/shuttle bus route that leads to most scenic overlooks and trail heads.

GETTING THERE/ACCESS POINTS   St. George and Cedar City are the closest towns with airport service. From either airport, it's easy to rent a car and drive to Zion. Utah 9 crosses Zion National Park, giving the main section of the park two entry gates—south and east. The drive into Zion Canyon (the main part of the park) from I-15 on the park's western side—following Utah 9 or Utah 17 and Utah 9 to the south entrance at Springdale, is the most popular, with two-thirds of park visitors arriving there. Most area lodgings and restaurants are in Springdale, and the park's two campgrounds and the Zion Canyon Visitor Center are just inside the south entrance. This approach has the added advantage of avoiding possible delays at the Zion–Mount Carmel Tunnel. However, this approach is much less scenic than the eastern approach.

From the east, it's a spectacularly scenic 24-mile drive from Mount Carmel on Utah 9, reached from either the north or south via U.S. 89. However, be aware that this route into the park drops over 2,500 feet in elevation, passes through the mile-long Zion–Mount Carmel Tunnel, and winds down six steep switchbacks. The tunnel is too small for two-way traffic that includes vehicles larger than standard passenger cars and pickup trucks. Buses, trucks, and most recreational vehicles must be driven down the center of the tunnel; therefore, all oncoming traffic must be stopped. This applies to all vehicles over 7 feet, 10 inches wide (including mirrors) or 11 feet, 4 inches tall (including luggage racks and so on). March through October, large vehicles are permitted in the tunnel only from 8am to 8pm daily; during other months, arrangements can be made at park entrances or by calling park headquarters (© **435/772-3256**). Affected vehicles must pay a $15 fee, good for two trips through the tunnel during a 7-day period. All vehicles over 13 feet, 1 inch tall and certain other particularly large vehicles are prohibited from driving anywhere on the park road between the east entrance and Zion Canyon.

You'll find Kolob Terrace Road, with additional viewpoints and trail heads, heading north off Utah 9 from the village of Virgin, about 15 miles west of the park's southern entrance. This road is closed in winter.

The Kolob Canyons section, in the park's northwest corner, can be reached via the short Kolob Canyons Road off I-15 exit 40.

The park is 83 miles southwest of Bryce Canyon National Park; 120 miles northwest of the north rim of Grand Canyon National Park, in northern Arizona; 309 miles south of Salt Lake City; and 158 miles northeast of Las Vegas, Nevada.

VISITOR INFORMATION   Contact Zion National Park, Utah 9, Springdale, UT 84767-1099 (© **435/772-3256;** www.nps.gov/zion). You can also purchase books, maps, and videos related to the park from the nonprofit **Zion Natural History Association,** Zion National Park, Springdale, UT 84767 (© **800/635-3959** or 435/772-3264; www.zion park.org).

The park has two visitor centers. The **Zion Canyon Visitor Center** (© **435/772-3256**), near the south entrance, has outdoor exhibits on the many resources available in the park and provides information on the shuttle operation. You can ask rangers questions; get backcountry permits; pick up free brochures; and purchase books, maps, videos, postcards, and posters. The smaller **Kolob Canyons Visitor Center** (© **435/586-9548**), in the northwest corner of the park off I-15, provides information, permits, books, and maps. Both visitor centers are open daily from 8am to 5pm in summer, with shorter varying hours the rest of the year (call to find out when).

WHEN TO GO   The park is open year-round 24 hours a day, although weather conditions such as extreme heat or icy trails may limit some activities at certain times.

If possible, try to avoid June, July, and August, when Zion receives almost half of its annual visitors. The quietest months are December, January, and February, but of course, it's cold and snowy then. A good compromise is to visit in April, May, September, or October, when the weather is usually good but the park is less crowded.

The best way to avoid crowds is to simply walk away from them. It's sad but true—most visitors never venture far from their cars, and you can enjoy a wonderful solitary experience if you're willing to expend a little energy. You can also avoid hordes of tourists by spending time in Kolob Canyons, in the far northwest section of the park; it's spectacular and gets surprisingly little use. In the summer, head to Kolob Terrace.

If you have only a day or two at the park, we recommend making one of the visitor centers your first stop. Then, if your visit is during the shuttle bus operating season, we suggest the following:

Hop on the free **shuttle bus,** which takes you to the major roadside viewpoints. You'll be able to get off, look at the formations, take a short walk if you like, and then catch the next shuttle for a ride to the next stop.

We recommend getting off the shuttle at the **Temple of Sinawava** and taking the 2-mile round-trip **Riverside Walk,** which follows the Virgin River through a narrow canyon past hanging gardens. Then take the shuttle back to the lodge (total time: 2–4 hr.). Stop by the gift shop and perhaps have lunch in the excellent restaurant.

Near the lodge, you'll find the trail head for the **Emerald Pools.** Especially pleasant on hot days, this easy walk through a forest of oak, maple, fir, and cottonwood trees leads to a waterfall, hanging garden, and the shimmering lower pool. This part of the walk should take about an hour round-trip, but those with a bit more time may want to add another hour and another mile to the loop by taking the moderately strenuous hike on a rocky, steeper trail to the upper pool. If you still have time and energy, head back to the south park entrance and stop at **Watchman** (east of Watchman Campground), for the 2-mile, 2-hour round-trip, moderately strenuous hike to a plateau with beautiful views of several rock formations and the town of Springdale. In the evening, try to take in a campground amphitheater program.

HIKING

Zion offers a wide variety of hiking trails, ranging from easy half-hour walks on paved paths to grueling overnight hikes over rocky terrain along steep drop-offs. Hikers with a fear of heights should be especially careful when choosing trails; many include steep, dizzying drop-offs. What follows are our hiking suggestions:

The **Weeping Rock Trail,** among the park's shortest and easiest rambles, is a .5-mile round-trip walk to a rock alcove with a spring and hanging gardens of ferns and wildflowers. Although paved, the trail is steep and not suitable for wheelchairs.

Another short hike is the **Lower Emerald Pools Trail,** which can be an easy 1-hour walk or a moderately strenuous 2-hour hike, depending on how much of the loop you choose to do. A .6-mile paved path from the Emerald Pools Parking Area, through a forest of oak, maple, fir, and cottonwood, leads to a waterfall, a hanging garden, and the Lower Emerald Pool, and is suitable for those in wheelchairs, with assistance. From here, a steeper, rocky trail continues past cactus, yucca, and juniper another .5 mile to Upper Emerald Pool, with another waterfall. A third pool, just above Lower Emerald Pool, offers impressive reflections of the cliffs.

A moderately strenuous but relatively short hike is the **Watchman Trail,** which starts near the Zion Canyon Visitor Center. This 3-mile round-trip hike gets light use, possibly because it can be very hot in the middle of the day. Climbing to a plateau near the base of the formation called the Watchman, it offers splendid views of lower Zion Canyon, the Towers of the Virgin, and West Temple formations.

Hiking the **Narrows** is not hiking a trail at all, but walking or wading along the bottom of the Virgin River, through a spectacular 1,000-foot-deep chasm that, at a mere 20 feet wide in spots, lives up to its name. Hikers pass fancifully sculpted sandstone arches, hanging gardens, and waterfalls. This moderately strenuous hike can be completed in 1 day or several. However, the Narrows are subject to flash flooding and can be very treacherous. Park Service officials remind hikers that they are responsible for their own safety and should check on current water conditions and weather forecasts. This hike is *not* recommended when rain is forecast or threatening. Permits are required for full-day and overnight hikes in the Narrows, but are not required for easy, short day hikes, which you can access from just beyond the end of the Riverside Walk, a 2-mile trail that starts at the Temple of Sinawava parking area.

WHERE TO CAMP

There are two large and one small **national park campgrounds.** Both of the main campgrounds, just inside the park's south entrance, have paved roads, well-spaced sites, lots of trees, and that national park atmosphere you came here to enjoy. Facilities include restrooms with flush toilets but no showers, a dump station, and a public telephone. The fee is $16 per night for basic sites, or $18 to $20 per night for sites with electric hookups. **South Campground** has 127 sites (no hookups), first-come, first-served, and is usually open from mid-March through October only; **Watchman Campground** (© 800/365-2267 or www.recreation.gov for reservations) has 145 sites, with electric hookups on two loops, and is open year-round (reservations available spring through early fall only).

Lava Point, with only six sites, is located on the Kolob Terrace. It has fire grates, tables, and toilets, but no water, and there's no fee. Vehicles are limited to 19 feet, and it's usually open from June through mid-October.

WHERE TO STAY

The only lodging in Zion National Park is at **Zion Lodge** (© 435/772-7700). For information and reservations, contact **Xanterra Parks & Resorts,** 6312 S. Fiddlers Green Circle, Ste. 600N, Greenwood Village, CO 80111 (© 888/297-2757 or 303/297-2757; www.zionlodge.com). Situated in a forest, with spectacular views of the park's rock cliffs, the charming cabins each have a private porch, stone (gas-burning) fireplace, two double beds, pine-board walls, and log beams. The comfortable motel units are basically just that. Rates from $151 double, cabins $161, suites $171.

Springdale, a village of some 350 people at the park's south entrance, has become the park's bedroom. Comfortable, affordable motel rooms are available at the **Canyon Ranch Motel,** 668 Zion Park Blvd. (© 866/946-6276 or 435/772-3357; www.canyonranch motel.com; $64–$94), where the rooms have spectacular views. More upscale are the moderately priced **Cliffrose Lodge & Gardens,** 281 Zion Park Blvd. (© 800/243-8824 or 435/772-3234; www.cliffroselodge.com; $139–$199 per unit), and the **Harvest House Bed & Breakfast at Zion,** 29 Canyon View Dr. (© 800/719-7501 or 435/772-3880; www.harvesthouse.net; $100–$135 double).

We especially like **Flanigan's Inn,** 428 Zion Park Blvd. (© 800/765-7787 or 435/772-3244; www.flanigans.com; $109–$139 double, $149–$259 suites), a very attractive complex just outside the park entrance. Parts of the inn date to 1947, but all rooms have been completely renovated, with Southwestern decor, wood furnishings, and local art. Flanigan's has a heated outdoor swimming pool and its own nature trail leading to a hilltop vista.

10 BRYCE CANYON NATIONAL PARK

If you could visit only one national park in your lifetime, we'd send you to Bryce Canyon. Here you'll find magic, inspiration, and spectacular beauty. The main draw of the park is the thousands of intricately shaped **hoodoos,** those silent rock sentinels and congregations

BRYCE CANYON NATIONAL PARK

gathered in colorful cathedrals, arranged in formations that invite your imagination to run wild.

Hoodoos, geologists tell us, are simply pinnacles of rock, often oddly shaped, left standing by the forces of millions of years of water and wind erosion. But perhaps the truth really lies in a Paiute legend. These American Indians, who lived in the area for several hundred years before being forced out by Anglo pioneers, told of a "Legend People" who lived here in the old days; because of their evil ways, they were turned to stone by the powerful Coyote, and even today they remain frozen in time.

Although the colorful hoodoos are the first things to grab your attention, it isn't long before you notice the deep amphitheaters that enfold them, with their cliffs, windows, and arches—all colored in shades of red, brown, orange, yellow, and white—that change and glow with the rising and setting sun. Beyond the rocks and light are the other faces of the park: three separate life zones, each with its own unique vegetation that changes with the elevation; and a kingdom of animals, from the busy chipmunks and ground squirrels to the stately mule deer and their archenemy, the mountain lion.

ESSENTIALS

GETTING THERE/ACCESS POINTS   Bryce Canyon Airport (© 435/834-5239; www.brycecanyoncountry.com/county/airport.html) is located several miles from the park entrance on Utah 12. There are no regularly scheduled direct flights to the airport, but charter service is available from **Bryce Canyon Airlines** (© 435/834-5341). Car rentals are available from **Hertz,** which is located at Ruby's Inn Chevron Station, 1 mile south of Utah 12 on Utah 63 (© 800/654-3131).

Situated in the mountains of southern Utah, the park is traversed east-west by Utah 12, with the bulk of the park, including the visitor center, accessible via Utah 63, which branches off from Utah 12 and goes south into the main portions of the park. Utah 89 runs north to south, west of the park, and Utah 12 heads east to Tropic and Escalante.

Entry into the park (for up to 7 days) costs $25 per private car, pickup truck, van, or RV, which includes unlimited use of the park shuttle (when it's operating). Campsites cost $10 per night. Backcountry permits are required for all overnight trips into the backcountry, and for up to 7 days cost $5 for one or two people.

VISITOR INFORMATION   Contact **Bryce Canyon National Park,** P.O. Box 170001, Bryce Canyon, UT 84717 (© 435/834-5322; www.nps.gov/brca).

The visitor center, at the north end as you enter the park, has exhibits and presents a short introductory slide show. Rangers can answer questions and provide backcountry permits. You can stock up on brochures, books, maps, DVDs, and postcards. The visitor center is open daily year-round except major holidays.

WHEN TO GO   Although Bryce Canyon National Park gets only two-thirds the number of annual visitors that pour into Zion, the park can still be crowded, especially from June to September. If you visit then, head for some of the lesser-used trails (ask rangers for recommendations) and start your hike as soon after sunrise as possible.

A better time to visit is spring or fall, and if you don't mind a bit of cold and snow, the park is practically deserted from December through February—and the sight of bright red hoodoos capped with fresh white snow is something you won't soon forget.

SEEING THE HIGHLIGHTS

Start at the visitor center, of course, and watch the short slide show that explains some of the area's geology. Then drive the 18-mile (each way) dead-end park road, stopping at

see the main section of the park on the shuttle bus, which operates from mid- to late May to early September. The shuttles run every 10 to 15 minutes, and you can get on and off as frequently as you want.

Whichever way you choose to get around, be sure to spend at least a little time at **Inspiration Point,** which offers a splendid (and, yes, inspirational) view into **Bryce Amphitheater** and its hundreds of statuesque pink, red, orange, and brown hoodoo stone sculptures. After seeing the canyon from the top down, it's time to walk at least partway down the **Queen's Garden Trail.** If you can spare 3 hours, hike down the Navajo Loop and return to the rim via Queen's Garden Trail. You can also enjoy a leisurely walk along the **Rim Trail,** which provides spectacular views down into the canyon, especially just after sunrise and about an hour before sunset.

Bryce Canyon Area Tours & Adventures (© 800/432-5383 or 435/834-5200; www. brycetours.com) offers 1¹/₂-hour sunrise and sunset tours, leaving from Bryce Canyon Resort next to the shuttle parking area outside the park entrance, at the intersection of the park entrance road and Utah 12. The tour has stops at some of the park's most scenic areas, timed to catch the rising or setting sun. Cost is $26 per passenger, and reservations are required.

HIKING

One of the things we like best about Bryce Canyon is that you don't have to be an advanced backpacker to really get to know the park. All trails below the rim have at least some steep grades, so you should wear hiking boots with a traction tread and good ankle support to avoid ankle injuries, the most common accidents in the park. During the hot summer months, you'll want to hike either early or late in the day; it gets hotter the deeper you go into the canyon.

The **Rim Trail,** which does not drop into the canyon but offers splendid views from above, meanders along the rim for over 5 miles. An easy-to-moderate walk, it includes a .5-mile section between two overlooks—Sunrise and Sunset—that is suitable for wheelchairs. Overlooking Bryce Amphitheater, the trail offers excellent views almost everywhere and is a good choice for an after-dinner walk, when you can watch the changing evening light on the rosy rocks below.

Your best bet for getting down into the canyon and seeing the most with the least amount of sweat is to combine two popular trails—**Navajo Loop** and **Queen's Garden.** The total distance is just less than 3 miles, with a 521-foot elevation change, and it takes most hikers from 2 to 3 hours. It's best to start at the Navajo Loop trail head at Sunset Point and leave the canyon on the less steep Queen's Garden Trail, returning to the rim at Sunrise Point, .5 mile to the north. A 2006 rockslide cut off one section of the Navajo Trail, but park officials say this is not necessarily a bad thing and that this work of nature actually gives visitors a unique opportunity to see the geologic forces that have helped create this park. The Navajo Loop section is fairly strenuous, while Queen's Garden is rated moderate. Along the Navajo Loop section, you'll pass Thor's Hammer, wonder why it hasn't fallen, and ponder the towering skyscrapers of Wall Street. Turning onto the Queen's Garden Trail, you'll see some of the park's most fanciful formations, including majestic Queen Victoria herself, for whom the trail was named, plus the Queen's Castle and Gulliver's Castle.

WHERE TO CAMP

The two campgrounds in the park offer plenty of trees, with a genuine "forest camping" experience, easy access to trails, and limited facilities. **North Campground** has 107 sites and **Sunset Campground** has 101 sites. A section of North Campground is open year-round, but Sunset Campground is open from May to September only. We prefer North Campground because it's closer to the Rim Trail—making it easier to rush over to catch those amazing sunrise and sunset colors. Neither has RV hookups or showers, but you will find modern restrooms with running water. Reservations are available from mid-May through September for North Campground (© 877/444-6777; www.recreation.gov) for an additional booking fee of $10, regardless of the number of days. Sunset Campground does not accept reservations, so get to the campground early to claim a site (usually by 2pm in summer). Cost is $10 per night at both campgrounds.

Showers ($2), a coin-operated laundry, a snack bar, bundles of firewood, food and camping supplies, and souvenirs are located at the **General Store** (for information, contact Bryce Canyon Lodge, © 435/834-5361), which is usually open daily from mid-April through October. The store is a healthy walk from either campground. The Park Service operates an RV dump station ($2 fee) in the summer. Tables on a covered porch run along one side of the building.

WHERE TO STAY

Our preferred lodging choice here is right in the park at the delightful **Bryce Canyon Lodge** (© 435/834-5361). For information and reservations, contact **Xanterra Parks & Resorts,** Central Reservations, 6312 S. Fiddlers Green Circle, Ste. 600N, Greenwood Village, CO 80111 (© 888/297-2757 or 303/297-2757; www.brycecanyonlodge.com; $120–$150 double). This is the perfect place to stay, allowing easy access to the trails and spectacular views. The handsome sandstone and ponderosa pine lodge, which opened in 1924, contains a busy lobby, with information desks for horseback riding and other activities. The luxurious lodge suites are wonderful, with white wicker furniture, ceiling fans, and separate sitting rooms. The motel rooms are just that, but they're pleasant and quite spacious. Our choice would be the "rustic luxury" of one of the cabins, which have been restored to their 1924 decor.

Nearby choices include **Best Western Ruby's Inn,** Utah 63, just outside the park entrance (© 866/866-6616 or 435/834-5341; www.rubysinn.com; $135–$159 double), where you'll find a large general store, a post office, and tour desks where you can arrange excursions. Outside are two gas stations. More-basic (and less expensive) motel units can be found at **Bryce View Lodge,** Utah 63, across from Best Western Ruby's Inn (© 888/279-2304 or 435/834-5180; www.bryceviewlodge.com; $78–$93 double); and **Bryce Valley Inn,** 199 Scenic Byway 12, Tropic (© 866/679-8811 or 435/679-8846; www.brycevalleyinn.com; $81–$99 double and suite).

11 CAPITOL REEF NATIONAL PARK

A relatively unknown gem, Capitol Reef offers more of that spectacular southern Utah scenery, but with a unique twist and a personality all its own. This is a place to let your imagination run wild, where you'll see the appropriately named Hamburger Rocks, sitting atop a white sandstone table; the tall, rust-red Chimney Rock; and the silent and eerie Temple of the Moon.

But Capitol Reef is more than just brilliant rocks and barren desert. Here the Fremont River has helped create a lush oasis in an otherwise unforgiving land, with cottonwoods and willows along its banks. In fact, 19th-century pioneers found the land so inviting

and the soil so fertile that they established a community here, planting orchards that have
been preserved by the Park Service.

ESSENTIALS

GETTING THERE   Capitol Reef National Park is about 224 miles south of Salt Lake City. It straddles Utah 24, which connects with I-70 both to the northeast and to the northwest. Entry into the park (for up to 7 days) costs $5 per vehicle or $3 per person on bike or foot. Free permits, available at the visitor center, are required for all overnight hiking trips into the backcountry.

VISITOR INFORMATION   Contact **Capitol Reef National Park,** HC 70 Box 15, Torrey, UT 84775-9602 (© **435/425-3791;** www.nps.gov/care). The visitor center is on the park access road at its intersection with Utah 24. A trail alongside the access road connects the visitor center and campground.

SEEING THE HIGHLIGHTS

Start at the visitor center, and watch the short slide show explaining the park's geology and history. From the visitor center, a 25-mile round-trip scenic drive leads into the park, offering good views of its dramatic canyons, colorful cliffs, and rock formations.

If the weather is dry, drive down the unpaved Capitol Gorge Road at the end of the paved scenic drive for a look at what many consider the best backcountry scenery in the park. It's a 6-mile round-trip drive. If you're up for a short walk, the flat 2-mile (round-trip) **Capitol Gorge Trail,** which starts at the end of Capitol Gorge Road, takes you to the historic Pioneer Register, a rock wall where traveling pioneers "signed in."

FROM PETROGLYPHS TO A PIONEER SCHOOLHOUSE: CAPITOL REEF'S HISTORIC SITES

Throughout the park, you'll find evidence of man's presence through the centuries. The Fremont people lived along the river as early as A.D. 700, staying until about 1300. Primarily hunters and gatherers, the Fremont also grew corn, beans, and squash. They lived in pit houses dug into the ground, and the remains of one can be seen from the Hickman Bridge Trail. Many of the Fremont's **petroglyphs** (images carved into rock) and some **pictographs** (images painted on rock) are still visible on the canyon walls. If we could read them, they might even tell us why these early Americans left the area, a puzzle that continues to baffle archaeologists.

Prospectors and other travelers passed through the Capitol Gorge section of the park in the late 1800s, leaving their names on the **Pioneer Register.** You can reach the Pioneer Register via an easy 2-mile (round-trip) hike.

Mormon pioneers established the community of **Fruita** in 1880. A tiny **schoolhouse,** built in 1896, also served as a church, social hall, and community-meeting hall. The school closed in 1941 but was restored by the National Park Service and is furnished with old wood and wrought-iron desks, a woodstove, a chalkboard, and textbooks. The orchards planted by the Mormon settlers continue to flourish, tended by park workers who invite you to sample the fruits of their labors.

SPORTS & ACTIVITIES

FOUR-WHEELING & MOUNTAIN BIKING   Capitol Reef has several so-called roads—actually little more than dirt trails—that provide exciting opportunities for those using 4×4s or pedal-power.

One recommended trip, the **Cathedral Valley Loop,** covers about 60 miles on a variety of surfaces, including dirt, sand, and rock, and requires the fording of the Fremont River, where water is usually 1 to $1^{1}/_{2}$ feet deep. But you'll be rewarded with unspoiled scenery, including sandstone monoliths and majestic cliffs, in one of the park's most remote areas. Access to this loop is from Utah 24, just outside the park, 12 miles east of the visitor center, or 19 miles east of the visitor center on the Caineville Wash Road.

For information on guided backpacking, hiking, mountain biking, and four-wheel-drive excursions (many with an emphasis on photo opportunities), contact **Wild Hare Expeditions** (© 888/304-4273 or 435/425-3999; www.wildhareexpeditions.com). Wild Hare also rents mountain bikes.

HIKING Trails through Capitol Reef National Park offer panoramas of colorful cliffs and domes, eerie journeys through desolate steep-walled canyons, and oases along the tree-shaded Fremont River. Watch for petroglyphs and other reminders of this area's first inhabitants. This is also the real Wild West, little changed from the way cowboys, bank robbers, settlers, and gold miners found it in the late 1800s.

Among our favorite short hikes here is the 2-mile round-trip **Capitol Gorge Trail.** It's easy, mostly level walking along the bottom of a narrow canyon, but looking up at the tall, smooth walls of rock conveys a strong sense of what the pioneers saw and felt 100 years ago. Starting at the end of the dirt Capitol Gorge Road, the hiking trail leads past the Pioneer Register, where early travelers carved their names.

Another short hike, but quite a bit more strenuous, is the 3.5-mile round-trip **Cassidy Arch Trail.** This offers spectacular views as it climbs steeply from the floor of Grand Wash to high cliffs overlooking the park. From the trail, you'll also get several perspectives of Cassidy Arch, a natural stone arch named for outlaw Butch Cassidy. The trail is off the Grand Wash Road, which branches off the east side of the highway about halfway down the park's scenic drive.

WHERE TO CAMP

The 71-site **Fruita Campground,** open year-round, offers modern restrooms, drinking water, picnic tables, fire grills, and an RV dump station (in summer only), but no showers or RV hookups. It's located along the main park road, 1 mile south of the visitor center. Camping costs $10; reservations are not accepted. The park also has two primitive campgrounds, free and open year-round on a first-come, first-served basis. Both have tables, fire grills, and pit toilets, but no water. Check road conditions before going, as unpaved roads may be impassable in wet weather. **Cedar Mesa Campground,** with five sites, is in the southern part of the park, and **Cathedral Valley Campground,** with six sites, is in the northern part of the park.

WHERE TO STAY

There are no lodging or dining facilities in the park itself, but the town of Torrey, just west of the park entrance, can take care of most needs.

Affordable accommodations include **Austin's Chuck Wagon Lodge,** 12 W. Main St. (© 800/863-3288 or 435/425-3335; www.austinschuckwagonmotel.com); **Best Western Capitol Reef Resort,** 2600 E. Utah 24 (© 888/610-9600 or 435/425-3761), which is only a mile from the park entrance; the **Capitol Reef Inn & Cafe,** 360 W. Main St. (Utah 24; © 435/425-3271; www.capitolreefinn.com); **Comfort Inn,** 2424 Utah 24 (© 800/424-6423 or 435/425-3866); and the **Super 8,** 600 E. Utah 24 (© 800/800-8000 or 435/425-3688). The **Skyridge Inn Bed & Breakfast,** on Utah 24, just east of its intersection with Utah 12 (© 800/448-6990 or 435/425-3222; www.bbiu.org/skyridge), offers a delightful alternative to the standard motel.

12 ARCHES NATIONAL PARK

Natural stone arches and fantastic rock formations, which look as if they were sculpted by an artist's hand, are the defining features of this park, and they exist in remarkable numbers and variety. Just as soon as you've seen the most beautiful, most colorful, most gigantic stone arch you can imagine, walk around the next bend and there's another—bigger, better, and more brilliant than the last. It would take forever to see them all, with more than 2,000 officially listed and more being discovered or "born" every day. And, as new ones are born, others gradually erode and collapse. In August 2008, Wall Arch, the 12th largest in the park, collapsed in a process that took thousands of years, if not longer.

Exploring the park is a great family adventure. The arches seem more accessible and less forbidding than the spires and pinnacles at Canyonlands and other southern Utah parks. Just down the road from Canyonlands National Park, Arches is much more visitor friendly, with relatively short, well-maintained trails leading to most of the park's major attractions.

ESSENTIALS

GETTING THERE   From Moab, drive 5 miles north on **U.S. 191.** Arches National Park is located 27 miles east of Canyonlands National Park's Island in the Sky Visitor Center, 233 miles southeast of Salt Lake City and 371 miles west of Denver, Colorado.

INFORMATION/VISITOR CENTERS   For advance information, contact **Arches National Park,** P.O. Box 907, Moab, UT 84532-0907 (© **435/719-2299;** www.nps.gov/arch).

The attractive **Arches National Park Visitor Center,** completed in 2005, is just inside the entrance gate. It offers maps, brochures, and other information, and a museum explains arch formation and other features of the park. From April through October, the visitor center is open daily from 7:30am to 6:30pm; the rest of the year, it's open daily from 8am to 4:30pm. On Christmas Day, the park is open, but the visitor center is closed.

Entry for up to 7 days costs $20 per private vehicle or $10 per person on foot, motorcycle, or bike. Campsites cost $20 per night. Required permits for overnight trips into the backcountry, available at the visitor center, are free.

March through October, rangers lead **guided hikes** on the Fiery Furnace Trail twice daily, as well as daily nature walks at various park locations. Evening campfire programs, April through October, are held on topics such as rock art, geological processes, and wildlife. A schedule of events is posted at the visitor center.

SEEING THE PARK'S HIGHLIGHTS BY CAR

Arches is the easiest of Utah's national parks to see in a day, if that's all you can spare. An 18-mile (one-way) **scenic drive** offers splendid views of countless natural rock arches and other formations, and several easy hikes reveal additional scenery. Allow 1¹/₂ hours for the round-trip drive, adding time for optional hikes. The main road is easy to navigate, even for RVs, but parking at some viewpoints is limited.

Start out by viewing the film *Secrets of Red Rock* at the **visitor center** to get a feel for what lies ahead. Then drive north past the Moab Fault to the overlook parking for **Park Avenue,** a solid rock "fin" that reminded early visitors of the New York skyline.

From here, your next stop is **La Sal Mountain Viewpoint,** where you look southeast to the La Sal Mountains, named by early Spanish explorers who thought the snow-covered mountains looked like huge piles of salt. In the overlook area is a "desert scrub" ecosystem, composed of sagebrush, saltbush, blackbrush, yucca, and prickly pear cactus. Animals that inhabit the area include the kangaroo rat, the black-tailed jackrabbit, the rock squirrel, several species of lizards, and the coyote.

Continuing on the scenic drive, you'll begin to see some of the park's major formations at **Courthouse Towers,** where large monoliths such as Sheep Rock, the Organ, and the Three Gossips dominate the landscape. Leaving Courthouse Towers, watch for the **Tower of Babel** on the east (right) side of the road, then proceed past the petrified sand dunes to **Balanced Rock,** a huge boulder weighing about 3,600 tons, perched on a slowly eroding pedestal.

Continue down a side road to the east (right) to the **Windows.** Created when erosion penetrated a sandstone fin, they can be seen after a short walk from the parking area. Also in this area are **Turret Arch** and the **Cove of Caves.** Erosion is continuing to wear away at the back of the largest cave, which means it will probably become an arch one day. A short walk from the parking lot takes you to **Double Arch,** which looks exactly like what its name implies. From the end of this trail, you can also see the delightful **Parade of Elephants.**

Return to the main park road, turn north (right), and drive to **Panorama Point,** which offers an expansive view of Salt Valley and the Fiery Furnace, which can really live up to its name at sunset.

Next, turn east (right) off the main road onto the Wolfe Ranch Road and drive to the **Wolfe Ranch** parking area. A short walk leads to what's left of this ranch. John Wesley Wolfe and his son Fred moved here from Ohio in 1898, and in 1907 were joined by John's daughter Flora, her husband, and their two children. The cabin seen here was built for Flora's family (John's cabin was destroyed by a flash flood). In 1910, the family packed up and returned to Ohio. If you follow the trail a bit farther, you'll see some Ute petroglyphs.

More ambitious hikers can continue for a moderately difficult 3-mile round-trip excursion to **Delicate Arch,** with a spectacular view at trail's end. If you don't want to take the hike, you can still see this lovely arch, albeit from a distance, by getting back in your car, continuing down the road for 1 mile, and walking a short trail (about 5 min.) to the **Delicate Arch Viewpoint.**

Returning to the park's main road, turn north (right) and go to the next stop, the **Salt Valley Overlook.** The various shades of color in this collapsed salt dome are caused by differing amounts of iron in the rock, as well as other factors.

Continue now to the viewpoint for **Fiery Furnace,** which offers a dramatic view of sandstone fins. This is the starting point for 2-hour ranger-guided hikes in summer.

From here, drive to a pullout for **Sand Dune Arch,** located down a short path from the road, where you'll find shade and sand along with the arch. This is a good place for kids to play. The trail leads across a meadow to Broken Arch (which isn't broken at all—it just looks that way from a distance).

Back on the road, continue to **Skyline Arch,** whose opening doubled in size in 1940 when a huge boulder tumbled out of it. The next and final stop is the often crowded parking area for the **Devils Garden Trail Head.** From here, you can hike to some of the most unique arches in the park, including **Landscape Arch,** which is among the longest natural rock spans in the world. It's a pretty easy 1.6-mile round-trip hike. From the trail head parking lot, it's 18 miles back to the visitor center.

Most trails here are relatively easy, although because of the hot summer sun and lack of shade, it's wise to carry a good amount of water on any jaunt of more than 1 hour.

One easy walk is to **Sand Dune Arch,** a good place to take kids who want to play in the sand. It's only .3 mile (round-trip). Sand Dune Arch is hidden among and shaded by rock walls, with a naturally created giant sandbox below the arch. Resist the temptation to climb onto the arch and jump down into the sand: Not only is it dangerous, but it can also damage the arch. Allow about 30 minutes to Sand Dune Arch and back.

From the **Devils Garden Trail,** you can see about 15 to 20 arches on a fairly long, strenuous, and difficult hike, or view some exciting scenery by following only part of the route. We suggest taking at least the easy-to-moderate 1.6-mile round-trip hike to **Landscape Arch,** a long, thin ribbon of stone that's one of the most beautiful arches in the park. Watch for mule deer along the way, and allow about an hour.

Considered by many to be the park's best and most scenic hike, the 3-mile round-trip **Delicate Arch Trail** is a moderate-to-difficult hike, with slippery slickrock, no shade, and some steep drop-offs along a narrow cliff. Hikers are rewarded with a dramatic and spectacular view of Delicate Arch. You'll see the John Wesley Wolfe ranch and have an opportunity to take a side trip to a Ute petroglyph panel that includes drawings of horses and what may represent a bighorn sheep hunt.

Continuing along the trail, watch for **Frame Arch,** off to the right. Its main claim to fame is that numerous photographers have used it to "frame" a photo of Delicate Arch in the distance. Just past Frame Arch, the trail gets a little weird, having been blasted out from the cliff. Allow 2 to 3 hours.

The **Fiery Furnace Guided Hike** is a difficult, strenuous 2-mile round-trip naturalist-led hike to some of the most colorful formations in the park. Guided hikes are given into this restricted area twice daily March through October by reservation, and last from 2¼ to 3 hours. Cost is $10 per adult, $6 per child from 6 to 12; reservations must be made in person up to 7 days in advance. Permits are required to enter the Fiery Furnace on your own ($2 adults, $1 children 6–12), but special restrictions apply and there are no marked trails, so you must first speak with a ranger at the visitor center. Unless you're an experienced hiker, it's best to join a guided hike.

CAMPING IN THE PARK

Devils Garden Campground, at the north end of the park's scenic drive, is Arches' only developed camping area. The 52 well-spaced sites are nestled among rocks, with plenty of piñon and juniper trees. From March through October, the campground accepts reservations (© **877/444-6777;** www.recreation.gov), with a $9 additional booking fee. In summer, the campground fills early, often by 9am, with people trying to garner the first-come, first-served sites, so either make reservations or get to the campground early. Sites costs $20 per night.

The Southwest

The Southwest is a land of extremes: from the rugged drama of the Grand Canyon and the haunting ruins of centuries-old cliff dwellings to the manicured fairways of some of the country's best golf courses and the neon-laden Las Vegas Strip. The stunning landscapes of red rock, the harsh and delicate beauty of the desert, the wild thrills of America's premier pleasure cities, and the vestiges of the Wild West are irresistible to many travelers. Whether you're a foodie seeking chic restaurants, a spa buff looking for luxurious pampering, a frustrated cowboy, or an art aficionado looking for the perfect piece, you'll hit the jackpot (maybe even literally in Reno and Vegas) in the American Southwest. Even for the pickiest travelers, the attractions in this part of the country have become the stuff of the classic road-trip vacation.

1 LAS VEGAS

Las Vegas is a true original; there is nothing like it in America or, arguably, the world. In other cities, hotels are built near the major attractions. Here, the hotels *are* the major attractions. And if you tire of hotel-hopping, you can enjoy great works of art, five-star world-renowned chefs, and rock clubs and arenas that attract significant and still-current acts. With so many options available, you don't have to gamble at all!

As if. Vegas is first and foremost a gambling destination. And though the hotels aren't undercharging anymore in an effort to lure you into gambling round-the-clock, they still do their best to separate you from your cash. The cheap buffets and meal deals still exist, as do some cut-rate rooms, but both are likely to prove the old adage about getting what you pay for. Nevertheless, free drinks are handed to anyone lurking near a slot, and if show tickets aren't in the budget, you won't lack for entertainment. Free lounge shows abound, and the people-watching opportunities never pall.

In its own way, Vegas is every bit as amazing as the nearby Grand Canyon and every bit as much a must-see. It's one of the Seven Wonders of the Artificial World. Everyone should experience it once—you might find yourself coming back for more.

ESSENTIALS

GETTING THERE **By Plane** Almost every major domestic airline, and some international airlines, fly into **McCarran International Airport,** 5757 Wayne Newton Blvd. (© **702/261-5211,** TTY 702/261-3111; www.mccarran.com), just a few minutes' drive from the southern end of the Strip.

Bell Trans (© **800/274-7433** or 702/739-7990; www.bell-trans.com) runs 20-passenger minibuses daily between the airport and all major Las Vegas hotels and motels (7:45am–midnight). The cost is $5 per person each way to Strip- and Convention Center–area hotels, $6.50 to Downtown or other off-Strip properties (anyplace north of the Sahara Hotel and west of I-15).

Taxis are plentiful and a ride to the Strip costs around $20, though we recommend you rent a car while you're in town; the major rental agencies have desks at the airport.

from the northeast (Salt Lake City) and southwest (Los Angeles and San Diego). Lots of folks drive up from Los Angeles, and thanks to the narrow two-lane highway, it can get very crowded on Friday and Sunday afternoons. Other major routes are **U.S. 93** from the southeast (Phoenix) and **U.S. 95** from the northwest (Reno).

VISITOR INFORMATION For advance information, call or write the **Las Vegas Convention and Visitors Authority,** 3150 Paradise Rd., Las Vegas, NV 89109 (© **877/ VISIT-LV** [847-4858] or 702/892-0711; www.visitlasvegas.com). They can send you a comprehensive information packet, map, show guide, events calendar, and attractions list; help you find a hotel that meets your specifications (and even make reservations); and tell you if a major convention is scheduled during the time you would like to visit Las Vegas. Or stop by when you're in town. They're open daily from 9am to 5pm.

Another excellent information source is the **Las Vegas Chamber of Commerce,** 3720 Howard Hughes Pkwy., #100, Las Vegas, NV 89109 (© **702/735-1616;** www.lvchamber. com). Ask them to send you their *Visitor Guide,* which contains extensive information about accommodations, attractions, excursions, children's activities, and more. They're open Monday through Friday from 8am to 5pm.

GETTING AROUND We highly recommend that visitors rent a car. The Strip is too spread out for walking (and Las Vegas is often too hot or too cold to make strolls pleasant), and public transportation is often ineffective in getting you from Point A to Point B. All the major Strip hotels offer free parking (and Downtown parking is cheap), so finding a spot won't be an issue. If, however, you plan to confine yourself to one part of the Strip or to Downtown, your feet will probably suffice. All the major rental-car agencies have desks at the airports, and rates are generally pretty good.

By Bus & Trolley The no. 301 bus operated by **CAT** (© **702/CAT-RIDE** [228-7433]; www.rtcsouthernnevada.com/cat) plies a route between the Downtown Transportation Center (at Casino Center Blvd. and Stewart Ave.) and a few miles beyond the southern end of the Strip. The fare is $2 for adults, 60¢ for seniors 62 and older and children 6 to 17, and free for those 5 and under. A low $5 buys an all-day pass. CAT buses run 24 hours a day and are wheelchair accessible. Exact change is required.

The Regional Transportation Commission (RTC) also operates a service called the **Deuce** (© **702/CAT-RIDE** [228-7433]; www.rtcsouthernnevada.com/deuce), a fleet of modern double-decker buses that run the length of the Strip into downtown and near the airport. A one-way ride is $2 for adults, $1 for seniors 62 and older and children 6 to 17, and free for those 5 and under. For $5, you get an all-day pass that lets you get on and off as many times as you like and also lets you ride all the other RTC buses all day. They even provide recorded color commentary as you sit in the mind-numbing traffic jams that plug up the Strip most of the time. Exact change is required.

By Monorail The first phase of the Strip monorail (opened in 2004) is a 4-mile route that runs from the MGM Grand at the southern end of the Strip to the Sahara at the northern end, with stops along the way. The trains make the end-to-end run in about 15 minutes, and operate from 7am until 2am (until 3am Fri–Sun). Fares are $5 (!!!) for a one-way ride (whether you ride from one end to the other or just to the next station), but discounts are available for round-trips and multiride/day passes.

There are also a number of free transportation services, courtesy of the casinos. A free monorail connects Mandalay Bay with Luxor and Excalibur, and a free tram shuttles between the Mirage and TI at the Mirage.

By Taxi Cabs line up in front of all major hotels and charge $3.20 at the meter drop and 25¢ for each additional ⅛ mile, plus an additional $1.20 fee for being picked up at the airport and time-based penalties if you get stuck in a traffic jam. A taxi between the Strip and Downtown costs about $12 to $15. You can often save money by sharing a cab with someone going to the same destination (up to five people can ride for the same fare). If you just can't find a taxi and want to call one, try the following companies: **Desert Cab Company** (𝒞 702/386-9102), **Whittlesea Blue Cab** (𝒞 702/384-6111), or **Yellow/ Checker Cab/Star Company** (𝒞 702/873-2000).

FAST FACTS Emergency services are available 24 hours a day at **University Medical Center,** 1800 W. Charleston Blvd., at Shadow Lane (𝒞 **702/383-2000;** www.umc-cares. org). **Sunrise Hospital and Medical Center,** 3186 Maryland Pkwy., between Desert Inn Road and Sahara Avenue (𝒞 **702/731-8080;** www.sunrisehospital.com), also has a 24-hour emergency room. There's a 24-hour **Walgreens** at 2280 N. Las Vegas Blvd. (𝒞 **702/649-1415**). The **sales tax** on meals, goods, and some services is 7.75%. Clark County hotel **room tax** is 9%.

WHAT TO SEE & DO

You can't sit at a slot machine forever. (Or maybe you can.) In any event, it's not too hard to find ways to fill your time between poker hands. The **hotels and casinos** are unquestionably the star attractions in Las Vegas. Where else in the world can you sail the canals of Venice, take in a joust at a medieval castle, and ascend the Eiffel Tower, all in the space of 1 block? Just strolling down the Strip at night when everything is awash in neon is an experience like no other.

Many of the hotels offer free entertainment in the form of light shows, animal-filled parks, and strolling musical performers. Can't-miss shows and attractions include the **Bellagio's dancing fountains,** a musical ballet of water and light that is the best free show in town, bar none; the almost-always-stunning floral displays at the **Bellagio Conservatory;** the **talking statues in Caesars' Forum Shops;** the Mardi Gras–style **Masquerade Show in the Sky** at the Rio; and the **Mirage's exploding "volcano."** Couch potatoes can watch the MGM Grand's 80-foot outdoor video screens, while adventurers head for a roller coaster celebrating that most daredevil of drivers—the New York cabbie. (This last one's not free, but that only heightens the reality of the experience.) And last but not least, the casinos offer one of the greatest free thrills of all— watching the high rollers win and lose big at the tables (nothing like watching someone else lose 50 grand).

Nevertheless, when you finally tire of Strip-gazing (or your brain shuts down from the overload), there are plenty of other things to see and do in Las Vegas.

The Atomic Testing Museum From 1951 until 1992, the Nevada Test Site was this country's primary location for testing nuclear weapons. Aboveground blasts in the early days were visible to the tourists and residents of Las Vegas. This well-executed museum (a Smithsonian affiliate), library, and gallery space offers visitors a fascinating glance at the test site from ancient days through modern times, with memorabilia, displays, official documents, videos, interactive displays, motion-simulator theaters (like sitting in a bunker, watching a blast), and emotional testimony from the people who worked there. It respectfully treads that tricky line between honoring the work done at the site and understanding its terrible implications. Not to be missed.

755 E. Flamingo Rd. 𝒞 **702/794-5151.** www.atomictestingmuseum.org. $12 adults; $9 seniors, military, students with ID, and Nevada residents; free for children 6 and under. Mon–Sat 9am–5pm; Sun 1–5pm.

Fremont Street Experience   The Fremont Street Experience in the heart of Downtown is a 5-block open-air pedestrian mall, a landscaped strip of outdoor cafes, vendor carts, and kiosks purveying food and merchandise. Overhead is a 90-foot-high steel-mesh "celestial vault"; at night, it is the successfully revamped **Viva Vision,** a high-tech light-and-laser show enhanced by a concert-hall-quality sound that takes place five times nightly. The canopy above you is equipped with more than 12.5 million lights. Not only does it provide shade, it cools the area through a misting system in summer and warms you with radiant heaters in winter. It's a place where you can stroll, eat, or even dance to the music under the lights. The crowd it attracts is more upscale than in years past, and of course, it's a lot less crowded than the hectic Strip.

Fremont St. (btw. Main St. and Las Vegas Blvd.), Downtown. www.vegasexperience.com. Free admission. Shows nightly.

Liberace Museum (Best)   You can keep your Louvres and Vaticans and Smithsonians; *this* is a museum. Housed, like everything else in Vegas, in a strip mall, this is a shrine to the glory and excess that was the art project known as Liberace. You've got your costumes (bejeweled), your cars (bejeweled), your pianos (bejeweled), and many jewels (also bejeweled). It just shows what can be bought with lots of money and no taste. This is a one-of-a-kind place that's better than ever after a costly renovation to make it even more gaudy and over-the-top. Unless you have an underdeveloped appreciation for camp, you shouldn't miss it.

1775 E. Tropicana Ave. (at Spencer St.). © **702/798-5595.** www.liberace.org. Admission $15 adults, $10 seniors 65 and over and students with ID, free for children 10 and under. Tues–Sat 10am–5pm; Sun noon–4pm. Closed Mon, Thanksgiving, Christmas, and New Year's Day.

Madame Tussaud's Celebrity Encounter (Kids) Even if you aren't a fan of wax museums, this one is probably worth a stop—if you can stomach the ridiculous price. Figures here are state-of-the-art, although some reproductions are considerably better than others. All the waxworks are free-standing, allowing—and indeed encouraging—guests to get up close and personal. Go ahead; lay your cheek next to Elvis's or Sinatra's and have your photo taken. The emphasis is on film, television, music, and sports celebrities, plus some Vegas icons, all housed in five themed rooms. There's also a behind-the-scenes look at the lengthy process involved in creating these figures.

In the Venetian, 3355 Las Vegas Blvd. S. © **702/862-7800.** www.mtvegas.com. Admission $24 adults, $18 seniors, $15 students, $14 children 7–12, free for children 6 and under. Daily 10am–10pm, but hours vary seasonally, and museum may close early for private events.

MGM Grand Lion Habitat (Value) (Kids) Hit this attraction at the right time—when the crowds aren't here—and it's one of the best freebies in town. Lions frolic during various times of day in its large, multilevel glass enclosure. In addition to regular viewing spots, you can walk through a glass tunnel and get a worm's-eye view of the underside of a lion (provided one is in position); note how very big Kitty's paws are.

In MGM Grand, 3799 Las Vegas Blvd. S. © **702/891-7777.** Free admission. Daily 11am–10pm.

Secret Garden of Siegfried & Roy and Mirage Dolphin Habitat (Kids) Get up close and personal with some of the famed duo's white tigers, lions, and plain old gray elephants, here at this minizoo; or better still, watch dolphins frolic in the neighboring Dolphin Habitat. There is nothing quite like the kick you get from seeing a baby dolphin play. If the knowledgeable staff isn't already, ask them to play ball with the dolphins; they toss large beach balls into the pools, and the dolphins hit them out with their noses—sometimes you can join in, too.

In the Mirage, 3400 Las Vegas Blvd. S. © **702/791-7111.** www.mirage.com. Admission $15 adults, $10 children 4–10, free for children 3 and under if accompanied by an adult. Memorial Day to Labor Day daily 10am–7pm; Labor Day to Memorial Day Mon–Fri 11am–5:30pm, Sat–Sun 10am–5:30pm. Hours subject to change.

SPEED: The Ride/Las Vegas Cyber Speedway This popular stop has two attractions. The first is a remarkable 8-minute virtual-reality ride, **Cyber Speedway,** featuring a three-quarter-size replica of a NASCAR race car. Hop aboard for an animated, simulated ride—either the Las Vegas Motor Speedway or a race around the streets of Las Vegas (start with the Strip, with all the hotels flashing by, and then through the Forum Shops—whoops! There goes Versace!—and so forth). **SPEED: The Ride** is a roller coaster that blasts riders out through a hole in the wall by the NASCAR Cafe, then through a loop, under the sidewalk, through the hotel's marquee, and finally straight up a 250-foot tower. At the peak, you feel a moment of weightlessness, and then you do the whole thing backward! Not for the faint of heart.

In the Sahara, 2535 Las Vegas Blvd. S. © **702/737-2111.** www.nascarcafelasvegas.com. $20 for all-day pass on both rides. Cyber Speedway (simulator) $10; $6 per re-ride (you must be at least 54 in. tall to ride);

Stratosphere Thrill Rides (Kids) Atop the 1,149-foot Stratosphere Tower are three marvelous thrill rides. The **Big Shot** is a breathtaking free-fall ride that thrusts you 160 feet in the air along a 228-foot spire at the top of the tower, then plummets back down again. Sitting in an open car, you seem to be dangling in space over Las Vegas. Amping up the terror factor is **X-Scream,** a giant teeter-totter-style device that propels you in an open car off the side of the 100-story tower and lets you dangle there weightlessly before returning you to relative safety. And now they have the aptly named **Insanity,** a spinning whirligig of a contraption that straps you into a seat and twirls you around 1,000 feet or so above terra firma. Insanity is right. *Note:* The rides are shut down in inclement weather and high winds.

Atop Stratosphere Las Vegas, 2000 Las Vegas Blvd. S. (© **702/380-7777.** www.stratospherehotel.com. Admission: $10 each for Big Shot, X-Scream, or Insanity, plus fee to ascend Tower: $12 adults; $8 locals, seniors, hotel guests, and children 4–12; free for children 3 and under and those dining in the buffet room or Top of the World. Multiride and all-day packages also available for varying costs. Sun–Thurs 10am–1am; Fri–Sat 10am–2am. Hours vary seasonally. Minimum height requirement for Big Shot is 48 in., minimum height requirement for X-Scream and Insanity is 52 in.

WHERE TO ROLL THE DICE

What? You didn't come to Las Vegas for the Liberace Museum? We are shocked. *Shocked.* Yes, there are gambling opportunities in Vegas. Let's not kid ourselves; gambling is what Vegas is about. The bright lights, shows, showgirls, and food—they are all there just to lure you in and make you open your wallet. You should casino-hop at least once to marvel (or get dizzy) at the decor/spectacle and the sheer excess of it all. Beyond decoration, there isn't too much difference. All the casinos have slot and video poker machines and offer games such as blackjack, roulette, craps, poker, Pai Gow, keno, and baccarat. If you're a novice, many casinos offer free gambling lessons that include low-stakes games, so you won't lose much while you learn.

Some notable places to gamble include the **MGM Grand,** the largest casino on the planet (you will get lost); the light, airy **Mandalay Bay,** which has the lowest claustrophobia factor in town; the tasteful **Venetian;** the **Las Vegas Hilton,** where the space-themed casino has light-beam-activated slots; **Harrah's,** where the "party pits" offer the most fun in town; **Paris–Las Vegas,** where you'll find a kitschy Disney-esque atmosphere; and **Binion's Horseshoe,** where all serious gamblers head, thanks to low minimum bets and the highest betting limits in town. Note, however, that when push comes to shove, you're going to love where you win and hate where you lose, no matter where you are. *Tip:* Whichever casino you pick, sign up for its free slot club and you'll be eligible for perks, including meals, shows, discounts on rooms, gifts, tournament invitations, discounts at hotel shops, and (more and more) cash rebates.

Remember that gambling is supposed to be entertainment. Pick a gaming table where the other players are laughing, slapping each other on the back, and enjoying themselves. Sometimes you can have a better time at one of the older places Downtown, where stakes are lower, pretensions are nonexistent, and the clientele are often friendlier. You don't have to be a high roller. You would not believe how much fun you can have with a nickel slot machine. You won't get rich, but neither will most of those guys playing the $5 slots, either.

If there's one thing Vegas has in spades, it's hotels. Big hotels. You'll find the 10 largest hotels in the United States, if not in the world, right here. And you'll find a whole lot of rooms: 140,000 rooms, give or take a few, at this writing. The hotels are the city's biggest tourist attraction, and they pack in the crowds accordingly. (Las Vegas usually has an occupancy rate of about 90%.) A last-minute Vegas vacation can turn into a housing nightmare. If possible, plan in advance so that you can have your choice: Ancient Egypt or Ancient Rome? New York or New Orleans? Strip or Downtown? Luxury or economy? Vegas has all that and way too much more.

First-time visitors will most likely stay on the Strip, although Downtown is a lot nicer than it used to be, and the rates there are cheaper. The **Las Vegas Convention and Visitors Authority** runs a room reservations hot line (© 877/VISIT-LV [847-4858] or 702/892-0711; www.visitlasvegas.com) that can be helpful. They can apprise you of room availability, quote rates, contact a hotel for you, and tell you when major conventions will be in town.

Vegas does have hotels that eschew the theme scheme. Unlike many of the casino hotels, they are far more likely to cater to kids, making them good choices for families. One great selection is the luxurious **Four Seasons** (© 877/632-5000 or 702/632-5000; www.fourseasons.com), inside the Mandalay Bay, although it has its own entrance and facilities. It offers a temporary respite from the Vegas hype since there's no casino, but guests who need a numbers fix can use Mandalay's. The same goes for **THEhotel at Mandalay Bay** (© 877/632-7800 or 702/632-7777; www.thehotelatmandalaybay. com), a chic and sophisticated all-suite part of the casino hotel with its own entrance. And last but not least, there's the **Palazzo** (© 877/883-6423 or 702/607-7777; www. palazzolasvegas.com), the latest *luxe* expansion of the Venetian, where the rooms are a tiny bit nicer than its sister, but prices are way higher.

All the usual budget chains have properties in Las Vegas. (See appendix D for their toll-free phone numbers and websites.)

Note: The following are a representative slice of the city's hotels (most of them on the Strip, which is where most first-timers stay) in various price categories. Most of them take Vegas's excess to heart, because, as one traveler who could afford the Four Seasons or Ritz-Carlton but never stays there when in Vegas told us, "Why would I want to stay in a hotel in Vegas that looks like it could be anywhere else in the U.S.?"

Many hotels offer fridges on request for an extra fee (usually $10–$20 per day); ask when you reserve if this is important to you. For the lowdown on all of the city's fabulous hotels (which would take dozens of pages), check out *Frommer's Las Vegas.*

Bellagio This $1.6-billion luxury resort ushered in the post-Vegas-is-for-families elegance epoch. Bellagio is not so much a romantic Italian village as its theme would suggest, but it's a big, grand, state-of-the-art Vegas hotel (with all the pluses and minuses therein). Here you'll find fabulous fountains, a magnificent floral conservatory, an art gallery, and the best collection of restaurants in town. There is even an 8-acre Lake Como stand-in out front, complete with a dazzling choreographed water ballet extravaganza (the best free show in town). Rooms are nicely decorated and the roomy bathrooms are even more luxurious. Service is surprisingly good, given the size of the place. The pool area is exceptional and the health club is marvelous, if overpriced. This is not much like a getaway to a peaceful, romantic Italian village. It's not the best value in town, but it's still the ultimate Vegas luxury resort experience.

3600 Las Vegas Blvd. S. (at the corner of Flamingo Rd.), Las Vegas, NV 89109. ✆ **888/987-6667** or
702/693-7111. Fax 702/693-8546. www.bellagio.com. 3,933 units. $169 and up double; $450 and up
suite. Extra person $35. No discount for children. AE, DC, DISC, MC, V. Free self- and valet parking. **Amenities:** 14 restaurants; 6 pools; health club; spa.

Caesars Palace

Caesars is the spectacle that every Vegas hotel should be. A combination of Vegas luxury and a good dose of kitsch, the hotel is graced by Roman colonnades, marble fountains, and staff members attired in gladiator outfits and togas. But the hotel has a confusing layout, and it takes forever to get anywhere—especially out to the Strip. Accommodations occupy six towers; the newest rooms are done in the sleek, unfussy neutrals that are all the rage and have all the modern gizmos. If you are looking for old-time Caesars romance, ask for rooms with a Greco-Roman theme (some have classical sculptures in niches); some may still have four-poster beds with mirrored ceilings. The pool area, the $100-million **Garden of the Gods,** is a tasteful, undeniably "Caesar-esque" masterpiece, and the spa is a knockout.

3570 Las Vegas Blvd. S. (just north of Flamingo Rd.), Las Vegas, NV 89109. ✆ **877/427-7243** or 702/731-7110. Fax 702/697-5706. www.caesarspalace.com. 3,348 units. $129 and up double; $549 and up suite. Extra person $30. No discount for children. AE, DC, DISC, MC, V. Free self- and valet parking. **Amenities:** 25 restaurants; 4 pools; health club; spa.

Circus Circus Hotel/Casino Ⓚⁱᵈˢ

The last bastion of family-friendly Las Vegas; which is not to say that it's a theme resort, a la Disney World—the fun still revolves around a casino. Nevertheless, the world's largest permanent circus and indoor theme park are still here (right by that casino!), and kids will love it. The newer tower rooms have just slightly better-than-average furnishings; the Manor section comprises five white three-story buildings out back, fronted by rows of cypresses. These rooms are usually among the least expensive in town, but we've said it before and we'll say it again: You get what you pay for. The hotel also has its own RV park.

2880 Las Vegas Blvd. S. (btw. Circus Circus Dr. and Convention Center Dr.), Las Vegas, NV 89109. ✆ **877/434-9175** or 702/734-0410. Fax 702/734-5897. www.circuscircus.com. 3,774 units. $59 and up double. Extra person $12. Children 16 and under stay free in parent's room. AE, DC, DISC, MC, V. Free self- and valet parking. **Amenities:** 7 restaurants; 2 outdoor pools.

The Flamingo Las Vegas

By Vegas standards, the Flamingo is Paleozoic, but not only is it hanging in there, some of the changes and renovations have made us reconsider Bugsy Siegel's "real class joint" entirely. All their dated rooms are getting upgraded; the first set of retro-style but tech-friendly rooms off the conveyor belt are terrific. No doubt the Rat Pack would have approved. The Flamingo's exceptional pool area encompasses fishponds, two water slides, five swimming pools, two whirlpools, waterfalls, and a flamingo enclave—plus its spa and tennis courts are a big draw.

3555 Las Vegas Blvd. S. (btw. Sands Ave. and Flamingo Rd.), Las Vegas, NV 89109. ✆ **800/732-2111** or 702/733-3111. Fax 702/733-3353. www.flamingolv.com. 3,517 units. $85 and up double; $350 and up suite. Extra person $30. Timeshare suites available. AE, DC, DISC, MC, V. Free self- and valet parking. **Amenities:** 8 restaurants; 5 outdoor pools; 4 night-lit tennis courts; health club; spa.

Golden Nugget

Always the standout hotel in the Downtown area, a recent face-lift has made it more appealing than ever, so while it's not the cheapest place Downtown, it is by far the nicest. A massive face-lift has made the place look terrific; a new color scheme has given it a rich, deep look that is most posh and fresh. Deluxe rooms are done in pretty floral schemes, and are attractive and comfortable enough that you don't need to splash out on the more contemporary gold-club rooms. The presence of a chic and snazzy pool (check out the water slide!) and general overall quality make this the best hotel Downtown for families, though it's not what we'd call family friendly.

129 E. Fremont St. (at Casino Center Blvd.), Las Vegas, NV 89101. © **800/846-5336** or 702/385-7111. Fax 702/386-8362. www.goldennugget.com. 1,907 units. $69 and up double; $275 and up suite. Extra person $20. No discount for children. AE, DC, DISC, MC, V. Free self- and valet parking. **Amenities:** 5 restaurants; outdoor pool; health club; spa.

Harrah's Las Vegas Though parts of Harrah's benefited from a remodeling a few years ago, the rest of it evokes the worst of old Las Vegas—as in, dark, dated, and claustrophobic. Still, there is much to like here, and occasional good rates might make the so-so bits worth overlooking. The rooms have undergone some cosmetic fluffing to the tune of good new mattresses and those white bed covers now more or less standard in most local hotels. The rooms aren't flashy, but they are reliable for what is ultimately a gamblers' hotel. Harrah's health club is one of the better ones on the Strip, but the pool is underwhelming. The casino is one of the friendliest in town.

3475 Las Vegas Blvd. S. (btw. Flamingo and Spring Mountain roads), Las Vegas, NV 89109. © **800/427-7247** or 702/369-5000. Fax 702/369-5283. www.harrahs.com. 2,526 units. $79 and up double; $199 and up suite. Extra person $30. No discount for children. AE, DC, DISC, MC, V. Free self- and valet parking. **Amenities:** 9 restaurants; pool; health club; spa.

Luxor Las Vegas Kitsch-worshipers were dealt a blow when the people behind this hotel came to the inexplicable decision to eliminate anything Egypt from it, casting aside identity in favor of generic luxury. Obviously, they can't get rid of certain elements—the main hotel is, after all, a 30-story onyx-hued pyramid, complete with a 315,000-watt light beam at the top. Replicas of Cleopatra's Needle and the Sphinx still dominate the exterior. But other than that, every other trace of the land of the Pharaohs is being obliterated. And some magic will be gone from Vegas. Now guests will be attracted only by the generally good prices, not by the giddy fun the theme produced. Decor renovations will likely produce more cookie-cutter blandness, though doubtless there will be welcome upgrades to the furnishings. High-speed "inclinator" elevators run on a 39-degree angle, making the ride up to the Pyramid rooms a bit of a thrill.

3900 Las Vegas Blvd. S. (btw. Reno and Hacienda aves.), Las Vegas, NV 89119. © **888/777-0188** or 702/262-4000. Fax 702/262-4478. www.luxor.com. 4,400 units. $69 and up double; $150 and up whirlpool suite; $249–$800 other suites. Extra person $30. Children 11 and under stay free in parent's room. AE, DC, DISC, MC, V. Free self- and valet parking. **Amenities:** 7 restaurants and a food court; 5 outdoor pools; health club; spa.

Main Street Station The Main Street Station, one of the best bargains in the city, is 2 short blocks away from Fremont Street in Downtown, barely a 3-minute walk. The overall look is turn-of-the-20th-century San Francisco, and the details, from the ornate chandeliers to the wood-paneled lobby, are outstanding. It's all very appealing and just plain pretty. The long and narrow rooms are possibly the largest in Downtown, though the ornate decorating downstairs does not extend up here. The bathrooms are small but well appointed. If you're a light sleeper, request a room on the south side.

200 N. Main St. (btw. Fremont St. and I-95), Las Vegas, NV 89101. © **800/465-0711** or 702/387-1896. Fax 702/386-4466. www.mainstreetcasino.com. 406 units. $59 and up double. AE, DC, DISC, MC, V. Free self- and valet parking. **Amenities:** 3 restaurants; use of outdoor pool next door at California Hotel.

Mandalay Bay ⓐBest It doesn't really evoke Southeast Asia, but the Mandalay Bay actually looks like a resort hotel rather than just a Vegas version of one, and we find a hotel whose theme doesn't bop you over the head refreshing. You don't have to walk

through the casino to get to the public areas or guest room elevators, the pool area is **735**
spiffy, and the whole complex is less confusing and certainly less overwhelming than
some neighboring behemoths. The freshly redone rooms are among the finest on the
Strip, spacious and subdued in decor. The large bathrooms, stocked with a host of fabulous amenities, are arguably the best in Vegas. The hotel's highly touted wave pool (set in
a veritable waterpark) offers a nice afternoon's relaxation.

3950 Las Vegas Blvd. S. (at Hacienda Ave.), Las Vegas, NV 89119. ☏ 877/632-7000 or 702/632-7000. Fax
702/632-7228. www.mandalaybay.com. 3,309 units (excluding THEhotel). $99 and up double; $149 and
up suite; $149 and up House of Blues Signature Rooms. Extra person $30. Children 14 and under stay free
in parent's room. AE, DC, DISC, MC, V. Free self- and valet parking. **Amenities:** 22 restaurants; 4 outdoor
pools; health club; spa.

MGM Grand Hotel/Casino   Set on 114 acres, the massive MGM Grand has a green
exterior and a casino the size of four football fields (you will get lost at least once). The
hotel management now downplays the once-touted "hugeness," trying to pretend that
the really big casino is actually several medium-big casinos. Whatever. Having said all of
that, we've grown fond of this hotel and have to admit that they've gone to some efforts
to make the size work to its advantage. The standard guest rooms are blandly upscale,
generously proportioned, and equipped with everything you might need. The West Wing
rooms are smaller but more memorable and stylish, with lots of mirrors and frosted green
glass in the bathroom, at least two flatscreen TVs (one in the bathroom), and electronic
gizmos like lamps that turn on and off if you touch them. The spa is a Zen-Asian minimalist wonder, and the pool area is wonderful.

3799 Las Vegas Blvd. S. (at Tropicana Ave.), Las Vegas, NV 89109. ☏ 800/929-1111 or 702/891-7777. Fax
702/891-1030. www.mgmgrand.com. 5,034 units. $99 and up standard double; $159 and up suite. Extra
person $30. Children 12 and under stay free in parent's room. AE, DC, DISC, MC, V. Free self- and valet
parking. **Amenities:** 15 restaurants; 5 outdoor pools; fitness center; spa.

The Mirage   The mother of all modern Vegas hotels has been somewhat eclipsed by
the very hotels whose presence it made possible, but we still really like this place. The
hotel, fronted by waterfalls and tropical foliage, centers on a very "active" volcano that
erupts every 15 minutes after dark. Inside you'll find a verdant rainforest, complete with
habitats for Siegfried and Roy's white tigers, and a bunch of Atlantic bottlenose dolphins.
Fresh renovations are sprucing up the rooms to keep with the hotel's new elegant, sleek,
Asian atmosphere, but there larger ones all over town and the bathrooms (though solid)
are a little too cramped for what's supposed to be a swanky hotel. The staff is genuinely
helpful; any problems that may arise are quickly smoothed out. The pool is one of the
best in Vegas.

3400 Las Vegas Blvd. S. (btw. Flamingo and Spring Mountain roads), Las Vegas, NV 89109. ☏ 800/627-
6667 or 702/791-7111. Fax 702/791-7446. www.mirage.com. 3,044 units. $109 and up double; $275 and
up suite. Extra person $30. No discount for children. AE, DC, DISC, MC, V. Free self- and valet parking.
Amenities: 11 restaurants; outdoor pool; fitness center; spa.

New York–New York Hotel & Casino   Here's one you'll either love or loathe (reactions tend to be strong on either side of the fence). The hotel looks like the New York
City skyline (complete with a taxicab-themed roller coaster running through it). Subtle
it isn't, but at least this property revels in a unique theme as many of its Strip brethren
do their best to embrace blandness. You can gamble in a casino done up as Central Park
or play games in the Coney Island arcade. You'll experience a true taste of the Big
Apple—including the noise and the (often claustrophobia-inducing) crowds. Rooms
come in 64 different styles and are decorated in a sophisticated modern color scheme of

earth tones and pale pastels; some are downright tiny and suffocating (just like New York). Light sleepers should request a room away from the roller coaster. If you're a pool person, go elsewhere—the one here is pretty mediocre.

Fax 702/740-6920. www.nynyhotelcasino.com. 2,023 units. $79 and up double. Extra person $30. No discount for children. AE, DC, DISC, MC, V. Free self- and valet parking. **Amenities:** 7 restaurants and a food court; outdoor pool; fitness center; spa.

Paris Las Vegas Casino Resort   *Sacre bleu!* The City of Light comes to Sin City in this Strip fantasy hotel. It's theme-run-amok time again, and we are so happy about it. You can stroll down a mini–Rue de la Paix, ride an elevator to the top of the Eiffel Tower, stop at an overpriced bakery for a baguette, take your photos by several very nice fountains, and snicker at dubious French signage ("le car rental"). Rooms are nice enough but disappointingly uninteresting, with furniture that only hints at mock French Regency, and with small but pretty bathrooms that have deep tubs. Try to get a Strip-facing room so you can see the Bellagio's fountains across the street; north-facing rooms give you nice Peeping Tom views right into neighboring Bally's. Overall, not a bad place to stay, but a great place to visit—*quelle hoot!*

3655 Las Vegas Blvd. S., Las Vegas, NV 89109. ✆ **888/BONJOUR** (266-5687) or 702/946-7000. www.parislv.com. 2,916 units. $119 and up double; $350 and up suites. Extra person $30. No discount for children. AE, DC, DISC, MC, V. Free self- and valet parking. **Amenities:** 12 restaurants; outdoor pool; health club; spa.

Planet Hollywood Resort & Casino   Those looking for the pop kitsch sensibility of the Planet Hollywood restaurants will be disappointed; the public areas here are actually kind of classy and design intensive. But you are going to come here for the rooms (make sure to ask for a remodeled one). Each has a movie or entertainment theme, such as *Pulp Fiction,* which might have John Travolta's suit in a glass case and a glass coffee table filled with more original memorabilia from the film. As gimmicks go, it's a catchy one, and a good use for all that junk the company's accumulated over the years. The Moroccan-themed spa may be aesthetically our hands-down local favorite. **Note:** *Do not self-park here because the lot is so far from the action*—follow the signs for casino valet parking, which is right outside the front desk.

3667 Las Vegas Blvd. S., Las Vegas, NV 89109. ✆ **877/333-9474** or 702/785-5555. Fax 702/785-5558. www.planethollywoodresort.com. 2,600 units. $99 and up double. Extra person $30. No discount for children. AE, DC, DISC, MC, V. Free self- and valet parking. **Amenities:** 19 restaurants; 2 pools; health club; spa.

Rio All Suite Hotel & Casino   Rio bills itself as a "carnival" atmosphere hotel, which in this case means hectic, crowded, and noisy; a recent edict requires the already Most Scantily Clad Waitresses in Town to burst into song and dance in between delivering beers. In addition to its tropically themed resort, the Rio has an immensely popular 41-story tower and Masquerade Village that simulate a European village, complete with shops, restaurants, and a bizarre live-action show in the sky. The "suites" are actually one rather large room with a sofa and coffee table. Rooms feature floor-to-ceiling windows that offer panoramic views of the Strip. Note that the hotel actively discourages guests from bringing children.

3700 W. Flamingo Rd. (just west of I-15), Las Vegas, NV 89103. ✆ **888/752-9746** or 702/777-7777. Fax 702/777-7611. www.riolasvegas.com. 2,582 units. $99 and up double-occupancy suite. Extra person $30. No discount for children. AE, DC, MC, V. Free self- and valet parking. **Amenities:** 12 restaurants; 4 pools; golf course; health club; spa. *In room:* Fridge.

Stratosphere Las Vegas (Kids) At 1,149 feet, the Stratosphere is the tallest building west of the Mississippi; it's also in the middle of nowhere on the Strip, which explains the lack of crowds. But if you are looking for a friendly place to hang your hat and don't need frills, it's a good choice. The panoramic views from the top of the tower and some amazing thrill rides (see "What to See & Do," earlier in this chapter) are the big attractions. The smaller-size rooms are basically motel rooms—nice motel rooms, but with that level of comfort and style. Perfect if you are coming to Vegas with no plans to spend time in your room except to sleep (if even that). That isn't to say there aren't other elements to like here, including a midway area with kiddie-oriented rides, a pool with a view, and some of the friendliest, most accommodating staff in town.

2000 Las Vegas Blvd. S. (btw. St. Louis and Baltimore aves.), Las Vegas, NV 89104. ℂ **800/998-6937** or 702/380-7777. Fax 702/383-5334. www.stratospherehotel.com. 2,444 units. $49 and up double; $109 and up suite. Extra person $20. Children 12 and under stay free in parent's room. AE, DC, DISC, MC, V. Free self- and valet parking. **Amenities:** 9 restaurants; pool.

TI–Treasure Island Originally the most modern family-friendly hotel on the Strip, the former Treasure Island was a blown-up version of Disneyland's Pirates of the Caribbean. But that's all behind them now, and the name change is there to make sure you understand this is a grown-up, sophisticated resort. Even its famous pirate stunt show out front has been revamped so that the pirates now "battle" scantily clad "strippers"—er, "sirens." The refit has spruced up the resort so much that we now rank it ahead of its sister, the Mirage. The good-size rooms are getting redone, and while they aren't breaking from the mold of geometric neutrals, they are more striking than some. Good bathrooms feature large soaking tubs. Best of all, Strip-side rooms have a view of the pirate battle—views are best from the sixth floor on up. You know, so you can see right down the sirens' dresses. The pool, alas, is not particularly memorable.

3300 Las Vegas Blvd. S. (at Spring Mountain Rd.), Las Vegas, NV 89109. ℂ **800/944-7444** or 702/894-7111. Fax 702/894-7446. www.treasureisland.com. 2,885 units. $89 and up double; $129 and up suite. Extra person $30. No discount for children. Inquire about packages. AE, DC, DISC, MC, V. Free self- and valet parking. **Amenities:** 6 restaurants; pool; fitness center; spa.

The Venetian The Venetian falls squarely between an outright adult Disneyland experience and the luxury resort sensibility of other Vegas hotels. The hotel impressively re-creates the city of Venice, including the artwork, the marble pillars and arches, and—unfortunately—the outrageous prices. A room makeover has pared the previously over-the-top fussy decor, which is a good thing, but then again, apart from the size, it's not as dreamily romantic on the eye. Rooms in the **Venezia Tower** are more lush—a plasma TV in the bathroom!—and worth the extra bucks. It's like a Four Seasons on human growth hormones, with over-the-top opulence. A branch of the famous Canyon Ranch SpaClub is on-site. If there's a weak point, it's the hotel's pool area, which is disappointing and bland.

3355 Las Vegas Blvd. S., Las Vegas, NV 89109. ℂ **888/283-6423** or 702/414-1000. Fax 702/414-4805. www.venetian.com. 4,027 units. $169 and up double. Extra person $35, $50 in executive level. Children 12 and under stay free in parent's room. AE, DC, DISC, MC, V. Free self- and valet parking. **Amenities:** 18 restaurants; 6 pools; health club; spa.

Wynn Las Vegas Vegas's newest and perhaps most trumpeted resort came with a $2.7-billion price tag. The result? Something that is at once pretty "wow" and a whole lot "It looks like Bellagio." In short, it was something many of us had, in fact, seen before, just down the street. There's quite a lot to like here. The rooms are the best on the Strip, the atrium is lovely, and the gym and spa are excellent. If you are new to town, it will look plenty spectacular. But just about everything here can generate sticker shock (even the "free" waterfall show is best viewed only from areas where you'll have to pony up money for an expensive drink) in all but those used to costly resorts, and the latter usually have one-tenth the number of rooms here. Still, this is a very adult hotel, in the best sense—classy and mature.

3131 Las Vegas Blvd. S. (corner of Spring Mountain Rd.), Las Vegas, NV 89109. (📞 **888/320-9966** or 702/770-7000. Fax 702/770-1571. www.wynnlasvegas.com. 2,716 units. $199 and up double. Extra person $50. No discount for children. AE, DC, DISC, MC, V. Free self- and valet parking. **Amenities:** 22 restaurants; 4 pools; health club; spa.

WHERE TO DINE

The dining scene in Las Vegas is a melting pot of midnight steak specials, cheap buffets, and gourmet rooms that rival those found in New York or Los Angeles. *One word of warning:* You can eat well in Vegas, and you can eat cheaply in Vegas, but you'll find it hard to do both. We list a few of the best bets in town, but the inexpensive ones can be hard to find.

Theme-restaurant buffs can chow down at **House of Blues,** in Mandalay Bay, 3950 Las Vegas Blvd. S. (📞 **702/632-7607**); the **Hard Rock Cafe,** at 4475 Paradise Rd., at Harmon Avenue (📞 **702/733-8400**); **ESPN,** at 3790 Las Vegas Blvd. S., in New York–New York Hotel & Casino (📞 **702/933-3776**); the **Harley Davidson Cafe,** 3725 Las Vegas Blvd. S., at Harmon Avenue (📞 **702/740-4555**); or the **Rainforest Café,** in the MGM Grand, 3799 Las Vegas Blvd. S. (📞 **702/891-8580**).

For those wanting to sample one of the many hotel buffets—and it's an essential part of the Las Vegas vacation—some of the better bets include **MORE—The Buffet at Luxor,** 3900 Las Vegas Blvd. S. (📞 702/262-4000); **Bellagio Buffet,** 3600 Las Vegas Blvd. S. (📞 877/234-6358); **Rio's Carnival World Buffet,** 3700 W. Flamingo Rd. (📞 702/252-7777); **Paris Le Village Buffet,** 3665 Las Vegas Blvd. S. (📞 888/266-5687); **Spice Market Buffet,** in the Planet Hollywood Resort, 3667 Las Vegas Blvd. S. (📞 702/785-5555); and **Main Street Station Garden Court,** 200 N. Main St. (📞 702/387-1896). The best Sunday brunch buffet is **Bally's Sterling Sunday Brunch,** 3645 Las Vegas Blvd. S. (📞 702/967-7999), which costs $75 per person.

Gourmands will also find plenty of dining options. Celebrity chefs Wolfgang Puck and Emeril Lagasse have 10 restaurants in town between them; multi-Michelin-starred chef Joël Robuchon opened two restaurants in the MGM Grand; master Italian chef Mario Batali has two; celeb chef Julian Serrano reigns at Bellagio's **Picasso;** Thomas Keller, the brains behind Napa Valley's French Laundry—considered by many to be the best restaurant in the United States—has a branch of his **Bouchon** bistro; legendary chef Alain Ducasse is behind **Mix** at THEhotel; and branches of L.A., New York, San Francisco, and Boston high-profile names such as **Pinot Brasserie, Le Cirque, Aureole, Olives, Border Grill, Nobu,** and others have all rolled into town.

Border Grill MEXICAN   For our money, here's the best Mexican food in town. This big cheerful space—like a Romper Room for adults—houses a branch of the much-lauded L.A. restaurant, conceived and run by the Food Network's "Two Hot Tamales," Mary Sue Milliken and Susan Feniger. This is truly authentic Mexican home-cooking. Consequently, don't expect precisely the same food you would encounter in your favorite corner joint, but do expect fresh and fabulous food, arranged as brightly on the plates as the decor on the walls. Don't miss the dense but fluffy Mexican chocolate cream pie (with a meringue crust).

Bouchon BISTRO   Here is where the whole celebrity chef concept bursts into full glory. Thomas Keller made his name with his Napa Valley restaurant, the French Laundry, considered by many to be the best restaurant in the United States. His Vegas restaurant is superlative as well. We tried nearly everything on the menu and can report that in almost every case they are gold-standard versions of classics. The sweet and supremely fresh Snow Creek oysters seem to melt on contact with your tongue. The beef bourguignon is exactly as you expect it to be, in the divine perfection sense.

In the Venetian, 3355 Las Vegas Blvd. S. ✆ **702/414-6200.** www.bouchonbistro.com. Reservations strongly recommended. Main courses $10–$20 at breakfast, $22–$45 at dinner; Sat–Sun brunch $21–$25. AE, DC, DISC, MC, V. Daily 7–10:30am and 5–11pm; Sat–Sun brunch 8am–2pm; oyster bar daily 3–11pm.

Bougainvillea ⟨Value⟩ DINER   Oh, how we love a Vegas coffee shop. You've got your all-day breakfasts, your graveyard-shift specials, your prime rib, and, of course, your full Chinese menu. And it's all hearty and well priced; we're talkin' build your own three-egg, three-ingredient omelet for around $5. You can get a full dinner entree or a nice light lunch of a large half-sandwich and soup, also for around $5. And 24-hour specials—a slab of meat, potato or rice, veggies, soup or salad, and a 12-ounce draft beer—are an astounding $10. Yep. That's the ticket.

In Terrible's, 4100 Paradise Rd. ✆ **702/733-7000.** Entrees $5–$13. AE, MC, V. Daily 24 hr.

Capriotti's SANDWICHES   It looks like a dump, but there's a reason that Capriotti's is one of the fastest-growing businesses in town. They roast their own beef and turkeys on the premises and stuff them (or Italian cold cuts, or whatever) into sandwiches mislabeled "small," "medium," and "large"—the latter clocks in at 20 inches, easily feeding two for under $10 total. And deliciously so; the "Slaw B Joe" (roast beef, coleslaw, and Russian dressing) is fabulous. They even have veggie varieties. We never leave town without a stop here, and you shouldn't, either.

322 W. Sahara Ave. (at Las Vegas Blvd. S.). ✆ **702/474-0229.** www.capriottis.com. Most sandwiches under $10. AE, MC, V. Mon–Fri 10am–5pm; Sat 11am–5pm.

Circo ITALIAN   Ignore the bright primary-color scheme, in favor of watching the dancing fountains outside. And then order the *mista di Campo,* a lovely little salad, both visually and in terms of taste; it's a creative construction of vegetables bound with cucumber and topped with a fab balsamic vinaigrette. Follow that with a perfect tagliatelle with rock shrimp—it comes loaded with various crustacean bits in a light sauce. Note that appetizer portions of pastas are filling and cheaper than full-size servings. Entrees usually include more elaborate dishes, such as breast of Muscovy duck with dried organic fruit in port-wine sauce. Save room for desserts such as *tutto cioccolato,* consisting of chocolate mousse, ice cream, and crumb cake.

In Bellagio, 3600 Las Vegas Blvd. S. ✆ **702/693-8150.** Reservations recommended. Main courses $16–$59. AE, DC, DISC, MC, V. Daily 5–10:30pm (last seating at 10pm).

Grand Wok ⟨Value⟩ ASIAN   No longer thoroughly Pan-Asian, but still a solid choice for sushi and, more importantly, budget fare in the form of the combo soup full of noodles and different kinds of meat. It's particularly nice and more affordable than the usual hotel restaurant—and the primarily Asian clientele clearly agrees. Note that soup portions are most generous; four people could easily split one order and have a nice and very inexpensive lunch, an unexpected bargain option for the Strip.

In MGM Grand, 3799 Las Vegas Blvd. S. ✆ **702/891-7777.** Reservations not accepted. Main courses $15–$38; sushi rolls and pieces $7–$30. AE, DC, DISC, MC, V. Restaurant Sun–Thurs 11am–10pm, Fri–Sat 11am–1am; sushi bar Mon–Thurs 5–10pm, Fri–Sat 11am–1am, Sun 11am–10pm.

Lawry's The Prime Rib STEAK/SEAFOOD   Yes, you can get prime rib all over town for under $5, but why (to mix food metaphors) have tuna when you can have caviar? If you love prime rib, head straight for this meat-lover's institution, with a 1930s-style dining room with Art Deco touches and big-band music on the sound system. Giant metal carving carts come to your table, and you name your cut (the regular Lawry's, the extra-large Diamond Jim Brady for serious carnivores, and the wimpy thin English cut) and specify how you'd like it cooked. Flavorful, tender, perfectly cooked, and lightly seasoned, this will be the best prime rib you will ever have. We kid you not! It comes with terrific Yorkshire pudding and some creamed horseradish that is combined with fluffy whipped cream, simultaneously sweet and tart.

4043 Howard Hughes Pkwy. (at Flamingo Rd., btw. Paradise Rd. and Koval Lane). ✆ **702/893-2223.** www.lawrysonline.com. Reservations recommended. Main courses $32–$49. AE, DC, DISC, MC, V. Sun–Thurs 5–10pm; Fri–Sat 5–11pm.

Lotus of Siam ⟨Value⟩ THAI   We don't feel guilty about dragging you out to a strip mall in the east end of Nowhere because here is what critic Jonathan Gold of *Gourmet* magazine called no less than the best Thai restaurant in North America. In addition to all the usual beloved Thai favorites, they have a separate menu featuring lesser-known dishes from northern Thailand—they don't routinely hand this one out (since most of the customers are here for the more pedestrian, if still excellent, $9 lunch buffet). Standouts include the Issan sausage, a grilled sour pork number; and *Sua Rong Hai* ("weeping tiger"), a dish of soft sliced and grilled marinated beef. If you insist on more conventional Thai, you certainly won't be disappointed.

In the Commercial Center, 953 E. Sahara Ave. ✆ **702/735-3033.** www.saipinchutima.com. Reservations strongly recommended for dinner; call at least a day in advance. Lunch buffet $9; other dishes $9–$20. AE, MC, V. Mon–Thurs 11:30am–2:30pm and 5:30–9:30pm; Fri–Sun 5:30–10pm.

Monte Carlo Pub & Brewery ⟨Kids⟩ PUB FARE   Lest you think we are big, fat foodie snobs who can't appreciate a meal unless it comes drenched in truffles and caviar, we direct you to this lively (and we mean lively) working microbrewery and its hearty, not-so-highfalutin' food. There's no romantic atmosphere, thanks to the 40 TV sets sprinkled around the room—but no fancy French frills and, best of all, no inflated prices. Earning recent raves were the short ribs in a fine barbecue sauce, cooked just right; the excellent appetizer of chicken fingers and shrimp fried in beer; and the avocado-and-shrimp salad. We also highly enjoyed the double-chocolate-fudge suicide brownie, though, really, what's not to love about something like that?

In Monte Carlo Resort & Casino, 3770 Las Vegas Blvd. S. ✆ **702/730-7777.** Reservations not accepted. Main courses $6–$15. AE, DC, DISC, MC, V. Wed–Sun 11am–11pm; Fri–Sat 11am–1am.

Picasso FRENCH   Madrid-born chef Julian Serrano's cooking stands proudly next to the $30 million worth of Picassos that pepper the dining room's walls, making a meal here a memorable experience. This may be the best restaurant in Vegas, and given the serious competition, that says a lot. The menu changes nightly and is always a choice between a four- or five-course fixed-price dinner or tasting menu. We were bowled over by roasted Maine lobster with a "trio" of corn—kernels, sauce, and flan. Hudson Valley foie gras was crusted in truffles and went down smoothly. For dessert, a molten chocolate cake leaves any other you may have tried in the dust.

In Bellagio, 3600 Las Vegas Blvd. S. ✆ **877/234-6358.** Reservations recommended. Prix-fixe 4-course dinner $113; 5-course degustation $123. AE, DC, DISC, MC, V. Wed–Mon 6–9:30pm.

Red Square CONTINENTAL/RUSSIAN The beheaded and pigeon-dropping-adorned statue of Lenin outside Red Square only hints at the near-profane delights on the interior. Inside you will a mix of Czarist and Communist trappings that only a capitalist could put together. And then there's the ice-covered bar—all the better to keep your drinks (they have 150 different kinds of vodka) chilled. If you can tear your eyes away from the theme-run-amok, you might notice that the menu is quite good. Blow your expense account on some caviar or, more affordably, try the Siberian nachos—smoked salmon, citron caviar, and crème fraîche. The chef's special is a Roquefort-crusted filet mignon; it's a grand piece of meat, one of the best in town and more cheaply priced than similarly ranked places. Desserts are worth saving room for, especially the warm chocolate cake with a liquid center and the strawberries Romanoff.

In Mandalay Bay, 3950 Las Vegas Blvd. S. ✆ **702/632-7407.** Reservations recommended. Main courses $22–$46. AE, DC, MC, V. Daily 4–10:30pm.

Rosemary's Restaurant ⟨Best⟩ AMERICAN A 15-minute (or so) drive down Sahara is all it takes to eat what the *Vegas-Review Journal* consistently calls the best food in Las Vegas (and we do, too). The brainchild of Michael and Wendy Jordan, both veterans of the New Orleans food scene, Rosemary's cuisine covers most regions of the U.S., though Southern influences dominate. Interesting sides include ultrarich blue cheese slaw and perfect cornmeal jalapeño hush puppies. A recent visit found the crispy striped bass fighting it out with the pan-seared honey-glazed salmon for the best fish dish I've ever had. Desserts are most pleasant. The restaurant, unusually, will give beer suggestions to pair with courses, including some fruity Belgian numbers; this is such a rare treat that if you drink, you must try some of their suggestions.

8125 W. Sahara. ✆ **702/869-2251.** www.rosemarysrestaurant.com. Reservations strongly recommended. Lunch $14–$17; dinner $27–$42. AE, DISC, MC, V. Mon–Fri 11:30am–2:30pm and 5:30–10:30pm; Sat–Sun 5:30–10:30pm.

Sensi ECLECTIC It's usually a truism, as far as restaurants go, "jack of all trades, master of none." Sensi seems to be an exception, given that its menu is made up of Italian (fancy pizzas and pastas), wood-grilled American options (burgers, fish, chicken), and Asian-influenced dishes (and they mean "Pan-Asian," thus tandoori and sushi both). And yet, it does it all very well indeed. You are probably best off here at lunchtime, sampling pizza al prosciutto or wok-fried shrimp, for more moderate prices than found at dinner. Best of all is the "Sensi 41," a healthy take on the bento box, featuring such things as miso-glazed Chilean sea bass, some tender sashimi, piquant rice, and, disconcertingly, mozzarella salad. They finish it up with two small, cunning servings of fancy ice cream in wee cones. And do try that homemade ginger ale. A fun menu in a fun-looking space, laid out to surround one very busy and versatile kitchen.

In Bellagio, 3600 Las Vegas Blvd. S. ✆ **877/234-6358.** Main courses $14–$22 at lunch, $22–$44 at dinner. AE, DC, DISC, MC, V. Daily 11am–2:30pm and 5–10:30pm.

LAS VEGAS AFTER DARK

Night is when it's happening in this 24-hour town. In fact, most bars and clubs don't even get going until close to midnight. You certainly won't lack for things to do when the sun sets. In addition to the free street shows (see "What to See & Do," earlier in this chapter), the hotels all have lounges, usually featuring live music, and you haven't truly done Vegas if you don't hit at least one showroom.

For up-to-date listings, contact the **Las Vegas Convention and Visitors Authority** (© **877/VISIT-LV** [847-4858] or 702/892-0711; www.visitlasvegas.com) and ask for a free copy of *Showguide* or *What's On in Las Vegas* (one or both of which will likely be in your hotel room). Plan well ahead if you have your heart set on seeing one of the most popular shows or a major headliner. Admission to shows runs the gamut, from about $25 for Mac King (comedy magic show at Harrah's) to $250 and more for top headliners. Prices occasionally include two drinks, but don't bet on it.

The Shows

There are shows all over town, ranging from traditional magic shows to cutting-edge acts such as *Mystère*. The showgirls remain, topless and otherwise. The trend in Vegas as we wrote this is toward celebrity showpieces (Bette Midler anyone?), sex (striptease-style shows), and anything Cirque du Soleil (the latest being *Believe*, a collaboration between the famous troupe and illusionist Criss Angel).

You won't go wrong seeing one of **Cirque du Soleil**'s productions—the best of that august group are *O,* at the Bellagio (© **888/488-7111** or 702/693-7722), which is a breathtaking mix of artistry and acrobatics over a 1.5-million-gallon pool; and *Mystère,* at TI (© **800/963-9634** or 702/796-9999), a sophisticated and surreal circus extravaganza. The most intelligent show in Vegas is definitely *Penn & Teller* at the Rio (© **888/746-7784**); it's got magic, juggling, acerbic comedy, mean stunts, and great quiet beauty. The **Blue Man Group** at the Venetian is performance art for the masses, but don't let that prevent you from going and laughing your head off (© **877/833-6423**). And if you want to see a classic Vegas topless revue—oh, why not?—check out *Jubilee!* at Bally's (© **800/237-7469** or 702/739-4567).

Magic fans will love **Lance Burton:** *Master Magician,* at the Monte Carlo (© **877/386-8224** or 702/730-7160), whose sleight-of-hand tricks are extraordinary. And for great afternoon (and cheap) entertainment, head straight for the magic and comedy of *Mac King* at Harrah's (© **800/427-7247**).

The Club & Bar Scene

Most Las Vegas bars and clubs don't even get going until close to midnight. To find out what's going on where, consult the *Las Vegas Weekly* (great club and bar descriptions in its listings; www.lasvegasweekly.com) and *City Life* (weekly, with listings of what's playing where all over town; www.lasvegascitylife.com). You can pick up both at local restaurants, bars, record and music stores, and hep retail stores.

At press time, our favorite club in Vegas is **Body English,** in the Hard Rock Hotel, 4455 Paradise Rd. (© **702/693-5000;** www.bodyenglish.com), which has long lines, a hefty price tag, and a clash of Anne Rice and Cher Gothic–themed wacky decadence that's exactly what a Las Vegas club should be. The **Bank,** at the Bellagio, 3600 Las Vegas Blvd. S. (© **702/693-8300**), is a grown-up nightclub that caters to the deep-pocket crowd and is the last word in high-end clubbing. **Privé and the Living Room,** in Planet Hollywood, 3667 Las Vegas Blvd. S. (© **702/492-3960**), is a user-friendly club that's hot but not intimidating—the VIP lines and attitude that are a hallmark of pretty much every other Vegas club are refreshingly absent here.

Gipsy, 4605 Paradise Rd. (© **702/731-1919**), is the gay dance club that draws the biggest crowds. For other gay nightlife, check out **www.gaylasvegas.com** or **www. gayvegas.com**.

It's still an honor for a comedian to play Vegas, and a number of good comedy clubs are on the Strip. The best of the bunch is the **Improv,** at Harrah's, 3475 Las Vegas Blvd. S. (© **800/392-9002**), which presents the top comics on the circuit, ones you're likely to see on Leno and Letterman.

2 RENO

There's the old adage that says you can't be all things to all people, but Reno sure tries to come close. The city has been marketing itself as **"America's Adventure Place,"** and whether your idea of adventure is on the slopes, on a single track, or at the slots, Reno won't disappoint. While gambling is still a big attraction, don't mistake this area for Las Vegas; if you're looking for a fantasy world of exotic casino-hotels, you're in the wrong end of the state. Here the gaming action is only a part of the experience. Sure, you can have a great time gambling 24 hours a day, but it's the combination of hotel bargains, great restaurants, myriad outdoor activities, and proximity to Lake Tahoe (p. 866) that makes Reno a fun and affordable tourist destination.

ESSENTIALS

GETTING THERE   By Air   Most major airlines offer service into **Reno-Tahoe International Airport** (© 775/328-6400; www.renoairport.com). A downtown casino shuttle service runs from the airport every half-hour. Look for the white minibuses outside of baggage claim marked DOWNTOWN HOTELS. Fare is $2.65. Rental cars from the major chains are available at the airport.

By Train   Amtrak (© 800/USA-RAIL [872-7245]; www.amtrak.com) trains pull into the station at 280 N. Center St. The *California Zephyr* connects Reno to Chicago (trip time: 45 hr.), Omaha (35 hr.), Denver (26 hr.), and Salt Lake City (10 hr.).

By Car   From San Francisco, take **I-80** East to Sacramento and on to Reno; from Salt Lake City, take I-80 West. From Los Angeles, take **I-5** through central California to Sacramento and then I-80 to Reno. Be prepared for winter snowstorms that can make I-80 a chain-required highway. For road conditions, contact the Nevada Department of Transportation's 24-hour **Road Reporting Service** (© **877/687-6237;** http://safetravel usa.com/nv).

VISITOR INFORMATION   For information on lodging, attractions, and more, contact the **Reno/Sparks Convention and Visitors Authority (RSCVA),** 4590 S. Virginia St., P.O. Box 837, Reno, NV 89502 (© **800/FOR-RENO** [367-7366] or 775/827-7600; www.visitrenotahoe.com).

GETTING AROUND   Pedestrian-friendly downtown Reno is easily navigable on foot. If you head out of the downtown area and don't want to rent a car, try **Yellow Cab** (© 775/355-5555), **Reno-Sparks Cab Co.** (© 775/333-3333), or **Whittlesea Checker Taxi** (© 775/322-2222). A number of the larger hotels and motels have free courtesy buses on call. Check with your hotel or motel for information.

FAST FACTS   **St. Mary's Regional Medical Center,** 235 W. 6th St. (© **775/770-3000**), is downtown just off I-80 near Circus Circus Reno Hotel Casino. There's a

24-hour Walgreens pharmacy at 750 N. Virginia St. (© **775/337-8703**). **Sales tax** in Reno is 7.375%; **hotel tax** is 13.5%.

WHAT TO SEE & DO

The **Historic Reno Preservation Society (HRPS),** P.O. Box 14003, Reno, NV 89533 (© **775/747-4478;** www.historicreno.org), offers a series of architectural and historical walking tours. You can stroll through the city's ethnic neighborhoods or bike through some of Reno's historic zones, each loaded with many examples of classic American architectural styles. Check the website for dates and times.

The Truckee River winds through downtown Reno, and the **Arts District (www. renoriver.org)** that's sprung up along its banks is worth a stroll. A walk beginning at Wingfield Park will lead you over the bridge onto West Street Plaza, where concerts are held. Shops line First Street with cinemas, coffeehouses, and art galleries. Follow Virginia Street to find the Riverside Hotel Artist Lofts, and the Pioneer Center for the Performing Arts. The third Saturday of each month the Downtown Merchants Association hosts **Wine Walk on the Riverwalk** from 2 to 5pm. For $20 participants get a commemorative glass and wine tastings at more than a dozen art galleries, specialty shops, restaurants, and theaters. The South end of the Truckee River Arts District, known as CalAve, is becoming a notable neighborhood with boutiques, restaurants and bars, and the formidable **Nevada Museum of Art.**

Fleischmann Planetarium and Science Center   At the north end of the University of Nevada Reno campus, the planetarium houses the Star Theater's SkyDome large-format movie system, as well as a free public observatory and the Hall of the Solar System featuring many fascinating exhibits, including a meteorite found in Nevada weighing in at a whopping ton.

900 N. Virginia St. © **775/784-4811.** www.planetarium.unr.nevada.edu. Free admission. SkyDome tickets $6 adults, $4 seniors and children 14 and under. Mon–Fri 11am–7pm; Sat–Sun 11:30am–7pm.

The National Automobile Museum   Travel back through time as you stroll through a century of automobiles. More than 220 antique, vintage, classic, special-interest, and "cars-of-the-stars" vehicles from the Harrah Collection are displayed in surroundings appropriate to their period. The museum's collection includes educational and historical exhibits relating to the automobile. Notable cars here include the Thomas Flyer, winner of the 1908 around-the-world race, James Dean's 1949 Mercury Coupe from *Rebel Without a Cause,* and a gold-plated 1981 De Lorean LK Sport Coupe.

10 S. Lake St. © **775/333-9300.** www.automuseum.org. Admission $10 adults, $8 seniors, $4 children 6–18, free for children 5 and under. Mon–Sat 9:30am–5:30pm; Sun 10am–4pm. Tours Mon–Sat at 10:30am and 1:30pm.

Nevada Historical Society   The state's oldest museum (it celebrated its 100th anniversary in 2004) displays memorabilia and historical information about Nevada. It's also home to the largest collection of Nevada-related library material in the country. Special programs augment the regular exhibits.

1650 N. Virginia St. © **775/688-1190.** Admission $3 adults, $2 seniors, free for 18 and under. Galleries Mon–Sat 10am–5pm.

The Nevada Museum of Art ⏥Best   You can't miss the museum's new and very distinctive headquarters downtown. The four-level structure inspired by the state's Black Rock Desert is a work of art in its own right. The permanent collection focuses on works

depicting nature and the environment; there's also a rooftop sculpture garden. Traveling
exhibitions are scheduled throughout the year.

160 W. Liberty St. (© **775/329-3333.** www.nevadaart.org. Admission $10 adults, $8 seniors, $1 children 6–12, free for children 5 and under. Tues–Sun 10am–5pm (Thurs until 8pm); closed Mon.

OUTDOOR ACTIVITIES

The Reno/Tahoe area abounds in winter and summer outdoor activities, with the major winter snow scene being centered around nearby Lake Tahoe (p. 866). The long spring, summer, and fall seasons provide ample opportunity to stretch the muscles with some adrenaline-pumping thrills to fill the daytime hours. For information on adventure tours and packages, contact the RSCVA (see above).

For those looking for a scenic and leisurely bike ride, the **Truckee River Trail** provides 14 miles of paved trails through downtown Reno/Sparks bordering the crystal-clear Truckee River.

For hikers, on the northwest side of Reno, **Peavine Mountain,** located in the Humboldt-Toiyabe National Forest (© **775/331-6444;** www.fs.fed.us/r4/htnf), is an area of solitude within minutes of paved city streets. Peavine Mountain features former mining roads and trails on Forest Service land that have been converted into a web of hiking and mountain-biking routes with extensive views of Reno and Sparks. The trails are of moderate difficulty and varied distances.

Sierra Adventures, 254 W. First St. (© **775/323-8928;** www.wildsierra.com), offers a variety of Reno-area adventure activities including hot-air ballooning, rock climbing, horseback riding, mountain biking, rafting, and more.

The **Truckee River Whitewater Park** (© **800/367-7366**) is a $1.5-million white-water and kayak park that's the first of its kind in Nevada. It's between First and Arlington streets in the heart of downtown. More than 2,600 feet long, the Class 3 white-water course includes north and south channels that surround a city park on an island in the river. It features 11 "drop pools," boulders for kayaking maneuvers, a slalom racing course, and 7,000 tons of smooth, flat rocks along the shores for easy river access. Best of all, the park is free and open to the public. **Sierra Nevada Outdoors** (© **800/881-6162;** www.sierranevadaoutdoors.com) offers professional kayak instruction for all levels. The "Intro to Kayak" class is a perfect overview for beginners. Two- and 3-day classes are also available for full immersion into the world of white-water kayaking.

GOLF   Golf is extremely popular in this mountain area (where the high altitude will put a little more zing in your drive). Reno's golf courses include the oldest in Nevada, the **Washoe County Golf Course,** 2601 W. Arlington Ave. (© **775/828-6640;** greens fees $30–$36), a par-72 course that was established in 1934. There are 50 other courses within a 90-minute drive of downtown Reno (many of them public courses with very reasonable greens fees); for course and golf package information, check out **www.visitrenotahoe.com/plan_your_trip/golf.**

SKIING   Skiing and snowboarding top the list of popular winter activities, with 18 ski resorts within a 90-mile radius. In fact, Reno-Tahoe boasts the highest concentration of resorts in North America. For resort and ski package information, check out **www.visitrenotahoe.com/plan_your_trip/ski.**

WHERE TO STAY

The casino hotels are the places to stay when in Reno. They are big, modern, and glitzy, with upscale dining rooms, bars, and showrooms. If you want something a little less busy and easier on the budget, there are numerous smaller motels and chain hotels in town. *Note:* Hotel rates here change almost daily and discounts are almost always available. In addition to the mainstream hotel discounters, **Reno Hotels** (© **888/682-0283;** www.renohotels.com) is a good option for obtaining discount hotel rooms.

Atlantis Casino Resort Spa

Just outside of the downtown district, this deluxe resort is notable for its friendly service and comfortable rooms with high-rise views of the city and mountains. The tropical-theme resort doesn't exactly resemble its namesake, but it makes for a good stay—provided you stick to rooms in the high-rise tower and avoid the cheap Motor Lodge rooms. Splurge on a Concierge Tower room (floors 21–27), which offers 20% more space, oversize tubs, terry robes, luxurious linens, and butler service. Recent renovations have included an all-new race and sports book, a new and expanded spa, and brand-new fitness center. The casino also claims Reno's only four-star, smoke-free poker room.

3800 S. Virginia St., Reno, NV 89502. © **800/723-6500** or 775/825-4700. Fax 775/825-1170. www.atlantis casino.com. 980 units. $46–$150 double; $125–$850 suite. Discounts available. Golf packages start at $89. Free self-parking. AE, DISC, MC, V. Pets allowed. **Amenities:** 8 restaurants; 2 pools (1 indoor); health club; spa.

Circus Circus Reno Hotel Casino (Value)(Kids)

If you're traveling with kids, this is the place to stay. The circus theme so popular in Las Vegas is carried over to this resort, where clowns and acrobats from China augment visiting headline acts from renowned companies such as Cirque du Soleil and Ringling Brothers. The high-flying acts perform for free above a midway housing carnival-style games and a video arcade. Don't let the circus theme fool you, however—there's a 65,000-square-foot casino, so your kids aren't the only ones feeding quarters into machines. The Victorian-style rooms are clean and comfortable; some offer mountain views. Jacuzzi suites feature a separate sitting area with a sofa bed and are good for families. On the downside, there is no pool, though for a fee you can use the one at a neighboring hotel.

500 N. Sierra St., Reno, NV 89503. © **800/648-5010** or 775/329-0711. Fax 775/328-9652. www.circus reno.com. 1,572 units. $39–$169 double; $69–$275 suite. Discount packages available. AE, DC, DISC, MC, V. Free self-parking. **Amenities:** 6 restaurants; exercise room.

Eldorado Hotel and Casino

Attached by a walkway to Circus Circus and the Silver Legacy, this hotel sports an upscale atmosphere with a relaxed vibe and a convenient location in the heart of downtown Reno. The Tower rooms feature a simple yet sophisticated decor, mountain views, and Judith Jackson toiletries in the bathrooms. The deluxe whirlpool suites toss in marble bathrooms, a Jacuzzi tub in the living area, and pop-up TVs. For the budget-minded traveler, the economy and standard rooms are a steal. The hotel casino also boasts nine award-winning restaurants, including a recent $5-million buffet renovation, 24-hour casino action, and a Broadway-style showroom that features a series of production shows alternating with headline artists. The **Brew Brothers** pub, with eight custom microbrews swings, plays live rock and blues nightly beginning at 9:30pm, and **Roxy's Bar & Lounge,** with its old-world charm and 102 versions of stiff martinis, is a popular gathering place with locals and tourists alike.

345 N. Virginia St., Reno, NV 89501. © **800/648-5966** or 775/786-5700. Fax 775/348-7513. www.eldorado reno.com. 816 units. $70–$80 double. 2-night golf packages from $115. AE, DISC, MC, V. Free valet and self-parking. **Amenities:** 9 restaurants; heated pool.

Grand Sierra Resort

The Grand Sierra Resort, formerly the Reno Hilton, is the newest and most chic resort property in Reno, with the first phase of a $90-million renovation project complete. The upper 11 floors have been transformed into a luxury condominium hotel called the Summit at Grand Sierra. The 825 suites are plush and worth the price. The rest of the resort is a destination in itself. One of Northern Nevada's largest resort properties, the GSR also boasts retail shopping, a cinema, a 50-lane championship bowling center, outdoor thrill rides, and an aqua golf driving range. Tapping into the region's "America's Adventure Place" brand, the resort also offers an adventure concierge, available to plan outdoor recreational activities for guests.

2500 E. Second St., Reno, NV 89595. (℗ **800/648-5080** or 775/789-2000. Fax 775/788-3703. www.grand sierraresort.com. 2,000 units. $39–$159 GSR; $115–$375 Summit suite. Golf Suites Starting at $100. AE, DISC, MC, V. Free valet and self-parking. Pet-friendly accommodations available. **Amenities:** 10 restaurants; pool; health club; spa.

Harrah's Reno   This branch of Harrah's, long a dominant player in the casino hotel market, is smack in the middle of downtown. The rooms are modern, clean, and comfortable; suites toss in Jacuzzi tubs and good views. The service, long a Harrah's hallmark, is excellent. Guests enjoy a variety of touches such as 24-hour room service, an extensive health club, pool, and in-house massage. Evening entertainment centers around **Sammy's** (named for Sammy Davis, Jr.), where Vegas-type shows feature topless gals and special guest entertainers. During the summer, Harrah's presents free concerts at the Plaza, a 65,000-square-foot outdoor venue.

219 N. Center St., Reno, NV 89501 (℗ **800/HARRAHS** (427-7247) or 775/786-3232. Fax 775/788-3703. www.harrahsreno.com. 952 units. $39–$159 double; $175–$375 suite. Golf packages start at $79. AE, DISC, MC, V. Free self-parking. Pet kennel service available. **Amenities:** 7 restaurants; pool; health club; spa.

Peppermill Hotel Casino (Best   Adjacent to a quiet park and lake about 2 miles south of downtown, this fun hotel consistently racks up awards as the city's best. With the newly opened $400-million Tuscan-themed expansion, it's even easier to see why. The new 600-suite Tuscany Tower features plush pillow-top king-size beds, European soaking tubs, and all the amenities you would expect. The Tower rooms are clean and spacious; king rooms feature a sofa. The new Tuscan Gardens, a year-round haven complete with pools and private cabanas, opened summer 2008, and there's also a fitness center, wedding chapels, Arcade Xtreme with all the latest and greatest in video games, and a three-story Roman baths–inspired spa. Free cabaret entertainment flows throughout the night, and there are 15 themed bars on the premises.

2707 S. Virginia St., Reno, NV 89502. (℗ **800/648-6992** or 775/826-2121. Fax 775/826-5205. www. peppermillreno.com. 1,635 units. $73–$140 double; $89–$249 suite. Golf packages start at $69. AE, DISC, MC, V. Free self-parking. **Amenities:** 11 restaurants; heated pool; health club; spa.

Siena Hotel Spa and Casino   Set on the banks of the Truckee River near downtown, this hotel offers a bit of Italian elegance and the best beds in the city. Come here if you want more intimate surroundings than the mammoth casino resorts. Rooms are decorated in modern Tuscan style and have views of the river or the mountains. The bathrooms feature Bath & Body Works toiletries, but it's the beds you'll remember— ultracomfy mattresses topped with Egyptian cotton linens and down comforters. Suites toss in more space and Jacuzzi tubs. The spa and rooftop pool are divine, the dining is grand (especially at the smoke-free **Enoteca** wine bar, which offers more than 35 wines by the glass), and the fitness center is free to guests.

One S. Lake St., Reno, NV 89501. (℗ **877/SIENA-33** (743-6233) or 775/32-SIENA (327-4362). Fax 775/321-5866. www.sienareno.com. 214 units. $79–$250 double; $200–$460 suite. AE, DISC, MC, V. Free self-parking. **Amenities:** 3 restaurants; pool; fitness center; spa. *In room:* Fridge.

Silver Legacy Resort Casino (Value)   The Silver Legacy Resort Casino is a Victorian-themed tour de force, with the largest center for gaming and entertainment in northern Nevada. The resort boasts six restaurants and eateries, Catch a Rising Star comedy club, 85,000 square feet of gaming space, and the world's largest composite dome. In the unlikely event you can't get your casino fix here, skywalks connect the hotel to Circus Circus on the north and to the Eldorado Hotel Casino on the south.

407 N. Virginia St., Reno, NV 89501. (𝒞 **800/687-8733** or 775/325-7401. Fax 775/325-7177. www.silverlegacy.com. 1,720 units. $55–$250 double; $100–$800 suite. AE, DISC, MC, V. Free self-parking. **Amenities:** 6 restaurants; pool; health spa.

WHERE TO DINE

Even though you'll find a seemingly endless array of restaurants inside the casino hotels, you won't want to miss some of these locals' favorites.

Beaujolais Bistro FRENCH   Reno lays claim to its own little corner of France in this small, charming bistro, near the Truckee River downtown. With its exposed brick walls, parquet floors, and dreamy atmosphere, Beaujolais Bistro is the perfect spot for an intimate dinner. Expect modern twists on classic French dishes such as beef bourguignon and duck a l'orange, and be sure to save room for one of the decadent desserts. There's an extraordinary selection of fine French and domestic wines.

130 West St. (𝒞 **775/323-2227.** www.beaujolaisbistro.com. Reservations recommended. Main courses $19–$34. AE, MC, V. Tues–Fri 11:30am–2pm; Tues–Sun 5–10pm.

Bertha Miranda's (Kids) MEXICAN   On the east side of town, this popular Mexican restaurant offers plenty of atmosphere in a three-tiered dining room lined with stone walls. Choose a booth or a table and try the Tamale Special or El Rancho Steak. In the evening there is live music in the bar/cocktail lounge.

336 Mill St. (𝒞 **775/786-9697.** www.berthamirandas.com. Reservations accepted Sun–Thurs only. Main courses $9–$15. MC, V. Daily 10am–10pm.

Charlie Palmer Steak AMERICAN   Renowned for his signature "Progressive American" cuisine, Charlie Palmer's culinary triumphs include restaurants in New York, Las Vegas, Sonoma, Washington, D.C.—and now Reno. Palmer landed on the Reno dining scene summer of 2007 with Charlie Palmer Steak, the third of his modern American steakhouses, at the Grand Sierra Resort. With an expansive dining room that seats over 200, an impeccable staff, and a decor that is industrial chic (an 18×21-foot, 2,000-lb. chandelier fashioned from beautifully ominous shards of metal looms over the room), Reno's newest steakhouse shouldn't be missed. Expect perfectly cooked Artisan meats, decadent sauces and accouterments, and delicious side dishes paired with an eclectic and well-priced wine list.

Inside Grand Sierra Resort. (𝒞 **775/789-2456.** www.charliepalmer.com. Reservations accepted. Main courses $21–$59. AE, DISC, MC, V. Daily 5:30–10:30pm.

Golden Fortune CHINESE   Serving up authentic high-style Hong Kong cuisine, Golden Fortune, inside the Eldorado Hotel Casino, is easily the best Asian fare in town. The extensive menu features more than 90 different specialties, including exotic dishes like braised sea cucumber with black mushrooms. The honey-glazed walnut prawns, a house specialty, is divine, as is the Peking duck. For the bold, allow the chef to present several dishes of his choosing and skip the menu altogether—it's well worth it.

Inside the Eldorado Hotel Casino. (𝒞 **775/786-5700.** www.eldoradoreno.com. Reservations recommended. Main courses $10–$25. AE, DISC, MC, V. Thurs–Mon 5–10pm.

Little Nugget Diner (Value) BURGERS/DINER   Pretty much every casino hotel in
Reno has a 24-hour diner, and this one (inside the Little Nugget Hotel) serves pretty
good coffee-shop fare, but that's not why it's always packed to the rafters. The crowds
flock here for one reason: the burgers, which are the undisputed champs in town. Practically a Reno institution is the Awful-Awful—a juicy $5.50 cheeseburger served with hot,
crispy fries that's been giving carnivores their burger fix for more than 5 decades. If you're
a burger fan, this diner a must.

Inside Nugget Hotel, 233 N. Virginia St. (C) **775/323-0716.** Reservations not accepted. Main courses
$3.50–$12. No credit cards. Daily 24 hr.

Rapscallion Seafood House & Bar SEAFOOD   Reno's local paper has named this
charming brick oasis the city's best seafood restaurant so many times, they might as well
retire the award. There are pasta and beef dishes on the daily-changing menu, but it's the
aquatic cuisine here that's truly memorable, from a perfectly grilled salmon to fresh oysters and prawns. A large mahogany bar with a scenic stained-glass backdrop along with
the fireplace also makes this a warm and cozy place to enjoy a predinner cocktail. Wine
is offered by the glass or bottle. Live music is offered Wednesday through Saturday in the
evenings.

1555 S. Wells Ave. (C) **775/323-1211.** www.rapscallion.com. Reservations recommended. Main courses
$15–$50. AE, MC, V. Mon–Fri 11:30am–4pm; Sun–Thurs 5–10pm; Fri–Sat 5–10:30pm; Sun 10am–2pm.

Silver Peak Grill and Tap Room (Value) BREWERY   Silver Peak Grill and Tap
Room is as popular for its ales and lagers as it is for its pub fare. With items such as
salmon fish and chips dipped in Red Ale batter, grilled-lamb burger with kalamata olives
and goat cheese, and their signature barley-crusted chicken-breast sandwich with apple-
wood-smoked bacon, this isn't your average bar menu. Located on the corner of First and
Sierra streets, across from the Century movie theater, Silver Peak is a popular meeting
spot, and the outdoor seating on the patio is a great place for people-watching.

First and Sierra sts. (C) **775/284-3300.** Reservations not accepted. Main courses $7–$10. AE, MC, V. Daily
11am–midnight.

Sushi Pier 2 (Value) SUSHI/JAPANESE   Visitors may be surprised to find top-quality,
fresh sushi in a desert town, but Sushi Pier 2 offers just that, and at an amazing value—
the all-you-can-eat lunch menu is $13. Opt for the dinner menu for just $5 more, and
you won't be disappointed. Sushi Pier 2 offers all the classics you would expect, plus a
few additions, like the baked-to-perfection mussels with a delicious cream sauce. With
two massive sushi bars, a full cocktail bar, and a large dining area, the wait is never too
long—even on the busiest nights.

1507 S. Virginia St. (C) **775/825-5225.** Reservations not accepted. Main courses $13–$18. AE, MC, V. Mon–
Sat 11am–9:30pm; Sun 11am–9pm.

Thai Chili (Value) THAI   This tiny restaurant south of the downtown area has already
made a big splash on the local restaurant scene. Decorated in true Thai fashion, with
loads of lacquered wood, bamboo, and rich fabrics, it offers a serene and atmospheric
dining experience at a very reasonable price. The seafood dumplings are spiced perfectly,
and the stir-fried Prik Khing plate of meat, garlic, bell peppers, Thai chili paste, and
string beans is excellent. The service and presentation are first-rate.

1030 S. Virginia St. (C) **775/786-7878.** Reservations accepted. Main courses $6–$14. MC, V. Daily 11am–
3pm and 5–9pm.

White Orchid CONTINENTAL   A fresh orchid on every table greets diners as they enter this award-winning haven of tranquillity. The menu changes every 2 weeks in order to take advantage of fresh seasonal produce, but typical entrees include elk medallions served with Maine lobster and winter vegetables, and Thai-barbecued salmon with Chinese long beans. A special five-course chef's menu (opt for the wine pairings) is the best way to sample it all and offers the most bang for your buck. *Wine Spectator* bestowed its Award of Excellence on the long and varied wine list.

Inside Peppermill Hotel & Casino, 2707 S. Virginia St. (C) **800/648-6992.** www.peppermillreno.com. Reservations recommended. Main courses $30–$47; 5-course chef's menu $55, $75 with wine pairings. AE, DISC, MC, V. Daily 5pm–closing.

Zagol (Value) ETHIOPIAN   This cheerful restaurant just east of downtown has a steadily increasing following. Reno's first and only foray into Ethiopian cuisine, Zagol serves traditional fare expertly seasoned with exotic spices to create authentic beef, chicken, lamb, and vegetarian dishes. The *zilzil tibs,* made from long strips of tender beef sautéed lightly in purified herbal butter and seasoned with onion and fresh rosemary, are especially flavorsome. Zagol also offers a fine selection of traditional Ethiopian beverages, from honey wines to hearty Ethiopian beer. All dishes are served "family style" and sans silverware. The staff will happily instruct patrons in the art of scooping up the tasty morsels using just *Injera*—a traditional Ethiopian flatbread made from teff flour. They will, however begrudgingly, provide silverware upon request.

855 E. 4th St. (C) **775/786-9020.** Reservations not accepted. Main courses $8–$14. MC, V. Tues–Sun 11am–3pm and 5–9pm.

RENO AFTER DARK

Reno's big action is in the casinos, and the major resorts have enough showrooms, cabaret lounges, and intimate bars to keep you entertained all night long. If you're staying in one of the big ones, you can usually find all the entertainment you want without leaving the premises. The new **Reno Events Center** has brought in such A-list entertainers as the Black Eyed Peas, Brooks & Dunn, and Tom Petty & The Heartbreakers. The Reno Events Center is 1 block north of National Bowling Stadium, bounded by Fourth and Fifth streets, and Center and Lake streets in downtown Reno. Check the RSCVA website at **www.visitrenotahoe.com** for up-to-date information about what's playing at the casino hotels and at the Reno Events Center.

PERFORMING ARTS   The **Theater Coalition** ((C) 775/786-2278; www.theatercoalition. org) gathers information about area theater, ballet, opera, and musical performances and lists them on its website.

The **Reno Philharmonic Orchestra,** 925 Riverside Dr. ((C) **775/323-6393;** www. renophilharmonic.com), presents a fall and winter concert season plus summer concerts in the park. On a smaller scale but no less talented is the **Reno Chamber Orchestra,** 925 Riverside Dr. ((C) **775/348-9413;** www.renochamberorchestra.org), which presents concerts at various times during the year. The **Pioneer Center,** 100 S. Virginia St. ((C) **775/686-6610;** www.pioneercenter.com), is the home for traveling Broadway companies, as well as the ballet and opera. The **Nevada Shakespeare Company,** 1 Booth St. ((C) **775/324-4198;** www.nevada-shakespeare.org), presents modern renditions of the Bard's famous plays, as well as original works.

CLUB & MUSIC SCENE   The 24-hour **Alturas Bar & Nightclub,** 1044 E. 4th St. ((C) 775/324-5050), is the place for the blues and also features top R&B entertainment and pool tables. A slew of hip clubs and ultra lounges have emerged as part of Reno's urban renaissance. **210North,** 210 N. Sierra St. (© **775/786-6210**), the largest entry on the club scene, features two distinct dance floors, plus two VIP lounges, VIP beds, and several full-service bars to ensure every glass is always full. **BuBinga Lounge,** inside the Eldorado Hotel (© **775/786-5700**), is an established favorite where DJs spin everything from electronica to rap and where the young and stylish congregate. **Divine Ultra Lounge,** 101 N. Sierra St. (© **775/329-8088**), offers an upscale experience on a more intimate scale. Also burning up the late-night scene is **Tonic,** 231 W. 2nd St. (© **775/337-6868**). A down-tempo lounge with an urban/chic decor, Tonic has lounge chairs and banquettes, local artists' work adorning the walls, and a large dance floor. It's a popular late-night spot with live jazz and DJs Thursday through Saturday, so expect the crowds on the weekends, particularly after 11pm.

Scruples Bar & Grill, 91 W. Plumb Lane (© **775/322-7171**), features a huge menu with the best bar food in town available 24/7, indoor/outdoor dining, live music on the patio in the summer, and the requisite big-screen TV for watching sports.

Tronix, 303 Kietzke Lane (© **775/333-9696**), caters mainly to the gay/lesbian community, while the **1099 Club,** 1099 S. Virginia St. (© **775/329-1099**), caters to Reno's drag set.

3 PHOENIX & SCOTTSDALE

Sprawling across more than 500 square miles of what once was cactus and creosote bushes, the greater Phoenix metropolitan area, also known as the Valley of the Sun, has become a sort of Los Angeles of the desert. The only thing missing is an ocean. The abundance of sunshine has made it a hot winter vacation spot, and adjacent Scottsdale has become one of the nation's top resort destinations, with dozens of challenging golf courses, health spas, and top resorts, many of which boast sprawling pool complexes complete with waterfalls. Downtown Phoenix has become something of a sports-and-entertainment district, with several museums, the America West Arena (home of the Phoenix Suns and Mercury), and the Arizona Diamondbacks' Bank One Ballpark, one of the country's few baseball stadiums with a retractable roof.

ESSENTIALS

GETTING THERE   By Plane   Major domestic and some international carriers fly into **Phoenix Sky Harbor International Airport** (© **602/273-3300;** www.phxskyharbor. com), 3 miles from downtown Phoenix.

SuperShuttle (© **800/BLUE-VAN** [258-3826] or 602/244-9000) offers 24-hour door-to-door van service to resorts, hotels, and homes throughout the valley. Per-person fares average $16 to $18 to the downtown and Tempe area, $18 to downtown Scottsdale, and $26 to $44 to north Scottsdale.

By Car   The major routes into Phoenix are **I-10** from the west (Los Angeles) and southeast (Tucson), and **I-17** from the north (Flagstaff).

VISITOR INFORMATION   The main visitor center is the **Greater Phoenix Convention & Visitors Bureau,** 50 N. Second St. (© **877/225-5749** or 602/452-6282; www. visitphoenix.com; Mon–Fri 8am–5pm), on the corner of Adams Street in downtown Phoenix. The **Visitor Information Line** (© **602/252-5588**) has recorded information about current events in Phoenix and is updated weekly.

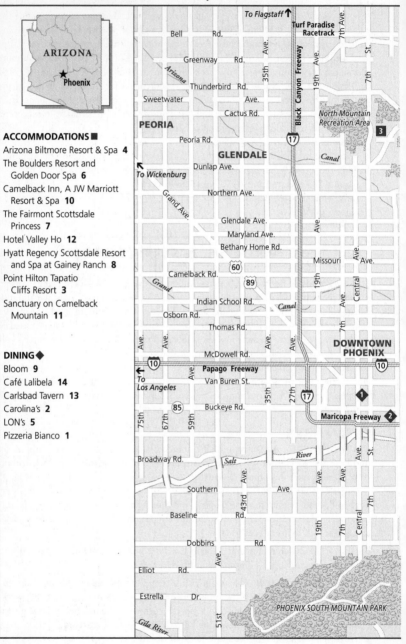

ACCOMMODATIONS ■

Arizona Biltmore Resort & Spa **4**

The Boulders Resort and
Golden Door Spa **6**

Camelback Inn, A JW Marriott
Resort & Spa **10**

The Fairmont Scottsdale
Princess **7**

Hotel Valley Ho **12**

Hyatt Regency Scottsdale Resort
and Spa at Gainey Ranch **8**

Point Hilton Tapatio
Cliffs Resort **3**

Sanctuary on Camelback
Mountain **11**

DINING ◆

Bloom **9**

Café Lalibela **14**

Carlsbad Tavern **13**

Carolina's **2**

LON's **5**

Pizzeria Bianco **1**

THE SOUTHWEST

11

PHOENIX & SCOTTSDALE

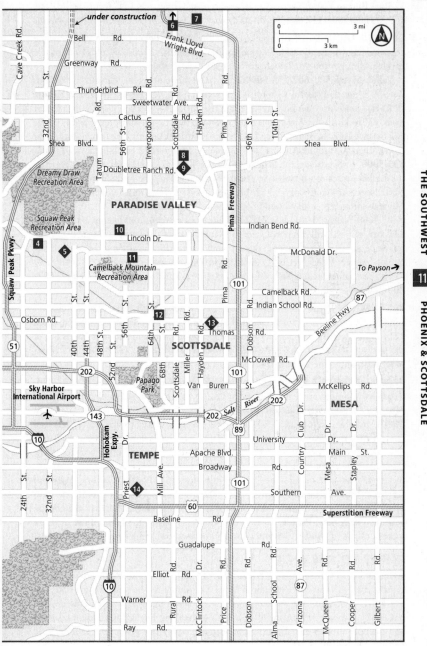

If you're staying in Scottsdale, you can get information at the **Scottsdale Convention & Visitors Bureau Visitor Center,** Galleria Corporate Center, 4343 N. Scottsdale Rd., Ste. 170 (© **800/782-1117** or 480/421-1004; www.scottsdalecvb.com; Mon–Fri 8am–5pm).

GETTING AROUND   If you want to make the best use of your time in this sprawling area, a car is a must. Outside downtown Phoenix, there's almost always plenty of free parking wherever you go. Rental-car rates tend to be relatively low.

Valley Metro (© 602/253-5000; www.valleymetro.org), the Phoenix public bus system, is not very useful to tourists. Instead, try the free **Downtown Area Shuttle (DASH),** which provides bus service within the downtown area Monday through Friday from 6:30am to 11pm. Attractions along the route include the state capitol and Heritage and Science Park. In Tempe, **Free Local Area Shuttle (FLASH)** buses provide a similar service on a loop around Arizona State University. For information on both, call © **602/253-5000.** In Scottsdale, the **Scottsdale Trolley** (© **480/421-1004;** www.valleymetro. org) shuttle buses run between Scottsdale Fashion Square, the Fifth Avenue shops, the Main Street Arts and Antiques district, and the Old Town district. These buses run Monday through Saturday 11am to 6pm (until 9pm Thurs).

By 2009, Valley Metro's new **METRO light-rail system** should be up and running. This new rail line will run down Central Avenue, through downtown Phoenix, and east to Tempe and Mesa, with stops at or near many of the major attractions. For more information, contact Valley Metro (© **602/253-5000;** www.valleymetro.org).

Cab companies include **Yellow Cab** (© **602/252-5252**) and **Discount Cab** (© **602/200-2000;** www.discountcab.com).

FAST FACTS   If you need a doctor, call the **Banner Health Physician & Resource Line** (© 602/230-2273) for a referral. The **Banner Good Samaritan Medical Center,** 1111 E. McDowell Rd., Phoenix (© **602/239-2000;** www.bannerhealth.com), is one of the largest hospitals in the Valley. Call © **800/WALGREENS** (925-4733) for a **pharmacy** near you; some are open 24 hours.

SPECIAL EVENTS & FESTIVALS   The **FBR Open Golf Tournament** (© 602/870-0163; www.fbropen.com) is a PGA event held in Scottsdale in late January. The **Heard Museum Guild Indian Fair and Market** (© **602/252-8848;** www.heard.org), held in March, includes performances of traditional dances and demonstrations of arts and crafts. **Cinco de Mayo** is celebrated in a big way, with food, music, and dancing.

In October, the **Arizona State Fair** (© **800/343-FAIR** [343-3247] or 602/268-FAIR [268-3247]; www.azstatefair.com) gets underway, with rodeos, entertainment, and ethnic food. Also that month, the Phoenix Art Museum hosts the **Cowboy Artists of America Annual Sale & Exhibition** (© **602/257-1222;** www.phxart.org), the most prestigious Western-art show in the region. The old year is ushered out on December 31 with the **Fiesta Bowl Parade,** followed on New Year's Day by the **Fiesta Bowl,** a college football classic (© **800/635-5748;** www.tostitosfiestabowl.com).

WHAT TO SEE & DO

Arizona Wing Commemorative Air Force   Fans of World War II bombers won't want to miss this small air museum in Mesa. The museum is home to *Sentimental Journey,* a B-17G bomber that was built in 1944 and is still flying today. The museum also has a B-25, a couple of Russian MIGs, and a F4 Phantom. Flights in *Sentimental Journey* and a couple of other aircraft can be arranged here, with tour prices ranging from $250 to $425 per person.

2017 N. Greenfield Rd., Mesa. ✆ **480/924-1940.** www.arizonawingcaf.com. Admission $7 adults, $3 <u>**755**</u> children 6–13, free for children 5 and under. Oct 15–May daily 10am–4pm; June–Oct 14 Wed–Sun 9am–3pm. Closed New Year's Day, Thanksgiving, and Christmas.

Desert Botanical Garden   Devoted exclusively to cacti and other desert plants, this botanic garden displays more than 20,000 plants from all over the world. The "Plants and People of the Sonoran Desert" trail is the state's best introduction to ethnobotany (human use of plants) in the Southwest. If you come late in the day, you can stay after dark and see night-blooming flowers and dramatically lit cacti. A cafe on the grounds serves surprisingly good food.

In Papago Park, 1201 N. Galvin Pkwy. ✆ **480/941-1225.** www.dbg.org. Admission $10 adults, $9 seniors, $5 students 13–18, $4 children 3–12. Oct–Apr daily 8am–8pm; May–Sept daily 7am–8pm. Closed July 4th, Thanksgiving, and Christmas. Bus: 3. METRO light rail: Priest Dr./Washington St.

Heard Museum ⟨Best⟩   This is one of the nation's finest museums dealing exclusively with Native American cultures, and the *Native Peoples of the Southwest* exhibit examines the culture of each of the region's major tribes. The Crossroads Gallery offers a fascinating look at contemporary Native American art. On many weekends there are performances by Native American singers and dancers, and throughout the week artists demonstrate their work. The museum has annexes in Scottsdale and the town of Surprise.

2301 N. Central Ave. ✆ **602/252-8848.** www.heard.org. Admission $10 adults, $9 seniors, $5 students, $3 children 6–12. Daily 9:30am–5pm. Closed major holidays. Bus: Blue (B), Red (R), or O. METRO light rail: Encanto Blvd./Central Ave.

Phoenix Art Museum   This is the largest art museum in the Southwest, with a collection spanning the major artistic movements from the Renaissance to the present. The selection of modern and contemporary art is particularly good, with works by Diego Rivera, Frida Kahlo, Pablo Picasso, Alexander Calder, Henry Moore, Georgia O'Keeffe, Henri Rousseau, and Auguste Rodin. The popular Thorne Miniature Collection consists of tiny rooms on a scale of 1 inch to 1 foot.

1625 N. Central Ave. (at McDowell Rd.). ✆ **602/257-1222.** www.phxart.org. Admission $10 adults, $8 seniors and students, $4 children 6–17; free on Tues 3–9pm and 1st Fri of each month 6–10pm. Tues 10am–9pm; Wed–Sun 10am–5pm (also 6–10pm on 1st Fri of each month). Closed major holidays. Bus: Blue (B), Red (R), or O. METRO light rail: McDowell Rd./Central Ave.

Scottsdale Museum of Contemporary Art   Scottsdale may be obsessed with art featuring lonesome cowboys and solemn Indians, but this boldly designed museum makes it clear that patrons of contemporary art are also welcome here. Cutting-edge art, from the abstract to the absurd, fills the galleries. In addition to the main building, there are several galleries in the adjacent Scottsdale Center for the Arts, which also has a pair of Dale Chihuly art-glass installations. The museum shop is excellent.

7374 E. Second St., Scottsdale. ✆ **480/994-ARTS** (994-2787). www.smoca.org. Admission $7 adults, $5 students, free for children 14 and under; free on Thurs. Sept 1–May 27 Tues–Wed and Fri–Sat 10am–5pm, Thurs 10am–8pm, Sun noon–5pm; May 28–Aug 31 Wed noon–5pm, Thurs 10am–8pm, Fri–Sat 10am–5pm, Sun noon–5pm. Closed major holidays. Bus: 41, 50, or 72. Also accessible via Scottsdale Trolley shuttle bus.

Taliesin West   Frank Lloyd Wright fell in love with the Arizona desert and, in 1937, opened a winter camp here that served as his office and school. Today Taliesin West is the headquarters of the Frank Lloyd Wright Foundation and School of Architecture. Tours explain the campus buildings and include a general introduction to Wright and his theories of architecture. Wright used local stone for the foundations and developed a number of innovative methods for dealing with the extreme desert climate.

12621 Frank Lloyd Wright Blvd. (at Cactus/114th St.), Scottsdale. (C) **480/860-8810** for information or 860-2700, ext. 494, for reservations. www.franklloydwright.org. Basic tours $27 adults, $23 seniors and students, $10 children 6–12. Daily 9am–4pm. Closed Easter, Thanksgiving, Christmas, New Year's Day, and occasional special events. From Scottsdale Rd., go east on Shea Blvd. to 114th St., then north 1 mile to the entrance road.

GOLF

With around 200 courses in the Valley of the Sun, golf is just about the most popular sport in Phoenix and one of the main reasons people flock here in winter. Sunshine, spectacular views, and the company of coyotes, quails, and doves make playing a round of golf here a truly memorable experience.

The only thing harder than getting a winter or spring tee time in the valley is facing the bill at the end of your 18 holes. Greens fees at most public and resort courses range from $90 to $185, with the top courses often charging $200 to $250 or more. Municipal courses, on the other hand, charge under $60. You can save money on many courses by opting for twilight play, which usually begins between 1 and 3pm.

You can get more information on Valley of the Sun golf courses from the **Greater Phoenix Convention & Visitors Bureau,** 50 N. Second St. (C) **877/225-5749** or 602/452-6282; www.visitphoenix.com).

It's a good idea to make reservations well in advance. You can avoid the hassle of booking tee times yourself by contacting **Golf Xpress** (C) **888/679-8246** or 602/404-GOLF [404-4653]; www.azgolfxpress.com), which can make reservations farther in advance than you could if you called the golf course directly, and can sometimes get you lower greens fees as well. This company also makes hotel reservations, rents golf clubs, and provides other assistance to golfers visiting the valley. For last-minute reservations, call **Stand-by Golf** (C) **800/655-5345;** www.discountteetimes.com).

The many resort courses are the favored fairways of valley visitors. For spectacular scenery, the two Jay Morrish–designed 18-hole courses at the **Boulders,** North Scottsdale Road and Carefree Highway, Carefree (C) **800/553-1717** or 480/488-9009), just can't be beat. Given the option, play the South Course, and watch out as you approach the tee box on the 7th hole—it's a real heart-stopper. Tee times for nonresort guests are very limited in winter and spring (try making reservations a month in advance if you aren't staying at the resort).

Jumping over to Litchfield Park, on the far west side of the valley, there's the **Wigwam Golf Resort & Spa,** 300 Wigwam Blvd. (C) **800/SAY-PUTT** [729-7888] or 623/935-3811), which has, count ['Jem, three championship 18-hole courses. The Gold Course is legendary, but even the Blue and Red courses are worth playing. These are traditional courses for purists who want vast expanses of green rather than cactuses and boulders. Reservations for nonguests can be made no more than 7 days in advance.

Way over on the east side of the valley, at the foot of the Superstition Mountains, is the **Gold Canyon Golf Resort,** 6100 S. Kings Ranch Rd., Gold Canyon (C) **800/827-5281** or 480/982-9449; www.gcgr.com), which has been rated the best public course in the state and has 3 of the state's best holes—the 2nd, 3rd, and 4th on the visually breathtaking, desert-style Dinosaur Mountain course. The Sidewinder course is more traditional and less dramatic, but much more economical. Reserve a week in advance. It's well worth the drive.

If you want to swing where the pros do, beg, borrow, or steal a tee time on the Tom Weiskopf and Jay Morrish–designed Stadium Course at the **Tournament Players Club**

www.playatpc.com), which hosts the FBR Open. The 18th hole has standing room for 40,000 spectators, but hopefully there won't be that many around the day you double-bogey this hole. The TPC's second 18, the Desert Course, is a municipal course, thanks to an agreement with the landowner, the Bureau of Land Management.

If you want a traditional course that has been played by presidents and celebrities alike, try to get a tee time at one of the two 18-hole courses at the **Arizona Biltmore Country Club,** 24th Street and Missouri Avenue (© **602/955-9655;** www.arizonabiltmore.com). The courses here are more relaxing than challenging, good to play if you're not yet up to par. Reservations can be made up to a month in advance. There's also a championship 18-hole putting course.

Of the Valley's many daily-fee courses, it's the two 18-hole courses at **Troon North Golf Club,** 10320 E. Dynamite Blvd., Scottsdale (© **888/TROON-US** [876-6687] or 480/585-7700; www.troonnorthgolf.com), seemingly carved out of raw desert, that garner the most local accolades. This is the finest example of a desert course that you'll find anywhere in the state, and with five tee boxes on each hole, golfers of all levels will be thoroughly challenged.

If you want to take a crack at a desert-style course or two but don't want to take out a second mortgage, try Dove Valley Ranch Golf Club or Rancho Mañana Golf Club. **Dove Valley Ranch Golf Club,** 33244 N. Black Mountain Pkwy., Cave Creek (© **480/488-0009;** www.dovevalleyranch.com), designed by Robert Trent Jones, Jr., was voted Arizona's best new public course when it opened in 1998. It's something of a merger of desert and traditional styles.

Of the municipal courses in Phoenix, **Papago Golf Course,** 5595 E. Moreland St. (© **602/275-8428**), at the foot of the red-sandstone Papago Buttes, offers fine views and a killer 17th hole. This is such a great course that it's used for Phoenix Open qualifying. **Encanto Golf Course,** 2605 N. 15th Ave. (© **602/253-3963**), is the third-oldest course in Arizona and, with its wide fairways and lack of hazards, is very forgiving. **Cave Creek Golf Course,** 15202 N. 19th Ave., in north Phoenix (© **602/866-8076**), is another good economical choice. For details on these courses, go to **http://phoenix.gov/SPORTS/golf.html**.

OTHER OUTDOOR ACTIVITIES

HIKING   The city's largest nature preserve, **South Mountain Park/Preserve** (© **602/534-6324;** www.phoenix.gov/PARKS/southmnt.html), said to be the largest city park in the world, contains miles of hiking, biking, and horseback riding trails, and the views of Phoenix from the Buena Vista Overlook are spectacular, especially at sunset. To reach the park, simply drive south on Central Avenue or 48th Street.

Perhaps the most popular hiking trail in the city is the trail to the top of **Camelback Mountain** (© **602/261-8318;** www.phoenix.gov/PARKS/hikecmlb.html), in Echo Canyon Recreation Area. This is the highest mountain in Phoenix, and the 1.25-mile trail to the summit is very steep. Don't attempt it in the heat of the day, and take at least a quart of water with you. The reward for your effort is the city's finest view. To reach the trail head, drive up 44th Street until it becomes McDonald Drive, then turn right on East Echo Canyon Drive and continue up the hill until the road ends at a parking lot.

HORSEBACK RIDING   Even in the urban confines of the Phoenix metro area, people like to play at being cowboys. On the south side of the city, try **Ponderosa Stables,** 10215 S. Central Ave. (© **602/268-1261;** www.arizona-horses.com), which leads rides into South Mountain Park and charges $26 for a 1-hour ride. On the east side of the Valley, you'll find **Don Donnelly Horseback Adventures,** 15371 Ojo Rd. (off Peralta Rd.), Gold Canyon (© 602/810-7029; www.dondonnelly.com), which charges $26 for a 1-hour ride.

HOT-AIR BALLOON RIDES   The still morning air of the Valley of the Sun is perfect for hot-air ballooning, and because of the stiff competition, prices are among the lowest in the country. **Over the Rainbow** (© 602/225-5666; www.letsgoballooning.com) charges only $135 for a 1- to 1½-hour flight, while **Adventures Out West** (© 800/755-0935 or 480/991-3666; www.adventuresoutwest.com) charges $185 (or $205 with transportation from your Scottsdale hotel) for a 1- to 1½-hour flight.

WATERPARKS   At **Phoenix Waterworld Safari,** 4243 W. Pinnacle Peak Rd. (© 623/581-8446; www.golfland.com), you can free-fall down the Kilimanjaro speed slide or catch a gnarly wave in the wave pool. **Mesa Golfland Sunsplash,** 155 W. Hampton Ave., Mesa (© 480/834-8319; www.golfland.com), has a wave pool and a water roller coaster. **Big Surf,** 1500 N. McClintock Rd., Tempe (© 480/947-2477; www.golfland.com), has the country's original wave pool and more.

WHITE-WATER RAFTING & TUBING   In the mountains to the northeast of Phoenix, the **Upper Salt River** flows wild and free and offers some exciting rafting. Most years from late February to late May, snowmelt from the White Mountains turns the river into a Class III and IV river filled with exciting rapids. Companies operating full-day, overnight, and multiday rafting trips on the Upper Salt River (conditions permitting) include **Wilderness Aware Rafting** (© 800/462-7238; www.inaraft.com), **Canyon Rio Rafting** (© 800/272-3353; www.canyonrio.com), and **Mild to Wild Rafting** (© 800/567-6745; www.mild2wildrafting.com). Prices range from $99 to $115 for a day trip.

Tamer river trips can be had from **Salt River Tubing & Recreation** (© 480/984-3305; www.saltrivertubing.com), which has its headquarters 20 miles northeast of Phoenix on Power Road at Usery Pass Road in Tonto National Forest. For $14, the company will rent you a large inner tube and will shuttle you upriver for the float down. The season runs from mid-May to September.

SHOPPING

Along the streets of Old Scottsdale, you'll find dozens of **art galleries.** On Main Street, you'll find primarily cowboy art, while on North Marshall Way, you'll find much more imaginative and daring contemporary art.

For contemporary art, try **Art One,** 4120 N. Marshall Way, Scottsdale (© 480/946-5076), specializing in work by art students and cutting-edge artists; or the **Lisa Sette Gallery,** 4142 N. Marshall Way, Scottsdale (© 480/990-7342), which represents international and local artists working in a wide mix of mediums.

The **Heard Museum Gift Shop,** in the Heard Museum, 2301 N. Central Ave. (© 602/252-8344), has an awesome collection of extremely well-crafted and very expensive Native American jewelry, art, and crafts of all kinds. For one of the finest selections of Navajo rugs in the valley, visit **John C. Hill Antique Indian Art,** 6962 E. First Ave., Scottsdale (© 480/946-2910).

WHERE TO STAY

During the winter, the Phoenix metro area has some of the highest room rates in the country. But keep in mind that most resorts offer a variety of weekend, golf, and tennis packages—it always pays to ask. Most places drop their rates in spring and fall, and prices really plummet for those who can take the summer heat.

While most people dreaming of a Phoenix vacation have visions of luxury resorts dancing in their heads, there are some bed-and-breakfasts around the Valley. **Mi Casa Su Casa** (© **800/456-0682** or 480/990-0682; www.azres.com) can book you into dozens of different homes in the Valley of the Sun, as can **Arizona Trails Travel Services** (© **888/799-4284** or 480/837-4284; www.arizonatrails.com), which also books tour and hotel reservations.

Arizona Biltmore Resort & Spa (Best)

For timeless elegance, a prime location, and historical character, no other resort in the valley can touch the Biltmore, which was partly designed by Frank Lloyd Wright. While the golf courses and spa are the main draws, the children's center also makes this a popular choice for families. The "resort rooms" are comfortable and have balconies or patios; villa suites are the most spacious and luxurious of all. Afternoon tea, a Phoenix institution, is served in the lobby.

2400 E. Missouri Ave., Phoenix, AZ 85016. © **800/950-0086** or 602/955-6600. Fax 602/381-7600. www. arizonabiltmore.com. 738 units. Jan to mid-May $575–$795 double, from $850 suite; mid-May to early Sept $279–$359 double, from $379 suite; early Sept to Dec $465–$585 double, from $615 suite. Rates do not include $25 daily service fee. Children 11 and under stay free in parent's room. AE, DC, DISC, MC, V. Valet parking $25; self-parking $10. Pets under 50 lb. accepted in cottage rooms ($100 deposit, $50 nonrefundable). **Amenities:** 4 restaurants; 8 pools; 2 18-hole golf courses; 7 tennis courts; health club; full-service spa. *In room:* Fridge.

The Boulders Resort and Golden Door Spa

Set amid a jumble of giant boulders 45 minutes north of Scottsdale, this prestigious golf resort epitomizes the Southwestern aesthetic. Adobe buildings blend unobtrusively into the desert, as do the two noted golf courses. Rooms continue the pueblo styling with stucco walls, beehive fireplaces, and beamed ceilings. Bathrooms are large and luxuriously appointed, with tubs for two and separate showers. If you can tear yourself away from the fairways, you can take advantage of the **Golden Door Spa** or even try rock climbing. In a commitment to being more eco-friendly, the Boulders is now emphasizing organic ingredients in its restaurants and has planted an organic herb-and-vegetable garden.

34631 N. Tom Darlington Dr. (P.O. Box 2090), Carefree, AZ 85377. © **866/397-6520** or 480/488-9009. Fax 480/488-4118. www.theboulders.com. 215 units. Late Dec to May $499 double, from $1,099 villa; May to early Sept $199 double, from $499 villa; early Sept to early Dec $349 double, from $799 villa; early to late Dec $299 double, from $899 villa. (There is an additional $29–$33 nightly service charge.) Children 16 and under stay free in parent's room. AE, DC, DISC, MC, V. Pets accepted ($100 deposit). **Amenities:** 6 restaurants; 4 pools; 2 18-hole golf courses; 8 tennis courts; exercise room; spa.

Camelback Inn, A JW Marriott Resort & Spa

Set at the foot of Mummy Mountain and overlooking Camelback Mountain, the Camelback Inn is one of the grande dames of the Phoenix hotel scene and abounds in traditional Southwestern character. Although the two 18-hole golf courses are the main attraction, the spa is among the finest in the state. Rooms are decorated with Southwestern furnishings and art, and all have balconies or patios. Some rooms even have their own private pools.

5402 E. Lincoln Dr., Scottsdale, AZ 85253. © **800/24-CAMEL** (242-2635) or 480/948-1700. Fax 480/951-8469. www.camelbackinn.com. 453 units. Jan to early June $299–$489 double, $570–$1,750 suite; early June to early Sept $179–$199 double, $260–$675 suite; early Sept to Dec $349–$399 double, $595–$1,250 suite. Children 17 and under stay free in parent's room. AE, DC, DISC, MC, V. Small pets accepted. **Amenities:** 7 restaurants; 2 pools; 2 18-hole golf courses; 6 tennis courts; exercise room; access to nearby health club; full-service spa.

The Fairmont Scottsdale Princess (Kids) This modern rendition of a Moorish palace offers an exotic atmosphere. It plays host to the FBR Open golf tournament and the city's top tennis tournament, and is also home to the **Willow Stream spa.** Located a 20-minute drive north of Old Town Scottsdale, this resort makes a good romantic hideaway, and a water playground (with two water slides) and a kids' fishing pond also make this resort a hit with families. Guest rooms are done in an elegant Southwestern style, and bathrooms have double vanities and separate showers and tubs.

7575 E. Princess Dr., Scottsdale, AZ 85255. (C) **800/344-4758** or 480/585-4848. Fax 480/585-0091. www. fairmont.com/scottsdale. 651 units. $159–$589 double; $319–$3,800 suite. Children 17 and under stay free in parent's room. AE, DC, DISC, MC, V. Valet parking $23. Pets accepted ($25 per night). **Amenities:** 4 restaurants; 5 pools; 2 18-hole golf courses; 7 tennis courts; exercise room; spa.

Hotel Valley Ho This Scottsdale grande dame dates from the 1950s, but in 2005, the hotel got a complete face-lift. What a looker she is now. The Valley Ho is hip and convenient, and has loads of outdoor space for soaking up the sun. Its big rooms are done in a bold contemporary style. The studio rooms have curtains to partition off the vanity area and an ultracool free-standing tub. Big balconies and patios provide plenty of space for lounging outdoors. When it's time to get even more relaxed, grab one of the plush, circular lounge chairs at the pool. Cool!

6850 E. Main St., Scottsdale, AZ 85251. (C) **866/882-4484** or 480/248-2000. Fax 480/248-2002. www. hotelvalleyho.com. 194 units. Jan–Apr $319–$389 double, $449–$899 suite; May and Sept $199–$259 double, $299–$699 suite; June–Aug $149–$179 double, $249–$699 suite; Oct–Dec $259–$299 double, $359–$899 suite. Children 17 and under stay free in parent's room. AE, DC, DISC, MC, V. Valet parking $12. Pets accepted. **Amenities:** 2 restaurants; pool; access to nearby health club; exercise room; full-service spa.

Hyatt Regency Scottsdale Resort & Spa at Gainey Ranch (Kids) With its gardens full of stately palm trees and an extravagant water playground that encompasses 10 swimming pools, a water slide, a sand beach, a water-volleyball pool, waterfalls, and a huge whirlpool spa, this luxurious resort is designed to astonish. A beautiful new lobby and lobby bar and the big new Spa Avania only enhance the resort's ability to awe. Guest rooms are luxurious and are designed to reflect the desert location. **Vu,** the resort's premier restaurant, has a sunken waterside gazebo, while **Ristorante Sandolo** features afterdinner gondola rides. The resort's Native American and Environmental Learning Center provides a glimpse into Sonoran Desert culture and ecology. Children's programs make this a super choice for families.

7500 E. Doubletree Ranch Rd., Scottsdale, AZ 85258. (C) **800/55-HYATT** (554-9288) or 480/444-1234. Fax 480/483-5550. www.scottsdale.hyatt.com. 490 units. Jan to mid-May $399 double, from $999 suite and casita; mid-May to mid-Sept $169 double, from $429 suite and casita; mid-Sept to Dec $359 double, from $899 suite and casita. Children 17 and under stay free in parent's room. AE, DC, DISC, MC, V. Valet parking $24. **Amenities:** 3 restaurants; 10 pools; 27-hole golf course; 4 tennis courts; health club; full-service spa.

Pointe Hilton Tapatio Cliffs Resort (Value) If you love to lounge by the pool, then this resort is a great choice. The Falls, a 3-acre water playground, includes two pools, a 138-foot water slide, 40-foot cascades, a whirlpool tucked into an artificial grotto, and rental cabanas. If you're a hiker, you can head out on the trails of the adjacent North Mountain Recreation Area. All rooms are spacious suites with Southwestern-inspired furnishings; corner units are particularly bright. This resort has steep walkways, so you need to be in good shape to stay here. At the top of the property is **Different Pointe of View,** a restaurant with one of the finest views in the city.

11111 N. Seventh St., Phoenix, AZ 85020. © **800/876-4683** or 602/866-7500. Fax 602/993-0276. www. pointehilton.com. 585 units. Jan to mid-May $169–$399 double; mid-May to mid-Sept $99–$209 double; mid-Sept to Dec $109–$299 double; year-round $1,500 grande suite. Rates do not include $9 daily resort fee. Children 17 and under stay free in parent's room. AE, DC, DISC, MC, V. Pets accepted ($75–$100 deposit). **Amenities:** 5 restaurants; 8 pools; golf course; 2 tennis courts; fitness center (extra charge); small full-service spa.

Radisson Fort McDowell Resort & Casino   You just can't stay any closer to the desert than at this beautiful resort a 30-minute drive from downtown Scottsdale but with a location that's hard to beat if you've come to the area to experience the desert. The resort is on the Fort McDowell Yavapai Nation, and, consequently, the tribe's Fort McDowell Casino is a big draw for many guests. The two 18-hole courses at the adjacent We-Ko-Pa Golf Club are also a major draw. For families, there's a children's water play area and, in summer, float trips down the nearby Verde River.

10438 N. Fort McDowell Rd., Fountain Hills, AZ 85264. © **800/333-3333** or 480/789-5300. Fax 480/789-5333. www.radisson.com/ftmcdowellaz. 246 units. Jan–Mar $269–$299 double; Apr $199–$210 double; May, Sept, and Dec $139–$159 double; June–Aug $109–$139 double; Oct–Nov $219–$239 double. Children 11 and under stay free in parent's room. AE, DC, DISC, MC, V. Pets accepted. **Amenities:** Restaurant; outdoor pool; 2 18-hole golf courses; exercise room; full-service spa.

Sanctuary on Camelback Mountain   Located high on the northern flanks of Camelback Mountain, the lushly landscaped property has unforgettable views across the Valley, especially from its restaurant and two bars. The extremely spacious guest rooms are divided between the more conservative deluxe casitas and the boldly contemporary spa casitas. With their dyed-cement floors, L-shaped couches, and streamline-moderne cabinetry, these latter units are absolutely stunning. Bathrooms are huge, and some have private outdoor soaking tubs. The resort's spa is gorgeous.

5700 E. McDonald Dr., Paradise Valley, AZ 85253. © **800/245-2051** or 480/948-2100. www.sanctuaryon camelback.com. 105 units. Jan to mid-May and late Dec $520–$725 double, $650–$1,580 suite; mid-May to mid-Sept $235–$415 double, $340–$935 suite; mid-Sept to mid-Dec $395–$620 double, $545–$1,370 suite. Children 16 and under stay free in parent's room. AE, DC, DISC, MC, V. Pets accepted. **Amenities:** Restaurant; 4 pools; 5 tennis courts; fitness center; full-service spa.

WHERE TO DINE

The Valley of the Sun boasts hundreds of excellent restaurants, with most of the best dining options concentrated in the Scottsdale Road and Biltmore Corridor areas. If you want to splurge on only one expensive meal while you're here, consider a resort restaurant that offers a view of the city lights.

Phoenix is a sprawling city and can be a real pain to have to drive around in search of a good lunch spot. If you happen to be visiting the Phoenix Art Museum, the Heard Museum, or the Desert Botanical Garden anytime around lunch, stay put for your noon meal. All three of these attractions have cafes serving decent, if limited, menus.

Bloom NEW AMERICAN   Bloom is big and always full of energy. The minimalist decor emphasizes flowers, an elegant wine bar serves a wide range of flights (tasting assortments), and the bistro-style menu has lots of great dishes in a wide range of prices. Among the entrees, the roast duck with a crisp potato nest and drunken cherry sauce is excellent.

8877 N. Scottsdale Rd. © **480/922-5666**. www.foxrc.com. Reservations recommended. Main courses $8–$17 lunch, $15–$29 dinner. AE, DC, DISC, MC, V. Mon–Thurs 11am–3pm and 5–10pm; Fri–Sat 11am–3pm and 5–10:30pm; Sun 5–9:30pm.

Bourbon Steak MODERN STEAKHOUSE Opened in 2008 by chef Michael Mina, who in 2005 was named chef of the year by *Bon Appétit* magazine, Bourbon Steak is one of the Valley's most expensive restaurants. If you have an appreciation for lobster, caviar, and foie gras, then you'll be glad this restaurant is here. Try the lobster potpie. Steaks are served a la carte, and there are lots of tempting sides. How about some truffled mac and cheese, or roasted marrow bones to accompany your main dish?

At the Fairmont Scottsdale Princess, 7575 E. Princess Dr. (about 12 miles north of downtown Scottsdale). *C* **480/585-2762.** www.michaelmina.net. Reservations highly recommended. Main courses $22–$60; steaks $32–$190; prix-fixe menus $85–$110. AE, DC, DISC, MC, V. Sun–Thurs 5:30–10pm; Fri–Sat 5:30–10:30pm.

Café Lalibela ETHIOPIAN/VEGETARIAN If you've never had Ethiopian food, this casual and inexpensive restaurant near Arizona State University is a good place to give it a try. The various stews, many of which are quite spicy, are eaten with pieces of a traditional Ethiopian crepelike bread called *injera*. For the best introduction to this flavorful cuisine, try the "Lalibela Exclusive" platter, which feeds three and comes with a dozen different dishes.

849 W. University Dr., Tempe. *C* **480/829-1939.** www.cafelalibela.com. Reservations recommended on weekends. Main courses $4.25–$14. AE, DC, DISC, MC, V. Tues–Thurs 11am–9pm; Fri 11am–10pm; Sat noon–10pm; Sun noon–9pm.

Carlsbad Tavern NEW MEXICAN Carlsbad Tavern blends the fiery tastes of New Mexican cuisine with a hip and humorous bat-theme atmosphere (a reference to Carlsbad Caverns). The menu lists traditional New Mexican dishes such as *carne adovada*, pork simmered in a fiery red-chili sauce, as well as contemporary Southwestern specialties such as poblano chilies stuffed with crab, and pasta with an unusual chipotle stroganoff. Cool off your taste buds with a prickly-pear margarita.

3313 N. Hayden Rd. (south of Osborn). *C* **480/970-8164.** www.carlsbadtavern.com. Reservations accepted for 5 or more. Main courses $9–$23. AE, DISC, MC, V. Daily 11am–2am (limited menu daily 10 or 11pm–2am).

Carolina's MEXICAN Carolina's is a Phoenix institution. As such you'll find everyone from Hispanic construction workers to downtown corporate types. Everyone enjoys the down-home Mexican cooking, but Carolina's flour tortillas are what really set this place apart. Order a burrito, perhaps with shredded beef in a spicy green sauce, and you'll be handed what feels like a down-filled pillow. Or get the tortillas to go and use them as the basis for a fun Phoenician picnic. There's a second Carolina's in north Phoenix at 2126 E. Cactus Rd. (*C* **602/275-8231**).

1202 E. Mohave St. *C* **602/252-1503.** www.carolinasmex.com. Main dishes $2.50–$5.75. AE, DISC, MC, V. Mon–Fri 7am–7:30pm; Sat 7am–6pm.

Digestif ITALIAN This is Peter Kasperski's first restaurant in the new waterfront development, and as the name implies, *digestifs* (after-dinner drinks) are an essential part of a meal. Sort of a reimagining of a basement eatery in New York's Little Italy, this place is casual yet hip. Don't miss the *bruschettone* with calamari, house-made chorizo, borlotti beans, and garlic. For the day's freshest produce, order the "farm to table" appetizer. Cheeses and cured meats are on the menu for late-night noshing.

7114 E. Stetson Dr., Scottsdale. *C* **480/425-WINE** (425-9463). www.digestifscottsdale.com. Reservations recommended. Main courses $13–$27. AE, DC, DISC, MC, V. Daily 11am–midnight.

LON'S at the hermosa AMERICAN REGIONAL   This old adobe hacienda surrounded by colorful gardens is one of the most "Arizonan" places in the Phoenix area. Entrees at both lunch and dinner are reliable, and if you peruse the menu closely, you'll turn up some interesting Southwestern ingredients, including prickly pear. Also be sure to ask about dishes made with Arizona-farmed shrimp. The bar is cozy and romantic, and the patio affords beautiful views of Camelback Mountain. Dishes often include herbs grown in the restaurant's own garden, and other ingredients are, as much as possible, from ecologically sound sources.

At the Hermosa Inn, 5532 N. Palo Cristi Rd. (📞 602/955-7878. www.lons.com. Reservations recommended. Main courses $11–$15 lunch, $22–$34 dinner. AE, DC, DISC, MC, V. Mon–Fri 11:30am–2pm and 5:30–10pm; Sat 5:30–10pm; Sun 10am–2pm (brunch) and 5:30–10pm.

Pizzeria Bianco PIZZA   Even though this historic brick building is smack-dab in the center of downtown Phoenix, the atmosphere is so cozy it feels like your neighborhood local. The wood-burning oven turns out deliciously rustic pizzas. Try one with red onion, Parmesan, rosemary, and crushed pistachios. Don't miss the fresh mozzarella, which can be ordered as an appetizer or on a pizza.

At Heritage Sq., 623 E. Adams St. (📞 602/258-8300. www.pizzeriabianco.com. Reservations accepted for 6–10 people. Pizzas $10–$14. AE, MC, V. Tues–Sat 5–10pm.

PHOENIX AFTER DARK

The weekly *Phoenix New Times* tends to have the most comprehensive listings for clubs and concert halls.

THE PERFORMING ARTS   Symphony Hall, 75 N. Second St. (📞 **602/262-7272;** www.ci.phoenix.az.us/CIVPLAZA/stages.html), is Phoenix's premier performance venue and is home to the Phoenix Symphony, Ballet Arizona, and the Arizona Opera Company. It also hosts touring Broadway shows and various concerts and productions.

With its sail-like shade canopies, sunken sculpture courtyard, numerous water features, and colorful architecture, the **Mesa Arts Center,** 1 E. Main St. (📞 **480/644-6500;** www.mesaartscenter.com), is the prettiest performing arts center in the Valley. In the cooler months, there are weekly free lunchtime concerts.

THE CLUB & MUSIC SCENE   Mill Avenue in Tempe is a good place to wander around in search of your favorite type of music. Packed into a couple of dozen blocks surrounding Old Town Scottsdale, near the corner of Camelback and Scottsdale roads, there are dozens of trendy dance clubs and chic bars. Clubs in this neighborhood tend to be the places to see and be seen.

At **Handlebar-J,** 7116 E. Becker Lane, Scottsdale (📞 **480/948-0110;** www.handlebarj. com), you'll hear live git-down two-steppin' music and can even get free dance lessons on Wednesday, Thursday, and Sunday. The beautiful **e4,** 4282 N. Drinkwater Blvd., Scottsdale (📞 **480/970-3325;** www.e4-az.com), is a nightclub with different spaces that are based on the four elements—earth, air, fire, and water.

THE BAR SCENE   The **Hyatt Regency Scottsdale Lobby Bar,** 7500 E. Doubletree Ranch Rd., Scottsdale (📞 480/991-3388), is a romantic spot for nightly live music. **Upstairs at Estate House,** 7134 E. Stetson Dr. (📞 480/970-4099), is the classiest bar in town; this is where the cocktail nation is headed. For the ultimate sports and rock bar, check out downtown Phoenix's **Alice Cooper'stown,** 101 E. Jackson St. (📞 602/253-7337), run by none other than Alice Cooper himself.

4 TUCSON

Melding Hispanic, Anglo, and Native American roots, Tucson is a city with a strong sense of identity—aware of its desert setting, confident in its style. Tucson supports an active cultural life, but it's the city's natural surroundings that set it apart. Four mountain ranges ring the city, and in those mountains and their foothills are giant saguaro cacti, a national park, an oasis, one of the finest zoos in the world, a ski area, and miles of hiking and horseback riding trails.

ESSENTIALS

GETTING THERE   By Plane   Tucson International Airport (© 520/573-8000; www.tucsonairport.org) is 6 miles south of downtown. Many resorts and hotels provide airport shuttle service. **Arizona Stagecoach** (© 520/889-1000; www.azstagecoach.com) operates 24-hour van service to downtown Tucson and the foothills resorts. One-way fares range from $22 to $41. A taxi to downtown costs around $23, to the resorts about $26 to $46.

Sun Tran (© 520/792-9222; www.suntran.com), the local public transit, operates a bus service to and from the airport, though you'll have to make a transfer to reach downtown. The fare is $1. Day passes are available on buses for $2.

By Train   Amtrak (© 800/USA-RAIL [872-7245]; www.amtrak.com) provides service from Los Angeles (trip time: 10 hr.), San Antonio (18 hr.), and New Orleans (32 hr.) to its station at 400 E. Toole St.

By Car   The major routes into Tucson are **I-10** from the northwest (Phoenix) and east (El Paso). **I-19** connects Tucson with the Mexican border at Nogales. If you're headed downtown, take the Congress Street exit off I-10. If you're headed for one of the foothills resorts north of downtown, take the Ina Road exit.

VISITOR INFORMATION   The **Metropolitan Tucson Convention & Visitors Bureau (MTCVB)**, 100 S. Church Ave. (at Broadway; © 800/638-8350 or 520/624-1817; www.visittucson.org), is an excellent source of information on Tucson and its environs. The visitor center is open Monday through Friday from 8am to 5pm, Saturday and Sunday from 9am to 4pm.

GETTING AROUND   Unless you plan to stay by the pool or on the golf course, you'll probably want to rent a car. Rates tend to be low. Downtown Tucson is still a relatively easy place to find a parking space, and parking fees are low. There are two parking lots on the south side of the Tucson Convention Center and plenty of metered parking downtown. Almost all Tucson hotels and resorts provide free parking.

Though they don't go very far, the restored electric streetcars of **Old Pueblo Trolley** (© 520/792-1802; www.oldpueblotrolley.org) are a fun way to get from the Fourth

No Exit to Downtown!

Until sometime in 2010, all downtown Tucson exits off I-10 are closed. Only Prince and 29th Street exits are open, so you'll have to use one or the other of these exits and then follow the frontage road to your cross street.

Avenue shopping district to the University of Arizona. The trolleys run Friday from 6 to 10pm, Saturday from noon to midnight, and Sunday from noon to 6pm. The fare is $1 for adults and 50¢ for children 6 to 12. The fare on Sunday is only 25¢ for all riders. Friday and Saturday all-day passes are $2.50 for adults and $1.25 for children.

For a taxi, phone **Yellow Cab** (☎ **520/624-6611**) or **Discount Cab** (☎ **520/388-9000**).

FAST FACTS For a doctor referral, call **University Medical Center** (☎ **520/694-8888**). The **University Medical Center** is at 1501 N. Campbell Ave. (☎ **520/694-0111**). Call ☎ **800/WALGREENS** (925-4733) for the Walgreens pharmacy that's nearest you or that's open 24 hours.

WHAT TO SEE & DO

Arizona-Sonora Desert Museum ⓑ Best ⓚ Kids The full spectrum of Sonoran Desert life—from plants to insects to fish to reptiles to mammals—is on display in natural settings at this world-class zoo. Coyotes and javelinas (peccaries) seem very much at home in their compounds, which are surrounded by almost invisible wire mesh fences. These display areas are along the Desert Loop Trail, which is also where you'll find the museum's newest exhibits. There are black bears, mountain lions, beavers, otters, frogs, fish, tarantulas, scorpions, prairie dogs, and desert bighorn sheep. Our favorite exhibit is the walk-in hummingbird aviary. The kid-oriented "Life on the Rocks" exhibit has finally opened after years of slow construction.

2021 N. Kinney Rd. ☎ 520/883-2702. www.desertmuseum.org. Admission Sept–May $12 adults, $4 children 6–12; June–Aug $9 adults, $2 children 6–12. Oct–Feb daily 8:30am–5pm; Mar–Sept daily 7:30am–5pm. From downtown Tucson, go west on Speedway Blvd., which becomes Gates Pass Rd., and follow the signs.

Center for Creative Photography Originally conceived by Ansel Adams, the center now holds more than 60,000 master prints by more than 2,000 of the world's best photographers, making it one of the best and largest collections in the world. The center mounts fascinating exhibits year-round and is also a research facility that preserves the photographic archives of more than 50 photographers, including Adams.

University of Arizona campus, 1030 N. Olive Rd. (east of Park Ave. and Speedway Blvd.). ☎ 520/621-7968. www.creativephotography.org. Admission by donation. Mon–Fri 9am–5pm; Sat–Sun noon–5pm. Closed major holidays. Bus: 1, 4, 5, or 6.

Mission San Xavier del Bac Called the White Dove of the Desert, Mission San Xavier de Bac, a blindingly white adobe building rising from a sere, brown landscape, is considered the finest example of mission architecture in the Southwest. The beautiful church, which was built between 1783 and 1797, incorporates Moorish, Byzantine, and Mexican Renaissance architectural styles. The church was never actually completed, which becomes apparent when the two bell towers are compared. One is topped with a dome, while the other has none. Restored murals cover the walls, and behind the altar are colorful and elaborate decorations.

1950 W. San Xavier Rd. ☎ 520/294-2624. www.sanxaviermission.org. Free admission; donations accepted. Daily 8am–5pm. Take I-19 S. 9 miles to exit 92 and turn right.

Old Tucson Studios ⓚ Kids Old Tucson was built as the set for the 1939 movie *Arizona* and since then has been used in the filming of countless movies, including *Tombstone* and *Geronimo*. Today Old Tucson is far more than just a movie set; it's a Wild West theme park with family-oriented activities and entertainment. Throughout the day, there are

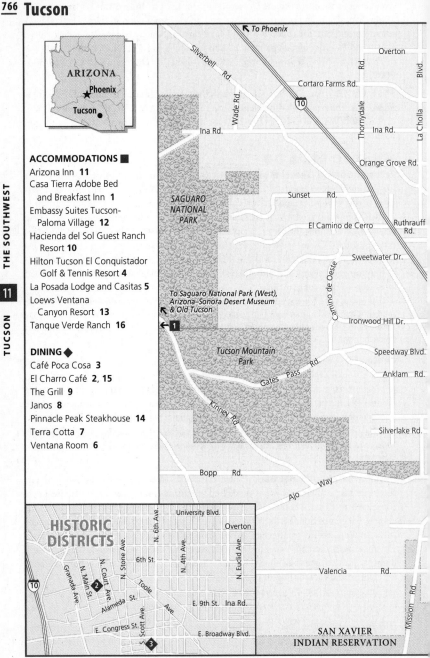

ARIZONA

Phoenix ★

Tucson ●

ACCOMMODATIONS ■

Arizona Inn **11**
Casa Tierra Adobe Bed
    and Breakfast Inn **1**
Embassy Suites Tucson-
    Paloma Village **12**
Hacienda del Sol Guest Ranch
    Resort **10**
Hilton Tucson El Conquistador
    Golf & Tennis Resort **4**
La Posada Lodge and Casitas **5**
Loews Ventana
    Canyon Resort **13**
Tanque Verde Ranch **16**

DINING ◆

Café Poca Cosa **3**
El Charro Café **2**, **15**
The Grill **9**
Janos **8**
Pinnacle Peak Steakhouse **14**
Terra Cotta **7**
Ventana Room **6**

THE SOUTHWEST

11

TUCSON

To Phoenix

Silverbell Rd.
Wade Rd.
Ina Rd.

SAGUARO
NATIONAL
PARK

To Saguaro National Park (West),
Arizona-Sonora Desert Museum
& Old Tucson

Tucson Mountain
Park

Gates   Pass   Rd.

Kinney Rd.

Bopp   Rd.

Overton
Cortaro Farms Rd.
Thorndale
La Cholla
Blvd.
Rd.
Ina Rd.
Orange Grove Rd.

Sunset   Rd.

El Camino de Cerro
Ruthrauff
Rd.

Sweetwater Dr.

Camino de Oeste

Ironwood Hill Dr.

Speedway Blvd.

Anklam   Rd.

Silverlake Rd.

Ajo   Way

HISTORIC
DISTRICTS

Granada Ave.
N. Main St.
N. Court Ave.
N. Stone Ave.
6th St.
N. 4th Ave.
N. 6th Ave.
University Blvd.
Overton
N. Euclid Ave.

Alameda   St.
Toole   Ave.
S. Scott Ave.
E. 9th St.   Ina Rd.
E. Congress St.
E. Broadway Blvd.

Valencia   Rd.

Mission Rd.

SAN XAVIER
INDIAN RESERVATION

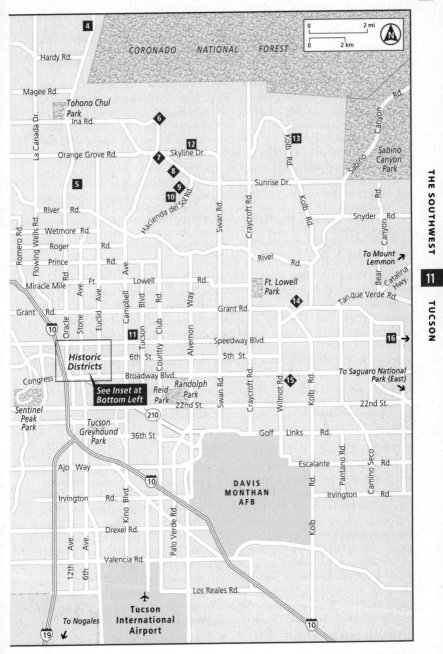

staged shootouts in the streets, stunt shows, a cancan revue, and other performances. Train rides, stagecoach rides, kiddie rides, educational shows, restaurants, and gift shops round out the experience.

201 S. Kinney Rd. ⓒ 520/883-0100. www.oldtucson.com. Admission $17 adults, $11 children 4–11. Daily 10am–4pm. Closed Thanksgiving, Dec 24–25, and occasional special events. Take Speedway Blvd. west, continuing in the same direction when it becomes Gates Pass Blvd., and turn left on S. Kinney Rd.

Sabino Canyon Recreation Area   Sabino Canyon is a desert oasis that has attracted people and animals for thousands of years. This spectacular and accessible corner of the desert contains not only impressive scenery, but also hiking trails and a stream. Many visitors come to splash in the canyon's waterfalls and pools, but for those who prefer just to gaze at the beauty of crystal-clear water flowing through a rocky canyon guarded by saguaro cacti, there are narrated tram rides through the lower canyon. There are also many trails and picnic tables. (Bring water if you want to hike.)

5900 N. Sabino Canyon Rd. ⓒ 520/749-8700, 749-2861 for shuttle information, or 749-2327 for moonlight shuttle reservations. www.fs.fed.us/r3/coronado or www.sabinocanyon.com. Parking $5 (also good for driving the Catalina Hwy.). Sabino Canyon tram ride $7.50 adults, $3 children 3–12; Bear Canyon tram ride $3 adults, $1 children 3–12. Park daily dawn–dusk. Sabino Canyon tram rides daily 9am–4:30pm (July to mid-Dec Mon–Fri 9am–4pm, Sat–Sun and holidays 9am–4:30pm); Bear Canyon tram rides daily 9am–4:30pm. Take Grant Rd. east to Tanque Verde Rd., continuing east; at Sabino Canyon Rd., turn north and watch for the sign.

Saguaro National Park   The massive, treelike saguaro cactus is the quintessential symbol of the American desert. Since 1933, saguaros (and all the other inhabitants of this part of the Sonoran Desert) have been preserved in the two sections of what is now Saguaro National Park. The most impressive stands of saguaros are to be found in the western district, near the Arizona–Sonora Desert Museum. In the area near the Red Hills Information Center is a water hole that attracts wild animals. The eastern section of the park contains an older area of forest at the foot of the Rincon Mountains. Both sections have visitor centers, loop roads, nature trails, hiking trails, and picnic grounds.

Rincon Mountain District visitor center: 3693 S. Old Spanish Trail. ⓒ 520/733-5153. Tucson Mountain District visitor center: 2700 N. Kinney Rd. ⓒ 520/733-5158. www.nps.gov/sagu. Entry fee $10 per car, $5 per hiker or biker. Daily 7am–sunset; visitor centers daily 9am–5pm; open to hikers 24 hr. a day. Visitor centers closed Christmas.

OUTDOOR ACTIVITIES

BICYCLING   Tucson is one of the best bicycling cities in the country, and the dirt roads and trails of the surrounding national forest and desert are perfect for mountain biking. Rentals at **Fair Wheel Bikes,** 1110 E. Sixth St. (ⓒ 520/884-9018; www.fairwheelbikes. com), go for $45 per day for road bikes and $45 to $65 per day for mountain bikes.

The number-one choice in town for cyclists in halfway decent shape is the road up **Sabino Canyon.** Keep in mind, however, that bicycles are allowed on this road only 5 days a week and then only before 9am and after 5pm (the road's closed to bikes all day on Wed and Sat). For a much easier ride, the **Rillito River Park path** currently has a 1-mile paved section between Swan and Craycroft roads and a 6-mile paved section between Campbell Avenue and I-10. The trail parallels River Road and the usually dry bed of the Rillito River, and if you've got knobby tires, you can link the two paved sections or continue west past La Cholla Road after the pavement ends.

BIRD-WATCHING   Southern Arizona has some of the best bird-watching in the country, and although the best spots are south of Tucson, there are a few places around the

city that birders will enjoy seeking out. Call the **Tucson Audubon Society's Rare Bird**
Alert (© 520/798-1005) to find out which birds have been spotted lately.

The city's premier birding spot is the **Sweetwater Wetland,** a man-made wetland just west of I-10 and north of Prince Road. These wetlands were created as part of a wastewater treatment facility and now have an extensive network of trails that wind past numerous ponds and canals. There are several viewing platforms and enough different types of wildlife habitat that the area attracts a wide variety of bird species. At **Roy P. Drachman Agua Caliente Park,** 12325 Roger Rd. (off N. Soldier Trail), the year-round warm springs here are a magnet for dozens of species. To find the park, follow Tanque Verde Road east 6 miles from the intersection with Sabino Canyon Road and turn left onto Soldier Trail. Watch for signs.

The best area for bird-watching is **Madera Canyon National Forest Recreation Area** (© 520/281-2296; www.fs.fed.us/r3/coronado), about 40 miles south of the city in the Coronado National Forest. Because of the year-round water here, Madera Canyon attracts a surprising variety of bird life. Avid birders flock to this canyon from around the country in hopes of spotting more than a dozen species of hummingbirds and an equal number of flycatchers, warblers, tanagers, buntings, grosbeaks, and many rare birds not found in any other state. However, before birding became a hot activity, this canyon was popular with families looking to escape the heat down in Tucson, and the shady picnic areas and trails still get a lot of use. If you're heading out for the day, arrive early—parking is very limited. To reach Madera Canyon, take the Continental Road/Madera Canyon exit off I-19; from the exit, it's another 12 miles southeast. The canyon is open daily from dawn to dusk for day use; there is a $5 day-use fee.

GOLF   Although there aren't quite as many golf courses in Tucson as in Phoenix, this is still a golfer's town. For last-minute tee-time reservations, contact **Stand-by Golf** (© 800/655-5345; www.discountteetimes.com). No fee is charged for this service.

In addition to the public and municipal links, there are numerous resort courses that allow nonguests to play. Perhaps the most famous of these are the two 18-hole courses at **Ventana Canyon Golf and Racquet Club,** 6200 N. Clubhouse Lane (© 520/577-4015). These Tom Fazio–designed courses offer challenging desert target–style play that is nearly legendary. The 3rd hole on the Mountain Course is one of the most photographed holes in the West.

As famous as Ventana Canyon courses are, it's the 27-hole **Omni Tucson National Golf Resort and Spa,** 2727 W. Club Dr. (© 520/575-7540; www.tucsonnational.com), a traditional course, that is perhaps more familiar to golfers as the site of the annual Tucson Open.

El Conquistador Country Club, 10555 N. La Cañada Dr., Oro Valley (© 520/544-1800; www.elconquistadorcc.com), with two 18-hole courses and a 9-hole course, offers stunning (and very distracting) views of the Santa Catalina Mountains.

There are many public courses around town. The **Arizona National,** 9777 E. Sabino Greens Dr. (© 520/749-3636; www.arizonanationalgolfclub.com), incorporates stands of cacti and rocky outcroppings into the course layout. **Heritage Highlands at Dove Mountain,** 4949 W. Heritage Club Blvd., Marana (© 520/579-7000; www.heritage highlands.com), is a championship desert course at the foot of the Tortolita Mountains.

Tucson Parks and Recreation operates five municipal golf courses, of which the **Randolph** and **Dell Urich,** 600 S. Alvernon Way (© 520/791-4161), are the premier courses. The former has been the site of Tucson's LPGA tournament. Other municipal courses include **El Rio,** 1400 W. Speedway Blvd. (© 520/791-4229); **Silverbell,** 3600

N. Silverbell Rd. (𝓒 520/791-5235); and **Fred Enke,** 8251 E. Irvington Rd. (𝓒 520/791-2539). This latter course is the city's only desert-style golf course. For general information and tee-time reservations for any of the municipal courses, visit **www.tucson citygolf.com**.

HIKING   Tucson is nearly surrounded by mountains, most of which are protected as city and state parks, national forest, or national park, and within these public areas are hundreds of miles of hiking trails. See the listings for Saguaro National Park and Sabino Canyon Recreation Area, above.

Tucson Mountain Park, at the end of Speedway Boulevard, is adjacent to Saguaro National Park and preserves a similar landscape. The parking area at Gates Pass, on Speedway, is a favorite sunset spot.

With Tucson's city limits pushing right out to the boundary of the Coronado National Forest, there are some excellent hiking options in Tucson's northern foothills. The **Ventana Canyon Trail** begins at a parking area adjacent to the Loews Ventana Canyon Resort (off Sunrise Dr., west of Sabino Canyon Rd.) and leads into the Ventana Canyon Wilderness. Over near the Westward Look Resort is the **Pima Canyon Trail,** which leads into the Ventana Canyon Wilderness and is reached off Ina Road just east of Oracle Road. Both of these trails provide classic desert canyon hikes of whatever length you feel like hiking (a dam at 3 miles on the latter trail makes a good turnaround point).

Catalina State Park, 11570 N. Oracle Rd. (𝓒 520/628-5798), is set on the rugged northwest face of the Santa Catalina Mountains, between 2,500 and 3,000 feet high. Hiking trails here lead into the Pusch Ridge Wilderness; however, the favorite park day hike is the 5.5-mile round-trip to **Romero Pools,** a refreshing destination on a hot day. Admission to the park is $6 per vehicle ($3 btw. Memorial Day and Labor Day). There are horseback riding stables adjacent to the park, and within the park is an ancient Hohokam ruin.

One of the reasons Tucson is such a livable city is the presence of the cool (and, in winter, snow-covered) pine forests of 8,250-foot Mount Lemmon. Within the **Mount Lemmon Recreation Area,** at the end of the Catalina Highway (also now called the Sky Island Scenic Byway), are many miles of trails, and the hearty hiker can even set out from down in the lowland desert and hike up into the Alpine forests. For a more leisurely excursion, drive to the top to start your hike. Keep in mind that in winter, when the weather is pleasant in Tucson, people may be skiing up here. There is a $5-per-vehicle charge to use any of the sites within this recreation area. Even if you only plan to pull off at a roadside parking spot and ogle the view, you'll need to stop at the roadside ticket kiosk at the base of the mountain and pay your fee.

HORSEBACK RIDING   In addition to renting horses and providing guided trail rides, the stables below offer sunset rides with cookouts. Reservations are a good idea.

Pusch Ridge Stables, 13700 N. Oracle Rd. (𝓒 520/825-1664; www.puschridge stables.com), is adjacent to Catalina State Park and Coronado National Forest. Rates are $35 for 1 hour, $55 for 2 hours, and $45 for a sunset ride.

Over on the east side, there's **Spanish Trail Outfitters** (𝓒 520/749-0167; www. spanishtrailoutfitters.com), which leads rides into the foothills of the Santa Catalina Mountains off Sabino Canyon Road. Rates are $35 for a 1-hour ride, $55 for a 2-hour or sunset ride.

HOT-AIR BALLOONING   The ballooning season in Tucson runs October through April. **Balloon America** (𝓒 520/299-7744; www.balloonridesusa.com) offers flights over the desert ($185) or a more adventurous trip over the foothills of the Santa Catalina

Mountains ($475). **Fleur de Tucson Balloon Tours** (© 520/529-1025; www.fleurde tucson.net) offers rides over the Tucson Mountains, Saguaro National Park, and the Avra Valley. Rates are $225 to $250 per person, including brunch and a champagne toast.

WILDFLOWER VIEWING Bloom time varies from year to year, but April and May are good times to view native wildflowers in the Tucson area. While the crowns of white blossoms worn by saguaro cacti are among the most visible blooms in the area, other cacti are far more colorful. **Saguaro National Park** and **Sabino Canyon Recreation Area** are among the best local spots to see saguaros, other cacti, and various wildflowers in bloom. If you feel like heading farther afield, the wildflower displays at **Picacho Peak State Park,** between Tucson and Casa Grande, are considered the most impressive in the state.

SHOPPING

El Presidio Historic District around the Tucson Museum of Art is the city's center for crafts shops. This area is home to Old Town Artisans and the Tucson Museum of Art museum shop. The **"Lost Barrio"** on the corner of Southwest Park Avenue and 12th Street (a block off Broadway) is a good place to look for Mexican imports and Southwestern-style home furnishings.

    Mark Sublette Medicine Man Gallery, Santa Fe Square, 7000 E. Tanque Verde Rd. (© 520/722-7798), has the best and biggest selection of old Navajo rugs in the city, as well as Mexican and other Hispanic textiles, Acoma pottery, basketry, and artwork by cowboy artists. With its museum-quality goods (antique Navajo rugs, kachinas, furniture, and a huge selection of old Native American jewelry), **Morning Star Traders,** 2020 E. Speedway Blvd. (© 520/881-2112), just may be the best store of its type in the entire state.

WHERE TO STAY

If you're looking to stay in a B&B, several agencies can help. The **Arizona Association of Bed and Breakfast Inns** (www.arizona-bed-breakfast.com) has several members in Tucson. **Mi Casa Su Casa** (© 800/456-0682 or 480/990-0682; www.azres.com) will book you into one of its many home stays (informal B&Bs) in the Tucson area or elsewhere in the state, as will **Arizona Trails Travel Services** (© 888/799-4284 or 480/837-4284; www.arizonatrails.com), which also books tour and hotel reservations.

Arizona Inn   With its pink-stucco buildings and immaculately tended gardens, the historic Arizona Inn is an absolute oasis. If you're searching for Old Arizona charm but also demand modern levels of comfort, then look no further. Most rooms have original or reproduction period furniture; some also have fireplaces. Most suites have private patios or enclosed sun porches. The main dining room is a casually elegant hall with plenty of outdoor seating as well.

2200 E. Elm St., Tucson, AZ 85719. © 800/933-1093 or 520/325-1541. Fax 520/881-5830. www.arizonainn.com. 95 units. Mid-Jan to mid-Apr from $319 double, from $469 suite; mid-Apr to May from $229 double, from $369 suite; June to mid-Sept from $179 double, from $289 suite; mid-Sept to mid-Dec from $229 double, from $369 suite; mid-Dec to mid-Jan $259 double, from $359 suite. Summer rates include full breakfast and complimentary evening ice-cream fountain. Children 12 and under stay free in parent's room. AE, MC, V. **Amenities:** 3 restaurants; heated outdoor pool; 2 tennis courts; well-equipped exercise room; access to nearby health club. *In room:* Fridge.

Casa Tierra Adobe Bed & Breakfast Inn   If you've come to Tucson to be in the desert, this modern adobe B&B is worth considering. Built to look as though it has been here since Spanish colonial days, Casa Tierra is surrounded by 5 cactus-studded acres on

(Best) **Two World-Class Spas**

Two of the world's greatest spas are located in and around Tucson. If you want to be pampered by the best, you can't go wrong at either of the following:

Canyon Ranch Health Resort, 8600 E. Rockcliff Rd. (© **800/742-9000** or 520/749-9000; www.canyonranch.com), offers the sort of complete spa experience that's available at only a handful of places around the country. On staff are doctors; psychotherapists; fitness instructors; massage therapists; and tennis, golf, and racquetball pros. Services offered include everything from health and fitness assessments and sports activities to facials and cooking demonstrations. Guests stay in a variety of spacious and very comfortable accommodations. Three gourmet, low-calorie meals are served daily with options for total daily caloric intake (don't worry, you won't go hungry). All this pampering does not come cheap—4-night packages here start at $3,520 double—but the rates do include all meals and a variety of spa services and programs.

Focusing on what it calls "life balancing," **Miraval Life in Balance Resort & Spa,** 5000 E. Via Estancia Miraval, Catalina (© **800/232-3969;** www.miraval resorts.com), one of the country's most exclusive health spas, emphasizes stress management, self-discovery, and relaxation rather than facials and mud baths. To this end, activities at the all-inclusive resort include meditation, tai chi, Pilates, and yoga; more active types can go hiking, mountain biking, and rock climbing (on an outdoor climbing wall). Such desert classics as horseback riding, tennis, and swimming are also available. Miraval also offers fitness/nutrition consultations, cooking demonstrations, exercise classes, and skin care and facials. Guest rooms, many of which have views of the Santa Catalina Mountains, are done in a Southwestern style. While very large, most of the bathrooms have showers but no tubs. In 2008, Miraval added 16 sustainable rooms; its dining room uses local and organic ingredients as much as possible.

Rates start at $1,480 double and include all meals, classes, and a $125 per-person per-day credit for spa service, a round of golf, or private consultation.

---

the west side of Saguaro National Park. Sunsets are enough to take your breath away. Rooms open onto a landscaped courtyard, which is surrounded by a covered seating area. The outdoor whirlpool makes a perfect stargazing spot.

11155 W. Calle Pima, Tucson, AZ 85743. © **866/254-0006** or 520/578-3058. www.casatierratucson.com. 4 units. $135–$195 double; $195–$285 suite. Rates include full breakfast. 2-night minimum stay. AE, DISC, MC, V. Closed June 16–Aug 14. **Amenities:** Exercise room. *In room:* Fridge, microwave.

Embassy Suites Tucson-Paloma Village Situated at the intersection of Skyline Drive and Campbell Road, this hotel is surrounded by upscale shopping centers and is close to some of Tucson's best restaurants. Although the suites here are small by Embassy Suites standards, you will still get two rooms, which makes this hotel a good choice for families on a budget. Some suites have mountain views, while others overlook the dense desert vegetation of a dry wash. The full breakfast and afternoon appetizers and drinks can help you save on meal costs.

3110 E. Skyline Dr., Tucson, AZ 85718. ✆ **800/EMBASSY** (362-2779) or 520/352-4000. Fax 520/352-4001.
www.tucsonpalomavillage.embassysuites.com. 120 units. Jan–Apr $220–$260 double; May and Sept–
Dec $150–$180 double; June–Aug $120–$140 double. Rates include full breakfast and evening social
hour. Children 17 and under stay free in parent's room. AE, DC, DISC, MC, V. **Amenities:** Outdoor pool;
exercise room. *In room:* Fridge, microwave.

Hacienda del Sol Guest Ranch Resort

With its colorful Southwestern styling, historical character, desert gardens, and ridge-top setting, Hacienda del Sol is one of the most distinctive hotels in Tucson. Rooms have rustic and colorful Mexican character, with a decidedly artistic flair. If you prefer more modern accommodations, ask for a suite; if you want loads of space, ask for a casita. The **Grill** (see below) is one of Tucson's best restaurants.

5601 N. Hacienda del Sol Rd., Tucson, AZ 85718. ✆ **800/728-6514** or 520/299-1501. www.haciendadel
sol.com. 30 units. Early Jan to May $175–$280 double, $345–$355 suite, $395–$495 casita; June–Sept
$109–$164 double, $175–$195 suite, $195–$310 casita; Oct to early Jan $165–$260 double, $330–$340
suite, $370–$495 casita. 2-night minimum stay weekends and holidays. AE, DC, DISC, MC, V. Pets
accepted ($50 fee). **Amenities:** Restaurant; outdoor pool; access to nearby health club; spa. *In room:*
Fridge.

Hilton Tucson El Conquistador Golf & Tennis Resort (Kids)

With the Santa Catalina Mountains as a backdrop, this resort in Tucson's northern foothills boasts a spectacular setting. Keep in mind that if you stay here, you'll be at least 30 minutes from downtown. Most guest rooms are built around a central courtyard with manicured lawns and a large oasis of swimming pools, one of which has a long water slide. Consequently, this place is a great choice for families. All units feature Southwestern-influenced furniture, marble bathrooms, and balconies or patios.

10000 N. Oracle Rd., Tucson, AZ 85704. ✆ **800/325-7832** or 520/544-5000. Fax 520/544-1222. www.
hiltonelconquistador.com. 428 units. Jan to late May $209–$319 double, from $359 suite; late May to
early Sept $119–$209 double, from $179 suite; early Sept to Dec $149–$259 double, from $239 suite.
Additional $10 daily service fee. Children 18 and under stay free in parent's room. AE, DC, DISC, MC, V.
Valet parking $11. Pets accepted ($50 fee). **Amenities:** 5 restaurants; 4 pools; 1 9-hole and 2 18-hole golf
courses; 31 tennis courts; 2 exercise rooms; spa services.

La Posada Lodge and Casitas

There are several different types of rooms here, but the best are the Western-style rooms, which have a sort of retro south-of-the-border decor that includes headboards painted with classic Mexican scenes. Casitas, which are the largest and most expensive rooms here, have a similar decor. There are also some fun rooms with a 1950s retro feel. The attractive rooms, pleasant pool area, and on-site Mexican restaurant together make this an excellent and economical choice.

5900 N. Oracle Rd., Tucson, AZ 85704. ✆ **800/810-2808** or 520/887-4800. Fax 520/293-7543. www.
laposadalodge.com. 72 units. $89–$149 double. Rates include continental breakfast. Children 17 and
under stay free in parent's room. AE, DC, DISC, MC, V. Pets accepted ($50 fee). **Amenities:** Restaurant;
pool; exercise room. *In room:* Fridge, microwave.

Loews Ventana Canyon Resort (Best)

For breathtaking scenery and superb facilities, no other Tucson accommodations can compare. The Santa Catalina Mountains rise behind the property, and despite its many amenities, the resort is firmly planted in the desert. Flagstone floors in the lobby give the public rooms a rugged but luxurious appeal. Guest rooms have balconies overlooking city lights or mountains; some have fireplaces. Bathrooms include tubs built for two. Both the **Ventana Room** and the **Flying V Bar & Grill** are among the best restaurants in Tucson. There are jogging and nature trails and a playground on the property.

7000 N. Resort Dr., Tucson, AZ 85750. © **800/234-5117** or 520/299-2020. Fax 520/299-6832. www.loews hotels.com/hotels/tucson. 398 units. Early Jan to late May $279–$429 double, from $750 suite; late May to early Sept $150–$295 double, from $295 suite; early Sept to early Jan from $279–$429 double, from $700 suite. Children 17 and under stay free in parent's room. AE, DC, DISC, MC, V. Pets accepted. **Amenities:** 5 restaurants; 2 pools; 2 18-hole golf courses; 8 tennis courts; exercise room; full-service spa. *In room:* Fridge.

Tanque Verde Ranch Tanque Verde, the most luxurious guest ranch in Tucson, borders both Saguaro National Park and the Coronado National Forest. The bird-watching here is excellent, and other activities include guided hikes, horseback rides, guided mountain-bike rides, and nature walks. Rooms are spacious and comfortable; many have fireplaces, patios, and fridges, but don't expect a TV. The casitas are absolutely huge and are among the most luxurious accommodations in the state.

14301 E. Speedway Blvd., Tucson, AZ 85748. © **800/234-DUDE** (234-3833) or 520/296-6275. Fax 520/721-9426. www.tanqueverderanch.com. 74 units. Mid-Dec to Apr $420–$640 double; May–Sept $330–$440 double; Oct to mid-Dec $370–$515 double. Rates include all meals and ranch activities. Children 3 and under stay free in parent's room. AE, DISC, MC, V. **Amenities:** Dining room; 3 pools (1 indoor); 5 tennis courts; exercise room; small full-service spa. *In room:* Fridge.

WHERE TO DINE

Foodies fond of the latest culinary trends will find plenty of spots to satisfy their cravings. Concentrations of creative restaurants can be found along East Tanque Verde Road and at foothills resorts and shopping plazas. On the other hand, if you're on a tight dining budget, look for early-bird dinners, which are quite popular with retirees.

Café Poca Cosa NEW MEXICAN   The food here is not just *any* Mexican food; it's imaginative and different and is served in a bold and angular space that belies the location on the ground floor of a parking garage. The cuisine consists of creations such as chicken with a dark mole sauce made with Kahlúa, chocolate, almonds, and chilies. The staff is courteous and friendly. It's an excellent value, especially at lunch.

110 E. Pennington St. © **520/622-6400.** www.cafepocacosainc.com. Reservations highly recommended. Main courses $13–$14 lunch, $19–$24 dinner. DC, DISC, MC, V. Tues–Thurs 11am–9pm; Fri–Sat 11am–10pm.

El Charro Café SONORAN MEXICAN   Located in an old stone building in El Presidio Historic District, El Charro is Tucson's oldest family-operated Mexican restaurant. Its specialty is *carne seca,* an air-dried beef similar to jerky. The cafe can be packed at lunch, so arrive early or late. The adjacent ¡**Toma!,** a colorful bar/cantina, is under the same ownership. There are other El Charro locations at 6310 E. Broadway (© **520/745-1922**), 4699 E. Speedway Blvd. (© **520/325-1922**), and 100 W. Orange Grove (© **520/615-1922**).

311 N. Court Ave. © **520/622-1922.** www.elcharrocafe.com. Reservations recommended for dinner. Main courses $6–$19. AE, DC, DISC, MC, V. Sun–Thurs 11am–9pm; Fri–Sat 11am–10pm.

The Grill REGIONAL   Located in a 1920s hacienda-style former dude ranch, the Grill is known for its classic Southwestern styling and great views of the city. For openers, consider the delicious wild-mushroom bisque, which comes with ancho chili–truffle crème fraîche. Despite the price, the dry-aged New York strip steak is deservedly the most popular entree on the menu and is big enough for two people to share. Sunday brunch here is a treat.

At the Hacienda del Sol Guest Ranch Resort, 5601 N. Hacienda del Sol Rd. ℭ **520/529-3500.** www.

haciendadelsol.com. Reservations recommended. Main courses $26–$38; Sun brunch $32. AE, DC, DISC, MC, V. Mon–Sat 5:30–10pm; Sun 10am–1:30pm and 5:30–10pm.

Janos (Best) SOUTHWESTERN/REGIONAL   Janos Wilder is the city's most cele-brated chef. The menu changes both daily and seasonally, with such offerings as Guaymas shrimp with morel cream sauce, beef tournedos with foie gras butter and truffle sauce, and lamb chops with a complex spicy Southwestern rub. This is about as formal a restau-rant as you'll find in this otherwise very casual city. No other restaurant in Tucson does as much to promote local and indigenous ingredients as Janos.

At the Westin La Paloma, 3770 E. Sunrise Dr. ℭ **520/615-6100.** www.janos.com. Reservations highly recommended. Main courses $28–$50; 5-course tasting menu $85 ($125 with wine). AE, DC, MC, V. Mon–Thurs 5:30–9pm; Fri–Sat 5:30–9:30pm.

McClintock's NEW AMERICAN   For classic Western ranch atmosphere, there is no place in Arizona to compare with this restaurant inside the exclusive Saguaro Ranch housing development. When you arrive, you'll even be escorted through the develop-ment to the restaurant. Be sure to make a reservation that will let you sit on the restau-rant's veranda and watch the sun go down over the rugged saguaro-covered hills. The view is gorgeous. As often as possible, dishes are made with natural or organic ingredi-ents, and the pastas and steaks are highlights.

In Saguaro Ranch, 3755 W. Conrad's Way. ℭ **520/579-2100.** www.mcclintocks-restaurant.com. Reserva-tions required. Main courses $28–$45. AE, DC, DISC, MC, V. Mon–Thurs & Sun, 5–10pm; Fri–Sat 5–11pm.

Pinnacle Peak Steakhouse (Kids) STEAKHOUSE   The Pinnacle Peak Steakhouse specializes in family dining in a fun cowboy atmosphere. Once through the doors, you'll be surprised at the authenticity of the place, which really does resemble a dining room in Old Tombstone. Be prepared for crowds—this place is popular with tour buses. Oh, and wear a necktie into this place, and it will be cut off! Actually, lots of people wear ties so they can have them added to the collection tacked to the ceiling.

6541 E. Tanque Verde Rd. ℭ **520/296-0911** or 296-4551. www.pinnaclepeaktucson.com. Reservations not accepted. Main courses $8–$20. AE, DC, DISC, MC, V. Mon–Thurs 5–9pm; Fri–Sat 4:30–10pm; Sun 4:30–9pm.

Terra Cotta SOUTHWESTERN   Terra Cotta is Arizona's original Southwestern res-taurant, offering a combination of creative cooking, casual atmosphere, and local art-work. A brick oven is used to make pizzas, while salads, sandwiches, small plates, and main dishes flesh out the long menu. With so many choices, it's often difficult to decide, but the must-have signature dish is garlic custard, served with a warm salsa vinaigrette and herbed hazelnuts. The poblano chilies rellenos stuffed with either shrimp or adobo pork are another can't-miss choice.

3500 E. Sunrise Dr. ℭ **520/577-8100.** www.dineterracotta.com. Reservations recommended. Main courses $10–$15 lunch, $16–$27 dinner. AE, DC, DISC, MC, V. Daily 4–10pm (call for seasonal lunch and Sun brunch hours).

Ventana Room NEW AMERICAN   *Ventana* means "window" in Spanish, and the views through the windows of this restaurant are every bit as memorable as the food that comes from the kitchen. Whether you're seated overlooking the resort's waterfall or the lights of Tucson far below, you'll likely have trouble concentrating on your food, but do

11

TUCSON

try; you wouldn't want to miss any of the subtle nuances of such dishes as the velvety Dover sole or grilled buffalo tenderloin with seared foie gras.

At Loews Ventana Canyon Resort, 7000 N. Resort Dr. ⓒ **520/615-5494.** www.ventanaroom.com. Reservations highly recommended. Jackets recommended for men. Prix-fixe menus $85–$120. AE, DC, DISC, MC, V. Tues–Thurs 6–9pm; Fri–Sat 6–10pm. Closed early July to early Sept.

Vero Amore ITALIAN   The brick oven at this little place turns out bubbly, thin-crust pizzas (try the margherita) that are made with fresh, house-made mozzarella and ingredients imported from Italy. You can also get that homemade mozzarella in panini and on salads. It even shows up baked on the Amore Cobb salad. Oh, and those panini are made with fresh bread baked in the same brick oven that turns out the pizzas.

3305 N. Swan Rd., Ste. 105. ⓒ **520/325-4122.** www.veroamorepizza.com. Reservations not accepted. Main courses $6.50–$11. DISC, MC, V. Sun–Thurs 11am–9pm; Fri–Sat 11am–10pm.

TUCSON AFTER DARK

The best place to look for entertainment listings is in the free *Tucson Weekly.*

The **Downtown Arts District** is home to the Temple of Music and Art, the Tucson Convention Center Music Hall, and several nightclubs. The **University of Arizona campus,** only a mile away, is another hot spot for entertainment.

THE PERFORMING ARTS   Tucson's largest performance venue is the **Tucson Convention Center (TCC) Music Hall,** 260 S. Church Ave. (ⓒ **520/791-4266**). It's the home of the **Tucson Symphony Orchestra** (ⓒ **520/882-8585** or 792-9155; www.tucson symphony.org) and is where the Arizona Opera Company and Ballet Arizona usually perform.

Originally opened in 1930, the **Fox Theatre,** 17 W. Congress St. (ⓒ **520/624-1515;** www.foxtucsontheatre.org), is a restored movie palace that is now the city's most beautiful place to catch live music, a play, or a classic or independent film. The box office is open Monday through Friday from 11am to 6pm and Saturday from 11am to 2pm.

THE CLUB & MUSIC SCENE   Tucson is the mariachi capital of the United States, and no one should visit without spending at least one evening listening to some of these strolling minstrels. **La Fuente,** 1749 N. Oracle Rd. (ⓒ **520/623-8659**), serves up good Mexican food, but what really draws the crowds is the nightly mariachi music. If you just want to listen and not have dinner, you can hang out in the lounge.

Club Congress, 311 E. Congress St. (ⓒ **520/622-8848**), is Tucson's main alternative-music venue, with usually a couple of nights of live music each week. With its tropical decor and overabundance of potted plants setting the mood, **El Parador** restaurant and dance club, 2744 E. Broadway (ⓒ **520/881-2808**), is Tucson's favorite spot for lively Latin jazz and salsa performances (salsa lessons on Fri nights).

THE BAR SCENE   ¡Toma!, 311 N. Court Ave. (ⓒ **520/622-1922**), always has a festive atmosphere and serves good margaritas. If you can't afford the lap of luxury, you can at least pull up a chair at **Flying V Bar & Grill,** in the Loews Ventana Canyon Resort, 7000 N. Resort Dr. (ⓒ **520/299-2020**). Set next to a waterfall, this watering hole has a grand view over the golf course and Tucson.

CASINOS   Casino del Sol, 7406 S. Camino de Oeste (ⓒ **800/344-9435;** www. casinodelsol.com), is southern Arizona's largest casino and offers slot machines, keno, bingo, and a card room.

THE VERDE VALLEY

The Verde Valley has long been a magnet for both wildlife and people. With its headwaters in the Juniper Mountains of the Prescott National Forest, the Verde River flows down through a rugged canyon before meandering slowly across the Verde Valley. Contact the **Cottonwood Chamber of Commerce,** 1010 S. Main St., Cottonwood (© 928/634-7593; http://cottonwood.verdevalley.com).

The **Verde Canyon Railroad,** 300 N. Broadway, Clarkdale (© 800/320-0718; www.verdecanyonrr.com), traverses unspoiled desert that's inaccessible by car. The views of the rocky canyon walls and green waters of the Verde River are quite dramatic, and if you look closely along the way, you'll see ancient Sinagua cliff dwellings. Tickets are $55 for adults, $50 for seniors, and $35 for children 2 to 12.

Consisting of two impressive stone pueblos, **Montezuma Castle National Monument,** exit 289 off I-17 (© 928/567-3322; www.nps.gov/moca), is among the best preserved of Arizona's **cliff dwellings.** The more intriguing pueblo is set in a shallow cave 100 feet up in a cliff overlooking Beaver Creek. Construction on this five-story, 20-room village began sometime in the early 12th century.

The **Hacienda de la Mariposa,** 3875 Stagecoach Rd., Camp Verde (© 888/520-9095 or 928/567-1490; www.lamariposa-az.com; $195–$235 double), is a modern Santa Fe–style inn set on the banks of Beaver Creek and is just up the road from Montezuma Castle National Monument. The almond croissants at **Old Town Café,** 1025 "A" N. Main St., downtown Cottonwood (© 928/634-5980), are the best we've ever had. If that isn't recommendation enough for you, there are also good salads and sandwiches, such as a grilled panini of smoked turkey, spinach, and tomatoes.

GETTING THERE   Take I-17 north from Phoenix or south from Flagstaff to Camp Verde. Then take Ariz. 260 north through the Verde Valley for 12 miles to Cottonwood.

JEROME

Clinging to the slopes of Cleopatra Hill high on Mingus Mountain, Jerome looks much as it did when it was an active mining town, and has been designated a National Historic Landmark. For information, contact the **Jerome Chamber of Commerce** (© 928/634-2900; www.jeromechamber.com).

Wandering the streets, soaking up the atmosphere, and shopping are the main pastimes here. You can also learn about the town's past at the **Jerome State Historic Park,** off U.S. 89A on Douglas Road (© 928/634-5381; www.azstateparks.com). Housed in a 1916 mansion, the Jerome State Historic Park has exhibits on mining and a few of the mansion's original furnishings. Admission is $3.

For that classic mining-town tourist-trap experience, follow the signs up the hill from downtown to the **Gold King Mine** (© 928/634-0053; www.goldkingmine.net), where you can see lots of old, rusting mining equipment and catch a demonstration. Admission is $5 for adults, $4 for seniors, and $3 for children ages 6 to 12.

The **Raku Gallery,** 250 Hull Ave. (© 928/639-0239; www.rakugallery.com), has gallery space on two floors and walls of glass across the back, with views of the red rocks of Sedona in the distance. Stop in at the **Jerome Artists Cooperative Gallery,** 502 Main St. (© 928/639-4276; www.jeromeartistscoop.com), on the west side of the street where Hull Avenue and Main Street fork as you come up the hill into town.

The **Connor Hotel of Jerome,** 164 Main St. (© **800/523-3554** or 928/634-5006; www.connorhotel.com; $90–$165 double), is a renovated historic hotel, with spacious rooms having large windows. The tiny **Flatiron Café,** at Main Street and Hull Avenue (© **928/634-2733**), serves breakfast and light meals.

GETTING THERE   Follow directions to the Verde Valley, above. Jerome is 8 miles west of Cottonwood on Ariz. 89A.

SEDONA & OAK CREEK CANYON

The town of Sedona claims the most beautiful setting in the Southwest. Red-rock buttes, eroded canyon walls, and mesas rise into blue skies. Off in the distance, the Mogollon Rim looms, its forests of juniper and ponderosa pine dark against the red rocks. With this drop-dead scenery and a plethora of resorts and good restaurants, Sedona makes an excellent base for exploring central Arizona.

Essentials

GETTING THERE   Sedona is on Ariz. 179 at the mouth of Oak Creek Canyon. From Phoenix, take I-17 to Ariz. 179 N. From Flagstaff, head south on I-17 until you see the turnoff for Ariz. 89A and Sedona.

VISITOR INFORMATION   The **Sedona Chamber of Commerce Visitor Center/ Uptown Gateway Visitor Center,** 331 Forest Rd. (© **800/288-7336** or 928/282-7722; www.visitsedona.com), operates a visitor center at the corner of Ariz. 89A and Forest Road in uptown Sedona. The visitor center is open Monday through Saturday from 8:30am to 5pm, and Sunday and holidays from 9am to 3pm.

SPECIAL EVENTS & FESTIVALS   In late September, **Sedona Jazz on the Rocks** (© **928/282-1985;** www.sedonajazz.com) brings world-class jazz to Sedona. From mid-November until early January, more than a million lights illuminate Los Abrigados Resort (© **800/521-3131** or 928/282-1777; www.redrockfantasy.com) in a **Red-Rock Fantasy.**

Red-Rock Country

Just south of Sedona, on Ariz. 179, you'll see the aptly named **Bell Rock** on the east side of the road. From Bell Rock, you can see **Cathedral Rock** to the west. Adjacent to Bell Rock is **Courthouse Rock,** and not far from Bell Rock and visible from Chapel Road are **Eagle Head Rock,** the **Twin Nuns,** and **Mother and Child Rock** (to the left of the Twin Nuns).

If you head west through Sedona on Ariz. 89A and turn left onto Airport Road, you'll drive up onto **Airport Mesa.** The views from here are among the best in the region, and there are some easy hiking trails.

One of the most beautiful areas around Sedona is **Boynton Canyon.** Drive west out of Sedona on Ariz. 89A, turn right on Dry Creek Road, take a left at the T intersection, and at the next T intersection take a right. On the way to Boynton Canyon, look north from Ariz. 89A and you'll see **Coffee Pot Rock,** rising 1,800 feet above Sedona. Three pinnacles, known as the **Three Golden Chiefs** by the Yavapai tribe, stand beside Coffee Pot Rock. As you drive up Dry Creek Road, on your right you'll see **Capitol Butte.** Just outside the gates of Enchantment Resort is a parking area for the **Boynton Canyon Trail.** From the parking area, the trail leads 3 miles up into the canyon.

In this same area, you can visit the Sinagua cliff dwellings at **Palatki Ruins.** To reach the ruins, follow the directions to Boynton Canyon, but instead of turning right at the second T intersection, turn left onto unpaved Boynton Pass Road (Forest Rd. 152). Follow this road to another T intersection and go right onto F.R. 125, then veer right onto F.R. 795. To visit the ruins, you'll need a Red Rock Pass, which costs $5 per car for a 1-day pass. Don't try this if the roads are at all muddy.

South of Ariz. 89A and a bit west of the turnoff for Boynton Canyon is Upper Red Rock Loop Road, which leads to **Crescent Moon Recreation Area,** a National Forest Service recreation area that has become a must-see spot. Hiking trails beginning here lead up to Cathedral Rock. Park admission is $8 per vehicle.

If you continue on Upper Red Rock Loop Road, it turns into Lower Red Rock Loop Road and reaches **Red Rock State Park** (© 928/282-6907; www.azstateparks.com). The views here take in many of the rocks above, and you have the additional bonus of being right on the creek. Park admission is $6 per vehicle.

Oak Creek Canyon

The **Mogollon Rim** is a 2,000-foot escarpment cutting diagonally across central Arizona and on into New Mexico. Of the many canyons cutting down from the rim, Oak Creek Canyon is the best known. Ariz. 89A runs through the canyon from Flagstaff to Sedona, winding its way down from the rim and paralleling Oak Creek. If you have a choice of how first to view Oak Creek Canyon, come at it from the north. Your first stop after traveling south from Flagstaff will be the **Oak Creek Canyon Vista,** which gives you a view far down the valley to Sedona and beyond.

The most popular spot in all of Oak Creek Canyon is **Slide Rock State Park** (© 928/282-3034). Located 7 miles north of Sedona on the site of an old homestead, this park preserves a natural water slide. Admission is $8 per vehicle ($10 during summer).

By far the most spectacular and popular hike in the canyon is the 6-mile round-trip up the **West Fork of Oak Creek.** Stop by the Sedona–Oak Creek Chamber of Commerce to pick up a free map.

What to See & Do Around Town

Sedona's most notable architectural landmark is the **Chapel of the Holy Cross,** south of town just off Ariz. 179 (© 928/282-4069; www.chapeloftheholycross.com). The chapel sits high above the road and is built right into the red rock.

The **Sedona Arts Center,** 15 Art Barn Rd., at Ariz. 89A (© 888/954-4442 or 928/ 282-3809; www.sedonaartscenter.com), near the north end of uptown Sedona, serves as a gallery for work by both local and regional artists.

You'll find the greatest concentration of galleries and shops in the uptown area of Sedona (along Ariz. 89A just north of the Y) and at **Tlaquepaque** (© 928/282-4838; www.tlaq.com), the arts-and-crafts village on Ariz. 179, at the bridge over Oak Creek on the south side of town.

Garland's Navajo Rugs, 411 Hwy. 179 (© 928/282-4070; www.garlandsrugs.com), has the largest selection of contemporary and antique Navajo rugs in the world. **Hoel's Indian Shop,** 9589 N. Hwy. 89A (© 928/282-3925; www.hoelsindianshop.com), is one of the finest Native American arts-and-crafts galleries in the region.

Where to Stay & Dine

If you're searching for tranquillity or a romantic retreat amid the cool shade of Oak Creek Canyon, the **Briar Patch Inn,** 3190 N. Hwy. 89A (© 888/809-3030 or 928/282-2342; www.briarpatchinn.com; $199–$395 double), is the place and offers good value. This inn's cottages are set amid beautiful shady grounds where bird songs and a babbling creek set the mood.

The **Enchantment Resort,** 525 Boynton Canyon Rd. (© **800/826-4180** or 928/ 282-2900; www.enchantmentresort.com; $350–$450 double), is pricey but more than lives up to its name. The setting is breathtaking, and the pueblo-style architecture of the hotel blends in with the canyon landscape. There are plenty of ways to keep busy—pools, tennis courts, a fitness center, hiking trails, and a putting green. The affiliated **Mii amo** spa is one of the finest in the state. **Sky Ranch Lodge,** Airport Road (© **888/708-6400** or 928/282-6400; www.skyranchlodge.com; $75–$189 double), a motel atop Airport Mesa, is another inexpensive place with fantastic views.

The **Cowboy Club Grille & Spirits,** 241 N. Hwy. 89A (© **928/282-4200**), may look like an ordinary steakhouse, but it's more than your average meat-and-potatoes joint. You can have fried cactus strips with black-bean caramel gravy, followed by grilled salmon with chipotle hollandaise. Because the view of Boynton Canyon is so much a part of the experience of dining at **Yavapai Restaurant,** at the Enchantment Resort, 525 Boynton Canyon Rd. (© **928/204-6000**), we recommend lunch or a sunset dinner. The menu focuses on Southwestern flavors and changes regularly.

6 FLAGSTAFF & THE GRAND CANYON

FLAGSTAFF: EN ROUTE TO THE GRAND CANYON

Perhaps best known as the jumping-off point for trips to the South Rim of the Grand Canyon, Flagstaff also has a wide variety of accommodations and restaurants, one of the state's finest museums, and a lively cultural community.

Essentials

GETTING THERE   By Plane   US Airways serves **Pulliam Airport,** 3 miles south of town off I-17.

By Train   Amtrak (© **800/USA-RAIL** [872-7245]; www.amtrak.com) provides daily service from Los Angeles (11 hr.) and Chicago (32 hr.) to its station at 1 E. Rte. 66. There are direct bus connections to the Grand Canyon (see below).

By Car   The main routes into Flagstaff are **I-40** from the east (Albuquerque) and west (Los Angeles), and **I-17** from the south (Phoenix). **Ariz. 89A** connects Flagstaff to Sedona by way of Oak Creek Canyon, and **U.S. 180** connects Flagstaff with the South Rim of the Grand Canyon.

VISITOR INFORMATION   Contact the **Flagstaff Visitor Center,** 1 E. Rte. 66 (© **800/842-7293** or 928/774-9541; www.flagstaffarizona.org).

What to See & Do

Flagstaff is northern Arizona's center for outdoor activities. Chief among them is snow skiing at **Arizona Snowbowl** (© **928/779-1951;** www.arizonasnowbowl.com) on the slopes of Mount Agassiz, from which you can see all the way to the North Rim of the Grand Canyon. All-day lift tickets are $48 for adults, $26 for seniors and children 8 to 12. In summer, you can ride a chairlift almost to the summit and enjoy the expansive views across seemingly all of northern Arizona. The round-trip lift-ticket price is $10 for adults, $6 for children 8 to 12.

When there's no snow on the ground, there are plenty of hiking trails throughout the San Francisco Peaks, and many national forest trails in the area are open to mountain bikes as well as to hikers. For information on the trails in the Coconino National Forest, contact the **Peaks Ranger District,** 5075 N. Hwy. 89, Flagstaff (© **928/526-0866;** www.fs.fed.us/r3/coconino).

Downtown Flagstaff along Route 66, San Francisco Street, Aspen Avenue, and Birch Avenue is the city's **historic district,** filled with interesting little shops. It's worth a walk even if you aren't shopping.

The small but thorough **Museum of Northern Arizona,** 3101 N. Fort Valley Rd. (© **928/774-5213;** www.musnaz.org), is the ideal first stop on an exploration of northern Arizona. Here you'll learn about the archaeology, ethnology, geology, biology, and fine arts of the region. Admission is $7 adults, $4 children 7 to 17.

Lowell Observatory, 1400 W. Mars Hill Rd. (© **928/774-3358;** www.lowell.edu), is one of the oldest astronomical observatories in the Southwest. The facility consists of several observatories, a large visitor center with fun and educational exhibits, and outdoor displays. Admission is $6 for adults, $3 for children 5 to 17.

Where to Stay & Dine
The **Inn at 410,** 410 N. Leroux St. (© **800/774-2008** or 928/774-0088; www.inn410. com; $170–$300 double), is one of the best B&Bs in Arizona and provides convenience, pleasant surroundings, comfortable rooms, and delicious breakfasts. One of Arizona's most unusual little B&Bs is in the middle of nowhere along the road from Flagstaff to the Grand Canyon. The **Shooting Star Inn,** 27948 N. Shooting Star Lane, Flagstaff (© **928/606-8070;** www.shootingstarinn.com; $175 double), a large log house, produces its own electricity from photovoltaic panels and offers guests a chance to gaze at the stars through a number of different telescopes.

For great food in a casual atmosphere, try **Cottage Place Restaurant,** 126 W. Cottage Ave. (© **928/774-8431**), which most people in Flagstaff agree serves the best food in town. Flagstaff now has a Tibetan restaurant (!) in **Himalyan Grill,** 801 S. Milton Ave. (© **928/213-5444;** www.himalayangrill.com), offering an inexpensive lunch buffet. People come to Flagstaff's counterculture hangout, **Macy's European Coffee House & Bakery,** 14 S. Beaver St. (© **928/774-2243**), for the espresso and baked goodies, but there are also decent vegetarian pasta dishes, soups, and salads.

The **Museum Club,** 3404 E. Rte. 66 (© **928/526-9434;** www.museumclub.com), is a Flagstaff institution and one of America's classic roadhouses. There's live music, predominantly country and western, most nights.

THE GRAND CANYON SOUTH RIM
A mile deep, 277 miles long, and up to 18 miles wide, the Grand Canyon is truly one of the great natural wonders of the world. By raft, by mule, on foot, and in helicopters and small planes, more than four million people each year come to gaze into this great chasm. You can expect parking problems and traffic congestion, but don't let these inconveniences dissuade you from visiting. Despite the crowds, the Grand Canyon more than lives up to its name and is one of the most amazing sights on earth.

Essentials
GETTING THERE   By Plane   Grand Canyon Airport, 6 miles south of Grand Canyon Village in Tusayan, primarily handles sightseeing tours and charters.

By Train   Amtrak (© **800/USA-RAIL** [872-7245]; www.amtrak.com) provides daily service to Flagstaff (see above) and Williams. From Flagstaff, there's a bus directly to

Grand Canyon Village; from Williams, the Grand Canyon Railway excursion train (see below) takes you to Grand Canyon Village.

By Bus   Bus service between Phoenix, Flagstaff, Williams, and Grand Canyon Village is provided by **Open Road Tours** (© **800/766-7117** or 602/997-6474; www.openroadtours. com). Between Phoenix and Flagstaff, adult fares are $42 one-way and $76 round-trip ($30 and $52 for children); between Flagstaff and the Grand Canyon (by way of Williams), fares are $27 one-way and $54 round-trip ($19 and $38 for children).

By Car   If at all possible, travel into the park by some means *other* than car and avoid the traffic. From Flagstaff, 78 miles away, you can take U.S. 180 directly to the South Rim or U.S. 89 to Ariz. 64 and the east entrance to the park.

VISITOR INFORMATION   You can get advance information by contacting **Grand Canyon National Park,** P.O. Box 129, Grand Canyon, AZ 86023 (© **928/638-7888;** www.nps.gov/grca). When you arrive at the park, stop by the **Canyon View Visitor Center,** at Canyon View Information Plaza, 6 miles north of the south entrance. The center is open daily 8am to 5pm. Unfortunately, the information plaza has no adjacent parking, so you'll have to park where you can and then walk or take a free shuttle bus. The nearest places to park are at Mather Point, Market Plaza, park headquarters, and Yavapai Observation Station. If you're parked anywhere in Grand Canyon Village, you'll want to catch the Village Route bus. If you happen to be parked at Yaki Point, you can take the Kaibab Trail Route bus.

GETTING AROUND   Taxi service is available to and from the airport, trail heads, and other destinations (© **928/638-2822**). The fare from the airport to Grand Canyon Village is $10 for up to two adults ($5 for each additional person).

Free shuttle buses operate on four routes within the park. The **Village Route** bus circles through Grand Canyon Village throughout the day, with frequent stops at the Canyon View Information Plaza, Market Plaza, hotels, campgrounds, restaurants, and other facilities. The **Hermit's Rest Route** bus takes visitors to eight canyon overlooks west of Bright Angel Lodge (this bus does not operate Dec–Feb). The **Kaibab Trail Route** bus stops at the Canyon View Information Plaza, Pipe Creek Vista, the South Kaibab Trailhead, and Yaki Point. The **Canyon View/Mather Point Route** is specifically for visitors who need mobility assistance and shuttles between the Mather Point parking lot and the Canyon View Information Center. There's also a Hikers' Express bus to the South Kaibab Trailhead. This bus stops at Bright Angel Lodge and the Back Country Information Office.

Ahhh! Fresh Air at Last

In 2008, Grand Canyon National Park replaced all of its old diesel and liquid natural gas (LNG) buses with more eco-friendly compressed natural gas (CNG) buses. Not only do these new buses not belch black smoke as the old diesel buses did, but they're also much quieter. The park has also announced that it will begin operating buses between Grand Canyon Village and the town of Tusayan, which is just outside the park's south entrance. Leave your car at your hotel and take the bus to avoid parking headaches, *and* get around in a "green" way.

shuttle service between the South Rim and the North Rim. The fare is $75 one-way; reservations are required.

FEES   The park entry fee is $25 per car and is good for 1 week. Remember not to lose the little paper receipt that serves as your admission pass.

Grand Canyon Village & Vicinity: Your First Look

Grand Canyon Village is the most crowded place in the park, but it also has the most overlooks and visitor services. **Mather Point** is the first overlook you reach if you enter through the south entrance, although just before Mather Point, you should now come to the Canyon View Information Plaza. Continuing west, you'll come to **Yavapai Point,** the site of the **Yavapai Observation Station.** This historic building houses a small museum and has excellent views.

Continuing west from Yavapai Point, you'll come to a parking lot at park headquarters and a side road that leads to parking at the Market Plaza, which is one of the closest parking lots to the Canyon View Information Plaza.

In the historic district, in addition to numerous canyon viewpoints, you'll find **El Tovar Hotel** and **Bright Angel Lodge.** Adjacent to El Tovar are two historic souvenir-and-curio shops. **Hopi House Gift Store and Art Gallery,** built in 1905 to resemble a Hopi pueblo, now sells Hopi and Navajo arts and crafts. The nearby **Verkamps Curios** is the main place to look for souvenirs and crafts.

To the west of Bright Angel Lodge, two buildings cling precariously to the rim of the canyon. These are the **Lookout** and **Kolb studios.**

Hermit Road

Hermit Road leads 8 miles west from Grand Canyon Village to Hermit's Rest. Because it is closed to private vehicles March through November, it is also one of the most pleasant places to do a little canyon viewing or easy hiking during the busiest times. Free shuttle buses stop at most of the overlooks. From December to February, you can drive your own vehicle, but keep in mind that winters usually mean a lot of snow.

The first two stops are **Trailview Overlook** and **Maricopa Point.** From both, you have a view of the Bright Angel Trail winding down into the canyon.

Powell Point, the third stop, is the site of a memorial to John Wesley Powell, the first person to navigate the Colorado River through the Grand Canyon.

Next along the drive is **Hopi Point,** from which you can see a long section of the Colorado River, and **Mohave Point,** where you can see Hermit Rapids.

The next stop is at the **Abyss,** the 3,000-foot drop created by the Great Mojave Wall. This vertiginous view is one of the most awe-inspiring in the park. Layers of erosion-resistant sandstone have formed the free-standing pillars that are visible from here.

From **Pima Point,** it's possible to see the remains of Hermit Camp on the Tonto Plateau. At the end of Hermit Road stands **Hermit's Rest,** a log-and-stone building that is listed on the National Register of Historic Places.

Desert View Drive

Desert View Drive extends for 25 miles from Grand Canyon Village to Desert View. The first stop is **Yaki Point;** the spectacular view from here encompasses a wide section of the central canyon.

Next, **Grandview Point** affords a view of Horseshoe Mesa. Next along the drive is **Moran Point,** from which you can see a bright-red layer of shale in the canyon walls.

The **Tusayan Museum** (free admission) is the next stop. This small museum is dedicated to the Hopi tribe and Ancient Pueblo People who inhabited the region 800 years ago.

At **Lipan Point,** you get one of the park's best views of the Colorado River. From here you can even see a couple of major rapids. From **Navajo Point,** the Colorado River and Escalante Butte are visible.

Desert View, with its trading post, general store, snack bar, service station, information center, bookstore, and watchtower, is the end of this scenic drive. The views are breathtaking from anywhere at Desert View, but the best lookout is from atop the Desert View Watchtower.

Other Ways to See the Canyon

MULE RIDES Mule rides into the canyon are one of the most popular activities at Grand Canyon Village. Trips of various lengths and to different destinations are offered. There are 1-day trips to Plateau Point and overnight trips to Phantom Ranch, the only lodge actually in the canyon. Make a reservation through **Xanterra Parks & Resorts** (© 888/297-2757 or 303/297-2757; www.grandcanyonlodges.com). If at the last minute (5 days or fewer from the day you want to ride) you decide you want to go on a mule trip, contact Grand Canyon National Park Lodges at its Arizona phone number (© 928/638-2631) for the remote possibility that there may be space available. If you arrive at the canyon without a reservation and decide that you'd like to go on a mule ride, stop by the Bright Angel Transportation Desk to get your name put on the next day's waiting list.

RIDING THE RAILS The **Grand Canyon Railway** (© 800/843-8724 or 928/773-1976; www.thetrain.com), which runs from Williams to the South Rim of the Grand Canyon at Grand Canyon Village, uses early-20th-century steam engines (during the summer) and 1950s-vintage diesel engines (during other months) to pull 1920s passenger cars and a dome coach car. The fun trip offers great scenery and a trip back in time, and allows you to avoid the traffic in Grand Canyon Village.

A BIRD'S-EYE VIEW Airplane and helicopter flights over the Grand Canyon remain one of the most popular ways to see these natural wonders. Companies offering tours by small plane include **Air Grand Canyon** (© 800/247-4726 or 928/638-2686; www.airgrandcanyon.com) and **Grand Canyon Airlines** (© 866/235-9422 or 928/638-2359; www.grandcanyonairlines.com). Helicopter tours are available from **Maverick Airstar Helicopters** (© 866/689-8687 or 702/262-6199; www.airstar.com) and **Grand Canyon Helicopters** (© 800/541-4537 or 928/638-2764; www.grandcanyonhelicoptersaz.com).

Hiking the Canyon

No visit to the canyon is complete without journeying below the rim. While the views don't get any better than they are from the top, they do change considerably. This is some of the most rugged and strenuous hiking anywhere in the United States, and for this reason anyone attempting even a short walk should be well prepared. Wear sturdy footgear and carry at least 1 to 2 quarts of water for even a short hike. A long hike into or out of the canyon in the heat can require drinking more than a gallon of water. Remember while hiking that mules have the right of way. Don't attempt to hike from the rim to the Colorado River and back in a day; many who have tried this have died.

DAY HIKES Loop-trail day hikes are not possible in the Grand Canyon. The easiest day hikes are those along the **Rim Trail.** Head out early and get off at the Abyss shuttle stop. From here, it's a 4-mile hike to Hermit's Rest, which makes a great place to take a break. You can catch a shuttle bus back to the village.

Trails leading down into the canyon include the **Bright Angel Trail, South Kaibab Trail, Grandview Trail,** and **Hermit Trail.** If you plan to hike for more than 30 minutes, carry 2 quarts of water per person.

BACKPACKING There are many miles of trails deep in the canyon and several established campgrounds for backpackers. The best times of year to backpack in the canyon are spring and autumn. Be sure to carry at least 2 quarts, and preferably 1 gallon, of water.

A **Backcountry Use Permit** is required of all hikers planning to overnight in the canyon unless you'll be staying at Phantom Ranch. Make reservations as soon as possible. Reservations are taken in person, by mail, by fax (but not by phone), and over the Internet. Contact the **Backcountry Information Center,** Grand Canyon National Park, P.O. Box 129, Grand Canyon, AZ 86023 (© **928/638-7875** Mon–Fri 1–5pm for information; fax 928/638-2125; www.nps.gov/grca). The office begins accepting reservations on the first of every month for the following 5 months.

There are **campgrounds** at Indian Garden, Bright Angel Campground (near Phantom Ranch), and Cottonwood, but hikers are limited to 2 nights per trip at each of these campgrounds (except Nov 15–Feb 28, when 4 nights are allowed at each campground).

The *Backcountry Trip Planner* contains information to help you plan your itinerary. It's available through the Backcountry Information Center (see contact information above). Maps are available through the **Grand Canyon Association,** P.O. Box 399, Grand Canyon, AZ 86023 (© **800/858-2808** or 928/638-2481; www.grandcanyon.org), and at bookstores and gift shops within the national park.

Where to Stay

Keep in mind that the Grand Canyon is one of the most popular national parks in the country; make reservations as far in advance as possible.

INSIDE THE PARK Xanterra Parks & Resorts, 6312 S. Fiddlers Green Circle, Ste. 600N, Greenwood Village, CO 80111 (© **888/297-2757** or 303/297-2757; www.grandcanyonlodges.com), operates the hotels inside the park. Reservations are taken up to 13 months in advance. It is *sometimes* possible, due to cancellations and no-shows, to get a same-day reservation by calling © **928/638-2631.**

El Tovar Hotel, completely renovated in 2005, is the park's premier lodge. Built of local rock and Oregon pine, it's a rustic yet luxurious mountain lodge that perches on the edge of the canyon and has awe-inspiring views from some rooms. If you want modern amenities and a fairly large room, **Thunderbird & Kachina Lodges** should be your in-park choice. **Bright Angel Lodge & Cabins** is the most affordable lodge in the park, but you'll pay more for a private bathroom. The rim cabins are the most popular and are usually booked a year in advance. **Phantom Ranch** (© **928/638-3283** for reconfirmations) is the only lodge at the bottom of the Grand Canyon and is very popular. The accommodations are in rustic stone-walled cabins or gender-segregated dormitories. Prices include meals, which must also be reserved ahead.

IN TUSAYAN (OUTSIDE THE SOUTH ENTRANCE) If you can't get a room in the park, this is the next closest place to stay. For lots of resort-style amenities, head to the **Best Western Grand Canyon Squire Inn** (© **800/622-6966** or 928/638-2681; www.grandcanyonsquire.com; $105–$205 double). With its mountain-lodge styling, Native American cultural shows, modern guest rooms, and large restaurant, the **Grand Hotel** (© **888/634-7263** or 928/638-3333; www.visitgrandcanyon.com; $79–$259 double) is the best choice in Tusayan.

Fifty-four miles north of Flagstaff on U.S. 89, the **Cameron Trading Post Motel** (© **800/338-7385** or 928/679-2231; www.camerontradingpost.com; $99–$109 double), offers some of the most attractive rooms anywhere in the vicinity of the Grand Canyon. Most have balconies and some have views of the Little Colorado River.

CAMPGROUNDS **Mather Campground,** in Grand Canyon Village, has over 300 campsites. Reservations can be made up to 5 months in advance and are required for stays between April and November (reservations not accepted for other months). Contact the **National Park Reservation Service** (© **800/365-2267** or 301/722-1257; www. recreation.gov). **Desert View Campground,** with 50 sites, is 25 miles east of Grand Canyon Village and open from mid-May to mid-October. No reservations are accepted. The **Trailer Village RV park,** with 80 RV sites, is in Grand Canyon Village. Reservations can be made up to 13 months in advance; contact **Xanterra South Rim/Xanterra Parks & Resorts** (© **888/297-2757** or 303/297-2757). www.grandcanyonlodges.com). For same-day reservations, call © **928/638-2631.**

Two miles south of Tusayan is the U.S. Forest Service's **Ten-X Campground,** open May through September. You can also camp just about anywhere within the **Kaibab National Forest,** which borders Grand Canyon National Park, as long as you are more than a quarter-mile away from Ariz. 64/U.S. 180. For more information, contact the **Tusayan Ranger District,** Kaibab National Forest, P.O. Box 3088, Grand Canyon, AZ 86023 (© **928/638-2443;** www.fs.fed.us/r3/kai).

Where to Dine

You'll find several restaurants just outside the south entrance in Tusayan. The best of these is the **Canyon Star Restaurant and Saloon** (© **928/638-3333**) at the Grand Hotel, and the **Coronado Room** (© **928/638-2681**) at the Best Western Grand Canyon Squire Inn. You'll also find a steakhouse and a pizza place, as well as familiar chains such as McDonald's, Taco Bell, Pizza Hut, and Wendy's.

For quick, inexpensive meals, try Grand Canyon Village's **Bright Angel Fountain,** at the back of the Bright Angel Lodge, which serves hot dogs, sandwiches, and ice cream. **Hermit's Rest Snack Bar** is at the west end of Hermit Road. At Desert View (near the east entrance to the park), there's the **Desert View Trading Post Cafeteria.**

El Tovar Dining Room, in El Tovar Hotel (© **928/638-2631,** ext. 6432), has one of the most awe-inspiring views in the world and serves up good, spicy Southwestern food. Book early.

THE GRAND CANYON NORTH RIM

If Grand Canyon Village sounds like it's going to be more human zoo than the wilderness experience you had expected, the North Rim will probably be much more to your liking. The North Rim is on the Kaibab Plateau, more than 8,000 feet high on average. The higher elevation of the North Rim means you'll find dense forests of ponderosa pines, Douglas firs, and aspens interspersed with large meadows.

Essentials

GETTING THERE From Flagstaff, take **U.S. 89** north to Bitter Springs, then **U.S. 89A** to Jacob Lake. From there take **Ariz. 67** (the North Rim Pkwy.) to the end at the North Rim.

Trans Canyon (© **928/638-2820**) operates a shuttle between the North Rim and the South Rim. The trip takes 5 hours; the fare is $75 one-way (reservations required).

www.nps.gov/grca). At the entrance gate, you'll be given a copy of *The Guide,* a small newspaper with information on park activities. There's also an **information desk** in the lobby of the Grand Canyon Lodge.

Note: Visitor facilities at the North Rim are open only from mid-May to mid-October. From mid-October to November (or until snow closes the road to the North Rim), the park is open for day use only. The campground may be open after mid-October, weather permitting.

For more information, see "Essentials" under "The Grand Canyon South Rim," earlier in this chapter.

Exploring the Area

The best spots for viewing the canyon are Bright Angel Point, Point Imperial, and Cape Royal. **Bright Angel Point** is the closest to Grand Canyon Lodge, and from here you can see and hear Roaring Springs, 3,600 feet below the rim and the North Rim's only water source. At 8,803 feet, **Point Imperial** is the highest point on the North Rim. A short section of the Colorado River can be seen far below, and off to the east the Painted Desert is visible.

Cape Royal, however, is the most spectacular setting on the North Rim, and along the 23-mile road to Cape Royal are several scenic overlooks. Across the road from the **Walhalla Overlook** are the ruins of an Ancestral Puebloan structure, and just before reaching Cape Royal you'll come to the **Angel's Window Overlook,** which gives you a breathtaking view of the natural bridge that forms Angel's Window. Once at Cape Royal, you can follow a trail across this natural bridge to a towering promontory overlooking the valley.

After simply taking in the views, hiking along the rim is the most popular activity. Day hikes of varying lengths are possible here.

If you want to see the canyon from a saddle, contact **Grand Canyon Trail Rides** (📞 **435/679-8665;** www.canyonrides.com), which offers mule rides varying in length from 1 hour to a full day.

Where to Stay & Dine

Perched right on the canyon rim, **Grand Canyon Lodge,** operated by Forever Resorts (📞 **877/386-4383;** http://foreverlodging.com), is listed on the National Register of Historic Places and is one of the most impressive lodges in the national park system. Accommodations vary from standard motel units to rustic mountain cabins to comfortable modern cabins.

Outside the park, you'll find numerous budget motels in Fredonia, Arizona (30 miles west of Jacob Lake), and Kanab, Utah (37 miles west of Jacob Lake). Located 5 miles north of the entrance to the North Rim, **Kaibab Lodge** (📞 **928/638-2389;** www. kaibablodge.com; doubles from $95) is on the edge of a large meadow where deer can often be seen grazing. The lodge's dining room serves all meals, and the kitchen also prepares box lunches.

CAMPGROUNDS Located just north of Grand Canyon Lodge, the **North Rim Campground,** with 75 sites and no hookups for RVs, is the only campground at the North Rim. The campground opens in mid-May and may stay open past the mid-October closing of other North Rim visitor facilities. Reservations can be made up to 6 months in advance by calling the National Recreation Reservation Service (© **877/444-6777** or 518/885-3639; www.recreation.gov).

There are two nearby campgrounds outside the park in the Kaibab National Forest. **DeMotte Park Campground,** the closest to the park entrance, has 23 sites, while **Jacob Lake Campground,** 30 miles north of the park entrance, has 53 sites. Neither takes reservations. You can also camp anywhere in the Kaibab National Forest as long as you're more than a quarter-mile from a paved road or water source.

7 MONUMENT VALLEY & CANYON DE CHELLY

MONUMENT VALLEY NAVAJO TRIBAL PARK

In its role as sculptor, nature has, in the north central part of the Navajo Reservation, created a garden of monoliths and spires unequaled anywhere on earth. You have almost certainly seen Monument Valley. This otherworldly landscape has served as a backdrop for countless commercials and movies.

Monument Valley is a vast flat plain punctuated by natural cathedrals of sandstone. These huge monoliths rise from the sagebrush with sheer walls that capture the light of the rising and setting sun and transform it into fiery hues. A 17-mile unpaved loop road winds among these 1,000-foot-tall buttes and mesas.

Human habitation has also left its mark. Within the park are more than 100 Ancient Pueblo People i archaeological sites, ruins, and petroglyphs dating from before A.D. 1300. The Navajo have been living in the valley for generations, herding their sheep through the sagebrush scrublands, and some families continue to live here today.

Essentials

GETTING THERE   Monument Valley is 200 miles northeast of Flagstaff. Take U.S. 89 north to U.S. 160 to Kayenta, which is 23 miles south of Monument Valley and 29 miles east of Navajo National Monument. Then drive north on U.S. 163.

VISITOR INFORMATION & FEES   For information, contact **Monument Valley Navajo Tribal Park** (© 435/727-5870; www.navajonationparks.org). May through September, the park is open daily from 6am to 8pm; between October and April, it's open daily from 8am to 5pm. Admission to the park is $5 per person (free for children 9 and under). *Note:* Because this is a tribal park and not a federal park, America the Beautiful passes are not valid here.

Exploring the Area

Because this is reservation land and people still live in Monument Valley, backcountry or off-road travel is prohibited unless you have a licensed guide. So basically the only way to see the park is from the overlook at the visitor center; by driving the park's scenic (but very rough) dirt road; or by taking a four-wheel-drive, horseback, or guided hiking tour.

At the valley overlook parking area in Monument Valley Navajo Tribal Park, you'll find a small museum, gift shop, restaurant, snack bar, campground, and numerous local Navajo guides who offer tours of the park.

Monument Valley Simpson's Trailhandler Tours (© **877/686-2848** or 435/727-3362; www.trailhandlertours.com), which charges $40 for a 2¹/₂-hour tour, is a reliable company to try, as is **Sacred Monument Tours** (© **435/727-3218** or 928/380-4527;

www.monumentvalley.net), which charges $57 for a 2¹/₂-hour jeep tour. A variety of **789** other tours are also available.

If you happen to be staying at Goulding's Lodge, then your best bet is to go out with **Goulding's Tours** (© **435/727-3231;** www.gouldings.com), which has its office right at the lodge (see "Where to Stay & Dine," below), just a few miles from the park entrance. Goulding's offers 3¹/₂-hour jeep tours ($40 for adults, $27 for children 7 and under) and full-day tours ($90 for adults, $70 for children).

You might want to visit **Goulding's Museum and Trading Post,** at Goulding's Lodge. It was the home of the Gouldings for many years and is set up as they had it back in the 1920s and 1930s. There are also displays about the many movies that have been shot here. The trading post hours vary with the seasons; admission is by donation. Inside Kayenta's Burger King, next door to the Hampton Inn, there's an interesting exhibit on the **Navajo code talkers** of World War II. The code talkers were Navajo soldiers who used their own language to transmit military messages.

Where to Stay & Dine
In addition to the lodgings listed here, you'll find numerous budget motels 22 miles north of Monument Valley in Mexican Hat, Utah.

Goulding's Lodge, Monument Valley, Utah (© **435/727-3231;** www.gouldings. com; $123–$180 double), is the only lodge actually in Monument Valley, and it offers superb views from the balconies of its rooms, which are furnished with Southwestern decor. A restaurant serves Navajo and American dishes.

Hampton Inn—Navajo Nation, U.S. 160, in Kayenta (© **800/HAMPTON** [426-7866] or 928/697-3170; www.hampton-inn.com; $115–$154 double), is built in a modern Santa Fe style and has spacious rooms.

CANYON DE CHELLY NATIONAL MONUMENT
Canyon de Chelly National Monument consists of two major canyons—**Canyon de Chelly** (pronounced "canyon duh *shay*" and derived from the Navajo word *tsegi,* meaning "rock canyon") and **Canyon del Muerto** (Spanish for "Canyon of the Dead")—as well as several smaller canyons. The canyons extend for more than 100 miles through the rugged slick-rock landscape of northeastern Arizona, draining the seasonal runoff from the snowmelt of the Chuska Mountains.

Canyon de Chelly's smooth sandstone walls of rich reds and yellows contrast sharply with the deep greens of corn, pasture, and cottonwood on the canyon floor. Vast stone amphitheaters form the caves in which the Ancient Pueblo People built their homes, and today there are more than 100 prehistoric dwelling sites in the area. For nearly 5,000 years, people have called these canyons home, and today the canyon is still lived in by Navajo farmers and sheepherders.

Essentials
GETTING THERE   From Flagstaff, the easiest route to Canyon de Chelly is **I-40** to **U.S. 191** to Ganado. At Ganado, drive west on Arizona 264 and pick up U.S. 191 North to Chinle. If you're coming down from Monument Valley or Navajo National Monument, **Indian Route 59,** which connects U.S. 160 and U.S. 191, is an excellent road with plenty of beautiful scenery. Take U.S. 191 south to Chinle.

VISITOR INFORMATION   Before leaving home, you can contact **Canyon de Chelly National Monument** (© **928/674-5500;** www.nps.gov/cach) for information. The visitor center is open daily May through September from 8am to 6pm (MST), and

October through April from 8am to 5pm. The monument itself is open daily from sunrise to sunset; admission is free.

Seeing the Canyon

Your first stop should be the **visitor center,** in front of which is an example of a traditional crib-style hogan, a hexagonal structure of logs and earth that Navajo use both as a home and as a ceremonial center. Inside, a small museum acquaints visitors with the history of Canyon de Chelly, and there's often a silversmith demonstrating Navajo jewelry-making techniques. From here most people tour the canyon by car.

The North and South Rim drives offer very different views of the canyon. The North Rim Drive overlooks Canyon del Muerto, and the South Rim Drive overlooks Canyon de Chelly. Each of the rim drives is around 20 miles in each direction, and with stops it can easily take 3 hours to visit each rim.

THE NORTH RIM DRIVE   The first stop on the North Rim is the **Ledge Ruin Overlook.** On the opposite wall, about 100 feet up from the canyon floor, you can see the Ledge Ruin. The Ancient Pueblo People occupied this site between A.D. 1050 and 1275. Nearby, at the **Dekaa Kiva Viewpoint,** you can see a lone kiva (circular ceremonial building). This structure was reached by means of toeholds cut into the soft sandstone cliff wall.

The second stop is the **Antelope House Overlook.** The Antelope House ruin takes its name from the paintings of antelopes on a nearby cliff wall. It's believed that the paintings were done in the 1830s. Beneath the ruins, archaeologists have found the remains of an earlier pit house dating from A.D. 693. Though most cliff dwellings of the Ancient Pueblo People were abandoned sometime after a drought began in 1276, Antelope House had already been abandoned by 1260, possibly because of flood damage. Across the wash from Antelope House, the Tomb of the Weaver was discovered in the 1920s by archaeologists. The ancient tomb contained the well-preserved body of an old man wrapped in a blanket of golden eagle feathers and accompanied by cornmeal, shelled and husked corn, pinyon nuts, beans, salt, and thick skeins of cotton. Also visible from this overlook is **Navajo Fortress,** a red-sandstone butte that the Navajo once used as a refuge from attackers. A steep trail leads to the top of Navajo Fortress, and through the use of log ladders that could be pulled up into the refuge, the Navajo were able to escape their attackers.

The third stop is at **Mummy Cave Overlook,** named for two mummies found in burial urns below the ruins. Archaeological evidence indicates that this amphitheater consisting of two caves was occupied from A.D. 300 to 1300. In the two caves and on the shelf between them there are 80 rooms, including three kivas. The central structure between the two caves includes a three-story building characteristic of the architecture in Mesa Verde, New Mexico. Archaeologists speculate that a group of Ancient Pueblo People migrated here from New Mexico. Much of the original plasterwork of these buildings is still intact and indicates that the buildings were colorfully decorated.

The fourth stop on the North Rim is at the **Massacre Cave Overlook.** The cave got its name after an 1805 Spanish military expedition killed more than 115 Navajo at this site. The Navajo had been raiding Spanish settlements that were encroaching on Navajo territory. Accounts of the battle at Massacre Cave differ. One claims that there were only women, children, and old men taking shelter in the cave, although the Spanish records claim 90 warriors and 25 women and children were killed. Also visible from this overlook is Yucca Cave, which was occupied about 1,000 years ago.

The South Rim Drive climbs slowly but steadily, and at each stop you're a little bit higher above the canyon floor.

Near the mouth of the canyon, you'll find the **Tunnel Overlook** and, nearby, the **Tsegi Overlook.** *Tsegi* means "rock canyon" in Navajo, and that's just what you'll see when you gaze down from this viewpoint. A short narrow canyon feeds into Chinle Wash, formed by the streams cutting through the canyons of the national monument.

The next stop is **Junction Overlook,** which overlooks the junction of Canyon del Muerto and Canyon de Chelly. Visible here is the Junction Ruin, with 10 rooms and one kiva. The Ancient Pueblo People occupied this ruin during the Great Pueblo Period, which lasted from around 1100 until the Ancient Pueblo People disappeared shortly before 1300. Also visible is First Ruin, perched on a long, narrow ledge. In this ruin are 22 rooms and two kivas.

The next stop, at **White House Overlook,** provides the only opportunity for descending into Canyon de Chelly without a guide or ranger. The **White House Ruins Trail** descends 600 feet to the canyon floor, crosses Chinle Wash, and approaches the White House Ruins. These buildings were constructed both on the canyon floor and 50 feet up the cliff wall in a small cave. You cannot enter the ruins, but you can get close enough to get a good look. You're not allowed to wander off this trail, and please respect the privacy of the Navajo living here. The 2.5-mile round-trip hike takes about 2 hours. Be sure to carry water. If you aren't inclined to hike the trail, you can view the ruins from the overlook. This is one of the largest ruins in the canyon and contains 80 rooms. It was inhabited between 1040 and 1275. Notice the black streaks on the sandstone walls above the White House Ruins. These streaks were formed by seeping water that reacted with the iron in the sandstone. Iron gives the walls their reddish hue. Ancient Pueblo artists used to chip away at this black patina to create petroglyphs. Later the Navajo would use paints to create pictographs, painted images of animals, and records of historic events such as the Spanish military expedition that killed 115 Navajo at Massacre Cave. Many of these petroglyphs and pictographs can be seen if you take one of the guided tours into the canyon.

The next stop is at **Sliding House Overlook.** These ruins are built on a narrow shelf and appear to be sliding down into the canyon. Inhabited from about 900 until 1200, Sliding House contained between 30 and 50 rooms. This overlook is already more than 700 feet above the canyon floor, with sheer walls giving the narrow canyon a foreboding appearance.

The **Face Rock Overlook** provides yet another dizzying glimpse of the ever-deepening canyon. Here you gaze 1,000 feet down to the bottom of the canyon. The last stop on the South Rim is one of the most spectacular: **Spider Rock Overlook.** This viewpoint overlooks the junction of Canyon de Chelly and Monument Canyon, and at this wide spot in the canyon stands the monolithic pinnacle called Spider Rock. Rising 800 feet from the canyon floor, the free-standing twin towers of Spider Rock are a natural monument, a geologic wonder. Across the canyon from Spider Rock stands the similarly striking **Speaking Rock,** connected to the far canyon wall.

Taking Photos on the Reservations

Before taking a photograph of a Navajo, always ask permission. If it's granted, a tip of $1 or more is expected. Photography is not allowed in Hopi villages.

Access to the floor of Canyon de Chelly is restricted, so to enter the canyon *you must be accompanied by either a park ranger or an authorized guide* (unless you're on the White House Ruins Trail). **Navajo guides** charge $15 to $25 per hour with a 3-hour minimum and will lead you into the canyon on foot or in your own four-wheel-drive vehicle. **De Chelly Tours** (© **928/674-3772;** www.dechellytours.com) charges $20 per hour, with a 3-hour minimum, to go out in your four-wheel-drive vehicle; if it supplies the vehicle, the cost goes up to $125 for three people for 3 hours.

Another way to see Canyon de Chelly and Canyon del Muerto is on what locals call **shake-and-bake tours,** via six-wheel-drive truck. In summer, these excursions really live up to the name. (In winter, the truck is enclosed to keep out the elements.) The trucks operate out of **Thunderbird Lodge** (© **800/679-2473** or 928/674-5841; www. tbirdlodge.com) and are equipped with seats in the bed. Tours make frequent stops for photographs and to visit ruins, Navajo farms, and rock art. Half-day trips cost $43 per person ($33 for children 12 and under).

If you'd rather use a more traditional means of transportation, you can go on a guided horseback ride. Stables offering horseback tours into the canyon include **Totsonii Ranch** (© **928/755-6209;** www.totsoniiranch.com), which charges $15 per group per hour for the guide and $15 per person per hour.

Where to Stay & Dine

The **Holiday Inn—Canyon de Chelly,** Indian Route 7, Chinle (© **800/HOLIDAY** [454-4329] or 928/674-5000; www.holiday-inn.com/chinle-garcia; $79–$129 double), is the top choice in Chinle. Rooms come with patios or balconies, most facing the cottonwood-shaded pool courtyard. The restaurant serves the best food in town.

Thunderbird Lodge (© **800/679-BIRD** [679-2473] or 928/674-5841; www. tbirdlodge.com; $106–$111 double), built on the site of an early trading post at the mouth of Canyon de Chelly, is the most appealing of the hotels in Chinle and the closest to the national monument. The red-adobe construction is reminiscent of ancient pueblos. American and Navajo meals are served.

Adjacent to the Thunderbird Lodge is the free **Cottonwood Campground,** which doesn't take reservations. In summer, the campground has water and restrooms, but in winter, you must bring your own water, and only portable toilets are available. On South Rim Drive 10 miles east of the Canyon de Chelly Visitor Center, you'll also find the private **Spider Rock Campground** (© **877/910-CAMP** [910-2267] or 928/674-8261; http://home.earthlink.net/~spiderrock), which charges $10 to $12 per night. This campground also has a couple of hogans for rent for $25 to $39 per night.

8 THE PETRIFIED FOREST & PAINTED DESERT

Though petrified wood can be found in almost every state, the "forests" of downed logs here in northeastern Arizona are by far the most spectacular. A 27-mile scenic drive winds through the petrified forest and a small corner of the Painted Desert, providing a fascinating high-desert experience.

At one time, this area this was a vast swamp. That was 225 million years ago, when dinosaurs and huge amphibians ruled earth and giant now-extinct trees grew on the high ground around the swamp. Fallen trees were washed downstream, gathered in piles in still backwaters, and were eventually covered over with silt, mud, and volcanic ash. As water seeped through this soil, it dissolved the silica in the volcanic ash and redeposited this silica inside the cells of the logs. Eventually, the silica recrystallized into stone to form petrified wood.

This region was later inundated with water, and thick deposits of sediment buried the logs ever deeper. Eventually, the land was transformed yet again as a geologic upheaval thrust the lake bottom up above sea level. This upthrust of the land cracked the logs into the segments we see today. Wind and water gradually eroded the landscape, once again exposing the now-petrified logs and creating the Painted Desert and the many other colorful and fascinating landscape features of northern Arizona.

Throughout the region you'll see petrified wood in all sizes and colors, natural and polished, being sold in gift stores. This petrified wood comes from private land, *not* the national park. No piece of petrified wood, no matter how small, may be removed from Petrified Forest National Park.

ESSENTIALS

GETTING THERE   Take **I-40** east from Flagstaff or west from Albuquerque. The north entrance to Petrified Forest National Park is 25 miles east of Holbrook on I-40. The south entrance is 20 miles east of Holbrook on **U.S. 180.**

VISITOR INFORMATION & FEES   For further information on the Petrified Forest or the Painted Desert, contact **Petrified Forest National Park,** P.O. Box 2217, Petrified Forest, AZ 86028 (© **928/524-6228;** www.nps.gov/pefo). For information on Holbrook and the surrounding region, contact the **Holbrook Chamber of Commerce,** 100 E. Arizona St. (© **800/524-2459** or 928/524-6558; www.gotouraz.com/holbrook). The park is open daily from 7am to 7pm in summer (call for hours other months). The entry fee is $10 per car.

EXPLORING A UNIQUE LANDSCAPE

Petrified Forest National Park has a north and a south entrance (and visitor centers at both). Connecting the two park entrances is a 27-mile scenic road with more than 20 overlooks. For the most enjoyable visit, start at the southern entrance and work your way north. That way, you'll see the most impressive displays of petrified logs early in your visit.

At the south entrance, you'll find the **Rainbow Forest Museum** (© **928/524-6228**), which has exhibits on the geology and human history of the park. A snack bar here serves sandwiches and ice cream. Just outside the museum is the **Giant Logs self-guided trail,** which winds across a hillside strewn with logs. Almost directly across the parking lot from the museum is the entrance to the **Long Logs** and **Agate House** areas. On the Long Logs trail, you can see more big trees, while at Agate House you will see the ruins of a pueblo built from colorful agatized wood.

Heading north, you pass by the unusual formations known as the **Flattops.** These structures are caused by the erosion of softer soil deposits from beneath a harder and more erosion-resistant layer of sandstone. This is one of the park's wilderness areas (both of the visitor centers issue the free permits necessary to backpack into the park's wilderness areas). The **Crystal Forest** is the next stop, named for the beautiful amethyst and quartz crystals that were once found in the cracks of petrified logs.

At the **Jasper Forest Overlook,** you can see logs that include petrified roots, and a bit farther north, at the **Agate Bridge** stop, you can see a petrified log that forms a natural agate bridge. Continuing north, you'll reach **Blue Mesa,** where pieces of petrified wood form capstones over easily eroded clay soils. As wind and water wear away at the clay beneath a piece of stone, the balance of the stone becomes more and more precarious until it eventually topples down. A 1-mile loop trail here leads into the park's badlands.

Erosion has played a major role in the formation of the Painted Desert, and to the north of Blue Mesa you'll see some of the most interesting erosional features of the area. It's quite evident why these hills of sandstone and clay are known as the **Teepees.** The layers of different color are due to different types of soils and stone and to minerals dissolved in the soil.

Human habitation of the area dates from more than 2,000 years ago, and at **Newspaper Rock,** you can see petroglyphs left by generations of Native Americans. At nearby **Puerco Pueblo,** which was probably constructed around 1400, you can see the remains of homes built by the people who created the park's petroglyphs.

North of Puerco Pueblo, the road crosses I-40. From here to the Painted Desert Visitor Center, there are eight overlooks onto the southernmost edge of the **Painted Desert.** Named for the vivid colors of the soil and stone that cover the land here, the Painted Desert is a dreamscape of pastel colors washed across a barren expanse of eroded hills. At Kachina Point, you'll find the historic **Painted Desert Inn,** open daily from 8am to 4pm. Just inside the park's northern entrance is the **Painted Desert Visitor Center,** which shows a short film explaining the process by which wood becomes fossilized. Adjacent to the visitor center are a cafeteria and a gas station.

WHERE TO STAY

Holbrook is the nearest town to Petrified Forest National Monument, and here you'll find lots of budget chain motels.

Although nearly 50 miles from the park, **La Posada,** 303 E. Second St., Winslow (© **928/289-4366;** www.laposada.org; $99–$149 double), a restored historic railroad hotel, is this region's best and most memorable hotel. The hotel is a reproduction of a Spanish colonial hacienda. If you're willing to sleep on a sagging mattress for the sake of reliving a bit of Route 66 history, consider the concrete wigwams at the **Wigwam Motel,** 811 W. Hopi Dr., Holbrook (© **800/414-3021** or 928/524-3048; www.galerie-kokopelli. com/wigwam; $48–$54 double). This unique motel was built in the 1940s, when unusual architecture was springing up all along Route 66.

---

9 ALBUQUERQUE

Albuquerque is the gateway to northern New Mexico, the portal through which most domestic and international visitors pass before traveling on to Santa Fe and Taos. But it's worth stopping here for a day or two in order to get a feel for the history of this area. Climbing out of the valley is the legendary Route 66, a major route from the East to California before the interstates were built. It's well worth a drive, if only to see the rust time has left. Old court hotels still line the street, many with their funky 1950s signage. In the University of New Mexico district are hip cafes and shops.

Farther downhill is downtown Albuquerque. During the day, this area is all suits and heels, but after dark it becomes a hip nightlife scene. Old Town is also worth a visit; though touristy, it's a unique Southwestern village with a graceful, intact Plaza.

GETTING THERE **By Plane** Albuquerque International Sunport (© 505/842-4366) is in the south-central part of the city, between I-25 on the west and Kirtland Air Force Base on the east, only about 4 miles from downtown. Most hotels have courtesy airport vans, and many car-rental agencies have desks here. **Airport Shuttle of Albuquerque** (© 505/765-1234; www.airportshuttleabq.com) runs services to and from city hotels. **ABQ Ride** (© 505/243-7433; **www.cabq.gov/transit**), Albuquerque's public bus system, also makes airport stops; it takes about 20 minutes. There is also efficient taxi service to and from the airport.

By Train Amtrak (© 800/USA-RAIL [872-7245]; www.amtrak.com) provides daily service from Chicago (trip time: 26 hr.), Flagstaff (5–6 hr.), and Los Angeles (26 hr.) to its station at 214 First St. SW.

By Car The major routes into Albuquerque are **I-40** from the east (Amarillo) and west (Flagstaff), and **I-25** from the north (Santa Fe and Denver) and south (El Paso).

VISITOR INFORMATION The main office of the **Albuquerque Convention and Visitors Bureau** is at 20 First Plaza NW (© 800/284-2282 or 505/842-9918; www. itsatrip.org). It's open Monday to Friday 8am to 5pm. There are information centers at the airport, open daily 9:30am to 8pm; and in Old Town at 303 Romero St. NW, Ste. 107, open daily 9am to 5pm.

GETTING AROUND ABQ Ride (© 505/243-7433) cloaks the arterials with its city bus network. Call for information on routes and fares. **Yellow Cab** (© 505/247-8888) serves the city and surrounding area 24 hours a day.

Parking is generally not difficult. Meters operate weekdays 8am to 6pm and are not monitored at other times. Only the large downtown hotels charge for parking. Traffic is a problem only at rush hours. Avoid I-25 and I-40 at the center of town around 5pm.

FAST FACTS For a doctor, call the **Greater Albuquerque Medical Association** (© 505/821-4583). **Presbyterian Hospital** is at 1100 Central Ave. SE (© 505/841-1234, or 841-1111 for emergency services). **Walgreens**, 5001 Montgomery St. (© 505/881-5210), runs a 24-hour pharmacy. In Albuquerque, the **sales tax** is 6.875%. An additional **hotel tax** of 6% will be added to your bill.

SPECIAL EVENTS & FESTIVALS The last weekend in June brings the **New Mexico Arts and Crafts Fair** (© 505/884-9043; www.nmartsandcraftsfair.org) to the State Fairgrounds. The fairgrounds also host the **New Mexico State Fair and Rodeo** (© 505/265-1791; http://exponm.com), one of America's top state fairs, for 17 days in early September. In mid-October, there's the **Albuquerque International Balloon Fiesta** (© 800/733-9918; www.balloonfiesta.com), the world's largest balloon rally, with races, contests, and special events.

WHAT TO SEE & DO

Albuquerque Museum of Art and History (Kids) In this museum on the outskirts of Old Town, you can take an interesting journey into New Mexico's past. A recent expansion has brought new gallery space, filled with impressive changing exhibits. The museum's art collection includes large canvases by Fritz Scholder, Peter Hurd, Ernest Blumenschein, and Georgia O'Keeffe. Downstairs you'll take a trip though history, represented by an impressive collection of Spanish colonial artifacts. In an old-style theater, two films on Albuquerque history are shown. An Old Town walking tour originates here at 11am Tuesday to Sunday during spring, summer, and fall.

2000 Mountain Rd. NW. (C) **505/243-7255.** www.albuquerquemuseum.com. Admission $4 adults, $2 seniors 65 and older, $1 children 4–12. Tues–Sun 9am–5pm. Closed major holidays.

American International Rattlesnake Museum   This unique museum, just off Old Town Plaza, has living specimens of common, uncommon, and rare rattlesnakes of North, Central, and South America in naturally landscaped habitats. More than 30 species can be seen, followed by a short film on this contributor to the ecological balance of our hemisphere. You'll also see rattlesnake artifacts from early American history, Native American culture, medicine, the arts, and advertising. You'll also find a gift shop that specializes in Native American jewelry, T-shirts, and other memorabilia related to the natural world and the Southwest, all with an emphasis on rattlesnakes.

202 San Felipe St. NW. (C) **505/242-6569.** www.rattlesnakes.com. Admission $3.50 adults, $3 seniors, $2.50 children. AE, DISC, MC, V. Summer Mon–Sat 10am–6pm, Sun 1–5pm; winter Mon–Sat 11:30am–5:30pm, Sun 1–5pm.

Balloon Museum (Kids)   With the Albuquerque International Balloon Fiesta drawing hundreds of brilliantly colored balloons to the city each October, this museum's time has come. Opened in 2005, it tells the history of ballooning, from the first flight in France in 1783, with a rooster, sheep, and duck as passengers, to the use of balloons in military, science, and aerospace research. Most poignant are displays of Albuquerque balloonists Maxie Anderson and Ben Abruzzo, who, with Larry Newman, completed the first manned crossing of the Atlantic Ocean in 1978. Kids will enjoy the flight simulator, which tests their ability to fly and land a balloon on target.

9201 Balloon Museum Dr., NE. (C) **505/768-6020.** www.cabq.gov/balloon.com. Admission $4 adults, $2 seniors 65 and older, $1 children 4–12, free for children 3 and under. Tues–Sun 9am–5pm. Closed Thanksgiving, Christmas, New Year's Day, and city holidays.

Indian Pueblo Cultural Center (Kids)   Owned and operated as a nonprofit organization by the 19 pueblos of New Mexico, this is a fine place to begin an exploration of Native American culture. Begin aboveground, where you'll find changing shows of contemporary Puebloan arts and crafts. Next, head downstairs, where a permanent exhibit depicts the evolution of the various pueblos from prehistory to present. On weekends, look for Native American dancers and artisans demonstrating their skills. A recent expansion has added a huge gift shop, which sells fine art and jewelry made by Native American artists, as well as books, posters and other souvenirs, and expanded the restaurant, which offers excellent lunches and fine dining at dinner.

2401 12th St. NW. (C) **866/855-7902** or 505/843-7270. www.indianpueblo.org. Admission $6 adults, $5.50 seniors, $1 students, free for children 4 and under. AE, DISC, MC, V. Daily 9am–5:30pm; restaurant Mon–Fri 8am–3pm; Fri–Sat 8am–10pm. Closed July 4, Labor Day, Thanksgiving, Christmas, and New Year's Day.

New Mexico Museum of Natural History and Science (Kids)   A trip through this museum will take you through 12 billion years of natural history. Begin by looking at a display of stones and gems, then stroll through the "Jurassic Super Giants" display, where you'll find dinosaur skeletons cast from the real bones. See the latest display "Triassic: Dawn of the Dinosaur." You can ride the **Evolator** (kids love this!), a simulated time-travel experience that moves and rumbles, taking you 1¼ miles up (or down) and through 38 million years of history. Be sure to check out the museum's Planetarium. Those exhibits, as well as the DynaTheater, which surrounds you with images and sound, cost an additional fee.

1801 Mountain Rd. NW. (C) **505/841-2800.** www.nmnaturalhistory.org. Admission $7 adults, $6 seniors, $4 children 3–12, free for children 2 and under. DynaTheater, Planetarium, and Virtual Voyages cost extra, with prices in the $7 range for adults and $4 range for children. Buying ticket combinations qualifies you

Sandia Peak Tramway (Best)   This is a fun half-day or evening outing with incredible views of the Albuquerque landscape and wildlife. The Sandia Peak tram is a "jigback"; in other words, as one car approaches the top, the other nears the bottom. The two pass halfway through the trip, in the midst of a 1^1/$_2$-mile "clear span" of unsupported cable between the second tower and the upper terminal. There are several hiking trails; La Luz Trail travels to the top of the Sandias and is very steep and scenic. *Note:* The trails on Sandia may not be suitable for children.

10 Tramway Loop NE. ✆ **505/856-7325.** Fax 505/856-6335. www.sandiapeak.com. Admission $18 adults, $15 seniors, $15 teens 13–20, $10 children 5–12, free for children 4 and under. Memorial Day to Labor Day daily 9am–9pm; spring and fall Wed–Mon 9am–8pm, Tues 5–8pm; ski season Wed–Mon 9am–8pm, Tues noon–8pm. Closed 2 weeks each spring and fall for maintenance; check the website for details. Parking $1 daily. AE, DISC, MC, V. To reach the base of the tram, take I-25 north to Tramway Rd. (exit 234), then proceed east about 5 miles on Tramway Rd. (N.M. 556); or take Tramway Blvd., exit 167 (N.M. 556), north of I-40 approx. 8^1/$_2$ miles.

Exploring Old Town

A maze of cobbled courtyard walkways leads to hidden patios and gardens, where many of Old Town's 150 galleries and shops are located. Adobe buildings, many refurbished in the Pueblo Revival style in the 1950s, are grouped around the tree-shaded **Plaza,** created in 1780. Pueblo and Navajo artisans often display their pottery, blankets, and jewelry on the sidewalks lining the Plaza. (Look especially for silver bracelets and strung turquoise. For something cheaper, buy a dyed corn necklace.)

When Albuquerque was established in 1706, the first building erected by the settlers was the cozy **Church of San Felipe de Neri,** with wonderful stained-glass windows and vivid *retablos* (religious paintings). Next door to the church is the **Rectory,** built about 1793. Also on the north Plaza is **Loyola Hall,** the Sister Blandina Convent, built originally of adobe in 1881 as a residence for Sisters of Charity teachers who worked in the region. When the Jesuit fathers built **Our Lady of the Angels School,** 320 Romero St., in 1877, it was the only public school in Albuquerque.

The **Antonio Vigil House,** 413 Romero St., is an adobe-style residence with traditional viga ends sticking out over the entrance door. The **Florencio Zamora Store,** 301 Romero St., was built in the 1890s of "pugmill" adobe for a butcher and grocer. The **Jesus Romero House,** 205 Romero St., was constructed by another grocer in 1915. Just down the street, the **Jesus Romero Store,** built in 1893, has Territorial and Queen Anne structural features. On the south Plaza, the **Manuel Springer House**'s hipped roof and bay windows are still visible under its present-day commercial facade. The adjacent **Cristobal Armijo House,** a banker's two-story adobe, combines Italianate and Queen Anne architectural styles.

Casa Armijo, in the 200 block of San Felipe Street, dates from before 1840; it was a headquarters for both Union and Confederate troops during the Civil War. The nearby **Ambrosio Armijo House and Store,** an 1882 adobe structure, once had the high false front of wooden boards typical of Old West towns in movies. The **Herman Blueher House,** 302 San Felipe St., built by a businessman in 1898, is a three-story Italianate mansion with fancy porches on two levels, now obscured by storefronts.

An excellent Old Town historical walking tour starts at the Albuquerque Museum of Art and History (see above) at 11am Tuesday through Sunday during spring, summer, and fall. The museum also publishes a brochure for a self-guided walking tour.

Visitors seeking regional specialties will find many **local artists** and **galleries** of interest in Albuquerque. If you want a real bargain in Native American arts and crafts, **Skip Maisel's,** 510 Central Ave. SW (© **505/242-6526**), is the place to shop. You'll find a broad range of quality and price here in goods such as pottery, weavings, and kachinas. Fifty artisans show their talents at the lovely cooperative **Amapola Gallery,** 205 Romero St. (© **505/242-4311**), off a cobbled courtyard. You'll find pottery, paintings, textiles, carvings, baskets, jewelry, and other items.

WHERE TO STAY

Hacienda Antigua   Hacienda Antigua, a 200-year-old adobe home that's a 20-minute drive from the airport, was once the first stagecoach stop out of Old Town in Albuquerque. Now it's one of Albuquerque's most elegant inns, with an artistically landscaped courtyard. Rooms are gracefully outfitted with antiques, fireplaces, custom toiletries, and VCRs. *Tip:* Light sleepers, beware—the Santa Fe Railroad runs by this inn, with one to three trains passing by each night.

6708 Tierra Dr. NW, Albuquerque, NM 87107. © **800/201-2986** or 505/345-5399. Fax 505/345-3855. www.haciendantigua.com. 8 units. $129–$209 double. Additional person $25. Rates include gourmet breakfast. AE, MC, V. Free parking. Pets welcome with $30 fee. **Amenities:** Pool. *In room:* Fridge.

Hotel Albuquerque at Old Town   This completely renovated hotel just 5 minutes from Old Town offers artfully decorated rooms with views and excellent service. No Albuquerque hotel is closer to top tourist attractions than this former Sheraton, which recently underwent a $16-million makeover. The cathedral-style lobby has Spanish colonial furnishings and art, a theme that carries into the guest rooms. They're medium-size, with comfortable beds and medium-size bathrooms with outer vanities.

800 Rio Grande Blvd. NW, Albuquerque, NM 87104. © **800/237-2133** (reservations only) or 505/843-6300. Fax 505/842-8426. www.hotelabq.com. 188 units. $99–$209 double; $149–$350 junior suite double. Children stay free in parent's room. AE, DC, DISC, MC, V. Free parking. **Amenities:** 2 restaurants; pool.

Hyatt Regency Albuquerque (Kids)   For a luxury stay right downtown, this is the place, pure shiny gloss and Art Deco. The lobby features a sky-lit and palm-shaded fountain, and the hotel's public areas feature an extensive art collection, including original Frederic Remington sculptures. Rooms are spacious, with views of the mountains. The hotel is located right next door to the Galeria, a shopping area, and has a number of shops itself.

330 Tijeras Ave. NW, Albuquerque, NM 87102. © **800/233-1234** or 505/842-1234. Fax 505/843-2710. www.hyatt.com. 395 units. Weekdays $225 double; weekends $105 double; $350–$700 suite. AE, DC, DISC, MC, V. Self-parking $12; valet $16. **Amenities:** Restaurant; pool; health club.

Hyatt Regency Tamaya Resort and Spa (Best)   This is the spot for a get-away-from-it-all luxury vacation. Set in the hills above the lush Rio Grande Valley on the Santa Ana Pueblo, this pueblo-style resort offers a 16,000-square-foot full-service spa and fitness center, an 18-hole Twin Warriors Championship Golf Course designed by Gary Panks, and views of the Sandia Mountains. Rooms are spacious, with large tile bathrooms. Request one that faces the mountains for one of the state's more spectacular vistas.

1300 Tuyuna Trail, Santa Ana Pueblo, NM 87004. © **800/55-HYATT** (554-9288) or 505/867-1234. www. tamaya.hyatt.com. 350 units. May–Oct $245–$415; Nov–Apr $199–$305, depending on the type of room. Suite rates available upon request. Inquire about spa, horseback riding, golf, and family packages. AE, DC, DISC, MC, V. Free parking. From I-25 take exit 242, following U.S. 550 west to Tamaya Blvd.; drive 1¹⁄₂ miles to the resort. **Amenities:** 2 restaurants; 3 pools; golf course; 2 tennis courts; health club; spa. *In room:* Fridge.

Nativo Lodge   This full-service hotel provides comfortable rooms with a Native American theme, utilizing high-tech elements as well. The five-story building has tan walls throughout the two-tiered lobby and standard-size guest rooms. The rooms are tastefully decorated with Native American geometric patterns creating a cozy feel, with comfortable beds and good linens, a desk, and small balcony. The bathrooms are small but functional. The service is thoughtful and efficient.

6000 Pan American Freeway NE, Albuquerque, NM 87109. ✆ **888/628-4861** or 505/798-4300. Fax 505/798-4305. www.nativolodge.com. $79–$139 double. AE, DC, DISC, MC, V. Free parking. **Amenities:** Restaurant; indoor/outdoor pool; exercise room.

WHERE TO DINE

Artichoke Cafe CONTINENTAL   An art gallery as well as a restaurant, this popular spot has modern paintings and sculptures set against azure walls. Start with an artichoke steamed with three dipping sauces or roasted and stuffed with forest mushrooms and rock shrimp. For lunch, there are a number of salads and gourmet sandwiches, as well as dishes such as garlic and lime prawns with orzo. At dinner, try the pumpkin ravioli with butternut squash, spinach, and ricotta filling. Recently the Artichoke has opened a wine bar on the premises.

424 Central Ave. SE. ✆ **505/243-0200.** www.artichokecafe.com. Reservations recommended. Main courses $9–$15 lunch, $18–$31 dinner. AE, DC, DISC, MC, V. Mon–Fri 11am–2:30pm; Mon 5:30–9pm; Tues–Sat 5:30–10pm; Sun 5–9pm.

Bien Shur INTERNATIONAL   On the top floor of the Sandia Resort & Casino, this fine-dining restaurant offers impressive views and delicious food, with a hint of Native America. Plan your meal at sunset for the most stunning effect. Service is excellent. Start with a marinated heirloom tomato salad with toasted focaccia, Maytag blue cheese, and basil dressing. For entrees, the rack of lamb with a garlic mint au jus is excellent, served with green beans and a Parmesan croquette. My favorite dessert here is a Southwestern take on pecan pie—made with piñon nuts! The wine list is eclectic.

30 Rainbow Rd. NE at Sandia Resort & Casino. ✆ **800/526-9366.** www.sandiaresort.com. Reservations recommended. Main courses $23–$75. AE, DC, DISC, MC, V. Daily 5–9pm.

Range Cafe Ⓚⓘⓓⓢ NEW MEXICAN/AMERICAN   This cafe, about 20 minutes north of Albuquerque, is a perfect place to stop on your way out of town. However, the food's so good you may just want to make a special trip. Housed in what was once an old drugstore, the restaurant has a pressed-tin ceiling and is decorated with Western touches. The cuisine ranges from enchiladas to chicken-fried steak to elegantly prepared meals. Taos Cow ice cream is a must for dessert. Two other branches of the restaurant in Albuquerque have similar food offerings (4200 Wyoming Blvd. NE, ✆ **505/293-2633;** and 2200 Menaul Blvd. NE, ✆ **505/888-1660**).

925 Camino del Pueblo (P.O. Box 1780), Bernalillo. ✆ **505/867-1700.** www.rangecafe.com. Reservations accepted for 8 or more. Breakfast and lunch $7–$13; dinner $10–$27. AE, DISC, MC, V. Summer Sun–Thurs 7:30am–10pm; winter Sun–Thurs 7:30am–9:30pm; a half-hour later on Fri–Sat. Closed Thanksgiving and Christmas.

Sadie's Ⓥⓐⓛⓤⓔ Ⓚⓘⓓⓢ NEW MEXICAN   Many New Mexicans lament the lost days when this restaurant was in a bowling alley. Though the current dining room is a little too big and the atmosphere a little too bright, the food is simply some of the best in New Mexico, with tasty sauces and large portions. Try the enchilada, either chicken or beef, or the stuffed sopaipilla dinner. There's a full bar, with excellent margaritas (and TV screens for you sports fans).

6230 4th St. NW. ✆ **505/345-5339.** Main courses $8–$17. AE, DC, DISC, MC, V. Mon–Sat 11am–10pm; Sun 10am–9pm.

ALBUQUERQUE AFTER DARK

Current listings appear in the two daily newspapers; detailed weekend arts calendars can be found in the Thursday *Tribune* and the Friday *Journal.* The monthly *On the Scene* also carries entertainment listings.

THE PERFORMING ARTS   The **New Mexico Symphony Orchestra** (✆ **800/251-6676** for tickets and information, or 505/881-9590; www.nmso.org) performs at Popejoy Hall, on the University of New Mexico campus; it also presents highly recommended outdoor concerts at the Rio Grande Zoo band shell. The **New Mexico Ballet Company** (✆ **505/292-4245;** www.nmballet.org) has several performances a year at Popejoy Hall.

THE CLUB & MUSIC SCENE   Top acts from each coast, including nationally televised comedians, are booked at **Laffs Comedy Cafe,** San Mateo Boulevard and Osuna Road (✆ **505/296-5653;** www.laffscomedy.com).

O'niell's Pub, 3211 Central NE (✆ **505/256-0564**), a favorite club in the University of New Mexico area, serves up good pub fare as well as live local music on Saturday nights and Celtic and bluegrass on Sunday evenings. **Burt's Tiki Lounge,** 313 Gold Ave. (✆ **505/243-BURT** [243-2878]), has the city's best variety of drinks. The club offers live music Thursday through Sunday.

THE SOUTHWEST

11

ALBUQUERQUE

(Best)   A Day Trip to Acoma Pueblo

This spectacular "Sky City," a walled adobe village perched high atop a sheer rock mesa 365 feet above the 6,600-foot valley floor, is believed to have been inhabited at least since the 11th century—the longest continuously occupied community in the United States. Both the pueblo and **San Estevan del Rey Mission** are National Historic Landmarks. Visits to Sky City are by guided tour only. In 2006, the **Sky City Cultural Center and Haak'u Museum** (✆ **800/747-0181;** http://acomaskycity.org) opened below Acoma, showcasing pottery, textiles, and other art from the tribe. Start your tour at the 40,000-square-foot museum, where you can get a meal at the excellent **Yaak'a Café.** Then board the **tour bus,** which climbs through a rock garden of 50-foot sandstone monoliths to the mesa's summit. There's no running water or electricity; drinking water is transported from below. Wood-hole ladders and mica windows are prevalent among the 300-odd structures. As you tour the village, you'll have opportunities to buy pottery and other pueblo treasures, and homemade snacks.

Admission for the tour is $12 for adults, $9 for children 6 to 17. The charge to take still photographs is $10; no video cameras are allowed. One-hour tours begin every 30 minutes, depending on the demand; the last tour is scheduled 1 hour before closing. Guided tours do not operate on the mesa during feast days. It's best to call ahead to make sure that the tour is available when you're visiting.

To reach Acoma from Albuquerque, drive west on I-40 approximately 52 miles to the Acoma–Sky City exit, then travel about 12 miles southwest.

10 WHITE SANDS NATIONAL MONUMENT

Arguably the most memorable natural area in this part of the Southwest, White Sands National Monument preserves the best part of the world's largest gypsum dune field, an area of 275 square miles of pure white gypsum sand reaching out over the floor of the Tularosa Basin in wavelike dunes. Plants and animals have evolved in special ways to adapt to the bright white environment here. Some creatures have a bleached coloration to match the whiteness all around them, and some plants have evolved means for surviving the smothering pressures of the blowing sands.

The surrounding mountains—the Sacramentos to the east, with their forested slopes, and the serene San Andres to the west—are composed of sandstone, limestone, sedimentary rocks, and pockets of gypsum. Over millions of years, rains and melting snows dissolved the gypsum and carried it down into Lake Lucero. Here the hot sun and dry winds evaporate the water, leaving the pure white gypsum to crystallize. Then the persistent winds blow these crystals, in the form of minuscule bits of sand, in a northeastern direction, adding them to growing dunes. As each dune grows and moves farther from the lake, new ones form in what seems an endless procession.

The dunes are especially enchanting at sunrise and under the light of a full moon, but you'll have to camp to experience this extraordinary sight (see below). If you're not camping, you'll probably want to spend only a couple of hours here.

ESSENTIALS

GETTING THERE The visitor center is 15 miles southwest of Alamogordo on **U.S. 70/82** (**Note:** Due to missile testing on the adjacent White Sands Missile Range, this road is sometimes closed for up to 2 hr. at a time.) The nearest major airport is El Paso International, 90 miles away. You can drive from there or take a commuter flight from Albuquerque to Alamogordo–White Sands Regional Airport. By car, take **I-25** south from Albuquerque or north from El Paso to Las Cruces. From there, take **U.S. 70** east to White Sands.

VISITOR INFORMATION Contact **White Sands National Monument,** P.O. Box 1086, Holloman AFB, NM 88330-1086 (© **505/479-6124;** www.nps.gov/whsa). When driving near or in the monument, tune your radio to 1610 AM for information on what's happening.

ADMISSION FEES & HOURS Admission is $3 for adults age 17 and over (free for children 16 and under). Memorial Day to Labor Day, the visitor center is open from 8am to 7pm, and Dunes Drive is open from 7am to 9pm. The rest of the year, the visitor center is open from 8am to 6pm, and Dunes Drive is open from 7am to sunset.

SEEING THE HIGHLIGHTS

The 16-mile **Dunes Drive** loops through the "heart of sands" from the visitor center. Information available at the center tells you what to look for on your drive. Sometimes the winds blow the dunes over the road, which must then be rerouted. The dunes are, in fact, all moving slowly to the northeast, pushed by prevailing southwest winds, some at the rate of as much as 20 feet a year.

In the center of the monument, the road itself is made of hard-packed gypsum (it can be especially slick after an afternoon thunderstorm, so drive cautiously!). Visitors are invited to get out of their cars at established parking areas and explore a bit; some like to climb a dune for a better view of the endless sea of sand. If you'd rather experience the park by hiking instead of the long drive, a good option right near the entrance is the **Big Dune Trail.** It takes you on a 45-minute loop along the edges of the dunes and then into their whiteness, ending atop a 60-foot-tall one.

The National Park Service emphasizes that (1) tunneling in this sand can be dangerous, for it collapses easily and could suffocate a person; (2) sand-surfing down the dune slopes, although permitted, can also be hazardous, so it should be undertaken with care, and never near an auto road; and (3) hikers can get lost in a sudden sandstorm should they stray from marked trails or areas.

We strongly recommend camping here, especially to see the dunes at sunrise or under a full moon. If you don't camp, you'll miss both because the park closes at dusk and doesn't reopen until after dawn. There are no campgrounds and no facilities, however, so this is strictly a backcountry adventure. Only tent camping is allowed, and you must register and get clearance from monument headquarters before you pitch yours. Call ✆ **505/479-6124** for information.

11 CARLSBAD CAVERNS NATIONAL PARK

One of the largest and most spectacular cave systems in the world, Carlsbad Caverns encompasses some 80 known caves that snake through the porous limestone reef of the Guadalupe Mountains. Fantastic and grotesque formations fascinate visitors, who find every shape imaginable sculpted in this underground world—frozen waterfalls, strands of pearls, soda straws, miniature castles, ice-cream cones, and everything in between.

ESSENTIALS

GETTING THERE   Take **U.S. 62/180** from either Carlsbad, New Mexico, which is 23 miles to the northeast, or El Paso, Texas (150 miles west). The scenic entrance road to the park is 7 miles long and originates at the park gate at Whites City.

VISITOR INFORMATION   For more information about the park, contact **Carlsbad Caverns National Park,** 3225 National Parks Hwy., Carlsbad, NM 88220 (✆ **800/967-CAVE** [967-2283] for tour reservations, 505/785-2232 for information about guided tours, or 785-3012 for bat flight information; www.nps.gov/cave).

ADMISSION FEES & HOURS   General admission to the park is $6 for adults, free for children ages 15 and under. Admission is good for 3 days and includes entry to the two self-guided walking tours. Guided tours range in price from $7 to $20, depending on the type of tour, and reservations are required. The visitor center and park are open daily from Memorial Day to mid-August from 8am to 7pm; the rest of the year they're open from 8am to 5pm. Closed Christmas.

WHAT TO SEE & DO

Two caves, Carlsbad Cavern and Slaughter Canyon, are open to the public. The National Park Service has provided facilities, including elevators, to make it easy for everyone to visit the cavern, and there is wheelchair access.

In addition to the options described below, ask at the visitor center about other ranger-guided tours, including climbing and crawling "wild" cave tours. Be sure to call in advance—some tours are offered only 1 day per week. **Reservations** (✆ **877/444-6777;** www.recreation.gov) are highly recommended for all guided tours. Spelunkers require special permission from the park superintendent.

CARLSBAD CAVERN TOURS You can tour the caverns in one of three ways, depending on your time, interest, and level of ability. The first, and least difficult, option is to take the elevator from the visitor center down 750 feet to the start of the self-guided tour of the Big Room. More difficult and time-consuming, but vastly more rewarding, is the 1-mile self-guided tour along the Natural Entrance route, which follows the traditional explorer's route, entering the cavern through the large historic natural entrance. The paved walkway through the natural entrance winds into the depths of the cavern and leads through a series of underground rooms; this tour takes about an hour. Parts of it are steep. At its lowest point, the trail reaches 750 feet below the surface, ending finally at an underground rest area.

Visitors who take the elevator or the Natural Entrance route begin the self-guided tour of the Big Room near the rest area. The floor of this room covers 14 acres; the tour, over a relatively level path, is 1¼ miles in length and takes about an hour.

The third option is the 1½-hour ranger-guided Kings Palace tour, which also departs from the underground rest area. This tour descends 830 feet beneath the surface of the desert to the deepest portion of the cavern open to the public. Reservations are required and an additional fee is charged.

TOUR TIPS Wear flat shoes with rubber soles and heels because of the slippery paths. A light sweater or jacket feels good in the constant temperature of 56°F (13°C), especially when it's 100°F (38°C) outside in the sun. The cavern is well lit, but you may want to bring along a flashlight as well. Rangers are stationed in the cave to answer questions.

SLAUGHTER CANYON CAVE TOUR Slaughter Canyon Cave was discovered in 1937 and was mined for bat guano until the 1950s. It consists of a corridor 1,140 feet long with many side passageways. The lowest point is 250 feet below the surface, and the passage traversed by the ranger-guided tours is 1¾ miles long, but more strenuous than hiking through the main cavern. There is also a strenuous 500-foot-rise hike from the parking lot to the cave mouth. The tour lasts about 2½ hours. No more than 25 people may take part, and by reservation only. Everyone needs a flashlight (make sure you have fresh batteries), hiking boots or shoes, and drinking water. Slaughter Canyon Cave is reached via U.S. 180 south 5 miles from Whites City, to a marked turnoff that leads 11 miles into a parking lot.

OTHER GUIDED TOURS Be sure to ask about the Left Hand Tunnel, Lower Cave, Hall of the White Giant, and Spider Cave tours. They vary in degree of difficulty and adventure, from **Left Hand,** which is an easy half-mile lantern tour; to **Spider Cave,** where you can expect tight crawlways and canyonlike passages; to **Hall of the White Giant,** a strenuous tour in which you're required to crawl long distances, squeeze through tight crevices, and climb up slippery flow-stone-lined passages. Call in advance for times of each tour. All depart from the visitor center.

THE SOUTHWEST

11

CARLSBAD CAVERNS NATIONAL PARK

The Bat Cave!

Every sunset from May to October, a crowd gathers at the natural entrance of the cave to watch a quarter of a million bats take flight for a night of insect feasting. (The bats winter in Mexico.) All day long the Mexican free-tailed bats sleep in the cavern; at night they all strike out on an insect hunt.

OTHER PARK ACTIVITIES   There's a 10-mile scenic loop drive through the Chihua-huan Desert to view **Rattlesnake** and **Upper Walnut canyons.** Picnickers can head for Rattlesnake Springs Picnic Area, on County Road 418 near Slaughter Canyon Cave, a water source for hundreds of years for the Native Americans of the area. Backcountry hikers must register at the visitor center before going out on the trails.

12 SANTA FE

With a strong local flavor that's made rich by vibrant Native American and Hispanic communities, Santa Fe has become increasingly sophisticated in recent decades. Visitors flock here for cutting-edge cuisine, world-class opera, first-run art films, and some of the finest artwork in the world, seen easily while wandering on foot from gallery to gallery, museum to museum. They're also enchanted by the city's setting, backed by rolling hills and the blue peaks of the Sangre de Cristo Mountains.

Santa Fe, the oldest capital city in the country, was founded by Spanish governor Don Pedro de Peralta, who built the Palace of the Governors as his capitol on the north side of the central Plaza, where it stands today as an excellent museum of the city's 4 centuries of history. The Plaza, once the terminus of the Santa Fe Trail from Missouri and of the earlier Camino Real from Mexico, is the focus of numerous bustling art markets and Santa Fe's early September fiesta, celebrated annually since 1770. It's also one of the major attractions in the Southwest, and under its portico, Native Americans sit cross-legged, selling their crafts to eager tourists, as they have done for decades.

ESSENTIALS

GETTING THERE   By Plane   Although you can fly to **Santa Fe Municipal Airport** (© 505/955-2900), it's easier to fly to **Albuquerque International Sunport** (© 505/842-4366; www.cabq.gov/airport) and drive from there. From the Santa Fe Municipal Airport, **Roadrunner Shuttle** (© 505/424-3367) meets every flight and takes visitors anywhere in Santa Fe. Car-rental options are also available.

By Train   Amtrak (© 800/USA-RAIL [872-7245]; www.amtrak.com) provides service from Albuquerque (trip time: 2 hr.), Chicago (24 hr.), and Los Angeles (19 hr.) to its station at nearby Lamy (approx. 20 miles from downtown Santa Fe).

By Car   The major route into Santa Fe is **I-25** from the south (Albuquerque) and north (Denver and Colorado Springs). For those coming from the northwest, the most direct route is via Durango, Colorado, on **U.S. 160** East, then **U.S. 84** South to Santa Fe.

VISITOR INFORMATION   The **Santa Fe Convention and Visitors Bureau** is downtown at 201 W. Marcy St. (P.O. Box 909), Santa Fe, NM 87504-0909 (© 800/777-**CITY** [777-2489] or 505/955-6200; www.santafe.org).

GETTING AROUND   The best way to see downtown Santa Fe is on foot. Street parking is difficult during summer months. You can pick up a wallet-size guide to parking areas at the visitor center. There's a metered parking lot near the federal courthouse, 2 blocks north of the Plaza; a city lot behind Santa Fe Village, a block south of the Plaza; and another city lot at Water and Sandoval streets.

The public bus system, **Santa Fe Trails** (© 505/955-2001; http://santafetrails.santafenm. gov), has seven routes. Most buses operate Monday to Friday 6am to 11pm and Saturday 8am to 8pm. **Capital City Cab** (© 505/438-0000) is the main taxi company.

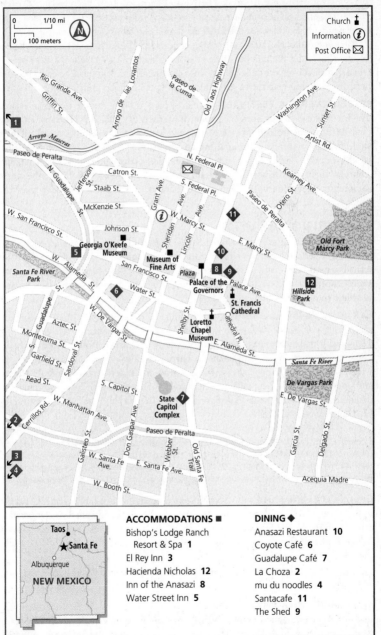

Church ✝
Information ⓘ
Post Office ✉

0   1/10 mi
0   100 meters

Map labels:

Rio Grande Ave.
Griffin St.
Arroyo de las Lovantos
Paseo de la Cuma
Old Taos Highway
Washington Ave.
Sunset St.
Arroyo Mancras
Paseo de Peralta
Artist Rd.
N. Guadalupe
Jefferson St.
Catron St.
Staab St.
McKenzie St.
Grant Ave.
S. Federal Pl.
N. Federal Pl.
Kearney Ave.
Otero St.
Paseo de Peralta
W. San Francisco St.
Johnson St.
Sheridan St.
W. Marcy St.
Lincoln Ave.
E. Marcy St.
Georgia O'Keefe Museum
Old Fort Marcy Park
W. Alameda St.
San Francisco St.
Museum of Fine Arts
Plaza
Palace of the Governors
Palace Ave.
Hillside Park
Santa Fe River Park
Water St.
Aztec St.
W. De Vargas St.
Shelby St.
St. Francis Cathedral
Loretto Chapel Museum
Cathedral Pl.
Guadalupe St.
Montezuma St.
Sandoval St.
Garfield St.
E. Alameda St.
Santa Fe River
De Vargas Park
Read St.
S. Capitol St.
E. De Vargas St.
Cerrillos Rd.
W. Manhattan Ave.
Don Gaspar Ave.
State Capitol Complex
Paseo de Peralta
Garcia St.
Delgado St.
Galisteo St.
W. Santa Fe Ave.
E. Santa Fe Ave.
Webber St.
Old Santa Fe Trail
Acequia Madre
W. Booth St.

Taos
Santa Fe
Albuquerque
NEW MEXICO

ACCOMMODATIONS ■

Bishop's Lodge Ranch Resort & Spa **1**
El Rey Inn **3**
Hacienda Nicholas **12**
Inn of the Anasazi **8**
Water Street Inn **5**

DINING ◆

Anasazi Restaurant **10**
Coyote Café **6**
Guadalupe Café **7**
La Choza **2**
mu du noodles **4**
Santacafe **11**
The Shed **9**

FAST FACTS   St. Vincent Hospital is at 455 St. Michael's Dr. (© 505/983-3361, or 995-3934 for emergency services). Del Norte Pharmacy, 1691 Galisteo St. (© 505/988-9797), offers delivery and emergency service. A sales tax of 7.937% is added to all purchases, with an additional 5% hotel tax for lodging bills.

Warning: Although the tourist district appears safe, Santa Fe is not on the whole a safe city; theft and the number of reported rapes have risen. Though the city's overall crime statistics do appear to be falling, when walking, guard your purse carefully because there are many bag-grab thefts, particularly during the summer tourist months.

SPECIAL EVENTS & FESTIVALS   Santa Fe Plaza is often the site of special events. The last weekend in July brings the Spanish Markets (© 505/982-2226), when more than 300 Hispanic artists from New Mexico and southern Colorado exhibit and sell their work. In August, there's the Annual Indian Market (© 505/983-5220), with artisans' booths, musical entertainment, tribal dancing, and crafts demonstrations. Beginning Thursday night after Labor Day is Fiesta de Santa Fe (© 505/988-7575), the oldest community celebration in the United States. Events include Masses, parades, mariachi concerts, and dances.

EXPLORING THE CITY

One of the oldest cities in the United States, Santa Fe has long been a center for the creative and performing arts, so it's not surprising that most of the city's major sights are related to local history and the arts. The city's Museum of New Mexico, art galleries and studios, historic churches, and cultural sights associated with local Native American and Hispanic communities all merit a visit.

El Rancho de las Golondrinas   This 200-acre ranch was once the last stopping place on the 1,000-mile El Camino Real from Mexico City to Santa Fe. Today it's a living 18th- and 19th-century Spanish village, comprising a hacienda, a village store, a schoolhouse, and several chapels and kitchens. There's also a working molasses mill, wheelwright and blacksmith shops, shearing and weaving rooms, a threshing ground, a winery and vineyard, and four water mills, as well as dozens of farm animals. Costumed volunteers demonstrate traditional trades. The Spring Festival (in June) and the Harvest Festival (in Oct) are the year's highlights.

334 Los Pinos Rd. © 505/471-2261. www.golondrinas.org. Admission $5 adults, $4 seniors and teens, $2 children 5–12, free for children 4 and under. Festival weekends $7 adults, $5 seniors and teens, $3 children 5–12. June–Sept Wed–Sun 10am–4pm; Apr–May and Oct open by advance arrangement. Closed Nov–Mar. From Santa Fe, drive south on I-25, taking exit 276, which will lead to N.M. 599 going north; turn left on W. Frontage Rd., drive ½ mile, turn right on Los Pinos Rd., and travel 3 miles to the museum.

Georgia O'Keeffe Museum   This museum contains the largest collection of O'Keeffes in the world: 117 oil paintings, drawings, watercolors, pastels, and sculptures. It's the only museum in the United States dedicated solely to one woman's work. The rich and varied collection includes such works as *Jimson Weed* (1932) and *Evening Star No. VII* (1917). You can also see an excellent film about her life.

217 Johnson St. © 505/946-1000. www.okeeffemuseum.org. Admission $8, free for students and youth 18 and under, free for all Fri 5–8pm. June–Oct daily 10am–5pm (Fri until 8pm); Nov–May closed Tues.

Museum of Indian Arts and Culture (Best)   A permanent interactive exhibit here makes this one of the most exciting Native American museum experiences in the Southwest. "Here, Now and Always" takes visitors through thousands of years of Native American history. More than 70,000 pieces of basketry, pottery, clothing, carpets, and

jewelry—much of it quite old—are on continual rotating display. The rest of the
museum houses a lovely pottery collection, as well as changing exhibits. Call for information on demonstrations of traditional skills, lectures on native traditions and arts, and performances of Native American music and dancing.

710 Camino Lejo. ℂ **505/476-1250.** www.miaclab.org. Admission $8 adults, free for kids 16 and under. 4-day passes (good at all 4 branches of the Museum of New Mexico and the Museum of Spanish Colonial Art) $18 for adults. Tues–Sun 10am–5pm. Drive southeast on Old Santa Fe Trail (beware: Old Santa Fe Trail takes a left turn; if you find yourself on Old Pecos Trail, you missed the turn). Look for signs pointing right onto Camino Lejo.

Museum of International Folk Art (Kids) With a collection of some 130,000 objects from more than 100 countries, this museum is the largest of its kind in the world. The special collections include Spanish colonial silver, traditional and contemporary New Mexican religious art, Mexican tribal costumes, Mexican majolica ceramics, Brazilian folk art, European glass, African sculptures, the marvelous Morris Miniature Circus, and American weather vanes and quilts. Children love to look at the hundreds of toys on display throughout the museum.

706 Camino Lejo. ℂ **505/476-1200.** www.moifa.org. Admission $8 adults, free for kids 16 and under. 4-day passes (good at all 4 branches of the Museum of New Mexico and at the Museum of Spanish Colonial Art) $18 for adults. Memorial Day to Labor Day daily 10am–5pm; rest of the year Tues–Sun 10am–5pm. The museum is about 2 miles southeast of the Plaza. Drive southeast on Old Santa Fe Trail (beware: Old Santa Fe Trail takes a left turn; if you find yourself on Old Pecos Trail, you missed the turn). Look for signs pointing right onto Camino Lejo.

New Mexico Museum of Art Opposite the Palace of the Governors, this was one of the first pueblo revival–style buildings constructed in Santa Fe (in 1917). The museum's permanent collection of more than 20,000 works emphasizes regional art and includes landscapes and portraits by all the Taos masters, *los Cincos Pintores* (a 1920s organization of Santa Fe artists), and contemporary artists.

107 W. Palace (at Lincoln Ave.). ℂ **505/476-5072.** www.museumofnewmexico.org. Admission $8 adults, free for seniors Wed, free for children 16 and under, free for all Fri 5–8pm. 4-day passes (good at all 4 branches of the Museum of New Mexico and the Museum of Spanish Colonial Art) $18 for adults. Tues–Sun 10am–5pm; Fri 10am–8pm. Closed Easter, Thanksgiving, Christmas, and New Year's Day.

Palace of the Governors Built in 1610 as the original capitol of New Mexico, the palace has been in continuous public use longer than any other structure in the United States. Today this museum chronicles 400 years of New Mexico's history. Highlights include a world-class collection of pre-Columbian art objects, with ceramics, gold, and stone work; a stagecoach and tools used by early Hispanic residents; a replica of a mid-19th-century chapel; and restored Mexican and 19th-century U.S. governors' offices.

North Plaza. ℂ **505/476-5100.** www.palaceofthegovernors.org. Admission $8 adults, free for children 16 and under, free for all Fri 5–8pm. 4-day passes (good at all 4 branches of the Museum of New Mexico and the Museum of Spanish Colonial Art) $18 for adults. Tues–Sun 10am–5pm. Closed Thanksgiving, Christmas, and New Year's Day.

St. Francis Cathedral Santa Fe's grandest religious structure, built in the style of the great cathedrals of Europe, is an architectural anomaly here. The small adobe Our Lady of the Rosary chapel on the northeast side is the only portion that remains from the original church, founded in 1610. Look for Our Lady of Peace, the oldest representation of the Madonna in the United States; and for the cathedral's front doors, featuring 16 carved panels memorializing the 38 Franciscan friars who were martyred during New Mexico's early years.

Cathedral Place at San Francisco St. ✆ **505/982-5619.** Donations appreciated. Open daily. Visitors may attend Mass Mon–Sat 7am and 5:15pm; Sun 8, 10am, noon, and 5:15pm. Free parking in city lot next to the cathedral to attend church services.

SHOPPING

Some call Santa Fe one of the top art markets in the world, and it's no wonder. Galleries speckle the downtown area, and as an artists' thoroughfare, Canyon Road is preeminent. Still, the greatest concentration of Native American crafts is displayed beneath the portal of the Palace of the Governors.

LewAllen Contemporary, 129 W. Palace Ave. (✆ **505/988-8997**), stocks bizarre and beautiful contemporary works in a range of mediums from granite to clay to twigs. **Shidoni Foundry, Gallery, and Sculpture Gardens,** Bishop's Lodge Road, Tesuque (✆ **505/988-8001**), is one of the area's most exciting spots for sculptors and sculpture enthusiasts. **Gerald Peters Gallery,** 1011 Paseo de Peralta (✆ **505/954-5700**), features the art of Georgia O'Keeffe, William Wegman, and the founders of the Santa Fe and Taos artists' colonies.

WHERE TO STAY

Year-round reservation assistance is available from **Santa Fe Hotels.com** (✆ 800/745-9910), the **Accommodation Hot Line** (✆ 800/338-6877), **All Santa Fe Reservations** (✆ 877/737-7366), and **Santa Fe Stay,** which specializes in casitas (✆ 800/995-2272). **Emergency Lodging Assistance** is available free after 4pm daily (✆ 505/986-0038).

Bishop's Lodge Ranch Resort & Spa (Kids) The 1,000-acre Bishop's Lodge is an active resort, and its many outdoor opportunities, including riding lessons, nature walks, and cookouts, make it an ideal place for families. In recent years, a $17-million renovation spruced up the place and added a spa. Rooms, spread through many buildings, feature handcrafted furniture and regional artwork. Deluxe units have traditional kiva fireplaces and private decks or patios. Some offer spectacular views of the Jemez Mountains.

Bishop's Lodge Rd. (P.O. Box 2367), Santa Fe, NM 87504. ✆ **505/983-6377.** Fax 505/989-8939. www. bishopslodge.com. 111 units. Summer $399–$489 double; fall and spring $299–$399 double; midwinter $189–$269 double. Villas $550–$1,500. Resort fee $15 per person per day. Additional person $15. Children 3 and under stay free in parent's room. Ask about packages that include meals. AE, DC, DISC, MC, V. Free parking. **Amenities:** Restaurant; outdoor pool; tennis courts; spa. *In room:* Fridge.

El Rey Inn Staying at "The King" makes you feel like you're traveling the old Route 66 through the Southwest. The two stories of suites around the Spanish colonial court-yard are a sweet deal. They feel like a Spanish inn, with carved furniture and cozy couches, and some have kitchenettes. Ten newer units offer more upscale amenities and gas log fireplaces. In the oldest section, the small rooms have style, with Art Deco tile in the bathrooms. Request a room as far back as possible from Cerrillos Road.

1862 Cerrillos Rd. (P.O. Box 4759), Santa Fe, NM 87502. ✆ **800/521-1349** or 505/982-1931. Fax 505/989-9249. www.elreyinnsantafe.com. 86 units. $99–$165 double; $125–$225 suite. Rates include continental breakfast. AE, DC, DISC, MC, V. Free parking. **Amenities:** Outdoor pool; exercise room. *In room:* Fridge.

Hacienda Nicholas This inn, a few blocks from the Plaza, has a delightful Southwestern hacienda feel. Rooms surround a sunny patio. All beds are comfortable, and bathrooms range from small with showers only to larger with tub/showers. A full breakfast—including such delicacies as house-made granola and red and green breakfast burritos—and afternoon wine and cheese are served in the lovely Great Room or on the patio, both with fireplaces. Service in this inn is excellent.

320 E. Marcy St., Santa Fe, NM 87501. © **888/284-3170** or 505/992-8385. www.haciendanicholas.com. Fax 505/982-8572. 7 units. $120–$240 double. Additional person $25. Rates include breakfast and afternoon wine and cheese. AE, DISC, MC, V. Free parking. Pets accepted with $20 fee.

Inn of the Anasazi (Best)   This fine luxury hotel, built in 1991 right off the Plaza, manages to suggest a feeling of grandness in a very limited space, and in 2006 a remodel added even finer touches, including new bedding and decor in the rooms, with bold splashes of color from indigenous rugs and hand-woven fabrics. The spacious rooms feature pearl-finished walls, cream-toned decor, iron sconces, four-poster beds, kiva gas fireplaces, and humidifiers. All rooms are quiet, though none have dramatic views. The Anasazi Restaurant (see below) serves creative Southwestern cuisine.

113 Washington Ave., Santa Fe, NM 87501. © **800/688-8100** or 505/988-3030. Fax 505/988-3277. www.innoftheanasazi.com. 57 units. Jan 5–Feb 26 $269–$469 double; Feb 27–Apr 28 $325–$525 double; Apr 29–Jan 4 $325–$525 double. AE, DC, DISC, MC, V. Valet parking $15 per day. **Amenities:** Restaurant.

Water Street Inn   An award-winning adobe restoration 4 blocks from the Plaza, this friendly inn features beautiful Mexican-tile bathrooms, several kiva fireplaces and woodstoves, and antique furnishings. A happy hour with quesadillas and margaritas is offered. Rooms are decorated in a Moroccan/Southwestern style and come with balconies or terraces, flatscreen TVs, DVD/VCR players, and CD players. Four suites have private patios with fountains. In the afternoons, a happy hour, with quesadillas and margaritas (on Fri), is offered in the living room or on the upstairs portal, where an extended continental breakfast is also served.

427 W. Water St., Santa Fe, NM 87501. © **800/646-6752** or 505/984-1193. Fax 505/984-6235. www.waterstreetinn.com. 12 units. $150–$250 double. Rates include continental breakfast and afternoon hors d'oeuvres and refreshments. AE, DISC, MC, V. Free parking. Children and pets welcome with prior approval.

WHERE TO DINE

Anasazi Restaurant CREATIVE SOUTHWESTERN/NATIVE AMERICAN   This is one of Santa Fe's more interesting dining experiences. All the food is inventive, and organic meats and vegetables are used whenever available. A new chef, Oliver Ridgeway, has brought new flavors to what has always been an imaginative menu, utilizing regional and seasonal ingredients. You might find a seasonal medley of wild mushrooms, with leek parpadelle and succotash. There are daily specials, as well as a nice list of wines by the glass and wines of the day. The Anasazi's patio dining is a great way to sample a variety of "small plates."

At the Inn of the Anasazi, 113 Washington Ave. © **505/988-3236.** www.innoftheanasazi.com. Reservations recommended. Main courses $7.50–$12 breakfast, $9.50–$15 lunch, $25–$36 dinner. AE, DISC, MC, V. Daily 7–10:30am, 11:30am–2:30pm, and 5:30–10pm.

Coyote Cafe CREATIVE SOUTHWESTERN/LATIN   World-renowned chef and cookbook author Mark Miller put this place on the map decades ago. Now under new ownership, it has gained new popularity as a place for innovative food in a festive environment. For a main course, look for delights such as pan-seared white miso halibut with roasted lobster jus, wasabi mashed potatoes, and braised baby bok choy. Coyote Café has an adjunct establishment: In summer, the place to be seen is **La Nueva Cantina,** where light Mexican fare and cocktails are served on a festively painted terrace. Try the jalapeño rellenos with buttermilk roasted garlic sauce.

132 Water St. © **505/983-1615.** www.coyotecafe.com. Reservations highly recommended. Main courses $6–$16 Rooftop Cantina, $19–$36 Coyote Café. AE, DC, DISC, MC, V. Rooftop Cantina: Daily 11:30am–9:30pm. Dining room: Daily 5:30–10pm.

Guadalupe Cafe NEW MEXICAN   This casually elegant cafe is in a white-stucco building that's warm and friendly, with a nice-size patio for dining in warmer months. For dinner, start with fresh roasted ancho chilies (filled with a combination of Montrachet and Monterey Jack cheese and pinyon nuts) and move on to the sour-cream chicken enchilada or any of the other Southwestern dishes. Order both red and green chili ("Christmas") so that you can sample some of the best sauces in town.

422 Old Santa Fe Trail. © **505/982-9762.** Breakfast $5.50–$9.75; lunch $6–$12; dinner $8–$17. DISC, MC, V. Tues–Fri 7am–2pm; Sat–Sun 8am–2pm; Tues–Sat 5:30–9pm.

La Choza ⓥ**alue** NEW MEXICAN   This warm, casual spot offers some of the best New Mexican food in town. The menu features enchiladas, tacos, and burritos on blue-corn tortillas, as well as green chili stew, chili con carne, and carne adovada. The portions are medium-size, so if you're hungry, start with guacamole or nachos. The cheese or chicken enchiladas are reliable favorites, though you might check out the blue-corn burritos served with *posole.* Vegetarians and children get their own menus.

905 Alarid St. © **505/982-0909.** Lunch or dinner $8.95–$12. AE, DISC, MC, V. Summer Mon–Sat 11am–9pm; winter Mon–Thurs 11am–8pm, Fri–Sat 11am–9pm.

mu du noodles PACIFIC RIM   If you're ready for a light, healthy meal with lots of flavor, head to this small restaurant, about an 8-minute drive from downtown. Of the two rooms, the back room is cozier, and the woodsy-feeling patio is worth requesting during warmer months. We recommend the Malaysian *laksa,* thick rice noodles in a blend of coconut milk, hazelnuts, onions, and red curry, stir-fried with chicken or tofu and julienne vegetables and sprouts. Wash it all down with the ginseng ginger ale.

1494 Cerrillos Rd. © **505/983-1411.** www.mudunoodles.com. Reservations for parties of 3 or larger only. Main courses $9–$18. AE, DC, DISC, MC, V. Tues–Sat 5:30–9pm (sometimes 10pm in summer).

Santacafé ⓑ**est** CREATIVE SOUTHWESTERN   Be prepared for spectacular bursts of flavor. The Southwestern food here has an Asian flair and is served amid a minimalist decor that accentuates the graceful architecture of the 18th-century Padre Gallegos House. The dishes change to take advantage of seasonal specialties: Shiitake and cactus spring rolls are served with green chili salsa, while achiote-marinated halibut comes with orange salsa and green rice.

231 Washington Ave. © **505/984-1788.** www.santacafe.com. Reservations recommended. Main courses $9–$15 lunch, $22–$40 dinner. AE, DISC, MC, V. Mon–Sat 11:30am–2pm; daily 5:30–10pm. Sun brunch served in summer, Easter, and Mother's Day.

The Shed NEW MEXICAN   During lunch, lines often form outside the Shed, a local institution since 1953. It occupies several rooms and the patio of a rambling hacienda built in 1692. Festive folk art adorns the doorways and walls. The food, like the cheese enchilada and the tacos and burritos, is some of the best in the state. All are served on blue-corn tortillas. The green chili soup is a local favorite. Don't leave without trying the mocha cake, possibly the best dessert you'll ever eat. Vegetarian and low-fat dishes are available, as is full bar service.

113¹/₂ E. Palace Ave. © **505/982-9030.** www.sfshed.com. Reservations accepted at dinner. Lunch $5.75–$9.50; dinner $8–$17. AE, DC, DISC, MC, V. Mon–Sat 11am–2:30pm and 5:30–9pm.

SANTA FE AFTER DARK

Santa Fe is a city committed to the arts, with a variety of cultural offerings. Current listings are published each Friday in the "Pasatiempo" section of *The New Mexican*

(www.sfreporter.com), published every Wednesday.

You can order tickets to most events by phone from **Ticketmaster** (© **505/883-7800**). Discount tickets may be available on the night of a performance.

THE PERFORMING ARTS   Many rank the **Santa Fe Opera** (© **800/280-4654** or 505/986-5900; www.santafeopera.org) second only to the Metropolitan Opera of New York as the finest company in the United States. The company performs in an open-sided venue on a wooded hilltop 7 miles north of the city off U.S. 84/285. It consistently attracts famed conductors, directors, and singers. The 8-week season runs from late June to late August.

The **Santa Fe Symphony Orchestra and Chorus** (© **800/480-1319** or 505/983-1414; www.sf-symphony.org) performs classical and popular works from October to May. An extraordinary group of artists comes to Santa Fe every summer for the **Santa Fe Chamber Music Festival** (© **505/983-2075** or 982-1890; www.sfcmf.org).

The oldest theater group in New Mexico, **Santa Fe Playhouse,** 142 E. de Vargas St. (© **505/988-4262;** www.santafeplayhouse.org), has a loyal audience for dramas, avant-garde theater, and musical comedy. The **Theater Grottesco** (© **505/474-8400;** www.theatergrottesco.org) troupe combines the best of comedy, drama, and dance in its original productions performed each spring, summer, or fall. You won't want to miss a performance of the **María Benitez Teatro Flamenco,** in the Maria Benitez Theater at the Radisson Hotel (© **888/435-2636** or 505/982-1237; www.mariabenitez.com).

THE BAR, CLUB & MUSIC SCENE   **El Farol,** 808 Canyon Rd. (© **505/983-9912**), is the place to head for Santa Fe's largest and most unusual selection of tapas. Jazz, swing, folk, and ethnic musicians, some of national note, perform most nights.

There's live entertainment nightly at the **Cowgirl Hall of Fame,** 319 S. Guadalupe St. (© **505/982-2565**): folk, rock, blues guitar, comedy, and cowboy poetry. In the summer, this is a great place to sit under the stars and listen to music.

You'll find everyone from businesspeople to bikers at **Evangelo's,** 200 W. San Francisco St. (© **505/982-9014**), a raucous downtown hangout with tropical decor and a mahogany bar. More than 60 varieties of imported beer are available, and pool tables are an added attraction. You might catch live rock, jazz, or reggae.

TOURING SOME PUEBLOS AROUND SANTA FE

The pueblos described in this section can easily be visited in a single day's round-trip from Santa Fe. Certain rules of etiquette should be observed in visiting the pueblos: These are personal dwellings and/or important historic sites, and must be respected as such. Don't climb on the buildings or peek into doors or windows. Don't enter sacred grounds, such as cemeteries and kivas. If you attend a dance or ceremony, remain silent while it's taking place and refrain from applause when it's over. Many pueblos prohibit photography or sketches; others require you to pay a fee for a permit.

Ohkay Owingeh (San Juan Pueblo)   This largest (pop. 1,950) and northernmost of the Tewa-speaking pueblos is on the east side of the Rio Grande—opposite the 1598 site of San Gabriel, the first Spanish settlement west of the Mississippi River and the first capital of New Spain. The annual **San Juan Fiesta** is held here on June 23 and 24, and the **turtle dance** is on December 26. The **Matachine dance,** performed Christmas Day, vividly depicts the subjugation of the Native Americans by the Catholic Spaniards. A crafts shop, **Ohkay Owingeh Arts and Crafts Cooperative** (© **505/852-2372**), specializes in local wares. This is a fine place to seek out San Juan's distinctive red pottery. Also for sale are seed, turquoise, and silver jewelry; wood and stone carvings; weavings; embroidery; and paintings.

On N.M. 74 about 4 miles north of Española. © **505/852-4400** or 852-4210. Free admission. Photography or sketching may be allowed with prior permission from the governor's office. Fishing $8 adults, $5 children and seniors. Daily during daylight hours.

San Ildefonso Pueblo   This pueblo has a broad, dusty plaza, with a kiva on one side, ancient dwellings on the other, and a church at the far end. It's nationally famous for its matte-finish black-on-black pottery, developed by tribeswoman María Martínez in the 1920s. A few shops surround the Plaza, and the **San Ildefonso Pueblo Museum** is tucked away in the governor's office beyond the Plaza. It's especially memorable to visit during ceremonial days. **San Ildefonso Feast Day,** on January 23, features the buffalo and Comanche dances in alternate years. **Corn dances,** held in late August or early September, commemorate a basic element in pueblo life, the importance of fertility in all creatures—humans as well as animals—and plants. The pueblo has a half-acre fishing lake surrounded by woodlands, open from April to October. Picnicking is encouraged, but camping is not allowed.

Rte. 5. © **505/455-3549.** Admission $5 per car. Still camera $10; video camera $20; sketching $25. Fishing $10 adults, $5 for kids 11 and under. Summer Mon–Fri 8am–5pm; call for weekend hours. Winter Mon–Fri 8am–4:30pm. Closed for major holidays and tribal events.

13 TAOS

New Mexico's favorite arts town is a place where its 5,000 residents combine 1960s hippiedom (thanks to communes set up in the hills back then) with the ancient culture of Taos Pueblo (some people still live without electricity and running water, as their ancestors did 1,000 years ago). It can be an odd place, where some completely eschew materialism and live "off the grid" in half-underground houses called earth ships.

But take a moment longer to look and you'll see a thriving art colony, not glitzy like Santa Fe, but real and down-to-earth, often with artists selling work out of their studios. You'll wander through amazing galleries, many displaying the town's rich history in a variety of art forms. And you'll eat some of the most inventive food in the Southwest, at very affordable prices.

Taos is 40 miles south of the Colorado border, about 70 miles north of Santa Fe, and 135 miles from Albuquerque. In addition to its arts scene, it's famous for the pueblo and for the nearby ski area, one of the most highly regarded in the Rockies.

ESSENTIALS

GETTING THERE   By Plane   The **Taos Municipal Airport** (© 505/758-4995) is about 8 miles northwest of town on U.S. 64. However, it's easier to fly into **Albuquerque International Sunport** (© 505/842-4366), rent a car, and drive from there (trip time: 2¹/₂ hr.). If you'd rather be picked up at Albuquerque International Sunport, call **Faust's Transportation, Inc.** (© 505/758-3410), which offers daily service, as well as taxi service between Taos and Taos Ski Valley.

By Car   From Santa Fe, take **U.S. 84/285** north, then **N.M. 68** to Taos. From Denver, take **I-25 South** to **U.S. 64,** then continue west about 95 miles to Taos.

VISITOR INFORMATION   The **Taos County Chamber of Commerce,** at the junction of N.M. 68 and N.M. 585 (P.O. Drawer I), Taos, NM 87571 (© **800/732-TAOS**

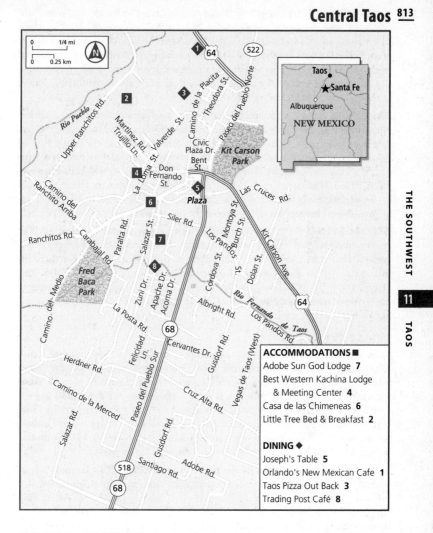

[732-8267] or 505/758-3873; www.taoschamber.com), is open in summer daily 9am to 5pm. It's closed on major holidays.

GETTING AROUND   **Chile Line Town of Taos Transit** (© **575/751-4459**) operates on the half-hour Monday to Saturday 7am to 7pm in summer, 7am to 6pm in winter, and on the hour Sunday 8am to 5pm. Two routes run southbound from Taos Pueblo and northbound from the Ranchos de Taos Post Office. Each route makes stops at the casino and various hotels in town, as well as at Taos RV Park. Bus fares are 50¢ one-way, $1 round-trip, $5 for a 7-day pass, and $20 for a 31-day pass.

   Faust's Transportation (© **505/758-3410**) has a taxi service linking town hotels and Taos Ski Valley, shuttle service, and on-call taxi service daily from 7am to 8:30pm, with fares of about $10 anywhere within the city limits for up to two people.

Parking can be difficult in summer. If you can't find a spot on the street or in the Plaza, check out some of the nearby roads. ***Safety tips:*** En route to many recreation sites, reliable paved roads can lead to poorer forest roads. Once you get off the main roads, you won't find gas stations or cafes. Four-wheel-drive vehicles are recommended on snow and much of the otherwise unpaved terrain of the region. If you're doing off-road adventuring, it's wise to go with a full gas tank, extra food and water, and warm clothing. Sudden summer snowstorms are not unheard of.

FAST FACTS You can get information on road conditions from the **State Highway Department** (© 800/432-4269); if you have a highway emergency, contact the Taos area state police at © 505/758-8878. **Holy Cross Hospital,** 1397 Weimer Rd., off Paseo del Canyon (© 505/758-8883), has 24-hour emergency service. **Sav-on Drug** (© 575/758-1203), **Smith's Pharmacy** (© 575/758-4824), and **Wal-Mart Pharmacy** (© 575/758-2743) are all on Pueblo Sur and are easily seen from the road.

Gross receipts tax for the city of Taos is 7.5%, and for Taos County it's 6.3%. There is an additional **lodgers' tax** of 5% in both the city of Taos and Taos County.

SPECIAL EVENTS & FESTIVALS May brings the **Taos Spring Arts Festival,** with gallery openings, studio tours, performances by visiting theatrical and dance troupes, musical events, traditional ethnic entertainment, readings, and more. For dates and tickets, contact the **Taos County Chamber of Commerce** (© 800/732-TAOS [732-8267] or 505/758-3873; www.taoschamber.com). From mid-August to early September, there's **Music from Angel Fire** (© 505/377-3233; www.angelfirenm.com), an acclaimed program of chamber music.

WHAT TO SEE & DO

If you'd like to visit five museums that comprise the Museum Association of Taos—Blumenschein Home, Martinez Hacienda, Harwood Museum, Millicent Rogers Museum, and Taos Art Museum—you'll save money by purchasing a **combination ticket** for $25 at any of the museums. For more information, call © 575/758-0505.

Given the town's historical associations with the arts, it isn't surprising that many visitors come to Taos to buy fine art. Some 50-odd galleries are within walking distance of the Plaza. The best-known modern artist in Taos is R. C. Gorman. His **Navajo Gallery,** 210 Ledoux St. (© 505/758-3250), is a showcase for his works.

Millicent Rogers Museum of Northern New Mexico This museum is small enough to introduce some of the Southwest's finest arts and crafts without being overwhelming. Included are Navajo and Pueblo jewelry, Navajo textiles, Pueblo pottery, Hopi and Zuni kachina dolls, paintings from the Rio Grande Pueblo people, and basketry from a wide variety of Southwestern tribes. The permanent collection also includes Anglo arts and crafts and Hispanic religious and secular arts and crafts.

Off U.S. 64, 4 miles north of Taos Plaza, on Millicent Rogers Rd. © 575/758-2462. www.millicentrogers. org. Admission $10 adults, $8 students and seniors, $2 children 6–16, $18 family rate. Daily 10am–5pm. Closed Mon Nov–Mar, Easter, Thanksgiving, Christmas, New Year's Day.

San Francisco de Asis Church From N.M. 68, about 4 miles south of Taos, this famous church looks like a modern adobe sculpture with no doors or windows. Visitors must walk through the garden on the east side of this remarkable two-story church to enter and get a full perspective of its massive walls, authentic adobe plaster, and beauty. A video presentation is given in the church office every hour on the half-hour. A few crafts shops surround the square.

4pm. Visitors may attend Mass Mon–Fri 5pm; Sat 6pm (Mass rotates from this church to the 3 mission chapels); Sun 7 (Spanish), 9, and 11:30am. Closed to the public 1st 2 weeks in June, when repairs are done; however, services still take place.

Taos Historic Museums   Two historic homes are operated as museums, affording visitors a glimpse of early Taos lifestyles.

The **Martinez Hacienda,** Lower Ranchitos Road, Hwy. 240, is remarkably beautiful, with thick, raw adobe walls and no exterior windows, to protect against raids by Plains tribes. The 21 rooms built around two interior courtyards give you a glimpse of the austerity of frontier lives. You'll see bedrooms, servants' quarters, stables, a kitchen, and a large fiesta room. The hacienda is also a living museum, with weavers, blacksmiths, and woodcarvers demonstrating their trades daily, more often during the **Taos Trade Fair** (in late Sept).

The **Ernest L. Blumenschein Home & Museum,** 222 Ledoux St., 1$^{1}/_{2}$ blocks south-west of the Plaza, re-creates the lifestyle of one of the founders of the Taos Society of Artists (founded 1915). Period furnishings include European antiques and handmade Taos furniture in Spanish colonial style. An extensive collection of works by early-20th-century Taos artists is on display in several rooms of the home.

222 Ledoux St. ⓒ **575/758-0505** (information for both museums can be obtained at this number). www.taoshistoricmuseums.org. Admission for each museum $8 adults, $4 children ages 6–16, free for children 5 and under. Summer daily 9am–5pm; call for winter hours.

Taos Pueblo (Best)   About 150 residents of Taos Pueblo live much as their ancestors did 1,000 years ago, and the village looks much as it did when a regiment from Coronado's expedition first came upon it in 1540. When you enter the pueblo, you'll see two large buildings, each with rooms piled on top of each other, forming structures that mimic Taos Mountain nearby. Here, a portion of Taos residents live without electricity and running water. The remaining residents of Taos Pueblo (nearly 2,000) live in conventional homes on the pueblo's 95,000 acres. In your explorations, you can visit the residents' studios, look into the **San Geronimo Chapel,** and wander past the fascinating ruins of the old church and cemetery. Ask permission from individuals before taking their photos; some will ask for a small payment. Kivas and other ceremonial underground areas are restricted.

The **Feast of San Geronimo** (the patron saint of Taos Pueblo), on September 29 and 30, is filled with dances, footraces, and artists and craftspeople. The **Taos Pueblo Pow-wow,** which brings together tribes from throughout North America, is held in July on tribal lands. Call for information on other special events.

Veterans Hwy. (P.O. Box 1846), Taos Pueblo. (From Paseo del Pueblo Norte, travel north 2 miles on Veterans Hwy.) ⓒ **575/758-1028.** www.taospueblo.com. Admission cost, as well as camera, video, and sketching fees, subject to change on a yearly basis; be sure to ask about telephoto lenses and digital cameras; photography not permitted on feast days. Daily 8am–4:30pm, with a few exceptions. Guided tours available. Closed for 45 consecutive days every year late winter or early spring (call ahead). Also, because this is a living community, you can expect periodic closures.

WHERE TO STAY
Southern Rockies Reservations (ⓒ **866/250-7313;** www.taosskitrips.com) will help you find accommodations ranging from bed-and-breakfasts to home rentals, hotels, and cabins throughout Taos, Taos Ski Valley, and northern New Mexico.

(Best) Hitting the Slopes of Taos

Five Alpine resorts are within an hour's drive of Taos; all offer complete facilities, including equipment rentals. Although exact opening and closing dates vary according to snow conditions, the season usually begins around Thanksgiving and continues into early April.

Taos Ski Valley (© **505/776-2291;** www.skitaos.org) is the preeminent ski resort in the southern Rockies, internationally renowned for its light, dry powder (320 in. annually), its superb ski school, and its personal, friendly service. Experienced skiers will most appreciate Taos Ski Valley's steep, high-Alpine, high-adventure skiing. The mountain is more intricate than it might seem at first glance, and it holds many surprises and challenges—even for the expert.

The area has an uphill capacity of 15,000 skiers per hour on its five double chairs, one triple, four quads, and one surface tow. Full-day lift tickets, depending on the season, cost $40 to $66 for adults, $30 to $55 for teens ages 13 to 17, $25 to $40 for children 7 to 12, $40 to $50 for seniors ages 65 to 79, and are free for seniors 80 and over and for children 6 and under with an adult ticket purchase. Full rental packages are $29 for adults and $20 for children. Taos Ski Valley is open daily 9am to 4pm from Thanksgiving to around the second week of April. *Note:* Taos Ski Valley has one of the best ski schools in the country, specializing in teaching people how to negotiate steep and challenging runs.

Adobe Sun God Lodge (Value)   For an economical stay with a New Mexico ambience, this is your best choice. This hotel, a 5-minute drive from the Plaza, has three distinct parts spread across 1½ acres of landscaped grounds. The oldest has some court-motel charm with a low ceiling and large windows. In a recently remodeled section, rooms are small but have little touches that make them feel cozy. The newest buildings have portal-style porches and balconies. Some rooms have kitchenettes; others have kiva fireplaces.

919 Paseo del Pueblo Sur, Taos, NM 87571. © **800/821-2437** or 575/758-3162. Fax 575/758-1716. www.sungodlodge.com. 53 units. $67–$92 double; $112–$145 suite. DISC, MC, V. Pets allowed for $15 per day.

Best Western Kachina Lodge & Meeting Center (Kids)   This lodge on the north end of town, within walking distance of the Plaza, has a lot of charm despite the fact that it's really a motor hotel. The Southwestern-style rooms surrounding a grassy courtyard are solidly built and quiet, and there's plenty of outdoor space for the kids. On summer nights, a family from Taos Pueblo builds a bonfire and performs, explaining the significance of the dances—a real treat.

413 Paseo del Pueblo Norte (P.O. Box NM), Taos, NM 87571. © **800/522-4462** or 575/758-2275. Fax 575/758-9207. www.kachinalodge.com. 118 units. $59–$159 double. Rates include full breakfast. Additional person $10. Children 11 and under stay free in parent's room. AE, DISC, MC, V. **Amenities:** 2 restaurants; pool.

Casa de las Chimeneas (Best)   This 82-year-old adobe home is a full-service luxury inn and a model of Southwestern elegance. The Rio Grande and Territorial rooms have heated saltillo-tile floors and Jacuzzi tubs. If you prefer a more antique-feeling room, the older section is delightful, and renovation in the Library Suite has made it worth

recommending. All have elegant bedding, private entrances, kiva fireplaces, and fridges **817**
stocked with complimentary beverages. Most look out onto flower and herb gardens.

405 Cordoba Rd., at Los Pandos Rd. (5303 NDCBU), Taos, NM 87571. © **877/758-4777** or 575/758-4777.
Fax 575/758-3976. www.visittaos.com. 8 units. $180–$320 double; $325 suite. Rates include breakfast
and light evening supper. AE, DC, DISC, MC, V. **Amenities:** Small exercise room; spa.

Little Tree Bed & Breakfast   Little Tree is one of our favorite Taos B&Bs, partly
because it has a beautiful, secluded setting (midway btw. Taos and the ski area), and partly
because it's constructed with real adobe that's been left in its raw state, lending the place an
authentic hacienda feel. The charming and cozy rooms have radiant heat under the floors,
queen-size beds (one with a king-size), nice medium-size bathrooms (one with a Jacuzzi tub),
and access to the portal and courtyard garden, at the center of which is the little tree for
which the inn is named. Some units are equipped with fireplaces and private entrances.

County Rd. B-143 (P.O. Box 509), Arroyo Hondo, NM 87513. © **800/334-8467** or 575/776-8467. www.
littletreebandb.com. 4 units. $135–$195 double. Rates include breakfast and afternoon snack. MC, V.

Snakedance Condominiums and Spa   A recent $3.5-million renovation has trans-
formed the rooms of this former hotel into comfortable condominiums. Skiers appreciate
the inn's location, just steps from the lift, as well as amenities such as ski storage and boot
dryers. All units have balconies with French doors and kitchens with granite counters and
a range, fridge, dishwasher, and microwave. Many feature wood-burning fireplaces.
Shuttle service is offered to and from nearby shops and restaurants.

110 Sutton Place (P.O. Box 89), Taos Ski Valley, NM 87525. © **800/322-9815** or 575/776-2277. Fax 575/
776-1410. www.snakedancecondos.com. 33 units. 1-bedroom condo $225–$400 double in winter, $95 in
summer; 2-bedroom condo $285–$600 for 4 people in winter, $120 in summer; 2-bedroom loft condo
$345–$725 for 6 people in winter, $150 in summer. Extra person $30 in winter, $10 in summer. Rates
include a complimentary continental breakfast. AE, DC, DISC, MC, V. Free parking at Taos Ski Valley parking lot. Closed mid-Apr to Memorial Day and mid-Oct to mid-Nov. **Amenities:** Restaurant; exercise room;
spa. *In room:* Kitchen.

WHERE TO DINE
Joseph's Table (Best) NEW AMERICAN/MEDITERRANEAN   This notable eatery
serves some of the most imaginative and precisely prepared food in northern New
Mexico. The setting is unique, with hand-hewn vigas (beams) on the ceiling and hardwood floors and some Asian-style tables along the back. Chef/owner Joseph Wrede creates such delicacies as a juicy green-chili buffalo burger served with homemade
sweet-potato chips or Mediterranean mussels in a pesto broth and Tuscan bread for
lunch. Dinner is equally inventive, if not for the faint of palate. It might start with marlin sashimi on fried kale and move on to steak au poivre with mashed potatoes and a
Madeira mushroom sauce.

In the Hotel La Fonda de Taos, 108-A South Taos Plaza. © **575/751-4512.** www.josephstable.com. Reservations recommended. Main courses $8–$18 lunch, $18–$35 dinner. AE, DISC, MC, V. May–Aug Mon–Sat
11:30am–2:30pm, daily 5:30–10pm; Sun brunch 10:30am–2:30pm. Hours are abbreviated in winter; call first.

Orlando's New Mexican Café (Value) NEW MEXICAN   Festivity reigns in this
spicy little cafe on the north end of town. Serving some of northern New Mexico's best
chili, this place has colorful tables set around a bustling open kitchen, as well as airy patio
dining during warmer months. Try Los Colores, their most popular dish, with three
enchiladas (chicken, beef, and cheese) smothered in chili and served with beans and
posole. The taco salad is another favorite. Portions are big, and you can order a Mexican
or microbrew beer, or a New Mexican or California wine.

114 Don Juan Valdez Lane. (1¾ miles north of the Plaza, off Paseo del Pueblo Norte.) 📞 **575/751-1450.** Reservations not accepted. Main courses under $12. MC, V. Daily 10:30am–3pm and 5–9pm.

Taos Pizza Out Back (Kids) PASTA/GOURMET PIZZA   At this raucous old adobe restaurant, the level of informality is high, the food is great, and the portions are huge. What to order? One word: *Pizza.* All come with a delicious thin crust. The variations are broad: from Thai chicken pizza (pineapple, peanuts, and a spicy sauce) to our favorite, the Florentine (spinach, basil, sun-dried tomatoes, chicken, mushrooms, capers, and garlic sautéed in white wine). Don't leave without trying the Taos Yum (a "mongo" chocolate-chip cookie with ice cream, whipped cream, and chocolate sauce).

712 Paseo del Pueblo Norte (just north of Allsup's). 📞 **575/758-3112.** Reservations recommended weekends and holidays. Pizzas $13–$28; pastas and calzones $10–$13. MC, V. Summer daily 11am–10pm; winter Sun–Thurs 11am–9pm, Fri–Sat 11am–10pm.

Trading Post Café ITALIAN/INTERNATIONAL   Ask folks in town where they most like to eat, and they'll probably name the Trading Post. What draws them is a gallery atmosphere, where rough plastered walls are set off by sculptures, paintings, and photographs from the Lumina Gallery. Be prepared to wait for a table, and don't expect quiet, unless you come at an off-time. Although the focus is on the fine food, diners feel comfortable trying three appetizers and skipping the main course. You've probably never had a Caesar salad as good as the one here, and if you like pasta, you'll find a nice variety on the menu. There are also fresh fish, stews, and soups.

4179 Paseo del Pueblo Sur, Ranchos de Taos. 📞 **575/758-5089.** Reservations accepted. Menu items $8–$30. AE, DC, DISC, MC, V. Tues–Sat 11:30am–9:30pm; Sun 4–9:30pm.

TAOS AFTER DARK

You can get information on current events in the *Taos News,* published every Thursday.

For a small town, Taos has its share of top entertainment. Performers are attracted to Taos because of the resort atmosphere and the arts community, and the city enjoys annual programs in music and literary arts. State troupes, such as the New Mexico Repertory Theater and New Mexico Symphony Orchestra, make regular visits. Many events are scheduled by the **Taos Center for the Arts (TCA),** 133 Paseo del Pueblo Norte (📞 **505/ 758-2052;** www.taoscenterforthearts.org), at the **Taos Community Auditorium** (📞 **505/ 758-4677**). The TCA imports local, regional, and national performers in theater, dance, and concerts.

A favorite gathering place for locals and visitors, the **Adobe Bar,** in the Historic Taos Inn, 125 Paseo del Pueblo Norte (📞 **505/758-2233**), often hosts live music—classical, jazz, folk, Hispanic, and acoustic. The bar features a wide selection of international beers, wines by the glass, light New Mexican dining, desserts, and an espresso menu.

The **Alley Cantina,** 121 Teresina Lane (📞 **505/758-2121**), is a hot late-night spot with a kitchen open until 11pm and games such as pool, chess, and backgammon. The **Sagebrush Inn,** Paseo del Pueblo Sur (📞 **505/758-2254**), has pure Old West atmosphere, with a rustic wooden dance floor and plenty of smoke. Dancers generally two-step to country performers nightly. The **Anaconda Bar,** in the new eco-resort El Monte Sagrado (📞 **505/758-3502**), is Taos's most happening nightspot, with live entertainment—jazz, blues, Native American flute, or country—playing nightly. An anaconda sculpture snaking across the ceiling and an 11,000-gallon fish tank set the contemporary tone of the place, where a variety of delectable tapas are served.

California

California's allure is understandable. It really is warm and sunny most of the year, movie stars *do* abound in Los Angeles, and you *can* leave your heart in San Francisco. This part of the California mystique—as exaggerated it may be—does exist.

But there's more—a lot more—to California that isn't scripted, sanitized, and broadcast to the world. Beyond the glitter and glamour is an incredibly diverse state that has it all: redwood forests, a verdant Central Valley, the Sierra Nevada mountains, deserts, a host of world-renowned cities, and hundreds of miles of stunning coastline.

Despite the crime, pollution, traffic, and earthquakes, it's still the golden child of the United States: America's spoiled rich kid everyone either loves or loathes. But, truth be told, natives really don't care. Californians *know* they live in one of the most diverse and interesting places in the world, and they're proud of the state they call home.

1 SAN FRANCISCO

San Francisco's reputation as a rollicking city where almost anything goes dates from the boom-or-bust days of the California Gold Rush. The result is a wee bit o' heaven for everyone. In a city that is so beautiful, exciting, and cosmopolitan there's always something enjoyable to see and do, no matter how long you're staying.

Enjoy the cool blast of salty air as you stroll across the Golden Gate. Stuff yourself with dim sum in Chinatown. Browse the secondhand shops along Haight Street. Recite poetry in a North Beach coffeehouse. Skate through Golden Gate Park, ride the cable cars, tour a Victorian mansion, explore Alcatraz Island, go to a Giants ballgame: Like an eternal world's fair, it's all happening in San Francisco, and everyone's invited.

ESSENTIALS

SAN FRANCISCO INTERNATIONAL AIRPORT   Almost four dozen major scheduled carriers serve **San Francisco International Airport** (*C* **650/821-8211;** www.flysfo.com; airport code **SFO**), 14 miles south of downtown on U.S. 101. Travel time to downtown during commuter rush hour is about 40 minutes; at other times, it's about 20 to 25 minutes.

The cheapest and often fastest way to get to the city is to take **BART** (Bay Area Rapid Transit; *C* **415/989-2278;** www.bart.gov), which offers stops in downtown San Francisco. This route, which takes about 35 minutes, avoids traffic and costs a lot less than taxis or shuttles (about $6 each way, depending on where you're going). Just jump on the airport's free shuttle bus to the International terminal, enter the BART station there, and you're on your way. Trains leave approximately every 15 minutes.

A **taxi** downtown from the airport is $30 to $35, plus tip. **SuperShuttle** (*C* **800/ BLUE-VAN** [258-3826] or 415/558-8500; www.supershuttle.com) will take you anywhere in town; it's $15 to a residence or business, and $8 to $15 for each additional person, depending on your destination. The shuttle requires pickup 2 hours before your flight (3 hr. during holidays).

About 5 miles south of downtown Oakland, **Oakland International Airport** (© 800/247-6255 or 510/563-3300; www.oakland airport.com; airport code **OAK**) primarily serves passengers with East Bay destinations. Some San Franciscans prefer this less-crowded airport during busy periods—especially because by car it takes around half an hour to get there from downtown San Francisco (traffic permitting). The airport is also accessible by BART.

Taxis from the Oakland airport to downtown San Francisco are expensive, costing approximately $50, plus tip. **Bayporter Express** (© 877/467-1800 or 415/467-1800; www.bayporter.com) shuttle service is $26 for the first person, $12 for each additional person, to downtown San Francisco; it costs more to the city's outlying neighborhoods.

The cheapest way to reach downtown San Francisco from either airport is to take the shuttle bus to **BART** (Bay Area Rapid Transit; © 510/464-6000; www.bart.gov). The AirBART shuttle bus runs about every 15 minutes Monday through Saturday from 5am to 12:05am and Sunday from 8am to 12:05am. It makes pickups in front of terminals 1 and 2 near the ground transportation signs. Tickets must be purchased at the Oakland Airport's vending machines prior to boarding. The cost is $2 for the 10-minute ride to BART's Coliseum station in Oakland. BART fares vary, depending on your destination; the trip to downtown San Francisco costs $3.15 and takes 15 minutes once you're on board.

BY TRAIN San Francisco–bound **Amtrak** (© 800/USA-RAIL [872-7245]; www.amtrak.com) trains leave from New York and cross the country via Chicago. The journey takes about $3^1/_2$ days, and seats sell quickly. At this writing, the lowest round-trip fare costs about $300 from New York and $270 from Chicago. Round-trip tickets from Los Angeles range from $120 to as much as $200. Trains arrive in Emeryville, just north of Oakland, and connect with buses to San Francisco's Ferry Building and the Caltrain station in downtown San Francisco.

Caltrain (© 800/660-4287 or 415/546-4461; www.caltrain.com) operates train service between San Francisco and the towns of the peninsula. The city depot is at 700 Fourth St., at Townsend Street.

BY CAR Major routes into San Francisco are **U.S. 101** and **Hwy. 1** from the north (Sonoma and the Napa Valley) and south (San Jose), and **I-80** and **I-580** from the northeast (Sacramento) and east, respectively.

VISITOR INFORMATION The **San Francisco Visitor Information Center,** on the lower level of Hallidie Plaza, 900 Market St., at Powell Street (© 415/391-2000; www.onlyinsanfrancisco.com), is the best source of information about the city. You might want to request the free *Visitors Planning Guide* and the *San Francisco Visitors* kit. The kit includes a 6-month calendar of events; a city history; shopping and dining information; several good, clear maps; plus lodging information.

GETTING AROUND The **San Francisco Municipal Transportation Agency,** better known as "Muni" (© 415/673-6864; www.sfmuni.com), operates the city's cable cars, buses, and streetcars. These three services crisscross the entire city. Fares for buses and streetcars are $1.50 for adults; 50¢ for seniors 65 and over, children 5 to 17, and riders with disabilities. Cable cars, which run from 6:30am to 12:50am, cost $5 for all people 56 and over ($1 for seniors and riders with disabilities 9pm–7am).

BART, an acronym for **Bay Area Rapid Transit** (© 650/992-2278), is a high-speed rail network that connects San Francisco with the East Bay. Fares range from $1.45 to $7.45. Trains run Monday through Friday from 4am to midnight, Saturday from 6am to midnight, and Sunday from 8am to midnight.

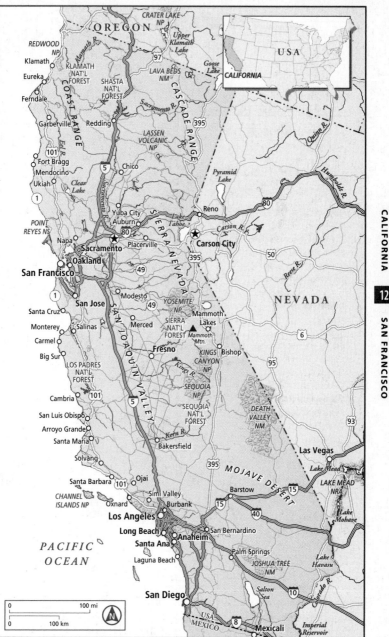

CALIFORNIA

12

SAN FRANCISCO

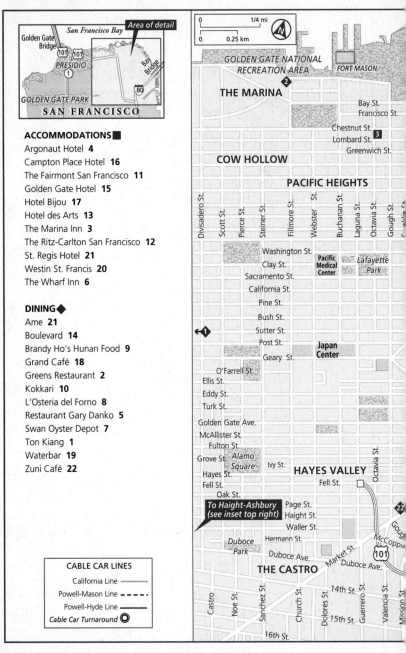

ACCOMMODATIONS ■
Argonaut Hotel **4**
Campton Place Hotel **16**
The Fairmont San Francisco **11**
Golden Gate Hotel **15**
Hotel Bijou **17**
Hotel des Arts **13**
The Marina Inn **3**
The Ritz-Carlton San Francisco **12**
St. Regis Hotel **21**
Westin St. Francis **20**
The Wharf Inn **6**

DINING ◆
Ame **21**
Boulevard **14**
Brandy Ho's Hunan Food **9**
Grand Café **18**
Greens Restaurant **2**
Kokkari **10**
L'Osteria del Forno **8**
Restaurant Gary Danko **5**
Swan Oyster Depot **7**
Ton Kiang **1**
Waterbar **19**
Zuni Café **22**

CABLE CAR LINES
California Line
Powell-Mason Line
Powell-Hyde Line
Cable Car Turnaround ◉

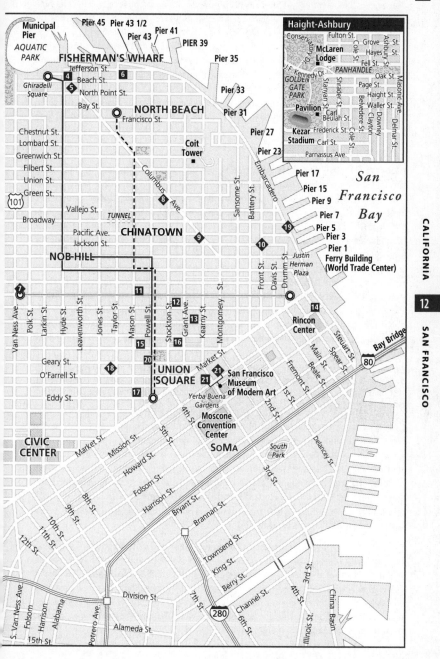

Municipal Pier
AQUATIC PARK
Ghiradelli Square
FISHERMAN'S WHARF
Pier 45
Pier 43 1/2
Pier 43
Pier 41
PIER 39
Pier 35
Jefferson St.
Beach St.
North Point St.
Bay St.
NORTH BEACH
Francisco St.
Pier 33
Pier 31
Pier 27
Pier 23
Chestnut St.
Lombard St.
Greenwich St.
Filbert St.
Union St.
Green St.
101
Broadway
Vallejo St.
TUNNEL
Pacific Ave.
Jackson St.
NOB-HILL
Coit Tower
Columbus Ave.
CHINATOWN
Sansome St.
Battery St.
Embarcadero
Pier 17
Pier 15
Pier 9
Pier 7
Pier 5
Pier 3
Pier 1
Ferry Building (World Trade Center)
Justin Herman Plaza
Front St.
Davis St.
Drumm St.

San Francisco Bay

Van Ness Ave.
Polk St.
Larkin St.
Hyde St.
Leavenworth St.
Jones St.
Taylor St.
Mason St.
Powell St.
Stockton St.
Grant Ave.
Kearny St.
Montgomery
St.
Rincon Center
Steuart St.
Main St.
Spear St.
Beale St.
Fremont St.
1st St.
2nd St.
Bay Bridge
80
Geary St.
O'Farrell St.
Eddy St.
UNION SQUARE
Market St.
San Francisco Museum of Modern Art
Yerba Buena Gardens
Moscone Convention Center
SoMa
South Park
Delancey St.
3rd St.
CIVIC CENTER
Market St.
Mission St.
Howard St.
Folsom St.
Harrison St.
Bryant St.
Brannan St.
8th St.
9th St.
10th St.
11th St.
12th St.
Townsend St.
King St.
Berry St.
3rd St.
4th St.
China Basin
S. Van Ness Ave.
Folsom
Harrison
Alabama
Potrero Ave.
15th St.
Division St.
Alameda St.
7th St.
6th St.
Channel St.
Illinois St.
280

Haight-Ashbury
Conservatory Dr.
Fulton St.
McLaren Lodge
Grove St.
Hayes St.
Fell St.
Cole St.
Ashbury St.
PANHANDLE
J.F. Kennedy Dr.
GOLDEN GATE PARK
Stanyan St.
Shrader St.
Oak St.
Page St.
Haight St.
Waller St.
Belvedere St.
Clayton
Downey
Cole St.
Masonic Ave.
Delmar St.
Pavilion
Carl Beulah St.
Kezar Stadium
Frederick St.
Carl St.
Parnassus Ave.

Saint Francis Memorial Hospital, 900 Hyde St., between Bush and Pine streets, Nob Hill (☎ 415/353-6000), provides 24-hour emergency care. The hospital also operates a physician-referral service (☎ 800/333-1355). The **Walgreens** on Divisadero Street at Lombard (☎ 415/931-6415) has a 24-hour pharmacy.

San Francisco, like any large city, has its fair share of crime and a serious homelessness problem. Exercise extra caution, particularly at night, in the Tenderloin, the Mission District (especially around 16th and Mission sts.), the lower Fillmore area, around lower Haight Street, and SoMa (south of Market St.).

An 8.5% **sales tax** is added to all goods and services. Hotel tax is charged on the room tariff only (which is not subject to sales tax) and is set by the city, ranging from 12% to 17% around Northern California.

WHAT TO SEE & DO

Alcatraz Island The sheer cliffs, treacherous tides and currents, and frigid temperatures of the surrounding water supposedly made "the Rock" an escape-proof prison. Among the famous gangsters who did time here were Al Capone, Robert Stroud (the Birdman of Alcatraz), and Machine Gun Kelly. In 1963, after an apparent escape in which no bodies were recovered, the government closed the prison, and in 1972 it became part of the Golden Gate National Recreation Area. Tours of Alcatraz include the ferry ride, an audio tour of the prison block, and a slide show. The excursion to Alcatraz is very popular and space is limited, so purchase tickets as far in advance as possible (up to 90 days) via the **Alcatraz Cruises** website at www.alcatrazcruises.com. You can also purchase tickets in person by visiting the Hornblower Alcatraz Landing ticket office at Pier 33. The first departure, called the "Early Bird," leaves at 9am, and ferries depart about every half-hour afterward until 2pm. Night tours (highly recommended) are also available Thursday through Monday and are a more intimate and wonderfully spooky experience.

Pier 41, near Fisherman's Wharf. ☎ 415/981-7625. www.alcatrazcruises.com or www.nps.gov/alcatraz. Admission (includes ferry trip and audio tour) $25 adults, $23 seniors 62 and older, $15 children 5–11. Night tours cost $32 adults, $29 seniors 62 and older, $19 children 5–11. Arrive at least 20 min. before departure time.

Cable Cars Designated official historic landmarks by the National Park Service, the city's beloved cable cars clank across the hills like mobile museum pieces. Each weighs about 6 tons and is hauled along by a steel cable under the street. They move at a constant 9½ mph. This may strike you as slow, but it doesn't feel that way when you're cresting an almost perpendicular hill and looking down at what seems like a bobsled dive straight into the ocean. But in spite of the thrills, they're perfectly safe.

Powell–Hyde and Powell–Mason lines begin at the base of Powell and Market sts.; California St. line begins at the foot of Market St. $5 per ride.

Coit Tower In a city known for its panoramic views and vantage points, Coit Tower is "The Peak." If it's a clear day, it's wonderful to get here by walking up the Filbert Steps. Inside the base of the tower are the impressive WPA murals titled *Life in California, 1934,* which were completed during the New Deal by more than 25 artists, many of whom had studied under master muralist Diego Rivera. You can see the murals for free, so we recommend not paying the admission to go to the top; the view is just as good from the parking area.

Telegraph Hill. ☎ 415/362-0808. Admission is free to enter; elevator ride to the top is $4.50 adults, $3.50 seniors, $2 children 6–12. Daily 10am–6pm. Bus: 39 (Coit).

The Exploratorium (Kids)   *Scientific American* magazine rated the Exploratorium "the best science museum in the world." This fun, hands-on science fair contains more than 650 permanent exhibits that explore everything from color theory to Einstein's theory of relativity. Every exhibit is designed to be used. You can whisper into a concave reflector and have a friend hear you 60 feet away, or design your own animated abstract art—using sound. Touch a tornado, shape a glowing electrical current, or take a sensory journey in total darkness in the **Tactile Dome** ($3 extra, and call ✆ 415/561-0362 to make advance reservations)—even if you spent all day here you couldn't experience everything. The museum is in the Marina District at the beautiful **Palace of Fine Arts,** the only building left standing from the Panama-Pacific Exposition of 1915. The adjoining park with lagoon—the perfect place for an afternoon picnic—is home to ducks, swans, seagulls, and grouchy geese—bring bread.

3601 Lyon St., in the Palace of Fine Arts (at Marina Blvd.). ✆ **415/EXPLORE** (397-5673) or 561-0360 (recorded information). www.exploratorium.edu. Admission $14 adults; $11 seniors, youth 13–17, visitors with disabilities, and college students with ID; $9 children 4–12; free for children 3 and under. AE, MC, V. Tues–Sun 10am–5pm. Closed Mon except Martin Luther King, Jr., Day, Presidents' Day, Memorial Day, and Labor Day. Free parking. Bus: 28, 30, or Golden Gate Transit.

Golden Gate Bridge   The year 2007 marked the 70th birthday of possibly the most beautiful, and certainly the most photographed, bridge in the world. Often half-veiled by the city's trademark fog, San Francisco's Golden Gate Bridge, named for the strait leading from the Pacific Ocean to the San Francisco Bay, spans tidal currents, ocean waves, and battering winds to connect the City by the Bay with the Redwood Empire to the north. The mile-long steel link reaches a height of 746 feet above the water and is an awesome bridge to cross. Millions of pedestrians brave the cold, wind, and vibrations each year; it's one of the best ways to experience the bridge's scale. You can walk out onto the span from either end. From Marin's Vista Point, you can look back on one of the most famous cityscapes in the world.

Hwy. 101 N. www.goldengatebridge.org. $5 cash toll collected when driving south. Bridge-bound Golden Gate Transit buses (✆ **511**) depart hourly during the day for Marin County, starting from Mission and First sts. (across the street from the Transbay Terminal and stopping at Market and Seventh sts., at the Civic Center, along Van Ness Ave., at Lombard and Fillmore sts., and at Francisco and Richardson sts.).

Golden Gate Park (Best)   From the Conservatory of Flowers near the eastern end to Ocean Beach on the western border, Golden Gate Park is an interactive, 1,017-acre botanical symphony—and anyone who likes can play in the orchestra. Spend a sunny day lounging on the grass along JFK Drive, have a read in the Shakespeare Garden, stroll around Stow Lake, or visit the M. H. de Young Museum's spectacular home.

The park is made up of hundreds of gardens and attractions linked by wooded paths and roads, so make your first stop the **McLaren Lodge and Park Headquarters** (✆ **415/ 831-2700**) for a detailed overview of information. The best gardens, among dozens in the park, are the Conservatory of Flowers, Rhododendron Dell, the Rose Garden, the Strybing Arboretum and, at the western edge in spring, the thousands of tulips and daffodils around the Dutch windmill. The AIDS Memorial Grove is a special, low-key place for reflection, near the northeastern side of the park.

The park also contains recreational facilities such as tennis courts; playing fields for baseball, soccer, and polo; a golf course; riding stables; and fly-casting pools.

Btw. Fulton St. and Lincoln Way; main entrance at Fell and Stanyan sts. ✆ **415/831-2700.** Bus: 16AX, BX, 5, 6, 7, 66, or 71.

The Legion of Honor   Designed as a memorial to California's World War I casualties, this neoclassical structure is a replica of the Legion of Honor Palace in Paris, down to the inscription HONNEUR ET PATRIE above the portal. The exterior's grassy expanses, cliff-side paths, and view of the Golden Gate and downtown make this a must-visit attraction before you even get in the door. The inside is equally impressive: The museum's collection covers 4,000 years of art and includes paintings, sculpture, and decorative arts from Europe, as well as tapestries, prints, and drawings. The chronological display of 4,000 years of ancient and European art includes one of the world's finest collections of Rodin sculptures.

In Lincoln Park (34th Ave. and Clement St.). (© **415/750-3600** or 863-3330 (recorded information). www. thinker.org. Admission $10 adults, $7 seniors 65 and over, $6 youths 13–17 and college students with ID, free for children 12 and under. Fees may be higher for special exhibitions. Free 1st Tues of each month. Tues–Sun 9:30am–5:15pm. Bus: 18.

Lombard Street   Known (erroneously) as the "crookedest street in the world," the whimsically winding block of Lombard Street puts smiles on the faces of thousands of visitors each year. The elevation is so steep that the road has to snake back and forth to make a descent possible. This short stretch is one-way, downhill, and fun to drive. You can also take staircases up or down on either side of the street.

Btw. Hyde and Leavenworth sts.

San Francisco Museum of Modern Art (SFMOMA)   MOMA's collection consists of more than 23,000 works, including close to 5,000 paintings and sculptures by artists such as Henri Matisse, Jackson Pollock, and Willem de Kooning. Other artists represented include Diego Rivera, Georgia O'Keeffe, Paul Klee, the Fauvists, and exceptional holdings of Richard Diebenkorn. MOMA was also one of the first to recognize photography as a major art form; its extensive collection includes more than 12,000 photographs by such notables as Ansel Adams, Alfred Stieglitz, Edward Weston, and Henri Cartier-Bresson. Whatever you do, check out the fabulous MuseumStore and cafe.

151 Third St. (2 blocks south of Market St., across from Yerba Buena Gardens). (© **415/357-4000.** www. sfmoma.org. Admission $13 adults, $8 seniors, $7 students 13 and over with ID, free for children 12 and under. Half-price for all Thurs 6–9pm; free to all 1st Tues of each month. Thurs 11am–8:45pm; Fri–Tues 11am–5:45pm. Closed Wed and major holidays. Bus: 15, 30, or 45. Streetcar: J, K, L, or M to Montgomery.

San Francisco Zoo (& Children's Zoo) (Kids)   Founded at its present site near the ocean in 1929, the zoo is spread over 100 acres and houses more than 930 animals, including some 245 species of mammals, birds, reptiles, amphibians, and invertebrates. Exhibit highlights include the Lipman Family Lemur Forest, a forest setting for five endangered species of lemurs from Madagascar that features interactive components for the visitor, and Jones Family Gorilla World, a tranquil setting for a family group of western lowland gorillas. The 6-acre Children's Zoo offers kids and their families opportunities for close-up encounters with domestic rare breeds of goats, sheep, ponies, and horses in the Family Farm. One of the Children's Zoo's most popular exhibits is the Meerkat and Prairie Dog exhibit, where kids can crawl through tunnels and play in sand, just like these burrowing species.

Great Highway btw. Sloat Blvd. and Skyline Blvd. (© **415/753-7080.** www.sfzoo.org. Admission $11 adults, $8 for seniors 65 and over and youth 12–17, $5 for children 3–11, free for children 2 and under. Free to all 1st Wed of each month, except $2 fee for Children's Zoo. Carousel $2. Daily 10am–5pm. Bus: 23 or 18. Streetcar: L from downtown Market St. to the end of the line.

One could easily contend that no urban shoreline is as stunning as San Francisco's. Wrapping around the northern and western edges of the city, the **Golden Gate National Recreation Area** is run by the National Park Service, which lets visitors fully enjoy it as a park. Several landmarks line the shore, from which visitors have views of both the bay and the ocean. Muni runs service to most sites, including Aquatic Park, the Cliff House, and Ocean Beach. For more information, contact the **National Park Service** (© 415/561-4700; www.nps.gov/goga).

At the northern end of Fillmore Street, **Marina Green** is a favorite spot for flying kites or watching the sailboats on the bay. Just west of here begins the 3.5-mile paved **Golden Gate Promenade,** a favorite biking and hiking path, which leads to the fantastic, recently reestablished marshland preserve **Crissy Field,** one of the city's favorite natural playgrounds. Make a point of seeing this spectacular destination, with sandy beach, lots of native birds, and jogging paths.

A national historic site under the Golden Gate Bridge, **Fort Point** (© 415/556-1693; www.nps.gov/fopo) was built in 1853 to protect the entrance to the harbor. Film buffs will recognize it from Alfred Hitchcock's *Vertigo.*

Lincoln Boulevard sweeps around the western edge of the bay to two of the most popular beaches in San Francisco. **Baker Beach,** a small and beautiful strand just outside the Golden Gate, is a fine spot for sunbathing (nudists flock here), walking, or fishing. It's usually packed, but if the cold water doesn't deter you from swimming here, the roaring currents will. Here you can pick up the **Coastal Trail,** which leads through the Presidio, and a short distance from Baker, **China Beach** is a small cove where swimming is permitted. Changing rooms, showers, a sun deck, and restrooms are available. But be warned: The water is crazy-cold!

A little farther around the coast, **Land's End** looks out to Pyramid Rock. A lower and upper trail provide varied hiking options amid wind-swept cypress trees and pines on the cliffs above the Pacific.

Point Lobos, the **Sutro Baths,** and the **Cliff House** lie still farther along the coast. The Cliff House has been serving refreshments to visitors since 1863. Here you can view the **Seal Rocks,** home to a colony of sea lions and marine birds. Only traces of the Sutro Baths remain today, northeast of the Cliff House. This popular swimming facility accommodated as many as 24,000 people before it burned down in 1966. A little farther inland, at the western end of California Street, **Lincoln Park** is home to a golf course and the Legion of Honor.

From the Cliff House, the Esplanade continues south along the 4-mile-long **Ocean Beach,** which is unsuitable for swimming but popular with brave surfers. At the southern end of Ocean Beach, around **Fort Funston,** an easy loop trail runs across the cliffs; for information, call the ranger station (© 415/239-2366).

Farther south along I-280, **Sweeney Ridge** is accessible only by car but affords sweeping views of the coastline from the trails that crisscross these 1,000 acres of land.

The **Presidio,** a 1,480-acre former military base, is now an urban park that combines historical, architectural, and natural aspects. It's adjacent to the Golden Gate National Recreation Area, but you could wander from one to the other without knowing it. The Presidio is popular with hikers, bikers, bird-watchers, golfers, and joggers. The National Park Service operates walking and biking tours around the Presidio, including the 2-mile **Ecology Loop Trail** through some of the Presidio's 60,000 trees, such as redwoods,

CALIFORNIA

12

SAN FRANCISCO

spruce, cypress, and acacias; and the 2.5-mile **Coastal Trail,** from the bluff top from Baker Beach to the southern base of the Golden Gate Bridge. Reservations are required.

SHOPPING

UNION SQUARE   San Francisco's most congested and popular shopping mecca is home to big department stores and many high-end specialty shops. Be sure to venture to Grant Avenue, Post and Sutter streets, and Maiden Lane.

If you're into art, pick up the *San Francisco Gallery Guide,* a comprehensive bimonthly publication listing the city's current shows. One of our favorite galleries is the **Catharine Clark Gallery,** on the second floor at 49 Geary St., between Kearny and Grant streets (© 415/399-1439; www.cclarkgallery.com). It exhibits up-and-coming contemporary artists, mainly from California, and nurtures beginning collectors by offering an unusual interest-free purchasing plan.

CHINATOWN   When you pass under the gate to Chinatown on Grant Avenue, say goodbye to the world of fashion and hello to a swarm of cheap tourist shops selling everything from linen and jade to plastic toys and $2 slippers. Grant Avenue is the main thoroughfare, but the real gems are on the side streets between Bush Street and Columbus Avenue, in small, one-person shops selling herbs, original art, and jewelry.

SOMA   Though this area isn't suitable for strolling, you'll find almost all the discount shopping in warehouse spaces south of Market. You can pick up a discount shopping guide at most major hotels. At the **SFMOMA MuseumStore,** 151 Third St. (© 415/357-4035; www.sfmoma.org), the array of cards, books, jewelry, housewares, and knick-knacks makes it one of the locals' favorite shops. It also offers far more tasteful mementos than most Fisherman's Wharf options. Fashionable bargain hunters head to **Jeremys,** 2 S. Park, at Second Street between Bryant and Brannan streets (© 415/882-4929; www.jeremys.com), where top designer fashions, from shoes to suits, sell at rock-bottom prices.

THE CASTRO   You could easily spend all day wandering through the home and men's clothing shops of the Castro. We also come here to visit our favorite chocolate shop, **Joseph Schmidt Confections,** 3489 16th St., at Sanchez Street (© 415/861-8682; www.josephschmidtconfections.com), where sinfully luscious sweets take on sculptural shapes so exquisite you'll be reluctant to bite into them. Prices are remarkably reasonable.

FISHERMAN'S WHARF & ENVIRONS   The tourist-oriented malls—Ghirardelli Square, PIER 39, the Cannery at Del Monte Square, and the Anchorage—run along Jefferson Street and include hundreds of shops, restaurants, and attractions. Standing out from the usual T-shirt shops and fudge emporiums is **Cost Plus World Market,** 2552 Taylor St., between North Point and Bay streets (© 415/928-6200), a vast warehouse crammed to the rafters with Chinese baskets, Indian camel bells, Malaysian batik scarves, and innumerable other items from Algeria to Zanzibar.

FILLMORE STREET   Some of the best shopping in town is packed into 5 blocks of Fillmore Street in Pacific Heights. **Zinc Details,** 1905 Fillmore St., between Bush and Pine streets (© 415/776-2100; www.zincdetails.com), offers an amazing collection of modern and contemporary handcrafted glass vases, pendant lights, ceramics, and furniture.

HAIGHT STREET   The shopping in the 6 blocks of upper Haight Street, between Central Avenue and Stanyan Street, reflects its green-haired, spiked-haired, and no-haired clientele, offering everything from incense and European and American street styles to furniture and antique clothing. **Recycled Records,** 1377 Haight St., between Central and Masonic streets (© 415/626-4075; www.recycled-records.com), easily one of the best used-record stores in the city, has a good selection of promotional CDs and used classic rock LPs.

NORTH BEACH   Along with a great cup of coffee, Grant and Columbus avenues cater to their hip clientele with a small but worthy selection of boutiques and specialty shops. Join the funky literary types who browse **City Lights Booksellers & Publishers,** 261 Columbus Ave., at Broadway (© **415/362-8193;** www.citylights.com), the famous bookstore owned by Beat poet Lawrence Ferlinghetti. The shelves here are stocked with a comprehensive collection of art, poetry, and political paperbacks, as well as more mainstream books.

WHERE TO STAY

Most of the hotels listed below are within easy walking distance of Union Square, the city's premier shopping and tourist district. Prices listed below do not include state and city taxes, which total 14%.

San Francisco Reservations, 360 22nd St., Ste. 300, Oakland, CA 94612 (© **800/ 677-1500** or 510/628-4450; www.hotelres.com), arranges reservations for more than 150 of San Francisco's hotels and often offers discounted rates. Their nifty website allows Internet users to make reservations online.

Argonaut Hotel (Kids)   The Kimpton Hotel Group is behind Fisherman's Wharf's best hotel, half a block from the bay. The four-story timber-and-brick landmark building features comfortable rooms and suites whimsically decorated in cheerful nautical colors. Luxurious touches include flatscreen TVs, DVD and CD players, and Aveda toiletries. Suites have killer views, telescopes, and spa tubs. Get a "view" room, which peers onto the wharf or bay (some overlook Alcatraz). Argonaut's friendly staff goes out of their way to make little ones feel at home, making this a great choice for families. All guests are welcome at nightly weekday wine receptions.

495 Jefferson St (at Hyde St.), San Francisco, CA 94109. © **866/415-0704** or 415/563-0800. Fax 415/563-2800. www.argonauthotel.com. 252 units. $189–$389 double; $489–$1,089 suite. Rates include evening wine in the lobby, daily newspaper, and kid-friendly perks like cribs and strollers. AE, DC, DISC, MC, V. Parking $39. Bus: 10, 30, or 47. Streetcar: F. Cable car: Powell–Hyde line. **Amenities:** Restaurant; fitness center.

Campton Place Hotel   This fabulous Union Square boutique hotel offers some of the best accommodations in town—and among the most expensive. Rooms are compact but comfy, with limestone, pear wood, and Italian modern decor. Discriminating guests will find superlative service, California king-size beds, exquisite bathrooms, bathrobes, top-notch toiletries, slippers, and every other necessity and extra that's made Campton Place a favored temporary address.

340 Stockton St. (btw. Post and Sutter sts.), San Francisco, CA 94108. © **866/332-1670** or 415/781-5555. Fax 415/955-5536. www.camptonplace.com. 110 units. $350–$485 double; $585–$2,000 suite. American breakfast $18. AE, DC, MC, V. Valet parking $38. Bus: 2, 3, 4, 30, 38, or 45. Cable car: Powell–Hyde or Powell–Mason lines (1 block west). BART: Market St. **Amenities:** Restaurant; outdoor fitness terrace.

The Fairmont San Francisco   The granddaddy of Nob Hill's ritzy hotels, the historic Fairmont was designed by the same architect who dreamed up Hearst Castle and wins top honors for the most awe-inspiring lobby in town. Even if you're not staying, come gape at its marble columns, vaulted ceilings, velvet chairs, gilded mirrors, and spectacular wraparound staircase. And yes, such decadence carries to the guest rooms, where luxuries abound: oversize marble bathrooms, thick down blankets, goose-down king pillows, extra-long mattresses, and large walk-in closets. Because it's perched at the top of Nob Hill, there are spectacular city views from every guest room

950 Mason St. (at California St.), San Francisco, CA 94108. ✆ **866/540-4491** or 415/772-5000. Fax 415/772-5086. www.fairmont.com. 591 units. Main building $229–$349 double; from $500 suite. Tower $289–$469 double; from $750 suite. Penthouse $12,500. Extra person $30. AE, DC, DISC, MC, V. Parking $43. Cable car: California St. line (direct stop). **Amenities:** 2 restaurants; health club (free for Fairmont President's Club members; $15 per day or $20 for 2 days nonmembers). *In room:* Kitchenette (in some units).

Golden Gate Hotel   The best thing about the 1913 Edwardian hotel—which has a B&B feel—is that it's family run: John and Renate Kenaston and daughter Gabriele are hospitable innkeepers who take pleasure in making their guests comfortable. Each individually decorated room has antique furnishings (plenty of wicker) from the early 1900s, quilted bedspreads, and fresh flowers. Request a room with a claw-foot tub if you enjoy a good, hot soak. Afternoon tea is served daily from 4 to 7pm, and guests are welcome to use the house fax and computer with wireless Internet free of charge.

775 Bush St. (btw. Powell and Mason sts.), San Francisco, CA 94108. ✆ **800/835-1118** or 415/392-3702. Fax 415/392-6202. www.goldengatehotel.com. 25 units, 14 with bathroom. $85–$105 double without bathroom; $150 double with bathroom. Rates include continental breakfast and afternoon tea. AE, DC, MC, V. Self-parking $20. Bus: 2, 4, 30, 38, or 45. Cable car: Powell–Hyde or Powell–Mason lines (1 block east). BART: Powell and Market. **Amenities:** Access to health club 1 block away.

Hotel Bijou ⓥ**alue**   Three words sum up this hotel: clean, colorful, and cheap. Once inside this gussied-up 1911 hotel, all's cheery, bright, and perfect for budget travelers who want a little style with their savings. There's lively decor, a Deco theater theme, and a lot of vibrant paint. To the left of the small lobby is a "theater" where guests can watch San Francisco–based double features (it has theater seating, though it's just a TV showing videos). Upstairs, rooms named after locally made films are small, clean, and colorful, and have all the basics, from clock radios, dressers, and small desks to tiny bathrooms (one of which is so small you have to close the door to access the toilet).

111 Mason St., San Francisco, CA 94102. ✆ **800/771-1022** or 415/771-1200. Fax 415/346-3196. www.hotelbijou.com. 65 units. $99–$159 double. Rates include continental breakfast. AE, DC, DISC, MC, V. Valet parking $27. Bus: All Market St. buses. Streetcar: Powell St. station.

Hotel des Arts ⓥ**alue**   The lobby of this Euro-style hotel hosts a rotating art gallery featuring works by emerging artists and is outfitted with groovy furnishings, while the guest rooms offer quality furnishings and tasteful accouterments. There's one suite that can sleep up to four persons at no additional charge. You'll love the location as well: across the street from the entrance to Chinatown and 2 blocks from Union Square. There's even a French brasserie downstairs. Rooms with a very clean shared bathroom start at $59, making it quite possibly the best budget hotel in the city.

447 Bush St. (at Grant St.), San Francisco, CA 94108. ✆ **800/956-4322** or 415/956-3232. Fax 415/956-0399. www.sfhoteldesarts.com. 51 units, 26 with private bathroom. $79–$159 double with bathroom; $59–$79 double without bathroom. Rates include continental breakfast. AE, DC, MC, V. Nearby parking $18. Cable car: Powell–Hyde and Powell–Mason lines. *In room:* Minifridge and microwave in many rooms.

The Marina Inn ⓥ**alue**   Each guest room in the 1924 four-story Victorian looks like something from a country furnishings catalog, complete with rustic pinewood furniture, a four-poster bed with silky-soft comforter, pretty wallpaper, and soothing tones of rose, hunter green, and pale yellow. You also get remote-control televisions discreetly hidden in pine cabinetry—all for as little as $75 a night. Combine that with continental breakfast, friendly service, free Wi-Fi, and a great location, and there you have it: one of the best low-priced hotels in town.

3110 Octavia St. (at Lombard St.), San Francisco, CA 94123. ⓒ **800/274-1420** or 415/928-1000. Fax **831**
415/928-5909. www.marinainn.com. 40 units. Nov–Feb $75–$115 double; Mar–May $85–$135 double;
June–Oct $95–$145 double. Rates include continental breakfast. AE, DC, DISC, MC, V. Bus: 28, 30, 43, or 76.

The Ritz-Carlton, San Francisco ⓑest   Ranked among the top hotels in the world
by readers of *Condé Nast Traveler,* the Ritz-Carlton has been the benchmark of Nob Hill's
luxury hotels since 1991, and it's the best in town. Just to make sure they stay on top,
the rooms were completely upgraded in 2007 to the tune of $13 million and now include
32-inch LCD TVs, DVD/CD players, and Wi-Fi. The Italian marble bathrooms offer
every possible amenity, including double sinks, name-brand toiletries, and plush terry
robes. Club rooms, on the top floors, have a dedicated concierge, separate elevator-key
access, and complimentary small plates throughout the day.

600 Stockton St. (btw. Pine and California sts.), San Francisco, CA 94108. ⓒ **800/241-3333** or 415/296-
7465. Fax 415/986-1268. www.ritzcarlton.com. 336 units. $445–$480 double; $600–$850 club-level double; from $750–$850 executive suite. Buffet breakfast $32; Sun champagne brunch $65. Weekend
discounts and packages available. AE, DC, DISC, MC, V. Parking $55. Cable car: California St. cable car line
(direct stop). **Amenities:** 2 restaurants; indoor pool; fitness center.

St. Regis Hotel   The latest in full-blown high-tech luxury is yours at this superchic
40-story SoMa tower near Yerba Buena Gardens. A shrine to urban luxury living, it
welcomes guests with a trendy lobby bar. Decor is minimalist, with sexy touches like
Barcelona benches, 42-inch plasma TVs, and leather paneling (in the suites). Bathrooms
beckon with soaking tubs, 13-inch LCD TVs, rainforest shower heads, and fancy toiletries. There's also the posh two-floor **Remède Spa** and restaurant **Ame,** where Chef Hiro
Sone presides over an Asian-influenced luxury menu.

125 Third St. (at Mission St.), San Francisco, CA 94103. ⓒ **877/787-3447** or 415/284-4000. Fax 415/284-
4100. www.stregis.com/sanfrancisco. 260 units. From $529–$679 double; from $1,050–$8,500 suite. AE,
DC, DISC, MC, V. Parking $45 per day. Bus: 15, 30, or 45. Streetcar: J, K, L, or M to Montgomery. **Amenities:**
2 restaurants; health club w/heated lap pool; spa.

Westin St. Francis Ⓚids   At the turn of the 20th century, Charles T. Crocker and a
few of his wealthy buddies decided that San Francisco needed a world-class hotel, and up
went the St. Francis. Since then, hordes of VIPs have hung their hats and hosiery here.
The older rooms of the main building vary in size and have more old-world charm than
the newer rooms, but the Tower is remarkable for its great views of the city (including
from the glass elevators) from above the 18th floor. The hotel has done massive renovations costing $185 million over the past decade, including adding the very expensive and
fancy **Michael Mina** restaurant.

335 Powell St. (btw. Geary and Post sts.), San Francisco, CA 94102. ⓒ **866/500-0038** or 415/397-7000.
Fax 415/774-0124. www.westinstfrancis.com. 1,195 units. Main building $229–$529 double; Tower
(Grand View) $219–$559 double; from $650 suite (in either building). Extra person $30. Continental
breakfast $15–$18. AE, DC, DISC, MC, V. Valet parking $42. Bus: 2, 3, 4, 30, 38, 45, or 76. Cable car: Powell–
Hyde or Powell–Mason lines (direct stop). Pets under 40 lb. accepted (dog beds available on request).
Amenities: 2 restaurants; elaborate health club and spa.

The Wharf Inn Ⓚids   For good-value/great-location lodging at Fisherman's Wharf, the
Wharf Inn offers above-average accommodations. The well-stocked rooms are done in
handsome tones of earth, muted greens, and burnt orange, and are smack-dab in the
middle of the wharf, 2 blocks from PIER 39 and the cable car turnaround, and within
walking distance of the Embarcadero and North Beach. The inn is ideal for car-bound
families because parking is free (that saves at least $25 a day right off the bat).

2601 Mason St. (at Beach St.), San Francisco, CA 94133. ✆ **877/275-7889** or 415/673-7411. Fax 415/776-2181. www.wharfinn.com. 51 units. $99–$209 double; $299–$439 penthouse. AE, DC, DISC, MC, V. Free parking. Bus: 10, 15, 39, or 47. Streetcar: F. Cable car: Powell–Mason or Powell–Hyde lines. **Amenities:** Access to nearby health club ($10 per day).

WHERE TO DINE

San Francisco's dining scene is one of the best in the world. Since our space is limited, we had to make tough choices, but the end result is a cross section of the best in every cuisine and price range. For top restaurants, make your reservation weeks in advance.

Ame ECLECTIC   Restaurateurs Hiro Sone and Lissa Doumani have blessed us foodies with a fantastic restaurant. On the ground level of the *très* chic St. Regis Hotel, the dining room, with its mesquite flooring, red accents, and long striped curtains, fits in with the hotel's minimalist theme. Sone, a master of Japanese, French, and Italian cuisines, offers an array of exotic selections that are utterly tempting, like grilled Wagyu beef with fried Miyagi oysters and rémoulade sauce. If you can't figure out where to start, opt for Sone's **A Taste of Ame,** an $81 five-course tasting menu that, for an additional $60, is paired with a bevy of wines by the glass. After dinner, be sure to enjoy an aperitif at the hotel's swank bar, where the city's elite congregate nightly.

689 Mission St. (at Third St.). ✆ **415/284-4040.** www.amerestaurant.com. Reservations recommended. Main courses $19–$25 lunch, $22–$35 dinner. AE, DC, DISC, MC, V. Daily 5:30–10pm. Valet parking $12 for the 1st 3 hr. Bus: 15, 30, or 45. Streetcar: J, K, L, or M to Montgomery.

Boulevard ⓑ**Best** AMERICAN   This SoMa spot is our pick for the best in the city. Why? The dramatic Belle Epoque interior combined with well-sculpted, mouthwatering dishes. The main courses might include grilled Pacific sea bass with fresh gulf prawns, grilled artichoke, spring asparagus, and green garlic purée. Vegetarian items, such as wild mushroom risotto with fresh chanterelles and Parmesan, are also offered. Three levels of formality—bar, open kitchen, and main dining room—keep things from getting too snobby. Although its prices are high, you'd be hard-pressed to find a better place for a special, fun-filled occasion.

1 Mission St. (btw. Embarcadero and Steuart sts.). ✆ **415/543-6084.** www.boulevardrestaurant.com. Reservations recommended. Main courses $14–$22 lunch, $28–$39 dinner. AE, DC, DISC, MC, V. Mon–Fri 11:30am–2pm; Sun–Thurs 5:30–10pm; Fri–Sat 5:30–10:30pm. Valet parking $12 lunch, $10 dinner. Bus: 12, 15, 30, 32, or 41. BART: Embarcadero.

Brandy Ho's Hunan Food ⓚ**Kids** CHINESE   Fancy black-and-white granite tabletops and a large, open kitchen are the first clues that the food at this casual, fun restaurant is a cut above the usual Hunan fare. Take my advice and start immediately with fried dumplings (in sweet-and-sour sauce) or cold chicken salad, and then move on to fish-ball soup with spinach, bamboo shoots, noodles, and other goodies. The best main course is Three Delicacies, a combination of scallops, shrimp, and chicken with onion, bell pepper, and bamboo shoots, seasoned with ginger, garlic, and wine, and served with black-bean sauce. Most dishes are hot and spicy, but the kitchen will adjust the level of heat to your specifications. A full bar includes Asian food–friendly libations such as plum wine and sake from 11:30am to 11pm.

217 Columbus Ave. (at Pacific Ave.). ✆ **415/788-7527.** www.brandyhos.com. Reservations recommended. Main courses $8–$13. AE, DISC, MC, V. Sun–Thurs 11:30am–11pm; Fri–Sat 11:30am–midnight. Paid parking available at 170 Columbus Ave. Bus: 15 or 41.

Grand Café FRENCH   If you want a huge dose of atmosphere with your seared salmon, Grand Café is your best bet. It's the most *grand* dining room in San Francisco, an enormous turn-of-the-20th-century ballroom–like dining oasis that's a magnificent combination of old Europe and Art Nouveau, and a festive (read: crowded) cocktail area. To match the surroundings, Chef Ron Boyd, a San Francisco native and Domaine Chandon alum, serves dressed-up French-inspired California dishes such as sautéed salmon with French lentils and house-cured bacon or salade niçoise. You can also drop by for a lighter meal in the more casual front room, the Petit Café, which offers a raw bar and similar dishes for about half the price.

501 Geary St. (at Taylor St., adjacent to the Hotel Monaco). ✆ **415/292-0101.** www.grandcafe-sf.com. Reservations recommended. Main courses $18–$28. AE, DC, DISC, MC, V. Mon–Fri 7–10:30am; Sat 8am–2:30pm; Sun 9am–2:30pm; Mon–Fri 11:30am–2:30pm; Sun–Thurs 5:30–10pm; Fri–Sat 5:30–11pm. Valet parking free at brunch, $15 for 3 hr. at dinner, $3 each additional half-hour. Bus: 2, 3, 4, 27, or 38.

Greens Restaurant VEGETARIAN   Knowledgeable locals swear by Greens, where Executive Chef Annie Somerville cooks with the seasons, using produce from local organic farms. In an old warehouse, with enormous windows overlooking the bridge and the bay, the restaurant is both a pioneer and a legend. Entrees run the gamut from pizza with wilted escarole, red onions, lemon, and Parmesan to Vietnamese yellow curry. Those interested in the whole shebang should make reservations for the $48 four-course dinner served Saturday only. Lunch and brunch are equally fresh and tasty. The adjacent Greens to Go sells sandwiches, soups, salads, and pastries.

Building A, Fort Mason Center (enter Fort Mason opposite the Safeway at Buchanan and Marina sts.). ✆ **415/771-6222.** www.greensrestaurant.com. Reservations recommended. Main courses $9.50–$14 lunch, $15–$20 dinner; fixed-price dinner $48; Sun brunch $8–$14. AE, DISC, MC, V. Tues–Sat noon–2:30pm; Sun 10:30am–9pm; Mon–Sat 5:30–9pm. Greens to Go Mon–Thurs 8am–8pm; Fri–Sat 8am–5pm; Sun 10:30am–4pm. Parking in hourly lot $4 for up to 2¹/₂ hr. Bus: 28 or 30.

Kokkari ⓥⓐⓛⓤⓔ GREEK   Kokkari (Ko-*car*-ee) takes Greek food to delicious contemporary heights—in both decor and flavor. The dining area is like a rustic living room, with a commanding fireplace and oversize furnishings. Delicious, traditional Aegean dishes include a moussaka (eggplant, lamb, potato, and béchamel) that's to die for, or the quail stuffed with winter greens served on oven-roasted leeks, orzo, and wild-rice *pilafi*.

200 Jackson St. (at Front St.). ✆ **415/981-0983.** www.kokkari.com. Reservations recommended. Main courses $14–$23 lunch, $19–$35 dinner. AE, DC, DISC, MC, V. Mon–Fri 11:30am–2:30pm; bar menu 2:30–5:30pm; Mon–Thurs 5:30–10pm; Fri 5:30–11pm; Sat 5–11pm. Valet parking (dinner only) $8. Bus: 12, 15, 41, or 83.

L'Osteria del Forno ITALIAN   It's not much bigger than a closet, but L'Osteria del Forno is one of the top Italian restaurants in North Beach. Peer in the window, and you'll probably see two Italian women sweating from the heat of the brick oven, which cranks out the best focaccia in the city. There's no pomp or circumstance: Locals come here strictly to eat. The menu features a variety of pizzas, salads, soups, and pastas, plus daily specials. Good news for folks on the go: You can get pizza by the slice.

519 Columbus Ave. (btw. Green and Union sts.). ✆ **415/982-1124.** www.losteriadelforno.com. Reservations not accepted. Sandwiches $6–$7; pizzas $10–$18; main courses $6–$14. No credit cards. Sun–Mon and Wed–Thurs 11:30am–10pm; Fri–Sat 11:30am–10:30pm. Bus: 15, 30, 41, or 45.

Restaurant Gary Danko MODERN CLASSIC   Gary Danko, who received the James Beard Foundation award for best chef in California, presides over this romantic yet unfussy dining room. The three- to five-course menu is freestyle, so whether you want a sampling of appetizers or a flight of meat courses, you need only ask. Top picks? Glazed oysters, which are as creamy as the light accompanying sauce graced with leeks and intricately carved "zucchini pearls." *Tip:* If you can't get a reservation and are set on dining here, slip in and grab a seat at the 10-stool first-come, first-served bar, where you can also order a la carte.

800 N. Point St. (at Hyde St.). ✆ 415/749-2060. www.garydanko.com. Reservations required except at walk-in bar. 3- to 5-course fixed-price menu $61–$89. AE, DC, DISC, MC, V. Daily 5:30–10pm. Bar open 5pm. Valet parking $10. Bus: 10. Streetcar: F. Cable car: Hyde.

Swan Oyster Depot SEAFOOD   Turning 96 years old in 2008, Swan Oyster Depot is a classic San Francisco dining experience you shouldn't miss. This tiny hole in the wall, run by the city's friendliest servers, is little more than a narrow fish market that decided to slap down some bar stools. Most patrons come for a quick cup of chowder or a plate of oysters on the half shell that arrive chilling on crushed ice. *Note:* Don't let the lunch-time line dissuade you—it moves fast.

1517 Polk St. (btw. California and Sacramento sts.). ✆ 415/673-1101. Reservations not accepted. Sea-food cocktails $7–$15; clams and oysters on the half-shell $7.95 per half-dozen. No credit cards. Mon–Sat 8am–5:30pm. Bus: 1, 19, 47, or 49.

Ton Kiang ⓚ **Kids** CHINESE/DIM SUM   Ton Kiang is the number-one place in the city to do dim sum. From stuffed crab claws, roast Peking duck, and a gazillion dumpling selections to the delicious and hard-to-find *doa miu* (snow-pea sprouts, flash-sautéed with garlic and peanut oil) and a mesmerizing mango pudding, every tray of morsels is an absolute delight. Though it's hard to get past the dim sum, which is served all day every day, the full menu of Hakka cuisine is worth investigation as well—flavorful soups; an array of seafood, beef, and chicken; and clay-pot specialties.

5821 Geary Blvd. (btw. 22nd and 23rd aves.). ✆ 415/387-8273. www.tonkiang.net. Reservations accepted for parties of 8 or more. Dim sum $2–$5.50; main courses $9–$25. AE, DC, DISC, MC, V. Mon–Thurs 10am–10pm; Fri 10am–10:30pm; Sat 9:30am–10:30pm; Sun 9am–10pm. Bus: 38.

Waterbar SEAFOOD   Renowned restaurant designer Pat Kuleto unleashed his imagination and created a most visually playful decor. The focal point is a pair of 19-foot floor-to-ceiling circular aquariums filled with fish and marine critters from the Pacific Ocean. The aquatic theme ebbs along with a glass "caviar" chandelier and a horseshoe-shaped raw bar. Even the open kitchen is visually—and aromatically—pleasing. The menu offers a wide selection of market-driven, sustainable seafood such as Dover sole served whole (a whopping $80), but more fun can be had at the raw bar. Either way, start off with the superb sea scallop seviche infused with sweet potato, smoked salt, and paprika. If the weather is agreeable, request a table on the patio.

399 Embarcadero (at Harrison St.). ✆ 415/284-9922. www.waterbarsf.com. Reservations recom-mended. Main courses $28–$36. AE, DISC, MC, V. Daily 11:30am–2pm and 5:30–10pm. Valet parking $15 lunch, $10 dinner. Bus: 1, 12, 14, or 41. Streetcar: F. BART: Embarcadero. Fri 11:30am–2pm; Mon–Sat 5:30–10:30pm; Sun 5:30–9:30pm. Bus: All Market St. buses.

Zuni Café MEDITERRANEAN   Trendsetting Zuni Café is, and probably always will be, a local favorite. Its expanse of windows and prime lower Castro location guarantee good people-watching, but even better is the incredibly satisfying menu. Stand at the bustling bar, order a glass of wine and a few oysters, and then take a seat amid the exposed-brick maze of little dining rooms. If you're there for lunch or after 10pm, the hamburger on grilled rosemary focaccia bread is a strong contender for the city's best. Whatever you decide, be sure to order a stack of shoestring potatoes.

1658 Market St. (at Franklin St.). ✆ 415/552-2522. www.zunicafe.com. Reservations recommended. Main courses $10–$19 lunch, $15–$29 dinner. AE, MC, V. Tues–Sat 11:30am–midnight; Sun 11am–11pm. Valet parking $10. Bus: 6, 7, or 71. Streetcar: All Market St. streetcars.

For up-to-date information, turn to the *San Francisco Weekly* (www.sfweekly.com) and the *San Francisco Bay Guardian* (www.sfbg.com), both of which run comprehensive listings. They are available free at bars and restaurants and from street-corner boxes all around the city. *Where* (www.wheresf.com), a free tourist-oriented monthly, also lists programs and performance times; it's available in most of the city's finer hotels. The Sunday edition of the *San Francisco Chronicle* features a "Datebook" section, printed on pink paper, with information on and listings of the week's events.

Tix Bay Area (also known as **TIX;** © **415/433-7827;** www.tixbayarea.org) sells half-price tickets on the day of performance and full-price tickets in advance to select Bay Area cultural and sporting events. Tickets are primarily sold in person, with some half-price tickets available on their website. A service charge, ranging from $1.75 to $6, is levied on each ticket, depending on its full price. You can pay with cash, traveler's checks, Visa, MasterCard, American Express, or Discover Card with photo ID. TIX, on Powell Street between Geary and Post streets, is open Tuesday through Thursday from 11am to 6pm, Friday from 11am to 7pm, Saturday from 10am to 7pm, and Sunday from 10am to 3pm. *Note:* Half-price tickets go on sale at 11am.

Get tickets to theater and dance events through **City Box Office,** 180 Redwood St., Ste. 100, between Golden Gate and McAllister streets off Van Ness Avenue (© **415/392-4400;** www.cityboxoffice.com). MasterCard and Visa are accepted.

For information on local theater, check out **www.bayareatheatre.org.**

THE PERFORMING ARTS The **American Conservatory Theater** (© **415/749-2ACT** [492-2228]; www.act-sf.org), one of the nation's premier theater ensembles, performs at the Geary Theater, 415 Geary St., at Mason Street, and features both classical and experimental works.

The **San Francisco Symphony** (© **415/864-6000;** www.sfsymphony.org), led by Michael Tilson Thomas, performs at Davies Symphony Hall, 201 Van Ness Ave., at Grove Street.

The War Memorial Opera House, 301 Van Ness Ave., at Grove Street, is home to performances of both the **San Francisco Ballet** (© **415/865-2000;** www.sfballet.org), the oldest professional ballet company in the nation, and the **San Francisco Opera** (© **415/864-3330;** www.sfopera.org), the first municipal opera in the United States.

COMEDY & CABARET A San Francisco tradition for 32 years, *Beach Blanket Babylon,* Club Fugazi, 678 Green St. (© **415/421-4222;** www.beachblanketbabylon.com), is known for its outrageous costumes and oversize headdresses. Almost every performance sells out, so get tickets well in advance.

JAZZ & BLUES CLUBS **Biscuits & Blues,** 401 Mason St. (© **415/292-2583;** www.biscuitsandblues.com), boasts a blow-your-eardrums-out sound system in a New Orleans–style basement speak-easy. **Lou's Pier 47 Club,** 300 Jefferson St. (© **415/771-5687;** www.louspier47.com), attracts few locals but hosts decent jazz, blues, rock, and country bands near the Wharf. If there's one good-time destination that's an anchor for the party people, it's Embarcadero's **Pier 23,** at the Embarcadero and Greenwich Street (© **415/362-5125;** www.pier23cafe.com). Part ramshackle patio spot and part dance floor, with a heavy dash of dive bar, here it's all about fun for a startlingly diverse clientele. Expect to boogie down shoulder-to-shoulder to live bands playing blues or funk. **Cafe du Nord,** 2170 Market St. (© **415/861-5016**), has been around since 1907, but only recently convinced a younger generation to appreciate it as a respectable jazz venue, with American fare, live music, and a front-room bar.

SUPPER CLUBS If you can eat dinner, listen to live music, and dance in the same room, we call it a supper club, and **Harry Denton's Starlight Room,** at the Sir Francis Drake Hotel, 450 Powell St., 21st floor (© **415/395-8595;** www.harrydenton.com), is one of the best. Everyone comes to this 1930s-era lounge-turned-nightclub to sip drinks at sunset and boogie to live swing and big-band tunes after dark. **Jazz at Pearls,** 256 Columbus Ave. (© **415/291-8255;** www.jazzatpearls.com), is one of the best supper clubs in town (its name is retained from a previous incarnation). Jazz at Pearl's combines a 1930s vibe, Spanish tapas, and great live music. With only 25 tables, advance tickets are recommended if you want to sit; general admission tickets are available as well but don't guarantee seating. Tickets range from $19 to $154 (for VIP seating).

DANCE CLUBS The **Endup,** 401 Sixth St. (© **415/357-0827;** www.theendup.com), is where the sleepless dance-all-day crowd comes after other clubs close (it's open Sat morning 6am–noon and then nonstop from Sat night around 10pm until Sun night/ Mon morning at 4am). Every night hosts a different theme, but you can always count on a huge heated outdoor deck (with waterfall and fountain), an indoor fireplace, and an eclectic clientele.

Within an 1890s Victorian playhouse previously known as the Stage Door, **Ruby Skye,** 420 Mason St. (© **415/693-0777;** www.rubyskye.com), hosts hundreds of party-ers who dance on the ballroom floor, mingle on the mezzanine, and puff freely in the smoking room. DJs or live music bring the dancing house down Thursday through Saturday. Big spenders should book the VIP lounge, which offers a glitzy place to hang and bird's-eye views of the whole club scene.

THE BAR SCENE **Bambuddha Lounge,** 601 Eddy St. (© **415/885-5088;** www. bambuddhalounge.com), adjoins the rock-'n'-roll Phoenix Hotel and is the hottest place for the young and the trendy to feast, flirt, or just be fabulous. The **Bubble Lounge,** 714 Montgomery St. (© **415/434-4204;** www.bubblelounge.com), serves 300 kinds of champagne (30 of them by the glass).

Over in North Beach, **Vesuvio,** 255 Columbus Ave. (© **415/362-3370**), has been catering to local writers, artists, and musicians since beatnik days (it's no coincidence that City Lights Bookstore is just across Jack Kerouac Alley). The convivial space consists of two stories of cocktail tables, complemented by exhibitions of local art.

Thirsty Bear Brewing Company, 661 Howard St. (© **415/974-0905;** www.thirsty bear.com), serves nine superb handcrafted varieties of beer and excellent Spanish food. The **San Francisco Brewing Company,** 155 Columbus Ave. (© **415/434-3344;** www. sfbrewing.com), is one of the city's few remaining old saloons, aglow with stained-glass windows, skylights, and a mahogany bar.

For cocktails with a view, try the **Carnelian Room,** 555 California St., on the 52nd floor of the Bank of America Building (© **415/433-7500;** www.carnelianroom.com). The restaurant has the most extensive wine list in the city, with 1,600 selections. They offer a four-course meal ($59 per person), as well as a la carte items ($24–$49 for main entrees). Jackets are required and ties are optional for men but encouraged. **Top of the Mark,** in the Mark Hopkins Intercontinental, 1 Nob Hill (© **415/616-6916**), is the most famous cocktail lounge in the city. During World War II, thousands of Pacific-bound servicemen toasted their farewells to the States here on the 19th floor.

9470), is one of the Castro's most famous gay hangouts. It caters to an older crowd but often has a mix of patrons and claims to be the first gay bar in America. The **Stud,** 399 Ninth St. (© **415/863-6623;** www.studsf.com), which has been around for almost 40 years, is one of the most successful gay bars in town. Music is a balanced mix of old and new, and nights vary from cabaret to oldies to disco-punk. When the **Café,** 2367 Market St. (© **415/861-3846;** www.cafesf.com), first got jumping, it was the only predominantly lesbian dance club on Saturday nights in the city. Today it's a happening mixed gay and lesbian scene, with three bars, two pool tables, a dance floor, and a small heated patio and balcony where smoking and schmoozing are allowed.

2 THE WINE COUNTRY

California's Napa and Sonoma valleys are two of the most famous winegrowing regions in the world. Hundreds of wineries are nestled among the vines, and most are open to visitors. But even if you don't want to wine-taste, the country air, beautiful countryside, and world-class restaurants and spas are reason enough to come. If you can, plan on spending more than a day here; you'll need a couple of days just to get to know one of the valleys (don't try to do both unless you've got several days free).

NAPA VALLEY

Napa Valley dwarfs Sonoma Valley in both population and number of wineries. It also has more spas (some at far cheaper rates), a superior selection of fine restaurants and hotels, and more traffic jams. But if your goal is to learn about the world of winemaking, world-class wineries such as Sterling and Robert Mondavi offer the most edifying wine tours in North America, if not the world.

Napa Valley is just 35 miles long, which means you can venture from one end to the other in around half an hour (traffic permitting). Most of the large wineries—as well as most of the hotels, shops, and restaurants—line a single road, **Hwy. 29,** which starts at the mouth of the Napa River, near the north end of San Francisco Bay, and continues north to Calistoga and the top of the growing region. Every Napa Valley town and winery can be reached from this main thoroughfare.

VISITOR INFORMATION In Napa Valley, stop at the **Napa Valley Conference & Visitors Bureau,** 1310 Town Center Mall, Napa, CA 94559 (© **707/226-7459,** ext. 106; www.napavalley.com), for the *Napa Valley Guide.* You can call or write for the *Napa Valley Guidebook,* which includes information on lodging, restaurants, wineries, and things to do, and a winery map; the bureau charges a $6 postage fee. If you don't want to pay for the hard copy, head to **www.napavalley.org**, the NVCVB's official site, which has lots of the same information for free.

TOURING THE TOP WINERIES

The Napa Valley has around 300 wineries—each with distinct wines, atmosphere, and experience—so touring the valley takes planning. Decide what interests you and chart your path from there. Don't plan to visit more than four wineries in a day. Above all, take it slowly. The Wine Country should never be rushed; like a great glass of wine, it should be savored.

Most wineries are open 10am to 5pm (some have extended hours during summer; most are closed on major holidays). Many offer tours daily from 10am to 4:30pm. Tours vary in length and formality; many are free.

No place in the valley brings together art and wine better than the **Hess Collection,** 4411 Redwood Rd., Napa (© **707/255-1144;** www.hesscollection.com). After acquiring the old Christian Brothers winery in 1978, Swiss art collector Donald Hess also funded a huge restoration and expansion project to honor wine and the fine arts. The result is a working winery interspersed with gloriously lit rooms that exhibit his truly stunning art collection. The self-guided tour is free, but the tasting fee is $10.

Domaine Chandon, 1 California Dr., at Hwy. 29, Yountville (© **707/944-2280;** www.chandon.com), is the valley's most renowned sparkling winery. It was founded in 1973 by French champagne house Moët et Chandon. Stroll the manicured gardens, sip sparkling wine on the patio, then glide into the dining room for lunch. Bubbly is sold by the glass ($9–$14); the comprehensive tour is worth the time.

Views, modern architecture, seclusion, and region-specific pinot noir flights make **Artesa Vineyards & Winery,** 1345 Henry Rd., Napa (© **707/224-1668;** www.artesa winery.com), one of my favorite stops. On days when the wind is blowing less than 10 mph, the fountains are captivating. Inside is a gift shop, a room outlining the history and details of the Carneros region, and a long bar with $10 to $15 flights of everything from chardonnays and pinot noirs to cabernet sauvignon and zinfandel.

At the magnificent mission-style **Robert Mondavi Winery,** 7801 St. Helena Hwy. (Hwy. 29), Oakville (© **800/MONDAVI** [666-3284] or 707/226-1395; www.robert mondaviwinery.com), almost every variable in the winemaking process is controlled by computer. After the 75-minute tour ($25), you can sample the results in selected current wines. There's also an "essence tasting" tour ($60), during which you compare wine with the scents of fruits, spices, nuts, and more. If you don't tour, you have to pay to taste. Reserve at least a week in advance in summer.

PlumpJack Winery, 620 Oakville Cross Rd., Oakville (© **707/945-1220;** www. plumpjack.com), stands out as the Todd Oldham of wine tasting—chic, colorful, a little wild, and popular with a young and old crowd. This playfully medieval winery is a welcome diversion. But there's some serious winemaking going on, too, and for $5 you can sample the impressive cabernet, chardonnay, and sangiovese. There are no tours or picnic spots, but this friendly facility will make you want to linger nonetheless.

Hollywood meets Napa Valley at the **Rubicon Estate,** 1991 St. Helena Hwy. (Hwy. 29), Rutherford (© **800/RUBICON** [782-4266] or 707/968-1100; www.rubiconestate. com), owned by director Francis Ford Coppola. Originally known as Inglenook Vineyards, it's now named after its most prestigious wine. You'll find some decent wine, produced on spectacular grounds. You'll have to fork over $25 to visit, but that includes a tasting of five wines, a tour of its historic properties, and valet parking.

Joseph Phelps Vineyards, 200 Taplin Rd., St. Helena (© **800/707-5789** or 707/ 963-4831; www.jpvwines.com), is a favorite stop for serious wine lovers. The winery was founded in 1973 and has become a major player both regionally and worldwide. The intimate tour and knockout tasting are available only by reservation, and the location—a quick, unmarked turn off the Silverado Trail in Spring Valley—makes it impossible to find unless you're looking for it.

Schramsberg, 1400 Schramsberg Rd., off Hwy. 29, Calistoga (© **707/942-2414;** www.schramsberg.com), is one of our favorite places. Schramsberg is the label that U.S. presidents serve when toasting foreign dignitaries, and there's plenty of memorabilia to prove it. The unintimidating tour of the 2-mile champagne caves ends in a charming tasting room, where you can sample varied selections of bubbly. Tastings are $25 per person, but it's money well spent. Tastings are offered only to those who take the free tour; you must reserve a spot in advance.

You don't need climbing shoes to reach **Sterling Vineyards,** 1111 Dunaweal Lane, off Hwy. 29, Calistoga (© **707/942-3344;** www.sterlingvineyards.com), a dazzling white Mediterranean-style winery, 300 feet up on a rocky knoll. Just hand over $15 ($10 for kids, which includes a goodie bag), and you'll arrive via aerial tram, which offers dazzling views along the way. Once on land, follow the valley's most comprehensive self-guided tour of the winemaking process. Samples at the panoramic tasting room are included in the tram fare.

Beyond the Wineries: What to See & Do in Napa Valley

ART GALLERIES   Anyone with an appreciation for art must visit the **di Rosa Preserve,** 5200 Sonoma Hwy., Napa (© **707/226-5991**). Rene and Veronica di Rosa's world-renowned collection of contemporary American art—more than 2,000 works by more than 900 Bay Area artists—is displayed throughout their 53-acre estate. Tours include a $10 1-hour overview at 10am and 11am (Tues–Fri), a $15 2-hour extended home tour at 1pm, and a $15 2-hour sculpture meadow tour. On Saturday you can take a guided 2¹/₂-hour tour for $15. Reservations are recommended. Drop-ins are welcome at the Gatehouse Gallery Tuesday through Friday from 9:30am to 3pm and Saturday by appointment ($3 suggested donation).

NATURAL WONDERS   **Old Faithful Geyser of California,** 1299 Tubbs Lane (© **707/942-6463;** www.oldfaithfulgeyser.com), is one of only three "old faithful" geysers in the world. The 350°F (176°C) water spews to a height of about 60 feet every 40 minutes, day and night. The performance lasts about 3 minutes, and you can watch as many times as you wish. Bring along a picnic to enjoy between spews. Admission is $8 for adults, $7 for seniors, $3 for children 6 to 12, and free for children 5 and under.

You'll find many petrified specimens at the **Petrified Forest,** 4100 Petrified Forest Rd., just north of Calistoga off Hwy. 128 (© **707/942-6667;** www.petrifiedforest.org). Volcanic ash blanketed this area after an eruption near Mount St. Helena three million years ago. You'll find redwoods that have turned to rock through the slow infiltration of silicas and other minerals, as well as petrified seashells, and marine life indicating that water covered this area before the redwood forest appeared. Admission is $6 for adults, $5 for seniors and youths 12 to 17, $3 for children 6 to 11, and free for children 5 and under.

SHOPPING   Shoppers head for St. Helena's **Main Street,** where you'll find trendy fashions, gifts, estate jewelry, and European home accessories. Most stores are open 10am to 5pm daily Shopaholics should also take the sharp turn off Hwy. 29, 2 miles north of St. Helena, to the **St. Helena Premier Outlets** (© **707/963-7282;** www.sthelena marketplace.com). Featured designers include Escada, Brooks Brothers, and Tumi. The stores are open daily from 10am to 6pm.

Another favorite is the **Napa Valley Olive Oil Manufacturing Company,** 835 Charter Oak Ave. (© **707/963-4173**), at the end of the road behind Tra Vigne restaurant. The tiny market presses and bottles its own oils and sells them at a fraction of the price you'd pay elsewhere. It also has an extensive selection of Italian cooking ingredients, imported snacks, great deals on dried mushrooms, and a picnic table in the parking lot. You'll love the age-old method for totaling the bill—which you must discover for yourself.

While we recommend staying in romantically pastoral areas such as St. Helena, you're going to find better deals in the towns of Napa or laid-back Calistoga.

Calistoga Ranch, 580 Lommel Rd., Calistoga (© **707/254-2800;** www.calistoga ranch.com), Napa Valley's hottest luxury resort, is tucked into the mountainside, on 157 pristine hidden-canyon acres. It's beautifully decorated and packed with every conceivable amenity (including fireplaces, outdoor patios along a wooded area, and cushy outdoor furnishings). Reasons not to leave include a giant swimming pool, reasonably large gym, beautifully designed indoor-outdoor spa with a natural thermal pool and individual pavilions with private-garden soaking tubs, and a breathtaking restaurant with stunning views of the property's petite Lake Lommel. Rates run from $600 to $3,200 double, including activities.

Meadowood Napa Valley, 900 Meadowood Lane, St. Helena (© **800/458-8080** or 707/963-3646; www.meadowood.com), is summer camp for wealthy grown-ups. Rooms, furnished with American country classics, have beamed ceilings, patios, stone fireplaces, and wilderness views. Many are individual suite-lodges. With golf, tennis, croquet, pools, hiking trails, and a spa on-site, you might never leave. Rates run from $475 to $975 double; from $900 to $1,700 one-bedroom suite.

Calistoga Spa Hot Springs, 1006 Washington St., Calistoga (© **866/822-5772** or 707/942-6269; www.calistogaspa.com), is one of very few hotels in the Wine Country that caters specifically to families with children. It's a great bargain ($136–$196 double), with comfortable rooms and spa facilities. Calistoga's best shops and restaurants are within easy walking distance, and you can whip up your own grub at the barbecue grills near the large pool and patio area.

Maison Fleurie, 6529 Yount St., Yountville (© **800/788-0369** or 707/944-2056; www.maisonfleurienapa.com), is one of the prettiest hotels in the Wine Country, a trio of 1873 brick-and-fieldstone buildings overlaid with ivy. Some rooms feature private balconies, patios, Jacuzzis, and fireplaces. A basic breakfast is served in the little dining room; afterward, you're welcome to wander the landscaped grounds or hit the wine-tasting trail, returning in time for afternoon hors d'oeuvres and wine. Rates are from $135 to $300 double, including full breakfast and afternoon hors d'oeuvres.

The Art Deco **El Bonita Motel,** 195 Main St., St. Helena (© **800/541-3284** or 707/963-3216; www.elbonita.com), was built a bit too close to Hwy. 29 for comfort, but the 2¹/₂ acres of beautifully landscaped gardens help even the score. The affordable rooms, while small, are spotlessly clean and decorated with comfy furnishings; some have kitchens or whirlpool tubs. Families like the larger bungalows with kitchenettes, but everybody loves the heated pool, Jacuzzi, and spa facility. Rates run from $89 to $259 double, including continental breakfast.

In addition to the listings above, check out **Napa Valley Railway Inn,** 6503 Washington St., Yountville, adjacent to the Vintage 1870 shopping complex (© **707/944-2000**), which rents private railway cars converted into adorable hotel rooms.

Where to Dine

To best enjoy Napa's restaurant scene, keep one thing in mind: *Reserve*—especially for seats in a more renowned room.

All Seasons Café, 1400 Lincoln Ave., Calistoga (© **707/942-9111;** www.allseasons napavalley.net), is the best restaurant downtown, balancing homey charm with sophisticated, seasonally inspired dishes. More than 400 wines are available from their adjoining wine shop. (Buy next door, pay the $15 corkage fee, and you're still drinking for far less than at most restaurants.)

ZuZu, 829 Main St., Napa (© **707/224-8555**), serves delicious affordable tapas for $3 to $13. The kitchen cranks out fantastic paella, sizzling prawns, and Moroccan barbecue lamb chops guaranteed to make you swoon.

Chef Richard Reddington's **Redd,** 6480 Washington St., Yountville (© **707/944-2222**), is one the best fine-dining experiences in the valley. Expect exceptional appetizers such as a delicate sashimi *hamachi* with *edamame,* cucumber, ginger, and sticky rice, and a cold foie gras trio with pistachios and brioche. For entrees, the Atlantic cod with chorizo, clams, and curry sauce manages to be rich *and* light. Desserts aren't quite as celestial, but they are lovely, with Meyer lemon *panna cotta* and rose water crème brûlée.

SONOMA VALLEY

Sonoma is often regarded as the "other" Wine Country. The truth, however, is that it's a distinct experience. Sonoma still manages to feel like backcountry, thanks to its lower density of wineries, restaurants, and hotels; because it's far less traveled than Napa, it offers a more genuine escape. Small, family-owned wineries are its mainstay. Tastings and tours on the Sonoma side of the Mayacamas Mountains are usually low-key, with plenty of friendly banter between staff and guests.

Stop by the **Sonoma Valley Visitors Bureau,** 453 First St. E. (© **866/996-1090** or 707/996-1090; www.sonomavalley.com). It's open Monday through Saturday from 9am to 5pm (6pm in the summer) and Sunday 10am to 5pm. If you prefer advance information from the bureau, contact them to order the free *Sonoma Valley Visitors Guide,* which lists almost every lodge, winery, and restaurant in the valley. An additional **Visitors Bureau** is a few miles south of the square at Cornerstone Festival of Gardens, at 23570 Arnold Dr. (Hwy. 121; © **866/996-1090**); it's open daily from 9am to 4pm, 5pm during summer.

Touring the Valley & Wineries

Sonoma Valley is home to about 40 wineries. They tend to be a little more spread out than those in Napa, so decide where you're going before you get on the road.

A visit to the **Benziger Family Winery,** 1883 London Ranch Rd., off Arnold Drive, Glen Ellen (© **888/490-2739** or 707/935-3000; www.benziger.com), confirms that this is indeed a "family" winery. At any given time, three generations of Benzigers may be running around tending to chores. The pastoral, user-friendly property features an exceptional self-guided tour. The fun, informative 45-minute tram tour ($15 for adults, $5 for kids), pulled by a beefy tractor, winds through the estate vineyards and into caves, and ends with a tasting of one estate wine. Tastings of the standard-release wines are $5. The winery has several scenic picnic spots.

Buena Vista Winery, 18000 Old Winery Rd., Sonoma (© **800/926-1266** or 707/265-1472; www.buenavistawinery.com), is the granddaddy of all California wineries, founded in 1857 by Count Agoston Haraszthy, the Hungarian émigré who returned from Europe in 1861 with 100,000 of the finest vine cuttings. The winery's tasting room is inside the restored 1862 Press House. Tastings are $5 for four wines; $10 for a flight of three of the really good stuff. You can take the free self-guided tour anytime during operating hours, but their $20 "Carneros Experience" requires a reservation and pairs five wines with a small plate of food, including cheeses.

(Best) The Finest Eating in the Land

Plainly put, the **French Laundry,** 6640 Washington St., at Creek Street, Yountville (© **707/944-2380;** www.thefrenchlaundry.com), is unlike any other dining experience. Part of its appeal has to do with intricate preparations, often finished table-side and always presented with uncommon artistry and detail, from the food itself to the surface it's delivered on.

Technically, the prix-fixe menu ($240, including service) offers a choice of nine courses (including a vegetarian menu), but after several presentations from the kitchen, everyone starts to lose count. Signature dishes include Keller's "tongue in cheek" (a marinated and braised round of sliced lamb tongue and tender beef cheeks) and "macaroni and cheese" (sweet butter-poached Maine lobster with creamy lobster broth and orzo with mascarpone cheese). Portions are small, but only because Keller wants his guests to taste as many things as possible. Trust me, nobody leaves hungry. The staff is well acquainted with the wide selection of regional wines; there's a $50 corkage fee if you bring your own, which is welcome only if it's not on the list. Reserve at least 2 months in advance; jackets are required for men.

When you've had it with chardonnays and pinots, visit **Gloria Ferrer Champagne Caves,** 23555 Carneros Hwy. (Calif. 121), Sonoma (© **707/996-7256;** www.gloria ferrer.com), home of Freixenet, the largest producer of sparkling wine in the world. To learn about *méthode champenoise,* take the $10 tasting and 30-minute tour of the fermenting tanks, bottling line, and caves brimming with racks of yeast-laden bottles. Afterward, retire to the tasting room and order a glass of one of seven sparkling wines ($4–$10 a glass) or tastes of their eight still wines ($2–$3 per taste).

Viansa Winery and Italian Marketplace, 25200 Arnold Dr. (Hwy. 121), Sonoma (© **800/995-4740** or 707/935-4700; www.viansa.com), is the brainchild of Sam and Vicki Sebastiani, who left the family dynasty to create their own temple to food and wine. The marketplace is crammed with a cornucopia of gourmet foods; the winery has quickly established a favorable reputation for its cabernet, sauvignon blanc, and chardonnay. Guided tours, held at 11am, 2pm, and 3pm, will set you back $10.

Where to Stay

If you're having trouble finding a vacancy, contact the **Sonoma Valley Visitors Bureau** (© **707/996-1090;** www.sonomavalley.com). They'll try to refer you to establishments with a room to spare, but they won't make reservations for you. Another option is the **Bed and Breakfast Association of Sonoma Valley** (© **800/969-4667**), which will refer you to a member B&B and make reservations for you.

At the **Fairmont Sonoma Mission Inn & Spa,** 101 Boyes Blvd., Sonoma (© **800/ 441-1414** or 707/938-9000; www.fairmont.com/sonoma), the naturally heated artesian mineral water is piped from underneath the spa into the temperature-controlled pools and whirlpools. Set on 12 meticulously groomed acres, the Sonoma Mission Inn consists of a massive three-story replica of a Spanish mission, built in 1927; an array of satellite wings with numerous superluxury suites; and world-class spa facilities. Rates run from $259 to $1,259 double, including a free wine tasting daily.

The century-old buttercup-yellow **Beltane Ranch,** 11775 Sonoma Hwy./Hwy. 12, Glen Ellen (© **707/996-650;** www.beltaneranch.com), has been everything from a bunkhouse to a brothel to a turkey farm. Rooms are decorated with American and European antiques, and all have sitting areas and separate entrances. A big country breakfast is served (included in the rates of $150–$220 double), and the 105-acre estate has hiking trails and a private tennis court.

The **Gaige House Inn,** 13540 Arnold Dr., Glen Ellen (© **800/935-0237** or 707/935-0237; www.gaige.com), recently taken over by the Thompson hotel group, remains Wine Country's finest B&B. The service, amenities, and decor are what you'd expect from an outrageously expensive resort, but without the snobbery. All rooms have private bathrooms and king- or queen-size beds; two rooms have Jacuzzi tubs, and several have fireplaces. The eight new, superfancy spa garden suites have, among other delights, granite soaking tubs. There's even a pool and outdoor hot tub on the manicured lawn out back. Summer rates are from $300 to $595 double, including full breakfast and wine in the evening.

The **Best Western Sonoma Valley Inn,** 550 Second St. W. (© **800/334-5784** or 707/938-9200; www.sonomavalleyinn.com), is perfect for families. Kids will love the large heated outdoor saltwater pool and in-room satellite TV, while perks for parents include continental breakfast delivered to your room and a gift bottle of Sonoma Valley wine (chilling in the fridge). Most rooms have either a balcony or a deck overlooking the inner courtyard. Rates are from $114 to $369 double.

Where to Dine

Though Sonoma Valley has far fewer visitors than Napa Valley, its restaurants are often as crowded, so be sure to make reservations in advance.

The **girl & the fig,** 110 W. Spain St. (© **707/938-3634;** www.thegirlandthefig.com), draws crowds nightly to its downtown digs. Figs are sure to be on the menu in one form or another, as in the wonderful winter fig salad made with arugula, pecans, dried figs, goat cheese, and fig-and-port vinaigrette.

If you just can't take another expensive, chichi meal, follow the locals to **Della Santina's,** 133 E. Napa St., just east of the square (© **707/935-0576;** www.dellasantinas. com). Every classic Tuscan dish is authentic and well flavored—without overbearing sauces or a *hint* of California pretentiousness. Don't worry about breaking the bank on a bottle of wine, as most of the choices here go for under $40.

Eclectic food, friendly owners, soothing atmosphere, and moderate prices make **Cafe La Haye,** 140 E. Napa St., Sonoma (© **707/935-5994**), a favorite. The small, straightforward menu offers just enough options, such as a risotto special, and pan-roasted chicken breast with caramelized shallot jus and fennel mashed potatoes.

If you're looking for picnic fare, head to the venerable **Sonoma Cheese Factory,** on the plaza at 2 Spain St. (© **707/996-1000**), which offers award-winning house-made cheeses and imported meats and cheeses. Also available are caviar, gourmet salads, pâté, and homemade Sonoma Jack cheese. Pick up some good, inexpensive sandwiches, such as fire-roasted pork loin or New York steak.

3 THE NORTHERN COAST

North of San Francisco, you can forget about California's fabled surf-and-bikini scene; instead, you'll find miles of rugged coastline with broad beaches and tiny bays harboring dramatic rock formations carved by the ocean. The best time to visit is in the spring or fall. In spring, the headlands are carpeted with wildflowers—golden poppy, iris, and sea foam—and in fall, the sun shines clear and bright. Summers are cool and windy, with the ubiquitous fog burning off by the afternoon. The water's too cold for much swimming this far north, but you can certainly enjoy the beaches, whether by strolling along the shore or taking in the panoramic views of cliffs and seascapes.

POINT REYES NATIONAL SEASHORE

This preserve is a 71,000-acre hammer-shaped peninsula jutting 10 miles into the Pacific and backed by Tomales Bay. It encompasses several surf-pounded beaches, bird estuaries, open swaths of land with roaming elk, and the Point Reyes Lighthouse, which offers spectacular views.

The infamous San Andreas Fault separates Point Reyes—the northernmost landmass on the Pacific Plate—from the rest of California, which rests on the North American Plate. In 1906, Point Reyes jumped north almost 20 feet in an instant, leveling San Francisco and jolting the rest of the state. The half-mile **Earthquake Trail,** near the Bear Valley Visitor Center, illustrates this geological drama with a loop through an area torn by the slipping fault. Shattered fences, rifts in the ground, and a barn knocked off its foundation by the quake illustrate how alive the earth is here.

Point Reyes is only 30 miles northwest of San Francisco, but it takes at least 90 minutes to reach by car (it's all the small towns, not the topography, that slow you down). The easiest route is via Sir Francis Drake Boulevard from U.S. 101 south of San Rafael. For a much longer but more scenic route, take the Stinson Beach/Hwy. 1 exit off U.S. 101 just south of Sausalito and follow Hwy. 1 north.

As soon as you arrive at Point Reyes, stop at the **Bear Valley Visitor Center** (© 415/ 464-5100; www.nps.gov/pore), on Bear Valley Road (look for the small sign posted just north of Olema on Hwy. 1), and pick up a free Point Reyes trail map. The rangers here are friendly and helpful. Be sure to check out the great natural history and cultural displays as well. It's open Monday through Friday from 9am to 5pm, Saturday and Sunday from 8am to 5pm. A websites with information about Point Reyes is www.point reyes.org.

Entrance to the park is free. Camping is $15 per site per night, and permits are required; reservations can be made up to 3 months in advance by calling © **415/663-8054** Monday through Friday from 9am to 2pm.

What to See & Do

The most popular attraction is the venerable **Point Reyes Lighthouse,** at the westernmost tip. Even if you plan to forego the 308 steps down to the lighthouse, it's worth the visit just to marvel at the scenery, which includes thousands of common murres and prides of sea lions basking on the rocks far below (binoculars come in handy). The lighthouse visitor center (© **415/669-1534**) is open Thursday through Monday from 10am to 4:30pm, weather permitting; admission is free.

The lighthouse is also the top spot on the California coast to see **gray whales** as they make their southward and northward migrations along the coast from January to April. The annual round-trip is 10,000 miles—one of the longest mammal migrations known. The whales head south in December and January, and return north in March. *Tip:* If you plan to drive out to the lighthouse to whale-watch, arrive early, as parking is limited. If possible, come on a weekday. On a weekend or holiday from December to April (weather permitting), it's wise to park at the Drake's Beach Visitor Center and take the shuttle bus to the lighthouse, which is $5 for adults and free for kids age 12 and under. Dress warmly—it's often quite cold and windy—and bring binoculars.

North and South **Point Reyes Beach** face the Pacific and withstand the full brunt of ocean tides and winds—the water is far too rough for even wading. Until a few years ago, entering the water was illegal, but persistent surfers went to court for their right to shred the mighty waves. Today the Park Service strongly advises against taking on the tides, so play it safe and be content to stroll the coastline. Along the southern coast, the waters of **Drake's Beach** can be as tranquil and serene as Point Reyes's are turbulent.

Some of the park's best—and least crowded—highlights can be approached only on foot, such as **Alamere Falls,** a freshwater stream that cascades down a 40-foot bluff onto Wildcat Beach, or **Tomales Point Trail,** which passes through the Tule Elk Reserve, a protected haven for herds of tule elk that once numbered in the thousands.

One of our favorite things to do in Point Reyes is paddle through placid **Tomales Bay,** a haven for migrating birds and marine mammals. **Blue Waters Kayaking** (© **415/669-2600;** www.bwkayak.com) organizes kayak trips, including 3-hour morning or sunset outings, oyster tours, day trips, and longer excursions. Instruction, clinics, and boat delivery are available, and all ages and levels are welcome. Prices for tours start at $68. Rentals begin at $30 per person. The launching points are at Hwy. 1 at the Marshall Boatworks in Marshall, 8 miles north of Point Reyes Station, and at Sir Francis Drake Boulevard, in Inverness, 5 miles west of Point Reyes Station. The Marshall site is open, weather permitting, on weekends from 9am to 5pm and by appointment. Call or visit their website to confirm.

Where to Stay & Dine

If you're having trouble finding a vacancy, **Inns of Marin** (© **800/887-2880** or 415/663-2000; www.innsofmarin.com), **Point Reyes Lodging Association** (© **800/539-1872** or 415/663-1872; www.ptreyes.com), and **West Marin Network** (© **415/663-9543**) are reputable services that will help you find accommodations, from one-room cottages to inns and vacation homes.

If there were ever a reason to pack your bags and leave San Francisco for a day or two, **Manka's Inverness Lodge,** 30 Callendar Way, Inverness (© **415/669-1034;** www.mankas. com), is it. A former hunting-and-fishing lodge, it's all romantic in a Jack London sort of way, and tastefully done. While the main lodge and restaurant were destroyed in a December 2006 fire, you can still eat like a prince: On a nightly basis, guests are invited to indulge in either a three- or four-course fireside supper or a private chef's meal that consists of seven or eight small courses. Doubles run from $215 to $385 double; it's $365 to $565 for a cabin and boathouse.

Finding an inexpensive place to stay in Point Reyes is next to impossible, but **Motel Inverness,** 12718 Sir Francis Drake Blvd. (© **888/669-6909** or 415/669-1081; www. motelinverness.com), is one exception. The homey, well-maintained property fronts Tomales Bay, and a giant great room with a fireplace and pool table is attached to the hotel. The two-bedroom suite with a kitchenette is ideal for families, as is the Dacha cottage, on the water, with three bedrooms. Rates are from $99 to $140 double, $150 to $200 suite, and $500 for the cottage.

The **Point Reyes Country Inn & Stables,** 12050 Hwy. 1, Point Reyes Station (© **415/663-9696;** www.ptreyescountryinn.com), is a ranch-style home on 4 acres that offers pastoral accommodations for two- and four-legged guests (horses only), plus access to plenty of trails. Each room has either a balcony or a garden. Also available are two studies (with kitchens) above the stables, plus two Tomales Bay cottages with decks, kitchens, fireplaces, and a shared dock. Rates are from $115 to $180 double, $185 to $225 in a cottage, and $10 to $15 per horse, including breakfast in the rooms and breakfast provisions in the cottages.

The **Station House Café,** Main Street, Point Reyes Station (© **415/663-1515;** www. stationhousecafe.com), has been a low-key favorite for more than 2 decades, thanks to its open kitchen, garden seating, and live music on weekends. Breakfast dishes range from a hangtown fry with local Johnson's oysters to mashed potato pancakes. Dinner specials might include fettuccine with fresh local mussels or two-cheese polenta served with fresh spinach sauté—all made from local produce, seafood, and organically raised Niman-Schell Farms beef.

Fresh, fast, good, and cheap: What more could you ask for in a restaurant? **Rosie's Cowboy Cookhouse** (formerly known as Taqueria La Quinta), 11285 Hwy. 1, at Third and Main streets (© **415/663-8868**), has been one of our favorite lunch stops in Point Reyes for years. Try the chile verde in a spicy tomatillo sauce with a side of handmade corn tortillas.

BODEGA BAY

Beyond the tip of the Point Reyes peninsula, the road curves around toward the coastal village of Bodega Bay, which supports a fishing fleet of around 300 boats. It's a good place to stop for lunch or a stroll around town. **Bodega Head State Park** is a great vantage point for whale-watching during the annual migration season from January to April. At **Doran Beach,** there's a large bird sanctuary, home to willets, curlews, godwits, and more.

The **Bodega Harbour Golf Links,** 21301 Heron Dr. (© **800/503-8158** or 707/875-3538; www.bodegaharbourgolf.com), enjoys a panoramic oceanside setting. It's an 18-hole Scottish-style course designed by Robert Trent Jones, Jr. A warm-up center and practice facility are free for registered golfers. Rates range from $60 with cart Monday through Thursday, $70 on Friday, and $90 on weekends. If golfing isn't your thing, you can go horseback riding through some spectacular coastal scenery by contacting **Chanslor Ranch** (© **707/875-3333;** www.chanslor.com), which also has pony rides for the kids. Open daily from 9am to 5pm.

One of the bay's major events is the **Fisherman's Festival** in April. Local fishing boats, decorated with ribbons and banners, sail out for a Blessing of the Fleet, while thousands of landlubbers enjoy music, a lamb-and-oyster barbecue, and an arts-and-crafts fair.

For details about this festival and other events, consult the **Bodega Bay Visitors Center,** 850 Hwy. 1, Bodega Bay, CA 94923 (© **707/875-3866;** www.bodegabay.com or www.visitsonomacoast.com). Open daily, it has lots of brochures, and maps of the Sonoma Coast State Beaches and the best fishing spots.

If you'd like to stay over, the upscale **Bodega Bay Lodge & Duck Club Restaurant,** 103 Hwy. 1 (© **800/368-2468** or 707/875-3525; www.bodegabaylodge.com), is easily the best choice. Each room has a fireplace and a balcony with sweeping views. Guests have access to a beautiful fieldstone spa and heated pool perched above the bay. The lodge's Duck Club Restaurant also enjoys a reputation as Bodega Bay's finest. Rates are $220 to $280 double Sunday through Thursday, $410 suite; $245 to $295 double Friday and Saturday, $460 suite.

The larger **Inn at the Tides,** 800 Coast Hwy. 1 (© **800/541-7788** or 707/875-2751; www.innatthetides.com), consists of a cluster of condolike complexes perched on the side of a gently sloping hill. The selling point here is the view; each unit is staggered just enough to guarantee a view of the bay across the highway. Summer rates are $189 to $259 Sunday through Thursday, $239 to $294 Friday and Saturday; winter rates drop about 20%. In summer, as many as 1,000 diners a day pass through the inn's **Tides Wharf Restaurant,** 835 Hwy. 1 (© **707/875-3652**). Back in the 1960s, it served as one of the settings for Hitchcock's *The Birds,* but renovation has enlarged and redecorated the place beyond recognition. The best tables offer views overlooking the ocean, and the bill of fare includes clam chowder and fish fresh from the cold blue waters offshore.

THE SONOMA COAST STATE BEACHES, JENNER & FORT ROSS STATE HISTORIC PARK

Along 13 winding miles of Calif. 1—from Bodega Bay to Goat Rock Beach in Jenner— stretch the Sonoma Coast State Beaches, ideal for walking, tide-pooling, abalone picking, fishing, and bird-watching. Each beach is clearly marked from the road, and numerous pullouts are available for parking. Even if you don't stop at any of the beaches, the drive alone is spectacular.

At **Jenner,** the Russian River empties into the ocean. **Penny Island,** in the river's estuary, is home to otters and many species of birds; a colony of harbor seals lives out on the ocean rocks. **Goat Rock Beach** is a popular breeding ground for the seals; pupping season is March through June.

From Jenner, a 12-mile drive along some dramatic coastline will bring you to **Fort Ross State Historic Park** (© 707/847-3286; www.parks.ca.gov/?page_id=449), a reconstruction of the fort that was established here in 1812 by the Russians as a base for seal and otter hunting. At the visitor center, you can view the silver samovars and elaborate table services the Russians used. The fenced compound contains several buildings, including the first Russian Orthodox church in North America outside Alaska. The park offers beach trails and picnic grounds on more than 1,000 acres. Admission to the park costs $6 per car per day.

North from Fort Ross, the road continues to **Salt Point State Park** (© 707/847-3221). This 3,500-acre expanse contains 30 campsites, 14 miles of trails, tide pools, a pygmy forest, and old Pomo village sites. Your best bet is to pull off the highway any place that catches your eye and start exploring on foot. At the north end of the park, head inland on Kruse Ranch Road to the **Kruse Rhododendron Reserve** (© 707/847-3221), where the wild purple and pink *Rhododendron californicum* grow to a height of 18 feet under the redwood-and-fir canopy.

MENDOCINO

Mendocino is, to our minds, *the* premier destination on California's north coast. Despite (or because of) its relative isolation, it emerged as one of Northern California's major centers for the arts in the 1950s. It's easy to see why artists were—and still are—attracted to this idyllic community, a cluster of New England–style sea captains' homes and small stores set on headlands overlooking the ocean.

At the height of the logging boom, Mendocino became an important and active port. Its population was about 3,500, and eight hotels were built, along with 17 saloons and more than a dozen bordellos. Today it has only about 1,000 residents, most of whom reside at the north end of town. On summer weekends, the population seems more like 10,000, as hordes of tourists drive up from the Bay Area—but despite the crowds, Mendocino manages to retain its small-town charm.

GETTING THERE The fastest route from San Francisco is via **U.S. 101** north to Cloverdale, then **Hwy. 128** west to **Hwy. 1,** then north along the coast. It's about a 4-hour drive. The most scenic route from the Bay Area, if you have the time and your stomach doesn't mind the twists and turns, is to take Hwy. 1 north along the coast the entire way; it's at least a 5- to 6-hour drive.

VISITOR INFORMATION Stock up on free brochures and maps at the **Fort Bragg/ Mendocino Coast Chamber of Commerce,** 332 N. Main St. (P.O. Box 1141), Fort Bragg, CA 95437 (✆ 800/726-2780 or 707/961-6300; www.mendocinocoast.com). Pick up a copy of the center's monthly magazine, *Arts and Entertainment,* which lists upcoming events. It's available at numerous stores and cafes. You can also do some pretrip research on Mendocino at **MendocinoFun.com**, a nifty online events and activities website/blog to the region.

What to See & Do

Stroll through town, enjoy the architecture, and browse through the dozens of galleries and shops. Our favorites include the **Highlight Gallery,** 45052 Main St. (✆ 707/937-3132; www.thehighlightgallery.com), for its handmade furniture, pottery, and other crafts; and the **Gallery Bookshop & Bookwinkle's Children's Books,** at Main and Kasten streets (✆ 707/937-2665; www.gallerybooks.com), one of the best independent bookstores in Northern California. Another popular stop is **Mendocino Jams & Preserves,** 440 Main St. (✆ 800/708-1196 or 707/937-1037; www.mendojams.com), which offers free tastings of its locally made gourmet wares.

After exploring the town, walk out on the headlands that wrap around the town and constitute **Mendocino Headlands State Park.** The visitor center is in Ford House on Main Street (✆ 707/937-5397). Three miles of trails wind through the park, giving visitors panoramic views of sea arches and hidden grottoes. If you're here at the right time of year, the area will be blanketed with wildflowers. The headlands are home to many unique species of birds, including black oystercatchers. Behind the Mendocino Presbyterian Church on Main Street is a trail leading to stairs that take you down to the beach, a small but picturesque stretch of sand.

In town, stop by the **Mendocino Art Center,** 45200 Little Lake St. (✆ 707/937-5818; www.mendocinoartcenter.org), the town's unofficial cultural headquarters. It's also known for its gardens, galleries, and shops that display and sell local fine arts and crafts. Admission is free; it's open daily from 10am to 5pm.

After a day of hiking, head to **Sweetwater Spa & Inn,** 44840 Main St. (✆ 800/300-4140 or 707/937-4140; www.sweetwaterspa.com), which offers group and private saunas and hot-tub soaks by the hour. Additional services include Swedish or deep-tissue massages. Reservations are recommended. Private tub prices are $15 per person per half-hour, $18 per person per hour. Group tub prices are $10 per person, with no time limit. Special discounts are available on Wednesday. The spa is open daily from noon to 10pm and Saturday from noon to 11pm.

Outdoor Activities

Explore the Big River by renting a canoe, kayak, or outrigger from **Catch a Canoe & Bicycles Too** (✆ 707/937-0273; www.stanfordinn.com), open daily from 9am to sunset, on the grounds of the Stanford Inn by the Sea. If you're lucky, you'll see osprey, blue herons, harbor seals, deer, and wood ducks. These same folks will also rent you a mountain bike so you can head up Hwy. 1 and explore the nearby state parks on two wheels.

Visitors can ride horseback (both English and Western style) on the beach and into the woods through **Ricochet Ridge Ranch,** 24201 N. Hwy. 1, Fort Bragg (© **888/873-5777** or 707/964-7669; www.horse-vacation.com). Prices range from $45 for a 1¹/₂-hour beach ride to $295 for an all-day private beach-and-redwoods trail ride.

In addition to Mendocino Headlands State Park, there are several other nearby state parks; all are within an easy drive or bike ride and make for a good day's outing. Information on all the parks' features, including maps, is found in a brochure called *Mendocino Coast State Parks,* available from the visitor center in Fort Bragg. These areas include **Manchester State Park,** located where the San Andreas Fault sweeps to the sea; **Jughandle State Reserve;** and **Van Damme State Park,** with a sheltered, easily accessible beach.

Our favorite of these parks, on Hwy. 1 just north of Mendocino, is **Russian Gulch State Park.** It's one of the region's most spectacular parks, where roaring waves crash against the cliffs that protect the coastal redwoods. The most popular attraction is the **Punch Bowl,** a collapsed sea cave that forms a tunnel through which waves crash, creating throaty echoes. Inland, there's a scenic paved bike path, and visitors can also hike along miles of trails. Admission is $6 and camping is $25 per night. Call © **800/444-7275** or log onto **ReserveAmerica** at www.reserveamerica.com for camping reservations; for general state park information, call © **707/937-5804** or visit www.cal-parks.ca.gov.

Where to Stay

Just south of town, the rustic but ever-so-sumptuous **Stanford Inn by the Sea,** North Hwy. 1 and Comptche Ukiah Road (© **800/331-8884** or 707/937-5615; www.stanford inn.com), has captivating grounds, with tiers of elaborate gardens, a pond for ducks and geese, and pastures containing horses, llamas, and gnarled old apple trees. There's a gorgeous solarium-style indoor hot tub and pool. Rooms offer down comforters, fresh flowers, fireplaces or stoves, stereos and VCRs, and private decks from which you can look out onto the Pacific. The inn has the only totally vegetarian restaurant on the Mendocino coast, a big hit with both guests and locals. Rates are from $195 to $305 double, $295 to $785 suite, including breakfast.

Less expensive is the **Agate Cove Inn,** 11201 N. Lansing St. (© **800/527-3111** or 707/937-0551; www.agatecove.com), with a vista of the waves crashing onto the bluffs. All but one of the 10 spacious units have views of the ocean, down comforters, CD players, VCRs, fireplaces, and private decks. Rates are $159 to $329 double, including full breakfast.

Right in the heart of town, the **Mendocino Hotel & Garden Suites,** 45080 Main St. (© **800/548-0513** or 707/937-0511; www.mendocinohotel.com), was built in 1878 and evokes California's gold-rush days. Rooms feature hand-painted French porcelain sinks with floral designs, quaint wallpaper, old-fashioned beds and armoires, and photographs of historic Mendocino. About half are located in four handsome small buildings behind the main house. Many of the deluxe rooms have fireplaces. Rates are $135 to $295 for a double with private bathroom, $325 to $395 suite.

The moderately priced **Joshua Grindle Inn,** 44800 Little Lake Rd. (© **800/GRIN-DLE** [474-6373] or 707/937-4143; www.joshgrin.com), is housed in a stately 1879 Victorian with a wraparound porch and large emerald lawns. Rates are $189 to $259 double, including full breakfast, afternoon tea, and wine.

In the nearby town of Albion is the modern, upscale **Albion River Inn and Restaurant,** North Hwy. 1 (𝓒 **800/479-7944** or 707/937-1919; www.albionriverinn.com), perched on a bluff some 90 feet above the Pacific. Most rooms have decks; all have ocean views, fireplaces, down comforters, fridges, and CD players. The restaurant serves up stellar cuisine and stellar views. Rates are $195 to $275 double, $325 spa suite, including full breakfast.

Where to Dine

Note: In addition to the following, see "Where to Stay," above, for hotel restaurants.

Café Beaujolais, 961 Ukiah St. (𝓒 **707/937-5614;** www.cafebeaujolais.com), is one of Mendocino's—if not Northern California's—top dining choices. The venerable French country–style tavern is set in a century-old house; rose-colored chandeliers add a burnish to the wood floors and the heavy oak tables adorned with flowers. On warm nights, request a table at the enclosed deck overlooking the gardens. The menu usually lists about six main courses, such as roast free-range duck with wild-huckleberry sauce.

Large but surprisingly cozy, the **955 Ukiah Street Restaurant,** 955 Ukiah St. (𝓒 **707/ 937-1955;** www.955restaurant.com), is accented with massive railway ties and vaulted ceilings. Ask for a window table overlooking the gardens. The cuisine is creative and reasonably priced, a worthy alternative to the perpetually booked Café Beaujolais next door.

The moderately priced **Bay View Café,** 45040 Main St. (𝓒 **707/937-4197**), is one of the most popular restaurants in town and serves a good breakfast. From the second-floor dining area, there's a sweeping view of the Pacific and faraway headlands. You'll find a menu with Southwestern selections, a good array of sandwiches, and the fresh catch of the day.

In the back of the **Little River Market** (𝓒 **707/937-5133**), directly across from the Little River Inn on Hwy. 1, a trio of tables overlooks the Mendocino coastline. Order a tamale, sandwich, hamburger, or whatever else is on the menu at the tiny deli, or buy a loaf of Café Beaujolais bread at the front counter and your favorite spread.

Mendo Burgers (𝓒 **707/937-1111**) is arguably the best burger joint on the Northern Coast, with patties of all stripes—beef, chicken, turkey, or veggie. A side of fresh-cut fries is mandatory. Hidden behind the Mendocino Bakery and Café at 10483 Lansing St., it's a little hard to find but well worth searching out.

THE AVENUE OF THE GIANTS & FERNDALE

From Fort Bragg, Hwy. 1 continues north along the shoreline for about 30 miles before turning inland to Leggett and the Redwood Highway (U.S. 101), which runs north to Garberville. Six miles beyond Garberville, the **Avenue of the Giants** (Hwy. 254) begins around Phillipsville. It's an alternate route that roughly parallels U.S. 101, and there are about a half-dozen interchanges between the two roads if you don't want to drive the whole thing. This stretch of Hwy. 254 is one of the most spectacular scenic routes in the West, cutting along the Eel River through the 51,000-acre **Humboldt Redwoods State Park.** The Avenue ends just south of Scotia; from here, it's only about 10 miles to the turnoff to Ferndale, about 5 miles west of U.S. 101. Since Redwoods National Park is so remote, we recommend this outing as a more convenient way to see California's majestic giants.

For more information or a detailed map of the area, go to the **Humboldt Redwoods State Park Visitor Center** in Weott (𝓒 **707/946-2263;** www.humboldtredwoods.org), in the center of the Avenue of the Giants.

Thirty-three miles long, the Avenue of the Giants was left intact for sightseers when the freeway was built. The giants, of course, are the majestic coast redwoods *(Sequoia sempervirens);* more than 50,000 acres of them make up the most outstanding display in the redwood belt. Their rough-bark columns climb 100 feet or more without a branch and soar to a total height of more than 340 feet. With their immunity to insects and fire-resistant bark, they have survived for thousands of years.

A few miles north of Weott is **Founders Grove,** named in honor of those who established the Save the Redwoods League in 1918. Farther north, close to the end of the Avenue, stands the 950-year-old **Immortal Tree,** just north of Redcrest. Near Pepperwood at the end of the Avenue, the **Drury Trail** and the **Percy French Trail** are two good short hikes. The park itself is also good for mountain biking. Ask the rangers for details. For more information, contact **Humboldt Redwoods State Park** (© **707/946-2409;** www.humboldtredwoods.org).

The state park has three **campgrounds** with 248 campsites: Hidden Springs, half a mile south of Myers Flat; Burlington, 2 miles south of Weott, near park headquarters; and Albee Creek State Campground, 5 miles west of U.S. 101 on the Mattole Road north of Weott. Reservations are advised in summer; you can make them by calling © **800/444-7275** or online via **ReserveAmerica** at www.reserveamerica.com. Remaining sites are on a first-come, first-served basis. You'll also come across picnic and swimming facilities, motels, resorts, restaurants, and rest areas with parking lots.

Near the southern entrance to the Avenue of the Giants is the **Benbow Inn,** 445 Lake Benbow Dr., Garberville (© **800/355-3301** or 707/923-2124; www.benbowinn.com), a National Historic Landmark overlooking the Eel River and surrounded by marvelous gardens. The sumptuous lobby has a huge fireplace surrounded by cushy sofas, grandfather clocks, and Oriental carpets. Rooms are tastefully decorated with period antiques; the deluxe units have fireplaces, Jacuzzis, private entrances and patios, and VCRs. Bicycles are available, and beautiful Benbow Lake State Park is right out the front door. Complimentary afternoon tea and scones are served in the lobby at 4pm, hors d'oeuvres in the lounge at 5pm, and port at 9pm—all very proper, of course. The dramatic high-ceilinged dining room opens onto a spacious terrace. Rates run from $90 to $330 for a double, $395 to $425 for a cottage.

The landmark village of **Ferndale,** beyond the Avenue of the Giants and west of U.S. 101, has many Victorian homes and storefronts (which include a smithy and a saddlery). Despite its unbearably cute shops, it is nonetheless a vital part of the northern coastal tourist circuit.

The small town has a number of artists in residence and is also home to one of California's oddest events, the **World Championship Great Arcata to Ferndale Cross-Country Kinetic Sculpture Race** (www.kineticuniverse.com), which draws more than 10,000 spectators every Memorial Day weekend. For 38 miles, over land, sand, mud, and water, participants race in whimsically designed, handmade, people-powered vehicles that have to be seen to be believed—dragons, Christmas trees, flying saucers, and pyramids, to mention but a few. Awards range from Best Art to Best Engineering to Best Bribe. Stop at the museum at 780 Main St. if you want to see a few past race entries.

If you'd like to stay over in Ferndale, try the **Gingerbread Mansion,** 400 Berding St. (© **800/952-4136** or 707/786-4000; www.gingerbread-mansion.com), a beautiful antiques-filled Victorian built in 1899. Some of the large rooms have claw-foot tubs for two; others offer fireplaces. Rates are from $135 to $285 double, $170 to $400 suite, including full breakfast and afternoon tea.

4 MONTEREY & BIG SUR

MONTEREY

The Monterey Peninsula and the Big Sur coast comprise one of the world's most spectacular shorelines, skirted with cypress trees, rugged shores, and crescent-shaped bays. Monterey reels in visitors with its world-class aquarium and array of outdoor activities. Pacific Grove is so peaceful that the butterflies choose it as their yearly mating ground. Big Sur's dramatic and majestic coast, backed by pristine redwood forests and rolling hills, is one of the most breathtaking, tranquil environments on earth. If you're traveling Hwy. 1 (which you should be), the coastline will guide you all the way through the region.

Monterey was one of the West Coast's first European settlements and the capital of California under the Spanish, Mexican, and American flags. A major whaling center in the 1800s, Monterey eventually became the sardine capital of the Western Hemisphere. By 1913, the boats were bringing in 25 tons of sardines a night to the 18 canneries. The gritty lives of the mostly working-class residents were captured by local hero John Steinbeck in his 1945 novel *Cannery Row.*

After the sardines disappeared, Monterey was forced to fish for tourist dollars, hence the array of boutiques, knickknack stores, and theme restaurants that now reside along the bay. The city's saving grace is its historic architecture, world-class aquarium, and beautiful Monterey Bay, where sea lions and otters still frolic in abundance. Lodgings here are far less expensive than the surrounding area, which makes it a great place to base yourself while exploring the coast.

Essentials

GETTING THERE   By Plane   Monterey Peninsula Airport (✆ 831/648-7000) is 3 miles east of Monterey on Hwy. 68. Many area hotels offer free airport shuttle service. A taxi will cost about $10 to $15 to get to a peninsula hotel.

By Car The major routes into Monterey are **Hwy. 1** from the north (Santa Cruz) and south (Carmel and Big Sur), and **Hwy. 68** from the east, which connects with U.S. 101 (San Francisco).

VISITOR INFORMATION The **Monterey Peninsula Visitors and Convention Bureau** (✆ 831/649-1770; www.montereyinfo.org) has two visitor centers: one in the lobby of the Maritime Museum at Custom House Plaza near Fisherman's Wharf, the other at Lake El Estero on Camino El Estero. Both locations, open daily, offer good maps and free pamphlets and publications, including an excellent visitors' guide and the magazine *Coast Weekly.*

GETTING AROUND The free **Waterfront Area Visitor Express (WAVE)** operates from Memorial Day weekend to Labor Day and takes passengers to and from the aquarium and other waterfront attractions. Stops are located at many hotels and motels in Monterey and Pacific Grove. For further information, call **Monterey Salinas Transit** (✆ 831/899-2555).

What to See & Do

The enormous **Monterey Bay Aquarium,** 886 Cannery Row (✆ 831/648-4800 or 648-4888; www.mbayaq.org), is home to more than 350,000 marine animals and plants. One of the main exhibits is a three-story, 335,000-gallon tank with clear acrylic walls; inside, hundreds of leopard sharks, sardines, anchovies, and other fish play hide-and-seek in a towering kelp forest. The Outer Bay exhibit features yellowfin tuna, large green sea turtles, barracuda, sharks, giant ocean sunfish, and schools of bonito. The jellyfish exhibit is guaranteed to amaze, and kids will love Flippers, Flukes, and Fun, a learning area for families. Mysteries of the Deep is the largest collection of live deep-sea species in the world. Everyone falls in love with the playful sea otters, and there's a petting pool where you can touch living bat rays and handle sea stars. Admission is $25 adults, $23 students and seniors, $16 visitors with disabilities and children 3 to 12, free for children 2 and under. Avoid lines by ordering tickets in advance via phone or online. It's open daily 10am to 6pm (9:30am–6pm May 28–Sept 5 and holidays).

Fisherman's Wharf, at 99 Pacific St. (© **831/649-6544;** www.montereywharf.com), is a wooden pier packed with gift shops, fish markets, and seafood restaurants. The natural surroundings are so beautiful that if you cast your view toward the bobbing boats and surfacing sea lions, you might not even notice the hordes of tourists. Grab some clam chowder in a sourdough bread bowl and find a perch along the pier. **Chris' Fishing Trips,** 48 Fisherman's Wharf (© **831/375-5951;** www.chrissfishing.com), offers excursions for cod, salmon, and whatever else is running. Call or log on to the website for a price list and departure schedule. Check-in is 45 minutes before departure, and equipment rental costs a bit extra.

Kayaks can be rented from several outfitters. Contact **Monterey Bay Kayaks,** 693 Del Monte Ave. (© **800/649-5357** or 831/373-5357; www.montereykayaks.com), north of Fisherman's Wharf, which offers instruction as well as natural history tours. Prices start at $45 for tours, $30 for rentals. For bike rentals, as well as kayak tours and rentals, contact **Adventures by the Sea,** 299 Cannery Row (© **831/372-1807;** www.adventures bythesea.com). Bikes cost $7 per hour or $24 per day, and kayaks are $30 per person or $50 for a 2½-hour tour. Adventures by the Sea has another location at 201 Alvarado Mall (© **831/648-7236**), at the Doubletree Hotel.

Once the center for an industrial sardine-packing operation immortalized by John Steinbeck, **Cannery Row,** between David and Drake avenues (© **831/373-1902;** www. canneryrow.com), is now a congested strip of tacky gift shops, overpriced seafood restaurants, and an overall parking nightmare. Curious tourists continue to visit the area, and, as the author himself put it, "They fish for tourists now, not pilchards, and that species they are not likely to wipe out."

The dozen or so historic buildings clustered around Fisherman's Wharf and the adjacent town collectively form the "Path of History," a tour that examines 1800s architecture and lifestyle (pick up a brochure detailing the route at the visitor center). Many of the buildings are a part of the **Monterey State Historic Park,** 20 Custom House Plaza (© **831/649-7118**).

The Monterey area has become an increasingly important and acclaimed winemaking region. Stop by **A Taste of Monterey,** 700 Cannery Row (© **888/646-5446** or 831/646-5446; www.tastemonterey.com), daily between 11am and 6pm, to learn about local wines and taste them in front of huge bayfront windows. The site also distributes maps and winery touring information.

Strolling Through Nearby Pacific Grove

Just next door to Monterey, Pacific Grove is a town to be strolled, so park the car, put on your walking shoes, and make an afternoon of it.

An excellent shorter alternative, or complement, to the 17-Mile Drive is the scenic drive or bike ride along Pacific Grove's **Ocean View Boulevard.** This coastal stretch starts near Monterey's Cannery Row and follows the Pacific around to the lighthouse point.

Here it turns into Sunset Drive, which runs along secluded **Asilomar State Beach** (© **831/648-3130**). Park on Sunset and explore the trails, dunes, and tide pools of this sandy stretch of shore. You might find purple shore crabs, green anemone, sea bats, starfish, and limpets.

Marine Gardens Park, a stretch of shoreline along Ocean View Boulevard on Monterey Bay and the Pacific, is renowned not only for its ocean views and colorful flowers, but also for its tide-pool seaweed beds. Walk out to Lover's Point and watch the sea otters playing and cracking open an occasional abalone for lunch.

Pacific Grove is known as "Butterfly Town, USA," a reference to the thousands of **monarchs** that migrate here from November to February, traveling from as far away as Alaska. Many settle in the Monarch Grove sanctuary, a eucalyptus stand on Grove Acre Avenue off Lighthouse Avenue.

Just as Ocean View Boulevard serves as an alternative to the 17-Mile Drive, the **Pacific Grove Municipal Golf Course,** 77 Asilomar Ave. (© **831/648-5777**), is a reasonably priced alternative to Pebble Beach. Views are panoramic, and the fairways and greens are better maintained than those of most semiprivate courses. Eighteen holes start at $40 Monday through Thursday and $45 Friday through Sunday and holidays; twilight rates are available. Optional carts cost $34.

Where to Stay

If you're having trouble finding a room, try calling **Resort 2 Me** (© **800/757-5646;** www.resort2me.com), a local reservations service that offers free recommendations of Monterey Bay–area hotels in all price ranges.

Although it's not waterfront (it's close to the wharf and across the street from the Monterey Conference Center), the **Hotel Pacific,** 300 Pacific St. (© **800/554-5542** or 831/373-5700; www.hotelpacific.com), is our favorite upscale choice in Monterey. Rooms are clustered around courtyards and gardens complete with spas and fountains. The cozy Southwestern-style suites have fluffy down comforters atop four-poster beds, terra-cotta floors, and fireplaces surrounded by cushy couches. Rates run from $179 to $389 for a suite for two, including continental breakfast and afternoon tea.

The **Old Monterey Inn,** 500 Martin St., off Pacific Avenue (© **800/350-2344** or 831/375-8284; www.oldmontereyinn.com), is an intimate, vine-covered, Tudor-style country inn. Though it's away from the surf, it's romantic, with rose gardens, a bubbling brook, and brick-and-flagstone walkways shaded by a panoply of oaks. Rates are from $250 to $365 double, from $430 cottage, including full breakfast, tea and cookies in the afternoon, and evening wine and hors d'oeuvres.

In Pacific Grove is the opulent **Seven Gables Inn,** 555 Ocean View Blvd. (© **831/372-4341;** www.pginns.com). In a compound of Victorian buildings constructed in 1886 by the Chase family (as in Chase Manhattan Bank), everything is luxurious and gilded, including the oceanview rooms, which are linked by verdant gardens. If the hotel's booked, ask about the Grand View Inn, a slightly less ornate but comparable B&B next door that's run by the same owners. Rates are $175 to $405 double, including breakfast and afternoon wine and cheese service.

Where to Dine

A historic 1833 adobe house has been converted into **Stokes Restaurant and Bar,** 500 Hartnell St., at Madison Street (© **831/373-1110;** www.stokesrestaurant.com). The rustic yet stylish interior is the perfect showcase for Chef Brandon Miller's carefully crafted California–Mediterranean fare.

The enormous dining room at **Montrio Bistro,** 414 Calle Principal, at Franklin (© **831/648-8880;** www.montrio.com), is definitely the sharpest in town, awash with the buzz of well-dressed diners. Enjoy crispy Dungeness crab cakes with spicy rémoulade, or succulent grilled pork chops with apple, pear, and currant compote.

On sunny afternoons, patrons at **Tarpy's Roadhouse,** 2999 Monterey-Salinas Hwy., at Hwy. 68 and Canyon del Rey near the airport (© **831/647-1444;** www.tarpys.com), relax under umbrellas on the huge outdoor patio, sipping margaritas and munching on Tarpy's legendary Caesar salad. Come nightfall, the place fills quickly with tourists and locals who pile in for the hefty plate of bourbon-molasses pork chops or Dijon-crusted lamb loin, all moderately priced.

If you want to take in the views at Fisherman's Wharf, avoid the many tourist traps and head for **Cafe Fina,** 47 Fisherman's Wharf (© **800/THE-FINA** [843-3462] or 831/372-5200; www.cafefina.com), where mesquite-grilled meats, well-prepared fish, brick-oven pizzas, and delicious salads and pastas give even locals a reason to head here.

In nearby Pacific Grove, Joe Rombi's, 208 17th St. (© **831/373-2416;** www.joe rombi.com), offers an intimate dining room and fresh Italian cuisine (pastas are made that day). At **Fandango,** 223 17th St. (© **831/372-3456;** www.fandangorestaurant. com), provincial Mediterranean specialties from Spain to Greece to North Africa spice up the menu. The five upstairs and downstairs dining rooms have roaring fires, wood tables, and antiqued walls. There's an award-winning international wine list. The **Fishwife at Asilomar Beach,** 1996$^1/_2$ Sunset Dr. (© **831/375-7107;** www.fishwife.com), is a casual, affordable, family-friendly spot offering terrific seafood. All main courses come with vegetables, bread, black beans, and rice or potatoes.

PEBBLE BEACH & THE 17-MILE DRIVE

Pebble Beach is a world unto itself, a pricey, elite golfers' paradise where endless grassy fairways are interrupted only by a few luxury resorts and cliffs where the ocean meets the land. In winter it's also the site of the AT&T Pebble Beach National Pro-Am, a celebrity tournament originally launched in 1937 by crooner Bing Crosby.

But even if you can't afford to stay here, come and check out the beautiful **17-Mile Drive** (which is also a great bike ride). You'll have to fork over $9 to enter the drive, but you'll get to see some of the most exclusive coastal real estate in California. The drive can be entered from any of five gates: two from Pacific Grove to the north, one from Carmel to the south, or two from Monterey to the east. The most convenient entrance from Hwy. 1 is just off the main road at the Holman Highway exit. You may beat traffic by entering at the Carmel Gate and doing the tour backward.

Admission to the drive includes an informative map that lists 26 points of interest. Aside from homes of the ultrarich, highlights include **Seal and Bird Rocks,** where you can see gulls, cormorants, and other offshore birds, as well as seals and sea lions; and **Cypress Point Lookout,** which gives you a 20-mile view all the way to the Big Sur Lighthouse on a clear day. From afar, you can also admire the famous **Lone Cypress** tree that has inspired many artists and photographers (it's no longer accessible on foot). The drive also traverses the **Del Monte Forest,** thick with tame black-tailed deer and often described as a "billionaire's private game preserve." *Note:* One of the best ways to see 17-Mile Drive is by bike. For more information and an interactive map, see **www.pebble beach.com** and click on "17-Mile Drive" at the bottom of the page.

Pebble Beach is synonymous with golf; guests of the posh resorts get first crack at preferred tee times. The most famous of all is the **Pebble Beach Golf Links** (© **800/ 654-9300;** www.pebblebeach.com) at the Lodge at Pebble Beach. Each year it hosts the

CALIFORNIA

12

MONTEREY & BIG SUR

AT&T Pebble Beach National Pro-Am, a celebrity-laden tournament televised world-wide. Jack Nicklaus has claimed, "If I could play only one course for the rest of my life, this would be it." Built in 1919, this 18-hole course is 6,799 yards and par 72; it's precariously perched over a rugged ocean. Greens fees are a staggering $475, and that doesn't include the cart fee for nonguests.

Also frequented by celebrities is the **Spyglass Hill Golf Course,** at Stevenson Drive and Spyglass Hill Road (© 800/654-9300; www.pebblebeach.com), one of the toughest courses in California. It's justifiably famous, at 6,859 yards and par 72 with 5 oceanfront holes. The rest reach deep into the Del Monte Forest. Greens fees are $315 plus cart. Reservations for nonguests should be made a month in advance. The excellent Grill Room restaurant is on the grounds.

Poppy Hills (© 831/622-8239; www.poppyhillsgolf.com), an 18-hole, 6,219-yard course designed by Robert Trent Jones, Jr., on 17-Mile Drive, was named one of the world's top 20 by *Golf Digest.* Fees are $195, plus $34 for the cart rental. You can make reservations 30 days in advance.

Lying on the north end of 17-Mile Drive at the Pebble Beach Resort and Inn at Spanish Bay, the **Links at Spanish Bay** (© 800/654-9300; www.pebblebeach.com) is the most easily booked course and perhaps the most challenging. Robert Trent Jones, Jr., Tom Watson, and Frank Tatum designed it to duplicate a Scottish links course. Greens fees are $250 plus a cart fee. Reservations accepted 60 days in advance.

The **Del Monte Golf Course,** 1300 Sylvan Rd. (© 831/373-2700; www.pebble beach.com), is the oldest course west of the Mississippi, charging some of the most "reasonable" greens fees: $110 per player, plus a cart rental of $20. The course, often cited in magazines for its "grace and charm," is relatively short—only 6,339 yards. This seldom-advertised course, which is at the Hyatt east of Monterey, is part of the Pebble Beach complex but is not along 17-Mile Drive.

Where to Stay & Dine

The **Inn at Spanish Bay,** 2700 17-Mile Dr. (© 800/654-9300 or 831/647-7500; www.pebblebeach.com), surrounded by its world-renowned golf course, is a plush, super-expensive low-rise set on 236 manicured acres. Half the rooms face the ocean and are more expensive than their counterparts, which overlook the forest. Each unit has a fireplace, four-poster bed with down comforter, and deck or patio. Roy Yamaguchi, Hawaii's celebrity chef, offers a Eurasian menu at **Roy's,** the best restaurant in Pebble Beach. A bagpiper strolls the terrace at dusk. Guests enjoy eight tennis courts, pro shops, a superb fitness center, an equestrian center, and a heated pool. Rates are from $580 to $925 double, from $1,075 suite.

For the combined cost of greens fees and a room at the **Lodge at Pebble Beach,** 1700 17-Mile Dr. (© 800/654-9300 or 831/624-3811; www.pebblebeach.com), you could easily create a professional putting green in your own backyard. But if you're a dedicated hacker, you've got to play here at least once. Your ultraplush room will have every conceivable amenity, including a wood-burning fireplace. Amenities include 12 tennis courts, a fitness room, horseback riding, a pool, and hiking trails. Rates are from $665 to $1,150 double; from $1,150 suite.

CARMEL-BY-THE-SEA

Once a bohemian artists' village, Carmel is today an adorable (albeit touristy) town that knows how to celebrate its surroundings. Vibrant wildflower gardens flourish along each residential street, and gnarled cypress trees reach up from white sandy beaches. It's still intimate enough that there's no need for street numbers. But a few hints such as Saks Fifth Avenue, intolerable traffic, and lofty B&B rates indicate we're not in Kansas any-more, but rather a well-preserved upscale tourist haven. If the prices here are too high, you can easily stay in nearby Monterey or Pacific Grove.

The **Carmel Business Association,** P.O. Box 4444, Carmel (© **831/624-2522;** www. carmelcalifornia.org), is on San Carlos Street between Fifth and Sixth streets. It distrib-utes local maps, brochures, and publications. You'll want to pick up the *Guide to Carmel* and a schedule of events. Hours are from 10am to 5pm daily.

What to See & Do

A wonderful stretch of white sand backed by cypress trees, **Carmel Beach City Park** is a bit of heaven on Earth (though the jammed parking lot can feel more like a car rally). There's room for families, surfers, and dogs with their owners (they can run off-leash). If the parking lot is full, try Ocean Avenue. It has some spaces, though they're mostly good for 90 minutes, and you will get a ticket if you park all day. Farther south around the promontory, **Carmel River State Beach** is a less crowded option, with white sand and a bird sanctuary.

If the tourists aren't lying on the beach, then they're probably shopping. This small town packs in more than 500 boutiques and a veritable cornucopia of art galleries. Most of the commercial action is along the small stretch of Ocean Avenue between Junipero and San Antonio.

The **Mission San Carlos Borromeo del Rio Carmelo,** on Basilica Rio Road at Lasuen Drive, off Hwy. 1 (© **831/624-1271;** www.carmelmission.org), is the burial ground of Father Junípero Serra and the second oldest of the 21 Spanish missions he established. The stone church, with its gracefully curving walls and Moorish bell tower, was begun in 1793. The old mission kitchen, the first library in California, the high altar, and the flower gardens are all worth visiting. More than 3,000 Native Americans are buried in the adjacent cemetery; their graves are decorated with seashells. The mission is open Monday through Saturday from 9:30am to 5pm, Sunday from 10:30am to 5pm. Admission is $5 for adults, $4 for seniors, $1 for youth, and free for children 6 and under. Docent-led tours are $7. Call the tour office (© **831/624-1271,** ext. 213) for schedules.

One of Carmel's prettiest homes and gardens is **Tor House,** 26304 Ocean View Ave. (© **831/624-1813;** www.torhouse.org), built by poet Robinson Jeffers. On Carmel Point, the house dates from 1918. Its 40-foot tower has stones embedded in the walls from around the world (including the Great Wall of China). Inside, an old porthole is reputed to have come from the ship on which Napoleon escaped from Elba in 1815. No photography is allowed. Admission is by guided tour only on Friday and Saturday from 10am to 3pm, and reservations are requested. It's $7 for adults, $4 for college students, and $2 for high-school students (no children 11 and under).

Where to Stay

The pricey, intimate **Carriage House Inn,** Junipero Street, between Seventh and Eighth avenues (© **800/433-4732** or 831/625-2585; www.ibts-carriagehouse.com), offers a luxurious atmosphere and lots of pampering. Each room comes with a VCR, fireplace, fridge, and king-size bed with down comforter. While most other choices in town are of the frill-and-lace variety, the Carriage House has a more mature, formal, yet cozy ambi-ence. Rates are from $299 to $369 double, including continental breakfast and afternoon wine and hors d'oeuvres.

MONTEREY & BIG SUR

If you want to stay a bit off the beaten track, consider **Mission Ranch,** 26270 Dolores St. (© **800/538-8221** or 831/624-6436), a converted 1850s dairy farm purchased and restored by Clint Eastwood. The accommodations are scattered amid different structures old and new, surrounded by wetlands and grazing sheep. As befits a ranch, rooms are decorated in a provincial style, with carved wooden beds with handmade quilts. Most are equipped with whirlpool tubs, fireplaces, and decks or patios. The restaurant is terrific. Rates are from $110 to $275 double, including continental breakfast.

Inland from Carmel, in sunny Carmel Valley, is the superplush, superexpensive **Quail Lodge Resort and Golf Club,** 8205 Valley Greens Dr. (© **888/828-8787** or 831/624-2888; www.quaillodge.com). In the foothills of the Santa Lucia Range, Quail Lodge is set on 850 acres of lakes, woodlands, and meadows. Rooms have balconies or terraces; some have fireplaces and wet bars. Guests enjoy an excellent 18-hole golf course, four tennis courts, two outdoor pools, a full-service spa, and hiking and jogging trails. Rates are from $365 to $380 double, $440 to $575 suite.

Back in Carmel, more moderately priced choices include the **Normandy Inn,** Ocean Avenue, between Monte Verde and Casanova streets, 3 blocks from the beach (© **800/343-3825** or 831/624-3825; www.normandyinncarmel.com). Rooms show their age a little but are well appointed, with French country decor and down comforters. The tiny heated pool is banked by a sweet flower garden. The three large family-style units are an especially good deal. Rates are from $98 to $220 double, $165 to $500 suite or cottage, including continental breakfast and afternoon sherry.

The **Cobblestone Inn,** on Junipero Street, between Seventh and Eighth avenues, 1½ blocks from Ocean Avenue (© **800/833-8836** or 831/625-5222; www.cobblestone inncarmel.com), is flowery, well kept, and cute, with hand-stenciled wall decorations and lots of teddy bears. Rooms vary in size; some can be small, and most have showers only, but the largest units include a wet bar, sofa, and separate bedroom. Rates are from $155 to $270 double, including full breakfast and afternoon wine and hors d'oeuvres.

A flower garden welcomes visitors to the **Sandpiper Inn by the Sea,** 2408 Bay View Ave. (© **800/590-6433** or 831/624-6433; www.sandpiper-inn.com), a quiet standby that's been in business for more than 60 years. Rooms are decorated with country antiques and fresh flowers, and Carmel's white-sand beaches are steps away. Rates are from $140 to $275 double, including extended continental breakfast and afternoon sherry and tea.

The **Carmel Sands Lodge** ($85–$199 double), San Carlos and Fifth streets (© **800/252-1255** or 831/624-1255; www.carmelsandslodge.com), and the **Carmel Village Inn** ($105–$245 double, with continental breakfast), Ocean Avenue and Junipero Street (© **800/346-3864** or 831/624-3864; www.carmelvillageinn.com), are well-maintained motor lodges with excellent locations. If you're traveling with pets, try the moderately priced **Cypress Inn,** Lincoln and Seventh (P.O. Box Y), Carmel-by-the-Sea, CA 93921 (© **800/443-7443** or 831/624-3871; www.cypress-inn.com), owned by actress Doris Day. Rates are from $150 to $445 for doubles, $455 to $575 suites, including continental breakfast.

Where to Dine

Though you may not spot owner Clint Eastwood, the **Restaurant at Mission Ranch,** 26270 Dolores St. (© **831/625-9040;** www.missionranchcarmel.com), delivers quality food and a merry atmosphere. Large windows accentuate the view of the marshlands and bay beyond. At happy hour, you'll find some of the cheapest drinks around (and Clint often stops by when he's in town). Prime rib with twice-baked potato and vegetables is the favored dish. At the piano bar, locals and tourists croon their favorites. The Sunday buffet brunch with live jazz piano is hugely popular.

Dark and romantic, the moderately priced **Flying Fish Grill,** in Carmel Plaza, Mission Street between Ocean and Seventh avenues (© 831/625-1962), features fresh seafood with Japanese accents, under the direction of Chef/Owner Kenny Fukumoto. Prepare for sensational main courses, like a savory rare peppered ahi, blackened and served with mustard-and-sesame-soy vinaigrette and angel-hair pasta.

Carmel Bakery, Ocean, between Dolores and Lincoln (© **831/626-8885**), serves inexpensive espresso, soup, sandwiches, and pastries. It's festive and well decorated, with a few tables and chairs, and music playing from speakers overhead. The food and the festive atmosphere at the **Rio Grill,** in the Crossroads Shopping Center, 101 Crossroads Blvd. (© **831/625-5436;** www.riogrill.com), have won over even the locals. The whimsical Santa Fe–style dining room belies the kitchen's serious preparations, which include homemade soups; a rich quesadilla with almonds, cheeses, and smoked-tomato salsa; and barbecue baby back ribs from a wood-burning oven.

BIG SUR

Though there is an actual Big Sur Village 25 miles south of Carmel, "Big Sur" refers to the 90-mile stretch of coastline between Carmel and San Simeon, blessed on one side by the majestic Santa Lucia Range and on the other by the rocky Pacific coastline. It's one of the most romantic and relaxing places on Earth, often misty and mysterious, and if you need respite from the rat race, we can recommend no better place.

Contact the **Big Sur Chamber of Commerce** (© 831/667-2100; www.bigsurcalifornia. org) for specialized information on places and events in Big Sur.

Most of this stretch is state park, and **Hwy. 1** runs its entire length, hugging the ocean the whole way. Restaurants, hotels, and sights are easy to spot—most are directly on the highway—but without major towns as reference points, their addresses can be obscure. For the purposes of orientation, we'll use the River Inn as our mileage guide. Located 29 miles south of Monterey on Hwy. 1, the inn is generally considered to mark the northern end of Big Sur.

Exploring the Big Sur Coast

Big Sur offers visitors tranquillity and natural beauty—ideal for hiking, picnicking, camping, fishing, and beachcombing. The inland **Ventana Wilderness,** maintained by the U.S. Forest Service, contains 167,323 acres straddling the Santa Lucia Mountains and is characterized by steep-sided ridges separated by V-shaped valleys. The streams that cascade through the area are marked by waterfalls, deep pools, and thermal springs. The wilderness offers 237 miles of hiking trails that lead to 55 designated trail camps—a backpacker's paradise. One of the easiest trails to access is the **Pine Ridge Trail** at Big Sur station (© 831/667-2315).

From Carmel, the first stop along Hwy. 1 is **Point Lobos State Reserve** (© 831/624-4909), 3 miles south of Carmel. Sea lions, harbor seals, sea otters, and thousands of seabirds reside in this 1,276-acre reserve. Between December and May, you can spot migrating California gray whales just offshore. Trails follow the shoreline and lead to hidden coves. Parking is limited; on weekends especially, arrive early.

From here, cross the Soberanes Creek, passing **Garrapata State Park** (© 831/624-4909), a 2,879-acre preserve with 4 miles of coastline. It's unmarked and undeveloped, though the trails are maintained. To explore them, you'll need to park at one of the turnouts on Hwy. 1 near Soberanes Point and hike in.

Ten miles south of Carmel, you'll arrive at North Abalone Cove. From here, Palo Colorado Road leads back into the wilderness to the first of the Forest Service camping areas at **Bottchers Gap** ($12 to camp, $5 to park overnight; C **805/434-1996;** www.campone.com).

Continuing south, about 13 miles from Carmel, you'll cross the **Bixby Bridge** and see the **Point Sur Lighthouse** off in the distance. The Bixby Bridge, one of the world's highest single-span concrete bridges, towers nearly 270 feet above Bixby Creek Canyon and offers gorgeous canyon and ocean views from several observation alcoves at regular intervals along the bridge. The lighthouse, which sits 361 feet above the surf on a volcanic rock promontory, was built in 1889, when only a horse trail provided access to this part of the world. Lighthouse tours, which take 2 to 3 hours and involve a steep half-mile hike, are scheduled on most weekends. Moonlight tours are offered as well; check the website for specific dates. For information, call C **831/625-4419** or visit www.pointsur.org. Admission is $8 for adults, $4 for youths ages 6 to 17, and free for kids 5 and under.

About 3 miles south of the lighthouse is **Andrew Molera State Park** (C **831/667-2315;** www.bigsurcalifornia.org), which is much less crowded than Pfeiffer–Big Sur. Miles of trails meander through meadows and along beaches and bluffs. **Molera Big Sur Trail Rides** (C **800/942-5486** or 831/625-5486; www.molerahorsebacktours.com) offers coastal trail rides for riders of all levels of experience. The 2¹/₂-mile-long beach is accessible via a mile-long path flanked in spring by wildflowers and offers excellent tidepooling. The park also has campgrounds.

Back on Hwy. 1, you'll soon reach the village of Big Sur, where commercial services are available.

About 26 miles south of Carmel you'll come to **Big Sur Station** (C **831/667-2315),** where you can pick up maps and other information about the region. It's a quarter-mile past the entrance to **Pfeiffer–Big Sur State Park** (C **831/667-2315),** an 810-acre park that offers 218 camping sites along the Big Sur River (C **800/444-7275** for camping reservations), picnicking, fishing, and hiking. It's a scenic park of redwoods, conifers, oaks, and open meadows, but often gets crowded. The **Big Sur Lodge** in the park has cabins with fireplaces and other facilities. Admission to the park is $5 per car, and it's open daily from dawn to dusk.

A mile south of the entrance to Pfeiffer–Big Sur State Park is the turnoff to Sycamore Canyon Road (unmarked), which will take you 2 winding miles down to beautiful **Pfeiffer Beach,** a great place to soak in the sun on the wide expanse of golden sand. It's open for day use only, there's no fee, and it's the only beach accessible by car (but not motor homes).

Back on Hwy. 1, the road travels 11 miles past Sea Lion Cove to Julia Pfeiffer Burns State Park. High above the ocean is the famous **Nepenthe** restaurant, the retreat bought by Orson Welles for Rita Hayworth in 1944. A few miles south is the **Coast Gallery** (C **800/797-6869** or 831/667-2301; www.coastgalleries.com), which shows lithographs of works by Henry Miller. The gallery's Coast Cafe offers simple serve-yourself lunches of soup, sandwiches, baked goods, and coffee drinks. Miller fans will also want to stop at the **Henry Miller Memorial Library** on Hwy. 1 (C **831/667-2574;** www.henrymiller.org), 30 miles south of Carmel and ¹/₄ mile south of Nepenthe restaurant. The library displays and sells books and artwork by Miller and houses a permanent collection of first editions. Admission is free; hours are from 11am to 6pm daily in the summer and 11am to 6pm Thursday through Sunday winter.

Julia Pfeiffer Burns State Park (© 831/667-2315; www.bigsurcalifornia.org) encompasses some of Big Sur's most spectacular coastline. To get a closer look, take the trail from the parking area at McWay Canyon, which leads under the highway to a bluff overlooking 80-foot-high McWay Waterfall, dropping directly into the ocean. It's less crowded here than at Pfeiffer–Big Sur, and there are miles of trails to explore in the 3,580-acre park. Scuba divers can apply for permits to explore the 1,680-acre underwater reserve.

From here, the road skirts the Ventana Wilderness, passing Anderson and Marble Peaks and the Esalen Institute, before crossing the Big Creek Bridge to Lucia and several campgrounds farther south. **Kirk Creek Campground,** about 3 miles north of Pacific Valley, offers camping with ocean views and beach access. Beyond Pacific Valley, the **Sand Dollar Beach** picnic area is a good place to stop and enjoy the coastal view and take a stroll. Two miles south of Sand Dollar is **Jade Cove,** a popular spot for rockhounds. From here, it's about another 27 miles past the Piedras Blancas Light Station to San Simeon.

Where to Camp

Big Sur is one of the most spectacular places in the state for camping. One of the most glorious settings can be found at **Pfeiffer–Big Sur State Park,** on Hwy. 1, 26 miles south of Carmel (© 831/667-2315), with hundreds of secluded sites in the redwood forest. Hiking trails, streams, and the river are steps away from your sleeping bag, and the most modern amenities are the 25¢ showers. Water faucets are located between sites, and each spot has its own picnic table and fire pit. There are, however, no RV hookups or electricity. At the entrance are a store, gift shop, restaurant, and cafe. Fees are $25 per night for family sites; call © 800/444-7275 or see www.reserveamerica.com for reservations.

The entrance to the **Ventana Campground,** on Hwy. 1, 28 miles south of Carmel and 4¹⁄₄ miles south of the River Inn (© 831/667-2712; www.ventanawildernesscampground. com), is adjacent to the Ventana Resort entrance, but the comparison stops there. This is pure rusticity. The 80 campsites, on 40 acres of a redwood canyon, are spaced well apart on a hillside and shaded by towering trees. Each has a picnic table and fire ring but no electricity, RV hookups, or river access. Three bathhouses have hot showers (25¢ fee). Reserve a space with a credit card for 1 night's deposit. Or mail a deposit check, the dates you'd like to stay, and a stamped, self-addressed envelope at least 2 weeks in advance (earlier during peak months). Rates are $35 for a site for two with one vehicle. An additional person is $5 extra, and it'll cost you $5 to bring Fido. Rates include the entrance fee for your car. Open March through October.

Big Sur Campground and Cabins is on Hwy. 1, 26 miles south of Carmel (© 831/667-2322; www.bigsurcalifornia.org/camping.html). Sites are cramped, so the feel is more like a camping village than an intimate retreat. However, it's well maintained and perfect for families, who love the playground, river swimming, and inner-tube rentals. Each campsite has its own wood-burning fire pit, picnic table, and freshwater faucet within 25 feet of the pitching area. There are also RV water and electric hookups. Facilities include bathhouses with hot showers, laundry facilities, an aged volleyball/ basketball court, and a grocery store. There are 81 tent sites (30 RV-ready with electricity and water hookup), plus 13 cabins (all with shower). The cabins have country furnishings, wood-burning ovens, patios, and full kitchens. Rates are $32 to $48 for a tent site for five people (plus $4 extra for electricity and water), $38 to $58 for an RV site for up to five people, $75 to $95 for a tent cabin (bed, but no heat or plumbing) for three, or

$115 to $345 for a cabin for six. Rates include the entrance for your car. MasterCard and Visa are accepted. Pets cost $4 for campsites and $12 for tent cabins; pets are not allowed in the other cabins. It's open year-round.

Where to Stay

Only a handful of Big Sur's accommodations offer the kind of pampering and luxury you'd expect in a fine urban hotel; even direct-dial phones and TVs are rare. Big Sur hotels are especially busy in summer, when advance reservations are required. If you're having trouble securing a room or a site, contact the **chamber of commerce** (© 831/667-2100; www.bigsurcalifornia.org) for other options.

In a class by itself is the incredibly expensive **Post Ranch Inn,** on Hwy. 1 (© 800/527-2200 or 831/667-2200; www.postranchinn.com), one of our favorite places to stay on the planet. Perched on 98 acres of pristine seaside ridges 1,200 feet above the Pacific, the wood-and-glass cottages are built around existing trees—some are elevated on stilts to avoid damaging native redwood root structures. Each room has a fireplace, terrace, massage table, CD player, and wet bar filled with complimentary goodies. There's also a small workout room, the best Jacuzzi we've ever encountered (it's on a cliff and seems to join the sky), a pool, as well as a number of spa services, and sun decks. The only drawback is that the vibe can be stuffy, which is due more to the clientele than the staff. The **Sierra Mar** restaurant is one of the best (and most expensive) dining choices in the area. Rates are from $550 to $1,485 double, including buffet breakfast.

Equally as expensive, but perhaps not delivering quite as much for your money, is the luxuriously rustic Ventana Inn and Spa, Hwy. 1 (© 800/628-6500 or 831/667-2331; www.ventanainn.com). On 243 mountainous oceanfront acres, Ventana has an elegance that's atypical of the region and attracts famous guests. The accommodations, in one- and two-story natural-wood buildings along winding, wildflower-flanked paths, blend in with the Big Sur countryside. Rooms are divinely decorated in warm, cozy luxury, with such amenities as VCRs, fridges, and terraces or balconies overlooking the ocean or forest. Most offer fireplaces; some have hot tubs and cathedral ceilings. A small fitness center offers the basics—but you'll be more inspired to hike the pastoral grounds, where you'll find a pool, a rustic library, and clothing-optional tanning decks and spa tubs. Rates run from $500 to $1,100 double, from $925 cottage, including continental breakfast and afternoon wine and cheese.

Affordable choices include the family-friendly **Big Sur Lodge,** in Pfeiffer–Big Sur State Park, Hwy. 1, 26 miles south of Carmel (© 800/424-4787 or 831/667-3100; www.bigsurlodge.com). The motel-style cabins are huge, clean, and heated. Some have fireplaces or kitchenettes. All offer porches or decks with views of the redwoods or the Santa Lucia Range. In addition, the lodge has its own pool, grocery store, and laundry facilities. Rates run from $199 to $249 cottage, $259 to $319 kitchen suite, $289 to $359 kitchen suite with fireplace; park entrance fee included.

Deetjen's Big Sur Inn, Hwy. 1 (© 831/667-2377; www.deetjens.com), is affordable and cute. Folks either love or hate the accommodations, which are in a redwood canyon. They're rustic and adorable, with their old-fashioned furnishings and down-home feel. But those who want extensive creature comforts should go elsewhere. Rooms are far from soundproof, so children 11 and under are allowed only if families reserve both rooms of a two-room building, and not all of the units have private bathrooms. There's no insulation, so prepare to crank up the fire or wood-burning stove. The cabins near the river offer the most privacy. The restaurant is a local favorite. Rates are from $95 to $200 double with private bathroom.

Cielo Restaurant, at the Ventana Inn and Spa (© 831/667-4242; www.ventanainn. com), is woodsy but extravagant. The airy cedar interior is divided into two spaces: the lounge, where a wooden bar and cocktail tables look onto a roaring fire and through picturesque windows; and the dining room, which overlooks the mountains and ocean. But in summer it's the patio, with its views of the Big Sur coast, that's the coveted spot. Lunch offers sandwiches, burgers, and an array of gourmet salads; dinner includes oak-grilled Kansas City steak au poivre and caramelized Maine Diver scallops in a red Thai curry–coconut milk broth.

Stop by **Nepenthe,** on Hwy. 1, 29 miles south of Carmel, 5 miles south of the River Inn (© 831/667-2345; www.nepenthebigsur.com), for the outrageous views. Sitting 808 feet above sea level along the cliffs overlooking the ocean, Nepenthe is naturally celestial. On a warm day, join the crowds on the terrace. On colder days, go the indoor route—the redwood-and-adobe structure offers an equally magical view, and with its fireplace, redwood ceilings, and bayfront windows, the atmosphere is something you can't find anywhere else. Unfortunately, that's not been our experience with the over-priced fare, so just come for lunch and spend big dinner bucks elsewhere.

One level below Nepenthe, **Café Kevah** (© 831/667-2345; www.nepenthebigsur. com) offers the same celestial view (at a fraction of the price), a more casual environment, and better food. Seating is entirely outdoors—a downside when the biting fog rolls in (bring a jacket), but perfect on a clear day. Fare here is more eclectic than Nepenthe's, with such choices as homemade granola, baby greens with broiled salmon and papaya, chicken brochettes, and new-potato hash.

The **Big Sur River Inn,** on Hwy. 1, 2 miles north of Pfeiffer–Big Sur State Park (© 831/667-2700; www.bigsurriverinn.com), is an unpretentious, rustic, down-home restaurant that's got something for all tastes. In winter, the wooden dining room is the prime spot; on summer days, some folks grab their patio chair and a cocktail and hang out literally midstream. Along with the local color, attractions include a full bar and good ol' American fare.

With the feel of an English farmhouse, **Deetjen's Big Sur Inn Restaurant,** on Calif. 1 (© 831/667-2377; www.deetjens.com), is the perfect venue for delicious comfort food and friendly service, including great breakfasts.

The **Big Sur Bakery and Restaurant,** on Hwy. 1, just past the post office and a mile south of Pfeiffer–Big Sur State Park (© 831/667-0520; www.bigsurbakery.com), offers healthy fare, ranging from wood-fired pizzas and portobello burgers at lunch to salmon, tuna, and chicken selections at dinner. Pastries are baked on the premises.

5 SAN SIMEON: HEARST CASTLE

Few places on Earth compare to **Hearst Castle.** The 165-room estate of publishing magnate William Randolph Hearst, high above the coastal village of San Simeon, atop a hill he called La Cuesta Encantada ("the Enchanted Hill"), is an ego trip par excellence. One of the last great estates of America's Gilded Age, it's an astounding, over-the-top monument to wealth—and to the power that money brings.

Hearst Castle is a sprawling compound, constructed over 28 years in a Mediterranean Revival architectural style, set in undeniably magical surroundings. The focal point of the estate is the you-have-to-see-it-to-believe-it **Casa Grande,** a 100-plus-room mansion brimming with priceless art and antiques. Hearst acquired most of his vast European collection via New York auction houses, where he bought entire rooms (including walls, ceilings, and floors) and shipped them here. Each week, railroad cars carrying fragments of Roman temples, lavish doors and carved ceilings from Italian monasteries, Flemish tapestries, ancient Persian rugs, and antique French furniture arrived—5 tons at a time—in San Simeon. The result is an old-world castle done in a priceless mix-and-match style.

Three opulent "guesthouses" also contain magnificent works of art. A lavish private movie theater was used to screen first-run films twice nightly—once for employees, and again for the guests and host. The ranch became a playground for the Hollywood crowd as well as dignitaries like Winston Churchill and George Bernard Shaw, who is said to have remarked of the estate, "This is the way God would have done it if He had the money."

And then there are the swimming pools. The Roman-inspired indoor pool has intricate mosaic work, Carrara-marble replicas of Greek gods and goddesses, and alabaster globe lamps that create the illusion of moonlight. The breathtaking outdoor Greco-Roman Neptune pool, flanked by marble colonnades that frame the distant sea, is one of the mansion's most memorable features.

In 1957, in exchange for a massive tax write-off, the Hearst Corporation donated the estate to the state of California (while retaining ownership of approx. 80,000 acres). The California Department of Parks and Recreation now administers it as a State Historic Monument.

ESSENTIALS

GETTING THERE   Hearst Castle is on Hwy. 1, about 42 miles north of San Luis Obispo, 94 miles south of Monterey, 250 miles north of Los Angeles, and 250 miles south of San Francisco. From San Francisco or Monterey, take U.S. 101 south to Paso Robles, then Hwy. 46 west to Hwy. 1, and Hwy. 1 north to the castle. From Los Angeles, take U.S. 101 north to San Luis Obispo, then Hwy. 1 north to the castle. Park in the visitor center lot; a bus takes guided tour guests up the hill to the estate. The movie theater and visitor center adjoin the parking lot and are easily accessible without heading up to the actual estate.

VISITOR INFORMATION   To get information about Hearst Castle, call ✆ **800/444-4445** or 805/927-2020, or log onto **www.hearstcastle.org**. For more information on nearby Cambria (see below), check out **www.cambria-online.com** or stop into the **Cambria Chamber of Commerce**'s visitor center at 767 Main St., in the west village (✆ **805/927-3624**; www.cambriachamber.org).

TOURING THE ESTATE

Hearst Castle can be visited only by guided tours, which are conducted daily beginning at 8:20am, except on New Year's Day, Thanksgiving, and Christmas. Two to six tours leave every hour, depending on the season. Allow 2 hours between starting times if you plan on taking more than one tour. Reservations are recommended and can be made up to 8 weeks in advance. Tickets can be purchased by phone or online at California Reservations (✆ **800/444-4445**; www.hearstcastle.org). If you're ordering tickets from outside the United States, call ✆ **916/414-8400**, ext. 4100. Tickets for the daytime tours are $24 for adults and $12 for kids 6 to 17. The evening tour is $30 for adults and $15 for kids. Children 5 and under are free. Prices are a few bucks cheaper during the off season, September 16 to May 14.

The **Experience Tour (Tour 1)** is ideal for first-time visitors and is the first to get filled up. In addition to the swimming pools, this tour visits several rooms on the ground floor taken during the castle's heyday.

Tour 2 focuses on Casa Grande's upper floors, including Hearst's opulent library, private suite of rooms, and lots of fabulous bathrooms. Tour 2 is a fine choice for first-timers if you're planning to take only one tour, particularly if your interest lies more in the home's private areas.

Tour 3, which delves into the construction and subsequent alterations of Hearst Castle, is fascinating for architecture buffs and detail hounds, but it shouldn't be the first and only tour if you've never visited the castle before.

From April to October, **Tour 4** is dedicated to the estate's gardens, terraces, and walk-ways, the Casa del Mar guesthouse, the wine cellar of Casa Grande, and the dressing rooms at the Neptune Pool. This tour does not visit any interiors of the main house.

Evening tours are held most Friday and Saturday nights during spring and fall, and usually nightly around Christmas (when the house, decked out for the holidays, is magical). Thirty minutes longer than the daytime tours, they visit highlights of the main house, the most elaborate guesthouse, and the illuminated pools and gardens.

No matter how many tours you take in a day, you must return to the visitor center each time and ride the bus back to the top of the hill with your tour group, so allow at least 2 hours between tours when you buy your tickets. You'll find plenty to keep you busy at the visitor center before, after, and in between tours: an observation deck of the Enchanted Hill, two gift shops, ballpark-quality food vendors, and a good small museum. The permanent William Randolph Hearst Exhibit focuses on the castle's history, art, and architecture.

Tip: Wear comfortable shoes—you'll walk about a half-mile per tour, each of which includes 150 to 400 steps. (Wheelchair tours are available by calling ✆ **800/444-4445** or 805/927-2020, with 10 days notice.)

You can visit the giant-screen **Hearst Castle National Geographic Theater** regardless of whether you take a tour. Larger-than-life films include the 40-minute *Hearst Castle: Building the Dream* and other films in five-story-high iWERKS format (just like IMAX) with seven-channel surround sound. Shows begin every 45 minutes throughout the day. The movie is included in the price of Tour 1; by itself it's $8 for adults, $6 for kids 6 to 17. For current information, call ✆ **805/927-6811** or visit their website at www.ng theater.com.

STAYING IN NEARBY CAMBRIA

Just south of San Simeon, Cambria, known as an artists' colony, is a charming town with little more than 4 blocks of art and antiques shops, restaurants, and a handful of B&Bs. It's the perfect escape and an ideal place to stay when visiting Hearst Castle.

Gray whales pass through the area from late December to early February, and since 1990, thousands of **elephant seals** have made the shore just north of the Hearst Castle entrance their year-round playground—much to the delight of locals and nature enthusiasts. Keep your distance from these mammoth mammals: They're a protected species and can be dangerous if approached. There is a parking lot, and docents are usually on hand to answer questions. The beaches and coves are also wonderful places for humans to play. For more information, see www.beachcalifornia.com/piedras.html. For more information on Cambria, check out **www.cambria-online.com.**

Our favorite B&B in the area is the **Olallieberry Inn,** 2476 Main St., Cambria (✆ **888/927-3222** or 805/927-3222; www.olallieberry.com), an 1873 Greek Revival house whose rates are on the high side of moderate. A berry motif reigns, and the guest rooms are lovingly and individually appointed. The grounds are manicured but bloom whimsically, in the afternoon the aromas of baking waft through the main house, and the staff does everything imaginable to make your stay special. Rates run from $130 to $200 double, including full breakfast and evening wine and hors d'oeuvres.

Other reliable lodging choices include the **Best Western Cavalier Oceanfront Resort,** 9415 Hearst Dr. (Hwy. 1), San Simeon (© 800/826-8168 or 805/927-4688; www. cavalierresort.com), a family-friendly place that is the only true oceanfront resort in the area (rates $159–$319 double), and the **Ragged Point Inn,** 19019 Hwy. 1 (© 805/927-4502; www.raggedpointinn.com), 21 miles north of Cambia, with sweeping ocean views from each basic motel-style room. Rates range from $149 to $329, depending on the day of the week and season.

---

6 LAKE TAHOE

Lake Tahoe has long been California's most popular recreational playground. In summer, you can enjoy boating and watersports, in-line skating, camping, ballooning, horseback riding, biking, parasailing—the list is endless. In winter, Lake Tahoe becomes one of the nation's premier ski destinations.

And then there's the lake. It's disputable whether Lake Tahoe is the most beautiful lake in the world, but it's certainly near the top of the list. It's famous for its pure water (a white dinner plate at a depth of 75 ft. would be visible from the surface) and its size (at 22 miles long and 12 miles wide, it's the largest Alpine lake in North America).

The north and south shores have about as much in common as snow cones and sand castles. The scenery is absolutely stunning on the less developed north shore, although the lake isn't quite as accessible on this side. South Lake Tahoe is brimming with developments: high-rise casinos, condos, and mini-malls. Which side you choose to stay on is important, as driving from one end of the lake to the other is a 1- to 2-hour affair on summer weekends and downright treacherous during snowstorms. So which side is for you? If you're here to gamble, stay south: The selection of casinos is better and the lodging more abundant. The south is also the place for families that are watching their wallets, as this is where you'll find the greatest concentration of affordable motels. The north shore offers a better selection of upscale lodgings and restaurants, and the scenery is more pristine.

ESSENTIALS

GETTING THERE   By Plane   **Reno-Tahoe International Airport** (45 min. to the north shore, 90 min. to the south shore; www.renoairport.com) is served by nearly a dozen major airlines. Rent a car or take a shuttle up to the lake: **No Stress Express** (© 888/4-SHUTTLE [474-8885]; www.nostressexpress.com) serves the north and west shores; **Tahoe Casino Express** (© 866/89-TAHOE [898-2463]; www.southtahoeexpress. com) serves the south shore (1-day advance reservations recommended). *Note:* For more on the airport and nearby Reno, see p. 743.

By Train   **Amtrak** (© 800/USA-RAIL [872-7245]; www.amtrak.com) stops in Truckee, 10 miles north of the lake. Public transportation (TART or Truce Trolley) is available, or you can take a taxi to the north shore.

By Car   It's a 4-hour drive from San Francisco; take **I-80 east** to Sacramento, then **U.S. 50** to the south shore, or I-80 east to **Calif. 89** or **Calif. 267** to the north shore. Be prepared for snow in the winter. During heavy storms, you won't be permitted to pass the

checkpoints without four-wheel-drive or chains. From Los Angeles, it's a 9-hour drive; take
I-5 through the Central Valley to Sacramento, then follow the directions above.

VISITOR INFORMATION   In Tahoe City, stop by the **Tahoe City Visitor Information Center,** 380 N. Lake Blvd. (© **800/824-6348;** www.PureTahoeNorth.com). In Incline Village, go to the **Incline Village/Crystal Bay Visitors Center,** 969 Tahoe Blvd. (© **800/468-2463** or 775/832-1606; www.gotahoe.com). Go to the **South Lake Tahoe Chamber of Commerce,** 3066 Lake Tahoe Blvd. (© **530/541-5255;** www.tahoeinfo. com). Many other websites offer information about Lake Tahoe, including www.virtual tahoe.com, www.skilaketahoe.com, www.laketahoeconcierge.com, www.gotahoenorth. com, and www.tahoevacationguide.com.

LAKE CRUISES

The *Tahoe Queen* (© **800/238-2463;** www.zephyrcove.com), which departs from the Marina Village at Ski Run Boulevard in South Lake Tahoe, is also an authentic paddle-wheeler offering Emerald Bay sightseeing tours ($46 adults, $22 children) and dinner/dance cruises ($106 adults, $71 children). Live music, buffet breakfast, dinner, and appetizers are all available on board.

The *Tahoe Gal* (© **800/218-2464** or 530/583-0141; www.tahoegal.com), departing from the Lighthouse Marina (behind Safeway) in Tahoe City, is the only cruise boat on the North Shore. Cruises include the Scenic Brunch Cruise ($34 adults, $16 children), Emerald Bay ($38 adults, $19 children), Happy Hour (4:30–6pm; $25 adults, $14 children), and Sunset Dinner ($35 adults, $16 children). *Note:* Prices are for the cruise only; food and beverages cost extra.

Woodwind Sailing Cruises (© **888/867-6394**) runs daily sightseeing tours ($32 adults, $15 children 3–12) and a Sunset Champagne Cruise ($42). *Woodwind I,* a 30-passenger Searunner trimaran, sails to Emerald Bay from Camp Richardson Marina in South Lake Tahoe. The *Woodwind II,* a 50-passenger Searunner catamaran, sails from Zephyr Cove Marina.

Tahoe Sailing Charters (© **530/583-6200;** www.tahoesail.com) offers scenic 2-hour afternoon ($50) or sunset cruises ($60) aboard the *Tahoe Cruz,* a sleek 50-foot Santa Cruz–class yacht with a 12-foot beam and plenty of elbowroom. Guests can take turns on the helm or just sit back, relax, and let captain and crew sail the deep blue. Complimentary refreshments and snacks are included with every voyage. The *Tahoe Cruz* sails daily from the Tahoe City Marina on Lake Tahoe's north shore.

A DRIVE AROUND THE LAKE

We'll start at the California–Nevada border in South Lake Tahoe and loop around the western shore on Hwy. 89 to Tahoe City and beyond. U.S. 50, which runs along the south shore, is an overdeveloped strip that obliterates any view of the lake, but keep heading west.

First stop is the **Tallac Historic Site,** a cluster of rustic 100-year-old mansions that provide a glimpse into Tahoe's past. Throughout the summer, the **Valhalla Festival of Arts and Music** (© **530/541-4975;** www.valhallatahoe.com) showcases jazz, bluegrass, rock, mariachi, and classical music.

From here, Hwy. 89 climbs northward. Soon you'll be peering down into beautiful **Emerald Bay,** a 3-mile-long inlet containing tiny Fanette Island, which has an old stone teahouse clearly situated at its peak. Across Hwy. 89 from Emerald Bay, there's another parking area. From here, it's a short, steep, quarter-mile hike to a footbridge above **Eagle Falls,** then about a mile to **Eagle Lake.**

It's not surprising that someone chose to build a mansion right here overlooking the bay—**Vikingsholm** (© 530/541-3030; www.vikingsholm.com), a 38-room replica of a medieval Viking castle. Tours of this unique structure are available from mid-June to Labor Day every half-hour between 10am and 4pm.

From here, it's only about 2 miles to **D. L. Bliss State Park** (© 530/525-7982), where you'll find one of the lake's best beaches, though it's crowded in summer. The park also contains 168 campsites and several trails, including one along the shoreline.

About 7 miles farther on, **Sugar Pine State Park** (© 530/525-7232) is the largest of the lake's parks and also the only one that has year-round camping. In summer, you can visit the beaches in the park plus a nature trail; in winter, there's cross-country skiing on well-maintained trails.

It's a clear drive through the small town of Homewood (site of the ski resort of the same name) to Tahoe City, which is smaller and more appealing than South Lake Tahoe, although it, too, has its share of strip development.

At Tahoe City, Hwy. 89 turns off to Truckee and to Alpine Meadows and Squaw Valley ski resorts. Squaw Valley is only 5 miles out, and a ride on the **Squaw Valley cable car** (© 530/583-6985) will reward you with incredible vistas from 2,000 feet above the valley floor. It runs year-round and costs $22 for adults, $17 for seniors, and $6 for children 12 and under.

If you continue around the lake on Hwy. 28, you'll reach Carnelian Bay, Tahoe Vista, and Kings Beach before crossing the state line into Nevada to Crystal Bay, Incline Village, the Ponderosa Ranch, and Sand Harbor Beach. **Kings Beach State Recreation Area** (© 530/546-7248), 12 miles east of Tahoe City, is a long, wide beach and picnic area, jammed in summer with sunbathers and swimmers.

As you approach **Crystal Bay,** you will immediately know, by the string of small casinos that suddenly appear, that you have crossed the state line. The **Cal-Neva Resort, Spa & Casino** on the right was once owned by Frank Sinatra and has a celebrity-studded history. The state line goes right through the lodge, and gambling is allowed only on the Nevada side (it's worth stopping to see). The east shore of the lake is largely undeveloped and scenic. Drive about 4 miles south of Incline Village to **Sand Harbor** (© 775/831-0494), one of the lake's best-loved beaches, home to the popular **Lake Tahoe Shakespeare Festival** (© 800/747-4697; www.tahoebard.com) every mid-July to August. In addition to turquoise water dotted with big boulders and a wide sandy beach, you'll find nature trails, picnic areas, and boating.

South of Sand Harbor, if you wish, you can turn inland to Spooner Lake and Carson City, or continue south along Hwy. 28 to an outcropping called **Cave Rock,** where the highway passes through 75 feet of solid stone. Farther along is **Zephyr Cove,** from which the tour boats depart. You'll then return to Stateline and South Lake Tahoe, your original starting point.

SUMMER ACTIVITIES

MOUNTAIN BIKING   A dizzying choice of mountain biking trails awaits mountain bikers in Lake Tahoe. For maps and information, check with one of the bicycle-rental shops. In North Lake Tahoe, try the **Olympic Bike Shop,** 620 N. Lake Blvd., Tahoe City (© 530/581-2500; www.olympicbikeshop.com), or **Tahoe Bike & Ski,** 8499 N. Lake Blvd., Kings Beach (© 530/546-7437; www.tahoebikeski.com). In South Tahoe, try **Anderson's Bike Rental,** 645 Emerald Bay Rd. (© 530/541-0500), or **Lakeview Sports,** 3131 Hwy. 50 at El Dorado Beach (© 530/544-0183).

Another great choice is **Cyclepaths Mountain Bike Adventures,** 1785 W. Lake Blvd. in Tahoe Park, a few miles south of Tahoe City (© **800/780-BIKE** [780-2453] or 530/581-1171; www.cyclepaths.com), where you can arrange a guided off-road tour. Whether you're into hard-core downhill single track or easygoing scenic outings, the expert guides will provide you with the necessary gear, food, and transportation.

BOAT RENTALS, WATERSPORTS & PARASAILING   Nothing beats actually getting out on the water. Take a guided tour, go off on your own, or just paddle around. Here are a few reliable choices: **Zephyr Cove Marina** (© **800/238-2463;** www.zephyrcove. com) is the lake's largest marina. Here you can parasail, charter sportfishing trips, or take guided tours. You can also rent motorized boats, pedal boats, kayaks, canoes, water-ski equipment, and jet skis. **Tahoe City Marina,** 700 N. Lake Blvd., Tahoe City (© **530/ 583-1039**), rents motorized boats, sailboats, and fishing boats. Sailboat cruises are available. This is also the location for **Lake Tahoe Parasailing** (© **530/583-7245**). **Tahoe Paddle and Oar,** North Lake Beach Center, 8299 N. Lake Blvd., Kings Beach (© **530/ 581-3029;** www.tahoepaddle.com), is a good place to rent kayaks, canoes, pedal boats, and windsurfing equipment. Paddling around in the clear waters of Crystal Bay is great fun.

FISHING   The cold, clear waters of Lake Tahoe are home to kokanee salmon and rainbow, brown, and Mackinaw trout. With lots of hiding places in the deep water, fishing here is a challenge, and many anglers opt to use a guide or charter boat. There are dozens of charter companies offering daily excursions. Rates run about $65 for a half-day to $95 for a whole day (bait, tackle, fish cleaning, and food included). On the North Shore, try **Mickey's Big Mack Charters** at the Sierra Boat Company in Carnelian Bay (© **800/ 877-1462** or 530/546-4444; www.mickeysbigmack.com). On the South Shore, try **Avid Fisherman,** Zephyr Cove (© **775/588-7675**); **Blue Ribbon Fishing Charters,** Tahoe Keys Marina (© **530/544-6552;** www.blueribbonfishing.com); or **Tahoe Sportfishing,** 900 Ski Run Blvd. (© **800/696-7797** or 530/541-5448; www.tahoesportfishing.com).

If you'd rather try your hand at fly-fishing, the **Northstar-at-Tahoe** resort (© **530/ 582-5393;** www.northstarattahoe.com) has a private 10-acre reservoir stocked with hundreds of rainbow trout, reserved for catch-and-release fly-fishing only. Equipment is available for guests at no extra cost, and there's a guide on-site daily to provide helpful hints.

GOLF   With its world-class golf courses, mild summer weather, and magnificent scenery, Lake Tahoe is a golfer's paradise. All of the following courses are very busy in the summer, so call *far* in advance for tee times. For more information about Tahoe-area golf courses, log on to **www.tahoesbest.com/Golf**.

The north end of the lake has four highly rated courses: **Incline Village Championship Course,** 955 Fairway Blvd.; the smaller **Incline Village Mountain (Executive) Course,** 690 Wilson Way (© **866/925-GOLF** [925-4653] for both; www.golfincline. com); **Northstar-at-Tahoe** (© **530/562-2490;** p. 871); and the **Resort at Squaw Creek** (© **800/327-3353;** p. 872).

In the south, **Edgewood,** U.S. 50 at Lake Parkway, Stateline (© **775/588-3566;** www.edgewood-tahoe.com), is home of the Celebrity Golf Championship; **Lake Tahoe Golf Course,** 2500 Emerald Bay Rd., South Lake Tahoe (© **530/577-0788;** www. laketahoegc.com), also has some good 9-hole municipal courses. There's also **Old Brockway Golf Course,** 7900 N. Lake Blvd., Kings Beach (© **530/546-9909;** www.oldbrockway. com); **Tahoe City Golf Course,** 251 N. Lake Blvd., Tahoe City (© **530/583-1516**); and **Bijou Municipal Golf Course,** 3464 Fairway Ave., South Lake Tahoe (© **530/542-6097**).

Most stables offer a variety of guided trail rides and lessons for individuals, families, and groups. Choose the one that appeals to your sense of adventure: 1- to 2-hour trail rides; breakfast, lunch, or dinner rides; half-day, full-day, overnight, and extended pack trips. Expect to pay $20 to $25 for a 1-hour ride, $6 for a half-hour pony ride. Saddle up and savor the scenery. Try **Alpine Meadows Stables,** 355 Alpine Meadows Rd., Tahoe City (© **530/583-3905**); **Squaw Valley Stables,** 1525 Squaw Valley Rd., north of Tahoe City (© **530/583-7433**); **Camp Richardson Corral,** Hwy. 89, South Lake Tahoe (© **530/541-3113**); or **Zephyr Cove Stables,** Zephyr Cove Resort, U.S. 50 at Zephyr Cove (© **775/588-5664;** www.zephyrcovestables.com).

RIVER RAFTING   For a swift but gentle ride down the Truckee River, try **Truckee River Raft Rental,** 185 River Rd., Tahoe City (© **530/583-0123;** www.truckeeriverraft. com). It's available only in the summer, and the rates are $35 for adults and $30 for children 6 to 12 (kids 5 and under are free). If you prefer a more exciting white-water experience, **Tributary Whitewater Tours** (© **800/672-3846;** www.whitewatertours. com) offers daily excursions (in season) down the Truckee River amid Class 2 to 3-plus rapids. It's exciting, but not dangerously so. For a half-day trip, rates range from $68 to $98 for adults and $60 to $70 for kids 7 and older.

SKIING

With the largest concentration of ski resorts in North America, Lake Tahoe is California's best skiing destination. The ski season typically lasts from November to May and frequently extends into the summer. Lift tickets last winter ranged from $44 to $75 per day for adults, and from free to $39 for children, with special rates for seniors. Ticket prices rise every year, but bargains are available, particularly midweek. Many resorts, hotels, and motels offer ski packages. Contact the visitor centers or visit the websites listed under "Visitor Information," above, to look for these values. The resorts offer instruction for adults and children, equipment rental, special courses for snowboarding, and restaurants. Most have free shuttles.

Six miles from Tahoe City, midsize **Alpine Meadows** (© 530/583-4232; www.ski alpine.com) is a great all-around performer, with something for everyone: unique kids' programs and a family ski zone, as well as its "wild side," for the double black diamond crowd.

Site of the 1960 Olympic Winter Games, **Squaw Valley USA** (© **800/545-4350** or 530/583-6985; www.squaw.com) offers the most challenging array of runs. Squaw's terrain is 70% for beginners and intermediates, 30% for the advanced, expert, and/or insane. The Cross-Country Ski Center at the Resort at Squaw Creek (© **530/583-6300**) has 400 acres of groomed trails.

Heavenly Resort (© **775/586-7000;** www.skiheavenly.com), which straddles the California-Nevada border, has the highest elevation (10,067 ft.) of any ski area at the lake. Skiers of all levels will find something here to challenge them, including 3 snowboard parks, 4,800 skiable acres, 30 lifts (including a 50-passenger aerial tram), and 86 runs. The Heavenly Gondola takes passengers from the south shore downtown area up to an observation deck at 9,200 feet.

Great choices for families include **Diamond Peak** (© **775/832-1177;** www.diamond peak.com), which is smaller, less crowded, and less expensive than many of the other choices. It's primarily a mountain for intermediates; kids love the snowboard park and sledding area. There's also cross-country skiing and snow shoeing, as well as dining and lodging in nearby Incline Village. Another family option is **Homewood Mountain**

Resort (© **530/525-2992;** www.skihomewood.com), a homey resort with gorgeous views of the lake. There's child care for 2- to 6-year-olds and there are also ski schools for kids 4 to 12. It's 6 miles south of Tahoe City and 19 miles north of South Lake Tahoe. **Northstar-at-Tahoe** (© **800/466-6784** or 530/562-1010; www.northstarattahoe.com) also has a full-time kids' program. It offers 2,420 acres of downhill skiing with 70 runs, plus sleigh rides, snowmobiling, and various snow toys.

The only real drawback of **Kirkwood,** off Hwy. 88 (© **209/258-6000;** www.kirkwood. com), is that it's 30 miles from South Lake Tahoe. Otherwise, this is one of the top ski areas in Tahoe, with lots of snow and excellent spring skiing on its 2,300 acres.

WHERE TO STAY & DINE

ON THE SOUTH SHORE   **MontBleu Resort Casino & Spa,** 55 U.S. 50 (© **888/829-7630** or 775/588-3515; www.montbleuresort.com), took over the Caesars Tahoe in 2006. Makeovers designed to attract a younger clientele include a chic new lobby that makes the other hotels on the strip look frumpy, seven stylin' new restaurants (tapas, anyone?), two hip new nightclubs, the 1,500-seat MontBleu Theatre featuring celebrity performers, a new outdoor sports arena hosting pro volleyball tournaments, a lagoon-style indoor pool, a Starbucks, and the new Onsen Spa.

In hot competition with MontBleu is **Harrah's Lake Tahoe,** U.S. 50 at Stateline Avenue (© **800/427-7247** or 775/588-6611; www.harrahstahoe.com), a glitzy, modern, Vegas-style palace. Rooms are among the largest in Tahoe, and most have bay windows overlooking the lake or the mountains. With families in mind, the casino has an enormous fun center with the latest in video and arcade games, virtual reality, and an indoor "playscape" for young children. Big names in showbiz headline at the casino's South Shore Room.

Harvey's Lake Tahoe Casino & Resort, U.S. 50 at Stateline Avenue (© **800/427-7247** or 775/588-2411; www.harrahs.com), is the largest (and possibly the ugliest) hotel in Tahoe, boasting an enormous casino, eight restaurants, and a cabaret with some of the most glittering, bespangled shows in town. Harvey's (owned by Harrah's) is like a city unto itself, with a pool, spa, salon, children's day camp, even a wedding chapel.

Perched near the state line, **Embassy Suites Lake Tahoe Hotel & Ski Resort,** 4130 Lake Tahoe Blvd., South Lake Tahoe (© **877/497-8483** or 530/544-5400; www.embassy tahoe.com), competes for the upscale gambling crowd and the convention business with Nevada's glittering casino hotels across the way. A château-style hotel of character, it offers an indoor pool and a basic gym. Accommodations are typical Embassy Suites, with fridges, microwaves, and VCRs. The resort's fine-dining restaurant, **Echo,** serves New American Cuisine for lunch and dinner. In summer, guests have access to a private beach.

Big, modern, and loaded with luxuries, the all-suites **Tahoe Seasons Resort,** 3901 Saddle Rd., off Ski Run Boulevard, South Lake Tahoe (© **800/540-4874** or 530/541-6700; www.tahoeseasons.com), lies in a relatively uncongested residential neighborhood at the base of the Heavenly Valley Ski Resort, 2 miles from Tahoe's casinos. Most suites have gas fireplaces, and all have huge whirlpools, VCRs, and fridges. Play a round of tennis on the roof or hop aboard the free casino shuttles.

More moderately priced choices include the **Best Western Station House Inn,** 901 Park Ave., South Lake Tahoe (© **800/822-5953** or 530/542-1101; www.stationhouse inn.com), one of the few hotels in town that has its own private "gated" beach on the lake. It offers free shuttle service to the casinos and most ski resorts. Rates run from $74 to $138 double, $135 to $165 suite, $200 to $300 cabin, including full breakfast. There's also an array of condo options at the **Lakeland Village Beach & Mountain Resort,** 3535 Lake Tahoe Blvd., South Lake Tahoe (📞 **800/822-5969** or 530/544-1685; www.lakeland-village.com).

ON THE NORTH SHORE   Part ski chalet, part boutique hotel, the **PlumpJack Squaw Valley Inn,** 1920 Squaw Valley Rd., off Hwy. 89, Olympic Valley (📞 **800/323-7666** or 530/583-1576; www.plumpjack.com), is easily Tahoe's most refined hotel and restaurant. Swirling sconces and sculpted metal accents are candy for the eyes, while the rest of your body parts are enveloped in thick hooded robes, slippers, and down comforters atop expensive mattresses. Rooms have mountain views. The sleek and sexy **PlumpJack Cafe** has a wonderful wine list and terrific food. Guests also enjoy ski rentals and storage, a pool, and two Jacuzzis. Rates run from $169 to $379 double (summer), $199 to $549 (winter).

The most deluxe resort on the lake, the **Resort at Squaw Creek,** 400 Squaw Creek Rd., Olympic Valley (📞 **800/327-3353** or 530/583-6300; www.squawcreek.com), boasts ski-in/ski-out access to Squaw Valley skiing (in fact, a chairlift lands just outside the door). Rooms are not particularly spacious, but they're well equipped. There are several dining options, including a steakhouse/sports bar with a pool table and live entertainment. Other perks include children's activities, an 18-hole golf course, three pools, two outdoor tennis courts, a fitness center, 20 miles of cross-country skiing trails (marked for hiking and biking in the summer), an ice-skating rink, and an equestrian center with riding stables. Rates are from $309 to $395 double, $450 to $1,900 suite.

The **Village at Squaw Valley,** 1985 Squaw Valley Rd., Olympic Valley (📞 **866/818-6963;** www.thevillageatsquaw.com), may look expensive, but it's one of the best deals in Tahoe. For as little as $150 per night, you can score a fully furnished condo—fireplace, full kitchen, deck, huge TV, sofa bed, DVD player—next to the ski lifts. The lodge's free perks are superb: underground parking, eight whirlpool spas, ski and snowboard lockers, a billiards lounge, and three fitness centers with saunas. After a day of skiing, there's no better way to finish off the day than with a Deluxe Deep Tissue massage at the **Trilogy Spa** (📞 **530/584-6125;** www.trilogyspa.com). And you'll never need to use your car during your stay because the best restaurants, bars, and shops are all within walking distance, including **Auld Dubliner** (📞 **530/584-6041;** www.aulddubliner.com), an authentic Irish Pub straight from Ireland (literally—the pub was built in Ireland, then dismantled, shipped over, and reassembled).

If you're looking for a romantic little B&B right on Lake Tahoe's shoreline, the **Shore House at Lake Tahoe,** 7170 N. Lake Blvd., Tahoe Vista (📞 **800/207-5160** or 530/546-7270; www.shorehouselaketahoe.com), is a real charmer. Each room has its own entrance, handmade log furniture, fridge, gas-log fireplace, and blissfully comfortable feather bed. All guests have access to a private beach and landscaped lawn, as well as a common hot tub. Rates are from $190 to $275 double, $275 to $310 cottage, including full breakfast.

Along the Truckee River, the **River Ranch Lodge & Restaurant,** on Hwy. 89, at Alpine Meadows Road, Tahoe City (📞 **800/535-9900** or 530/583-4264; www.riverranchlodge.com), is a bargain, with rates from $115 to $200 double, including continental breakfast. It's minutes away from the Alpine Meadows and Squaw Valley ski resorts. All rooms have a mountain-home decor; the best feature private balconies overlooking the river. In summer, guests relax on the patio, downing burgers while watching rafters float by. During ski season, the circular lounge and dining area, which cantilevers over the river, is a popular après-ski hangout. Also a big hit is the River Ranch Lodge Restaurant, which serves seafood, steaks, and rack of lamb.

Built as a private home in 1908, the **Sunnyside Lodge,** 1850 W. Lake Blvd., off Hwy. 89, Tahoe City (© **800/822-2754** or 530/583-7200; www.sunnysideresort.com), is one of the few grand old lodges left on the lake and has a popular restaurant. It looks very much like a giant wooden cabin, complete with dormers and steep pitched roofs; a large deck fronts a tiny marina. The place is rustic but fairly sophisticated. Rates are from $135 to $295 double, including continental breakfast and afternoon tea.

The 14 cabins at the **Tahoma Meadows Bed & Breakfast,** 6821 W. Lake Blvd., on Hwy. 89, 8¹/₂ miles from Tahoe City in Homewood (© **866/525-1553** or 530/525-1553; www.tahomameadows.com), are perched on a gentle forest slope. The largest cabins, Treehouse and Sugar Pine, sleep six and are ideal for families. In the main lodge is the highly recommended Stoneyridge Cafe, serving breakfast, lunch, and dinner. Nearby activities include skiing at Ski Homewood (including shuttle service), fly-fishing at a private trout-stocked lake, and sunbathing at the lakeshore just across the street. Rates are from $109 to $375 double, including full breakfast.

TAHOE AFTER DARK

Tahoe is not known for its nightlife, although something is always going on in the show-rooms of the major casinos on the South Shore. Call **Harrah's** (© **775/588-6611**), **Harveys** (© **775/588-2411**), **MontBleu** (© **775/588-3515**), and the **Horizon** (© **775/588-6211**) for current show schedules and prices. Most cocktail shows cost $20 to $55. On the North Shore, **Sandy's Pub,** at the Resort at Squaw Creek (© **530/581-6617**), hosts live music nightly. If it's just a casual cocktail you're after, my favorite spot is the fireside lounge at **River Ranch Lodge,** which cantilevers over a turbulent stretch of the Truckee River, on Hwy. 89 at the entrance to Alpine Meadows (© **530/583-4264**).

---

7 YOSEMITE NATIONAL PARK

It was in Yosemite that naturalist John Muir found "the most songful streams in the world . . . the noblest forests, the loftiest granite domes, the deepest ice sculpted canyons." Even today, despite the impact that hordes of people and cars have made, few visitors would disagree with Muir's early impressions as they explore this land of towering cliffs, Alpine lakes, river beaches, and fields of snow in winter.

YOSEMITE'S GATEWAYS

Towns on each gateway's periphery are virtually built around the tourism industry. They offer plenty of places to stay and eat, and have natural wonders of their own. The bad news: If you stay here, reaching any point within the park requires at least a half-hour drive (usually closer to an hour), which is especially frustrating during high season, when congestion causes traffic to move at a snail's pace.

But there's no shortage of options to encourage you to help the environment by leaving your car at your lodging or a parking area and entering the park on convenient, inexpensive buses (and then moving around the valley floor on free, readily available shuttles). The **Yosemite Area Regional Transit System (YARTS;** © **877/989-2787;** www.yarts.com) runs round-trip transit from communities within Mariposa, Merced, and Mono counties to Yosemite. Fares for riding vary but range from $7 to $25 round-trip for adults, including park entrance, with discounts for children and seniors. Summer routes originate at Coulterville, Mammoth Lake and Lee Vining, and Wawona. For information on the Hwy. 120 East service (Mammoth Lakes to Yosemite Valley), call ℂ 877/989-2787 from May until it snows (Sept or Oct).

Big Oak Flat Entrance

Among the string of small communities along the way is charming **Groveland** (24 miles from the park's entrance), a throwback to gold-mining days, complete with the oldest saloon in the state. It'll take about an hour to reach the park entrance from Groveland, but there's some extracurricular activity, should you choose to hang around. If you're driving from San Francisco, take **I-580** (which turns into I-205) to Manteca, then **Hwy. 120 East.** Contact the **Yosemite Chamber of Commerce** (ℂ 800/449-9120 or 209/962-0429; www.groveland. org) for an exhaustive list of hotels, motels, cabins, RV parks, and campsites in the area.

Our favorite accommodations here are the affordable cabins at **Evergreen Lodge,** 33160 Evergreen Rd., at Hwy. 120, Groveland (ℂ 800/935-6343 or 209/379-2606; www.evergreenlodge.com). It's 8 miles from Yosemite's entrance. There are hiking trails and, in summer, access to Camp Mather's tennis courts, pool, and horseback riding. Though officially in Groveland, the lodge is 40 minutes east of downtown. Rates vary with season and cabin size: $79 to $249 for 1- and 2-bedroom cabins.

The moderately priced **Groveland Hotel,** 18767 Main St., Groveland (ℂ 800/273-3314 or 209/962-4000; www.groveland.com), is a historic choice that complements the surroundings of the Wild West–like town. Rooms are sweetly appointed with antiques as well as modern amenities; the suite has a spa tub and fireplace. The staff is accommodating, and the restaurant (the best and most expensive in town) is surprisingly sophisticated. Rates from $145 to $285 double, including extended continental breakfast.

Yosemite National Park gets crowded during summer months, so it's wise to stay outside the park at a quiet B&B like the **Berkshire Inn Bed & Breakfast,** 19950 Hwy. 120, Groveland (ℂ 888/225-2064 or 209/962-6744; www.berkshireinn.net), then make day trips into the park. This sprawling open-beam lodge sits on 20 wooded acres just outside Groveland and consists of six spacious, pleasant guest rooms and four

Burgers & Bullets: The Iron Door Saloon

Walk through the English iron doors that were shipped around the Horn, and step into a bar that has been serving whiskey to thirsty travelers for more than 150 years. Built from solid blocks of granite, the Iron Door Saloon is a must-stop on your way to Yosemite. They say Black Bart enjoyed a tumbler or two here and put a few bullets in the walls to keep the locals jumpy (keep looking). Thousands of dollar bills are tacked to the ceiling, and a stuffed buffalo's head hangs on the wall to remind guests of the house special—a thick, juicy, char-broiled buffalo burger served with pickles, tomato, onions, and house-made coleslaw. Espressos, cappuccinos, and lattes are available as well. At 18761 Main St. in downtown Groveland, it's open daily for lunch and dinner (ℂ 209/962-8904; www.iron-door-saloon.com). Live music acts (with both local and national artists) regularly play at the saloon—a remnant perk from the days when the owners used to work for concert promoter Bill Graham.

minisuites, all with private entrances and bathrooms. Rates from $135 to $180 double, **875** including continental breakfast.

Arch Rock Entrance
Arch Rock is 75 miles northeast of Merced. If you're driving from central California, take I-5 to Hwy. 99 to Merced, then Hwy. 140 east.

The **Yosemite View Lodge,** 11136 Hwy. 140, El Portal (© **888/742-4371** or 209/ 379-2681; www.yosemite-motels.com), is a gargantuan compound set amid the otherwise awesome natural surroundings. This 279-room megamotel is scheduled to eventually offer around 500 rooms. The motel-style units include fridges and microwaves; some offer river views, balconies, and fireplaces. There's also a general store, along with two restaurants, two pools, and four hot tubs. Rates from $104 to $209 double.

South Entrance
The South Entrance is 332 miles north of Los Angeles and 190 miles east of San Francisco. Fish Camp and Oakhurst are the closest towns to the south entrance at Wawona. If you're driving from Los Angeles, take **I-5** to **Hwy. 99 North,** then **Hwy. 41 North.** For more options, contact the **Yosemite Sierra Visitors Bureau,** 40637 Hwy. 41, Oakhurst (© **559/683-4636;** www.yosemitethisyear.com). Ask for the helpful brochure on the area, and be sure to check out the excellent online guide.

The estate of **Château du Sureau,** 48688 Victoria Lane, Oakhurst (© **559/683-6860;** www.chateaudusureau.com), is the sine qua non of luxurious lodging, decadent dining, and exclusivity. The main house resembles a French château, with turret and terra-cotta tile roof. The interior is exquisitely furnished with antiques, rugs, and fabrics. Each individually decorated room has a wood-burning fireplace and a wrought-iron balcony. Canopy beds are covered in Italian linens and goose-down comforters; several rooms have whirlpool tubs. Rates from $445 to $575 double, including full breakfast. The restaurant, **Erna's Elderberry House** (© **559/683-6800**), is famous in its own right, offering impeccable food, ambience, and service. The six-course prix-fixe menu changes daily.

For moderately priced accommodations, check out the **Narrow Gauge Inn,** 48571 Hwy. 41, Fish Camp (© **888/644-9050** or 559/683-7720; www.narrowgaugeinn.com), 4 miles south of the park entrance. Rates $140 to $195 double; November to March $79 to $109 double, including continental breakfast. All of the superclean motel-style units have a rustic cabin feel, with little balconies or decks, antiques, quilts, and lace curtains. On the property are a pool, a hot tub, and hiking trails, as well as a wonderfully old-fashioned lodge-style restaurant.

The **Tenaya Lodge,** 1122 Hwy. 41, Fish Camp (© **888/514-2167** or 559/683-6555; www.tenayalodge.com), is idyllic for families, as it's set on 35 acres of forest a few miles outside of the national park. The decor is a cross between an Adirondack hunting lodge and a Southwestern pueblo, with a lobby dominated by a massive river-rock fireplace rising three stories; rooms are ultramodern. Extras include restaurants, two pools, and a spa. Rates in winter from $129 double, summer from $255 double.

YOSEMITE NATIONAL PARK
Yosemite is a place of record-setting statistics: the highest waterfall in North America and 3 of the world's 10 tallest (Upper Yosemite Fall, Ribbon Fall, and Sentinel Falls), the tallest and largest granite monolith in the world (El Capitan), the most recognizable mountain (Half Dome), one of the world's largest trees (the Grizzly Giant in the Mariposa

Grove), and thousands of rare plant and animal species. But trying to explain its majesty is impossible: This is a place you simply must experience firsthand.

Bears, too, are at home in the valley. Grizzlies are gone from the park now, but black bears are plentiful—and hungry for your food. They don't actually come begging by daylight, but they make their presence known through late-night ransacking of ice chests and have been known to rip into cars that have even the smallest treats inside.

Right in the middle of the valley's thickest urban cluster is the **Yosemite Valley Visitor Center** (© 209/372-0200; www.nps.gov/yose), with exhibits that will teach you about glacial geology, history, and the park's flora and fauna. Check out the **Yosemite Museum** next door for insight into what life in the park was once like. Excellent exhibits highlight the Miwok and Paiute cultures that thrived here. The **Ansel Adams Gallery** (© 209/372-4413; www.adamsgallery.com) displays the famous photographer's prints, as well as other artists' works. You'll also find much history and memorabilia from the career of nature writer John Muir, one of the founders of the conservation movement.

Tenaya Lake and Tuolumne Meadows are two of the most popular high-country destinations, as well as starting points for many great trails to the backcountry. Since this area of the park is under snow November through June, summer is really more like spring. From snowmelt to the first snowfall, the high country explodes with wildflowers and long-dormant wildlife trying to make the most of the short season.

Essentials

ENTRY POINTS There are four main entrances to the park. Most valley visitors enter through the **Arch Rock Entrance** on Hwy. 140. The best entrance for Wawona is the **South Entrance** on Hwy. 41 from Oakhurst. If you're going to the high country, you'll save a lot of time by coming in through the **Big Oak Flat Entrance,** which puts you straight onto Tioga Road without forcing you to deal with the congested valley. The **Tioga Pass Entrance** is open only in summer and is only really relevant if you're coming from the east side of the Sierra (in which case, it's your only choice). A fifth, little-used entrance is the **Hetch Hetchy Entrance,** in the euphonious Poopenaut Valley, on a dead-end road. *Note:* There are no gas stations in Yosemite Valley, so be sure to fill up your tank before entering the park.

It costs $20 per car per week to enter the park, or $10 per person per week (15 and younger free). Annual Yosemite Passes are a steal at $40. Wilderness permits are free, but reserving them requires a $5 fee per person. If you are 62 or older you may purchase a lifetime Golden Age Passport for $10.

VISITOR CENTERS & INFORMATION For general information, call the central, 24-hour recorded information line for the park (© 209/372-0200) or log onto the park's main website (**www.nps.gov/yose**). All visitor-related service lines, including hotels and information, can be accessed by phone at © 209/372-1000, or at www.yosemitepark.com. Another good resource is **Yosemite Area Travelers Information** (© 209/723-3153; www.yosemite.com). For details on lodgings within Yosemite National Park, contact **Yosemite Reservations,** P.O. Box 578, Yosemite National Park, California 95389 (© 801/559-5000; www.yosemitepark.com).

The biggest visitor center is the **Valley Visitor Center** (© 209/372-0200). For trail advice and biological and geological displays about the High Sierra, the **Tuolumne Meadows Visitor Center** (© 209/372-0263) is great (closed in winter). All can provide you with maps, plus more newspapers, books, and photocopied leaflets than you'll ever read.

Yosemite's wonderful rangers also take time to lead a number of educational and
interpretive programs ranging from backcountry hikes to fireside talks to snow-country survival clinics. Call the main park information number with specific requests for the season and park area you'll be visiting.

WHEN TO GO   Winter is one of the nicest times to visit the valley. It isn't crowded, as it is during summer, and a dusting of snow provides a stark contrast to all that granite. To see the waterfalls at their best, come in spring when snowmelt is at its peak. Fall can be cool, but it's beautiful and much less crowded than summer. Sunshine seekers will love summer—if they can tolerate the crowds. The high country is under about 20 feet of snow November through May, so unless you're snow camping, summer is pretty much the only season to pitch a tent. Even in summer, thundershowers are a frequent occurrence, sometimes with a magnificent lightning show. Mosquitoes can be a plague during the peak of summer, but the plague gets better after the first freeze.

Popularity isn't always the greatest thing for wild places. Over the last 20 years, Yosemite Valley has set records for the worst crowding, noise, crime, and traffic in any California national park. Our best advice is to try to come before Memorial Day or after Labor Day. If you must come in summer, do your part to help out. Once you're here, park your car, then bike, hike, or ride the shuttle buses. **Curry Village** (© **209/372-8319**) and **Yosemite Lodge** (© **209/372-1208**) both offer bicycle rentals in summer. It may take longer to get from point A to point B, but you're in one of the most gorgeous places on Earth—so why hurry?

Seeing the Highlights
The Valley

First-time visitors are often completely dumbstruck as they enter the valley from the west. The first two things you'll see are the delicate and beautiful **Bridalveil Fall** and the immense face of **El Capitan,** a stunning and anything-but-delicate 3,593-foot-tall solid-granite rock. A short trail leads to the base of Bridalveil, which, at 620 feet tall, is only a medium-size fall by park standards, but one of the prettiest.

It's a good idea to buy the excellent *Map and Guide to Yosemite Valley* for $2.50; it describes many hikes and short nature walks. Then go take a look. Walking and biking are the best ways to get around. To cover longer distances, the park shuttles run frequently around the east end of the valley.

A variety of **guided tram and bus tours** are available. You can buy tickets at Yosemite Lodge, the Ahwahnee, Curry Village, or beside the Village Store in Yosemite Village. Advanced reservations are suggested for all tours; space can be reserved in person or by phone (© **209/372-1240**). Always double-check for updated schedules and prices. Most tours depart from Yosemite Lodge, the Ahwahnee, or Curry Village, and most tours are about $75 for adults for full-day trips. Children's rates are usually 40% to 50% less, and most tours offer discounts for seniors. The 2-hour **Valley Floor Tour** is a great way to get acclimated to the park, with a good selection of photo ops, including El Capitan, Tunnel View, and Half Dome.

The best single view in the valley is from **Sentinel Bridge** over the Merced River. At sunset, Half Dome's face functions as a projection screen for all the sinking sun's hues, from yellow to pink to dark purple, and the river reflects it all. Ansel Adams took one of his most famous photographs from this very spot.

VALLEY WALKS & HIKES   Yosemite Falls is within a short stroll of the visitor center. You can actually see it better elsewhere in the valley, but it's really impressive to stand at the base of all that falling water. The wind, noise, and blowing spray generated when millions of gallons catapult 2,425 feet through space onto the rocks below are sometimes so overwhelming you can barely stand on the bridge.

If you want more, the **Upper Yosemite Fall Trail** zigzags 3.5 miles from Sunnyside Campground to the top of Upper Yosemite Fall. This trail gives you an inkling of the weird, vertically oriented world entered by climbers when they head up Yosemite's sheer walls. As you climb this narrow switchback trail, the valley floor drops away until people below look like ants, but the top doesn't appear any closer. It's a little unnerving at first, but braving it promises indescribable rewards. Plan on spending all day on this 7-mile round-trip because of the incredibly steep climb.

A mile-long trail leads from the Valley Stables (take the shuttle; no car parking) to **Mirror Lake.** The already-tiny lake is gradually becoming a meadow as it fills with silt, but the reflections of the valley walls and sky on its surface remain one of the park's most memorable sights.

Also accessible from the Valley Stables or nearby Happy Isles is the best valley hike of all—the **John Muir Trail** to Vernal and Nevada falls. It follows the Sierra crest 200 miles south to Mount Whitney, but you only need go 1.5 miles round-trip to get a great view of 317-foot **Vernal Fall.** Add another 1.5 miles and 1,000 vertical feet for the climb to the top of Vernal Fall on the **Mist Trail,** where you'll get wet as you climb directly alongside the falls. On top of Vernal and before the base of Nevada Fall is a beautiful little valley and deep pool. For a truly outrageous view of the valley and one heck of a workout, continue on up the Mist Trail to the top of Nevada Fall. From 2,000 feet above Happy Isles where you began, it's a dizzying view straight down the face of the fall. To the east is an interesting profile perspective of Half Dome. Return either by the Mist Trail or by the slightly easier John Muir Trail for a 7-mile round-trip hike.

Half Dome may look insurmountable to anyone but an expert rock climber, but thousands every year take the popular cable route up the backside. It's almost 17 miles round-trip and a 4,900-foot elevation gain from Happy Isles on the John Muir Trail. Many do it in a day, starting at first light and rushing home to beat nightfall. A more relaxed strategy is to camp in the backpacking campground in Little Yosemite Valley just past Nevada Fall. From here the summit is within easy striking distance of the base of Half Dome. If you plan to spend the night, you must have a Wilderness Pass (see "Where to Camp," below). You must climb up a very steep granite face using steel cables installed by the Park Service. In summer, boards are installed as crossbeams, but they're still far apart. Wear shoes with lots of traction and bring your own leather gloves for the cables (your hands will thank you). The view from the top is an unbeatable vista of the high country, Tenaya Canyon, Glacier Point, and the awe-inspiring abyss of the valley below. When you shuffle up to the overhanging lip for a look down the face, be extremely careful not to kick rocks or anything else onto the climbers below, who are earning this view the hard way.

The Southwest Corner

This corner of the park is densely forested and gently sculpted in comparison to the stark granite that makes up so much of Yosemite. Coming from the valley, Hwy. 41 passes through a long tunnel. Just before the entrance is **Tunnel View,** the subject of another famous Ansel Adams photograph, and the best scenic outlook of the valley accessible by car. The whole valley is laid out below: Half Dome and Yosemite Falls straight ahead in the distance, Bridalveil to the right, and El Capitan to the left.

A few miles past the tunnel, Glacier Point Road turns off to the east. Closed in winter, this winding road leads to a picnic area at **Glacier Point,** site of another fabulous view of the valley, this time 3,000 feet below. Schedule at least an hour to drive here from the valley and an hour or two to absorb the view. This is a good place to study the glacial scouring of the valley below; the Glacier Point perspective makes it easy to picture the valley filled with sheets of ice.

Some 30 miles south of the valley on Hwy. 41 are the **Wawona Hotel** and the **Pioneer Yosemite History Center.** The Wawona was built in 1879 and is the oldest hotel in the park. Its Victorian architecture evokes a time when travelers spent several days in horse-drawn wagons to get here. The Pioneer Center is a collection of early homesteading log buildings across the river from the Wawona.

One of the primary reasons Yosemite was first set aside as a park was the **Mariposa Grove** of giant sequoias. (Many good trails lead through the grove.) These huge trees have personalities that match their gargantuan size. Single limbs on the biggest tree in the grove, the Grizzly Giant, are 10 feet thick. The tree itself is 209 feet tall, 32 feet in diameter, and more than 2,700 years old. Totally out of proportion with the size of the trees are the tiny cones of the sequoia. Smaller than a baseball and tightly closed, the cones won't release their cargo of seeds until opened by fire.

The High Country

The high country of Yosemite is stunning: Dome after dome of beautiful crystalline granite reflects the sunlight above deep-green meadows and ice-blue rivers.

Tioga Pass is the gateway to the high country. At times it clings to the side of steep rock faces; in other places it weaves through canyon bottoms. Several good campgrounds make it a pleasing overnight alternative to fighting summertime crowds in the valley, although use is increasing here, too.

Near the top of Tioga Pass is beautiful **Tuolumne Meadows.** This meadow covering several square miles is bordered by the Tuolumne River on one side and spectacular granite peaks on the other. The meadow is cut by many stream channels full of trout, and herds of mule deer are almost always present. The **Tuolumne Meadows Lodge** and store is a welcome counterpoint to the overdeveloped valley. In winter, the canvas roofs are removed and the buildings fill with snow. You can buy last-minute backpacking supplies here, and there's a basic burgers-and-fries cafe.

TUOLUMNE MEADOWS HIKES & WALKS   So many hikes lead from here into the backcountry that it's impossible to do them justice. A good trail passes an icy-cold spring and traverses several meadows.

On the far bank of the Tuolumne from the meadow, a trail leads downriver, eventually passing through the grand canyon of the Tuolumne and exiting at Hetch Hetchy. Shorter hikes will take you downriver past rapids and cascades.

An interesting geological quirk is the **Soda Springs** on the far side of Tuolumne Meadow from the road. This bubbling spring gushes carbonated water from a hole in the ground; a small log cabin marks its site.

For a great selection of Yosemite high-country hikes and backpacking trips, consult some of the specialized guidebooks to the area. Two of the best are published by Wilderness Press: *Tuolumne Meadows,* a hiking guide by Jeffrey B. Shaffer and Thomas Winnett, and *Yosemite National Park,* by Thomas Winnett and Jason Winnett.

SPORTS & OUTDOOR ACTIVITIES

BICYCLING   With 10 miles of bike paths in addition to the valley roads, biking is an ideal way to get around the park. You can rent bikes at the **Yosemite Lodge** (© 209/372-1208) or **Curry Village** (© 209/372-8319) for about $7.50 per hour or $24 per day.

You can also rent bike trailers for little kids at $14 per hour or $42 per day. All hiking trails in the park are closed to mountain bikes.

FISHING   Trout season begins on the last Saturday in April and continues through November 15. The Merced River from Happy Isles downstream to the Pohono Bridge is catch-and-release only for native rainbow trout, and barbless hooks are required. Everyone 16 years old or more must display a California license to fish. Get licenses at the Yosemite Village Sport Shop (② 209/372-1286). Guided fly-fishing trips in Yosemite for all levels are available from **Yosemite Guides** (② 866/922-9111 or 209/379-2231; www.yosemiteguides.com). *Note:* Yosemite Valley has special fishing regulations; get information at the visitor centers.

HORSEBACK RIDING   Three stables offer day rides and multiday excursions in the park. **Yosemite Valley Stables** (② 209/372-8348) is open spring through fall. The other two—**Wawona** (② 209/375-6502) and **Tuolumne Stables** (② 209/372-8427)—operate only in summer. Day rides run from about $55 to $95, depending on length. Multiday backcountry trips cost roughly $100 per day and must be booked almost a year in advance. The park wranglers can also be hired to make resupply drops at any of the High Sierra Camps if you plan an extended trip. Log onto www.yosemiteparktours.com (click on "Activities") for more information.

ICE-SKATING   The **Curry Village Ice Rink** (② 209/372-8319) is fun in winter. It's outdoors, however, and melts quickly when the weather warms up. Rates are $8 for adults and $6 for children 11 and under. Skate rentals are $3.

ROCK CLIMBING   Much of the most technical advancement in rock climbing grew out of the highly competitive Yosemite Valley climbing scene of the 1970s and 1980s. Other places have since stepped into the limelight, but Yosemite is still one of the most desirable climbing destinations in the world. The **Yosemite Mountaineering School** (② 209/372-8344; www.yosemitemountaineering.com) runs classes for beginning through advanced climbers. Considered one of the best climbing schools in the world, it offers private lessons that will teach you basic body moves and rappelling, and will take you on a single-pitch climb. Classes run from early spring to early October in the valley, and during summer in Tuolumne Meadows.

SKIING & SNOWSHOEING   Opened in 1935, **Badger Pass** (② 209/372-8430; www.yosemitepark.com) is the oldest operating ski area in California and great for families. Four chairs and one rope tow cover a compact mountain, with beginner and intermediate runs. At $38 for adults, $32 for youths from 13 to 17, and $15 for children from 7 to 12 (kids 6 and under free with adult), it's a great place to learn how to ski or snowboard. Naturalists lead special winter children's programs, and the facility provides babysitting.

Yosemite is popular with **cross-country skiers and snowshoers.** Both the Badger Pass ski school and the mountaineering school run trips and lessons for all abilities, ranging from basic technique to trans-Sierra crossings. Two ski huts can accommodate anyone taking guided cross-country tours, including the **Glacier Point Hut** (② 209/372-8444), with its massive stone fireplace, beamed ceilings, and bunk beds; and the **Ostrander Hut** (② 209/379-2646; www.ostranderhut.com) with 25 bunks. You have to pack in your own supplies. If you're on your own, Crane Flat is a good place to go, as is the groomed track up to Glacier Point, a 20-mile-round-trip self-guided tour.

Campgrounds in Yosemite can be reserved up to 5 months in advance through the **National Park Reservation Service** (© 877/444-6777; www.recreation.gov). *Be warned:* During busy season, all valley campsites sell out within hours of becoming available on the service.

Backpacking into the wilderness and camping there is the least crowded option and takes less planning than reserving a campground. If you plan to camp in the wilderness, you must get a free **Wilderness Pass** (and pay the park entrance fee). At least 40% of each trail-head quota is allocated up to 24 hours in advance; the rest is available by mail. Write to the Yosemite Association, P.O. Box 545, Yosemite, CA 95389; specify the dates and trail heads of entry and exit, the destination, number of people, and any accompanying animals; and include $5 per person.

Valley Campgrounds

Until January 1997, the park had five car campgrounds that were always full except in the dead of winter. Now the park has half the number of campsites, and getting a reservation on short notice takes a minor miracle. (Yosemite Valley lost almost half of its 900 camping spaces in a freak winter storm in 1997 that washed several campsites downstream and buried hundreds more beneath a foot of silt.)

The two and a half remaining campgrounds—**North Pines, Upper Pines,** and half of **Lower Pines**—charge $20 to $30 per night. All have drinking water, flush toilets, pay phones, fire pits, and heavy ranger presence. Showers are available for a small fee at Curry Village. Upper Pines, North Pines, and Lower Pines allow small RVs (less than 40 ft. long). If you're expecting a real nature experience, skip camping in the valley unless you like doing so with 4,000 strangers.

Camp 4 (previously named Sunnyside campground) is a year-round, walk-in campground that fills quickly since it's only $5 per night. Hard-core climbers used to live here for months at a time. The Park Service has stopped them, but this site still has a more bohemian atmosphere than any of the other campgrounds.

Campgrounds Elsewhere in the Park

Outside the valley, things open up for campers. Two-car campgrounds near the South Entrance of the park, **Wawona** and **Bridalveil Creek,** offer a total of 210 sites with all the amenities. Wawona is open year-round, and reservations are required May through September; otherwise, it's first-come, first-served. Family sites at Wawona are $20 per night, and group sites, which hold up to 30 people, are $40 per night. Because it sits well above the snow line, at more than 7,000 feet, Bridalveil is open only in summer. Rates are $14 per night for first-come, first-served sites, and $40 for group sites.

Crane Flat, Hodgdon Meadow, and Tamarack Flat are all in the western corner of the park near the Big Oak Flat Entrance. **Crane Flat** is the nearest to the valley, about a half-hour drive away, with 166 sites, water, flush toilets, and fire pits. Its rates are $20 per night, and it's open July through September. **Hodgdon Meadow** is directly adjacent to the Big Oak Flat Entrance, at 4,800 feet elevation. It's open year-round, charges $20 per night, and requires reservations May through September, through the National Park Reservation Service. Facilities include flush toilets, running water, a ranger station, and pay phones. It's one of the least crowded low-elevation car campgrounds, but you won't find lots to do here. **Tamarack Flat** is a waterless 52-site campground with pit toilets. Open June through October, it's a bargain at $8 per night.

Tuolumne Meadows, White Wolf, Yosemite Creek, and Porcupine Flat are all above 8,000 feet, open only in summer. **Tuolumne Meadows** is the park's largest campground, with more than 300 spaces. It absorbs the crowd well and has all the amenities, including campfire programs and slide shows in the outdoor amphitheater. You will, however, feel sardine-packed between hundreds of other visitors. Half of the sites are reserved in advance; the rest are set aside on a first-come, first-served basis. Rates are $18 per night.

White Wolf, west of Tuolumne Meadows, is the other full-service campground in the high country, with 74 sites available for $12 per night for family sites, $40 for group sites. It offers a drier climate than the meadow and doesn't fill up as quickly. Sites are available on a first-come, first-served basis.

Two primitive camps, **Porcupine Flat** and **Yosemite Creek,** are the last to fill up in the park. Both have pit toilets but no running water, and charge $10 per night on a first-come, first-served basis.

WHERE TO STAY IN THE PARK

All hotel reservations can be made exactly 366 days in advance. Call **Yosemite Concessions Services** at ✆ **801/559-5000** in the morning 366 days before your intended arrival for the best chance of securing a spot. If you don't plan that far in advance, it's still worth calling, because cancellations may leave openings. You may also book reservations online through **www.yosemitepark.com**. Reservations without a deposit must be confirmed on the day of arrival by 4pm. Otherwise, you'll lose your reservation. An intriguing option bridging the gap between backpacking and staying in a hotel is Yosemite's five backcountry **High Sierra Camps** (✆ 559/253-5674). Due to the popularity of these camps, reservations are booked by lottery. Applications are accepted from October 15 to November 30. The lottery is then held in December and the winning applicants are notified by the end of March.

The Ahwahnee Hotel (Best)   A National Historic Landmark noted for its granite-and-redwood architecture and soaring lobby, the six-story Ahwahnee is one of the most romantic and beautiful hotels in California; it's a special-occasion sort of affair. Try to reserve one of the more spacious cottages, which cost the same as rooms in the main hotel. For the price you're paying, the hotel's guest rooms, although pleasant in warm woods and Indian motif fabrics, may seem simple to the point of austerity. On the other hand, where else in the world can you look out your window and see Half Dome, Yosemite Falls, or Glacier Point? The **Ahwahnee Restaurant** is a colossal and impressive chamber highlighted by 50-foot-tall, floor-to-ceiling leaded windows. It's more noteworthy, however, for its ambience than for its expensive cuisine.

✆ **209/372-1489.** www.yosemitepark.com. 99 units, 24 cottages. $408–$984 double. Children 12 and under stay free in parent's room. AE, DC, DISC, MC, V. Pets are not accepted, but they can board in the kennel at the park stables. **Amenities:** Restaurant; heated outdoor pool; nearby golf course; 2 tennis courts. *In room:* No A/C in cottages, fridge in cottages.

Wawona Hotel   If the Ahwahnee doesn't fit your plans or your pocketbook, the Wawona is the next best thing. Also a National Historic Landmark, the Wawona is a romantic throwback to another century. However, old-world charm has its ups and downs. Private bathrooms were not a big hit in the 19th century, rooms were small to hold in heat, there were no TVs or phones, and walls were thin—and all of the above still applies today. Still, the Wawona is less commercial than other accommodations on the valley floor.

private bathroom; $198 double with private bathroom. Children 12 and under stay free in parent's room. Extra person $16. AE, DC, DISC, MC, V. **Amenities:** Restaurant; swimming tank; golf course; tennis court. *In room:* No phone.

Yosemite Lodge at the Falls   The next step down in valley accommodations, Yosemite Lodge is not actually a lodge, but a large, more modern complex with two types of accommodations. The larger "Lodge" rooms with balconies have striking views of Yosemite Falls. Indeed, the largest bonus—and curse—is that every room's front yard is the valley floor, which means you're near glorious larger-than-life natural attractions and equally gargantuan crowds.

801/559-5000. www.yosemitepark.com. 249 units. $113–$180 double. Children 12 and under stay free in parent's room. Extra person $10–$12. AE, DC, DISC, MC, V. **Amenities:** 2 restaurants; food court; heated outdoor pool; nearby golf course.

8 SANTA BARBARA

Nestled between palm-lined Pacific beaches and sloping foothills, this prosperous resort community presents a mosaic of red tile roofs and a gracious, relaxed attitude.

ESSENTIALS
GETTING THERE   By Car   U.S. 101 runs right through Santa Barbara; it's the fastest and most direct route from north or south (1½ hr. from Los Angeles, 6 hr. from San Francisco).

By Train   Amtrak (**② 800/USA-RAIL** [872-7245]; www.amtrak.com) offers daily service to Santa Barbara. Trains arrive and depart from the **Santa Barbara Rail Station,** 209 State St. (**② 805/963-1015**). Fares can be as low as $29 (round-trip) from Los Angeles's Union Station.

VISITOR INFORMATION   The **Santa Barbara Conference and Visitors Bureau,** 1601 Anacapa St. (**② 805/966-9222;** www.santabarbaraca.com), distributes maps, brochures, an events calendar, and information. It's open Monday through Saturday from 9am to 5pm, and Sunday from 10am to 5pm. Pick up a copy of *The Independent,* Santa Barbara's free weekly; and *Explore Santa Barbara,* a compact visitor's guide published by the local paper, the *Santa Barbara News-Press.* Both are also available at shops and sidewalk racks throughout town.

WHAT TO SEE & DO
State Street is the city's main thoroughfare and has the largest concentration of cafes, boutiques, antiques stores, and more. Electric shuttle buses (25¢) run up and down State Street. At the harbor end is the city's 1872-vintage Stearns Wharf, offering a small collection of souvenir shops, attractions, and restaurants, plus terrific inland views and fishing.

The town has an array of beaches. **Arroyo Burro Beach County Park,** also known as **Hendry's Beach,** at the end of Cliff Drive, is popular with families, boogie boarders, and sunset strollers. **East Beach** is a wide swath of clean white sand that hosts beach umbrellas, sand-castle builders, and spirited volleyball games.

A relatively flat, palm-lined, 2-mile coastal pathway runs along the beach and is perfect for biking and skating. More adventurous riders can pedal through town, up to the mission, or to Montecito, the next town over. **Wheel Fun Rentals,** 101 State St. (just off

Cabrillo Blvd.; ℂ **805/966-2282;** www.wheelfunrentals.com), rents well-maintained beach cruisers, mountain bikes, tandem bikes, and an Italian four-wheel surrey that seats three adults; rates vary. It's open daily from 8am to 8pm.

Santa Barbara's most distinctive attraction is the 1786 **Old Mission Santa Barbara,** at Laguna and Los Olivos streets (ℂ **805/682-4149;** www.sbmission.org), whose graceful Spanish-Moorish style earned it the title "Queen of the Missions." It overlooks the town and the sea beyond. Admission is $4 for adults, free for children 11 and under; open daily from 9am to 5pm.

The **Red Tile Tour** of downtown (ask for details at the visitor center) passes many historic and architectural highlights, including the 1929 **Santa Barbara County Courthouse,** 1100 Anacapa St. (ℂ **805/962-6464;** www.santabarbaracourthouse.org). You've seen its facade on TV during the Michael Jackson trial. The observation deck atop the clock tower affords great views of the ocean, the mountains, and the courthouse's outstanding gardens.

WHERE TO STAY

The free one-stop reservations service **Hot Spots** (ℂ **800/793-7666** or 805/564-1637) keeps an updated list of availability for most of the area's hotels, motels, inns, and B&Bs. The service will have the latest information on last-minute vacancies at reduced rates. Reservationists are available Monday through Saturday from 9am to 9pm, and Sunday from 9am to 4pm.

In addition to the listings below, there are moderately priced rooms ($119–$309 double) at the **Casa del Mar Inn at the Beach,** 18 Bath St. (ℂ **800/433-3097** or 805/ 963-4418; www.casadelmar.com), and the **Franciscan Inn** ($165–$180 double), 109 Bath St. (ℂ **800/663-5288** or 805/963-8845; www.franciscaninn.com).

Four Seasons Resort, The Biltmore Santa Barbara (Best)   This grand Spanish-style hacienda, once patronized by such Hollywood golden age celebs as Greta Garbo and Errol Flynn, manages to adhere to the most elegant standards of hospitality without making anyone feel unwelcome. Rooms have an airy feel, heightened by white plantation shutters and marble bathrooms with all the modern amenities. Guests can amuse themselves with a putting green, shuffleboard, and croquet courts. The hotel's most recent addition is the Spa, a multimillion-dollar, 10,000-square-foot Spanish-style annex that houses numerous treatment rooms, a swimming pool and two huge whirlpool tubs, a state-of-the-art fitness center, and, for the big spenders, 10 oceanview deluxe suites with fireplaces, in-room bars, changing rooms, and twin massage tables (essentially, your own private treatment room).

1260 Channel Dr. (at the end of Olive Mill Rd.), Santa Barbara, CA 93108. ℂ **800/819-5053** or 805/969-2261. Fax 805/565-8323. www.fourseasons.com/santabarbara. 207 units. $550–$8,000 double; from $1,250 suite. Extra person $55. Children age 18 and under stay free in parent's room. Special midweek and package rates available. AE, DC, MC, V. Valet parking $20; free self-parking. **Amenities:** 4 restaurants; 2 outdoor heated pools; 3 lit tennis courts; health club; salon/spa.

Hotel Oceana   The 2¹/₂-acre Spanish mission–style property consists of four adjacent motels built in the 1940s that have been merged and renovated into one sprawling hotel. The result is a wide range of charmingly old-school accommodations—everything from apartments with real daybeds (great for families) to courtyard rooms and deluxe oceanview suites—with bright modern furnishings. Each guest room is appointed with soft Frette linens, down comforters, ceiling fans, CD players, cozy duvets, and Aveda bath products. Along with the size and location of your room, you get to choose from four color schemes—soothing blue or green, racy red, and a cheery yellow. The beach and jogging path are right across the street, and the huge lawn is perfect for picnic lunches.

202 W. Cabrillo Blvd., Santa Barbara, CA 93101. ⓒ **800/965-9776** or 805/965-4577. Fax 805/965-9937. www.hoteloceana.com. 122 units. $250–$360 double. 2-night minimum for weekend reservations. AE, DC, DISC, MC, V. **Amenities:** Denny's restaurant adjacent; 2 swimming pools; fitness room; spa. *In room:* No A/C, fridge.

Simpson House Inn Bed & Breakfast
Rooms in the 1874 Historic Landmark house are decorated to Victorian perfection, with extras ranging from a claw-foot tub to French doors; cottages are nestled throughout the grounds. Accommodations have everything you could possibly need (including VCRs), but most impressive are the extras: the Mediterranean hors d'oeuvres and Santa Barbara wines, the enormous video library, and the heavenly gourmet breakfast. Fact is, the Simpson House goes the distance—and then some—to create the perfect stay.

121 E. Arrellaga St. (btw. Santa Barbara and Anacapa sts.), Santa Barbara, CA 93101. ⓒ **800/676-1280** or 805/963-7067. Fax 805/564-4811. www.simpsonhouseinn.com. 15 units. $255–$615 double; $595–$605 suite and cottage. 2-night minimum on weekends. Rates include full gourmet breakfast, evening hors d'oeuvres, and wine. AE, DISC, MC, V.

The Upham Victorian Hotel and Garden Cottages
This conveniently located inn combines the intimacy of a B&B with the service of a small hotel. Built in 1871, the Upham is the oldest continuously operating hostelry in Southern California. Somewhere the management made time for upgrades, though, because guest accommodations are complete with all the modern comforts. The hotel is constructed of redwood, with sweeping verandas and a Victorian cupola on top. It also has a warm lobby and a cozy restaurant.

1404 De La Vina St. (at Sola St.), Santa Barbara, CA 93101. ⓒ **800/727-0876** or 805/962-0058. Fax 805/963-2825. www.uphamhotel.com. 50 units. $195–$290 double; from $340 suite and cottage. Rates include continental breakfast and afternoon wine and cheese. AE, DC, MC, V. **Amenities:** Restaurant.

WHERE TO DINE

bouchon ⟮Best⟯ CALIFORNIA   This warm and inviting restaurant serves a seasonal menu inspired by the wines of the Santa Barbara countryside—*bouchon* is French for "wine cork." Past delights have included smoked Santa Barbara albacore "carpaccio," and monkfish saddle fragrant with fresh herbs and accompanied by a creamy fennel-Gruyère gratin. Request a table on the romantic patio, and don't miss the chocolate soufflé.

9 W. Victoria St. (off State St.). ⓒ **805/730-1160.** www.bouchonsantabarbara.com. Reservations recommended. Main courses $25–$35. AE, DC, MC, V. Daily 5:30–10pm.

Brophy Bros. Clam Bar & Restaurant SEAFOOD
This place is most known for its unbeatable view of the marina, but the fresh seafood keeps tourists and locals coming back. Favorites include New England clam chowder and cioppino. The scampi-and-garlic-baked clams are good, as is all the fresh fish, which comes with soup or salad, coleslaw, and pilaf or french fries. A great deal is the hot-and-cold shellfish platter for $13. Ask for a table on the narrow deck overlooking the harbor. **Be forewarned:** The wait at this small place can be up to 2 hours on a weekend night.

119 Harbor Way (off Cabrillo Blvd. in the Waterfront Center). ⓒ **805/966-4418.** www.brophybros.com. Reservations not accepted. Main courses $9–$19. AE, MC, V. Sun–Thurs 11am–10pm; Fri–Sat 10am–11pm.

La Super-Rica Taqueria ⟮Value⟯ MEXICAN
Looking at this street-corner shack, you'd never guess it's blessed with the Nobel Prize of cuisine: an endorsement by the late

Julia Child. The tacos here are no-nonsense, generous portions of filling piled onto fresh, grainy corn tortillas. Sunday's special is *pozole,* a stew of pork and hominy in red chili sauce. On Friday and Saturday, the specialty is freshly made tamales.

622 N. Milpas St. (btw. Cota and Ortega sts.). ✆ **805/963-4940.** Most menu items $4–$10. No credit cards. Daily 11am–9pm.

Wine Cask CALIFORNIA/ITALIAN   Take a 20-year-old wine shop, a 1920s land-mark dining room, outstanding Italian fare, and an attractive clientele, and you've got the Wine Cask. You'll be treated to comforting creations by Chef John Pettitt, such as pan-roasted arctic char in a Dijon-artichoke emulsion. Other options include Australian lamb chops, or pasta with chanterelle mushrooms, baby artichokes, and gold beets. The wine list reads like a novel, with more than 2,000 wines ($14–$1,400), and has deservedly received the *Wine Spectator* award for excellence.

In El Paseo Center, 813 Anacapa. ✆ **800/436-9463** or 805/966-9463. www.winecask.com. Reservations recommended. Lunch $12–$17; dinner main courses $29–$36. AE, DC, MC, V. Mon–Thurs 11:30am–2pm and 5:30–10pm; Fri 11:30am–2pm and 5:30–11pm; Sat 5:30–11pm; Sun 5:30–10pm.

9 LOS ANGELES & ENVIRONS

The allure of L.A.—for better or for worse—is undeniable. Los Angelenos know their city will never have the style of Paris or the history of London, but they cheerfully lay claim to living in the most entertaining city in the country, if not the world.

This part of the L.A. mystique—however exaggerated it may be—truly does exist, and it's not hard to find. In fact, it's fitting that L.A. is home to the world's first amusement park, because it feels like one, as the line between fantasy and reality is often obscured. From the unattainable, anachronistic glamour of Beverly Hills to the vibrant street energy of Venice, each of the city's neighborhoods is like a mini theme park, offering its own kind of adventure. Drive down Sunset Boulevard and you'll see what we mean: the billboards are racier, the fashions trendier, the cars fancier, the bodies sexier, and the energy higher than anyplace you've ever been. Darlin', you ain't in Kansas anymore—you're in La-La Land.

ESSENTIALS

GETTING THERE   By Plane   Most visitors fly into **Los Angeles International Airport** (✆ 310/646-5252; www.lawa.org/lax), known as LAX. Situated ocean-side just off I-405, LAX is minutes away from the city's beach communities and about a half-hour from Westside, Hollywood, or downtown. **Travelers Aid of Los Angeles** (✆ 310/646-2270; www.travelersaid.org) operates booths in each terminal.

The flat price between LAX and downtown Los Angeles is $42. Expect to pay at least $35 to Hollywood, $25 to Beverly Hills, $20 to Santa Monica, and $50 to $60 to the Valley and Pasadena. You'll also pay an airport surcharge of $2.50 for trips originating from LAX.

For some travelers, one of the area's smaller airports might be more convenient than LAX. **Bob Hope Airport,** 2627 N. Hollywood Way, Burbank (✆ 818/840-8840; www.bobhopeairport.com), is the best place to land if you're headed for Hollywood or the valleys—and it's closer to downtown L.A. than LAX. The small airport has good links to Las Vegas and other Southwestern cities. **Long Beach Municipal Airport,** 4100 Donald Douglas Dr., Long Beach (✆ 562/570-2600; www.lgb.org), south of LAX, is the best place to land if you're visiting Long Beach or northern Orange County and want to avoid L.A. **John Wayne Airport,** 19051 Airport Way N., Anaheim (© 949/252-5200; www. ocair.com), is closest to Disneyland, Knott's Berry Farm, and other Orange County attractions.

By Train Amtrak (© 800/USA-RAIL [872-7245]; www.amtrak.com) serves **Union Station,** 800 N. Alameda St. (© 213/617-0111), on downtown's northern edge. There's frequent service from San Diego (trip time: 3 hr.), as well as daily service from Santa Barbara (3 hr.), Oakland (12 hr.), and Chicago (30 hr.).

By Car Los Angeles is well connected to the rest of the United States by several major highways. Among them are **I-5,** which enters the state from the north; **I-10,** which originates in Jacksonville, Florida, and terminates in Los Angeles; and **U.S. 101,** a scenic route that follows the coast from Los Angeles north to the Oregon state line.

VISITOR INFORMATION The **Los Angeles Convention and Visitors Bureau** (or **LA INC.;** © 800/228-2452 or 213/624-7300; www.discoverlosangeles.com) is the city's main source for information. In addition to maintaining an informative website, answering telephone inquiries, and sending free visitors kits, the bureau has two **walk-in visitor centers:** downtown at 685 S. Figueroa St. at West Seventh Street (Mon–Fri 9am–5pm), and in Hollywood at the Hollywood & Highland Center, 6801 Hollywood Blvd. at Highland Avenue (daily 10am–11pm).

Many Los Angeles–area communities also have their own visitor centers, including the **Beverly Hills Visitors Bureau** (© 800/345-2210 or 310/248-1015; www.beverlyhills cvb.com); the **Pasadena Convention and Visitors Bureau,** 171 S. Los Robles Ave. (© 626/795-9311; www.pasadenacal.com); and the **Santa Monica Convention and Visitors Bureau** (© 800/544-5319 or 310/393-7593; www.santamonica.com).

Web-surfers should visit @ **L.A.**'s website, **www.at-la.com**; its exceptional search engine provides links to more than 23,000 sites in the greater L.A. region.

GETTING AROUND Forget about trying to get around the city by the slow and inconvenient public transportation system. Despite its hassles (L.A.'s traffic problems are the stuff of legend), driving is still the only way to go. L.A. is one of the cheapest places in the United States to rent a car. All car-rental agencies have locations at LAX.

FAST FACTS The centrally located **Cedars-Sinai Medical Center,** 8700 Beverly Blvd., Los Angeles (© 310/423-3277), has a 24-hour emergency room. Chances are good that there's either a **Walgreens** (www.walgreens.com) or **Rite Aid** (www.riteaid. com) within a mile of where you're staying.

The combined Los Angeles County and California state **sales taxes** amount to 8.25%; **hotel taxes** range from 12% to 17%, depending on the municipality you're in.

SPECIAL EVENTS & FESTIVALS New Year's Day is greeted by the spectacular **Tournament of Roses** (© 626/449-4100; www.tournamentofroses.com) parade in Pasadena, with lavish floats, music, and extraordinary equestrian entries, followed by the Rose Bowl Game.

In early May, **Cinco de Mayo** (© 213/485-6855) ushers in a weeklong celebration throughout the city. The fiesta's carnival-like atmosphere is created by large crowds, live music, dances, and food. The main festivities are held in El Pueblo de Los Angeles State Historic Park, downtown, with other events around the city.

The **Los Angeles County Fair** (© 909/623-3111; www.fairplex.com), held at the Los Angeles County Fair and Exposition Center in Pomona, usually runs throughout

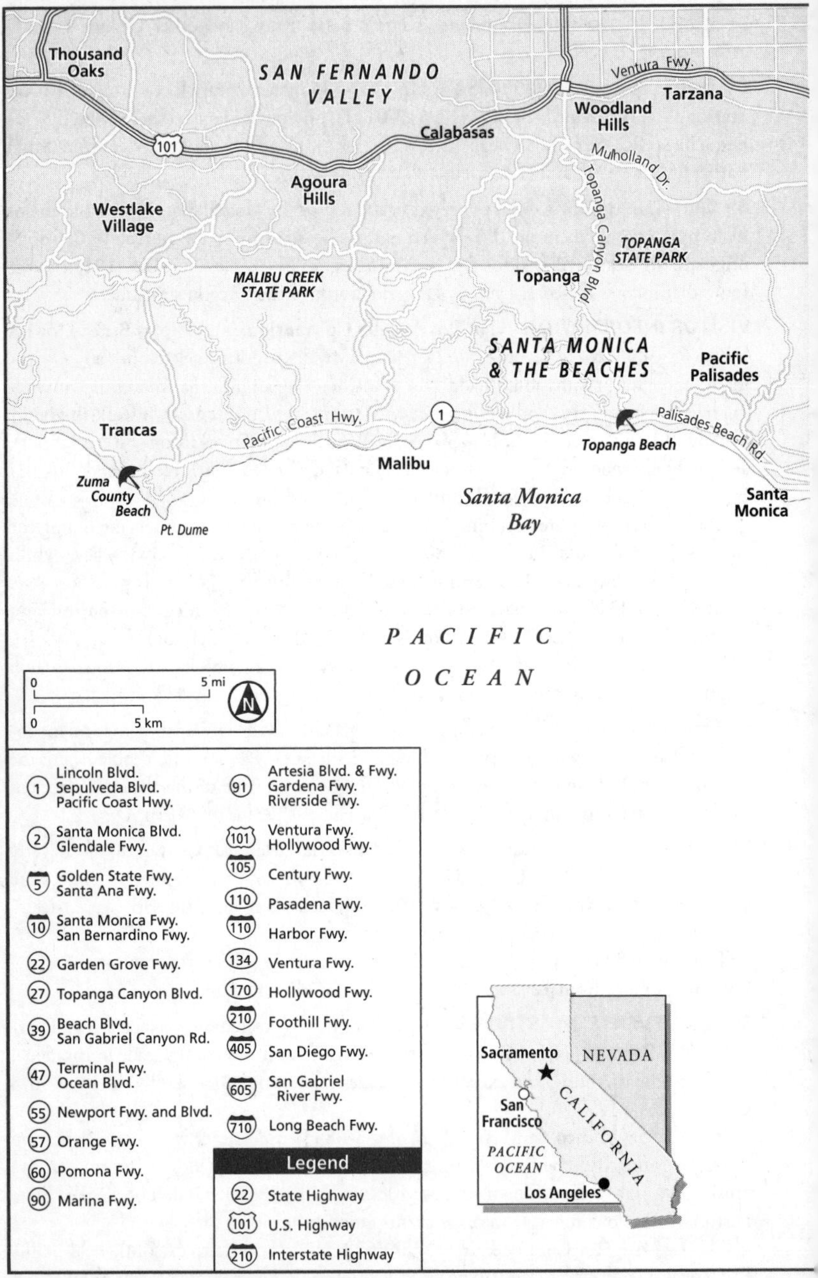
Thousand Oaks
SAN FERNANDO VALLEY
Ventura Fwy.
Tarzana
Woodland Hills
Calabasas
101
Mulholland Dr.
Agoura Hills
Westlake Village
Topanga Canyon Blvd.
TOPANGA STATE PARK
MALIBU CREEK STATE PARK
Topanga
SANTA MONICA & THE BEACHES
Pacific Palisades
1
Pacific Coast Hwy.
Palisades Beach Rd.
Trancas
Topanga Beach
Malibu
Zuma County Beach
Pt. Dume
Santa Monica Bay
Santa Monica
PACIFIC OCEAN
0
5 mi
0
5 km
N
1 Lincoln Blvd. Sepulveda Blvd. Pacific Coast Hwy.
2 Santa Monica Blvd. Glendale Fwy.
5 Golden State Fwy. Santa Ana Fwy.
10 Santa Monica Fwy. San Bernardino Fwy.
22 Garden Grove Fwy.
27 Topanga Canyon Blvd.
39 Beach Blvd. San Gabriel Canyon Rd.
47 Terminal Fwy. Ocean Blvd.
55 Newport Fwy. and Blvd.
57 Orange Fwy.
60 Pomona Fwy.
90 Marina Fwy.
91 Artesia Blvd. & Fwy. Gardena Fwy. Riverside Fwy.
101 Ventura Fwy. Hollywood Fwy.
105 Century Fwy.
110 Pasadena Fwy.
110 Harbor Fwy.
134 Ventura Fwy.
170 Hollywood Fwy.
210 Foothill Fwy.
405 San Diego Fwy.
605 San Gabriel River Fwy.
710 Long Beach Fwy.
Legend
22 State Highway
101 U.S. Highway
210 Interstate Highway
Sacramento
NEVADA
CALIFORNIA
San Francisco
PACIFIC OCEAN
Los Angeles

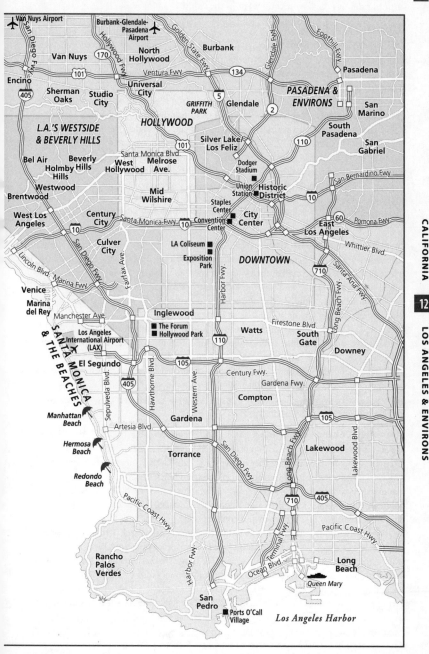

September, with horse racing, arts, agricultural displays, celebrity entertainment, and carnival rides. It's the largest county fair in the world.

WHAT TO SEE & DO

California Science Center (Kids)   A $130-million renovation—reinvention, actually—has turned the former Museum of Science and Industry into Exposition Park's most popular attraction. Using high-tech sleight of hand, the center stimulates kids of all ages with lessons about the world. One of the museum's highlights is Tess, a 50-foot animatronic woman whose muscles, bones, organs, and blood vessels are revealed, demonstrating how the body reacts to a variety of conditions. The **Air and Space Gallery** is a seven-story space where real air- and spacecraft are suspended overhead. There are nominal fees, ranging from $2 to $5, to enjoy the science center's more thrilling attractions—try the zero-gravity Space Docking Simulator. The IMAX theater screens surround-sound movies in 2-D and 3-D throughout the day until 9pm.

700 State Dr., Exposition Park. ✆ **323/724-3623;** IMAX theater ✆ **213/744-7400.** www.casciencectr. org. Free admission to the museum; IMAX theater $8 adults, $5.75 seniors 61 and over and children ages 13–17, $4.75 ages 4–12. Multishow discounts available. Daily 10am–5pm. Closed Thanksgiving, Christmas, and New Year's Day. Parking $6.

Farmers Market & The Grove (Kids)   The original Depression-era farmers' stands have slowly grown into permanent buildings topped by a trademark clock tower and have evolved into a sprawling marketplace with a carnival atmosphere. About 100 restaurants, shops, and grocers cater to a mix of locals and visitors. Retailers sell greeting cards, kitchen implements, candles, and souvenirs, but everyone comes for the food stands, which offer oysters, Cajun gumbo, fresh-squeezed orange juice, fresh-pressed peanut butter, and all kinds of international fast foods. Don't miss **Kokomo Café** (✆ **323/933-0773**), a "gourmet" outdoor coffee shop that has become a power breakfast spot for showbiz types. At the eastern end of the Farmers Market is the **Grove,** a massive 575,000-square-foot Vegas-style retail complex composed of various architectural styles ranging from Art Deco to Italian Renaissance.

6333 W. Third St. (at Fairfax Ave.), Hollywood. ✆ **888/315-8883** or 323/900-8080. www.thegrovela.com. Mon–Thurs 10am–9pm; Fri–Sat 10am–10pm; Sun 11am–8pm.

The Getty Center Los Angeles (Best) (Kids)   Since opening in 1997, the Richard Meier–designed Getty Center has quickly assumed its place as a cultural cornerstone and international mecca. Museum galleries display J. Paul Getty's enormous art collection, which includes antiquities, Impressionist paintings, French decorative arts, illuminated manuscripts, contemporary photography, and graphic arts. One of the museum's finest holdings is van Gogh's *Irises.* A new addition is the Fran and Ray Stark Sculpture Collection. This collection of 28 modern and contemporary outdoor sculptures features works by Roy Lichtenstein, Joan Miró, and Isamu Noguchi. Realizing that fine-art museums can be boring for kids, the center also provides several clever programs, including exploratory games such as *Perplexing Paintings* and *The Getty Art Detective;* and a Family Room filled with puzzles, computers, picture books, and games. Visitors park at the base of the hill and ascend via an electric tram. On clear days, the sensation is of being in the clouds, gazing across Los Angeles and the Pacific Ocean. *Tip:* Avoid the crowds by visiting in the late afternoon or evening.

1200 Getty Center Dr., Los Angeles. ✆ **310/440-7300.** www.getty.edu. Free admission. Tues–Thurs and Sun 10am–6pm; Fri–Sat 10am–9pm. Closed major holidays. Parking $8.

The Getty Villa Malibu ⓥalue   After 8 years and $275 million, the Getty Villa is receiving guests again. This former residence of oil tycoon J. Paul Getty, built in 1974 on the edge of a Malibu bluff with dazzling views of the ocean, was modeled after a first-century Roman country house buried by the eruption of Mt. Vesuvius in A.D. 79. The museum's collection of Greek, Roman, and Etruscan artifacts—from 6,500 B.C. to A.D. 400—includes more than 1,200 works in 23 galleries arranged by theme, and five additional galleries for changing exhibitions. Highlights include the *Statue of a Victorious Youth,* a large-scale bronze discovered in an Adriatic shipwreck. For a more enlightening museum experience, I suggest you rent a $3 GettyGuide Audio Player, which features commentary from curators and conservators on over 150 works (it's available at the Pick-Up Desk on Floor 1). Admission to the Villa is free, but, unlike the Getty Center, advance tickets are required and can be obtained online or by phone.

17985 Pacific Coast Hwy. (1 mile north of Sunset Blvd.), Malibu. ⓒ **310/440-7300.** www.getty.edu. Free admission, but tickets required. Thurs–Mon 10am–5pm. Closed major holidays. Parking $8.

Grauman's Chinese Theatre   One of the world's great movie palaces, the Chinese Theatre was opened in 1927 by entertainment impresario Sid Grauman, a brilliant promoter who's credited with originating the idea of the paparazzi-packed movie premiere. Original Chinese heavenly doves top the facade, and two of the theater's columns once propped up a Ming Dynasty temple. Visitors flock to the theater for its famous entry court, where stars like Elizabeth Taylor, Ginger Rogers, Humphrey Bogart, Frank Sinatra, Marilyn Monroe, and about 160 others set their signatures and hand- and footprints in concrete.

6925 Hollywood Blvd. (btw. Highland and La Brea Ave.). ⓒ **323/464-8111.** www.manntheaters.com/chinese. Movie tickets $11. Call for showtimes.

Griffith Observatory   Closed for renovation for what seemed like forever, it reopened in 2006 after a $93-million renovation. The central dome houses the 300-seat **Samuel Oschin Planetarium,** where hourly screenings of a narrated half-hour projection show called "Centered in the Universe" reveal the stars and planets that are hidden from the naked eye by the city's ubiquitous lights and smog. The Observatory also features 60 space-related exhibits designed to "sparkle your imagination," the highlight being the largest astronomically accurate image ever produced—a 20×152-foot porcelain enamel dazzler that's cleverly called "The Big Picture." Made world-famous in the film *Rebel Without a Cause,* Griffith Observatory's bronze domes have been Hollywood Hills landmarks since 1935. Most visitors don't go inside; they come to this spot on the south slope of Mount Hollywood for unparalleled city views.

2800 E. Observatory Rd. (in Griffith Park, at the end of Vermont Ave.). ⓒ **213/473-0800.** www.griffith observatory.org. Planetarium tickets $7 adults, $5 seniors 60 or older and students with ID, $3 children ages 5–12. Tues–Fri noon–10pm; Sat–Sun 10am–10pm. Call or check website for planetarium show-times.

The HOLLYWOOD Sign   These 50-foot-high, white sheet-metal letters have come to symbolize both the movie industry and the city itself. Erected in 1923 as an advertisement for a real-estate development, the full text originally read HOLLYWOODLAND. A thorny hiking trail leads to the sign from Durand Drive near Beachwood Drive, but the best view is from down below, at the corner of Sunset Boulevard and Bronson Avenue. For more information, call the Griffith Park headquarters at ⓒ **323/913-4688.**

12

LOS ANGELES & ENVIRONS

Huntington Library, Art Collections & Botanical Gardens This is the jewel in Pasadena's crown. Industrialist and railroad magnate Henry E. Huntington collected such rarities as Shakespeare first editions, Benjamin Franklin's handwritten autobiography, and a Gutenberg Bible. If you prefer canvas to parchment, Huntington also put together a terrific 18th-century British and French art collection, including Gainsborough's *The Blue Boy.* These and other works are displayed in a stately Italianate mansion, so you can also get a glimpse of its splendid furnishings. But it's the botanical gardens that draw most locals. The Japanese Garden comes complete with a koi-filled stream and Zen garden. The cactus garden is exotic, the jungle garden is intriguing, and the lily ponds are soothing. A popular English high tea (☏ **626/683-8131** for reservations) is served in the charming tearoom overlooking the Rose Garden. It's a genteel bargain even for hearty appetites, at $20 per person.

1151 Oxford Rd., San Marino. ☏ **626/405-2100**. www.huntington.org. Admission $15 adults, $12 seniors 65 and over, $10 students and children ages 12–18, $6 children ages 5–11, free to children 4 and under; free to all the 1st Thurs of each month. Sept–May Mon and Wed–Fri noon–4:30pm, Sat–Sun 10:30am–4:30pm; June–Aug Wed–Mon 10:30am–4:30pm. Closed major holidays. Free parking.

La Brea Tar Pits & Page Museum (Kids) The La Brea Tar Pits are an awesome, primal sight on Museum Row, where hot tar has been bubbling from the earth for more than 40,000 years. The glistening pools have enticed thirsty animals throughout history. Thousands of mammals, birds, amphibians, and insects crawled into the sticky sludge and stayed forever. In 1906, scientists began a systematic removal and classification of entombed specimens, including ground sloths, giant vultures, mastodons, camels, and even prehistoric relatives of today's superrats. The best finds are on display in the adjacent **George C. Page Museum of La Brea Discoveries,** which also shows an entertaining 15-minute film documenting the recoveries.

5801 Wilshire Blvd. (east of Fairfax Ave.), Los Angeles. ☏ **323/934-7243**. www.tarpits.org. Museum admission $7 adults, $4.50 seniors 62 and older and students with ID, $2 children ages 5–12, free for kids 4 and under; free for everyone the 1st Tues of every month. Mon–Fri 9:30am–5pm; Sat–Sun 10am–5pm (museum). Parking $6 with validation.

Los Angeles County Museum of Art For more than 50 years the LACMA has been one of the finest art museums in the nation, housing a 110,000-piece collection that includes works by Degas, Rembrandt, Hockney, and Monet. The 20-acre complex has been expanded even more with the opening of the $56-million, three-story **Broad Contemporary Art Museum** (also known as BCAM). It's the first new art museum built in L.A. since the Getty Center opened in 1997. Installations include works by contemporary artists like Richard Serra, Jeff Koons, Jasper Johns, Andy Warhol, and Roy Lichtenstein. Other highlights include LACMA's **Pavilion for Japanese Art,** which has exterior walls made of Kalwall, a translucent material that permits the entry of soft natural light. The **Ahmanson Building** houses everything from 2,000-year-old pre-Columbian Mexican ceramics to 19th-century portraiture, to a glass collection spanning the centuries. Free 50-minute guided tours of many of LACMA's exhibitions are offered weekly—check the museum's online calendar for times and locations.

5905 Wilshire Blvd. ☏ **323/857-6000**. www.lacma.org. Admission $12 adults, $8 students and seniors ages 62 and over, free for children 17 and under; regular exhibitions free for everyone after 5pm and all day the 2nd Tues of each month. Mon–Tues and Thurs noon–8pm; Fri noon–9pm; Sat–Sun 11am–8pm. Parking $5.

Museum of the American West   Located north of downtown in Griffith Park, this is one of the country's most comprehensive museums of the American West. More than 78,000 artifacts showcasing the history of the region west of the Mississippi River are displayed. Evocative exhibits illustrate the lives of early pioneers, not only with antique firearms, tools, saddles, and the like, but with hands-on displays that stir the imagination and the heart, including footage from Buffalo Bill's Wild West Show, movie clips from the silent days, contemporary films, the works of Wild West artists, and plenty of memorabilia from Gene "The Singing Cowboy" Autry's film and TV projects. Docent-led tours are generally scheduled on Saturday at 11am and noon.

4700 Western Heritage Way (in Griffith Park). ✆ **323/667-2000.** www.autrynationalcenter.org. Admission $9 adults, $5 seniors 60 and over and students ages 13–18, $3 children ages 2–12, free for children 1 and under; free to all Thurs after 4pm. Tues–Sun 10am–5pm (Thurs until 8pm). Free parking.

Norton Simon Museum of Art   Architect Frank Gehry helped remodel the galleries at what has become one of California's most important museums. The Norton Simon displays one of the finest private collections of European, American, and Asian art in the world. Comprehensive collections of masterpieces by Degas, Picasso, Rembrandt, and Goya are augmented by sculptures by Henry Moore and Auguste Rodin. The "Blue Four" collection of works by Kandinsky, Jawlensky, Klee, and Feininger is impressive, as are the superb Southeast Asian sculptures. One of the most popular pieces is *The Flower Vendor/Girl with Lilies,* by Diego Rivera.

411 W. Colorado Blvd., Pasadena. ✆ **626/449-6840.** www.nortonsimon.org. Admission $8 adults, $4 seniors, free for students and kids 17 and under; free for everyone the 1st Fri of each month 6–9pm. Wed–Mon noon–6pm (Fri until 9pm). Free parking.

Universal Studios Hollywood & CityWalk (Kids)   Universal is more than just one of the largest movie studios in the world—it's one of the biggest amusement parks. The main attraction is the **Studio Tour,** a 1-hour guided tram ride that gives you a peek at stars' dressing rooms, production offices, and back-lot sets. Along the way, the tram encounters several staged "disasters." The **Simpsons Ride** allows guests to join Homer, Marge, Bart, Lisa, and Maggie as they soar above the fictional "Krustyland" theme park in a "virtual roller coaster," creating the sensation of thrilling drops and turns and a full 360-degree loop. **Revenge of the Mummy** is a high-tech indoor roller coaster that whips you backward and forward through a dark Egyptian tomb filled with creepy Warrior Mummies. **Shrek 4D** is one of the park's best attractions, a multisensory animated show that combines 3-D effects, a humorous story line, and "surprise" special effects. On the **Animal Actors Stage,** trained monkeys, pigs, hawks, and other animals perform various entertaining tricks (well, most of the time). Located just outside the gate of Universal Studios Hollywood is **Universal CityWalk** (✆ **818/622-4455;** www.citywalkhollywood.com), a 3-block long pedestrian promenade with stores, restaurants, clubs, and more attractions. Entrance to CityWalk is free; it's open until 9pm on weekdays and until midnight Friday and Saturday.

Hollywood Fwy. (Universal Center Dr. or Lankershim Blvd. exits), Universal City. ✆ **800/UNIVERSAL** (864-8377) or 818/622-3801. www.universalstudioshollywood.com. Admission $65 adults, $55 children under 48 in. tall, free for kids 2 and under. Parking $10. Winter 10am–6pm; summer 9am–7pm. Hours are subject to change.

Venice Beach's Ocean Front Walk (Kids)   No visit to Los Angeles would be complete without a stroll along Venice's famous beach path, an almost surreal assemblage of every L.A. stereotype—and then some. Among stalls and stands selling cheap sunglasses and Mexican blankets swirls a carnival of humanity that includes bikini-clad in-line skaters, tattooed bikers, muscle-bound pretty boys, panhandling vets, beautiful wannabes, and plenty of tourists and gawkers. On any given day, you're bound to come across all kinds of performers: mimes, buskers, chain-saw jugglers, talking parrots, and the occasional apocalyptic evangelist.

On the beach, btw. Venice Blvd. and Rose Ave., Venice. www.venicebeach.com.

MORE HIGHLIGHTS
TV Tapings

Being part of the audience for the taping of a television show might be the quintessential L.A. experience. Timing is important here—remember that most series productions go on hiatus from March to July. Tickets to the top shows are in greater demand than others, so getting your hands on them usually takes advance planning—and possibly some time waiting in line.

Request tickets as far in advance as possible. In addition to the suppliers listed below, tickets are sometimes given away to the public outside popular tourist sites like Grauman's Chinese Theatre in Hollywood and Universal Studios in the Valley; L.A.'s visitor centers in downtown and Hollywood often have tickets as well. But if you're determined to see a particular show, contact the following sources.

Audiences Unlimited, Inc. (© 818/753-3470; www.tvtickets.com), is a good place to start. It distributes tickets for most of the top sitcoms, including *Two And A Half Men,* *Wizards of Waverly Place,* and more. This service is organized and informative (as is its website), and sanctioned by production companies and networks. ABC no longer handles ticket distribution, but refers all inquiries to Audiences Unlimited, Inc. **TVTIX.COM** (© 323/653-4105; www.tvtix.com) also distributes tickets for numerous talk and game shows, including *The Tonight Show* and *Jeopardy!.*

Hitting the Beach

Los Angeles County's 72-mile coastline sports more than 30 miles of beaches, most of which are operated by the **Department of Beaches & Harbors,** 13837 Fiji Way, Marina del Rey (© 310/305-9503). County-run beaches usually charge for parking ($4–$8). Alcohol, bonfires, and pets are prohibited. For recorded **surf conditions** (and coastal weather forecast), call © 310/457-9701. The following are the county's best beaches, listed from north to south.

Jampacked on warm weekends, L.A. County's largest beach park, **Zuma Beach County Park,** is off the Pacific Coast Highway (Hwy. 1), a mile past Kanan Dume Road. While it can't claim to be the loveliest beach in the Southland, Zuma has the most comprehensive facilities: plenty of restrooms, lifeguards, playgrounds, volleyball courts, and snack bars. The southern stretch, toward Point Dume, is Westward Beach, separated from the noisy highway by sandstone cliffs. A trail leads over the point's headlands to Pirate's Cove, once a popular nude beach.

Malibu Lagoon State Beach is not just a pretty white-sand beach, but an estuary and wetlands area as well. The entrance is on the Pacific Coast Highway (Hwy. 1), south of Cross Creek Road, and there's a small admission fee. Marine life and shorebirds teem where the creek empties into the sea, and the waves are mild. The historic Adamson House is here, a showplace of Malibu tile operating as a museum.

L.A.'s best waves roll ashore at **Surfrider Beach.** One of the city's most popular surfing spots, this beach is between the Malibu Pier and the lagoon. Few "locals-only" wave wars are ever fought here—surfing is not as territorial here as it can be in other areas, where out-of-towners can be made to feel unwelcome. Surfrider is surrounded by all of Malibu's hustle and bustle, so don't come here for peace and quiet.

Three miles along the Pacific Coast Highway (Hwy. 1), between Sunset Boulevard and the Santa Monica border, are named for American humorist Will Rogers, whose ranch-turned-state-historic-park is nestled above the palisades that provide the backdrop for the popular **Will Rogers State Beach.** Facilities include a pay parking lot, restrooms, lifeguards, and a snack hut in season. While the surfing is not the best, the waves are friendly for swimmers and there are always competitive volleyball games to be found.

Santa Monica State Beach, encompassing the beaches on either side of the Santa Monica Pier, is popular for its white sands and easy accessibility. There are big parking lots, eateries, and lots of restrooms. A paved beach path runs along here, allowing you to walk, bike, or skate to Venice and points south. Colorado Boulevard leads to the pier; turn north on the Pacific Coast Highway (Hwy. 1) below the coastline's bluffs, or south along Ocean Avenue.

Moving south from Santa Monica, the pedestrian Promenade along **Venice Beach** becomes Ocean Front Walk and gets progressively weirder until it reaches an apex at Washington Boulevard and the Venice fishing pier. Although there are people who swim and sunbathe, Venice Beach's character is defined by the sea of humanity that gathers here, plus the bevy of boardwalk vendors and old-fashioned pedestrian streets a block away. Park on the side streets or in the plentiful lots west of Pacific Avenue.

A wide white-sand beach with tons to recommend it, **Hermosa City Beach** extends to either side of the pier and includes "The Strand," a pedestrian lane that runs its entire length. Main access is at the foot of Pier Avenue, which is lined with shops. There's plenty of street parking, as well as restrooms, lifeguards, volleyball courts, a fishing pier, playgrounds, and good surfing.

ORGANIZED TOURS

STUDIO TOURS   **Universal Studios** offers daily tram tours of their studio lot as part of the general admission price to their amusement park. See the listing on p. 893 above for more information.

Paramount Pictures, 5555 Melrose Ave., Hollywood (© 323/956-1777; www.paramount.com), the only studio still in Hollywood, offers a 2-hour "cart" tour that's both a historical ode to filmmaking and a real-life look at a working studio. Chances of spotting a celebrity are pretty good, though every tour is different. The $35 tours depart Monday through Friday by advance reservations only. Cameras, recording equipment, and children 11 and under are not allowed.

NBC Studios, 3000 W. Alameda Ave., Burbank (© 818/840-3537), offers guided 70-minute tours Monday through Friday from 9am to 3pm that feature a behind-the-scenes look at *The Tonight Show* set; wardrobe, makeup, and set-building departments; and several sound studios. The tour includes some cool video demonstrations of special effects. Tours are $8.50 adults, $7.50 seniors 60 and over, $5 children ages 5 to 12.

Warner Brothers Studios, 3400 Riverside Dr., Burbank (© 818/972-8687; www.wbstudiotour.com), has the most comprehensive—and the least theme-park-like—of the studio tours. The 2-hour drive-and-walk jaunt goes around the studio's faux streets, including stops (whenever possible) at working film and television sets. Whether it's an orchestra scoring a film or a TV show being taped or edited, you'll get a glimpse of how it's all done. Tours are $45 (kids 7 and under not admitted) and are offered Monday through Friday from 8:30am to 4pm. Reservations are required.

SIGHTSEEING TOURS L.A. Tours' (© 323/460-6490; www.latours.net) plush shuttle buses pick up riders from major hotels for morning or afternoon tours of Sunset Strip, the movie studios, the Farmers Market, Hollywood, and homes of the stars. Tours vary in length from a half-day Beaches & Shopping tour to a full-day Grand City tour. Advance reservations are required.

GREAT SHOPPING AREAS

Serious shoppers often make Santa Monica their first stop; the seaside end of L.A. offers many diverse shopping neighborhoods, including **Third Street Promenade** (www.thirdst. com), a pedestrians-only outdoor mall boasting trendy stores and boutiques, as well as dozens of restaurants and a movie theater. The Promenade bustles on into the evening with an assortment of street performers and shoppers.

Main Street, between Pacific Street and Rose Avenue, is another good strip for strolling, boasting a healthy combination of mall standards as well as left-of-center boutiques and casually hip cafes; Main Street's relaxed, beach-community vibe sets it apart, straddling the fashion fence between upscale trendy and beach-bum edgy.

And there's **Montana Avenue,** between Seventh and 17th streets, a breezy, slow-traffic stretch where specialty shops still outnumber the chains. Look around and you'll see upscale moms with strollers shopping for designer fashions, country-home decor, and gourmet takeout.

Elsewhere in L.A., check out **West Third Street,** between Fairfax Avenue and Robertson Boulevard: You can shop 'til you drop on this trendy strip, anchored on the east end by the Farmers Market. *Fun* is more the catchword than *funky,* and the shops (including the vintage-clothing stores) tend a bit more to the refined. Nearby, **La Brea Avenue,** north of Wilshire Boulevard, is L.A.'s artsiest shopping strip. Anchored by the giant **American Rag, Cie** alterna-complex (© 323/935-3157), La Brea is home to lots of urban antiques stores dealing in Deco, Arts and Crafts, 1950s modern, and the like. You'll also find vintage clothiers, furniture galleries, and other warehouse-size stores, as well as some of the city's hippest restaurants, such as Campanile.

Everyone knows about **Rodeo Drive,** the city's most famous shopping street. Couture shops from high fashion's old guard—like Gucci and Hermès—are here, along with plenty of newer high-end labels. The 16-square-block area surrounding Rodeo is known as Beverly Hills' **"Golden Triangle."** Shops off Rodeo are generally not as name-conscious as those on the strip, but they're nevertheless plenty upscale.

Although stretches of **Melrose Avenue** are showing some wear, this is still one of the most exciting shopping streets in the country for cutting-edge fashions—and some eye-popping people-watching, to boot. There are scores of shops selling the latest in clothes, gifts, jewelry, and accessories. Melrose is a playful stroll, dotted with plenty of hip restaurants and funky shops that are sure to shock. Where else could you find green patent-leather cowboy boots, a working 19th-century pocket watch, an inflatable girlfriend, and glow-in-the-dark condoms in the same shopping spree?

If you're a shopping rookie, you might consider an outing with **Urban Shopping Adventures** (© 213/683-9715; www.urbanshoppingadventures.com), which offers custom guided shopping tours to the Fashion District—90 sprawling blocks loaded with wholesale and retail venues—and the trendy Melrose Heights Shopping District.

WHERE TO STAY

In sprawling Los Angeles, location is everything. Choosing the right neighborhood as a base can make or break your vacation. If you plan to spend your days at the beach but stay downtown, for example, you're going to lose a lot of valuable relaxation time on the freeway. But wherever you stay, count on doing a good deal of driving—no hotel in Los Angeles is convenient to everything.

In addition to the listings below, other good bets near the beach include the **Cal Mar Hotel Suites** ($129–$229 suite), 220 California Ave., Santa Monica (© **800/776-6007** or 310/395-5555; www.calmarhotel.com), whose garden apartments are lovingly cared for; and the **Best Western Marina Pacific Hotel & Suites** ($189–$309 double, including continental breakfast), 1697 Pacific Ave., Venice (© **800/786-7789** or 310/452-1111; www.mphotel.com), a haven of smart value just off the newly renovated Venice Boardwalk.

The **Beverly Laurel Motor Hotel** ($107–$150 double), 8018 Beverly Blvd. (© **800/962-3824** or 323/651-2441), is a great choice for wallet-watching travelers who want a central location and a room with more style than your average motel.

Beverly Hills Hotel and Bungalows   Behind the famous facade of the "Pink Palace" (pictured on the cover of the Eagles' *Hotel California*) lies this star-studded haven where legends were, and still are, made. The hotel's grand lobby and impeccably landscaped grounds retain their over-the-top glory, while the lavish rooms boast state-of-the-art luxuries such as marble bathrooms, CD players, VCRs, and butler service at the touch of a button. Many units feature private patios, Jacuzzis, and kitchens. Dining options include the iconic Polo Lounge, the famous Fountain Coffee Shop, and the alfresco Cabana Club Cafe.

9641 Sunset Blvd. (at Rodeo Dr.), Beverly Hills, CA 90210. © **800/283-8885** or 310/276-2251. Fax 310/887-2887. www.beverlyhillshotel.com. 204 units. $485–$665 double; from $1,025 suite or bungalow. AE, DC, MC, V. Parking $23. Pets accepted in bungalows only. **Amenities:** 3 restaurants; Olympic-size outdoor heated pool; 2 outdoor tennis courts (lit for night play); fitness center; full spa services. *In room:* Kitchens (in some).

Casa del Mar   Housed in a former 1920s Renaissance Revival beach club, this Art Deco stunner is a dream of a resort hotel, radiating period glamour. The villalike building's shape awards ocean views to most of the guest rooms, whose luxuries include sumptuously dressed beds, big Italian marble bathrooms with extra-large whirlpool tubs and separate showers, CD players, VCRs, and playful treats such as rubber duckies. Its **Catch Restaurant** has earned justifiable kudos (and more than a few celebrity fans) for its beautiful setting, great service, and finest seasonal seafood.

1910 Ocean Way (next to the Santa Monica Pier), Santa Monica, CA 90405. © **800/898-6999** or 310/581-5533. Fax 310/581-5503. www.hotelcasadelmar.com. 129 units. $460–$735 double; from $1,085 suite. AE, DC, DISC, MC, V. Valet parking $26. **Amenities:** Restaurant; cafe; heated outdoor pool; plunge pool; state-of-the-art health club w/spa services.

Casa Malibu   Evoking the heyday of Malibu's golden age, this modest, low-rise inn on the beach is a refreshing alternative to sleek, impersonal resorts. Wrapped around a palm-studded inner courtyard, the rooms are comfortable, charming, and thoughtfully outfitted in a timeless "California beach cottage" look. Many have been upgraded with air-conditioning and VCRs, but even the older ones are in great shape and boast top-quality bedding, robes, and fridges. Some units have fireplaces, kitchenettes, and CD players. A handsome brick sun deck faces the blue Pacific, while wooden stairs lead to the hotel's private beach.

22752 Pacific Coast Hwy. (about ¼ mile south of Malibu Pier), Malibu, CA 90265. © **800/831-0858** or 310/456-2219. Fax 310/456-5418. 21 units. $129–$229 garden or oceanview double; $289–$299 beachfront double; $269–$429 suite. Rates include continental breakfast. Extra person $15. AE, MC, V. Free parking. **Amenities:** Access to nearby private health club. *In room:* Fridge.

Chamberlain West Hollywood   This four-story boutique hotel, in a tree-lined, residential West Hollywood neighborhood, looks and feels much like a high-quality Manhattan apartment building. The location is reason enough to stay here: It's 2 blocks from the Sunset Strip and Santa Monica Boulevard. Each guest room is a suite with a separate living and sleeping area, a king-size bed with Mascioni 250-count sheets, gas-log fireplace, balcony, flatscreen TV, DVD/VCR combo, CD player, and large desk with Internet access. The rooftop pool and cabana is ideal for sunbathing, with a view of the city, and the small restaurant and bar is good for drinks and appetizers.

1000 Westmount Dr. (1 block west of La Cienega Blvd.), West Hollywood, CA 90069. (C) **800/201-9652** or 310/657-7400. Fax 310/854-6744. www.chamberlainwesthollywood.com. 112 units. $289–$389 studio to 1-bedroom suites. AE, DC, DISC, MC, V. Valet parking $24 with in/out privileges. **Amenities:** Restaurant; heated rooftop pool; fitness center.

Figueroa Hotel (Value)   With an artistic eye and a heartfelt commitment to budget travelers—particularly from Europe and Japan—this former 1925-vintage YWCA has been transformed into L.A.'s best budget hotel. This enchanting 12-story property sits in an increasingly gentrified corner of downtown. The big, airy lobby exudes a Spanish colonial–Gothic vibe with beamed ceilings and soaring columns, tile flooring, ceiling fans, Moroccan chandeliers, and medieval-style furnishings. Elevators lead to equally artistic guest rooms, which, though a bit dark and small, are comfortable.

939 S. Figueroa St. (at Olympic Blvd.), Los Angeles, CA 90015. (C) **800/421-9092** or 213/627-8971. Fax 213/689-0305. 285 units. $144 double; $245 Casablanca suite; $195–$205 other suites. www.figueroa hotel.com. AE, DC, MC, V. Parking $8. **Amenities:** Restaurant; outdoor pool area. *In room:* Fridge.

Hotel Angeleno Los Angeles   This L.A. landmark building is the last of a breed of circular hotels from the 1960s and 1970s. It was bought by the Joie de Vivre hotel group that made its name by revamping tired hotels into hip, modern destinations, and this is the company's first L.A. venture. The location alone is a good reason to stay here: It's beside the city's busiest freeway, a short hop from the popular Getty Center and centrally located between the beaches, Beverly Hills, and the San Fernando Valley. Each pie-shape room comes with a private balcony and double-paned glass to keep most of the freeway din at bay, while comfort comes in the form of 300-count Italian linens, feather duvets, and pillow-top mattresses. Little extras like 30-inch plasma TVs, wireless Internet access, and great views add to the panache. Also a hot spot is the 17-story hotel's penthouse-level **West** supper club and cocktail lounge, the city's first Italian steakhouse. *Tip:* Check the website for good package deals.

170 N. Church Lane (at intersection of Sunset Blvd. and I-405), Los Angeles, CA 90049. (C) **866/ANGELENO** (264-3536) or 310/476-6411. Fax 310/472-1157. www.hotelangeleno.com. 209 units. $189–$239 double; from $295 suite. Rates include evening wine reception. AE, DC, DISC, MC, V. Valet parking $18. **Amenities:** Rooftop restaurant; lobby cafe; heated outdoor pool; fitness center.

Le Parc Suite Hotel   On a quiet street, this stylish all-suite hotel attracts an interesting mix of clientele: Designers stay because it's a few minutes' walk to the Pacific Design Center; music-industry celebs stay for its low-key location; patients and medical consul- tants check in because it's close to Cedars-Sinai; and tourists enjoy being near the Farmers Market, the Beverly Center, and Museum Row. The renovated apartment-like units are extra large—studios are 650 square feet, one-bedrooms 875 to 1,000 square feet— and each has a well-outfitted kitchenette, a dining area, a living room with a fireplace, and a balcony. What the hotel lacks in views it makes up for in value and elbowroom, and the rooftop night-lit tennis court is a rare perk in this area. The hotel's bistro-style restaurant,

Knoll, is a gem, offering good contemporary American cuisine and romantic alfresco
seating at the rooftop dining area.

733 N. West Knoll Dr., West Hollywood, CA 90069. ☎ **800/578-4837** or 310/855-8888. Fax 310/659-7812. www.leparcsuites.com. 154 units. $215–$500 junior or 1-bedroom suite. Check for theater and bed-and-breakfast packages. AE, DC, DISC, MC, V. Parking $18. Pets accepted for $75 fee. **Amenities:** Restaurant; outdoor heated pool; rooftop night-lit tennis court; exercise room w/sauna; access to nearby health club. *In room:* Kitchenette.

Magic Castle Hotel (Value) (Kids)　A stone's throw from Hollywood Boulevard's attractions, this garden-style hotel/motel at the base of the Hollywood Hills offers L.A.'s best cheap sleeps and is ideal for wallet-watching families or long-term stays. The rooms are done in high Levitz style—but the units are spacious, comfortable, and well kept. Named for the Magic Castle, the illusionist club just uphill, the hotel was once an apartment building; it still feels private and insulated from Franklin Avenue's constant stream of traffic. The units are situated around a central swimming pool. Most are large apartments with fully equipped kitchens complete with a microwave and coffeemaker. *Tip:* The Magic Castle Club is renowned as a magician's mecca and is very exclusive—you can get in only by invitation from a member . . . or if you happen to be a guest of the hotel.

7025 Franklin Ave. (btw. La Brea and Highland aves.), Hollywood, CA 90028. ☎ **800/741-4915** or 323/851-0800. Fax 323/851-4926. www.magiccastlehotel.com. 40 units. $129 double; $149–$239 suite. Extra person $10. Off-season and other discounts available. Free continental breakfast. AE, DC, DISC, MC, V. Parking $8. **Amenities:** Outdoor heated pool. *In room:* Kitchen.

The Mosaic Hotel Beverly Hills (Best)　The owners pumped $3 million into renovating this boutique hotel, and the result is spectacular. The lobby is a showcase of functional art, with tile mosaics; fabrics in deep, rich tones; and a profusion of artfully arranged orchids. A wall has been removed to allow direct access from the check-in desk to the bar and lounge, where guests are encouraged to sample the house special—a Mosaic sake martini. The guest rooms offer 300-count linens, goose-down comforters and piles of pillows, windows that open onto the street or garden courtyard, stocked minibars, and bathrooms with Bulgari bath products and rain shower heads. Other perks include free high-speed Internet access, poolside cabanas, CD players, and DVD players in the suites. *Tip:* The corner deluxe rooms are worth the extra $15.

125 S. Spalding Dr., Beverly Hills, CA 90212. ☎ **800/463-4466** or 310/278-0303. Fax 310/278-1728. www.mosaichotel.com. 49 units. $285–$520 double; from $600 suite. AE, DC, MC, V. Parking $15. Small pets accepted. **Amenities:** Restaurant; heated outdoor pool; exercise room w/sauna. *In room:* Fridge.

Sheraton Universal Hotel　The 21-story Sheraton is considered *the* Universal City hotel of choice for tourists, businesspeople, and industry folks visiting the studios. It has a spacious 1960s feel, with updated styling and amenities. Choose a Lanai room for balconies that overlook the pool area, or a Tower room for stunning views and solitude. The hotel is close to the Hollywood Bowl, and you can practically roll out of bed and into the theme park (via free shuttle). An extra $35 per night buys a Club Level room—worth the money for the extra in-room amenities and free continental breakfast and afternoon hors d'oeuvres.

333 Universal Hollywood Dr., Universal City, CA 91608. ☎ **800/325-3535** or 818/980-1212. Fax 818/985-4980. www.sheraton.com/universal. 436 units. $209–$239 double; from $420 suite. Children stay free in parent's room. Ask about AAA, AARP, and corporate discounts; also inquire about packages that include theme-park admission. AE, DC, DISC, MC, V. Valet parking $21; self-parking $16. **Amenities:** Restaurant; outdoor pool; health club.

Shutters on the Beach This Cape Cod–style luxury hotel is on the beach, a block from Santa Monica Pier. The beach-cottage rooms are more desirable than those in the towers. All units have balconies, VCRs, and CD players; some have fireplaces and/or whirlpool tubs; and all have floor-to-ceiling windows that open. The marble bathrooms come with waterproof radios and toy whales. Despite this welcome whimsy, there's a relaxed and elegant ambience throughout the contemporary art-filled hotel. The small pool and the sunny lobby lounge are two great celebrity-spotting perches.

1 Pico Blvd., Santa Monica, CA 90405. ✆ **800/334-9000** or 310/458-0030. Fax 310/458-4589. www.shutters onthebeach.com. 198 units. $490–$785 double; from $1,175 suite. AE, DC, DISC, MC, V. Valet parking $26. **Amenities:** Restaurant; cafe; outdoor heated pool; health club w/spa services.

Venice Beach House Listed on the National Register of Historic Places, this two-story, ivy-covered 1911 Craftsman bungalow is a homey bed-and-breakfast on one of Venice's unique sidewalk streets, a block from the beach. The interior has a lived-in look that adds charm for romantics but won't live up to the expectations of travelers who like designer appointments. What's more, the inn hums noisily with activity when there's a full house. Still, the huge repeat-clientele base doesn't seem to mind. My favorite room is the Venice Pier Suite—light and airy, with a wood-burning fireplace, king-size bed, private bathroom, and sitting room. An expanded continental breakfast with homemade baked goods is served in the sunroom overlooking a splendid garden.

15 30th Ave. (at Speedway, 1 block west of Pacific Ave.), Venice, CA 90291. ✆ **310/823-1966.** Fax 310/823-1842. www.venicebeachhouse.com. 9 units, 5 with private bathroom. $145 double with shared bathroom; $170–$235 double with private bathroom. Extra person after 2 people $20. Rates include expanded continental breakfast. AE, MC, V. On-site parking $12 a day.

WHERE TO DINE

The Apple Pan (Value) SANDWICHES/AMERICAN There are no tables, just a U-shaped counter, at this classic American burger shack and L.A. landmark. Open since 1947, the Apple Pan is a diner that looks—and acts—the part. It's famous for juicy burgers, speedy service, and authentic frills-free atmosphere. The hickory burger is best, though the tuna sandwich also has its share of fans. Definitely order fries and, if you're in the mood, the home-baked apple pie.

10801 Pico Blvd. (east of Westwood Blvd.). ✆ **310/475-3585.** Most menu items under $6. No credit cards. Tues–Thurs and Sun 11am–midnight; Fri–Sat 11am–1am. Free parking.

Café Santorini GREEK In Pasadena's crowded Old Town, this second-story gem has a secluded Mediterranean ambience, due in part to its historic brick building with patio tables overlooking the plaza below. In the evening, lighting is subdued and romantic, but ambience is casual. The food is terrific and affordable, featuring grilled meats and kabobs, pizzas, fresh and tangy hummus, warm pita, and other staples of Greek cuisine. The menu includes regional flavors such as lamb, feta cheese, spinach, or Armenian sausage; the vegetarian baked butternut squash is filled with fluffy rice and smoky roasted vegetables.

64 W. Union St. (main entrance at the shopping plaza at the corner of Fair Oaks and Colorado), Pasadena. ✆ **626/564-4201.** www.cafesantorini.com. Reservations recommended on weekends. Main courses $9–$29. AE, DC, DISC, MC, V. Mon–Thurs 11:30am–10pm; Fri–Sat 11:30am–midnight; Sun 11am–10pm. Valet or self-parking $7.

El Cholo MEXICAN El Cholo has been serving up south-of-the-border comfort food in this festive hacienda since 1927, even though the surrounding mid-Wilshire neighborhood has become Koreatown. Their expertly blended margaritas, invitingly messy nachos, and classic combination dinners don't break new ground, but the kitchen has

perfected these standards over 70 years (we wish they bottled their rich enchilada sauce).
The creative sizzling vegetarian fajitas go way beyond just eliminating the meat. The atmosphere is festive, as people from all parts of town dine happily in the many rambling dining rooms.

1121 S. Western Ave. (south of Olympic Blvd.). ✆ 323/734-2773. www.elcholo.com. Reservations suggested. Main courses $8–$15. AE, DC, DISC, MC, V. Mon–Sat 11am–10pm; Sun 11am–9pm. Free self-parking; valet parking $5.

Jar MODERN CHOP HOUSE Jar offers everything you could hope for in a restaurant: a warm and relaxed setting, excellent service, and generous servings of reliably fantastic food. Flavorful meat dishes such as braised Kurobuta pork shank and Kobe filet of beef are perfectly cooked, simply seasoned, and divinely flavorful. Among the most popular dishes are the Neiman Ranch Char Sui pork chops and an unparalleled pot roast with caramelized onions and carrots. An extensive wine list and martini menu are two good reasons to arrive early and stay for a nightcap at the beautiful Parisian-style bar. *Tip:* Sunday brunch is one of the best in the city.

8225 Beverly Blvd. (at Harper Ave.), Los Angeles. ✆ 323/655-6566. www.thejar.com. Reservations recommended. Main courses $21–$48. AE, DC, DISC, MC, V. Mon–Thurs 5:30–10pm; Fri–Sat 5:30–11pm; Sun 10am–2pm and 5:30pm–9:30pm. Valet parking $6.

Joe's Restaurant (Value) AMERICAN ECLECTIC Chef/Owner Joseph Miller excels in simple cuisine, particularly grilled fish and roasted meats accented with piquant herbs. Formerly a tiny, quirky storefront, the restaurant has been gutted and completely remodeled (the best tables are on the patio, complete with waterfall). Entrees are sophisticated: fallow deer wrapped in bacon, served in a black currant sauce; monkfish in a saffron broth; wild striped bass with curried cauliflower coulis. A four-course prix-fixe menu is $61, and a tasting menu for $75.

1023 Abbot Kinney Blvd., Venice. ✆ 310/399-5811. www.joesrestaurant.com. Reservations required. Main courses dinner $18–$28, lunch $14–$18. AE, MC, V. Tues–Thurs noon–2:30pm and 6–10pm; Fri noon–2:30pm and 6–11pm; Sat 11am–2:30pm and 6–11pm; Sun 11:30am–2:30pm and 6–10pm. Free street parking or valet parking in rear of building.

Koi (Best) ASIAN-FUSION If your goal is to spot Hollywood's A-list of celebrities, make a reservation at Koi: Stars from George Clooney to Madonna are all spotted here regularly. Or just make a reservation because the food—brilliant fusions of Japanese and California cuisine—is so good. Incorporating feng shui elements of trickling water, votive candles, open-air patios, and soft lighting, the minimalist earthen-hued interior has a calming ambience. Start with the cucumber *sunomono* tower flavored with sweet vinegar and edible flowers, followed by a baked crab roll with edible rice paper (fantastic), the tuna tartare and avocado on crispy wontons, the yellowtail carpaccio delicately flavored with grape-seed oil, and the house specialty of black cod bronzed with miso that's warm-butter soft and exploding with sweet flavor.

730 N. La Cienega Blvd. (btw. Melrose Ave. and Santa Monica Blvd.), West Hollywood. ✆ 310/659-9449. www.koirestaurant.com. Reservations recommended. Main courses $13–$27. AE, DC, DISC, MC, V. Sun–Thurs 6–10pm; Fri–Sat 6pm–midnight. Valet parking $5.

Lucques FRENCH/MEDITERRANEAN Pronounced *Luke*, this quietly sophisticated restaurant has a clubby style and handsome enclosed patio. Chef Suzanne Goin cooks with bold flavors, fresh-from-the-farm produce, and an instinctive feel for the food of the Mediterranean. The short menu makes the most of unusual ingredients, such as salt cod and oxtail. Lucques's bar menu and tantalizing hors d'oeuvres are a godsend for late-night diners. *Tip:* On Sunday, Lucques offers a bargain $40 prix-fixe three-course dinner from a weekly changing menu.

8474 Melrose Ave. (east of La Cienega), West Hollywood. (C) **323/655-6277.** www.lucques.com. Reservations recommended. Main courses $18–$30. AE, DC, MC, V. Mon 6–10pm; Tues–Sat noon–2:30pm and 6–11pm; Sun 5–10pm. Metered street parking or valet ($5.50).

Matsuhisa JAPANESE/PERUVIAN   Chef/Owner Nobuyuki Matsuhisa is a true master of fish cookery, creating fantastic dishes by combining Japanese flavors with South American spices and salsas. Broiled sea bass with black truffles is one example of the masterfully prepared delicacies, in addition to nigiri and creative sushi rolls. Matsuhisa is popular with celebrities and foodies, so reserve early. *Tip:* Feeling adventurous? Ask for *omakase* and the chef will compose a selection of eclectic dishes.

129 N. La Cienega Blvd. (north of Wilshire Blvd.), Beverly Hills. (C) **310/659-9639.** www.nobumatsuhisa. com. Reservations recommended. Main courses $15–$50; sushi $4–$13 per order; full *omakase* dinner from $75. AE, DC, MC, V. Mon–Fri 11:45am–2:15pm; daily 5:45–10:15pm. Valet parking $5.

The Palm STEAKS/LOBSTER   Every great American city has a renowned steak-house; in Los Angeles it's the Palm. The child of the famous New York restaurant of the same name, the Palm is regarded by local foodies as one of the best traditional American eateries in the city. The glitterati seem to agree, as stars and their handlers are regularly in attendance. In both food and ambience, this West Coast apple hasn't fallen far from the proverbial tree. The restaurant is brightly lit, bustling with energy, and playfully decorated with dozens of celebrity caricatures on the walls.

9001 Santa Monica Blvd. (btw. Doheny Dr. and Robertson Blvd.), West Hollywood. (C) **310/550-8811.** www.thepalm.com. Reservations recommended. Main courses dinner $17–$41, lobsters $18 per pound; lunch $10–$19. AE, DC, MC, V. Mon–Fri noon–10:30pm; Sat 5–10:30pm; Sun 5–9:30pm. Valet parking $5.

Pink's Hot Dogs (Value) (Kids) SANDWICHES/BURGERS/HOT DOGS   This crusty corner stand isn't your typical hot dog shack; name another stand that has its own valet parking attendant. This L.A. icon grew around the late Paul and Betty Pink, who opened for business in 1939 selling 10¢ wieners from a hot dog cart. Now 2,000 of them are served every day on Pink's soft steamed rolls. There are 24 varieties of dogs, many of the them named for the celebrities who order them (try the Martha Stewart). Even though the dogs are churned out every 30 seconds, expect to wait in line even at mid-night—you'll invariably meet a true crossroads of Los Angeles cultures. Pray that greedy developers spare this little nugget of Americana.

709 N. La Brea Ave. (at Melrose Ave.). (C) **323/931-4223.** www.pinkshollywood.com. Chili dog $2.85. No credit cards. Sun–Thurs 9:30am–2am; Fri–Sat 9:30am–3am.

Providence MODERN AMERICAN SEAFOOD   After 6 years at Water Grill, Chef Michael Cimarusti and his multilingual Italian compatriot, Donato Poto, have fulfilled their dream to create the city's preeminent seafood experience. Relax in this sleek, mod-ern space, which, like the sauces, is not overpowering. Because Cimarusti visits the fish market daily for the choicest seafood, I recommend asking the waiter which are the evening's best dishes or inquire if Michael has time to make a brief visit to your table and offer his advice. If you're in a mood to splurge, go with the $140 Market Menu: nine memorable courses paired with superb wines. And order anything Cimarusti makes with sea urchin—especially if you don't like it. He'll convert you.

5855 Melrose Ave. (at N. Cahuenga Blvd.), Los Angeles. (C) **323/460-4170.** www.providencela.com. Reservations recommended. Main courses $32–$49. AE, MC, V. Fri noon–2:30pm; Mon–Fri 6–10pm; Sat 5:30–10pm; Sun 5:30–9pm. Valet parking $6.

Your best bet for current entertainment info is the *L.A. Weekly* (www.laweekly.com), a free weekly paper available at sidewalk stands, shops, and restaurants. It has all the most up-to-date news on what's happening in Los Angeles's playhouses, cinemas, museums, and live-music venues. The Sunday **"Calendar"** and Thursday **"Weekend"** sections of the *Los Angeles Times* (www.calendarlive.com) are also a good source of information for what's going on throughout the city.

Ticketmaster (© 213/480-3232; www.ticketmaster.com) is L.A.'s major charge-by-phone ticket agency, selling tickets to concerts, sporting events, plays, and special events, but beware of the absurdly high processing fees.

THE PERFORMING ARTS   It's a little-known fact that on any given night, there's more live theater to choose from in Los Angeles than in New York. The all-purpose **Music Center of Los Angeles County,** 135 N. Grand Ave., downtown, houses the **Ahmanson Theatre** and **Mark Taper Forum** (© 213/628-2772; www.taperahmanson. com). You've probably already heard of the **Kodak Theatre,** 6834 Hollywood Blvd. (© 323/308-6300; www.kodaktheater.com), home of the Academy Awards. And the recently restored **Pantages Theatre,** 6233 Hollywood Blvd. between Vine and Argyle streets (© 323/468-1770), reflects the full Art Deco glory of L.A.'s theater scene.

The city is also home to nearly 200 small and medium-size theaters and theater companies. Across town, the **Geffen Playhouse,** 10886 Le Conte Ave., Westwood (© 310/208-5454; www.geffenplayhouse.com), presents work by prominent and emerging writers. One of L.A.'s most venerable landmarks, the **Orpheum Theatre,** 842 S. Broadway (at 9th St.; © 877/677-4386; www.laorpheum.com), reopened after a 75-year hiatus. **Actors Circle Theater,** 7313 Santa Monica Blvd., West Hollywood (© 323/882-8043), is a 47-seater that's as acclaimed as it is tiny.

The world-class **Los Angeles Philharmonic** (© 323/850-2000; www.laphil.org), led by Finnish-born Esa-Pekka Salonen, just moved into its breathtaking new Frank Gehry–designed home—the **Walt Disney Concert Hall,** 111 S. Grand Ave. (© 213/972-7200), with a summer season at the **Hollywood Bowl,** 2301 N. Highland Ave., Hollywood (© 323/850-2000; www.hollywoodbowl.org), an elegant Greek-style natural outdoor amphitheater. The Hollywood Bowl also hosts jazz, pop, and virtuoso performances in summer.

Slowly but surely, the **Los Angeles Opera** (© 213/972-8001; www.losangelesopera. com), which performs at the **Dorothy Chandler Pavilion,** is gaining respect and popularity with inventive stagings of classic and modern operas.

Finally, the **UCLA Center for the Performing Arts** (© 310/825-2101; www. performingarts.ucla.edu) has presented music, dance, and theatrical performances of unparalleled quality for more than 60 years, and continues to be a major presence in the local and national cultural landscape.

THE CLUB & MUSIC SCENE   Veteran record producer/executive Lou Adler opened the **Roxy Theatre,** 9009 W. Sunset Blvd., West Hollywood (© 323/276-2222; www. theroxyonsunset.com), in the 1970s, and it's remained among the top showcase venues in Hollywood ever since. There are plenty of reasons music fans and industry types keep coming back to the **House of Blues,** 8430 Sunset Blvd., West Hollywood (© 323/848-5100; www.hob.com). Night after night, audiences are dazzled by hot national acts, ranging from the Black Eyed Peas to Motorhead.

(Value) Free Morning Music At Hollywood Bowl

It's not widely known, but the Bowl's morning rehearsals are open to the public and absolutely free. On Tuesday, Thursday, and Friday from 9:30am to 12:30pm you can see the program scheduled for that evening. So bring some coffee and doughnuts (the concession stands aren't open) and enjoy the best seats in the house (© **323/850-2000;** www.hollywoodbowl.org).

Nearby is the **Troubadour,** 9081 Santa Monica Blvd. (© **310/276-6168;** www. troubadour.com), the infamous West Hollywood mainstay that radiates rock history. This beer- and sweat-soaked club likes it loud. Louder still is the hip **Viper Room,** 8852 Sunset Blvd., West Hollywood (© **310/358-1881;** www.viperroom.com), owned by Johnny Depp. With an often star-filled scene, the club is known for late-night surprise performances from such powerhouses as Tom Petty, Slash, and Trapt.

In south central L.A.'s up-and-coming Leimert Park, **Babe's & Ricky's Inn,** 4339 Leimert Blvd., Leimert Park (© **323/295-9112;** www.bluesbar.com), stands out as an original, a place where we can imagine B. B. King himself would have played before he became famous. Mama Laura Gross is the cultivator of the fabulous, endangered sound and the house goddess. Great guitarists are the rule, not the exception here.

The legendary bi-level **Whisky A Go-Go,** 8901 Sunset Blvd., West Hollywood (© **310/652-4202,** ext. 15; www.whiskyagogo.com), personifies L.A. rock 'n' roll, from Jim Morrison and X to Guns N' Roses and Beck. Every trend has passed through this club, and it continues to be the most vital venue of its kind. With the hiring of an in-house booker a few years ago, the Whisky began showcasing local talent on free-admission Monday nights.

Straight from New York, a West Coast branch of the **Knitting Factory,** 7021 Hollywood Blvd., Hollywood (© **323/463-0204;** www.theknittingfactory.com), sees such diverse bookings as Kristin Hersh, Pere Ubu, and Jonathan Richman. On the fringe of east Hollywood, **Spaceland,** 1717 Silver Lake Blvd., Silver Lake (© **323/661-4380;** www.club spaceland.com), has become a club where you're likely to see the next big thing, with a history of presenting acts like Arctic Monkeys, Scissor Sisters, and the Decemberists.

When you've gotta dance, head for **El Floridita,** 1253 N. Vine St., Hollywood (© **323/871-8612;** www.elfloridita.com), a Cuban restaurant and salsa joint that's hot, hot, hot. The **Derby,** 4500 Los Feliz Blvd., Los Feliz (© **323/663-8979;** www.the-derby. com), attracts dancers who come dressed to the nines to swing the night away to such musical acts as Big Bad Voodoo Daddy and the Royal Crown Revue.

COMEDY CLUBS You can't go wrong at the **Comedy Store,** 8433 Sunset Blvd., West Hollywood (© **323/650-6268;** www.comedystore.com). New comics develop their material, and established ones work out the kinks, at this landmark venue owned by Mitzi Shore (Pauly's mom). The talent here is always first-rate and includes comics who regularly appear on *The Tonight Show.*

For more edgy fare, head to the **Groundling Theater,** 7307 Melrose Ave. (© **323/ 934-4747;** www.groundlings.com), the most innovative group in town. The Groundlings were the springboard to fame for former *Saturday Night Live* stars Jon Lovitz, the late Phil Hartman, and Julia Sweeney.

clubs.com), a showcase for top stand-ups since 1975, features the likes of Jay Leno and Billy Crystal more often than you'd expect. But even if the comedians on the bill are all unknowns, they won't be for long.

10 THE DISNEYLAND RESORT

There are newer and larger Disneyland parks in Florida, Tokyo, and even France, but the original still opens its gates in Anaheim, California, every day, proudly proclaiming itself "The Happiest Place on Earth." Smaller than Walt Disney World (see "Walt Disney World & Orlando," p. 334), Disneyland—which opened in 1955 on a 107-acre tract surrounded by orange groves—has always capitalized on being the world's first family-oriented mega theme park. The Disney difference—the one that keeps the park fresh and fantastic, whether you're 6 or 60—is *imagination.* Disneyland is about more than rides and shows . . . it's fantasy elevated to an art form.

In 2001, Disney unveiled a brand-new theme park, Disney's California Adventure, and revamped its own name to "The Disneyland Resort," reflecting a greatly expanded array of entertainment options.

ESSENTIALS

GETTING THERE   Disneyland is about an hour's drive south of Los Angeles, or 90 minutes north of San Diego. Follow **I-5** until you see signs for Disneyland; offramps from both directions lead into parking lots and surrounding streets.

VISITOR INFORMATION   For information on the **Disneyland Resort,** log onto its official website at **www.disneyland.com**. For general information on the entire Anaheim region, contact the **Anaheim/Orange County Visitor and Convention Bureau,** 800 W. Katella Ave., inside the Anaheim Convention Center ($\textcircled{c}$ **714/765-8888;** www.anaheim oc.org). It's open Monday to Friday from 8:30am to 5:30pm. They can fill you in on area activities and shopping, as well as send you their *Official Visitors Guide* and the AdventureCard, which offers discounts at dozens of local attractions, hotels, restaurants, and shops.

ADMISSION & HOURS   As of press time, admission to *either* Disneyland or Disney's California Adventure, including unlimited rides and all festivities and entertainment, is $66 for adults and children 10 and over, $56 for children 3 to 9, and free for children 2 and under. Parking is $11. A 1-Day Park Hopper ticket is $91 for adults and $81 for children. A 2-day Park Hopper ticket, which allows you to go back and forth as much as you'd like each day, is $132 for adults and children over 9, and $112 for children 3 to 9. Be sure to check the Disney website, **www.disneyland.com**, for seasonal ticket specials.

Disneyland and Disney's California Adventure are open every day of the year, but operating hours vary, so be sure to call for information that applies to the specific day(s) of your visit ($\textcircled{c}$ **714/781-7290**).

DISNEYLAND

Once in the park, many visitors tackle Disneyland (or Disney's California Adventure) systematically, beginning at the entrance and working their way clockwise around the park. My advice: Arrive early and run to the most popular rides—the Indiana Jones

(Value)   **CityPass Savings**

If your vacation includes a visit to San Diego, look into purchasing a **Southern California CityPass** (www.citypass.com). It includes a 3-Day Park Hopper ticket to Disneyland and Disney's California Adventure, plus a 1-day admission to Universal Studios Hollywood, SeaWorld Adventure Park, and the San Diego Zoo or Wild Animal Park. It costs $247 for adults and $199 for children, and if you visit all these attractions, you'll save more than $90.

Adventure, Star Tours, Big Thunder Mountain Railroad, Splash Mountain, the Haunted Mansion, and Pirates of the Caribbean, all in Disneyland; and Twilight Zone Tower of Terror, Soarin' Over California, California Screamin', Grizzly River Run, and It's Tough to Be a Bug rides in Disney's California Adventure. Waits for these rides can last an hour or more in the middle of the day.

This time-honored plan of attack may eventually become obsolete, thanks to Disney's **FASTPASS** system. Here's how it works: Say you want to ride Space Mountain, but the line is long—*so* long the current wait sign indicates a 75-minute standby. Instead, you can head to the FASTPASS ticket dispenser, where you pop in your park ticket to receive a voucher listing a computer-assigned boarding time later that day. When you return at the assigned time, you enter through the FASTPASS gate and only have to wait about 10 minutes. The hottest features at Disney's California Adventure had FASTPASS built in from the start; for a complete list for each park, check your official map/guide when you enter and look for the red FP symbol. *Note:* You can obtain a FASTPASS for only one attraction at a time. And only a limited supply of FASTPASSes are available for each attraction on a given day.

Only 1 day in the park? Then start by riding the most popular rides first—or get a FASTPASS early—so you don't waste time in line. If you've got smaller children, concentrate on Fantasyland, a kids' paradise with fairy-tale-derived rides like **King Arthur Carousel, Dumbo the Flying Elephant, Casey Jr. Circus Train, Mr. Toad's Wild Ride, Peter Pan's Flight, Alice in Wonderland, Pinocchio's Daring Journey,** and the Disney signature ride, **It's a Small World,** a boat ride through a saccharine nightmare of all the world's children singing the song everybody loves to hate. Elsewhere in the park, little ones will enjoy clambering through **Tarzan's Treehouse. Mickey's Toontown** is a wacky, gag-filled world inspired by the *Roger Rabbit* films, featuring endless amusement for young imaginations.

If high-speed thrills are your style, then follow the **Indiana Jones Adventure** into the Temple of the Forbidden Eye, or jump on one of Disneyland's "mountain"-themed action roller coasters. There's perennial favorite, the newly revamped **Space Mountain,** a pitch-black indoor roller coaster; **Splash Mountain,** a water flume ride (with a big, wet splash at the end) based on the Disney movie *Song of the South;* the **Matterhorn Bobsleds,** a zippy coaster through the landmark mountain's chilled caverns and drifting fog banks; and **Big Thunder Mountain Railroad,** where runaway railroad cars careen through a deserted 1870s gold mine. **Star Tours** is a *Star Wars*–inspired Tomorrowland simulation ride.

A longtime Disneyland highlight is the more-funny-than-scary **Haunted Mansion,** which showcases the brilliant eye for details of the Disney "imagineers"; and the new-look

Pirates of the Caribbean, where Captain Jack Sparrow and his cohorts from the hit film franchise now appear in the ride that inspired their movie.

If you've got more than 1 day, you'll have the luxury of enjoying some Disney extras not essential enough to pack into a single day. Avoid the midday crush by strolling along **Main Street U.S.A.,** shopping for souvenirs, enjoying some ice cream or candy, and a mixed-media attraction that combines a presentation on the life of Walt Disney (*The Walt Disney Story*) with a remembrance of Abraham Lincoln. The **parades and shows** draw huge crowds. There's also a nighttime **fireworks** spectacular above Sleeping Beauty's Castle, and the after-dark pyrotechnic show *FANTASMIC!*

DISNEY'S CALIFORNIA ADVENTURE

With a grand entrance designed to resemble one of those "Wish you were here" scenic postcards, the 55-acre Disney's California Adventure starts out with a bang. You walk beneath the scale model of the Golden Gate Bridge into **Sunshine Plaza,** anchored by a perpetual wave fountain and an enormous gold titanium "sun" that shines all day (it follows the real sun's path). Visitors can head into four themed "districts," each containing rides, attractions, shows, and dining, snacking, and shopping opportunities.

The **Golden State** represents California's history, heritage, and physical attributes. The park's splashiest attractions are here. The ride **Soarin' Over California** combines suspended seats with a spectacular IMAX-style movie (use FASTPASS for this one), while the **Grizzly River Run** is a wet gold-country ride through caverns and mine shafts. **Pacific Wharf,** inspired by Monterey's Cannery Row, features mouthwatering demonstration attractions by Boudin Sourdough Bakery and Mission Tortillas.

A Bug's Land encompasses **Flik's Fun Fair, Bountiful Valley Farm,** and *It's Tough to Be a Bug,* an interactive 3-D film that takes *A Bug's Life* characters on an underground romp with bees, termites, grasshoppers, spiders, and a few surprises. **Bountiful Farm** pays tribute to California's agriculture and includes the park's most upscale eatery, the **Vineyard Room,** a great place to sip champagne and watch Disney's Electrical Parade.

At **Paradise Pier,** highlights include the **California Screamin'** roller coaster; the **Maliboomer,** a trio of towers that catapults riders to the tiptop bell, then lets them down bungee style; the **Orange Stinger,** a whooshing swing ride inside an enormous orange; and **Mulholland Madness,** a wild trip along L.A.'s precarious hilltop street. In 2008 the **Toy Story Mania** ride debuted. Guests donning 3-D glasses are "shrunk" to the size of a toy for a fanciful ride that twists along a midway-themed route.

The **Hollywood Pictures Backlot** features the **Disney Animation** building, where visitors can learn how stories become animated features, and the **Hyperion Theater,** which presents a live-action tribute to classic Disney films. The resort's hottest attraction is the **Twilight Zone Tower of Terror.** The Backlot's other main attraction is **Playhouse Disney—Live on Stage!,** starring the characters from the popular *Playhouse Disney* kids' program on the Disney Channel. Other popular shows include **Monsters, Inc. Mike & Sulley to the Rescue!;** and *Jim Henson's MuppetVision 3D,* an on-screen comedy romp featuring Kermit, Miss Piggy, Gonzo, Fozzie Bear—and even hecklers Waldorf and Statler.

DOWNTOWN DISNEY   This is a colorful (and sanitized) "street scene" filled with restaurants, shops, and entertainment. The promenade begins at the park gates and stretches toward the Disneyland Hotel; there are nearly 20 shops and boutiques, restaurants, live music venues, and entertainment options from **House of Blues** to **Ralph Brennan's Jazz Kitchen,** and **World of Disney,** one of the biggest Disney shopping experiences anywhere, with a vast range of toys, souvenirs, and collectibles.

11 SAN DIEGO

San Diego, California's first city, is best known for its benign climate and fabulous beaches. On sunny days, the city is one big outdoor playground—you can choose from swimming, snorkeling, windsurfing, kayaking, bicycling, skating, and tons of other fun in or near the water. The city is also home to top-notch attractions, including three world-famous animal parks and splendid Balboa Park. Growth has been fast and furious over the last decade, and although it has been awkward at times, as growth can be, San Diego now finds itself with a new skyline and a new attitude. Restored historic districts draw a stylish crowd that's updating the face of San Diego dining, shopping, and entertainment. Welcome to California's grown-up beach town.

ESSENTIALS

GETTING THERE **By Plane** **San Diego International Airport,** 3707 N. Harbor Dr. (© **619/231-2100;** www.san.org), locally known as Lindbergh Field, is 2 miles from downtown. If you're driving into the city from the airport, take Harbor Drive south to Broadway and turn left. All the major car-rental agencies have offices at the airport, and we recommend renting a car if you plan to explore the city in any depth.

If you don't want to rent a car, several **shuttles** run regularly from the airport to downtown hotels, charging around $8 per person. **Taxis** line up outside both terminals and charge around $10 (plus tip) to take you to a downtown location.

By Train **Amtrak** (© **800/872-7245;** www.amtrak.com) connects San Diego to the rest of the country via Los Angeles. Trains pull into San Diego's mission-style **Santa Fe Train Depot,** 1050 Kettner Blvd. (at Broadway), within walking distance of some downtown hotels and the Embarcadero. It's $29 one-way from L.A.

By Car From Los Angeles, you'll enter San Diego via coastal route **I-5.** From northeast of the city, you'll come down on **I-15** and **Hwy. 163** south to drive into downtown (where 163 turns into 10th Ave.), or hook up with **I-8** west for the beaches.

VISITOR INFORMATION You'll find staffed information booths at the airport, train station, and cruise ship terminal. Downtown, the Convention & Visitors Bureau's **International Visitor Information Center** (© **619/236-1212;** www.sandiego.org) is at 1040¹/₃ W. Broadway at Harbor Drive. Daily summer hours are from 9am to 5pm; it's open 9am to 4pm daily the rest of the year. The bureau offers great info and deals on its website, but you can also get your hands on the glossy *Official Visitors Planning Guide* from the information center. The guide includes information on dining, activities, attractions, tours, and transportation. ConVis also publishes *San Diego Travel Values,* which is full of discount coupons for hotels, restaurants, and attractions (it's available online, too).

To find out what's playing, pick up a copy of the *San Diego Weekly Reader* (www.sdreader.com), a free newspaper available all over the city every Thursday. "Night & Day," the entertainment supplement in the *San Diego Union-Tribune* (www.signon sandiego.com), the city's main daily newspaper, appears on Thursday; the free alternative weekly *San Diego CityBeat* comes out on Wednesday.

GETTING AROUND San Diego traffic can be problematic. It's not L.A., but the construction of dense, outlying suburbia over the last 20 years has made morning and evening rush-hour traffic a headache. Aside from that, it's car friendly and easy to navigate. For up-to-the-minute traffic info, dial © **511.**

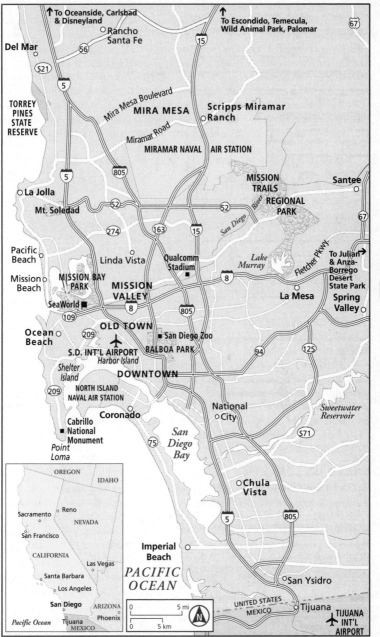

To Oceanside, Carlsbad & Disneyland

To Escondido, Temecula, Wild Animal Park, Palomar

67

Del Mar

Rancho Santa Fe

56

15

S21

5

TORREY PINES STATE RESERVE

Mira Mesa Boulevard

MIRA MESA

Scripps Miramar Ranch

Miramar Road

MIRAMAR NAVAL   AIR STATION

MISSION TRAILS

Santee

5

805

La Jolla

Mt. Soledad

52

52

REGIONAL PARK

San Diego River

67

Pacific Beach

274

163

15

Lake Murray

Fletcher Pkwy.

To Julian & Anza-Borrego Desert State Park

Linda Vista

Qualcomm Stadium

8

Mission Beach

MISSION BAY PARK

MISSION VALLEY

La Mesa

Spring Valley

SeaWorld

8

805

109

Ocean Beach

209

OLD TOWN

San Diego Zoo

BALBOA PARK

94

125

S.D. INT'L AIRPORT

Harbor Island

DOWNTOWN

Shelter Island

209

NORTH ISLAND NAVAL AIR STATION

Coronado

National City

Sweetwater Reservoir

Cabrillo National Monument

75

San Diego Bay

S71

Point Loma

Chula Vista

5

805

CALIFORNIA

12

SAN DIEGO

OREGON

IDAHO

Sacramento

Reno

NEVADA

San Francisco

CALIFORNIA

Las Vegas

Santa Barbara

Los Angeles

San Diego

ARIZONA

Pacific Ocean

Tijuana

Phoenix

MEXICO

Imperial Beach

PACIFIC OCEAN

San Ysidro

UNITED STATES

MEXICO

Tijuana

TIJUANA INT'L AIRPORT

0   5 mi

0   5 km

Downtown, many streets run one-way, and finding a parking space can be tricky. There are several centrally located parking lots, where prices fluctuate wildly according to the day and time. Free parking is the rule in Balboa Park and Old Town.

Both city buses and the San Diego Trolley are operated by the **San Diego Metropolitan Transit System** (MTS; ✆ **800/266-6883** or 619/233-3004; www.sdcommute. com). The website offers timetables, maps, and fares online, and provides information on how the transit system accommodates travelers with disabilities. Or visit the system's **Transit Store,** 102 Broadway, at First Avenue (✆ **619/234-1060**), a complete public-transportation information center, supplying travelers with passes, tokens, timetables, maps, and brochures. The store is open Monday through Friday from 9am to 5pm. A $5 **Day-Tripper pass** allows for 1 day of unlimited rides (a 2-day pass is $9, a 3-day pass is $12, or a 4-day pass is $15); it's available from the Transit Store, at all trolley ticket vending machines, or online.

The **San Diego Trolley** runs south to the Mexican border (a 40-min. trip), north to Old Town, and east to the city of Santee. Trolleys stop at many popular locations; fares range from $1.25 to $3.

FAST FACTS   The most conveniently located hospital emergency room is at **UCSD Medical Center—Hillcrest,** 200 W. Arbor Dr. (✆ **619/543-6222**).

Of the 10 largest cities in the United States, San Diego historically has had the lowest incidence of violent crime, per capita. Still, it never hurts to take precautions. Caution is advised in Balboa Park, in areas not frequented by regular foot traffic. Parts of the city that are usually safe on foot at night include the Gaslamp Quarter, Hillcrest, Old Town, Mission Valley, La Jolla, and Coronado.

Sales tax in restaurants and shops is 7.75%. Hotel tax is 10.5%, or 12.5% for lodgings with more than 70 rooms.

SPECIAL EVENTS & FESTIVALS   From mid-June to early July, the whole county heads to the Del Mar Fairgrounds for the **San Diego County Fair** (✆ **858/755-1161;** www.sdfair.com), a 3-week event with livestock competitions, rides, flower and garden shows, food and crafts booths, carnival games, and home-arts exhibits; concerts by name performers are included with admission.

The first weekend after Labor Day, the **San Diego Street Scene** (✆ **619/557-0505;** www.street-scene.com) transforms the Gaslamp Quarter with a 3-day extravaganza featuring food, dance, international character, and live music. The festival is all-ages, with certain shows restricted to 21 and older.

WHAT TO SEE & DO

The **Old Town Trolley** (✆ **619/298-TOUR** [298-8687]; www.historictours.com) isn't a trolley at all; it's a privately operated open-air tour bus that travels in a continuous loop around the city. You can hop on and off throughout the day. Major stops include Old Town, Presidio Park, Bazaar del Mundo, Balboa Park, the San Diego Zoo, the Embarcadero, Seaport Village, and the Gaslamp Quarter. Tours operate daily from 9am to 4pm (until 5pm in summer); they cost $30 for adults and $15 for children 4 to 12.

LEGOLAND California (Kids)   This is the ultimate monument to the world's most famous plastic building blocks. In addition to 5,000 LEGO models, the Carlsbad park is beautifully landscaped with 1,360 bonsai trees and other plants from around the world, and features more than 50 rides, shows, and attractions. Attractions include hands-on interactive displays, a life-size menagerie of animals, and scale models of international landmarks (the Eiffel Tower, Sydney Opera House, and so on)—all constructed of real LEGO bricks. There are three relatively tame coaster rides (don't worry, they're built from steel), but the park is geared toward children ages 2 to 12. A whole new sister park opened in 2008: **Sea Life LEGOLAND California Resort** is an interactive, educational aquarium experience, focusing on the creatures (the real things—not models) found in regional waters from the Sierra Mountains to the depths of the Pacific. Separate admission is required ($19 adults, $16 seniors, $12 kids).

1 Legoland Dr. ✆ **877/534-6526** or 760/918-5346. www.legoland.com. $59 adults, $47 seniors and kids 3–12, free for children 2 and under. AE, DISC, MC, V. Summer (late June to Aug) daily 10am–8pm; off season Thurs–Mon 10am–5 or 6pm. Closed Tues–Wed Sept–May, but open daily during winter and spring vacation periods. Parking $10. From I-5 take Cannon Rd. exit east, follow signs for Legoland Dr.

San Diego Wild Animal Park (Best) (Kids)

Located 34 miles north of San Diego, this 1,800-acre park features 3,500 animals, many of them endangered species, roaming freely—it's the humans who are enclosed. This living arrangement encourages breeding colonies, so it's not surprising that you'll find the largest crash of rhinos at any zoological facility in the world here. Several other species that had vanished from the wilds have been reintroduced to their natural habitats from stocks bred here. The best way to see the animals is by riding the 5-mile **monorail** (included in the price of admission), a 50-minute ride through areas resembling Africa and Asia. Other exhibits bring you closer to the animals, like the three self-guided **walking tours,** which visit various habitats. The San Diego Zoo may be more famous, but we actually enjoy this park more. For a real up-close experience, take one of the park's **Photo Caravans** (call for details and current prices).

15500 San Pasqual Valley Rd., Escondido. ✆ **760/747-8702.** www.wildanimalpark.org. Admission $29 adults, $18 children 3–11, free for children 2 and under and military. AE, DISC, MC, V. Daily 9am–4pm (grounds close at 5pm); extended hours during summer and Festival of Lights (2 weekends in Dec). Parking $9, $14 RVs. Bus: 386 (Mon–Sat). Take I-15 to Via Rancho Pkwy.; follow signs for about 3 miles.

San Diego Zoo (Kids)

More than 4,000 animals reside at this world-famous zoo. The zoo is one of only four in the U.S. with giant pandas, but there are many other animals worth seeing: cuddly koalas from Australia, wild Przewalski's horses from Mongolia, lowland gorillas from Africa, and giant tortoises from the Galápagos. The usual lions, elephants, giraffes, and tigers are present, too, housed in barless, moated enclosures designed to resemble their natural habitats. There's a **Children's Zoo,** with a nursery for baby animals and a petting area where kids can cuddle up to sheep, goats, and the like. The zoo offers **bus tours,** which provide a narrated overview and show you about 75% of the park. You can get an aerial perspective via the **Skyfari.**

2920 Zoo Dr., Balboa Park. ✆ **619/234-3153** (recorded info), or 231-1515. www.sandiegozoo.org. Admission $25 adults, $17 children 3–11, free for military in uniform; "Best Value" package (admission, guided bus tour, round-trip Skyfari aerial tram) $34 adults, $31 seniors, $24 children. AE, DISC, MC, V. Sept to mid-June daily 9am–4pm (grounds close at 5 or 6pm); mid-June to Aug daily 9am–8pm (grounds close at 9pm). Bus: 7. I-5 south to Pershing Dr., follow signs.

SeaWorld San Diego (Kids)

This 165-acre aquatic playground may be your main reason for visiting California. Several successive 4-ton black-and-white killer whales have functioned as the park's mascot, Shamu. At its heart, SeaWorld is a family entertainment center where the performers are dolphins, otters, sea lions, walruses, and seals. Shows run continuously throughout the day, while visitors can rotate through the various theaters. A small collection of rides is led by **Journey to Atlantis,** a roller coaster and log flume; **Shipwreck Rapids** is a splashy adventure on raftlike inner tubes, and **Wild Arctic** is a simulated helicopter trip to the frozen North. Enjoy a passel of new *Sesame Street*–related attractions, including rides, a musical production *(Big Bird's Beach Party),* and a "4-D"

(Value) Lots of Animals on a Budget!

San Diego's three main animal attractions have joined forces with combo ticket deals that reward big savings to visitors with recreational stamina. Here's how it works: If you plan to visit both the zoo and the Wild Animal Park, a two-park ticket (the "Best Value" zoo package, plus Wild Animal Park admission) is $60 for adults, $43 for children 3 to 11. You get unlimited visits to each attraction, to be used within 5 days of purchase. Throw in SeaWorld within the same 5 days, and the combo works out to $109 for adults, $89 children ages 3 to 9.

interactive movie experience. SeaWorld's real specialties are simulated marine environments, like the **arctic research station,** surrounded by beluga whales and polar bears. Other animal environments worth seeing are **Manatee Rescue, Shark Encounter,** and **Penguin Encounter.**

500 SeaWorld Dr., Mission Bay. (©) **800/257-4268** or 619/226-3901. www.seaworld.com. Admission $59 adults, $49 children 3–9, free for children 2 and under. AE, DISC, MC, V. Hours vary seasonally, but always at least daily 10am–5pm; most weekends and during summer 9am–11pm. Parking $10, $15 RVs. Bus: 8 or 9. From I-5, take SeaWorld Dr. exit; from I-8, take W. Mission Bay Dr. exit to SeaWorld Dr.

Exploring Balboa Park

Balboa Park is one of the nation's largest and loveliest city parks, boasting walkways, gardens, historic buildings, a restaurant, an ornate pavilion with one of the world's largest outdoor organs, and the world-famous San Diego Zoo. Stroll along **El Prado,** the park's main street, and admire the distinctive Spanish/Mediterranean buildings, which house an amazing array of museums. El Prado is also popular with musicians and other performers whose busking provides an entertaining backdrop.

Entry to the park is free, but most of its museums have admission charges, ranging from $6 to $13 for adults, and varying open hours. A free tram transports you around the park. Get details from the **Balboa Park Visitor Center,** in the House of Hospitality (© **619/239-0512;** www.balboapark.org). *Note:* Most Balboa Park attractions are open free of charge one Tuesday each month; there's a rotating schedule, so two or three participate each Tuesday (the visitor center has a schedule). If you plan to visit more than three of the park's museums, buy the **Passport to Balboa Park,** which allows entrance to 13 major museums; it's valid for 1 week and costs $39 for adults, $21 for children 3 to 12.

The **San Diego Aerospace Museum,** 2001 Pan American Plaza (© **619/234-8291;** www.aerospacemuseum.org), celebrates great achievers and achievements in the history of aviation and aerospace with a superb collection of aircraft and artifacts.

The impressive painting and sculpture collections at the **San Diego Museum of Art,** 1450 El Prado (© **619/232-7931;** www.sdmart.com), include outstanding Italian Renaissance and Dutch and Spanish baroque art, along with an impressive collection of works by Toulouse-Lautrec.

The **Museum of Contemporary Art San Diego,** 700 Prospect St. (© **858/454-3541;** www.mcasd.org), focuses on works produced since 1950 and is known internationally for its permanent collection and thought-provoking exhibitions. The 3,000-plus holdings represent every major art movement of the past half-century, with a strong showing by California artists. The MCASD now has a third facility, across the street from its downtown once historic Santa Fe Depot's "baggage building."

The **Museum of Photographic Arts,** 1649 El Prado (© **619/238-7559;** www.mopa. org), is one of a few in the United States. If the names of Ansel Adams, Margaret Bourke-White, Imogen Cunningham, Edward Weston, and Henri Cartier-Bresson stimulate your interest, then don't miss this 7,000-plus image collection.

The best exhibits in the **San Diego Natural History Museum,** 1788 El Prado (© **619/232-3821;** www.sdnhm.org), focus on the plants, animals, and minerals of the Southwest. The interactive installation *Fossil Mysteries* includes life-size models of prehistoric animals, including the megalodon shark, the largest predator the world has ever known.

The **Reuben H. Fleet Science Center,** 1875 El Prado (© **619/238-1233;** www. rhfleet.org), features five galleries with hands-on exhibits as intriguing for grown-ups as for kids, plus SciTours, a simulator ride that voyages into space and the worlds of science and biology. Equally popular is the OMNIMAX movie theater, surrounding viewers with breathtaking adventure travelogues.

Old Town: A Look at California's Beginnings

The birthplace of San Diego is Old Town, the hillside where the Spanish Presidio and Father Junípero Serra's mission (the first in California) were built. By protecting the remaining adobes and historic buildings, **Old Town State Historic Park** brings to life Mexican California, which existed here until the mid-1800s. Much of the surrounding area, however, has become a mini Mexican theme park. Free walking tours leave daily at 11am and 2pm from **Robinson-Rose House** (© **619/220-5422;** www.parks.ca.gov).

BEACHES & OUTDOOR ACTIVITIES
Hitting the Beach

San Diego County is blessed with 70 miles of sandy coastline. The following are some of our favorite San Diego beaches, arranged geographically from south to north.

Lovely, wide, and sparkling white, **Coronado Beach** is conducive to strolling and lingering, especially in the late afternoon. It fronts Ocean Boulevard and is especially pretty in front of the Hotel del Coronado.

The northern end of **Ocean Beach** is known as "Dog Beach" and is one of only two in San Diego where your pooch can roam freely on the sand. Surfers congregate around the Ocean Beach Pier. Rip currents are strong here and discourage most swimmers from venturing beyond waist depth. To get here, take West Point Loma Boulevard all the way to the end.

In the 4,600-acre aquatic playground of **Mission Bay Park,** you'll find 27 miles of bayfront; 17 miles of oceanfront beaches; picnic areas; playgrounds; and paths for biking, roller skating, and jogging. The bay lends itself to windsurfing, sailing, water-skiing, and fishing. One of the most popular access points is off I-5 at Clairemont Drive, where there's a visitor center.

Pacific Beach is the home of Tourmaline Surfing Park, where the sport's old guard gathers to surf waters where swimmers are prohibited, and there's always some action along Ocean Front Walk, a paved promenade featuring a human parade akin to that at L.A.'s Venice Beach boardwalk. It runs along Ocean Boulevard (just west of Mission Blvd.), north of Pacific Beach Drive.

The protected, calm waters of **La Jolla Cove**—praised as the clearest along the California coast—attract swimmers, snorkelers, divers, and families. There's a small sandy beach and, on the cliffs above, the Ellen Browning Scripps Park. The cove's "look but don't touch" policy protects the colorful marine life in this Underwater Park. La Jolla Cove can be accessed from Coast Boulevard.

The wide, flat mile of sand at **La Jolla Shores** is popular with joggers, swimmers, and beginning body- and board surfers, as well as with families. Weekend crowds can be enormous, quickly occupying both the sand and the metered parking spaces in the beach's lot.

More Places to Play

Mission Bay and Coronado are especially good for leisurely biking. The boardwalks in Pacific Beach and Mission Beach can get very crowded, especially on weekends. For rentals, call **Bike Tours San Diego,** 509 Fifth Ave. (© 619/238-2444), which offers delivery ($5) as far north as Del Mar. Rates for a city/hybrid bike start at $20 a day and include helmets, locks, maps, and roadside assistance. Other rental outlets include **Mission Beach Surf & Skate,** 704 Ventura Place, off Mission Boulevard at Ocean Front Walk, for one-speed beach cruisers (© 858/488-5050); and **Cheap Rentals** on Mission Boulevard for mountain bikes and more (© 858/488-9070).

If you have sailing or boating experience, there are options for nonchartered rentals. **Seaforth Boat Rental,** 1641 Quivira Rd., Mission Bay (© 888/834-2628 or 619/223-1681; www.seaforthboatrental.com), has a variety of boats for bay or ocean. **Mission Bay Sportcenter,** 1010 Santa Clara Place (© 858/488-1004; www.missionbaysportcenter.com), rents sailboats, catamarans, sailboards, kayaks, and motorboats. Prices range from $18 to $90 an hour, with discounts for 4-hour and full-day rentals.

GOLF San Diego County has 90-plus courses, and more than 50 open to the public. For a full listing of area courses, visit **www.golfsd.com,** or request the *Golf Guide* from the San Diego Convention and Visitors Bureau (© 619/236-1212; www.sandiego.org). **San Diego Golf Reservations** (© 866/701-4653 or 858/964-5980; www.sandiegogolf.com) can arrange tee times. The city's most famous links are at the **Torrey Pines Golf Course,** a pair of 18-hole championship courses on the cliffs between La Jolla and Del Mar. Setting for the 2008 U.S. Open, tee times are taken 8 to 90 days in advance by automated telephone system ($37 booking fee); first-come, first-served tee times are offered from sunrise to 7:30am. Greens fees on the south course are $145 weekdays, $181 weekends; the north course is $85 weekdays, $106 weekends. Cart rentals are $30, and twilight rates are available. For automated reservations, call © 877/581-7171; for information, call © 800/985-4653 or go to www.torreypinesgolfcourse.com.

If you prefer to watch other people play, head for $474-million **PETCO Park.** The 42,000-seat ballpark incorporates seven historic structures into the stadium, including the Western Metal Supply building, a four-story brick edifice dating from 1909 that now sprouts left-field bleachers from one side. The **San Diego Padres** play April through September. PETCO parking is limited and costly—take the San Diego Trolley. For schedules, information, and tickets, call © 877/374-2784 or 619/795-5000, or visit **www.padres.com.**

SHOPPING

Horton Plaza (© 619/238-1596; www.westfield.com/hortonplaza) is the Disneyland of shopping malls, in the heart of the revitalized city center. Within a colorful, and often confusing, series of paths and bridges, the complex has tons of shops, including galleries, several fun shops for kids, a 14-screen cinema, three major department stores, and a variety of restaurants. Other downtown shopping opportunities include **Seaport Village,**

on Harbor Drive (© **619/235-4014;** www.seaportvillage.com), a Cape Cod–style "village" of shops snuggled alongside San Diego Bay; it's worth a visit for the 1890 carousel
imported from Coney Island.

In Old Town State Historic Park, **Plaza del Pasado,** 2754 Calhoun St. (© **619/297-3100;** www.plazadelpasado.com), maintains the park's old *Californio* theme and has 11
specialty shops, 3 restaurants, and a boutique hotel. Costumed employees, special events
and activities, and strolling musicians heighten the festive atmosphere.

San Diego's greatest concentration of antiques stores is in the **Ocean Beach Antique District,** along the 4800 block of Newport Avenue. Several stores are mall-style, with
multiple dealers. **Newport Ave. Antique Center,** 4864 Newport Ave. (© **619/222-8686**), has 18,000 square feet of retail and a small espresso bar. Most of the O.B.
antiques stores are open daily from 10am to 6pm, with reduced hours Sunday.

Shopping in **La Jolla** tends toward the conservative and costly: Swiss watches, tennis
bracelets, and pearl necklaces sparkle at you from windows along every street.

WHERE TO STAY

The **San Diego Convention & Visitors Bureau** is a good place to start looking for hotel
deals (© **619/232-3101;** www.sandiego.org), while the **San Diego Bed & Breakfast Guild** (© **800/619-7666;** www.bandbguildsandiego.org) is a helpful resource if you are
interested in staying someplace cozy.

Near Old Town there's the **Heritage Park Bed & Breakfast Inn** ($125–$295 double,
including full breakfast and afternoon tea), 2470 Heritage Park Row (© **800/995-2470**
or 619/299-6832; www.heritageparkinn.com). The **La Jolla Village Lodge,** 1141 Silverado St. (© **877/551-2001** or 858/551-2001; www.lajollavillagelodge.com), is a basic
motel that's a good value in La Jolla, with rooms as low as $90 midweek. Well located
and a good value, the **Village Inn** ($85–$95 double, including continental breakfast),
1017 Park Place (© **619/435-9318;** www.coronadovillageinn.com), is within walking
distance of Coronado's sights.

For those on a budget: Room rates at properties on Hotel Circle in Mission Valley (an
area loaded with chain properties) are significantly cheaper than those in many other
parts of the city. One good choice with some character is the **Crowne Plaza San Diego**
($147–$189 double), 2270 Hotel Circle N. (© **800/733-5466** or 619/297-1101; www.
cp-sandiego.com), a comfort-conscious yet sophisticated Polynesian-themed hotel whose
rooms sport contemporary furnishings and conveniences.

Crystal Pier Hotel (Kids)   This historic, charming, and unique cluster of cottages sits
literally over the surf on the vintage Crystal Pier. Each self-contained hideaway has a
living room, bedroom, full kitchen, and private patio with breathtaking ocean views. The
sound of waves is soothing, but the boardwalk action is only a few steps away. Guests
drive right out and park beside their cottages, a real boon on crowded weekends. Boogie
boards, fishing poles, beach chairs, and umbrellas are all available.

4500 Ocean Blvd. (at Garnet Ave.), San Diego, CA 92109. © **800/748-5894** or 858/483-6983. Fax 858/
483-6811. www.crystalpier.com. 29 units. $300–$375 double; $500 for larger units sleeping 4 or 6. 3-night
minimum in summer, 2-night minimum in winter. DISC, MC, V. Free parking. Bus: 8, 9, 27, or 30. Take I-5
to Grand/Garnet exit; follow Garnet to the pier. *In room:* Kitchen.

The Grand Del Mar   A faux Tuscan villa nestled in the foothills of Del Mar, this new
resort features ornate, Vegas-style luxury and high-end comforts. Liberally accented with
fountains, courtyards, terraces, sweeping staircases, and outdoor fireplaces, the hotel is
grandly European. It even has a canyon-side walking path overlooking the golf course

(dramatically lit at night), tennis courts, four swimming pools, a tricked-out kids' activity center, and a 21,000-square-foot spa. The signature restaurant, **Addison,** is one of San Diego's most sumptuous dining rooms: Plush, elegant, and refined, it serves cuisine to match—and the wine list is more fairly described as a wine novel. This is simply San Diego's most opulent resort.

5300 Grand Del Mar Court, San Diego, CA 92130. ✆ **888/314-2030** or 858/314-2000. Fax 858/314-2001. www.thegranddelmar.com. 249 units. From $575 double; from $1,100 suite. Children 17 and under stay free in parent's room. Packages available. AE, DC, DISC, MC, V. Valet parking. From I-5 merge onto Ted Williams Pkwy. east, exit Carmel Country Rd. and turn right, left at Meadows Del Mar. **Amenities:** 4 restaurants; 4 swimming pools; 18-hole golf course; 2 tennis courts; fitness center; spa.

Hilton San Diego Gaslamp Quarter

With a location at the foot of the Gaslamp Quarter, the Hilton is a great place for guests who want to be close to the action (which includes loads of restaurants, nightlife, and the ballpark within a few blocks) but not get lost in the shuffle. Built on the site of the old Bridgeworks building, much of the brick facade was incorporated into the hotel's polished design. Standard rooms boast upmarket furniture, down comforters, and pillow-top mattresses. The snazziest picks are rooms in the intimate Enclave wing, which features 30 oversize guest rooms (the handsomest in town) with towering ceilings, custom furnishings, Frette linens, and lavish bathrooms sporting whirlpool tubs.

401 K St. (at Fourth Ave.), San Diego, CA 92101. ✆ **800/445-8667** or 619/231-4040. Fax 619/231-6439. 282 units. $329 double; from $399 suite. Children 11 and under stay free in parent's room. AE, DC, DISC, MC, V. Valet parking $30. Trolley: Gaslamp Quarter or Convention Center. **Amenities:** 2 restaurants; outdoor pool; health club and full-service spa.

Holiday Inn on the Bay (Kids)

This better-than-average Holiday Inn is reliable and nearly always offers great deals. Rooms, while basic, always seem to sport clean new furnishings and plenty of thoughtful comforts. Although rooms are identical inside, you can choose either marvelous bay views or a look at San Diego's still-evolving skyline. In either case, request the highest floor possible.

1355 N. Harbor Dr. (at Ash St.), San Diego, CA 92101-3385. ✆ **800/465-4329** or 619/232-3861. Fax 619/232-4924. www.holiday-inn.com/san-onthebay. 600 units. $224 double; from $339 suite. Children 17 and under stay free in parent's room. AE, DC, MC, V. Valet parking $26; self-parking $20. Bus: 2, 210, 810, 820, 850, 860, 923, or 992. Trolley: American Plaza. Pets accepted with $25 nonrefundable fee and $100 deposit. **Amenities:** 4 restaurants; outdoor heated pool; exercise room.

Horton Grand

A cross between an elegant hotel and a charming inn, the Horton Grand combines two historic 1880s hotels connected by an airy atrium lobby. Each room is utterly unique, with vintage furnishings, gas fireplaces, and business-savvy features. Rooms overlook either the city or the fig tree–filled courtyard. The suites (really just large studio-style rooms) are located in a newer wing; choosing one means sacrificing historical character for a sitting area/sofa bed and minibar with microwave.

311 Island Ave. (at Fourth Ave.), San Diego, CA 92101. ✆ **800/542-1886** or 619/544-1886. Fax 619/239-3823. www.hortongrand.com. 132 units. $169–$199 double; from $269 suite. Extra person $20. Children 17 and under stay free in parent's room. AE, DC, MC, V. Valet parking $24. Bus: 3, 11, or 120. Trolley: Convention Center. **Amenities:** Restaurant.

Hotel del Coronado (Best) (Kids)

Opened in 1888 and designated a National Historic Landmark, the "Hotel Del" is the last of California's grand old seaside hotels. Legend has it that the Duke of Windsor met his duchess here, and Marilyn Monroe frolicked here in *Some Like It Hot.* This monument to Victorian grandeur boasts cupolas, turrets, and gingerbread trim, all spread over 26 acres (including some contemporary tower additions). Rooms run the gamut from compact to extravagant, and all are packed with antique charm. The best have balconies fronting the ocean. Since 2001, the Del has done nonstop restoration and upgrading, most recently adding a state-of-the-art **spa** and creating Beach Village, a collection of 78 "coastal cottages." Even if you don't stay here, take a stroll through the grand wood-paneled lobby or along the pristine beach.

1500 Orange Ave., Coronado, CA 92118. ✆ **800/468-3533** or 619/435-6111. Fax 619/522-8238. www. hoteldel.com. 757 rooms. $300–$545 double; from $780 suite. Extra person $25. Children 17 and under stay free in parent's room. Minimum stay requirements apply most weekends. $25 per day resort fee. AE, DC, DISC, MC, V. Valet parking $30; self-parking $23. Bus: 901 or 904. From Coronado Bridge, turn left onto Orange Ave. **Amenities:** 5 restaurants; 2 outdoor pools; health club; spa.

Keating House This grand 1880s Bankers Hill mansion, between downtown and Hillcrest and 4 blocks from Balboa Park, has been meticulously restored by two energetic innkeepers with a solid background in architectural preservation. Doug Scott and Ben Baltic not only know old houses, but are also neighborhood devotees filled with historical knowledge. Breakfast is served in a sunny setting; special dietary needs are cheerfully considered. The classy, not frilly, inn draws guests ranging from Europeans to businesspeople, avoiding the cookie-cutter ambience of a chain hotel.

2331 Second Ave. (btw. Juniper and Kalmia sts.), San Diego, CA 92101. ✆ **800/995-8644** or 619/239-8585. Fax 619/239-5774. www.keatinghouse.com. 9 units. $115–$165 double. Rates include full breakfast. AE, DISC, MC, V. Bus: 1, 3, 11, or 25. From the airport, take Harbor Dr. toward downtown; turn left on Laurel St., then right on Second Ave. *In room:* No phone.

La Pensione Hotel (Value) Offering modern amenities, remarkable value, a convenient location, and a friendly staff, the three-story La Pensione feels like a small European hotel. The decor throughout is modern and streamlined, with minimal furniture and plenty of sleek black and metallic surfaces. Rooms, while not overly large, make the most of their space. Try for a bay or city view rather than the view of the concrete courtyard. La Pensione is in Little Italy, within walking distance of eateries and nightspots.

606 W. Date St. (at India St.), San Diego, CA 92101. ✆ **800/232-4683** or 619/236-8000. Fax 619/236-8088. www.lapensionehotel.com. 75 units. $90 double. AE, DC, DISC, MC, V. Limited free underground parking. Bus: 83. Trolley: Little Italy.

Pacific Terrace Hotel The best modern hotel on the boardwalk sports a soothing South Seas ambience and upscale atmosphere that make it stand apart from the casual beach pads in the area. Large guest rooms come with balconies or terraces; about half have kitchenettes. Management keeps cookies, coffee, and iced tea at the ready throughout the day; the lushly landscaped pool and hot tub overlook a relatively quiet stretch of beach. Several local restaurants allow meals to be billed to the hotel, but there's no restaurant on the premises.

610 Diamond St., San Diego, CA 92109. ✆ **800/344-3370** or 858/581-3500. Fax 858/274-3341. www. pacificterrace.com. 73 units. $359–$500 double; from $490 suite. Children 12 and under stay free in parent's room. 2- to 4-night minimums apply in summer. Rates include continental breakfast and afternoon wine reception. AE, DC, DISC, MC, V. Parking $20; limited free parking in off-street lot. Bus: 30. Take I-5 to Grand/Garnet exit and follow Grand or Garnet west to Mission Blvd., turn right (north) and then left (west) onto Diamond. **Amenities:** Pool; fitness room.

Paradise Point Resort & Spa (Kids) This Mission Bay hotel complex is as much a theme park as its closest neighbor, SeaWorld (a 3-min. drive). Single-story accommodations are spread across 44 acres of lagoons, gardens, and swim-friendly beaches; all have private patios and plenty of thoughtful conveniences like fridges and coffeemakers. It's been recently updated to keep its 1960s charm but lose tacky holdovers. And despite daunting high-season rack rates, there's usually a deal to be had. The upscale waterfront restaurant, **Baleen,** features fine dining in a contemporary, fun space, and a stunning Indonesian-inspired spa offers cool serenity and aroma-tinged Asian treatments.

1404 Vacation Rd. (off Ingraham St.), San Diego, CA 92109. ℂ **800/344-2626** or 858/274-4630. Fax 858/581-5924. www.paradisepoint.com. 462 units. $356–$421 double; from $421 suite. Extra person $20. Children 17 and under stay free in parent's room. AE, DC, DISC, MC, V. Parking $20. Bus: 8 or 9. Follow I-8 west to Mission Bay Dr. exit; take Ingraham St. north to Vacation Rd. **Amenities:** 2 restaurants; 5 outdoor pools; 18-hole putting course; tennis courts; fitness center; full-service spa.

WHERE TO DINE

If you've got a sweet tooth, the city's top dessert emporium is aptly monikered **Extraordinary Desserts,** with locations in Little Italy, 1430 Union St. (ℂ **619/294-7001**), and adjacent to Balboa Park, 2929 Fifth Ave. (ℂ **619/294-2132**). Both locations stay open late (midnight Fri–Sat, 11pm Sun–Thurs). Proprietor Karen Krasne produces exquisite cakes and pastries garnished with edible gold and flowers.

Noteworthy in the Gaslamp for those on a budget is the hip, bohemian **Café Lulu,** 419 F St. (ℂ **619/238-0114**), a coffee bar with light meals; the spot is open until 1am (3am Fri–Sat).

Bread & Cie. LIGHT FARE/MEDITERRANEAN   The traditions of European artisan bread-making and attention to the fine points of texture and crust catapulted Bread & Cie. to local stardom—they supply bread to more than 75 local restaurants. Some favorites are available daily, like anise and fig, black olive, and jalapeño and cheese. Order one of the many Mediterranean-inspired sandwiches. A specialty coffee drink, delivered in a bowl-like mug, perfectly accompanies a light breakfast of fresh scones, muffins, or homemade granola with yogurt.

350 University Ave. (at Fourth St.), Hillcrest. ℂ 619/683-9322. www.breadandcie.com. Reservations not accepted. Sandwiches and light meals $4–$9. DISC, MC, V. Mon–Fri 7am–7pm; Sat 7am–6pm; Sun 8am–6pm. Bus: 1, 3, 10, 11, or 120.

Cafe Pacifica CALIFORNIA   Inside this cozy Old Town casita, the decor is cleanly contemporary (but still romantic) and the food anything but Mexican. Cafe Pacifica serves upscale, imaginative seafood. Signature items include Hawaiian ahi with shiitake mushrooms and ginger butter, and the "Pomerita," a pomegranate margarita. Patrons tend to dress up, though it's not required.

2414 San Diego Ave., Old Town. ℂ 619/291-6666. www.cafepacifica.com. Reservations recommended. Main courses lunch $12–$30, dinner $13–$30. AE, DC, DISC, MC, V. Wed–Fri 11:30am–2pm; Mon–Sat 5–10pm; Sun 4:30–9:30pm. Valet parking $5. Bus: 8, 9, 10, 14, 28, or 30. Trolley: Old Town.

Chez Loma FRENCH   You'd be hard-pressed to find a more romantic dining spot than this intimate Victorian cottage filled with antiques and candlelight. Tables are scattered throughout the house and on the enclosed terrace; an upstairs wine salon is a cozy spot for coffee. Among the creative entrees are salmon with smoked tomato vinaigrette and roast duckling with green peppercorn sauce. Chez Loma's service is attentive, the herb rolls addictive, and early birds enjoy special prices—$25 for a three-course meal before 6pm and all night on Tuesday.

1132 Loma (off Orange Ave.), Coronado. ℂ 619/435-0661. www.chezloma.com. Reservations recommended. Main courses $23–$36. AE, DC, DISC, MC, V. Tues–Sun 5–10pm. Bus: 901 or 904.

Chive CALIFORNIAN   This big-city-style Gaslamp venue introduced San Diego to the sleek and chic dining rooms of the East Coast, and to daring culinary adventures. In 2006, the restaurant took a new tack, moving away from traditional three-course meals. They now concentrate on small shared plates (with some available as entree-size portions). The cuisine is as modern as the decor, taking a global approach with dishes like a Moroccan-spiced chicken kabob and Kung Pao–style sweetbreads, while still making room for unique comfort food like the crab mac 'n' cheese. The wine list offers many intriguing selections by "cork" or "stem" from around the world. One lament: The cement floors and other hard surfaces amplify the noise level.

558 Fourth Ave. (at Market St.), Gaslamp Quarter. ✆ 619/232-4483. www.chiverestaurant.com. Reservations recommended. Main courses $10–$36. AE, DISC, MC, V. Sun–Thurs 5–10pm; Fri–Sat 5–11pm. Valet parking Thurs–Sat $12–$17. Bus: 3, 11, or 120. Trolley: Convention Center.

El Agave Tequileria MEXICAN   Don't be misled by this restaurant's less than impressive location above a liquor store—this warm, bustling eatery offers the best regional Mexican cuisine in the city and a rustic elegance that leaves the touristy fajitas-and-*cerveza* joints of Old Town far behind. If you like tequila, the restaurant boasts more than 850 boutique and artisan tequilas from throughout the Latin world. But even tee-totalers will enjoy the restaurant's authentically flavored mole sauces or the signature beef filet with goat cheese and dark tequila sauce. Lunches are simpler affairs without the exotic sauces, and inexpensive.

2304 San Diego Ave., Old Town. ✆ 619/220-0692. www.elagave.com. Reservations recommended. Main courses $8–$11 lunch, $16–$32 dinner. AE, MC, V. Daily 11am–10pm. Street parking. Bus: Numerous Old Town routes, including 8, 9, 10, 14, 28, and 30. Trolley: Old Town.

Filippi's Pizza Grotto (Value)(Kids) ITALIAN   To get to the dining area of this "Little Italy" tradition, which is decorated with chianti bottles and red-checked tablecloths, you walk through a "cash and carry" Italian grocery store and deli. The intoxicating smell of pizza wafts into the street; Filippi's has more than 15 varieties (including vegetarian), plus pasta. Children's portions are available. The Friday and Saturday evening line to get in can look intimidating, but it moves quickly. This is the original of a dozen branches throughout the county; the other locations include one in **Pacific Beach** at 962 Garnet Ave. (✆ **858/483-6222**).

1747 India St. (btw. Date and Fir sts.), Little Italy. ✆ 619/232-5094. www.realcheesepizza.com. Reservations Mon–Thurs for groups of 8 or more. Main courses $6–$13. AE, DC, DISC, MC, V. Sun–Mon 11am–10pm; Tues–Thurs 11am–10:30pm; Fri–Sat 11am–11:30pm. Deli opens daily at 8am. Free parking. Bus: 83. Trolley: Little Italy.

The Fishery SEAFOOD   You're guaranteed fresh-off-the-boat seafood at this off-the-beaten-track establishment, which is really a wholesale warehouse and retail fish market with a restaurant attached. Menu favorites include spicy mahimahi, chargrilled and topped with jalapeño butter, or—the favorite—sea bass, charbroiled with a soy-ginger marinade. You can keep it simple at lunch or dinner with bacon-wrapped scallops over a delectable salad, or the reliable fish and chips; a couple of vegetarian stir-fry entrees are always available. *Note:* As of this writing, the Fishery was undergoing renovations that will add two dozen more seats and a small wine bar.

5040 Cass St. (at Opal, ³/₄ mile north of Garnet), Pacific Beach. ✆ **858/272-9985.** www.pacshell.com. Reservations recommended for dinner. Main courses $8–$21 lunch, $9–$28 dinner. AE, DC, DISC, MC, V. Daily 11am–10pm. Street parking usually available. Bus: 30.

Georges California Modern CALIFORNIA   La Jolla's signature restaurant has it all: ocean views, style, impeccable service, and a world-class chef. Georges closed briefly in 2007 for a $2.5-million renovation. It reemerged with a new name (it had been called George's at the Cove since 1984) and a new design-forward environment. Most importantly, Trey Foshee can still be found in the kitchen. Foshee, named one of America's top-10 chefs by *Food & Wine,* has been set loose stylistically—the menu is larger and more adventurous than before (still driven by the freshest local ingredients), incorporating more cross-cultural influences. Those seeking fine food and at more modest prices can head upstairs to the **Ocean Terrace** and **George's Bar.**

1250 Prospect St., La Jolla. ☎ **858/454-4244.** www.georgesatthecove.com. Reservations strongly recommended. Main courses $26–$90. AE, DC, DISC, MC, V. Sun–Thurs 5:30–10pm; Fri–Sat 5–10:30pm. Ocean Terrace Bistro main courses $10–$15 lunch, $16–$29 dinner. Daily 11am–10pm (Fri–Sat 'til 10:30pm). Valet parking $7. Bus: 30.

Jack's La Jolla AMERICAN   Jack's La Jolla is a three-floor Epicurean fun house that rises from sidewalk coffee stop to rooftop oyster bar, with a fine-dining component and a couple of bars and lounges (with live music and DJs) thrown in for good measure. Jack's is built around an open-air courtyard that can take full advantage of sunny days and mild nights. Jack's is also built around the talents and modern American cuisine of Chef/Owner Tony DiSalvo, formerly executive chef at Jean-Georges in New York City. The middle level features the chic Wall Street Bar and the Dining Room at Jack's. Jack's Grille provides more casual, less expensive dining.

7863 Girard Ave., La Jolla. ☎ **858/456-8111.** www.jackslajolla.com. Reservations recommended. The Dining Room main courses $22–$44. AE, DC, DISC, MC, V. Sun 5:30–8:30pm; Tues 5:30–9pm; Wed–Sat 5:30–10pm. Jack's Grille main courses $10–$44. Sun–Wed 5–9:30pm; Thurs–Sat 5–11pm. Ocean Room main courses $11–$14 lunch, $22–$40 dinner. Daily 11:30am–2:30pm; Sun–Wed 5:30–9:30pm; Thurs–Sat 5:30–11pm. Sidewalk Cafe Sun–Tues 8am–8pm; Wed–Thurs 8am–10pm; Fri–Sat 8am–11pm. Bars and lounges 'til 2am Thurs–Sat (Wall St. Bar and sushi bar closed Mon). Valet parking Tues–Sun 11:30am–close $5. Bus: 30.

Laurel Restaurant & Bar ⓑest FRENCH/MEDITERRANEAN   Given its stylish decor, pedigreed chefs, prime Balboa Park location, and well-composed menu of country French dishes with a Mediterranean accent, it's no wonder this restaurant is at the top of its game. It's a rewarding splurge for a special occasion. Tantalizing choices include mouthwatering crisp duck confit with applewood bacon and green lentil, and New Zealand lamb loin with Japanese eggplant and wild rice. Laurel offers a wonderful cassoulet; a main-course vegetable sampler; a seven-course chef's tasting meal; and a daily three-course, prix-fixe meal from 5 to 6:30pm for $35.

505 Laurel St. (at Fifth Ave.), Hillcrest. ☎ **619/239-2222.** www.laurelrestaurant.com. Reservations recommended. Main courses $22–$34. AE, DC, DISC, MC, V. Daily 5–10pm.

SAN DIEGO AFTER DARK

The San Diego Convention and Visitors Bureau's **Art + Sol** campaign publishes a calendar of performing and visual arts events; check it out at www.sandiegoartandsol.com. The San Diego Performing Arts League produces the *What's Playing?* guide every 2 months. You can pick one up at the ARTS TIX booth (see below) or view it online (☎ **619/238-0700;** www.sandiegoperforms.com).

Half-price tickets to theater, music, and dance events are available at the **ARTS TIX** booth, in Horton Plaza Park at Broadway and Third Avenue. For a daily roster of offerings, call ☎ **619/497-5000** or visit www.sandiegoperforms.com.

THE PERFORMING ARTS   Some of the finest theater in the U.S. can be found in San Diego. Near the entrance to Balboa Park, the Tony Award–winning **Old Globe** (© 619/ 234-5623; www.theoldglobe.org) is a complex of three performance venues. High-profile actors, writers, and directors are often involved with productions here. Another Tony winner, the **La Jolla Playhouse,** 2910 La Jolla Village Dr. (© 858/550-1010; www. lajollaplayhouse.com), has originated such productions as *Jersey Boys* and *The Who's Tommy* that eventually ended up winning lots of awards on Broadway.

Also noteworthy are **San Diego Repertory Theatre**, which mounts plays and musicals at the Lyceum Theatre in Horton Plaza (© 619/544-1000; www.sandiegorep.com); **Lamb's Players Theatre** (© 619/437-0600; www.lambsplayers.org), a resident-professional company based in Coronado; iconoclastic **Sledgehammer Theatre** (© 619/544-1484; www.sledgehammer.org); and **Cygnet Theatre** (© 619/337-1525; www.cygnet theatre.com), which produces work at the **Old Town Theatre,** 4040 Twiggs St., as well as at its original space, the **Rolando Theatre,** 6663 El Cajon Blvd., near San Diego State University.

THE CLUB & BAR SCENE   The **Casbah,** 2501 Kettner Blvd., near the airport (© 619/232-4355; www.thecasbah.com), is a divey joint with a rep for breakthrough alternative and rock bands. **Croce's Restaurant & Jazz Bar,** 802 Fifth Ave., at F Street (© 619/233-4355; www.croces.com), features jazz and rhythm and blues. **Humphrey's,** 2241 Shelter Island Dr. (© 619/523-1010; www.humphreysconcerts.com), is a 1,300-seat outdoor venue set on the water and has a seasonal lineup that ranges from rock to folk to international. The Gaslamp Quarter is the epicenter for the city's hottest dance clubs, including **Sevilla,** 555 Fourth Ave. (© 619/233-5979), where you can salsa and merengue to Brazilian dance music. **belo** (© 619/231-9200; www.belosandiego.com), below street level in the Gaslamp on E St., between Fourth and Fifth avenues, is a huge three-room space with retro design.

Stingaree, 454 Sixth Ave. at Island Street (© 619/544-0867), has three levels, a cool rooftop lounge, and 22,000 square feet of party space. Opening at press time is the city's latest über-club, **Universal,** 1202 University Ave., in Hillcrest (© 619/544-9704; www. universalhillcrest.com). **Beach,** the rooftop bar of the W Hotel at 421 B St. downtown (© 619/398-3100; www.wbeachbar.com), features a heated sand floor, cabanas, and fire pit. Hypermodern **Thin** and its downstairs sister club, the **Onyx Room,** 852 Fifth Ave., Gaslamp Quarter (© 619/235-6699), let you to move from a contemporary vibe to classic lounge. The Onyx Room also has live jazz on Tuesday.

12 PALM SPRINGS

Palm Springs, once known for polyester-clad golfing retirees and college-age spring breakers, has been quietly changing its image and attracting a whole new crowd. These days, the city fancies itself a European-style resort with a dash of good ol' American small town thrown in for good measure, and Hollywood's young glitterati are returning to "the Springs." One thing hasn't changed: Swimming, sunbathing, golfing, and playing tennis are still the primary pastimes in this convenient little oasis.

ESSENTIALS
GETTING THERE   By Plane   You can fly into **Palm Springs Regional Airport,** 3400 E. Tahquitz Canyon Way (© 760/323-8161). Flights from LAX take about 40 minutes.

By Car   Most visitors drive to Palm Springs, a trip that takes about 2 hours from either Los Angeles (via **I-10 East** and **Hwy. 111**) or San Diego (via **I-15 North** to connect with **I-10 East**).

VISITOR INFORMATION   Be sure to pick up *Palm Springs Life* magazine's free monthly, *Desert Guide.* It contains copious visitor information, including a comprehensive calendar of events. Copies are distributed in hotels and newsstands and by the **Palm Springs Desert Resorts Convention & Visitors Authority,** 70–100 Hwy. 111, Rancho Mirage, CA 92270 (© **800/967-3767** or 760/770-9000). The bureau's office staff can help with maps, brochures, and advice Monday through Friday from 8:30am to 5pm. They also operate a website (www.palmspringsusa.com).

The **Palm Springs Visitors Information Center,** 2901 N. Palm Canyon Dr., Palm Springs, CA 92262 (© **800/34-SPRINGS** [347-7746]; www.palm-springs.org), has maps, brochures, advice, souvenirs, and a free hotel reservation service. The office is open Monday through Saturday from 9am to 5pm, and Sunday from 8am to 4pm.

SPECIAL EVENTS & FESTIVALS   Golf takes center stage in the desert at two high-profile events each year: January's **Bob Hope Chrysler Classic** (© **888/MR-BHOPE** [672-4673]; www.bhcc.com), which features a celebrity-studded Pro-Am; and March's **Kraft Nabisco Championship** (© **760/324-4546;** www.kncgolf.com), an LPGA event that coincides with a legendary lesbian convention in the desert. Other only-in-the-desert happenings include the 2-week **National Date Festival** (© **800/811-3247;** www.datefest.org) in February, an Arabian Nights–esque pageant and fair celebrating the area's most abundant fruit.

WHAT TO SEE & DO

GOLF   The Palm Springs area is a world-famous mecca for golfers, with 115 courses. If you're planning a golf vacation, you're best off staying at one of the valley's many golf resorts (most are outside Palm Springs), where you can enjoy the proximity of your hotel's facilities, as well as smart package deals that can give you a taste of country club membership. See "Where to Stay," below.

Tee times at many resort courses cannot be booked more than a few days in advance for nonguests, but some companies are able to make arrangements several months earlier or even construct a custom package with accommodations, golf, meals, and other extras. Among them is **Golf à la Carte** (© **877/887-6900** or 760/772-9330; www.palmsprings golf.com).

One of our favorite desert courses is the **PGA West TPC Stadium Course,** La Quinta Resort & Club, 49499 Eisenhower Dr., La Quinta (© **760/564-7111**), which received *Golf* magazine's 1994 Gold Medal Award for the total golf-resort experience. The par-3 17th has a picturesque island green where Lee Trevino made Skins Game history with a spectacular hole-in-one. The rest of Pete Dye's 7,261-yard design is flat, with huge bunkers, lots of water, and severe mounding throughout. Also open for semiprivate play is the **Mountain Course at La Quinta,** another Dye design that regularly appears on U.S. top-100 lists. It's set dramatically against the rocky mountains, which thrust into fairways to create tricky doglegs, and its small Bermuda greens are well guarded by boulders and deep bunkers. Greens fees for nonguests vary seasonally, from $190 to $209 on weekends, including the required cart.

Recommended public courses include **Tommy Jacobs' Bel-Air Greens,** 1001 El Cielo, Palm Springs (© **760/322-6062;** www.tommyjacobsbelairgreens.com), a scenic

9-hole, par-32 executive course well suited for beginners and high-handicappers. Greens **923** fees are $20, less for a replay.

Slightly more advanced amateurs will like **Tahquitz Creek Golf Resort,** 1885 Golf Club Dr., Palm Springs (© **760/328-1005**), whose two diverse courses both appeal to mid-handicappers; greens fees, including cart, range from $59 to $109, depending on the day of the week.

The **Classic Club** (75-200 Northstar Resort Pkwy., north of I-10 at Cook St. exit, Palm Desert; © **760/601-3601;** www.classicclubgolf.com) is a new 7,305-yard Arnold Palmer–designed course that won critical praise from the pros at the Bob Hope Classic. Greens fees in winter are $175 to $195, which includes a cart and a driving range; summer fees are half that.

OTHER OUTDOOR ACTIVITIES Within an hour's drive of Palm Springs is **Joshua Tree National Park,** named for the curious shaggy succulent found only in California's Mojave Desert. A mecca for hikers, campers, and rock climbers, the park's intriguing geology and abundant spring wildflowers can also be easily appreciated by car and make for a wonderful day's outing. For more information, contact the **Park Superintendent's Office,** 74485 National Park Dr., Twentynine Palms, CA 92277 (© **760/367-5525;** www.nps.gov/jotr).

Desert Adventures (© **888/440-JEEP** [440-5337] or 760/340-2345; www.red-jeep. com), 74794 Lennon Place, Palm Desert, offers four-wheel-drive eco-tours led by naturalist guides. Your off-road adventure may take you to a replica of an ancient Cahuilla village, the Santa Rosa Mountain roads overlooking the Coachella Valley, or picturesque ravines on the way to the San Andreas Fault. Tours run from 3 to 5 hours and cost from $129 to $150. Advance reservations are required.

Elite Land Tours (© **800/514-4866** or 760/318-1200; www.elitelandtours.com) offers a new way to visit the desert region: eco-exploration of the backcountry from the air-conditioned comfort of a Hummer H2. Tours can include desert and mountain regions, exploration of ancient cultures, wildlife, and geological wonders. A Safari Trax Tour offers an up-close experience with two Siberian tigers, Asian leopards, and a caracal plus a safari lunch ($249 per person in a four-person group).

OTHER ATTRACTIONS The **Living Desert Zoo & Gardens,** 47–900 Portola Ave., Palm Desert (© **760/346-5694;** www.livingdesert.org), is a 1,200-acre desert reserve designed to acquaint visitors with the unique habitats of California deserts. You can walk or take a tram, learning about bighorn sheep, mountain lions, rattlesnakes, lizards, owls, golden eagles, and the ubiquitous roadrunner. Admission is $12 adults, $11 seniors/military, $7.50 children 3 to 12. Open in summer daily from 8am to 1:30pm, the rest of the year daily from 9am to 5pm.

To gain a bird's-eye perspective of the Coachella Valley, try the **Palm Springs Aerial Tramway,** off Hwy. 111 (© **888/515-TRAM** [515-8726] or 760/325-1391; www.ps tramway.com), a 14-minute, $2^1/_2$-mile ascent to the top of Mount San Jacinto. At the top you'll find Alpine scenery, a ski-lodge-style restaurant and gift shop, and temperatures typically 40° cooler than the desert floor. Guided mule rides and cross-country ski equipment are available. Tickets $22 for adults, $20 seniors, $15 children 3 to 12; a Ride 'n' Dine combination is available. It runs Monday through Friday from 10am to 8pm, Saturday and Sunday from 8am to 8pm.

Unlikely though it may sound, the well-endowed **Palm Springs Desert Museum,** 101 Museum Dr. (© **760/325-7186;** www.psmuseum.org), is a must-see. Exhibits include world-class Western and Native American art, plus extensive artifacts of the local Cahuilla tribe. Plays, lectures, and other events are presented in the museum's Annenberg Theater. Admission is $13 for adults, $11 for seniors, and $5 for children 6 to 17. Open Tuesday through Saturday from 10am to 5pm, Sunday from noon to 5pm.

SHOPPING   Downtown Palm Springs revolves around **North Palm Canyon Drive;** many art galleries, souvenir shops, and restaurants are here, along with a couple of large-scale hotels and shopping centers. This wide, one-way boulevard is designed for pedestrians, with many businesses set back from the street itself—don't be shy about poking around the little courtyards you'll encounter. The northern section of Palm Canyon is becoming known for vintage collectibles and is being touted as the **Antique and Heritage Gallery District.**

Down in Palm Desert lies the delicious excess of **El Paseo,** a glitzy cornucopia of high-rent boutiques, salons, and upscale restaurants reminiscent of Rodeo Drive in Beverly Hills, along with a dozen or more major shopping malls just like back home.

WHERE TO STAY

Some of the best golf resorts in the country are in the resort towns just beyond Palm Springs. We've listed La Quinta below, but there are other equally fabulous choices, all with great golf, tennis, and complete resort services. Many fine resorts offer generous golf packages, among them **Marriott's Desert Springs Spa & Resort** in Palm Desert (© 760/341-2211), **Marriott's Rancho Las Palmas Resort & Spa** in Rancho Mirage (© 760/568-2727), the **Hyatt Grand Champions** in Indian Wells (© 760/341-1000), and **La Quinta Resort & Club** in La Quinta (© 760/564-4111).

Casa Cody   Once owned by "Wild" Bill Cody's niece, this 1920s casa with a double courtyard has been restored to fine condition. It now sports a vaguely Southwestern decor and peaceful grounds marked by large lawns and mature fruit trees. You'll feel more like a houseguest than a hotel client here, in a residential area a couple of blocks from Palm Canyon Drive. All units have fridges; many have fireplaces and kitchens. Breakfast is served poolside.

175 S. Cahuilla Rd. (btw. Tahquitz Way and Arenas Rd.), Palm Springs, CA 92262. © **800/231-2639** or 760/320-9346. Fax 760/325-8610. www.casacody.com. 27 units. $69–$189 double; $209–$279 suite; $429 2-bedroom house; $639 4-bedroom house. Rates include expanded continental breakfast. AE, DC, DISC, MC, V. Pets accepted for $15 extra per night. **Amenities:** 2 outdoor heated pools. In room: Fridge.

La Quinta Resort & Club (Best)   A luxury resort set amid citrus trees, towering palms, and cacti at the base of the rocky Santa Rosa Mountains, La Quinta is *the* place to be if you're serious about your golf or tennis game. Rooms are in single-story, Spanish-style buildings; each unit has a VCR, patio, and access to one of several dozen small pools, enhancing the feeling of privacy. Some rooms have fireplaces or Jacuzzis. The tranquil lounge in the original hacienda hearkens back to the early days of the resort, when Clark Gable, Greta Garbo, and other luminaries chose La Quinta as their hideaway. The resort is renowned for its five championship golf courses. Spa La Quinta has 35 treatment rooms for every pampering luxury.

49499 Eisenhower Dr., La Quinta, CA 92253. © **800/598-3828** or 760/564-4111. Fax 760/564-7656. www.laquintaresort.com. 796 units. $329–$629 double; from $1,000 suite. $27 resort fee per night. Extra person $25. Children 17 and under stay free in parent's room. Packages available. AE, MC, V. Free self-parking; valet parking. Pets welcome for a fee. **Amenities:** 5 restaurants; 41 outdoor pools; 23 outdoor tennis courts (10 lit); full-service spa.

Gay & Lesbian Life in Palm Springs

The Palm Springs area is a major destination for GLBT travelers, who will want to check out *The Bottom Line* (**www.psbottomline.com**), the desert's free biweekly magazine of articles, events, and community guides for the gay reader; it's available at hotels and newsstands and from select merchants.

Throughout the year, events are held that transcend the gay community to include everyone. In March, the **Desert AIDS Walk** benefits the Desert AIDS Project, while one of the world's largest organized gatherings of lesbians—the **Dinah Shore Weekend** (www.clubskirts.com)—coincides with the LPGA's **Kraft Nabisco Championship** in March. The predominantly male **White Party** (www.jeffreysanker.com), the area's largest circuit party event, takes place Easter weekend. **Greater Palm Spring Pride** occurs the first weekend in November, with a parade and 2-day fair (© **760/416-8711;** www.pspride.org).

Palm Mountain Resort and Spa (Kids) Within easy walking distance of Palm Springs's main drag, this former Holiday Inn welcomes kids 17 and under free in their parent's room, making it a good choice for families. The rooms are in the two- or the three-story wing, and many have a patio or balcony, with a view of the mountains or the large Astroturf courtyard. Midweek and summer rates can be as low as $99. For the best rates, book online or ask for "Great Rates."

155 S. Belardo Rd., Palm Springs, CA 92262. © **800/622-9451** or 760/325-1301. Fax 760/323-8937. www.palmmountainresort.com. 119 units. Jan–Apr $109–$209 double; May–Sept $69–$139 double; Oct–Dec $99–$169 double. Rates include continental breakfast. Children 17 and under stay free in parent's room. AE, DC, DISC, MC, V. Free parking. **Amenities:** Restaurant; heated pool; spa. *In room:* Fridge.

Spa Resort Casino One of the more unusual choices in town, this resort is on Indian-owned land above the city's eponymous mineral springs, believed by the Cahuilla to have healing properties. Today's travelers still come here to pamper both body and soul in this sleekly modern facility. There are three pools—one a conventional outdoor swimming pool, the other two filled from the underground natural springs. Inside the extensive spa are private marble tubs and many pampering treatments. Despite the addition of an adjoining Vegas-style casino, the Cahuilla have truly managed to integrate modern hotel comforts with the ancient healing and Indian spirit this land represents.

100 N. Indian Canyon Dr., Palm Springs, CA 92263. © **888/999-1995** or 760/325-1461. Fax 760/325-3344. www.sparesortcasino.com. 228 units. $189–$259 double; $369–$1,500 suite. AE, DC, MC, V. Free parking. **Amenities:** 3 restaurants; outdoor heated pool; fitness center; spa. *In room:* Fridge.

Villa Royale This charming inn, 5 minutes from downtown Palm Springs, evokes a European cluster of villas, complete with climbing bougainvillea and antiques-filled rooms. Uniform luxuries (down comforters and other pampering touches) appear throughout. Rooms vary widely in size and ambience; larger isn't always better, as some of the most appealing rooms are in the more affordable range. Many rooms have fireplaces, patios with Jacuzzis, or kitchens. The inn's **Europa Restaurant** is the finest in the area.

1620 Indian Trail (off E. Palm Canyon), Palm Springs, CA 92264. © **800/245-2314** or 760/327-2314. Fax 760/322-3794. www.villaroyale.com. 30 units. $200–$275 suite; $350–$450 villa. Rates include full breakfast. AE, DC, DISC, MC, V. Free parking. **Amenities:** Restaurant; 2 outdoor heated pools.

Europa Restaurant ⓑest CALIFORNIA/CONTINENTAL   Long advertised as the "most romantic dining in the desert," Europa is a sentimental favorite of many regulars among an equally gay and straight clientele. Whether you sit on the garden patio or in subdued candlelight indoors, you'll savor dinner prepared by one of Palm Springs's most dedicated kitchens. Standouts are filet mignon on a bed of crispy onions with garlic butter, and a show-stopping salmon baked in parchment with crème fraîche and dill. For dessert, don't miss the signature chocolate mousse.

1620 Indian Trail (at the Villa Royale). ℭ **760/327-2314.** Reservations recommended. Main courses $26–$42. AE, DC, DISC, MC, V. Tues–Sun 5–10pm. Closed Mon.

Murph's Gaslight PAN-FRIED CHICKEN   Join those in the know at this budget-saving lunch-and-dinner meeting place, where the chicken just keeps coming, with all the trimmings: black-eyed peas, mashed potatoes, corn bread, hot biscuits, country gravy, and fruit cobbler. Call ahead for takeout or join the family-style crowd, on a first-come, first-served basis. An early-bird special starts at 5pm for $10. If there's a wait, relax in Murph's Irish Pub.

79-860 Ave. 42, next to the airport in Bermuda Dunes near Jefferson. ℭ **760/345-6242.** $16 for full dinner. MC, V. Mon–Sat 11am–3pm and 5–9pm; Sun 3–9pm.

Sammy's Woodfired Pizza PIZZA   In the same mall complex as Tommy Bahama's is a great inexpensive restaurant for families. The large room with booths and tables is fronted by a misted outdoor patio. Choose from 21 wood-fired pizzas drizzled with chili oil, such as the N.Y. pizza: homemade tomato sauce, sautéed mushrooms, pepperoni, salami, and Italian sausage for $13. The menu also has a variety of salads and pasta. Beer and wine are available.

73595 El Paseo (at Larkspur Ave.). ℭ **760/836-0500.** Pizzas $9.75–$13; salads $9.50–$17; pastas $13–$17. AE, MC, V. Daily 11am–9pm.

PALM SPRINGS AFTER DARK

Good sources for information are *The Desert Guide* and *The Bottom Line* (a biweekly gay magazine). On Thursday nights, **VillageFest** turns Palm Canyon Drive into an outdoor party with vendors and colorful entertainment.

The **Fabulous Palm Springs Follies,** at Plaza Theatre, 128 S. Palm Canyon Dr., Palm Springs (ℭ **760/327-0225;** www.psfollies.com), is a vaudeville-style show filled with production numbers. Guest stars and international vaudeville acts join the Follies' world-renowned line of Long-Legged Lovelies and Follies Gentlemen, all ranging in age from 55 to 85. The season runs November through May. Tickets range from $42 to $95. Matinees are at 1:30pm, evening shows at 7pm.

13 DEATH VALLEY NATIONAL PARK

The forty-niners, whose suffering gave the valley its name, would have howled at the notion of Death Valley National Park. Americans looking for gold in California's mountains in 1849 were forced to cross the burning sands to avoid severe snowstorms in the nearby Sierra Nevada. Some perished along the way, and the land became known as Death Valley.

Mountains stand naked, unadorned. The bitter waters of saline lakes evaporate into bizarre, razor-sharp crystal formations. Jagged canyons jab deep into the earth. Ovenlike heat, frigid cold, and the driest air imaginable combine to make this one of the most inhospitable locations in the world.

Human nature being what it is, however, it's not surprising that people have long been drawn to challenge the power of Mother Nature. Man's first foray into tourism began in 1925. It probably would have begun sooner, but the valley had been consumed with lucrative borax mining since the late 1880s.

Today's visitor drives in air-conditioned comfort, stays in comfortable hotel rooms or at well-maintained campgrounds, orders meals and provisions at park concessions, even quaffs a cold beer at the local saloon. You can take a swim in the Olympic-size pool, tour a Moorish castle, shop for souvenirs, and enjoy the desert landscape while hiking along a nature trail with a park ranger.

ESSENTIALS

ACCESS POINTS   There are several routes into the park, all of which involve crossing one of the mountain ranges that isolate Death Valley from, well, everything. Perhaps the most scenic entry to the park is via **Calif. 190,** east of **Calif. 178** from Ridgecrest. Another scenic drive to the park is by way of **Calif. 127** and **Calif. 190** from Baker. The $15-per-car entrance fee is valid for 7 days.

VISITOR CENTER & INFORMATION   The **Furnace Creek Visitor Center & Museum,** 15 miles inside the eastern park boundary on Calif. 190 (© **760/786-3200**), offers interpretive exhibits and an hourly slide program. Ask at the information desk for ranger-led nature walks and evening naturalist programs. The center is open daily from 8am to 6pm in winter (to 5pm in summer).

SEEING THE HIGHLIGHTS

A good first stop after checking in at the main park visitor center in Furnace Creek is the **Harmony Borax Works**—a rock-salt landscape as tortured as you'll ever find. Death Valley prospectors called borax "white gold"; this profitable—though unglamorous— substance was mined here until 1928. The famous 20-mule teams hauled huge loaded wagons 165 miles to the rail station at Mojave.

Badwater—at 282 feet below sea level, the lowest point in the Western Hemisphere— is also one of the hottest places in the world, with regularly recorded summer temperatures of 120°F (38°C).

Salt Creek is the home of the **Salt Creek pupfish,** found nowhere else on Earth. This little fish, which has made some amazing adaptations to survive in this arid land, can be glimpsed from a wooden-boardwalk nature trail.

Before sunrise, photographers set up their tripods at **Zabriskie Point** and aim their cameras down at the magnificent panoramic view of Golden Canyon's pale mudstone hills and the great valley beyond. For another grand vista, check out **Dante's View,** a 5,475-foot viewpoint looking out over the shimmering Death Valley floor, backed by the high Panamint Mountains.

Just south of Furnace Creek is the 9-mile loop of **Artists Drive,** an easy must-see for visitors (except those in RVs, which can't negotiate the sharp, rock-bordered curves in the road). From the highway, you can't see the splendid palette of colors splashed on the rocks behind the foothills; once inside, continue through to aptly named **Artists Palette,** where an interpretive sign explains the source of nature's rainbow.

Scotty's Castle & the Gas House Museum (© 760/786-2392), the 1930s Mediterranean hacienda in the northern part of the park, is Death Valley's premier tourist attraction. Visitors are wowed by the elaborate Spanish tiles, well-crafted furnishings, and innovative construction that included solar water heating. The 1-hour walking tour is excellent, both for its inside look at the mansion and for what it reveals about the eccentricities of the millionaire who built the "castle." Tours fill up quickly; arrive early for the first available spots ($11 adult, $9 senior, and $6 child).

Near Scotty's Castle is **Ubehebe Crater.** It's known as an explosion crater—one look and you'll know why. When hot magma rose from the depths of earth to meet the groundwater, the resultant steam blasted out a crater and scattered cinders.

WHERE TO CAMP & STAY

The park's nine campgrounds are at elevations ranging from below sea level to 8,000 feet. In Furnace Creek, **Sunset** offers 1,000 spaces with water and flush toilets. **Furnace Creek Campground** has 200 similarly appointed spaces. **Stovepipe Wells** has 200 spaces with water and flush toilets. Reservations can be made online at **http://reservations.nps.gov** or by calling © **800/365-2267.**

Like an oasis in the middle of Death Valley, the **Furnace Creek Inn's** (© **800/236-7916** or 760/786-2345; www.furnacecreekresort.com) red-tiled roofs and sparkling blue mineral-spring-fed swimming pool hint at the elegance within. The hotel has equipped its 66 deluxe rooms and suites with every modern amenity while successfully preserving the charm of this 1930s resort. Rates run $250 to $375 double.

The **Furnace Creek Ranch** (© **760/786-2345;** www.furnacecreekresort.com), a private in-holding within the park, has 224 no-frills cottage units with air-conditioning and showers ($141–$191). The swimming pool is a popular hangout. Nearby are a coffee shop, saloon, steakhouse, and general store. **Stovepipe Wells Village** (© **760/786-2387**) has 74 modest rooms with air-conditioning and showers, plus a casual dining room that closes between meals ($75–$115).

The only lodging in the park not run by the official concessionaire is the **Panamint Springs Resort** (© **775/482-7680;** www.deathvalley.com), a rustic motel, cafe, and snack shop an hour east of Furnace Creek ($89–$167). Because accommodations in Death Valley are limited and expensive, you might consider the money-saving (but inconvenient) option of spending a night at one of the two gateway towns: **Lone Pine,** on the west side of the park, or **Baker,** on the south. **Beatty, Nevada,** which has inexpensive lodging, is an hour's drive from the park's center. The restored **Amargosa Hotel** (© **760/852-4441**) in Death Valley Junction offers 14 rooms in a historic, out-of-the-way place, 40 minutes from Furnace Creek ($67–$84).

Tip: Meals and groceries are exceptionally costly at Death Valley due to the remoteness of the park. If possible, consider bringing a cooler with some snacks, sandwiches, and beverages to last the duration of your visit. Ice is easily obtainable, and you'll also be able to keep water chilled.

The Pacific Northwest

Washington and Oregon, situated in the northwest corner of the nation, are an amalgam of American life and landscapes; within their boundaries, these two states reflect a part of almost every region of the country. Take a bit of New England's rural beauty: covered bridges, steepled churches, and familiar place names such as Portland and Springfield. Temper the climate to that of the upper South to avoid harsh winters. Now bring in some low rolling mountains similar to the Appalachians; rugged, glaciated mountains like those in the Rockies; and even volcanoes, as in Hawaii. Add a river as large and important as the Mississippi. Toss in a coastline as rugged as California's, and an island-filled inland sea that offers as many sailing and kayaking opportunities as the coast of Maine. Even the deserts of the Southwest and wheat fields of the Midwest could be added. The wine country of California would be a nice touch, and so would some long sandy beaches. On top of all this, there should be a beautiful city, one with hills and a waterfront like those in San Francisco. Mix all these things together, and you have a portrait of the Northwest.

1 SEATTLE

Imagine yourself seated at a table on the Seattle waterfront, a tall latte and an almond croissant close at hand. The snowy peaks of the Olympic Mountains shimmer on the far side of Puget Sound, and the ferryboats come and go across Elliott Bay. It just doesn't get much better than this, unless, of course, you swap the latte for a microbrew and catch a 9:30pm summer sunset. No wonder people love this town so much.

ESSENTIALS

GETTING THERE **By Plane** Seattle–Tacoma International Airport (© 206/433-5388; www.portseattle.org/seatac), most commonly referred to simply as "Sea-Tac," is about 14 miles south of Seattle.

Inside the arrivals terminal, you'll find a **Visitor Information Desk** (© 206/433-5218) in the baggage-claim area across from carousel no. 11. It's open daily from 9am to 5pm. You'll also find branches of all the major car-rental companies (for further details see "Getting Around," below).

A **taxi** into downtown Seattle will cost you about $35 ($28 for the return ride to the airport). There are usually plenty of taxis around, but if not, call **Yellow Cab** (© 206/622-6500) or **Farwest Taxi** (© 206/622-1717). The flag-drop charge is $2.50; after that, it's $2 per mile.

Gray Line Airport Express (© 800/426-7532 or 206/626-6088; www.graylineof seattle.com) is your best bet for getting downtown. These shuttle vans provide service between the airport and downtown Seattle daily, every 30 minutes from 5:30am (5am from downtown) to 11pm. Fares are $11 one-way for adults, $18 round-trip. **Shuttle Express** (© 800/487-7433 or 425/981-7000; www.shuttleexpress.com) provides 24-hour service between Sea-Tac and the Seattle, north Seattle, and Bellevue areas. It's $28 for one or two adults, $36 for three, and $48 for four. Children 12 and under ride free.

Metro Transit (© **800/542-7876** in Washington, or 206/553-3000; http://transit. metrokc.gov) operates two public buses between the airport and downtown. Bus trips to downtown take 40 to 50 minutes, depending on conditions. The fare is $1.50 during off-peak hours, $2.25 during peak hours.

By Train   **Amtrak** (© **800/872-7245** or 206/382-4125; www.amtrak.com) trains stop at King Street Station, 303 S. Jackson St., within a few blocks of the historic Pioneer Square neighborhood. Any bus running north on First, Second, Third, or Fourth avenues will take you to within a few blocks of most downtown hotels. The Waterfront Streetcar also stops within a block of King Street Station.

By Car   The major routes into Seattle are **I-5** from the north (Vancouver) and south (Portland), and **I-90** from the east (Spokane). **I-405,** Seattle's east-side bypass, leads to the cities of Bellevue, Redmond, and Kirkland; **Wash. 520** connects I-405 with Seattle north of downtown; and **Wash. 99,** the Alaskan Way Viaduct, is another major north-south highway through downtown and the waterfront.

VISITOR INFORMATION   Visitor information on the Seattle area is available from **Seattle's Convention and Visitors Bureau Citywide Concierge Center,** Washington State Convention and Trade Center, Eighth Avenue and Pike Street, main level (© **206/461-5888;** www.seeseattle.org). To find it, walk up Pike Street to the Convention Center (the street is covered by a huge arched glass ceiling in front of the convention center).

GETTING AROUND   Seattle's **Metro** buses (© **800/542-7876** in Washington, or 206/553-3000; http://transit.metrokc.gov) are free if you ride only in the downtown area between 6am and 7pm. The **Ride Free Area** is between Alaskan Way (the waterfront) in the west, Sixth Avenue and I-5 in the east, Battery Street in the north, and South Jackson Street in the south. Within this area are Pioneer Square, the waterfront attractions, Pike Place Market, the Seattle Art Museum, and almost all of the city's major hotels. The Ride Free Area also encompasses the Metro Tunnel, which extends from the International District in the south to the Convention Center in the north and allows buses to drive underneath downtown Seattle.

Outside the Ride Free Area, fares range from $1.50 to $2.25, depending on distance and time of day. (The higher fares are incurred during commuter hours.) *Note:* When traveling out of the Ride Free Area, you pay when you get off the bus; when traveling into the Ride Free Area, you pay when you get on the bus. Exact change is required; dollar bills are accepted.

In addition to the bus system, **Metro** operates old-fashioned streetcars that follow a route along the waterfront from Pier 70 to Pioneer Square and then east to the corner of Fourth Avenue South and South Jackson Street, on the edge of the International District. The fare is $1.75 for adults and 50¢ for seniors and students. Exact change is required. If you plan to transfer to a Metro bus, you can get a transfer good for 90 minutes. They are wheelchair accessible. Streetcars run every 15 minutes and operate Monday through Thursday from 6am to 9pm, Friday and Saturday from 6am to 11pm, and Sunday and holidays from 10am to 7pm.

The **Seattle Monorail** (© **206/905-2600;** www.seattlemonorail.com) connects Seattle Center with the Westlake Center mall (Fifth Ave. and Pine St.). The elevated train covers the 1¼ miles in 2 minutes and passes through the middle of the Experience Music Project, the Frank Gehry–designed rock-music museum. The monorail operates daily

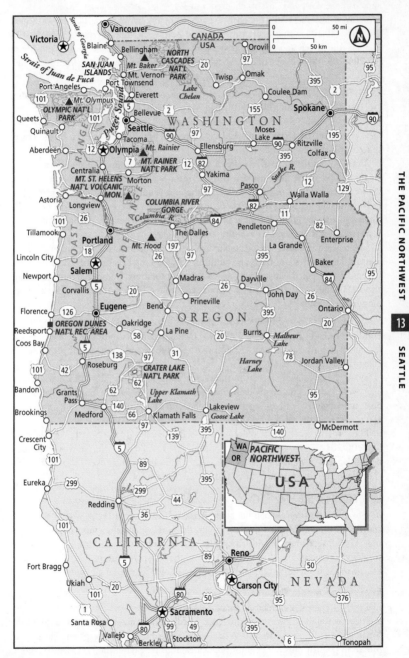

from 9am to 11pm. Departures are every 10 minutes. The one-way fare is $2 for adults and $1 for seniors, and 75¢ for children 5 to 12.

Between late April and October, a water taxi runs between the downtown Seattle waterfront (Pier 55) and Seacrest Park in West Seattle, providing access to West Seattle's popular Alki Beach and adjacent paved path. For a service schedule, check with Metro (© 206/205-3866; http://transit.metrokc.gov). The one-way fare is $3 (free for children 5 and under), $1 with a valid bus transfer, free with all-day pass.

FAST FACTS   Hospitals convenient to downtown include **Swedish Medical Center,** 747 Broadway (© 206/386-6000), and **Virginia Mason Hospital and Clinic,** 925 Seneca St. (© 206/583-6433 for emergencies, or 624-1144 for information). For 24-hour service, try **Bartell Drug Store,** 600 First Ave. N. (© 206/284-1353), in the Lower Queen Anne neighborhood.

Although Seattle is a relatively safe city, it has its share of crime. The most questionable neighborhood you're likely to visit is the Pioneer Square area, which is home to more than a dozen bars and nightclubs. By day, this area is quite safe, but late at night, when the bars are closing, keep your wits about you. And keep an eye on your wallet or purse when you're in the crush of people at Pike Place Market. Whenever possible, try to park your car in a garage, instead of on the street, at night.

Seattle has a 9% **sales tax.** In restaurants, there's an additional .5% **food-and-beverage tax.** The **hotel-room tax** is an additional 7%, for a total tax on hotel rooms of 16%. On rental cars, you'll pay not only an 18.5% **car-rental tax,** but also, if you rent at the airport, an additional 10% to 12% **airport concession fee** (plus other fees, for a whopping total of around 45%!).

SPECIAL EVENTS & FESTIVALS   Memorial Day weekend brings the **Northwest Folklife Festival** (© 206/684-7300; www.nwfolklife.org), with dozens of national and regional folk musicians, crafts, and plenty of good food and dancing. All performances take place at Seattle Center.

By far the city's biggest event of the year is **Seafair** (© 206/728-0123; www.seafair. org), with festivities occurring daily from early July to early August: parades, hydroplane boat races, the navy's Blue Angels, a Torchlight Parade, ethnic festivals, sporting events, and open house on naval ships.

The city's second-most-popular festival is **Bumbershoot, the Seattle Arts Festival** (© 206/281-7788; www.bumbershoot.org). Rock, folk, jazz, rap, and world music performances draw crowds into Seattle Center and other venues over Labor Day weekend. You'll also find arts and crafts, film, theater, and more.

WHAT TO SEE & DO

The Seattle waterfront, which lies along Alaskan Way between Yesler Way in the south and Bay Street and Myrtle Edwards Park in the north, is the city's most popular attraction. Yes, it's very touristy, with tacky gift shops, saltwater taffy, T-shirts galore, and lots of overpriced restaurants, but it's also home to the Seattle Aquarium, Odyssey Maritime Discovery Center, and Ye Olde Curiosity Shop (king of the tacky gift shops).

Experience Music Project (Best   The brainchild of Microsoft co-founder Paul Allen and designed by architect Frank Gehry, this rock-'n'-roll museum is a massive multicolored blob at the foot of the Space Needle. The museum encompasses all of the Northwest's rock scene (from "Louie Louie" to grunge) and the general history of American popular music. The most popular exhibits here (after the Jimi Hendrix room)

are the interactive rooms. In one room you can play guitars, drums, keyboards, or even **933**
DJ turntables. In another, you can experience what it's like to be onstage performing in
front of adoring fans. Another exhibit focuses on the history of guitars and includes some
of the first electric guitars, which date from the early 1930s. In the museum's main hall,
known as the **Sky Church,** there are regularly scheduled concerts. Expect long lines in
the summer and leave plenty of time to see this unusual museum.

Seattle Center, 325 Fifth Ave. N. (C) **877/367-7361** or 206/770-2702. www.emplive.org. Admission (valid
for Science Fiction Museum) $15 adults, $12 seniors and children 5–17. Free admission 1st Thurs of each
month 5–8pm. Memorial Day to Labor Day daily 10am–7pm; rest of year Wed–Mon 10am–5pm (until
8pm 1st Thurs of each month). Closed Thanksgiving and Christmas. Bus: 1, 2, 3, 4, 13, 15, 16, 18, 24, 30, or
33. Monorail: From Westlake Center at Pine St. and Fourth Ave.

Flying Heritage Collection   Because of the Boeing connection, the Seattle area has
an abundance of airplane-related attractions. At the Flying Heritage Collection, you can
marvel at the 15 immaculately restored fighter planes that belong to Microsoft co-
founder Paul Allen. Old fighter planes are another of Allen's interests, along with professional football (he owns the Seattle Seahawks) and rock music and science fiction (he
owns the Experience Music Project and the Science Fiction Museum). Many of the rare
planes in this collection are in flyable condition, and twice a month during the summer,
planes take to the air over Paine Field.

Paine Field, 3407 109th St. SW, Everett. (C) **877/342-3404.** www.flyingheritage.com. Admission $12
adults, $10 seniors, $8 children 6–15, free for children 5 and under. Memorial Day to Labor Day daily
10am–5pm; other months closed Mon. Closed Thanksgiving and Christmas.

Hiram M. Chittenden (Ballard) Locks   Locks don't provide panoramic views and
aren't nearly as dramatic as waterfalls, but a lot of people are intrigued by the concept of
two side-by-side bodies of water on two different levels, and these locks are one of the
city's most popular attractions. From June through September (July–Aug are the peak
months), you can view salmon as they leap up the locks' fish ladder and through underwater observation windows. These locks connect Lake Union and Lake Washington with
the waters of Puget Sound. Here you can stroll the grounds of the **Carl S. English, Jr.
Botanical Gardens,** a park filled with unusual shrubs and trees. March through November, there are free tours of the grounds Monday through Friday at 1 and 3pm, Saturday
and Sunday at 11am and 1 and 3pm.

3015 NW 54th St. (C) **206/783-7059.** Free admission. Daily 7am–9pm (visitor center: May–Sept daily
10am–6pm; Oct–Apr Thurs–Mon 10am–4pm). Bus: 17.

Odyssey Maritime Discovery Center (Kids)   Sort of an interactive promotion for
modern fishing and shipping, this facility at the north end of the Seattle waterfront is
aimed primarily at kids and has more than 40 hands-on exhibits highlighting Seattle's
modern working waterfront and its links to the sea. Exhibits include a kid-size fishing
boat, a virtual kayak trip through Puget Sound, and a live radar center that allows you to
track the movement of vessels in Elliott Bay. In another exhibit, you can use a simulated
crane to practice loading a scale model of a cargo ship.

Pier 66 (Bell St. Pier), 2205 Alaskan Way. (C) **206/374-4000.** www.ody.org. Admission $7 adults, $5 seniors
and students 5–18, $2 children 2–4, free for children 1 and under. Tues–Thurs 10am–3pm; Fri 10am–4pm;
Sat 11am–5pm. Closed New Year's Day, July 4, Thanksgiving, and Christmas. Bus: 15, 18, 21, 22, or 56 to
Bell St. Waterfront Streetcar Bus (99): Bell St./Pier 66 stop.

Pacific Science Center (Kids)   Although its exhibits are aimed primarily at children,
the Pacific Science Center is fun for all ages. There are life-size robotic dinosaurs, a

THE PACIFIC NORTHWEST

13

SEATTLE

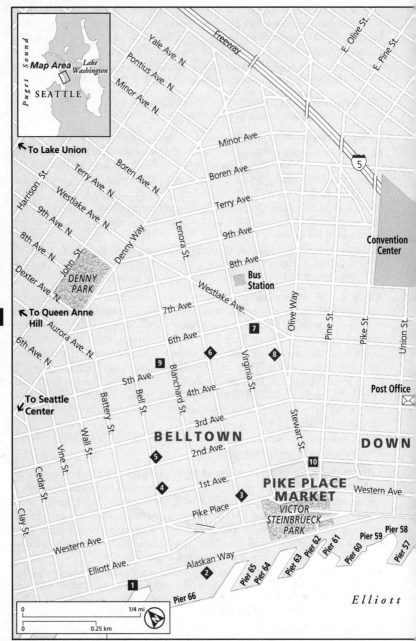

Map Area
Lake Washington
Puget Sound
SEATTLE

To Lake Union

Freeway

Yale Ave. N.
Pontius Ave. N.
Minor Ave. N.

E. Olive St.
E. Pine St.

Boren Ave. N.
Terry Ave. N.
Westlake Ave. N.
Harrison St.
9th Ave. N.
8th Ave. N.
Dexter Ave. N.

John St.

DENNY PARK

Denny Way

To Queen Anne Hill

Aurora Ave. N.

6th Ave. N.

To Seattle Center

Minor Ave.
Boren Ave.
Terry Ave.
9th Ave.
8th Ave.

Lenora St.

Westlake Ave.

7th Ave.

6th Ave.

5th Ave.

Battery St.

Bell St.

Blanchard St.

4th Ave.

3rd Ave.

2nd Ave.

Wall St.

Vine St.

Cedar St.

Clay St.

BELLTOWN

1st Ave.

Pike Place

Western Ave.

Elliott Ave.

Alaskan Way

Bus Station

Virginia St.

Olive Way

Pine St.

Pike St.

Union St.

Convention Center

I-5

Stewart St.

Post Office

DOWN

PIKE PLACE MARKET

VICTOR STEINBRUECK PARK

Western Ave.

Pier 66

Pier 65
Pier 64
Pier 63
Pier 62
Pier 61
Pier 60
Pier 59
Pier 58
Pier 57

Elliott

0   1/4 mi
0   0.25 km

1 2 3 4 5 6 7 8 9 10

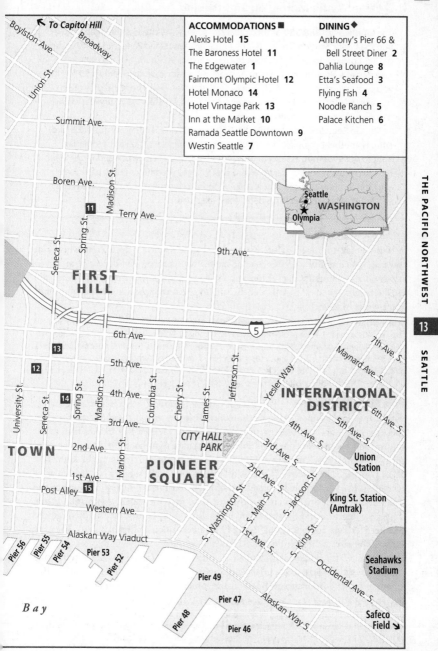

ACCOMMODATIONS ■

Alexis Hotel **15**
The Baroness Hotel **11**
The Edgewater **1**
Fairmont Olympic Hotel **12**
Hotel Monaco **14**
Hotel Vintage Park **13**
Inn at the Market **10**
Ramada Seattle Downtown **9**
Westin Seattle **7**

DINING ◆

Anthony's Pier 66 &
   Bell Street Diner **2**
Dahlia Lounge **8**
Etta's Seafood **3**
Flying Fish **4**
Noodle Ranch **5**
Palace Kitchen **6**

To Capitol Hill

Boylston Ave.
Broadway
Union St.
Summit Ave.
Boren Ave.
Madison St.
Terry Ave.
9th Ave.
Spring St.
Seneca St.

FIRST HILL

WASHINGTON
Seattle
Olympia

6th Ave.
5th Ave.
4th Ave.
3rd Ave.
2nd Ave.
1st Ave.
Post Alley
Western Ave.
Alaskan Way Viaduct

University St.
Seneca St.
Spring St.
Madison St.
Marion St.
Columbia St.
Cherry St.
James St.
Jefferson St.
Yesler Way

TOWN

PIONEER SQUARE

CITY HALL PARK

INTERNATIONAL DISTRICT

Maynard Ave. S.
7th Ave. S.
6th Ave. S.
5th Ave. S.
4th Ave. S.
3rd Ave. S.
2nd Ave. S.
S. Washington St.
S. Main St.
S. Jackson St.
1st Ave. S.
S. King St.
Occidental Ave. S.

Union Station

King St. Station (Amtrak)

Seahawks Stadium

Safeco Field ↘

Pier 56
Pier 55
Pier 54
Pier 53
Pier 52
Pier 49
Pier 48
Pier 47
Pier 46

Alaskan Way S.

Bay

(Value) **Saving Money on Sightseeing**

The **CityPass** (© **888/330-5008** or 208/787-4306; www.citypass.com) gets you into the Pacific Science Center, Seattle Aquarium, Woodland Park Zoo, and Museum of Flight or Experience Music Project/Science Fiction Museum, and also lets you take a boat tour of the harbor with Argosy Cruises, at a savings of almost 50% if you paid individual fees at each. The passes, good for 9 days from the date of first use, cost $44 for adults and $29 for children 3 to 12. Purchase your CityPass at any of the participating attractions.

The **Go Seattle Card** (© **800/887-9103** or 617/671-1001; www.goseattlecard. com) is another option for the see-it-all, do-it-all travelers. It takes careful planning to get your money's worth out of this card, but it can be done. You pay $55 ($35 for children ages 3–12) for a card that will get you into as many participating attractions as you can visit in 1 day. There's a discount for 2-, 3-, 5-, and 7-day cards, and your best bet is probably the 3-day card.

butterfly house and insect village (with giant robotic insects), a **Tech Zone** where kids can play virtual-reality soccer or play tic-tac-toe with a robot, and dozens of other fun hands-on exhibits addressing the biological sciences, physics, and chemistry. There's also a planetarium and an IMAX theater. Be sure to check the schedule for special exhibits when you're in town.

Seattle Center, 200 Second Ave. N. © **206/443-2001,** 443-4629 for IMAX information, or 443-2850 for laser-show information. www.pacsci.org. Admission $11 adults, $9.50 seniors, $8 ages 6–12, $6 ages 3–5, free for children 2 and under. IMAX $8–$11 adults, $7.50–$9.75 seniors, $7–$8.75 ages 6–12, $6–$8.75 ages 3–5, free for children 2 and under. Laser show $5–$8. Various discounted combination tickets available. Mon–Fri 10am–5pm; Sat–Sun 10am–6pm. Closed Christmas. Bus: 1, 2, 3, 4, 13, 15, 16, 18, 24, 30, or 33. Monorail: From Westlake Center at Pine St. and Fourth Ave.

Pike Place Market **(Best)** This 9-acre National Historic District is a bustling market with farmers and fishmongers, craftspeople and artists, restaurants, some of the city's best specialty shops, and entertaining street performers. Pick up a free market map at the information booth below the large Pike Place Market sign. Look for *Rachel,* the giant piggy bank that's raised more than $100,000 over the years, and the flying fish at the Pike Place Fish stall. The market's **"Gum Wall"** is a bit of a sticky subject. No one can agree whether it is art or just a disgusting form of litter. You'll find the chewing-gum-covered wall just down Pike Street (actually a cobbled alley) from the market information booth. To get a glimpse behind the scenes and learn all about its history, take a 1-hour guided **Market Heritage Tour** (© **206/774-5249** for information and reservations). Tours are offered Wednesday through Friday at 11am and Saturday at 9:30am; the cost is $10 for adults and $7 for seniors and children 17 and under. Reservations are required and should be made at least a day in advance (by noon on Fri for Sat tours). Tours depart from the market's **Information Booth** at the corner of Pike Street and First Avenue.

Btw. Pike and Pine sts. at First Ave. © 206/682-7453. www.pikeplacemarket.org. Pike Place/First Ave. businesses Mon–Sat 10am–6pm, Sun 11am–5pm; Down Under stores daily 11am–5pm; many produce vendors open at 8am in summer; restaurant hours vary. Closed New Year's Day, Thanksgiving, and Christmas. Bus: 10, 12, 15, 18, 21, or 22. Waterfront Streetcar Bus (Route 99): Pike St. Hillclimb stop.

Seattle Aquarium Although it's not as large as the Monterey Bay Aquarium or the Oregon Coast Aquarium, the Seattle Aquarium is a fabulous introduction to the sea life of the Northwest. The "Window on Washington Waters" exhibit, a huge tank just inside the entrance, is a highlight, especially when divers feed the fish. There's also a tank that generates crashing waves, and, in the *Life on the Edge* tide-pool exhibit that focuses on life along Washington's shores, you can reach into the water to touch starfish, sea cucumbers, and anemones. The aquarium's main focus is on the water worlds of the Puget Sound region, but there are also fascinating exhibits of sea life from around the world, including a beautiful coral-reef tank. The star attractions are the playful **river otters** and **sea otters,** as well as the giant **octopus.** Each September you can watch salmon return up a fish ladder to spawn.

Pier 59, 1483 Alaskan Way. (✆) **206/386-4300.** www.seattleaquarium.org. Admission $15 adults, $10 children 4–12, free for children 3 and under. Daily 9:30am–5pm. Bus: 10, 12, 15, or 18 and then walk through Pike Place Market to the waterfront. Waterfront Streetcar Bus (99): Pike St. stop.

Seattle Art Museum (SAM) This large museum verges on world-class and should not be missed. Before you even step inside the museum, you'll come face to faceless silhouette with Jonathon Borofsky's shadowy *Hammering Man,* an animated three-story steel sculpture that pounds out a silent beat in front of the museum. Once you get inside the museum proper, you'll find one of the nation's premier collections of Northwest Coast Indian art and artifacts, and an equally large collection of African art. The museum is particularly strong in modern and contemporary art, but there are also good collections of European and American art ranging from ancient Mediterranean works to pieces from the medieval, Renaissance, and baroque periods. Of course, the Northwest contemporary art collection is also quite extensive.

1300 First Ave. (✆) **206/654-3100.** www.seattleartmuseum.org. Admission $13 adults, $10 seniors, $7 children 13–17, free for children 12 and under. Free for all on 1st Thurs of each month; free for seniors on 1st Fri of each month; free for teens on 2nd Fri of each month 5–9pm. Tues–Wed and Sat–Sun 10am–5pm; Thurs–Fri 10am–9pm. Closed Columbus Day, Thanksgiving, Christmas Eve, Christmas, New Year's Eve, and New Year's Day (open some holiday Mon). Bus: 10, 12, 15, 18, 21, 22, 39, or 42.

Seattle Asian Art Museum In an Art Deco building in Volunteer Park, the collection at this museum places an emphasis on Chinese and Japanese art, but also includes works from Korea, Southeast Asia, South Asia, and the Himalayas. Among the museum's most notable pieces are Chinese terra-cotta funerary art, Chinese snuff bottles, and Japanese *netsuke* (belt decorations). Rooms are devoted to Japanese and Chinese ceramics. The central hall contains stone religious sculptures from South Asia (primarily India). If you'd like to learn more about the Asian-American experience in Seattle, visit the **Wing Luke Asian Museum,** 719 S. King St. (✆) **206/623-5124;** www.wingluke.org), in the Chinatown/International District. Parts of the museum's interior are designed to resemble narrow alleyways.

Volunteer Park, 1400 E. Prospect St. (✆) **206/654-3100.** www.seattleartmuseum.org. Admission $5 adults, $3 seniors and youths 13–17, free for children 12 and under. Free admission for all on 1st Thurs of each month; free for seniors on 1st Fri of each month; free for families on 1st Sat of each month 5–9pm. Tues–Wed and Fri–Sun 10am–5pm; Thurs 10am–9pm. Closed New Year's Eve, New Year's Day, Columbus Day, Thanksgiving, and Dec 24–25. Bus: 10.

Space Needle From a distance, it looks like a flying saucer on a tripod, and when it was built for the 1962 World's Fair, the 605-foot-tall Space Needle was meant to suggest future architectural trends. Today the Space Needle is the quintessential symbol of Seattle, and at 520 feet above ground level, its observation deck provides superb views of the city and its surroundings. If you don't mind standing in line and paying quite a bit for an elevator ride, make this your first stop in Seattle so that you can orient yourself.

Seattle Center, 400 Broad St. ✆ **206/905-2100.** www.spaceneedle.com. Admission $16 adults ($20 for day-and-night ticket); $14 seniors ($18 for day-and-night ticket); $8 ages 4–13 ($12 for day-and-night ticket); free for children 3 and under. No charge if dining in the SkyCity restaurant. Sun–Thurs 9am–11pm; Fri–Sat 9am–midnight. Valet parking $12 for all-day parking. Bus: 1, 2, 3, 4, 13, 15, 16, 18, 24, 30, or 33. Monorail: From Westlake Center at Pine St. and Fourth Ave.

Woodland Park Zoo (Kids)   This sprawling zoo has outstanding exhibits focusing on Alaska, tropical Asia, the African savanna, and the tropical rainforest. The brown-bear enclosure, one of the zoo's best exhibits, is a realistic reproduction of Alaskan stream and hillside. In the savanna, zebras gambol and giraffes graze contentedly near a reproduction of an African village. An elephant forest provides plenty of space for the zoo's pachyderms. A large walk-through butterfly house is open during the summer months. Kids like the **Zoomazium,** an interactive educational play area where they can see what it's like to be wild animals.

750 N. 50th St. ✆ **206/548-2500.** www.zoo.org. Admission May–Sept $15 adults, $13 seniors, $10 children 3–12, free for children 2 and under; Oct–Apr $11 adults, $9 seniors, $8 children 3–12, free for children 2 and under. May–Sept daily 9:30am–6pm; Oct–Apr daily 9:30am–4pm. Parking $4.50. Bus: 5 or 44.

PARKS & PUBLIC GARDENS

For serious communing with nature, head for **Discovery Park,** 3801 W. Government Way (✆ **206/386-4236**). Occupying a high bluff and sandy point jutting into Puget Sound, this is Seattle's largest and wildest park. You can easily spend a day wandering the trails and beaches here. The park's visitor center is open Tuesday through Sunday from 8:30am to 5pm. To reach the park, follow the waterfront north from downtown Seattle toward the Magnolia neighborhood and watch for signs to the park.

Up on Capitol Hill, at East Prospect Street and 14th Avenue East, you'll find **Volunteer Park,** 1247 15th Ave. E. (✆ **206/684-4075**), which is surrounded by the mansions of Capitol Hill. It's a popular spot for sunning and playing Frisbee, and it's home to the Seattle Asian Art Museum (p. 937), an amphitheater, a water tower with a superb view of the city, and a conservatory filled with tropical and desert plants.

Any avid gardener should be sure to make a trip across one of Seattle's two floating bridges to the city of Bellevue and the **Bellevue Botanical Garden,** Wilburton Hill Park, 12001 Main St. (✆ **425/452-2750;** www.bellevuebotanical.org). This 36-acre garden has become one of the Northwest's most-talked-about perennial gardens. The summertime displays of flowers, in expansive mixed borders, are absolutely gorgeous. Admission is free; take the Northeast Fourth Street exit off I-405.

The **Japanese Garden,** Washington Park Arboretum, 1075 Lake Washington Blvd. E., north of East Madison Street (✆ **206/684-4725;** bus: 11), is a perfect little world unto itself, with babbling brooks, a lake rimmed with Japanese irises and filled with colorful koi (Japanese carp), and a cherry orchard (for spring color). A special tea garden encloses a teahouse where, on the third Saturday of each month between April and October, you can attend a traditional tea ceremony ($10). Unfortunately, noise from a nearby road can be distracting at times. Admission is $5 adults and $3 seniors, persons with disabilities, and children 6 to 17. It's closed December through February.

Acres of trees and shrubs stretch from the far side of Capitol Hill all the way to the Montlake Cut, a canal connecting Lake Washington to Lake Union. Within the 230-acre

Washington Park Arboretum, 2300 Arboretum Dr. E. (© **206/543-8800;** http://depts. washington.edu/wpa/general.htm; bus: 11, 43, or 48), there are 4,600 varieties of plants and quiet trails that are pleasant throughout the year but are most beautiful in spring, when the azaleas, cherry trees, rhododendrons, and dogwoods are all in flower. The north end of the arboretum, a marshland that is home to ducks and herons, is popular with kayakers, canoeists (see "Outdoor Activities," below, for places to rent a canoe or kayak), and bird-watchers. Free tours are offered the first and third Sundays of each month at 1pm. Admission is free. Enter on Lake Washington Boulevard off East Madison Street; or follow Wash. 520 off I-5 north of downtown, take the Montlake Boulevard exit, and go straight through the first intersection.

ORGANIZED TOURS

If you have an appreciation for off-color humor and are curious about the seamier side of Seattle history, the **Underground Tour,** 608 First Ave. (© **206/682-4646;** www. undergroundtour.com), will likely entertain and enlighten you. The tours lead down below street level in the Pioneer Square area, where you can still find the vestiges of Seattle businesses built before the great fire of 1889. Tours are held daily. The cost is $14 for adults, $12 for seniors and students 13 to 17 or with college ID, and $7 for children 7 to 12; children 6 and under are discouraged.

For an insider's glimpse of life in Seattle's International District, hook up with **Chinatown Discovery Tours** (© **425/885-3085;** www.seattlechinatowntour.com). On these walking tours, which last from 1¹/₂ to 3¹/₄ hours, you'll learn the history of this colorful and historic neighborhood; some tours include a six-course lunch or eight-course banquet. Rates (for four or more on a tour) start from $17 for adults and $11 for children ages 5 to 11.

Seattle is surrounded by water; if you'd like to see it from this perspective, contact **Argosy Cruises** (© **800/642-7816** or 206/623-1445; www.argosycruises.com), which offers everything from a 1-hour harbor jaunt to a cruise around Lake Washington that will take you past Bill Gates's fabled waterfront Xanadu.

If you opt for only one tour while in Seattle, the **Tillicum Village Tour,** Pier 55 (© **800/426-1205** or 206/933-8600; www.tillicumvillage.com), should be it. The tour includes a boat excursion, a salmon dinner, and Northwest Coast Indian masked dances. The dinner is pretty good, and the traditional dances are fascinating. Afterward, you can strike out on forest trails to explore the island (you can return on a later boat if you want to spend a couple of extra hours hiking). Tours are $80 for adults, $73 for seniors, $30 for children 5 to 12, and free for children 4 and under. They're offered daily from May to September, and on a more limited basis (usually weekends only) October through December and March through April. You can also just opt to ride the boat out to Blake Island and skip the meal and dancing. This option costs $40 for adults, $37 for seniors, and $12 for children 5 to 12.

OUTDOOR ACTIVITIES

See "Parks & Public Gardens," above, for a rundown of great places to play.

BIKING **Montlake Bicycle Shop,** 2223 24th Ave. E. (© **206/329-7333;** www. montlakebike.com), rents bikes by the day for $25 to $85. This shop is just south of the Montlake Bridge and is convenient to the **Burke-Gilman/Sammamish River Trail,** a 27-mile paved pathway created mostly from an old railway bed. This immensely popular path is a great place to take the family for a bike ride or to get in a long, vigorous ride

(Value) Money-Saving Tip

The **Ticket/Ticket** booth under the big clock at Pike Place Market sometimes has boat tour tickets available at discounted prices. If your schedule is flexible, be sure to check here first.

without having to deal with traffic. The Burke-Gilman portion of this trail starts in the Ballard neighborhood of north Seattle, but the most convenient place to start a ride is at **Gas Works Park** on the north shore of Lake Union. From here you can ride north and east to **Kenmore Logboom Park** at the north end of Lake Washington. There are lots of great picnicking spots along both trails. The West Seattle bike path along **Alki Beach** is another good place to ride and offers great views of the sound and the Olympics.

SEA KAYAKING   If you'd like to try your hand at **sea kayaking,** head to the **Northwest Outdoor Center,** 2100 Westlake Ave. N. (© **800/683-0637** or 206/281-9694; www.nwoc.com), on the west side of Lake Union. You can rent a sea kayak for between $13 and $18 per hour. You can also opt for guided tours lasting from a few hours to several days, and there are plenty of classes available. **Moss Bay Rowing, Kayaking and Sailing Center,** 1001 Fairview Ave. N. (© **206/682-2031;** www.mossbay.net), rents sea kayaks, rowing shells, and sailboats at the south end of Lake Union near Chandler's Cove. Rates range from $12 per hour for a single kayak to $17 per hour for a double. Because this rental center is a little closer to downtown Seattle, it's a better choice if you are here without a car.

SHOPPING

The heart of Seattle's shopping district is the corner of **Pine Street** and **Fifth Avenue.** Within 2 blocks of this intersection are two major department stores (**Nordstrom** and **Macy's**) and two upscale urban shopping malls (**Westlake Center** and **Pacific Place**). The most famous shopping area is **Pike Place Market** (see "What to See & Do," above). **Pioneer Square,** Seattle's historic district, is filled with art galleries and antiques stores. **Capitol Hill** is the center of both the gay community and the city's youth culture, and has the most eclectic selection of shops in the city. Even funkier is the **Fremont** neighborhood just north of Lake Union, filled with retro stores selling vintage clothing, collectibles, and curious crafts.

A couple of miles east of Fremont there's **Wallingford,** which is anchored by an old schoolhouse that has been converted into a shopping arcade with crafts, fashions, and gifts. The **University District,** also in north Seattle, has everything to support a student population and goes upscale at the University Village shopping center.

If antiques are your passion, you won't want to miss the opportunity to spend a day browsing the many antiques stores in the historic farm town of **Snohomish,** located roughly 30 miles north of Seattle off I-5. The town has more than 400 antiques dealers and is without a doubt the antiques capital of the Northwest.

In business since 1933, the **Legacy Ltd.,** 1003 First Ave. (© **800/729-1562** or 206/624-6350; www.thelegacyltd.com), is Seattle's finest gallery of contemporary and historic Northwest Coast Indian and Alaskan Eskimo art and artifacts.

REI (Recreational Equipment, Inc.), 222 Yale Ave. N. (© **888/873-1938** or 206/223-1944; www.rei.com), was founded in Seattle back in 1938 and today is the nation's largest co-op selling outdoor gear. Its awesome flagship store, just off I-5, is a cross between a high-tech warehouse and a mountain lodge, with a 65-foot climbing pinnacle, a rain room for testing rain gear, a trail for test-riding mountain bikes, even a play area for kids.

For the way-offbeat experience, **Ye Olde Curiosity Shop,** Pier 54, 1001 Alaskan Way (© **206/682-5844;** www.yeoldecuriosityshop.com), is a cross between a souvenir store and *Ripley's Believe It or Not!* It's weird! It's wacky! It's tacky! The collection of oddities was started in 1899 by Joe Standley, who developed a more-than-passing interest in strange curios. See Siamese-twin calves, a natural mummy, the Lord's Prayer on a grain of rice, a narwhal tusk, shrunken heads, a 67-pound snail, fleas in dresses—all the stuff that may have fascinated you as a kid.

WHERE TO STAY

If you're willing to head out a bit from downtown (usually booked solid in July–Aug), you'll find prices a little easier to swallow. Room rates are almost always considerably lower October through April (the rainy season), and downtown hotels often offer substantially reduced prices on weekends.

If you're having a hard time finding a room in your price range, consider using the services of **Pacific Northwest Journeys** (© 800/935-9730 or 206/935-9730; www. pnwjourneys.com). It charges $45 per reservation, but you can usually make that up in savings on just a 2-night stay. You might also want to check with **Seattle Super Saver** (© **800/535-7071** or 206/461-5882; www.seattlesupersaver.com), a reservation service operated by Seattle's Convention and Visitors Bureau. Rates are comparable to what you might find at online booking sites.

We list some of our favorite Seattle B&Bs (often less expensive than downtown hotels) in the pages that follow, but to find out about other good B&Bs in Seattle, contact the **Seattle Bed & Breakfast Association** (© 800/348-5630 or 206/547-1020; www.seattle bandbs.com) or **A Pacific Reservation Service** (© **800/684-2932** or 206/439-7677; www.seattlebedandbreakfast.com), which represent dozens of accommodations in the Seattle area, including B&Bs and houseboats on Lake Union.

Alexis Hotel   This century-old building is a sparkling gem in an enviable location: halfway between Pike Place Market and Pioneer Square, and 3 blocks from the waterfront and the Seattle Art Museum. Throughout the hotel, both in guest rooms and in public spaces, are numerous original works of art. The cheerful, personalized service and the pleasant mix of contemporary and antique furnishings give the Alexis a lovely atmosphere. In the guest rooms, classic styling with a European flavor prevails. About a quarter of the rooms are suites, and the spa suites are real winners, offering whirlpool tubs in exceedingly luxurious bathrooms. The hotel also has complimentary evening wine tastings.

1007 First Ave. (at Madison St.), Seattle, WA 98104. © **866/356-8894** or 206/624-4844. Fax 206/621-9009. www.alexishotel.com. 121 units. $299–$319 double; $355–$549 suite. Rates include evening wine reception. Children 17 and under stay free in parent's room. AE, DC, DISC, MC, V. Valet parking $30. Pets accepted. **Amenities:** Restaurant; exercise room and access to nearby health club; Aveda day spa.

The Baroness Hotel (Value)   The Baroness is an apartment hotel primarily used by people in Seattle for medical reasons. It is a great value if you are not a demanding traveler. Rooms, though a bit dowdy, are comfortable, and some have kitchens. The surrounding neighborhood is quite pretty. Downtown Seattle starts 4 blocks downhill. Although the rooms are not centrally air-conditioned, air conditioners can be requested.

1005 Spring St., Seattle, WA 98104. ✆ **800/283-6453** or 206/624-0787. Fax 206/447-9553. www.baroness hotel.com. 58 units. $85–$107 double; $114–$122 suite. Children 17 and under stay free in parent's room. AE, DISC, MC, V. Parking $13. *In room:* Fridge.

The Edgewater

On a pier at the north end of the waterfront, the Edgewater is Seattle's only true waterfront hotel, and somehow it captures the feel of a classic Northwest wilderness retreat. The views are among the best in Seattle, and sunsets can be mesmerizing. On a clear day, you can see the Olympic Mountains across Puget Sound. The mountain-lodge theme continues in the rooms, which feature fireplaces and lodge-pole-pine furniture. It's worth it to spring for a water view. The rooms with balconies are a bit smaller than other rooms, although the premium waterview rooms, with claw-foot tubs and walls that open out to those great views, are hard to beat.

Pier 67, 2411 Alaskan Way, Seattle, WA 98121. ✆ **800/624-0670** or 206/728-7000. Fax 206/441-4119. www.edgewaterhotel.com. 223 units. $269–$589 double; $629–$2,500 suite. Children 17 and under stay free in parent's room. AE, DISC, MC, V. Valet parking $28. Pets accepted. **Amenities:** Restaurant exercise room and access to nearby health club; courtesy bikes.

Fairmont Olympic Hotel (Best)

If you're looking for classically elegant surroundings, excellent service, and great amenities, then head here, to a gorgeous facsimile of an Italian Renaissance palace. This hotel has the grandest lobby in Seattle. Gilt-and-crystal chandeliers hang from the arched ceiling, while ornate moldings grace the hand-burnished oak walls and pillars. Although many of the guest rooms tend to be rather small, all are very elegant. If you crave extra space, opt for one of the suites, of which there are more than 200. The **Georgian** is the most elegant restaurant in Seattle, with a menu that combines Northwest and Continental cuisines. Of all Seattle's luxury hotels, the Fairmont works the hardest at being eco-friendly.

411 University St., Seattle, WA 98101. ✆ **800/223-8772**, 800/821-8106 (in Washington), 800/268-6282 (in Canada), or 206/621-1700. Fax 206/682-9633. www.fairmont.com/seattle. 450 units. $419–$429 double; $449–$3,500 suite. Children 18 and under stay free in parent's room. AE, DC, DISC, MC, V. Valet parking $30. Pets accepted. **Amenities:** 2 restaurants; health club w/indoor pool, exercise machines, Jacuzzi, and saunas.

The Gaslight Inn

Anyone enamored of Craftsman bungalows and the Arts and Crafts movement of the early 20th century should enjoy a stay in this 1906 home. The common rooms are spacious and attractively decorated with a combination of Western and Northwestern flair, and throughout the inn are lots of art-glass pieces. In summer, guests can swim in the backyard pool or lounge on the deck. Guest rooms continue the design themes of the common areas, with lots of oak furnishings and heavy, peeled-log beds in some units. The innkeepers here can provide a wealth of information about the surrounding Capitol Hill neighborhood, which is the center of Seattle's gay scene.

1727 15th Ave., Seattle, WA 98122. ✆ **206/325-3654.** Fax 206/328-4803. www.gaslight-inn.com. 8 units, 3 with shared bathroom. $88–$98 double with shared bathroom; $108–$158 double with private bathroom. Rates include continental breakfast. AE, MC, V. No children allowed. **Amenities:** Small heated outdoor pool.

Hotel Deca (Value)

The 16-story Hotel Deca is one of Seattle's hippest hotels, and it offers excellent value. You'll be surrounded by modern Art Deco style, and the retro look is elegant, playful, and reminiscent of the 1930s. You'll also enjoy views of downtown Seattle, distant mountains, and various lakes and waterways. Every room is a corner unit, which means plenty of space to spread out. Small bathrooms are the biggest drawback. Hotel Deca is much cheaper than comparable downtown options, and if you need to be near the university, it's the top choice in the neighborhood.

4507 Brooklyn Ave. NE, Seattle, WA 98105. ✆ **800/899-0251** or 206/634-2000. Fax 206/545-2103. www. hoteldeca.com. 158 units. June–Sept $149–$249 double; Oct–May $119–$189 double. Rates include continental breakfast. Children 16 and under stay free in parent's room. AE, DC, DISC, MC, V. Parking $6. **Amenities:** Restaurant; exercise room.

Hotel Monaco   The Monaco is one of downtown's most stylish hotels, attracting a young, affluent clientele. If you appreciate cutting-edge style, you'll go for the eclectic, over-the-top, retro-contemporary design. The lobby has reproductions of ancient Greek murals, while in the guest rooms, you'll find wild color schemes, bold-striped wallpaper, flat-panel LCD TVs, DVD and CD players, and animal-print terry-cloth robes. Miss your pet back home? Call the front desk, and a staff member will send up a pet goldfish for the night. **Sazerac,** the hotel's Southern-inspired restaurant, is as boldly designed as the rest of the place.

1101 Fourth Ave., Seattle, WA 98101. ✆ **800/945-2240** or 206/621-1770. Fax 206/621-7779. www. monaco-seattle.com. 189 units. $179–$319 double; $229–$349 suite. Rates include evening wine and beer tasting. Children 17 and under stay free in parent's room. AE, DC, DISC, MC, V. Valet parking $30. Pets accepted. **Amenities:** Restaurant; exercise room and access to nearby health club.

Hotel Vintage Park   Small, classically elegant, and exceedingly romantic, the Vintage Park is a must for both lovers and wine lovers. Guests stay in rooms named for Washington wineries and enjoy a complimentary wine tasting each evening. Rooms vary quite a bit here, but when you see the plush draperies framing the beds and the neo-Victorian furnishings in the deluxe units, you'll likely want to spend your days luxuriating amid the sumptuous surroundings. Deluxe rooms have the best views. Standard rooms, though smaller, are still very comfortable.

1100 Fifth Ave., Seattle, WA 98101. ✆ **800/624-4433** or 206/624-8000. Fax 206/623-0568. www.hotel vintagepark.com. 125 units. $139–$394 double; $475–$595 suite. Children 17 and under stay free in parent's room. AE, DC, DISC, MC, V. Valet parking $30. Pets accepted. **Amenities:** Restaurant; exercise room.

Inn at the Market   For romance, convenience, and the chance to immerse yourself in the Seattle aesthetic, it's hard to beat this hotel in Pike Place Market. A rooftop deck overlooking Elliott Bay provides a great spot to soak up the sun. Don't look for a grand entrance or large sign; there's only a small plaque on the wall to indicate that the building houses a tasteful and understated luxury hotel. Be sure to ask for one of the waterview rooms, which have large windows overlooking the bay. **Campagne,** the formal main dining room, serves French cuisine, while **Café Campagne** offers country-style French food amid casual surroundings.

86 Pine St., Seattle, WA 98101. ✆ **800/446-4484** or 206/443-3600. Fax 206/728-1955. www.innatthemarket. com. 70 units. $235–$490 double; $625 suite. Children 18 and under stay free in parent's room. AE, DC, DISC, MC, V. Parking $25. **Amenities:** 3 restaurants; access to nearby health club.

Ramada Seattle Downtown   Right on the monorail route and a few blocks from downtown Seattle's main shopping district, this hotel may not look like much from the outside, but it has a pretty lobby that belies the hotel's age. Guest rooms were all completely renovated in 2007 and are comfortable and functional. You just won't find a more reliable budget hotel in downtown Seattle. Ask for a room with a view of the Space Needle; you just might get lucky.

2200 Fifth Ave., Seattle, WA 98121. ✆ **800/272-6232** or 206/441-9785. Fax 206/448-0924. www.ramada. com. 120 units. $119–$169 double. Children 17 and under stay free in parent's room. AE, DC, DISC, MC, V. Parking $12. **Amenities:** Restaurant; exercise room and access to nearby health club.

Residence Inn by Marriott Seattle Downtown/Lake Union   Across the street from Lake Union, this is a good bet that's slightly removed from the city center. A seven-story atrium floods the hotel's plant-filled lobby court with light, while the sound of a waterfall soothes traffic-weary nerves. All accommodations, which were redone in 2008 in a bright, modern style, are suites, so you get more space for your money than at downtown hotels. Suites have full kitchens, so you can prepare your own meals, if you like (though breakfast is provided).

800 Fairview Ave. N., Seattle, WA 98109. ✆ **800/331-3131** or 206/624-6000. Fax 206/223-8160. www. marriott.com/sealu. 234 units. $199–$299 1-bedroom suite; $289–$429 2-bedroom suite. Rates include full breakfast. Children 17 and under stay free in parent's room. AE, DC, DISC, MC, V. Parking $19. Pets accepted ($10 per night). **Amenities:** Indoor lap pool; exercise room. *In room:* Kitchen.

Westin Seattle (Kids)   With its distinctive cylindrical towers, the 47-story Westin is the tallest hotel in Seattle, and, consequently, rooms on the upper floors offer breathtaking vistas of the city and surrounding mountains. Guest rooms here are some of the nicest in town, and both the north and south towers of the hotel have undergone extensive renovations. Couple those great views (seen through unusual curved walls of glass) with the Westin's plush "Heavenly Beds," and you'll be sleeping on clouds both literally and figuratively. The hotel, unlike most downtown properties, has a pool, making it a good choice for families.

1900 Fifth Ave., Seattle, WA 98101. ✆ **800/937-8461** or 206/728-1000. Fax 206/728-2259. www.westin. com/seattle. 891 units. $169–$399 double; from $495 suite. Children 17 and under stay free in parent's room. AE, DC, DISC, MC, V. Valet parking $38; self-parking $35. Pets accepted. **Amenities:** 2 restaurants; large indoor pool; exercise room and access to nearby health club.

WHERE TO DINE

As everyone on Earth must know by now, Seattle takes coffee *very* seriously. This is where **Starbucks** got its start, and though they are now ubiquitous everywhere, there was a time when there was only one Starbucks—if you feel the need to make a pilgrimage, the first-ever store is still at Pike Place Market.

Anthony's Pier 66 & Bell Street Diner   SEAFOOD   The Anthony's chain has several outposts around the Seattle area, but this is the most convenient and versatile. It has not only an upper-end, stylish seafood restaurant with good waterfront views, but also a moderately priced casual restaurant and a walk-up counter. The upscale crowd heads upstairs for Asian- and Southwestern-inspired seafood dishes, while the more cost-conscious stay downstairs at the Bell Street Diner, where meals are much easier on the wallet (though far less creative). You can save money with the $19 four-course sunset dinners that are served Monday through Friday between 4 and 6pm.

2201 Alaskan Way. ✆ **206/448-6688.** www.anthonys.com. Reservations recommended at Pier 66, not taken at Bell Street Diner. Pier 66 main courses $8–$40; Bell Street Diner main courses $7–$19. AE, DISC, MC, V. Pier 66 Mon–Thurs 5–9:30pm, Fri–Sat 5–10pm, Sun 5–9pm; Bell Street Diner Mon–Thurs 11am–10pm, Fri–Sat 11am–10:30pm, Sun 11am–9pm.

Canlis NORTHWEST   Canlis has been around since 1950, yet still manages to keep up with the times. Its stylish interior mixes contemporary decor with Asian antiques; its Northwest cuisine, with Asian and Continental influences, keeps both traditionalists and more adventurous diners content. Steaks from the copper grill are perennial favorites. To finish, have the Grand Marnier soufflé. They also have one of the best wine lists in town.

A Sporting Town

With professional football, baseball, and basketball teams, Seattle is definitely a city of sports fans, and it's a great place to take in a game.

Of all of Seattle's major league sports teams, none is more beloved than baseball's **Seattle Mariners** (**(** **206/346-4000** or 346-4001; www.seattle mariners.com). The Mariners' beautiful, retro-style **Safeco Field** is one of only a handful of stadiums with a retractable roof, allowing the Mariners a real grass field without the worry of getting rained out.

If you're wondering where the Seattle SuperSonics went, it was Oklahoma City, where new owners moved them in 2008. Pro hoops are still represented, however, by the WNBA's **Seattle Storm** (**(** **877/WNBA-TIX** [962-2849] or 206/217-WNBA [217-9622]; www.storm.wnba.com), league champions in 2004 led by stars like Olympic gold medalist Sue Bird and MVP Lauren Jackson.

Although the NFL's **Seattle Seahawks** (**(** **888/NFL-HAWK** [635-4295] or 206/381-7816; www.seahawks.com) didn't win the Superbowl in 2006, they came close, and best of all, they developed a little respect in their hometown. The Seahawks play at **Qwest Field,** Occidental Avenue South, on the site of the old Kingdome.

Ticketmaster (**(** **206/628-0123;** www.ticketmaster.com) sells tickets to almost all sporting events in the Seattle area. You'll find Ticketmaster outlets at area Fred Meyer stores and Tower Records.

2576 Aurora Ave. N. (**(** **206/283-3313.** www.canlis.com. Reservations highly recommended. Main courses $28–$72; chef's tasting menu $85 ($130 with wines). AE, DC, DISC, MC, V. Mon–Thurs 5:30–9pm; Fri–Sat 5:30–10pm.

Dahlia Lounge PAN-ASIAN/NORTHWEST   One bite of any dish will convince you that this is one of Seattle's finest restaurants. Mouthwatering Dungeness crab cakes, a bow to chef Tom Douglas's Delaware roots, are the house specialty and should not be missed. The menu—influenced by the far side of the Pacific Rim—changes regularly, with the lunch menu featuring some of the same offerings at lower prices. It's way too easy to fill up on the restaurant's breads, which are baked in the adjacent Dahlia Bakery, and for dessert, it takes a Herculean effort to resist the crème caramel and the coconut-cream pie.

2001 Fourth Ave. (**(** **206/682-4142.** www.tomdouglas.com. Reservations highly recommended. Main courses $12–$32 lunch, $22–$38 dinner. AE, DC, DISC, MC, V. Mon–Fri 11:30am–2:30pm; Sun–Thurs 5–10pm; Fri–Sat 5–11pm.

Etta's Seafood SEAFOOD   Tom Douglas's strictly seafood (well, almost) restaurant, Etta's, is smack in the middle of the Pike Place Market neighborhood and, of course, serves Douglas's signature crab cakes, which are not to be missed (and if they're not on the menu, just ask). Don't ignore your side dishes, either; they can be exquisite and are usually enough to share around the table. Stylish contemporary decor sets the mood, making this place as popular with locals as it is with tourists.

2020 Western Ave. ✆ **206/443-6000.** www.tomdouglas.com. Reservations recommended. Main courses $12–$34 lunch, $12–$34 dinner. AE, DC, DISC, MC, V. Mon–Thurs 11:30am–9:30pm; Fri 11:30am–10:30pm; Sat 9am–3pm and 4–10pm; Sun 9am–3pm and 4–9pm.

Flying Fish NORTHWEST/SEAFOOD   Flying Fish is the main stage for celebrity chef Christine Keff, and not only does this restaurant offer bold combinations of vibrant flavors, but it also serves dinner until 1am nightly. Every dish is a work of art, and with small plates, large plates, and platters for sharing, diners can sample a wide variety of the kitchen's creations. The menu changes daily, so you can be sure that the latest seasonal ingredients will show up. Desserts are festive little miniature parties on each plate, and the wine list is vast.

2234 First Ave. ✆ **206/728-8595.** www.flyingfishseattle.com. Reservations recommended. Main courses $11–$15 lunch, $18–$38 dinner. AE, MC, V. Mon–Fri 11:30am–2pm; daily 5pm–1am.

Noodle Ranch PAN-ASIAN   This Belltown hole in the wall serves Pan-Asian cuisine for the hip but financially challenged crowd. It's a lively scene, and the food is packed with intense and often unfamiliar flavors. The Mekong grill—rice noodles with a rice-wine/vinegar-and-herb dressing topped with grilled pork, chicken, beef, or tofu—is a must. You'll also find Laotian cucumber salad and other vegetarian options. Although the place is frequently packed, the wait's not usually too long.

2228 Second Ave. ✆ **206/728-0463.** Reservations not accepted. Main courses $8.25–$14. AE, DISC, MC, V. Mon–Fri 11am–10pm; Sat noon–10pm.

Palace Kitchen AMERICAN REGIONAL/MEDITERRANEAN   Aside from Serious Pie, Tom Douglas's pizza place, this is the most casual of Douglas's five Seattle restaurants. The atmosphere is urban chic, with cement pillars, simple wood booths, and a few tables in the front window, which overlooks the monorail tracks. The menu is short and features a nightly selection of unusual cheeses and different preparations from the apple-wood grill. Entrees are usually simple and delicious, ranging from the Palace burger royale (one of the best burger in Seattle) to apple-wood grilled *wagyu* flank steak. For dessert, the coconut-cream pie is an absolute must.

2030 Fifth Ave. ✆ **206/448-2001.** www.tomdouglas.com. Reservations accepted only for parties of 6 or more. Main courses $13–$30. AE, DC, DISC, MC, V. Daily 5pm–1am.

Palisade NORTHWEST   With a panorama that sweeps from downtown to West Seattle and across the sound to the Olympic Mountains, Palisade has one of the best views of any Seattle waterfront restaurant and is always my choice for a splurge. It also happens to have fine food and inventive interior design (incorporating a saltwater pond, complete with fish, sea anemones, and starfish, right in the middle of the dining room). The menu features both fish and meats prepared in both a wood-fired oven and a wood-fired rotisserie. The three-course sunset dinners, served before 6pm, cost $30 and are a great way to enjoy this place on a budget. Palisade also has an excellent and very popular Sunday brunch. *Note:* The restaurant is not easy to find; call for directions or to have the restaurant's complimentary limo pick you up at your hotel.

Elliott Bay Marina, 2601 W. Marina Place. ✆ **206/285-1000.** www.palisaderestaurant.com. Reservations recommended. Main courses $11–$18 lunch, $18–$59 dinner; Sun brunch $28. AE, DC, DISC, MC, V. Mon–Fri 11:15am–2pm; Mon–Thurs 5–9pm; Fri 5–10pm; Sat 4–10pm; Sun 9:30am–2pm and 4–9pm.

Rover's NORTHWEST/VEGETARIAN   In a quaint clapboard house behind a chic little shopping center in Madison Valley, Rover's is one of Seattle's most acclaimed restaurants. Thierry Rautureau, its award-winning chef, received classical French training before falling in love with the Northwest. *Voilà!* Northwest cuisine with a French accent. The delicacies on the frequently changing menu are enough to send the most jaded of gastronomes into fits of indecision. Luckily, you can opt for one of the fixed-price dinners. Notable creations include scrambled eggs with lime crème fraîche and caviar, and hibiscus-infused sorbet. Vegetarians, take note: You won't find many vegetarian feasts to compare with what's served here.

2808 E. Madison St. ✆ **206/325-7442.** www.rovers-seattle.com. Reservations required. Main courses $17–$23; prix-fixe 3-course lunch $35; 5-course menu degustation $80 (vegetarian) and $95; chef's 8-course grand menu $130. AE, MC, V. Tues–Thurs 6–9:30pm; Fri noon–1:30pm and 5:30–9:30pm; Sat 5:30–9:30pm.

Serafina ITALIAN   A bit off the beaten tourist track but close to downtown, Serafina is one of our favorites. It has a touch of sophistication, but overall it's a relaxed neighborhood place where the rustic, romantic atmosphere underscores the earthy, country-style dishes. It's hard to resist ordering at least one of the bruschetta appetizers. Among the pasta offerings, don't pass up the delicious veal meatballs in a green olive–tomato sauce served over penne. Live music (mostly jazz and Latin) plays Friday through Sunday nights and for Sunday brunch.

2043 Eastlake Ave. E. ✆ **206/323-0807.** www.serafinaseattle.com. Reservations recommended. Main courses $10–$17 lunch, $18–$28 dinner. AE, MC, V. Mon–Fri 11:30am–2:30pm; Sun 10am–2pm; Sun–Thurs 5:30–10pm; Fri–Sat 5:30–11pm (bar menu nightly until midnight).

Tilth NEW AMERICAN   Tilth is one of the nation's only restaurants to receive organic certification from Oregon Tilth (an organization that sets organic standards), but don't confuse organic with granola-crunchy hippie food. Chef Maria Hines's menu emphasizes fresh, seasonal ingredients in dishes that seem simple yet are packed with flavor. While the menu changes with the seasons, you can almost always count on finding the mini duck burgers on the menu. One of my favorite aspects of the menu here is that everything is available as an appetizer or an entree, so if you want to try several dishes, you can.

1411 N. 45th St. ✆ **206/633-0801.** www.tilthrestaurant.com. Reservations recommended. Main courses $22–$28; Mon-only 4-course dinner $45 ($65 with wine). MC, V. Mon–Thurs 5–10pm; Fri 5–10:30pm; Sat 10am–2pm and 5–10:30pm; Sun 10am–2pm and 5–10pm.

SEATTLE AFTER DARK

To find out what's on when you're in town, pick up a free copy of *Seattle Weekly* (www. seattleweekly.com), Seattle's arts-and-entertainment newspaper. You'll find it in bookstores, convenience stores, grocery stores, newsstands, and newspaper boxes around downtown and other neighborhoods. On Friday, the *Seattle Times* includes a section called "Ticket," a guide to the week's arts-and-entertainment offerings.

Ticketmaster (✆ **206/292-ARTS** [292-2787]; www.ticketmaster.com) sells tickets to a wide variety of performances and events in the Seattle area. For half-price day-of-show tickets (and 1-day advance tickets for matinees) to a wide variety of performances, stop by **Ticket/Ticket** (✆ **206/324-2744;** www.ticketwindowonline.com), which has four sales booths in the Seattle area: one in Pike Place Market, one in Pacific Place mall, one on Capitol Hill, and one in Bellevue. The Pike Place location, in the Market information booth at First Avenue and Pike Street, and the Pacific Place location are open Tuesday through Sunday from noon to 6pm. The Capitol Hill booth is in the Broadway Market, 401 Broadway E., and is open Tuesday through Saturday from noon to 7pm and Sunday from noon to 6pm. The Bellevue booth is in the Meydenbauer Center, 11100 NE Sixth

St. (at 112th Ave.), and is open Tuesday through Sunday from noon to 6pm. Ticket/Ticket charges a small service fee, the amount of which depends on the ticket price.

THE PERFORMING ARTS   The **Seattle Opera** (© **800/426-1619** or 206/389-7676; www.seattleopera.org), which performs at Seattle Center's Marion Oliver McCaw Hall, is considered one of the finest opera companies in the country, and *the* Wagnerian opera company in the United States. In addition to classical operas, the season usually includes a more contemporary production.

The 90-musician **Seattle Symphony** (© **866/833-4747** or 206/215-4747; www.seattlesymphony.org), which performs in the acoustically superb Benaroya Hall, offers an amazingly diverse musical season that runs from September to July.

The **Seattle Repertory Theatre** (© **877/900-9285** or 206/443-2222; www.seattlerep.org), which performs at the Bagley Wright and Leo K. theaters, Seattle Center, 155 Mercer St., is one of the top regional theaters in the country and has originated many award-winning plays. The Rep's season runs from September to May, and productions range from classics to world premieres.

With a season that runs from April to December, the **Intiman Theatre** (© **206/269-1900**; www.intiman.org), which performs at the Intiman Playhouse, Seattle Center, 201 Mercer St., fills in the gap left by those months when the Seattle Rep's lights are dark. Performing in the historic Eagles Building theater adjacent to the Washington State Convention and Trade Center, **A Contemporary Theater (ACT),** Kreielsheimer Place, 700 Union St. (© **206/292-7676**; www.acttheatre.org), offers slightly more adventurous productions than the other major theater companies in Seattle, though it's not nearly as avant-garde as some of the smaller companies. The season runs from March to December.

The **Pacific Northwest Ballet,** Marion Oliver McCaw Hall, 301 Mercer St. (© **206/441-2424**; www.pnb.org), is Seattle's premier dance company. During the season, which runs from September to June, the company presents a range of classics, new works, and (the company's specialty) pieces choreographed by George Balanchine. This company's performance of *The Nutcracker,* with outstanding dancing and sets and costumes by children's book author Maurice Sendak, is the highlight of every season. **On the Boards,** Behnke Center for Contemporary Performance, 100 W. Roy St. (© **206/217-9888**; www.ontheboards.org), is the area's best modern-dance venue.

THE CLUB & MUSIC SCENE   If you want to go clubbing and barhopping, there's no better place to start than **Pioneer Square.** Good times are guaranteed, whether you want to hear a live band, hang out in a good old-fashioned bar, or dance. Keep in mind that this neighborhood tends to attract a very rowdy crowd (lots of frat boys) and can be pretty rough late at night. **Belltown,** north of Pike Place Market, is another good place to club-hop. Clubs here are way more style-conscious than those in Pioneer Square and tend to attract 20- and 30-something trendsetters.

With a demented-looking clown for a logo and located in a space that has housed numerous clubs over the years, **Neumo's,** 925 E. Pike St. (© **206/709-9467**; www.neumos.com), is Seattle's leading club for indie rock bands that haven't yet developed a big enough following to play the Showbox.

The **Showbox at the Market,** 1426 First Ave. (© **206/628-3151**; www.showboxonline.com), books a variety of rock acts, many with a national following. Cool and sophisticated, **Dimitriou's Jazz Alley,** 2033 Sixth Ave. (© **206/441-9729**; www.jazzalley.com), has been Seattle's premier jazz club for more than 25 years, featuring only the best performers. The classic **Century Ballroom,** 915 E. Pine St. (© **206/324-7263**; www.centuryballroom.com), plays host to some of the best touring acts to come to town.

This is Seattle's top spot for swing and salsa dancing. Established in 1892, the **Central** **Saloon,** 207 First Ave. S. (© **206/622-0209;** www.centralsaloon.com), is a Seattle institution. It's a must-stop during a night out in Pioneer Square. You might catch sounds ranging from funk to reggae.

THE BAR SCENE   Belltown's **Virginia Inn,** 1937 First Ave. (© **206/728-1937**), has a decidedly old Seattle feel, due in large part to the fact that this place has been around since 1903. Best of all, this is a nonsmoking bar and it serves French food! **Marcus' Martini Heaven,** 88 Yesler Way (© **206/624-3323;** www.marcusmartiniheaven.com), is hidden down a flight of stairs just off First Avenue in Pioneer Square. Search this place out, and you'll be drinking with the ghosts of the city's past and the lounge lizards of today.

You might see members of the Seahawks or Mariners at Pioneer Square's **FX McRory's,** 419 Occidental Ave. S. (© **206/623-4800;** www.fxmcrorys.com), an upscale sports bar with an oyster bar and a large selection of bourbons and microbrews. For good stout and strong ales at a local brewpub, try Capitol Hill's **Elysian Brewing Company,** 1221 E. Pike St. (© **206/860-1920;** www.elysianbrewing.com). South of Pioneer Square and popular before or after sports events is **Pyramid Ale House,** 1201 First Ave. S. (© **206/682-3377;** www.pyramidbrew.com), part of the brewery that makes Thomas Kemper lagers and Pyramid ales.

THE GAY & LESBIAN SCENE   Capitol Hill is Seattle's main gay neighborhood, where you'll find the greatest concentration of gay and lesbian bars and dance clubs. Look for the readily available *Seattle Gay News* (© **206/324-4297;** www.sgn.org), where you'll find ads for many of the city's gay bars and nightclubs. For dancing, head to **Neighbours,** 1509 Broadway Ave. (© **206/324-5358;** www.neighboursonline.com). A longtime favorite of the lesbian community is **Wildrose,** 1021 E. Pike St. (© **206/324-9210;** www.thewildrosebar.com), a friendly restaurant/bar that claims to be the oldest lesbian bar on the West Coast.

2 THE SAN JUAN ISLANDS

There's something magical about traveling to the San Juans. Some people say it's the light, some say it's the sea air, some say it's the weather (temperatures are always moderate, and rainfall is roughly half what it is in Seattle). Whatever it is that so entrances, the San Juans have become the favorite getaway of urban Washingtonians, and if you make time to visit these idyllic islands, we think you, too, will fall under their spell. On the downside, the islands have been discovered by tourists and, in summer, there can be waits of several hours to get on a ferry with your car. One solution is to come over on foot or with a bicycle. You can then get around by renting a car or bike, hopping on the island shuttle buses, or calling taxis.

The San Juans consist of at least 175 named islands, or up to 786 if you include all the rocks and reefs that poke above the water at low tide. Only three (San Juan, Orcas, and Lopez) have anything in the way of tourist accommodations. *Warning:* Don't expect to find a place to stay in summer if you come out here without a room reservation.

ESSENTIALS

GETTING THERE   **By Boat**   **Washington State Ferries** (© **800/84-FERRY** [843-3779] or 888/808-7977 in Washington, or 206/464-6400; www.wsdot.wa.gov/ferries) operates ferries between Anacortes and four of the San Juan Islands (Lopez, Shaw, Orcas, and San Juan) and Sidney, British Columbia (on Vancouver Island near Victoria). Foot passengers are welcome. There are also passenger-ferry services from several cities around the region. **Victoria Clipper** (© **800/888-2535,** 206/448-5000, or 250/382-8100; www.victoriaclipper.com) operates excursion boats between Seattle and Friday Harbor on San Juan Island. There are also boats that go to Victoria, British Columbia. *Note:* To cross into Canada and return to the United States by ferry, you will need either a **passport** or both proof of citizenship and a government-issued photo ID (such as a driver's license).

By Plane **Kenmore Air** (© **866/435-9524** or 425/486-1257; www.kenmoreair.com) offers floatplane flights that take off from either Lake Union or the north end of Lake Washington. Flights go to Friday Harbor and Roche Harbor on San Juan Island; Rosario Resort, Deer Harbor, and West Sound on Orcas Island; and the Lopez Islander on Lopez Island. You can also get from Sea-Tac Airport or downtown Seattle to the San Juan Islands ferry terminal in Anacortes on the **Airporter Shuttle** (© **866/235-5247** or 360/380-8800; www.airporter.com).

VISITOR INFORMATION For information on all the islands, contact the **San Juan Islands Visitors Bureau,** P.O. Box 1330, Friday Harbor, WA 98250 (© **888/468-3701;** www.visitsanjuans.com).

GETTING AROUND Cars can be rented from **Susie's Mopeds,** 125 Nichols St. (© **800/532-0087** or 360/378-5244; www.susiesmopeds.com), which is 1 block from the top of the ferry lanes in Friday Harbor. Susie's rents scooters and mopeds as well, for $25 to $50 per hour or $65 to $130 per day. **San Juan Transit** (© **800/887-8387,** or 360/378-8887 on San Juan Island; www.sanjuantransit.com) operates a shuttle bus on San Juan during the summer. To rent a car on Orcas Island, contact **M&W Auto Sales** (© **800/323-6037** or 360/378-2886; www.interisland.net/mandw).

SAN JUAN ISLAND

San Juan Island is the most populous and touristy of the islands. **Friday Harbor,** where the ferry docks, is the county seat for San Juan County and the only real town on all the islands. Friday Harbor's simple wood-frame buildings date back to the turn of the 20th century and now house numerous shops, restaurants, motels, and inns.

Whale-watching is one of the most popular summer activities in the San Juans. Stop by the **Whale Museum,** 62 First St. N. (© **360/378-4710;** www.whale-museum.org), where you can see whale skeletons and models of whales, and learn all about the area's pods of orcas (also known as killer whales). Admission is $6 for adults, $5 for seniors, and $3 for students and children 5 to 18.

San Juan Vineyards, 3136 Roche Harbor Rd. (© **360/378-9463;** www.sanjuan vineyards.com), makes wines both from grapes grown off the island and from its own estate-grown Siegrebbe and Madeline Angevine grapes. The tasting room is housed in an old schoolhouse built in 1896. It's open daily in summer.

A little farther north, you'll come to **Roche Harbor,** once the site of large limestone quarries that supplied lime to much of the West Coast. Many of the quarries' old structures are still visible, giving this area a decaying industrial look, but amid the abandoned machinery stands the historic **Hotel de Haro,** a simple whitewashed wooden building with verandas across its two floors. Stop to admire the old-fashioned marina and colorful gardens; the deck of the hotel's lounge is one of the best places on the island to linger over a drink. In an old pasture on the edge of the resort property, you'll find the **Westcott Bay Sculpture Park** (© **360/370-5050;** www.wbay.org), a park that includes more than

100 works of art set in grassy fields and along the shores of a small pond. Back in the woods near the resort is an unusual **mausoleum,** which was erected by the founder of the quarries and the Hotel de Haro.

South of Roche Harbor, on West Valley Road, you'll come to the **English Camp** unit of **San Juan Island National Historical Park** (© 360/378-2902; www.nps.gov/sajh). The park commemorates San Juan Island Pig War, one of North America's most unusual and least remembered confrontations. San Juan Island nearly became the site of a battle between the British and the Americans in 1859, when a British pig on San Juan Island decided to have dinner in an American garden while the two countries were having a border dispute.

The English Camp unit of the park is set amid shady trees and spacious lawns; the camp is the picture of British civility. There's even a formal garden surrounded by a white picket fence. You can look inside the reconstructed buildings and imagine the days when this was one of the most far-flung corners of the British Empire. If you're full of energy, hike up to the top of 650-foot **Mount Young** for a beautiful panorama of the island. An easier hike is out to the end of **Bell Point.**

South of English Camp, watch for the Mitchell Bay Road turnoff. This connects to the Westside Road, which leads down the island's west coast. Along here, you'll find **San Juan County Park,** a great spot for a picnic. A little farther south, you'll come to **Lime Kiln Point State Park** (© 360/378-2044; www.parks.wa.gov), the country's first whale-watching park and a great place to spot these gentle giants in summer.

Outdoor Activities

BIKING   Winding country roads are ideal for leisurely trips. If you didn't bring your own wheels, you can rent a bike in Friday Harbor from **Island Bicycles,** 380 Argyle St. (© 360/378-4941; www.islandbicycles.com), which charges $9 to $18 per hour (2-hr. minimum) or $36 to $72 per day.

SEA KAYAKING   Between mid-April and mid-October, sea-kayak tours are offered by **San Juan Outfitters** (© 866/810-1483 or 360/378-1962; www.sanjuanislandoutfitters. com), which operates out of Roche Harbor, at the north end of the island. You'll pay $69 for a 3-hour tour and $85 for a 5-hour tour. This company also operates out of Friday Harbor. **Crystal Seas Kayaking** (© 877/732-7877 or 360/378-4223; www.crystalseas. com), which paddles the waters off the west side of San Juan, does anything from 3-hour tours ($69) and sunset tours ($69) to all-day tours ($89) and multiday trips.

WHALE-WATCHING   In the summer, 3- to 4-hour whale-watching cruises from Friday Harbor are offered by **San Juan Safaris** (© 800/450-6858 or 360/378-1323; www. sanjuansafaris.com), which charges $69 for adults and $49 for children 2 to 12. If you're staying up at the north end of the island, you can go out with **San Juan Outfitters** (© 866/810-1483 or 360/378-1962; www.sanjuanislandoutfitters.com), which offers 3- to 4-hour whale-watching tours for $69 adults, $49 children ages 2 to 12. For a speedier and more personalized whale-watching excursion, book a tour with **Maya's Westside Charters** (© 360/378-7996; www.mayaswhalewatch.biz), which operates the fastest whale-watching boat in the islands and takes out only six people at a time. A 3-hour tour costs $69 for adults and $59 for children 12 and under.

WHERE TO STAY & DINE

Friday Harbor House, 130 West St., Friday Harbor (© 866/722-7356 or 360/378-8455; www.fridayharborhouse.com), is a luxurious contemporary hotel. The bluff-top location ensures excellent views, and rooms contain fireplaces, whirlpool tubs, and balconies. In some rooms, you can relax in your tub and gaze at both the view out the window and your own crackling fire. The dining room is one of the best on the island, offering a seasonal menu with an emphasis on Northwest cuisine. Rates run $205 to $325 double in summer and include continental breakfast.

Olympic Lights Bed & Breakfast, 146 Starlight Way, Friday Harbor ((🕐) **888/211-6195** or 360/378-3186; www.olympiclights.com), on San Juan's dry southwestern tip, is a Victorian farmhouse surrounded by windswept meadows. The Ra Room has a bay window with a glorious view. Rates ($145–$155 double in summer) include full breakfast; the B&B doesn't take credit cards.

The **Place Bar & Grill,** 1 Spring St. ((🕐) **360/378-8707**), is the island's finest waterfront restaurant. It aims to attract the upscale Seattle market with its regularly changing seafood menu. Main courses run $20 to $40. A new favorite eatery—**Coho Restaurant,** 120 Nichols St. ((🕐) **360/378-6330;** www.cohorestaurant.com)—is a tiny place that serves very fresh and very creative cuisine.

ORCAS ISLAND

Shaped like a horseshoe and named for an 18th-century Mexican viceroy (not for the area's orca whales, as is commonly assumed), Orcas Island has long been a popular summer vacation spot and is the most beautiful of the San Juan Islands. Orcas is a particular favorite of nature lovers, who come to enjoy the views of green rolling pastures, forested mountains, and fjordlike bays. **Eastsound** is the largest town on the island, with several interesting shops and good restaurants.

Several pottery shops are located around the island. A few miles west of Eastsound off Enchanted Forest Road is **Orcas Island Pottery,** 338 Old Pottery Rd. ((🕐) **360/376-2813;** www.orcasislandpottery.com), the oldest pottery studio in the Northwest. Between Eastsound and Orcas on Horseshoe Highway is **Crow Valley Pottery,** 2274 Orcas Rd. ((🕐) **360/376-4260;** www.crowvalley.com), housed in an 1866 log cabin. And on the east side of the island in the community of Olga, you'll find **Orcas Island Artworks,** Horseshoe Highway ((🕐) **360/376-4408;** www.orcasisland.com/artworks), which is full of beautiful work by island artists.

Outdoor Activities

Covering 5,252 acres of the island, **Moran State Park** ((🕐) **360/902-8844;** www.parks. wa.gov) is the largest park in the San Juans and the main destination for most island visitors. If the weather is clear, you'll enjoy great views from the summit of Mount Constitution, which rises 2,409 feet above Puget Sound. There are also five lakes, 33 miles of hiking trails, and an environmental learning center. Popular park activities include fishing, hiking, boating, mountain biking, and camping (for campsite reservations, contact **Washington State Parks** at (🕐) **888/226-7688;** www.parks.wa.gov/reserve.asp). The park is off Horseshoe Highway, approximately 13 miles from the ferry landing.

BIKING Although Orcas is considered the most challenging of the San Juan Islands for biking, plenty of cyclists pedal the island's roads. **Dolphin Bay Bicycles** ((🕐) **360/376-4157;** www.rockisland.com/~dolphin), located just to the right as you get off the ferry, has long been our favorite place in the islands to rent a bike. Bikes rent for $30 per day, $70 for 3 days, and $100 per week. Guided bike rides are also sometimes available.

WHALE-WATCHING If you want to see some of the orca whales for which the San Juans are famous, you can take a whale-watching excursion with **Deer Harbor Charters** ((🕐) **800/544-5758** or 360/376-5989; www.deerharborcharters.com), which operates out

Odd Fellows, Good Food!

Eastsound's **Odd Fellows Hall,** 112 Haven Rd. (© **360/376-5640;** www.oddshall. org), a block off Main Street on the road to picturesque Madrona Point, has for years been a starting point for creative Orcas Island cooks. From year to year, you never know what sort of restaurant you'll find here in this historic building, but it's almost always good and a well-guarded local secret.

of both Deer Harbor and Rosario Resort, and charges $49 to $69 for adults and $35 to $44 for children 13 and under; or with **Orcas Island Eclipse Charters** (© **800/376-6566** or 360/376-6566; www.orcasislandwhales.com), which operates out of the Orcas Island ferry dock and charges $64 for adults and $42 for children.

Where to Stay & Dine

The **Spring Bay Inn,** Olga (© 360/376-5531; www.springbayinn.com), is one of the only waterfront B&Bs in the San Juans. Innkeepers Sandy Playa and Carl Burger, both retired park rangers, make a stay here both fun and educational. You can soak in the hot tub on the beach, spot bald eagles, hike on the nature trails, and go for a guided sea-kayak tour. Four rooms have fireplaces, two have views from their tubs, and two have balconies; all have fridges. Rates ($240–$280 double) include continental breakfast, brunch, and a daily kayak tour. The **Turtleback Farm Inn,** 1981 Crow Valley Rd., Eastsound (© **800/376-4914** or 360/376-4914; www.turtlebackinn.com), is a restored farmhouse overlooking 80 idyllic acres of farmland at the foot of Turtleback Mountain. Simply furnished with antiques, the rooms range from cozy to spacious. The four rooms in the Orchard House are among the biggest and most luxurious on the island (with gas fireplaces, claw-foot tubs, balconies, wood floors, and fridges). Rates ($100–$245 double) include full breakfast.

Café Olga, Horseshoe Highway, Olga (© 360/376-5098), is the best place for breakfast or lunch. Everything here is homemade, using fresh local produce whenever possible. Try the blackberry pie with Lopez Island Creamery ice cream. This building also houses Orcas Island Artworks, a gallery representing more than 70 local artists. Main courses run $10 to $18. You can now get decent Thai food in Eastsound at **Thai Sisters Café,** 529 Shaner Lane (© **360/376-3993**).

3 THE OLYMPIC PENINSULA

Olympic National Park is unique in the Lower 48 for its temperate rainforests, which are found in the valleys of the Hoh, Queets, Bogachiel, Clearwater, and Quinault rivers. Rainfall here can exceed 150 inches per year, trees grow nearly 300 feet tall, and mosses hang from every limb. Trails lead from these valleys (and other points around the peninsula) into the interior of the park, providing access to hundreds of miles of hiking trails. In fact, trails are the only access to most of the park, which has fewer than a dozen roads, none of which lead more than a few miles into the park.

Within a few short miles of the park's rainforests, the jagged, snowcapped Olympic Mountains rise to the 7,965-foot peak of Mount Olympus and produce an Alpine zone where no trees can grow. Together, elevation and heavy rainfall combine to form 60 glaciers within the park. It is these glaciers that have carved the Olympic Mountains into the jagged peaks that mesmerize visitors and beckon to hikers and climbers. Rugged and spectacular sections of the coast have also been preserved as part of the park, and offshore waters have been designated the Olympic Coast National Marine Sanctuary. June through September are much less wet than the other months. In winter, the road to Hurricane Ridge can be iffy, as it's plowed only Saturday through Monday.

ESSENTIALS

GETTING THERE   By Plane   Kenmore Air Express (© 866/435-9524 or 425/486-1257; www.kenmoreair.com) flies between Seattle's Boeing Field and Port Angeles's William Fairchild Airport (with a free shuttle from Seattle-Tacoma International Airport to Boeing Field). Rental cars are available in Port Angeles from **Budget** (© 800/527-0700; www.budget.com).

By Car   U.S. 101 circles Olympic National Park with main park entrances south of Port Angeles, at Lake Crescent, at Sol Duc, and at the Hoh River. The Port Angeles park entrance is 48 miles west of Port Townsend and 55 miles east of Forks.

VISITOR INFORMATION   For information on the park, contact **Olympic National Park,** 600 E. Park Ave., Port Angeles, WA 98362 (© 360/565-3130 or 565-3131; www.nps.gov/olym). For information on Port Angeles and the rest of the Olympic Peninsula, contact the **Olympic Peninsula Visitor Bureau,** 338 W. First St., Ste. 104 (P.O. Box 670), Port Angeles, WA 98362 (© 800/942-4042 or 360/452-8552; www.olympic peninsula.org), or the **Port Angeles Regional Chamber of Commerce Visitor Center,** 121 E. Railroad Ave., Port Angeles, WA 98362 (© 360/452-2363; www.portangeles.org). The park entry fee is $15 per vehicle.

Port Angeles is also home to the national park headquarters and the **Olympic National Park Visitor Center,** 3002 Mount Angeles Rd. (© 360/565-3130), on the south edge of town. In addition to offering lots of information, maps, and books about the park, the center has exhibits on the park's flora and fauna. It's open daily throughout the year, with hours varying with the seasons.

The park entry fee is $15 per motor vehicle or $5 per person for pedestrians, motorcyclists, and bicyclists.

SEEING THE HIGHLIGHTS
The North Side

From the **Olympic Park National Visitor Center,** continue 17 miles up to Hurricane Ridge, which offers breathtaking views of the park. Several trails lead into the park from here, and several day hikes are possible. The 3-mile **Hurricane Hill Trail** and the 1-mile **Meadow Loop Trail** are the most scenic. Stop by the **Hurricane Ridge Visitor Center** to see its exhibits on plants and wildlife; this is a good place to learn about the fragile nature of this beautiful Alpine landscape.

West of Port Angeles on U.S. 101 lies **Lake Crescent,** a glacier-carved lake. Near the east end of the lake, you'll find the 1-mile trail to 90-foot-high **Marymere Falls** and the **Storm King Ranger Station** (© 360/928-3380). You can rent boats during the warmer months at several places on the lake. **Lake Crescent Lodge** has rowboats for rent ($9 per hr.), while the **Fairholm General Store** (© 360/928-3020), at the lake's west end, has both rowboats and kayaks ($9 per hr.) available.

Continuing west from Lake Crescent, watch for the turnoff to **Sol Duc Hot Springs** (© 866/4-SOLDUC [476-5382]; www.visitsolduc.com). For 14 miles, the road follows the Soleduck River, passing the Salmon Cascades along the way. Sol Duc Hot Springs were for centuries considered healing waters by local Indians, and after white settlers arrived in the area, the springs became a popular resort. In addition to the hot swimming pool and soaking tubs, you'll find cabins, a campground, a restaurant, and a snack bar. The springs are open daily from early March to late October; admission is $11 for adults, $8 for children ages 4 to 12. A 4.5-mile loop trail leads from the hot springs to **Sol Duc Falls,** which are among the most photographed falls in the park.

The West Side

The western regions of Olympic National Park can be divided into two sections—the rugged coastal strip and the famous rainforest valleys. Of course, these are the rainiest areas within the park, and many a visitor has called short a vacation here because of rain. Well, what do you expect? It is, after all, a *rainforest.* Come prepared to get wet.

Just outside the northwest corner of the park on U.S. 101, the timber town of Forks serves as the gateway to Olympic National Park's west side. It is the largest community in this northwest corner of the Olympic Peninsula. For more information on the Forks area, contact the **Forks Chamber of Commerce,** 1411 S. Forks Ave. (P.O. Box 1249), Forks, WA 98331 (*C* **800/443-6757** or 360/374-2531; www.forkswa.com). The Forks area is home to quite a few artists' studios and galleries. You can pick up an **Olympic West Arttrek** guide and map to these studios and galleries at the chamber office.

Just west of Forks is the first place you can drive to the Pacific Ocean. At the end of a spur road, you come to the **Quileute Indian Reservation** and the community of La Push. Right in town there's a beach at the mouth of the Quillayute River; however, before you reach La Push, you'll see signs for **Third Beach** and **Second Beach,** which are two of the prettiest beaches on the peninsula. Third Beach is a 1.5-mile walk and Second Beach is just over half a mile from the trail head. **Rialto Beach,** just north of La Push, is another beautiful and rugged beach; it's reached from a turnoff east of La Push. On any of these beaches, keep an eye out for bald eagles, seals, and sea lions.

Hoh River Valley & Ruby Beach

Roughly 8 miles south of Forks is the turnoff for the Hoh River Valley. It's 17 miles up this side road to the **Hoh Rain Forest Visitor Center** (*C* **360/374-6925**), campground, and trail heads. This valley receives an average of 140 inches of rain per year—and as much as 190 inches per year—making it the wettest region in the continental United States. At the visitor center, you can learn all about the natural forces that cause this tremendous rainfall.

To see the effect of so much rain on the landscape, walk the .8-mile **Hall of Mosses Trail,** where the trees (primarily Sitka spruce, western red cedar, and western hemlock) tower 200 feet tall. Here you'll see big-leaf maple trees with limbs draped in thick carpets of mosses. If you're up for a longer walk, try the **Spruce Nature Trail.** If you've come with a backpack, there's no better way to see the park and its habitats than by hiking the **Hoh River Trail,** which is 17 miles long and leads to Glacier Meadows and Blue Glacier on the flanks of Mount Olympus. A herd of elk calls the Hoh Valley home and can sometimes be seen along these trails.

Continuing south on U.S. 101, before crossing the Hoh River, you'll come to a secondary road (Oil City Rd.) that heads west from the Hoh Oxbow campground. From the end of the road, it's a hike of less than a mile to a rocky beach at the **mouth of the Hoh River.** You're likely to see sea lions or harbor seals feeding just offshore, and to the north are several haystack rocks that are nesting sites for numerous seabirds. Primitive camping is permitted on this beach, and from here backpackers can continue hiking for 17 miles north along a pristine wilderness of rugged headlands and beaches.

U.S. 101 finally reaches the coast at **Ruby Beach,** noted for its pink sand. The highway parallels the wave-swept coastline for another 17 miles. Along this stretch are pull-offs and short trails down to six numbered beaches. Near the south end, you'll find Kalaloch Lodge, which also has a gas station, and the **Kalaloch Ranger Station** (② 360/962-2283), which is usually open only in summer.

Shortly beyond Kalaloch, the highway turns inland again, passing through the community of **Queets** on the river of the same name. If you'd like to do some rainy valley hiking away from the crowds, head up the gravel road to the **Queets campground** to find the trail leading up the valley.

A long stretch of clear-cuts and tree farms, mostly on the Quinault Indian Reservation, will bring you to **Lake Quinault.** Surrounded by forested mountains, this deep lake offers boating and freshwater fishing, as well as more rainforests to explore. This is also a good area for spotting Roosevelt elk.

OUTDOOR ADVENTURES & GUIDED TOURS

With its rugged beaches, rainforest valleys, Alpine meadows, and mountaintop glaciers, the park offers a variety of **hiking** opportunities. Day hikes, overnight trips, and longer backpacking trips are all possible. For several of the most popular backpacking destinations in Olympic National Park (the Ozette Coast Loop, Grand Valley, Royal Basin, Badger Valley, Flapjack Lakes, and Lake Constance), advance-reservation hiking permits are required or highly recommended between May 1 and September 30, and can be made up to 30 days in advance. Reservations can be made by contacting the **Wilderness Information Center** (② 360/565-3100). If you'd like to have a llama carry your gear, contact **Kit's Llamas,** P.O. Box 116, Olalla, WA 98359 (② 253/857-5274; www.northolympic.com/llamas).

The rivers of the Olympic Peninsula are well known for their fighting salmon, steelhead, and trout, and in Lake Crescent and Lake Ozette, you can **fish** for such elusive species as Beardslee and Crescenti trout. No fishing license is necessary to fish for trout on national park rivers and streams or in Lake Crescent or Lake Ozette. However, you will need a state punch card—available wherever fishing licenses are sold—to fish for salmon or steelhead.

If you're more interested in heading out on open water to do a bit of salmon or deep-sea fishing, numerous charter boats operate out of Sekiu and Neah Bay. In Neah Bay, try **King Fisher Charters** (② 888/622-8216; www.kingfisherenterprises.com). Expect to pay from $180 to $220 per person for a day of fishing.

WHERE TO STAY
In & Around Port Angeles

As the peninsula's biggest town and a base for families exploring the national park, Port Angeles abounds in budget hotels. You'll find dozens along U.S. 101 east of downtown. Beyond town, accommodations are scarce, and the places worth recommending tend to be popular. Reserve before heading west from Port Angeles.

Domaine Madeleine, 146 Wildflower Lane, 7 miles east of Port Angeles (② 888/811-8376 or 360/457-4174; www.domainemadeleine.com), is a secluded B&B with a waterfront setting. Rooms are in several different buildings surrounded by colorful gardens, and all have views of the Strait of Juan de Fuca and the mountains beyond. All units have fireplaces and VCRs; four have whirlpool tubs. Rates ($140–$310 double) include full breakfast.

Historic **Lake Crescent Lodge,** 416 Lake Crescent Rd. (© **360/928-3211;** www. lakecrescentlodge.com), 20 miles west of Port Angeles on Lake Crescent, contains rustic wood paneling, a stone fireplace, and a sunroom. Rooms in the main lodge are the oldest, with shared bathrooms. More modern motel-style rooms and cottages are available, some with fireplaces and all with a lake or mountain view. None of the rooms have phones, but the lodge does offer free Wi-Fi. The lodge features a dining room, a lounge, and rowboat rentals. Rates run $68 to $99 for a double without bathroom, $106 to $158 for a double with bathroom, and $132 to $231 for a cottage.

Long a popular family vacation spot, the **Sol Duc Hot Springs Resort,** Sol Duc Road (© **866/4-SOLDUC** [476-5382]; www.visitsolduc.com), 40 miles west of Port Angeles, attracts campers, day-trippers, and resort guests to its three hot spring–fed swimming pools. The grounds are grassy and open, but the forest is at arm's reach. The modern cabins are comfortable, if not spacious. There's an excellent restaurant, a poolside deli, an espresso bar, a grocery store, and massage service. Closed late October to early March. Rates run from $141 to $172 for a cabin for two, including full breakfast.

In the Forks Area

The town of Forks has several inexpensive motels and is a good place to look if you happen to be out this way without a reservation.

Perched on a bluff above the Pacific Ocean, the **Kalaloch Lodge,** 157151 U.S. 101 (© **866/525-2562;** www.visitkalaloch.com), 35 miles south of Forks, has a breathtaking setting and is the national park's only waterfront hotel. Rooms in the old cedar-shingled lodge are the least expensive, but the oceanview bluff cabins are the most in demand. For modern comforts, there are motel-like rooms in the Sea Crest House. You'll find a coffee shop, dining room, general store, and gas station. Book at least 4 months ahead. Rates run from $149 to $159 for a double and $169 to $279 for a cabin in season.

Set on Lake Quinault in the southwest corner of the park, **Lake Quinault Lodge,** 345 S. Shore Rd., Quinault (© **800/562-6672** or 360/288-2900; www.visitlakequinault. com), is the grande dame of the Olympic Peninsula. It possesses an ageless tranquillity, with towering firs and cedars shading the rustic lodge and deck. Some rooms have balconies or fireplaces, but none have TVs or phones. You'll also find a dining room, an indoor pool, a sauna, lawn games, boat rentals, and massages. Rates run from $90 to $175 double in season.

Where to Camp

For general information on national park campgrounds, contact **Olympic National Park** (© **360/565-3130**). Make reservations at the Kalaloch Campground at **Recreation. gov** (© **877/444-6777** or 518/885-3639; www.recreation.gov).

The national park's **Heart o' the Hills Campground** (105 campsites), on Hurricane Ridge Road 5 miles south of the Olympic National Park Visitor Center, is the most convenient campground for exploring the Hurricane Ridge area. On Olympic Hot Springs Road, you'll find both **Elwha Campground** (40 campsites) and **Altair Campground** (30 campsites). The only campground on Lake Crescent is **Fairholme** (88 campsites), at the west end of the lake. The nearby **Sol Duc Campground** (82 campsites), set amid impressive stands of old-growth trees, is adjacent to Sol Duc Hot Springs. The national park's remote **Ozette Campground** (15 campsites), on the north shore of Lake Ozette, is a good choice for people wanting to day-hike out to the beaches on either side of Cape Alava.

The national park's **Mora Campground** (94 campsites) is near Rialto Beach at the mouth of the Quillayute River west of Forks. If you want to say you've camped at the wettest campground in the contiguous United States, head for **Hoh Campground** (88 campsites), in the Hoh River Valley. South of the Hoh River, along the only stretch of U.S. 101 right on the beach, you'll find **Kalaloch Campground** (170 campsites), the national park's largest campground and the only one that takes reservations.

WHERE TO DINE

The casual **Bella Italia,** 118 E. First St. (© **360/457-5442;** www.bellaitaliapa.com), is in the basement of a natural foods store in downtown Port Angeles and serves reliable Italian food. Local seafood makes it onto the menu, including smoked salmon ravioli and steamed mussels and clams. There are also some interesting pizzas, a good selection of wines, and plenty of excellent Italian desserts. Main courses cost $9 to $30.

You can't miss the strikingly painted **C'est Si Bon,** 23 Cedar Park Rd. (© **360/452-8888;** www.cestsibon-frenchcuisine.com), 4 miles south of Port Angeles off U.S. 101. Inside you'll find classic decor, European artwork, chandeliers, and deftly prepared Gallic standards such as French onion soup and escargot. Whatever you have, it will likely be tasty and fresh. Main courses run $24 to $36.

4 MOUNT RAINIER NATIONAL PARK

At 14,410 feet, Mount Rainier is the highest point in Washington, and to the sun-starved residents of Seattle, the dormant volcano is a giant weather gauge. Either "the Mountain" is out and the weather is good, or it isn't (out or good). And when it's out, all eyes turn to admire its broad slopes, which remain snow-covered year-round. The region's moisture-laden air has made Mount Rainier one of the snowiest spots in the country; record snowfalls have created glaciers on the mountain's flanks, and one of these, the Carbon Glacier, is the lowest-elevation glacier in the Lower 48.

Snow and glaciers notwithstanding, Rainier has a heart of fire. Steam vents at the mountain's summit are evidence that, although this volcanic peak has been dormant for more than 150 years, it could erupt again at any time. However, scientists believe that Rainier's volcanic activity occurs in 3,000-year cycles—and luckily, we have another 500 years to go before there's another big eruption.

ESSENTIALS

For advance information, contact **Mount Rainier National Park,** Tahoma Woods, Star Route, Ashford, WA 98304-9751 (© **360/569-2211,** ext. 3314; www.nps.gov/mora). We recommend visiting the park as early in the day as possible, especially on summer weekends, when traffic and crowds can be daunting. Keep in mind that, during the winter, only the Henry M. Jackson Memorial Visitor Center at Paradise is open, and then only on weekends and holidays. Park entrances other than the Nisqually entrance are closed by snow throughout the winter.

The entry fee to Mount Rainier National Park is $15 per motor vehicle.

EXPLORING THE PARK

Just past the main southwest (Nisqually) entrance, you'll come to **Longmire,** site of the National Park Inn, the Longmire Museum (with exhibits on the park's natural and human history), a hiker information center that issues backcountry permits, and a ski-touring center where you can rent cross-country skis and snowshoes in winter.

The road then climbs to **Paradise** (elevation 5,400 ft.), the aptly named mountainside aerie that affords a breathtaking close-up view of the mountain. Paradise, 110 miles southeast of Seattle and 150 miles northeast of Portland, is the park's most popular destination, so expect crowds. In July and August, the meadows here are ablaze with wildflowers. The circular **Henry M. Jackson Memorial Visitor Center** provides 360-degree panoramic views and includes exhibits on the flora, fauna, and geology of the park, as well as a display on mountain climbing. (*Note:* It's not unusual to find plenty of snow at Paradise as late as July. In 1972, the area set a world's record for snowfall in 1 year: 94 ft.!)

A 1.2-mile walk from the visitor center leads to a spot from which you can look down on the **Nisqually Glacier.** Many miles of other trails lead out from Paradise, looping through meadows and up onto snowfields above timberline.

In summer, you can continue to the **Ohanapecosh Visitor Center,** where you can walk through a forest of old-growth trees, some more than 1,000 years old.

Continuing around the mountain, you'll reach the turnoff for **Sunrise.** At 6,400 feet, Sunrise is the highest spot in the park accessible by car, and a beautiful old log lodge serves as the visitor center. From here you can see not only Mount Rainier, seemingly at arm's length, but also Mount Baker and Mount Adams. Some of the park's most scenic trails begin here at Sunrise. This area is usually less crowded than Paradise.

If you want to avoid the crowds and see a bit of dense old-growth forest, head for the park's **Carbon River entrance** in the northwest corner. This is the least visited region of the park because it offers views only to those willing to hike several miles uphill. At 3 miles, there's a glacier plowing through the middle of the rainforest, and at about 5 miles, you reach meadows and in-your-face views of the northwest flank of Mount Rainier. The road into this area is in bad shape and has washed out twice in recent years. Currently, high-clearance vehicles are recommended, but regular passenger vehicles have been getting through by driving very slowly.

If you don't have a car but still want to visit Mount Rainier National Park, book an all-day tour through **Seattle Tours** (© **888/293-1404** or 206/768-1234; www.seattle citytours.com), which charges $87 for adults and $59 for children 3 to 12 for a 10-hour tour. These tours spend most of that time in transit, but you get to see the mountain up close and even get in a couple of hours of hiking at Paradise.

OUTDOOR ACTIVITIES

Hikers have more than 240 miles of trails to explore within the park. The 5-mile **Skyline Trail** is the highest trail at Paradise and climbs above the tree line, with views of Mount Adams, Mount St. Helens, and the Nisqually Glacier. The **Lakes Trail,** of similar length, heads downhill to the Reflection Lakes, which have picture-perfect views of the mountain reflected in their waters. The park's single-most memorable low-elevation hike is the **Grove of the Patriarchs Trail.** This 1.5-mile round-trip trail is fairly flat (good for kids) and leads through a forest of huge old trees to a grove of 1,000-year-old red cedars on an island in the Ohanapecosh River. The trail head for this hike is near the Steven Canyon park entrance (southeast entrance).

In winter, miles of trails are open for **snowshoeing** and **cross-country skiing,** but there is limited access because of road closures. At Longmire, you'll find a **rental shop** at the National Park Inn (© **360/569-2411**) with skis and snowshoes. There are also guided snowshoe walks at Paradise. Just outside the northeast corner of the park, off

THE PACIFIC NORTHWEST

13

MOUNT RAINIER NATIONAL PARK

Wash. 410, **Crystal Mountain** (© 360/663-2265 for information, or 888/754-6199 for snow conditions; www.skicrystal.com) is the state's best all-around downhill ski area. Experienced backcountry skiers will also find some challenging cross-country skiing here at Crystal Mountain. Call for hours and current lift ticket prices.

WHERE TO STAY & CAMP

Built in 1916 high on the flanks of Mount Rainier in the area aptly known as Paradise, **Paradise Inn** (© 360/569-2275; http://rainier.guestservices.com) should be your first choice of accommodations in the park. Cedar-shake siding, exposed beams, cathedral ceilings, and a gigantic stone fireplace make this the quintessential mountain retreat. Offering breathtaking views of the mountain, the inn is also the starting point for miles of trails that in summer wander through flower-filled meadows. The inn reopened in May 2008 after a 2-year rehabilitation and renovation. Rates are from $104 double with shared bathroom, $155 to $235 double with private bathroom. It's closed from early October to mid-May.

The 25-room **National Park Inn** (© 360/569-2275; http://rainier.guestservices. com) is in Longmire, at the southwest corner of the park. The inn's front veranda does have a view of the mountain, and guests often gather here at sunset on clear days. Because this lodge stays open year-round, it's popular with cross-country skiers. Rooms vary in size and contain rustic furnishings, but are not the most memorable part of a stay here. Rates ($110 double with shared bathroom; $149–$205 double with private bathroom) from late October to late April include breakfast.

There are also several **campgrounds.** Two of these—Cougar Rock and Ohanapecosh—take reservations, which should be made several months in advance for summer weekends. To make reservations, contact **Recreation.gov** (© 877/444-6777 or 518/885-3639; www.recreation.gov).

5 MOUNT ST. HELENS

Mount St. Helens was once considered the most perfect of the Cascade peaks, a snow-covered cone rising above lush forests. Then on May 18, 1980, a violent eruption blew out the side of the volcano and removed the top 1,300 feet of the peak, causing the largest landslide in history. More than 540 million tons of ash traveled nearly 16 miles into the atmosphere, raining down as far away as Denver, and laid waste to the immediate area.

In the fall of 2004, the volcano awoke from many years of relative quiet and the lava dome inside the volcano's crater began growing again. Plumes of ash can once again be seen billowing from the volcano on an irregular basis. In response to the volcanic activity within the crater of the volcano, summit climbs are sometimes halted and parts of the monument are occasionally closed. The monument continues to closely monitor the volcano's activity, and if things heat up again, you can count on more closures. However, for the time being, the volcano's visitor centers are open for business.

ESSENTIALS

The monument is about 160 miles south of Seattle, off I-5 (take the Castle Rock exit). Admission to the monument's two main visitor centers is $8 for adults and free for children 15 and under. If you just want to park at one of the monument's trail heads and go for a hike, all you need is a valid Northwest Forest Pass, which costs $5 per day. In winter you'll need a Sno-Park permit, which costs $10 to $11 per day. For more information, contact

Exploring the Park

The best place to start exploring is the **Mount St. Helens Visitor Center at Silver Lake** (© **360/274-0962;** www.parks.wa.gov/mountsthelens.asp), operated by Washington State Parks at Silver Lake, 5 miles east of Castle Rock on Wash. 504. The visitor center houses exhibits on the eruption and its effects on the region. May through September, it's open daily from 9am to 5pm (until 4pm in other months). Admission is $3 for adults, $1 for children 7 to 17. A family pass is $8.

Continuing east from the visitor center, at Milepost 27, you'll come to the **Hoffstadt Bluffs Visitor Center** (© **360/274-7750;** www.mt-st-helens.com). This is primarily a snack bar and takeoff site for 30-minute helicopter flights over Mount St. Helens ($165 per person), but it also has great views. July and August, this visitor center is open daily from 9:30am to 6:30pm; June and September, it's open daily 10am to 6pm; and October through May, call for hours.

Just past Milepost 33 is the **Charles W. Bingham Forest Learning Center at Mount St. Helens** (© **360/414-3439;** www.mountsthelens.com/Forest-Learning-Center.html), open mid-May through mid-October daily from 10am to 6pm (until 5pm in Oct). In a theater designed to resemble an ash-covered landscape, you can watch a short, fascinating video about the eruption. Outside both the Hoffstadt Bluffs Visitor Center and the Forest Learning Center, you can usually see numerous elk on the floor of the Toutle River Valley far below.

None of the visitor centers offers a more awe-inspiring view than the **Johnston Ridge Observatory** (© **360/274-2140**). Built into the mountainside and designed to blend into the landscape, this observatory houses the equipment that is still used to monitor activity within Mount St. Helens. The observatory is open from mid-May to October daily from 10am to 6pm. If you're up for a bit of hiking, the best choice on this side of the monument is the **Boundary Trail,** which heads east from the Johnston Ridge Observatory, with a jaw-dropping view of the blast zone the entire way.

Drive around to the monument's east side for a close-up view of how the eruption affected the surrounding lands. For the best views, take U.S. 12 east from exit 68 off I-5. In Randle, head south on Local Route 25 and then take Local Route 26. At Meta Lake, Route 26 joins Route 99, which continues to the **Windy Ridge Viewpoint,** where visitors get their closest look at the crater. The 1-mile **Harmony Trail** leads down to the shore of Spirit Lake and is a very worthwhile hike; just keep in mind that it's a 600-foot climb back up to the trail head parking lot.

On the south side of the monument, you can explore the **Ape Cave,** a 2-mile lava tube formed 1,900 years ago when lava poured from the volcano. At Ape Headquarters, open from late June to early September, you can join a regular ranger-led exploration of the cave or rent a lantern to explore on your own.

If you'd like to turn a visit to Mount St. Helens into a learning vacation, check the schedule of seminars being offered by the **Mount St. Helens Institute,** 42218 NE Yale Bridge Rd., Amboy, WA 98601 (© **360/449-7887;** www.mshinstitute.org).

WHERE TO STAY & CAMP

You'll find nearly a dozen campgrounds near the monument. For reservations at state campgrounds, contact **Washington State Parks Reservations** (© **888/226-7688;** www.parks.wa.gov). For information on national forest campgrounds, contact the **Cowlitz**

Valley Ranger District, 10024 U.S. 12 (P.O. Box 670), Randle (© **360/497-1100**). For national forest campground reservations, contact the **National Recreation Reservation Service** (© **800/280-CAMP** [280-2267]; www.reserveusa.com).

Blue Heron Inn Bed & Breakfast, 2846 Spirit Lake Hwy., Castle Rock (© **800/959-4049** or 360/274-9595; www.blueheroninn.com), is a modern B&B on the road to the Coldwater and Johnston Ridge visitor centers. It has an excellent view of Mount St. Helens and is by far the best choice for accommodations in the area. Rates run $159 to $209 double, including full breakfast.

---

6 PORTLAND

At the confluence of the Willamette and Columbia rivers, Portland is a city of discreet charms. Strolling through the tranquil Japanese Garden on a misty May morning, people-watching at Pioneer Courthouse Square, perusing the acres of books at Powell's, shopping for arts and crafts at the Saturday Market, sampling beer at one of the many brewpubs, or leaving the city for a quick trip to the beach or Oregon wine country—these are the quintessential Portland experiences to seek out and savor.

ESSENTIALS

GETTING THERE   By Plane   Portland International Airport, 7000 NE Airport Way (**PDX;** © **877/739-4636** or 503/460-4040; www.flypdx.com), is 10 miles northeast of downtown, adjacent to the Columbia River. Many hotels near the airport provide courtesy shuttle service; be sure to ask when you make a reservation.

If you're driving to central Portland from the airport, follow signs for downtown, which will take you first onto **I-205** and then **I-84** west. Take the Morrison Bridge exit to cross the Willamette River. The trip into town takes about 20 minutes.

If you haven't rented a car at the airport, the best way to get into town is to take the **Airport MAX (Red Line)** light-rail system, which operates daily every 15 minutes between 5am and midnight (11:30pm on Sun), and takes about 40 minutes to make the trip from the airport to downtown Portland. The fare is $2.05. For information on this service, contact **TriMet** (© **503/238-7433;** www.trimet.org).

A taxi to downtown generally costs between $20 and $25.

By Train   Amtrak (© **800/872-7245;** www.amtrak.com) serves **Union Station,** 800 NW Sixth Ave., about 10 blocks from the heart of downtown, with daily service from Seattle (trip time: $3^1/2$ hr.), Spokane (8 hr.), Chicago (37 hr.), Oakland (19 hr.), and Los Angeles (31 hr.).

By Car   The major routes into Portland are **I-5** from the north (Seattle) and south (Sacramento), and **I-84** from the east (Boise). **I-405** arcs around the west and south of downtown, **I-205** bypasses the city to the east, and **U.S. 26** runs west to the coast.

VISITOR INFORMATION   The **Travel Portland Visitor Information and Services Center,** 701 SW Sixth Ave., Portland, OR 97205 (© **877/678-5263** or 503/275-8355; www.travelportland.com), is underneath Pioneer Courthouse Square near Starbucks. Hours are Monday through Friday from 8:30am to 5:30pm, Saturday from 10am to 4pm, and Sunday from 10am to 2pm. There are also two information booths in the baggage claim area at Portland Airport.

elsewhere, and because the entire downtown area covers only about 15×32 blocks, it's easy to explore on foot. Because the city is committed to keeping this area uncongested, it has invested heavily in public transportation. **TriMet public buses,** the **MAX (Metropolitan Area Express) light-rail system,** and the **Portland Streetcar** are all free within Fareless Square, the area between I-405 on the south and west, Hoyt Street on the north, and the Willamette River on the east. There is also a Fareless Square extension that allows free rides across the Willamette River (on buses and the MAX) to the Lloyd Center area, which is the site of a large shopping mall, the Portland Convention Center, and the Rose Garden arena.

Outside Fareless Square, adult fares on both TriMet buses and MAX are $1.75 or $2.05, depending on distance. A $4.25 all-day ticket, available from any MAX ticket-vending machine or bus driver, is good for travel to all zones and is valid on buses, streetcars, and MAX. Transfers between the bus, the streetcar, and MAX are free. Pick up bus route and schedule information at the **TriMet Ticket Office** (© **503/238-7433;** www.trimet.org), behind the waterfall fountain at Pioneer Courthouse Square, open Monday through Friday from 8:30am to 5:30pm. The **Portland Streetcar** (www. portlandstreetcar.org) runs from the waterfront south of downtown, through downtown and the trendy Pearl District, to the Northwest shopping and restaurant district. It costs $1.75 outside of Fareless Square.

Because Portland is fairly compact, getting around by taxi is not too expensive. Wait at a taxi stand at one of the major hotels, or contact **Broadway Cab** (© **503/227-1234;** www.broadwaycab.com) or **Radio Cab** (© **503/227-1212;** www.radiocab.net). Fares are $2.50 for the first mile, $2.50 for each additional mile, and $1 for additional passengers.

FAST FACTS   Three area hospitals are **Legacy Good Samaritan,** 1015 NW 22nd Ave. (© **503/413-7711;** www.legacyhealth.org); **Providence Portland Medical Center,** 4805 NE Glisan St. (© **503/215-1111;** www.providence.org); and the **Oregon Health Sciences University Hospital,** 3181 SW Sam Jackson Park Rd. (© **503/494-8311;** www.ohsu.edu). If you need a physician referral, call the **Legacy Referral Service** (© **503/335-3500;** www.legacyhealth.org).

Central Drug, 538 SW Fourth Ave. (© **503/226-2222;** www.centraldrugportland. com), is a pharmacy convenient to most downtown hotels. It's open Monday through Friday from 9am to 6pm, Saturday from 10am to 4pm.

Portland is a relatively safe city. Take extra precautions, however, if you venture into the entertainment district along West Burnside Street or into Chinatown at night. If you plan to go hiking in Forest Park, don't leave anything valuable in your car. This holds true in the Skidmore Historic District (Old Town) as well.

Portland is a shopper's paradise—there's no sales tax. However, there is a 12.5% tax on hotel rooms in the city. (Outside the city limits, the room tax varies.) On car rentals, there is a 12.5% tax, and if you pick your car up at the airport, there is an additional fee of around 10%. You can avoid all of these car-rental taxes by renting your car over on the west side of the metro area in Beaverton, Tigard, or Hillsboro.

SPECIAL EVENTS & FESTIVALS   Celebrated annually since 1907, the **Portland Rose Festival** (© **503/227-2681;** www.rosefestival.org) has blossomed into the city's biggest celebration. The festivities span 1¹/₂ weeks and include a rose show, two parades, a rose queen contest, fireworks, and dragon boat races. Most events take place during the first week of June. Contact **Ticketmaster** (© **503/224-4400;** www.ticketmaster.com) for tickets to specific events.

The last full weekend in July brings the **Oregon Brewers Festival** (© **503/778-5917;** www.oregonbrewfest.com) to Tom McCall Waterfront Park. This is one of the country's largest festivals of independent craft brewers and features plenty of local and international microbrews, as well as food and music.

WHAT TO SEE & DO

Pioneer Courthouse Square, at the corner of Southwest Broadway and Yamhill Street, is the heart of downtown Portland and acts as an outdoor stage for everything from flower displays to protest rallies. The square, with its waterfall fountain and free-standing columns, is the city's favorite gathering spot, especially at noon when the Weather Machine, a mechanical sculpture, forecasts the weather for the upcoming 24 hours. Keep your eyes on the square's brick pavement for some surprising names.

A few blocks away, at 1120 SW Fifth Ave., stands *Portlandia,* the symbol of the city and the second-largest hammered bronze statue in the country (only the Statue of Liberty is larger).

International Rose Test Garden   Covering $4^1/_2$ acres of hillside in the West Hills above downtown Portland, and planted with nearly 7,000 rose bushes, this garden was established in 1917 and is one of the largest and oldest rose test gardens in the United States. The American Rose Society uses the garden as a testing ground for new varieties of roses. Although you will likely see some familiar roses in the Gold Medal Garden, most of the 400 varieties on display are new hybrids. These acres of roses give Portland its nickname: "City of Roses." Allow 1 hour.

400 SW Kingston Ave. (in Washington Park). © **503/823-3636.** www.rosegardenstore.org. Free admission (donations accepted). Daily 7:30am–9pm. Bus: 63.

Japanese Garden (Best)   Considered the finest example of a Japanese garden in North America, Portland's Japanese Garden is one of the city's most popular attractions. There are five different styles of Japanese gardens scattered over $5^1/_2$ acres, and a view of volcanic Mount Hood, which has a strong resemblance to Mount Fuji. This is a very tranquil spot and is even more peaceful on rainy days when the crowds stay away, so don't pass up a visit just because it's drizzling. Many special events, exhibits, and demonstrations are held here throughout the year. Allow 2 hours.

611 Kingston Ave. (in Washington Park). © **503/223-1321.** www.japanesegarden.com. Admission $8 adults, $6.25 seniors and college students, $5.25 youths 6–17. Apr–Sept Mon noon–7pm, Tues–Sun 10am–7pm; Oct–Mar Mon noon–4pm, Tues–Sun 10am–4pm. Closed Thanksgiving, Christmas, and New Year's Day. Bus: 63. MAX: Washington Park Station (late May to early Sept, take the shuttle bus).

Oregon History Museum   This museum is a great introduction to Oregon. The state's history, from before the arrival of the first Europeans to contemporary times, is chronicled in fascinating exhibits, including "Oregon My Oregon," which utilizes two theaters and lots of interactive displays to make the state's history accessible. Temporary exhibits change frequently and might include a display of contemporary art by Oregon artists or a traveling exhibit on loan from the Smithsonian Institution. Museum docents are often on hand to answer questions. Allow 2 hours.

1200 SW Park Ave. © **503/306-5198.** www.ohs.org. Admission $10 adults, $8 seniors and college students, $5 youths 6–18 (free for all 3rd Sat of each month). Tues–Sat 10am–5pm; Sun noon–5pm. Closed July 4, Thanksgiving, Christmas, and New Year's Day. Bus: 6 or 63. MAX: Library Station. Portland Streetcar: Art Museum (northbound); 11th Ave. and Jefferson St. (southbound).

Hitting the Water

If you want to check out the Portland skyline from water level, arrange for a sea kayak tour through the **Portland River Company,** 0315 SW Montgomery St. ((*C*) **888/238-2059** or 503/229-0551; www.portlandrivercompany.com). A 2¹/₂-hour tour ($45–$47) circles nearby Ross Island. The company also rents sea kayaks for independent use and offers raft trips.

Oregon Museum of Science and Industry (OMSI)   On the east bank of the Willamette River, this modern science museum has six huge halls filled with exhibits aimed at youngsters but often of interest to adults as well. This is a hands-on museum, and the motion simulator and tornado-like air vortex are perennial favorites. The museum also has an OMNIMAX theater and the Kendall Planetarium, which features laser-light shows and astronomy presentations. The USS *Blueback* submarine is docked here, and tours are given daily. Allow 2 to 3 hours.

1945 SE Water Ave. (*C*) **800/955-6674** or 503/797-4000. www.omsi.edu. Museum: $11 adults, $9 seniors and children 3–13. OMNIMAX shows: $8.50 adults, $6.50 seniors and children. Submarine tours, planetarium shows, or laser-light show matinees: $5.50. Evening laser light shows: $7.50 (discounted combination tickets available). Mid-June to Aug daily 9:30am–7pm; Sept to mid-June Tues–Sun 9:30am–5:30pm (open holiday Mon). Closed Thanksgiving and Christmas. Bus: 33.

Oregon Zoo   The Oregon Zoo is best known for its large breeding herd of elephants. It also has an excellent African exhibit, which includes a rainforest and a savanna. The Cascade Crest exhibit includes mountain goats, while the Steller Cove exhibit has sea lions and sea otters. In Eagle Canyon, there are eagles and salmon, and the Amazon Flooded Forest displays everything from poisonous dart frogs to two-toed sloths. In the summer, there are outdoor concerts. A scaled-down train connects the zoo with the International Rose Test Garden and the Japanese Garden. Allow 2 to 3 hours.

4001 SW Canyon Rd., Washington Park. (*C*) **503/226-1561.** www.oregonzoo.org. Admission $9.75 adults, $8.25 seniors, $6.75 children ages 3–11. Apr 15–Sept 15 daily 9am–6pm (Memorial Day to Labor Day 8am–6pm); Sept 16–Apr 14 daily 9am–4pm. Closed Christmas. Parking $2. Bus: 63. MAX: Washington Park Station.

Portland Art Museum   This is the oldest art museum in the Northwest, and it has an excellent collection of modern and contemporary art. This collection begins with European Impressionists and moves right up to the present. However, the best reason to visit is to see the extensive collection of Native American art and artifacts. There's also a good collection of Northwest contemporary art that includes a fascinating two-story wall of "artifacts" by glass artist William Morris. Other collections include European, Asian, and American art. The Portland Art Museum is frequently the Northwest stop for touring blockbuster exhibits. Allow 2 hours.

1219 SW Park Ave. (*C*) **503/226-2811.** www.portlandartmuseum.org. Admission $10 adults, $9 seniors and college students, free for youths 17 and under. Tues–Wed and Sat 10am–5pm; Thurs–Fri 10am–8pm; Sun noon–5pm. Closed major holidays. Bus: 6 or 63. MAX: Library Station. Portland Streetcar: Art Museum (northbound); 11th Ave. and Jefferson St. (southbound).

Portland Classical Chinese Garden   With its rare plants and unusual imported limestone rocks, this classically styled Chinese garden is designed to evoke the wild mountains of China. The garden, located in Portland's Chinatown, takes up an entire

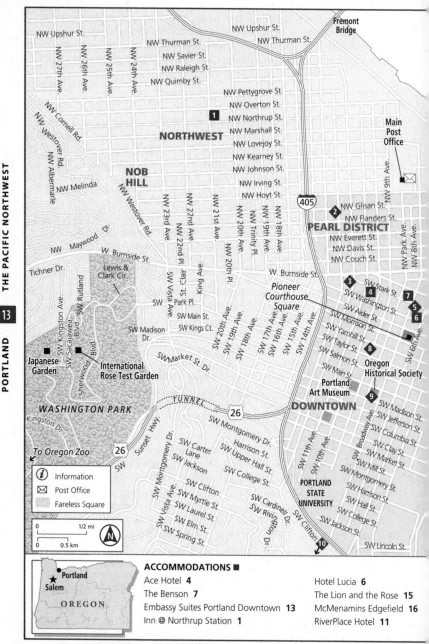

NW Upshur St.
NW Thurman St.
NW Savier St.
NW Raleigh St.
NW Quimby St.
NW 27th Ave.
NW 26th Ave.
NW 25th Ave.
NW 24th Ave.
NW Cornell Rd.
NW Westover Rd.
NW Albermarle
NW Melinda
NW Maywood Dr.
NW Westover Rd.

NW Upshur St.
NW Thurman St.
NW Pettygrove St.
NW Overton St.
NW Northrup St.
NW Marshall St.
NW Lovejoy St.
NW Kearney St.
NW Johnson St.
NW Irving St.
NW Hoyt St.
NW Glisan St.
NW Flanders St.
NW Everett St.
NW Davis St.
NW Couch St.

Fremont Bridge

NORTHWEST

NOB HILL

PEARL DISTRICT

Main Post Office

NW 23rd Ave.
NW 22nd Ave.
NW 21st Ave.
NW 20th Ave.
NW 19th Ave.
NW 18th Ave.
NW Trinity Pl.
NW 22nd Pl.
NW 20th Pl.
King Ave.
NW Park Ave.
NW 8th Ave.
NW 9th Ave.

Tichner Dr.
Lewis & Clark Cir.
W. Burnside St.
W. Burnside St.

Pioneer Courthouse Square

SW Stark St.
SW Washington St.
SW Alder St.
SW Morrison St.
SW Yamhill St.
SW Taylor St.
SW Salmon St.
SW Main St.

Oregon Historical Society

Portland Art Museum

DOWNTOWN

SW Vista Ave.
SW St. Clair
Park Pl.
SW Main St.
SW Kings Ct.
SW Madison Dr.
SW Market St. Dr.
SW 20th Ave.
SW 19th Ave.
SW 18th Ave.
SW 17th Ave.
SW 16th Ave.
SW 15th Ave.
SW 14th Ave.

Japanese Garden

International Rose Test Garden

WASHINGTON PARK

SW Kingston Ave.
SW Sacajawea Blvd.
SW Rutland
Sherwood Blvd.

Kingston Dr.
To Oregon Zoo

TUNNEL

SW Montgomery Dr.
SW Carter Lane
SW Upper Hall St.
Harrison St.
SW College St.
SW Jackson

PORTLAND STATE UNIVERSITY

SW Madison St.
SW Jefferson St.
SW Columbia St.
SW Clay St.
SW Market St.
SW Mill St.
SW Montgomery St.
SW Harrison St.
SW Hall St.
SW College St.
SW Jackson St.
SW Lincoln St.

Broadway Ave.
SW 11th Ave.
SW 10th Ave.

SW Montgomery Dr.
SW Vista Ave.
SW Clifton
SW Myrtle St.
SW Laurel St.
SW Elm St.
SW Spring St.
SW Cardinell Dr.
SW River...
SW Clifton
SW Clifton Dr.

(i) Information
✉ Post Office
Fareless Square

0   1/2 mi
0   0.5 km

N

★ Portland
Salem

OREGON

ACCOMMODATIONS ■

Ace Hotel **4**

The Benson **7**

Embassy Suites Portland Downtown **13**

Inn @ Northrup Station **1**

Hotel Lucia **6**

The Lion and the Rose **15**

McMenamins Edgefield **16**

RiverPlace Hotel **11**

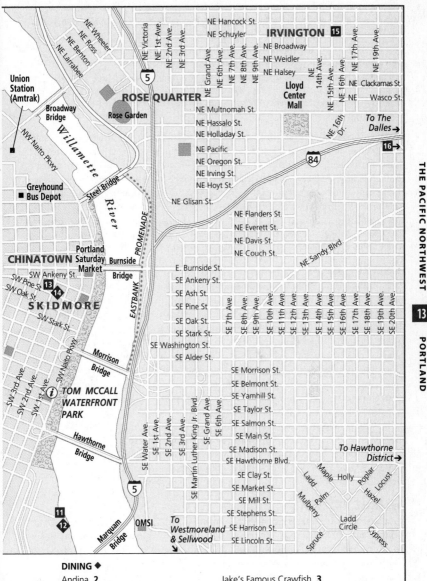

DINING ◆

Andina **2**

Bijou Café **14**

Chart House **10**

Higgins **9**

Jake's Famous Crawfish **3**

Marina Fish House **12**

Southpark Seafood Grill & Wine Bar **8**

Typhoon! **5**

city block and is surrounded by walls that separate the tranquil, timeless Chinese oasis from the buzz of 21st-century urban life that surrounds it. To fully appreciate this garden, quietly stroll the winding paths, stop in the many viewing pavilions, and gaze at the reflections in the garden's tiny lake. It's easy to imagine that you have been transported to China. Try to visit as soon as the gardens open in the morning, before the crowds descend and the guided tours start circulating; also be sure to stop and have a cup of tea and maybe a snack in the garden's tearoom. Allow 1 to 2 hours.

NW Everett St. and NW Third Ave. ✆ 503/228-8131. www.portlandchinesegarden.org. Admission $8.50 adults, $7.50 seniors, $6.50 students, free for children 5 and under. Apr–Oct daily 9am–6pm; Nov–Mar daily 10am–5pm. Closed Thanksgiving, Christmas, and New Year's Day. Bus: 1, 4, 5, 8, 10, 16, 33, 40, or 77. MAX: Skidmore Fountain.

Portland Saturday Market   For decades, the Northwest has attracted artists and craftspeople, and on Saturday and Sunday throughout most of the year, hundreds of them can be found selling their creations at this outdoor market. Most of the art and crafts sold here are fairly inexpensive and small enough to fit into a suitcase. These days the market seems to appeal primarily to teenagers and 20-somethings. There are also food vendors and performances by local bands.

108 W. Burnside St. (underneath the west end of the Burnside Bridge on SW Naito Pkwy.). ✆ **503/222-6072.** www.portlandsaturdaymarket.com. Free admission. 1st weekend in Mar to Christmas Eve Sat 10am–5pm, Sun 11am–4:30pm. Bus: 12, 19, or 20. MAX: Skidmore Fountain.

SHOPPING

The blocks around **Pioneer Courthouse Square** are Portland's main upscale shopping streets. Here you'll find Nordstrom, Saks Fifth Avenue, the upscale Pioneer Place shopping mall, and numerous boutiques. The city's prettiest shopping area is the **Nob Hill/Northwest** neighborhood along Northwest 23rd Avenue beginning at West Burnside Street. Here you'll find block after block of interesting boutiques. For art galleries and shops with a hip, urban aesthetic, head to the **Pearl District,** which is north of West Burnside Street between Northwest 9th Avenue and Northwest 15th Avenue. For funkier shops, head out to the **Hawthorne District,** the city's main counterculture shopping area, on the east side of the Willamette River along Hawthorne Boulevard between 17th and 43rd avenues.

No visit to Portland is complete without a stop at the humongous **Powell's City of Books,** 1005 W. Burnside St. (✆ **800/878-7323** or 503/228-4651; www.powells.com), the bookstore to end all bookstores. Covering an entire city block three floors deep, Powell's is unusual in that it shelves new and used books together. You can easily spend hours browsing here.

WHERE TO STAY

The largest concentrations of hotels are downtown, which is the most convenient for visitors, and near the airport. Reserve as far in advance as possible. If you can't find a room, contact **Travel Portland** (✆ **877/678-5263;** www.travelportland.com), which offers a reservations service for the metro area as well as information on B&Bs.

Ace Hotel   Bauhaus meets industrial salvage at this überhip hotel a block from Powell's City of Books. Young creative types will adore this fun and funky place. In the lobby, an old industrial door serves as a giant coffee table, while just off the lobby you can get some of Portland's best espresso. Every guest room is different, but all have unusual murals. Platform beds have Pendleton blankets, and in rooms with private bathrooms, you might find an old apple crate serving as a step up into the claw-foot tub. Ask for a room in back if you're a light sleeper.

1022 SW Stark St., Portland, OR 97205. ✆ **503/228-2277.** Fax 503/228-2297. www.acehotel.com. 79 units (10 with shared bathroom). $95 double with shared bathroom; $140 double with private bathroom; $250 suite. AE, DC, DISC, MC, V. Parking $20. Pets accepted. **Amenities:** 3 restaurants.

The Benson Built in 1912, the Benson exudes old-world sophistication and elegance. In the French baroque lobby, walnut paneling frames a marble fireplace, Austrian crystal chandeliers hang from the ornate plasterwork ceiling, and a marble staircase allows for grand entrances. These are the poshest digs in Portland, and guest rooms are luxuriously furnished in a plush Euro-luxe styling. Rooms vary considerably in size, but most of the deluxe kings are particularly spacious. The corner junior suites, which are large and have lots of windows, are the hotel's best deal. All the guest rooms have Tempur-Pedic mattresses (with pillow-top mattresses available upon request).

309 SW Broadway, Portland, OR 97205. ✆ **888/523-6766** or 503/228-2000. Fax 503/471-3920. www. bensonhotel.com. 287 units. $154–$234 double; $209–$304 junior suite; $450–$1,200 suite. AE, DC, DISC, MC, V. Valet parking $28. Pets accepted ($75 fee). **Amenities:** 2 restaurants; exercise room.

Embassy Suites Portland Downtown Located in the restored 1912 Multnomah Hotel, the Embassy Suites rivals the Benson hotel for the plushness of its lobby. This is a historic hotel in the grand style, with gilded plasterwork and potted palms in the lobby. Units are primarily two-room suites with classically styled furnishings and lots of space (a rarity in downtown hotels). The location is only a couple of blocks from the waterfront and the Portland Saturday Market. You'll find everyone from couples to families to business travelers here.

319 SW Pine St., Portland, OR 97204-2726. ✆ **800/EMBASSY** [362-2779] or 503/279-9000. Fax 503/497-9051. www.embassyportland.com. 276 units. $159–$229 double. Rates include full breakfast. AE, DC, DISC, MC, V. Valet parking $28; self-parking $18. **Amenities:** Restaurant; indoor pool; spa. *In room:* Fridge, microwave.

Hotel Lućia With guest rooms and public spaces decorated with contemporary art and black-and-white photos by Pulitzer Prize–winning presidential photographer David Hume Kennerly, this is downtown Portland's truly hip hotel, and it attracts stylish young visitors and business travelers. Guest rooms boast dreamy beds with down comforters and bathrooms with gorgeous modern sinks. Try to get one of the corner rooms, which have lots of big windows and a bit more space than other rooms. The location puts you within walking distance of most of the city's top attractions.

400 SW Broadway, Portland, OR 97205. ✆ **877/225-1717** or 503/225-1717. Fax 503/225-1919. www. hotellucia.com. 127 units. $189–$729 double. AE, DC, DISC, MC, V. Valet parking $24. Pets accepted ($35 fee). **Amenities:** Restaurant; exercise room.

Inn @ Northrup Station This hotel in the Nob Hill neighborhood is located on the Portland Streetcar line, which makes it convenient for exploring the city. The colorful retro decor also sets this all-suite hotel apart from other hotels around town. If you appreciate bright colors and contemporary styling, this should be your first choice in town. Many of the suites here have full kitchens, and most also have a balcony or a patio. The hotel's location in a quiet residential neighborhood is a plus, and the hotel is also within a few blocks of some of Portland's top restaurants.

2025 NW Northrup St., Portland, OR 97209. ✆ **800/224-1180** or 503/224-0543. Fax 503/273-2102. www. northrupstation.com. 70 units. $149–$219 double. Rates include continental breakfast. Children 11 and under stay free in parent's room. AE, DISC, MC, V. Free parking. *In room:* Kitchen (in some), fridge, microwave.

Lion and the Rose This Queen Anne–style Victorian inn is in the Irvington District 1 block off Northeast Broadway, and restaurants, cafes, eclectic boutiques, and a huge shopping mall are all within 4 blocks. In the Lavonna Room, there's a turret sitting area, while in the Starina Room you'll find an imposing Edwardian bed and armoire. Both the Garden Room and the Avandel Room have bathrooms with claw-foot tubs. If you have problems climbing stairs, ask for the ground floor's Rose Room, which has a whirlpool tub. The Victorian parlors and dining room are beautiful.

1810 NE 15th Ave., Portland, OR 97212. ✆ **800/955-1647** or 503/287-9245. Fax 503/287-9247. www. lionrose.com. 7 units. $134–$224 double. AE, DISC, MC, V. Children 10 and older welcome.

McMenamins Edgefield Ideally situated for exploring the Columbia Gorge and Mount Hood, this flagship of the McMenamin microbrewery empire is the former Multnomah County poor farm. Today the property includes not only tastefully decorated guest rooms with antique furnishings, but a brewery, a pub, a restaurant, a movie theater, a winery, a wine-tasting room, a distillery, two golf courses, a day spa, a soaking pool, and extensive gardens. With so much in one spot, this makes a great base for exploring the area. The beautiful grounds give this inn the feel of a remote retreat, though you are still within 20 miles of Portland.

2126 SW Halsey St., Troutdale, OR 97060. ✆ **800/669-8610** or 503/669-8610. www.mcmenamins.com. 114 units (100 with shared bathroom). $60–$105 double with shared bathroom; $80–$145 double with private bathroom; $40 per person for a bed in the hostel. Children 6 and under stay free in parent's room. AE, DC, DISC, MC, V. **Amenities:** 3 restaurants; 2 golf courses; day spa. *In room:* No TV, no phone.

RiverPlace Hotel (Best) With the Willamette River at its back doorstep and the sloping lawns of Waterfront Park to one side, the RiverPlace is one of Portland's only waterfront hotels and is hands down the best place to stay for a luxurious vacation. Understated contemporary furnishings and plush beds make this a very comfortable choice. More than half the rooms are suites, and some have wood-burning fireplaces and whirlpool tubs The river-view standard king rooms are the best deal. The quiet boutique-hotel atmosphere tends to attract affluent couples and business travelers.

1510 SW Harbor Way, Portland, OR 97201. ✆ **800/227-1333** or 503/228-3233. Fax 503/295-6161. www. riverplacehotel.com. 84 units. $199–$249 double; $229–$525 suite. Children 17 and under stay free in parent's room. AE, DC, DISC, MC, V. Valet parking $26. Pets accepted ($50 fee). **Amenities:** Restaurant; access to nearby health club. *In room:* Fridge.

WHERE TO DINE

Andina PERUVIAN If you've never had Peruvian food, don't miss an opportunity to eat at Andina. If you have had Peruvian food, don't miss an opportunity to eat at Andina. I just can't get enough of the spicy bread-dipping sauces, the grilled octopus, and the beautifully presented *causa* (mashed purple potatoes flavored with lime and layered with savory fillings). I suggest trying lots of the small plates. Also be sure to have a glass of the unusual *chicha morada*, a juice made from purple corn.

1314 NW Glisan St. ✆ **503/228-9535.** www.andinarestaurant.com. Reservations recommended. Small plates $7.50–$15; main courses $16–$29. AE, DISC, MC, V. Mon–Thurs 11:30am–2:30pm and 4–9:30pm (tapas until 11pm); Fri–Sat 11:30am–2:30pm and 4–10:30pm (tapas until midnight); Sun 11:30am–2:30pm and 5–9:30pm.

Bijou Café NATURAL FOODS Although the Bijou is ostensibly just a breakfast joint, the folks who run the restaurant take food very seriously. The fresh oyster hash is an absolutely unforgettable way to start the day, as is the brioche French toast. Other big hits include the sautéed potatoes and the muffins, which come with full breakfasts; don't leave without trying them. Local and organic products are used as often as possible at this **971** comfortably old-fashioned yet thoroughly modern cafe.

132 SW Third Ave. ✆ **503/222-3187.** Breakfast and lunch $5.25–$14. MC, V. Mon–Fri 7am–2pm; Sat–Sun 8am–2pm.

Chart House SEAFOOD   Although this place is part of a national restaurant chain, it also happens to boast the finest view of any restaurant in Portland. While you savor the best New England clam chowder in the city, you can marvel at the views of the Willamette River, Mount Hood, Mount St. Helens, and nearly all of Portland's east side. Fresh fish (grilled, baked, or blackened) is the house specialty.

5700 SW Terwilliger Blvd. ✆ **503/246-6963.** Reservations recommended. Main courses $10–$22 lunch, $20–$45 dinner. AE, DC, DISC, MC, V. Mon–Thurs 11:30am–9:30pm; Fri 11:30am–10pm; Sat 5–10pm; Sun 5–9pm.

Higgins (Best) NORTHWEST/MEDITERRANEAN   Higgins has long been one of Portland's top restaurants and strikes a balance between contemporary and classic in its decor and its cuisine. The menu, which changes frequently, explores the contemporary culinary landscape, with the flavors of Asia and the Mediterranean emphasized. Dishes are inventive, yet homey and satisfying. Be sure to leave room for dessert. Although the main dining room is formal, the bar in the back is a casual spot with a less expensive menu (you can also order off the main menu in the bar).

1239 SW Broadway. ✆ **503/222-9070.** Reservations recommended. Main courses $9–$18 lunch, $19–$37 dinner. AE, DC, DISC, MC, V. Mon–Fri 11:30am–midnight; Sat 4pm–midnight; Sun 4–11:30pm or midnight.

Jake's Famous Crawfish SEAFOOD   This place is a Portland institution and has been serving up crawfish since 1909 at an address that has housed a restaurant or bar since 1892. The noise level after work, when the bar is packed, can be high, and the wait for a table can be long if you don't have a reservation, but don't let these obstacles dissuade you from visiting. A daily menu lists a dozen or more specials, but there's really no question about what to eat here: crawfish, which are served a variety of ways.

401 SW 12th Ave. ✆ **888/344-6861** or 503/226-1419. www.jakesfamouscrawfish.com. Reservations recommended. Main courses $7.50–$19 lunch, $15–$40 dinner. AE, DC, DISC, MC, V. Mon–Thurs 11am–11pm; Fri 11am–midnight; Sat noon–midnight; Sun 3–11pm.

Marina Fish House SEAFOOD   This restaurant has the best location of any restaurant in town—floating on the Willamette River. Located in the marina at RiverPlace shopping-and-dining complex, the Marina Fish House provides views of the river and the city skyline. Popular with young couples, families, and boaters, this place exudes a cheery atmosphere, and service is efficient. Nearly everything on the menu has some sort of seafood in it, even the sandwiches, salads, and pastas.

RiverPlace Marina, 0425 SW Montgomery St. ✆ **503/227-3474.** www.marinafishhouse.com. Reservations recommended. Main courses $9–$17 lunch, $10–$35 dinner. AE, DISC, MC, V. Sun–Thurs 11am–10pm; Fri–Sat 11am–11pm.

Southpark Seafood Grill & Wine Bar MEDITERRANEAN/SEAFOOD   The wine bar here is a contemporary interpretation of late-19th-century Paris, and the main dining room is both comfortable and classy. For a starter, don't pass up the fried calamari and vegetables served with spicy tomato sauce. Equally delicious is the butternut-squash-and-ricotta-filled ravioli with toasted hazelnuts, which comes in a rich sauce that begs to be sopped up with the crusty bread. An extensive wine list presents some compelling choices, and the desserts are consistently delicious.

Typhoon! THAI   This sophisticated downtown restaurant has long been one of my favorites in town for its many unusual menu offerings. Start a meal with the *miang kum,* which consists of dried shrimp, tiny chilies, ginger, lime, peanuts, shallots, and toasted coconut with a sweet-and-sour sauce and wrapped up in a spinach leaf. The burst of flavors on your taste buds is astounding. There is an extensive tea list. There's another **Typhoon!** at 2310 NW Everett St. (© **503/243-7557**).

In Hotel Lúcia, 410 SW Broadway. (© **503/224-8285.** www.typhoonrestaurants.com. Reservations recommended. Main courses $9–$24. AE, DC, DISC, MC, V. Mon–Fri 6am–2pm and 4–10pm; Sat 6am–10:30pm; Sun 6am–9:30pm.

PORTLAND AFTER DARK

To find out what's going on, pick up a copy of *Willamette Week* or the "A&E" section of Friday's *Oregonian.* Tickets for many events can be purchased through **Ticketmaster** (© **503/224-4400;** www.ticketmaster.com) or **Tickets West** (© **800/992-8499** or 503/224-8499; http://ticketswest.rdln.com).

THE PERFORMING ARTS   For the most part, the Portland performing arts scene revolves around the **Portland Center for the Performing Arts,** 1111 SW Broadway (© **503/248-4335;** www.pcpa.com), which is comprised of five theaters in three different buildings.

Founded in 1896, the **Oregon Symphony** (© **800/228-7343** or 503/228-1353; www.orsymphony.org) is the oldest symphony orchestra on the West Coast. The diverse season runs September through May. Performances are held at the Arlene Schnitzer Concert Hall, 1037 SW Broadway at Main Street, an immaculately restored 1920s Italian Rococo Revival movie palace. The **Oregon Ballet Theatre** (© **888/922-5538** or 503/222-5538; www.obt.org), which performs primarily at the Keller Auditorium, is best loved for its December performances of *The Nutcracker.*

Portland Center Stage, Gerding Theater at the Armory, 128 NW Eleventh Ave. (© **503/445-3700;** www.pcs.org), is the city's largest professional theater company. The season runs October through early June.

THE CLUB & MUSIC SCENE   The **Crystal Ballroom,** 1332 W. Burnside St. (© **503/225-0047;** www.mcmenamins.com), has over the years seen everyone from James Brown to the Grateful Dead. The theater is noted for its "floating" dance floor (set on hidden rollers so that it bounces). The **Aladdin Theater,** 3017 SE Milwaukie Ave. (© **503/233-1994;** www.aladdin-theater.com), is one of the city's main venues for touring performers such as Richard Thompson and Brian Wilson. A diverse performance calendar usually includes blues, rock, country, folk, and jazz.

THE BAR SCENE   At the **Rogue Ales Public House,** 1339 NW Flanders St. (© **503/222-5910;** www.rogue.com), you can sample the beers of one of Oregon's most diverse and eclectic breweries. Don't miss the Old Crustacean ale. With two levels of brewpubs, a restaurant, and a bakery, **Bridgeport Brewpub + Bakery,** 1313 NW Marshall St. (© **503/241-3612;** www.bridgeportbrew.com), in the trendy Pearl District, is Portland's oldest microbrewery. The Pearl District's other big brewpub is the **Deschutes Brewery & Public House,** 210 NW 11th Ave. (© **503/296-4906;** www.deschutesbrewery.com), a satellite of a popular central Oregon brewery. For organic beers, head to **Roots**

Organic Brewing Company, 1520 SE Seventh Ave. (© **503/235-7668;** www.roots
organicbrewing.com).

If you want to taste some Oregon pinot noirs, drop by **Oregon Wines on Broadway,** 515 SW Broadway (© **800/943-8858** or 503/228-4655; www.oregonwinesonbroadway. com), which usually has 30 red wines available for tasting or by the glass. For the best cocktails with a view (and a great happy hour), head to the bar at **Portland City Grill,** 111 SW Fifth Ave. (© **503/450-0030;** www.portlandcitygrill.com), on the 30th floor of the US Bancorp Tower.

7 THE OREGON COAST

One of the most beautiful coastlines in the United States, the spectacular Oregon coast is this state's top tourist destination. Beginning less than 2 hours from Portland, the coast has everything from rugged coves to long sandy beaches, from artists' communities to classic family beach towns.

The quickest route from Portland to the coast is via **U.S. 26,** also called the Sunset Highway.

ASTORIA

If you're interested in history and historic towns, turn north at the junction with U.S. 101 and proceed 20 minutes to Astoria. Situated on the banks of the Columbia River just inland from the river's mouth, this is the oldest American community west of the Mississippi. More a river town than a beach town, Astoria boasts hillsides of restored Victorian homes and scenic views across the Columbia to the hills of southwestern Washington. However, the town's biggest claim to fame is that it was here Lewis and Clark's Corps of Discovery spent the winter of 1805–06 at a log structure they named Fort Clatsop. A restoration of their "fort" can be seen a few miles southwest of town at **Lewis and Clark National Historical Park,** 92343 Fort Clatsop Rd. (© **503/861-2471;** www. nps.gov/lewi). Not far from Fort Clatsop, near the mouth of the Columbia River, there are miles of wide sand beaches and bike trails at **Fort Stevens State Park** (© **503/861-1671;** www.oregonstateparks.org).

In downtown Astoria, you'll find the impressive **Columbia River Maritime Museum,** 1792 Marine Dr. (© **503/325-2323;** www.crmm.org), several smaller historical museums, and numerous art galleries, boutiques, and good restaurants.

Astoria's most luxurious lodging choice is the **Cannery Pier Hotel,** 10 Basin St. (© **888/325-4996** or 503/325-4996; www.cannerypierhotel.com; $179–$299 double), which is built at the end of a 600-foot-long pier on the Columbia River. For historic accommodations, try the stylish **Hotel Elliott,** 357 12th St. (© **877/378-1924** or 503/ 325-2222; www.hotelelliott.com; $109–$350).

For more information, contact the **Astoria-Warrenton Area Chamber of Commerce,** 111 W. Marine Dr. (P.O. Box 176), Astoria, OR 97103 (© **800/875-6807** or 503/325-6311; www.oldoregon.com).

CANNON BEACH

Cannon Beach is the artsiest town on the Oregon coast and lies just off U.S. 101 a few miles south of the junction with U.S. 26. Before you reach the town, detour to **Ecola Beach State Park** for some of the most spectacular views on the coast. Several trails lead through the park's lush forest, which contains stands of old-growth spruce, hemlock, and Douglas fir. The park's Indian Beach is popular with surfers.

What makes Cannon Beach truly memorable are the views of offshore rocks, most of which are protected as nesting grounds for colorful **tufted puffins** and other seabirds. The most famous of these monoliths is the massive 235-foot-tall **Haystack Rock,** the most photographed rock on the coast. At low tide, Haystack Rock is popular with beach-combers and tide-pool explorers.

In mid-June, **Sand Castle Day** attracts sand sculptors and thousands of appreciative viewers, and throughout the year, the winds are ideal for kite flying. For many visitors, **shopping** is the town's greatest attraction. You'll find dozens of galleries and shops along Hemlock Street, selling everything from fine crafts to casual fashions.

Three miles south of town on U.S. 101, watch for the pretty little **Arcadia Beach Wayside.** Another mile farther south, you'll come to **Hug Point State Recreation Site,** which has picnic tables and a sheltered beach. Rugged and remote **Oswald West State Park,** 10 miles south of Cannon Beach, is one of our favorites. A short trail takes you through dense forest to a driftwood-strewn beach on a small cove. Hiking trails lead to headlands on either side of the cove. The waves here are popular with surfers, and there are plenty of picnic tables.

The **Stephanie Inn,** 2740 S. Pacific St. (© 800/633-3466 or 503/436-2221; www.stephanie-inn.com; $369–$529 double), a classic Cape Cod–style lodge, is one of the most romantic inns on the Oregon coast; rooms have fireplaces, Jacuzzi tubs, and DVD players. **Cannon Beach Hotel Lodgings,** 1116 S. Hemlock St. (© 800/238-4107 or 503/436-1392; www.cannonbeachhotel.com; $85–$240 double), has a wide variety of rooms that fit a broad range of budgets.

For more information, contact the **Cannon Beach Chamber of Commerce,** 207 N. Spruce St. (P.O. Box 64), Cannon Beach, OR 97110 (© 503/436-2623; www.cannonbeach.org).

TILLAMOOK COUNTY

U.S. 101 continues south from Oswald West State Park and climbs over **Neahkahnie Mountain.** Legend has it that the survivors of a wrecked Spanish galleon buried a fortune in gold at the base of this ocean-side mountain. Keep your eyes open for elk, which frequently graze in the meadows here.

Just below the mountain is the quiet resort village of **Manzanita.** Tucked under the fir, spruce, and hemlock trees are attractive summer homes. There's not much to do here except walk along the sandy beach, which is precisely the appeal of the place.

Just before reaching the busy town of **Tillamook,** which lies inland from the Pacific at the south end of Tillamook Bay, you'll come to the **Tillamook Cheese Factory,** 4175 U.S. 101 N. (© 503/815-1300; www.tillamookcheese.com). Since 1854, Tillamook has been producing cheese, and today this factory turns out a substantial portion of the cheese consumed in the Northwest. Each year, hundreds of thousands of visitors watch the cheese-making process through large windows. The store sells an assortment of tasty cheeses and ice creams.

From Tillamook, the **Three Capes Scenic Route** leads to Cape Meares, Cape Lookout, and Cape Kiwanda, all of which provide stunning vistas of rocky cliffs, misty mountains, and booming surf.

Cape Meares State Park is the site of the Cape Meares Lighthouse, built in 1890 and open to the public. Continuing around the cape, you'll come to the village of Oceanside.

If you walk north along the beach, you'll find a pedestrian tunnel through the headland that protects this hillside community. Through the tunnel is another beautiful stretch of beach.

A few miles south of Oceanside is **Cape Lookout State Park.** A breathtaking trail leads to the end of Cape Lookout, which is an excellent spot for whale-watching in the spring and fall. **Cape Kiwanda,** which lies just outside the town of Pacific City, is the last of the three capes on this scenic loop. This sandstone headland is backed by a huge sand dune that is fun to run down. At the base of the cape is the staging area for Pacific City's beach-launched dory fishing fleet. Located right on the beach and boasting a terrific view, the **Pelican Pub & Brewery,** 33180 Cape Kiwanda Dr. (© **503/965-7007;** www.pelicanbrewery.com), is a good spot to grab a burger and a beer.

With its artfully designed modern cabins, **Coast Cabins,** 635 Laneda Ave. (© **800/ 435-1269** or 503/368-7113; www.coastcabins.com; $125–$375 double), is our favorite lodging in Manzanita. There's also the romantic **Inn at Manzanita,** 67 Laneda Ave. (© **503/368-6754;** www.innatmanzanita.com; $120–$180 double), where double whirlpool tubs sit between the fireplace and the bed in every room, and balconies look out through shady pines to the ocean. In Pacific City, the **Inn at Cape Kiwanda,** 33105 Cape Kiwanda Dr. (© **888/965-7001;** www.innatcapekiwanda.com; $169–$249 double), a cedar-shingled modern (and romantic) hotel, has rooms with great views of Pacific City's Haystack Rock.

For more information on the area, contact the **Tillamook Area Chamber of Commerce,** 3705 U.S. 101 N., Tillamook, OR 97141 (© **503/842-7525;** www.tillamook chamber.org).

LINCOLN CITY

Lincoln City, 44 miles south of Tillamook, is not really a city, but a collection of five small towns that stretch for miles along the coast. Over the years, these towns have all grown together as this area has become the state's most popular beach destination.

Family vacationers will love Lincoln City's 7$^{1}/_{2}$-mile-long sandy beach. The water may be too cold for swimming, but the steady winds here offer the best **kite flying** on the Oregon coast. The Summer Kite Festival takes place in late June, while the Fall Kite Festival is held in early October.

Adding to the appeal of the Lincoln City beach area is **Devil's Lake,** which drains across the beach by way of the D River, the world's shortest river. Boating, sailing, waterskiing, boardsailing, swimming, fishing, and camping are popular activities here.

Nearby Gleneden Beach is home to the largest full-service resort on the coast, the **Salishan Spa & Golf Resort,** 7760 U.S. 101 N. (© **800/452-2300** or 541/764-3600; www.salishan.com; $160–$350 double), which has a fine-dining restaurant and an excellent golf course.

For more information on the area, contact the **Lincoln City Visitor and Convention Bureau,** 801 SW U.S. 101, Ste. 1, Lincoln City, OR 97367 (© **800/452-2151** or 541/ 996-1274; www.oregoncoast.org).

DEPOE BAY

Depoe Bay, 13 miles south of Lincoln City, calls itself the smallest harbor in the world, and although the tiny harbor covers only 6 acres, it's home to more than 100 fishing boats. Just outside the harbor mouth, storm waves cause the impressive fountains of Depoe Bay's famous spouting horns. These geyserlike fountains send plumes of water into the air when waves break in the narrow fissures of the area's rocky coastline.

On U.S. 101, you'll find a row of garish souvenir shops, plus several family restaurants as well as charter-fishing and whale-watching companies.

The road south from Depoe Bay winds its way through grand, rugged scenery and passes small picturesque coves. Several miles south of town, watch for signs to the **Otter Crest State Scenic Viewpoint,** atop Cape Foulweather. Keep an eye out for sea lions sunning themselves on offshore rocks.

Just south of Cape Foulweather, you'll find **Devils Punchbowl State Natural Area.** The site of a collapsed sea cave becomes a cauldron of churning foam during high tides or stormy seas. A short path here leads to an area known as the marine gardens, where you can explore numerous tide pools containing various sea creatures.

Channel House Inn, 35 Ellingson St., Depoe Bay (© **800/447-2140** or 541/765-2140; www.channelhouse.com; $100–$330 double), is a luxurious inn built above the narrow channel into Depoe Bay; all rooms have whirlpool tubs and fireplaces.

Contact the **Depoe Bay Chamber of Commerce,** 223 SW U.S. 101, Ste. B (P.O. Box 21), Depoe Bay, OR 97341 (© **877/485-8348** or 541/765-2889; www.depoebay chamber.org).

NEWPORT

As coastal towns go, Newport has a split personality. Dockworkers unloading fresh fish mingle with vacationers licking ice-cream cones as freeloading sea lions wait for their next meal from the processing plants along the waterfront. Many of the town's old cottages and late-19th-century buildings still stand, and despite downtown's souvenir shops, galleries, and restaurants, Newport is also home to the largest commercial fishing fleet on the Oregon coast.

Newport is home to the **Oregon Coast Aquarium,** 2820 SE Ferry Slip Rd. (© **541/867-3474;** www.aquarium.org), the Oregon coast's top attraction. There are seals, otters, sea lions, tufted puffins, jellyfish, a giant octopus, and a huge walk-through tank full of sharks. Admission is $14 adults, $12 seniors, and $8.75 children 3 to 12. Memorial Day to Labor Day daily, the aquarium is open from 9am to 6pm, the rest of the year daily from 10am to 5pm.

Beaches in the Newport area range from tiny rocky coves where you can search for agates, to long, wide stretches of sand perfect for kite flying. Right in town, north and west of the Yaquina Bay Bridge, you'll find **Yaquina Bay State Recreation Site,** which borders both the ocean and the bay. North of Newport is **Agate Beach,** which has a stunning view of Yaquina Head. This latter spot has a historic lighthouse and is preserved as the **Yaquina Head Outstanding Natural Area.** Two miles south of Newport, you'll find **South Beach State Park,** a wide, sandy beach with picnic areas and a large campground that rents yurts (if you haven't brought your own tent).

Six miles south of Newport, you'll find **Ona Beach State Park,** a sandy beach with a picnic area under the trees. Beaver Creek, a fairly large stream, flows through the park and across the beach to the ocean. **Seal Rock State Recreation Site** is another 2 miles south. Here a long wall of rock rises from the waves and sand, creating numerous tide pools and fascinating nooks and crannies to explore.

North of town in a grove of fir trees on the edge of a cliff, the condos at **Starfish Point,** 140 NW 48th St. (© **800/870-7795** or 541/265-3751; www.starfishpoint.com; $150–$215 double), are our favorite rooms in the area. The bathrooms here are extravagant, with double whirlpool tubs and skylights or big windows. For unique accommodations, book a stateroom on the *Newport Belle* **Bed & Breakfast,** Newport South Beach Marina

(© **800/348-1922** or 541/867-6290; www.newportbelle.com; $135–$165 double), a reproduction paddle-wheeler moored near the Oregon Coast Aquarium. The **Sylvia Beach Hotel,** 267 NW Cliff St. (© **888/795-8422** or 541/265-5428; www.sylviabeach hotel.com; $70–$193 double), has rooms named for different authors, and in each you'll find memorabilia, books, and decor that reflects these writers' lives, times, and works. The hotel's restaurant is a local favorite.

Contact the **Greater Newport Chamber of Commerce,** 555 SW Coast Hwy., Newport, OR 97365 (© **800/262-7844** or 541/265-8801; www.newportchamber.org).

YACHATS

Located 26 miles south of Newport, the village of Yachats (pronounced *Yah*-hots) is known as something of an artists' community—small but sophisticated and a little bit funky. The town is set on a pretty cove with adjoining rocky beaches and the Yachats River flowing into the surf. To the east, steep mountains rise up on the edge of town.

Looming over the town is the bulk of **Cape Perpetua,** which, at 800 feet, is the highest spot on the Oregon coast. The **Cape Perpetua Interpretive Center** (© **541/547-3289;** www.fs.fed.us/r6/siuslaw), located up a steep road off U.S. 101, houses displays on the cape's natural history and the Native Americans who harvested its seafood for hundreds of years. Within the Cape Perpetua Scenic Area are more than 25 miles of hiking trails, tide pools, ancient forests, scenic overlooks, and a campground.

If you're looking for wide, sandy **beaches,** continue south to the Stonefield Beach State Recreation Site, Muriel O. Ponsler Memorial State Scenic Viewpoint, or Carl G. Washburne Memorial State Park. Washburne offers 2 miles of beach, plus hiking trails and a campground. At Heceta Head Lighthouse State Scenic Viewpoint, you'll find a pretty little cove, a historic lighthouse, and 7 miles of hiking trails.

The **Shamrock Lodgettes,** 105 U.S. 101 S. (© **800/845-5028** or 541/547-3312; www.shamrocklodgettes.com; $69–$189 double), classic log cabins set amid spacious lawns and old fir trees at the mouth of the Yachats River, are just bewitching, if a bit old-fashioned. For luxury, we recommend the romantic **Overleaf Lodge,** 280 Overleaf Lodge Lane (© **800/338-0507** or 541/547-4880; www.overleaflodge.com; $125–$265 double). South of Yachats, there's the **Heceta Head Keeper's House,** 92072 U.S. 101 S. (© **866/547-3696;** www.hecetalighthouse.com; $133–$315 double), a B&B housed in a historic lighthouse keeper's home at Heceta Head Lighthouse State Scenic Viewpoint. Just south of this park, there is a stupendous view of Heceta Head Lighthouse.

Contact the **Yachats Area Chamber of Commerce,** 241 U.S. 101 (P.O. Box 728), Yachats, OR 97498 (© **800/929-0477** or 541/547-3530; www.yachats.org).

FLORENCE

Florence (www.florencechamber.com), 50 miles south of Newport, has long been a popular vacation spot for families. However, with few roads providing access to the ocean's shore, this area is known more for its lakes than for its beaches. Sand dunes, the Siuslaw River, and 17 freshwater lakes offer an abundance of recreational opportunities. Many area lakes are ringed with summer homes and public campgrounds. Popular activities include water-skiing, four-wheeling through the sand dunes, and fishing.

Florence's **Old Town,** on the north bank of the Siuslaw River, has quite a bit of charm, with many restored wood and brick buildings, interesting boutiques and galleries, and waterfront seafood restaurants.

13

Barking Up a Storm with the Sea Lions

Approximately 10 miles south of Yachats, you'll find **Sea Lion Caves**, 91560 U.S. 101 N. (© **541/547-3111;** www.sealioncaves.com), the only year-round mainland home for Steller sea lions, hundreds of which reside here. Admission is $10 adults, $9 seniors, $6 children 3 to 12, free for children 2 and under. The cave is open daily from 9am to 5:30pm (6pm in summer).

THE OREGON DUNES NATIONAL RECREATION AREA

The **Oregon Dunes National Recreation Area** (© 541/271-6000; www.fs.fed.us/r6/siuslaw), more than 14,000 acres of sand dunes, stretches for more than 40 miles along the coast between Florence and Coos Bay. Within this vast area of shifting sands are dunes more than 500 feet tall, numerous lakes both large and small, living forests, and skeletal forests of trees that were long ago "drowned" beneath drifting sands. It is here that you'll find the longest unbroken publicly owned stretches of Oregon's coast.

Jessie M. Honeyman Memorial State Park (www.oregonstateparks.org), 3 miles south of Florence, is a unique spot with a beautiful forest-bordered lake and towering sand dunes. The park offers camping, picnicking, hiking trails, and access to Cleawox and Woahink lakes. Cleawox Lake has a swimming area and boat rentals, and adjacent dunes are open to off-road vehicles.

On the **Taylor Dunes Trail,** which begins at the Carter Lake Campground, 7¹/₂ miles south of Florence, a platform overlooks the dunes. It's an easy half-mile walk to the platform. If you want to get your shoes full of sand but have time for only a quick walk, you can continue on to the beach, which is less than a mile beyond the viewing platform; roughly half this distance is through dunes.

At the **Oregon Dunes Overlook,** 10 miles south of Florence, you'll find viewing platforms high atop a forested sand dune overlooking a vast expanse of bare sand. A 3.5-mile loop trail leads from this overlook out to the beach by way of Tahkenitch Creek. Another 2.5 miles south of the Dunes Overlook, you'll find the trail head for the **Tahkenitch Dunes Trail,** which gives you access to an 8.5-mile network of trails that wander through dunes, forest, marshes, and meadows.

For truly impressive dunes, the best route is the **John Dellenback Dunes Trail;** its trail head is half a mile south of **Eel Creek Campground,** which is 11 miles south of Reedsport (32 miles south of Florence). This 3-mile round-trip trail leads through an area of dunes 2 miles wide by 4 miles long. Don't get lost!

BANDON

Once known as the cranberry capital of Oregon, **Bandon** (www.bandon.com) is a seaside village set on one of the most breathtaking pieces of coastline in the Northwest. The beach is littered with boulders, monoliths, and haystack rocks that seem to have been strewn by some giant hand. About 20 miles north of town, near the town of Coos Bay, three state parks together preserve more breathtaking shoreline. The Coquille River empties into the Pacific here at Bandon, and at the river's mouth stands a picturesque little lighthouse.

Coquille Point, at the end of 11th Street, is one of the best places to view Bandon's famous rocks. Here you'll find a short paved interpretive trail atop a bluff overlooking the beach, rock monoliths, and the river's mouth. From nearby **Face Rock Viewpoint,** you can see the area's most famous rock, which resembles a face gazing skyward.

At **Sunset Bay State Park,** 20 miles north of Bandon, you'll find a small bay almost completely surrounded by sandstone cliffs. The entrance to the bay is narrow, which means the waters here stay fairly calm. This is one of the few beaches in Oregon where the water gets warm enough for swimming. Picnicking and camping are available in the park, and there are lots of tide pools to explore.

Another 3 miles southwest brings you to **Shore Acres State Park,** once the estate of a local shipping tycoon who spent years developing his gardens. The park includes formal English and Japanese gardens atop sandstone cliffs overlooking the Pacific and a tiny cove. Along the shoreline, rock walls rise from the water and have been sculpted by the waves into unusual shapes.

Continue a little farther along the same road and you'll come to **Cape Arago State Park.** Just offshore from the rugged cape are Shell Island and the rocks and small islands of Simpson Reef, which together offer numerous sunbathing spots for hundreds of seals (including elephant seals) and sea lions. Their barking can be heard from hundreds of yards away. The best viewing point is the **Simpson Reef Viewpoint.** *Tip:* Information on all three state parks is available online at **www.oregonstateparks.org.**

The **Bandon Dunes Golf Resort,** 57744 Round Lake Dr. (© **888/345-6008** or 541/347-4380; www.bandondunesgolf.com; $100–$360 double), offers the most tasteful and luxurious accommodations on the Oregon coast. However, the emphasis is so entirely on the golf course that anyone not interested in the game will feel like an interloper. Dozens of Bandon's famous monoliths rise from the sand and waves in front of the **Sunset Oceanfront Lodgings,** 1865 Beach Loop Dr. (© **800/842-2407** or 541/347-2453; www.sunsetmotel.com; $50–$160 double), making sunsets from the Sunset memorable. Although many of the rooms are dated, the view can't be beat.

For more information, contact the **Bandon Chamber of Commerce,** 300 Second St. (P.O. Box 1515), Bandon, OR 97411 (© **541/347-9616;** www.bandon.com).

8 THE COLUMBIA RIVER GORGE & MOUNT HOOD

Formed when 1,000-foot-high ice-age floodwaters raged down the Columbia River, the Columbia River Gorge is a landscape of rare beauty that has been preserved as the Columbia River Gorge National Scenic Area. Within this flood-carved landscape, sheer basalt cliffs rise from the river and diaphanous waterfalls cascade down dark, forested heights. The Gorge is the only sea-level gap along the entire length of the Cascade Range, which stretches from California to Canada, and consequently, this massive opening in the mountains serves as a sort of natural wind tunnel that funnels air between the cool, moist coastal regions and the hot, dry interior.

Although I-84 runs beside the river on the Oregon side, and Wash. 14 follows the Washington shore, a leisurely drive along U.S. 30, the **Historic Columbia River Highway,** is the preferred way to see the Gorge. This winding highway parallels I-84 for 22 miles at the west end of the Gorge and for 15 miles at the east end. Along the way there are close-up views of waterfalls, scenic vistas, and opportunities for hiking.

Rising to the south of the Gorge is 11,235-foot **Mount Hood,** Oregon's highest peak and a popular destination in both summer and winter. A drive up the Gorge can easily be combined with a loop around the mountain, and from Timberline, on the southern flanks of the mountain, you can get close-up views of Mount Hood, do a bit of hiking, and visit the historic Timberline Lodge.

From Portland, head east on I-84. At Troutdale, take the exit marked HISTORIC COLUMBIA RIVER HIGHWAY. This winding highway is an engineering marvel, but it's dwarfed by the spectacular vistas that present themselves at every turn. To learn more about the road and how it was built, stop at **Vista House** (© 503/695-2230; www.vista house.com), 733 feet above the river on Crown Point. Here you'll find interpretive displays and a spectacular view that includes Beacon Rock, an 800-foot-tall monolith on the far side of the river.

There are some 77 waterfalls in the Columbia Gorge, but **Multnomah Falls** is the most impressive and best known. At 620 feet from the lip to the pool, it's also the tallest waterfall in Oregon and the second-tallest year-round waterfall in the United States. A paved trail leads to the top of the falls and a dizzying view from an observation platform.

Near **Ainsworth State Park** (© 503/695-2301; www.oregonstateparks.org), the western segment of the Historic Columbia River Highway comes to an end. Five miles east of here on I-84, you'll come to **Bonneville Lock and Dam** (© 541/374-8820; www.nwp.usace.army.mil/op/b/home.asp). In operation since 1938, this is the oldest dam on the river. Thousands of visitors come each year to see its fish ladder, which allows salmon and other fish to migrate upstream. June and September are the best months to observe salmon. Also be sure to visit the trout and sturgeon ponds.

Just east of the dam is the **Bridge of the Gods,** which connects Oregon and Washington at the site where an old Indian legend says a natural bridge once stood. Geologists believe that the legend has its basis in fact. There is evidence that 500 years ago a massive rock slide blocked the river at this point.

On the Washington side of the Columbia, east of the Bridge of the Gods, is the **Columbia Gorge Interpretive Center Museum,** 990 SW Rock Creek Dr., Stevenson (© 800/991-2338 or 509/427-8211; www.columbiagorge.org). This museum is the single best introduction to the natural and human history of the Columbia Gorge; it also boasts an awesome view. Admission is $7 adults, $6 seniors and students, and $5 children 6 to 12. Hours are daily from 10am to 5pm.

Just beyond Bridge of the Gods on the Oregon side is **Cascade Locks** where, in 1896, navigational locks were built so that river traffic could avoid the treacherous passage through the cascades that once existed at this spot. There are two small museums here, one of which also holds the ticket office for **Portland Spirit** (© 800/224-3901 or 503/224-3900; www.portlandspirit.com), which operates the stern-wheeler *Columbia Gorge.* This tour boat makes regular trips on the river between May and October. Sightseeing excursions are $26 for adults and $16 for children. Dinner and brunch cruises are also offered.

Anyone who windsurfs has likely heard of the town of Hood River. Because of the strong winds that blow through the gorge in summer, the Hood River section of the Columbia River is one of the most popular windsurfing spots in the world. If you want to try this thrilling sport, stop by one of the many board shops downtown for rental and instruction information. In recent years, kite-surfing, which uses a kite instead of a sail, has also become very popular here.

The **Mount Hood Railroad,** 110 Railroad Ave., Hood River (© 800/872-4661 or 541/386-3556; www.mthoodrr.com), is an excursion train that uses vintage rail cars to carry passengers up the Hood River Valley from the town of Hood River to Odell and Parkdale and back. Fares for the 4-hour excursion are $30 adults, $26 seniors, and $18 children 2 to 12. The train runs from April to late December (mid-Apr to late June and Sept–Oct Wed–Sun; July–Aug Tues–Sun; Nov–Dec, schedule varies).

If you continue heading east on I-84 from Hood River, you'll come to the **Dalles,** which was an important stop on the Oregon Trail. Here in the Dalles, you can learn more about the Columbia Gorge at the **Columbia Gorge Discovery Center,** 5000 Discovery Dr. (© **541/296-8600;** www.gorgediscovery.org). Among the displays here are reproduced historic storefronts and Native American artifacts. Admission is $8 adults, $7 seniors, and $4 children ages 6 to 16. Hours are daily from 9am to 5pm.

If you turn south on Ore. 35 at Hood River, you'll pass through thousands of acres of apple, pear, and cherry orchards. Shortly after Ore. 35 merges into U.S. 26, turn right onto the road to **Timberline Lodge.** As the name implies, this lodge is at the timberline, and a July or August walk on one of the trails in the vicinity will lead you through wildflower-filled meadows. Because of the glacier and snowfields above the lodge, you can ski and snowboard here all summer long.

WHERE TO STAY & DINE

The **Columbia Gorge Hotel,** 4000 Westcliff Dr., just west of Hood River (© **800/345-1921** or 541/386-5566; www.columbiagorgehotel.com), which perches 200 feet above the Columbia River atop a cliff, opened in 1921 and is the grande dame hotel of the gorge. While the rooms tend to look a bit dated, the gardens and the views make this one of your best options in the area. Rates run $199 to $249 double.

Constructed during the Depression as a WPA project, the classic Alpine-style **Timberline Lodge,** Timberline (© **800/547-1406** or 503/272-3391; www.timberlinelodge.com), boasts a stone fireplace, exposed beams, wide plank floors, woodcarvings, wrought-iron fixtures, hand-hooked rugs, and handmade furniture. Rooms vary in size, with the smallest lacking private bathrooms ($99–$105 double); some have fireplaces. The Cascade Dining Room serves pricey (but good) Northwest cuisine; however, service can be glacially slow. Rates for rooms with bathroom run $105 to $285.

On the Washington side of the Columbia River, **Skamania Lodge,** 1131 SW Skamania Lodge Way (© **800/221-7117** or 509/427-7700; www.skamania.com), in Stevenson, has the most spectacular vistas of any hotel in the Gorge, and the only golf course. The interior features a cathedral-ceilinged lobby, stone fireplace, and Native American artwork and artifacts. The dining room serves good Northwest cuisine amid views of the Gorge. Facilities include a spa, tennis courts, an indoor pool, whirlpools, a sauna, an exercise facility, nature trails, and bikes for guests to use. Guest rooms not facing the parking lot feature wonderful views. Rates from $159 to $319 double.

9 WILLAMETTE VALLEY WINE COUNTRY

Oregon's Willamette Valley, which stretches south from Portland, is one of the country's premier wine-producing regions. Pinot noir, some of which rivals that of France's Burgundy region, is what has put Oregon on the world's wine map, but area wineries also produce pinot gris, pinot blanc, chardonnay, and even sparkling wines.

Although the Willamette Valley now has plenty of large "corporate" wineries, many of the region's wineries are still small, family-owned and -operated businesses that produce moderately priced wines in limited quantities. Even many of the wineries along busy Ore. 99W, the main route through wine country, are small affairs compared to the wineries of

Napa Valley. While some of these latter wineries seem geared toward providing beach-bound vacationers with a bit of distraction and some less-than-impressive wine, there are also some good wines and good values to be found.

Wine country begins less than an hour southwest of Portland near the town of Newberg, and all along Ore. 99W, which runs through the heart of wine country, you'll see blue road signs directing you to nearby wineries. At most wineries in the region, you can pick up a map of Willamette Valley wineries. Alternatively, you can get a copy of this map by contacting **Willamette Valley Wineries,** P.O. Box 25162, Portland, OR 97298 (© **503/646-2985;** www.willamettewines.com).

In between visiting wineries, you can visit McMinnville's **Evergreen Aviation & Space Museum,** 500 NE Capt. Michael King Smith Way (© **503/434-4180;** www.spruce goose.org), which is home to Howard Hughes's famous "Spruce Goose" flying boat, an SR-71A Blackbird, and a 3-D IMAX theater.

The town of McMinnville makes the best base for exploring the north Willamette Valley wine country. Although it is part of a regional microbrew empire, the simply furnished yet artistically designed **McMenamins Hotel Oregon,** 310 NE Evans St. (© **888/472-8427** or 503/472-8427; www.mcmenamins.com; $50–$121 double), with its rooftop bar overlooking the valley, is a good place to stay. For more luxurious all-suite accommodations surrounded by the vineyards above the town of Dundee, try the **Black Walnut Inn,** 9600 NE Worden Hill Rd. (© **866/429-4114** or 503/429-4114; www. blackwalnut-inn.com; $180–$430 double). The most unusual inn in the area is **Abbey Road Farm,** 10501 NE Abbey Rd., Carlton (© **503/852-6278;** www.abbeyroadfarm. com), which has luxurious guest rooms in three large metal silos.

10 CRATER LAKE NATIONAL PARK

At 1,943 feet deep, Crater Lake is the deepest lake in the United States and one of the deepest in the world. But depth alone is not what makes this one of the most visited spots in the Northwest—it's the startling sapphire-blue waters that are mesmerizing.

The **caldera** (crater) that today holds the serene lake was born in an explosive volcanic eruption 7,700 years ago. When the volcano now known as Mount Mazama erupted, its summit (thought to have been around 12,000 ft. high) collapsed, leaving a crater 4,000 feet deep. Thousands of years of rain and melting snow created cold, clear Crater Lake, which today is surrounded by walls nearly 2,000 feet high.

Don't despair as you drive through uninteresting forest en route to the lake. The drive into the park winds through forests that don't provide a glimpse of the lake. With no warning except the signs leading to Rim Village, you'll suddenly find yourself gazing down into a vast bowl full of blue water. Toward one end of the lake rises the cone of Wizard Island, the tip of a volcano that has been slowly building since the last eruption of Mount Mazama.

Crater Lake is 57 miles north of Klamath Falls via U.S. 97 and Ore. 62, and 71 miles northeast of Medford via Ore. 62. In winter, only the south entrance is open. Due to deep snowpack, the north entrance usually doesn't open until sometime in late July.

Park admission (good for 7 days) is $10 per vehicle. For information, contact **Crater Lake National Park,** P.O. Box 7, Crater Lake, OR 97604 (© **541/594-3100;** www.nps. gov/crla).

After your first breathtaking view of the lake, you may want to stop by one of the park's two visitor centers—**Steel Visitor Center** and **Rim Visitor Center.** The park is open year-round, but in winter, when deep snows blanket the region, only the road to **Rim Village** is kept clear. In summer (beginning roughly in late June), the 39-mile Rim Drive provides stunning views.

Boat trips around the lake are the park's most popular activity. These tours last $1^3/_4$ hours and begin at Cleetwood Cove, at the bottom of a very steep 1.1-mile trail that descends 700 feet from the rim to the lakeshore. Be sure you're in good enough physical condition to make the steep climb back up to the rim. Bring warm clothes, as it can be quite a bit cooler on the lake than on the rim. A naturalist on each boat provides a narrative on the ecology and history of the lake; all tours include a stop on Wizard Island. Tours are offered from early July to mid-September and cost $26 for adults ($36 if you want to get dropped off on Wizard Island) and $16 for children 3 to 11 ($20 for drop-off on Wizard Island).

Many miles of **hiking trails** can be found in the park, but the Cleetwood Trail is the only one that leads down to the lakeshore. The trail to the top of Mount Scott, although a rigorous 2.5 miles, is the park's most rewarding hike. Shorter trails with good views include the .7-mile trail to the top of the Watchman, which overlooks Wizard Island, and the 1.7-mile trail up Garfield Peak. The short Castle Crest Wildflower Trail is best hiked in late July and early August, when the wildflowers are at the height of their glory. Backpackers can hike the length of the park on the Pacific Crest Trail.

In winter, **cross-country skiing** is popular on the park's snow-covered roads. Skiers in good condition can usually make the entire circuit of the lake in 2 days but must be prepared to camp in the snow. Spring, when the weather is warmer and there are fewer severe storms, is actually the best time to ski around the lake.

WHERE TO STAY & CAMP

The park contains two lodging options. Overlooking the lake from the rim, **Crater Lake Lodge** (© 541/830-8700; www.craterlakelodges.com) has the look and feel of a historic mountain lodge, and though it boasts many modern conveniences, guest rooms do not have telephones, televisions, or air-conditioning. About half the rooms overlook the lake. The dining room serves creative Northwest cuisine and provides a view of both Crater Lake and the Klamath River basin. Rates run $143 to $267 double. A short drive away, the **Cabins at Mazama Village** (© 541/830-8700; www.craterlakelodges.com) is, despite the name, a collection of motel-style rooms in 10 buildings that are designed to resemble traditional mountain cabins. Once again, there are no TVs, telephones, or air-conditioning. Rates are $122 double. Both lodges are closed from mid-October to late May.

Tent camping and RV spaces are available on the south side of the park at the **Mazama Campground,** which is open mid-June through early October. There are also tent sites at **Lost Creek Campground** on the park's east side. This latter campground is open mid-July through early October. Reservations are accepted only at Mazama Campground (contact Crater Lake Lodge, see above).

14

Alaska & Hawaii

They're not part of the Lower 48, but the newest United States (both admitted in 1959), can be considered domestic *and* exotic destinations. In 2008, both were noteworthy for providing half the Democrat and Republican top candidates in the national elections. As destinations, both offer an abundance of natural beauty—admittedly of different types—not found anywhere else in the country.

Alaska, geographically the largest state in the country (twice the size of Texas!), has more unexplored wilderness and arctic beauty than any other state in the nation. Few won't gasp in amazement when they see a chunk of ice the size of a building fall from a glacier, a bear, or caribou grazing in one of the numerous state parks, or an orca feeding in the waters off the southeast coast. It's the ultimate destination for those who like their terrain rugged and unspoiled.

If arctic glaciers and rugged outdoor sports attract visitors to Alaska, then sun-soaked beaches, loads of water fun, and breathtaking, lush greenery lure travelers (nearly seven million of them each year) to **Hawaii.** There's no place quite like this handful of sun-drenched mid-Pacific islands, remote no matter what continent you live on. The possibilities for adventure—and relaxation—are endless, whether you want to surf a wave, snorkel in pristine waters, or hike a volcano.

Note: We discuss many of the best spots for the first-time visitor in this chapter, but it's admittedly the tip of the iceberg—covering the cream of the crop in each state would take an entire book. If you plan to visit either state, we highly recommend getting detailed guidebooks such as *Frommer's Alaska* and *Frommer's Hawaii*.

1 SOUTHEAST ALASKA

The Southeast Panhandle is the relatively narrow strip of mountains and islands between Canada and the Gulf of Alaska. It's a land of huge rainforest trees, glacier-garbed mountains, and countless islands, all of it reachable by the ferry system or cruise ships along the waterway known as the **Inside Passage.** This land of ice and forest may not look as large on the map as other parts of Alaska, but the better you know it, the bigger it becomes, until you have to surrender to its immensity. Nearly all of Southeast Alaska, stretching 500 miles from Ketchikan to Yakutat, is in **Tongass National Forest.** The towns sit in small pockets of private land surrounded by 17 million acres of land controlled by the U.S. Forest Service—an area nearly as large as the state of Maine, and considerably larger than any other national forest or any national park in the U.S. Southeast contains **Juneau,** Alaska's capital and third-largest city; and **Ketchikan,** next in size to Juneau. Southeast's towns are as quaint and historic as any in Alaska, especially **Sitka,** which preserves the story of Russian America and its conflict with the indigenous Native people. Alaska **Native culture**—Tlingit and Haida—is rich and close at hand, as is the history of the region's **gold rush,** which towns have turned into perpetual performance art. No other region is richer in opportunities for boating or seeing marine wildlife. The weather is wet and temperate.

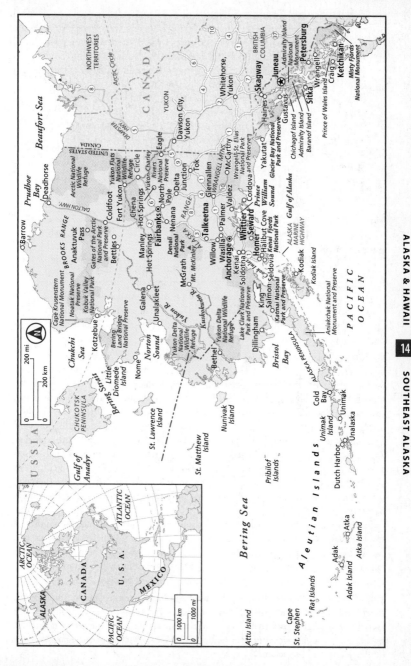

Arriving by Cruise Ship

Most visitors to Southeast Alaska (and many visitors headed to Anchorage) arrive by cruise ship, stopping at the port towns by day and allowing the ship to do the traveling for them by night. It's by far the easiest and most comfortable way of seeing the state, though what you save in convenience you obviously give back in lack of control and spontaneity. Where the ship goes, you go, and on shore you're rarely out of a crowd.

Covering all of the cruise options available for Alaska would literally take an entire book, so if you're interested in visiting Alaska in this manner, contact the **Alaska Travel Industry Association,** 2600 Cordova St., Ste. 201, Anchorage, AK 99503 (© **907/929-2842;** www.travelalaska.com), the state's official visitor information agency. Or get a dedicated guidebook, such as *Frommer's Alaska Cruises & Ports of Call.*

ESSENTIALS

GETTING THERE   By Plane   Since most of Southeast Alaska's towns are not linked by road, anyone traveling to or around the region does so by plane or boat. Major towns without road access have jet service, provided by **Alaska Airlines** (© 800/252-7522; www.alaskaair.com), the region's only major airline. **Juneau International Airport** (www. juneau.org/airport) is Southeast Alaska's travel hub. Ketchikan and Sitka each have a few flights a day.

By Ferry   The state-run **Alaska Marine Highway System** (© 800/642-0066 or 907/ 465-3941, or 800/764-3779 TTY; www.ferryalaska.com) is a subsidized fleet of big, blue-hulled ferries whose mission is to connect the roadless coastal towns of Alaska for roughly the same cost you'd pay if there were roads and you were driving. Call for a free schedule, or download it from the website. If you're bringing a vehicle or need a cabin, be sure to make reservations as early as possible. Rates vary widely depending on your destination, whether you're bringing a vehicle, whether you're reserving a cabin, and so on. Call or consult the website to get current rates. One way around the state's reservation system is to call **Viking Travel,** in Petersburg (**800/327-2571** or 907/772-3818; www. alaskaferry.com), which will accept, without additional service charges, your booking before the official reservation system opens, then reserve it the first day the system becomes available.

In the summer, on-board Forest Service guides offer interpretive talks in Southeast's Inside Passage and in Prince William Sound. The system's weaknesses are the crowds during the July peak season, the fact that if they're late they can be many hours late (although they're usually on time), and a shortage of cabins, which means that most people have to camp on deck or in chairs during overnight passages.

VISITOR INFORMATION   The **Southeast Alaska Discovery Center,** 50 Main St., Ketchikan, AK 99901 (© **907/228-6220;** www.fs.fed.us/r10/tongass), is much more than a visitor center. Located a block from the cruise ship dock, the center is the best museum in the region when it comes to illustrating the interaction of the region's ecology and human society, including traditional Native and contemporary uses. Admission to these facilities in summer costs $5, free ages 15 and under, with a $15 family maximum; in winter it's free. Without paying, you can get guidance about planning your time and activities. An information kiosk is located near the entrance. The center is open May through September daily from 8am to 5pm, October through April Tuesday through Friday noon to 4pm and Saturday 10:30am to 4:30pm.

GETTING AROUND   Planes and boats are your two options. See "By Ferry" under "Getting There," above, for information on the ferry. **Wings of Alaska** (© **907/789-0790;** www.ichoosewings.com) offers many flights to surrounding communities and an active flightseeing operation.

KETCHIKAN

Not so long ago, Ketchikan was a rugged and exotic intersection of cultures built on the profits of logging Southeast's rainforest, but in a decade it has transformed itself into a tourist center. The rough waterfront streets and boardwalk red-light district of rainy Ketchikan have been prettified and packaged for the cruise ship crowds, who cram streets of gift shops when the ships dock. But when they leave, history's ghosts still lurk in the twisting streets, and the totem poles look on with their forbidding magic. Tlingit and Haida culture are close at hand, as well as outdoor water attractions.

What to See & Do

Tip: Pick up a copy of the **Official Historic Ketchikan Walking Tour Map,** available all over town, which gives you three different routes through town and loads of information about sites of interest on the way. In 2008 the town also posted handy directional signs and maps at intersections all over the downtown area.

Stop first at the **Southeast Alaska Discovery Center,** 50 Main St., Ketchikan, AK 99901 (© **907/228-6220,** or 907/288-6237 TTY; fax 907/228-6234; www.fs.fed.us/r10/tongass).

Creek Street was Ketchikan's red-light district; now it's a quaint tourist mall. **Dolly's House** (© **907/225-6329**), a museum dedicated to a prostitute who had a long career here, is amusing, mildly racy, and a little sad. Admission is $5; it's open daily from 8am to 4pm during the summer. The attractively situated **Tongass Historical Museum** (© **907/225-5600**) presents the history and Native heritage of Ketchikan ($2 admission, free in winter).

Following the creek upstream, take a look at the **fish ladder** at the Park Avenue bridge, then continue to the **Deer Mountain Tribal Hatchery & Eagle Center,** 1158 Salmon

---

Fishing in Southeast

There is great fishing in Southeast Alaska. The best fishing is away from the roads. The **Alaska Department of Fish and Game,** 2030 Sea Level Dr., Ste. 205, Ketchikan, AK 99901 (© **907/465-4100;** www.alaska.gov/adfg, click on "Sport Fishing," then on the Southeast region on the map), produces fishing guides for most of Southeast Alaska's major towns, including Ketchikan and Sitka. The guides detail where to find fish in both fresh water and salt water, and include maps of favorite fishing areas. You can pick up a copy at the Southeast Alaska Discovery Center (see "Visitor Information," above).

Rd. (© **800/252-5158** or 907/225-6760), a small king and silver salmon hatchery where you can see fry swimming in large tubs and even feed them. The eagle center exhibits captive bald eagles and other raptors in indoor cages and a large outdoor eagle enclosure. Admission costs $9 adults, kids 12 and under free.

Beyond the hatchery is **City Park,** where Ketchikan Creek splits into a maze of ornamental pools and streams once used as a hatchery. You'll find the **Totem Heritage Center** (© **907/225-5900**) here. Admission is $5 in summer to see the largest collection of original 19th-century totem poles in existence.

Two major totem pole sites that shouldn't be missed will require you to have transportation or join a tour. The excellent **Totem Bight State Historical Park,** 10 miles out of town on North Tongass Highway (© **907/247-8574**), presents poles and a clan house carved since 1938 by elders working with traditional tools to copy fragments of historic poles that had mostly rotted away. The setting, the site of a traditional fish camp, is a peaceful spot on the edge of Tongass Narrows, at the end of a short walk through the woods, so the experience is both aesthetic and educational. Admission is free. The **Saxman Native Village Totem Pole Park,** 2¹/₂ miles south of Ketchikan on the South Tongass Highway (© **907/225-4846**), has artifacts similar to those at Totem Bight Park, but with an added resource: You can watch carvers work in the building to the right of the park. The park offers 2-hour tours ($35 adults, $18 children 12 and under), which include entry to the clan house, a short performance of a Tlingit legend, and traditional dance and song by the Cape Fox Dancers. Or you can buy a pamphlet ($3) and tour the park yourself for free, though this is the kind of place that warrants a guided tour.

The islands, coves, and channels around Ketchikan create protected waters rich with life and welcoming for exploration by kayak. **Southeast Sea Kayaks** (© **800/287-1607** or 907/225-1258; www.kayakketchikan.com) rents kayaks and guides day trips and overnights. Tours start at $89 adults for a 2¹/₂-hour paddle.

Where to Stay & Dine

In addition to the places listed below, the **Ketchikan Reservation Service,** 412 D-1 Loop Rd., Ketchikan, AK 99901 (© **800/987-5337** or ©/fax 907/247-5337; www.ketchikan-lodging.com), books many B&Bs and outfitted apartments online. **Alaska Travelers Accommodations, LLC** (© **800/928-3308** or 907/247-7117; www.alaskatravelers.com), is a Ketchikan-based service of long standing that handles lodgings here, in Juneau, and scattered in other Southeast communities.

Ⓑest **Lodging in Luxury**

The **Cape Fox Lodge,** 800 Venetia Way, Ketchikan (© **800/325-4000** or 907/225-8001; www.westcoasthotels.com), is the most beautiful hotel in Southeast Alaska. A sheer drop-off and tall rainforest trees create the lofty feeling of a treehouse in the rooms and restaurant. (The Heen Kahidi is the best in town, and offers great views along with a menu of steak and seafood at lunch and dinner.) The hotel has an understated but inspired design; masterpieces of Tlingit art lend a sense of the peace and spirit of the rainforest. Rooms are large and airy, appointed in rich-toned wood, and have attractively tiled bathrooms. All but a dozen share a view of Ketchikan and the sea and islands beyond. Rates for doubles run $200 to $230 in high season.

Salmon Falls Resort, 16707 N. Tongass Hwy. (P.O. Box 5700), Ketchikan, AK 99901 (© **800/247-9059** or 907/225-2752; www.salmonfallsresort.net), has its own waterfall where salmon spawn in August, plus a dock on Clover Passage. The resort is flawlessly managed by new owners who took over in 2008, improving on already good facilities, including freshening the bedrooms and adding a spa. A 3-day minimum stay includes all meals. It's $1,859 per person double occupancy for a 3-day stay with 2 days on the water with guide, $1,259 per person without guide, $760 room and board only.

The rooms at **Captain's Quarters Bed & Breakfast,** 325 Lund St., Ketchikan, AK 99901 (© **907/225-4912;** www.captainsquartersbb.com), rival the best hotel rooms in Ketchikan but cost half as much. All have a sweeping view of the city and the ocean. It's $105 to $115 double in high season, including continental breakfast.

The **New York Hotel/The Inn at Creek Street,** 207 Stedman St., Ketchikan, AK 99901 (© **800/225-0246;** www.thenewyorkhotel.com), have the perfect central location just off Creek Street. The quirky hotel building has antiques-furnished rooms that look out on a small boat harbor. It is on the National Register of Historic Places, and the owners have done a good job of adding modern comforts consistent with its pedigree. The inn consists of spacious, modern luxury suites with kitchens, excellent amenities, and lots of privacy. It's $119 to $129 double in high season.

Ocean View Restaurante, 1831 Tongass Ave. (© **907/225-7566**), is a lively local favorite, featuring reasonably priced, tasty dishes. The restaurant offers Mexican and Italian cuisine. Service is friendly and efficient. The pizza, delivered free, is the best in town. Expect to pay around $7 to $9 at lunch, $6 to $16 at dinner.

SITKA

Sitka's history is Alaska's richest, and there's more of interest in this town than any other you might visit. Once the capital of Russian America—and the site of a historic battle between the Russian colonists and the Tlingit tribe—Sitka retains much of the influence of both of its formative cultures. Historical photographs bear a surprising resemblance to today's city. Even a brief exploration of the attractions takes a day, and that's without time for the out-of-the-way points of interest or the outdoors. Besides its historical significance, Sitka is fun to visit. Somehow it has retained a friendly, authentic feel, despite the crush of visitors (though there are fewer than in many other Alaska towns because cruise ships can't get easy access to its harbor).

GETTING AROUND We recommend walking in this town. You can hoof it to all the sites, and it's a beautiful place to explore. The **Visitor Transit Bus** operated by the Sitka Tribe makes a continuous circuit of the sites from May to September when large cruise ships are in town. The fare is $5 round-trip or $10 all day.

What to See & Do

A kiosk in the city-operated **Harrigan Centennial Hall,** 330 Harbor Dr., next to the Crescent Boat Harbor (© **907/747-3225**), is a walk-in information stop. It is staffed 9am to 4pm daily in the summer, and you may be able to ask questions of hall staff other times. The hall is open Monday through Friday from 8am to 10pm, Saturday and Sunday 8am to 5pm. The **Sitka Convention and Visitors Bureau,** at P.O. Box 1226, Sitka, AK 99835 (© **907/747-5940**), maintains a useful website at **www.sitka.org**.

The **Sitka National Historical Park Visitor Center,** 106 Metlakatla St., Sitka, AK 99835 (© **907/747-0110;** www.nps.gov/sitk), run by the National Park Service, which maintains key historic sites in Sitka, is an essential stop to gather information and learn about what happened here. The center is open daily from 8am to 5pm in summer, Monday through Saturday from 8am to 5pm in winter. For more on the park, see below.

At the **Sitka Tribe of Alaska's Community House,** you can sign up for walking or bus tours, kayaking, trail hikes, and other activities. **Sitka Tribe Dance Performances** presents traditional dances by members of the tribe at 200 Katlian St. (© **888/270-8687** or 907/747-7290; www.sitkatribe.org). Tickets cost $6 adults, $5 kids.

Most of Alaska's historic buildings are within walking distance. Up the road to your left, at Lincoln and Cathedral streets, **St. Michael's Cathedral** (© **907/747-8120**) is the first Russian Orthodox cathedral built in the New World—or at least a facsimile of the 1848 building, which burned in 1966. The icons, saved from the fire, date from the 16th century. A $2 donation is requested.

Continue on Lincoln Street to **Castle Hill,** where the American flag first rose over Alaska in 1867. In the opposite direction on Lincoln Street, at Monastery Street, the **Bishop's House** is Alaska's most interesting historic site. Downstairs is a self-guided museum; upstairs, the bishop's quarters are furnished with original and period pieces. It's an extraordinary window into an alternate stream of American history, from a time before the founding of Seattle or San Francisco, when Sitka was the most important city on North America's Pacific Coast. The tour concludes with a visit to a beautiful little chapel with many original icons from Russia. Admission is $4.

Farther on, at Lincoln Street and College Drive, the **Sheldon Jackson Museum** (© **907/747-8981;** www.museums.state.ak.us) houses one of the best collections of Alaska Native art anywhere. Admission is $4. A few blocks down Lincoln Street you reach the must-see **Sitka National Historical Park** (© **907/747-0110**), the site of the 1804 battle in which the Russians won Southeast Alaska from its Tlingit owners. The visitor center contains a museum explaining the history and the art of totem carving and a series of workshops in which to see Native artisans at work. Outside, explore the rain-forest battlefield on trails lined with a collection of totem poles. Admission is $4.

At 1000 Raptor Way, not far from the park, the nonprofit **Alaska Raptor Center** (© **907/747-8662;** www.alaskaraptor.org) heals bald eagles, owls, and other injured birds of prey. You'll have the opportunity to see the impressive birds up close in large enclosures; the highlight is an extraordinary flight-training center, built in 2003 at a cost of $3 million. Admission is $12 for adults, $6 for kids 12 and under.

The **Sitka Wildlife Quest,** operated by Allen Marine Tours (© **888/747-8101** or 907/747-8100; www.allenmarinetours.com), does terrific wildlife boat tours, guided by well-trained naturalists. Cruises start at $59 adults, $39 children. Sitka's waters and intricate shorelines are perfect for sea kayaking. Various companies offer guided paddles. Beginners will do well with **Sitka Sound Ocean Adventures** (© **907/747-6375;** www.ssoceanadventures.com).

Where to Stay & Dine

Carol and Bill Denkinger have a passion for making the **Alaska Ocean View Bed & Breakfast,** 1101 Edgecumbe Dr. (© **907/747-8310;** www.sitka-alaska-lodging.com), a place to remember. Amenities include a covered outdoor Jacuzzi. The inn has a view of the Gulf of Alaska and is about a mile from the historic district. Rates from $149 to $249 double in high season, including full breakfast.

The **Westmark Atika,** 330 Seward St. (© **800/544-0970** or 907/747-56241; www.westmarkhotels.com), overlooks Crescent Harbor in the heart of the historic district. The lobby suggests the building style of Northwest Native Americans; the rooms have furniture of warm wood and all the expected amenities. Rates from $140–$160 double. The

Raven Dining Room restaurant shares the hotel's view and is one of the best places in town for an evening meal.

The **Galley Deli,** near the big fuel tanks on the waterfront at the end of Lincoln Street (© 907/747-9997), produces huge sandwiches on homemade bread, delicious wraps and salads, and rich chowder of local clams. **Pizza Express,** 236 Lincoln St. (© 907/966-2428), has a Mexican menu, but they also serve and deliver good pizza.

JUNEAU

Impossibly tucked into the mountains along the Gastineau Channel, Juneau (*June*-oh) is the nation's most remote state capital and surely its most beautiful. Eagles wheel over downtown streets and land on mountainside rainforest roosts just blocks from the capitol. Yet the town also bustles like no other Alaskan city, the downtown streets echoing with the shopping sprees of cruise-ship passengers in the summer and the whispered intrigues of the politicians during the winter legislative session.

Downtown, the crush of visitors can be overwhelming when several cruise ships are in port at once. The streets around the docks have been taken over by shops and other touristy businesses, but only a few blocks away are mountainside neighborhoods of houses with mossy roofs, and the woods and mountains, populated by bears, eagles, and salmon. The city's many government workers make it the most cosmopolitan town between Vancouver and Anchorage, a place where you can get a great meal at the end of a day's mountain hike or kayak paddle.

GETTING AROUND A car is a hindrance in compact downtown Juneau, but if you're going to the Mendenhall Glacier or to any of the attractions out the road or on Douglas Island, renting a car for a day or two is a good idea. Hertz, Avis, Budget, Alamo, and National are based at Juneau's airport. If you can handle hills, bikes make good sense in Juneau. The 24-mile round-trip to Mendenhall Glacier keeps you on a bike path almost all the way. Bikes are for rent at the **Driftwood Lodge,** 435 Willoughby Ave. (© 800/544-2239 or 907/586-2280; www.driftwoodalaska.com), for $25 a day, $15 for a half-day.

What to See & Do

The **Visitor Information Center** is in the Centennial Hall at 101 Egan Dr., near the State Museum (© 888/581-2201 or 907/586-2201; fax 907/586-6304; www.travel juneau.com). The center is open in summer Monday through Friday from 8:30am to 5pm, and Saturday and Sunday from 9am to 5pm; in winter Monday through Friday from 9am to 4pm. Volunteers also staff a **visitor information desk** at the airport and at the Auke Bay ferry terminal. During summer, centers are staffed at the cruise-ship terminal and at Marine Park.

You can see a good many of Juneau's sights, and some of its nature, within walking distance of the cruise-ship dock. The bronze statue of **Patsy Ann** on the dock represents a bull terrier famous in the 1930s for greeting all arriving boats. To the right, as you face the mountains, the **Mount Roberts Tramway,** 490 S. Franklin St. (© 888/461-8726 or 907/463-3412; www.goldbelttours.com), whisks passengers from tourist-clogged Franklin Street to clear air, expansive trails, and overwhelming views at the tree line. It costs $24 adults, $14 children ages 6 to 12, and free for kids 5 and under. Don't bother spending the money if it's a cloudy day. Closed October through April.

The interesting **Alaska State Museum,** below the state office building at 395 Whittier St. (© 907/465-2901; www.museums.state.ak.us), puts the whole state in context with its huge collection of Alaskan art and Alaska Native artifacts. Summer admission is $5 adults, free for ages 18 and under. After tackling the museum, head to the intersection of Fourth and Main streets, the center of the city, where you'll find the state capitol, courthouse, state office building, and **Juneau–Douglas City Museum** (© **907/586-3572;** www.juneau.org/parksrec/museum). This fun little museum is worth a visit to learn about Tlingit culture and the city's pioneer and mining history. The plaza in front is where the 49-star U.S. flag was first raised in 1959, when Alaska got its statehood before Hawaii did. Summer admission is $4. About 3 blocks away, at Fifth and Gold, the tiny, octagonal **St. Nicholas Russian Orthodox Church** is a landmark built in 1893 by local Tlingits who, under pressure to convert to Christianity, chose the only faith that allowed them to keep their language. Admission $2.

The **Macaulay Salmon Hatchery,** 2697 Channel Dr., 3 miles from downtown (© **877/463-2486** or 907/463-4810; www.dipac.net), was designed to allow visitors to watch from outdoor decks the entire process of harvesting and fertilizing eggs. From mid-June to October, salmon swim up a 450-foot fish ladder, visible through a window. Inside, large saltwater aquariums show off the area's marine life as it looks in the natural environment. Admission is $3.25 adults, $1.75 kids 12 and under.

A truly impressive sight is the state's third-most-visited attraction, **Mendenhall Glacier,** at the head of Glacier Spur Road (from Egan Dr., turn right on Mendenhall Loop Rd. to Glacier Spur; visitor center © **907/789-0097**). Mendenhall is the most easily accessible glacier in Alaska, with great views from the parking lot across the lake to the glacier's face, and a wheelchair-accessible trail that leads to the water's edge. Simply standing in front of the blue ice and feeling its cool breath is worth the stop, but also check out the visitor center, a sort of glacier museum with explanatory models, computerized displays, and ranger talks. Excellent hiking trails start from here, ranging from a half-mile nature trail loop to two steep 3.5-mile hikes approaching each side of the glacier. Those with experience and the proper equipment can hike on the glacier. In summer, admission is $3 for adults, free for children 15 and under.

Where to Stay & Dine

Hotel rooms can be tight in the summer, so book ahead. Bed-and-breakfasts are a good way to get a better deal and have more fun. Lodging rates are high and room reservations tight in Juneau. The Juneau Convention and Visitors Bureau's *Juneau Guide & Travel Planner* and website contain listings of the hotels and B&Bs with links (© **888/581-2201;** www.traveljuneau.com).

Set in a historic building that once functioned as a branch of the state capitol, the **Baranof Hotel,** 127 N. Franklin St. (© **800/544-0970** or 907/586-2660; www.westmark hotels.com), has the feel of a grand hotel, although some rooms are a bit small. The upper-floor rooms have great views on the water side. Its restaurant, the **Gold Room,** offers the best fine dining in Juneau. Rates run $139 to $169 double in high season. The business-oriented **Goldbelt Hotel Juneau,** 51 W. Egan Dr. (© **888/478-6909** or 907/586-6900; www.goldbelttours.com), is decorated with masterpieces of Tlingit art, including a totem pole out front and a huge yellow cedar bas-relief by Nathan Jackson in the lobby-restaurant area. The large rooms are noticeably silent and immaculate. Rates from $179 to $189 double in summer. **Pearson's Pond Luxury B&B Inn and Adventure Spa,** 4541 Sawa Circle (© **888/658-6328** or 907/798-3772; www.pearsonspond. com), has every amenity, from yoga, laptops, and fishing rods to VCRs, a separate hot tub in the garden (and maybe one in your room, too), and kitchenettes stocked with food, wine, and the owner's home-baked bread. Rates from $249 to $449 double in high season.

The **Driftwood Lodge,** 435 Willoughby Ave. (© **800/544-2239** or 907/586-2280; www.driftwoodalaska.com), offers modernized two-bedroom suites with full kitchens for the same price that other hotels charge for a regular room (though the lodge has standard rooms, too). Rates from $94 to $100 double, high season.

The **Hangar,** handy to the docks at 2 Marine Way (© **907/586-5018**), is a fun bar and grill with great sea views. Literally across the hall from the Hangar, **Pizzeria Roma** (© **907/723-4658**) serves fantastic pizza—the best in Southeast Alaska—and tasty Italian cuisine. **Zyphyr Restaurant,** 200 Seward St. (© **907/780-2221**), once an old-fashioned grocery store, was remodeled with restraint and a magnificent sense of style. Dishes are from the traditional fine-dining palette of colors: calamari, pasta puttanesca, or veal scallopini. **Hot Bite,** at the Auke Bay boat harbor, is a local secret, serving charcoal-broiled hamburgers and halibut burgers and mind-blowing milkshakes. Take out or sit at one of six indoor tables.

SOUTHEAST ALASKA'S NATURAL WONDERS
Glacier Bay National Park

What you can see in Glacier Bay you can see few other places. Humpback whales often frequent the waters right in front of the visitor center and lodge, jumping out of the water as if putting on performances for sea kayakers, and glaciers of bright blue drop immense hunks of ice into the ocean at the head of the bay. And there's the land itself. Crushed under a mile-thick wall of ice less than 2 centuries ago, today it's an impossibly rugged 65-mile-long fjord. Mankind has left no mark on this new land; there are no roads or buildings beyond the edge of the park.

Most of the cruise ships on Inside Passage itineraries visit Glacier Bay, although the National Park Service limits their number to protect the whales, so some lines skip it. Independent travelers can visit by day boat, fly over in a small plane, or join a sea-kayaking adventure.

Exploring the Park

Glacier Bay Lodge (© **888/229-8687** or 907/697-4000; www.visitglacierbay.com) is the only place to stay in the park. The wood-paneled rooms have a bit of rustic charm, but they're mainly just comfortable lodgings in a pleasant setting. The buildings are set amid the soothing quiet of large rainforest trees and are reached from the main lodge by boardwalks and steps. Laundry facilities and rental of bikes and fishing gear are available. Rates are from $174 to $202 double, and inquire about all-inclusive packages, which include lodging, meals, activities, and transfers from the airport.

VISITOR INFORMATION   Contact the **Glacier Bay National Park and Preserve** at P.O. Box 140, Gustavus, AK 99826 (© **907/697-2230;** www.nps.gov/glba). The Park Service interprets the park mainly by placing well-prepared rangers on board most cruise and tour vessels entering the bay. The park also maintains a visitor center with displays on the park on the second floor of the lodge at Bartlett Cove. Pick up the park map and handy guide, *The Fairweather.* Nearby are the park's offices, a free campground, a backcountry office, a few short hiking trails, a dock, sea kayak rental, and other park facilities. During the summer, rangers lead a daily nature walk and present an evening program.

BY TOUR BOAT   Most independent travelers take a day boat to see the vast majority of Glacier Bay. The boat is operated by a park concessionaire called **Glacier Bay Lodge and Tours,** with offices at 241 North C St., Anchorage, AK 99501 (© **888/229-8687** or 907/264-4600; fax 907/258-3668; www.visitglacierbay.com), or, locally, in the summer only, at P.O. Box 179, Gustavus, AK 99826 (© **907/697-4000;** fax 907/697-4001). The boat leaves from the dock in Bartlett Cove and sails to the fjords' very head and the Grand Pacific Glacier. The 8-hour voyage is too long for many children. There's a snack bar, and a simple lunch is provided. Bring binoculars, good rain gear, and layers of warm clothing. A Park Service employee does the commentary, so you can count on accuracy and a didactic approach missing from most commercial tours. The fare is $182 for adults, half-price for children 2 to 12.

The company offers a same-day trip from Juneau, but it makes for too long a day, and the schedule leaves no shore time in Glacier Bay or Gustavus, or time for whale-watching in Icy Strait. A better choice is to book one of their multiday packages, which may save money over separate transportation and room rates, and include all the transfers and details.

BY SEA KAYAK   You won't forget seeing a breaching humpback whale from a sea kayak, sitting just inches off the water. It happens around here. When we breathlessly told our innkeepers about the experience, they smiled politely. They hear the same descriptions all the time.

Inexperienced paddlers should choose a guided trip. **Glacier Bay Sea Kayaks,** based in Gustavus (© **907/697-2257;** www.glacierbayseakayaks.com), offers half-day and all-day paddles in Bartlett Cove good for beginners. Although the trips go nowhere near the glaciers, the paddlers stand a good chance of seeing whales, sometimes quite close up. Any fit person can enjoy it. A half-day costs $85, full day $135, including a lunch. The same folks rent kayaks for day trips in the cove. These self-guided outings begin with a briefing, and novices are welcome. The cost is $30 half-day, $40 full day. Longer tours are available as well.

Tracy Arm & Endicott Arm

About 50 miles due south of Juneau, these long, deep, and almost claustrophobically narrow fjords reach back into the coastal mountains to active glaciers—the **Sawyer Glacier** in Tracy Arm and **Dawes Glacier** in Endicott. Both calve ice constantly, sometimes discarding blocks of such size that they clog the narrow fjord passages, making navigation difficult. A passage up either fjord offers stunning views of high, cascading waterfalls; tree- and snow-covered mountain valleys; and wildlife that might include Sitka black-tailed deer, bald eagles, sea lions, harbor seals, and possibly even the odd black bear or whale.

The scenery and wildlife viewing in Tracy Arm easily rival Glacier Bay, and for those not riding a cruise ship, Tracy Arm has a significant advantage: It's much easier and less expensive to visit. **Adventure Bound Alaska,** at 76 Egan Dr., Juneau (© **800/228-3875** or 907/463-2509; www.adventureboundalaska.com), is a family business operating a 56-foot single-hull boat with deck space all the way around. They charge $140 adults, $90 ages 4 to 17; children must be at least 4 to go.

Misty Fjords National Monument

President Jimmy Carter set aside these 2.3 million acres of inviolate wilderness as a national monument in 1978, and they're still waiting to be discovered. The monument's **Rudyerd Bay** is like a place where the earth shattered open: The cliffs in its Punchbowl Cove rise vertically 3,150 feet from the surface of water that's 900 feet deep—topography in a league with the Grand Canyon. Waterfalls pound down out of the bay's granite. The glaciers of the northern part of the monument are also impressive, although they require a plane to visit.

Visits to the monument are by tour boat, floatplane, or sea kayak. It isn't a cheap place to go, and you don't see much wildlife. By boat, you don't see glaciers, although glaciated mountains are a spectacular feature of the flights. Unlike Glacier Bay or Tracy Arm—places with more wildlife and more glaciers at sea level—the experience at Misty is pure geology: You go for the scenery.

Two companies offer boat tours to Misty's Punchbowl Cove, Rudyerd Bay, and back, and both include meals. Sitka-based **Allen Marine** (© **877/686-8100** or 907/225-8100; www.allenmarinetours.com) has some distinct advantages. The fast, quiet boat makes the round-trip in 4¹/₂ hours. All seats face forward. A knowledgeable naturalist interprets the scenery. Adult passengers can peruse regional books, while children work with craft boxes and activities. Tickets are $145 adults, $95 children. Sailings every day in the summer coordinate with the cruise ships' dockings. **Alaska Travel Adventures** (© **800/323-5757** or 907/247-5295; www.bestofalaskatravel.com) offers the opportunity see the fjords from above by float plane and return to Ketchikan by water for $269 adult, $229 child; taking the boat both ways is $139 adult and $89 child.

Visiting the fjords by kayak is advisable only for those who already know they enjoy this mode of travel, but I can think of few more spectacular places to paddle. **Southeast Exposure** (© **907/225-8829;** www.southeastexposure.com) does guided paddles, and has for 20 years. Their 6-day trip is $1,150 per person.

2 DENALI NATIONAL PARK

Denali (Den-*al*-ee) National Park gives regular people easy access to real wilderness. This is Alaska's most visited—environmentalists say overvisited—wilderness area, with almost one million people a year entering annually to soak up the park's scenic splendor. It's got sweeping tundra vistas, abundant wildlife, and North America's tallest mountain, **Mount McKinley** (commonly known to Alaskans by its original Native name, *Denali,* which means the "Great One"), all in a pristine natural environment where truly wild animals live in a complete ecosystem pretty much without human interference. A single National Park Service decision makes this possible: The only road through the park is closed to the public. This means that to get into the park, you must ride a crowded bus over a dusty gravel road hour after hour, but it also means that the animals are still there to watch, and their behavior remains essentially normal. From the window of the bus, you're likely to see grizzly bears doing what they would be doing even if you weren't there.

What's even more unique is that you can get off the bus whenever you want to and walk away across the tundra, out of sight of the road, to be alone in this primeval wilderness. When you're ready to return to civilization, you can just walk to the road and catch the next bus—they come every half-hour.

VISITOR INFORMATION

The most important resource for setting up a trip is the concessionaire: **Doyon/ARA-MARK Joint Venture,** 241 W. Ship Creek Ave., Anchorage, AK 99501 (© **800/622-7275** or 907/272-7275; fax 907/264-4684; at Denali, May 15 through the visitor season, the number is © 907/683-8200; www.reservedenali.com). The concession is operated by a joint venture of ARAMARK and the Doyon Native corporation. They handle the reservations system for the campgrounds and shuttle buses, as well as two hotels, bus tours, a rafting operation, and a dinner theater.

Getting to the Park by Train

The **Alaska Railroad** (© **800/544-0552** or 907/265-2494; www.alaskarailroad. com) pioneered tourism to the park before the George Parks Highway was built in 1972. The cars are luxurious; you'll follow a historic, unspoiled route through beautiful countryside; the commentary by well-trained Alaska high school students is engaging; and the food is good.

In summer, trains leave both Anchorage and Fairbanks daily at 8:15am, arriving at the park from Anchorage at 3:45pm and from Fairbanks at 12:15pm, crossing and going on to the opposite city for arrival at 8pm in each. The basic fare from Anchorage to Denali is $135 one-way for adults, from Fairbanks $59, half-price for children ages 2 to 11, free 1 and under. First-class "Gold Star" seats are $85 more per leg. During the winter, the Alaska Railroad runs a single passenger car from Anchorage to Fairbanks and back once a week—a truly spectacular, truly Alaskan experience.

Reservations by Internet or mail open for the whole summer on December 1 of the preceding year. Reservations by phone open in mid-February. Lines are answered daily from 7am to 5pm Mountain Standard Time (that's 2 hr. later than Alaska Standard Time, where the hours would be 5am–3pm, and 2 hr. earlier than Eastern Standard Time, where they would be 9am–7pm). By booking online, you can get a big jump on those who call for reservations. Payment online is by credit card.

The easiest place to make in-person contact with the concessionaire or the Park Service itself is the **Wilderness Access Center** on Denali Park Road, ¹/₂ mile from the park entrance (P.O. Box 9), Denali National Park, AK 99755 (© **907/683-2294;** www.nps. gov/dena). It's open from mid-May to mid-September daily from 5am to 7pm (reservation desks don't open until 7am). Here you will find the Denali Park Resorts reservation and ticketing desks and the park backcountry desk. Since there's no park entrance station, this center is also the stop for the park map, a copy of the *Alpenglow* park newspaper, and other handouts.

Park entrance fees are $20 per family (up to eight) or $10 per person, good for 7 days. There is no entrance station to collect the fee, but it is automatically added to your bill when you make shuttle or campground reservations. If you have one of the national passes for seniors, those with disabilities, or frequent park users, you can get a refund when you get to the park. Entrance fees are in place year-round and are collected at the Murie Science and Learning Center during winter months.

Warning: Reserving shuttle-bus seats and a space at one of the campground sites in advance is **essential** if you want to guarantee yourself entrance into the park. Only 35% of shuttle seats and any leftover car-camping sites are opened to walk-ins, 2 days before date of entrance. You could easily get shut out of a visit. For information on reserving ahead of time, as well as walk-in procedures, contact Doyon/ARAMARK (see above), or check out the park's website (**www.nps.gov/dena**).

WHAT TO SEE & DO

There are no reserved seats on the park buses, but if you arrive early, choose a place on the left side, which has the best views on the way out. Most buses will see grizzly bears, caribou, Dall sheep, moose, and, occasionally, wolves.

Service information handouts to confirm times of the guided walks):

Mile 9: In clear weather, this is the closest spot to the park entrance with a view of Mount McKinley. This section also is a likely place to see moose, especially in the fall rutting season.

Mile 29: An hour and 10 minutes into the drive, a large rest stop overlooks the Teklanika River. The Teklanika, like many other rivers on Alaska's glacier-carved terrain, is a braided river—a stream wandering in a massive gravel streambed that's much too big for it.

Mile 34: Craggy Igloo Mountain is a likely place to see Dall sheep. Without binoculars, they'll just look like white dots. Manageable climbs on Igloo, Cathedral, and Sable mountains take off along the road in the section from Igloo Creek to Sable Pass.

Miles 38–43: Sable Pass, a critical habitat area for bears, is closed to people. A half-eaten sign helps explain why. Bears show up here mostly in the fall. This is the start of the road's broad Alpine vistas.

Mile 46: The top of 5-mile-wide Polychrome Pass, the most scenic point on the ride, and a toilet break, is 2 hours and 25 minutes into the trip. Caribou look like specks when they pass in the great valley below you. Note how the mountains of colored rock on either side of the plain match up—they were once connected before glacial ice carved this valley. Huge rocks on its floor are glacial erratics, plucked from the bedrock by moving ice and left behind when it melted.

Mile 53: The Toklat River, another braided river, is a flat plain of gravel with easy walking. The glaciers that feed the river are 10 miles upstream. The river bottom is habitat for bears, caribou, and wolves, and a good place for picnics.

Mile 58: Highway Pass is the highest point on the road. In good weather, dramatic views of Mount McKinley start here. The Alpine tundra from here to the Eielson Visitor Center is inviting for walking, but beware: Tundra is soft underfoot and can conceal holes and declivities that can twist an ankle.

Mile 64: Thorofare Pass, where the road becomes narrow and winding, is a good area to look for bears and caribou.

Mile 68.5: The rugged terrain to the north is the earth and vegetation covering Muldrow Glacier. The ice extends to McKinley's peak and was the early and arduous route for climbers. McKinley's glaciers, falling 15,000 vertical feet and extending up to 45 miles in length, are among the world's greatest. The Ruth Glacier has carved the Great Gorge on the south side, which is almost 6,000 feet deep above the ice and another 4,000 below—almost twice the depth of the Grand Canyon. The park road comes within a mile of the Muldrow's face, then continues through wet, rolling terrain past beaver ponds, and finally descends into a small spruce patch near Mile 82.

Mile 86: Wonder Lake campground is the closest road point to Mount McKinley, 27 miles away. The fact that McKinley looks so massive from this considerable distance, dominating the sky, is a testament to its stupendous size. You'll likely never see a larger object on this planet. From its base (elevation here is only 2,000 ft.) to its top is an elevation gain greater than that of any other mountain on earth. Other mountains are taller overall, but they stand on higher ground.

WHERE TO CAMP, STAY & DINE

There are a number of campgrounds in and around Denali, bookable through ARAMARK (see "Visitor Information," above). **Riley Creek campground,** near the visitor center, is near the store, showers, a bus stop for the free front-country shuttle, and a pay phone. Nightly rates are $20 for vehicle sites, $12 for walk-in sites. **Savage River,** on Denali Park Road, 13 miles from the entrance, is a campground with unforgettable views. Sites are $20 per night.

The **Denali Bluffs Hotel,** at Mile 238.4 on the Parks Highway (© 866/683-8500 or 907/683-8500; www.denalialaska.com), looks down on the Nenana Canyon area from above the highway. Rooms are light and tastefully decorated. Rates from $239 double in high season. **Denali Crow's Nest Log Cabins,** at Mile 238.5 on the Parks Highway (© 888/917-8130 or 907/683-2723; www.denalicrowsnest.com), is a series of roomy and comfortable cabins perched in five tiers on the side of a mountain above the Nenana Canyon area. Rates start at $199 per cabin per night for two people.

The **Denali Park Salmon Bake** (© 907/683-2733; www.denaliparksalmonbake. com) in Glitter Gulch is a casual, friendly place. It's a hot spot for live music as well. The **Overlook Bar and Grill,** at Mile 238.5 on the Parks Highway (© 907/683-2641), is a fun, noisy place with the feeling of a classic bar and grill. A variety of craft beers is available, with several on tap. The **Perch/Panorama Pizza Pub,** at Mile 224 on the Parks Highway (© 888/322-2523 or ©/fax 907/683-2523; www.denaliperchresort.com), is a friendly place serving a simple steak-and-seafood menu. The home-baked bread is noteworthy. The Pizza Pub has a bakery/deli that packs lunches in cloth tote bags for the park bus.

3 ANCHORAGE

Anchorage, which started as a tent camp for workers building the Alaska Railroad in 1914, stands between the Chugach Mountains and the waters of upper Cook Inlet. It was a sleepy railroad town until World War II, when a couple of military bases livened things up. Anchorage did not start becoming a city in earnest until the 1950s, when the Cold War (and Alaska's proximity to the ol' Evil Empire) spurred a huge investment in infrastructure. Today Anchorage boasts good restaurants, good museums, and a nice little zoo; fancy ski resorts such as Mount Alyeska; and cultural attractions such as the world-class Alaska Native Heritage Center, a 26-acre celebration of the region's five major Native groups. And always, of course, there is wilderness, so close that moose regularly annoy gardeners, and bears sometimes amble though town.

Anchorage's downtown area is about 8×20 blocks near Ship Creek, but the rest of the city spreads some 5 miles east and 15 miles south. Most visitors spend a day or two in town before going somewhere more remote. The downtown area is pleasant, but we recommend you try to see more than just the streets of tourist-oriented shops. Check out the **Coastal Trail** and the **museums,** and if you have time, plan a day trip about 50 miles south along the incredibly scenic inlet known as **Turnagain Arm.**

ESSENTIALS

GETTING THERE By Plane If you're arriving or leaving by plane, you'll land at the **Ted Stevens Anchorage International Airport.** It's within the city limits, a 15-minute drive from downtown. Taxis run about $15 for the trip. The **People Mover** city bus also has an airport route, for those whose priority is saving money. Bus fares all over town are $1.75 for adults, $1 for ages 5 to 18, 50¢ for seniors.

By Car By car, there is only one road into Anchorage from the rest of the world: the **Glenn Highway.** The other road out of town, the **Seward Highway,** leads to the Kenai Peninsula.

VISITOR INFORMATION   The **Anchorage Convention and Visitor Bureau,** 524 W. 4th Ave., Anchorage, AK 99501-2212 (**©** **907/276-4118;** fax 907/278-5559; www. anchorage.net), offers information on the whole state at its centers and extensive website. The main location is the **Log Cabin Visitor Information Center,** downtown at 4th Avenue and F Street (**©** **907/274-3531;** open daily June–Aug 7:30am–7pm, May and Sept 8am–6pm, Oct–Apr 9am–4pm). If it's crowded, go to the storefront office right behind it.

For an extensive listing of the city's major events and festivals (there's something happening in town almost every day of the year), check **www.anchorage.net**.

FAST FACTS   There's no sales tax in Anchorage. The **bed tax** is 12%.

GETTING AROUND   Most **car-rental** companies operate at the airport. Advanced bookings are recommended. It takes a long time to go far using the **People Mover** bus system (**©** **907/343-6543;** www.peoplemover.org), but if you have the time, it's inexpensive and covers most of the city.

WHAT TO SEE & DO

At the **Anchorage Museum at Rasmuson Center,** 121 W. Seventh Ave. (**©** **907/343-4326;** www.anchoragemuseum.org), the Alaska Gallery offers an informative and enjoyable walk through the state's history and anthropology. In the art galleries, you can see what's happening in art in Alaska today; Alaska art isn't all scenery and walrus ivory, but the grandeur of the place does influence almost every work. A $100-million expansion project is underway but will not be completed until 2010. Admission is $8 adults, $7 seniors 65 and older, free for children 17 and under.

Alaska Native Heritage Center, near the intersection of the Glenn Highway and Muldoon Road (**©** **800/315-6608** or 907/330-8000; www.alaskanative.net), is Alaska's best cultural site. Alaska Natives built this extraordinary center to bring their cultures to visitors. What makes it so memorable is not the graceful building or the professional and informative displays, but the Native people themselves, real village people, who make a personal connection with visitors. The center takes most of a day to absorb. Attractions include storytellers, dance performances, and a series of workshops where artisans practice traditional crafts. Finally, there's a pond surrounded by five traditional Native dwellings representing each cultural group, each hosted by a member of that group. Admission is $24 adults, $16 children ages 7 to 16. Open daily from 9am to 5pm in summer.

At the **Alaska Zoo,** 4731 O'Malley Rd. (**©** **907/346-3242;** www.alaskazoo.org), gravel paths wander through the woods past large enclosures with natural flora for bears, seals, otters, musk oxen, mountain goats, moose, caribou, and waterfowl. Two-hour Naturalist tours take place every day at noon and include some backstage stops (for an additional fee). Admission is $10 adults, $8 seniors, $6 children 12 to 17, $4 children 3 to 12, free 2 and under. Drive out the New Seward Highway to O'Malley Road, then turn left and go 2 miles. In summer, there's a free shuttle bus from downtown.

Earthquake Park, on the west end of Northern Lights Boulevard, offers a sculpture and excellent interpretive signs commemorating and explaining the 1964 Good Friday earthquake (North America's largest earthquake ever) and pointing out its few remaining marks on the land. It is also a good access point to the **Coastal Trail,** which leads 10 miles from the western end of Second Avenue along the shore to **Kincaid Park.** It's a unique pathway to a natural environment from the heart of downtown. You can join the wide, paved trail at various points; downtown, **Elderberry Park,** at the western end of Fifth Avenue, is the most popular. From there, you might see beluga whales swimming along the trail at high tide. Moose are sometimes spotted toward the Kincaid Park end of the trail.

The **Eklutna Historical Park,** about 26 miles out the Glenn Highway (© **907/688-6026;** www.eklutna.com), has a fascinating old cemetery, still in use, in which each grave is enclosed by a decorated spirit house the size of a large dollhouse. The practice evolved in the melding of Athabascan and Russian Orthodox beliefs. There are two Russian Orthodox churches on the site, including the **St. Nicholas Orthodox Church.** Built north of here before 1870, it is among the oldest buildings in the Southcentral region. Walk through the park by yourself or take an informative 30-minute tour for the same price: $5 adults, $3 children ages 10 to 18 and seniors, free 9 and under. Take the Glenn Highway to the Eklutna exit, then go left across the overpass.

For information on outdoors options from Anchorage, stop by the **Alaska Public Lands Information Center,** located at 605 W. 4th Ave., Ste. 105, in the 1930s concrete federal building across the intersection from the log cabin at 4th Avenue and F Street (© **907/271-2737;** www.nps.gov/aplic), where staff can offer guidance for anyone planning to spend time in the outdoors anywhere in Alaska. You can buy ferry tickets from the Alaska Marine Highway System, there's an excellent selection of trail and field guides, and the rangers behind the desk know what they're talking about.

WHERE TO STAY

A decent hotel room under $150 a night is hard to find in summer. To visit economically, choose a B&B or small inn. Dozens of B&Bs are listed on a website maintained by the cooperative **Anchorage Alaska Bed and Breakfast Association (www.anchorage-bnb. com).** You can search by area of town or preferred amenities, or browse alphabetically.

The **Hotel Captain Cook,** 4th Avenue and K Street (© **800/843-1950** or 907/276-6000; www.captaincook.com), is Alaska's great grand hotel, where royalty and rock stars stay. Rates run $250 to $260 double. The **Anchorage Grand Hotel,** 505 W. 2nd Ave. (© **888/800-0640** or 907/929-8888; www.anchoragegrand.com), is an all-suite hotel (each suite has a kitchen) with a central location. Rates from $205, including continental breakfast.

The small, unpretentious **Voyager Hotel,** 501 K St. (© **800/247-9070** or 907/277-9501; www.voyagerhotel.com), has large, light rooms with kitchens and gets consistent raves from travelers. Rooms go for $189 double; smoking is not permitted. The **Downtown Guest House,** 1238 G St. (© **907/279-2359;** www.downtownguesthouse.com), is a single two-bedroom apartment, beautifully decorated and with many amenities, for only $150 double in the summer. The owner is one of Alaska's most noted photographers.

WHERE TO DINE

The **Marx Brothers Cafe,** 627 W. 3rd Ave. (© **907/278-2133;** www.marxcafe.com), began as a hobby among three friends and sets the standard of excellence in the state. The cuisine is varied and creative, ranging from Asian to Italian, but everyone orders the Caesar salad, prepared tableside. The decor and style are studied casual elegance. Main courses run $18 to $36. Despite its Italian name, **Orso,** 737 W. 5th Ave. (© **907/222-3232;** www.orsoalaska.com), offers superb wood-grilled steaks and locally caught seafood as well as excellent pastas, all in an elegant, comfortable setting. Main courses cost $12 to $33.

For an active, hardy experience, the **Glacier Brewhouse,** 737 W. 5th Ave. (© **907/274-BREW** [274-2739]; www.glacierbrewhouse.com), offers a tasty, eclectic, and ever-changing menu served in a large dining room with lodge decor, where the pleasant scent

Main courses cost $9 to $34.

The best pizza and beer in Anchorage undoubtedly come from the fun and friendly **Moose's Tooth Pub and Pizzeria,** 3300 Old Seward Hwy. (© **907/258-2537;** www. moosestooth.net). The microbrewery came first, but the pizza really is the greater accomplishment. It has a soft, light crust like Italian pizza, but with the oomph of the American version. Dine inside (perhaps in the "hippie pad") or at picnic tables outside in a tent that's open year-round. A large pie will run you between $13 and $25.

Simon and Seafort's Saloon and Grill, 420 L St. (© **907/274-3502**), is one of Anchorage's great dinner houses, with a turn-of-the-20th-century decor, a cheerful atmosphere, and fabulous sunset views of Cook Inlet. Prime rib and seafood are the specialties. To enjoy the place on a budget, order a sandwich and soup for lunch in the well-stocked bar. Main courses run $16 to $42.

---

4 HONOLULU & OAHU

It's astounding to spend hours flying across the barren blue of the Pacific and then suddenly see below you the 26-mile-long metropolis of Honolulu, with its bright city lights, five-star restaurants, world-class shopping, and grand old hotels. Most visitors end up along the canyonlike streets of Waikiki, Honolulu's well-known hotel district and its most densely populated neighborhood. Some days, it seems like the entire world is sunning itself on Waikiki's famous beach.

Out in the country, the island of Oahu can be as down-home as a slack-key guitar. Here's where you'll find a big blue sky, perfect waves, empty beaches, rainbows, waterfalls, sweet tropical flowers, and fiery Pacific sunsets.

ESSENTIALS

GETTING THERE **Honolulu International Airport** sits on the south shore of Oahu, west of downtown Honolulu and Waikiki near Pearl Harbor. **Airport Waikiki Express** (© **800/831-5541;** www6.hawaii.gov/dot/airports/hnl) offers 24-hour service every day of the year between the airport and all 350 hotels and condos in Waikiki. You'll find the shuttle at street level outside baggage claim. A one-way trip from the airport to Waikiki in one of the company's air-conditioned vans costs $9 per person ($15 round-trip). **TheBus** nos. 19 and 20 (Waikiki Beach and Hotels) take about an hour from the airport to downtown Honolulu and Waikiki. The one-way fare is $2 for adults and $1 for students ages 6 to 19; exact change only. You can bring a small suitcase, as long as it fits under your seat. **Taxi** fare is about $20 from Honolulu International to downtown Honolulu, about $25 to $35 to Waikiki.

VISITOR INFORMATION The **Hawaii Visitors & Convention Bureau (HVCB),** 2270 Kalakaua Ave., Ste. 801, Honolulu, HI 96815 (© **800/GO-HAWAII** [464-2924] or 808/923-1811; www.gohawaii.com), supplies free brochures, maps, accommodations guides, and *Islands of Aloha,* the official HVCB magazine. The **Oahu Visitors Bureau,** 733 Bishop St., Ste. 1520, Honolulu, HI 96813 (© **877/525-OAHU** [525-6248] or 808/524-0722; fax 808/521-1620; www.visit-oahu.com), distributes a free travel planner and map.

GETTING AROUND Traffic can be extremely heavy on Oahu's mostly two-lane roads. You can avoid gridlock by driving between 9am and 3pm or after 6pm.

Taking **TheBus** (© 808/848-5555, or 296-1818 for recorded information; www.thebus.org) is often easier than parking your car. TheBus goes around the whole island for $2. The most popular route is no. 8, which shuttles between Waikiki and Ala Moana Center every 10 minutes (trip time: 15–20 min.).

The fun, open-air, motorized **Waikiki Trolley** (© 800/824-8804 or 808/593-2822; www.waikikitrolley.com) loops around Waikiki and downtown Honolulu, stopping every 40 minutes at 12 key places, with commentary along the way. A 1-day pass ($25 for adults, $12 for kids 4–11) allows you to jump on and off all day long.

The major cab companies offer islandwide service; vehicles with wheelchair lifts (there's a $5 charge for wheelchairs) are available. **Star Taxi** (© 800/671-2999 or 808/942-STAR [942-7827]; www.startaxihawaii.com) offers a discount taxi service at the fixed price of $25 to Waikiki for up to five passengers, and no charge for baggage.

FAST FACTS   Hospitals with 24-hour emergency care include **Queens Medical Center,** 1301 Punchbowl St. (© 808/538-9011), and **Moanalua Medical Center,** 3288 Moanalua Rd. (© 808/834-5333). Central Oahu has **Wahiawa General Hospital,** 128 Lehua St. (© 808/621-8411). **Straub Doctors on Call** (© 808/971-6000) can dispatch a van if you need help getting to any of its numerous clinics.

Although Oahu is generally safe, there has been a series of purse-snatching incidents there. Thieves in slow-moving cars or on foot have snatched handbags from female pedestrians. The most common crime against tourists is rental-car break-in. Never leave any valuables in your car, not even in your trunk. Be especially leery of high-risk areas, such as beaches and resorts. And don't carry valuables or large amounts of cash in Waikiki and other tourist zones, including the USS *Arizona,* a high-theft area.

The **general excise tax** is 4%. **Hotel and room taxes** total about 12%.

HITTING THE BEACH

No beach anywhere is as famous as **Waikiki Beach,** a narrow, 1¹⁄₂-mile-long crescent of sand at the foot of a string of high-rise hotels. Home to the world's longest-running beach party, Waikiki is fabulous for swimming, board- and bodysurfing, diving, sailing, and snorkeling. Go early—it gets crowded.

Gold-sand **Ala Moana Beach Park,** on sunny Mamala Bay, stretches for more than a mile between downtown and Waikiki. This 76-acre midtown park has spreading lawns, a lagoon, a yacht harbor, tennis courts, and more. The water is calm almost year-round. Oahu's most popular snorkeling spot is **Hanauma Bay,** a marine-life conservation district with a small gold-sand beach that's packed with people year-round. TheBus runs frequent shuttles from Waikiki. Closed Tuesdays. Two-mile-long **Kailua Beach** is a 35-acre golden strand with dunes, palms, and panoramic views. The waters are great for swimming, windsurfing, bodysurfing, and kayaking. Postcard-perfect **Lanikai Beach** is good for sailing, windsurfing, and kayaking, and perfect for swimming in the crystal-clear lagoon. Because it's in a residential neighborhood, Lanikai has fewer crowds. There are no facilities or lifeguards.

OUTDOOR ACTIVITIES

GOLF   For last-minute and discount tee times, call **Stand-by Golf** (© 888/645-BOOK [645-2665]; www.stand-bygolf.com), which offers discounted tee times for same-day or next-day golfing. Call between 7am and 11pm for a guaranteed tee time with up to a 50% discount off greens fees.

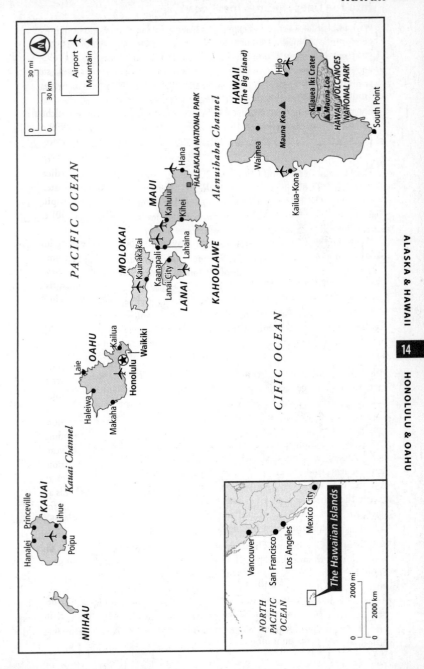

Into the Deep: Submarine Rides

Want to play Jules Verne and experience Hawaii's underwater world from the comfort of a submarine? **Atlantis Submarines** (© **800/548-6262** or 808/973-9811; www.go-atlantis.com) offers visitors the chance to explore the state's aquatic life in their natural habitat by plunging 100 feet below the surface of the sea in a state-of-the-art, high-tech submarine. Rates are $95 to $113 for adults, $80 to $98 for kids 12 and under (children must be at least 36 in. tall). *Tip:* Book online for discount rates. *Warning:* Though the ride is safe for everyone, skip it if you suffer from claustrophobia.

The **Makaha Resort Golf Club,** 84–627 Makaha Valley Rd., Waianae, 45 miles west of Honolulu (© **800/695-7111** or 808/695-5239; www.makahavalleycc.com; greens fees $85), is "The Best Golf Course on Oahu," according to *Honolulu* magazine. The challenging par-72, 7,091-yard course meanders toward the ocean before turning and heading into the valley; sheer volcanic walls tower above.

The North Shore's **Turtle Bay Resort** (© **808/293-8574** or 293-9094; www.turtle bayresort.com; greens fees $160–$195 for nonguests) is home to two of Hawaii's top courses. The challenging 18-hole **Arnold Palmer Course** was designed by Arnold Palmer and Ed Seay. The front 9 holes play like a British Isles course, with rolling terrain and lots of wind. The back 9 have narrower, tree-lined fairways and water. A more forgiving choice is the **George Fazio–designed 9-hole course,** which can be played twice for a regulation par-71, 6,200-yard course. The course has two sets of tees, one designed for men and one for women, so you can get a slightly different play if you decide to tackle 18 holes.

HIKING A moderate but steep 1½-hour, 1.4-mile walk leads to the summit of Hawaii's most famous landmark: **Diamond Head Crater,** a 760-foot volcanic cone that affords 360-degree views of Oahu. The hike, which costs $1 per person, starts at Monsarrat and 18th avenues on the crater's inland side. Take TheBus no. 58 from the Ala Moana Shopping Center, or drive to the intersection of Diamond Head Road and 18th Avenue. Follow the road through the tunnel and park in the lot. The trail head proceeds along a paved walkway as it climbs the slope. You'll pass old World War I and II pillboxes, gun emplacements, and tunnels built as part of the Pacific defense network. Several steps take you up to the top observation post on Point Leahi. The views are indescribable. Wear decent shoes (sneakers are fine) and bring a flashlight (for the tunnels you'll walk through), water, a hat, and binoculars. Try to head out just after the 6:30am opening, before the noonday sun starts beating down.

WATERSPORTS Because Oahu's greatest dives are offshore, your best bet is to book a two-tank dive from a dive boat. Hawaii's oldest and largest outfitter is **Aaron's Dive Shop,** 307 Hahani St., Kailua (© **808/262-2333;** www.hawaii-scuba.com), which offers boat and beach dive excursions off the coast. The boat dives start at $115 per person ($99 if you book online), including two tanks and transportation from the Kailua shop. The beach dive off the North Shore in summer or the Waianae Coast in winter is the same price as a boat dive, including all gear and transportation, so Aaron's recommends the boat dive.

For snorkelers, Hanauma Bay has clear, warm, protected waters and an abundance of friendly fish. The bay has two reefs, an inner and an outer—the first for novices, the other for experts. Closed on Tuesday. The uninitiated can take a lesson and a 2-hour snorkel tour with **Surf-N-Sea** (© 808/637-9887; www.surfnsea.com). Snorkel rentals are available at most dive shops and beach activity centers.

Summer is surf season in Waikiki, the best place on Oahu to learn how to surf. For lessons, go early to **Aloha Beach Service,** next to the Sheraton Moana Surfrider (© 808/922-3111). The beach boys offer group lessons for $30 an hour; board rentals are $10 for the first hour and $5 for every hour after that. You must know how to swim.

Surfboards are also available for rent at **Surf-N-Sea,** 62–595 Kamehameha Hwy., Haleiwa (© 808/637-9887; www.surfnsea.com).

More experienced surfers should drop by any surf shop or call the **Surf News Network Surfline** (© 808/596-SURF [596-7873]) to get the latest conditions. A good spot for advanced surfers is the **Cliffs,** at the base of Diamond Head.

In winter, you can watch the serious surfers at the beach near **Kalalua Point.**

THE TOP ATTRACTIONS

The forbidding, four-story Romanesque lava-rock structure that houses the **Bishop Museum,** 1525 Bernice St. (© 808/847-3511; www.bishopmuseum.org), holds a vast collection of natural and cultural artifacts from Hawaii and the Pacific, including insect specimens, ceremonial spears, and pre-industrial Polynesian art. Daily cultural shows and demonstrations enrich the experience. Admission is $15 adults, $12 kids 4 to 12 and seniors. *Note:* A "mini" version of the Bishop Museum, at 2005 Kalia Rd. (© 808/946-9478), is just right for visitors who want to get an insider's view of Hawaiian culture but are pressed for time ($1^{1}/_{2}$ hr. will do). You can participate in a variety of interactive, hands-on activities, from lei making to playing a Hawaiian instrument. Admission costs $16 adults, $13 for seniors and kids 4 to 12.

You can experience the natural beauty and culture of the vast Pacific at the **Polynesian Cultural Center,** 55–370 Kamehameha Hwy. (© 800/367-7060, 808/293-3333, or 923-2911; www.polynesia.com), a living museum of seven islands. You "travel" through the 42-acre park by foot or canoe on a man-made freshwater lagoon. Each re-created village is "inhabited" by native students from Polynesia, who attend Hawaii's Brigham Young University. The park, which is operated by the Mormon Church, also features a variety of stage shows celebrating the music, dance, history, and culture of Polynesia; there's a luau every evening. Since a visit can take up to 8 hours, it's a good idea to arrive before 2pm. Basic admission costs $58 adults, $47 children 3 to 11.

At **Pearl Harbor** (© 808/422-0561 or 422-2771; www.nps.gov/usar), you can't miss the USS *Arizona* **Memorial,** built right above the shallow water where the ship was sunk on December 7, 1941; or the battleship **USS *Missouri*** (© 808/423-2263; www.uss missouri.com), on the decks of which peace was declared. Admission is free to the USS *Arizona* Memorial, with an audio tour available for $5; it costs $16 adults, $8 kids 4 to 12 for the USS *Missouri.* What you may not notice, and should, is the **USS *Bowfin* Submarine Museum & Park** (© 808/423-1341; www.bowfin.org). This National Historic Landmark offers a rare glimpse into the thrill and danger of life aboard a submarine. Admission is $10 adults, $4 kids 4 to 12.

WHERE TO STAY

The moderately priced **Ohana Hotels & Resorts** offer dependable, clean, well-appointed rooms and terrific deals for budget travelers. The chain's price structure (from $179) is based entirely on location, room size, and amenities. Check the Internet site where "best available rates" start at $199 (true bargain in Waikiki!). They also offer other deals, including air and car-rental packages; for information, call © **800/462-6262,** or visit www.ohanahotels.com.

The 80-room **Aqua Coconut Waikiki** (formerly the Aston Coconut Plaza), 450 Lewers St. (© **866/406-2782** or 808/923-8828; www.aquaresorts.com/aqua-coconut-plaza), has recently emerged from a huge renovation with free high-speed Internet and flatscreen TVs in every room. Rates from $200 to $285 double.

For the ultimate heavenly Hawaii vacation, **Halekulani,** 2199 Kalia Rd. (© **800/367-2343** or 808/923-2311; www.halekulani.com), is *the* best place on the island. The luxury resort features five buildings spread out over 5 acres of prime Waikiki beachfront interconnected by courtyards and lush, tropical gardens. Rooms, 90% of which face the ocean, are huge, with separate sitting areas, furnished lanais, and fridges. Bathrooms have deep soaking tubs, separate showers, and luxurious robes. Rates from $445 to $555 double.

At the low-rise **Hawaiiana Hotel,** 260 Beach Walk (© **800/367-5122** or 808/923-3811; www.hawaiianahotelatwaikiki.com), you'll find a pineapple waiting for you at check-in, complimentary Kona coffee and tropical juice served poolside each morning, and flower leis at checkout. Each concrete hollow-tiled room contains a kitchenette, two beds (a double and a single), a fridge, and a view of the gardens and pools. Rates from $125 to $215 double.

The best place to stay with the kids, the **Hilton Hawaiian Village Beach Resort & Spa,** 2005 Kalia Rd. (© **800/HILTONS** [445-8667] or 808/949-4321; www.hilton hawaiianvillage.com), is Waikiki's biggest resort, with nearly 3,000 rooms spread over 20 acres. You'll find gardens dotted with exotic birds, award-winning restaurants, a lagoon, and a gorgeous stretch of Waikiki Beach. Accommodations in the four towers range from lovely to ultradeluxe; rooms are large and beautifully furnished. The **Mandara Spa** is top-notch. Rates from $279 to $429 double.

Step back in time at Waikiki's first hotel, the **Moana Surfrider, a Westin Resort,** 2365 Kalakaua Ave. (© **800/325-3535** or 808/922-3111; www.moana-surfrider.com), a National Historic Landmark that dates from 1901. The aloha spirit pervades this classy and charming place. You'll even see female employees wearing traditional Victorian-era muumuus. Most rooms have ocean views; all come with fridges and plush robes. The hotel sits on a prime stretch of beach. Daily activities include Hawaiian arts and crafts. From $299 to $675 double.

The **ResortQuest Waikiki Joy Hotel,** 320 Lewers St. (© **877/997-6667** or 808/923-2300; www.resortquesthawaii.com), is a hidden jewel that offers not only outstanding personal service, but also a Jacuzzi in every room. The marble-accented open-air lobby and the tropical veranda set the tone for the beautifully decorated rooms. All rooms come with a fridge and lanai. A downside: The beach is a 10- to 15-minute walk away. Doubles from $139 to $205 double; check the website for specials.

WHERE TO DINE

Cozy, busy, casual, and occasionally smoky, with a tiny tatami room for small groups, **Akasaka,** 1646B Kona St. (© **808/942-4466**), wins high marks for sushi, sizzling tofu and scallops, miso-clam soup, and the quality of its cuisine. During soft-shell crab season, you can order these spiny delicacies in sushi—a novel, tasty treat. Ordering specials, noodles, or other less-expensive a la carte items helps ease the bite of the bill.

Chef/owner George Mavrothalassitis (a James Beard award winner), a native of Provence, runs the warm and elegant **Chef Mavro Restaurant,** 1969 S. King St. (© **808/944-4714;** www.chefmavro.com), in an accessible, nontouristy neighborhood in McCully. Hints of Tahitian vanilla, lemon grass, ogo, rosemary, and Madras curry add exotic flavors to the French-inspired cooking and fresh island ingredients. A prix-fixe menu runs $65 to $150 ($98–$154 with wine pairings).

Named after fabled surfer Duke Kahanamoku, the casual, all-day, upbeat, oceanfront **Duke's Waikiki,** in the Outrigger Waikiki on the Beach at 2335 Kalakaua Ave. (© **808/ 922-2268;** www.hulapie.com), buzzes with diners and Hawaiian-music lovers throughout the day. Open-air dining gives a front-row view of the sunset. Dinner fare is steak and seafood, with high marks for the prime rib, macadamia-crab wontons, and several preparations of the daily catch. Duke's is also loved for its Barefoot Bar with top-notch island entertainment and its island-style ambience.

Honolulu's most sumptuous and expensive dining takes place at **La Mer,** in the Halekulani hotel, 2199 Kalia Rd. (© **808/923-2311**), the only AAA Five-Diamond restaurant in the state. Classical French influences meld with fresh island ingredients in this second-floor, open-sided ocean-side room with views of Diamond Head and the sunset. The menu is prix-fixe only, starting at $90 for three courses, $120 for four courses, $135 for five courses, $150 for nine courses, $190 for "Ultimate" dinner.

Roy's Restaurant, 6600 Kalanianaole Hwy. (© **808/396-7697;** www.roysrestaurant. com), was the first of Roy Yamaguchi's six signature restaurants in Hawaii. It is still the flagship and many people's favorite, true to its Euro-Asian roots and Yamaguchi's winning formula: open kitchen, fresh ingredients, and a good dose of nostalgia mingled with European techniques. The menu changes nightly, but you can generally count on individual pizzas, and entrees such as lemon grass–roasted chicken and several types of fresh fish.

Sam Choy's Breakfast, Lunch, Crab & Big Aloha Brewery, 580 Nimitz Hwy. (© **808/545-7979;** www.samchoy.com), is a happy, carefree eatery—elegance and cholesterol be damned. The menu ensures delightfully messy dining such as beef stew and fried rice at breakfast, the Hawaiian plate and fresh fish at lunch, and the featured attraction—crab—at dinner. A 2,000-gallon live-crab tank lines the open kitchen. The eight varieties of "Big Aloha Beer," brewed on-site, go well with the crab and poke.

The **Sushi Sasabune,** 1419 S. King St. (© **808/947-3800**), serves "trust-me" sushi: Obey the chef, eat what's served, and may God help you if you drop a grain of rice or dip something in wasabi without permission. There is no California roll, nothing that's not authentically Japanese. If you wish to order from the menu, grab a table; if you're brave enough to sit at the sushi bar, you'll receive what the chef serves. This is an extraordinary experience for sushi aficionados, and worth the expense.

5 MAUI

This 727-square-mile island has three peaks more than a mile high, thousands of waterfalls, 120 miles of shoreline, more than 80 golden-sand beaches, great seaside hotels, and a historic port town teeming with fine restaurants, B&Bs, and art galleries. Next to Waikiki, Maui is Hawaii's most popular destination, welcoming 2.5 million people each year to its sunny shores.

ALASKA & HAWAII

14

MAUI

Maui's microclimates offer distinct variations on the tropical-island theme: It's as lush as an equatorial rainforest in Hana; as dry as the Arizona desert in Makena; as hot as Mexico in Lahaina; and cool and misty, like Oregon, up in Kula.

ESSENTIALS

GETTING THERE   Several major carriers offer direct service from the U.S. mainland to **Kahului Airport.** Other major carriers fly to Honolulu, where you'll have to pick up an interisland flight (where you'll invariably have a couple-hour layover). You can avoid Kahului altogether by taking Island Air to **Kapalua–West Maui Airport,** which is only a 10- to 15-minute drive to most hotels in West Maui, as opposed to an hour from Kahului. All of the airports have car-rental desks.

SpeediShuttle (© **800/977-2605** or 808/661-6667; www.speedishuttle.com) runs between Kahului Airport and all major resorts. Rates vary, but figure on $39 for one person to Wailea (one-way), $54 one-way to Kaanapali, and $74 one-way to Kapalua. Be sure to call ahead to arrange pickup.

VISITOR INFORMATION   The **Maui Visitors Bureau** is at 1727 Wili Pa Loop, Wailuku, Maui, HI 96793 (© **800/525-MAUI** [525-6284] or 808/244-3530; fax 808/244-1337; www.visitmaui.com).

GETTING AROUND   The only way to really see Maui is by rental car. All of the major rental firms have offices on the island.

FAST FACTS   **Maui Memorial Hospital,** in central Maui, is at 221 Mahalani, Wailuku (© **808/244-9056**). East Maui's **Hana Medical Center** is on Hana Highway (© **808/248-8924**). In upcountry Maui, **Kula Hospital** is at 204 Kula Hwy., Kula (© **808/878-1221**).

HITTING THE BEACH

Four-mile-long **Kaanapali Beach** is one of Maui's best, with grainy gold sand as far as the eye can see. A paved beach walk links hotels, open-air restaurants, and the Whalers Village shopping center, but the beach is crowded only in pockets. Summertime swimming is excellent; the best snorkeling is around Black Rock, in front of the Sheraton.

Kapalua Beach, the cove that fronts the Kapalua Bay Hotel and the Coconut Grove Villas, is the stuff of dreams and one of the best in Hawaii: a golden crescent bordered by two palm-studded points. Protected from strong winds and currents, Kapalua's calm waters are great for snorkelers and swimmers of all ages and abilities.

Wailea Beach is the best gold-sand crescent on Maui's sunny south coast. It's big, wide, and protected on both sides by black-lava points. The view out to sea, framed by the islands of Kahoolawe and Lanai, is magnificent. The waves are just the right size for gentle riding, with or without a board.

The hard, constant wind and endless waves at **Hookipa Beach Park,** 2 miles past Paia, make it one of the most famous windsurfing sites in the world. A grassy cliff provides a natural amphitheater for spectators. Weekdays are the best time to watch the daredevils fly over the waves; winter weekends host regular competitions.

OUTDOOR ACTIVITIES

GOLF   Weekdays are your best bet for tee times. For last-minute and discount tee times, call **Stand-by Golf** (© **888/645-BOOK** [645-2665] or 808/874-0600; www.stand-bygolf.com) from 7am to 9pm. It offers discounted (up to 50%) guaranteed tee times for same-day or next-day golfing.

Golf Club Rentals (© **808/665-0800;** www.mauiclubrentals.com) has custom-built clubs for men, women, and juniors (both right- and left-handed), which can be delivered island-wide; the rates are $25 a day.

The views from the championship **Kapalua Resort Courses,** off Hwy. 30 (© **877/ KAPALUA** [527-2582]; www.kapaluamaui.com; greens fees $185–$295), are worth the greens fees alone. The par-72, 6,761-yard **Bay Course** (© **808/669-8820**), designed by Arnold Palmer and Ed Seay, is a bit forgiving, but its greens are difficult to read. The par-71, 6,632-yard **Village Course** (© **808/669-8830**), another Palmer/Seay design, is the most scenic. The par-73, 6,547-yard **Plantation Course** (© **808/669-8877**), a Ben Crenshaw/Bill Coore design set on a rolling hillside, is excellent for developing your low shots and precise chipping.

At the **Makena Courses,** Makena Alanui Drive, just past the Maui Prince Hotel (© **808/879-3344;** www.makenagolf.com; greens fees $150–$190), you'll find 36 holes of "Mr. Hawaii Golf"—Robert Trent Jones, Jr.—at its best, with great views of Molokini and humpback whales. The par-72, 6,876-yard South Course has a couple of holes you'll never forget, while the par-72, 6,823-yard North Course is more difficult and even more spectacular.

Wailea Courses, Wailea Alanui Drive (© **888/328-MAUI** [328-6284] or 808/875-7540; www.waileagolf.com; greens fees $165–$225), offers three courses to choose from, two designed by Robert Trent Jones, Jr. The par-72 Gold Course is the toughest, with narrow fairways and several tricky dogleg holes.

WATERSPORTS Snorkel Bob's (www.snorkelbob.com) has snorkel gear, boogie boards, and other ocean toys at four locations: 1217 Front St., Lahaina (© **808/661-4421**); Napili Village, 5425-C Lower Honoapiilani Hwy., Napili (© **808/669-9603**); Azeka Place II, 1279 S. Kihei Rd. #310 (© **808/875-6188**); and Kamaole Beach Center, 2411 S. Kihei Rd., Kihei (© **808/879-7449**). All locations are open daily from 8am to 5pm. If you're island hopping, you can rent from a Snorkel Bob's location on one island and return to a branch on another.

Boss Frog's Dive and Surf Shops (www.maui-vacation.net) has six locations for rental and other gear: Napili Plaza, next to Subway, in Napili (© 808/669-4949); Kahana Manor Shops, next to Dollies Pizza, in Kahana (© 808/669-6700); Kaanapali, 3636 L. Honoapiilani Rd. (© 808/665-1200); 150 Lahainaluna Rd., in Lahaina (© 808/661-3333); Longs Drugs Shopping Center, 1215 Kihei Rd., in North Kihei (© 808/891-0077); and Dolphin Plaza, 2395 S. Kihei Rd., behind Pizza Hut, in South Kihei (© 808/875-4477).

Trilogy (© **888/MAUI-800** [628-4800] or 808/TRILOGY [874-5649]; www.sail trilogy.com) offers our favorite Hawaiian boat trip: a sail to Lanai for snorkeling, swimming, and whale-watching (in season). This is the only cruise that offers a personalized ground tour of the island of Lanai.

Ed Robinson's Diving Adventures (© **800/635-1273** or 808/879-3584; www.maui scuba.com), one of the best on Maui, offers specialized charters for small groups. If Ed is booked, call **Mike Severns Diving** (© **808/879-6596;** www.mikeseversdiving.com), for small, personal tours. Mike and his wife are both biologists who make diving in Hawaii not only fun, but educational.

If fishing is more your thing, marlin, tuna, ono, and mahimahi await you in Maui's coastal and channel waters. No license is required; just book a sportfishing vessel out of Lahaina or Maalaea harbors. The best booking desk in the state is **Sportfish Hawaii** (© **877/388-1376** or 808/396-2607; www.sportfishhawaii.com), which books boats not only on Maui, but on all islands. These fishing vessels have been inspected and must meet rigorous criteria. Prices range from $595 to $1,000 for a full-day exclusive charter (you, plus five friends, get the entire boat to yourself); it's $395 to $700 for a half-day exclusive.

Want to catch a wave? Experts visit Maui in winter, when the surf's really up. The best beaches include **Honolua Bay,** north of Kapalua Resort; **Maalaea,** just outside the break-water of Maalaea Harbor; and **Hookipa Beach,** where surfers get the waves until noon (after that, the windsurfers take over). Always wanted to learn to surf but didn't know whom to ask? Call the **Nancy Emerson School of Surfing,** 358 Papa Place, Ste. F, Kahului (© **808/244-SURF** [244-7873] or 808/662-4445; www.surfclinics.com). Nancy has been surfing since 1961 and has even been a stunt performer in various mov-ies. She's pioneered an instructional technique called "Learn to Surf in One Lesson." It's $85 per person for a 2-hour group lesson; private 2-hour classes are $175.

The best time to **whale-watch** is from mid-December to April: Just look out to sea. For a close-up look, take a whale-watching cruise; try **Maui Classic Charters** in Maalaea Harbor (© **800/736-5740** or 808/879-8188; www.mauicharters.com), which offers a 3¹/₂-hour whale-watching trip for $42 for adults and $30 for children ages 3 to 12; price includes beverages.

Maui has Hawaii's best **windsurfing** beaches. In winter, windsurfers flock to **Hookipa Beach,** site of several world-championship contests. **Hawaiian Island Surf and Sport,** 415 Dairy Rd., Kahului (© **800/231-6958** or 808/871-4981; www.hawaiianisland.com), offers lessons (from $79), rentals, and repairs.

HOUSE OF THE SUN: HALEAKALA NATIONAL PARK

Haleakala National Park, extending from the summit of Mount Haleakala down the volcano's southeast flank to Maui's eastern coast, is Maui's main natural attraction. More than 1.3 million people a year go up the 10,023-foot-high mountain to peer down into the crater of the world's largest dormant volcano—a hole that would hold Manhattan. Just going up the mountain is an experience in itself. Where else can you climb from sea level to 10,000 feet in just 37 miles, or a 2-hour drive? The snaky road passes through puffy cumulus clouds to offer magnificent views of the isthmus of Maui, the West Maui Mountains, and the Pacific Ocean.

ACCESS POINTS   There are actually two separate and distinct destinations within the park: Haleakala Summit and the Kipahulu coast. No road links the summit and the coast; you have to approach them separately. **Haleakala Summit** is 37 miles, or a 1¹/₂- to 2-hour drive, from Kahului. Take Hwy. 37 to Hwy. 377 to Hwy. 378. (See "Driving to the Summit," below.) The **Kipahulu** section of the park is on Maui's east end near Hana, 60 miles from Kahului on Hwy. 36 (the Hana Hwy.). Due to traffic and rough road conditions, plan on 4 hours, one-way.

At both entrances to the park, the admission fee is $10 per car, good for a week of unlimited entry.

INFORMATION & VISITOR CENTERS   Contact **Haleakala National Park,** Box 369, Makawao, HI 96768 (© **808/572-4400;** www.nps.gov/hale). On the island, a mile from the park entrance, at 7,000 feet, is **Haleakala National Park Headquarters** (© **808/ 572-4400**), which provides information on park programs and activities, camping per-mits, restrooms, a pay phone, and drinking water. It's open daily from 7:30am to 4pm. The **Haleakala Visitor Center,** open daily from sunrise to 3pm, is near the summit, 11 miles from the park entrance. It offers a panoramic view, exhibits on the area, restrooms, and water.

A Word of Warning About the Weather

The weather at 10,000 feet can change suddenly and without warning. Come prepared for cold, high winds, rain, and even snow in winter. Temperatures can range from 77°F down to 26°F (25°C to –3°C), and high winds are frequent. Rainfall varies from 40 inches a year on the western end of the crater to more than 200 inches on the eastern side. Bring boots, waterproof gear, extra layers, and lots of sunscreen—the sun shines very brightly up here. For the latest weather information, call ✆ **808/871-5054.**

DRIVING TO THE SUMMIT   Hwy. 378, also known as **Haleakala Crater Road,** is one of the few roads in the world that climbs from sea level to 10,000 feet, in just 37 miles. It has at least 33 switchbacks; passes through numerous climate zones; goes under, in, and out of clouds; and offers a view that extends more than 100 miles.

Going to the summit takes 1¹/₂ to 2 hours from Kahului. Follow Hwy. 37 (Haleakala Hwy.) to Pukalani, where you'll pick up Hwy. 377 (also Haleakala Hwy.), which you'll take to Hwy. 378. Along the way, expect fog, rain, and wind. Fill up your gas tank before you go—Pukalani is the last town with services. There are no facilities beyond the ranger stations. Bring your own food and water.

Remember, you're entering a high-altitude wilderness area. Some people get dizzy due to the lack of oxygen; you may also suffer lightheadedness, shortness of breath, nausea, and headaches. People with asthma, pregnant women, heavy smokers, and those with heart conditions should be especially careful. Bring water and a jacket or a blanket, especially if you go up for sunrise.

Beyond headquarters are two overlooks. Stop at **Leleiwi Overlook,** just beyond mile marker 17. If you feel dizzy or drowsy, consider heading back down. A short trail leads to a panoramic view of the crater.

Two miles farther is **Kalahaku Overlook,** the best place to see a rare silversword. You can turn into this overlook only when you are descending from the top. The silversword, which grows only in Hawaii, has silvery bayonets displaying tiny purple bouquets; it takes from 4 to 50 years to bloom.

Continue on and you'll quickly reach **Haleakala Visitor Center,** which offers spectacular views. But don't turn around here; the actual summit's a little farther on, at **Puu Ulaula Overlook** (also known as Red Hill), the volcano's highest point. If you do go up for the sunrise, the building at Puu Ulaula Overlook is the best viewing spot.

Tip: When driving down the Haleakala Crater Road, be sure to put your car in low gear; that way, you won't destroy your brakes by riding them the whole way down.

HIKING IN THE PARK   Hiking into Maui's dormant volcano is really the way to see it. There are some 27 miles of hiking trails, two camping sites, and three **cabins,** which are so popular that requests for them must be made 3 months in advance—and that only gets you into a lottery system. For more on camping in the park, contact the park directly (✆ **808/572-4400;** www.nps.gov/hale).

Park rangers offer free guided hikes several times a week. If you opt to take one (and they're great), wear sturdy shoes and be prepared for wind, rain, and intense sun. Bring water and a hat. Options include full-moon hikes and star program hikes. *Always call in advance:* The hikes and briefing sessions are subject to change, so check first. For details and schedules, call the park at ℂ **808/572-4400,** or visit **www.nps.gov/hale**.

For those venturing out on their own, the best route takes in two trails: into the crater along **Sliding Sands Trail,** which begins on the rim at 9,800 feet and descends to the valley floor at 6,600 feet; and back out along **Halemauu Trail.** Hardy hikers can consider making the 11-mile, one-way descent, which takes 9 hours, and the equally long return ascent, in a day. The rest of us will need to extend this steep hike to 2 days. The descending and ascending trails aren't loops; the trail heads are miles apart, so you'll need to make transportation arrangements in advance. Before you set out, stop at park headquarters to get camping and hiking updates.

A shorter, easier option is the half-mile walk down the **Hosmer Grove Nature Trail,** or a mile or two down **Sliding Sands Trail** for a hint of what lies ahead. A good day hike is Halemauu Trail to Holua Cabin and back, an 8-mile, half-day trip.

WHERE TO STAY

Maui has accommodations to fit every kind of vacation, from deluxe oceanfront resorts to reasonably priced condos to historic bed-and-breakfasts. You'll get your money's worth at the **Fairmont Kea Lani Maui,** 4100 Wailea Alanui Dr. (ℂ **800/659-4100** or 808/875-4100; www.fairmont.com/kealani), plus a few extras. This all-suite luxury hotel has 840-square-foot suites with kitchenettes; a living room with high-tech media center and pullout sofa bed (great if you have the kids in tow); a marble wet bar; an oversize bathroom with separate shower big enough for a party; a separate spacious bedroom; and a large lanai overlooking the pools and lawns, right down to the white-sand beach. Rates from $525 to $1,200 suite.

If money's not a factor, the **Four Seasons Resort Maui at Wailea,** 3900 Wailea Alanui Dr. (ℂ **800/334-MAUI** [334-6284] or 808/874-8000; www.fourseasons.com/maui), a Hawaiian palace by the sea, is the place to spend it. The spacious (about 600-sq.-ft.) rooms feature furnished lanais with ocean views, along with grand bathrooms containing deep marble tubs, showers for two, hair dryers, and plush terry robes. Service is attentive but not cloying. Rates from $475 to $990 double.

The **Kahana Sunset,** 4909 Lower Honoapiilani Hwy. (ℂ **800/669-1488** or 808/669-8011; www.kahanasunset.com), a series of wooden condo units, stair-steps down the side of a hill to a postcard-perfect white-sand beach. The location, nestled between the coastline and road above, makes it very private. In the midst of the buildings lies a small pool and Jacuzzi; down by the sandy beach are gazebos and picnic areas. The units are great for families, with full kitchens, washer/dryers, large lanais with terrific views, and sofa beds. Rates from $165 to $290, one-bedroom.

Across the street from the ocean, **Koa Resort,** 811 S. Kihei Rd. (ℂ **800/541-3060** or 808/879-3328; www.bellomaui.com), consists of five two-story wooden buildings on 5½ acres of landscaped grounds. The spacious, privately owned one-, two-, and three-bedroom units come equipped with kitchens, large lanais, ceiling fans, and washer/dryers. For maximum peace and quiet, ask for a unit far from Kihei Road. High-season rates from $115 one-bedroom, $120 to $145 two-bedroom, $180 to $225 three-bedroom.

The spacious condo units at the **Outrigger Maui Eldorado,** 2661 Kekaa Dr. (ℂ **800/688-7444** or 808/661-0021; www.outrigger.com), feature full kitchens, washer/dryers, and daily maid service. The Outrigger chain has managed to keep prices down to reasonable levels, especially if you come in spring or fall. This is a great choice for families, with grassy areas and a beachfront that's usually safe for swimming. Rates from $279 to $329 studio double, $335 to $365 one-bedroom.

(Best) The Ritziest Ritz?

The **Ritz-Carlton Kapalua,** 1 Ritz-Carlton Dr. (© **800/262-8440** or 808/669-6200; www.ritzcarlton.com), may be the best Ritz-Carlton in the world. In 2008, it reopened after an extensive $16-million renovation that transformed the place into an even more elegant property, adding an Environmental Education Center and the 17,500-square-foot **Waihua Spa**. It rises proudly on a knoll, in a spectacular setting between the rainforest and the sea. Rooms have private lanais. Hospitality is the keynote here; you'll find exemplary Ritz service seasoned with good old-fashioned Hawaiian aloha. From $599 to $649 double.

If you can't decide between the privacy of a condo and the conveniences of a hotel, try the **ResortQuest Maui Hill,** 2881 S. Kihei Rd. (© **866/77-HAWAII** [774-2924] or 808/879-6321; www.resortquesthawaii.com). This Spanish-style resort is on a hill above the heat of Kihei town. It combines the amenities of a hotel—large pool, hot tub, tennis courts, putting green, Hawaiiana classes, daily maid service—with the luxury of large condos that have full kitchens, lots of space, and plenty of privacy. Nearly all units offer ocean views, washer/dryers, sofa beds, and big lanais. Rates from $220 to $325 one-bedroom.

One of Maui's best-value finds is the two-story **Napili Bay,** 33 Hui Dr. (© **877/782-5642;** www.alohacondos.com), on Napili's white-sand beach. The place is great for a romantic getaway. The studio apartments have everything you need, from full kitchens to roomy lanais. Though there is no air-conditioning, louvered windows and ceiling fans keep the units cool. Book early. Rates from $120 to $315.

The **Noelani Condominium Resort,** 4095 Lower Honoapiilani Rd. (© **800/367-6030** or 808/669-8374; www.noelani-condo-resort.com), is a great value. Everything is first class, from the furnishings to the location—on the ocean with a sandy cove next door at the new county park. There's good snorkeling off the cove, which is frequented by spinner dolphins and turtles in summer and humpback whales in winter. All units feature complete kitchens, entertainment centers, and spectacular views. Our favorites are in the Anthurium Building, where the one-, two-, and three-bedrooms have ocean-front lanais. Rates from $125 to $175 studio double, $175 to $197 one-bedroom.

A lovingly restored 1924 former plantation manager's home, **Old Wailuku Inn at Ulupono,** 2199 Kahookele St. (© **800/305-4899** or 808/244-5897; www.mauiinn.com), offers a genuine Old Hawaii experience. The theme centers around 1920s and 1930s Hawaii, with decor, design, and landscaping to match. The spacious rooms are gorgeously outfitted with exotic ohia-wood floors, high ceilings, and traditional Hawaiian quilts. Some of the mammoth bathrooms have claw-foot tubs; others have Jacuzzis. In the "Vagabond House," rooms feature all the modern amenities you can imagine (TV/VCR, air-conditioning, and an ultra-luxurious multihead shower). Rates from $150 to $180 double, including full breakfast.

Terrific facilities and the best location on Kaanapali Beach make the beautiful **Sheraton Maui Resort,** 2605 Kaanapali Pkwy. (© **800/782-9488** or 808/661-0031; www.sheraton-maui.com), a great place to stay. It's built into the side of the cliff on the white-sand cove next to Black Rock (an 80-ft.-high lava formation); a new lagoonlike pool features lava-rock waterways and an open-air spa. The new emphasis is on family appeal, with a class of rooms dedicated to those traveling with kids. Every unit is outfitted with amenities galore. Rates from $500 to $770 double.

In the heart of Kaanapali, right on the world-famous beach, lies the **Whaler on Kaanapali Beach,** 2481 Kaanapali Pkwy. (© **800/922-7866** or 808/661-4861; www.astonhotels.com), an oasis of elegance, privacy, and luxury. Each of the gorgeous units has a full kitchen, washer/dryer, 10-foot beamed ceilings, and lanai. The spectacular views take in Kaanapali's gentle waves and the peaks of the West Maui Mountains. Rates from $255 to $330 studio double.

WHERE TO DINE

More than a decade after opening the **Haliimaile General Store,** Haliimaile Road (© **808/572-2666;** www.haliimailegeneralstore.com), Bev Gannon, one of the 12 original Hawaii Regional Cuisine chefs, is still going strong at her foodie haven in the pineapple fields. You'll dine at tables set on old wood floors under high ceilings (sound ricochets fiercely here), in a room emblazoned with works by local artists. The food, a blend of eclectic American with ethnic touches, puts an innovative spin on Hawaii Regional Cuisine. Sip the lilikoi lemonade and nibble the notable sashimi napoleon.

Mañana Garage, 33 Lono Ave. (© **808/873-0220**), serves incomparable Latin American fare and has introduced exciting new flavors to Maui's dining scene. The restaurant's industrial motif features table bases like hubcaps, blown-glass chandeliers, and gleaming chrome and cobalt walls with orange accents. The menu is brilliantly conceived and executed. The seviche perfectly balances flavors and textures: lime, cilantro, chili, coconut, and fresh fish.

Nick's Fishmarket Maui, in the Fairmont Kea Lani Hotel at 4100 Wailea Alanui (© **808/879-7224;** www.tristarrestaurants.com), has a perfect balance of visual sizzle and memorable food. Stefanotis vines create shade on the terrace, where the sunset views are superb. We love the onion vichyssoise with taro swirl and a hint of *tobiko* (flying-fish roe). Bow-tied waiters and almond-scented cold towels add an extra touch to this oceanside phenomenon—as well as the lavish wine list and torch lighting at sunset.

Despite the lack of dramatic view and an upstairs location in a shopping mall, **Roy's Kahana Bar & Grill,** in the Kahana Gateway Shopping Center at 4405 Honoapiilani Hwy. (© **808/669-6999;** www.roysrestaurant.com), remains crowded and extremely popular for one reason—fabulous food. Young, hip, impeccably trained servers deliver

---

(Best) **A Night to Remember: Maui's Top Luau**

The nightly **Old Lahaina Luau** (© **800/248-5828** or 808/667-1998; www.old lahainaluau.com), staged at a 1-acre site just oceanside of the Lahaina Cannery, is the indisputable champ of Maui's luaus. Local craftspeople display their wares. Seating is provided on lauhala mats for those who wish to dine as the traditional Hawaiians did, but there are also tables.

The luau begins at sunset and features Tahitian and Hawaiian entertainment, including ancient, missionary-era, and modern hula. The entertainment is riveting. The food is as much Pacific Rim as authentically Hawaiian. No watered-down mai tais, either; these are the real thing. The cost is $96 for adults, $65 for children 12 and under.

Euro-Asian fare such as blackened ahi, rack of lamb, and fresh seafood (usually eight or nine choices) to tables of satisfied customers.

Furiously fusion, part Hawaii Regional Cuisine, and all parts sushi, **Sansei Seafood Restaurant & Sushi Bar,** Kapalua Shops, 115 Bay Dr. (© **808/669-6286;** www.sansei hawaii.com), is tirelessly creative, with a menu that scores higher with the adventurous than the purists. Maki is the mantra here. Other choices include panko-crusted ahi sashimi and traditional Japanese tempura. There's also simpler fare, such as pastas and wok-tossed vegetables. Desserts, including the macadamia nut tempura fried ice cream, are not to be missed.

The best Italian food on Maui is served at the exquisite **Vino Italian Tapas & Wine Bar,** at the Kapalua Resort (© **808/661-VINO** [661-8466]), overlooking the rolling hills of the Kapalua Golf Course and run by famed chef D. K. Kodama and Hawaii's only master sommelier Chuck Furuya. The menu changes constantly, but it's always pure Italian—lots of homemade pastas, classic and contemporary preparations of poultry and meat, and special fish and seafood dishes nightly. And every dish is perfectly paired with wine (the list is exceptional).

6 THE BIG ISLAND

The Big Island of Hawaii—the island that lends its name to the entire 1,500-mile-long archipelago—is where Mother Nature pulled out all the stops. Simply put, it's spectacular. The island looks like the inside of a barbecue pit on one side and a lush jungle on the other, with fiery volcanoes and sparkling waterfalls, black-lava deserts and snowcapped mountain peaks, tropical rainforests and Alpine meadows, a glacial lake and miles of beaches filled with a rainbow of black, green, and golden sands. A 50-mile drive will take you from snowy winter to sultry summer, passing through spring or fall along the way. Five volcanoes—one still erupting—have created this continental island, which is expanding every day.

The Big Island is not for everyone, however. Some tourists are taken aback at the sight of stark fields of lava or black-sand beaches, and you may have to go out of your way if you're looking for traditional tropical beauty, such as a white-sand beach.

ESSENTIALS

GETTING THERE   The Big Island has two major airports: **Kona International Airport,** on the west coast, and **Hilo International Airport,** on the east. The Kona Airport receives direct overseas flights from Japan as well as direct mainland flights from Los Angeles and San Francisco. Otherwise, you'll have to pick up an interisland flight in Honolulu. All major rental companies have cars available at both airports.

VISITOR INFORMATION   The **Big Island Visitors Bureau** (© **800/648-2441;** www. bigisland.org) has two offices on the Big Island: one at 250 Keawe St., Hilo, HI 96720 (© **808/961-5797;** fax 808/961-2126), and one on the other side of the island at 250 Waikoloa Beach Dr., Waikoloa, HI 96738 (© **808/886-1655;** fax 808/886-1652). The Big Island's best free tourist publications are *This Week,* the *Beach and Activity Guide,* and *101 Things to Do on Hawaii the Big Island.* All three offer lots of useful information, as well as discount coupons on a variety of island adventures. Copies are easy to find all around the island.

You'll need a rental car here, where taxis can take you anywhere but are prohibitively expensive. All the major car-rental firms have agencies at both the airports and the Kohala Coast resorts.

FAST FACTS **Kona Community Hospital,** on the Kona Coast in Kealakekua (© **808/322-9311**), has a 24-hour urgent-care facility. If you need a doctor, call **Hualalai Urgent Care,** 75–1028 Henry St., Kona (© **808/327-HELP** [327-4357]).

BEACHES

Too young geologically to have many great beaches, the Big Island instead has an odd collection of unusual ones: brand-new black-sand beaches, green-sand beaches, salt-and-pepper beaches, and even a rare white-sand beach.

Just off Queen Kaahumanu Highway, south of the Hapuna Beach Prince Hotel, is the golden crescent of **Hapuna Beach**—big, wide, and a half-mile long. In summer, when the beach is widest, the ocean calmest, and the crowds biggest, this is the island's best beach for swimming, snorkeling, and bodysurfing. But beware in winter, when its thundering waves, rip currents, and lack of lifeguards can be dangerous.

A coconut grove sweeps around **Kaunaoa Beach (Mauna Kea Beach),** at the foot of Mauna Kea Beach Hotel, where the water is calm and protected by two black-lava points. The sandy bottom slopes gently into the bay, which often fills with schools of tropical fish, sea turtles, and manta rays. Swimming is excellent year-round, except in rare winter storms. Snorkelers prefer the rocky points, where fish thrive in the surge.

The Big Island makes up for its dearth of beaches with a few spectacular ones, such as **Anaehoomalu Bay** (or **A-Bay,** as the locals call it). This peppered, gold-sand beach, fringed by palms and backed by royal fishponds, fronts the Outrigger Waikoloa Beach Resort. The beach slopes gently from shallow to deep water; swimming, snorkeling, diving, kayaking, and windsurfing are all excellent. At the far edge of the bay is a turtle cleaning station, where snorkelers and divers can watch endangered green sea turtles line up, waiting their turn to have small fish clean them.

OUTDOOR ACTIVITIES

The not-for-profit group **Friends for Fitness,** P.O. Box 1671, Kailua-Kona, HI 96745 (© **808/322-0033**), offers a free brochure on physical activities (from aerobic classes to dancing to yoga) in West Hawaii; they will gladly mail it to you upon request.

GOLF For last-minute and discount tee times, call **Stand-by Golf** (© **888/645-BOOK** [645-2665] or 808/322-BOOK [322-2665]) between 7am and 11pm. Stand-by Golf offers discounted (10%–40%), guaranteed tee times for same-day or next-day golfing.

Designed by Arnold Palmer and Ed Seay, the 18-hole championship **Hapuna Golf Course,** Hapuna Prince Beach Resort, off Hwy. 19 near mile marker 69 (© **808/880-3000;** www.hapunabeachprincehotel.com; greens fees $165), has been named the most environmentally sensitive course by *Golf* magazine. The 6,027-yard links-style course extends from the shoreline to 700 feet above sea level, with views of the pastoral Kohala Mountains and sweeping vistas of the Kohala coastline.

The beautiful, par-72, 7,114-yard **Mauna Kea Golf Course,** Mauna Kea Beach Resort, Hwy. 19 near mile marker 68 (© **808/882-5400;** www.maunakeabeachhotel.com; greens fees $210), designed by Robert Trent Jones, Jr., is consistently rated one of the top courses in the U.S. As we went to press, Mauna Kea's greens, tees, fairways, and

levels of both resort and professional golfers. The bunkers were being restored to their original configuration. Plans call for the course to reopen by 2009; call ahead for updates.

The **Mauna Lani Frances I'i Brown Championship Courses** are on Mauna Lani Drive, off Hwy. 19, 20 miles north of Kona Airport (© **808/885-6655;** www.mauna lani.com; greens fees $210). The par-72, 7,029-yard Mauna Lani South Course has an unforgettable ocean hole: the downhill, 221-yard, par-3 7th, which is bordered by the sea, a salt-and-pepper sand dune, and lush kiawe trees. The North Course's more extensive indigenous vegetation gives it a Scottish feel.

WATERSPORTS   If you want to rent beach toys (snorkel gear, boogie boards), the beach concessions at all the big resorts, as well as tour desks and dive shops, offer equipment rentals and sometimes lessons for beginners. The cheapest place to get great rental equipment is **Snorkel Bob's,** in the parking lot of Huggo's Restaurant at 75–5831 Kahakai Rd., at Alii Drive, Kailua-Kona (© **808/329-0770;** www.snorkelbob.com).

There are nearly two dozen dive operators on the west side of the island, offering everything from certification courses to guided boat dives. **BottomTime Hawaii,** 74–5590 Luhia St. (© **866/GO-DIVEN** [463-4836] or 808/331-1858; www.bottom timehawaii.com), takes their 34-foot catamaran (complete with showers, TV, and restrooms) to unusual dive sites, and also offers free introductory dives in enriched air (Nitrox) for $130 and two-tank dives for $130.

One of Kona's oldest dive shops, **Jack's Diving Locker,** 75–5819 Alii Dr. (© **800/ 345-4807** or 808/329-7585; www.jacksdivinglocker.com), offers the classic two-tank for $125, and a two-tank manta-ray night dive for $145.

The year-round calm waters along the Kona and Kohala coasts are home to spectacular marine life. Some of the best areas include the secret little **Hapuna Beach Cove,** at the foot of the Hapuna Beach Prince Hotel. If you're a first-time snorkeler, you can simply wade in and look down at **Kahaluu Beach Park.** The best snorkeling for all levels is in **Kealakekua Bay.** The calm waters of this underwater preserve teem with a wealth of marine life. Kealakekua is reachable only by boat or kayak.

If you want to fish, it doesn't get any better than the Kona Coast, known internationally as the marlin capital of the world. Nearly 100 charter boats with professional captains and crew offer fishing charters out of **Keauhou, Kawaihae, Honokohau,** and **Kailua Bay harbors.** If you're not an expert angler, the best way to arrange a charter is through a booking agency such as the **Charter Desk at Honokohau Marina** (© **888/KONA-4-US** [566-2487] or 808/329-5735; www.charterdesk.com) or **Charter Services Hawaii** (© **800/567-2650** or 808/334-1881; www.konazone.com).

Most surfing off the Big Island is for the experienced only. **Ocean Eco Tours** (© **808/324-SURF** [324-7873]; www.oceanecotours.com) is one of the few companies on the Big Island that teaches surfing. Your only choice for surfboard rentals is **Pacific Vibrations,** 75–5702 Likana Lane, just off Alii Dr., across from the pier, Kailua-Kona (© **808/329-4140;** www.laguerdobros.com/pacvib/pacificv.html).

HAWAII VOLCANOES NATIONAL PARK

Hawaii Volcanoes National Park is a work in progress, thanks to Kilauea volcano, which pours red-hot lava into the sea and adds land to the Big Island every day. Hawaii's eruptions produce slow-moving, oozing lava that provides excellent, safe viewing most of the

Dressing for Volcano-Watching

Thanks to its higher elevation and windward (rainier) location, the volcanic area is always colder than it is at the beach. In the winter months, expect temperatures to be in the 40s or 50s (5°–15°C), and dress accordingly. Always have rain gear on hand, especially in winter.

time. You can see the highlights by car (the park has 50 miles of good roads, some of them often covered by lava flows) if you have only a day to spare, or allow at least 3 days to fully explore the park, which has hiking trails, rainforests, and campgrounds in addition to some of the world's weirdest landscapes.

ACCESS POINTS   Hawaii Volcanoes National Park is 29 miles from Hilo, on Hawaii Belt Road (Hwy. 11). From Kailua-Kona, it's 100 miles, or about a 2¹/₂-hour drive. At press time, admission was still $10 per vehicle, but the park was proposing to double that to $20 per car. Hikers and bicyclists pay $5; bikes are allowed on roads and paved trails only.

INFORMATION & VISITOR CENTERS   For advance information, contact **Hawaii Volcanoes National Park,** P.O. Box 52, Hawaii Volcanoes National Park, HI 96718 (© 808/985-6000; www.nps.gov/havo). If you want to camp or hike in the park, be sure to inquire about them in advance or check out *Frommer's Hawaii* for detailed information. **Kilauea Visitor Center** is at the entrance to the park, just off Hwy. 11; it's open daily from 7:45am to 5pm.

Everything you wanted to know about Hawaii's volcanoes is at **http://volcano.wr. usgs.gov/kilaueastatus.php**. The site is divided into areas on Kilauea (the currently erupting volcano), Mauna Loa (which last erupted in 1984), and Hawaii's other volcanoes. Each section provides photos, maps, eruption summaries, and historical information.

You can also get the latest on volcanic activity in the park by calling the park's **24-hour hot line** (© 808/985-6000). Updates on volcanic activity are posted daily on the bulletin board at the visitor center.

Seeing the Highlights

Your first stop should be **Kilauea Visitor Center,** just inside the park entrance, where you can get the latest reports on the volcano's activity and learn how volcanoes work. Walk across the street to **Volcano House;** go through the lobby and out the other side, where you can have a good look at **Kilauea Caldera,** a 2¹/₂-mile-wide, 500-foot-deep pit. It used to be a bubbling pit of lava; today, you can still see wisps of steam.

Now get out on the highway and drive by the **Sulphur Banks,** which smell like rotten eggs, and the **Steam Vents,** where trails of smoke, once molten lava, rise from within the inner reaches of the earth. It's one of the few places where you can feel that the volcano is truly alive. Stop at the **Thomas A. Jaggar Museum** (daily 8:30am–5pm; free admission), which shows eruption videos, explains the Pele legend, and monitors earthquakes (a precursor of eruptions).

Next, drive around the caldera to the other side, park, and take the short walk to Halemaumau Crater's edge to stand at the overlook and stare at this once-fuming and bubbling old fire pit, which still generates ferocious heat out of vestigial vents. If you feel the need to cool off, go to the Thurston Lava Tube, the coolest place in the park. You'll hike down into a natural bowl, a forest preserve the lava didn't touch, and see a black hole in the earth; step in. It's dripping and cool, with bare roots hanging down.

A BIRD'S-EYE VIEW OF THE VOLCANO   The best way to see the volcano is from up high, in a helicopter. This view puts the enormity of it all into perspective. The best outfitter is **Blue Hawaiian Helicopter** (© **800/745-BLUE** [745-2583] or 808/886-1768; www.bluehawaiian.com), a professionally run, locally based company with an excellent safety record, comfortable copters, and extremely knowledgeable pilots. The 45-minute **Circle of Fire** flight from Hilo takes you over the boiling volcano and then on to a bird's-eye view of the destruction the lava has caused and remote beaches ($210 per person, or $169 online). Our favorite trip, from Waikoloa, is the 2-hour **Big Island** **Spectacular,** starring the volcano, tropical valleys, Hamakua Coast waterfalls, and the Kohala Mountains (from $424, or $364 online, and worth every penny!).

WHERE TO STAY

For additional information on bed-and-breakfasts, contact the **Hawaii Island B&B** **Association,** P.O. Box 1890, Honokaa, HI 96727 (no phone; www.stayhawaii.com).

Relax in the lap of luxury at **Four Seasons Resort Hualalai at Historic Kaupulehu,** Kailua-Kona (© **888/340-5662** or 808/325-8000; www.fourseasons.com/hualalai), the best hotel on the island. Low-rise clusters of villas nestle between the sea and the greens of a fabulous golf course. The rooms are furnished in Pacific tropical style; some have bathrooms with private outdoor gardens (surrounded by black-lava rock), so you can shower under the sun or the stars. The spa has been selected by *Condé Nast Traveler* magazine as the world's best resort spa. From $725 to $1,155 double.

The **Kona Village Resort,** Kailua-Kona (© **800/367-5290** or 808/325-5555; www. konavillage.com), which had begun to fall into disrepair, was recently sold, and it appears that the new owners are pouring much-needed funds into maintenance of this oceanside Polynesian village, where the thatched-roof bungalows lack air-conditioning, TVs, and phones (they do have fully stocked fridges and some have an outdoor hot tub). The room rate includes breakfast, lunch, and dinner—the luau here is fabulous—plus all snorkeling equipment, other beach toys, and scheduled activities throughout the day for kids and teens. Rates from $660 to $1,475 double.

The serene **Mauna Lani Bay Hotel & Bungalows,** 68–1400 Mauna Lani Dr., Kohala Coast (© **800/367-2323** or 808/885-6622; www.maunalani.com), offers sandy beaches and lava tide pools, plus gracious hospitality. The plush rooms, each with lanai, are arranged to capture the best ocean views. The two-bedroom, 4,000-square-foot bunga-lows come with private pools. Rates from $445 to $935 double.

The elegant, upscale **Fairmont Orchid,** 1 N. Kaniku Dr., Kohala Coast (© **800/845-****9905** or 808/885-2000; www.fairmont.com/orchid), which underwent a major renova-tion in 2006, is *the* place for watersports nuts, families, or those who just want to relax. The spacious rooms feature ocean views (all have lanais), sitting areas, and marble bath-rooms. The beach and watersports facilities are extensive, and the excellent Hawaiiana program covers everything from paddling a canoe to strumming a ukulele. Rates from $399 to $839 double.

The inexpensive, 60-unit **Kona Billfisher,** Alii Drive (across from Royal Kona Resort), Kailua-Kona (© **800/622-5348** or 808/329-3333; www.konahawaii.com), is our favorite of all the affordable condos on this coast. Each well-maintained unit comes with a full kitchen and a balcony, and features new furnishings and king-size beds. Book well in advance. High-season rates from $150 one-bedroom, $165 two-bedroom.

The comfortable, spacious condos at **Outrigger Kanaloa at Kona,** 78–261 Manukai St., Kailua-Kona (© **800/688-7444** or 808/322-9625; www.outrigger.com), border the rocky coast beside Keauhou Bay, 6 miles south of Kailua-Kona. They're ideal for families; the huge bathrooms have whirlpool bathtubs and spacious lanais. Rates from $249 to $365 one-bedroom apartment.

If you're going to Volcanoes National Park, you'll really need to stay 3 days to take in the park properly. The best way to do this is to rent a cottage or house, and the best rental agency is **Hawaii Volcano Vacations,** P.O. Box 913, Volcano, HI 96785 (© **800/709-0907** or 808/967-7271; www.hawaiivolcanovacations.com). Manager Aurelia Gutierrez selects only the top cottages, cabins, and houses in Volcano and makes sure that they are perfect for you. Very reasonably priced, her units range from $99 to $200, and each one is outfitted with a full kitchen, plus an outdoor grill, cooler, flashlight, umbrella, and fresh flower arrangement.

WHERE TO DINE

Huggo's on the Rocks, a mound of thatch, rock, and grassy, sandy ground right next to **Huggo's,** 75–5828 Kahakai Rd. (© **808/329-1493;** www.huggos.com), is a sunset-lover's nirvana. At sundown, it's choked with people either on chaises or at the 50-seat thatched bar, sipping mai tais and noshing on salads, poke, sandwiches, plate lunches, sashimi, and fish and chips.

The **Beach Tree Bar and Grill,** Four Seasons Resort Hualalai, Queen Kaahumanu Highway, Kaupulehu-Kona (© **808/325-8000**), is an example of outstanding cuisine in a perfect setting—without being fancy, expensive, or fussy. The bar on the sand is a sunset paradise, and the sandwiches, seafood, and grilled items at the casual outdoor restaurant (a few feet from the bar) are simple, excellent, and prepared with imagination and no shortcuts.

Great food, crisp air, and a sweeping ocean view make the **Coffee Shack,** Hwy. 11, 1 mile south of Captain Cook (© **808/328-9555**), one of South Kona's finds. Besides trying its fabulous breakfasts, come here for lunch: imported beers, sandwiches on home-baked breads, and hearty salads made with organic greens.

When it comes to dining on the Big Island, **Merriman's,** Opelu Plaza, Hwy. 19 in Waimea (© **808/885-6822**), is peerless. At dinner, choose from the signature wok-charred ahi, lamb from nearby Kahua Ranch, and a noteworthy vegetarian selection. The restaurant's famous platters of seafood and meats are among the many reasons this is the best dining spot in Waimea.

Appendix A:
The Best of the Rest

There's no way we're doing Frommer's U.S.A. without mentioning something in every single state! There's plenty to see and do in Arkansas, Iowa, Kansas, North Dakota, and West Virginia (and we have that pesky limit of putting together a book you don't need a wheelbarrow to carry around). So here is a bird's-eye view of some of the excellent attractions and some of the best scenery in these particular United States. Best of all, the lack of major crowds in many of these areas means you can explore in relative peace and quiet, and you won't get hit with the high prices so common in major tourist zones. If you're looking for the "real" America, here are five more places to look.

1 ARKANSAS

Once on the eastern edge of the American frontier, Arkansas was once a rough-and-ready territory comprised of plantations and settlements of poor immigrants from nearby Appalachia. The Civil War brought an end to slavery, but racial tensions remained until desegregation was forced on the state in 1957. Industrialization improved the economic plight of residents somewhat during the same time period. Today the Natural State is best known for its fabulous outdoor recreational opportunities, exceptional hot springs, and glorious mountain scenery. For history buffs, there are many sites and attractions dealing with the civil rights movement, rural Ozark mountain culture, and Bill Clinton (who remains a favorite son, and built his Presidential Library & Museum in Little Rock). All in all, the state offers a good deal of variety—and a lot of good value.

ESSENTIALS

VISITOR INFORMATION Contact the **Arkansas Department of Parks & Tourism,** 1 Capitol Mall, Little Rock, AR 72201 (© **800/NATURAL** [628-8725] or 501/682-7777; www.arkansas.com),

and request the state's comprehensive vacation kit, which includes a map, visitor's guide, and calendar of events.

Fourteen tourist information centers are located at strategic entry points and long major road routes within the state. The centers are open 8am to 5pm daily (they are closed on several major holidays; summer hours extended by 1 hr.) and are staffed by travel counselors who will gladly dispense attractions and sightseeing information.

GETTING THERE By Plane Arkansas's largest commercial airport, **Little Rock National Airport** (© **501/372-3439;** www.lrn-airport.com), which spent $170 million upgrading facilities in the 1990s, is served by nine major domestic and discount carriers. Most of the major car-rental agencies have desks at the airport.

By Train Amtrak's *Texas Eagle* train (© **800/872-7245;** www.amtrak.com) makes stops at several cities in Arkansas, including Little Rock and Texarkana, as it travels from Chicago to Dallas.

By Car **I-40** enters the state out of Tennessee and continues west into Little Rock, then shifts slightly northward and heads in the direction of the Ozark region and Oklahoma. **I-30** enters the southwest corner of the state from Texas and ends in Little Rock. **I-540** and **U.S. 71** both offer lots of scenery as they run through the Ozarks. *Note:* A major portion of the state's 655-mile interstate network is currently undergoing a $950-million renovation that will add an **I-69** and **I-555** (see **www.arkansasinterstates.com** for updates). It's scheduled to run until 2010.

SPECIAL EVENTS Held in mid-October, the **Arkansas State Fair and Livestock Show,** at the State Fairgrounds and Barton Coliseum in Little Rock (© **501/ 372-8341;** www.arkansasstatefair.com), will celebrate its 70th anniversary in 2009. The festivities include educational exhibits, concerts, a rodeo, a carnival, a midway with rides and games, arts and crafts, clowns, magicians, strolling musicians, and talent contests.

WHERE TO STAY The state offers a host of accommodations, ranging from full-scale resorts to park lodges to motels to quaint inns. An online directory of available accommodations in cities throughout the state is available at **www. arkansas.com**. Noteworthy hotels in the state include Eureka Springs's historic **1886 Crescent Hotel and Spa** (© **877/ 342-9766** or 479/253-9766; www.crescent-hotel.com), a Historic Hotel of America; and Little Rock's **Peabody Hotel** (© **501/ 906-4000;** www.peabodylittlerock.com), a branch of the famous luxury hotel group which features its own set of marching ducks.

Arkansas features a plethora of bed-and-breakfasts, many of them situated in historic buildings and woodsy cabins. The **Bed & Breakfast Association of Arkansas** (**www.bedandbreakfastarkansas.com**) publishes a free directory listing all 63 of its member inns.

HIGHLIGHTS OF ARKANSAS

Dubbed "The Natural State," Arkansas features first-class parks and recreation areas. Outdoor enthusiasts will find more activities than anyone could hope to fit into one vacation. For information on all of the state's outdoor and recreational opportunities, contact the **Arkansas Department of Parks & Tourism** (see above), the **Division of State Parks** (© **888/287-2757;** www.arkansasstate parks.com), or the **National Park Service** (www.nps.gov).

In 2004, the $160-million **Clinton Presidential Center & Library** (© 501/ 374-4242; www.clintonfoundation.org) opened inside downtown Little Rock's River Market District off I-30. America's 12th presidential library contains the largest collection of presidential papers and artifacts in U.S. history. The **River Market District** (© 501/375-2552) itself is worth a stop. The city took an abandoned warehouse district and turned it into an area that is now home to numerous restaurants, businesses, museums, shops, and galleries; a riverside park and amphitheater; and vibrant nightlife.

Located in Little Rock's historic MacArthur Park, the **Arkansas Art Center,** at 9th and Commerce streets (© **501/372-4000;** www.arkarts.com), is the state's largest cultural institution and features exhibits spread over seven galleries. It encompasses the **Arkansas Museum of Art,** whose noteworthy collection includes some Renaissance-era drawings, and the **Arkansas Children's Theater.**

Do visit the **State Capitol,** at Woodlane Drive and Capitol Avenue (© **501/682-5080;** www.sosweb.state.ar.us), a striking neoclassical structure of limestone and marble, whose six brass doors—ordered from Tiffany's—are worth an estimated $250,000 each. Organized and self-guided tours are available.

(Best) Soaking in Hot Springs

A remarkable array of thermal springs in a valley of the Ouachita Mountains in western Arkansas prompted Congress in 1832 to set aside the valley known today as **Hot Springs** as a federal reservation. People have used the hot-spring-water therapeutic baths for more than 200 years to treat rheumatism and other ailments. The reservation developed into a well-known resort nick-named "the American Spa" because it attracted not only the famous (Al Capone and Harry S. Truman), but also indigent health seekers from around the world.

Though it officially became America's 18th national park in 1921, **Hot Springs National Park,** off I-70 and Hwy. 7 (© **501/624-2701;** www.nps.gov/hosp), is actually the oldest in the national park system protected by law. On Bathhouse Row, the park's most celebrated feature, the **Fordyce Bathhouse,** serves as the park's visitor center and a museum of the thermal bathing indus-try. The park also features a working bathhouse, the **Buckstaff Bathhouse;** a mountain observation tower; an open cascade spring; and hiking trails. Stop in at the visitor center, located in downtown Hot Springs on Hwy. 7 North (Central Ave.). They distribute a pamphlet detailing the city's associations with former President Bill Clinton, who spent much of his childhood in Hot Springs.

For more information on the park and the many sights and activities avail-able in Hot Springs, contact the **Hot Springs Convention & Visitors Bureau** (© **800/543-2284;** www.hotsprings.org) and request their free visitor's guide.

A major U.S. civil rights landmark, the **Little Rock Central High School National Historic Site,** 2125 W. Daisy L. Gatson Bates Dr. (© **501/374-1957**), is still a working school. In 1957, when the state's governor tried to block the school's first African-American students—the famous Little Rock Nine—from being admitted, President Eisenhower sent federal troops to intervene. The **Central High Museum and Visitor Center,** located in a renovated Mobil Service Station across the street from the school, features a perma-nent exhibit, detailing the events of the 1957 desegregation crisis at the school.

Fans of *Gone With the Wind* should head to the **Old Grist Mill** (© **501/758-1424**), a National Historic Landmark at McCain Boulevard and Lakeshore Drive in North Little Rock. An authentic repro-duction of an old water-powered gristmill, this striking structure, built in 1933 but

designed to look as if it were constructed in the 1800s, appears in the opening scene of the classic film and is believed to be the only building used in the movie that's still standing.

If diamonds are a girl's best friend, then **Crater of Diamonds State Park,** off Ark. 301 near Murfreesboro (© **870/285-3113;** www.craterofdiamondsstatepark.com), is a bastion of female goodwill. The world's only public diamond mine lets visitors prospect for their own shiny souvenirs; if you find one (more than 25,000 have got-ten lucky since 1972), you can keep it. Exhibits at the park trace the history of Arkansas's diamonds.

On U.S. 278, just northwest of Hope, is **Old Washington Historic State Park** (© **870/983-2684;** www.oldwashington statepark.com), a National Historic Land-mark established on the site of the town of Washington, which came into being in

1824. Today visitors can explore over 30 carefully restored historic structures, including classic examples of southern Greek Revival and Federal architecture, as well as hand-hewn timber-framed cottages. Tour the public buildings and homes; see the remarkable collections of antiques, guns, and knives (the blacksmith shop here was where the famous Bowie knife was first forged); and visit with guides in period attire who will greet you at each stop.

Off Ark. 14, you'll find **Blanchard Springs Cavern,** a limestone formation located deep in the Ozark National Forest,

15 miles north of Mountain View. It is operated by the U.S. Forest Service and is open throughout the year. Lighted walkways lead to stunning formations and massive rooms, one as large as six football fields. Nearby, Blanchard Springs Recreational Use Area provides scenic campgrounds, picnic areas, hiking trails, a massive natural spring, and a trout lake. For information, call the U.S. Forest Service at © **202/205-8333** or head online to **www.fs.fed.us**.

For information on the historic and charming city of **Eureka Springs,** see "A Side Trip to Eureka Springs," on p. 556.

2 IOWA

No, it isn't heaven, no matter what the Oscar-nominated *Field of Dreams* may imply. But the 29th state admitted to the Union is a cool place to visit. The movie's famous baseball field is here (and you can play on it), as are cornfields galore, one of the country's oldest and most celebrated state fairs, and the famous covered bridges of Madison County. And of course, Iowa's caucuses are where presidential dreams begin (or don't take off at all!). Only one Iowa native's managed to make it all the way to the White House—Herbert Hoover, whose unfortunate presidency dovetailed with the Great Depression. It's also the home state of Grant Wood, the artist whose *American Gothic* is one of the most famous pieces of art on the planet (that particular work isn't in Iowa, but 5,000 or so of his other works are scattered throughout the state). And, it's the future birthplace of USS *Enterprise* captain James T. Kirk, who, according to *Star Trek* lore, will be born there in March 2228, in Riverside.

Love the great outdoors? Iowans do, and visitors reap the benefits of the local passion for recreation. Iowa offers a wide variety of outdoor activities, including an abundance of fishing, hiking, hunting, camping, and biking. The state even has the largest number of golfers per capita in the country, and they tee up on some of America's best public courses. Native minigolfers are so devoted to getting in their strokes, they even play on ice in the winter (bring spikes!). And before the snow starts falling, the state offers some beautiful fall foliage-watching (and prices that aren't as sky-high as those in states better known for their seasonal coloring). In other words, Iowa is a hidden bargain that hasn't yet been discovered.

ESSENTIALS

VISITOR INFORMATION For a calendar of events, map, and comprehensive travel guide, contact the **Iowa Tourism Office,** 200 E. Grand Ave., Des Moines, IA 50309 (© **888/472-6035** or 515/242-4705; www.traveliowa.com). A good website featuring lots of information on the state can be found at **www.iowa.com**.

The Tourism Office runs 19 welcome centers dispensing tourist information at strategic points along major roads and border crossings, and in small towns throughout the state. For locations, check **www.traveliowa.com**.

GETTING THERE By Plane The state's major airport is **Des Moines International** (© 515/256-5100; www.dsm airport.com), just 10 minutes outside of Des Moines. It's serviced by most domestic carriers and car-rental agencies.

By Car The major east-west route through the state is **I-80,** which enters from Illinois and passes through Des Moines before heading southwest toward Omaha. **I-35** runs from the northern Minnesota border before intersecting with I-80 just above Des Moines and continuing southward to Kansas City. I-29 weaves through the state's western border with Nebraska. Road conditions, especially during the winter, can change in a hurry. Before setting out on a long drive, call © 511 in Iowa, or 800/288-1047 from outside the state. You can also go online to **www.511ia.org**.

SPECIAL EVENTS Iowa's largest event, the **Iowa State Fair,** in Des Moines (© 800/545-3247 or 515/262-3111; www.iowa statefair.org), is one of the oldest (at over 150 years and counting) in the country, and one of the best (both *Esquire* and *USA Today* have named it one of the country's best summer experiences). Highlights include a livestock show, the state's largest arts show, tons of wacky contests, performances by nationally renowned artists (ranging from Rick Springfield to Blake Shelton), tons of food, fireworks, and more.

WHERE TO STAY The majority of the state's accommodations are of the chain variety; consult the Iowa Tourism Office (see above) for information on lodging and reservations. Noteworthy hotels in Iowa include Des Moines's **Suites of 800 Locust Hotel & Spa** (© 515/288-5800; www.800locust.com), the city's only boutique property and its best hotel; and, just

40 minutes north of Des Moines in the city of Perry, the **Hotel Pattee** (© 888/424-4268 or 515/465-3511; www.hotel pattee.com), a luxury property and National Historic Landmark whose 40 rooms and suites are individually decorated to pay tribute to historical figures from the Midwest.

Iowa's B&Bs range in style from historic properties to farmhouses. For information on available options, contact the **Iowa Bed & Breakfast Guild,** 9001 Hickman Rd., Ste. 220, Des Moines, IA 50322 (© 800/743-4692; www.ia-bednbreakfast-inns. com). One especially lovely choice in Des Moines is the multi-award-winning **Butler House on Grand** (© 866/455-4096 or 515/255-4096; www.butlerhouseon grand.com), whose romantic and exquisitely decorated rooms have been cited by many, including being named one of the top 10 B&B's for business travelers by *USA Today.*

HIGHLIGHTS OF IOWA

In the capital city of Des Moines, the **Des Moines Art Center,** 4700 Grand Ave. (© 515/277-4405; www.desmoinesart center.org), is a masterpiece designed by not one, but three renowned architects: I. M. Pei, Eliel Saarinen, and Richard Meier. It houses a world-class collection of contemporary modern art featuring works by Matisse, O'Keeffe, Rothko, and Richter, and sculptures by Rodin. It's hard to miss the gold-leaf-covered dome of the century-old **Iowa State Capitol,** East 12th Street and Grand Avenue (© 515/281-5129; www.legis.state.ia.us). Do go on one of the hour-long tours of the premises, which take in, among other things, an absolutely delightful collection of First Lady dolls. On the grounds you'll find several monuments and memorials to armed forces personnel who fell during various wars. For the lowdown on the state's history, check out the **State Historical Building,** 600 E. Locust St. (© 515/281-5111;

A Little Piece of Baseball Heaven

Okay, so there really is a little piece of heaven in Iowa. Baseball heaven, that is. In the town of Dyersville, Iowa, you'll find the famous cornfield-based baseball diamond immortalized in the Oscar-nominated film *Field of Dreams*. The **Field of Dreams Movie Site,** 28963 Lansing Rd., off Hwy. 136 South (© **888/875-8404;** www.fieldofdreamsmoviesite.com), was opened to the public in 1989 and, true to form, they built it and fans came. The field is open for play April through November, 9am to 6pm daily, and admission is free. If you're a baseball fan, it's worth the pilgrimage—just don't forget to bring your bat and glove. Go the distance!

www.iowahistory.org), whose ultramodern building houses interactive exhibits on native wildlife, American Indian and pioneer artifacts, military history, and an extensive collection of Iowa's historical records. A favorite exhibit traces the history of the woolly mammoth; the highlight of the exhibit is a complete skeleton of one of the extinct creatures.

Cedar Rapids, just north of Iowa City off I-380, is home to the **Cedar Rapids Museum of Art,** 410 Third Ave. SE (© **319/366-7503;** www.crma.org), which was seriously damaged by floods in the summer of 2008 that left most of the city under water. The museum reopened at the end of August, and the **Grant Wood Studio** on Turner Street is also open again, after a major renovation that survived the flood. The CRMA is home to the world's largest collection of works by native Iowan artist Grant Wood (1892–1942), best known for the iconic *American Gothic.* The city is also home to the **National Czech & Slovak Museum & Library,** 30 16th Ave. SW (© **319/362-8500;** www. ncsml.org), the country's foremost museum covering Czech and Slovak history and culture, which is set in Czech Village, an area along the Cedar River that is loaded with old-world European charm. The state is home to a large population of Czech immigrants; a highlight of the museum is a restored 19th-century immigrant home.

About 10 miles west of Iowa City in the small community of West Branch is the **Herbert Hoover Presidential Library, Museum, and National Historic Site,** 210 Parkside Dr. (© **319/643-5301;** www.hoover.archives.gov), where you can tour the birthplace cottage of former president Hoover, his father's blacksmith shop, a Quaker meetinghouse, a pioneer schoolhouse, and the president's gravesite. Other exhibits detail the life of former First Lady Lou Henry Hoover, and President Hoover's diminishing reputation during the days of the Great Depression.

In the city of West Bend (2¹/₂ hr. from Des Moines), the dream of Catholic priest Father Paul Dobberstein, the **Grotto of the Redemption** (© **515/887-2371;** www.westbendgrotto.com) is a religious shrine composed of nine exceptionally designed grottoes depicting the life of Christ. It has been hailed by critics as "a miracle in stone" and took 45 years to build. The on-premises museum includes a large display of precious and semiprecious stones from throughout the world (its geological value is approx. $4.3 million). Tours are given daily May 1 through October 16.

Set alongside the Iowa River, you'll find the **Amana Colonies,** settled in the 19th century (they celebrated their 150th anniversary in 2005) by Inspirationists, a German religious sect. Though the original colonists' descendants voted to end their communal lifestyle in 1932, they left behind seven colonies, a virtually intact district of 500 historical buildings (including barns, kitchens, a mill, and factories—among them the famous appliance factory that bears the colonies' name) that's a National Historic Landmark. To begin your visit, head for the **Amana Colonies Welcome Center,** 622 46th Ave. in Amana (© **800/579-2294** or 319/622-7622; www.amanacolonies.com).

Fans of Robert James Waller's novels should head to picturesque Winterset in **Madison County,** off U.S. 92 (© **515/ 462-1185;** www.madisoncounty.com). Its five covered bridges date from the 1880s and are National Historic Landmarks. The best time to visit is October, when fall foliage is at its peak and the Covered Bridge Festival takes place. Also notable in Winterset is the **birthplace of John Wayne,** 216 S. 2nd St. (© **515/462-1044;** www. johnwaynebirthplace.org). You can visit the four-room house in which the legendary actor was born; it's loaded with memorabilia and photos.

3 KANSAS

Rightly or wrongly, no state has come to signify the American heartland in the way that Kansas does. This picturesque land of rolling prairies and wheat fields is where all-American Superman grew up (sorry, there is no actual Smallville) and the place the *Wizard of Oz*'s Dorothy Gale called home. But there's more to Kansas than Aunt Em and apple pie. This is the state of Bleeding Kansas, where pro- and antislavery forces fought long and hard against each other before Kansas finally joined the Union as a free state in 1860; it was also a major battleground for civil rights when desegregation was challenged here in 1954. It's the home of the Chisholm Trail, the Santa Fe Trail, the pioneers, and the Pony Express; of plains and grasslands that saw many an Indian skirmish and relocation; and of Dodge City, where many of the gunslingers of the Old West made their reputations. The state is also a major center of aviation and features several top-notch space- and aeronautics-related attractions. It may not be home, but Kansas has got a ton of interesting options for visitors.

ESSENTIALS

VISITOR INFORMATION For the state's comprehensive *Visitors' Guide,* contact the Kansas Department of Commerce's Travel & Tourism Development Division (© **785/296-2009;** www.travelKS. com). For information on the state's many parks and outdoor facilities, try the **Kansas Department of Wildlife & Parks** (© **620/672-5911;** www.kdwp.state.ks.us). History buffs can get the scoop on the state's many historical sites from the **Kansas State Historical Society** (© **785/272-8681;** www.kshs.org). Golfers can get the inside scoop on the state's best courses from the **Kansas Golf Association** (© **785/ 842-4833;** www.kansasgolf.org).

If you're driving, you'll find two visitor centers scattered along some of the state's major travel corridors: along I-35, just north of the Oklahoma border (© **620/ 326-5123**), and off I-70, east of the Colorado state line (© **785/899-6695**). The friendly staff dispenses travel and touring advice, as well as maps and brochures.

GETTING THERE By Plane The state's major airport is **Kansas City International Airport** (www.flykci.com); it's serviced by several major domestic carriers. For general information call © **816/ 243-5237.** Most major car-rental agencies have desks at the airport.

By Train Amtrak (© 800/872-7245; www.amtrak.com) trains stop at several cities, including Topeka, Lawrence, and Kansas City.

By Car The major road route is **I-70,** which runs west from St. Louis, Missouri, passing through the entire state before moving on to Colorado and Denver. **I-35** runs north to Kansas City out of Oklahoma City. Two scenic and historic routes in the state that originate in Dodge City are **U.S. 50** (moving west along the old Santa Fe Trail) and **U.S. 56** (heading north). Note that road conditions can change in a moment; call the **Road & Weather Conditions Hotline** (© 877/511-5368) before setting out on a long drive.

SPECIAL EVENTS The **Kansas City Renaissance Festival** (© 800/373-0357 or 913/721-2110; www.kcrenfest.com), one of the largest of its kind in the country, kicks off on 16 acres in Bonner Springs (15 min. outside Kansas City) on Labor Day, runs for 7 consecutive weekends, and then ends on Columbus Day. Each weekend features its own theme, lots of food, a mock-up of a 16th-century English village, live entertainment, tons of shopping, and 500 costumed characters. It's a royal hoot.

We're also fans of the **Amelia Earhart Festival** (www.atchisonkansas.net), held annually in Atchison (as in "The Atchison, Topeka, and Santa Fe"). The famous aviatrix spent much of her girlhood in this eastern Kansas town, which retains many Victorian structures (some of which are now B&Bs). Earhart's girlhood home is restored, and available for tour by costumed docents. There are also a parade, musical performances, and flyovers.

Cowboys and wannabes shouldn't miss one of the state's many rodeos. Dates vary, so consult **www.travelKS.com** for up-to-the-minute event information.

HIGHLIGHTS OF KANSAS

Most of Kansas's major sights are set along the state's historic I-70 corridor.

In Topeka, stop in at the **Brown vs. Board of Education National Historic Site,** 1515 Monroe St. (© 785/354-4273; www.nps.gov/brvb), a National Historic Site commemorating the landmark 1954 Supreme Court decision that originated in the city's Monroe school and ended segregation in the United States. The site opened in 2004 in time for the decision's 50th anniversary. While you're in town, also check out the **Kansas State Capitol,** 300 SW 10th St. (© 785/296-3966; www.kshs.org), noted for its impressive dome and famous mural of abolitionist John Brown. Free tours of the building are offered on weekdays.

A former cow town on the Chisholm Trail, Wichita is now home to some of the state's best cultural attractions. The newly renovated **Wichita Art Museum,** 1400 W. Museum Blvd. (© 316/268-4921; www.wichitaartmuseum.org), features an excellent collection of American art. Don't miss the stunning Dale Chihuly Persian Seafoam Installation hanging in the lobby. For a look at the Native American experience in Kansas, take in the **Mid-America All-Indian Center & Museum,** 650 N. Seneca (© 316/262-5221; www.theindiancenter.org), which allows visitors to experience Native American culture and cuisine, artwork exhibitions, and artifacts.

Architecture aficionados should head over to the **Allen Lambe House Museum,** 255 N. Roosevelt St. (© 316/687-1027), the last of the prairie houses designed by Frank Lloyd Wright; the interior and many of the furnishings are still intact. Kansas has always been a major player in the aviation industry, and Wichita's **Kansas Aviation Museum,** 3350 George Washington Blvd. (© 316/683-9242; www.kansasaviationmuseum.org), is a must for any airplane buff. Set inside

(Best) Rising from the Ashes

The historic **Eldridge Hotel,** 701 Massachusetts St., in Lawrence, Kansas (© **800/527-0909** or 785/749-5011; www.eldridgehotel.com), has a never-die attitude. It began life in 1855 as the Free State Hotel, its name a clear statement by its New England–born owners about their preference for Kansas's admittance to the Union as a nonslave state. It didn't take long for proslavery forces to express their own inclination—by burning the building to the ground in 1856. That same year, Col. Shalor Eldridge vowed to rebuild—again and again if he had to. This time, the building managed to last until 1863, when Quantrill's raiders did the hotel in, along with pretty much everything else in the city. Not one to be cowed, Colonel Eldridge did indeed rebuild, and his hotel stood until 1926, when the structure was torn down due to deterioration. It was rebuilt again and remained a hotel until 1970, when it was closed and converted into apartments. A massive renovation campaign begun in 1985 restored it to its former glory as a fitting symbol of a city whose motto is "From ashes to immortality."

A stay at this National Landmark will steep you in history. The all-suite hotel's lobby evokes it with its old-style lighting, dark woods, and rich fabrics. Each of the 48 suites offers separate sitting areas, old-style elegance, and refrigerators. The hotel's spa offers a full range of treatments, as well as in-room spas. Rates run $125 to $315 double, including breakfast. Stay here in early December to catch the hotel's famed Christmas Parade featuring nearly 100 old-fashioned horse-drawn buggies, wagons, and carriages.

Wichita's old municipal airport building (built in 1935), the museum showcases over 40 of the aircraft built by many of the state's famous manufacturers, including Cessna, Boeing, and Learjet. For an out-of-this-world experience, head 60 miles northwest out of Wichita to Hutchinson's **Kansas Cosmosphere and Space Center,** 1100 N. Plum St. (© **800/397-0330** or 620/662-2305; www.cosmo.org). The Smithsonian-affiliated center has an impressive array of space- and aeronautics-related exhibits, including the only Soviet *Vostok* craft in the West, the *Apollo 13* spacecraft ("Houston, we have a problem . . ."), and the gloves Neil Armstrong wore on the moon. There's also an IMAX theater.

The city of Abilene is home to the **Eisenhower Center,** 200 SE 4th St. (© **877/746-4453** or 785/263-6700;

www.eisenhower.archives.gov), which celebrates native son Dwight D. Eisenhower's presidency. The complex includes the family home where the Eisenhowers lived from 1898 to 1946; the burial site of the president, his First Lady, and their son; the Eisenhower Presidential Library; a museum; and a visitor center. Also in the area is the **Dickinson County Heritage Center,** 412 S. Campbell St. (© **785/263-2681;** www.heritagecenterdk.com), which features exhibits on prairie life, the Chisholm Trail, and the area's Native Americans—and also has a splendid 1901 C. W. Parker carousel that's a National Historic Landmark.

The tallgrass prairies of the Great Plains are rapidly disappearing, and one of the few places you can still see them in their natural glory is **Tallgrass National Prairie**

Preserve, Hwy. 177, Strong City (𝒞 **620/ 273-8494;** www.nps.gov/tapr). The only preserve of its kind encompasses the remains of a 19th-century ranch and its surrounding grassland. There are several self-guided and ranger-led hikes to choose from, and a number of living history programs are offered several times a year.

The city of Lawrence was founded by abolitionists in 1854 and eventually became an important stop on the underground railroad. Most of the city was destroyed in 1863 by Quantrill's Raiders, but today's Lawrence is home to the University of Kansas and offers a beautiful downtown historic district loaded with 19th-century architecture that's well worth a stroll. Be sure to stop in at the **Spencer Art Museum,** 1301 Mississippi St.

(𝒞 **785/864-4710;** www.spencerart.ku. edu), whose varied collections include works by Dale Chihuly, Claude Monet, Jean Fragonard, Georgia O'Keeffe, and Ansel Adams. It's one of the best university art museums in the country.

Historic Dodge City is renowned for its Old West roots (Wyatt Earp and Bat Masterson both made their reputations here during the city's rough-and-tumble heyday during the late 19th c.). Head first to the **Boot Hill Museum,** Front Street (𝒞 **620/ 227-8188;** www.boothill.org), a living-history reconstruction of Dodge City's notorious Front Street in 1876, with lots of authentic artifacts, the infamous Boot Hill Cemetery, exhibits on several Indian tribes, and historical reenactments.

4 NORTH DAKOTA

Quick: Name the state whose scenic landscape so inspired Teddy Roosevelt that he went on to do his darnedest to preserve America's great parklands by creating the National Forest Service. If you answered North Dakota, pat yourself on the back. This sparsely populated corner of the Great Plains has a lot going for it—picturesque farmland and wheat fields, the stark beauty of the Badlands, numerous historic sites, and so on—but it also has something of an identity problem: Even the movie that put one of its major cities on the map, the Coen brothers' Oscar-winning *Fargo,* was filmed elsewhere. So impassioned have North Dakotans become about forging their own path that it seems to be a sport for residents to try and rename the state every couple of years to prevent it from being that "other Dakota" (no luck so far). Still, outside of Alaska, the Rough Rider State has more unexplored and untouched wilderness than any other. This is truly the final frontier.

ESSENTIALS

VISITOR INFORMATION Contact the **North Dakota Tourism Division,** 1600 E. Century Ave., Ste. 2, P.O. Box 2057, Bismarck, ND 58502-2057 (𝒞 **800/435-5663** or 701/328-2525; www.ndtourism. com), and request a free visitor travel guide. Several welcome centers are scattered at strategic points along the state's major road routes; for operating hours and exact locations, contact the Tourism Division. *Note:* Road conditions can change in a moment; call 𝒞 **701/328-7623** (or 511 when in North Dakota) before heading out on a long drive.

GETTING THERE By Plane The two major airports are **Bismarck Municipal Airport** (𝒞 **800/453-4244;** www. bismarckairport.com) and **Minot International Airport** (𝒞 **701/857-4724;** http://web.ci.minot.nd.us/airport). **Northwest** is the domestic airline that offers the most service to North Dakota.

By Train Amtrak's *Empire Builder* (© 800/872-7245; www.amtrak.com) services six cities in North Dakota, including Grand Forks, Devils Lake, and Minot, on its way from Chicago to Seattle.

By Car The major east-west corridor is **I-94,** which enters the state from Minnesota at Fargo and runs through Bismarck and on to Medora before exiting into Montana. **I-29** enters from Canada along the eastern edge of the state and runs south through Grand Forks and Fargo into South Dakota.

SPECIAL EVENTS The **North Dakota State Fair (www.ndstatefair.com)** is held annually in Minot in late July. Visitors will enjoy live entertainment from top national artists, a parade, rodeo events, a car show, a carnival, lots of local and native cuisine, and a host of juried competitions involving everything from wine to rabbits. The **United Tribes International Pow Wow** (© 701/255-3285; www.unitedtribespowwow.com), held annually in Bismarck on the weekend after Labor Day, is one of the largest powwows in the United States. Representatives from over 70 tribes, including more than 1,500 dancers and drummers, take part in numerous concerts and performances.

WHERE TO STAY Most of the accommodations in the state are of the chain variety. For information on North Dakota B&Bs, check out the website of the **North Dakota Bed & Breakfast Association** (www.ndbba.com).

HIGHLIGHTS OF NORTH DAKOTA

Lewis and Clark spent more time in North Dakota than in any other state; it was here that they met up with an Indian woman named Sakakawea (note the correct spelling of her Hidatsa name), who would end up on the back of the country's current dollar coin. The State Historical Society of North Dakota has identified and marked

27 locations of significance to Lewis and Clark's expedition. For details on visiting these preserved sites on the Lewis & Clark Trail, contact the Tourism Division (see "Visitor Information," above).

The **North Dakota Heritage Center,** 612 E. Boulevard Ave., Bismarck (© 701/328-2666; www.state.nd.us/hist/hcenter.htm), is the state's largest museum and features an exceptional collection of Plains Indian artifacts and interpretive exhibits that feature North Dakota's varied American Indian, military, and agricultural history. A statue of Sakakawea is located near the entrance. The 19-story Art Deco **North Dakota State Capitol,** 600 E. Boulevard Ave. (© 701/328-2471; www.nd.gov), was constructed in 1933 and contains unique woods and materials from many states and countries.

Fort Abraham Lincoln State Park, 4480 Fort Lincoln Rd. (© 800/807-4723 or 701/667-6340; www.ndparks.com), 7 miles south of Mandan on Hwy. 1806, is a former cavalry post that is rich in both military and early Native American history. It was from here that Custer and the Seventh Cavalry rode out on their ill-fated expedition against the Sioux at Little Big Horn. Portions of the military post, including the Custer House, have been reconstructed, and there is also a reconstructed Indian village. Visitors have a panoramic vista of the Missouri River from the park's nature and historic trails.

The **Dakota Dinosaur Museum,** 200 Museum Dr., Dickinson (© 701/225-3466; www.dakotadino.com), about 100 miles west of Bismarck, features 14 full-scale dinosaur skeletons (including a triceratops), numerous fossils (check out the new Great White Shark tooth!), and mineral exhibits.

The historic city of **Medora (www.medorand.com)** is a restored cow town founded by a French nobleman, the Marquis de Mores, in 1883. The most popular attraction in North Dakota, the city still

(Best) The Park That Launched Them All

Theodore Roosevelt once claimed, "I never would have been President if it had not been for my experiences in North Dakota." Roosevelt, who spent a great deal of time in the North Dakota Badlands, was appalled by the increasing amount of destruction being inflicted upon the land and its wildlife habitats. His subsequent conservation efforts as president led to the founding of the National Park Service. North Dakota's best attraction, **Theodore Roosevelt National Park** (**www.nps.gov/thro**), was created in 1947 as a memorial to the man responsible for its very existence.

The park is actually comprised of two areas—the North Unit and the South Unit—separated by about 70 miles of highway. The **South Unit** is the more visited of the two and lies along I-94 in Medora. It features a 36-mile scenic driving route, numerous wildlife and hiking trails, a petrified forest, and the spectacular Painted Canyon (check out the scenic overlook at exit 32). A small visitor center with restrooms, picnic shelters, tables, and water is open at the canyon April through October. Be sure to stop in at the main **Medora Visitor's Center**, at exit 24 (© **701/623-4466**), year-round, where rangers can advise you on your touring and activity options. A small museum there exhibits some of Roosevelt's personal items, ranching artifacts, and natural history displays.

The more isolated **North Unit**, off U.S. Hwy. 85, 16 miles south of Watford City (© **701/842-2333**), is usually less crowded, giving it a more serene feel. It, too, features lots of wildlife viewing, as well as several hiking trails. Stop in at the **North Unit Visitor Center** at the park's entrance to get maps and park information and to see a movie on the park's famous badlands. Be sure to take the 14-mile Scenic Drive that runs from the entrance to the Oxbow Overlook, with turnouts and interpretive signs along the way.

No matter where you go in each park, you'll see tons of wildlife—bison, mule deer, coyote, bighorn sheep, elk, and dozens of bird species. There are also several campgrounds, ranger-led programs, and biking trails.

offers a lot of Western flavor; stroll its streets and soak up the atmosphere, then go see the *Medora Musical* (© 800/633-6721; www.Medora.com), an entertaining and patriotic musical extravaganza about Roosevelt and the Wild West (it's staged only in summer in the Burning Hills Badlands Amphitheater). **Château De Mores State Historic Site,** on the southwestern edge of Medora (© 701/623-4355; www.state.nd.us/hist/sites), is a 26-room two-story frame building that was built in 1883 as the summer residence of the Marquis de Mores family. The château is now

a historic house museum. The historic von Hoffman House, on the National Register of Historic Places, is home to the **Medora Doll House** (© 800/633-6721 or 701/623-4444; www.medora.com), which features unique exhibits of antique dolls and toys. The **Badlands Museum,** 195 Third Ave. (© 800/633-6721), features numerous Native American artifacts and exhibits on the area's wildlife and pioneer heritage.

Knife River Indian Villages National Historic Site, Stanton (**www.nps.gov/knri**), is the only National Park Service site that preserves and protects the heritage of the Northern Plains Indians. There are the remains of three Hidatsa village sites within the park boundaries. A state-of-the-art museum dedicated to preserving the culture of the Hidatsa, Mandan, and Arikara tribes is located at the visitor center.

Devils Lake, 152 S. Duncan Rd., Devils Lake State Park (© **701/766-4015,** or 800/807-4723 for camping reservations; www.ndparks.com), is one of North Dakota's most scenic regions. The sprawling lake with its hidden bays is an angler's paradise, and the surrounding woodlands are home to numerous forms of wildlife. It's also known for its incredible ice fishing in winter.

Want to see what life was like for the pioneers of the prairies? **Bonanzaville**

USA, 1351 Main Ave. W., West Fargo (© **701/282-2822;** www.bonanzaville. org), is a living history museum and village that shows what life was like in the Dakota Territory of the late 19th century. The village is home to over 400,000 artifacts, several museums, and 40 historic or re-created buildings gathered here from points in the Midwest and the Great Plains. While in Fargo, check out the fully restored 1926 Art Moderne **Fargo Theatre,** 314 Broadway (© **701/239-8385;** www.fargotheatre.com), and the collections at the **Plains Art Museum,** 704 First Ave. (© **701/232-3821;** www.plainsart. org), the region's largest fine arts museum.

5 WEST VIRGINIA

Yes, this is the land of *Deliverance* and the Hatfields and the McCoys. But to chalk up West Virginia as a punch line to a hillbilly joke is to do the state an incredible disservice. For those who love the great outdoors, there are few states that can match this corner of Appalachia for scenic beauty and challenging terrain. (The state's nickname, "The Mountain State," is well earned.) Indeed, West Virginia ranks just behind Colorado in the quality of its white-water rapids and offers splendid skiing—and it's a whole lot cheaper than Colorado to visit. You'll find plenty of history, too. Harpers Ferry, site of one of the most famous raids in American history, is located here; the raid helped chart West Virginia's course of secession from Virginia and its entrance as a separate state into the Union in 1863. And if you prefer relaxation, the state is home to one of the country's most renowned resorts, the Greenbrier, and to the historic spa city of Berkeley Springs, where the Founding Fathers liked to get away from all—and

you can, too. For sheer value, few states in the country can beat this one.

ESSENTIALS

VISITOR INFORMATION Contact the **West Virginia Division of Tourism** (© **800/CALL-WVA** [225-5982] or 304/558-2200; www.callwva.com) for its very comprehensive travel guide, as well as maps and other travel information. Very knowledgeable travel counselors will offer advice, suggest travel ideas, and make reservations for you if you so desire.

Eight welcome centers, staffed daily from 9am to 5pm November to April and 8am to 6pm May to October, are strategically placed along major road routes and state borders. For exact locations, contact the Division of Tourism.

For information on the state's myriad outdoor recreational activities, contact the Division of Tourism or head to the website of **West Virginia State Parks (www. wvstateparks.com).**

GETTING THERE **By Plane** West Virginia has nine commercial airports. For more information on flying into the state, consult the **West Virginia Department of Transportation Aeronautics Commission** (© 304/558-3436; www.wvdot. com).

By Train Amtrak (© 800/872-7245; www.amtrak.com) provides service to several major cities, including White Sulphur Springs and Charleston, via its *Cardinal* train. **MARC commuter rail service** (© 866/743-3682; www.mtamaryland. com) is available from Washington, D.C., to Harpers Ferry.

By Car The major north-south interstate is the four-lane **I-77,** which runs south out of Cleveland, through West Virginia, and down to Charlotte. The other major interstate is **I-79,** which enters the state just north of Morgantown from Pittsburgh and runs southwest until Charleston, where it intersects with **I-64,** which runs from Virginia to Charleston and on into Kentucky. **I-81** runs from Maryland through the northeast corner of the state and into Virginia.

SPECIAL EVENTS The annual **State Fair of West Virginia** (© 304/645-1090; www.wvstatefair.com) has featured family-friendly livestock exhibits, a carnival, concerts, food, and other fun for over 80 years. It's staged in mid-August at the State Fairgrounds in Lewisburg. On **West Virginia Day,** commemorating the date the state was granted admittance to the Union (June 20, 1863), celebrations, concerts, parades, and fireworks are staged in various cities all over the state. For more information, check out **www.callwva. com.**

WHERE TO STAY For information on B&Bs throughout the state, contact the **Mountain State Association of Bed & Breakfasts** (www.wvbedandbreakfasts. com).

HIGHLIGHTS OF WEST VIRGINIA

The top historical attraction in the state is **Harpers Ferry National Historic Park** (© 304/535-6029; www.nps.gov/hafe), whose 2,300 acres actually cover three states, though the primary historic sites are in West Virginia, in the historic town of Harpers Ferry. It was here that abolitionist John Brown launched a raid of the federal arsenal (which supplied guns for Lewis and Clark's famous expedition), as an attack on slavery. It was also here that Stonewall Jackson secured the largest surrender of Union troops (over 12,000 of them) during the Civil War. The town still looks as it did in the 19th century, and many of the historic buildings are open to the public; there are lots of quaint shops and restaurants as well. Stop in at the **Cavaliers Visitors Center,** off U.S. 340 (© 304/535-6298), for assistance in planning your visit. Park admission is $6 per vehicle, $4 per pedestrian or cyclist. The fee includes the shuttle bus from the visitor center to the town proper and is good for 3 days.

Hikers should head for the **Appalachian Trail Conference,** 799 Washington St., Harpers Ferry (© 304/535-6331; www.appalachiantrail.org), the headquarters for the Appalachian Trail, for information, maps, and advice on hiking the famous trail.

Once you've worked your muscles into a frenzy, head to historic **Berkeley Springs** (© 800/447-8797 or 304/258-9147; www.berkeleysprings.com), a quirky town that's a haven for artists, and where massage therapists outnumber lawyers three to one. George Washington was among the first of many visitors who came to "take the waters" at the first spa town in the country. Today it's still a popular place to kick back and relax. **Berkeley Springs Historic State Park** (© 304/258-2711;

John Brown's Body: A Bloody Pre–Civil War Raid

On October 16, 1859, John Brown—already notorious from a bloody raid against slaveholders in Kansas—enlisted 19 men to raid the federal arsenal at Harpers Ferry, intent on arming the nation's slaves and starting a rebellion. Frederick Douglass warned Brown that the arsenal, in a town wedged between mountains and the Shenandoah and Potomac rivers, would be impossible to hold with so few men, and, as Douglass had foreseen, the raid failed. Brown and his men captured the arsenal but were unable to raise any significant number of slaves into rebellion. They were soon pinned in the arsenal's firehouse (later to be known as John Brown's Fort), and Brown was captured when U.S. Marines under Lt. Col. Robert E. Lee stormed the building. Brown was tried and convicted of "conspiring with slaves to commit treason and murder," for which he was hanged. His action polarized the nation and was one of the sparks that ignited the war. Harpers Ferry later witnessed the largest surrender of Federal troops during the Civil War; it also opened one of the earliest integrated schools in the U.S.

The **John Brown Museum,** on Shenandoah Street, offers exhibits and displays on the abolitionist and tracks the course of his raid, capture, and conviction. The **Harper House** is a restored dwelling that sits at the top of the stone stairs, above High Street. The oldest remaining structure in Harpers Ferry, it was built between 1775 and 1782, and served as a tavern for such guests as Thomas Jefferson and George Washington.

www.berkeleyspringssp.com), whose bathhouse opened in 1930, is still a working mineral spa today. Luxuriate in the Roman-style baths or take advantage of the health treatments; prices are extremely reasonable. Once you've soaked and relaxed, browse the town's many art galleries and antiques shops.

For those of a more scientific bent, the state's Potomac Highlands region is home to the **National Radio Astronomy Observatory,** Route 92/28 in Green Bank (© **304/456-0211;** www.nrao.edu/epo), which houses the world's largest radio telescope and several hands-on exhibits dealing with radio waves and space exploration. Tours of the facility are offered daily in summer.

When it comes to outdoor recreation, West Virginia offers more activities and opportunities than most outdoor enthusiasts can hope to take advantage of. More than

three million visitors a year take advantage of some of the best wildlife viewing, hiking, mountain biking, and horseback riding in the state at the exceptional **Monongahela National Forest,** 200 Sycamore St., Elkins (© **304/636-1800;** www.fs.fed.us/r9/mnf). Civil War buffs can also drive the park's **Auto Tour,** featuring stops at historic sites such as Fort Summit and Camp Allegheny. Be sure to stop at the park's **Seneca Rocks Discovery Center** (© **304/567-2827**), at the base of the exceptionally scenic Seneca Rocks cliffs off I-33, which attract rock climbers from all over the country.

Two state parks just north of the National Forest on Hwy. 32—**Canaan Valley Resort** (© **800/622-4121** or 304/866-4121; www.canaanresort.com) and **Backwater Falls State Park** (© **304/259-5216;** www.blackwaterfalls.com)—offer first-class downhill and cross-country

(Best) A Hotel Fit for Congress

Since 1778, visitors have trooped to the town of White Sulphur Springs to restore their health in the curative waters that flow from the town's spring. Today the spring in question is the centerpiece of the **Greenbrier,** 300 W. Main St. (© **800/453-4858;** www.greenbrier.com), a magnificent 6,500-acre resort that is rich in both history (it's hosted 26 presidents) and luxury.

Once the most fashionable summer resort in the South where Robert E. Lee built a summer home, it was forced to close during the Civil War when, depending on which side was occupying the property, it served as a hospital or as a military headquarters. At the end of the war, the resort once again rose to prominence, only to switch identities once more during World War II, when it was purchased by the U.S. Army and turned into a hospital. Following the war, the building was transformed into a luxury resort by noted designer Dorothy Draper (the exterior of the magnificent Georgian main building strongly resembles the White House), and counted the legendary Sam Snead as its golf pro (establishing the resort as a premiere golf destination) until his death in 2002.

But perhaps the most interesting bit of Greenbrier history is this: In the 1950s, the government built a secret underground Emergency Relocation Center under the resort that, for nearly 30 years, was maintained to serve as the emergency location of Congress should an international crisis ever force the legislative branch out of Washington. The shelter was finally closed down in 1995 (you can tour it along with other notable portions of this National Historic Landmark's interior and grounds on guided tours).

Today a stay at the Greenbrier features luxurious accommodations, unbelievable service, first-class dining, and an amazing array of recreational activities, ranging from the Falconry Academy and *Golf Digest* Academy to state-of-the-art fitness and tennis centers and a world-renowned spa. There's also a specialized diagnostic and health evaluation clinic. The resort renovates each of its guest rooms at least once every 4 years, which means that all of them—from the small but elegant standard rooms to the two-bedroom cottages—are exquisitely decorated and kept in tiptop condition. Don't miss having at least one meal in the elegant main dining room, renowned for its classical cuisine.

skiing in winter, and fabulous mountain biking and hiking trails in summer. The best skiing in the Southeast and Mid-Atlantic states, as well as superior mountain biking trails, can be found at **Snowshoe Mountain,** 10 Snowshoe Dr., Snowshoe (© **877/441-4386;** www.snowshoemtn.com), an 11,000-acre resort in the scenic Allegheny Mountains.

If you prefer watersports, head straight for the southeast section of the state to the **New River Gorge National River Recreation Area,** off I-64 (© **304/574-2115** or 466-0417; www.nps.gov/neri). Here you'll find the best white-water rapids in the eastern U.S., as well as numerous other recreational activities, from horseback riding and hiking, to fishing and boating. Be sure to stop at the year-round **Canyon Rim Visitor Center,** off Route 19 just north of the New River Gorge Bridge, where you'll find exhibits on the natural and cultural history of the area, and several rangers who dispense valuable information and offer guided walks several times a year. Contact the Tourism Division (see "Visitor Information," above) for information on the numerous reputable outfitters who service the region if you're interested in a guided raft trip or other organized tour.

For a different sort of scenic tour, head over to Cass Scenic Railroad State Park, Route 66 (© 304/456-4300; www.cass railroad.com), which encompasses a historic early-20th-century logging town, but whose prime attraction is a vintage steam train ride amid the West Virginia mountains. Head here in the fall for breathtaking foliage.

Appendix B:
State Tourism Offices

Alabama Bureau of Tourism & Travel
P.O. Box 4927
Montgomery, AL 36103-4927
℡ 800/ALABAMA (252-2262)
℡ 334/242-4169
www.alabama.travel

Alaska Travel Industry Association
2600 Cordova St., Ste. 201
Anchorage, AK 99503
℡ 800/862-5275
www.travelalaska.com

Arizona Office of Tourism
1110 W. Washington St., Ste. 155
Phoenix, AZ 85007
℡ 866/275-5816
www.arizonaguide.com

Arkansas Department of Parks & Tourism
1 Capitol Mall
Little Rock, AR 72201
℡ 800/NATURAL (628-8725)
℡ 501/682-7777
www.arkansas.com

California Travel and Tourism Commission
P.O. Box 1499
Sacramento, CA 95812-1499
℡ 800/GO-CALIF (462-2543)
℡ 916/444-4429
www.visitcalifornia.com

Colorado Tourism Office
1625 Broadway, Ste. 2700
Denver, CO 80202
℡ 800/COLORADO (265-6723)
www.colorado.com

Connecticut Commission on Culture & Tourism
1 Financial Plaza
755 Main St.
Hartford, CT 06103
℡ 888/CT-VISIT (288-4748)
℡ 860/270-8080
www.ctvisit.com

Delaware Tourism Office
99 King's Hwy.
Dover, DE 19901
℡ 866/284-7483
℡ 302/739-4271
www.visitdelaware.com

Washington, DC Convention & Tourism Corporation
901 7th St. NW, 4th Floor
Washington, DC 20001
℡ 800/422-8644
www.washington.org

Visit Florida
661 E. Jefferson St., Ste. 300
Tallahassee, FL 32301
℡ 888/7-FLA-USA (735-2872)
℡ 850/488-5607
www.visitflorida.com

Georgia Department of Economic Development
75 5th St. NW, Ste. 1200
Atlanta, GA 30308
℡ 800/VISIT-GA (847-4842)
℡ 404/962-4000
www.exploregeorgia.org

Hawaii Visitors & Convention Bureau
2270 Kalakaua Ave., Ste. 801
Honolulu, HI 96815
℡ 800/464-2924
www.gohawaii.com

Idaho Department of Commerce
700 W. State St.
Boise, ID 83720
℡ 800/842-5858
℡ 208/334-2470
www.visitid.org

Illinois Bureau of Tourism
100 W. Randolph, Ste. 3-400
Chicago, IL 60601
℡ 800/2-CONNECT (226-6632)
℡ 312/814-4732
www.enjoyillinois.com

Indiana Department of Commerce/ Tourism
1 N. Capitol Ave., Ste. 100
Indianapolis, IN 46204
℡ 800/677-9800
www.in.gov/visitindiana

Iowa Division of Tourism
200 E. Grand Ave.
Des Moines, IA 50309
℡ 888/472-6035
℡ 515/242-4705
www.traveliowa.com

Kansas Travel & Tourism Division
Department of Commerce and Housing
1000 SW Jackson St., Ste. 100
Topeka, KS 66612
℡ 800/2-KANSAS (252-6727)
℡ 785/296-2009
www.travelks.com

Kentucky Department of Tourism
Capital Plaza Tower, 22nd Floor
500 Metro St.
Frankfort, KY 40601
℡ 800/225-8747
℡ 502/564-4930
www.kentuckytourism.com

Louisiana Office of Tourism
P.O. Box 94291
Baton Rouge, LA 70804
℡ 800/677-4082
℡ 225/342-8100
www.louisianatravel.com

Maine Office of Tourism
59 State House Station
Augusta, ME 04333
℡ 888/624-6345
www.visitmaine.com

Maryland Office of Tourism Development
217 E. Redwood St., 9th Floor
Baltimore, MD 21202
℡ 866/639-3526
www.mdisfun.org

Massachusetts Office of Travel & Tourism
10 Park Plaza, Ste. 4510
Boston, MA 02116
℡ 800/227-MASS (227-6277)
www.massvacation.com

Travel Michigan
300 N. Washington Sq., 2nd Floor
Lansing, MI 48913
℡ 888/784-7328
www.michigan.org

Explore Minnesota Tourism
100 Metro Sq., 121 7th Place E.
St. Paul, MN 55101
℡ 888/TOURISM (868-7476)
℡ 651/296-5029
www.exploreminnesota.com

Mississippi Division of Tourism Development
P.O. Box 849
Jackson, MS 39205
℡ 866/733-6477
℡ 601/359-3297
www.visitmississippi.org

Missouri Division of Tourism
Box 1055
Jefferson City, MO 65102
℡ 800/519-2100
℡ 573/751-4133
www.visitmo.co

Travel Montana
301 South Park
P.O. Box 200533
Helena, MT 59620
☎ 800/VISIT-MT (847-4868)
☎ 406/841-2870
http://visitmt.com

Nebraska Division of Tourism & Travel
P.O. Box 98907
Lincoln, NE 68509-8907
☎ 877/NEBRASKA (632-7275)
www.visitnebraska.org

Nevada Commission on Tourism
401 N. Carson St.
Carson City, NV 89701
☎ 800/NEVADA-8 (638-2328)
www.travelnevada.com

New Hampshire Office of Travel & Tourism
172 Pembroke Rd.
P.O. Box 1856
Concord, NH 03302-1856
☎ 800/386-4664
☎ 603/271-2665
www.visitnh.gov

New Jersey Division of Travel & Tourism
P.O. Box 820
Trenton, NJ 08625-0820
☎ 800/VISIT-NJ (847-4865)
☎ 609/777-0885
www.visitnj.org

New Mexico Department of Tourism
491 Old Santa Fe Trail
Santa Fe, NM 87501
☎ 800/733-6396
☎ 505/827-7400
www.newmexico.org

New York State Division of Tourism
30 S Pearl St.
Main Concourse, Room 110
Albany, NY 12246
☎ 800/CALL-NYS (225-5697)
☎ 518/474-4116
www.iloveny.com

North Carolina Division of Travel & Tourism
301 N. Wilmington St.
Raleigh, NC 27699-4301
☎ 800/VISIT-NC (847-4862)
www.visitnc.com

North Dakota Tourism Division
Century Center
1600 E. Century Ave., Ste. 2
P.O. Box 2057
Bismarck, ND 58502-2057
☎ 800/HELLO-ND (435-5663)
www.ndtourism.com

Ohio Division of Travel & Tourism
P.O. Box 1001
Columbus, OH 43216-1001
☎ 800/BUCKEYE (282-5393)
www.discoverohio.com

Oklahoma Travel & Tourism Division
P.O. Box 52002
Oklahoma City, OK 73152
☎ 800/652-6552
☎ 405/230-8400
www.travelok.com

Oregon Tourism Commission
670 Hawthorne SE, Ste. 240
Salem, OR 97301
☎ 800/378-8850
☎ 503/378-8850
www.traveloregon.com

Pennsylvania Tourism Marketing Office
400 North St., 4th Floor
Harrisburg, PA 17120-0225
☎ 800/VISIT-PA (847-4872)
☎ 717/787-5453
www.visitpa.com

Rhode Island Tourism Division
1 W. Exchange St.
Providence, RI 02903
☎ 800/556-2484
☎ 401/222-2601
www.visitrhodeisland.com

South Carolina Department of Parks, Recreation, and Tourism
1205 Pendleton St.
Columbia, SC 29201
📞 866/224-9339
📞 803/734-1700
www.discoversouthcarolina.com

South Dakota Department of Tourism
711 E. Wells Ave.
Pierre, SD 57501-5070
📞 800/S-DAKOTA (732-5682)
📞 605/773-3301
www.travelsd.com

Tennessee Department of Tourism Development
Wm. Snodgrass/Tennessee Tower
312 8th Ave. N., 25th Floor
Nashville, TN 37243
📞 800/GO-2-TENN (462-8366)
📞 615/741-2159
www.tnvacation.com

Texas Department of Commerce, Tourist Division
P.O. Box 12428
Austin, TX 78711
📞 800/888-8TEX (888-8839)
www.traveltex.com

Utah Travel Council
P.O. Box 147420
Salt Lake City, UT 84114-7420
📞 800/200-1160
📞 801/538-1030
www.utah.com

Vermont Department of Tourism
National Life Building, 6th Floor,
Drawer 20
Montpelier, VT 05620-0501
📞 800/VERMONT (837-6668)
📞 802/828-3237
www.vermontvacation.com

Virginia Tourism Corporation
901 E. Byrd St.
Richmond, VA 23219
📞 800/VISIT-VA (847-4882)
📞 804/545-5500
www.virginia.org

Washington State Tourism
128 10th Ave. SW
Olympia, WA 98504
📞 800/544-1800
📞 360/753-4470
www.experiencewashington.com

West Virginia Division of Tourism
90 MacCorkle Ave. SW
South Charleston, WV 25303
📞 800/CALL-WVA (225-5982)
📞 304/558-2200
www.callwva.com

Wisconsin Division of Tourism
201 W. Washington Ave.
P.O. Box 8690
Madison, WI 53708
📞 800/432-TRIP (432-8747) outside
Wisconsin
📞 608/266-2161
www.travelwisconsin.com

Wyoming Tourism
I-25 at College Dr., Dept. WY
Cheyenne, WY 82002
📞 800/225-5996
📞 307/777-7777
www.wyomingtourism.org

Appendix C:
For International Visitors

1 PREPARING FOR YOUR TRIP

PASSPORTS

New regulations issued by the Department of Homeland Security now require virtually every air traveler entering the U.S. to show a passport. As of January 23, 2007, all persons, including U.S. citizens, traveling by air between the United States and Canada, Mexico, Central and South America, the Caribbean, and Bermuda are required to present a valid passport. As of January 31, 2008, U.S. and Canadian citizens entering the U.S. at land and sea ports of entry from within the Western Hemisphere will need to present government-issued proof of citizenship, such as a birth certificate, along with a government-issued photo ID, such as a driver's license. A passport is not required for U.S. or Canadian citizens entering by land or sea, but it is highly encouraged to carry one.

VISAS

The U.S. State Department has a **Visa Waiver Program (VWP)** allowing citizens of the following countries to enter the United States without a visa for stays of up to 90 days: Andorra, Australia, Austria, Belgium, Brunei, Denmark, Finland, France, Germany, Iceland, Ireland, Italy, Japan, Liechtenstein, Luxembourg, Monaco, the Netherlands, New Zealand, Norway, Portugal, San Marino, Singapore, Slovenia, Spain, Sweden, Switzerland, and the United Kingdom. (*Note:* This list was accurate at press time; for the most up-to-date list of countries in the VWP, consult **www.travel. state.gov/visa**.)

Even though a visa isn't necessary, in an effort to help U.S. officials check travelers against terror watch lists before they arrive at U.S. borders, as of January 12, 2009, visitors from VWP countries must register online before boarding a plane or a boat to the U.S. Travelers will complete an electronic application providing basic personal and travel eligibility information. The Department of Homeland Security recommends filling out the form at least 3 days before traveling. Authorizations will be valid for up to 2 years or until the traveler's passport expires, whichever comes first. Currently, there is no fee for the online application. Canadian citizens may enter the United States without visas; they will need to show passports (if traveling by air) and proof of residence, however. *Note:* Any passport issued on or after October 26, 2006, by a VWP country must be an **e-Passport** for VWP travelers to be eligible to enter the U.S. without a visa. Citizens of these nations also need to present a round-trip air or cruise ticket upon arrival. E-Passports contain computer chips capable of storing biometric information, such as the required digital photograph of the holder. (You can identify an e-Passport by the symbol on the bottom center cover of your passport.) If your passport doesn't have this feature, you can still travel without a visa if it is a valid passport issued before October 26, 2005, and includes a machine-readable zone, or between October 26, 2005, and October 25, 2006, and includes a digital photograph. For more information, go to **www.travel.state.gov/visa**.

Citizens of all other countries must have (1) a valid passport that expires at least 6 months later than the scheduled end of their visit to the U.S. and (2) a tourist visa. To obtain a visa, applicants must schedule an appointment with a U.S. consulate or embassy, fill out the application forms (available from www.travel.state.gov/visa), and pay a $131 fee. Wait times can be lengthy, so it's best to initiate the process as soon as possible.

As of January 2004, many international visitors traveling on visas to the United States will be photographed and finger-printed on arrival at Customs in airports and on cruise ships in a program created by the Department of Homeland Security called **US-VISIT.** Exempt from the extra scrutiny are visitors entering by land or those (mostly in Europe; p. 1042) that don't require a visa for short-term visits. For more information, go to the Homeland Security website at **www.dhs.gov/dhspublic**.

For specifics on how to get a visa, and where to apply for a passport in your home country if you are not a U.S. citizen, go to the "**Passports**" section under "**Fast Facts: For the International Traveler**" later in this chapter.

MEDICAL REQUIREMENTS If you have a medical condition that requires **syringe-administered medications,** carry a valid signed prescription from your physician—the **Federal Aviation Administration (FAA)** no longer allows airline passengers to pack syringes in their carry-on baggage without documented proof of medical need. If you have a disease that requires treatment with **narcotics,** you should also carry documented proof with you—smuggling narcotics aboard a plane is a serious offense that carries severe penalties in the U.S.

Unless you're arriving from an area known to be suffering from an epidemic (particularly cholera or yellow fever), inoculations or vaccinations are not required for entry into the United States.

DRIVER'S LICENSES Foreign driver's licenses are mostly recognized in the U.S., although you may want to get an international driver's license if your home license is not written in English.

CUSTOMS
What You Can Bring into the U.S.

Every visitor more than 21 years of age may bring in, free of duty, the following: (1) 1 liter of wine or hard liquor; (2) 200 cigarettes, 100 cigars (but not from Cuba), or 3 pounds of smoking tobacco; and (3) $100 worth of gifts. These exemptions are offered to travelers who spend at least 72 hours in the United States and who have not claimed them within the preceding 6 months. It is forbidden to bring into the country almost any meat products (including canned, fresh, and dried meat products such as bullion and soup mixes). Generally, condiments including vinegars, oils, spices, coffee, tea, and some cheeses and baked goods are permitted. Avoid rice products, as rice can often harbor insects. Bringing fruits and vegetables is not advised, though not prohibited. Customs will allow produce depending on where you got it and where you're going after you arrive in the U.S. Foreign tourists may carry in or out up to $10,000 in U.S. or foreign currency with no formalities; larger sums must be declared to U.S. Customs on entering or leaving, which includes filing form CM 4790. For details regarding U.S. Customs and Border Protection, consult your nearest U.S. embassy or consulate, or **U.S. Customs (www.customs.ustreas.gov)**.

What You Can Take Home from the U.S.

Canadian Citizens: For a clear summary of Canadian rules, write for the booklet *I Declare,* issued by the Canada Border Services Agency (© 800/461-9999 in Canada, or 204/983-3500; www.cbsa-asfc. gc.ca).

U.K. Citizens: For information, contact **HM Customs & Excise** at © 0845/010-9000 (from outside the U.K., 020/8929-0152), or consult their website at **www.hmce.gov.uk**.

Australian Citizens: A helpful brochure available from Australian consulates or Customs offices is *Know Before You Go.* For more information, call the **Australian Customs Service** at © 1300/363-263, or log on to **www.customs.gov.au**.

New Zealand Citizens: Most questions are answered in a free pamphlet available at New Zealand consulates and Customs offices: *New Zealand Customs Guide for Travellers, Notice no. 4.* For more information, contact **New Zealand Customs,** The Customhouse, 17–21 Whitmore St., Box 2218, Wellington (© 04/473-6099 or 0800/428-786; **www.customs.govt.nz**).

HEALTH INSURANCE

International visitors to the U.S. should note that, unlike many European countries, the United States does not usually offer free or low-cost medical care to its citizens or visitors. Doctors and hospitals are expensive and, in most cases, will require advance payment or proof of coverage before they render their services. Good policies will cover the costs of an accident, repatriation, or death. Packages such as **Europ Assistance's "Worldwide Healthcare Plan"** are sold by European automobile clubs and travel agencies at attractive rates. **Worldwide Assistance Services, Inc.** (© 800/777-8710; www.worldwideassistance.com), is the agent for Europ Assistance in the United States. Though lack of health insurance may prevent you from being admitted to a hospital in nonemergencies, don't worry about being left on a street corner to die: The American way is to fix you now and bill the daylights out of you later.

Canadians should check with their provincial health plan offices or call **Health Canada** (© 866/225-0709; www.hc-sc. gc.ca) to find out the extent of their coverage and what documentation and receipts they must take home in case they are treated in the United States.

Travelers from the U.K. should carry their **European Health Insurance Card (EHIC),** which replaced the E111 form as proof of entitlement to free or reduced-cost medical treatment abroad (© 0845 606 2030; www.ehic.org.uk). Note, however, that the EHIC covers only "necessary medical treatment," and for repatriation costs, lost money, baggage, or cancellation, travel insurance from a reputable company should always be sought (www.travelinsuranceweb. com).

MONEY

CURRENCY The most common bills are the $1 (a "buck"), $5, $10, and $20 denominations. There are also $2 bills (seldom encountered), $50 bills, and $100 bills (the last two are usually not welcome as payment for small purchases).

Coins come in seven denominations: 1¢ (1 cent, or a penny); 5¢ (5 cents, or a nickel); 10¢ (10 cents, or a dime); 25¢ (25 cents, or a quarter); 50¢ (50 cents, or a half-dollar); the gold-colored Sacagawea coin, worth $1; and the rare silver dollar.

Leave any currency other than U.S. dollars at home—"foreign-exchange bureaus" common in Europe are rare even at airports in the United States, and it's best not to change foreign money at local banks.

CREDIT CARDS & ATMS Credit cards are the most widely used form of payment in the United States: **Visa** (Barclaycard in Britain), **MasterCard** (Eurocard in Europe, Access in Britain, Chargex in Canada), **American Express, Diners Club,** and

Discover. There are, however, some stores and restaurants that do not take credit cards, so be sure to ask in advance. (*Note:* Businesses may require a minimum purchase, usually around $10, to use a credit card.)

It is strongly recommended that you bring at least one major credit card. You must have a credit or charge card to rent a car. Hotels and airlines usually require a credit card imprint as a deposit against expenses, and in an emergency, a credit card can be priceless.

You'll find **automated teller machines (ATMs)** on just about every block in every city across the country. Some ATMs will allow you to draw U.S. currency against your bank and credit cards. Check with your bank before leaving home, and remember that you will need your personal identification number (PIN) to do so. Most accept Visa, MasterCard, and American Express, as well as ATM cards from other U.S. banks. The **Cirrus** (© 800/424-7787; www.mastercard.com) and **PLUS** (© 800/843-7587; www.visa.com) networks span the country; you can find them even in remote regions. Look at the back of your bank card to see which network you're on, then call or check online for ATM locations at your destination. Expect to be charged up to $5 per transaction, however, if you're not using your own bank's ATM.

ATM cards with major credit card backing, known as "debit cards," are a commonly acceptable form of payment in most stores and restaurants. Debit cards draw money directly from your checking account. Some stores enable you to receive "cash back" on your debit card purchases as well (you can also get money back at U.S. post offices with debit card purchases).

TRAVELER'S CHECKS Though traveler's checks are widely accepted, foreign-currency checks are often difficult to exchange. The most popular traveler's checks are offered by **American Express**

(© **800/807-6233,** or 800/221-7282 for cardholders—this number accepts collect calls, offers service in several foreign languages, and exempts Amex gold and platinum cardholders from the 1% fee); **Visa** (© **800/732-1322**)—AAA members can obtain Visa checks for a $9.95 fee (for checks up to $1,500) at most AAA offices or by calling © **866/339-3378;** and **MasterCard** (© **800/223-9920**). Most businesses are pretty good about taking traveler's checks, but you're better off cashing them at a bank and paying in cash.

SAFETY

GENERAL SUGGESTIONS Although tourist areas are generally safe, U.S. urban areas can be less safe than many in Europe or Japan. This is particularly true of large American cities. If you're in doubt about which neighborhoods are safe, don't hesitate to make inquiries with the hotel front desk staff or the local tourist office. Avoid deserted areas, especially at night, and don't go into public parks after dark unless there's a concert or similar occasion that will attract a crowd.

Avoid carrying valuables with you on the street, and keep expensive cameras or electronic equipment bagged up or covered when not in use. If you're using a map, try to consult it inconspicuously. Hold on to your pocketbook, and place your billfold in an inside pocket. In theaters, restaurants, and other public places, keep your possessions in sight.

DRIVING SAFETY If you have an accident, even on the highway, stay in your car with the doors locked until you assess the situation or until the police arrive. If you're bumped from behind on the street or are involved in a minor accident with no injuries, and the situation appears to be suspicious, motion to the other driver to follow you. Never get out of your car in such situations. Go directly to the nearest police precinct, well-lit service station, or 24-hour store.

Park in well-lit and well-traveled areas whenever possible. Always keep your car doors locked, whether the vehicle is attended or unattended. Never leave any packages or valuables in sight. If someone attempts to rob you or steal your car, don't try to resist the thief or carjacker. Report the incident to the police department immediately by calling ⓒ **911.**

Many car-rental agencies now offer the option of renting a cellphone for the duration of your car rental (if your own cellphone doesn't work in the U.S.); check with the rental agent when you pick up the car. Otherwise, contact **InTouch USA** at ⓒ **800/872-7626** or www.intouchusa.com for short-term cellphone rental.

2 GETTING TO THE U.S.

IMMIGRATION & CUSTOMS CLEARANCE International visitors arriving by air, no matter what the port of entry, should cultivate patience and resignation before setting foot on U.S. soil. U.S. airports have considerably beefed up security clearances in the years since the terrorist attacks of September 11, 2001, and clearing Customs and Immigration can take as long as 2 hours.

In some Caribbean and European destinations, it is possible to go through U.S. Customs at the airport before you depart. Check with your airline.

3 GETTING AROUND THE U.S.

BY PLANE Some large airlines (as well as the "Star Alliance" of about 24 domestic and international airlines) offer travelers on their transatlantic or transpacific flights special discount tickets under the name **Visit USA,** allowing mostly one-way travel from one U.S. destination to another at very low prices. These discount tickets are not on sale in the United States and must be purchased abroad in conjunction with your international ticket. This system is the best, easiest, and fastest way to see the United States at low cost. You should obtain information well in advance from your travel agent or the office of the airline concerned, since the conditions attached to these discount tickets can be changed without advance notice. For more information, visit **www.staralliance.com/en/travellers/fare_products/north_american_airpass.html**.

BY TRAIN International visitors (excluding Canada) can also buy a **USA Rail Pass,** good for 15 or 30 days of unlimited travel on Amtrak (ⓒ **800/USA-RAIL** [872-7245]; www.amtrak.com). The pass is available through many overseas travel agents and at Amtrak offices nationwide. See Amtrak's website for the cost of travel within the western, eastern, or northwestern United States. With a foreign passport, you can also buy passes direct from some Amtrak locations, including San Francisco, Los Angeles, Chicago, New York, Miami, Boston, and Washington, D.C. Reservations are generally required and should be made as early as possible. Regional rail passes are also available.

BY BUS Bus travel is often the most economical form of public transit for short hops between U.S. cities, but it can also be slow and uncomfortable—certainly not an option for everyone (particularly when Amtrak, which is far more luxurious, offers similar rates). **Greyhound/Trailways** (ⓒ **800/231-2222;** www.greyhound.com), the sole nationwide bus line, offers several pass and discount options. Their

Discovery Pass (www.discoverypass.com) covers travel on all Greyhound routes in the U.S. and some in Canada.

BY CAR Unless you plan to spend the bulk of your vacation time in a city where walking is the best and easiest way to get around, the most cost-effective, convenient, and comfortable way to travel around the United States is by car. A list of the major rental-car companies in the United States can be found in appendix D, "Useful Toll-Free Numbers & Websites." Foreign driver's licenses are usually recognized in the U.S., but you should get an international one if your home license is not in English.

If you plan to rent a car in the United States, you probably won't need the services of an additional automobile organization. If you're planning to buy or borrow a car, automobile-association membership is recommended. **AAA**, the **American Automobile Association** (② **800/222-4357;** http://travel.aaa.com), is the country's largest auto club and supplies its members with maps, insurance, and, most importantly, emergency road service. The cost of joining starts at $58 for a single driver, but if you're a member of a foreign auto club with reciprocal arrangements, you can enjoy free AAA service in America.

For more information and tips about the ins and outs of car rental, see the "By Car" section in "Getting Around the United States" in chapter 1. It starts on p. 14.

4 FAST FACTS: INTERNATIONAL TRAVELERS

BUSINESS HOURS Offices are usually open weekdays from 9am to 5pm. Banks are open weekdays from 9am to 3pm or later and sometimes Saturday mornings. Stores typically open between 9 and 10am and close between 5 and 6pm Monday through Saturday. Stores in shopping complexes or malls tend to stay open late: until about 9pm on weekdays and weekends. Many malls and larger department stores are open on Sunday.

DRINKING LAWS The legal age for purchase and consumption of alcoholic beverages is 21; proof of age is required and often requested at bars, nightclubs, and restaurants, so it's always a good idea to bring ID when you go out. Beer and wine often can be purchased in supermarkets, but liquor laws vary from state to state. A county or city which prohibits the sale of alcohol is called "dry."

Do not carry open containers of alcohol in your car or any public area that isn't zoned for alcohol consumption. The police can fine you on the spot. And nothing will ruin your trip faster than getting a citation for DUI ("driving under the influence"), so don't even think about driving while intoxicated.

ELECTRICITY Like Canada, the United States uses 110–120 volts AC (60 cycles), compared to 220–240 volts AC (50 cycles) in most of Europe, Australia, and New Zealand. If your small appliances use 220–240 volts, you'll need a 110-volt transformer and a plug adapter with two flat parallel pins to operate them here. Downward converters that change 220–240 volts to 110–120 volts are difficult to find in the United States, so bring one with you.

EMBASSIES & CONSULATES All embassies are located in the nation's capital, Washington, D.C. Some consulates are located in major U.S. cities, and most nations have a mission to the United Nations in New York City. If your country isn't listed below, call for directory information in Washington, D.C. (② **202/555-1212**), or log on to **www.embassy.org/embassies**.

The embassy of **Australia** is at 1601 Massachusetts Ave. NW, Washington, DC 20036 (© 202/797-3000; www.austemb. org). There are consulates in New York, Honolulu, Houston, Los Angeles, and San Francisco.

The embassy of **Canada** is at 501 Pennsylvania Ave. NW, Washington, DC 20001 (© 202/682-1740; www.canadian embassy.org). Other Canadian consulates are in Buffalo (NY), Detroit, Los Angeles, New York, and Seattle.

The embassy of **Ireland** is at 2234 Massachusetts Ave. NW, Washington, DC 20008 (© 202/462-3939; www.ireland emb.org). Irish consulates are in Boston, Chicago, New York, San Francisco, and other cities. See website for complete listing.

The embassy of **Japan** is at 2520 Massachusetts Ave. NW, Washington, DC 20008 (© 202/238-6700; www.emb japan.org). Japanese consulates are located in many cities, including Atlanta, Boston, Detroit, New York, San Francisco, and Seattle.

The embassy of **New Zealand** is at 37 Observatory Circle NW, Washington, DC 20008 (© 202/328-4800; www.nzemb. org). New Zealand consulates are in Los Angeles, Salt Lake City, San Francisco, and Seattle.

The embassy of the **United Kingdom** is at 3100 Massachusetts Ave. NW, Washington, DC 20008 (© 202/588-7800; www.britainusa.com). Other British consulates are in Atlanta, Boston, Chicago, Cleveland, Houston, Los Angeles, New York, San Francisco, and Seattle.

EMERGENCIES Call © 911 to report a fire, call the police, or get an ambulance anywhere in the United States. This is a toll-free call.

If you encounter serious problems, contact **Traveler's Aid International** (© 202/546-1127; www.travelersaid.org). This nationwide, nonprofit, social-service organization geared to helping travelers in difficult straits offers services that might include reuniting families separated while traveling, providing food and/or shelter to people stranded without cash, or even emotional counseling. If you're in trouble, seek them out.

GASOLINE (PETROL) Petrol is known as gasoline (or simply "gas") in the United States, and petrol stations are known as both gas stations and service stations. British, European, and Australian visitors will find it less expensive than at home. Taxes are already included in the printed price. One U.S. gallon equals 3.8 liters or .85 imperial gallons.

HOLIDAYS Banks, government offices, post offices, and many stores, restaurants, and museums are closed on the following legal national holidays: January 1 (New Year's Day), the third Monday in January (Martin Luther King, Jr., Day), the third Monday in February (Presidents' Day, Washington's Birthday), the last Monday in May (Memorial Day), July 4 (Independence Day), the first Monday in September (Labor Day), the second Monday in October (Columbus Day), November 11 (Veterans Day/Armistice Day), the fourth Thursday in November (Thanksgiving Day), and December 25 (Christmas).

LEGAL AID If you are "pulled over" for a minor infraction (such as speeding), never attempt to pay the fine directly to a police officer; this could be construed as attempted bribery, a much more serious crime. Pay fines by mail, or directly into the hands of the clerk of the court. If accused of a more serious offense, say and do nothing before consulting a lawyer. Here the burden is on the state to prove a person's guilt beyond a reasonable doubt, and everyone has the right to remain silent, whether he or she is suspected of a crime or actually arrested. Once arrested, a person can make one telephone call to a party of his or her choice. International visitors should call their embassy or consulate.

MAIL Generally found at intersections, mailboxes are blue with a red-and-white stripe and carry the inscription U.S. MAIL.

At press time, domestic postage rates were 27¢ for a postcard and 42¢ for a letter. For international mail, a first-class letter of up to 1 ounce costs 94¢ (72¢ to Canada and Mexico); a first-class postcard costs the same as a letter. For more information, go to **www.usps.com** and click on "Calculate Postage."

If you aren't sure what your address will be in the United States, mail can be sent to you, in your name, c/o General Delivery at the main post office of the city or region where you expect to be. (Call ✆ **800/275-8777** for information on the nearest post office.) The addressee must pick up mail in person and must produce proof of identity (driver's license, passport, or similar document). Most post offices will hold your mail for up to 1 month, and are open Monday to Friday from 8am to 6pm and Saturday from 9am to 3pm.

Always include zip codes when mailing items in the U.S. If you don't know your zip code, visit www.usps.com/zip4.

PASSPORTS The websites listed provide downloadable passport applications as well as the current fees for processing applications. *Note:* Children are required to present a passport when entering the United States at airports.

For Residents of Australia You can pick up an application from your local post office or any branch of Passports Australia, but you must schedule an interview at the passport office to present your application materials. Call the **Australian Passport Information Service** at ✆ **131-232,** or visit the government website at www.passports.gov.au.

For Residents of Canada Passport applications are available at travel agencies throughout Canada or from the central

Passport Office, Department of Foreign Affairs and International Trade, Ottawa, ON K1A 0G3 (✆ **800/567-6868;** www. ppt.gc.ca). *Note:* Canadian children who travel must have their own passport. However, if you hold a valid Canadian passport issued before December 11, 2001, that bears the name of your child, the passport remains valid for you and your child until it expires.

For Residents of Ireland You can apply for a 10-year passport at the **Passport Office,** Setanta Centre, Molesworth Street, Dublin 2 (✆ **01/671-1633;** www. irlgov.ie/iveagh). Those under age 17 and those 66 and over apply for a 3-year passport. You can also apply at 1A South Mall, Cork (✆ **21/494-4700**) or at most main post offices.

For Residents of New Zealand You can pick up a passport application at any New Zealand Passports Office or download it from their website. Contact the **Passports Office** at ✆ **0800/225-050** in New Zealand or 04/474-8100, or log on to www.passports.govt.nz.

For Residents of the United Kingdom To pick up an application for a standard 10-year passport (5-year passport for children 15 and under, visit your nearest passport office, major post office, or travel agency, or contact the **United Kingdom Passport Service** at ✆ **0870/521-0410** or search its website at www.ukpa. gov.uk.

TAXES The United States has no value-added tax (VAT) or other indirect tax at the national level. Every state, county, and city has the right to levy its own local tax on all purchases, including hotel and restaurant checks, airline tickets, and so on. These taxes will not appear on price tags.

TELEPHONES Many convenience stores, drugstores, and newsstands sell **prepaid calling cards** in denominations up to $50; for international visitors, these can be the least expensive way to call home. Many public pay phones at airports now accept American Express, MasterCard, and Visa credit cards. **Local calls** made from pay phones in most locales cost either 25¢ or 50¢ (no pennies, please). Most long-distance and international calls can be dialed directly from any phone. **For calls within the United States and to Canada,** dial 1 followed by the area code and the seven-digit number. **For other international calls,** dial 011 followed by the country code, city code, and the number you are calling.

If you're not from the U.S., you may be stymied by the limitations of our **GSM (Global System for Mobile Communications) wireless network.** Your phone will probably work in most major U.S. cities; it definitely won't work in many rural areas. To see where GSM phones work in the U.S., check out www.t-mobile.com/coverage. And you may or may not be able to send SMS (text messages). Check with your home provider to see if you need a different SIM chip or setting before coming to North America. And if your phone doesn't work here, consider buying a cheap pay-as-you-go phone.

Calls to area codes **800, 888, 877,** and **866** are toll-free. However, calls to area codes **700** and **900** (chat lines, bulletin boards, "dating" services, and so on) can be very expensive—usually a charge of 95¢ to $3 or more per minute, and they sometimes have minimum charges that can run as high as $15 or more.

For **reversed-charge or collect calls,** and for person-to-person calls, dial the number 0, then the area code and number; an operator will come on the line, and you should specify whether you are calling collect, person-to-person, or both. If your operator-assisted call is international, ask for the overseas operator.

For **local directory assistance** ("information"), dial 411; for long-distance information, dial 1, then the appropriate area code and 555-1212.

TIME The continental United States is divided into **four time zones:** Eastern Standard Time (EST), Central Standard Time (CST), Mountain Standard Time (MST), and Pacific Standard Time (PST). Alaska and Hawaii have their own zones. For example, when it's 9am in Los Angeles (PST), it's 7am in Honolulu (HST),10am in Denver (MST), 11am in Chicago (CST), noon in New York City (EST), 5pm in London (GMT), and 2am the next day in Sydney.

Daylight saving time takes effect at 2am the second Sunday in March until 2am the first Sunday in November, except in Arizona, Hawaii, the U.S. Virgin Islands, and Puerto Rico. Daylight saving moves the clock 1 hour ahead of standard time.

TIPPING Tips are a very important part of certain workers' income, and gratuities are the standard way of showing appreciation for services provided. (Tipping is certainly not compulsory if the service is poor!) In hotels, tip **bellhops** at least $1 per bag ($2–$3 if you have a lot of luggage) and tip the **chamber staff** $1 to $2 per day (more if you've left a disaster area for him or her to clean up).

Tip the **doorman** or **concierge** only if he or she has provided you with some specific service (for example, calling a cab for you or obtaining difficult-to-get theater tickets). Tip the **valet-parking attendant** $1 every time you get your car.

In restaurants, bars, and nightclubs, tip **service staff** 15% to 20% of the check, tip **bartenders** 10% to 15%, tip **checkroom attendants** $1 per garment, and tip **valet-parking attendants** $1 per vehicle.

As for other service personnel, tip **cab-drivers** 15% of the fare; tip **skycaps** at airports at least $1 per bag ($2–$3 if you have a lot of luggage); and tip **hairdressers** and **barbers** 15% to 20%.

TOILETS You won't find public toilets, or "restrooms," on the streets in most U.S.

cities, but they can be found in hotel lobbies, bars, restaurants, museums, department stores, railway and bus stations, and service stations. Large hotels and fast-food restaurants are often the best bet for clean facilities. Restaurants and bars in resorts or heavily visited areas may reserve their restrooms for patrons.

Department of State Travel Advisory ✆ 202/647-5225 (staffed 24 hr.)

U.S. Passport Agency ✆ 202/647-0518.

U.S. Centers for Disease Control International Traveler's Hotline ✆ 404/332-4559.

Appendix D: Toll-Free Numbers & Websites

MAJOR U.S. AIRLINES

(*flies internationally as well)

Alaska Airlines/Horizon Air
℗ 800/252-7522
www.alaskaair.com

American Airlines*
℗ 800/433-7300 (in U.S. and Canada)
℗ 020/7365-0777 (in U.K.)
www.aa.com

Cape Air
℗ 800/352-0714
www.flycapeair.com

Continental Airlines*
℗ 800/523-3273 (in U.S. and Canada)
℗ 084/5607-6760 (in U.K.)
www.continental.com

Delta Air Lines*
℗ 800/221-1212 (in U.S. and Canada)
℗ 084/5600-0950 (in U.K.)
www.delta.com

Hawaiian Airlines*
℗ 800/367-5320 (in U.S. and Canada)
www.hawaiianair.com

Midwest Airlines
℗ 800/452-2022
www.midwestairlines.com

Nantucket Airlines
℗ 800/635-8787
www.nantucketairlines.com

Northwest Airlines
℗ 800/225-2525 (in U.S.)
℗ 870/0507-4074 (in U.K.)
www.nwa.com

PenAir (The Spirit of Alaska)
℗ 800/448-4226 (in U.S.)
www.penair.com

United Airlines*
℗ 800/864-8331 (in U.S. and Canada)
℗ 084/5844-4777 in U.K.
www.united.com

US Airways*
℗ 800/428-4322 (in U.S. and Canada)
℗ 084/5600-3300 (in U.K.)
www.usairways.com

Virgin America*
℗ 877/359-8474
www.virginamerica.com

BUDGET AIRLINES

Frontier Airlines
✆ 800/432-1359
www.frontierairlines.com

go!
✆ 888/435-9462
www.iflygo.com
(Hawaii based)

JetBlue Airways
✆ 800/538-2583 (in U.S.)
✆ 801/365-2525 (in U.K. and Canada)
www.jetblue.com

MAJOR HOTEL & MOTEL CHAINS

Best Western International
✆ 800/780-7234 (in U.S. and Canada)
✆ 0800/393-130 (in U.K.)
www.bestwestern.com

Clarion Hotels
✆ 800/CLARION (252-7466) or
877/424-6423 (in U.S. and Canada)
✆ 0800/444-444 (in U.K.)
www.choicehotels.com

Comfort Inns
✆ 800/228-5150
✆ 0800/444-444 (in U.K.)
www.ChoiceHotels.com

Courtyard by Marriott
✆ 888/236-2427 (in U.S.)
✆ 0800/221-222 (in U.K.)
www.marriott.com/courtyard

Crowne Plaza Hotels
✆ 888/303-1746
www.ichotelsgroup.com/crowneplaza

Days Inn
✆ 800/329-7466 (in U.S.)
✆ 0800/280-400 (in U.K.)
www.daysinn.com

Doubletree Hotels
✆ 800/222-TREE (222-8733) (in U.S. and Canada)
✆ 087/0590-9090 (in U.K.)
www.doubletree.com

Southwest Airlines
✆ 800/435-9792 (in U.S., U.K., and Canada)
www.southwest.com

Spirit Airlines
✆ 800/772-7117
www.spiritair.com

WestJet
✆ 800/538-5696 (in U.S. and Canada)
www.westjet.com

Econo Lodge
✆ 800/55-ECONO (552-3666)
www.choicehotels.com

Embassy Suites
✆ 800/EMBASSY (362-2779)
www.embassysuites.hilton.com

Fairfield Inn by Marriott
✆ 800/228-2800 (in U.S. and Canada)
✆ 0800/221-222 (in U.K.)
www.marriott.com/fairfieldinn

Four Seasons
✆ 800/819-5053 (in U.S. and Canada)
✆ 0800/6488-6488 (in U.K.)
www.fourseasons.com

Hampton Inn
✆ 800/HAMPTON (426-4766)
www.hamptoninn.hilton.com

Hilton Hotels
✆ 800/HILTONS (445-8667) (in U.S. and Canada)
✆ 087/0590-9090 (in U.K.)
www.hilton.com

Holiday Inn
✆ 800/315-2621 (in U.S. and Canada)
✆ 0800/405-060 (in U.K.)
www.holidayinn.com

Howard Johnson
✆ 800/446-4656 (in U.S. and Canada)
www.hojo.com

D

Hyatt
- ✆ 888/591-1234 (in U.S. and Canada)
- ✆ 084/5888-1234 (in U.K.)
- www.hyatt.com

InterContinental Hotels & Resorts
- ✆ 800/424-6835 (in U.S. and Canada)
- ✆ 0800/1800-1800 (in U.K.)
- www.ichotelsgroup.com

La Quinta Inns and Suites
- ✆ 800/642-4271 (in U.S. and Canada)
- www.lq.com

Loews Hotels
- ✆ 800/23LOEWS (235-6397)
- www.loewshotels.com

Marriott
- ✆ 877/236-2427 (in U.S. and Canada)
- ✆ 0800/221-222 (in U.K.)
- www.marriott.com

Motel 6
- ✆ 800/4MOTEL6 (466-8356)
- www.motel6.com

Omni Hotels
- ✆ 888/444-OMNI (444-6664)
- www.omnihotels.com

Quality
- ✆ 877/424-6423 (in U.S. and Canada)
- ✆ 0800/444-444 (in U.K.)
- www.ChoiceHotels.com

Radisson Hotels & Resorts
- ✆ 888/201-1718 (in U.S. and Canada)
- ✆ 0800/374-411 (in U.K.)
- www.radisson.com

Ramada Worldwide
- ✆ 888/2-RAMADA (272-6232) (in U.S. and Canada)
- ✆ 080/8100-0783 (in U.K.)
- www.ramada.com

Red Carpet Inns
- ✆ 800/251-1962
- www.bookroomsnow.com

Red Lion Hotels
- ✆ 800/RED-LION (733-5466)
- www.redlion.rdln.com

Red Roof Inns
- ✆ 866/686-4335 (in U.S. and Canada)
- ✆ 614/601-4075 (international)
- www.redroof.com

Renaissance
- ✆ 888/236-2427
- www.marriott.com

Residence Inn by Marriott
- ✆ 800/331-3131
- ✆ 800/221-222 (in U.K.)
- www.marriott.com/residenceinn

Rodeway Inns
- ✆ 877/424-6423
- www.RodewayInn.com

Sheraton Hotels & Resorts
- ✆ 800/325-3535 (in U.S.)
- ✆ 800/543-4300 (in Canada)
- ✆ 0800/3253-5353 (in U.K.)
- www.starwoodhotels.com/sheraton

Super 8 Motels
- ✆ 800/800-8000
- www.super8.com

Travelodge
- ✆ 800/578-7878
- www.travelodge.com

Vagabond Inns
- ✆ 800/522-1555
- www.vagabondinn.com

Westin Hotels & Resorts
- ✆ 800/937-8461 (in U.S. and Canada)
- ✆ 0800/3259-5959 (in U.K.)
- www.starwoodhotels.com/westin

Wyndham Hotels & Resorts
- ✆ 877/999-3223 (in U.S. and Canada)
- ✆ 050/6638-4899 (in U.K.)
- www.wyndham.com

INDEX

FROMMER'S® COMPLETE TRAVEL GUIDES

FROMMER'S® DAY BY DAY GUIDES

PAULINE FROMMER'S GUIDES: SEE MORE. SPEND LESS.

FROMMER'S® PORTABLE GUIDES

Acapulco, Ixtapa & Zihuatanejo
Amsterdam
Aruba, Bonaire & Curacao
Australia's Great Barrier Reef
Bahamas
Big Island of Hawaii
Boston
California Wine Country
Cancún
Cayman Islands
Charleston
Chicago
Dominican Republic

Florence
Las Vegas
Las Vegas for Non-Gamblers
London
Maui
Nantucket & Martha's Vineyard
New Orleans
New York City
Paris
Portland
Puerto Rico
Puerto Vallarta, Manzanillo &
    Guadalajara

Rio de Janeiro
San Diego
San Francisco
Savannah
St. Martin, Sint Maarten, Anguila &
    St. Bart's
Turks & Caicos
Vancouver
Venice
Virgin Islands
Washington, D.C.
Whistler

FROMMER'S® CRUISE GUIDES

Alaska Cruises & Ports of Call

Cruises & Ports of Call

European Cruises & Ports of Call

FROMMER'S® NATIONAL PARK GUIDES

Algonquin Provincial Park
Banff & Jasper
Grand Canyon

National Parks of the American West
Rocky Mountain
Yellowstone & Grand Teton

Yosemite and Sequoia & Kings
    Canyon
Zion & Bryce Canyon

FROMMER'S® WITH KIDS GUIDES

Chicago
Hawaii
Las Vegas
London

National Parks
New York City
San Francisco

Toronto
Walt Disney World® & Orlando
Washington, D.C.

FROMMER'S® PHRASEFINDER DICTIONARY GUIDES

Chinese
French

German
Italian

Japanese
Spanish

SUZY GERSHMAN'S BORN TO SHOP GUIDES

France
Hong Kong, Shanghai & Beijing
Italy

London
New York
Paris

San Francisco
Where to Buy the Best of Everything.

FROMMER'S® BEST-LOVED DRIVING TOURS

Britain
California
France
Germany

Ireland
Italy
New England
Northern Italy

Scotland
Spain
Tuscany & Umbria

THE UNOFFICIAL GUIDES®

Adventure Travel in Alaska
Beyond Disney
California with Kids
Central Italy
Chicago
Cruises
Disneyland®
England
Hawaii

Ireland
Las Vegas
London
Maui
Mexico's Best Beach Resorts
Mini Mickey
New Orleans
New York City
Paris

San Francisco
South Florida including Miami &
    the Keys
Walt Disney World®
Walt Disney World® for
    Grown-ups
Walt Disney World® with Kids
Washington, D.C.

SPECIAL-INTEREST TITLES

Athens Past & Present
Best Places to Raise Your Family
Cities Ranked & Rated
500 Places to Take Your Kids Before They Grow Up
Frommer's Best Day Trips from London
Frommer's Best RV & Tent Campgrounds in the U.S.A.

Frommer's Exploring America by RV
Frommer's NYC Free & Dirt Cheap
Frommer's Road Atlas Europe
Frommer's Road Atlas Ireland
Retirement Places Rated